4/
07

THE QUR'ĀN

with

Annotated Interpretation in Modern English

THE QUR'ĀN

with

Annotated Interpretation in Modern English

by
Ali Ünal

Light

New Jersey
2006

Published by The Light, Inc.
26 Worlds Fair Dr. Suite C
Somerset, New Jersey, 08873, USA
www.thelightpublishing.com

Library of Congress Cataloging-in-Publication Data

Unal, Ali
   The Qur'an with annotated interpretation in modern English / by Ali Unal.
      p. cm.
   Includes bibliographical references and index.
   ISBN-13: 978-1-59784-000-2
   1. Koran--Criticism, interpretation, etc. I. Title.
BP130.4.U48 2006
297.1'227--dc22

                              2006006298

Printed by

SİSTEM MATBAACILIK
Yılanlı Ayazma Sk. No:8
Davutpaşa - Zeytinburnu / İST.
Tel.: (0212) 482 11 01 (3 Hat)
İstanbul

Çağlayan A.Ş., Izmir - Turkey
June 2006

Contents

SŪRAH

FOREWORD

All praise is for God, the Lord of the worlds, may His Majesty be exalted, and peace and blessings be upon the Prophet Muḥammad, his household, Companions and the righteous servants among the inhabitants of the heaven and earth.

The movement of returning to the Qur'ān which began in the Muslim world around a century ago, is continuing with its ups and downs, and right and wrong aspects. As is known, the Qur'ān was revealed to the Prophet Muḥammad, upon him be peace and blessings, in 23 years 14 centuries ago mostly on different occasions. This last "version" of the Divine Word which was planted in the Last Prophet as a seed and, growing swiftly, "raised on its stem, put out its shoots" (Qur'ān, 48: 29) came to leaf, blossomed and yielded fruit in all aspects of life. Almost one third of the world having lived a peaceful life under its calm, serene shade for many centuries, the Qur'ān was veiled by the neglect and unfaithfulness of its "friends" and the hostility of its "enemies." However, after a few centuries of misery, the Muslims all over the Muslim world felt the dire need of returning to the Qur'ān and found that this Word of God is as fresh as it was first revealed and "growing younger as time gets older."

The very essence of their being deeply injured by the poison injected by materialistic trends, humanity are in quest of immediate cure. It is the Word of God which has this cure. However, it is in anticipation of "doctors" who will present it. The future of humanity is dependent on the efforts of these doctors to present this cure. If the Qur'ān had been fully and accurately understood and practiced effectively in life, the poisons produced in modern times would not have been able to find Muslim customers in considerable number, no matter if they have been presented in golden cups. Whereas, unfortunately, in addition to these poisons being easily injected in many believing bodies, some so-called Muslim "doctors" who should have defied them with the Qur'ān, have taken them as if antidote. They even have gone so far as to identify the cure of the Qur'ān with them and, further, have ventured to test it in the tubes in the laboratories where the poisons are produced.

WHAT IS THE QUR'ĀN; HOW CAN IT BE DEFINED?

According to the majority of scholars, the word Qur'ān is an infinitive form of the verb QaRaA meaning reading or reciting. Therefore it literally means a thing recited by adding letters and words to one another.

The verb QaRaA has another infinitive form qar'u which means to collect. So, some are of the opinion that qur'ān means "the thing which collects." It is narrated from 'Abdullāh ibn 'Abbās that the word qur'ān in the verse, *Surely it is for Us to collect it (in your heart) and enable you to recite it (by heart)* (75: 17), means being collected and established in the heart. For this reason, some assert that since the Qur'ān collects and contains in it the "fruit" of the previous Scriptures and the whole of knowledge, it is called Qur'ān.

Some other scholars affirm that the word *qur'ān* was not derived from any word. It is the proper name given to the Book which God, may His Majesty be exalted, sent to His Last Messenger, upon him be peace and blessings. Imam Shāfi'ī held this opinion (Abu'l-Baqā, 287; Rāghib al-Isfahānī, 402; as-Ṣāliḥ [translated], 15-18).

The Qur'ān is the Word of God and therefore eternal and not created. But as a book conveyed to the Prophet by the Archangel Gabriel and composed of letters and words, recited, touched, and listened to, is not eternal (Çetin, 30-32).

The general definition of the Qur'ān is as follows:

> The Qur'ān is the miraculous Word of God which was revealed to the Prophet Muḥammad, upon him be peace and blessings, written down on sheets, and transmitted to the succeeding generations by numerous reliable channels, and whose recitation is an act of worship and obligatory in daily Prayers. (Karaman, 63)

The Qur'ān describes some of its features as follows:

> *The month of Ramaḍān (is the month), in which the Qur'ān was sent down as guidance for people, and as clear signs of guidance and the Criterion (between truth and falsehood).* (2: 185)

> *And this Qur'ān is not such that it could possibly be fabricated by one in attribution to God, but it is a (Divine Book) confirming (the Divine origin of and the truths that are still contained by) the Revelations prior to it, and an explanation of the essence of all Divine Books – wherein there is no doubt, from the Lord of the worlds.* (10: 37)

> *We send it down as a qur'ān (discourse) in Arabic so that (using your reason to reflect) you may understand.* (12: 2)

> *This Qur'ān surely guides (in all matters) to that which is most just and right and gives the believers who do good, righteous deeds the glad tidings that for them is a great reward.* (17: 9)

> *And indeed (by revealing it through human language) We have made the Qur'ān easy for remembrance (of God and for taking heed), then is there any that remembers and takes heed?* (54: 17)

> *Most certainly it is a Qur'ān (recited) most honorable, in a Book well-guarded.* (56: 77-78)

The Qur'ān has other titles each of which describes it in one of its aspects and therefore can be regarded an attribute of its. Some of them are: The Book, the Criterion, the Remembrance, the Advice, the Light, the Guidance, the Healer, the Noble, the Mother of the Book, the Truth, the Admonishment, the Good Tiding, the Book Gradually Revealed, the Knowledge, and the Clear (Çetin, 32-36).

The Qur'ān aims to guide all people to truth and has four main purposes: demonstrating God's Existence and Unity, establishing Prophethood, and proving and elucidating afterlife with all its aspects and dimensions, and promulgating worship of God and essentials of justice. The verses of the Qur'ān mainly dwell on these purposes. There are, based on these main purposes, the principles of creed, rules to govern human life, detailed information on the Resurrection and afterlife, prescripts of worship of God, moral standards, direct or indirect information on some scientific facts, principles of the formation and decay of civilizations, outlines of the histories of many previous peoples, an so on. The Qur'ān is also a source of healing; its application in life provides cure for almost all psychological and social illnesses. It is also a cosmology, epistemology, ontology, sociology, psychology, and law. It was revealed to regulate human life in the world. It is not limited to any time, place, or people. It is for all times and for all peoples.

The Prophet Muḥammad, upon him be peace and blessings, declares:

> The Qur'ān is more lovable to God than the heavens and earth and those in them. The superiority of the Qur'ān over all other words and speeches is like God's superiority over His creatures. (at-Tirmidhī, "Faḍāil al-Qur'ān," 25)
>
> The Qur'ān is a definite decree distinguishing between the truth and falsehood. It is not for pastime. Whoever rejects it because of his or her despotism, God breaks his or her neck. It contains the history of previous peoples, the tiding of those to come after you, and the judgment on the disagreements among you. Whoever searches for guidance in something other than it, God leads him or her astray. It is God's strong rope. It is the wise instruction. It is the Straight Path. It is a book which desires cannot deviate and tongues cannot confuse, and which scholars are not fed up with, never worn-out by repetition, and has uncountable admirable aspects. It is such a book that they could not help but say: "We have indeed heard a wonderful Qur'ān, guiding to what is right in belief and action and so we have believed in it." Whoever speaks based on it speaks truth; whoever judges by it judges justly and whoever calls to it calls to truth. (at-Tirmidhī, "Thawāb al-Qur'ān," 14)

We close this topic with the definition of the Qur'ān by Bediüzzaman Said Nursi, an illustrious Muslim scholar who started an Islamic revival movement in Turkey during the first half of the twentieth century:

> The Qur'an is an eternal translation of the great Book of the Universe and the everlasting translator of the "languages" in which the Divine laws of the universe's creation and operation are "inscribed;" the interpreter of the books of the visible, material world and the World of the Unseen; the discloser of the immaterial treasuries of the Divine Names hidden on the earth and in the heavens; the key to the truths lying beneath the lines of events; the World of the Unseen's tongue in the visible, material one; the treasury of the All-Merciful's favors and the All-Glorified's eternal addresses coming from the World of the Unseen beyond the veil of this visible world; the sun of Islam's spiritual and intellectual worlds, as well as its foundation and plan; the sacred map of the Hereafter's worlds; the expounder, lucid interpreter, articulate proof, and clear translator of the Divine Essence, Attributes, Names and acts; the educator and trainer of humanity's world and the water and light of Islam, the true and greatest humanity; and the true wisdom of humanity and the true guide leading them to happiness.

For humanity, it is a book of law, prayer, wisdom, worship and servanthood to God, commands and invitation, invocation and reflection. It is a holy book containing books for all of our spiritual needs; a heavenly book that, like a sacred library, contains numerous booklets from which all saints, eminently truthful people, all purified and discerning scholars, and those well-versed in knowledge of God have derived their own specific ways, and which illuminate each way and answer their followers' needs.

Having come from God's Supreme Throne, originated in His Greatest Name, and issued from each Name's most comprehensive rank, the Qur'an is God's word (as regards His being the Lord of the worlds) and His decree (in respect of His having the title of Deity of all creatures). It is a discourse in the name of the Creator of the heavens and the earth, a speech from the view of absolute Divine Lordship, and an eternal sermon on behalf of the All-Glorified One's universal Sovereignty. It is also a register of the All-Merciful's favors from the viewpoint of all-embracing Mercy; a collection of messages, some of which begin with a cipher; and a holy book that, having descended from the Divine Greatest Name's surrounding circle, looks over and surveys the circle surrounded by His Supreme Throne.

This is why the title "the Word of God" has been (and will always be) given to the Qur'an. After the Qur'an come the Books and Scrolls sent to other Messengers. Some of the other countless Divine words are inspirations coming as particular manifestations of a particular aspect of Divine Mercy, Sovereignty, and Lordship under a particular title and with a particular regard. The inspirations coming to angels, human beings, and animals vary greatly with regard to their universality or particularity.

The Qur'ān is a heavenly book, which contains in brief the Scriptures revealed to the previous Messengers in different ages, and the content of the treatises of all the saints with different temperaments, and the works of all the purified scholars each following a way particular to himself; the six sides of which are bright and absolutely free of the darkness of doubts and whimsical thoughts; whose point of support is with certainty Divine Revelation and the Divine eternal Word, whose aim is manifestly eternal happiness, and whose inside is manifestly pure guidance. And it is surrounded and supported: from above by the lights of faith, from below by proof and evidence, from the right by the submission of the heart and the conscience, and from the left by the admission of reason and other intellectual faculties. Its fruit is with absolute certainty the mercy of the All-Merciful, and Paradise; and it has been accepted and promoted by angels and innumerable people and jinn through the centuries. (*The Words*, "the 25th Word," 388-389)

THE RECORDING OF THE QUR'ĀN AND ITS PRESERVATION

It is commonly accepted that during the human history God the Almighty sent 124,000 Prophets. According to the Islamic definition, a Prophet is one who comes with important tidings, "the tidings of the Religion" which are based on faith in the Existence and Unity of God and His angels, the mission or office of Prophethood and Prophets, Revelation and Divine Scriptures, the Resurrection and afterlife, and Divine Destiny including human free will. The "tidings" also include offering a life to be based on this belief, and promises and warning with respect to accepting this belief and offering or not. It frequently happened during history that the Religion was considerably corrupted, which caused a Prophet to be chosen to revive and restore the Religion and make some amendments in its rules or make new laws concerning the daily life. This Prophet, who was usually given a Book, is called Messenger, and his mission, Messengership. Five of the Messengers, namely Noah, Abraham, Moses, Jesus, and Muḥammad, upon them be peace, are mentioned in a verse in *Sūrat ash-Shūrā* (42: 13) and accepted as the greatest of all Messengers.

The name of the Religion which God the Almighty sent to all the Messengers during history is Islam. Just as the laws in the order and operation of the universe are the same and constant, and, similarly, there is no difference between the first human being on the earth and all the human beings of today with respect to their being human with the same peculiarities, essential needs and the final destination awaiting them, so too, it is natural that the religion should be one and the same based on the same essentials of faith, worship and morality. As this Religion was corrupted or altered or contaminated with borrowings from false creeds, God sent different Messengers in different epochs of history. He sent the Prophet Muḥammad, upon him be peace and blessings, as the last of the Messengers with the perfected and last form of the Religion and "undertook" the preservation of its Book: *Indeed it is We, We Who send down the Reminder in parts, and it is indeed We Who are its Guardian* (15: 9). Since after Moses, upon him be peace, the religion he communicated came to be called Judaism, and after Jesus, upon him be peace, Christianity, Islam has remained as the name of the perfected, preserved form of the Divine Religion which the Prophet Muḥammad, upon him be peace and blessings, communicated.

In this world, God the Almighty acts behind natural or material causes. So He has created and will create causes or means to preserve the Qur'ān. One of these means and one of the reasons why the Almighty allowed His previous Scriptures to be corrupted and "undertook" to preserve the Qur'ān is that the Companions of the Prophet, may God be pleased with them, and the succeeding Muslim generations were devoted to their Book more than any other people being devoted to their own, and tried their utmost to preserve it without the least alteration. With the Prophet Muḥammad, upon him be peace and blessings, God perfected Islam in a way to be able to address all levels of knowledge of understanding to exist and solve the problems of humankind to appear until the Last Day. Therefore, there would be no need for another Prophet to revive or restore the Religion and no Book to be revealed. So, as the first step to preserve the Qur'ān, it was written down during the life of the Prophet Muḥammad, upon him be peace and blessings, under his direct supervision. It is due to this that not one word of its text has been deleted, added, or mutilated. There is not a single difference among the copies of the Qur'ān that have been circulating throughout the world during the 14 centuries of Islam.

In considering the fact that, unlike other Scriptures preceding it, the Qur'ān has been preserved in its original form or text, without a single alteration, addition, or deletion, the following points are of considerable significance:

- The Qur'ān was revealed in parts. God the Almighty undertook not only the preservation of the Qur'ān but also its due recitation and the arrangement of its parts as a book. He revealed to His Messenger where each verse and chapter revealed would be placed:

> *Move not your tongue to hasten it (for safekeeping in your heart).*
> *Surely it is for Us to collect it (in your heart) and enable you to recite it*
> *(by heart). So when We recite it, follow its recitation; thereafter, it is for*
> *Us to explain it. (75: 16-19)*

> *Absolutely Exalted is God, the Supreme Sovereign, the Ultimate Truth*
> *and Ever-Constant. Do not show haste (O Messenger) with (the receiving*
> *and memorizing of any Revelation included in) the Qur'an (the receiving*
> *and memorizing of it) before it has been revealed to you in full, but say:*
> *"My Lord, increase me in knowledge." (20: 114)*

- The Almighty emphasizes that no falsehood can approach the Qur'ān and there will be nothing to cause doubt about its authenticity as the Book of God:

> *It is surely a glorious, unconquerable Book. Falsehood can never have*
> *access to it, whether from before it or from behind it (whether by argu-*
> *ments and attitudes based on philosophies to be invented or by attacks*
> *from the past based on earlier Scriptures; it is) the Book being sent down*
> *in parts from the One All-Wise, All-Praiseworthy (to Whom all praise*
> *and gratitude belong). (41: 41-42)*

- The Messenger of God, upon him be peace and blessings, once a year used to review with the Archangel Gabriel the portion of the Qur'ān that had been revealed until that year. In his last year, after the completion of the Qur'ān's revelation, Gabriel came twice for this purpose. The Messenger concluded from this that his emigration to the other world was near (Yıldırım, 43, 62-63).
- From the very beginning of its revelation, the Prophet's Companions, may God be pleased with them, paid utmost attention to the Qur'ān, and tried their best to understand, memorize, and learn it. This was, in fact, the order of the Qur'ān:

> *And so, when the Qur'ān is recited, give ear to it and listen in silence*
> *so that you may be shown mercy. (7: 204)*

- There were few Muslims who knew how to read and write in the starting period of the Qur'ān's revelation. It was decreed after the Battle of Badr, which was the first encounter between the Muslims and the Makkan polytheists, that the prisoners of war would be emancipated on condition that each should teach ten Muslims of Madīnah how to read and write. Those who learned to read and write first attempted to memorize the Qur'ān. They attempted to do so because recitation of some portion out of the Qur'ān is obligatory in the Prescribed Prayers; because the Qur'ān was very original for them; and because it purified their minds of prejudices and wrong assertions, and their hearts of sins, and illuminated them; and because it built a society out of illuminated minds and purified hearts.

- In order to understand the extent of the efforts the Companions exerted to memorize the Qur'ān and the number of those who memorized it, it suffices to mention that in the disaster of *Bi'r al-Ma'ūnah* which took place just a few years after the Emigration, 70 Companions who had memorized the Qur'ān were martyred. Another 70 or so memorizers of the Qur'ān were also martyred in other similar events and battles during the life of the Prophet, upon him be peace and blessings (as-Ṣāliḥ, 55). When the Prophet died, there were several Companions who knew the Qur'ān by heart such as 'Ali ibn Abī Ṭālib, 'Abdullāh ibn Mas'ūd, 'Abdullāh ibn 'Abbās, 'Abdullāh ibn 'Amr, Hudayfah ibn al-Yamān, Sālim, Mu'adh ibn Jabal, Abū'd-Dardā, Ubeyy ibn Ka'b, Ā'ishah and Umm Salamah, the wives of the Prophet. When a person was converted into Islam or emigrated to Madīnah, the Prophet, upon him be peace and blessings, sent him to a Companion to teach him the Qur'ān. Since a humming raised when the learners of the Qur'ān began reciting, the Prophet asked them to lower their voices not to confuse one another (as-Ṣāliḥ, 57, reporting from az-Zarkānī).

- The Qur'ān was revealed in parts mostly on certain occasions. Whenever a verse or chapter or a group of verses was revealed, it was both memorized by many people, and God's Messenger, upon him be peace and blessings, had it written down. He instructed where it would be placed in the Qur'ān. (The Qur'ān was revealed within 23 years. However, it was called the Qur'ān since the beginning of its revelation.) Those whom the Messenger employed in the writing-down of the Qur'ān were called the Scribes of the Revelation. Histories give the names of 40 or so among them. In addition to writing down the parts of the Qur'ān revealed, the Scribes copied them for themselves and preserved them (as-Ṣāliḥ, 61, reporting from *al-Burhān* by az-Zarkashī).

- When the Prophet, upon him be peace and blessings, died, several Companions such as 'Ali ibn Abī Ṭālib, Mu'adh ibn Jabal, Abū'd-Dardā, and Ubayy ibn Ka'b had already collected the portions of the Qur'ān as a complete book. 'Ali had arranged them according to the revelation time of the chapters (M.M. Pūye, 95–8, reporting from *al-Itqān* by as-Suyūṭī, and also from aṭ-Ṭabarānī and Ibn al-Asākīr). Following the death of the Prophet, when around 700 memorizers of the Qur'ān were martyred in the Battle of Yamāmah, U'mar ibn al-Khaṭṭāb applied to the Caliph Abū Bakr with the request that they should have an "official" copy of the Qur'ān since the memorizers of the Qur'ān were being martyred in the battles. Zayd ibn Thābit, one of the leading scholars and memorizers of the Qur'ān at that time, was chosen for the task. After a meticulous work, Zayd prepared the official collection, which was called the *Muṣḥaf* (Yıldırım, 62–66; as-Ṣāliḥ, 62–65).

- The Almighty openly declares in *Sūrat al-Qiyāmah*: *Surely it is for Us to collect it (in your heart) and enable you to recite it (by heart)* (75: 17). All the verses and chapters of the Qur'ān were arranged and collected as a book by the instructions of the Prophet himself, upon him be peace and blessings, as guided by the Revelation. After the Battle of Yamāmah an official copy was brought about and many copies of this version were produced and sent out to all cities during the time of the Third Caliph 'Uthmān, may God be pleased with him (Yıldırım, 66–70; as-Ṣāliḥ, 65–73).

- One of the foremost reasons of the Qur'ān coming down to us through many centuries without a single distortion or change is that it has been preserved in its own original language. No one in the Muslim world has ever thought to supersede it with any translation of it, with the result that it has been protected from being exposed to what the previous Scriptures were.

In conclusion: The authenticity and genuineness of the copy of the Qur'ān now in our hands, in the sense that it is in the very words which were uttered by God's Messenger, upon him be peace and blessings, is so evident that no Muslim scholar of any standard has ever doubted its genuineness or the fact that each and every letter, word or sentence, verse or chapter was uttered by the Messenger, as the part of the Qur'ān. In other words, the version we have in our hands is undoubtedly the Qur'ān as recited by the Messenger, upon him be peace and blessings. (For further explanations, see *sūrah* 15, note 3.)

THE QUR'ĀN'S STYLES

The Qur'ān is a book conveyed by the Prophet Muḥammad, upon him be peace and blessings, as the Word of God and which testifies to his Prophethood. It is also his greatest miracle which challenges not only the Arabs of his time but all people to come until the Last Day to produce a like of not the whole but a single chapter of it. The Qur'ān is also unparalleled among the Divine Scriptures in being preserved and transmitted to the later generations without the slightest alteration. There is not a single difference among the copies of the Qur'ān which have been circulating in the world since its first revelation.

Although there is no problem of any theological value which the Qur'ān has not dealt with, and it surpasses all scriptural records of pre or post Islamic ages in the abundant variety of its contents, yet its method of approach, presentation and solution is exclusively unique in itself. Rather than dealing any topic in the common, so-called systematic way used by any author of theology or by an apostolic writer, it expressly says that it has adopted a special manifold method of its own which may be called "taṣrīfī." That is, it displays varieties or changing the topics and shifting from one subject to another or reverting to the previous one and repeating deliberately and purposefully one and the same subject in unique and peculiar rhythmic and recitative forms to facilitate the understanding, learning and remembering of it.

> *Look, how We set out the signs (of God's Existence and Unity and other truths of faith) in diverse ways, so that it may be that they will penetrate the essence of matters and understand.* (6: 65)

The Qur'ān exhibits the order of the universe. As almost all varieties of existing things present themselves side by side or mingled before our eyes, the Qur'ān displays varieties linked together with a rhythm of peculiar pitch. This is to show forth the signs of the Unity of God. Although itself openly expresses that this changing attitude may cause some opponents of it to put forth doubts about its Divine authorship (6: 106), it gives the reason for this as to stir up the depth of human intellect to reflect on the unity in variety and harmony in diversity. As a matter of fact, the holy Qur'ān deals in each chapter of particular rhythm with various topics in various ways. This variety adds only to its unique beauty and matchless eloquence. An attentive reciter or an intelligent audience of the holy Qur'ān while passing through these varieties of rhythmical pitch, enjoys to the extent that the Qur'ān itself declares:

> *God sends down in parts the best of the words as a Book fully consistent in itself, and whose statements corroborate, expound and refer to one another. The skins of those who stand in awe of their Lord tingle at (the hearing and understanding of) it. Then, their skins and their hearts come to rest in the Remembrance of God (the Qur'ān). This is God's guidance, by which He guides whomever He wills. And whoever God leads astray, there is no guide for him.* (39: 23)

In addition to this unique style of the Qur'ān, the arrangement of its verses and chapters does not follow a chronological order. You find some verses that were revealed together and put in the same place in the Qur'ān but are preceded and followed by other verses. Some chapters and verses are lengthy while some others are very short. Although this arrangement is one of the aspects of the Qur'ān's miraculousness, one of the most important reasons why many orientalists and their imitators in the Muslim world venture to criticize the Qur'ān on the pretext that there is not consistency among its verses is this:

The Qur'ān exhibits the order of the universe. Just as there is both a whole-part and holistic-partial or universal-particular relation among the things or elements in the universe, the same relation is also true for the verses of the Qur'ān. That is, a body is a whole and the head, arms, legs, and other organs are its parts. Any of these parts cannot wholly represent the body because whatever there is in the body is not to be wholly found in any of its parts. However, each part is a whole in itself. Whereas humankind or any species in existence are holistic or universal. That is, each species is composed of the members that each contains all the features of the species and therefore represents the species. A human being is an exact specimen of humankind in structure.

It is just like this that each of the Qur'ānic verses is a whole in itself and has an independent existence. Most of them can be put in any place in the Qur'ān without harming either the composition or the meaning. In addition, there is an intrinsic relation among all the verses of the Qur'ān or between a verse and all the others. In the words of Bediüzzaman Said Nursi:

> The verses of the Qur'ān are like stars in a sky among which there are visible and invisible ropes and relationships. It is as if each of the verses of the Qur'ān has an eye which sees most of the verses, and a face which looks towards them, so that it extends to them the immaterial threads of relationship to weave a fabric of miraculousness. A single *sūrah* can contain the whole 'ocean' of the Qur'ān in which the whole of the universe is contained. A single verse can comprehend the treasury of that *sūrah*. It is as if most of the verses are each a small *sūrah*, and most of the *sūrah*s, each a little Qur'ān.

It is a commonly accepted fact that the whole of the Qur'ān is contained in *Sūrat al-Fātiḥah*, and *Sūrat al-Fātiḥah* in the *Basmalah*." (*The Words*, "the 25ᵗʰ Word," 394)

There are verses in the Qur'ān which at first glance seem to be contradictory. However, there is not a single contradiction in the Qur'ān. As mentioned above, the "taṣrīfī" arrangement of the verses may cause such "apparent" contradiction. However, the Qur'ān is like an organism all parts of which are interlinked with one another. Both because of this arrangement and the whole-part and wholistic-partial relationship among the verses make, in most cases, a correct understanding of a verse dependent upon the understanding of the whole of the Qur'ān. This is another characteristic particular to the Qur'ān which is another aspect of its miraculousness and demonstrates its Divine authorship. This characteristic is very important in interpretation of the Qur'ān. Since the Qur'ān is the written counterpart of the universe and the human; since, according to Muslim sages, the Qur'ān, the universe, and the human are the three "copies" of the same book – the first being the "revealed and written universe and the human" and the second and third are each a "created Qur'ān," it also teaches us how we can view the human and the universe. Therefore, what a careless human being sees as contradiction in the Qur'ān is, in reality, the contradiction in his or her viewpoint. One whose being has been unified with the Qur'ān will see no contradiction in it, as such a one has been freed from all contradictions. If one views the Qur'ān from the windows of one's particular world full of contradictions, he or she will absolutely see contradiction in it. This is why a human being who attempts to approach the Qur'ān must first be freed from all kinds of contradiction.

The Qur'ān was revealed in the language of Arabic. The Qur'ān's language is its outer body. It should not be forgotten that religion does not solely consist in neither a philosophy nor a theology. It is a method of unifying all the dimensions of our being. Therefore, as pointed out above, the language of the Qur'ān is one of the essential, inseparable elements of the Qur'ān. It was revealed in Arabic not only because the Arabs of the time of its revelation could understand it. Rather, a universal religion must have a universal language. The Qur'ān views the world as the cradle of human brotherhood and sisterhood. It envisages to unite all races, colors, and beliefs as brothers-sisters and servants of One God. Its language is one of the basic factors that help a human being not only ponder over religious realities but also unite all the dimensions of his or her being according to the Divine standards. Translations of the Qur'ān cannot be recited in the Prescribed Prayers, since any of its translations is not identical with it. Without Arabic, one can be a good Muslim but can understand only a little of the Qur'ān.

The Qur'ān is the source of all knowledge in Islam, not only the religious and spiritual but also social and scientific knowledge and good morals, law, and philosophy.

UNDERSTANDING THE QUR'ĀN

The first step to understand the Qur'ān is understanding its language. The language has the same meaning for a text as the bodily features have for a human being. The essential existence of a text lies in its meaning, as that of a human being in his or her spirit. The bodily features are the externalized form the spirit of a human being has taken on, and therefore serve as a mirror in which to see into his or her character. It is like this that the language and styles of the Qur'ān are the form of its meaning and therefore cannot be separated from it.

The second step to understand the Qur'ān is penetrating its meaning, which requires practicing it in the daily life. Although its language constitutes its outer form and structure and therefore very important in penetrating its meaning, restriction to its language in understanding the Qur'ān means restriction to the form or formalism. One can penetrate the meaning of the Qur'ān, in which its essential existence lies, through his or her "heart" which is the seat of his/her spirit. This requires that the heart should be purified by refraining from sins and evils, doing the necessary acts of worship and living a pious life.

The Qur'ān is, in the words of the late Professor Haluk Nurbaki, a Turkish scientist, "like a rose which continuously grows petals in the womb of time" (Nurbaki, 14). As sciences develop and contribute to penetrating through its depths of meaning, the Qur'ān becomes more and more in bloom and grows younger and fresher. This is why, besides having sufficient knowledge of the topics such as "abrogation of laws, laws and principles dependent on certain conditions and unconditioned, general and particular rules and the occasions on which the verses were revealed," knowing the general principles of natural sciences is also of great importance. In addition, since it is the Prophet Muḥammad, upon him be peace and blessings, who received the Qur'ān and taught and practiced it first of all in the daily life as an infallible authority, knowing his Sunnah, the way he practiced the Qur'ān, and the example he set in living Islam, is indispensable to understanding the Qur'ān.

The Qur'ān is not a book of sciences, nor a book of history, nor a book of morality only. Nor is it a book in the sense that the word "book" signifies. It is a book to be practiced; it came to guide people to truth, to educate people both intellectually and spiritually and to govern their life in both the individual and social realm. Therefore it can be understood by practicing it in the daily life. This point can be better understood when we consider that the Qur'ān was not revealed on one occasion only; it was revealed on many diverse occasions during the 23 years of Muḥammad's Prophethood. Separating the Qur'ān and the practical life means reducing the Qur'ān to being only a book to read. It does not unfold itself much to those who approach it as if it was only a book to "read."

Another point to stress concerning understanding the Qur'ān is this:

The Qur'ān is a book of medium-size and, at first glance, contains repetitions. However, it declares that there is nothing "wet and dry" but it is in a Manifest Book, that is, the Qur'ān itself (6: 59). As stated in a Prophetic saying, it contains the history of previous peoples, the tidings of those to come after its revelation and the solutions to the disagreements between people. It addresses all levels of understanding and knowledge in all places at all times, and satisfies them. Hundreds of interpreters who have written commentaries on it during the 14 centuries of Islam have derived different meanings from it but none of them has ever claimed that he or she has been able to comprehend the whole of it. Thousands of jurists have inferred laws from it and based their juridical reasoning on it but no one among them has ever asserted that he or she has been able to infer all the laws contained in it and understand all the reasons behind its injunctions and prohibitions. All the pure, exacting scholars who have been able to "marry" the mind and heart, all the revivers – the greatest, saintly scholars who have come at certain times to revive and restore Islam – have found their ways in it, all saints have derived from it their sources of inspiration and ways of purification, and all the paths of Sufism have depended on it, but, like a source of water which increases as it flows, it has remained as if untouched.

It is due to its miraculous eloquence that the Qur'ān has such depth and richness of meaning. One of the elements on which the Qur'ān's eloquence is based is its creative style rich in arts. It frequently speaks in parables and adopts a figurative, symbolic rhetoric using metaphors and similes. This is natural because it contains knowledge of all things and addresses all levels of understanding and knowledge.

Ignoring such symbolic and artistic style of the Qur'ān in contentment with the outward meaning of its expressions caused the appearance of a superficial, narrow-minded current called *Ẓāhiriyyah*. Just opposite this is another current called *Bāṭiniyyah* (esotericism), which searches for the whole of truth in symbols in negligence of the outward meaning of the expressions. Both currents are harmful. The middle way is always preferable.

IS A FULL, EXACT TRANSLATION OF THE QUR'ĀN POSSIBLE?

The question "Is a full, exact translation of the Qur'ān possible?" has been the cause of hot debates in the Muslim world for almost a century. This is a question asked without due consideration. For, first of all, a language is not a set of molds made up of letters and words. As his or her style of speech or writing gives a human being away, the language of a nation is a mirror to that nation's character molded by their culture, history, religion, and even the land where they live. It is almost impossible that any word used in a language is not the exact counterpart of the word used for the same meaning in another. That word has different connotations and associations particular to each people using it and different impressions on each. For example, according to the majority of Muslim scholars, the word *qur'ān* is derived from the verb *qirā'ah* meaning reading or reciting, and means recitation. Although *Qur'ān* has been the proper name for the book sent to the Prophet, upon him be peace and blessings, even as a common noun in the infinitive form, it is not the exact counterpart of "reading" or "recitation" in English or another word used for the same meaning in another language. A language with all its words is a living entity changing forms and undergoing adaptations during the history of the people using it.

Second, Arabic is a strictly grammatical language. The rules of its grammar is established. It is the richest language of the world in conjugation and derivation. For example, there are three different types of infinitive in Arabic, and, in addition, a verb has 35 different infinitive forms, each of which has different connotations and implications. Again, the tenses do not always have the same meaning and usage in every language. For instance, the Qur'ān describes the events of the Judgment Day in the past tense, although the Judgment Day will come in the future. Besides other reasons of this usage, the simple past tense in Arabic is also used to give the meaning that a future event will doubtlessly take place. Also, the present tense is not the same in Arabic and in English. Let alone such differences between any two languages, there are differences in using the present perfect tense in the British and American English. As another characteristic of language, while in Arabic nouns are classified into two genders (masculine and feminine), in English there are three forms of gender. In English nouns have two forms of number: singular and plural, while adjectives and verbs do not have no plural forms. As for Arabic, it has three forms of number for both nouns and adjectives and verbs: singular, dual, and plural. In addition, in Arabic nouns have many plural forms, each of which has differences of implications.

The Qur'ān has another important peculiarity which makes its exact translation into another language almost impossible.

The Qur'ān has made many of its words each into a concept. Besides the word *qur'ān*, many other words such as *rabb* (lord), *ilāh* (deity), *malik* (sovereign), *kitāb* (book), *waḥy* (revelation), *dīn* (religion), *millah* (nation, way), *sharī'ah*, *'ibādah* (worship, adoration), *taqwā* (piety and righteousness), *iḥsān* (perfect goodness or excellence, doing something fully aware that God is seeing His servants), *waliyy* (friend, saint), *nūr* (light), *nabiyy* (prophet), *rasūl* (messenger), *islām*, *īmān* (faith, belief) and other words with the addition that the words which gave rise to a branch of knowledge or science called the Sciences of the Qur'ān, such as *muḥkam* (the established, the decisive), *mutashābih* (the parabolical, the allegorical), *tafsīr* (interpretation), *ta'wīl* (exegesis), *nāsikh* (the abrogator) and *mansūkh* (the abrogated) are each a concept which it is impossible to render in another language without necessary explanations.

The reasons why the exact translation of the Qur'ān into another language is not possible are not limited to those mentioned here. That is why no rendering of the Qur'ān can be substituted for it and recited in the Prayers.

ON THIS STUDY OF INTERPRETATION

So far many studies have been made to be able to render the meaning of the Qur'ān in other languages. Each study surely is superior to others in many respects, yet in many others inferior to them. Nevertheless, it is also true that in many of those studies, in addition to many shortcomings, there may be mistakes of understanding.

We do not have any claim that this study, which is partly based on the interpretation of venerable Suat Yıldırım, the renowned professor of the Qur'ānic interpretation in Turkey, is superior to others. However, it differs from them in the following, important points:

- As mentioned earlier, as almost every verse of the Qur'ān has an independent existence, it also has intrinsic relation with every other verse and the totality of the Qur'ān. Therefore, understanding and interpreting a verse requires having a complete knowledge and understanding of the Qur'ān as a whole and considering the totality of it. It should not be forgotten that the main interpreter of the Qur'ān is the Qur'ān itself; as verses interpret one another, the Qur'ān as a whole also interprets each of them. We have tried to strictly observe this unique feature of the Qur'ān.

- Bediüzzaman Said Nursi frequently draws the attention to the depths of the meaning the wording of the Qur'ān has as one of the aspects of its being miraculous. For example, since in Arabic, the definite article *al* adds inclusiveness to the word, he interprets "*al-ḥamdu* – the praise" at the beginning of *Sūrat al-Fātiḥah*: "All praise and gratitude that everyone has given to others since the beginning of the human life on the earth for any reason on any occasion and will give until the Last Day, are for God."

• Also, from the characteristics of the words used and the word-order in the sentence, *Out of what We have provided for them* (of wealth, knowledge, power, etc.,) *they spend* (to provide sustenance for the needy and in God's cause, purely for the good pleasure of God and without placing others under obligation), that comes in the 3rd verse of *Sūrat al-Baqarah*, the 2nd *sūrah*, he infers the following rules or conditions of giving alms:

1. In order to make their alms-giving acceptable to God, believers must give out of their belongings such amount that they themselves will not have to need to receive alms. *Out of* in *Out of what* expresses this condition.

2. Believers must not transfer to the needy from another's goods, but they must give out of their own belongings. The phrase, *what We have provided for them* points to this condition. The meaning is: "Believers give out of what We have provided for *them*, (not out of what We have provided for others)."

3. Believers must not remind those to whom they have given of the kindness they have done to them. *We* in *We have provided* indicates this condition, for it means: "It is We who have provided for you wealth out of which you give to the poor as sustenance. Therefore, by giving to a servant of Ours out of Our property, you cannot put them under obligation."

4. Believers must not fear that they may become poor because they give others. The pronoun *We* in *We have provided* points to this. Since it is God Who provides for us and commands us to spend for others, He will not cause us to become poor because of giving others.

5. Believers must give to those who will spend it for their livelihood. It is not acceptable to give to those who will dissipate it. The phrase, *They spend to provide sustenance*, points to this condition.

6. Believers must give for God's sake. *We have provided for them*, states this condition. It means: "Essentially, it is Our property out of which you spend, therefore you must spend in Our Name."

7. The word *what* in *Out of what* signifies that whatever God provides for a person is included in the meaning of *rizq* (provision.) Therefore, one must spend not only out of one's goods, but also out of whatever one has. Therefore a good word, an act of help, a piece of advice, and teaching are all included in the meaning of provision and spendin as sustenance for others (*İşârâtü'l-Îcâz*, 40).

Together with all these conditions, the meaning of the expression, the original of which comprises three words, becomes: "Out of what We have provided for them of wealth, knowledge, and power, etc., believing that it is We Who provide and therefore without feeling any fear that they may become poor because of giving and without putting those to whom they give under obligation, they spend both in God's cause and to provide sustenance for the needy who are sensible enough not to dissipate what is given to them, such amount that they themselves will not have to need to receive alms."

In this study of interpretation, we have tried to consider such depths of meaning to the extent that the scope of the study allows.

- It is of considerable significance that the Qur'ān was revealed within 23 years on certain occasions. Therefore its due, correct understanding caused the birth of an important science called The Sciences of the Qur'ān, which includes a wide range of the topics such as abrogation of a law or verse by others, generalization or particularization of the meaning because of certain occasions or conjuncture, and the occasions on which verses were revealed. If these points are not given due consideration in interpreting the Qur'ān, one with a superficial view can have the impression that there are contradictions in the Qur'ān. In order to prevent such an impression, we have tried to take these points into consideration. For example:

> O you who believe! If you follow those who disbelieve (the hypocrites and Jews in Madīnah who spread negative propaganda concerning the events at Uhud), they will drive you back on your heels (into unbelief), and you will turn utter losers (in both this world and the next). (3: 149)

This verse commands that the believers should not obey the unbelievers. However, like many commandments in the Qur'ān, this one has also relative aspects according to time and conditions. Besides, the verse must have a connection with the verses before and after it. To see this connection sometimes requires knowing the reason for its revelation.

After the Battle of Uhud the hypocrites and Jews began to propagate that had Muḥammad been a true Prophet, he would not have suffered the reverse at Uhud. They tried to persuade the Muslims to turn back into their former state of unbelief. The Muslims this verse addressed in Madīnah knew what specifically it was about. For this reason, in order to clarify the meaning and the direct purpose for the verse's revelation, it requires to have interpretation with explanations. However, in doing this, we should never forget that with respect to its meaning, connotations and the commandments it contains, a verse can in no way be restricted to the occasion on which it was revealed. "It does not prevent the commandment a verse contains from having a general, inclusive area of enforcement that it was revealed on a certain occasion," is a rule in both the Qur'ānic interpretation and Islamic Jurisprudence.

- The structure and character of the words used in the Qur'ān are the source of diverse meanings. For example, the being that refused to prostrate before Adam was Iblīs but it was Satan when it approached Adam to deceive him in the Garden. It is possible to deduce from this word what happened between its refusal to prostrate before Adam and its approaching to deceive him, and this should be shown in a study of interpretation. So the shortest meaning of the verse 2: 36 is as follows:

> *(Iblis was inherently devoid of good, and defeated by his vainglory, disobeyed God's command and was driven out from the Garden, becoming Satan despair of God's mercy and accursed Satan. Tempting Adam and Eve to the forbidden tree despite Our pre-warning,) Satan caused them both to deflect therefrom and brought them out of the (happy) state in which they were; and We said, 'Go down, all of you, (and henceforth you will live a life,) some of you being the enemies of the others. There will be for you on the the earth (where you have already been appointed as vicegerent) a habitation and provision until an appointed time.*

Unfortunately, we have not been able make the whole of this study with such broadness.

- The explanatory words that we have had to put (usually in brackets) before or within the translations of the verses are not additions to, nor any sort of adaptations of, the meaning of the verses. They express the full normal meaning of the words, understood individually and in context. By "context" we mean both the context of the passage or the *sūrah* or the Qur'ān as a whole, and also the historical context, the situation that is the background to the verses. Also, we should be aware that the Qur'ān is miraculous in its power of concision, of conveying much in few words. Sometimes this concision is achieved through the powerful compactness of the structures and syntax of the language of Arabic, raised to inimitable perfection in the Qur'ān. A relatively uninflected language like English simply cannot reproduce the full meaning without explanations to convey the meaning that is carried in the words of the Arabic by their inflection, position in the sentence, etc. Sometimes the concision of the Qur'ān is achieved through ellipsis, that is, through omission of what is already known or easily knowable to one familiar with the language and the subject-matter (see the next point).

  The occasions on which the verses were revealed require explanatory additions (as well as notes) because the historical context is not known to us in the way that it was known to the first addressees of the Qur'ān. However, it is important to clarify that, while the historical context is important for the meaning of the verses and, equally important, for the links between them, it does not restrict their meaning. Everyone should respond to the Qur'ān as if its words and meanings were being revealed to them as the first addressees of the Revelation. Knowing the historical context of certain verses or passages in fact enhances understanding of their present and permanent relevance, it does not diminish or restrict it.

- It is impossible to find a single ample word in the Qur'ān. While narrating the events, without getting into detail, it gives the main points and refers the detail to the mind. The listener or reader can supply what is missing from familiarity with the story and/or ordinary common sense. For example, in the verse 2: 35, the Divine command to Adam and Eve not to approach the (forbidden) tree is

followed by Satan's causing them to "stumble." Several incidents happened between these two events. These should be given in a study of interpretation.
To cite another example:

> *Now after all that time, of the two (prisoners) the one who had been*
> *delivered remembered (what Joseph had asked him to remember) and he*
> *said: "I will inform you of its meaning, so send me forth!" "Joseph, O man*
> *of truth!..."* (12: 45–46)

Between *so send me forth* and *Joseph, o man of truth!*, there are several
events that the narrative omits: "So send me forth to Joseph so that I may ask
him about the dream's interpretation. They sent him. He left the king's court to
get to the prison. He arrived there and, on receiving permission from the prison
guard to enter, did so. He came to Joseph and, after exchanging greetings with
him, said: Joseph, o man of truth!" By omitting these events, the Qur'ān narrates
briefly and to the point without any loss of clarity. However, in this study we
have tried to mention some of such omitted events in brackets to make it easy
for the reader to understand.

- The Qur'ān's verses interpret one another, so in order to understand the exact
  and complete meaning of a verse, we should consider the verses particularly
  related to it. For example, the verse 2: 42 should be interpreted taking into consideration the verses 2: 71, 79, 140, 174, 179; 3: 167; 4: 13, 46; 5: 106:

> *Do not confound the truth by mixing it with falsehood, and do not*
> *conceal the truth while you know (the meaning and outcome of what*
> *you do, and that what you strive to hide is true, and that Muḥammad*
> *is the Messenger of God, the Messenger whose coming you have been*
> *anticipating).*

In many of the Qur'ānic interpretations, interpreters are content with making a literal translation. For example, in this verse, they do not mention what
it is that the Children of Israel know and conceal. However, we have tried to
make the meaning as clear as possible either through annotations or putting
explanations in brackets.

- The tenses used and passing from one tense to the other, the nouns being definite
  and indefinite, and the kind of the clauses (noun or verb – a clause beginning
  with a verb is a verb clause), and the adressee being in the second or the third
  person – the person in absence – all of these make important contributions to
  the meaning. For example, from the verse 2: 30 downward, God addresses Adam
  directly, but in the verse 37 coming after the verse telling his approaching the
  forbidden tree, He addresses him in the third person. This means that Adam got
  into a new way of relationship with his Lord. Also, the verb *telaqqā* used in the
  meaning of receiving connotes perceiving to be inspired. So the shades of meaning that all such features of language contribute to the verses should be given in
  a study of the Qur'ānic interpretation. The shortest of this verse is as follows:

> *(Aware of his lapse and in the hope of retrieving his error, rather than attempting to find excuses for it,) Adam received from his Lord, (with Whom he got into a new way of relationship,) words (that he perceived to be inspired into him because of his remorse), and (asked for God's forgiveness through them.) In return, He accepted His repentance. He is the One Who truly returns repentance with liberal forgiveness, the All-Compassionate.*

- Another important point:

  The shortest meaning of the verse 2: 27 provided by the character of the words is as follows:

> *(Those) who break God's covenant (which is a rope of light woven of the threads of Divine Will, Wisdom and Favor, and responsible for the order in the universe, and able to establish peace, order and harmony in human life) after its solemn binding, and sever the bonds God commanded to be joined (among the relatives as a requirement of blood relationship, and among people as required by human social needs), and (in an attempt to spread their vices in the whole community, even in the whole world, like one who, having caught a contagious disease, desires to pass it to others) cause disorder and corruption on earth. Such are those who are the losers (in both this world and the next).*

The meanings given in brackets are not commentary; they are the meanings provided by the words used in the verse and their order, as well as the grammar rules and styles. For example, the original word translated as "break" is *NeQaḌa*, which means raveling a thick, strong rope. This implies that God's Covenant is a strong rope binding people together and humanity to God. The word *mīthāq* translated as binding corroborates this meaning. God's Covenant is a rope of light woven of His Will, Wisdom, Knowledge, and Favoring, and which extends from the eternity in the past to the eternity in the future. Being responsible for the magnificent order in the universe and establishing the relationship among all creatures, one of its ends was given to the hand of humanity. The present environmental pollution and the state of things in the world are the result of breaking God's Covenant. The verse uses God's Covenant, which is a rope binding people together and humanity to God, together with the bonds (among people, including particularly among the relatives) to be joined.

In this study, we have preferred to give these meanings sometimes in brackets and sometimes as notes.

- While narrating the series of events or God's blessings, the Qur'ān follows such a style that it provokes minds to ask questions and the suceeding event or the blessing provides an answer to them. For example, while mentioning the blessings of Paradise in the verse 2: 25, one who lives in a palace surrounded by trees among which rivers flow will not be saved from feeling lonely and need a companion. The Qur'ān presents to the view pure spouses. If there is something to cloud such a blessing, it is death, and the Qur'ān removes this worry by immediately adding that the life in Paradise is eternal. So, the meaning of this verse is as follows:

Give glad tidings to those who believe and do good, righteous deeds: for them are Gardens beneath (the palaces and through the trees of) which rivers flow. Every time they are provided with fruits (of different color, shape, taste, and smell and that are constantly renewed) therefrom, they say, "This is what we were provided with before." For they are given to them in resemblance (to what was given to them both in the world, and just before in the Gardens, familiar in shape and color so that they may not be unattractive because unknown). Furthermore, for them are spouses eternally purified (of all kinds of worldly uncleanliness.) They will abide there (forever).

- As mentioned before, the verses of the Qur'ān interpret each other and make references to one another through the same words and expressions. Besides, there are words and conceptions functioning as the frame of the Qur'ān's meaning, such as *Rabb* (Lord), *taqwā* (piety and righteousness), *iḥsān* (perfect goodness or excellence, doing something fully aware that God is seeing His servants), *'ibādah* (worship), *islām* (submission to God), *kufr* (unbelief; concealing the truth willingly and rejecting it), and so on. Although these conceptions should be interpreted in their full meaning, we have not been able to do so thinking that it would be too long for the readers to follow making it difficult to concentrate on.

  To sum up: The features of the Qur'ān's style and aspects of its miraculousness caused paranthetical explanations in this study. They are all the meanings the verses contain, not our additions.

- Another point to mention is that some of the precepts or practices in Islam – such as slavery, *jihād* (holy strife in God's cause), permission to war and women's share in inheritance – have been made the subject of biased criticism by its enemies and a hot debate by its friends and defenders. Throughout this study, we have tried to clarify these points.

During the study, despite his chronic illnesses, occupations, and being surrounded by many negative factors, venerable Fethullah Gülen Hocaefendi has never refrained from sparing his encouragement, support, guidance, and corrections. Therefore I am much grateful to him and other friends because of their generous help. I also thank Mr. Jamil Qureshi from Oxford, England, and Mrs. Jane Louise Kandur for editing the English text.

Again, I am thankful to Hüseyin Bingül for his valuable proofreading, and to Fikret Yaşar, Hakan Yeşilova, Ekrem Tez, and İbrahim Akdağ for their technical assistance.

It is on us to strive and it is the Almighty Who will give success, if He wills. I close with begging prayers from all believers for this humble servant for sincerity, purity of intention, conviction in the pillars of faith and obtaining the approval and good pleasure of our Lord, our Creator.

ON THE HOLY QUR'ĀN AND ITS INTERPRETATION

M. Fethullah Gülen

The Qur'ān is God's miraculous, matchless message that has been sent to all humanity via His last Messenger. With the Qur'ān God has shown humanity, one last time, a short-cut to His good pleasure. He has communicated to us about His Essence, Attributes, and Names. He has expressed in the most explicit way, leaving no room for any misunderstanding, His will to be known and recognized in the correct way, to be believed in and worshipped. Almighty God has put emphasis on the duties and responsibilities of believers, while enthusing hearts and agitating souls with His warrant for punishment and promise for reward. He has presented the Qur'ān as a sign for perfection and completion and as an orbit to rotate around for His good pleasure, while condescending to offer this gift to us as a compliment greater than any that has been or will ever be granted to anyone else. The Qur'ān is the most radiant and enduring of the hundreds of miracles bestowed upon the Master of creation, upon him be the best of blessings and peace. In addition to its wondrous discourse, articulation, and styles of expression, with its social discipline, legal rulings, principles of good morality, and education, its analysis of the whole creation including especially humanity, with its many allusions and indications to the essentials of almost all the sciences, which are sometimes even presented as manifest expressions, and the alternative solutions it offers for many administrative, economic, and political problems, the Qur'ān is the ultimate source of reference for everyone and for all times. It is an untainted fountain with an infinite resource; it is a vast ocean which can never be dimmed by even the most complicated and filthy of eras.

With all respect for its grandeur, I have to confess my inability and insufficiency to elaborate on the depth of meaning and richness of expression and style of the Qur'ān. A considerable number of studies have been dedicated to the Qur'ān, and many more studies will be carried out on this topic. There is no doubt that all these studies have presented valuable content for any seeking person to grasp the gist of what the Qur'ān stands for and to believe in its message, and they mirror the order of Islam in its true essence. However, it would not be right for anyone to claim that they have come up with a perfect interpretation of the endless content of this expository atlas of humankind, the universe and the truth of Divinity. The Qur'ān can be interpreted only to the extent that a heavenly and Divine word can be interpreted by human perception. Thus, although it does not seem to be possible to spell out this huge atlas within the measures of an article, we cannot stay indifferent to or neglect studying the Qur'ān with the excuse that our interpretations are deficient or the power of our discourse is inadequate. Everyone has the right to study the Qur'ān, more than that, it is a duty upon those equipped with necessary, accurate knowledge. We should work harder to better understand the Qur'ān, while the learned should wield all their perceptiveness and sensations toward understanding it and conveying its message, allowing a wider audience to learn more from it. Indeed, the Qur'ān is the greatest gift from the Mercy of God to the human mind to be understood and to be conveyed to others. Understanding the Qur'ān is both a duty and an act of gratitude, whereas conveying its message to those hearts in need of its light is a prerequisite of respect and fidelity.

The Qur'ān is a miracle of eloquence honored with the merit of being the voice of all ages. It is the most luminous expression of the Divine Speech, around whose light the angels hover like moths. If we take into consideration its Source and purpose of revelation, its first representative(s) and the impact it leaves on hearts, then we must realize that it is not a book to put to one side. When the Qur'ān speaks, angels fall deep into a silent vigilance, spirit beings fall prostrate, and the jinn, enchanted with its voice, set out to the deserts to meet it.

The Qur'ān is the expression and explanation of God's laws of creation or "nature," and the strongest and immutable source of religious rules and pillars. The Qur'ān is the indisputable Book that includes the most reliable criteria for studying existence (the whole universe and humankind), thus for all individual, familial, social, or ethical problems we must seek wisdom and illumination from the Qur'ān; it cries out that its source is the all-encompassing Knowledge of the One Who knows everything with their causes and results. The Qur'ān has captivated everyone to whom its voice has reached – provided they were not prejudiced – with its holistic perspective, comprehensive discourse and style, the vastness of its content and meaning, its delicate expressions, its magical expounding in proportion to the different levels of knowledge and understanding, and its capacity to penetrate souls. Neither its friends nor its foes have been able to come up with something in a similar style or an utterance that is equal in grandiosity, the former motivated for imitation, the latter in fury to choke off its voice, despite their efforts for almost fourteen centuries, even when they use the same material and concentrate on the same issues. Their works have never been able to overcome artificiality, they have never been appreciated by masters of literary skills, and they have never evoked any lasting or effective influence.

The Qur'ān has such a musical harmony and delicate correlations between the topics it deals with, be they interrelated or apparently unrelated with each other, so that one is able to realize, with only the slightest effort of comprehensive thinking, that many apparently unrelated topics have points of junction. The mastership of discourse belongs to the Qur'ān, which no literary personality can challenge, and enables those of its audience who are unprejudiced and can judge with some reason to obtain some things from it, introducing them to deeper contemplation beyond their horizons of thought. If once they can judge fairly and let their souls delve into this heavenly waterfall of expression, all other speech-like voices will immediately turn into nothing but rumblings.

Above all, the Qur'ān has come from an all-encompassing Knowledge; it contains and explains the meaning and content of human and non-human existence, of humankind, nature, and all the worlds; it is both their language and interpreter of their purpose of creation. It speaks to multifarious dimensions of its audience all at the same time: while addressing the mind, it does not neglect to speak to the heart in its own language; when it calls out to the consciousness, it does not push emotions aside; while conversing with the faculties of reasoning and logic, it does not leave the soul without any favor. All faculties and senses, external and internal, benefit from the Qur'ān, which gives each its share without giving rise to any deprivation and contradiction. They all receive their share from this heavenly table, each to the extent of its capacity, and enjoy a most harmonious composition.

All Divine Scriptures, especially before human interpolations were mixed with the original texts, possessed the same holistic approach and all-embracing quality; nevertheless the superiority and widest comprehension of the Qur'ān are evident in proportion to the profundity of the spirit of the Prophet Muḥammad, upon him be peace and blessings. It is by no means possible to show any other heavenly or man-made book which excels it with its content and extensiveness. It is by no means an exaggeration to claim its uniqueness in dealing with humanity, the universe and Divinity in the most comprehensive, as well as the most exquisite fashion, while interpreting them in the best forms of synthesis and analysis in its own way.

All of the topics that the Qur'ān deals with are the most valuable treasures of the truths pertaining to Divinity and the realm of creation. Some of these truths are decisive or explicit in meaning and content, and others are concise, metaphorical, and allegorical, the explanation of which has been entrusted to the one who brought the Qur'ān, upon him be peace and blessings, and the scholars favored with inspiration. The Qur'ān never complicates any of the matters it presents or analyzes. It presents topics concerned with the essentials of faith, worship, and morality, and basic principles of individual and social life clearly and succinctly; while for matters requiring comprehensive thinking, reflection, and careful consideration, it demands deeper examination and scrutiny, and suggests turning to God, without approving of burdening oneself with grave matters that one cannot shoulder. Like a magical chandelier which continuously shines brighter, it is a means for brand new discoveries at diverse wavelengths as hearts and minds go deeper in thought, thus offering Divine gifts of all kinds to our internal and external senses. With its blessings and inspirations augmenting in excess, and light rain becoming a deluge, and with its endless beauty and glittering lights, the Qur'ān showers banquets one within another to those who ponder and study it.

True understanding of existence and what lies beyond the sensed dimension of the cosmos, and also humankind with its spiritual depths is possible only through the Qur'ān. They discover in its bright realm straight thinking and real sources of reflection, and are thereby saved from the vicious circles of deception and misjudgments based on probabilities. There is no other source of knowledge that is not mistaken or not entrusted to uncertainty or doubt other than this miraculous Speech from God, the All-Knowing of the Unseen. The Qur'ān explains and presents everything explicitly, plainly, and correctly. It enables us to understand that it is we who make errors in evaluating the issues, giving rise to contradictory judgments and in filling in the gaps entrusted to reflection. Understanding and interpreting the Qur'ān correctly is not only a duty upon us, but also a requirement of our fidelity to it. The fulfillment of this duty and fidelity is closely related with the erudition of every capable and well-equipped individual and in their living in devotion to God. Such individuals dive into this vast ocean with utmost sincerity and commitment for the good pleasure of God, uncovering the truth so that it flourishes. They proceed toward this infinite horizon with caution, composure, comprehensive thought, and without surrendering to their carnality. The Messenger, who brought the Qur'ān from God, is their first and greatest guide; they follow the pious scholars among the earliest generations of Islam in the light of its expressions, which are decisive and explicit in meaning and content. They are less likely to err; their efforts to attain the pleasure of God are rewarded with special treatment. Their interpretations and explanations of the Qur'ān are each a hue and adornment of Qur'ānic uniqueness.

On the other hand, the Qur'ān cannot be explained as it deserves in consideration of its position and loftiness with rudimentary Arabic and the limited scope of dictionaries; such an attempt would also be manifest disrespect to this heavenly monument of speech. It should be rendered in other languages as is required. Anything concerning Qur'ānic expositions (*tafsīr*) should be very well versed and before they are launched, every *tafsīr* should be tested against the exalted Islamic sciences. What falls to us is not to bring the Divine Word down to our level of perception and expression in its immeasurable immensity and depth, excusing such an act as we have translated it for the benefit of everyone.

While it is a duty, an appreciation of, or an act of respect toward the Qur'ān for experts to make the Qur'ān known to everyone via exposition, interpretation, or a commentary, such an attempt would be paramount to insolence if one did not have a high command of Arabic grammar, the principles of rhetoric or eloquence, knowledge of the study of Qur'anic exposition (*tafsīr*), the methodology of *hadīth* studies (Traditions of Prophet) and Islamic jurisprudence (*fiqh*). The Qur'an cannot be translated as a novel is; even the translation of a novel calls for an expertise in its own genre.

Forging the way toward a sound interpretation of the Qur'an, it would be better to discuss first what a "translation" is, and what *tafsīr* (exposition) and *ta'wīl* (commentary) mean.

Translation is the rendering of a text or statement in one language into another language, while preserving the meaning. An accurate translation would be to transfer the exact meaning of every word – if this is ever possible – while preserving the relationships between word combinations. On the other hand, a literal translation of the words only, or an exclusively semantic translation would be a deficient translation.

To a certain extent we can also talk about translation software; however, the current technology or even more advanced technology to come is not able to help very much in the translation of substantial literary works. Consider the situation when the text is the Word of God, which addresses all times, conditions, and levels and therefore the exposition of which with all its depths is considerably dependent on time, inspiration, and circumstances. Some works of literature are said to be impossible to accurately render; then it is clear that there is no way that the Holy Qur'ān, with its immense profundity, can be expressed by an ordinary translation.

Many Muslim scholars, including Bediüzzaman Said Nursi, are of the opinion that it is impossible to translate the Qur'ān, due to the aforementioned and many other considerations. Some other scholars, on the other hand, approach the matter cautiously, but more moderately, provided that the prerequisites underscored above have been abided with.

The late Hamdi Yazır,[1] one of the greatest contemporary expounders of the Qur'ān, states that the translation must exactly correspond to the original text in terms of explicitness and indications, conciseness and comprehensiveness, generalizations and specifics, restrictedness or exclusiveness and inclusiveness, powerfulness, and appropriateness, and eloquence and style. Therefore, prose or poetry can be translated into another language which is as developed as the original language, with the condition that the translator is well-versed with the subtleties of both languages; however such a translation is hardly possible for a book which addresses the mind and heart, the soul and all the senses together, with all its diverse literary delicacy, and its vigor and exuberance. And what happens if the book to be translated is a work of God that transcends all other books Divine or non-Divine with its dimensions beyond time and space, and speaks to all ages?!...

The Qur'ān is, in the words of Bediüzzaman Said Nursi, a Divine interpretation of the book of existence; it is the voice and breath of the laws of creation, the true interpreter of things and events that bear multifarious meanings, a candid expounder of this world and the world to come, the revealer of the treasure of the Divine Names hidden in the heavens and on the earth, the mysterious key to the mysteries beyond all things, the plain language of the beyond manifested in this world; the sun, the foundation, and the geometry of the spiritual world of Islam, the sacred map that explicitly lays out the worlds of the Hereafter with clearly drawn lines, the voice and clearest interpreter of the Divine Essence, Attributes, and Names, the most reliable teacher of all humanity; the air, the water, and the light of the Islamic world, and the Word of the All-Exalted, All-Majestic Being, Who is the Creator and Lord of all worlds, and His decree and address.

This is not to say that the Qur'ān cannot be understood; on the contrary and most importantly of all, it was revealed to humanity to be understood and to be lived by. However, its phrases are so deep and have so many meanings, its content is so multilayered, that even if we can know and understand the meaning of every single word, and sense certain things from word combinations, we will certainly miss many truths that are contained in styles, indications, suggestions, connotations, and purposes, that cannot be fully reflected in any translation.

I am of the opinion that every person who approaches the Qur'an with an open mind can perceive all of the above characteristics, and thus appreciate that its sublimity and transcendence cannot be confided to a simple translation. A translation might certainly have some value in proportion to the translator's learning, knowledge, horizon of perception, and skills; however, it can never convey the Qur'ān in all its profundity; therefore no translation, nor no commentary or interpretation can be called the Qur'ān itself.

---

1   Hamdi Yazır is a twentieth century Turkish scholar of Islam who is most renowned for his Qur'anic interpretation, *Hak Dini Kur'an Dili* ("The Qur'ān; The Language of the Religion of Truth").

TAFSĪR AND *TA'WĪL*

We all have a need for the Qur'ān and thus are obliged to understand it, even if at different levels. In order to penetrate its essence and understand it according to what it really and essentially is we must study it following a comprehensive exposition (*tafsīr*) that has been prepared in accordance with the methodology of the science of *tafsīr* by learned scholars. We should not narrow down its content, which is as extensive as all the worlds, to the level of our inadequate learning, knowledge, and perception.

Tafsīr is an exposition which entails an effort to reflect the content of a text. A Qur'ānic *tafsīr* is an exposition of the Divine Word that takes into account the grammar, the principles of eloquence, and the explanations of God's Messenger and the earliest Muslim generations (the Messenger's Companions), as well as an exposition illuminated by the light of the mind and the rays of the heart. Most of the *tafsīr*s prepared so far can be said to comply with this. Any given *tafsīr* can be defined according to the dominance of any feature given above. For instance, if the *tafsīr* is based in various ways upon the commentaries and explanations of the Messenger of God, as well as on the opinions of the Companions who best understood the language of the time, then this is a "*tafsīr* based on Traditions or knowledge reported (from the Messenger and his Companions)" (*at-tafsīr ar-riwāyah*). A "*tafsīr* by expert knowledge" (*at-tafsīr ad-dirāyah*), on the other hand, is an exposition based on, in addition to reported knowledge, a direct or indirect studying of linguistics, literature, and other relevant fields of science.

In earlier times, the Qur'ān was primarily expounded by recourse to the Qur'ān itself, with the Sunnah being the second source of its exposition. The explanations of the Prophet, upon him be peace and blessings, were always the most reliable source from which the Companions benefited. Most of the Companions already had a good command of the language, therefore they encountered few problems. Those issues which needed explanation were either referred to the Prophet or clarified by the Prophet himself without any recourse.

In later times, large volumes that compiled such statements, explanations, and expositions were gathered, an effort which was initially started earlier by some Companions. A very rich heritage was left behind by the *Tābi'ūn* (the generation of Muslims who came after the Companions) to the following centuries. Verifying scholars, such as Muḥammad ibn Jarīr aṭ-Ṭabarī, made great use of this heritage from the tenth century onwards. Alongside the explanations of the Prophet, upon him be peace and blessings, the collections composed of the reports from the Companions and the next two generations have always constituted a reliable source for scholars.

Az-Zamakhsharī, a scholar of Mu'tazilah and a master of the language, is considered to be one of the pioneers of the "*tafsīr* by expert knowledge" with his *al-Kashshāf* ("The Discoverer"). Fakhru'd-Dīn ar-Rāzī's *Mafātīḥ al-Ghayb* ("The Keys to the Unseen") is one of the most powerful voices of the Sunnī *tafsīr* approach and trend, and is considered to be one of the greatest representatives of this tradition. Bayḍāwī's *Anwar at-Tanzīl wa Asrār at-Ta'wīl* ("The Lights of the Revelation and the Mysteries in Its Meaning") is one of the significant links in the chain of *tafsīr*s; this is of particular significance as it contains answers to Zamakhsharī's Mu'tazilī thoughts and considerations.

Subsequent centuries witnessed a number of *tafsīr* studies within the framework of Sufism and jurisprudence. Ebu'l-Lays as-Samarkandī, Baghawī, İbn Kathīr, Jalālu'd-Dīn as-Suyūṭī, Ebu's-Suūd, Kemalpaşazade, İsmail Hakkı Bursevî, Ālūsī al-Baghdādī, Konyalı Vehbî and Allame Hamdi Yazır are some of the distinguished figures who have preserved this sacred tradition.

A majority of these figures and others have dedicated utmost care to their expositions; they did whatever needed to be done with superhuman effort in order to accurately understand the Divine purposes in the Qur'ān. They carefully studied word by word how the Companions, who constituted the first row of its audience, understood and interpreted the Qur'ān; their studies were based on the essentials of the Religion in their studies and approach to the Qur'ān and they tested their personal opinions against the disciplines of the Qur'ānic study and the authentic Sunnah. Thus, they discarded distorted crumbs of information which had been put forward by the enemies of the Qur'ān as commentary and explanations. Their effort was a marvelous feat by which we are better able to understand the will of God.

It is also worth noting at this point Hamdi Yazır's thoughts on *tafsīr*: *Tafsīr*, he says, is opening something that is closed and revealing it, therefore a Qur'ānic *tafsīr* is an effort to disclose the meanings of God's Word in accordance with His will.

With its wording and meaning of immeasurable profundity, each word of which gives its share to everyone in every age, the Qur'ān is a unique, matchless Book. It addresses different ages, different nations, and people of different intellectual levels all at the same time. It is a book of wisdom that is easily understood by its readers, yet at the same time has veiled, difficult, terse, or concise, as well as metaphorical or allegorical aspects. The profundity and secretiveness of the first three aspects can be revealed through agreement among the scholars, whereas the fourth is entrusted to the interpretation and commentary of the verifying scholars well-versed in knowledge, who remain faithful to the essentials of the Qur'ān and Islam, and have the capacity to understand what is figurative and allegorical.

Although almost every individual who knows its language can grasp something from the Qur'ān, a true and comprehensive understanding of it can be achieved by those experts of exposition and commentary who have attained the required and correct level of knowledge. These experts take into consideration the linguistic rules, and pay necessary attention to the methodology of *tafsīr* in understanding what is veiled, difficult, or abstruse. They exert endless efforts in reflection, contemplation, and meditation in order to be able to attain a correct understanding of the Divine purpose or what God really means. They resort to the explanations of God's Messenger in order to expound the concise verses (*mujmal*), and explore the depths of reported knowledge with expert knowledge and vice versa. Throughout history, the genuine commentators and expounders have always followed this same path.

As for *ta'wīl* (commentary), it means referring a word, an attitude, or an action to or explaining it with one of its probable meanings. Some have defined *ta'wīl* as expounding words and actions to the contrary of what reason superficially judges; in other words, it is also possible to say that *ta'wīl* is expounding something read or seen or heard with other than what first comes to the mind and with a rational knowledge that is not instantly comprehended. Imam Abū Manṣūr al-Māturidī makes the distinction that *tafsīr* is the exposition of the Qur'ān by the Companions, and *ta'wīl* is the commentaries and interpretations made by the *tābi'ūn* and succeeding generations.

Ta'wīl comes from the root *AWL* and due to the fact that it implies the preference of one of the probable meanings, it would be wrong to propose meaning(s) which is/are in no way related with the wording of the Qur'ān as *tafsīr* or *ta'wīl*.

It is also essential that there should be some sign that provides evidence for the meaning proposed, or a rational or transmitted proof that supports the idea put forward. It would be wrong to load different meanings on words or sentences on the grounds of "figurativeness" or "allusion" without a sign or proof while ignoring what the word or sentence apparently means. Such loading of different meanings has no real value in any case.

The end-result or product of *ta'wīl* is called a *me'āl* (interpretation). We can define this as the preference of one of the meanings. A Qur'ānic interpretation is neither just a translation nor a *tafsīr*. An interpretation might include points or issues that are typically found in a *tafsīr*; however, it does not go beyond this framework.

From the first centuries of Islam, alongside many high or low quality translations, there have been, and will be, many interpretations and *tafsīrs*. We applaud all sincere efforts dedicated to voice the spirit of the Qur'ān and to reveal the Divine purpose. We particularly applaud the efforts which do not ignore the passage of time and the aspects of Qur'ānic content and meanings that address themselves to each part of time, the circumstances that prevail in every age and environment, the essential purposes of the Religious Law and efforts which adhere to them in accordance with the spirit of the Qur'ān and the authentic Sunnah, the thoughts enriched with the passage of time and through developments in human life, and new discoveries and attainments in sciences and human thought.

ON THIS STUDY OF INTERPRETATION

Taking this opportunity, I would like to express my due appreciation for the services of Ali Ünal to the Qur'ān and I hope that he will be able to produce many other good works.

I personally think of this fellow brother as one of those figures who can read our age well, who seeks solutions for the problems of our day, as one who is imbued with love for the truth and a desire for learning. There are quite a few people today who study the Qur'ān and try to uncover the Divine purposes in the same way as the pioneers (the Companions) did. It is without a doubt that Ali Ünal is one of these. Above everything else, he is not a stranger to the Message of the Qur'ān, and I assuredly express my confidence in his overall approach to Islamic issues. He is an intellectual who confronts himself frequently and is filled with the courage to voice his beliefs confidently. His perseverance to attain the truth in religious matters, the importance he lays on consultation, his concern to avoid doing wrong and his readiness to return from error are indications of his proximity to the Almighty Lord.

He has never claimed that his work is the best in the interpretation of the Qur'ān. As a matter of fact, no one should make such a claim. His efforts and services to the Qur'ān, as well as those of his predecessors and his successors who followed and will follow the same way, are in proportion to their knowledge and sincerity, and to God's favor and help.

In this work, he has paid careful attention to the disciplines of *tafsīr* methodology, like many other contemporary commentators, and has answered the criticisms of those many hypocrites who harbor incessant animosity to Islam and to many furious aggressors. His answers are to the point and, sometimes, having recourse to contemporary interpretations and commentaries, he has articulated important things in today's language. He has always taken side with the Qur'ān with sincerity and unpretentiousness. While expressing his views, he is humble, but determined and persistent, resolved to attain the truth, but always open to correction.

In his interpretation, he has consulted a variety of Sunni-Shi'ite sources, whether classical or contemporary. I see this not as a luxury, but as an endeavor to find a worthwhile inference or comment that could have been inspired by God Almighty. Motivated by the idea that "Wisdom is the lost property of a believer; a believer should obtain it wherever he finds it," Ali Ünal has aimed to present, for the benefit of everyone, any truth which he has found to be in compliance with the essentials of Islam.

Together with the requirements mentioned for a good *tafsīr*, *ta'wīl*, and *me'āl* (interpretation), God's special help or favor is incomparably important in order to discover His purposes and what He means in His Speech. Without this favor, nothing can be truly discovered, comprehended, or voiced. In my humble opinion, Ali Ünal has made the utmost endeavor to correctly understand and render the Qur'ān comprehensible for us; he is filled with a desire and diligence to carry out the necessary research in order to answer any old or new objections and accusations made against Islam; in the face of efforts made by a positivist group to reduce every truth into material experience and observation, his confidence and trust in God's Word is exactly as it should be in a believer. Nevertheless, all these positive attitudes and features can earn their value by Divine help and special favor, and we hope that everything written and expressed here has been realized through this help and favor.

A number of books have been written about Qur'ānic interpretation and commentary, while objections to the Qur'ān and some of its contents have been repeatedly addressed. Many more interpretations and commentaries will continue to be prepared in the future too, just as many new objections will be answered, and this will perhaps continue until the end of time. How many new doubts will be manufactured about the Qur'ān; how many more times will minds be exposed to contamination; what new unthinkable plots will Satan, our eternal enemy, play on weak believers; what new scenarios, unheard of until today, will the devils of humankind and jinn put on the stage to tempt humanity; how many more times will they induce suspicion with regards to our values and agitate people? Such animosity has always existed and will continue to exist. Thankfully, hundreds of people like Ali Ünal, with zeal to serve the Religion, will always stand to face them by exploring new depths of that Book of lofty truths and strive to interpret that Eternal Speech, which they hold in the greatest esteem. The mischievous organizations of Satan and his companions will always be challenged by the companions of the Qur'ān.

The Interpretation in your hands can be perceived as a product of the aforementioned efforts. At certain points, the work goes beyond the limits of a restricted interpretation to include answers to doubts that have been put forward by some deniers, and some orientalists and their ignorant imitators, and presents satisfactory information to remove doubts in hearts with frequent references to the invincible power of the Qur'ān.

The fundamental elements of the Qur'ān are constantly emphasized in this work: the Unity of God (*tawḥīd*), Prophethood (*nubuwwah*), Resurrection, and worship (together with justice) are discussed in keeping with the approach of Bediüzzaman Said Nursi. The essence of faith and the ways in which it flourishes are frequently brought to mind, together with topics concerning the spirit and meaning of worship.

The work presents to its reader much new material about faith, unbelief, and hypocrisy, as well as former and new representatives of these attitudes. The *Sūrah Baqarah* (the Cow) is studied in the scope of a large *tafsīr*, delving into the history of the Children of Israel, and issues of war and peace. The truth of Jesus and *Āl 'Imrān* (the Family of 'Imrān), the rights of women, and issues concerning the lawful and forbidden are also broadly presented. Paradise, Hell, and the world in-between are told of together with instances of wisdom. The answers given to distorted thoughts are wise and based on accurate knowledge. It is clear that a serious effort has been made to discover the instances of wisdom in the narratives. Issues such as the Night Journey and Ascension of God's Messenger, the Companions of the Cave, the companionship of Moses and al-Khadr, and the campaigns of Dhu'l-Qarnayn are all studied in detail and in a manner which is found in *tafsīrs*. The whole of the work gives the impression that it is as if Ali Ünal has tried to compress the content of the Qur'ānic *tafsīrs* and commentaries into a single volume of interpretation.

It is impossible to cite all the distinguished aspects of this work, but we will give some examples from the last chapters.

In *Sūrat al-Mulk* (The Sovereignty) the fourth verse is interpreted in the style of Bediüzzaman, and many things are whispered to our hearts that transcend the scope of an ordinary interpretation. It says: "Perfect artistry in creation despite abundance, perfect order despite absolute ease, perfect measure, proportion, and firmness despite incredible speed, perfect individualization despite world-wide distribution, the highest price and value despite the greatest economy, perfect distinction despite absolute integration and similarity – all point to the One, Single Creator and Lord, Who has absolute Will, Power, and Knowledge."

Another example is from a footnote to the first verse of *Sūrat al-Insān* (Human): "Humankind is the fruit of the Tree of Creation and therefore contained in its seed. So the Tree of Creation has grown out of the seed of humankind. In other words, as a tree is the grown or developed form of its seed, humankind carries in its body and being the nature and all original elements of other beings. What meaning a seed bears with respect to a tree, humankind has with respect to the universe. Science should concentrate on this point while investigating how life began on earth and how humankind was originated."

There are references to modern scientific discoveries, and we are given as much knowledge as can be found in a *tafsīr*. For instance, the 1993 report of the International Meteor Organization is referred to in connection with the fifth verse of *Sūrat al-Mulk*: "The Perseid meteor shower observed almost every year suggests that those meteors are shot for certain, important purposes, for they surprise the observers by showing great diversity. The observations made in, for example, 1993, demonstrate the fact that the structure of the shower is yet little understood." Such verses are significant sources of knowledge, but it is difficult to say that we have ever been able to benefit well from them.

Metaphorical or allegorical verses are interpreted within the Sunni approach and understanding, their exact nature, however, being referred to the Knowledge of God Almighty. For example, verse 16 in *Sūrat al-Mulk* is interpreted in this way: *And yet, are you secure that He Who is above everything will not cause the earth to swallow you up then, when it is in a state of commotion?*

In many cases, and distinct from similar studies of Qur'ānic interpretation, this work presents meanings beyond the words and phrases that are suggested by the context and the whole of the Qur'ān. Although this entails numerous explanations inside parentheses within the text, it is hoped that the meaning and content are thus better disclosed for the reader. Verse 18 in *Sūrat al-Qalam* is an example from among many: *They made no allowance (in their oaths, being oblivious of the rights of the needy and oblivious of God's will).*

Sūrat al-Jinn (The Jinn) 72: 18 is interpreted: *All places of worship (and all parts of the body with which one prostrates) are for God, and all worship is due to Him alone, so do not worship anyone along with God.* The interpretation of *Sūrat al- Muzzammil* (The Enwrapped One) 73: 4 is: *Or add to it (a little); and pray and recite the Qur'ān calmly and distinctly (with your mind and heart concentrated on it).* There are many other examples, but let these few suffice for now.

The author sometimes quotes directly from great commentators of the past, preferring their way of understanding to his own. For example, in interpreting verse 17 in *Sūrat a-Ḥāqqah* (The Sure Reality), he provides noteworthy information transmitted by Hamdi Yazır from Ibn 'Arabī and others, concerning the eight angels carrying the Throne of God Almighty.

The author stands firmly at various places where others might speculate and tries to prevent distorted understandings. For instance, for verse Noah 71: 17: *And God has caused you to grow from earth like a plant*, he footnotes the following explanation: "The verse alludes to the first origin of the father of humanity from the elements of the earth – soil, air, and water – and also the material origin of every human being, which are the same elements that are made into particular biological entities in human body. As Elmalılı Hamdi Yazır points out, the word *nabātan*, which comes at the end of the verse as an adverbial complement to 'grow' denotes the particular way of human creation and growth. So, it allows no room for any inclination toward the Darwinian theory of evolution."

The work emphasizes the role of *asbāb an-nuzul* (reasons for and occasions on the revelation of verses) in understanding the Qur'ān, but it never confines the interpretation to them. It can approach many issues from a different, wider perspective without diverting from the rules of the methodology of *tafsīr*. For instance, this work suggests some other probable considerations in interpreting the initial verses of *Sūrah Abasa* (He Frowned).

I personally believe that the reader will benefit from this interpretation of the Qur'ān at least as much as they do from others. I pray that the endeavor dedicated for this work may become a means for Divine blessings and seek forgiveness from God Almighty for our mistakes and misdeeds.

بِسْمِ اللهِ الرَّحْمٰنِ الرَّحِيمِ ۝ الْحَمْدُ لِلّٰهِ رَبِّ الْعَالَمِينَ ۝٢ الرَّحْمٰنِ الرَّحِيمِ ۝٣ مَالِكِ يَوْمِ الدِّينِ ۝٤ اِيَّاكَ نَعْبُدُ وَاِيَّاكَ نَسْتَعِينُ ۝٥ اِهْدِنَا الصِّرَاطَ الْمُسْتَقِيمَ ۝٦ صِرَاطَ الَّذِينَ اَنْعَمْتَ عَلَيْهِمْ غَيْرِ الْمَغْضُوبِ عَلَيْهِمْ وَلَا الضَّالِّينَ ۝٧

بِسْمِ اللهِ الرَّحْمٰنِ الرَّحِيمِ

الٓمٓ ۚ ﴿١﴾ ذٰلِكَ الْكِتَابُ لَا رَيْبَ ۛ فِيهِ ۛ هُدًى لِّلْمُتَّقِينَ ﴿٢﴾ الَّذِينَ يُؤْمِنُونَ بِالْغَيْبِ وَيُقِيمُونَ الصَّلَاةَ وَمِمَّا رَزَقْنَاهُمْ يُنفِقُونَ ﴿٣﴾ وَالَّذِينَ يُؤْمِنُونَ بِمَا أُنزِلَ إِلَيْكَ وَمَا أُنزِلَ مِن قَبْلِكَ وَبِالْآخِرَةِ هُمْ يُوقِنُونَ ﴿٤﴾ أُولَٰئِكَ عَلَىٰ هُدًى مِّن رَّبِّهِمْ ۖ وَأُولَٰئِكَ هُمُ الْمُفْلِحُونَ ﴿٥﴾

I seek refuge in God from Satan eternally rejected (from God's Mercy).[1]

1. The Qur'ān (16: 98) commands: *When you recite the Qur'ān, seek refuge in God from Satan eternally rejected (from God's Mercy).* Accordingly, before beginning to recite the Qur'ān, one should say: "I seek refuge in God from Satan eternally rejected (from God's Mercy)." This is a prayer for God's protection and help during the recitation against evil suggestions from Satan.

SŪRAH 1

AL-FĀTIḤAH (THE OPENING)
Makkah period

It is commonly accepted that this *sūrah* was revealed during the Makkah period of Muḥammad's Prophethood. Some Traditions say that it was also revealed on a second occasion in Madīnah. The majority of scholars hold that the first *sūrah* to be revealed in its entirety is *Sūrat al-Fātiḥah*. In one respect, the *Basmalah* is the "seed" of *Sūrat al-Fātiḥah*, which, in turn, is the "seed" of the whole Qur'ān. With its marvelously terse and comprehensive words, it balances praise and petition perfectly, and it establishes four main themes or purposes of the Qur'ānic guidance – (1) establishing the Existence and Unity of God, (2) Prophethood, (3) the Resurrection and afterlife, and (4) worship and justice. It is called *Sūrat al-Fātiḥah* because it is the opening chapter of the Qur'ān. It also has other names such as "the Seven Doubly-Repeated (Verses)" because of its glory and distinction and because it must be recited in the first two *rak'ah*s of each of the Prescribed Prayers (the *Ṣalāh*); "the Mother of the Book" because it is the seed of the whole Qur'ān; and "the Treasure" because it contains many precious truths.

[1]In the Name[2] of God,[3] the All-Merciful,[4] the All-Compassionate.[5]

All praise and gratitude[6] (whoever gives them to whomever for whatever reason and in whatever way from the first day of creation until eternity) are for God, the Lord[7] of the worlds,[8]

The All-Merciful, the All-Compassionate,

The Master[9] of the Day of Judgment.[10]

[11]You alone do We worship[12] and from You alone do we seek help.[13]

Guide[14] us to the Straight Path,[15]

The Path of those whom You have favored,[16] not of those who have incurred (Your) wrath (punishment and condemnation),[17] nor of those who are astray.[18]

1. This blessed phrase (*Bi 'smi-llāhi 'r-Raḥmāni 'r-Raḥīm* translated as "in the Name of God, the All-Merciful, the All-Compassionate," called the *Basmalah*), is one of the symbols of Islam. Muslims begin every good deed by uttering it. All things and beings come to life and survive through it. The particle *bi-* here means both *in* and *with* so that everything, dependent on the laws of the All-Merciful, does whatever it does in and with His Name. A minute seed under earth germinates and pushes through soil and stone to grow into the sunlight, depending on the laws of the All-Merciful and begging the (special) compassion of the All-Compassionate. Human beings, favored with free will, should always do good and do so in God's Name and to please Him, beginning the effort in and with the Name of God.

According to some scholars, the *Basmalah* is counted as the first verse of every Qur'ānic *sūrah* (chapter) except the ninth. According to the Ḥanafī school of Law, it is a verse, but not counted as the first verse of every *sūrah*. It is the first verse of *Sūrah al-Fātiḥah*, the opening *sūrah* of the Qur'ān, and it is written before every *sūrah* because of its importance and its being blessed, and so as to separate the *sūrah*s from each other. It is, in any case, a rope of light extending from the Supreme Throne of God to the hearts of people. Whoever holds fast to it in awareness of its meaning and is enlightened by it can rise to the highest point of human perfection.

2. The word "name" translates the Arabic *ism*. It is derived from the root *SaMā* (s-m-v) meaning to be high, exalted, or *VaSaMa*, meaning to be a sign. (We may call to mind *samāwât* meaning skies or heavens because of their being high.) The nominal phrase "the name of God" reminds us that God is exalted as the Divine Being having names, One Whom we may address, and we mean and remember only that Divine Being when we mention the name God.

Knowledge of God (in the sense of the Arabic *ĩlm*) is impossible in respect of His Being or Essence (*Dhāt*). Because there is none like or comparable to Him, it is therefore impossible to grasp or comprehend His Essence. However, we can recognize God or have some knowledge of Him (in the sense of the Arabic *maʿrifah*) through His works, acts, Names, Attributes and Essential Qualities (*shuʿūn*). Awareness of His works (what we see in the world, His creation) leads us to become aware of His acts, and that awareness leads us to His Names and Attributes which, in turn, lead us to His Essential Qualities, and thence to awareness of the One Who has these Qualities.

Journeying to the Divine Being can be through either reflection on God's works – the universe, including human beings in particular, with the physical and psychological composition particular to each – or through the disciplines of the "heart," following a Ṣūfī way. Combining the two is always safer and preferable. (On the Ṣūfī way or Islamic Sufism, see Fethullah Gülen, *Key Concepts in the Practice of Sufism* (translated).

3. *Allāh*, translated as God, is the proper Name of the Divine Being Who creates and administers His creatures, individually and as a whole, Who provides, brings up, sustains, protects, guides each and all, Who causes to perish and revives each and all, Who rewards or punishes, etc. All His Attributes are Attributes of absolute perfection, and He is absolutely free from any and all defect. He is Unique and Single, having no like or resemblance and nothing is comparable to Him. He is absolutely beyond any human conception: *Eyes comprehend Him not, but He comprehends all eyes* (6: 103).

God is the Unique, Single Being with the exclusive right to be worshipped and to be made the sole aim of life. He is loved in and of Himself. Everything is dependent on Him and subsists by Him. Every truth has its source in Him. His Existence is so manifest that one may doubt one's own existence but one cannot and should not doubt His. Eyes cannot see Him because of the density and plenitude of His manifestations. His Light is a veil before the eyes. He is worshipped because He is worthy of it as God; not the other way round – that is He is God because He is the object of worship.

Without (belief in) God, life is torment within torment, intellect is pure retribution, ambitions are pure pain, attainments are losses, union is separation, love is suffering, pleasure is distress, and knowledge is whim. He is the cure for the afflicted, and remedy for the wounded hearts. Hearts attain peace and come to rest by remembering and mentioning Him. Whoever has found Him, has found everything; whoever has lost Him, has lost everything.

4. The expression "the All-Merciful" translates the Arabic *ar-Raḥmān*. *ar-Raḥmān* is an essential Attribute of God, precise rendering of which into another language is impossible. Though an Attribute in essence, *ar-Raḥmān* can be used almost interchangeably with the name God, for it is applied to none other than God. It means the One with infinite mercy Who embraces the whole of creation with mer-

cy, grace and favor including all of humanity, without discrimination between believers and unbelievers, giving life, maintaining, providing, and endowing with the capacities necessary for each. God has created the universe out of, and as the manifestation of, the mercy embodied by His Name, the All-Merciful.

The universe is the work of the All-Merciful, and God's Mercy embodied by the All-Merciful embraces the creation in its entirety. There are two aspects of Divine manifestation pertaining to the universe. One is His universal manifestation with all of His Names related to the universe. It may be understood by analogy with the sun's manifestation throughout the world with its light including the seven colors in it and heat. This is called the manifestation of Oneness (*at-tajallī al-Wāhidiyah*). The (attributive) Name the All-Merciful is the source of this manifestation. It is the source of the magnificent order of the universe such that everything is in absolute obedience to God, bound by the laws of the All-Merciful. A particular instance and visible symbol of it is the enlivening of the earth, with the plants and animals therein, together with the provision and sustaining and administration thereof in perfect harmony and mercy. All of that is owed to and dependent on the manifestation of God as the All-Merciful.

5. The other aspect of Divine manifestation may be understood by analogy with the sun's particular manifestation on each thing according to the capacity of that thing. This is God's particular manifestation on each thing with one or a few of His Names, with the other Names subordinated to them. This manifestation is the result of God's being *ar-Rahīm*, translated as "the All-Compassionate," and is called the manifestation of Unity (*at-tajallī al-Ahadiyah*). God embraces the whole of creation as *ar-Rahmān* (the All-Merciful) without discrimination between belief and unbelief, truth and falsehood, right and wrong, beauty and ugliness, good and evil, while as *ar-Rahīm* (the All-Compassionate) He has special mercy for faith, justice, truth, right, beauty and good both in this world and, particularly, in the Hereafter. No one has any part in their com-

ing into existence, the determination of their place or date of birth and death, race, color, physical features and the functioning of their body. These are all dependent on the absolute choice of God as the All-Merciful and therefore cannot be the grounds of superiority or inferiority, of discrimination, among people. By contrast, the conscious inhabitants of the earth (jinn and humankind) have a choice between belief and unbelief, justice and injustice, right and wrong, good and evil, truth and falsehood, exercised by their free wills, and are therefore accountable for their preference. Being *ar-Rahīm*, God helps those who prefer faith, right, justice, and good in this world and rewards them with eternal happiness in the Hereafter. But for *ar-Rahmān* (the All-Merciful), we would not have come into the world. But for *ar-Rahīm* (the All-Compassionate), we would not be able to use our free will to make the right preference, comprehend the marvelous works of God's art, know what faith, religion and Prophethood are, and attain true, eternal happiness in Paradise.

6. As one must understand the Qur'ānic concepts in order to understand the Qur'ān, we give a brief explanation.

The Arabic word translated as "praise and gratitude" is *hamd*. It encompasses both meanings, and carries other connotations as well. We give praise on account of some particular praiseworthy achievements or qualities; we feel gratitude for some particular good done. But in relation to God, *hamd* affirms that God is eternally worthy of praise and gratitude because He is God eternally, eternally merciful and the Lord of all creation. Whether His favors are recognized as such by His creatures or not, He must be praised and thanked. Thanking is required by loyalty to God because of His favors, while praise is required by being a sincere servant aware of Who God is and what servanthood means.

It should be noted that all praise and thanks are due to God alone, are His alone. Wherever beauty, excellence and perfection occur, the ultimate source is God. No created beings, whether angels or humans, heavenly or earthly objects, have other than a dependent excellence, beauty or perfection. Where these qualities occur, they are in reality favors from God. Thus, if there is one to whom we should feel indebted and grateful, it is the Creator of everything, Who is in reality the Creator of that to which we respond with praise and gratitude, and not its apparent possessor.

When we say *All praise and gratitude are for God*, we also mean that it is God in Whom we seek refuge when we are in danger, to Whom we pray for help when we are in difficulty or in need, and Whom alone we adore and worship.

7. The word "Lord" is used to translate *Rabb*. It has three sets of related meanings: (i) Upbringer, Trainer, Sustainer, Nourisher; (ii) Lord and Master; (iii) He Who directs and controls.

God's being *Rabb* means that every being (and every part of every being) – from elements or inanimate objects to plants, animals and humanity, and all other beings in other worlds – is raised, sustained, directed and controlled by Him until it achieves its particular perfection, the purpose of its creation. This means that what we commonly call "natural laws" are in reality designations or descriptions for God's exercise of His Lordship, of His being *Rabb*. A complementary kind of God's bringing up or training of humanity is His sending Prophets and religions. It follows that, in affirming God as the sole Upbringer, Trainer, Sustainer, Nourisher, Lord and Master of all beings (*at-tawḥīd ar-Rubūbiyah*), we affirm another dimension of faith in God's Oneness and Unity.

8. "Worlds" translates the Arabic *ʿālamīn* (singular, *ʿālam*). The word comes from *ʿalam, ʿalāmah*, meaning something by which another thing is known. Thus, in this perspective, every individual thing or set of things, from the tiniest sub-atomic particles to the largest nebulae and galaxies, is a "world" and indicates God. The plural form (*ʿālamīn*) is particularly used for conscious beings, giving the sense that everything that is created is as if conscious, and signifying that its pointing to God's Existence, Unity and Lordship is ex-

tremely clear for conscious beings.

From another perspective, the "worlds" are classified as *Lāhūt* (the High Empyrean: the pure, immaterial world of pure Divine Realities), *Jabarūt* (another of the immaterial worlds where Divine realities are manifested in their pure, immaterial forms), *Malakūt* (the world of the pure inner dimension of existence), *Mithāl* (the world of the symbols or ideal, immaterial forms of things) and *Shahādah* (the corporeal world, including the visible world and the firmaments.) These worlds should be thought of as dimensions rather than distinct locations: the Divine truths or realities manifested in material forms in this world are manifested in other worlds in the forms peculiar to each.

The "worlds" are also classified as the world of spirits, this world, the immaterial world between this and the next *(al-ʿĀlam al-Barzakh)*, and the eternal world of the Hereafter.

The "worlds" may also be taken to refer to different domains or "kingdoms" within this earthly world, and other worlds beyond this earth.

9. The word *Mālik*, here translated as "Master," means both owner and sovereign. Although God allows the existence of sovereigns in this world because He has endowed humankind with free will, He will be the sole, absolute Sovereign on the Day of Judgment: *Whose is the absolute Sovereignty on that Day? It is God's, the One, the All-Overwhelming (with absolute sway over all that exist* (40: 16). In addition, ownership of the other world with all its regions or sub-worlds, such as the Place of Supreme Gathering, the Bridge, Paradise and Hell, belongs to God exclusively.

10. The "Day of Judgment" translates the Arabic phrase *Yawm ad-Dīn*. The word *dīn* is usually rendered in English as "religion," being derived from the verb *Dā-Na* (from *d-y-n*) meaning to profess a religion. From the same radicals (*d-y-n*), the verb *Dā-Na* has another, connected set of meanings – to borrow or be indebted, to be subjected or bound, to owe allegiance, to be called to account, judged, con-

victed. (The related noun is *dayn*, a debt or liability, an obligation.) The Islamic concept of religion (*dīn*) encompasses all these meanings. God has brought us from the darkness of nonexistence into the light of existence, created us in the best pattern and raised us to the highest point in the hierarchy of creation. He has included in the dough of our existence certain elements that, however seemingly negative or destructive, will, when disciplined, cause us to rise to higher ranks of perfection. So that we might discipline them with His help, and not be defeated by them, and so that we might use all our capacities and the positive elements in our existence in the right way, He sent Prophets and revealed through them and through Books the rules of how we should conduct ourselves. These are God's trust or gifts to us for which we owe Him the debt of gratitude. Paying this debt requires, first of all, designing our life in accordance with the rules God has established. In this sense, religion or *dīn* is the assemblage of Divine rules that human beings must observe in order to attain to good and salvation. A day will come when we will be called to account for our efforts in this regard, and we will be judged as to how we acted in this world, and rewarded or punished accordingly. Of that day, the sole Master is God.

As the lifetime of this universe is referred to as a "day," so too the time when we are raised to life after death and judged and eternally recompensed for what we did in this world, is also referred to as a "day." That time is also the time when the realities of religion will become clearly and fully manifest. That is another of the reasons why the Qur'ān calls that "day" *Yawm ad-Dīn*, the Day of Judgment.

11. It is reported from God's Messenger, upon him be peace and blessings, that God said: "The half of *al-Fātiḥah* belongs to Me, while the other half to My servant" (Muslim, "Ṣalāh," 38). The part up to this verse (i.e. verses 1–4) belongs to God. In it the servant addresses God as it were in the third person, praising Him. These four verses of praise serve as a ladder to rise to His Presence and there attain the dignity of addressing Him in the second person (verses 5–7).

At this point, the servant addresses a petition to the One praised with His most comprehensive Attributes in the preceding verses. According to the Tradition mentioned above, verse 5 belongs to both God and the servant, whereas the following verses (6 and 7), when the servant prays to God for his/her most pressing need (i.e. right guidance), belong to the servant.

12. The words "we worship" translate the Arabic *na budu*, first person plural in the imperfect tense of the verb *'ABaDa*. It means doing something with energy and determination. *Ibādah* is derived from it and, as a term, means adoration and submission. The verb *'ABaDa* has two other important infinitives both of which are deeply related with worshipping. *Ubūdah* means humility and submission, and *ubūdiyah*, doing the duty of worship in a systematic way. "You alone do we worship" translates the meaning of the Arabic construction *iyyā-ka na budu*, which puts the pronoun "You" in an emphatic position; the same emphasis is found in the next phrase also: *iyyā-ka nasta'īnu* (instead of the usual *nasta'īnu-ka*). Thus, the meaning here is we worship God in awe and with utmost submission, sincerity and humility, and in a systematic way. In so doing we express our total devotion, submission and subjection to God and declare our faith that none other than God deserves worship, which expresses *at-tawḥīd al-'ubūdiyah*. The fact that *na budu* is in the first person plural, and in the imperfect tense, means that the duty of worship is not restricted to one occasion only or discharged once only, rather that it is due always and due collectively as well as individually. Indeed, worship in congregation is preferable. The collective aspect refers to (i) the individual person with all the systems and cells of his/her body, (ii) the group(s) of believers who have come together at any place or time to worship God, and (iii) the whole body of believers throughout the world who have turned to the Ka'bah to worship.

13. Since the relationship between the worshipping servant and God as the One Worshipped is not maintained in other religions with the

strict clarity proper to it – especially given the influence of modern trends of humanism and individualism – it may give rise to certain misconceptions, which we will try to clarify:

Servanthood in Islam means freedom from all other kinds of servitude and slavery. The response of Rabī' ibn 'Āmir, the envoy of the Muslim army's commander, before the battle of Qadīsiyah, when asked by the commander of the Persian armies about the meaning and message the Muslims sought to proclaim, expresses well what servanthood means in Islam: "We invite people from servanthood to false deities to servanthood to One God, from the suffocating dungeon of the world to the exhilarating expanse of the heavens, and from the darkness of false religions to the light of Islam" (Ahmed Cevdet Paşa, 1: 391).

Servanthood in Islam is the only means to true human freedom and dignity. No one is greater than any other in being a servant and therefore not worthy of worship and adoration. All created beings, whether a Prophet or a common human, are equally removed from being objects of worship. The Prescribed Prayer (the Ṣalāh) and the Pilgrimage (the Hajj) are public occasions that demonstrate this most clearly.

> One who claims human freedom in rebellion to God may be a Pharaoh-like tyrant, but he is one who will abase himself, in order to serve his interest, so far as to bow in worship before the meanest thing. He may be haughty and arrogant, and yet so wretched as to accept degradation for the sake of a momentary pleasure; unyielding in self-esteem and yet so ignoble as to kiss the feet of devilish people for the sake of some trivial advantage. He may be conceited and domineering, but since he can find no point of support in his heart against death, misfortunes and innumerable enemies, he knows himself within as an impotent, vainglorious tyrant. He may be a self-centered egoist who, in striving to gratify his own carnal desires or personal interests or the advantage of his racial or cultural group, quickly becomes a slave to those desires and interests.

> As for the sincere servant of God, he is a worshipping servant, who does not degrade himself to bow in worship even before the greatest of the creatures. He is dignified and does not regard as the goal of worship a thing of even the greatest benefit like Paradise. Also, though modest, mild and gentle, he does not lower himself before anybody other than his Creator. He is indeed weak and in want, and aware of his weakness and neediness. Yet he is independent of others, owing to the spiritual wealth that his Munificent Owner has provided for him, and he is powerful in that he relies on the infinite power of his Master. He acts and strives purely for God's sake, for God's pleasure, and to be endowed with virtues. (The Words, "the 12th Word," 147)

14. *Ihdi-nā* translated as "guide us" is from the verb *HaDā* which means taking by the hand and leading and guiding rightly, and gently. The noun *hidāyah* derived from it usually means true or right guidance, and is the opposite of deviation or being astray.

The verb *HaDā* is used both transitively and intransitively. God guides one either directly or through a means. In most cases, He kindles faith in the hearts of people as a result of their using their will and striving to find guidance. However, although God wants His servants to desire guidance and strive for it, their desiring and striving are not the cause of being guided. This seeming paradox is well expressed in the anonymous saying: "Although He is not to be found by searching, only those who search for Him find Him." The primary means of guidance is Prophets and Divine Books. In the absence of a Prophet, those who, without deviation, follow in the footsteps of the Prophets, serve the same function. Their character is made clear in the next verse.

15. The Arabic word translated as Path is *ṣirāt*. It is a way having ups and downs, one wide in some of it parts and narrow in others, and difficult to walk on. It is described in a Prophetic Tradition as a path or bridge with ups and downs, one having walls on its sides, and doors and windows opening on the outside.

The walls are the rules of the Islamic Sharī'ah, which protect it from external attacks and save those following it from veering off. The doors and windows are the openings to things forbidden. Those following the Path should not follow these openings lest they go astray (Ibn Hanbal, 4: 182–183).

Ṣirāṭ is used in the Qur'ān in singular; the word has no plural. This tells us that it is the one and only road leading to God although there are many roads (*sabīl*) leading to the Path. It is qualified with the adjective straight, meaning that the Straight Path is the way of the Qur'ān with no crookedness at all (18: 1). It is the middle way having nothing to do with any extremes. It is equally far from communism and capitalism in economy, from absolutism and anarchism in politics, from realism and idealism in philosophy, from materialism and spiritualism in belief, and from being exclusively this-worldly or exclusively other-worldly in world-view. It is the middle way considering human psychology and the realities of life and creation. In educating people, it disciplines and ennobles the intellect, saving it from the extremes of demagogy, cunning and stupidity, and so leads to sound knowledge and wisdom. The disciplining and ennobling of the faculty of anger and impulse of defense saves that faculty from wrongdoing, oppression and cowardice, and leads to justice and valor. The power or impulse of lust is saved through discipline from dissipation and hedonism and grows into chastity.

16. Even if one can, by studying creation and reflecting on it, work out that there must be One Who has created it, none can discover what the Straight Path is through reasoning alone.

Human beings have a distinguished place amongst created beings. They are usually drawn to and desire what is the most beautiful. Meeting even their everyday needs requires multifarious skills and crafts. As social beings, they are obliged to share and exchange the products of their labor with others. However, their innate impulses and powers, such as intellect, anger, passion and lust, are unrestricted and therefore need some discipline. It follows that human beings must be guided to a universal straight way far from all extremes, a way that contains the correct rules to guarantee their happiness in both worlds. Even if all people came together to establish these rules, they could not do so, for it requires knowing all human beings with the character, ambitions and fears of each, as well as the conditions of both worlds. This is possible only for a universal intellect, which has been manifested as Divine religion throughout history.

The greatest favor or blessing of God for humanity is the Religion. People attain happiness in both worlds through it, and realize the aim of their creation. In order to be able to find and follow the true Religion, God points us towards some persons He has chosen among people. He describes them as those whom He has favored. He presents the Straight Path as their way, and He publicizes their identity in another verse (4: 69): *Whoever obeys God and the Messenger (as they must be obeyed), then those are (and in the Hereafter will be, in Paradise) in the company of those whom God has favored (with the perfect guidance) – the Prophets, and the truthful ones (loyal and truthful in whatever they do and say), and the witnesses (those who see the hidden Divine truths and testify thereto with their lives), and the righteous ones (in all their deeds and sayings and dedicated to setting everything right). How excellent they are for companions!* One who sincerely searches for such people, finds them, because they shine in the spiritual and intellectual "heaven" of humankind.

17. The Qur'ān forbids us to follow the ways of two groups: those who have incurred God's wrath (punishment and condemnation), and those who are astray.

God's wrath does not mean that God becomes angry in some way analogous to us. Rather, His wrath means punishment and condemnation. We read in the Qur'ān that those who kill a believer intentionally (4: 93), those who cherish evil thoughts about God (48: 6), those who flee the battlefield (8: 16), those who have disbelieved after their belief (16: 106), and those who argue concerning God after He has been acknowledged (42: 16) have incurred God's punishment and condemnation. Again, those who disbelieved in God and kill His Prophets (2: 61); those who refused to believe in the Prophet Muḥammad because of envy and racist tendencies, even though they knew and recognized that he was a Prophet (2: 90); those who took a calf for worship after they believed in God (7: 152, 20: 86); and those who showed disrespect to the Sabbath, also incurred God's wrath (punishment and condemnation) Since those Jews who committed the sins and crimes mentioned had incurred God's punishment and condemnation, God's Messenger, upon him be peace and blessings, interpreted *those who have incurred (Your) punishment and condemnation*, as referring to those Jews (at-Tirmidhī, "Tafsīr al-Qur'ān," 2; Ibn Hanbal, 4: 378). However, this is to exemplify a general truth – it does not exclude others who commit the same crimes and share the same characteristics from the meaning of the expression. Those who are of the same character as those Jews who incurred God's punishment and condemnation, who follow the same way without being Jews, are certainly included in the meaning of the expression.

We should note that most of the crimes of those Jews mentioned in the Qur'ān and their incurring God's punishment and condemnation are presented in the Old Testament in much severer terms (*Numbers*, 16: 12–24, 31–35, 41–50; 21: 4–6; *Deuteronomy*, 4: 25–29; 9: 9–29). The Prophet Moses, upon him be peace, reproached them in *Deuteronomy*, 9: 24: "You have been rebellious against the Lord ever since I have known you."

And, according to the report of the New Testament, Jesus reproached them with still harsher words: *Matthew*, 12: 34–35; 23: 2–7, 23–33.

18. The verbal noun meaning "astray" (*ḍalāl*) can refer to a broad range of straying from the path – from the slightest lapse of a believer to complete deviation from the Straight Path. As a term, it denotes returning to unbelief after belief and exchanging unbelief for belief (2: 108), associating partners with God either in His Essence or His Attributes or acts (4: 116), and rejecting faith in all or any of the pillars of faith, namely believing in the Existence and Unity of God (including Destiny), in angels, in all the Divine Scriptures and Prophets without making any distinction among them with respect to believing in them, and in the Resurrection and afterlife. The followers of Jesus had first obeyed Jesus and followed his way heroically despite persecutions of the severest kind. However, since many among later lapsed into deviations, God's Messenger, upon him be peace and blessings, interpreted *those who are astray* as referring to those Christians (at-Tirmidhī, "Tafsīr al-Qur'ān," 2).

The Messenger made clear to the Muslims how, through their particular beliefs and ways of acting, people incur God's punishment and condemnation and go astray. This is his warning to the Muslims not to follow the same ways, so that they may be saved from being included in those two groups.

SŪRAH 2

AL-BAQARAH (THE COW)

Madīnah period

T his *sūrah* of 286 verses is the longest in the Qur'ān, and may be regarded as a detailed summary of it. The *sūrah* began to be revealed just after the Emigration (*Hijrah*) to Madīnah and continued to be revealed over almost ten years until all elements of it were completed. As pointed out in the Preface, whenever a verse or group of verses was revealed, God's Messenger, upon him be peace and blessings, had it written and inserted in the place in the *sūrah* to which it belonged, and where it had to be, by God's order.

In the Name of God, the All-Merciful, the All-Compassionate.

1. *Alif. Lām. Mīm.*[1]
2. This is the (most honored, matchless) Book: there is no doubt about it (its Divine authorship and that it is a collection of pure truths throughout). A perfect guidance for the God-revering, pious, who keep their duty to God.[2]
3. Those who believe in the Unseen,[3] establish the Prayer in conformity with its conditions, and out of what We have provided for them (of wealth, knowledge, power, etc.,) they spend (to provide sustenance for the needy and in God's cause, purely for the good pleasure of God and without placing others under obligation).
4. And those who believe in what is sent down to you, and what was sent down before you (such as the Torah, Gospel and Psalms, and the Scrolls of Abraham); and in the Hereafter they have certainty of faith.[4/5]
5. Those (illustrious ones) stand on true guidance (originating in the Qur'ān) from their Lord; and they are those who are the prosperous.[6]

1. If the *lām -alif* (a compound letter) is counted, the Qur'ānic alphabet has 29 letters, otherwise 28. The Qur'ān uses half of these at the beginning of 29 *sūrah*s, either singly like *qāf* (as in *Sūrah Qāf*) and *ṣād* (as in *Sūrah Ṣād*) or in two-, three-, four- or five-letter combinations. These letters are called *ḥurūf al-muqaṭṭa'āt*, disjunct, isolated or abbreviated letters.

Much has been said and written about their meaning:

- Spelling these letters means that people had just begun to learn how to read and write. So, their presence at the beginning of some *sūrah*s shows that the Qur'ān was sent down to an illiterate people.

- They imply that the Qur'ān is a book composed of words and letters, which it is impossible for a person like the Prophet Muḥammad who neither reads nor writes, upon him be peace and blessings, to have produced. As the Qur'ān is a book, the universe is also a book. This is why Muslim sages call the former "the Revealed and Written Universe," and the latter "the Created Book." A letter has no meaning of itself; rather, it functions in a word and points to its writer in many ways. Each creature in the universe functions in a similar way by likewise pointing to its Creator.

- The characters of the Arabic alphabet are variant forms, extended and curved, of the first letter *alif*, which is itself described as the extended form of the *nuktah* or "point." This is a symbol of the reality that, like the letters, words and sentences of the Qur'ān, all the creatures of the universe originate in a single source and are interrelated. From this we may understand that, in order to be able to produce even a single atom in the universe or a word in the Qur'ān in its proper place, one must have the knowledge and power to produce the whole universe and the whole Qur'ān.

- These letters are like ciphers between the Revealer – God – and the Messenger, the exact and complete meaning of which is known to the Messenger only. However, this does not mean no one else can grasp some of their meanings. Scholars well-versed in the science of the mysteries of the letters and exacting scholars have drawn many mysterious conclusions from them and discovered in them such truths that, in their view, these letters form a most brilliant miracle. For example, Imam Rabbānī Ahmad Fārūq al-Sirhindī (1564?-1624) discovered the signs of many future events in them.

2. The word translated as "the God-revering, pious, who keep their duty to God" is *muttaqī*. It is derived from *taqwā* from *wiqāyah*, meaning protection, self-defense and averting (danger). *Taqwā* is one of the most important concepts used to characterize a Muslim believer. It denotes refraining from sins in utmost reverence for God and receiving His protection against deviations and His punishment. God has two sets of laws: one the "religious" laws (including the pillars of faith, and principles of worship and morality) governing human individual and social life, the other the Divine laws of the creation and operation of the universe studied by the natural sciences (which we wrongly call "laws of nature"). God's protection depends on acting in accordance with both of these sets of laws. The recompense for complying or not

with the former usually comes in the Hereafter, while for the latter, in this world. *Taqwā*, which we will render as "piety, righteousness, and reverence for God" in this commentary, is the only criterion of human distinction or nobility in God's sight: *Surely the noblest, most honorable of you in God's sight is the one best in taqwā (piety, righteousness, and reverence for God)* (49: 13).

3. The word translated as "the Unseen" is *ghayb*. Its opposite, *shahādah*, means what is observable or sensed. So, the *ghayb* denotes that which is not directly sensed or is beyond the physical senses. It has two categories: one absolute, the other limited or relative. The absolute *ghayb*, from the perspective of this world, denotes God, the Divine Being with His Attributes and Names, and the worlds of the Hereafter. The worlds of angels, jinn, spirits and other immaterial beings can also be included in the absolute *ghayb* for the common people – "common" from the perspective of spiritual development. The exact knowledge of the absolute *ghayb* belongs to God exclusively. However, He may impart some of it to whomever He wishes amongst His servants, including primarily His Messengers, in whatever way He wills. As for the limited or relative *ghayb*, it denotes all that we cannot "sense" within the present conditions we are in, of which the most obvious case is occurrences in the past and future. For example, the Qur'ān uses the term "the tidings of the *ghayb*" when narrating the histories of bygone peoples. This class of the *ghayb* can be known through study and investigation and, in respect of the future, with the passage of time.

It is of great significance that the Qur'ān praises the believers, first of all, for their belief in the *ghayb*. This means that existence is not restricted to what is sensed and observed. This corporeal realm is the manifestation of the Unseen and unobservable according to the measures particular to it. So the truth or full reality of every phenomenon in this world lies in the world of the *ghayb*. By mentioning the believers' faith in the *ghayb* at the outset, the Qur'ān teaches us how we must view things and events, providing us with the true criterion and viewpoint.

This world is like a book whose meaning lies in the *ghayb* and which makes its Author known to us. Believers are those who study this Book and discover its Author. They view every thing and event in this world from this perspective and base all their studies upon this foundation. This is the point at which Islamic epistemology departs from modern epistemology.

4. The word translated as "certainty of faith" is *yaqīn*. It means having no doubt about the truth of a matter and arriving at accurate, doubt-free knowledge. This knowledge can come from either Revelation or study and verification. *Yaqīn* has three degrees: first, that which comes from knowledge (*'ilm al-yaqīn*); second, that which depends on seeing and observation (*'ayn al-yaqīn*); and third, that which comes from direct experience (*ḥaqq al-yaqīn*). For example, rising smoke is the sign of fire and gives us some certainty about the existence of a fire where it is rising. This certainty is that which is based on knowledge. When we go to where the smoke is rising and see the fire with our own eyes, our certainty of the fire's existence is the kind coming from direct observation. If we put our hand into the fire and feel its burning quality, then we obtain experienced certainty about the existence and quality of fire.

One may acquire certainty about or certain faith in the Hereafter through Revelation or discovery or through the seeing of the "heart" (the spiritual intellect), through intellectual deduction or reasoning or through some sort of contact with the spirits of the dead (provided that this last is done through authentic ways); through true dreams or through scientific studies. In all these cases, it will be certainty based on knowledge, that is, certainty of the first degree.

5. By describing the qualities of believers in a few, concise phrases, the Qur'ān summarizes the main essentials of Islam. Islam is based on believing in the meta-physical – including first and foremost the reality of God with all His Attributes and Names, which is the source of all truths. Believing in one of the pillars of the

Islamic faith requires believing in the others, because one cannot be conceived of without the others. For example, believing in God requires believing in the Messengership, because, first of all, it is only through Messengership that we can have accurate knowledge about God and receive answers to the basic questions we all ask as human beings: Who am I? What is this world all about? What is the essence, nature, and meaning of life? Who sent me to this world and why? What do life and death ask of me? What is my final destination? Who is my guide in this journeying of life? Believing in Messengership requires believing in Revelation, Divine Books, and angels. Finally, the afterlife is both the inevitable, eternal consequence of this life and a requirement of God's being eternal with all His Attributes and Names.

Second, as stated in a Prophetic Tradition, the Prescribed Prayer constitutes the central pillar of Islamic life (ad-Daylamī, 2: 204). Without it, one cannot establish the building of Islam. Giving to those in need is the bridge between people, a bridge that fills the space between social classes. Believing in all the Prophets and Divine Books make all believers from the time of Adam brothers and sisters. Islam is the consummation of all Divine religions and the Prophet Muḥammad, upon him be peace and blessings, was heir to all his predecessors. Faith in the Hereafter extends life and time to eternity and embraces all believers among humankind, jinn, and angels, in a single, eternal embrace.

6. Prosperity (*falāḥ*) has many degrees and types according to the needs and aspirations of people and the degrees of their spiritual enlightenment. For example, some want to be saved from eternal punishment, while others desire Paradise. There are still some who aim at the higher ranks in Paradise and others who aspire to obtain God's good pleasure. By ending the account of the believers' virtues with prosperity but without specifying it, the Qur'ān allows that there are various degrees in faith, sincerity, purity of intention, and good deeds, and corresponding degrees in the final prosperity achieved.

2   سُورَةُ البَقَرَة   ٢

إِنَّ الَّذِينَ كَفَرُوا سَوَآءٌ عَلَيْهِمْ ءَأَنذَرْتَهُمْ أَمْ لَمْ تُنذِرْهُمْ
لَا يُؤْمِنُونَ ۞ خَتَمَ اللَّهُ عَلَىٰ قُلُوبِهِمْ وَعَلَىٰ سَمْعِهِمْ وَعَلَىٰٓ
أَبْصَٰرِهِمْ غِشَٰوَةٌ وَلَهُمْ عَذَابٌ عَظِيمٌ ۞ وَمِنَ النَّاسِ
مَن يَقُولُ ءَامَنَّا بِاللَّهِ وَبِالْيَوْمِ الْأَخِرِ وَمَا هُم بِمُؤْمِنِينَ
۞ يُخَٰدِعُونَ اللَّهَ وَالَّذِينَ ءَامَنُوا وَمَا يَخْدَعُونَ إِلَّآ
أَنفُسَهُمْ وَمَا يَشْعُرُونَ ۞ فِى قُلُوبِهِم مَّرَضٌ فَزَادَهُمُ
اللَّهُ مَرَضًا وَلَهُمْ عَذَابٌ أَلِيمٌ بِمَا كَانُوا يَكْذِبُونَ ۞ وَإِذَا قِيلَ
لَهُمْ لَا تُفْسِدُوا فِى الْأَرْضِ قَالُوٓا إِنَّمَا نَحْنُ مُصْلِحُونَ ۞ أَلَآ إِنَّهُمْ
هُمُ الْمُفْسِدُونَ وَلَٰكِن لَّا يَشْعُرُونَ ۞ وَإِذَا قِيلَ لَهُمْ ءَامِنُوا
كَمَآ ءَامَنَ النَّاسُ قَالُوٓا أَنُؤْمِنُ كَمَآ ءَامَنَ السُّفَهَآءُ أَلَآ إِنَّهُمْ
هُمُ السُّفَهَآءُ وَلَٰكِن لَّا يَعْلَمُونَ ۞ وَإِذَا لَقُوا الَّذِينَ ءَامَنُوا
قَالُوٓا ءَامَنَّا وَإِذَا خَلَوْا إِلَىٰ شَيَٰطِينِهِمْ قَالُوٓا إِنَّا مَعَكُمْ إِنَّمَا نَحْنُ
مُسْتَهْزِءُونَ ۞ اللَّهُ يَسْتَهْزِئُ بِهِمْ وَيَمُدُّهُمْ فِى
طُغْيَٰنِهِمْ يَعْمَهُونَ ۞ أُوْلَٰٓئِكَ الَّذِينَ اشْتَرَوُا الضَّلَٰلَةَ
بِالْهُدَىٰ فَمَا رَبِحَت تِّجَٰرَتُهُمْ وَمَا كَانُوا مُهْتَدِينَ ۞

---

6. (Despite the commitment and energy you show in striving to help people to believe,) those who willfully persist in unbelief: it is alike to them whether you warn them or do not warn them (of the end waiting for them); (although it is your mission to warn them and you do it without any neglect,) they will not believe.

7. God has set a seal upon their hearts and on their hearing, and on their eyes is a covering.[7] For them is a mighty punishment (in the Hereafter).[8]

8. [9]Among people are some who say, "We believe in God and in the Last Day," although they are not believers.

9. They would trick God and those who believe, and they trick only their own selves (of which they are enamored), but they do not perceive.

10. In the very center of their hearts is a sickness (that dries up the source of their spiritual life, extinguishes their power of understanding and corrupts their character), and (because of their moral corruption and the tricks they deploy out of envy and malice) God has increased them in sickness.[10] For them is a painful punishment because they habitually lie.

11. (Because of the disorder they intend to provoke with their lies), whenever they are told (as part of the duty enjoined upon the believers to promote good and forbid evil), "Do not cause disorder and corruption on earth," they say: "Why! We indeed are the ones who set things right."

12. Beware, they themselves are those who cause disorder and corruption but they are unaware (of what they do and ignorant of what setting things right is and what causing disorder is).

13. Again, whenever they are told (as a duty of calling to faith), "Believe as the people believe," (in a way to demonstrate their self-pride and disparagement of the people) they say: "Shall we believe as the fools[11] believe!?" Beware, they themselves are the fools, but they do not know (seeing that they have no true knowledge to distinguish between truth and falsehood, sincere faith and hypocrisy, right and wrong).[12]

14. When they meet those who believe, they declare (hypocritically), "We believe;" but when they are alone in secret with their (apparently human) satans (to whom they hasten in need to renew their unbelief and their pledge to them for fear of losing their support), they say: "Assuredly we are with you; we only mock (those others)."

15. (Since what they do only means demanding straying and ridicule,) God returns their mockery, leaving them to wander blindly on in their rebellion.

16. Such are the ones who have bought straying in exchange for guidance, but their trade has brought no profit, and they have no way out to escape it.

7. The three most important reasons for unbelief are self-pride, wrongdoing or injustice, and prejudice causing deviancy in thought and action. Under the influence of these, the heart, which has been created to serve as a mirror to God, is darkened and polluted. Just as institutions or buildings that have operated in a way contrary to the law or the lawful purpose of their construction are sealed up, so does God seal up a heart which has lost its ability to believe internally.

If the heart is protected against sins, wrongdoing, prejudice, self-pride, and the mercilessness that does injustice, the senses of hearing and seeing through which the heart establishes its relationship with the outer world, function properly. Besides, such a heart has a "point of affirmation." That is, the verses of Revelation coming into it through the ears and the evidences the eyes obtain from the universe cause the light of faith to be kindled in it. But if a heart loses its essential identity for the reasons mentioned above, it is useless to look for a point of affirmation in it. As a result, the ears become deaf to Revelation, and since the heart has no longer a point of affirmation, the eyes' observation or study of the universe increase only unbelief in it. Perhaps that is why in many science circles, where the science is pursued on the modern Western pattern, some still insist on atheism.

8. Unbelief is an immeasurable, unpardonable crime, because it is:

- an unforgivable ingratitude in the face of infinite Divine favors;
- a limitless disrespect to God and His Attributes;
- a rejection of and contempt for the innumerable signs of God in the universe;
- an accusation of lying and deceit against numberless beings who have believed in God, among whom are angels, believing jinn and human beings, more than a hundred thousand Prophets and millions of saints and scholars, who have never lied;

- an everlasting destruction of human conscience, which has been created for eternity and therefore aspires to it.
- Just as faith results in eternal happiness and bliss, so does unbelief in the sense of rejecting any of the pillars of faith have the potential to result in an eternal, painful punishment.

9. After describing the believers and unbelievers in a few comprehensive statements, the Qur'ān starts to depict the hypocrites in thirteen verses. This is because:

- A hypocrite is a deceiving, secret enemy. An undeclared enemy is the more dangerous – if cheating and dishonest, more malicious and seditious, and if internal to the community, more harmful. The crimes of hypocrisy in the Muslim world have always been greater and more destructive. A little attention to the characteristics described in these verses will suffice to call to mind the committees of evil, the underground gangs and secret circles who have been "setting fire" to this world for centuries.
- Evil attributes and acts such as derision, trickery, lying, and ostentation are found more in hypocrites than unbelievers. This is another reason why the Qur'ān has described the hypocrites in detail and warned the Muslims against acquiring such attributes through unguarded association with them.
- On the other hand, since hypocrites live among the believers, it is possible that long and repeated description of their characteristics may cause the hypocrites to perceive the evil of hypocrisy, and the *Kalimat at-Tawḥīd* (the declaration of faith in God's Unity, namely "There is no deity but God, and Muḥammad is His Messenger"), which they pronounce with their tongues, may find a way to their hearts.

10. Qur'ānic statements such as God has "increased them in sickness", "set a seal on their hearts and hearing", and "left them to wan-

der blindly" do not by an means signify that human beings have no will-power and therefore no responsibility for their acts of deviancy. Rather, such statements clarify the true nature of Divine pre-determination or Destiny and human free will.

A person gets his or her just deserts in recompense for his or her inclinations, thought and actions. A person *wills* and *acts*, and God *creates*. *Creating* human deeds means giving "external" existence or reality to human will and human actions. The Qur'ānic statements cited above mean that, in response to people using their will-power in a certain direction and acting in that direction, God has given "external" or "visible, material" existence to their intentions, choices, and actions.

Having confused human acting with Divine creation and supposed that there are two kinds of destiny – one for the cause, and the other for the effect – the school of the *Jabriyyah* (fatalists) denied human free will, while the school of the *Mu'tazilah* (rationalists) accorded creative effect to human will and agency, concluding that it is human beings who create their actions.

11. Elsewhere (63: 4) the Qur'ān describes the hypocrites in these words: *When you see them, their outward form pleases you, and (their posture and speech are attractive and effective so that) you give ear to their words when they speak. (In reality) they are like blocks of wood propped up and (draped over) in striped cloaks.* Throughout history, puffed up by their wealth, social status, and physique, the leaders of unbelievers and hypocrites have usually belittled specially weak and poor believers as *fools*, as *the lowliest among them* and *as those without reflection*. But the truth is clearly the opposite.

This verse also clarifies that, besides being the shelter for the weak and poor, Islam defends and supports right and truth, and destroys haughtiness and self-pride. Islam has also established the true criteria for perfection, nobility and honor so that the Religion cannot be made a means of oppression at the hands of worldly people and rulers. It is hypocrisy and unbelief that give rise to haughtiness, conceit, egotism, hatred, and enmity.

12. The verse points out that only through knowledge and a sound viewpoint can one distinguish between truth and falsehood, between the way of faith and that of hypocrisy. Such other admonitions of the Qur'ān as "Do they not use their intellect?", "Do they not reason and understand?", "Do they not reflect?", and "Do they not reflect and be mindful?", signify that the appeal of Islam is based on knowledge, sound reasoning and wisdom, so that anyone with a sound intellect and capable of reflection is expected to accept Islam. By contrast, ignorance, falsehood, blind imitation and subjection to prejudice are characteristic of a disposition to superstition or unbelief and hypocrisy.

مَثَلُهُمْ كَمَثَلِ الَّذِى اسْتَوْقَدَ نَارًا فَلَمَّا أَضَاءَتْ مَا حَوْلَهُ ذَهَبَ اللَّهُ بِنُورِهِمْ وَتَرَكَهُمْ فِى ظُلُمَاتٍ لَا يُبْصِرُونَ ۝ صُمٌّ بُكْمٌ عُمْىٌ فَهُمْ لَا يَرْجِعُونَ ۝ أَوْ كَصَيِّبٍ مِنَ السَّمَاءِ فِيهِ ظُلُمَاتٌ وَرَعْدٌ وَبَرْقٌ يَجْعَلُونَ أَصَابِعَهُمْ فِى آذَانِهِمْ مِنَ الصَّوَاعِقِ حَذَرَ الْمَوْتِ وَاللَّهُ مُحِيطٌ بِالْكَافِرِينَ ۝ يَكَادُ الْبَرْقُ يَخْطَفُ أَبْصَارَهُمْ كُلَّمَا أَضَاءَ لَهُمْ مَشَوْا فِيهِ وَإِذَا أَظْلَمَ عَلَيْهِمْ قَامُوا وَلَوْ شَاءَ اللَّهُ لَذَهَبَ بِسَمْعِهِمْ وَأَبْصَارِهِمْ إِنَّ اللَّهَ عَلَى كُلِّ شَيْءٍ قَدِيرٌ ۝ يَا أَيُّهَا النَّاسُ اعْبُدُوا رَبَّكُمُ الَّذِى خَلَقَكُمْ وَالَّذِينَ مِنْ قَبْلِكُمْ لَعَلَّكُمْ تَتَّقُونَ ۝ الَّذِى جَعَلَ لَكُمُ الْأَرْضَ فِرَاشًا وَالسَّمَاءَ بِنَاءً وَأَنْزَلَ مِنَ السَّمَاءِ مَاءً فَأَخْرَجَ بِهِ مِنَ الثَّمَرَاتِ رِزْقًا لَكُمْ فَلَا تَجْعَلُوا لِلَّهِ أَنْدَادًا وَأَنْتُمْ تَعْلَمُونَ ۝ وَإِنْ كُنْتُمْ فِى رَيْبٍ مِمَّا نَزَّلْنَا عَلَى عَبْدِنَا فَأْتُوا بِسُورَةٍ مِنْ مِثْلِهِ وَادْعُوا شُهَدَاءَكُمْ مِنْ دُونِ اللَّهِ إِنْ كُنْتُمْ صَادِقِينَ ۝ فَإِنْ لَمْ تَفْعَلُوا وَلَنْ تَفْعَلُوا فَاتَّقُوا النَّارَ الَّتِى وَقُودُهَا النَّاسُ وَالْحِجَارَةُ أُعِدَّتْ لِلْكَافِرِينَ ۝

17. They are like him who (while traveling with company in the desert, halted for the night and) kindled a fire (for light and warmth and protection). However, when the fire had just lit all around him (and the company had become comfortable but were not properly appreciative of the fire and failed to guard it against wind, the fire was extinguished. Thus) God took away their light and left them in darkness, unseeing.

18. They are utterly deaf, dumb, and blind; they can no longer recover.[13]

19. Or like (those caught in) a rainstorm from the sky, accompanied by veils of darkness, thunderclaps and flashes of lightning. (Terrified by the thunder, and as if they might thereby evade a possible stroke of lightning), they press their fingers into their ears in fear of death. This is how God has encompassed the unbelievers from all sides.

20. The lightning almost snatches away their sight. Whenever it gives them light, they take a few steps in it, and when the darkness covers them, they stand still. Had God so willed,[14] indeed He would have taken away their hearing and sight. Surely God has full power over everything.

21. Now O humankind! Worship your Lord Who has created you as well as those before you (and brought you up in your human nature and identity), so that you may attain reverent piety towards Him and His protection (against any kind of straying and its consequent punishment in this world and the Hereafter);

22. And Who has made the earth a bed (comfortable, couch-like floor) for you, and the sky a canopy. He sends down from the sky water, with which He brings forth fruits for your provision.[15] So do not set up rivals to God (as deities, lords and objects of worship)[16] when you know (that there can be no deities, lords, creators, and providers at all to worship save God).[17]

23. If you are in doubt about the Divine authorship of what We have been sending down on Our servant (Muḥammad) (and claim that it is the work of a human being like Muḥammad who can neither read nor write), then produce just a *sūrah* like it and call for help to all your supporters, all those (to whom you apply for help apart from God), if you are truthful in your doubt and claim.[18]

24. If you fail to do that – and you will most certainly fail – then guard yourselves against the Fire whose fuel is human beings and stones (that you have shaped into idols to adore), prepared for the unbelievers.

13. A fuller interpretation is as follows:

> (Since no voice is heard in the darkness of night and their hearing has long been closed to any "good, beneficial" voice,) they are utterly deaf; (since they cannot hear, they are) dumb (who have no possibility to speak and shout for help;) and (since their eyes are veiled to light by darkness, they are) blind; they can no longer recover (from the state they are in).

Verses 17–20 illustrate the condition and consequence of hypocrisy in the heart by means of two comparisons or similes. Both contain wonderfully effective and abrupt transitions from general truth to concrete representation and vice versa. Without due consideration of this, the statement here describing the hypocrites as *deaf, dumb, and blind* may seem at variance with the later one (verse 20) in which it is said that, had God willed, He would have taken away their hearing and sight. The two similes describe the hypocrites from different viewpoints.

14. It points to an important truth that God did not will to take away their sight and hearing. The eternal Divine Will is, in one respect, identical to Divine Knowledge. That is, with His Eternal Knowledge Which encompasses all time or in Which all time ends, God knew eternally what people would do and "wrote" it. People do not do something because God (pre-)determined or (pre-)wrote it but God (pre-)wrote it because He eternally knew that people would do it. So, since it is part of what the hypocrites have deserved that they suffer from the dreadful condition they are in, God did not will to take away their sight and hearing out of justice. He does not take away their sight and hearing also to give them respite so that they may yet see their pitiful condition and give up their way. However, it should particularly be pointed out that it is solely God Who determines what consequence people face in return for what deed. This "determinism" which is prevalent in the world of conscious beings where knowledge and will have a significant place points decisively to an all-encompassing Knowledge and Will, and therefore to God's Existence and Uni-

ty. That is why the Qur'ān presents the Divine Will as a link between cause and effect and human free will and its consequences.

15. The atmosphere surrounds the earth as the rind of an orange surrounds and protects the fruit within it. The layer of the atmosphere nearest to the earth is the layer of air. It preserves the earth from the harmful rays coming from different parts of the sky. By allowing only the rays beneficial to life to pass through, it functions like a sort of filter or screen providing shade. Clouds and rain are formed in this layer of the atmosphere.

16. This verse shows that unbelief is not based on true knowledge. However, it also points to the fact that knowing does not always prevent unbelief. As pointed out above, the main reasons for unbelief are haughtiness, self-pride, wrongdoing, prejudice, and deviancy in thought and action. Even if unbelief is not always based on ignorance, it causes ignorance. One whose heart is lacking in "a point of affirmation" may have specialist knowledge of all the natural and social sciences but, for want of that opening to faith, this knowledge increases him or her only in ignorance of Divine truths. According to the Qur'ān, only the knowledge which leads to "knowing" God and belief in Him is true knowledge: *Of all His servants, only those possessed of true knowledge have awe of God* (35: 28). Any knowledge polluted by haughtiness, self-pride, wrongdoing, prejudice, and deviancy in thought and action, is worthy only of being a piece of information.

17. These two verses, as well as expressing many other truths, establish God's Oneness in Divinity, Lordship, and His being the Sole Object of Worship, and describe what this means. Believing in God's Oneness requires that He must be affirmed as the only Creator, Nourisher, Provider, as the One Who brings up every creature and equips it with the necessary systems, organs, and faculties in accordance with its functions and duties in life, and the One Who deserves worship exclusively. All phenomena in the universe – from humanity's creation to the earth's being made like a comfort-

able, couch-like floor, and from the sky's being built like a dome-like ceiling for us to the
rain and all kinds of vegetation brought forth
to feed us – are enough to establish these three
requirements of belief in God's Oneness.

18. After mentioning some of the phenomena demonstrating God's Oneness, the Qur'ān
presents another proof as clear as daylight to
establish both God's Unity and the Messengership of Muḥammad, upon him be peace and
blessings, and its Divine authorship. This proof
is presented in the form of a challenge that humankind are absolutely unable to produce even
the like of one of its sūrahs.

When the Qur'ān was revealed, eloquence,
oratory, and poetry were held in the highest regard among the Arabs. In order to prove its Divine authorship and the main purposes it pursues, the Qur'ān challenged first the literary
geniuses of the time and then the whole of humankind until the Last Day:

> O men and jinn! If you have doubts
> concerning the Divine authorship of the
> Qur'ān and fancy it to be the product of a
> human mind, come forward and let an il-
> literate one among you like the one whom
> you call Muḥammad, the Trustworthy,
> produce a like of the Qur'ān. If he (or
> she) cannot do that, let the most famous
> of your writers or scholars try it. If they
> too cannot do it, let them all work to-
> gether and deploy the whole legacy of the
> past, and call on their deities to help. Let
> all of your scientists, philosophers, soci-
> ologists, theologians, and men of letters
> try their utmost to produce the like of the
> Qur'ān. If they too cannot do it, then let
> them try – leaving aside the miraculous
> aspects of the Qur'ān's meaning, which
> are inimitable – to produce a work which
> can match the Qur'ān in the eloquence of
> its word order and composition.

By *Then produce ten invented sūrahs
like it* (11: 13), the Qur'ān means: "It is
not stipulated that the meaning of what
you invent should be true, you may fabricate legends, myths, or stories. If you
cannot do that, not the like of the whole
Qur'ān, produce a work which can

match only ten *sūrah*s of it. If you cannot do that either, then produce a work
like only one *sūrah* of it. If that also is
too difficult, then produce a work like
one of its short *sūrah*s.

If you cannot do that either – and you
will never be able to – although you are
in dire need of doing so because your
honor, religion, nationality, and even
lives will otherwise be at risk, you will
perish in the world in utter humiliation,
and as stated in the verse, *Then guard
yourselves against the Fire, whose fuel is human beings and stones (that you
have shaped into idols to adore)*, (2: 24),
you will go to Hell. Since you have now
understood that you are absolutely unable, you must admit that the Qur'ān
is the miraculous Word of God. (*The
Words*, "the 25th Word," 404–405)

Those self-conceited people were unable to
argue with the Qur'ān in words. Although it
was the easier and safer course for them to obstruct and falsify its message, they chose to
fight against it with the sword, which was the
perilous and most difficult course. If those intelligent people had been able to argue with the
Qur'ān in words, they would not have chosen
to put their property and lives at risk. However,
as al-Jāhiz remarked, since they could not argue with it in words, they were compelled to
argue with their swords, taking the risk of losing their lives and properties.

Like the parts of an organism, all the verses, even individual words, of the Qur'ān are interrelated. Among its verses, there is both the
relation of whole and parts, and the relation
of universal and particular. That is, most of
the verses are each an independent part of the
Qur'ān – wherever you put it, you will see it
fitted. Yet most verses have an essential link to
all other verses and represent the whole of the
Qur'ān. The Qur'ān has many other aspects of
miraculousness which make it impossible for
humankind to produce even the like of one of
its verses.

4   سُورَةُ البَقَرَة   ٤

وَبَشِّرِ الَّذِينَ ءَامَنُوا وَعَمِلُوا الصَّالِحَاتِ أَنَّ لَهُمْ جَنَّاتٍ
تَجْرِي مِن تَحْتِهَا الْأَنْهَارُ كُلَّمَا رُزِقُوا مِنْهَا مِن
ثَمَرَةٍ رِّزْقًا قَالُوا هَٰذَا الَّذِي رُزِقْنَا مِن قَبْلُ وَأُتُوا بِهِ
مُتَشَابِهًا وَلَهُمْ فِيهَا أَزْوَاجٌ مُّطَهَّرَةٌ وَهُمْ فِيهَا
خَالِدُونَ ۝ إِنَّ اللَّهَ لَا يَسْتَحْيِ أَن يَضْرِبَ مَثَلًا مَّا
بَعُوضَةً فَمَا فَوْقَهَا فَأَمَّا الَّذِينَ ءَامَنُوا فَيَعْلَمُونَ
أَنَّهُ الْحَقُّ مِن رَّبِّهِمْ وَأَمَّا الَّذِينَ كَفَرُوا فَيَقُولُونَ
مَاذَا أَرَادَ اللَّهُ بِهَٰذَا مَثَلًا يُضِلُّ بِهِ كَثِيرًا وَيَهْدِي بِهِ
كَثِيرًا وَمَا يُضِلُّ بِهِ إِلَّا الْفَاسِقِينَ ۝ الَّذِينَ يَنقُضُونَ
عَهْدَ اللَّهِ مِن بَعْدِ مِيثَاقِهِ وَيَقْطَعُونَ مَا أَمَرَ
اللَّهُ بِهِ أَن يُوصَلَ وَيُفْسِدُونَ فِي الْأَرْضِ أُوْلَٰئِكَ هُمُ الْخَاسِرُونَ
۝ كَيْفَ تَكْفُرُونَ بِاللَّهِ وَكُنتُمْ أَمْوَاتًا فَأَحْيَاكُمْ
ثُمَّ يُمِيتُكُمْ ثُمَّ يُحْيِيكُمْ ثُمَّ إِلَيْهِ تُرْجَعُونَ ۝ هُوَ الَّذِي
خَلَقَ لَكُم مَّا فِي الْأَرْضِ جَمِيعًا ثُمَّ اسْتَوَىٰ إِلَى السَّمَاءِ
فَسَوَّاهُنَّ سَبْعَ سَمَاوَاتٍ وَهُوَ بِكُلِّ شَيْءٍ عَلِيمٌ ۝

———❧———

25. [19]Give glad tidings to those who believe and do good, righteous deeds:[20] for them are Gardens through which rivers flow. Every time they are provided with fruits (of different color, shape, taste, and fragrance and that are constantly renewed) therefrom, they say, "This is what we were provided with before." For they are given to them in resemblance (to what was given to them both in the world, and just before in the Gardens, familiar in shape and color so that they may not be unattractive because unknown). Furthermore, for them are spouses eternally purified (of all kinds of worldly uncleanliness); and therein they will abide.[21]

26. God does not disdain to strike any parable – (that of) something like a gnat or something greater or lower than it.[22] Those who have already believed know that it is the truth from their Lord. As to those whose unbelief has long been established in their hearts, they say, "What does God mean by such a parable?" Thereby He leads many astray, and thereby He guides many. He thereby leads none astray save the transgressors;[23]

27. (Those) who break God's covenant after its solemn binding, and sever the bonds God commanded to be joined, and cause disorder and corruption on earth.[24] Such are those who are the losers (in both this world and the next.)

28. How can you disbelieve in God, seeing that you were dead, and He gave you life.[25] Then He causes you to die.[26] Then He will bring you to life again; and then you will be returned to Him.[27]

29. It is He Who (prepared the earth for your life before He gave you life, and) created all that is in the world for you (in order to create you – the human species – and make the earth suitable for your life); then He directed (His Knowledge, Will, Power, and Favor) to the heaven,[28] and formed it into seven heavens.[29] He has full knowledge of everything.

---

19. In addition to being a miracle of eloquence, the Qur'ān is also miraculous in maintaining the balance among both the truths of divinity and the absolute and relative truths in the universe. It also maintains the balance between encouraging people to do good deeds in the hope and expectation of pleasing God and earning His reward, and discouraging them from doing evil ones for fear of His punishment. Following the presentation of the characteristics of believers, unbelievers and hypocrites, it warns those who are willfully determined in their unbelief against the Fire. Now it directs attention to the result of faith and doing good deeds

with most pleasant and exhilarating expressions, and in so doing, it both relieves the fearful souls and encourages faith and good deeds.

20. There are many deeds and attitudes, such as believing, establishing the Prayer, giving alms, and helping others, that are praised as good and enjoined by the Qur'ān and God's Messenger, upon him be peace and blessings. There are other deeds and attitudes which can either be virtuous or evil according to the time and occasions when they are done. Besides, the qualities or "virtues" that are often associated with good deeds and good character are best judged according to the rightness of intention and the particular circumstances in which it is expressed.

For example, the self-respect that a weak person should wear before a powerful one becomes, if the powerful one assumes it before a weak one, self-conceit. The humility which a powerful person should wear before a weak one becomes, if assumed by a weak one, self-abasement. The solemn or strict bearing of an administrator in the exercise of his or her duties of office is dignity, while humility in that situation would be self-abasement. The same solemnity in his or her house would be self-conceit, whereas humility there would indeed be humility. Forbearance and forgiving the evils done to one is good and a virtue; but when done on behalf of others, it is bad and a treason: a person may and perhaps should bear patiently whatever is done to him or her personally; but it is impermissible for that person to, for example, bear patiently wrongs being done to the society or nation. Conversely, whereas pride and indignation on behalf of the nation are commendable, on one's own behalf they are not.

Believing and doing good deeds are mentioned together but distinguished in the verse. This implies that doing good deeds is not a part of faith, yet faith alone without good deeds is not enough for the final salvation in the Hereafter.

21. The verse signifies that there will be Gardens for every believer within Paradise, and depicts them. The greatest blessing in Paradise is obtaining God's approval and good pleasure and (as indicated by some verses and explicitly stated in some *hadith*s) "seeing God," though this is a "seeing" beyond all our measures of quality and modality. However, since such wholly spiritual blessings are related to the elite among the believers, the Qur'ān usually presents the blessings of Paradise in a language that can appeal to pleasures of the body. A human being is a tripartite being composed of the spirit, the carnal soul, and the flesh or physical body. Since the body and carnal soul serve the believer in this world, and, in order to be disciplined and trained, have to endure some hardships and deprivation of some worldly pleasures, the believer will be rewarded with the pleasures appropriate to the body and the carnal soul. It should, however, not be thought that such pleasures are purely corporeal. The spiritual contentment they will give is greater than the corporeal. For example, every person needs a friend, a companion. What most satisfies this human need is having an intimate life-companion with whom to share love, joys, and sorrows. Since the kindest, most compassionate and generous of hearts is the heart of a woman, the Qur'ān mentions women among the greatest blessings of Paradise for men, rather than vice versa. This does not mean that the women will be left there without companions. The pleasure coming from mutual helping, sharing joys and grieves, companionship, love, affection, and intimacy is much greater that the bodily pleasures men and women may satisfy in each other. However, those who have been defeated by the bodily pleasures of this world, and who are therefore unaware of the spiritual pleasures accompanying them, may see Paradise as a realm of sensual enjoyment.

22. Like the Divine Scriptures prior to it, the Qur'ān uses parables and comparisons to convey abstract truths. This is because, people in general do not understand abstractions unless they have had some preparation in the specialized terms and specialized discourse appropriate to the presentation of abstract concepts. The Qur'ān addresses itself to all of humanity from the first day of its revelation until the

Last Day, and accordingly deploys the full re-sources of language in a style that is forceful, clear, accessible, and effective in communicating its message. The accessibility of the Revelation is, like the intelligibility of the "book" of creation, an aspect of God's mercy to His creatures, of His grace in making His will knowable and known to humankind.

A second point to note here is that what human beings may see as "small" or insignificant is not always so, conversely what they see as "great" is not always so. It may sometimes be completely the other way round. Indeed, in many respects the smaller a thing is, the greater the artistry it manifests. In terms of artistry, there is no difference between the solar system on the one hand, and, on the other, the eye of a gnat or the belly of a flea. It could be argued that the artistry of the latter is greater in that they are constituent organs of living creatures.

23. The verse confirms once more the truth explained in the note 10 above. One of the principal reasons why God creates straying for someone or why He leads them to straying, is transgression. This word translates *fisq*. Used as a term, it means deviating from what is true, going beyond the limit, and abandoning the path leading to the eternal life of happiness. *Fisq* originates in using the three principal human drives or faculties – namely reason, lust, and anger – in the wrong way, a way that leads to demagogy, craftiness, hedonism, wrongdoing, and oppression. The next verse mentions the main reasons for unbelief, which is the greatest transgression.

24. The shortest meaning of this verse provided by the character of the words is as follows:

(Those) who break God's covenant (which is a rope of light woven of the threads of Divine Will, Wisdom, and Favor, and responsible for the order in the universe, and able to establish peace, order, and harmony in human life) after its solemn binding, and sever the bonds God commanded to be joined (among the relatives as a requirement of blood relationship, and among people as required by

human social needs), and (in an attempt to spread their vices in the whole community, even in the whole world, like one who, having caught a contagious disease, desires to pass it to others) cause disorder and corruption on earth. Such are those who are the losers (in both this world and the next).

The words given in brackets are not additional commentary; they indicate the meanings carried in the words used in the verse, in their order, and in their structure and style. For example, the word translated as "break up" is from the verb *NaQaDa* which means unraveling a thick, strong rope. This implies that God's covenant is a strong rope binding people together and humanity to God. The word *mīthāq* translated as binding corroborates this meaning.

God's covenant is a "rope of light" woven of His Will, Wisdom, Knowledge, and Favoring, and which extends from the eternity in the past to the eternity in the future. This rope holds together the magnificent order in the universe and establishes the relationship among all creatures. One end of it was given into the hand of humankind. This led to the implanting of the seeds of many capabilities in the human spirit. The seeds should germinate and be developed by human beings themselves into "good trees yielding ever-fresh fruits" according to the principles of Sharī‘ah. Loyalty to God's covenant is possible by developing these capabilities and using them in the way established by Islam. Breaking the covenant means breaking this "rope of light" into pieces. Denying any of the Prophets and Divine Books, rejecting some of the commandments of Islam while accepting others, approving some of the verses of the Qur'ān while disapproving others, and similar attitudes or approaches mean breaking this rope into pieces. Such destruction results in environmental imbalance as well as imbalance and disorder in human relations. The present environmental crisis and the state of relations between people(s) and nations in the world are the result of breaking God's covenant.

25. In order to better understand the truth presented in the verse, we should provide a fuller

translation derived from the character of the words used and other relevant verses (i.e., 22: 5; 23: 12-14; 76: 1):

> How can you disbelieve in God, seeing you were dead (the particles or atoms that had long been appointed to constitute the body of each of you were dispersed in air, water, and earth, then transferred to the worlds of plants and animals according to certain laws and principles, and, taken as food, formed into sperm in the loins of your fathers, thereafter placed as a drop of seed in the wombs of your mothers. Having undergone several stages, they came to the point of formation where God breathed into them out of His Spirit) and He gave you life. (You live until the hour He appointed for each of you, and) then He causes you to die. Then (you stay as long as He wills in the world of the grave, between this world and the next, until, following many mighty revolutions) He will you back to life; and then (passing through a series of tremendous revolutions and several worlds), you will be returned to Him.

In order to establish belief in the Existence and Unity of God in the minds and hearts of people, the Qur'ān draws attention to His being the Creator and how humanity was brought to life. Life is the most pleasant and fascinating miracle of God, as well as being one of His greatest blessings. It also provides a bright evidence for the eternal Existence and Unity of God and other pillars of faith. The simplest of the degrees of life visible to ordinary observation is the life of plants, the beginning of which is germination under the soil. Despite its being apparently common and observable, the origin and nature of life is still unknown to humanity. The sphere of relationship of a lifeless body, even if it is as big as a mountain, is restricted to the spot where it is located. By contrast, a living creature so small as a honeybee establishes relationship with the whole world and can say, "The world is my property, my garden." When life attains the degree of the human being, it can travel through all times and places and perhaps beyond on the wings of

mind, heart and imagination. Containing the material, biological, spiritual dimensions of life, as well as its mineral, vegetable, and animal divisions, human life encompasses all kinds and degrees of life. Since it is pure and transparent in both its outer and inner dimensions, there is not the veil of "natural" causes between life and God's Power. That is, the "natural" causes have no part in God's creating life.

26. Like life, death is also created by God and therefore as great a blessing as life itself. It may even be said that death is a greater blessing than life. Every degree of earthly life results in death, but death in every degree results in a greater degree of life. For example, consumed in animal and human bodies, plants attain by dying the degree of animal and human life, while the animals consumed in human bodies acquire by dying the degree of human life in the human body. A seed annihilating itself under the soil develops into a plant or tree which will yield thousands of its exact like. By dying and going into the earth, a person starts his or her eternal life. In that perspective, death is good and as great a blessing as, or one greater than, life.

27. Some claim that, together with the verse, *Our Lord! You have made us die twice, and given us life twice* (40: 11), this verse provides an evidence for reincarnation. However, both that verse and this one utterly refute reincarnation. For, first of all, reincarnation is not restricted to two cycles of re-birth. Secondly, reincarnation is restricted to unbelievers or evil persons, but the verse discussed is not (for the interpretation of verse 40: 11, consult itself where it exists). Thirdly, there are several verses stating that there is no return to the world after death. In response to the desire of the unbelievers to be returned to the world so that they may believe and do good, righteous deeds in order to be saved from the Fire, God will say: *No, never!* (23: 99-100).

The expression *You were dead*, implies that each member of humankind has some sort of existence in the world of atoms or particles. It has already been determined in God's Knowledge which atoms in the worlds of elements, plants, and animals will constitute the body of which person. So there is no room for chance and coincidences in the motion of the particles that constitute human bodies. The expression also suggests that since death follows life, those particles are themselves devoid of what we recognize as life, which is a direct gift of God pointing to Him clearly. Again, the verse draws attention to the fact that it is God Who deals both death and life with no one and nothing else having any part in it. It signifies: "You were lifeless in the world of elements because God willed you to be so and made you so."

28. While this verse and the verses 41: 9–12 apparently imply that the earth was created prior to the heavens, verses 79: 27–30 suggest the opposite, and verse 21: 30 seems to be saying that they were created together at the same time. However, when considered together, they mean:

In the primeval stages of creation, the heavens or the solar system and the earth were like a piece of dough that the Hand of Power kneaded of ether, which resembles water in spreading and permeation and in its being the medium for God's creation in the beginning as water is the medium for life on the earth. This fact is what the verse, *His Supreme Throne was upon the water* (11: 7), refers to. Out of this matter – ether – God made atoms and molecules, and intensified and solidified some part of it, making this part into the earth. In its being solidified and crusted with a cover, the creation of the earth was prior to the heavens. However, before the earth was solidified and crusted with a cover, there was a single heaven in the form of clouds of gaseous elements. The fashioning of these clouds of gaseous elements, the primal form of the heavens, into "seven heavens" and adorning them with the sun, moon, and stars followed the formation of the earth, while the preparation of the earth for human life was after the fashioning of the heavens.

What the Qur'ān means by *seven heavens* has been interpreted in different ways, the most significant of which are as follows:

- This extremely broad space is filled with ether, the existence of which physics once admitted without, however, establishing it. This ether serves as the medium to transmit heat, light and the like, and establish the relationship among the laws God established for the movement of the heavenly bodies. Like water changing into vapor and ice without losing its essential nature, this ether has also similar kinds of formation. What the Qur'ān means by "seven heavens" may be these different kinds of formation of ether.

- It is a known fact that there are many galaxies, of which the Milky Way is but one, their exact number being (as yet) unknown.

- Just as ash, coal, and diamond are substances produced from the same mineral during the process of its working, fire generates flames and smoke, so too, different levels or layers could have been formed of the same matter during its being fashioned. Since in Arabic usage (as in other languages) such numbers as seven, seventy, and seven hundred signify different degrees of multiplicity, there may be more than seven heavens.

- The Qur'ān calls the heaven where the sun, moon, and stars are *the nearest heaven* or *the heaven of the world* (67: 5). The other six heavens may be the heavens of the worlds of the Hereafter. (God knows the best.)

29. In respect of how the Qur'ān deals with issues that are the subject-matter of sciences, the following points should be noted:

- The Qur'ān is not a book of sciences like physics, chemistry, biology, and astronomy.

- The Qur'ān aims to establish in minds and hearts the pillars of faith and the truths of worshipping and justice.

- The Qur'ān mentions scientific facts only parenthetically and uses them as evidences of the truths it conveys. For this reason, it prefers a style accessible and adapted to every level of understanding from its revelation until the Last Day.

- Since the Qur'ān uses such matters as evidence and evidence cannot be more abstruse than the thesis propounded, it gives consideration to the people's understanding and sense-perceptions.

- The Qur'ān was revealed fourteen centuries ago, when little was known about the issues sciences study. Seeing that humanity has made continuous progress in scientific studies and discoveries since then, the Qur'ān would obviously have to use a language impossible to contradict in any age.

- In point of fact, all the Qur'ānic expressions that allude to realities as studied in the sciences are absolutely true. However, what the Qur'ān means by them is, in most cases, open to interpretation. In this way, the Qur'ān, opens the door to scientific study and encourages it.

- Science is an assemblage of hypotheses, tested and disproved, partially or wholly, then replaced by other hypotheses, calling for further testing, and so on. It can be said that the sciences are still far away from knowing "the human" thoroughly and may always remain so. They will never be able to solve the mystery of creation and the origin of life, two mighty issues beyond the scope of scientific experiment and verification. For this reason, on the basis of present knowledge, no one can or should object to the Qur'ānic expressions that allude

to realities as studied in the science. If there is any appearance of contradiction, one should wait for what future studies will reveal and confirm about the meaning of the Qur'ānic expressions. There are three principles concerning the Qur'ānic expressions which are allegorical and ambiguous:

- The expression is God's word.
- What God means by it is absolutely true.
- What God means by it may be "such and such."

Confirming the first two principles is a requirement of faith, the denial of which amounts to unbelief. The third indicates that what *God* means by a particular expression is open to study and interpretation and, within certain conditions, different opinions may be put forward. The conditions are: (i) having excellent knowledge of Qur'ānic Arabic and its rules and modes of eloquence, and always considering them; (ii) having excellent knowledge of the essential principles of Islam and the main, clear pronouncements of the Qur'ān; (iii) having sufficient expertise in the subject-matter in question; and (iv) having no intention whatever other than to find out the truth and do so purely to obtain God's approval. If these conditions are met, any opinion may be respected and appreciated as true, at least in part, or as contributing to the effort to arrive at the truth.

وَإِذْ قَالَ رَبُّكَ لِلْمَلَٰٓئِكَةِ إِنِّى جَاعِلٌ فِى ٱلْأَرْضِ خَلِيفَةً ۖ قَالُوٓا۟ أَتَجْعَلُ فِيهَا مَن يُفْسِدُ فِيهَا وَيَسْفِكُ ٱلدِّمَآءَ وَنَحْنُ نُسَبِّحُ بِحَمْدِكَ وَنُقَدِّسُ لَكَ ۖ قَالَ إِنِّىٓ أَعْلَمُ مَا لَا تَعْلَمُونَ ۝ وَعَلَّمَ ءَادَمَ ٱلْأَسْمَآءَ كُلَّهَا ثُمَّ عَرَضَهُمْ عَلَى ٱلْمَلَٰٓئِكَةِ فَقَالَ أَنۢبِـُٔونِى بِأَسْمَآءِ هَٰٓؤُلَآءِ إِن كُنتُمْ صَٰدِقِينَ ۝ قَالُوا۟ سُبْحَٰنَكَ لَا عِلْمَ لَنَآ إِلَّا مَا عَلَّمْتَنَآ ۖ إِنَّكَ أَنتَ ٱلْعَلِيمُ ٱلْحَكِيمُ ۝ قَالَ يَٰٓـَٔادَمُ أَنۢبِئْهُم بِأَسْمَآئِهِمْ ۖ فَلَمَّآ أَنۢبَأَهُم بِأَسْمَآئِهِمْ قَالَ أَلَمْ أَقُل لَّكُمْ إِنِّىٓ أَعْلَمُ غَيْبَ ٱلسَّمَٰوَٰتِ وَٱلْأَرْضِ وَأَعْلَمُ مَا تُبْدُونَ وَمَا كُنتُمْ تَكْتُمُونَ ۝ وَإِذْ قُلْنَا لِلْمَلَٰٓئِكَةِ ٱسْجُدُوا۟ لِءَادَمَ فَسَجَدُوٓا۟ إِلَّآ إِبْلِيسَ أَبَىٰ وَٱسْتَكْبَرَ وَكَانَ مِنَ ٱلْكَٰفِرِينَ ۝ وَقُلْنَا يَٰٓـَٔادَمُ ٱسْكُنْ أَنتَ وَزَوْجُكَ ٱلْجَنَّةَ وَكُلَا مِنْهَا رَغَدًا حَيْثُ شِئْتُمَا وَلَا تَقْرَبَا هَٰذِهِ ٱلشَّجَرَةَ فَتَكُونَا مِنَ ٱلظَّٰلِمِينَ ۝ فَأَزَلَّهُمَا ٱلشَّيْطَٰنُ عَنْهَا فَأَخْرَجَهُمَا مِمَّا كَانَا فِيهِ ۖ وَقُلْنَا ٱهْبِطُوا۟ بَعْضُكُمْ لِبَعْضٍ عَدُوٌّ ۖ وَلَكُمْ فِى ٱلْأَرْضِ مُسْتَقَرٌّ وَمَتَٰعٌ إِلَىٰ حِينٍ ۝ فَتَلَقَّىٰٓ ءَادَمُ مِن رَّبِّهِۦ كَلِمَٰتٍ فَتَابَ عَلَيْهِ ۚ إِنَّهُۥ هُوَ ٱلتَّوَّابُ ٱلرَّحِيمُ ۝

───────✦───────

30. [30](Remember) when your Lord said to the angels:[31] "I am setting on the earth a vicegerent." The angels asked: "Will you set therein one who will cause disorder and corruption on it and shed blood, while we glorify You with Your praise (proclaim that You are absolutely above having any defect and that all praise belongs to You exclusively), and declare that You alone are All-Holy and to be worshipped as God and Lord." He said: "Surely I know what you do not know."

31. (Having brought him into existence, God) taught Adam the names, all of them.[32] Then (in order to clarify the supremacy of humankind and the wisdom in their being created and made vicegerent on the earth), He presented them (the things and beings that had been taught to Adam with their names) to the angels, and

said: "Now tell Me the names of these, if you are truthful (in your praising, worshipping, and sanctifying Me as My being God and Lord deserves)."

32. (In acknowledgement of their imperfection, and their perception of the truth of the matter, the angels) said: "All-Glorified are You (in that You are absolutely above having any defect and doing anything meaningless, and Yours are all the attributes of perfection). We have no knowledge save what You have taught us. Surely You are the All-Knowing, the All-Wise."

33. (In order to demonstrate the superiority of humankind more clearly, God) said: "O Adam, inform them of these things and beings with their names." When he (Adam) informed them with their names, He said (to the angels), "Did I not tell you that I know the unseen of the heavens and the earth, and I know all that you reveal and all that you have been concealing?"[33]

34. [34]And (remember) when We said to the angels: "Prostrate before Adam!"[35] They all prostrated, but Iblīs did not; he refused, and grew arrogant, and displayed himself as an unbeliever.[36]

35. "O Adam! Dwell you, and your spouse, in the Garden,[37] and eat (of the fruits) thereof to your hearts' content where you desire, but do not approach this tree,[38] or you will both be among the wrongdoers.[39]

36. But Satan[40] (tempting them to the forbidden tree despite Our forewarning,) caused them both to deflect therefrom and brought them out of the (happy) state in which they were. And We said, "Go down, (all of you,) (and henceforth you will live a life,) some of you being the enemies of others. There shall be for you on the earth a habitation and provision until an appointed time."[41]

37. (Aware of his lapse and in the hope of retrieving his error, rather than attempting to find excuses for it,) Adam received from his Lord words that he perceived to be inspired in him (because of his remorse, and he pleaded through them for God's forgiveness). In return, He accepted his repentance. He is the One Who accepts repentance and returns it with liberal forgiveness and additional reward, the All-Compassionate (especially towards His believing servants).[42]

---

30. The Qur'ān presented the creation of the heaven and the earth, and the formation of the heavens, as the most manifest signs of God's Existence and Unity in the outer world. Then, as signs in their inner world, it showed how humankind was brought into life. It now proceeds to explain what kind of beings humans are and why they were created and how they can fulfill the purpose of their creation. For we need to know why so valued a being was created and wherein the value lies.

31. The primary reason why God informed the angels of His will to set a vicegerent on the earth was to indicate the better way of counseling and to teach the angels the wisdom in His making humankind vicegerent on the earth. The angels knew that this vicegerent would cause disorder and corruption because the jinn, beings who resemble humankind in having free will and powers of intellect, anger, and lust, had caused sedition and bloodshed on the earth before.

Angels are among the beings in the universe endowed with a life different in kind from life in the earthly kinds directly known to us. That different kinds of life-forms can exist in the universe should not surprise us. Yet, there was surprise when, in 1993, nearly 300 animal species, almost all of them previously unknown, were discovered living around hydrothermal vents formed where sea-water, leaking through the ocean floor at spreading ridges, is heated by the underlying magma and rushes into the cold ocean. Until then scientists had thought that there could be no life without solar energy, and few organisms were known to survive without a direct or indirect way to tap it. Perhaps this "most startling discovery of twentieth century biology" will strengthen our willingness to recognize that there can be life in other forms and conditions than those known to us. If scientists had given ear to the Qur'ān, and not defined life by the earthly forms known to them, they might have acknowledged that there can be different kinds of life in other parts and dimensions of the universe, particular to each part or dimension, and so given a truer direction to their sciences.

Angels are spiritual beings, of subtle forms created from "light" (Muslim, "Zuhd," 10); they have different kinds or species but are not differentiated as male or female (37: 149–150; 43: 19; 53: 27; *The Essentials*, 64). Being servants of God with no evil-commanding soul, they obey the commandments issuing from the Eternal Will and Creative Power that rules the universe. There is nothing to cause quarrels or disputes among them because they are innocent, their realm is vast, their nature is pure, and their stations are fixed. Each of the heavenly bodies is a place of worship for the angels (*The Words*, "the 29th Word," 532–533).

They ask no reward for their services; their reward is the spiritual contentment of nearness to their Creator. Their worship varies according to their different natures and functions. No event in the universe can be conceived of or occurs without the function of the angels. There are angels representing or responsible for every event in the universe and every species on the earth. For example, some of them, the chief of whom is Michael, are responsible for the growth of vegetation. Michael superintends the growth of all kinds of corn and provision by leave and Power of God, and, if one may put it in such terms, he is the head of all the angels who may be likened to farmers. There is another great angel who, by God's leave, Command and Power, is the chief of the "incorporeal shepherds" of all animals. They look on God's acts with wonder and admiration and present to Him the glorification and worship of each species of creature offered in the language of its nature and disposition.

There are still other kinds or species of angels such as Gabriel who carried Revelation to the Messengers, and 'Azrāīl and his aides whom God employs in taking the lives of people, and Isrāfīl who will blow the Trumpet during the final destruction of the world and the resurrection of the dead. The Qur'ān also mentions the angels who record people's deeds (82: 11); and angels who carry out a variety of tasks of awesome majesty and power (77: 1–4; 79: 1–5; 82: 11).

32. The primary reason why humankind was accorded superiority over the angels is that they were taught the names. The duty of humankind on the earth is vicegerency or *khilāfah*, meaning succession. This indicates another species or kind of beings on the earth preceding humankind. These were the jinn, who were succeeded by humankind because of their unending conflicts and revolts against God.

As a term, *khilāfah* or vicegerency denotes improving the earth, on the basis of knowledge of things and the laws of creation (which we wrongly call the "laws of nature"), and ruling on the earth according to the dictates of God, thus establishing justice. Carrying out this duty requires scientific knowledge and religion. Humankind can acquire scientific knowledge by studying nature and are given religion through God's Messengers. The Books given or revealed to the Messengers, in addition to containing the religious principles, are in one respect like discourses describing nature and its meaning. That is why in Islam the universe or nature is seen as the "Created Book" and its laws as the laws of the creation and operation of the universe issuing from the Divine Attributes of Will and Power. The Qur'ān is the "Revealed Book," the set of Divine laws and principles issuing from God's Attribute of Speech. For this reason, there can and should be no dichotomy or conflict between science and the Religion.

The names taught to Adam are the names of both things and his descendants. We know this from the use of the pronoun *hum* – meaning "their" in the compound "their names" – which is used for conscious beings. It shows that Adam's descendants are included among the "names" taught to him. There must be a relation between this event, which took place in the World of the Unseen (*Ghayb*), and the event (referred to in 7: 172) when God brought forth from the children of Adam, from their loins, their seed, and made them testify to His being their Lord, which also must have taken place in the Unseen. The angels must have fully comprehended Adam's supremacy and the wisdom in his vicegerency, not merely because of his being taught the names that they had not been taught, but also because they saw the illustrious members of humankind among the descendants of Adam – such as the Prophets, saints, and pure, exacting scholars, who would change the earth into gardens of Paradise through their faith, knowledge, and morality.

The knowledge of things was given to Adam in summarized form and then, during the course of history, was taught to the Messengers in relative detail according to the mission of each. That is why the Messengers became also the forerunners of scientific knowledge and progress, in addition to their being guides in spirituality and morality. The Qur'ān, which consummates all the previous Scriptures, sheds light on future scientific studies and discoveries, and indicates their final point of advancement in its narrations of the miracles of the Messengers.

The names taught to Adam also signify the potentiality of learning bestowed on humankind. Giving a name means knowing, for one can give a name only to something one knows. Animals come, or rather, are sent, to the world as if taught and trained in another world. They are adapted to the conditions of their life within a very short period as if they knew them already. By contrast, it takes human beings on average one year to learn how to walk, and many more years to learn the conditions of life, to distinguish securely between what is harmful and what is beneficial for them. This learning indeed continues until death, an evidence that learning has a fundamental place in human life and progress.

As pointed out above, vicegerency denotes humankind's ruling on the earth and improving it by using all that is subjected to them in accordance with the dictates of God. If humankind attribute to themselves what God has given them of knowledge, power, the ability of learning, and various other capacities, and then attempt to act independently of God, it is then that disorder and bloodshed begin on the earth. For this reason, their happiness, dignity, and the improvement of the earth lie in acknowledging their innate weakness, poverty, and ignorance before God and, attributing whatever they have and their accomplishments to God, becoming to His infinite Power, Absolute Sufficiency, and Knowledge.

33. Historically, humankind have not avoided bloodshed nor ceased to cause disorder, from the beginning of their earthly existence. Furthermore, the majority of people have been those who follow false doctrines or beliefs and associate partners with God. However, this does not mean that the creation of humankind and their being appointed as vicegerent on the earth has proved evil and ugly. The following simple analogy will explain:

For example: 100 seeds of fruit have the value of 100 seeds while they are seeds. But once they are planted, if even 80 out of the 100 rot away while the remaining 20 germinate and grow to bear fruit, the value of those 20 will far exceed that of the 100 seeds.

If the human race had remained existent only in God's Knowledge without developing their potential on the earth, the Tree of Creation would not have yielded more than 100,000 Prophets, millions of saints, pure, exacting scholars, heroes of good morals, and other virtuous members of humankind. The good that these illustrious fruits have added to existence far exceeds the evil of the rest. The angels at first could not discern this outcome, but when the potential of the human race was clear to them, they admitted its supremacy with full contentment of heart.

34. After the potential supremacy of humankind to the angels became evident, it can be said that an arena of trial was opened for both humankind and the angels and other conscious beings, among whom was Satan. This also im-

plied that the earthly life of humankind was about to begin. The motor of this life would be human free will. Having free will meant making a choice between at least two contrary alternatives. The individual and collective life of humankind, as well as human history, is the history of the conflicts of choices.

Besides the Attributes essential to His being God, namely Existence, having no beginning, Permanence, Oneness, being unlike the created, and Self-Subsistence, God has another kind of Attributes called the Positive Attributes which are Life, Knowledge, Will, Power, Hearing, Seeing, Speech, and Creating. These Attributes are the origin of the Names such as Giver of life and the All-Reviver, the All-Knowing, the All-Willing, the All-Powerful, the All-Hearing, the All-Seeing, the All-Speaking, and the Creator, etc. Having such absolute, unrestricted Attributes and all-beautiful Names means that their manifestation is "inevitable." One Who exists in and of Himself, and Whose Existence is absolutely perfect, will manifest Himself, as "required" by His very "nature." Thus, the universe is the collection of the manifestations of God's Attributes and Names, and those manifestations are focused on humankind. It is as if God Almighty drew an imaginary veil before His Attributes and Names and created humankind as the theater where almost all of His Attributes and Names are manifested. This demonstrates the high value accorded to humankind.

35. The prostration mentioned here signifies the angels' admission of the superiority of humankind and their obedience to the Divine purpose for the creation of Adam and his being made vicegerent on the earth. Prostration in the meaning of worship is done exclusively before God. By obeying God's order to prostrate before Adam, the angels were, in reality, prostrating to Him.

36. The angels (as explained in note 30 above) are beings created from "light," always busy with worshipping God and almost unable to commit sins. Since they do not have to struggle against sins, they do not progress spiritually. Satan and his progeny represent the opposite

pole to the angels. The Qur'ān mentions Satan in the course of narrating his refusal to prostrate before Adam as Iblīs and subsequently as Satan. Iblīs belonged to the jinn (18: 50) and had free will. He had not been tested until he was ordered to prostrate before Adam. Defeated by his vainglory, he attempted to justify his refusal on the pretext that he had been created from smokeless fire while Adam was created from clay. In other words, he considered himself superior by virtue of his physical composition, whereas no one should claim superiority on the basis of something in which they have no part. What brings superiority is righteous acts done freely, without compulsion. Such things as physical structure, wealth, status, position, and the like, cannot be the basis of a reasonable claim to superiority. Because of this the Qur'ān openly decrees: *Surely the noblest, most honorable of you in God's sight is the one best in "taqwā" (piety, righteousness, and reverence for God).* (49: 13). Unlike Adam, Satan did not acknowledge his error and so appeared as the embodiment of haughtiness and malicious enmity towards humankind. It is clear that he had been inwardly defeated by the attributes that cause unbelief, such as wrong viewpoint, prejudice, and self-pride. In the very first test he was set, these attributes swallowed him up and caused him to be an obstinate, refractory unbeliever.

As pointed out above, Satan was called Iblīs at the stage of his rebellion against God's order to prostrate before Adam. Iblīs means one who is desperate. After that event, he was called Satan, meaning one expelled from God's Presence and Mercy and burning with envy and passion. As Adam is the father of humankind, Satan has also progeny. The unbelieving human beings who share the same character with Satan and are always busy misleading people from the path of God are also called "satans" in the Qur'ān. The "satans" of the hypocrites, referred to in 2: 14, are an example.

37. There are different opinions about whether the Garden mentioned here was a Paradise-like corner of the earth or the Paradise to which the believers will go in the Hereafter by God's grace. There is another point of view worthy of

consideration: The significant events narrated in 2: 30–39 – Adam being created and presented as the prototype of humankind, taught the names by God, the angels prostrating to him as God commanded; Iblīs (the embodiment of wickedness and prototype of devils) refusing to prostrate – all these events took place in the Unseen. Similarly, the event (7: 172) when God brought forth from the children of Adam, from their loins, their seed, and they testified to His being their Lord, must have taken place in the Unseen. If Adam's being placed in the Garden with Eve also happened in one of the worlds of the Unseen, then that Garden might be a Garden belonging to those worlds, some aspect or dimension of the manifestation of the Paradise in the Hereafter, which must even now be existing as a "seed." What we should dwell on here is the lessons that God wills to teach us by such events. From this perspective, the Garden may be a realm where the parents of humankind stayed for some time or a stage they had to pass through on the way to being fully "human" in order to reside on the earth.

38. There are again different opinions about the forbidden tree. When we reflect on how Satan tempted Adam and Eve – *O Adam, shall I lead you to the tree of eternity and a kingdom that will never decay?* (20: 120) – and the inevitable results to come from approaching the forbidden tree (experiencing toil, hunger, nakedness, thirst, and exposure to the sun's heat [20: 117–119], and that after they ate of it, their shameful parts revealed to them [20: 121]), we may conclude that the forbidden tree indicates the act of sexual union, which would later be allowed, or a kind of food or something else that caused them to become aware of their full physical and biological humanity with all the needs, feelings, and passions attendant upon it. We can deduce that this prohibition would have been only for a limited time, as in fasting or during the Ḥajj or during post-childbirth bleeding. But they showed haste and disobeyed.

39. The word here translated as wrongdoer is ẓālim derived from ẓulm meaning darkness. It is the opposite of light and the reason or symbol of non-existence as opposed to existence. For

this reason, it is used as a Qur'ānic term for acts causing the darkening and extinction of the faculties of the heart ("seeing" and "hearing" in the sense of verse 2: 7). The main feature of such acts is transgressing the bounds established by the Religion and behaving without considering the time, place, and conditions. Having a very wide area of usage, it ranges from putting something in the wrong place to associating partners with God. People harm, first of all, themselves by committing *zulm*. This is why the Qur'ān says that people wrong themselves by transgressing the bounds. The wrongdoing mentioned in this verse is such an act. (This will be clearer in the words Adam received from his Lord, explained below in note 41.)

40. Although Satan is the embodiment of evil and always tries to cause evil in human life, his being created is not evil. God is the only Creator Who creates all things and beings, along with their good or evil deeds, and whatever He creates is good either in itself or with respect to its result. The angels never do evil and Satan never does good, but humankind have been endowed with the ability to do both good and evil. They are responsible for using and developing their ability to do good, resisting their potentiality for evil and channeling it towards what is good. For example, envy can be channeled into competitiveness in doing good; obstinacy can be turned into steadfastness on the path of right and truth. By both doing good and, especially, by struggling against the temptations of Satan and the carnal, evil-commanding soul, and against the potentiality for evil, a person evolves spiritually, while the ranks or stations of the angels are fixed because they are free from the seduction of Satan and have no evil tendency to struggle against. The inclusion in creation of relative evil – there is nothing absolutely evil in creation – is the wheel of both spiritual, intellectual, and scientific development in human life. That is why the creation of Satan and other apparent evils is not evil. Against the argument that many people deviate and many evils appear in human life because of the temptations of Satan, readers may refer to

the analogy in note 33. Unaware of this highly significant truth, the Magians in Iran attributed the creation of evil to a second deity, and within the civilization of Islam, the Mu'tazilites attributed it to humankind themselves.

Some think that Satan is a being who "fulfills a specific function in God's plan," namely tempting humankind so that they can exercise their God-given freedom of choice. Therefore his rebellion is merely apparent and has a purely symbolic significance as the outcome of the function assigned to him. This is a grave misconception, impossible to reconcile with the explicit statements of the Qur'ān, and therefore impossible to accept.

41. While it was Adam and his spouse tested in the Garden, we understand from the Qur'ān's usage of the plural form in the order, *Go down, all of you!* that more than two people received the order: *Go down, all of you, (henceforth you will live a life,) some of you being the enemies of others*. Those addressed by this order must be Adam, Eve, Satan, and their future progeny.

42. Unlike Satan, Adam did not offer to defend himself with excuses for his lapse. Rather, he felt great remorse and thus opened the door to being forgiven. In return for his remorse, God Almighty inspired in him some words – *talaqqā* here translated as "received", connotes "inspired"– through which he, together with his spouse, pleaded for God's forgiveness. It is agreed by the majority of the interpreters of the Qur'ān, that these words were those given in 7: 23: *Our Lord! We have wronged ourselves, and if You do not forgive us and do not have mercy on us, we will surely be among those who have lost!*

Some (probably under the influence of narrations from Israelite sources) have argued that Eve led Adam to be deceived by Satan. Since this is the approach in the Old Testament (*Genesis*, 3: 1–6), woman was considered evil and held in disgrace in medieval Christianity. The Qur'ān presents the event centered on Adam; that is why it was he who received the words and, even more than Eve, had to implore God's forgiveness, although they both did so.

6 سورة البقرة ٦

قُلْنَا اهْبِطُوا مِنْهَا جَمِيعًا فَإِمَّا يَأْتِيَنَّكُم مِنِّي هُدًى فَمَن تَبِعَ
هُدَايَ فَلَا خَوْفٌ عَلَيْهِمْ وَلَا هُمْ يَحْزَنُونَ ۞ وَالَّذِينَ كَفَرُوا
وَكَذَّبُوا بِـَٔايَٰتِنَا أُوْلَٰٓئِكَ أَصْحَٰبُ النَّارِ هُمْ فِيهَا خَٰلِدُونَ ۞
يَٰبَنِيٓ إِسْرَٰٓءِيلَ اذْكُرُوا نِعْمَتِيَ الَّتِيٓ أَنْعَمْتُ عَلَيْكُمْ وَأَوْفُوا بِعَهْدِيٓ
أُوفِ بِعَهْدِكُمْ وَإِيَّٰيَ فَارْهَبُونِ ۞ وَءَامِنُوا بِمَآ أَنزَلْتُ مُصَدِّقًا
لِّمَا مَعَكُمْ وَلَا تَكُونُوٓا أَوَّلَ كَافِرٍۭ بِهِۦ وَلَا تَشْتَرُوا بِـَٔايَٰتِي ثَمَنًا
قَلِيلًا وَإِيَّٰيَ فَاتَّقُونِ ۞ وَلَا تَلْبِسُوا الْحَقَّ بِالْبَٰطِلِ وَتَكْتُمُوا
الْحَقَّ وَأَنتُمْ تَعْلَمُونَ ۞ وَأَقِيمُوا الصَّلَوٰةَ وَءَاتُوا الزَّكَوٰةَ
وَارْكَعُوا مَعَ الرَّٰكِعِينَ ۞ أَتَأْمُرُونَ النَّاسَ بِالْبِرِّ
وَتَنسَوْنَ أَنفُسَكُمْ وَأَنتُمْ تَتْلُونَ الْكِتَٰبَ أَفَلَا تَعْقِلُونَ ۞
وَاسْتَعِينُوا بِالصَّبْرِ وَالصَّلَوٰةِ وَإِنَّهَا لَكَبِيرَةٌ إِلَّا عَلَى الْخَٰشِعِينَ
۞ الَّذِينَ يَظُنُّونَ أَنَّهُم مُّلَٰقُوا رَبِّهِمْ وَأَنَّهُمْ إِلَيْهِ رَٰجِعُونَ ۞
يَٰبَنِيٓ إِسْرَٰٓءِيلَ اذْكُرُوا نِعْمَتِيَ الَّتِيٓ أَنْعَمْتُ عَلَيْكُمْ وَأَنِّي فَضَّلْتُكُمْ
عَلَى الْعَٰلَمِينَ ۞ وَاتَّقُوا يَوْمًا لَّا تَجْزِي نَفْسٌ عَن نَّفْسٍ شَيْـًٔا
وَلَا يُقْبَلُ مِنْهَا شَفَٰعَةٌ وَلَا يُؤْخَذُ مِنْهَا عَدْلٌ وَلَا هُمْ يُنصَرُونَ ۞

through your Prophets),[48] so that I fulfill your covenant,[49] and of Me alone be in awe and fear (in awareness of My Power and of your being My servants).

41. Believe in that which I have sent down (the Qur'ān), confirming what (of the truth) you already possess, and do not be the first to disbelieve in it. And (you scribes, fearful of losing your status and the worldly benefit accruing from it) do not sell My Revelations for a trifling price (such as worldly gains, status, and renown); and in Me alone seek refuge through reverence for Me and piety.

42. Do not confound the truth by mixing it with falsehood,[50] and do not conceal the truth while you know (the meaning and outcome of what you do, and that what you strive to hide is true, and that Muḥammad is the Messenger of God, whose coming you have been anticipating).[51]

43. Establish the Prayer in conformity with its conditions, and pay the Prescribed Purifying Alms (the Zakāh); and bow (in the Prayer, not by forming a different community or congregation, but) together with those who bow (the Muslims).[52]

44. Do you enjoin upon people godliness and virtue but forget your own selves, (even) while you recite the Book (and see therein the orders, prohibitions, exhortations, and warnings)? Will you not understand and come to your senses?[53]

45. Seek help through patience[54] (and fasting, which requires and enables great patience), and through the Prayer. Indeed the Prayer is burdensome, but not for those humbled by their reverence of God:

46. Those who feel as if always in the Presence of their Lord, having met with Him; and are certain of following the way to return to Him.[55]

38. [43]We said: "Go down, all of you, from there!" (and executed Our order). If, henceforth, a guidance (like a Book through a Messenger) comes to you from Me, and whoever follows My guidance (and turns to Me with faith and worship), they will have no fear (for they will always find My help and support with them), nor will they grieve."

39. But those who disbelieve and deny Our signs (the verses of the revealed Book of guidance as well as the signs in both their inner world and the outer world establishing My Existence and Unity and other pillars of faith), they will be the companions of the Fire; therein they will abide.[44]

40. [45]O Children of Israel![46] Remember My favor[47] that I bestowed upon you, and fulfill My covenant (which I made with you

47. O Children of Israel! Remember My

favor that I bestowed upon you, and that I once exalted you above all peoples;

48. And be fearful of and strive to be guarded against a Day when (everybody will be seeking a means to save himself, and when) no soul will pay on behalf of another, nor will any intercession (of the sort common in the world but which does not meet with God's permission and approval) be accepted from any of them, nor will compensation be received from them, nor will they be helped.

---

43. The acceptance of the repentance of Adam and Eve, following their appeal to God for forgiveness, did not mean that God's decree that they would descend to the earth would not be implemented. Rather, it meant that they started their earthly life cleansed of their error – without any blemish or "original sin" to be passed on to their descendants – as all newborns begin their life free of sin.

44. With its wonderful eloquence and concision, the Qur'ān has, thus far in this *sūrah*, informed us about guidance, faith, and Islam, and the pillars and main principles thereof, then about unbelief and hypocrisy and the reasons for them, together with a description of the different qualities of the believers, unbelievers, and hypocrites. Then, it has presented decisive and comprehensive proofs, in the inner world of human beings and in the outer world around them, of God's Existence and Unity, the Divine authorship of the Qur'ān, the Messengership of Muḥammad, upon him be peace and blessings, and about the Hereafter, Paradise, and Hell. It has then explained the nature and duty of humankind and how they started their earthly life. The Qur'ān has in this way summarized its main purposes before beginning to narrate the earthly adventure of humankind and human communities, which will illustrate those purposes with concrete, historical examples. In verses 38 and 39 it has extended a rope to the beginning of the *sūrah*, binding the whole together. It makes direct reference to the guidance mentioned at the beginning of the *sūrah* with the mention of guidance in verse 38. It interprets or expands on the prosperity mentioned in verse 5 with the explanation in verse 38: *They will have no fear (in this world and the next, for they will always find My help and support with them), nor will they grieve.* In addition, by stating that the unbelievers and those who deny God's Revelations and signs will be the companions of the Fire to abide therein, it recalls verses 23 and 24, which threaten those who deny the Divine authorship of the Qur'ān with the Fire *whose fuel is human beings and the stones (that they have shaped into idols to adore).*

45. The history of the Children of Israel narrated in the Qur'ān is an example of the general history of humankind or of all nations. It is both for this reason and because of the significant part that the Israelites and their descendants would play in the future history of Islam and humankind, that the Qur'ān draws attention to certain aspects of their story.

In presenting and praising the true believers at the beginning of the *sūrah*, the Qur'ān opened a door on the history of previous peoples with the verse, *Those who believe in what is sent down to you, and what was sent down before you (such as the Torah, Psalms, and Gospel, and the Scrolls of Abraham)* (2: 4). This door is opened for several reasons: because of the importance of the part the Children of Israel played in the past, and would play in the future history of humankind; because of the important position the Jews enjoyed in Madīnah during the Madīnah period of the Messengership of Muḥammad, upon him be peace and blessings; and to warn the nascent Muslim community and all the Muslims to come in the future against lapsing into the same deviancy and error as the Children of Israel fell. For these reasons, the Qur'ān recounts notable events in the history of the Jews, at the same time urging them to believe in Muḥammad and enter the Muslim community.

46. "Israel" was a title of the Prophet Jacob, upon him be peace, meaning a pure servant of God. In Muslim history, the Jews are usually referred to as *Yahūdī*, meaning one who belongs to Yahūda –Judah in the Old Testament. Judah – *Yehudah* in Hebrew – is the name of one of the two kingdoms which emerged with the division of Prophet Solomon's kingdom after his death, and takes this name from Judah, one of the sons of Jacob. According to another opinion, *Yahūdī* means one who follows the Law established by Judah, an Israelite jurist who lived in the second century after Jesus. The Jews themselves name their religion – Judaism – after Judah. The Qur'ān uses the term *Yahūdī* for the most rigid enemies of Muslims among the Children of Israel and those who regard and call themselves as *Yahūdī* among them (6: 82; 2: 62). By referring to them as the children of a Prophet, a pure servant of God, the Qur'ān means that they are expected to believe in the Prophet Muḥammad and so fulfill their covenant with God. This usage also establishes an important principle of good manners, especially in calling people to the Straight Path, that one should address people with the titles they like to be addressed with.

47. Here there is a reference to the favor mentioned in *Sūrat al-Fātiḥah*. When used in a general sense, it means being favored with the Religion, a Divine Book, a Prophet, guidance, and following the Straight Path without deviancy. It specifically means here God's choosing Prophets and Messengers from amongst the Children of Israel and granting them a great kingdom, and giving them a Book, guiding them to the Straight Path, and making them inhabit the land promised to them.

48. The covenant God made with the Children of Israel was that when a Messenger came after the Prophets, they would believe in him and help him, and therefore they would believe in the Prophet Muḥammad, upon him be peace and blessings, whom God had mentioned with his particular attributes and the good tidings of whose coming He had given in the Book He

had sent to them, and whom they therefore knew very well.

49. The covenant of the Children of Israel – *your covenant* in the verse – is that they would continue to receive His favor if they reformed themselves and were steadfast in following His way after so many calamities striking them in return for their rebellions and transgressions.

For the covenant between God and the Children of Israel, see also 17: 4–8.

50. About the ways in which the Children of Israel confounded the truth by mixing it with falsehood, see 2: 71, 79, 140, 174, 179; 3: 167; 4: 13, 46; 5: 106. (They made additions or changes in the Book and then attributed them to God; they willfully misinterpreted its words; and they hid the truths which they thought did not serve their purposes. They also confounded it through false testimony and wrong judgment.)

51. Elmalılı Hamdi Yazır (1877–1942), one of the greatest Muslim interpreters of the Qur'ān, made the following comment on confounding the truth by mixing it with falsehood:

> Were it not for another verse concerning this subject, this verse alone would suffice to teach us how we must act in the matter of the translation and interpretation of the Qur'ān and in similar other issues of the religious sciences. It must never be forgotten how important it is that the Qur'ān should remain and be preserved in its original form, and its translation, interpretation, or commentary in any other language can never replace and be substituted for the Qur'ān. We must avoid such expressions as the Turkish Qur'ān or the Persian Qur'ān. No matter into how many languages the Qur'ān is translated or in how many languages it is interpreted or commented on, none of them can be the Qur'ān, nor can they substitute for it. God Almighty declares explicitly: *Do not confound the truth by mixing it with falsehood.* (Yazır, 1: 336)

This point should be considered especially with reference to the controversies about whether the extant versions of the earlier Scriptures are (or could be) exactly the same as their originals. As is well known, the earlier Scriptures were not preserved in their original language and only translations of them are extant.

52. The Qur'ān orders the Children of Israel to do, not their Prayer which lacks the rite of bowing – they must have changed it during their long history – but the Prayer God taught the Muslims through the Prophet Muḥammad, upon him be peace and blessings. The Qur'ān draws particular attention to the bowing (rukū') in the Prayer. This tells us that bowing has a special importance in the Prayer, and because of this, every cycle of the Prayer is called rak'ah, a word derived from the same root as rukū'. In addition, the verse is alluding to the importance of establishing the Prescribed Prayer in congregation, which is a means and an expression of the solidarity and unity of the Muslims. This is a warning against forming separate congregations on the basis of differences of opinion about minor legal or other secondary matters. The verse is also inviting the Children of Israel to join the Muslim community. We can infer from this verse that they had become negligent about the duties of the Prayer and the Prescribed Purifying Alms (the Zakāh). The latter is a tax at fixed rate in proportion to the value of property or wealth above a certain minimum, and its proper expenditure is decreed in sūrah 9: 60.

53. Enjoining godliness on others but forgetting one's own self means knowingly exposing oneself to perdition and consenting to punishment. Not acting on the advice one gives to others means contradicting oneself and degrading the knowledge and authority on which that advice is based. Obviously, it can have little or no effect on others to recommend and enjoin on others what one does not do oneself. So, enjoining the good on others but not doing it is sheer stupidity and absurdity.

Like earlier Israelite Prophets who severely admonished and scolded their people, we also see in the Gospels that the Prophet Jesus, upon him be peace, addressed many among the Jewish scholars of his time in terms much harsher than the Qur'ān. For example:

Brood of vipers, how can you, being evil, speak good things? For out of the abundance of the heart the mouth speaks. A good man out of the good treasure of the heart brings forth good things: and an evil man out of the evil treasure brings forth evil things. (Matthew, 12: 34–35)

. . .saying, The scribes and the Pharisees sit in Moses' seat: Therefore whatever they tell you observe, that observe and do; but do not do according to their works: for they say, and do not do. For they bind heavy burdens, hard to bear, and lay them on men's shoulders; but they themselves will not move them with one of their fingers. But all their works they do for to be seen by men: they make their phylacteries broad, and enlarge the borders of their garments. They love the best places at feasts, the best seats in the synagogues, greetings in the market places, and to be called by men, 'Rabbi, Rabbi.' But you, do not be called 'Rabbi'; for One is your Teacher, the Christ; and you are all brethren.

But woe to you, scribes and Pharisees, hypocrites! For you shut up the kingdom of heaven against men: for you neither go in yourselves, nor do you allow those who are entering to go in. Woe to you, scribes and Pharisees, hypocrites! For you devour widows' houses, and for a pretense make long prayers: therefore you will receive the greater damnation. Woe to you, scribes and Pharisees, hypocrites! For you travel land and sea to win one proselyte, and when he is won, you make him twice as much a son of hell as yourselves. Woe to you, blind guides, who say, 'Whosoever swears by the temple, it is nothing; but whoever swears by the gold of the temple, he is obliged to perform it!' . . . Woe to you, scribes and Pharisees, hypocrites! For you pay tithe of mint and anise and cumin, and have neglected the weightier matters of the law, justice and mercy and faith. These you ought to have done, without leaving the others undone. . .

Blind Pharisee, first cleanse the inside of the cup and dish, that the outside of them may be clean also. Woe to you, scribes and Pharisees, hypocrites! For you are like unto whitewashed tombs which indeed appear beautiful outwardly, but inside are full of dead *men's* bones and all uncleanness. . . Woe to you, scribes and Pharisees, hypocrites! Because you build the tombs of the prophets and adorn the monuments of the righteous, and say, 'If we had lived in the days of our fathers, we would not have been partakers with them in the blood of the prophets.' Therefore you are witnesses against yourselves that you are the sons of those who murdered the prophets. Fill up, then, the measure of your fathers' guilt. 'Serpents, brood of vipers, how can you escape the damnation of hell? (*Matthew*, 23: 2-8; 13-16, 23, 26-27, 29, 31-33)

The Qur'ān's warnings are not addressed only to the scholars and leading representatives of a certain religion; they are directed to all those who represent a heavenly religion, including, of course, Muslim scholars.

54. It can be said that patience is the half of Islam, the other half being thankfulness. The patience shown just at the moment when misfortune strikes is true patience. With respect to the situations requiring it, patience can be divided into the following categories:

- enduring difficulties of fulfilling the duty of servanthood to God or steadfastness in performing regular acts of worship;

- resisting the temptations to sin of the carnal soul and Satan;

- enduring heavenly or earthly calamities, which entails resignation to Divine decrees;

- steadfastness in following the Straight Path without deviancy in spite of worldly attractions and distractions;

- showing no haste in pursuing those of one's hopes or plans that require a stretch of time to achieve.

Because fasting requires prohibiting to the carnal soul the things of which it is most enamored – eating, drinking, and sexual relations, as well as lying, backbiting, and gossip – it strengthens and deepens the believer's willpower. Accordingly, fasting as a duty of worship has come to be regarded as identical with patience. For this reason, the meaning of *patience* in the verse includes fasting.

55. God's guidance is based on compassion, knowledge, evidence, logic, reasoning, warning, giving good tidings, and illustration. Here, again, the Qur'ān refers to the beginning of the *sūrah*: it relates the topic here to faith, establishing the Prescribed Prayer, paying the Purifying Alms-giving, and spending in God's cause, reverence for God, and the afterlife – all of which were treated at the beginning. By recounting the history of the Children of Israel and the favors God bestowed upon them, the Qur'ān continues to send its rays of guidance to their minds and hearts.

49. And (remember) that We saved you from the clan (the court and military aristocracy) of the Pharaoh,[56] afflicting you with the most evil suffering (by enslaving you to such laborious tasks as construction, transportation and farming[57]), slaughtering your sons and letting live your womenfolk (for further humiliation and suffering). In that was a grievous trial from your Lord.[58]

50. And remember when (after years of struggle to escape Egypt, you had just reached the sea with the army of the Pharaoh in close pursuit and) We parted the sea for you and saved you, and (as sheer grace from Us, which you had no part in) caused the clan of the Pharaoh to drown while you were looking on.

51. And when on another occasion We appointed with Moses forty nights,[59] then (during the time he stayed on Mount Sinai,) you adopted the (golden) calf as deity and worshipped it after him; and you were wronging yourselves thereby with a most heinous wrong.

52. Then (even though adopting as deity any other than God is an unpardonable sin, We accepted your atonement and) We pardoned you after that, that you might (acknowledge Our many and great favors to you and) give thanks (believing in God and worshipping Him alone, and carrying out His commandments).

53. And (remember) when We granted Moses (while he was on Mount Sinai for forty nights) the Book[60] and the Criterion (to distinguish between truth and falsehood, and the knowledge, and power of judgment to put it into effect),[61] that you might be guided to truth and abide by it.[62]

54. [63]And when Moses said to his people: "O my people, assuredly you have wronged yourselves by adopting the (golden) calf as deity; so turn in repentance to your All-Holy Creator (Who is absolutely above having any partners), and kill amongst yourselves those who have committed that great offense, thus purifying yourselves of this tremendous sin.[64] That will be best for you in the sight of your All-Holy Creator, and He will accept your repentance and pardon you. Surely He is the One Who accepts repentance and returns it with liberal forgiveness and additional reward, the All-Compassionate.[65]

55. And (despite all that had occurred and the manifest signs of your Lord that you witnessed over many years, a time came) when you said: "Moses, we will never believe in you (whether the commandments you have brought are really from God) unless we plainly see God (speaking to you)."

Thereupon the thunderbolt (that you saw come unexpectedly) seized you. Motionless as if dead, you were gazing.[66]

56. Then after that death-like state (and your spiritual death), We revived you (recovering you from the death-like state) so that you might give thanks.

57. And (since, unaided, you would not be able to survive in the desert without shelter and food) We caused the cloud (which you plainly saw was assigned for you) to shade you, and sent down upon you manna and quails: "Eat of the pure, wholesome things that We have provided for you." Yet (in breaking the laws, in refusing to obey the injunctions about even those foods) they did not wrong Us but they were wronging themselves.[67]

---

56. When the Prophet Joseph, upon him be peace, was taken to Egypt as a slave, the Hyksos dynasty ruled Egypt. They were a northwestern Arab or mixed Arab–Asiatic people who came to Egypt from Syria sometime between 1720 and 1710 BC and subdued the Middle Kingdom. The Muslim historians call them al-Amālik. From the time of Joseph (roughly mid-seventeenth century BC) the Divine Religion represented by the Children of Israel (Prophet Jacob) became prevalent and they had the authority in Egypt (Qur'ān, 5: 20). However, within two centuries thereafter, the native Copts took over rule. Their kings were called Pharaoh. As understood from the Qur'ān, the Pharaoh ruled in Egypt with his clan, army, and a privileged aristocracy. What the Qur'ān means by Āl-i Fir'awn is this ruling oligarchy.

57. *The Bible*, "Exodus," 1: 11–14.

58. The Qur'ān uses the term *balā'* (trial) for the tormented life of the Children of Israel in Egypt. God tries people with both good and evils. When He tries with good such as success, wealth, high position, and physical beauty, it requires gratitude to God and attributing it to Him. When He tries with evils such as a misfortune, illness, or poverty, it requires patience without complaint. This, however, does not mean that one stricken by an evil should not try to escape from it. Being tried with evil is usually the result of a sin. Therefore, it also requires repentance and seeking forgiveness. Whether a believer is tried with good or evil it is good with respect to its consequence, provided it is met with gratitude in case of the former and patience without complaint in case of the latter. In addition to serving for the forgiveness of the sin committed and bringing extra good, trial causes the stricken people to be saved from wrong conceptions, beliefs, and assertions, and it matures and perfects them. The trial of the Children of Israel resulted in their escaping a life of torment in Egypt and being favored with God's guidance and a great kingdom.

59. The night (because it is quieter and there are fewer distractions than in the day) is particularly favored for spiritual journeying in God's cause. We read in the Qur'ān that the Last Messenger of God, upon him be peace and blessings, was commanded long night vigils especially at the beginning of his mission because night is more suitable for prayer and night vigils are more impressive, with the recitation in them being more certain and upright (73: 2–6; 76: 26). The Messenger's miraculous journey to Jerusalem and his Ascension also took place at night.

60. The Book wherein was light, guidance, mercy, and the solution to all the problems that would confront them. See 5: 44; 6: 91, 154; 7: 145.

61. The word translated as "the Criterion to distinguish between truth and falsehood, and the knowledge, insight, and power of judgment to put it into effect" is *al-Furqān*, as it is the means to distinguish truth and falsehood, right and wrong, and lawful and unlawful. In another verse (8: 29), the Qur'ān declares that if those who believe keep their duty to God in fear and respect in order to deserve His protection, He will assign them a *furqān*. Here it

means an inner sense or faculty of insight, discernment, inspiration, and power of judgment to distinguish between right and wrong. *Al-Furqān* is also one of the titles of the Qur'ān. God's Messenger said: "I have been given the Qur'ān and its like together with it" (Abū Dāwūd, "Sunnah," 5). The "like of the Qur'ān" is the Sunnah of the Messenger. In addition to its other functions, the Sunnah interprets the Qur'ān. In order to understand the Qur'ān correctly and fully, especially its commandments, we must of necessity depend upon the Sunnah. For this reason, as the Sunnah may be a *furqān*, the *Furqān* given to the Prophet Moses, upon him be peace, may be his Sunnah in the sense of the criteria by which to practice the Book in daily life.

62. The previous verse concludes with the need to give thanks – a comprehensive concept that includes carrying out God's commands and refraining from His prohibitions – for forgiveness after apostasy and returning to *tawḥīd*, while this verse, which mentions that God gave Moses the Book and the *Furqān*, ends with being guided to truth and abiding by it. This points to a very significant fact: the only way to find the Straight Path and follow it without deviancy is by obeying the Book in accordance with the *Furqān* – the Divine criteria. The concept includes both the Divine commandments in the Book and the criteria to apply them, namely the Sharī'ah. The rules and principles of the Sharī'ah are the citadel of religion. It is also the Sharī'ah which determines the limits and principles of the spiritual ways leading to God. Any spiritual or esoteric journeying trespassing its limits ends in a marsh of deviancy. It is worthwhile noting that "Torah" means "law."

63. In a few verses, the Qur'ān has summarized the history of the Children of Israel from their life of slavery in Egypt to Moses being given the Book and the *Furqān* on Mount Sinai, reminding them of God's past favors to them. It has invited them to believe in the Prophet Muḥammad, upon him be peace and blessings, about whom the Bible states that he resembles the Prophet Moses (*Deuteronomy*, 18: 18; also see the introduction to *Sūrat al-*

Qasas), and thereby reform themselves to follow the Straight Path. At this point, it enters into certain details and mentions particular events in order to strengthen its encouragement and give greater contentment to minds and hearts. While following these events, we will note how the Qur'ān bases all the topics it discusses on belief in God, the Messenger, and the Last Day, and on worshipping and doing good deeds.

64. After many eventful years, the Prophet Moses, believing that his people had attained to the stage of forming a civilized community on the basis of the Divine laws, went to Mount Sinai to receive the Torah. However, the Children of Israel adopted as deity the calf – one amongst them (called as-Sāmiriyy in the Qur'ān) made it of jewelry – and they began worshipping it. This demonstrated that belief in God as the only Lord to be worshipped was not yet ingrained in their hearts, and they were still enthralled by the impressions they had received in Egypt, where the cow was one of the deities. Moses postponed putting the Torah into effect and attempted to suppress this doctrinal uprising. He ordered them to "kill amongst yourselves those who have committed that great offense, thus purifying yourselves of this tremendous sin." Some interpreters are of the opinion that this order meant for them to kill their carnal, evil-commanding souls, that is, to reform themselves. However, it may well mean that an internal conflict ensued between those who remained loyal to the Divine Oneness and the apostates, and Moses ordered the killing of the latter. (Also, see note 70.) Killing the carnal, evil-commanding souls might be a consequence of this. The Bible is full of accounts of such punishments as mass-killing, exile, and malaria or bubonic plague that came in return for certain grave sins. It records that 3000 people were killed because of taking to themselves the calf (*Exodus*, 32: 28).

65. In earlier verses, God draws attention to His favors by using the pronoun "We." This verse presents the orders of the Prophet Moses, upon him be peace, to his people. It indicates that after receiving the Book and the *Furqān*,

Moses became a "Prophet-ruler." Moses' command, *kill amongst yourselves those who have committed that great offense, thus purifying yourselves of this tremendous sin*, as recorded in the Qur'ān, marks this change.

66. In order to petition God probably not to inflict another greater punishment on his people for their adopting the calf as deity, Moses, upon him be peace, chose seventy from amongst his people and took them to Mount Sinai (7: 155). He also desired that they might witness God's orders and persuade their people of the Divine origin of the orders. Although the Almighty did not speak to them directly, they witnessed the manifest, convincing signs of God's revealing to Moses His orders (Yazır, 4: 2292–2293). Despite this, they demanded to openly see God speaking to Moses, upon him be peace. Thereupon a thunderbolt seized them.

Although the seventy people or some amongst them made this demand and the thunderbolt seized them, since they represented the whole of the people and the people themselves had the same mood of deviancy, the Qur'ān attributes the offense to the Children of Israel as a whole. If the collective duties that fall upon the whole community and must be carried out by at least a group of responsible people are totally neglected, the punishment comes to the community as a whole. The verse, *And beware and guard yourselves against a trial that will surely not smite exclusively those among you who are engaged in wrongdoing; and know that God is severe in retribution* (8: 25), points to this fact. For this reason, the elite of any Islamic movement should continuously scrutinize themselves and their actions more than others.

67. God bestowed the three favors mentioned here on the Children of Israel for many years in the desert. A cloud constantly provided them with shade, quails poured down wherever they were in the evening, and manna came in abundance in the morning. Despite this, and despite the fact that the quails and manna came on the sixth day of the week in double the quantity of other days because they were forbidden to work on the seventh day (Sabbath) and therefore could not collect them, many of them went out to collect on that day. Also, though they were ordered not to leave the food they collected in the evening for the next day, some left it only to go bad, and still others collected more than their need (*Exodus*, 16: 4–31). In addition to many other wise purposes, these commandments surely aimed to purify their hearts of such evil attributes as avarice, hoarding, and selfishness, in order to perfect them morally and spiritually.

وَإِذْ قُلْنَا ادْخُلُوا هَٰذِهِ الْقَرْيَةَ فَكُلُوا مِنْهَا حَيْثُ شِئْتُمْ رَغَدًا

وَادْخُلُوا الْبَابَ سُجَّدًا وَقُولُوا حِطَّةٌ نَغْفِرْ لَكُمْ خَطَايَاكُمْ

وَسَنَزِيدُ الْمُحْسِنِينَ ۝ فَبَدَّلَ الَّذِينَ ظَلَمُوا قَوْلًا غَيْرَ الَّذِي

قِيلَ لَهُمْ فَأَنْزَلْنَا عَلَى الَّذِينَ ظَلَمُوا رِجْزًا مِنَ السَّمَاءِ بِمَا

كَانُوا يَفْسُقُونَ ۝ وَإِذِ اسْتَسْقَىٰ مُوسَىٰ لِقَوْمِهِ فَقُلْنَا اضْرِبْ

بِعَصَاكَ الْحَجَرَ فَانْفَجَرَتْ مِنْهُ اثْنَتَا عَشْرَةَ عَيْنًا قَدْ عَلِمَ

كُلُّ أُنَاسٍ مَشْرَبَهُمْ كُلُوا وَاشْرَبُوا مِنْ رِزْقِ اللَّهِ وَلَا تَعْثَوْا

فِي الْأَرْضِ مُفْسِدِينَ ۝ وَإِذْ قُلْتُمْ يَا مُوسَىٰ لَنْ نَصْبِرَ عَلَىٰ

طَعَامٍ وَاحِدٍ فَادْعُ لَنَا رَبَّكَ يُخْرِجْ لَنَا مِمَّا تُنْبِتُ الْأَرْضُ

مِنْ بَقْلِهَا وَقِثَّائِهَا وَفُومِهَا وَعَدَسِهَا وَبَصَلِهَا

قَالَ أَتَسْتَبْدِلُونَ الَّذِي هُوَ أَدْنَىٰ بِالَّذِي هُوَ خَيْرٌ

اهْبِطُوا مِصْرًا فَإِنَّ لَكُمْ مَا سَأَلْتُمْ وَضُرِبَتْ عَلَيْهِمُ

الذِّلَّةُ وَالْمَسْكَنَةُ وَبَاءُوا بِغَضَبٍ مِنَ اللَّهِ ذَٰلِكَ

بِأَنَّهُمْ كَانُوا يَكْفُرُونَ بِآيَاتِ اللَّهِ وَيَقْتُلُونَ

النَّبِيِّينَ بِغَيْرِ الْحَقِّ ذَٰلِكَ بِمَا عَصَوْا وَكَانُوا يَعْتَدُونَ ۝

---

58. And remember (after you had been wandering in the desert, how We guided you to a town) when We commanded: "Enter this town and eat (of the fruits) thereof as you may desire to your hearts' content.[68] Enter it (not through different ways with the aim of plundering and massacring its people but) through its gate humbly and in utmost submission to God. Say words of imploring forgiveness and loyalty to Him,[69] that We forgive you your misdeeds." We will increase the reward for those devoted to doing good, aware that God is seeing them.

59. Then those who persisted in wrongdoing changed what had been said to them (regarding humility, imploring forgiveness, submission, and loyalty) for another saying (and so acted contrarily to how they had been ordered.) So We sent down upon those who did wrong a scourge from heaven because they were continually transgressing .[70]

60. Again (remember) when Moses (on an occasion when his people were without water in the desert) beseeched water for his people, so We told him: "Strike the rock with your staff!" (As soon as he struck) there gushed forth from it twelve springs. Each tribe knew their drinking place.[71] Eat and drink of that which God has provided, and do not go about acting wickedly on earth, causing disorder and corruption.

61. And (remember) when you said: "Mo-

ses, we will no longer be able to endure one sort of food. Pray for us to your Lord that He may bring forth for us of all that the soil produces – its green herbs, and its cucumbers, and its corn, and its lentils, and its onions." He (Moses) responded: "Would you have in exchange what is meaner for what is better? Get you down to Egypt (or some city); surely there is for you there what you ask for."[72] So (in the end) ignominy and misery were pitched upon them, and they earned wrath (a humiliating punishment) from God. That was because they were persistently disbelieving in Our Revelations and rejecting Our signs (despite continuously observing them in their lives), and killing the Prophets against all right and truth. That was because they disobeyed and kept on exceeding the bounds (of the Law).[73]

68. There is a clear link between the command in this verse and the command given to Adam (2: 35): *Dwell you, and your spouse, in the Garden, and eat (of the fruits) thereof to your hearts' content where you desire.*

69. It is not certain (either from the Qur'ān or from the Bible) what town this was. In recounting historical events, the Qur'ān focuses on the lessons to be taken from them, rather than chronicling details of the place, time, or individuals involved. What is of importance here is that, on entering a town triumphantly after a battle or with the aim of settling, one should enter humbly, as our Prophet did when entering Madīnah during the *Hijrah* and Makkah during its conquest, and giving praise, glory, and thanks to God, with loyal submission to His commands, and seeking His forgiveness for one's sins, and not thinking of plundering and massacring. The orders recorded in the Bible (*Leviticus*, 25, 26; *Numbers*, 15: 1–41) to be carried out while entering a town, such as keeping the Sabbath and offering sacrifice to the Lord, are of the same import. Beyond such commandments is the consciousness of being seen by God and therefore doing good with greater sincerity and diligence. God exhorts the believers to this level of spiritual awareness in doing good.

70. The scourge sent down from heaven was probably the bubonic plague in which, according to the Bible, 14,700 people died (*Numbers*, 16: 46–49). The Qur'ān describes a pestilence, the causes of which are known, as a scourge sent down from heaven, and a means of suppressing an uprising against a Prophetic order. This teaches us to regard calamities (whether they strike individually or collectively) from the viewpoint of their real causes and the Divine wisdom in them, rather than their apparent "natural" causes. They come as the result of our negligence in God's laws governing our religious and "natural" lives, and of our transgressing the bounds established by Him. The great scholar Hamdi Yazır remarks:

> God Almighty is the One of Majesty Who is powerful enough to pull up the mountains and demolish them over the heads of people. He can change in an instant the gravity between things or objects. Those who have some sense should not forget how great and irresistible a force earthquake and volcanic eruption demonstrate. Some think that such events have nothing to do with the transgressions of humankind. This is a manifest error. Although it cannot be said that all of them are punitive, all of them are certainly linked to the life and actions of humankind. (Yazır, 4: 2322)

The function and dignity of humankind as vicegerent require this to be so.

71. The staff of Moses served as a means for many of his miracles. The gushing forth of water from the rock was one of them. This rock is still to be found in the Sinai and attracts tourists. It bears the signs of slits and cracks made by the springs (al-Mawdūdī, 1, note:75).

> By this miracle, the Almighty conveys the message that it is possible to benefit from the hidden treasuries of His Mercy, and even to cause "the water of life" to gush forth from a place as hard as a rock, with simple tools such as a staff. In addition, He encourages humankind: O humankind! I gave to the hand of a servant of Mine who had perfect trust in Me such a staff that he could summon by it the "water of life" when he wished. If you rely on My Mercy and your studies are founded upon Its laws, you can discover an instrument like that staff. So, come on and discover! (*The Words*, "the 20th Word," 261–262)

This verse contains two other messages. One is that there is a "natural" cause, no matter how slight, in every miracle because humankind are tested in this world, not compelled. If there were no "natural" causes, then all would be compelled to believe. The Almighty opens a door to faith for human reason but does not make it compelled to pass through that door. Given their free will, human beings choose and determine their way and therefore get their des-

erts. The second message the verse conveys is
that one who prays to God for any need should
do whatever is normally required to attain the
end desired. For example, if one is ill, one should
both go to a doctor and pray. If one desires success, one should both work and pray. When
Moses prayed for water, God could have sent
down water from the sky, but He ordered him
to strike a rock with his staff. Moses did what
he was ordered without the slightest hesitation
about whether water could or would come out
from the rock. He had perfect reliance on God
and was perfectly certain of his mission.

72. "Egypt (or some city)" translates *misr*,
which can mean either. It might be a city that
the Children of Israel passed on the way to Palestine, or it might be Egypt, which they had
left. Their demand indicates that they still felt
longing for their life in Egypt and was a sign
of ignobility of character. That is why Moses,
upon him be peace, might have meant in a sa-
tirically warning manner, "Get you down to
Egypt where there was what you ask for, and
return to your previous life of slavery."

73. What the Children of Israel asked for
was not in itself sinful. But by saying "your
Lord" instead of "our Lord," they manifested a sign of unbelief. Second, as a people on
the way to becoming a civilized society under the leadership of a great Messenger, they
were expected to make demands required by
a civilized life. By drawing attention to the
ignominy and misery pitched upon them,
and to their crimes even after they became
settled and founded a great kingdom during
the reigns of the Prophets David and Solomon, upon them be peace, the Qur'ān illustrates how they relapsed into their character of
slavery. In telling of the humiliating punishment they earned from God's wrath, the verse
links back to and interprets "those who have
incurred (Your) wrath" in *Sūrat al-Fātiḥah*.

Considered in the light of this verse, the
Prophetic saying warning the Muslims against
the causes of ignominy and misery, becomes
more apt: "When you let yourselves go into
speculative transactions and are occupied with
animal-breeding only and content with agri-
culture and abandon striving in God's cause to
preach His religion, God will subject you to
such a humiliation that He will not remove it
from you until you return to your Religion"
(Abū Dāwūd, "Buyū'," 54; Ibn Hanbal, 2: 84).

It may serve as a comparison that the apostles of Jesus, upon him be peace, made a similar
demand from him, also using the expression,
"your Lord." However, while the Children of
Israel demanded what the soil produces, Jesus'
apostles demanded a table from heaven (5: 112).

إِنَّ الَّذِينَ آمَنُوا وَالَّذِينَ هَادُوا وَالنَّصَارَىٰ وَالصَّابِئِينَ
مَنْ آمَنَ بِاللَّهِ وَالْيَوْمِ الْآخِرِ وَعَمِلَ صَالِحًا فَلَهُمْ أَجْرُهُمْ
عِندَ رَبِّهِمْ وَلَا خَوْفٌ عَلَيْهِمْ وَلَا هُمْ يَحْزَنُونَ ۝ وَإِذْ
أَخَذْنَا مِيثَاقَكُمْ وَرَفَعْنَا فَوْقَكُمُ الطُّورَ خُذُوا مَا آتَيْنَاكُم
بِقُوَّةٍ وَاذْكُرُوا مَا فِيهِ لَعَلَّكُمْ تَتَّقُونَ ۝ ثُمَّ تَوَلَّيْتُم مِّن
بَعْدِ ذَٰلِكَ فَلَوْلَا فَضْلُ اللَّهِ عَلَيْكُمْ وَرَحْمَتُهُ لَكُنتُم مِّنَ
الْخَاسِرِينَ ۝ وَلَقَدْ عَلِمْتُمُ الَّذِينَ اعْتَدَوْا مِنكُمْ فِي السَّبْتِ
فَقُلْنَا لَهُمْ كُونُوا قِرَدَةً خَاسِئِينَ ۝ فَجَعَلْنَاهَا نَكَالًا لِّمَا
بَيْنَ يَدَيْهَا وَمَا خَلْفَهَا وَمَوْعِظَةً لِّلْمُتَّقِينَ ۝ وَإِذْ قَالَ مُوسَىٰ
لِقَوْمِهِ إِنَّ اللَّهَ يَأْمُرُكُمْ أَن تَذْبَحُوا بَقَرَةً ۖ قَالُوا أَتَتَّخِذُنَا
هُزُوًا ۖ قَالَ أَعُوذُ بِاللَّهِ أَنْ أَكُونَ مِنَ الْجَاهِلِينَ ۝ قَالُوا
ادْعُ لَنَا رَبَّكَ يُبَيِّن لَّنَا مَا هِيَ ۚ قَالَ إِنَّهُ يَقُولُ إِنَّهَا بَقَرَةٌ لَّا فَارِضٌ
وَلَا بِكْرٌ عَوَانٌ بَيْنَ ذَٰلِكَ ۖ فَافْعَلُوا مَا تُؤْمَرُونَ ۝ قَالُوا
ادْعُ لَنَا رَبَّكَ يُبَيِّن لَّنَا مَا لَوْنُهَا ۚ قَالَ إِنَّهُ يَقُولُ إِنَّهَا بَقَرَةٌ
صَفْرَاءُ فَاقِعٌ لَّوْنُهَا تَسُرُّ النَّاظِرِينَ ۝

---

instructions so that you may attain rever-ent piety towards God and His protection (against any kind of straying and its con-sequent punishment in this world and the Hereafter)."

64. Then, after that, you turned away again (breaking your promise and disobey-ing the commandments of the Book). So, had it not been for the grace of God to you and His mercy (overlooking your offens-es and forgiving you), surely you would have been of the losers (in this world and the next).

65. You surely know of those among you who exceeded the bounds with respect to the Sabbath, and so We said to them, "Be you apes, miserably slinking and reject-ed."[75]

66. We made it a severe affliction exem-plary for their own generations and those to follow them, and instruction and guid-ance for the God-revering, pious.

67. And (remember) when Moses told his people: "God commands you to sacrifice a cow." They responded: "Are you making fun of us?" He replied: "I seek refuge in God lest I should be among the ignorant (by making fun of anybody)."[76]

68. They said, "Pray for us to your Lord that He may make clear to us what it should be like." (Moses) answered: "He says, it should be a cow neither old nor virgin, middling between the two. So do what you are commanded."

69. They (continuing to make trouble about the matter) responded: "Pray for us to your Lord that He may make clear to us what color it should be." (Moses) an-swered: "He says, it should be a yellow cow, radiant its color, gladdening those who see."

62. (The truth is not as they – the Jews – claim, but this:) Those who believe (i.e. professing to be Muslims) or those who declare Judaism, or the Christians or the Sabaeans (or those of some other faith) – whoever truly believes in God and the Last Day and does good, righteous deeds, surely their reward is with their Lord, and they will have no fear, nor will they grieve.[74]

63. And (remember) when We took your promise (to keep Our covenant) and (in order to stress the importance of both the covenant and keeping it, and warn you against breaking it,) We raised the Mount (causing it to tower) over you: "Hold firm-ly to what We haven given you (of the Book) and study its commandments and

74. The aim of the verse is to repudiate the illusion cherished by the Jews that, by virtue of their being Jews, they have a monopoly of salvation. They had long asserted their belief that a special and exclusive relationship existed between them and God. They thought that Jews as Jews were predestined to salvation, regardless of their beliefs and actions, whereas all non-Jews were predestined to serve as fuel for the Fire.

The context of the verse makes it clear that it does not aim to enumerate in full all the articles of faith in which one should believe in order to be saved. They are mentioned elsewhere, in the appropriate places. No one should conclude from this verse that for the eternal salvation it is not compulsory to believe in the Prophet Muḥammad, upon him be peace and blessings, and follow his way. There is a clear relationship between this verse and verse 38 – *If, henceforth, a guidance (like a Book through a Messenger) comes to you from Me, and whoever follows My guidance (and turns to Me with faith and worship), they will have no fear (in this world and the next, for they will always find My help and support with them), nor will they grieve.*– and the beginning of the *sūrah* where belief in the Qur'ān and the previous Books, together with establishing the Prayer and spending in God's cause, are mentioned as the attributes of the believers who prosper. Verses 41, 42, 43 – *Believe in that which I have sent down (the Qur'ān), confirming that which is with you (of the truth), and do not be the first to disbelieve in it. And (you scribes, fearful of losing your status and the worldly benefit accruing from it) do not sell My Revelations for a trifling price (such as worldly gains, status and renown); and in Me alone seek refuge through piety and reverence for Me. Do not confound the truth by mixing it with falsehood, and do not conceal the truth while you know (the meaning and outcome of what you do, and that what you strive to hide is true, and that Muḥammad is the Messenger of God, the Messenger whose coming you have been anticipating). Establish the Prayer* in conformity with its conditions, and pay the Prescribed Purifying Alms (the Zakāh); and bow (in the Prayer, not by forming a different community or congregation, but) together with those who bow (the Muslims). – explicitly address the Jews and explicitly invite them to believe in the Prophet Muḥammad, upon him be peace and blessings.

In order to fully understand the message of this verse, verse 22: 17 should also be taken into consideration.

75. The event outlined here is told in detail in 7: 163–166.

It was laid down that the Children of Israel should consecrate the Sabbath – Saturday – for rest and worship. They were required to abstain from all worldly acts. The injunctions in this connection were so strict that breaking the Sabbath was punishable by death (*Exodus*, 31: 12–17).

Some have commented on *Be you apes, miserably slinking and rejected!* that they were invested with the characteristic of apes, becoming "like" apes in character, thought, and conduct, in other words, that the transformation was a moral (and not a physical) one. However – quite aside from the fact that there were many similar unusual events in the history of the Israelites – its being meant to serve as a severe affliction, exemplary for their own generation and those to follow them (see the verse to come), reinforces the opinion that the transformation into apes was physical. It may be that while their minds were allowed to remain intact, their bodies were changed into those of apes, so they were driven away wherever they were encountered.

There are several passages in the Old Testament concerning the Sabbath (*Exodus*, 16: 21–30; 20 :8–11; 31: 12–17; *Deuteronomy*, 5: 12–15). As can be understood from *Deuteronomy*, one of the reasons for its consecration may have been that the Children of Israel should not forget their life of slavery in Egypt and be mindful of perceiving God's blessings upon them, as well as serving as a day of respite for slaves and animals.

God's "saying" an order is identical with expressing and executing His will: *When He wills a thing to be, He but says to it "Be!" and (in the selfsame instant) it is* (36: 82).

76. Despite numerous signs of God through many eventful years, the Children of Israel began, very soon after Moses went to Mount Sinai to receive the Torah, to worship a calf made of jewelry. This deviancy, happening in defiance of the Prophet Aaron, demonstrated the extent to which the Israelites had absorbed the attitudes of the native people of Egypt, in particular their sanctifying cattle. As may be understood from their demanding of Moses what the soil produces – the green herbs, cucumbers, corn, lentils, and onions – their occupation as farm laborers in Egypt may also have contributed to their veneration of the cow. By commanding them to sacrifice a cow, God willed to disabuse them of this attitude. However, it is with great difficulty that human nature can free itself from long and deeply ingrained prejudices. Accordingly, the Israelites, who had been expected to sacrifice any cow, chose to make trouble about it. Although the useless questions they asked and the expressions they used such as "your Lord" that displayed their disrespect for God brought them to the door of perdition, the mercy and gentle forbearance of God rescued them once more, and they were able to carry out the order. There are lessons for Muslim guides to take from this event.

As pointed out before, establishing faith in the Hereafter in minds and hearts is one of the four cardinal purposes of the Qur'ān. For this reason, while narrating an event even from a different perspective or for a different purpose, if it is possible to open a way through it to one of its main purposes or essentials of faith, the Qur'ān always does so. The main reason for the order of sacrificing a cow was, as we said, to disabuse the Israelites of their reverence for cattle. However, in order to disclose the identity of a murderer which they had been hiding, God created a miracle. Upon His order, they smote the corpse with some part of the sacrificed cow and the corpse, restored to life, told who his murderer was. This showed that God can restore the dead to life in any way He wills, so it is foolishness to doubt or question whether God can revive the dead. Such doubts and questions indicate a deficiency in the use of reason or its abuse.

10

سُوْرَةُ الْبَقَرَةِ

١٠

قَالُوا ادْعُ لَنَا رَبَّكَ يُبَيِّنْ لَنَا مَا هِيَ إِنَّ الْبَقَرَ تَشَابَهَ عَلَيْنَا وَإِنَّا إِنْ شَاءَ اللّهُ لَمُهْتَدُونَ ۞ قَالَ إِنَّهُ يَقُولُ إِنَّهَا بَقَرَةٌ لَا ذَلُولٌ تُثِيرُ الْأَرْضَ وَلَا تَسْقِي الْحَرْثَ مُسَلَّمَةٌ لَا شِيَةَ فِيهَا قَالُوا الْآنَ جِئْتَ بِالْحَقِّ فَذَبَحُوهَا وَمَا كَادُوا يَفْعَلُونَ ۞ وَإِذْ قَتَلْتُمْ نَفْسًا فَادَّارَأْتُمْ فِيهَا وَاللّهُ مُخْرِجٌ مَا كُنْتُمْ تَكْتُمُونَ ۞ فَقُلْنَا اضْرِبُوهُ بِبَعْضِهَا كَذَلِكَ يُحْيِ اللّهُ الْمَوْتَى وَيُرِيكُمْ آيَاتِهِ لَعَلَّكُمْ تَعْقِلُونَ ۞ ثُمَّ قَسَتْ قُلُوبُكُمْ مِنْ بَعْدِ ذَلِكَ فَهِيَ كَالْحِجَارَةِ أَوْ أَشَدُّ قَسْوَةً وَإِنَّ مِنَ الْحِجَارَةِ لَمَا يَتَفَجَّرُ مِنْهُ الْأَنْهَارُ وَإِنَّ مِنْهَا لَمَا يَشَّقَّقُ فَيَخْرُجُ مِنْهُ الْمَاءُ وَإِنَّ مِنْهَا لَمَا يَهْبِطُ مِنْ خَشْيَةِ اللّهِ وَمَا اللّهُ بِغَافِلٍ عَمَّا تَعْمَلُونَ ۞ أَفَتَطْمَعُونَ أَنْ يُؤْمِنُوا لَكُمْ وَقَدْ كَانَ فَرِيقٌ مِنْهُمْ يَسْمَعُونَ كَلَامَ اللّهِ ثُمَّ يُحَرِّفُونَهُ مِنْ بَعْدِ مَا عَقَلُوهُ وَهُمْ يَعْلَمُونَ ۞ وَإِذَا لَقُوا الَّذِينَ آمَنُوا قَالُوا آمَنَّا وَإِذَا خَلَا بَعْضُهُمْ إِلَى بَعْضٍ قَالُوا أَتُحَدِّثُونَهُمْ بِمَا فَتَحَ اللّهُ عَلَيْكُمْ لِيُحَاجُّوكُمْ بِهِ عِنْدَ رَبِّكُمْ أَفَلَا تَعْقِلُونَ ۞

70. They (still unwilling to carry out the order) replied: "Pray for us to your Lord that He may make clear to us what it should be like; cows are much alike to us; and if God wills, we will then be guided (to find the precise type of cow we are commanded to sacrifice, and sacrifice it)."

71. (Moses) answered: "He says, it is a cow unyoked to plough the earth or water the tillage, one kept secure and sound, with no blemish on it." "Now you have brought the truth," they answered; and they sacrificed it, though they all but did not.

72. And (remember also) when you had killed a living soul, and were accusing one another to deny the responsibility, but God would disclose what you were concealing.

73. So We commanded: "Strike him (the corpse) with part of it (the sacrificed cow)." (So they did and the corpse, brought to life, informed of the murderer.) Even so God brings to life the dead, and shows you the signs (of His Power, Oneness and way of acting), that you may understand the truth, (and have no doubt at all, concerning the essentials of faith).[77]

74. Then, a while after that, your hearts became hardened; they were like rocks, or even harder, for there are rocks from which rivers come gushing; there are some that split and water issues from them; and there are still others that roll down for fear and awe of God. (Whereas your hearts are harder than rocks, and) God is not unaware and unmindful of what you do.[78]

75. (O community of the believers!) Do you hope that those people (whose hearts have become more hardened than rocks and who have continually shown disloyalty to God) will believe you (and believe in the Prophet Muḥammad, and in the Book he brought and the Religion he preaches)? (It is surely not possible) when there has been a party among them that hear the Word of God, and then, after they reasoned and judged it (to be the Word of God), have tampered with it knowingly.[79]

76. When they meet those who believe, they declare (hypocritically), "We believe (in what you believe in);" but when they are alone with one another in private, they say (chiding each other): "Will you tell them what God has disclosed to you that they might use it as an argument against you before your Lord? Do you have no sense?"[80]

77. Like every other Prophetic miracle, this miracle also marks a horizon for scientific advances. In the future, it may well become possible to discover, for example, the murderer of a victim by "interrogating" some of the cells of the brain that remain alive for some time after death, or trace the murderer through some other element of the victim's body, analogous to the way that traces of the murderer's DNA found on the victim or at the crime scene can lead to definitive identification.

78. Hard rocks give way to the roots and fibers of plants. Those fibers, though as soft as silk, can, saying "In the Name of God", pierce and pass through hard stones and earth. By their mentioning the Name of God, the Name of the Merciful, everything becomes subjected to them.

As a result of the awesome manifestations of Divine Majesty in the form of earthquakes and other abrupt geological events, we can see huge rocks fall from the high summits of mountains (mostly formed, long ago, from thickened and cooled molten fluid) and shatter. Some of these crumble and disintegrate further to become soil for plantation. Others remain as rocks, and are scattered down to the valleys and plains. They serve many uses in the works of the earth's inhabitants, as in their houses. In submission to the Divine Power and Wisdom that foresees hidden purposes and benefits, mountains and rocks are thus ever ready and willing to be used in accordance with the principles of the Divine Wisdom. It is neither in vain nor accidental that, out of awe of God, they leave their lofty positions at the summits and choose the lower places in humility and become the means of those significant benefits. Rocks are so wonderfully subjugated to God's commands that rivers do appear to gush out of them. However, it is not possible that the mountains could be the actual source of the mighty rivers in the world such as the Tigris, Euphrates, and the Nile. Even if the mountains were made up entirely and only of water, like a sort of giant conical reservoirs, the swift and abundant flow of those great rivers would exhaust their supply of water in only a few months. Also, the rain, which only penetrates about a meter into the earth, cannot be sufficient income for that high expenditure. In fact, reason cannot yet satisfactorily explain the sources and flow of these rivers in terms of "natural causes." The All-Majestic Creator makes the rivers flow forth in truly wonderful fashion from an unseen "treasury."

By drawing attention to the benefits of rocks and by comparing the rocks favorably with the hardened hearts of the Israelites, the Qur'ān gives the following instruction to all humankind:

> O Children of Israel and O children of Adam! Despite your weakness and impotence, what sort of hearts do you have that in their hardness they resist the commands of the Divine Being? By contrast, massive formations of rocks carry out their subtle tasks perfectly in darkness in utmost submission to His commands. Indeed, the rocks act as a store and conduit for water (and other means of life) for all the living creatures on the earth. In the hand of Power of the All-Wise One of Majesty the hard rocks become, unresistingly, as malleable as wax or air, making way for the flowing waters, and the delicate roots and silk-like fibers of plant life, which, also, are acting under the command of God.

> O Children of Israel and children of Adam! Through hardness of heart and lack of feeling, you disobey the commandments of One of such awesome Majesty and life-giving Power; through heedlessness you close your eyes to the light of the Knowledge of such an Everlasting Sun. He makes mighty rivers like the Nile gush from solid rocks and makes the land of Egypt fertile –and yet you fail to notice and take heed. He produces for the heart of the universe and the mind of the earth miracles of His Power, and witnesses to His Oneness as strong and abundant as those mighty rivers, and makes them flow to the hearts and minds of the jinn and humankind. How then is it that you

are blind to the light of His Knowledge and do not see the truth? (*The Words*, "the 20th Word," 262)

79. One of the aims of the Qur'ān in presenting diverse aspects of the history of the Children of Israel is to make them known to the nascent Muslim community in Madīnah and the succeeding Muslim generations. Prior to the Emigration (*Hijrah*), the Jewish communities in Madīnah were better off than the native Arab tribes, al-Aws and Khazraj, being more knowledgeable of worldly affairs and belonging to a heavenly religion. Whenever a conflict arose between them and the Arabs, they threatened that a Prophet would appear among them and that, under his leadership, they would triumph over them. Thus, they had been anticipating the coming of the Last Prophet. However, when he appeared not among them but among the Arabs, they refused to believe in him. It was partly because of this background that the Muslims of Madīnah had expected that they would be the first to believe in the Prophet Muḥammad, upon him be peace and blessings. Accordingly, the Muslim converts among the Arab tribes approached their Jewish friends and neighbors and invited them to embrace Islam. When the Jews declined to do so, this was exploited by the hypocrites and other enemies of Islam as an argument for creating doubts about the truth of Islam. In order to warn the new Muslim converts against such doubts and the mischief the Jewish communities might bring about, the Qur'ān

draws attention to their character and past history, and the real reasons for their reluctance to embrace Islam.

80. Among the Jewish rabbis were some who partly preserved their loyalty to their religion. They had told the members of al-Aws and Khazraj tribes about the attributes of the Last Prophet they had been anticipating. Since all of these attributes were seen in the Prophet Muḥammad, upon him be peace and blessings, 'Abdullāh ibn Salām, the greatest among them, accepted Islam. It was because of such factors that at least some among them felt compelled to admit faith when they encountered the Muslims. However, when they were alone with one another, they chided each other or those who admitted faith, saying: "God had disclosed to you some secrets about the Last Prophet in the Book He sent to you. By telling the Muslims these secrets, would you like it if they use them as an argument against you in the presence of your Lord?" In thinking and acting in this way, they demonstrated that they did not have true knowledge of God, and had a conception of Him such that He does not know what people keep secret. Also, by using the expression "your Lord," they demonstrated that they believed that they had a Lord exclusive to themselves. (This is a false conception: either it means that God is not the Lord of all, or, equally bad, it means that God practices a sort of "favoritism" on behalf of some of His creatures to the neglect or detriment of others.)

أَوَلَا يَعْلَمُونَ أَنَّ اللَّهَ يَعْلَمُ مَا يُسِرُّونَ وَمَا يُعْلِنُونَ ۝ وَمِنْهُمْ أُمِّيُّونَ لَا يَعْلَمُونَ الْكِتَابَ إِلَّا أَمَانِيَّ وَإِنْ هُمْ إِلَّا يَظُنُّونَ ۝ فَوَيْلٌ لِلَّذِينَ يَكْتُبُونَ الْكِتَابَ بِأَيْدِيهِمْ ثُمَّ يَقُولُونَ هَٰذَا مِنْ عِنْدِ اللَّهِ لِيَشْتَرُوا بِهِ ثَمَنًا قَلِيلًا فَوَيْلٌ لَهُمْ مِمَّا كَتَبَتْ أَيْدِيهِمْ وَوَيْلٌ لَهُمْ مِمَّا يَكْسِبُونَ ۝ وَقَالُوا لَنْ تَمَسَّنَا النَّارُ إِلَّا أَيَّامًا مَعْدُودَةً قُلْ أَتَّخَذْتُمْ عِنْدَ اللَّهِ عَهْدًا فَلَنْ يُخْلِفَ اللَّهُ عَهْدَهُ أَمْ تَقُولُونَ عَلَى اللَّهِ مَا لَا تَعْلَمُونَ ۝ بَلَىٰ مَنْ كَسَبَ سَيِّئَةً وَأَحَاطَتْ بِهِ خَطِيئَتُهُ فَأُولَٰئِكَ أَصْحَابُ النَّارِ هُمْ فِيهَا خَالِدُونَ ۝ وَالَّذِينَ آمَنُوا وَعَمِلُوا الصَّالِحَاتِ أُولَٰئِكَ أَصْحَابُ الْجَنَّةِ هُمْ فِيهَا خَالِدُونَ ۝ وَإِذْ أَخَذْنَا مِيثَاقَ بَنِي إِسْرَائِيلَ لَا تَعْبُدُونَ إِلَّا اللَّهَ وَبِالْوَالِدَيْنِ إِحْسَانًا وَذِي الْقُرْبَىٰ وَالْيَتَامَىٰ وَالْمَسَاكِينِ وَقُولُوا لِلنَّاسِ حُسْنًا وَأَقِيمُوا الصَّلَاةَ وَآتُوا الزَّكَاةَ ثُمَّ تَوَلَّيْتُمْ إِلَّا قَلِيلًا مِنْكُمْ وَأَنْتُمْ مُعْرِضُونَ ۝

---

77. Do they not know that surely God knows what they keep concealed and what they disclose?

78. Among them are the unlettered folk who do not know anything about the Book except fancies from hearsay, and merely follow their conjectures.

79. Woe, then, to those who write the Book with their hands (interpolating into it their readings of the Scriptures and their explanatory notes thereto, stories from their national history, superstitious ideas and fancies, philosophical doctrines and legal rules) and then in order to sell it for a trifling price (such as worldly benefit, status, and renown), they declare: "This is from God." So woe to them for what their hands have written and woe to them for what they have earned (of the worldly income and the sin thereby).[81]

80. They say (despite all that): "The Fire will not touch us at all except for a certain number of days."[82] Say, then, (to them): "Have you made a covenant with God and received a promise from Him? If so, God will never break His covenant. Or do you say things against God that you do not know?"

81. (It is indeed the case that you speak in ignorance. The truth is,) rather, that whoever earns an evil (by his free will) and his vices engulf him – those are the companions of the Fire;[83] therein they will abide.

82. While those who believe and do good, righteous deeds, those are the companions of Paradise; they will abide therein.

83. And (remember) when We took a promise from the Children of Israel: You shall worship none save God (as the only Deity, Lord, and Sovereign), and do good to parents in the best way possible, and to the near (relatives), to the orphans, and to the destitute; and speak kindly and well to the people; and establish the Prescribed Prayer in conformity with its conditions; and pay the Prescribed Purifying Alms (the Zakāh). But then you turned away in aversion, all except a few of you; in fact you are a people always avoiding your compacts and responsibilities.[84]

---

81. In addition to interpreting the Book of God according to their wishes for the sake of fame, status, and worldly gain, the rabbis interpolated into it their own readings of the Scriptures, stories from their national history, superstitious ideas and fancies, philosophical doctrines and legal rules, and attributed these to God. This caused what was human and what was Divine to be confounded. Furthermore, they expected others to believe in whatever there was in the Book and regarded rejection of their additions as identical with unbelief. As pointed

out in verse 78, the common people were un-lettered. They tended to believe in whatever they were told in the name of religion and were dragged along into conjectures and fancies through mere imitation.

As in other similar verses, this one contains significant warning for the learned scholars and the unlearned Muslims of this community. As pointed out by Bediüzzaman Said Nursi, the religious books written by scholars should serve as "binoculars" to look at the Qur'ān, not substitute for it. This and similar verses also shed light on why God's Messenger, upon him be peace and blessings, showed some reluctance in the early years of his mission to have his sayings written down.

82. Left without any means to object to the Qur'ān's unveiling their past and inner world, some Jewish rabbis attempted to defend themselves by claiming that the Fire would not touch the Israelites except for a definite number of days – as many days as they had worshipped the calf. They put forward as an excuse their being Jewish and a nation exalted above others, whereas this was not in terms of supremacy in virtue, and was for a determined period when they were granted a great kingdom during the reigns of the Prophets David and Solomon, upon them be peace. They even went so far as to claim that they were – God forbid! – the children of God and His beloved ones (5: 18). The only true criterion in the sight of God in judging people is *taqwā*; as stressed in verse 2: 62, being a Jew, Christian, or Muslim by name does not suffice for salvation.

83. There is a close relation between this and the following verse (82) and verses 2: 28 and 29. This verse is also linked to verse 24 which threatens those who reject belief in the Qur'ān. The words and expressions used here – evil, earning evil, vices, and vices engulfing the person – describe the people of Hell, who are deprived of faith and engulfed in sins. The verse

also implies a warning for those Jews that the sins they committed in their past history and were still committing in Madīnah were of the kind that, contrary to their claim that the Fire would not touch them except for a certain number of days, had contaminated their very being and would doom them to being companions of the Fire eternally.

84. When the noble Messenger of God, upon him be peace and blessings, emigrated to Madīnah, three Jewish tribes were living there, namely Banū Qurayzah (the Children of Qurayzah), Banū Qaynuqa' and Banū Nadīr. The Messenger made a written contract with each of them, as co-citizens of the city-state of Madīnah, then in process of establishment. None of these tribes remained loyal to the contract and went so far as to attempt to kill God's Messenger, and to make secret agreements with the enemy forces during the Battle of the Trench against the Muslims. The verses in this *sūrah* recounting God's favors to the Children of Israel, inviting them to believe in the Prophet Muḥammad, upon him be peace and blessings, and making them known to the Muslim community, did not come on a single occasion but covered a period of at least five or six years. They were intended to warn the nascent Muslim community in Madīnah and all the Muslims to come until the Last Day against any conspiracy to put doubt in the mind concerning the tenets of Islam. They were also intended to invite and encourage the Jews to believe in the Prophet Muḥammad and follow him. To this end, by reminding them of God's favors to them during their history, stressing their continual disloyalty, and drawing their attention to the calamities that struck them because of their transgressions, these verses would have stirred their inner human resources – to return good with good, to take lessons from past experiences, to feel remorse for wrongs done and to reform themselves.

وَإِذْ أَخَذْنَا مِيثَاقَكُمْ لَا تَسْفِكُونَ دِمَاءَكُمْ وَلَا تُخْرِجُونَ أَنفُسَكُم مِّن دِيَارِكُمْ ثُمَّ أَقْرَرْتُمْ وَأَنتُمْ تَشْهَدُونَ ۝ ثُمَّ أَنتُمْ هَـٰؤُلَاءِ تَقْتُلُونَ أَنفُسَكُمْ وَتُخْرِجُونَ فَرِيقًا مِّنكُم مِّن دِيَارِهِمْ تَظَاهَرُونَ عَلَيْهِم بِالْإِثْمِ وَالْعُدْوَانِ وَإِن يَأْتُوكُمْ أُسَارَىٰ تُفَادُوهُمْ وَهُوَ مُحَرَّمٌ عَلَيْكُمْ إِخْرَاجُهُمْ أَفَتُؤْمِنُونَ بِبَعْضِ الْكِتَابِ وَتَكْفُرُونَ بِبَعْضٍ فَمَا جَزَاءُ مَن يَفْعَلُ ذَٰلِكَ مِنكُمْ إِلَّا خِزْيٌ فِي الْحَيَاةِ الدُّنْيَا وَيَوْمَ الْقِيَامَةِ يُرَدُّونَ إِلَىٰ أَشَدِّ الْعَذَابِ وَمَا اللَّهُ بِغَافِلٍ عَمَّا تَعْمَلُونَ ۝ أُولَـٰئِكَ الَّذِينَ اشْتَرَوُا الْحَيَاةَ الدُّنْيَا بِالْآخِرَةِ فَلَا يُخَفَّفُ عَنْهُمُ الْعَذَابُ وَلَا هُمْ يُنصَرُونَ ۝ وَلَقَدْ آتَيْنَا مُوسَى الْكِتَابَ وَقَفَّيْنَا مِن بَعْدِهِ بِالرُّسُلِ وَآتَيْنَا عِيسَى ابْنَ مَرْيَمَ الْبَيِّنَاتِ وَأَيَّدْنَاهُ بِرُوحِ الْقُدُسِ أَفَكُلَّمَا جَاءَكُمْ رَسُولٌ بِمَا لَا تَهْوَىٰ أَنفُسُكُمُ اسْتَكْبَرْتُمْ فَفَرِيقًا كَذَّبْتُمْ وَفَرِيقًا تَقْتُلُونَ ۝ وَقَالُوا قُلُوبُنَا غُلْفٌ بَل لَّعَنَهُمُ اللَّهُ بِكُفْرِهِمْ فَقَلِيلًا مَّا يُؤْمِنُونَ ۝

---

84. And (remember also) when We took a promise from you: you shall not shed blood among yourselves, and shall not expel one another from your habitations. You confirmed it, and you yourselves were (and still must be) witnesses to it.

85. Then, here you are, killing one another, and expelling a party of your own from their habitations, conspiring against them in iniquity and enmity. If you take them as captives, you hold them to ransom, and if they are brought to you as captives, you ransom them; yet their expulsion was made religiously forbidden to you.[85] Then (like a people having no sense) do you believe in part of the Book, and disbelieve in part? What else, then, could be the recompense of those of you who act thus than dis-

grace in the life of this world? On the Day of Resurrection, they will be consigned to the severest of punishment. God is not unaware and unmindful of what you do.

86. Such are the ones who have bought the present, worldly life (the life of corporeal desires and ambitions) in exchange for the Hereafter. So (in consequence of this exchange) the punishment will not be lightened for them, nor will they be helped (not saved from the punishment in any of the ways they resort to in the world such as bribery, influence, or unjust intercession).

87. (That is their just deserts. For) We assuredly granted Moses the Book, and after him sent succeeding Messengers (in the footsteps of Moses to judge according to the Book, and thus We have never left them without guides and the light of guidance.) And (in the same succession) We granted Jesus son of Mary the clear proofs of the truth (and of his Messengership), and confirmed him with the Spirit of Holiness.[86] Is it (ever so) that whenever a Messenger comes to you with what (as a message and commandments) does not suit your selves, you grow arrogant, denying some of them (the Messengers) and killing others?

88. (Despite all such favors, affection, forgiveness, advice, and truths, they refuse to believe, and by way of excuse they ask derisively: "Do we need any of what you have to tell?" Recognizing that what they are told has no effect on them) they say: "Our hearts have become covered (callous, no longer having any ability to believe)." No! Rather, because of their unbelief God has cursed them (excluded them from His mercy and set a seal on their hearts and hearing and a veil on their eyes.) So, little do they believe (or can admit of the truth).

85. The style of the verses is of a nature to guide to a historical review and understanding of events. Past and present are linked and brought together in a meaningful juxtaposition. This is how narration of the past becomes, instead of a random chronicling of events, meaningful history – an account of life still vivid and relevant for the present, full of lessons connected with its continuing effects. In addition, since the characters of the past and those of the present share the same attitudes and qualities, all the events, those of the past and the present, give the impression that they occur around the same characters. That is why in the foreground we see the persons, with their characteristics, intentions, and attributes, rather than the events.

Before the emigration of God's Messenger to Madīnah, the Jewish tribes had concluded an alliance with the Arab tribes of al-Aws and Khazraj, who were then polytheists. When fighting broke out between the Arab tribes, each Jewish tribe fought against another on the side of its allies, which led to fratricide and therefore to a violation of the Divine Book. Furthermore, when the war ended the captives were ransomed. They justified the ransom on the basis of scriptural arguments. They venerated the Book when it allowed the ransom of captives, but when it came to its prohibition of mutual feuding, they paid no heed to it.

86. Different views have been put forward about the Spirit of Holiness with which Jesus, upon him be peace, was confirmed. Literally meaning the spirit of extraordinary purity, cleanliness, and blessing, it is, according to some, a spirit from God, while some are of the opinion that it is one of the Greatest Names of God, and still others maintain that it is the Gospel. Others hold that it is the Archangel Gabriel, upon him be peace, whom the Qur'ān calls the Spirit of Holiness (16: 102) and One Trustworthy (81: 21). Still some others opine that the Spirit whose holiness is stressed with respect to Jesus and both holiness and trustworthiness with respect to the Prophet Muḥammad, is the same being or entity. According to Imam al-Ghazzālī, he is an angel (or angel-like being) whom God employs in breathing each one's spirit into his/her body. Bediüzzaman Said Nursi maintains that there is a spirit representing every thing, every being. In the light of these opinions, it can be said that there is a Spirit which functions differently according to the particular mission of each Prophet. It is a Spirit of Law for the Prophet Moses, a Spirit of Holiness and Trustworthiness for the Prophet Muḥammad, and a Spirit of Holiness for the Prophet Jesus. The Qur'ān's mentioning of Jesus being confirmed with the Spirit of *Holiness* is because spirituality had precedence in Jesus' mission. Muḥammad's mission is distinguished with both holiness and trustworthiness, more than the missions of other Prophets. (Also see *sūrah* 70, note 1.)

وَلَمَّا جَآءَهُمْ كِتَـٰبٌ مِّنْ عِندِ اللَّهِ مُصَدِّقٌ لِّمَا مَعَهُمْ وَكَانُوا

مِن قَبْلُ يَسْتَفْتِحُونَ عَلَى الَّذِينَ كَفَرُوا فَلَمَّا جَآءَهُم

مَّا عَرَفُوا كَفَرُوا بِهِۦ فَلَعْنَةُ اللَّهِ عَلَى الْكَافِرِينَ ۝ بِئْسَمَا

اشْتَرَوْا بِهِۦ أَنفُسَهُمْ أَن يَكْفُرُوا بِمَآ أَنزَلَ

اللَّهُ بَغْيًا أَن يُنَزِّلَ اللَّهُ مِن فَضْلِهِۦ عَلَىٰ مَن يَشَآءُ مِنْ

عِبَادِهِۦ فَبَآءُو بِغَضَبٍ عَلَىٰ غَضَبٍ وَلِلْكَافِرِينَ عَذَابٌ مُّهِينٌ ۝

وَإِذَا قِيلَ لَهُمْ ءَامِنُوا بِمَآ أَنزَلَ اللَّهُ قَالُوا نُؤْمِنُ بِمَآ أُنزِلَ

عَلَيْنَا وَيَكْفُرُونَ بِمَا وَرَآءَهُۥ وَهُوَ الْحَقُّ مُصَدِّقًا لِّمَا مَعَهُمْ

قُلْ فَلِمَ تَقْتُلُونَ أَنبِيَآءَ اللَّهِ مِن قَبْلُ إِن كُنتُم

مُّؤْمِنِينَ ۝ وَلَقَدْ جَآءَكُم مُّوسَىٰ بِالْبَيِّنَـٰتِ ثُمَّ

اتَّخَذْتُمُ الْعِجْلَ مِنۢ بَعْدِهِۦ وَأَنتُمْ ظَالِمُونَ ۝ وَإِذْ

أَخَذْنَا مِيثَـٰقَكُمْ وَرَفَعْنَا فَوْقَكُمُ الطُّورَ خُذُوا

مَآ ءَاتَيْنَـٰكُم بِقُوَّةٍ وَاسْمَعُوا قَالُوا سَمِعْنَا وَعَصَيْنَا

وَأُشْرِبُوا فِى قُلُوبِهِمُ الْعِجْلَ بِكُفْرِهِمْ قُلْ بِئْسَمَا

يَأْمُرُكُم بِهِۦٓ إِيمَـٰنُكُمْ إِن كُنتُم مُّؤْمِنِينَ ۝

---

89. And when there has (now) come to them a Book from God, confirming what (of the truth) they already possess – and though before that they were asking for a victory over the (tribes of al-Aws and Khazraj who were then) unbelievers, (saying: "The Last Prophet will come and we will defeat and destroy you under his leadership") – and when there has come to them what they recognize (as well as their own sons), they have disbelieved in it. Then God's curse (rejection) is on the unbelievers.

90. How evil is that for which they have sold themselves: (they have disbelieved in what God has sent down) begrudging that God should send down out of His grace the Book (and bestow Messengership) on whomever He wills of His servants. So they have earned wrath upon wrath. And

(as with other unbelievers who, defeated by their haughtiness, malicious envy, racial prejudice, worldly desires, and ambitions, knowingly reject the truth,) for those unbelievers is a shameful, humiliating punishment.

91. And when they are told (since the sign of a believer is believing in whatever God has sent down): "Believe in that which He has sent down (on Muḥammad, namely the Qur'ān)," they retort: "We believe in only what was sent down on us," and they disbelieve in what is beyond that, though it is the truth, confirming what (of the truth) they already possess.[87] Say (to them, O Messenger): "Why then did you kill the Prophets of God before, if indeed you are believers (loyal to what was sent down on you)?"

92. Assuredly Moses came to you with clear proofs of the truth. Then however, very soon after he left you, you adopted the calf as deity, proving yourselves to be wrongdoers (who were continually committing such sins as breaking your covenants with God and serving false deities in His place).

93. And (remember) when We took your promise (to keep Our covenant) and (in order to stress the importance of both the covenant and keeping it, and warn you against breaking it) We raised the Mount (and caused it to tower) above you: Hold firmly to what We haven given you (of the Book) and give ear (to Our commandments and obey Moses). They replied: "We give ear," (but by doing the opposite of what they were commanded, they meant) "we disobey." Because of their unbelief, they were made to drink into their hearts (love of) the calf (with then no place left therein for faith). Say (to them): "How evil is that which your belief enjoins on you, if you are believers."[88]

87. Every unfair, unjust individual and community surely acts in this way. For them faith is no more than a mere assertion by which they make a display of themselves. They will not acknowledge a Prophet or a scholar as such, if he does not belong to their community or nation. It has often been this self-centered haughtiness, this kind of racist nationalism, which has brought about rifts within a people and led them to associate partners with God, and to oppose right with sophistry and intrigue or brute force. It was the same kind of attitude that caused Iblīs to be expelled from the Presence and Mercy of God.

88. Even if action is not a part, an essential element of faith, faith exhibits itself through actions commanded or required by it. Actions are the mirror that show whether one is a believer or not.

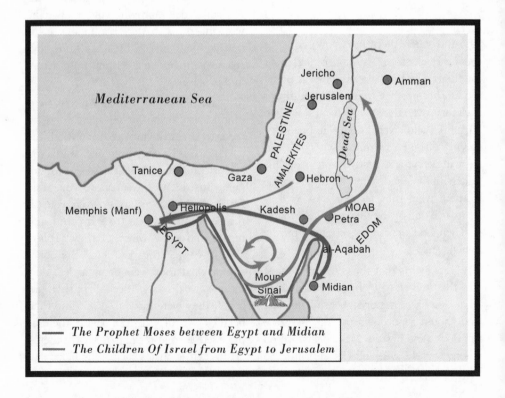

—— *The Prophet Moses between Egypt and Midian*
—— *The Children Of Israel from Egypt to Jerusalem*

14 ١٤

ners with God. Everyone of them wishes if only he might be spared for a thousand years,[89] yet his being spared to live will not remove him from the punishment. God sees well all that they do.

97. (This is not all. They feel enmity towards Gabriel because he brings the Qur'ān to you, not to one among them.) Say (O Messenger, to them): "(The Lord of the worlds, my and your Lord, declares:) 'Whoever is an enemy to Gabriel (should know that) it is he who brings down the Qur'ān on your heart by the leave of God, (not of his own accord), confirming (the Divine origin of and the truths still contained in) the Revelations prior to it, and (serving as) guidance and glad tidings for the believers.' "[90]

98. (Enmity to Gabriel, who does nothing other than what he is commanded to do by God, means enmity to God and to His will.) Whoever is an enemy to God and His angels and His Messengers and (so) Gabriel and Michael, (should know that) God is surely an enemy to the unbelievers.

99. (O Messenger, do not grieve about their persistence in unbelief!) Assuredly We have sent down to you truths so manifest (that they both prove your Messengership and the Divine authorship of the Qur'ān as brightly as the sunlight). None disbelieve in them except transgressors (who have strayed from the Straight Path in belief, thought, and conduct).

100. Is it not ever so that whenever they (those transgressors) make a covenant, a party of them set it aside? (Indeed, they do so, and they are not a small party,) rather, most of them do not believe (so that they might be expected to keep their covenant).

94. Say: "If (as you claim, you are the beloved ones of God and the sole followers of the Straight Path, and therefore) the abode of the Hereafter with God is reserved for you alone, excluding other people, then long for death, if you are sincere in your belief and truthful in your claim."

95. But because of what they have forwarded with their own hands (to the Hereafter, namely the sins and offenses which have destroyed the desire in them to meet God), they will never long for it. God has full knowledge of the wrongdoers (who wrong their own selves by what they have done).

96. And you will undoubtedly find them the greediest of all people for life, more greedy than even those who associate part-

101. (This is not all.) When (finally) there has come to them a Messenger from God, confirming what (of the truth) they already possess, a party of those who were given the Book (the Torah) have (instead of paying heed to what it contains concerning the Last Messenger) flung the Book of God (the Qur'ān) behind their backs, as if they did not know (that it is a Book from God and that the Messenger who has brought it is the Last Prophet they have been anticipating.)

---

89. God's Messenger warns: "Love of the world is the source of all errors and sins" (al-Bayhaqī, 7: 338).

90. The link between this verse and the opening verses of the *sūrah* describing the praiseworthy qualities of the believers is explicit. The believers mentioned here are as described in those verses, that is, they believe in the Unseen, establish the Prayer, and spend, out of whatever God provides for them, to help those in need, and who believe in what has been sent down to the Messenger, upon him be peace and blessings, and what was sent down before him, and who have certain faith in the Hereafter. The opening verses of every *sūrah* are of pivotal importance to an understanding of its meaning.

Gabriel (*Jibrīl* in the Qur'ān) denotes the angelic existence above every other power with the exception of the Divine, and the spirit that no material force can resist, and whose works are irreversible and indispensable. Since Revelation has an absolute certainty with no room for the intervention of any mortal being, the name *Jibrīl* (by which the angel bringing it is called) also serves as a definition of that angel. He has other titles as well (e.g., a Spirit from God, the Trustworthy Spirit, and even the Spirit of Holiness according to some: see note 85), and is described in the Qur'ān as a noble, honored messenger, mighty, having a high, secured position with the Lord of the Supreme Throne, obeyed by other angels, and trustworthy (81: 18–21) (Yazır, 1: 432).

وَاتَّبَعُوْا مَا تَتْلُوا الشَّيَاطِيْنُ عَلٰى مُلْكِ سُلَيْمٰنَ وَمَا كَفَرَ سُلَيْمٰنُ
وَلٰكِنَّ الشَّيَاطِيْنَ كَفَرُوْا يُعَلِّمُوْنَ النَّاسَ السِّحْرَ وَمَا
اُنْزِلَ عَلَى الْمَلَكَيْنِ بِبَابِلَ هَارُوْتَ وَمَارُوْتَ وَمَا يُعَلِّمٰنِ
مِنْ اَحَدٍ حَتّٰى يَقُوْلَا اِنَّمَا نَحْنُ فِتْنَةٌ فَلَا تَكْفُرْ
فَيَتَعَلَّمُوْنَ مِنْهُمَا مَا يُفَرِّقُوْنَ بِهٖ بَيْنَ الْمَرْءِ وَزَوْجِهٖ
وَمَا هُمْ بِضَآرِّيْنَ بِهٖ مِنْ اَحَدٍ اِلَّا بِاِذْنِ اللّٰهِ وَيَتَعَلَّمُوْنَ
مَا يَضُرُّهُمْ وَلَا يَنْفَعُهُمْ وَلَقَدْ عَلِمُوْا لَمَنِ اشْتَرٰىهُ
مَا لَهٗ فِى الْاٰخِرَةِ مِنْ خَلَاقٍ وَلَبِئْسَ مَا شَرَوْا بِهٖ
اَنْفُسَهُمْ لَوْ كَانُوْا يَعْلَمُوْنَ ۝ وَلَوْ اَنَّهُمْ اٰمَنُوْا
وَاتَّقَوْا لَمَثُوْبَةٌ مِّنْ عِنْدِ اللّٰهِ خَيْرٌ لَوْ كَانُوْا يَعْلَمُوْنَ
۝ يٰٓاَيُّهَا الَّذِيْنَ اٰمَنُوْا لَا تَقُوْلُوْا رَاعِنَا وَقُوْلُوا انْظُرْنَا
وَاسْمَعُوْا وَلِلْكٰفِرِيْنَ عَذَابٌ اَلِيْمٌ ۝ مَا يَوَدُّ الَّذِيْنَ
كَفَرُوْا مِنْ اَهْلِ الْكِتَابِ وَلَا الْمُشْرِكِيْنَ اَنْ يُّنَزَّلَ
عَلَيْكُمْ مِّنْ خَيْرٍ مِّنْ رَّبِّكُمْ وَاللّٰهُ يَخْتَصُّ
بِرَحْمَتِهٖ مَنْ يَّشَآءُ وَاللّٰهُ ذُو الْفَضْلِ الْعَظِيْمِ ۝

———————❦———————

102. And (just as their ancestors did) they follow the fictions the satans invented and spread about the rule of Solomon (falsely attributing his employment of the jinn, devils, and animals in his kingdom to sorcery). But (ascribing creativity or creative effect to sorcery is a kind of unbelief and) Solomon (being a Prophet and excellent servant of God) never disbelieved. Rather, the satans (who spread false things about his rule) disbelieved, teaching people sorcery and the (distorted form of the) knowledge that was sent down on Hārūt and Mārūt, the two angels in Babylon. And they (these two angels charged with teaching people some occult sciences such as breaking a spell and protection against sorcery) never taught them to anyone without first warning, "We are a trial, so do not disbelieve (– It is risky to learn the knowledge given to us, therefore use it in lawful ways, and beware of committing an act of unbelief

by abusing it)." And (yet) they (those who followed the falsehoods of the satans) learned from them (the two angels) that by which they might divide a man and his wife. But (though they wrongly attributed creative power to sorcery, in fact) they could not harm anyone thereby save by the leave of God. And they learned what would harm them, not what would benefit them. Assuredly they knew well that he who bought it (in exchange for God's Book) will have no (happy) portion in the Hereafter. How evil was that for which they sold their selves; and if only they had known (acted like people of true knowledge and understanding).[91]

103. And if only they had believed and, in fear and reverence of God, sought to deserve His protection (against their straying and His punishment), a reward from God (of which they could not conceive) would have been absolutely good; if only they had known (acted like people of true knowledge and understanding).[92]

104. O you who believe![93] Do not say (in your relationship and conversations with God's Messenger,) *rāʿinā* (please attend to us), but say, *unẓurnā*[94] (favor us with your attention), and pay heed to him. (And be assured that) for the unbelievers (who are disrespectful to God's Messenger) is a painful punishment.

105. Those who disbelieve among the People of the Book (by denying any of the Prophets or Divine Books or associating partners with God or cherishing enmity to His angels or in another way), and those who associate partners with God (among the people of Makkah and others) love not that there should be sent down on you any good from your Lord. But God singles out for His mercy (of favoring with Prophethood or another similar mission) whom He wills. God is of tremendous grace and bounty.

91. In addition to many miracles and miraculous achievements, the Prophet Solomon, upon him be peace, was distinguished by his ability, by leave of God, to subjugate the jinn and satans to his command and employ them in diverse tasks. Once they made an attempt to revolt against him but failed. After his death, satans began to whisper to their intimates among the devilish people that Solomon had derived his power from sorcery. When moral and material decline set in among the Children of Israel, they turned increasingly to black magic, sorcery, and charms in order to ensure the achievement of their desired ends.

During their life of exile in Babylon, a very ancient center of science, especially the science of astronomy, God sent them two angels, called Hārūt and Mārūt, in order to teach them some occult sciences so that they might be protected against sorcery and the evils it caused. The angels, as dutiful servants of God with power to assume the form most fitting for the specific task assigned to them, must have come to them in human form, just as the angels sent to the Prophet Lot came in the form of handsome youths (11: 69–81). While teaching people some occult knowledge, they warned them, saying: "Any knowledge is indeed a trial and temptation. So what we teach you may be used for undesirable ends by some evil ones. Beware that they do not lead you to any act of unbelief." Any knowledge, indeed even elements as essential to human life as fire and water, can be turned into a means for evil in the hands of evil people. The evil ones among the Israelites were interested only in how they could sow discord between a man and his wife. This indicates the depth of moral corruption to which these people had fallen.

The Prophet Muḥammad, upon him be peace and blessings, said: "Satan sends his agents to all parts of the world. On their return these agents report their accomplishments, each mentioning his own special evil act. But Satan is not satisfied with any of them. It is only when an agent reports that he was able to separate a wife from her husband that Satan becomes joyful and embraces him" (al-Bukhārī, "Talaq," 25).

We might consider the teaching of the Kabala and certain similar esoteric doctrines and rituals of some secret organizations in the light of this verse. (We may note in passing that, there was a deity called Madruk among the deities of Babylon, a deity of magic.)

92. Both this and the preceding verse conclude with the words literally meaning, *If only they had known.* However, in the light of – *Assuredly they knew very well that he who bought it (in exchange for God's Book) has no share, (no happy portion) in the Hereafter* – these words mean that these people *did* know, but they did not act according to what they knew as men of true knowledge and understanding. We can conclude that any knowledge which does not lead its possessors to act according to it is of no benefit to them, is not regarded as "true knowledge" by the Qur'ān. Another point to note here is that in some of its verses (e.g. 3: 19), the Qur'ān refers to the Divine Book or Revelation as "knowledge." Therefore, those who do not act according to this "knowledge," are ignorant, even though they may be knowledgeable in some other matters. All that we would wish to explain here is succinctly expressed by the verse (35: 28): *Of all His servants, only those possessed of true knowledge have awe of God.* The pre-Islamic period is called the "Age of Ignorance" (*Jāhiliyyah*). This is not because the people living in that era were ignorant, but because they believed and acted like people without (true) knowledge and understanding.

93. In the Qur'ān, the phrase, *O you who believe!* occurs in some eighty places. This address is to those who declare their belief (with their tongue) and perform the Prescribed Prayer (the *Salāḥ*) in congregation with the Muslims, pay the Prescribed Purifying Alms (the *Zakāh*) due on their wealth including property held in the open (such as livestock and agricultural produce), and eat of the animals sacrificed by the Muslims. Obeying the commandments that follow the use of this address

is a requirement of being a believer. Only one who sincerely believes in the essentials of faith and obeys the prescribed commandments from the heart, purely for the good pleasure and approval of God, is a true believer.

94. In their conversation with God's Messenger, upon him be peace and blessings, the Companions, may God be pleased with them, sometimes used the expression *ra'inā*, meaning "kindly lend ear to us" or "please attend to us," when they wanted to request a short pause. However, when some Jews visited the Messenger, they tried to vent their spite by using ambiguous expressions in their greetings and conversation. They either used words with double meanings, one innocent and the other offensive, or changed the pronunciation of the expressions used by the Companions, may God be pleased with them. They would pronounce *ra'inā* to sound like a Hebrew word meaning "Listen, may you become deaf", and sometimes like an Arabic word meaning "our shepherd." To prevent the expression *ra'inā* from being abused in this way, the Muslims were asked to avoid it and use instead the straightforward expression *unẓurnā*, meaning "kindly favor us with your attention" or "kindly grant us a while to follow." The verse draws attention to the importance of showing the necessary respect to God's Messenger, upon him be peace and blessings, and paying heed to his teaching.

106. (Though they would exploit the abrogation of some rules of secondary degree to challenge your authority, the truth is that) We do not abrogate any verse or omit it (leaving it to be forgotten) but We bring one better than it or the like of it (more suited to the time and conditions in the course of perfecting the Religion and completing Our favor upon you).[95] Do you not know (and surely you do know) that God has full power over everything?

107. Do you not know (and surely you do know) that God is He to Whom belongs the sovereignty (absolute ownership and dominion) of the heavens and the earth (with all that is therein)? (He acts as He wills in His dominion, and you are His servants wholly submitted to Him. Given this, and unless He wills,) you have, apart from God, neither a guardian (to whom you can entrust your affairs) nor a helper.

108. Or do you desire (prompted by the unbelievers among the People of the Book and without perceiving the wisdom in the abrogation of some verses) to harass your Messenger with senseless questions and unanswerable demands (such as seeing God plainly) as Moses was harassed before? Whoever exchanges faith for unbelief has surely strayed from the right, even way.

109. Many among the People of the Book, out of the envy ingrained in their souls, wish they could restore you as unbelievers after you have believed, after the truth was clear to them (that the Qur'ān is God's Word and Muḥammad is the last, awaited Messenger). Yet pardon and overlook them (avoiding useless debates and polemics with them) until God brings in His verdict about them. Surely God has full power over everything.

110. (Let your concern be to) establish the Prayer in conformity with its conditions and pay the Prescribed Purifying Alms. Whatever good you send ahead (to your future life in this world and the next) to your own souls' account, you will find it with God. Whatever (good or evil) you do, surely God sees it well.

111. They (Jews or Christians) say that none will enter Paradise unless he be a Jew or a Christian. That is their wishfulness (vain desires and fancies). Say: "Produce your proof if you are truthful (in and convinced of your claim)!"

112. No! Rather, whoever submits his whole being to God (and does so) as one devoted to doing good, aware that God is seeing him, his reward is with his Lord, and all such will have no fear (for they will always find My help and support with them), nor will they grieve.[96]

95. With regard to legislation, Islam followed three principal ways:

- It retained the commandments that pre-existed it, in the previous Books or in the custom and practice of the community in which Islam appeared, and were not contradictory with its essential principles.
- It corrected or amended the ones that were not in conformity with its principles.
- It made new legislations.

In making new legislations, it considered life's unchanging (essential) and changing (temporal) aspects. In the second case, it laid down rules that could be revised when necessary according to time and conditions and in conformity with its essentials of faith, worship, and morality; and established legal principles to maintain this process. The best known and most important of these are analogy (*qiyās*); deducing new laws through reasoning based on the Qur'ān and Sunnah (*ijtihād*); adoption of what is good and beneficial (*istiḥsān*); maintaining without change what has already been approved (*istiṣḥāb*); taking what is suited to the public benefit and discarding what is harmful *(maṣāliḥ al-mursalah)*; and blocking corruption and what is unlawful (*sadd az-zarāʾiʿ*). The same procedure was followed also in the time of the Prophet himself, during which

the Qur'ān was revealed. God abrogated some verses either with the injunction contained in their wording or with both their wording and the command they contained. This process was called *naskh*, and the verses abrogated, *mansūkh*, and the new ones substituting the previous ones, *nāsikh*.

Scholars differ over the number of abrogated verses. However, remember that the Qur'ān has absolute authority until Judgment Day and that human life consists of ups, downs, and twists. Given this, there may be times when some of the commands replacing or abrogating others should be temporarily neglected or viewed as not-yet-revealed, especially in preaching Islam to people. This process of *naskh* contributes a great deal to Islam's dynamism, for preaching Islam and transforming people into true and perfect Muslims is a process. Also, the principles or commands conveyed to new believers or those who are interested have different priorities.

96. We sometimes need to stress the relationships between verses and how the *sūrah* turns round its opening verses. The relationship between this verse and verses 2: 38 and 62 is manifest. These three verses are especially important with respect to linking the events narrated to the pivot or main theme of the *sūrah* and drawing attention to that link.

113. The Jews say the Christians have nothing (from God) to be based on, and the Christians say the Jews have nothing (from God) to be based on; yet they (both) recite the Book. So too those who have no knowledge (from God) say the like of their word. God will judge between them on the Day of Resurrection concerning what they have been disputing.

114. Who is more in the wrong than he who bars God's places of worship, so that His Name be not mentioned and invoked in them, and strives to ruin them?[97] Such people might never enter them, save in fear (whether because of their alienation from the Religion or because they try to destroy them owing to their animosity against God). For them is disgrace in the world, and in the Hereafter a mighty punishment.[98]

115. (They attempt to exploit the issue of *qiblah* – the direction of the Prayer – as a pretext to bar God's places of worship so that His Name be not mentioned in them.) To God belong the east and the west (and therefore the whole earth: wherever you are, you can turn to Him in the Prayer). Then, to whatever direction you turn, there is the "Face" of God.[99] God is All-Embracing (with His Mercy), All-Knowing.

116. And (despite this fact and that God is infinite, with nothing to restrict Him, and therefore has no equal or like) they claim that God has taken to Him a son. All-Glorified is He (in that He is absolutely above having any attributes particular to those contained in time and space). Rather, to Him belongs all that is in the heavens and the earth (under His absolute rule;)[100] all are (by their very nature as beings created by Him) subservient to Him.

117. The Originator of the heavens and the earth with nothing preceding Him to imitate. When He decrees a thing, He does but say to it "Be!" and it is.[101]

118. Those who have no knowledge (from Him, and therefore lead an ignorant life) say: "Why does not God speak to us (directly) or a manifest sign (a miracle) come to us?" So spoke those before them, a word like theirs. Their hearts are alike. Yet We have made clear the signs (and the Revelations establishing the Unity and Sovereignty of God, the Messengership of Muḥammad, and the Divine authorship of the Qur'ān) to a people who seek certainty (with open, inquiring minds).

119. (Let not what they say grieve you.) Surely We have sent you as a Messenger with the truth as a bearer of glad tidings (of prosperity in return for faith and righteousness) and as a warner (against the consequences of straying and transgression). You (carry out your duty perfectly, and therefore) will not be questioned concerning the companions of the Blazing Flame.

97. The verse asks rhetorically if there is a greater wrongdoing than barring God's places of worship so that His Name is not extolled there, and strive to ruin them. This does not mean that it is uniquely the greatest wrongdoing. Rather, it is one of the greatest offenses, some others being concealing a truth revealed and established by God concerning faith (2: 140), knowingly denying God's Revelations (6: 21, 93), and turning away from God's Revelations in purposeful denial (32: 22). Each of these is among the greatest wrongdoings.

98. This verse severely denounces any offenses against God's places of worship, and alludes to such historical examples as the Bayt al-Maqdis in Jerusalem being ruined by the Assyrian kings, by Nebuchadnezzar, the Babylon king, and the Roman emperor Titus and other Roman rulers such as Adrianus. It also refers to the Muslims being prevented from worshipping in the Ka'bah. In general, it warns against any attempt in the future to close down places of worship or ban people from worshipping in them.

99. The Laws of the previous Prophets stated that worship should be performed in specific places. For example, Jews worship in synagogues and Christians in churches. But Islam allows worship in any clean place (al-Bukhārī, "Tayammum," 1; "Salāh," 56). This verse also clarifies that God's "Face" is not connected with a specific direction, for God is not contained by time or space. Specifying a certain spot, such as the Ka'bah, was done only to establish unity and solidarity among Muslims in the Prayer and all other matters.

100. Since absolutism was prevalent among ancient peoples, they held that any son they attributed to a deity must also be a deity, as the son of a king succeeded to his father's rank and powers. By categorically refuting the doctrine that God might have a son and clarifying that God, being the Infinite, cannot have any like, the Qur'ān decisively rejects Christians' attributing Divine sonship to Jesus and some Jews' attributing the same to Ezra. Just as God cannot have a like, so too there cannot be any partner of Him in the dominion of the heavens and the earth, for it is He Who originated them without any help from any other and without any precedent or example to follow.

101. There is no contradiction between God's saying to a thing "Be" when He wills to create it – indicating that creation is instantaneous – and creation's appearing to us in our perspectives to be a process that takes time:

Existence has two dimensions, one corporeal, where matter and material causes and time and space have their relevance, and the other purely spiritual and transcendental, where neither matter and material causes nor time and space have any part at all, and where thought and action are almost identical. The Divine Power mainly operates in this second dimension in the act of creation, making it dependent on or linking it to matter and material causes, as well as time and space. Any corporeal thing comes into existence in that way because the Divine Wisdom requires it to be so.

Second, neither matter and material causes nor time and space can put any constraint on the Divine Being of God nor on His Power. Above the corporeal realm or dimension are many other realms or dimensions, all of which are spiritual and transcendent to varying degrees, and in each of which the measure of time is completely different. All of these realms are infinitely contained by the Divine "Realm," where any aspect of corporeality is out of the question. The operations of the Divine Power originating in this "Realm" are manifested in the other realms according to the characteristic of each realm.

As many saintly scholars such as Muhyi'd-Dīn ibn al-'Arabī (1165–1240) and Mawlānā Jalālu'd-Dīn ar-Rūmī (1207–1273) have observed in several places in their works and as – in different terms – modern quantum physics also asserts, what we see as a solid, corporeal world really consists in continuous movement. The universe is in a continuous cycle of appearance and disappearance by God's Power.

We witness even in this corporeal or material world that things come into existence as if all at once. Especially when we observe the lack of proportion between causes and effects – that is, Almighty God makes the existence of huge things dependent on their minute seeds, or causes minute things to end in great consequences – we can conclude that the manifestation of the Divine Power even in this world is also instantaneous. (Also see 36: 83, note 27.)

120. Never will the Jews be pleased with you, nor the Christians, unless you follow their way of faith and life.[102] Say (to them, O Messenger): "God's guidance (represented by the Qur'ān) is the true guidance." If (supposing the impossible) you were to follow their desires and fancies after the knowledge[103] that has come to you, you will have against God neither a guardian (who can protect you from His punishment) nor a helper.

121. Those (people) to whom We gave the Book (and who) recite it with true recitation, (following its commandments without making any changes or distortions in it): they have (ever-strengthening) faith in it. Whoever disbelieves in it (conceals and distorts the truths the Book contains): they are the losers (in both this world and the Hereafter).

122. O Children of Israel! Remember My favor that I bestowed upon you (by choosing Prophets and Messengers from amongst you and granting you a great kingdom, and by giving you a Book and guiding you to the Straight Path), and that I once exalted you above all peoples.

123. And be fearful and strive to be guarded against a day when (everybody will be seeking a means to save himself, and when) no soul will pay on behalf of another, nor will compensation be accepted from any of them, nor will any intercession (of the sort common in the world but which does not meet with God's permission and approval) be of use to them, nor will they be helped.

124. (You refuse to believe in and follow Muḥammad chiefly because Prophethood was not retained with you and so he did not appear amongst you. But you surely do admit Abraham's Prophethood, so)[104] remember that his Lord tested Abraham with commands and ordeals (such as his

being thrown into a fire, the destruction of the people of his kinsman Lot, and his being ordered to sacrifice his son Ishmael), and he fulfilled them thoroughly. He said: "Indeed I will make you an imām for all people." He (Abraham) pleaded: "(Will You appoint imāms) also from my offspring?" (His Lord) answered: "(I will appoint from among those who merit it. But) My covenant does not include the wrongdoers."[105]

125. Remember, again, that We made the House (the Ka‘bah in Makkah) a resort for people, and a refuge of safety (a sanctuary, that is, a sign of the truth). Stand in the Prayer (O believers, as you did in earlier times) in the Station of Abraham. And We imposed a duty on Abraham and Ishmael: "Purify My House for those who go around it as a rite of worship, and those who abide in devotion, and those who bow and prostrate (in the Prayer)."[106]

126. And (remember) once Abraham prayed: "My Lord! Make this (untilled valley) a land of security, and provide its people with the produce of earth, such of them as believe in God and the Last Day."[107] He (his Lord) answered: "(I will bestow provision upon both believers and unbelievers. But) whoever is thankless and disbelieves, I will provide for him to enjoy himself for a short while (in this life), then I will compel him to the punishment of the Fire – how evil a destination to arrive at!

---

102. The word *millah*, here translated as "way of belief and life", comes from the infinitive *imlāl*, meaning dictation or writing down from memory. As a term, it means the way followed, whether it be straight or twisted and crooked. The Qur'ān uses it in the meaning of a system of faith and conduct, a life-style. For this reason, it is attributed to people, not to God. We say, for example, the *millah* of Abraham, not the *millah* of God.

103. As we said in note 91 above, by "knowledge" the Qur'ān refers primarily to either the knowledge based on the Divine Revelation or the Revelation itself. Its opposite is the output of human desires and fancies based on nothing certain or proven, and conjectures having nothing to do with established knowledge (see 3: 4, 157; 10: 36, 66; 53: 23, 28). Thus, the first and primary source of knowledge in Islam is Divine Revelation or the Qur'ān and the established Sunnah – the sayings and actions of the Prophet, upon him be peace and blessings. The other sources are sound intellect or reason and sound perceptions, and therefore observation and experiment.

104. The explanatory words that we put (usually in brackets) before or within the translations of the verses are not additions to, nor any sort of adaptations of, the meaning of the verses. They express the full normal meaning of the words, understood individually and in context. By "context" we mean both the context of the passage or the *sūrah* or the Qur'ān as a whole, and also the historical context, the situation that is the background to the verses. Also, we should be aware that the Qur'ān is miraculous in its power of concision, of conveying much in few words. Sometimes this concision is achieved through the powerful compactness of the structures and syntax of Arabic, raised to inimitable perfection in the Qur'ān. A relatively uninflected language like English simply cannot reproduce the full meaning without adding words to convey the meaning that is carried in the words of the Arabic by their inflection, position in the sentence, etc. Sometimes the concision of the Qur'ān is achieved through ellipsis, that is, through omission of what is already known or easily knowable to one familiar with the language and the subject-matter. Concision by ellipsis is most briefly illustrated from narrative passages, such as in the wonderful *Sūrah Yūsuf* ("the best of narratives"): For example, between verse 12: 45 (*Then said he – of the two [prisoners] the one who was released – remembering after a long time, "I will inform you of its meaning, so send me forth*) and the next verse (12: 46, beginning *Joseph, O man of truth!*) a number of events are passed over because they are not immediately relevant to the meaning being conveyed, and because the listener or reader can supply what is missing from familiarity with the story and/or ordinary common sense: "He left the king's court to get to the prison. He arrived there and, on receiving permission from the prison guard to enter, did so. He came to Joseph and, after exchanging greetings with him, said: 'Joseph, O man of truth. . .' ."

The occasions on which the verses were revealed require explanations (as well as notes) because the historical context is not known to us in the way that it was known to the first addressees of the Qur'ān. However, it is important to clarify that, while the historical context is important for the meaning of the verses and, equally important, for the links between them, it does not restrict their meaning. Everyone should respond to the Qur'ān as if its words and meanings were being revealed to them as the first addressees of the Revelation. Knowing the historical context of certain verses or passages in fact enhances understanding of their present and permanent relevance, it does not diminish or restrict it.

105. God accorded to Abraham a very high rank and charged him with a very significant function: imamate for people. The meaning of *imāmah* includes any important leadership function, from leading others in the Prayer to leading a formally constituted group or institution in specific matters, to leading the Muslim community as a whole in all matters. The main function of imamate is acting as a means for the guidance of people in God's cause (21: 73; 32: 24). Being a very important mission requiring competence and qualification, it usually comes, as stated in this verse and 32: 24, after great tests and trials demanding patience, and needs, as stressed in the same verse, expert knowledge. So one who will lead the Muslims in all matters should have certainty in matters of faith, scholarly expertise in the religious sciences, and discernment in the outer and inner meaning of things and events. It is significant that the Qur'ān describes as "wrongdoers" those who are not worthy of such a mission. In the terminology of the Qur'ān, "wrongdoing" (*zulm*) includes a wide of range of wrong actions from deviancy in a small matter to the unforgivable sin of associating partners with God. It literally means putting something in what is not its place, or doing something not at the proper time and place and in the wrong way. One who has come to be known as a "wrongdoer" (*zālim*) cannot be an imam. The verse allusively explains why Prophethood and imamate were not retained with the Children of Israel, who, though descendants of Abraham through Isaac and Jacob, all of whom were appointed as imams, did every kind of wrong, including adoption of the calf as deity and attributing a son to God.

The Shī'ah, especially the so-called Twelver-Shī'ah, typically rest their doctrine of imamate on this verse. They claim that imamate was accorded to Abraham, upon him be peace, after he became a Prophet and Messenger, and therefore imamate is a greater rank than both Prophethood and Messengership. As is well-known, a Messenger is a Prophet who usually receives a Book or Scrolls and is charged with preaching God's Message, while a Prophet usually follows in the footstep of the Messenger preceding him. The Shī'ah, therefore, argue that the Twelve Imams, the first of whom is 'Ali, the fourth caliph and the cousin and son-in-law of the Prophet Muḥammad, upon him be peace and blessings, the others having come from the line of Imam Husayn, the son of 'Ali, are greater than all the Prophets and Messengers except the Prophet Muḥammad. However, their argument contradicts their doctrine of imamate, as none of the Twelve is either a Prophet or a Messenger. Second, according to the Qur'ān, imamate is, rather than an office or institution, a function. It is for this reason that all of the Prophets and Messengers were also imams. Third, the Qur'ān never associates the concepts of Prophet and Messenger with a negative value, whereas the concept of imam, because it is a function, is associated in that way: for example, there may be imams "of unbelief" (9: 12) and imams "calling to the Fire" (28: 41).

106. The Station of Abraham is (the place of) the stone on which Abraham reportedly stood while building the Ka'bah. By mentioning that in older times people used to visit the Ka'bah for the purpose of worship, going around it and abiding there in devotion, the verse refers to the fact that the real and historical center of the true religion that God chose for humankind is the Ka'bah. It therefore prepares hearts and minds for the changing of the *qiblah* (the direction to which people turn in Prayer) from Bayt al-Maqdis in Jerusalem to the Ka'bah. It also prepares the way for the commandment of the *Ḥajj* (the Pilgrimage to the Ka'bah), which is the fifth pillar of Islam.

The Ka'bah was the first building to be

built in the world. It was built by the Prophet Adam, upon him be peace. The Prophets Abraham and Ishmael, upon them be peace, re-built it upon its original foundations. Abraham's rebuilding it with his son Ishmael, the forefather of the Prophet Muḥammad, upon him be peace and blessings, not with Isaac, is an important symbol and sign that the Last Prophet, who would make the Ka'bah the focus for his followers in religion, was to appear among the descendants of Ishmael.

107. Believing in God and believing in the Last Day are two of the cardinal elements of Islamic faith. That does not mean that the essentials of faith are restricted to these two elements. Nor does it lead to the conclusion that salvation is possible without believing in the other essentials – notably, believing in Moses and the Torah during the time of Moses, together with the Prophets and Books preceding him, in Jesus and the Gospel during Jesus' time, together with those preceding him, and finally, in the Prophet Muḥammad and the Qur'ān as the seal of the Prophets and Divine Books, without excluding all other Prophets and Books in their original forms.

The Ka'bah toward the end of the 19th century. (A painting by R. Yazdani, reproduced from a photo from the Yıldız Sarayı archives in Istanbul.)

127. And when Abraham, and Ishmael with him, raised the foundations of the House (they were praying): "Our Lord! Accept (this service) from us. Surely You are the All-Hearing, the All-Knowing.

128. "Our Lord! Make us Muslims, submissive to You, and of our offspring a community Muslim, submissive to You. Show us our rites of worship (including particularly the rites of the Pilgrimage) and accept our repentance (for our inability to worship You as worshipping You requires). Surely You are the One Who accepts repentance and returns it with liberal forgiveness and additional reward, the All-Compassionate.

129. "Our Lord! Raise up among that community a Messenger of their own, reciting to them Your Revelations, and instructing them in the Book (that You will reveal to him) and the Wisdom,[108] and purifying them (of false beliefs and doctrines, of sins and all kinds of uncleanness). Surely You are the All-Glorious with irresistible might, the All-Wise."

130. Who (therefore) shrinks from the Way of Abraham, save him who makes himself a fool. Indeed We chose him as one pure and distinguished in the world, and he is surely among the righteous in the Hereafter.

131. When his Lord told him, "Submit yourself wholly (to your Lord)," he responded: "I have submitted myself wholly to the Lord of the worlds."[109]

132. Abraham bequeathed and enjoined this submission to his sons (Ishmael and Isaac) and (to his grandson) Jacob, saying: "My sons, God has chosen for you (from different ways of faith and life) the Religion (of Islam,[110] based on submission to Him and absolutely free from any kind

of associating partners with Him). Therefore, make sure that you do not die except as Muslims (those submitted to Him)."

133. Or were you (O Children of Israel, of Jacob) witnesses when death came to Jacob (so that you might claim that he bequeathed and enjoined a religion otherwise than as Abraham did, to give yourselves an excuse for refusing Islam,) when he said to his sons: "What will you worship after me?" They answered: "We will worship your God and the God of your fathers, Abraham, Ishmael, and Isaac, One God; we are Muslims submitted to Him."

134. Those were a people that passed away. Theirs is what they earned, and yours is what you earn. You will not be called to account for what they used to do.

108. By "the Wisdom" is meant the ways of understanding the Book and the ways of practicing or applying it in daily life. In this meaning, "the Wisdom" is almost synonymous with the Sunnah of the Messenger, and this is why many scholars have interpreted it as the Sunnah. It also includes knowing the meaning of things and events in the universe, in the human realm in particular. (For a detailed explanation, see note 159.)

109. This very short verse is a wonderfully concise summary of the Prophet Abraham's life from the beginning of his mission in Babylon to his being made an imam for all people and rebuilding the Ka'bah. God presents Himself as "his" Lord when He orders him to submit to Him. This signifies the initial phase of Abraham's mission: initially his relationship was with God as "his" Lord when he had not yet been charged with preaching. After this, he acquired knowledge of the outer and inner dimensions of existence, began preaching the Religion, and passed through many severe tests. Finally, he attained to the universal rank of relationship with God as the Lord of the worlds, and he was appointed as an imām for people. This is a significant point to help differentiate sainthood and Prophethood and various ranks in each. Saints, no matter what their "station," can build relationship with God only as the Lord of the heart of each. But a Prophet, especially one who is also a Messenger, has relationship, according to his degree, with God as the Lord of his people, of all humankind, and all existence as a whole. This explains in what sense the Prophet Muḥammad, upon him be peace and blessings, as the heir to the missions of all the Prophets and Messengers before him, is the greatest of all, as his mission began in the universal relation with God as Lord of the worlds, for he was sent to all of humankind and the jinn and as a mercy for the whole of creation.

110. The religion which God Almighty sent from the time of Adam is Islam. In its essentials – the pillars of faith, the principles of devotion or worship, moral and ethical standards for individual and collective behavior – it has remained the same. It is only with respect to the changing aspects of life that, as explained in note 95, it laid down rules subject to revision in the light of both changed conditions and the unchanging essentials of faith, worship, and morality, and it established legal principles to maintain this process.

At the cosmic level, Islam is the religion or universal system which the whole of existence, including the very bodies of the unbelievers, follow unconditionally. That is, the whole universe maintains its life in perfect and unconditional submission to God's laws. This is why there is a perfect stability, order and harmony throughout it. What falls on humankind is to follow the counterparts of these laws in their lives not unconditionally but of their free will. If they do that, the same stability, order, and harmony will prevail in their lives and their relationships with each other, individually and collectively, and with their "natural" environment. As is well known, the word islām means, as well as submission to God, peace, harmony, order, and serenity.

135. And they (the Jews) say, "Be Jews" or (the Christians say,) "Be Christians (*hūdan aw naṣārā*),[111] that you may be rightly guided." Say: "Rather, the Way of Abraham of pure faith (is what we choose, the Way free from unbelief, associating partners with God and hypocrisy, that we may be rightly guided)." Abraham was never of those who associate partners with God.

136. (O Muslims! You) declare: "We have believed in God (without associating any partners with Him), and that which has been sent down to us, and that which was sent down to Abraham, Ishmael, Isaac, Jacob, and the Prophets who were raised in the tribes, and that which was given to Moses and Jesus, and that (knowledge, wisdom and Prophethood) which was given to all other Prophets from their Lord. We make no distinction between any of them (in believing), and we are Muslims (submitted to Him wholly and exclusively)."

137. If (the Jews and Christians who claim to be guided) believe in the same as that which you believe in, they are rightly guided; but if they turn away, then they are in schism. God suffices you against them. He is the All-Hearing, the All-Knowing.

138. (O Muslims, say: "We take) the "color" of God (the "color" that He has put on the whole universe, not the color some party put upon themselves through some rites in the name of religion[112])." Who is better than God in coloring, (and whose color is better than God's)? And We are those who worship Him (as He is to be worshipped,) exclusively."

139. Say: "Do you dispute with us concerning God (as if He had said Paradise is only for the Jews or the Christians) seeing that He is our Lord and your Lord (He has created and provides for us as well as for you). (Whatever He commands us to believe, He also commands you to believe. Yet if you persist in disputing and asserting your superiority, we say) to us are accounted our deeds, and to you, your deeds. It is we who are sincere to Him (in believing in Him and worshipping Him exclusively)."

140. Or do you claim that Abraham, Ishmael, Isaac, Jacob, and the Prophets who were raised in the tribes were "Jews" or "Christians?" Say (to them): "Do you know better, or does God?" (They know well that any of the Prophets were neither "Jews" nor "Christians," but they conceal the truth.) Who is more in the wrong than he who conceals the testimony he has from God? God is never unaware and unmindful of what you do.

141. Those were a people that passed away. Theirs is what they earned, and yours is what you earn. You will not be called to account for what they used to do.

111. The Qur'ān does not typically use the term "Jews." Rather, as is clear from many preceding verses, it prefers the honorific phrase "Children of Israel" to designate the Jews. As we briefly explained in note 46, the Qur'ān uses the term Jews for those among the Children of Israel who describe themselves as such. As for the term *Nazarenes* (Christians), it was invented by pagan Romans as a pejorative term to designate the followers of "Jesus of Nazareth." The Qur'ān prefers the term "the People of the Book" for both the Christians and Jews as an honorary title and to encourage them to obey the commandments of the Books given to each and therefore accept Islam.

112. The Arab Christians used to mix a dye or color in the baptismal water, signifying that the person baptized took on a new color in life.

سَيَقُولُ السُّفَهَآءُ مِنَ النَّاسِ مَا وَلَّىٰهُمْ عَن قِبْلَتِهِمُ الَّتِى
كَانُوا عَلَيْهَا قُل لِّلَّهِ الْمَشْرِقُ وَالْمَغْرِبُ يَهْدِى مَن يَشَآءُ
إِلَى صِرَاطٍ مُّسْتَقِيمٍ ۞ وَكَذَٰلِكَ جَعَلْنَاكُمْ أُمَّةً وَسَطًا
لِّتَكُونُوا شُهَدَآءَ عَلَى النَّاسِ وَيَكُونَ الرَّسُولُ عَلَيْكُمْ
شَهِيدًا وَمَا جَعَلْنَا الْقِبْلَةَ الَّتِى كُنتَ عَلَيْهَآ إِلَّا لِنَعْلَمَ مَن
يَتَّبِعُ الرَّسُولَ مِمَّن يَنقَلِبُ عَلَىٰ عَقِبَيْهِ وَإِن كَانَتْ لَكَبِيرَةً إِلَّا
عَلَى الَّذِينَ هَدَى اللَّهُ وَمَا كَانَ اللَّهُ لِيُضِيعَ إِيمَانَكُمْ إِنَّ
اللَّهَ بِالنَّاسِ لَرَءُوفٌ رَّحِيمٌ ۞ قَدْ نَرَىٰ تَقَلُّبَ وَجْهِكَ
فِى السَّمَآءِ فَلَنُوَلِّيَنَّكَ قِبْلَةً تَرْضَاهَا فَوَلِّ وَجْهَكَ شَطْرَ
الْمَسْجِدِ الْحَرَامِ وَحَيْثُ مَا كُنتُمْ فَوَلُّوا وُجُوهَكُمْ شَطْرَهُ
وَإِنَّ الَّذِينَ أُوتُوا الْكِتَابَ لَيَعْلَمُونَ أَنَّهُ الْحَقُّ مِن رَّبِّهِمْ وَمَا
اللَّهُ بِغَافِلٍ عَمَّا يَعْمَلُونَ ۞ وَلَئِنْ أَتَيْتَ الَّذِينَ أُوتُوا
الْكِتَابَ بِكُلِّ آيَةٍ مَّا تَبِعُوا قِبْلَتَكَ وَمَآ أَنتَ بِتَابِعٍ قِبْلَتَهُمْ
وَمَا بَعْضُهُم بِتَابِعٍ قِبْلَةَ بَعْضٍ وَلَئِنِ اتَّبَعْتَ أَهْوَآءَهُم
مِّنۢ بَعْدِ مَا جَآءَكَ مِنَ الْعِلْمِ إِنَّكَ إِذًا لَّمِنَ الظَّالِمِينَ ۞

142. The (hypocritical) fools among the people will say, "What has turned them from the direction they were facing in the Prayer?" Say (O Messenger): "To God belong the east and the west (and therefore the whole earth with its easts and wests; in whatever direction He wants us to turn, we turn). He guides whomever He wills to a straight path."

143. And in that way (O Community of Muḥammad, whereas others turn in different directions and, straying from the Straight Path, falter between extremes in thought and belief) We have made you a middle-way community, that you may be witnesses for the people (as to the ways they follow), and that the (most noble) Messenger may be a witness for you.[113] We formerly appointed (the Bayt al-Maqdis in Jerusalem) the direction to turn in the Prayer (and now are changing it) so that We may mark out and distinguish who truly follows the Messenger from him who turns back on his heels (when the Messenger's way does not suit his desires). And indeed that testing is burdensome, save for those whom God has guided (and made steadfast in faith). God will never let your faith go to waste.[114] Surely God is for humankind All-Pitying, All-Compassionate.

144. Certainly We have seen you (O Messenger) often turning your face to heaven (in expectation of a Revelation. Do not worry, for) We will surely turn you towards a direction that will please and satisfy you. (Now the time has come, so) turn your face towards the Sacred Mosque. (And you, O believers) turn your faces towards it wherever you are. Surely those who were given the Book (before, no matter if the hypocrites or the foolish among

them deny or object to it) do know (the coming of this Prophet and this change of qiblah) to be true (commandments) from their Lord.[115] God is not unaware, nor unmindful, of whatever they do.

145. Even if (O Messenger) you were to bring to those who were given the Book (before) all kinds of signs and evidences, they would not follow your direction (qiblah). Indeed you are not a follower of their direction, nor are they followers of one another's direction. (Theirs is an attitude arising from their fancies and desires, not from knowledge.) Were you to follow their lusts and fancies after the knowledge that has come to you, then you would surely be among the wrongdoers (those who wrong themselves because of the errors they have done).

113. The most distinguishing characteristic of Islam and, when loyal to that characteristic, of the community of Muḥammad, upon him be peace and blessings, is that it is far from all kinds of extremism. Islam represents the middle way in all aspects of life. For example, it is neither spiritualism nor materialism, neither realism nor idealism, neither capitalism nor socialism, neither individualism nor étatism, neither absolutism nor anarchism, neither this-worldly and hedonist, nor purely other-worldly or monastic. As it is unique in its worldview and social, economic, and political aspects, it is also unique in the moral education it gives to individuals. The human being has three cardinal drives or faculties, namely the intellect or reasoning power, lust or worldly appetite, and anger or the impulse to self-assertion or defense. Each of these faculties has an upper or lower extreme. For example, the extremes of the intellect are demagogy or deceitful reasoning, and the refusal or failure to reason, namely stupidity; the extreme conditions of lust are wanton self-indulgence and listlessness, and of anger arrogant, thoughtless rashness, and self-abasing cowardice. The teachings of Islam discipline and balance these faculties. The disciplining of the intellect enables the acquisition of knowledge that is sound and functions as wisdom. The disciplining of lust results in the development of the virtues of restraint and chastity and, subsequently, of forbearance. The disciplining of anger results in the ability to live and act with courage in the cause of right and justice. Representing the middle way in its creed, its rites of worship, its social, economic and political principles, and the moral training it gives to people, Islam as a way of life means peace, balance, harmony, and salvation.

Islam being the consummation or final, universal form of the Divine religion, which corrects the deviations into which the earlier communities had lapsed during the course of history, the community of Muḥammad will bear witness on behalf of the communities of the previous Prophets in the Hereafter, and the Prophet Muḥammad, upon him be peace and blessings, on behalf of them.

114. The sentence, "God will never let your faith go to waste" has usually been interpreted to mean "God will never let the Prayers you did turning to the Bayt al-Maqdis go to waste." However, it also conveys more general and important truths, such as:

- Faith cannot be separated from action. One's way of life and acting demonstrate whether one is a believer or not.
- The Prayer has an essential relation with faith. The Prayer, together with the intention in it and the way of doing it, is a definite sign of the character and depth of one's faith.
- Good deeds or actions done only for the good pleasure of God and based on faith will profit in the Hereafter. Whatever is done as a requirement of faith never goes to waste, provided one preserves one's faith and goes to the other world with that faith strong and intact.

115. The expression "true (commandments) from their Lord", that is, the Lord of those who were given the Book before, is to stress that the Prophet Muḥammad was predicted in the previous Divine Books with all his attributes including that he would turn in the Prayer towards the Sacred Mosque (the Mosque of the Kaʿbah) in Makkah.

22   سُورَةُ الْبَقَرَة   ٢٢

الَّذِينَ ءَاتَيْنَٰهُمُ الْكِتَٰبَ يَعْرِفُونَهُۥ كَمَا يَعْرِفُونَ أَبْنَآءَهُمْ وَإِنَّ فَرِيقًا
مِّنْهُمْ لَيَكْتُمُونَ الْحَقَّ وَهُمْ يَعْلَمُونَ ۝ الْحَقُّ مِن رَّبِّكَ فَلَا تَكُونَنَّ
مِنَ الْمُمْتَرِينَ ۝ وَلِكُلٍّ وِجْهَةٌ هُوَ مُوَلِّيهَا فَاسْتَبِقُوا
الْخَيْرَٰتِ أَيْنَ مَا تَكُونُوا يَأْتِ بِكُمُ اللَّهُ جَمِيعًا إِنَّ اللَّهَ
عَلَىٰ كُلِّ شَىْءٍ قَدِيرٌ ۝ وَمِنْ حَيْثُ خَرَجْتَ فَوَلِّ وَجْهَكَ
شَطْرَ الْمَسْجِدِ الْحَرَامِ وَإِنَّهُۥ لَلْحَقُّ مِن رَّبِّكَ وَمَا اللَّهُ
بِغَٰفِلٍ عَمَّا تَعْمَلُونَ ۝ وَمِنْ حَيْثُ خَرَجْتَ فَوَلِّ وَجْهَكَ
شَطْرَ الْمَسْجِدِ الْحَرَامِ وَحَيْثُ مَا كُنتُمْ فَوَلُّوا وُجُوهَكُمْ
شَطْرَهُۥ لِئَلَّا يَكُونَ لِلنَّاسِ عَلَيْكُمْ حُجَّةٌ إِلَّا الَّذِينَ ظَلَمُوا
مِنْهُمْ فَلَا تَخْشَوْهُمْ وَاخْشَوْنِي وَلِأُتِمَّ نِعْمَتِي عَلَيْكُمْ
وَلَعَلَّكُمْ تَهْتَدُونَ ۝ كَمَا أَرْسَلْنَا فِيكُمْ رَسُولًا مِّنكُمْ
يَتْلُوا عَلَيْكُمْ ءَايَٰتِنَا وَيُزَكِّيكُمْ وَيُعَلِّمُكُمُ الْكِتَٰبَ
وَالْحِكْمَةَ وَيُعَلِّمُكُم مَّا لَمْ تَكُونُوا تَعْلَمُونَ ۝ فَاذْكُرُونِي
أَذْكُرْكُمْ وَاشْكُرُوا لِي وَلَا تَكْفُرُونِ ۝ يَٰٓأَيُّهَا الَّذِينَ
ءَامَنُوا اسْتَعِينُوا بِالصَّبْرِ وَالصَّلَوٰةِ إِنَّ اللَّهَ مَعَ الصَّٰبِرِينَ ۝

146. Those to whom We gave the Book (before) know him (the Messenger with all his distinguishing attributes including the direction he will turn to in the Prayer) as they know their own sons. Yet a party among them conceal the truth and they do it knowingly.[116]

147. It (your turning towards the Sacred Mosque, O Messenger,) is the truth from your Lord, and only that which is from your Lord is the truth; be not, then, among the doubters.

148. Every people has a direction towards which they turn, (a goal they turn to in life, and those who turn to the Sacred Mosque have a way they follow to their goal). So strive together as if in a race, (O community of believers,) towards all that is good. Wherever you may be, God will bring you all together.[117] Surely God has full power over everything.

149. From wherever you go out (for journeying), turn your face (O Messenger) towards the Sacred Mosque (in the Prayer). This is the truth from your Lord. (O you who believe! Do the same, for) God is not unaware and unmindful of what you do.

150. From wherever you go out (for journeying), turn your face (O Messenger) towards the Sacred Mosque (in the Prayer). Wherever you may be, (O you who believe,) turn your faces towards it, that the people may not have an argument against you – unless they be those immersed in wrongdoing; and hold not them in awe, but stand in awe of Me – and that I may complete My favor (of faith and Islam) upon you, and that you may be wholly guided (in Islam to the truth).

151. As We have sent among you a Messenger of your own, reciting to you Our Revelations, and purifying you (of false beliefs and doctrines, and sins, and all kinds of uncleanness), and instructing you in the Book and the Wisdom, and instructing you in whatever you do not know.

152. So always remember and make mention of Me (when service to Me is due), that I may remember and make mention of you (when judgment and recompense are due); and give thanks to Me, and do not be ungrateful to Me.[118]

153. O you who believe! Seek help (against all kinds of hardships and tribulations) through persevering patience and the Prayer; surely God is with the persevering and patient.[119]

116. The Jews and Christians of that time recognized God's Messenger, upon him be peace and blessings. After his conversion, 'Umar asked 'Abdullāh ibn as-Salām, the most renowned Jewish scholar of the time, who converted after the Messenger's emigration to Madīnah, if he had recognized God's Messenger. "I recognized him," Ibn as-Salām answered and added, "I may doubt my children – my wife might have deceived me – but I have no doubt about God's Messenger being the Last Prophet.' (aṣ-Ṣābūnī, 1: 140)

For the indications to the Prophet Muḥammad's coming that still exist in the Bible, see Appendix 1.

117. The sentence *Wherever you may be, God will bring you all together* has a wide range of meaning, such as:

- The Muslims will be scattered throughout the world and turn towards the Ka'bah in the Prayer as a single community.
- Islam will spread throughout the world extensively, among many diverse peoples and societies, having superiority or dominance over other religions.
- God will bring all the people together in the Place of Supreme Gathering and judge them.

118. Thankfulness or gratitude is the door to faith, and ingratitude the way to unbelief. The Qur'ān uses the same word – *kufr* – for both unbelief and ingratitude. *Kufr* (unbelief) literally means overlaying or concealing, and as a term, it means concealing and rejecting or denying any of the pillars of faith and the established religious commandments. Denying God or not recognizing Him with His essential Attributes such as His being the Creator, the Provider, the absolute Ruler and Governor of the universe, the Sustainer, and the Self-Subsisting One, etc., is primarily included in *kufr*. Those who do not recognize God with His Attributes, will attribute anything good or praiseworthy in their lives to themselves, instead of attributing them to God. Such an attitude is obviously identical with ingratitude.

119. The verse's ending with *God is with the persevering and patient*, not "God is with those who establish the Prayer and those who are persevering and patient," indicates that establishing the Prayer properly itself requires persevering patience (as, indeed, it also enables it). As mentioned in note 54, enduring the difficulties of the duty of servanthood to God or steadfastness in regular worship is one of the categories of patience. The verse's ending also links it to the verses to come that announce how God tests His servants. Being successful in the test obviously demands patience.

154. And say not of those who are killed in God's cause: "They are dead." Rather they are alive,[120] but you are not aware.

155. We will certainly test you with something of fear and hunger and loss of wealth, and lives, and fruits (earnings);[121] but give glad tidings to the persevering and patient:

156. Those who, when a disaster befalls them, say, "Surely we belong to God (as His creatures and servants) and surely to Him we are bound to return." (And they act accordingly.)[122]

157. Such are those upon whom are blessings from their Lord (such as forgiveness, answering their calls, and satisfying their needs) and mercy (to come in the form of help in both this world and Hereafter, and favors in Paradise beyond human imagination); and they are those who are rightly guided.

158. [123](The hills of) aṣ-Ṣafā and Marwah are among the emblems God has appointed (to represent Islam and the Muslim community).[124] Hence whoever does the *Ḥajj* (the Major Pilgrimage) to the House (of God, the Ka‘bah) or the *‘Umrah* (the Minor Pilgrimage), there is no blame on him to run between them (and let them run after they go round the Ka‘bah as an obligatory rite). And whoever does a good work voluntarily (such as additional going-round the Ka‘bah and running between aṣ-Ṣafā and Marwah, and other kinds of good works), surely God is All-Responsive to thankfulness, All-Knowing.

159. Those who conceal anything of the clear truths (concerning the fundamentals of the Religion, including Muḥammad's Messengership in particular) and (the Revelations conveying) the guidance (that We have sent down), after We have made them clear in the Book – God curses such people (excludes them from His mercy) and so do all who (have any authority to) curse.

160. Except those who repent and mend their ways, and openly declare (those truths and Revelations) – for those, I return their repentance with forgiveness. I am the One Who accepts repentance and returns it with liberal forgiveness and additional reward, the All-Compassionate.

161. But those who reject faith (demonstrated in their persisting in concealing the truths) and die unbelievers, on them is the curse of God and the angels, and of all humankind.[125]

162. Abiding therein (in the Fire, the consequence or place of the curse); the punishment will not be lightened for them, nor will they be reprieved.

163. (So, O people, refrain from concealing the truths and from disbelieving, and do not seek in vain another source of help and a refuge for yourselves. For) Your God is One God; there is no deity but He, the All-Merciful, the All-Compassionate.[126]

120. Human life has five degrees:

- Our life which depends on certain conditions and the fulfillment of certain needs.

- The life of Khidr and Ilyās (Elijah) which is free to some extent from the necessities of our life. They (Khidr and Elijah) can be present in different places at the same time.

- The life of the Prophets Jesus and Enoch. These two Prophets live in heaven free of the necessities of human life in their "astral" bodies.

- The life of martyrs – those who are killed in God's cause. Martyrs do not feel the pangs of death and know themselves to be transferred into a better world where they enjoy the blessings of God.

- The life of the dead. Death means one's being discharged from worldly duties with the soul set free. (See *The Letters*, "the 1st Letter," 1-3.)

121. The believers, both individually and collectively, pass through one or some of these tests. These include the religious obligations which would come after the revelation of this verse, such as war, which causes fear and the loss of wealth and lives, and the fasting of Ramadan. The main purpose for testing is to mature and perfect the believers both as individuals and as a community, purify them, distinguish the true believers among them from the hypocritical ones, develop their capacities, prepare them for the future and make them worthy of Paradise.

122. This is the reaction of a sincere believer when visited by one of the tests mentioned in the previous verse. It signifies the highest spiritual degree, which is complete resignation to what God has decreed for the believer. The following verse explains the glad tidings (the door to which was opened in the preceding verses, 2: 153–55) given to those who have attained this degree.

123. The verses up to here have followed a line of argument that, either through exhortation or admonition, urges the Children of Israel to accept Islam and thereby re-discover their original way. They also contain warnings for the young Muslim community against dangers that may originate within itself and/or from within the communities of the Jews and Christians. Besides, these verses prepare minds and hearts for the kind of *jihad* with their possessions and persons that may become unavoidable for the Muslims.

The approach and style the Qur'ān deploys are miraculous and unique to it. The Qur'ān turns around its main purposes, namely God's Oneness, Prophethood, the Hereafter, and worship and justice. It deals with religion and life as a whole and with different aspects of each. Just as we can see our "natural" environment both as a whole and in its constituent elements when we look at it, so too the Qur'ān directs our minds and hearts through all the elements of life. As a matter of fact, the best of styles or the highest degree of eloquence can be attained by approximating the way the natural world impresses itself upon ours senses and understanding. The Qur'ān is, in fact, a perfect translation or another copy of the "books" of the universe and humanity, which is the miniature specimen of the universe.

124. Aṣ-Ṣafā and al-Marwah are two hills near the Ka'bah in Makkah. The Prophet Abraham, upon him be peace, left his wife Hagar together with his son Ishmael near these two hills. In order to find water or see whether there was a caravan nearby, Hagar ran between these two hills. Pilgrims run between these two hills, four times from aṣ-Ṣafā to al-Marwah and three times the other way. This is called *sa'y* (speedy walking). Emblems (*shi'ār*), like the call to the Prayer, Prayer in congregation, most particularly the congregational prayers of *Jumu'ah* and the two 'Īds, the *Ḥajj* with its rituals, mosques, sacrifice, etc., are (as well as having their religious meaning for the individual and the community) public symbols that identify Islam and the Muslim community. Such emblems or public symbols, even those established by the Prophet himself, not directly by God, are more important than the individual obligatory

prayers or rituals for the life and maintenance of the Muslim community.

125. This verse explains the phrase "all who curse" at the end of 2: 159. They are the angels who are extremely averse to unbelief, polytheism, hypocrisy, and other sins. The curse of all humankind may rather be related to the Hereafter when all the truths will be manifest. All kinds of relations between people, especially between the unbelievers, such as ties of blood, of economic or political interest, of being leaders of others or followers, will be severed. They will curse and blame each other. The curse of God means His excluding from His forgiveness and special mercy, while the curse of the angels, who continuously pray for the believers, denotes their asking God to exclude those deserving the curse from His mercy and condemn them to punishment.

126. This verse marks a conclusion in respect of the topics discussed up to this point. It links all those topics with the *Basmalah* (In the Name of God, the All-Merciful, the All-Compassionate), which is the seed of Islam, and the Opening Chapter (the *Fātiḥah*, the core of the Book), and the initial verses of this *sūrah*.

24   سُوْرَةُ الْبَقَرَةِ   ٢٤

إِنَّ فِى خَلْقِ السَّمَوَاتِ وَالْأَرْضِ وَاخْتِلَافِ الَّيْلِ وَالنَّهَارِ وَالْفُلْكِ الَّتِى تَجْرِى فِى الْبَحْرِ بِمَا يَنفَعُ النَّاسَ وَمَا أَنزَلَ اللَّهُ مِنَ السَّمَاءِ مِنْ مَاءٍ فَأَحْيَا بِهِ الْأَرْضَ بَعْدَ مَوْتِهَا وَبَثَّ فِيهَا مِنْ كُلِّ دَابَّةٍ وَتَصْرِيفِ الرِّيَاحِ وَالسَّحَابِ الْمُسَخَّرِ بَيْنَ السَّمَاءِ وَالْأَرْضِ لَآيَاتٍ لِقَوْمٍ يَعْقِلُونَ ۝ وَمِنَ النَّاسِ مَن يَتَّخِذُ مِن دُونِ اللَّهِ أَندَادًا يُحِبُّونَهُمْ كَحُبِّ اللَّهِ ۖ وَالَّذِينَ آمَنُوا أَشَدُّ حُبًّا لِلَّهِ ۗ وَلَوْ يَرَى الَّذِينَ ظَلَمُوا إِذْ يَرَوْنَ الْعَذَابَ أَنَّ الْقُوَّةَ لِلَّهِ جَمِيعًا وَأَنَّ اللَّهَ شَدِيدُ الْعَذَابِ ۝ إِذْ تَبَرَّأَ الَّذِينَ اتُّبِعُوا مِنَ الَّذِينَ اتَّبَعُوا وَرَأَوُا الْعَذَابَ وَتَقَطَّعَتْ بِهِمُ الْأَسْبَابُ ۝ وَقَالَ الَّذِينَ اتَّبَعُوا لَوْ أَنَّ لَنَا كَرَّةً فَنَتَبَرَّأَ مِنْهُمْ كَمَا تَبَرَّءُوا مِنَّا ۗ كَذَٰلِكَ يُرِيهِمُ اللَّهُ أَعْمَالَهُمْ حَسَرَاتٍ عَلَيْهِمْ ۖ وَمَا هُم بِخَارِجِينَ مِنَ النَّارِ ۝ يَا أَيُّهَا النَّاسُ كُلُوا مِمَّا فِى الْأَرْضِ حَلَالًا طَيِّبًا وَلَا تَتَّبِعُوا خُطُوَاتِ الشَّيْطَانِ ۚ إِنَّهُ لَكُمْ عَدُوٌّ مُبِينٌ ۝ إِنَّمَا يَأْمُرُكُم بِالسُّوءِ وَالْفَحْشَاءِ وَأَن تَقُولُوا عَلَى اللَّهِ مَا لَا تَعْلَمُونَ ۝

---

164. Surely in the creation of the heavens and the earth, and the alternation of night and day (with their periods shortening and lengthening), and the vessels sailing in the sea with profit to people, and the water that God sends down from the sky, therewith reviving the earth after its death and dispersing therein all kinds of living creatures, and His disposal of the winds, and the clouds subservient between the sky and earth – surely there are signs (demonstrating that He is the One God deserving worship, and the sole Refuge and Helper) for a people who reason and understand.

165. Yet there are among humankind those who take to themselves objects of worship as rivals to God, loving them with a love like that which is the due of God only – while those who truly believe are firmer in their love of God. If only those who commit this (greatest) wrong could see – as they will see when they behold the punishment – that the power altogether belongs to God, and that God is severe in punishment.[127]

166. At that time when (they see it) those who were followed (in the world as elders, heads, or leaders and loved as only God is to be loved) disown those who followed them and declare themselves innocent of their evil deeds, and they see the punishment, and the relations between them are cut off.

167. And those who followed say: "If only we might return (to the world) and disown them, as they have disowned us." Thus does God show them their deeds in a manner that will cause them bitter regrets. Never will they come out of the Fire.

168. O humankind! (Observe whatever God commands you. He has made you dwell on the earth, so) eat of what is on the earth provided it is lawful, and pure and wholesome (in composition and religiously); and do not follow in the footsteps of Satan (who deceives both those who are followed and those who follow); indeed he is a manifest enemy to you.

169. He only commands you to evil and indecency and that you should speak against God the things about which you have no (sure) knowledge.[128]

---

127. The verses emphasize the Oneness of God as the only Object of Worship, and the sole Refuge and Helper of humanity. None other than God is worthy of being worshipped and being regarded as a deity. Those who love their

Prophets or leaders or elders with a love due to God only, and go so far as to see in them attributes belonging exclusively to God, and obey them willingly in their orders contrary to those of God, have rebelled against God and associated partners with Him, and therefore committed the greatest wrong. Such people are those who do not use their reason and cannot see the uncountable manifest signs in the universe and in human life that demonstrate God and His Oneness. It is only when they see the punishment of God that they will perceive that the power altogether belongs to God. This verse also refers to the absolute necessity of following God's Messenger, upon him be peace and blessings, and accepting him as the leader, the fact announced in the verse (3: 31): *Say (O Messenger): "If you indeed love God, then follow me, so that God will love you and forgive you your sins."*

128. Satan deceives people. He continuously whispers evils and indecency into their hearts, urges them to utter what they do not know concerning God, and invites them to disbelieve in Him or to associate partners with Him. He is insistent in this whispering and draws people under his influence to the extent that the Qur'ān describes this as "commanding." Another important point included in the meaning of Satan's "commanding" is that those who follow in the footsteps of Satan are, so to speak, acting on his authority as his officials and agents. What Satan commands them to utter about God without any knowledge are wrong conceptions of God's very Being or Essence, and errors of thought, attitude, and action in relation to His Attributes, acts, and commandments.

وَإِذَا قِيلَ لَهُمُ اتَّبِعُوا مَا أَنزَلَ اللّهُ قَالُوا بَلْ نَتَّبِعُ مَا أَلْفَيْنَا عَلَيْهِ آبَاءَنَا أَوَلَوْ كَانَ آبَاؤُهُمْ لَا يَعْقِلُونَ شَيْئًا وَلَا يَهْتَدُونَ ۞ وَمَثَلُ الَّذِينَ كَفَرُوا كَمَثَلِ الَّذِي يَنْعِقُ بِمَا لَا يَسْمَعُ إِلَّا دُعَاءً وَنِدَاءً صُمٌّ بُكْمٌ عُمْيٌ فَهُمْ لَا يَعْقِلُونَ ۞ يَا أَيُّهَا الَّذِينَ آمَنُوا كُلُوا مِن طَيِّبَاتِ مَا رَزَقْنَاكُمْ وَاشْكُرُوا لِلّهِ إِن كُنتُمْ إِيَّاهُ تَعْبُدُونَ ۞ إِنَّمَا حَرَّمَ عَلَيْكُمُ الْمَيْتَةَ وَالدَّمَ وَلَحْمَ الْخِنزِيرِ وَمَا أُهِلَّ بِهِ لِغَيْرِ اللّهِ فَمَنِ اضْطُرَّ غَيْرَ بَاغٍ وَلَا عَادٍ فَلَا إِثْمَ عَلَيْهِ إِنَّ اللّهَ غَفُورٌ رَّحِيمٌ ۞ إِنَّ الَّذِينَ يَكْتُمُونَ مَا أَنزَلَ اللّهُ مِنَ الْكِتَابِ وَيَشْتَرُونَ بِهِ ثَمَنًا قَلِيلًا أُولَٰئِكَ مَا يَأْكُلُونَ فِي بُطُونِهِمْ إِلَّا النَّارَ وَلَا يُكَلِّمُهُمُ اللّهُ يَوْمَ الْقِيَامَةِ وَلَا يُزَكِّيهِمْ وَلَهُمْ عَذَابٌ أَلِيمٌ ۞ أُولَٰئِكَ الَّذِينَ اشْتَرَوُا الضَّلَالَةَ بِالْهُدَىٰ وَالْعَذَابَ بِالْمَغْفِرَةِ فَمَا أَصْبَرَهُمْ عَلَى النَّارِ ۞ ذَٰلِكَ بِأَنَّ اللّهَ نَزَّلَ الْكِتَابَ بِالْحَقِّ وَإِنَّ الَّذِينَ اخْتَلَفُوا فِي الْكِتَابِ لَفِي شِقَاقٍ بَعِيدٍ ۞

170. When it is said to them (who follow in the footsteps of Satan), "Follow what God has sent down," they respond: "No, but we follow that (the traditions, customs, beliefs, and practices) which we found our forefathers in." What! even though their forefathers had no understanding of anything, and were not rightly guided?

171. The likeness of those who refuse to believe is that of those who hear, from the one who is calling them, nothing except a shouting and crying out – they are deaf, dumb and blind, and so they have no understanding of (what is said to them).[129]

172. O you who believe! (Without concern for the rules the unbelievers contrive in regard to food) eat of the pure, wholesome things that We have provided for you, and (in return) give thanks to God, if you worship Him alone.

173. He has made unlawful to you only carrion, and blood, and the flesh of swine, and that which is offered in the name of other than God. Yet whoever is constrained by dire necessity to eat of them, provided he does not covet (that which is unlawful) nor exceed the bounds of necessity, no sin shall be on him. Surely God is All-Forgiving, All-Compassionate.

174. Those who conceal the truths and commandments in the Book that God has sent down, and sell them for a trifling price (such as worldly benefit, status, and renown), they eat nothing but fire in their bellies. And God will not speak to them on the Day of Resurrection (when they will be in dire need to speak to Him to implore forgiveness and mercy), nor will He absolve them to pronounce them pure. For them is a painful punishment.

175. Such are the ones who have bought straying in exchange for guidance, and punishment in exchange for forgiveness. How they persevere in their striving to reach the Fire (and enduring it)![130]

176. That is so because God is sending down the Book with the truth, and there is nothing false in it. Those who are at variance regarding the Book (believing in part of it, disbelieving in part, and believing in one or some of the Divine Books, while disbelieving in the others), have certainly veered far (from the truth) into wide schism.

129. This parable has two aspects. On the one hand, it suggests that the unbelievers are like animals that only follow their herdsmen and obey them without knowing and understanding why. On the other hand, it also suggests that when the truth is preached to them, they show such insensitivity to it that one may as well be addressing animals that merely comprehend sounds but are incapable of understanding their meaning. "Shouting and crying" allude to the fact that the call is "loud" enough to be easily registered as sound, but they are incapable of any effort to make sense of it.

130. Those unbelievers who have no patience when it comes to heeding the truth, doing good, and refraining from the unlawful pleasures of the world, are nevertheless steadfast and persevering in deserving the Fire, which it is impossible to endure. This is an astonishing disposition, impossible to understand.

26   سُوْرَةُ الْبَقَرَة   ٢٦

لَّيْسَ الْبِرَّ أَن تُوَلُّوا وُجُوهَكُمْ قِبَلَ الْمَشْرِقِ وَالْمَغْرِبِ
وَلَكِنَّ الْبِرَّ مَنْ آمَنَ بِاللهِ وَالْيَوْمِ الْآخِرِ وَالْمَلَائِكَةِ
وَالْكِتَابِ وَالنَّبِيِّنَ وَآتَى الْمَالَ عَلَى حُبِّهِ ذَوِي الْقُرْبَى وَالْيَتَامَى
وَالْمَسَاكِينَ وَابْنَ السَّبِيلِ وَالسَّائِلِينَ وَفِي الرِّقَابِ وَأَقَامَ
الصَّلَوةَ وَآتَى الزَّكَوةَ وَالْمُوفُونَ بِعَهْدِهِمْ إِذَا عَاهَدُوا
وَالصَّابِرِينَ فِي الْبَأْسَاءِ وَالضَّرَّاءِ وَحِينَ الْبَأْسِ أُولَئِكَ الَّذِينَ
صَدَقُوا وَأُولَئِكَ هُمُ الْمُتَّقُونَ ۝ يَا أَيُّهَا الَّذِينَ آمَنُوا كُتِبَ
عَلَيْكُمُ الْقِصَاصُ فِي الْقَتْلَى الْحُرُّ بِالْحُرِّ وَالْعَبْدُ بِالْعَبْدِ وَالْأُنثَى
بِالْأُنثَى فَمَنْ عُفِيَ لَهُ مِنْ أَخِيهِ شَيْءٌ فَاتِّبَاعٌ بِالْمَعْرُوفِ وَأَدَاءٌ إِلَيْهِ
بِإِحْسَانٍ ذَلِكَ تَخْفِيفٌ مِنْ رَبِّكُمْ وَرَحْمَةٌ فَمَنِ اعْتَدَى بَعْدَ
ذَلِكَ فَلَهُ عَذَابٌ أَلِيمٌ ۝ وَلَكُمْ فِي الْقِصَاصِ حَيَوةٌ يَا أُولِي
الْأَلْبَابِ لَعَلَّكُمْ تَتَّقُونَ ۝ كُتِبَ عَلَيْكُمْ إِذَا حَضَرَ
أَحَدَكُمُ الْمَوْتُ إِنْ تَرَكَ خَيْرًا الْوَصِيَّةُ لِلْوَالِدَيْنِ وَالْأَقْرَبِينَ
بِالْمَعْرُوفِ حَقًّا عَلَى الْمُتَّقِينَ ۝ فَمَنْ بَدَّلَهُ بَعْدَ مَا سَمِعَهُ فَإِنَّمَا
إِثْمُهُ عَلَى الَّذِينَ يُبَدِّلُونَهُ إِنَّ اللهَ سَمِيعٌ عَلِيمٌ ۝

—————— ∽ ——————

177. Godliness and virtue is not that you should turn your faces in the direction of the east and west; but he is godly and virtuous who believes in God and the Last Day, the angels, the Book, and the Prophets, and gives away of his property with pleasure, although he loves it, to relatives, orphans, the destitute, the wayfarer, and those who have to beg (or who need a loan), and for the liberation of slaves, and establishes the Prayer, and pays the Prescribed Purifying Alms. And those (are godly and virtuous) who fulfill their covenant when they have engaged in a covenant, and who are patient

and persevering in hardship, and disease, and at the time of stress (such as battle between the truth and falsehood). Those are they who are true (in their faith), and those are they who have achieved righteousness, piety, and due reverence for God.

178. O you who believe! Prescribed for you is retaliation in cases of (deliberate, unjust) killing: freeman for freeman, slave for slave, female for female. Yet if he (the murderer) is granted some remission by his brother (any of the heirs of the victim), then what falls on the pardoning side is fulfilling in fairness what has been agreed on, and the other side is making the payment kindly enough to please the other side.[131] This is a lightening from your Lord, and a mercy. Whoever offends after that, for him is a painful punishment.

179. There is life for you in retaliation, (if you understand,) O people of discernment, so it may be that you (will perceive it and fulfill God's command and in so doing) attain the desired piety and righteousness and deserve His protection.

180. Prescribed for you, when any of you is visited by death, if he leaves behind wealth, is to make testament in favor of his parents and near relatives according to customary good and religiously approvable practice[132] – a duty for the truly God-revering, pious.

181. Then if anyone changes the will after hearing it (and the will is not carried out as it must be), then the sin thereof is on those who change it. Surely God is All-Hearing, All-Knowing.

---

131. The law of retaliation was also prescribed in the Bible: "He who strikes a man, so that he dies, shall surely be put to death." (Exodus, 21: 12) "And he who strikes his father or his mother shall surely be put to death. And

he who kidnaps a man and sells him, of if he is found in his hand, shall surely be put to death." (Exodus, 21: 15–6) However, there is no law of remission in the Bible. Islamic law decrees retaliation but also decrees that if the injured parties (or in cases of murder, the heirs of the deceased) pardon the guilty person either outright or in return for some compensation, then retribution is not executed. Insofar as modern law reserves the right to punish to the state, it denies that right to the victim. This is, on the face of it, an offense against natural justice. Whoever is the victim of the offense, he or she must have the right of punishing or pardoning.

Although some countries recognize and apply the death penalty, imprisonment is the usual mode of punishment for murder in the West. However, to make a brief, general comparison, although an offense is something concrete, imprisonment is not. Second, an offense and its punishment should be considered together in the same context, and they should be of the same sort, like a dirt of oil being cleaned with soap made from oil. Third, an offense and its punishment must be of the same nature. For example, killing and stealing are two offenses of different nature. The modern law gives the same kind and nature of punishment for both, namely imprisonment. The difference is only in quantity. However, quantity can never serve as a substitute for quality or nature. As for Islam, the punishment it gives for any offense is of the same nature as the offense. Fourth, the criminal law of Islam is based on justice and mercy. According to the declaration in the next verse, *There is life for you in retaliation, (if you understand,) O people of discernment*, it takes into consideration both the criminal and the victim and the society and the fundamental moral and spiritual values all together, and is of the nature that it trains, reforms, prevents, and satisfies the victim. But there is none of these in imprisonment. It is not reformative and preventive, and it is not satisfactory for the victim either. In addition, it destroys the spirit and personality, and excludes the person from social life.

In conclusion, like all of its other laws, the criminal law of Islam is reformative, and based on justice, balance, and mercy.

Although Islam allows retaliation or retaliation in case of wrong as a requirement of jus-

tice, as inviolate values demand retaliation and equal respect (2: 194), it advises an individual to forgive an offense done to himself or herself, or better, to repel it with what is better. For a discussion of this matter, see *sūrah* 22, note 18.

The expressions *freeman for freeman, slave for slave, female for female* do not mean that a freeman will not be liable to retaliation for a crime against a slave, or that a man will not be liable to retaliation for a crime against a woman. On the contrary, the Qur'ān put an end to a practice widespread in pre-Islamic Arabia and still existing in the present world – if a respected member of the tribe was killed by an ordinary member of another, they would kill several members of the murderer's tribe as well as the murderer himself. Also, if the murderer was a man of high standing, the pre-Islamic Arabs were unwilling to permit the murderer to be executed. Even today, those nations that are supposedly the most civilized often proclaim that if one of their citizens is killed, they will execute scores of the killer's compatriots.

132. This commandment relates to the period when there were no rules for the distribution of inheritance. Thus everyone was required to make testament in order not to deprive his parents and nearest relatives of some inheritance from him that would otherwise have been distributed, most probably, only among his children. Later when God revealed a set of laws regarding the distribution of the inheritance (4: 11-12), the Prophet, upon him be peace and blessings, clarified the laws relating to testaments and inheritance. These may be summarized as follows:

Provisions in a will cannot be made in favor of any of an individual's legal heirs, i.e. those whose different portions are specified in the Qur'ān, as no changes can be made therein. Second, the will may specify the distribution of only one-third of the deceased's whole estate. When a person has died, his or her debts (if any) are cleared, the person's last will and testament (within the limitations just mentioned) is carried out, and then the estate is divided among the legal heirs according to the Qur'ānic injunctions.

فَمَنْ خَافَ مِنْ مُوصٍ جَنَفًا أَوْ إِثْمًا فَأَصْلَحَ بَيْنَهُمْ
فَلَآ إِثْمَ عَلَيْهِ إِنَّ اللَّهَ غَفُورٌ رَّحِيمٌ ۝ يَٰٓأَيُّهَا
الَّذِينَ ءَامَنُوا كُتِبَ عَلَيْكُمُ الصِّيَامُ كَمَا كُتِبَ عَلَى الَّذِينَ مِن
قَبْلِكُمْ لَعَلَّكُمْ تَتَّقُونَ ۝ أَيَّامًا مَّعْدُودَٰتٍ فَمَن كَانَ
مِنكُم مَّرِيضًا أَوْ عَلَىٰ سَفَرٍ فَعِدَّةٌ مِّنْ أَيَّامٍ أُخَرَ وَعَلَى الَّذِينَ
يُطِيقُونَهُ فِدْيَةٌ طَعَامُ مِسْكِينٍ فَمَن تَطَوَّعَ خَيْرًا فَهُوَ خَيْرٌ لَّهُ
وَأَن تَصُومُوا خَيْرٌ لَّكُمْ إِن كُنتُمْ تَعْلَمُونَ ۝
شَهْرُ رَمَضَانَ الَّذِي أُنزِلَ فِيهِ الْقُرْءَانُ هُدًى لِّلنَّاسِ
وَبَيِّنَٰتٍ مِّنَ الْهُدَىٰ وَالْفُرْقَانِ فَمَن شَهِدَ مِنكُمُ
الشَّهْرَ فَلْيَصُمْهُ وَمَن كَانَ مَرِيضًا أَوْ عَلَىٰ سَفَرٍ فَعِدَّةٌ
مِّنْ أَيَّامٍ أُخَرَ يُرِيدُ اللَّهُ بِكُمُ الْيُسْرَ وَلَا يُرِيدُ
بِكُمُ الْعُسْرَ وَلِتُكْمِلُوا الْعِدَّةَ وَلِتُكَبِّرُوا
اللَّهَ عَلَىٰ مَا هَدَىٰكُمْ وَلَعَلَّكُمْ تَشْكُرُونَ ۝ وَإِذَا
سَأَلَكَ عِبَادِي عَنِّي فَإِنِّي قَرِيبٌ أُجِيبُ دَعْوَةَ الدَّاعِ إِذَا دَعَانِ
فَلْيَسْتَجِيبُوا لِي وَلْيُؤْمِنُوا بِي لَعَلَّهُمْ يَرْشُدُونَ ۝

—⁓—

182. But if anyone fears from the testator an injustice or sin and brings about a settlement between the parties (by making the necessary change), then no sin will be on him. Surely God is All-Forgiving, All-Compassionate.

183. O you who believe! Prescribed for you is the Fast, as it was prescribed for those before you, so that you may deserve God's protection (against the temptations of your carnal soul) and attain piety.

184. (Fasting is for) a fixed number of days. If any of you is so ill that he cannot fast, or on a journey, he must fast the same number of other days. But for those who can no longer manage to fast, there is a redemption (penance) by feeding a person in destitution (for each day missed or giving him the same amount in money). Yet better it is for him who volunteers greater good (by either giving more or fasting in case of recovery), and that you should fast (when you are able to) is better for you, if you but knew (the worth of fasting).

185. The month of Ramaḍān (is the month) in which the Qur'ān was sent down as guidance for people, and as clear truths of the guidance and the Criterion (between truth and falsehood). Therefore whoever of you is present this month, must fast it, and whoever is so ill that he cannot fast or on a journey (must fast the same) number of other days. God wills ease for you, and He does not will hardship for you, so that you can complete the number of the days required, and exalt God for He has guided you, and so it may be that you will give thanks (due to Him).

186. And when (O Messenger) My servants ask you about Me, then surely I am near: I answer the prayer of the suppliant when he prays to Me.[133] So let them respond to My call (without hesitation), and believe and trust in Me (in the way required of them), so that they may be guided to spiritual and intellectual excellence and right conduct.

---

133. Prayer or supplication is the essence of worship or servanthood to God. What rises to God from the whole creation is prayer. It has kinds and degrees:

- The first kind is the prayer of all organisms, plant, animal and human, through the natural disposition of their bodies and their functioning in line with their duties in creation. This kind of prayer is always acceptable.

- The second kind is that which is uttered by all organisms, plant, animal, and human, in the tongue of vital needs. God meets these needs just on time, with the exception that plants, and the animals relatively weaker and less intelligent (as compared to others, such as wolves and foxes), are nourished more easily than the others. The more powerful and intelligent and more self-subsisting a creature feels, the greater hardship it suffers to get nourishment. All that a baby has to do in order to procure its need is cry.

- The third kind of prayer is that which is done by human beings. This falls into two categories:
- The first category is the active prayer. It means complying with the laws that God has set for life. For example, a farmer's plowing the soil is knocking on the door of Divine providence. A patient's going to the doctor's is appealing to God for cure. This kind of prayer is usually accepted.

- The second category is the verbal prayer that we do. This kind of prayer is also answered. But answering is different from accepting. God answers all the prayers done sincerely. However, He answers sometimes by giving whatever is asked for, sometimes by giving what is better, sometimes by postponing giving to the afterlife, and sometimes by not giving at all, since it will not turn out in favor of the one who prays. The way that God answers a prayer depends on His Wisdom. (See *The Words*, "the 23rd Word," 333-334.)

28   سُورَةُ الْبَقَرَة   ٢٨

بِسْمِ اللَّهِ الرَّحْمَٰنِ الرَّحِيمِ

ing the period when you are in retreat in the mosques. These are the bounds set by God; do not draw near them (keep a safe distance away from them).[135] Thus does God make His Revelations clear to people so that they may attain piety and be protected against the punishment therefor.

188. (Eat and drink, but do the kinds of worship that help you to control your soul such as the Fast.) And do not consume your wealth among yourselves in false ways (in vanities, sins, and crimes such as theft, usurpation, bribery, usury, and gambling); nor proffer it to those in authority so that you may sinfully consume a portion of other people's goods, and that knowingly.

189. They ask you (O Messenger) about the new moons (because of the month of Ramaḍān). Say: "They are appointed times (markers) for the people (to determine time periods) and for the Pilgrimage." (Do not link them to superstitions and superstitious behavior like entering dwellings by the back rather than the front.) It is not virtue that you enter dwellings from the backs of them, but virtue is (the state of) one who (truly believing in God) strives to attain righteousness and piety (by carrying out His commandments and refraining from His prohibitions). So come to dwellings (in the normal way) by their doors. (Do everything according to the rule and establish relations with your leader and among yourselves in proper terms.) And strive to obey God in due reverence and piety so that you may prosper.[136]

187. It is made lawful for you to go in to your wives on the night of the Fast. (There is such intimacy between you that) they are a garment for you (enfolding you to protect you against illicit relations and beautifying you) and you are (in the same way for the same reasons) a garment for them. God knows that (you felt that) you were betraying yourselves (by doing what you supposed was prohibited), and has turned to you in lenience (and protected you from possible sins by not legislating such a prohibition). So now associate in intimacy with them and seek what God has ordained for you. And (you are permitted to) eat and drink until you discern the white streak of dawn against the blackness of night; then observe the Fast until night sets in.[134] But do not associate in intimacy with them (your wives) dur-

190. Fight in God's cause (in order to exalt His Name) against those who fight against you, but do not exceed the bounds (set by God),[137] for surely God loves not those who exceed the bounds.

134. In fixing the time of obligatory rites, God has decreed what is so clear and simple that people in all times and places, and at any stage of scientific development, can observe them. Accordingly the timing of the rites is done with reference to conspicuous and familiar natural phenomena.

Some people argue that this method is not feasible in zones close to the poles, where night and day each last for about six months. However, in these zones, signs of morning and evening do appear with unfailing regularity and the people know them. It is on the basis of these signs that people time their sleeping and waking patterns. In the days before watches were common, the inhabitants of countries like Finland, Norway, and Greenland used to fix the hours of the day and night by means of various signs that appeared on the horizon. Just as those signs helped them to determine their schedules in other matters, so they should enable them to time their various prayers, the pre-fast meal and the breaking of the Fast.

135. The phrase *in retreat in the mosques* refers to the practice of spending some time in Ramaḍān in a mosque in devotion to God. God's Messenger used to dedicate the last ten days of Ramaḍān to such retreat in the mosque. While in this state, known as *iʿtikāf*, one may go out of the mosque for only the absolutely necessary requirements of life, and one must refrain from gratifying sexual desire.

136. The waxing and waning of the moon attracted people's attention in the pre-Islamic era, as it still does today, and some fanciful ideas and superstitions were associated with it. The moon was considered the basis of good and bad omens. The Qur'ān warns against such superstitious notions.

It also draws attention to another important matter, namely propriety and good sense in controlling curiosity, so that it does not become nor lead to idle or vain preoccupation. It is unbecoming to believers that they ask pointless questions and become preoccupied with useless things. But if such questions are put, the teacher or leader should give an answer that will, rather than satisfying their curiosity, keep the questioners curious but direct their curiosity towards more worthy or useful matters.

As to the questions put to the Messenger about the waxing and waning of the moon: the worthwhile, useful element of the questioners' curiosity is indicated in the response of God: it is necessary for them to know the beginning and end of months and periods between, so that the time of the great religious rites can be determined by reference to phenomena literally visible or knowable by all human beings. That tells us what the waxing and waning is for and how the knowledge thereof helps us. It also tells us that such knowledge should be useful and open – it should not become difficult, secret, mysterious, and therefore liable to degenerate into superstition among the ignorant, and malicious manipulation of the ignorant by the knowledgeable. Any questions related to *how* the moon waxes and wanes or *why* it does so could not, at that time, have been answered in any way both accurate and intelligible to the questioners. Indulging curiosity of this kind is precisely what breeds ignorance and superstition. Curiosity needs to be disciplined so that it approaches what is unknown through questions that can be answered intelligibly in a way that sustains the questioning – questions that, if asked and answered truthfully, increase the stock of human knowledge and strengthen the pillars of faith in the knowledge and wisdom of the Creator Who made this world, made it intelligible and made human beings, within certain limitations, capable of understanding it.

The verse uses the occasion of the Prophet's being asked about the new moons to establish or emphasize the proper rules and norms in people's relations among themselves and with their leader/teacher. It invites them again to true piety and godliness. Clearly the verse has a fundamental connection with all the verses of the *sūrah* to this point, especially 2: 177 and the opening verses describing "those who prosper" (2: 1–5). Next, the Qur'ān goes on to lay down important principles concerning war in order to put an end to the *Jāhiliyyah* wars that recognized no rules, and to educate the believers, as individuals and a community, in the best conduct.

137. For a detailed explanation concerning Islam and war, see Appendix 2.

وَاقْتُلُوهُمْ حَيْثُ ثَقِفْتُمُوهُمْ وَأَخْرِجُوهُم مِّنْ حَيْثُ أَخْرَجُوكُمْ وَالْفِتْنَةُ أَشَدُّ مِنَ الْقَتْلِ وَلَا تُقَاتِلُوهُمْ عِندَ الْمَسْجِدِ الْحَرَامِ حَتَّى يُقَاتِلُوكُمْ فِيهِ فَإِن قَاتَلُوكُمْ فَاقْتُلُوهُمْ كَذَلِكَ جَزَاءُ الْكَافِرِينَ ۝ فَإِنِ انتَهَوْا فَإِنَّ اللَّهَ غَفُورٌ رَّحِيمٌ ۝ وَقَاتِلُوهُمْ حَتَّى لَا تَكُونَ فِتْنَةٌ وَيَكُونَ الدِّينُ لِلَّهِ فَإِنِ انتَهَوْا فَلَا عُدْوَانَ إِلَّا عَلَى الظَّالِمِينَ ۝ الشَّهْرُ الْحَرَامُ بِالشَّهْرِ الْحَرَامِ وَالْحُرُمَاتُ قِصَاصٌ فَمَنِ اعْتَدَى عَلَيْكُمْ فَاعْتَدُوا عَلَيْهِ بِمِثْلِ مَا اعْتَدَى عَلَيْكُمْ وَاتَّقُوا اللَّهَ وَاعْلَمُوا أَنَّ اللَّهَ مَعَ الْمُتَّقِينَ ۝ وَأَنفِقُوا فِي سَبِيلِ اللَّهِ وَلَا تُلْقُوا بِأَيْدِيكُمْ إِلَى التَّهْلُكَةِ وَأَحْسِنُوا إِنَّ اللَّهَ يُحِبُّ الْمُحْسِنِينَ ۝ وَأَتِمُّوا الْحَجَّ وَالْعُمْرَةَ لِلَّهِ فَإِنْ أُحْصِرْتُمْ فَمَا اسْتَيْسَرَ مِنَ الْهَدْيِ وَلَا تَحْلِقُوا رُءُوسَكُمْ حَتَّى يَبْلُغَ الْهَدْيُ مَحِلَّهُ فَمَن كَانَ مِنكُم مَّرِيضًا أَوْ بِهِ أَذًى مِّن رَّأْسِهِ فَفِدْيَةٌ مِّن صِيَامٍ أَوْ صَدَقَةٍ أَوْ نُسُكٍ فَإِذَا أَمِنتُمْ فَمَن تَمَتَّعَ بِالْعُمْرَةِ إِلَى الْحَجِّ فَمَا اسْتَيْسَرَ مِنَ الْهَدْيِ فَمَن لَّمْ يَجِدْ فَصِيَامُ ثَلَاثَةِ أَيَّامٍ فِي الْحَجِّ وَسَبْعَةٍ إِذَا رَجَعْتُمْ تِلْكَ عَشَرَةٌ كَامِلَةٌ ذَلِكَ لِمَن لَّمْ يَكُنْ أَهْلُهُ حَاضِرِي الْمَسْجِدِ الْحَرَامِ وَاتَّقُوا اللَّهَ وَاعْلَمُوا أَنَّ اللَّهَ شَدِيدُ الْعِقَابِ ۝

---

191. (While at war) kill them wherever you come upon them, and drive them out from where they drove you out (thus recovering your lands from their usurpation). (Though killing is something you feel aversion to) disorder (rooted in rebellion against God and recognizing no laws) is worse than killing.[138] Do not fight against them in the vicinities of the Sacred Mosque unless they fight against you there; but if they fight against you (there), kill them – such is the recompense of the (rebellious) unbelievers.

192. Then if they desist (from fighting), surely God is All-Forgiving, All-Compassionate.

193. (But if they persist in causing disorder, continue to) fight against them until there is no longer disorder (rooted in rebellion against God), and the religion (the right for worship and the authority to or-

der the way of life) is recognized for God. However, if they desist, then there is no hostility except to the wrongdoers.[139]

194. A sacred month is retributive for another sacred month, and the inviolate values demand retaliation. So whoever attacks you, attack them in like manner as they attacked you. Nevertheless, fear God and remain within the bounds of piety and righteousness, and know that God is with the God-revering, pious.[140]

195. (Just retaliation, as well as war or other defensive measures to maintain your existence, are not possible without expense. So) spend in God's cause (out of whatever you have) and do not ruin yourselves by your own hands (by refraining from spending. Whatever you do,) do it in the best way in the awareness that God sees it. Surely God loves those who are devoted to doing good, aware that God is seeing them.

196. Complete the Ḥajj (the Major Pilgrimage) and the ʿUmrah (the Minor Pilgrimage) for God, and if you are impeded (after you have already put on the Pilgrimage attire), then send (to Makkah) a sacrificial offering you can afford. Do not shave your heads (to mark the end of the state of consecration for the Pilgrimage) until the offering has reached its destination and is sacrificed. However, if any of you is ill (so that he is obliged to leave the state of consecration) or has an ailment of the head, he must make redemption by fasting, or giving alms, or offering a sacrifice. When you are secure (when the Pilgrimage is not impeded, or the impediment is removed), then whoever takes advantage of the ʿUmrah before the Ḥajj, must give a sacrificial offering he can afford. For whoever cannot afford the offering, a fast for three days during the Ḥajj, and for seven days when you return home, that is, ten days in all. This is for those whose families do not live in the environs of the Sa-

cred Mosque. Act in due reverence for God and piety (avoiding disobedience to Him and obeying His ordinances), and know that God is severe in retribution.

138. The verse regards *fitnah* (here translated as "disorder [rooted in rebellion against God and recognizing no laws]") as one of the most prominent reasons for war. War is something undesired and abhorrent; nevertheless, situations do arise that will make it inevitable. *Fitnah* is just such a situation or, rather, all such situations share characteristics that may be summed up as *fitnah*. In most Qur'ānic contexts, it denotes associating partners with God and adopting this as a life-style, spreading unbelief and apostasy, committing major sins with willful, insolent abandon, open hostilities to Islam, causing public disorder, and oppression, all of which are worse than killing. Although each of these can constitute a reason for war, the term *fitnah* covers all of them.

139. Believing in God's Oneness entails accepting Him as the sole Deity, Lord, and Object of Worship. That in turn means recognizing Him as having the exclusive authority to make things lawful or unlawful. So His laws must prevail in human life. If some people, exploiting any means available to them, attempt to usurp this authority and establish a social order according to their own desires and moreover force others to obey them, this is the *fitnah* which the Muslims are ordered to fight against. Islam seeks to eradicate *fitnah* and set up a stable environment of justice and freedom for all, without excuses for injustice, oppression, violation of essential human rights, for anarchy, and terror. Under the rule of Islam, properly constituted and administered, everyone is allowed to live according to their faith and practice their religion individually and collectively.

140. The months of Dhu'l-Qa'dah, Dhu'l-Hijjah, Muharram, and Rajab (the 11th, 12th, and the 1st and 7th months of the lunar year) were consecrated, and warfare, killing, and pillage were prohibited during these months. However, in order to have an advantage over others, the polytheist Arabs frequently violated the sanctity of these months and tried to compensate for this violation by substituting one of the other months for the violated sacred month.

In order not to allow them this advantage over the Muslims and because of the principle expressed in *the inviolate values demand retaliation*, the Qur'ān permitted the Muslims to attack their enemies in whichever month they attacked them.

This verse establishes an important principle in social life, in the penal code, and in international relations. The Islamic Law recognized as priorities the protection of religion, life, reason, family and lineage, and private property. Whoever is killed while defending one of them dies a martyr. It is because of the sanctity of these five things that offending religion and religious values (apostasy and blasphemy), killing and murder, alcohol and narcotics (which enfeeble reason), fornication and adultery (which dishonor as well as confounding lineage), and theft and usurpation, are among the major sins. The life or property of no one individual or nation or race is more sacred than another. So, since there is equality between these things that the Qur'ān calls *the inviolate values*, it requires that any violation is reciprocated only within the strict measure of just and equal retaliation. This is also what natural justice demands. However, an individual may forgive anything wrong done to him or her; such forgiving is praised and commended by the Qur'ān as virtue. However, one does not have the right to pardon on behalf of others, to pardon an offense against public order or property or against national values or security.

Islam allows retaliation but prohibits doing harm or returning harm with harm. That is, if someone or some group does wrong or evil, the victims of the wrong are not licensed to do the same, still less is the wrong or evil to be accepted as the normal way of doing things. Retaliation must be for the sake of restoring justice and must be strict as to means and proportionality. Islam strives for peace and for the removal of violations. That is why the verse continues with the command to remain within the bounds of piety, meaning that any further offense or exceeding the bounds in repelling an attack is prohibited.

30 سورة البقرة ٢ ٣٠

الْحَجُّ أَشْهُرٌ مَّعْلُومَاتٌ فَمَن فَرَضَ فِيهِنَّ الْحَجَّ
فَلَا رَفَثَ وَلَا فُسُوقَ وَلَا جِدَالَ فِي الْحَجِّ وَمَا تَفْعَلُوا
مِنْ خَيْرٍ يَعْلَمْهُ اللهُ وَتَزَوَّدُوا فَإِنَّ خَيْرَ الزَّادِ
التَّقْوَىٰ وَاتَّقُونِ يَٰٓأُولِي الْأَلْبَابِ ۝ لَيْسَ عَلَيْكُمْ
جُنَاحٌ أَن تَبْتَغُوا فَضْلًا مِّن رَّبِّكُمْ فَإِذَآ أَفَضْتُم
مِّنْ عَرَفَاتٍ فَاذْكُرُوا اللهَ عِندَ الْمَشْعَرِ الْحَرَامِ
وَاذْكُرُوهُ كَمَا هَدَىٰكُمْ وَإِن كُنتُم مِّن قَبْلِهِ لَمِنَ
الضَّآلِّينَ ۝ ثُمَّ أَفِيضُوا مِنْ حَيْثُ أَفَاضَ النَّاسُ
وَاسْتَغْفِرُوا اللهَ إِنَّ اللهَ غَفُورٌ رَّحِيمٌ ۝ فَإِذَا
قَضَيْتُم مَّنَاسِكَكُمْ فَاذْكُرُوا اللهَ كَذِكْرِكُمْ
ءَابَآءَكُمْ أَوْ أَشَدَّ ذِكْرًا فَمِنَ النَّاسِ مَن يَقُولُ
رَبَّنَآ ءَاتِنَا فِي الدُّنْيَا وَمَا لَهُ فِي الْآخِرَةِ مِنْ
خَلَاقٍ ۝ وَمِنْهُم مَّن يَقُولُ رَبَّنَآ ءَاتِنَا فِي الدُّنْيَا حَسَنَةً
وَفِي الْآخِرَةِ حَسَنَةً وَقِنَا عَذَابَ النَّارِ ۝ أُوْلَٰٓئِكَ
لَهُمْ نَصِيبٌ مِّمَّا كَسَبُوا وَاللهُ سَرِيعُ الْحِسَابِ ۝

———❧———

197. The Ḥajj is in the months well-known.[141] Whoever undertakes the duty of Ḥajj in them, there is no sensual indulgence, nor wicked conduct, nor disputing during the Ḥajj. Whatever good you do (all that you are commanded and more than that, especially to help others), God knows it. Take your provisions for the Ḥajj (and do not be a burden upon others). In truth, the best provision is righteousness and piety, so be provided with righteousness and piety to guard against My punishment, O people of discernment!

198. There is no blame on you that you should seek of the bounty of your Lord (by trading during the Ḥajj but beware of preoccupation to the extent of neglecting any of the rites of the Ḥajj.) When you press on in multitude from 'Arafāt (after you have stayed there for some time,) mention God at Mash'ar al-Harām (al-Muzdalifah); mention Him aware of how He has guided you, for formerly you were surely of those astray.

199. Then (do not choose to remain in Muzdalifah without climbing 'Arafat in order to refrain from mixing with other people because of vanity. Instead,) press on in multitude from where all the (other) people press on, and implore God's forgiveness (for your opposing Him in any way before now and for the mistakes you have made during the Ḥajj). Surely God is All-Forgiving, All-Compassionate (especially towards His believing servants).

200. And when you have performed those rites, mention God, as you mentioned your fathers (with the merits you approve of in them), or yet more intensely. For there are, among humankind, those who pray, "Our Lord, grant us in the world," and they have no share in the Hereafter.

201. And among them are those who pray, "Our Lord, grant us in the world what is good, and in the Hereafter what is good, and protect us from the punishment of the Fire."

202. Those people – for them is a portion, each according to what they have earned. God is swift at reckoning.

---

141. The months of the Ḥajj are Shawwāl, Dhu'l-Qa'dah, and Dhu'l-Hijjah. The Ḥajj cannot be performed in another month than these ones. One of the two pillars of the Ḥajj is staying for some time on the mount of 'Arafāt. This is done on the ninth day of Dhu'l-Hijjah, the eve of the 'Īd al-aḍhā (the religious festival of the day of sacrifice). The time of performing the other pillar, which is the Circumambulation of ifāḍah – the obligatory going round the Ka'bah seven times – begins on the first of the three days of 'Īd al-aḍhā.

وَاذْكُرُوا اللهَ فِىٓ اَيَّامٍ مَعْدُودَاتٍ فَمَنْ تَعَجَّلَ فِى يَوْمَيْنِ
فَلَآ اِثْمَ عَلَيْهِ وَمَنْ تَاَخَّرَ فَلَآ اِثْمَ عَلَيْهِ لِمَنِ اتَّقٰى
وَاتَّقُوا اللهَ وَاعْلَمُوٓا اَنَّكُمْ اِلَيْهِ تُحْشَرُونَ ۞ وَمِنَ النَّاسِ
مَنْ يُّعْجِبُكَ قَوْلُهُ فِى الْحَيٰوةِ الدُّنْيَا وَيُشْهِدُ اللهَ عَلٰى مَا فِى قَلْبِهِ ۙ
وَهُوَ اَلَدُّ الْخِصَامِ ۞ وَاِذَا تَوَلّٰى سَعٰى فِى الْاَرْضِ لِيُفْسِدَ
فِيْهَا وَيُهْلِكَ الْحَرْثَ وَالنَّسْلَ ۗ وَاللهُ لَا يُحِبُّ الْفَسَادَ
۞ وَاِذَا قِيلَ لَهُ اتَّقِ اللهَ اَخَذَتْهُ الْعِزَّةُ بِالْاِثْمِ
فَحَسْبُهُ جَهَنَّمُ ۗ وَلَبِئْسَ الْمِهَادُ ۞ وَمِنَ النَّاسِ مَنْ يَّشْرِى
نَفْسَهُ ابْتِغَاءَ مَرْضَاتِ اللهِ ۗ وَاللهُ رَؤُفٌ بِالْعِبَادِ
۞ يٰٓاَيُّهَا الَّذِينَ اٰمَنُوا ادْخُلُوا فِى السِّلْمِ كَافَّةً ۖ
وَلَا تَتَّبِعُوا خُطُوَاتِ الشَّيْطَانِ ۗ اِنَّهُ لَكُمْ عَدُوٌّ
مُبِينٌ ۞ فَاِنْ زَلَلْتُمْ مِّنْ بَعْدِ مَا جَاءَتْكُمُ
الْبَيِّنَاتُ فَاعْلَمُوٓا اَنَّ اللهَ عَزِيزٌ حَكِيمٌ ۞ هَلْ
يَنْظُرُونَ اِلَّآ اَنْ يَّاْتِيَهُمُ اللهُ فِى ظُلَلٍ مِّنَ الْغَمَامِ
وَالْمَلٰئِكَةُ وَقُضِيَ الْاَمْرُ ۗ وَاِلَى اللهِ تُرْجَعُ الْاُمُورُ ۞

203. Mention God during the (three) appointed days (of *Īd al-aḍḥā*). Whoever is in haste and content with two days (of mentioning God, having performed the rite of throwing pebbles at Satan), it is no sin for him; and whoever delays (continuing the rite to the third day), it is no sin for him, for him who is careful of the bounds of piety. Keep from disobedience to God in due reverence for Him and piety, and know that you will be gathered to Him.

204. Among the people there is he whose conversation on (the affairs of) the present, worldly life fascinates you, and he calls on God to bear testimony to what is in his heart, yet he is most fierce in enmity.

205. When he leaves (you) or attains authority, he rushes about the land to foment disorder and corruption therein and to ruin the sources of life and human generations. Surely God does not love disorder and corruption.

206. When he is told "Be fearful of your duty to God (and so follow His commands)," vainglory seizes and thrusts him towards (greater) sin. Hell will settle the account for him – how evil a cradle indeed it is!

207. And (in contrast, there is) among the people one who sells himself in pursuit of God's good pleasure. God is All-Pitying towards His servants (and therefore commends to them reverent piety and fear of His punishment).

208. O you who believe! Come in full submission to God, all of you, (without allowing any discord among you due to worldly reasons), and do not follow in the footsteps of Satan, for indeed he is a manifest enemy to you (seeking to seduce you to rebel against God with glittering promises).

209. If you stumble and fall back (from following God's way to realize peace and agreement) after the clear proofs of the truth have come to you, then know that God is All-Glorious with irresistible might, All-Wise.[142]

210. What do those (who fail to come in full submission to God) look for but that God('s command of destruction) should come to them in the shades of clouds with angels, and the matter be settled? To God are all matters ultimately referred, (and whatever He wills occurs).

142. The conclusions of verses are particularly important to understanding their meaning. For example, this verse concludes with the declaration that God is *'Azīzun Ḥakīm* (All-Glorious with irresistible might, All-Wise). It reminds us that it can neither harm nor benefit God whether we are submitted to Him and therefore able to come to peace and agreement among ourselves, or not. In whatever way we act, God is All-Glorious with irresistible might and does whatever He wills. While we cannot do anything to Him, He can, if He wills, punish and destroy us. However, He is also All-Wise; there are many instances of wisdom in whatever He does. He tests us in this world. That is why life here has laws particular to itself. For this reason, while evaluating the events and outcomes of human history, we should be ever mindful that God is All-Wise as well as All-Glorious with irresistible might. We may make judgments in partial or complete ignorance of our own and others' motives, of the near and far consequences of the conditions and events in which we are immersed, but God sees the whole future as He sees the whole past, and His Power and Wisdom are manifested throughout. The following verse sheds further light on this point.

سُوْرَةُ الْبَقَرَة

سَلْ بَنِيَ اِسْرَآءِيْلَ كَمْ اٰتَيْنَاهُمْ مِّنْ اٰيَةٍ بَيِّنَةٍ ۖ وَمَنْ يُّبَدِّلْ نِعْمَةَ اللّٰهِ مِنْ بَعْدِ مَا جَآءَتْهُ فَاِنَّ اللّٰهَ شَدِيْدُ الْعِقَابِ ۞ زُيِّنَ لِلَّذِيْنَ كَفَرُوا الْحَيٰوةُ الدُّنْيَا وَيَسْخَرُوْنَ مِنَ الَّذِيْنَ اٰمَنُوْا ۘ وَالَّذِيْنَ اتَّقَوْا فَوْقَهُمْ يَوْمَ الْقِيٰمَةِ ۗ وَاللّٰهُ يَرْزُقُ مَنْ يَّشَآءُ بِغَيْرِ حِسَابٍ ۞ كَانَ النَّاسُ اُمَّةً وَّاحِدَةً ۖ فَبَعَثَ اللّٰهُ النَّبِيّٖنَ مُبَشِّرِيْنَ وَمُنْذِرِيْنَ ۖ وَاَنْزَلَ مَعَهُمُ الْكِتٰبَ بِالْحَقِّ لِيَحْكُمَ بَيْنَ النَّاسِ فِيْمَا اخْتَلَفُوْا فِيْهِ ۚ وَمَا اخْتَلَفَ فِيْهِ اِلَّا الَّذِيْنَ اُوْتُوْهُ مِنْ بَعْدِ مَا جَآءَتْهُمُ الْبَيِّنٰتُ بَغْيًا بَيْنَهُمْ ۚ فَهَدَى اللّٰهُ الَّذِيْنَ اٰمَنُوْا لِمَا اخْتَلَفُوْا فِيْهِ مِنَ الْحَقِّ بِاِذْنِهٖ ۗ وَاللّٰهُ يَهْدِيْ مَنْ يَّشَآءُ اِلٰى صِرَاطٍ مُّسْتَقِيْمٍ ۞ اَمْ حَسِبْتُمْ اَنْ تَدْخُلُوا الْجَنَّةَ وَلَمَّا يَأْتِكُمْ مَّثَلُ الَّذِيْنَ خَلَوْا مِنْ قَبْلِكُمْ ۖ مَّسَّتْهُمُ الْبَأْسَآءُ وَالضَّرَّآءُ وَزُلْزِلُوْا حَتّٰى يَقُوْلَ الرَّسُوْلُ وَالَّذِيْنَ اٰمَنُوْا مَعَهٗ مَتٰى نَصْرُ اللّٰهِ ۗ اَلَا اِنَّ نَصْرَ اللّٰهِ قَرِيْبٌ ۞ يَسْئَلُوْنَكَ مَاذَا يُنْفِقُوْنَ ۖ قُلْ مَا اَنْفَقْتُمْ مِّنْ خَيْرٍ فَلِلْوَالِدَيْنِ وَالْاَقْرَبِيْنَ وَالْيَتٰمٰى وَالْمَسٰكِيْنِ وَابْنِ السَّبِيْلِ ۗ وَمَا تَفْعَلُوْا مِنْ خَيْرٍ فَاِنَّ اللّٰهَ بِهٖ عَلِيْمٌ ۞

211. Ask the Children of Israel how many clear proofs We gave to them (and what happened when they heeded them or did not heed them). Whoever tampers with God's blessing after it has come to him (whoever alters the guidance or exchanges it for straying): surely God is severe in retribution.[143]

212. The present, worldly life is decked out to be appealing to those who are ungrateful to God's blessing and disbelieve, and they deride those who believe (and attach no importance to the worldly life). But those who obey God in due reverence for Him and piety will be above them on the Day of Resurrection. God provides whomever He wills without reckoning.

213. Humankind were (in the beginning) one community (following one way of life without disputing over provision and other similar things. Later on differences arose and) God sent Prophets as bearers of glad tidings (of prosperity in return for faith and righteousness) and warners (against the consequences of straying and transgression), and He sent down with them the Book with the truth (containing nothing false in it) so that it might judge between the people concerning that on which they were differing. And only those who were given it differed concerning it, after the most manifest truths came to them, because of envious rivalry and insolence among themselves. God has guided by His leave those who have believed (in the Book and the Prophets, those who now believe in the Qur'ān and Muḥammad) to the truth about that on which they were differing. God guides whomever He wills to a straight path.[144]

214. (Given the history of humankind in this world,) do you think that you will enter Paradise while there has not yet come upon you the like of what came upon those who passed away before you? They were visited by such hardships and adversities, and were so shaken as by earthquake that the Messenger and those who believed in his company nearly cried out: "When comes God's help?" Beware! the help of God is surely near![145]

215. They ask you what they will spend (to provide sustenance for the needy). Say: "Whatever you spend of your wealth is for (your) parents and the near relatives, and the (needy) orphans, the destitute, and the wayfarer. Whatever good you do, surely God has full knowledge of it.[146]

143. The punishment that the Qur'ān mentions in return for the sins or crimes that people commit or for the discord among them arising from tampering with God's blessing of guidance should not be understood as restricted in reference to the Hereafter. God has laws that He has established for the worldly life of humankind. A person gets the recompense for obedience to those laws, or for disobedience to them, more in this world than in the Hereafter. Conversely, for the laws of God as presented through the *Dīn* or Religion, human compliance or non-compliance is for the most part recompensed in the Hereafter. Whether as individuals or as a community, human beings meet their just deserts both in this world and Hereafter. Accordingly, we should understand God's punishment to include the consequences of our actions in both this world and in the Hereafter.

The verses above warn the believers against discord and disagreements which may arise from failure in full submission to God. The shades of clouds in verse 210 may be alluding to various kinds of disasters they may suffer because of the disagreements among them. The verse to come (212) explains the cardinal cause for failure in full submission to God. It is attachment to the allurements of the worldly life, which is also the principal cause for unbelief.

144. This verse explains the right understanding or philosophy of history. God declared in 2: 38–39, with which this verse has a clear link, that He would send guidance to humankind, who were destined to live on the earth – that is, He would show them the way they should follow. In the early period of their earthly life, they followed a way under the leadership of Prophet Adam, to whom some Divine Scrolls was reportedly given. As alluded to in the previous verse (2: 212), there was no competition among them about how to share the products of their labor and what the earth yielded. When such competition eventually arose, it resulted in differences, clashes, and bloodshed. God, out of compassion, raised up Messengers among them and sent Books with some and Scrolls with some others so that they might live in justice and be guided to the truth in what they differed on. He also raised up Prophets in the footsteps of the Messengers to continue their

way. Nevertheless, because of rivalry, greed and envy, those who were given the Book differed on it, and this history continued so until, finally, the Prophet Muḥammad, upon him be peace and blessings, came with the Qur'ān. Some of those who had been given the Book before believed in him and some did not.

This verse clarifies that the primary reason for the conflicts among the peoples of the Book, as well as among other peoples, is envious rivalry. It also clarifies that the final source or reference for the solution of the problems among people is the Qur'ān and the Prophet Muḥammad, upon him be peace and blessings.

There have been differences of opinion among the Muslims in understanding some verses and commandments of the Qur'ān. This is very natural. The recourse for the settlement of these differences is the Sunnah of the Prophet. The Sunnah interprets the Qur'ān, expanding on what is brief in it, particularizing what is general in it, and generalizing what is particular in it. It also has the authority to make new legislation. For this reason, opposing, even attacking, the Sunnah means opposing and attacking one of the two foundations of Islam.

145. This verse points to way marks in the history of those following the Straight Path. This Path is no easy route. It passes through privations, persecutions, and even sufferings of war to the point where the believers all but cry out, "When comes the help of God?" This point, when the followers of the Straight Path are convinced that it is only God Who gives success, is also the point when God's help is at hand, and which leads on to the final triumph or prosperity in both worlds. However, testing of the quality of faith and obedience continues: it requires thankfulness and controlling the drives of the carnal soul, so as to guard against rebellion.

146. Even if the verses seem independent of each other, they are linked in that they draw attention to the important marks of the way leading to the final triumph and Paradise, and teach how to follow that way. It requires patience through all hardships and privations and, as mentioned in the preceding verse, spending in God's cause for the relatives and needy – in other words, building "social" bridges between various strata in society.

216. Prescribed for you is fighting, though it is disliked by you. It may well be that you dislike a thing but it is good for you, and it may well be that you like a thing but it is bad for you. God knows, and you do not know.

217. They ask you about the Sacred Month and fighting in it. Say: "Fighting in it is a grave sin; but barring people from the way of God, unbelief in Him, and denying entry into the Sacred Mosque, and expelling its inmates from it, are far graver and more sinful in the sight of God; disorder (rooted it rebellion to God and recognizing no laws) is even far graver and more sinful than killing. And they will not cease fighting against you until they turn you from your Religion, if they can. Whoever of you turns away from his Religion and dies an unbeliever – those are they whose works have been wasted in both the world and the Hereafter, and those are the companions of the Fire; therein they will abide.

218. Surely those who believe, those who emigrate and strive in God's cause[147] – they are the ones who may hope for the mercy of God. God is All-Forgiving, All-Compassionate.

219. They ask you about intoxicating drinks and games of chance. Say: "In both

٣٣

زُجُزُٱلثَّانِی

33

بِسْمِ اللّٰهِ الرَّحْمٰنِ الرَّحِيمِ

كُتِبَ عَلَيْكُمُ الْقِتَالُ وَهُوَ كُرْهٌ لَّكُمْ وَعَسَىٰٓ أَن تَكْرَهُوا۟ شَيْـًٔا
وَهُوَ خَيْرٌ لَّكُمْ وَعَسَىٰٓ أَن تُحِبُّوا۟ شَيْـًٔا وَهُوَ شَرٌّ لَّكُمْ وَاللّٰهُ
يَعْلَمُ وَأَنتُمْ لَا تَعْلَمُونَ ﴿٢١٦﴾ يَسْـَٔلُونَكَ عَنِ الشَّهْرِ الْحَرَامِ
قِتَالٍ فِيهِ قُلْ قِتَالٌ فِيهِ كَبِيرٌ وَصَدٌّ عَن سَبِيلِ اللّٰهِ
وَكُفْرٌۢ بِهِ وَالْمَسْجِدِ الْحَرَامِ وَإِخْرَاجُ أَهْلِهِ مِنْهُ أَكْبَرُ عِندَ
اللّٰهِ وَالْفِتْنَةُ أَكْبَرُ مِنَ الْقَتْلِ وَلَا يَزَالُونَ يُقَاتِلُونَكُمْ
حَتَّىٰ يَرُدُّوكُمْ عَن دِينِكُمْ إِنِ اسْتَطَاعُوا۟ وَمَن يَرْتَدِدْ
مِنكُمْ عَن دِينِهِ فَيَمُتْ وَهُوَ كَافِرٌ فَأُو۟لَٰٓئِكَ حَبِطَتْ
أَعْمَالُهُمْ فِي الدُّنْيَا وَالْآخِرَةِ وَأُو۟لَٰٓئِكَ أَصْحَابُ النَّارِ
هُمْ فِيهَا خَالِدُونَ ﴿٢١٧﴾ إِنَّ الَّذِينَ آمَنُوا۟ وَالَّذِينَ هَاجَرُوا۟
وَجَاهَدُوا۟ فِي سَبِيلِ اللّٰهِ أُو۟لَٰٓئِكَ يَرْجُونَ رَحْمَتَ اللّٰهِ
وَاللّٰهُ غَفُورٌ رَّحِيمٌ ﴿٢١٨﴾ يَسْـَٔلُونَكَ عَنِ الْخَمْرِ وَالْمَيْسِرِ
قُلْ فِيهِمَآ إِثْمٌ كَبِيرٌ وَمَنَافِعُ لِلنَّاسِ وَإِثْمُهُمَآ أَكْبَرُ
مِن نَّفْعِهِمَا وَيَسْـَٔلُونَكَ مَاذَا يُنفِقُونَ قُلِ الْعَفْوَ
كَذَٰلِكَ يُبَيِّنُ اللّٰهُ لَكُمُ الْآيَاتِ لَعَلَّكُمْ تَتَفَكَّرُونَ ﴿٢١٩﴾

there is great evil, though some use for people, but their evil is greater than their usefulness." They also ask you what they should spend (in God's cause and for the needy). Say: "What is left over (after you have spent on your dependents' needs). Thus does God make clear to you His Revelations, that you may reflect[148]

---

147. *Jihād* denotes, literally, doing one's utmost to achieve something. It is not the equivalent of war, for which the Arabic and Qur'ānic word is *qitāl*. Jihad does not mean Holy War either; in fact that term was coined during the Crusades, meaning a war against Muslims. It does not have a counterpart in Islam, and *jihad* is certainly not its translation. Although warfare is contained in the meaning of *jihād*, the root meaning is doing one's best to achieve something.

Jihād has a wider connotation and embraces every kind of striving in God's cause for His good pleasure. *Mujāhids* (those who do *jihād*) are sincerely devoted to the cause of Islam, expend the utmost of their intellect and spirit in its service, and deploy all the force at their command to defend Islam against aggression, and, whenever necessary, they do not hesitate to risk their very lives for Islam. All this is *jihād*. *Jihād* in God's cause is that striving in which a person engages exclusively to win

God's good pleasure, and to make His Word superior to all other words.

There are two aspects of *jihād*. One is fighting against superstitions and wrong convictions and also against carnal desires and evil inclinations, and is therefore a seeking of enlightenment, both intellectual and spiritual. This is called the *greater jihād*. The other is encouraging others to seek and achieve the same objective and it is called the *lesser jihād*.

The *lesser jihād*, which has usually been taken to mean fighting for God's cause, does not refer only to the form of striving done on battlefields. The term is comprehensive. It includes every action, from speaking out when necessary (for example, to challenge tyranny) to presenting oneself on the battlefield – provided the effort is done for God's sake. Whether speaking or keeping silent, smiling or making a sour face, joining a meeting or leaving it, every action taken to ameliorate the lot of humanity, whether by individuals or communities, is also included in the meaning of the *lesser jihād*.

While the *lesser jihād* depends on the mobilization of outward or material facilities and is done in the outer world, and the *greater jihād* is an inward struggle against the carnal soul, the two forms of *jihād* cannot really be separated from each other. Only those who are sincere in battling their carnal selves can initiate and sustain the *lesser jihād* in the right way, which, in turn, helps them to succeed in the *greater jihād*.

The Prophet Muḥammad, upon him be peace and blessings, combined these two aspects of *jihād* in the most perfect way in his person. He displayed monumental courage in communicating God's Message, and he was the most devoted in worshipping God. He was consumed with love and fear of God in his Prayer, and those who saw him felt great tenderness towards him. He frequently fasted every other day or even on successive days. Sometimes he would spend almost the whole night in the Prayer and his feet would swell up as a result of long periods of standing in the Prayer. As recorded in *al-Bukhārī*, 'Ā'ishah,

thinking his persistence in the Prayer excessive, once asked him why he exhausted himself so, considering that all his sins had been forgiven. He said in reply: *Shall I not be a servant grateful to God?*

As explained above, striving in God's cause entails, besides conveying the Message to others, a believer's struggle with the carnal soul to build a true spiritual character, overflowing with faith and ardent with the love of God. A believer's struggle in God's cause, with these two dimensions of it, continues, in the individual sphere, until the believer's death, and up to the Last Day in the collective sphere.

Islam did not come to cause dissension among humankind; it came to establish spiritual contentment in the inner worlds of human beings and to make them at peace with God, with each other, with nature, and with the whole of being as such, in its entirety. It came to eradicate injustice and corruption on the earth, and to "unite" the earth with the heavens in peace and harmony. Islam calls people to the faith with wisdom and fair exhortation, and does not resort to force until those who desire to maintain the corrupted order they built on injustice, oppression, self-interest and exploitation of others and usurpation of their rights, resist it with force, determined to prevent its being preached.

148. Alcohol and games of chance were deeply established and widespread among the Arabs in the pre-Islamic era (the *Jāhiliyyah* or "Age of Ignorance"). It is not easy to eradicate such evil habits in a community. As in almost all other such matters, the Qur'ān followed a step-wise approach in forbidding alcohol and gambling: instead of forbidding them outright, it first persuaded the believers of their evil. When the final commandment of prohibition came, there was no one among the believers who did not willingly renounce these habits. The same procedure was followed in establishing new patterns of conduct. For example, before commanding the women to wear the head-scarf or veil, the Qur'ān first persuaded the Muslim community of the value and good of women wearing head-scarves. Several people

came to the Messenger, upon him be peace and blessings, and asked him when he would order the women to veil themselves. When the order of veiling came, as stated by 'Ā'ishah, may God be pleased with her, all the women without exception put on the veil willingly.

As another important example, the next two verses instruct the Muslims on how to treat the orphans and manage their affairs, and forbid the Muslims to marry idolaters. Although seemingly disconnected, these two verses together prepared the hearts of the believers to marry orphan girls. Before verse 3 in *Sūrat al-Nisā'* was revealed, which allowed marriage to more than one woman, these verses encouraged wealthy men to prefer orphans if they were considering more than one marriage.

This is the Qur'ān, the Word of God, the Lord of the worlds. While God's Word is available to instruct humankind, minds and hearts should be turned to it with the utmost attentiveness, so that we may reform ourselves and our societies according to His will, Who created us, and provides us. The Muslims, especially those who feel responsibility to guide and teach others, should avoid being diverted by fashionable theories and agendas with little connection to the Qur'ānic foundations of thought, faith, worship, morality, social and political relationships, and economy. They should strive to return to those foundations. In particular, they should heed the Qur'ān's way of guiding, its way of teaching, and achieving vital reforms. No effort exerted in the name of Islam, but not based upon the Qur'ān and not permitted by it, can be successful.

34　سُورَةُ الْبَقَرَة　٣٤

بِسْمِ اللَّهِ الرَّحْمَنِ الرَّحِيمِ
(Arabic Qur'anic text)

even though she pleases and attracts you (with her beauty, wealth, status, or family). Nor marry (your believing women) to the men who associate partners with God until they believe. A believing slave is better than a (free) man who associates partners with God, even though he pleases and attracts you. Those call to the Fire, while God calls to Paradise and forgiveness (of your sins) by His leave. He makes clear His Revelations for people, that they may reflect and be mindful (of their duty to God).

222. They also ask you about (the injunctions concerning) menstruation. Say: "It is a state of hurt (and ritual impurity), so keep away from them during their menstruation and do not approach them until they are cleansed.[149] When they are cleansed, then (you can) go to them inasmuch as God has commanded you (according to the urge He has placed in your nature and within the terms He has enjoined upon you). Surely God loves those who turn to Him in sincere repentance (of past sins and errors), and He loves those who cleanse themselves.[150]

223. Your women are like a tilth for you (where you plant seed to obtain produce) so come to your tilth as you wish, and send ahead (good issue) for (the future of) your souls. Act in due reverence for God, keeping within the bounds of piety and obedience to Him (both in your relations with your women and bringing up offspring, as in all other matters).[151] And know that you are to meet with Him; and give glad tidings to the believers (of what they will find in His Presence).

224. (Do not make thoughtless oaths by God,) and do not (in striving to keep your oaths) make Him a hindrance by your oaths to doing greater good, acting from piety, and making peace among people. And God is All-Hearing, All-Knowing.

---

220. Upon this world and the Hereafter (with all the truths related to both). And they ask you about (how they should act in regard to) orphans. Say (to them): "(Rather than doing nothing for fear of doing wrong) set their affairs aright for their good, that is the best. If you intermix (your expenses) with theirs, (there is no harm in that) for they are your brothers(-in-religion, and brotherhood demands doing what is good for one's brothers). God knows well him who causes disorder from him who sets aright. Had God willed, He would have imposed on you exacting conditions. Indeed He is All-Glorious with irresistible might, All-Wise.

221. Do not marry the women who associate partners with God until they believe. A believing slave-girl is better than a (free) woman who associates partners with God,

149. A woman during her menstrual period cannot perform the Prayer, fast, enter the mosque, nor do the Pilgrimage. Neither can they touch the Qur'an and recite it except the petitionary sentences in it with the intention of saying prayer. This is because menstruation signals ritual impurity, like the state of needing to do ablution.

150. As the Qur'ān draws attention to the spiritual garment of piety where it mentions bodily dress (7: 26), and spiritual nourishment where it mentions provision (2: 197), so here it draws attention to spiritual purity or being cleansed of sins through repentance, where it mentions being clean of body. This is because true beauty and good rest not in "turning one's face towards east or west" but in the proper orientation of the heart and spirit. The form is something shaped by the essence and revealing it. The commandments of the Religion are intended to lead humanity to intellectual and spiritual excellence and purity, and therefore to personal integrity.

151. In a few concise statements, this verse reminds that the true purpose of marital relations is not carnal pleasures but reproduction and having good issue, that is, bringing up children properly. The satisfaction of carnal desires is a sort of advance reward to encourage the realization of this purpose. As mentioned in some related verses (2: 187), there are other instances of wisdom in marriage – for example, that the spouses are a garment for each other (to protect each other from unlawful relations and to enhance each other's spiritual beauty), that they become life-companions sharing each other's joys and sorrows. For this reason, as implied in this verse and stated in a *hadith* (al-Bukhārī, "Nikāḥ," 15), sincere piety is the best quality to look for in a marriage partner. After that, as also pointed out by the Messenger, upon him be peace and blessings, the spouses should be as closely matched as possible in knowledge, culture, and similar qualities, so that their companionship may be richer and more respectful (at-Tirmidhī, "Nikāḥ," 3).

٣٥   أَلْجُزْءُالثَّانِى   35

لَا يُؤَاخِذُكُمُ اللّٰهُ بِاللَّغْوِ فِىٓ أَيْمَانِكُمْ وَلٰكِن يُؤَاخِذُكُم بِمَا كَسَبَتْ قُلُوبُكُمْ ۗ وَاللّٰهُ غَفُورٌ حَلِيمٌ ۞ لِلَّذِينَ يُؤْلُونَ مِن نِّسَآئِهِمْ تَرَبُّصُ أَرْبَعَةِ أَشْهُرٍ ۖ فَإِن فَآءُو فَإِنَّ اللّٰهَ غَفُورٌ رَّحِيمٌ ۞ وَإِنْ عَزَمُوا الطَّلَاقَ فَإِنَّ اللّٰهَ سَمِيعٌ عَلِيمٌ ۞ وَالْمُطَلَّقَاتُ يَتَرَبَّصْنَ بِأَنفُسِهِنَّ ثَلَاثَةَ قُرُوٓءٍ ۚ وَلَا يَحِلُّ لَهُنَّ أَن يَكْتُمْنَ مَا خَلَقَ اللّٰهُ فِىٓ أَرْحَامِهِنَّ إِن كُنَّ يُؤْمِنَّ بِاللّٰهِ وَالْيَوْمِ الْآخِرِ ۚ وَبُعُولَتُهُنَّ أَحَقُّ بِرَدِّهِنَّ فِى ذٰلِكَ إِنْ أَرَادُوٓا إِصْلَاحًا ۚ وَلَهُنَّ مِثْلُ الَّذِى عَلَيْهِنَّ بِالْمَعْرُوفِ ۚ وَلِلرِّجَالِ عَلَيْهِنَّ دَرَجَةٌ ۗ وَاللّٰهُ عَزِيزٌ حَكِيمٌ ۞ الطَّلَاقُ مَرَّتَانِ ۖ فَإِمْسَاكٌ بِمَعْرُوفٍ أَوْ تَسْرِيحٌ بِإِحْسَانٍ ۗ وَلَا يَحِلُّ لَكُمْ أَن تَأْخُذُوا مِمَّا آتَيْتُمُوهُنَّ شَيْئًا إِلَّآ أَن يَخَافَآ أَلَّا يُقِيمَا حُدُودَ اللّٰهِ ۖ فَإِنْ خِفْتُمْ أَلَّا يُقِيمَا حُدُودَ اللّٰهِ فَلَا جُنَاحَ عَلَيْهِمَا فِيمَا افْتَدَتْ بِهِ ۗ تِلْكَ حُدُودُ اللّٰهِ فَلَا تَعْتَدُوهَا ۚ وَمَن يَتَعَدَّ حُدُودَ اللّٰهِ فَأُولٰٓئِكَ هُمُ الظَّالِمُونَ ۞ فَإِن طَلَّقَهَا فَلَا تَحِلُّ لَهُ مِن بَعْدُ حَتَّىٰ تَنكِحَ زَوْجًا غَيْرَهُ ۗ فَإِن طَلَّقَهَا فَلَا جُنَاحَ عَلَيْهِمَآ أَن يَتَرَاجَعَآ إِن ظَنَّآ أَن يُقِيمَا حُدُودَ اللّٰهِ ۗ وَتِلْكَ حُدُودُ اللّٰهِ يُبَيِّنُهَا لِقَوْمٍ يَعْلَمُونَ ۞

---

225. God does not take you to task for a slip in your oaths, but He takes you to task for what your hearts have earned (through intention). And God is All-Forgiving, All-Clement.

226. For those who vow abstinence from their wives there is a respite of four months. Then, if they go back on their vow (within this period by atoning), then surely God is All-Forgiving, All-Compassionate.

227. But if (the period ends and) they resolve on divorce, (know that) God is All-Hearing, All-Knowing (well aware of what they say and do).

228. Divorced women shall keep themselves in waiting for three menstrual courses, and it is not lawful for them, if they believe in God and the Last Day, to conceal what God has created in their wombs. In such time their husbands have better right to take them back, if they desire a settlement. According to customary good and religiously approvable practice, women have rights similar to those against them (that men have), but men (in respect of their heavier duty and responsibility) have a degree above them (which they must not abuse). And God is All-Glorious with irresistible might, All-Wise.

229. Divorce is (to be) pronounced twice. Then (at the end of each pronouncement) the husband should either retain (his wife) without offending her honor and in a fair manner, or release (her) kindly and in a manner fairer and pleasing (to her). (In the event of divorce) it is not lawful for you to take back anything of what you have given them (as bridal-due or wedding gift or gifts on other occasions), unless both fear that they might not be able to keep within the bounds set by God. If you fear that they might not be able to keep within the bounds set by God (and deviate into unlawful acts particularly because of the wife's disgust with the husband), there is no blame on them that the wife might pay some compensation to be released from the marriage tie. Those are the bounds set by God, therefore do not exceed them. Whoever exceeds the bounds set by God, such are wrongdoers.

230. If he divorces her (finally, for the third time), she will no longer be lawful to him unless she marries another husband (of her own volition). (If she and her new husband do not get along well and) if he divorces her, there is no blame on them (the woman and her first husband, if they agree) to return to each other if they think that they can keep within the bounds set by God. These are the bounds set by God; He makes them clear for a people who know (the wisdom and benefit in the bounds prescribed for them by their Creator).

231. And when you divorce women and they reach the end of their waiting term, then either retain them without offending their honor and in a fair manner, or release them without offending their honor and in a fair manner. Do not retain them to their hurt and to transgress (their rights). Whoever does that, surely he has wronged himself. Do not take God's Revelations for a mockery (by not paying them due heed), and remember God's favor on you and what He has sent down on you of the Book and the Wisdom wherewith He exhorts you (to guidance). Keep from disobedience to God in due reverence for Him and piety, and know that God has full knowledge of everything.

232. When you divorce women and they have reached the end of their waiting term, (then, you judges, and you who are guardians of either party,) do not debar them from marrying their (former) husbands, (and O former husbands of them), from marrying other men if they have come to an agreement between them on equitable terms.[152] This is an admonition to whoever among you truly believes in God and the Last Day; that is a cleaner and purer way for you. And God knows, and you do not know.[153]

233. Mothers (whether married or divorced) are to suckle their children for two complete years if the fathers wish that the period be completed. It is incumbent upon him who fathered the child to provide the mothers (during this period) with sustenance and clothing according to customary good and religiously approvable practice. But no soul is charged save to its capacity; a mother should not be made to suf-

fer because of her child, nor the one who fathered the child because of his child. The same duty (towards the suckling mother) rests with the heir (of a father who has died). If the couple desire by mutual consent and consultation to wean the child (before the completion of the two years' period), then there is no blame on them. And if you desire to seek nursing for your children, there is no blame on you (O fathers), provided you pay what is due from you according to customary good and religiously approvable practice. Keep from disobedience to God and try to act within the bounds of piety, and know that whatever you do, surely God sees it well.

---

152. Islam makes divorce possible when it is established beyond doubt that the spouses cannot get along with each other and marriage has

lost its meaning and function. Nevertheless, as is clear in the verses, Islam makes the arrangement of divorce difficult inasmuch as the arrangement contains the opportunity for both spouses to re-think and again re-think their decision. Also, God's Messenger, upon him be peace and blessings, said: "Of the permitted things, the most abhorrent to God is divorce." (Abū Dāwūd, "Talaq," 3)

Divorce initiated by the husband is in this way: he pronounces divorce at a time when his wife has no period. The wife then waits for three monthly courses, during which the husband is obliged to provide for her and may not force her to leave home. They may turn to each other during this period. If they do so, they do not have to renew the marriage contract. If they turn to each other after the end of this period, they do. The divorce may be pronounced a second time, but if it is repeated for the third time, they can no longer be reunited unless the woman marries another man and divorces or is divorced by him.

The wife also has a right to initiate divorce. If she feels disgust at her husband, and it is feared that either or both of them may deviate into unlawful ways, she can refer the matter to the judge and demand divorce. In the event of such a divorce, the woman pays something to the husband, whereas when the husband initiates divorce he cannot claim anything of what he gave her by way of dower or after marriage.

153. For a brief outline of the status of women in Islam, see Appendix 4.

وَالَّذِينَ يُتَوَفَّوْنَ مِنكُمْ وَيَذَرُونَ أَزْوَاجًا يَتَرَبَّصْنَ بِأَنفُسِهِنَّ

أَرْبَعَةَ أَشْهُرٍ وَعَشْرًا فَإِذَا بَلَغْنَ أَجَلَهُنَّ فَلَا جُنَاحَ عَلَيْكُمْ

فِيمَا فَعَلْنَ فِي أَنفُسِهِنَّ بِالْمَعْرُوفِ وَاللَّهُ بِمَا تَعْمَلُونَ خَبِيرٌ ۝

وَلَا جُنَاحَ عَلَيْكُمْ فِيمَا عَرَّضْتُم بِهِ مِنْ خِطْبَةِ النِّسَاءِ

أَوْ أَكْنَنتُمْ فِي أَنفُسِكُمْ عَلِمَ اللَّهُ أَنَّكُمْ سَتَذْكُرُونَهُنَّ

وَلَكِن لَّا تُوَاعِدُوهُنَّ سِرًّا إِلَّا أَن تَقُولُوا قَوْلًا مَّعْرُوفًا

وَلَا تَعْزِمُوا عُقْدَةَ النِّكَاحِ حَتَّى يَبْلُغَ الْكِتَابُ أَجَلَهُ وَاعْلَمُوا

أَنَّ اللَّهَ يَعْلَمُ مَا فِي أَنفُسِكُمْ فَاحْذَرُوهُ وَاعْلَمُوا

أَنَّ اللَّهَ غَفُورٌ حَلِيمٌ ۝ لَّا جُنَاحَ عَلَيْكُمْ إِن طَلَّقْتُمُ

النِّسَاءَ مَا لَمْ تَمَسُّوهُنَّ أَوْ تَفْرِضُوا لَهُنَّ فَرِيضَةً وَمَتِّعُوهُنَّ

عَلَى الْمُوسِعِ قَدَرُهُ وَعَلَى الْمُقْتِرِ قَدَرُهُ مَتَاعًا بِالْمَعْرُوفِ

حَقًّا عَلَى الْمُحْسِنِينَ ۝ وَإِن طَلَّقْتُمُوهُنَّ مِن قَبْلِ أَن تَمَسُّوهُنَّ

وَقَدْ فَرَضْتُمْ لَهُنَّ فَرِيضَةً فَنِصْفُ مَا فَرَضْتُمْ إِلَّا أَن يَعْفُونَ

أَوْ يَعْفُوَ الَّذِي بِيَدِهِ عُقْدَةُ النِّكَاحِ وَأَن تَعْفُوا أَقْرَبُ لِلتَّقْوَى

وَلَا تَنسَوُا الْفَضْلَ بَيْنَكُمْ إِنَّ اللَّهَ بِمَا تَعْمَلُونَ بَصِيرٌ ۝

234. Those among you who die, leaving behind their wives: they (the wives) shall keep themselves in waiting for four months and ten days,[154] (during which they should refrain from marrying and from self-adornment with a view to presenting themselves for marriage). When they have reached the end of the waiting term, then there is no blame on you for what they may do by themselves within (the bounds of) decency. God is fully aware of all that you do.

235. There is no blame on you that (during this waiting period) you indicate a marriage proposal to such women or keep it hidden in yourselves. God knows that you will think of them (with such proposals in mind), but do not make any secret engagement with them, except that you speak it properly in decent words. Do not resolve on the marriage tie until the ordained term has come to its end. Know that God knows what is in your hearts, so be careful about Him; and know that God is All-Forgiving, All-Clement, (Who shows no haste in punishing).

236. There is no blame on you if you divorce women (with whom you made a marriage contract,) while as yet you have not touched them nor appointed any bridal-due for them. Yet, make some provision for them, the affluent according to his means, and the straitened according to his means – a provision according to custom-ary good and religiously approvable practice, as a duty upon those devoted to doing good, aware that God is seeing them.

237. If you divorce them before you have touched them but have already appointed for them a bridal-due, then (give them) half of what you appointed, unless they make remission and forgo it or he in whose hand the marriage tie is makes remission (and pays the full amount). If you make remission, this is nearer and more suited to piety, and do not forget magnanimity among yourselves. Whatever you do, surely God sees it well.

---

154. A pregnant widow is exempted from this rule. Her waiting period expires with childbirth, irrespective of whether the time between the husband's death and the birth is shorter or longer than the waiting period here prescribed.

38　سُوْرَةُ الْبَقَرَةِ　٣٨

حَافِظُوْا عَلَى الصَّلَوَاتِ وَالصَّلٰوةِ الْوُسْطٰى وَقُوْمُوْا
لِلّٰهِ قَانِتِيْنَ ۝ فَاِنْ خِفْتُمْ فَرِجَالًا اَوْ رُكْبَانًا فَاِذَآ
اَمِنْتُمْ فَاذْكُرُوا اللّٰهَ كَمَا عَلَّمَكُمْ مَّا لَمْ تَكُوْنُوْا تَعْلَمُوْنَ
۝ وَالَّذِيْنَ يُتَوَفَّوْنَ مِنْكُمْ وَيَذَرُوْنَ اَزْوَاجًا ۖ وَّصِيَّةً
لِّاَزْوَاجِهِمْ مَّتَاعًا اِلَى الْحَوْلِ غَيْرَ اِخْرَاجٍ ۚ فَاِنْ خَرَجْنَ
فَلَا جُنَاحَ عَلَيْكُمْ فِيْ مَا فَعَلْنَ فِيْٓ اَنْفُسِهِنَّ مِنْ مَّعْرُوْفٍ ۗ
وَاللّٰهُ عَزِيْزٌ حَكِيْمٌ ۝ وَلِلْمُطَلَّقٰتِ مَتَاعٌ ۢ بِالْمَعْرُوْفِ ۗ
حَقًّا عَلَى الْمُتَّقِيْنَ ۝ كَذٰلِكَ يُبَيِّنُ اللّٰهُ لَكُمْ اٰيٰتِهٖ
لَعَلَّكُمْ تَعْقِلُوْنَ ۝ اَلَمْ تَرَ اِلَى الَّذِيْنَ خَرَجُوْا مِنْ
دِيَارِهِمْ وَهُمْ اُلُوْفٌ حَذَرَ الْمَوْتِ ۖ فَقَالَ لَهُمُ
اللّٰهُ مُوْتُوْا ۖ ثُمَّ اَحْيَاهُمْ ۗ اِنَّ اللّٰهَ لَذُوْ فَضْلٍ عَلَى
النَّاسِ وَلٰكِنَّ اَكْثَرَ النَّاسِ لَا يَشْكُرُوْنَ ۝ وَقَاتِلُوْا فِيْ سَبِيْلِ
اللّٰهِ وَاعْلَمُوْٓا اَنَّ اللّٰهَ سَمِيْعٌ عَلِيْمٌ ۝ مَنْ ذَا الَّذِيْ يُقْرِضُ
اللّٰهَ قَرْضًا حَسَنًا فَيُضٰعِفَهٗ لَهٗٓ اَضْعَافًا كَثِيْرَةً ۗ
وَاللّٰهُ يَقْبِضُ وَيَبْصُۜطُ ۖ وَاِلَيْهِ تُرْجَعُوْنَ ۝

---

without expulsion. If they themselves leave (of their own accord), there is no blame on you for what they may do of lawful deeds by themselves. Surely God is All-Glorious with irresistible might, All-Wise.

241. Likewise, there should be a provision for the divorced women according to customary good and religiously approvable practice, as a duty upon the God-revering pious.

242. Thus does God make His Revelations (and signpost of His way) clear to you, that you may reason and understand (where your benefit lies and act accordingly).

243. Do you not call to mind those who went forth from their habitations for fear of death even though they were in thousands? God said to them "Die!", then He restored them to life. Indeed God is gracious to humankind, but most of humankind do not give thanks.

244. (Do not act in fear of death; rather,) fight in God's cause, and know that God is All-Hearing, All-Knowing.

245. Who is he that (by spending out of his wealth purely in God's cause) lends to God a handsome loan that He will return after multiplying it for him manifold? God straitens (your means of livelihood), and He enlarges it; (in either case) you are being returned to Him.

238. Be ever mindful and protective of the Prescribed Prayers, and the middle Prayer, and stand in the presence of God in utmost devotion and obedience.

239. If you are exposed to danger (and it is impossible for you to perform the Prayer standing in a place, then pray) afoot or mounted. When you are secure, mention God (and establish the Prayer) as He has taught you what you did not know (of faith, Book, and the Prayer).[155]

240. Those of you who (are about to) die leaving behind wives should make testament in their favor of one year's provision

---

155. Having explained the rules for a happy family and social life, God rounds off this address by emphasizing the Prayer, for the

Prayer has an indispensable function in the spiritual education of humanity. It instills the ideals of goodness and purity and it nurtures the disposition to obey the ordinances of God; it fosters adherence to piety and religious seriousness; and it forbids indecency and iniquities (29: 45). The order to be ever mindful and protective of the prescribed Prayers gains greater importance in light of verse 239. For a Muslim can in no wise neglect the Prayer. Even in dangers one must perform it whether "afoot or mounted." One can only postpone it during actual fighting on battlefield.

There are different opinions on the "middle Prayer." According to the majority of scholars, it is the Afternoon Prayer, i.e. *'asr*. Since this is the time of the day when daily work draws to its end, people may neglect the Prayer prescribed for this time. Being the third of the five daily Prayers, the Afternoon Prayer may also be the middle Prayer in that sense. However, given that, in the Islamic tradition, the day is usually considered to start after sunset, the third or middle Prayer could then be the Morning Prayer (*fajr*).

اَلَمْ تَرَ اِلَى الْمَلَاِ مِنْ بَنِيْ اِسْرَآءِيْلَ مِنْ بَعْدِ مُوْسَى اِذْ قَالُوْا

لِنَبِيٍّ لَهُمُ ابْعَثْ لَنَا مَلِكًا نُّقَاتِلْ فِىْ سَبِيْلِ اللّٰهِ

قَالَ هَلْ عَسَيْتُمْ اِنْ كُتِبَ عَلَيْكُمُ الْقِتَالُ اَلَّا

تُقَاتِلُوْا قَالُوْا وَ مَا لَنَآ اَلَّا نُقَاتِلَ فِىْ سَبِيْلِ اللّٰهِ

وَقَدْ اُخْرِجْنَا مِنْ دِيَارِنَا وَاَبْنَآئِنَا فَلَمَّا كُتِبَ

عَلَيْهِمُ الْقِتَالُ تَوَلَّوْا اِلَّا قَلِيْلًا مِّنْهُمْ وَ اللّٰهُ

عَلِيْمٌ بِالظّٰلِمِيْنَ وَقَالَ لَهُمْ نَبِيُّهُمْ اِنَّ اللّٰهَ

قَدْ بَعَثَ لَكُمْ طَالُوْتَ مَلِكًا قَالُوْا اَنّٰى يَكُوْنُ لَهُ الْمُلْكُ

عَلَيْنَا وَنَحْنُ اَحَقُّ بِالْمُلْكِ مِنْهُ وَلَمْ يُؤْتَ سَعَةً مِّنَ

الْمَالِ قَالَ اِنَّ اللّٰهَ اصْطَفٰهُ عَلَيْكُمْ وَزَادَهُ بَسْطَةً فِى

الْعِلْمِ وَالْجِسْمِ وَاللّٰهُ يُؤْتِىْ مُلْكَهُ مَنْ يَّشَآءُ وَاللّٰهُ

وَاسِعٌ عَلِيْمٌ وَقَالَ لَهُمْ نَبِيُّهُمْ اِنَّ اٰيَةَ

مُلْكِهٖ اَنْ يَّأْتِيَكُمُ التَّابُوْتُ فِيْهِ سَكِيْنَةٌ مِّنْ رَّبِّكُمْ

وَبَقِيَّةٌ مِّمَّا تَرَكَ اٰلُ مُوْسٰى وَاٰلُ هٰرُوْنَ تَحْمِلُهُ الْمَلٰئِكَةُ

اِنَّ فِىْ ذٰلِكَ لَاٰيَةً لَّكُمْ اِنْ كُنْتُمْ مُّؤْمِنِيْنَ

246. Do you not consider what happened with the elders of the Children of Israel after Moses: once they appealed to a Prophet chosen for them, saying: "Set up for us a king and we will fight in God's cause." He said: "Is it possible you would hold back from fighting if fighting were prescribed for you?" They said: "Why should we not fight in God's cause when we have been driven from our habitations and our children?" But when fighting was prescribed for them, they did turn away, except a few of them. God has full knowledge of (such) wrongdoers.

247. Their Prophet said to them: "God has set up Saul (Ṭālūt) for you as king." They said: "How can he have kingdom over us when we are more deserving of kingdom than him, seeing that he has not been given abundance of wealth?" He said: "God has chosen him over you and increased him abundantly in knowledge and physical power (so that he can execute his decrees). God bestows kingdom on whomever He wills, and God is All-Embracing (with His mercy), All-Knowing.

248. Their Prophet added: "The sign of his kingdom is that the Ark will come to you, in which there is inward peace and assurance from your Lord, and a remnant of what the house of Moses and the house of Aaron left behind, the angels bearing it. Truly in that is a sign for you if you are (true) believers.

40   سُوْرَةُ الْبَقَرَة   ٤٠

فَلَمَّا فَصَلَ طَالُوتُ بِالْجُنُودِ قَالَ اِنَّ اللّٰهَ مُبْتَلِيكُمْ
بِنَهَرٍ فَمَنْ شَرِبَ مِنْهُ فَلَيْسَ مِنِّي وَمَنْ لَمْ يَطْعَمْهُ
فَاِنَّهُ مِنِّي اِلَّا مَنِ اغْتَرَفَ غُرْفَةً بِيَدِهِ فَشَرِبُوا مِنْهُ
اِلَّا قَلِيلًا مِنْهُمْ فَلَمَّا جَاوَزَهُ هُوَ وَالَّذِيْنَ اٰمَنُوا
مَعَهُ قَالُوا لَا طَاقَةَ لَنَا الْيَوْمَ بِجَالُوتَ وَجُنُوْدِهِ
قَالَ الَّذِيْنَ يَظُنُّوْنَ اَنَّهُمْ مُلَاقُوا اللّٰهِ كَمْ مِنْ
فِئَةٍ قَلِيلَةٍ غَلَبَتْ فِئَةً كَثِيرَةً بِاِذْنِ اللّٰهِ وَاللّٰهُ
مَعَ الصّٰبِرِيْنَ ۞ وَلَمَّا بَرَزُوا لِجَالُوتَ وَجُنُوْدِهِ قَالُوا
رَبَّنَا اَفْرِغْ عَلَيْنَا صَبْرًا وَثَبِّتْ اَقْدَامَنَا وَانْصُرْنَا
عَلَى الْقَوْمِ الْكَافِرِيْنَ ۞ فَهَزَمُوهُمْ بِاِذْنِ
اللّٰهِ وَقَتَلَ دَاوُدُ جَالُوتَ وَاٰتٰهُ اللّٰهُ الْمُلْكَ
وَالْحِكْمَةَ وَعَلَّمَهُ مِمَّا يَشَاءُ وَلَوْلَا دَفْعُ اللّٰهِ
النَّاسَ بَعْضَهُمْ بِبَعْضٍ لَفَسَدَتِ الْاَرْضُ وَلٰكِنَّ
اللّٰهَ ذُو فَضْلٍ عَلَى الْعَالَمِيْنَ ۞ تِلْكَ اٰيَاتُ اللّٰهِ
نَتْلُوهَا عَلَيْكَ بِالْحَقِّ وَاِنَّكَ لَمِنَ الْمُرْسَلِيْنَ ۞

———✦———

249. And when Saul (Ṭālūt) set out with the army and said (to them): "God will put you to a test by (means of) a river: whoever then drinks of it is not of my company, and whoever does not taste it, he is of my company; but forgiven will he be who takes thereof in the hollow of his hand. But they drank thereof, all save a few of them; and when he crossed it, he and those who believed with him, (those who, with weak faith, took of the river in the hollow of their hands) said: "Today we have no power against Goliath and his forces." But those who had certainty of their meeting with God and felt as if always standing in His Presence said: "Many a small company has overcome a numerous company by God's leave." God is with the patient and persevering.

250. And when they went forth against Goliath and his forces, they prayed: "Our Lord, pour out upon us steadfastness, and set our feet firm, and help us to victory over the disbelieving people."

251. So they routed them by God's leave, and David killed Goliath, and God granted him kingdom and Wisdom, and taught him of that which He willed. Were it not that God repelled people, some by means of others, the earth would surely be cor-

rupted; but God is gracious for all the worlds.[156]

252. Those are the Revelations of God and His signs (demonstrating Him with His Names and Attributes) that We recite to you in truth, for indeed you (O Muḥammad) are one of the Messengers (sent with the Book and receiving Revelation).

---

156. The event described in these verses, which reveal the wisdom in war as a reality of human history, and an important part of the dynamics of the believers' prevailing over the unbelievers, was a turning-point in the history of the Children of Israel. God had delivered them from the oppression of the Pharaohs in Egypt and guided them towards Palestine. However, never inwardly free from the influence of their life as slaves in Egypt, their hearts had not revived spiritually. After many years spent in the desert, new generations brought up in the climate of Divine Revelation replaced the old ones. The verse 2: 243 may be referring to this fact.

After Moses, upon him be peace, they conquered Jericho under the leadership of the Prophet Joshua (Yūshā), upon him be peace. Then came the period of the Judges, which lasted almost five centuries. During this period, the Children of Israel sometimes got the upper hand over their enemies and sometimes lost ground to them. The event described in these verses happened during the period of the Prophet Samuel. The Israelites defeated the pagan Philistines and founded the greatest and most powerful state in their history. David, upon him be peace, became the first Prophet-Caliph of this state.

The Ark referred to in 2: 248, was, as mentioned in various places of the Old Testament (*Exodus*, 25: 10–16, 40: 20–21; *Deuteronomy*, 10: 1–5; *Joshua*, 3: 3) and mentioned by some interpreters of the Qur'ān (See al-Qurṭubī), a wooden coffer containing the tablets on which the Torah was inscribed, and some "remnant of what the house of Moses and the house of Aaron left behind." The Israelites carried it ahead of them in their marches in the desert and military campaigns. It was an emblem of their triumph. It had been lost during the centuries following Moses, or it may have been captured by their enemies.

تِلْكَ الرُّسُلُ فَضَّلْنَا بَعْضَهُمْ عَلَىٰ بَعْضٍ مِّنْهُم مَّن كَلَّمَ اللَّهُ
وَرَفَعَ بَعْضَهُمْ دَرَجَاتٍ وَءَاتَيْنَا عِيسَى ابْنَ مَرْيَمَ الْبَيِّنَاتِ
وَأَيَّدْنَاهُ بِرُوحِ الْقُدُسِ وَلَوْ شَاءَ اللَّهُ مَا اقْتَتَلَ الَّذِينَ مِنْ
بَعْدِهِم مِّن بَعْدِ مَا جَاءَتْهُمُ الْبَيِّنَاتُ وَلَٰكِنِ اخْتَلَفُوا فَمِنْهُم
مَّنْ ءَامَنَ وَمِنْهُم مَّن كَفَرَ وَلَوْ شَاءَ اللَّهُ مَا اقْتَتَلُوا وَلَٰكِنَّ اللَّهَ
يَفْعَلُ مَا يُرِيدُ ۞ يَا أَيُّهَا الَّذِينَ ءَامَنُوا أَنفِقُوا مِمَّا رَزَقْنَاكُم
مِّن قَبْلِ أَن يَأْتِيَ يَوْمٌ لَّا بَيْعٌ فِيهِ وَلَا خُلَّةٌ وَلَا شَفَاعَةٌ
وَالْكَافِرُونَ هُمُ الظَّالِمُونَ ۞ اللَّهُ لَا إِلَٰهَ إِلَّا هُوَ الْحَيُّ الْقَيُّومُ
لَا تَأْخُذُهُ سِنَةٌ وَلَا نَوْمٌ لَّهُ مَا فِي السَّمَاوَاتِ وَمَا فِي الْأَرْضِ مَن
ذَا الَّذِي يَشْفَعُ عِندَهُ إِلَّا بِإِذْنِهِ يَعْلَمُ مَا بَيْنَ أَيْدِيهِمْ وَمَا
خَلْفَهُمْ وَلَا يُحِيطُونَ بِشَيْءٍ مِّنْ عِلْمِهِ إِلَّا بِمَا شَاءَ وَسِعَ كُرْسِيُّهُ
السَّمَاوَاتِ وَالْأَرْضَ وَلَا يَئُودُهُ حِفْظُهُمَا وَهُوَ الْعَلِيُّ
الْعَظِيمُ ۞ لَا إِكْرَاهَ فِي الدِّينِ قَد تَّبَيَّنَ الرُّشْدُ مِنَ الْغَيِّ
فَمَن يَكْفُرْ بِالطَّاغُوتِ وَيُؤْمِن بِاللَّهِ فَقَدِ اسْتَمْسَكَ
بِالْعُرْوَةِ الْوُثْقَىٰ لَا انفِصَامَ لَهَا وَاللَّهُ سَمِيعٌ عَلِيمٌ ۞

---

253. Of those Messengers, some We have exalted above others (in some respects). Among them are those to whom God spoke, and He raised some others in degrees. We granted Jesus son of Mary the clear proofs (of his Messengership), and confirmed him with the Spirit of Holiness. Had God willed (to deny humankind free will and compelled them to act in a predetermined way), those who came after them would not have fought one against the other after the most manifest truths had come to them; but they differed among themselves, some of them believing and some disbelieving. Yet had God so willed, they would not have fought one against the other, but God does whatever He wills.

254. O you who believe! (So that you may enjoy solidarity and discipline, as a cohesive, peaceful community) spend (in God's cause and for the needy) out of what We have provided for you (of wealth, power, and knowledge, etc.) before there comes a Day when there will be no trading nor friendship (which will bring any benefit), nor intercession (of the sort you resort to unjustly in the world). The unbelievers – it is they who are wrongdoers (those unable to discern the truth, who darken both their inner and outer world, and who wrong, first and most of all, themselves).

255. God, there is no deity but He; the All-Living, the Self-Subsisting (by Whom all subsist). Slumber does not seize Him, nor sleep. His is all that is in the heavens and all that is on the earth. Who is there that will intercede with Him save by His leave? He knows what lies before them and what lies after them (what lies in their future and in their past, what is known to them and what is hidden from them); and they do not comprehend anything of His Knowledge save what He wills. His Seat (of dominion) embraces the heavens and the earth, and the preserving of them does not weary Him; He is the All-Exalted, the Supreme.

256. There is no compulsion in the Religion. The right way stands there clearly distinguished from the false. Hence he who rejects the *tāghūt* (false deities and powers of evil that institute patterns of faith and rule in defiance of God) and believes in God (as the only Deity, Lord, and Object of Worship) has indeed taken hold of the firm, unbreakable handle; and God is All-Hearing, All-Knowing.

42   سُوْرَةُ الْبَقَرَة   ٤٢

اللَّهُ وَلِيُّ الَّذِينَ ءَامَنُوا يُخْرِجُهُم مِّنَ الظُّلُمَاتِ إِلَى النُّورِ
وَالَّذِينَ كَفَرُوا أَوْلِيَاؤُهُمُ الطَّاغُوتُ يُخْرِجُونَهُم مِّنَ
النُّورِ إِلَى الظُّلُمَاتِ أُوْلَئِكَ أَصْحَابُ النَّارِ هُمْ فِيهَا
خَالِدُونَ ۝ أَلَمْ تَرَ إِلَى الَّذِى حَاجَّ إِبْرَاهِيمَ فِى رَبِّهِ أَنْ ءَاتَاهُ
اللَّهُ الْمُلْكَ إِذْ قَالَ إِبْرَاهِيمُ رَبِّيَ الَّذِى يُحْيِى وَيُمِيتُ قَالَ
أَنَا أُحْيِي وَأُمِيتُ قَالَ إِبْرَاهِيمُ فَإِنَّ اللَّهَ يَأْتِى بِالشَّمْسِ مِنَ
الْمَشْرِقِ فَأْتِ بِهَا مِنَ الْمَغْرِبِ فَبُهِتَ الَّذِى كَفَرَ
وَاللَّهُ لَا يَهْدِى الْقَوْمَ الظَّالِمِينَ ۝ أَوْ كَالَّذِى مَرَّ عَلَى
قَرْيَةٍ وَهِيَ خَاوِيَةٌ عَلَى عُرُوشِهَا قَالَ أَنَّى يُحْيِى هَذِهِ
اللَّهُ بَعْدَ مَوْتِهَا فَأَمَاتَهُ اللَّهُ مِائَةَ عَامٍ ثُمَّ بَعَثَهُ
قَالَ كَمْ لَبِثْتَ قَالَ لَبِثْتُ يَوْمًا أَوْ بَعْضَ يَوْمٍ قَالَ بَل
لَّبِثْتَ مِائَةَ عَامٍ فَانظُرْ إِلَى طَعَامِكَ وَشَرَابِكَ لَمْ يَتَسَنَّهْ
وَانظُرْ إِلَى حِمَارِكَ وَلِنَجْعَلَكَ ءَايَةً لِّلنَّاسِ وَانظُرْ
إِلَى الْعِظَامِ كَيْفَ نُنشِزُهَا ثُمَّ نَكْسُوهَا لَحْمًا
فَلَمَّا تَبَيَّنَ لَهُ قَالَ أَعْلَمُ أَنَّ اللَّهَ عَلَى كُلِّ شَيْءٍ قَدِيرٌ ۝

---

257. God is the guardian of those who believe (to Whom they can entrust their affairs and on Whom they can rely), bringing them out from all kinds of (intellectual, spiritual, social, economic, and political) darkness into the light, and keeping them firm therein. And those who disbelieve, their guardians are the *ṭāghūt*; bringing them out from the light into all kinds of darkness.[157] Those are companions of the Fire; therein they will abide.

258. Do you not consider the one who remonstrated with Abraham about his Lord (in defiance of Him) because of the kingdom God had granted him? When Abraham said, "My Lord is He Who gives life and causes to die," he retorted: "I give life and cause to die." Said Abraham: "Surely God causes the sun to rise in the east, now you cause it to rise in the west." Thus was the unbeliever utterly confounded.[158] God does not guide (such) wrongdoing people.

259. Or (as another proof that it is God alone Who gives and takes life, and will restore life to the dead, call to mind) him who passed by a town that had fallen into utter ruin, and asked himself (in bewilderment): "How will God restore life to this town that is now dead?" So God made him remain dead for a hundred years and then raised him to life, and asked him: "How long did you remain in this state?" He said: "I remained so for a day or part of a day." God said: "No, you have rather remained thus for a hundred years. But look at your food and drink: it has not spoiled; and look at your donkey! So We would make you a sign for the people (that they might understand how We have created them and will restore them to life after their death.) And look at the bones, how We will set them up, and then clothe them with flesh." Thus when the truth became clear to him, he said: "I know that God has full power over everything."

---

157. The verse may cause one to ask whether the unbelievers whom the *ṭāghūt* bring out from the light into all kinds of darkness were in the light. So this statement has been interpreted that, first, it came by way of comparison with the previous statement: *God brings* the believers out from all kinds of darkness into the light. Secondly, the *ṭāghūt* call the believing people to darkness (unbelief, associating partners with God, transgression, etc.) and try to cause them to fall into it. Thirdly, as stated in a *hadith*, everyone is born with a disposition to be a Muslim, but his parents (and environment) cause them to accept other faiths (al-Bukhārī, "Janā'iz," 80, 93). This is what the *ṭāghūt* do, that is, they strive to mislead generations.

158. This event (not recounted in the Bible) is told in the Talmud in considerable harmony with the Qur'ānic description. The exchange referred to must have taken place between the Prophet Abraham and the Chaldaean king, Nimrod, who ruled at that time over Mesopotamia. According to the Talmud, the father of Abraham held a high office in the government of Nimrod. When Abraham began preaching *tawḥīd*, belief in God's Oneness, and smashed the idols in the temple, his father lodged a complaint against him before the king. This was followed by the conversation mentioned here.

All disbelieving peoples from the earliest times have either rejected God's Existence, being materialists or atheists in a general sense, or associated partners with Him. Some of those who associate partners with God share out His absolute authority in the universe among physical things (such as natural forces) or nominal entities (such as the so-called "laws of nature"), or other things or beings (such as angels, spirits, and heavenly bodies). Some others who accept God's universal authority nevertheless invent for themselves religions or systems for the direction of human life in all its aspects and force others to obey them. They attempt to appropriate for themselves God's absolute sovereignty in the human realm. As is understood from the verse, Nimrod associated himself as a partner with God in ruling the people in his kingdom. He desired absolute rule over them. For this reason, he stood utterly confounded when Abraham, upon him be peace, moved from giving and taking life in the particular field of humanity to the universal field. The earth is a part of the universe, and humankind are a part of all beings: whoever owns true sovereignty in the cosmic realm, must also own it in the human realm. Seeing that human beings regard themselves as being so powerful as to dispute with God concerning sovereignty, yet have no part (to say nothing of the creation and maintenance of the universe) in even their own coming into existence, the time and place of their birth and death, their family environment, the specific features and operation of their bodies, or the characteristics of their personalities, what falls on them is to submit to God's authority. This is what the Prophet Abraham, the breaker of idols, declared before the Pharaoh of his time, and it was universally pronounced and preached and inculcated in minds and hearts by his most illustrious descendant, the Prophet Muḥammad, upon him be peace and blessings.

بِسْمِ اللّٰهِ الرَّحْمٰنِ الرَّحِيْمِ

وَإِذْ قَالَ إِبْرَاهِيمُ رَبِّ أَرِنِي كَيْفَ تُحْيِ الْمَوْتَىٰ قَالَ أَوَلَمْ تُؤْمِنْ قَالَ بَلَىٰ وَلَٰكِن لِّيَطْمَئِنَّ قَلْبِي قَالَ فَخُذْ أَرْبَعَةً مِّنَ الطَّيْرِ فَصُرْهُنَّ إِلَيْكَ ثُمَّ اجْعَلْ عَلَىٰ كُلِّ جَبَلٍ مِّنْهُنَّ جُزْءًا ثُمَّ ادْعُهُنَّ يَأْتِينَكَ سَعْيًا وَاعْلَمْ أَنَّ اللّٰهَ عَزِيزٌ حَكِيمٌ ۝ مَّثَلُ الَّذِينَ يُنفِقُونَ أَمْوَالَهُمْ فِي سَبِيلِ اللّٰهِ كَمَثَلِ حَبَّةٍ أَنبَتَتْ سَبْعَ سَنَابِلَ فِي كُلِّ سُنبُلَةٍ مِّائَةُ حَبَّةٍ وَاللّٰهُ يُضَاعِفُ لِمَن يَشَاءُ وَاللّٰهُ وَاسِعٌ عَلِيمٌ ۝ الَّذِينَ يُنفِقُونَ أَمْوَالَهُمْ فِي سَبِيلِ اللّٰهِ ثُمَّ لَا يُتْبِعُونَ مَا أَنفَقُوا مَنًّا وَلَا أَذًى لَّهُمْ أَجْرُهُمْ عِندَ رَبِّهِمْ وَلَا خَوْفٌ عَلَيْهِمْ وَلَا هُمْ يَحْزَنُونَ ۝ قَوْلٌ مَّعْرُوفٌ وَمَغْفِرَةٌ خَيْرٌ مِّن صَدَقَةٍ يَتْبَعُهَا أَذًى وَاللّٰهُ غَنِيٌّ حَلِيمٌ ۝ يَا أَيُّهَا الَّذِينَ آمَنُوا لَا تُبْطِلُوا صَدَقَاتِكُم بِالْمَنِّ وَالْأَذَىٰ كَالَّذِي يُنفِقُ مَالَهُ رِئَاءَ النَّاسِ وَلَا يُؤْمِنُ بِاللّٰهِ وَالْيَوْمِ الْآخِرِ فَمَثَلُهُ كَمَثَلِ صَفْوَانٍ عَلَيْهِ تُرَابٌ فَأَصَابَهُ وَابِلٌ فَتَرَكَهُ صَلْدًا لَّا يَقْدِرُونَ عَلَىٰ شَيْءٍ مِّمَّا كَسَبُوا وَاللّٰهُ لَا يَهْدِي الْقَوْمَ الْكَافِرِينَ ۝

for whom He wills. God is All-Embracing (with His mercy), All-Knowing.

262. Those who spend their wealth in God's cause and then do not follow up what they have spent with putting (the receiver) under obligation and taunting, their reward is with their Lord, and they will have no fear, nor will they grieve.

263. A kind word and forgiving (people's faults) are better than almsgiving followed by taunting. God is All-Wealthy and Self-Sufficient, (absolutely independent of the charity of people), All-Clement (Who shows no haste in punishing.)

264. O you who believe! Render not vain your almsgiving by putting (the receiver) under an obligation and taunting – like him who spends his wealth to show off to people and be praised by them, and believes not in God and the Last Day. The parable of his spending is that of a rock on which there is soil; a heavy rain falls upon it, and leaves it barren. They have no power (control) over what they have earned. God guides not such disbelieving people (to attain their goals).

260. And recall when Abraham said: "My Lord, show me how You will restore life to the dead!" God said: "Why? Do you not believe?" Abraham said: "Yes, but that my heart may be at rest." (His Lord) said: "Then take four of the birds (of different kinds), and tame them to yourself to know them fully. Then (cut them into pieces and mix the pieces with each other, and) put on every one of the hills a piece from each, and then summon them, and they will come to you flying. Know that surely God is All-Glorious with irresistible might, All-Wise.

261. The parable of those who spend their wealth in God's cause is like that of a grain that sprouts seven ears, and in every ear there are a hundred grains. God multiplies

44   سُوْرَةُ البَقَرَة   ٤٤

وَمَثَلُ الَّذِينَ يُنفِقُونَ أَمْوَالَهُمُ ابْتِغَاءَ مَرْضَاتِ اللَّهِ وَتَثْبِيتًا مِّنْ أَنفُسِهِمْ كَمَثَلِ جَنَّةٍ بِرَبْوَةٍ أَصَابَهَا وَابِلٌ فَآتَتْ أُكُلَهَا ضِعْفَيْنِ فَإِن لَّمْ يُصِبْهَا وَابِلٌ فَطَلٌّ وَاللَّهُ بِمَا تَعْمَلُونَ بَصِيرٌ ۝

265. The parable of those who spend their wealth in pursuit of where God's good pleasure lies and to make their hearts firmly established (in faith) is that of a garden on a hilltop: a heavy rain falls upon it, and it yields its produce twofold; even if no heavy rain falls upon it, yet a light shower suffices. Whatever you do, God sees it well.

266. Would any of you wish to have a garden of palms and vines with rivers flowing in it, where he has all kinds of crops, and that, when old age has come upon him while he has offspring still too small (to look after their affairs), a fiery whirlwind should smite it, and it should be burnt up? Thus does God make clear to you the Revelations (and signs of truth), that you may reflect (on them and act accordingly.)

267. O you who believe! Spend (in God's cause and for the needy) out of the pure, wholesome things you have earned and of what We have produced for you from the earth, and do not seek after the bad things to spend thereof (in alms and in God's cause) when you would not take it save with disdain; and know that God is All-Wealthy and Self-Sufficient (absolutely independent of the charity of people), All-Praiseworthy (as your Lord, Who provides

for you and all other beings and meets all your needs).

268. Satan frightens you with poverty and bids you into indecencies, whereas God promises you forgiveness from Himself and bounty. God is All-Embracing (with His Mercy), All-Knowing.

269. He grants the Wisdom[159] to whomever He wills, and whoever is granted the Wisdom, has indeed been granted much good. Yet none except people of discernment reflect and are mindful.

---

159. Although the term has a broad range of meanings, "the Wisdom" basically signifies insight, discernment, and knowledge of creation, life, right and wrong, and of the Divine system prevailing in the universe, so as to enable persuasive, convincing answers for such questions as "Who am I? What is the purpose for my existence in this world? Who has sent me

to this world and why? Where did I come from and where am I heading? What does death ask of me?" It also signifies the true nature of and purpose behind the things and events in the universe, including especially human life; in other words, it may be regarded, from one perspective, as harmony with Divine Destiny or knowledge of It. The Qur'ān is the source of knowledge in all these vital matters. The Sunnah of the Prophet Muḥammad, upon him be peace and blessings, being the system or principles by which to understand and practice the Qur'ān in daily life, comes to mind first of all when speaking of "the Wisdom."

Deceived by Satan, worldly people believe that it is the height of wisdom to be constantly concerned with saving out of one's earnings and to be perpetually on the look-out for a higher income. But those granted wisdom aim at eternal happiness in the eternal world, which requires spending in God's cause and giving to the needy for a balanced, happy social life.

٤٥   45

وَمَآ أَنفَقْتُم مِّن نَّفَقَةٍ أَوْ نَذَرْتُم مِّن نَّذْرٍ فَإِنَّ
اللَّهَ يَعْلَمُهُ وَمَا لِلظَّٰلِمِينَ مِنْ أَنصَارٍ ۗ ﴿٢٧٠﴾ إِن تُبْدُوا
الصَّدَقَاتِ فَنِعِمَّا هِيَ ۖ وَإِن تُخْفُوهَا وَتُؤْتُوهَا الْفُقَرَآءَ
فَهُوَ خَيْرٌ لَّكُمْ ۚ وَيُكَفِّرُ عَنكُم مِّن سَيِّئَاتِكُمْ ۗ
وَاللَّهُ بِمَا تَعْمَلُونَ خَبِيرٌ ﴿٢٧١﴾ لَّيْسَ عَلَيْكَ هُدَاهُمْ وَلَٰكِنَّ
اللَّهَ يَهْدِى مَن يَشَآءُ ۗ وَمَا تُنفِقُوا مِنْ خَيْرٍ
فَلِأَنفُسِكُمْ ۚ وَمَا تُنفِقُونَ إِلَّا ابْتِغَآءَ وَجْهِ
اللَّهِ ۚ وَمَا تُنفِقُوا مِنْ خَيْرٍ يُوَفَّ إِلَيْكُمْ وَأَنتُمْ
لَا تُظْلَمُونَ ﴿٢٧٢﴾ لِلْفُقَرَآءِ الَّذِينَ أُحْصِرُوا فِى سَبِيلِ
اللَّهِ لَا يَسْتَطِيعُونَ ضَرْبًا فِى الْأَرْضِ يَحْسَبُهُمُ
الْجَاهِلُ أَغْنِيَآءَ مِنَ التَّعَفُّفِ ۖ تَعْرِفُهُم بِسِيمَاهُمْ
لَا يَسْـَٔلُونَ النَّاسَ إِلْحَافًا ۗ وَمَا تُنفِقُوا مِنْ خَيْرٍ فَإِنَّ
اللَّهَ بِهِ عَلِيمٌ ﴿٢٧٣﴾ الَّذِينَ يُنفِقُونَ أَمْوَٰلَهُم بِالَّيْلِ
وَالنَّهَارِ سِرًّا وَعَلَانِيَةً فَلَهُمْ أَجْرُهُمْ عِندَ
رَبِّهِمْ وَلَا خَوْفٌ عَلَيْهِمْ وَلَا هُمْ يَحْزَنُونَ ﴿٢٧٤﴾

270. Whatever you spend (whether little or much, good or bad, in God's cause or in the way of Satan) and whatever vow you make, God surely knows it. (Even though they may regard their future as secured) the wrongdoers have no helpers (with regard to their ultimate future).

271. If you dispense your alms openly, it is well, but if you conceal it and give it to the poor (in secret), this is better for you; and God will (make it an atonement to) blot out some of your evil deeds. God is fully aware of all that you do.

272. (O Messenger! Your mission is to convey all such commandments, so) it is not your duty to secure their guidance (in every matter); but God guides whomever He wills. Whatever good you spend in alms is to your own benefit, and (as believers) you do not spend but in search of God's "Face" (seeking to be worthy of His favor). Whatever good you spend will be repaid to you in full, and you will not be wronged.

273. That (which you spend) is for the poor who, having dedicated themselves to God's cause, are in distressed circumstances. They are unable to move about the earth (to render service in God's cause and earn their livelihood). Those who are unaware (of their circumstances) suppose them wealthy because of their abstinence and dignified bearing, but you will know them by their countenance – they do not beg of people importunately. And whatever good you spend, surely God has full knowledge of it.

274. Those who spend their wealth night and day, secretly and in public, their reward is with their Lord, and they will have no fear, nor will they grieve.

46　　　سورة البقرة　　　٤٦

الَّذِينَ يَأْكُلُونَ الرِّبَوا لَا يَقُومُونَ إِلَّا كَمَا يَقُومُ الَّذِي يَتَخَبَّطُهُ الشَّيْطَانُ مِنَ الْمَسِّ ذَلِكَ بِأَنَّهُمْ قَالُوا إِنَّمَا الْبَيْعُ مِثْلُ الرِّبَوا وَأَحَلَّ اللَّهُ الْبَيْعَ وَحَرَّمَ الرِّبَوا فَمَن جَاءَهُ مَوْعِظَةٌ مِّن رَّبِّهِ فَانتَهَى فَلَهُ مَا سَلَفَ وَأَمْرُهُ إِلَى اللَّهِ وَمَنْ عَادَ فَأُوْلَئِكَ أَصْحَابُ النَّارِ هُمْ فِيهَا خَالِدُونَ ۝ يَمْحَقُ اللَّهُ الرِّبَوا وَيُرْبِي الصَّدَقَاتِ وَاللَّهُ لَا يُحِبُّ كُلَّ كَفَّارٍ أَثِيمٍ ۝ إِنَّ الَّذِينَ آمَنُوا وَعَمِلُوا الصَّالِحَاتِ وَأَقَامُوا الصَّلَوٰةَ وَآتَوُا الزَّكَوٰةَ لَهُمْ أَجْرُهُمْ عِندَ رَبِّهِمْ وَلَا خَوْفٌ عَلَيْهِمْ وَلَا هُمْ يَحْزَنُونَ ۝ يَا أَيُّهَا الَّذِينَ آمَنُوا اتَّقُوا اللَّهَ وَذَرُوا مَا بَقِيَ مِنَ الرِّبَوا إِن كُنتُم مُّؤْمِنِينَ ۝ فَإِن لَّمْ تَفْعَلُوا فَأْذَنُوا بِحَرْبٍ مِّنَ اللَّهِ وَرَسُولِهِ وَإِن تُبْتُمْ فَلَكُمْ رُءُوسُ أَمْوَالِكُمْ لَا تَظْلِمُونَ وَلَا تُظْلَمُونَ ۝ وَإِن كَانَ ذُو عُسْرَةٍ فَنَظِرَةٌ إِلَى مَيْسَرَةٍ وَأَن تَصَدَّقُوا خَيْرٌ لَّكُمْ إِن كُنتُمْ تَعْلَمُونَ ۝ وَاتَّقُوا يَوْمًا تُرْجَعُونَ فِيهِ إِلَى اللَّهِ ثُمَّ تُوَفَّى كُلُّ نَفْسٍ مَّا كَسَبَتْ وَهُمْ لَا يُظْلَمُونَ ۝

―――――※―――――

275. As to those who consume interest, (even though they seem, for a time, to be making a profit), they turn out like one whom Satan has bewitched and confounded by his touch, (and they will rise up (from their graves in the same way before God). That is because they say interest is just like trading, whereas God has made trading lawful, and interest unlawful.[160] To whomever an instruction comes from his Lord, and he desists (from interest), he may keep his past gains (legally), and his affair is committed to God (– if he repents sincerely and never again reverts to taking interest, he may hope that God will forgive him). But whoever reverts to it (by judging to be lawful), they are companions of the Fire; therein they will abide.

276. God deprives interest (which is thought to increase wealth) of any blessing, and blights it, but makes alms-giving (which is thought to decrease wealth) productive. God does not love any obstinate unbeliever (who regards what God has made lawful as unlawful or vice versa), any obstinate sinner.

277. Those who believe and do good, righteous deeds, and establish the Prayer in conformity with its conditions, and pay the Prescribed Purifying Alms, their reward is with their Lord, and they will have no fear, nor will they grieve.

278. O you who believe! Keep from disobedience to God and try to attain piety in due reverence for Him, and give up what remains (due to you) from interest if you are (in truth) believers.

279. If you do not (and you persist in taking interest, whether regarding it as lawful or not), be warned of war from God and His Messenger. If you sincerely repent (and give up all interest transactions completely), you will have your principal. Then you will neither be doing wrong nor being wronged.

280. If the debtor is in straitened circumstances, let him have respite until the time of ease; if you make any remission (of his debt) by way of charity, this is better for you, if only you knew.

281. And guard yourselves against a Day in which you will be brought back to God (with all your deeds referred to His judgment). Then every soul will be repaid in full what it has earned (while in the world), and they will not be wronged.

160. As with the implementation of other Islamic injunctions, interest was forbidden gradually, and all kinds of interest transactions were utterly stopped during the Farewell Pilgrimage just three months before the death of God's Messenger, upon him be peace and blessings. Bediüzzaman Said Nursi writes on interest very succinctly as follows:

> The cause of all revolutions and social corruption, and the root of all moral failings, are these two attitudes:
>
> First: I do not care if others die of hunger so long as my own stomach is full.
>
> Second: You must bear the costs of my ease – you must work so that I may eat.
>
> The cure for the first attitude is the obligation of the *Zakāh*, the Purifying Alms prescribed by the Qur'ān. The cure for the second attitude is the prohibition of all interest transactions. The justice of the Qur'ān stands at the door of the world and turns away interest, proclaiming: No! You have no right to enter. Humankind did not heed this prohibition and have suffered terrible blows in consequence. Let them heed it now to avoid still greater suffering. (*The Words*, "the 25th Word," 427-428)

As will be seen in the following verses, the Qur'ān is extremely strict on interest, so much so that regarding it as lawful amounts to persistence in unbelief and sin, and still taking interest while regarding it as unlawful because of God's prohibition of it amounts to warring with from God and His Messenger.

Interest is the principal mechanism for the concentration of wealth, for making the rich richer and the poor poorer. The present state of the world, where the poor countries are crushed under the burden of loans to the rich ones, and the rich people live on the poor, is an example of this. Interest is the means of the maintenance of oppression both on a world scale and within a country. In addition to the corruption it causes in the economy, by its very nature, interest breeds meanness, selfishness, apathy, and cruelty towards others. It leads to the worship of money, to the valuing of it for its own sake, and destroys fellow-feeling and the spirit of altruistic cooperation among people. Thus it is ruinous for humankind from both an economic and a moral viewpoint.

When Islam is fully applied, there is no need for interest-based loans and transactions. Islamic economics encourages partnership-based investment, in which participants share directly in the profit or loss of a venture, and mutual helping, cooperation, and altruism. The prohibition of interest reduces the cost of such ventures, and also suppresses inflation. Money is a means of exchanging goods. To make money itself a subject of (what is in practice) risk-free trade is irrational, exploitative, and generates a host of essentially parasitic attitudes and activities.

٤ ٧   الجُزْءُ الثَّالِثُ   47

يَا أَيُّهَا الَّذِينَ آمَنُوا إِذَا تَدَايَنتُم بِدَيْنٍ إِلَى أَجَلٍ مُّسَمًّى
فَاكْتُبُوهُ وَلْيَكْتُب بَّيْنَكُمْ كَاتِبٌ بِالْعَدْلِ وَلَا يَأْبَ
كَاتِبٌ أَن يَكْتُبَ كَمَا عَلَّمَهُ اللَّهُ فَلْيَكْتُبْ وَلْيُمْلِلِ
الَّذِي عَلَيْهِ الْحَقُّ وَلْيَتَّقِ اللَّهَ رَبَّهُ وَلَا يَبْخَسْ مِنْهُ شَيْئًا
فَإِن كَانَ الَّذِي عَلَيْهِ الْحَقُّ سَفِيهًا أَوْ ضَعِيفًا أَوْ لَا يَسْتَطِيعُ
أَن يُمِلَّ هُوَ فَلْيُمْلِلْ وَلِيُّهُ بِالْعَدْلِ وَاسْتَشْهِدُوا شَهِيدَيْنِ
مِن رِّجَالِكُمْ فَإِن لَّمْ يَكُونَا رَجُلَيْنِ فَرَجُلٌ وَامْرَأَتَانِ مِمَّن
تَرْضَوْنَ مِنَ الشُّهَدَاءِ أَن تَضِلَّ إِحْدَاهُمَا فَتُذَكِّرَ إِحْدَاهُمَا
الْأُخْرَى وَلَا يَأْبَ الشُّهَدَاءُ إِذَا مَا دُعُوا وَلَا تَسْأَمُوا أَن
تَكْتُبُوهُ صَغِيرًا أَوْ كَبِيرًا إِلَى أَجَلِهِ ذَلِكُمْ أَقْسَطُ عِندَ
اللَّهِ وَأَقْوَمُ لِلشَّهَادَةِ وَأَدْنَى أَلَّا تَرْتَابُوا إِلَّا أَن تَكُونَ
تِجَارَةً حَاضِرَةً تُدِيرُونَهَا بَيْنَكُمْ فَلَيْسَ عَلَيْكُمْ جُنَاحٌ أَلَّا
تَكْتُبُوهَا وَأَشْهِدُوا إِذَا تَبَايَعْتُمْ وَلَا يُضَارَّ كَاتِبٌ
وَلَا شَهِيدٌ وَإِن تَفْعَلُوا فَإِنَّهُ فُسُوقٌ بِكُمْ وَاتَّقُوا
اللَّهَ وَيُعَلِّمُكُمُ اللَّهُ وَاللَّهُ بِكُلِّ شَيْءٍ عَلِيمٌ ﴿٢٨٢﴾

282. O you who believe! When you contract a debt between you for a fixed term, record it in writing. Let a scribe write it down between you justly, and let no scribe refuse to write it down: as God has taught him (through the Qur'ān and His Messenger), so let him write. And let the debtor dictate, and let him avoid disobeying God, his Lord (Who has created him and brought him up with mercy and grace) and curtail no part of it. If the debtor be weak of mind or body, or incapable of dictating, let his guardian dictate justly. And call upon two (Muslim) men among you as witnesses. If two men are not there, then let there be one man and two women,[161] from among those of whom you approve as witnesses, that if either of the two women errs (through forgetfulness), the other may remind her. Let the witnesses not refuse when they are summoned (to give evidence). And (you, O scribes) be not loath to write down (the contract) whether it be small or great, with the term of the contract. Your doing so (O you who believe), is more equitable in the sight of God, more upright for testimony, and more likely that you will not be in doubt. If it be a matter of buying and selling concluded on the spot, then there will be no blame on you if you do not write it down; but do take witnesses when you settle commercial transactions with one another, and let no harm be done to either scribe or witness (nor let either of them act in a way to injure the parties). If you act (in a way to harm either party or the scribe and witnesses), indeed it will be transgression on your part. (Always) act in due reverence for God and try to attain piety. God teaches you (whatever you need in life and the way you must follow in every matter); God has full knowledge of everything.

---

161. The reason why the Qur'ān demands two women in place of one man in commercial transactions is straightforward. It does not at all mean that the Qur'ān regards a woman as half of a man. For what is important here is not the relative status of women or men but reliability, justice, and equity in business transactions, particularly transactions involving debt.

Typically, across the diverse cultures in the world, men engage in business more than women, and men are directly responsible for the livelihood of the family. Furthermore, again typically (therefore, not always), women are more emotional than men and more susceptible to forgetting. Accordingly, it is reasonable to expect that, in matters wherein they are not typically engaged, women will be more susceptible to erring or forgetting than men. Of course, there will always be some women with a keener memory than some men, and some men more emotional than some women. However, rather than exceptions, the norm and the typical majority are considered in matters relating to institutions for the community.

Islam does not demand two women in place of one man in all cases of bearing testimony. For example, whether it be a wife or husband, whoever accuses his/her spouse of adultery, he or she must swear by God four times. Likewise, there is no difference between a man and woman in scanning the sky and bearing testimony to seeing the crescent in order to establish whether a lunar month has begun or ended. In addition, the testimony of two women is not sought in place of a man in the matters in which women have greater knowledge or specialty than men.

It is of considerable significance that this verse contains the rules necessary for the establishment of the office of "notary public." It is one of the many proofs for the universality of the Qur'ān, for its being timeless, that it established these rules at a time when, and for a society in which, there were few who knew how to read and write and there was almost no paper to write on. These rules are based on justice, equity, ensuring accuracy in testimony, and removing all doubts concerning the terms of the transaction, thus reducing the potential for future disagreement.

48   سُورَةُ الْبَقَرَةِ   ٤٨

وَإِن كُنتُمْ عَلَىٰ سَفَرٍ وَلَمْ تَجِدُواْ كَاتِبًا فَرِهَانٌ مَّقْبُوضَةٌ فَإِنْ أَمِنَ بَعْضُكُم بَعْضًا فَلْيُؤَدِّ ٱلَّذِى ٱؤْتُمِنَ أَمَانَتَهُ وَلْيَتَّقِ ٱللَّهَ رَبَّهُۥ وَلَا تَكْتُمُواْ ٱلشَّهَٰدَةَ وَمَن يَكْتُمْهَا فَإِنَّهُۥٓ ءَاثِمٌ قَلْبُهُۥ وَٱللَّهُ بِمَا تَعْمَلُونَ عَلِيمٌ ۞ لِّلَّهِ مَا فِى ٱلسَّمَٰوَٰتِ وَمَا فِى ٱلْأَرْضِ وَإِن تُبْدُواْ مَا فِىٓ أَنفُسِكُمْ أَوْ تُخْفُوهُ يُحَاسِبْكُم بِهِ ٱللَّهُ فَيَغْفِرُ لِمَن يَشَآءُ وَيُعَذِّبُ مَن يَشَآءُ وَٱللَّهُ عَلَىٰ كُلِّ شَىْءٍ قَدِيرٌ ۞ ءَامَنَ ٱلرَّسُولُ بِمَآ أُنزِلَ إِلَيْهِ مِن رَّبِّهِۦ وَٱلْمُؤْمِنُونَ كُلٌّ ءَامَنَ بِٱللَّهِ وَمَلَٰٓئِكَتِهِۦ وَكُتُبِهِۦ وَرُسُلِهِۦ لَا نُفَرِّقُ بَيْنَ أَحَدٍ مِّن رُّسُلِهِۦ وَقَالُواْ سَمِعْنَا وَأَطَعْنَا غُفْرَانَكَ رَبَّنَا وَإِلَيْكَ ٱلْمَصِيرُ ۞ لَا يُكَلِّفُ ٱللَّهُ نَفْسًا إِلَّا وُسْعَهَا لَهَا مَا كَسَبَتْ وَعَلَيْهَا مَا ٱكْتَسَبَتْ رَبَّنَا لَا تُؤَاخِذْنَآ إِن نَّسِينَآ أَوْ أَخْطَأْنَا رَبَّنَا وَلَا تَحْمِلْ عَلَيْنَآ إِصْرًا كَمَا حَمَلْتَهُۥ عَلَى ٱلَّذِينَ مِن قَبْلِنَا رَبَّنَا وَلَا تُحَمِّلْنَا مَا لَا طَاقَةَ لَنَا بِهِۦ وَٱعْفُ عَنَّا وَٱغْفِرْ لَنَا وَٱرْحَمْنَآ أَنتَ مَوْلَىٰنَا فَٱنصُرْنَا عَلَى ٱلْقَوْمِ ٱلْكَٰفِرِينَ ۞

——————❀——————

283. If you are (in circumstances like being) on a journey and cannot find a scribe, then a pledge in hand will suffice. But if you trust one another, let him (the debtor) who is trusted fulfill his trust, and let him act in piety and keep from disobedience to God, his Lord, (by fulfilling the conditions of the contract). And do not conceal the testimony; he who conceals it, surely his heart (which is the center of faith) is contaminated with sin. God has full knowledge of what you do.

284. To God belongs all that is in the heavens and the earth; whether you reveal what is within yourselves (of intentions, plans) or keep it secret, God will call you to account for it. He forgives whom He wills (either from His grace or His grace responding to the repentance of the sinful), and He punishes whom He wills (as a requirement of His justice). God has full power over everything.

285. The Messenger believes in what has been sent down to him from his Lord, and so do the believers; each one believes in God, and His angels, and His Books, and His Messengers: "We make no distinction between any of His Messengers (in believing in them)." And they say: "We have heard (the call to faith in God) and (unlike some of the people of Moses) obeyed. Our Lord, grant us Your forgiveness, and to You is the homecoming."

286. (O believers, if you are worried that God will take every soul to account even for what the soul keeps within it of intentions and plans, know that) God burdens no soul except within its capacity: in its favor is whatever (good) it earns, and against it whatever (evil) it merits. (So, pray thus to your Lord:) "Our Lord, take us not to task if we forget or make mistake. Our Lord, lay not on us a burden[162] such as You laid on those gone before us. Our Lord, impose not on us what we do not have the power to bear. And overlook our faults, and forgive us, and have mercy upon us. You are our Guardian and Owner (to Whom We entrust our affairs and on Whom we rely), so help us and grant us victory against the disbelieving people!"[163]

---

162. The burden which was laid upon the previous communities was some commandments required by the education they had to receive according to the time and conditions and to their disposition. (Also see *sūrah* 7, note 38.)

163. The last two verses were revealed to God's Messenger during the Ascension. It is a highly meritorious Sunnah act to recite them before going to bed every night. The Messenger advises the parents to teach them to their children.

SŪRAH 3

ĀL ʿIMRĀN
(THE FAMILY OF ʿIMRĀN)

Madīnah period

T his *sūrah* takes its name from the family of Virgin Mary. It was revealed in Madīnah and consists of 200 verses. It deals with many matters concerning the relations of the Muslims with the People of the Book, in particular, the Christians. It clarifies some important points regarding Jesus, including his birth, the miracles he performed, and his mission. It discusses at length the lessons to be taken from the Battle of Uhud and teaches the believers about many important points with respect to belief, reliance on God, preference of the other world over the present one, and the wisdom contained in historical events.

In the Name of God, the All-Merciful, the All-Compassionate.

1. *Alif. Lām. Mīm.*

2. God, there is no deity but He; the All-Living, the Self-Subsisting (by Whom all subsist).

3. He sends down on you the Book in parts with the truth, confirming (the Divine origin of, and the truths still contained by) the Revelations prior to it; and He sent down the Torah and the Gospel

4. In time past, as guidance for the people; and He has sent down the Criterion (to distinguish between truth and falsehood, and the knowledge, and power of judgment to put it into effect).[1] Those who disbelieve in the Revelations of God, for them is a severe punishment. God is All-Glorious with irresistible might, Ever-Able to Requite.

5. Surely God – nothing whatever on the earth and in the heaven is hidden from Him.

6. It is He Who fashions you in the wombs as He wills. There is no deity but He, the All-Glorious with irresistible might, the All-Wise.

7. It is He Who has sent down on you this Book, in which there are verses explicit in meaning and content and decisive: they are the core of the Book, others being allegorical.[2] Those in whose hearts is swerving pursue what is allegorical in it, seeking (to cause) dissension, and seeking to make it open to arbitrary interpretation, although none knows its interpretation save God. And those firmly rooted in knowledge say: "We believe in it (in the entirety of its verses, both explicit and allegorical); all is from our Lord;" yet none derives admonition except the people of discernment.

8. (They entreat God:) "Our Lord, do not let our hearts swerve after You have guided us, and bestow upon us mercy from Your Presence. Surely You are the All-Bestowing.

9. "Our Lord, You it is Who will gather humankind for a Day about (the coming of) which there is no doubt. Surely God does not fail to keep the promise."

---

1. For the Criterion, refer to 2: 53, note 60.

As for the Torah and the Gospel, which are confirmed by the Qur'ān: the Torah, in the Qur'ānic usage, signifies the Book which was given to the Prophet Moses, upon him be peace, and included the Ten Commandments, which were handed over to him inscribed on tablets on Mount Sinai. Moses took down the rest of the revealed injunctions and handed over one copy to each of the tribes, and one copy to the Levites for safe-keeping. It is this book which was known as the Torah and it existed until the first destruction of Jerusalem. The copy entrusted to the Levites was put beside the Ark (of the Covenant) along with the Commandments tablets, and the Israelites knew this as the Torah. The Jews, however, neglected the Book: during the reign of Josiah, the king of Judah, the Temple of Solomon was under repair and the high priest, Hilkiah, chanced to find the Book lying in the construction area. He gave it to the King's secretary, Shaphan, who in turn took it to the King; they acted as if this were a strange object to find (see: *II Kings*, 22: 8–13).

Hence, when the Babylonian king, Nebuchadnezzar, conquered Jerusalem and razed it and the Temple of Solomon to the ground, the Israelites lost forever the few original copies of the Torah which they had possessed. At the time of Ezra, some Israelites returned from captivity in Babylon, and when Jerusalem was rebuilt, the entire history of Israel, which comprises the first 14 books of the Old Testament, was recorded by Ezra with the assistance of some other elders of the community. Four of these books, Exodus, Leviticus, Numbers and Deuteronomy, consist of a biographical narrative of Moses. In this biography, those verses of the Torah available to Ezra and the other elders were also recorded, along with the contexts in which they were revealed. The present Torah, therefore, comprises fragments of the original book interspersed throughout with a biography of Moses (composed in the manner described above).

In locating these fragments of the original Torah there are certain expressions which help us. These are interspersed between the different pieces of biographical narrative and usually open with words such as: "Then the Lord said to Moses," and "Moses said, the Lord your God commands you." These expressions, then, are most probably fragments of the original Torah. When the biographical narration re-commences, however, we can be sure that the fragments of the true Torah ceases. Wherever authors and editors of the Bible have added anything of their own accord, by way of their elaboration or elucidation, it becomes very difficult for an ordinary reader to distinguish the original from the explanatory additions. Those with insight into Divine Scripture, however, do have the capacity to distinguish between the original revealed fragments and the later human interpolations.

It is the original Book revealed to Moses, some of the verses of which are to be found in the Bible, which the Qur'ān terms as the Torah, and it is this which it confirms. When these fragments are compared with the Qur'ān, there is no difference between the two as regards the fundamental teachings. Whatever differences exist relate to legal matters and are of secondary importance. Even today, a careful reader can appreciate that the Torah and the Qur'ān have sprung from the same Divine source.

Likewise, the *Injīl* signifies the inspired orations and utterances of Jesus (upon him be peace), which he delivered during the last three years of his life in his capacity as a Messenger. There are no certain means by which we can definitely establish whether or not his statements were recorded during his lifetime. It is possible that some people took notes of them and that some followers committed them to memory. After a period of time, however, several treatises on the life of Jesus were written. The authors of these treatises recorded, in connection with the biographical account, those sayings of his which they had received from the previous generation of co-religionists, in the form of either oral traditions or written notes about events in his life. As a result, the Gospels of Matthew, Mark, Luke, and John, whose authors belonged to the second or third generation after Jesus, and which were chosen from among more than 300 other similar versions and accepted by the Church as the Canonical Gospels, are not identical with the *Injīl*. Rather, the *Injīl* consists of those statements by Jesus which form part of these Gospels. Unfortunately, we have no means of distinguishing the fragments of the original *Injīl* from the pieces written by the authors themselves. All we can say is that only those sections explicitly attributed to Jesus, for example statements such as: "And Jesus said" and "And Jesus taught," most probably constitute the true *Injīl*. It is the totality of such fragments which is designated as the *Injīl* by the Qur'ān, and it is the teachings contained in these fragments that the Qur'ān confirms. If these fragments are put together and compared with the teachings of the Qur'ān, one notices very few discrepancies between the two, and any discrepancies that are found can be resolved easily by unbiased reflection (Largely quoted from al-Mawdūdī, 1: 233—234).

2. *Muḥkam* means that which has been made firm and perfect, while *mutashābih* derives from the root *shibh,* which means resemblance. All the verses of the Qur'ān are *muḥkam* in the sense that there is no doubt about their Divine authorship, yet they are *mutashābih* as well in the sense that they are interrelated with one another. Nevertheless, what is meant in this verse by *muḥkam* and *mutashābih* is as follows:

The *muḥkam* verses are those verses whose meaning is so clear that they are not open to any ambiguity or equivocation. Such verses are the core of the Qur'ān. They embody admonition and instruction, as well as the refutation of erroneous doctrines. They also contain the essentials of the true faith, teachings related to faith, worship, daily life and morality, and the mandatory duties and prohibitions. These are the verses which will guide the genuine seeker of the truth, which will guide those who turn to the Qur'ān in order to find out what they ought or ought not to do.

The *mutashābih* verses are those which, having more than one meaning, require other evidence in order to be understood. The reason for these multiple meanings is that time progresses, conditions change, human information increases, and there are as many levels of understanding as there are people. The Qur'ān, being the Word of God, addresses all levels of understanding from the time of its revelation to the Day of Resurrection. It explains to people matters which cannot be easily understood by using metaphors, similes, personifications, and parables. This way of explanation does not harm the unchanging, essential truths of religion, for God has clearly informed us of what He demands from us relating to faith, worship, morality, and the mandatory duties and prohibitions. The *mutashābih* (allegorical) verses contain relative truths which can be understood by considering the relevant verses and referring to the *muḥkam* ones.

Because of the realities of human life in this world, the relative truths are more in number than the absolute, unchanging ones. In order to understand this point, let us take a crystal chandelier as an example. While the light remains the same, those sitting around it perceive different colors or light of varying strength as their positions change. Such differences arise from the different shapes of the crystals in the chandelier, and the different angles of the crystals. In the same way, God Almighty included in the Qur'ān several allegorical verses in order to provide unlimited meanings with limited words to all people, whatever their level of knowledge or understanding might be, in order to teach them until the Last Day; in this way they are invited to reflect on the Book and to be guided to the truth. It should not be forgotten that an exact resemblance is not sought between that which is compared and that to which it is being compared.

Since the allegorical verses have multiple meanings, the interpreters of the Qur'ān may be able to discover one or more of those meanings. Each of their discoveries can be regarded as being true, provided it is in conformity with the *muḥkam* verses and the essentials of Islam, the rules of Qur'ānic Arabic and the rules of the science of interpretation. But whatever true meaning is arrived at by a scholar, the exact meaning of these verses is always referred to God, the All-Knowing; this is exegesis.

50 سورة آل عمران ٥.

إِنَّ الَّذِينَ كَفَرُوا لَنْ تُغْنِيَ عَنْهُمْ أَمْوَالُهُمْ وَلَا أَوْلَادُهُمْ مِنَ اللهِ شَيْئًا ۖ وَأُولَٰئِكَ هُمْ وَقُودُ النَّارِ ۝ كَدَأْبِ آلِ فِرْعَوْنَ وَالَّذِينَ مِنْ قَبْلِهِمْ ۚ كَذَّبُوا بِآيَاتِنَا فَأَخَذَهُمُ اللهُ بِذُنُوبِهِمْ ۗ وَاللهُ شَدِيدُ الْعِقَابِ ۝ قُلْ لِلَّذِينَ كَفَرُوا سَتُغْلَبُونَ وَتُحْشَرُونَ إِلَىٰ جَهَنَّمَ ۚ وَبِئْسَ الْمِهَادُ ۝ قَدْ كَانَ لَكُمْ آيَةٌ فِي فِئَتَيْنِ الْتَقَتَا ۖ فِئَةٌ تُقَاتِلُ فِي سَبِيلِ اللهِ وَأُخْرَىٰ كَافِرَةٌ يَرَوْنَهُمْ مِثْلَيْهِمْ رَأْيَ الْعَيْنِ ۚ وَاللهُ يُؤَيِّدُ بِنَصْرِهِ مَنْ يَشَاءُ ۗ إِنَّ فِي ذَٰلِكَ لَعِبْرَةً لِأُولِي الْأَبْصَارِ ۝ زُيِّنَ لِلنَّاسِ حُبُّ الشَّهَوَاتِ مِنَ النِّسَاءِ وَالْبَنِينَ وَالْقَنَاطِيرِ الْمُقَنْطَرَةِ مِنَ الذَّهَبِ وَالْفِضَّةِ وَالْخَيْلِ الْمُسَوَّمَةِ وَالْأَنْعَامِ وَالْحَرْثِ ۗ ذَٰلِكَ مَتَاعُ الْحَيَاةِ الدُّنْيَا ۖ وَاللهُ عِنْدَهُ حُسْنُ الْمَآبِ ۝ قُلْ أَؤُنَبِّئُكُمْ بِخَيْرٍ مِنْ ذَٰلِكُمْ ۚ لِلَّذِينَ اتَّقَوْا عِنْدَ رَبِّهِمْ جَنَّاتٌ تَجْرِي مِنْ تَحْتِهَا الْأَنْهَارُ خَالِدِينَ فِيهَا وَأَزْوَاجٌ مُطَهَّرَةٌ وَرِضْوَانٌ مِنَ اللهِ ۗ وَاللهُ بَصِيرٌ بِالْعِبَادِ ۝

---

10. Those who disbelieve, neither their wealth nor their offspring will avail them at all against God; they are fuel for the Fire.

11. It is just as that which happened to the clan (the court and military aristocracy) of the Pharaoh, and those before them. They denied Our signs and Revelations, and so God seized them for their sins. God is severe in retribution.

12. Say to those who disbelieve: "You will soon be overpowered and gathered into Hell!" – How evil a cradle it is!

13. Indeed there has been a manifest sign (of the truth of God's way) and lesson for you in the two hosts that encountered (at the Battle of Badr): one host fighting in God's cause, and the other disbelieving, who saw with their very eyes (the host of the believers) as twice their actual number (during fighting). God confirms with His help and victory whom He wills. Surely in that is a lesson for those who have the power of seeing.

14. Made innately appealing to men are passionate love for women, children, (hoarded) treasures of gold and silver, branded horses, cattle, and plantations. Such are enjoyments of the present, worldly life; yet with God is the best of the goals to pursue.

15. Say (to them): "Shall I inform you of what is better than those (things that you so passionately seek to obtain)? For those who keep from disobedience to God in due reverence for Him and piety there are, with their Lord, Gardens through which rivers flow, wherein they will abide, and spouses purified, and God's good pleasure (with them). God sees the servants well.

الَّذِينَ يَقُولُونَ رَبَّنَا إِنَّنَا آمَنَّا فَاغْفِرْ لَنَا ذُنُوبَنَا وَقِنَا
عَذَابَ النَّارِ ۞ الصَّابِرِينَ وَالصَّادِقِينَ وَالْقَانِتِينَ وَالْمُنْفِقِينَ
وَالْمُسْتَغْفِرِينَ بِالْأَسْحَارِ ۞ شَهِدَ اللَّهُ أَنَّهُ لَا إِلَهَ إِلَّا هُوَ
وَالْمَلَائِكَةُ وَأُولُوا الْعِلْمِ قَائِمًا بِالْقِسْطِ لَا إِلَهَ إِلَّا هُوَ
الْعَزِيزُ الْحَكِيمُ ۞ إِنَّ الدِّينَ عِندَ اللَّهِ الْإِسْلَامُ
وَمَا اخْتَلَفَ الَّذِينَ أُوتُوا الْكِتَابَ إِلَّا مِن بَعْدِ مَا جَاءَهُمُ
الْعِلْمُ بَغْيًا بَيْنَهُمْ وَمَن يَكْفُرْ بِآيَاتِ اللَّهِ فَإِنَّ اللَّهَ
سَرِيعُ الْحِسَابِ ۞ فَإِنْ حَاجُّوكَ فَقُلْ أَسْلَمْتُ وَجْهِيَ لِلَّهِ
وَمَنِ اتَّبَعَنِ وَقُل لِّلَّذِينَ أُوتُوا الْكِتَابَ وَالْأُمِّيِّينَ
أَأَسْلَمْتُمْ فَإِنْ أَسْلَمُوا فَقَدِ اهْتَدَوْا وَإِن تَوَلَّوْا فَإِنَّمَا
عَلَيْكَ الْبَلَاغُ وَاللَّهُ بَصِيرٌ بِالْعِبَادِ ۞ إِنَّ الَّذِينَ
يَكْفُرُونَ بِآيَاتِ اللَّهِ وَيَقْتُلُونَ النَّبِيِّينَ بِغَيْرِ حَقٍّ
وَيَقْتُلُونَ الَّذِينَ يَأْمُرُونَ بِالْقِسْطِ مِنَ النَّاسِ فَبَشِّرْهُم
بِعَذَابٍ أَلِيمٍ ۞ أُولَئِكَ الَّذِينَ حَبِطَتْ أَعْمَالُهُمْ
فِي الدُّنْيَا وَالْآخِرَةِ وَمَا لَهُم مِّن نَّاصِرِينَ ۞

——◆——

16. Those (the God-revering, pious) pray: "Our Lord, we do indeed believe, so forgive us our sins and guard us against the punishment of the Fire."

17. Those who are persevering (in misfortune and steadfast in fulfilling God's commandments and in refraining from sins), and truthful (in their words and actions, and true to their covenants), and devoutly obedient, and who spend (out of what God has provided for them, in His cause and for the needy), and who implore God's forgiveness before daybreak.

18. God (Himself) testifies that there surely is no deity but He, and so do the angels and those of knowledge, being firm in upholding truth and uprightness: (these all testify that) there is no deity but He, the All-Glorious with irresistible might, the All-Wise.[3]

19. The (true) religion with God is Islam. Those who were given the Book before differed only after the knowledge (of truth) came to them because of envious rivalry and insolence among themselves. Whoever disbelieves in the Revelations of God (should know that) God is swift at reckoning.

20. If they still remonstrate with you, say (to them, O Messenger): "I have submitted my whole being to God, and so have those who follow me." And ask those who were given the Book before, and the common folk who know nothing about the Book: "Have you also submitted (to God)?" If they have submitted, then they are indeed rightly guided; but if they turn away, then what rests with you is only to convey the Message fully and clearly. God sees the servants well.

21. Those who disbelieve in the Revelations of God, and frequently kill the Prophets (sent to them) against all right, and who kill those who advocate and try to establish equity and justice – give them the glad tidings of a painful punishment.

22. Those are the ones whose works have been wasted in both this world and the Hereafter, and they have no helpers (to restore their works to their benefit and save them from punishment).

3. This verse, by virtue of its being the greatest evidence of God's Existence and Oneness, of being the verse that is the most expressive of this, is regarded as being equal to God's Greatest Name.

Everything in the universe, from the minutest particles to the most expansive galaxies, and every event that takes place in it, bears decisive evidence of the Existence and Oneness of God. For with a thing's coming into existence, its life and particularities, and with the function it fulfills in the general network of existence, every creature and every object points to a single Deity Who has absolute and infinite Attributes, including, in particular, Knowledge, Power, and Will.

Imagine that you are standing by a river at midday. In each of the bubbles floating by on this river there can be seen a tiny, shining sun. When those bubbles go into a distant tunnel, the tiny suns can no longer be seen. But in the bubbles that are passing in front of us at that moment we can still see the same tiny suns. This proves that the suns found in the bubbles do not actually belong to the bubbles themselves, nor are they of their own making. They are the reflections of the one, single sun in the sky. This is how each bubble bears witness to the existence and oneness of the sun. It also shows that the sun provides light. (If we look at the sun through a prism, we are able to discern the light of the sun in different colors.) The tiny suns continuing to be reflected in new bubbles that pass us by while others are getting lost in the tunnel – all this goes to demonstrate that the sun is a permanent object.

Thus, all the things in the universe are like a bubble. The coming into existence of these things, provided as they are with the necessary equipment for life in the proper environment, goes to prove the Existence of a Creator Who has full knowledge of both the object and the universe, for every object has a relationship with almost everything else in the whole of the universe. The power that those living creatures have to see and hear indicates that the Creator sees and hears, and their ability to satisfy their vital needs proves that the Creator is All-Providing. The death of living beings and their being replaced by new ones show that the Creator is Permanent. Likewise, the order of the universe and the reality that its components mutually help one another also indicate the fact that the Creator is One. For example, in order for a morsel of food to enter the human body as sustenance, the sun, soil, water, and the plant from which the morsel has been produced, and all the organs of the human body must cooperate. This can only be explained by attributing this cooperation to a Unique Being Who has full knowledge of and power over all these things. It is clear that whoever has created and directs the solar system has also created the human body and directs it. Among creatures, humanity has will and consciousness. Despite this, no human being plays a role in their coming into this world, in the choice of their family, color or race, nor in the time or their place of birth and death. Moreover, human beings have the minutest part even in their most ordinary acts, like eating and drinking. It is not we who make it necessary for us to eat or drink; someone else has designed this body, which works automatically, outside of our free will; someone else has placed us in this welcoming environment and has determined the relationship between our body and the environment, including what is edible and what is not. The part we play in eating only consists of putting the morsel in our mouth and chewing. All this clearly demonstrates that the One Who has designed the human body with all its vital needs and organs is the same Being as the One Who has created its environment including the sun, the soil, water and plants, and Who has undertaken to meet these vital needs. That Being is One Who has full knowledge of the universe and humanity and has enough power to create and direct them all at the same time, with an absolutely free will.

Apart from this "objective" reality, there is the fact that human beings feel in their conscience the Existence of God as a point of reliance, especially in instances when they are left with nothing to resort to in order to achieve their desire or to be saved from a calamity; it is at this time that they ask for help. Humans feel that there must be One Who can help them to achieve their desires or save them from danger. Even if they do not encounter difficult situations, all humans have an innate feeling for His Existence.

In short, it is absolutely impossible to explain existence without the Existence of God. His Existence is more manifest than anything else in the universe. The person who denies Him is no different from one who closes their eyes at midday and claims that there is no sun in the universe. God's Existence is even more manifest than that of the sun. A person can act like a sophist and doubt their own existence, but they cannot doubt God's Existence or Oneness. Certain factors, such as vainglory, wrongdoing, having an incorrect perspective of existence because of, for example, the education that one has had, or the environment in which one has grown up, or the life-style that one leads and one's personal interests, may have sealed the faculties of "seeing", "hearing," and "thinking," which lead some to denial of God. Whereas, the angels and those possessed of "knowledge" who view and study things and events with eyes that are able to "see," with ears that are able to "hear," with a heart that is keen and lively enough to understand, and with a pure conscience, and those who rely on the knowledge that the Prophets received from God through Revelation, witness that God exists and that He is One.

4. Literally, Islam means submission, salvation, and peace. It is possible only through submission to God that one can attain the peace in both individual and social spheres,

and salvation in both this world and the next. This is why all the Prophets came with the same doctrine of faith, the same precepts of worship and good conduct, and the same principles for regulating social life. It is only in some secondary matters of law that they differed; and this was only in connection with the time and conditions in which they lived. The name of the religion that encompasses this doctrine and these precepts and principles is Islam. Names such as Judaism and Christianity were given to this religion by either its followers or by its opponents, and they were given some time after Moses and Jesus had left this world. What this means is that all the Prophets came with Islam and communicated it, but their followers failed to observe and preserve it, making changes in it over time. It was communicated for the final time by the Prophet Muḥammad, upon him be peace and blessings, in a way that would *embrace all people until the end of time*. So it is only "the Islam" which the Prophet Muḥammad preached that is approved by God as the true religion: *Say (O Messenger): "We have believed in God (without associating any partners with Him), and that which has been sent down on us, and that which was sent down on Abraham, Ishmael, Isaac, Jacob, and the Prophets who were raised in the tribes, and that which was given to Moses, Jesus, and all other Prophets from their Lord; we make no distinction between any of them (in believing), and we are Muslims (submitted to Him exclusively). Whoever seeks as religion other than Islam, it will never be accepted from him, and in the Hereafter he will be among the losers"* (3: 84–85).

52   سُورَةُ آلِ عِمرَان   ٥٢

الَمْ تَرَ إِلَى الَّذِينَ أُوتُوا نَصِيبًا مِّنَ الْكِتَابِ يُدْعَوْنَ
إِلَى كِتَابِ اللَّهِ لِيَحْكُمَ بَيْنَهُمْ ثُمَّ يَتَوَلَّى فَرِيقٌ مِّنْهُمْ وَهُم
مُّعْرِضُونَ ۝ ذَلِكَ بِأَنَّهُمْ قَالُوا لَن تَمَسَّنَا النَّارُ إِلَّا أَيَّامًا
مَّعْدُودَاتٍ وَغَرَّهُمْ فِي دِينِهِم مَّا كَانُوا يَفْتَرُونَ ۝ فَكَيْفَ
إِذَا جَمَعْنَاهُمْ لِيَوْمٍ لَّا رَيْبَ فِيهِ وَوُفِّيَتْ كُلُّ نَفْسٍ مَّا كَسَبَتْ
وَهُمْ لَا يُظْلَمُونَ ۝ قُلِ اللَّهُمَّ مَالِكَ الْمُلْكِ تُؤْتِي الْمُلْكَ
مَن تَشَاءُ وَتَنزِعُ الْمُلْكَ مِمَّن تَشَاءُ وَتُعِزُّ مَن تَشَاءُ وَتُذِلُّ
مَن تَشَاءُ بِيَدِكَ الْخَيْرُ إِنَّكَ عَلَى كُلِّ شَيْءٍ قَدِيرٌ ۝ تُولِجُ اللَّيْلَ
فِي النَّهَارِ وَتُولِجُ النَّهَارَ فِي اللَّيْلِ وَتُخْرِجُ الْحَيَّ مِنَ الْمَيِّتِ وَتُخْرِجُ
الْمَيِّتَ مِنَ الْحَيِّ وَتَرْزُقُ مَن تَشَاءُ بِغَيْرِ حِسَابٍ ۝ لَّا يَتَّخِذِ
الْمُؤْمِنُونَ الْكَافِرِينَ أَوْلِيَاءَ مِن دُونِ الْمُؤْمِنِينَ وَمَن يَفْعَلْ ذَلِكَ
فَلَيْسَ مِنَ اللَّهِ فِي شَيْءٍ إِلَّا أَن تَتَّقُوا مِنْهُمْ تُقَاةً
وَيُحَذِّرُكُمُ اللَّهُ نَفْسَهُ وَإِلَى اللَّهِ الْمَصِيرُ ۝ قُلْ إِن تُخْفُوا مَا فِي
صُدُورِكُمْ أَوْ تُبْدُوهُ يَعْلَمْهُ اللَّهُ وَيَعْلَمُ مَا فِي السَّمَاوَاتِ
وَمَا فِي الْأَرْضِ وَاللَّهُ عَلَى كُلِّ شَيْءٍ قَدِيرٌ ۝

---

23. Do you not consider those who were given a portion from the Book? They are called to the Book of God to judge between them, and then, (after the judgment was given,) a party of them turn away in aversion.

24. (They venture to do so) because they claim: "The Fire will not touch us at all, except for a certain number of days." (The false beliefs) that they used to invent have deluded them in their religion.

25. How then will they fare when We gather them all together for a (terrible) Day about (the coming of) which there is no doubt, and when every soul will be repaid in full for what it earned (while in the world), and none will be wronged?

26. Say: "O God, Master of all dominion! You give dominion to whom You will, and take away dominion from whom You will, and You exalt whom You will, and abase whom You will; in Your hand is all good; surely You have full power over everything.

27. "You make the night pass into the day and You make the day pass into the night, (and so make each grow longer or shorter); You bring forth the living out of the dead, and You bring the dead out of the living, and You provide whomever You will without reckoning."

28. Let not the believers take the unbelievers for friends, guardians, and councilors in preference to the believers. Whoever does that is not on a way from God and has no connection with Him, unless it be to protect yourselves against them and take precautions (against the danger of being persecuted and forced to turn away from your Religion or betray your community, or of losing your life). And God warns you that you beware of Himself; and to God is the homecoming.[5]

29. Say (to the believers): "Whether you keep secret what is in your bosoms or reveal it, God knows it. He knows whatever is in the heavens and whatever is on the earth. God has full power over everything."

5. This verse does not forbid believers to treat others well; even if the others are unbelievers, the believers should do good to them. Obeying the law, remaining faithful to promises and covenants, earnestness and trustworthiness in transactions, doing good for others and showing mercy, are all requirements of the faith. But believers cannot prefer unbelievers, especially if they are openly hostile to Islam and to Muslims, in the deputation of their affairs, nor take them as confidants, councilors, governors, or friends. They cannot establish a relationship with them in a way that will harm Islam or the Muslim community. Only in order to protect Islam, the Muslim community, and their sacred values, and only in cases of imminent danger of being wronged and persecuted, can they take them for intimate friends and guardians, and only provided that their hearts are wholly content with faith (16: 106). However, this kind of relationship requires that the limits set by God should be observed.

يَوْمَ تَجِدُ كُلُّ نَفْسٍ مَّا عَمِلَتْ مِنْ خَيْرٍ مُّحْضَرًا وَمَا عَمِلَتْ مِن سُوٓءٍ
تَوَدُّ لَوْ أَنَّ بَيْنَهَا وَبَيْنَهُۥٓ أَمَدًۢا بَعِيدًا وَيُحَذِّرُكُمُ اللَّهُ نَفْسَهُۥ
وَاللَّهُ رَءُوفٌۢ بِالْعِبَادِ ۝ قُلْ إِن كُنتُمْ تُحِبُّونَ اللَّهَ فَاتَّبِعُونِى
يُحْبِبْكُمُ اللَّهُ وَيَغْفِرْ لَكُمْ ذُنُوبَكُمْ وَاللَّهُ غَفُورٌ
رَّحِيمٌ ۝ قُلْ أَطِيعُوا اللَّهَ وَالرَّسُولَ فَإِن تَوَلَّوْا فَإِنَّ اللَّهَ لَا يُحِبُّ
الْكَٰفِرِينَ ۝ إِنَّ اللَّهَ اصْطَفَىٰٓ ءَادَمَ وَنُوحًا وَءَالَ إِبْرَٰهِيمَ
وَءَالَ عِمْرَٰنَ عَلَى الْعَٰلَمِينَ ۝ ذُرِّيَّةًۢ بَعْضُهَا مِنۢ بَعْضٍ
وَاللَّهُ سَمِيعٌ عَلِيمٌ ۝ إِذْ قَالَتِ امْرَأَتُ عِمْرَٰنَ رَبِّ إِنِّى نَذَرْتُ
لَكَ مَا فِى بَطْنِى مُحَرَّرًا فَتَقَبَّلْ مِنِّىٓ إِنَّكَ أَنتَ السَّمِيعُ الْعَلِيمُ
فَلَمَّا وَضَعَتْهَا قَالَتْ رَبِّ إِنِّى وَضَعْتُهَآ أُنثَىٰ وَاللَّهُ أَعْلَمُ بِمَا
وَضَعَتْ وَلَيْسَ الذَّكَرُ كَالْأُنثَىٰ وَإِنِّى سَمَّيْتُهَا مَرْيَمَ وَإِنِّىٓ أُعِيذُهَا بِكَ
وَذُرِّيَّتَهَا مِنَ الشَّيْطَٰنِ الرَّجِيمِ ۝ فَتَقَبَّلَهَا رَبُّهَا بِقَبُولٍ
حَسَنٍ وَأَنۢبَتَهَا نَبَاتًا حَسَنًا وَكَفَّلَهَا زَكَرِيَّا كُلَّمَا دَخَلَ عَلَيْهَا
زَكَرِيَّا الْمِحْرَابَ وَجَدَ عِندَهَا رِزْقًا قَالَ يَٰمَرْيَمُ أَنَّىٰ لَكِ هَٰذَا قَالَتْ
هُوَ مِنْ عِندِ اللَّهِ إِنَّ اللَّهَ يَرْزُقُ مَن يَشَآءُ بِغَيْرِ حِسَابٍ ۝

---

30. The Day when every soul will find whatever good it has done brought forward, and whatever evil it has done. It will wish that there were a far space between it and that evil. God warns you that you beware of Himself; and God is All-Pitying for the servants.

31. Say (to them, O Messenger): "If you indeed love God, then follow me, so that God will love you and forgive you your sins." God is All-Forgiving, All-Compassionate.[6]

32. Say (again): "Obey God, and the Messenger." If they still turn away, (then know that only the unbelievers turn away from this call, and let them know that) God does not love the unbelievers.

33. (They refuse faith in you and some of the Prophets because you did not appear among them, but God favors whomever He wishes with Messengership, and) God made pure Adam and Noah and the House of Abraham and the House of 'Imrān, choosing them above all humankind,

34. As descendants of one another, (and they were following the same way. Therefore, do not, in respect of believing in them as Prophets, make any distinction between the Prophets and do not think or speak ill of God's preference). God is All-Hearing, All-Knowing.[7]

35. (Remember) when the wife of 'Imrān entreated: "My Lord, I have dedicated that which is in my womb to Your exclusive service. Accept it, then, from me. Surely You are the All-Hearing, the All-Knowing."

36. When she was delivered of it she said: "My Lord, I have given birth to a female." – God knew best of what she was delivered, (so she did not need to be sorry, because) the male child (she expected) could not be the same as (the) female child (whom We bestowed on her and would honor with a great favor). – I have named her Mary and commend her and her offspring to You for protection from Satan eternally rejected (from God's Mercy)."

37. (In response to her mother's sincerity and purity of intention in dedicating the child,) her Lord accepted her with gracious favor and enabled to her a good growth (upbringing), and entrusted her to the care of Zachariah. Whenever Zachariah went in to her in the Sanctuary, he found her provided with food. "Mary," he asked, "how does this come to you?" "From God," she answered. Truly God provides to whomever He wills without reckoning.

6. This verse alone would be enough to proclaim the infallibility of God's Messenger, upon him be peace and blessings, and the importance of following his Sunnah, even if there were no other verse of equal importance.

Love is the very substance of existence and the link amongst all its parts. With all His essential Qualities originating in His very Essence, and Attributes, Names and acts, the Creator of existence is absolutely perfect. Any perfection is loved because of itself. Since God is All-Perfect and the source of all perfection in existence, He is worthy of love above everything else. Being the All-Loving, He loves Himself in a way suitable for His all-sacred and all-holy Essence. This love is the origin of existence or the universe. That is, due to His sacred love of Himself, He has created the universe and loves all of His creatures beyond all comparison. This infinite love is focused, first of all, on the Prophet Muhammad, upon him be peace and blessings, as he is both the seed and most illustrious fruit of creation; one who has manifested God with his whole life and the religion he preached. He made God known to people and loved by them, thus realizing the purpose for God's creation of the universe. Humanity has the loftiest position and is expected to respond to God's love of creatures, including, in particular, humanity itself, with a recognition and love for Him. Love of God requires loving His most beloved servant and Messenger – the Prophet Muhammad – because the door to the love of God opens through him. Loving him shows itself by following him and designing one's life according to the religion he preached. People cannot be sincere in their claim of love unless they follow the practices of the Prophet Muhammad in their daily life and practice Islam. The following verse confirms this point.

7. Muslim scholars, such as Muhyi'd-dīn ibn al-'Arabī and Bediüzzaman Said Nursi compare creation to a tree. A tree grows from a seed. This seed contains the laws God has established to govern the future life of the tree. The program and the general future form of the tree, with all its parts, are also encapsulated

or encoded in the seed. The main substance or essence of the tree encoded or encapsulated in the seed is gradually refined and develops until it yields fruit. Just as the life of a tree begins with and ends in a seed, humanity is not only the fruit, but also the seed of the Tree of Creation.

The roots of the Tree of Creation are in the heavens. This Tree first produced its main two branches as the spiritual/metaphysical and material/physical worlds. The physical worlds are divided into two: the heavens and the earth, each being filled with its own inhabitants. The Tree of Creation finally yielded humanity as the main fruit.

Since the fruit contains the seed, and the seed, as pointed out above, contains all the characteristics of the tree, this means that in addition to humanity having particular aspects, such as will-power and speech as a developed system of communication, it also has both angelic and satanic, heavenly and earthly, elemental, vegetable, and animal aspects.

Although a tree yields much fruit, it grows from a single seed. Since humanity is endowed with free will and human beings vary in capacity, there are among them as many degrees in mental and spiritual progress as there are human beings. The Prophets are the most developed and perfect among human beings, these fruits of the Tree of Creation. They descended from the Families of Abraham and 'Imrān, the two being related, and their history dates back to Noah and Adam. Therefore, all the Prophets are the descendants of Adam, and after him, Noah, and after him, they are from the family of Abraham and the family of 'Imrān. The family of 'Imrān was the family from which Jesus descended, while the family of Abraham is that from which the Prophet Muhammad came. The chain of the Prophets was selected among all of humanity and finally, at the point of greatest perfection and purity, ended in the Prophet Muhammad, upon him be peace and blessings. This means that as the Prophet Muhammad is the most perfect and the purest fruit of the Tree of Creation, his nature and essence is the seed of the Tree of Creation.

The fact that the Prophets are the descendants of one another does not mean that one family or dynasty is given priority. The line to which the Prophets belong spreads throughout the Tree of Creation; in this way one or more Prophets came to every people. This is made quite clear in the Qur'ān, which declares that God will not punish a people unless He has raised a Prophet among them (17: 15) and that He raised almost every Prophet among his own people (26: 106, 124, 142, 161, 176).

The fact that all of the Prophets, upon them be peace, are pure and are chosen above all other people makes them distinguished by certain important qualities or characteristics, known as the characteristics of the Prophets. These characteristics are: absolute truthfulness and trustworthiness, intellect and sagacity to the highest degree, sinlessness, communication of the Divine Message, and being exempt from all mental and bodily defects (*The Messenger of God*, 43).

هُنَالِكَ دَعَا زَكَرِيَّا رَبَّهُ قَالَ رَبِّ هَبْ لِى مِن لَّدُنكَ ذُرِّيَّةً
طَيِّبَةً إِنَّكَ سَمِيعُ الدُّعَآءِ ۞ فَنَادَتْهُ الْمَلَٰٓئِكَةُ وَهُوَ
قَآئِمٌ يُصَلِّى فِى الْمِحْرَابِ أَنَّ اللَّهَ يُبَشِّرُكَ بِيَحْيَىٰ مُصَدِّقًا
بِكَلِمَةٍ مِّنَ اللَّهِ وَسَيِّدًا وَحَصُورًا وَنَبِيًّا مِّنَ
الصَّالِحِينَ ۞ قَالَ رَبِّ أَنَّىٰ يَكُونُ لِى غُلَٰمٌ وَقَدْ بَلَغَنِىَ الْكِبَرُ
وَامْرَأَتِى عَاقِرٌ قَالَ كَذَٰلِكَ اللَّهُ يَفْعَلُ مَا يَشَآءُ ۞ قَالَ
رَبِّ اجْعَل لِّى ءَايَةً قَالَ ءَايَتُكَ أَلَّا تُكَلِّمَ النَّاسَ ثَلَٰثَةَ أَيَّامٍ
إِلَّا رَمْزًا وَاذْكُر رَّبَّكَ كَثِيرًا وَسَبِّحْ بِالْعَشِيِّ وَالْإِبْكَٰرِ ۞
وَإِذْ قَالَتِ الْمَلَٰٓئِكَةُ يَٰمَرْيَمُ إِنَّ اللَّهَ اصْطَفَىٰكِ وَطَهَّرَكِ
وَاصْطَفَىٰكِ عَلَىٰ نِسَآءِ الْعَٰلَمِينَ ۞ يَٰمَرْيَمُ اقْنُتِى
لِرَبِّكِ وَاسْجُدِى وَارْكَعِى مَعَ الرَّٰكِعِينَ ۞ ذَٰلِكَ مِنْ أَنۢبَآءِ الْغَيْبِ
نُوحِيهِ إِلَيْكَ وَمَا كُنتَ لَدَيْهِمْ إِذْ يُلْقُونَ أَقْلَٰمَهُمْ أَيُّهُمْ
يَكْفُلُ مَرْيَمَ وَمَا كُنتَ لَدَيْهِمْ إِذْ يَخْتَصِمُونَ ۞ إِذْ قَالَتِ
الْمَلَٰٓئِكَةُ يَٰمَرْيَمُ إِنَّ اللَّهَ يُبَشِّرُكِ بِكَلِمَةٍ مِّنْهُ اسْمُهُ الْمَسِيحُ
عِيسَى ابْنُ مَرْيَمَ وَجِيهًا فِى الدُّنْيَا وَالْآخِرَةِ وَمِنَ الْمُقَرَّبِينَ ۞

38. At that point, Zachariah turned to his Lord in prayer and said: "My Lord, bestow upon me out of Your grace a good, upright offspring. Truly, You are the All-Hearing of prayer."

39. It was when he stood praying in the Sanctuary after some time that the angels called to him: "God gives you the glad tidings of John to confirm a Word from God, and as one lordly, perfectly chaste, a Prophet, among the righteous."

40. "Lord," said he (Zachariah), "How shall I have a son when old age has overtaken me, and my wife is barren?" "Just so," he (the angel) said, "God does whatever He wills."

41. "Lord," he (Zachariah) entreated, "appoint a sign for me." "Your sign," He said, "is that you will not be able to speak to people for three days except by gesture. And (meanwhile) remember and mention your Lord much and glorify Him in the afternoon and the early hours of morning."

42. And (in due time came the moment) when the angels said: "Mary, God has chosen you and made you pure, and exalted you above all the women in the world.

43. "Mary, be devoutly obedient to your Lord, prostrate and bow (in the Prayer and devotion to Him) with those who bow!"

44. (O Messenger!) That is of the tidings of the things of the unseen (the things that took place in the past and have remained hidden from people with all their truth), which We reveal to you, for you were not present with them when they drew lots with their pens about who should have charge of Mary; nor were you present with them when they were disputing (about the matter).

45. And (remember) when the angels said: "Mary, God gives you the glad tidings of a Word from Him, to be called the Messiah, Jesus son of Mary, highly honored in the world and the Hereafter, and one of those near-stationed to God.

وَيُكَلِّمُ ٱلنَّاسَ فِي ٱلْمَهْدِ وَكَهْلًا وَمِنَ ٱلصَّالِحِينَ ۝ قَالَتْ رَبِّ أَنَّىٰ يَكُونُ لِي وَلَدٌ وَلَمْ يَمْسَسْنِي بَشَرٌ قَالَ كَذَٰلِكِ ٱللَّهُ يَخْلُقُ مَا يَشَاءُ إِذَا قَضَىٰ أَمْرًا فَإِنَّمَا يَقُولُ لَهُ كُنْ فَيَكُونُ ۝ وَيُعَلِّمُهُ ٱلْكِتَابَ وَٱلْحِكْمَةَ وَٱلتَّوْرَاةَ وَٱلْإِنْجِيلَ ۝ وَرَسُولًا إِلَىٰ بَنِي إِسْرَائِيلَ أَنِّي قَدْ جِئْتُكُم بِآيَةٍ مِّن رَّبِّكُمْ أَنِّي أَخْلُقُ لَكُم مِّنَ ٱلطِّينِ كَهَيْئَةِ ٱلطَّيْرِ فَأَنفُخُ فِيهِ فَيَكُونُ طَيْرًا بِإِذْنِ ٱللَّهِ وَأُبْرِئُ ٱلْأَكْمَهَ وَٱلْأَبْرَصَ وَأُحْيِ ٱلْمَوْتَىٰ بِإِذْنِ ٱللَّهِ وَأُنَبِّئُكُم بِمَا تَأْكُلُونَ وَمَا تَدَّخِرُونَ فِي بُيُوتِكُمْ إِنَّ فِي ذَٰلِكَ لَآيَةً لَّكُمْ إِن كُنتُم مُّؤْمِنِينَ ۝ وَمُصَدِّقًا لِّمَا بَيْنَ يَدَيَّ مِنَ ٱلتَّوْرَاةِ وَلِأُحِلَّ لَكُم بَعْضَ ٱلَّذِي حُرِّمَ عَلَيْكُمْ وَجِئْتُكُم بِآيَةٍ مِّن رَّبِّكُمْ فَٱتَّقُوا ٱللَّهَ وَأَطِيعُونِ ۝ إِنَّ ٱللَّهَ رَبِّي وَرَبُّكُمْ فَٱعْبُدُوهُ هَٰذَا صِرَاطٌ مُّسْتَقِيمٌ ۝ فَلَمَّا أَحَسَّ عِيسَىٰ مِنْهُمُ ٱلْكُفْرَ قَالَ مَنْ أَنصَارِي إِلَى ٱللَّهِ قَالَ ٱلْحَوَارِيُّونَ نَحْنُ أَنصَارُ ٱللَّهِ آمَنَّا بِٱللَّهِ وَٱشْهَدْ بِأَنَّا مُسْلِمُونَ ۝

to the Children of Israel (saying to them, by way of explaining his mission): 'Assuredly I have come to you with a clear proof from your Lord: I fashion for you out of clay something in the shape of a bird, then I breathe into it, and it becomes a bird by God's leave. And I heal the blind from birth and the leper, and I revive the dead, by God's leave. And I inform you of what things you eat, and what you store up in your houses. Surely in this is a clear proof for you (demonstrating that I am a Messenger of God), if you are sincere believers (as you claim.)[8]

50. 'And confirming (the truth contained in) the Torah that was revealed before me, and to make lawful for you certain things that had been forbidden to you. Be sure that I have come to you with a clear proof (demonstrating that I am a Messenger of God) from your Lord. So keep from disobedience to God in due reverence for Him and piety, and obey me.

51. 'Surely, God is my Lord and your Lord, so worship Him. This is a straight path (to follow).' "[9]

52. (Having preached his message in this way for a long time) Jesus perceived their willful persistence in unbelief (and open hostility), and called out: "Who will be my helpers (on this way) to God?" The disciples answered: "We are the helpers of God('s cause). We believe in God, and (we call you to) bear witness that we are Muslims (submitted to Him exclusively).

---

46. "He will speak to people in the cradle and in manhood, and he is of the righteous."

47. "Lord," said Mary, "how shall I have a son seeing no mortal has ever touched me?" "That is how it is," he (the Spirit who appeared before her) said, "God creates whatever He wills; when He decrees a thing, He does but say to it 'Be!' and it is.

48. "And He will teach him the Book and the Wisdom – and the Torah and the Gospel,

49. "(And He will make him) a Messenger

---

8. While explaining the meaning of the Names taught to Adam, it was pointed out (note 32 to the previous *sūrah*) that the knowledge of things was given to Adam in a summarized form and was taught to the Messengers in relative details during the course of history according to the mission of each. This is why the

Messengers also became the forerunners in scientific knowledge and progress, in addition to their being guides in spirituality and morality. The knowledge given to the Prophets to make them the forerunners in scientific knowledge and progress was usually manifested as miracles. The miracles a Prophet worked, by God's leave, usually concerned the science that was being studied the most at that time. So, just as the miracles left the scientists of the time helpless in creating a similar miracle, they also marked the final point of progress which that science would be able to realize by the Last Day.

Through Jesus' miracles, such as healing the congenitally blind and the lepers, or in bringing the dead back to life by His leave, God Almighty means:

> I gave two gifts to one of My servants who renounced the world for My sake: the remedy for spiritual ailments, and the cure for physical sicknesses. Dead hearts were quickened through the light of guidance, and sick people, who were like the dead, found health through his breath and cure. You may find the cure for all illnesses in My "pharmacy" in nature, where I attached many important purposes to each thing. Work and find it. (*The Words*, "the 20th Word," 268)

Thus, this verse marks the final point of medical development, which is far ahead of the present level, and urges us towards it.

The Prophetic Traditions that inform us that Jesus will return to the world towards the end of time suggest that the science of medicine will be in great demand and will have realized significant progress. The community of believers who will represent the Messianic spirit at that time will have to not only revive the dead hearts with the light of faith, but also find cures for almost every illness.

Jesus' insistence on repeating "by God's leave" while presenting his miracles is a serious warning that it is not Jesus who created all such miracles, rather it is God, underlining the fact that Jesus is only a human being, not a deity or son of a deity.

9. The verses both refute those among the Jews who rejected the Prophethood of Jesus and reject the "divinity" of Jesus or relationship of a "son" that is claimed by some Christians. If he had been an imposter, not designated by God, Jesus would surely have attempted to make use of his miracles to found an independent religion. He believed in, and confirmed, the validity of the teachings of the original religion preached by the earlier Prophets. This is also clear in his statements in the existing Gospels: "Do not think not that I came to destroy the Law or the Prophets: I did not come to destroy but to fulfill" (*Matthew*, 5: 17). When a Jewish lawyer asked, "Teacher, which *is* the great commandment in the Law?" he replied: "You shall love the Lord your God with all your heart, and with all your soul, and with all your mind. This is *the* first and great commandment. And the second *is* like it, You shall love your neighbor as yourself. On these two commandments hang all the Law and the Prophets" (*Ibid.*, 22: 35–40).

The fundamental points of Jesus' mission were the same as those of the other Prophets and were as follows:

- Humanity should believe, first of all, in the Existence and Oneness of God, and acknowledge His exclusive sovereignty, which demands absolute service and obedience to Him.
- Humanity should obey the Prophets since they have been designated by God to convey His religion.
- God also establishes the law which orders human life.

56

٥٦

رَبَّنَا آمَنَّا بِمَا أَنزَلْتَ وَاتَّبَعْنَا الرَّسُولَ فَاكْتُبْنَا مَعَ الشَّاهِدِينَ ۝ وَمَكَرُوا وَمَكَرَ اللَّهُ وَاللَّهُ خَيْرُ الْمَاكِرِينَ ۝ إِذْ قَالَ اللَّهُ يَا عِيسَى إِنِّي مُتَوَفِّيكَ وَرَافِعُكَ إِلَيَّ وَمُطَهِّرُكَ مِنَ الَّذِينَ كَفَرُوا وَجَاعِلُ الَّذِينَ اتَّبَعُوكَ فَوْقَ الَّذِينَ كَفَرُوا إِلَى يَوْمِ الْقِيَامَةِ ثُمَّ إِلَيَّ مَرْجِعُكُمْ فَأَحْكُمُ بَيْنَكُمْ فِيمَا كُنتُمْ فِيهِ تَخْتَلِفُونَ ۝ فَأَمَّا الَّذِينَ كَفَرُوا فَأُعَذِّبُهُمْ عَذَابًا شَدِيدًا فِي الدُّنْيَا وَالْآخِرَةِ وَمَا لَهُم مِّن نَّاصِرِينَ ۝ وَأَمَّا الَّذِينَ آمَنُوا وَعَمِلُوا الصَّالِحَاتِ فَيُوَفِّيهِمْ أُجُورَهُمْ وَاللَّهُ لَا يُحِبُّ الظَّالِمِينَ ۝ ذَلِكَ نَتْلُوهُ عَلَيْكَ مِنَ الْآيَاتِ وَالذِّكْرِ الْحَكِيمِ ۝ إِنَّ مَثَلَ عِيسَى عِندَ اللَّهِ كَمَثَلِ آدَمَ خَلَقَهُ مِن تُرَابٍ ثُمَّ قَالَ لَهُ كُن فَيَكُونُ ۝ الْحَقُّ مِن رَّبِّكَ فَلَا تَكُن مِّنَ الْمُمْتَرِينَ ۝ فَمَنْ حَاجَّكَ فِيهِ مِن بَعْدِ مَا جَاءَكَ مِنَ الْعِلْمِ فَقُلْ تَعَالَوْا نَدْعُ أَبْنَاءَنَا وَأَبْنَاءَكُمْ وَنِسَاءَنَا وَنِسَاءَكُمْ وَأَنفُسَنَا وَأَنفُسَكُمْ ثُمَّ نَبْتَهِلْ فَنَجْعَل لَّعْنَتَ اللَّهِ عَلَى الْكَاذِبِينَ ۝

---

self) and raise you up to Myself, and will purify you of (the groundless slanders of) those who disbelieve, and set your followers above those who disbelieve until the Day of Resurrection.[10] Then to Me you will all return, and I will judge between you concerning all that on which you were used to differ.

56. "As for those who disbelieve, I will punish them with a severe punishment in the world and the Hereafter; and they will have no helpers (against My punishment).

57. "As for those who believe and do good, righteous deeds, He will pay their rewards in full. God does not love the wrongdoers (and Himself never does wrong)."

58. Thus (O Messenger,) all this that We recite to you consists of Revelations and is from the Wise Reminder (the Qur'ān).

59. (The creation of) Jesus in reference to God resembles (the creation of) Adam. He created him from earth, then said He to him, "Be!" and he is.[11]

60. (As the truth always consists in what your Lord wills and decrees,) so is this the truth from your Lord (in this matter); do not then be, (and you are never expected to be,) of those who doubt.

61. After the (true) knowledge has come to you, whoever still disputes with you about him (Jesus), say (in challenging them): "Come, then! Let us summon our sons and your sons, and our women and your women, our selves and your selves, and then let us pray and invoke God's curse upon those who lie."

---

53. "Our Lord! We believe in what You have sent down and we follow the Messenger, so write us down among the witnesses (of Your Oneness and Lordship, and of the truth You have revealed)."

54. And they (the unbelievers) schemed (against Jesus), but God put His will into effect (and brought their scheme to nothing). God wills what is the best (for His believing servants) and makes His will prevail.

55. (It was part of His executing His will) when God said: "Jesus, (as your mission has ended) I will take you back (to My-

---

10. Like his coming into the world, Jesus' departure from the world was unusual. He did not die as other people do, but God took back his spirit and body, which took on the form of, or changed into, an "astral" body. This can

be analogous with the Ascension of Prophet Muḥammad, upon him be peace and blessings. However, while Prophet Muḥammad returned to the world again to complete his mission, Jesus did not return, leaving the completion of his mission to a time just before the Last Day. (Also refer to the note 31 in *Sūrat an-Nisā'*.)

The Divine will that Jesus' followers will be above the unbelievers until the Day of Judgment has two meanings:

- The people of pure monotheism, including primarily the community of Muḥammad, will generally be above the unbelievers until the Day of Resurrection. (Such rules are general, having certain exceptions, but an exception does not nullify the rule.)
- Those who believe and follow Jesus, even with some errors and deviations, will generally be above the Jews who reject him.

History has confirmed this Divine will for 2000 years and will continue to do so until the Last Day.

11. The particles or atoms that formed Adam's body existed in the ground, water and air. As mentioned in note 7 above, the essence of humanity, which constitutes the essence or seed of the Tree of Creation, was inherent in the "roots, trunk," and the "main branches" of the corporeal and immaterial worlds during the process of its continual refinement. The corporeal or visible world ramified into the branches of the heavens and the earth. As understood from a supplication of the Prophet Muḥammad, which contains, "All-Glorified is He Who has laid soil over a fluid solidified," the earth was initially a hot fluid. The fluid was later solidified into a rock stratum and formed a crust. The rock stratum crumbled over a long period, and the soil stratum was formed. This stratum was prepared for life with rain that descended from the direction of the heaven. The essence or seed of the Tree of Creation, which under-

went a continual process of refinement, during which it grew into many worlds inhabited by animate and inanimate beings that are particular to each, yielded the elements, vegetables, and animals as its twigs, leaves, and blossoms, each of which serve the other as source or main material in coming into existence and as food for its survival. At the final point of the refinement process and as the fruit of the Tree of Creation on the branch of the earth, God created Adam and Eve. The verse, *Did there pass (– and surely there passed –) over human a stretch of time when he was a thing not mentioned and remembered (as human)?* (76: 1, also see note 1) indicates this process of refinement during which the human essence existed at its center or origin, although there was as yet no mention of humanity.

In order to remove the doubts concerning creation which existed at that time (and still continue to exist in different forms today), as well as to balance the Jewish materialism with an accurate spiritualism of the Divine Religion, and to demonstrate His Will and Power in a more obvious way, God created Jesus as He had created Adam. Out of the same elements from which He fashioned Adam in the "womb" of the earth, He fashioned Jesus in the womb of a virgin. The difference between this type of fashioning and the fashioning of other humans is that God, out of wisdom, uses sperm in the creation of the latter.

While narrating Adam's creation, the verse uses the past tense, but concludes with "*fe-yekūn*," meaning "becomes" or "is." This is done in order to stress that it is God alone Who creates and gives life; nothing else plays any part. This is the same for all living beings, including Adam and Jesus. The verse also implies that God creates every thing and every being separately and individually.

ٱلْجُزْءُ الثَّالِث   ٥٧   57

إِنَّ هَٰذَا لَهُوَ ٱلْقَصَصُ ٱلْحَقُّ ۚ وَمَا مِنْ إِلَٰهٍ إِلَّا ٱللَّهُ ۚ وَإِنَّ ٱللَّهَ
لَهُوَ ٱلْعَزِيزُ ٱلْحَكِيمُ ۞ فَإِن تَوَلَّوْا۟ فَإِنَّ ٱللَّهَ عَلِيمٌۢ بِٱلْمُفْسِدِينَ
۞ قُلْ يَٰٓأَهْلَ ٱلْكِتَٰبِ تَعَالَوْا۟ إِلَىٰ كَلِمَةٍ سَوَآءٍۭ بَيْنَنَا
وَبَيْنَكُمْ أَلَّا نَعْبُدَ إِلَّا ٱللَّهَ وَلَا نُشْرِكَ بِهِۦ شَيْـًٔا وَلَا
يَتَّخِذَ بَعْضُنَا بَعْضًا أَرْبَابًا مِّن دُونِ ٱللَّهِ ۚ فَإِن تَوَلَّوْا۟
فَقُولُوا۟ ٱشْهَدُوا۟ بِأَنَّا مُسْلِمُونَ ۞ يَٰٓأَهْلَ ٱلْكِتَٰبِ لِمَ تُحَآجُّونَ
فِىٓ إِبْرَٰهِيمَ وَمَآ أُنزِلَتِ ٱلتَّوْرَىٰةُ وَٱلْإِنجِيلُ إِلَّا مِنۢ بَعْدِهِۦٓ ۚ أَفَلَا
تَعْقِلُونَ ۞ هَٰٓأَنتُمْ هَٰٓؤُلَآءِ حَٰجَجْتُمْ فِيمَا لَكُم بِهِۦ عِلْمٌ فَلِمَ
تُحَآجُّونَ فِيمَا لَيْسَ لَكُم بِهِۦ عِلْمٌ ۚ وَٱللَّهُ يَعْلَمُ وَأَنتُمْ
لَا تَعْلَمُونَ ۞ مَا كَانَ إِبْرَٰهِيمُ يَهُودِيًّا وَلَا نَصْرَانِيًّا وَلَٰكِن
كَانَ حَنِيفًا مُّسْلِمًا وَمَا كَانَ مِنَ ٱلْمُشْرِكِينَ ۞ إِنَّ أَوْلَى ٱلنَّاسِ
بِإِبْرَٰهِيمَ لَلَّذِينَ ٱتَّبَعُوهُ وَهَٰذَا ٱلنَّبِىُّ وَٱلَّذِينَ ءَامَنُوا۟ ۗ وَٱللَّهُ
وَلِىُّ ٱلْمُؤْمِنِينَ ۞ وَدَّت طَّآئِفَةٌ مِّنْ أَهْلِ ٱلْكِتَٰبِ لَوْ يُضِلُّونَكُمْ
وَمَا يُضِلُّونَ إِلَّآ أَنفُسَهُمْ وَمَا يَشْعُرُونَ ۞ يَٰٓأَهْلَ
ٱلْكِتَٰبِ لِمَ تَكْفُرُونَ بِـَٔايَٰتِ ٱللَّهِ وَأَنتُمْ تَشْهَدُونَ ۞

---

62. This is indeed the true narrative; and there is no deity but God, and truly God is the All-Glorious with irresistible might, the All-Wise.

63. If they (still) turn away, be assured that God has full knowledge of those engaged in causing disorder and corruption.

64. Say (to them, O Messenger): "O People of the Book, come to a word common between us and you, that we worship none but God, and associate none as partner with Him, and that none of us take others for Lords, apart from God." If they (still) turn away, then say: "Bear witness that we are Muslims (submitted to Him exclusively)."[12]

65. O People of the Book (Jews and Christians)! Why do you dispute concern-ing Abraham (whether he was a Jew or a Christian), when both the Torah and the Gospel were not sent down save after him? Will you ever not reason and understand?

66. Indeed, you are such people that you dispute concerning even a matter about which you have knowledge; why, then, should you dispute on a matter about which you have no knowledge? God knows, but you do not know.

67. Abraham was not a Jew, nor a Christian; but he was one pure of faith and Muslim (who submitted to God with a sound heart). He was never of those who associate partners with God.[13]

68. Surely those of humankind who have the best claim to relationship with Abraham are those who followed him (during the term of his mission), and this (most illustrious) Prophet, and those (in his company) who believe. God is the guardian of the believers (to Whom they can entrust their affairs and on Whom they can rely).

69. A party of the People of the Book wish that they could lead you astray; yet they lead none astray except themselves, but they do not perceive (that this is so).

70. O People of the Book! Why do you disbelieve[14] in God's Revelations (the clear proofs of truth), when you yourselves bear witness (to their truth in your own Books)?

12. This call, made by Islam 14 centuries ago to the People of the Book, is still being made to the People of the Book and people of learning today; it is of great significance, especially from the following viewpoints:

- In conveying Islam to others we should seek a common point on which to meet the audience. If it is worshipping One God without associating any partners with Him in relation to People of the Book, then when dealing with atheists it can be sharing the same human nature and destiny on the earth.

- Using an attractive, gentle style, and endearments are of great importance. If we can liken Islam to a magnificent palace that has as many roads to reach it as there are in the whole of creation and as many portals to enter it as there are human beings, then there is a door for each human being to enter it and what we must do is to be able to detect to whom we must show which door (*Kur'an'dan İdrake*, 109–110).

- Despite their deliberately refractory attitude, the Qur'ān does not cut off dialogue with the People of the Book and indicates that the common points should be given priority in this dialogue.

- "The verse has shown how various consciences, nations, religions, and books can unite in one essential conscience and word of truth, and how Islam has instructed the human realm in such a wide, open, and true path of salvation and law of freedom. It has been shown fully that this is not limited to Arab or non-Arab. Religious progress is possible not by narrow consciences or by being separate from one another, but by being universal and broad" (Yazır, 2: 1131–32).

- Worshipping God without associating any partners with Him in His Divinity and Lordship (His being the One Who nurtures, raises and trains all creation and the One Who has exclusive right to be worshipped and sole authority to establish the fundamental rules and principles to govern human life) is the primary condition of believing in One God and following His religion.

13. The Jews claimed that their religion was the true religion and therefore Abraham was a Jew, whereas the Christians claimed that their religion was the true one and therefore Abraham was a Christian. Naturally this was impossible. While they could not agree on several matters contained by their Books and the matters like that of Jesus, it was completely senseless that they made claims and disputed about matters about which they had no knowledge. It is impossible that Abraham should be a Jew or a Christian, because both the Torah and Gospel were revealed centuries after Abraham. So since there cannot be two true religions at the same time, either or both of Judaism and Christianity could be true. Historically, Judaism and Christianity are the names given to the religions revealed to Moses and Jesus respectively by either their followers or opponents centuries later. So, Abraham was neither a Jew nor a Christian but a Muslim who followed Islam, which is the unique Religion revealed by God to all the Prophets during history.

14. The Holy Qur'ān has broadened the meaning of many words and has introduced them as concepts. For this reason, it is almost impossible to render them in other languages with only one word. Such words require explanation or description when translated. The original of unbelief is "*kufr.*" It means concealing a truth and rejecting it willfully. In most cases, it originates in vainglory and egotism, obstinacy, mental and spiritual deviation, wrongdoing, having an incorrect viewpoint, seeking self-interest, and gratifying one's ambitions.

71. O People of the Book! Why do you confound the truth (by mixing it) with falsehood and conceal the truth knowingly?

72. (In attempting a trick on the believers,) a party of the People of the Book say (to each other): "Feign belief at the beginning of the day in what has been sent down upon those who believe, and disbelieve at the end of it, that they may thus (doubt their Religion and) turn back (to their former condition).

73. "But do not believe in any but him who follows your religion –Say (O Messenger): "Surely the only guidance is God's guidance"– that anyone should be given the like of what you were given, or that they should argue against you before your Lord." Say: "Surely all grace and bounty is in God's Hand; He gives it to whomever He wills." God is All-Embracing (with His Mercy), All-Knowing.

74. He singles out for His mercy (of favoring with Prophethood or another calling) whom He wills. God is of tremendous grace and bounty.

75. Among the People of the Book are some who, if you entrust them with a weight of treasure, restore it to you; and among them are some who, if you entrust them with one gold piece, do not restore it unless you keep standing over them. That is because they claim: "We have no responsibility towards the unlettered (those who do not have a Book like ours and follow our religion)." Thus they speak lies in attribution to God, and do so knowingly.

76. On the contrary (what God decrees is this): Whoever fulfills his pledge and keeps from disobedience to God in due reverence for Him and piety, surely God loves the God-revering, pious.

77. As to those who sell God's covenant and their oaths for a trifling price, there will be no share for them in the Hereafter; and God will not speak to them nor look upon them (with mercy) on the Day of Resurrection, nor will He purify them (of their sins to absolve them). And for them is a painful punishment.

وَإِنَّ مِنْهُمْ لَفَرِيقًا يَلْوُونَ أَلْسِنَتَهُم بِالْكِتَابِ لِتَحْسَبُوهُ مِنَ الْكِتَابِ وَمَا هُوَ مِنَ الْكِتَابِ وَيَقُولُونَ هُوَ مِنْ عِندِ اللّهِ وَمَا هُوَ مِنْ عِندِ اللّهِ وَيَقُولُونَ عَلَى اللّهِ الْكَذِبَ وَهُمْ يَعْلَمُونَ ۞ مَا كَانَ لِبَشَرٍ أَن يُؤْتِيَهُ اللّهُ الْكِتَابَ وَالْحُكْمَ وَالنُّبُوَّةَ ثُمَّ يَقُولَ لِلنَّاسِ كُونُوا عِبَادًا لِّي مِن دُونِ اللّهِ وَلَٰكِن كُونُوا رَبَّانِيِّينَ بِمَا كُنتُمْ تُعَلِّمُونَ الْكِتَابَ وَبِمَا كُنتُمْ تَدْرُسُونَ ۞ وَلَا يَأْمُرَكُمْ أَن تَتَّخِذُوا الْمَلَائِكَةَ وَالنَّبِيِّينَ أَرْبَابًا أَيَأْمُرُكُم بِالْكُفْرِ بَعْدَ إِذْ أَنتُم مُّسْلِمُونَ ۞ وَإِذْ أَخَذَ اللّهُ مِيثَاقَ النَّبِيِّينَ لَمَا آتَيْتُكُم مِّن كِتَابٍ وَحِكْمَةٍ ثُمَّ جَاءَكُمْ رَسُولٌ مُّصَدِّقٌ لِّمَا مَعَكُمْ لَتُؤْمِنُنَّ بِهِ وَلَتَنصُرُنَّهُ قَالَ ءَأَقْرَرْتُمْ وَأَخَذْتُمْ عَلَىٰ ذَٰلِكُمْ إِصْرِي قَالُوا أَقْرَرْنَا قَالَ فَاشْهَدُوا وَأَنَا مَعَكُم مِّنَ الشَّاهِدِينَ ۞ فَمَن تَوَلَّىٰ بَعْدَ ذَٰلِكَ فَأُولَٰئِكَ هُمُ الْفَاسِقُونَ ۞ أَفَغَيْرَ دِينِ اللّهِ يَبْغُونَ وَلَهُ أَسْلَمَ مَن فِي السَّمَاوَاتِ وَالْأَرْضِ طَوْعًا وَكَرْهًا وَإِلَيْهِ يُرْجَعُونَ ۞

78. And among them is a party twisting (the words of) the Book with their tongues (during their reading in order to distort its meaning), so that you may suppose it part of the Book, when it is not part of the Book; and they say it is from God's Presence, when it is not from God's Presence. They speak lies in attribution to God, and do so knowingly.

79. It is not (conceivable) that God should give a human being the Book, authority with sound, wise Judgment, and Prophethood, and then he should say to people: "Be servants to me, apart from God." Rather (he would say): "Be pure, dedicated servants of the Lord in that you teach the Book and in that you study it."

80. And he never commands you to take the angels and the Prophets for Lords. Would he command you to unbelief, when you have (answered his call and) become Muslims (submitted to God exclusively)?

81. And when God took compact with the Prophets: "That I have given you a Book and Wisdom; then there will come to you a Messenger confirming what (of the Divine Revelations) you already possess – you shall certainly believe in him and you shall certainly help him."[15] So saying, He asked: "Have you affirmed this and agreed to take up My burden (that I lay upon you) in this matter?" They answered: "We have affirmed (it)." He said: "Then bear witness (you and your communities), and I will be with you among the witnesses."

82. Then whoever after this turns away, those are the transgressors.

83. Do they now seek a religion other than God's, when to Him submits whoever is in the heavens and on the earth, willingly or unwillingly,[16] and to Him they are being returned?

15. In a general sense, a Prophet is one who receives Revelation from God and has the duty of communicating it to people. In this sense, Messengership is included in the meaning of Prophethood. In a more particular sense, a Prophet is one who receives Divine Revelation, and follows the Book and the Law that the Messenger prior to him brought or follows a contemporary Messenger, without himself having received a separate Book. What is meant by the Book in the verse must be the Book or the part of it to which a Prophet becomes heir. Every Messenger is also a Prophet, but not vice versa.

Prior to the Prophet Muhammad, upon him be peace and blessings, in former communities, there used to be several Prophets at the same time, even in the same place. When circumstances required a Messenger to come with a new Book, or Law, or some amendment, God sent one. After the Prophet Muhammad, upon him be peace and blessings, meticulous, pure scholars and great spiritual masters have carried on the mission of the Prophets, without, of course, receiving Revelation, and great "revivers," who combined both scholarship and spiritual mastery, have become heirs to the mission of Messengership. The saying, "The scholars of my community are like the Prophets of the Children of Israel," attributed to the Prophet Muhammad, is not reliable due to its chain of narration, but it still remains true in that scholars and spiritual masters have done what the previous Prophets and Messengers did, with the exception that there is no longer any need for a new Book to be sent. No scholar or spiritual master, however great and virtuous he may be, can be on the same level with a Prophet in virtue.

16. God has two kinds of laws, one related to the creation and operation of the universe, including each separate being, and to human (biological) life; the other established to govern human individual and social life. The former constitutes the subject matter of sciences (physics, chemistry, astronomy, biology, sociology, psychology, etc). Some aspects of human social life are also included in the scope of this kind of laws. For example, the fruit of working is usually wealth or success, while that of laziness is poverty. The second kind of laws can be summed up as being religion. The whole of creation absolutely obeys the first kind of laws, while obeying the second is optional. However, it is also God Who determines the results of obeying or disobeying both kinds of laws. Therefore, the whole universe, including the human kingdom, is subject to God's laws and no one can escape them.

60 ٦٠

قُلْ ءَامَنَّا بِاللَّهِ وَمَآ أُنزِلَ عَلَيْنَا وَمَآ أُنزِلَ عَلَىٰٓ إِبْرَٰهِيمَ
وَإِسْمَٰعِيلَ وَإِسْحَٰقَ وَيَعْقُوبَ وَالْأَسْبَاطِ وَمَآ أُوتِيَ
مُوسَىٰ وَعِيسَىٰ وَالنَّبِيُّونَ مِن رَّبِّهِمْ لَا نُفَرِّقُ بَيْنَ أَحَدٍ
مِّنْهُمْ وَنَحْنُ لَهُۥ مُسْلِمُونَ ۞ وَمَن يَبْتَغِ غَيْرَ الْإِسْلَٰمِ
دِينًا فَلَن يُقْبَلَ مِنْهُ وَهُوَ فِي الْأَخِرَةِ مِنَ الْخَٰسِرِينَ ۞ كَيْفَ
يَهْدِي اللَّهُ قَوْمًا كَفَرُوا بَعْدَ إِيمَٰنِهِمْ وَشَهِدُوٓا أَنَّ
الرَّسُولَ حَقٌّ وَجَآءَهُمُ الْبَيِّنَٰتُ وَاللَّهُ لَا يَهْدِي الْقَوْمَ الظَّٰلِمِينَ ۞
أُوْلَٰٓئِكَ جَزَآؤُهُمْ أَنَّ عَلَيْهِمْ لَعْنَةَ اللَّهِ وَالْمَلَٰٓئِكَةِ وَالنَّاسِ
أَجْمَعِينَ ۞ خَٰلِدِينَ فِيهَا لَا يُخَفَّفُ عَنْهُمُ الْعَذَابُ وَلَا هُمْ
يُنظَرُونَ ۞ إِلَّا الَّذِينَ تَابُوا مِنۢ بَعْدِ ذَٰلِكَ وَأَصْلَحُوا
فَإِنَّ اللَّهَ غَفُورٌ رَّحِيمٌ ۞ إِنَّ الَّذِينَ كَفَرُوا بَعْدَ إِيمَٰنِهِمْ
ثُمَّ ازْدَادُوا كُفْرًا لَّن تُقْبَلَ تَوْبَتُهُمْ وَأُوْلَٰٓئِكَ هُمُ
الضَّآلُّونَ ۞ إِنَّ الَّذِينَ كَفَرُوا وَمَاتُوا وَهُمْ كُفَّارٌ
فَلَن يُقْبَلَ مِنْ أَحَدِهِم مِّلْءُ الْأَرْضِ ذَهَبًا وَلَوِ افْتَدَىٰ بِهِ
أُوْلَٰٓئِكَ لَهُمْ عَذَابٌ أَلِيمٌ وَمَا لَهُم مِّن نَّٰصِرِينَ ۞

---

84. Say: "We have believed in God (without associating any partners with Him), and that which has been sent down on us, and that which was sent down on Abraham, Ishmael, Isaac, Jacob and the Prophets who were raised in the tribes, and that which was given to Moses, Jesus, and all other Prophets from their Lord; we make no distinction between any of them (in believing), and we are Muslims (submitted to Him wholly and exclusively)."

85. Whoever seeks as religion other than Islam, it will never be accepted from him, and in the Hereafter he will be among the losers.[17]

86. How would God guide a people who have disbelieved after their belief, and after they have borne witness that the Messenger is true and after the clear proofs (of His Messengership and the Divine origin of the Book he has brought) have come to them? God guides not wrongdoing people.

87. For those – their recompense is that on them rests the curse of God, and of angels, and of humankind, all together.[18]

88. Therein will they abide. Neither will their punishment be lightened, nor will they be granted any respite.

89. Save those who afterwards repent and mend their ways. Surely God is All-Forgiving, All-Compassionate.

90. But those who have disbelieved after their (profession of) belief[19] and then have hardened in unbelief, (they have lost the capacity for believing so they can no longer return to faith, nor repent until they are held in the jaws of death, and) their repentance (at that moment) will not be accepted. And they are those who are altogether astray.

91. Assuredly, those who disbelieve and die as unbelievers, no ransom even if it was as much gold as to fill the earth will be accepted from any of them. Such are those for whom is a painful punishment, and they will have no helpers (against it).

17. Verse 83 declares that the only, authentic religion is God's Religion, because whoever is in the heavens and the earth submits to God willingly or unwillingly. In Verse 84 it is stated that all the Prophets followed and conveyed this Religion, and this verse gives its name: Islam. As is explicit in the verses, Islam is the only religion in God's sight and it is based on unconditional submission to God. The verses also make it clear that Islam is, first of all, the religion of all things and beings that are outside the human realm, as they are submitted to God willingly and unwillingly and because they lead their lives according to the laws that God has established. Second, human life, except in its aspects related to human free will, is also ruled by Islam. Third, Islam is the religion that God wants human beings to follow in life, but through their free will. As mentioned above, all the Prophets followed and conveyed Islam, and the other religions, such as Judaism and Christianity, are the forms it took on over time after being preached by Moses and Jesus, respectively. Moreover, these names, at least in case of Christianity, were given to them by others, rather than by their own followers.

As the whole universe is submitted to and strictly follows the laws of One God as the Single Deity, Lord, and Sovereign, in it there is a magnificent peace, balance, and harmony. What humanity must do as a part of existence that enjoys free will is to take part in this chorus of peace, balance, and harmony with its free will and attain true happiness in both worlds. Any other belief or act would result in nothing more than corruption, unrest, anarchy, and wrongdoing in the world and torment and darkness upon darkness in the Hereafter.

18. Even though the majority of people have not usually been true believers, the human conscience does not admit or confirm unbelief, wrongdoing, and transgression. A human being falls into unbelief only after they follow their evil-commanding carnal souls and silence their conscience. However, as the human conscience rejects unbelief, and wrongdoing, and transgression, the destruction that they cause in the individual and human social life never remains hidden. For this reason, succeeding generations have cursed their predecessors who have transgressed. This is why the Prophets are remembered and mentioned with feelings of blessing, even after thousands of years, and why the unjust tyrants of human history are always cursed. Such people will be cursed by God, the angels, and all humankind, especially in the Hereafter.

God's cursing means excluding from His mercy and condemning to punishment. Cursing by others denotes their asking God to exclude those deserving the curse from His mercy and condemn them to punishment.

19. Like unbelief, belief or faith is an act of confirmation by the heart. So, both have two aspects, one true, and the other apparent and related to the law. A human being who professes belief and fulfills the legal requirements of being a Muslim member of a Muslim community (such as giving the Prescribed Alms – the *Zakāh*) is regarded as a believer and a Muslim. Whether he or she is truly so must be referred to God. The Qur'ān includes such people in its address of "O you who believe" and by doing so, it encourages believers to do what they are expected to as professors of the faith. It is hoped that they may confirm their profession of their faith through their actions, and belief may be implanted in their hearts. Despite their never-ending conspiracies, God's Messenger, upon him be peace and blessings, always treated the hypocrites as believers and Muslims unless ordered to do otherwise by God; an example of such a case is the matter of 'Abdullāh ibn Ubayy ibn Salūl, the chief of the hypocrites. When he died, the Messenger was forbidden by the Revelation to perform the funeral prayer for him.

لَنْتَنَالُوا الْبِرَّحَتَّى تُنْفِقُوا مِمَّا تُحِبُّونَ ۞ وَمَاتُنْفِقُوامِنْ شَيْءٍ فَإِنَّ
اللَّهَ بِهِ عَلِيمٌ ۞ كُلُّ الطَّعَامِ كَانَ حِلًّا لِبَنِي اِسْرَآئِيلَ اِلَّا
مَاحَرَّمَ اِسْرَآئِيلُ عَلَى نَفْسِهِ مِنْ قَبْلِ اَنْ تُنَزَّلَ التَّوْرٰيةُ قُلْ فَأْتُوا
بِالتَّوْرٰيةِ فَاتْلُوهَا اِنْ كُنْتُمْ صَادِقِينَ ۞ فَمَنِ افْتَرٰى عَلَى اللَّهِ
الْكَذِبَ مِنْ بَعْدِ ذٰلِكَ فَأُولٰئِكَ هُمُ الظَّالِمُونَ ۞ قُلْ صَدَقَ اللَّهُ
فَاتَّبِعُوا مِلَّةَ اِبْرٰهِيمَ حَنِيفًا وَمَاكَانَ مِنَ الْمُشْرِكِينَ ۞ اِنَّ
اَوَّلَ بَيْتٍ وُضِعَ لِلنَّاسِ لَلَّذِي بِبَكَّةَ مُبَارَكًا وَهُدًى لِلْعَالَمِينَ ۞
فِيهِ اٰيَاتٌ بَيِّنَاتٌ مَقَامُ اِبْرٰهِيمَ وَمَنْ دَخَلَهُ كَانَ اٰمِنًا وَلِلَّهِ
عَلَى النَّاسِ حِجُّ الْبَيْتِ مَنِ اسْتَطَاعَ اِلَيْهِ سَبِيلًا وَمَنْ كَفَرَ فَإِنَّ اللَّهَ
غَنِيٌّ عَنِ الْعَالَمِينَ ۞ قُلْ يَا اَهْلَ الْكِتَابِ لِمَ تَكْفُرُونَ بِاٰيَاتِ اللَّهِ
وَاللَّهُ شَهِيدٌ عَلَى مَا تَعْمَلُونَ ۞ قُلْ يَا اَهْلَ الْكِتَابِ
لِمَ تَصُدُّونَ عَنْ سَبِيلِ اللَّهِ مَنْ اٰمَنَ تَبْغُونَهَا عِوَجًا
وَاَنْتُمْ شُهَدَآءُ وَمَا اللَّهُ بِغَافِلٍ عَمَّا تَعْمَلُونَ ۞
يَا اَيُّهَا الَّذِينَ اٰمَنُوا اِنْ تُطِيعُوا فَرِيقًا مِنَ الَّذِينَ اُوتُوا
الْكِتَابَ يَرُدُّوكُمْ بَعْدَ اِيمَانِكُمْ كَافِرِينَ ۞

92. You will never be able to attain godliness and virtue until you spend of what you love (in God's cause or to provide sustenance for the needy). Whatever you spend, God has full knowledge of it.[20]

93. All (kinds of) food (that are lawful in the Law revealed to Muḥammad) were lawful to the Children of Israel (in the beginning) except what Israel (i.e. Prophet Jacob) forbade for himself before the Torah was sent down. Say (to them, O Messenger): "Bring the Torah and recite it, if you are truthful (in your claim that there is no abrogation in it).[21]

94. So whoever fabricates falsehood in attribution to God after that (statement, above, of the truth of the matter) – such are the wrongdoers.

95. Say: "God speaks the truth." Therefore follow the way of Abraham as people of pure faith (a faith free of unbelief, of associating partners with God, and of hypocrisy). He was never of those who associate partners with God.

96. Behold, the first House (of Prayer) established for humankind is the one at Bakkah (Makkah), a blessed place and a (center or focus of) guidance for all peoples.

97. In it there are clear signs (demonstrating that it is a blessed sanctuary, chosen by God as the center of guidance), and the Station of Abraham. Whoever enters it is in security (against attack and fear). Pilgrimage to the House is a duty owed to God by all who can afford a way to

it. And whoever refuses (the obligation of the Pilgrimage) or is ungrateful to God (by not fulfilling this command), God is absolutely independent of all creatures.

98. Say: "O People of the Book! Why do you conceal and disbelieve in God's Revelations, God being witness to all that you do?"

99. Say: "O People of the Book! Why do you bar from God's way those who believe, seeking to make it appear crooked, when you yourselves are witnesses (to its being the right way)? God is not unaware and unmindful of all that you do."

100. O you who believe! Were you to obey a party of those who were given the Book, they would turn you, after your faith, into unbelievers.

20. *Birr*, which it is preferable to translate as "godliness," is an elevated rank in goodness and virtue. Those who have attained this rank are called the *barr* (plural *abrār*). Love of God and seeking out His approval or good pleasure lie in the essence of worship. In order to be regarded among the *abrār*, a believer must have acquired the spiritual refinement that enables one to spend in God's way or to give others of what one loves. Godliness, or virtue, or piety, cannot be attained only by fulfilling certain formalities.

21. When the *qiblah* was changed from Bayt al-Maqdis in Jerusalem to the Kaʿbah in Makkah, some Israelite rabbis objected, claiming that this was an abrogation (*naskh*) and that there had been no abrogation in the Torah. Whereas, this verse, which openly declares the Torah to be a witness, announces that all kinds of food that are lawful in the Law revealed to Prophet Muḥammad were lawful to the Children of Israel in the beginning except what the Prophet Jacob forbade for himself before the Torah was sent down. However, verse 4: 160 says that, because of the wrong committed by the Jews, God made unlawful for them many pure, wholesome things which had (hitherto) been lawful for them, and verse 6: 146, that unto those who are Jews God has made unlawful every animal with claws; and of oxen and sheep He has made unlawful to them their fat save that upon their backs or the entrails, or that which is mixed with the bone, and that it was because He recompensed them for their insolence and defiance. So, all this shows explicitly that there has been abrogation in the Torah as well. (Also see *Leviticus*, 7: 23-26.)

وَكَيْفَ تَكْفُرُونَ وَأَنتُمْ تُتْلَىٰ عَلَيْكُمْ ءَايَاتُ اللَّهِ
وَفِيكُمْ رَسُولُهُ وَمَن يَعْتَصِم بِاللَّهِ فَقَدْ هُدِيَ إِلَىٰ صِرَاطٍ مُّسْتَقِيمٍ
﴿١٠١﴾ يَا أَيُّهَا الَّذِينَ ءَامَنُوا اتَّقُوا اللَّهَ حَقَّ تُقَاتِهِ وَلَا تَمُوتُنَّ إِلَّا وَأَنتُم
مُّسْلِمُونَ ﴿١٠٢﴾ وَاعْتَصِمُوا بِحَبْلِ اللَّهِ جَمِيعًا وَلَا تَفَرَّقُوا ۚ وَاذْكُرُوا
نِعْمَتَ اللَّهِ عَلَيْكُمْ إِذْ كُنتُمْ أَعْدَاءً فَأَلَّفَ بَيْنَ قُلُوبِكُمْ
فَأَصْبَحْتُم بِنِعْمَتِهِ إِخْوَانًا وَكُنتُمْ عَلَىٰ شَفَا حُفْرَةٍ مِّنَ النَّارِ
فَأَنقَذَكُم مِّنْهَا ۗ كَذَٰلِكَ يُبَيِّنُ اللَّهُ لَكُمْ ءَايَاتِهِ لَعَلَّكُمْ تَهْتَدُونَ
﴿١٠٣﴾ وَلْتَكُن مِّنكُمْ أُمَّةٌ يَدْعُونَ إِلَى الْخَيْرِ وَيَأْمُرُونَ بِالْمَعْرُوفِ
وَيَنْهَوْنَ عَنِ الْمُنكَرِ ۚ وَأُولَٰئِكَ هُمُ الْمُفْلِحُونَ ﴿١٠٤﴾ وَلَا تَكُونُوا
كَالَّذِينَ تَفَرَّقُوا وَاخْتَلَفُوا مِن بَعْدِ مَا جَاءَهُمُ الْبَيِّنَاتُ ۚ وَأُولَٰئِكَ
لَهُمْ عَذَابٌ عَظِيمٌ ﴿١٠٥﴾ يَوْمَ تَبْيَضُّ وُجُوهٌ وَتَسْوَدُّ وُجُوهٌ ۚ فَأَمَّا
الَّذِينَ اسْوَدَّتْ وُجُوهُهُمْ أَكَفَرْتُم بَعْدَ إِيمَانِكُمْ فَذُوقُوا الْعَذَابَ
بِمَا كُنتُمْ تَكْفُرُونَ ﴿١٠٦﴾ وَأَمَّا الَّذِينَ ابْيَضَّتْ وُجُوهُهُمْ فَفِي
رَحْمَةِ اللَّهِ هُمْ فِيهَا خَالِدُونَ ﴿١٠٧﴾ تِلْكَ ءَايَاتُ اللَّهِ
نَتْلُوهَا عَلَيْكَ بِالْحَقِّ ۗ وَمَا اللَّهُ يُرِيدُ ظُلْمًا لِّلْعَالَمِينَ ﴿١٠٨﴾

101. How do you disbelieve, seeing you are the ones to whom God's Revelations are recited and His Messenger is amidst you? Whoever holds fast to God, he has certainly been guided to a straight path.

102. O you who believe! Keep from disobedience to God in reverent piety with all the reverence that is due to Him, and see that you do not die save as Muslims (submitted to Him exclusively).

103. And hold fast all together to the rope of God and never be divided. Remember God's favor upon you: you were once enemies and He reconciled your hearts so that through His favor you became like brothers. You stood on the brink of a pit of fire, and He delivered you from it. Thus God makes His signs of truth (Revelations) clear to you that you may be guided (to the Straight Path in all matters and be steadfast on it).

104. There must be among you a community calling to good, and enjoining and promoting what is right and good and forbidding and trying to prevent evil (in appropriate ways). They are those who are the prosperous.

105. Be not as those who split into parties and followed different ways after the manifest truths had come to them. Those are the ones for whom is a tremendous punishment.

106. On the Day when some faces turn bright and some faces turn dark: and as to those whose faces have turned dark (they will be told): "What! did you disbelieve after having believed? Taste, then, the punishment because you used to follow the way of unbelief!"

107. As for those whose faces have turned bright, they are (embraced) in God's mercy, therein abiding forever.

108. These are God's Revelations: We recite them to you in truth, and God wills not any wrong to the world's people.[22]

22. These verses inform the Muslim nation, a nation that is, and indeed should be, a solid, well-compacted structure under a leader, of the keys to true success and prosperity in both worlds:

- In order to maintain their existence and unity and be able to follow the Straight Path without any deviation, Muslims must regard as good whatever God has decreed good and as evil whatever He has decreed evil. They must always depend on the Qur'ān and the Sunnah and the principles originating from these two main sources, and refrain from referring to another source or confirming and imitating the People of the Book in their mistaken creeds and false ways.

- The Sunnah of God's Messenger, upon him be peace and blessings, is a highway upon which all Muslims come together to form a strong united body.

- Following the Sunnah leads one to hold fast to God.

- Piety of the highest degree – refraining from disobeying God and doing one's best to perform His commands – guarantees that one follows the Sunnah and holds fast to God.

- By following the Sunnah and thereby by holding fast to God and the highest degree of piety, a Muslim offers God an irrefutable petition to be able to remain a Muslim until the time of their death and to accomplish the goal of dying a Muslim (submitted to Him exclusively).

- By following the Sunnah, a Muslim follows the Qur'ān and, in a general sense, the religion of Islam based on these two cardinal sources. The Sunnah, in the broadest sense, is how God's Messenger understood and practiced Islam dependent on the Qur'ān in both the life of the individual and society, and the principles God established for this purpose.

- Remembering God's favors as often as possible and paying the required thanks and thus being a thankful servant saves a Muslim against falling into unbelief after having believed. In this way, Muslims are also protected from any sort of misleading errors.

- Enjoining and preventing what is right or good and forbidding what is evil means teaching and advising people whatever God and His Messenger commanded and what the public view, based on the Qur'ān and Sunnah, regards as good, and preventing the spread of evil in the community. This important duty can and should be performed by every individual in a proper way. However, for this purpose a group should be formed of individuals who have the requisite qualities, or an institution or a governmental department should be established.

- If people go astray after they have seen and experienced the clear truths, this is because they have followed their evil-commanding carnal souls. This leads people to do wrong and to oppress one another, causing the appearance of different factions, each of which pursues its own interests. This is the main cause of the appearance of different ways followed in the name of the same religion; the consequence of this is a fatal disease that threatens both the life of the individual and society.

- Belief in the Hereafter, the realm where everyone will be called to account for whatever they have done in the world and where everyone will see the consequences of their actions, is the most effective way for preventing sins and evil in both the life of the individual and society.

٦٣

الجزءالرابع

63

وَلِلّٰهِ مَا فِى السَّمٰوَاتِ وَمَا فِى الْأَرْضِ وَإِلَى اللّٰهِ تُرْجَعُ
الْأُمُورُ ۝ كُنْتُمْ خَيْرَ أُمَّةٍ أُخْرِجَتْ لِلنَّاسِ تَأْمُرُونَ
بِالْمَعْرُوفِ وَتَنْهَوْنَ عَنِ الْمُنْكَرِ وَتُؤْمِنُونَ بِاللّٰهِ وَلَوْ اٰمَنَ
أَهْلُ الْكِتَابِ لَكَانَ خَيْرًا لَهُمْ مِنْهُمُ الْمُؤْمِنُونَ وَأَكْثَرُهُمُ
الْفَاسِقُونَ ۝ لَنْ يَضُرُّوكُمْ إِلَّا أَذًى وَإِنْ يُقَاتِلُوكُمْ
يُوَلُّوكُمُ الْأَدْبَارَ ثُمَّ لَا يُنْصَرُونَ ۝ ضُرِبَتْ عَلَيْهِمُ
الذِّلَّةُ أَيْنَ مَا ثُقِفُوا إِلَّا بِحَبْلٍ مِنَ اللّٰهِ وَحَبْلٍ
مِنَ النَّاسِ وَبَآءُو بِغَضَبٍ مِنَ اللّٰهِ وَضُرِبَتْ عَلَيْهِمُ الْمَسْكَنَةُ
ذٰلِكَ بِأَنَّهُمْ كَانُوا يَكْفُرُونَ بِاٰيَاتِ اللّٰهِ وَيَقْتُلُونَ
الْأَنْبِيَاءَ بِغَيْرِ حَقٍّ ذٰلِكَ بِمَا عَصَوْا وَكَانُوا يَعْتَدُونَ ۝
لَيْسُوا سَوَاءً مِنْ أَهْلِ الْكِتَابِ أُمَّةٌ قَائِمَةٌ يَتْلُونَ اٰيَاتِ
اللّٰهِ اٰنَاءَ الَّيْلِ وَهُمْ يَسْجُدُونَ ۝ يُؤْمِنُونَ بِاللّٰهِ وَالْيَوْمِ
الْأَخِرِ وَيَأْمُرُونَ بِالْمَعْرُوفِ وَيَنْهَوْنَ عَنِ الْمُنْكَرِ وَيُسَارِعُونَ
فِى الْخَيْرَاتِ وَأُولٰئِكَ مِنَ الصَّالِحِينَ ۝ وَمَا يَفْعَلُوا
مِنْ خَيْرٍ فَلَنْ يُكْفَرُوهُ وَاللّٰهُ عَلِيمٌ بِالْمُتَّقِينَ ۝

---

109. (How could that be so, seeing that) to God belongs whatever is in the heavens and on the earth, and to God are all matters ultimately referred, (and whatever He wills occurs).

110. (O Community of Muḥammad!) You are the best community ever brought forth for (the good of) humankind, enjoining and promoting what is right and good and forbidding and trying to prevent the evil, and (this you do because) you believe in God.[23] If only the People of the Book believed (as you do), this would be sheer good for them. Among them there are believers, but most of them are transgressors.

111. They will never be able to harm you except hurting a little (mostly with their tongues). If they fight against you, they will turn their backs in flight; then they will not be helped (to victory over you).

112. Ignominy has been their (the Jews') portion wherever they have been found except for (when they held on to) a rope from God or a rope from other peoples; and they were visited with a wrath (humiliating punishment) from God, and misery has been pitched upon them[24] – and all this because they were persistently disbelieving in Our Revelations, rejecting Our signs of truth (that they continually observed in their lives), and killing the Prophets

against all right; and all this because they disobeyed and kept on transgressing (the bounds of the Law).

113. (Yet) they are not all alike: among the People of the Book there is an upright community, reciting God's Revelations in the watches of the night and prostrating (themselves in worship).

114. They believe in God and the Last Day, and enjoin and promote what is right and good and forbid and try to prevent the evil, and hasten to do good deeds as if competing with one another. Those are of the righteous ones.

115. Whatever good they do, they will never be denied the reward of it; and God has full knowledge of the God-revering, pious.

23. The Muslims, when they truly and sincerely follow Islam, are the best people among humankind in terms of character and morals, and they have developed in theory and practice the qualities essential for truly righteous leadership, namely the commitment to promoting good and suppressing evil and the acknowledgement of the One True God as their Lord and Master. In view of the mission entrusted to them, they should become conscious of their responsibilities and avoid the mistakes committed by their predecessors.

24. So long as they continue to have the qualities mentioned in notes 22 and 23 above, God has promised that no power in the world can harm the Muslims; and history bears witness that God has fulfilled His promise.

Bediüzzaman Said Nursi explains why Israel presently enjoys the upper hand against the Muslim Arabs: The Jews are much more obedient to the commandments of their religion, even if it has been abrogated, than the Muslims are to Islam, and more respectful of their religious heritage. They are also supported by many governments throughout the world. That is, the Jews are now holding on to a rope both from God and from other nations. As for the Christians, they, especially the administrative elite of Christendom, are more respectful of their religion than the Muslim governments are of Islam, and Christianity plays a specific part in their policies. Moreover, as mentioned before, God has two kinds of law, one governing the universe and the other which has been manifested as religion. Christendom has discovered God's laws governing the universe and human life – even if they call them the laws of nature – and lives according to them. This is why, as well as the Jews, the Christians have enjoyed a certain degree of supremacy over the Muslims for the last two or three centuries.

إِنَّ الَّذِينَ كَفَرُوا لَنْ تُغْنِيَ عَنْهُمْ أَمْوَالُهُمْ وَلَا أَوْلَادُهُمْ مِنَ اللَّهِ شَيْئًا وَأُولَئِكَ أَصْحَابُ النَّارِ هُمْ فِيهَا خَالِدُونَ ۝ مَثَلُ مَا يُنْفِقُونَ فِي هَذِهِ الْحَيَاةِ الدُّنْيَا كَمَثَلِ رِيحٍ فِيهَا صِرٌّ أَصَابَتْ حَرْثَ قَوْمٍ ظَلَمُوا أَنْفُسَهُمْ فَأَهْلَكَتْهُ وَمَا ظَلَمَهُمُ اللَّهُ وَلَكِنْ أَنْفُسَهُمْ يَظْلِمُونَ ۝ يَا أَيُّهَا الَّذِينَ آمَنُوا لَا تَتَّخِذُوا بِطَانَةً مِنْ دُونِكُمْ لَا يَأْلُونَكُمْ خَبَالًا وَدُّوا مَا عَنِتُّمْ قَدْ بَدَتِ الْبَغْضَاءُ مِنْ أَفْوَاهِهِمْ وَمَا تُخْفِي صُدُورُهُمْ أَكْبَرُ قَدْ بَيَّنَّا لَكُمُ الْآيَاتِ إِنْ كُنْتُمْ تَعْقِلُونَ ۝ هَا أَنْتُمْ أُولَاءِ تُحِبُّونَهُمْ وَلَا يُحِبُّونَكُمْ وَتُؤْمِنُونَ بِالْكِتَابِ كُلِّهِ وَإِذَا لَقُوكُمْ قَالُوا آمَنَّا وَإِذَا خَلَوْا عَضُّوا عَلَيْكُمُ الْأَنَامِلَ مِنَ الْغَيْظِ قُلْ مُوتُوا بِغَيْظِكُمْ إِنَّ اللَّهَ عَلِيمٌ بِذَاتِ الصُّدُورِ ۝ إِنْ تَمْسَسْكُمْ حَسَنَةٌ تَسُؤْهُمْ وَإِنْ تُصِبْكُمْ سَيِّئَةٌ يَفْرَحُوا بِهَا وَإِنْ تَصْبِرُوا وَتَتَّقُوا لَا يَضُرُّكُمْ كَيْدُهُمْ شَيْئًا إِنَّ اللَّهَ بِمَا يَعْمَلُونَ مُحِيطٌ ۝ وَإِذْ غَدَوْتَ مِنْ أَهْلِكَ تُبَوِّئُ الْمُؤْمِنِينَ مَقَاعِدَ لِلْقِتَالِ وَاللَّهُ سَمِيعٌ عَلِيمٌ ۝

116. As to those who disbelieve, their riches will not avail them in the least, nor their children, against God; and those are the companions of the Fire; therein they will abide.

117. Their spending (to attain their goals in humanitarian or religious guises) in this life of the world is like a biting wind accompanied with frost that smites the harvest of a people who wronged themselves (by their wrong belief and their wrong actions), and devastates it. God has never wronged them but they do wrong themselves.

118. O you who believe! Take not for intimates from among others than your own people, for those (who especially cherish hostility towards you) spare no effort to ruin you, and yearn for you to always suffer. Hatred has shown itself by their mouths, and what their bosoms conceal is even greater. Now We have told you the manifest truths, if you reason and understand.

119. You are such (frank, clear-hearted) people that you love them (even those who are enemies to you), but they do not love you; and you believe in the whole of the Book (without making any distinction between the verses, and believe in all of the God-revealed Books). When they meet you, they say (hypocritically), "We believe;"

but when they find themselves alone, they gnaw their fingers in rage against you. Say (to them): "Perish in your rage!" Assuredly God has full knowledge of what lies hidden in the bosoms.

120. If anything good happens to you, this grieves them; if any evil befalls you, they rejoice at it. Yet if you endure and persevere in your way and act in piety keeping from evil and any injustice, their guile will never harm you. Surely God fully encompasses (with His Knowledge and Power) all that they do.

121. (Remember, O Messenger,) when you set forth from your home at dawn to place the believers in battle order – God is All-Hearing, All-Knowing (He heard and knew all that was happening and being talked about on that day).[25]

25. The verses to come up to 175 are concerned with the Battle of Uhud, the attitudes of the hypocrites during the war, its aftermath, and the lessons to get from it.

The victory of Badr alerted Arabia's hostile forces. The Muslims were in a state of unease, and endured the wrath of most neighboring societies.

The Quraysh were still smarting from their defeat in the Battle of Badr. Their women were mourning their dead warriors almost daily, and encouraging the survivors to revenge themselves. In addition, the Jewish efforts to rouse their feelings of revenge were like pouring oil on flames. Within a year, the Quraysh attacked Madīnah with an army of 3,000 soldiers, including 700 in coats of mail and 200 cavalrymen.

Informed of the Makkans' march upon Madīnah, the Messenger, upon him be peace and blessings, consulted with his Companions about how to meet this threat. He knew that the Makkan army was coming to fight on open ground, but himself thought that they should defend themselves within Madīnah's boundaries. If they defended themselves within Madīnah, the Makkan army could not mount a long siege. However, several young people who had not fought at Badr and longed for martyrdom they wanted to fight the enemy outside of Madīnah. The Messenger gave in to this ultimately majority demand (Ibn Hishām, 3: 64–67).

Having decided to follow the majority, the Messenger and 1,000 warriors left Madīnah for Uhud, a volcanic hill only a few miles from its western outskirts. Its main feature was a plain that stretched out before it. When they were only half way there, however, 'Abdullah ibn Ubayy ibn Salūl, the chief of the hypocrites, turned back with his 300 men (*Ibid.*, 3: 68). This event, coming just before the battle began, caused such perplexity and confusion that the Banū Salamah and Banū Hārithah tribes also wanted to turn back. Eventually, they were persuaded to remain.

The Messenger advanced with the remaining ill-equipped 700 Muslims. He lined them up at the foot of Mount Uhud so that the mountain was behind them and the Makkan army in front of them. The enemy could launch a surprise attack from only one mountain pass. The Messenger posted 50 archers there under the command of 'Abdullah ibn Jubayr. He told him not to let anyone approach or move from that spot, adding: "Even if you see birds fly off with our flesh, do not move from this place" (al-Bukhārī, "Jihād," 164).

Muṣ'ab ibn 'Umayr was the standard bearer, Zubayr ibn 'Awwām commanded the cavalry, and Hamzah commanded the infantry. The army was ready to fight. To encourage his Companions, the Prophet brought forth a sword and asked: "Who would like to have this sword in return for giving its due?" Abu Dujānah asked: "What is its due?" "To fight with it until it is broken," the Prophet said (Muslim, "Faḍāil aṣ-Ṣaḥābah," 128). Abu Dujānah took it and fought. Sa'd ibn Abī Waqqāṣ and 'Abdullah ibn Jahsh prayed to God to let them meet the strongest enemy soldiers. Hamzah, the Prophet's uncle and "Lion of God," wore an ostrich feather on his chest.

٦٥   65

اِذْهَمَتْ طَّآئِفَتَانِ مِنكُمْ اَنْ تَفْشَلَا وَاللهُ وَلِيُّهُمَا وَعَلَى
اللهِ فَلْيَتَوَكَّلِ الْمُؤْمِنُونَ ۞ وَلَقَدْ نَصَرَكُمُ اللهُ بِبَدْرٍ وَاَنتُمْ
اَذِلَّةٌ فَاتَّقُوا اللهَ لَعَلَّكُمْ تَشْكُرُونَ ۞ اِذْ تَقُولُ
لِلْمُؤْمِنِينَ اَلَنْ يَكْفِيَكُمْ اَنْ يُمِدَّكُمْ رَبُّكُم بِثَلَاثَةِ اٰلَافٍ
مِنَ الْمَلَٰٓئِكَةِ مُنْزَلِينَ ۞ بَلَىٰ اِنْ تَصْبِرُوا وَتَتَّقُوا وَيَأْتُوكُم مِنْ فَوْرِهِمْ
هٰذَا يُمْدِدْكُمْ رَبُّكُم بِخَمْسَةِ اٰلَافٍ مِنَ الْمَلَٰٓئِكَةِ مُسَوِّمِينَ ۞ وَمَا جَعَلَهُ
اللهُ اِلَّا بُشْرَىٰ لَكُمْ وَلِتَطْمَئِنَّ قُلُوبُكُم بِهِ وَمَا النَّصْرُ
اِلَّا مِنْ عِنْدِ اللهِ الْعَزِيزِ الْحَكِيمِ ۞ لِيَقْطَعَ طَرَفًا مِنَ الَّذِينَ
كَفَرُوا اَوْ يَكْبِتَهُمْ فَيَنْقَلِبُوا خَائِبِينَ ۞ لَيْسَ لَكَ مِنَ
الْاَمْرِ شَيْءٌ اَوْ يَتُوبَ عَلَيْهِمْ اَوْ يُعَذِّبَهُمْ فَاِنَّهُمْ ظَالِمُونَ ۞
وَلِلّٰهِ مَا فِي السَّمَاوَاتِ وَمَا فِي الْاَرْضِ يَغْفِرُ لِمَنْ يَشَاءُ وَيُعَذِّبُ
مَنْ يَشَاءُ وَاللهُ غَفُورٌ رَحِيمٌ ۞ يَا اَيُّهَا الَّذِينَ اٰمَنُوا
لَا تَأْكُلُوا الرِّبَا اَضْعَافًا مُضَاعَفَةً وَاتَّقُوا اللهَ لَعَلَّكُمْ
تُفْلِحُونَ ۞ وَاتَّقُوا النَّارَ الَّتِي اُعِدَّتْ لِلْكَافِرِينَ ۞
وَاَطِيعُوا اللهَ وَالرَّسُولَ لَعَلَّكُمْ تُرْحَمُونَ ۞

---

122. When two parties of you were about to lose heart, although God was their helper and protector; and in God let the believers put all their trust.

123. For sure God had helped you to victory at Badr when you were a despised (small) force. So observe your duty to God in due reverence for Him, that you may be thankful.

124. When you said to the believers: "Does it not suffice you that your Lord will come to your help with three thousand angels sent down?"

125. Surely it does. (More than that), if you are steadfast and act in piety to deserve His protection, and the enemy should fall upon you all at once, your Lord will come to your help with five thousand angels swooping down.

126. God did not ordain this save as a message of good hope for you, and so that thereby your hearts might be at peace and rest. Victory comes only from God, the All-Glorious with irresistible might, the All-Wise.

127. And that (through you) He might cut off a (leading) party of those who disbelieved, or overwhelm them, so that they (and others) would retreat in utter disappointment.

128. (O Messenger, you are a servant charged with a certain duty, therefore) it is not a matter for you whether He turns towards them in mercy (to accept their repentance for their unbelief, and grants

them faith) or punishes them because they are wrongdoers.

129. To God belongs whatever is in the heavens and whatever is on the earth; He forgives whom He wills and punishes whom He wills. And God is All-Forgiving, All-Compassionate.

130. O you who believe! Do not consume usury, doubled and redoubled; and act in piety, keeping from disobedience to Him in reverence for Him, so that you may prosper (in both worlds).[26]

131. And (be careful of your acts and transactions and) guard yourselves against the Fire, prepared for the unbelievers.

132. Obey God and the Messenger so that you may be shown mercy (granted a good, virtuous life in this world and eternal happiness in the Hereafter).

26. It is highly significant that an admonition is given while war is being discussed. It should be stressed, before everything else, that the Qur'ān takes a holistic, not a fragmentary, view of life and the universe. It does not consider the matters relating to individuals as being separate from social matters, nor does it see social matters as being apart from the economy, or the economy from spirituality and other internal matters, such as education and security, and from foreign relations. None of these can be viewed or treated as being separate from the others. In view of this, the use of interest is no longer only an economic matter; it is also deeply connected with the life of the society and the individual. It affects both the spiritual and moral nature of the individual, and their participation in the social and economic life of the society. Therefore, interest will have a significant effect on a person's attitude to war, which requires them to take away egotism and worldliness from their heart. Interest destroys social solidarity, and the desire to help one another, as well as undermining confidence within a society; these are all important factors if a nation wants to succeed in a war. So, this verse, which, when viewed superficially, may seem to be out of place, is actually just where it should be. It warns us that, instead of making our limited minds or reason the criterion or judge when approaching the Qur'ān, we should design our thinking system according to the Qur'ān.

66   سُورَةُ آلِ عِمْرَان   ٦٦

وَسَارِعُوٓا إِلَىٰ مَغْفِرَةٍ مِّن رَّبِّكُمْ وَجَنَّةٍ عَرْضُهَا السَّمَـٰوَٰتُ وَالْأَرْضُ أُعِدَّتْ لِلْمُتَّقِينَ ۝ الَّذِينَ يُنفِقُونَ فِى السَّرَّآءِ وَالضَّرَّآءِ وَالْكَـٰظِمِينَ الْغَيْظَ وَالْعَافِينَ عَنِ النَّاسِ وَاللَّهُ يُحِبُّ الْمُحْسِنِينَ ۝ وَالَّذِينَ إِذَا فَعَلُوا فَـٰحِشَةً أَوْ ظَلَمُوٓا أَنفُسَهُمْ ذَكَرُوا اللَّهَ فَاسْتَغْفَرُوا لِذُنُوبِهِمْ وَمَن يَغْفِرُ الذُّنُوبَ إِلَّا اللَّهُ وَلَمْ يُصِرُّوا عَلَىٰ مَا فَعَلُوا وَهُمْ يَعْلَمُونَ ۝ أُوْلَـٰٓئِكَ جَزَآؤُهُم مَّغْفِرَةٌ مِّن رَّبِّهِمْ وَجَنَّـٰتٌ تَجْرِى مِن تَحْتِهَا الْأَنْهَـٰرُ خَـٰلِدِينَ فِيهَا وَنِعْمَ أَجْرُ الْعَـٰمِلِينَ ۝ قَدْ خَلَتْ مِن قَبْلِكُمْ سُنَنٌ فَسِيرُوا فِى الْأَرْضِ فَانظُرُوا كَيْفَ كَانَ عَـٰقِبَةُ الْمُكَذِّبِينَ ۝ هَـٰذَا بَيَانٌ لِّلنَّاسِ وَهُدًى وَمَوْعِظَةٌ لِّلْمُتَّقِينَ ۝ وَلَا تَهِنُوا وَلَا تَحْزَنُوا وَأَنتُمُ الْأَعْلَوْنَ إِن كُنتُم مُّؤْمِنِينَ ۝ إِن يَمْسَسْكُمْ قَرْحٌ فَقَدْ مَسَّ الْقَوْمَ قَرْحٌ مِّثْلُهُ وَتِلْكَ الْأَيَّامُ نُدَاوِلُهَا بَيْنَ النَّاسِ وَلِيَعْلَمَ اللَّهُ الَّذِينَ آمَنُوا وَيَتَّخِذَ مِنكُمْ شُهَدَآءَ وَاللَّهُ لَا يُحِبُّ الظَّـٰلِمِينَ ۝

133. And hasten, as if competing with one another, to forgiveness from your Lord, and to a Garden as spacious as the heavens and the earth, prepared for the God-revering, pious.

134. They spend (out of what God has provided for them) both in ease and hardship, ever-restraining their rage (even when provoked and able to retaliate), and pardoning people (their offenses). God loves (such) people who are devoted to doing good, aware that God is seeing them.

135. They are also the ones who, when they have committed a shameful deed or wronged themselves (through any kind of sinful act), immediately remember God and implore Him to forgive their sins – for who will forgive sins save God? – and do not persist knowingly in whatever (evil) they have committed.

136. Such are the ones whose reward is forgiveness from their Lord and Gardens through which rivers flow, to abide therein. How excellent is the reward of those who always do good deeds!

137. Assuredly, before you have passed many ways of life and practices (that illustrate the law God has established for the life of human societies). Go about, then, on the earth and behold how the outcome was for those who denied (God's manifest signs and Messengers).

138. This (history of peoples past) is a plain exposition (of the truth) for all people, and a clear guidance (to a more substantial faith and devotion) and an instruction for the God-revering, pious.

139. Do not, then, be faint of heart, nor grieve, for you are always the superior side if you are (true) believers.

140. If a wound has touched you (at Uhud), (you know that) a similar wound touched those (disbelieving) people (at Badr). Such (historic, eventful) days – We deal them out in turns among people so that God may mark out those who (truly) believe and select from among you such as bear witness to the truth (with their lives); – (it is a fact that) God does not love the wrongdoers (and in the end He punishes wrong and makes the truth superior) –

وَلِيُمَحِّصَ اللّٰهُ الَّذِينَ اٰمَنُوا وَيَمْحَقَ الْكَافِرِينَ ۞ أَمْ حَسِبْتُمْ
أَنْ تَدْخُلُوا الْجَنَّةَ وَلَمَّا يَعْلَمِ اللّٰهُ الَّذِينَ جَاهَدُوا مِنْكُمْ
وَيَعْلَمَ الصَّابِرِينَ ۞ وَلَقَدْ كُنْتُمْ تَمَنَّوْنَ الْمَوْتَ مِنْ
قَبْلِ أَنْ تَلْقَوْهُ فَقَدْ رَأَيْتُمُوهُ وَأَنْتُمْ تَنْظُرُونَ ۞ وَمَا
مُحَمَّدٌ إِلَّا رَسُولٌ قَدْ خَلَتْ مِنْ قَبْلِهِ الرُّسُلُ أَفَإِنْ مَاتَ
أَوْ قُتِلَ انْقَلَبْتُمْ عَلَى أَعْقَابِكُمْ وَمَنْ يَنْقَلِبْ عَلَى عَقِبَيْهِ
فَلَنْ يَضُرَّ اللّٰهَ شَيْئًا وَسَيَجْزِي اللّٰهُ الشَّاكِرِينَ ۞ وَمَا
كَانَ لِنَفْسٍ أَنْ تَمُوتَ إِلَّا بِإِذْنِ اللّٰهِ كِتَابًا مُؤَجَّلًا وَمَنْ يُرِدْ
ثَوَابَ الدُّنْيَا نُؤْتِهِ مِنْهَا وَمَنْ يُرِدْ ثَوَابَ الْاٰخِرَةِ نُؤْتِهِ مِنْهَا
وَسَنَجْزِي الشَّاكِرِينَ ۞ وَكَأَيِّنْ مِنْ نَبِيٍّ قَاتَلَ مَعَهُ
رِبِّيُّونَ كَثِيرٌ فَمَا وَهَنُوا لِمَا أَصَابَهُمْ فِي سَبِيلِ اللّٰهِ
وَمَا ضَعُفُوا وَمَا اسْتَكَانُوا وَاللّٰهُ يُحِبُّ الصَّابِرِينَ ۞ وَمَا
كَانَ قَوْلَهُمْ إِلَّا أَنْ قَالُوا رَبَّنَا اغْفِرْ لَنَا ذُنُوبَنَا وَإِسْرَافَنَا فِي
أَمْرِنَا وَثَبِّتْ أَقْدَامَنَا وَانْصُرْنَا عَلَى الْقَوْمِ الْكَافِرِينَ ۞ فَاٰتَاهُمُ اللّٰهُ
ثَوَابَ الدُّنْيَا وَحُسْنَ ثَوَابِ الْاٰخِرَةِ وَاللّٰهُ يُحِبُّ الْمُحْسِنِينَ
۞

---

141. And that He may purify the believers (individually, of all base metal, and collectively, of the hypocrites among them) and gradually blot out the unbelievers.

142. Did you suppose that you should enter Paradise without God marking out those among you who really strive hard (in His cause), and marking out the patient and steadfast?

143. You did indeed long for death (for God's cause) before you came face to face with it; now you have faced it (on the battlefield), only observing it with your own eyes (without doing anything to meet it).

144. (Did you think that this cause of Islam subsisted not by God but while Muḥammad was alive among you? If so, know that this cause depends on God and as for his part in it, know that) Muḥammad is but a Messenger, and Messengers passed away before him. If, then, he dies or is killed, will you turn back on your heels? Whoever turns back on his heels can in no way harm God. But God will (abundantly) reward the thankful ones (those who are steadfast in God's cause).

145. It never occurs that a soul dies save by God's leave, at a time appointed. So whoever desires the reward of this world, We give him of it (in the world); and whoever desires the reward of the Hereafter, We give him of it; and We will soon reward the thankful.

146. And how many a Prophet has had to fight (for God's cause), followed by numbers of godly, dedicated servants of God; and they did not become faint of heart for all that befell them in God's cause, nor did they weaken, nor did they abase themselves (before the enemy). And God loves the patient and steadfast.

147. What they said (when they encountered the enemy) was: "Our Lord! Forgive us our sins and any wasteful act we may have done in our duty, and set our feet firm, and help us to victory over the disbelieving people!"

148. So God granted them the reward of this world as well as the best reward of the Hereafter. Indeed God loves those devoted to doing good, aware that God is seeing them

Views from Mount Uhud (photo by H. Akarsu)

68　　　سورة آل عمران　　　٦٨

يَـٰٓأَيُّهَا الَّذِينَ ءَامَنُوٓا إِن تُطِيعُوا الَّذِينَ كَفَرُوا
يَرُدُّوكُمْ عَلَىٰٓ أَعْقَابِكُمْ فَتَنقَلِبُوا
خَاسِرِينَ ۝ بَلِ اللَّهُ مَوْلَىٰكُمْ وَهُوَ خَيْرُ
النَّاصِرِينَ ۝ سَنُلْقِى فِى قُلُوبِ الَّذِينَ كَفَرُوا
الرُّعْبَ بِمَآ أَشْرَكُوا بِاللَّهِ مَا لَمْ يُنَزِّلْ بِهِ سُلْطَانًا
وَمَأْوَىٰهُمُ النَّارُ وَبِئْسَ مَثْوَى الظَّالِمِينَ ۝
وَلَقَدْ صَدَقَكُمُ اللَّهُ وَعْدَهُ إِذْ تَحُسُّونَهُم
بِإِذْنِهِ حَتَّىٰٓ إِذَا فَشِلْتُمْ وَتَنَازَعْتُمْ فِى الْأَمْرِ وَعَصَيْتُم
مِّنۢ بَعْدِ مَآ أَرَىٰكُم مَّا تُحِبُّونَ مِنكُم مَّن يُرِيدُ الدُّنْيَا
وَمِنكُم مَّن يُرِيدُ الْآخِرَةَ ثُمَّ صَرَفَكُمْ عَنْهُمْ لِيَبْتَلِيَكُمْ
وَلَقَدْ عَفَا عَنكُمْ وَاللَّهُ ذُو فَضْلٍ عَلَى الْمُؤْمِنِينَ
۝ إِذْ تُصْعِدُونَ وَلَا تَلْوُونَ عَلَىٰٓ أَحَدٍ وَالرَّسُولُ
يَدْعُوكُمْ فِىٓ أُخْرَىٰكُمْ فَأَثَابَكُمْ غَمًّا
بِغَمٍّ لِّكَيْلَا تَحْزَنُوا عَلَىٰ مَا فَاتَكُمْ
وَلَا مَآ أَصَابَكُمْ وَاللَّهُ خَبِيرٌ بِمَا تَعْمَلُونَ ۝

───────❧───────

149. O you who believe! If you follow those who disbelieve (the hypocrites and Jews in Madīnah who spread negative propaganda concerning the events at Uhud), they will drive you back on your heels (into unbelief), and you will turn utter losers (in both this world and the next).[27]

150. But God is your Guardian and Owner, and He is the best of helpers.

151. We will throw alarm into the hearts of those who disbelieve because they as-

sociate with God partners, for which He has sent no authority at all; and their refuge will be the Fire; and how evil is the dwelling of the wrongdoers!

152. God did indeed fulfill His promise to you when you routed them by His leave, up to (the point) when you lost heart, and disagreed about the order (given to the archers among you not to leave their positions), and disobeyed, after He had brought you within sight of that (victory) for which you were longing. Among you were such as cared for this world, and among you were such as cared for the Hereafter. Then He diverted you from them (the enemy), that He might try you. But He has surely pardoned you: God has grace and bounty for the believers.[28]

153. When you were running off (from the battlefield), paying no heed to anyone, and at your rear the Messenger was calling out to you (to stay in the battle), then God requited you with grief after grief so that you might not grieve either for what escaped you, or for what befell you.[29] God is fully aware of all that you do.

───────────────────────

27. As mentioned in the Foreword, the occasion on which a verse was revealed is important in correctly understanding it. If the occasion were not known, it would be possible for us to incorrectly interpret the verse and to overlook some of the significant aspects of the meaning of the verse. For example, this verse commands that the

believers should not obey the unbelievers. However, like many commandments in the Qur'ān, this one also has relative aspects, according to time and conditions. Moreover, the verse is connected with the verses that precede and follow it. Seeing this connection sometimes requires knowing the reason for the revelation of the verse.

After the Battle of Uhud, the hypocrites and the Jews began to propagate the idea that had Muḥammad been a true Prophet, he would not have suffered the reverse he faced at Uhud. They tried to persuade the Muslims to turn back to their former state of unbelief. The Muslims to whom this verse was addressed in Madīnah understood what the verse was about specifically. For this reason, in order to clarify the meaning and the direct purpose of the verse's revelation, in translation, explanatory additions are necessary. However, by doing this, we should not forget that with respect to its meaning, connotations and the commandments contained, a verse can never be restricted only to the occasion on which it was revealed. "The fact that a verse was revealed on a certain occasion does not prevent the commandment contained in the verse from having a general, inclusive enforcement," is a rule in both Qur'ānic interpretation and Islamic jurisprudence.

28. In the first stage of the Battle of Uhud, the Muslims defeated the enemy so easily that Abu Dujānah, with the sword the Prophet had given him, pushed into the center of the Makkan army. There he met Abū Sufyan's (the Makkan commander) wife Hind. He tried to kill her but, "in order not to dirty the sword given by the Prophet with a woman's blood," spared her (al-Haythamī, 6: 109). All who carried the enemy standard were killed one after the other. Self-sacrificing heroes of the Muslim army flung themselves upon the enemy and routed them.

When the enemy began to flee, the Muslims gathered the spoils. The archers on the mountain pass saw this and said to themselves: "God has defeated the enemy, and our brothers are collecting the spoils. Let's join them." 'Abdullāh ibn Jubayr reminded them of the Prophet's order, but they said: "He ordered us to do that without knowing the outcome of the battle." All but a few left their posts and began to collect booty. Khālid ibn Walīd, still an unbeliever and commander of the Makkan cavalry, seized this opportunity to lead his men around Mount Uhud and attacked the Muslims' flank through the pass. 'Abdullāh ibn Jubayr's depleted forces could not repel them.

The fleeing enemy soldiers came back and joined the attack from the front. Now, the battle turned against the Muslims. Both of these sudden attacks by superior forces caused great confusion among the Muslims. The enemy wanted to seize the Messenger alive or kill him, and so attacked him from all sides with swords, spears, arrows, and stones. Those who defended him fought heroically. Hamzah, the Messenger's uncle, was martyred.

Ibn Kāmi'ah martyred Muṣ'ab ibn 'Umayr, the Muslims' standard-bearer who had been fighting in front of the Messenger, upon him be peace and blessings. Mus'ab resembled God's Messenger in build and complexion, and this caused Ibn Kāmi'a to announce that he had killed the Messenger. Meanwhile, the Messenger had been wounded by a sword and some stones. Falling into a pit and bleeding profusely, he stretched his hands and prayed: "O God, forgive my people, because they do not know (the truth)" (Qadi 'Iyad, 1: 78–79).

The rumor of the Prophet's martyrdom led many Companions to lose courage. However, several among them fought self-sacrificingly. Some Muslim women heard the rumor and rushed to the battlefield. Sumayrā, of the Banū Dinār tribe, had lost her husband, father, and brother. All she asked about was the Messenger. When she saw him, she said: "All misfortunes mean nothing to me as long as you are alive, O Messenger!" (Ibn Hishām, 3: 99)

Umm 'Umārah fought before the Messenger so heroically that he asked her: "Who else can endure all that you endure?" That pride of womanhood took this opportunity to ask him to pray for her: "O Messenger of God, pray to God that I may be in your company in Paradise!" The Messenger did so, and she responded: "Whatever happens to me from now on does not matter" (Ibn Sa'd, 8: 415).

Despite the indescribable resistance of the Muslim warriors such as 'Ali, Abū Dujānah, Sahl ibn Hunayf, Talhah ibn 'Ubaydullāh, Anas ibn Naḍr, and 'Abdullāh ibn Jahsh, around the Messenger, defeat seemed inevitable until Ka'b ibn Mālik, seeing the Messenger, shouted: "O Muslims! Good tidings for you! This is the

Messenger, here!" The scattered Companions advanced towards him from all sides, rallied around him, and led him to the safety of the mountain.

29. This verse states a very significant aspect of human psychology: if a person is visited by successive hardships and disasters, the later one causes the previous one to be forgotten. This helps a person to develop immunity towards disasters and realize that one should neither grieve for losing anything of this world or for the disasters that befall one nor rejoice excessively at any good. Even though disasters usually befall a believer in return for their sins or errors, such events are accompanied by several rewards. For example, God forgives believers the sins or errors which caused the disaster and repays it with future rewards; this helps the believers to develop endurance against disasters and come to know the true nature of the worldly life. What is expected of a believer when visited by a disaster is that they should show patience, especially at the first moment and they should preserve their faith, confidence, and trust in God.

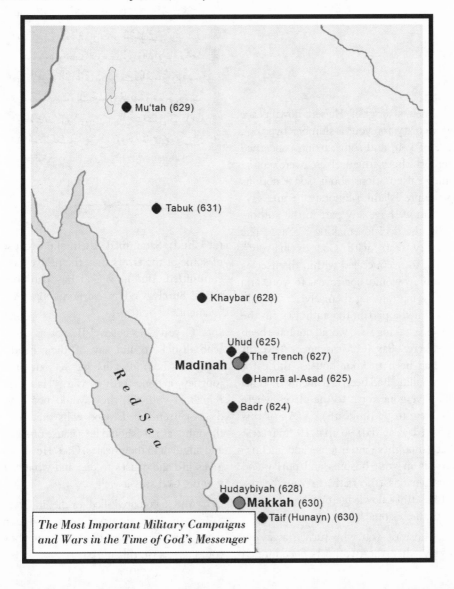

● Mu'tah (629)

● Tabuk (631)

Red Sea

● Khaybar (628)

Uhud (625)
● ●The Trench (627)
Madīnah ○
● Hamrā al-Asad (625)

◆ Badr (624)

Hudaybiyah (628)
● ○**Makkah** (630)
●Tāif (Hunayn) (630)

The Most Important Military Campaigns and Wars in the Time of God's Messenger

نَّثَمَّ أَنزَلَ عَلَيْكُم مِّنۢ بَعْدِ ٱلْغَمِّ أَمَنَةً نُّعَاسًا يَغْشَىٰ طَآئِفَةً مِّنكُمْ ۖ
وَطَآئِفَةٌ قَدْ أَهَمَّتْهُمْ أَنفُسُهُمْ يَظُنُّونَ بِٱللَّهِ غَيْرَ ٱلْحَقِّ ظَنَّ
ٱلْجَٰهِلِيَّةِ ۖ يَقُولُونَ هَل لَّنَا مِنَ ٱلْأَمْرِ مِن شَىْءٍ ۗ قُلْ إِنَّ ٱلْأَمْرَ كُلَّهُۥ
لِلَّهِ ۗ يُخْفُونَ فِىٓ أَنفُسِهِم مَّا لَا يُبْدُونَ لَكَ ۖ يَقُولُونَ لَوْ كَانَ
لَنَا مِنَ ٱلْأَمْرِ شَىْءٌ مَّا قُتِلْنَا هَٰهُنَا ۗ قُل لَّوْ كُنتُمْ فِى بُيُوتِكُمْ
لَبَرَزَ ٱلَّذِينَ كُتِبَ عَلَيْهِمُ ٱلْقَتْلُ إِلَىٰ مَضَاجِعِهِمْ ۖ وَلِيَبْتَلِىَ
ٱللَّهُ مَا فِى صُدُورِكُمْ وَلِيُمَحِّصَ مَا فِى قُلُوبِكُمْ ۗ وَٱللَّهُ
عَلِيمٌۢ بِذَاتِ ٱلصُّدُورِ ۝ إِنَّ ٱلَّذِينَ تَوَلَّوْا۟ مِنكُمْ يَوْمَ
ٱلْتَقَى ٱلْجَمْعَانِ إِنَّمَا ٱسْتَزَلَّهُمُ ٱلشَّيْطَٰنُ بِبَعْضِ مَا كَسَبُوا۟ ۖ
وَلَقَدْ عَفَا ٱللَّهُ عَنْهُمْ ۗ إِنَّ ٱللَّهَ غَفُورٌ حَلِيمٌ ۝ يَٰٓأَيُّهَا ٱلَّذِينَ
ءَامَنُوا۟ لَا تَكُونُوا۟ كَٱلَّذِينَ كَفَرُوا۟ وَقَالُوا۟ لِإِخْوَٰنِهِمْ إِذَا ضَرَبُوا۟
فِى ٱلْأَرْضِ أَوْ كَانُوا۟ غُزًّى لَّوْ كَانُوا۟ عِندَنَا مَا مَاتُوا۟ وَمَا قُتِلُوا۟
لِيَجْعَلَ ٱللَّهُ ذَٰلِكَ حَسْرَةً فِى قُلُوبِهِمْ ۗ وَٱللَّهُ يُحْىِۦ وَيُمِيتُ ۗ
وَٱللَّهُ بِمَا تَعْمَلُونَ بَصِيرٌ ۝ وَلَئِن قُتِلْتُمْ فِى سَبِيلِ ٱللَّهِ
أَوْ مُتُّمْ لَمَغْفِرَةٌ مِّنَ ٱللَّهِ وَرَحْمَةٌ خَيْرٌ مِّمَّا يَجْمَعُونَ ۝

---

154. Then, after grief, He sent down peace and security for you: a slumber overtook some of you; and some, being concerned (merely) about themselves, were entertaining false notions about God – notions of (the pre-Islamic) Ignorance – and saying: "Do we have any part in the authority (in the decision-making)?" Say: "The authority rests with God exclusively." Indeed, they concealed within themselves what they would not reveal to you, and were saying (among themselves): "If only we had had a part in the authority (in the decision-making), we would not have been killed here." Say (O Messenger): "Even if you had been in your houses, those for whom killing had been ordained would indeed have gone forth to the places where they were to lie (in death)."[30] (All of this happened as it did) so that He may test what (thoughts, intentions, and inclinations) is in your bosoms and purify and prove what is (the faith) in your hearts. God has full knowledge of what lies hidden in the bosoms.

155. Those of you who turned away on the day when the two hosts encountered (at Uhud), Satan made them slip because of some of the errors they themselves had committed. But now God has pardoned them. Surely God is All-Forgiving, All-Clement.

156. O you who believe! Be not as those who disbelieve and say of their brothers who (died) after having set out on a journey or gone forth to war, "Had they remained with us, they would not have died or been killed." God wills that such thoughts as this should be a cause of sighs and anguish in their hearts. God (He alone) gives life and causes to die; and whatever you do, God sees it well.

157. And if you are killed, or die, in God's cause, then forgiveness from God and mercy are far better than all that they could amass (in this life).

30. This verse teaches three significant points concerning Divine Destiny and human free will: (1) In one respect, Destiny is identical with God's eternal Knowledge, so knowing something beforehand does not mean that it compels that thing to take place. God knows beforehand how each person will use their free will, and He has determined their fate. (2) Destiny considers the cause and its effect or result together; there are not two separate destinies, one for the cause and the other for the effect. If God has destined for a person to be killed in a battle, considering, of course, how that person uses their free will, they will set out for the battle and will be killed. (3) The past and any misfortunes are and should be considered from the viewpoint of Destiny. We should take the necessary lessons from these events, but not spend time regretting them in vain and we should avoid mutual accusations for them.

The verse also teaches us that if a decision reached after consultation does not give the expected result, we should not criticize it or the consultative assembly.

70 سُوْرَةُ العِمْرَان V.

وَلَئِنْ مُّتُّمْ أَوْ قُتِلْتُمْ لَإِلَى اللّٰهِ تُحْشَرُوْنَ ۞ فَبِمَا رَحْمَةٍ مِّنَ اللّٰهِ لِنْتَ لَهُمْ ۖ وَلَوْ كُنْتَ فَظًّا غَلِيْظَ الْقَلْبِ لَانْفَضُّوْا مِنْ حَوْلِكَ ۖ فَاعْفُ عَنْهُمْ وَاسْتَغْفِرْ لَهُمْ وَشَاوِرْهُمْ فِى الْأَمْرِ ۖ فَإِذَا عَزَمْتَ فَتَوَكَّلْ عَلَى اللّٰهِ ۚ إِنَّ اللّٰهَ يُحِبُّ الْمُتَوَكِّلِيْنَ ۞ إِنْ يَّنْصُرْكُمُ اللّٰهُ فَلَا غَالِبَ لَكُمْ ۚ وَإِنْ يَّخْذُلْكُمْ فَمَنْ ذَا الَّذِى يَنْصُرُكُمْ مِّنْ بَعْدِهِ ۗ وَعَلَى اللّٰهِ فَلْيَتَوَكَّلِ الْمُؤْمِنُوْنَ ۞ وَمَا كَانَ لِنَبِىٍّ أَنْ يَّغُلَّ ۚ وَمَنْ يَّغْلُلْ يَأْتِ بِمَا غَلَّ يَوْمَ الْقِيٰمَةِ ۚ ثُمَّ تُوَفّٰى كُلُّ نَفْسٍ مَّا كَسَبَتْ وَهُمْ لَا يُظْلَمُوْنَ ۞ أَفَمَنِ اتَّبَعَ رِضْوَانَ اللّٰهِ كَمَنْ بَآءَ بِسَخَطٍ مِّنَ اللّٰهِ وَمَأْوٰىهُ جَهَنَّمُ ۚ وَبِئْسَ الْمَصِيْرُ ۞ هُمْ دَرَجٰتٌ عِنْدَ اللّٰهِ ۗ وَاللّٰهُ بَصِيْرٌ بِمَا يَعْمَلُوْنَ ۞ لَقَدْ مَنَّ اللّٰهُ عَلَى الْمُؤْمِنِيْنَ إِذْ بَعَثَ فِيْهِمْ رَسُوْلًا مِّنْ أَنْفُسِهِمْ يَتْلُوْا عَلَيْهِمْ اٰيٰتِهِ وَيُزَكِّيْهِمْ وَيُعَلِّمُهُمُ الْكِتٰبَ وَالْحِكْمَةَ ۚ وَإِنْ كَانُوْا مِنْ قَبْلُ لَفِىْ ضَلٰلٍ مُّبِيْنٍ ۞ أَوَلَمَّا أَصَابَتْكُمْ مُّصِيْبَةٌ قَدْ أَصَبْتُمْ مِّثْلَيْهَا ۙ قُلْتُمْ أَنّٰى هٰذَا ۖ قُلْ هُوَ مِنْ عِنْدِ أَنْفُسِكُمْ ۗ إِنَّ اللّٰهَ عَلٰى كُلِّ شَىْءٍ قَدِيْرٌ ۞

158. And, assuredly, if you die or are killed, it is to God that you will be gathered.

159. It was by a mercy from God that (at the time of the setback), you (O Messenger) were lenient with them (your Companions). Had you been harsh and hard-hearted, they would surely have scattered away from about you. Then pardon them, pray for their forgiveness, and take counsel with them in the affairs (of public concern), and when you are resolved (on a course of action), put your trust in God.[31] Surely God loves those who put their trust (in Him).

160. If God helps you, there will be none who can overcome you; if He forsakes you, who is there that can help you thereafter? In God, then, let the believers put all their trust.

161. It is not conceivable that a Prophet defrauds; and whoever defrauds (by stealing from public property or war-gains) will come with what he gained by his fraud on the Day of Resurrection. Then every soul shall be repaid in full what it has earned (while in the world), and they will not be wronged.

162. What! is he who strives after God's good pleasure and approval like him who is laden with God's condemnation and whose refuge is Hell? How evil a destination to arrive at!

163. They are in varying grades in God's sight, and God sees well all that they do.

164. Assuredly God has done the believers a great kindness by raising among them a Messenger of their own, reciting to them His Revelations, and purifying them (of false beliefs and doctrines, and sins, and all kinds of uncleanness), and instructing them in the Book and the Wisdom. Whereas, before that, they were lost in obvious error.

165. And do you, now that a disaster has befallen you, though you inflicted the double (of that on your foes at Badr), say: "Whence is this?" Say (to them, O Messenger): "It is from your own selves." Surely God has full power over everything.

31. Like many other verses, this verse also contains several important principles.

- It is of great significance that a leader should be lenient towards those around him after any attempt made with a good intention has ended in failure due to unintentional mistakes.

- In addition to establishing devotion to One God, promoting what is good and right and preventing evil, establishing justice through the rule of law, obedience to the leader save in sin and rebellion to God, freedom of thought and speech, provided they are not against the public benefit and what is good or right, and an advisory system of government – all these make up essential articles of the Constitution of Islamic rule. When a decision has been reached through counsel, the leader or the head of the government implements the decision in complete reliance on God. If the leader turns back under the pressure of those who have different opinions or have changed their minds, this will cause a confusion of views and faltering among the people.

- The Prophet, upon him be peace and blessings, sought counsel with his Companions about how to handle the approaching enemy before the Battle of Uhud. Although he and the elder Companions were of the opinion that they should face the enemy outside Madīnah and lead a defensive war, the young members of the army, who formed the majority, insisted on fighting in the open field. After consultation, the elders warned the younger ones and pressed them to change their minds. They came to the Messenger and informed him that the young people had changed their minds. The Messenger, who had already donned his armor, responded: "When a Prophet has donned his armor, he does not take it off" (al-Bukhārī, "I'tiṣām," 28).

- Although one of the reasons for the setback at the Battle of Uhud was the decision to go out to face the enemy upon the insistence of the younger members during consultation, it is highly significant for the importance of consultation that God still orders it even after such a setback.

- One of the points that attract our attention is that the Qur'ān uses historical events to teach important lessons, make significant warnings and create new legislations. This teaches us that action and thought should go side by side, the former engendering thought and the latter leading to action.

وَمَا أَصَابَكُمْ يَوْمَ الْتَقَى الْجَمْعَانِ فَبِإِذْنِ اللهِ وَلِيَعْلَمَ الْمُؤْمِنِينَ ۝ وَلِيَعْلَمَ الَّذِينَ نَافَقُوا وَقِيلَ لَهُمْ تَعَالَوْا قَاتِلُوا فِي سَبِيلِ اللهِ أَوِ ادْفَعُوا قَالُوا لَوْ نَعْلَمُ قِتَالًا لَاتَّبَعْنَاكُمْ هُمْ لِلْكُفْرِ يَوْمَئِذٍ أَقْرَبُ مِنْهُمْ لِلْإِيمَانِ يَقُولُونَ بِأَفْوَاهِهِمْ مَّا لَيْسَ فِي قُلُوبِهِمْ وَاللهُ أَعْلَمُ بِمَا يَكْتُمُونَ ۝ الَّذِينَ قَالُوا لِإِخْوَانِهِمْ وَقَعَدُوا لَوْ أَطَاعُونَا مَا قُتِلُوا قُلْ فَادْرَءُوا عَنْ أَنْفُسِكُمُ الْمَوْتَ إِنْ كُنْتُمْ صَادِقِينَ ۝ وَلَا تَحْسَبَنَّ الَّذِينَ قُتِلُوا فِي سَبِيلِ اللهِ أَمْوَاتًا بَلْ أَحْيَاءٌ عِنْدَ رَبِّهِمْ يُرْزَقُونَ ۝ فَرِحِينَ بِمَا آتَاهُمُ اللهُ مِنْ فَضْلِهِ وَيَسْتَبْشِرُونَ بِالَّذِينَ لَمْ يَلْحَقُوا بِهِمْ مِنْ خَلْفِهِمْ أَلَّا خَوْفٌ عَلَيْهِمْ وَلَا هُمْ يَحْزَنُونَ ۝ يَسْتَبْشِرُونَ بِنِعْمَةٍ مِنَ اللهِ وَفَضْلٍ وَأَنَّ اللهَ لَا يُضِيعُ أَجْرَ الْمُؤْمِنِينَ ۝ الَّذِينَ اسْتَجَابُوا لِلّهِ وَالرَّسُولِ مِنْ بَعْدِ مَا أَصَابَهُمُ الْقَرْحُ لِلَّذِينَ أَحْسَنُوا مِنْهُمْ وَاتَّقَوْا أَجْرٌ عَظِيمٌ ۝ الَّذِينَ قَالَ لَهُمُ النَّاسُ إِنَّ النَّاسَ قَدْ جَمَعُوا لَكُمْ فَاخْشَوْهُمْ فَزَادَهُمْ إِيمَانًا وَقَالُوا حَسْبُنَا اللهُ وَنِعْمَ الْوَكِيلُ ۝

---

166. What befell you on the day when the two hosts met (in battle) was by God's leave, and that He might mark out the (true) believers.

167. And that He might mark out those who acted in hypocrisy: when they were told, "Come and fight in God's cause, or defend yourselves (actively, in order to keep the enemy outside the city)," they said: "If we but knew there would be fighting, we would indeed follow you." They that day were nearer to unbelief than to faith, uttering with their mouths what was not in their hearts. God knows very well what they were concealing.

168. They who, having themselves held back (from fighting), say of their (slain) brothers, "Had they but paid heed to us, they would not have been killed." Say (to them, O Messenger): "Avert, then, death from yourselves, if you are truthful (in your claim)."

169. Do not think at all of those killed in God's cause as dead. Rather, they are alive; with their Lord they have their sustenance,

170. Rejoicing in what God has granted them out of His bounty, and joyful in the glad tidings for those left behind who have not yet joined them, that (in the event of martyrdom) they will have no fear, nor will they grieve.

171. They are joyful in the glad tidings of God's blessing and bounty (that He has prepared for the martyrs), and in (the promise) that God never leaves to waste the reward of the believers.[32]

172. Those who responded to the call of God and the Messenger after the hurt had befallen them – for all those of them who persevered in doing good, aware that God was seeing them, and acted in reverence for God and piety, there is a tremendous reward.

173. Those to whom some people said: "Look, those people have gathered against you, therefore be fearful of them." But it increased them only in faith, and they responded: "God is sufficient for us; how excellent a Guardian He is!"

32. Why the Muslims experienced a setback can be summarized as follows:

- The Messenger, the commander-in-chief, thought they should stay within Madīnah. The younger Companions, inexperienced and excited, urged him to march out of the city. This was a mistake, even though for the sake of martyrdom in the way of God, since the Messenger tended to apply different tactics in battles and knew in advance that the Quraysh army was coming to fight in an open field.

- The archers posted to defend the army left their posts. They misinterpreted the Messenger's order not to leave for any reason and went to collect booty.

- 300 Hypocrites, one-third of the army, deserted half-way and returned to Madīnah. This undermined the morale of the Banūh Salamah and Banū Hārithah tribes, who were persuaded only with difficulty not to leave. Moreover, a small group of hypocrites demoralized the Muslims during the battle.

- Several Companions became impatient. They acted, in certain respects, inconsistently with the dictates of piety and were lured by material wealth.

- Some believers thought that as long as the Messenger was with them, and as long as they enjoyed God's support and help, the unbelievers could never beat them. However true this was, the setback taught them that deserving God's help requires, besides belief and devotion, deliberation, strategy, and steadfastness. They also perceived that the world is a field of testing and trial.

- Those who had not taken part in Badr sincerely prayed to God for martyrdom. They were deeply devoted to Islam and longed to meet God. Some, like Hamzah, 'Abdullah ibn Jahsh, Anas ibn Nadr, Sa'd ibn Rabi', and 'Amr ibn Jamūh tasted the pleasure of martyrdom; the martyrdom of the others was delayed.

- Any success or triumph lies with God, Who does whatever He wills and cannot be questioned. Belief in God's Unity means that believers must always ascribe their accomplishments to God and never appropriate anything good for themselves. If the decisive victory of Badr gave some Muslims a sort of self-pride, and if they imputed the victory to their own prudence, wise arrangement, or some material causes, this would have been part of the reason for their setback.

- Among the Makkan army were several eminent soldiers and commanders (such as Khālid ibn Walīd, Ikrimah ibn Abī Jahl, 'Amr ibn al-'As, and Ibn Hishām) who were destined by God to be great servants of Islam in the future. They were the ones most esteemed and respected among the people. For the sake of their future service, God may not have willed to hurt their feelings of honor completely. So, as expressed by Bediüzzaman Said Nursi, the Companions of the future defeated the Companions of the present (*Lemalar* ["The Gleams"], 28). (*The Messenger of God*, 233–235)

72 سُورَةُ العِمْرَان ٧٢

فَانقَلَبُوا بِنِعْمَةٍ مِّنَ اللَّهِ وَفَضْلٍ لَّمْ يَمْسَسْهُمْ سُوٓءٌ وَاتَّبَعُوا رِضْوَانَ اللَّهِ وَاللَّهُ ذُو فَضْلٍ عَظِيمٍ ۝ إِنَّمَا ذَٰلِكُمُ الشَّيْطَٰنُ يُخَوِّفُ أَوْلِيَآءَهُۥ فَلَا تَخَافُوهُمْ وَخَافُونِ إِن كُنتُم مُّؤْمِنِينَ ۝ وَلَا يَحْزُنكَ الَّذِينَ يُسَٰرِعُونَ فِي الْكُفْرِ إِنَّهُمْ لَن يَضُرُّوا اللَّهَ شَيْـًٔا يُرِيدُ اللَّهُ أَلَّا يَجْعَلَ لَهُمْ حَظًّا فِي الْءَاخِرَةِ وَلَهُمْ عَذَابٌ عَظِيمٌ ۝ إِنَّ الَّذِينَ اشْتَرَوُا الْكُفْرَ بِالْإِيمَٰنِ لَن يَضُرُّوا اللَّهَ شَيْـًٔا وَلَهُمْ عَذَابٌ أَلِيمٌ ۝ وَلَا يَحْسَبَنَّ الَّذِينَ كَفَرُوٓا أَنَّمَا نُمْلِي لَهُمْ خَيْرٌ لِّأَنفُسِهِمْ إِنَّمَا نُمْلِي لَهُمْ لِيَزْدَادُوٓا إِثْمًا وَلَهُمْ عَذَابٌ مُّهِينٌ ۝ مَّا كَانَ اللَّهُ لِيَذَرَ الْمُؤْمِنِينَ عَلَىٰ مَآ أَنتُمْ عَلَيْهِ حَتَّىٰ يَمِيزَ الْخَبِيثَ مِنَ الطَّيِّبِ وَمَا كَانَ اللَّهُ لِيُطْلِعَكُمْ عَلَى الْغَيْبِ وَلَٰكِنَّ اللَّهَ يَجْتَبِي مِن رُّسُلِهِۦ مَن يَشَآءُ فَـَٔامِنُوا بِاللَّهِ وَرُسُلِهِۦ وَإِن تُؤْمِنُوا وَتَتَّقُوا فَلَكُمْ أَجْرٌ عَظِيمٌ ۝ وَلَا يَحْسَبَنَّ الَّذِينَ يَبْخَلُونَ بِمَآ ءَاتَىٰهُمُ اللَّهُ مِن فَضْلِهِۦ هُوَ خَيْرًا لَّهُم بَلْ هُوَ شَرٌّ لَّهُمْ سَيُطَوَّقُونَ مَا بَخِلُوا بِهِۦ يَوْمَ الْقِيَٰمَةِ وَلِلَّهِ مِيرَٰثُ السَّمَٰوَٰتِ وَالْأَرْضِ وَاللَّهُ بِمَا تَعْمَلُونَ خَبِيرٌ ۝

───────⊰❦⊱───────

174. So they returned with favor and bounty from God, having suffered no harm. They strove after God's good pleasure by acting in the way He approved of. God is of tremendous grace and bounty.[33]

175. It was but that (human) devil who, (by provoking alarm,) desires to make you fearful of his allies. So do not fear them, but fear Me,[34] if you are (true) believers.[35]

176. Let not those who rush in unbelief as if competing with one another grieve you; they can in no way harm God (and His true friends). God wills that they will have no share in (the blessings of) the Hereafter. For them is a tremendous punishment.

177. Those who have bought unbelief in exchange for faith can in no way harm God (and His true friends who fear and rely on Him). For them is a tremendous punishment.

178. And let not those who disbelieve think that Our giving them rein is good for them. We give them rein only that they may grow in sin and wickedness (and deserve God's punishment).[36] For them is a shameful, humiliating punishment.

179. It was not (the will) of God to leave the believers in the state you are now in (with the people of true faith indistinguishable from the hypocrites), until He distinguishes the corrupt from the pure. Nor was it (the will of God) that He would make you aware of the Unseen (so that you would know your future and have insight into the hearts of people). But God chooses of His Messengers whom He wills (and imparts to him some

of the knowledge of the Unseen and completes the test to which He puts you in the world). So believe in God and His Messengers: if you (truly) believe and live in piety, keeping from disobedience to Him and to His Messenger, then there is for you a tremendous reward.

180. Let not those who are niggardly with what God has granted them out of His bounty think that it is good for them: rather, it is bad for them. What they are niggardly with, they will have it hung about their necks on the Day of Resurrection. (Why are they niggardly, seeing that to God belongs the absolute ownership of the heavens and the earth, and) He will inherit them in the end. And God is fully aware of all that you do.

33. After the Muslims' setback in the Battle of Uhud, the Makkan army returned and headed for Makkah. However, the Messenger worried that they might return and launch another attack on Madīnah. On the second day of Uhud, therefore, he ordered those who had fought the day before to gather together and pursue the unbelievers. Some of the Banū 'Abdi'l-Qays, appointed by Abū Sufyan, the commander of the Makkan army, tried to discourage this line of action by saying: "Those people have gathered against you, therefore be fearful of them." But this only increased the faith of the believers, who retorted: "God is sufficient for us; how excellent Guardian He is!"

Most were seriously wounded; some could not stand and had to be carried by their friends. At this highly critical moment, they girded up their loins and prepared to lay down their lives at the Messenger's behest. They accompanied him to Hamra' al-Asad, eight miles from Madīnah. The Makkan polytheists had halted and were talking about a second attack on Madīnah. However, when they saw the believers they had supposedly just defeated coming towards them, they could not muster sufficient courage and so continued on to Makkah. The Messenger's prudence and military genius had turned a defeat into a victory (Ibn Hishām, 3: 240–242).

34. While returning from the Battle of Uhud, Abū Sufyan had challenged the Muslims to another encounter at Badr the following year. But when the appointed time arrived, Abū Sufyan's courage failed him to fight against God's Messenger. As a face-saving device he sent an agent, Nu'aym ibn Mas'ud, who was then an unbeliever, to Madīnah who spread the rumor that the Quraysh were making tremendous war preparations and that they were gathering a huge army which no other power in the whole of Arabia would resist. However, when the Messenger, upon him be peace and blessings, reached Badr with an army of fifteen hundred fighters, they found there no one to fight with them. They stayed at Badr for eight days awaiting the threatened encounter, and

when no sign of the Quraysh army appeared, they returned to Madīnah. This campaign was called *Badr al-Sughrā* (Badr the Minor).

35. It is not possible to find this relationship between God and the servant in other religions. Belief in only One God, bowing before Him alone, and both a fear and a love of Him, liberate and save the servant from fearing and bowing before any other power – such as other human beings, Satan, death, and the so-called natural forces and (evil) spirits – and from suffering all other kinds of fruitless love. One who serves God is a servant, but such servants do not degrade themselves to serve even the greatest of the created, they are so dignified that they do not even pursue Paradise in return for service. They are humble, and only humble themselves voluntarily to their Creator, never exceeding what He has permitted. They are aware of their inherent weaknesses and needs, but are independent of all creation because of what the Munificent Owner has prepared for them in the Hereafter. Relying on the infinite Power of their Master, they are powerful. Their fear of Him makes them fearless of everything else and, as it draws them to Him, is as pleasant as love of Him.

36. As mentioned before, the Qur'ānic expressions used for this kind of God's way of acting and which give the impression as if God wished for the perdition of some people, should be viewed according to His law of the creation and operation of the universe and the human individual and social life. That is, God has laws which He has established for the life of the individual and the society and humanity, which are followed out of free will, or which are obeyed or disobeyed and which receive the requital of this obedience or disobedience. Since it is God Who has established these laws and since it is the whole of creation, including humanity, which lives within their limits, the Qur'ān uses such expressions. So, the above verse actually says: "These people use the rein We give them only to increase in sin and wickedness in such a way that they deserve God's punishment."

لَّقَدْ سَمِعَ اللّهُ قَوْلَ الَّذِينَ قَالُوٓاْ إِنَّ اللّهَ فَقِيرٌ وَنَحْنُ
أَغْنِيَآءُ سَنَكْتُبُ مَا قَالُواْ وَقَتْلَهُمُ الْأَنۢبِيَآءَ بِغَيْرِ
حَقٍّ وَنَقُولُ ذُوقُواْ عَذَابَ الْحَرِيقِ ۞ ذَٰلِكَ بِمَا قَدَّمَتْ
أَيْدِيكُمْ وَأَنَّ اللّهَ لَيْسَ بِظَلَّامٍ لِّلْعَبِيدِ ۞ الَّذِينَ
قَالُوٓاْ إِنَّ اللّهَ عَهِدَ إِلَيْنَآ أَلَّا نُؤْمِنَ لِرَسُولٍ حَتَّىٰ يَأْتِيَنَا
بِقُرْبَانٍ تَأْكُلُهُ النَّارُ قُلْ قَدْ جَآءَكُمْ رُسُلٌ مِّن قَبْلِى
بِالْبَيِّنَاتِ وَبِالَّذِى قُلْتُمْ فَلِمَ قَتَلْتُمُوهُمْ إِن كُنتُمْ
صَادِقِينَ ۞ فَإِن كَذَّبُوكَ فَقَدْ كُذِّبَ رُسُلٌ مِّن قَبْلِكَ
جَآءُو بِالْبَيِّنَاتِ وَالزُّبُرِ وَالْكِتَابِ الْمُنِيرِ ۞ كُلُّ نَفْسٍ
ذَآئِقَةُ الْمَوْتِ وَإِنَّمَا تُوَفَّوْنَ أُجُورَكُمْ يَوْمَ الْقِيَامَةِ فَمَن
زُحْزِحَ عَنِ النَّارِ وَأُدْخِلَ الْجَنَّةَ فَقَدْ فَازَ وَمَا الْحَيَوٰةُ
الدُّنْيَآ إِلَّا مَتَاعُ الْغُرُورِ ۞ لَتُبْلَوُنَّ فِىٓ أَمْوَالِكُمْ
وَأَنفُسِكُمْ وَلَتَسْمَعُنَّ مِنَ الَّذِينَ أُوتُواْ الْكِتَابَ
مِن قَبْلِكُمْ وَمِنَ الَّذِينَ أَشْرَكُوٓاْ أَذًى كَثِيرًا وَإِن
تَصْبِرُواْ وَتَتَّقُواْ فَإِنَّ ذَٰلِكَ مِنْ عَزْمِ الْأُمُورِ ۞

181. God has indeed heard the saying of those who said, "God is poor, and we are rich." We will record what they have said, as well as their killing the Prophets against all right; and We will say (to them): "Taste the punishment of the scorching fire!"

182. This is because of (the unrighteous deeds) that your own hands have forwarded, for never does God do the least wrong to the servants.

183. (Also it is) they who said: "God made covenant with us, that we believe not in any Messenger unless he brings us an offering which (as a sign of its being accepted by God) a fire (from heaven) will consume." Say (to them, O Messenger): "Before me there came to you Messengers with the clear proofs (of their Messengership) and with that (same miracle) which you describe: why, then, did you kill them, if you are true in your claim?"

184. (O Messenger!) If they deny you, (do not grieve!) For in the same way Messengers were denied before you, who came with the clear proofs (of their Messengership), Scrolls (full of wisdom and advice), and the Book (the Torah and the Gospel) enlightening (their minds and hearts, and) illuminating (their way).

185. (No one will live forever doing what they do:) Every soul is bound to taste death.[37] So (O people) you will but be repaid in full on the Day of Resurrection (for whatever you have done in the world). Whoever is spared the Fire and admitted into Paradise has indeed prospered and triumphed. (Know that) the present, worldly life is nothing but a transient enjoyment of delusion.

186. (So, O believers, as a requirement of the wisdom in and purpose for your worldly life,) you will surely be tested in respect of your properties and your selves, and you will certainly hear many hurtful things from those who were given the Book before you and those who associate partners with God. If you are patient steadfast (in your Religion and observe the bounds set by God in your relations with them) and keep within the limits of piety (in obeying God and in your conduct towards them), (know that) this is among meritorious things requiring great resolution to fulfill.

37. *Nafs* (translated as soul) has two meanings: (1) the self of a living being, whether transcendent and incorporeal like that of God or that composed of a spirit and body; and (2) the faculty which is the source or mechanism of the worldly life possessed by humankind and the jinn. So, considered from the viewpoint of its first meaning, the souls meant in the following phrase, "Every soul is bound to taste death" are those of humankind and the jinn. This is also corroborated by the context.

The idea of a soul (in the meaning of the self of the living being) tasting death also implies that the living being has a part of it which tastes the death, but does not itself die. This entails that while the body dies, the spirit is transferred to the other world alive. However, the verse,

Everything is perishable (and so perishing) except His "Face" (His eternal Self and what is done in seeking His good pleasure) (28: 88) alludes to the idea that the spirits and spiritual beings, like angels, will also taste death, even though for only a short while. On the other hand, if, by the expression *Except those whom God wills (to exempt)* in the verse, *The Trumpet will be blown, and so all who are in the heavens and all who are on the earth will fall dead, except those whom God wills (to exempt* (39: 68), the absolute authority of the Divine Will is not intended to be emphasized; i.e., if God wills, He may cause whomever He wills to live without tasting death, it can be said that in some cases there will be some living beings who will never taste death. God knows best.

187. (Remember) when God took a covenant from those who were given the Book: "You shall make clear to the people (the whole truth of all that is in) the Book (including mention of the Last, promised Prophet), and not conceal it." But they paid no heed to it, flinging it behind their backs, and sold it for a trifling price (such as worldly advantage and position, status and renown). How evil a bargain they made!

188. Never suppose that those who rejoice in what they have thus contrived, and who love to be (famed and) praised for what they have not achieved (such as being devout and pious and defenders of God's law) – never suppose that they have saved themselves from the punishment: for them is a painful punishment.

189. And God's is the sovereignty (absolute ownership and dominion) of the heavens and the earth, and God has full power over everything.

190. Surely in the creation of the heavens and the earth and the alternation of night and day (with their periods shortening and lengthening) there are signs (manifesting the truth) for the people of discernment.

191. They remember and mention God (with their tongues and hearts), standing and sitting and lying down on their sides (whether during the Prayer or not), and reflect on the creation of the heavens and the earth. (Having grasped the purpose of their creation and the meaning they contain, they conclude and say): "Our Lord, You have not created this (the universe) without meaning and purpose. All-Glorified are You (in that You are absolutely above doing anything meaningless and purposeless), so save us from (having wrong conceptions of Your acts and acting against Your purpose for creation, and so deserving) the punishment of the Fire!

192. "Our Lord! Whomever You admit into the Fire, indeed You have brought him to disgrace. (Having concealed or rejected God's signs in the heavens and on the earth and so denied God or fallen into associating partners with Him,) the wrongdoers will have no helpers (against the Fire).

193. "Our Lord! Indeed We have heard a caller calling to faith, saying: 'Believe in your Lord!', so we did believe. Our Lord, forgive us, then, our sins, and blot out from us our evil deeds, and take us to You in death in the company of the truly godly and virtuous.

194. "Our Lord! Grant us what You have promised us through Your Messengers. Do not disgrace us on the Day of Resurrection; indeed You never break Your promise."

195. And thus does their (All-Gracious and Generous) Lord answer them: "I do not leave to waste the work of any of you (engaged in doing good), whether male or female. (As males and females following the same way) you are all one from the other. Hence, those who have emigrated (in My cause) and been expelled from their homelands and suffered hurt in My cause, and have fought and been killed, indeed I will blot out from them their evil deeds and will admit them into Gardens through which rivers flow, as a reward from God (with infinite Mercy and Power to fulfill whatever He promises)." With God lies the best reward.

196. Let it not deceive you (O Messenger) that those who disbelieve strut about the land in pomp and show of dominion.

197. It is but a brief enjoyment, with Hell thereafter as their final refuge: how evil a cradle it is!

198. Whereas those who keep from disobedience to their Lord (Who created and raised them, and sustains them, and Who has sent them the best of laws to order their lives), and act within the limits of piety – for them are Gardens through which rivers flow, therein to abide: a hospitality from the Presence of God; and that which is with God is best for the truly godly and virtuous.

199. And, behold, among the People of the Book are those who believe in God and what has been sent down to you, and what was sent down to them, those humbling themselves before God in reverence, not selling God's Revelations for a trifling price. Such are those whose reward is with their Lord. God is swift at reckoning.

200. O you who believe! Be patient (persevere through what befalls you in the world in God's cause); encourage each other to patience vying in it with one another and outdoing all others in it; and observe your duties to God in solidarity, and keep from disobedience to God in due reverence for Him and piety, so that you may prosper (in both worlds).

SŪRAH 4

AN-NISĀ' (WOMEN)

Madīnah period

This *sūrah*, which has 176 verses, was revealed around the 6th year of the *Hijrah*. It is the first of two *sūrah*s that begin with the phrase "O humankind!". When the Qur'ān is divided into two equal parts, *Sūrat an-Nisā'* is the fourth *sūrah* of the first part, while *Sūrah Ḥajj*, the second *sūrah* that begins with "O humankind!" is the fourth *sūrah* of the second part. After addressing us in this way, the *sūrah* draws attention to the origin or beginning of humankind; *Sūrah Ḥajj*, in contrast, focuses on the afterlife. Most of the principles that were revealed to govern Muslim civil life are found in this *sūrah*.

In the Name of God, the All-Merciful, the All-Compassionate.

1. O humankind! In due reverence for your Lord, keep from disobedience to Him Who created you from a single human self, and from it created its mate, and from the pair of them scattered abroad a multitude of men and women. In due reverence for God, keep from disobedience to Him in Whose name you make demands of one another, and (duly observe) the rights of the wombs (i.e. of kinship, thus observing piety in your relations with God and with human beings). God is ever watchful over you.[1]

2. Restore their property to the orphans (in your custody, when they come of age), and do not exchange the corrupt for the good (the unlawful for the lawful), nor consume their property by mixing it up with your own. For doing that would be a great crime (whereby you risk the spiritual reward you hope for by caring for them).

3. If you fear that you will not be able to observe their rights with exact fairness

when you marry the orphan girls (in your custody), you can marry, from among other women (who are permitted to you in marriage and) who seem good to you, two, or three, or four.[2] However, if you fear that (in your marital obligations) you will not be able to observe justice among them, then content yourselves with only one, or the captives that your right hands possess.[3] Doing so is more likely that you will not act rebelliously.

4. Give to the women (whom you marry) their bridal-due (*mahr*) willingly and for good (i.e. without expecting a return); however, if of their own accord they remit any part of it to you, then you are welcome to enjoy it gladly.

5. Do not give to those of weak mind your property that God has put in your charge (as a means of support for you and for

the needy), but feed and clothe them out of it (especially with the profit you will make by exploiting it), and speak to them kindly and words of honest advice.

6. (Care for and) test the orphans well until they reach the age of marriage. Then, if you find them to be mature of mind, hand over to them their property; and do not consume it by wasteful spending, nor do so in haste fearing that they will come of age (and so take it over). If the guardian is rich (enough to support himself and his family), let him abstain (from his ward's property); but if he is poor, let him consume thereof in a just and reasonable manner. When you hand (their property) over to them, let there be witnesses on their behalf. God suffices as One Who reckons and settles the accounts (of His servants).

---

1. From many different aspects this verse is very significant. However, due to the scope of this study we can only discuss a few points here:

The original Arabic that has been translated as "a single human self" is *nafs wāhidah* (literally, a single self or soul). As mentioned before, *nafs* has two basic meanings: the self of a being and the faculty which is the source or mechanism of the worldly life possessed by humankind and the jinn. When both meanings are taken into consideration, the phrase "a single human self" is preferable as a translation for *nafs wāhidah*.

There are similar verses in the Qur'ān that support such a choice. For example: *And among His signs is that He has created for you, from your selves, mates, that you may incline towards them and find rest in them, and He has engendered love and tenderness between you* (30: 21); *God has made for you, from your selves, mates (spouses), and has made for you from your mates children and grandchildren, and has provided you with good, wholesome things* (16: 72); *The Originator of the heavens and the earth each with particular features; He has made for you, from your selves, mates, and from the cattle mates (of their own kind)* .... (42: 11). What these verses are referring to by the phrase "your selves" is humankind, or the human self or nature. These verses draw our attention to the fact that everything exists in the universe in pairs, as is made clear in the verse: *And all things We have created in pairs, so that you may reflect and be mindful* (51:49).

Some are of the opinion that what the verse refers to by "a single human self" is Adam. This is not contrary to the preference made in this study, for the Qur'ān presents Adam in the Garden before his earthly life as one who represents humankind or the human self, rather than as an individual man. However, Adam being used as the representative of the human self is a very subtle point. It is the male that inseminates and is the primary factor in reproduction. Insemination can result in either a male child or a female child. That is, a male can beget both a male or female. If nature has a creative power, as materialists or naturalists claim, a male cannot beget a female; for nature is regularity and constancy. A female is neither a "natural" product or a continuation of a male, nor vice versa. The male and female are the two halves or mates of a whole; these two halves complete each other and each has features that are peculiar to itself. The existence of each depends solely on the Creator's Will and Power, which are absolute. Nature is not an originator nor a creative power; it is a creation, a model, a regular system established by the Creator.

Since the male has the inseminating function in reproduction in pairs and the human self from which its mate was created is represented primarily by Adam, women mean more as a blessing for men than men mean for women. As pointed out before (*sūrah* 2, note 21), it is from this perspective that the Qur'ān mentions women as being among the primary blessings of Paradise for men. The fact that the male has the inseminating function in reproduction in pairs means men have a more dominant position and are charged naturally with responsibilities required by this position.

Sūrat an-Nisā' is, in addition to including other aspects, the source of Islamic civil law. This is why it is of great significance that it begins with the address, "O humankind!" With such an address, the Qur'ān appeals to human feelings, and brings out the need for being human in relationships. What is meant is that: "Each of you is a human being that shares the same human nature. You are all the offspring of the same father and mother, and therefore are all brothers and sisters. This requires that you treat each other as brothers and sisters, without making any discrimination based on color, race, or language." By focusing attention on the rights of kinship, this verse underlines this point, and by mentioning these rights along with the observation of God's rights, it stresses their importance.

2. Some people wrongfully criticize Islam because it allows polygamy. Such a criticism, from several perspectives, is not justifiable; some of these perspectives are as follows:

- Polygamy is a very ancient practice found in many human societies. The Bible did not condemn polygamy. On the contrary, the Old Testament and Rabbinic writings frequently attest to the legality of polygamy. King Solomon and King David had many wives and concubines (*2 Samuel*, 5: 13). According to Father Eugene Hillman in his insightful book, *Polygamy Reconsidered*, "Nowhere in the New Testament is there any explicit commandment that marriage should be monogamous or any explicit commandment forbidding polygamy." Moreover, Jesus did not speak against polygamy, even though it was practiced by the Jews in his society. Father Hillman stresses the fact that the Church in Rome banned polygamy in order to conform to the Greco-Roman culture (which prescribed only one legal wife while tolerating concubinage and prostitution). The Qur'ān, contrary to the Bible, limits the maximum number of wives to four, and

imposes the strict condition that all the wives be treated equally and justly. This should not be seen as the Qur'ān exhorting believers to practice polygamy, or that polygamy is considered as an ideal state. In other words, the Qur'ān tolerates or allows polygamy, and nothing more. But why is polygamy permissible? The answer is simple: there are places and times in which there are compelling social and moral reasons for polygamy. Islam as a universal religion suitable for all places and all times cannot ignore these compelling reasons.

- In most human societies, females outnumber males. In America today there are at least eight million more women than men. In a country like Guinea there are 122 females for every 100 males. In Tanzania, there are 95.1 males per 100 females (Hillman, 88–93). What should a society do when faced with such an unbalanced sex ratio? There are various solutions; some might suggest celibacy, others prefer female infanticide (which does happen in even some "civilized" societies in the world today!) Others may think the only solution is that society should tolerate all manners of sexual permissiveness: prostitution, infidelity, homosexuality, etc.

- Such an imbalance in the sex ratios becomes truly problematic in times of war. Native American Indian tribes used to suffer highly unbalanced sex ratios after military losses. The women in these tribes, who in fact enjoyed a fairly high status, accepted polygamy as being the best protection against indulgence in indecent activities. After the Second World War, there were 7,300,000 more women than men in Germany (3.3 million of them were widows). Many of these women needed a man not only as a companion, but also as a provider for the household in a time of unprecedented misery and hardship. What is more dignified for a woman? To be an accepted and respected second wife, as in the native Indians' approach, or to be nothing more than a prostitute? In 1987, a poll conducted by the student newspaper at the University of California at Berkeley asked the students whether they agreed that men should be allowed by law to have more than one wife. This question was posed in response to a perceived shortage of male marriage candidates in California. Almost all of the students polled approved of the idea (J. Lang, *Struggling to Surrender*, 172).

- Up to the present day, polygamy continues to be a viable solution for some of the social ills in modern society. Philip Kilbride, an American anthropologist with a Roman Catholic background, proposes polygamy as a solution to some of the ills found in American society in his provocative book, *Plural Marriage For Our Time*. He argues that plural marriage may serve as a potential alternative for divorce in many cases, where it would obviate the damaging impact that divorce has on many children (Kilbride, 118).

- It should be noted that in many Muslim societies today the practice of polygamy is rare, since there is a better balance between the ratio of the sexes. One can safely say that the rate of polygamous marriages in the Muslim world is much less than the rate of extramarital affairs in the West. In other words, men in the Muslim world today are far more monogamous, in the absolute sense of the word, than men in the Western world.

- Billy Graham, the eminent Christian evangelist has recognized this fact: "Christianity cannot compromise on the question of polygamy. If present-day Christianity cannot do so, it is to its own detriment. Islam has permitted polygamy as a solution to social ills and has allowed a certain degree of latitude to human nature, but only within the strictly defined framework of the law.

Christian countries make a great show of monogamy, but actually they practice polygamy. No one is unaware of the part mistresses play in Western society. In this respect Islam is a fundamentally honest religion, and permits a Muslim to marry a second wife if he must, but strictly forbids all clandestine amatory associations in order to safeguard the moral probity of the community" ('Abd ar-Raḥmān Doi, *Woman in Shari'ah*, 76).

- There are even psychological factors calling for polygamy. For example, many young African brides, whatever their religion, would prefer to marry a man who has already proved himself to be a responsible husband. Many African wives urge their husbands to get a second wife so that they will not feel lonely (Hillman, 92–97). A survey of over six thousand women, ranging in age from 15 to 59, conducted in the second largest city in Nigeria showed that 60 percent of these women would be pleased if their husbands took another wife. In a survey undertaken in rural Kenya, 25 out of 27 women considered polygamy to be better than monogamy. These women felt polygamy can be a happy and beneficial experience if the co-wives cooperate with each other (Kilbride, 108–109).

- Modern civilization rejects polygamy as unwise and disadvantageous to social life. As observed even in animals and plants, the purpose for and wisdom in sexual relations is reproduction. The resulting pleasure is a small payment determined by Divine Mercy to realize this duty. Marriage is for reproduction and the perpetuation of the species. Being able to give birth at most once a year, able to become pregnant during half of a month, and entering menopause around 50, a woman is, reproductively inferior to a man, who can sometimes impregnate women until the age of 70 or more. That is why, in most cases, modern civilization is obliged to find new ways of impregnation at great cost. Even if the purpose of marriage were sexual gratification, polygamy would be a lawful way to realize it. (Summarized from Sherif Muḥammad.)

3. The following points should be considered when viewing the matter of (female-)slavery from within the matrix of Islam:

- Islam did not invent or establish the institution of (female-)slavery; rather it found itself in an international arena where (female-)slavery was practiced in the most abominable manner. Islam viewed the matter as related to wartime and dealt with this subject as if it were a matter of how to treat prisoners of war. Although (female-)slavery, in various forms, was in practice until recently, Islam adopted a process to abolish it over the course of time, fourteen centuries ago. It was not Islam, but those who related themselves to Islam, that were responsible for certain objectionable practices that have been witnessed in some Muslim communities over the previous centuries.

- While international law in the modern world does not date back to more than a few centuries, Islam established principles and laws in matters concerning international relations, such as war and the treatment of the prisoners-of-war over fourteen centuries ago. Imam Muḥammad al-Shaybānī, who lived twelve centuries ago, was the first to write a book on international law, *al-Siyar al-Kabīr*. This book is based on the relevant injunctions in the Qur'ān and on the practice of the Prophet, upon him be peace and blessings.

- Islam forbade the killing of prisoners-of-war, and in place of this, instructed that they be distributed among Muslim families. Great importance was attached to their education and their "owners" were advised to marry the women

among them. Such "prisoners-of-war" were to be given the status of free women when they gave birth to a child. Islam aims at their final emancipation and the eradication of (female-)slavery. As recompense for many sinful acts, such as breaking fast before the proper time, Islam required the emancipation of a (female-)slave, and exhorted believers to emancipate their (female-)slaves, stating that this is a very meritorious act.

- Without making any gender discrimination, Islam attaches great value to humankind. It aims at elevating all human beings to the true rank of humanity, as this is the best pattern of creation. It regards the women who have attained this rank with their level of education, character and virtuousness, as being *muḥṣan* (protected women). A woman devoid of such lofty moral and spiritual values, one who presents herself as merely a physical object of sex cannot be a *muḥṣan*. Attaining this rank requires true education, and Islam has established rules for each stage or grade. Therefore the matter of (female-)slavery has educational and psychological dimensions, in addition to social and international ones.

- As pointed out before (*Sūrah: 2, note: 95*), with regard to legislation, Islam follows three principal ways: It retains the commandments that existed in previous Books or that prevailed in the community in which it appeared and which were not contradictory to its essential principles. It corrected or amended the ones that were not in conformity with its principles; and finally, it made new legislations. In each of these ways, Islam followed a gradual process, especially in matters that required a long time to eradicate old habits or establish a new approach. The matter of (female-)slavery is one such issue, especially due to its international dimension.

لِلرِّجَالِ نَصِيبٌ مِّمَّا تَرَكَ الْوَالِدَانِ وَالْأَقْرَبُونَ وَلِلنِّسَاءِ نَصِيبٌ مِّمَّا تَرَكَ الْوَالِدَانِ وَالْأَقْرَبُونَ مِمَّا قَلَّ مِنْهُ أَوْ كَثُرَ ۚ نَصِيبًا مَّفْرُوضًا ۝ وَإِذَا حَضَرَ الْقِسْمَةَ أُولُوا الْقُرْبَىٰ وَالْيَتَامَىٰ وَالْمَسَاكِينُ فَارْزُقُوهُم مِّنْهُ وَقُولُوا لَهُمْ قَوْلًا مَّعْرُوفًا ۝ وَلْيَخْشَ الَّذِينَ لَوْ تَرَكُوا مِنْ خَلْفِهِمْ ذُرِّيَّةً ضِعَافًا خَافُوا عَلَيْهِمْ فَلْيَتَّقُوا اللَّهَ وَلْيَقُولُوا قَوْلًا سَدِيدًا ۝ إِنَّ الَّذِينَ يَأْكُلُونَ أَمْوَالَ الْيَتَامَىٰ ظُلْمًا إِنَّمَا يَأْكُلُونَ فِي بُطُونِهِمْ نَارًا ۖ وَسَيَصْلَوْنَ سَعِيرًا ۝ يُوصِيكُمُ اللَّهُ فِي أَوْلَادِكُمْ ۖ لِلذَّكَرِ مِثْلُ حَظِّ الْأُنثَيَيْنِ ۚ فَإِن كُنَّ نِسَاءً فَوْقَ اثْنَتَيْنِ فَلَهُنَّ ثُلُثَا مَا تَرَكَ ۖ وَإِن كَانَتْ وَاحِدَةً فَلَهَا النِّصْفُ ۚ وَلِأَبَوَيْهِ لِكُلِّ وَاحِدٍ مِّنْهُمَا السُّدُسُ مِمَّا تَرَكَ إِن كَانَ لَهُ وَلَدٌ ۚ فَإِن لَّمْ يَكُن لَّهُ وَلَدٌ وَوَرِثَهُ أَبَوَاهُ فَلِأُمِّهِ الثُّلُثُ ۚ فَإِن كَانَ لَهُ إِخْوَةٌ فَلِأُمِّهِ السُّدُسُ ۚ مِنْ بَعْدِ وَصِيَّةٍ يُوصِي بِهَا أَوْ دَيْنٍ ۗ آبَاؤُكُمْ وَأَبْنَاؤُكُمْ لَا تَدْرُونَ أَيُّهُمْ أَقْرَبُ لَكُمْ نَفْعًا ۚ فَرِيضَةً مِّنَ اللَّهِ ۗ إِنَّ اللَّهَ كَانَ عَلِيمًا حَكِيمًا ۝

———❧———

7. For the male heirs is a share out of what parents and near kindred leave behind, and for the female heirs is a share of what parents and near kindred leave behind, whether it (the inheritance) be little or much – a share ordained by God.[4]

8. If some from among other relatives (who do not have a legally defined share), and orphans, and the destitute are present at the division (of the inheritance), give them something thereof (for their provision), and speak to them kindly and pleasing words.

9. Let those fear (be anxious for the rights of the orphans) who, if they themselves were to leave behind weak offspring, would be fearful on their account – and let them keep from disobedience to God for fear of His punishment, and let them

speak the truth and proper words (in respect of the division of the inheritance and their treatment of the orphans.)

10. Surely those who consume the property of orphans wrongfully, certainly they consume a fire in their bellies; and soon they will be roasting in a Blaze (the like of which you have never seen and the degree of whose intensity none knows except God).

11. God commands you in (the matter of the division of the inheritance among) your children: for the male is the equivalent of the portion of two females. If there are more than two females (with no males), for them is two-thirds of the inheritance; if there is only one, then the half. As for the parents (of the deceased): for each of the two is one-sixth of the inheritance, in case of his having left a child; but if he has left no children and his parents are his only heirs, then for his mother is one-third. If he has (a surviving mother and, together with or without sisters,) two or more (surviving) brothers, then for his mother is one-sixth – (all these commands to be put into effect) after deduction for any bequest he may have made (provided such bequest is in conformity with the relevant teachings of Islam) and any debt (incurred by him) (– first the debt is paid, then the bequest is fulfilled, and then the inheritance is shared). Your parents and your children: you do not know which of them is nearer to you in (bringing you) benefit. This (law of inheritance) is an ordinance from God (that you must absolutely obey). Surely God is All-Knowing (of your affairs and what benefits or harms you), and All-Wise.

4. This short verse contains the basic principles of the Islamic law of inheritance established by the Qur'ān, as well as a significant warning:

- Like men, women also have a share in inheritance.
- The property left behind by a deceased person is inherited, no matter the amount.
- It makes no difference whether the inherited property is movable or immovable.
- Any children, parents, grandparents or other near relatives can inherit from another person. If there are near kindred, those who are of collateral relations cannot inherit.
- Heirs cannot be deprived of inheritance, except for exceptional cases such as they have killed their testator (at-Tirmidhī, "Farā'iḍ," 17) (Suat Yıldırım, *Kur'an-ı Hakim*, 77).

The significant warning that is contained in the verse is as follows: In the pre-Islamic age women were forbidden from inheriting. By mentioning women or female heirs separately, in the same way that male heirs are mentioned, i.e. by reiteration, an emphasis is made, stressing that whether the inheritance is great or small, women cannot be deprived of it on any pretext, such as the amount being insignificant.

12. And for you is a half of what your wives leave behind if they have no children, but if they have a child, then you shall have one-fourth of what they leave behind – after deduction for any bequest they may have made and any debt (incurred by them). And for them is one-fourth of what you leave behind, if you have no children; but if you have a child, then they shall have one-eighth of what you leave behind – after deduction for any bequest you may have made and any debt (incurred by you). And if a man or a woman has no heir in the direct line, but has a brother or a sister (on the mother's side), for him or her is one-sixth; but if there are two or more, then they shall be sharers in one-third – after deduction for any bequest that may have been made or debt; neither (bequest or debt) intending harm (to the rights of the heirs in such ways as declaring fictitious debts or bequeathing more than one-third of one's estate). A commandment from God. God is All-Knowing (of all your intentions, actions, and outcomes), All-Clement (not hasty to punish the errors of His servants).[5]

13. These are the bounds set by God. Whoever obeys God and His Messenger (by remaining within these bounds), God will admit him into Gardens through which rivers flow, abiding therein. That is the supreme triumph.

14. But whoever disobeys God and His Messenger and exceeds His bounds, God will admit him into a Fire, to abide therein, and for him is a shameful, humiliating punishment.

5. In these last two verses, the basic principles and standards of the Islamic law of inheritance are laid down; the precise details have been established on these standards and on the practice of the Prophet and his Companions. Before elucidating some points, we should consider the fact that these two verses present the Islamic law of inheritance as God's absolute command, and in their conclusive pronouncements declare that they are based on God's Knowledge and Wisdom. Therefore, what we should do is to try to find instances of His Divine Wisdom in them. Breaching these orders means disobedience to God and His Messenger, while rejecting them amounts to unbelief. Secondly, Islam is not a religion that takes up a position of answering objections. Whatever it decrees, is right and just. So, our intention, while explaining Islam's position in matters that have been made the target of objections during recent times, is to illuminate sincere minds.

• According to the Islamic law of inheritance, with the exception of the father and mother, and in some cases, the brothers and sisters, a son receives twice as much as a daughter, a brother twice as much as a sister and a husband twice as much as a wife.

- Islam is universal, taking into consideration and addressing the conditions of all ages and communities. Its worldview is holistic and deals with particular matters in a universal frame. So, when viewing its law of inheritance, we should consider many psychological and sociological factors, such as the psychology of women and men, their positions and financial responsibilities in the family and society, and their contribution to the economy. We should evaluate every matter with respect to its own nature and within its own framework, and not be misled by theoretical abstractions disconnected from lived reality, such as absolute equality, the pursuit of which can often result in loss of equity and balance.

- In order to understand the rationale behind why Islam in some cases gives women half the share of men, one must take into account the fact that the financial obligations of men in Islam far exceed those of women. A bridegroom must provide his bride with a marriage gift. This gift becomes her exclusive property and remains so even if she is later divorced. The bride is under no obligation to present any gifts to her husband. Moreover, the Muslim husband is charged with the maintenance of his wife and children. The wife, on the other hand, is not obliged to help him in this regard. Her property and earnings are for her use alone, except what she may voluntarily offer her husband. Moreover, one has to realize that Islam strongly advocates family life. It positively encourages young people to get married and discourages divorce. Therefore, in a truly Islamic society, family life is the norm, while single life is the rare exception. That is, almost all women and men of a marriageable age will be married in an Islamic society. In light of these facts, one can appreciate that Muslim men, in general, have greater financial bur-

dens than Muslim women, and the inheritance rules take account of this reality (See Sherif Muḥammad).

- When a woman inherits less than a man does, she is not actually deprived of anything for which she has worked. Any property that is inherited is not the result of her earning or her endeavors. It is something that comes from a neutral source, something additional or extra. It is something that neither the man nor the woman has struggled for. It is a sort of aid, and any aid has to be distributed according to the most urgent needs and responsibilities, especially when the distribution is regulated by God's law (http://www.thewaytotruth.org/womaninislam/financial.html).

- The Qur'ānic injunction of inheritance is a perfect mercy for women, in addition to its being perfectly just. Because a girl is delicate, and vulnerable; she must be looked on with affection by her father. Thanks to the Qur'ānic injunction concerning inheritance, the father does not see her as a child who will cause him loss by carrying away to others half of his wealth. In addition, her brothers feel compassion for her and protect her, without feeling envy; they do not consider her as a rival in the division of the family possessions. Thus, the affection and compassion which the girl enjoys through her family compensates for her apparent loss in inheritance.

- Some still object that a woman's share should, from the beginning, be equal to that of man, and then we would not be compelled to compensate her by allowing her a dowry and maintenance on the part of her husband.

Those who make this objection think that the dowry and the maintenance are the results of women's peculiar position with regard to inheritance, whereas the reality is just the opposite. Furthermore, they seem to be under the impression that the financial aspect is the only consideration. Had that been the only consideration, obviously there would have been neither a need for the system of dowry and maintenance, nor would there be a disparity between the shares of men and women. As we have mentioned earlier, Islam has taken into consideration many aspects, some of them natural and others psychological. In most cases, in her parents' house her contribution to the family income is much less than that of her brother(s). Also, a son has to look after his mother if the father dies, the mother will not have to support herself from this portion, nor will any unmarried daughter have to support herself from her share in an Islamic society, therefore, their shares are for their personal use. Other psychological and social aspects, which help in the consolidation of domestic relations have also been considered (M. Mutahhari).

- It is for this reason that it would be a severe injustice, not at all a kindness, to institute a larger share for a girl or woman; to give her more than is her due, merely out of compassion. This is unrealistic, because no one can be more compassionate than God. Rather, if the Qur'ānic bounds are exceeded, women may become, for the reasons we have given, vulnerable to exploitation and tyranny in the family, especially in view of the barbaric selfishness of certain times. As for the Qur'ānic injunctions, all of them, like those pertaining to inheritance, prove the truth expressed in the verse, *We have not sent you (O Muḥammad) but as an unequalled mercy for all the worlds* (21: 107).

- Islam does not support the idea that wealth is a fortune circulated among a small minority. It wants the wealth to be distributed among as many people as possible. Concerning inheritance, considering that God's grace and bountifulness have a share in it, it is strongly advised, even ordered, that distant relatives, orphans, and the poor should also benefit from any wealth.

وَالَّتِي يَأْتِينَ الْفَاحِشَةَ مِنْ نِسَآئِكُمْ فَاسْتَشْهِدُوا عَلَيْهِنَّ
أَرْبَعَةً مِنْكُمْ فَإِنْ شَهِدُوا فَأَمْسِكُوهُنَّ فِي الْبُيُوتِ حَتَّى
يَتَوَفَّاهُنَّ الْمَوْتُ أَوْ يَجْعَلَ اللهُ لَهُنَّ سَبِيلًا ۝ وَالَّذَانِ
يَأْتِيَانِهَا مِنْكُمْ فَآذُوهُمَا فَإِنْ تَابَا وَأَصْلَحَا
فَأَعْرِضُوا عَنْهُمَآ إِنَّ اللهَ كَانَ تَوَّابًا رَحِيمًا
۝ إِنَّمَا التَّوْبَةُ عَلَى اللهِ لِلَّذِينَ يَعْمَلُونَ السُّوءَ
بِجَهَالَةٍ ثُمَّ يَتُوبُونَ مِنْ قَرِيبٍ فَأُولَئِكَ يَتُوبُ
اللهُ عَلَيْهِمْ وَكَانَ اللهُ عَلِيمًا حَكِيمًا ۝ وَلَيْسَتِ
التَّوْبَةُ لِلَّذِينَ يَعْمَلُونَ السَّيِّئَاتِ حَتَّى إِذَا حَضَرَ أَحَدَهُمُ
الْمَوْتُ قَالَ إِنِّي تُبْتُ الْآنَ وَلَا الَّذِينَ يَمُوتُونَ وَهُمْ كُفَّارٌ
أُولَئِكَ أَعْتَدْنَا لَهُمْ عَذَابًا أَلِيمًا ۝ يَا أَيُّهَا الَّذِينَ آمَنُوا
لَا يَحِلُّ لَكُمْ أَنْ تَرِثُوا النِّسَاءَ كَرْهًا وَلَا تَعْضُلُوهُنَّ
لِتَذْهَبُوا بِبَعْضِ مَا آتَيْتُمُوهُنَّ إِلَّا أَنْ يَأْتِينَ بِفَاحِشَةٍ
مُبَيِّنَةٍ وَعَاشِرُوهُنَّ بِالْمَعْرُوفِ فَإِنْ كَرِهْتُمُوهُنَّ فَعَسَى
أَنْ تَكْرَهُوا شَيْئًا وَيَجْعَلَ اللهُ فِيهِ خَيْرًا كَثِيرًا ۝

15. Such of your women as have committed indecency (unlawful sex), there must be four male witnesses of you who (having seen them in the act) will testify against them (within one succeeding month in towns and six succeeding months in the rural areas). If they do bear witness, then confine those women to their houses until death takes them away or God opens some way for them.

16. When two from among you have committed it, then punish them both by scolding and beating; but if they are remorseful and repent, and make amends, then withdraw from them.⁶ Surely God is He Who accepts repentance and returns it with liberal forgiveness and additional reward, All-Compassionate.

17. God's acceptance of repentance is only for those who commit evil due to ignorance (an instance of defeat to the evil-commanding soul), and then (pull themselves together and) repent shortly afterwards. It is they whose repentance God returns with forgiveness; and God is All-Knowing (of what everyone does and why), and All-Wise.

18. But of no avail is the repentance of those who commit evil (for a lifetime) until, when one of them is visited by death, he says, "Indeed now I repent." Nor (likewise does the repentance avail) of those who (spend their lives in unbelief and offer to repent just at the time of death,

but) die as unbelievers (since such repentance is not acceptable). For such We have prepared a painful punishment.

19. O you who believe! It is not lawful for you to become inheritors, against their will, of women (of your deceased kinsmen, marrying them against their will, without paying their bridal-due, or forcing them to marry others in return for their bridal-due as though they were a part of heritable property); nor should you constrain your wives in order to take away anything of what you have given them (as bridal-due or bridal gift), unless they be guilty of indecency in an obvious manner (such as to justify divorce). Consort with them in a good manner, for if you are not pleased with them, it may well be that you dislike something but God has set in it much good.

6. Unjust killing, fornication and adultery, theft and usurpation, anarchy and terror, open and rebellious apostasy, slander and partaking of intoxicating substances, including drugs, are the most grievous crimes in Islam. Muslim Law aims at the protection of the faith, the mind, life, property, and healthy reproduction; the most severe punishments are applied for their violation.

Although there are different opinions concerning these two verses, the view which has been most widely accepted is that they are complementary to one another. While verse 15 is concerned only with Muslim women guilty of indulging in unlawful sex, verse 16 concerns the act of unlawful sex, the partners of which are known. The reason why the Qur'ān has established the matter in this way and mentions women separately must be that, just as there are brothels and similar places in modern societies, women engaged in prostitution were also around during the pre-Islamic period of *Jāhiliyyah*. So, as an important step on the way to the decisive banning and prevention of prostitution and any other kind of unlawful sex, the Qur'ān mentions women separately. Then, it proceeds to mention individual cases of unlawful sex where the partners are known to have committed this act.

As with several other commandments, Islam followed a gradual process in laying down the final penalty for unlawful sex. First, in these two verses, it prescribed that the Muslims who had committed such an act should be scolded and beaten and that the female partners be kept in houses in order to prevent prostitution. The expression, *or God opens some way for them,* which meant that a new, final commandment would be revealed, resulted in the execution of the adulterous married couples according to the Prophet's practice, and striking the unmarried ones with a whip 100 times (See 24: 2).

In note 131 in *Sūrat al-Baqarah*, the basic principles upon which the Islamic Penal Law is based were summarized. Taking into consideration the penalty for adultery, we should add the following points:

- During the Makkan period, it was revealed to the believers (18: 26, 31-35, 59): give relatives, the needy and wayfarers their due; kill nobody unjustly, including children; refrain from adultery; do not consume the property of orphans; and do not deceive in weighing and measuring. These came as principles of Wisdom, in return for whose violation no penalty was prescribed. However, in Madīnah, where an Islamic government was established after the Companions' swearing a pledge to the Messenger, these provisions became articles of law, the violation of which brought a penalty. This shows that the Islamic Penal Law was put into effect in a system established on the basis of the Islamic creed, worldview, worship, behavior, standards of morality, and social and economic structure. Thus, the penal law should be evaluated within the entirety of Islam.

- Islam followed a gradual process in laying down the final penalty for crimes, such as adultery and the consumption of alcohol, and the penalties prescribed before the final one were not removed from the Qur'ān, despite their being abrogated. This means that an Islamic community is one that is gradually perfected along with the implementation of Islamic rules. It resembles a healthy body. Every crime committed in such a community is like a disease threatening the body, according to its nature and degree. Rebellious apostasy, killing, anarchy, terror, adultery, consuming intoxicating substances, slander, theft and usurpation are the most deadly of diseases. Just as some diseases require medicine for recovery, while others need radiotherapy, and still others require an operation, so too, the diseases that threaten a healthy social body require the same kind of therapies, each according to its nature and degree of intensity.

- With its principles of creed, worship, good conduct or behavior, morality, and social and economic structure, Islam prevents people from committing crimes. It can be

said that Islam makes it 95% more difficult to commit deadly sins or crimes, and
leaves the remaining 5% to human free will.
Therefore, it is clear that those who commit
the grave crimes mentioned in the previous
note are diseased elements in a truly Islamic society.

- Islam has made it considerably difficult
to establish and prove adultery and to im-
plement the prescribed penalty. The number of those who have been proven to be
guilty of adultery or theft and who have
been punished during the thirteen centuries of Islam until the 14th century after
the *Hijrah*, was extremely small. The incidents of adultery and theft that occur in
a single year in one so-called modern, civilized country, and the complications, such
as divorce, the collapse of families, suicide,
murder, and depression, caused by such
events, far exceed the number of such incidents during the thirteen centuries of Islamic history throughout all the Muslim
lands. Should not those who criticize Islam for the penalties it prescribes for grievous crimes view the matter from this perspective at least, if they are not ignorant of
the truth of the matter or prejudiced opponents of Islam?

- In the Bible, there are many examples of
adultery, all of which were punished either
by stoning or burning, or in some other
way. Furthermore, these kinds of punishment were not restricted only to adultery;
if a man married a woman and her daughter at the same time, all three were killed
by burning (*Leviticus*, 20: 10–21). There is
no commandment in the Gospels that abrogates these laws. We can only find an episode in *John* (8: 3-11) where Jesus refused
to judge on the stoning of an adulterous
woman brought before him. The reason
why he did this is quite clear: The teachers
of the Law and the Pharisees brought in a
woman caught in adultery. They made her
stand before the group and said to Jesus,
"Teacher, this woman was caught in the act

of adultery. In the Law, Moses commanded us to stone such women. Now what do
you say?" They were using this question as
a trap, in order to have a basis for accusing
him. If Jesus had ordered her to be stoned,
they would have objected: "Did you not order mercy?" If he had not, they would have
protested: "Did you not declare that you accepted Moses' Law?" Jesus started to write
on the ground with his finger, and said: "If
any one of you is without sin, let him be
the first to throw a stone at her." By so
doing, he taught a lesson. At his time the
Jewish community was highly contaminated by sins. Those who wanted to make him
exercise a commandment were the same
persons who were foremost in disobedience to the Law, yet it was they who had
to preserve it and judge by it. There was
no ground propitious for implementing the
Law, nor was Jesus in the position to im-
plement it. So, this event is not one that
shows there was no penalty for adultery in
the Gospels, but rather one which demonstrates the spirit of the religious – Islamic
– Penal Law, which is what we have been
trying to explain.

Furthermore, The Prophet Jesus, upon him be peace, brought more strict moral and spiritual sanctions against adultery:
"You have heard that it was said to those of
old: '*You shall not commit adultery*.' But I
say to you that whoever looks at a woman to lust for her has already committed
adultery with her in his heart. If your right
eye causes you to sin, pluck it out and cast
it from you; for it is more profitable for
you that one of your members perish, than
for your whole body to be cast into hell"
(*Matthew*, 5: 27-29).

- Islam is not aimed at the satisfaction of animal appetites at any cost, as are secular,
materialist civilizations, but rather it urges the spirit to true human perfection and
the bringing up of virtuous generations,
whose minds are enlightened with scientific knowledge and whose hearts are illuminated with pure spiritual values.

80   سُوۡرَۃُ النِّسَآء   ٨٠

وَإِنۡ أَرَدتُّمُ اسۡتِبۡدَالَ زَوۡجٍ مَّكَانَ زَوۡجٍ وَآتَيۡتُمۡ
إِحۡدَىٰهُنَّ قِنطَارًا فَلَا تَأۡخُذُوا مِنۡهُ شَيۡـًٔا أَتَأۡخُذُونَهُ
بُهۡتَانًا وَإِثۡمًا مُّبِينًا ۞ وَكَيۡفَ تَأۡخُذُونَهُ وَقَدۡ
أَفۡضَىٰ بَعۡضُكُمۡ إِلَىٰ بَعۡضٍ وَأَخَذۡنَ مِنكُم مِّيثَاقًا غَلِيظًا
۞ وَلَا تَنكِحُوا مَا نَكَحَ آبَاؤُكُم مِّنَ النِّسَآءِ إِلَّا
مَا قَدۡ سَلَفَ إِنَّهُ كَانَ فَاحِشَةً وَمَقۡتًا وَسَآءَ
سَبِيلًا ۞ حُرِّمَتۡ عَلَيۡكُمۡ أُمَّهَاتُكُمۡ وَبَنَاتُكُمۡ
وَأَخَوَاتُكُمۡ وَعَمَّاتُكُمۡ وَخَالَاتُكُمۡ وَبَنَاتُ الۡأَخِ
وَبَنَاتُ الۡأُخۡتِ وَأُمَّهَاتُكُمُ الَّاتِي أَرۡضَعۡنَكُمۡ
وَأَخَوَاتُكُم مِّنَ الرَّضَاعَةِ وَأُمَّهَاتُ نِسَآئِكُمۡ
وَرَبَائِبُكُمُ الَّاتِي فِي حُجُورِكُم مِّن نِّسَآئِكُمُ
الَّاتِي دَخَلۡتُم بِهِنَّ فَإِن لَّمۡ تَكُونُوا دَخَلۡتُم بِهِنَّ
فَلَا جُنَاحَ عَلَيۡكُمۡ وَحَلَائِلُ أَبۡنَائِكُمُ الَّذِينَ
مِنۡ أَصۡلَابِكُمۡ وَأَن تَجۡمَعُوا بَيۡنَ الۡأُخۡتَيۡنِ إِلَّا
مَا قَدۡ سَلَفَ إِنَّ اللَّهَ كَانَ غَفُورًا رَّحِيمًا ۞

———————⟨≫⟩———————

20. But if you still decide to dispense
with a wife and marry another and you
have given the former (even so much as
amounts to) a treasure, do not take back
anything thereof. Would you take it back
by slandering (for the purpose of contriving the kind of divorce that allows you
to take it back) and so committing a flagrant sin?

21. Then, how could you take it back
when you have gone in to each other, and
they (the married women) have taken
from you a most solemn pledge (of honoring their rights)?

22. And do not marry the women whom
your fathers married – except what has
happened (of that sort) in the past (before
your conversion: such occurrences are forgivable provided you rectify your conduct
and terminate any such contract of marriage). This was indeed a shameful deed
and hateful thing, and how evil a way!

23. Forbidden to you (O believing men)
are your mothers (including stepmoth-
ers and grandmothers) and daughters (including granddaughters), your sisters (including full sisters and half-sisters), your
aunts paternal and maternal, your brothers' daughters, your sisters' daughters,
your mothers who have given suck to
you, your milk-sisters (all those as closely related to you through milk as through
descent[7]), your wives' mothers, your step-
daughters – who are your foster-children,
born of your wives with whom you have
consummated marriage; but if you have
not consummated marriage with them,
there will be no blame on you (should you
marry their daughters) – and the spouses
of your sons who are of your loins, and to
take two sisters together in marriage (including a niece and her aunt maternal or
paternal)[8] – except what has happened (of
that sort) in the past. Surely God is All-
Forgiving, All-Compassionate.

7/8. Marrying not only milk-mothers and
milk-sisters but all of those who have as close
a relationship through milk as through descent
(i.e. nieces or nephews from milk), and marry-

ing a niece and her aunt together were prohibited by the Messenger, upon him be peace and
blessings, based either on the Revelation or by
inference from this verse.

٨١   اَلْجُزْءُ الْخَامِسُ   81

وَالْمُحْصَنَاتُ مِنَ النِّسَاءِ اِلَّا مَا مَلَكَتْ اَيْمَانُكُمْ
كِتَابَ اللهِ عَلَيْكُمْ وَاُحِلَّ لَكُمْ مَا وَرَاءَ ذٰلِكُمْ اَنْ
تَبْتَغُوا بِاَمْوَالِكُمْ مُحْصِنِيْنَ غَيْرَ مُسَافِحِيْنَ فَمَا اسْتَمْتَعْتُمْ
بِهِ مِنْهُنَّ فَاٰتُوهُنَّ اُجُوْرَهُنَّ فَرِيْضَةً وَلَا جُنَاحَ عَلَيْكُمْ فِيْمَا
تَرَاضَيْتُمْ بِهِ مِنْ بَعْدِ الْفَرِيْضَةِ اِنَّ اللهَ كَانَ عَلِيْمًا حَكِيْمًا ۝
وَمَنْ لَمْ يَسْتَطِعْ مِنْكُمْ طَوْلًا اَنْ يَنْكِحَ الْمُحْصَنَاتِ
الْمُؤْمِنَاتِ فَمِنْ مَا مَلَكَتْ اَيْمَانُكُمْ مِنْ فَتَيَاتِكُمُ
الْمُؤْمِنَاتِ وَاللهُ اَعْلَمُ بِاِيْمَانِكُمْ بَعْضُكُمْ مِنْ بَعْضٍ
فَانْكِحُوْهُنَّ بِاِذْنِ اَهْلِهِنَّ وَاٰتُوْهُنَّ اُجُوْرَهُنَّ
بِالْمَعْرُوْفِ مُحْصَنَاتٍ غَيْرَ مُسَافِحَاتٍ وَلَا مُتَّخِذَاتِ
اَخْدَانٍ فَاِذَا اُحْصِنَّ فَاِنْ اَتَيْنَ بِفَاحِشَةٍ فَعَلَيْهِنَّ نِصْفُ
مَا عَلَى الْمُحْصَنَاتِ مِنَ الْعَذَابِ ذٰلِكَ لِمَنْ خَشِيَ الْعَنَتَ مِنْكُمْ
وَاَنْ تَصْبِرُوْا خَيْرٌ لَكُمْ وَاللهُ غَفُوْرٌ رَّحِيْمٌ ۝
يُرِيْدُ اللهُ لِيُبَيِّنَ لَكُمْ وَيَهْدِيَكُمْ سُنَنَ الَّذِيْنَ
مِنْ قَبْلِكُمْ وَيَتُوْبَ عَلَيْكُمْ وَاللهُ عَلِيْمٌ حَكِيْمٌ ۝

24. And (also forbidden to you are) all married women save those (captives) whom your right hands possess (and whose ties with their husbands have practically been cut off). This is God's decree, binding upon you. Lawful for you are all beyond those mentioned, that you may seek, offering them of your wealth, taking them in sound chastity (i.e. in marriage), and not in licentiousness. And whomever of them you seek to enjoy in marriage (under these conditions), give them their bridal-due as a duty. But there is no blame on you for what you do by mutual agreement after the duty (has been done). Surely God is All-Knowing (of what you do and why), and All-Wise.

25. If any of you cannot afford to marry free, believing women, (let them marry) believing maidens from among those whom your right hands possess. (Do not regard marriage to such believing maidens as a degradation. Rather, degradation is deviating into licentiousness without marrying.) God knows well all about your faith (and measures you by it); and (whether you be free or slaves) you are one from another (belonging, as believers, to the same faith and community). Marry them, then, with the leave of their guardians, and give them their bridal-due according to religiously lawful and custom-ary good practice, they being women who give themselves in honest chastity, not in licentiousness, nor having secret love-companions.[9] Then if they commit indecency after they have entered into wed-lock, they shall be liable to half the penalty to which free (unmarried) women are liable. That (permission to marry bonds-maids) is for those of you who fear to fall into sin (by remaining unmarried). But if you persevere (in self-restraint with no fear of falling into sin), that is better for you. And God is All-Forgiving, All-Com-passionate.

26. God wills to explain to you (His com-mandments in which your happiness lie), and to guide you to the (righteous) ways of life of those who preceded you, and to turn to you (with mercy and favor). God is All-Knowing, All-Wise.

9. In these last two verses, the Qur'ān indicates an important social reality and clarifies an aspect of female slavery. While the previous verse warns men who will marry believing, free women not to stray into ways of indecency, like adultery, this verse admonishes that female slaves should also refrain from such deviations. It also mentions the matter of marrying female slaves in the case of men who fear deviation into unlawful ways if they were to remain unmarried. What we can understand from this is that men are more susceptible to deviation than women. A free Muslim woman is so far from falling that it is not even contemplated; such a woman is extremely careful about her chastity. A believing female slave may be susceptible.

We conclude from this that in the view of Islam a free, Muslim, chaste woman is the ideal of respectable womanhood; others who, even though believers, may not be careful about their chastity, therefore do not enjoy the same status or respect. A woman loses her right to respect when she indulges in indecency or if she presents herself as a sexual object, using her physical charms to allure; this means that she has fallen from the rank of true, perfect humanity. Similarly, respected members of a pure, Islamic society cannot perceive of women as sexual objects. Islam regards indecencies such as fornication, adultery, and prostitution as the most abominable things, and sees these as the cause of people falling lower than animals. The sexual drive in animals is directed at reproduction; it is not just a desire to be satisfied in any way at any means. For example, bull-camels smell the urine of a she-camel in order to learn whether the camel has been inseminated or not. They will not mate otherwise.

82   سُوْرَةُ النِّسَاءِ   ٨٢

وَاللّٰهُ يُرِيدُ أَنْ يَتُوبَ عَلَيْكُمْ وَيُرِيدُ الَّذِينَ
يَتَّبِعُونَ الشَّهَوَاتِ أَنْ تَمِيلُوا مَيْلاً عَظِيمًا ۝ يُرِيدُ
اللّٰهُ أَنْ يُخَفِّفَ عَنْكُمْ وَخُلِقَ الْإِنْسَانُ ضَعِيفًا ۝
يَا أَيُّهَا الَّذِينَ آمَنُوا لَا تَأْكُلُوا أَمْوَالَكُمْ بَيْنَكُمْ
بِالْبَاطِلِ إِلَّا أَنْ تَكُونَ تِجَارَةً عَنْ تَرَاضٍ مِنْكُمْ
وَلَا تَقْتُلُوا أَنْفُسَكُمْ إِنَّ اللّٰهَ كَانَ بِكُمْ رَحِيمًا ۝ وَمَنْ يَفْعَلْ
ذَلِكَ عُدْوَانًا وَظُلْمًا فَسَوْفَ نُصْلِيهِ نَارًا وَكَانَ ذَلِكَ عَلَى
اللّٰهِ يَسِيرًا ۝ إِنْ تَجْتَنِبُوا كَبَائِرَ مَا تُنْهَوْنَ عَنْهُ نُكَفِّرْ
عَنْكُمْ سَيِّئَاتِكُمْ وَنُدْخِلْكُمْ مُدْخَلاً كَرِيمًا ۝
وَلَا تَتَمَنَّوْا مَا فَضَّلَ اللّٰهُ بِهِ بَعْضَكُمْ عَلَى بَعْضٍ لِلرِّجَالِ
نَصِيبٌ مِمَّا اكْتَسَبُوا وَلِلنِّسَاءِ نَصِيبٌ مِمَّا اكْتَسَبْنَ وَسْئَلُوا
اللّٰهَ مِنْ فَضْلِهِ إِنَّ اللّٰهَ كَانَ بِكُلِّ شَيْءٍ عَلِيمًا ۝
وَلِكُلٍّ جَعَلْنَا مَوَالِيَ مِمَّا تَرَكَ الْوَالِدَانِ
وَالْأَقْرَبُونَ وَالَّذِينَ عَقَدَتْ أَيْمَانُكُمْ فَآتُوهُمْ
نَصِيبَهُمْ إِنَّ اللّٰهَ كَانَ عَلَى كُلِّ شَيْءٍ شَهِيدًا ۝

27. God wills to turn to you (with mercy and favor by explaining to you His commandments and guiding you to the Straight Path), whereas those who follow (their) lusts (for women, offspring, wealth, fame, status, and position) desire you to deviate greatly (from the Straight Path).

28. God wills to lighten for you (your burdens), for human has been created weak (liable to err).[10]

29. O you who believe! Do not consume one another's wealth in wrongful ways (such as theft, extortion, bribery, usury, and gambling), except it be dealing by mutual agreement; and do not destroy yourselves (individually or collectively by following wrongful ways like extreme asceticism and idleness. Be ever mindful that) God has surely been All-Compassionate towards you (particularly as believers).

30. Whoever acts wrongfully through enmity (towards others) and by way of deliberate transgression and wronging (both himself and others), We will surely land him in a Fire to roast therein (the like of which you have never seen and the degree of whose intensity none knows except God); that indeed is easy for God.

31. If you avoid the major sins[11] which you have been forbidden, We will blot out from you your minor evil deeds and make you enter by a noble entrance (to an abode of glory).

32. (People differ from each other in capacity and means of livelihood; nor is it in your hands to be born male or female. Therefore) do not covet that in which God has made some of you excel others (thus envying others in such things as status or wealth or physical charms and so objecting to God's distribution). Men shall have a share according to what they have earned (in both material and spiritual terms), and women shall have a share according to what they have earned. (On the other hand, do not refuse effort and aspiration; instead of envying others,) ask God (to give you more) of His bounty (through lawful labor and through prayer). Assuredly God has full knowledge of everything.

33. And to everyone We have appointed heirs to what the parents and near kindred might leave behind. (As those heirs have defined portions in the inheritance that must be given them,) so to those with whom you have made a solemn covenant, give them their due share. God is indeed a witness over everything.

10. Humanity is, so to speak, riddled with many weak spots. So we must be educated and liberated from our weak points. An important dimension of education is to keep the sphere of permission so wide as to satisfy the vital needs and lawful human desires and lay down such prohibitions that will prevent people from going to extremes. Religious prohibitions and other responsibilities are not a burden on humanity; rather, they serve to lighten a burden which would otherwise crush them. The sphere of permission in Islam is wide enough for humanity to lead a perfect, human life, and to remove all possibility of conflict between the human spirit and bodily desires. So any kind of satisfaction sought outside that sphere is a great burden for the human heart and spirit to bear, and a torment upon torment, and a means of suffering and disasters for the family and social life.

11. The major sins are those in return for committing which God or His Messenger threatens a severe punishment in the Hereafter, and for some of which there is (also) a prescribed punishment in the world. Disbelieving in God and/or associating partners with Him are the greatest of the major sins. The others are: being despair of God's mercy, regarding oneself as secure from His punishment, disrespecting one's parents and unobserving their rights, unjust killing, fornication and adultery, consuming the property of others, especially that of orphans, theft, engaging in usury, turning back (as a soldier) when the army advances or fleeing from battle-front, slandering the reputation of chaste women, sorcery, drinking alcohol, gambling, exchanging God's covenant and the oaths taken in His Name for worldly advantages, betraying public trusts, giving false evidence in a court, not carrying out any of the obligatory religious duties (such as abandoning the Prescribed Prayer, not paying the *Zakāh* (Prescribed Purifying Alms), not fasting the Ramaḍān, not going to the Major Pilgrimage), and barring people from God's way.

It is said that no sin for which one has sincerely repented and asked for God's forgiveness is great, and no sin that has been committed continuously and without repentance is considered to be minor.

اَلرِّجَالُ قَوَّامُونَ عَلَى النِّسَاءِ بِمَا فَضَّلَ اللّٰهُ
بَعْضَهُمْ عَلَىٰ بَعْضٍ وَبِمَا أَنْفَقُوا مِنْ أَمْوَالِهِمْ
فَالصَّالِحَاتُ قَانِتَاتٌ حَافِظَاتٌ لِلْغَيْبِ بِمَا حَفِظَ اللّٰهُ
وَالَّتِي تَخَافُونَ نُشُوزَهُنَّ فَعِظُوهُنَّ وَاهْجُرُوهُنَّ
فِي الْمَضَاجِعِ وَاضْرِبُوهُنَّ فَإِنْ أَطَعْنَكُمْ
فَلَا تَبْغُوا عَلَيْهِنَّ سَبِيلًا إِنَّ اللّٰهَ كَانَ عَلِيًّا كَبِيرًا ۝
وَإِنْ خِفْتُمْ شِقَاقَ بَيْنِهِمَا فَابْعَثُوا حَكَمًا مِنْ أَهْلِهِ وَحَكَمًا مِنْ
أَهْلِهَا إِنْ يُرِيدَا إِصْلَاحًا يُوَفِّقِ اللّٰهُ بَيْنَهُمَا إِنَّ اللّٰهَ
كَانَ عَلِيمًا خَبِيرًا ۝ وَاعْبُدُوا اللّٰهَ وَلَا تُشْرِكُوا بِهِ
شَيْئًا وَبِالْوَالِدَيْنِ إِحْسَانًا وَبِذِي الْقُرْبَىٰ وَالْيَتَامَىٰ
وَالْمَسَاكِينِ وَالْجَارِ ذِي الْقُرْبَىٰ وَالْجَارِ الْجُنُبِ وَالصَّاحِبِ
بِالْجَنْبِ وَابْنِ السَّبِيلِ وَمَا مَلَكَتْ أَيْمَانُكُمْ إِنَّ اللّٰهَ
لَا يُحِبُّ مَنْ كَانَ مُخْتَالًا فَخُورًا ۝ الَّذِينَ يَبْخَلُونَ
وَيَأْمُرُونَ النَّاسَ بِالْبُخْلِ وَيَكْتُمُونَ مَا آتَاهُمُ اللّٰهُ
مِنْ فَضْلِهِ وَأَعْتَدْنَا لِلْكَافِرِينَ عَذَابًا مُهِينًا ۝

---

34. Men (those who are able to carry out their responsibilities) are the protectors and maintainers of women inasmuch as God has endowed some of humankind (in some respects) with greater capacity than others and inasmuch as they (the men) spend of their wealth (for the family's maintenance). Good, righteous women are the devoted ones (to God) and observant (of their husbands' rights), who guard the secrets (family honor and property, their chastity, and their husband's rights, especially where there is none to see them and in the absence of men) as God guards and keeps undisclosed (what should be guarded and private). As for those women from whose determined disobedience and breach of their marital obligations you have reason to fear, admonish them (to do what is right); then, (if that proves to be of no avail), remain apart from them in beds; then (if that too proves to be of no avail) beat them (lightly without beating them in their faces). Then if they obey you (in your directing them to observe God's rights and their marital obligations) do not seek ways against them (to harm them). (Be ever mindful that) God is indeed All-Exalted, All-Great.[12]

35. And if you fear that a breach might occur between a couple, appoint an arbiter from among his people and an arbiter from among her people. If they both want to set things aright, God will bring about reconciliation between them. Surely God is All-Knowing, All-Aware.

36. And (as the essential basis of contentment in individual, family and social life,) worship God and do not associate anything as a partner with Him; and do good to your parents in the best way possible, and to the relatives, orphans, the destitute, the neighbor who is near (in kinship, location, faith), the neighbor who is distant (in kinship and faith), the companion by your side (on the way, in the family, in the workplace, etc.), the wayfarer, and those who are in your service. (Treat them well and bring yourself up to this end, for) God does not love those who are conceited and boastful;

37. Those who act meanly (in spending out of what God has granted them) and urge others to be mean, and conceal the things God has granted them out of His bounty (such as wealth or knowledge, and certain truths in their Book). We have prepared for (such) unbelievers a shameful, humiliating punishment.

12. This verse is highly significant for male–female relationships and family law. It draws attention to the following cardinal points:

- God has not created all people exactly the same in all respects, but rather has given each person a form of superiority in some respect to others; this is a requirement of social life and is the origin of the division of labor and the need for variety of occupation. Although it is not true to the same degree with all men and women, He has created men, in some respects, superior to women, while He has also given women superiority over men in other respects.

- As a general rule, God has given men greater physical strength then women and endowed them with a greater capacity for management, and He has charged them with the financial responsibility of the family. Again, this is not true to the same degree for all men and women; there will of course be some women who are better managers than some men. This is why He has made men the head of the family. However, this does not mean that men have absolute authority in the family; rather, this authority must be exercised according to the Prophetic principle: *The master of a people is he who serves them.* But responsibility is proportionate to authority, and authority is proportionate to responsibility.

- Men are responsible for the education of the family members, especially in bringing them up to prosper in the other world (66: 6), and in the management of the family. So while the verse directs men as to how they should treat rebellious women who are of bad conduct, it guides them to a gradual means of education: admonish them (to do what is right); then, (if that proves to be of no avail), remain apart from them in beds; then (if that too proves to be of no avail) beat them (lightly without slapping them in their faces).

It should be noted that these measures are aimed at education and saving the marriage from collapse in case of a wife's rebelliousness. It is not a matter of *women* being beaten only because they are women, but rather this punishment is only applicable to a truly rebellious person who is of evil conduct, a person who displays obstinacy, not only not doing her duty in the home but also one who does not care about good moral conduct; in short, such a woman is not only wronging her family, she is also wronging herself.

God's Messenger, upon him be peace and blessings, interpreted the verse to mean that the beating should be light and only employed as a last resort in extreme cases such as lewdness committed by the wife; he warned men to refrain from beating as much as possible, and slapping in the faces (at-Tirmidhī, "Kitāb at-Tafsīr, Tawbah," 1; Abū Dāwūd, "Nikāḥ," 42). The last part of the verse is also of the same import. Furthermore, the Messenger condemned any unjustifiable beating. He exhorted men to be good to their families, saying: "The best of you is he who is best to his family, and I am the best among you to my family" (Ibn Mājah, "Nikāḥ" 50). He advised a Muslim woman, Fātimah bint Qays, not to marry a man known for beating women (Muslim, "Talaq," 36).

On the other hand, Islam never leaves women unprotected in the face of men's harsh treatment and negligence of their family duties. First, it advises reconciliation: *If a woman fears from her husband ill-treatment or (such breach of marital obligations as) his turning away in aversion, then there will be no blame on them to set things right peacefully between them; peaceful settlement is better.... (O husbands) if you do good in consciousness of God and act in reverence for Him and piety (in observing the rights of women), then surely God is fully aware of what you do* (4: 128). However, it does not advise women to resort to the two measures of leaving their husbands in bed and beating. This must be because it seeks to protect the wife from a violent physical reaction by her already misbehaving husband. But it recognizes the woman the right to re-sort to the court and even demand divorce. Muslim scholars suggest that the court can apply the same three measures in question against the husband on the wife's behalf.

- No system or religion has a right to ask Is-lam to apologize for any of its command-ments, including this one concerning wom-en. On the contrary, all surveys conduct-ed show that women have been subject-ed to abuse in almost all other "religions" and systems, and this still continues in the modern, "civilized" world. In contrast, the periods when Islam was being practiced consciously were a golden age for women. To cite a single example, what foreign trav-elers and observers wrote during the first quarter of the 18th century – a time when all the Muslim world, including the Otto-man State, was in decline, is enough to clar-ify this point:

No one locks their house in the city where about one million people live be-cause no theft has ever been reported. You do not see a vagabond, nor a beg-gar, nor one who shouts loudly in the streets. Women receive the greatest re-spect at home and enjoy certain authori-ty. There is nothing more abominable to stare at a woman walking in the street, and especially raising a hand to beat them. It is impossible to describe the beauty of the Turkish women (Djevad, 35-36 [Quoted from Mr. Porter, British Ambassador to Turkey]).

84　سُورَةُ النِّسَاءِ　٨٤

وَالَّذِينَ يُنفِقُونَ أَمْوَالَهُمْ رِئَاءَ النَّاسِ وَلَا يُؤْمِنُونَ بِاللَّهِ وَلَا بِالْيَوْمِ الْآخِرِ وَمَن يَكُنِ الشَّيْطَانُ لَهُ قَرِينًا فَسَاءَ قَرِينًا ۝ وَمَاذَا عَلَيْهِمْ لَوْ آمَنُوا بِاللَّهِ وَالْيَوْمِ الْآخِرِ وَأَنفَقُوا مِمَّا رَزَقَهُمُ اللَّهُ وَكَانَ اللَّهُ بِهِمْ عَلِيمًا ۝ إِنَّ اللَّهَ لَا يَظْلِمُ مِثْقَالَ ذَرَّةٍ وَإِن تَكُ حَسَنَةً يُضَاعِفْهَا وَيُؤْتِ مِن لَّدُنْهُ أَجْرًا عَظِيمًا ۝ فَكَيْفَ إِذَا جِئْنَا مِن كُلِّ أُمَّةٍ بِشَهِيدٍ وَجِئْنَا بِكَ عَلَىٰ هَٰؤُلَاءِ شَهِيدًا ۝ يَوْمَئِذٍ يَوَدُّ الَّذِينَ كَفَرُوا وَعَصَوُا الرَّسُولَ لَوْ تُسَوَّىٰ بِهِمُ الْأَرْضُ وَلَا يَكْتُمُونَ اللَّهَ حَدِيثًا ۝ يَا أَيُّهَا الَّذِينَ آمَنُوا لَا تَقْرَبُوا الصَّلَاةَ وَأَنتُمْ سُكَارَىٰ حَتَّىٰ تَعْلَمُوا مَا تَقُولُونَ وَلَا جُنُبًا إِلَّا عَابِرِي سَبِيلٍ حَتَّىٰ تَغْتَسِلُوا وَإِن كُنتُم مَّرْضَىٰ أَوْ عَلَىٰ سَفَرٍ أَوْ جَاءَ أَحَدٌ مِّنكُم مِّنَ الْغَائِطِ أَوْ لَامَسْتُمُ النِّسَاءَ فَلَمْ تَجِدُوا مَاءً فَتَيَمَّمُوا صَعِيدًا طَيِّبًا فَامْسَحُوا بِوُجُوهِكُمْ وَأَيْدِيكُمْ إِنَّ اللَّهَ كَانَ عَفُوًّا غَفُورًا ۝ أَلَمْ تَرَ إِلَى الَّذِينَ أُوتُوا نَصِيبًا مِّنَ الْكِتَابِ يَشْتَرُونَ الضَّلَالَةَ وَيُرِيدُونَ أَن تَضِلُّوا السَّبِيلَ ۝

38. And (likewise) those who spend their wealth (in charity or other good cause) to make a show of it to people (so as to be praised by them) when they believe neither in God nor in the Last Day: whoever has Satan for a comrade, how evil a comrade he is!

39. Why, what (harm) would fall upon them, if they believed in God and the Last Day and spent out of what God has provided for them (purely for the pleasure of God), and God has full knowledge of them (of what they believe in and what they spend)?

40. Assuredly, God wrongs (no-one) not even so much as an atom's weight; while if there is a good deed, He multiplies it (with respect to its outcomes and the reward it will bring), and grants (its doer) a tremendous reward purely from His Presence (beyond what it may have merited).

41. How, then, will it be (with people on the Day of Judgment) when We bring forward a witness from every community (to testify against them and that God's Religion was communicated to them), and bring you (O Messenger) as a witness against all those (whom your Message may have reached)?

42. On that Day those who disbelieved (in this life and died in unbelief) and disobeyed the Messenger wish that the earth might be leveled with them (so as to leave no trace or record of them); but they will not be able to conceal from God any telling (of what they said or did).

43. O you who believe! Do not come forward to (stand in) the Prayer while you are in (any sort of) state of drunkenness until you know what you are saying, nor while you are in the state of ritual impurity (requiring the total ablution) – save when you are on a journey (and then unable to bathe) – until you have bathed (done the total ablution). But if you are ill, or on a journey, or if any of you has just satisfied a call of nature, or you have had contact with women, and can find no water, then betake yourselves to pure earth, passing with it lightly over your face and hands (and forearms up to and including the elbows). Surely God is One Who grants remission, All-Forgiving.

44. Do you not see and reflect upon those who were given a portion from the Book? They are occupied with buying straying and desire that you too should stray from the (right) way.

45. (O believers!) God knows best who your enemies are; and God suffices as Guardian and Protecting Friend, and God suffices as Helper.

46. Among those who have become Jews (Judaized) are some who alter the words from their context to distort their meanings, and say: "We have heard and we disobey," and, "Do hear us, may you turn dumb," (while pretending to say: "Will you hearken to us, O respected one!"), and "Listen to us! May you become deaf, O shepherd!" (while pretending to say: "Attend to us!") – thus making a malicious play with their tongues and seeking to revile the (True) Religion. Had they but said, "We have heard and we obey," and "Listen to us," and "Favor us with your attention!", it would indeed have been for their own good, and more upright. But God has cursed them (excluded them from His mercy) because of their (willful, persistent) unbelief, and, but for a few, scarcely do they believe.

47. O you who were given the Book (before)! Believe (sincerely) in (the whole of) what We have been sending down (on Muḥammad), confirming what (of the truth) you already possess, before We obliterate faces so as to deprive them of seeing, hearing, speaking and smelling, or exclude them from Our mercy as We excluded the Sabbath-breakers. (Bear in mind that) God's command is always executed.

48. Assuredly God does not forgive that partners be associated with Him; less than that He forgives to whomever He wills (whomever He has guided to repentance and righteousness either out of His pure grace or as a result of the person's choosing repentance and righteousness by his free will). Whoever associates any partner with God has indeed fabricated a most heinous sin.

49. Do you (O Messenger) not consider those who regard themselves pure and sanctified? No! Rather, it is God Who makes pure and sanctifies whomever He wills (considering the free will of each), and none is wronged even by as much as a tiny hair.

50. Look! how they fabricate falsehood in attribution to God; and that suffices for a flagrant sin (to lead them to their perdition.)

51. Do you not consider those who were given a portion of the Book, how they believe in any false deity and all manner of powers of evil (that institute patterns of faith and rule in defiance of God), and say about those (idolaters) who disbelieve that they are more rightly guided (in the way they follow) than those who believe?

86 سُورَةُ النِّسَاء ٨٦

بِسْمِ اللَّهِ الرَّحْمَنِ الرَّحِيمِ

52. Such are the ones whom God has cursed (excluded from His mercy), and he whom God excludes from His mercy, you shall never find one to help and save him.

53. Or do they have a share in the sovereignty (ownership and dominion of the heavens and the earth, so that they claim some privileged position in God's sight and a right to guidance, Prophethood, and rule on the earth)? If that were so, they would not give people even as much as (would fill) the groove of a date-stone.

54. Or do they envy others for what God granted them out of His grace and bounty? Yet We did grant the Family of Abraham (including the progeny of Ishmael proceeding from him, as well as that of Isaac) the Book and the Wisdom, and We granted them a mighty kingdom (in both the material and spiritual realm).

55. Among them (those belonging to Abraham's progeny) have been and are such as truly believe in him (and therefore they believe in Muḥammad who has the best claim to a relationship with Abraham, and believe in the Qur'an revealed to him), and among them are such as bar people from him (like some from among those who were given the Book before). (For the latter) Hell suffices for a blaze.

56. Those who (knowingly) conceal and reject Our Revelations, We will land them in a Fire to roast there. Every time their skins are burnt off, We will replace them with other skins, that they may taste the punishment. Surely God is All-Glorious with irresistible might, and All-Wise.

57. But those who believe and do good, righteous deeds, We will admit them into Gardens through which rivers flow, therein abiding forever. Therein for them will be spouses purified, and We will admit them to an all-protecting shade (ease and contentment).

58. God commands you to deliver trusts (including public and professional duties of service) to those entitled to them, and when you judge between people, to judge with justice. How excellent is what God exhorts you to do; surely God is All-Hearing, All-Seeing.

59. O you who believe! Obey God and obey the Messenger, and those from among you who are invested with authority; and if you are to dispute among yourselves about anything, refer it to God and the Messenger, if indeed you believe in God and the Last Day. This is the best (for you) and fairest in the end.[13]

13. These last two verses lay down the fundamental principles for a sound Islamic social system:

- The entrusting of all public duties and positions to those qualified for them,

- Ensuring justice in public affairs and judgment,

- Having absolute obedience to God and His Messenger,

- Ensuring that especially the critical posts and positions are assigned to the believers qualified for them, and ensuring that their commands are obeyed, provided they are in conformity with the Qur'ān and the Sunnah of the Messenger,

- Referring controversial matters and differences to the Qur'ān and the Sunnah,

- and, as the most influential sanction for the maintenance of the system, having real belief in God and the Last Day.

The command of *obeying* being mentioned twice, once for God and once for the Messenger, indicates that the Messenger is infallible and has the right to legislate alongside the Qur'ān. He must be obeyed in his orders, both as a President and a Prophet; his orders or prohibitions and way of life comprise his Sunnah, which is to be strictly followed until the Last Day, while his presidency ended with his death. The command of obeying is not mentioned for administrators specifically. This means that obedience to them is conditional. The Messenger clarified this point by saying that there is no obedience in sin or rebellion against God (al-Bukhārī, "Aḥkām," 4; Muslim, "'Imârah," 46). They must be obeyed in their orders as long as they are not contrary to the Sharī'ah. However, disobedience does not mean revolt. It is laid out in relevant books of Islamic law what Muslim people can do to protest against their administrators.

Another point to note here is that Islam refers all the functions fulfilled by modern democratic or undemocratic systems of government to the Muslim community itself. This means that these functions are duties that are to be shared and fulfilled by the community as a whole. The institution of swearing allegiance in Islam also demonstrates this. The system of government is a kind of social contract and division of labor.

أَلَمْ تَرَ إِلَى الَّذِينَ يَزْعُمُونَ أَنَّهُمْ آمَنُوا بِمَا أُنْزِلَ
إِلَيْكَ وَمَا أُنْزِلَ مِنْ قَبْلِكَ يُرِيدُونَ أَنْ يَتَحَاكَمُوٓا
إِلَى الطَّاغُوتِ وَقَدْ أُمِرُوٓا أَنْ يَكْفُرُوا بِهِ وَيُرِيدُ
الشَّيْطَانُ أَنْ يُضِلَّهُمْ ضَلَالًا بَعِيدًا ۝ وَإِذَا قِيلَ لَهُمْ
تَعَالَوْا إِلَى مَا أَنْزَلَ اللَّهُ وَإِلَى الرَّسُولِ رَأَيْتَ الْمُنَافِقِينَ
يَصُدُّونَ عَنْكَ صُدُودًا ۝ فَكَيْفَ إِذَا أَصَابَتْهُمْ مُصِيبَةٌ
بِمَا قَدَّمَتْ أَيْدِيهِمْ ثُمَّ جَآءُوكَ يَحْلِفُونَ بِاللَّهِ إِنْ أَرَدْنَآ إِلَّا
إِحْسَانًا وَتَوْفِيقًا ۝ أُولَٰئِكَ الَّذِينَ يَعْلَمُ اللَّهُ مَا فِي قُلُوبِهِمْ
فَأَعْرِضْ عَنْهُمْ وَعِظْهُمْ وَقُلْ لَهُمْ فِي أَنْفُسِهِمْ
قَوْلًا بَلِيغًا ۝ وَمَآ أَرْسَلْنَا مِنْ رَسُولٍ إِلَّا لِيُطَاعَ
بِإِذْنِ اللَّهِ وَلَوْ أَنَّهُمْ إِذْ ظَلَمُوٓا أَنْفُسَهُمْ
جَآءُوكَ فَاسْتَغْفَرُوا اللَّهَ وَاسْتَغْفَرَ لَهُمُ الرَّسُولُ
لَوَجَدُوا اللَّهَ تَوَّابًا رَحِيمًا ۝ فَلَا وَرَبِّكَ لَا يُؤْمِنُونَ
حَتَّىٰ يُحَكِّمُوكَ فِيمَا شَجَرَ بَيْنَهُمْ ثُمَّ لَا يَجِدُوا
فِي أَنْفُسِهِمْ حَرَجًا مِمَّا قَضَيْتَ وَيُسَلِّمُوا تَسْلِيمًا ۝

---〜❧〜---

60. Do you not consider those who assert that they believe in what has been sent down to you and what was sent before you, and yet desire to go for judgment in their disputes to (the rule of) the powers of evil (that institute patterns of faith and rule in defiance of God), when they were expressly commanded to reject it.[14] Truly, Satan desires to lead them far astray.

61. When they were told: "Come to that which God has sent down and to the Messenger (and submit to God's judgment)," you see the hypocrites turn away from you with disgust.

62. But how then, when a disaster befalls them because of what they have forwarded with their own hands (to their future), they come to you, swearing by God and say: "We intended only goodwill and conciliation!"

63. Such are the ones – God knows what is in their hearts; so withdraw from them (do not care what they say and do), and (continue to) admonish them, and say to them profound words touching their very souls.

64. (Everyone should know well that) We have never sent a Messenger but that he should be obeyed by God's leave. If, when they wronged themselves (by committing a sin), they but came to you and implored God to forgive them – with the Messenger praying to God for their forgiveness – they would find that God is One Who accepts repentance and returns it with liberal forgiveness and additional reward, and All-Compassionate.

65. But no! By your Lord, they do not (truly) believe unless they make you the judge regarding any dispute between them, and then find not the least vexation within themselves over what you have decided, and surrender in full submission.[15]

14. The Qur'ān is a miracle of eloquence and conciseness from beginning to the end. One of the aspects of its eloquence is that while reporting an incident, it uses the incident as a reason to promulgate a new rule or declare a universal truth, without drifting away from the incident.

The word *tāghūt* (powers of evil that institute patterns of faith and rule in defiance of God) is used both in singular and plural. In this verse, in the clause *when they were expressly commanded to reject him* the Qur'ān refers to a particular person included in the meaning of *tāghūt* and who was known to its first addressees during the time of the Messenger. By mentioning an incident, it presents an important aspect of hypocrisy, which is that although hypocrites claim to believe in God's Book and therefore must practice it in their daily lives, they also continue to ignore justice and what is right, seeking other authorities whose judgment they hope will be to their advantage. By presenting an incident which took place during the Messenger's time, the Qur'ān draws attention to this aspect of hypocrisy and declares a very important truth or requirement of faith: If you believe in God's Book, you must refer to its judgment in the disputes among you and submit to it wholeheartedly. You cannot seek another authority in the settlement of the issues among you.

15. The facts expressed in the verses above are very important for both the health of a person's faith and for an Islamic society. First of all, it should be known that the Messenger of God legislates just as the Qur'ān does. Moreover, his way of living or practicing Islam is the principal standard for believers to follow. Secondly, the Qur'ān and the way of the Messenger – Sunnah – are the unquestionable and absolutely authorized sources of Islam which must be obeyed. All other ways that are not authorized by them will lead to heresy.

The Qur'ān frequently calls God's Messenger *The Prophet* or *The Messenger*. Naming him thus means that the Prophet Muḥammad, upon him be God's blessings and peace, is the greatest of the Prophets and Messengers. When we mention someone with their title without mentioning their name, and with the definite article attached then we are saying that they are the most distinguished among those sharing that title and that they are the greatest representative of the mission or institution whose members bear that title. So when we hear or say *The Prophet* or *The Messenger*, we refer to the Prophet Muḥammad, upon him be peace and blessings; it is he who represents the Prophethood and the Messengership in the best way as the greatest of the Prophets and Messengers.

88

سُوۡرَةُ النِّسَاء

٨٨

وَلَوۡ أَنَّا كَتَبۡنَا عَلَيۡهِمۡ أَنِ اقۡتُلُوٓاْ أَنفُسَكُمۡ أَوِ اخۡرُجُواْ مِن
دِيَارِكُم مَّا فَعَلُوهُ إِلَّا قَلِيلٌ مِّنۡهُمۡ وَلَوۡ أَنَّهُمۡ فَعَلُواْ مَا يُوعَظُونَ
بِهِۦ لَكَانَ خَيۡرًا لَّهُمۡ وَأَشَدَّ تَثۡبِيتًا ۞ وَإِذًا لَّءَاتَيۡنَـٰهُم
مِّن لَّدُنَّآ أَجۡرًا عَظِيمًا ۞ وَلَهَدَيۡنَـٰهُمۡ صِرَٰطًا مُّسۡتَقِيمًا ۞
وَمَن يُطِعِ اللَّهَ وَالرَّسُولَ فَأُوْلَـٰٓئِكَ مَعَ الَّذِينَ أَنۡعَمَ اللَّهُ
عَلَيۡهِم مِّنَ النَّبِيِّـۧنَ وَالصِّدِّيقِينَ وَالشُّهَدَآءِ وَالصَّـٰلِحِينَ
وَحَسُنَ أُوْلَـٰٓئِكَ رَفِيقًا ۞ ذَٰلِكَ الۡفَضۡلُ مِنَ اللَّهِ
وَكَفَىٰ بِاللَّهِ عَلِيمًا ۞ يَـٰٓأَيُّهَا الَّذِينَ ءَامَنُواْ خُذُواْ حِذۡرَكُمۡ
فَانفِرُواْ ثُبَاتٍ أَوِ انفِرُواْ جَمِيعًا ۞ وَإِنَّ مِنكُمۡ لَمَن
لَّيُبَطِّئَنَّ فَإِنۡ أَصَـٰبَتۡكُم مُّصِيبَةٌ قَالَ قَدۡ أَنۡعَمَ اللَّهُ
عَلَيَّ إِذۡ لَمۡ أَكُن مَّعَهُمۡ شَهِيدًا ۞ وَلَئِنۡ أَصَـٰبَكُمۡ
فَضۡلٌ مِّنَ اللَّهِ لَيَقُولَنَّ كَأَن لَّمۡ تَكُنۢ بَيۡنَكُمۡ وَبَيۡنَهُۥ مَوَدَّةٌ يَـٰلَيۡتَنِي
كُنتُ مَعَهُمۡ فَأَفُوزَ فَوۡزًا عَظِيمًا ۞ فَلۡيُقَـٰتِلۡ فِي سَبِيلِ اللَّهِ
الَّذِينَ يَشۡرُونَ الۡحَيَوٰةَ الدُّنۡيَا بِالۡءَاخِرَةِ وَمَن يُقَـٰتِلۡ
فِي سَبِيلِ اللَّهِ فَيُقۡتَلۡ أَوۡ يَغۡلِبۡ فَسَوۡفَ نُؤۡتِيهِ أَجۡرًا عَظِيمًا ۞

───────◈───────

66. If We were to ordain for them, "Lay down your lives (in God's cause so that you may be purified of your sins)" or "Leave your habitations (that you have contaminated with your sins and emigrate to another land in God's cause)," they would not do that save a few of them. But if they had done what was urged upon them (before things had come to this point) – if only they would do it from now on – it would indeed have been (and would be) for their own good and (more apt for them) to be more securely established (in the land).[16]

67. And then We would surely have granted them from Our Presence a tremendous reward;

68. And indeed guided them to a straight path (in belief, thought, feeling, and action).

69. Whoever obeys God and the Messenger (as they must be obeyed), then those are (and in the Hereafter will be, in Paradise) in the company of those whom God has favored (with the perfect guidance) – the Prophets, and the truthful ones (loyal to God's cause and truthful in whatever they do and say), and the witnesses (those who see the hidden Divine truths and testify thereto with their lives), and the righteous ones (in all their deeds and sayings and dedicated to setting everything right). How excellent they are for companions![17]

70. Such is the grace that is from God, and God suffices as One All-Knowing (of how great that grace is, who deserves it, and the rank of those favored with it).

71. O you who believe! (While such great grace is there) be fully prepared, then (as circumstance demands) either go forward in (small) consolidated groups (on military expeditions) or go forward all together.

72. There are indeed among you such as him who lags behind. Then, if a disaster befalls you, he says: "Indeed God bestowed His favor upon me that I was not present with them."

73. But if some bounty from God comes to you, he is sure to say – just as if there had never been any tie of affection between you and him, (and therefore as if there had been an obstacle to his going forth with you) – "Oh, if only I had been with them, I would have come by a great gain."

74. So let those who trade the life of this world for the Hereafter fight in God's cause Whoever fights in God's cause, whether he is killed or victorious, We will grant him a tremendous reward.

16. The words and style adopted by this verse lead us to understand that it is connected with what verse 2: 54 and similar verses teach.

17. This verse refers to four classes of people who act as guides for others throughout the history of humankind. It has a direct connection with and explains verses 1: 6–7. What is meant by *favor* is perfect guidance; each class of people mentioned here is favored with this.

وَمَا لَكُمْ لَا تُقَاتِلُونَ فِي سَبِيلِ اللّٰهِ وَالْمُسْتَضْعَفِينَ مِنَ الرِّجَالِ
وَالنِّسَاءِ وَالْوِلْدَانِ الَّذِينَ يَقُولُونَ رَبَّنَا أَخْرِجْنَا مِنْ هٰذِهِ الْقَرْيَةِ
الظَّالِمِ أَهْلُهَا وَاجْعَلْ لَنَا مِنْ لَدُنْكَ وَلِيًّا وَاجْعَلْ لَنَا مِنْ لَدُنْكَ نَصِيرًا
٧٥ الَّذِينَ آمَنُوا يُقَاتِلُونَ فِي سَبِيلِ اللّٰهِ وَالَّذِينَ كَفَرُوا يُقَاتِلُونَ
فِي سَبِيلِ الطَّاغُوتِ فَقَاتِلُوا أَوْلِيَاءَ الشَّيْطَانِ إِنَّ كَيْدَ الشَّيْطَانِ
كَانَ ضَعِيفًا ٧٦ أَلَمْ تَرَ إِلَى الَّذِينَ قِيلَ لَهُمْ كُفُّوا أَيْدِيَكُمْ
وَأَقِيمُوا الصَّلَوٰةَ وَآتُوا الزَّكَوٰةَ فَلَمَّا كُتِبَ عَلَيْهِمُ الْقِتَالُ إِذَا فَرِيقٌ
مِنْهُمْ يَخْشَوْنَ النَّاسَ كَخَشْيَةِ اللّٰهِ أَوْ أَشَدَّ خَشْيَةً وَقَالُوا
رَبَّنَا لِمَ كَتَبْتَ عَلَيْنَا الْقِتَالَ لَوْلَا أَخَّرْتَنَا إِلَى أَجَلٍ قَرِيبٍ قُلْ مَتَاعُ الدُّنْيَا
قَلِيلٌ وَالْآخِرَةُ خَيْرٌ لِمَنِ اتَّقَى وَلَا تُظْلَمُونَ فَتِيلًا ٧٧ أَيْنَمَا تَكُونُوا
يُدْرِكْكُمُ الْمَوْتُ وَلَوْ كُنْتُمْ فِي بُرُوجٍ مُشَيَّدَةٍ وَإِنْ تُصِبْهُمْ
حَسَنَةٌ يَقُولُوا هٰذِهِ مِنْ عِنْدِ اللّٰهِ وَإِنْ تُصِبْهُمْ سَيِّئَةٌ يَقُولُوا
هٰذِهِ مِنْ عِنْدِكَ قُلْ كُلٌّ مِنْ عِنْدِ اللّٰهِ فَمَالِ هٰؤُلَاءِ الْقَوْمِ لَا يَكَادُونَ
يَفْقَهُونَ حَدِيثًا ٧٨ مَا أَصَابَكَ مِنْ حَسَنَةٍ فَمِنَ اللّٰهِ وَمَا أَصَابَكَ
مِنْ سَيِّئَةٍ فَمِنْ نَفْسِكَ وَأَرْسَلْنَاكَ لِلنَّاسِ رَسُولًا وَكَفَى بِاللّٰهِ شَهِيدًا ٧٩

---

75. Why, then, should you not fight in the cause of God and and of the oppressed, helpless men, women, and children, who cry out: "O Lord! Bring us out of this land whose people are oppressors, and appoint for us from Your Presence a protector, and appoint for us from Your Presence a helper!"

76. Those who (truly) believe fight in God's cause, while those who disbelieve fight in the cause of *tāghūt* (powers of evil who institute patterns of faith and rule in defiance of God). So (O believers) fight against the friends and allies of Satan. Assuredly, Satan's guile is ever feeble.

77. Do you not consider those who were told, "Restrain your hands (from war and similar endeavor), and do the Prayer in conformity with its conditions, and pay the Prescribed Purifying Alms (at which time they insistently asked you when they would be allowed to fight)? But as the time has come and fighting has been ordained for them, a party among them fear people as one should fear God, or with even greater fear, and say: "O Lord! Why have You ordained fighting for us? If only You had granted us a little more respite!" Say (to them, O Messenger): "The enjoyment of the world is short-lived, whereas the Hereafter is the best for him who keeps from disobedience to God in reverence for Him and piety, and you will not be wronged by so much as a tiny hair."

78. Wherever you may be, death will overtake you, even though you be in towers built up strong and high. Yet, when some good happens to them, they say: "This is from God;" and when an evil befalls them, they say: "This is because of you." Say: "All is from God." But how is it with these people that they do not grasp the truth of anything said (or anything that has happened)!

79. (O human being!) Whatever good happens to you, it is from God; and whatever evil befalls you, it is from yourself. We have sent you (O Messenger) to humankind as a Messenger, and God suffices for a witness.[18]

18. The last two verses explain some important things concerning Divine Destiny and human free will, such as the following:

- Be it good or bad, whatever happens to a person has been determined by the Divine Eternal Will, Which considers human free will in all Its determinations.
- It is God Who established what cause (thought, belief, and action) brings about what result, and humanity cannot escape this framework. It is also in this sense that it is said that whatever happens to humanity is from God.
- As a requirement of the free will He has granted to humanity, God creates whatever His servants will. So, it is God Who creates whatever happens to them, whether it be good or bad, and it is in this meaning that whatever happens to a person is from God.
- God never wills evil for His servants. He always wills good for them and directs them to it. So, whatever good thing happens to a person, it is because God has willed it for them and directs their free will towards it.

This means that since God has willed it, He has directed a person's free will towards this action, enabling them to do it, and creating it; therefore any good that happens to a person is solely from God.

- A person becomes the source and doer of whatever evil befalls them by preferring evil and doing it despite God's orienting their free will towards good. So, whatever evil befalls a person is from themselves.
- In addition to the fact that whatever good happens to a person is from God, God rewards that good and admits His good servants into Paradise. So, God's rewarding a person and admitting him or her into Paradise is purely out of His bounty and grace. Whereas misfortune will befall a person in the world and they will earn Hellfire in the Hereafter because of their obstinacy in unbelief or polytheism or their transgressions despite God's infinite compassion, forgiveness, and His exhorting people to good. So, the placing of a person in Hell is merely justice that is embedded in the compassion of God.

90   سُوۡرَةُ النِّسَاءِ   ٩٠

مَنۡ يُّطِعِ الرَّسُوۡلَ فَقَدۡ اَطَاعَ اللّٰهَ ۚ وَمَنۡ تَوَلّٰى فَمَاۤ اَرۡسَلۡنٰكَ
عَلَيۡهِمۡ حَفِيۡظًا ۞ وَيَقُوۡلُوۡنَ طَاعَةٌ ۖ فَاِذَا بَرَزُوۡا مِنۡ
عِنۡدِكَ بَيَّتَ طَآئِفَةٌ مِّنۡهُمۡ غَيۡرَ الَّذِىۡ تَقُوۡلُ ۚ وَاللّٰهُ يَكۡتُبُ
مَا يُبَيِّتُوۡنَ ۚ فَاَعۡرِضۡ عَنۡهُمۡ وَتَوَكَّلۡ عَلَى اللّٰهِ ۚ وَكَفٰى بِاللّٰهِ
وَكِيۡلًا ۞ اَفَلَا يَتَدَبَّرُوۡنَ الۡقُرۡاٰنَ ۚ وَلَوۡ كَانَ مِنۡ عِنۡدِ غَيۡرِ اللّٰهِ
لَوَجَدُوۡا فِيۡهِ اخۡتِلَافًا كَثِيۡرًا ۞ وَاِذَا جَآءَهُمۡ اَمۡرٌ مِّنَ الۡاَمۡنِ
اَوِ الۡخَوۡفِ اَذَاعُوۡا بِهٖ ۚ وَلَوۡ رَدُّوۡهُ اِلَى الرَّسُوۡلِ وَاِلٰٓى اُولِى الۡاَمۡرِ مِنۡهُمۡ
لَعَلِمَهُ الَّذِيۡنَ يَسۡتَنۡۢبِطُوۡنَهٗ مِنۡهُمۡ ۚ وَلَوۡلَا فَضۡلُ اللّٰهِ عَلَيۡكُمۡ
وَرَحۡمَتُهٗ لَاتَّبَعۡتُمُ الشَّيۡطٰنَ اِلَّا قَلِيۡلًا ۞ فَقَاتِلۡ فِىۡ سَبِيۡلِ اللّٰهِ ۚ
لَا تُكَلَّفُ اِلَّا نَفۡسَكَ وَحَرِّضِ الۡمُؤۡمِنِيۡنَ ۚ عَسَى اللّٰهُ اَنۡ يَّكُفَّ
بَاۡسَ الَّذِيۡنَ كَفَرُوۡا ۚ وَاللّٰهُ اَشَدُّ بَاۡسًا وَّاَشَدُّ تَنۡكِيۡلًا
۞ مَنۡ يَّشۡفَعۡ شَفَاعَةً حَسَنَةً يَّكُنۡ لَّهٗ نَصِيۡبٌ مِّنۡهَا ۚ
وَمَنۡ يَّشۡفَعۡ شَفَاعَةً سَيِّئَةً يَّكُنۡ لَّهٗ كِفۡلٌ مِّنۡهَا ۚ وَكَانَ اللّٰهُ
عَلٰى كُلِّ شَىۡءٍ مُّقِيۡتًا ۞ وَاِذَا حُيِّيۡتُمۡ بِتَحِيَّةٍ فَحَيُّوۡا بِاَحۡسَنَ
مِنۡهَاۤ اَوۡ رُدُّوۡهَا ؕ اِنَّ اللّٰهَ كَانَ عَلٰى كُلِّ شَىۡءٍ حَسِيۡبًا ۞

---

80. He who obeys the Messenger (thereby) obeys God, and he who turns away from him (and his way), (do not be grieved, O Messenger, for) We have not sent you as a keeper and watcher over them (to prevent their misdeeds and be accountable for them).

81. They say (when in your presence, to every command of yours), "By all means!" But when they leave your presence, a party of them make secret plans against what you say. God records whatever secret plans they make. So withdraw from them, and put your trust in God. God suffices as the One to be relied on, to Whom affairs should be referred.

82. Do they not contemplate the Qur'an (so that they may be convinced that it is from God)? Had it been from any other than God, they would surely have found in it much inconsistency.[19]

83. Whenever any news comes to them, related to (public) security or alarm, they go about spreading it (without ascertaining if the news is true or not and without thinking about whether it is beneficial or harmful to spread it). Whereas if they would but refer it to the Messenger and to those among them (in the community) who are entrusted with authority, those from among them who are competent to investigate it would bring to light what it is really about. (O believers!) And but for God's grace and mercy upon you (in illuminating your way and guiding you with Revelation and His Messenger, and protecting you against your enemies and wrong ways), all but a few (of you) would have been (deceived by the hypocrites and) following Satan.

84. Fight (therefore, O Messenger) in God's cause – for (in the same way that every individual is responsible for himself) you are (first of all) responsible for none except yourself. (Even left by yourself alone, fulfill your responsibility) – and urge on the believers (to take their responsibility). It may be that God will (thereby) restrain the force of those who disbelieve. Indeed God is strongest in might and strongest in repressing and punishing.[20]

85. Whoever intercedes, mediates and helps for a good cause will have a share in its blessings, and whoever intercedes, mediates, and helps for an evil cause shares in its burden. God has full watch over all things.

86. When (whether traveling or at home, or in war or at peace) you are greeted with a greeting (of peace and goodwill), answer with one better, or (at least) with the same. Surely God keeps account of all things.

19. Consider the following facts:

- Although the Qur'ān was revealed in parts over 20 years, to fulfill different needs and purposes, it has perfect harmony, as if it had all been revealed at the same time.
- Although the Qur'ān was revealed over 20 years on different occasions, its parts are so mutually supportive that it is as if it had been revealed on only one occasion.
- Although the Qur'ān came in answer to different, repeated questions, its parts are so united and harmonious with one another that it is as if it had been in answer to a single question.
- Although the Qur'ān came to judge diverse cases and events, it displays such a perfect order that it is as if it were a judgment delivered on a single case or event.
- Although the Qur'ān was revealed by Divine courtesy in styles varied to suit innumerable people who had or have different levels of understanding, moods, and temperament, its parts exhibit so beautiful a similarity, correspondence, and fluency that it is as if it were addressing one level of understanding and temperament.
- Although the Qur'ān speaks to an infinite variety of people, all distant from one another in time, space, and character, it has such a fluent way of explanation, such a pure style, and a clear way of description that it is as if it were addressing only one homogenous group, each different group thinking that it is being addressed uniquely and specifically.
- Although the Qur'ān was revealed to enable the gradual guidance of different peoples with various purposes, it has such a perfect straightforwardness, sensitive balance, and beautiful order that it is as if it were pursuing only one purpose.
- Rather than being reasons for confusion, these factors add to the miraculousness of the Qur'ān's explanations and to its fluency of style and harmony. Anyone with a sound heart, conscience, and good taste can see the graceful fluency, exquisite proportion, pleasant harmony, and matchless eloquence in its explanations. Anyone with a sound power of sight and insight can see that the Qur'ān presents an eye with which to see the whole universe, with all its inner and outer dimensions, like a single page on which all the meanings contained can be read (*The Words*, "the 25th Word," 433).

20. For the Qur'ān's attitude towards war and the rules it established concerning war, see, 2: 190, 191, 194, 216, and notes 137 (Appendix 2), 138, 140, and 147 in *Sūrat al-Baqarah*.

اللَّهُ لَا إِلَٰهَ إِلَّا هُوَ لَيَجْمَعَنَّكُمْ إِلَىٰ يَوْمِ الْقِيَٰمَةِ لَا رَيْبَ فِيهِ
وَمَنْ أَصْدَقُ مِنَ اللَّهِ حَدِيثًا ۞ فَمَا لَكُمْ فِي الْمُنَافِقِينَ فِئَتَيْنِ
وَاللَّهُ أَرْكَسَهُم بِمَا كَسَبُوا ۚ أَتُرِيدُونَ أَن تَهْدُوا مَنْ أَضَلَّ
اللَّهُ ۖ وَمَن يُضْلِلِ اللَّهُ فَلَن تَجِدَ لَهُ سَبِيلًا ۞ وَدُّوا لَوْ تَكْفُرُونَ
كَمَا كَفَرُوا فَتَكُونُونَ سَوَاءً ۖ فَلَا تَتَّخِذُوا مِنْهُمْ أَوْلِيَاءَ حَتَّىٰ
يُهَاجِرُوا فِي سَبِيلِ اللَّهِ ۚ فَإِن تَوَلَّوْا فَخُذُوهُمْ وَاقْتُلُوهُمْ حَيْثُ
وَجَدتُّمُوهُمْ ۖ وَلَا تَتَّخِذُوا مِنْهُمْ وَلِيًّا وَلَا نَصِيرًا ۞
إِلَّا الَّذِينَ يَصِلُونَ إِلَىٰ قَوْمٍ بَيْنَكُمْ وَبَيْنَهُم مِّيثَاقٌ
أَوْ جَاءُوكُمْ حَصِرَتْ صُدُورُهُمْ أَن يُقَاتِلُوكُمْ أَوْ يُقَاتِلُوا
قَوْمَهُمْ ۚ وَلَوْ شَاءَ اللَّهُ لَسَلَّطَهُمْ عَلَيْكُمْ فَلَقَاتَلُوكُمْ ۚ فَإِنِ
اعْتَزَلُوكُمْ فَلَمْ يُقَاتِلُوكُمْ وَأَلْقَوْا إِلَيْكُمُ السَّلَمَ فَمَا جَعَلَ
اللَّهُ لَكُمْ عَلَيْهِمْ سَبِيلًا ۞ سَتَجِدُونَ آخَرِينَ يُرِيدُونَ أَن يَأْمَنُوكُمْ
وَيَأْمَنُوا قَوْمَهُمْ كُلَّ مَا رُدُّوا إِلَى الْفِتْنَةِ أُرْكِسُوا فِيهَا ۚ فَإِن لَّمْ يَعْتَزِلُوكُمْ
وَيُلْقُوا إِلَيْكُمُ السَّلَمَ وَيَكُفُّوا أَيْدِيَهُمْ فَخُذُوهُمْ وَاقْتُلُوهُمْ
حَيْثُ ثَقِفْتُمُوهُمْ ۚ وَأُولَٰئِكُمْ جَعَلْنَا لَكُمْ عَلَيْهِمْ سُلْطَانًا مُّبِينًا ۞

──────────❧──────────

87. God, there is no deity but He. He will gather you all together on the Day of Resurrection, about (the coming of) which there is no doubt. Who can be truer in statement than God?

88. (O believers!) How is it with you that you are in two groups regarding the hypocrites (from Makkah and other tribes who claim to be Muslims yet take part in the hostile machinations of their people against you), seeing that God has thrown them back (to unbelief) on account of what they have earned (by their sins)? Do you seek to guide him whom God has led astray? Whoever God has led astray, for him you cannot find a (safe) way (to follow).

89. They yearn that you should disbelieve just as they disbelieved so that you might be all alike. Do not, therefore, take from among them confidants and allies until they emigrate (to Madīnah and join you) in God's cause. But if they turn away (from this call and continue their hostility against you), seize them and kill them wherever you find them; and do not take to yourselves any of them as confidant, nor as helper.[21]

90. Except those who seek refuge in a people between whom and you there is a treaty (of peace or alliance), or (those who) come to you with hearts shrinking from fighting against you as well as fighting against their own people. Had God willed, He would certainly have given them power over you and they would have fought against you. If they withdraw from you and do not fight against you, and offer you peace, then God allows you no way (to war) against them.

91. You will find others who wish to be secure from you (by signing treaty with you) and to be secure from their people (by breaking their treaty with you and joining them): every time they are called back to conspiracy and hostility against you, they plunge into it headlong. Hence, if they do not withdraw from you, nor offer you peace, nor restrain their hands (from hurting you), then seize them and kill them wherever you come upon them. It is against such that We have given you a clear sanction.

21. As recorded in the sources, the last two verses refer to those people who belonged to the tribes of Ghatfan and Asad; they professed faith in Madīnah, but returned to unbelief and cooperated with the Makkan polytheists against the Muslims when they returned to their lands. However, since a verse being revealed with respect to a specific event does not mean that it is restricted to that event, the Qur'ān is here presenting a typical hypocrisy. Hypocrites, who were constantly worried whether time would progress in their favor or disfavor, professed faith when they came to Madīnah in order to secure the Muslims' confidence in them, but when they returned home they displayed the unbelief in their hearts and took part in all the hostile machinations against Islam and the Muslims. Emigration to Madīnah was of crucial importance and a sign of true belief in that period when the Muslims suffered from the pressures and constraints imposed on them by the unbelievers. So, by revealing the hypocrisy in the hearts and attitudes of such people, the Qur'ān warns the believers against them.

92   سُورَةُ النِّسَاء   ٩٢

وَمَا كَانَ لِمُؤْمِنٍ أَن يَقْتُلَ مُؤْمِنًا إِلَّا خَطَأً وَمَن قَتَلَ
مُؤْمِنًا خَطَأً فَتَحْرِيرُ رَقَبَةٍ مُّؤْمِنَةٍ وَدِيَةٌ مُّسَلَّمَةٌ إِلَىٰ
أَهْلِهِ إِلَّا أَن يَصَّدَّقُوا ۚ فَإِن كَانَ مِن قَوْمٍ
عَدُوٍّ لَّكُمْ وَهُوَ مُؤْمِنٌ فَتَحْرِيرُ رَقَبَةٍ مُّؤْمِنَةٍ ۖ وَإِن
كَانَ مِن قَوْمٍ بَيْنَكُمْ وَبَيْنَهُم مِّيثَاقٌ فَدِيَةٌ
مُّسَلَّمَةٌ إِلَىٰ أَهْلِهِ وَتَحْرِيرُ رَقَبَةٍ مُّؤْمِنَةٍ ۖ فَمَن
لَّمْ يَجِدْ فَصِيَامُ شَهْرَيْنِ مُتَتَابِعَيْنِ تَوْبَةً مِّنَ
اللَّهِ ۗ وَكَانَ اللَّهُ عَلِيمًا حَكِيمًا ۝ وَمَن يَقْتُلْ
مُؤْمِنًا مُّتَعَمِّدًا فَجَزَاؤُهُ جَهَنَّمُ خَالِدًا فِيهَا وَغَضِبَ
اللَّهُ عَلَيْهِ وَلَعَنَهُ وَأَعَدَّ لَهُ عَذَابًا عَظِيمًا ۝
يَا أَيُّهَا الَّذِينَ آمَنُوا إِذَا ضَرَبْتُمْ فِي سَبِيلِ اللَّهِ فَتَبَيَّنُوا
وَلَا تَقُولُوا لِمَنْ أَلْقَىٰ إِلَيْكُمُ السَّلَامَ لَسْتَ مُؤْمِنًا
تَبْتَغُونَ عَرَضَ الْحَيَاةِ الدُّنْيَا فَعِندَ اللَّهِ مَغَانِمُ
كَثِيرَةٌ ۚ كَذَٰلِكَ كُنتُم مِّن قَبْلُ فَمَنَّ اللَّهُ عَلَيْكُمْ
فَتَبَيَّنُوا ۚ إِنَّ اللَّهَ كَانَ بِمَا تَعْمَلُونَ خَبِيرًا ۝

———❧———

92. Yet (be circumspect), it is not for a believer to kill another believer unless it be by mistake. He who has killed a believer by mistake must set free a believing slave, and pay blood-money to his family (legal heirs), unless they forgo it as a freewill offering. If he (the victim), while himself a believer, belonged to a people hostile to you (between whom and you there is no treaty), then (the expiation is to) set free a believing slave. If he (the victim) belonged to a (non-Muslim) people between whom and you there is a treaty, then (the expiation is to) pay blood-money to his heirs, and to set free a believing slave. But he who has no means (to make such expiation), must fast for two consecutive months – a penance from God (a way of repentance).[22] God is All-Knowing (of everything including what is in your bosoms), All-Wise.

93. Whoever kills a believer intentionally, his recompense (in the Hereafter) is Hell, therein to abide; and God has utterly condemned him, excluded him from His mercy, and prepared for him a tremendous punishment.

94. O you who believe! When you go forth (to war) in God's cause, investigate with care until the situation becomes fully clear to you, and do not say to anyone who offers you (the greeting of) peace (thereby indicating his being a Muslim), "You are not a believer," seeking the fleeting gains of the present, worldly life; for with God are gains abundant. Even thus (as he now is) were you before (ignorant of faith and what being a Muslim is, and you too entered Islam with a similar word); but God has since then been gracious to you. So investigate with care until the situation becomes fully clear to you. Surely God is fully aware of all that you do.

22. Setting free a believing slave is a duty to God and the Muslim community, while paying blood-money is a duty to the heirs of the victim. Emancipating a believing slave means, in one respect, granting the slave (free) life in atonement for killing a believer by mistake. This explicitly shows the great value Islam attaches to freedom. The Messenger, upon him be peace and blessings, fixed the blood-money at 100 camels or at the market value of the same. However, the heirs of the victim are allowed to forgo the blood-money or to reduce it. The killer should also turn to God in remorse and repentance, so that his sin may be pardoned and his soul secured against the recurrence of similar mistakes.

٩٣   أَلْجُزْءُ الْخَامِسُ   93

لَا يَسْتَوِى الْقَاعِدُونَ مِنَ الْمُؤْمِنِينَ غَيْرُ أُولِى الضَّرَرِ وَالْمُجَاهِدُونَ فِى سَبِيلِ اللَّهِ بِأَمْوَالِهِمْ وَأَنفُسِهِمْ فَضَّلَ اللَّهُ الْمُجَاهِدِينَ بِأَمْوَالِهِمْ وَأَنفُسِهِمْ عَلَى الْقَاعِدِينَ دَرَجَةً وَكُلًّا وَعَدَ اللَّهُ الْحُسْنَى وَفَضَّلَ اللَّهُ الْمُجَاهِدِينَ عَلَى الْقَاعِدِينَ أَجْرًا عَظِيمًا ۝ دَرَجَاتٍ مِّنْهُ وَمَغْفِرَةً وَرَحْمَةً وَكَانَ اللَّهُ غَفُورًا رَّحِيمًا ۝ إِنَّ الَّذِينَ تَوَفَّاهُمُ الْمَلَائِكَةُ ظَالِمِى أَنفُسِهِمْ قَالُوا فِيمَ كُنتُمْ قَالُوا كُنَّا مُسْتَضْعَفِينَ فِى الْأَرْضِ قَالُوا أَلَمْ تَكُنْ أَرْضُ اللَّهِ وَاسِعَةً فَتُهَاجِرُوا فِيهَا فَأُولَٰئِكَ مَأْوَاهُمْ جَهَنَّمُ وَسَاءَتْ مَصِيرًا ۝ إِلَّا الْمُسْتَضْعَفِينَ مِنَ الرِّجَالِ وَالنِّسَاءِ وَالْوِلْدَانِ لَا يَسْتَطِيعُونَ حِيلَةً وَلَا يَهْتَدُونَ سَبِيلًا ۝ فَأُولَٰئِكَ عَسَى اللَّهُ أَن يَعْفُوَ عَنْهُمْ وَكَانَ اللَّهُ عَفُوًّا غَفُورًا ۝ وَمَن يُهَاجِرْ فِى سَبِيلِ اللَّهِ يَجِدْ فِى الْأَرْضِ مُرَاغَمًا كَثِيرًا وَسَعَةً وَمَن يَخْرُجْ مِن بَيْتِهِ مُهَاجِرًا إِلَى اللَّهِ وَرَسُولِهِ ثُمَّ يُدْرِكْهُ الْمَوْتُ فَقَدْ وَقَعَ أَجْرُهُ عَلَى اللَّهِ وَكَانَ اللَّهُ غَفُورًا رَّحِيمًا ۝ وَإِذَا ضَرَبْتُمْ فِى الْأَرْضِ فَلَيْسَ عَلَيْكُمْ جُنَاحٌ أَن تَقْصُرُوا مِنَ الصَّلَاةِ إِنْ خِفْتُمْ أَن يَفْتِنَكُمُ الَّذِينَ كَفَرُوا إِنَّ الْكَافِرِينَ كَانُوا لَكُمْ عَدُوًّا مُّبِينًا ۝

95. Not equal are those of the believers who (when not all believers are required to mobilize for God's cause) sit still without justifiable excuse (and without doing any harm to God's cause), and those who strive (and fight) in God's cause with their wealth and their persons. God has exalted in rank those who strive with their wealth and their persons over those who sit still. To each God has promised the best reward (Paradise), and yet God has exalted those who strive above those who sit still by a tremendous reward.

96. For them are ranks from Him (differing according to the degree of the sincerity and striving of each), and forgiveness, and mercy (to bring unforeseen blessings). God is All-Forgiving, All-Compassionate.

97. As to those whose souls the angels (charged with taking the souls of people) take in the state of wronging themselves (by continuing to live in unbelief without suffering to emigrate to a land where they would be able to attain faith): They (the angels) ask them: "What situation were you in (so that you were not with the believers)?" They say: "We were under such oppression in this land that we could not find way to faith." They (the angels) say: "Was God's earth not wide enough for you to emigrate in it?" Such are those whose refuge is Hell: how evil a destination to arrive at!

98. Except those truly oppressed among the men, and the women, and the children altogether without means and not guided to a way (to emigrate, and including those who, in their lifetime, have not had a means to be guided to faith).

99. For those (while their circumstanc-es are unchanged, it is expected that) God will not hold them accountable and will excuse them. Assuredly God is One Who excuses much, All-Forgiving.

100. Whoever emigrates in God's cause will find on the earth enough room for refuge and plentiful resources. He who leaves his home as an emigrant to God and His Messenger and whom death overtakes (while still on the way), his reward is due and sure with God. God is indeed All-Forgiving, All-Compassionate.

101. (O believers!) When you go forth on the earth, there is no blame on you that you shorten the (Prescribed) Prayers, if you fear that those who disbelieve might cause you harm (by attacking you). Assuredly the unbelievers are a manifest enemy to you.

94　　　سورة النساء　　　٩٢

وَإِذَا كُنتَ فِيهِمْ فَأَقَمْتَ لَهُمُ الصَّلَوٰةَ فَلْتَقُمْ طَآئِفَةٌ مِّنْهُم مَّعَكَ وَلْيَأْخُذُوٓا۟ أَسْلِحَتَهُمْ فَإِذَا سَجَدُوا۟ فَلْيَكُونُوا۟ مِن وَرَآئِكُمْ وَلْتَأْتِ طَآئِفَةٌ أُخْرَىٰ لَمْ يُصَلُّوا۟ فَلْيُصَلُّوا۟ مَعَكَ وَلْيَأْخُذُوا۟ حِذْرَهُمْ وَأَسْلِحَتَهُمْ وَدَّ الَّذِينَ كَفَرُوا۟ لَوْ تَغْفُلُونَ عَنْ أَسْلِحَتِكُمْ وَأَمْتِعَتِكُمْ فَيَمِيلُونَ عَلَيْكُم مَّيْلَةً وَٰحِدَةً وَلَا جُنَاحَ عَلَيْكُمْ إِن كَانَ بِكُمْ أَذًى مِّن مَّطَرٍ أَوْ كُنتُم مَّرْضَىٰٓ أَن تَضَعُوٓا۟ أَسْلِحَتَكُمْ وَخُذُوا۟ حِذْرَكُمْ إِنَّ اللَّهَ أَعَدَّ لِلْكَٰفِرِينَ عَذَابًا مُّهِينًا ۝ فَإِذَا قَضَيْتُمُ الصَّلَوٰةَ فَاذْكُرُوا۟ اللَّهَ قِيَٰمًا وَقُعُودًا وَعَلَىٰ جُنُوبِكُمْ فَإِذَا اطْمَأْنَنتُمْ فَأَقِيمُوا۟ الصَّلَوٰةَ إِنَّ الصَّلَوٰةَ كَانَتْ عَلَى الْمُؤْمِنِينَ كِتَٰبًا مَّوْقُوتًا ۝ وَلَا تَهِنُوا۟ فِي ابْتِغَآءِ الْقَوْمِ إِن تَكُونُوا۟ تَأْلَمُونَ فَإِنَّهُمْ يَأْلَمُونَ كَمَا تَأْلَمُونَ وَتَرْجُونَ مِنَ اللَّهِ مَا لَا يَرْجُونَ وَكَانَ اللَّهُ عَلِيمًا حَكِيمًا ۝ إِنَّآ أَنزَلْنَآ إِلَيْكَ الْكِتَٰبَ بِالْحَقِّ لِتَحْكُمَ بَيْنَ النَّاسِ بِمَآ أَرَىٰكَ اللَّهُ وَلَا تَكُن لِّلْخَآئِنِينَ خَصِيمًا ۝

――――✧――――

102. When you (O Messenger) are among the believers (who are on an expedition and in fear that the unbelievers might harm them) and stand (to lead) the Prayer for them, let a party of them stand in the Prayer with you and retain their arms with them (while the other party maintain their positions against the enemy). When the first party have done the prostrations (finished the *rak 'ah*), let them go to the rear of your company (and there hold positions against the enemy), and let the other party who have not prayed come forward and pray with you, being fully prepared against danger and retaining their arms. Those who disbelieve wish that you should be heedless of your weapons and your equipment, so that they might swoop upon you in a single (surprise) attack. But there will be no blame on

you if you lay aside your arms (during the Prayer) if you are troubled by rain (and the ground impedes your movement), or if you are ill; however, be fully prepared against danger. Surely God has prepared for the unbelievers a shameful, humiliating punishment.

103. When you have finished the Prayer (especially considering you have shortened your Prayers when journeying and in the state of fear), remember and mention God (with your tongues and hearts), standing and sitting and lying down on your sides (and even while at war). Then when you are once again secure, do the Prayer in conformity with all its conditions (and do the Prayers you had to omit just at the time of actual fighting).[23] (Know that) the Prayer (being the most important kind of worship) is prescribed for the believers at fixed times.[24]

104. Do not be faint of purpose in pursuing these people (who fight with you, and keep them under pressure as long as the state of war continues between you and them). If you are suffering (having to endure hardships), they too are suffering just as you are, but you hope (to receive) from God what they cannot hope for. God is indeed All-Knowing (of the states and conditions of all things), All-Wise.

105. Surely We have sent down to you the Book with the truth (embodying it, with nothing false in it), so that you should judge between people according to how God has shown you. So do not be a pleader on behalf of those who betray their trust.

23. With its miraculous eloquence, the Qur'ān exhorts the believers to emigrate and strive in God's way, implying that the most valuable journeying in God's sight is that which is made for God's cause, such as emigration and going forth to serve God's cause. By mentioning the Prescribed Prayer between the verses in which it stresses the significance of emigration (*hijrah*) and striving in God's cause (*jihād*), including fighting the enemy, it both legislates how Prayer should be performed during the journey and in a state of war and draws attention to the fundamental relation between success in striving for God's cause and the Prayer, including the recitations of God's glorification, praise, and exaltation after the Prayer, which are the seeds of faith.

The Prescribed Prayers are shortened during a journey or when in a state of fear or insecurity, including times of war or disaster, such as fire and flood. Those Prayers performed in a state of fear are called Prayers of Fear (*as-Ṣalāt al-Khawf*), while those prayed during a journey are known as the Prayers of Journey. For the Prayers that consist of four *rak'ah*, the Prayer of Journey is performed with two *rak'ah*s, while the others – those of morning and evening – remain the same. Although there are differences of opinion among jurists on how many *rak'ah*s for the Prayers that normally consist of four *rak'ah*s should be prayed for a Prayer of Fear, by mentioning them together with those of the journey, the Qur'ān seems to imply that both are the same. However, the forms of their praying are different. The Prayers of Journey that consist of two *rak'ah*s are prayed like the Morning Prayer, while those of Fear are prayed as described in the verse 102: A group of soldiers pray one *rak'ah* while the other group take their positions against the enemy, and then this other group also pray one *rak'ah*, each behind the Prayer-leader. Subsequently, each of the two groups comes, in turn, to complete the Prayer by performing one more *rak'ah* individually. This is the view of the Ḥanafī School.

24. Although the five times of the Prescribed Prayer were fixed by the Messenger upon the instruction of Archangel Gabriel, they can be deduced from the relevant verses of the Qur'ān: *Establish the Prayer from the declining of the sun to the darkness of the night, and (be ever observant of) the recitation of the Qur'ān at dawn* (17: 78); *Establish the Prayer at the beginning and the end of the day, and in the watches of the night near to the day* (11: 114); *Glorify your Lord with praise before sunrise and before sunset, and glorify Him during some hours of the night – as well as glorifying (Him) at the ends of the day* (20: 130); *So glorify God when you enter the evening and when you enter the morning; and (proclaim that) all praise and gratitude in the heavens and on the earth are for Him – and in the afternoon and when you enter the noon time* (30: 17–18). It is possible also to see the time of the late night Prayers (*Tahajjud* and *Witr*) in both the verses mentioned and in 73: 2–4; 17: 79; 51: 17; 76: 26. Both these verses and that which has just been interpreted above (103) emphasize in particular the importance of the recitations of God's glory, praise, and exaltation after each Prayer. This last verse also stresses the importance of observing the prescribed times for the Prayer and performing it on time.

وَٱسْتَغْفِرِ ٱللَّهَ إِنَّ ٱللَّهَ كَانَ غَفُورًا رَّحِيمًا ۞ وَلَا تُجَٰدِلْ
عَنِ ٱلَّذِينَ يَخْتَانُونَ أَنفُسَهُمْ إِنَّ ٱللَّهَ لَا يُحِبُّ مَن كَانَ خَوَّانًا
أَثِيمًا ۞ يَسْتَخْفُونَ مِنَ ٱلنَّاسِ وَلَا يَسْتَخْفُونَ مِنَ ٱللَّهِ
وَهُوَ مَعَهُمْ إِذْ يُبَيِّتُونَ مَا لَا يَرْضَىٰ مِنَ ٱلْقَوْلِ وَكَانَ ٱللَّهُ
بِمَا يَعْمَلُونَ مُحِيطًا ۞ هَٰٓأَنتُمْ هَٰٓؤُلَآءِ جَٰدَلْتُمْ عَنْهُمْ
فِى ٱلْحَيَوٰةِ ٱلدُّنْيَا فَمَن يُجَٰدِلُ ٱللَّهَ عَنْهُمْ يَوْمَ ٱلْقِيَٰمَةِ
أَم مَّن يَكُونُ عَلَيْهِمْ وَكِيلًا ۞ وَمَن يَعْمَلْ سُوٓءًا أَوْ يَظْلِمْ نَفْسَهُۥ ثُمَّ
يَسْتَغْفِرِ ٱللَّهَ يَجِدِ ٱللَّهَ غَفُورًا رَّحِيمًا ۞ وَمَن يَكْسِبْ إِثْمًا
فَإِنَّمَا يَكْسِبُهُۥ عَلَىٰ نَفْسِهِۦ وَكَانَ ٱللَّهُ عَلِيمًا حَكِيمًا ۞
وَمَن يَكْسِبْ خَطِيٓئَةً أَوْ إِثْمًا ثُمَّ يَرْمِ بِهِۦ بَرِيٓئًا
فَقَدِ ٱحْتَمَلَ بُهْتَٰنًا وَإِثْمًا مُّبِينًا ۞ وَلَوْلَا فَضْلُ ٱللَّهِ
عَلَيْكَ وَرَحْمَتُهُۥ لَهَمَّت طَّآئِفَةٌ مِّنْهُمْ أَن يُضِلُّوكَ
وَمَا يُضِلُّونَ إِلَّآ أَنفُسَهُمْ وَمَا يَضُرُّونَكَ مِن
شَىْءٍ وَأَنزَلَ ٱللَّهُ عَلَيْكَ ٱلْكِتَٰبَ وَٱلْحِكْمَةَ وَعَلَّمَكَ
مَا لَمْ تَكُن تَعْلَمُ وَكَانَ فَضْلُ ٱللَّهِ عَلَيْكَ عَظِيمًا ۞

from God, whereas He is always with them when they hold night counsels displeasing to Him. God indeed encompasses (with His Knowledge, Seeing, Hearing and Power) all that they do.

109. Ah! You (O believers) might well plead on their behalf in the life of this world, but who will plead with God on their behalf on the Day of Resurrection, or who will then be their defender and guardian?

110. Yet whoever does an evil or wrongs himself (by committing sins to harm himself spiritually), and then implores God for forgiveness will find God All-Forgiving, All-Compassionate.

111. Whereas whoever earns a sin (failing to seek forgiveness for it), earns it only against himself (to his own loss only). And God is All-Knowing, All-Wise.

112. And he who earns a wrong or sin and then throws the blame on an innocent person, has thereby laid upon himself (the additional burden of) a calumny and a flagrant sin.

113. But for God's grace and favor upon you and His mercy, one party of them determined to mislead you, yet they mislead none but themselves, and cannot harm you in any way. (How could they do so, seeing that) God has sent down on you the Book and the Wisdom, and taught you what you did not know. God's grace and favor upon you is tremendous indeed.[25]

106. Pray God for forgiveness. Surely God is All-Forgiving, All-Compassionate.

107. And do not plead on behalf of those who betray themselves (by lying to conceal the truth of the matter brought before you). Surely God does not love whoever betrays trust and persists in sin.

108. They strive to hide (their evil deeds) from people but they do not strive to hide

25. "There are good lessons to be learned from the incidents in connection with which the four verses above were revealed. A Muslim named Ta'imah ibn Ubayraq from the tribe of Ẓafar was suspected of having stolen a suit of armor. When he feared detection, he planted the stolen property in the house of a Jew, where it was found. The Jews denied the charge and accused Ta'imah, but some among the Muslims sympathized with Ta'imah because of his nominal profession of Islam. When the case came for trial, Islamic justice prevailed and the case turned against Ta'imah. Realizing that his punishment was imminent, he fled and left Islam" (Özek et al., 95).

سُوۡرَةُ النِّسَاۤء ٩٦

لَّاخَيْرَ فِى كَثِيرٍ مِّنْ نَّجْوَيٰهُمْ اِلَّا مَنْ اَمَرَ بِصَدَقَةٍ اَوْ مَعْرُوفٍ اَوْ اِصْلَاحٍ بَيْنَ النَّاسِ وَمَنْ يَّفْعَلْ ذٰلِكَ ابْتِغَآءَ مَرْضَاتِ اللّٰهِ فَسَوْفَ نُؤْتِيهِ اَجْرًا عَظِيمًا ۞ وَمَنْ يُّشَاقِقِ الرَّسُولَ مِنْ بَعْدِ مَا تَبَيَّنَ لَهُ الْهُدٰى وَيَتَّبِعْ غَيْرَ سَبِيلِ الْمُؤْمِنِينَ نُوَلِّهِ مَا تَوَلّٰى وَنُصْلِهِ جَهَنَّمَ وَسَآءَتْ مَصِيرًا ۞ اِنَّ اللّٰهَ لَا يَغْفِرُ اَنْ يُّشْرَكَ بِهِ وَيَغْفِرُ مَا دُونَ ذٰلِكَ لِمَنْ يَّشَآءُ وَمَنْ يُّشْرِكْ بِاللّٰهِ فَقَدْ ضَلَّ ضَلَالًا بَعِيدًا ۞ اِنْ يَّدْعُونَ مِنْ دُونِهِ اِلَّا اِنَاثًا وَاِنْ يَّدْعُونَ اِلَّا شَيْطَانًا مَّرِيدًا ۞ لَّعَنَهُ اللّٰهُ وَقَالَ لَاَتَّخِذَنَّ مِنْ عِبَادِكَ نَصِيبًا مَّفْرُوضًا ۞ وَّلَاُضِلَّنَّهُمْ وَلَاُمَنِّيَنَّهُمْ وَلَاٰمُرَنَّهُمْ فَلَيُبَتِّكُنَّ اٰذَانَ الْاَنْعَامِ وَلَاٰمُرَنَّهُمْ فَلَيُغَيِّرُنَّ خَلْقَ اللّٰهِ وَمَنْ يَّتَّخِذِ الشَّيْطَانَ وَلِيًّا مِّنْ دُونِ اللّٰهِ فَقَدْ خَسِرَ خُسْرَانًا مُّبِينًا ۞ يَعِدُهُمْ وَيُمَنِّيهِمْ وَمَا يَعِدُهُمُ الشَّيْطَانُ اِلَّا غُرُورًا ۞ اُولٰئِكَ مَأْوَاهُمْ جَهَنَّمُ وَلَا يَجِدُونَ عَنْهَا مَحِيصًا ۞

114. No good is there in most of their secret counsels except for him who exhorts to a deed of charity, or kind equitable dealings and honest affairs, or setting things right between people. Whoever does that seeking God's good pleasure, We will grant to him a tremendous reward.

115. While whoever cuts himself off from the Messenger after the guidance (to what is truest and best in thought, belief, and conduct) has become clear to him, and follows a way other than that of the believers (for whom it is impossible to agree unanimously on a way that leads to error), We leave him (to himself) on the way he has turned to, and land him in Hell to roast there: how evil a destination to arrive at!

116. Indeed God does not forgive that partners be associated with Him; less than that He forgives to whomever He wills (whomever He has guided to repentance and righteousness as a result of his choosing repentance and righteousness by his free will). Whoever associates partners with God has indeed strayed far away (from the Straight Path).

117. In His stead, they invoke female deities – (in so doing) they in fact invoke none but a haughty, rebellious Satan,[26]

118. One who is accursed by God (excluded from His mercy). Once he said: "Of Your servants I will surely take a share to be assigned to me (by their following me).

119. "I will surely lead them astray and surely engross them in vain desires (superstitious fancies and false conceptions); and I will surely command them, and they

will surely slit the ears of cattle (to mark them out as meant for their idols and as forbidden to themselves to eat, thus making a lawful thing unlawful); and also I will surely command them and they will surely alter God's creation."[27] Whoever takes Satan for a confidant and guardian instead of God has indeed suffered a manifest loss.

120. (In reality, however, Satan has no authority over people against God.) He makes promises to them and fills them with vain desires (superstitious fancies and false conceptions), and what he promises them is nothing but delusion.

121. Such (as those deluded by Satan): their shelter is Hell, and they will find no way to escape from it.

26. Many among those who reject belief in One God often adopt male and female deities. While they often choose a masculine one as their supreme deity, their other deities are feminine. This is because they adore their own selves and consider, first of all, the satisfaction of their interests and animal desires. Since men's primary appetite is for women and since they tend to exploit these deities to satisfy their needs, they choose many of their deities from among women. They desire to see a physically handsome woman wherever they look and tend to eternalize them by making them into statutes and pictures. This is the most abominable way of degrading the standing of women and is nothing more than viewing women as only a physical object. For them women are no more than simple objects involved in the gratification of their desires and interests. Women are no longer given any respect or affection when they need them most.

Humankind also suffer from many different fears. They feel awe before the things they fear. This is why they generally conceive of their supreme deity, before whom they feel awe, as being masculine, and fawn on him. Even if such people may be Pharaoh-like tyrants, it makes no difference; such people degrade themselves to kiss the feet of any power above themselves and in whose hands they see the satisfaction of their needs and desires.

The verse clarifies that those who invent deities other than God in fact call upon Satan as deity, as it is Satan who drives them to do so.

27. The alteration of God's creation means changing an original or natural form by artificial means and using a thing outside of the purpose for which it was created by God. All acts done in violation of a thing's true or intrinsic nature are included in this. For example: the sterilization of men or women, turning males into eunuchs, surgically altering one's physical appearance, turning women from the functions that were entrusted to them, because of their nature, and causing them to carry out the functions for which men are created, sodomy and other kinds of illicit relations, making lawful what God has made unlawful and vice versa, etc.

وَالَّذِينَ ءَامَنُوا وَعَمِلُوا الصَّالِحَاتِ سَنُدْخِلُهُمْ جَنَّاتٍ
تَجْرِى مِن تَحْتِهَا الْأَنْهَارُ خَالِدِينَ فِيهَآ أَبَدًا وَعْدَ اللَّهِ
حَقًّا وَمَنْ أَصْدَقُ مِنَ اللَّهِ قِيلًا ۝ لَيْسَ بِأَمَانِيِّكُمْ
وَلَا أَمَانِيِّ أَهْلِ الْكِتَابِ مَن يَعْمَلْ سُوءًا يُجْزَ بِهِ
وَلَا يَجِدْ لَهُ مِن دُونِ اللَّهِ وَلِيًّا وَلَا نَصِيرًا ۝ وَمَن
يَعْمَلْ مِنَ الصَّالِحَاتِ مِن ذَكَرٍ أَوْ أُنثَىٰ وَهُوَ مُؤْمِنٌ فَأُولَٰئِكَ
يَدْخُلُونَ الْجَنَّةَ وَلَا يُظْلَمُونَ نَقِيرًا ۝ وَمَنْ أَحْسَنُ
دِينًا مِّمَّنْ أَسْلَمَ وَجْهَهُ لِلَّهِ وَهُوَ مُحْسِنٌ وَاتَّبَعَ مِلَّةَ
إِبْرَاهِيمَ حَنِيفًا وَاتَّخَذَ اللَّهُ إِبْرَاهِيمَ خَلِيلًا ۝ وَلِلَّهِ
مَا فِي السَّمَوَاتِ وَمَا فِي الْأَرْضِ وَكَانَ اللَّهُ
بِكُلِّ شَيْءٍ مُّحِيطًا ۝ وَيَسْتَفْتُونَكَ فِي النِّسَاءِ قُلِ اللَّهُ
يُفْتِيكُمْ فِيهِنَّ وَمَا يُتْلَىٰ عَلَيْكُمْ فِي الْكِتَابِ فِي يَتَامَى النِّسَاءِ
اللَّاتِي لَا تُؤْتُونَهُنَّ مَا كُتِبَ لَهُنَّ وَتَرْغَبُونَ أَن تَنكِحُوهُنَّ
وَالْمُسْتَضْعَفِينَ مِنَ الْوِلْدَانِ وَأَن تَقُومُوا لِلْيَتَامَى بِالْقِسْطِ
وَمَا تَفْعَلُوا مِنْ خَيْرٍ فَإِنَّ اللَّهَ كَانَ بِهِ عَلِيمًا ۝

122. As for those who believe and do good, righteous deeds, We will admit them into Gardens through which rivers flow, therein abiding forever. This is God's promise in truth. Who can be truer than God in speech?

123. It is not according to your fancies, nor according to the fancies of the People of the Book. (No one has a privilege in God's sight by virtue of being nominally a Muslim or Jew or Christian. Rather, the truth is this:) Whoever does an evil will be recompensed for it, and he will not find for himself, apart from God, a guardian or a helper (to guard or help him against the consequence of that evil).

124. And whoever does deeds of righteousness, whether male or female, and is a (true) believer – such will enter Paradise, and they will not be wronged by even so little as (would fill) the groove of a date-stone.

125. Who is better in religion than he who has submitted his whole being to God (seeking only His good pleasure, as one devoted to) doing good, aware that God is seeing him, and who follows the way (*millah*) of Abraham being of pure faith (free of unbelief, of associating partners with God, and of hypocrisy). God accepted Abraham as a friend (one close and trusted).

126. To God belongs whatever is in the heavens and whatever is on the earth, and God encompasses everything (with His Knowledge and Power).

127. (O Messenger!) They ask you to pronounce laws concerning women. Answer them: "God pronounces to you the laws concerning them and it is recited to you in this Book concerning female orphans, to whom you do not give what has been ordained for them (as bridal-due or for their maintenance), and yet desire to marry them (out of greed to get their charms or wealth for yourselves, or by refusing to let them marry to continue benefiting from their wealth); and also concerning the weak, helpless children (whose rights should be protected), and that you must be assiduous in observing the rights of orphans." Whatever good you do – surely God has full knowledge of it.

98   سورة النساء   ٩٨

وَإِنِ امْرَأَةٌ خَافَتْ مِنْ بَعْلِهَا نُشُوزًا أَوْ إِعْرَاضًا فَلَا جُنَاحَ عَلَيْهِمَا أَن يُصْلِحَا بَيْنَهُمَا صُلْحًا وَالصُّلْحُ خَيْرٌ وَأُحْضِرَتِ الْأَنفُسُ الشُّحَّ وَإِن تُحْسِنُوا وَتَتَّقُوا فَإِنَّ اللَّهَ كَانَ بِمَا تَعْمَلُونَ خَبِيرًا ۝ وَلَن تَسْتَطِيعُوا أَن تَعْدِلُوا بَيْنَ النِّسَاءِ وَلَوْ حَرَصْتُمْ فَلَا تَمِيلُوا كُلَّ الْمَيْلِ فَتَذَرُوهَا كَالْمُعَلَّقَةِ وَإِن تُصْلِحُوا وَتَتَّقُوا فَإِنَّ اللَّهَ كَانَ غَفُورًا رَّحِيمًا ۝ وَإِن يَتَفَرَّقَا يُغْنِ اللَّهُ كُلًّا مِّن سَعَتِهِ وَكَانَ اللَّهُ وَاسِعًا حَكِيمًا ۝ وَلِلَّهِ مَا فِي السَّمَاوَاتِ وَمَا فِي الْأَرْضِ وَلَقَدْ وَصَّيْنَا الَّذِينَ أُوتُوا الْكِتَابَ مِن قَبْلِكُمْ وَإِيَّاكُمْ أَنِ اتَّقُوا اللَّهَ وَإِن تَكْفُرُوا فَإِنَّ لِلَّهِ مَا فِي السَّمَاوَاتِ وَمَا فِي الْأَرْضِ وَكَانَ اللَّهُ غَنِيًّا حَمِيدًا ۝ وَلِلَّهِ مَا فِي السَّمَاوَاتِ وَمَا فِي الْأَرْضِ وَكَفَى بِاللَّهِ وَكِيلًا ۝ إِن يَشَأْ يُذْهِبْكُمْ أَيُّهَا النَّاسُ وَيَأْتِ بِآخَرِينَ وَكَانَ اللَّهُ عَلَىٰ ذَٰلِكَ قَدِيرًا ۝ مَّن كَانَ يُرِيدُ ثَوَابَ الدُّنْيَا فَعِندَ اللَّهِ ثَوَابُ الدُّنْيَا وَالْآخِرَةِ وَكَانَ اللَّهُ سَمِيعًا بَصِيرًا ۝

128. If a woman fears from her husband ill-treatment or (such breach of marital obligations as) his turning away in aversion, then there will be no blame on them to set things right peacefully between them; peaceful settlement is better. (Bear in mind that) human souls are prone to selfish avarice, so (O husbands) if you do good in consciousness of God and act in reverence for Him and piety (in observing the rights of women), then surely God is fully aware of what you do.

129. You will never be able to deal between your wives with absolute equality (in respect of love and emotional attachment), however much you may desire to do so. But do not turn away altogether (from any one of them), so as to leave her in a dangling state (uncertain if she has or does not have a husband). If you act righ-

teously (between them) and act in piety (fearful of doing any deliberate wrong to any of them), then surely God is All-Forgiving, All-Compassionate.

130. If (despite every effort to reconcile them, it is no longer possible to sustain marriage, and) the couple do separate, (let neither fear to become poor and helpless, for) God suffices all by His abundance. God is All-Embracing (in His bounty), All-Wise.

131. And to God belongs whatever is in the heavens and whatever is on the earth. And assuredly We commanded those who were given the Book before you, and (We command) you (O Muslims) to act in piety and reverence for God, fearful of disobedience to Him (in all matters including especially observing your mutual rights). Yet if you disbelieve (and despite this admonishment act with ingratitude to Him, then bear in mind that) to God belongs whatever is in the heavens and whatever is on the earth: (if you believe in Him and thank Him, this adds nothing to Him, or if you disbelieve in Him and become ungrateful to Him, this does not diminish anything from Him. For) God is All-Wealthy and Self-Sufficient (absolutely independent of all His creatures), All-Praiseworthy (as your Lord, Who provides for you and all other beings and meets all your needs).

132. (Again, know that) to God belongs whatever is in the heavens and whatever is on the earth; and God suffices as One on Whom to rely and to Whom all affairs should be referred.

133. If He wills, He can remove you, O humankind, and bring in others in your place. God is entirely Able to do that.

134. If one desires the reward of this world, (let him know that) with God is the reward of this world and the Hereafter. God is indeed All-Hearing, All-Seeing.

يَٰٓأَيُّهَا ٱلَّذِينَ ءَامَنُوا۟ كُونُوا۟ قَوَّٰمِينَ بِٱلْقِسْطِ شُهَدَآءَ لِلَّهِ
وَلَوْ عَلَىٰٓ أَنفُسِكُمْ أَوِ ٱلْوَٰلِدَيْنِ وَٱلْأَقْرَبِينَ إِن يَكُنْ غَنِيًّا أَوْ فَقِيرًا
فَٱللَّهُ أَوْلَىٰ بِهِمَا فَلَا تَتَّبِعُوا۟ ٱلْهَوَىٰٓ أَن تَعْدِلُوا۟ وَإِن تَلْوُۥٓا۟
أَوْ تُعْرِضُوا۟ فَإِنَّ ٱللَّهَ كَانَ بِمَا تَعْمَلُونَ خَبِيرًا ۞ يَٰٓأَيُّهَا
ٱلَّذِينَ ءَامَنُوٓا۟ ءَامِنُوا۟ بِٱللَّهِ وَرَسُولِهِۦ وَٱلْكِتَٰبِ ٱلَّذِى نَزَّلَ عَلَىٰ
رَسُولِهِۦ وَٱلْكِتَٰبِ ٱلَّذِىٓ أَنزَلَ مِن قَبْلُ وَمَن يَكْفُرْ بِٱللَّهِ
وَمَلَٰٓئِكَتِهِۦ وَكُتُبِهِۦ وَرُسُلِهِۦ وَٱلْيَوْمِ ٱلْءَاخِرِ فَقَدْ ضَلَّ ضَلَٰلًۢا بَعِيدًا
۞ إِنَّ ٱلَّذِينَ ءَامَنُوا۟ ثُمَّ كَفَرُوا۟ ثُمَّ ءَامَنُوا۟ ثُمَّ كَفَرُوا۟ ثُمَّ ٱزْدَادُوا۟
كُفْرًا لَّمْ يَكُنِ ٱللَّهُ لِيَغْفِرَ لَهُمْ وَلَا لِيَهْدِيَهُمْ سَبِيلًۢا ۞
بَشِّرِ ٱلْمُنَٰفِقِينَ بِأَنَّ لَهُمْ عَذَابًا أَلِيمًا ۞ ٱلَّذِينَ يَتَّخِذُونَ
ٱلْكَٰفِرِينَ أَوْلِيَآءَ مِن دُونِ ٱلْمُؤْمِنِينَ أَيَبْتَغُونَ عِندَهُمُ
ٱلْعِزَّةَ فَإِنَّ ٱلْعِزَّةَ لِلَّهِ جَمِيعًا ۞ وَقَدْ نَزَّلَ عَلَيْكُمْ فِى ٱلْكِتَٰبِ
أَنْ إِذَا سَمِعْتُمْ ءَايَٰتِ ٱللَّهِ يُكْفَرُ بِهَا وَيُسْتَهْزَأُ بِهَا فَلَا تَقْعُدُوا۟
مَعَهُمْ حَتَّىٰ يَخُوضُوا۟ فِى حَدِيثٍ غَيْرِهِۦٓ إِنَّكُمْ إِذًا مِّثْلُهُمْ إِنَّ
ٱللَّهَ جَامِعُ ٱلْمُنَٰفِقِينَ وَٱلْكَٰفِرِينَ فِى جَهَنَّمَ جَمِيعًا ۞

---

135. O you who believe! Be upholders and standard-bearers of justice, bearing witness to the truth for God's sake, even though it be against your own selves, or parents or kindred. Whether the person concerned be rich or poor, (bear in mind that) God is nearer to them (than you are and more concerned with their well-being). So do not (in expectation of some gain from the rich or out of misplaced compassion for the poor) follow your own desires lest you swerve from justice. If you distort (the truth) or decline (to bear truthful witness), then know that God is fully aware of all that you do.

136. O you who believe! Believe in God and His Messenger (Muḥammad) and the Book He has been sending down on His Messenger in parts and the (Divine) Books He sent down before. Whoever disbelieves in God, and His angels, and His Books, and His Messengers, and the Last Day, has indeed gone far astray.[28]

137. Those who have believed and then disbelieved, then believed, and again disbelieved, and thereafter grown more intense in unbelief, God will never forgive them,

nor will He guide them to a way (leading to the ultimate triumph and salvation).

138. To the hypocrites (who are as just described) give glad tidings that for them is a painful punishment.

139. (The hypocrites are) those who take unbelievers for confidants, guardians and allies in preference to the believers: do they seek might and glory in being together with them? (If so, let them know that) might and glory belong altogether to God.

140. He has already revealed to you in the Book that when you hear the Revelations of God being rejected and mocked, no longer sit with them (show your disagreement) until they engage in some other talk, or else you will surely become like them. Surely God will gather the hypocrites and the unbelievers all together in Hell.

28. By using the phrase "O you who believe," which includes a verb, instead of "O believers," the Qur'ān is addressing all who have verbally confessed belief and entered the sphere of faith and Islam. The hypocrites are included in this address. By commanding to believe after this address, it stresses that true faith does not consist in a verbal confession alone.

Truly, faith does not consist in a simple acceptance or confession. Just as there are many stages or degrees in the growth of a tree (for example, the date tree) from its seed until its fully-grown, fruit-bearing state, and just as there are countless degrees and ranks in the manifestations of the sun from its manifestations of light and heat in all things on the earth up to its reflection on the moon and then back to itself, so too does faith have almost uncountable degrees and ranks, from a simple acknowledgment of reason and confirmation of the heart, up to degrees of penetration in all the parts and faculties of the body that control and the degrees that direct the entire life of a person – from the faith of a common person to that of the greatest of the Messengers. The first degree or rank of faith is simply believing in the essentials mentioned in this verse, and then comes the deepening of and being steadfast in faith. This is why the Qur'ān usually commands or prohibits some things after the address "O you who believe!"; i.e., confession of belief requires obeying these commandments, which in turn causes them to be stronger and deeper.

The essentials of faith require and corroborate one another. The verse does not mention Divine Destiny as an article or essential of faith. This is because it is included in recognizing and believing in God with all His Qualities essential to Him as God, and His Attributes, Names and acts.

100

سُورَةُ النِّسَاءِ

١٠٠

الَّذِينَ يَتَرَبَّصُونَ بِكُمْ فَإِن كَانَ لَكُمْ فَتْحٌ مِّنَ اللَّهِ قَالُوٓاْ أَلَمْ نَكُن مَّعَكُمْ وَإِن كَانَ لِلْكَٰفِرِينَ نَصِيبٌ قَالُوٓاْ أَلَمْ نَسْتَحْوِذْ عَلَيْكُمْ وَنَمْنَعْكُم مِّنَ ٱلْمُؤْمِنِينَ فَٱللَّهُ يَحْكُمُ بَيْنَكُمْ يَوْمَ ٱلْقِيَٰمَةِ وَلَن يَجْعَلَ ٱللَّهُ لِلْكَٰفِرِينَ عَلَى ٱلْمُؤْمِنِينَ سَبِيلًا ۞ إِنَّ ٱلْمُنَٰفِقِينَ يُخَٰدِعُونَ ٱللَّهَ وَهُوَ خَٰدِعُهُمْ وَإِذَا قَامُوٓاْ إِلَى ٱلصَّلَوٰةِ قَامُواْ كُسَالَىٰ يُرَآءُونَ ٱلنَّاسَ وَلَا يَذْكُرُونَ ٱللَّهَ إِلَّا قَلِيلًا ۞ مُّذَبْذَبِينَ بَيْنَ ذَٰلِكَ لَآ إِلَىٰ هَٰٓؤُلَآءِ وَلَآ إِلَىٰ هَٰٓؤُلَآءِ وَمَن يُضْلِلِ ٱللَّهُ فَلَن تَجِدَ لَهُۥ سَبِيلًا ۞ يَٰٓأَيُّهَا ٱلَّذِينَ ءَامَنُواْ لَا تَتَّخِذُواْ ٱلْكَٰفِرِينَ أَوْلِيَآءَ مِن دُونِ ٱلْمُؤْمِنِينَ أَتُرِيدُونَ أَن تَجْعَلُواْ لِلَّهِ عَلَيْكُمْ سُلْطَٰنًا مُّبِينًا ۞ إِنَّ ٱلْمُنَٰفِقِينَ فِى ٱلدَّرْكِ ٱلْأَسْفَلِ مِنَ ٱلنَّارِ وَلَن تَجِدَ لَهُمْ نَصِيرًا ۞ إِلَّا ٱلَّذِينَ تَابُواْ وَأَصْلَحُواْ وَٱعْتَصَمُواْ بِٱللَّهِ وَأَخْلَصُواْ دِينَهُمْ لِلَّهِ فَأُوْلَٰٓئِكَ مَعَ ٱلْمُؤْمِنِينَ وَسَوْفَ يُؤْتِ ٱللَّهُ ٱلْمُؤْمِنِينَ أَجْرًا عَظِيمًا ۞ مَّا يَفْعَلُ ٱللَّهُ بِعَذَابِكُمْ إِن شَكَرْتُمْ وَءَامَنتُمْ وَكَانَ ٱللَّهُ شَاكِرًا عَلِيمًا ۞

───❧───

141. (The hypocrites are) those who wait to see what befalls you: thus if a victory comes to you from God, they say, "Were we not with you?" but if the unbelievers meet with a success, they say (to them): "Did we not gain leverage over you (by not joining the believers and weakening them from within) and did we not defend you from the believers?" God will judge between you (and them) on the Day of Resurrection, and never will God allow the unbelievers to find a way (to triumph) over the (true) believers.[29]

142. The hypocrites would trick God, whereas it is God who "tricks" them (by causing them to fall into their own traps). When they rise to do the Prayer, they rise lazily, and to be seen by people (to show them that they are Muslims); and they do not remember God (within or outside the Prayer) save a little.

143. Vacillating between (the believers) and (the unbelievers), neither with these, nor with those. Whoever God leads astray, for him you can never find a sound way (to follow).

144. O you who believe! Do not take the unbelievers for guardians and confidants in preference to the believers; or do you want to offer God a manifest proof against yourselves (of being hypocrites and so incur His punishment)?

145. Surely the hypocrites will be in the lowest depth of the Fire; and you will never find for them any helper (against the Fire).

146. Except those who repent and mend their ways and hold fast to God and practice their Religion purely and sincerely for God's sake: those (who repent) are counted with the believers, and in time God will grant to the believers a tremendous reward.

147. What should God punish you if you are grateful (to Him) and believe (in Him)?[30] God is Ever-Responsive to gratitude, All-Knowing.

29. This last sentence, "and never will God allow the unbelievers to find a way (to triumph) over the (true) believers," has several meanings and implications:

- In the Hereafter, the believers will be on the winning side, while the unbelievers will be complete losers.
- Islam has two wings on which the believers fly: one is God's laws and decrees that we call "religion," the other is His laws of life and the creation and operation of the universe, which are the subject-matter of (physical) sciences. As long as the believers obey these two kinds of God's laws, victory will always be on their side. Whereas, if they fall behind the unbelievers in obeying the second kind of God's laws and show neglect in obeying the former, the unbelievers can gain the upper hand over them.
- The unbelievers may at times gain the upper hand, but the final victory always belongs to the believers.
- Although the believers may sometimes be on the losing side, they are always, with respect to the truth of their beliefs, ideas, and spiritually, on the winning side. It is enough to see and prove this fact to look at the phenomenon that during the past few hundred years, when the unbelievers enjoyed supremacy in political, economic, and military fields throughout the world, few have left Islam to enter another religion, while many from other religions have continued to embrace it.
- This statement indicates a very important goal for the believers: They must never allow the unbelievers to gain advantage or find a way to triumph over them. If they fail, they will be accountable before God and have to bear the consequences of such a failure, both in this world and in the world to come.

30. While being ungrateful is a door to unbelief and even may be identical with it (in Arabic, both are derived from the same root), being thankful or grateful (*shukr*) is a door to faith and identical with it. This is because:

The attitude of gratefulness to God consists of acknowledging that whatever good a person has and whatever achievement they have realized is purely from God. It also consists in acknowledging God's benediction and blessings in their heart, confessing it in their speech and manifesting it in their deeds. Their hearts should be overflowing with love for, and loyalty to, the Benefactor, and they should not attribute real creative effect to apparent causes in His benedictions reaching them. They should also use whatever God has granted to them in His way and according to His directives.

لَا يُحِبُّ ٱللَّهُ ٱلْجَهْرَ بِٱلسُّوٓءِ مِنَ ٱلْقَوْلِ إِلَّا مَن ظُلِمَ وَكَانَ ٱللَّهُ
سَمِيعًا عَلِيمًا ۝ إِن تُبْدُواْ خَيْرًا أَوْ تُخْفُوهُ أَوْ تَعْفُواْ عَن سُوٓءٍ
فَإِنَّ ٱللَّهَ كَانَ عَفُوًّا قَدِيرًا ۝ إِنَّ ٱلَّذِينَ يَكْفُرُونَ بِٱللَّهِ
وَرُسُلِهِ وَيُرِيدُونَ أَن يُفَرِّقُواْ بَيْنَ ٱللَّهِ وَرُسُلِهِ وَيَقُولُونَ
نُؤْمِنُ بِبَعْضٍ وَنَكْفُرُ بِبَعْضٍ وَيُرِيدُونَ أَن يَتَّخِذُواْ بَيْنَ ذَٰلِكَ
سَبِيلًا ۝ أُوْلَٰئِكَ هُمُ ٱلْكَافِرُونَ حَقًّا وَأَعْتَدْنَا لِلْكَافِرِينَ
عَذَابًا مُّهِينًا ۝ وَٱلَّذِينَ ءَامَنُواْ بِٱللَّهِ وَرُسُلِهِ وَلَمْ يُفَرِّقُواْ
بَيْنَ أَحَدٍ مِّنْهُمْ أُوْلَٰئِكَ سَوْفَ يُؤْتِيهِمْ أُجُورَهُمْ وَكَانَ ٱللَّهُ
غَفُورًا رَّحِيمًا ۝ يَسْـَٔلُكَ أَهْلُ ٱلْكِتَٰبِ أَن تُنَزِّلَ عَلَيْهِمْ كِتَٰبًا
مِّنَ ٱلسَّمَآءِ فَقَدْ سَأَلُواْ مُوسَىٰٓ أَكْبَرَ مِن ذَٰلِكَ فَقَالُوٓاْ أَرِنَا ٱللَّهَ
جَهْرَةً فَأَخَذَتْهُمُ ٱلصَّٰعِقَةُ بِظُلْمِهِمْ ثُمَّ ٱتَّخَذُواْ ٱلْعِجْلَ
مِنۢ بَعْدِ مَا جَآءَتْهُمُ ٱلْبَيِّنَٰتُ فَعَفَوْنَا عَن ذَٰلِكَ وَءَاتَيْنَا
مُوسَىٰ سُلْطَٰنًا مُّبِينًا ۝ وَرَفَعْنَا فَوْقَهُمُ ٱلطُّورَ
بِمِيثَٰقِهِمْ وَقُلْنَا لَهُمُ ٱدْخُلُواْ ٱلْبَابَ سُجَّدًا وَقُلْنَا لَهُمْ
لَا تَعْدُواْ فِي ٱلسَّبْتِ وَأَخَذْنَا مِنْهُم مِّيثَٰقًا غَلِيظًا ۝

148. God does not like any harsh speech to be uttered save by one who has been wronged (and therefore has the right to express that in appropriate language). God is indeed All-Hearing, All-Knowing.

149. Whether you do some good openly or do it in secret, or pardon an evil (done to you, even though you have the right to legal retaliation, know that) God is All-Pardoning, Ever-Able (to punish or forgive).

150. Those (deserving punishment) are they who disbelieve in God (not recognizing Him at all or not as He should be) and His Messengers (denying Messengership altogether or denying some of the Messengers), and who seek to make distinction between God and His Messengers (by claiming belief in God but denying Messengership or denying some of the Messengers), and say, "We believe in some and deny others," seeking to take a way in between.

151. Such are in truth unbelievers, and We have prepared for the unbelievers a shameful, humiliating punishment.

152. But as for those who believe in God and His Messengers and make no distinction between them (between God and His Messengers or between the Messengers themselves), to them God will grant their rewards (in full). God is indeed All-Forgiving, All-Compassionate.

153. The People of the Book ask you to cause a Book to be sent down on them from heaven. (O Messenger, let this not shock you, for) they asked an even greater thing than this of Moses, when they said, "Show God to us openly," and the thun-derbolt seized them for their wrong-doing. Then they adopted the (golden) calf as deity – and this after the (miracles and other) clear proofs of the truth had come to them. Yet We (accepted their atonement and) pardoned them that; and We granted Moses (the Book and the Criterion, and thereby) a clear proof and authority.

154. (Moreover) We raised the Mount to tower above them to secure their promise (to hold firmly to the Book), and (on another occasion when We guided them to a town) We commanded them, "Go into it through its gate prostrating (humbly in utmost submission to God)"; and again We once commanded them, "Do not exceed the bounds with respect to the Sabbath," and We took from them a most solemn pledge.

102 سُوْرَةُ النِّسَاء ١٠٢

differ about this matter and about Jesus are indeed confused; they have no definite knowledge thereof, following mere conjecture; and of a certainty, they did not kill him.

158. But God raised him to Himself. God is All-Glorious with irresistible might, All-Wise.

159. Yet there is none of the People of the Book but will, before the moment of his death, (grasp the truth about Jesus and) believe in him (though that belief will be of no benefit to them then); and on the Day of Resurrection he will be a witness against them.[32]

160. So, because of the wrong committed by the Jews We made unlawful for them many pure, wholesome things which had (hitherto) been lawful for them, and because of their barring many from God's way;

161. And because of their taking interest although it had been forbidden to them, and consuming the wealth of people in wrongful ways (such as usury, theft, usurpation, bribery, gambling, and selling God's Revelations); and We have prepared for the unbelievers among them (those who persisted in unbelief despite all the many warnings) a painful punishment.

162. But those of them firmly rooted in Knowledge, and the (true) believers believe in what has been sent down to you (O Messenger) and what was sent down before you; and especially those who do the Prayer in conformity with its conditions, and those who pay the Prescribed Purifying Alms, and the believers in God and the Last Day (as both must be believed in): to them will We grant a tremendous reward.

155. And so because of their breaking their pledge, and their intentional ignoring of God's signs (in the universe and in themselves) and their rejection of His Revelations, and their killing certain Prophets against all right, and their saying, "Our hearts have become callous (no longer having any ability to believe)." No! Rather, God has set a seal on their hearts because of their persistent unbelief, so that, with the exception of few, scarcely do they believe.[31]

156. And because of their (persistence in) unbelief and speaking against Mary a tremendous calumny;

157. And their saying "We killed the Messiah, Jesus son of Mary, the Messenger of God " – whereas they did not kill him, nor did they crucify him, but the matter was made dubious to them. Those who

31. For the events mentioned here, see: 2: 51–55, 58, 61, 63–66, 79, 83, 84–88, 92–93.

32. There are various views on Jesus' departure from the world and the Prophetic Traditions about his return to the world before the Day of Resurrection. The following points may be closer to the truth in these two matters:

- Neither the Jews nor the Romans were able to kill or crucify Jesus. According to some interpreters of the Qur'ān, one of his disciples, Judas, was likened to Jesus and substituted for him by God because of his betrayal. However, the late Muḥammad Asad, a Muslim convert from Judaism regards this as only legend. According to him, "in the course of time, long after the time of Jesus, a legend somehow grew up (possibly under the then-powerful influence of Mithraistic beliefs) to the effect that Jesus had died on the cross in order to atone for the 'original sin' with which mankind is allegedly burdened; and this legend became so firmly established among the latter-day followers of Jesus that even his enemies, the Jews, began to believe it – albeit in a derogatory sense (for crucifixion was, in those times, a heinous form of the death-penalty, reserved for the lowest of criminals) (*The Message of the Qur'ān*, 134). Whether M. Asad is right or not, many of the doctrines found in modern Christianity, such as original sin, blood atonement and the Trinity, were essential to Mithraism, which was very widespread in Asia Minor in the years when Christianity began to spread there, and entered Rome long before Christianity did. What is a fact in this matter is that Jesus was not killed, nor crucified, but the matter became ambiguous to those who put forth such assertions.
- If we deal with verse 158 along with 3: 55, and as pointed out in footnote 10 regarding verse 3: 55, and mentioned by Bediüzzaman Said Nursi (*The Letters* "the 1st Letter"), we can say on this matter of God's raising Jesus

to himself: Just as he came into the world in an unusual manner, so too did Jesus depart from the world in an unusual manner. He did not die as other people do, but God took him back with his spirit and body, which took on the form or changed into an "astral" body or energetic envelope. This can be analogous with the Ascension of the Prophet Muḥammad, upon him be God's blessings and peace. However, while the Prophet Muḥammad returned to the world again to complete his mission, Jesus remained where he was taken.

- Among the greatest Messengers – Noah, Abraham, Moses, Jesus, and Muḥammad, upon them be peace – Noah resembled Moses in nature and character, and Abraham resembled Jesus. While God's Attributes of Majesty were more manifest than those of Grace in the former two due to their mission, with Abraham and Jesus it is the other way. Noah and Moses were distinguished with their great sternness towards unbelievers, Abraham and Jesus were better known for their affection and compassion. the Prophet Muḥammad, due to the universality of his mission, combined both in a balanced degree, but according to time and conditions, sometimes majesty and sternness and sometimes affection and compassion had priority. The circumstances before the end of time will make it imperative that Muslims be equipped more with affection, compassion, love, and dialogue. Christianity will be purified of the doctrines that have filtered into it over time, and there will be a coming together between the Muslims and Christians against the onslaught of the trends of materialism and similar ideologies. This will enable God's religion to triumph over atheism and materialism throughout the world. This is what several modern Muslim scholars understand from the Prophetic Traditions that Jesus will return to the world before the end of time and practice the Islamic Law.

إِنَّا أَوْحَيْنَا إِلَيْكَ كَمَا أَوْحَيْنَا إِلَى نُوحٍ وَالنَّبِيِّنَ مِنْ بَعْدِهِ وَأَوْحَيْنَا إِلَى إِبْرَاهِيمَ وَإِسْمَاعِيلَ وَإِسْحَاقَ وَيَعْقُوبَ وَالْأَسْبَاطِ وَعِيسَى وَأَيُّوبَ وَيُونُسَ وَهَارُونَ وَسُلَيْمَانَ وَآتَيْنَا دَاوُودَ زَبُورًا ۝ وَرُسُلًا قَدْ قَصَصْنَاهُمْ عَلَيْكَ مِنْ قَبْلُ وَرُسُلًا لَمْ نَقْصُصْهُمْ عَلَيْكَ وَكَلَّمَ اللَّهُ مُوسَى تَكْلِيمًا ۝ رُسُلًا مُبَشِّرِينَ وَمُنْذِرِينَ لِئَلَّا يَكُونَ لِلنَّاسِ عَلَى اللَّهِ حُجَّةٌ بَعْدَ الرُّسُلِ وَكَانَ اللَّهُ عَزِيزًا حَكِيمًا ۝ لَكِنِ اللَّهُ يَشْهَدُ بِمَا أَنْزَلَ إِلَيْكَ أَنْزَلَهُ بِعِلْمِهِ وَالْمَلَائِكَةُ يَشْهَدُونَ وَكَفَى بِاللَّهِ شَهِيدًا ۝ إِنَّ الَّذِينَ كَفَرُوا وَصَدُّوا عَنْ سَبِيلِ اللَّهِ قَدْ ضَلُّوا ضَلَالًا بَعِيدًا ۝ إِنَّ الَّذِينَ كَفَرُوا وَظَلَمُوا لَمْ يَكُنِ اللَّهُ لِيَغْفِرَ لَهُمْ وَلَا لِيَهْدِيَهُمْ طَرِيقًا ۝ إِلَّا طَرِيقَ جَهَنَّمَ خَالِدِينَ فِيهَا أَبَدًا وَكَانَ ذَلِكَ عَلَى اللَّهِ يَسِيرًا ۝ يَا أَيُّهَا النَّاسُ قَدْ جَاءَكُمُ الرَّسُولُ بِالْحَقِّ مِنْ رَبِّكُمْ فَآمِنُوا خَيْرًا لَكُمْ وَإِنْ تَكْفُرُوا فَإِنَّ لِلَّهِ مَا فِي السَّمَوَاتِ وَالْأَرْضِ وَكَانَ اللَّهُ عَلِيمًا حَكِيمًا ۝

---

163. We have revealed to you (O Messenger) as We revealed to Noah and the Prophets after him; and We revealed to Abraham, Ishmael, Isaac, Jacob and the Prophets who were raised in the tribes, and Jesus, Job, Jonah, Aaron, and Solomon; and We gave David the Psalms.[33]

164. And Messengers We have already told you of (with respect to their mission) before, and Messengers We have not told you of; and God spoke to Moses in a particular way.[34]

165. Messengers (have been sent as) bearers of glad tidings and warners, so that people might have no argument against God after the Messengers (had come to them). And God is All-Glorious with irresistible might, All-Wise.

166. (Whether people believe or not) God bears witness to (the truth of) what He has sent down to you. And He has sent it down from, based on and together with, His Knowledge. And the angels also bear witness (to it) though God suffices for a witness.

167. Surely those who (in defiance of that testimony) disbelieve and bar (people) from God's way, have indeed gone far astray.

168. Surely those who disbelieve and do wrong (to people by barring them from God's way, and to God and His Messengers and angels, and to all believers and all creatures bearing witness to the truth, and to their own conscience, by accusing them of lying and deception) – God will indeed not forgive them nor will He guide them to a road

169. Except the road of Hell, to abide therein forever; and that is easy for God.

170. O humankind! The (most illustrious) Messenger has come to you with the truth from your Lord: believe, then, for your own good. And if you disbelieve, then (know that your unbelief will in no way harm Him, for) to God belongs whatever is in the heavens and on the earth. And God is All-Knowing, All-Wise.

33. Abu'l-A'lā al-Mawdūdī has the following note on this verse:

The 'Psalms' embodied in the Bible are not the Psalms of David. The Biblical version contains many 'psalms' by others and they are ascribed to their actual authors. The 'psalms' which the Bible does ascribe to David do indeed contain the characteristic luster of truth. The book called 'Proverbs,' attributed to Solomon, contains many assertions, and the last two chapters, in particular, are undoubtedly spurious. A great many of these proverbs, however, do have a ring of truth and authenticity. Another book of the Bible is ascribed to Job. Even though it contains many gems of wisdom, it is difficult to believe that the book attributed to Job could in fact be his. For the portrayal of Job's character in that book is quite contrary to the wonderful patience for which he is applauded in the Qur'ān and for which he is praised in the beginning of the Book of Job itself. The Book of Job, quite contrary to the Qur'ānic portrayal of him, presents him as one who was so full of grievance and annoyance with God throughout the entire period of his tribulation that his companions had to try hard to convince him that God was not unjust.

In addition to these, the Bible contains seventeen other books of the Israelite Prophets. The greater part of these seem to be authentic. In Jeremiah, Isaiah, Ezekiel, Amos and certain other books, in particular, one often encounters whole sections which stir and move one's soul. These sections, without doubt, have the luster of Divine Revelation. While going through them one is struck by the vehemence of moral admonition, the powerful opposition to polytheism, the forceful exposition of monotheism, and the strong denunciation of the moral corruption of the Israelites which characterize them. One inevitably senses that these books, the orations of Jesus embodied in the Gospels, and the glorious Qur'ān are like springs which have arisen from one and the same Divine source (al-Mawdūdī, 2: 113–114, note 205).

34. As mentioned in 42: 51, Revelation occurs in three ways:

1. God puts the meaning in the Prophet's heart in a way that the Prophet knows with certainty that it is from God.
2. God speaks to the Prophet without mediation, but without being seen and from behind a veil, as God spoke to Moses from a tree.
3. God sends an angel who communicates God's message to the Prophet. He always sent Gabriel to communicate His messages contained in His Books (aṣ-Ṣaliḥ, 22).

As mentioned in 2: 253, God exalted and distinguished some Prophets in some respects due to the mission of each, meaning that, with the exception of the Prophet Muḥammad, who represented all aspects of Prophethood in the most perfect manner because of the universality of his mission, every Prophet is superior to others in one or more respects. The Prophet Moses was distinguished by being addressed by God without mediation. But although direct address by God was a special favor, it is not the most superior way of Revelation. God sent His messages forming His Book through the angel Gabriel; therefore the most superior way of Revelation is via Gabriel. It is for this reason that the Torah is not formed of God's direct Revelations to Moses.

104   سُوْرَةُ النِّسَاء   ١٠٤

يَا أَهْلَ الْكِتَابِ لَا تَغْلُوا فِي دِينِكُمْ وَلَا تَقُولُوا عَلَى
اللّٰهِ إِلَّا الْحَقَّ إِنَّمَا الْمَسِيحُ عِيسَى ابْنُ مَرْيَمَ رَسُولُ
اللّٰهِ وَكَلِمَتُهُ أَلْقَاهَا إِلَى مَرْيَمَ وَرُوحٌ مِنْهُ فَآمِنُوا
بِاللّٰهِ وَرُسُلِهِ وَلَا تَقُولُوا ثَلَاثَةٌ انْتَهُوا خَيْرًا لَكُمْ إِنَّمَا
اللّٰهُ إِلَٰهٌ وَاحِدٌ سُبْحَانَهُ أَنْ يَكُونَ لَهُ وَلَدٌ لَهُ مَا فِي السَّمَاوَاتِ
وَمَا فِي الْأَرْضِ وَكَفَى بِاللّٰهِ وَكِيلًا ۞ لَنْ يَسْتَنْكِفَ الْمَسِيحُ
أَنْ يَكُونَ عَبْدًا لِلّٰهِ وَلَا الْمَلَائِكَةُ الْمُقَرَّبُونَ وَمَنْ
يَسْتَنْكِفْ عَنْ عِبَادَتِهِ وَيَسْتَكْبِرْ فَسَيَحْشُرُهُمْ إِلَيْهِ جَمِيعًا ۞
فَأَمَّا الَّذِينَ آمَنُوا وَعَمِلُوا الصَّالِحَاتِ فَيُوَفِّيهِمْ أُجُورَهُمْ
وَيَزِيدُهُمْ مِنْ فَضْلِهِ وَأَمَّا الَّذِينَ اسْتَنْكَفُوا وَاسْتَكْبَرُوا
فَيُعَذِّبُهُمْ عَذَابًا أَلِيمًا وَلَا يَجِدُونَ لَهُمْ مِنْ دُونِ
اللّٰهِ وَلِيًّا وَلَا نَصِيرًا ۞ يَا أَيُّهَا النَّاسُ قَدْ جَاءَكُمْ
بُرْهَانٌ مِنْ رَبِّكُمْ وَأَنْزَلْنَا إِلَيْكُمْ نُورًا مُبِينًا ۞
فَأَمَّا الَّذِينَ آمَنُوا بِاللّٰهِ وَاعْتَصَمُوا بِهِ فَسَيُدْخِلُهُمْ فِي رَحْمَةٍ
مِنْهُ وَفَضْلٍ وَيَهْدِيهِمْ إِلَيْهِ صِرَاطًا مُسْتَقِيمًا ۞

servant to God, nor do the angels near-stationed to Him. Whoever disdains to worship God as a servant and feels his pride (puffed up by arrogance, should know that) God will gather them all to Himself (and call them to account).

171. O People of the Book! Do not go beyond the bounds in your religion, and do not say anything of God but the truth. The Messiah, Jesus son of Mary, was but a Messenger of God, and a Word of His (Power) which He conveyed to Mary, and a spirit from Him.[35] So believe in God (as the One, Unique God), and His Messengers (including Jesus, as Messenger); and do not say: (God is one of) a trinity. Give up (this assertion) – (it is) for your own good (to do so). God is but One God; All-Glorified is He in that He is absolutely above having a son. To Him belongs whatever is in the heavens and whatever is on the earth. And God suffices as the One to be relied on, to Whom affairs should be referred.

172. The Messiah never disdains to be a

173. To those who believe and do good, righteous deeds He will grant their rewards in full, and will give them yet more out of His bounty; but as to those who are disdainful and arrogant, He will punish them with a painful punishment, and they will not find for them, against God, a guardian and protector, nor a helper.

174. O humankind! Now a Proof has come to you from your Lord, and We have sent down to you a clear Light (to illuminate your way and show you everything clearly).

175. So those who believe in God (as taught by this Proof and Light), and hold fast to Him – He will admit them into a (great) mercy from His Presence, and a bounty, and guide them direct to Him on a straight path.

35. God has two kinds of words, one issuing from His Attribute of Speech, the other from His Power. His words that issue from His Attribute of Speech are His Books and Scrolls that He sent to some of His Messengers. His words that issue from His Attribute of Power are all of His works – His creatures and all events in the universe. Why then does God mention Jesus especially as one of His Words (of His Power) is that God, due to His Grandeur and Honor, acts in this world from behind cause and effect. He does so because this world is the world of Wisdom and some people, unable to discern the good behind every act of God, would otherwise ascribe to God the things displeasing to them, which could lead them to perish. God acts from behind the veil of cause and effect so that people can ascribe displeasing things, such as illnesses, death, and misfortunes, to their "natural" causes and not complain of God. But since the other world is the world of Power, God will act there without any veils; everything will happen there instantly. The creation of Jesus was different from that of other people, and God created him without a father. So, in Jesus His law of Power was manifested, rather than His law of Wisdom. The Prophet Adam was also created without parents, but God did not call him

His Word. Adam was the first to be created as a human being; but Jesus' creation was completely unusual after so many centuries during which all people came to the world with a father and mother.

The idea of Jesus being a spirit from God should also be considered from this viewpoint. Since he was a Word of God's Power, in the meaning of being created not based on cause and effect, as all other people are, but rather by being breathed into Virgin Mary by or through an angel who is purely a spiritual being, the spiritual dimension weighs more in his creation. Why this was so for Jesus is that he came to spiritually revive the Children of Israel who had been drowned in materialism and who were selling God's Revelations for trifling prices. So Jesus' mission gave priority to the spiritual dimension of the Divine Religion. Unfortunately, most of his followers overstepped the bounds of truth in their religion in later years and in their hands "the spirit *from* God" became "the spirit *of* God," and "the spirit of holiness" with which he was confirmed (2: 87) was interpreted to mean God's own Spirit which became incarnate in Jesus. Thus, along with God and Jesus, there developed the third person of God – the Holy Ghost. The Qur'ān categorically refutes all such assertions.

176. They ask you (O Messenger) to pronounce a ruling. Say (to them): God pronounces to you the ruling concerning inheritance from those who have left behind no lineal heirs (*kalalah*): should a man die childless but have a sister, for her is the half of what he has left behind; and the brother will inherit from her if the sister dies childless. If the heirs are two sisters, for them is two-thirds of what he has left behind. And if the heirs are brothers and sisters, then for the male is the equivalent of the portion of two females. God makes (His commandments) clear to you lest you go astray. God has full knowledge of everything.

SŪRAH 5

AL-MĀIDAH (THE TABLE)

Madīnah period

This *sūrah* is one of the last chapters of the Qur'ān to be revealed. It consists of 120 verses, and takes its name from the table (verse 112) which Jesus' disciples asked God to send them from heaven. In addition to several other topics, it contains rulings concerning daily life.

In the Name of God, the All-Merciful, the All-Compassionate.

1. O you who believe! Fulfill the bonds (you have entered into with God and with people). Lawful for you is the flesh of cattle (grazing beasts of the flock), save what is mentioned to you (herewith), and unlawful (for you is) hunted game when you are in the state of pilgrim sanctity. Surely God decrees as He wills.

2. O you who believe! Do not violate the sanctity of the public symbols (of Islam) set up by God (such as *Jumu'ah* and *'Īd* Prayers, the call to the Prayer, the Sacrifice, and attendant rites of the Pilgrimage), nor of the Sacred Months (during which fighting is forbidden except when you are attacked), nor of the animals (brought to the Sacred House for sacrifice), nor of the collars (put on the animals marked for sacrifice), nor of those who have set out for the Sacred House seeking from their Lord bounty and His good pleasure. But once you leave your pilgrim sanctity (and the sacred precincts of Makkah), you are free to hunt. And never let your detestation for a people because they barred you from the Sacred Mosque, move you to commit violations (acts of aggression or injustice). Rather, help one another in virtue, goodness, righteousness, and piety, and do not help one another in sinful, iniquitous acts and hostility. Keep from disobedience to God in reverence for Him and piety, seeking His protection. Surely God is severe in retribution.

106 سُوۡرَةُ الۡمَآئِدَة ١٠٦

[Arabic Quranic text]

حُرِّمَتۡ عَلَيۡكُمُ الۡمَيۡتَةُ وَالدَّمُ وَلَحۡمُ الۡخِنۡزِيۡرِ وَمَا أُهِلَّ لِغَيۡرِ اللّٰهِ بِهِ وَالۡمُنۡخَنِقَةُ وَالۡمَوۡقُوۡذَةُ وَالۡمُتَرَدِّيَةُ وَالنَّطِيۡحَةُ وَمَا أَكَلَ السَّبُعُ إِلَّا مَا ذَكَّيۡتُمۡ وَمَا ذُبِحَ عَلَى النُّصُبِ وَأَنۡ تَسۡتَقۡسِمُوۡا بِالۡأَزۡلَامِ ذٰلِكُمۡ فِسۡقٌ الۡيَوۡمَ يَئِسَ الَّذِيۡنَ كَفَرُوۡا مِنۡ دِيۡنِكُمۡ فَلَا تَخۡشَوۡهُمۡ وَاخۡشَوۡنِ الۡيَوۡمَ أَكۡمَلۡتُ لَكُمۡ دِيۡنَكُمۡ وَأَتۡمَمۡتُ عَلَيۡكُمۡ نِعۡمَتِيۡ وَرَضِيۡتُ لَكُمُ الۡإِسۡلَامَ دِيۡنًا فَمَنِ اضۡطُرَّ فِيۡ مَخۡمَصَةٍ غَيۡرَ مُتَجَانِفٍ لِّإِثۡمٍ فَإِنَّ اللّٰهَ غَفُوۡرٌ رَّحِيۡمٌ ۞ يَسۡـَٔلُوۡنَكَ مَاذَا أُحِلَّ لَهُمۡ قُلۡ أُحِلَّ لَكُمُ الطَّيِّبَاتُ وَمَا عَلَّمۡتُمۡ مِّنَ الۡجَوَارِحِ مُكَلِّبِيۡنَ تُعَلِّمُوۡنَهُنَّ مِمَّا عَلَّمَكُمُ اللّٰهُ فَكُلُوۡا مِمَّا أَمۡسَكۡنَ عَلَيۡكُمۡ وَاذۡكُرُوا اسۡمَ اللّٰهِ عَلَيۡهِ وَاتَّقُوا اللّٰهَ إِنَّ اللّٰهَ سَرِيۡعُ الۡحِسَابِ ۞ الۡيَوۡمَ أُحِلَّ لَكُمُ الطَّيِّبَاتُ وَطَعَامُ الَّذِيۡنَ أُوۡتُوا الۡكِتَابَ حِلٌّ لَّكُمۡ وَطَعَامُكُمۡ حِلٌّ لَّهُمۡ وَالۡمُحۡصَنَاتُ مِنَ الۡمُؤۡمِنَاتِ وَالۡمُحۡصَنَاتُ مِنَ الَّذِيۡنَ أُوۡتُوا الۡكِتَابَ مِنۡ قَبۡلِكُمۡ إِذَا آتَيۡتُمُوۡهُنَّ أُجُوۡرَهُنَّ مُحۡصِنِيۡنَ غَيۡرَ مُسَافِحِيۡنَ وَلَا مُتَّخِذِيۡ أَخۡدَانٍ وَمَنۡ يَّكۡفُرۡ بِالۡإِيۡمَانِ فَقَدۡ حَبِطَ عَمَلُهُ وَهُوَ فِي الۡآخِرَةِ مِنَ الۡخَاسِرِيۡنَ ۞

---

3. Unlawful to you (for food) are carrion, and blood, and the flesh of swine, and that (the animal) offered in the name of any other than God, and the animal strangled, and the animal beaten down, and the animal fallen to death, and the animal gored, and that devoured by wild beasts – save that which you make lawful (by slaughtering properly while it was still alive) – and that which has been sacrificed to anything serving the function of idols and at the places consecrated for offerings to other than God. And (also unlawful is) that divided and obtained through divining arrows (and the like, such as lotteries and throwing dice). (Eating of any of) that (just mentioned) is transgression. – This day those who disbelieve have lost all hope of (preventing the establishment of) your Religion, so do not hold them in awe, but stand in awe of Me. This day I have perfected for you your

Religion (with all its rules, commandments and universality), completed My favor upon you,[1] and have been pleased to assign for you Islam as Religion. – Then, whoever is constrained by dire necessity (and driven to what is forbidden), without purposely inclining to sin – surely God is All-Forgiving, All-Compassionate.

4. They ask you (O Messenger) what is lawful for them (including, in particular, the game caught by trained hunting animals). Say: "Lawful for you are all pure, wholesome things;" and as for such hunting animals as you have trained as hounds teaching them from what God has taught you: you may eat of what they have caught for you (and brought to you dead or alive without themselves having eaten thereof). And pronounce God's Name (while dispatching them to hunt for you). Keep from disobedience to God in reverence for Him and piety. Surely God is swift at reckoning.

5. This day all pure, wholesome things have been made lawful for you. And the food of those who were given the Book before (including the animals they slaughter unless, of course, they invoke the name of any other than God) is lawful for you, just as your food (including the animals you slaughter) is lawful for them. And (lawful for you in marriage) are chaste women from among the believers and chaste women from among those who were given the Book before, provided that you give them their bridal-due, taking them in honest wedlock, and not in debauchery, nor as secret love-companions. (That is the ordinance regarding your relations with the People of the Book in this world. But know this:) Whoever rejects (the true) faith (and rejects following God's way as required by faith), all his works are in vain, and in the Hereafter he will be among the losers.

1. During the Caliphate of 'Umar, a Jew said: "There is a verse in your Book that if it had been revealed to us, we would have celebrated the day it was revealed as a religious festival," and recited: *This day I have perfected for you your Religion (with all its rules, commandments and universality), completed My favor upon you...* This section of the verse, which seems to have no direct relation with the other parts, declares the dominion of Islam and secures its future. So its importance should be sought in the Prophetic declaration: "This day I leave to you two precious things: as long as you hold fast to them, you will never go astray. They are God's Book and the Family of His Messenger." This *hadith*, which exists in books of the authentic Traditions such as *Ṣaḥīḥ* Muslim, *Sunan* at-Tirmidhī, *Sunan* an-Nasāī, and *Musnad* Ahmad ibn Hanbal, reads in *al-Muwaṭṭa* by Imām Mālik: .... "God's Book and the Sunnah of His Messenger." However, these two versions do not contradict each other; rather they interpret each other. For, as pointed out by Bediüzzaman Said Nursi, what is meant by the Messenger's Family is His Sunnah. That is, the progeny of the Messenger are, first and most of all, responsible for the maintenance and practice of the Sunnah. Moreover, during the history of Islam, the overwhelming majority of the greatest Muslim scholars, spiritual masters, and revivers (those who have come to revive Islam) have all descended from the Prophet's Family. God's Messenger, upon him be peace and blessings, encouraged his *Ummah* to gather around his family and declared that the Qur'ān and his Family, which retains and represents his Sunnah, his way, would never be separated from one another.

١٠٧   الجزء السادس   107

يَٰٓأَيُّهَا ٱلَّذِينَ ءَامَنُوٓاْ إِذَا قُمۡتُمۡ إِلَى ٱلصَّلَوٰةِ فَٱغۡسِلُواْ
وُجُوهَكُمۡ وَأَيۡدِيَكُمۡ إِلَى ٱلۡمَرَافِقِ وَٱمۡسَحُواْ بِرُءُوسِكُمۡ
وَأَرۡجُلَكُمۡ إِلَى ٱلۡكَعۡبَيۡنِۚ وَإِن كُنتُمۡ جُنُبًا فَٱطَّهَّرُواْۚ
وَإِن كُنتُم مَّرۡضَىٰٓ أَوۡ عَلَىٰ سَفَرٍ أَوۡ جَآءَ أَحَدٌ مِّنكُم
مِّنَ ٱلۡغَآئِطِ أَوۡ لَٰمَسۡتُمُ ٱلنِّسَآءَ فَلَمۡ تَجِدُواْ مَآءً فَتَيَمَّمُواْ
صَعِيدًا طَيِّبًا فَٱمۡسَحُواْ بِوُجُوهِكُمۡ وَأَيۡدِيكُم مِّنۡهُۚ
مَا يُرِيدُ ٱللَّهُ لِيَجۡعَلَ عَلَيۡكُم مِّنۡ حَرَجٍ وَلَٰكِن يُرِيدُ
لِيُطَهِّرَكُمۡ وَلِيُتِمَّ نِعۡمَتَهُۥ عَلَيۡكُمۡ لَعَلَّكُمۡ
تَشۡكُرُونَ ۞ وَٱذۡكُرُواْ نِعۡمَةَ ٱللَّهِ عَلَيۡكُمۡ
وَمِيثَٰقَهُ ٱلَّذِي وَاثَقَكُم بِهِۦٓ إِذۡ قُلۡتُمۡ سَمِعۡنَا وَأَطَعۡنَاۖ وَٱتَّقُواْ
ٱللَّهَۚ إِنَّ ٱللَّهَ عَلِيمٌۢ بِذَاتِ ٱلصُّدُورِ ۞ يَٰٓأَيُّهَا ٱلَّذِينَ ءَامَنُواْ كُونُواْ
قَوَّٰمِينَ لِلَّهِ شُهَدَآءَ بِٱلۡقِسۡطِۖ وَلَا يَجۡرِمَنَّكُمۡ شَنَـَٔانُ قَوۡمٍ
عَلَىٰٓ أَلَّا تَعۡدِلُواْۚ ٱعۡدِلُواْ هُوَ أَقۡرَبُ لِلتَّقۡوَىٰۖ وَٱتَّقُواْ
ٱللَّهَۚ إِنَّ ٱللَّهَ خَبِيرٌۢ بِمَا تَعۡمَلُونَ ۞ وَعَدَ ٱللَّهُ ٱلَّذِينَ ءَامَنُواْ
وَعَمِلُواْ ٱلصَّٰلِحَٰتِ لَهُم مَّغۡفِرَةٌ وَأَجۡرٌ عَظِيمٌ ۞

———⟨❧⟩———

6. O you who believe! When you rise up for the Prayer, (if you have no ablution) wash your faces and your hands up to (and including) the elbows, and lightly rub your heads (with water) and (wash) your feet up to (and including) the ankles. And if you are in the state of major ritual impurity (requiring total ablution), purify yourselves (by taking a bath). But if you are ill, or on a journey, or if any of you has just satisfied a want of nature, or you have had contact with women, and can find no water, then betake yourselves to pure earth, passing with it lightly over your face and your hands (and forearms up to and including the elbows). God does not will to impose any hardship upon you, but wills to purify you (of any kind of material and spiritual filth), and to com-

plete His favor upon you, so that you may give thanks (from the heart and in speech, and in action by fulfilling His commandments).

7. And remember God's favor upon you and the pledge by which He bound you when you said: "We have heard and we obey." Keep from disobedience to God in reverence for Him and piety. Surely God has full knowledge of what lies hidden in the bosoms.

8. O you who believe! Be upholders and standard-bearers of right for God's sake, being witnesses for (the establishment of) absolute justice. And by no means let your detestation for a people (or their detestation for you) move you to (commit the sin of) deviating from justice. Be just: this is nearer and more suited to righteousness and piety. Seek righteousness and piety and always act in reverence for God. Surely God is fully aware of all that you do.

9. God has promised those who believe and do good, righteous deeds that for them is forgiveness and a tremendous reward.

108   سُورَةُ المَّائِدَةِ   ١٠٨

وَٱلَّذِينَ كَفَرُوا وَكَذَّبُوا بِـَٔايَٰتِنَآ أُوْلَٰٓئِكَ أَصۡحَٰبُ ٱلۡجَحِيمِ ۞ يَٰٓأَيُّهَا ٱلَّذِينَ ءَامَنُوا ٱذۡكُرُوا نِعۡمَتَ ٱللَّهِ عَلَيۡكُمۡ إِذۡ هَمَّ قَوۡمٌ أَن يَبۡسُطُوٓا إِلَيۡكُمۡ أَيۡدِيَهُمۡ فَكَفَّ أَيۡدِيَهُمۡ عَنكُمۡ وَٱتَّقُوا ٱللَّهَ وَعَلَى ٱللَّهِ فَلۡيَتَوَكَّلِ ٱلۡمُؤۡمِنُونَ ۞ وَلَقَدۡ أَخَذَ ٱللَّهُ مِيثَٰقَ بَنِيٓ إِسۡرَٰٓءِيلَ وَبَعَثۡنَا مِنۡهُمُ ٱثۡنَيۡ عَشَرَ نَقِيبٗاۖ وَقَالَ ٱللَّهُ إِنِّي مَعَكُمۡۖ لَئِنۡ أَقَمۡتُمُ ٱلصَّلَوٰةَ وَءَاتَيۡتُمُ ٱلزَّكَوٰةَ وَءَامَنتُم بِرُسُلِي وَعَزَّرۡتُمُوهُمۡ وَأَقۡرَضۡتُمُ ٱللَّهَ قَرۡضًا حَسَنٗا لَّأُكَفِّرَنَّ عَنكُمۡ سَيِّـَٔاتِكُمۡ وَلَأُدۡخِلَنَّكُمۡ جَنَّٰتٖ تَجۡرِي مِن تَحۡتِهَا ٱلۡأَنۡهَٰرُۚ فَمَن كَفَرَ بَعۡدَ ذَٰلِكَ مِنكُمۡ فَقَدۡ ضَلَّ سَوَآءَ ٱلسَّبِيلِ ۞ فَبِمَا نَقۡضِهِم مِّيثَٰقَهُمۡ لَعَنَّٰهُمۡ وَجَعَلۡنَا قُلُوبَهُمۡ قَٰسِيَةٗۖ يُحَرِّفُونَ ٱلۡكَلِمَ عَن مَّوَاضِعِهِۦ وَنَسُوا حَظّٗا مِّمَّا ذُكِّرُوا بِهِۦۚ وَلَا تَزَالُ تَطَّلِعُ عَلَىٰ خَآئِنَةٖ مِّنۡهُمۡ إِلَّا قَلِيلٗا مِّنۡهُمۡۖ فَٱعۡفُ عَنۡهُمۡ وَٱصۡفَحۡۚ إِنَّ ٱللَّهَ يُحِبُّ ٱلۡمُحۡسِنِينَ ۞

10. Whereas those who deny Our Revelations (coming as verses of the Book), as well as Our signs (both in their inner world and in the outer world) – such are companions of the Blazing Flame.

11. O you who believe! Remember God's favor upon you: when a people were minded to stretch out their hands against you but He restrained their hands from you. Keep from disobedience to God in reverence for Him and piety so as to always deserve His protection. And in God the believers should put their trust.

12. And, indeed, God took a solemn pledge from the Children of Israel and raised up from among them twelve leaders and representatives (one from each tribe, to look after their affairs and as spiritual mentors). God said: "Surely I am with you: if indeed you establish the Prayer in conformity with its conditions, and pay the Prescribed Purifying Alms, and believe in all of My Messengers, and honor and support them, and lend God a good loan (by spending out of your wealth in God's cause), I will surely blot out from you your evil deeds and will certainly admit you into Gardens through which rivers flow. But whoever among you disbelieves after this and is ungrateful has surely strayed from the right, even way.

13. Then, because of their breaking their pledge, We cursed them (excluded them from Our mercy and exposed them to many disasters), and caused their hearts to harden. They alter the words (in their Book) from their context (in order to distort their meanings), and they have forgotten a (most important) portion of what they were admonished about. You will not cease to light upon some act of treachery from them, except a few of them. Yet pardon them, and overlook (their misdeeds). Surely God loves those devoted to doing good, aware that God is seeing them.

وَمِنَ ٱلَّذِينَ قَالُوٓا۟ إِنَّا نَصَـٰرَىٰٓ أَخَذْنَا مِيثَـٰقَهُمْ
فَنَسُوا۟ حَظًّا مِّمَّا ذُكِّرُوا۟ بِهِۦ فَأَغْرَيْنَا بَيْنَهُمُ
ٱلْعَدَاوَةَ وَٱلْبَغْضَآءَ إِلَىٰ يَوْمِ ٱلْقِيَـٰمَةِ وَسَوْفَ
يُنَبِّئُهُمُ ٱللَّهُ بِمَا كَانُوا۟ يَصْنَعُونَ ۝ يَـٰٓأَهْلَ ٱلْكِتَـٰبِ
قَدْ جَآءَكُمْ رَسُولُنَا يُبَيِّنُ لَكُمْ كَثِيرًا مِّمَّا كُنتُمْ
تُخْفُونَ مِنَ ٱلْكِتَـٰبِ وَيَعْفُوا۟ عَن كَثِيرٍ
قَدْ جَآءَكُم مِّنَ ٱللَّهِ نُورٌ وَكِتَـٰبٌ مُّبِينٌ ۝
يَهْدِى بِهِ ٱللَّهُ مَنِ ٱتَّبَعَ رِضْوَٰنَهُۥ سُبُلَ ٱلسَّلَـٰمِ
وَيُخْرِجُهُم مِّنَ ٱلظُّلُمَـٰتِ إِلَى ٱلنُّورِ بِإِذْنِهِۦ
وَيَهْدِيهِمْ إِلَىٰ صِرَٰطٍ مُّسْتَقِيمٍ ۝ لَّقَدْ كَفَرَ
ٱلَّذِينَ قَالُوٓا۟ إِنَّ ٱللَّهَ هُوَ ٱلْمَسِيحُ ٱبْنُ مَرْيَمَ قُلْ
فَمَن يَمْلِكُ مِنَ ٱللَّهِ شَيْـًٔا إِنْ أَرَادَ أَن يُهْلِكَ
ٱلْمَسِيحَ ٱبْنَ مَرْيَمَ وَأُمَّهُۥ وَمَن فِى ٱلْأَرْضِ
جَمِيعًا وَلِلَّهِ مُلْكُ ٱلسَّمَـٰوَٰتِ وَٱلْأَرْضِ وَمَا بَيْنَهُمَا
يَخْلُقُ مَا يَشَآءُ وَٱللَّهُ عَلَىٰ كُلِّ شَىْءٍ قَدِيرٌ ۝

and passing over many things (in order not to put you to further shame). Assuredly there has come to you from God a light (which enlightens your minds and hearts, and illuminates your way), and a Book clear in itself and clearly showing the truth,

16. Whereby God guides whoever strives after His good pleasure (by acting in the way He approves) to the ways of peace, salvation, and safety. And He leads them by His leave out of all kinds of (intellectual, spiritual, social, economic, and political) darkness into light, and guides them to a straight path (in belief, thought, and action).

17. They have indeed disbelieved who declare: God is the Messiah, son of Mary. Say: "Who then has the least power against God, if He had willed to destroy the Messiah, son of Mary, and his mother, and all those who are on the earth?" To God belongs the sovereignty of the heavens and the earth and all that is between them. He creates whatever He wills. God has full power over everything.

14. And from those who said, "We are *Naṣārā* (Helpers),"[2] We also took a solemn pledge, but they have forgotten a (most important) portion of what they were admonished about. So We have stirred up among them enmity and hatred till the Day of Resurrection; then God will cause them to understand what they have been contriving.

15. O People of the Book! Now there has indeed come to you Our Messenger, making clear to you many things you have been concealing of the Book (the Bible),

---

2. Some assert that the word *Naṣārā* (Helpers) is derived from the word *Nāṣirah* (Nazareth), which is the home town of the Prophet Jesus, upon him be peace. On the contrary, this word is derived from the word *nuṣrah* (help); this

derivation is based on the question posed by Jesus to his disciples: "Who will my helpers (*anṣār*) on this way to God?" The disciples answered: "We are the helpers of God's cause" (3: 52). The Qur'ān uses this word here either to refer to this incident and thereby to remind the Christians of their original creed and basic responsibilities, warning them, or only to remind them of their assertion that they are the helpers.

The Prophet Jesus, upon him be peace, never claimed that he had introduced a new religion under the name of Christianity, nor did he call his followers "Christians." He came to revive the Prophet Moses' religion and to follow his Law (*Matthew*, 5: 17). He also gave the glad tidings of the advent of the Last Prophet (*Qur'ān*, 61: 6; *John*, 14: 25–27, 30; 15: 26; 16: 7–8, 12–15). Likewise, his early followers neither regarded themselves as being a separate community from the Israelites nor did they adopt any distinctive name or symbol. They worshipped in the temple along with other Jews and considered themselves to be followers of the Mosaic Law (*Acts*, 3: 1–10; 21: 14–15). Later on, Paul asserted that observing the Law was not required and faith in Christ was all that one needed for salvation (*Romans*, 3: 21–24, 27; 5: 1; 6: 14...). Even in those days, Jesus' followers called themselves "those who believed," "disciples," and "brethren" (*Acts*, 2: 44; 4: 32; 9: 26; 11: 29; 13: 52; 15: 1, 4; 23: 1). The Jews sometimes designated them as "Galileans" and as "the sect of Nazarenes" (*Luke*, 13: 2; *Acts*, 24 :5). The label "Christians" was flung at them by their opponents in Antioch in 43 or 44 CE only to taunt and mock them (*Acts*, 11: 26), and this appellation gradually became established (al-Mawdūdī, 2, note 36).

110   سُورَةُ الْمَائِدَة   ١١٠

وَقَالَتِ الْيَهُودُ وَالنَّصَارَىٰ نَحْنُ أَبْنَاءُ اللَّهِ وَأَحِبَّاؤُهُ قُلْ
فَلِمَ يُعَذِّبُكُم بِذُنُوبِكُم بَلْ أَنتُم بَشَرٌ مِّمَّنْ خَلَقَ يَغْفِرُ لِمَن يَشَاءُ
وَيُعَذِّبُ مَن يَشَاءُ وَلِلَّهِ مُلْكُ السَّمَٰوَٰتِ وَالْأَرْضِ وَمَا بَيْنَهُمَا
وَإِلَيْهِ الْمَصِيرُ ۩ يَٰٓأَهْلَ الْكِتَٰبِ قَدْ جَاءَكُمْ رَسُولُنَا
يُبَيِّنُ لَكُمْ عَلَىٰ فَتْرَةٍ مِّنَ الرُّسُلِ أَن تَقُولُوا مَا جَاءَنَا
مِن بَشِيرٍ وَلَا نَذِيرٍ فَقَدْ جَاءَكُم بَشِيرٌ وَنَذِيرٌ وَاللَّهُ
عَلَىٰ كُلِّ شَيْءٍ قَدِيرٌ ۩ وَإِذْ قَالَ مُوسَىٰ لِقَوْمِهِ يَٰقَوْمِ
اذْكُرُوا نِعْمَةَ اللَّهِ عَلَيْكُمْ إِذْ جَعَلَ فِيكُمْ أَنبِيَاءَ وَجَعَلَكُم
مُّلُوكًا وَءَاتَىٰكُم مَّا لَمْ يُؤْتِ أَحَدًا مِّنَ الْعَٰلَمِينَ ۩ يَٰقَوْمِ
ادْخُلُوا الْأَرْضَ الْمُقَدَّسَةَ الَّتِي كَتَبَ اللَّهُ لَكُمْ وَلَا تَرْتَدُّوا
عَلَىٰ أَدْبَارِكُمْ فَتَنقَلِبُوا خَٰسِرِينَ ۩ قَالُوا يَٰمُوسَىٰ إِنَّ فِيهَا
قَوْمًا جَبَّارِينَ وَإِنَّا لَن نَّدْخُلَهَا حَتَّىٰ يَخْرُجُوا مِنْهَا فَإِن يَخْرُجُوا مِنْهَا
فَإِنَّا دَٰخِلُونَ ۩ قَالَ رَجُلَانِ مِنَ الَّذِينَ يَخَافُونَ أَنْعَمَ اللَّهُ
عَلَيْهِمَا ادْخُلُوا عَلَيْهِمُ الْبَابَ فَإِذَا دَخَلْتُمُوهُ فَإِنَّكُمْ
غَٰلِبُونَ وَعَلَى اللَّهِ فَتَوَكَّلُوا إِن كُنتُم مُّؤْمِنِينَ ۩

———❧———

18. The Jews and Christians assert, "We are God's children and His beloved ones." Say: "Why, then, does He punish you for your sins? No. You are but mortals that (just like others) He has created. He forgives whom He wills, and He punishes whom He wills. To God belongs the sovereignty of the heavens and the earth and all that is between them, and to Him is the homecoming.

19. O People of the Book! Now, after a long interlude during which no Messengers have appeared, there has indeed come to you Our Messenger, making the whole truth clear to you, lest you should say, "There has not come to us any bearer of good tidings, nor any warner." Indeed, there has come to you a bearer of good tidings and a warner. And God has full power over everything.

20. And (remember) when Moses warned his people, saying: "O my people! Remember God's favor upon you,[3] for He appointed among you Prophets, and appointed (among you) rulers (while in Egypt; and made you free to manage your own affairs), and He granted to you favors such as He had not granted to anyone else in the worlds.

21. "O my people! Enter the holy land which God has prescribed for you and commanded you to enter;[4] and do not turn back (from faith to your previous state), for then you will turn about as losers (in both this world and the Hereafter)."

22. They said: "Moses, therein live a people of exceeding strength: we cannot enter it unless they depart from it; so if they depart from it, then we will surely enter it."

23. Said two men from among those who feared (God's punishment for disobedience to Him), and whom God had favored (with faith, sagacity, and devotion): "Enter upon them through the gate (by frontal attack). For once you have entered it, you will surely be the victors. And in God you must put your trust if you are truly believers."

3. It can be said that true humanity lies in two important virtues, which may serve as the means for a person's guidance. One of them is that people acknowledges their innate weakness and poverty, and the errors they have committed, and pray for forgiveness. The other is that they feel gratitude for any good they receive from others. Haughtiness and ingratitude are usually reasons for unbelief. One who never feels remorse or asks forgiveness for their errors and is unaware of gratitude or being thankful cannot be regarded as being truly human. A person whose conscience has not been fully darkened does not refrain from acknowledging their errors, and is appreciative of any good they receive. This is why the Qur'ān, on the one hand, reminds people of God's favors upon them, thereby arousing in them a feeling of gratitude and thankfulness, while on the other hand, it calls on them to acknowledge their errors and sins and to ask for forgiveness. This is very important, both in being truly human and in making people accept Divine truths and guidance.

4. This verse refers to Palestine, which had been the homeland of the Prophets Abraham, Isaac and Jacob (upon them and all other Prophets be peace). At that time, the Divine trust – the representation and promotion of God's religion, which has always been Islam – rested on the shoulders of the Children of Israel. It is for this reason that God Almighty prescribed that land for them and commanded them to enter it and make Islam prevalent there. So this prescription is not for the Children of Israel as a race, or as the followers of the Jewish religion, or Judaism. It is for those who represent Islam and shoulder its promotion and exaltation at all times.

قَالُوا يَا مُوسَىٰٓ إِنَّا لَن نَّدْخُلَهَآ أَبَدًا مَّا دَامُوا فِيهَا ۖ فَاذْهَبْ أَنتَ
وَرَبُّكَ فَقَاتِلَآ إِنَّا هَٰهُنَا قَاعِدُونَ ۝ قَالَ رَبِّ
إِنِّي لَآ أَمْلِكُ إِلَّا نَفْسِي وَأَخِي ۖ فَافْرُقْ بَيْنَنَا وَبَيْنَ الْقَوْمِ
الْفَاسِقِينَ ۝ قَالَ فَإِنَّهَا مُحَرَّمَةٌ عَلَيْهِمْ ۛ أَرْبَعِينَ سَنَةً ۛ
يَتِيهُونَ فِي الْأَرْضِ ۚ فَلَا تَأْسَ عَلَى الْقَوْمِ الْفَاسِقِينَ ۝ وَاتْلُ
عَلَيْهِمْ نَبَأَ ابْنَيْ آدَمَ بِالْحَقِّ إِذْ قَرَّبَا قُرْبَانًا فَتُقُبِّلَ مِنْ أَحَدِهِمَا
وَلَمْ يُتَقَبَّلْ مِنَ الْآخَرِ قَالَ لَأَقْتُلَنَّكَ ۖ قَالَ إِنَّمَا يَتَقَبَّلُ اللَّهُ
مِنَ الْمُتَّقِينَ ۝ لَئِن بَسَطتَ إِلَيَّ يَدَكَ لِتَقْتُلَنِي مَآ
أَنَا بِبَاسِطٍ يَدِيَ إِلَيْكَ لِأَقْتُلَكَ ۖ إِنِّي أَخَافُ اللَّهَ
رَبَّ الْعَالَمِينَ ۝ إِنِّي أُرِيدُ أَن تَبُوءَ بِإِثْمِي وَإِثْمِكَ فَتَكُونَ
مِنْ أَصْحَابِ النَّارِ ۚ وَذَٰلِكَ جَزَاءُ الظَّالِمِينَ ۝ فَطَوَّعَتْ لَهُ
نَفْسُهُ قَتْلَ أَخِيهِ فَقَتَلَهُ فَأَصْبَحَ مِنَ الْخَاسِرِينَ ۝ فَبَعَثَ اللَّهُ
غُرَابًا يَبْحَثُ فِي الْأَرْضِ لِيُرِيَهُ كَيْفَ يُوَارِي سَوْءَةَ أَخِيهِ ۚ
قَالَ يَا وَيْلَتَا أَعَجَزْتُ أَنْ أَكُونَ مِثْلَ هَٰذَا الْغُرَابِ
فَأُوَارِيَ سَوْءَةَ أَخِي ۖ فَأَصْبَحَ مِنَ النَّادِمِينَ ۝

———❧———

24. They said: "O Moses! By no means will we enter it as long as they are there. Go forth, then, you and your Lord, and fight, both of you. (As for ourselves) we will be sitting just here!"

25. He (Moses) said (turning to His Lord with entreaty): "O my Lord! I have power over none except my own self and my brother (Aaron) only; so You judge and separate between us and this transgressing people!"

26. He (God) said (passing this judgment): "Then, this (land) shall now be forbidden to them for forty years, while they shall wander about on the earth, bewildered. Do not grieve over that transgressing people."

27. Narrate to them (O Messenger) in truth the exemplary experience of the two sons of Adam, when they each offered a sacrifice, and it was accepted from one of them, and not accepted from the other. "I will surely kill you," said (he whose sacrifice was not accepted). "God accepts only from the sincere and truly pious," said the other.

28. "Yet if you stretch out your hand against me to kill me, I will not stretch out my hand against you to kill you. Surely I fear God, the Lord of the worlds.

29. "(In refusing to fight you and remembering to fear God) I desire indeed (to warn you) that you will bear the burden of my sin (were I to take part in fighting you) and your own sin (for seeking to kill me) and so you will be among the companions of the Fire.[5] For that is the recompense of wrongdoers."

30. (This warning served only to fuel the other's passion:) His carnal, evil-commanding soul prompted him to kill his brother, and he killed him, thus becoming among the losers.

31. (He did not know what to do with the dead body of his brother.) Then God sent forth a raven, scratching in the earth, to show him how he might cover the corpse of his brother. (So seeing) he cried: "Oh, alas for me! Am I then unable even to be like this raven, and so find a way to cover the corpse of my brother?" And he became distraught with remorse.[6]

5. This part of the verse literally means: "I desire that you should be laden with both my sin and yours, and so will be among the companions of the Fire." However, this is not the expression of a desire, but rather a reality and a serious warning. The Messenger, upon him be peace and blessings, declares: "When two Muslims attempt to kill each other, both the killer and the killed will go to Hell. Because the one killed would have killed the other if he had been able to." (Muslim, "Kitāb al-Fitan," 14; Ibn Māʾjah, "Kitāb al-Farāiḍ," 8) He also declares: "When two people set out to slander one another, the one who starts the slander shall bear the burden of the sin of both because he has caused mutual slandering, as long as the other does not exceed him in slander" (Muslim, "Kitāb al-Birr wa's-Silah," 68; at-Tirmidhi, "Kitāb al-Birr," 51). This is what the answer of Adam's wronged son is based on. What is meant is: "I do not desire to bear the burden of both my own and your sin, which will happen if I attempt to kill you." This brother, known as Abel in the Bible also warns his brother: "Be careful not to bear the burden of the sins of two people and thus become among the companions of Hell." He (Abel) never desired that his sibling should kill him and thus, laden with the sin of two men, go to Hell.

6. Some events, even though seemingly minor and isolated, reveal universal realities and laws. For example, once the Messenger, upon him be peace and blessings, left his house, thinking about which day the Night of Power might fall on. When he saw some Muslims fiercely disputing, he forgot what he had been thinking about. This particular event indicated an important reality: Dispute and discord, to which Muslims are inclined, are perilous to the Muslim community. Similarly, the event which took place between the two sons of Adam, whose names are mentioned as Cain and Abel in the Bible (*Genesis*: 4), discloses an important aspect of human nature. As narrated in the Bible, Abel kept sheep, while Cain worked the soil. (In order to get near to God,) Cain offered some of the fruits of the soil, while Abel brought fat portions from some of the first-born of his flock. Offering a sacrifice means getting near (to God) and is done to be near to God. Even though it was established and is practiced in Islam as the sacrifice of a sheep or of a cow, the main purpose for such an action is to become nearer to God and to attain true piety. The Qurʾan declares: *Bear in mind that neither their flesh nor their blood reaches God, but only piety and consciousness of God reach Him from you.* (22: 37). Since Cain was devoid of true piety and most probably made the offering with ulterior motives, God did not accept this sacrifice from him. This aroused jealousy in him, a trait that is common to humankind, and eventually it caused the first bloodshed in human history.

Life is extremely important and valuable in God's sight. This is why Islam has established the principle: Right is to be esteemed and observed because it is right, even if it is small. The right of an individual cannot be sacrificed for the society. Taking the life of a human being is the same as if one were to take the lives of all humankind, and sparing or restoring the life of one person is the same as sparing and restoring the life of all. Rights and inviolate values are of equal worth and demand retaliation.

112　　سُورَةُ الْمَائِدَة　　١١٢

مِنْ أَجْلِ ذَٰلِكَ كَتَبْنَا عَلَىٰ بَنِى إِسْرَآءِيلَ أَنَّهُ مَنْ قَتَلَ نَفْسًا
بِغَيْرِ نَفْسٍ أَوْ فَسَادٍ فِى الْأَرْضِ فَكَأَنَّمَا قَتَلَ النَّاسَ
جَمِيعًا وَمَنْ أَحْيَاهَا فَكَأَنَّمَا أَحْيَا النَّاسَ جَمِيعًا وَلَقَدْ
جَاءَتْهُمْ رُسُلُنَا بِالْبَيِّنَاتِ ثُمَّ إِنَّ كَثِيرًا مِنْهُمْ بَعْدَ ذَٰلِكَ
فِى الْأَرْضِ لَمُسْرِفُونَ ۞ إِنَّمَا جَزَٰٓؤُا الَّذِينَ يُحَارِبُونَ
اللَّهَ وَرَسُولَهُ وَيَسْعَوْنَ فِى الْأَرْضِ فَسَادًا أَنْ يُقَتَّلُوٓا
أَوْ يُصَلَّبُوٓا أَوْ تُقَطَّعَ أَيْدِيهِمْ وَأَرْجُلُهُمْ مِنْ
خِلَافٍ أَوْ يُنْفَوْا مِنَ الْأَرْضِ ذَٰلِكَ لَهُمْ خِزْيٌ فِى
الدُّنْيَا وَلَهُمْ فِى الْآخِرَةِ عَذَابٌ عَظِيمٌ ۞ إِلَّا الَّذِينَ
تَابُوا مِنْ قَبْلِ أَنْ تَقْدِرُوا عَلَيْهِمْ فَاعْلَمُوٓا أَنَّ
اللَّهَ غَفُورٌ رَحِيمٌ ۞ يَٰٓأَيُّهَا الَّذِينَ آمَنُوا اتَّقُوا
اللَّهَ وَابْتَغُوٓا إِلَيْهِ الْوَسِيلَةَ وَجَاهِدُوا فِى سَبِيلِهِ
لَعَلَّكُمْ تُفْلِحُونَ ۞ إِنَّ الَّذِينَ كَفَرُوا لَوْ أَنَّ لَهُمْ
مَا فِى الْأَرْضِ جَمِيعًا وَمِثْلَهُ مَعَهُ لِيَفْتَدُوا بِهِ مِنْ
عَذَابِ يَوْمِ الْقِيَامَةِ مَا تُقُبِّلَ مِنْهُمْ وَلَهُمْ عَذَابٌ أَلِيمٌ ۞

---❦---

32. It is because of this that We ordained for (all humankind, but particularly for) the Children of Israel: He who kills a soul unless it be (in legal punishment) for murder or for causing disorder and corruption on the earth will be as if he had killed all humankind; and he who saves a life will be as if he had saved the lives of all humankind. Assuredly there came to them Our Messengers (one after the other) with clear proofs of the truth (so that they might be revived both individually and as a people). Then (in spite of all this), many of them go on committing excesses on the earth.

33. The recompense of those who fight against God and His Messenger, and hasten about the earth causing disorder and corruption: they shall (according to the nature of their crime) either be execut-ed, or crucified, or have their hands and feet cut off alternately, or be banished from the land. Such is their disgrace in the world, and for them is a mighty punishment in the Hereafter.

34. Except for those who repent (and desist from their crimes against order) before you have overpowered them, (although the judgment as to specific crimes against individuals is left to those individuals or to their heirs). Know that God surely is All-Forgiving, All-Compassionate (especially towards His servants who turn to Him in repentance).

35. O you who believe! Keep from disobedience to God in reverence for Him and piety, and seek the means to come closer to Him, and strive in His cause, so that you may prosper (in both worlds).

36. As to those who persist in unbelief: even if they owned the whole of what is on the earth, and the like with it, to offer as ransom from the punishment on the Day of Resurrection, it would not be accepted from them. For them is a painful punishment.

يُرِيدُونَ أَن يَخْرُجُوا مِنَ ٱلنَّارِ وَمَا هُم بِخَارِجِينَ
مِنْهَا وَلَهُمْ عَذَابٌ مُّقِيمٌ ۝ وَٱلسَّارِقُ وَٱلسَّارِقَةُ
فَٱقْطَعُوٓا أَيْدِيَهُمَا جَزَآءًۢ بِمَا كَسَبَا نَكَٰلًا مِّنَ ٱللَّهِ
وَٱللَّهُ عَزِيزٌ حَكِيمٌ ۝ فَمَن تَابَ مِنۢ بَعْدِ ظُلْمِهِۦ وَأَصْلَحَ فَإِنَّ
ٱللَّهَ يَتُوبُ عَلَيْهِ إِنَّ ٱللَّهَ غَفُورٌ رَّحِيمٌ ۝ أَلَمْ تَعْلَمْ أَنَّ
ٱللَّهَ لَهُۥ مُلْكُ ٱلسَّمَٰوَٰتِ وَٱلْأَرْضِ يُعَذِّبُ مَن يَشَآءُ
وَيَغْفِرُ لِمَن يَشَآءُ وَٱللَّهُ عَلَىٰ كُلِّ شَىْءٍ قَدِيرٌ ۝ يَٰٓأَيُّهَا
ٱلرَّسُولُ لَا يَحْزُنكَ ٱلَّذِينَ يُسَٰرِعُونَ فِى ٱلْكُفْرِ مِنَ
ٱلَّذِينَ قَالُوٓا ءَامَنَّا بِأَفْوَٰهِهِمْ وَلَمْ تُؤْمِن قُلُوبُهُمْ وَمِنَ
ٱلَّذِينَ هَادُوا سَمَّٰعُونَ لِلْكَذِبِ سَمَّٰعُونَ لِقَوْمٍ
ءَاخَرِينَ لَمْ يَأْتُوكَ يُحَرِّفُونَ ٱلْكَلِمَ مِنۢ بَعْدِ مَوَاضِعِهِۦ
يَقُولُونَ إِنْ أُوتِيتُمْ هَٰذَا فَخُذُوهُ وَإِن لَّمْ تُؤْتَوْهُ
فَٱحْذَرُوا وَمَن يُرِدِ ٱللَّهُ فِتْنَتَهُۥ فَلَن تَمْلِكَ لَهُۥ مِنَ ٱللَّهِ
شَيْـًٔا أُو۟لَٰٓئِكَ ٱلَّذِينَ لَمْ يُرِدِ ٱللَّهُ أَن يُطَهِّرَ قُلُوبَهُمْ لَهُمْ فِى
ٱلدُّنْيَا خِزْىٌ وَلَهُمْ فِى ٱلْءَاخِرَةِ عَذَابٌ عَظِيمٌ ۝

37. They will wish to come out of the Fire, but they shall not come out of it; theirs is a punishment enduring.

38. And for the thief, male or female: cut off their hands as a recompense for what they have earned (of evil), and an exemplary deterrent punishment from God. God is All-Glorious with irresistible might, All-Wise.

39. But he who repents after having done wrong, and mends his ways, surely God accepts His repentance. For God is All-Forgiving, All-Compassionate.[7]

40. Do you not know that surely to God belongs the sovereignty of the heavens and the earth? He punishes whom He wills and forgives whom He wills. He has full power over everything.[8]

41. O Messenger! Let them not grieve you who would rush in unbelief, as if competing with one another in a race, such of them as say with their mouths, "We believe," but their hearts do not believe, and those of them who are Jews. They are eagerly listening out for falsehoods (especially about you) and eagerly listening out (spying) on behalf of other people who have never come to you (even to learn the essence of your Message); altering any words (whether pertaining to God or not) from their contexts to distort their meanings. They say (about matters referred to you for judgment): "If such and such judgment is given to you, accept it; but if it is not given to you, then beware!" Whoever God has willed to put to a trial (to prove his nature, and has failed in this trial), you have no power in anything on his behalf against God. Such are those whose hearts (because of their rushing in unbelief) God does not will to purify. For them is disgrace in the world, and in the Hereafter a mighty punishment.

7. As has been pointed out where the occasion required, the penal law is not the fundamental law upon which a complete system of life has been founded. Rather it is a collection of sanctions and cautions that help to maintain a healthy system. For this reason, it is very important for a penal law to act as a deterrent. So, in evaluating any penal law we should consider to what extent it deters people from committing crimes and how often and widely such crimes are committed in the community where the law is to be enforced. Another important point to note is that the severity or lightness of penalties demonstrates the degree of importance attached to the values that have been brought under protection by the means of such laws. The penalties Islam legislated for the crimes committed against basic human rights and freedoms, such as the right to life, personal property, belief, reproduction, and individual and public security, and basic values like chastity and innocence, and those verses that legislate for crimes against mental and physical health show the importance Islam attaches to these values and their protection. In addition, any penal law should be considered within the whole body of the system, with all its social, economic, and political dimensions, and its principles of creed, worship, morality, and law. Also, by stressing and giving particular importance to repentance and reformation, Islam approaches the matter as one of education and upbringing, showing that it aims to enable individuals to attain human perfection. For this reason, without limiting itself to legal sanctions, Islam brings piety, reverence for God, and life to the forefront.

As a legal term in the Penal Law of Islam, the punishment of cutting off a hand for theft should have the following elements:

The thief should possess legal discretion; i.e., they must have committed the crime purely with their own free will, without any compulsion; they must have taken possession of the thing stolen, thereby depriving its rightful owner of it; they must have stolen it from the place where it was kept, not in an open place where they could enter freely; they must not have had any right to it; and the stolen thing should be of the kind of thing that Islam regards as goods; the value of the goods should be above a certain amount; and it should not be fruit, vegetables, or grain that are not stored in a barn. There is another condition; the person who steals should not be constrained to steal out of dire necessity. Caliph 'Umar, may God be pleased with him, did not enforce this punishment at times of famine. However, such exemptions do not mean that the person who steals will not be punished. Under these circumstances, the judge can determine a punishment for the thief, but cannot decide to have their hand cut off.

8. Such statements in the Qur'ān are of extreme importance. What they mean can be summarized as follows:

- Being the sole Creator of everything, God has absolute sovereignty over everything; He decrees whatever He wills.
- God is also absolutely Merciful, Forgiving, and Wise. Whatever He does and decrees has many instances of wisdom. Nothing he does is in vain. What we must do, after acknowledging that He has absolute sovereignty over everything and absolute power to do whatever He wills, is to try to find the instances of wisdom in His decrees and acts.
- God's absolute Will is, in one respect, identical with His Knowledge. This means that He "knows" with His Eternal Knowledge whatever will happen in the future, and has "pre-recorded" it. Whatever He knows and pre-records takes place when its time is due. But He records an event with its causes and results all together, and also takes into consideration the partial will that He granted to us in His "pre-determinations" that concern us.
- We are confronted by the results of our intentions and deeds, whether they are good or bad. However, since He always wills good for us, guides us to it, and enables us to do it, whatever good we meet is from Him. But whatever misfortune happens to us, it is from our selves (see 4, note 18).

114

سُوْرَةُ الْمَائِدَة   ١١٤

سَمَّاعُونَ لِلْكَذِبِ أَكَّالُونَ لِلسُّحْتِ فَإِنْ جَآءُوكَ فَاحْكُمْ بَيْنَهُمْ أَوْ أَعْرِضْ عَنْهُمْ وَإِنْ تُعْرِضْ عَنْهُمْ فَلَنْ يَضُرُّوكَ شَيْئًا وَإِنْ حَكَمْتَ فَاحْكُمْ بَيْنَهُمْ بِالْقِسْطِ إِنَّ اللّٰهَ يُحِبُّ الْمُقْسِطِينَ ۞ وَكَيْفَ يُحَكِّمُونَكَ وَعِنْدَهُمُ التَّوْرٰيةُ فِيهَا حُكْمُ اللّٰهِ ثُمَّ يَتَوَلَّوْنَ مِنْ بَعْدِ ذٰلِكَ وَمَا أُولٰئِكَ بِالْمُؤْمِنِينَ ۞ إِنَّآ أَنْزَلْنَا التَّوْرٰيةَ فِيهَا هُدًى وَنُورٌ يَحْكُمُ بِهَا النَّبِيُّونَ الَّذِينَ أَسْلَمُوا لِلَّذِينَ هَادُوا وَالرَّبَّانِيُّونَ وَالْأَحْبَارُ بِمَا اسْتُحْفِظُوا مِنْ كِتَابِ اللّٰهِ وَكَانُوا عَلَيْهِ شُهَدَآءَ فَلَا تَخْشَوُا النَّاسَ وَاخْشَوْنِ وَلَا تَشْتَرُوا بِآيَاتِي ثَمَنًا قَلِيلًا وَمَنْ لَمْ يَحْكُمْ بِمَا أَنْزَلَ اللّٰهُ فَأُولٰئِكَ هُمُ الْكَافِرُونَ ۞ وَكَتَبْنَا عَلَيْهِمْ فِيهَآ أَنَّ النَّفْسَ بِالنَّفْسِ وَالْعَيْنَ بِالْعَيْنِ وَالْأَنْفَ بِالْأَنْفِ وَالْأُذُنَ بِالْأُذُنِ وَالسِّنَّ بِالسِّنِّ وَالْجُرُوحَ قِصَاصٌ فَمَنْ تَصَدَّقَ بِهِ فَهُوَ كَفَّارَةٌ لَهُ وَمَنْ لَمْ يَحْكُمْ بِمَآ أَنْزَلَ اللّٰهُ فَأُولٰئِكَ هُمُ الظَّالِمُونَ ۞

42. Listening out for lies and falsehood eagerly, and consuming unlawful earnings greedily! If they come to you (for judgment), you may either judge between them or turn away from them (and decline to give judgment). If you turn away from them, they cannot harm you in any way. But if you judge, judge between them with equity and justice. Surely God loves the scrupulously equitable.

43. But how is it that they ask you for judgment when they have the Torah, in which there is God's judgment (concerning murder), and still thereafter turn away (from that and from your judgment)? The fact is: those are not believers.

44. Surely We did send down the Torah, in which there was guidance and a light (to illuminate people's minds, hearts, and ways of life). Thereby did the Prophets, who were fully submitted to God, judge for the Jews; and so did the masters (self-dedicated to God and educating people) and the rabbis (teachers of law), as they had been entrusted to keep and observe the part of God's Book (revealed up to

their time);[9] and they were all witnesses to its truth. (Concerning judging by God's Book and observing It, We warned them saying): Do not hold people in awe, but stand in awe of Me; and do not sell My Revelations for a trifling price. Whoever (declines to confirm and) does not judge by what God has sent down, those are indeed unbelievers.

45. And We prescribed for them in it (concerning murder): A life for a life, and an eye for an eye, and a nose for a nose, and an ear for an ear, and a tooth for a tooth, and a (like) retaliation for all wounds (the exact retaliation of which is possible). But whoever remits (the retaliation), it will be an act of expiation for him. Whoever does not judge by what God has sent down, those are indeed wrongdoers.[10]

9. By the expression "*the part* of God's Book" it is implied that the Torah did not encompass the whole of God's Revelation, and that more was yet to be revealed. There are several other books in the Old Testament and it is natural that every Rabbi and jurist was responsible for judging by and observing the part of the Revelation which had been revealed up to his time.

10. Retaliation is based on absolute equality of rights – whether the rights are those of the president or a common citizen, the richest and noblest of people or the poorest of the poor – and therefore is absolutely just. This is why the Qur'ān declares that there is life for people in retaliation (2: 179). As retaliation is based on justice and absolute equality, only the injuries for which an exact retaliation is possible can fall under the system of retaliation. For this reason, as it would be risky to retaliate for a broken bone or injury to the skin, such injuries are punishable by indemnification.

Although retaliation means absolute justice and equality, it is not good in itself and is aimed only at securing basic individual rights and providing compensation for the violation of the same. So one whose rights have been violated can either demand retaliation as a legal right or forgo that right. The Qur'ān encourages people to forgo retaliation and gives the glad tiding that a person who forgoes their right of retaliation has done a good deed which will atone for their sins, in accordance with the greatness of the right that has been forgone. For example, a person who saves the life of another shall be considered as having saved the lives of all humankind; in the same way, if a person has the right to demand retaliation for a murder but forgoes it, they will gain as great reward as if they had forgiven the whole of humankind or they will have their sins forgiven to that extent.

In addition to being based on absolute justice and equality, the Divine Commandments also consider and attach great merit to forgiveness and mutual sacrifice in society; God knows best His servants (human beings) and what is good or bad for them. For this reason, no one person or system can be better or equal to God in establishing commandments or making laws. Those who do not accept and judge by His Commandments are unbelievers, wrongdoers, and transgressors. If they accept these laws, but do not judge by them while they are able to do so, they are both wrongdoers and transgressors.

For retaliation in the Bible, see *Exodus*, 21: 23–25; *Leviticus*, 25: 17–22.

وَقَفَّيْنَا عَلَىٰٓ ءَاثَٰرِهِم بِعِيسَى ٱبْنِ مَرْيَمَ مُصَدِّقًا لِّمَا بَيْنَ يَدَيْهِ مِنَ
ٱلتَّوْرَىٰةِ وَءَاتَيْنَٰهُ ٱلْإِنجِيلَ فِيهِ هُدًى وَنُورٌ وَمُصَدِّقًا لِّمَا بَيْنَ
يَدَيْهِ مِنَ ٱلتَّوْرَىٰةِ وَهُدًى وَمَوْعِظَةً لِّلْمُتَّقِينَ ۝ وَلْيَحْكُمْ
أَهْلُ ٱلْإِنجِيلِ بِمَآ أَنزَلَ ٱللَّهُ فِيهِ وَمَن لَّمْ يَحْكُم بِمَآ أَنزَلَ ٱللَّهُ
فَأُو۟لَٰٓئِكَ هُمُ ٱلْفَٰسِقُونَ ۝ وَأَنزَلْنَآ إِلَيْكَ ٱلْكِتَٰبَ
بِٱلْحَقِّ مُصَدِّقًا لِّمَا بَيْنَ يَدَيْهِ مِنَ ٱلْكِتَٰبِ وَمُهَيْمِنًا عَلَيْهِ
فَٱحْكُم بَيْنَهُم بِمَآ أَنزَلَ ٱللَّهُ وَلَا تَتَّبِعْ أَهْوَآءَهُمْ عَمَّا جَآءَكَ مِنَ
ٱلْحَقِّ لِكُلٍّ جَعَلْنَا مِنكُمْ شِرْعَةً وَمِنْهَاجًا وَلَوْ شَآءَ ٱللَّهُ
لَجَعَلَكُمْ أُمَّةً وَٰحِدَةً وَلَٰكِن لِّيَبْلُوَكُمْ فِى مَآ ءَاتَىٰكُمْ
فَٱسْتَبِقُوا۟ ٱلْخَيْرَٰتِ إِلَى ٱللَّهِ مَرْجِعُكُمْ جَمِيعًا فَيُنَبِّئُكُم
بِمَا كُنتُمْ فِيهِ تَخْتَلِفُونَ ۝ وَأَنِ ٱحْكُم بَيْنَهُم بِمَآ أَنزَلَ ٱللَّهُ
وَلَا تَتَّبِعْ أَهْوَآءَهُمْ وَٱحْذَرْهُمْ أَن يَفْتِنُوكَ عَنۢ بَعْضِ مَآ أَنزَلَ ٱللَّهُ
إِلَيْكَ فَإِن تَوَلَّوْا۟ فَٱعْلَمْ أَنَّمَا يُرِيدُ ٱللَّهُ أَن يُصِيبَهُم بِبَعْضِ ذُنُوبِهِمْ
وَإِنَّ كَثِيرًا مِّنَ ٱلنَّاسِ لَفَٰسِقُونَ ۝ أَفَحُكْمَ ٱلْجَٰهِلِيَّةِ
يَبْغُونَ وَمَنْ أَحْسَنُ مِنَ ٱللَّهِ حُكْمًا لِّقَوْمٍ يُوقِنُونَ ۝

─────────────◈─────────────

46. And in the footsteps of those (earlier Prophets) We sent Jesus son of Mary, confirming (the truth of) the Torah revealed before him, and We granted to him the Gospel, in which there was guidance and a light (to illuminate people's minds, hearts and ways of life), confirming what was revealed before it in the Torah (except for a few unlawful things that it made lawful), (and serving as) a guidance and an instruction for the God-revering, pious.

47. (And We commanded:) Let the People of the Gospel judge by what God sent down therein; and whoever does not judge by what God has sent down, those are indeed the transgressors.

48. We have sent down to you (O Messenger) the Book with the truth (embodying it, and with nothing false in it), confirming (the Divine authorship of and the truths that are still contained in) whatever of the Book was revealed before it, and guarding over (all the true teachings in) it. Judge, then, between them by what God has sent down (to you), and do not follow their lusts and fancies away from the truth that has come to you. For each (community to which a Messenger was sent with a Book) have We appointed a clear way of life and a comprehensive system (containing the principles of that way and how to follow it). And if God had so willed, He would surely have made you a single community (following the same way of life and system surrounded by the same conditions throughout all history); but (He willed it otherwise) in order to test you by what He granted to you (and thereby made you subject to a law of

progress). Strive, then, together as if competing in good works. To God is the return of all of you, and He will then make you understand (the truth) about what you have differed on.[11]

49. (Thus did We command you:) Judge between them with what God has sent down and do not follow their lusts and fancies, and beware of them lest they tempt you away from any part of what God has sent down to you. If they turn away, then know that God wills only to afflict them for some of their sins. And many among human beings are indeed transgressors.

50. Or is it the law of the (pagan) Ignorance that they seek (to be judged and ruled by)? Who is better than God as law-giver and judge for a people seeking certainty (and authoritative knowledge)?

11. Similar to 2: 213, these last verses draw attention to some historical and sociological principles and realities. There are two kinds of differences between people: one is the "natural" difference in intelligence, ability, ambition and desire in life, and character. These are the differences that lead people to take up different occupations and which lead to scientific and technological progress. The other kind of difference comes from conflicts of interest and the parceling out of the world's riches. Although these changes too may incite progress, they also cause unrest, clashes and corruption on the earth. The changing conditions of life caused by scientific and technological progress were one of the basic reasons why different Messengers were sent with different Books, although all agreed on the essentials of faith, worship, morality, and the fundamental rules of what is lawful or unlawful.

Since humanity was living what was, in many respects, an age of childhood until the time of the Prophet Muḥammad, upon him be peace and blessings, every Messenger to come before that time had been sent to a certain people and for a certain period. In the Abrahamic line, Moses, upon him be peace, came to the Children of Israel with the Torah, and Jesus, upon him be peace, with the Gospel, which confirmed the Torah in the essentials of faith, worship, morality, and the fundamental rules of the lawful and unlawful, but which made some unlawful things lawful. So, when Jesus came, the Children of Israel, who had followed the Torah until then, should have believed in him and all the previous Prophets and Books, and taken into account the changes which the Gospel introduced in the commandments of the Torah. Many of them, however, did not. When the Prophet Muḥammad, upon him be peace and blessings, came with the Qur'ān at a time when there was no longer any need for another Prophet after him or Book to be sent, both the Jews and Christians should have believed in him and all the previous Prophets and Books,

and followed the Qur'ān. Unfortunately, many of them did not, and thus there came to be three different religions and ways where there should have been only one. The conclusion of verse 48, *To God is the return of all of you, and He will then make you understand (the truth) about what you have differed on,* is extremely important and contains a threat that is directly linked to the existence of these three major religions and ways.

The verses above mention the Books prior to the Qur'ān, giving the name of each. In verse 48 the expression *whatever of the Book* is used, and the Qur'ān is mentioned as the Book. This means that, although there are some differences in the laws, the Qur'ān encompasses all the truths contained in the previous Books. Concerning the Law, the Qur'ān retained the commandments contained in other Books which it did not abrogate. This caused the Muslim jurists to establish the rule, "The unabrogated laws of the previous communities to which a Divine Book was sent are also ours." Although all people must follow the Qur'ān, the People of the Book may live as autonomous communities and follow their own books under the rule of Islam.

Islam has a very comprehensive, dynamic methodology of law that is unparalleled in human history. This law originates in the Qur'ān and Sunnah, and Muslim jurists have developed several other legal procedures that are based on them, such as Analogy (*qiyās*), the principle of deducing new laws through reasoning based on the Qur'ān and Sunnah (*ijtihād*), adoption of what is good and beneficial (*istiḥsān*), maintaining something approvable without changing it (*istiṣḥāb*), taking what is suited to the public benefit and discarding what is harmful (*maṣāliḥ al-mursalah*), barring the road that leads to corruption and what is unlawful (*sadd al-zarāï*), and customary law and tradition acceptable to Islam's basic essentials *('urf)*. (See also notes 2 and 95 on this *sūrah*.)

51. O you who believe! Take not the Jews and Christians for guardians and confidants (in their Judaism and Christianity). Some among them are guardians and confidants to some others. Whoever among you takes them for guardians and confidants will eventually become one of them (and be counted among them in the Hereafter). Surely God does not guide such wrongdoers.

52. Yet you (O Messenger) see those, in whose hearts there is a sickness (that dries up the source of their spiritual life, extinguishes their power of understanding and corrupts their character), hastening towards them (to get their friendship and patronage) as if competing with one another, saying, "We fear lest a turn of fortune should befall us." But it may be that God will bring about (for the believers) victory or some other outcome of His own will (to punish those hypocrites or the wrongdoers whose friendship and patronage they seek). And then they will find themselves utterly regretful for the secrets they (as hypocrites) sought to keep hidden in their selves.

53. And those who believe will say (to each other): "Are those the self-same people who swore by God their most solemn oaths that they were indeed with you?" Their works have gone to waste and they have become losers.

54. O you who believe! Whoever of you turns away from his Religion, (know that) in time God will raise up a people whom He loves, and who love Him, most humble towards the believers, dignified and commanding in the face of the unbelievers, striving (continuously and in solidarity) in God's cause, and fearing not the censure of any who censure. That is God's grace and bounty, which He grants to whom He wills. God is All-Embracing (with His profound grace), All-Knowing.[12]

55. Your guardian and confidant is none but God, and His Messenger, and those who, having believed, establish the Prayer in conformity with all its conditions, and pay the Prescribed Purifying Alms (the Zakāh), and they bow (in humility and submission to Him).

56. Whoever takes God and His Messenger and those who believe for guardian and confidant, then surely the party of God (that they constitute), they are the victors.

57. O you who believe! Do not take for guardians and confidants such of those who were given the Book before you as make a mockery and sport of your Religion, and the unbelievers (who reject the Messenger, Divine Revelation, and the Last Day). Keep from disobedience to God in reverence for Him and piety, if you are truly believers.

12. This verse, which contains a great promise for the distant future of Islam, is of great importance because of the following points:

- No one can detract from Islam by renouncing it. It is God Himself Who preserves it, and He will make it prevail over all other faiths and systems.

- God acts behind the veil of cause and effect in the world; the world is the realm of wisdom. So, if the nation or community which God has favored with the responsibility of shouldering Islam fails to maintain it, God will raise up another people whom He keeps concealed in His treasury of the Unseen. Such are those whom God chose in pre-eternity because of the performance they will exhibit in the future. He loves them and because of this love, they love Him.

- In praising the Companions of the Prophet Muḥammad, upon him be peace and blessings, God presents the following four virtues for us to consider (48: 29):

  1. continuously being in the Messenger's company to support him and share his sufferings;
  2. being stern and implacable against the unbelievers; in that period of ignorance and savagery triumphing over these people was possible by being strong and unyielding;
  3. being merciful among themselves;
  4. being sincere and devoted to gaining God's good pleasure and approval.

Since Abū Bakr, 'Umar, 'Uthmān and 'Alī were, in turn, at the forefront in having these four virtues respectively, they were the greatest among the Companions.

However, a time comes when humanity progresses from ignorance and savagery to science and some sort of civilization, and in that era, when unbelief arises from science and philosophy, the following four virtues, in degree of importance, become prominent and be the most desired in the company which God favors with the responsibility of shouldering Islam:

1. being most humble towards the believers;
2. being able to give orders, command respect, and being dignified (not the same as being "stern" as described above) in the face of the unbelievers, aware that honor and dignity lie in following Islam.
3. constantly striving in utmost solidarity in God's way to make Him known by people and to be a means for their guidance;
4. not fearing the censure of any who will censure them for their struggle to make God known by people.

وَإِذَا نَادَيْتُمْ إِلَى الصَّلَوٰةِ اتَّخَذُوهَا هُزُوًا وَلَعِبًا ذَٰلِكَ بِأَنَّهُمْ قَوْمٌ لَّا يَعْقِلُونَ ۝ قُلْ يَٰٓأَهْلَ الْكِتَٰبِ هَلْ تَنقِمُونَ مِنَّآ إِلَّآ أَنْ ءَامَنَّا بِاللّٰهِ وَمَآ أُنزِلَ إِلَيْنَا وَمَآ أُنزِلَ مِن قَبْلُ وَأَنَّ أَكْثَرَكُمْ فَٰسِقُونَ ۝ قُلْ هَلْ أُنَبِّئُكُم بِشَرٍّ مِّن ذَٰلِكَ مَثُوبَةً عِندَ اللّٰهِ مَن لَّعَنَهُ اللّٰهُ وَغَضِبَ عَلَيْهِ وَجَعَلَ مِنْهُمُ الْقِرَدَةَ وَالْخَنَازِيرَ وَعَبَدَ الطَّٰغُوتَ أُوْلَٰٓئِكَ شَرٌّ مَّكَانًا وَأَضَلُّ عَن سَوَآءِ السَّبِيلِ ۝ وَإِذَا جَآءُوكُمْ قَالُوٓا ءَامَنَّا وَقَد دَّخَلُوا بِالْكُفْرِ وَهُم قَدْ خَرَجُوا بِهِ وَاللّٰهُ أَعْلَمُ بِمَا كَانُوا يَكْتُمُونَ ۝ وَتَرَىٰ كَثِيرًا مِّنْهُمْ يُسَٰرِعُونَ فِى الْإِثْمِ وَالْعُدْوَٰنِ وَأَكْلِهِمُ السُّحْتَ لَبِئْسَ مَا كَانُوا يَعْمَلُونَ ۝ لَوْلَا يَنْهَٰهُمُ الرَّبَّٰنِيُّونَ وَالْأَحْبَارُ عَن قَوْلِهِمُ الْإِثْمَ وَأَكْلِهِمُ السُّحْتَ لَبِئْسَ مَا كَانُوا يَصْنَعُونَ ۝ وَقَالَتِ الْيَهُودُ يَدُ اللّٰهِ مَغْلُولَةٌ غُلَّتْ أَيْدِيهِمْ وَلُعِنُوا بِمَا قَالُوا بَلْ يَدَاهُ مَبْسُوطَتَانِ يُنفِقُ كَيْفَ يَشَآءُ وَلَيَزِيدَنَّ كَثِيرًا مِّنْهُم مَّآ أُنزِلَ إِلَيْكَ مِن رَّبِّكَ طُغْيَٰنًا وَكُفْرًا وَأَلْقَيْنَا بَيْنَهُمُ الْعَدَٰوَةَ وَالْبَغْضَآءَ إِلَىٰ يَوْمِ الْقِيَٰمَةِ كُلَّمَآ أَوْقَدُوا نَارًا لِّلْحَرْبِ أَطْفَأَهَا اللّٰهُ وَيَسْعَوْنَ فِى الْأَرْضِ فَسَادًا وَاللّٰهُ لَا يُحِبُّ الْمُفْسِدِينَ ۝

---

58. When you recite the call to the Prayer, they take it for a mockery and sport – that is because they are a people who do not reason and understand.

59. Say: "O People of the Book! Is it not that you begrudge us only because we believe in God and what has been sent down to us and what was sent down before, and because most of you are transgressors?"

60. Say: "Shall I tell you of a case the worst of all for recompense with God? Those whom God has cursed (excluded from His mercy), and whom He has utterly condemned, and some of whom He turned into apes, and swine, and servants of powers of evil (that institute patterns of faith and rule in defiance of God) – they are worse situated and further astray from the right, even way."

61. Whenever those (of the same character and life-pattern and the hypocrites following in their footsteps) come to you, they declare (hypocritically), "We believe," whereas in fact they enter with unbelief (in their hearts), and so they depart with it. God knows very well what (unbelief and hypocrisy) they have been concealing.

62. You see many among them rushing as if competing in sinful, iniquitous acts, and enmity, and consuming unlawful earnings. How evil indeed is what they have been doing!

63. Why is it that the masters (self-dedicated to God and educating people), and the rabbis (teachers of law) do not forbid them from sinful utterances and consuming unlawful earnings? How evil indeed is what they have been contriving!

64. The Jews say: "God's Hand is fettered" (thus attributing their humiliation and misery to Him). Be their hands fettered and be they excluded from His mercy for saying so! No indeed! both His Hands are spread out wide in bounty, bestowing as He wills. And (the Revelation and bounties) that are sent down to you from your Lord indeed increase many of them in rebellion and unbelief. However (according to the laws We established for human life in the world), We have cast enmity and hateful rancor among them to last until the Day of Resurrection: as often as they kindle a fire of war (against Islam to overcome and put it off), God extinguishes it (without allowing them to attain to their goal). They hasten about the earth causing disorder and corruption, and God does not love those who cause disorder and corruption.

118   سُوْرَةُ الْمَائِدَة   ١١٨

وَلَوْ أَنَّ أَهْلَ الْكِتَابِ ءَامَنُوا وَاتَّقَوْا لَكَفَّرْنَا عَنْهُمْ سَيِّئَاتِهِمْ وَلَأَدْخَلْنَاهُمْ جَنَّاتِ النَّعِيمِ ۞ وَلَوْ أَنَّهُمْ أَقَامُوا التَّوْرَىٰةَ وَالْإِنجِيلَ وَمَا أُنزِلَ إِلَيْهِم مِّن رَّبِّهِمْ لَأَكَلُوا مِن فَوْقِهِمْ وَمِن تَحْتِ أَرْجُلِهِم مِّنْهُمْ أُمَّةٌ مُّقْتَصِدَةٌ وَكَثِيرٌ مِّنْهُمْ سَاءَ مَا يَعْمَلُونَ ۞ يَا أَيُّهَا الرَّسُولُ بَلِّغْ مَا أُنزِلَ إِلَيْكَ مِن رَّبِّكَ وَإِن لَّمْ تَفْعَلْ فَمَا بَلَّغْتَ رِسَالَتَهُ وَاللَّهُ يَعْصِمُكَ مِنَ النَّاسِ إِنَّ اللَّهَ لَا يَهْدِي الْقَوْمَ الْكَافِرِينَ ۞ قُلْ يَا أَهْلَ الْكِتَابِ لَسْتُمْ عَلَىٰ شَيْءٍ حَتَّىٰ تُقِيمُوا التَّوْرَىٰةَ وَالْإِنجِيلَ وَمَا أُنزِلَ إِلَيْكُم مِّن رَّبِّكُمْ وَلَيَزِيدَنَّ كَثِيرًا مِّنْهُم مَّا أُنزِلَ إِلَيْكَ مِن رَّبِّكَ طُغْيَانًا وَكُفْرًا فَلَا تَأْسَ عَلَى الْقَوْمِ الْكَافِرِينَ ۞ إِنَّ الَّذِينَ ءَامَنُوا وَالَّذِينَ هَادُوا وَالصَّابِئُونَ وَالنَّصَارَىٰ مَنْ ءَامَنَ بِاللَّهِ وَالْيَوْمِ الْآخِرِ وَعَمِلَ صَالِحًا فَلَا خَوْفٌ عَلَيْهِمْ وَلَا هُمْ يَحْزَنُونَ ۞ لَقَدْ أَخَذْنَا مِيثَاقَ بَنِي إِسْرَائِيلَ وَأَرْسَلْنَا إِلَيْهِمْ رُسُلًا كُلَّمَا جَاءَهُمْ رَسُولٌ بِمَا لَا تَهْوَىٰ أَنفُسُهُمْ فَرِيقًا كَذَّبُوا وَفَرِيقًا يَقْتُلُونَ ۞

---

65. If only the People of the Book would believe (in the Prophet Muḥammad and what is revealed to him), and keep from disobedience to God in piety so as to deserve His protection, We would certainly blot out from them their (previous) evil deeds and admit them for sure into Gardens of bounty and blessing.

66. If only they had truly observed the Torah and the Gospel, and all that was sent down to them from their Lord (without introducing distortions therein, and therefore would believe in Muḥammad and follow his way), they would have been fed from above them and from beneath their feet (as God would have poured forth His blessings upon them from both heaven and earth).[13] Among them there are just, moderate people who hold to the

right course, but many of them – evil indeed is what they do!

67. O Messenger (you who convey and embody the Message in the best way)! Convey and make known in the clearest way all that has been sent down to you from your Lord. For, if you do not, you have not conveyed His Message and fulfilled the task of His Messengership. And God will certainly protect you from the people. God will surely not guide the disbelieving people (to attain their goal of harming or defeating you).[14]

68. Say: "O People of the Book! You do not stand on anything valid (in God's sight) unless you truly observe the Torah and the Gospel (in their preserved and unabrogated commandments), and all that has been sent down to you from your Lord, (and doing that you would believe in me and the Qur'ān, and follow my way)."[15] However, what is sent down to you from your Lord surely increases many of them in rebellion and unbelief. But grieve not for the disbelieving people.

69. Surely be they of those who declare faith (in Muḥammad and what he brings from God) or be they of those who are the Jews or the Sabaeans or the Christians (or of another faith) – whoever truly and sincerely believes in God and the Last Day and does good, righteous deeds – they will have no fear, nor will they grieve.

70. We did indeed make a covenant with the Children of Israel and (accordingly) We sent them Messengers (one after the other). But whenever a Messenger came to them with what did not suit (the desires of) their souls – some they would deny and some they would kill.

13. The following verses of the Old Testament are of the same import as this verse:

> If you walk in My statutes and keep My commandments, and perform them, I will give you rain in its season, the land shall yield its produce, and the trees of the field shall yield their fruit. Your thresh-ing shall last till the time of vintage, and the vintage shall last till the time of sow-ing; you shall eat your bread to the full, you dwell in your land safely (*Leviticus*, 26: 3–5).

The same meaning is explained in Moses' sermon in *Deuteronomy*, chapter 28.

These two last verses of the *sūrah* point to an important truth related to the concep-tion of *taqwā* (keeping from disobedience to God in reverence for Him and piety in order to deserve His protection). As mentioned be-fore, God has two sets of laws, one which we call religion, the other being those which God has established for the life and operation of the universe, and which are the subject-matter of sciences. While one gets a return for obey-ing or disobeying the former, usually in the Hereafter, the return for obeying or disobeying the latter usually comes in this world. *Taqwā* requires obeying both.

14. This verse explains one of the numerous miracles of the Qur'ān. It openly declares and predicts that God will protect His Messenger, Muḥammad, upon him be peace and blessings, from all his enemies, allowing him to convey His Message to the end and not allowing oth-ers to harm him. Although surrounded by fierce enemies from among the polytheists of Makkah and the desert, from among the Jews, hypocrites, Christians, and many others, the Messenger fulfilled his mission without any fear and died in his bed after having carried his mission to victory.

This promise of God is also true for the heirs to the mission of the Messenger in subse-quent centuries, especially towards the end of time when conditions to live Islam and convey it will be as difficult as they were in Makkah during the early years of Islam. God will also protect these Muslims from their enemies who will be unable to prevent them from fulfilling their mission. Also see: 33: 39.

15. This verse signifies three important things:

- The Jews and Christians meant nothing and did not stand for anything valid in the sight of God or in the name of the Religion unless, for the Jews, they had been ob-serving the Torah and other books sent to them, including the Gospel, and for the Christians, unless they had been observing the Gospel. They should have believed in and followed the Qur'ān when it began to be revealed.

- Even though the Jews and Christians do not believe in the Qur'ān and the Prophet Muḥammad, upon him be peace and bless-ings, Islam regards them as the People of the Book and they are expected to observe the Torah and the Gospel (in their true commandments). If they do not, they will have no right to claim to have been given anything by God.

- Although the Qur'ān clearly explained to them the way of guidance and ultimate sal-vation, since it revealed how they ill-treat-ed their books, they grew more stubborn in their rejection of it and Muḥammad's Messengership.

١١٩　　　　الجزء السادس　　　　119

وَحَسِبُوٓا۟ أَلَّا تَكُونَ فِتْنَةٌ فَعَمُوا۟ وَصَمُّوا۟ ثُمَّ تَابَ ٱللَّهُ
عَلَيْهِمْ ثُمَّ عَمُوا۟ وَصَمُّوا۟ كَثِيرٌ مِّنْهُمْ وَٱللَّهُ
بَصِيرٌۢ بِمَا يَعْمَلُونَ ۝ لَقَدْ كَفَرَ ٱلَّذِينَ قَالُوٓا۟ إِنَّ ٱللَّهَ
هُوَ ٱلْمَسِيحُ ٱبْنُ مَرْيَمَ وَقَالَ ٱلْمَسِيحُ يَٰبَنِىٓ إِسْرَٰٓءِيلَ ٱعْبُدُوا۟ ٱللَّهَ
رَبِّى وَرَبَّكُمْ إِنَّهُۥ مَن يُشْرِكْ بِٱللَّهِ فَقَدْ حَرَّمَ ٱللَّهُ
عَلَيْهِ ٱلْجَنَّةَ وَمَأْوَىٰهُ ٱلنَّارُ وَمَا لِلظَّٰلِمِينَ مِنْ أَنصَارٍ ۝
لَّقَدْ كَفَرَ ٱلَّذِينَ قَالُوٓا۟ إِنَّ ٱللَّهَ ثَالِثُ ثَلَٰثَةٍ وَمَا مِنْ
إِلَٰهٍ إِلَّآ إِلَٰهٌ وَٰحِدٌ وَإِن لَّمْ يَنتَهُوا۟ عَمَّا يَقُولُونَ لَيَمَسَّنَّ
ٱلَّذِينَ كَفَرُوا۟ مِنْهُمْ عَذَابٌ أَلِيمٌ ۝ أَفَلَا يَتُوبُونَ إِلَى
ٱللَّهِ وَيَسْتَغْفِرُونَهُۥ وَٱللَّهُ غَفُورٌ رَّحِيمٌ ۝
مَّا ٱلْمَسِيحُ ٱبْنُ مَرْيَمَ إِلَّا رَسُولٌ قَدْ خَلَتْ مِن قَبْلِهِ ٱلرُّسُلُ
وَأُمُّهُۥ صِدِّيقَةٌ كَانَا يَأْكُلَانِ ٱلطَّعَامَ ٱنظُرْ كَيْفَ
نُبَيِّنُ لَهُمُ ٱلْءَايَٰتِ ثُمَّ ٱنظُرْ أَنَّىٰ يُؤْفَكُونَ ۝
قُلْ أَتَعْبُدُونَ مِن دُونِ ٱللَّهِ مَا لَا يَمْلِكُ لَكُمْ
ضَرًّا وَلَا نَفْعًا وَٱللَّهُ هُوَ ٱلسَّمِيعُ ٱلْعَلِيمُ ۝

───※───

71. They calculated that there would be no trial (of them as a result of what they did), and so became as if blind and deaf (to truth and all Divine admonitions). Then God (having guided them to waken their consciences, and turn to Him in repentance so that they could reform themselves) relented towards them (in gracious forgiveness). Then (again, in spite of that) many of them became as if blind and deaf. And God sees well all that they do.

72. Assuredly they have disbelieved who say: God is the Messiah, son of Mary, whereas the Messiah himself proclaimed: "O Children of Israel! Worship God, my Lord and your Lord." Whoever associates partners with God, God has surely made Paradise forbidden to him, and his refuge is the Fire. And the wrongdoers will have no helpers.

73. Assuredly they also have disbelieved who say: God is the third of the Three, whereas there is no deity save the One God. If they desist not from their saying so, there shall touch those of them who persist in unbelief (and die unbelievers) a painful punishment.

74. Will they not turn to God in repentance and (being resolved never again to commit the same wrong) ask Him for forgiveness? God is All-Forgiving, All-Compassionate.

75. The Messiah, son of Mary, was but a Messenger; Messengers had passed away before him; and his mother was an upright one wholly devoted to God; both of them ate food (as do all mortals). Look, how We make the truths clear to them, then look how they are turned away from the truth and make false claims!

76. Say (to them, O Messenger): "Do you worship, apart from God, that which (in and of itself) has no power to harm or to benefit you – when God is He Who is the All-Hearing, the All-Knowing?"

77. Say: "O People of the Book! Do not go beyond the bounds in your Religion, (straying towards) other than the truth, and do not follow the lusts and fancies of a people who went astray before, and led many others astray, and they strayed (as again others do now) from the right, even way."[16]

78. Those of the Children of Israel who disbelieved were cursed by the tongue of David and Jesus son of Mary. That was because they disobeyed and kept on exceeding the bounds (of the Law).

79. They would not restrain one another from doing the evil they did: indeed evil was what they used to do.

80. You see many of them (the Jews) taking those who disbelieve as allies and friends (instead of allying with the Messenger and the believers). Evil indeed is what they themselves send ahead for themselves (for their future and for the life hereafter), so that God will condemn them, and they will abide in the punishment.

81. Had they truly believed in God and the (most illustrious) Prophet (Muḥammad) and what has been sent down to him, they would not have taken them (the unbelievers) for allies and friends; but many of them are transgressors.

82. You will most certainly find that, of the people (of unbelief), the most violent in enmity towards the believers (the Muslims) are the Jews and those who associate part-

ners with God. And you will most certainly find that the nearest of them in affection to the believers (the Muslims) are those who say: "We are Christians." This is because there are among them (the Christians) hermits (who devote themselves to worshipping God, especially at night) and monks (who struggle with their carnal souls, ever fearful of God's punishment), and because they are not arrogant.[17]

16. This verse warns the Christians particularly against certain peoples of antiquity and some sectarian ones among the Jews who followed ways other than God's Straight Path. It also warns, allusively, the Muslims and, more particularly, the "lettered ones" of our age – the expression "People of the Book" containing an allusion to educated people. It is impossible not to see the part that those peoples played in the alterations of the essentials of Christian faith and worship, or in the revolts and disturbances that broke out in the Muslim Community in its early period, which gave rise to the emergence of several groups that had strayed from the true path, and the part which they have played in the certain anti-religious ideologies that have appeared in recent centuries. Similar warnings are found in the Bible.

In the article titled 'Christianity' in the Encyclopedia Britannica (14th edition), a Christian theologian Reverend George William Knox touches on the same fact while writing about the essential beliefs of the Church:

> Its moulds of thought are those of Greek philosophy, and into these were run the Jewish teachings. We have thus a peculiar combination – the religious doctrines of the Bible, as culminating in the person of Jesus, run through the forms of an alien philosophy.

In the same work, Charles Anderson Scott writes under the title of "Jesus Christ:"

> There is nothing in these three Gospels (*Matthew, Mark, Luke*) to suggest that their writers thought of Jesus as other than human, a human being especially endowed with the Spirit of God and standing in an unbroken relation to God which justified his being spoken of as the 'Son of God.' Even *Matthew* refers to him as the carpenter's son – [According to Matthew, the carpenter Joseph was the step-father of Jesus. Jesus came to the world without a father-AÜ] – and records that after Peter had acknowledged him as Messiah he 'took Him aside and began to rebuke him' (*Matthew*, 16: 22). And in *Luke*, the two disciples on the way to Emmaus can still speak of him as 'a prophet mighty in deed and word before God and all the people' (*Luke*, 24: 19)... It is very singular, that in spite of the fact that before *Mark* was composed, 'the Lord' had become the description of Jesus common among Christians; he is never so described in the second Gospel (nor yet in the first, though the word is freely used to refer to God). All three relate the Passion of Jesus with a fullness and an emphasis of its great significance; but except the 'ransom' passage (*Mark*, 10: 45) and certain words at the Last Supper there is no indication of the meaning which was afterwards attached to it. It is not even suggested that the death of Jesus had any relation to sin or forgiveness.
>
> He (Jesus) frequently referred to himself as the Son of Man... Certain words of Peter spoken at the time of Pentecost, 'A man approved of God', described Jesus as he was known and regarded by his contemporaries... From them (the Gospels) we learn that Jesus passed through the stages of development, physical and mental, that he hungered, thirsted, was weary and slept, that he could be surprised and require information, that he suffered pain and died. He not only made no claim to omniscience, he distinctly waived it... There is still less reason to predicate omnipotence to Jesus. There is no indication that he ever acted independently of God, or as an independent God. Rather does he acknowledge dependence upon God, by his habit of prayer...He even repudiates the ascription to himself of goodness in the absolute sense in which it belongs to God alone.

William Knox, quoted above, writes about ascribing divinity to Jesus:

> ... before the close of the 3rd century, his deity was still widely denied... At the Council of Nicaea in 325 the deity of Christ received official sanction... but controversy continued for some time (more). (For the quotations see al-Mawdūdī, 2, note 101.)

17. This verse points to many facts, such as follows:

- Arrogance and transgression (committing sins openly, without feeling any shame) are obstacles to belief, while modesty and self-criticism are doors opened to it.

- Because of the nature of his mission, The Prophet Jesus, upon him be peace, attached more importance to the spiritual aspect of the Divine Religion than to its other aspects, and this gave rise to many hermits and monks appearing in his community.

- Islam is a middle way; but since modesty, humility, worship, and struggling against the carnal soul are also essential to Islam, there must be a natural closeness between Muslims and the followers of Jesus.

- The mildness and humility of some hermits and monks caused their accepting Islam and the Qur'ān when they heard God's Messenger, upon him be peace and blessings.

١٢١   الجزء السابع   121

وَإِذَا سَمِعُوا مَا أُنزِلَ إِلَى الرَّسُولِ تَرَىٰ أَعْيُنَهُمْ تَفِيضُ مِنَ الدَّمْعِ مِمَّا عَرَفُوا مِنَ الْحَقِّ يَقُولُونَ رَبَّنَا آمَنَّا فَاكْتُبْنَا مَعَ الشَّاهِدِينَ ۝ وَمَا لَنَا لَا نُؤْمِنُ بِاللَّهِ وَمَا جَاءَنَا مِنَ الْحَقِّ وَنَطْمَعُ أَن يُدْخِلَنَا رَبُّنَا مَعَ الْقَوْمِ الصَّالِحِينَ ۝ فَأَثَابَهُمُ اللَّهُ بِمَا قَالُوا جَنَّاتٍ تَجْرِي مِن تَحْتِهَا الْأَنْهَارُ خَالِدِينَ فِيهَا وَذَٰلِكَ جَزَاءُ الْمُحْسِنِينَ ۝ وَالَّذِينَ كَفَرُوا وَكَذَّبُوا بِآيَاتِنَا أُولَٰئِكَ أَصْحَابُ الْجَحِيمِ ۝ يَا أَيُّهَا الَّذِينَ آمَنُوا لَا تُحَرِّمُوا طَيِّبَاتِ مَا أَحَلَّ اللَّهُ لَكُمْ وَلَا تَعْتَدُوا إِنَّ اللَّهَ لَا يُحِبُّ الْمُعْتَدِينَ ۝ وَكُلُوا مِمَّا رَزَقَكُمُ اللَّهُ حَلَالًا طَيِّبًا وَاتَّقُوا اللَّهَ الَّذِي أَنتُم بِهِ مُؤْمِنُونَ ۝ لَا يُؤَاخِذُكُمُ اللَّهُ بِاللَّغْوِ فِي أَيْمَانِكُمْ وَلَٰكِن يُؤَاخِذُكُم بِمَا عَقَّدتُّمُ الْأَيْمَانَ فَكَفَّارَتُهُ إِطْعَامُ عَشَرَةِ مَسَاكِينَ مِنْ أَوْسَطِ مَا تُطْعِمُونَ أَهْلِيكُمْ أَوْ كِسْوَتُهُمْ أَوْ تَحْرِيرُ رَقَبَةٍ فَمَن لَّمْ يَجِدْ فَصِيَامُ ثَلَاثَةِ أَيَّامٍ ذَٰلِكَ كَفَّارَةُ أَيْمَانِكُمْ إِذَا حَلَفْتُمْ وَاحْفَظُوا أَيْمَانَكُمْ كَذَٰلِكَ يُبَيِّنُ اللَّهُ لَكُمْ آيَاتِهِ لَعَلَّكُمْ تَشْكُرُونَ ۝

83. When they hear what has been sent down to the Messenger, you see their eyes brimming over with tears because of what they know of the truth (from their own Books); and they say: "Our Lord! We do believe (in Muḥammad and the Qur'ān); so inscribe us among the witnesses (of the truth in the company of his community).

84. "Why should we not believe in God and what has come to us of the truth? And we fervently desire that our Lord admit us among the righteous people."

85. So God (judged that He would) reward them for their saying so with Gardens through which rivers flow, therein to abide. Such is the reward of those who are devoted to doing good, aware that God is seeing them.

86. As to those who disbelieve and deny Our signs and Revelations, those are companions of the Blazing Flame.

87. O you who believe! Do not hold as unlawful the pure, wholesome things that God has made lawful to you, and do not exceed the bounds (either by making forbidden what is lawful, or by over-indulgence in the lawful). God does not love those who exceed the bounds.

88. Eat as lawful, pure and wholesome from that which God has provided for you; and keep from disobedience to God, in Whom you have faith.

89. God does not take you to task for a slip (or blunder of speech) in your oaths, but He takes you to task for what you have concluded by solemn, deliberate oaths. The expiation (for breaking such oaths) is to feed ten destitute persons (or one person for ten days) with the average of the food you serve to your families, or to clothe them, or to set free a slave. If anyone does not find (the means to do that), let him fast for three days. That is the expiation for your oaths when you have sworn (and broken them). But be mindful of your oaths (do not make them lightly, and when you have sworn them, fulfill them). Thus God makes clear to you His Revelations (the lights of His way), that you may give thanks (from the heart and in speech, and in action by fulfilling His commandments).

122   سُوْرَةُ الْمَائِدَة   ١٢٢

يَٰٓأَيُّهَا الَّذِينَ ءَامَنُوٓا إِنَّمَا الْخَمْرُ وَالْمَيْسِرُ وَالْأَنصَابُ وَالْأَزْلَٰمُ

رِجْسٌ مِّنْ عَمَلِ الشَّيْطَٰنِ فَاجْتَنِبُوهُ لَعَلَّكُمْ تُفْلِحُونَ ۝ إِنَّمَا

يُرِيدُ الشَّيْطَٰنُ أَن يُوقِعَ بَيْنَكُمُ الْعَدَٰوَةَ وَالْبَغْضَآءَ فِى الْخَمْرِ

وَالْمَيْسِرِ وَيَصُدَّكُمْ عَن ذِكْرِ اللَّهِ وَعَنِ الصَّلَوٰةِ فَهَلْ أَنتُم مُّنتَهُونَ

۝ وَأَطِيعُوا اللَّهَ وَأَطِيعُوا الرَّسُولَ وَاحْذَرُوا فَإِن تَوَلَّيْتُمْ فَاعْلَمُوٓا

أَنَّمَا عَلَىٰ رَسُولِنَا الْبَلَٰغُ الْمُبِينُ ۝ لَيْسَ عَلَى الَّذِينَ ءَامَنُوا وَعَمِلُوا الصَّٰلِحَٰتِ

جُنَاحٌ فِيمَا طَعِمُوٓا إِذَا مَا اتَّقَوا وَّءَامَنُوا وَعَمِلُوا الصَّٰلِحَٰتِ ثُمَّ اتَّقَوا

وَّءَامَنُوا ثُمَّ اتَّقَوا وَّأَحْسَنُوا وَاللَّهُ يُحِبُّ الْمُحْسِنِينَ ۝ يَٰٓأَيُّهَا الَّذِينَ

ءَامَنُوا لَيَبْلُوَنَّكُمُ اللَّهُ بِشَيْءٍ مِّنَ الصَّيْدِ تَنَالُهُۥٓ أَيْدِيكُمْ

وَرِمَاحُكُمْ لِيَعْلَمَ اللَّهُ مَن يَخَافُهُۥ بِالْغَيْبِ فَمَنِ اعْتَدَىٰ بَعْدَ ذَٰلِكَ فَلَهُۥ

عَذَابٌ أَلِيمٌ ۝ يَٰٓأَيُّهَا الَّذِينَ ءَامَنُوا لَا تَقْتُلُوا الصَّيْدَ وَأَنتُمْ حُرُمٌ وَمَن

قَتَلَهُۥ مِنكُم مُّتَعَمِّدًا فَجَزَآءٌ مِّثْلُ مَا قَتَلَ مِنَ النَّعَمِ يَحْكُمُ بِهِۦ ذَوَا عَدْلٍ

مِّنكُمْ هَدْيًۢا بَٰلِغَ الْكَعْبَةِ أَوْ كَفَّٰرَةٌ طَعَامُ مَسَٰكِينَ أَوْ عَدْلُ ذَٰلِكَ

صِيَامًا لِّيَذُوقَ وَبَالَ أَمْرِهِۦ عَفَا اللَّهُ عَمَّا سَلَفَ وَمَنْ عَادَ

فَيَنتَقِمُ اللَّهُ مِنْهُ وَاللَّهُ عَزِيزٌ ذُو انتِقَامٍ ۝

---

90. O you who believe! Intoxicants, games of chance, sacrifices to (anything serving the function of) idols (and at places consecrated for offerings to other than God), and (the pagan practice of) divination by arrows (and similar practices) are a loathsome evil of Satan's doing; so turn wholly away from it so that you may prosper (in both worlds).

91. Satan only seeks to provoke enmity and hatred among you by means of intoxicants and games of chance, and to bar you from the remembrance of God and from the Prayer. So, then, will you abstain?[18]

92. Obey God and obey the Messenger, (whose commands are based on Divine Revelation), and be on the alert (against opposing them). If you turn away (from obedience to them), then know that what

rests with Our Messenger is only to convey the Message fully and clearly.

93. There is no sin on those who believe and do good, righteous deeds for what they might have partaken (in their pre-Islamic past), provided (henceforth) they fear (the end of their previous creeds and misdeeds) and come to faith and do good, righteous deeds, then keep from disobedience to God in reverence for Him and piety and believe (more profoundly), then be more meticulous in obeying God in greater reverence for Him and piety and be devoted to doing good: God loves those who are devoted to doing good, aware that God is seeing them.

94. O you who believe! God will certainly try you with something of the game that you can take with your hands or your lances (while you are on the Pilgrimage), so that He may prove those who fear Him (though) unseen. Whoever, after that, exceeds the bounds, for him is a painful punishment.

95. O you who believe! Do not kill game while you are in the state of pilgrim sanctity or in the sacred precincts of Makkah. Whoever of you kills it, then its recompense is the like of what he has killed, from livestock, to be judged by two men among you of equity and probity, and to be brought to the Ka‘bah as an offering; or (there shall be) an expiation by way of giving (as much) food to the destitute (as the value of the game killed), or fasting (a number of days) equivalent (to the number of the persons to be fed or the shares assigned for them). (That is ordained) so that he may taste the evil consequences of his deed. God has pardoned what is past; but for one who re-offends, God will take retribution from him. And God is All-Glorious with irresistible might, Ever-Able to requite (wrong).

18. These two last verses, which contain significant principles for human life in this world and the next, draw attention to dangers, such as alcohol, drugs, gambling and all other kinds of games of chance, and a predilection for erecting monuments and statutes of an idolatrous nature, which are an embodiment of ostentation, pride, worldliness, and the vain desires of immortality. They also present to us enmity, hatred, and the crimes caused by these. When we consider that the "mafia" type organizations are the breeding grounds of such and many other kinds of sins and illicit relationships, such as prostitution, uncontrollable black marketing, drug addiction and smuggling, and that these are loathsome evils of Satan's doing, the warning of the verses becomes more significant. Also, it is extremely important to understand what losses can be incurred by ignoring even one verse of the Qur'ān; for example many traffic accidents that take lives and property arise from alcohol.

أُحِلَّ لَكُمْ صَيْدُ الْبَحْرِ وَطَعَامُهُ مَتَاعًا لَكُمْ وَلِلسَّيَّارَةِ

وَحُرِّمَ عَلَيْكُمْ صَيْدُ الْبَرِّ مَا دُمْتُمْ حُرُمًا وَاتَّقُوا اللّٰهَ

الَّذِيٓ إِلَيْهِ تُحْشَرُونَ ۝ جَعَلَ اللّٰهُ الْكَعْبَةَ الْبَيْتَ الْحَرَامَ

قِيَامًا لِّلنَّاسِ وَالشَّهْرَ الْحَرَامَ وَالْهَدْيَ وَالْقَلَائِدَ ذٰلِكَ

لِتَعْلَمُوٓا أَنَّ اللّٰهَ يَعْلَمُ مَا فِي السَّمٰوٰتِ وَمَا فِي الْأَرْضِ وَأَنَّ اللّٰهَ

بِكُلِّ شَيْءٍ عَلِيمٌ ۝ اِعْلَمُوٓا أَنَّ اللّٰهَ شَدِيدُ الْعِقَابِ وَأَنَّ اللّٰهَ

غَفُورٌ رَّحِيمٌ ۝ مَا عَلَى الرَّسُولِ إِلَّا الْبَلَاغُ وَاللّٰهُ

يَعْلَمُ مَا تُبْدُونَ وَمَا تَكْتُمُونَ ۝ قُلْ لَّا يَسْتَوِي الْخَبِيثُ

وَالطَّيِّبُ وَلَوْ أَعْجَبَكَ كَثْرَةُ الْخَبِيثِ فَاتَّقُوا اللّٰهَ

يَٰٓأُولِي الْأَلْبَابِ لَعَلَّكُمْ تُفْلِحُونَ ۝ يَٰٓأَيُّهَا الَّذِينَ اٰمَنُوا لَا تَسْـَٔلُوا

عَنْ أَشْيَآءَ إِنْ تُبْدَ لَكُمْ تَسُؤْكُمْ وَإِنْ تَسْـَٔلُوا عَنْهَا حِينَ يُنَزَّلُ الْقُرْاٰنُ

تُبْدَ لَكُمْ عَفَا اللّٰهُ عَنْهَا وَاللّٰهُ غَفُورٌ حَلِيمٌ ۝ قَدْ

سَأَلَهَا قَوْمٌ مِّنْ قَبْلِكُمْ ثُمَّ أَصْبَحُوا بِهَا كَافِرِينَ ۝ مَا جَعَلَ اللّٰهُ

مِنْ بَحِيرَةٍ وَلَا سَآئِبَةٍ وَلَا وَصِيلَةٍ وَلَا حَامٍ وَلٰكِنَّ الَّذِينَ كَفَرُوا

يَفْتَرُونَ عَلَى اللّٰهِ الْكَذِبَ وَأَكْثَرُهُمْ لَا يَعْقِلُونَ ۝

---

96. (To hunt and eat) the game in the sea, and its (fish and other) edibles are lawful for you, a provision for you and for travelers (whom you want to feed). However, while you are in the state of pilgrim sanctity, you are forbidden to hunt on land (or slaughter and eat of animals that you get others to hunt for you). Keep from disobedience to God in reverence for Him and piety, to Whom you will be gathered.

97. God has made the Ka‘bah, the Sacred House, a standard and maintenance for the people, and also the Sacred Months (during which fighting is forbidden), and the animals for sacrificial offering, and the (camels wearing the sacrificial) collars. That is so that you may know that God knows whatever is in the heavens and whatever is on the earth, and that God has full knowledge of everything.

98. Know (also) that God is severe in pun-

ishment, and that God is All-Forgiving, All-Compassionate.

99. Nothing rests with the Messenger but to convey the Message fully and clearly. (It is your responsibility to act in accordance therewith) and God knows whatever you reveal and do openly and whatever you conceal and do secretly.

100. Say: "The bad and the good are not alike," even though the abundance of the bad (the sheer quantity of the corrupt) amazes you. So keep from disobedience to God in reverence for Him and piety, O people of discernment (so that you may rightly distinguish quality and quantity and so) that you may prosper (in both worlds).[19]

101. O you who believe! (Practice as you are admonished to practice, and) do not ask about things which, if made manifest to you, would give you trouble (and make the practice of the Religion difficult for you). Even so, if you ask about them while the Qur'ān is being sent down, they (what is necessary to be made manifest) will be made manifest to you (to the extent that God wills). (Many things that you have either asked or want to ask about, but which God has left unspoken) God has absolved you thereof: God is All-Forgiving, All-Clement.

102. Indeed a people before you used to ask such questions (and demanded from their Prophet such things as particular miracles), and thereafter they fell into unbelief (through not carrying out the commandments given in answer to their questions or through willfully disbelieving in their Prophet despite the miracles worked).

103. God has not ordained anything (in the nature) of a *bahīrah*, nor a *sā'ibah*, nor a *waṣīlah*, nor *ḥām*. But those who disbelieve fabricate falsehoods against God – most of them do not reason and indeed are devoid of sense.[20]

19. This verse enunciates a very important standard of evaluation and judgment. Since the world and whatever is in it are not capable of receiving and reflecting what is perfect, and due to their innate deficiencies that are essential to their nature, they can only reflect many absolute truths in relative ways, degrees, or colors. That is why, both from a perspective of relativity and in actual fact, the ugly, bad, and corrupt (unbelievers, hypocrites, transgressors, unlawful earnings, wrong thoughts and false beliefs, etc.) exist in the world more abundantly than the beautiful, good, and pure (believers, sincere and just persons, lawful earnings, right thoughts and sound beliefs). For this reason, it is wrong to judge by quantity; what is important is nature and quality. It sometimes occurs that a single person may represent right and truth in a community. So, except for things which are open to question and which are true relative to circumstances, what is right and true cannot be judged by quantity. The source of absolute truths is God. Whatever He judges to be true and right is true and right. Thinking and acting otherwise brings failure, not success and salvation. Both history and the present world bear witness to this.

20. *Bahīrah*: a she-camel, whose milk the pagans dedicated to idols after she gave birth to five young, the fifth being a male; *sā'ibah*: a camel let loose, whose milk the pagans forbade themselves, consecrating it to express gratitude for successful fulfillment of a vow; *wasīlah*: cattle which gave birth to twins, one male, the other female, and whose male young was let loose and dedicated to idols; *hām*: a male camel which the pagans forbade themselves after it had inseminated ten females.

The conclusion of the verse points to a very important truth: God never does anything in vain or anything that is useless, and anyone who can use their reason, anyone who has sufficient intellect, can grasp at least some of the wisdom in every command of God.

Islam makes reason or intellect bear witness to the fact that every one of its commands is reasonable, but this does not mean that reason or intellect can discover and establish these commands. In order to discover or establish these commands in their proper place requires an "intellect" which, as stated in verse 97 above, knows whatever is in the heavens and whatever is on the earth, and which has full knowledge of everything – an intellect which knows the structure of the whole universe along with its relationships with all the parts and everything and every event, with all of time and space, and which knows humanity with all its needs, nature, and which understands the web of relationships. There is only one such "intellect:" God. So, the duty of humanity is to discover the wisdom in God's commands and to use our reason or intellect to deduce the secondary principles and commandments that are mutable according to time and circumstances.

Another point to mention here is that those who disregard any Islamic commandment because they consider it to be incompatible with reason and therefore prefer other commandments to them are either devoid of sufficient knowledge, intellectual capacity and reasoning, or they have some other purposes.

124 سُورَةُ الْمَائِدَة ١٢٤

وَإِذَا قِيلَ لَهُمْ تَعَالَوْا إِلَى مَا أَنزَلَ اللّهُ وَإِلَى الرَّسُولِ
قَالُوا حَسْبُنَا مَا وَجَدْنَا عَلَيْهِ ءَابَآءَنَا أَوَلَوْ كَانَ ءَابَآؤُهُمْ لَا يَعْلَمُونَ
شَيْئًا وَلَا يَهْتَدُونَ ۞ يَـٰٓأَيُّهَا الَّذِينَ ءَامَنُوا عَلَيْكُمْ أَنفُسَكُمْ
لَا يَضُرُّكُم مَّن ضَلَّ إِذَا اهْتَدَيْتُمْ إِلَى اللّهِ مَرْجِعُكُمْ جَمِيعًا
فَيُنَبِّئُكُم بِمَا كُنتُمْ تَعْمَلُونَ ۞ يَـٰٓأَيُّهَا الَّذِينَ ءَامَنُوا شَهَـٰدَةُ
بَيْنِكُمْ إِذَا حَضَرَ أَحَدَكُمُ الْمَوْتُ حِينَ الْوَصِيَّةِ اثْنَانِ ذَوَا عَدْلٍ
مِّنكُمْ أَوْ ءَاخَرَانِ مِنْ غَيْرِكُمْ إِنْ أَنتُمْ ضَرَبْتُمْ فِي الْأَرْضِ
فَأَصَابَتْكُم مُّصِيبَةُ الْمَوْتِ تَحْبِسُونَهُمَا مِنۢ بَعْدِ الصَّلَوٰةِ فَيُقْسِمَانِ
بِاللّهِ إِنِ ارْتَبْتُمْ لَا نَشْتَرِي بِهِ ثَمَنًا وَلَوْ كَانَ ذَا قُرْبَىٰ
وَلَا نَكْتُمُ شَهَـٰدَةَ اللّهِ إِنَّا إِذًا لَّمِنَ الْآثِمِينَ ۞ فَإِنْ عُثِرَ عَلَىٰٓ
أَنَّهُمَا اسْتَحَقَّآ إِثْمًا فَـَٔاخَرَانِ يَقُومَانِ مَقَامَهُمَا مِنَ الَّذِينَ اسْتَحَقَّ عَلَيْهِمُ
الْأَوْلَيَانِ فَيُقْسِمَانِ بِاللّهِ لَشَهَـٰدَتُنَآ أَحَقُّ مِن شَهَـٰدَتِهِمَا وَمَا
اعْتَدَيْنَآ إِنَّآ إِذًا لَّمِنَ الظَّـٰلِمِينَ ۞ ذَٰلِكَ أَدْنَىٰٓ أَن يَأْتُوا بِالشَّهَـٰدَةِ
عَلَىٰ وَجْهِهَآ أَوْ يَخَافُوٓا أَن تُرَدَّ أَيْمَـٰنٌۢ بَعْدَ أَيْمَـٰنِهِمْ وَاتَّقُوا
اللّهَ وَاسْمَعُوا وَاللّهُ لَا يَهْدِي الْقَوْمَ الْفَـٰسِقِينَ ۞

---

104. When it is said to them, "Come (in obedience) to what God has sent down and to the Messenger (to whom the Qur'ān is being revealed), they (refuse to think, and instead) say: "Enough for us (are the ways) that we found our forefathers on." What! even if their forefathers knew nothing and were not guided (and so did not follow a right way)?

105. O you who believe! (Do not busy yourselves with those who follow different ways!) Your responsibility is your selves (so consider how you are faring along your own way). Those who go astray can do you no harm if you yourselves are rightly guided (and so follow your right way without deviation). To God is the return of all of you, and He will make you understand all that you used to do (and call you to account for it).

106. O you who believe! Let there be witnesses among you when death approaches you, at the time of making bequests – two straightforward and trustworthy persons from among your own people (the Muslim community), or two other persons from among people other than your own (from among the People of the Book) if you are on a journey (and there are no Muslims) when the affliction of death befalls you. Then if any doubt arises (concerning their testimony), have the two of them stay (in the mosque) after the Prayer, and they shall swear by God: "We will not sell our testimony for any price, even if it concerns one near of kin, nor will we conceal the testimony of God (namely, the truth), for then we would surely be among the sinful."

107. Then if it is discovered later that the two (witnesses) have been guilty of (that very) sin (of not giving true testimony), then have two others stand in their place from among those (rightful heirs of the deceased) whom the first two have deprived of their right, and these shall swear by God: "Our testimony is truer than the testimony of the other two, and we have not exceeded the bounds (of what is right, nor violated the rights of any others), for then we would indeed be among the wrongdoers."

108. That (way) it is more likely that people will offer correct testimony or else they will (at least) fear that their oaths will be rebutted by other oaths. Keep from disobedience to God in reverence for Him and piety and pay heed (to His commandments). God does not guide transgressing people.[21]

21. These last verses contain important principles concerning Islamic jurisprudence, good morals and social order. They are:

- (Although we should always hold a good opinion of believers,) the transactions in society must be based on legal procedures.
- Bearing witness is extremely important. Refraining from this and bearing false testimony are among the major, cardinal sins.
- The testimony of non-Muslims, especially that of the People of the Book, can be acceptable in cases of necessity.
- If contradictory evidence is discovered after a court has passed judgment, a new trial must begin.
- If it is discovered that the executors did not tell the truth, they are dismissed and in their place two people are appointed from among the rightful heirs of the deceased person.
- Both the executors and the heirs are asked to swear an oath.
- Those whom people regard as trustworthy and straightforward may always not be so. We should regard everybody as trustworthy until contradictory evidence emerges, and we can only decide another person is untrustworthy on concrete evidence.
- The law has principles of its own, but in order for them to prevail and become operative as we expect, belief in and respect for God, Who sees everybody and what everybody does and Who will call them to account in another world, and belief in the Hereafter, where people will see the return of what they did in this world, are paramount. Belief in, respect for, and fear of God are the primary conditions to ensure a happy social life.

يَوْمَ يَجْمَعُ ٱللَّهُ ٱلرُّسُلَ فَيَقُولُ مَاذَآ أُجِبْتُمْ قَالُوا۟ لَا عِلْمَ لَنَآ
إِنَّكَ أَنتَ عَلَّٰمُ ٱلْغُيُوبِ ۝ إِذْ قَالَ ٱللَّهُ يَٰعِيسَى ٱبْنَ مَرْيَمَ
ٱذْكُرْ نِعْمَتِى عَلَيْكَ وَعَلَىٰ وَٰلِدَتِكَ إِذْ أَيَّدتُّكَ بِرُوحِ ٱلْقُدُسِ
تُكَلِّمُ ٱلنَّاسَ فِى ٱلْمَهْدِ وَكَهْلًا وَإِذْ عَلَّمْتُكَ ٱلْكِتَٰبَ
وَٱلْحِكْمَةَ وَٱلتَّوْرَىٰةَ وَٱلْإِنجِيلَ وَإِذْ تَخْلُقُ مِنَ ٱلطِّينِ
كَهَيْـَٔةِ ٱلطَّيْرِ بِإِذْنِى فَتَنفُخُ فِيهَا فَتَكُونُ طَيْرًا
بِإِذْنِى وَتُبْرِئُ ٱلْأَكْمَهَ وَٱلْأَبْرَصَ بِإِذْنِى وَإِذْ تُخْرِجُ
ٱلْمَوْتَىٰ بِإِذْنِى وَإِذْ كَفَفْتُ بَنِىٓ إِسْرَٰٓءِيلَ عَنكَ إِذْ جِئْتَهُم
بِٱلْبَيِّنَٰتِ فَقَالَ ٱلَّذِينَ كَفَرُوا۟ مِنْهُمْ إِنْ هَٰذَآ إِلَّا سِحْرٌ
مُّبِينٌ ۝ وَإِذْ أَوْحَيْتُ إِلَى ٱلْحَوَارِيِّـۧنَ أَنْ ءَامِنُوا۟ بِى وَبِرَسُولِى
قَالُوٓا۟ ءَامَنَّا وَٱشْهَدْ بِأَنَّنَا مُسْلِمُونَ ۝ إِذْ قَالَ ٱلْحَوَارِيُّونَ
يَٰعِيسَى ٱبْنَ مَرْيَمَ هَلْ يَسْتَطِيعُ رَبُّكَ أَن يُنَزِّلَ عَلَيْنَا
مَآئِدَةً مِّنَ ٱلسَّمَآءِ قَالَ ٱتَّقُوا۟ ٱللَّهَ إِن كُنتُم مُّؤْمِنِينَ
۝ قَالُوا۟ نُرِيدُ أَن نَّأْكُلَ مِنْهَا وَتَطْمَئِنَّ قُلُوبُنَا وَنَعْلَمَ
أَن قَدْ صَدَقْتَنَا وَنَكُونَ عَلَيْهَا مِنَ ٱلشَّٰهِدِينَ ۝

---

109. The day when God will gather the Messengers and ask them: "What was the response you received (from the people to whom you were appointed to convey My Message)?" They say: "We have no (exact) knowledge (of the truth of their response); You and You alone have knowledge of the Unseen (of all that lies beyond the reach of any created being's perception)."

110. When God says: "O Jesus son of Mary! Remember My favor upon you and upon your mother, when I confirmed you with the Spirit of Holiness so that you talked to people in the cradle and in manhood; and when I taught you of the Book[22] and Wisdom, and the Torah and the Gospel; and when you fashioned out of clay something in the shape of a bird by My leave, then you breathed into it,

and it became a bird by My leave, and you healed the blind from birth and the leper by My leave; and when you raised the dead by My leave; and when I restrained the Children of Israel from you when you came to them with clear proofs (of the truth and miracles demonstrating Your Messengership), and those of them who disbelieved said: 'This is clearly nothing but sorcery.'

111. "And when I revealed to the disciples (through you, and inspired in their hearts), 'Believe in Me and My Messenger!', they said: 'We believe, and bear witness that we are (Muslims) submitted exclusively to Him.' "

112. And once the disciples said: "Jesus son of Mary, is your Lord able to send down on us a table (of food) from heaven?"[23] (Jesus) answered: "Fear God (as He should be feared, and so desist from making such demands lest He punish you) if you are (truly) believers."

113. They said: "We desire to eat thereof and that our hearts might be set at rest (with certainty of God's being our Lord and of your being His Messenger), and so that we might know that you speak the truth to us, and so that we might be among the witnesses (to the meaning and truth of what is demonstrated to us)."

22. The verse mentioning the Torah and the Gospel in addition to the Book, as in 3: 48, has led some to interpret the Book (al-kitāb) as meaning "writing." However, when we consider another fact, namely that the Torah and the Gospel contain or even are embodiments of the Wisdom as Divine Books, we can conclude that by the Book and the Wisdom the verse refers to the Divine Book and the Wisdom generally, and particularize or specify them to be the Torah and the Gospel.

23. The wording of this demand which the disciples made to have greater certainty of faith, contains several points that go against the good manners that a believer must have before God and His Messenger:

- While they should have addressed Jesus as God's Messenger, which would demonstrate their faith in and respect for him, they displayed bad manners and doubted him concerning his Messengership.
- By saying "your Lord," they implied that their faith in God had not been established in their hearts, thus behaving in a rude manner.
- By saying "Is your Lord able...?" they demonstrated that they had no true judgment of God as His right (in being God) requires.
- By demanding a miracle after they claimed faith, they displayed doubt and another kind of rudeness.

However, we should note that the disciples which the Qur'ān highly praised in some other verses (i.e., 3: 52, 5: 111), may have made this demand at a time when faith had not yet been fully established in their hearts and before they had responded to Jesus' calling, "Who will be my helpers (on this way) to God?" by saying: "We are the helpers of God('s cause). We believe in God, and bear witness that we are (Muslims), submitted exclusively to Him." (3: 52)

It should also be noted that none of the Companions of the Prophet Muhammad, upon him be peace and blessings, made such a demand after they had entered into the fold of Islam. Not only did they not make any such demand, they also attached no greater importance to the miracles that God's Messenger worked than one might have expected from within the milieu of Islam. An example of such a miracle is the time when there was no other means to obtain water or food, and the Prophet was able to make water flow from his fingers and he was able to multiply the small amount of food available so that it sufficed for hundreds of soldiers to partake of. (For a detailed explanation of the miracles of the Prophet Muhammad, see *The Letters*, "The 19th Letter.") The Companions focused on and devoted themselves to reporting the rules of the Religion and deemed it sufficient that such miracles be reported by only a few.

126　　سُورَةُ الْمَائِدَةِ　　١٢٦

قَالَ عِيسَى ابْنُ مَرْيَمَ اللَّهُمَّ رَبَّنَا أَنْزِلْ عَلَيْنَا مَائِدَةً مِنَ السَّمَاءِ تَكُونُ لَنَا عِيدًا لِأَوَّلِنَا وَآخِرِنَا وَآيَةً مِنْكَ وَارْزُقْنَا وَأَنْتَ خَيْرُ الرَّازِقِينَ ۝ قَالَ اللَّهُ إِنِّي مُنَزِّلُهَا عَلَيْكُمْ فَمَنْ يَكْفُرْ بَعْدُ مِنْكُمْ فَإِنِّي أُعَذِّبُهُ عَذَابًا لَا أُعَذِّبُهُ أَحَدًا مِنَ الْعَالَمِينَ ۝ وَإِذْ قَالَ اللَّهُ يَا عِيسَى ابْنَ مَرْيَمَ أَأَنْتَ قُلْتَ لِلنَّاسِ اتَّخِذُونِي وَأُمِّيَ إِلَهَيْنِ مِنْ دُونِ اللَّهِ قَالَ سُبْحَانَكَ مَا يَكُونُ لِي أَنْ أَقُولَ مَا لَيْسَ لِي بِحَقٍّ إِنْ كُنْتُ قُلْتُهُ فَقَدْ عَلِمْتَهُ تَعْلَمُ مَا فِي نَفْسِي وَلَا أَعْلَمُ مَا فِي نَفْسِكَ إِنَّكَ أَنْتَ عَلَّامُ الْغُيُوبِ ۝ مَا قُلْتُ لَهُمْ إِلَّا مَا أَمَرْتَنِي بِهِ أَنِ اعْبُدُوا اللَّهَ رَبِّي وَرَبَّكُمْ وَكُنْتُ عَلَيْهِمْ شَهِيدًا مَا دُمْتُ فِيهِمْ فَلَمَّا تَوَفَّيْتَنِي كُنْتَ أَنْتَ الرَّقِيبَ عَلَيْهِمْ وَأَنْتَ عَلَى كُلِّ شَيْءٍ شَهِيدٌ ۝ إِنْ تُعَذِّبْهُمْ فَإِنَّهُمْ عِبَادُكَ وَإِنْ تَغْفِرْ لَهُمْ فَإِنَّكَ أَنْتَ الْعَزِيزُ الْحَكِيمُ ۝ قَالَ اللَّهُ هَذَا يَوْمُ يَنْفَعُ الصَّادِقِينَ صِدْقُهُمْ لَهُمْ جَنَّاتٌ تَجْرِي مِنْ تَحْتِهَا الْأَنْهَارُ خَالِدِينَ فِيهَا أَبَدًا رَضِيَ اللَّهُ عَنْهُمْ وَرَضُوا عَنْهُ ذَلِكَ الْفَوْزُ الْعَظِيمُ ۝ لِلَّهِ مُلْكُ السَّمَاوَاتِ وَالْأَرْضِ وَمَا فِيهِنَّ وَهُوَ عَلَى كُلِّ شَيْءٍ قَدِيرٌ ۝

―――――❦―――――

114. Jesus son of Mary said (in entreaty to his Lord): "O God, our Lord! Send down on us a table (of food) from heaven, that shall be an ever-recurring (religious) festival for us – for the first and the last of us – and a sign from You; and provide us sustenance, for You are the Best to be sought as provider with the ultimate rank of providing."

115. God said: "I send it down on you. Then if any of you should henceforth disbelieve, surely I inflict on him a punishment that I never inflict on anyone in the worlds."[24]

116. And (remember) when God will say: "Jesus son of Mary, is it you who said to people: 'Take me and my mother for deities beside God?' " and he will answer: "All-Glorified are You (in that You are absolutely above having a partner, as having any need or deficiency whatever)! It is not for me to say what I had no right to! Had I said it, You would already have known it. You know all that is within myself, whereas I do not know what is within Yourself. Surely You and You alone have knowledge of the Unseen (of all that lies beyond the reach of any created being's perception).

117. "I did not say to them except what You commanded me to (say): 'Worship God, my Lord and your Lord.' I was a witness over them so long as I remained among them; and when You took me back, You were Yourself the Watcher over them. Indeed, You are Witness over everything.

118. "If You punish them, they are Your servants; and if You forgive them, You are the All-Glorious with irresistible might, the All-Wise."[25]

119. God will say: "This is the Day when their truthfulness (faithfulness and steadfastness) will benefit all who were true to their word (to God). For them are Gardens through which rivers flow, therein to abide forever. God is well-pleased with them, and they are well-pleased with Him. That is the supreme triumph."

120. To God belongs the sovereignty of the heavens and the earth and all that is in them. And He has full power over everything.

24. By concluding the event without specifying whether the table was sent down or not, the Qur'ān shows that the purpose for relating these events is either to reinforce the main purposes within them or to give a lesson through them. By relating this event, the Qur'ān is showing us that what leads people to believe in the Messengers and the Message they brought is not primarily the miracles they worked. Rather, it is the persons of the Messengers themselves, their deep spirituality, the high morals they have, and the rationality and truth of their Message and its compatibility with the unblemished human conscience. This shows that both belief and unbelief are a conscious choice. So, instead of expecting miracles, people should study the universe, which is, in fact, an exhibition of "miracles" from top to bottom, and the character and lives of the Prophets, along with the Books they brought, and one's conscience should not be allowed to be contaminated with such things as prejudices, carnal desires, sins, wrongdoing, wrong viewpoints, and arrogance, each of which is an obstacle to faith.

25. The answer that The Prophet Jesus, upon him be peace, will give displays his mission and character. By saying, "If You punish them, they are Your servants; and if You forgive them, You are the All-Glorious with irresistible might, the All-Wise." he exhibits his absolute respect for God, while, with the expression "they are Your servants," he appeals to God's compassion. Although it seems more reasonable to refer the matter to God's being the All-Forgiving and All-Compassionate, where forgiving is mentioned, that illustrious Prophet, who refers this matter to God's being the All-Glorious with irresistible might and to His being the All-Wise, displays his deep submission to God's absolute Authority and Wisdom.

On one occasion our Prophet, upon him be peace and blessings, mentions Abraham and Jesus, upon them be peace, together and likens them to one another. Abraham appealed to God on behalf of his people who disobeyed him, by saying, "He who follows me is truly of me; while he who disobeys me, surely You are All-Forgiving, All-Compassionate" (14: 36).

SŪRAH 6

AL-AN'ĀM (CATTLE)

Makkah period

This *sūrah* was revealed in its entirety during the final year of the Makkah period of Islam. Coming in order in the Qur'ān after *al-Baqarah*, *Āl 'Imrān*, *an-Nisā'*, and *al-Mā'idah*, all of which were revealed in Madīnah, this *sūrah* dwells on such themes as rejecting polytheism and unbelief, the establishment of *Tawḥīd* (pure monotheism), the Revelation, Messengership, and Resurrection.

In the Name of God, the All-Merciful, the All-Compassionate.

1. All praise and gratitude are for God, Who has created the heavens and the earth, and (as a dimension of their existence and result of their movement) brought into being veils of darkness and the light. Yet those who disbelieve ascribe equals to their Lord (Who raises, sustains, and maintains them such things as idols, certain celestial bodies, and certain people).[1]

2. He it is Who has created you from clay (in the beginning, and the material origin of every one of you is clay), and then decreed a term (of life for you), and there is with Him another unchanging term determined by and known to Him.[2] Yet, you are in doubt (concerning these manifest truths, some of which you experience and some others you can deduce).

3. He is (the One, True) God (executing His absolute sovereignty and manifesting His Attributes and Names) both in the heavens and on the earth. He knows what you keep concealed and what you declare (and do) openly, and He knows what you earn (of good or bad – what you are doing in your life).

4. Yet whenever any of their Lord's signs and Revelations comes to them, they turn away from it in aversion.

5. And so they willfully deny the truth (embodied by the Qur'ān) when it has come to them (and mock the truths, warnings, and especially the tidings of the Resurrection). Even so, they will come to understand what it was they were mocking.

6. Do they not see (even though they pass by the ruins on their journeys) how many a generation We have destroyed before them, whom We established on the earth more firmly than We ever established you (We gave them means and possibilities such as We have not given you), and upon whom We showered blessings from heaven (above them), and from beneath them We made rivers flow. And yet We destroyed them for their sins, and after them We raised up another generation.

7. Had We sent down on you (O Messenger) a book on parchment such that they touched it with their hands, yet those who persist in their unbelief would indeed have said: "This is clearly nothing but sorcery."

8. "Why has not an angel been sent down on him?" they say. Yet, had We sent down an angel (i.e. one they could see, as We did to some of the previous peoples such as those of Lot), then the matter would surely have long been decided and they would have been allowed no respite (since angels coming in this way heralds the destruction).

---

1. The verse uses *creating* for the heavens and the earth, and *bringing into being* or *appointing* for darkness and light. This means that darkness and light are not things that have been created as independent entities, but are rather the result of the movement of the heavens (or certain heavenly objects) and the earth as a dimension of their existence.

The fact that darkness is mentioned before light signifies that non-existence precedes existence in the life of the universe and that it has an existence in God's Knowledge. For this reason, the start of the day actually begins with the fall of night.

Both darkness and light are used in their spiritual connotation also. Since the sources and kinds of "spiritual" darkness (materialism, atheism, agnosticism, polytheism of all sorts, and hypocrisy) are numerous, while the "spiritual" light is one and comes from the same, single source, darkness is used in the plural, and light in the singular. This also explains the reason why, even though philosophers and thinkers differ in their ideas greatly, as they have all based their thinking on their own reasoning, all the Prophets, numbering more than 100,000, throughout human history have agreed on the same principles.

In addition to all the shades of meaning mentioned, by referring to those who disbelieve in rejecting polytheism and emphasizing that God is the Lord of also unbelievers, the verse points out that every kind of polytheism amounts to unbelief and even if many people associate partners, rivals, equals to God, God is the Lord – the Creator, Sustainer, Raiser, the Provider – of the whole of creation, including humankind, and therefore polytheism has absolutely no sound, justifiable basis. Thus, this short, single verse summarizes the whole of the *sūrah*.

2. For an indirect explanation of this verse and the relevant theological terms *ajal* or *al-qadar al-mu'allaq* (the term or destiny suspended) and *ajal musammā* (the term determined) or *al-qadar al-mubram (the destiny decisive)*, see note 13 in this *sūrah*, and *sūrah* 13, note 13, and *sūrah* 10, note 19.

Some interpreters of the Qur'ān are of the opinion that the first term mentioned in the verse is the "natural" term determined by God for beings. For example, a doctor can say of a patient in view of the kind and gravity of their sickness: "He (or she) will die within ten days," but the patient can live for many years more. The term presumed by the doctor is the "natural" term. But the final term of the patient is known to God only.

128   ١٢٨   سُوْرَةُ الأَنْعَامِ

وَلَوْ جَعَلْنَاهُ مَلَكًا لَّجَعَلْنَاهُ رَجُلًا وَلَلَبَسْنَا عَلَيْهِم مَّا يَلْبِسُونَ ۞ وَلَقَدِ اسْتُهْزِئَ بِرُسُلٍ مِّن قَبْلِكَ فَحَاقَ بِالَّذِينَ سَخِرُوا مِنْهُم مَّا كَانُوا بِهِ يَسْتَهْزِئُونَ ۞ قُلْ سِيرُوا فِي الْأَرْضِ ثُمَّ انظُرُوا كَيْفَ كَانَ عَاقِبَةُ الْمُكَذِّبِينَ ۞ قُل لِّمَن مَّا فِي السَّمَاوَاتِ وَالْأَرْضِ قُل لِّلَّهِ كَتَبَ عَلَى نَفْسِهِ الرَّحْمَةَ لَيَجْمَعَنَّكُمْ إِلَى يَوْمِ الْقِيَامَةِ لَا رَيْبَ فِيهِ الَّذِينَ خَسِرُوا أَنفُسَهُمْ فَهُمْ لَا يُؤْمِنُونَ ۞ وَلَهُ مَا سَكَنَ فِي الَّيْلِ وَالنَّهَارِ وَهُوَ السَّمِيعُ الْعَلِيمُ ۞ قُلْ أَغَيْرَ اللَّهِ أَتَّخِذُ وَلِيًّا فَاطِرِ السَّمَاوَاتِ وَالْأَرْضِ وَهُوَ يُطْعِمُ وَلَا يُطْعَمُ قُلْ إِنِّي أُمِرْتُ أَنْ أَكُونَ أَوَّلَ مَنْ أَسْلَمَ وَلَا تَكُونَنَّ مِنَ الْمُشْرِكِينَ ۞ قُلْ إِنِّي أَخَافُ إِنْ عَصَيْتُ رَبِّي عَذَابَ يَوْمٍ عَظِيمٍ ۞ مَن يُصْرَفْ عَنْهُ يَوْمَئِذٍ فَقَدْ رَحِمَهُ وَذَٰلِكَ الْفَوْزُ الْمُبِينُ ۞ وَإِن يَمْسَسْكَ اللَّهُ بِضُرٍّ فَلَا كَاشِفَ لَهُ إِلَّا هُوَ وَإِن يَمْسَسْكَ بِخَيْرٍ فَهُوَ عَلَىٰ كُلِّ شَيْءٍ قَدِيرٌ ۞ وَهُوَ الْقَاهِرُ فَوْقَ عِبَادِهِ وَهُوَ الْحَكِيمُ الْخَبِيرُ ۞

------◈------

9. Had We appointed an angel (as Our Messenger) We would surely have made him (since he would have to guide humankind in all aspects of life, in the form of) a man, and thus We would have confused for them what they themselves are confusing.

10. Messengers indeed were mocked before you (O Messenger), but what they used to mock overwhelmed those who scoffed (at the Messengers to humiliate them).

11. Say: "Go about on the earth and look: how was the outcome for those who denied (God's signs and Messengers)?³

12. Say: "To whom belongs all that is in the heavens and on the earth?", and say: "To God." He has bound Himself to mercy (so that, despite the errors and false beliefs of His servants, He sustains all that

is in the heavens and on the earth by His Mercy. He does not leave anybody to their own devices and, as a requirement of His Mercy) He will assuredly gather you together on the Day of Resurrection, about (the coming of) which there is no doubt: yet those who ruin their own selves (by misusing and corrupting their primordial nature, sound reasoning and the capacity to believe, which are their capital share in God's Mercy) – they do not believe.

13. And His is whatsoever dwells in the night and the day; and He is the All-Hearing, the All-Knowing.

14. Say: "Shall I take for guardian and confidant anyone other than God, the Originator of the heavens and the earth each with particular features, and He Who feeds and Himself never needs to be fed?" Say: "Moreover, I have surely been ordered to be the foremost in submitting to Him wholly, and (I have been warned): 'Do not be among those who associate partners with Him'."

15. Say: "Indeed I fear, if I should disobey my Lord, the punishment of an awesome Day."

16. Whoever has been spared punishment on that Day, surely God has had mercy on him; and that is the manifest triumph.

17. If God touches you with affliction, there is none who can remove it but He; and if He touches you with good – it is He Who has full power over everything.

18. He is the All-Omnipotent over His servants; He is the All-Wise, the All-Aware.

3. Having demonstrated the truth with substantial, indisputable arguments along the way, the *sūrah* now invalidates unbelief and polytheism, establishing pure monotheism by presenting the end that awaited those who did not follow God's way. The arguments are made clear by providing historical and sociological foundations. This verse severely warns the polytheists and consoles the Messenger, upon him be peace and blessings. It continues with concrete and incontestable truths concerning God's Divinity and Lordship.

The Qur'ān draws attention to and takes the human mind and heart through all the fields and aspects of life, as a bee goes from flower to flower to collect nectar, and leaves its audience face to face with the unquestionable proofs of the truths it propounds. This style is called *taṣrīf*. Whatever subject the Qur'ān deals with, be it from individual life to the earth, from the heavens to social life, from human conscience to human history, it extracts the water with a miraculous "staff" to quench the thirst of the human intellect, heart and all the other faculties. It is the human soul that spreads a veil of conjecture made up of arrogance, prejudices, incorrect viewpoints, and wrongdoing over the Qur'ānic truths; these truths, when apparent, are such that the human conscience, heart, and intellect cannot but concede. It is this blanketing attitude of the human soul that the Qur'ān calls *kufr*, meaning 'to veil' and which is rendered in English as "unbelief." When a person disbelieves, that is, when they veil the truths, they are not able to cancel or obliterate these truths. Unbelief is the same as closing one's eyes to the sun and claiming that there is neither a sun nor sunlight, and that everywhere is dark. Those who destroy themselves by misusing their innate, God-given faculties, such as the intellect and the potential to believe and possess a sound nature – these are then people who do not believe.

قُلْ أَيُّ شَىْءٍ أَكْبَرُ شَهَادَةً قُلِ اللّٰهُ شَهِيدٌ بَيْنِى وَبَيْنَكُمْ وَأُوحِىَ إِلَىَّ هَذَا الْقُرْآنُ لِأُنذِرَكُم بِهِ وَمَنۢ بَلَغَ أَئِنَّكُمْ لَتَشْهَدُونَ أَنَّ مَعَ اللّٰهِ ءَالِهَةً أُخْرَىٰ قُل لَّآ أَشْهَدُ قُلْ إِنَّمَا هُوَ إِلَهٌ وَاحِدٌ وَإِنَّنِى بَرِىٓءٌ مِّمَّا تُشْرِكُونَ ۝ ٱلَّذِينَ ءَاتَيْنَاهُمُ الْكِتَابَ يَعْرِفُونَهُ كَمَا يَعْرِفُونَ أَبْنَاءَهُمُ ٱلَّذِينَ خَسِرُوٓا أَنفُسَهُمْ فَهُمْ لَا يُؤْمِنُونَ ۝ وَمَنْ أَظْلَمُ مِمَّنِ ٱفْتَرَىٰ عَلَى اللّٰهِ كَذِبًا أَوْ كَذَّبَ بِآيَاتِهِ إِنَّهُ لَا يُفْلِحُ ٱلظَّالِمُونَ ۝ وَيَوْمَ نَحْشُرُهُمْ جَمِيعًا ثُمَّ نَقُولُ لِلَّذِينَ أَشْرَكُوٓا أَيْنَ شُرَكَاؤُكُمُ ٱلَّذِينَ كُنتُمْ تَزْعُمُونَ ۝ ثُمَّ لَمْ تَكُن فِتْنَتُهُمْ إِلَّآ أَن قَالُوا وَاللّٰهِ رَبِّنَا مَا كُنَّا مُشْرِكِينَ ۝ ٱنظُرْ كَيْفَ كَذَبُوا عَلَىٰٓ أَنفُسِهِمْ وَضَلَّ عَنْهُم مَّا كَانُوا يَفْتَرُونَ ۝ وَمِنْهُم مَّن يَسْتَمِعُ إِلَيْكَ وَجَعَلْنَا عَلَىٰ قُلُوبِهِمْ أَكِنَّةً أَن يَفْقَهُوهُ وَفِىٓ ءَاذَانِهِمْ وَقْرًا وَإِن يَرَوْا كُلَّ ءَايَةٍ لَّا يُؤْمِنُوا بِهَا حَتَّىٰٓ إِذَا جَآءُوكَ يُجَادِلُونَكَ يَقُولُ ٱلَّذِينَ كَفَرُوٓا إِنْ هَٰذَآ إِلَّآ أَسَاطِيرُ ٱلْأَوَّلِينَ ۝ وَهُمْ يَنْهَوْنَ عَنْهُ وَيَنْأَوْنَ عَنْهُ وَإِن يُهْلِكُونَ إِلَّآ أَنفُسَهُمْ وَمَا يَشْعُرُونَ ۝ وَلَوْ تَرَىٰٓ إِذْ وُقِفُوا عَلَى ٱلنَّارِ فَقَالُوا يَالَيْتَنَا نُرَدُّ وَلَا نُكَذِّبَ بِآيَاتِ رَبِّنَا وَنَكُونَ مِنَ ٱلْمُؤْمِنِينَ ۝

────~◈~────

19. Say: "What is most weighty in testimony?" Say: "God: a witness between me and you; and to me is being revealed this Qur'ān so that I may warn you thereby, and whomever it may reach." (O you who associate partners with God:) Do you truly testify that there are deities besides God? Say (to them): "I give no such testimony." Say: "He is only One God, and surely I am absolutely free from your association of partners with Him and from whatever you associate with Him as partners."

20. Those who were given the Book (before) know him (the Messenger with all his distinguishing attributes) as they know their own sons; yet those who ruin their own selves (by concealing this truth, being overcome by their lusts and worldly interests) – they do not believe.

21. Who is more in wrong than he who fabricates falsehood in attribution to God

and denies His signs (in the universe and their own selves pointing to Him) and His Revelations. Assuredly, the wrongdoers will not prosper.

22. A Day will come when We raise them all from the dead and gather them together, and then ask those who (while they were in the world) associated partners with God: "Where, now, are those of yours whom you asserted to have a part in Divinity?"

23. Then they will have no argument except to say: "By God, our Lord, we were not of those who associated partners with God."

24. Look! – How they lie against themselves, and (how) what they fabricated as partners (to worship besides God) has failed them!

25. There are among them such as could not help but listen to you (reciting the Qur'ān), but We have laid veils over their hearts (made by their ill-intention, wrongdoing, and arrogance, which caused them to lose the capacity to believe) so that they do not comprehend it (and so cannot believe), and in their ears, heaviness: even if they see whatever manifest sign (pointing to God's Unity and other truths of faith), they will not believe in it – so much so that when they come to you (only in order) to dispute with you, they, who have disbelieved, say: "This is nothing but fables of the ancients."

26. They bar others from it (the Qur'ān), as they themselves keep afar from it; and in doing so, they destroy only their own selves, though they do not perceive it.[4]

27. If you (O Messenger) could see them when they are made to stand by the Fire, and (in dread of being thrown into it, as if they forgot that they denied their associating partners with God) they say: "Oh, would that we were brought back (to the world)! Then we would not deny the signs and Revelations of our Lord and would be among the believers!"

4. The attitude of those who resist the truths of faith has never changed during human history: derision, claiming that the truths of faith are nothing but myth, falsehood, or legend, making out that the believers are a band of reactionary, regressive people with uncultivated, arid minds, preventing others from listening to them, silencing those who speak for them, and if all else fails, resorting to force – imprisonment, exile, and assassinations. Whatever the unbelievers resort to, it only indicates that they are devoid of sufficient thought and knowledge to compete with the truths of faith, and it only demonstrates their weakness, ignorance, and mental inadequacy. They lack the consciousness to perceive that what they do will ultimately cause their ruin; all this, despite the fact that there may even be sociologists, historians, and anthropologists among them who study history and events. What is important for the believers is that they should perceive this fact and, without being influenced by cultural pressure, they should always pursue the truth in Islam. It must never be forgotten that the greatest power of the unbelievers feeds upon the weakness of the believers in belief and submission.

130　سورة الأنعام ٦　١٣٠

بَلْ بَدَا لَهُمْ مَّا كَانُوا يُخْفُونَ مِنْ قَبْلُ ۖ وَلَوْ رُدُّوا لَعَادُوا لِمَا نُهُوا عَنْهُ وَإِنَّهُمْ لَكَاذِبُونَ ۝ وَقَالُوٓا إِنْ هِيَ إِلَّا حَيَاتُنَا الدُّنْيَا وَمَا نَحْنُ بِمَبْعُوثِينَ ۝ وَلَوْ تَرَىٰ إِذْ وُقِفُوا عَلَىٰ رَبِّهِمْ ۚ قَالَ أَلَيْسَ هَٰذَا بِالْحَقِّ ۚ قَالُوا بَلَىٰ وَرَبِّنَا ۚ قَالَ فَذُوقُوا الْعَذَابَ بِمَا كُنْتُمْ تَكْفُرُونَ ۝ قَدْ خَسِرَ الَّذِينَ كَذَّبُوا بِلِقَاءِ اللَّهِ ۖ حَتَّىٰ إِذَا جَاءَتْهُمُ السَّاعَةُ بَغْتَةً قَالُوا يَا حَسْرَتَنَا عَلَىٰ مَا فَرَّطْنَا فِيهَا وَهُمْ يَحْمِلُونَ أَوْزَارَهُمْ عَلَىٰ ظُهُورِهِمْ ۚ أَلَا سَاءَ مَا يَزِرُونَ ۝ وَمَا الْحَيَاةُ الدُّنْيَا إِلَّا لَعِبٌ وَلَهْوٌ ۖ وَلَلدَّارُ الْآخِرَةُ خَيْرٌ لِّلَّذِينَ يَتَّقُونَ ۗ أَفَلَا تَعْقِلُونَ ۝ قَدْ نَعْلَمُ إِنَّهُ لَيَحْزُنُكَ الَّذِي يَقُولُونَ ۖ فَإِنَّهُمْ لَا يُكَذِّبُونَكَ وَلَٰكِنَّ الظَّالِمِينَ بِآيَاتِ اللَّهِ يَجْحَدُونَ ۝ وَلَقَدْ كُذِّبَتْ رُسُلٌ مِّنْ قَبْلِكَ فَصَبَرُوا عَلَىٰ مَا كُذِّبُوا وَأُوذُوا حَتَّىٰ أَتَاهُمْ نَصْرُنَا ۚ وَلَا مُبَدِّلَ لِكَلِمَاتِ اللَّهِ ۚ وَلَقَدْ جَاءَكَ مِنْ نَبَإِ الْمُرْسَلِينَ ۝ وَإِنْ كَانَ كَبُرَ عَلَيْكَ إِعْرَاضُهُمْ فَإِنِ اسْتَطَعْتَ أَنْ تَبْتَغِيَ نَفَقًا فِي الْأَرْضِ أَوْ سُلَّمًا فِي السَّمَاءِ فَتَأْتِيَهُمْ بِآيَةٍ ۚ وَلَوْ شَاءَ اللَّهُ لَجَمَعَهُمْ عَلَى الْهُدَىٰ ۚ فَلَا تَكُونَنَّ مِنَ الْجَاهِلِينَ ۝

----

until, as the Hour comes upon them all of a sudden, they cry, "Alas for us! how negligent we have been in this regard," when they have already loaded their burdens on to their backs. Evil indeed is the burden they are loading themselves with!

32. And the present, worldly life is nothing but a play and a pastime, and better is the abode of the Hereafter for those who keep from disobedience to God in reverence for Him and piety. Will you not, then, reason and understand?⁵

33. (O Messenger!) We know indeed that the things (lies, mockery, and slanders) that they say grieve you: yet, it is not you that they deny (they cannot very well call you a liar since they themselves have called you 'the trustworthy one'); rather, it is the signs and Revelations of God that the wrongdoers obstinately reject.

34. (Do not be grieved at what they do!) Indeed, Messengers before you were denied (regarding the Message they brought), but they endured with patience the charge of falsehood and the hurt done to them, until Our help reached them: there is none that can change God's words (alter His decrees and His execution of them). And, indeed, some account of those Messengers has already come to you.

35. If their recalcitrance is distressful for you, then if you are able, seek a way down into the earth or a ladder up to the heavens to bring them a sign (a miracle of the kind that they ask you to bring) – then know that had God so willed, He could surely have gathered them all to the true guidance (whether by a single miracle or by some other means. Seeing that God wills otherwise: that the truth be set before people with its supporting arguments through Messengers, and people should choose their way by exercise of their free will and judgment, then) do not be among those who act as if ignorant (of this fact).⁶

28. No! Rather, they say this because what they used to hide (the manifest truth, and their own evil intentions and intrigues in response to it) has become obvious to them; and if they were brought back to the world, they would revert to the very thing they were forbidden: indeed, they are just liars.

29. (They always behaved so whenever they got into distress while in the world, but when relieved of it) they would say: "There is no life beyond our present life of the world, and we are not to be raised (from the dead)."

30. But if you could see when they are made to stand in their Lord's Presence: He says: "Is not this (your being raised from the dead and gathered in My Presence) the truth?" They say: "Yes indeed, by our Lord!" He says: "Taste, then, the punishment for what you used to disbelieve."

31. Assuredly those have lost who deny the (truth of the final) meeting with God

5. The world has three aspects. The first aspect looks to the fact that it is the realm where God's Names are manifested and therefore, whatever is there and whatever takes place in it is a mirror to God with His Attributes and Names. The second aspect, which looks to the Hereafter, is that the world is the tillage for the Hereafter. The building-blocks to make up one's Paradise or Hell in the Hereafter are the seeds of one's belief or unbelief and the deeds that one sows here. With these two aspects the world is very important and is regarded as being the equal of the heavens; in fact, the Qur'ān mentions it alongside of the heavens. The third aspect of the world is that which looks to our carnal desires, passions, lusts, and ambitions. It is this aspect that the Qur'ān condemns, as these consist of games, pastimes, greed (hoarding things), and competing in having more goods; in short, the source of all vice and evil.

6. In addition to the deep desire which God's Messenger had to guide people and His endless efforts and the great success he exhibited in conveying God's Message, these verses also show the intensity of the suffering he endured, the hardships he encountered, and the obstinate resistance of the unbelievers, which all made heavy impressions on his human spirit. The following verses will interpret and elucidate these; they express the greatness of God's Messenger along with demonstrating his profound knowledge of God, his perfect conviction of the truth of the Message he brought, and his deep concern for the guidance and salvation of people. It is these verses which consoled him and kept in check the intense passion he felt for the salvation of people.

١٣١ الجُزْءَ السَّابِع 131

بِسْمِ اللَّهِ الرَّحْمَنِ الرَّحِيمِ

preme Ever-Preserved Tablet, which is the source of all books, and the Book of Creation: We have created everything just in its place and for a purpose, so that the universe is maintained in perfect balance and order). Then, (a Day will come when the universe will be changed into a new one, and) they will be raised from the dead and gathered to their Lord.

39. Those who deny Our signs and Revelations are deaf and dumb in veils of darkness. Whomever God wills, He leads astray, and whomever He wills, He sets on a straight path.[9]

40. Say (to them): "Do you ever consider: if some punishment of God comes upon you or the Last Hour comes upon you, do you then invoke other than God? (Answer that) if you are truthful (and admit the voice of your conscience)"!

41. (No indeed!) Rather, it is Him alone that you invoke – then He may, if He wills, remove that which caused you to invoke Him[10] – and you forget (then) whatever partners you have been associating with Him.

42. And We did indeed send Messengers to the communities before you, and We seized those (communities) with trials and tribulations so that they might invoke Us with humility (seeking the truth and forgiveness).

43. If only, when Our trial came upon them, they had invoked Us with humility! But their hearts grew hard and Satan decked out whatever they were doing as appealing to them.

44. Then, when they forgot (the advice and warnings) that they were reminded of, We opened for them the gates of all things, until, even while they were rejoicing in what they were granted, We seized them suddenly, so then they were plunged into despair.[11]

36. Only they who have the ability to hear can respond (to a call); as for the dead, God will raise them to life, and then to Him they will be returned.[7]

37. And they say: "Why is not a miraculous sign (of the kind we desire) sent down on him from his Lord?" Say (to them): "Surely God has the power to send down a sign (of any kind)." But most of them have nothing to do with knowledge (so that they would know the nature of the signs, Revelation, and Prophethood, and the purpose for them).

38. (Should not those whose ears are closed to the Qur'ān look around themselves to see the signs of the truth?) No living creature is there moving on the earth, no bird flying on its two wings, but they are communities like you.[8] We have neglected nothing in the Book (the Qur'ān, the Su-

7. Using many literary arts, such as metaphor, simile, comparison, and allusion, the verses of the Qur'ān attain various depths of meaning. This short verse contains several meanings and truths, as well as an admonition:

- There are people through whose ears the Qur'ān cannot penetrate to their hearts and who resist faith; these are the "spiritually" deaf. A deaf person cannot hear the call nor can they respond to it.
- One who has the ability to hear cannot be indifferent to the Qur'ān. One who can remain indifferent to the Qur'ān and its call can only be "deaf."
- Those through whose ears the Qur'ān does not enter are no different from the dead, for like the dead, they have no life in their heart, and one whose heart is not "alive" is "dead," even if they are physically alive. The true life is the life of the heart. The same is true for biological life, which depends on the health of the heart.
- No one will be saved by dying and no one will stay in the grave eternally. God will raise all of the dead, gathering them together in His Presence and the truth in which they believed or rejected while in the world will appear in their faces. This second life is eternal, either in bliss or despair.

8. "God, Who does not leave the bees without a queen nor the ants without a leader, does not leave humankind without a Prophet" (*The Letters*, 2: 303).

9. It is sometimes necessary to explain what making one's guidance or misguidance by God's absolute Will means. Here we will give a brief overview:

- The original word rendered as "will" is *Mashīah*. God has two kinds of will, one *Mashīah*, the other *Irādah*. God does not will (*irādah*) unbelief, polytheism, hypocrisy, and sins, but these are all, like faith, good deeds, and virtues, included in His *Mashīah*, which is associated with His Knowledge or which can be regarded as "Pre-knowledge."
- As knowledge depends on what is known, and since it is eternally known to God how

each person will use their free will, God's *Mashīah* encompasses human free will. In other words, as God cannot be contained by time, as He is beyond all time and space, and therefore, as He knows how each person will use their free will, He wills accordingly.

- A person uses their free will to believe or not to believe. But it is God Who puts human free will into effect and Who creates the deeds of people.
- Human choices and inclinations, including every thing and every event in the universe, even the movement of a leaf, occur within the universal system that God has established. So, nothing is excluded from God's Knowledge and Will (*Mashīah*).

10. This part of the verse expresses a very important truth:

We should not expect God to give us exactly what we pray for. God dominates and rules the whole universe by manifesting all of His Names. That is, He has universal rules derived from all His Names which compose the magnificent universal order with its manifestations. These rules encompass everything within the universal frame and operate according to His universal Wisdom. The wheel of the universe does not turn according to the wishes of each thing or person. So God gives what is asked for in compliance with this Wisdom.

However, this does not mean that God does not have special concern for each thing or being; this concern stems from His Compassion. But this concern does not require that He will give exactly the thing that is asked for. He gives whatever is good for the person who prays. For example, a patient who has undergone a medical operation may ask for water, even though this may be very dangerous for them. The doctor does the patient good by refusing them water. Similarly, God gives what is good for His servant who prays to Him, and this is why He sometimes does not give us what we desire in this world, but rather delays it to the Hereafter.

11. These last verses discuss some recurring patterns in the history of different peoples and societies:

- If the Divine Message begins to spread in a place, varying conditions, such as abundance or famine appear there, according to the devotion of its followers and their efforts to spread it, and the attitude of the opposing side.

- Usually God Almighty first sends misfortune and hardship to the people among whom the Divine Message has begun to be spread. This is in order to urge them to renounce their false beliefs and wrong ways and to accept the Message; in most cases, especially for uncivilized peoples, force and hardship are more effective than gentle persuasion. This method also aims at perfecting those who had believed in the Message first, equipping them with the necessary patience to endure all future hardships.

- If people do not renounce their ways, despite the hardships and misfortune they are suffering, and if they remain deaf and blind to the Message, God will then provide them with abundance. That is, as a result of their being lost in the world and exerting all their abilities and strength to achieve a luxurious life, God opens the gates of the world to them. This causes many of them to become extremely rich at the cost of many others, who grow poorer, and these blind people increase in their dissipation, debauchery, corruption, and similar evils.

- The loss of balance in society and the increase in dissipation and corruption all herald general misfortune or disaster. If there is a formidable group that can shoulder the Divine Message and apply it to life, the destruction that will befall society results in the rising of this group. If there is no such group, the destruction becomes more encompassing.

- If, despite all their vices and sins, a person grows in prosperity with nothing adverse befalling them, and if there is welfare in society despite all the wrongdoing, injustices, dissipation and corruption prevalent in it, this means a misfortune or destruction is imminent for that society, and that that person will see the consequence of their misdeeds.

سُوَرةُ الأنْعَام   132

فَقُطِعَ دَابِرُ الْقَوْمِ الَّذِينَ ظَلَمُوا ۚ وَالْحَمْدُ لِلَّهِ رَبِّ الْعَالَمِينَ ۞ قُلْ
أَرَأَيْتُمْ إِنْ أَخَذَ اللَّهُ سَمْعَكُمْ وَأَبْصَارَكُمْ وَخَتَمَ عَلَىٰ قُلُوبِكُم
مَّنْ إِلَٰهٌ غَيْرُ اللَّهِ يَأْتِيكُم بِهِ ۗ انظُرْ كَيْفَ نُصَرِّفُ الْآيَاتِ ثُمَّ هُمْ
يَصْدِفُونَ ۞ قُلْ أَرَأَيْتَكُمْ إِنْ أَتَاكُمْ عَذَابُ اللَّهِ بَغْتَةً أَوْ جَهْرَةً
هَلْ يُهْلَكُ إِلَّا الْقَوْمُ الظَّالِمُونَ ۞ وَمَا نُرْسِلُ الْمُرْسَلِينَ إِلَّا
مُبَشِّرِينَ وَمُنذِرِينَ ۖ فَمَنْ آمَنَ وَأَصْلَحَ فَلَا خَوْفٌ عَلَيْهِمْ
وَلَا هُمْ يَحْزَنُونَ ۞ وَالَّذِينَ كَذَّبُوا بِآيَاتِنَا يَمَسُّهُمُ
الْعَذَابُ بِمَا كَانُوا يَفْسُقُونَ ۞ قُل لَّا أَقُولُ لَكُمْ
عِندِي خَزَائِنُ اللَّهِ وَلَا أَعْلَمُ الْغَيْبَ وَلَا أَقُولُ لَكُمْ إِنِّي مَلَكٌ ۖ
إِنْ أَتَّبِعُ إِلَّا مَا يُوحَىٰ إِلَيَّ ۚ قُلْ هَلْ يَسْتَوِي الْأَعْمَىٰ وَالْبَصِيرُ ۚ
أَفَلَا تَتَفَكَّرُونَ ۞ وَأَنذِرْ بِهِ الَّذِينَ يَخَافُونَ أَن
يُحْشَرُوا إِلَىٰ رَبِّهِمْ ۙ لَيْسَ لَهُم مِّن دُونِهِ وَلِيٌّ وَلَا شَفِيعٌ لَّعَلَّهُمْ
يَتَّقُونَ ۞ وَلَا تَطْرُدِ الَّذِينَ يَدْعُونَ رَبَّهُم بِالْغَدَاةِ وَالْعَشِيِّ
يُرِيدُونَ وَجْهَهُ ۖ مَا عَلَيْكَ مِنْ حِسَابِهِم مِّن شَيْءٍ وَمَا مِنْ حِسَابِكَ
عَلَيْهِم مِّن شَيْءٍ فَتَطْرُدَهُمْ فَتَكُونَ مِنَ الظَّالِمِينَ ۞

45. And so (in the end) were uprooted those people who had persisted in wrong-doing. All praise and gratitude are for God, the Lord of the worlds!

46. Say: "What do you think, if God should take away your hearing and your sight and set a seal upon your hearts, what deity but God is there that could restore it[12] to you?" Look, how We set out the Revelations and signs (of God's Existence and Unity and other truths of faith) in diverse ways, and yet they turn away.

47. Say: "What do you think, if God's punishment comes upon you unawares or perceptibly (so that you see its approach), will any be destroyed but the people of wrong-doing?

48. We do not send the Messengers except as bearers of glad tidings (of prosperity in return for faith and righteousness) and warners (against the consequences of misguidance). So whoever believes and mends his way, they will have no fear, nor will they grieve.

49. And as for those who deny Our manifest signs and Revelations, the punishment will touch them on account of their transgressing (the bounds in belief and conduct).

50. Say (to them, O Messenger): "(You want me to do miracles. However,) I never tell you that with me are the treasures of God, or that I know the Unseen; nor do I tell you that I am an angel. I only follow what is revealed to me." And say: "Are the blind and the seeing alike? Will you not, then, reflect?"

51. Warn with this (Qur'ān) those who (whether they already have true faith or not yet) are fearful in their hearts because they will be raised from the dead and gathered to their Lord, that they have, apart from Him, no guardian and confidant, nor intercessor, so that they may keep from disobedience to God in reverence for Him and piety, and be protected against His punishment.

52. And do not (in the hope of persuading the chieftains of the unbelievers) drive away any of those (poor believers of humble social standing) who, in the morning and afternoon, call upon their Lord, seeking His "Face" (i.e. the meeting with Him hereafter and His eternal, good pleasure). You are not accountable for them in anything just as they are not accountable for you in anything, that you should drive them away, and so become among the wrongdoers.

12. Like many other verses which present physical and spiritual elements together, this verse also contains and presents such elements in both a literal and figurative way. The hearing, sight and heart mentioned here are our both the physical and spiritual powers of hearing and seeing and the center of our physical and spiritual life. As it is God Who created our ears, eyes, and hearts and as there is nobody else who can create them or restore them to us when we lose them, it is also He Who makes them spiritually alive.

This verse in its Arabic original uses the sense of hearing in the singular form (sem'), while the sense of seeing is expressed in the plural (absār). This means that the duty of the ears with respect to faith is hearing and listening to the Divine Revelation and that there is a single source of Revelation. By contrast, there are innumerable signs of faith which a person can see with their eyes. In the excerpt, *What deity but God is there that could restore it to you?*, the verse uses the singular pronoun *it* for the powers of hearing and seeing and the heart; in short, in order to attain faith the powers of hearing and sight, and the heart must be alive and all these faculties must work together.

133

53. And it is in this way that We try people through one another: so that they (who think that such things as wealth and social status are the means of superiority) say (of the believers who are poor and lacking in recognized social status): "Are these the ones among us on whom God has bestowed His favor?" Does God not know best who are the thankful (who recognize the real source and bestower of every good thing one receives, and act accordingly)?

54. When those who believe in all of Our Revelations and signs (whenever they come to them,) come to you, say in welcome: "Peace be upon you! Your Lord has bound Himself to mercy (to treat His servants with mercy) – so that if any of you does a bad deed due to ignorance (an instance of defeat to the evil-commanding soul), and thereafter repents and mends his way and conduct, surely He is All-Forgiving, All-Compassionate."

55. Thus We set out in detail the signposts of Our way and the relevant Revelations (included in the Qur'ān), and (We do so) so that the path of the disbelieving criminals might become distinct (from that of the righteous believers).

56. Say (to those associating partners with God): "I have been forbidden to worship those beings whom you deify and invoke apart from God." Say: "I do not follow your lusts and fancies – or else I would go astray and would not be of those who are rightly guided."

57. Say: "I take my stand on clear evidence from my Lord, whereas you deny it. Not within my power is what you (derisively) ask to be hastened, (saying: 'If there is such a punishment with which you threaten us, let it come immediately'). (In the absolute sense) judgment and authority rest with none but God alone. He always relates the truth, and He is the best judge between truth and falsehood.

58. Say: "If it were within my power (to bring) what you ask to be hastened, the matter between me and you would have been decided." God best knows the wrongdoers.

59. With Him are the keys to the Unseen; none knows them but He. And He knows whatever is on land and in the sea; and not a leaf falls but He knows it; and neither is there a grain in the dark layers of earth, nor anything green or dry, but is (recorded) in a Manifest Book.[13]

13. The Qur'ān mentions the Manifest Book and Manifest Record (36: 12).

The universe displays a magnificent and perfect order; God has created and creates everything perfectly and in exactly the right place. This demonstrates that the universe is based on a universal, perfect knowledge and determination, which we call Divine Destiny. To better understand this subtle point, we should consider the following two examples:

Before setting out to write a book, a writer has the necessary information in their head; this can be regarded as the archetype of the book. Then the writer makes a plan and divides the knowledge in their mind into chapters and sections, which is the "destined" existence of the book. Afterwards, they write the book; i.e. they create the book's material existence. For another example, before constructing a building, an architect builds it in their mind; i.e. they create the essential or archetypal existence of the building. Afterwards, they draw a plan of the building, which is the "destined" existence of the building. Then, they build it according to the plan they have made.

Similarly, the universe with all the things and events in it, from the first day until the last, has an archetypal existence in God's Eternal Knowledge. God destined (when considered from the perspective of the universe contained in time and space) or destines (when considered from God's perspective, as He is beyond all time and space) a particular form, life-time, and function for each thing or being. This second type of the determined existence of the universe in God's Knowledge, with everything and every event in it is called the Manifest Record or the Supreme Ever-Preserved Tablet. This is, in one respect, identical with God's Knowledge. Destiny gives form to the archetypes, and Divine Power brings them into material existence.

God duplicates the "destined" existence of each thing. One of the copies is included in its seed. For example, when God turns the embryo in the mother into another (human) creation, the destiny of this new human creature has already been determined (for the relation between Destiny and human free will, see note 8 in this *sūrah*, and in *sūrah* 2, notes 10, 14, *sūrah* 3, notes 30, 36, and *sūrah* 4, note 18). Likewise, the future life of every plant or tree is encapsulated in its seed. The life-history of the plant or tree from the time of its germination under soil until it yields fruit is the developed form of its seed. We call this active life-history of a living thing or being its Destiny Practical or the Manifest Book. With every thing and event being included in it, the universe has its own "universal" Destiny Practical, which is the "universal" Manifest Book. The Manifest Record relates to the origins of things or beings and Divine Knowledge, while the Manifest Book contains their entire life-histories and is a notebook written by the Divine Power.

60. He it is Who recalls your souls at night (while you sleep, a state comparable to death), and He knows what You already worked in the daytime. Then He raises you to life therein (the next daytime) so that the exact term appointed by Him is fulfilled. (He causes you to die after the completion of this term, and, just as He raises you again to life each day after sleep, He will raise you from the dead when the appointed time is due.) Your final return is to Him; and then He will make you understand what you were doing (and call you to account for it).

61. He is the All-Omnipotent over His servants; and He sends to you (angel) guardians (who watch over, and keep a record of, whatever you do). When death finally approaches any of you, Our envoys (the angels assigned to this duty) take his soul, and they do not neglect (any part of their tasks).

62. Then they are restored to God, their All-True Master and Protector. Indeed His alone is the judgment, and He is the most swift in reckoning.

63. Say: "Who is it that saves you from the veils of darkness on land and the sea, (when) you call upon Him most humbly and in the secrecy of your hearts: 'If You but save us from this (distress), we will most certainly be among the thankful (who turn to You in faith and righteousness)!'?"

64. Say: "God alone saves you from this and from every distress, but then you associate partners with Him (instead of being thankful to Him by believing in and obeying Him)."

65. Say: "He it is Who has the power to send punishment upon you from above you or from beneath your feet, or to confound you by splitting you into hostile groups and make you taste the violence of one an-

other. Look, how We set out the signs (of God's Existence and Unity and other truths of faith) in diverse ways, so that they may ponder and grasp the truth.

66. And yet, your people (O Messenger) deny the Qur'ān, even though it is the truth. Say: "I am not one appointed as a guardian over you to assume your responsibility for you."

67. Every tiding (from God) has a term appointed for its fulfillment; and in time you will come to know (the truth).

68. When you meet such as indulge in (blasphmeous or derisive) talk about Our Revelations, turn away from them until they engage in some other talk. And should Satan cause you to forget, no longer remain, after recollection, in the company of such wrongdoing people.

١٣٥   الجُزْءُ السَّابِع   135

وَمَا عَلَى الَّذِينَ يَتَّقُونَ مِنْ حِسَابِهِم مِّن شَىْءٍ وَلَٰكِن
ذِكْرَىٰ لَعَلَّهُمْ يَتَّقُونَ ۝ وَذَرِ الَّذِينَ اتَّخَذُوا دِينَهُمْ
لَعِبًا وَلَهْوًا وَغَرَّتْهُمُ الْحَيَوٰةُ الدُّنْيَا ۚ وَذَكِّرْ بِهِ أَن
تُبْسَلَ نَفْسٌ بِمَا كَسَبَتْ لَيْسَ لَهَا مِن دُونِ اللَّهِ
وَلِيٌّ وَلَا شَفِيعٌ وَإِن تَعْدِلْ كُلَّ عَدْلٍ لَّا يُؤْخَذْ مِنْهَا ۗ أُولَٰئِكَ
الَّذِينَ أُبْسِلُوا بِمَا كَسَبُوا ۖ لَهُمْ شَرَابٌ مِّنْ حَمِيمٍ وَعَذَابٌ
أَلِيمٌ بِمَا كَانُوا يَكْفُرُونَ ۝ قُلْ أَنَدْعُوا مِن دُونِ اللَّهِ
مَا لَا يَنفَعُنَا وَلَا يَضُرُّنَا وَنُرَدُّ عَلَىٰٓ أَعْقَابِنَا بَعْدَ إِذْ هَدَىٰنَا اللَّهُ
كَالَّذِي اسْتَهْوَتْهُ الشَّيَاطِينُ فِي الْأَرْضِ حَيْرَانَ لَهُ
أَصْحَابٌ يَدْعُونَهُ إِلَى الْهُدَى ائْتِنَا ۗ قُلْ إِنَّ هُدَى اللَّهِ
هُوَ الْهُدَىٰ ۖ وَأُمِرْنَا لِنُسْلِمَ لِرَبِّ الْعَالَمِينَ ۝ وَأَنْ أَقِيمُوا
الصَّلَوٰةَ وَاتَّقُوهُ ۚ وَهُوَ الَّذِيٓ إِلَيْهِ تُحْشَرُونَ ۝ وَهُوَ الَّذِي
خَلَقَ السَّمَٰوَٰتِ وَالْأَرْضَ بِالْحَقِّ ۖ وَيَوْمَ يَقُولُ كُن
فَيَكُونُ ۚ قَوْلُهُ الْحَقُّ ۚ وَلَهُ الْمُلْكُ يَوْمَ يُنفَخُ فِي الصُّورِ
عَالِمُ الْغَيْبِ وَالشَّهَٰدَةِ ۚ وَهُوَ الْحَكِيمُ الْخَبِيرُ ۝

---

69. Those who keep from disbodience to God in reverence for Him and piety are not accountable for them in anything. But (what rests with them is) to remind and thereby admonish them so that they may fear (the evil of what they do) and avoid it.

70. Quit those who take their Religion (the one appointed for them by God) for a play and pastime (and have made play and fun their own religion), and whom the present, worldly life has deluded. But remind them (through the Qur'ān) lest any soul should be given up to destruction for what it has earned, for there will neither be any protecting friend nor intercessor apart from God, and even though it may offer any ransom (in return for its unforgivable sins such as unbelief and associating partners with God), it will not

be accepted from it. They are those who are given up to destruction for what they have earned; for them is a drink of boiling water and a painful punishment because they were persistently disbelieving.

71. Say: "Shall we invoke, apart from God, the things that can neither benefit us (when we invoke them) nor harm us (when we do not invoke them), and (thus) be turned back on our heels, after God has guided us – like the one whom the satans have infatuated on earth so that they blunder about in valleys of misguidance, though he has companions calling him to the guidance, saying: 'Come to us!'?" Say: "Surely God's guidance is the (only true) guidance, and we have been commanded to submit with all our being to the Lord of the worlds;

72. "And to establish the Prayer in conformity with its conditions, and keep from disobedience to Him in reverence for Him and piety." He it is to Whom you will be gathered.

73. He it is Who has created the heavens and the earth in truth (meaningfully, and for definite purpose, and on solid foundations of truth). Whenever He says "Be!" it is. His word is the truth. And His is the sovereignty on the day when the Trumpet is blown,[14] the Knower of the Unseen and the witnessed. He is the All-Wise, the All-Aware.[15]

14. We do not know the exact nature of the Trumpet and what is really meant by its being blown. It will be blown twice (see also 39: 68, note 22) by the archangel Isrāfīl, and when it is blown the first time, the entire order of the universe will be disrupted, and on its second blowing, all the dead will be raised in a completely fresh world and order.

God has absolute ownership and dominion over the whole creation, even in this world. But, since this world is the world of Wisdom, His acts are screened by some apparent causes; that is, He allows things to occur according to certain (apparent) causes, and beings like humans and the jinn, endowed with free will, are allowed to have property and exercise some sort of dominion, and are tested. Whereas, in the next world, which will be the world of Power and where there will be no causes nor time or duration for a thing to occur, He will act without the intervention of causes and no one will be allowed to enjoy any dominion.

15. The verses which so far have concentrated on the pillars of faith, in particular the two most cardinal, namely belief in God's Existence and Unity and in the Resurrection, present us with observable, manifest truths and evidence:

- It is God Who has created the heavens and the earth and, in connection with them, brings darkness and light into existence. It is also He Who gives existence to people's will and preference for belief or unbelief, along with the causes of these.
- God also created the first human being from clay, a material propitious for cultivation, and all succeeding men and women from the food that is obtained from earth. He appoints for each person, as well as appointing for humanity, a fixed term in this world; after the completion of this term, He takes them into another, eternal world.
- God has not left the universe and humankind to their own devices after creating them. He is the All-Omnipotent and has full sway over them. He knows whatever happens in the universe, down to the fall of a leaf, and He knows all the deeds, thought,

and intentions of humankind. His appointed angels record these, and people will be called to account for these acts in the other world. To avoid punishment, people must follow the way He has established for them through His Messengers.

Having presented the cardinal pillars of faith along with their indisputable proofs, which the Qur'ān calls "signs," that are understandable to and observable by everybody, the verses proceed to reject polytheism in all its forms and consolidate the truths of faith with manifold proofs:

- Despite the evidence of belief that is observable by everybody, God also sent Messengers to people to teach them and bring the message to their attention. But, unfortunately, most people, particularly those who have some status in society, such as the wealthy, aristocrats, the governing elite and some intellectuals, willfully reject the messages brought by the Messengers, as well as their manifest signs that are derived from the universe and life, including the miracles which the Messengers work when necessary and when God allows them to do so.
- There is not a single truth for those who reject the truths of faith and their proofs on which to base their claims. This is why they attempt to oppose the Messengers with derision, demanding that they work miracles, and claiming that the miracles they work are nothing but magic. This openly shows their intellectual defeat and bankruptcy when placed before the truth brought by the Messengers. The true reason for their unbelief and resistance against the Divine Message is that they fear losing their status, they cannot give up their life-style or bear to be together with those they have despised as being poor and lacking status in society; that is, arrogance, having the wrong viewpoint and world-view, wrongdoing and luxury prevent them from believing. These attitudes have caused them to lose their senses of hearing and seeing, and they can no longer hear the revealed message nor see

its manifest evidence (signs) in life and the universe, and, as a consequence, they lose the capacity to believe, a capacity which God has ingrained in their nature.

- The life of the world is not only transient; it also consists of play and pastime in respect to human carnal life. The wealth, posts and positions, and social status, to which people tend to attach much importance and on which they depend, are not lasting. God, Who gives these favors as a means of testing people, may take them away at an unexpected time. History is full of instances of this giving and taking away; there are many lessons to be learned from destroyed civilizations and the lost wealth and positions of our ancestors.

- God is, first of all, the All-Merciful, the All-Compassionate; all His acts are based on mercy. For this reason, He provides for every living thing in the world without discriminating between believers and unbelievers, maintaining the lives of everything. So it should not be expected that He will immediately destroy those who are bent on unbelief, those who associate partners with Him, and those who indulge in sins. The place where people are rewarded or punished for their belief and deeds is the Hereafter. God has special laws for the worldly life and people usually see the consequences of their deeds in the world according to these laws. However, this does not mean that God does not have special concern and compassion for His believing, righteous servants in the world. He helps them according to His Wisdom, accepts their repentance, forgives them, and protects them as long as they remain devoted to His cause and religion. When wrongdoing and transgression exceed all limits, God punishes people in the world through calamities, such as earthquakes, floods, volcanic eruptions, epidemics, or wars, internal conflicts, anarchy, terror, or causing them to lose their wealth, status or jobs. But since this punishment usually appears to be in accordance with the (sociological) laws of life

and "(physical) laws of nature," not everyone can see the Divine Hand behind them.

- God is not of the same kind as the created, so He cannot be conceived of in terms of the created. He never eats and drinks, nor does He need anything. He feeds, sustains, and provides. His Existence and Unity are more manifest than anything else, and it is rationally impossible to accept the existence of anything without accepting His Existence. The universe, with whatever is and happens in it, testifies to this, as does the Qur'ān, the other Divine Scriptures, tens of thousands of Prophets, and billions of people who followed them throughout history. Those who deny Him have nothing substantial on which to base their claims, for denial cannot be proved, and therefore it has no rational or scientific weight. Denial consists in mere conjecture and hypothesis.

- Even if a person denies the truths of faith, defeated by their carnal soul, they will see, when they die, the true nature of those truths that are manifested in our world with their outer dimensions, and they will understand the truth of the other life clearly; yet, it is of no use for this person to feel remorse. They desire to be returned to the world, but it is of no avail! Even if they were allowed to return, they would not act otherwise. No one can go to the Hereafter with a valid excuse for their wrong beliefs and acts. Everybody feels the existence of a Supreme Power in their conscience, especially when they are facing danger or death. They invoke only God with both their tongue and their conscience, for God has inculcated in the conscience of everyone a point where we seek help and a point where we seek support. Both of these manifest themselves, especially when there is no apparent, material means to escape from peril or difficulties, and this causes a person to turn to God alone. Every person has had this experience several times in their life. But most people, upon reaching safety, behave as if they have had no such experience. They pursue their ambitions, and under the pressure of such attitudes as arrogance, wrongdoing and having the wrong viewpoint of things and events, they insist on unbelief or the association of partners with God.

- In order to show people that the way they follow is wrong and to warn them against its consequences, God Almighty repeatedly presents to them evidence and He renews His admonitions. A time comes when He will expose them to different hardships and disasters, such as famine and warfare, in order to help them to come to their senses, and at other times He will pour on them His bounties in order to stir up feelings of gratitude in them. But, if a person has already lost their inborn capacity to believe, none of these will be of any avail. Furthermore, they are deluded by Satan into seeing their way as being good.

- Those who persist in unbelief or polytheism are too arrogant to find themselves side by side with those whom they see as being devoid of any social status and attempt to excuse their own unbelief by mocking the belief of those others. This is because they are beguiled by Satan into judging the degree of intelligence and worth of a human by the post, wealth and social status one has, and therefore think of themselves as much more intelligent and better than those who are poor and devoid of status. This leads such people to conclude that if the Message brought by the Prophet is true, then they should have been among the first to accept it. But this is Satan's trickery; they become the victims of their carnal selves; wealth and social status are not the criterion to judge one's intelligence or worth. There are many people who are very knowledgeable and intelligent, but who are poor and have no positions and social status. Imam Ghazzālī calls the intelligence that grasps worldly affairs the intelligence of worldly life. It can never be asserted that one who is advanced in the intelligence of worldly life is also advanced in grasping the perennial truths and principles that lie at the root

of and govern life, existence, things and events, and their meaning. Moreover, the Divine criteria to judge people are different. At the foremost of these criteria comes the grasping of the truths and principles mentioned, which automatically lead to believing in God and to the other pillars of faith, and living according to these truths and principles in reverence for God and piety; this is what the Qur'ān calls *taqwā*. If life and existence consisted only of economy, then there would be no philosophy, religion and contemplative thought, nor even art and literature, which are the elevated products of the human mind and heart. Human thought should be based on and guided by the truths and principles mentioned here so that there will be no deviation in thought and belief; these deviations are what lead to unbelief or associating partners with God.

- As mentioned above, God is not, as some think, "a passive deity" who created the universe and humanity and left everyone to their own devices. He has full knowledge of everything, is fully aware of whatever one thinks, intends, and does, and the reins of all things and events are in His Hand. Whatever happens in the world occurs by His commanding "Be!" He makes His appointed angels record all the deeds of human beings, and will call people to account in the other world for what they have done in this world. Going to sleep every night and waking up every morning is evidence of the fact that we will one day be raised from the dead; it is a means of comparison for us.

After all these truths and all the evidence which has been presented in this *sūrah*, the Qur'ān goes on to narrate a very significant event from the life of the Prophet Abraham, upon him be peace, one of the greatest heroes of the truth of *Tawḥīd* (believing in and declaring God's Oneness), from whom all the greatest Messengers descended, including Muḥammad, Jesus and Moses, upon them be peace.

136   سُوْرَةُ الأَنْعَام   ١٣٦

[Arabic Quranic text]

وَإِذْ قَالَ إِبْرَاهِيمُ لِأَبِيهِ آزَرَ أَتَتَّخِذُ أَصْنَامًا آلِهَةً إِنِّي أَرَاكَ وَقَوْمَكَ فِي ضَلَالٍ مُبِينٍ ۝ وَكَذَلِكَ نُرِي إِبْرَاهِيمَ مَلَكُوتَ السَّمَاوَاتِ وَالْأَرْضِ وَلِيَكُونَ مِنَ الْمُوقِنِينَ ۝ فَلَمَّا جَنَّ عَلَيْهِ اللَّيْلُ رَأَى كَوْكَبًا قَالَ هَذَا رَبِّي فَلَمَّا أَفَلَ قَالَ لَا أُحِبُّ الْآفِلِينَ ۝ فَلَمَّا رَأَى الْقَمَرَ بَازِغًا قَالَ هَذَا رَبِّي فَلَمَّا أَفَلَ قَالَ لَئِنْ لَمْ يَهْدِنِي رَبِّي لَأَكُونَنَّ مِنَ الْقَوْمِ الضَّالِّينَ ۝ فَلَمَّا رَأَى الشَّمْسَ بَازِغَةً قَالَ هَذَا رَبِّي هَذَا أَكْبَرُ فَلَمَّا أَفَلَتْ قَالَ يَا قَوْمِ إِنِّي بَرِيءٌ مِمَّا تُشْرِكُونَ ۝ إِنِّي وَجَّهْتُ وَجْهِيَ لِلَّذِي فَطَرَ السَّمَاوَاتِ وَالْأَرْضَ حَنِيفًا وَمَا أَنَا مِنَ الْمُشْرِكِينَ ۝ وَحَاجَّهُ قَوْمُهُ قَالَ أَتُحَاجُّونِّي فِي اللَّهِ وَقَدْ هَدَانِ وَلَا أَخَافُ مَا تُشْرِكُونَ بِهِ إِلَّا أَنْ يَشَاءَ رَبِّي شَيْئًا وَسِعَ رَبِّي كُلَّ شَيْءٍ عِلْمًا أَفَلَا تَتَذَكَّرُونَ ۝ وَكَيْفَ أَخَافُ مَا أَشْرَكْتُمْ وَلَا تَخَافُونَ أَنَّكُمْ أَشْرَكْتُمْ بِاللَّهِ مَا لَمْ يُنَزِّلْ بِهِ عَلَيْكُمْ سُلْطَانًا فَأَيُّ الْفَرِيقَيْنِ أَحَقُّ بِالْأَمْنِ إِنْ كُنْتُمْ تَعْلَمُونَ ۝

---

74. And (call to mind) when Abraham spoke to his father Āzar: "Do you take idols for deities? Indeed, I see you and your people lost in obvious error."[16]

75. Thus (he spoke and acted for) We had showed Abraham (the ugliness and irrationality of polytheism and) the inner dimension of (the existence of) the heavens and the earth, and the eternal truth (which this outer, corporeal dimension manifests and depends upon) – this We had done so that he might be one of those who have achieved certainty of faith (that he might attain the final degree in his certainty as a Messenger of God):

76. When the night overspread over him, he saw a star; and he exclaimed: "This is my Lord, (is it)?" But when it set (sank from sight), he said: "I love not the things that set."[17]

77. And when (on another night), he beheld the full moon rising in splendor, he said: "This is my Lord, (is it)?" But when it set, he said: "Unless my Lord guided me, I would surely be among the people gone astray."

78. Then, when he beheld the sun rising in all its splendor, he said: "This is my Lord, (is it)? This one is the greatest of all!"[18] But when it set, he said: "O my people! Surely I am free from your association of partners with God and from whatever you associate with Him as partners."

79. "I have turned my face (my whole being) with pure faith and submission to the One Who has originated the heavens and the earth each with particular features, and I am not one of those associating partners with God."[19]

80. His people set out to remonstrate with him. Abraham said: "Do you remonstrate with me concerning God, when He has guided me? I do not fear those that you associate with Him as partners (and that cannot even benefit or harm themselves, so what do I have to fear of your threats?). Whatever my Lord wills happens, and no evil befalls me unless He so wills. My Lord embraces all things in His Knowledge. Will you not, then, reflect and take heed?

81. "And how should I fear those that you associate with God as partners when you do not fear to associate partners with Him without His having sent down on you any authority (to do so)? (Tell me,) then, which of the two parties has right to feel secure, if you have anything of knowledge?

16. The nation that Abraham was sent to as a Messenger was that of the ancient Chaldeans, who lived in modern day Iraq. Abraham began his mission in Ur, the capital of the state and located in southern Iraq, in around 2100 BC. The founder of the ruling dynasty was Ur-Nammu, who established a vast kingdom that stretched from Susa in the east, to Lebanon in the west, and which extended a little beyond the boundaries of modern day Iraq to the north. This dynasty was called Nammu, becoming Nimrud in Arabic.

It was estimated that between 250,000 and 500,000 people lived in Ur at that time. The majority of these people were merchants and craftsmen; these people had a purely materialistic outlook on life. They were comprised of three classes: (1) the priests and government and military officers; (2) the merchants, craftsmen, and farmers; and (3) slaves. Abraham's family belonged to the first class and his father had a high position in the government.

The people worshipped about 5,000 deities. The chief deity of Ur was Nannar (the moon god). The idol carved in its image was kept in a palace-like building. Every night a female worshipper went to the bedroom of the god, adorned as a bride. A great number of women were consecrated in the name of this deity; they were considered as a means to salvation, and it was generally the priests who made most use of this institution.

The other major city was Larsa, which later replaced Ur as the capital. Its chief deity was Shamash (the sun deity). Under these major deities there was a myriad of minor deities; these were generally chosen from among the heavenly bodies. Polytheism in this state, as in almost all others, did not consist merely of a set of religious beliefs and polytheistic rites; it also provided the foundation on which the order of economic, cultural, social, and political life rested.

Even though we are not exactly sure of the impact of Abraham's teachings on the people and the state, after his emigration, both the ruling dynasty and the nation of Ur were subjected to a succession of disasters. First, the Elamites sacked Ur and captured Nimrud along with the idols of Nannar. Later on, an Elamite state was established in Larsa, which governed Ur as well. Later still, Babylon prospered under a dynasty of Arabian origin and both Larsa and Ur came under its dominion. The laws which were codified by the Babylonian king Hammurabi in 1910 BC. show the impression of the prophetic influence (al-Mawdūdī, 2: 246–248, note 52, from Leonard Wooley, *Abraham*, London 1935).

17. "This verse, which illustrates the decay of the universe uttered by the Prophet Abraham, made me weep. The eyes of my heart wept bitter tears for it. Each tear was so bitterly sad that it caused others to fall, as though the tears themselves were weeping. Those tears make up the lines that follow. They are like a commentary on the words of that wise Prophet of God contained in the Qur'ān:

"A beloved one who disappears is not beautiful, for one doomed to decline cannot be truly beautiful. It is not, and should not be, loved in the heart, for the heart is created for eternal love and mirrors the Eternally-Besought-of-All. A desired one doomed to disappear is unworthy of the heart's attachment or the mind's preoccupation. It cannot be the object of desire, and is unworthy of being missed. So why should the heart adore and be attached to it?

I do not seek or desire anything mortal, for I am myself mortal.

I am impotent, so I do not desire the impotent.

I surrendered my spirit to the All-Merciful One, so I desire no one else.

I want only One Who will remain my friend forever.

I am but an insignificant particle, but I desire an everlasting sun.

I am nothing in essence, but I wish for the whole of creation.

"I do not invoke or seek refuge with something that will decay, for I am infinitely needy and impotent. That which is powerless cannot cure my endless pain or solve my infinitely deep wounds. How can anything subject to decay be an object of worship? A mind obsessed with appearance wails upon seeing that which it adores begin to decay, while the spirit, which seeks an eternal beloved, also wails, saying: 'I love not the things that set.'

"I do not want or desire separation, for I cannot endure it. Meetings followed immediately by separation are not worthy of thought or longing. Just as the disappearance of pleasure is painful, imagining it is also painful. The works of lovers (poetry on metaphorical love for the opposite sex) are lamentations caused by the pain that arises from imagining this disappearance. If you condensed their spirit, this lament would flow from each. The pain coming from such meetings and painful metaphorical loves causes my heart to cry out, like Abraham: 'I love not the things that set.'

"If you desire permanence in this transient world, permanence is born out of self-annihilation. Annihilate your evil-commanding soul so that you may gain permanence. Free yourself of bad morals, the basis of worldly adoration, and realize self-annihilation. Sacrifice what is under your control in the way of the True Beloved. See the end of beings, which marks extinction. The way leading from this world to permanence passes through self-annihilation.

"The human mind, absorbed in causality, laments the upheavals caused by the world's decay. The conscience, desiring true existence, wails like Abraham: 'I love not the things that set.' It severs the connection with metaphorical lovers and decaying beings, and attaches itself to the Truly Existent One, the Eternal Beloved.

"O my base soul. This world and all beings are mortal. However, you may find two ways to the All-Permanent Being in each mortal thing, and may discern two glimpses or mysteries of the manifestations of the Undying Beloved's Grace – if you sacrifice your mortal being.

"The act of bestowing is discerned, and the All-Merciful's favor is perceived in each bounty. If you discern this act through what is bestowed, you will find the Bestower. Each work of the Eternally-Besought-of-All indicates the Names of the All-Majestic Maker, like a missive. If you understand the meaning through the inscription, the Names will lead you to the One called by those Names. If you can find the kernel, the essence, of these transient things, obtain

it. Discard their meaningless shells into the flood of mortality. Every item that exists is a word of embodied meaning and shows many of the Names of the All-Majestic Maker. Since beings are words of Divine Power, understand their meanings and place them in your heart. Fearlessly cast the letters left without meaning into the wind of transience and forget about them.

"The worldly mind, preoccupied with appearance and whose capital consists only of knowledge of the material world, cries out in bewilderment and frustration as its chains of thought end in nothingness and non-existence. It seeks a true way leading to truth. Since the heart has withdrawn from what sets and what is mortal and has abandoned the deceiving beloveds, and since the conscience has turned away from transitory beings, you, my wretched soul, must seek help in: 'I love not the things that set,' and be saved.

"See how well Mawlānā Jāmi', who was intoxicated with the "wine" of love as if created from love, expressed it:

> Want only One (the rest are not worth wanting)
> Call One (the others will not help you)
> Seek One (the others are not worth seeking)
> See and follow One (the others are not seen all the time; they become invisible behind the veil of mortality)
> Know One (knowledge other than that which adds to your knowledge of Him is useless)
> Mention One (words not concerning Him are useless).

"O Jāmi', I admit that you spoke the truth. The True Beloved, the True Sought One, the True Desired One, and the True Object of Worship is He alone. In the mighty circle of remembering and reciting God's Names, this universe and its inhabitants declare, in various tongues and tones: 'There is no deity but God,' and testify to Divine Oneness. It salves the wound caused by those that set, and points to the Undying Beloved (*The Words*, "the 17th Word," 229–231)."

18. This verse hints at an important reality through a grammatical rule which is impossible

to render in translation: The sun is a feminine word in Arabic; whereas the Prophet Abraham, upon him be peace, used a masculine pronoun when pointing to it. This means that his people, like almost all other polytheist peoples, considered their greatest deity as being male. It was pointed out in 4: 117, note 25, that whatever they may claim, in nearly all communities that reject Divine Religion in the establishment of their society, women are only objects exploited by men for their interest and tools used to satisfy their carnal desires. Men hold the sovereignty. This is because those who reject God's authority depend on and adore force and might; this is possessed and represented by men, rather than women. Therefore a (supreme) god, in such a system, cannot be seen as being female.

19. The conclusion of the verse 3: 67, *He (Abraham) was never of those who associate partners with God* removes a serious misunderstanding concerning the verses above. Unfor-tunately, some interpreters of the Qur'ān have misunderstood from the Prophet Abraham's mentioning a star, and then the moon, and then the sun, as his Lord, that he took these heavenly objects as Lord for a short time one after the other before being chosen as Prophet. Whereas the verses are explicit about the fact he made a mental and spiritual journeying in the *malakūt* (the inner dimension of existence) to have certainty of faith, not faith simply, according to his rank as one near-stationed to God. In addition, He mentioned them as his Lord also to demonstrate to his people that none of the heavenly objects could be the Lord. He openly declared before he beheld the sun and said that it was his Lord: "Unless my Lord guided me, I would surely be among the people gone astray." If he had not yet found his true Lord – God Almighty, he would not have said: "Unless my Lord guided me." And the conclusion of the verse 3: 67 quoted above explicitly states that Abraham was never of the idolaters.

الَّذِينَ ءَامَنُوا وَلَمْ يَلْبِسُوٓا إِيمَٰنَهُم بِظُلْمٍ أُوْلَٰٓئِكَ لَهُمُ ٱلْأَمْنُ وَهُم مُّهْتَدُونَ ۝ وَتِلْكَ حُجَّتُنَآ ءَاتَيْنَٰهَآ إِبْرَٰهِيمَ عَلَىٰ قَوْمِهِ نَرْفَعُ دَرَجَٰتٍ مَّن نَّشَآءُ إِنَّ رَبَّكَ حَكِيمٌ عَلِيمٌ ۝ وَوَهَبْنَا لَهُۥٓ إِسْحَٰقَ وَيَعْقُوبَ كُلًّا هَدَيْنَا وَنُوحًا هَدَيْنَا مِن قَبْلُ وَمِن ذُرِّيَّتِهِۦ دَاوُۥدَ وَسُلَيْمَٰنَ وَأَيُّوبَ وَيُوسُفَ وَمُوسَىٰ وَهَٰرُونَ وَكَذَٰلِكَ نَجْزِي ٱلْمُحْسِنِينَ ۝ وَزَكَرِيَّا وَيَحْيَىٰ وَعِيسَىٰ وَإِلْيَاسَ كُلٌّ مِّنَ ٱلصَّٰلِحِينَ ۝ وَإِسْمَٰعِيلَ وَٱلْيَسَعَ وَيُونُسَ وَلُوطًا وَكُلًّا فَضَّلْنَا عَلَى ٱلْعَٰلَمِينَ ۝ وَمِنْ ءَابَآئِهِمْ وَذُرِّيَّٰتِهِمْ وَإِخْوَٰنِهِمْ وَٱجْتَبَيْنَٰهُمْ وَهَدَيْنَٰهُمْ إِلَىٰ صِرَٰطٍ مُّسْتَقِيمٍ ۝ ذَٰلِكَ هُدَى ٱللَّهِ يَهْدِي بِهِۦ مَن يَشَآءُ مِنْ عِبَادِهِۦ وَلَوْ أَشْرَكُوا لَحَبِطَ عَنْهُم مَّا كَانُوا يَعْمَلُونَ ۝ أُوْلَٰٓئِكَ ٱلَّذِينَ ءَاتَيْنَٰهُمُ ٱلْكِتَٰبَ وَٱلْحُكْمَ وَٱلنُّبُوَّةَ فَإِن يَكْفُرْ بِهَا هَٰٓؤُلَآءِ فَقَدْ وَكَّلْنَا بِهَا قَوْمًا لَّيْسُوا بِهَا بِكَٰفِرِينَ ۝ أُوْلَٰٓئِكَ ٱلَّذِينَ هَدَى ٱللَّهُ فَبِهُدَىٰهُمُ ٱقْتَدِهْ قُل لَّآ أَسْـَٔلُكُمْ عَلَيْهِ أَجْرًا إِنْ هُوَ إِلَّا ذِكْرَىٰ لِلْعَٰلَمِينَ ۝

─────◈─────

82. "Those who have believed and not obscured their faith with any wrongdoing (of which, associating partners with God is the most grave, unforgivable kind)[20] – they are the ones for whom there is true security, and they are rightly guided."

83. That was Our argument which We granted to Abraham against his people. We raise in degrees whom We will. Your Lord is All-Wise (having many wise purposes for what He does), All-Knowing (whatever He does is based on His absolutely comprehensive Knowledge).

84. And later, We bestowed upon him (a son) Isaac and (a grandson) Jacob, and each of them We guided (and distinguished them with Prophethood). Earlier We had guided Noah (and distinguished him with Prophethood). And of Abraham's descen-

dants (We guided and distinguished with Prophethood) David and Solomon, Job, Joseph, Moses and Aaron. Thus do We reward those devoted to doing good as if seeing God.

85. And Zachariah, John, Jesus and Elijah: every one of them was of the righteous.

86. And Ishmael, Elisha, Jonah, and Lot: every one of them We favored above all other people.

87. And some from among their forefathers, and their descendants, and their brothers: We chose them and guided them to a straight path (which has characteristics particular to each according to his epoch).

88. That is God's guidance with which He guides whomever He wills of His servants.[21] And had they (the ones mentioned above) associated partners with God, then all that they did (of good and the recompense they had earned) would have gone to waste.

89. Those are the (illustrious) ones to whom We granted the Book and authority with sound, wise judgment, and Prophethood. Then if those (people of yours, O Messenger,) disbelieve in it (Our guidance which We have sent them with you), then certainly We entrust it to a people who are disbelievers in it.

90. Those are the (illustrious) ones whom God guided. Follow, then, their guidance, and say (to your people): "I ask of you no wage for it (for conveying the Message); it is but a reminder (an admonition and advice) for all created, conscious beings (humankind and the jinn)."

20. God's Messenger, upon him be peace and blessing, explained that what is meant by wrongdoing in this verse is the association of partners with God. Literally meaning not putting a thing in its place, *ẓulm* (wrongdoing) has many degrees, the worst of which is unbelief and the association of partners with God. Denying the Existence of God or associating partners with Him without having a correct judgment of Him with His Attributes and acts is the greatest error one can ever commit in life, and causes darkness upon darkness in one's heart and mind. This darkness also envelops one's whole life and causes one to always remain in darkness in the grave and in the other world.

Associating partners with God is of various kinds and degrees. Ascribing divinity or lordship with Divine functions and absolute sovereignty in the heavens and the earth, including the human realm, to others is one of the gravest forms of associating partners with God; hypocrisy, ostentation and desiring others to hear of the good things one does are also forms of associating partners with Him, especially for people who are spiritually evolved. Not aiming to obtain God's good pleasure in the thing one does in the name of religion or not doing it only because God wants it to be done, taking credit for one's abilities and accomplishments and feeling proud of them, and making use of religion for worldly purposes, such as acquiring wealth and positions and satisfying one's feeling of superiority – each of these is a kind of wrongdoing that obscures one's belief. For this reason, belief that is free from all such kinds of wrongdoing – associating partners with God – means true security for those who have it.

21. Even though Prophethood and being chosen are a special grace and favor of God which He bestows upon His servants as He wills, this does not mean that human free will has no part in it. Since God knew (beforehand) how those chosen people would act in the world and in what direction they would use their free will, He determined and decreed for them accordingly. Like all other people, the Prophets are also tested in the world; their testing is more stringent, according to the degree of each. They are not a "privileged class" of human beings in God's sight. The second part of the verse corroborates this.

138   سورة الأنعام   ١٣٨

وَمَا قَدَرُوا اللَّهَ حَقَّ قَدْرِهِ إِذْ قَالُوا مَا أَنزَلَ اللَّهُ عَلَىٰ
بَشَرٍ مِّن شَىْءٍ قُلْ مَنْ أَنزَلَ الْكِتَابَ الَّذِي جَاءَ بِهِ مُوسَىٰ نُورًا وَهُدًى
لِّلنَّاسِ تَجْعَلُونَهُ قَرَاطِيسَ تُبْدُونَهَا وَتُخْفُونَ كَثِيرًا وَعُلِّمْتُم
مَّا لَمْ تَعْلَمُوا أَنتُمْ وَلَا ءَابَاؤُكُمْ قُلِ اللَّهُ ثُمَّ ذَرْهُمْ فِي خَوْضِهِمْ
يَلْعَبُونَ ۝ وَهَٰذَا كِتَابٌ أَنزَلْنَاهُ مُبَارَكٌ مُّصَدِّقُ الَّذِي بَيْنَ
يَدَيْهِ وَلِتُنذِرَ أُمَّ الْقُرَىٰ وَمَنْ حَوْلَهَا وَالَّذِينَ يُؤْمِنُونَ بِالْآخِرَةِ
يُؤْمِنُونَ بِهِ وَهُمْ عَلَىٰ صَلَاتِهِمْ يُحَافِظُونَ ۝ وَمَنْ أَظْلَمُ
مِمَّنِ افْتَرَىٰ عَلَى اللَّهِ كَذِبًا أَوْ قَالَ أُوحِيَ إِلَيَّ وَلَمْ يُوحَ إِلَيْهِ شَىْءٌ
وَمَن قَالَ سَأُنزِلُ مِثْلَ مَا أَنزَلَ اللَّهُ وَلَوْ تَرَىٰ إِذِ الظَّالِمُونَ
فِي غَمَرَاتِ الْمَوْتِ وَالْمَلَائِكَةُ بَاسِطُوا أَيْدِيهِمْ أَخْرِجُوا أَنفُسَكُمُ
الْيَوْمَ تُجْزَوْنَ عَذَابَ الْهُونِ بِمَا كُنتُمْ تَقُولُونَ عَلَى اللَّهِ غَيْرَ
الْحَقِّ وَكُنتُمْ عَنْ ءَايَاتِهِ تَسْتَكْبِرُونَ ۝ وَلَقَدْ جِئْتُمُونَا فُرَادَىٰ
كَمَا خَلَقْنَاكُمْ أَوَّلَ مَرَّةٍ وَتَرَكْتُم مَّا خَوَّلْنَاكُمْ وَرَاءَ ظُهُورِكُمْ
وَمَا نَرَىٰ مَعَكُمْ شُفَعَاءَكُمُ الَّذِينَ زَعَمْتُمْ أَنَّهُمْ فِيكُمْ شُرَكَاؤُكُمْ
لَقَد تَّقَطَّعَ بَيْنَكُمْ وَضَلَّ عَنكُم مَّا كُنتُمْ تَزْعُمُونَ ۝

---

91. And they (some of the Jews) had no true judgment of God, such as His being God requires, when they say: "God has not sent anything down on any human being." Say: "Then, who sent down the Book which Moses brought as a light and guidance for the people (you know), and which you put into, and treat as, mere leaves of paper to make show of, while you conceal much of it, and you have been taught (by it) what neither you knew nor your forefathers?" Say: "God (sent it down)," and then leave them to their game of plunging into vanities.

92. And this (the Qur'ān) is a (Divine) Book that We send down – blessed and full of blessing, confirming (the Divine authorship of) whatever was revealed before it – so that you may warn (the people of) the Mother of Cities (Makkah) and those around it. Those who believe in the Hereafter do believe in it; and they are ever mindful guardians of their Prayers.

93. Who is more in wrong than he who fabricates falsehood in attribution to God, or says, "I receive Revelation from God," when nothing has been revealed to him, and he who claims, "I will produce the like of what God has sent down"? If you could but see how it will be when those wrongdoers find themselves in the agonies of death when the angels (appointed to take their souls), stretching forth their hands (say): "Yield up your souls! Today you will be recompensed with the punishment of ignominy for having continuously and persistently spoken about God other than the truth, and in persistent arrogance scorned His Revelations."

94. (God says:) "Now assuredly you (having died and been buried alone) have come to us quite alone, as We created you in the first instance; and you have left behind all that We bestowed upon you (in the world). And We do not see with you any of those "intercessors" (whom you associated with God as partners, and) of whom you supposed that they had shares in you (i.e. authority to order your life in certain ways). Indeed, all the bonds between you and them have now been severed, and all that you supposed (to be God's partners in your affairs) has failed you.

95. God is He Who splits the grain and the fruit-stone (so that they germinate by His command). He brings forth the living from the dead, and He is One Who brings forth the dead from the living; Such is God: how then are you turned away from the truth and make false claims?[22]

96. He it is Who splits the dawn (from the darkness of night). He has made the night for repose, and the sun and the moon a means for reckoning (the divisions of time). This is the ordaining of the All-Glorious with irresistible might, the All-Knowing.

97. He it is Who has made for you the stars (in their present conditions and positions) so that you may find your way by them in the darkness of the land and the sea. Assuredly We have set out in detail the signs and proofs (of the truth) for a people seeking knowledge.

98. He it is Who developed you from a single human self, and has appointed (in each station of your journeying from mother's womb to eternal life) for each of you a lodging-place where, and time-limit during which, you will stay and then be transferred. We have certainly set out in detail the signs and proofs (of the truth) for a people seeking to attain profound understanding.

99. He it is Who sends down water from the sky, and therewith We bring forth vegetation of every kind (from their seeds under the soil), and then from it We bring forth a lively shoot, from which We bring forth close-packed and compounded ears of grain, and from the palm-tree – from the spathe of it – dates thick-clustered hanging (ready to the hand), and gardens of vines, and the olive tree, and the pomegranate: alike (in the fundamentals of life and growth) and diverse (in structure,

look, taste, and smell). Look at their fruit, when they begin to fruit and as they ripen. Surely in that there are signs for those who will believe and who will deepen in faith (as they see new signs).

100. Yet they associate the jinn as partners with God, although He created them, and, devoid of any knowledge, they invent for Him sons and daughters. All-Glorified is He, and absolutely Exalted above what they attribute (to Him).

101. The Originator of the heavens and the earth with nothing before Him to imitate. How can He have a child, when there is for Him no consort; and He has created all things (so as the Eternal, self-existent Creator it is inconceivable for Him to have a consort and children)? And He has full knowledge of everything.

22. Life and death form a cycle. Death is an inevitable end that awaits every living being; it is a reality more manifest than life. For this reason, the verse uses the simple present tense with respect to God's bringing forth the living from the dead, which denotes repetition and renewal; it uses the present participle and noun clause with respect to His bringing forth the dead from the living, which denotes stability and constancy.

The verse also points out that living beings are in a state of death before they are brought to life. This is what the verse *How can you disbelieve in God, seeing that you were dead* (2: 28), indicates. By being brought to the worldly life, living beings attain the first life or, in other words, they are raised to life while they are dead. So life in every phase is the result of death and death is the foundation of life. Water, carbon dioxide, hydrogen and inorganic salts in soil change into organic substances forming the life-substance in plants and animals by means of sunlight, vegetation, and certain bacteria. Inorganic elements die in plants, and in animal and human bodies, and become vegetable, animal and human life respectively, and plants die in animal and human bodies to become animal and human life, and animals whose flesh is edible by human beings die in human bodies to become part of human life. This leads one to understand that human beings falling into soil like seed will wake up into a higher rank of life in another world.

Bringing forth the living from the dead and bringing forth the dead from the living is also observed in the life of the earth in the cycles of day and night, and spring and winter, and in the lives of individuals and communities. Individuals frequently change spiritual states and are guided to belief from unbelief or turn to unbelief from belief. Small seed-like communities grow into great states and civilizations, which, in time, are gradually destroyed. It is God Who causes all these to happen and the events in which human free will has a part also happen according to the (psychological, sociological, and historical) laws that God has established. Nevertheless, most people waste away in the valleys of misguidance despite this manifest reality.

102. Such is God, your Lord; there is no deity but He, the Creator of all things; therefore worship Him alone. He holds all things in His care and control.

103. Eyes comprehend Him not, but He comprehends all eyes. He is the All-Subtle (penetrating everything no matter how small), the All-Aware.[23]

104. Lights of discernment and insight have come to you from your Lord. Whoever therefore (by choosing to open the eye of his heart and place his eyes in its service) discerns, does so for his own good; and whoever chooses to be blind (to the truth), does so to his own harm. And (O Messenger, say to them): "I am not a keeper and watcher over you."

105. Thus do We set out the signs of the truth and Revelations in diverse ways, so that they (who choose blindness) say, "You have learned it (from somebody else);" this We do in order that We may make it (the truth, the Qur'ān) clear to a people seeking knowledge.

106. Follow (O Messenger) what has been revealed to you from your Lord; there is no deity but He; and withdraw from those who associate partners with God (do not care what they say and do).

107. Yet if God had so willed (and not enabled their free choice), they would not have associated partners with Him, (so do not torment yourself to death with grief because they do not believe). And We have not made you a keeper over them, and you are not one charged with care and control of them.

108. And do not (O believers) revile the things or beings that they have, apart from God, deified and invoke, lest (if you do so) they attempt to revile God out of spite and in ignorance. Thus have We made their deeds seem fair to every people;[24] then to their (true) Lord is the return of all of

them, and He will make them understand what they were doing (and call them to account for it).

109. They swear by God with their most solemn oaths that if a miracle (of the kind they desire) is shown to them, they will believe in it. Say: "Miracles are in God's power alone (His is the sole authority to produce them or not)." (O believers, who think that if such a miracle were produced, the unbelievers would believe:) Are you not aware that even if such a miracle were shown to them, they would not believe?

110. Just as they did not believe in it before (despite many evidences sufficient to convince one who really means to believe), and (because of their attitudes preventing them from belief,) We confound their hearts and eyes, and leave them blindly wandering in their rebellion.

23. Based on this verse, the Mu'tazilah, the Shī'ah, and some others who trust in their reason have claimed that God will not be seen in the Hereafter. Yet, this verse states that God is not a 'body' whom people are able to see, to comprehend, with their eyes, and relates God's comprehending all eyes not to His being the All-Seeing (Al-Basīr) but to His being the All-Subtle penetrating everything no matter how small (Al-Laṭīf), and to His being the All-Aware (Al-Khabīr). So God is beyond all physical conceptions and people can only "see" Him, have knowledge of Him, with the "eye of the heart" or with insight and through knowledge.

Secondly, it is clear that seeing in the Hereafter will not be the same as seeing here in this world. It is not the eyes which see, even in this world, and how we see is still not fully understood by science. Seeing means comprehending something with its outer dimensions, and it is neither the eyes nor the brain which comprehends this. Eyes are totally blind to the inner dimension of existence. Yet, eyes can serve for penetrating the inner dimension of existence if the spirit or heart, which is what truly "sees,"

can be refined and acquire sufficient keenness. However, when people die, the veil preventing them from seeing the metaphysical dimension of existence is removed and people will acquire in the Hereafter a keen sight and the ability to penetrate beyond the obvious. Believers will observe God beyond all qualitative and quantitative conceptions with their eyes, which will be equipped with the required ability according to the conditions of the Hereafter; they will observe God to the extent of their insight and knowledge of Him that they have obtained in this world and as a reward of this insight and knowledge. However, this does mean that they will comprehend or encompass God with their eyes. God, being all infinite, is exalted above comprehension or encompassing.

As with the verse, *Indeed it is not the eyes that have become blind, it is rather the hearts in the breasts that are blind* (22: 46), the following verse illustrates the same truth dealt with here.

24. That is, it is in the nature of human to see their beliefs and deeds as good, even as the best and the only true ones.

111. Even if We were to send down angels to them (whenever they wished it), and the dead were to speak to them, and We were to assemble before them, face to face, all the creatures (to bear witness to the truth of the Message you bring), they would still not believe, unless God so willed (and came to their aid out of His pure grace); but most of them are ignorant (they pursue worldly pleasures completely unaware of faith and mindless of their own selves).

112. And thus it is that (as a dimension of human earthly life taking place according to Our eternal Will embracing human free will, and according to the wisdom in sending the Religion) We have set against every Prophet a hostile opposition from among the satans of humankind and the jinn, whispering and suggesting to one another specious words, by way of delusion. Yet had your Lord willed (and compelled everybody to behave in the way He wills), they would not do it. So leave them alone with what they have been fabricating.

113. And the hearts of those who do not believe in the Hereafter incline towards it (their deluding speech) and take pleasure in it, and they continue perpetrating the evils that they have long been perpetrating.

114. (Say to them, O Messenger:) "What! shall I seek other than God for judge (to settle the matters between you and me), when it is He Who has sent down to you this (unique, most perfect) Book (in which truth and falsehood, right and wrong are) fully distinguished?" (The scholars among) those to whom We gave the Book before know that it is one being sent down in parts in truth by your Lord. So never be among the doubters (concerning the truth of your way).

115. The Word of your Lord (which He sent down in parts in different periods considering the conditions of each period) is perfected (with the Qur'ān) as the embodiment of truth (with respect to the essentials of faith, principles of worship and good conduct, the rules to govern human life, and all the tidings it gives considering the past and future including the Hereafter), and of justice (regarding all the commandments it contains): there is no altering of His words (the laws He has established for life and the operation of the universe; attempting to interfere with them will bring about great disasters, so no one must ever attempt to change His commandments, which are contained in the Book). He is the All-Hearing, the All-Knowing (Who knows every need of every creature, every requirement of every age, just as He knows how you respond to His commandments).

116. And if you pay heed to the majority of those on the earth, they will lead you astray from God's way. They follow only conjecture (not knowledge), and they themselves do nothing but make guesses (they pronounce and act according to their fancies, selfish interests, and personal value judgments).

117. Indeed your Lord is He Who knows best who goes astray from His way, and He knows best (those who are) the rightly-guided.

118. Eat, then, of (the flesh of) that over which God's Name has been pronounced, if you are sincere believers in His Revelations.

وَمَا لَكُمْ اَلَّا تَأْكُلُوا مِمَّا ذُكِرَ اسْمُ اللهِ عَلَيْهِ وَقَدْ فَصَّلَ
لَكُمْ مَّا حَرَّمَ عَلَيْكُمْ اِلَّا مَا اضْطُرِرْتُمْ اِلَيْهِ ؕ وَاِنَّ كَثِيْرًا
لَّيُضِلُّوْنَ بِاَهْوَآئِهِمْ بِغَيْرِ عِلْمٍ ؕ اِنَّ رَبَّكَ هُوَ اَعْلَمُ بِالْمُعْتَدِيْنَ
۝ وَذَرُوْا ظَاهِرَ الْاِثْمِ وَبَاطِنَهٗ ؕ اِنَّ الَّذِيْنَ يَكْسِبُوْنَ الْاِثْمَ
سَيُجْزَوْنَ بِمَا كَانُوْا يَقْتَرِفُوْنَ ۝ وَلَا تَأْكُلُوْا مِمَّا لَمْ يُذْكَرِ اسْمُ
اللهِ عَلَيْهِ وَاِنَّهٗ لَفِسْقٌ ؕ وَاِنَّ الشَّيَاطِيْنَ لَيُوْحُوْنَ اِلٰٓى
اَوْلِيَآئِهِمْ لِيُجَادِلُوْكُمْ ۚ وَاِنْ اَطَعْتُمُوْهُمْ اِنَّكُمْ لَمُشْرِكُوْنَ
۝ اَوَمَنْ كَانَ مَيْتًا فَاَحْيَيْنَاهُ وَجَعَلْنَا لَهٗ نُوْرًا يَّمْشِيْ بِهٖ
فِى النَّاسِ كَمَنْ مَّثَلُهٗ فِى الظُّلُمَاتِ لَيْسَ بِخَارِجٍ مِّنْهَا ؕ
كَذٰلِكَ زُيِّنَ لِلْكَافِرِيْنَ مَا كَانُوْا يَعْمَلُوْنَ ۝ وَكَذٰلِكَ
جَعَلْنَا فِى كُلِّ قَرْيَةٍ اَكَابِرَ مُجْرِمِيْهَا لِيَمْكُرُوْا فِيْهَا ؕ
وَمَا يَمْكُرُوْنَ اِلَّا بِاَنْفُسِهِمْ وَمَا يَشْعُرُوْنَ ۝ وَاِذَا
جَآءَتْهُمْ اٰيَةٌ قَالُوْا لَنْ نُّؤْمِنَ حَتّٰى نُؤْتٰى مِثْلَ مَا اُوْتِيَ رُسُلُ
اللهِ ؕ اَللهُ اَعْلَمُ حَيْثُ يَجْعَلُ رِسَالَتَهٗ ؕ سَيُصِيْبُ الَّذِيْنَ اَجْرَمُوْا صَغَارٌ
عِنْدَ اللهِ وَعَذَابٌ شَدِيْدٌ ؕ بِمَا كَانُوْا يَمْكُرُوْنَ ۝

---

119. And why should you not eat of (the flesh of) that over which God's Name has been pronounced, seeing that He has clearly spelled out to you what He has made unlawful to you unless you are constrained to it by dire necessity?[25] But, indeed many people lead others astray, driven by their lusts and fancies without any knowledge (from God). Indeed your Lord is He Who knows best those who exceed the bounds.

120. Abstain from sinning, whether done in public or secret, (and the intentions and attitudes that accompany either). Indeed, those who record sins to their account will be recompensed for what they have earned.

121. And do not eat of that which is slaughtered in the name of other than God and over which God's Name has not been pronounced (at the time of its slaughtering), for that is indeed a transgression. And the satans do whisper and make suggestions to their confidants to contend with you. If you obey them, you are indeed those who associate partners with God.[26]

122. Is he who was dead (in spirit), and We raised him to life and set for him a light by which he moves (without any

deviancy) among people, (is then he) like the one who is as one lost in depths of darkness, from which he cannot get out? (But) thus it is: to the unbelievers are the things they have been doing decked out to be appealing.

123. And in that way have We set up in every township as leaders its most prominent criminals so that they scheme (against the believers). But they scheme only against their own selves – and they do not perceive it.

124. When a Revelation is conveyed to them, they say: "We will not believe unless we are given the like of what God's Messengers were given." God knows best upon whom to place His Message. Soon will an abasement from God's Presence befall these criminals and a severe punishment for their scheming.

25. In order to emphasize the sensitivity which people should have in eating and drinking, the Qur'ān refers to these activities after it has stressed the importance of accepting and obeying God's commandments. This is because people are easily lost to their carnal desires and act carelessly in the matter of eating and drinking. Also, many nations have imposed on themselves superfluous religious rules in this matter. If left to their own judgment, every people, or those with authority, will make some things lawful and others unlawful, according to their caprices and own interests. In addition, eating and drinking have an important place in one's personal, social, and spiritual life.

26. As in the part of verse 112 above, *We have set against every Prophet a hostile opposition from among the satans of humankind and the jinn, whispering and suggesting to one another specious words, by way of delusion,* in this verse, too, the Qur'ān refers to satans and their whispering and suggestions to their confidants. This reference is especially significant on two points and contains an important warning to the believers of every age:

There has been and will always be a group composed of the satans of the jinn and some people who are opposed to Islam and its message being conveyed; these people are open to the suggestions of the satans, and they have been like Satan in their opposition to Islam and in the evils that they have committed. The struggle on the earth is between humankind and Satan, and some people are deluded by Satan and his agents, unfortunately becoming like Satan in their enmity towards God and His Religion.

This group frequently holds meetings in secret places (also see: 2: 14) and decide on new methods and ways to struggle against Islam and Muslims, and suggest them to the men they employ in this struggle. What Muslims must do is to know such people well, be on the alert against their tricks and intrigues, and to never obey them. Such people will always try to make Muslims to fall back and turn away from Islam, and those who make "idols" out of their carnal desires, personal interests, fondness for posts and fame, ostentation, some systems or ideologies, and certain other people will follow and obey them. Their doing so means associating partners with God.

125. Thus, whomever God wills to guide, He expands his breast to Islam, and whomever He wills to lead astray, He causes his breast to become tight and constricted, as if he were climbing towards the heaven.[27] Thus God lays ignominy upon those who do not believe (despite many signs and evidences).

126. And this (the way of Islam) is the Straight Path of your Lord. We have assuredly set out in detail the signs (of the right and wrong ways) for a people who reflect and are mindful.

127. For them is the Abode of Peace with their Lord (where they will enjoy perfect bliss, peace, and safety), and He is their Guardian because of what they have been doing.

128. On the Day when He will raise to life and gather them (the jinn and humankind, believers and unbelievers) all together, (He says): "O you assembly of the jinn! You have seduced a good many of humankind (and included them in your company)." Their closest fellows from among humankind will (confess and) say: "Our Lord! We enjoyed one another (in self-interested fellowship, serving one another's selfish ends), and now we have reached the end of our term that You appointed for us." He (God) will say: "The Fire is now your dwelling to abide therein – God decrees however He wills." Indeed your Lord is All-Wise, All-Knowing (Whose every decree and act are based on absolute wisdom and knowledge).

129. In this manner We cause the wrongdoers to befriend and help one another (with seduction and sinning) because of what they are engaged in earning.

130. "O assembly of the jinn and human-kind! Did there never come to you Messengers from among yourselves, relating to you My signs and Revelations, and warning you of encountering this Day of yours?" They say: "We bear witness against ourselves." The life of the world had deluded them, and (just as their speeches and actions in the world testified to their unbelief, so) they have borne witness against themselves that they were unbelievers.

131. Clearly it is not the way of your Lord that He would destroy lands unjustly without their people being warned (beforehand of the consequence of their way of life) and therefore unmindful (of the distinctions between right and wrong, truth and falsehood).

---

27. It is possible to see here a Qur'ānic miracle concerning scientific developments. As we now know, as we ascend a mountain, or go up in the air, the amount of oxygen diminishes, the air pressure decreases, and breathing becomes impossible without special equipment.

The Qur'ān describes the state of one who feels depressed in the face of Islam and insists on not believing in it, despite many signs and all the evidence that they see, in the terms of a physical fact, thus alluding to a scientific fact which would be discovered centuries later.

144   سُوْرَةُ الْأَنْعَامِ   ١٤٤

وَلِكُلٍّ دَرَجَاتٌ مِّمَّا عَمِلُوْا ۚ وَمَا رَبُّكَ بِغَافِلٍ عَمَّا
يَعْمَلُوْنَ ۞ وَرَبُّكَ الْغَنِيُّ ذُو الرَّحْمَةِ ۚ اِنْ يَّشَأْ
يُذْهِبْكُمْ وَيَسْتَخْلِفْ مِنْ بَعْدِكُمْ مَّا يَشَاءُ
كَمَا أَنْشَأَكُمْ مِّنْ ذُرِّيَّةِ قَوْمٍ اٰخَرِيْنَ ۞ اِنَّ
مَا تُوْعَدُوْنَ لَاٰتٍ ۚ وَمَا أَنْتُمْ بِمُعْجِزِيْنَ ۞ قُلْ يَا قَوْمِ
اعْمَلُوْا عَلٰى مَكَانَتِكُمْ اِنِّيْ عَامِلٌ ۚ فَسَوْفَ تَعْلَمُوْنَ
مَنْ تَكُوْنُ لَهُ عَاقِبَةُ الدَّارِ ۚ اِنَّهُ لَا يُفْلِحُ الظَّالِمُوْنَ
۞ وَجَعَلُوْا لِلّٰهِ مِمَّا ذَرَأَ مِنَ الْحَرْثِ وَالْأَنْعَامِ نَصِيْبًا
فَقَالُوْا هٰذَا لِلّٰهِ بِزَعْمِهِمْ وَهٰذَا لِشُرَكَائِنَا
فَمَا كَانَ لِشُرَكَائِهِمْ فَلَا يَصِلُ اِلَى اللّٰهِ ۚ وَمَا كَانَ
لِلّٰهِ فَهُوَ يَصِلُ اِلٰى شُرَكَائِهِمْ ۚ سَاءَ مَا
يَحْكُمُوْنَ ۞ وَكَذٰلِكَ زَيَّنَ لِكَثِيْرٍ مِّنَ
الْمُشْرِكِيْنَ قَتْلَ أَوْلَادِهِمْ شُرَكَاؤُهُمْ
لِيُرْدُوْهُمْ وَلِيَلْبِسُوْا عَلَيْهِمْ دِيْنَهُمْ ۚ وَلَوْ شَاءَ
اللّٰهُ مَا فَعَلُوْهُ ۖ فَذَرْهُمْ وَمَا يَفْتَرُوْنَ ۞

─────※─────

132. For everyone there are (different) ranks according to what they have done (of right and wrong). Your Lord is not unmindful of what they do.[28]

133. Your Lord, having boundless, all-encompassing mercy, is the All-Wealthy and Self- Sufficient (with no need of any kind, including His servants' belief and worship). If He so wills, He can put you away and cause whom He wills to succeed you just as He produced you from the seed of another people.

134. What you have been promised (and warned of, concerning your future and the Hereafter), is indeed bound to happen, and you have no power at all to frustrate it.

135. Say: "O my people! Do all that lies within your power, indeed I (too) am at work (doing my task). So in time you will come to know to whom the ultimate abode of happiness will belong. Indeed the wrong-doers do not prosper and attain their goals.

136. They assign to God, of the produce and cattle that He has created, a portion, and they say: "This is God's" – so they assert – "and this (the rest) is for our associate-deities." Then (acting in what they deem to their own interest), what is assigned for their "associate-deities" does not reach God, while what is assigned for God reaches their "associate-deities." How evil is what they ordain as laws (and how badly they enforce them)!

137. And, in the way they follow, their associate-deities (their association of partners with God or their idol-worshipping, and satans of the jinn and humankind they obey,) deck out the killing of their children to be appealing to many among those who associate partners with God, so as to bring them to ruin and confound them in their religion. If God had so willed (if He had not decreed freedom of will to humankind, thus compelling them to act in a particular way like other beings), they would not be doing all this. So, leave them alone with what they have been fabricating.

───────────────────

28. *For everyone there are (different) ranks according to what they have done (of right and wrong)*, means that people are not of the same rank. People differ in rank from one another according to whether they are believers, unbelievers, hypocrites, believers but sinful, or unbelievers who are actively fighting against belief and

truth, etc. This also means that not everybody will have the same reward for the same actions. The reward for an action differs according to how it is done, the intention of doing it, the degree of sincerity in doing it, the time when and the conditions where it is done, the care shown in doing it, and similar other factors.

وَقَالُوا هَـٰذِهِۦٓ أَنْعَامٌ وَحَرْثٌ حِجْرٌ لَّا يَطْعَمُهَآ إِلَّا مَن
نَّشَآءُ بِزَعْمِهِمْ وَأَنْعَامٌ حُرِّمَتْ ظُهُورُهَا وَأَنْعَامٌ لَّا
يَذْكُرُونَ اسْمَ اللَّهِ عَلَيْهَا ٱفْتِرَآءً عَلَيْهِ ۚ سَيَجْزِيهِم بِمَا
كَانُوا۟ يَفْتَرُونَ ۝ وَقَالُوا۟ مَا فِى بُطُونِ هَـٰذِهِ ٱلْأَنْعَـٰمِ
خَالِصَةٌ لِّذُكُورِنَا وَمُحَرَّمٌ عَلَىٰٓ أَزْوَٰجِنَا ۖ وَإِن يَكُن
مَّيْتَةً فَهُمْ فِيهِ شُرَكَآءُ ۚ سَيَجْزِيهِمْ وَصْفَهُمْ
إِنَّهُ حَكِيمٌ عَلِيمٌ ۝ قَدْ خَسِرَ ٱلَّذِينَ قَتَلُوٓا۟
أَوْلَـٰدَهُمْ سَفَهًۢا بِغَيْرِ عِلْمٍ وَحَرَّمُوا۟ مَا رَزَقَهُمُ ٱللَّهُ
ٱفْتِرَآءً عَلَى ٱللَّهِ ۚ قَدْ ضَلُّوا۟ وَمَا كَانُوا۟ مُهْتَدِينَ ۝
وَهُوَ ٱلَّذِىٓ أَنشَأَ جَنَّـٰتٍ مَّعْرُوشَـٰتٍ وَغَيْرَ مَعْرُوشَـٰتٍ
وَٱلنَّخْلَ وَٱلزَّرْعَ مُخْتَلِفًا أُكُلُهُۥ وَٱلزَّيْتُونَ وَٱلرُّمَّانَ
مُتَشَـٰبِهًا وَغَيْرَ مُتَشَـٰبِهٍ ۚ كُلُوا۟ مِن ثَمَرِهِۦٓ إِذَآ أَثْمَرَ وَءَاتُوا۟
حَقَّهُۥ يَوْمَ حَصَادِهِۦ ۖ وَلَا تُسْرِفُوٓا۟ ۚ إِنَّهُۥ لَا يُحِبُّ ٱلْمُسْرِفِينَ ۝
وَمِنَ ٱلْأَنْعَـٰمِ حَمُولَةً وَفَرْشًا ۚ كُلُوا۟ مِمَّا رَزَقَكُمُ ٱللَّهُ
وَلَا تَتَّبِعُوا۟ خُطُوَٰتِ ٱلشَّيْطَـٰنِ ۚ إِنَّهُۥ لَكُمْ عَدُوٌّ مُّبِينٌ ۝

138. (Putting some of the produce and cattle to one side,) they say: "These animals and crops are taboo; none can eat of them save those whom we will – so they assert – and there are cattle whose backs they declare are forbidden (to bear loads), and cattle over which they do not pronounce God's Name. (Their attributing these customs to God) is a lie against Him. He will soon recompense them for all that they fabricate in attribution to God.[29]

139. They also say (concerning certain other cattle they consecrate): "All that is in the wombs of these cattle is (if they are born alive) exclusively for our males and is unlawful for our wives. If it (the newborn) is born dead or dies soon after birth, all of them (men and women) may share therein." He will soon recompense them for their attributing (these rules falsely to Him). Surely He is All-Wise (in Whose every act and commandment are many instances of wisdom), All-Knowing (whose every act is based on absolute knowledge).[30]

140. Assuredly those are lost who, in folly and without knowledge, kill their children (either in the wombs of their mothers or after birth), and make unlawful (the lawful and pure, wholesome things) that God has provided them as sustenance, falsely attributing that to God. Assuredly they have gone astray, and have never been able to find the right way.

141. (Ever providing you with lawful, pure, and wholesome food), He it is Who produces gardens (and vineyards, and orchards) trellised and untrellised, and date-palms, and crops varying in taste, and olives, and pomegranates, resembling one another and yet so different. Eat of their fruits when they come to fruition, and give (to the poor and the needy) the due thereof on harvest day. And do not be wasteful (by over-eating or other unnecessary consumption, or by giving to others so much as to leave in need those whose maintenance is your responsibility); indeed He does not love the wasteful.

142. And of the cattle (He has created) some for carrying loads, and some for the sake of their flesh, and skins and fur. Consume from what God has provided for you as sustenance, and do not follow in the footsteps of Satan (by laying down rules other than those of God and adopting ways other than God's); surely he is a manifest enemy to you.

29. Just as the recompense or punishment mentioned can come in the Hereafter, it may also come in this world. This can be understood from the fact that the verse uses a tense that indicates the near future. Those who make false attributions to God or fabrications may lose their dominion, positions, wealth, even their lives or they may be subject to certain natural-seeming calamities or their system may be replaced by a new one. Muslims have been suffering the same punishment for their neglect in practicing Islam and for not paying due respect to it.

30. For a sound state, based on law and which is truly accepted by its people, the principles of wisdom, the laws of the government, the rules of right, and the directives of power should all be in accord with and support one another. Otherwise, no one thing could be influential on the people by itself and it would not be possible to talk of a state of law that is approved of by people nor of solidarity between them.

بِسْمِ

143. Eight in pairs of cattle: two of sheep, two of goats. Say (to them, O Messenger): "Is it the two males that God has made unlawful or the two females, or what the wombs of the two females may contain? Inform me about this with sound, authoritative knowledge, if you are truthful (in your claim that God has made them unlawful)."

144. And likewise of camels there are two, and of oxen there are two. Say: "Is it the two males that God has made unlawful or the two females, or what the wombs of the two females may contain? Or were you present there to witness when God laid down this (the commandment you attribute to Him) for you?" Who is more in wrong than he who fabricates falsehood in attribution to God, and thus leads people astray without sound, authoritative knowledge? Indeed, God does not guide wrongdoing people (to the truth and the attainment of their goals).

145. Say (O Messenger): "I do not find in what has been revealed to me anything made unlawful to one who would eat except it be carrion or blood outpoured (not that which is left in the veins of such organs as the liver and spleen), or the flesh of swine, which is loathsome and unclean, or that which is profane having been slaughtered in the name of other than God (or without pronouncing God's Name over it).[31] Yet whoever is constrained by dire necessity (to eat thereof) provided he does not covet nor exceed the bounds (of the necessity): (no sin shall be on him). Your Lord is indeed All-Forgiving, All-Compassionate.

146. And for those who are Jews We have made unlawful all beasts with claws, and of oxen and sheep We have made unlawful for them their fat, save that which is in their backs or entrails or that which is mixed with the bone. Thus did We recompense them for their continuous rebellion.[32] And We are indeed true (in all Our decrees and deeds).

31. When this verse is considered alongside those of 2: 173, 5: 3, and 16: 115, it will be seen that they elucidate each other, and there are no differences between them in declaring the things that are unlawful to eat. For example, the flesh of the animals that is mentioned in 5: 3 along with their ways of dying or being killed that are forbidden is included in carrion.

The animals or kinds of meat that are forbidden are not only these. The forbidden things mentioned in these two verses pertain only to domestic animals – sheep and cattle. Based on the Revelation, God's Messenger informed us of the other animals that we are forbidden to eat. They can be found in the relevant books of Islamic law. Also see 22: 30, note 9.

32. The Qur'an is a miracle of eloquence throughout. Seeing that this verse begins with the phrase "to those who are (had become) Jews," it can be understood that the commandment mentioned was in the nature of recompense. For the Jews mentioned deviated from their way and made several things unlawful for themselves, and as a punishment God allowed these to remain unlawful. (See also 4: 160; 3: 93). These include birds with claws, such as the ostrich, seagull and water-hen, and also the fat of oxen and sheep. Prohibitions of these kinds have been interpolated among the injunctions of the Torah (See *Leviticus*, 3: 17, 22–3; 11: 16–18; *Deuteronomy*, 14: 14–16). This point can be considered as being the same as that which was explained in the note 26 above.

فَإِنْ كَذَّبُوكَ فَقُل رَّبُّكُمْ ذُو رَحْمَةٍ وَاسِعَةٍ وَلَا يُرَدُّ بَأْسُهُ عَنِ الْقَوْمِ الْمُجْرِمِينَ ۝ سَيَقُولُ الَّذِينَ أَشْرَكُوا لَوْ شَاءَ اللَّهُ مَا أَشْرَكْنَا وَلَا آبَاؤُنَا وَلَا حَرَّمْنَا مِن شَيْءٍ كَذَلِكَ كَذَّبَ الَّذِينَ مِن قَبْلِهِمْ حَتَّىٰ ذَاقُوا بَأْسَنَا قُلْ هَلْ عِندَكُم مِّنْ عِلْمٍ فَتُخْرِجُوهُ لَنَا إِن تَتَّبِعُونَ إِلَّا الظَّنَّ وَإِنْ أَنتُمْ إِلَّا تَخْرُصُونَ ۝ قُلْ فَلِلَّهِ الْحُجَّةُ الْبَالِغَةُ فَلَوْ شَاءَ لَهَدَاكُمْ أَجْمَعِينَ ۝ قُلْ هَلُمَّ شُهَدَاءَكُمُ الَّذِينَ يَشْهَدُونَ أَنَّ اللَّهَ حَرَّمَ هَٰذَا فَإِن شَهِدُوا فَلَا تَشْهَدْ مَعَهُمْ وَلَا تَتَّبِعْ أَهْوَاءَ الَّذِينَ كَذَّبُوا بِآيَاتِنَا وَالَّذِينَ لَا يُؤْمِنُونَ بِالْآخِرَةِ وَهُم بِرَبِّهِمْ يَعْدِلُونَ ۝ قُلْ تَعَالَوْا أَتْلُ مَا حَرَّمَ رَبُّكُمْ عَلَيْكُمْ أَلَّا تُشْرِكُوا بِهِ شَيْئًا وَبِالْوَالِدَيْنِ إِحْسَانًا وَلَا تَقْتُلُوا أَوْلَادَكُم مِّنْ إِمْلَاقٍ نَّحْنُ نَرْزُقُكُمْ وَإِيَّاهُمْ وَلَا تَقْرَبُوا الْفَوَاحِشَ مَا ظَهَرَ مِنْهَا وَمَا بَطَنَ وَلَا تَقْتُلُوا النَّفْسَ الَّتِي حَرَّمَ اللَّهُ إِلَّا بِالْحَقِّ ذَٰلِكُمْ وَصَّاكُم بِهِ لَعَلَّكُمْ تَعْقِلُونَ ۝

147. Then, if they still deny you (O Messenger), say to them: "Your Lord (Who creates, nourishes, and provides you,) has an all-embracing mercy (and so does not immediately punish you for your acts of insolence but gives you respite so that you may repent and ask Him for forgiveness). However, (if you do not mend your ways, know that) His punishment cannot be averted from disbelieving criminals.

148. Those who persist in associating partners with God will say: "Had God willed, neither we nor our forefathers would have associated partners with Him, nor would we have declared anything (which God has made lawful) unlawful." Even so did those who lived before them deny (their Prophets with similar false excuses) until they tasted Our mighty punishment. Say (to them): "Do you have any sound, authoritative knowledge (to support your claim)? (If you have) then bring it out for us! In fact you follow only conjecture, and you yourselves are only making false surmises (you pronounce judgments and act only according to your fancies, interests and personal value judgments)."

149. Say: "(As against what you argue) God's is the final, conclusive argument. And had He so willed (and compelled you act in a certain way, rather than letting you associate partners with Him and make unlawful what He has made lawful), He would have guided you all together to the truth.[33]

150. Say: "Bring forward your witnesses who could testify that God has made unlawful (what you claim to be forbidden.)" Then if they bear witness (falsely), do not bear witness with them, and do not follow the lusts and fancies of those who deny Our signs and Revelations, who do not believe in the Hereafter, and who (as the main source of their unbelief in other essentials of faith) ascribe equals to their Lord.[34]

151. Say: "Come, let me recite what your Lord has made unlawful for you: that you associate nothing with Him; and (do not offend against but, rather) treat your parents in the best way possible; and that you do not kill your children for fear of poverty – it is We Who provide for you as well as for them; and that you do not draw near to any shameful thing (like adultery, fornication, and homosexuality), whether committed openly or secretly; and that you do not kill any soul, which God has made sacred and forbidden, except in just cause. All this He has enjoined upon you, that you may reason (and so believe, know right from wrong, and follow His way).

33. God presents signs and evidence of the truth so clearly that human reason and conscience cannot help but confess the truth of the essentials of faith, in particular that of God's Existence and Unity, but He never compels people to believe. He leaves the choice to believe or not to believe up to human free will.

34. Each essential of faith demands the existence of the others. One who believes in God should believe in Messengership, for Divine Lordship requires Messengership to make Itself known and to convey Its demands to conscious beings. Messengership cannot be conceived of without Books, which cannot be thought of without the mediation of angels which bring them to the Messengers. The Divine Names, such as the All-Compassionate, the Lord (One Who creates, sustains, and brings up), the All-Just, the All-Munificent, the All-Generous, the All-Gracious, the All-Beautiful, and the All-Recording and Preserving require the Hereafter. For absolute beauty and perfection are loved. The One Who creates all-beautifully and Who does best whatever He does, makes Himself known and loved more perfectly in the eternal world, not in this fleeting world where His beauties are manifested behind many veils. This perfect Tree of Creation, which has been created in order to yield humanity as its final fruit, cannot be confined to this transient life, for otherwise many things in it would be in vain and a waste, whereas God is absolutely free from doing anything in vain. We see that in the world full justice cannot be established in many cases – oppressors die without suffering the necessary punishment, with many oppressed people leaving the world without having their rights restored. God is absolutely Just, and this requires absolute justice, which in turn demands another world where it will be realized. The seeds of plants and trees are a way for us to see that everything is recorded, as within them is encapsulated the whole life-history of the plants and trees; human memory also shows us that everything is recorded. Human beings have not been sent to this world for no purpose and they have not been left to their own devices. The faculties with which they have been equipped, such as reason, spirit, will-power, and the senses and feelings, demonstrate that humanity has an important duty in life. This is why all the deeds and sayings of humanity are recorded along with the intentions and the degree of sincerity in performing the action and in saying it; the consequences of these will become apparent in another, eternal world. Like all these, the perfect order and magnificent accord in the universe display an all-encompassing knowledge and a perfect plan made by that knowledge. Every thing or being is clothed with a body particular to itself, which is appropriate to its duties or functions in life. In addition, almost every human being has a dream of some future events. All these show that there is a Divine determination, which we call Destiny. To conclude, belief in God requires other essentials of faith, and these require one another.

152. "And do not draw near to the property of the orphan except in the best way (such as to improve and increase it) until he comes of age. Weigh and balance with full measure and equity." We do not burden any soul beyond its capacity. "And when you speak, be just, even though it be against one near of kin; and fulfill God's covenant (and the covenants you make with one another in God's Name). All this He has enjoined upon you, that you may reflect and be mindful.

153. "This is my straight path, so follow it, and do not follow other paths, lest they scatter you from His Path. This He has enjoined upon you, that you keep from disobedience to Him in reverence for Him and piety to deserve His protection."

154. And once again: We gave Moses the Book, completing Our favor upon those devoted to doing good deeds in the awareness that God sees them, and detailing everything (concerning truth and falsehood, and right and wrong), and as a guidance and mercy, that they may have ever-deepening faith in the (final) meeting with their Lord.

155. And likewise, this (Qur'ān) is a Book We have sent down, blessed and giving blessing; so follow it and keep from disobedience to it, that you may be shown mercy (to be granted a virtuous life in this world and eternal happiness in the Hereafter).

156. (We have sent it down) lest you should say (as an excuse), "The Book was sent down only on the two groups of people before us and indeed we were unaware of what they were taught by it."

157. Or lest you should say, "Had the Book been sent down on us, we would surely have been more rightly guided than they are." Now there has come to you a manifest proof from your Lord, and a guidance, and a mercy.[35] Who, then, is more in wrong than he who denies God's Revelations and turns away from them? We will recompense those who turn away from Our Revelations with an evil punishment for turning away.

---

35. It is very interesting that in verse 154 above God mentions the Book sent to Moses, upon him be peace, as a Book *given as* a guidance and a mercy. That is, that Book *functioned* as a guidance and a mercy, and being a guidance and mercy was an attribute of it. But He mentions the Qur'ān as the Book which itself is a guidance and mercy. That is, guidance and mercy are not merely attributes of the Qur'ān, rather the Qur'ān is completely the guidance in and of itself and it is a mercy in and of itself.

١٤٩   الجُزْءُ الثَّامِنُ   149

هَلْ يَنظُرُونَ إِلَّا أَن تَأْتِيَهُمُ ٱلْمَلَٰٓئِكَةُ أَوْ يَأْتِيَ رَبُّكَ أَوْ يَأْتِيَ بَعْضُ ءَايَٰتِ رَبِّكَ يَوْمَ يَأْتِي بَعْضُ ءَايَٰتِ رَبِّكَ لَا يَنفَعُ نَفْسًا إِيمَٰنُهَا لَمْ تَكُنْ ءَامَنَتْ مِن قَبْلُ أَوْ كَسَبَتْ فِىٓ إِيمَٰنِهَا خَيْرًا قُلِ ٱنتَظِرُوٓاْ إِنَّا مُنتَظِرُونَ ۝ إِنَّ ٱلَّذِينَ فَرَّقُواْ دِينَهُمْ وَكَانُواْ شِيَعًا لَّسْتَ مِنْهُمْ فِى شَىْءٍ إِنَّمَآ أَمْرُهُمْ إِلَى ٱللَّهِ ثُمَّ يُنَبِّئُهُم بِمَا كَانُواْ يَفْعَلُونَ ۝ مَن جَآءَ بِٱلْحَسَنَةِ فَلَهُۥ عَشْرُ أَمْثَالِهَا وَمَن جَآءَ بِٱلسَّيِّئَةِ فَلَا يُجْزَىٰٓ إِلَّا مِثْلَهَا وَهُمْ لَا يُظْلَمُونَ ۝ قُلْ إِنَّنِى هَدَىٰنِى رَبِّىٓ إِلَىٰ صِرَٰطٍ مُّسْتَقِيمٍ دِينًا قِيَمًا مِّلَّةَ إِبْرَٰهِيمَ حَنِيفًا وَمَا كَانَ مِنَ ٱلْمُشْرِكِينَ ۝ قُلْ إِنَّ صَلَاتِى وَنُسُكِى وَمَحْيَاىَ وَمَمَاتِى لِلَّهِ رَبِّ ٱلْعَٰلَمِينَ ۝ لَا شَرِيكَ لَهُۥ وَبِذَٰلِكَ أُمِرْتُ وَأَنَا۠ أَوَّلُ ٱلْمُسْلِمِينَ ۝ قُلْ أَغَيْرَ ٱللَّهِ أَبْغِى رَبًّا وَهُوَ رَبُّ كُلِّ شَىْءٍ وَلَا تَكْسِبُ كُلُّ نَفْسٍ إِلَّا عَلَيْهَا وَلَا تَزِرُ وَازِرَةٌ وِزْرَ أُخْرَىٰ ثُمَّ إِلَىٰ رَبِّكُم مَّرْجِعُكُمْ فَيُنَبِّئُكُم بِمَا كُنتُمْ فِيهِ تَخْتَلِفُونَ ۝ وَهُوَ ٱلَّذِى جَعَلَكُمْ خَلَٰٓئِفَ ٱلْأَرْضِ وَرَفَعَ بَعْضَكُمْ فَوْقَ بَعْضٍ دَرَجَٰتٍ لِّيَبْلُوَكُمْ فِى مَآ ءَاتَىٰكُمْ إِنَّ رَبَّكَ سَرِيعُ ٱلْعِقَابِ وَإِنَّهُۥ لَغَفُورٌ رَّحِيمٌ ۝

———⟨❧⟩———

158. Do they wait only for the angels to come to them (to take their souls or bring them a disaster), or for your Lord to judge them (and bring forth Hell for them), or for some clear signs of your Lord to appear (such as rocks pouring down on them, which they want you to show them, or signs signaling the final destruction of the world)? When some clear signs of your Lord appear, believing will be of no avail to anyone who did not believe before, or who has earned no good through his belief. Say (to them, O Messenger): "Wait on, we too are waiting!"

159. Those who have made divisions in their Religion (whereas they must accept it in its totality), and have been divided into different parties – you have nothing to do with them. Their case rests with God, and then He will make them understand what they were doing, (and call them to account).

160. Whoever comes to God with a good deed will have ten times as much, and whoever comes with an evil deed, will be recompensed with only the like of it; and they will not be wronged.

161. Say: "Surely my Lord has guided me to a Straight Path, being an upright Religion leading to prosperity (in both worlds), the way of Abraham based on pure faith (free from unbelief, associating partners with God and hypocrisy). He was never of those associating partners with God."

162. Say: "My Prayer, and all my (other) acts and forms of devotion and worship, and my living and my dying are for God alone, the Lord of the worlds.

163. "He has no partners; thus have I been commanded, and I am the first and foremost of the Muslims (who have submitted to Him exclusively)."

164. Say: "Am I, then, to seek after someone other than God as Lord when He is the Lord of everything?" Every soul earns only to its own account; and no soul, as bearer of burden, bears and is made to bear the burden of another. Then, to your Lord is the return of all of you, and He will then make you understand (the truth) concerning all that on which you have differed.

165. He it is Who has appointed you vicegerents on the earth (to improve it and rule over it according to God's commandments), and has exalted some of you over others in degrees (of intelligence, capacity, and then wealth and status): thus He tries you in what He has granted you. (Always bear in mind that) your Lord is the most swift in retribution (when it is due), and surely He is the All-Forgiving, the All-Compassionate (especially towards those who turn to Him in repentance as His believing servants).[36]

36. Working around God's Oneness and other essentials of faith from the beginning to the end, the *sūrah* ends with the threat that God is most swift in delivering punishments and with the glad tidings that God is the All-Forgiving, the All-Compassionate (especially towards those who turn to Him in repentance and to His believing servants). However, the glad tidings come last, and His being the All-Forgiving, the All-Compassionate is stressed and confirmed. This is because God's Mercy is greater than His punishment and God has bound Himself to mercy and treating His creatures with mercy; it is also intended to encourage His servants to repent and take refuge in His Forgiveness and Mercy.

SŪRAH 7

AL-A'RĀF (THE HEIGHTS)

Makkah period

S̲ūrat al-A'rāf was revealed in Makkah and consists of 206 verses. It takes its title from the word al-a'rāf, which occurs in verses 46 and 48. Al-A'rāf is the heights between Paradise and Hell. Following Sūrat al-An'ām, which discusses the Oneness of God and other essentials of faith, this sūrah also is concerned with the same themes, as well as focusing on the basis of human nature and the lives of some of the Messengers. It concentrates on the consequences in both this and the next world of following the way of faith in God's Oneness or of following polytheism.

In the Name of God, the All-Merciful, the All-Compassionate.

1. *Alif. Lām. Mīm. Ṣād.*

2. This is a Book sent down to you (O Messenger) – so let there be no tightness in your breast in respect of it (in conveying it to people and fearing that they may not believe in it) – that thereby you may warn (people against any deviation), and as an admonition and advice to the believers.

3. Follow what has been sent down to you (O humankind) from your Lord, and, do not follow as confidants and guardians other than Him. How little you reflect and take heed!

4. How many a township We have destroyed (because they did not pay heed to Our warning). Our scourge fell upon them at night or when they were taking their ease in the noontime.

5. And there was no appeal from them when Our scourge fell upon them, except for their saying: "Indeed, we have been wrongdoers."

6. So We will surely question those to whom Messengers were sent (as to how they responded to them), and We will surely question the Messengers (concerning their duty of conveying it and how their peoples reacted to it).

7. Then We will surely relate to them (the full account of their worldly lives) with (full, accurate) knowledge; We were not absent (while they were doing their deeds and so we have a perfect record).

8. The weighing on that Day shall be the truth (complete and accurate), and he whose scales (of good deeds) are heavy – they will be the prosperous.

9. And he whose scales are light (because they have no acceptable good deeds) –

they will be those who have ruined their own selves because they wrongfully treated Our Revelations and signs (in both the universe and themselves).

10. Indeed, We have established you on the earth (O humankind, endowed you with great potential) and arranged for your livelihood in it. Scarcely do you give thanks![1]

11. We brought you into existence, then We gave you each a form (perfectly suited to your nature), and then We said to the angels (to signify that they affirm the degree of knowledge and superiority of Adam and his deserving vicegerency, and that they will help him to perform his duty on the earth): "Prostrate before Adam!" They all prostrated, but Iblīs did not; he was not of those who prostrated.

---

1. When we look about the earth and at the universe from the earth, we can easily see what great bounties humankind have been endowed with. The earth has been prepared for humankind, and we have been endowed with what is necessary to live on the earth, being equipped in a way that will satisfy both our material needs and all our outer and inner senses. Furthermore, not only the earth, but the heavens with the sun, the moon, and the stars are at the service of the earth and humankind, even though the earth is no bigger than a dot when compared to the heavens. Humankind has an innate tendency to thank anyone who does them some good, so how ungrateful it would be not to give thanks to God Who has spread before us the earth like a table and made the universe a palace in which we can reside. Giving thanks to God is based on acknowledging that whatever humankind has and whatever we acquire in our earthly life is from God, and to follow the way He has established for us. Thankfulness, which we can say consists largely of belief and worship in all its forms, is a duty to be performed not for the sake of a future reward, but in return for the bounties already granted. That is, belief and worship are not a cause for God to give further rewards to humankind, like eternal bliss in Paradise; rather, they are a duty required by the bounties which have already been granted. Eternal bliss in Paradise is only given out of God's grace and mercy. For this reason, the Qur'ān expresses the attitude of those who have entered Paradise as being *All praise and gratitude are for God, the Lord of the worlds*! (39: 75); this is felt in their hearts and emerges as speech from their mouths.

قَالَ مَا مَنَعَكَ أَلَّا تَسْجُدَ إِذْ أَمَرْتُكَ قَالَ أَنَا خَيْرٌ مِنْهُ خَلَقْتَنِي مِن نَّارٍ
وَخَلَقْتَهُ مِن طِينٍ ۝ قَالَ فَاهْبِطْ مِنْهَا فَمَا يَكُونُ لَكَ أَن
تَتَكَبَّرَ فِيهَا فَاخْرُجْ إِنَّكَ مِنَ الصَّاغِرِينَ ۝ قَالَ أَنظِرْنِي إِلَىٰ
يَوْمِ يُبْعَثُونَ ۝ قَالَ إِنَّكَ مِنَ الْمُنظَرِينَ ۝ قَالَ فَبِمَا أَغْوَيْتَنِي
لَأَقْعُدَنَّ لَهُمْ صِرَاطَكَ الْمُسْتَقِيمَ ۝ ثُمَّ لَآتِيَنَّهُم مِّن بَيْنِ أَيْدِيهِمْ
وَمِنْ خَلْفِهِمْ وَعَنْ أَيْمَانِهِمْ وَعَن شَمَائِلِهِمْ وَلَا تَجِدُ أَكْثَرَهُمْ
شَاكِرِينَ ۝ قَالَ اخْرُجْ مِنْهَا مَذْءُومًا مَّدْحُورًا لَّمَن تَبِعَكَ
مِنْهُمْ لَأَمْلَأَنَّ جَهَنَّمَ مِنكُمْ أَجْمَعِينَ ۝ وَيَا آدَمُ اسْكُنْ أَنتَ
وَزَوْجُكَ الْجَنَّةَ فَكُلَا مِنْ حَيْثُ شِئْتُمَا وَلَا تَقْرَبَا هَٰذِهِ الشَّجَرَةَ
فَتَكُونَا مِنَ الظَّالِمِينَ ۝ فَوَسْوَسَ لَهُمَا الشَّيْطَانُ لِيُبْدِيَ لَهُمَا مَا وُورِيَ
عَنْهُمَا مِن سَوْآتِهِمَا وَقَالَ مَا نَهَاكُمَا رَبُّكُمَا عَنْ هَٰذِهِ الشَّجَرَةِ إِلَّا أَن
تَكُونَا مَلَكَيْنِ أَوْ تَكُونَا مِنَ الْخَالِدِينَ ۝ وَقَاسَمَهُمَا إِنِّي لَكُمَا لَمِنَ النَّاصِحِينَ
۝ فَدَلَّاهُمَا بِغُرُورٍ فَلَمَّا ذَاقَا الشَّجَرَةَ بَدَتْ لَهُمَا سَوْآتُهُمَا وَطَفِقَا
يَخْصِفَانِ عَلَيْهِمَا مِن وَرَقِ الْجَنَّةِ وَنَادَاهُمَا رَبُّهُمَا أَلَمْ أَنْهَكُمَا عَن
تِلْكُمَا الشَّجَرَةِ وَأَقُل لَّكُمَا إِنَّ الشَّيْطَانَ لَكُمَا عَدُوٌّ مُّبِينٌ ۝

───── ❧ ─────

12. He (God) said: "What prevented you from prostrating, when I commanded you to do so?" Iblīs said: "I am better than he, for You have created me from fire, and him You have created from clay."

13. (God) said: "Then go down from it; it is not for you to act haughtily there! So be gone! Surely you are of the degraded."

14. (Iblīs) said: "Grant me respite till the Day when they are raised from the dead."

15. (God) said: "You shall be among the ones (humankind) granted respite (so long as they remain on the earth)."

16. (Iblīs) continued: "Now that You have allowed me to rebel and go astray, I will surely lie in wait for them on Your Straight Path (to lure them from it).

17. "Then I will come upon them from before them and from behind them, and from their right and from their left.[2] And You will not find most of them thankful."

18. (God) said: "Get out from there, disgraced and disowned! Those of them that follow you, surely I will fill Hell with you all!"

19. (To Adam, He said): "O Adam! Dwell, you and your spouse, in the Garden, and eat (of the fruits) thereof where you desire, but do not approach this tree, or you will both be among the wrongdoers."

20. Then Satan made an evil suggestion to both of them that he might reveal to them their private parts that had remained hidden from them (and waken their carnal impulses), and he said: "Your Lord has forbidden you this tree only lest you should become sovereigns, or lest you should become immortals."

21. And he swore to them: "Truly, I am for you a sincere adviser."

22. Thus he led them on by delusion; and when they tasted the tree, their private parts (and all the apparently shameful, evil impulses in their creation) were revealed to them, and both began to cover themselves with leaves from the Garden. And their Lord called out to them: "Did I not prohibit you from that tree, and did I not say to you that Satan is a manifest enemy to you?"[3]

2. That is:

- I will come upon them from before them, and sow in them worry and hopelessness concerning their future; I will invite them not to pay the *Zakāh* or do any supererogatory forms of charity in fear of becoming poor; I will urge them to hoard their wealth; I will provoke them to disbelieve in the Hereafter and show them a dark future; I will present to them the way of the Prophets as reactionary and regressive, and I will call them into valleys of misguidance through the promises I make to them about their future.

- I will come upon them from behind them, and show them the past as a dark cemetery; and by showing them both the past and the present as dark, I will drive them to pessimism and distress after distress; I will incite them to turn away from the way of the Prophets, and to condemn and reject their past while following this way, encouraging them to revive their former (ancient) past when they had worshipped many so-called deities and had lived a corrupt life of sheer ignorance, and to see all this as progress.

- I will come upon them from their right and show them their religious devotions as being perfect, driving them to ostentation, self-pride, and to the desire that their religious life be known and praised by others, thereby causing all their good deeds to go to waste. I will also provoke them to attach more importance to secondary matters in religion, while neglecting the essentials, thus provoking them to disagree and causing conflict. Again, I will cause them to use religion for their worldly interests and ambitions, and for the satisfaction of their carnal desires, but will whisper to them that they do so for the sake of religion, and try my best in order that they may go to the Hereafter devoid of any good deeds.

- I will come upon them from their left, and incite them to reject God's Existence, the Hereafter, and other essentials of faith, and to search different systems of belief or ideology; I will urge them to struggle and even fight against God's religion and those who follow it; I will invite them to dive into the swamp of sins, such as adultery, prostitution, drinking alcohol, and gambling and similar games of chance; I will provoke them to unlawful transactions, like bribery, usury, corruption, theft, robbery, and deception, and other forms of wrong, such as injustice, oppression, murder, disrespect to parents, and the violation of basic human rights, and I will call them to present all these under the titles of justice, peace, humanism, progress, and civilization, etc.

3. The relationship between Adam or humankind and Iblīs or/and Satan, some of the important points of which were mentioned in *Sūrat al-Baqarah* (verses 34–39, notes 34–44), is narrated here with further details that are related to the main topic of this *sūrah*. In order to be able to understand the nature of humanity and its earthly life well, this relationship should be made clear. The main aspects of this relationship can be summed up as follows:

- Although they have free will, however weak it may be, the angels do not have the capacity to do evil, while Satan is a being who has completely lost his capacity to do good. Contrary to this, human beings have the capacity to do both good and evil because of our dual nature that arises from our belonging to both the physical and the metaphysical realm and our having both spiritual, or angelic, and satanic dimensions. However, evil means destruction; the absence of only one part of something will suffice for its destruction; good means existence, and the existence of something is dependent upon the existence of all of its parts. Therefore, humanity can cause great destruction and can even excel Satan in doing harm, yet we have very little power and ability to do good. We need help and support in doing good, and this is why God has established senses that ask for help and support in our hearts. These senses lead humankind to God.

- The dual nature of humankind and our being equipped with free will are the reasons why our inner world is an arena of struggle between good and evil. We feel the two opposing calls or invitations, one coming from God and the angels, the other coming from Satan and the carnal, evil-commanding soul. Real humanity lies in this struggle. Since the angels have no capacity to do evil, and therefore do not struggle with any inherent evil force, they do not progress spiritually; their stations are fixed. But the human struggle with evil forces stimulates the potential of humankind and causes them to progress both scientifically and spiritually. For this reason, this struggle is the engine that powers the spiritual evolution of human beings.

- What caused Satan to be excluded from God's mercy was his arrogance and vanity. Like many modern people, he thought that superiority lay in physical composition and opposed God's command. He insisted on his defiance and tried to excuse himself for it. This caused him to lose his ability to reform himself and forced him to be subjected to eternal condemnation. In contrast, Adam and Eve felt immediate remorse after their lapse and pleaded with God for forgiveness. This teaches us that we must repent and ask God for forgiveness for any evil we have committed. In order to be able to do this, we must understand our innate poverty and helplessness before God and we must be able to comprehend how always we need His help and support. We must also abandon all arrogance and be humble.

- We must always be on the alert against the seductions of the satans found among humankind and the jinn, and we must never give in to their invitations.

152   سُوۡرَةُ الۡاَعۡرَافِ   ۱۰۲

قَالَا رَبَّنَا ظَلَمۡنَآ اَنۡفُسَنَا وَاِنۡ لَمۡ تَغۡفِرۡ لَنَا وَتَرۡحَمۡنَا لَنَكُوۡنَنَّ
مِنَ الۡخَاسِرِيۡنَ ۞ قَالَ اهۡبِطُوۡا بَعۡضُكُمۡ لِبَعۡضٍ عَدُوٌّ وَلَكُمۡ
فِى الۡاَرۡضِ مُسۡتَقَرٌّ وَمَتَاعٌ اِلٰى حِيۡنٍ ۞ قَالَ فِيۡهَا تَحۡيَوۡنَ وَفِيۡهَا
تَمُوۡتُوۡنَ وَمِنۡهَا تُخۡرَجُوۡنَ ۞ يٰبَنِىۤ اٰدَمَ قَدۡ اَنۡزَلۡنَا عَلَيۡكُمۡ
لِبَاسًا يُّوَارِىۡ سَوۡاٰتِكُمۡ وَرِيۡشًا وَلِبَاسُ التَّقۡوٰى ذٰلِكَ خَيۡرٌ ذٰلِكَ مِنۡ
اٰيٰتِ اللّٰهِ لَعَلَّهُمۡ يَذَّكَّرُوۡنَ ۞ يٰبَنِىۤ اٰدَمَ لَا يَفۡتِنَنَّكُمُ الشَّيۡطٰنُ
كَمَآ اَخۡرَجَ اَبَوَيۡكُمۡ مِّنَ الۡجَنَّةِ يَنۡزِعُ عَنۡهُمَا لِبَاسَهُمَا لِيُرِيَهُمَا
سَوۡاٰتِهِمَا اِنَّهٗ يَرٰىكُمۡ هُوَ وَقَبِيۡلُهٗ مِنۡ حَيۡثُ لَا تَرَوۡنَهُمۡ
اِنَّا جَعَلۡنَا الشَّيٰطِيۡنَ اَوۡلِيَآءَ لِلَّذِيۡنَ لَا يُؤۡمِنُوۡنَ ۞ وَاِذَا
فَعَلُوۡا فَاحِشَةً قَالُوۡا وَجَدۡنَا عَلَيۡهَآ اٰبَآءَنَا وَاللّٰهُ اَمَرَنَا بِهَا قُلۡ
اِنَّ اللّٰهَ لَا يَأۡمُرُ بِالۡفَحۡشَآءِ اَتَقُوۡلُوۡنَ عَلَى اللّٰهِ مَا لَا تَعۡلَمُوۡنَ
۞ قُلۡ اَمَرَ رَبِّىۡ بِالۡقِسۡطِ وَاَقِيۡمُوۡا وُجُوۡهَكُمۡ عِنۡدَ كُلِّ مَسۡجِدٍ
وَادۡعُوۡهُ مُخۡلِصِيۡنَ لَهُ الدِّيۡنَ كَمَا بَدَاَكُمۡ تَعُوۡدُوۡنَ ۞ فَرِيۡقًا
هَدٰى وَفَرِيۡقًا حَقَّ عَلَيۡهِمُ الضَّلٰلَةُ اِنَّهُمُ اتَّخَذُوا الشَّيٰطِيۡنَ
اَوۡلِيَآءَ مِنۡ دُوۡنِ اللّٰهِ وَيَحۡسَبُوۡنَ اَنَّهُمۡ مُّهۡتَدُوۡنَ ۞

---

23. They said (straightaway): "Our Lord! We have wronged ourselves, and if You do not forgive us and do not have mercy on us, we will surely be among those who have lost!"

24. He said: "Go down, (all of you,) (and henceforth you will live a life,) some of you being the enemies of others. There shall be for you on the earth a habitation and provision until an appointed time."

25. He said: "You will live there, and there you will die, and from it you will be brought forth (on the Day of Resurrection)."

26. O children of Adam! Assuredly We have sent down on you a garment[4] to cover your private parts, and garments for adornment. However, (remember that) the garment of piety and righteousness – it is the best of all.[5] That is from God's signs, that they may reflect and be mindful.

27. Children of Adam! Never let Satan seduce you (and cause you to fail in similar trials) as he caused your (ancestral) parents to be driven out of the Garden, pulling off from them their garment and revealing to them their private parts (and the carnal impulses ingrained in them). He sees you, he and his host (see you), from where you do not see them. We have made satans the confidants and fellow-criminals of those who do not believe.

28. And whenever they commit an indecency, they say (attempting to excuse themselves): "We found our fathers doing that (and follow in their footsteps), and this is what God has enjoined upon us." Say: "Indeed, God does not enjoin indecency. Or is it that you speak about God things you have no knowledge of?"

29. Say: "My Lord enjoins right and justice." Turn towards Him your faces (i.e. your whole being) whenever you rise to perform the Prayer, and call upon Him, sincere in your faith in Him and practicing the Religion for His sake. As He initiated you (in existence), so to Him you are returning.

30. A party He has guided (to the right way), and for another party straying in error is their just due: they have taken satans, rather than God, for confidants, supporters, and guardians, yet they suppose that they are rightly-guided.[6]

4. The use of the phrase "sending down" for the things human beings need in life, such as garments and, as appears later in the Qur'ān (57: 25), iron, means that these are all bounties of God which He has created especially for the benefit of humankind.

5. We cover our private parts and the whole of our body with other garments, but the garment of piety and righteousness transforms the apparently negative elements and impulses in our nature and channels them into means of virtues that adorn us.

6. The last two verses, especially the sentences *As He initiated you (in existence), so to Him you are returning*, and *A party He has guided (to the right way), and for another party straying in error is their just due*, indicate significant truths:

• While all creatures have an archetypal existence in God's Knowledge, Destiny determines their nature, and (the Divine) Power clothes them in the kind of existence that is peculiar to each. Being transferred from one world to another and clothed in the physical existence of this world, humankind has started on the road that leads to the Hereafter; this journey started when they first stepped into this world. Humans will be stripped of the garment of the body when they die and will be raised into another realm on the Resurrection Day, when this world will be destroyed and rebuilt. The world of every one in this new realm will be built upon their deeds in this world.

• In addition to indicating this journeying of humankind that consists of coming down from high, transcendental worlds and of ascending towards the same worlds, the expression, *As He initiated you (in existence), so to Him you are returning*, also alludes to the fact that time progresses not linearly, but in cycles, just like the earth, the sun and the solar system that go onward or progress in orbit, each around itself. This expression also refers to the fact that day and night, winter and spring, and winter or night-like periods and spring or day-like periods exist in the lives of individuals and communities, one progressing after the other.

• The sentence, *A party He has guided (to the right way), and for another party straying in error is their just due*, teaches that guidance to the right way is from God, but it is the persons themselves that cause straying. This is because guidance means existence and construction. The existence of something depends on the existence of all its parts. Therefore, human beings are totally incapable of creating the conditions necessary for guidance and in dire need of God and His help for their guidance. In contrast, to stray or be misguided means non-existence and destruction. Seeing that the destruction of something is possible by the destruction or non-existence of one of its parts, humanity can outstrip the satans in destruction. So, in order to be saved from destruction and straying, human beings also need the help of God, and should never give up taking care or practicing self-criticism. Bediüzzaman Said Nursi gives us a golden criterion in this respect: "Take asking God for forgiveness for your sins in one of your hands, and prayer in the other. Asking for forgiveness severs evils and sins from their roots, while prayer encourages doing good" (*The Words*, "the 26th Word," 485). That is, a person should always ask God for forgiveness for their sins and pray to Him, while also trying to be saved from sins and evils.

31. O children of Adam! Dress cleanly and beautifully for every act of worship; and (without making unlawful the things God has made lawful to you) eat and drink, but do not be wasteful (by over-eating or consuming in unnecessary ways): indeed, He does not love the wasteful.

32. Say: "Who is there to make unlawful the beautiful things (obtained from plants, animals and minerals) that God has brought forth for His servants, and the pure, wholesome things from among the means of sustenance?" Say: "They are for (the enjoyment of) the believers in the life of the world (without excluding others), and will be exclusively theirs on the Day of Resurrection." Thus We set out in detail Our signs (showing Our way) and Revelations for a people seeking knowledge.[7]

33. Say: "My Lord has made unlawful only indecent, shameful deeds (like fornication, adultery, prostitution, and homosexuality), whether those of them that are apparent and committed openly or those that are committed secretly; and any act explicitly sinful;[8] and insolence and offenses (against the Religion, life, personal property, others' chastity, and mental and bodily health), which is openly unjustified; and (it is also forbidden) that you associate partners with God for which He has sent no authority at all, and that you speak against God the things about which you have no sure knowledge.[9]

34. And (know that) for every community there is a term appointed (by God considering their free will); and when the end of the term falls, they can neither delay it by a single moment, nor can they hasten it.[10]

35. O children of Adam! (As to your earthly life, the term of which has already been appointed, We decreed): Whenever there come to you Messengers from among yourselves, relating to you My Revelations, then whoever keeps from disobedience to

Me and them so as to deserve My protection and mends his ways, thus acting for the general peace in the community, they will have no fear, nor will they grieve.

36. But those who deny Our Revelations and turn arrogantly from them, they are the companions of the Fire, and therein they will abide.

37. Who is more in wrong than he who fabricates falsehood in attribution to God and denies His Revelations and signs (in the universe and their selves)? Their full portion of God's decree (concerning life and providence) will reach them, until Our envoys (angels assigned for this duty) come to them to take their souls, and say: "Where, now, are those beings whom you deified and invoked apart from God?" They say: "They have failed us," and thus bear witness against themselves that they were (always) unbelievers.

7. Great misunderstandings and incorrect behavior have been caused by the fact that some specific matters are generalized. One of these matters is the categorical condemnation of the world and the concept of asceticism.

Human beings have the function or duty to be vicegerent on the earth. This function or duty entails the right to interfere with things within the bounds (the ecological equilibrium and the universal laws of "nature") set up by God and to improve the earth, ruling on it in the name of God according to the laws He has established. It goes without saying that this duty falls on, first of all, the believers. The denial of God or irreligion severs the link between God and human beings, turning humanity into the kind of being that sheds blood and causes unrest on the earth. Since the maintenance of human existence in the world depends on there being a formidable group of believers that has the potential to bear the Divine Trust, the Divine bounties on the earth belong, first of all, to these people, and it is their duty to administer and distribute the same justly among people. This means it is the believers' right to make use of the bounties on the earth within the limits established by Islam, and it is their duty to administer and distribute these bounties justly among people, and to thank God in return. However, it is forbidden for them to go beyond the lawful limits in benefiting from these bounties, and to make eating and drinking the goal of their lives. Over-consumption not only causes competition and conflict over the things that are eaten and drunk, it also means that the accumulated energy of human beings is being spent without measure, causing some destructive sins, such as adultery and prostitution. If one is inclined to overindulge in eating and drinking, then one is more likely to seek the gratification of other desires in an indulgent manner. So, in order to protect against such destruction, individuals can seek shelter in asceticism, and it is even advisable that they do so. But the Muslim community cannot leave the earthly bounties and their administration and distribution to others in the name of asceticism. As Bediüzzaman puts it, believers must not set their hearts on the world, but they must work and earn to maintain themselves, uphold the Word of God, and spend in God's cause.

8. Examples of explicitly sinful acts are consuming intoxicants, blood, carrion, the flesh of swine; taking part in games of chance, bribery, usurpation, corruption, and theft, etc.

9. See also 5: 3, and 6: 151–152.

10. This verse does not mean that an absolute determinism prevails in history. Rather, the Qur'ān sees human beings as the "motor" of history, contrary to the fatalistic approaches of some nineteenth century Western historical philosophies, such as dialectical materialism and historicism. Such philosophies assert that time and conditions direct human history and the only thing that people must do is to keep up with the stream of time, which progresses independently of human will. Whereas, according to the Qur'ān, just as every individual's will and behavior determine the outcome of their life in this world and in the Hereafter, a society's progress or decline is determined by the will, world-view, and lifestyle of its inhabitants. The Qur'ān says (13: 11): *God does not change the condition of a people unless they change what is in themselves (their beliefs, world-view, and lifestyle)*. In other words, each society holds the reins of its fate in its hands. A prophetic Tradition emphasizes this idea: "You will be ruled according to how you are" (al-Hindī, 6: 89). Therefore, this verse should be viewed in the light of human free will in its relationship with the Divine Eternal Will, and in other verses and our explanations that concern it (see *sūrah* 2: 20, note 13; *sūrah* 4, note 18; *sūrah* 5: 40, note 8; *sūrah* 6: 39, 112, 137, note: 8). Since God is absolutely independent of time and sees everything, witnessing all times as if they were no more than one point, He cannot be viewed in terms of the past, the present, or the future. His Will is, in some respect, identical with His Knowledge, and every event takes place according to the law of cause and effect, which His Will has appointed. Therefore, the verse mentions a phenomenon, rather than a compelling, determining law. The verses to come will clarify the matter.

154

سُورَةُ الأَعْرَافِ

١٥٤

> قَالَ ادْخُلُوا فِي أُمَمٍ قَدْ خَلَتْ مِن قَبْلِكُم مِّنَ الْجِنِّ
> وَالْإِنسِ فِي النَّارِ كُلَّمَا دَخَلَتْ أُمَّةٌ لَّعَنَتْ أُخْتَهَا حَتَّى إِذَا
> ادَّارَكُوا فِيهَا جَمِيعًا قَالَتْ أُخْرَاهُمْ لِأُولَاهُمْ رَبَّنَا هَـٰؤُلَاءِ
> أَضَلُّونَا فَآتِهِمْ عَذَابًا ضِعْفًا مِّنَ النَّارِ قَالَ لِكُلٍّ ضِعْفٌ
> وَلَـٰكِن لَّا تَعْلَمُونَ ۞ وَقَالَتْ أُولَاهُمْ لِأُخْرَاهُمْ فَمَا كَانَ لَكُمْ
> عَلَيْنَا مِن فَضْلٍ فَذُوقُوا الْعَذَابَ بِمَا كُنتُمْ تَكْسِبُونَ ۞
> إِنَّ الَّذِينَ كَذَّبُوا بِآيَاتِنَا وَاسْتَكْبَرُوا عَنْهَا لَا تُفَتَّحُ لَهُمْ أَبْوَابُ
> السَّمَاءِ وَلَا يَدْخُلُونَ الْجَنَّةَ حَتَّى يَلِجَ الْجَمَلُ فِي سَمِّ الْخِيَاطِ وَكَذَٰلِكَ
> نَجْزِي الْمُجْرِمِينَ ۞ لَهُم مِّن جَهَنَّمَ مِهَادٌ وَمِن فَوْقِهِمْ غَوَاشٍ
> وَكَذَٰلِكَ نَجْزِي الظَّالِمِينَ ۞ وَالَّذِينَ آمَنُوا وَعَمِلُوا الصَّالِحَاتِ
> لَا نُكَلِّفُ نَفْسًا إِلَّا وُسْعَهَا أُولَـٰئِكَ أَصْحَابُ الْجَنَّةِ هُمْ فِيهَا
> خَالِدُونَ ۞ وَنَزَعْنَا مَا فِي صُدُورِهِم مِّنْ غِلٍّ تَجْرِي مِن
> تَحْتِهِمُ الْأَنْهَارُ وَقَالُوا الْحَمْدُ لِلَّهِ الَّذِي هَدَانَا لِهَـٰذَا وَمَا كُنَّا
> لِنَهْتَدِيَ لَوْلَا أَنْ هَدَانَا اللَّهُ لَقَدْ جَاءَتْ رُسُلُ رَبِّنَا بِالْحَقِّ
> وَنُودُوا أَن تِلْكُمُ الْجَنَّةُ أُورِثْتُمُوهَا بِمَا كُنتُمْ تَعْمَلُونَ ۞

38. (God) says: "Enter in company with the communities of the jinn and human-kind that went before you into the Fire!" Every time a community enters the Fire, it curses its fellow-community (that went before it) – so much so that, when they all have gathered there one after another, those who came later say of those who came earlier: "Our Lord! Those are the ones who led us astray: give them, there-fore, double suffering through fire!" (God) says: "For each is double (since those who went earlier both strayed themselves and led others astray, and those who came later both strayed themselves and imitated the others blindly), but you do not know."

39. Then the preceding ones among them say to the succeeding ones: "You are in no wise superior to us, so taste the punish-ment for all (the sins) that you were busy earning (through your belief and deeds)!"

40. Those who deny Our Revelations and turn arrogantly from them – for them, the gates of Heaven will indeed not be opened (i.e. God will not accept even their good deeds) and they will enter Paradise no fur-ther than a camel can pass through the eye of a needle. Thus do We recompense the disbelieving criminals.

41. For them is a bed of Hellfire and, over them, is a covering (of the same fire).[11] Thus do We recompense the wrongdoers.

42. But those who believe and do good, righteous deeds – We do not burden any soul beyond its capacity – they are the companions of Paradise; and therein they will abide.

43. We will strip away whatever is in their bosoms of rancor and any jealousy (they may have felt against other believers while in the world). Rivers flowing beneath them (and themselves overflowing with gratitude), they say: "All praise and grati-tude are for God, Who has guided us to this (prosperity as a result of the guidance with which He favored us in the world). If God had not guided us, we would cer-tainly not have found the right way. The Messengers of our Lord did indeed come with the truth." And a voice calls to them: "That is the Paradise that you have been made to inherit in return for what you used to do (in the world)."

11. Using an extraordinarily eloquent style, the verse implies that those described are fond of lying in comfortable beds under comfortable coverings. One's recompense is given in the same form as the crime. Those fond of lying in comfortable beds are also fond of eating and entertainment, and give in to their sexual impulses. Here we can remember the Prophetic saying, "Concerning my community, I fear a large stomach, oversleeping, idleness and a lack of certainty" (al-Hindī, 3: 460). In addition to being an obstacle to believing, such a life also impinges on the rights of others. It is significant that the verse depicts these people as wrongdoers. They wrong both others and their own selves.

وَنَادَىٰٓ أَصْحَٰبُ ٱلْجَنَّةِ أَصْحَٰبَ ٱلنَّارِ أَن قَدْ وَجَدْنَا مَا وَعَدَنَا رَبُّنَا حَقًّا فَهَلْ وَجَدتُّم مَّا وَعَدَ رَبُّكُمْ حَقًّا قَالُوا نَعَمْ فَأَذَّنَ مُؤَذِّنٌۢ بَيْنَهُمْ أَن لَّعْنَةُ ٱللَّهِ عَلَى ٱلظَّٰلِمِينَ ﴿٤٤﴾ ٱلَّذِينَ يَصُدُّونَ عَن سَبِيلِ ٱللَّهِ وَيَبْغُونَهَا عِوَجًا وَهُم بِٱلْءَاخِرَةِ كَٰفِرُونَ ﴿٤٥﴾ وَبَيْنَهُمَا حِجَابٌ وَعَلَى ٱلْأَعْرَافِ رِجَالٌ يَعْرِفُونَ كُلًّۢا بِسِيمَىٰهُمْ وَنَادَوْا أَصْحَٰبَ ٱلْجَنَّةِ أَن سَلَٰمٌ عَلَيْكُمْ لَمْ يَدْخُلُوهَا وَهُمْ يَطْمَعُونَ ﴿٤٦﴾ وَإِذَا صُرِفَتْ أَبْصَٰرُهُمْ تِلْقَآءَ أَصْحَٰبِ ٱلنَّارِ قَالُوا رَبَّنَا لَا تَجْعَلْنَا مَعَ ٱلْقَوْمِ ٱلظَّٰلِمِينَ ﴿٤٧﴾ وَنَادَىٰٓ أَصْحَٰبُ ٱلْأَعْرَافِ رِجَالًا يَعْرِفُونَهُم بِسِيمَٰهُمْ قَالُوا مَآ أَغْنَىٰ عَنكُمْ جَمْعُكُمْ وَمَا كُنتُمْ تَسْتَكْبِرُونَ ﴿٤٨﴾ أَهَٰٓؤُلَآءِ ٱلَّذِينَ أَقْسَمْتُمْ لَا يَنَالُهُمُ ٱللَّهُ بِرَحْمَةٍ ٱدْخُلُوا ٱلْجَنَّةَ لَا خَوْفٌ عَلَيْكُمْ وَلَآ أَنتُمْ تَحْزَنُونَ ﴿٤٩﴾ وَنَادَىٰٓ أَصْحَٰبُ ٱلنَّارِ أَصْحَٰبَ ٱلْجَنَّةِ أَنْ أَفِيضُوا عَلَيْنَا مِنَ ٱلْمَآءِ أَوْ مِمَّا رَزَقَكُمُ ٱللَّهُ قَالُوٓا إِنَّ ٱللَّهَ حَرَّمَهُمَا عَلَى ٱلْكَٰفِرِينَ ﴿٥٠﴾ ٱلَّذِينَ ٱتَّخَذُوا دِينَهُمْ لَهْوًا وَلَعِبًا وَغَرَّتْهُمُ ٱلْحَيَوٰةُ ٱلدُّنْيَا فَٱلْيَوْمَ نَنسَىٰهُمْ كَمَا نَسُوا لِقَآءَ يَوْمِهِمْ هَٰذَا وَمَا كَانُوا بِـَٔايَٰتِنَا يَجْحَدُونَ ﴿٥١﴾

---

44. And the companions of Paradise call out to the companions of the Fire: "Now we have found what our Lord promised us to be true. Have you (also) found true what your Lord promised you?" They say, "Yes!" And an announcer announces among them: "God's curse (rejection and condemnation) is the due of all wrongdoers!"

45. (The wrongdoers are) those who bar people from God's way and seek to make it crooked; and they are persistent unbelievers in the Hereafter.

46. And between the two there is a barrier, and on the Heights (between Paradise and Hell) are some men,[12] recognizing each by their countenances. They – not yet entering Paradise, but longing for it – call out to the companions of Paradise: "Peace be upon you!"

47. And when their eyes are turned towards the companions of Hell, they say (in dread of that state): "Our Lord! Do not include us among the wrongdoing people!"

48. The people of the Heights call out to some men (who were the leaders of unbelief in the world, and) whom they recognize by their marks (on their countenances), saying: "(Now you see that) neither your numbers and the wealth you amassed nor your growing arrogance and vanity have availed you!"

49. (Pointing to the companions of Paradise, they continue): "Are those not the ones of whom you swore that God would not favor them with mercy?" (For now it is they who have been told:) "Enter Paradise; you will have no fear, nor will you grieve."

50. And the companions of the Fire call out to the companions of Paradise: "Pour out some water upon us, or something of what God has provided for you!" They say: "Indeed God has forbidden both to the unbelievers."

51. (The unbelievers are) those who took their Religion (the one appointed for them by God) for a play and pastime (and have made play and fun their own religion), and the present, worldly life deluded them. So We are oblivious of them today (concerning forgiveness and favoring), as they were oblivious of the encounter of this Day of theirs, and were obstinately rejecting Our Revelations.

12. Some interpreters of the Qur'ān are of the opinion that those men mentioned are Prophets and other beloved servants of God who have drawn near to Him. Others defend the idea that they are the believers whose good and bad deeds are equal and who therefore expect God's forgiveness. Fethullah Gülen, a contemporary Turkish scholar and activist, offers a good explanation: "Whatever misfortune happens to a believer, it serves as a means of forgiveness for some of their sins. God forgives some of His believing servants' sins by making them suffer death pangs, some by making them suffer in the grave, some through tribulations in the Plain of Supreme Gathering, some while their deeds are being weighed, and there are still those who remain whose sins are to be forgiven by being kept on the Heights of the wall between Paradise and Hell. So, those people mentioned in this verse may be the believers whose remaining sins will be forgiven by being kept between Paradise and Hell in suspense and fear of being thrown in Hell, while they also expect God's forgiveness and admission to Paradise" (*Tereddütler* 4: 133–136). God knows best.

سُوۡرَةُ الۡاَعۡرَافِ ١٥٦

وَلَقَدۡ جِئۡنَاهُمۡ بِكِتَابٍ فَصَّلۡنَاهُ عَلٰى عِلۡمٍ هُدًى وَّرَحۡمَةً
لِّقَوۡمٍ يُّؤۡمِنُوۡنَ ۞ هَلۡ يَنۡظُرُوۡنَ اِلَّا تَاۡوِيۡلَهٗ يَوۡمَ يَاۡتِيۡ
تَاۡوِيۡلُهٗ يَقُوۡلُ الَّذِيۡنَ نَسُوۡهُ مِنۡ قَبۡلُ قَدۡ جَآءَتۡ رُسُلُ رَبِّنَا
بِالۡحَقِّ فَهَلۡ لَّنَا مِنۡ شُفَعَآءَ فَيَشۡفَعُوۡا لَنَاۤ اَوۡ نُرَدُّ فَنَعۡمَلَ غَيۡرَ
الَّذِيۡ كُنَّا نَعۡمَلُ قَدۡ خَسِرُوۡۤا اَنۡفُسَهُمۡ وَضَلَّ عَنۡهُمۡ مَّا كَانُوۡا
يَفۡتَرُوۡنَ ۞ اِنَّ رَبَّكُمُ اللّٰهُ الَّذِيۡ خَلَقَ السَّمٰوٰتِ وَالۡاَرۡضَ
فِيۡ سِتَّةِ اَيَّامٍ ثُمَّ اسۡتَوٰى عَلَى الۡعَرۡشِ يُغۡشِى الَّيۡلَ النَّهَارَ يَطۡلُبُهٗ
حَثِيۡثًا وَّالشَّمۡسَ وَالۡقَمَرَ وَالنُّجُوۡمَ مُسَخَّرَاتٍ بِاَمۡرِهٖ اَلَا لَهُ
الۡخَلۡقُ وَالۡاَمۡرُ تَبَارَكَ اللّٰهُ رَبُّ الۡعَالَمِيۡنَ ۞ اُدۡعُوۡا رَبَّكُمۡ
تَضَرُّعًا وَّخُفۡيَةً اِنَّهٗ لَا يُحِبُّ الۡمُعۡتَدِيۡنَ ۞ وَلَا تُفۡسِدُوۡا فِى
الۡاَرۡضِ بَعۡدَ اِصۡلَاحِهَا وَادۡعُوۡهُ خَوۡفًا وَّطَمَعًا اِنَّ رَحۡمَتَ اللّٰهِ
قَرِيۡبٌ مِّنَ الۡمُحۡسِنِيۡنَ ۞ وَهُوَ الَّذِيۡ يُرۡسِلُ الرِّيَاحَ بُشۡرًا
بَيۡنَ يَدَيۡ رَحۡمَتِهٖ حَتّٰۤى اِذَاۤ اَقَلَّتۡ سَحَابًا ثِقَالًا سُقۡنَاهُ
لِبَلَدٍ مَّيِّتٍ فَاَنۡزَلۡنَا بِهِ الۡمَآءَ فَاَخۡرَجۡنَا بِهٖ مِنۡ كُلِّ
الثَّمَرَاتِ كَذٰلِكَ نُخۡرِجُ الۡمَوۡتٰى لَعَلَّكُمۡ تَذَكَّرُوۡنَ ۞

52. Assuredly We have brought them a Book (the meaning and commandments of) which We set out in detail with knowledge, as guidance and mercy for people who will believe and who have already believed.

53. Are they waiting but for the final end of the call to that Book? On the Day when this end comes, those, who until then have been oblivious of it, say: "The Messengers of our Lord assuredly came with the truth (but we did not pay heed). Have we, then, any intercessors who will now intercede on our behalf? Or can we be returned (to the world) that we might do otherwise than we used to do (when we were in the world)? They have certainly ruined their selves and what they fabricated (of false deities) has failed them.

54. Indeed your Lord is God, Who has created the heavens and the earth in six days, then He has established Himself on the Supreme Throne, covering the day with the night, each pursuing the other swiftly, with the sun, the moon, and the stars obedient to His command. Know well that His is the creation and His is the command. Blessed and Supreme is God, the Lord of the worlds.[13]

55. Call upon your Lord (O humankind) with humility and in the secrecy of your hearts. Indeed your Lord does not love those who exceed the bounds.

56. (Keep within the bounds He has decreed:) Do not cause disorder and corruption on the earth seeing that it has been so well ordered, and call upon Him with fear (of His punishment) and longing (for His forgiveness and mercy). God's mercy is indeed near to those devoted to doing good, aware that God is seeing them.

57. And He it is Who sends forth the merciful winds as glad tidings in advance of His mercy – so that, when they carry heavy clouds, We drive them towards a dead land, then We cause thereby water to descend, and bring forth thereby fruits (crops) of every kind. Even so We make the dead come forth (on Judgment Day), that you may reflect and be mindful.

13. This verse and those that follow show humankind traveling in the outer world and their inner world to demonstrate to them God's absolute dominion. A person first focuses on their own private world. It is God, our Lord, Who creates all of us with all our features, and nourishes us and governs our lives and bodies. The verse, therefore, draws our attention to this fact, and therefore we must accept Him as our Lord Who has the right to direct us in all aspects of our lives. Then it has us travel in the outer world and explains why the right to rule or command belongs to God both in our world and the universe as a whole. Since it is He Who has created the heavens and the earth, He owns them and has the absolute right to rule over them. Seeing that a person claims exclusive ownership over their private property in which they have only one share out of a thousand, the others belonging to God, God will surely have the total right to execute dominion over His property.

The verse also states that God has created the heavens and the earth in six days and established Himself on the Supreme Throne. The Qur'ān uses the word *day* not only in the sense of our normal day, but also as time unit and period. Another verse (32: 5) mentions that one day is like 1,000 years in our reckoning, and another mentions a day which lasts 50,000 years (70: 4). This shows that the concept of day is relative. The "world" does not consist in our world or the visible universe. Rather there are worlds or dimensions one within another. Just as time is different in the world of dreams, so is it also different in the worlds of the spirit and imagination, as well as in the world of immaterial forms and the High Empyrean (*Jabarūt*). It can even be said that the whole lifespan of the universe, from its creation to its final destruction, is a day, and as mentioned in the Qur'ān, the lifetime in the other world is also a day. So, what the Qur'ān means by six days may be the geological eras of the earth or the creational periods of the universe, which still continue, or the periods from the beginning of the creation of the universe until the time it took its present form.

'Arsh (translated as the Supreme Throne) literally means anything constructed high like a roof, a dome, an arch, or pavilion. However, since the Qur'ān addresses all levels of understanding through all ages, it tends to present certain abstract truths, like those pertaining to Divinity, with concrete expressions and uses metaphors and comparisons. It presents the *Kursiyy* (Seat: see 2: 256) as if it were a platform or seat, and the *'Arsh* as if it were a throne and God were the ruler of the universe seated on His throne, governing all creation. By so doing, the Qur'ān establishes in our minds God's supreme authority and dominion. God is not just the Creator of the universe, but is also its Sovereign and Ruler. Having created the universe, He did not detach Himself from it, nor become indifferent to His creation. On the contrary, He effectively rules over the universe as a whole, as well as controlling every small part of it. All power and sovereignty rest with Him. Everything in the universe is fully in His grasp and is subservient to His Will and Power. Bediüzzaman says that *'Arsh* is the composition of God's Names the First, the Last, the Outward, and the Inward. Also, deducing from his description of water as the *'Arsh* (throne) of mercy and earth, the throne of life, we can say that *'Arsh* (the Supreme Throne) implies God's full control of and authority over the universe. Elements such as water and earth are things that conduct God's decrees or media by which they are manifested and executed.

وَالْبَلَدُ الطَّيِّبُ يَخْرُجُ نَبَاتُهُ بِإِذْنِ رَبِّهِ وَالَّذِي خَبُثَ لَا يَخْرُجُ إِلَّا نَكِدًا كَذَٰلِكَ نُصَرِّفُ الْآيَاتِ لِقَوْمٍ يَشْكُرُونَ ۝ لَقَدْ أَرْسَلْنَا نُوحًا إِلَىٰ قَوْمِهِ فَقَالَ يَا قَوْمِ اعْبُدُوا اللَّهَ مَا لَكُم مِّنْ إِلَٰهٍ غَيْرُهُ إِنِّي أَخَافُ عَلَيْكُمْ عَذَابَ يَوْمٍ عَظِيمٍ ۝ قَالَ الْمَلَأُ مِن قَوْمِهِ إِنَّا لَنَرَاكَ فِي ضَلَالٍ مُّبِينٍ ۝ قَالَ يَا قَوْمِ لَيْسَ بِي ضَلَالَةٌ وَلَٰكِنِّي رَسُولٌ مِّن رَّبِّ الْعَالَمِينَ ۝ أُبَلِّغُكُمْ رِسَالَاتِ رَبِّي وَأَنصَحُ لَكُمْ وَأَعْلَمُ مِنَ اللَّهِ مَا لَا تَعْلَمُونَ ۝ أَوَعَجِبْتُمْ أَن جَاءَكُمْ ذِكْرٌ مِّن رَّبِّكُمْ عَلَىٰ رَجُلٍ مِّنكُمْ لِيُنذِرَكُمْ وَلِتَتَّقُوا وَلَعَلَّكُمْ تُرْحَمُونَ ۝ فَكَذَّبُوهُ فَأَنجَيْنَاهُ وَالَّذِينَ مَعَهُ فِي الْفُلْكِ وَأَغْرَقْنَا الَّذِينَ كَذَّبُوا بِآيَاتِنَا إِنَّهُمْ كَانُوا قَوْمًا عَمِينَ ۝ وَإِلَىٰ عَادٍ أَخَاهُمْ هُودًا قَالَ يَا قَوْمِ اعْبُدُوا اللَّهَ مَا لَكُم مِّنْ إِلَٰهٍ غَيْرُهُ أَفَلَا تَتَّقُونَ ۝ قَالَ الْمَلَأُ الَّذِينَ كَفَرُوا مِن قَوْمِهِ إِنَّا لَنَرَاكَ فِي سَفَاهَةٍ وَإِنَّا لَنَظُنُّكَ مِنَ الْكَاذِبِينَ ۝ قَالَ يَا قَوْمِ لَيْسَ بِي سَفَاهَةٌ وَلَٰكِنِّي رَسُولٌ مِّن رَّبِّ الْعَالَمِينَ ۝

---

58. And the good, pure land: its vegetation comes forth in abundance by its Lord's leave, whereas from the bad, corrupt land, it comes forth but poorly (like thorny bushes). Thus do We in diverse ways set out the signs (of God's Existence and Unity and other truths of faith) for the people who give thanks (from the heart and in speech, and in action by fulfilling God's commandments).[14]

59. Indeed We sent Noah to his people as Messenger (to convey Our Message to them), and he said: "O my people! Worship God alone: you have no deity other than Him. Indeed I fear for you the punishment of an awesome day!"

60. The leading ones among his people said: "We see that you are surely lost in obvious error."

61. (Noah) said: "O my people! There is no error in me. Rather, I am a Messenger from the Lord of the worlds.

62. "I convey to you the messages of my Lord, give you sincere advice, and I know from God that which you do not know.

63. "What! do you deem it strange that a reminder from your Lord has come to you through a man from among yourselves that he may warn you (against the consequences of your way of life), and that you may guard against His punishment, and so that you may be favored with His grace and mercy?"

64. And yet they (instead of paying heed to Noah's warning) denied him. And so We saved him and those who were with

him in the Ark, and caused to drown those who denied all the Revelations and signs (of Our Existence and Unity). They were indeed a blind people.[15]

65. And to the (people of) 'Ād We sent their brother Hūd.[16] He said: "O my people! Worship God alone: you have no deity other than Him. Will you not, then, keep from disobedience to Him and deserve His protection?"

66. The leading ones among his people who were persisting in unbelief said: "We see you to be indeed foolish and weak-minded, and we are certain that you are a liar."

67. (Hūd) said: "O my people! There is no folly and weak-mindedness in me, rather I am a Messenger from the Lord of the worlds.

14. The Qur'ān mentions "natural" truths along with sociological truths and those that pertain to human spiritual life, in order that the more familiar truths (natural truths, which surround us in our everyday life) can provide an example for the other truths. These verses provide one of the best instances of this aspect of the Qur'ānic style. They mention the creation of the heavens and the earth, and the fact that the celestial bodies are subservient to God's command to present the absolute sovereignty of God, calling on humanity to submit to this sovereignty and worship and to pray to Him. Both in the spiritual life of people, and in the lives of communities and the life of the earth, the days and nights (light and darkness), winter and spring (winter-like and spring-like periods), dearth and abundance follow one another. It is God Almighty Who will change night to daytime, winter to spring, and dearth to abundance, and the duty that falls upon human beings is to turn to God sincerely and entreat Him with fear (of His punishment) and expectation (of His forgiveness and mercy), remaining within the bounds which He has established for us. In the same way that He accepts the prayers the "dead" earth recites in the language of need and disposition, and as He moves the winds and clouds of rain to revive it, so too, exhausted or dead hearts and communities are revived with the rain of Revelation, mercy, and are favored as a result of turning to God. What is important here is that the earth, and our minds and hearts should be fertile and pure (uncontaminated by prejudices, not clinging to wrong viewpoints, wrongdoings, or having attachments to worldly ambitions). Then the fertile, pure earth and our minds and hearts are favored with a rain of mercy that helps to produce an abundance of good, fresh vegetation and delicious fruit (faith, true and enlightening knowledge, good morals, and virtues). If this is not the case, our infertile, unclean earth, and our contaminated minds and hearts will only produce thorny bushes (false beliefs and misleading thoughts and ideologies), no matter how much the rain of mercy pours from the heavens.

After such expressions, full of meaning and messages, and after presenting what is abstract and what is concrete, after discussing the physical realities alongside sociological and spiritual ones, the *sūrah* continues by giving concrete examples from history.

15. The Qur'ānic allusions and Biblical statements lead us to conclude that the Prophet Noah lived in Iraq around Mosul (Nineveh). This is also supported by the inscriptions belonging to pre-Biblical times discovered during archaeological excavations. Kurdish and Armenian traditions also corroborate this account. Some relics ascribed to Noah can still be found in the vicinity of Mount Ararat. The people of Nakhichevan believe that their city was founded by Noah.

Traditions similar to the story of Noah and the Flood are also found in classical Greek, Egyptian, Indian, and Chinese literature. Moreover, stories of identical import have been popular since time immemorial in Burma, Malaya, the East Indies, Australia, New Guinea and various parts of Europe and America. This is a good indication that this story was either learned from the Messengers sent to these areas or that the people in the company of Noah and their descendants dispersed to different parts of the world after the Flood. It is also possible that both these events happened.

16. The people of 'Ād were an ancient Arab people known throughout Arabia for their legendary prosperity. There were many references to them in pre-Islamic (*Jāhiliyyah*) poetry, and their stories circulated widely, so much so that the word *ādī*, in the sense of ancient things, and *ādiyāt* in the sense of archeological remnants, found their way into Arabic as derivatives from the name of this people. The region called Ahqāf that is situated between Hijaz, Yemen, and Yamāmah is their native land; they scattered as far as the western coasts of Yemen and expanded their dominion to Oman, Hadramawt, and Iraq. A few remnants found in the southern Arabian Peninsula and a grave in Hadramawt are attributed to this tribe. In 1837, James R. Wellested, a British naval officer, found an inscription in Hisn al-Ghurab where the name of Hūd was mentioned. It clearly belonged to those who followed the religion of Hūd (al-Mawdūdī, 3: 42–43, note 51).

158 سُورَةُ الأَعْرَافِ ١٥٨

68. "I convey to you the messages of my Lord, and I am a trustworthy counselor to you.

69. "Why, do you deem it strange that a reminder (a message and guidance) from your Lord has come to you through a man from among you that he may warn you (against the consequences of your way)? Remember and be mindful that He has made you successors (on the earth) after Noah's people and increased you in stature and power. Remember and be mindful, then, of God's bounties, that you may prosper (in both worlds, and attain your goals)."

70. They said: "Have you come to us (with the command) that we should worship God alone and forsake what our forefathers used to worship? Then bring about what you have threatened us with, if you are truthful!"

71. (Hūd) said: "Already abhorrence and anger (i.e. idol-worship in blind imitation of your forefathers) from your Lord have befallen you. What! do you dispute with me about mere designations which you and your forefathers invented and for which God has not sent down any author-

ity? (If that is the case) then wait, as indeed I too am among those who wait."

72. Then, through mercy from Us, We saved him and those who were in his company, while we uprooted those who denied Our signs and Revelations and were not believers.

73. And to (the people of) Thamūd (We sent) their brother Ṣāliḥ.[17] He said (conveying the same message): "O my people! Worship God alone: you have no deity other than Him. Assuredly a manifest proof has come to you from your Lord: this is a she-camel from God as a sign for you (of the truth of my Messengership). So leave her to pasture on God's earth, and touch her with no harm lest a painful punishment should seize you.

17. The Thamūd were another ancient Arab people almost as famous as the 'Ād. Their name was frequently mentioned in pre-Islamic poetry and Greek, Alexandrian, and Roman histories and geographies. The Roman historians recorded that they joined the Roman armies against the Nabateans. They lived in Ḥijr in the north-west of Arabia and their main city was Madā'in Ṣāliḥ, situated along the route of the famous Hijāz railway. Some remnants of this city can still be found. The Makkan merchants passed by this area on their journeys to Syria. It was during the Tabuk Campaign that the Messenger passed by there with his army; he did not halt there because it was a region where God's scourge had fallen. He told his Companions to reflect on it and to take lessons from it (al-Mawdūdī, 3: 45–46, note 57).

The she-camel appeared as the result of the demand of the Thamūd chieftains to have a sign or miracle to prove Ṣāliḥ's Messengership. There is nothing in the Qur'ān or authenticated Ḥadīth literature to indicate how this camel came into existence. However, she was an extraordinary creature and recognized by the people as a sign or miracle. Some wicked person killed her, and the other unbelievers, instead of opposing him, supported him. This was the final atrocity of the Thamūd that brought upon them God's punishment. It caused their ruin.

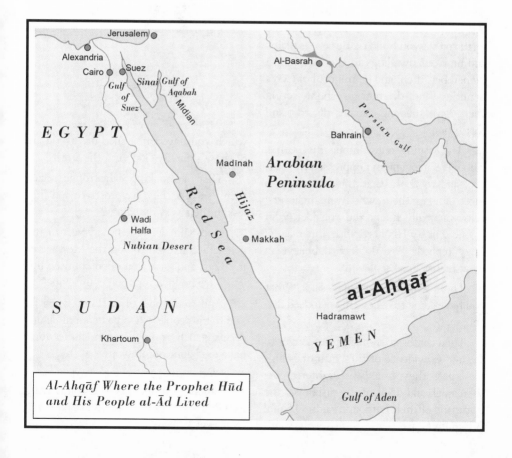

Al-Ahqāf Where the Prophet Hūd and His People al-Ād Lived

وَاذْكُرُوا إِذْ جَعَلَكُمْ خُلَفَاءَ مِنْ بَعْدِ عَادٍ
وَبَوَّأَكُمْ فِي الْأَرْضِ تَتَّخِذُونَ مِنْ سُهُولِهَا
قُصُورًا وَتَنْحِتُونَ الْجِبَالَ بُيُوتًا فَاذْكُرُوا آلَاءَ
اللَّهِ وَلَا تَعْثَوْا فِي الْأَرْضِ مُفْسِدِينَ ۞ قَالَ الْمَلَأُ الَّذِينَ
اسْتَكْبَرُوا مِنْ قَوْمِهِ لِلَّذِينَ اسْتُضْعِفُوا لِمَنْ آمَنَ
مِنْهُمْ أَتَعْلَمُونَ أَنَّ صَالِحًا مُرْسَلٌ مِنْ رَبِّهِ قَالُوا إِنَّا بِمَا
أُرْسِلَ بِهِ مُؤْمِنُونَ ۞ قَالَ الَّذِينَ اسْتَكْبَرُوا إِنَّا بِالَّذِي
آمَنْتُمْ بِهِ كَافِرُونَ ۞ فَعَقَرُوا النَّاقَةَ وَعَتَوْا عَنْ أَمْرِ
رَبِّهِمْ وَقَالُوا يَا صَالِحُ ائْتِنَا بِمَا تَعِدُنَا إِنْ كُنْتَ مِنَ
الْمُرْسَلِينَ ۞ فَأَخَذَتْهُمُ الرَّجْفَةُ فَأَصْبَحُوا فِي دَارِهِمْ
جَاثِمِينَ ۞ فَتَوَلَّى عَنْهُمْ وَقَالَ يَا قَوْمِ لَقَدْ أَبْلَغْتُكُمْ رِسَالَةَ
رَبِّي وَنَصَحْتُ لَكُمْ وَلَكِنْ لَا تُحِبُّونَ النَّاصِحِينَ ۞ وَلُوطًا
إِذْ قَالَ لِقَوْمِهِ أَتَأْتُونَ الْفَاحِشَةَ مَا سَبَقَكُمْ بِهَا
مِنْ أَحَدٍ مِنَ الْعَالَمِينَ ۞ إِنَّكُمْ لَتَأْتُونَ الرِّجَالَ
شَهْوَةً مِنْ دُونِ النِّسَاءِ بَلْ أَنْتُمْ قَوْمٌ مُسْرِفُونَ ۞

---

74. "And remember and be mindful that He made you successors of the people of 'Ād and established you securely on the earth so that you build castles on its plains and hew out dwellings in the mountains. Remember, then, and be mindful of God's bounties, and do not go about acting wickedly in the land, causing disorder and corruption."

75. The leading ones among his people, who were arrogant and oppressed the others, said to those that they scorned, to those among them who were believers: "Do you really know and consider Ṣāliḥ as one sent by His Lord with a message?" They replied: "We do indeed believe in what he has been sent with."

76. Those who were arrogant said: "What you have come to believe in we indeed disbelieve."

77. Then (without enduring any longer to see her as evidence of the truth of Ṣāliḥ's message), they cruelly slaughtered the she-camel, and disdainfully disobeyed the command of their Lord, and said: "O Ṣāliḥ! Bring upon us that (punishment) with

which you have threatened us, if you are of those sent (by God with the truth)!"

78. Then a shocking catastrophe seized them, so that they lay prostrate and lifeless in their very dwellings.

79. And Ṣāliḥ left them, saying: "O my people! I conveyed to you the Message of my Lord and gave you good counsel; but you have no love for good counselors."

80. And (remember) Lot (Lūt), when he said to his people[18]: "Do you commit an indecency such as no people in all the world have ever done before you?

81. "You come to men with lust in place of women. You are a people committing excesses and wasteful (of your God-given faculties)."

18. The people of Lot lived in the region lying to the southeast of the Dead Sea. According to archeologists, this area was very prosperous between 2300 and 1900BC. It has been estimated that Abraham, the uncle of Lot, lived around 2000 BC. The people of Lot were destroyed during Abraham's lifetime (15: 51–60).

The land in which they lived was very verdant; it was resplendent with gardens and orchards, appearing as if a single garden, and fascinated those who saw it. The most fertile and populous part of the region was the area called the "Valley of Siddim." The major cities were Sodom, Gomorrah, Admah, Zeboim, and Zo'ar.

These cities were devastated on account of the major sins that were indulged in there, in particular homosexuality, which had almost become a general way of life. The valley sank and was covered by the Dead Sea. The rain mentioned in verse 84 was a rain of stones. According to the Bible, when Abraham heard about what had befallen Lot's people, he traveled from Hebron and observed: "The smoke of the land rose like the smoke from a furnace" (*Genesis*, 19: 28).

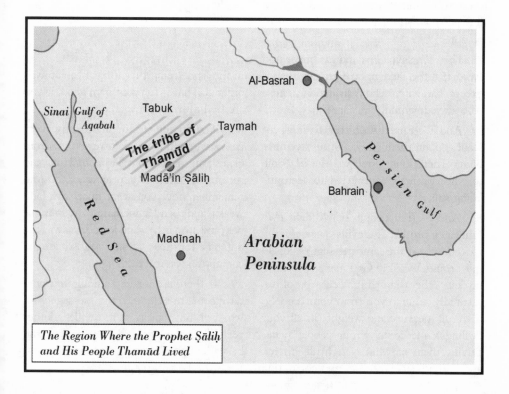

The Region Where the Prophet Ṣāliḥ and His People Thamūd Lived

160 سُورَةُ الأَعْرَافِ ١٦٠

وَمَا كَانَ جَوَابَ قَوْمِهِ إِلَّا أَن قَالُوٓا أَخْرِجُوهُم
مِّن قَرْيَتِكُمْ إِنَّهُمْ أُنَاسٌ يَتَطَهَّرُونَ ۝ فَأَنجَيْنَاهُ
وَأَهْلَهُۥٓ إِلَّا ٱمْرَأَتَهُۥ كَانَتْ مِنَ ٱلْغَابِرِينَ ۝ وَأَمْطَرْنَا
عَلَيْهِم مَّطَرًا فَٱنظُرْ كَيْفَ كَانَ عَاقِبَةُ
ٱلْمُجْرِمِينَ ۝ وَإِلَىٰ مَدْيَنَ أَخَاهُمْ شُعَيْبًا قَالَ يَا
قَوْمِ ٱعْبُدُوا۟ ٱللَّهَ مَا لَكُم مِّنْ إِلَٰهٍ غَيْرُهُۥ قَدْ جَآءَتْكُم
بَيِّنَةٌ مِّن رَّبِّكُمْ فَأَوْفُوا۟ ٱلْكَيْلَ وَٱلْمِيزَانَ وَلَا
تَبْخَسُوا۟ ٱلنَّاسَ أَشْيَآءَهُمْ وَلَا تُفْسِدُوا۟ فِى ٱلْأَرْضِ
بَعْدَ إِصْلَاحِهَا ذَٰلِكُمْ خَيْرٌ لَّكُمْ إِن كُنتُم مُّؤْمِنِينَ ۝
وَلَا تَقْعُدُوا۟ بِكُلِّ صِرَاطٍ تُوعِدُونَ وَتَصُدُّونَ
عَن سَبِيلِ ٱللَّهِ مَنْ ءَامَنَ بِهِۦ وَتَبْغُونَهَا عِوَجًا وَٱذْكُرُوٓا۟
إِذْ كُنتُمْ قَلِيلًا فَكَثَّرَكُمْ وَٱنظُرُوا۟ كَيْفَ كَانَ
عَاقِبَةُ ٱلْمُفْسِدِينَ ۝ وَإِن كَانَ طَآئِفَةٌ مِّنكُمْ ءَامَنُوا۟
بِٱلَّذِىٓ أُرْسِلْتُ بِهِۦ وَطَآئِفَةٌ لَّمْ يُؤْمِنُوا۟ فَٱصْبِرُوا۟
حَتَّىٰ يَحْكُمَ ٱللَّهُ بَيْنَنَا وَهُوَ خَيْرُ ٱلْحَاكِمِينَ ۝

82. But his people's response was only that they said (to one another): "Banish them from your township, for they are a few persons who make themselves out to be pure!"

83. Then We saved Lot and his household (who left the land upon Our command) except his wife, who was among those who stayed behind.

84. And We rained a destructive rain (of stones) upon them (those who stayed behind). Then, look, how was the outcome for the criminals committed to accumulating sins.

85. And to (the people of) Midian (We sent) their brother Shu'ayb as Messenger.[19] He (conveying the same message) said: "O my people! Worship God alone: you have no deity other than Him. A clear proof has assuredly come to you from your Lord. So give full measure and weight (in all your dealings), and do not wrong people by depriving them of what is rightfully theirs, and do not cause disorder and corruption in the land seeing that it has been so well ordered. That is for your own good, if you are (to be) true believers.

86. "And do not lurk in ambush by every pathway, seeking to overawe and bar from God's way one who believes in Him, and seeking to make it appear crooked. And remember how you were once few (and weak), and then He increased you in number (and strength). And look, how was the outcome for those who cause disorder and corruption (on the earth).

87. "If there are a party among you who have come to believe in the message with which I have been sent, while another party do not believe, then persevere and be patient until God judges between us. He is the Best in judging."

19. The territory of Madyan (Midian) lay to the north-west of Hijāz and south of Palestine on the coast of the Red Sea and the Gulf of ‘Aqabah; part of the territory stretched to the northern border of the Sinai Peninsula. The towns were situated at the crossroads of the trade routes from Yemen through Makkah and Yanbu‘ to Syria along the Red Sea coast, and from Iraq to Egypt. Midian was, therefore, quite well known to the Arabs. The Midianites related themselves to Midyan, a son of the Prophet Abraham, born of his third wife, Qatūrā. Initially they were Muslims, but later contaminated their pure faith with polytheism, and their economic life with corruption and dishonesty.

The destruction of Midian remained well-known in Arabia for a long time. As such, the following lines in *Psalms* are significant:

> For they have consulted together with one consent;
> They form a confederacy against You:
> ...
> Deal with them as *with* Midian,
> As *with* Sisera,
> As *with* Jabin at the Brook Kishon,
> Who perished at En Dor
> *Who* became *as* refuse on the earth.
> ...
> O my God, make them like the whirling dust,
> Like the chaff before the wind! (*Psalms*, 83: 5, 9–10, 13).

(al-Mawdūdī, 3: 53, note 69)

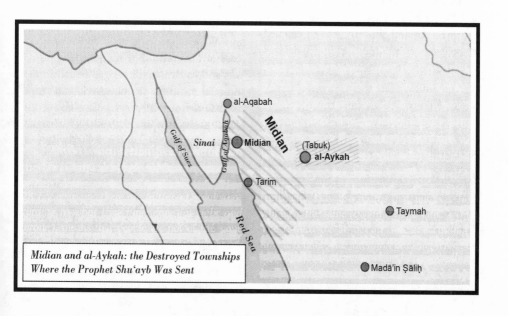

Midian and al-Aykah: the Destroyed Townships
Where the Prophet Shu‘ayb Was Sent

88. The leading ones among his people who were arrogant and oppressed the others said: "We will surely banish you, O Shu'ayb, and those who believe in your company from our township, or else you will return to our way (of faith and life)." (Shu'ayb) said: "What? Even though we abhor it?

89. "Should we return to your way after God has saved us from it, then most certainly we would be fabricating lies in attribution to God. It is not for us to turn back to it, unless God, our Lord, should so will.[20] Our Lord embraces all things within His Knowledge. In God do we put our trust. Our Lord! Judge between us and our people, making the truth manifest, for You are the Best in judging to make the truth manifest."

90. The leading ones who persisted in unbelief said (so as to put pressure upon the others among his people): "Should you follow Shu'ayb, you will then surely be the losers!"

91. Then a shocking catastrophe seized them, so that they lay prostrate and lifeless in their very dwellings –

92. Those who denied Shu'ayb – as though they had not lived there in abundance – those who denited Shu'ayb (and threatened the believers with loss and ruin), it was they who were the losers.

93. And Shu'ayb left them, saying: "O my people! I conveyed to you the messages of my Lord and gave you good counsel. How, then, could I mourn for a people ungrateful and persistent in unbelief?"[21/22]

94. And We did not send a Prophet to a town-

ship but We seized its people with distress and hardship so that they might (wake from heedlessness and) be humble (invoking Us for forgiveness and turning to the truth.)

95. Then (after this phase of trial and training) We changed the affliction into good (ease of life) until they increased (in numbers and wealth, and indulged in comforts) and said (without taking any lesson from it): "Sometimes distress and sometimes happiness visited our forefathers (whereas we are living an easy life". So We seized them all of a sudden without their being aware (of what was coming).[23]

---

20. That is: "We will never turn back to your way, but we cannot know what God, our Lord, has in store for us in His Will and Knowledge. We cannot do anything unless He wills it, and He embraces all things within His Knowledge."

21. The Messengers whose stories are narrated in the Qur'ān are those who lived and conveyed the Divine Message in the places which, particularly, the people of Makkah passed through during their travels to the south, north, and the

north-east. Their stories were known to a certain extent in the region. In addition, they were the greatest of the Prophets who, if we can make such a comparison, were like great persons founding the spiritual orders and schools of law, each being an important link in the chain of Messengers, and guiding our Prophet, upon him be peace and blessings, especially during the Makkan period of his mission. Though all were endowed with the necessary characteristics, capacities, and attributes that are found in a Messenger, some exceeded others in patience, some in gratitude, some in mildness, some in knowledge, and some in their ability to administer; these particular strengths were in relation to what was required by each mission, and each set an example for the last Messenger of God. Having progressed in their footsteps during a certain period of his mission, the Messenger, upon him be peace and blessings, exceeded them all later and became the universal guide, as required by his universal mission.

Just as with God's final Messenger, upon him be peace and blessings, all the preceding Messengers, upon them be peace, conveyed, first of all, God's Oneness as the bedrock of God's Religion, and then they conveyed the other pillars of faith and Divine worship, along with principles of good morality and behavior. These are the roots of the universal tree of Islam, providing irrefutable proof for the Messengership of the Last Prophet. Nevertheless, it should be pointed out that, due to the conditions in which the previous Messengers lived and the restrictions of their mission to a certain time and people, each tended to attach more importance to certain dimensions of God's Religion that were of paramount importance in their time, while other things were more briefly explained. It is the last form of this Religion, namely the Islam communicated by the Last Messenger, upon him be peace and blessings, that expounded and established this Religion with all its dimensions, giving each matter the importance it needed to be given, and which has grown into a blessed, universal tree encompassing all times and places. The Qur'ān having provided the roots and the principles and laws of

its growth, this blessed tree grew up, making a strong trunk consisting of the life and practices of the Messenger, which we call Sunnah, and has become a tree which has yielded its everfresh fruits during all times in Islamic history. The great contribution that Muslim statesmen, commanders, scholars in every field of religious knowledge, scientists, and spiritual masters have made to Islamic civilization cannot be forgotten or neglected. Those who claim to return to the Messenger's Age of Happiness omit this magnificent history, and then go so far as to criticize the Sunnah and even the Qur'ān itself; these are people who recognize no bounds and who invite ruin upon themselves.

The Qur'ān relates stories of the previous Messengers as examples of guidance to be used during the period when Islam was first conveyed by God's Messenger, upon him be peace and blessings, and during later times. So it presents these stories in dimensions that are related to the main subject of the *sūrah* where they occur. It never aims to make reiterations or to tell stories. These stories are like a prism which reflects a different, but complementary view, within a whole.

22. The stories of the Messengers mentioned demonstrate that there are points shared among all the destroyed peoples and that are peculiar to each:

- Manifest polytheism was common among all. However, this was not something that was mentioned in relation to the people of Lot, but which was particularly ingrained in the peoples of Noah, Hūd, and Ṣāliḥ. For this reason, all of the Messengers mentioned except Lot based their mission on the precept: *Worship God alone: you have no deity other than Him.*

- There are other important social and economic diseases other than polytheism that are fatal, mentioned as afflicting the peoples of Ṣāliḥ and Shu'ayb. In the former, there is a fondness for luxury and the problems that accompany such indulgence, while in the latter the economic life is based on deception, injustice, and total corruption. The people of Shu'ayb gave no respite to those who attempted to oppose them and reform the economic life.

- In all of these communities there was a leading elite or class. However, at the time of Noah, this class was merely a "leading elite," and the whole of the people with the exception of the believers were equally persistent in their unbelief and polytheism. The leading elite among the people of 'Ād led others in associating partners with God and forced them to follow them. During the time of Ṣāliḥ (the Thamūd), this elite group formed a small, despotic oligarchy that indulged in vices and tyrannized over the people. Likewise, during the time of Shu'ayb this class became a despotic oligarchy leading the people in unbelief.

- During the time of Lot, moral corruption demonstrated itself, more than other vices, in the homosexuality that had become the way people satisfied their lusts; at that time this was the most prevalent problem, more than polytheism. The people as a whole had been engulfed by it; in fact they showed no inclination to stop this behavior.

23. The last two verses express an important historical and sociological truth. When the Divine Message begins to be conveyed to a people by a Prophet or by a person or community qualified to be heir to a Prophet, distress and hardship (like diseases, wars, famine, and poverty) would appear among that people so that they may make their hearts softer and turn to God. If, despite this, people insist on unbelief and

wrongdoing and struggle against the preaching of Islam, God changes this adversity to ease and abundance: abundant rain replaces famine, new ways of treatment are discovered, wars come to an end, etc. This both means a destruction is on its way to the wrongdoers and is in order to stimulate a feeling of thankfulness in people and to remind them of the blessings that have come along with the Divine Message. People tend to perceive and appreciate a blessing more if it follows adversity. Repletion after hunger, health after disease, and wealth after poverty make these blessings more appreciated. Nevertheless, if a people cannot see the Divine Hand and wisdom behind these blessings and continue to resist the Divine Message, and if those who represent it and try to communicate it are too weak to carry it to a victory, then Divine punishment comes.

These two verses contain another important message. Ease and abundance also follow after the Divine Message has been accepted by a people and when this message has become a way of life. However, if succeeding generations lead a life of ease, forgetting that this easy life is the result of the acceptance of the Divine Message and, instead of continuing to fulfill their duties towards God in thankfulness, attribute it to their own ability to indulge in luxuries, then this is a grave error, and heedless behavior. This will be the start of a decline, which will pervade all the community like a cancer. The time when the corruption has almost entirely encompassed the entire community is when its death is imminent.

162 سُورَةُ الأَعْرَافِ ١٦٢

وَلَوْ أَنَّ أَهْلَ الْقُرَى آمَنُوا وَاتَّقَوْا لَفَتَحْنَا عَلَيْهِمْ بَرَكَاتٍ
مِنَ السَّمَاءِ وَالْأَرْضِ وَلَكِنْ كَذَّبُوا فَأَخَذْنَاهُمْ بِمَا
كَانُوا يَكْسِبُونَ ۝ أَفَأَمِنَ أَهْلُ الْقُرَى أَنْ يَأْتِيَهُمْ بَأْسُنَا
بَيَاتًا وَهُمْ نَائِمُونَ ۝ أَوَأَمِنَ أَهْلُ الْقُرَى أَنْ يَأْتِيَهُمْ بَأْسُنَا
ضُحًى وَهُمْ يَلْعَبُونَ ۝ أَفَأَمِنُوا مَكْرَ اللَّهِ فَلَا يَأْمَنُ مَكْرَ
اللَّهِ إِلَّا الْقَوْمُ الْخَاسِرُونَ ۝ أَوَلَمْ يَهْدِ لِلَّذِينَ يَرِثُونَ الْأَرْضَ
مِنْ بَعْدِ أَهْلِهَا أَنْ لَوْ نَشَاءُ أَصَبْنَاهُمْ بِذُنُوبِهِمْ وَنَطْبَعُ عَلَى
قُلُوبِهِمْ فَهُمْ لَا يَسْمَعُونَ ۝ تِلْكَ الْقُرَى نَقُصُّ عَلَيْكَ
مِنْ أَنْبَائِهَا وَلَقَدْ جَاءَتْهُمْ رُسُلُهُمْ بِالْبَيِّنَاتِ فَمَا
كَانُوا لِيُؤْمِنُوا بِمَا كَذَّبُوا مِنْ قَبْلُ كَذَلِكَ يَطْبَعُ
اللَّهُ عَلَى قُلُوبِ الْكَافِرِينَ ۝ وَمَا وَجَدْنَا لِأَكْثَرِهِمْ
مِنْ عَهْدٍ وَإِنْ وَجَدْنَا أَكْثَرَهُمْ لَفَاسِقِينَ ۝ ثُمَّ بَعَثْنَا
مِنْ بَعْدِهِمْ مُوسَى بِآيَاتِنَا إِلَى فِرْعَوْنَ وَمَلَئِهِ فَظَلَمُوا
بِهَا فَانْظُرْ كَيْفَ كَانَ عَاقِبَةُ الْمُفْسِدِينَ ۝ وَقَالَ
مُوسَى يَا فِرْعَوْنُ إِنِّي رَسُولٌ مِنْ رَبِّ الْعَالَمِينَ ۝

96. If the peoples of those townships had but believed and, in order to deserve His protection, had kept from disobedience to God in reverence for Him and piety, We would surely have opened up for them blessings from heaven and earth; but they denied (the Messengers and the Divine Message they brought), and so We seized them for what they habitually earned (through their deeds).

97. Did the peoples of the townships feel secure that Our mighty punishment would not come upon them at night while they are sleeping?

98. Or did the peoples of the townships feel secure that Our mighty punishment would not come upon them in the daytime while they have indulged in worldly play?

99. Or did they feel secure from God's designing (against them some unexpected disaster)? But none feels secure from God's designing (against them some unexpected affliction) save the people of loss and self-ruin.

100. Has it not, then, become clear to those who have inherited the earth in the wake of former generations that, if We so willed, We could strike them for their sins? But (they are unresponsive to the meaning of events because, in consequence of their wrongdoing, their misguided attitudes and arrogance, and the grave sins they commit) We impress their hearts with a seal so that they cannot hear (the revealed truths and any admonition).

101. Those townships – We relate to you some tidings of them by way of exemplary histories (to teach you this): assuredly the Messengers came to them (chosen by God) from among themselves with clear proofs of the truth but they did not believe in that which they used to deny before. Thus does God impress the hearts of the unbelievers with a seal (that shuts them off from the affects of admonition).

102. We did not find in most of them any (faithfulness to) covenant; indeed We found most of them to be transgressors.

103. Then, after those (early Messengers) We sent Moses to the Pharaoh and his chiefs with Our Revelations and signs (miracles to support him), but they treated them wrongfully. So look, how was the outcome for those causing disorder and corruption!

104. And Moses said: "Pharaoh! I am a Messenger from the Lord of the worlds,

حَقِيقٌ عَلَىٰ أَنْ لَّا أَقُولَ عَلَى اللهِ إِلَّا الْحَقَّ قَدْ جِئْتُكُمْ
بِبَيِّنَةٍ مِّنْ رَّبِّكُمْ فَأَرْسِلْ مَعِيَ بَنِيٓ إِسْرَآئِيلَ ۞ قَالَ إِنْ كُنْتَ
جِئْتَ بِـَٔايَةٍ فَأْتِ بِهَآ إِنْ كُنْتَ مِنَ الصَّادِقِينَ ۞ فَأَلْقَىٰ
عَصَاهُ فَإِذَا هِيَ ثُعْبَانٌ مُّبِينٌ ۞ وَنَزَعَ يَدَهُ فَإِذَا هِيَ
بَيْضَآءُ لِلنَّاظِرِينَ ۞ قَالَ الْمَلَأُ مِنْ قَوْمِ فِرْعَوْنَ إِنَّ هٰذَا
لَسَاحِرٌ عَلِيمٌ ۞ يُرِيدُ أَنْ يُّخْرِجَكُمْ مِّنْ أَرْضِكُمْ فَمَاذَا
تَأْمُرُونَ ۞ قَالُوٓا أَرْجِهْ وَأَخَاهُ وَأَرْسِلْ فِي الْمَدَآئِنِ حَاشِرِينَ
۞ يَأْتُوكَ بِكُلِّ سَاحِرٍ عَلِيمٍ ۞ وَجَآءَ السَّحَرَةُ فِرْعَوْنَ
قَالُوٓا إِنَّ لَنَا لَأَجْرًا إِنْ كُنَّا نَحْنُ الْغَالِبِينَ ۞ قَالَ نَعَمْ وَإِنَّكُمْ
لَمِنَ الْمُقَرَّبِينَ ۞ قَالُوا يَا مُوسَىٰ إِمَّا أَنْ تُلْقِيَ وَإِمَّا أَنْ
نَّكُونَ نَحْنُ الْمُلْقِينَ ۞ قَالَ أَلْقُوا فَلَمَّآ أَلْقَوْا سَحَرُوٓا
أَعْيُنَ النَّاسِ وَاسْتَرْهَبُوهُمْ وَجَآءُو بِسِحْرٍ عَظِيمٍ ۞
وَأَوْحَيْنَآ إِلَىٰ مُوسَىٰ أَنْ أَلْقِ عَصَاكَ فَإِذَا هِيَ تَلْقَفُ
مَا يَأْفِكُونَ ۞ فَوَقَعَ الْحَقُّ وَبَطَلَ مَا كَانُوا يَعْمَلُونَ ۞
فَغُلِبُوا هُنَالِكَ وَانْقَلَبُوا صَاغِرِينَ ۞ وَأُلْقِيَ السَّحَرَةُ سَاجِدِينَ ۞

105. "Bound in truth to say nothing about God except the truth. I have surely come to you with a clear proof from your Lord (Who creates, nourishes, and sustains you). So, let the Children of Israel go with me!"

106. He (the Pharaoh) said: "If you have come with a sign, then bring it forth, if you are truthful!"

107. Then he (Moses) threw down his staff, and thereupon it was a serpent manifest (clear for all to see as a sign).

108. And he drew forth his (right) hand (from his armpit where he had put it), and thereupon it was shining white to those looking on.[24]

109. The chiefs among the people of the Pharaoh said, (discussing the matter among themselves): "This is indeed, (as the Pharaoh says,) a learned, skillful sorcerer,

110. "Who seeks to drive you out from your land. Then, what do you advise (to do)?"

111. They said (to the Pharaoh): "Put him and his brother off for a while, and (in the meantime) send forth heralds to all cities

112. "To bring to your presence every learned, skillful sorcerer."

113. The sorcerers came to the Pharaoh and said: "We must surely have a reward, if we are the victors."

114. (The Pharaoh) answered: "Yes, and you will indeed be among those near-stationed to me."

115. They (the sorcerers) said: "Moses! Either you throw first or we will be the first to throw!"

116. He answered: "Throw!" And when they threw (whatever they held in their hands to make spells) they cast a spell upon the people's eyes (i.e. overawed and deluded them), and produced a mighty sorcery.

117. We revealed to Moses: "Throw down your staff!" and behold! it swallowed up their false devices.

118. Thus was the truth made victorious and all that they (the sorcerers) were doing was proved false.

119. Thus were they (the Pharaoh and his chiefs) defeated there (in front of everyone's eyes), and brought low.

120. And the sorcerers threw themselves down, prostrating,

24. We must approach the Divine Being, existential reality, the universe and the things and events in it from two viewpoints: one from a viewpoint related to God, the other from our own viewpoint. When we approach the matter from the viewpoint related to God, the concepts of time, space, and dimensions no longer exist; everything consists in God's manifestations and deeds beyond time, space, and dimension. For this reason, the Qur'ān usually relates events connected to the Resurrection and Judgment Day in the past tense. In addition to this is the fact that the past tense in Arabic expresses the certainty of an event's having taken place; such a usage also indicates that for God there is no difference between that which took place and that which is taking place and that which will take place.

When we approach existential reality, the universe, and things and events in it from our viewpoint, restrictions such as time, space, and dimension intervene, as do human free will and its functions. Moreover, causality is added to these restrictions, which exist so that we can follow events by including some principles that we call "law," and order our life accordingly. These function as veils before God's manifestations and actions that are beyond all dimensions; we deal with whatever takes place before the outermost veil in the framework of causality and the principles which we call "laws." This is one of the most important points that cause materialists and naturalists to err. Since the outer five senses of human beings cannot penetrate the veils, those who restrict themselves to the perceptions of their five senses accept only those things that are in front of the veils

as being existent and real. Whereas, a person who merely considers only their own being can easily perceive that this being has many "mental worlds;" for example, the imagination, and the "worlds" of concepts, thoughts, ideals, and intentions, and – even if they do not believe in the existence of spirit – there are other innermost worlds, like those of consciousness, willpower, emotions, and the heart, all one within another, each one more spacious than the last. These are reflections or examples of the worlds beyond the material one.

The phenomena that the Qur'ān calls "signs" and theologians "miracles" are God's certain executions and acts of creation which, from the human viewpoint of things and events, exceed the frame of causality and other laws, and are therefore extraordinary. Although they are miracles from our viewpoint, they are actually only some "ordinary" actions of God, Who holds the universe in His Grasp of Power and governs it as He wills, manifesting, along with other Attributes, His Attributes of Knowledge, Wisdom, Absolute Will, and Favor. For those who view things and events with the eye of faith, everything and every event in the universe is a miracle that is no less than the miracles worked by the Prophets. For this reason, addressing the period of human history where reason and science have much greater prominence and importance, the Qur'ān and *the Islam* in the form perfected through the Prophet Muḥammad, upon him be peace and blessings, give prominence to knowledge and such mental faculties as thought, reflection, and reasoning, as well as spiritual aspects of these and other human faculties.

121. And they said: "We have come to believe in the Lord of the worlds,

122. "The Lord of Moses and Aaron."

123. The Pharaoh said: "What! Do you believe in Him before I give you permission? This is indeed a plot you have contrived in the city that you may drive out its (native) people from it. But you shall come to know!

124. "I will certainly have your hands and feet cut off alternately, and then I will certainly have you crucified all together."

125. They responded: "Indeed, to our (true and everlasting) Lord are we bound to return.

126. "You take vengeance on us only because we have come to believe in our Lord's messages when they came to us."[25] "Our Lord! Pour out upon us persevering patience and take our souls to You as Muslims (wholly submitted to You)!"

127. The chiefs among the Pharaoh's people said: "Will you (O Pharaoh) leave Moses and his people to cause disorder and corruption in the country, and forsake you and your deities?" He replied: "We will kill their sons and let live their womenfolk (to serve and satisfy our desires). And indeed we hold irresistible sway over them."

128. Moses said to his people: "Seek help from God and be patient, persevering. The earth belongs indeed to God, and He makes it an inheritance for whom He wills of His servants. The (final, happy) outcome is in favor of the God-revering, pious."

129. They (having been subjected to persecutions by the Pharaoh) said: "We suffered hurt before you came to us, and since you came to us." (Moses) replied: "It may well be that your Lord is going to destroy your enemy and make you the inheritors of rule in (some part of) the earth: and then He will look to see how you act (when you hold power)."

130. And We certainly seized the clan (the court and military aristocracy) of the Pharaoh with years of famine and scarcity of corps, so that they might reflect and be mindful.

---

25. Throughout history the opposing side has always attempted to take vengeance on believers merely because they declare, "Our Lord is God alone!" Such actions have been concealed behind many false excuses; for example, the believers have been disturbing the order, exploiting religion and religious sentiments for personal interests, or dividing people in the name of religion, to mention a few of the spurious claims that have been made over time.

فَإِذَا جَاءَتْهُمُ الْحَسَنَةُ قَالُوا لَنَا هَٰذِهِ وَإِنْ تُصِبْهُمْ سَيِّئَةٌ
يَطَّيَّرُوا بِمُوسَىٰ وَمَنْ مَعَهُ أَلَا إِنَّمَا طَائِرُهُمْ عِنْدَ اللَّهِ
وَلَٰكِنَّ أَكْثَرَهُمْ لَا يَعْلَمُونَ ۝ وَقَالُوا مَهْمَا تَأْتِنَا بِهِ
مِنْ آيَةٍ لِتَسْحَرَنَا بِهَا فَمَا نَحْنُ لَكَ بِمُؤْمِنِينَ ۝ فَأَرْسَلْنَا
عَلَيْهِمُ الطُّوفَانَ وَالْجَرَادَ وَالْقُمَّلَ وَالضَّفَادِعَ وَالدَّمَ
آيَاتٍ مُفَصَّلَاتٍ فَاسْتَكْبَرُوا وَكَانُوا قَوْمًا مُجْرِمِينَ ۝
وَلَمَّا وَقَعَ عَلَيْهِمُ الرِّجْزُ قَالُوا يَا مُوسَى ادْعُ لَنَا رَبَّكَ
بِمَا عَهِدَ عِنْدَكَ لَئِنْ كَشَفْتَ عَنَّا الرِّجْزَ لَنُؤْمِنَنَّ لَكَ
وَلَنُرْسِلَنَّ مَعَكَ بَنِي إِسْرَائِيلَ ۝ فَلَمَّا كَشَفْنَا عَنْهُمُ الرِّجْزَ
إِلَىٰ أَجَلٍ هُمْ بَالِغُوهُ إِذَا هُمْ يَنْكُثُونَ ۝ فَانْتَقَمْنَا مِنْهُمْ
فَأَغْرَقْنَاهُمْ فِي الْيَمِّ بِأَنَّهُمْ كَذَّبُوا بِآيَاتِنَا وَكَانُوا عَنْهَا غَافِلِينَ
۝ وَأَوْرَثْنَا الْقَوْمَ الَّذِينَ كَانُوا يُسْتَضْعَفُونَ مَشَارِقَ
الْأَرْضِ وَمَغَارِبَهَا الَّتِي بَارَكْنَا فِيهَا وَتَمَّتْ كَلِمَتُ رَبِّكَ
الْحُسْنَىٰ عَلَىٰ بَنِي إِسْرَائِيلَ بِمَا صَبَرُوا وَدَمَّرْنَا مَا كَانَ
يَصْنَعُ فِرْعَوْنُ وَقَوْمُهُ وَمَا كَانُوا يَعْرِشُونَ ۝

---

131. But whenever prosperity came their way, they would say: "This is but our due and by our deserving," and whenever evil befell them, they would attribute it to the evil auspices (they alleged) of Moses and whoever was in his company. Beware! their auspice (whether evil or good) was decreed by God, but most of them did not know (being ignorant of true knowledge).

132. And they would say: "Whatever sign you produce before us to cast a spell on us, we are not going to believe you."

133. So, (in order that they might reflect and be mindful) We sent upon them floods and (plagues of) locusts and vermin, and frogs, and (water turning into) blood: distinct signs one after another. Yet they remained arrogant, and they were a criminal people committed to accumulating sins.

134. Each time a plague befell them, they would say: "O Moses, pray for us to your Lord for the covenant He has made with you (of servanthood and Messengership with respect to His Lordship): for sure, if you remove this plague from us, we will surely believe in you, and we will surely let the Children of Israel go with you."

135. But when We removed the plague from them for a term in which they were to fulfill (what they promised), they then broke their promise.

136. So We inflicted Our retribution on them (just as they deserved), and so caused them to drown in the sea, as they denied Our signs (with willful persistence) and were heedless of them.[26]

137. And We made the people who had been persecuted and oppressed (for centuries) inherit all the easts and wests (the whole length and breadth) of the land that We had blessed (with benefits for humankind). And your Lord's gracious word to the Children of Israel was fulfilled,[27] for they had endured patiently; and We obliterated what the Pharaoh and his people had produced (by art or industry) and what they had erected (of castles, palaces, gardens, and the like).[28]

---

26. Prior to our Prophet, upon him be peace and blessings, many well-developed, strong communities were totally destroyed by what seemed to be "natural catastrophes." It may be asked why the same kind of total destruction has not taken place since this time. The first

thing to be said in reply to such a question is that the Prophet Muḥammad, upon him be peace and blessings, was sent as mercy for the whole of creation. As he is a mercy for all creation, the religion he brought and the Qur'ān also provide universal mercy for all beings.

This means that as long as the Qur'ān and Islam exist, an overall, sudden destruction like those witnessed in the pre-Islamic era will not occur. When there are almost no Muslims and when the Qur'ān is no longer heeded, the final destruction of the world will occur.

Secondly, the pre-Islamic era communities were crude and uncivilized to a great extent. They were very obstinate, refractory, and unyielding. The vices causing their destruction were so widespread that they became almost a life-style. Only a few people believed in the Prophets that had been sent and these were too weak to carry out the requirements of the Divine Religion.

Thirdly, it is difficult to say that there is no destruction. The communities in the pre-Islamic era were *totally* destroyed by calamities such as earthquakes, volcanic eruptions, floods, and whirlwinds; we refer these to nature and call them natural calamities. When such calamities take place, costing many lives and even towns, we try to explain them away by referring them to nature. However, these are also a type of punishment sent by God in recompense for disobedience to God's Religion and laws of life and operation of the universe. In addition to these, there are disturbances, in particular world wars, internal conflicts and coups, economic imbalances, and revolutions costing millions of lives, and instances of famines; these are also punishment from God. But we attempt to explain these on the basis of their apparent reasons and never try to discover their real reasons or understand their meaning.

It may be asked here why these destructions may also encompass the believers. Such destructions, unlike the *total* destructions that came in the early ages purely to punish the criminals, come *partially* both as a punishment and as an admonition. Not only the disbelieving criminals but also the believers may also need admonition and deserve punishment. In addition, admonition comes in a way that it appeals to reason to take heed but does not compel human will to believe and submit. If the calamities were to encompass only the disbelieving criminals, this would be like the miracles which were given to earlier Prophets. When their peoples did not believe despite all the miracles, they were de-

stroyed. So, if the calamities were to come to the disbelieving criminals exclusively, and then if other peoples did not believe, this would cause the coming of greater calamities. God saves humanity from such greater calamities due to some important reasons. A powerful reason is that it is hoped that many people will embrace Islam in the future. Thirdly, the destruction of the believers causes the forgiveness of their sins and is a kind of martyrdom for them, and the destruction of their goods cause them to gain the merit of giving charity. Fourthly, it may be argued that the destruction of some "good" believers who are ever ready to sacrifice themselves for the good of others may serve for the salvation of believers from greater destructions for their sins and failure in representing Islam.

As an example for Muslims, the defeat of the Ottoman State in the First World War resulting in its collapse has some apparent reasons. But Bediüzzaman Said Nursi deals with the real reason, the reason why Divine Destiny judged this collapse necessary, in two categories:

• Based on His Attribute of Will, God has a way or a form of acting in creating and governing the universe with whatever there is in it, the events, and human individual and collective life. Since this way or form of acting is apparently constant, we can reach certain conclusions as the result of our study of "nature" and human life and call them "laws of nature, laws of sociology" and "history," and "principles of science." Obeying or disobeying God with respect to these laws and principles has recompense in the world, such as prosperity or poverty, winning or loss, success or defeat, or development or regress. As Muslims, we tend to neglect these laws while the part of the world that has equipped itself with the power of science and technology obeys them, consciously or unconsciously, taking the upper hand.

• To the degree which we have unforgivably neglected obeying the laws of the first category, we also neglect to obey the second collection of Divine laws, which issue from God's Attribute of Speech and which He has sent as Religion. God ordered us to assign approximately one hour of our day to performing the prescribed five daily Prayers, but we were negligent in the last centuries preceding the First World War, and in return He prostrated us during the war, (and unfortunately we have not been able to raise our heads from this prostration yet). He ordered us to fast for a single month in Ramaḍān each year, but we neglected, pitying our souls. In return, He made us fast for five years during the war (and additionally the next 25 years. In many parts of the Muslim world, we still suffer this punishment of fasting!) He ordered us to give the *Zakāh* (Prescribed Purifying Alms) at a rate of 1 out of 40 or 30 or 20 or 10 or 5 – varying according to the kind of the property – of the property He provided for us. We neglected this and acted niggardly, and in return He took back for five years all of our belongings that had accumulated as the *Zakāh*, (and since we have not been able to be saved from this niggardliness, our wealth still continues to be plundered by world powers). God ordered those who could to go on the Pilgrimage; this is a very important, multi-dimensional form of worship. We neglected this and in return He drove us from one front to another for five years, (and we still continue to seek our livelihood in foreign lands) (*Sözler*, "Lemaat," 667).

When we approach the matter from the perspective of the main truth, other truths disclose themselves.

27. This word was what is mentioned in *sūrah* 28: 5–6: *We willed to bestow Our favor upon those who were being humiliated and oppressed in the land (of Egypt), and make of them (exemplary) leaders (to guide people on the way to God and in their lives), and make them inheritors (of the glory of the Pharaoh and the land in which We produced blessings for people), and to establish them in the land with power.*

28. This verse expresses another important historical and sociological principle: Doing wrong or carrying out an injustice, and anything based on these cannot be enduring. God has made an enduring promise to the oppressed believers who, without submitting to unjust systems of polytheism or unbelief, adhere to God's Religion, carrying out its commandments within the principles that God has established and who, without yielding to persecutions, are able to show "active patience" in serving God after the way of His Messengers, and refrain from sins. In this verse, the Qur'ān informs us of the final triumph God bestowed upon the Children of Israel that came with Prophets David and Solomon, upon them be peace, almost five centuries after their escape from the Egypt of the Pharaohs under the leadership of the Prophet Moses, upon him be peace. It is emphasized that this came about as the result of their patience, described above. In *Sūrat al-Baqarah* some episodes are given that took place during this span of five centuries (50–61, 63–74, etc.) and will be given in the following verses, in a suitable style and according to the main topics of the *sūrah* and to the conditions prevalent in Makkah at the time when these verses were revealed.

وَجَاوَزْنَا بِبَنِي إِسْرَآءِيلَ ٱلْبَحْرَ فَأَتَوْا عَلَىٰ قَوْمٍ يَعْكُفُونَ
عَلَىٰٓ أَصْنَامٍ لَّهُمْ قَالُوا يَا مُوسَى ٱجْعَل لَّنَا إِلَٰهًا كَمَا لَهُمْ
ءَالِهَةٌ قَالَ إِنَّكُمْ قَوْمٌ تَجْهَلُونَ ۝ إِنَّ هَٰٓؤُلَآءِ مُتَبَّرٌ مَّا هُمْ فِيهِ
وَبَاطِلٌ مَّا كَانُوا يَعْمَلُونَ ۝ قَالَ أَغَيْرَ ٱللَّهِ أَبْغِيكُمْ
إِلَٰهًا وَهُوَ فَضَّلَكُمْ عَلَى ٱلْعَالَمِينَ ۝ وَإِذْ أَنجَيْنَاكُم
مِّنْ ءَالِ فِرْعَوْنَ يَسُومُونَكُمْ سُوٓءَ ٱلْعَذَابِ يُقَتِّلُونَ
أَبْنَآءَكُمْ وَيَسْتَحْيُونَ نِسَآءَكُمْ وَفِي ذَٰلِكُم بَلَآءٌ
مِّن رَّبِّكُمْ عَظِيمٌ ۝ وَوَاعَدْنَا مُوسَىٰ ثَلَاثِينَ لَيْلَةً
وَأَتْمَمْنَاهَا بِعَشْرٍ فَتَمَّ مِيقَاتُ رَبِّهِ أَرْبَعِينَ
لَيْلَةً وَقَالَ مُوسَىٰ لِأَخِيهِ هَٰرُونَ ٱخْلُفْنِي فِي قَوْمِي وَأَصْلِحْ وَلَا
تَتَّبِعْ سَبِيلَ ٱلْمُفْسِدِينَ ۝ وَلَمَّا جَآءَ مُوسَىٰ لِمِيقَاتِنَا وَكَلَّمَهُ رَبُّهُ
قَالَ رَبِّ أَرِنِيٓ أَنظُرْ إِلَيْكَ قَالَ لَن تَرَانِي وَلَٰكِنِ ٱنظُرْ إِلَى
ٱلْجَبَلِ فَإِنِ ٱسْتَقَرَّ مَكَانَهُ فَسَوْفَ تَرَانِي فَلَمَّا تَجَلَّىٰ رَبُّهُ
لِلْجَبَلِ جَعَلَهُ دَكًّا وَخَرَّ مُوسَىٰ صَعِقًا فَلَمَّا أَفَاقَ
قَالَ سُبْحَانَكَ تُبْتُ إِلَيْكَ وَأَنَا أَوَّلُ ٱلْمُؤْمِنِينَ ۝

---

138. And We led the Children of Israel across the sea, and then they came upon a people who were devoted to the worship of some idols that they had (particular to themselves). They said: "O Moses! Make for us a deity even as they have deities!"[29] He replied: "You are indeed a people given to ignorance.

139. "As for those people – what they are engaged in (by way of religion) is bound to destruction, and false and vain is all they have been doing (by way of worship)".

140. He said: "What! shall I seek a deity for you other than God, when He has exalted you above all other people (through faith and the true Religion with which He has favored you)?"

141. And (remember, O Children of Israel,) when We saved you from the the clan of the Pharaoh, who were afflicting you with the most evil suffering (by enslaving you to such laborious tasks as construction, transportation and farming), slaughtering your sons and letting live your womenfolk (for further humiliation and suffering). In that was a grievous trial from your Lord.

142. And (so that you would be favored with the Torah to order your affairs) We appointed with Moses thirty nights, to which We added ten, so he completed the term of forty nights set by His Lord (for him to spend in devotion).[30] (Before leaving his people in order to come to Our Presence) Moses had said to his brother (Aaron): "Take my place among my people (act to reform them and set things right), and do not follow the way of those who provoke disorder and corruption."

143. And when Moses came to Our appointed time, his Lord spoke to him. (Then, in the rapture of nearness to God arising from his being addressed by Him) he said: "My Lord, show me Yourself, so that I may look upon You!" (God) said: "You cannot see Me (with your eyes in the world). But look at that mountain: if it remains firm in its place, then you will see Me." And the moment his Lord manifested His glorious Majesty to the mountain, He made it crumble to dust, and Moses fell down in a faint (as if struck by lightning). When he awoke, he said: "All-Glorified are You (in that You are absolutely above having any defects and any resemblance with the created)! I turn to You in repentance (for my desire to see You), and I am the first of the (true) believers (who realize that You are beyond any resemblance to any creature and beyond the grasp of any creature's senses).[31]

29. This shows how slavery can degenerate a people. The Children of Israel, descended from Prophet Jacob, upon him be peace, were Muslims who had submitted to God for centuries. But after they had been enslaved by the Pharaohs they lost their identity. This degeneration showed itself frequently during their lives. The sight of a temple would be enough to stir up in them what they had observed among their former masters. Even though, according to the Bible, they had been taught by Moses for 40 years and by Joshua for nearly 30 years after their exodus from Egypt, Joshua still addressed them as follows:

> Now therefore, fear the Lord, serve Him in sincerity and in truth, and put away the gods which your fathers served on the other side of the River and in Egypt. Serve the Lord. And it seems evil to you to serve the Lord, choose for yourselves this day whom you will serve, whether the gods which your fathers served that were on the other side of the River, or the gods of the Amorites, in whose land you dwell. But as for me and my house, we will serve the Lord (*Joshua*, 24: 14–15).

For the influence of slavery on the Children of Israel, see also: *sūrah* 2, notes 62, 71, 72, 74, 155; and *sūrah* 4, note 3.

30. As God also ordered the Prophet Muhammad, upon him be peace and blessings, to keep long vigils at night due to the fact that devotion at night is more impressive (73: 1–8; 76: 26), it can be concluded that the time of devotion that brings a human being nearer to God is the night-time. It is because of this that the Qur'ān mentions 30 and 40 nights, not days. Assigning 40 nights (yet meaning a 24 hour period) for devotion, ascetic discipline, and reflection is very important in following a spiritual path to God in Muslim Sufism. It is called *'arba'in* (Arabic) or *chilah* (Persian), which means 40. The Sufis attach great importance to 40 days also as being the time period required to acquire a second nature or form a habit and be saved from a bad habit or sin.

31. Each Prophet bears some traits peculiar to his people and as required by his mission. An educator will be more successful in matters in which they have personal experience and which they share with their students. This explains why the Children of Israel (2: 55) among nations and the Prophet Moses, upon him be peace, among Prophets, desired to see God. However, there is a great difference between the two desires. While the demand of the Children of Israel arose from doubt in God's Existence, despite all the evidence that they had observed until then, Moses displayed the ardent desire that every lover of God has to see Him. That is why God responded to the demand of the Israelites by nearly killing them with a thunderbolt followed by revival, while He answered Moses' desire with an exclusive manifestation upon a mountain, making it crumble to dust. Moses fell down in a swoon in the face of this manifestation.

The Prophet Moses, upon him be peace, was favored with and distinguished by receiving a particular manifestation of God's Speech. However, it should be noted that this manifestation came according to the receiving capacity of his spirit. When he desired a manifestation beyond the degree of that which he was favored with, he could not bear it. As stated in the verse to come, God told him by way of compliment that He had favored him with bearing His Messages and being His addressee and therefore, without aspiring to something higher, he should be thankful for what he had been granted. We should, however, point out here that Fethullah Gülen comments on Moses' falling down in a swoon as being the result of his utter amazement and shock in the face of God's partial manifestation of His Majesty in all Its transcendence and above all corporeality (*Key Concepts*, 2: 41).

God Almighty manifests Himself with His Names and Attributes behind numerous veils. Neither anything in the universe nor the universe in its totality is able to bear His manifestation beyond that. Those who feel His particular manifestations in their hearts, each according to the capacity of their hearts, are enraptured or intoxicated like Prophet Moses.

But some among them cannot measure these manifestations according to the rules and criteria of the Sharī'ah, and they utter some words for which they would be held accountable if they were to utter them in a normal state. The utterance of Hallāj al-Mansūr, a Muslim Sūfī "I am the Truth," is an example. Nevertheless, there are many who demonstrate sainthood or see themselves as saints and utter the same kinds of words; they will be held accountable for such words. There are still some who think that they have attained great ranks when they feel favored with a few slight manifestations in return for their devotion or ascetic discipline, and who cannot balance their words and acts, with the result that they finally deviate and lead others to deviation. Bediüzzaman Said Nursi writes: "I have observed that the deviating sectarian groups have all been led to deviation by their leaders. Those leaders follow a spiritual path. When they advance a little, they think that they have reached the final station and turn back, deviating and leading others to deviation" (*Mathnawī an-Nūriyah*, 224). For this reason, any spiritual path must be followed in the light of the rules of the Sharī'ah.

قَالَ يَامُوسَىٰٓ إِنِّى ٱصْطَفَيْتُكَ عَلَى ٱلنَّاسِ بِرِسَالَٰتِى وَبِكَلَٰمِى فَخُذْ مَآ ءَاتَيْتُكَ وَكُن مِّنَ ٱلشَّٰكِرِينَ ۝ وَكَتَبْنَا لَهُۥ فِى ٱلْأَلْوَاحِ مِن كُلِّ شَىْءٍ مَّوْعِظَةً وَتَفْصِيلًا لِّكُلِّ شَىْءٍ فَخُذْهَا بِقُوَّةٍ وَأْمُرْ قَوْمَكَ يَأْخُذُوا بِأَحْسَنِهَا سَأُوْرِيكُمْ دَارَ ٱلْفَٰسِقِينَ ۝ سَأَصْرِفُ عَنْ ءَايَٰتِىَ ٱلَّذِينَ يَتَكَبَّرُونَ فِى ٱلْأَرْضِ بِغَيْرِ ٱلْحَقِّ وَإِن يَرَوْا كُلَّ ءَايَةٍ لَّا يُؤْمِنُوا بِهَا وَإِن يَرَوْا سَبِيلَ ٱلرُّشْدِ لَا يَتَّخِذُوهُ سَبِيلًا وَإِن يَرَوْا سَبِيلَ ٱلْغَىِّ يَتَّخِذُوهُ سَبِيلًا ذَٰلِكَ بِأَنَّهُمْ كَذَّبُوا بِـَٔايَٰتِنَا وَكَانُوا عَنْهَا غَٰفِلِينَ ۝ وَٱلَّذِينَ كَذَّبُوا بِـَٔايَٰتِنَا وَلِقَآءِ ٱلْءَاخِرَةِ حَبِطَتْ أَعْمَٰلُهُمْ هَلْ يُجْزَوْنَ إِلَّا مَا كَانُوا يَعْمَلُونَ ۝ وَٱتَّخَذَ قَوْمُ مُوسَىٰ مِنۢ بَعْدِهِۦ مِنْ حُلِيِّهِمْ عِجْلًا جَسَدًا لَّهُۥ خُوَارٌ أَلَمْ يَرَوْا أَنَّهُۥ لَا يُكَلِّمُهُمْ وَلَا يَهْدِيهِمْ سَبِيلًا ٱتَّخَذُوهُ وَكَانُوا ظَٰلِمِينَ ۝ وَلَمَّا سُقِطَ فِىٓ أَيْدِيهِمْ وَرَأَوْا أَنَّهُمْ قَدْ ضَلُّوا قَالُوا لَئِن لَّمْ يَرْحَمْنَا رَبُّنَا وَيَغْفِرْ لَنَا لَنَكُونَنَّ مِنَ ٱلْخَٰسِرِينَ ۝

possible). I will soon show you the (ultimate) abode of the transgressors.

146. I will turn away from My Revelations and signs those who act with haughtiness on the earth against all right. And though they see every sign (of the truth), they do not believe in it; and though they see the way of right guidance, they do not take it as a way to follow. But if they see the way of error and rebellion against the truth, they take it as a way to follow. That is because they deny Our Revelations and are ever heedless of them.

147. Those who deny Our Revelations and the meeting of the Hereafter – their works have wasted. Or are they to be recompensed for anything but what they used to do?

148. The people of Moses, after he (had left them to meet with his Lord), adopted for worship a calf (in effigy, made) of their ornaments, which gave out a lowing sound.[33] Did they not see that it neither spoke to them nor guided them to a way? They adopted it for worship and so became wrongdoers (acting contrary to all the truths of creation and Divine commandments, and thereby wronging their very selves).[34]

149. When they realized in remorse that they earned nothing but ruin, and perceived that they had gone astray, they said: "If our Lord does not have mercy on us and forgive us, we will certainly be among the losers."[35]

144. He (God) said: "O Moses! Indeed I have chosen you above people by virtue of My Messages (that I have entrusted to you) and My speaking (to you). So (without aspiring to what is not for you), hold fast to what I have granted you, and (in return, with your every word and action) be of the thankful!"[32]

145. (Moses completed the term appointed by his Lord for him to be favored with the Book to order his people's affairs.) And We recorded for him on the Tablets whatever is necessary as instruction and guidance (to follow the way to God), and as explanation for all matters. And (We said): "Hold fast to them with strength, and command your people to hold fast to the best thereof (fulfill the commandments in the best way

32. This verse gives a very important lesson: God the Almighty reminds even the Prophet Moses, who is one of His greatest Messengers, that he should not crave for what is beyond the favors bestowed on him. He means: "Be pleased with what I have favored you with, and try to do the duty of thanksgiving it requires." That is, God the Almighty bestows upon each and every one the exact favor which each can receive, and the favor bestowed upon each without the part of their free will, (such as capacities, lifespan, physical structure, race and family, and the time and place of birth, and the like,) is that which is best for each. So what everyone must do is that they should be pleased with the favor bestowed upon them and, without making objections like why certain other favors have not been bestowed upon them also, try to fulfill the duty of thanksgiving required by that favor.

33. This verse contains three allusions to the character of the Children of Israel:

- The ancient Egyptians, among whom the Children of Israel lived for centuries, were mainly farmers and due to the importance of animals in farming, they worshipped cattle. This idolatry penetrated their hearts so deeply that, as we can also see in verse 138 above, it would frequently reveal itself, despite the education Moses was providing. They still carried the traces of slavery in their souls.
- The Children of Israel were a people inclined to easy corruption and therefore required strict control.
- They were deeply attached to the world

and material wealth meant a great deal to them.

34. It is significant that in this verse speech and guidance are mentioned in connection with the Deity. God spoke to the Children of Israel through Moses, whom He had specially favored with His address, and constantly guided them along their way from Egypt to Palestine. They openly witnessed these two great favors of God upon themselves. Despite this and despite the fact that anything which cannot grant such favors cannot be a deity, they adopted the calf as a deity. This was a grave sin, no less than treating all the truths of creation, the universe, and Deity unjustly and therefore they wronged themselves.

35. As can clearly be seen in verses 137 and 142, as well as in this verse, the Qur'ān sometimes mentions the result of something first and then proceeds to narrate the events that led up to it, thus teaching us eloquence in the name of guidance. Verse 137 mentions the final result which would come about five centuries later, along with the more immediate one, namely the Exodus from Egypt. It then proceeds to relate some important events that took place after the Exodus. Verse 142 presents Moses' instruction to his brother before leaving for the mountain; this is described after mentioning his term of 40 days spent in the mountain, and the verses that follow relate his experiences on the mountain and what happened to his people in his absence. As for this verse, it draws attention to the consequence of worshipping the calf, while the verses that follow mention certain events prior to this event.

168 ١٦٨

سُوْرَةُ الْأَعْرَافِ

وَلَمَّا رَجَعَ مُوسَى إِلَى قَوْمِهِ غَضْبَانَ أَسِفًا قَالَ بِئْسَمَا خَلَفْتُمُونِى مِنْ بَعْدِى أَعَجِلْتُمْ أَمْرَ رَبِّكُمْ وَأَلْقَى الْأَلْوَاحَ وَأَخَذَ بِرَأْسِ أَخِيهِ يَجُرُّهُ إِلَيْهِ قَالَ ابْنَ أُمَّ إِنَّ الْقَوْمَ اسْتَضْعَفُونِى وَكَادُوا يَقْتُلُونَنِى فَلَا تُشْمِتْ بِىَ الْأَعْدَاءَ وَلَا تَجْعَلْنِى مَعَ الْقَوْمِ الظَّالِمِينَ ۝ قَالَ رَبِّ اغْفِرْ لِى وَلِأَخِى وَأَدْخِلْنَا فِى رَحْمَتِكَ وَأَنْتَ أَرْحَمُ الرَّاحِمِينَ ۝ إِنَّ الَّذِينَ اتَّخَذُوا الْعِجْلَ سَيَنَالُهُمْ غَضَبٌ مِنْ رَبِّهِمْ وَذِلَّةٌ فِى الْحَيَوةِ الدُّنْيَا وَكَذَٰلِكَ نَجْزِى الْمُفْتَرِينَ ۝ وَالَّذِينَ عَمِلُوا السَّيِّئَاتِ ثُمَّ تَابُوا مِنْ بَعْدِهَا وَآمَنُوا إِنَّ رَبَّكَ مِنْ بَعْدِهَا لَغَفُورٌ رَحِيمٌ ۝ وَلَمَّا سَكَتَ عَنْ مُوسَى الْغَضَبُ أَخَذَ الْأَلْوَاحَ وَفِى نُسْخَتِهَا هُدًى وَرَحْمَةٌ لِلَّذِينَ هُمْ لِرَبِّهِمْ يَرْهَبُونَ ۝ وَاخْتَارَ مُوسَى قَوْمَهُ سَبْعِينَ رَجُلًا لِمِيقَاتِنَا فَلَمَّا أَخَذَتْهُمُ الرَّجْفَةُ قَالَ رَبِّ لَوْ شِئْتَ أَهْلَكْتَهُمْ مِنْ قَبْلُ وَإِيَّايَ أَتُهْلِكُنَا بِمَا فَعَلَ السُّفَهَاءُ مِنَّا إِنْ هِىَ إِلَّا فِتْنَتُكَ تُضِلُّ بِهَا مَنْ تَشَاءُ وَتَهْدِى مَنْ تَشَاءُ أَنْتَ وَلِيُّنَا فَاغْفِرْ لَنَا وَارْحَمْنَا وَأَنْتَ خَيْرُ الْغَافِرِينَ ۝

—✦—

150. And when Moses (having received the Tablets and learned that his people had adopted a calf to worship) returned to his people, full of wrath and sorrow, he said: "Evil is the course you have followed after me! Have you forsaken your Lord's commandment so hastily to hasten your destruction?" And he threw down the Tablets (to postpone enforcement of the laws therein until he put an end to this rebellion against faith in God's absolute Oneness), and laid hold of his brother's head, dragging him towards himself. He (Aaron) said: "Son of my mother! Indeed the people deemed me weak, and almost killed me. So let not my

enemies gloat over me, and do not count me among the wrongdoing people."

151. He (Moses) said: "My Lord! Forgive me and my brother, and admit us in Your special Mercy, for You are the Most Compassionate of the Compassionate."

152. Those who adopted the calf for worship – a severe punishment and condemnation from their Lord will indeed overtake them, and humiliation in this life of the world. Thus do We recompense those who fabricate falsehood (in attribution to God).[36]

153. But as for those who do evil deeds, but later turn to God in repentance and (truly) believe – after that (effort of self-reform) your Lord is assuredly All-Forgiving, All-Compassionate (especially towards His servants who turn to Him).

154. And so when the anger subsided from Moses, He took up the Tablets (to put them into force). Inscribed on them was guidance and mercy for those who have awe of their Lord.

155. Moses chose of his people seventy men (to represent them) for Our appointment (on the mountain, in order to ask God for forgiveness for the calf-worship of some among them and to renew their covenant with Him). Then, when the shocking catastrophe seized them,[37] Moses said: "My Lord! Had You so willed, You would have destroyed them before, and me (along with them). Will You now destroy us for what the fools among us have done? This is a trial from You whereby You lead whom You will astray, and whom You will You guide. You are Our Guardian (to Whom we entrust our affairs and on Whom we rely), so forgive us and have mercy on us! You are the Best in forgiving.

36. God punished those who adopted the calf for worship, but forgave the others. The others had not prevented the calf-worshippers from this deviance or apostasy. However, they repented after Moses' return and God forgave them (See, 2: 54; 4: 153).

37. This shocking catastrophe was an earthquake. It came because, despite all the manifest signs they had witnessed, the seventy men refused to believe that the commandments Moses brought were indeed from God unless they openly saw God speak to him.

وَاكْتُبْ لَنَا فِى هٰذِهِ الدُّنْيَا حَسَنَةً وَفِى الْأَخِرَةِ إِنَّا هُدْنَآ

إِلَيْكَ قَالَ عَذَابِى أُصِيبُ بِهِ مَنْ أَشَآءُ وَرَحْمَتِى

وَسِعَتْ كُلَّ شَىْءٍ فَسَأَكْتُبُهَا لِلَّذِينَ يَتَّقُونَ

وَيُؤْتُونَ الزَّكَوٰةَ وَالَّذِينَ هُم بِأَيَاتِنَا يُؤْمِنُونَ ۝ الَّذِينَ يَتَّبِعُونَ الرَّسُولَ النَّبِىَّ الْأُمِّىَّ الَّذِى يَجِدُونَهُ مَكْتُوبًا

عِندَهُمْ فِى التَّوْرَاةِ وَالْإِنجِيلِ يَأْمُرُهُم بِالْمَعْرُوفِ وَيَنْهَاهُمْ

عَنِ الْمُنكَرِ وَيُحِلُّ لَهُمُ الطَّيِّبَاتِ وَيُحَرِّمُ عَلَيْهِمُ الْخَبَائِثَ

وَيَضَعُ عَنْهُمْ إِصْرَهُمْ وَالْأَغْلَالَ الَّتِى كَانَتْ عَلَيْهِمْ

فَالَّذِينَ ءَامَنُوا بِهِ وَعَزَّرُوهُ وَنَصَرُوهُ وَاتَّبَعُوا النُّورَ

الَّذِى أُنزِلَ مَعَهُ أُولَٰئِكَ هُمُ الْمُفْلِحُونَ ۝ قُلْ يَأَيُّهَا النَّاسُ

إِنِّى رَسُولُ اللّٰهِ إِلَيْكُمْ جَمِيعًا الَّذِى لَهُ مُلْكُ

السَّمَٰوَاتِ وَالْأَرْضِ لَا إِلَٰهَ إِلَّا هُوَ يُحْىِ وَيُمِيتُ

فَآمِنُوا بِاللّٰهِ وَرَسُولِهِ النَّبِىِّ الْأُمِّىِّ الَّذِى يُؤْمِنُ بِاللّٰهِ

وَكَلِمَاتِهِ وَاتَّبِعُوهُ لَعَلَّكُمْ تَهْتَدُونَ ۝ وَمِن

قَوْمِ مُوسَىٰ أُمَّةٌ يَهْدُونَ بِالْحَقِّ وَبِهِ يَعْدِلُونَ ۝

---

156. "Ordain for us good in this world as well as in the Hereafter, for we have turned to You, following Your way." (God) said: "My punishment – I afflict with it whom I will (and no one can escape it except that I have mercy on him), and My Mercy embraces all things; and so, (although in the world every being has a share in My Mercy, in the Hereafter) I will ordain it for those who act in reverence for Me and piety and pay their Prescribed Purifying Alms, and they are those who truly believe in all of Our Revelations and signs.

157. They follow the (most illustrious) Messenger, the Prophet who neither reads nor writes (and has therefore remained preserved from any traces of the existing written culture and is free from any intellectual and spiritual pollution), whom they find described (with all his distinguishing features) in the Torah and the Gospel (that are) with them. He enjoins upon them what is right and good and forbids them what is evil; he makes pure, wholesome things lawful for them, and bad, corrupt things unlawful. And he relieves them of their burdens (remaining of their own Law) and the restraints that were upon them. So those who believe in him (with all sincerity), honor and support him, and help him, and follow the Light (the Qur'ān) which has been sent down with him – they are those who are the prosperous."[38]

158. Say (O Messenger to all humankind): "O humankind! Surely I am a Messenger of God to all of you, of Him to Whom belongs the sovereignty of the heavens and the earth. There is no deity but He. He gives life and causes to die." Believe, then, in God and His Messenger, the Prophet who neither reads nor writes, who believes in God and His words (all His Books, commandments, and deeds); and follow him so that you may be rightly-guided.

159. And of the people of Moses there was a community who guided by the truth (by God's leave) and dispensed justice by it.

38. The Qur'ān suddenly and in a purposeful style jumps to the period of God's Messenger – the Prophet Muḥammad, upon him be peace and blessings – and makes the acceptance of Moses' prayer for those who live in the Messenger's period dependent upon believing in and following him and the Qur'ān. It gently reminds the People of the Book, especially the Children of Israel, of the fact that following their own Prophets and Books requires following God's Messenger and the Qur'ān, or in other words, believing in and following God's Messenger and the Qur'ān is the same as believing in and following their own Prophets and Books. It also warns that true prosperity can only be achieved by so doing, and thus once more refers to the initial verses of *Sūrat al-Baqarah*. The verse to come will announce that the mission of the Prophet Muḥammad, upon him be peace and blessings, includes all human beings, and will explain the foundation upon which his mission is based.

Another point that is emphasized in this verse is that there were strict commandments in the Torah that were there due to the conditions of the time and the character of the Children of Israel; these commandments are what the Qur'ān describes as burdens and fetters. The Prophet Jesus, upon him be peace, modified and lightened some of them (3: 50). God's Messenger removed all of them, and it is for this reason that Islam is described as the pure, primordial religion which is easy to follow. In the last verse of *Sūrat al-Baqarah*, the believers are taught to pray: "Our Lord, lay not on us a burden such as You laid on those gone before us (as required by the education they had to receive according to the time and conditions and to their disposition)."

وَقَطَّعْنَاهُمُ اثْنَتَيْ عَشْرَةَ أَسْبَاطًا أُمَمًا وَأَوْحَيْنَا إِلَىٰ
مُوسَىٰٓ إِذِ اسْتَسْقَاهُ قَوْمُهُ أَنِ اضْرِب بِّعَصَاكَ الْحَجَرَ
فَانبَجَسَتْ مِنْهُ اثْنَتَا عَشْرَةَ عَيْنًا قَدْ عَلِمَ كُلُّ أُنَاسٍ
مَّشْرَبَهُمْ وَظَلَّلْنَا عَلَيْهِمُ الْغَمَامَ وَأَنزَلْنَا عَلَيْهِمُ
الْمَنَّ وَالسَّلْوَىٰ كُلُوا مِن طَيِّبَاتِ مَا رَزَقْنَاكُمْ
وَمَا ظَلَمُونَا وَلَٰكِن كَانُوٓا أَنفُسَهُمْ يَظْلِمُونَ ۝
وَإِذْ قِيلَ لَهُمُ اسْكُنُوا هَٰذِهِ الْقَرْيَةَ وَكُلُوا مِنْهَا حَيْثُ
شِئْتُمْ وَقُولُوا حِطَّةٌ وَادْخُلُوا الْبَابَ سُجَّدًا
نَّغْفِرْ لَكُمْ خَطِيٓئَاتِكُمْ سَنَزِيدُ الْمُحْسِنِينَ ۝ فَبَدَّلَ
الَّذِينَ ظَلَمُوا مِنْهُمْ قَوْلًا غَيْرَ الَّذِي قِيلَ لَهُمْ
فَأَرْسَلْنَا عَلَيْهِمْ رِجْزًا مِّنَ السَّمَاءِ بِمَا كَانُوا
يَظْلِمُونَ ۝ وَسْـَٔلْهُمْ عَنِ الْقَرْيَةِ الَّتِي كَانَتْ حَاضِرَةَ
الْبَحْرِ إِذْ يَعْدُونَ فِي السَّبْتِ إِذْ تَأْتِيهِمْ حِيتَانُهُمْ
يَوْمَ سَبْتِهِمْ شُرَّعًا وَيَوْمَ لَا يَسْبِتُونَ لَا تَأْتِيهِمْ
كَذَٰلِكَ نَبْلُوهُم بِمَا كَانُوا يَفْسُقُونَ ۝

160. We divided Moses' people into twelve tribes, forming them into communities. We revealed to Moses when his people asked him for water (on the occasion that they were left without water in the desert), saying: "Strike the rock with your staff!" And (as soon as he struck) there gushed forth from it twelve springs. Each tribe knew their drinking place. And We caused the cloud to shade them, and sent down upon them manna and quails: "Eat of the pure, wholesome things that We have provided for you." And (by disobeying Our commandments) they wronged not Us, but themselves they used to wrong.

161. And when they were told, "Dwell in this town and eat (of the fruits) thereof as you may desire, and say words of imploring forgiveness and loyalty to Him, and enter it (not through different ways with the aim of plundering it and massacring its people, but) through its gate humbly and in utmost submission to God, so that We forgive you your misdeeds." We will in-

crease the reward for those devoted to doing good, aware that God is seeing them.

162. But those among them who persisted in wrongdoing changed what had been said to them (regarding humility, imploring forgiveness, submission, and loyalty) for another saying (and acted contrarily to how they had been ordered). So We sent down on them a scourge from heaven because they were persistent in wrongdoing.[39]

163. Ask them about the township that was by the sea: how its people were violating the Sabbath when their fish came swimming to them on the day of their Sabbath, but on the day they did not keep Sabbath, they did not come to them. Thus did We try them as they were transgressing (all bounds).[40]

39. See also 2: 57–60, notes 67–71.

40. God never tests a person or a people in order to mislead them. God has established the laws for the operation of the universe and life. Religion is also a collection of the laws God has established to order our personal and collective life and which He has conveyed to us through His Messengers. Just as these laws include our relationship with and duty towards all other creatures, they also include our relationship and duty towards our Creator, God. We come to know what will happen as a consequence of what we do either through the teachings of God sent to us through the Messengers or from the Books He has sent to them, or through our study of the universe and life. Everyone sees the consequence of their decisions and actions in life. We meet the consequences of both types of God's laws, the laws for the operation of the universe and life and the laws comprising religion. This is what God calls testing or trial. In this sense, all life is a collection of trials.

If a person or community continuously performs good deeds, they will find themselves in a "virtuous circle," where good deeds give rise to good results which, in turn, lead to good deeds again. If they continue to do evil, this time a vicious circle appears where evil deeds yield evil results which, in turn, lead to evil deeds again. Either of these circles becomes "second nature" in a person. The Qur'ān also indicates this fact with expressions like *Thus did We test them as they were transgressing all bounds* (7: 163); *so taste the punishment for all (the sins) that you were busy earning (through your belief and deeds)* (7: 39); *That is the Paradise that you have been made to inherit in return for what you used to do (in the world)* (7: 43); etc.

اَلْجُزْءُالتَّاسِعُ

وَإِذْقَالَتْ أُمَّةٌ مِّنْهُمْ لِمَ تَعِظُونَ قَوْمَّا ٱللّٰهُ مُهْلِكُهُمْ أَوْمُعَذِّبُهُمْ
عَذَابًا شَدِيدًا قَالُوا مَعْذِرَةً إِلَىٰ رَبِّكُمْ وَلَعَلَّهُمْ يَتَّقُونَ ١٦٤
فَلَمَّا نَسُوا مَا ذُكِّرُوا بِهِۦٓ أَنجَيْنَا ٱلَّذِينَ يَنْهَوْنَ عَنِ
ٱلسُّوٓءِ وَأَخَذْنَا ٱلَّذِينَ ظَلَمُوا بِعَذَابٍۭ بَئِيسٍۭ بِمَا كَانُوا
يَفْسُقُونَ ١٦٥ فَلَمَّا عَتَوْا عَن مَّا نُهُوا عَنْهُ قُلْنَا لَهُمْ كُونُوا
قِرَدَةً خَاسِئِينَ ١٦٦ وَإِذْ تَأَذَّنَ رَبُّكَ لَيَبْعَثَنَّ عَلَيْهِمْ إِلَىٰ يَوْمِ
ٱلْقِيَٰمَةِ مَن يَسُومُهُمْ سُوٓءَ ٱلْعَذَابِ إِنَّ رَبَّكَ لَسَرِيعُ ٱلْعِقَابِ وَإِنَّهُۥ
لَغَفُورٌ رَّحِيمٌ ١٦٧ وَقَطَّعْنَٰهُمْ فِى ٱلْأَرْضِ أُمَمًا مِّنْهُمُ
ٱلصَّٰلِحُونَ وَمِنْهُمْ دُونَ ذَٰلِكَ وَبَلَوْنَٰهُم بِٱلْحَسَنَٰتِ
وَٱلسَّيِّئَاتِ لَعَلَّهُمْ يَرْجِعُونَ ١٦٨ فَخَلَفَ مِنۢ بَعْدِهِمْ خَلْفٌ
وَرِثُوا ٱلْكِتَٰبَ يَأْخُذُونَ عَرَضَ هَٰذَا ٱلْأَدْنَىٰ وَيَقُولُونَ
سَيُغْفَرُ لَنَا وَإِن يَأْتِهِمْ عَرَضٌ مِّثْلُهُۥ يَأْخُذُوهُ أَلَمْ يُؤْخَذْ عَلَيْهِم
مِّيثَٰقُ ٱلْكِتَٰبِ أَن لَّا يَقُولُوا عَلَى ٱللّٰهِ إِلَّا ٱلْحَقَّ وَدَرَسُوا مَا فِيهِ
وَٱلدَّارُ ٱلْأَخِرَةُ خَيْرٌ لِّلَّذِينَ يَتَّقُونَ أَفَلَا تَعْقِلُونَ ١٦٩ وَٱلَّذِينَ
يُمَسِّكُونَ بِٱلْكِتَٰبِ وَأَقَامُوا ٱلصَّلَوٰةَ إِنَّا لَا نُضِيعُ أَجْرَ ٱلْمُصْلِحِينَ ١٧٠

164. And when a community of people among them asked (others who tried to restrain the Sabbath-breakers): "Why do you preach to a people whom God will destroy or punish with a severe punishment?" They said: "So as to have an excuse before your Lord and so that they might keep from such disobedience in reverence for God."

165. Then, when they became heedless of all that they had been reminded of, We saved those who had tried to prevent the evil-doing, and seized the others who had been doing wrong with an evil punishment for their transgressions.

166. Then, when they disdainfully persisted in doing what they had been forbidden to do, We said to them: "Be apes miserably slinking and rejected!"[41]

167. And (remember) when your Lord proclaimed that He would, until the Day of Resurrection, send forth against them those who would afflict them with the most evil of suffering. Your Lord is indeed swift in retribution (when it is due), and He is indeed the All-Forgiving, the All-Compassionate (especially towards those who turn to Him in repentance and His believing servants).[42]

168. And We have split them up on the earth as separate communities. Among them are those who are righteous, and those who are not; and We have tried them with blessings as well as with afflictions, that they might turn back (to the right way from the misleading paths they follow).

169. And there have succeeded after them new generations who inherited the Book, taking the gains of this low life (for which they sell it), and saying: "We will be forgiven." (Although by saying so they recognize what they do as a sin), if there comes to them the same sort of fleeting gains, they are ready to take them (instead of refraining). Was there not taken from them the promise concerning the Book that they should say of God nothing but the truth? and they (are people who) have studied and taught what is therein. But the abode of the Hereafter is better for those who keep from disobedience to God in reverence for Him and piety. Will you not, then, reason and understand?

170. And as for those who hold fast to the Book sincerely and establish the Prayer in conformity with its conditions – indeed We do not let waste the reward of those who are ever reforming (themselves and society), and setting things right.

41. For an explanation, see: 2: 65, note 75.

42. This proclamation of God is restricted by both the conclusion of the verse which declares that God is the All-Forgiving and the All-Compassionate, and the verse: *Ignominy has been their (the Jews') portion wherever they have been found except for (when they hold on to) a rope from God or a rope from other peoples* (see *sūrah* 3: 112, note 24). So the verse means: And (remember) when your Lord proclaimed that He would, until the Day of Resurrection, send forth against them those who would afflict them with the most evil of suffering, (so long as they persist in their wrongdoing and transgressions and do not hold on to a rope from God or a rope from other peoples).

171. And (remember) when We shook the Mount above them as if it were a canopy, and they thought that it was going to fall upon them. (We said:) "Hold firmly to (the Book) that We haven given you and be mindful of (the commands and warnings) that it contains, that you may attain piety and due reverence for God, so deserving His protection (against any kind of deviancy and its consequent punishment in both this world and the Hereafter)."

172. And (remember, O Messenger,) when your Lord brought forth from the children of Adam, from their loins, their offspring, and made them bear witness against themselves (asking them:) "Am I not your Lord?" They said: "Yes, we do bear witness." (That covenant was taken) lest you should say on the Day of Resurrection, "We were indeed unaware of this (fact that you are our Lord)."

173. Or lest you should say (in trying to excuse yourselves): "Our forefathers used to associate partners with God before us, and we were their offspring just following after them. Will You, then, ruin us for what those did who rejected Your Lordship and invented that false way (of associating partners with You)?"[43]

174. And thus do We set out in detail the signposts of Our way and the relevant Revelations (included in the Qur'ān), so that they may turn back (from their wrong ways to Us).

175. Tell them (based on Our Revelation) the story of him whom We made well-informed of Our signs and Revelations, but he cast them off, and Satan overtook him, and he became of those (followers of Satan) who rebel (against God's way) and go astray.

176. If We had willed (to impede the way he chose by his free will), We could indeed have lifted him (towards the heaven of perfections enabled by faith) through those signs and Revelations, but (by his own free choice) he clung to the earth and followed his desires. So (in his being surrendered to greed), his likeness is that of a dog: if you move to drive it away, it pants with its tongue lolling out (still hoping to be fed more), or if you leave it, it pants with its tongue lolling out. Such is the likeness of those who deny Our signs and Revelations. So tell them this narrative so that they may (be stirred to) reflect.

177. How evil an example are the people who deny Our signs and Revelations, and (in so doing) are ever wronging themselves.

178. He whom God guides, he is indeed rightly guided; and he whom He leads astray – they are the losers.

43. The event mentioned in verse 172 is of great significance in understanding the existential position of humanity and its relationship with God. We can summarize its meaning and importance as follows:

- As God cannot be contained in time or space, nothing exists and no event takes place in relation to Him within the framework of the past, the present, or the future. It is human beings that are contained in time and space, and it is we who view all things and events within the framework of time and space. So, in relation to God, it is meaningless to ask when and where He spoke to us.

- When viewed from our perspective and within the framework of time and space, creation follows a descending and ascending line that passes through many stages or realms. Just as an article, for instance, has many stages of existence, like existing in the mind of the writer, and then as a plan, and then in a written form, every being has a primordial existence in God's Knowledge, and as a general form determined by Destiny, and then in the stages of its material existence. Since our consciousness comes not from our corporeal being, but rather from our spiritual existence, it is completely possible that God may have spoken to us before He sent us, or may speak after He has sent us, to the world through our spirit or our nature. Some people whom God has enabled to acquire such spiritual refinement that they are able to live at the life-level of the spirit and heart, and therefore able to travel in these realms, can remember the incident mentioned in the verse, namely God taking from them the primordial covenant mentioned in the verse.

- It is very important to note that the covenant God received from all human beings is binding on them, to the extent that we must remember it and cannot defend ourselves in the Hereafter by saying that we were unaware of it. Therefore, this covenant must have an objective reality. We can find this reality in the Prophetic Tradition: "Every new born child is born with a primordial nature and disposition inclined to Islam (al-Bukhārī, "Janāiz," 80)." Despite this, as stated in the continuation of this same Prophetic Tradition, the human disposition to find God and the innate inclination to find Him can be obscured by the family, environment and education received, and in many verses such as *Say (to them): "Tell me, if some punishment of God comes upon you or the Last Hour comes upon you, do you then invoke other than God? (Answer that) if you are truthful (and admit the voice of your conscience)"!* (6: 40); the Qur'ān stresses that the human conscience cannot help but be aware of Him in certain circumstances. God has inculcated in everyone's conscience a point where we seek help and a point where we seek support. Both manifest themselves at various times, especially when one is left with no apparent, material means of escape from danger or difficulties, and feels that there is no way out other than turning to God. Even if most people behave as if they have had no such experience when they reach safety, every one has had some such experience several times in their lives. A person can deny God when they are under the influence of their carnal soul, directed by Satan, but every truth, becomes manifest when they die and are left with no other choice but to acknowledge that they have felt deeply and many times during their worldly life the Existence of God and that He is their Lord, and protected them during their worldly life many times against dangers that appear unexpectedly.

- The expression *made them bear witness against themselves*, draws our attention to the fact that, although we are innately aware of God's Existence and His being our Lord, our carnal soul never wants to accept and acknowledge His Existence or His being our Lord. This is because it desires to live in whatever way it wishes, satisfying all of its ambitions and appetites without recognizing any power that may be able to restrict it. But the carnal soul cannot prevent its owner, the human being, from feeling and acknowledging God's Existence and being aware of the fact that He is their Lord in their conscience, although this acknowledgment goes against the carnal soul.

وَلَقَدْ ذَرَأْنَا لِجَهَنَّمَ كَثِيرًا مِنَ الْجِنِّ وَالْإِنْسِ لَهُمْ قُلُوبٌ لَا يَفْقَهُونَ
بِهَا وَلَهُمْ أَعْيُنٌ لَا يُبْصِرُونَ بِهَا وَلَهُمْ آذَانٌ لَا يَسْمَعُونَ بِهَا أُولَٰئِكَ
كَالْأَنْعَامِ بَلْ هُمْ أَضَلُّ أُولَٰئِكَ هُمُ الْغَافِلُونَ ۝ وَلِلَّهِ
الْأَسْمَاءُ الْحُسْنَىٰ فَادْعُوهُ بِهَا وَذَرُوا الَّذِينَ يُلْحِدُونَ فِي أَسْمَائِهِ
سَيُجْزَوْنَ مَا كَانُوا يَعْمَلُونَ ۝ وَمِمَّنْ خَلَقْنَا أُمَّةٌ يَهْدُونَ
بِالْحَقِّ وَبِهِ يَعْدِلُونَ ۝ وَالَّذِينَ كَذَّبُوا بِآيَاتِنَا سَنَسْتَدْرِجُهُمْ
مِنْ حَيْثُ لَا يَعْلَمُونَ ۝ وَأُمْلِي لَهُمْ إِنَّ كَيْدِي مَتِينٌ ۝ أَوَلَمْ
يَتَفَكَّرُوا مَا بِصَاحِبِهِمْ مِنْ جِنَّةٍ إِنْ هُوَ إِلَّا نَذِيرٌ مُبِينٌ ۝
أَوَلَمْ يَنْظُرُوا فِي مَلَكُوتِ السَّمَاوَاتِ وَالْأَرْضِ وَمَا خَلَقَ اللَّهُ
مِنْ شَيْءٍ وَأَنْ عَسَىٰ أَنْ يَكُونَ قَدِ اقْتَرَبَ أَجَلُهُمْ فَبِأَيِّ حَدِيثٍ بَعْدَهُ
يُؤْمِنُونَ ۝ مَنْ يُضْلِلِ اللَّهُ فَلَا هَادِيَ لَهُ وَيَذَرُهُمْ فِي
طُغْيَانِهِمْ يَعْمَهُونَ ۝ يَسْأَلُونَكَ عَنِ السَّاعَةِ أَيَّانَ مُرْسَاهَا
قُلْ إِنَّمَا عِلْمُهَا عِنْدَ رَبِّي لَا يُجَلِّيهَا لِوَقْتِهَا إِلَّا هُوَ ثَقُلَتْ فِي
السَّمَاوَاتِ وَالْأَرْضِ لَا تَأْتِيكُمْ إِلَّا بَغْتَةً يَسْأَلُونَكَ كَأَنَّكَ حَفِيٌّ عَنْهَا
قُلْ إِنَّمَا عِلْمُهَا عِنْدَ اللَّهِ وَلَٰكِنَّ أَكْثَرَ النَّاسِ لَا يَعْلَمُونَ ۝

179. Surely, among the jinn and mankind are many that We have created (and destined for) Hell (knowing that they would deserve it). They have hearts with which they do not seek the essence of matters to grasp the truth, and they have eyes with which they do not see, and they have ears with which they do not hear. They are like cattle (following only their instincts) – rather, even more astray (from the right way and in need of being led). Those are the unmindful and heedless.

180. To God belong the All-Beautiful Names so call and pray to Him by them.[44] And keep aloof from those who blaspheme (and distort the meaning of) His Names. They will be recompensed for what they are doing.

181. And of those whom We have created there are people who, (in due recognition of God with His Names,) guide by the truth (by God's leave) and dispense justice by it.

182. Whereas those who deny Our signs and Revelations, (as the consequence of their way,) We will step by step lead them on to perdition in ways they do not know.

183. I grant them respite. My designing is firm and irresistible.

184. And do they not reflect (by all that they witness in the Messenger and the Revelations coming to him) that there is no madness in their companion (the Prophet Muḥammad)? He is but a plain warner.

185. And do they never consider the inner dimension of the heavens and the earth and God's absolute dominion over them, and what things God has created, and that the end of their appointed term may already have approached? In what other discourse than this (warning contained in the Qur'ān) will they believe?

186. Whomever God leads astray there is no one to guide him; and He leaves them wandering blindly in their rebellion.

187. They ask you about the Hour, when it will come to anchor. Say: "It is my Lord alone Who knows it; none will disclose it in its time but He. It weighs heavily on the heavens and the earth. It does not come to you except unawares." They ask you as if you (being a Messenger required or meant that you) were well-informed of it. Say: "It is indeed God alone Who knows it, but most people have no knowledge (of this)."

44. A perfectly written article demonstrates the perfection of the act or work of writing, which, in turn, demonstrates the perfection of the title "author." This title is a sign of the perfection of the attribute of authorship, which, in turn, demonstrates the perfection of the talent for or ability in writing possessed by the author. And this capacity indicates the perfect writer who has written the article. Similarly, the perfection of creation or the universe demonstrates the perfection of the act of creation which, in turn, indicates the perfection of the title of the Creator. The perfection of the title is a sign of the perfection of the attribute of creativity, which, in turn, demonstrates the perfection of the essential, indispensable quality of having the "ability" to create. And the perfection of this indispensable quality or ability shows the perfection of the Being Who has it.

An article displays many other abilities or qualities, such as knowledge, fluency in writing, eloquence, the will to write, and the abilities to write, to arrange, and to express one's opinions; in short, there are many titles such as scholar, author, and organizer. The universe displays many Attributes and Titles or Names of God in the same way. Since it must be the product of only a perfect, infinite knowledge, will and power, we can deduce from this that God is All-Knowing, All-Willing, and All-Powerful. Similarly, as the universe also displays the acts of forming, giving shape, and adorning, etc., and many attributes, such as infinite

mercy, munificence, justice, wisdom, grace, and purity, etc., we can deduce that God is All-Merciful, All-Munificent, All-Just, All-Wise, All-Gracious, and All-Pure. This means that the universe, with whatever is in it, points to the Names of God which originate in His Attributes. These, in turn, originate in His Essential, Indispensable Qualities of being God, and these qualities have their source in God Himself, as the Divine Essence or Being. One or some of these Names are more manifested in a being, with other Names being subordinate; this is what gives it its essence with its particular characteristics. This causes differences among beings. For example, human beings on whom the Divine Name the All-Generous is more manifested than on others are potentially more generous; those on whom the Name All-Knowing is more manifested become more knowledgeable potentially, and those on whom the Name the All-Wise is more manifested, generally become wiser, and so on.

We call and must call God by His Names which He taught us, and can and must never call Him by names that are not compatible with His absolute perfection. Also, we pray to Him by mentioning His Names. For example, if we are ill and pray to Him for recovery, we pray to Him as the All-Healing, and mention this Name. If we feel we need provision and compassion, we pray to Him as or mentioning His Names the All-Providing and the All-Merciful. This is what is meant in this verse.

188. Say: "It is not within my power (to deal benefit and harm, so) unless God wills (and allows me to), I can neither bring benefit to, nor avert harm from, even myself. Had I knowledge of the Unseen, I would always be in profit (with no loss at all), and no adversity would ever touch me. I am only a warner (against the evil consequences of misguidance) and a bearer of glad tidings (of prosperity in return for faith and righteousness) for a people who will believe and who have already believed."

189. He it is Who created you from a single human self, and made from it its mate, so that he (inclining with love towards his mate) may find rest in her. And so, when he has covered her, she conceives a light burden, and continues to bear it. Then, when she grows heavy (with child), both (feel the need to) turn to God, their Lord, with prayer: "If You indeed grant us a righteous child, we will most certainly be among the thankful."

190. Then when He grants the couple a righteous child, they begin to associate partners with God in respect of what He has granted them.[45] Infinitely is He exalted above their association of partners with Him and whatever they associate with Him as partners.

191. Do they associate as partners with Him those who create nothing and themselves are created,

192. And who have no power to give them any help, nor can help themselves?

193. And if you call them in the direction of guidance, they do not follow you: It is the same for you whether you call to them or remain silent.

194. Those whom you deify and invoke apart from God are subservient beings created by God just like yourselves. (If you think and claim otherwise) then call on them and let them answer you, if you are truthful![46]

195. (How can you expect that they will answer:) have they feet on which they could walk; or have they hands with which they could grasp; or have they eyes with which they could see; or have they ears with which they could hear? Say (to them): "Call upon those you associate with God as partners, then scheme against me, and give me no respite!

---

45. Parents associate partners with God in respect of their children in the ways such as attributing them to nature or "natural laws" and causes or by ascribing their children's looks or

intelligence or achievements in life to themselves or to their children themselves, forgetting God and their debt and duty towards Him because of their children.

46. Some elementary school teachers in some Muslim lands used to enter the rooms with sweets in their pockets and, in order to avert young minds from belief in God, would ask the students, "Ask God for sweets and see whether He will give you any!" When, naturally, the students did not receive their sweets, using the most primitive method of dialectics, the teacher then would say: "Now ask me and see whether I will give you any!" This was the basest and most primitive way of thinking that history has ever seen, conceiving of God as being of the same as the created. Like Abraham's challenging Nimrod to make the sun rise from the west, as opposed to how God makes it rise from the east, this verse, too, provides an answer to such primitive modes of thinking. The operation of the universe, like its creation, is included in God's acts; they are not based on partial wisdom taking into consideration individual entities as being independent from others, but are based on the universal wisdom considering the universe both as a whole and with every individual entity in it and the universe's relationships with individual entities and the relationships among those entities.

Among beings, humankind has the most developed consciousness and the greatest ability to do or bring about something; yet most aspects of our lives are independent of us. For example, we have no say in the matter of our color, race, family, physique, and the date and place of our birth and death. Our bodies work automatically, according to a system established by the Creator and independently of us. Our vital needs, such as hunger, thirst, respiration, and sleeping keep us always under their grip and therefore we cannot overcome them; rather we are compelled to live bound to these needs. However, we observe a magnificent, perfect coordination and harmony between our lives, needs, the composition and working of our bodies, and the "natural" environment that surrounds us. If, despite all this and the magnificent order of the universe with whatever is in it that demonstrates the existence of an absolute, all-including knowledge, will, and power, we deny that there is One Who possesses them, then this is nothing less than self-deception. Denial of God is the deepest abyss into which we can fall, the darkest ignorance, the basest choice, the meanest lie, and means abandoning being endowed with reason, consciousness and the power of thought.

God makes humankind aware of His Existence in many other ways. Everyone has experienced that some of their needs have been met unexpectedly; some of our inward prayers, those that appear in the form of desires, have been answered; an unseen hand has come to our aid in an impossible situation or we have been saved from a danger when left without any other means. But, in order to be able to deny the Existence of a Supreme Being, people attribute all these to chance or coincidence; both are in fact nothing more than mere designations, and attributing the creation and direction of the universe and events to them is the greatest and most shameful of crimes. In the face of such an unforgivable crime, committed by many in the world, including many scientists, it is not possible to perceive and acknowledge how great a blessing belief is, how valuable a gift He grants us almost for nothing.

The verse to come will explain that anything substituted for God – be it nature or chance or matter or causality or an idol – must possess power, seeing, and hearing. In the universe there are beings, like animals and humanity, which have these powers. Seeing that it is not these beings themselves who create with such faculties, and seeing that their lives pass independently of themselves to a great extent, seeing that anyone who does not have these powers cannot impart them to others, there must be one who possesses them and imparts them to others. What a great pity it is that in the present age, which we call the age of science, many scientists cannot see this most manifest reality; this is a reality which even the people who lived in the most "primitive" ages could see. The reason many refuse to see this nowadays is merely in order to deny the Existence of God, and to attribute existence to such idols as matter, nature, chance, and causality, which have no knowledge, consciousness, seeing, or hearing. This is a most heinous deception on their part and a trick that their carnal selves, caprices, and satans play on them.

إِنَّ وَلِيِّ َ اللهُ الَّذِى نَزَّلَ الْكِتَابَ وَهُوَ يَتَوَلَّى الصَّالِحِينَ ۞ وَالَّذِينَ تَدْعُونَ مِنْ دُونِهِ لَا يَسْتَطِيعُونَ نَصْرَكُمْ وَلَا أَنفُسَهُمْ يَنصُرُونَ ۞ وَإِن تَدْعُوهُمْ إِلَى الْهُدَى لَا يَسْمَعُوا ۖ وَتَرَىٰهُمْ يَنظُرُونَ إِلَيْكَ وَهُمْ لَا يُبْصِرُونَ ۞ خُذِ الْعَفْوَ وَأْمُرْ بِالْعُرْفِ وَأَعْرِضْ عَنِ الْجَاهِلِينَ ۞ وَإِمَّا يَنزَغَنَّكَ مِنَ الشَّيْطَانِ نَزْغٌ فَاسْتَعِذْ بِاللهِ ۚ إِنَّهُ سَمِيعٌ عَلِيمٌ ۞ إِنَّ الَّذِينَ اتَّقَوْا إِذَا مَسَّهُمْ طَائِفٌ مِنَ الشَّيْطَانِ تَذَكَّرُوا فَإِذَا هُم مُّبْصِرُونَ ۞ وَإِخْوَانُهُمْ يَمُدُّونَهُمْ فِى الْغَىِّ ثُمَّ لَا يُقْصِرُونَ ۞ وَإِذَا لَمْ تَأْتِهِم بِآيَةٍ قَالُوا لَوْلَا اجْتَبَيْتَهَا ۚ قُلْ إِنَّمَا أَتَّبِعُ مَا يُوحَى إِلَىَّ مِن رَّبِّى ۚ هَٰذَا بَصَائِرُ مِن رَّبِّكُمْ وَهُدًى وَرَحْمَةٌ لِقَوْمٍ يُؤْمِنُونَ ۞ وَإِذَا قُرِئَ الْقُرْآنُ فَاسْتَمِعُوا لَهُ وَأَنصِتُوا لَعَلَّكُمْ تُرْحَمُونَ ۞ وَاذْكُر رَّبَّكَ فِى نَفْسِكَ تَضَرُّعًا وَخِيفَةً وَدُونَ الْجَهْرِ مِنَ الْقَوْلِ بِالْغُدُوِّ وَالْآصَالِ وَلَا تَكُن مِّنَ الْغَافِلِينَ ۞ إِنَّ الَّذِينَ عِندَ رَبِّكَ لَا يَسْتَكْبِرُونَ عَنْ عِبَادَتِهِ وَيُسَبِّحُونَهُ وَلَهُ يَسْجُدُونَ ۞

196. "Indeed, my Guardian is God Who sends down the Book in parts, and He be-friends and protects the righteous.

197. "Whereas those you deify and invoke, apart from Him, have no power to help you, nor can they help themselves.

198. If you call them to the guidance, they will not hear. And you see them looking at you (and may suppose that they have the power of seeing), but they do not see (having no insight or perceptiveness)."

199. (Even so, O Messenger) adopt the way of forbearance and tolerance, and enjoin what is good and right, and withdraw from the ignorant ones (do not care what they say and do).

200. And if a prompting from Satan should cause you hurt (as you carry out your mission or during worship or in your everyday life), seek refuge in God. He is All-Hearing, All-Knowing.

201. Those who keep from disobedience to God in reverence for Him and piety: when a suggestion from Satan touches them – they are alert and remember God, and then they have clear discernment.

202. Whereas their brothers (the brothers of the satans in the form of human beings) – satans draw them deeper into error and do not give over relax in their efforts.

203. When you (O Messenger) do not produce for them a sign (a miracle of the kind they desire, or Revelation temporarily ceases), they say, "Were you unable to make one up?" Say: "I only follow what-

ever is revealed to me from my Lord. This (the Qur'ān) is the light of discernment and insight (into the truth) from your Lord (Who creates, sustains, and protects you), and guidance and mercy for people will believe and who have already believed."

204. And so, when the Qur'ān is recited, give ear to it and listen in silence so that you may be shown mercy.

205. Remember and mention your Lord within yourself (in the depths of your heart), most humbly and in awe, not loud of voice, at morning and evening. And do not be among the neglectful.

206. Those (angels) who are in your Lord's Presence never turn away from His service out of pride, and they glorify Him, and prostrate before Him.

SŪRAH 8

AL-ANFĀL (GAINS OF WAR)

Madīnah period

This *sūrah* was revealed during the Madīnah period of Islam, just after the Battle of Badr, the first major confrontation between the Muslims of Madīnah and the polytheists of Makkah. It takes its name from the word *al-anfāl* found in the first verse. *Al-Anfāl* has the meaning of "extra, addition," but here refers to the spoils taken in war. The *sūrah* deals for the most part with the Battle of Badr and the lessons that are to be taken from it, and instructs believers in topics such us *jihād*, *hijrah* (emigration for God's sake), the law of war, treaties, gains of war, patience, mutual helping and solidarity, and reliance on God.

In the Name of God, the All-Merciful, the All-Compassionate.

1. They (the believers) ask you about the gains of war. Say: "The gains of war belong to God and the Messenger (and they distribute them as they will)." So keep from disobedience to God in reverence for Him and piety, and set things right among yourselves to allow no discord; and obey God and His Messenger if you are true believers.[1]

2. The true believers are only those who, when God is mentioned, their hearts tremble with awe, and when His Revelations are recited to them, it strengthens them in faith, and they put their trust in their Lord.

3. They establish the Prayer in conformity with its conditions, and out of whatever We have provided for them (of wealth, knowledge, power, etc.,) they spend (to provide sustenance for the needy, and in God's cause, purely for the good pleasure of God and without placing others under obligation.)

4. Those (illustrious ones) are they who are truly believers. For them are ranks with their Lord (to be granted one after the other), and forgiveness (to bring unforeseen blessings), and generous, honorable provision.

5. Just so, your Lord caused you to go forth from your home for a true cause (which He had already determined would be realized); and yet a group from among the believers were averse (to the direction that events took).

6. They argued with you concerning the truth (of the matter which God had already decided would be realized) even after it (the direction that developments would take) had been manifest, as if they

were being driven toward death with their eyes wide open.

7. Even when God had promised you that one of the two hosts (the trade caravan and the Makkan army approaching) would fall to you, you still wished that other than the powerful, armed one should fall into your hands – whereas God willed to prove

the truth to be true by His decrees and make it triumphant, and uproot the unbelievers (by causing their leaders to die).

8. (He willed it so) so as to prove the truth to be true and make it triumphant, and the falsehood to be false, however hateful this might be to the disbelieving criminals.[2]

---

1. The original word *anfāl* translated as "gains of war" is the plural form of *nafl*. This word means extra, voluntary service when used in relation to a servant, and extra or additional reward when used for God. It is my humble opinion that any worldly reward coming as the result of services rendered in God's cause is included in this meaning. The majority of scholars are in agreement that here it denotes the gains of war. However, the word *ghanā'im* (plural of *ghanīmah*) is used for the gains of war in verse 41; *anfāl* has a more comprehensive meaning. It also includes the idea of *fay* (gains of war taken without fighting: 59: 6).

A believer aims only to obtain God's approval and good pleasure in their services in His way. They have no other expectations. Even when they have to fight against God's enemies, they only aim to obtain God's good pleasure and uphold His Word, without expecting anything worldly. No worldly aims, such as spoils, fame, or position can have a place in the believer's heart. The gains of war are extra rewards that come as the result of fighting in His way, so they belong to God and the Messenger. They can distribute them as they will and the believers must accept their distribution. It is because of this that the *sūrah* begins with orienting the believers' hearts according to this general principle. It stresses that a believer cannot fight for the gains of war, and teaches that if a believer has captured even a needle in war, they must hand it over to the commander or state before what has been gained is distributed.

2. These verses are concerned with the events

that led up to the Battle of Badr. After the emigration to Madīnah, the Prophet Muhammad, upon him be peace and blessings, made a treaty with the Jewish tribes which gave the city the status of a multi-communal city-state. Then he organized a new market that would help to establish the economic independence of the Muslims. In Madīnah there were powerful Jewish tribes, polytheist Arabs, and hypocrites; each posed a threat to the new Muslim community, and in the surrounding desert were polytheist tribes who recognized the Quraysh as their leaders. The Makkans threatened 'Abdullah ibn Ubayy ibn Salūl, the chief hypocrite in Madīnah, that unless he were to expel the Prophet Muhammad from Madīnah they would attack the city. They would organize sudden attacks on the suburbs of the city and plunder and shed blood. Under such adverse conditions, the Prophet Muhammad, upon him be peace and blessings, felt obliged to provide security, in order to maintain the existence of Islam, and to be able to continue to communicate the message. For this purpose, he organized military campaigns in the desert, sometimes under the leadership of his commanders, sometimes under his own leadership. He never allowed for there to be any bloodshed. With these campaigns, he also aimed to make the neighboring tribes aware of the existence of Muslims and to prevent them from gathering around the polytheist Quraysh.

The Makkans usurped whatever the emigrating Muslims had left behind. They dispatched a trade caravan to Syria, the merchandise of which consisted mainly of the property of the Muslims. God's Messenger decided to take repossession of their property while the caravan was en route to Makkah. As can be understood from these verses, God Almighty willed that the Makkans, who were extremely uneasy about the development of Islam, should be determined to guard the caravan and to undergo a military encounter with the Muslims. The events developed as God had willed. Most likely having sensed God's will, God's Messenger consulted his army about the matter; his army was comprised of only about 310 men, most of them on foot, except for two or three mounted on horses and about 50 on camels. Some insisted that they should march upon the caravan, as the Makkan army was very powerful, comprised of 1,000 men, 600 armored with more than 100 horsemen. However, the speeches of Miqdād ibn 'Amr and Sa'd ibn Mu'ādh, who said that they would follow the Messenger wherever he led them, pleased the Messenger and greatly encouraged the believers. In the end, the two armies came face to face in Badr, situated between Madīnah and Makkah on the 17th of Ramaḍān (or, according to some authorities on the 19th or 21st,) in the second year of *Hijrah* (624).

إِذْ تَسْتَغِيثُونَ رَبَّكُمْ فَاسْتَجَابَ لَكُمْ أَنِّي مُمِدُّكُمْ
بِأَلْفٍ مِّنَ الْمَلَٰٓئِكَةِ مُرْدِفِينَ ۞ وَمَا جَعَلَهُ اللَّهُ إِلَّا بُشْرَىٰ
وَلِتَطْمَئِنَّ بِهِ قُلُوبُكُمْ وَمَا النَّصْرُ إِلَّا مِنْ عِندِ اللَّهِ إِنَّ اللَّهَ
عَزِيزٌ حَكِيمٌ ۞ إِذْ يُغَشِّيكُمُ النُّعَاسَ أَمَنَةً مِّنْهُ وَيُنَزِّلُ عَلَيْكُم
مِّنَ السَّمَآءِ مَآءً لِّيُطَهِّرَكُم بِهِ وَيُذْهِبَ عَنكُمْ رِجْزَ الشَّيْطَٰنِ
وَلِيَرْبِطَ عَلَىٰ قُلُوبِكُمْ وَيُثَبِّتَ بِهِ الْأَقْدَامَ ۞ إِذْ يُوحِي رَبُّكَ
إِلَى الْمَلَٰٓئِكَةِ أَنِّي مَعَكُمْ فَثَبِّتُوا الَّذِينَ ءَامَنُوا سَأُلْقِي فِي
قُلُوبِ الَّذِينَ كَفَرُوا الرُّعْبَ فَاضْرِبُوا فَوْقَ الْأَعْنَاقِ
وَاضْرِبُوا مِنْهُمْ كُلَّ بَنَانٍ ۞ ذَٰلِكَ بِأَنَّهُمْ شَآقُّوا اللَّهَ
وَرَسُولَهُ وَمَن يُشَاقِقِ اللَّهَ وَرَسُولَهُ فَإِنَّ اللَّهَ شَدِيدُ
الْعِقَابِ ۞ ذَٰلِكُمْ فَذُوقُوهُ وَأَنَّ لِلْكَٰفِرِينَ عَذَابَ
النَّارِ ۞ يَٰٓأَيُّهَا الَّذِينَ ءَامَنُوا إِذَا لَقِيتُمُ الَّذِينَ كَفَرُوا
زَحْفًا فَلَا تُوَلُّوهُمُ الْأَدْبَارَ ۞ وَمَن يُوَلِّهِمْ يَوْمَئِذٍ
دُبُرَهُ إِلَّا مُتَحَرِّفًا لِّقِتَالٍ أَوْ مُتَحَيِّزًا إِلَىٰ فِئَةٍ فَقَدْ
بَآءَ بِغَضَبٍ مِّنَ اللَّهِ وَمَأْوَىٰهُ جَهَنَّمُ وَبِئْسَ الْمَصِيرُ ۞

9. When you were imploring your Lord for help (as a special mercy), and He responded to you: "I will help you with a thousand angels, coming host after host."

10. God did that only as glad tidings (of your imminent victory), and that your hearts thereby might be at rest. For help and victory come from God alone. Surely God is All-Glorious with irresistible might, All-Wise.

11. When (at the time that you most needed courage), He caused a slumber to enfold you as a reassurance from Him, and sent down water upon you from the sky, that thereby He might cleanse you (of all actual or ritual impurities, by enabling you to do the minor and major ablution), and take away from you the polluting whisperings of Satan, and through it make your hearts strong, and your steps steady.

12. When (in the meantime) your Lord revealed to the angels: "I am certainly with you, so make firm the feet of those who believe. I will cast fear into the hearts of those who disbelieve. So strike at their necks and strike at every finger (which holds a sword or bow).

13. "Do so because they defied God and His Messenger." Whoever defies God and His Messenger: (let everyone know that) God is severe in retribution.

14. That is (by your deserving, O enemies of God), so taste it, and (let everyone know that) for the unbelievers there is also the punishment of the Fire.

15. O you who believe! When you encounter in battle those who disbelieve, do not turn your backs on them in flight.

16. For whoever turns his back on them on the day of such an engagement – except that it be tactical maneuvering to fight again or joining another troop of believers (or taking up a position against another enemy host) – has indeed incurred God's condemnation, and his final refuge is the Fire; how evil a destination to arrive at!

178 سُورَةُ الأَنْفَال ١٧٨

فَلَمْ تَقْتُلُوهُمْ وَلَٰكِنَّ اللَّهَ قَتَلَهُمْ وَمَا رَمَيْتَ إِذْ رَمَيْتَ
وَلَٰكِنَّ اللَّهَ رَمَىٰ وَلِيُبْلِيَ الْمُؤْمِنِينَ مِنْهُ بَلَاءً حَسَنًا إِنَّ اللَّهَ
سَمِيعٌ عَلِيمٌ ۝ ذَٰلِكُمْ وَأَنَّ اللَّهَ مُوهِنُ كَيْدِ الْكَافِرِينَ ۝
إِنْ تَسْتَفْتِحُوا فَقَدْ جَاءَكُمُ الْفَتْحُ وَإِنْ تَنْتَهُوا فَهُوَ خَيْرٌ
لَكُمْ وَإِنْ تَعُودُوا نَعُدْ وَلَنْ تُغْنِيَ عَنْكُمْ فِئَتُكُمْ
شَيْئًا وَلَوْ كَثُرَتْ وَأَنَّ اللَّهَ مَعَ الْمُؤْمِنِينَ ۝ يَا
أَيُّهَا الَّذِينَ آمَنُوا أَطِيعُوا اللَّهَ وَرَسُولَهُ وَلَا تَوَلَّوْا عَنْهُ وَأَنْتُمْ
تَسْمَعُونَ ۝ وَلَا تَكُونُوا كَالَّذِينَ قَالُوا سَمِعْنَا وَهُمْ لَا يَسْمَعُونَ
۝ إِنَّ شَرَّ الدَّوَابِّ عِنْدَ اللَّهِ الصُّمُّ الْبُكْمُ الَّذِينَ لَا
يَعْقِلُونَ ۝ وَلَوْ عَلِمَ اللَّهُ فِيهِمْ خَيْرًا لَأَسْمَعَهُمْ
وَلَوْ أَسْمَعَهُمْ لَتَوَلَّوْا وَهُمْ مُعْرِضُونَ ۝ يَا أَيُّهَا
الَّذِينَ آمَنُوا اسْتَجِيبُوا لِلَّهِ وَلِلرَّسُولِ إِذَا دَعَاكُمْ
لِمَا يُحْيِيكُمْ وَاعْلَمُوا أَنَّ اللَّهَ يَحُولُ بَيْنَ الْمَرْءِ وَقَلْبِهِ وَأَنَّهُ
إِلَيْهِ تُحْشَرُونَ ۝ وَاتَّقُوا فِتْنَةً لَا تُصِيبَنَّ الَّذِينَ ظَلَمُوا
مِنْكُمْ خَاصَّةً وَاعْلَمُوا أَنَّ اللَّهَ شَدِيدُ الْعِقَابِ ۝

───◆───

17. You (O believers) did not kill them (by yourselves in the battle), but God killed them;[3] and when you (O Messenger) threw (dust at them at the start of the battle), it was not you who threw but God threw.[4] (He did all this) so that He might put the believers to a test by a fair testing from Him (so that could attain to their goal and should know that victory is from God). Surely, God is All-Hearing, All-Knowing.

18. That is (how He treats you) and (let everyone know that) God it is Who undermines the schemes of the unbelievers.

19. If you (O unbelievers) sought a judgment (through battle to see which party is in the right), then surely a judgment has come to you. If you cease (hostilities towards the believers), it is what will be to your good. But if you revert (to hostilities), We will also revert (to what We did to you in that battle). And never will your being a great host be of any avail to you, however numerous it be, and (let everyone know) that God is with the believers.[5]

20. O you who believe! Obey God and His Messenger, and do not turn away from him when you are hearing (from him God's Revelations).

21. And do not be like those who say, "We hear," but in truth they do not hear.

22. Indeed the worst kind of all living creatures in God's sight are the deaf and dumb, who do not reason and understand.

23. And had God seen any good in them, He would certainly have made them hear, but (being as they are) even if He made them hear, they would surely turn away in aversion.

24. O you who believe! Respond to God and to the Messenger when the Messenger calls you (in the Name of God) to that which gives you life; and know well that surely God "intervenes" between a person and his heart (to cause his heart to swerve); and that He it is to Whom you will be gathered.

25. And beware and guard yourselves against a trial that will surely not smite exclusively those among you who are engaged in wrongdoing; and know that God is severe in retribution.

3. That is, "but for God's plan and help, you could not have killed them and won the war." This is a warning to those who thought with pride that they won the war by their valor and war skills.

4. This phrase refers to the occasion when the Muslim and Makkan armies stood face to face in the Battle of Badr. At that moment, God's Messenger (upon him be peace and blessings) threw a handful of dust at the enemy saying, "May their faces be scorched," and every enemy soldier felt as if he had became blind. (Ibn Hishām, 1: 668)

5. The Muslims were very few and were persecuted in a variety of ways in Makkah. God Almighty saved them and provided them with a refuge in Madīnah. However, since they had to leave all their belongings in Makkah, they suffered great deprivations in Madīnah in the early years, despite the peerless sacrifices of the Anṣār, the Muslims of Madīnah. They were also surrounded by totally unfavorable conditions. In such circumstances, the caravan that was en route to Makkah from Syria, which contained their belongings that they had had to leave in Makkah, was a chance for them to restore some of their usurped property. Yet, God

willed that they should encounter the strong Makkan army, which included all the leaders of polytheism except Abū Lahab, and which was three times greater in number than them. If we consider that around 600 of the opposing army were armored and that there were more than 100 horsemen, while the Muslim army consisted of about 310 men, and only two or three horsemen, with none of them wearing armor, and also that the battles in those days were hand-to-hand combat, it can be easily understood what a terrible position the Muslims found themselves in. They were in dire need of God's help. The Qur'ān quite explicitly states that they won this war with God's help; in fact God attributes to Himself the killing of the enemy soldiers, almost all of whom were the leaders of the polytheists, and also the efficacy of the dust thrown at them by the Messenger. He also sent angels to encourage the Muslims. They struck at the necks and fingers of the enemy soldiers to make it difficult for them to remain standing and to use their swords, arrows and spears. In addition to these things mentioned above, God helped the Muslims in many other ways. These will be mentioned later, as the occasion necessitates.

وَاذْكُرُوٓا اِذْ اَنْتُمْ قَلِيلٌ مُّسْتَضْعَفُوْنَ فِي الْاَرْضِ
تَخَافُوْنَ اَنْ يَّتَخَطَّفَكُمُ النَّاسُ فَاٰوٰىكُمْ وَاَيَّدَكُمْ بِنَصْرِهٖ
وَرَزَقَكُمْ مِّنَ الطَّيِّبٰتِ لَعَلَّكُمْ تَشْكُرُوْنَ ۞ يٰٓاَيُّهَا
الَّذِيْنَ اٰمَنُوْا لَا تَخُوْنُوا اللّٰهَ وَالرَّسُوْلَ وَتَخُوْنُوٓا اَمٰنٰتِكُمْ
وَاَنْتُمْ تَعْلَمُوْنَ ۞ وَاعْلَمُوٓا اَنَّمَاۤ اَمْوَالُكُمْ وَاَوْلَادُكُمْ
فِتْنَةٌ وَّاَنَّ اللّٰهَ عِنْدَهٗٓ اَجْرٌ عَظِيْمٌ ۞ يٰٓاَيُّهَا الَّذِيْنَ اٰمَنُوٓا
اِنْ تَتَّقُوا اللّٰهَ يَجْعَلْ لَّكُمْ فُرْقَانًا وَّيُكَفِّرْ عَنْكُمْ سَيِّاٰتِكُمْ
وَيَغْفِرْ لَكُمْ وَاللّٰهُ ذُو الْفَضْلِ الْعَظِيْمِ ۞ وَاِذْ يَمْكُرُ
بِكَ الَّذِيْنَ كَفَرُوْا لِيُثْبِتُوْكَ اَوْ يَقْتُلُوْكَ اَوْ يُخْرِجُوْكَ وَيَمْكُرُوْنَ
وَيَمْكُرُ اللّٰهُ وَاللّٰهُ خَيْرُ الْمٰكِرِيْنَ ۞ وَاِذَا تُتْلٰى عَلَيْهِمْ اٰيٰتُنَا
قَالُوْا قَدْ سَمِعْنَا لَوْ نَشَاءُ لَقُلْنَا مِثْلَ هٰذَاۤ اِنْ هٰذَاۤ اِلَّاۤ اَسَاطِيْرُ الْاَوَّلِيْنَ
۞ وَاِذْ قَالُوا اللّٰهُمَّ اِنْ كَانَ هٰذَا هُوَ الْحَقَّ مِنْ
عِنْدِكَ فَاَمْطِرْ عَلَيْنَا حِجَارَةً مِّنَ السَّمَاۤءِ اَوِ ائْتِنَا بِعَذَابٍ
اَلِيْمٍ ۞ وَمَا كَانَ اللّٰهُ لِيُعَذِّبَهُمْ وَاَنْتَ فِيْهِمْ وَمَا
كَانَ اللّٰهُ مُعَذِّبَهُمْ وَهُمْ يَسْتَغْفِرُوْنَ ۞

---

26. And remember (with gratitude) when you were few and deemed weak in the land (and oppressed), fearing that people would snatch you away, how He provided you with refuge, and strengthened you with His help, and provided for you sustenance out of the pure, wholesome things, that you might give thanks (to Him from the heart and in speech, and in action by fulfilling His commandments).

27. O you who believe! Do not betray God and His Messenger, that you should not betray the trusts in your keeping while you know (what doing so means).[6]

28. Know that your possessions and your children are but a trial and temptation, and God is He with Whom there is a tremendous reward.

29. O you who believe! If you keep from disobedience to God in reverence for Him and piety to deserve His protection, He will make a criterion for you (in your hearts to distinguish between truth and falsehood, and right and wrong), and blot out from you your evil deeds, and forgive you. God is of tremendous grace and bounty.

30. And (recall, O Messenger,) how those who disbelieve schemed against you to take you captive, or kill you, or drive you away (from Makkah). Thus were they scheming, but God put His will into effect (and brought their scheme to nothing). God wills what is the best (for His believing servants) and makes His will prevail.[7]

31. When Our Revelations are recited to them, they say: "We have heard (the like of this before many times); if we wish, we can speak the like of this; this is nothing but fables of the ancients."

32. And when they said (even this): "O God! If this is indeed the truth from You, then rain down upon us stones from the sky or bring upon us another painful punishment!"

33. But God would not punish them so long as you were among them; and God is not to punish them (or other people) while they implore Him for forgiveness for their sins.[8]

6. Betraying God and His Messenger by disobeying them means self-betrayal and results in betraying trusts in one's keeping such as the confidences, the lives, properties, and chastity of others, and the public affairs, duties, and posts and positions in his or her care.

7. Verses 20–30 contain serious advice and reminders for the new Muslim community in Madīnah and for all Muslims in all ages and places. Verse 30 is concerned with a favor granted to God's Messenger, upon him be peace and blessings, and to the Muslim community through him.

The Battle of Badr proved to be the turning point and one of the greatest victories in Muslim history, perhaps even the greatest. It was won purely with God's help. As the Muslims had won after having been in such an unenviable position, it is highly likely that the victorious heroes of Badr felt some pride in their achievement. In addition, some of them had been reluctant to fight, and some began to collect booty without first routing the enemy or asking whether it was permissible to collect booty (M. Asim Köksal, 2: 146, 171–73). So, verses 20–30 contain warnings and serious advice for these people, and for all Muslims to come until Judgment Day. These warnings and advice can be summed up as follows:

- Victory and defeat are purely in the hand of God. In order to deserve victory, people must do whatever is necessary to gain it.
- Although people do whatever they can to gain or deserve victory, God is never obliged to make them victorious. As with any good that comes to people, victory is also a blessing from God. Therefore, we must always be thankful to God.
- In all His commandments, people must obey God and His Messenger. They must obey these commandments and not act as if they had not heard anything. They must obey what God and His Messenger command and sincerely carry out these orders.
- Those to whose ears God's and His Messenger's commands have not found a way, or who act as if they had not been told anything, are spiritually dead. These people, therefore, are just like lifeless objects, deaf and dumb, not able to understand or use their reason.

- There are certain things which make people deaf, dumb, and senseless in the face of Divine Revelation, such as having prejudices, indulging in vainglory and arrogance, holding the wrong viewpoint, being controlled by their carnal desires and worldly ambitions, and wrongdoing. Because of such things, people lose all their spiritual senses and faculties, and their ability to believe.

- Believers must always give respond positively to the call of God and His Messenger. The Messenger conveys to them God's call to the truth; this is what makes them spiritually alive. If they do not give positive responses to this call, God "intervenes" between them and their hearts, and causes their hearts to swerve, leading them to perdition and bringing about their doom in the Hereafter.

- If believers fail to respond positively to the call of God through His Messenger this will not only cause their doom in the Hereafter, but also give rise to an internal conflict in society. This is a decisive test, enabling them to distinguish those who are sincere from those who are not. They may lose their lives, property, and beloved ones in this conflict and, what is worse, although once being sincere brothers and sisters, they begin to kill each other as sworn enemies. Internal security and mutual trust no longer exist, and public affairs and posts are given to those who are not qualified. This may result in falling under the control of a despotic government or foreign dominion, or being subject to other kinds of calamities.

- Believers must always pursue God's good pleasure and approval and try to obtain it in all their words and actions. They must never think of gaining worldly advantages, in particular through religious acts or services.

- Whatever a person has in the world, whether it be social status, a post, smart and successful children, or wealth, is a means of testing to determine what "carat" a person is. That is our possessions, the things that we take pride in, are a test for us. God provides us with all our gifts, and therefore we must attribute them to God and give constant thanks to God from the heart, verbally and through our life-style. If we act in such a way, God will reward us greatly in the Hereafter and may also increase what He has provided in the world for us as well. Otherwise, whatever a person has may be a means of self-ruin for them in the other world or even in this world.

- Believers must always be God-conscious and act in piety and utmost reverence for God, fearing that they might make a mistake or commit a sin. If they do so sincerely, God will equip them with a criterion which they will feel in their hearts. By this criterion they can distinguish between what is right and wrong, and true and false, without applying to a mufti or another scholar. So long as they do whatever they must to deserve God's protection,

God will protect them against thinking and doing wrong, from internal conflicts, and from defeat by other powers.

It should also be noted here that, while the verses that were revealed after the Battle of Uhud console the believers due to the reverse they experienced in the second stage of the battle and even contain compliments for them to lift their wounded spirits, these verses, as they came after the victory of Badr, do not contain any congratulatory words; rather we find warning and advice. This is important, particularly with respect to guidance and education.

8. This verse implies that so long as the religion – Islam – brought by God's Messenger, upon him be peace and blessings, continues to be practiced and to order the life of the community in a way that is pleasing to God Almighty, and as long as people go on living in consciousness of God and imploring Him for forgiveness whenever they commit sins, God will not inflict any grievous suffering on them.

151   سورة الأنفال   ١٨٠

وَمَالَهُمْ اَلَّا يُعَذِّبَهُمُ اللهُ وَهُمْ يَصُدُّونَ عَنِ
الْمَسْجِدِ الْحَرَامِ وَمَا كَانُوٓا اَوْلِيَآءَهُ إِنْ اَوْلِيَآؤُهُ اِلَّا
الْمُتَّقُونَ وَلٰكِنَّ اَكْثَرَهُمْ لَا يَعْلَمُونَ ۞ وَمَا كَانَ صَلَاتُهُمْ
عِنْدَ الْبَيْتِ اِلَّا مُكَآءً وَتَصْدِيَةً فَذُوقُوا الْعَذَابَ بِمَا
كُنْتُمْ تَكْفُرُونَ ۞ اِنَّ الَّذِينَ كَفَرُوا يُنْفِقُونَ
اَمْوَالَهُمْ لِيَصُدُّوا عَنْ سَبِيلِ اللهِ فَسَيُنْفِقُونَهَا ثُمَّ
تَكُونُ عَلَيْهِمْ حَسْرَةً ثُمَّ يُغْلَبُونَ وَالَّذِينَ كَفَرُوٓا
اِلٰى جَهَنَّمَ يُحْشَرُونَ ۞ لِيَمِيزَ اللهُ الْخَبِيثَ مِنَ الطَّيِّبِ
وَيَجْعَلَ الْخَبِيثَ بَعْضَهُ عَلٰى بَعْضٍ فَيَرْكُمَهُ جَمِيعًا
فَيَجْعَلَهُ فِي جَهَنَّمَ اُولٰئِكَ هُمُ الْخَاسِرُونَ ۞ قُلْ لِلَّذِينَ
كَفَرُوٓا اِنْ يَنْتَهُوا يُغْفَرْ لَهُمْ مَا قَدْ سَلَفَ وَاِنْ يَعُودُوا
فَقَدْ مَضَتْ سُنَّتُ الْاَوَّلِينَ ۞ وَقَاتِلُوهُمْ حَتّٰى لَا تَكُونَ
فِتْنَةً وَيَكُونَ الدِّينُ كُلُّهُ لِلهِ فَاِنِ انْتَهَوْا فَاِنَّ
اللهَ بِمَا يَعْمَلُونَ بَصِيرٌ ۞ وَاِنْ تَوَلَّوْا فَاعْلَمُوٓا اَنَّ
اللهَ مَوْلٰيكُمْ نِعْمَ الْمَوْلٰى وَنِعْمَ النَّصِيرُ ۞

34. What plea do they have that God should not punish them, seeing that they bar (the believers) from the Sacred Mosque, although they are not qualified to own and guard it? Its qualified, rightful guardians are only the pious who keep from disobedience to God in reverence for Him, but most of them (those unbelievers) do not know.

35. Their Prayer at the House (in the Sacred Mosque) is nothing but whistling and hand-clapping. Then, taste the punishment because you persistently disbelieve.[9]

36. Those who are persistent in unbelief spend their wealth in order that they may bar from God's way. They will continue to spend it so until it becomes for them a source of sighs and anguish, and then they will be vanquished. Those who are persistent in unbelief will finally be gathered into Hell.

37. Thus does God separate the corrupt from the pure, and make all those who are corrupt into a pile one upon another, and then place them in Hell. Those are indeed the losers.

38. Tell those persistent in unbelief that if they cease (to disbelieve themselves and prevent others from entering the fold of Islam), what is past will be forgiven them; but if they revert (to their hostilities), then it is manifest by what happened to the people of old times (what their fate must be).

39. And (if they still persist in unbelief and hostilities), fight against them until there is no longer disorder and oppression rooted in rebellion against God, and the whole of religion (the full authority to order the way of life is recognized) for God exclusively. If they cease (to persist in unbelief and continue hostilities toward the believers), then surely God sees well all that they do.[10]

40. If they still follow their own way, know that God is your Owner and Guardian. How excellent a Guardian and an Owner He is, how excellent a Helper.

9. The punishment mentioned here is not of the kind referred to in verse 32 above and which usually follows as a "natural" calamity. It is either their defeat at the hands of the Muslims or some social catastrophes or Divine punishment in the Hereafter. It may indeed refer to all.

10. The Qur'ān mentions *fitnah* as being the most important reason for going to war. As also mentioned in 2: 191 and explained in note 138 to that *sūrah* (al-Baqarah), *fitnah* means unbelief, associating partners with God, hypocrisy, wrongdoing, transgression, and the chaotic atmosphere or disorder that gives rise to these or that is caused by these. It may be truer to define *fitnah* as corruption, including all these evils mentioned.

God Almighty wills that peace, justice, security, and belief in and submission to Him should prevail on the earth; these are the conditions that are essential to humanity. So what the believers must do is to strive to put an end to *fitnah* or the dominion of unbelief, the association of partners with God, and wrongdoing. This is one legitimate reason for entering a war; the other one is in the case of self-defense. Once *fitnah* has been eradicated, people can adopt different world-views and the followers of other faiths such as Christianity, Judaism, Zoroastrianism, and Sabeanism are free to live according to their own religions. But public order should not be harmed by any of these faiths. (See also 2: 190–93, 256, notes 138–39.)

وَٱعْلَمُوٓا أَنَّمَا غَنِمْتُم مِّن شَىْءٍ فَأَنَّ لِلَّهِ خُمُسَهُ وَلِلرَّسُولِ وَلِذِى ٱلْقُرْبَىٰ وَٱلْيَتَامَىٰ وَٱلْمَسَاكِينِ وَٱبْنِ ٱلسَّبِيلِ إِن كُنتُمْ ءَامَنتُم بِٱللَّهِ وَمَآ أَنزَلْنَا عَلَىٰ عَبْدِنَا يَوْمَ ٱلْفُرْقَانِ يَوْمَ ٱلْتَقَى ٱلْجَمْعَانِ وَٱللَّهُ عَلَىٰ كُلِّ شَىْءٍ قَدِيرٌ ۝ إِذْ أَنتُم بِٱلْعُدْوَةِ ٱلدُّنْيَا وَهُم بِٱلْعُدْوَةِ ٱلْقُصْوَىٰ وَٱلرَّكْبُ أَسْفَلَ مِنكُمْ وَلَوْ تَوَاعَدتُّمْ لَٱخْتَلَفْتُمْ فِى ٱلْمِيعَادِ وَلَٰكِن لِّيَقْضِىَ ٱللَّهُ أَمْرًا كَانَ مَفْعُولًا لِّيَهْلِكَ مَنْ هَلَكَ عَن بَيِّنَةٍ وَيَحْيَىٰ مَنْ حَىَّ عَن بَيِّنَةٍ وَإِنَّ ٱللَّهَ لَسَمِيعٌ عَلِيمٌ ۝ إِذْ يُرِيكَهُمُ ٱللَّهُ فِى مَنَامِكَ قَلِيلًا وَلَوْ أَرَىٰكَهُمْ كَثِيرًا لَّفَشِلْتُمْ وَلَتَنَازَعْتُمْ فِى ٱلْأَمْرِ وَلَٰكِنَّ ٱللَّهَ سَلَّمَ إِنَّهُ عَلِيمٌ بِذَاتِ ٱلصُّدُورِ ۝ وَإِذْ يُرِيكُمُوهُمْ إِذِ ٱلْتَقَيْتُمْ فِىٓ أَعْيُنِكُمْ قَلِيلًا وَيُقَلِّلُكُمْ فِىٓ أَعْيُنِهِمْ لِيَقْضِىَ ٱللَّهُ أَمْرًا كَانَ مَفْعُولًا وَإِلَى ٱللَّهِ تُرْجَعُ ٱلْأُمُورُ ۝ يَٰٓأَيُّهَا ٱلَّذِينَ ءَامَنُوٓا إِذَا لَقِيتُمْ فِئَةً فَٱثْبُتُوا وَٱذْكُرُوا ٱللَّهَ كَثِيرًا لَّعَلَّكُمْ تُفْلِحُونَ ۝

41. And know that whatever you take as gains of war, to God belongs one fifth of it, and to the Messenger, and the near kinsfolk, and orphans, and the destitute, and the wayfarer (one devoid of sufficient means of journeying).[11] (This you must observe) if you truly believe in God and what We sent down on our Servant on the day when the truth and falsehood were distinguished from each other, the day when the two hosts met in battle. God has full power over everything.

42. (Remember the day) when you were at the nearer end of the valley (of Badr on the Madīnah side) and they were at the farther end and the caravan below you (on the coastal plain). If you had mutually made an appointment to meet for battle in such circumstances, indeed you would not have been able to hold to the appointment. But (God caused you to meet for battle in such circumstances) so that God might accomplish a thing that He had already decreed in order that he who was to perish should perish by a clear evidence (of his deserving perishing because he followed falsehood), and he who survived might survive by a clear evidence (of his deserving survival because of his devotion to the truth). Surely God is All-Hearing, All-Knowing.

43. (And recall, O Messenger) when God showed them to you in your dream as few. If He had showed them to you as numerous (as they really were), you (O believers) would surely have lost heart, and would surely have disagreed with one another about the matter. But God saved (you from that). God surely has full knowledge of what lies hidden in the bosoms.

44. And when He made them appear as few in your eyes when you met them in the battle just as He lessened you in their eyes, so that God might accomplish a thing that He had already decreed. And to God are all affairs ultimately referred, (and whatever He wills occurs).

45. O you who believe! When you meet a host in battle, stand firm and remember and mention God much, that you may triumph.

11. This *sūrah* began by emphasizing the basic principle that the gains of war belong to God and His Messenger and it has prepared the hearts of the believers to willingly accept the distribution that God will make. This verse describes how the gains of war will be distributed and assigns one-fifth to God first; that is to public services, and then mentions the people who represent these services: the Messenger, his near kinsfolk, orphans, the destitute and the wayfarer who does not have sufficient means to complete the journey. The remainder is distributed among the warriors.

The Messenger, upon him be peace and blessings, devoted all his life to communicating Islam to others and to the service of the people. He was not in a position to provide for the poor among his kinsfolk. In addition, there were many other places or items of expenditure for which the Messenger had to pay as both a Messenger and the head of the state. The share assigned to him may, in some respects, be likened to the funds assigned for the special expenditure of heads of state.

It is a historical fact that the Messenger, upon him be peace and blessings, spent his first wife Khadījah's wealth on the cause of calling to Islam, while he, his family and his kinsfolk lived as the poorest of all Muslims. They also spent all the shares of the gains of war that were assigned to them on Islamic services and the needy.

182   سورة الأنفال   ١٨٢

وَأَطِيعُوا اللّٰهَ وَرَسُولَهُ وَلَا تَنَازَعُوا فَتَفْشَلُوا وَتَذْهَبَ
رِيحُكُمْ وَاصْبِرُوا إِنَّ اللّٰهَ مَعَ الصَّابِرِينَ ۞ وَلَا تَكُونُوا
كَالَّذِينَ خَرَجُوا مِنْ دِيَارِهِمْ بَطَرًا وَرِئَاءَ النَّاسِ وَيَصُدُّونَ
عَنْ سَبِيلِ اللّٰهِ وَاللّٰهُ بِمَا يَعْمَلُونَ مُحِيطٌ ۞ وَإِذْ زَيَّنَ
لَهُمُ الشَّيْطَانُ أَعْمَالَهُمْ وَقَالَ لَا غَالِبَ لَكُمُ الْيَوْمَ مِنَ
النَّاسِ وَإِنِّي جَارٌ لَكُمْ فَلَمَّا تَرَاءَتِ الْفِئَتَانِ نَكَصَ
عَلَىٰ عَقِبَيْهِ وَقَالَ إِنِّي بَرِيءٌ مِنْكُمْ إِنِّي أَرَىٰ مَا لَا تَرَوْنَ
إِنِّي أَخَافُ اللّٰهَ وَاللّٰهُ شَدِيدُ الْعِقَابِ ۞ إِذْ يَقُولُ
الْمُنَافِقُونَ وَالَّذِينَ فِي قُلُوبِهِمْ مَرَضٌ غَرَّ هٰؤُلَاءِ دِينُهُمْ وَمَنْ
يَتَوَكَّلْ عَلَى اللّٰهِ فَإِنَّ اللّٰهَ عَزِيزٌ حَكِيمٌ ۞ وَلَوْ تَرَىٰ إِذْ
يَتَوَفَّى الَّذِينَ كَفَرُوا الْمَلَائِكَةُ يَضْرِبُونَ وُجُوهَهُمْ
وَأَدْبَارَهُمْ وَذُوقُوا عَذَابَ الْحَرِيقِ ۞ ذٰلِكَ بِمَا قَدَّمَتْ
أَيْدِيكُمْ وَأَنَّ اللّٰهَ لَيْسَ بِظَلَّامٍ لِلْعَبِيدِ ۞ كَدَأْبِ
آلِ فِرْعَوْنَ وَالَّذِينَ مِنْ قَبْلِهِمْ كَفَرُوا بِآيَاتِ اللّٰهِ
فَأَخَذَهُمُ اللّٰهُ بِذُنُوبِهِمْ إِنَّ اللّٰهَ قَوِيٌّ شَدِيدُ الْعِقَابِ ۞

---

46. And obey God and His Messenger, and do not dispute with one another, or else you may lose heart and your power and energy desert you; and remain steadfast. Surely, God is with those who remain steadfast.

47. Be not like those (unbelievers) who went forth from their habitations swaggering boastfully and to show off to people, and bar (others) from God's way. And God fully encompasses (with His Knowledge and Power) all that they do.

48. Satan decked out their deeds to be appealing to them, and said: "Today no power among humankind can overcome you, and for sure I am your supporter." But when the two hosts came within sight of each other, he turned on his heels to run away and said: "Indeed I am quit of you; surely I see that which you do not see. Indeed, I fear God."[12] And God is severe in retribution.

49. And (remember) when the hypocrites and those in whose hearts there is a sickness (that dries up the source of their spiritual life) were saying (of the believers): "Their religion has deluded those (people)." But whoever puts his trust in God, truly God is All-Glorious with irresistible might, All-Wise.

50. If you could but see how it will be when the angels take the souls of those who disbelieve, striking them on the fac-

es and the backs, and (saying): "Taste the punishment of the scorching Fire!

51. This is because of (the evil deeds) that you forwarded with your own hands, for never does God do the least wrong to the servants."

52. Just as that which happened to the clan (the court and military aristocracy) of the Pharaoh, and those before them: they disbelieved in God's Revelations, and so God seized them for their sins. Surely God is All-Strong, severe in retribution.

---

12. When Satan perceived that the Muslim army was supported by angels and would defeat the polytheists, he chose to flee, as he feared receiving blows. His words "Surely I am quit of you," and "In addition, I fear God," are only excuses for his flight.

ذَلِكَ بِأَنَّ اللَّهَ لَمْ يَكُ مُغَيِّرًا نِّعْمَةً أَنْعَمَهَا عَلَى قَوْمٍ حَتَّى
يُغَيِّرُوا مَا بِأَنفُسِهِمْ وَأَنَّ اللَّهَ سَمِيعٌ عَلِيمٌ ۞ كَدَأْبِ ءَالِ
فِرْعَوْنَ وَالَّذِينَ مِن قَبْلِهِمْ كَذَّبُوا بِآيَاتِ رَبِّهِمْ فَأَهْلَكْنَاهُم
بِذُنُوبِهِمْ وَأَغْرَقْنَا ءَالَ فِرْعَوْنَ وَكُلٌّ كَانُوا ظَالِمِينَ ۞ إِنَّ شَرَّ
الدَّوَابِّ عِندَ اللَّهِ الَّذِينَ كَفَرُوا فَهُمْ لَا يُؤْمِنُونَ ۞ الَّذِينَ
عَاهَدتَّ مِنْهُمْ ثُمَّ يَنقُضُونَ عَهْدَهُمْ فِي كُلِّ مَرَّةٍ وَهُمْ
لَا يَتَّقُونَ ۞ فَإِمَّا تَثْقَفَنَّهُمْ فِي الْحَرْبِ فَشَرِّدْ بِهِم مَّنْ
خَلْفَهُمْ لَعَلَّهُمْ يَذَّكَّرُونَ ۞ وَإِمَّا تَخَافَنَّ مِن قَوْمٍ خِيَانَةً
فَانبِذْ إِلَيْهِمْ عَلَى سَوَاءٍ إِنَّ اللَّهَ لَا يُحِبُّ الْخَائِنِينَ ۞ وَلَا
يَحْسَبَنَّ الَّذِينَ كَفَرُوا سَبَقُوا إِنَّهُمْ لَا يُعْجِزُونَ ۞ وَأَعِدُّوا
لَهُم مَّا اسْتَطَعْتُم مِّن قُوَّةٍ وَمِن رِّبَاطِ الْخَيْلِ تُرْهِبُونَ
بِهِ عَدُوَّ اللَّهِ وَعَدُوَّكُمْ وَءَاخَرِينَ مِن دُونِهِمْ لَا
تَعْلَمُونَهُمُ اللَّهُ يَعْلَمُهُمْ وَمَا تُنفِقُوا مِن شَيْءٍ فِي سَبِيلِ
اللَّهِ يُوَفَّ إِلَيْكُمْ وَأَنتُمْ لَا تُظْلَمُونَ ۞ وَإِن جَنَحُوا لِلسَّلْمِ
فَاجْنَحْ لَهَا وَتَوَكَّلْ عَلَى اللَّهِ إِنَّهُ هُوَ السَّمِيعُ الْعَلِيمُ ۞

---

53. That (happened so) because God never changes a favor that He has bestowed upon a people unless they change what is in themselves (their belief, life-style, world-view, and devotion to God's laws embodied in religion and in the creation, life and operation of the universe). And God is indeed All-Hearing, All-Knowing.

54. Just as that which happened to the court and military aristocracy of the Pharaoh, and those before them: they denied the Revelations of their Lord, and so We destroyed them for their sins, and We caused the court and military aristocracy of the Pharaoh to drown. All of those peoples (destroyed in the past) were wrongdoers (in that they rebelled against their Lord, oppressed people, and so wronged themselves).

55. Indeed the worst kind of living creatures in God's sight are those who are so rooted in unbelief that they cannot believe.

56. Those of them with whom you have made a treaty, and who break their treaty on every occasion without fearing God.

57. If you meet them in war, deal with them in such a manner as to deter those behind them (who follow them and those who will come after them), so that they may reflect and be mindful.

58. If you have strong reason to fear treachery from a people (with whom you have a treaty), return it to them (i.e. publicly declare to them, before embarking on any action against them, that you have dissolved the treaty) so that both parties should be informed of its termination. Surely God does not love the treacherous.[13]

59. And let not those who disbelieve ever think that they can outdo the believers or otherwise escape Our punishment. They can never frustrate Our will.

60. (Believers:) make ready against them whatever you can of force and horses assigned (for war), that thereby you may dismay the enemies of God and your enemies and others besides them, of whom (and the nature of whose enmity) you may be unaware. God is aware of them (and of the nature of their enmity). Whatever you spend in God's cause will be repaid to you in full, and you will not be wronged.[14]

61. And if they (the enemies) incline to peace, incline to it also, and put your trust in God. Surely, He is the All-Hearing, the All-Knowing.

13. Islam is a system of values and all its principles are aimed at preserving these values and governing life according to them in justice. This verse lays down a basic rule of Islamic international law: When two nations have made a treaty with each other that will last for a certain period of time, both sides should remain true to the treaty until its termination. If one party contravenes the treaty, the other side should make it known to them that the treaty has been dissolved before starting any hostile actions, so that both parties will know where things stand. The Messenger, upon him be peace and blessings, says: "Whoever is bound in a treaty with a people cannot dissolve this treaty until either the term is up or until he publicly declares that it has been annulled" (Abū Dāwūd, "Jihād," 2: 75). In another saying, he declares: "Do not be treacherous, even to him who is treacherous to you" (Abū Dāwūd, "Kitāb al-Buyū'," 2: 75). Even today's "civilized" nations do not comply with this principle, established fourteen centuries ago by Islam; rather they work on the principle, "Whoever launches a surprise attack first will win."

14. This verse contains important advice and warnings for the Muslims:

- Until Doomsday there will always be enemies of belief and Islam. For this reason, Muslims must always be on the alert against any enmity and be powerful enough to deter it.
- The next verse (61) is especially important as it follows verses concerned with warfare, verses that state that a Muslim state must always be ready for war since such readiness can act as a deterrent. Whereas in verse 61, it is stated that Muslims are peaceful and that they must live peacefully and be representatives of universal peace. So, their acting as a deterrent in the power balance is one of the most important factors in bringing peace to the world and in preserving this peace. For this reason, if Muslims are not powerful enough to do this, and if, because of this, others shed innocent blood in the world, it is also the Muslims who will be held accountable for that blood by God.

- There are many kinds of enemies of belief and Islam. Some of them are overt enemies of God and religion, and thus display their enmity and are known. Some others maintain enmity against Islam and Muslims for other reasons, in addition to their being Muslims. There are some enemies that the Muslims may not be aware of because they are usually found among the Muslims and they conceal their enmity. These people are hypocrites, or they live in Muslim society because they see their interests lie in so doing; sometimes such a person may not yet have their belief ingrained in their hearts, and therefore may easily change sides, even for an insignificant reason. God knows these people well. Muslims must also take these people into account, trying to accumulate the necessary power to overwhelm them.

- Muslims must be powerful. Islam holds individuals and societies responsible for their own fate; therefore, people must be responsible for governing themselves. The Qur'ān addresses society with such phrases as: "O people!" and "O believers!" The duties entrusted to modern states are those that Islam refers to society and classifies, in order of importance, as "absolutely necessary, relatively necessary, and commendable to perform." Such a system causes Muslims to establish the institutions necessary to fulfill these duties. One of the ways to be powerful is that everyone should expend in God's cause of whatever they have. This usually occurs by way of the *Zakāh* (Prescribed Purifying Alms), and, when necessary, by imposing new taxes in addition to the *Zakāh*, and, again when necessary, by way of general mobilization.

184　　سُوۡرَةُ الۡاَنۡفَال　　١٨٤

وَإِن يُرِيدُوٓاْ أَن يَخۡدَعُوكَ فَإِنَّ حَسۡبَكَ ٱللَّهُ هُوَ ٱلَّذِىٓ أَيَّدَكَ بِنَصۡرِهِۦ وَبِٱلۡمُؤۡمِنِينَ ۞ وَأَلَّفَ بَيۡنَ قُلُوبِهِمۡ لَوۡ أَنفَقۡتَ مَا فِى ٱلۡأَرۡضِ جَمِيعًا مَّآ أَلَّفۡتَ بَيۡنَ قُلُوبِهِمۡ وَلَٰكِنَّ ٱللَّهَ أَلَّفَ بَيۡنَهُمۡۚ إِنَّهُۥ عَزِيزٌ حَكِيمٌ ۞ يَٰٓأَيُّهَا ٱلنَّبِىُّ حَسۡبُكَ ٱللَّهُ وَمَنِ ٱتَّبَعَكَ مِنَ ٱلۡمُؤۡمِنِينَ ۞ يَٰٓأَيُّهَا ٱلنَّبِىُّ حَرِّضِ ٱلۡمُؤۡمِنِينَ عَلَى ٱلۡقِتَالِۚ إِن يَكُن مِّنكُمۡ عِشۡرُونَ صَٰبِرُونَ يَغۡلِبُواْ مِاْئَتَيۡنِۚ وَإِن يَكُن مِّنكُم مِّاْئَةٌ يَغۡلِبُوٓاْ أَلۡفًا مِّنَ ٱلَّذِينَ كَفَرُواْ بِأَنَّهُمۡ قَوۡمٌ لَّا يَفۡقَهُونَ ۞ ٱلۡـَٰٔنَ خَفَّفَ ٱللَّهُ عَنكُمۡ وَعَلِمَ أَنَّ فِيكُمۡ ضَعۡفًاۚ فَإِن يَكُن مِّنكُم مِّاْئَةٌ صَابِرَةٌ يَغۡلِبُواْ مِاْئَتَيۡنِۚ وَإِن يَكُن مِّنكُمۡ أَلۡفٌ يَغۡلِبُوٓاْ أَلۡفَيۡنِ بِإِذۡنِ ٱللَّهِۗ وَٱللَّهُ مَعَ ٱلصَّٰبِرِينَ ۞ مَا كَانَ لِنَبِىٍّ أَن يَكُونَ لَهُۥٓ أَسۡرَىٰ حَتَّىٰ يُثۡخِنَ فِى ٱلۡأَرۡضِۚ تُرِيدُونَ عَرَضَ ٱلدُّنۡيَا وَٱللَّهُ يُرِيدُ ٱلۡأَخِرَةَۗ وَٱللَّهُ عَزِيزٌ حَكِيمٌ ۞ لَّوۡلَا كِتَٰبٌ مِّنَ ٱللَّهِ سَبَقَ لَمَسَّكُمۡ فِيمَآ أَخَذۡتُمۡ عَذَابٌ عَظِيمٌ ۞ فَكُلُواْ مِمَّا غَنِمۡتُمۡ حَلَٰلًا طَيِّبًاۚ وَٱتَّقُواْ ٱللَّهَۚ إِنَّ ٱللَّهَ غَفُورٌ رَّحِيمٌ ۞

──────◈──────

62. And if they seek (thereby only) to deceive you (O Messenger), surely God is sufficient for you. He it is Who has strengthened you with His help and with the believers.

63. He has attuned their (the believers') hearts. If you had spent all that is on the earth, you could not have attuned their hearts, but God has attuned them. Surely He is All-Glorious with irresistible might, All-Wise.

64. O (most illustrious) Prophet! God is sufficient for you and the believers who follow you.

65. O (most illustrious) Prophet! Rouse the believers to fighting. If there be twenty of you who are steadfast, they will vanquish two hundred; and if there be of you

a hundred, they will vanquish a thousand of those who disbelieve, for they (the disbelievers) are a people who do not ponder and seek to penetrate the essence of matters in order to grasp the truth.

66. For now (while you lack in necessary equipment and training), God has lightened your burden, for He knows that there is weakness in you. So if there be a hundred of you who are strong-willed and steadfast, they will vanquish two hundred; and if there be a thousand of you, they will vanquish two thousand by God's leave. God is with those who are steadfast.[15]

67. It is not for a Prophet to have captives until he has widely exhausted the enemies in the land. You (O believers) seek the fleeting gains of the present, worldly life, but God wills that the Hereafter will be yours. God is All-Glorious with irresistible might, All-Wise.

68. Had there not been a previous decree from God (concerning that gains of war are lawful and captives can be released in return for ransom), a tremendous punishment would surely have touched you because of what you took (the gains of war, and the captives taken in expectation of ransom, before the enemies' power in the land had been sufficiently suppressed and exhausted).

69. (But since such a decree has already come) now enjoy as lawful and pure and wholesome of what you have obtained (as gains of war and ransom); and keep from disobedience to God in all your actions. Surely God is All-Forgiving, All-Compassionate (especially toward His believing, pious servants).

15. These last two verses should not be mis-read. When all is equal, i.e. equipment, re-sources, etc., then the believers can be ten times more powerful than the unbelievers, ow-ing to their sources of power, such as their be-lief in God and eternal life, their fearlessness of death, their strength of will that they have acquired by regular worship, their resistance against the temptations of their carnal selves, their dependence on God, patience, and the fact that they expect the eternal bliss of Paradise and God's being pleased with them. These are things which the unbelievers do not possess. But the Muslims at that time – the time when this *sūrah* was revealed just after the Battle of Badr – did not have enough material pow-er, nor did they have military training. That is why they were able to overcome an enemy that was twice as powerful as them. They won the Battle of Badr against an enemy that was more than three times as powerful as they were re-inforced with the help of God. However, when they had the same equipment and military training as their enemies they were able to re-sist and even overcome their enemies, many of whom were five, ten, twenty or even thir-ty times as powerful as they in later years in the Battles of Mū'tah, Yarmuk, Qadīsiyah, and in many other wars. The verses here state the minimum limit.

These two verses also present some mili-tary standards. It is preferable that the smallest army unit should contain 20 soldiers when the believers are powerful and 100 soldiers when they are weak. While steadfastness and having strong will-power is one of the sources of su-periority in war, penetrating and discerning the essence of matters is another source.

يَا أَيُّهَا النَّبِيُّ قُل لِّمَن فِي أَيْدِيكُم مِّنَ الْأَسْرَىٰ إِن يَعْلَمِ اللَّهُ فِي قُلُوبِكُمْ خَيْرًا يُؤْتِكُمْ خَيْرًا مِّمَّا أُخِذَ مِنكُمْ وَيَغْفِرْ لَكُمْ وَاللَّهُ غَفُورٌ رَّحِيمٌ ۝ وَإِن يُرِيدُوا خِيَانَتَكَ فَقَدْ خَانُوا اللَّهَ مِن قَبْلُ فَأَمْكَنَ مِنْهُمْ وَاللَّهُ عَلِيمٌ حَكِيمٌ ۝ إِنَّ الَّذِينَ آمَنُوا وَهَاجَرُوا وَجَاهَدُوا بِأَمْوَالِهِمْ وَأَنفُسِهِمْ فِي سَبِيلِ اللَّهِ وَالَّذِينَ آوَوا وَّنَصَرُوا أُولَٰئِكَ بَعْضُهُمْ أَوْلِيَاءُ بَعْضٍ وَالَّذِينَ آمَنُوا وَلَمْ يُهَاجِرُوا مَا لَكُم مِّن وَلَايَتِهِم مِّن شَيْءٍ حَتَّىٰ يُهَاجِرُوا وَإِنِ اسْتَنصَرُوكُمْ فِي الدِّينِ فَعَلَيْكُمُ النَّصْرُ إِلَّا عَلَىٰ قَوْمٍ بَيْنَكُمْ وَبَيْنَهُم مِّيثَاقٌ وَاللَّهُ بِمَا تَعْمَلُونَ بَصِيرٌ ۝ وَالَّذِينَ كَفَرُوا بَعْضُهُمْ أَوْلِيَاءُ بَعْضٍ إِلَّا تَفْعَلُوهُ تَكُن فِتْنَةٌ فِي الْأَرْضِ وَفَسَادٌ كَبِيرٌ ۝ وَالَّذِينَ آمَنُوا وَهَاجَرُوا وَجَاهَدُوا فِي سَبِيلِ اللَّهِ وَالَّذِينَ آوَوا وَّنَصَرُوا أُولَٰئِكَ هُمُ الْمُؤْمِنُونَ حَقًّا لَّهُم مَّغْفِرَةٌ وَرِزْقٌ كَرِيمٌ ۝ وَالَّذِينَ آمَنُوا مِن بَعْدُ وَهَاجَرُوا وَجَاهَدُوا مَعَكُمْ فَأُولَٰئِكَ مِنكُمْ وَأُولُو الْأَرْحَامِ بَعْضُهُمْ أَوْلَىٰ بِبَعْضٍ فِي كِتَابِ اللَّهِ إِنَّ اللَّهَ بِكُلِّ شَيْءٍ عَلِيمٌ ۝

---

70. O (most illustrious) Prophet! Say to the captives in your hands: "If God knows any good in your hearts (any readiness to believe in and surrender to God), He will grant you something better than what has been taken from you, and He will forgive you." God is All-Forgiving, All-Compassionate (especially towards His servants who return to Him in repentance).

71. But if they seek to betray you (O Messenger) – well, they were treacherous to God before (and the outcome thereof is plain to see): God has given you power over them. God is All-Knowing, All-Wise.

72. Those who have believed and emigrated (to the home of Islam) and striven hard with their wealth and persons in God's cause, and those who give refuge (to them) and help (them) – those (illustrious ones) are friends and protectors of one another, and can inherit from one another.[16] But those who believe but have not emigrated – you have no duty of protection towards them until they emigrate[17] and inheritance is not permissible between them and you. Yet, if they ask you for help in the matter of religion, it is your duty to provide help except against a people between whom and you there is a treaty. God sees well all that you do.

73. Those who disbelieve – they are friends and protectors of one another (especially against you). Unless you do it also (i.e. maintain solidarity among the believers) there will be unrest on the earth and great corruption.

74. Those who have believed and emigrated (to the home of Islam) and striven (with their wealth and persons) in God's cause, and those who give refuge (to them) and help (them) – those (illustrious ones) are the believers in truth. For them is forgiveness (to bring unforeseen blessings) and honorable, generous provision.

75. And those who believe after (the Prophet's emigration) and emigrate and strive hard alongside you, they also belong to you. And those related by blood are nearer to one another according to God's ordinance (with respect to inheritance). Surely God has full knowledge of every thing.

16. When God's Messenger emigrated to Madīnah with the Makkan Muslims, he established brotherhood among the Muslims from Madīnah and those from Makkah. They could inherit from each other even though they had no blood relation. This continued for some until the emigrating Muslims had certain means to earn their livelihood in Madīnah. Verse 75 which came later abolished this institution of formal brotherhood and restricted inheritance to blood relationship.

17. This judgment concerns, rather than all times inclusively, a time when emigration to and settling in the center of Islam is compulsory for all Muslims.

186   سُورَةُ التَّوبَةِ   ١٨٦

بِسْمِ اللَّهِ الرَّحْمَٰنِ الرَّحِيمِ

﴿بَرَآءَةٌ مِّنَ اللَّهِ وَرَسُولِهِ إِلَى الَّذِينَ عَاهَدتُّم مِّنَ الْمُشْرِكِينَ ١ فَسِيحُوا فِي الْأَرْضِ أَرْبَعَةَ أَشْهُرٍ وَاعْلَمُوا أَنَّكُمْ غَيْرُ مُعْجِزِي اللَّهِ وَأَنَّ اللَّهَ مُخْزِي الْكَافِرِينَ ٢ وَأَذَانٌ مِّنَ اللَّهِ وَرَسُولِهِ إِلَى النَّاسِ يَوْمَ الْحَجِّ الْأَكْبَرِ أَنَّ اللَّهَ بَرِيءٌ مِّنَ الْمُشْرِكِينَ وَرَسُولُهُ فَإِن تُبْتُمْ فَهُوَ خَيْرٌ لَّكُمْ وَإِن تَوَلَّيْتُمْ فَاعْلَمُوا أَنَّكُمْ غَيْرُ مُعْجِزِي اللَّهِ وَبَشِّرِ الَّذِينَ كَفَرُوا بِعَذَابٍ أَلِيمٍ ٣ إِلَّا الَّذِينَ عَاهَدتُّم مِّنَ الْمُشْرِكِينَ ثُمَّ لَمْ يَنقُصُوكُمْ شَيْئًا وَلَمْ يُظَاهِرُوا عَلَيْكُمْ أَحَدًا فَأَتِمُّوا إِلَيْهِمْ عَهْدَهُمْ إِلَىٰ مُدَّتِهِمْ إِنَّ اللَّهَ يُحِبُّ الْمُتَّقِينَ ٤ فَإِذَا انسَلَخَ الْأَشْهُرُ الْحُرُمُ فَاقْتُلُوا الْمُشْرِكِينَ حَيْثُ وَجَدتُّمُوهُمْ وَخُذُوهُمْ وَاحْصُرُوهُمْ وَاقْعُدُوا لَهُمْ كُلَّ مَرْصَدٍ فَإِن تَابُوا وَأَقَامُوا الصَّلَاةَ وَآتَوُا الزَّكَاةَ فَخَلُّوا سَبِيلَهُمْ إِنَّ اللَّهَ غَفُورٌ رَّحِيمٌ ٥ وَإِنْ أَحَدٌ مِّنَ الْمُشْرِكِينَ اسْتَجَارَكَ فَأَجِرْهُ حَتَّىٰ يَسْمَعَ كَلَامَ اللَّهِ ثُمَّ أَبْلِغْهُ مَأْمَنَهُ ذَٰلِكَ بِأَنَّهُمْ قَوْمٌ لَّا يَعْلَمُونَ ٦﴾

―――――✺―――――

SŪRAH 9

AT-TAWBAH (REPENTANCE)

Madīnah period

According to the majority of scholars, this *sūrah* was revealed in Madīnah in the 9th year of the *Hijrah*. It deals with almost the same topics as those dealt with in *Sūrat al-Anfāl*. It is the only *sūrah* in the Qur'ān which does not begin with the usual opening formula, *In the Name of God, the All-Merciful, the All-Compassionate*. In contrast to all other *sūrah*s, God's Messenger, upon him be peace and blessings, did not order that this formula should be put at the beginning of this *sūrah*. Among the explanations put for-

ward for his not doing so, the most commonly accepted one is that, like the Islamic salutation, *Peace be upon you*, *In the Name of God, the All-Merciful, the All-Compassionate* expresses security and the giving of quarter to those addressed. However, *Sūrat al-Tawbah* begins with an ultimatum to certain polytheists in Arabia. It deals, for the most part, with a re-evaluation of the relations with the polytheists, who were frequently violating their agreements, the campaign to Tabuk, a disclosure of the intrigues of the hypocrites in Madīnah, the importance of *jihād* in God's cause, and relationships with the People of the Book.

―――――✺―――――

1. This is an ultimatum from God and His Messenger to those who associate partners with God with whom you have made a treaty.

2. (O you polytheists who always break the treaties you have entered into!) You may go about freely in the land for four months (making whatever war preparations you wish). But know that you can never escape (the Power of God, nor frustrate His will), and that God will bring disgrace upon the unbelievers.

3. And a proclamation from God and His Messenger to all people on this day of the Major Pilgrimage: that God disavows those who associate partners with Him (and break their treaty), and His Messenger likewise (disavows them). But if you repent and give up hostilities, this will be for your good; but if you turn away again, know that you will never be able to escape God and frustrate His will in any way. Give glad tidings (O Messenger) of a painful punishment to those who insist on unbelief.

4. Excepting those among the people who associate partners with God with whom

you made a treaty, and who have not thereafter failed to fulfill their obligations towards you (required by the treaty), nor have backed anyone against you. Observe, then, your treaty with them until the end of the term (that you agreed with them). Surely God loves the God-revering, pious (who keep their duties to Him).

5. Then, when the (four) sacred months (of respite, during which fighting with those who associate partners with God and violate their treaties was prohibited to you,) are over, then (declare war on them and) kill them wherever you may come upon them, and seize them, and confine them, and lie in wait for them at every conceivable place. Yet if they repent and (mending their ways) establish the Prescribed Prayer and pay the Prescribed Purifying Alms, let them go their way. Surely God is All-Forgiving, All-Compassionate.

6. And if any of those who associate partners with God seeks asylum of you (O Messenger), grant him asylum, so that he may hear the Word of God, and then convey him to his place of security. That (is how you should act) because they are a people who have no knowledge (of the truth about Islam).[1]

---

1. When considered together with other relevant verses of the Qur'ān, the verses present ent significant principles concerned with the Islamic view of war. See Appendix 3.

كَيْفَ يَكُونُ لِلْمُشْرِكِينَ عَهْدٌ عِندَ ٱللَّهِ وَعِندَ
رَسُولِهِ إِلَّا ٱلَّذِينَ عَاهَدتُّمْ عِندَ ٱلْمَسْجِدِ ٱلْحَرَامِ فَمَا
ٱسْتَقَامُوا لَكُمْ فَٱسْتَقِيمُوا لَهُمْ إِنَّ ٱللَّهَ يُحِبُّ
ٱلْمُتَّقِينَ ﴿٧﴾ كَيْفَ وَإِن يَظْهَرُوا عَلَيْكُمْ لَا يَرْقُبُوا فِيكُمْ
إِلًّا وَلَا ذِمَّةً يُرْضُونَكُم بِأَفْوَٰهِهِمْ وَتَأْبَىٰ
قُلُوبُهُمْ وَأَكْثَرُهُمْ فَٰسِقُونَ ﴿٨﴾ ٱشْتَرَوْا بِـَٔايَٰتِ
ٱللَّهِ ثَمَنًا قَلِيلًا فَصَدُّوا عَن سَبِيلِهِ إِنَّهُمْ سَآءَ مَا كَانُوا
يَعْمَلُونَ ﴿٩﴾ لَا يَرْقُبُونَ فِي مُؤْمِنٍ إِلًّا وَلَا ذِمَّةً وَأُوْلَٰٓئِكَ
هُمُ ٱلْمُعْتَدُونَ ﴿١٠﴾ فَإِن تَابُوا وَأَقَامُوا ٱلصَّلَوٰةَ وَءَاتَوُا
ٱلزَّكَوٰةَ فَإِخْوَٰنُكُمْ فِي ٱلدِّينِ وَنُفَصِّلُ ٱلْآيَٰتِ لِقَوْمٍ يَعْلَمُونَ
﴿١١﴾ وَإِن نَّكَثُوٓا أَيْمَٰنَهُم مِّنۢ بَعْدِ عَهْدِهِمْ وَطَعَنُوا فِي
دِينِكُمْ فَقَٰتِلُوٓا أَئِمَّةَ ٱلْكُفْرِ إِنَّهُمْ لَآ أَيْمَٰنَ لَهُمْ لَعَلَّهُمْ
يَنتَهُونَ ﴿١٢﴾ أَلَا تُقَٰتِلُونَ قَوْمًا نَّكَثُوٓا أَيْمَٰنَهُمْ وَهَمُّوا
بِإِخْرَاجِ ٱلرَّسُولِ وَهُم بَدَءُوكُمْ أَوَّلَ مَرَّةٍ أَتَخْشَوْنَهُمْ
فَٱللَّهُ أَحَقُّ أَن تَخْشَوْهُ إِن كُنتُم مُّؤْمِنِينَ ﴿١٣﴾

———◦———

7. How could there be a covenant with those who associate partners with God (and recognize no laws and treaty) on the part of God and His Messenger? – excepting those with whom you made a treaty in the vicinity of the Sacred Mosque: (as for the latter) so long as they remain true to you, be true to them. Surely God loves the God-revering, pious (who keep their duties to Him).[2]

8. How (could there be a covenant with the others) when, if they were to prevail against you, they would observe towards you neither any bond, nor law, nor agreement, they seek to please you with their mouths but in their hearts they are averse; and most of them are transgressors (who habitually disregard all bounds of equity).

9. (As well as breaking their treaties) they have sold God's Revelations (concerning treaties) for a trifling price and they barred people from His way. How evil is what they do!

10. They observe neither any bond, nor law, nor agreement towards the believers. They are those who exceed all bounds.

11. Yet if they repent so as to mend their ways and establish the Prescribed Prayer and pay the Prescribed Purifying Alms, they are your brothers in religion. Thus We set out in detail Our Revelations (the signposts of Our way, included in the Qur'ān) for a people seeking knowledge.

12. But if they break their pledges after their treaty (with you) and assail your religion, then fight with those leaders of unbelief – surely they have no trustworthy pledges – so that they may desist (from aggression).

13. Will you not fight against the people who have broken their pledges and have done all they could to drive the Messenger (from where he chooses to dwell), and initiated hostilities against you? Do you hold them in awe? But, assuredly God has greater right to be held in awe, if you are sincere believers.

---

2. The polytheists mentioned in this verse as those with whom the Muslims had made a treaty in the vicinity of the Sacred Mosque are the same people mentioned in verse 4; i.e. those who did not fail to fulfill their obligations towards the Muslims as required by the treaty made between them. Both of the verses warn the Muslims not to treat those polytheists in the same way as the others, and to regard adhering to the agreement as a form of piety. It is therefore highly significant that both verses end in *Surely God loves the God-revering, pious (who keep their duties to Him)*.

188 سُورَةُ التَّوبَة ١٨٨

قَاتِلُوهُمْ يُعَذِّبْهُمُ اللَّهُ بِأَيْدِيكُمْ وَيُخْزِهِمْ وَيَنْصُرْكُمْ عَلَيْهِمْ وَيَشْفِ صُدُورَ قَوْمٍ مُؤْمِنِينَ ۝ وَيُذْهِبْ غَيْظَ قُلُوبِهِمْ وَيَتُوبُ اللَّهُ عَلَى مَن يَشَاءُ وَاللَّهُ عَلِيمٌ حَكِيمٌ ۝ أَمْ حَسِبْتُمْ أَن تُتْرَكُوا وَلَمَّا يَعْلَمِ اللَّهُ الَّذِينَ جَاهَدُوا مِنكُمْ وَلَمْ يَتَّخِذُوا مِن دُونِ اللَّهِ وَلَا رَسُولِهِ وَلَا الْمُؤْمِنِينَ وَلِيجَةً وَاللَّهُ خَبِيرٌ بِمَا تَعْمَلُونَ ۝ مَا كَانَ لِلْمُشْرِكِينَ أَن يَعْمُرُوا مَسَاجِدَ اللَّهِ شَاهِدِينَ عَلَى أَنفُسِهِمْ بِالْكُفْرِ أُولَئِكَ حَبِطَتْ أَعْمَالُهُمْ وَفِي النَّارِ هُمْ خَالِدُونَ ۝ إِنَّمَا يَعْمُرُ مَسَاجِدَ اللَّهِ مَنْ آمَنَ بِاللَّهِ وَالْيَوْمِ الْآخِرِ وَأَقَامَ الصَّلَاةَ وَآتَى الزَّكَاةَ وَلَمْ يَخْشَ إِلَّا اللَّهَ فَعَسَى أُولَئِكَ أَن يَكُونُوا مِنَ الْمُهْتَدِينَ ۝ أَجَعَلْتُمْ سِقَايَةَ الْحَاجِّ وَعِمَارَةَ الْمَسْجِدِ الْحَرَامِ كَمَنْ آمَنَ بِاللَّهِ وَالْيَوْمِ الْآخِرِ وَجَاهَدَ فِي سَبِيلِ اللَّهِ لَا يَسْتَوُونَ عِندَ اللَّهِ وَاللَّهُ لَا يَهْدِي الْقَوْمَ الظَّالِمِينَ ۝ الَّذِينَ آمَنُوا وَهَاجَرُوا وَجَاهَدُوا فِي سَبِيلِ اللَّهِ بِأَمْوَالِهِمْ وَأَنفُسِهِمْ أَعْظَمُ دَرَجَةً عِندَ اللَّهِ وَأُولَئِكَ هُمُ الْفَائِزُونَ ۝

14. Fight against them: God will punish them by your hands and humiliate them, and (know) that He will help you to victory over them, and soothe the bosoms of the believing people (oppressed and suffering at their hands as well as at the hands of other oppressors).

15. And He will remove the wrath in their hearts (by making right and justice prevail). And God guides whomever He wills to turn to Him in repentance. God is All-Knowing (with full knowledge of him who deserves guidance), All-Wise (in Whose every decree and act there are many instances of wisdom).[3]

16. Or did you think that you would be left (without being tried through suffering and hardship) unless God marks out those among you who really strive (in His way), and who take none as intimate friend other than God and His Messenger and the believers to seek help and solidarity? God is fully aware of all that you do.

17. It is not for those who associate partners with God to maintain God's houses of worship while they are witnesses against themselves of unbelief (and do not worship God in those houses of worship). They are those whose works have been wasted, and they will abide in the Fire.

18. Only he will maintain God's houses of worship (using them for the purposes for which they are built) who believes in God and the Last Day, and establishes the Prescribed Prayer, and pays the Prescribed Purifying Alms, and stands in awe of none but God. It is hoped that such (illustrious) persons will be among the ones guided to achieve their expectations (especially in the Hereafter).

19. Do you consider providing water to the pilgrims and tending the Sacred Mosque as equal in value to one who believes in God and the Last Day, and strives in God's cause? They are not equal in God's sight. And God does not guide (to truth) the wrongdoing folk (whose measure and judgment are wrong).

20. Those who believe and have emigrated (to the home of Islam in God's cause), and strive in God's cause with their wealth and persons are greater in rank in God's sight, and those are the ones who are the triumphant.

3. The last two verses mention five secondary aims of war and draw our attention to a significant point:

- The world is the domain where God acts behind the law of causality according to His Wisdom which has established the order of the universe, formed the general plan, and turns the wheel of all events. Although this Wisdom considers the whole of the universe when turning its wheel, this does not mean that it neglects any one part, not even the smallest. This Wisdom requires that people should see the consequences of their actions. So, God usually punishes the oppressors at the hands of other people. The believers are required to struggle with the oppressors and, when necessary, to fight against them.

- The oppressors who act in the world in arrogance, as if they were its sole rulers and owners, and who oppress others should be humbled.

- The believers are duty-bound to make right and justice prevail in the world and thus they must fight against oppressors whenever necessary. God will help them and grant them victory.

- The oppressed, suffering people should be saved from the hands of the oppressors and relieved of their burdens.

- When right and justice have been made to prevail, the rage of the oppressed is removed from their hearts and this prevents them from adopting worse ideologies or systems and going to excesses to cause greater disorder and injustice in the world, as they did (went to excesses) during communist uprisings and regimes.

After mentioning these five secondary aims of war, the last verse draws our attention to the following point:

Since God never wills that any of His servants should go astray and deserve eternal punishment, He always keeps the door to repentance open; He is extremely pleased when a servant turns to Him in repentance.

21. Their Lord gives them glad tidings of mercy from Him (to bring unforeseen blessings), and His being pleased with them, and of Gardens wherein is everlasting bounty for them;

22. Therein to dwell forever. Surely, with God is a tremendous reward.

23. O you who believe! Do not take your fathers and your brothers for confidants and guardians (to whom you can entrust your affairs), if they choose unbelief in preference to belief. Whoever of you takes them for confidants and guardians, those are wrongdoers (who have wronged themselves by committing a great error).

24. Say: "If your fathers, and your children, and your brothers and sisters, and your spouses, and your kindred and clan, and the wealth you have acquired, and the commerce you fear may slacken, and the dwellings that you love to live in, are dearer to you than God and His Messenger and striving in His way, then wait until God brings about His decree. God does not guide the transgressing people (who prefer worldly things to Him, His Messenger and striving in His way, to truth and true happiness in both the world and the Hereafter).[4]

25. God has already helped you on many fields, and on the day of Hunayn, when your multitude was pleasing to you, but it

availed you nothing, and the earth, for all its vastness, was too narrow for you, and you turned back, retreating.

26. Then God sent down His gift of inner peace and reassurance on His Messenger and the believers, and sent (to your aid) hosts that you did not see, and punished those who disbelieved. Such is the recompense of unbelievers.

---

4. As mentioned before, Muslims are responsible for improving this world and living here according to God's religion, as well as being responsible for striving to communicate the religion to others. They can demand and own worldly favors provided they use them for this purpose and fulfill the duty of thanksgiving. They should also distribute the worldly bounties justly and therefore fulfill a significant role in the power balance in the world. However, there is a point to note here: worldly riches seduce people. In order to avoid this, Muslims should not demand the world from their heart, not should they leave it to the oppressors and transgressors. Being able to establish an equilibrium between these two extremes, namely being seduced by the world and renouncing it and leaving it to the oppressors, requires living a life according to the commandments of God and His Messenger, and striving for the whole of one's life to convey God's Message throughout the world.

190   سُوۡرَةُ التَّوۡبَة   ۱۹۰

ثُمَّ يَتُوبُ اللّٰهُ مِنۢ بَعۡدِ ذٰلِكَ عَلٰى مَنۡ يَّشَآءُ ۚ وَاللّٰهُ
غَفُوۡرٌ رَّحِيۡمٌ ۝ يٰٓاَيُّهَا الَّذِيۡنَ اٰمَنُوۡٓا اِنَّمَا الۡمُشۡرِكُوۡنَ
نَجَسٌ فَلَا يَقۡرَبُوا الۡمَسۡجِدَ الۡحَرَامَ بَعۡدَ عَامِهِمۡ هٰذَا ۚ
وَاِنۡ خِفۡتُمۡ عَيۡلَةً فَسَوۡفَ يُغۡنِيۡكُمُ اللّٰهُ مِنۡ فَضۡلِهٖٓ اِنۡ
شَآءَ ۚ اِنَّ اللّٰهَ عَلِيۡمٌ حَكِيۡمٌ ۝ قَاتِلُوا الَّذِيۡنَ لَا
يُؤۡمِنُوۡنَ بِاللّٰهِ وَلَا بِالۡيَوۡمِ الۡاٰخِرِ وَلَا يُحَرِّمُوۡنَ
مَا حَرَّمَ اللّٰهُ وَرَسُوۡلُهٗ وَلَا يَدِيۡنُوۡنَ دِيۡنَ الۡحَقِّ مِنَ
الَّذِيۡنَ اُوۡتُوا الۡكِتَابَ حَتّٰى يُعۡطُوا الۡجِزۡيَةَ عَنۡ يَّدٍ
وَّهُمۡ صَاغِرُوۡنَ ۝ وَقَالَتِ الۡيَهُوۡدُ عُزَيۡرٌ ۨ ابۡنُ اللّٰهِ
وَقَالَتِ النَّصَارَى الۡمَسِيۡحُ ابۡنُ اللّٰهِ ۚ ذٰلِكَ قَوۡلُهُمۡ
بِاَفۡوَاهِهِمۡ ۚ يُضَاهِـُٔوۡنَ قَوۡلَ الَّذِيۡنَ كَفَرُوۡا مِنۡ قَبۡلُ ۚ
قَاتَلَهُمُ اللّٰهُ ۖ اَنّٰى يُؤۡفَكُوۡنَ ۝ اِتَّخَذُوۡٓا اَحۡبَارَهُمۡ
وَرُهۡبَانَهُمۡ اَرۡبَابًا مِّنۡ دُوۡنِ اللّٰهِ وَالۡمَسِيۡحَ ابۡنَ
مَرۡيَمَ ۚ وَمَاۤ اُمِرُوۡٓا اِلَّا لِيَعۡبُدُوۡٓا اِلٰهًا وَّاحِدًا ۚ
لَاۤ اِلٰهَ اِلَّا هُوَ ۚ سُبۡحَانَهٗ عَمَّا يُشۡرِكُوۡنَ ۝

──────〜──────

27. Then after all this, God guides whom He wills to repentance (turning to Islam from unbelief). God is All-Forgiving, all Compassionate (especially to His servants who turn to Him in repentance).[5]

28. O you who believe! Those who associate partners with God are (nothing) but impure. So, after the expiry of this year, let them not approach the Sacred Mosque.[6] And should you fear poverty (because of the possible reduction in your income due to their not coming to Makkah in the season of the *Hajj*), God will enrich you out of His bounty if He so wills. Surely, God is All-Knowing, All-Wise.

29. Fight against those from among the People of the Book who (despite being People of the Book) do not believe in God and the Last Day (as they should be believed in), and do not hold as unlawful that which God and His Messenger have decreed to be unlawful, and do not adopt and follow the Religion of truth, until they pay the *jizyah* (tax of protection and exemption from military service) with a willing hand in a state of submission.[7]

30. And those Jews (who came to you) say (as did some Jews who lived before): "Ezra ('Uzayr) is God's son;" and (as a general assertion) the Christians say: "The Messiah is God's son." Such are merely their verbal assertions in imitation of the utterances of some unbelievers who preceded them. May God destroy them! How can they be turned away from the truth and make such assertions?

31. The Jews take their rabbis (teachers of law), and the Christians take their monks, as well as the Messiah, son of Mary, for Lords besides God (by holding as lawful or unlawful what the teachers of law and monks decree to be lawful or unlawful, as against God's decree), whereas they were commanded to worship none but the One God. There is no deity but He.[8] All-Glorified He is in that He is absolutely above their association of partners with Him.

5. The Arab tribes were awaiting the settlement of the conflict between the Quraysh and the Muslims before they would accept Islam, saying: "If Muḥammad prevails over his people, he would indeed be a Prophet." Consequently, when this was finally accomplished, people began to join Islam in throngs. This caused the Hawāzīn and the Thaqīf tribes in Ṭā'if, who were famous for their courage and archery skills, to prepare a great expedition to Makkah. Informed of their movements, God's Messenger, upon him be peace and blessings, left Makkah with 12,000 Muslims. This was the greatest army the Muslims had ever gathered and some among the Companions were pleased and assured. However, Muslims must always rely on God, without ever forgetting that it is God Who takes one to victory. Their self-assurance cost them a setback in the first stage of the war, which took place in the valley of Hunayn between Makkah and Ṭā'if. The enemy laid an ambush in which the advance guard of the Muslim forces was caught, and the rear forces fell into confusion under a shower of enemy arrows. The Prophet, as ever, was calm in his faith and wisdom in that hour of danger and spurred his horse forward. He cried: "Now war has been kindled. I am the Prophet; that is no lie. I am the descendant of 'Abd al-Muttalib" (al-Bukhārī, "Jihad," 52; Muslim, "Jihad," 78). 'Abbās, the Prophet's uncle, also called out at the top of his voice to the retreating Companions to return. Thereupon, from all sides the Companions responded *"Labbayk!"* (at your service), and rallied to the Prophet. The enemy, who had pushed themselves into the center of the Muslim army, were surrounded on all sides. The courage, wisdom, and steadfastness of God's Messenger snatched victory from the jaws of defeat by God's leave. It was by God's help that the Muslims won the day.

The routed enemy took refuge in Ṭā'if. The Muslim victory persuaded the desert tribes to accept Islam and shortly thereafter the rebel tribes and Ṭā'if also surrendered and entered Islam.

6. Because of their beliefs, morals, practices, and customs, and since they do not make ab-

lutions (*wudū'*) for Prayer nor total ablution in case of canonical impurity, those who associate partners with God are spiritually and canonically unclean. Just as those without ablution cannot perform Prayer and read the Qur'ān, so the polytheists, who are totally unclean, cannot approach the Sacred Mosque.

Islam attaches extreme importance to cleanliness, including spiritual, moral, bodily, and material cleanliness. The source of spiritual cleanliness is true belief, sincerity, purity of heart, and wishing all well. Moral cleanliness comes from avoiding all kinds of vices, such as illicit relationships like fornication, adultery, prostitution, and homosexuality, and unlawful transactions and ways of income and expenditure, and deception, lying, slander, backbiting, etc. Bodily and all kinds of material cleanliness, such as that of clothes, dwelling places, and the environment are also important. To cite only one example, if one's clothes or the rug or place on which one prays are fouled with any liquid dirt, such as urine, to the amount that fills the palm of one's hand, or with any solid filth to the amount of three grams, the prayer is invalid.

7. The People of the Book are the people such as the Jews and Christians who were given a Divine Book. So, when God sent the Prophet Muḥammad, upon him be peace and blessings, with the last, universal form of Islam, the Religion of truth with which He sent all the Messengers during history, the People of the Book were expected to believe in and follow the Prophet Muḥammad and the Qur'ān, which was revealed to him as a consummation of the previous Divine Books, and accordingly to have true faith in God and the Last Day (and in other essentials of faith), and to hold lawful what God and His Messenger decreed to be lawful, and unlawful what they decreed to be unlawful. But when, despite their claim to belong to the People of the Book, they acted contrarily to what they were expected to do, and were hostile towards Islam and Muslims and collaborated against them with the polytheists, God allowed the Muslim state to fight against them. However, He commanded that once it had subdued them, it should

accord them full protection of all their civic rights, including the protection of life, wealth, reproduction, mental and bodily health, and religious freedom. Moreover, the People of the Book were exempted from military service and fighting enemies; this was something for which Muslim citizens were responsible. Muslim citizens also had to pay the *Zakāh*, the prescribed alms-due. In place of the *Zakāh*, the non-Muslim citizens of the Muslim state, who were called the *ahl adh-dhimmah*, the protected people, were charged with the payment of the *jizyah*, which was the tax of protection and exemption from military service.

It should be noted here that only a Muslim state can declare and carry out war; no Muslim individual or group has the right or authority to do this.

Muslims can eat the meat of animals slaughtered by the People of the Book and it is permissible for a Muslim man to marry a woman from among them.

8. Being the Lord means creating, bringing up, sustaining, and giving each creature a structure and nature according to its duty in creation. It also includes the authority to determine what is (religiously) lawful and unlawful in human life. Being divine (deity) or possessing divinity means having the exclusive right to be worshipped. By mentioning divinity (being a deity) and being the Lord together, this verse explains that only One who is God can be Lord and that the One Who is the Lord is also God; therefore belief in God as One God requires confessing that He is both Lord and God.

يُرِيدُونَ أَن يُطْفِئُوا نُورَ اللَّهِ بِأَفْوَاهِهِمْ وَيَأْبَى
اللَّهُ إِلَّا أَن يُتِمَّ نُورَهُ وَلَوْ كَرِهَ الْكَافِرُونَ ۞
هُوَ الَّذِي أَرْسَلَ رَسُولَهُ بِالْهُدَىٰ وَدِينِ الْحَقِّ لِيُظْهِرَهُ
عَلَى الدِّينِ كُلِّهِ وَلَوْ كَرِهَ الْمُشْرِكُونَ ۞ يَا أَيُّهَا
الَّذِينَ آمَنُوا إِنَّ كَثِيرًا مِّنَ الْأَحْبَارِ وَالرُّهْبَانِ
لَيَأْكُلُونَ أَمْوَالَ النَّاسِ بِالْبَاطِلِ وَيَصُدُّونَ عَن سَبِيلِ
اللَّهِ وَالَّذِينَ يَكْنِزُونَ الذَّهَبَ وَالْفِضَّةَ وَلَا
يُنفِقُونَهَا فِي سَبِيلِ اللَّهِ فَبَشِّرْهُم بِعَذَابٍ أَلِيمٍ
۞ يَوْمَ يُحْمَىٰ عَلَيْهَا فِي نَارِ جَهَنَّمَ فَتُكْوَىٰ بِهَا جِبَاهُهُمْ
وَجُنُوبُهُمْ وَظُهُورُهُمْ هَٰذَا مَا كَنَزْتُمْ لِأَنفُسِكُمْ
فَذُوقُوا مَا كُنتُمْ تَكْنِزُونَ ۞ إِنَّ عِدَّةَ الشُّهُورِ عِندَ
اللَّهِ اثْنَا عَشَرَ شَهْرًا فِي كِتَابِ اللَّهِ يَوْمَ خَلَقَ السَّمَاوَاتِ
وَالْأَرْضَ مِنْهَا أَرْبَعَةٌ حُرُمٌ ذَٰلِكَ الدِّينُ الْقَيِّمُ فَلَا
تَظْلِمُوا فِيهِنَّ أَنفُسَكُمْ وَقَاتِلُوا الْمُشْرِكِينَ كَافَّةً كَمَا
يُقَاتِلُونَكُمْ كَافَّةً وَاعْلَمُوا أَنَّ اللَّهَ مَعَ الْمُتَّقِينَ ۞

---

32. They seek (with renewed plans and stratagems) to extinguish God's light (His favor of Islam, as if by the breath issuing) from their mouths. Whereas God refuses but to complete His light, however hateful this may be to the unbelievers.

33. He it is Who has sent His Messenger with the guidance and the Religion of truth that He may make it prevail over all religions, however hateful this may be to those who associate partners with God.[9]

34. O you who believe! Many among the rabbis and monks do indeed consume the wealth of people in legally invalid, wrongful ways (such as changing the Book's commandments in return for worldly benefit, bribery, and using religion as a means of worldly gain) and bar them from God's way. Those who hoard up gold and silver and do not spend it in God's cause (to exalt His cause and help the poor and needy): give them (O Messenger) the glad tidings of a painful punishment.

35. On that day, it (that hoarded wealth) will be heated in the fire of Hell and therewith their foreheads and their sides and their backs will be branded (and they will hear): "This is the treasure which

you hoarded up for yourselves; taste now what you were busy hoarding!"[10]

36. The number of the months, in God's sight, is twelve as determined and decreed by God on the day when He created the heavens and the earth (and set them moving in the present conditions). Four of them are sacred (in that fighting is forbidden during them). This is the upright, ever-true Religion (the order that God has established for the operation of the universe and life of humanity). Do not, therefore, wrong yourselves with respect to these months. Nevertheless, fight all together against those who associate partners with God just as they fight against you all together; and know well that God is with the God-revering, pious who keep their duties to Him.

9. The last two verses give important guides to understanding Islam and its history. With all its essentials of faith, pillars of worship, standards of morality, principles of conduct, and its sociological, economic, and administrative teachings, Islam is a pure light that illuminates minds and hearts, indeed the whole world; with respect to the world, it is like the sun. Those who oppose this light are like those who close their ears, eyes, hearts, and minds to the truth and enlightenment, or to the "sun" and He Who created it, thereby darkening their own worlds. This attitude is what is meant by unbelief in Islamic literature. Those who do not believe, whether they are among those who associate partners with God, or if they belong to the People of the Book (see note 7, above), or if they recognize no faith at all, have sought throughout history to extinguish this "sun" of Islam with ever-renewed plans and strategies. But just as they were unable to prevent its being completed in its dawning during the Messenger's life (see 5: 3), they have never been able to take its place with all its splendor, even at times when they have seen it almost setting. Any plan or strategy carried out to extinguish this "sun" has no greater weight than a mere breath.

It may sometimes happen that those who identify themselves with Islam, although they are unable to represent or practice it fully in its true meaning and content, are lost to the world of unbelief. However, this never means the defeat of Islam by other religions or unbelief. Islam is always triumphant over all other religions and ideologies. Even in the last centuries, when the Muslims passed through the darkest period of their history and the world of Islam was uninterruptedly subjected to concerted attacks from all fronts by its opponents throughout the world, opponents equipped with the most sophisticated means, there have been few who have renounced Islam in favor of another religion, while many people have continued to convert to Islam from all other religions. In spite of the fact that the Muslims of today suffer from a multitude of deficiencies, even in their performance of the rites

of worship as commanded by Islam, with a thousand mistakes and without true spiritual fulfillment, and in spite of every effort made by the opponents of Islam to distort its image, many people in the West are still affected by it, whether they are religious or not. The comments of Western observers who are aware of Islam's dynamism and inextinguishable nature are very interesting. For example, Caesar E. Farah wrote the following on this subject:

> Putting aside the obstacles it met and the infrequent cases of apostasy, Islam has always shown an unlimited ability to live and spread, even under difficult conditions. This capability can be explained by its essential hidden dynamism and flexibility that can go immediately into action when the need arises. The attractive qualities of Islam that bound great masses to its ranks in the early centuries continued to attract people to the same ranks even when it lost political power. (al-Ezzati, 345)

Furthermore, while other religions, such as Christianity and Buddhism, have been defeated by atheistic, materialistic, and communist ideologies in several parts of the world, Islam has not lost ground. On this point the observations of E.H. Jurji are significant:

> With all its consistency, self-sufficiency and realism, and its determination that gave precedence to solidarity against racial and Marxist ideologies, with its mental rigging that can show the way to Western thought, with its determined attitude against imperialism and pillage, with its brave defense based on Qur'ānic faith that impedes all critical attacks and the plainness and authenticity of the message it brings to humanity that has strayed from the path, Islam appears before the modern world with a very special sense of responsibility. This sense of duty, which has not been spoiled by theological debates drowned in details, involved in confusing speculations, or fossilized under heavy layers of dogma, takes its strength from doctrines based on revelation. (al-Ezzati, 348)

In short, Islam always prevails over all other religions. This is what God has decreed. It is there with all its purity and continues to shine in all its dimensions.

10. The last two verses contain a serious warning. God's Religion can never be made a means of worldly gain; it cannot be exploited for such things as show, fame, acquiring wealth, status, or political aims. What people are commanded to do is to practice Islam purely to please God; this is the duty of His servants and this must be done because God has commanded us to do so (98: 5). For this reason, it is severely prohibited to attempt to use Islam for ulterior motives, i.e. to use it for reasons other than why it has been sent; this is especially pertinent to religious scholars and spiritual masters who are expected to represent and convey Islam in its purity, not to exploit it. Such leaders have a place and status in the people's eyes and they are more liable than others to exploit this status for worldly aims. 'Ali, the Fourth Caliph and cousin of the Messenger, says of some types of scholars, whom the Messenger had said would exploit God's religion for their selfish benefits toward the end of time: "Know, O community of brothers! The worst of people at that time are the scholars who, for the sake of worldly benefits, approve the innovations invented against the religion." Such scholars are called the "evil scholars" in Islamic literature. God's Messenger, upon him be peace and blessings, talked about 70,000 men who would wear turbans (i.e. religious scholars) who will support the practices of the Dajjāl (the man or a collective personality that is expected to appear toward the end of time and will try to eradicate Islam from the social life of Muslims) for worldly benefits.

In addition to the ways mentioned above, the scholars and spiritual masters may also exploit religion for selfish motives by distorting some rules of religion and arbitrarily interpreting some of its commandments. In whatever way they exploit religion, such attitudes on the part of religious scholars and spiritual masters cause people to grow antipathetic towards religion and prevent its being taught correctly. A scholar or spiritual master who sells religion for material gain cannot help but distort it. Holding such attitudes is what is meant by barring people from God's way.

Hoarding up money and goods without spending them in God's cause to promote God's cause and to help the poor and needy is one of the major sins. The foremost duty with respect to wealth is paying the Prescribed Alms (the Zakāh). Some scholars are of the opinion that any wealth out of which the Prescribed Alms is given cannot be considered hoarded wealth. However, this opinion has not received welcome from the majority of scholars. The standard by which to judge whether any accumulation of money is regarded as hoarded wealth is the general living standard of all Muslims and the conditions that affect the Islamic world. In another verse (59: 7), the Qur'ān openly declares that wealth should not be a means of prosperity circulated among the rich only. At a time when the majority of Muslims are poor and Islam is left without support, any wealth exceeding the limit of richness according to Islam (which is the amount out of which the Prescribed Alms should be given) and some amount of which is not spent in God's cause, is regarded as hoarded wealth, and is the object of the threat in the verse. The verse clearly mentions hoarded wealth and the failure to spend it in God's cause.

192   سُورَةُ التَّوبَةِ   ١٩٢

إِنَّمَا النَّسِيءُ زِيَادَةٌ فِي الْكُفْرِ يُضَلُّ بِهِ الَّذِينَ
كَفَرُوا يُحِلُّونَهُ عَامًا وَيُحَرِّمُونَهُ عَامًا لِّيُوَاطِئُوا
عِدَّةَ مَا حَرَّمَ اللَّهُ فَيُحِلُّوا مَا حَرَّمَ اللَّهُ زُيِّنَ لَهُمْ سُوءُ
أَعْمَالِهِمْ وَاللَّهُ لَا يَهْدِي الْقَوْمَ الْكَافِرِينَ ۞
يَا أَيُّهَا الَّذِينَ آمَنُوا مَا لَكُمْ إِذَا قِيلَ لَكُمُ انفِرُوا
فِي سَبِيلِ اللَّهِ اثَّاقَلْتُمْ إِلَى الْأَرْضِ أَرَضِيتُم
بِالْحَيَاةِ الدُّنْيَا مِنَ الْآخِرَةِ فَمَا مَتَاعُ الْحَيَاةِ الدُّنْيَا
فِي الْآخِرَةِ إِلَّا قَلِيلٌ ۞ إِلَّا تَنفِرُوا يُعَذِّبْكُمْ
عَذَابًا أَلِيمًا وَيَسْتَبْدِلْ قَوْمًا غَيْرَكُمْ وَلَا
تَضُرُّوهُ شَيْئًا وَاللَّهُ عَلَى كُلِّ شَيْءٍ قَدِيرٌ ۞ إِلَّا تَنصُرُوهُ
فَقَدْ نَصَرَهُ اللَّهُ إِذْ أَخْرَجَهُ الَّذِينَ كَفَرُوا ثَانِيَ
اثْنَيْنِ إِذْ هُمَا فِي الْغَارِ إِذْ يَقُولُ لِصَاحِبِهِ
لَا تَحْزَنْ إِنَّ اللَّهَ مَعَنَا فَأَنزَلَ اللَّهُ سَكِينَتَهُ عَلَيْهِ
وَأَيَّدَهُ بِجُنُودٍ لَّمْ تَرَوْهَا وَجَعَلَ كَلِمَةَ الَّذِينَ كَفَرُوا
السُّفْلَى وَكَلِمَةُ اللَّهِ هِيَ الْعُلْيَا وَاللَّهُ عَزِيزٌ حَكِيمٌ ۞

───────⟪──────

37. The postponement of a sacred month, and therefore making changes (for such aims as to make fighting in the Sacred Months lawful and cause the season of the Pilgrimage to fall in the period of the year they wish) is but an increase in unbelief (for it means making the unlawful lawful and changing the nature of many lawful and unlawful acts done in those months and therefore recognizing no law). By doing so, those who disbelieve are (further) misled, declaring it (the month they postpone) permitted in one year and forbidden in another, in order that they may conform to the number of the months that God has declared as sacred, (without caring) that they thereby make lawful what God has made unlawful. The evil of their deeds is decked out to be appealing to them. God does not guide the disbelieving people (to truth and to the attainment of their aims).

38. O you who believe! What excuse do you have that when it is said to you: "Mobilize (for the campaign of Tabuk)[11] in God's cause!" you cling heavily to the earth? Are you content with the present, worldly life, rather than the Hereafter? Yet slight is the enjoyment of the worldly life as compared with the Hereafter.

39. If you do not mobilize (as you are commanded), He will punish you grievously, and instead of you He will substitute another people, and you will in no way harm Him. God has full power over everything.

40. If you do not help him (the Messenger), yet for certain God helped him when those who disbelieve drove him out (of his home during the *Hijrah*), the second of the two when they were in the cave (with those in pursuit of them having reached the mouth of the cave), and he said to his companion (with utmost trust in God and no worry at all): "Do not grieve. God is surely with us."[12] Then God sent down His gift of inner peace and reassurance on him, supported him with hosts you cannot see, and brought the word (the cause) of the unbelievers utterly low. And God's word (His cause) is (always and inherently) supreme. God is All-Glorious with irresistible might, All-Wise.

11. The outcome of the Muslim–Byzantine encounter in Mu'tah came as a shock to Arabia and the Middle East, for the Romans did not gain the upper hand over the Muslims, even though they outnumbered the Muslims thirty-three to one. Ultimately, thousands of people from the semi-independent Arab tribes living in Syria and adjoining areas converted to Islam. To avenge himself for Mu'tah and to prevent the advance of Islam, the Byzantine Emperor ordered military preparations to invade Arabia.

God's Messenger, who always kept himself abreast of developments bearing on his mission, promptly decided to challenge the Byzantines on the battlefield. Any show of Muslim weakness might have given fresh life to the dying forces of Arabian polytheism and hostility, which had received a crushing blow at Hunayn. Such a development could also encourage the hypocrites in and around Madīnah to cause serious damage to Islam from within. They were already in touch with the Ghassanid Christian prince and with the Byzantine Emperor, and had built a mosque, which the Qur'ān calls the Mosque of *Dhirār* (Dissension) (9: 107), near Madīnah to serve as their operational base.

Realizing the gravity of the situation, God's Messenger, upon him be peace and blessings, publicly appealed to the Muslims to prepare for war and, contrary to his usual practice, declared that the Romans were his target.

It was mid-summer, the scorching heat was at its peak, the harvest season had just arrived, and there was a shortage of material resources. Moreover, the enemy was one of the two superpowers of the time. Despite all this, the Companions responded ardently to the Prophet's call and commenced their war preparations, all contributing much more than their financial means warranted.

In Rajab 9 AH (after *Hijrah*)/631 AD. God's Messenger and 30,000 soldiers left Madīnah and marched to Tabuk, quite close to what was then the Byzantine territory in Syria. The Byzantine Emperor, who had begun amassing a huge army, abandoned his plans and withdrew his army, for the Messenger arrived before he was expected and well before the Byzantine troop concentrations were completed (Ibn Sa'd, 2: 165–168; aṭ-Ṭabarī, 3: 100–111).

The Messenger stayed in Tabuk for 20 days, during which several buffer states under Byzantine hegemony agreed to pay the protection and exemption tax (*jizyah*) and live under his rule. Many Christian tribes embraced Islam willingly (*al-Bidāyah*, 5: 13). This bloodless victory also enabled the Muslims to consolidate their position before a prolonged conflict with the Byzantines, and altogether shattered the power of both the unbelievers and the Hypocrites in Arabia.

12. The verse refers to the *Hijrah*. The Messenger's reliance on God made him fearless. He appeared in the heartland of a desert inhabited by one of the most uncivilized peoples of the world. Despite their harsh treatment, and the strident hostility of one of his own uncles, he challenged the whole world and, through complete trust in God, carried his mission to victory. He had only a handful of supporters, and his victory came in a very short period – an unparalleled achievement.

The Quraysh were so eager to kill him that just before his emigration to Madīnah they selected one man from each clan. These numbered roughly 200, led by Abū Jahl and Abū Lahab, then besieged his house. God's Messenger told his cousin 'Ali to spend the night in his bed and, throwing some dust at the 200 hostile men while reciting: *And We have set a barrier before them and a barrier behind them, and (thus) We have covered them from all sides, so that they cannot see* (36: 9), he departed without being seen. He left Makkah with his closest friend, Abū Bakr, and reached the cave of Thawr, which is at the top of a steep mountain. Finding him gone, the chiefs of the Quraysh sent out search parties. One of these climbed the mountain up to the cave. Abū Bakr became anxious, fearing for the life of God's Messenger. However, the latter comforted him: *Do not grieve. God is surely with us*, and added: "What do you think of the two men beside whom God is the third?" (al-Bukhārī, "Tafsīr," 9; Ibn Hanbal, 1: 4).

انْفِرُوا خِفَافًا وَثِقَالًا وَجَاهِدُوا بِأَمْوَالِكُمْ وَأَنْفُسِكُمْ فِى سَبِيلِ اللَّهِ ذَٰلِكُمْ خَيْرٌ لَّكُمْ إِن كُنتُمْ تَعْلَمُونَ ۝ لَوْ كَانَ عَرَضًا قَرِيبًا وَسَفَرًا قَاصِدًا لَّاتَّبَعُوكَ وَلَٰكِن بَعُدَتْ عَلَيْهِمُ الشُّقَّةُ وَسَيَحْلِفُونَ بِاللَّهِ لَوِ اسْتَطَعْنَا لَخَرَجْنَا مَعَكُمْ يُهْلِكُونَ أَنفُسَهُمْ وَاللَّهُ يَعْلَمُ إِنَّهُمْ لَكَاذِبُونَ ۝ عَفَا اللَّهُ عَنكَ لِمَ أَذِنتَ لَهُمْ حَتَّىٰ يَتَبَيَّنَ لَكَ الَّذِينَ صَدَقُوا وَتَعْلَمَ الْكَاذِبِينَ ۝ لَا يَسْتَأْذِنُكَ الَّذِينَ يُؤْمِنُونَ بِاللَّهِ وَالْيَوْمِ الْآخِرِ أَن يُجَاهِدُوا بِأَمْوَالِهِمْ وَأَنفُسِهِمْ وَاللَّهُ عَلِيمٌ بِالْمُتَّقِينَ ۝ إِنَّمَا يَسْتَأْذِنُكَ الَّذِينَ لَا يُؤْمِنُونَ بِاللَّهِ وَالْيَوْمِ الْآخِرِ وَارْتَابَتْ قُلُوبُهُمْ فَهُمْ فِى رَيْبِهِمْ يَتَرَدَّدُونَ ۝ وَلَوْ أَرَادُوا الْخُرُوجَ لَأَعَدُّوا لَهُ عُدَّةً وَلَٰكِن كَرِهَ اللَّهُ انبِعَاثَهُمْ فَثَبَّطَهُمْ وَقِيلَ اقْعُدُوا مَعَ الْقَاعِدِينَ ۝ لَوْ خَرَجُوا فِيكُم مَّا زَادُوكُمْ إِلَّا خَبَالًا وَلَأَوْضَعُوا خِلَالَكُمْ يَبْغُونَكُمُ الْفِتْنَةَ وَفِيكُمْ سَمَّاعُونَ لَهُمْ وَاللَّهُ عَلِيمٌ بِالظَّالِمِينَ ۝

———◦———

41. Mobilize whether you are equipped lightly or heavily (and whether it be easy or difficult for you); and strive with your wealth and persons in God's cause. Doing so is what is for your good, if you but know it.

42. Had there been an immediate gain, and an easy journey, those (who stayed behind because of hypocrisy) would surely have followed you, but the difficult journey was too distant for them. Yet they will swear by God: "If only we had been able to, we would surely have gone forth with you." They destroy their own selves, for God knows that they are truly liars.

43. May God give you grace! Why did you give them leave to stay behind until it became clear to you who was speaking the truth and you came to know the liars.[13]

44. Those who believe in God and the Last Day do not ask you for leave to be excused from striving in God's cause with their wealth and persons. God has full knowledge of the God-revering, pious who keep their duty to Him.

45. Only they ask you for leave who do not truly believe in God and the Last Day and whose hearts are doubting, so that in their doubting they waver between one thing and another.

46. Had they truly meant to go forth for war, they would surely have made certain preparation (demonstrating their intent). But God was averse to their rising to fight (unwillingly and without sincerity of purpose), and so He caused them to hold back, and it was decreed for them: "Stay at home with the stay-at-homes (women and children)."

47. If they had gone forth among you, they would have brought no addition to you except trouble, and would have run about in your midst seeking to stir up sedition among you. Among you were some who were prone to heed them. God has full knowledge of the wrongdoers.

13. In the statement *until it became clear to you who was speaking the truth and you came to know the liars*, there are subtle points and legal principles to be noted:

- If a person known to be truthful says something, they should be believed. However, this does not remove the probability that they may have lied. But, while a verbal statement is enough to judge that a person is truthful in a matter, judging their speech as a lie must be based on certain knowledge. For this reason, while the verse uses the expression *become clear* for judging a person to be speaking the truth, it uses the expression *to come to know* to judge whether he or she is telling a lie.

- The verse uses a verb – speak – for those who spoke the truth when asking the Messenger to be excused from the war, while it uses a noun – liar – for those who did not speak the truth. A noun implies constancy and so a liar is one who habitually lies.

Therefore those who told lies in this matter were liars, and therefore the hypocrites in the community – because habitual lying is a sign of hypocrisy. However, since a single act of lying is enough to damage reliability or trustworthiness, a believer must always avoid lying, as a believer is, most of all, one reliable and trustworthy.

- The verse using a verb – speak – for those who spoke the truth but a noun – liar – for the others also implies that we cannot judge a person to be always and absolutely truthful by their saying the truth in a matter, although we cannot suspect them of being liars.

At this point, it would be useful to note that rendering such subtleties of the Qur'ān in its original language into other languages is often impossible. It is for this reason that the Qur'ān cannot be fully and exactly translated into another language and any translation of it cannot be regarded as being the Qur'ān.

194 سُورَةُ التَّوۡبَة ١٩٤

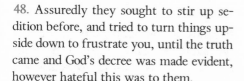

48. Assuredly they sought to stir up sedition before, and tried to turn things upside down to frustrate you, until the truth came and God's decree was made evident, however hateful this was to them.

49. Among them is one who says: "Give me leave (not to participate in this campaign) and do not expose me to temptation." Oh, but surely, they have already fallen into temptation (because of their hypocrisy and transgressions)! And surely Hell encompasses the unbelievers.

50. If something good comes to you (O Messenger), this grieves them; and if a disaster befalls you, they say, "We have taken due care of our affairs in good time," and turn away, exultant.

51. Say: "Nothing befalls us except what God has decreed for us; He is our Guardian and Owner; and in God let the believers put all their trust.

52. Say (to the hypocrites): "Or else are you are expecting for us other than one of the two best things (namely, victory or martyrdom in God's cause)? But what we expect for you is that God will inflict punishment upon you from Himself or by our hands! Wait, then, and we too are waiting with you."

53. (Respond to their unwilling donation and) say: "Whether you give willingly or unwillingly, (pretending that you give in God's cause), it will never be acceptable (to God) from you. Surely, you are a transgressing people."

54. Nothing hinders their offerings being accepted from them, except that they disbelieve in God and His Messenger, and whenever they come to the Prescribed Prayer they do so indolently (i.e. with reluctance), and they do not offer contributions except as averse (to doing so).

اَلْجُزْءُ الْعَاشِرْ

فَلَا تُعْجِبْكَ أَمْوَالُهُمْ وَلَآ أَوْلَادُهُمْ إِنَّمَا يُرِيدُ اللّٰهُ لِيُعَذِّبَهُمْ
بِهَا فِى الْحَيٰوةِ الدُّنْيَا وَتَزْهَقَ أَنْفُسُهُمْ وَهُمْ كَافِرُونَ
۞ وَيَحْلِفُونَ بِاللّٰهِ إِنَّهُمْ لَمِنْكُمْ وَمَا هُمْ مِنْكُمْ وَلٰكِنَّهُمْ
قَوْمٌ يَفْرَقُونَ ۞ لَوْ يَجِدُونَ مَلْجَأً أَوْ مَغَارَاتٍ أَوْ مُدَّخَلًا
لَوَلَّوْا إِلَيْهِ وَهُمْ يَجْمَحُونَ ۞ وَمِنْهُمْ مَنْ يَلْمِزُكَ فِى
الصَّدَقَاتِ فَإِنْ أُعْطُوا مِنْهَا رَضُوا وَإِنْ لَمْ يُعْطَوْا مِنْهَآ
إِذَا هُمْ يَسْخَطُونَ ۞ وَلَوْ أَنَّهُمْ رَضُوا مَآ أٰتٰىهُمُ اللّٰهُ وَرَسُولُهُ
وَقَالُوا حَسْبُنَا اللّٰهُ سَيُؤْتِينَا اللّٰهُ مِنْ فَضْلِهِ وَرَسُولُهُ إِنَّا
إِلَى اللّٰهِ رَاغِبُونَ ۞ إِنَّمَا الصَّدَقَاتُ لِلْفُقَرَاءِ وَالْمَسَاكِينِ
وَالْعَامِلِينَ عَلَيْهَا وَالْمُؤَلَّفَةِ قُلُوبُهُمْ وَفِى الرِّقَابِ
وَالْغَارِمِينَ وَفِى سَبِيلِ اللّٰهِ وَابْنِ السَّبِيلِ فَرِيضَةً
مِنَ اللّٰهِ وَ اللّٰهُ عَلِيمٌ حَكِيمٌ ۞ وَمِنْهُمُ الَّذِينَ
يُؤْذُونَ النَّبِيَّ وَيَقُولُونَ هُوَ أُذُنٌ قُلْ أُذُنُ خَيْرٍ
لَكُمْ يُؤْمِنُ بِاللّٰهِ وَيُؤْمِنُ لِلْمُؤْمِنِينَ وَرَحْمَةٌ لِلَّذِينَ آمَنُوا
مِنْكُمْ وَالَّذِينَ يُؤْذُونَ رَسُولَ اللّٰهِ لَهُمْ عَذَابٌ أَلِيمٌ ۞

55. Let neither their wealth nor their children impress you. God only wills thereby to punish them in the life of this world and that their souls will depart while they are unbelievers.[14]

56. They swear by God that they are indeed of you (belonging with the believers), yet they are not of you. They are only a people ridden by fear (and thereby pretending to be of you).

57. If they could but find a place of refuge, or any cavern, or any place to creep into to hide, they would turn about and make a bolt for it.

58. Among them is one who finds fault with you concerning (the distribution of) alms. If they are given something thereof, they are pleased; but if they are not given anything, they are consumed with rage.

59. If only they were content with what God and His Messenger give them and would say, "God is sufficient for us! God will give us more out of His grace and bounty, and so will His Messenger. Surely we are supplicants before God (seeking His good pleasure, with no right or cause of complaint)."

60. The Prescribed Purifying Alms (the *Zakāh*) are meant only for the poor, and the destitute (albeit, out of self-respect, they do not give the impression that they are in need), and those in charge of collecting (and administering) them, and those whose hearts are to be won over (for support of God's cause, including those whose hostility is to be prevented), and to free those in bondage (slavery and captivity), and to help those over-burdened with debt, and in God's cause (to exalt God's word, to provide for the warriors and students, and to help the pilgrims), and for the wayfarer (in need of help). This is an ordinance from God. God is All-Knowing, All-Wise.

61. Among them (the hypocrites) are those who hurt the Prophet and say (of him): "He is all ear (listening to everyone and disposed to believe them)." Say: "Yes, he is all ear, listening to what is best for you; he believes in God, and trusts the believers, and a great mercy for those among you who believe." Those who hurt God's Messenger – for them is a painful punishment.

14. It should once more be pointed out that God does not will unbelief or punishment for anybody. He is pleased only with the belief and well-being of His servants. However, such statements mean that God has recognized a field of free movement for human free will, and whatever a person wills He brings it into existence through that person. He is never pleased with the unbelief or hypocrisy or transgression of His servants, and in order for them to find true guidance He sent Messengers, and with them He sent down Books. After the Prophets, He creates great persons who represent His religion and convey it to people. Despite all this, those who persist in unbelief and transgression deserve punishment in accordance with the laws God has established for human life. Wealth and children are causes of trouble and anxiety for those who do not believe in God and the Hereafter and who assign all their efforts to this worldly life. All their lives are spent trying to earn their livelihood and bring up their children; yet they make their living without any lofty ideals. They never think of the other life and they die as they have lived, as unbelievers.

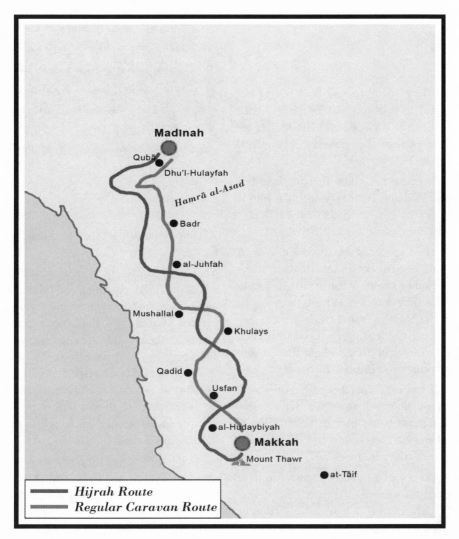

The route God's Messenger followed in his emigration from Makkah to Madīnah

196   سُوۡرَةُ التَّوۡبَة   ١٩٦

يَحۡلِفُونَ بِاللّٰهِ لَكُمۡ لِيُرۡضُوكُمۡ وَاللّٰهُ وَرَسُولُهُ
اَحَقُّ اَنۡ يُّرۡضُوهُ اِنۡ كَانُوۡا مُؤۡمِنِيۡنَ ۞ اَلَمۡ يَعۡلَمُوۡۤا اَنَّهُ
مَنۡ يُّحَادِدِ اللّٰهَ وَرَسُولَهُ فَاَنَّ لَهُ نَارَ جَهَنَّمَ خَالِدًا
فِيۡهَا ذٰلِكَ الۡخِزۡىُ الۡعَظِيۡمُ ۞ يَحۡذَرُ الۡمُنٰفِقُوۡنَ اَنۡ
تُنَزَّلَ عَلَيۡهِمۡ سُوۡرَةٌ تُنَبِّئُهُمۡ بِمَا فِىۡ قُلُوۡبِهِمۡ قُلِ
اسۡتَهۡزِءُوۡا اِنَّ اللّٰهَ مُخۡرِجٌ مَّا تَحۡذَرُوۡنَ ۞ وَلَئِنۡ سَاَلۡتَهُمۡ
لَيَقُوۡلُنَّ اِنَّمَا كُنَّا نَخُوۡضُ وَنَلۡعَبُ قُلۡ اَبِاللّٰهِ وَاٰيٰتِهٖ
وَرَسُوۡلِهٖ كُنۡتُمۡ تَسۡتَهۡزِءُوۡنَ ۞ لَا تَعۡتَذِرُوۡا قَدۡ كَفَرۡتُمۡ
بَعۡدَ اِيۡمَانِكُمۡ اِنۡ نَّعۡفُ عَنۡ طَآئِفَةٍ مِّنۡكُمۡ نُعَذِّبۡ
طَآئِفَةً بِاَنَّهُمۡ كَانُوۡا مُجۡرِمِيۡنَ ۞ اَلۡمُنٰفِقُوۡنَ وَالۡمُنٰفِقٰتُ
بَعۡضُهُمۡ مِّنۡ بَعۡضٍ يَاۡمُرُوۡنَ بِالۡمُنۡكَرِ وَيَنۡهَوۡنَ عَنِ
الۡمَعۡرُوۡفِ وَيَقۡبِضُوۡنَ اَيۡدِيَهُمۡ نَسُوا اللّٰهَ فَنَسِيَهُمۡ
اِنَّ الۡمُنٰفِقِيۡنَ هُمُ الۡفٰسِقُوۡنَ ۞ وَعَدَ اللّٰهُ الۡمُنٰفِقِيۡنَ
وَالۡمُنٰفِقٰتِ وَالۡكُفَّارَ نَارَ جَهَنَّمَ خَالِدِيۡنَ فِيۡهَا
هِىَ حَسۡبُهُمۡ وَلَعَنَهُمُ اللّٰهُ وَلَهُمۡ عَذَابٌ مُّقِيۡمٌ ۞

62. They swear to you by God (O believers) so that you may be pleased with them, while it is God and His Messenger whose pleasure they should seek, if indeed they are believers.

63. Do they not know that whoever opposes God and His Messenger, for him is the fire of Hell to abide therein. That is the tremendous disgrace.

64. The hypocrites are afraid lest a *sūrah* should be sent down against them making plainly known what is in their hearts (while they do not hold back from mocking the Messenger and the believers). Say (to them, O Messenger): "Go on mocking. God will surely bring to light that (whose disclosure) you dread."

65. If you ask them (about what they were saying), they will say: "We were merely jesting and being playful." Say: "Was it God and His Revelations and His Messenger that you were mocking?"

66. Do not make excuses now! You have indeed disbelieved after your (declaration of) faith. Even if We pardon a section of you (those whose idle talk was not intended to mock God and His Messenger), We will surely punish another section of you for they have been criminals.

67. The hypocrites, both men and women, are all of a kind: enjoining and promoting what is evil and forbidding and trying to prevent what is right and good, and they withhold their hands (from doing good and spending in God's cause). They are oblivious of God (with respect to faith and worship and serving in His cause), and so He is oblivious of them (with respect to rewarding). Assuredly, the hypocrites are those who are the transgressors.

68. God has promised the hypocrites, both men and women, and the unbelievers, the fire of Hell, therein to abide: it is (recompense) to suffice them. God has excluded them from His mercy, and for them is a lasting punishment.

كَالَّذِينَ مِن قَبْلِكُمْ كَانُوٓا۟ أَشَدَّ مِنكُمْ قُوَّةً وَأَكْثَرَ
أَمْوَٰلًا وَأَوْلَٰدًا فَٱسْتَمْتَعُوا۟ بِخَلَٰقِهِمْ فَٱسْتَمْتَعْتُم
بِخَلَٰقِكُمْ كَمَا ٱسْتَمْتَعَ ٱلَّذِينَ مِن قَبْلِكُمْ بِخَلَٰقِهِمْ
وَخُضْتُمْ كَٱلَّذِى خَاضُوٓا۟ أُو۟لَٰٓئِكَ حَبِطَتْ أَعْمَٰلُهُمْ فِى
ٱلدُّنْيَا وَٱلْءَاخِرَةِ وَأُو۟لَٰٓئِكَ هُمُ ٱلْخَٰسِرُونَ ۝ أَلَمْ يَأْتِهِمْ
نَبَأُ ٱلَّذِينَ مِن قَبْلِهِمْ قَوْمِ نُوحٍ وَعَادٍ وَثَمُودَ وَقَوْمِ
إِبْرَٰهِيمَ وَأَصْحَٰبِ مَدْيَنَ وَٱلْمُؤْتَفِكَٰتِ أَتَتْهُمْ رُسُلُهُم
بِٱلْبَيِّنَٰتِ فَمَا كَانَ ٱللَّهُ لِيَظْلِمَهُمْ وَلَٰكِن كَانُوٓا۟ أَنفُسَهُمْ
يَظْلِمُونَ ۝ وَٱلْمُؤْمِنُونَ وَٱلْمُؤْمِنَٰتُ بَعْضُهُمْ أَوْلِيَآءُ بَعْضٍ
يَأْمُرُونَ بِٱلْمَعْرُوفِ وَيَنْهَوْنَ عَنِ ٱلْمُنكَرِ وَيُقِيمُونَ ٱلصَّلَوٰةَ
وَيُؤْتُونَ ٱلزَّكَوٰةَ وَيُطِيعُونَ ٱللَّهَ وَرَسُولَهُۥٓ أُو۟لَٰٓئِكَ
سَيَرْحَمُهُمُ ٱللَّهُ إِنَّ ٱللَّهَ عَزِيزٌ حَكِيمٌ ۝ وَعَدَ ٱللَّهُ
ٱلْمُؤْمِنِينَ وَٱلْمُؤْمِنَٰتِ جَنَّٰتٍ تَجْرِى مِن تَحْتِهَا ٱلْأَنْهَٰرُ
خَٰلِدِينَ فِيهَا وَمَسَٰكِنَ طَيِّبَةً فِى جَنَّٰتِ عَدْنٍ
وَرِضْوَٰنٌ مِّنَ ٱللَّهِ أَكْبَرُ ذَٰلِكَ هُوَ ٱلْفَوْزُ ٱلْعَظِيمُ ۝

69. Just like the peoples before you (O hypocrites and unbelievers) who were greater than you in power and more abundant in wealth and children. They enjoyed their lot (in the world) for a while; and you have been enjoying your lot just as those who preceded you enjoyed their lot, and you have plunged in self-indulgence as others who plunged. Such (hypocrites and unbelievers) are those whose works have been wasted in both this world and the Hereafter, and those – they are the losers.

70. Have there not reached them the exemplary histories of those who lived before them – the people of Noah, the Ād, the Thamūd, and the people of Abraham, and the dwellers of Madyan (Midian), and the overthrown cities (of Sodom and Gomorrah)? Their Messengers came to them with the clear proofs (of the truth, in which they would not believe.) It was not, then, God who wronged them but they wronged their own selves.

71. The believers, both men and women, they are guardians, confidants, and helpers of one another. They enjoin and promote what is right and good and forbid and try to prevent the evil, and they establish the Prescribed Prayer in conformity with its conditions, and pay the Prescribed Purifying Alms. They obey God and His Messenger. They are the ones whom God will treat with mercy. Surely God is All-Glorious with irresistible might, All-Wise.

72. God has promised the believers, both men and women, Gardens through which rivers flow, therein to abide, and blessed dwellings in Gardens of perpetual bliss; and greater (than those) is God's being pleased with them. That indeed is the supreme triumph.

198

سورة التوبة

١٩٨

يَا أَيُّهَا النَّبِيُّ جَاهِدِ الْكُفَّارَ وَالْمُنَافِقِينَ وَاغْلُظْ
عَلَيْهِمْ وَمَأْوَاهُمْ جَهَنَّمُ وَبِئْسَ الْمَصِيرُ ۝ يَحْلِفُونَ
بِاللَّهِ مَا قَالُوا وَلَقَدْ قَالُوا كَلِمَةَ الْكُفْرِ وَكَفَرُوا بَعْدَ
إِسْلَامِهِمْ وَهَمُّوا بِمَا لَمْ يَنَالُوا وَمَا نَقَمُوا إِلَّا أَنْ أَغْنَاهُمُ
اللَّهُ وَرَسُولُهُ مِنْ فَضْلِهِ فَإِنْ يَتُوبُوا يَكُ خَيْرًا لَهُمْ
وَإِنْ يَتَوَلَّوْا يُعَذِّبْهُمُ اللَّهُ عَذَابًا أَلِيمًا فِي الدُّنْيَا وَالْآخِرَةِ
وَمَا لَهُمْ فِي الْأَرْضِ مِنْ وَلِيٍّ وَلَا نَصِيرٍ ۝ وَمِنْهُمْ مَنْ عَاهَدَ
اللَّهَ لَئِنْ آتَانَا مِنْ فَضْلِهِ لَنَصَّدَّقَنَّ وَلَنَكُونَنَّ مِنَ
الصَّالِحِينَ ۝ فَلَمَّا آتَاهُمْ مِنْ فَضْلِهِ بَخِلُوا بِهِ وَتَوَلَّوْا
وَهُمْ مُعْرِضُونَ ۝ فَأَعْقَبَهُمْ نِفَاقًا فِي قُلُوبِهِمْ إِلَى يَوْمِ
يَلْقَوْنَهُ بِمَا أَخْلَفُوا اللَّهَ مَا وَعَدُوهُ وَبِمَا كَانُوا يَكْذِبُونَ
۝ أَلَمْ يَعْلَمُوا أَنَّ اللَّهَ يَعْلَمُ سِرَّهُمْ وَنَجْوَاهُمْ وَأَنَّ
اللَّهَ عَلَّامُ الْغُيُوبِ ۝ الَّذِينَ يَلْمِزُونَ الْمُطَّوِّعِينَ مِنَ
الْمُؤْمِنِينَ فِي الصَّدَقَاتِ وَالَّذِينَ لَا يَجِدُونَ إِلَّا جُهْدَهُمْ
فَيَسْخَرُونَ مِنْهُمْ سَخِرَ اللَّهُ مِنْهُمْ وَلَهُمْ عَذَابٌ أَلِيمٌ ۝

73. O (most illustrious) Prophet! Strive against the unbelievers and the hypocrites (in the way required by time and conditions),[15] and be stern against them. Their final refuge is Hell: how evil a destination to arrive at!

74. They swear by God that they have said nothing (blasphemous), whereas they certainly did utter blasphemies (the word of unbelief), and they fell into unbelief after having entered the fold of Islam, and they purposed and attempted what they could not achieve. They are spiteful against (Islam and the Messenger) for no other reason than that God enriched them and (caused) His Messenger (to enrich them) out of His grace and bounty! Even so, if they repent, it will be to their good; but if they still turn away, God will punish them painfully in the world and the Hereafter. They have on earth no protecting guardian nor helper (against God's punishment).

75. Among them are some who vowed to God: "Surely, if God grants us out of His grace and bounty, we will most certainly (pay the Prescribed Alms and) spend in alms for His sake, and we will most certainly be among the righteous."

76. Then God granted them out of His grace and bounty, but they clung to it in niggardly fashion and turned about, swerving away (from what they had vowed).

77. So as a consequence He has caused hypocrisy to be in their hearts (and to remain rooted therein) until the day when they will meet Him (at death), because they have broken their word to God that they promised Him, and because they were lying habitually.

78. Do they not know that God knows what they keep concealed and their private counsels and gossips, and that God has full knowledge of the whole of the Unseen (all that lies beyond the reach of any created being's perception).

79. They taunt the believers, who give for God's sake more than they are duty-bound to give, as well as those who can find nothing to give except (what they earn through) their hard toil, and they scoff at them. God causes their scoffing to rebound on themselves, and for them is a painful punishment.[16]

15. The expression "in the way required by time and conditions" does not exist in the original text of the verse. However, first of all, as mentioned in many other verses, the Qur'ān discriminates among the opponents of Islam, and even the unbelievers, the People of the Book, and the polytheists themselves, as we saw at the beginning of this *sūrah*. It never orders that all the unbelievers and hypocrites be treated in the same way. It sometimes orders that the Muslims should treat them with patience, sometimes with forgiveness, and sometimes by overlooking their ill-treatment of the Prophet and the believers. There even comes a time when the believers are ordered to converse with them in the best way possible and call them to the truth with fair exhortation and wisdom. What is important is that we should know what kinds of unbelievers and hypocrites are being discussed, and under what conditions the verse orders the Messenger, and therefore the Muslims, to strive hard and be stern against them. We should, finally, point out that the ways of striving against the unbelievers and that of striving against the hypocrites differ from one another. For example, since the hypocrites are Muslim in appearance and are regarded as such, Muslims cannot fight against them as long as they obey the government and fulfill their duties of citizenship. (See also verse 123, note 28.)

16. The verses reveal how disgusting hypocrisy is and warns people against it. The last verse describes a typical aspect of hypocrisy. Those who have no praiseworthy virtues taunt the worthy people because of their merits. For example, as mentioned in the verse, those who cannot spend out of their wealth for the good of the community and in God's cause, attempt to find fault with those who can do that and taunt them with making show. The hypocrites during the Messenger's time accused the wealthy believers who donated a large amount of insincerity and ostentation, and scoffed at the poor believers who donated modest amounts out of their scanty earnings through their hard toil, saying, "Will the strongholds of Byzantium be destroyed with what those give!?" They derided them by making signs with their eyes and eyebrows. This was the reflection of the hypocrisy in their hearts. The attitudes, such as derision, scoffing and taunting, which some display when they see others who have merits that they do not have, demonstrate the hypocrisy in their hearts. Even though we cannot say that anyone who does this is a hypocrite, it is certain that such attitudes are in fact attitudes that belong to hypocrites.

اسْتَغْفِرْ لَهُمْ أَوْ لَا تَسْتَغْفِرْ لَهُمْ إِن تَسْتَغْفِرْ لَهُمْ سَبْعِينَ مَرَّةً
فَلَن يَغْفِرَ اللَّهُ لَهُمْ ذَٰلِكَ بِأَنَّهُمْ كَفَرُوا بِاللَّهِ وَرَسُولِهِ وَاللَّهُ
لَا يَهْدِي الْقَوْمَ الْفَاسِقِينَ ۝ فَرِحَ الْمُخَلَّفُونَ بِمَقْعَدِهِمْ
خِلَافَ رَسُولِ اللَّهِ وَكَرِهُوا أَن يُجَاهِدُوا بِأَمْوَالِهِمْ وَأَنفُسِهِمْ
فِي سَبِيلِ اللَّهِ وَقَالُوا لَا تَنفِرُوا فِي الْحَرِّ قُلْ نَارُ جَهَنَّمَ أَشَدُّ
حَرًّا لَّوْ كَانُوا يَفْقَهُونَ ۝ فَلْيَضْحَكُوا قَلِيلًا وَلْيَبْكُوا كَثِيرًا
جَزَاءً بِمَا كَانُوا يَكْسِبُونَ ۝ فَإِن رَّجَعَكَ اللَّهُ إِلَىٰ طَائِفَةٍ مِّنْهُمْ
فَاسْتَأْذَنُوكَ لِلْخُرُوجِ فَقُل لَّن تَخْرُجُوا مَعِيَ أَبَدًا وَلَن تُقَاتِلُوا مَعِيَ
عَدُوًّا إِنَّكُمْ رَضِيتُم بِالْقُعُودِ أَوَّلَ مَرَّةٍ فَاقْعُدُوا مَعَ الْخَالِفِينَ
۝ وَلَا تُصَلِّ عَلَىٰ أَحَدٍ مِّنْهُم مَّاتَ أَبَدًا وَلَا تَقُمْ عَلَىٰ قَبْرِهِ إِنَّهُمْ
كَفَرُوا بِاللَّهِ وَرَسُولِهِ وَمَاتُوا وَهُمْ فَاسِقُونَ ۝ وَلَا
تُعْجِبْكَ أَمْوَالُهُمْ وَأَوْلَادُهُمْ إِنَّمَا يُرِيدُ اللَّهُ أَن يُعَذِّبَهُم بِهَا
فِي الدُّنْيَا وَتَزْهَقَ أَنفُسُهُمْ وَهُمْ كَافِرُونَ ۝ وَإِذَا أُنزِلَتْ سُورَةٌ
أَنْ آمِنُوا بِاللَّهِ وَجَاهِدُوا مَعَ رَسُولِهِ اسْتَأْذَنَكَ أُولُوا
الطَّوْلِ مِنْهُمْ وَقَالُوا ذَرْنَا نَكُن مَّعَ الْقَاعِدِينَ ۝

80. Whether you (O Messenger) pray for their forgiveness or do not pray for their forgiveness, even if you pray for their forgiveness seventy times, God will not forgive them. That is because they disbelieve in God and His Messenger. God will not guide the transgressing people.

81. Those who were left behind in opposition to God's Messenger rejoiced at staying at home, and abhorred striving with their wealth and persons in God's cause. And they said: "Do not go forth to war in this heat." Say (O Messenger): "The fire of Hell is fiercer in heat." If only they had been able to ponder and penetrate the essence of matters to grasp the truth!

82. So let them laugh little and weep much, in recompense for what they have been earning.

83. If God brings you back (from the Campaign) and a party of them ask your leave to go forth to war with you, say to them: "Never will you go forth with me any more, nor will you fight an enemy in my company. You were content to stay at home on that first occasion, so continue to stay at home with those who are (naturally) bound to remain behind!"

84. And never do the funeral Prayer over any of them who dies, nor stand by his grave to pray for him. They surely disbelieved in God and His Messenger and died transgressors.

85. Let neither their wealth nor their children impress you; God only wills thereby to punish them in this world and that their souls should depart while they are unbelievers.[17]

86. (Indeed they are unbelievers, and never want to go forth to war in God's cause.) Whenever a *surah* is sent down (calling them): "Believe in God and strive in God's cause in the company of His Messenger," (even) those of them who are well able (to go to war) ask you to excuse them, saying: "Leave us to be with those who are to stay at home."

---

17. See verse 55, note 14.

200 سورة التوبة ٢..

وَرَضُوا بِأَن يَكُونُوا مَعَ الْخَوَالِفِ وَطُبِعَ عَلَىٰ قُلُوبِهِمْ فَهُمْ لَا يَفْقَهُونَ ۝ لَٰكِنِ الرَّسُولُ وَالَّذِينَ ءَامَنُوا مَعَهُ جَاهَدُوا بِأَمْوَالِهِمْ وَأَنفُسِهِمْ وَأُوْلَٰئِكَ لَهُمُ الْخَيْرَٰتُ وَأُوْلَٰئِكَ هُمُ الْمُفْلِحُونَ ۝ أَعَدَّ اللَّهُ لَهُمْ جَنَّٰتٍ تَجْرِى مِن تَحْتِهَا الْأَنْهَٰرُ خَٰلِدِينَ فِيهَا ذَٰلِكَ الْفَوْزُ الْعَظِيمُ ۝ وَجَآءَ الْمُعَذِّرُونَ مِنَ الْأَعْرَابِ لِيُؤْذَنَ لَهُمْ وَقَعَدَ الَّذِينَ كَذَبُوا اللَّهَ وَرَسُولَهُ سَيُصِيبُ الَّذِينَ كَفَرُوا مِنْهُمْ عَذَابٌ أَلِيمٌ ۝ لَيْسَ عَلَى الضُّعَفَآءِ وَلَا عَلَى الْمَرْضَىٰ وَلَا عَلَى الَّذِينَ لَا يَجِدُونَ مَا يُنفِقُونَ حَرَجٌ إِذَا نَصَحُوا لِلَّهِ وَرَسُولِهِ مَا عَلَى الْمُحْسِنِينَ مِن سَبِيلٍ وَاللَّهُ غَفُورٌ رَّحِيمٌ ۝ وَلَا عَلَى الَّذِينَ إِذَا مَا أَتَوْكَ لِتَحْمِلَهُمْ قُلْتَ لَا أَجِدُ مَا أَحْمِلُكُمْ عَلَيْهِ تَوَلَّوا وَّأَعْيُنُهُمْ تَفِيضُ مِنَ الدَّمْعِ حَزَنًا أَلَّا يَجِدُوا مَا يُنفِقُونَ ۝ إِنَّمَا السَّبِيلُ عَلَى الَّذِينَ يَسْتَأْذِنُونَكَ وَهُمْ أَغْنِيَآءُ رَضُوا بِأَن يَكُونُوا مَعَ الْخَوَالِفِ وَطَبَعَ اللَّهُ عَلَىٰ قُلُوبِهِمْ فَهُمْ لَا يَعْلَمُونَ ۝

───────◈───────

87. They are well-pleased to be with those (women and children) bound to stay behind, and a seal has been set upon their hearts, so they cannot ponder and penetrate the essence of matters to grasp the truth.

88. But the Messenger and those who believe in his company have striven in God's cause with their wealth and persons. They are those for whom is all good, and they are those who are the prosperous.

89. God has prepared for them Gardens through which rivers flow, therein to abide. That is the supreme triumph.

90. Some among the Bedouin Arabs having true excuses came (to the Messenger) to ask leave to stay behind, whereas those who are false to God and His Messenger (in their covenant and claim of adherence) stayed at home (without taking part in the campaign). A painful punishment will befall those of them who disbelieve.

91. There is no blame on those too weak to go forth to war, and the sick, and on those who cannot find the means (with which to equip and maintain themselves if they go forth), provided that they are true to God and His Messenger. There can be no way (of blame) against those who are devoted to doing good, aware that God is seeing them. God is All-Forgiving, All-Compassionate.

92. Nor (can there be any way to blame) those who, when they came to you to provide them with mounts, and you said, "I cannot find anything whereon to mount you," they returned, their eyes overflowing with tears for sorrow that they could not find anything to spend (to prepare themselves for the campaign).

93. The way (of blame) is open only against those who sought leave to stay behind even though they are wealthy (well able to equip themselves for the campaign). They were well-pleased to be with those (women and children) bound to stay behind. God has set a seal on their hearts, so that they do not know (the truth and what is really beneficial to them).

يَعْتَذِرُونَ إِلَيْكُمْ إِذَا رَجَعْتُمْ إِلَيْهِمْ قُل لَّا تَعْتَذِرُوا لَن نُّؤْمِنَ لَكُمْ قَدْ نَبَّأَنَا اللَّهُ مِنْ أَخْبَارِكُمْ وَسَيَرَى اللَّهُ عَمَلَكُمْ وَرَسُولُهُ ثُمَّ تُرَدُّونَ إِلَىٰ عَالِمِ الْغَيْبِ وَالشَّهَادَةِ فَيُنَبِّئُكُم بِمَا كُنتُمْ تَعْمَلُونَ ۞ سَيَحْلِفُونَ بِاللَّهِ لَكُمْ إِذَا انقَلَبْتُمْ إِلَيْهِمْ لِتُعْرِضُوا عَنْهُمْ فَأَعْرِضُوا عَنْهُمْ إِنَّهُمْ رِجْسٌ وَمَأْوَاهُمْ جَهَنَّمُ جَزَاءً بِمَا كَانُوا يَكْسِبُونَ ۞ يَحْلِفُونَ لَكُمْ لِتَرْضَوْا عَنْهُمْ فَإِن تَرْضَوْا عَنْهُمْ فَإِنَّ اللَّهَ لَا يَرْضَىٰ عَنِ الْقَوْمِ الْفَاسِقِينَ ۞ الْأَعْرَابُ أَشَدُّ كُفْرًا وَنِفَاقًا وَأَجْدَرُ أَلَّا يَعْلَمُوا حُدُودَ مَا أَنزَلَ اللَّهُ عَلَىٰ رَسُولِهِ وَاللَّهُ عَلِيمٌ حَكِيمٌ ۞ وَمِنَ الْأَعْرَابِ مَن يَتَّخِذُ مَا يُنفِقُ مَغْرَمًا وَيَتَرَبَّصُ بِكُمُ الدَّوَائِرَ عَلَيْهِمْ دَائِرَةُ السَّوْءِ وَاللَّهُ سَمِيعٌ عَلِيمٌ ۞ وَمِنَ الْأَعْرَابِ مَن يُؤْمِنُ بِاللَّهِ وَالْيَوْمِ الْآخِرِ وَيَتَّخِذُ مَا يُنفِقُ قُرُبَاتٍ عِندَ اللَّهِ وَصَلَوَاتِ الرَّسُولِ أَلَا إِنَّهَا قُرْبَةٌ لَّهُمْ سَيُدْخِلُهُمُ اللَّهُ فِي رَحْمَتِهِ إِنَّ اللَّهَ غَفُورٌ رَّحِيمٌ ۞

94. They will offer excuses to you (O believers) when you return to them. Say (to them, O Messenger): "Do not offer excuses: we will never believe you. God has informed us (of the truth) about you. And God will observe your (future) conduct, and so will His Messenger, and then you will be brought back to the Knower of the Unseen and the witnessed, and He will make you understand what you used to do (and call you to account).

95. When you return to them, they will (out of fear of punishment) swear to you in the Name of God, (repeating their excuses) so that you may leave them be. So leave them be and withdraw from them. They are loathsome, and their final refuge is Hell as a recompense for what they have been earning.

96. They will swear to you so that you may be pleased with them. But even should you be pleased with them, God will not be pleased with the transgressing people.

97. The Bedouin Arabs are (by nature) more stubborn in unbelief and hypocrisy (than the city-dwellers), and more liable to be unaware of the bounds prescribed by God in what He has sent down on His Messenger. God is All-Knowing (of the nature and state of His servants), All-Wise.[18]

98. Among the Bedouin Arabs there are such as take what they spend (as Prescribed Alms and the contributions they are called on to make in God's cause) as a fine, and wait for some misfortune to befall you; theirs will be the evil turn. God is All-Hearing, All-Knowing.

99. Among the Bedouin Arabs there are also those who believe in God and the Last Day, and take what they spend (as Prescribed Alms and the contributions they are called on to make in God's cause) as a means of drawing them near to God and of the Messenger's praying (to God for them). Indeed, it is a means for them to draw near to God. God will admit them into His mercy. Surely, God is All-Forgiving, All-Compassionate.

18. The Bedouin Arabs were those who lived a nomadic life in the desert or in villages. They were rude, obstinate, and ignorant. They could not find time to visit the Messenger and listen to him. So it was difficult for them to change their centuries-old world-view, beliefs, and life-style.

We should note here that history tells us that both the unbelievers and hypocrites who lived during the Messenger's life were the most refractory of all times. Both the people of Makkah and Madīnah were extremely courageous, arrogant, merciless, deeply devoted to their centuries-old cultures, beliefs, and life-styles, and therefore were extremely difficult to deal with. But the Prophet Muḥammad, upon him be peace and blessings, educated them in such a way that he raised from them the greatest, most merciful, wise, virtuous, and knowledgeable community of all times. They came to be known and respected as the Companions and became the teachers of all future Muslim generations. This is one of the greatest miracles of the Messenger, which is unparalleled in human history. Said Nursi writes:

> Consider how he quickly eradicated his people's fanatic attachment to their evil and savage customs and immoral qualities. See how he equipped and adorned the Peninsula's disparate, wild, and unyielding peoples with all praiseworthy virtues and made them teachers and masters of the world, especially to the civilized nations. Moreover, this domination was not outward – he conquered and subjugated minds, spirits, hearts, and souls. He became the beloved of hearts, the teacher of minds, the trainer of souls, and the ruler of spirits.
>
> You know that a small habit like smoking in a small community can be removed permanently only by a powerful ruler and with great effort. But the Prophet quickly removed numerous ingrained habits from large obsessed communities with little outward power and effort. In their place, he implanted and inculcated exalted qualities that became inherent in their being. Many more such miraculous accomplishments can be credited to him. To those who refuse to see the testimony of this blessed age, let them go to the present "civilized" Arabian peninsula with hundreds of philosophers, sociologists, and psychologists, and strive for 100 years. I wonder if they can achieve in that period even a small fraction of what the Prophet achieved in a year (*The Words*, "the 19th Word," 249–250).

In viewing the Qur'ānic passages about the unbelievers among the hypocrites, this point should never be forgotten.

202

سُورَةُ التَّوۡبَةِ ٢٠٢

وَالسَّابِقُونَ الْأَوَّلُونَ مِنَ الْمُهَاجِرِينَ وَالْأَنْصَارِ وَالَّذِينَ اتَّبَعُوهُم بِإِحْسَانٍ رَّضِيَ اللَّهُ عَنْهُمْ وَرَضُوا عَنْهُ وَأَعَدَّ لَهُمْ جَنَّاتٍ تَجْرِي تَحْتَهَا الْأَنْهَارُ خَالِدِينَ فِيهَا أَبَدًا ذَٰلِكَ الْفَوْزُ الْعَظِيمُ ۞ وَمِمَّنْ حَوْلَكُم مِّنَ الْأَعْرَابِ مُنَافِقُونَ وَمِنْ أَهْلِ الْمَدِينَةِ مَرَدُوا عَلَى النِّفَاقِ لَا تَعْلَمُهُمْ نَحْنُ نَعْلَمُهُمْ سَنُعَذِّبُهُم مَّرَّتَيْنِ ثُمَّ يُرَدُّونَ إِلَىٰ عَذَابٍ عَظِيمٍ ۞ وَآخَرُونَ اعْتَرَفُوا بِذُنُوبِهِمْ خَلَطُوا عَمَلًا صَالِحًا وَآخَرَ سَيِّئًا عَسَى اللَّهُ أَن يَتُوبَ عَلَيْهِمْ إِنَّ اللَّهَ غَفُورٌ رَّحِيمٌ ۞ خُذْ مِنْ أَمْوَالِهِمْ صَدَقَةً تُطَهِّرُهُمْ وَتُزَكِّيهِم بِهَا وَصَلِّ عَلَيْهِمْ إِنَّ صَلَاتَكَ سَكَنٌ لَّهُمْ وَاللَّهُ سَمِيعٌ عَلِيمٌ ۞ أَلَمْ يَعْلَمُوا أَنَّ اللَّهَ هُوَ يَقْبَلُ التَّوْبَةَ عَنْ عِبَادِهِ وَيَأْخُذُ الصَّدَقَاتِ وَأَنَّ اللَّهَ هُوَ التَّوَّابُ الرَّحِيمُ ۞ وَقُلِ اعْمَلُوا فَسَيَرَى اللَّهُ عَمَلَكُمْ وَرَسُولُهُ وَالْمُؤْمِنُونَ وَسَتُرَدُّونَ إِلَىٰ عَالِمِ الْغَيْبِ وَ الشَّهَادَةِ فَيُنَبِّئُكُم بِمَا كُنتُمْ تَعْمَلُونَ ۞ وَآخَرُونَ مُرْجَوْنَ لِأَمْرِ اللَّهِ إِمَّا يُعَذِّبُهُمْ وَإِمَّا يَتُوبُ عَلَيْهِمْ وَاللَّهُ عَلِيمٌ حَكِيمٌ ۞

---

100. The first and foremost (to embrace Islam and excel others in virtue) among the Emigrants and the Helpers, and those who follow them in devotion to doing good, aware that God is seeing them – God is well-pleased with them, and they are well-pleased with Him, and He has prepared for them Gardens throughout which rivers flow, therein to abide for ever. That is the supreme triumph.[19]

101. Among the Bedouin Arabs who dwell around you there are hypocrites, and among the people of Madīnah (too) there are such as have grown more artful and insidious in hypocrisy: you (O Messenger) do not know them (unless We inform you of them). We know them all (and the threat they pose). We will punish them doubly, and then they will be returned to a mighty punishment (in the Hereafter).

102. Others (there are who) have admitted their sins: they have mixed a righteous deed with an evil one. It may be that God will return their repentance with forgiveness. Surely God is All-Forgiving, All-Compassionate.

103. Take alms (prescribed or voluntary) out of their wealth so that you (O Messenger) may thereby cleanse them and cause them to grow in purity and sincerity, and pray for them. Indeed your prayer is a source of comfort for them. God is All-Hearing, All-Knowing.

104. Do they not know that surely God is He Who welcomes His servants' turning to Him in repentance, and accepts what is offered as charity (prescribed or voluntary) for His sake, and that surely God is He Who accepts repentance and returns it with liberal forgiveness and additional reward, the All-Compassionate (especially towards His believing servants)?

105. Say: "Work, and God will see your work, and so will His Messenger and the true believers; and you will be brought back to the Knower of the Unseen and the witnessed, and He will make you understand all that you were doing (and call you to account for it).

106. And yet others (there are, about whom) God's decree is awaited: whether He will punish them or guide them to repentance to forgive them.[20] God is All-Knowing, All-Wise.

19. This verse is enough to show the merit of the Messenger's Companions. The Muslim scholars unanimously agree that the Companions of Muḥammad, upon him be peace and blessings, are the most meritorious of all people after the Prophets. It should be noted that while the Qur'ān uses the preposition *min* (functioning to exclude some part from a whole) in describing the Gardens all other believers will be admitted into, it does not do so in this verse. So, while there are rivers in other Gardens flowing through them, the Gardens into which the Companions will be admitted have rivers flowing throughout them. This means that they are richer than the others in blessings and bounties.

According to the definition of the scholars, a Companion is "a believer who saw and heard the Messenger at least once and died as a believer" (al-Asqalānī, 1: 7). Scholars have divided them into twelve ranks, according to their precedence in accepting and serving Islam, which are as follows: (Some Companions, particularly those who were the first to accept Islam, are included in many of the ranks. For example, nine of the ten who were promised Paradise while they were alive and comprised the first rank are also included in the second. So, each rank should be considered with respect to those who are included in it particularly.)

- The four Rightly Guided Caliphs (Abū Bakr, 'Umar, 'Uthmān, and 'Ali), and the rest of the ten who were promised Paradise while still alive (Zubayr ibn al-'Awwām, Abū 'Ubaydah ibn al-Jarrāḥ, 'Abdurraḥmān ibn al-'Awf, Talḥah ibn 'Ubaydullāh, Sa'd ibn Abī Waqqāṣ, and Sa'īd ibn Zayd).
- Those who believed prior to 'Umar's conversion and met secretly in Zayd ibn Arqām's house to listen to the Messenger.
- Those who migrated to Abyssinia.
- The Helpers (Anṣār) who swore their allegiance to the Messenger at al-'Aqabah.
- The Helpers who swore their allegiance at al-'Aqabah the following year.
- The Emigrants who joined the Messenger during the *Hijrah* before his arrival in Madīnah from Qūba, where he stayed for a short while.
- The Companions who fought at Badr.
- Those who emigrated to Madīnah between the Battle of Badr and the Treaty of Hudaybiyah.
- The Companions who swore allegiance under a tree during the expedition to Hudaybiyah.
- Those who converted and emigrated to Madīnah after the Treaty of Hudaybiyah.
- Those who became Muslims after the conquest of Makkah.
- Children who saw the Messenger any time or any place after the conquest of Makkah (al-Ḥākim, 22–24).

Some interpreters of the Qur'ān understand from the expression *The first and foremost among the Emigrants and the Helpers* to be indicating the first two or three ranks among the Emigrants and the Helpers, and the expression *those who follow them in devotion to doing good aware that God is seeing them*, denoting the others. But some are of the opinion that the preposition *min* translated as "among" here functions as an explanation and therefore *the Emigrants and the Helpers* are in apposition to *the first and foremost*. According to these scholars, all of the Emigrants and Helpers are the first and foremost in Islam and *those who follow them in devotion in doing good, aware that God is seeing them* are the two generations which followed the Companions. The Messenger declared: "The best people are those living in my time. Then come those who follow them, and then come those who follow them. Those will be followed by a generation whose witness is sometimes true, sometimes false" (al-Bukhārī, "Fadā'il al-Aṣḥāb," 1; Muslim, "Fadā'il aṣ-Ṣaḥābah," 212).

20. There are some events which function as decisive criteria in clearly distinguishing people from one another, in helping to understand their character and values, and in judging them. The campaign to Tabuk during the Messenger's time was one of these events. It

explicitly showed that there are groups among the Muslims of different ranks.

As pointed out above in note 1 (appendix 3), there are basically two kinds of Muslims: the real ones who believe in whatever must be believed, and the false ones who are legally Muslims or Muslim citizens of an Islamic state. If a person verbally declares faith and attends the congregational prayer, in particular the Friday Prayer, and pays the Prescribed Alms, then they are regarded as Muslim. But such a person may well be a hypocrite who is inwardly an unbeliever. The campaign to Tabuk displayed the existence of three groups of Muslims:

- True believers: They took part in the campaign willingly, or if they did not take part this was because they could not, due either to lacking the necessary means or being ill or too weak. These believers always remained true to God and His Messenger, and made free donations each according to their capacity. Among these believers there were also ranks. Some excelled others in embracing Islam and serving it, while others followed them sincerely and in devotion to doing good.
- The believers who did not take part in the campaign but immediately repented. God forgave them.
- The believers who did not participate in the campaign and yet showed no repentance. Their case was deferred until a time when God would pass His judgment on them.

They were those verse 118 would tell that they also repented sincerely. They were also forgiven.

- The hypocrites: They did not believe in the essentials of faith, but declared faith verbally. Even though reluctantly and lazily, they attended the congregational prayers, in particular the Friday Prayer, and, if they were wealthy enough, they paid the Prescribed Alms. But they frequently lied, never missed any opportunity to cause harm to Islam, the Messenger, and the believers. Some of them were more artful and insidious in their hypocrisy. But the matchless sagacity, insight and intelligence of the Prophet, as well as the fact that he was supported by Divine Revelation, prevented all their plans from being successful. However, since they did not do anything that would have legally classified them as unbelievers or apostates, they were regarded as Muslims. The Messenger did not disclose their identity. He only told Hudayfah ibn al-Yamān about them. After he was prohibited from performing their funeral prayer (9: 84), the Messenger did not perform the funeral prayer for any hypocrite when they died. After the Messenger, the other Companions, including 'Umar in particular, followed the lead of Hudayfah as to whether a funeral prayer should be performed for a person, and if Hudayfah did not participate in someone's funeral prayer, then they did not participate either.

٢٠٣   اَلْجُزْءُ الْحَادِى عَشَرَ   203

وَالَّذِينَ اتَّخَذُوا مَسْجِدًا ضِرَارًا وَكُفْرًا وَتَفْرِيقًا بَيْنَ
الْمُؤْمِنِينَ وَإِرْصَادًا لِّمَنْ حَارَبَ اللَّهَ وَرَسُولَهُ مِن
قَبْلُ وَلَيَحْلِفُنَّ إِنْ أَرَدْنَا إِلَّا الْحُسْنَىٰ وَاللَّهُ يَشْهَدُ إِنَّهُمْ
لَكَاذِبُونَ ۝ لَا تَقُمْ فِيهِ أَبَدًا لَّمَسْجِدٌ أُسِّسَ عَلَى التَّقْوَىٰ
مِنْ أَوَّلِ يَوْمٍ أَحَقُّ أَن تَقُومَ فِيهِ فِيهِ رِجَالٌ يُحِبُّونَ أَن
يَتَطَهَّرُوا وَاللَّهُ يُحِبُّ الْمُطَّهِّرِينَ ۝ أَفَمَنْ أَسَّسَ بُنْيَانَهُ عَلَىٰ
تَقْوَىٰ مِنَ اللَّهِ وَرِضْوَانٍ خَيْرٌ أَم مَّنْ أَسَّسَ بُنْيَانَهُ عَلَىٰ
شَفَا جُرُفٍ هَارٍ فَانْهَارَ بِهِ فِي نَارِ جَهَنَّمَ وَاللَّهُ لَا يَهْدِي الْقَوْمَ
الظَّالِمِينَ ۝ لَا يَزَالُ بُنْيَانُهُمُ الَّذِي بَنَوْا رِيبَةً فِي
قُلُوبِهِمْ إِلَّا أَن تَقَطَّعَ قُلُوبُهُمْ وَاللَّهُ عَلِيمٌ حَكِيمٌ
۝ إِنَّ اللَّهَ اشْتَرَىٰ مِنَ الْمُؤْمِنِينَ أَنفُسَهُمْ وَأَمْوَالَهُم
بِأَنَّ لَهُمُ الْجَنَّةَ يُقَاتِلُونَ فِي سَبِيلِ اللَّهِ فَيَقْتُلُونَ
وَيُقْتَلُونَ وَعْدًا عَلَيْهِ حَقًّا فِي التَّوْرَاةِ وَالْإِنجِيلِ
وَالْقُرْآنِ وَمَنْ أَوْفَىٰ بِعَهْدِهِ مِنَ اللَّهِ فَاسْتَبْشِرُوا
بِبَيْعِكُمُ الَّذِي بَايَعْتُم بِهِ وَذَٰلِكَ هُوَ الْفَوْزُ الْعَظِيمُ ۝

109. Is he better, who founded his building (religion and personal world) on piety and reverence for God, and the aim to please God, or he who founded his building on the edge of a water-worn, crumbling river-bank so that it tumbles with him into the Hell-fire? God does not guide wrongdoing people.

110. The building (systems, plans, and life-styles) which the hypocrites have founded will never cease to be doubt and disquiet in their hearts (that are crushed by fear and anxieties) unless their hearts are cut into pieces (and they themselves die).[22] God is All-Knowing (of their states of mind and conspiracies), All-Wise (in Whose every act and decree there are many instances of wisdom).

111. God has bought from the believers their selves and wealth because Paradise is for them.[23] They fight in God's cause, and they kill or are killed. This is a promise with which God has bound Himself in the Torah and in the Gospel and in the Qur'ān.[24] Who could be more faithful to his covenant than God? So (O believers) glad tidings to you because of the bargain you have made with Him! That indeed is the supreme triumph.

107. Some among the hypocrites – who have adopted a mosque out of dissension and unbelief, in order to cause division among the believers, and use as an outpost to collaborate with him who before made war on God and His Messenger – will certainly swear: "We mean nothing but good (in building this mosque)", whereas God bears witness that they are surely liars.[21]

108. Do not stand in that mosque to do the Prayer. The mosque that was founded on piety and reverence for God from the very first days (in Madīnah) is worthy that you should stand in it for the Prayer. In it are men who love to be purified (of all spiritual and moral blemishes). God loves those who strive to purify themselves.

21. This verse mentions a very important point. Despite the Qur'ān's emphatic warnings, Muslims have been unable to perceive the conspiracies of hypocrites, except during the Age of Happiness, including to a certain extent the period of the first Four Rightly Guided Caliphs; many acts of hypocrisy have been sources of the greatest danger for Muslims.

In their unceasing struggle against Islam in Madīnah, the hypocrites built a mosque. It was meant to divide the Muslim Community. They invited the Messenger to inaugurate it by leading the first prayer in it. However, the Messenger excused himself from this, as he was busy with the preparations for the campaign to Tabuk.

There was a man called Abū 'Āmir who had become a Christian before the Messenger's emigration to Madīnah and who desired to be the chief. But, since he had not been able to realize his plans once the Messenger emigrated there, he had become the enemy of the Messenger and began to fight against him. He finally went to the Emperor of Byzantium to provoke him against the Muslims. By building the mosque, the hypocrites also intended to use it as a base to collaborate with these enemies. The Messenger, who knew the real purpose for the construction of that mosque, ordered its destruction on his return from Tabuk.

Many bands of hypocrisy under the guise of Islam have conspired against Muslims during the history of Islam. As well as having played a great part in the emergence of many of the heterodox sects, it has also been such bands that caused the destruction of the Ottoman State and have conspired against Muslims throughout the world since that time. Although Muslims in name, they usually belong to different faiths or are anti-religious, and are refractory enemies of Islam. Among them, some have appeared who have built mosques and infiltrated some Muslim organizations. It is unfortunate that in recent centuries in particular the Muslims have lacked the insight to recognize these people.

22. This verse describes the inner worlds of the hypocrites in an extraordinarily figurative style. All the systems that they devise and the plans that they make and the outposts they build to struggle with Islam are nothing but a source of disquiet and fear for them. For they feign to be Muslims while their hearts are like nests of snakes and scorpions. Since they are traitors, they are fearful. They constantly feel fear of being discovered and of their plans being brought to light. This fear pounds in their chests. It is evident to what extent such a fear can be harmful to the heart. If the bands of hypocrisy have been successful to certain extent in their conspiracies against the Muslims, particularly in recent centuries, this is because the Muslims have fallen away from Islam and have lost the discernment that Islam provides for them. In truth, hypocrisy is a dungeon or prison for a hypocrite.

23. It is God Who has created humankind and prepared all the conditions for our life. So, He is our absolute Owner. However, He has distinguished and honored us with free will and, without leaving us to be lost in the "wasteland" of the world, He has informed us of what consequences we will meet in return for what we do.

As the very being of humankind belongs to God, His share in what they suppose to be their wealth is more than 999/1000. For example, air and water are two of the three basic essentials for human life; these belong solely to God and almost nothing of them is the property of human beings or the result of their effort. It is also God Who creates the wheat seed and Who equips it with the ability to germinate, and Who creates air, water, earth, and solar light, which are essential to its growth, and brings about the necessary co-operation among these elements. Again, it is He Who creates human beings with the power and ability to obtain this wheat. Therefore, their share in the bread they make from it is even less than 1 in a 1000.

Though humankind, with their very being and their wealth, belong absolutely to God, God offers them a bargain: He will buy from them what He has and has deposited in them in return for eternal happiness. He will also safeguard them and save themselves from being troubled because of these things. This is a bargain completely in their favor. Nevertheless, our ignorance and heedlessness can prevent us from willingly accepting such a bargain.

While the Qur'ān mentions first wealth and then the person of human beings in the places where it talks about striving in God's cause, in this verse it gives precedence to the being or persons of human beings. This is because it is these beings themselves that will enjoy the eternal happiness in Paradise (*The Words*, "the 6th Word;" *Kur'an'dan İdrake*, 1: 182–183).

24. The verse explicitly informs us of a promise to the believers, which is mentioned in the Torah, the Gospel, and in the Qur'ān. However, although there are many passages in the Gospel that concern Paradise, sometimes under the title of the Kingdom of Heaven, such as in the verse "Blessed are those who are persecuted for righteousness' sake, for theirs is the kingdom of heaven" (*Matthew*, 5: 10), and some times under the title of eternal life, such as in the verse, "And everyone who has left houses or brothers or sisters or father or mother or wife or children or lands, for My name's sake, shall receive a hundredfold, and inherit eternal life" (*Matthew*, 19: 29). The Torah in its present form does not contain any explicit promise of Paradise. It is shorn of the notion of life after death, of the Day of Judgment, and of Divine reward and punishment, even though belief in the Hereafter is the second pillar of

faith in all God-revealed religions. Although the original Torah certainly contained passages concerning this pillar, since the present Torah is the product of a time in Jewish history when the Jews became too worldly, all the promises of the eternal life of Paradise were taken to mean triumph in this worldly life and the descriptions of Paradise were interpreted as being descriptions of Palestine. For example, in the Qur'ān 48: 15, Paradise is described as a place that has been promised to the pious in which there are rivers of pure, unpolluted water, of milk, of delicious, non-intoxicant wine (fruit juice), and of pure honey. But in the present Torah, the land with milk and honey (*Deuteronomy*, 6: 3) has come to be taken to mean Palestine.

However, there are some Jews who regard the Resurrection and afterlife as being "the thirteenth foundation" of the Jewish religion. For example: The Thirteenth Foundation is the resurrection of the dead. The following is a translation of what the Ramba'm writes on this subject: The resurrection of the dead is a foundation from the foundations of Moshe our Teacher, may peace be upon him. There is no faith and no connection to the Jewish religion for one who does not believe this. But the resurrection is only for the righteous. And so we find the Sages teach: "The rains are for the righteous and the wicked, and the resurrection of the dead is for the righteous alone." (http://members.aol.com/LazerA/13yesodos.html)

سُورَةُ التَّوبَة

٢٠٤

اَلتَّائِبُونَ الْعَابِدُونَ الْحَامِدُونَ السَّائِحُونَ الرَّاكِعُونَ
السَّاجِدُونَ الْآمِرُونَ بِالْمَعْرُوفِ وَالنَّاهُونَ عَنِ
الْمُنْكَرِ وَالْحَافِظُونَ لِحُدُودِ اللهِ وَبَشِّرِ الْمُؤْمِنِينَ
۞ مَاكَانَ لِلنَّبِيِّ وَالَّذِينَ آمَنُوٓا أَن يَسْتَغْفِرُوا
لِلْمُشْرِكِينَ وَلَوْ كَانُوٓا أُوْلِي قُرْبَىٰ مِنۢ بَعْدِ مَا تَبَيَّنَ لَهُمْ
أَنَّهُمْ أَصْحَابُ الْجَحِيمِ ۞ وَمَا كَانَ اسْتِغْفَارُ إِبْرَٰهِيمَ
لِأَبِيهِ إِلَّا عَن مَّوْعِدَةٍ وَعَدَهَآ إِيَّاهُ فَلَمَّا تَبَيَّنَ لَهُۥٓ أَنَّهُۥ عَدُوٌّ
لِّلَّهِ تَبَرَّأَ مِنْهُ إِنَّ إِبْرَٰهِيمَ لَأَوَّٰهٌ حَلِيمٌ ۞ وَمَا كَانَ
اللهُ لِيُضِلَّ قَوْمًۢا بَعْدَ إِذْ هَدَىٰهُمْ حَتَّىٰ يُبَيِّنَ لَهُم مَّا يَتَّقُونَ إِنَّ
اللهَ بِكُلِّ شَيْءٍ عَلِيمٌ ۞ إِنَّ اللهَ لَهُۥ مُلْكُ السَّمَٰوَٰتِ
وَالْأَرْضِ يُحْيِۦ وَيُمِيتُ وَمَا لَكُم مِّن دُونِ
اللهِ مِن وَلِيٍّ وَلَا نَصِيرٍ ۞ لَّقَد تَّابَ اللهُ عَلَى النَّبِيِّ
وَالْمُهَٰجِرِينَ وَالْأَنصَارِ الَّذِينَ اتَّبَعُوهُ فِي سَاعَةِ
الْعُسْرَةِ مِنۢ بَعْدِ مَا كَادَ يَزِيغُ قُلُوبُ فَرِيقٍ مِّنْهُمْ
ثُمَّ تَابَ عَلَيْهِمْ إِنَّهُۥ بِهِمْ رَءُوفٌ رَّحِيمٌ ۞

112. Those who return in repentance to God, and those who worship God, and those who praise God, and those who travel (with such aims as conveying God's Message or studying and making investigations for God's sake or reflecting on God's signs), and those who bow down in awe of God, and those who prostrate themselves before God in submission, and those who enjoin and promote what is right and good and forbid and try to prevent evil, and those who keep to the bounds set by God: give glad tidings to the believers.

113. It is not for the Prophet and those who believe to ask God for the forgiveness of those who associate partners with God even though they be near of kin, after it has become clear to them that they (died polytheists and therefore) are condemned to the Blazing Flame.

114. The prayer of Abraham for the forgiveness of his father was only because of a promise which he had made to him. But when it became clear to him that he was an enemy of God, he (Abraham) dissociated himself from him.[25] Abraham was most tender-hearted, most clement.

115. It is not God's way to lead people astray after He has guided them, without having made clear to them what they should beware of (so as to guard against straying).[26] Surely God has full knowledge of everything.

116. God is He to Whom belongs the sovereignty of the heavens and the earth. He gives life and causes to die. And you have, apart from God, neither a guardian (who will protect you and to whom you can entrust your affairs) nor a helper.

117. God has assuredly turned in mercy to the Prophet, as well as to the Emigrants and the Helpers who followed him in the time of hardship, when the hearts of a party among them had well-nigh swerved but God turned (also) to them in mercy (and protected against swerving). Surely for them He is All-Pitying, All-Compassionate.

25. It is a controversial matter whether Āzar, whom the Qur'ān mentions as Abraham's father, was his real father or foster father. The Qur'ān always uses the term *ab* for him, which can mean either real father or foster father. Abraham promised him that he would ask God for his forgiveness (19: 47). In order to fulfill his promise, he asked for his forgiveness (26: 86). Then it became clear to Abraham that Āzar was the enemy of God, he stopped praying for him. However, we also read in the Qur'ān that toward the end of his life when he begot both Ishmael (Ismāīl) and Isaac (Ishāq), Abraham prayed for his parents, saying: *Our Lord! Forgive me, and my parents* (14: 41). The Qur'ān uses here the word *wālidayn* (parents), not *abawayn*. While *ab* may mean real father or foster father, the word *wālid* means real father. We conclude from this that Āzar was not the real father of the Prophet Abraham, upon him be God's peace.

26. After He has guided a people, God never lets them go astray without having made fully clear to them what attitudes may result in their going astray. So, those who deviate from the right path after God has guided them to it are those whose hearts God swerves because they themselves swerve from the right path (61: 5), and who change their inner worlds, world-views, and life-styles (13: 11).

118. And (He turned in mercy also) to the three left behind and whose cases had been deferred (because they had not taken part in the campaign of Tabuk): (they felt such remorse that) the earth was too narrow for them despite all its vastness, and their souls became utterly constricted for them, and they came to perceive fully that there is no refuge from God except in Him. Then He turned to them in mercy that they might repent and recover their former state (in Islam). Surely God is the One Who truly returns repentance with liberal forgiveness and additional reward, the All-Compassionate (especially towards His believing servants.)

119. O you who believe! Keep from disobedience to God in reverence for Him and piety, and keep the company of the truthful (those who are also faithful to their covenant with God).

120. It does not behove the people of Madīnah and the Bedouin Arabs around them to fail to follow God's Messenger and to care for their own selves more than for him. That is because they suffer neither from thirst, nor weariness, nor hunger in God's cause, nor take a step which enrages the unbelievers, nor win some gain from the enemy, but a righteous deed is thereby recorded for them (to their account). Indeed, God does not leave to waste the reward of those devoted to doing good, aware that God is seeing them.

121. Nor do they spend any amount for God's sake, small or great, nor do they

وَعَلَى الثَّلَاثَةِ الَّذِينَ خُلِّفُوا حَتَّىٰٓ إِذَا ضَاقَتْ عَلَيْهِمُ الْأَرْضُ بِمَا رَحُبَتْ وَضَاقَتْ عَلَيْهِمْ أَنفُسُهُمْ وَظَنُّوٓا أَن لَّا مَلْجَأَ مِنَ اللَّهِ إِلَّآ إِلَيْهِ ثُمَّ تَابَ عَلَيْهِمْ لِيَتُوبُوٓا إِنَّ اللَّهَ هُوَ التَّوَّابُ الرَّحِيمُ ۞ يَٰٓأَيُّهَا الَّذِينَ ءَامَنُوا اتَّقُوا اللَّهَ وَكُونُوا مَعَ الصَّٰدِقِينَ ۞ مَا كَانَ لِأَهْلِ الْمَدِينَةِ وَمَنْ حَوْلَهُم مِّنَ الْأَعْرَابِ أَن يَتَخَلَّفُوا عَن رَّسُولِ اللَّهِ وَلَا يَرْغَبُوا بِأَنفُسِهِمْ عَن نَّفْسِهِ ذَٰلِكَ بِأَنَّهُمْ لَا يُصِيبُهُمْ ظَمَأٌ وَلَا نَصَبٌ وَلَا مَخْمَصَةٌ فِي سَبِيلِ اللَّهِ وَلَا يَطَئُونَ مَوْطِئًا يَغِيظُ الْكُفَّارَ وَلَا يَنَالُونَ مِنْ عَدُوٍّ نَّيْلًا إِلَّا كُتِبَ لَهُم بِهِۦ عَمَلٌ صَٰلِحٌ إِنَّ اللَّهَ لَا يُضِيعُ أَجْرَ الْمُحْسِنِينَ ۞ وَلَا يُنفِقُونَ نَفَقَةً صَغِيرَةً وَلَا كَبِيرَةً وَلَا يَقْطَعُونَ وَادِيًا إِلَّا كُتِبَ لَهُمْ لِيَجْزِيَهُمُ اللَّهُ أَحْسَنَ مَا كَانُوا يَعْمَلُونَ ۞ وَمَا كَانَ الْمُؤْمِنُونَ لِيَنفِرُوا كَآفَّةً فَلَوْلَا نَفَرَ مِن كُلِّ فِرْقَةٍ مِّنْهُمْ طَآئِفَةٌ لِّيَتَفَقَّهُوا فِي الدِّينِ وَلِيُنذِرُوا قَوْمَهُمْ إِذَا رَجَعُوٓا إِلَيْهِمْ لَعَلَّهُمْ يَحْذَرُونَ ۞

cross a valley (while traveling in God's cause), but it is recorded for them (to their account) so that God may repay them the best reward for what they used to do .

122. And the believers should not go forth to war all together. But why should not a party from every community of them mobilize to acquire profound, correct knowledge and understanding of religion and warn their people when they return to them so that they may beware (of wrongful attitudes)?[27]

---

27. Islam is a religion of perfect balance, each part of which is exactly where it should be. While exhorting the believers to mobilize against one of the two superpowers of the time, the Qur'ān does not neglect an important dimension. It orders the Muslim community that there must be some among these people who are well-versed in Islam. If the warriors are victorious, they may feel proud and adopt some undesirable attitudes in the society, while if they are defeated, this may cause them to despair for the future. So they may need a warning from someone well-versed in Islam. Secondly, the army members may not have enough time to learn the commandments of the religion. All this requires that there must be a scholarly group who will teach them. The verse uses the word "*tafakkuh*" for the group that is to be mobilized in order to instruct in the religion. This means to penetrate the essence of a matter, to attain a deep and correct understanding and discernment. Only such people can grasp the religion accurately and these people are called *faqīh*.

123. O you who believe! Fight against those unbelievers who are in your vicinity (and pose an immediate threat to you and the preaching of Islam), and let them find in you sternness.[28] Know that God is with the God-revering, pious who keep their duty to Him.

124. Whenever a *sūrah* is sent down, there are some among them (the hypocrites) who say: "Which of you has this strengthened in his faith?"[29] As for those who believe, it does strengthen them in faith and they rejoice in its being sent down and in the glad tidings (they receive thereby).

125. But as for those in whose hearts there is a sickness (that dries up the source of their spiritual life, extinguishes their power of understanding and corrupts their character), it increases them in foulness added

to their foulness, and they die while they are unbelievers.

126. Do they not see that they are tried time and again every year (by coming face to face with such decisive events and situations as reveal to them their inner world and remind them that they should turn to God in repentance and mend their ways)? Yet they neither repent (and mend their ways) nor take warning (from all that befalls them).

127. Whenever a *sūrah* is sent down (and the Messenger is reciting it in the presence of the Muslims), they glance at each other (as though saying), "Is there anyone who sees you?" and then they slip away. God has turned their hearts away (from the truth) because they are a people who do not ponder and try to grasp the truth.

128. There has come to you (O people) a Messenger from among yourselves; extremely grievous to him is your suffering, full of concern for you is he, and for the believers full of pity and compassion.

129. Still, if they turn away from you (O Messenger), say: "God is sufficient for me; there is no deity but He. In Him have I put my trust, and He is the Lord of the Supreme Throne (as the absolute Ruler and Sustainer of the universe and all creation, Who maintains and protects it)."

28. There is a relationship with this verse and verse 73. In verse 73 it is ordered that the believers must strive hard (do *jihād*) against the unbelievers and the hypocrites and be stern against them. This verse orders fighting against the unbelievers and being stern against them. When the two verses are considered together, we understand that the unbelievers and hypocrites against whom they ordered the Prophet (and the believers) to strive hard and be stern were particularly those in and around Madīnah. Just as the Messenger was ordered to begin preaching Islam with his nearest kindred (26: 214), so it is natural that priority in fighting should be given to those who are in the neighborhood and pose an immediate threat. This was also required by the fact that the very center of Islam had to be secure against every attack.

While verse 73 orders doing *jihād* against both the unbelievers and the hypocrites and being stern against them, this verse orders *fighting* against the unbelievers only and being stern against them. This explicitly shows the difference between *jihād* and fighting (*qitāl*). Since the hypocrites are legally regarded as Muslims, the Muslims are not allowed to fight them unless they cause disorder and dissension and rebel against the public order. But the Muslims must do *jihād* against both the unbelievers and the hypocrites.

29. At first a person usually believes in the essentials of faith superficially. But when they continue to order their life in the light of their faith, carrying out their religious duties, regularly worshiping God, reflecting on the essentials and truths of faith based on the evidence that they collect from "nature," events and their conscience and heart, increasing in knowledge about them, then they increasingly deepen their understanding and knowledge. Thus the truths of faith are increasingly expanded in their mind and heart with the result that, like a bud blossoming into an elaborate flower with full-grown petals, their faith constantly develops. Imam Rabbānī Ahmad al-Fārūqī al-Sirhindī (d. 1624), one of the greatest scholars and Sūfī masters in Islam, who lived in India, says: "I would prefer to make one matter of faith known in plain terms than attain thousands of spiritual pleasures and ecstasies and work wonders." He also says: "The final station of all spiritual journeying is to attain the full perception of the truths of faith" (*The Letters*, "the 5th Letter," 22). This knowledge and perception cause faith to grow stronger and deeper.

بِسْمِ اللَّهِ الرَّحْمَٰنِ الرَّحِيمِ

الٓرٰ تِلْكَ ءَايَٰتُ الْكِتَٰبِ الْحَكِيمِ ۝ أَكَانَ لِلنَّاسِ عَجَبًا أَنْ أَوْحَيْنَآ إِلَىٰ رَجُلٍ مِّنْهُمْ أَنْ أَنذِرِ النَّاسَ وَبَشِّرِ الَّذِينَ ءَامَنُوٓا۟ أَنَّ لَهُمْ قَدَمَ صِدْقٍ عِندَ رَبِّهِمْ قَالَ الْكَٰفِرُونَ إِنَّ هَٰذَا لَسَٰحِرٌ مُّبِينٌ ۝ إِنَّ رَبَّكُمُ اللَّهُ الَّذِي خَلَقَ السَّمَٰوَٰتِ وَالْأَرْضَ فِي سِتَّةِ أَيَّامٍ ثُمَّ اسْتَوَىٰ عَلَى الْعَرْشِ يُدَبِّرُ الْأَمْرَ مَا مِن شَفِيعٍ إِلَّا مِنۢ بَعْدِ إِذْنِهِ ذَٰلِكُمُ اللَّهُ رَبُّكُمْ فَاعْبُدُوهُ أَفَلَا تَذَكَّرُونَ ۝ إِلَيْهِ مَرْجِعُكُمْ جَمِيعًا وَعْدَ اللَّهِ حَقًّا إِنَّهُ يَبْدَؤُا۟ الْخَلْقَ ثُمَّ يُعِيدُهُ لِيَجْزِيَ الَّذِينَ ءَامَنُوا۟ وَعَمِلُوا۟ الصَّٰلِحَٰتِ بِالْقِسْطِ وَالَّذِينَ كَفَرُوا۟ لَهُمْ شَرَابٌ مِّنْ حَمِيمٍ وَعَذَابٌ أَلِيمٌۢ بِمَا كَانُوا۟ يَكْفُرُونَ ۝ هُوَ الَّذِي جَعَلَ الشَّمْسَ ضِيَآءً وَالْقَمَرَ نُورًا وَقَدَّرَهُ مَنَازِلَ لِتَعْلَمُوا۟ عَدَدَ السِّنِينَ وَالْحِسَابَ مَا خَلَقَ اللَّهُ ذَٰلِكَ إِلَّا بِالْحَقِّ يُفَصِّلُ الْآيَٰتِ لِقَوْمٍ يَعْلَمُونَ ۝ إِنَّ فِي اخْتِلَٰفِ الَّيْلِ وَالنَّهَارِ وَمَا خَلَقَ اللَّهُ فِي السَّمَٰوَٰتِ وَالْأَرْضِ لَآيَٰتٍ لِّقَوْمٍ يَتَّقُونَ ۝

———❧———

SŪRAH 10

YŪNUS (JONAH)

Makkah period

This *sūrah* was revealed in Makkah and is composed of 109 verses. It takes its name from verse 98, where an incident related to Jonah's people is recounted. The *sūrah* as a whole deals with the essentials of faith – in particular the Divine origin of the Qur'ān – and mentions certain events from the missions of the Prophets Moses and Noah related to the essentials of faith.

In the Name of God, the All-Merciful, the All-Compassionate.

1. *Alif. Lām. Rā.* These are the Revelations included in the Book full of wisdom.

2. Does it seem strange to people that We reveal to a man from among them, saying: "Warn all humankind (of the conse-

quences of the way they follow), and give those who believe the glad tidings that they have a sure footing with their Lord (on account of t heir belief, faithfulness, and righteous deeds)."[1] (Is it because of this that) the unbelievers say: "This (man) is clearly a sorcerer?"

3. Surely your Lord is God, Who has created the heavens and the earth in six days, then He established Himself on the Supreme Throne,[2] directing all affairs (as the sole Ruler of creation). There is none to intercede with God unless after He grants leave. That is God, Your Lord, so worship Him. Will you still not reflect (on this fundamental truth) and be mindful?

4. To Him you are all bound to return: a promise from God in truth (therefore certain to happen). He originates creation, then He brings it forth anew (in another world) to the end that He may reward with equity those who believe and do good, righteous deeds. Whereas, for those who disbelieve (and die as unbelievers) there is a drink of boiling water and a painful punishment because they persistently disbelieve.

5. He it is Who has made the sun a radiant, illuminating light, and the moon a light reflected, and has determined for it stations, that you might know (how to compute) the number of the years and to measure (time). God has not created that but with truth (for a definite purpose and meaningfully). He sets out in detail the signs (and proofs of the truth) for a people seeking knowledge.

6. In the alternation of night and day (with their periods shortening and lengthening), and all that He has created in the heavens and the earth, surely there are signs (manifesting truth) for a people who keep from disobedience to Him in reverence for Him.

1. The initial verses of a *sūrah* disclose the main theme that will be dealt with. The first two verses of this *sūrah* indicate that it will dwell mainly on the Divine origin of the Qur'ān and the evidence presented will be based on wisdom. The evidence to be drawn from the universe, human life, history, and events as the manifestations of the Divine Name the All-Wise, will address human intellect, thought, and power of reasoning, and present to our views the instances of wisdom in the creation of human and the universe.

2. For the creation of the heavens and the earth in six days, the meaning of the Supreme Throne and God's establishing Himself thereon, see 2: 28, note 28-29; 7: 54, note 13; 41, note 2.

208   سُورَة يُونُسَ   ٢٠٨

إِنَّ الَّذِينَ لَا يَرْجُونَ لِقَاءَنَا وَرَضُوا بِالْحَيَوةِ الدُّنْيَا وَاطْمَأَنُّوا بِهَا وَالَّذِينَ هُمْ عَنْ ءَايَـٰتِنَا غَـٰفِلُونَ ۝ أُوْلَـٰئِكَ مَأْوَىٰهُمُ النَّارُ بِمَا كَانُوا يَكْسِبُونَ ۝ إِنَّ الَّذِينَ ءَامَنُوا وَعَمِلُوا الصَّـٰلِحَـٰتِ يَهْدِيهِمْ رَبُّهُم بِإِيمَـٰنِهِمْ تَجْرِى مِن تَحْتِهِمُ الْأَنْهَـٰرُ فِى جَنَّـٰتِ النَّعِيمِ ۝ دَعْوَىٰهُمْ فِيهَا سُبْحَـٰنَكَ اللَّهُمَّ وَتَحِيَّتُهُمْ فِيهَا سَلَـٰمٌ وَءَاخِرُ دَعْوَىٰهُمْ أَنِ الْحَمْدُ لِلَّهِ رَبِّ الْعَـٰلَمِينَ ۝ وَلَوْ يُعَجِّلُ اللَّهُ لِلنَّاسِ الشَّرَّ اسْتِعْجَالَهُم بِالْخَيْرِ لَقُضِىَ إِلَيْهِمْ أَجَلُهُمْ فَنَذَرُ الَّذِينَ لَا يَرْجُونَ لِقَاءَنَا فِى طُغْيَـٰنِهِمْ يَعْمَهُونَ ۝ وَإِذَا مَسَّ الْإِنسَـٰنَ الضُّرُّ دَعَانَا لِجَنبِهِ أَوْ قَاعِدًا أَوْ قَائِمًا فَلَمَّا كَشَفْنَا عَنْهُ ضُرَّهُ مَرَّ كَأَن لَّمْ يَدْعُنَا إِلَىٰ ضُرٍّ مَّسَّهُ كَذَٰلِكَ زُيِّنَ لِلْمُسْرِفِينَ مَا كَانُوا يَعْمَلُونَ ۝ وَلَقَدْ أَهْلَكْنَا الْقُرُونَ مِن قَبْلِكُمْ لَمَّا ظَلَمُوا وَجَاءَتْهُمْ رُسُلُهُم بِالْبَيِّنَـٰتِ وَمَا كَانُوا لِيُؤْمِنُوا كَذَٰلِكَ نَجْزِى الْقَوْمَ الْمُجْرِمِينَ ۝ ثُمَّ جَعَلْنَـٰكُمْ خَلَـٰئِفَ فِى الْأَرْضِ مِن بَعْدِهِم لِنَنظُرَ كَيْفَ تَعْمَلُونَ ۝

──────◦≫◦──────

greeting (to each other and from God and the angels) will be: "Peace!" And their invocation will close with "All praise and gratitude are for God, the Lord of the worlds!"

11. If God were to hasten for human beings the ill (which they have earned) in the same manner as they hasten (the coming to them of what they consider to be) the good, their term would indeed have been decreed over for them. But We leave those who do not expect to encounter Us in their rebellion blindly wandering.

12. When affliction befalls (such) a person, he invokes Us (in every situation), lying down on his side or sitting or standing; but when We remove his affliction from him, he goes his way as if he had never invoked us for an affliction that befell him. So to those wasteful ones (who have wasted their God-given faculties and committed excesses) are the things they have been doing decked out to be appealing.

13. Assuredly We destroyed many generations before you when they committed wrongs (in their deeds, in their measures and judgments, and in their response to the truth): the Messengers raised from among them came to them with the clear proofs of the truth, but it was plain that they would not believe. Thus do We recompense the guilty people committed to accumulating sins.

14. Then We made you successors after them on the earth, so that We might behold how you act.

7. Those who have no expectations to meet Us and are well-pleased with the present, worldly life and (neither looking nor seeing beyond it) are content with it, and those who are heedless of Our Revelations and Our signs (manifested to them in their inner worlds and in the outer world):

8. Those are they whose final refuge is the Fire because of what they have been earning.

9. Surely for those who believe and do good, righteous deeds, their Lord will guide them by virtue of their belief to a happy end: rivers will flow at their feet in the Gardens of bounty and blessing.

10. Therein their invocation will be: "All-Glorified You are, O God! (You are absolutely exalted above having any defects and doing anything wrong.)" And their

وَإِذَا تُتْلَىٰ عَلَيْهِمْ ءَايَاتُنَا بَيِّنَاتٍ قَالَ الَّذِينَ
لَا يَرْجُونَ لِقَآءَنَا ائْتِ بِقُرْءَانٍ غَيْرِ هَـٰذَآ أَوْ بَدِّلْهُ قُلْ مَا
يَكُونُ لِى أَنْ أُبَدِّلَهُ مِن تِلْقَآئِ نَفْسِى إِنْ أَتَّبِعُ إِلَّا مَا يُوحَىٰ
إِلَيَّ إِنِّى أَخَافُ إِنْ عَصَيْتُ رَبِّى عَذَابَ يَوْمٍ عَظِيمٍ ۝ قُل لَّوْ
شَآءَ اللَّهُ مَا تَلَوْتُهُ عَلَيْكُمْ وَلَآ أَدْرَىٰكُم بِهِ فَقَدْ
لَبِثْتُ فِيكُمْ عُمُرًا مِّن قَبْلِهِ أَفَلَا تَعْقِلُونَ ۝ فَمَنْ
أَظْلَمُ مِمَّنِ افْتَرَىٰ عَلَى اللَّهِ كَذِبًا أَوْ كَذَّبَ بِـَٔايَاتِهِ إِنَّهُ
لَا يُفْلِحُ الْمُجْرِمُونَ ۝ وَيَعْبُدُونَ مِن دُونِ اللَّهِ مَا لَا
يَضُرُّهُمْ وَلَا يَنفَعُهُمْ وَيَقُولُونَ هَـٰٓؤُلَآءِ شُفَعَاؤُنَا
عِندَ اللَّهِ قُلْ أَتُنَبِّئُونَ اللَّهَ بِمَا لَا يَعْلَمُ فِى السَّمَاوَاتِ
وَلَا فِى الْأَرْضِ سُبْحَانَهُ وَتَعَالَىٰ عَمَّا يُشْرِكُونَ ۝
وَمَا كَانَ النَّاسُ إِلَّا أُمَّةً وَاحِدَةً فَاخْتَلَفُوا وَلَوْلَا
كَلِمَةٌ سَبَقَتْ مِن رَّبِّكَ لَقُضِىَ بَيْنَهُمْ فِيمَا فِيهِ
يَخْتَلِفُونَ ۝ وَيَقُولُونَ لَوْلَآ أُنزِلَ عَلَيْهِ ءَايَةٌ مِّن رَّبِّهِ فَقُلْ إِنَّمَا
الْغَيْبُ لِلَّهِ فَانتَظِرُوٓا إِنِّى مَعَكُم مِّنَ الْمُنتَظِرِينَ ۝

15. When Our Revelations, clear as evidence and in meaning are recited (and conveyed) to them, those who have no expectations to meet Us say (in response to Our Messenger): "Either bring a Qur'ān other than this or alter it." Say: "It is not for me to alter it of my own accord. I only follow what is revealed to me. Indeed I fear, if I should rebel against my Lord, the punishment of an Awful Day."

16. Say (also): "If God had so willed, I would not have recited it to you, nor would He have brought it to your knowledge. I lived among you a whole lifetime before it (began to be revealed to me). Will you not reason and understand?"

17. Who is more in the wrong than he who fabricates falsehood in attribution to God or denies His Revelations and His signs (in the universe and in their own selves). Surely the disbelieving criminals will not prosper.[3]

18. They worship, apart from God, things or beings that can neither harm nor benefit them, and they say: "These are our intercessors with God." Say: "Would you inform God of something in the heavens or the earth that He does not know? All-Glorified is He, and absolutely exalted above all that they associate with Him."

19. Humankind (in the beginning) were but one community following one single way but later they differed and began following different ways. Had it not been for a decree already issued by your Lord (postponing the final, decisive judgment until an appointed term), it would indeed have been judged between them in respect of all that they differ on.

20. They say: "Why isn't a miraculous sign (of a different sort) sent down on him from his Lord?" Say, then: "The Unseen belongs to God alone (He does whatever He wills and only He knows what the future will bring): therefore, wait and see, indeed I too am with you among those who wait."

---

3. For the Prophet Muḥammad among his people before and during his mission as evidence for his Prophethood, see Appendix 5.

210   سُوْرَةُ يُوْنُسَ   ٢١٠

وَإِذَآ أَذَقْنَا ٱلنَّاسَ رَحْمَةً مِّنۢ بَعْدِ ضَرَّآءَ مَسَّتْهُمْ إِذَا لَهُم
مَّكْرٌ فِىٓ ءَايَاتِنَا ۚ قُلِ ٱللَّهُ أَسْرَعُ مَكْرًا ۚ إِنَّ رُسُلَنَا يَكْتُبُونَ
مَا تَمْكُرُونَ ۝ هُوَ ٱلَّذِى يُسَيِّرُكُمْ فِى ٱلْبَرِّ وَٱلْبَحْرِ ۖ حَتَّىٰٓ إِذَا كُنتُمْ
فِى ٱلْفُلْكِ وَجَرَيْنَ بِهِم بِرِيحٍ طَيِّبَةٍ وَفَرِحُوا بِهَا جَآءَتْهَا رِيحٌ
عَاصِفٌ وَجَآءَهُمُ ٱلْمَوْجُ مِن كُلِّ مَكَانٍ وَظَنُّوٓا أَنَّهُمْ
أُحِيطَ بِهِمْ دَعَوُا۟ ٱللَّهَ مُخْلِصِينَ لَهُ ٱلدِّينَ لَئِنْ أَنجَيْتَنَا مِنْ
هَٰذِهِۦ لَنَكُونَنَّ مِنَ ٱلشَّٰكِرِينَ ۝ فَلَمَّآ أَنجَىٰهُمْ إِذَا هُمْ يَبْغُونَ فِى
ٱلْأَرْضِ بِغَيْرِ ٱلْحَقِّ ۗ يَٰٓأَيُّهَا ٱلنَّاسُ إِنَّمَا بَغْيُكُمْ عَلَىٰٓ أَنفُسِكُم مَّتَٰعَ
ٱلْحَيَوٰةِ ٱلدُّنْيَا ۖ ثُمَّ إِلَيْنَا مَرْجِعُكُمْ فَنُنَبِّئُكُم بِمَا كُنتُمْ تَعْمَلُونَ ۝
إِنَّمَا مَثَلُ ٱلْحَيَوٰةِ ٱلدُّنْيَا كَمَآءٍ أَنزَلْنَٰهُ مِنَ ٱلسَّمَآءِ فَٱخْتَلَطَ بِهِۦ نَبَاتُ
ٱلْأَرْضِ مِمَّا يَأْكُلُ ٱلنَّاسُ وَٱلْأَنْعَٰمُ حَتَّىٰٓ إِذَآ أَخَذَتِ ٱلْأَرْضُ
زُخْرُفَهَا وَٱزَّيَّنَتْ وَظَنَّ أَهْلُهَآ أَنَّهُمْ قَٰدِرُونَ عَلَيْهَآ
أَتَىٰهَآ أَمْرُنَا لَيْلًا أَوْ نَهَارًا فَجَعَلْنَٰهَا حَصِيدًا كَأَن لَّمْ تَغْنَ
بِٱلْأَمْسِ ۚ كَذَٰلِكَ نُفَصِّلُ ٱلْءَايَٰتِ لِقَوْمٍ يَتَفَكَّرُونَ ۝ وَٱللَّهُ
يَدْعُوٓا۟ إِلَىٰ دَارِ ٱلسَّلَٰمِ وَيَهْدِى مَن يَشَآءُ إِلَىٰ صِرَٰطٍ مُّسْتَقِيمٍ ۝

---

so that they are sure that they are encompassed (by death with no way out), they call upon God, sincerely believing in Him alone (as the only Deity, Lord, and Sovereign): "If You save us from this, we will most certainly be among the thankful."

23. But when He has saved them, they behave rebelliously on earth, offending against all right. O humankind! Your rebellion is only against yourselves. (What you seek and get by all your offenses is only) the enjoyment of the present, worldly life, thereafter to Us is your return, then We will make you understand what you were doing (and call you to account).

24. The present, worldly life is like this: We send down water from the sky, and the earth's vegetation, of which humans and animals eat, mingles with it, until, when the earth has taken on her ornaments and has been embellished,[4] and its inhabitants suppose that they are its masters with a free hand over the earth, Our command comes upon it by night or day unexpectedly, and We cause it to become like a field mown down, as if it had not flourished the previous day. Thus We set out in detail the signs (the signposts of Our way and the relevant commands and guidance included in the Qur'ān) for a people who reflect (on them and draw the necessary lesson).

25. And God invites to the Abode of Peace (where they will enjoy perfect bliss, peace, and safety,) and He guides whomever He wills to a Straight Path.

---

21. Whenever We let the (unbelieving) people taste an act of grace after a hardship which has visited them, they at once contrive some plot against Our Revelations. Say: "God is more swift in enforcing His will (and making any plot rebound on those who conceived it)." Surely Our (heavenly) envoys (angels) are recording what they are devising.

22. He it is Who conveys you on the land and the sea. And when you are in the ship, and the ships run with their voyagers with a fair breeze, and they rejoice in it, there comes upon them a tempest, and waves surge towards them from all sides,

---

4. The Qur'ān is a miracle of eloquence. This verse draws a portrait of an attractive, elaborately dressed lady, decked out in all her ornaments. In fact, the world is often compared to an alluring, unfaithful woman. By using a feminine pronoun for the earth, the Qur'ān adds a new dimension to this comparison. But the riches and beauties of the physical world, like the physical beauty of a woman, are also transient.

بِسْمِ اللّٰه الرَّحْمٰنِ الرَّحِيْم

لِلَّذِيْنَ اَحْسَنُوا الْحُسْنٰى وَزِيَادَةٌ وَلَا يَرْهَقُ وُجُوْهَهُمْ قَتَرٌ
وَلَا ذِلَّةٌ اُولٰٓئِكَ اَصْحَابُ الْجَنَّةِ هُمْ فِيْهَا خَالِدُوْنَ ۞ وَالَّذِيْنَ
كَسَبُوا السَّيِّاٰتِ جَزَاۤءُ سَيِّئَةٍ بِمِثْلِهَا وَتَرْهَقُهُمْ
ذِلَّةٌ مَا لَهُمْ مِنَ اللّٰهِ مِنْ عَاصِمٍ كَاَنَّمَا اُغْشِيَتْ وُجُوْهُهُمْ
قِطَعًا مِنَ الَّيْلِ مُظْلِمًا اُولٰٓئِكَ اَصْحَابُ النَّارِ هُمْ فِيْهَا خَالِدُوْنَ ۞
وَيَوْمَ نَحْشُرُهُمْ جَمِيْعًا ثُمَّ نَقُوْلُ لِلَّذِيْنَ اَشْرَكُوْا مَكَانَكُمْ اَنْتُمْ
وَشُرَكَاۤؤُكُمْ فَزَيَّلْنَا بَيْنَهُمْ وَقَالَ شُرَكَاۤؤُهُمْ مَا كُنْتُمْ اِيَّانَا
تَعْبُدُوْنَ ۞ فَكَفٰى بِاللّٰهِ شَهِيْدًا بَيْنَنَا وَبَيْنَكُمْ اِنْ كُنَّا
عَنْ عِبَادَتِكُمْ لَغَافِلِيْنَ ۞ هُنَالِكَ تَبْلُوا كُلُّ نَفْسٍ مَّا
اَسْلَفَتْ وَرُدُّوٓا اِلَى اللّٰهِ مَوْلٰىهُمُ الْحَقِّ وَضَلَّ عَنْهُمْ مَا كَانُوْا يَفْتَرُوْنَ
۞ قُلْ مَنْ يَّرْزُقُكُمْ مِنَ السَّمَاۤءِ وَالْاَرْضِ اَمَّنْ يَّمْلِكُ السَّمْعَ وَالْاَبْصَارَ
وَمَنْ يُّخْرِجُ الْحَيَّ مِنَ الْمَيِّتِ وَيُخْرِجُ الْمَيِّتَ مِنَ الْحَيِّ وَمَنْ يُّدَبِّرُ
الْاَمْرَ فَسَيَقُوْلُوْنَ اللّٰهُ فَقُلْ اَفَلَا تَتَّقُوْنَ ۞ فَذٰلِكُمُ
اللّٰهُ رَبُّكُمُ الْحَقُّ فَمَاذَا بَعْدَ الْحَقِّ اِلَّا الضَّلَالُ فَاَنّٰى تُصْرَفُوْنَ
۞ كَذٰلِكَ حَقَّتْ كَلِمَتُ رَبِّكَ عَلَى الَّذِيْنَ فَسَقُوٓا اَنَّهُمْ لَا يُؤْمِنُوْنَ ۞

26. For those who do good, aware that God is seeing them is the best (of the rewards that God has promised for good deeds), and still more. Neither stain nor ignominy will cover their faces. They are the companions of Paradise; they will abide therein.

27. And for those who have earned evil deeds, the recompense of an evil deed will be the like of it; and ignominy will cover them – nor will they have anyone to defend them against God – it is as though their faces were veiled with patches of darkest night. Those are the companions of the Fire, they will abide therein.[5]

28. On that Day We will raise them all to life and gather them all together, and then We will order those who associated partners with God: "Get to your place, you and your (so-called) associates (of God)!" So did We distinguish between them and the believers, and separate them from their associates. Their associates say to them: "It was not us that you worshipped.

29. "God is sufficient as a witness between us and you: we were certainly unaware of your worshipping (us)."

30. There every soul will experience what it did before (in the world). They have been returned to God, their true Owner and Master; and those that they fabricated to worship besides God have failed them.

31. Say: "Who is it that provides for you from heaven and earth, or Who is it that possesses full power over (your) hearing and eyes, or Who is it that brings forth the living from the dead and brings forth the dead from the living, and Who directs the whole affair (the universe)?" They will say, "It is God."[6] Then, say: "Will you not then keep your duty to him in reverence for Him and in fear of His punishment?"

32. That is God (Who does all these), Your rightful Lord, the Ultimate Truth and Ever-Constant. What is there, after the truth, but error?[7] Then, how are you turned about (to different ways, removed from the Straight Path)?

33. Thus has the word of your Lord proved true with regard to those who transgress: that they will not believe.

5. God rewards a good deed done with sincerity at least tenfold (6: 160). This reward can multiply as much as 700 times (2: 261) or even more, according to the depth of the sincerity in doing it, how well it is done, and the conditions under which it is done. In addition to this, God gives more than that in Paradise, purely out of His grace. We cannot imagine what this surplus reward will be like because Paradise is full of the bounties of God, bounties that no eyes have ever seen and of which no ears have ever heard and which no minds have ever conceived. The believers will also be favored there with the vision of God, the nature of which is beyond our grasp and knowledge here in this world.

While God returns a good deed with multiple rewards, the recompense of an evil deed is only the like of it.

6. The Makkan polytheists admitted that God was the Creator and Governor of the universe, but associated partners with Him in ordering their own lives. They did not accept a power above themselves with which to order their lives. It was they who devised deities for themselves and, although they imbued their (false) deities with some power, it was not their deities that ruled them, but, rather like all other polytheists throughout history, including today, they themselves exploited their deities in their own interests.

There have been, and of course there still are, such people who will not give the answer "It is God" to the questions posed in this verse. But as they do not have a definite alternative answer, they will cite different things or mention some hypotheses. They will never be able to convince themselves of the truth of their answers and their consciences will not be at rest with the hypotheses they have put forward. So many of them will take refuge in agnosticism. For this reason, even if their carnal selves attempt to give different answers to the questions asked in the verse, the answer which almost everyone's conscience will be comfortable with, especially under the conditions mentioned in verse 22, will be, "It is God." However, this answer emanating from the conscience, especially under particular conditions, is not faith, for faith is confirmation and conviction with the heart (and reason), willingly and knowingly.

7. The true, straight way is one, while the ways of error are almost as numerous as the people who are in error. All of the Prophets who came during human history agreed on the same essentials of faith, worship, good conduct, and the basic rules of law, and on the same worldview, the same view of things and events. They gave the same answer to the basic questions of life, questions which everyone asks themselves and which philosophers and thinkers have tried to answer, namely: "Who am I?" "What is the meaning of life and death and what do they demand from me?" "Who has sent me to the world and for what purpose?" "Who is my guide in this earthly journey?" The fact that all of the Prophets gave the same answers to these questions demonstrates that their source is one and the same. Therefore, their answer should also be the same; indeed, the answer provided by all the Prophets is the same, yet nearly all philosophers and thinkers have given different answers to these questions. This fact demonstrates that the way of truth is one and is that which is represented by the Prophets and those who follow them, while the ways of error are numerous.

34. Say: "Is there any of your (so-called) associates (of God) who originates creation and then reproduces it, and will bring it forth anew (in another world)?" Say: "God originates creation and then reproduces it, and He will bring it forth anew. How then are you turned away from the truth and make false claims?

35. Say: "Is there any of your (so-called) associates (of God) who guides to the truth?" Say: "God alone guides to the truth. Which, then, is worthy to be followed: He Who guides to the truth or he who cannot find the true way unless he is guided? What, then, is the matter with you, and how do you judge (so wrongly)?"

36. Most of them follow only conjecture. Surely conjecture can never substitute for anything of the truth. God surely has full knowledge of all that they do.

37. And this Qur'ān is not such that it could possibly be fabricated by one in attribution to God, but it is a (Divine Book) confirming (the Divine origin of and the truths that are still contained by) the Revelations prior to it, and an explanation of the Essence of all Divine Books – wherein there is no doubt,[8] from the Lord of the worlds.

38. Or do they say that he (the Messenger) has fabricated it? Say: "(If it is possible for a mortal to fabricate it) then produce a *sūrah* like it and call for help on anyone you can, apart from God, if you are truthful (in your doubt and the claim you base upon it)."

39. No (they are not truthful in their doubt and claim), but they have denied a thing (the Qur'ān) whose knowledge they could not encompass and whose exposition (through the fulfillment of its promises and threats) has not reached them. Even so did those who were before them

deny (the Books sent to them). So look! how was the outcome for the wrong-doers (who judged and acted wrongly)?

40. Among them (the people of Makkah) there are such as have believed and will believe in it, just as among them there are such as have not believed and will not believe in it. Your Lord has full knowledge of those who provoke disorder and corruption.

41. If (O Messenger) they continue to deny you (regarding the Message you bring), say: "To me are accounted my deeds, and to you, your deeds. You are quit of all that I do, and I am quit of all that you do."

42. Among them are such as come to listen to you, but how can you make the deaf hear, if they do not use their reason (to make sense of it)?

8. There are no differences among the Divine Books – the Qur'ān, the Torah, the Gospel, and others – with respect to the essentials on which they are based. So, as the Prophet Muḥammad, upon him be peace and blessings, testifies that all the previous Prophets were on God's way and carried out the missions imposed on them by God, and as the Muslim Community testifies that all those who followed the previous Prophets correctly were on the right way in the footsteps of the Prophets, so too does the Qur'ān bear witness that all the previous Divine Books are books revealed by God. So, the passages found in their present copies contrary to the basic principles of the Divine Religion on which all the missions of the Prophets and the Divine Books are based, are only interpolations and alterations made by human hands. The Prophet Muḥammad, the Qur'ān, and the Muslim Community acquit all the previous Prophets, Books, and believing communities of any possible accusations arising from the incorrect understanding and practices of those who follow them and who attribute themselves to them.

Another point to cite here is that all the previous Divine Books confirm the Divine origin of the Qur'ān, and along with all the previous Prophets, the Prophethood and Messengership of the Prophet Muḥammad, upon him be peace and blessings.

وَمِنْهُمْ مَنْ يَنْظُرُ إِلَيْكَ أَفَأَنْتَ تَهْدِى الْعُمْيَ وَلَوْ كَانُوا لَا يُبْصِرُونَ ۞ إِنَّ اللّٰهَ لَا يَظْلِمُ النَّاسَ شَيْئًا وَلٰكِنَّ النَّاسَ أَنْفُسَهُمْ يَظْلِمُونَ ۞ وَيَوْمَ يَحْشُرُهُمْ كَأَنْ لَمْ يَلْبَثُوا إِلَّا سَاعَةً مِّنَ النَّهَارِ يَتَعَارَفُونَ بَيْنَهُمْ قَدْ خَسِرَ الَّذِينَ كَذَّبُوا بِلِقَاءِ اللّٰهِ وَمَا كَانُوا مُهْتَدِينَ ۞ وَإِمَّا نُرِيَنَّكَ بَعْضَ الَّذِى نَعِدُهُمْ أَوْ نَتَوَفَّيَنَّكَ فَإِلَيْنَا مَرْجِعُهُمْ ثُمَّ اللّٰهُ شَهِيدٌ عَلٰى مَا يَفْعَلُونَ ۞ وَلِكُلِّ أُمَّةٍ رَسُولٌ فَإِذَا جَاءَ رَسُولُهُمْ قُضِيَ بَيْنَهُمْ بِالْقِسْطِ وَهُمْ لَا يُظْلَمُونَ ۞ وَيَقُولُونَ مَتٰى هٰذَا الْوَعْدُ إِنْ كُنْتُمْ صَادِقِينَ ۞ قُلْ لَا أَمْلِكُ لِنَفْسِى ضَرًّا وَلَا نَفْعًا إِلَّا مَا شَاءَ اللّٰهُ لِكُلِّ أُمَّةٍ أَجَلٌ إِذَا جَاءَ أَجَلُهُمْ فَلَا يَسْتَأْخِرُونَ سَاعَةً وَلَا يَسْتَقْدِمُونَ ۞ قُلْ أَرَأَيْتُمْ إِنْ أَتٰيكُمْ عَذَابُهُ بَيَاتًا أَوْ نَهَارًا مَاذَا يَسْتَعْجِلُ مِنْهُ الْمُجْرِمُونَ ۞ أَثُمَّ إِذَا مَا وَقَعَ آمَنْتُمْ بِهِ آلْآنَ وَقَدْ كُنْتُمْ بِهِ تَسْتَعْجِلُونَ ۞ ثُمَّ قِيلَ لِلَّذِينَ ظَلَمُوا ذُوقُوا عَذَابَ الْخُلْدِ هَلْ تُجْزَوْنَ إِلَّا بِمَا كُنْتُمْ تَكْسِبُونَ ۞ وَيَسْتَنْبِئُونَكَ أَحَقٌّ هُوَ قُلْ إِى وَرَبِّى إِنَّهُ لَحَقٌّ وَمَا أَنْتُمْ بِمُعْجِزِينَ ۞

---

43. Among them are such as look towards you, but how can you guide the blind (to the right way), if they are lacking the power of (in)sight?[9]

44. Surely God does not wrong humankind in anything, but humankind wrong their own selves.

45. On the Day when God will raise to life and gather them together, it will seem to them that they had not tarried in the world but a short while of the day, knowing one another. Assuredly, those who deny (the truth) that they must encounter God have ruined themselves and have never been guided.

46. Whether We let you (O Messenger) witness the fulfillment of some of what We have promised them, or We cause you to die (before it befalls them), still to Us is their return. And God is witness to all that they do.

47. Every community has its Messenger:[10] when their Messenger comes, (some believe in him and the others not) and it is judged between them with absolute justice, and they are not wronged.

48. And they say: "When will this promise be fulfilled if you (O believers) are truthful?"

49. Say (O Messenger): "I have no power to harm or benefit myself, except by God's will. For every community there is an appointed term; and when the end of the term falls in, they can neither delay it by any period of time, however short, nor can they hasten it."[11]

50. Say: "Have you ever considered: what

(could you do) if God's punishment should come to you by night (unexpectedly) or by day (and you saw it come)? What do the disbelieving criminals have in prospect that they wish it to be hastened?"

51. What! Is it only when it has come to pass that you will believe in it? (That day it will be said to you:) "What? (Do you believe in it) now, after you had (in your contemptuous unbelief) wished it to be hastened?"

52. Then it will be said to those who wronged (themselves through unbelief and wrong judgments): "Taste the punishment everlasting! Are you recompensed for anything other than what you used to earn?"

53. They ask you, "Is it true?" Say: "Yes, by my Lord, it is surely true; and you cannot evade it."

9. The eyeball is of no use without the retina. In seeing the truth, the mind is like the eyeball, and the heart is the retina. The light of the heart is reflected on the mind just like the moon reflects the light of the sun. The mind without the light of the heart is left in darkness. The place of faith is the heart, and it is reflected on the mind. The doubts that attack the mind encourage people to investigate and to base their faith on established knowledge. The evidence provided by the universe and the inner and outer world of humankind and which is presented by the Qur'ān functions as a broom to sweep away all doubts. So the mind protects the belief in the heart from being pestered by doubts coming from all directions. If the mind were to be the place of faith instead of the heart, then faith would have been exposed to a variety of attacks which would harm conviction (Sözler ("The Words"), "Lemaât," 658).

10. Throughout human history, God sent a Messenger to every nation – i.e., a separate community that shares the same life-style and culture and that speaks the same language – to convey His Message to them. The Message was one, although tailored in some details of social and ritual practices in order to meet local cultural needs. After the Messengers, the Message was gradually forgotten or seriously distorted, and therefore God raised Prophets to revive the Message or restore it to its original purity, and apply it to daily life. However, the time came when almost all the world was in darkness, oblivious of God's Message, and human beings had reached a stage when a single Messenger and Book would be sufficient for the whole of them; this was when God sent the Prophet Muhammad as the Seal of the Prophets and Messengers along with the Qur'ān.

Since the religions prior to Islam were of a national character, their followers tended to believe that they were chosen peoples.

The Christians acknowledge only the Prophets of Israel, while the Jewish people reject the Prophethood of Jesus. Islam says, however, that it would be a denial of the universal providence of God to assert that Messengers and Prophets were raised for one nation only. According to the Holy Qur'ān, God is the Lord and Sustainer of all the worlds. As He has not discriminated between nations in sending His Revelations, so Muslims make no distinctions between any of His Messengers in their belief in them (2: 285).

Islam is the consummation of all Divine religions. By accepting the Prophets and Scriptures of all nations, Islam affirms the unity and universal providence of God and the universality of religious experience, and also seeks to bring together people of all races and creeds in a single all-embracing faith and brotherhood. Further, a Muslim is also the true follower of all Prophets, including Moses and Jesus, upon them be peace. Such being the case, while the term Christian means one who follows Jesus Christ and Judaism has turned into the racial religion of the Jewish people only, Muslims totally reject the term of Muhammadanism, a term used only by non-Muslims to refer to them. To understand Islam as its adherents do, one should purge the word Muhammadan or Muhammadanism from one's vocabulary. The labelling of Islam as Muhammadanism is the result of a false analogy with Christianity. Muslims do not worship Muhammad as Christians worship Christ. Muhammad was neither a god, nor an incarnation, nor the son of God. He never claimed to be anything more than a man who had received Revelations from God. He did not make Islam, he simply received the Message of Islam.

11. For the explanation of *for every community there is an appointed term; and when the end of the term falls in, they can neither delay it by any period of time, however short, nor can they hasten it*, see 7: 34, note 10.

214 سورة يونس ٢١٤

وَلَوْ أَنَّ لِكُلِّ نَفْسٍ ظَلَمَتْ مَا فِي الْأَرْضِ لَافْتَدَتْ بِهِ ۗ وَأَسَرُّوا النَّدَامَةَ لَمَّا رَأَوُا الْعَذَابَ ۖ وَقُضِيَ بَيْنَهُم بِالْقِسْطِ وَهُمْ لَا يُظْلَمُونَ ۝ أَلَا إِنَّ لِلَّهِ مَا فِي السَّمَاوَاتِ وَالْأَرْضِ ۗ أَلَا إِنَّ وَعْدَ اللَّهِ حَقٌّ وَلَٰكِنَّ أَكْثَرَهُمْ لَا يَعْلَمُونَ ۝ هُوَ يُحْيِي وَيُمِيتُ وَإِلَيْهِ تُرْجَعُونَ ۝ يَا أَيُّهَا النَّاسُ قَدْ جَاءَتْكُم مَّوْعِظَةٌ مِّن رَّبِّكُمْ وَشِفَاءٌ لِّمَا فِي الصُّدُورِ وَهُدًى وَرَحْمَةٌ لِّلْمُؤْمِنِينَ ۝ قُلْ بِفَضْلِ اللَّهِ وَبِرَحْمَتِهِ فَبِذَٰلِكَ فَلْيَفْرَحُوا هُوَ خَيْرٌ مِّمَّا يَجْمَعُونَ ۝ قُلْ أَرَأَيْتُم مَّا أَنزَلَ اللَّهُ لَكُم مِّن رِّزْقٍ فَجَعَلْتُم مِّنْهُ حَرَامًا وَحَلَالًا قُلْ آللَّهُ أَذِنَ لَكُمْ ۖ أَمْ عَلَى اللَّهِ تَفْتَرُونَ ۝ وَمَا ظَنُّ الَّذِينَ يَفْتَرُونَ عَلَى اللَّهِ الْكَذِبَ يَوْمَ الْقِيَامَةِ ۗ إِنَّ اللَّهَ لَذُو فَضْلٍ عَلَى النَّاسِ وَلَٰكِنَّ أَكْثَرَهُمْ لَا يَشْكُرُونَ ۝ وَمَا تَكُونُ فِي شَأْنٍ وَمَا تَتْلُو مِنْهُ مِن قُرْآنٍ وَلَا تَعْمَلُونَ مِنْ عَمَلٍ إِلَّا كُنَّا عَلَيْكُمْ شُهُودًا إِذْ تُفِيضُونَ فِيهِ ۚ وَمَا يَعْزُبُ عَن رَّبِّكَ مِن مِّثْقَالِ ذَرَّةٍ فِي الْأَرْضِ وَلَا فِي السَّمَاءِ وَلَا أَصْغَرَ مِن ذَٰلِكَ وَلَا أَكْبَرَ إِلَّا فِي كِتَابٍ مُّبِينٍ ۝

54. If every soul that has committed wrong (through unbelief and thereby wronged itself) possessed all that is on the earth, it would surely offer that as ransom (to be saved from the punishment); and when they see the punishment, they will even be unable to express their remorse. It is judged between them in equity, and they are not wronged.

55. Know well that to God belongs all that is in the heavens and on the earth. Know well that God's promise is surely true, but most of them do not know.

56. He gives life and causes to die, and you are on the way to return to Him.

57. O humankind! There has come to you an instruction from your Lord, and a cure for what (of sickness or doubt) is in the breasts, and guidance and mercy for the believers.

58. Say: "In the grace and bounty of God and in His mercy – in this, then, let them rejoice. That is better than what they amass (of worldly goods and riches)."

59. Say: "Have you considered the provision God has sent down[12] on you, and you have (of your own accord, at your own whim) made some of it lawful and some of it unlawful?" Say: "Has God given you leave, or do you (make laws of your own accord and) attribute to God falsely?

60. What do those who falsely attribute (their own inventions) to God think will be (their situation) on the Day of Resur-

rection? Indeed God has grace and bounty for humankind, but most of them do not give thanks.

61. Whatever your preoccupation (O Messenger), and whatever discourse from Him in this (Qur'ān) you may be reciting, and whatever work you (O people) may be doing, We are certainly witness over you while you are engaged in it. Not an atom's weight of whatever there is in the earth or in the heaven escapes your Lord, nor is there anything smaller than that, or greater, but it is (recorded) in a Manifest Book.[13]

---

12. The Qur'ān, by saying *the provision God has sent down*, emphasizes that the real source of all provision is God's mercy and bounty, and therefore it comes from a very exalted source. It also alludes to the fact that almost all the

provision with which living beings are maintained requires rain and that this rain comes from on high.

13. For the Manifest Book, see *sūrah* 6: 59, note 13.

الآ إِنَّ أَوْلِيَاءَ اللّٰهِ لَا خَوْفٌ عَلَيْهِمْ وَلَا هُمْ يَحْزَنُونَ ۝ الَّذِينَ آمَنُوا وَكَانُوا يَتَّقُونَ ۝ لَهُمُ الْبُشْرَىٰ فِي الْحَيَوٰةِ الدُّنْيَا وَفِي الْأَخِرَةِ ۚ لَا تَبْدِيلَ لِكَلِمَاتِ اللّٰهِ ۚ ذَٰلِكَ هُوَ الْفَوْزُ الْعَظِيمُ ۝ وَلَا يَحْزُنْكَ قَوْلُهُمْ ۘ إِنَّ الْعِزَّةَ لِلّٰهِ جَمِيعًا ۚ هُوَ السَّمِيعُ الْعَلِيمُ ۝ الآ إِنَّ لِلّٰهِ مَنْ فِي السَّمٰوَاتِ وَمَنْ فِي الْأَرْضِ ۗ وَمَا يَتَّبِعُ الَّذِينَ يَدْعُونَ مِنْ دُونِ اللّٰهِ شُرَكَاءَ ۚ إِنْ يَتَّبِعُونَ إِلَّا الظَّنَّ وَإِنْ هُمْ إِلَّا يَخْرُصُونَ ۝ هُوَ الَّذِي جَعَلَ لَكُمُ اللَّيْلَ لِتَسْكُنُوا فِيهِ وَالنَّهَارَ مُبْصِرًا ۚ إِنَّ فِي ذَٰلِكَ لَآيَاتٍ لِقَوْمٍ يَسْمَعُونَ ۝ قَالُوا اتَّخَذَ اللّٰهُ وَلَدًا ۗ سُبْحَانَهُ ۖ هُوَ الْغَنِيُّ ۖ لَهُ مَا فِي السَّمٰوَاتِ وَمَا فِي الْأَرْضِ ۚ إِنْ عِنْدَكُمْ مِنْ سُلْطَانٍ بِهَٰذَا ۚ أَتَقُولُونَ عَلَى اللّٰهِ مَا لَا تَعْلَمُونَ ۝ قُلْ إِنَّ الَّذِينَ يَفْتَرُونَ عَلَى اللّٰهِ الْكَذِبَ لَا يُفْلِحُونَ ۝ مَتَاعٌ فِي الدُّنْيَا ثُمَّ إِلَيْنَا مَرْجِعُهُمْ ثُمَّ نُذِيقُهُمُ الْعَذَابَ الشَّدِيدَ بِمَا كَانُوا يَكْفُرُونَ ۝

---

62. Know well that the friends (saintly servants) of God[14] – they will have no fear, nor will they grieve.

63. They are those who believe and keep from disobedience to God in reverence for Him and piety.

64. For them is the glad tiding (of prosperity) in the life of this world and in the Hereafter. No change can there be in God's decrees. That indeed is the supreme triumph.

65. Do not let their sayings grieve you (O Messenger). Might and glory belong to God entirely. He is the All-Hearing, the All-Knowing.

66. Know well that to God belongs whoever is in the heavens and whoever is on the earth (His creatures and servants). Those who invoke, apart from God, (do not do so because they really have found deities and lords that can be partners with God in His Divinity and Lordship, and so) follow those partners. They do but follow only conjecture (not authoritative knowledge), and they do nothing except making up suppositions.[15]

67. It is He Who has made for you the night so that you may rest in it, and the day, sight-giving (for you to work in). Surely in this are signs (manifesting the truth) for people who hear and pay heed (to God's Revelations, and view things and events in their light).

68. They (the polytheists) assert that God has taken to Himself a child. All-Glorified is He; He is Self-Sufficient (beyond any need of anything). To Him belongs all that is in the heavens and all that is on the earth. You have no authority, nor evidence, for this (assertion). Are you, then, saying things about God that you do not know (anything about)?

69. Say: "Surely those who fabricate falsehood in attribution to God will never prosper."

70. A brief enjoyment in the world; then to Us is their return, and then We will make them taste the severe punishment because they habitually disbelieved (in whatever truth was conveyed to them in God's Name).

14. Above all else, all the believers are friends of God, for God is the guardian and confidant of believers, as is mentioned in many verses (2: 257; 3: 68; 5: 55; 6: 127; 7: 155; 34, 41, etc.) Likewise, Satan and the unbelievers, especially those who are more deeply rooted in unbelief, are the friends and guardians of one another. Another point to be made here is that the believers are friends and guardians of one another (3: 28; 8: 72; 9: 71, etc.), just as in the same way some of the unbelievers and some of the People of the Book are friends and guardians of each other, especially against the believers (5: 51; 8: 73; 45: 9, etc).

In addition to this general meaning of God being the guardian and confidant of the believers and the believers being His friends, the original word *waliyy* (the plural of which is *awliyā*) has another special meaning. The believers are not of the same degree in believing and doing what is required by this belief, nor are they of the same degree in nearness to God. Some among them are more advanced than the others and accordingly are nearer to God. In common Islamic literature, when we say *waliyy* or *awliyā*, this special meaning is usually what is meant. The following verse sheds light on the subject, allowing us to better understand this concept:

God is the confidant and guardian of those who believe (to Whom they can entrust their affairs and on Whom they can rely), bringing them out from all kinds of (intellectual, spiritual, social, economic and political) darkness into the light and keeping them firm therein. (2: 257).

The most manifest function of God being the confidant and guardian of the believers is that He brings them out of all the different kinds of existing darkness (intellectual, spiritual, social, economic, and political) into the light. So, those among the believers who try their best, with utmost sincerity, so that people can be brought out of all the different kinds of darkness into the light are nearer to God and are His special friends. This is the main mission of the Messengers and the Prophets, and those who follow them in their missions. This requires that one has knowledge, the deepest conviction of the essentials of faith, and that one lives according to these essentials, sincerely worshipping God, refraining from sins, and that one has praiseworthy qualities or virtues, while being dedicated to God's cause (*Key Concepts*, 2: 60-65).

15. That is, they judge and speak according to their passing fancies, interests and personal value judgments.

216   سُورَةُ يُونُسَ   ٢١٦

وَاتْلُ عَلَيْهِمْ نَبَأَ نُوحٍ إِذْ قَالَ لِقَوْمِهِ يَا قَوْمِ إِن كَانَ كَبُرَ
عَلَيْكُم مَّقَامِي وَتَذْكِيرِي بِآيَاتِ اللَّهِ فَعَلَى اللَّهِ تَوَكَّلْتُ
فَأَجْمِعُوا أَمْرَكُمْ وَشُرَكَاءَكُمْ ثُمَّ لَا يَكُنْ أَمْرُكُمْ
عَلَيْكُمْ غُمَّةً ثُمَّ اقْضُوا إِلَيَّ وَلَا تُنظِرُونِ ۝ فَإِن تَوَلَّيْتُمْ
فَمَا سَأَلْتُكُم مِّنْ أَجْرٍ إِنْ أَجْرِيَ إِلَّا عَلَى اللَّهِ وَأُمِرْتُ
أَنْ أَكُونَ مِنَ الْمُسْلِمِينَ ۝ فَكَذَّبُوهُ فَنَجَّيْنَاهُ وَمَن مَّعَهُ
فِي الْفُلْكِ وَجَعَلْنَاهُمْ خَلَائِفَ وَأَغْرَقْنَا الَّذِينَ كَذَّبُوا بِآيَاتِنَا
فَانظُرْ كَيْفَ كَانَ عَاقِبَةُ الْمُنذَرِينَ ۝ ثُمَّ بَعَثْنَا مِنْ بَعْدِهِ رُسُلًا
إِلَى قَوْمِهِمْ فَجَاءُوهُم بِالْبَيِّنَاتِ فَمَا كَانُوا لِيُؤْمِنُوا بِمَا كَذَّبُوا
مِن قَبْلُ كَذَٰلِكَ نَطْبَعُ عَلَى قُلُوبِ الْمُعْتَدِينَ ۝ ثُمَّ بَعَثْنَا مِنْ
بَعْدِهِم مُّوسَى وَهَارُونَ إِلَىٰ فِرْعَوْنَ وَمَلَئِهِ بِآيَاتِنَا فَاسْتَكْبَرُوا
وَكَانُوا قَوْمًا مُّجْرِمِينَ ۝ فَلَمَّا جَاءَهُمُ الْحَقُّ مِنْ عِندِنَا قَالُوا إِنَّ
هَٰذَا لَسِحْرٌ مُّبِينٌ ۝ قَالَ مُوسَىٰ أَتَقُولُونَ لِلْحَقِّ لَمَّا جَاءَكُمْ أَسِحْرٌ هَٰذَا
وَلَا يُفْلِحُ السَّاحِرُونَ ۝ قَالُوا أَجِئْتَنَا لِتَلْفِتَنَا عَمَّا وَجَدْنَا عَلَيْهِ آبَاءَنَا
وَتَكُونَ لَكُمَا الْكِبْرِيَاءُ فِي الْأَرْضِ وَمَا نَحْنُ لَكُمَا بِمُؤْمِنِينَ ۝

cepting it will gain me nothing) I ask you for no wage; my wage is only due from God, and I have been commanded to be of the Muslims (those who have submitted to Him)."

73. And yet they denied him, and so We saved him and all who were with him in the Ark, and made them successors (to inherit the earth), while We caused to drown those who denied Our Revelations and all other signs (pointing to Our Existence and Unity).Look, then, how was the outcome for those who were warned (but never paid heed)?

74. Then, after him, We sent forth Messengers to their people; and they came to them with the clear signs of the truth but they would not believe in that which they used to deny before. Thus do We impress a seal on the hearts of those who exceed the bounds.[16]

75. Then, after them, We sent forth Moses and Aaron to the Pharaoh and his chiefs with Our signs (miracles to support them), but they grew arrogant (in the face of those signs), and (demonstrated that) they were a guilty people committed to accumulating sins.

76. When the truth came to them from Us, they said: "Surely this is clearly nothing but sorcery."

77. Moses said: "Do you speak of the truth like this when it has come to you? Is this sorcery? But sorcerers do not prosper."

78. They said: "Have you come to us to turn us away from what we found our forefathers following, and that high authority in this land may belong to you two? Never will we believe in you two!"

---

71. Relate to them the exemplary history of Noah when he said to his people: "O my people! If my presence (among you) and my reminding (you) by God's Revelations are offensive to you – well, in God have I put my trust. So, coming together, decide upon your course of action, and (call to your aid) your (so-called) associates of God, then let not your affair be a worry to you, and then carry out against me (whatever you have decided), and give me no respite!

72. "Then if you turn away (from the Message that I convey to you), then (know that it will cause me no loss, just as your ac-

---

16. For the exemplary histories of those Messengers, see, 7: 65–102, and the related notes.

وَقَالَ فِرْعَوْنُ ائْتُوْنِى بِكُلِّ سَاحِرٍ عَلِيْمٍ ۞ فَلَمَّا جَآءَ
السَّحَرَةُ قَالَ لَهُمْ مُّوْسٰى اَلْقُوْا مَآ اَنْتُمْ مُّلْقُوْنَ ۞ فَلَمَّآ
اَلْقَوْا قَالَ مُوْسٰى مَا جِئْتُمْ بِهِ السِّحْرُ اِنَّ اللّٰهَ سَيُبْطِلُهُ اِنَّ
اللّٰهَ لَا يُصْلِحُ عَمَلَ الْمُفْسِدِيْنَ ۞ وَيُحِقُّ اللّٰهُ الْحَقَّ بِكَلِمٰتِهِ
وَلَوْ كَرِهَ الْمُجْرِمُوْنَ ۞ فَمَآ اٰمَنَ لِمُوْسٰى اِلَّا ذُرِّيَّةٌ مِّنْ قَوْمِهِ عَلٰى
خَوْفٍ مِّنْ فِرْعَوْنَ وَمَلَائِهِمْ اَنْ يَّفْتِنَهُمْ وَاِنَّ فِرْعَوْنَ لَعَالٍ فِى
الْاَرْضِ وَاِنَّهُ لَمِنَ الْمُسْرِفِيْنَ ۞ وَقَالَ مُوْسٰى يٰقَوْمِ اِنْ كُنْتُمْ اٰمَنْتُمْ
بِاللّٰهِ فَعَلَيْهِ تَوَكَّلُوْٓا اِنْ كُنْتُمْ مُّسْلِمِيْنَ ۞ فَقَالُوْا عَلَى
اللّٰهِ تَوَكَّلْنَا رَبَّنَا لَا تَجْعَلْنَا فِتْنَةً لِّلْقَوْمِ الظّٰلِمِيْنَ ۞
وَنَجِّنَا بِرَحْمَتِكَ مِنَ الْقَوْمِ الْكٰفِرِيْنَ ۞ وَاَوْحَيْنَآ اِلٰى مُوْسٰى
وَاَخِيْهِ اَنْ تَبَوَّءَا لِقَوْمِكُمَا بِمِصْرَ بُيُوْتًا وَّاجْعَلُوْا بُيُوْتَكُمْ
قِبْلَةً وَّاَقِيْمُوا الصَّلٰوةَ وَبَشِّرِ الْمُؤْمِنِيْنَ ۞ وَقَالَ مُوْسٰى رَبَّنَآ
اِنَّكَ اٰتَيْتَ فِرْعَوْنَ وَمَلَاَهُ زِيْنَةً وَّاَمْوَالًا فِى الْحَيٰوةِ الدُّنْيَا رَبَّنَا
لِيُضِلُّوْا عَنْ سَبِيْلِكَ رَبَّنَا اطْمِسْ عَلٰٓى اَمْوَالِهِمْ وَاشْدُدْ عَلٰى
قُلُوْبِهِمْ فَلَا يُؤْمِنُوْا حَتّٰى يَرَوُا الْعَذَابَ الْاَلِيْمَ ۞

79. And the Pharaoh said: "Bring me every learned, skillful sorcerer!"

80. When the sorcerers came, Moses said to them: "Throw down what you will throw."

81. When they had thrown (whatever they had in their hands and produced a mighty sorcery), Moses said: "What you have brought is but sorcery. Surely God will bring it to nothing and prove it false. God never validates and sets right the work of those who cause disorder and corruption.

82. "And God proves by His decrees the truth to be true and makes it triumph, however hateful this is to the criminals."

83. None save a young generation among his people believed in Moses for (they were in) fear that the Pharaoh and the chiefs among them (who collaborated with the Pharaoh in order not to lose their wealth) would subject them to persecutions. The Pharaoh was indeed a haughty tyrant in the land and he was indeed one of those who commit excesses.

84. And Moses said (in earnest advice to his people): "If you believe in God, then put your trust in Him, if you are Muslims (who have wholly submitted themselves to Him)."

85. They invoked (verbally and by their actions): "In God we put our trust. Our Lord! Do not make us a target of persecution for the wrongdoing people!

86. "And save us through Your mercy from those unbelieving people!"

87. We revealed to Moses and his brother: "Appoint houses for your people in Egypt (as places of refuge and coming together in God's cause), and (as a whole community) make your homes places to turn to God, and establish the Prescribed Prayer in conformity with its conditions. And (O Moses,) give glad tidings to the believers!"

88. Moses prayed to God: "Our Lord! Surely You have granted the Pharaoh and his chiefs splendor and riches in the life of this world, and so, our Lord, they lead people astray from Your way. Our Lord! Destroy their riches, and press upon their hearts, for they do not believe until they see the painful punishment."

218

سُوۡرَةُ يُوۡنُسَ ٢١٨

قَالَ قَدۡ اُجِيبَتۡ دَّعۡوَتُكُمَا فَاسۡتَقِيمَا وَلَا تَتَّبِعَآنِّ سَبِيلَ الَّذِينَ لَا يَعۡلَمُونَ ۞ وَجَاوَزۡنَا بِبَنِىۡٓ اِسۡرَآءِيۡلَ الۡبَحۡرَ فَاَتۡبَعَهُمۡ فِرۡعَوۡنُ وَجُنُوۡدُهٗ بَغۡيًا وَّعَدۡوًا حَتّٰىٓ اِذَآ اَدۡرَكَهُ الۡغَرَقُ قَالَ اٰمَنۡتُ اَنَّهٗ لَآ اِلٰهَ اِلَّا الَّذِىٓ اٰمَنَتۡ بِهٖ بَنُوۡٓا اِسۡرَآءِيۡلَ وَاَنَا مِنَ الۡمُسۡلِمِيۡنَ ۞ اٰلۡـٰٔنَ وَقَدۡ عَصَيۡتَ قَبۡلُ وَكُنۡتَ مِنَ الۡمُفۡسِدِيۡنَ ۞ فَالۡيَوۡمَ نُنَجِّيۡكَ بِبَدَنِكَ لِتَكُوۡنَ لِمَنۡ خَلۡفَكَ اٰيَةً وَّاِنَّ كَثِيۡرًا مِّنَ النَّاسِ عَنۡ اٰيٰتِنَا لَغٰفِلُوۡنَ ۞ وَلَقَدۡ بَوَّاۡنَا بَنِىۡٓ اِسۡرَآءِيۡلَ مُبَوَّاَ صِدۡقٍ وَّرَزَقۡنٰهُمۡ مِّنَ الطَّيِّبٰتِ فَمَا اخۡتَلَفُوۡا حَتّٰى جَآءَهُمُ الۡعِلۡمُ اِنَّ رَبَّكَ يَقۡضِىۡ بَيۡنَهُمۡ يَوۡمَ الۡقِيٰمَةِ فِيۡمَا كَانُوۡا فِيۡهِ يَخۡتَلِفُوۡنَ ۞ فَاِنۡ كُنۡتَ فِىۡ شَكٍّ مِّمَّآ اَنۡزَلۡنَآ اِلَيۡكَ فَسۡـَٔلِ الَّذِينَ يَقۡرَءُوۡنَ الۡكِتٰبَ مِنۡ قَبۡلِكَ لَقَدۡ جَآءَكَ الۡحَقُّ مِنۡ رَّبِّكَ فَلَا تَكُوۡنَنَّ مِنَ الۡمُمۡتَرِيۡنَ ۞ وَلَا تَكُوۡنَنَّ مِنَ الَّذِينَ كَذَّبُوۡا بِاٰيٰتِ اللّٰهِ فَتَكُوۡنَ مِنَ الۡخٰسِرِيۡنَ ۞ اِنَّ الَّذِينَ حَقَّتۡ عَلَيۡهِمۡ كَلِمَتُ رَبِّكَ لَا يُؤۡمِنُوۡنَ ۞ وَلَوۡ جَآءَتۡهُمۡ كُلُّ اٰيَةٍ حَتّٰى يَرَوُا الۡعَذَابَ الۡاَلِيۡمَ

---

89. God said: "The prayer of you two (O Moses and Aaron) has indeed been answered; so, (since the realization of your goals is dependent upon your way of conduct,) continue steadfastly on the Straight Path, and do not follow the way of those who have no knowledge (of right and wrong) and act in ignorance."

90. And We brought the Children of Israel across the sea, and the Pharaoh and his hosts pursued them with vehement insolence and hostility, until (they were overwhelmed by the waters of the sea opened for Moses and his people to cross,) and when the drowning overtook the Pharaoh, he exclaimed: "I have come to believe that there is no deity save Him in whom the Children of Israel believe, and I am of the Muslims (those who have submitted themselves wholly to Him)."

91. Now? – (You surrender now) when before this you always rebelled and were of those engaged in causing disorder and corruption?

92. So this day (as a recompense for your belief in the state of despair which will be of no avail to you in the Hereafter), We will save only your body, that you may be a sign for those to come after you.[17] Surely, a good many people among humankind are heedless of Our signs (full of clear warning and lessons).

93. And indeed We settled the Children of Israel in a proper place of dwelling, and provided them with pure, wholesome things. They did not suffer discord until after the knowledge came to them (of the way they would have to follow and of what they would meet as a result of what they did). Your Lord will surely judge among them on the Day of Resurrection concerning that on which they used to differ.[18]

94. If you are in doubt about the truth of what We have sent down on you (concerning what happened between Moses and the Pharaoh), then ask those who have been reading the Book (which was given to them) before you. Surely the truth has come to you from your Lord, so be not among those who feel doubt.

95. And neither be among those who deny God's signs and Revelations, for then you will be among the losers.[19]

96. Those for whom the truth of your Lord's decree (that they will die unbelievers and go to Hell) has been confirmed – they will not believe,

97. Even though every proof should come to them, until they see the painful punishment.

17. With this verse about the Pharaoh's drowning the Qur'ān suggests the following: All the Pharaohs believed in reincarnation, therefore, they mummified their bodies in the hopes of eternalizing themselves. Thus, their bodies have survived to the present day. Although not mummified, the body of the Pharaoh who lived during the time of Moses and drowned while pursuing Moses with his army was found prostrate beside the Nile in the final years of the nineteenth century. This is an explicit Qur'ānic miracle, which was foretold centuries before in the above verse (*The Words*, "the 25${}^{\text{th}}$ Word," 420; al-Mawdūdī, 2, note 92).

18. The Qur'ān mentions the story of the Children of Israel which, for the most part, is based mainly on the mission of Moses, in many of its *sūrah*s as this story is a rounded exemplary history for the progress of all nations and provides an indication of the importance of the place the Children of Israel hold in human history. The Qur'ān deals with their story every time in relation to the main themes of the *sūrah* in which it is recounted. For example, in this *sūrah*, while the story of the Prophet Noah, upon him be peace, is described with the challenge he gave to his people, his deep reliance on God and his confidence in his mission, and with God's saving him and the believers in his company while destroying all of the unbelievers, and while the stories of the Messengers Hūd, Ṣāliḥ, Lot, and Shu'ayb, upon them be peace, are referred to only in one verse with their end and the reason why that end occurred, the story of the Children of Israel is narrated in its aspect of the basic dimension of Moses' message, the intellectual and final material defeat of the Pharaoh and his chiefs, who were opposed to that message, as well as the final triumph of the Children of Israel and the main factor that led to that triumph. The main idea behind all the stories mentioned in this *sūrah* is:

All of the Messengers came with the same fundamental message based on Divine Oneness, and God equipped them with miracles and other manifest signs or evidence to prove that they were God's Messengers. Those who opposed them had nothing valid in their hands to justify their opposition; rather their opposition was out of sheer ignorance, based on prejudices governed by their worldly interests and carnal desires, as well as their arrogance and incorrect viewpoints. They persecuted the Messengers and the believers in their company, but the latter endured all their persecutions, relying solely on God. In the end, the Messengers and their followers were saved and triumphed while their opponents were defeated and ruined themselves. The believers will enjoy eternal happiness in Paradise in the other world but the unbelievers will suffer unending punishment in Hell.

Mentioning these stories from this perspective in this *sūrah*, God consoles the Prophet Muḥammad, upon him be peace and blessings, and his followers, confirming them in their belief, strengthening their patience, reminding them of the main characteristic of the way they are destined to follow, and, finally, giving them a mild warning against any discord which may break out among themselves after their final victory against their enemies.

19. These verses do not mean that the Messenger had any doubts concerning his mission, the Revelation he received, or the stories of the previous Messengers narrated in the Qur'ān. When the verses are considered in the light of the context in which they exist, the meaning is clear:

God's Messenger, upon him be peace and blessings, was very grieved in the face of the persecutions and derisions he suffered at the hands of the unbelievers who persisted in unbelief. He told the people who were obstinate in their rejection of the truth and who knew nothing of Revelation and Messengership, and who were confined to this world with all their being, about the realms beyond the sensed world, the Divine Revelation, contact with God, Who is beyond all conceptions and other metaphysical realities, as well as the histories of bygone peoples about whom he had neither read nor heard anything substantial before. It is clear what kind of reaction he faced. It was not easy to talk about such matters, to challenge formidable, stubborn enemies and to claim that the future would belong to the believers at a time when they were too few and weak. But he related all these with utmost confidence in his mission and without any doubt.

It was essential that the believers should also believe with unwavering certainty in whatever he said and in whatever news he gave, so that they should be reinforced, increasing their endurance. So, in addressing the Messenger, the Almighty consoled and reinforced the believers, and in addressing one who had absolute certainty in what he had received from God and conveyed to others, He was also warning the believers that they should feel no doubts about their faith and should not be influenced by the opposition of the unbelievers. He also reminded the Messenger and the believers of the fact that all that had occurred indicated that the way they were going was the same way that had been trodden by previous nations.

The meaning of what God says here is: "Just as the Pharaoh, one of the most refractory tyrants of history, and his chiefs did not believe, yet had to believe when he saw one of many of God's earthly punishments at a time when believing was of no use, so too will all those who resist God's Message – in the way that the Pharaoh and previous peoples did – have to declare faith, even if it will be of no use to them. So, their unbelief should not discourage you or cause you to waver in your faith. Besides, as believers, you will not be discouraged by the resistance and power of your enemies. For God is the All-Powerful and will make you triumphant so long as you continue your way without wavering. "

98. If only there had been a community that believed (just when God's decree of punishment was issued) and profited by their belief – there was none except the people of Jonah. When they came to believe We withdrew from them the punishment of disgrace in the life of this world, and We allowed them to enjoy life for a term.[20]

99. If your Lord had so willed (and, denying them free will, compelled humankind to believe), all who are on the earth would surely have believed, all of them. Would you, then, force people until they become believers?

100. It is not for any person to believe save by God's leave. God sets those who do not use their reason in a mire of uncleanness.[21]

101. Say: "Consider what there is (and what happens) in the heavens and on the earth." But all such signs (of the truth of the essentials of faith) and the warnings cannot avail a people who will not believe.

102. For what do they watch and wait but the like of the days of punishment which befell those (unbelievers) who passed away before them? Say: "Then watch and wait, and I will be with you watching and waiting."

103. Then We save Our Messengers and those who believe (as We always did be-

fore). We have bound Ourselves to save the believers.

104. Say: "O humankind! If you are in doubt about my religion, then (know that) I do not worship those whom you worship apart from God, but I worship God alone, Who causes you all to die. I have been commanded to be of the believers.

105. "(I have also been commanded:) Set all your being exclusively to the true religion as one with pure faith (free from unbelief and hypocrisy), and never be among those who associate partners with God.

106. And do not invoke, apart from God, that which can neither benefit you nor harm you; if you did so, then you would be of the wrongdoers (who wrong themselves by committing the greatest wrong of associating partners with God).

20. As has been pointed out several times before, as God is beyond all time and space, His (pre-) ordaining means His knowing all things and events beforehand. Therefore, a people are not compelled to do something against their own free will. (We feel obliged to use expressions such as "pre-ordaining" and "beforehand," which denote time, since we have to bring the concepts of Divinity within our understanding, which is constrained by time and space.) For this reason, Islam does not recognize determinism in human history. If we talk about determinism established by God, it is that God has determined what consequence people will meet in return for what they do. Causality is a law established by God. He has explicitly informed people of this through the Messengers He has sent and the Books He has revealed.

Another important "law" concerning God's way of acting and the way He has established for people to follow, according to their own free will, is that He may withdraw His decree for a person or people. This law is called the law of God's special grace or sparing. This is like detonating a missile before it attains its target. God sometimes informs a person or people of what will befall them, either through true dreams or presentiments, or in some other way. If that person or people can understand this warning and implore God for forgiveness, give in charity, and mend their ways, then God may spare them. Many peoples throughout history, such as those of the 'Ād, the Thamūd, and the Pharaoh's people, deserved to be destroyed because of their persistence in associating partners with God, dissolute lifestyles, and the injustices and atrocities they inflicted on others despite all the warnings made to them. However, the Prophet Jonah's people, upon him be peace, turned to God with utmost sincerity and deep repentance, and morally reformed themselves after they saw the signs of impending destruction. As a result, God spared them the penalty of disgrace in the worldly life, and allowed them to enjoy life for a term. Emphasizing this point, God's Messenger, upon him be peace and blessings, said: "Fear does not prevent misfortunes, rather prayer and charity do" (al-Hindī, *hadīth* no. 3123).

The Prophet Jonah, upon him be peace, lived about eight centuries before Jesus and was sent to Nineveh during the early years of the second Asyyrian Empire. Despite his years of preaching God's Message, his people persisted in their association of partners with God, and despairing of his people's ability to believe, he left them without having been ordered to do so by God, believing that God would always guard and provide him wherever he was (21: 87). According to what we conclude from the Qur'ān (37: 140), the ship he had boarded was about to sink in a storm because of the weight of its load, and the sailors felt constrained to lighten it. They cast lots to decide who should be thrown into the sea and the lot fell to Jonah. So, they cast him into the sea.

A large fish swallowed him. Jonah was a beloved servant of God who had always glorified Him. He glorified God in the fish also and asked for His forgiveness. In the end, by God's leave, the fish threw him out on the shore. When Jonah left his people and the signs of God's impending punishment appeared, they implored Him for forgiveness for days, and God withdrew His decree of punishment. Jonah returned to his people and more than 100,000 people believed in his message (37: 137–148). Jonah's suffering must have had a share in the sparing of his people. For every misfortune generally comes upon a believer as a result of a sin committed or fault made and, when they ask God for forgiveness for those sins or faults, this serves as a means of two rewards, one coming immediately, the other later on.

Some people who approach the Qur'ān and the miracles of the Prophets purely from a rationalistic viewpoint tend to interpret Jonah's being swallowed by a fish and then being saved from it by God in a metaphorical way. Whereas a similar event took place centuries later. A hunter of whales in England called James Bartly fell into the sea while fishing on a boat called Star of East in August 1891 and was swallowed by a whale. The whale was found dead two days later, the fisherman was taken out of its belly alive, after 60 hours (*Urdu Digest*, February 1964, quoted in *Tefhim*, 5: 41, note 82).

21. The Qur'ān attaches great importance to the intellectual activities or faculties, all of which it relates to the "heart;" these faculties are reflection, using the reason, considering, knowledge, insight and "hearing," etc. It regards anyone who is devoid of these as being dead. Even if we relate all these to the heart, or each to a different faculty, the way to keep these alive is to refrain from being pre-conditioned, to avoid prejudices, incorrect viewpoints, evil intentions, sins, wrongdoing, arrogance, and selfishness. These are the vices which prevent one from believing. The last two verses both complement and also give a mild warning to God's Messenger because he wished for all people to believe; in fact, this was such a strong desire in him that he would torment himself nearly to death with grief if they would not believe (18: 6). This verse also relates belief to God's leave, which He relates to whether or not people's intellectual faculties are alive. Those who do not use their intellectual faculties or those who use them in improper ways are devoid of God's leave to believe.

SŪRAH 11

HŪD

Makkah period

This *surah* was revealed in Makkah, and consists of 123 verses. It takes its name from the story of the Prophet Hūd, which has special importance here due to the topics dealt with. Like *Sūrah Yūnus*, this *surah* deals with the essentials of faith, including in particular the Divine origin of the Qur'ān, and it mentions the stories of the Messengers (narrated also in *Sūrat al-A ʿrāf*), giving details that pertain to the main themes and the conditions that prevailed at the time it was revealed. As the *surah* begins with the Divine Names the All-Wise and the All-Aware, the stories in it can also be approached from this perspective.

In the Name of God, the All-Merciful, the All-Compassionate.

1. *Alif. Lām. Rā.* A Book whose Revelations in verses have been made firm (absolutely free of doubt, alteration, or annulment) and full of wisdom, and arranged in sequence and distinctly detailed. It is from One All-Wise, All-Aware.

2. So that you worship none but God. (Say, O Messenger:) "Surely I am a warner for you (O people, against the evil consequences of all kinds of misguidance) and a bearer of glad tidings (of prosperity in return for faith and righteousness)."

3. And that you ask your Lord for forgiveness (for the sins you have so far committed), then turn to Him repentant and sincerely, so that He may enable for you a

107. If God touches you with affliction, there is none who can remove it but He; and if He wills any good for you, then there is none who can hold back His bounty. He causes it to reach whomever He wills of His servants. He is the All-Forgiving, the All-Compassionate."

108. Say: "O humankind! Assuredly there has come to you the truth from your Lord. Whoever, therefore, chooses the right way, follows it but for his own good; and whoever chooses to go astray, goes astray but to his own harm. I am not one appointed as a guardian over you to assume your responsibility."

109. And follow what is revealed to you, and remain patient and steadfast in your way until God gives His judgment. And He is the best in giving judgment.

good life for a term appointed, and bestow His grace and bounty more abundantly on whoever is more advanced in virtue and devotion. But if you turn away, then, surely I fear for you the punishment of a mighty Day.

4. To God is your final return. He has full power over everything.

5. Beware! surely they (who associate partners with God) lean over their breasts (as if in respect for you, but in reality they are) seeking to hide (from God the unbelief and hostility) in their hearts. Beware! at the very time that they cover themselves with their garments (or hide themselves in their houses behind shut doors and curtained windows) God knows well all that they keep concealed as well as all that they disclose. Surely God has full knowledge of what lies hidden in the bosoms.

وَمَا مِن دَآبَّةٍ فِي الْأَرْضِ إِلَّا عَلَى اللَّهِ رِزْقُهَا وَيَعْلَمُ مُسْتَقَرَّهَا وَمُسْتَوْدَعَهَا ۚ كُلٌّ فِي كِتَابٍ مُّبِينٍ ۝ وَهُوَ الَّذِي خَلَقَ السَّمَاوَاتِ وَالْأَرْضَ فِي سِتَّةِ أَيَّامٍ وَكَانَ عَرْشُهُ عَلَى الْمَاءِ لِيَبْلُوَكُمْ أَيُّكُمْ أَحْسَنُ عَمَلًا ۗ وَلَئِن قُلْتَ إِنَّكُم مَّبْعُوثُونَ مِن بَعْدِ الْمَوْتِ لَيَقُولَنَّ الَّذِينَ كَفَرُوا إِنْ هَٰذَا إِلَّا سِحْرٌ مُّبِينٌ ۝ وَلَئِنْ أَخَّرْنَا عَنْهُمُ الْعَذَابَ إِلَىٰ أُمَّةٍ مَّعْدُودَةٍ لَّيَقُولُنَّ مَا يَحْبِسُهُ ۚ أَلَا يَوْمَ يَأْتِيهِمْ لَيْسَ مَصْرُوفًا عَنْهُمْ وَحَاقَ بِهِم مَّا كَانُوا بِهِ يَسْتَهْزِئُونَ ۝ وَلَئِنْ أَذَقْنَا الْإِنسَانَ مِنَّا رَحْمَةً ثُمَّ نَزَعْنَاهَا مِنْهُ إِنَّهُ لَيَئُوسٌ كَفُورٌ ۝ وَلَئِنْ أَذَقْنَاهُ نَعْمَاءَ بَعْدَ ضَرَّاءَ مَسَّتْهُ لَيَقُولَنَّ ذَهَبَ السَّيِّئَاتُ عَنِّي ۚ إِنَّهُ لَفَرِحٌ فَخُورٌ ۝ إِلَّا الَّذِينَ صَبَرُوا وَعَمِلُوا الصَّالِحَاتِ أُولَٰئِكَ لَهُم مَّغْفِرَةٌ وَأَجْرٌ كَبِيرٌ ۝ فَلَعَلَّكَ تَارِكٌ بَعْضَ مَا يُوحَىٰ إِلَيْكَ وَضَائِقٌ بِهِ صَدْرُكَ أَن يَقُولُوا لَوْلَا أُنزِلَ عَلَيْهِ كَنزٌ أَوْ جَاءَ مَعَهُ مَلَكٌ ۚ إِنَّمَا أَنتَ نَذِيرٌ ۚ وَاللَّهُ عَلَىٰ كُلِّ شَيْءٍ وَكِيلٌ ۝

6. No living creature is there moving on the earth but its provision depends on God,[1] and He knows its every lodging and disposition (every stage of its life), and the duration of its stay and the moment of its transition therefrom. All is in a Manifest Book.

7. He it is Who has created the heavens and the earth in six days – His Supreme Throne was upon the water[2]– that He might make trial of you to manifest which of you is best in conduct. Yet, if you say (to people), "(Your proper abode is the Hereafter, where you will be either in bliss or suffering according to your conduct in the world. That is why) you are bound to be raised after death," those who persist in unbelief will say: "This is clearly nothing but an enchanting delusion."

8. Seeing that We postpone the punishment (with which We threaten them) until an appointed term, they are sure to say (in mockery): "What detains it that it does not come?" Beware! on the Day when it befalls them, it will not be averted from them, and that which they have been mocking at will overwhelm them.

9. If We let human taste some mercy from Us, and then take it away from him, he becomes hopeless, and thankless (forgetting all Our favors to him).

10. And if We let him taste ease and plenty after some hardship has visited him, he says: "Gone is all affliction from me!" Surely he is prone to vain exultation and self-glorifying.

11. Except those who are persevering and patient (neither despairing in affliction, nor exultant and self-glorifying in success), and do good, righteous deeds; it is they for whom is forgiveness and a great reward.[3]

12. Now it may be that you (O Messenger) are drawn to abandon some part of what is revealed to you (such as the verses concerning your Messengership), and your breast is constricted thereby, on account of their saying: "Why has a treasure not been sent down upon him, or an angel accompanying him (visible to us)?" But you are only a warner. It is God Who has everything in His care and under His control.

1. God has (pre-)ordained the provision each living being will consume during the life which He has appointed for it, and He has bound Himself to supply it. The plants have no power to move from one place to another; in other words, they are wholly submitted to God, their provision is ready beneath their feet. Animals labor to find their provision which has been (pre-)assigned for them, and when they are too young to do this they are fed by their mothers. As for new-born human beings, their provision is likewise sent to them through the breasts of their mothers by the Hand of Mercy. From the time when they begin to feel strong enough to find their own provision, they labor to procure it. No living being can obtain more than what was assigned for them by the All-Providing, nor do they die without having consumed it all.

It is a fact that one who works gains, while another who is lazy suffers deprivation. But this is not contrary to God's (pre-)assignment of every being's provision. For Destiny takes the cause and effect into consideration together. That is, God destines that a particular effect will come into being as a result of a particular cause. In any case, God has bound Himself to provide the essential, vital provision for every being.

It is also important to point out that although the explanations for Destiny and human free will are enough to convince human reason, the matter of Destiny and provision are not purely rational or scientific. It has a deep dimension of mystery relating to the Divine Being which cannot be perceived by reason. One can catch some glimpses of it only after having a certain degree of knowledge of God (*maʿrifah*) and spiritual experiences. Destiny and human free will mark the farthest point of perfect belief and submission, and are related to the inner experiences and spiritual states of the believers. Humanity has not been given the equipment with which to perceive every matter concerning the Divine Essence. If this had been the case, then the line between Divinity and humanity or between the Creator and the created would not have existed. So such matters as Destiny and provision have dimensions that pertain solely to God as two of His mysteries, and human beings can have

knowledge about them only to the extent that is needed to convince their reason.

2. For the creation of the heavens and the earth and the nature of the Supreme Throne, see *sūrah* 2: 28, note 28; *sūrah* 7: 54, note 13.

The statement, *His Supreme Throne was upon the water*, is either a continuation of *He has created the heavens and the earth in six days*, or adds an additional meaning to it, or it has both functions, which seems to be more befitting of the Qur'ān's matchless eloquence. In the first case, the meaning is: *He has created the heavens and the earth in six days and His Supreme Throne was upon the water*. When considered together with *We have made every living thing from water* (21: 30), this verse is indicating the stage where the heavens and the earth were created and the earth was made ready for life, denoting that it is water which lies at the essence of every thing and being. As is known, the main element in all things, including solid objects, is water. In a prayer recited by God's Messenger, upon him be peace and blessings, it is said: "All-Glorified is He Who has laid soil upon a fluid solidified." This means that rocks and mountains were formed as a result of this solidification and their crumbling into parts over time has formed the stratum of soil.

In the second case, the meaning is: *He it is Who has created the heavens and the earth in six days while His Supreme Throne was upon the water*. This denotes that there was water before the creation of the heavens and the earth. Considering that the Qur'ān sometimes uses the word *mā* (water) to mean fluid and liquid, the water here may mean a fluid substance which was the origin of both the heavens and the earth. According to some physicists, this substance is ether. The Prophetic Tradition, "God's Will and Favoring was upon *amā* both below and above of which there was no air," (at-Tirmidhī, "Tafsīr Hūd," HN: 3108) clarifies this point. It is possible that *amā* may be ether (*Tereddütler* 1: 219).

3. God wills good for humankind, but humankind incur evil. For an explanation, see Appendix 7.

222　سورة هود　٢٢٢

بِسْمِ اللّٰهِ

16. It is they for whom there is nothing in the Hereafter but the Fire. All that they produced in it (this world) has come to nothing and all that they were doing is fruitless, vain.

17. So, (how can you compare others with) one who stands on a clear evidence from his Lord (the Qur'ān), and is supported by a witness guided by Him,[5] and there was (revealed) before it the Book of Moses (confirming it) as a guide and mercy? Those (who make and understand the comparison) believe in it (the Qur'ān); while whoever from the diverse parties (belonging to different nations and faiths, knowingly) disbelieves[6] in it – the Fire will be their promised place. And so you should not have the least doubt of it (being revealed by God). Surely, it is the truth from your Lord, though most of the people do not believe.

18. Who is greater in doing wrong than he who fabricates falsehood in attribution to God? Such will be brought before their Lord, and the witnesses will say, "Those are they who lied in attribution to God. Surely, it is the due of the wrongdoers that God has excluded them from His mercy."

19. The ones who bar people from God's way and seek to make it crooked (wishing they could distort it);[7] and they, they are those who persistently disbelieve in the Hereafter.

───◈───

13. Or they say (about the Messenger): "He fabricates it (the Qur'ān)"? Say (to them): "Then produce ten invented *sūrah*s like it (in eloquence, meaningfulness and truth), and call to your aid whomever you can, apart from God, if you are truthful (in your claim, not deluded or just making up excuses to justify your unbelief).[4]

14. "If they (whom you call to your aid) cannot answer your call, then know that it (the Qur'ān) is sent down as based on God's Knowledge, and that there is no deity save Him. Will you, then, submit to God as Muslims?"

15. Whoever desires the present, worldly life and its outward shows, We recompense them for all that they do therein, and they are not deprived of their just due therein.

4. At a time in history when eloquence was most highly prized, the Qur'ān of miraculous exposition was revealed. Just as God Almighty had endowed Moses and Jesus, upon them be peace, with the miracles which were most suitable to their times, He used eloquence as the most notable aspect of the Qur'ān, the chief miracle of Prophet Muḥammad, upon him be peace and blessings. At the time that the Qur'ān was revealed, it first challenged the literary figures of the Arabian peninsula, and then all the people throughout the ages and at every level of knowledge and understanding until Judgment Day. For its challenging and some aspects of its miraculousness, see Appendix 6.

5. Although there have been different views concerning the evidence and the witness, what is meant by evidence, in our view, is the Qur'ān and what is meant by witness is a person or persons who are learned in the Divine Books. Verse 3: 18, which states that God, the angels, and those possessed of knowledge bear witness that there is no deity but He, and verse 46: 10, which states that a witness – 'Abdullāh ibn Salām – from among the Children of Israel bears witness to Muḥammad's Prophethood and the Divine origin of the Qur'ān, corroborate this meaning.

This meaning is also corroborated by the verse to come. It mentions the witnesses who testify against the unbelievers on Judgment Day. Verse 4: 41 also mentions such witnesses: *How, then, will it be (with people on the Day of Judgment) when We bring forward a witness from every community (to testify against them and that God's Rreligion was communicated to them), and bring you (O Messenger) as a witness against all those (whom your Message may have reached)?* Although the witnesses mentioned here may be the individual Messengers sent to their peoples, it also confirms the meaning that any witness mentioned in the Qur'ān with such import is a learned one, whether he is a Prophet or not.

6. The word translated as "disbelieving" is *kufr*, which means to cover. So, *kufr* in Islamic terminology means covering the truth knowingly; that it is covering the truth while under the influence of different factors, such as carnal desires, personal interests, prejudices, incorrect view-points, incorrect judgment, arrogance, ill intentions, and wrongdoing. Secondly, in order to judge someone as a *kāfir* (unbeliever), the truths of faith should have been conveyed to this person to the extent that, left to their (carnal) soul and conscience they can make a free choice between belief and unbelief, or this person should be in such a position that they can make the necessary investigations, being aware of belief and unbelief. The Islamic term for this action of conveying the truths of faith is *tablīgh*, meaning conveying a message fully and as clearly as possible. Those whom the Qur'ān condemns as unbelievers and the eternal inhabitants of the Fire are the people to whom the truths of faith have been thoroughly conveyed, to the extent that they have been convinced, yet they still prefer unbelief freely, being under the kinds of influences mentioned above.

7. God's way is a straight path that has been established by Him. What human beings must do is to know this path well in all its aspects and principles and to infer new rules in the secondary matters of law, which are subject to change in parallel with the change of time and place, according to the main, unchangeable principles of this path. But those who do not believe in it and the hypocrites have always wished that this path were crooked, in accordance with their desires in order to serve their interests. So, to attempt to make changes in this path (Islam) or to make it appear different from what it really is so that its enemies may approve of it – such attempts, however intensive or extensive, have always been in vain – is only a betrayal of the path.

أُوْلَٰٓئِكَ لَمْ يَكُونُوا۟ مُعْجِزِينَ فِى ٱلْأَرْضِ وَمَا كَانَ لَهُم مِّن دُونِ
ٱللَّهِ مِنْ أَوْلِيَآءَ ۘ يُضَٰعَفُ لَهُمُ ٱلْعَذَابُ ۚ مَا كَانُوا۟ يَسْتَطِيعُونَ
ٱلسَّمْعَ وَمَا كَانُوا۟ يُبْصِرُونَ ۝ أُوْلَٰٓئِكَ ٱلَّذِينَ خَسِرُوٓا۟
أَنفُسَهُمْ وَضَلَّ عَنْهُم مَّا كَانُوا۟ يَفْتَرُونَ ۝ لَا جَرَمَ
أَنَّهُمْ فِى ٱلْءَاخِرَةِ هُمُ ٱلْأَخْسَرُونَ ۝ إِنَّ ٱلَّذِينَ ءَامَنُوا۟ وَعَمِلُوا۟
ٱلصَّٰلِحَٰتِ وَأَخْبَتُوٓا۟ إِلَىٰ رَبِّهِمْ أُوْلَٰٓئِكَ أَصْحَٰبُ ٱلْجَنَّةِ ۖ هُمْ فِيهَا
خَٰلِدُونَ ۝ مَثَلُ ٱلْفَرِيقَيْنِ كَٱلْأَعْمَىٰ وَٱلْأَصَمِّ وَٱلْبَصِيرِ
وَٱلسَّمِيعِ ۚ هَلْ يَسْتَوِيَانِ مَثَلًا ۚ أَفَلَا تَذَكَّرُونَ ۝ وَلَقَدْ أَرْسَلْنَا
نُوحًا إِلَىٰ قَوْمِهِۦٓ إِنِّى لَكُمْ نَذِيرٌ مُّبِينٌ ۝ أَن لَّا تَعْبُدُوٓا۟ إِلَّا
ٱللَّهَ ۖ إِنِّىٓ أَخَافُ عَلَيْكُمْ عَذَابَ يَوْمٍ أَلِيمٍ ۝ فَقَالَ ٱلْمَلَأُ ٱلَّذِينَ
كَفَرُوا۟ مِن قَوْمِهِۦ مَا نَرَىٰكَ إِلَّا بَشَرًا مِّثْلَنَا وَمَا نَرَىٰكَ ٱتَّبَعَكَ
إِلَّا ٱلَّذِينَ هُمْ أَرَاذِلُنَا بَادِىَ ٱلرَّأْىِ وَمَا نَرَىٰ لَكُمْ عَلَيْنَا
مِن فَضْلٍ بَلْ نَظُنُّكُمْ كَٰذِبِينَ ۝ قَالَ يَٰقَوْمِ أَرَءَيْتُمْ
إِن كُنتُ عَلَىٰ بَيِّنَةٍ مِّن رَّبِّى وَءَاتَىٰنِى رَحْمَةً مِّنْ عِندِهِۦ فَعُمِّيَتْ
عَلَيْكُمْ أَنُلْزِمُكُمُوهَا وَأَنتُمْ لَهَا كَٰرِهُونَ ۝

―――――⊷―――――

way of false deities to worship besides God) have failed them.

22. Without doubt, in the Hereafter they will be the greatest losers.

23. As for those who believe and do good, righteous deeds, and have humbled themselves before their Lord, they are the companions of Paradise; they will abide therein.

24. These two classes of people are like the blind and deaf, and the seeing and hearing. Can they be likened to each other? Will you not, then, reflect and be mindful?

25. And assuredly We sent Noah to his people as Messenger (with the same message that he preached): "Surely, I am for you a plain warner (advising you for your good):

26. "That you worship none but God. Indeed I fear for you the punishment of a painful Day!"

27. The leading ones who disbelieved from among his people said: "We do not see you but as a mortal like ourselves, and we do not see that any follow you save those who are but the lowliest of us, without an opinion worthy of consideration; and we do not see you (and your followers) having any superiority over us;[8] rather, we consider that you are liars."

28. Noah said: "O my people! What do you think – if I stand on a clear evidence from my Lord, and He has granted me a mercy[9] from His Presence to which you have remained blind – can we force you to accept it when you are averse to it?

20. Those can never frustrate on earth (whatever God wills for it), nor can they find any guardians, apart from God, able to protect them against God. For them the punishment will be doubled (in the Hereafter). (Having wasted the faculties of hearing and seeing that God granted them), they have no longer been able to listen to (the revealed truths), nor have they any longer had sight to see.

21. Such are they who have ruined their selves, and all that they fabricated (by

8. Throughout history it has been typical of all disbelieving opponents of the Divine Religion that they have always seen the believers as being devoid of knowledge and thought, while they have acclaimed themselves as being intelligent and knowledgeable. This is partly because of their arrogance and self-pride, which,

is in fact, a reflection of an inferiority complex from which they have never been able to escape, and partly because the viewpoint of the unbelievers, based on material goods, personal interests, and this fleeting world, has always been different from that of the believers, which is established by God and based on belief in and worship of One God, and belief in the Unseen and the other pillars of faith, and universal moral values. The status of such unbelievers that derives from their posts, positions, and wealth, as well as their worldly interests, have blinded them to the Divine truths, and they have always acted vainly and in arrogance that arises from their riches and positions. For such people, superiority lies in wealth, higher position, race, or color, or physical constitution. However, in the end it has always been clear that it is the believers who hold the true viewpoint, who think correctly, and who are truly superior to the others; for them superiority lies in consciousness of God, true knowledge, and moral values.

In order to make a brief comparison between the civilizations set up by the believers and unbelievers, the following points need to be focused on:

The civilization of unbelievers is mostly founded upon five negative principles: It is based upon power, and power is inclined toward oppression; it seeks to realize individual self-interest, even though this causes people to rush about madly trying to earn possessions; it considers life as a struggle, which causes internal and external conflict; it unifies through national and/or racial separatism, and feeds this selfish solidarity by swallowing the resources and territories of "others," both of which engender terrible conflict; and it strives to satisfy novel caprices or aroused desires (whether the satisfaction is real or not), and so brutalizes people's tastes and aspirations.

Islamic civilization rests upon right (not power), which requires justice and balance; it encourages virtue, which spurs mutual affection and love; it considers life as consisting of mutual help, which leads to unity and solidarity; it unifies people through a common religion in a common state, leading them to internal peace, and brotherhood and sisterhood, and it creates a willing self-defense against external enemies, guiding people to the truth. It elevates people, through knowledge and moral perfection, to higher ranks of humanity.

If we compare a believer with an unbeliever, the following points come to our attention:

Haughty, refractory unbelievers, such as those (we see) opposing the Messengers are usually Pharaoh-like tyrants, yet they abuse themselves by bowing in worship before the meanest things if they perceive it to be in their interest to do so. They are stubborn, misleading, and unyielding, but so wretched that they accept endless degradation for the attainment of one pleasure; they are unbending, but so mean as to kiss the feet of evil people for a base advantage. They are conceited and domineering, but unable to find any point of support in their hearts, are utterly impotent and vainglorious tyrants. Such people are nothing less than self-centered egoists who strive to gratify their material and carnal desires, pursuers of personal interests and certain national interests.

On the other hand, the sincere believers are worshipping servants of God, but they do not degrade themselves by bowing in worship before even the greatest of the created. They are dignified servants who do not worship in order to obtain a benefit, even Paradise. They are modest, mild, and gentle, but only lower themselves voluntarily before their Creator, never exceeding what He has permitted. They are aware of their innate weaknesses and needs as created beings, but are independent because the Munificent Owner provides them with wealth. Relying on their Master's infinite Power, they are powerful. They act and strive purely for the sake and pleasure of God, and so as to be graced with virtue (*The Words*, "the 12th Word," 147).

9. Evidence here means the things which confirm the Divine Messengership, such as the Divine Book, miracles, and the Messengers' laudable morals, and the special mercy granted to them. The special mercy granted to them constitutes Messengership, with all its attributes, such as absolute certainty in belief, truthfulness, trustworthiness, intelligence, knowledge, receiving Revelation, and being free from all kinds of intellectual and bodily defects.

224　سُورَةُ هُودٍ　٢٢٤

وَيَاقَوْمِ لَآ أَسْـَٔلُكُمْ عَلَيْهِ مَالًا إِنْ أَجْرِىَ إِلَّا عَلَى اللَّهِ وَمَآ أَنَا۠
بِطَارِدِ الَّذِينَ ءَامَنُوٓا۟ إِنَّهُم مُّلَٰقُوا۟ رَبِّهِمْ وَلَٰكِنِّىٓ أَرَىٰكُمْ قَوْمًا
تَجْهَلُونَ ۝ وَيَاقَوْمِ مَن يَنصُرُنِى مِنَ اللَّهِ إِن طَرَدتُّهُمْ ۚ أَفَلَا
تَذَكَّرُونَ ۝ وَلَآ أَقُولُ لَكُمْ عِندِى خَزَآئِنُ اللَّهِ وَلَآ أَعْلَمُ
الْغَيْبَ وَلَآ أَقُولُ إِنِّى مَلَكٌ وَلَآ أَقُولُ لِلَّذِينَ تَزْدَرِىٓ
أَعْيُنُكُمْ لَن يُؤْتِيَهُمُ اللَّهُ خَيْرًا ۖ اللَّهُ أَعْلَمُ بِمَا فِىٓ أَنفُسِهِمْ ۖ
إِنِّىٓ إِذًا لَّمِنَ الظَّٰلِمِينَ ۝ قَالُوا۟ يَٰنُوحُ قَدْ جَٰدَلْتَنَا فَأَكْثَرْتَ
جِدَٰلَنَا فَأْتِنَا بِمَا تَعِدُنَآ إِن كُنتَ مِنَ الصَّٰدِقِينَ ۝
قَالَ إِنَّمَا يَأْتِيكُم بِهِ اللَّهُ إِن شَآءَ وَمَآ أَنتُم بِمُعْجِزِينَ ۝
وَلَا يَنفَعُكُمْ نُصْحِىٓ إِنْ أَرَدتُّ أَنْ أَنصَحَ لَكُمْ إِن كَانَ اللَّهُ يُرِيدُ
أَن يُغْوِيَكُمْ ۚ هُوَ رَبُّكُمْ وَإِلَيْهِ تُرْجَعُونَ ۝ أَمْ يَقُولُونَ
افْتَرَىٰهُ ۖ قُلْ إِنِ افْتَرَيْتُهُ فَعَلَىَّ إِجْرَامِى وَأَنَا۠ بَرِىٓءٌ مِّمَّا تُجْرِمُونَ
۝ وَأُوحِىَ إِلَىٰ نُوحٍ أَنَّهُۥ لَن يُؤْمِنَ مِن قَوْمِكَ إِلَّا مَن قَدْ
ءَامَنَ فَلَا تَبْتَئِسْ بِمَا كَانُوا۟ يَفْعَلُونَ ۝ وَاصْنَعِ الْفُلْكَ بِأَعْيُنِنَا
وَوَحْيِنَا وَلَا تُخَٰطِبْنِى فِى الَّذِينَ ظَلَمُوٓا۟ ۚ إِنَّهُم مُّغْرَقُونَ ۝

---

29. "O my people! I ask of you no wealth for it (for conveying the Message to you); my wage is due only from God. I will not drive away those who believe; they are destined to meet their Lord (Who will treat them as they should be treated) – whereas I see you as a people acting in ignorance.

30. "O my people! Who could help me against God were I to drive them away? Will you not then reflect and be mindful?

31. "And I do not say to you that with me are the treasures of God, nor do I know the Unseen (what is stored in the future), nor do I say that I am an angel, nor do I say of those, whom your eyes hold in contempt, that God will not grant them some good. God knows best whatever is in their bosoms (what kind of people they are in their inner worlds). (If I drove them away or spoke ill of them), then I would indeed be among the wrongdoers."

32. They said: "O Noah! You have argued with us, and have prolonged your arguments; so stop arguing with us and, if you are telling the truth, bring upon us what you have been threatening us with!"

33. Noah said: "Only God can bring it upon you, if He wills; and you can never be frustrators (of His will).

34. "My counsel – much as I would counsel you – will not benefit you, if God has willed that you be and remain misguided. He is your Lord (Who created you, and nurtures, sustains and protects you), and you are on the way to return to Him."

35. Do they (the idolaters) say (of you, O Messenger): "He has fabricated it (invented all those stories and the Qur'ān containing them)?" Say: "If indeed I fabricate it, then upon me falls my sin, but (as you are slandering me to excuse your own willful persistence in unbelief, know that) I am free of the sins you have been committing."

36. And it was revealed to Noah (by Us): "Never will any of your people believe except those who have already believed. Then, do not be distressed because of what they have been doing.

37. "Build the Ark (which We have described to you) under Our eyes and in accordance with Our instructions to be revealed (to you), and do not plead with Me for those who have persisted in wrongdoing. They are bound to be drowned."

٢٢٥   ٱلْجُزْءُ ٱلثَّانِى عَشَرَ   225

وَيَصْنَعُ الْفُلْكَ وَكُلَّمَا مَرَّ عَلَيْهِ مَلَأٌ مِّن قَوْمِهِ سَخِرُوا مِنْهُ
قَالَ إِن تَسْخَرُوا مِنَّا فَإِنَّا نَسْخَرُ مِنكُمْ كَمَا تَسْخَرُونَ ۞
فَسَوْفَ تَعْلَمُونَ مَن يَأْتِيهِ عَذَابٌ يُخْزِيهِ وَيَحِلُّ عَلَيْهِ عَذَابٌ
مُّقِيمٌ ۞ حَتَّىٰ إِذَا جَاءَ أَمْرُنَا وَفَارَ التَّنُّورُ قُلْنَا احْمِلْ فِيهَا
مِن كُلٍّ زَوْجَيْنِ اثْنَيْنِ وَأَهْلَكَ إِلَّا مَن سَبَقَ عَلَيْهِ الْقَوْلُ
وَمَنْ آمَنَ وَمَا آمَنَ مَعَهُ إِلَّا قَلِيلٌ ۞ وَقَالَ ارْكَبُوا فِيهَا
بِسْمِ اللَّهِ مَجْرَاهَا وَمُرْسَاهَا إِنَّ رَبِّي لَغَفُورٌ رَّحِيمٌ ۞ وَهِيَ
تَجْرِي بِهِمْ فِي مَوْجٍ كَالْجِبَالِ وَنَادَىٰ نُوحٌ ابْنَهُ وَكَانَ فِي
مَعْزِلٍ يَا بُنَيَّ ارْكَب مَّعَنَا وَلَا تَكُن مَّعَ الْكَافِرِينَ ۞ قَالَ
سَآوِي إِلَىٰ جَبَلٍ يَعْصِمُنِي مِنَ الْمَاءِ قَالَ لَا عَاصِمَ الْيَوْمَ
مِنْ أَمْرِ اللَّهِ إِلَّا مَن رَّحِمَ وَحَالَ بَيْنَهُمَا الْمَوْجُ فَكَانَ مِنَ
الْمُغْرَقِينَ ۞ وَقِيلَ يَا أَرْضُ ابْلَعِي مَاءَكِ وَيَا سَمَاءُ أَقْلِعِي وَغِيضَ
الْمَاءُ وَقُضِيَ الْأَمْرُ وَاسْتَوَتْ عَلَى الْجُودِيِّ وَقِيلَ بُعْدًا
لِّلْقَوْمِ الظَّالِمِينَ ۞ وَنَادَىٰ نُوحٌ رَّبَّهُ فَقَالَ رَبِّ إِنَّ ابْنِي مِنْ
أَهْلِي وَإِنَّ وَعْدَكَ الْحَقُّ وَأَنتَ أَحْكَمُ الْحَاكِمِينَ ۞

---

38. And so Noah set to building the Ark. And every time the leading ones among his people passed by him, they mocked at him. He said: "Now you are mocking us, but (a day will come when) we mock you just as you mock us.

39. "And so shall you know upon whom will come a punishment which will disgrace him, and upon whom will alight a lasting punishment (in the Hereafter)."

40. (And so it went on) until the time when Our command came and the boiler started boiling over.[10] We said (to Noah): "Embark in it a pair of each kind (of living creature), and your family, except those against whom Our sentence has already been passed, and those who believe." And those who believed with him were few.

41. Noah said, "Board it!" (and all the people and the pairs of creatures God willed should be saved were settled in the Ark). "In God's Name be its course and its mooring. Surely my Lord is All-Forgiving, All-Compassionate."

42. So the Ark floated with them amid waves like mountains, and Noah cried out to a son of his who was standing apart: "Embark with us, my son, and do not be with the unbelievers!"

43. He said: "I will betake myself to a mountain that will protect me from the waters!"[11] He (Noah) said: "Today there is no protection from God's judgment except for him on whom He has mercy." And the waves came between them, and he (the son) was among the drowned.

44. And it was said: "O earth, swallow up your waters! And, O sky, cease (your rain)!"[12] And the waters were made to subside, and (by God's will) the affair was accomplished. Then the Ark came to rest on al-Jūdī, and it was said: "Away with the wrongdoing people!"

45. Noah called out to his Lord, saying: "O my Lord, my son was of my family (as a believer), and Your promise is surely true (for my believing family members), and You are the Most Just of judges."

10. Different comments have been made on *fāra 't-tannūr*, which literally means "the oven spurted out (of water)." Some commentators such as Ibn Jarīr at-Tabarī and Ibn al-Kathīr are of the opinion that since *tannūr* also means the surface of the earth, the expression literally means that water gushed over the face of the earth. According to Ibn Kathīr, the gushing waters turned the earth into springs. Elmalılı Hamdi Yazır, a great Turkish interpreter of the twentieth century, deals with all such views from a linguistic viewpoint and concludes that *fāra 't-tannūr* marks the start of the Flood and therefore means that the oven or kiln of the Ark was heated to run the Ark.

This expression alludes to the notion that Noah's Ark was powered by steam. It is this point which leads some modern commentators to think that *fāra 't-tannūr* cannot mean that the oven (functioning as a boiler) boiled over. They assert that it is impossible that a steam-powered ship was built at the time of Noah. Modern historians and scientists tend to see the Flood as a legend, although this is contrary to the modern concept of science. Science requires that it should be investigated. In addition, an ark, which could accommodate one or two pairs from all animals, or at least from all domesticated animals, as well as Noah's family and the believers, however few they were, and which was able to sail among mountain-like waves, as will be mentioned in verse 42 below, could not be a mere sailboat or a simple vessel. According to some who base their theory on the *fulk*, the original word for Ark, also means fleet; therefore Noah's Ark was in actual fact a fleet. It was built under God's "Eyes" and in accordance with His revealed instructions. Although it was Noah's miracle, it also shows to what extent science and technology, especially engineering, had advanced during the time of this Prophet.

11. This response is typical of a materialist or naturalist who does not believe in God and His supreme dominion over the entire universe, and displays the characteristic of Noah's people and how persistent unbelievers they were.

12. A word should be considered from the perspectives, "Who said it?" To whom it was said?" and "Why was it said?" The one who can order the earth "O earth, swallow up your waters!", and the sky, "O sky, cease (your rain)!" can only be one who has absolute dominion over both the sky and the earth. This one can only be God. Such orders given by any other than God would be absurd. Both the sky and the earth are under God's dominion and since they obey Him alone and work under His absolute rule, they continue to exist in order and balance. Even if they sometimes are set to move, the extent of the sins and wrongs committed has not yet reached the point of their destruction. When the wrong, unbelief, and rebellion come to the point where they will completely destroy the order and balance on earth, then it will be Doomsday.

The verse emphasizes that it was the sky which sent the rain and the earth which caused the waters to gush. Such a style is meaningful from two perspectives: one is that the entire universe obeys God as if it were a conscious being. The other is that the sky and the earth or, rather, the angels that represent these things before God and who are in charge of them, and other spirit beings that inhabit the heavens became angry at the unbelief and rebellion of human beings. Verse 44: 29 states that neither the heaven nor the earth shed tears over the drowning of the Pharaoh and his army. It may also be that the sky and the earth, together with whatever there is in them, are affected in some way by the thoughts, beliefs, attitudes, and actions of conscious beings living on the earth.

سُوۡرَةُ هُوۡد

٢٢٦

قَالَ يَا نُوحُ إِنَّهُ لَيْسَ مِنْ أَهْلِكَ إِنَّهُ عَمَلٌ غَيْرُ صَالِحٍ فَلَا تَسْأَلْنِ
مَا لَيْسَ لَكَ بِهِ عِلْمٌ إِنِّيٓ أَعِظُكَ أَنْ تَكُونَ مِنَ الْجَاهِلِينَ
۞ قَالَ رَبِّ إِنِّيٓ أَعُوذُ بِكَ أَنْ أَسْأَلَكَ مَا لَيْسَ لِي بِهِ عِلْمٌ
وَإِلَّا تَغْفِرْ لِي وَتَرْحَمْنِيٓ أَكُنْ مِنَ الْخَاسِرِينَ ۞ قِيلَ يَا نُوحُ
اهْبِطْ بِسَلَامٍ مِنَّا وَبَرَكَاتٍ عَلَيْكَ وَعَلَىٰٓ أُمَمٍ مِمَّنْ مَعَكَ وَأُمَمٌ
سَنُمَتِّعُهُمْ ثُمَّ يَمَسُّهُمْ مِنَّا عَذَابٌ أَلِيمٌ ۞ تِلْكَ مِنْ أَنْبَاءِ
الْغَيْبِ نُوحِيهَآ إِلَيْكَ مَا كُنْتَ تَعْلَمُهَآ أَنْتَ وَلَا قَوْمُكَ مِنْ قَبْلِ
هَٰذَا فَاصْبِرْ إِنَّ الْعَاقِبَةَ لِلْمُتَّقِينَ ۞ وَإِلَىٰ عَادٍ أَخَاهُمْ هُودًا
قَالَ يَا قَوْمِ اعْبُدُوا اللَّهَ مَا لَكُمْ مِنْ إِلَٰهٍ غَيْرُهُ إِنْ أَنْتُمْ
إِلَّا مُفْتَرُونَ ۞ يَا قَوْمِ لَآ أَسْأَلُكُمْ عَلَيْهِ أَجْرًا إِنْ
أَجْرِيَ إِلَّا عَلَى الَّذِي فَطَرَنِيٓ أَفَلَا تَعْقِلُونَ ۞ وَيَا قَوْمِ
اسْتَغْفِرُوا رَبَّكُمْ ثُمَّ تُوبُوٓا إِلَيْهِ يُرْسِلِ السَّمَآءَ عَلَيْكُمْ
مِدْرَارًا وَيَزِدْكُمْ قُوَّةً إِلَىٰ قُوَّتِكُمْ وَلَا تَتَوَلَّوْا
مُجْرِمِينَ ۞ قَالُوا يَا هُودُ مَا جِئْتَنَا بِبَيِّنَةٍ وَمَا نَحْنُ بِتَارِكِيٓ
آلِهَتِنَا عَنْ قَوْلِكَ وَمَا نَحْنُ لَكَ بِمُؤْمِنِينَ ۞

46. (God) said: "O Noah! he (being an unbeliever) is not of your family. He is one of unrighteous conduct (which embodied his unbelief). So do not ask of Me what you have no knowledge of. I admonish you so that you do not behave as one among the ignorant."[13]

47. (Noah) said: "O my Lord! I seek refuge in You, lest I should ask of You what I have no knowledge of. And unless You forgive me and have mercy on me, I will indeed be among the losers."

48. He was told: "O Noah! Get you down in peace and safety from Us, and with blessings upon you and upon the communities (of believers) who are with you (and those to descend from you and them). (There will also be other) communities (of unbelievers) – We will provide for them to enjoy themselves for a term and then there will visit them from Us a painful punishment."[14]

49. Those are accounts of some exemplary events of the unseen (a time and realm beyond any created's perception) that We reveal to you, (O Messenger). Neither you nor your people knew them before this.[15] Then (seeing that there is no substantial difference between the conditions in which the Messengers carried out their missions and the reactions they encountered) be patient (with their reactions and their persistence in unbelief). The (final, happy) outcome is in favor of the God-revering, pious.

50. And to (the people of) 'Ād We sent their brother Hūd. He said: "O my people! Worship God alone: you have no deity other than Him. You are only fabrica-

tors of falsehood (in attributing partners to Him).

51. "O my people! I ask of you no wage for it (for conveying the Message to you); my wage is due from only Him Who originated me with a particular character. Will you not use your reason?

52. "O my people! Implore your Lord to forgive you (for the sins you have so far committed) and turn to Him repentant that He may cause the sky to pour down upon you abundant rain, and add strength to your strength. So, do not turn your backs (on this message that I convey to you), as disbelieving criminals!"

53. "O Hūd!" they said: "You have brought us no clear sign (– a miracle to prove your Messengership). We are not going to forsake our deities on your mere saying so, the more so as we do not believe you.

13. The Prophet Noah, upon him be God's peace, is one of the five greatest Messengers mentioned in the Qur'ān (42: 13). He prayed to God to forgive him, his parents, and those who believed among his family, and all believers, men and women (71: 28). Just before the Flood started, as mentioned above (verse: 40), God ordered him to take into the Ark those who believed from among his family and other believers. He saw one of his sons standing aloof and he invited him to embark. He thought his son was a believer because he had not seen any signs of unbelief in him. We understand from his prayer that he was aware that there were some among his family who were not believers. For this reason, he prayed not for all of his family; but for only those who believed among them. It can easily be concluded from his prayer and his statement that, "My son was of my family," that he thought of his son as a believer. His son was obviously a believer in appearance, but not in truth. He did not display any sign of unbelief which he had concealed in his heart; that is, he was a hypocrite. This is also evident from the Almighty's answer "what you have no knowledge of." In the original of Noah's statement which has been translated as *O my Lord, my son was of my family (as a believer), and Your promise is surely true (for my believing family members), and You are the Most Just of judges,*" the parenthetical phrases (*as a believer*) and (*for my believing family members*) are not there, but they are implied. So his purpose for calling out in this way was to discover the Divine purpose for or wisdom in the drowning of a person whom he thought to be a believer. God Almighty informed him of the fact that his son was not a believer, and forewarned him against making any requests on behalf of a disbelieving one.

Though a miracle of eloquence, the reason why such a detail in the story of Noah should be included in the Qur'ān must be sought in its purpose for narrating the exemplary phases of the Messengers' missions. When this *sūrah* was revealed, many families in Makkah were divided into believers and unbelievers. However important a blood relationship is with respect to certain mutual rights and matters of law, such as guardianship and inheritance, the relationship that emanates from faith is more important. Although it has no part in legal matters, such as inheritance, it forms the basic foundation upon which the relationship among believers is based. The blood relationship should provide a support for it. In addition, a difference in faith invalidates the legal rights or responsibilities, such as guardianship and inheritance. A disbelieving child cannot inherit from believing parents. Any disbelieving member of a family cannot be preferred over any believing one even though they do not belong to that family (58: 22).

14. It is controversial whether the Flood stretched throughout the earth or if it was localized. As far as we can understand from this verse, the Flood took place in the inhabited part of the world and encompassed all the existing people.

It has been pointed out before (*sūrah* 7, note 15) that the Flood took place in Iraq and neighboring regions. However, there are some differences of opinion about the mountain upon which the Ark came to rest. According to the Bible, it was Mt. Ararat. The Qur'ān names it as al-Jūdī. Al-Jūdī means the heights, and this does not contradict the statement that it was Mt. Ararat. On the other hand, there is a mountain located south of Lake Van in Turkey that rises to a height of 7,700 feet which is known as Mount Judi. The local tribesmen there maintain that the Ark drifted to a high point on the Judi mountain chain and that the remains of it are still located at the top.

Mt. Judi overlooks the all-important Mesopotamian plain and is notable for the many archaeological ruins found in and around the mountain. There are also many references to this mountain in ancient history. Sennacherib (700 BC), the Assyrian king, carved relieves of himself in the rock on the side of the mountain. The Nestorians (a Christian sect) built several monasteries around the mountain, including one at the summit, known as "The Cloister of the Ark." It was destroyed by lightning in 766

AD. In 1910, Gertrude Bell explored the area and found a stone structure still at the summit in the shape of a ship, which was known by the locals as "Sefîne-i Nebî Nuh" (The Ship of Noah). Bell also reported that on September 14 every year Christians, Jews, Muslims, Sabaeans, and Yezidis gather on the mountain to commemorate Noah's sacrifice. As late as 1949 two Turkish journalists claimed to have seen the Ark on this mountain, a ship measuring 500 feet in length!

There is another mountain in Turkey called Judi, which is located 32 kilometers from Mount Ararat. In the Jan 16 1994 issue, *The Observer* (London) published the news that a team of scientists had found Noah's Ark on that mountain. Some investigators, both Muslims and Christians, are of the opinion that the Ararat mentioned in the Bible is the name of, not a mountain, but the region where Mount Ararat is located, and therefore the Ark having come to rest upon al-Jūdī or on Ararat is not contradictory (www.arksearch.com/najudi/htm; www.trustthebible.com/ark.htm).

15. From one perspective, the Qur'ān presents a lot of history of bygone nations and predictions about the near or distant future. Some of its predictions are explicit while some others are implicit, or alluded to. It is impossible to contradict its accounts of historical events, therefore, whatever it predicts either has come true or will come true when its time is due. What researchers should do is to carry out studies in the light of the Qur'ān.

As pointed out in the verse, it was impossible for God's Messenger to know the histories of the Prophets and their peoples. But, based on Divine Revelation and with utmost confidence in his mission, he conveyed both the histories of bygone nations and many predictions concerning future important events. This is a challenge to all ages and peoples, including historians and other researchers, and is one of the undeniable proofs of His Prophethood.

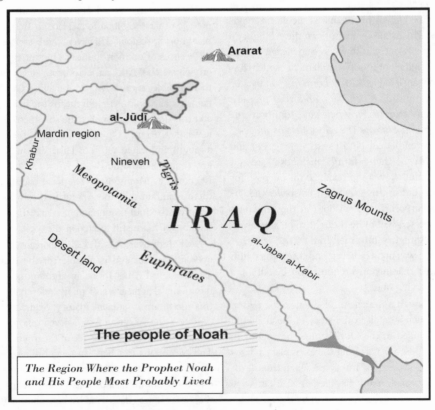

The people of Noah

The Region Where the Prophet Noah and His People Most Probably Lived

إِن نَّقُولُ إِلَّا اعْتَرَاكَ بَعْضُ الِهَتِنَا بِسُوءٍ قَالَ إِنِّي أُشْهِدُ اللَّهَ وَاشْهَدُوا أَنِّي بَرِيٓءٌ مِّمَّا تُشْرِكُونَ ۝ مِن دُونِهِ فَكِيدُونِي جَمِيعًا ثُمَّ لَا تُنظِرُونِ ۝ إِنِّي تَوَكَّلْتُ عَلَى اللَّهِ رَبِّي وَرَبِّكُم مَّا مِن دَابَّةٍ إِلَّا هُوَ ءَاخِذٌ بِنَاصِيَتِهَا إِنَّ رَبِّي عَلَىٰ صِرَاطٍ مُّسْتَقِيمٍ ۝ فَإِن تَوَلَّوْا فَقَدْ أَبْلَغْتُكُم مَّآ أُرْسِلْتُ بِهِ إِلَيْكُمْ وَيَسْتَخْلِفُ رَبِّي قَوْمًا غَيْرَكُمْ وَلَا تَضُرُّونَهُ شَيْئًا إِنَّ رَبِّي عَلَى كُلِّ شَيْءٍ حَفِيظٌ ۝ وَلَمَّا جَآءَ أَمْرُنَا نَجَّيْنَا هُودًا وَالَّذِينَ ءَامَنُوا مَعَهُ بِرَحْمَةٍ مِّنَّا وَنَجَّيْنَاهُم مِّنْ عَذَابٍ غَلِيظٍ ۝ وَتِلْكَ عَادٌ جَحَدُوا بِآيَاتِ رَبِّهِمْ وَعَصَوْا رُسُلَهُ وَاتَّبَعُوٓا أَمْرَ كُلِّ جَبَّارٍ عَنِيدٍ ۝ وَأُتْبِعُوا فِي هَٰذِهِ الدُّنْيَا لَعْنَةً وَيَوْمَ الْقِيَامَةِ أَلَآ إِنَّ عَادًا كَفَرُوا رَبَّهُمْ أَلَا بُعْدًا لِّعَادٍ قَوْمِ هُودٍ ۝ وَإِلَىٰ ثَمُودَ أَخَاهُمْ صَالِحًا قَالَ يَا قَوْمِ اعْبُدُوا اللَّهَ مَا لَكُم مِّنْ إِلَٰهٍ غَيْرُهُ هُوَ أَنشَأَكُم مِّنَ الْأَرْضِ وَاسْتَعْمَرَكُمْ فِيهَا فَاسْتَغْفِرُوهُ ثُمَّ تُوبُوٓا إِلَيْهِ إِنَّ رَبِّي قَرِيبٌ مُّجِيبٌ ۝ قَالُوا يَا صَالِحُ قَدْ كُنتَ فِينَا مَرْجُوًّا قَبْلَ هَٰذَآ أَتَنْهَانَآ أَن نَّعْبُدَ مَا يَعْبُدُ ءَابَآؤُنَا وَإِنَّنَا لَفِي شَكٍّ مِّمَّا تَدْعُونَآ إِلَيْهِ مُرِيبٍ ۝

54. "We say only that some of our deities have possessed you with evil." Hūd said: "Surely I call God to witness, and you too be witnesses, that I am free of what you associate (with God as partners with Him),

55. "Apart from Him (I only take Him as Deity and Lord). So, scheme against me all together, and then give me no respite!

56. "I have put my trust in God, my Lord and your Lord. No living creature is there but He holds it by its forelock and keeps it under His complete control. Surely, my Lord is on a straight path (He governs all that exists and carries out His decrees rightly and with absolute justice).

57. "If you turn your backs (on the Message I convey to you, know that) I have conveyed to you what I was sent with to you. My Lord will (if you continue in your rejection) cause another people to take your place, whereas you cannot harm Him in the least. Surely, my Lord keeps watch and record of all things."

58. And when Our judgment came to pass (because the people of 'Ād did continue in their rejection), We saved Hūd and those who believed with him out of a mercy from Us (because of their faith, righteousness and patience): We saved them from a harsh punishment.

59. Such were the 'Ād. They obstinately rejected the Revelations of their Lord (the signs and miracles proving His Oneness and all other essentials of faith) and they rebelled against His Messengers (by rejecting the Messenger – Hūd – sent to them), and followed every stubborn tyrant.

60. And a curse was made to pursue them in this world and on the Day of Resurrection. Beware! the 'Ād disbelieved in their Lord with ingratitude; so away with the 'Ād, the people of Hūd!

61. And to (the people of) Thamūd (We sent) their brother Ṣāliḥ (as Messenger to convey the same message): "O my people! Worship God alone: you have no deity other than Him. He has raised you from the earth and settled you in it, enabling your dignity and prosperity. So, ask forgiveness of Him (for the sins you have so far committed) and turn to Him repentant. Assuredly, my Lord is All-Near, All-Responsive (to the call of all beings that call upon Him)."

62. They said: "O Ṣāliḥ! Before this, you were a source of hope among us. Would you now seek to prevent us from worshipping what our forefathers used to worship? Indeed we are in real doubt concerning what you call us to."

228   سُوۡرَةُ هُوۡدٍ   ٢٢٨

قَالَ يَٰقَوۡمِ أَرَءَيۡتُمۡ إِن كُنتُ عَلَىٰ بَيِّنَةٖ مِّن رَّبِّي وَءَاتَىٰنِي مِنۡهُ رَحۡمَةٗ
فَمَن يَنصُرُنِي مِنَ ٱللَّهِ إِنۡ عَصَيۡتُهُۥ ۖ فَمَا تَزِيدُونَنِي غَيۡرَ تَخۡسِيرٖ ۝
وَيَٰقَوۡمِ هَٰذِهِۦ نَاقَةُ ٱللَّهِ لَكُمۡ ءَايَةٗ فَذَرُوهَا تَأۡكُلۡ فِيٓ أَرۡضِ ٱللَّهِ
وَلَا تَمَسُّوهَا بِسُوٓءٖ فَيَأۡخُذَكُمۡ عَذَابٞ قَرِيبٞ ۝ فَعَقَرُوهَا
فَقَالَ تَمَتَّعُواْ فِي دَارِكُمۡ ثَلَٰثَةَ أَيَّامٖ ذَٰلِكَ وَعۡدٌ غَيۡرُ مَكۡذُوبٖ
۝ فَلَمَّا جَآءَ أَمۡرُنَا نَجَّيۡنَا صَٰلِحٗا وَٱلَّذِينَ ءَامَنُواْ مَعَهُۥ
بِرَحۡمَةٖ مِّنَّا وَمِنۡ خِزۡيِ يَوۡمِئِذٍ ۗ إِنَّ رَبَّكَ هُوَ ٱلۡقَوِيُّ ٱلۡعَزِيزُ
۝ وَأَخَذَ ٱلَّذِينَ ظَلَمُواْ ٱلصَّيۡحَةُ فَأَصۡبَحُواْ فِي دِيَٰرِهِمۡ
جَٰثِمِينَ ۝ كَأَن لَّمۡ يَغۡنَوۡاْ فِيهَآ ۗ أَلَآ إِنَّ ثَمُودَاْ كَفَرُواْ رَبَّهُمۡ ۗ
أَلَا بُعۡدٗا لِّثَمُودَ ۝ وَلَقَدۡ جَآءَتۡ رُسُلُنَآ إِبۡرَٰهِيمَ بِٱلۡبُشۡرَىٰ
قَالُواْ سَلَٰمٗا ۖ قَالَ سَلَٰمٞ ۖ فَمَا لَبِثَ أَن جَآءَ بِعِجۡلٍ حَنِيذٖ
۝ فَلَمَّا رَءَآ أَيۡدِيَهُمۡ لَا تَصِلُ إِلَيۡهِ نَكِرَهُمۡ وَأَوۡجَسَ
مِنۡهُمۡ خِيفَةٗ ۚ قَالُواْ لَا تَخَفۡ إِنَّآ أُرۡسِلۡنَآ إِلَىٰ قَوۡمِ
لُوطٖ ۝ وَٱمۡرَأَتُهُۥ قَآئِمَةٞ فَضَحِكَتۡ فَبَشَّرۡنَٰهَا
بِإِسۡحَٰقَ وَمِن وَرَآءِ إِسۡحَٰقَ يَعۡقُوبَ ۝

---

63. He said: "O my people! What do you think – if I stand on a clear evidence from my Lord, and He has granted me a mercy from Himself – who could help me against God were I to disobey Him? You would add to me nothing but ruin.

64. "O my people! This is the she-camel from God as a sign for you (of the kind you demand to see before you believe). So leave her alone to pasture on God's earth, and touch her with no evil lest an imminent punishment should seize you."

65. But (unable to bear to see her as an evidence of the truth of Ṣāliḥ's message) they cruelly slaughtered her. Then he (Ṣāliḥ) said: "Enjoy the life in your habitations three days more, (then will be your ruin). This is a threat that will not be proved false."

66. So when Our judgment came to pass, We saved Ṣāliḥ and those who believed with him out of mercy from Us (because of their faith, righteousness, and patience), from the ignominy of that day. Surely your Lord is the All-Powerful, the All-Glorious with irresistible might.

67. And the awful blast seized those who committed the greatest wrong (by associating partners with God), so that they lay prostrate lifeless in their very dwellings,

68. As though they had never lived there in prosperity. Beware! The Thamūd disbelieved in their Lord (and were ungrateful for His favors), so away with the Thamūd!

69. And Our (heavenly) envoys came (in human form) to Abraham with glad tidings. They said "Peace!", and he (returning the greeting) said "Peace!" Without delay, he brought them a roasted calf.

70. But when he saw that their hands did not reach out to it, he was doubtful of them (deeming their conduct strange) and became apprehensive of them.[16] They said: "Do not fear! We have been sent to the people of Lot."

71. Meanwhile his (old, infertile) wife, standing by, felt she was menstruating (and smiled); and We gave her the glad tidings of (the birth of) Isaac and, after Isaac, of (his son) Jacob.

---

16. According to the existing traditions where the Prophet Abraham lived, if a guest held back from eating food that was offered, it meant that that person had an evil intention. That is why the Prophet Abraham became apprehensive of the guests.

قَالَتْ يَاوَيْلَتَىٰٓ ءَاَلِدُ وَاَنَا۠ عَجُوزٌ وَهٰذَا بَعْلِى شَيْخًا ۖ اِنَّ
هٰذَا لَشَىْءٌ عَجِيبٌ ۞ قَالُوٓا اَتَعْجَبِينَ مِنْ اَمْرِ اللّٰهِ ۖ رَحْمَتُ
اللّٰهِ وَبَرَكَاتُهُ عَلَيْكُمْ اَهْلَ الْبَيْتِ ۚ اِنَّهُ حَمِيدٌ مَجِيدٌ ۞ فَلَمَّا ذَهَبَ
عَنْ اِبْرٰهِيمَ الرَّوْعُ وَجَاءَتْهُ الْبُشْرٰى يُجَادِلُنَا فِى قَوْمِ لُوطٍ ۞
اِنَّ اِبْرٰهِيمَ لَحَلِيمٌ اَوَّاهٌ مُنِيبٌ ۞ يَآ اِبْرٰهِيمُ اَعْرِضْ عَنْ هٰذَا ۖ اِنَّهُ
قَدْ جَآءَ اَمْرُ رَبِّكَ ۖ وَاِنَّهُمْ اٰتِيهِمْ عَذَابٌ غَيْرُ مَرْدُودٍ ۞ وَلَمَّا جَآءَتْ
رُسُلُنَا لُوطًا سِيٓءَ بِهِمْ وَضَاقَ بِهِمْ ذَرْعًا وَقَالَ هٰذَا يَوْمٌ عَصِيبٌ
۞ وَجَآءَهُ قَوْمُهُ يُهْرَعُونَ اِلَيْهِ وَمِنْ قَبْلُ كَانُوا يَعْمَلُونَ السَّيِّئَاتِ ۚ
قَالَ يَا قَوْمِ هٰٓؤُلَآءِ بَنَاتِى هُنَّ اَطْهَرُ لَكُمْ فَاتَّقُوا اللّٰهَ وَلَا
تُخْزُونِ فِى ضَيْفِى ۖ اَلَيْسَ مِنْكُمْ رَجُلٌ رَشِيدٌ ۞ قَالُوا لَقَدْ
عَلِمْتَ مَا لَنَا فِى بَنَاتِكَ مِنْ حَقٍّ ۚ وَاِنَّكَ لَتَعْلَمُ مَا نُرِيدُ
۞ قَالَ لَوْ اَنَّ لِى بِكُمْ قُوَّةً اَوْ اٰوِى اِلٰى رُكْنٍ شَدِيدٍ ۞ قَالُوا
يَا لُوطُ اِنَّا رُسُلُ رَبِّكَ لَنْ يَصِلُوٓا اِلَيْكَ ۖ فَاَسْرِ بِاَهْلِكَ بِقِطْعٍ
مِنَ الَّيْلِ وَلَا يَلْتَفِتْ مِنْكُمْ اَحَدٌ اِلَّا امْرَاَتَكَ ۖ اِنَّهُ مُصِيبُهَا
مَآ اَصَابَهُمْ ۚ اِنَّ مَوْعِدَهُمُ الصُّبْحُ ۚ اَلَيْسَ الصُّبْحُ بِقَرِيبٍ ۞

---

72. She said: "Oh, woe is me! Shall I bear a child, now that I am an old woman, and this my husband is an old man? That would be a strange thing indeed!"

73. They (the envoys) said: "Are you surprised at God's command? The mercy of God and His blessings be upon you, O people of the house! Surely He is All-Praiseworthy (as the Lord Who meets all needs of His servants), All-Sublime."

74. So when the apprehension left Abraham and the glad tiding was conveyed to him, he began to argue with Our envoys to plead with Us on behalf of the people of Lot.

75. Abraham was indeed most clement, tender-hearted, ever-turning to God with all his heart.

76. "O Abraham! Cease from this! For sure, the command of your Lord has already gone forth; and there is coming upon them a punishment not to be turned back."[17]

77. And when Our envoys came to Lot, he was troubled on their account and felt himself powerless to protect them, and he said: "This is a distressful day."

78. His people came rushing to him, driven by their perverted desire, as they had before that been committing such abominations. Lot said: "O my people! Here are my daughters; they are utterly clean for you (to satisfy your desires in wedlock). Have fear of God, and do not disgrace me in respect of my guests. Is there not among you one right-minded man?"

79. They said: "You know well that we have no claim on your daughters; and you surely know well what we desire."

80. He said: "O! would that I had power to resist you, or that I could lean upon some strong support!"

81. They (the envoys) said: "O Lot! We are envoys of your Lord. They will not reach you. So, set out with your family in a part of the night, and let no one among you turn round – all save your wife, for that which is to befall them will befall her as well.[18] Their appointed time is the morning. Is the morning not near?"

7. While narrating some important episodes from the earlier Prophets' lives in connection with the main themes of this *sūrah*, the Qur'ān of miraculous expression includes this episode from the life of Abraham, upon him be God's peace. This hints that even amid the greatest destructions there is always a hope for the future of faith, like a seed destined to grow into a great tree. While many peoples were destroyed because of their stubborn unbelief, evil deeds, immoralities, and the unrest and corruption they caused on earth, Abraham begot two sons – Ishmael and Isaac – from whom two branches would issue bearing Messengers, and by whose grace human history would enter a completely new phase. So, with this episode from the life of Abraham, the father of all the great Messengers to come after him, the Qur'ān both consoles the Last Messenger, upon him be peace and blessings, and his friends who suffered great persecutions at the hands of the Makkan polytheists, and gives glad tiding of a new seed which had already germinated under the earth to grow into a magnificent tree. This is true for all similar periods until the Day of Resurrection.

18. Noah's son and Lot's wife were among the unbelievers who were destroyed. This is an extremely significant warning for all people. In order to be saved, we must always seek refuge in God and implore Him to protect our hearts from all kinds of deviation from the Straight Path.

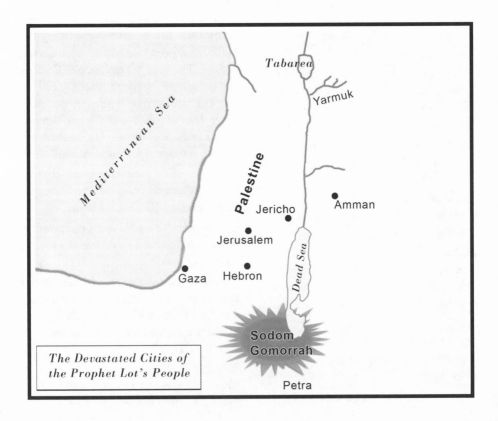

The Devastated Cities of the Prophet Lot's People

فَلَمَّا جَآءَ أَمۡرُنَا جَعَلۡنَا عَالِيَهَا سَافِلَهَا وَأَمۡطَرۡنَا عَلَيۡهَا

حِجَارَةً مِّن سِجِّيلٍ مَّنضُودٍ ۝ مُّسَوَّمَةً عِندَ رَبِّكَ وَمَا هِيَ

مِنَ الظَّالِمِينَ بِبَعِيدٍ ۝ وَإِلَىٰ مَدۡيَنَ أَخَاهُمۡ شُعَيۡبًا قَالَ

يَٰقَوۡمِ اعۡبُدُوا اللَّهَ مَا لَكُم مِّنۡ إِلَٰهٍ غَيۡرُهُ وَلَا تَنقُصُوا

الۡمِكۡيَالَ وَالۡمِيزَانَ إِنِّيٓ أَرَىٰكُم بِخَيۡرٍ وَإِنِّيٓ أَخَافُ عَلَيۡكُمۡ عَذَابَ

يَوۡمٍ مُّحِيطٍ ۝ وَيَٰقَوۡمِ أَوۡفُوا الۡمِكۡيَالَ وَالۡمِيزَانَ بِالۡقِسۡطِ

وَلَا تَبۡخَسُوا النَّاسَ أَشۡيَآءَهُمۡ وَلَا تَعۡثَوۡا فِي الۡأَرۡضِ مُفۡسِدِينَ

بَقِيَّتُ اللَّهِ خَيۡرٌ لَّكُمۡ إِن كُنتُم مُّؤۡمِنِينَ وَمَآ

أَنَا عَلَيۡكُم بِحَفِيظٍ ۝ قَالُوا يَٰشُعَيۡبُ أَصَلَوٰتُكَ

تَأۡمُرُكَ أَن نَّتۡرُكَ مَا يَعۡبُدُ ءَابَآؤُنَآ أَوۡ أَن نَّفۡعَلَ فِيٓ

أَمۡوَٰلِنَا مَا نَشَٰٓؤُا۟ إِنَّكَ لَأَنتَ الۡحَلِيمُ الرَّشِيدُ ۝ قَالَ

يَٰقَوۡمِ أَرَءَيۡتُمۡ إِن كُنتُ عَلَىٰ بَيِّنَةٍ مِّن رَّبِّي وَرَزَقَنِي

مِنۡهُ رِزۡقًا حَسَنًا وَمَآ أُرِيدُ أَنۡ أُخَالِفَكُمۡ إِلَىٰ مَآ

أَنۡهَىٰكُمۡ عَنۡهُ إِنۡ أُرِيدُ إِلَّا الۡإِصۡلَٰحَ مَا اسۡتَطَعۡتُ

وَمَا تَوۡفِيقِيٓ إِلَّا بِاللَّهِ عَلَيۡهِ تَوَكَّلۡتُ وَإِلَيۡهِ أُنِيبُ ۝

―――✽―――

82. So when Our judgment came to pass, We overturned (those sinful towns), and rained down on them stones of baked clay one after another,

83. (Each stone) marked out by your Lord (for a particular individual). And they are never far from wrongdoers (in all times and places).[19]

84. And (to the people of) Midian (We sent as Messenger) their brother Shu'ayb. He said (conveying the same message): "O my people! Worship God: you have no deity other than Him. Do not give short measure and weight (in your dealings). Surely I see you affluent (in wealth which you have gained in unlawful ways), and I fear for you the punishment of an all-encompassing Day.

85. "O my people! Give full measure and weight, with perfect equity, and do not t wrong people by depriving them of what is rightfully theirs, and do not go about acting wickedly in the land, causing disorder and corruption.

86. "What God leaves with you (as lawful profit) is better for you, if you are believers.[20] I am not a keeper and watcher over you."

87. They said: "O Shu'ayb! Does your Prayer-rite command you that we should forsake all that our forefathers used to worship, or that we should cease doing whatever we wish with our property? Surely you are one mild-mannered, and one right-minded."

88. He answered: "O my people! What do you think – if I stand on a clear evidence from my Lord, and out of His provision He provides for me? I do not (in hope of worldly gain and provoking disorder) act in opposition to you (myself doing) what I ask you to avoid. What I seek is only to set things right so far as I am able. My success in my task depends on God alone. In Him have I put my trust, and to Him do I always turn with all my heart.

19. The Qur'ānic presentation of the destruction of ancient peoples, especially those of Lot, points to calamities which we today label as "natural" and which we think we understand and attribute to nature. It seems as if the people of Lot were destroyed by a terrible volcanic eruption, probably in conjunction with a severe earthquake. The land where those people lived sank into the earth; it could be said that the site was wiped clean.

Whatever the calamity was with which they were destroyed, it is God Who judged their destruction and Who brought it about. But since the world is the realm of wisdom and human beings are equipped with free will, God acts behind the veil of causes. Angels represent His acts in the world and act as His "officials." Every occurrence in "nature" is connected with an angel, to the extent that even a rain drop falls with the an angel, to the extent that even a rain drop falls with the angel in charge of it. Nothing can be attributed to chance for God's all-inclusive Will prevails. It is He Who creates everything and nothing occurs without His control or permission.

One of the reasons why God acts in this world behind the veil of causes or causes-and-effects is that human reason cannot see the ultimate beauty in some happenings, such as death, illnesses, and misfortune. If God were directly involved in such happenings, people might attribute to Him the apparent ugliness inherent in them, and therefore more readily commit great sins. But, as God has mercy on us, He has put causes between Him and the happenings and saved us from falling into such error. People ascribe to certain causes such seemingly ugly happenings as death, illness, and misfortune. But this should not prevent us from searching for the Divine purposes behind all these happenings in order to ask God for forgiveness for our sins and pray to Him to receive blessings.

As with the peoples mentioned in the Qur'ān, if an evil encompasses all people, God may destroy them. However, in many cases we see that, rather than the unbelievers, it is the believers who are subjected to Divine punishment that arises in the form of what we wrongly call natural disasters. This is because major cases and great crimes are referred to and tried and judged by high courts, while minor ones are decided in ordinary ones. Similarly, the punishment for the greater part of the sins of unbelievers has been postponed to the Last, Supreme Judgment, while the believers are mostly punished in this world as an atonement for their sins and failures in following God's laws of the Religion and life. However, as with the peoples mentioned in the Qur'ān, if the sins and crimes committed exceed certain limits, God may punish the unbelievers in this world as well.

God does not usually choose between the good and the evil or the innocent and guilty in disasters that result from the wrongdoing of the majority, in such calamities as earthquakes or floods that come as a form of destruction. Such calamities befall everyone, for they are part of the tests and trials prepared for us. We are tested in this world, where God opens the door to reason in order to know and believe in Him but, since He has given free will to humankind, He never acts in a way that would compel us to believe. If He were to choose between the believers and unbelievers in every calamity, this

would be as if He had written His Name in the sky with the stars, and everyone would feel obliged to believe. But it is very important that everyone should believe with their own free will.

In return for undergoing such calamities, good and innocent people will receive a great reward in the Hereafter. For them there is another kind of mercy: just as the lost property of the innocent becomes like alms given to the poor and thereby gains permanence, their death in a disaster may be regarded as a kind of martyrdom and therefore will gain them an eternal life of happiness. For this reason, having gained for them a great and perpetual profit from a relatively trivial and temporary difficulty or torment, such calamities are, for them, an instance of Divine mercy hidden within wrath. Nevertheless, it should also be stressed that sometimes God uses such calamities to punish people because they have not tried to enjoin what is good and prevent what is evil. In addition, most people may have participated in some sinful actions of the sinful majority, either actively or by giving them direct or indirect support, or in some other way.

In connection with the exemplary history of Lot's people, we should also indicate that as a sinless Messenger of God, Lot was free of all sins, major or minor. The misconduct attributed to Lot in the Bible (*Genesis*, 19: 30–38) are monstrous absurdities, and contradicted by what the same text recounts – that he and his daughters, precisely because they were exemplary in their conduct, were saved from the destruction that befell the people on account of their sexual immorality.

20. Islam determines the lawful and the unlawful to order relationships among people. It is extremely careful of dealings between people, of not wronging others, gaining by lawful ways, and of absolutely refraining from gaining through unlawful ways such as deception, interest, lying, and all other kinds of corrupt practices. Although, in general terms, Islam allows prices to be determined by free and lawful marketing, it does not permit selling goods for a price grossly in excess of the normal market price. It strictly forbids any deception, or the giving of deficient measure or weight. Although people may think that they are profiting by gaining in such unlawful ways, in truth, they are in loss. Only one who acts in conformity with God's laws has an advantage, and therefore it is better for everybody to be honest in their dealings.

وَيَا قَوْمِ لَا يَجْرِمَنَّكُمْ شِقَاقِيٓ أَن يُصِيبَكُم مِّثْلُ مَآ أَصَابَ قَوْمَ نُوحٍ أَوْ قَوْمَ هُودٍ أَوْ قَوْمَ صَالِحٍ ۚ وَمَا قَوْمُ لُوطٍ مِّنكُم بِبَعِيدٍ ۝ وَٱسْتَغْفِرُوا۟ رَبَّكُمْ ثُمَّ تُوبُوٓا۟ إِلَيْهِ ۚ إِنَّ رَبِّي رَحِيمٌ وَدُودٌ ۝ قَالُوا۟ يَٰشُعَيْبُ مَا نَفْقَهُ كَثِيرًا مِّمَّا تَقُولُ وَإِنَّا لَنَرَىٰكَ فِينَا ضَعِيفًا ۖ وَلَوْلَا رَهْطُكَ لَرَجَمْنَٰكَ ۖ وَمَآ أَنتَ عَلَيْنَا بِعَزِيزٍ ۝ قَالَ يَٰقَوْمِ أَرَهْطِىٓ أَعَزُّ عَلَيْكُم مِّنَ ٱللَّهِ وَٱتَّخَذْتُمُوهُ وَرَآءَكُمْ ظِهْرِيًّا ۖ إِنَّ رَبِّي بِمَا تَعْمَلُونَ مُحِيطٌ ۝ وَيَٰقَوْمِ ٱعْمَلُوا۟ عَلَىٰ مَكَانَتِكُمْ إِنِّي عَٰمِلٌ ۖ سَوْفَ تَعْلَمُونَ مَن يَأْتِيهِ عَذَابٌ يُخْزِيهِ وَمَنْ هُوَ كَٰذِبٌ ۖ وَٱرْتَقِبُوٓا۟ إِنِّي مَعَكُمْ رَقِيبٌ ۝ وَلَمَّا جَآءَ أَمْرُنَا نَجَّيْنَا شُعَيْبًا وَٱلَّذِينَ ءَامَنُوا۟ مَعَهُۥ بِرَحْمَةٍ مِّنَّا وَأَخَذَتِ ٱلَّذِينَ ظَلَمُوا۟ ٱلصَّيْحَةُ فَأَصْبَحُوا۟ فِي دِيَٰرِهِمْ جَٰثِمِينَ ۝ كَأَن لَّمْ يَغْنَوْا۟ فِيهَآ ۗ أَلَا بُعْدًا لِّمَدْيَنَ كَمَا بَعِدَتْ ثَمُودُ ۝ وَلَقَدْ أَرْسَلْنَا مُوسَىٰ بِـَٔايَٰتِنَا وَسُلْطَٰنٍ مُّبِينٍ ۝ إِلَىٰ فِرْعَوْنَ وَمَلَإِي۟هِۦ فَٱتَّبَعُوٓا۟ أَمْرَ فِرْعَوْنَ ۖ وَمَآ أَمْرُ فِرْعَوْنَ بِرَشِيدٍ ۝

89. "O my people! Let your dissent from me not cause you to sin so that there befall you the like of what befell the people of Noah, or the people of Hūd, or the people of Ṣāliḥ. And the people of Lot (who were subjected to the same doom) did not live far from you.

90. "Implore your Lord to forgive you (for the sins you have so far committed) and turn to Him repentant. Surely my Lord is All-Compassionate (especially towards His servants who turn to Him), All-Loving."

91. "O Shu'ayb!" they said: "We do not understand much of what you say, and we see you indeed as a weak one among us. And, were it not for your tribe (esteemed among us), we would most certainly have stoned you to death. Know well that we do not hold you in esteem as having power over us."

92. He replied: "O my people! Do you hold my tribe in greater esteem than God, that you take Him as something to cast behind you and forget? But surely my Lord encompasses (with His Knowledge and Power) all that you do.

93. "O my people! Do then all that may be within your power, while I am at work (doing my task). In time you will come to see and know who it is that will be visited by a punishment to disgrace him, and who it is that speaks falsehood and will be contradicted in his speech. Wait and watch, then, and I am watching with you!"

94. And so when Our judgment came to pass, We saved Shu'ayb and those who believed in his company out of a mercy from Us (because of their faith, righteousness, and patience), and the awful blast seized those who acted wrongly to their own ruin, so that they lay prostrate lifeless in their own dwellings,

95. As though they had never lived there in affluence. So, away with the (people of) Midian, just as the Thamūd have been done away with!

96. And We indeed sent Moses with Our clear signs (miracles to support him), and a manifest authority (from Us),

97. To the Pharaoh and his chiefs, but they (his chiefs, his own people, and many among the Children of Israel) followed the rule of the Pharaoh; and the rule of the Pharaoh was by no means a guide right and just (and no tyrant in the mould of the Pharaoh has ever done differently).[22]

---

22. The subtle meaning discovered by the great Turkish interpreter of the Qur'ān, Elmalılı Hamdi Yazır, is quite beautiful. Since the title "the Pharaoh" is used in the first part of the verse, the pronoun "he" in reference to him is expected in the second part. But we see that the title "the Pharaoh" is repeated. So, the first "the Pharaoh" refers to the Egyptian tyrant, to whom Moses was sent, the second "Pharaoh" is, rather than a proper name, a denomination referring to all Pharaoh-like tyrants and their rules.

232   سُوۡرَةُ هُوۡدٍ   ٢٣٢

بَقۡدُمُ قَوۡمَهٗ يَوۡمَ الۡقِيَٰمَةِ فَأَوۡرَدَهُمُ النَّارَ وَبِئۡسَ الۡوِرۡدُ الۡمَوۡرُودُ ۝ وَأُتۡبِعُوا فِى هَٰذِهِۦ لَعۡنَةً وَيَوۡمَ الۡقِيَٰمَةِ بِئۡسَ الرِّفۡدُ الۡمَرۡفُودُ ۝ ذَٰلِكَ مِنۡ أَنۢبَآءِ الۡقُرَىٰ نَقُصُّهُۥ عَلَيۡكَ مِنۡهَا قَآئِمٌ وَحَصِيدٌ ۝ وَمَا ظَلَمۡنَٰهُمۡ وَلَٰكِن ظَلَمُوٓا أَنفُسَهُمۡ فَمَآ أَغۡنَتۡ عَنۡهُمۡ ءَالِهَتُهُمُ الَّتِى يَدۡعُونَ مِن دُونِ اللَّهِ مِن شَىۡءٍ لَّمَّا جَآءَ أَمۡرُ رَبِّكَ وَمَا زَادُوهُمۡ غَيۡرَ تَتۡبِيبٍ ۝ وَكَذَٰلِكَ أَخۡذُ رَبِّكَ إِذَآ أَخَذَ الۡقُرَىٰ وَهِىَ ظَٰلِمَةٌ إِنَّ أَخۡذَهُۥٓ أَلِيمٌ شَدِيدٌ ۝ إِنَّ فِى ذَٰلِكَ لَءَايَةً لِّمَنۡ خَافَ عَذَابَ الۡءَاخِرَةِ ذَٰلِكَ يَوۡمٌ مَّجۡمُوعٌ لَّهُ النَّاسُ وَذَٰلِكَ يَوۡمٌ مَّشۡهُودٌ ۝ وَمَا نُؤَخِّرُهُۥٓ إِلَّا لِأَجَلٍ مَّعۡدُودٍ ۝ يَوۡمَ يَأۡتِ لَا تَكَلَّمُ نَفۡسٌ إِلَّا بِإِذۡنِهِۦ فَمِنۡهُمۡ شَقِىٌّ وَسَعِيدٌ ۝ فَأَمَّا الَّذِينَ شَقُوا فَفِى النَّارِ لَهُمۡ فِيهَا زَفِيرٌ وَشَهِيقٌ ۝ خَٰلِدِينَ فِيهَا مَا دَامَتِ السَّمَٰوَٰتُ وَالۡأَرۡضُ إِلَّا مَا شَآءَ رَبُّكَ إِنَّ رَبَّكَ فَعَّالٌ لِّمَا يُرِيدُ ۝ وَأَمَّا الَّذِينَ سُعِدُوا فَفِى الۡجَنَّةِ خَٰلِدِينَ فِيهَا مَا دَامَتِ السَّمَٰوَٰتُ وَالۡأَرۡضُ إِلَّا مَا شَآءَ رَبُّكَ عَطَآءً غَيۡرَ مَجۡذُوذٍ ۝

---

98. He will go before his people on the Day of Resurrection and lead them to the Fire (as cattle are led to water)! How evil a "watering-place" to be led to!

99. And a curse was made to pursue them in this world, and on the Day of Resurrection. How evil is the gift offered!

100. That is something of the accounts of some townships (that were destroyed in the past). We relate it to you (O Messenger). Among them are some still standing, and some extinct like a mown field.

101. We did not wrong them, but they wronged themselves. When the judgment of your Lord came to pass, their deities which they used to invoke apart from God proved of no avail to them, and they increased them not save in ruin.

102. That is how your Lord seizes the townships when He seizes them when they are wrongdoers. His seizing is indeed painful, severe.

103. Surely in that is a sign (lesson and warning) for those who fear the punishment of the Hereafter. That is a Day when all humankind will be gathered together, and that is a Day bound to be witnessed (experienced by all living creatures in their whole being).

104. We do not postpone it beyond a term already appointed (by Us).

105. On the Day when it comes no one will speak unless by His leave. Among those (gathered together) some are wretched and some happy.

106. As for those who will be wretched (on that Day, on account of the deeds they have earned), they will be in the Fire, wherein moaning and wailing will be their lot,

107. Abiding there so long as the heavens and the earth endure, except as your Lord wills. Surely your Lord is the Sovereign Doer of what He wills.

108. And as for those who are happy (having been blessed by God with faith and good deeds), they will be in Paradise, abiding there so long as the heavens and the earth endure, except as your Lord wills[24] – as a gift unceasing.

23. The verse compares the Pharaoh to a blind cowherd and those who followed him blindly to cattle, and thereby warns us against blind imitation and not using our reason and free will to find and follow the right path. See also 7: 179.

24. The expression *except as your Lord wills* is included in the last two verses especially in order to stress that God is a (sovereign) Doer of whatever He wills, as mentioned in verse 107. No one can compel Him, nor is He Himself obliged to do anything. He does whatever He wills. If there is enduring bliss in Paradise, this is because God has willed it so; if there is enduring punishment in Hell, again this is because God has willed it so.

As for the statement, *so long as the heavens and the earth endure*, this is an idiomatic statement in Arabic denoting eternity. On Doomsday, the earth will be transformed into another earth peculiar to the other world, and there will also be heavens there (14: 48).

فَلَا تَكُ فِي مِرْيَةٍ مِمَّا يَعْبُدُ هَٰؤُلَاءِ مَا يَعْبُدُونَ إِلَّا كَمَا
يَعْبُدُ ءَابَاؤُهُم مِّن قَبْلُ وَإِنَّا لَمُوَفُّوهُمْ نَصِيبَهُمْ غَيْرَ مَنقُوصٍ
﴿١٠٩﴾ وَلَقَدْ ءَاتَيْنَا مُوسَى الْكِتَابَ فَاخْتُلِفَ فِيهِ وَلَوْلَا كَلِمَةٌ
سَبَقَتْ مِن رَّبِّكَ لَقُضِيَ بَيْنَهُمْ وَإِنَّهُمْ لَفِي شَكٍّ مِّنْهُ
مُرِيبٍ ﴿١١٠﴾ وَإِنَّ كُلًّا لَّمَّا لَيُوَفِّيَنَّهُمْ رَبُّكَ أَعْمَالَهُمْ إِنَّهُ بِمَا
يَعْمَلُونَ خَبِيرٌ ﴿١١١﴾ فَاسْتَقِمْ كَمَا أُمِرْتَ وَمَن تَابَ مَعَكَ وَلَا
تَطْغَوْا إِنَّهُ بِمَا تَعْمَلُونَ بَصِيرٌ ﴿١١٢﴾ وَلَا تَرْكَنُوا إِلَى الَّذِينَ ظَلَمُوا
فَتَمَسَّكُمُ النَّارُ وَمَا لَكُم مِّن دُونِ اللَّهِ مِنْ أَوْلِيَاءَ ثُمَّ
لَا تُنصَرُونَ ﴿١١٣﴾ وَأَقِمِ الصَّلَاةَ طَرَفَيِ النَّهَارِ وَزُلَفًا
مِّنَ اللَّيْلِ إِنَّ الْحَسَنَاتِ يُذْهِبْنَ السَّيِّئَاتِ ذَٰلِكَ
ذِكْرَىٰ لِلذَّاكِرِينَ ﴿١١٤﴾ وَاصْبِرْ فَإِنَّ اللَّهَ لَا يُضِيعُ أَجْرَ الْمُحْسِنِينَ
﴿١١٥﴾ فَلَوْلَا كَانَ مِنَ الْقُرُونِ مِن قَبْلِكُمْ أُولُوا بَقِيَّةٍ
يَنْهَوْنَ عَنِ الْفَسَادِ فِي الْأَرْضِ إِلَّا قَلِيلًا مِّمَّنْ أَنجَيْنَا مِنْهُمْ
وَاتَّبَعَ الَّذِينَ ظَلَمُوا مَا أُتْرِفُوا فِيهِ وَكَانُوا مُجْرِمِينَ ﴿١١٦﴾
وَمَا كَانَ رَبُّكَ لِيُهْلِكَ الْقُرَىٰ بِظُلْمٍ وَأَهْلُهَا مُصْلِحُونَ ﴿١١٧﴾

109. So do not be in doubt of anything that those (misguided people) worship. They but worship as their forefathers worshipped in time past; and We will most certainly pay them their due in full, undiminished.

110. And, indeed, We granted Moses the Book, and discord arose about it, (just as your people, O Messenger, differ concerning the Book We are revealing to you. So do not be grieved). Had it not been for a decree already issued by your Lord (postponing the final, decisive judgment until an appointed term),[25] it would indeed have been judged between them. They (your people) are surely in serious doubt, truly uncertain, concerning it (the Qur'ān).

111. And surely for each of them – your Lord will certainly pay them in full for their deeds. He is indeed fully aware of all that they do.

112. Pursue, then, what is exactly right (in every matter of the Religion) as you are commanded (by God), and those who, along with you, have turned (to God with faith, repenting their former ways, let them do likewise); and do not rebel against the bounds of the Straight Path (O believers)! He indeed sees well all that you do.

113. And do not incline towards those who do wrong (against God by associating partners with Him and against people by violating their rights), or the Fire will touch you. For you have no guardians and true friends apart from God, (but if you should incline towards those who do wrong,) you will not be helped (by Him).

114. Establish the Prayer (O Messenger) at the beginning and the end of the day, and in the watches of the night near to the day. Surely good deeds wipe out evil deeds.[26] This is advice and a reminder for the mindful who reflect.

115. And be patient, persevering (in doing good, avoiding mistakes, and against all kinds of persecution you are made to suffer in God's cause), for surely God never leaves to waste the reward of those devoted to doing good, aware that God is seeing them.

116. If only there had been among the generations before you (of whom some We destroyed) people with lasting qualities (such as faith, knowledge, virtue, and good deeds, whose goal was what is lasting with God, the eternal life of the Hereafter, and) who would warn against disorder and corruption on earth! Among them only a few, included among those whom We saved, did this. But those who did wrong (against God by associating partners with Him, and against people by violating their rights) were lost in the pursuit of pleasures, and were criminals committed to accumulating sins.

117. And it has never been the way of your Lord to destroy the townships unjustly while their people were righteous, dedicated to continuous self-reform and setting things right in the society.

---

25. This decree is that there will be for humankind on the earth, where they have been appointed as vicegerent to improve it, a habitation and provision until the Day of Resurrection (2: 36), and that recompense for obedience or disobedience to the Religion is generally deferred to the Hereafter.

26. In one respect, this verse circumscribes the five prescribed Prayers, although it does specify the exact time of each.

The Prayers to be established at the beginning and end of the day may be seen as the Noon and Afternoon Prayers. If so, what is meant by day is broad daylight. The original word for "watches of the night near to the day" is *zulef*, which is in the plural. In Arabic the plural must include at least three things, so it can be concluded that the word *zulef* refers to the three Prayers to be established during the night; i.e. the Evening, Late Evening and Dawn or Morning Prayers. Although this is the apparent meaning of the verse, which indicates five times for Prayer in a day, these times may not be the exact times of the daily Prescribed Prayers.

Praying five times a day was prescribed for the Muslims during the Messenger's Ascension in the eleventh year of his mission. Therefore, the five times mentioned in the verse may be only for the Messenger, and one of the three times in the night may be the time of *Tahajjud*, the Late Night Prayer which was prescribed for the Messenger, not the time of dawn or early morning.

The Prescribed Prayer is the pillar of the Religion and the best of good deeds. One who does not perform the Prescribed Prayer cannot construct the building of the Religion on the foundation of faith. A foundation on which a building has not been built is easily removed. The Messenger, upon him be peace and blessings, taught that the Prayer is like a river running by one's house. One who bathes in it five times a day is cleaned of all dirt (which may have attached to them during the intervening periods). He also taught that the Prescribed Prayers can serve as atonement for the minor sins committed between the times (Muslim, "Tahārah," 16). The Qur'ān declares that the Prescribed Prayer prevents one from committing indecencies and other kinds of evil deeds (29: 45). Also, it serves as repentance and a means of asking God for forgiveness. Similarly, any good deed done just after an evil one may cause the evil one to be forgiven. So it is highly advisable that one should do good immediately after any evil committed. Of course, this does not mean that we may willfully do evil so long as we pray immediately afterwards. Rather, like the Prescribed Prayer, the doing of a good deed after an evil one is intended to train and restrain one from committing further evil. This is what is indicated to in the sentence *Surely good deeds wipe out evil deeds*, in the verse.

118. If your Lord had so willed (and withheld from humankind free will), He would have made all humankind one single community (with the same faith, worldview, and life-pattern). But (having free choice) they never cease to differ (and follow diverse paths diverging from the Straight Path),

119. Save those on whom your Lord has mercy (and guides to the Straight Path because of the merits they have).[27] It is for that He created them. And thus the word of your Lord will have been fulfilled: "I will fill Hell with all those (deserving it) among the jinn and humankind."[28]

120. All that We relate to you of the exemplary narrative of (the lives of some of the earlier) Messengers is in order that whereby We make firm your heart. In all these accounts there comes to you the truth, as well as an instruction and a reminder for the believers.

121. Say to those who do not believe: "Do all that may be within your power, while we too are doing (our task).

122. "And wait on, we too are waiting."

123. To God belongs (absolute dominion and full knowledge of) the unseen of the

the whole matter referred (for final judgment). So worship Him, and put your trust in Him. Your Lord is by no means unaware and unmindful of what you do.

---

27. God, as the All-Just, and more than that, the All-Merciful Whose Mercy encompasses everything, never wrongs His creatures, or discriminates between them. Rather, He always wishes good for them. What we must do is to use our free will on the right course. Some virtues, such as truthfulness, modesty, humility, altruism, generosity, being free of prejudices, and keeping from such evils as lying, deception, wronging others, illicit sexual relations, and the like, are petitions presented to God for faith and salvation. On the other hand, vices such as wrongdoing, arrogance, being prejudiced, selfishness, miserliness, and indulgence in pleasures are obstacles before faith and salvation. God's Messenger replied to one of his Companions who asked him about whether people would benefit

from the good deeds they had done in the period of *jāhiliyyah* (pre-Islamic era) said: "Why else do you think God has guided you to Islam?" (al-Bukhārī, "Zakāh," 24).

For the conflicts among humankind, their meaning, and place in human life and history, and the Divine wisdom contained in them see: 2: 213, note 143; 3: 19, note 4; 5: 48, note 11; 10: 93, not: 14.

28. This word has already been given in 7: 18 with reference to Satan's followers: *He (God) said: "Go away from there, disgraced and disowned! Those of them that follow you, surely I will fill Hell with you all!"* God will fill Hell with Satan and his followers among the jinn and humankind who have ultimately become "satanic." Time has demonstrated that Paradise is not easy to deserve, nor is Hell useless.

SŪRAH 12

YŪSUF (JOSEPH)

Makkah period

This *surah*, revealed toward the end of the Makkan period of Islam and comprising 111 verses, takes its name from the Prophet Joseph, whose life and mission it recounts. Unlike the accounts of other Messengers, different elements and aspects of which are related in different *surah*s, the life-history of Joseph, upon him be God's peace, is narrated in this *surah* only, in full and in chronological order. This *surah*, which also tells us of the truth contained in dreams, presents many principles of how to serve Islam by relating the life-history of a Messenger, who became the most renowned and respected figure in the country to which he had been sold as a slave.

In the Name of God, The All-Merciful, The All-Compassionate.

1. *Alif. Lām, Rā.* These are the Revelations of the Book clear in itself and clearly showing the truth.

2. We send it down as a *qur'ān* (discourse) in Arabic so that you may reflect (on both its meaning and wording) and understand.[1]

3. We are about to relate to you (O Messenger) the best of narratives (of the past) by Our revealing to you this Qur'ān. Before this, indeed you were unaware of it.[2]

4. When Joseph said to his father: "O my father! I saw in a dream eleven stars,[3] as well as the sun and the moon: I saw them prostrating themselves before me."[4]

---

1. The Qur'ān – the word *qur'ān* literally means recitation, something to be recited, or a discourse – was revealed in Arabic. Being a universal religion, Islam addresses all people, regardless of differences in race, color, and language, and embraces whoever accepts it whatever background or language they have. But, naturally, it must have a language and the language of Arabic was chosen. However, this in no way means that those who enter the fold of Islam from other languages must learn Arabic in order to be Muslims. Knowing a language is a scientific matter, and is different from speaking it and reading books written in it. Every Muslim is expected to be able to read (i.e. phonetically pronounce the words) the Qur'ān, and they can learn to read it within a month, which is one of the miraculous aspects of the Qur'ān. However, knowing Arabic and studying and understanding the Qur'ān is a scientific matter. Just as a native English speaker who speaks English does not necessarily know the grammar rules of English or the English that is studied in schools as a branch of science, so too, not every native Arabic speaker is thought to know Arabic well enough to understand the Qur'ān. Likewise, just as every one who knows English well is not expected to have learned physics or chemistry or medicine merely by reading books that were written in English, or even to be able to understand books about them written in English, so too someone who knows Arabic well does not necessarily know or understand the Qur'ān; understanding and knowing the Qur'ān is a scientific matter that involves many other sciences. Just as everyone cannot be a physicist or chemist or a historian, and just as each branch of science requires special study, so too, it is an obvious fact that there will be scholars of the Qur'ān who must instruct others in it.

God sent every Messenger with the language he and his people spoke. So, one of the primary reasons why the Qur'ān was revealed in Arabic is that God's Messenger appeared among the Arabs and the people to whom the Qur'ān first addressed itself were the Arabs. There must be other reasons some of which we can know, while others we cannot. One of these other reasons may be that Arabic is the most appropriate language in human realm for a Divine discourse. God calls people to reflect on the fact that the Qur'ān was revealed in Arabic, and being in Arabic is an essential dimension of the Qur'ān.

2. *Sūrah* Yūsuf (Joseph) exhibits its beauty from the very beginning. We can understand why it is called the best of narratives in this way:

- Only the Qur'ān can tell these events in the best way. That is, it tells them most comprehensively and concisely, and presents the full historical, psychological, moral and spiritual meaning of those events and how they unfolded.

- It cannot be told so beautifully in any other book than in this Arabic Qur'ān because of the unique beauties and felicities of the Qur'anic Arabic.

- The best of the narratives concerning the lives of the previous Messengers which consoled the Prophet Muḥammad, upon him be peace and blessings, and his Companions in Makkah, and also enlightened their way, is the one that is presented in this *sūrah*.

- While almost all of the other narratives contain elements of destruction, all the persons involved in the events described in this *sūrah* come to understand their mistakes and find the truth in the end.

- While all other narratives are scattered throughout different *sūrah*s, the narrative in *Sūrah* Yūsuf is given in one *sūrah* in its entirety, and in greater detail.

- In this narrative it is possible to find an anatomy of the character of humanity, with both its negative and positive aspects. We are also presented with how the complete process of the overall reformation of a country from within is possible. This process is one which will enlighten the ways of believers until the Resurrection Day.

- The mission of Prophet Joseph, upon him be peace, marks the appearance and first development in history of the descendents of Isaac, son of Abraham. This mission opened the way for the Children of Israel, descending from Jacob, Isaac's son and Joseph's father, to settle in Egypt and rise to a leading position there. This history descends from Prophet Joseph, who stood at the starting point of their history, and then enters a new phase with Prophet Moses, rising to its zenith with David and Solomon, upon them all be peace.

- The spiritual beauty of Joseph, reflected in his physical beauty and his representation of such important virtues as chastity and devotion to doing good, add to the beauty of the narrative of his life and mission.

- It was impossible for God's Messenger Muḥammad, upon him be peace and blessings, who was unlettered, to know of Joseph's life, especially in the particular detail recounted in the Qur'ān. So, among the histories of the lives and missions of the Messengers, the completeness and perfection of the narrative in this *sūrah* is among the greatest proofs of Muḥammad's Messengership.

3. The original word for "stars"– *kawkab* – also means "planets." From this we may conclude that if the earth is included, there are actually twelve planets, although as yet only ten of them have been discovered. In the dream, Joseph is symbolized by the earth, which, due to the significance it possesses as the habitat for humankind, is the "spiritual" center of the solar system. It is explicitly stated in the Qur'ān several times that whatever there is in the heavens and the earth, including the sun and the moon, has been made subservient to God's laws for the benefit of human beings (*sūrah* 13: 33; *sūrah* 16: 12; *sūrah* 31: 20).

4. While you sleep with your eyes closed, your ears deaf, your tongue silent, and your arms and legs at rest, how do you travel, meet people, and do many things in a few minutes or even seconds? When you get up in the morning, you feel deeply influenced by that few seconds' adventure. Although Freud and his followers attribute dreams to the workings of the subconscious mind, to thoughts and desires, impulses and past experiences, how can this explain dreams that inform of a future event with which one has had no contact or even thought about?

When we sleep, our spirit enters the world of ideal forms or symbols where to some extent past, present, and future are combined, without completely breaking its connection to the body. It continues this connection through a cord. As a result, it may experience a past event or witness a future one. However, since things in that world exist in ideal forms or symbols, the spirit usually receives symbols that require interpretation. For example, clear water in that world may correspond to knowledge in this world. The metaphors, similes, and parables found in the Qur'ān and the Prophetic sayings, and sometimes popular sayings may provide significant keys to interpret dreams. However, some dreams are so clear that no interpretation is needed.

Dreams are of three kinds. Two are included in the category of "jumbled dreams" (the Qur'ānic expression in 12: 44). In these dreams, either the imagination gives form to the deviations of a bad temper or the mind remembers an exciting event which happened some time ago, and produces it in a new and different form, and the dreams that a person has in such moods are "jumbled ones," as will be mentioned in verses 43–44, 47–49 of this sūrah. Despite being jumbled, some of these dreams may also have some significant meaning, but need to be interpreted.

The other type of dream has nothing to do with the subconscious self. Such dreams carry important messages: either they are glad tidings from God, which encourage us to do good things and guide us, or warnings concerning the evils we have done or will do. Those dreams, which we call true dreams, are very clear and unforgettable. In an authenticated narration God's Messenger says that true dreams are one of the forty-six aspects of Prophethood. (That is, since God's Messenger had true dreams in the initial six months of his twenty-three years of Prophethood, true dreams are a type of Divine inspiration.) This means that true dreams contain elements of truth.

Several scientific or technological discoveries were first seen in dreams. Elias Howe, while trying to figure out how to thread a sewing machine, dreamed that he was being held prisoner by a tribe who were thrusting spears at him. Puzzled and in mortal fear, he suddenly saw holes at the top end of his captors' spears. He woke up and made a little "spear" with a hole at the sharp end of the needle, and thus made sewing by machine possible. Niels Bohr, who was studying atomic structures, dreamed of planets connected to the sun with threads that were spinning around it. When he woke up, he conceived of a resemblance between what he had dreamed of and atomic structures.

قَالَ يَٰبُنَىَّ لَا تَقْصُصْ رُءْيَاكَ عَلَىٰٓ إِخْوَتِكَ فَيَكِيدُوا لَكَ كَيْدًا ۖ إِنَّ الشَّيْطَٰنَ لِلْإِنسَٰنِ عَدُوٌّ مُّبِينٌ ۝ وَكَذَٰلِكَ يَجْتَبِيكَ رَبُّكَ وَيُعَلِّمُكَ مِن تَأْوِيلِ الْأَحَادِيثِ وَيُتِمُّ نِعْمَتَهُ عَلَيْكَ وَعَلَىٰٓ ءَالِ يَعْقُوبَ كَمَآ أَتَمَّهَا عَلَىٰٓ أَبَوَيْكَ مِن قَبْلُ إِبْرَٰهِيمَ وَإِسْحَٰقَ ۚ إِنَّ رَبَّكَ عَلِيمٌ حَكِيمٌ ۝ لَّقَدْ كَانَ فِي يُوسُفَ وَإِخْوَتِهِۦٓ ءَايَٰتٌ لِّلسَّآئِلِينَ ۝ إِذْ قَالُوا لَيُوسُفُ وَأَخُوهُ أَحَبُّ إِلَىٰٓ أَبِينَا مِنَّا وَنَحْنُ عُصْبَةٌ إِنَّ أَبَانَا لَفِي ضَلَٰلٍ مُّبِينٍ ۝ اقْتُلُوا يُوسُفَ أَوِ اطْرَحُوهُ أَرْضًا يَخْلُ لَكُمْ وَجْهُ أَبِيكُمْ وَتَكُونُوا مِنۢ بَعْدِهِۦ قَوْمًا صَٰلِحِينَ ۝ قَالَ قَآئِلٌ مِّنْهُمْ لَا تَقْتُلُوا يُوسُفَ وَأَلْقُوهُ فِي غَيَٰبَتِ الْجُبِّ يَلْتَقِطْهُ بَعْضُ السَّيَّارَةِ إِن كُنتُمْ فَٰعِلِينَ ۝ قَالُوا يَٰٓأَبَانَا مَا لَكَ لَا تَأْمَنَّا عَلَىٰ يُوسُفَ وَإِنَّا لَهُۥ لَنَٰصِحُونَ ۝ أَرْسِلْهُ مَعَنَا غَدًا يَرْتَعْ وَيَلْعَبْ وَإِنَّا لَهُۥ لَحَٰفِظُونَ ۝ قَالَ إِنِّي لَيَحْزُنُنِيٓ أَن تَذْهَبُوا بِهِۦ وَأَخَافُ أَن يَأْكُلَهُ الذِّئْبُ وَأَنتُمْ عَنْهُ غَٰفِلُونَ ۝ قَالُوا لَئِنْ أَكَلَهُ الذِّئْبُ وَنَحْنُ عُصْبَةٌ إِنَّآ إِذًا لَّخَٰسِرُونَ ۝

---

5. He (Jacob) said: "O my son! Do not relate your dream to your brothers, lest (out of envy) they devise a scheme against you. For Satan is a manifest enemy to humankind (and can incite them to do such a thing).

6. "So will your Lord choose you and impart to you some knowledge of the inner meaning of all happenings (including dreams),[5] and complete His favor upon you and upon the family of Jacob, as He completed it formerly upon your forefathers Abraham and Isaac.[6] Surely, your Lord is All-Knowing, All-Wise.[7]

7. Assuredly, in (this account of) Joseph and his brothers there are many signs (messages) for seekers of truth.

8. When they (the brothers addressing one another) said: "Joseph and his brother are indeed more loved by our father than we are,[8] even though we are a powerful band (of greater use to him). Surely, our father is manifestly mistaken."

9. (One of them said:) "Kill Joseph, or cast him out in some distant land so that your father's attention should turn only to you, and after that you may again become righteous people."

10. Another of them, putting forward his view, said: "Do not kill Joseph, but rather, cast him into the depth of the well (that you know of), that some caravan may pick him up – (do that) if you are seriously intending to take action."

11. They said (having agreed on this) to their father: "Our father! Why will you not trust Joseph with us, while we are his sincere well-wishers?

12. "Let him go out with us tomorrow, that he may enjoy himself and play; surely we will take good care of him."

13. He (Jacob) said: "Indeed, it grieves me that you should take him with you, and I fear lest a wolf should devour him while you are inattentive of him."

14. They said: "If a wolf should devour him when we are so strong a company, then we should surely be lost!"

5. Every thing and event has a substantial inner meaning in the general context of the universe. Nothing exists or happens by chance. Every thing and event is a knot or weft in the general fabric of things and events. Moreover, God has an ultimate purpose for the existence of every thing and every happening, so no thing and no event is meaningless. They bear messages for conscious beings – humankind, angels, and the jinn. Although all the Prophets and even some distinguished saintly people can have knowledge of the meaning and messages of events and what they are intended for, the Prophet Joseph has a special place among them.

6. As in the Bible, the Qur'ān shows that the Prophet Jacob understood the meaning of the dream with all its deeper implications, with the eleven stars symbolizing his brothers, and the sun and the moon his parents. But the Bible relates that the Prophet Jacob, upon him be peace, assumed that Joseph's dream was the outcome of wishful thinking and rebuked Joseph for having such a dream (*Genesis*, 37: 10). Moreover, there are other serious differences between the account of the Prophet Joseph's life in the Qur'ān and that of the Bible.

It is unfortunate that the Bible contains many such grave accusations against the Prophets; some are even worse than the one given above. For example, see: *Genesis*, 19: 30–38; 27; 32: 25–31; *II Samuel* 11; *I Kings* 11.

If the Qur'ān had not been revealed, we could not be sure whether the other Prophets really had been sincere, devout, and thankful servants of God. So, all the previous Prophets, the Books which were sent through some of them, and the religion they brought are greatly indebted to the Qur'ān, to the Prophet Muḥammad, upon him be peace and blessings, and to *the Islam* he brought.

7. The verse concluding with God's being All-Knowing and All-Wise shows that this *sūrah* is based mainly on these two Names and that the Prophet Joseph, upon him be peace, was favored with them. He was particularly a wise, knowledgeable Prophet.

8. As a matter of fact, the Prophet Jacob, upon him be peace, did not discriminate in showing his sons love, but as he discerned the potential in Joseph and what kind of mission he was destined for, he therefore paid greater attention to him.

15. And so they went away with him, and decided to put Joseph in the depth of the well,[9] (which they did). We revealed to him: "You will most certainly remind them of this deed of theirs while they are unaware (neither knowing nor understanding all that has transpired)."

16. And at nightfall they returned to their father, weeping.

17. They said: "Our father! We went off racing with one another, and left Joseph behind by our things, then a wolf devoured him. But we know that you will not believe us, even though we speak the truth."

18. They had brought his shirt back with false blood on it. Jacob said: "Rather, your (evil-commanding) souls have tempted you to do something evil. So (the proper recourse for me is) a becoming patience (a patience that endures without complaint).[10] God it is Whose help is sought against (the situation) that you have described."[11]

19. And there came a caravan, and they sent forth one among them to fetch water. He let down his bucket (into the well). "Good luck!" he exclaimed: "(There is) a youth here!" So they hid and preserved him as merchandise to sell. God had full knowledge of what they were doing.

20. And they sold him for a paltry price – a few silver coins – so little did they value him.

21. The man who bought him in Egypt said to his wife: "Give him honorable, good lodging. It may be that he will prove use- ful to us or we may adopt him as a son."[12] Thus did We establish Joseph in the land (Egypt), that We would impart to him knowledge and understanding of the inner meaning of events, including dreams. God always prevails in whatever be His will, but most people do not know (that it is so).

22. When Joseph reached his full manhood, We granted him authority with sound, wise judgment, and special knowledge. Thus do We reward those devoted to doing good as if seeing God.

---

9. While reflecting on the reasons for which the Qur'ān was sent down in Arabic, we should also be mindful of the fact that, more than any other language, the pronunciation of the words in Arabic is in accord with their meaning. In other words, the pronunciation of the words and the conjugation of the verbs call to mind the meaning. For example, in the Qur'ānic statement, *O earth, swallow up your waters!* (11: 44), the word translated "swallow" is *ebli'ī*, word associated with the act of swallowing. Similarly the word here translated as "depth," *ghay''ābah*, calls to mind a disappearance in depth by its sound, and the word translated as "well," *jubb*, calls to mind the sound made when one falls into a well. It is possible to find many other examples of this linguistic feature in the Qur'ān.

10. It is worth noting that Jacob, as a Prophet of God, never complained to or of God when he had apparently lost Joseph. He did not shout nor did he chide his sons, but only hinted that he did not believe them. He reacted with utmost serenity and referred the matter to God in perfect reliance on Him as the true Helper of His servants.

Both being Messengers raised among the same community, the attitudes of Jacob and Moses are worth noting. As mentioned before (7: 150), Moses, having received the Tablets and learned that his people had adopted a calf to worship, returned to his people, full of wrath and sorrow, and rebuked them, saying: *Evil is the course you have followed after me! Have you forsaken your Lord's commandment so hastily to hasten your destruction?* (7: 150). And then he threw down the Tablets, and laid hold of his brother's head, dragging him toward himself. The great difference between these two attitudes should be sought in the "misfortune" each faced. It appeared as if the Prophet Jacob had lost his son. It was God who gave him this son as a gift and it was God Who could take him back. What a father should do in such a case is to show the proper patience, which the Prophet Jacob did in the best way. By contrast, Moses faced apostasy after many years during which God's favors had poured down upon the people, and at a time when he hoped he could apply God's laws in his community. So, both of the Messengers did what they were expected to do,

11. Jacob's sons were the first ancestors of the Children of Israel. It is possible to find in them the traces of the character of the Children of Israel as a nation. Three traits seem to be predominant in their character: jealousy, dependence on power and riches and adopting these as criteria in judging people, and deception.

Every human being may have such traits. God has equipped humankind with three major powers: lust for the opposite sex, offspring, money, earning, and the comforts of life; the power of anger to protect themselves and their values, and intellect. Moreover, they are, by nature, fallible, forgetful, neglectful, fond of disputing, obstinate, selfish, and envious, among many other negative traits. Since human beings are distinguished from other conscious beings, like angels, by being endowed with free will, these powers, faculties, and apparently negative qualities have not been restricted in creation. However, in order to attain happiness as a social being, both in their individual and collective life, in the world and in the Hereafter, and to rise to higher and higher ranks of humanity, they should either discipline these traits according to certain precepts or channel them into virtues. For example, obstinacy can be channeled into steadfastness in right and truth, and envy into a feeling of competition to do good things. The happiness and perfection of a person lies in their struggling against the negative aspects of their nature and restricting these aspects or channeling them into virtues and in acquiring a distinction with their good qualities, thus becoming good, worshipping servants of God, and useful members of society. The Last Messenger of God, upon him be peace and blessings, said: "I have been sent to perfect the standards and beauties of good morals" (at-Ṭabarānī, 7: 74).

We should point out that the sons of the Prophet Jacob were able, later on, under the education of their father, to transform the three traits mentioned into virtues.

12. While describing events, the Qur'ān displays what kind of people the characters involved were. As we see from verses 19 and 20, the Qur'ān's complaint about the members of the caravan, who were apparently low, rough people lacking in discernment and so unaware of the true value things and persons have; this verse in contrast shows the nobility of the man who bought Joseph in Egypt.

13. The original words *ḥukm* and *'ilm*, which we translate here as "sound, wise judgment" and "special knowledge" respectively, are used in the indefinite form. This implies that the judgment and knowledge given to the Prophet Joseph, as well as to other Prophets, are of a special kind peculiar to the Prophets which cannot be acquired through studying. Some people may acquire a portion of this through self-purification of their sins and by spiritual contact with God through worship and reflection, as the conclusion of the verse, *Thus do We reward those devoted to doing good as if seeing God*, suggests.

ورَاوَدَتْهُ الَّتِي هُوَ فِي بَيْتِهَا عَن نَّفْسِهِ وَغَلَّقَتِ الْأَبْوَابَ
وَقَالَتْ هَيْتَ لَكَ قَالَ مَعَاذَ اللَّهِ إِنَّهُ رَبِّي أَحْسَنَ
مَثْوَايَ إِنَّهُ لَا يُفْلِحُ الظَّالِمُونَ ۞ وَلَقَدْ هَمَّتْ بِهِ
وَهَمَّ بِهَا لَوْلَا أَن رَّأَى بُرْهَانَ رَبِّهِ كَذَلِكَ لِنَصْرِفَ عَنْهُ
السُّوءَ وَالْفَحْشَاءَ إِنَّهُ مِنْ عِبَادِنَا الْمُخْلَصِينَ ۞ وَاسْتَبَقَا
الْبَابَ وَقَدَّتْ قَمِيصَهُ مِن دُبُرٍ وَأَلْفَيَا سَيِّدَهَا لَدَى الْبَابِ
قَالَتْ مَا جَزَاءُ مَنْ أَرَادَ بِأَهْلِكَ سُوءًا إِلَّا أَن يُسْجَنَ أَوْ
عَذَابٌ أَلِيمٌ ۞ قَالَ هِيَ رَاوَدَتْنِي عَن نَّفْسِي وَشَهِدَ شَاهِدٌ مِّنْ
أَهْلِهَا إِن كَانَ قَمِيصُهُ قُدَّ مِن قُبُلٍ فَصَدَقَتْ وَهُوَ مِنَ الْكَاذِبِينَ
۞ وَإِن كَانَ قَمِيصُهُ قُدَّ مِن دُبُرٍ فَكَذَبَتْ وَهُوَ مِنَ الصَّادِقِينَ
۞ فَلَمَّا رَأَى قَمِيصَهُ قُدَّ مِن دُبُرٍ قَالَ إِنَّهُ مِن كَيْدِكُنَّ
إِنَّ كَيْدَكُنَّ عَظِيمٌ ۞ يُوسُفُ أَعْرِضْ عَنْ هَـٰذَا
وَاسْتَغْفِرِي لِذَنبِكِ إِنَّكِ كُنتِ مِنَ الْخَاطِئِينَ ۞ وَقَالَ
نِسْوَةٌ فِي الْمَدِينَةِ امْرَأَتُ الْعَزِيزِ تُرَاوِدُ فَتَاهَا عَن نَّفْسِهِ
قَدْ شَغَفَهَا حُبًّا إِنَّا لَنَرَاهَا فِي ضَلَالٍ مُّبِينٍ ۞

23. And the woman in whose house he was living sought to enjoy herself by him. She bolted the doors and said, "Come, please!" He said: "God forbid! My lord (your husband) has given me honorable, good lodging. Assuredly, wrongdoers never prosper."

24. Certainly, she was burning with desire for him; and he would have desired her had it not been that he had already seen the argument and proof of his Lord (concerning chastity and good conduct, and so was anxious only about how to escape her). We did it in that way (We showed to him Our argument and proof) so that We might avert from him an evil and indecency. For he was one of Our servants endowed with perfect sincerity and purity of intention in faith and practicing the Religion.[14]

25. So they raced to the door and she tore his shirt from the back, and they met her master (husband) by the door. She cried: "What should be the recompense for him who purposes evil against your household – except imprisonment or a grievous punishment?"

26. He (Joseph) said: "She it was who sought to enjoy herself by me." And one of those present, a member of her household, said: "If his shirt has been torn from

the front, she is telling the truth, and he is a liar.

27. "But if it is torn from the back, then she is lying, and he is truthful."

28. So when he (her husband) saw that his shirt was torn from the back, he (turned to his wife and) said: "This is from the guile of you women; for sure your guile is great."

29. (To Joseph) he said "Do not mention this (to anyone)." (To his wife) he said: "Ask forgiveness for your sin; for surely you have committed a sin."

30. Women (gossiping) in the city said: "The minister's wife has sought to enjoy herself by her slave-boy. Certainly it (her desire for him) has pierced her heart with love. We see that she has plainly lost her wits and her way."[15]

14. When God excluded Satan from His mercy eternally, he took permission from God to come upon human beings, claiming that he would lead astray all except those endowed with sincerity in faith and practicing the Religion (15: 40; 38: 83). It is true that the Qur'ān mentions only the pure and sincere ones as being those whose salvation is guaranteed, and these are only the Prophets (37: 40, 74, 128). However, this does not mean that everybody else will go astray under the influence of Satan and perish. But everybody other than a Prophet is at risk and can be seduced by Satan. So we must continuously be on the alert against Satan's seduction and whenever we feel driven by Satan, we must immediately turn to God in repentance. The Prophets are, however, sinless and exempt from Satan's influence. Having overcome their carnal selves eternally by always using their free will in the right direction, they are secured by God against any deviation.

God orders sincerity; that is, believing and practicing the Religion only for His sake. Whatever God has ordered us to do we must do it because God wants us to do it and in order to obtain His approval. Those who act so, who seek devotion to God in purity of intention and sincerity, are the *mukhlis*, those who always seek sincerity. As for the Prophets, they are the *mukhlas*, those whom God has favored with purity of intention and sincerity. Since they always sought His good pleasure and used their free will in the direction that would please God, God has established them on the peak of sincerity. The Prophet Joseph, upon him be peace, was among those servants, one whom the Qur'ān mentions as a person who was endowed with sincerity in faith and practicing the Religion (*mukhlas*) and who was devoted to doing good as if seeing God (*muhsin*).

15. In Arabic when the subject is feminine, the verb is in feminine form. Another grammatical rule is that any noun that is in the plural is regarded as being feminine. However, in this verse, although the subject – women – is feminine and it is also in the plural – that is, although the subject is doubly in the feminine form, the verb in the original text is in the masculine. This means that when there is a strong solidarity in a community or group – even though this is a group of women – that group or community acquires "manly" power (*Lem'alar* ("The Gleams"), 161). This usage in the verse implies that there was a strong society of women which had dominance in the capital of Egypt while Joseph was a slave there.

238

فَلَمَّا سَمِعَتْ بِمَكْرِهِنَّ أَرْسَلَتْ إِلَيْهِنَّ وَأَعْتَدَتْ لَهُنَّ مُتَّكَأً وَآتَتْ كُلَّ وَاحِدَةٍ
مِنْهُنَّ سِكِّينًا وَقَالَتِ اخْرُجْ عَلَيْهِنَّ فَلَمَّا رَأَيْنَهُ أَكْبَرْنَهُ وَقَطَّعْنَ
أَيْدِيَهُنَّ وَقُلْنَ حَاشَ لِلَّهِ مَا هَذَا بَشَرًا إِنْ هَذَا إِلَّا مَلَكٌ كَرِيمٌ
۝ قَالَتْ فَذَلِكُنَّ الَّذِي لُمْتُنَّنِي فِيهِ وَلَقَدْ رَاوَدتُّهُ عَن نَّفْسِهِ
فَاسْتَعْصَمَ وَلَئِن لَّمْ يَفْعَلْ مَا آمُرُهُ لَيُسْجَنَنَّ وَلَيَكُونًا مِّنَ
الصَّاغِرِينَ ۝ قَالَ رَبِّ السِّجْنُ أَحَبُّ إِلَيَّ مِمَّا يَدْعُونَنِي إِلَيْهِ
وَإِلَّا تَصْرِفْ عَنِّي كَيْدَهُنَّ أَصْبُ إِلَيْهِنَّ وَأَكُن مِّنَ الْجَاهِلِينَ
۝ فَاسْتَجَابَ لَهُ رَبُّهُ فَصَرَفَ عَنْهُ كَيْدَهُنَّ إِنَّهُ هُوَ السَّمِيعُ
الْعَلِيمُ ۝ ثُمَّ بَدَا لَهُم مِّن بَعْدِ مَا رَأَوُا الْآيَاتِ لَيَسْجُنُنَّهُ
حَتَّى حِينٍ ۝ وَدَخَلَ مَعَهُ السِّجْنَ فَتَيَانِ قَالَ أَحَدُهُمَا
إِنِّي أَرَانِي أَعْصِرُ خَمْرًا وَقَالَ الْآخَرُ إِنِّي أَرَانِي أَحْمِلُ فَوْقَ رَأْسِي
خُبْزًا تَأْكُلُ الطَّيْرُ مِنْهُ نَبِّئْنَا بِتَأْوِيلِهِ إِنَّا نَرَاكَ مِنَ الْمُحْسِنِينَ
۝ قَالَ لَا يَأْتِيكُمَا طَعَامٌ تُرْزَقَانِهِ إِلَّا نَبَّأْتُكُمَا بِتَأْوِيلِهِ
قَبْلَ أَن يَأْتِيَكُمَا ذَلِكُمَا مِمَّا عَلَّمَنِي رَبِّي إِنِّي تَرَكْتُ
مِلَّةَ قَوْمٍ لَّا يُؤْمِنُونَ بِاللَّهِ وَهُم بِالْآخِرَةِ هُمْ كَافِرُونَ ۝

31. When she heard of their sly whispers, she sent for them, and prepared for them a place of reclining for a sumptuous meal. She gave to each one of them a knife and said (to Joseph): "Come out before them!" When they saw him, they were so stricken with admiration of him that they cut their hands, exclaiming: "God save us! This is no human mortal; he is but a noble angel!"

32. She said: "This is the one about whom you have been taunting me. And, indeed, I did seek to enjoy myself by him, but he was resolute in his chastity. Yet if he continues to refuse what I command him, he shall certainly be imprisoned, and shall certainly find himself among the humbled!"

33. He (imploring God) said: "My Lord! Prison is dearer to me than what they bid me to. If You do not avert their guile from me, I might incline towards them and become one of the ignorant (those who succumb to such temptations)."[16]

34. So his Lord answered him and averted from him their guile. Surely He it is Who is the All-Hearing, the All-Knowing.

35. It occurred to them (the noblemen and his household), even after they had seen the signs (of Joseph's innocence), that they should imprison him for a time.

36. And there entered the prison with him two young men. One of them said (to Joseph one day): "I dreamed that I was pressing grapes for wine." The other said: "I dreamed that I was carrying bread upon my head, of which birds were eating." "Inform us of their meaning. For sure we see that you are of those endowed with the best qualities."

37. He said: "There does not come to you any food that you will be given but I can inform you of what kind of food it is before it comes to you. This is of the knowledge that my Lord has taught me. Surely I have totally rejected the way of a people who do not have faith in God (as they ought to have faith), and who do not believe in the Hereafter.[17]

16. These verses show clearly what the Egyptian community was like. There were shadowy remnants of the Divine Religion and those in authority could talk about sin and asking forgiveness. But this was no more than habit. Even though they knew about God and had some belief in Him, they associated partners with Him. Like their counterparts in the present in many countries, the ruling class and the high society of the Capital were morally corrupt. The women indulged in gossip, giving banquets, arranging amusements and competing for worldly things. They enjoyed control in their houses and husbands could react to their improper behavior only by giving advice. Laws were ignored in favor of the interest of the ruling class and there was injustice throughout society.

It is in such circumstances that the Prophet Joseph, upon him be peace, succeeded in all the tests to which he was put. Though a slave in the palace, he rejected the invitation of noble, rich, and beautiful women. He willingly preferred imprisonment to committing sin. In the end, the ruling class had to admit his innocence, wisdom, knowledge, ability to judge in all affairs, and his performance of good deeds.

17. The Prophet Joseph, upon him be peace, like all the other Messengers of God, lost no opportunity to convey his message to those around him. He teaches us that we should use all convenient opportunities to do the same.

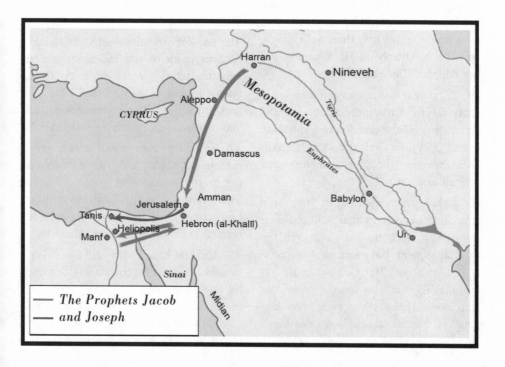

The Prophets Jacob and Joseph

وَاتَّبَعْتُ مِلَّةَ اٰبَآئِيْ اِبْرٰهِيمَ وَاِسْحٰقَ وَيَعْقُوبَ مَاكَانَ لَنَآ اَنْ نُّشْرِكَ بِاللّٰهِ مِنْ شَيْءٍ ذٰلِكَ مِنْ فَضْلِ اللّٰهِ عَلَيْنَا وَعَلَى النَّاسِ وَلٰكِنَّ اَكْثَرَ النَّاسِ لَا يَشْكُرُوْنَ ۞ يٰصَاحِبَيِ السِّجْنِ ءَاَرْبَابٌ مُّتَفَرِّقُوْنَ خَيْرٌ اَمِ اللّٰهُ الْوَاحِدُ الْقَهَّارُ ۞ مَاتَعْبُدُوْنَ مِنْ دُوْنِهٖٓ اِلَّآ اَسْمَآءً سَمَّيْتُمُوْهَآ اَنْتُمْ وَاٰبَآؤُكُمْ مَّآ اَنْزَلَ اللّٰهُ بِهَا مِنْ سُلْطَانٍ اِنِ الْحُكْمُ اِلَّا لِلّٰهِ اَمَرَ اَلَّا تَعْبُدُوْٓا اِلَّآ اِيَّاهُ ذٰلِكَ الدِّيْنُ الْقَيِّمُ وَلٰكِنَّ اَكْثَرَ النَّاسِ لَا يَعْلَمُوْنَ ۞ يٰصَاحِبَيِ السِّجْنِ اَمَّآ اَحَدُكُمَا فَيَسْقِيْ رَبَّهٗ خَمْرًا وَاَمَّا الْاٰخَرُ فَيُصْلَبُ فَتَأْكُلُ الطَّيْرُ مِنْ رَأْسِهٖ قُضِيَ الْاَمْرُ الَّذِيْ فِيْهِ تَسْتَفْتِيٰنِ ۞ وَقَالَ لِلَّذِيْ ظَنَّ اَنَّهٗ نَاجٍ مِّنْهُمَا اذْكُرْنِيْ عِنْدَ رَبِّكَ فَاَنْسٰىهُ الشَّيْطٰنُ ذِكْرَ رَبِّهٖ فَلَبِثَ فِي السِّجْنِ بِضْعَ سِنِيْنَ ۞ وَقَالَ الْمَلِكُ اِنِّيْٓ اَرٰى سَبْعَ بَقَرٰتٍ سِمَانٍ يَّأْكُلُهُنَّ سَبْعٌ عِجَافٌ وَّسَبْعَ سُنْبُلٰتٍ خُضْرٍ وَّاُخَرَ يٰبِسٰتٍ يٰٓاَيُّهَا الْمَلَاُ اَفْتُوْنِيْ فِيْ رُءْيَايَ اِنْ كُنْتُمْ لِلرُّءْيَا تَعْبُرُوْنَ ۞

38. "I have followed the way of my fathers Abraham, Isaac, and Jacob. It is not for us to associate anything with God as partner. This (His teaching and calling us to belief in Him without associating any partners with Him) is from God's grace and bounty on us and on all people, but most people do not give thanks (in return, by believing firmly in His Oneness and worshipping Him alone).

39. "O my two fellow-prisoners! Are many diverse lords more reasonable and better (to attribute creation to and believe in and obey), or God, the One, the All-Overwhelming (holding absolute sway over all that exists)?[18]

40. "What you worship apart from Him is nothing but names that you and your forefathers made up for them. (In the absolute sense) judgment and authority rest with none but God alone: He has commanded that you worship none but Him alone. This is the upright, ever-true Religion, but most people do not know (and they act from their ignorance).

41. "(As for your dreams:) O my fellow-prisoners! One of you will again give his lord (the king) wine to drink. As to the other, he will be hanged, and birds will peck at his head. The matter about which you inquired has already been decided."[19]

42. He said to the one of the two whom he deemed would be delivered: "Mention me in the presence of your lord." But Satan caused him to forget to mention him to his lord, and so he (Joseph) remained in prison some more years.

43. And the king[20] said one day: "I saw in a dream seven fat cows being devoured by seven lean ones, and seven green ears of grain and another (seven) dry. O you courtiers! Enlighten me about my dream, if you know how to interpret dreams."

18. For the Existence and Unity of God and having this belief, see Appendix 8.

19. The interpreters of the Qur'ān have inferred from the verse that the second person did not have a dream, but rather that he had lied. When he heard the meaning of his dream, he admitted that he had not had a dream, but had invented it. However, this was of no avail concerning its result; the Prophet Joseph, upon him be peace, concluded: "*The matter about which you inquired has already been decided.*"

Inventing dreams is a two-fold lie and is a grave sin. For we do not dream by our free will; rather God causes us to dream, so inventing dreams means attributing a lie to God. When someone with exact knowledge about the meaning of dreams has interpreted a dream – particularly if that person is a Prophet or another one near to God although not a Prophet – it is expected that that dream will come true. So we should relate our dreams to those who have exact knowledge of their meaning and refrain from relating our "evil" dreams. God's Messenger, upon him be peace and blessings, advises us that when we have an evil dream,

we should pray to God to save us from any evil likely to befall us, and that we should give something in charity.

20. This king was most probably one of the Hyksos rulers who ruled Egypt from about 1700 to 1550 BC. They were a northwestern Arab or mixed Arab-Asiatic people who entered Egypt sometime between 1720 and 1710 BC, and subdued the Middle Kingdom. They used Avaris-Tanis in the Nile delta as their capital rather than the Egyptian capital of Thebes. Under their hegemony, which lasted over a century, they established a powerful kingdom that included Syria and Palestine, and maintained peace and prosperity in their territories, to which the Prophet Joseph must have made the greatest contribution. They introduced the horse-drawn chariot and the composite bow, and their successful conquests were furthered by a type of rectangular fortification of beaten earth used as a fortress; archaeologists have uncovered examples of these mounds at Jericho, Shechem, and Lachish. The Hyksos were crushed by Amasis I at the battle of Tanis in 1550 BC.

44. They said: "Jumbles of dream images. And we are not knowledgeable in the interpretation of dream images."

45. Now after all that time, of the two (prisoners) the one who had been delivered remembered (what Joseph had asked him to remember) and he said: "I will inform you of its meaning, so send me forth!"

46. (Coming to Joseph in the prison, he said): "Joseph, O man of truth! Enlighten us about seven fat cows being devoured by seven lean ones, and seven green ears of grain and another (seven) dry[21] – so that I can return to the people (of the court). And it may be that (after I have told them your interpretation of the dreams) they will come to know (what manner of man you are and the injustice done to you)."

47. He said: "You shall sow for seven years as usual, but that which you have harvested, leave it in the ear, all save a little which you eat.

48. "Then will come after that seven hard years, which will consume what you have laid up for them, all but a little you should keep in store (to use as seed stock).

49. "And thereafter will come a year in which the people will be relieved (with abundance in place of scarcity), and in which they will press (fruit for drink and oil, and milk from their cattle)."

50. (Informed of the meaning of his dream,) the king said, "Bring him to me!" When the messenger (of the king) came to him, Joseph said: "Go back to your lord and ask him to find out the facts of the case about the women who cut their hands. For sure my Lord has full knowledge of their guile (and my innocence)."

51. (The king had the woman assem-

bled before him and) he said: "What happened (between you and Joseph) when you sought to enjoy yourselves by him?" They said: "God save us! We perceived no evil at all on his part!" And the wife of the minister said: "Now the truth has come to light. It was I who sought to enjoy myself by him. He was indeed truthful (in all he said and true to his lord)."

52. (Joseph was informed of the women's confessions and the declaration of his innocence. He explained why he had asked for the inquiry:) "This was so that he (my former lord) should know that I did not betray him in his absence, and that God never guides the schemes of the treacherous (to success).

---

21. Dreams should be narrated exactly as they were, and the words used to narrate them are of great importance with respect to their meaning and interpretation. For this reason,

the Qur'ān mentions the dream of the king in exactly the same words in two different places where it quotes it from the king himself and his cupbearer.

٢٤١   آلْجُزْءُ الثَّالِثَ عَشَر   241

وَمَآ أُبَرِّئُ نَفْسِيٓ إِنَّ النَّفْسَ لَأَمَّارَةٌ بِالسُّوٓءِ إِلَّا مَا رَحِمَ رَبِّيٓ إِنَّ رَبِّي
غَفُورٌ رَّحِيمٌ ۝ وَقَالَ الْمَلِكُ ائْتُونِي بِهِۦ أَسْتَخْلِصْهُ لِنَفْسِي
فَلَمَّا كَلَّمَهُۥ قَالَ إِنَّكَ الْيَوْمَ لَدَيْنَا مَكِينٌ أَمِينٌ ۝ قَالَ اجْعَلْنِي
عَلَىٰ خَزَآئِنِ الْأَرْضِ إِنِّي حَفِيظٌ عَلِيمٌ ۝ وَكَذَٰلِكَ مَكَّنَّا لِيُوسُفَ
فِي الْأَرْضِ يَتَبَوَّأُ مِنْهَا حَيْثُ يَشَآءُ نُصِيبُ بِرَحْمَتِنَا مَن
نَّشَآءُ وَلَا نُضِيعُ أَجْرَ الْمُحْسِنِينَ ۝ وَلَأَجْرُ الْأَخِرَةِ خَيْرٌ
لِّلَّذِينَ ءَامَنُوا۟ وَكَانُوا۟ يَتَّقُونَ ۝ وَجَآءَ إِخْوَةُ يُوسُفَ
فَدَخَلُوا۟ عَلَيْهِ فَعَرَفَهُمْ وَهُمْ لَهُۥ مُنكِرُونَ ۝ وَلَمَّا جَهَّزَهُم
بِجَهَازِهِمْ قَالَ ائْتُونِي بِأَخٍ لَّكُم مِّنْ أَبِيكُمْ ۚ أَلَا تَرَوْنَ أَنِّيٓ
أُوفِي الْكَيْلَ وَأَنَا۠ خَيْرُ الْمُنزِلِينَ ۝ فَإِن لَّمْ تَأْتُونِي بِهِۦ فَلَا كَيْلَ
لَكُمْ عِندِي وَلَا تَقْرَبُونِ ۝ قَالُوا۟ سَنُرَٰوِدُ عَنْهُ أَبَاهُ وَإِنَّا
لَفَاعِلُونَ ۝ وَقَالَ لِفِتْيَانِهِ اجْعَلُوا۟ بِضَاعَتَهُمْ فِي رِحَالِهِمْ
لَعَلَّهُمْ يَعْرِفُونَهَآ إِذَا انقَلَبُوٓا۟ إِلَىٰٓ أَهْلِهِمْ لَعَلَّهُمْ يَرْجِعُونَ
۝ فَلَمَّا رَجَعُوٓا۟ إِلَىٰٓ أَبِيهِمْ قَالُوا۟ يَٰٓأَبَانَا مُنِعَ مِنَّا الْكَيْلُ
فَأَرْسِلْ مَعَنَآ أَخَانَا نَكْتَلْ وَإِنَّا لَهُۥ لَحَٰفِظُونَ ۝

———⟨⟩———

53. "Yet I do not claim my self free of error, for assuredly the human soul always commands evil, except that my Lord has mercy (which saves us from committing evil acts). Surely my Lord is All-Forgiving, All-Compassionate (especially toward His believing servants)."[22]

54. The king said: "Bring him to me, so that I may appoint him to myself (as my personal counselor)." And when he had conversed with him, he said: "From this day you shall be of high standing with us, established and trusted."

55. He (Joseph) said: "Place me in charge over the store-houses of the land, for I am a good custodian, a knowledgeable one."[23]

56. Thus We established Joseph in the land (of Egypt) with authority. He was fully accepted therein, able to go and execute his authority wherever he willed. We visit with Our mercy whomever We will. We do not leave to waste the reward of those devoted to doing good as if seeing God.

57. However, certainly the reward of the Hereafter is better for those who believe and keep from disobedience to God in reverence for Him and piety.

58. And (after some years) Joseph's brothers came to Egypt and presented themselves before him: he knew them (at once), they did not recognize him.

59. When he provided them with their provisions, he said: "Bring me (when you come next time) that (step) brother of yours by your father. Do you not see that I fill up the measure and I am the best of hosts?

60. "But if you do not bring him, I will no longer have any measure of provisions to give you, and you shall not be given leave to come near me."

61. They said: "We will try to win him from his father, indeed we will do our utmost."

62. He (Joseph) said to his servants: "Put back their merchandise (with which they had bartered) into their saddlebags, so that they may find it there when they have returned home, and hence will (be more eager to) return."

63. So when they went back to their father, they said: "O our father! We will be denied any measure (of provisions unless we take our brother), so send our brother with us that we may obtain our measure. For we will surely take every care of him."

22. These words display the deep devotion of a Prophet to God Almighty and his announcement that it is not possible for a person to find the right way and be steadfast on it without God's special succor. These words of the Prophet Joseph may be considered along with those of the Last Messenger: "No one can enter Paradise by virtue of their own deeds. Nor do I. However, my Lord has embraced me in His mercy" (al-Bukhārī, "Riqāq," 18).

23. The Prophet Joseph, upon him be peace, teaches us very important lessons. He had a lofty ideal, which was to convey God's Eternal Message to the people wherever he was. He had the opportunity to convey it to his fellow-prisoners after they came to know how perfect a man he was. Now, in order to convey it to all people, he first wanted his innocence and trustworthiness to be openly acknowledged by them. Secondly, he asked for a job about which he had the best and most expert knowledge. Thirdly, he asked for the job, not for its own sake or for the sake of worldly advantages, but in order to be able to convey his message in the best and most influential way possible. Innocence, virtue, wishing the best for all and doing good for them, trustworthiness, truthfulness, and special knowledge are essential to Prophethood; those who are in a position to convey God's Message in every age and place should try to equip themselves with these characteristics as much as possible.

242

﷽

قَالَ هَلْ اٰمَنُكُمْ عَلَيْهِ اِلَّا كَمَا اَمِنْتُكُمْ عَلٰٓى اَخِيهِ مِنْ قَبْلُ فَاللّٰهُ خَيْرٌ حَافِظًا ۖ وَهُوَ اَرْحَمُ الرَّاحِمِينَ ۞ وَلَمَّا فَتَحُوْا مَتَاعَهُمْ وَجَدُوْا بِضَاعَتَهُمْ رُدَّتْ اِلَيْهِمْ ۖ قَالُوْا يٰٓاَبَانَا مَا نَبْغِيْ ۖ هٰذِهِ بِضَاعَتُنَا رُدَّتْ اِلَيْنَا ۖ وَنَمِيرُ اَهْلَنَا وَنَحْفَظُ اَخَانَا وَنَزْدَادُ كَيْلَ بَعِيرٍ ۖ ذٰلِكَ كَيْلٌ يَسِيرٌ ۞ قَالَ لَنْ اُرْسِلَهُ مَعَكُمْ حَتّٰى تُؤْتُوْنِ مَوْثِقًا مِّنَ اللّٰهِ لَتَأْتُنَّنِيْ بِهٖٓ اِلَّآ اَنْ يُحَاطَ بِكُمْ ۖ فَلَمَّآ اٰتَوْهُ مَوْثِقَهُمْ قَالَ اللّٰهُ عَلٰى مَا نَقُوْلُ وَكِيلٌ ۞ وَقَالَ يٰبَنِيَّ لَا تَدْخُلُوْا مِنْ بَابٍ وَّاحِدٍ وَّادْخُلُوْا مِنْ اَبْوَابٍ مُّتَفَرِّقَةٍ ۖ وَمَآ اُغْنِيْ عَنْكُمْ مِّنَ اللّٰهِ مِنْ شَيْءٍ ۖ اِنِ الْحُكْمُ اِلَّا لِلّٰهِ ۖ عَلَيْهِ تَوَكَّلْتُ ۖ وَعَلَيْهِ فَلْيَتَوَكَّلِ الْمُتَوَكِّلُوْنَ ۞ وَلَمَّا دَخَلُوْا مِنْ حَيْثُ اَمَرَهُمْ اَبُوْهُمْ ۖ مَا كَانَ يُغْنِيْ عَنْهُمْ مِّنَ اللّٰهِ مِنْ شَيْءٍ اِلَّا حَاجَةً فِيْ نَفْسِ يَعْقُوْبَ قَضٰىهَا ۖ وَاِنَّهُ لَذُوْ عِلْمٍ لِّمَا عَلَّمْنٰهُ وَلٰكِنَّ اَكْثَرَ النَّاسِ لَا يَعْلَمُوْنَ ۞ وَلَمَّا دَخَلُوْا عَلٰى يُوْسُفَ اٰوٰٓى اِلَيْهِ اَخَاهُ ۖ قَالَ اِنِّيْ اَنَا اَخُوْكَ فَلَا تَبْتَئِسْ بِمَا كَانُوْا يَعْمَلُوْنَ ۞

---

64. He said: "Shall I to entrust him to you as I once entrusted his brother to you before? However, God is the Best as protector and He is the Most Merciful of the merciful."

65. Then when they opened their packs, they found that their merchandise had been returned to them. "Father," they said, "What more should we ask for? Here is our merchandise returned to us. So we will again be able to get provisions for our family! We will guard our brother and (his being with us) we will have an additional camel-load. That will be an easy gain."

66. He said: "Never will I send him with you until you give me a solemn pledge in God's Name that you will indeed bring him back to me, unless you are (in some insurmountable way) overwhelmed. Then, when they gave him their solemn pledge, he said: "God is witness to and watcher over all that we say (and only on Him can we rely to fulfill our pledges)."

67. He said (by way of advice at the time of their departure): "O my sons! Do not enter the city by one gate (in a single company), but enter by different gates. Yet I can be of no avail whatever to you against anything God wills. Judgment and authority rest with none but God alone. In Him have I put my trust, and whoever would entrust themselves should put their trust in Him."

68. They entered the city in the manner their father had enjoined on them, although this would have proved of no avail whatever to them against anything God had willed; it was but a need in Jacob's soul, which he thus satisfied. For he was possessed of knowledge because We had taught it to him, but most people do not know (nor do they act according to the knowledge from God).[24]

69. And when they presented themselves before Joseph, he welcomed his brother to himself, and (having taken him aside) said: "Surely it is I – I am your brother, so do not grieve over what they did."

24. We do not know what Destiny has in store for us, so we must behave according to the apparent conditions. If we behave according to the Divine rules, we have behaved in accordance with Destiny.

Jacob's sons were well-built and good-looking. Their entering the capital of a foreign state all together may have attracted the attention of both people and the government. Therefore, they may have been exposed to some harm. For this reason, Jacob advised them to enter the city through different gates in order not to draw attention to themselves. This was what he had to do as a precaution. However, in order to remind us of God's absolute sovereignty and of the fact that if He wills something people cannot prevent it from taking place, God stresses the dominion of His Will while approving of Jacob's attitude. As a Messenger of God, Jacob was well aware of the relationship between human free will and willed actions and God's absolute sovereignty and Destiny.

243

74. They said: "What, then, shall be the penalty for it if you are proved liars?"

75. They said: "The penalty for it is: the (freedom of the) one in whose saddlebag it is found is the penalty for it. That is how we recompense the wrongdoers (who steal)."

76. (So they were brought back before Joseph to be searched.) He began with their sacks before his brother's sack; and then he brought the drinking-cup out of his brother's sack. In this way We made an arrangement for Joseph. Under the king's law, he could not have detained his brother, had not God so willed. Whomsoever We will, We raise in ranks. Above every owner of knowledge there is (always) one more knowledgeable (until God Who is the All-Knowing).[25/26]

77. They (the other brothers) said: "If he has stolen – well, a brother of his stole before." But Joseph (endured their false accusation in silence and) held it secret in his soul and did not disclose it to them. He said (to himself): "You are indeed in a bad situation (now and say so). God has full knowledge of (the truth of) what you allege."

78. "O minister!" they said: "He has a father, a very old man; so take one of us in his place. We see that you are indeed of those devoted to selfless kindness."

70. Then when he had provided them with their provisions, he put the drinking-cup (belonging to him) in his brother's saddlebag (as a gift). Then, (as they had just departed on their return) a herald called out: "O you people of the caravan! You are surely thieves!"

71. They said, turning towards them (the herald and his companions): "What is it that you are missing?"

72. They said: "We are missing the king's goblet, and whoever brings it shall receive a camel-load (as reward)." (And the herald added:) "I have pledged myself to recovering it."

73. They (the brothers) said: "By God! Certainly you know well that we did not come to provoke disorder and corruption in this land, and we have never been thieves!"

25. This verse contains lessons, such as the following:

- Muslims must not cause corruption and unrest where they stay, especially when they are given accommodation.
- The original word used for law in the phrase "under the king's law" is *dīn* – religion. This means that *dīn* ('religion' in Islam) includes the laws ordering human worldly life.
- No one should claim to have the final say in a matter about which they do not have full, verified knowledge, and they should always consider that there may be one who is more knowledgeable than them. There are degrees of knowledge, reaching up until God's all-encompassing Knowledge. A Prophet's knowledge is based on God's Knowledge and teaching.
- By saying *Above every owner of knowledge there is one more knowledgeable,* not "Above every scholar," the verse differentiates between those who have some (piece of) knowledge and those who are scholars or well-versed in knowledge. This difference is like the difference between one who teaches science at a school and a scientist. Bediüzzaman Said Nursi says: "Any piece of knowledge that has not been fully digested should not be taught. A true, guiding scholar acts like a sheep, not like a bird. A sheep feeds its lambs on its milk, a fully-digested and processed substance, whereas a bird feeds its chicks on what it has half-chewed and then regurgitated" (Sözler, ["The Words"], 658).

26. Different comments have been made on the arrangement mentioned in these verses. The gist of the matter must be as follows:

The Prophet Joseph, who enjoyed full authority on behalf of the king, put the drinking-cup which was known to belong to the king, but which Joseph himself used or might have been given as a present, in the saddle-bag of his brother as a gift. The courtiers noticed that the cup was missing and, without finding it despite searching, promised a camel load of grain to whoever could bring it. When it could not be found in the court, those who set out to find it with the hope of receiving the reward promised, became suspicious of the caravans that had come to buy wheat.

When the sacks of Jacob's sons were searched, the goblet was found in the sack of Joseph's brother. As explicitly stated in verse 76, this was the arrangement of God, not Joseph, so that Joseph could retain his brother with himself. Although Joseph knew that his brother was innocent, the result was in both his and his brother's favor and would serve for his cause. Joseph's brother would have to endure the accusation only for a while, just as Joseph had endured a great slander and imprisonment for a long time.

Destiny always wills good for believers. On the way to the good or the desired result He has ordained for them, God may subject believers to the stones of Destiny because of the crimes they have committed. Such stones cause their crimes to be forgiven, if they repent and ask for God's forgiveness. Joseph's brothers paid for the wrong they had done to Joseph by being accused of theft and having to leave their brother in Egypt, despite the pledge they had given to their father. The following verse (77) shows that they still nurtured bad feelings for Joseph, thus proving that they deserved a stone from Destiny. However, in the end, everything turned to be good for them, because it caused them to see the truth, to understand why their father was more concerned for Joseph, and to submit to God's judgment for them and their brother Joseph, allowing their sin to be forgiven. They would settle in Egypt, occupying high positions (5: 20), and God's Religion would prevail there for a certain time. It was Jacob and Joseph, upon them be peace, who had to bear the greatest sufferings to that end, as they were God's Messengers charged with that great, lofty mission.

244   سورة يوسف   ٢٤٤

قَالَ مَعَاذَ اللهِ أَن نَّأْخُذَ إِلَّا مَن وَجَدْنَا مَتَاعَنَا عِندَهُ

إِنَّآ إِذًا لَّظَالِمُونَ ۝ فَلَمَّا اسْتَيْـَٔسُوا مِنْهُ خَلَصُوا نَجِيًّا

قَالَ كَبِيرُهُمْ أَلَمْ تَعْلَمُوٓا أَنَّ أَبَاكُمْ قَدْ أَخَذَ عَلَيْكُم

مَّوْثِقًا مِّنَ اللهِ وَمِن قَبْلُ مَا فَرَّطتُمْ فِي يُوسُفَ فَلَنْ أَبْرَحَ

الْأَرْضَ حَتَّىٰ يَأْذَنَ لِيٓ أَبِيٓ أَوْ يَحْكُمَ اللهُ لِي وَهُوَ خَيْرُ الْحَاكِمِينَ

۝ ارْجِعُوٓا إِلَىٰٓ أَبِيكُمْ فَقُولُوا يَٰٓأَبَانَآ إِنَّ ابْنَكَ سَرَقَ

وَمَا شَهِدْنَآ إِلَّا بِمَا عَلِمْنَا وَمَا كُنَّا لِلْغَيْبِ حَافِظِينَ

۝ وَسْـَٔلِ الْقَرْيَةَ الَّتِي كُنَّا فِيهَا وَالْعِيرَ الَّتِيٓ أَقْبَلْنَا

فِيهَا وَإِنَّا لَصَادِقُونَ ۝ قَالَ بَلْ سَوَّلَتْ لَكُمْ أَنفُسُكُمْ

أَمْرًا فَصَبْرٌ جَمِيلٌ عَسَى اللهُ أَن يَأْتِيَنِي بِهِمْ جَمِيعًا

إِنَّهُ هُوَ الْعَلِيمُ الْحَكِيمُ ۝ وَتَوَلَّىٰ عَنْهُمْ وَقَالَ يَٰٓأَسَفَىٰ

عَلَىٰ يُوسُفَ وَابْيَضَّتْ عَيْنَاهُ مِنَ الْحُزْنِ فَهُوَ كَظِيمٌ

۝ قَالُوا تَاللهِ تَفْتَؤُا تَذْكُرُ يُوسُفَ حَتَّىٰ تَكُونَ حَرَضًا

أَوْ تَكُونَ مِنَ الْهَالِكِينَ ۝ قَالَ إِنَّمَآ أَشْكُوا بَثِّي

وَحُزْنِيٓ إِلَى اللهِ وَأَعْلَمُ مِنَ اللهِ مَا لَا تَعْلَمُونَ ۝

---

79. He said: "God forbid that we take any other but him with whom we found our merchandise; (if we did otherwise) then surely we (too) would be wrongdoers."

80. So, when they lost hope of moving him, they withdrew to take counsel among themselves. The eldest of them said: "Do you not know how your father took a solemn pledge from you in God's Name, and how, before

---

that, you failed with regard to Joseph? Never will I depart from this land, until my father gives me leave, or God judges for me (by ending my life or enabling me to win back my brother). And He is the Best of judges.

81. "Return to your father, and say: 'Our father! Your son stole. We do not testify (to anything) except what we know; and we are not keepers of the Unseen.[27]

82. 'Inquire in the township where we were, and the caravan with whom we traveled hither. We are certainly telling the truth.' "

83. (When they had returned to their father and made that speech to him) he said: "No! Rather, your (evil-commanding) souls have tempted you to something. So (the proper recourse for me now is, again,) a becoming patience (a patience that endures without complaint). It may be that God will bring them back to me all together.[28] He it is Who is the All-Knowing, the All-Wise."

84. He turned away from them and said: "Alas, my grief for Joseph!" And his eyes turned white because of the grief. And he was restraining (any resentment toward his other sons, never displaying it to them).[29]

85. They said: "By God! You will not cease mentioning Joseph until you are consumed, or you perish!"

86. He said: "I only disclose my anguish and sorrow to God,[30] and I know from God what you do not know."

---

27. That is: We only judge according to what we see. We could not have known what would happen when we had promised you to protect him, and we make no claim about anything that we have not witnessed.

28. As a Messenger of God with deep insight and sagacity, the Prophet Jacob, upon him be peace, felt that there was a Divine mystery in all that took place, and events were advancing to a good end. When events start to worsen, this means, for the believers who follow God's

way without deviation and with pure intention, that the happy end is approaching. The final end of darkness is the dawn of light.

29. What the Prophet Jacob felt deeply for his son Joseph was fatherly affection. Affection is keen, pure, and sublime. It enables one to manifest the Divine Name of the All-Compassionate. It is so comprehensive that people's affection for their own children makes them feel some affection for all children and all living beings. They can become comprehensive mirrors

in which the Divine Name, the All-Compassionate manifests Itself.

Also, affection is a sincere feeling with no ulterior motive and seeks no return. Even the lowest type of sincere affection (such as that felt by animals for their young) proves that affection does not demand any return. It directs us to the Divine Names, the All-Merciful and the All-Compassionate and shows that the way of affection leads to Divine Compassion. These two great Divine Names seem to own a light so comprehensive and splendid that it envelops the universe, satisfying everyone's needs forever, securing them against all hostility. They can enlighten people if they understand their poverty and helplessness vis-à-vis God's Riches and Power and, in return, thank Him for His limitless Compassion and Mercy. This is the way of sincere devotion to God and humility.

The remedy for the ailments of affection is the truth expressed in the concept that *God is the Best as protector and He is the Most Merciful of the merciful* (12: 64) (*The Letters*, "the 8th Letter," 1: 33–34).

30. Those enduring great suffering find the remedy for it in the suffering itself. They say, "I used to seek a remedy for my suffering, and I came to know that the remedy for my suffering is my suffering itself." Muhammad Lütfi of Alvar expresses his similar feelings as follows:

I used to seek a remedy for my inward suffering, until they said: "The remedy for your suffering is your suffering itself."

Bediüzzaman Said Nursi is one of those who have written the most on this topic. While he was in exile in Barla, a village in the southwestern Turkey, he felt inward, acute pain when he found himself in exile in a mountain, especially in the evenings, in autumn, and in his old age; he suffered separation from all his beloved ones and felt his heart groan out the following:

O Lord, I am a stranger, I am lonely and weak,
Impotent, old, and ill, and I have no choices;
O God, I beg Your mercy, ask Your forgiveness,
And I cry for help from Your Throne of Grace!

At just that point, the light of faith, the Qur'ān's effusive grace, and the All-Gracious Be-

ing's favor came to his aid and changed five kinds of separation into five circles of warm companionship. As he recited: *God is sufficient for us; and how excellent a Guardian He is* (3: 173), his heart recited: *If they turn away from you, say: "God is sufficient for me; there is no deity but He. In Him have I put my trust, and He is the Lord of the Supreme Throne (as the absolute Ruler and Sustainer of the universe and all creation, Who maintains and protects it)"* (9: 129).

Also his soul, weeping and wailing in its fearful sorrow, was persuaded by his intellect, which told it:

O helpless one, give up wailing and trust God,
For this wailing is an error that causes many troubles;
If you have found the One Who makes you suffer, then
This suffering changes into a gift bringing peace and happiness.
So thank God instead of complaining; do not think that
Nightingales and roses smile because they are always happy.
But if you do not find Him, then the whole world
Is a place of suffering and misfortune.
When you suffer from a world-wide responsibility,
Why are you wailing over an insignificant misfortune?
Come, put your trust in God and smile at the face of misfortune
So that it may also smile, for as it smiles, it lessens and changes.

After that, Bediüzzaman quotes from Jalālu'd-Dīn ar-Rūmī,

He asked: "Am I not (your Lord)?"
And you responded: "Yes!"
How can one thank Him for that "yes"?
By suffering misfortune!
What is the mystery of that "yes"?
That you say: "I am the leader of the circle of dervishes
In the lodge of poverty and perishing."

and then from 'Atā'ullāh al-Iskandarānī:

What has he found who has lost God?
And what has he lost who has found God?

(*The Letters*, "the 6th Letter," 1: 26–27)

بِسْمِ اللَّهِ الرَّحْمَٰنِ الرَّحِيمِ

يَٰبَنِيَّ اذْهَبُوا۟ فَتَحَسَّسُوا۟ مِن يُوسُفَ وَأَخِيهِ وَلَا تَا۟يْـَٔسُوا۟ مِن رَّوْحِ اللَّهِ إِنَّهُۥ لَا يَا۟يْـَٔسُ مِن رَّوْحِ اللَّهِ إِلَّا ٱلْقَوْمُ ٱلْكَٰفِرُونَ ﴿٨٧﴾ فَلَمَّا دَخَلُوا۟ عَلَيْهِ قَالُوا۟ يَٰٓأَيُّهَا ٱلْعَزِيزُ مَسَّنَا وَأَهْلَنَا ٱلضُّرُّ وَجِئْنَا بِبِضَٰعَةٍ مُّزْجَىٰةٍ فَأَوْفِ لَنَا ٱلْكَيْلَ وَتَصَدَّقْ عَلَيْنَآ إِنَّ ٱللَّهَ يَجْزِى ٱلْمُتَصَدِّقِينَ ﴿٨٨﴾ قَالَ هَلْ عَلِمْتُم مَّا فَعَلْتُم بِيُوسُفَ وَأَخِيهِ إِذْ أَنتُمْ جَٰهِلُونَ ﴿٨٩﴾ قَالُوٓا۟ أَءِنَّكَ لَأَنتَ يُوسُفُ قَالَ أَنَا۠ يُوسُفُ وَهَٰذَآ أَخِى قَدْ مَنَّ ٱللَّهُ عَلَيْنَآ إِنَّهُۥ مَن يَتَّقِ وَيَصْبِرْ فَإِنَّ ٱللَّهَ لَا يُضِيعُ أَجْرَ ٱلْمُحْسِنِينَ ﴿٩٠﴾ قَالُوا۟ تَٱللَّهِ لَقَدْ ءَاثَرَكَ ٱللَّهُ عَلَيْنَا وَإِن كُنَّا لَخَٰطِـِٔينَ ﴿٩١﴾ قَالَ لَا تَثْرِيبَ عَلَيْكُمُ ٱلْيَوْمَ يَغْفِرُ ٱللَّهُ لَكُمْ وَهُوَ أَرْحَمُ ٱلرَّٰحِمِينَ ﴿٩٢﴾ ٱذْهَبُوا۟ بِقَمِيصِى هَٰذَا فَأَلْقُوهُ عَلَىٰ وَجْهِ أَبِى يَأْتِ بَصِيرًا وَأْتُونِى بِأَهْلِكُمْ أَجْمَعِينَ ﴿٩٣﴾ وَلَمَّا فَصَلَتِ ٱلْعِيرُ قَالَ أَبُوهُمْ إِنِّى لَأَجِدُ رِيحَ يُوسُفَ لَوْلَآ أَن تُفَنِّدُونِ ﴿٩٤﴾ قَالُوا۟ تَٱللَّهِ إِنَّكَ لَفِى ضَلَٰلِكَ ٱلْقَدِيمِ ﴿٩٥﴾

87. (He said when once more seeing off his sons): "O my sons, go forth and seek earnestly for Joseph and his brother; and do not despair of God's Mercy, for none ever despairs of God's Mercy, except people who disbelieve in Him."

88. They (went back to Egypt and once more) presented themselves before Joseph, saying: "O minister! Hardship has visited us and our family, and we have brought only merchandise of scant worth; but fill up for us the measure and be charitable to us. Surely God rewards the charitable."

89. He said: "Do you know what you did to Joseph and his brother at that time when you acted as if ignorant (of right and wrong)?"

90. They said: "Is it indeed you who are Joseph?" He said: "I am Joseph, and this is my brother. God has indeed been gracious to us. Surely whoever keeps from disobedience to God in reverence for Him and piety, and is patient – surely God will not leave to waste the reward of those devoted to doing good as if seeing God."

91. "By God," they responded, "God has indeed preferred you above us, and certainly we were sinful."[31]

92. He said: "No reproach this day shall be on you. May God forgive you; indeed He is the Most Merciful of the merciful.[32]

93. "Go with this shirt of mine and lay it over my father's face, and he shall recover his sight; and come to me with all your people."

94. At the time that the (brothers') caravan set out, their father said (to those around him): "Surely, I sense the fragrance of Joseph, unless you would consider me a dotard."[33]

95. "By God," they said, "you are indeed still lost in your old error."

31. Based on this confession of Joseph's brothers, Ziya Pasha, a famous Turkish poet and politician who lived in the second half of the nineteenth century, says:

> A day certainly comes when the Power of God causes the wrongdoers to confess:
>
> "God has indeed preferred you above us!"

32. It is possible to see the manners of a Prophet in all the words and actions of Joseph, upon him be peace. His response to those who acknowledged their wrongdoing to him was to pardon them; he did not reproach them nor did he leave them feeling guilty. This attitude, which is the manifestation of adopting the way God acts, was manifested by the Last Messenger, upon him be peace and blessings, in the greatest, most perfect degree. After 21 years of persecution by the Makkan polytheists – the most stubborn unbelievers of history who subjected him to derision, slander, boycotting, and all kinds of harsh treatment, attempting to kill him, compelling him to leave his homeland, waging wars on him many times, and killing many of his most beloved friends – he conquered Makkah without bloodshed. To his diehard enemies who awaited his judgment on the day of the conquest, he said: "Today I will say to you what Joseph said to his brothers: *No reproach this day shall be on you. May God forgive you; indeed He is the Most Merciful of the merciful.*" Muslim conquerors usually displayed this same attitude, which they inherited from the Prophets, toward the conquered people. It was Mehmed II who displayed the most striking example of this nobility when he conquered Istanbul and repeated the same words to the Byzantine people who were gathered in Haghia Sophia. He provided them with the security of life and property and the freedom to live according to their own religion. This is the way of Islam.

The Qur'ān teaches important lessons through this narrative, which is the best of the narratives concerning the past. Having been revealed in Makkah at a time when the Muslims were suffering the most at the hands of the Makkan polytheists, this *sūrah*, in addition to giving the Muslims the glad tidings of the final victory, informed the Makkan polytheists that the result of their brutal resistance to the Prophet Muḥammad, upon him be peace and blessings, would not differ from the result of the matter between Joseph and his brothers. It reminded both sides that the Makkans would be obliged to acknowledge their error and reassured them that there was no reason to fear the punishment of the Prophet Muḥammad if he were to be finally victorious; his treatment would not be any different from that of the Prophet Joseph, upon him be peace.

33. As has been mentioned before, the miracles of the Prophets mark the final point of scientific progress. It was stated that the Prophet Jacob's eyes had turned white, i.e. that he was suffering from cataracts. We can conclude from these last two verses that there is a substance which removes cataract-like obstacles from the eye, and that like images and sounds, scent can also be transmitted. The Qur'ān encourages humankind to find that substance and to try to transmit scent.

Said Nursi answers a possible question which may arise concerning Jacob's perception of Joseph's scent from far away:

> The Prophet Ya'qūb (Jacob) was asked why he had not seen Yūsuf (Joseph) in a nearby well in Canaan, although the fragrance of his shirt reached him from Egypt. He replied:
>
> Our state, especially with regard to miracle-working, is like lightning that is sometimes visible and at other times hidden. Sometimes it is as if we were sitting on the highest point with the whole universe spread out before us, but at other times we cannot see what lies just ahead of us (*The Letters*, "the 15th Letter," 1: 72).

It is God Who creates the miracles at the hand of the Prophets. Therefore, without His leave, even Prophets cannot work miracles whenever they wish.

246   سُوْرَةُ يُوْسُفَ   ٢٤٦

فَلَمَّآ أَن جَآءَ ٱلۡبَشِيرُ أَلۡقَىٰهُ عَلَىٰ وَجۡهِهِۦ فَٱرۡتَدَّ بَصِيرٗاۖ قَالَ أَلَمۡ
أَقُل لَّكُمۡ إِنِّيٓ أَعۡلَمُ مِنَ ٱللَّهِ مَا لَا تَعۡلَمُونَ ۝ قَالُواْ يَٰٓأَبَانَا
ٱسۡتَغۡفِرۡ لَنَا ذُنُوبَنَآ إِنَّا كُنَّا خَٰطِـِٔينَ ۝ قَالَ سَوۡفَ
أَسۡتَغۡفِرُ لَكُمۡ رَبِّيٓۖ إِنَّهُۥ هُوَ ٱلۡغَفُورُ ٱلرَّحِيمُ ۝ فَلَمَّا دَخَلُواْ عَلَىٰ
يُوسُفَ ءَاوَىٰٓ إِلَيۡهِ أَبَوَيۡهِ وَقَالَ ٱدۡخُلُواْ مِصۡرَ إِن شَآءَ
ٱللَّهُ ءَامِنِينَ ۝ وَرَفَعَ أَبَوَيۡهِ عَلَى ٱلۡعَرۡشِ وَخَرُّواْ لَهُۥ سُجَّدٗاۖ
وَقَالَ يَٰٓأَبَتِ هَٰذَا تَأۡوِيلُ رُءۡيَٰيَ مِن قَبۡلُ قَدۡ جَعَلَهَا
رَبِّي حَقّٗاۖ وَقَدۡ أَحۡسَنَ بِيٓ إِذۡ أَخۡرَجَنِي مِنَ ٱلسِّجۡنِ وَجَآءَ بِكُم
مِّنَ ٱلۡبَدۡوِ مِنۢ بَعۡدِ أَن نَّزَغَ ٱلشَّيۡطَٰنُ بَيۡنِي وَبَيۡنَ
إِخۡوَتِيٓۚ إِنَّ رَبِّي لَطِيفٞ لِّمَا يَشَآءُۚ إِنَّهُۥ هُوَ ٱلۡعَلِيمُ ٱلۡحَكِيمُ ۝
رَبِّ قَدۡ ءَاتَيۡتَنِي مِنَ ٱلۡمُلۡكِ وَعَلَّمۡتَنِي مِن تَأۡوِيلِ ٱلۡأَحَادِيثِۚ
فَاطِرَ ٱلسَّمَٰوَٰتِ وَٱلۡأَرۡضِ أَنتَ وَلِيِّۦ فِي ٱلدُّنۡيَا وَٱلۡأٓخِرَةِۖ
تَوَفَّنِي مُسۡلِمٗا وَأَلۡحِقۡنِي بِٱلصَّٰلِحِينَ ۝ ذَٰلِكَ مِنۡ أَنۢبَآءِ
ٱلۡغَيۡبِ نُوحِيهِ إِلَيۡكَۖ وَمَا كُنتَ لَدَيۡهِمۡ إِذۡ أَجۡمَعُوٓاْ أَمۡرَهُمۡ وَهُمۡ
يَمۡكُرُونَ ۝ وَمَآ أَكۡثَرُ ٱلنَّاسِ وَلَوۡ حَرَصۡتَ بِمُؤۡمِنِينَ ۝

~◈~

---

96. But when the bearer of the good tidings came (with Joseph's shirt), Jacob laid it over his face and he regained his sight. (Soon the caravan of the brothers reached home.) Jacob said: "Did I not tell you that I know from God what you do not know?"[34]

97. (Jacob's sons confessed what they had done.) They said: "O our father! Ask God to forgive us our sins; surely we have been sinful."

98. He said: "I will ask my Lord to forgive you.[35] Surely He it is Who is the All-Forgiving, the All-Compassionate."

99. (When Jacob's family reached Egypt,) they presented themselves before Joseph (who had come out to welcome them). He embraced his parents,[36] and said (addressing all those who came): "Enter Egypt by God's will in security (free from fear of privation or grief)!"

100. He raised his parents on the throne and they all bowed down before Joseph (as a sign of loyalty to him). He said: "O my father! This is the meaning of my dream of long ago; my Lord has made it come true. He has indeed been gracious to me: He freed me from prison, and He brought you all from the desert after Satan had sown discord between me and my brothers. Truly, my Lord is subtly kind in the way He brings about whatever He wills. Surely, He it is Who is the All-Knowing, the All-Wise.

101. "My Lord! You have indeed granted me some important part of the rule and imparted to me some knowledge of the inner meaning of all happenings (including dreams). O You, Originator of the heavens and the earth each with particular features! You are my Owner and Guardian in this world and in the Hereafter. Take my soul to You a Muslim, and join me with the righteous."[37]

102. That is an account of some exemplary events of the unseen (a realm and time beyond the reach of any created being's perception) that We reveal to you, (O Messenger). You were not with them when those agreed upon their plans, and then were scheming (against Joseph).

103. Yet, be you ever so eager, most people will not believe.

---

34. It is usually the fate of great persons like Prophets that those around them usually are not aware of them nor can they understand them, and thus they suffer remoteness in parallel with their physical nearness. The physical nearness and the familiarity produced by it is like a veil over their eyes and hearts.

35. Concerning the Prophet Muḥammad, upon him be peace and blessings, and his community, the Qur'ān declares: *If, when they wronged themselves (by committing a sin), they but came to you and implored God to forgive them – with the Messenger praying to God for their forgiveness – they would find that God is One*

Who returns the repentance of His servants with acceptance and additional reward, and All-Compassionate (4: 64). It also says: *(O Messenger!).... Pray for them. Indeed your prayer is a source of comfort for them. God is All-Hearing, All-Knowing* (9: 103). It is of great importance that a Prophet prays for his community and asks God to forgive their sins. First of all, his prayer is more acceptable to God. Secondly, his prayer for his community and asking God to forgive their sins mean that he is pleased with them. God is pleased with those with whom a Prophet is pleased, and does not reject a prayer for those with whom a Prophet is pleased. It is for this reason that Jacob's sons asked their father to pray to God to forgive their sins. However, this does not mean that they themselves did not need to ask for God's forgiveness. Rather, every believer should pray to God themselves and ask Him to forgive their sins. However, one's sincere admission of one's sins and showing remorse for them, and calling for another who is regarded as being nearer to God to ask for God's forgiveness for them, especially if that one is a Prophet, means repentance.

It is worth noting that the Prophet Jacob postponed asking God to forgive the sins of his sons. This might be because a Prophet does not pray and ask for God's forgiveness for even his children without God's leave and without being fully aware of their inner state. As mentioned before (9: 144; 11: 46), the Almighty forbade Noah and Abraham to ask for forgiveness for their nearest relatives since those relatives were unbelievers. So, in order to wait for both God's leave and to observe his sons, the Prophet Jacob postponed asking for God's forgiveness.

36. The interpreters of the Qur'ān are of the opinion that the mother mentioned in this *sūrah* was Joseph's step-mother. The use here of *abawayn* not *wālidayn* (for the difference between these two expressions, see *sūrah* 9, note 24) for parents may indicate this.

37. *Make me die a Muslim (one wholly submitted to You), and join me with the righteous* marks the end of the story of the Prophet Joseph, upon him be peace. This contains, in a vivid fashion, the following significant truth concerning human life and glad tidings:

Every Prophet was sent with an important mission, conveying God's Message, and when he fulfills this mission, he asks for death since there is no further meaning in or purpose for living. When his dream came true, the Prophet Joseph thought that his mission was over. Similarly, when some jinn believed in him in Makkah, the Prophet Muḥammad, upon him be peace and blessings, also thought that his mission was over and that his death was near because some among both humankind and the jinn believed in him. God has a purpose for the creation of every being and He has created humankind and the jinn to worship Him. Moreover, every believer has some part in the mission of the Prophets, and they must order their life according to this vital purpose of their life. When there is no longer anything to do for this purpose, it means that no important meaning in remaining alive has been left. (See *The Messenger of God*, 25–26, 75.)

As for the glad tidings the verse contains:

The pleasure received from a happy story ends in deep sorrow because of final separation or death. Or, it arouses more sorrow when we learn that the people involved encounter separation or death just after finding ease and happiness. But the verse quoted above, even if it contemplates Joseph's death when he became Egypt's 'Azīz (grand vizier or chancellor) and was reunited with his parents and brothers (the happiest moment in his life), shows it in a different light. It declares: "To receive a far greater happiness, Joseph asked God for death." This means that a more attractive and pleasure-giving bliss than the greatest happiness of this world waits on the other side of the grave. Knowing this, Joseph asked for death, by all appearances an unpleasant thing, when he was enjoying the world's greatest happiness.

Another benefit of such an ending is that it encourages us to strive for the other side of the grave, where we will find real happiness and pleasure. It also shows Joseph's exalted truthfulness and announces that even the most joyful and brightest condition of the worldly life could not captivate him; rather, it led him to ask for death and the other life. (See *The Letters*, "the 23rd Letter," 2: 86–87.).

247

وَمَاتَسْأَلُهُمْ عَلَيْهِ مِنْ أَجْرٍ إِنْ هُوَ إِلَّا ذِكْرٌ لِّلْعَالَمِينَ ۝ وَكَأَيِّنْ مِّنْ ءَايَةٍ فِي السَّمَاوَاتِ وَالْأَرْضِ يَمُرُّونَ عَلَيْهَا وَهُمْ عَنْهَا مُعْرِضُونَ ۝ وَمَا يُؤْمِنُ أَكْثَرُهُم بِاللَّهِ إِلَّا وَهُم مُّشْرِكُونَ ۝ أَفَأَمِنُوٓا۟ أَن تَأْتِيَهُمْ غَاشِيَةٌ مِّنْ عَذَابِ اللَّهِ أَوْ تَأْتِيَهُمُ السَّاعَةُ بَغْتَةً وَهُمْ لَا يَشْعُرُونَ ۝ قُلْ هَٰذِهِۦ سَبِيلِىٓ أَدْعُوٓا۟ إِلَى اللَّهِ عَلَىٰ بَصِيرَةٍ أَنَا۠ وَمَنِ اتَّبَعَنِى وَسُبْحَانَ اللَّهِ وَمَآ أَنَا۠ مِنَ الْمُشْرِكِينَ ۝ وَمَآ أَرْسَلْنَا مِن قَبْلِكَ إِلَّا رِجَالًا نُّوحِىٓ إِلَيْهِم مِّنْ أَهْلِ الْقُرَىٰٓ أَفَلَمْ يَسِيرُوا۟ فِي الْأَرْضِ فَيَنظُرُوا۟ كَيْفَ كَانَ عَاقِبَةُ الَّذِينَ مِن قَبْلِهِمْ وَلَدَارُ الْأَخِرَةِ خَيْرٌ لِّلَّذِينَ اتَّقَوْا۟ أَفَلَا تَعْقِلُونَ ۝ حَتَّىٰٓ إِذَا اسْتَيْـَٔسَ الرُّسُلُ وَظَنُّوٓا۟ أَنَّهُمْ قَدْ كُذِبُوا۟ جَآءَهُمْ نَصْرُنَا فَنُجِّىَ مَن نَّشَآءُ وَلَا يُرَدُّ بَأْسُنَا عَنِ الْقَوْمِ الْمُجْرِمِينَ ۝ لَقَدْ كَانَ فِى قَصَصِهِمْ عِبْرَةٌ لِّأُو۟لِى الْأَلْبَٰبِ مَا كَانَ حَدِيثًا يُفْتَرَىٰ وَلَٰكِن تَصْدِيقَ الَّذِى بَيْنَ يَدَيْهِ وَتَفْصِيلَ كُلِّ شَىْءٍ وَهُدًى وَرَحْمَةً لِّقَوْمٍ يُؤْمِنُونَ ۝

is my way: I call to God on clear evidence and with sure knowledge – I and those who follow me. All-Glorified is God (in that He is absolutely above having any partners) – and I am not one of those who associate partners with Him."

109. We did not send before you as Messengers any but men to whom We revealed, from amongst the people of the townships (where We raised them). Have they never traveled about the earth and beheld how was the outcome for those who came before them (those who persisted in associating partners with Him and in wrongdoing and transgression)? Assuredly, the abode of the Hereafter is best for those who keep from disobedience to God in reverence for Him and piety. Will you not, then, reason and understand?

110. So far so that when they (the earlier Messengers who all had to suffer much persecution for a long time) nearly lost hope and were convinced that they were denied, Our help came to them. And whoever We willed was saved. But Our mighty punishment cannot be averted from the guilty people committed to accumulating sins.

111. Indeed, in their exemplary life-stories there is a significant lesson for people of discernment. It (the Qur'ān, which contains them) is not a discourse fabricated, but (a Divine Book revealed as) a confirmation of (the Divine authorship of and the truths still contained by) the Revelations prior to it, and an explanation of everything, and a guidance and mercy for people who will and do believe.

104. You do not ask them any wage for it (for conveying the Qur'ān to them). It is but a message and reminder to all conscious beings.

105. How many a sign there is in the heavens and earth that they pass by, being unmindful of the signs and giving no consideration to them.

106. And most of them do not even believe in God without associating partners with Him.[38]

107. Do they deem themselves secure that there will not come upon them an overwhelming punishment of God, which will envelop them thoroughly, or that the Last Hour will not come upon them all of a sudden, without their being aware (of its coming)?

108. Say (to them, O Messenger): "This

38. The Qur'ān regards associating partners with God as the greatest wrongdoing (31: 13) and belief in God without associating partners with Him as a means of the ultimate salvation (6: 82). It is not easy to remain free from associating partners with God. It has many forms and types:

• Accepting another creator besides God or helpers with Him in creation;

• admitting any part in the creation and administration of the universe to persons or some nominal principles called natural laws or to nature and so-called natural forces or to matter or to spirit or to something else;

• associating partners with Him in the government of human life;

• recognizing some powers other than He as absolute authority to make things lawful or unlawful;

• ascribing to Him certain attributes essential to created beings, such as begetting or being begotten;

• believing that He takes the form of any created being (incarnation) or that any mortal can join Him and become one with Him (union);

• ascribing to any mortal being qualities belonging to Him exclusively such as creating, taking the soul, having no beginning and end, self-sufficiency, and absolute sovereignty, etc.;

• supposing that He may have some deficiencies, such as impotence and need;

• supposing Him to be a spirit permeating the universe or the universe as His outward manifestation (Monism and Pantheism);

In short, *having no true judgment of Him* and ascribing to Him attributes that are not befitting for Him means associating partners with Him. Also,

• worshipping other than Him;

• regarding any beings other than Him as having the absolute power to give benefit or harm to themselves or others without His leave and enabling, and bowing before them in a way that indicates adoration or worship;

• praying to another being or power are also forms of associating partners with Him.

Again,

• intending to please other than He in any act of worship or in the practice of any rule or principle of religion;

• using religion for worldly benefits or personal purposes such as being known or praised means associating partners with Him.

So, there are many people who claim faith, but who cannot free themselves from associating partners with God. This is a very subtle and important point that requires great care.

248   سورة الرعد   ٢٤٨

SŪRAH 13

AR-RA'D (THUNDER)

Makkah period

Revealed in Makkah, this *sūrah* consists of 43 verses. It takes its name from the word *ar-Ra'd* (thunder) which is found in verse 13. Like other Makkan *sūrah*s, it also dwells on the essentials of faith and the arguments for them found in "nature" and humanity.

In the Name of God, the All-Merciful, the All-Compassionate.

1. *Alif. Lām. Mīm. Rā.* These are the Revelations of the Book; and what has been sent down on you from your Lord is the truth – yet most people do not believe.

2. God it is Who has raised the heavens without pillars you can see,[1] then He established Himself on the Supreme Throne;[2] and He made the sun and the moon subservient to His command, each running its course for a term appointed by Him. He directs all affairs (as the sole Ruler of creation); He sets out in detail the signs of the truth and the relevant Revelations included in the Book, that you may have certainty in the meeting with your Lord (on Judgment Day).

3. And it is He Who has spread the earth wide and set therein firm mountains and rivers, and of fruit of every kind He has made mated pairs.[3] He covers the day with the night. Surely in that are signs (manifesting the truth) for a people who reflect.

4. And on the earth are tracts close by one another (and yet different from one another), and gardens of vines, and cultivated fields, and date-palms growing in clusters from one root but standing alone, (all) watered with the same water, and yet as sustenance We have made some preferable to others (in certain respects).[4] Surely in that are signs of truth for a people who reason and understand.

5. If there is something for you to find strange, how strange their saying is: "What! After we have become dust, will we indeed be (raised up again) in a new creation?" Those are they who disbelieve in their Lord, and around whose necks are fetters (by which they are being dragged into the Fire). They are the companions of the Fire; they will abide therein.

---

1. All celestial bodies move in order, balance, and harmony. They are held and supported by invisible pillars, some of which are repulsion or centrifugal forces: *Do you not consider that God has made all that is on earth to be of service to you, and the ships that run upon the sea by* His command? And that He holds the heaven so that it may not fall upon the earth otherwise than by His leave? Surely God is for humankind All-Pitying, All-Compassionate (22: 65).

At any moment, the heavens could fall upon the earth. That the All-Mighty does not allow this to happen is yet another instance of universal obedience to His Word. Modern science explains this as a balance of centripetal and centrifugal forces. What is of far greater importance for us, however, is that we focus our minds on that obedience and on the Divine Mercy that holds the universe in its reliable motion, rather than deciding to follow Newton's or Einstein's theories about the mechanical and mathematical terms of that obedience (*The Essentials*, 244).

2. For the meaning of the Supreme Throne and God's establishing Himself thereon, see 2: 28, note 29; 7: 54, note 11.

3. By using *therein* in the meaning of "in the earth," the verse indicates that the mountains have roots within the earth. And all the rivers gushing out of the mountains show how wonderfully and miraculously rocks are susceptible and subjugated to the Divine commands of creation. To awakened, attentive hearts, this means:

The mountains cannot be the actual source of such mighty rivers, for even if they were formed completely of water, they could supply such a river for only a few months. To cite a single example, even if all the mountains on earth were to be formed of water, they could not supply even just the Nile, a river which is more than 3,000 miles long and which has been flowing from time immemorial through the deserts. Also rain, which can penetrate only about a meter underground, cannot be a sufficient source for such high expenditure. No ordinary reason, natural cause, or chance can explain the sources of these rivers and their flow. The All-Majestic Creator makes them flow forth in truly wonderful fashion from an unseen "treasury."

A source of one of the Nile's main branches is found in the Mountains of the Moon, while the Tigris' main branch starts in a cave in Turkey, and one of the main streams of the Euphrates rises in the foothills of a mountain in Diyadin. It is scientifically established that mountains are rocks solidified from liquid matter. One of the Prophet's glorifications – *All-Glorified is He Who has laid soil on a fluid solidified* – testifies that the original formation of the earth is as follows: Some liquid matter solidified at Divine command and became rock, and then the rock became soil. In other words, the liquid matter was too soft to settle on, and the rock was too hard to benefit from. Therefore, the All-Wise and Compassionate One spread soil over the rock and made it a place of habitation for living beings.

(For further meanings of such expressions, see 2: 74, note 78; 50: 6-11; 78: 6-8, notes 2-3.)

4. Look at the seal God has put on life, through which one thing is made into many, and many things are made into one. He transforms the water we drink into a means for forming innumerable animal organs and systems. Through His command, a single entity becomes "many." Conversely, He changes varieties of foods into a particular body or skin, a whole system or subsystem. Thus "many" things become, by God's command, a single entity. Whoever has an intellect, consciousness, and a heart must conclude that making a single, simple entity from many things and using a single entity to make many things is a seal unique to the Creator of all things.

On the surface of the earth, we observe acts of ever-original and purposeful creation. These occur in infinite abundance together with beautiful and perfect artistry; with absolute ease and in perfect order and arrangement; at incredible speed with no loss of proportion, firmness, or substantiality; and in an infinite distribution of species together with the infinite beauty of each individual. These acts occur with the greatest economy or at the lowest cost imaginable, yet every individual is priceless and unique while there is the highest correspondence and similarity between and among species, despite the vast distances of time and space. They are in balance with an absolute variety, a perfect individualization of characters and features though generated from similar, or even the same materials, structural principles, and organization.

Perfect artistry despite abundance, perfect order despite absolute ease, perfect measure, proportion, and firmness despite incredible speed, perfect individualization despite worldwide distribution, the highest price and value despite the greatest economy, and perfect distinguishing despite absolute mixedness and similarity point to the One, Single Creator. (See *Mathnawī an-Nūriyah*, 51.)

وَيَسْتَعْجِلُونَكَ بِالسَّيِّئَةِ قَبْلَ الْحَسَنَةِ وَقَدْ خَلَتْ
مِنْ قَبْلِهِمُ الْمَثُلَاتُ وَإِنَّ رَبَّكَ لَذُو مَغْفِرَةٍ لِلنَّاسِ عَلَى
ظُلْمِهِمْ وَإِنَّ رَبَّكَ لَشَدِيدُ الْعِقَابِ ۝ وَيَقُولُ الَّذِينَ
كَفَرُوا لَوْلَا أُنْزِلَ عَلَيْهِ آيَةٌ مِنْ رَبِّهِ إِنَّمَا أَنْتَ مُنْذِرٌ وَلِكُلِّ
قَوْمٍ هَادٍ ۝ اللَّهُ يَعْلَمُ مَا تَحْمِلُ كُلُّ أُنْثَى وَمَا تَغِيضُ
الْأَرْحَامُ وَمَا تَزْدَادُ وَكُلُّ شَيْءٍ عِنْدَهُ بِمِقْدَارٍ ۝ عَالِمُ
الْغَيْبِ وَالشَّهَادَةِ الْكَبِيرُ الْمُتَعَالِ ۝ سَوَاءٌ مِنْكُمْ مَنْ
أَسَرَّ الْقَوْلَ وَمَنْ جَهَرَ بِهِ وَمَنْ هُوَ مُسْتَخْفٍ بِاللَّيْلِ وَسَارِبٌ
بِالنَّهَارِ ۝ لَهُ مُعَقِّبَاتٌ مِنْ بَيْنِ يَدَيْهِ وَمِنْ خَلْفِهِ
يَحْفَظُونَهُ مِنْ أَمْرِ اللَّهِ إِنَّ اللَّهَ لَا يُغَيِّرُ مَا بِقَوْمٍ حَتَّى
يُغَيِّرُوا مَا بِأَنْفُسِهِمْ وَإِذَا أَرَادَ اللَّهُ بِقَوْمٍ سُوءًا فَلَا مَرَدَّ لَهُ
وَمَا لَهُمْ مِنْ دُونِهِ مِنْ وَالٍ ۝ هُوَ الَّذِي يُرِيكُمُ الْبَرْقَ خَوْفًا
وَطَمَعًا وَيُنْشِئُ السَّحَابَ الثِّقَالَ ۝ وَيُسَبِّحُ الرَّعْدُ بِحَمْدِهِ
وَالْمَلَائِكَةُ مِنْ خِيفَتِهِ وَيُرْسِلُ الصَّوَاعِقَ فَيُصِيبُ بِهَا
مَنْ يَشَاءُ وَهُمْ يُجَادِلُونَ فِي اللَّهِ وَهُوَ شَدِيدُ الْمِحَالِ ۝

---

6. They challenge you to hasten the coming upon them of the evil instead of the good, although there have indeed come to pass before them many exemplary punishments. Your Lord is indeed rich in forgiveness for humankind despite their wrongdoing, and your Lord is indeed severe in retribution.

7. Those who disbelieve say: "Why is not a miraculous sign (of the kind we desire) sent down on him from his Lord?" You are (O Messenger) but a warner, and for each people there is a guide (appointed by God).

8. God knows what any female bears (in her womb with all its traits from her conception of it until delivery, and the future awaiting it), and what the wombs diminish and what they increase, (and by how much they may fall short in gestation,

and by how much they may increase the average period), and everything with Him is by a determined measure.

9. The Knower of the Unseen and the witnessed (all that lies in the hidden and visible realms and beyond and within the reach of any created being's perception), the All-Great, the All-Transcending.

10. (To Him) the one who holds his opinion in secret and the one who declares it are the same, and the one who hides himself (and his plans) under cover of night and the one who sallies out in the daylight.

11. (Every person advances through varying states before and after, and) by God's command attendant angels succeeding one another accompany him before and after him to guard him (and record his deeds). God does not change the condition of a people unless they change what is in themselves.[5] When God wills evil for a people (in consequence of their own evil deeds), it cannot be averted, and apart from Him, they have no protector.

12. He it is Who displays before you the lightning, giving rise to both fear (of being struck) and hopeful expectation (of rain), and builds the clouds heavy (with rain).[6]

13. The thunder glorifies Him with His praise (in that He is absolutely above having any partners, and that all praise belongs to Him exclusively) and so do the angels, in awe of Him. And He lets loose the thunderbolts and strikes with them whom He wills. Yet they stubbornly argue about God, (notwithstanding all evidence that) He is severe in repelling and retribution.

5. Almost all of the nineteenth and even twentieth-modern century Western philosophies of history, including dialectical materialism and historicism, were based on:

- Whether along a line or in cycles, humanity is progressing continually toward a definite end.
- This progress depends on history's deterministic and irresistible laws, all of which are completely independent of us. All that we can do is to discover and obey them, for if we do not we will be eliminated.
- All stages (e.g., primitive, feudal, or capitalistic) through which we inevitably pass should not be criticized, for we have no choice but to pass through them.

Such philosophies of history imply that the present socio-economic and even political conditions are inevitable, because they have been dictated by nature and history, which decree the survival of the most powerful. If this reality favors the West, communities that choose to survive must concede to Western dominion.

Although post-modernist philosophies of history and historicism give precedence to relativism in parallel to developments in physics, the genuine, irreversible laws of history are still emphasized.

The Qur'ān views history from completely different perspectives. First of all, it views it from the perspective of unchanging principles, while all of the other philosophies mentioned interpret past events and present situations in order to build their theories. Secondly, contrary to the fatalism of those philosophies, the Qur'ān stresses the individual's free choice and moral responsibility.

According to the Qur'ān, we sow the field of this world or the present time in order to harvest in the near (this world) and far future (the next world or eternal life). Given this, history is made up of our own choices and not laid out by a compelling will.

Islam considers a society to be composed of conscious individuals who are equipped with free will and who have a responsibility toward both themselves and others (God and other living and non-living beings). It sees humanity as the "motor" of history. Just as, without excluding God's forgiveness, mercy, and extra aids, every individual's will and behavior determine the outcome of their life in this world and in the Hereafter, a society's progress or decline is determined by the will, world-view, and lifestyle of its members. The verse means God will not change the state of a people unless they change themselves (with respect to their beliefs, world-view, and lifestyle). In other words, each society holds the reins of its fate in its own hands. A Prophetic Tradition emphasizes this idea: "You will be ruled according to how you are (– how you believe, live, and behave)."

6. Even if we may sometimes see an apparent interruption in the Qur'ānic verses, the actual fact is that there is a deep, fundamental relevance and continuity between them. Reflection on this verse and the preceding and succeeding ones in the light of the explanations in *sūrah* 7, note 14, reveals what a beautiful, meaningful, and deep relation exists among them.

250   سُوۡرَةُ الرَّعۡد   ٢٥٠

لَهٗ دَعۡوَةُ الۡحَقِّ وَالَّذِيۡنَ يَدۡعُوۡنَ مِنۡ دُوۡنِهٖ لَا يَسۡتَجِيۡبُوۡنَ لَهُمۡ بِشَىۡءٍ
اِلَّا كَبَاسِطِ كَفَّيۡهِ اِلَى الۡمَآءِ لِيَبۡلُغَ فَاهُ وَمَا هُوَ بِبَالِغِهٖ وَمَا دُعَآءُ
الۡكَافِرِيۡنَ اِلَّا فِىۡ ضَلَالٍ ۞ وَلِلّٰهِ يَسۡجُدُ مَنۡ فِى السَّمٰوٰتِ وَالۡاَرۡضِ
طَوۡعًا وَّكَرۡهًا وَّظِلَالُهُمۡ بِالۡغُدُوِّ وَالۡاٰصَالِ ۩ قُلۡ مَنۡ رَّبُّ
السَّمٰوٰتِ وَالۡاَرۡضِ قُلِ اللّٰهُ قُلۡ اَفَاتَّخَذۡتُمۡ مِّنۡ دُوۡنِهٖۤ
اَوۡلِيَآءَ لَا يَمۡلِكُوۡنَ لِاَنۡفُسِهِمۡ نَفۡعًا وَّلَا ضَرًّا قُلۡ هَلۡ يَسۡتَوِى
الۡاَعۡمٰى وَالۡبَصِيۡرُ اَمۡ هَلۡ تَسۡتَوِى الظُّلُمٰتُ وَالنُّوۡرُ اَمۡ جَعَلُوۡا لِلّٰهِ
شُرَكَآءَ خَلَقُوۡا كَخَلۡقِهٖ فَتَشَابَهَ الۡخَلۡقُ عَلَيۡهِمۡ قُلِ اللّٰهُ
خَالِقُ كُلِّ شَىۡءٍ وَّهُوَ الۡوَاحِدُ الۡقَهَّارُ ۞ اَنۡزَلَ مِنَ السَّمَآءِ مَآءً
فَسَالَتۡ اَوۡدِيَةٌۢ بِقَدَرِهَا فَاحۡتَمَلَ السَّيۡلُ زَبَدًا رَّابِيًا وَمِمَّا يُوۡقِدُوۡنَ
عَلَيۡهِ فِى النَّارِ ابۡتِغَآءَ حِلۡيَةٍ اَوۡ مَتَاعٍ زَبَدٌ مِّثۡلُهٗ كَذٰلِكَ يَضۡرِبُ اللّٰهُ
الۡحَقَّ وَالۡبَاطِلَ فَاَمَّا الزَّبَدُ فَيَذۡهَبُ جُفَآءً وَاَمَّا مَا يَنۡفَعُ النَّاسَ فَيَمۡكُثُ
فِى الۡاَرۡضِ كَذٰلِكَ يَضۡرِبُ اللّٰهُ الۡاَمۡثَالَ ۞ لِلَّذِيۡنَ اسۡتَجَابُوۡا لِرَبِّهِمُ
الۡحُسۡنٰى وَالَّذِيۡنَ لَمۡ يَسۡتَجِيۡبُوۡا لَهٗ لَوۡ اَنَّ لَهُمۡ مَّا فِى الۡاَرۡضِ جَمِيۡعًا وَّمِثۡلَهٗ مَعَهٗ
لَافۡتَدَوۡا بِهٖ اُولٰٓئِكَ لَهُمۡ سُوۡٓءُ الۡحِسَابِ وَمَاۡوٰىهُمۡ جَهَنَّمُ وَبِئۡسَ الۡمِهَادُ ۞

———◦———

14. To Him alone is made the call of truth and the prayer of truth addressed). Those to whom they pray and call others (to pray), apart from Him, cannot answer them in any way – (so that he who prays to them is) but like one who stretches out his hands to water (praying) that it may come to his mouth, but it never comes to it. The prayer of the unbelievers is but destined to go to waste.

15. To God prostrate all that are in the heavens and the earth, willingly or unwillingly, as do their shadows in the mornings and the evenings.[7]

16. Say: "Who is the Lord of the heavens and the earth?" Say: "God." Say (also): "Do you then take for guardians, apart from Him, such as have no power to bring benefit to or avert harm from even them-selves?" Say: "Are the blind and the seeing equal or are the depths of darkness and the light equal?" Or have they assigned to God partners who create the like of His creation so that the creation (that they make and God's creation) seem alike to them (that they cannot distinguish the true Creator?)" Say: "God is the Creator of all things, and He is the One, the All-Overwhelming."

17. He sends down water from the sky, and the valleys flow (in abundance) each according to its measure, and the flood carries a swelling foam (on its surface). And out of what they smelt in the fire in order to make ornaments or utensils, there rises a scum like it. Thus does God strike a parable to illustrate truth and falsehood. For, as for the scum, it vanishes as does all dross, but that which is of use to people abides on earth. In this way does God strike parables.[8]

18. For those who respond to (the call of) their Lord there is the fairest reward; and those who do not respond to Him – even if they possessed all that is on earth and its like besides, they would offer it as ransom (to be spared the punishment). Such are those whose is the most evil reckoning, and their final refuge is Hell: how evil a resting-place!

7. The lengths of the shadow varying according to the position of the sun in relation to the earth – the shadow's lengthening and contraction – is a very beautiful and meaningful image of how creation prostrates in submission to its Creator.

Everything is assigned a place in the grand scheme of the universe, which works in a magnificent harmony and interconnectedness. The sun, the moon, stars, and all heavenly bodies are knit together in a splendid system, following an unalterable law, and never deviating from their ordained course. Everything in the world, from electrons to nebulae, follows its own laws. The birth of a human, its growth and life, and all the bodily organs, from small tissues to the heart and brain, are also governed by the laws prescribed for them. (Once more we should remember that what we call laws are but certain principles which we have deduced by observing "natural" events. They are in fact designations for God's executions of His commands or acts.)

This is why we say that Islam is the religion of the universe, for Islam is nothing other than obedience and submission to God, the Lord of the universe. The sun, the moon, the earth, and all (other) heavenly bodies are Muslim, as are the air, water, heat, stones, trees, and animals, for everything in existence obeys God by submitting to His laws. Even unbelievers and atheists are Muslim, in so far as their bodily existence is concerned, for each part of their body follows the course God established for it, from birth until death and dissolution. In this meaning, whatever and whoever – whether a believer or an unbeliever – is in the heavens and the earth prostrates before God or submits to Him willingly or unwillingly; this is obligatory, there is no choice.

Secondly, as pointed out before in several places (4: 79, note 18; 5: 40, note 8; 6: 38, note 8), God has absolute sovereignty over every-

thing. He decrees however He wills. Although we are endowed with free will, and meet the results of our intentions and deeds, since it is He Who established the law of causality in this corporeal world, since it is He Who determined which cause brings about which effect or result, His absolute Will is the sole authority in our actions as well. It is God Who established which cause (thought, belief, or action) brings about which result, and humankind cannot escape this framework. It is also in this meaning that whatever and whoever is in the heavens and the earth prostrates to Him.

8. The comparisons and expressions in this verse and in verses 12 and 13 are like those found in 7: 54–58. Water or rain symbolizes Divine Revelation and the valleys represent the minds and hearts, which differ in their capacity to receive and benefit from the Revelation. Just as minds and hearts or human souls are like the valleys or river-beds that receive rain and flow each according to its measure, so too are people like raw materials or metal to be worked. Those who convey the Divine Revelation and educate people based on it work upon human souls to refine and make them silver, gold, diamond, or platinum, each according to its capacity. In both cases, that is, on the water that is carried by floods and on the metal worked in the fire, there rises a scum, which symbolizes any useless attribute or undesirable thing that is innate in the human soul; these things must be eliminated through education. Scum exists on the surface and usually obscures the water flowing beneath. Falsehood is like this scum. This is why people think that it dominates over truth. But this is only so in appearance and is deceitful, for, just like the scum, falsehood is destined and bound to vanish when the truth comes (17: 81). Truth is lasting and is like the water which flows beneath the scum and which carries life wherever it reaches.

أَفَمَن يَعْلَمُ أَنَّمَا أُنزِلَ إِلَيْكَ مِن رَّبِّكَ الْحَقُّ كَمَنْ هُوَ أَعْمَىٰ إِنَّمَا يَتَذَكَّرُ
أُوْلُواْ الْأَلْبَابِ ۞ الَّذِينَ يُوفُونَ بِعَهْدِ اللَّهِ وَلَا يَنقُضُونَ الْمِيثَاقَ
۞ وَالَّذِينَ يَصِلُونَ مَا أَمَرَ اللَّهُ بِهِ أَن يُوصَلَ وَيَخْشَوْنَ رَبَّهُمْ وَيَخَافُونَ
سُوٓءَ الْحِسَابِ ۞ وَالَّذِينَ صَبَرُواْ ابْتِغَآءَ وَجْهِ رَبِّهِمْ وَأَقَامُواْ
الصَّلَوٰةَ وَأَنفَقُواْ مِمَّا رَزَقْنَاهُمْ سِرًّا وَعَلَانِيَةً وَيَدْرَءُونَ بِالْحَسَنَةِ
السَّيِّئَةَ أُوْلَٰئِكَ لَهُمْ عُقْبَى الدَّارِ ۞ جَنَّاتُ عَدْنٍ يَدْخُلُونَهَا وَمَن
صَلَحَ مِنْ ءَابَآئِهِمْ وَأَزْوَاجِهِمْ وَذُرِّيَّاتِهِمْ وَالْمَلَٰئِكَةُ يَدْخُلُونَ
عَلَيْهِم مِّن كُلِّ بَابٍ ۞ سَلَامٌ عَلَيْكُم بِمَا صَبَرْتُمْ فَنِعْمَ عُقْبَى الدَّارِ
۞ وَالَّذِينَ يَنقُضُونَ عَهْدَ اللَّهِ مِنْ بَعْدِ مِيثَاقِهِ وَيَقْطَعُونَ مَا أَمَرَ
اللَّهُ بِهِ أَن يُوصَلَ وَيُفْسِدُونَ فِي الْأَرْضِ أُوْلَٰئِكَ لَهُمُ اللَّعْنَةُ
وَلَهُمْ سُوٓءُ الدَّارِ ۞ اللَّهُ يَبْسُطُ الرِّزْقَ لِمَن يَشَآءُ وَيَقْدِرُ
وَفَرِحُواْ بِالْحَيَوٰةِ الدُّنْيَا وَمَا الْحَيَوٰةُ الدُّنْيَا فِي الْآخِرَةِ إِلَّا مَتَاعٌ
۞ وَيَقُولُ الَّذِينَ كَفَرُواْ لَوْلَآ أُنزِلَ عَلَيْهِ ءَايَةٌ مِّن رَّبِّهِ قُلْ إِنَّ
اللَّهَ يُضِلُّ مَن يَشَآءُ وَيَهْدِي إِلَيْهِ مَنْ أَنَابَ ۞ الَّذِينَ ءَامَنُواْ
وَتَطْمَئِنُّ قُلُوبُهُم بِذِكْرِ اللَّهِ أَلَا بِذِكْرِ اللَّهِ تَطْمَئِنُّ الْقُلُوبُ ۞

---

adversities they face in God's cause) in pursuit of where God's good, eternal pleasure lies, and they establish the Prayer in conformity with its conditions, and spend of whatever We provide for them secretly and openly, and repel the evil with good.[9] Such are those for whom there is the ultimate (everlasting) abode:

23. Gardens of perpetual bliss which they will enter, along with all who are righteous from among their ancestors, their spouses, and their descendants; and the angels will come to them from every gate, (saying):

24. "Peace be upon you, for that you endured patiently. How excellent is the ultimate (everlasting) abode!"

25. But those who break God's covenant after its solemn binding, and sever the bonds God commanded to be joined, and cause disorder and corruption on the earth – such are those for whom there is curse (exclusion from God's Mercy), and for them there is the most evil abode.

26. God enlarges provision for whom He wills, and straitens it (for whom He wills). They (the unbelievers who have indulged in the present, worldly life oblivious of God and the Hereafter) rejoice in the present, worldly life, whereas the present, worldly life is but a fleeting enjoyment as compared with the Hereafter.

27. Those who disbelieve say: "Why is not a miraculous sign (of the kind we desire) sent down on him from his Lord?" Say: "Surely God leads astray whomever He wills,[10] and guides to Himself all who turn (to Him whole-heartedly),"

28. Those who have believed (and become established in faith), and whose hearts find rest and contentment in remembrance of and whole-hearted devotion to God. Be aware that it is in the remembrance of and whole-hearted devotion to God that hearts find rest and contentment.

---

19. Is the one who knows that what is sent down to you from your Lord is the truth – is that one like him who is blind? Surely only people of discernment reflect and be mindful.

20. Those who fulfill God's covenant (responsible for the order in the universe, and able to establish the peace, order and harmony in human life) and do not break the pledge (that they shall worship none save God, and fulfill all other obligations resulting from believing in and worshipping only One God);

21. And those who unite the bonds God has commanded to be joined (among kin as a requirement of blood relationship, and among people as required by human social interdependence), and stand in awe of their Lord, and fearful of (facing) the most evil reckoning;

22. And those who endure patiently (all

9. This last phrase has several meanings:

- Whatever evil a person has done or whatever sin they have committed, they repel (its effect) immediately by repentance.
- Whatever evil they have done, they immediately do a good deed in atonement for it.
- They repel the evil done to them by doing good to those who did evil to them.
- "When they are deprived (of anything), they give; and when they are wronged, they forgive."

Fethullah Gülen writes vividly about this matter:

> Return good for evil, and disregard discourteous treatment. An individual's character is reflected in their behavior. Choose tolerance, and be magnanimous toward the ill-mannered.
>
> The most distinctive feature of a soul overflowing with faith is to love all types of love that are expressed in deeds, and to feel enmity for all deeds in which enmity is expressed. To hate everything is a sign of insanity or of infatuation with Satan.
>
> Accept how God treats you. Make it the measure by which you treat others, so that you may represent the truth among them and be free from the fear of loneliness in either world (*Pearls of Wisdom*, 75–76).

He writes about the reflection of this praiseworthy quality in education:

> Improving a community is possible only by elevating the young generations to the rank of humanity, not by obliterating the bad ones. Unless a seed composed of religion, tradition, and historical consciousness is germinated throughout the country, new evil elements will appear and grow in the place of each eradicated bad one (*Ibid.*, 39).

10. For God's leading whomever He wills astray, see *sūrah* 2, note 10; 26-27, note 23; *sūrah* 6: 39, note 9.

252   سورة الرعد   ٢٥٢

الَّذِينَ آمَنُوا وَعَمِلُوا الصَّالِحَاتِ طُوبَى لَهُمْ وَحُسْنُ مَآبٍ ۞ كَذَلِكَ
أَرْسَلْنَاكَ فِي أُمَّةٍ قَدْ خَلَتْ مِنْ قَبْلِهَا أُمَمٌ لِتَتْلُوَا عَلَيْهِمُ الَّذِي
أَوْحَيْنَا إِلَيْكَ وَهُمْ يَكْفُرُونَ بِالرَّحْمَٰنِ قُلْ هُوَ رَبِّي لَآ إِلَٰهَ إِلَّا هُوَ
عَلَيْهِ تَوَكَّلْتُ وَإِلَيْهِ مَتَابِ ۞ وَلَوْ أَنَّ قُرْآنًا سُيِّرَتْ بِهِ الْجِبَالُ
أَوْ قُطِّعَتْ بِهِ الْأَرْضُ أَوْ كُلِّمَ بِهِ الْمَوْتَى بَلْ لِلَّهِ الْأَمْرُ جَمِيعًا أَفَلَمْ
يَايْئَسِ الَّذِينَ آمَنُوا أَنْ لَوْ يَشَآءُ اللَّهُ لَهَدَى النَّاسَ جَمِيعًا وَلَا
يَزَالُ الَّذِينَ كَفَرُوا تُصِيبُهُمْ بِمَا صَنَعُوا قَارِعَةٌ أَوْ تَحُلُّ قَرِيبًا
مِنْ دَارِهِمْ حَتَّى يَأْتِيَ وَعْدُ اللَّهِ إِنَّ اللَّهَ لَا يُخْلِفُ الْمِيعَادَ
۞ وَلَقَدِ اسْتُهْزِئَ بِرُسُلٍ مِنْ قَبْلِكَ فَأَمْلَيْتُ لِلَّذِينَ
كَفَرُوا ثُمَّ أَخَذْتُهُمْ فَكَيْفَ كَانَ عِقَابِ ۞ أَفَمَنْ هُوَ
قَائِمٌ عَلَى كُلِّ نَفْسٍ بِمَا كَسَبَتْ وَجَعَلُوا لِلَّهِ شُرَكَآءَ قُلْ
سَمُّوهُمْ أَمْ تُنَبِّئُونَهُ بِمَا لَا يَعْلَمُ فِي الْأَرْضِ أَمْ بِظَاهِرٍ مِنَ
الْقَوْلِ بَلْ زُيِّنَ لِلَّذِينَ كَفَرُوا مَكْرُهُمْ وَصُدُّوا عَنِ السَّبِيلِ
وَمَنْ يُضْلِلِ اللَّهُ فَمَا لَهُ مِنْ هَادٍ ۞ لَهُمْ عَذَابٌ فِي الْحَيَوةِ
الدُّنْيَا وَلَعَذَابُ الْآخِرَةِ أَشَقُّ وَمَا لَهُمْ مِنَ اللَّهِ مِنْ وَاقٍ ۞

———— ∝◊∝ ————

29. Those (whose hearts have attained to
rest and contentment,) who have believed
and do good, righteous deeds – for them is
the greatest happiness and the most beautiful of destinations.

30. For that end We have raised you as
Messenger among a community before
whom other (similar) communities have
come and gone, that you may recite (and
convey) to them what We reveal to you,
whereas (in their ignorance) they disbelieve in the All-Merciful. Say: "He is my
Lord. There is no deity save Him. In Him
I have put my trust, and to Him is my
recourse."

31. If at all through a Divine Book mountains were moved, or the earth were torn
apart, or the dead were made to speak, (all
would be only through this Qur'ān so that
the unbelievers would be compelled, hav-

ing no choice but, to believe). No, but to
God belongs the whole command (to decide what shall be and how it shall be). Do
not yet those who believe know that, if
God had so willed, He would indeed have
guided all humankind (to faith)? Those
who disbelieve will not cease to be struck
by severe blows for what they have been
contriving, or these will alight close to
their homes (to afflict them), until God's
promise (of the final victory of Islam or
Judgment Day) is fulfilled.[11] Surely God
does not fail to keep the promise.

32. Messengers were certainly mocked before you. Yet (despite all that they did), I
gave respite to those who disbelieved, but
then I seized them (with terrible destructions). Then, (see) how was My retribution!

33. Is He Who watches over every soul
and whatever it earns (to be denied or disobeyed)? Yet they associate partners with
God. Say: "Name them (if anything can
be a deity merely by calling it so)! Do you
(presume to) inform Him of something
(existent) on earth that He does not know?
Or are you just uttering mere words (with
neither meaning nor reference to anything
existent and real)? No, but their own fictions are decked out to be appealing to
those who disbelieve, and they are kept
away from the right way. Whoever God
leads astray, for him there is no guide.

34. For them is punishment in the life
of this world, but the punishment of the
Hereafter is yet more grievous, and they
have none to guard them against God.

11. This expression is highly significant for understanding many important events in human history. In rejection of the truth and God's true way, the unbelievers continue to contrive new ways and produce new things to satisfy their selfish desires. The verb used to express their contrivances, *ṢaNe'A*, is also the root word of *ṣana ỳi'*, meaning industry. Although what the Qur'ān primarily means here by *those who disbelieve* is the Makkan unbelievers, it is also referring to all of the unbelievers to come until Judgment Day. Unbelievers have never ceased to contrive new ways to struggle against Islam or to develop new devices to satisfy their carnal appetites and exploit the natural resources of wealth throughout the world; they have struggled until they have built up gigantic industries, including the weapons industry. However, they have also never ceased to be visited by severe blows from all sides, like wars, including especially the two world wars. Just as the Makkan unbelievers did not cease to be visited by blows until their final defeat and surrender to Islam, the contemporary unbelievers will not cease to be struck by blows until they surrender to Islam or are utterly destroyed. In the end, the Last Day will seize them severely.

253

مَثَلُ الْجَنَّةِ الَّتِي وُعِدَ الْمُتَّقُونَ تَجْرِي مِن تَحْتِهَا الْأَنْهَارُ
أُكُلُهَا دَآئِمٌ وَظِلُّهَا تِلْكَ عُقْبَى الَّذِينَ اتَّقَوا وَّعُقْبَى الْكَافِرِينَ
النَّارُ ۞ وَالَّذِينَ اتَيْنَاهُمُ الْكِتَابَ يَفْرَحُونَ بِمَا أُنزِلَ
إِلَيْكَ وَمِنَ الْأَحْزَابِ مَن يُنكِرُ بَعْضَهُ قُلْ إِنَّمَا أُمِرْتُ
أَنْ أَعْبُدَ اللَّهَ وَلَا أُشْرِكَ بِهِ إِلَيْهِ أَدْعُوا وَإِلَيْهِ مَآبِ ۞
وَكَذَٰلِكَ أَنزَلْنَاهُ حُكْمًا عَرَبِيًّا وَلَئِنِ اتَّبَعْتَ أَهْوَآءَهُم
بَعْدَ مَا جَآءَكَ مِنَ الْعِلْمِ مَالَكَ مِنَ اللَّهِ مِن وَلِيٍّ وَلَا وَاقٍ
۞ وَلَقَدْ أَرْسَلْنَا رُسُلًا مِّن قَبْلِكَ وَجَعَلْنَا لَهُمْ أَزْوَاجًا وَذُرِّيَّةً
وَمَا كَانَ لِرَسُولٍ أَن يَأْتِيَ بِآيَةٍ إِلَّا بِإِذْنِ اللَّهِ لِكُلِّ أَجَلٍ كِتَابٌ
۞ يَمْحُوا اللَّهُ مَا يَشَآءُ وَيُثْبِتُ وَعِندَهُ أُمُّ الْكِتَابِ ۞ وَإِن
مَّا نُرِيَنَّكَ بَعْضَ الَّذِي نَعِدُهُمْ أَوْ نَتَوَفَّيَنَّكَ فَإِنَّمَا عَلَيْكَ الْبَلَاغُ
وَعَلَيْنَا الْحِسَابُ ۞ أَوَلَمْ يَرَوْا أَنَّا نَأْتِي الْأَرْضَ نَنقُصُهَا مِنْ
أَطْرَافِهَا وَاللَّهُ يَحْكُمُ لَا مُعَقِّبَ لِحُكْمِهِ وَهُوَ سَرِيعُ الْحِسَابِ
۞ وَقَدْ مَكَرَ الَّذِينَ مِن قَبْلِهِمْ فَلِلَّهِ الْمَكْرُ جَمِيعًا يَعْلَمُ
مَا تَكْسِبُ كُلُّ نَفْسٍ وَسَيَعْلَمُ الْكُفَّارُ لِمَنْ عُقْبَى الدَّارِ ۞

---

35. The Paradise promised to the God-revering, pious ones can be likened to a garden through which rivers flow. Its produce is everlasting, and so its shade. That is the ultimate outcome for those who keep from disobedience to God in reverence for Him and piety, just as the ultimate outcome for the unbelievers is the Fire.

36. Those to whom We granted the Book before rejoice in what is sent down to you. (Some do so because they believe that it is the expected final Revelation, and some because it contains passages confirming their Books and Prophets.)[12] Yet among those parties (responding to the Book), some deny some of it (because it discloses their interpolations in their Books and does not serve their interests). Say (O Messenger): "I have only been commanded to worship

God and not to associate any partners with Him. To Him I call (all people), and to Him is my destined return."

37. And so (as a Book, whose message is founded on faith in and worship of One God, and which should therefore be accepted by all who were given the Book before) We have sent down (this Qur'ān) as a final judgment in the Arabic tongue. And, indeed, if you were to follow their lusts and fancies after what has come to you of the Knowledge, you would have none to defend and protect you against God.

38. Most certainly We sent Messengers before you, and (like every other man) appointed wives and children for them. It was not (the way) for a Messenger to work a miracle (as a sign of his being a Messenger) except by God's leave. Every appointed term has its own Revelation and law.

39. God effaces what He wills (of things and events He has created, and laws He has established), and He confirms and establishes (what He wills): with Him is the Mother of the Book.[13]

40. Whether We let you (O Messenger) witness the fulfillment of some of what We have promised them, or whether We cause you to die (before it happens), still yours (by way of duty and command from Us) is only to convey the Message, and Ours is the reckoning.

41. Do they not see how We deal with the earth, reducing it of its outlying parts?[14] God judges, and (when He has judged) there is none to revise His judgment. And He is swift at reckoning.

42. Those who were before them schemed (just as their descendants now do), but all schemes are owned by God (Who brings them to nothing and enforces His own will). He knows what every soul earns (by its intentions and deeds). So the unbelievers will know whose is the ultimate, everlasting abode.

12. As pointed out in the Qur'ān in such verses as *sūrah* 7: 159, *sūrah* 28: 52, and *sūrah* 46: 10, there were some People of the Book who believed in Islam in the Makkan period and in the early years of *Hijrah*, for example, some Christians in Abyssinia and a few Jews in Madīnah. There were also some others who welcomed only some passages of the Qur'ān because they confirmed their Books as being of Divine origin and their Prophets. This verse refers to them.

13. The origins, sources, and seeds from which God Almighty shapes things and/or beings with perfect order and art show that they are arranged according to a "book of principles" contained in Divine Knowledge. The seeds contain the plans and programs of beings or things that will come into existence. To give a more concrete example, a seed contains or even constitutes the plan and program according to which a tree may be formed and, furthermore, is a miniature embodiment of the Divine principles that cause the tree to come into existence and determine this plan and program. This archetypal plan and program of the Tree of Creation as a whole, which spreads its branches through the past and future and into the World of the Unseen, is called the Manifest Record, and the Divine principles that determine this plan and program constitute what the Qur'ān calls the Supreme Ever-Preserved Tablet that is contained in Divine Knowledge (see also 6: 59, note 12).

The life-history of, for example, a plant or tree from its germination under soil until it yields fruit is the developed form of its seed, and this complete life-history with all its cycles is summed up in its fruit, rather in each seed in its fruits. We call this active life-history of a living thing or being its Destiny Practical or Manifest Book. With everything and event in it, the universe has its own "universal" Destiny Practical, which is the "universal" Manifest Book. The Manifest Record, which is written by Divine Knowledge, relates to the origins of things or beings, while the Manifest Book relates to their entire life-histories and is a notebook written by the Divine Power.

Through the dictates of the Manifest Record, that is, through the decree and instruction of the Divine Destiny, the Divine Power uses atoms to create or manifest the chain of beings, each link of which is His sign, on the metaphorical page of time, which is called the Tablet of Effacement (Canceling) and Confirmation. Thus, atoms are set to move so that beings may be transferred from the World of the Unseen to the material, visible world, from (the Realm of) Knowledge to the (Realm of) Power.

The Tablet of Effacement and Confirmation is the Tablet on which events and things or/and beings are inscribed and then removed or effaced according to the dictates of the Supreme Ever-Preserved Tablet contained in Divine Eternal Knowledge. Therefore, it displays continuous change. The Tablet of Effacement and Confirmation constitutes the essence of time. Time, a mighty river which flows through existence, has its essence in the Divine Power's inscription of beings and in the "ink" It uses.

Similarly, God also has archetypal principles for human social life, all of which are called the Mother of the Book. He lays down these principles as commandments or laws during human history as suited to the particular needs of the time and the people concerned. For this reason, every age or appointed term has its own Revelation and laws. God sent them down with succeeding Messengers in a way that culminated in the Qur'ān as the final form of the Divine Message.

So, with regard to legislation, Islam as the final message and the consummation of all the Divine messages followed three principal ways:

- It retained the commandments that existed in the previous Books or prevailed in the community in which they appeared and that were not contradictory to its essential principles.
- It corrected or amended those that were not in conformity with its principles.
- It made new legislation.

In making new legislation, it considered both the unchanging, essential aspects of life and those that change over the course of time.

With respect to the changing aspects of life, it laid down rulings that were open to revision in the light of both new conditions and its essentials of faith, worship, and morality, as well as establishing legal principles to maintain this process (see 6: 59, note 13). The same procedure was followed also in the time of the Prophet himself, during which the Qur'ān was revealed. Some verses were abrogated or annulled by God Himself, either with the injunctions they contained with their wording preserved or with both their wording and the commandments. This process was called *naskh*, and the verses abrogated are known as *mansūkh*, with the new ones that substituted the previous ones as *nāsikh*.

14. This expression has several meanings and connotations suggested by interpreters of the Qur'ān. It means:

- We are visiting with Our punishment the lands of the unbelievers, gradually curtailing them from all sides. It suggests that Arabia is gradually being conquered by the Muslims. It also prophesies the subsequent conquests of the Muslims, as well as their final victory throughout the world.

- We make destruction follow prosperity on the earth, death after life, humiliation after glory, poverty after richness, fall after rise... So no one, no nation can be sure that God will not change their prosperity into abjection.

- God gradually deprives a land, especially toward the time of its destruction, of the best among people – the scholars, spiritual guides, thinkers, good rulers, and great leaders, and so on.

- The earth is gradually being compressed at the poles.

- Lands and mountainous areas are eroded by the wind and rain, and coastal areas by the sea; agricultural land is gradually being eroded and becoming desert.

43. Those who disbelieve say: "You are not a Messenger sent by God." Say (to them): "God suffices for a witness between me and you, and (as witnesses) those who have true knowledge of the Book."

SŪRAH 14

IBRĀHĪM (ABRAHAM)

Makkah period

This *sūrah* of 52 verses was revealed in the closing years of the Makkan period of Islam. Taking its name from the Prophet Abraham, whose prayer concerning Makkah and its future people is mentioned in verses 35–41. In verse 5 Moses' mission is mentioned as leading *his people* out of the depths of darkness into the light, while in its initial verse it declares that the Qur'ān was sent to the Prophet Muḥammad to lead *humankind* out of the depths of darkness into the light, thus stressing the universality of his mission.

In the Name of God, the All-Merciful, the All-Compassionate.

1. *Alif. Lām. Rā.* (This is) a Book which We have sent down to you so that you may lead humankind, by their Lord's leave, out of all kinds of (intellectual, spiritual, social, economic, and political) darkness into the light, to the Path of the All-Glorious with irresistible might, the All-Praiseworthy (Who provides for them and all other beings and meets all their needs),

2. God, to Whom belongs whatever is in the heavens and whatever is on the earth; and woe to the unbelievers because of a severe punishment.

3. They choose the present, worldly life in preference to the Hereafter and bar (people)

from God's way, and seek to make it appear crooked – those have indeed gone far astray.

4. We have sent no Messenger save with the tongue of his people, that he might make (the Message) clear to them. Then God leads whomever He wills astray, and He guides whomever He wills.[1] He is the All-Glorious with irresistible might, the All-Wise.

5. And, certainly, We sent Moses as Messenger with Our Revelations and signs (miracles to support him), saying: "Lead your people from all kinds of darkness into the light, and remind them (thereby preaching Our Message) of the Days of God.[2] Surely in that are signs for all who are greatly patient and persevering (in God's cause) and greatly thankful (to God).

---

1. For God's leading whomever He wills astray, and guiding whomever He wills, see *sūrah* 2, note 10; verses 26–27, note 23; *sūrah* 6: 39, note 9.

2. The phrase *Days of God* refers to momentous historical events, such as destructions of previous communities, turning-points in history, and eschatological events.

وَإِذْ قَالَ مُوسَىٰ لِقَوْمِهِ اذْكُرُوا نِعْمَةَ اللَّهِ عَلَيْكُمْ إِذْ أَنجَىٰكُم مِّنْ آلِ فِرْعَوْنَ يَسُومُونَكُمْ سُوءَ الْعَذَابِ وَيُذَبِّحُونَ أَبْنَاءَكُمْ وَيَسْتَحْيُونَ نِسَاءَكُمْ وَفِي ذَٰلِكُم بَلَاءٌ مِّن رَّبِّكُمْ عَظِيمٌ ۞ وَإِذْ تَأَذَّنَ رَبُّكُمْ لَئِن شَكَرْتُمْ لَأَزِيدَنَّكُمْ وَلَئِن كَفَرْتُمْ إِنَّ عَذَابِي لَشَدِيدٌ ۞ وَقَالَ مُوسَىٰ إِن تَكْفُرُوا أَنتُمْ وَمَن فِي الْأَرْضِ جَمِيعًا فَإِنَّ اللَّهَ لَغَنِيٌّ حَمِيدٌ ۞ أَلَمْ يَأْتِكُمْ نَبَأُ الَّذِينَ مِن قَبْلِكُمْ قَوْمِ نُوحٍ وَعَادٍ وَثَمُودَ وَالَّذِينَ مِن بَعْدِهِمْ لَا يَعْلَمُهُمْ إِلَّا اللَّهُ جَاءَتْهُمْ رُسُلُهُم بِالْبَيِّنَاتِ فَرَدُّوا أَيْدِيَهُمْ فِي أَفْوَاهِهِمْ وَقَالُوا إِنَّا كَفَرْنَا بِمَا أُرْسِلْتُم بِهِ وَإِنَّا لَفِي شَكٍّ مِّمَّا تَدْعُونَنَا إِلَيْهِ مُرِيبٍ ۞ قَالَتْ رُسُلُهُمْ أَفِي اللَّهِ شَكٌّ فَاطِرِ السَّمَاوَاتِ وَالْأَرْضِ يَدْعُوكُمْ لِيَغْفِرَ لَكُم مِّن ذُنُوبِكُمْ وَيُؤَخِّرَكُمْ إِلَىٰ أَجَلٍ مُّسَمًّى قَالُوا إِنْ أَنتُمْ إِلَّا بَشَرٌ مِّثْلُنَا تُرِيدُونَ أَن تَصُدُّونَا عَمَّا كَانَ يَعْبُدُ آبَاؤُنَا فَأْتُونَا بِسُلْطَانٍ مُّبِينٍ ۞

more; but if you are ungrateful, surely My punishment is severe."

8. And Moses said: "Even if you and whoever else is on the earth were unbelieving and ungrateful, surely God is All-Wealthy and Self-Sufficient (as Owner of everything, so independent of all creation), All-Praiseworthy (to Whom belong all praise and gratitude)."[4]

9. Has any account not reached you of the exemplary histories of those who lived before you – the people of Noah, and the 'Ād and Thamūd – and those who came after them? None save God has true knowledge about them. Their Messengers came to them with clear signs of the truth, but they thrust their hands into their mouths (in derision and anger, and frustrated by their inability to refute them), and said: "We certainly disbelieve in what you have been sent, and indeed we are in serious doubt about that to which you call us."

10. Their Messengers said: "Can there be any doubt about (the Existence, Oneness, and absolute Sovereignty of) God, the Originator of the heavens and the earth? He calls you so that He may forgive you your sins and grant you respite until a term appointed by Him (not destroying you because of your sins)."[5] But they said: "You are but mortals like us; you desire to bar us from what our forefathers used to worship: well, then, bring us some clear authority."

6. And (recall) when Moses said to his people: "Remember God's favor upon you when He saved you from the clan of the Pharaoh, who were afflicting you with the most evil suffering (by enslaving you to such laborious tasks as construction, transportation and farming), slaughtering your sons and letting live your womenfolk (for further humiliation and suffering). In that was a grievous trial from your Lord.[3]

7. And (remember also) when your Lord proclaimed: "If you are thankful (for My favors), I will most certainly give you

---

3. For an explanation of this verse, see *sūrah* 2: 49, notes 56–58.

4. See *sūrah* 1: 2, note 6.

5. For God's sparing and reprieving a people to a term appointed by God, see *sūrah* 10: 98,

note 20. This shows that neither an individual nor a people are subject to some sort of absolute determinism. God Almighty judges them, their lives and the conditions surrounding them according to their own choice, lifestyle, and deeds.

256

سُورَةُ اِبْرٰهِيمَ

٢٥٦

قَالَتْ لَهُمْ رُسُلُهُمْ اِنْ نَحْنُ اِلَّا بَشَرٌ مِّثْلُكُمْ وَلٰكِنَّ اللّٰهَ يَمُنُّ عَلٰى مَنْ يَّشَآءُ مِنْ عِبَادِهِ ۖ وَمَا كَانَ لَنَا اَنْ نَّأْتِيَكُمْ بِسُلْطَانٍ اِلَّا بِاِذْنِ اللّٰهِ ۖ وَعَلَى اللّٰهِ فَلْيَتَوَكَّلِ الْمُؤْمِنُونَ ۝ وَمَا لَنَا اَلَّا نَتَوَكَّلَ عَلَى اللّٰهِ وَقَدْ هَدٰىنَا سُبُلَنَا ۖ وَلَنَصْبِرَنَّ عَلٰى مَا اٰذَيْتُمُونَا ۖ وَعَلَى اللّٰهِ فَلْيَتَوَكَّلِ الْمُتَوَكِّلُونَ ۝ وَقَالَ الَّذِينَ كَفَرُوا لِرُسُلِهِمْ لَنُخْرِجَنَّكُمْ مِّنْ اَرْضِنَا اَوْ لَتَعُودُنَّ فِي مِلَّتِنَا ۖ فَاَوْحٰى اِلَيْهِمْ رَبُّهُمْ لَنُهْلِكَنَّ الظّٰلِمِينَ ۝ وَلَنُسْكِنَنَّكُمُ الْاَرْضَ مِنْ بَعْدِهِمْ ۖ ذٰلِكَ لِمَنْ خَافَ مَقَامِي وَخَافَ وَعِيدِ ۝ وَاسْتَفْتَحُوا وَخَابَ كُلُّ جَبَّارٍ عَنِيدٍ ۝ مِّنْ وَّرَآئِهِ جَهَنَّمُ وَيُسْقٰى مِنْ مَّآءٍ صَدِيدٍ ۝ يَتَجَرَّعُهُ وَلَا يَكَادُ يُسِيغُهُ وَيَأْتِيهِ الْمَوْتُ مِنْ كُلِّ مَكَانٍ وَمَا هُوَ بِمَيِّتٍ ۖ وَمِنْ وَّرَآئِهِ عَذَابٌ غَلِيظٌ ۝ مَثَلُ الَّذِينَ كَفَرُوا بِرَبِّهِمْ اَعْمَالُهُمْ كَرَمَادٍ اشْتَدَّتْ بِهِ الرِّيحُ فِي يَوْمٍ عَاصِفٍ ۖ لَا يَقْدِرُونَ مِمَّا كَسَبُوا عَلٰى شَيْءٍ ۚ ذٰلِكَ هُوَ الضَّلٰلُ الْبَعِيدُ ۝

---

11. Their Messengers said to them: "We are indeed only mortals like yourselves, but God has been specially gracious to whom He wills of His servants. It is not for us to bring you some authority (for our mission), unless it be by God's leave; and so it is in God that the believers must put their trust.

12. "What reason do we have that we should not put our trust in God, seeing that He has guided us to our ways (that we follow)? So, we will surely endure patiently whatever hurt you may do us; and let all those who entrust themselves put their trust in God."

13. Those who disbelieve said to their Messengers: "Assuredly we will banish you from our land, unless you return to our faith and way of life." Then their Lord revealed to the Messengers: "Most certainly, We will destroy the wrongdoers,

14. "And most certainly We will make you dwell in the land after them. That is (My promise) for him who fears Me as (the All-Majestic, All-Powerful) God, and who fears My threat."

15. They (both the Messengers and unbelievers) sought a judgment (through test of right and might), and in the end every stubborn tyrant was frustrated (made to fail),

16. And Hell is awaiting him, and he is made to drink of oozing pus,[6]

17. Sipping it little by little, yet hardly able to swallow it, and death besets him from every side though he cannot die, and a still harsher punishment lies ahead of him.

18. The parable of those who disbelieve in their Lord: all their works are as ashes on which the wind blows fiercely on a stormy day (and so scatters). They have no control of anything that they have earned (to benefit from). That indeed is utmost error and failure.

6. In particular, some modern commentators, such as Muḥammad Asad, tend to take almost all the expressions describing the other world metaphorically. For example, he renders *oozing pus* as "water of most bitter distress." This is due to the presupposition that the other life is a "spiritual" one which will be experienced by the spirit only. The truth is otherwise. That is, humankind will be both bodily and spiritually resurrected and experience the other life both bodily and spiritually. But it is not possible for us to be able to perceive the exact nature of that life according to this life, so the Qur'ān presents that life with the familiar expressions we use in this life. Ibn 'Abbās when interpreting the Qur'ānic expression, *Every time they are provided with fruits (of different color, shape, taste, and fragrance and that are constantly renewed) therefrom, they say, "This is what we were provided with before." For they are given to them in resemblance (to what was given to them both in the world, and just before in the Gardens, familiar in shape and color so that they may not be unattractive because unknown)* (2: 25), says that all the provisions of Paradise resemble those in the world, but they are completely different. For example, there are all kinds of drink and food in Paradise (which are fitting for it), including water, milk, honey, fruit, etc., with which we are provided here in this world, but they are completely unique to the other world, and we cannot perceive their exact nature. We will taste them both bodily and spiritually in our existence that is purely unique to the other world. Similarly, in Hell, there will be oozing pus and boiling water and other elements of punishment mentioned in the Qur'ān, but they will also be unique to the other world. For this reason, rendering the rewards of Paradise and forms of punishment of Hell figuratively or metaphorically is not correct. It means "pursuing that which we have no knowledge of," which is forbidden in the Qur'ān (17: 36), and forgetting that "the hearing, the sight, and the heart will be called to account for it."

الٓمَ تَرَ أَنَّ اللَّهَ خَلَقَ السَّمَوَاتِ وَالْأَرْضَ بِالْحَقِّ إِن يَشَأْ يُذْهِبْكُمْ وَيَأْتِ بِخَلْقٍ جَدِيدٍ ۝ وَمَا ذَٰلِكَ عَلَى اللَّهِ بِعَزِيزٍ ۝ وَبَرَزُوا لِلَّهِ جَمِيعًا فَقَالَ الضُّعَفَٰٓؤُا لِلَّذِينَ اسْتَكْبَرُوٓا إِنَّا كُنَّا لَكُمْ تَبَعًا فَهَلْ أَنتُم مُّغْنُونَ عَنَّا مِنْ عَذَابِ اللَّهِ مِن شَيْءٍ قَالُوا لَوْ هَدَىٰنَا اللَّهُ لَهَدَيْنَٰكُمْ سَوَآءٌ عَلَيْنَآ أَجَزِعْنَآ أَمْ صَبَرْنَا مَا لَنَا مِن مَّحِيصٍ ۝ وَقَالَ الشَّيْطَٰنُ لَمَّا قُضِيَ الْأَمْرُ إِنَّ اللَّهَ وَعَدَكُمْ وَعْدَ الْحَقِّ وَوَعَدتُّكُمْ فَأَخْلَفْتُكُمْ وَمَا كَانَ لِيَ عَلَيْكُم مِّن سُلْطَٰنٍ إِلَّآ أَن دَعَوْتُكُمْ فَاسْتَجَبْتُمْ لِي فَلَا تَلُومُونِي وَلُومُوٓا أَنفُسَكُم مَّآ أَنَا۠ بِمُصْرِخِكُمْ وَمَآ أَنتُم بِمُصْرِخِيَّ إِنِّي كَفَرْتُ بِمَآ أَشْرَكْتُمُونِ مِن قَبْلُ إِنَّ الظَّٰلِمِينَ لَهُمْ عَذَابٌ أَلِيمٌ ۝ وَأُدْخِلَ الَّذِينَ ءَامَنُوا وَعَمِلُوا الصَّٰلِحَٰتِ جَنَّٰتٍ تَجْرِي مِن تَحْتِهَا الْأَنْهَٰرُ خَٰلِدِينَ فِيهَا بِإِذْنِ رَبِّهِمْ تَحِيَّتُهُمْ فِيهَا سَلَٰمٌ ۝ أَلَمْ تَرَ كَيْفَ ضَرَبَ اللَّهُ مَثَلًا كَلِمَةً طَيِّبَةً كَشَجَرَةٍ طَيِّبَةٍ أَصْلُهَا ثَابِتٌ وَفَرْعُهَا فِي السَّمَآءِ ۝

19. Do you not see that God has created the heavens and the earth with truth (meaningfully, and with definite purpose, and on solid foundations of truth)? If He so wills (for the fulfillment of His purpose in creation), He can put you away and bring another generation (of humankind in your place).

20. And that is surely no great matter for God.

21. They will appear before God all together. Then those who were weak (in the world and followed the arrogant oppressors in their misguidance) will say to those who were arrogant and oppressed others: "We used to follow your lead: can you now avert from us anything of God's punishment?" The others will answer: "If God had guided us (to the way to be saved), we would indeed have guided you to it. It is all the same for us now whether we are anguished (about it) or endure with patience; there is no escape for us!"

22. And Satan will say when the matter is decided: "Surely God promised you something that was bound to come true; I too promised but I failed you. And I had no power over you, except that I appealed to you, and you answered me. So do not blame me, but blame yourselves. I cannot respond to your cry for help, nor can you respond to my cry for help. I reject your associating me as a partner with God (in belief or worship) in the past." Surely, for the wrongdoers (who have wronged and ruined themselves by denying God or associating partners with Him) there is a painful punishment.

23. But those who believed and did good, righteous deeds are admitted to the Gardens through which rivers flow, therein to abide by their Lord's leave. Their greeting therein (among themselves and from God and the angels) will be "Peace!"

24. Do you not see how God strikes a parable of a good word: (a good word is) like a good tree – its roots holding firm (in the ground) and its branches in heaven;

258   سُورَةُ إِبْرَٰهِيمَ   ٢٥٨

نُؤْتِىٓ أُكُلَهَا كُلَّ حِينٍ بِإِذْنِ رَبِّهَا ۗ وَيَضْرِبُ اللَّهُ الْأَمْثَالَ
لِلنَّاسِ لَعَلَّهُمْ يَتَذَكَّرُونَ ۝ وَمَثَلُ كَلِمَةٍ خَبِيثَةٍ كَشَجَرَةٍ
خَبِيثَةٍ اجْتُثَّتْ مِن فَوْقِ الْأَرْضِ مَا لَهَا مِن قَرَارٍ ۝
يُثَبِّتُ اللَّهُ الَّذِينَ آمَنُوا بِالْقَوْلِ الثَّابِتِ فِى الْحَيَوٰةِ
الدُّنْيَا وَفِى الْآخِرَةِ ۖ وَيُضِلُّ اللَّهُ الظَّالِمِينَ ۚ وَيَفْعَلُ اللَّهُ
مَا يَشَاءُ ۝ أَلَمْ تَرَ إِلَى الَّذِينَ بَدَّلُوا نِعْمَتَ اللَّهِ
كُفْرًا وَأَحَلُّوا قَوْمَهُمْ دَارَ الْبَوَارِ ۝ جَهَنَّمَ يَصْلَوْنَهَا ۖ
وَبِئْسَ الْقَرَارُ ۝ وَجَعَلُوا لِلَّهِ أَندَادًا لِّيُضِلُّوا عَن سَبِيلِهِ ۗ
قُلْ تَمَتَّعُوا فَإِنَّ مَصِيرَكُمْ إِلَى النَّارِ ۝ قُل لِّعِبَادِىَ الَّذِينَ
آمَنُوا يُقِيمُوا الصَّلَوٰةَ وَيُنفِقُوا مِمَّا رَزَقْنَاهُمْ سِرًّا وَعَلَانِيَةً
مِّن قَبْلِ أَن يَأْتِىَ يَوْمٌ لَّا بَيْعٌ فِيهِ وَلَا خِلَالٌ ۝ اللَّهُ الَّذِى
خَلَقَ السَّمَاوَاتِ وَالْأَرْضَ وَأَنزَلَ مِنَ السَّمَاءِ مَاءً فَأَخْرَجَ
بِهِ مِنَ الثَّمَرَاتِ رِزْقًا لَّكُمْ ۖ وَسَخَّرَ لَكُمُ الْفُلْكَ لِتَجْرِىَ
فِى الْبَحْرِ بِأَمْرِهِ ۖ وَسَخَّرَ لَكُمُ الْأَنْهَارَ ۝ وَسَخَّرَ لَكُمُ
الشَّمْسَ وَالْقَمَرَ دَائِبَيْنِ ۖ وَسَخَّرَ لَكُمُ اللَّيْلَ وَالنَّهَارَ ۝

─────❦─────

25. It yields its fruit in every season due by its Lord's leave. So God strikes parables for human beings in order that they may reflect on them and infer the necessary lessons.

26. And the parable of a corrupt word is that of a corrupt tree uprooted from upon the earth, having no constancy.

27. God keeps firm those who believe by the true, firm word in the life of this world and in the Hereafter; and God leads the wrongdoers astray. And God does whatever He wills.[7]

28. Do you ever consider those who exchanged God's blessing (of thankfulness and faith) for ingratitude and unbelief, and caused their people to settle in the abode of ruin –

29. Hell – wherein they land to be roasted? How evil a place to settle in!

30. They have set up rivals to God (as deities, lords, and objects of worship), and so they have led (themselves and other people) astray from His way. Say: "Enjoy yourselves (in this world). Your journey's end is the Fire."

31. Tell those of My servants who believe that they must establish the Prayer in conformity with its conditions, and spend out of what We have provided for them (of wealth, power, and knowledge, etc.) secretly and openly (and in God's cause and for the needy), before there comes a Day when there will be no trading nor friendship (that will bring any benefit).

32. God is He Who has created the heavens and the earth, and sends down water from the sky with which He brings forth fruits for your provision. And He has made the ships serviceable for you, so that they run upon the sea by His command, and He has made the rivers serviceable for you;

33. And He has made the sun and the moon constant in their courses, (and so) serviceable for you, and He has made the night and the day of service to you.

7. The good word is any word uttered and/or any action done purely for God's sake and in compliance with His commandments. The best of words is the declaration of faith, which is *Lā ilāha illa-llāh* (There is no deity but God).

It is the seed of Islam planted in the believer's heart, as well as in the ground. This tree of faith grows elaborate through practice, so that it has its branches in "celestial worlds." It continuously yields its produce of virtue and laudable works and causes the blossoming of a magnificent civilization, for the heart which is connected to the higher worlds is always receiving the influx of Divine gifts.

The good word or faith is the truth and therefore cannot be uprooted from the world. It is well-established and lasting. Like water flowing beneath the scum (13: 17), it causes

life wherever it passes and is of great use to people.

The good word, besides its metaphorical meaning, is also used in its first, literal meaning. Every good word, in particular when accompanied by good deeds, causes the growth of good "trees" in hearts (35: 10).

What is meant by the true, firm word is also the truth of faith. It is established and unchanging. Therefore, believers are firm in their belief and conduct. They do not waver amidst different currents, and they are also firm and persevering in their endeavors on God's way. On the other hand, wrongdoers are those who do wrong in their deeds, who waver in their thoughts and stray from true belief. Any "wind" is enough to bend and even uproot them.

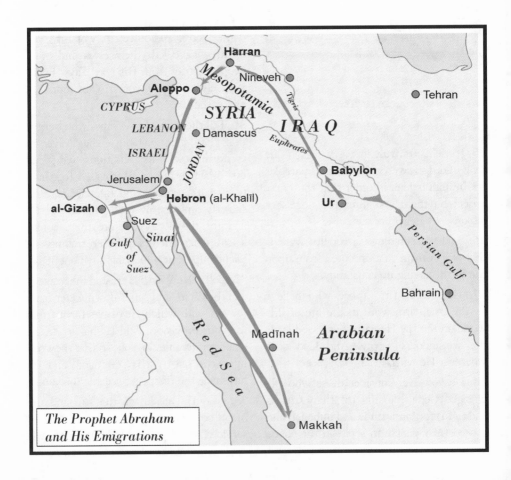

The Prophet Abraham and His Emigrations

وَءَاتَىٰكُم مِّن كُلِّ مَا سَأَلْتُمُوهُ ۚ وَإِن تَعُدُّوا۟ نِعْمَتَ ٱللَّهِ لَا تُحْصُوهَآ ۗ إِنَّ ٱلْإِنسَـٰنَ لَظَلُومٌ كَفَّارٌ ۝ وَإِذْ قَالَ إِبْرَٰهِيمُ رَبِّ ٱجْعَلْ هَـٰذَا ٱلْبَلَدَ ءَامِنًا وَٱجْنُبْنِى وَبَنِىَّ أَن نَّعْبُدَ ٱلْأَصْنَامَ ۝ رَبِّ إِنَّهُنَّ أَضْلَلْنَ كَثِيرًا مِّنَ ٱلنَّاسِ ۖ فَمَن تَبِعَنِى فَإِنَّهُۥ مِنِّى ۖ وَمَنْ عَصَانِى فَإِنَّكَ غَفُورٌ رَّحِيمٌ ۝ رَّبَّنَآ إِنِّىٓ أَسْكَنتُ مِن ذُرِّيَّتِى بِوَادٍ غَيْرِ ذِى زَرْعٍ عِندَ بَيْتِكَ ٱلْمُحَرَّمِ رَبَّنَا لِيُقِيمُوا۟ ٱلصَّلَوٰةَ فَٱجْعَلْ أَفْـِٔدَةً مِّنَ ٱلنَّاسِ تَهْوِىٓ إِلَيْهِمْ وَٱرْزُقْهُم مِّنَ ٱلثَّمَرَٰتِ لَعَلَّهُمْ يَشْكُرُونَ ۝ رَبَّنَآ إِنَّكَ تَعْلَمُ مَا نُخْفِى وَمَا نُعْلِنُ ۗ وَمَا يَخْفَىٰ عَلَى ٱللَّهِ مِن شَىْءٍ فِى ٱلْأَرْضِ وَلَا فِى ٱلسَّمَآءِ ۝ ٱلْحَمْدُ لِلَّهِ ٱلَّذِى وَهَبَ لِى عَلَى ٱلْكِبَرِ إِسْمَـٰعِيلَ وَإِسْحَـٰقَ ۚ إِنَّ رَبِّى لَسَمِيعُ ٱلدُّعَآءِ ۝ رَبِّ ٱجْعَلْنِى مُقِيمَ ٱلصَّلَوٰةِ وَمِن ذُرِّيَّتِى ۚ رَبَّنَا وَتَقَبَّلْ دُعَآءِ ۝ رَبَّنَا ٱغْفِرْ لِى وَلِوَٰلِدَىَّ وَلِلْمُؤْمِنِينَ يَوْمَ يَقُومُ ٱلْحِسَابُ ۝ وَلَا تَحْسَبَنَّ ٱللَّهَ غَـٰفِلًا عَمَّا يَعْمَلُ ٱلظَّـٰلِمُونَ ۚ إِنَّمَا يُؤَخِّرُهُمْ لِيَوْمٍ تَشْخَصُ فِيهِ ٱلْأَبْصَـٰرُ ۝

———— ❧ ————

34. He has granted you from all that you ask Him. Were you to attempt to count God's blessings, you could not compute them. But for sure humankind are much prone to wrongdoing (sins and errors of judgment) and to ingratitude.

35. And (remember) when Abraham prayed: "O my Lord! Make this land (Makkah) secure, and preserve me and my children (my sons and their descendants) from ever worshipping idols.

36. "My Lord! They have indeed caused many among humankind to go astray. So, he who follows me is truly of me; while he who disobeys me, surely You are All-Forgiving, All-Compassionate.[8]

37. "O our Lord! I have settled some of my offspring (Ishmael and his descendants) in an uncultivable valley near Your Sacred House, so that, our Lord, they may establish the Prayer; so make the hearts of people incline towards them, and provide them with the produce of earth (by such means as trade), so that they may give thanks (constantly from the heart and in speech, and in action by fulfilling Your commandments).[9]

38. "O our Lord! Surely You know all that we keep secret as well as all that we disclose; nothing whatever, whether it be on earth or in heaven, is hidden from God.

39. "All praise and gratitude are for God, Who has granted me, despite my old age, Ishmael and Isaac. Indeed, my Lord is the Hearer of prayer.

40. "O my Lord! Make me one who establishes the Prayer in conformity with its conditions, and (likewise) from my offspring (those who are not wrongdoers),[10] Our Lord, and accept my prayer!

41. "O our Lord! Forgive me, and my parents, and all the believers, on the Day on which the Reckoning will be established."[11]

42. Never reckon that God is unaware of what the wrongdoers are doing. He only defers them to a day when their eyes will stare (in terror);

8. For a similar prayer of the Prophet Jesus, upon him be peace, see 5: 118, note 26.

9. While Abraham says in verse 35 of this *sūrah Make this land secure*, he says in 2: 126: *Make this (untilled valley) a land of security*. This shows that he made the prayer in 2: 126, before the one found in this *sūrah*. As can be understood from the relevant verses, he settled Hagar and his son Ishmael in Makkah upon God's order and returned to Palestine. He came back a while later, and upon seeing that some people had already settled in the valley of Makkah, which was on its way to growing into a settled land, he prayed: *My Lord! Make this (untilled valley) a land of security, and provide its people with the produce of earth, such of them as believe in God and the Last Day* (2: 126). Then he came once more to Makkah and built the Ka'bah with Ishmael and made the prayers mentioned in 2: 127–129. After that, he paid a last visit to Makkah toward the end of his life and saw that it had already grown into a land of residence and said the prayers and supplications mentioned in this *sūrah*, verses 35–41. Either he observed idol-worshipping among some of the people or he was worried that idol-worshipping might appear there and prayed to God to save him and his progeny from it. It seems as if these prayers and supplications are the last prayers he made in Makkah. The Prophet Ishmael and his children had already made a home there and had begun to grow in number. This is explicit in that the verb "establish" in *establishing the Prayer* is plural, which in Arabic indicates that the subject is at least three people.

10. See 2: 124, note 106.

11. This prayer of the Prophet Abraham, as one of the five greatest Messengers and one whom God praises as a community (16: 120) because of his consideration for all people, and as the forefather of the Prophets Moses, Jesus, and Muḥammad, upon all of them be peace, has been fully accepted by God Almighty. Some significant points in his prayer merit special attention:

- When he prays for himself, his parents, and his progeny, he addresses God Almighty as *my Lord*, while He addresses Him as *our Lord* when he prays for all believers. Thus, he teaches us how to address God.

- He lays much stress on the daily Prescribed Prayer as one of the most important forms of worship, and he regards it as the bedrock of servanthood to God and the purpose for life. This is because the Prayer is, in the words of God's Messenger, upon him be peace and blessings, the pillar of Islam, without which the building of Islam cannot be erected (al-Bayhaqī, *Shu'ab al-Īmān*, 3: 39).

- He sees provision, or being provided by God, as the reason for thankfulness to Him. That is, God wills thankfulness in people when He provides for them. Thankfulness is both the door that opens on faith and its main token. Thankfulness means seeing the source of all that one has and attributing it to its real Owner. This shatters the idol of self-worship and leads one to believe in God and worship Him. The pleasure God has placed in provision – food, drink, clothes, and other things – serves to arouse thankfulness to God in people.

The Prophet Abraham, upon him be peace, cannot include all of his offspring in his prayer for God to make them of those who establish the Prayer; rather he says, *from my offspring*. As referred to in note 10 above, this is an allusion to 2: 124, which says: *Remember that his Lord tested Abraham with commands and ordeals (such as his being thrown into a fire, the destruction of the people of his kinsman Lot, and his being ordered to sacrifice his son Ishmael), and he fulfilled them thoroughly. He said: "Indeed I will make you an imām for all people." He (Abraham) pleaded: "(Will You appoint imāms) also from my offspring?" He (his Lord) answered: "(I will appoint from among those who merit it. But) My covenant does not include the wrongdoers."* Abraham knew that all of his offspring would not be able to be righteous and establish the Prayer. This shows that being a descendant of a righteous one, even if that one be a great Messenger, is not enough to make one of the virtuous; none can claim to belong to a chosen people. This was also explicit in his prayer, *"Our Lord! Make us Muslims, submissive to You, and of our offspring a community Muslim, submissive to You"* (2: 128).

260   سُوۡرَةُ اِبۡرٰهِيۡمَ   ٢٦٠

مُّهۡطِعِيۡنَ مُقۡنِعِىۡ رُءُوۡسِهِمۡ لَا يَرۡتَدُّ اِلَيۡهِمۡ طَرۡفُهُمۡ وَاَفۡـِٕدَتُهُمۡ هَوَآءٌ ۞ وَاَنۡذِرِ النَّاسَ يَوۡمَ يَاۡتِيۡهِمُ الۡعَذَابُ فَيَقُوۡلُ الَّذِيۡنَ ظَلَمُوۡا رَبَّنَاۤ اَخِّرۡنَاۤ اِلٰٓى اَجَلٍ قَرِيۡبٍ ۙ نُّجِبۡ دَعۡوَتَكَ وَنَتَّبِعِ الرُّسُلَ ؕ اَوَلَمۡ تَكُوۡنُوۡۤا اَقۡسَمۡتُمۡ مِّنۡ قَبۡلُ مَا لَكُمۡ مِّنۡ زَوَالٍ ۞ وَّسَكَنۡتُمۡ فِىۡ مَسٰكِنِ الَّذِيۡنَ ظَلَمُوۡۤا اَنۡفُسَهُمۡ وَتَبَيَّنَ لَكُمۡ كَيۡفَ فَعَلۡنَا بِهِمۡ وَضَرَبۡنَا لَكُمُ الۡاَمۡثَالَ ۞ وَقَدۡ مَكَرُوۡا مَكۡرَهُمۡ وَعِنۡدَ اللّٰهِ مَكۡرُهُمۡ ؕ وَاِنۡ كَانَ مَكۡرُهُمۡ لِتَزُوۡلَ مِنۡهُ الۡجِبَالُ ۞ فَلَا تَحۡسَبَنَّ اللّٰهَ مُخۡلِفَ وَعۡدِهٖ رُسُلَهٗ ؕ اِنَّ اللّٰهَ عَزِيۡزٌ ذُوانۡتِقَامٍ ۞ يَوۡمَ تُبَدَّلُ الۡاَرۡضُ غَيۡرَ الۡاَرۡضِ وَالسَّمٰوٰتُ وَبَرَزُوۡا لِلّٰهِ الۡوَاحِدِ الۡقَهَّارِ ۞ وَتَرَى الۡمُجۡرِمِيۡنَ يَوۡمَئِذٍ مُّقَرَّنِيۡنَ فِى الۡاَصۡفَادِ ۞ سَرَابِيۡلُهُمۡ مِّنۡ قَطِرَانٍ وَّتَغۡشٰى وُجُوۡهَهُمُ النَّارُ ۞ لِيَجۡزِىَ اللّٰهُ كُلَّ نَفۡسٍ مَّا كَسَبَتۡ ؕ اِنَّ اللّٰهَ سَرِيۡعُ الۡحِسَابِ ۞ هٰذَا بَلٰغٌ لِّلنَّاسِ وَلِيُنۡذَرُوۡا بِهٖ وَلِيَعۡلَمُوۡۤا اَنَّمَا هُوَ اِلٰهٌ وَّاحِدٌ وَّلِيَذَّكَّرَ اُولُوا الۡاَلۡبَابِ ۞

how We had dealt with them, and We made examples for you (to enable you to grasp the truth and mend your ways)."

46. They contrived their schemes, but their schemes were in God's disposition (entirely encompassed by His Knowledge and Power), even though their schemes were such as to shock mountains.

47. So do not reckon that God will fail to keep His promise to His Messengers. Surely God is All-Glorious with irresistible might, Ever-Able to Requite (all wrongs).

48. On the Day when the earth is changed into another earth, and the heavens (also), they all appear before God, the One, the All-Overwhelming.

49. On that Day you will see all the disbelieving criminals linked together in shackles,

50. Clothed in garments of pitch and their faces covered by the Fire,

51. That God may recompense every soul for what it has earned. God is indeed swift at reckoning.

52. This is a clear message for humankind that they may be warned by it, and that they should know that He is One God, and that people of discernment may reflect and be mindful.

43. Hurrying on in fear with necks outstretched and heads upraised, and their eyes are fixed on a point from which they are unable to look away, and their hearts are void (as if filled with air).

44. And warn humankind of the Day when the punishment will come upon them; and those who did wrong (by associating partners with God and other grave sins) will say: "Our Lord! Grant us respite for a short while – we will answer your call and follow the Messengers!" (And their entreaty will get the response:) "Did you not use to swear before that there would be no decline and fall for you?

45. "And you dwelt in the dwelling-places of those who wronged themselves (by associating partners with God and other grave sins), and it became clear to you

SŪRAH 15

AL-ḤIJR

Makkah period

This *surah*, consisting of 99 verses, was revealed in Makkah. Its main theme is the evidence of God's Existence and Oneness, and the Divine authorship of the Qur'ān. It mentions some of the exemplary events of previous peoples. It derives its name from the name of the Arabian region mentioned in verse 80, al-Ḥijr, where the people of Ṣāliḥ lived.

In the Name of God, the All-Merciful, the All-Compassionate.

1. *Alif. Lām. Rā.* These are the Revelations of the Book, a Qur'ān clear in itself and clearly showing the truth.

2. Again and again will those who disbelieve wish that they had been Muslims.

3. Leave them that they may continue to eat and enjoy themselves, and that hope (for a long, easy life) distract them (from considering their main duty in life and considering their end). In time they will come to know (the truth).

4. And We did not destroy any township unless it had a known and recorded decree.[1]

5. No community can ever hasten on the end of its term, nor can they delay it.[2]

6. They say: "O you, on whom the Reminder (the Book of advice, warning, and instructions) is sent down, truly you are a madman.

7. "Why do you not bring down the angels to us if you are truthful (in your claim)!"

8. We do not send down the angels save with the truth (for a just reason and with wisdom, not to satisfy vain caprice or curiosity, and once the angels are sent down, the matter is decided, and) then they are allowed no (further) respite.

9. Indeed it is We, We Who send down the Reminder in parts, and it is indeed We Who are its Guardian.[3]

10. Certainly We sent Messengers before you among the communities of old.

11. And there never came to them a Messenger but they did mock him.

12. Just so, We cause it (the Qur'ān) to pass unheeded through the hearts of the disbelieving criminals:

13. They do not believe in it: for certain the pattern of life of the (sinful) peoples of old has already passed.

14. Even if (as a miracle of the kind they desire) We opened to them a gate in heaven and they kept ascending through it all the while,

15. They would say, "Our eyes are but spellbound; rather, we have been bewitched!"[4]

1. That is, its people were made well aware of what they would meet in consequence of the way they chose to follow, and the period of respite allowed them was determined and laid down by God.

2. For an explanation of this verse, see 7: 34, note 10.

3. The text of the Qur'ān was preserved in four different ways during the lifetime of the Messenger of God, upon him be peace and blessings:

- The Prophet had the whole text of the Divine Messages, from the beginning to the end, committed to writing by the scribes of Revelations.
- Many of the Companions learned the whole text of the Qur'ān, every syllable, by heart.
- All the illustrious Companions, without exception, had memorized at least some portions of the Holy Qur'ān, for the simple reason that it was obligatory for them to recite it during worship.
- A considerable number of the literate Companions kept a private record of the text of the Qur'ān and satisfied themselves as to the purity of their record by reading it out to the Messenger, upon him be peace and blessings.

There are many incidents during the Messenger's life-time that prove that there were also copies of the parts of the Qur'ān that had been revealed up until the time of the recording. For example, the Prophet provided visitors to Madīnah, who came to learn about Islam, with copies of chapters of the Qur'ān to read and learn. To cite just one example, a Tradition from Saḥīḥ Muslim ("Kitāb al-'Imārah," 24) states that Ibn 'Umar was asked by the Prophet not to take the Qur'ān on a journey with him, for he was afraid that it might fall into the hands of the enemy.

Following the death of the Prophet, when numerous memorizers of the Qur'ān were martyred at the Battle of Yamāmah, 'Umar ibn al-Khattāb made a request to the Caliph Abū Bakr that they should have an "official" col-

lection of the Qur'ān, since the memorizers of the Qur'ān were being martyred in the battles. Zayd ibn Thābit, one of the leading scholars and memorizers of the Qur'ān at that time, was chosen for this task. After meticulous work, Zayd prepared the official collection, which was called the Muṣḥaf.

During the time of 'Uthmān, the 3rd Caliph, some Companions appealed to him to have new copies of the Muṣḥaf produced so that they may be sent to the provinces. So 'Uthmān ordered Zayd ibn Thābit, 'Abdullāh ibn az-Zubayr, Sa'īd ibn al-'Āṣ, and 'Abdurraḥmān ibn Hārith ibn Hishām to produce new copies of the Muṣḥaf.

According to Jalālu'd-Dīn as-Suyūtī, a fifteenth-century scholar of Egypt, five copies of the Qur'ān were made at the time of 'Uthmān. This excludes the copy that 'Uthmān kept for himself. The cities of Makkah, Damascus, Kūfah, Basrah, and Madīnah each received a copy.

Al-Kindī (d. around 236/850) wrote in the early third century that the copy sent to Damascus was still kept at his time in Malatya, Turkey. Ibn Baṭṭutah (779/1377) said that he had seen copies made from the copies of the Qur'ān prepared under 'Uthmān in Granada, Marrakesh, Basrah, and other cities.

Ibn Jubayr (d. 614/1217) saw the Madīnah manuscript in the Mosque of Madīnah in the year 580/1184. It remained in Madīnah until the Turks took it from there in 1334/1915. It has been reported that this copy was removed by the Turkish authorities to Istanbul, from where it went to Berlin during World War I. The Treaty of Versailles, which concluded that war, contains the following clause:

> Article 246: Within six months from the coming into force of the present Treaty, Germany will restore to His Majesty, King of Hedjaz, the original Koran of Caliph 'Uthman, which was removed from Madina by the Turkish authorities and is stated to have been presented to the ex-Emperor William II (Israel, Fred L. [ed.]: *Major Peace Treaties of Modern History*, New York, Chelsea House Pub., 2: 1418).

As for the "Imām" Manuscript, which is the name used for the copy which 'Uthmān kept himself, and which he was reading when he was killed, the Umayyads took it to Andalusia, from where it went to Morocco and, according to Ibn Baṭṭuṭah, it was there in the eighth century after the *Hijrah*, with traces of blood still on it. From Morocco, it might have found its way to Samarqand. There is presently a copy in Tashkent (Uzbekistan). It may be the Imām Manuscript, or one of the other copies made at the time of 'Uthmān.

This copy came to Samarqand in 890 *Hijrah* (1485) and remained there till 1868. Then it was taken to St. Petersburg by the Russians in 1869. It remained there till 1917. A Russian orientalist gave a detailed description of it, saying that many pages were damaged and some were missing. Some 50 facsimiles of this *muṣḥaf* were produced by S. Pisareff in 1905. A copy was sent to the Ottoman Sultan 'Abdul Hamid, to the Shah of Iran, to the Amīr of Bukhārah, to Afghanistan, to Morocco and to some other important Muslim personalities. One copy can now be found in the Columbia University Library (U.S.A.) (*The Muslim World*, vol . 30 [1940], pp. 357–358).

The manuscript was afterwards returned to its former place and reached Tashkent in 1924, where it has remained ever since. Apparently the Soviet authorities have made further copies, which are presented from time to time to visiting Muslim heads of state and other important personalities. In 1980, photocopies of such a facsimile were produced in the United States, with a two-page foreword by M. Hamidullah. Makhdūm, the writer of the *History of the Muṣḥaf of 'Uthmān in Tashkent*, gives a number of reasons that support the authenticity of this manuscript. They are, excluding various historical reports which suggest this, as follows:

- The fact that the *muṣḥaf* is written in the script that was used in the first half of the first century of the *Hijrah*.
- The fact that it is written on parchment made from gazelle, while later copies of the Qur'ān were written on paper-like sheets.
- The fact that it does not have any diacritical

marks which were introduced around the eighth decade of the first century; hence the manuscript must have been written before that.

- The fact that it does not have the vowel symbols introduced by Abu'l-Aswad ad-Du'alī, who died in 68 *Hijrah*; hence it is earlier than this. (http://www.muhammad.net/quran/ulumulQuran/004.htm)

In other words: two of the copies of the Qur'ān which were originally prepared in the time of Caliph 'Uthmān are still available to us today and their text and arrangement can be compared, by anyone who cares to, with any other copy of the Qur'ān, be it in print or manuscript, from any place or period of time. They will be found to be identical.

To sum up: God Almighty has guarded the Qur'ān against any corruption. The Qur'ān that we have now, anywhere in the world, has remained exactly the same over the last fourteen centuries and there is not the slightest difference between the one that was recited during the earliest period of Islam and any other printed and recited now in any part of the Muslim world. (For the preservation of the Qur'ān, also see Foreword, "The Recording of the Qur'ān and Its Preservation.")

4. As we have pointed out in some places of this commentary (*sūrah* 2: 7, 22, notes 7, 16; *sūrah* 5: 115, note 24), the main reasons for unbelief are conceit, self-pride, wrongdoing, misjudgment, incorrect viewpoints, deviation in thought and action, and indulgence in carnal appetites. Demanding different kinds of miracles from the Messengers is only an excuse for persistence in unbelief. Instead of presenting the miracles to view, the Qur'ān, as will be mentioned below, draws attention to God's works and acts in the universe, each of which means more than a miracle for one who has "eyes" to see with, "ears" to hear with, and "hearts" to perceive and believe with.

For another explanation of unbelief and the cardinal reasons for it, and for the arguments in favor of faith in the Qur'ān, see 6: 73, note 15.

وَلَقَدْ جَعَلْنَا فِى السَّمَاءِ بُرُوجًا وَزَيَّنَّاهَا لِلنَّاظِرِينَ ۞ وَحَفِظْنَاهَا مِن كُلِّ شَيْطَانٍ رَّجِيمٍ ۞ إِلَّا مَنِ اسْتَرَقَ السَّمْعَ فَأَتْبَعَهُ شِهَابٌ مُّبِينٌ ۞ وَالْأَرْضَ مَدَدْنَاهَا وَأَلْقَيْنَا فِيهَا رَوَاسِىَ وَأَنبَتْنَا فِيهَا مِن كُلِّ شَىْءٍ مَّوْزُونٍ ۞ وَجَعَلْنَا لَكُمْ فِيهَا مَعَايِشَ وَمَن لَّسْتُمْ لَهُ بِرَازِقِينَ ۞ وَإِن مِّن شَىْءٍ إِلَّا عِندَنَا خَزَائِنُهُ وَمَا نُنَزِّلُهُ إِلَّا بِقَدَرٍ مَّعْلُومٍ ۞ وَأَرْسَلْنَا الرِّيَاحَ لَوَاقِحَ فَأَنزَلْنَا مِنَ السَّمَاءِ مَاءً فَأَسْقَيْنَاكُمُوهُ وَمَا أَنتُمْ لَهُ بِخَازِنِينَ ۞ وَإِنَّا لَنَحْنُ نُحْيِى وَنُمِيتُ وَنَحْنُ الْوَارِثُونَ ۞ وَلَقَدْ عَلِمْنَا الْمُسْتَقْدِمِينَ مِنكُمْ وَلَقَدْ عَلِمْنَا الْمُسْتَأْخِرِينَ ۞ وَإِنَّ رَبَّكَ هُوَ يَحْشُرُهُمْ إِنَّهُ حَكِيمٌ عَلِيمٌ ۞ وَلَقَدْ خَلَقْنَا الْإِنسَانَ مِن صَلْصَالٍ مِّنْ حَمَإٍ مَّسْنُونٍ ۞ وَالْجَانَّ خَلَقْنَاهُ مِن قَبْلُ مِن نَّارِ السَّمُومِ ۞ وَإِذْ قَالَ رَبُّكَ لِلْمَلَائِكَةِ إِنِّى خَالِقٌ بَشَرًا مِّن صَلْصَالٍ مِّنْ حَمَإٍ مَّسْنُونٍ ۞ فَإِذَا سَوَّيْتُهُ وَنَفَخْتُ فِيهِ مِن رُّوحِى فَقَعُوا لَهُ سَاجِدِينَ ۞ فَسَجَدَ الْمَلَائِكَةُ كُلُّهُمْ أَجْمَعُونَ ۞ إِلَّا إِبْلِيسَ أَبَىٰ أَن يَكُونَ مَعَ السَّاجِدِينَ ۞

---

16. (As evidence for a people open to faith) We have assuredly set in the heaven great constellations, and We have made it (the heaven) beautiful for those beholding;

17. And We have made it secure against every accursed Satan rejected (from God's mercy),

18. Excepting one who listens by stealth; but it is immediately pursued (and destroyed) by a shooting-star clear to see.[5]

19. And the earth – We have spread it out and set therein firm mountains, and caused to grow therein of every kind in balance and proportion (and in a measured quantity);

20. And We have provided means of livelihood therein for you, and for those for whom you do not provide (such as beasts, birds, and fish).

21. There is not a thing but the stores (for its life and sustenance) are with Us, and We do not send it down except in due, determined measure.

22. And We send the winds to fertilize,[6] and so We send down water from the sky, and give it to you to drink (and use in other ways); it is not you who are the keepers of its stores (under earth).

23. Surely it is also We, We Who give life and cause to die, and We are the Inheritors (it is We Who remain after all others have passed away).

24. And well do We know those of you who have gone before and those who are to come later.

25. And your Lord – He will surely raise to life and gather them together (on Judgment Day). He is All-Wise, All-Knowing.

26. Assuredly We have created humankind from dried, sounding clay, from molded dark mud.

27. And the jinn We had created before, from smokeless, scorching fire penetrating through the skin.[7]

28. And (remember) when your Lord said to the angels: "I am creating a mortal from dried, sounding clay, from molded dark mud.

29. "When I have fashioned him in due proportions and breathed into him out of My Spirit, then fall down prostrating before him (as a token of respect for him and his superiority)."[8]

30. So the angels prostrated, all of them together,

31. But Iblīs did not; he refused to be among those who prostrated.[9]

5. The original of constellation – *burj* – means stronghold, citadel, or tower. It also means the constellations, which are the names of some fixed star-groups. During its annual revolution around the sun, the earth passes through this belt of constellations (familiarly called the Zodiac). It has been widely accepted from ancient times that this has some affect upon the world and those living in it. Although there may be some truth in this claim, it has been carried to such a point that fortune-telling has arisen from this belief. The misuse of astrology has also contributed to such beliefs.

In some types of fortune-telling, the contact between fortune-tellers and the jinn and/or satans (devils) has a certain place. The jinn and/or satans sometimes attempt to rise to the heaven to eavesdrop on the angels' conversations about human beings and their future. But they have never succeeded in doing this. Rather, they whisper some things to those who have contact with them as if they had been able to overhear the conversation of the angels, and as if they had some information about the future. Yet God never allows them to steal information from the heavens. For a detailed explanation of this point and of these jinn and satans being repelled with meteors, see 67: 5 and the corresponding note.

We should add here that the jinn live much longer than human beings. Also, due to the refinement of the matter of which they are created, they can move much more speedily and communicate to those who are in contact with them some information about history and what is taking place in other parts of the world. This is also true for mediums and similar types of people. But neither the jinn nor medium-like people can ever be trusted; the unbelieving jinn set out to deceive people. For every truth they utter, they tell hundreds of lies. None of them have any true knowledge about the future.

6. Some interpreters of the Qur'ān hold that winds fertilize plants by carrying and spreading pollen. This is true. However, it is clearer in the verse that the winds fertilize through their action on the clouds, that is, through their role in the formation of rain. Ibn Jarīr aṭ-Ṭabarī (244/839–310/923), one of the most outstanding figures in Islamic jurisprudence, history, and Qur'ānic interpretation, mentioned this and wrote about how the winds fertilize the clouds so that rain falls.

Scientists recently discovered that clouds are charged with electricity and that rain forms only when the positive and negative poles in the clouds form a circuit, which is brought about by means of the winds.

God causes rain to be held in reservoirs or water sources under the earth. It is cleaned by passing through salts and soil and is presented to living beings to drink and use in other ways.

7. The Qur'ān has many references to the creation of humankind out of clay or earth, both of which signify the lowly material of their origin, as well as the fact that the human body is composed of elements that are derived from the earth, air, and water. This in part implies that the true value of humankind lies in the immaterial dimension of their existence. As for the jinn, beings that resemble humankind in that they have free will and powers of intellect, anger, and lust, their origin is mentioned in the Qur'ān as being smokeless fire that penetrates through the skin. Some interpret this fire as something that resembles energy or X-rays, or the high-temperature fire that fuses things together (55: 16). The jinn are the beings which caused sedition and bloodshed on the earth before the creation of humanity.

The following reflections, written by Bediüzzaman Said Nursi at the beginning of the 1930s, give us much insight into the origin and creation of angels, the jinn, and humankind:

> Life perfects a thing's existence, for life is the real basis and light of existence. Consciousness, in turn, is the light of life.... Since life and consciousness are so important, and a perfect harmony prevails over all creation, the universe displays a firm cohesion. As our small rotating planet is full of countless living and intelligent beings, those heavenly castles and

lofty constellations must have conscious living inhabitants unique to themselves. Just as fish live in water, those spirit beings may exist in the heat of the sun. Fire does not consume light; rather, fire makes light brighter. We observe that the Eternal Power creates countless living beings from inert, solid substances and transforms the densest matter into subtle living compounds with life. Thus It radiates the light of life everywhere in great abundance and furnishes most things with the light of consciousness.

From this, we can conclude that the All-Powerful, All-Wise One would not make such subtle forms of matter as light and ether, which are close to and fitting for the spirit, without life and consciousness. He creates countless animate and conscious beings from light and darkness, ether and air, and even from meanings (conceived) and words (uttered). As He creates numerous animal species, He also creates different spirit creatures from subtle forms of matter. Some of these are angels, various spirit beings, and the jinn (*The Words*, "the 29th Word," 528).

Half a century later, nearly 300 animal species, almost all of them previously unknown, have been discovered living around the hydrothermal vents that form when sea-water leaks through the ocean floor where the spreading ridges are heated by the underlying magma which rushes into the cold ocean. Verena Tunniclife writes:

All life requires energy, and nearly all life on the earth looks to the sun as the source. But solar energy is not the only kind of energy available on the earth. Consider the energy that drives the movement and eruption of the planet's crust. When you look at an active volcano, you are witnessing the escape of heat that has been produced by radioactive decay in the earth's interior and is finally reaching the surface. Why should there not be biological communities associated with the same nuclear energy that moves continents and makes mountains? And why could not whole communities be fuelled by chemical, rather than, solar energy?

... Most of us associate the escape of heat from the interior of the earth with violent events and unstable physical conditions, with extreme high temperatures and the release of toxic gasses –circumstances that are hardly conducive to life. The notion that biologic communities might spring up in a geologically active environment once seemed fantastic. And until recently, few organisms were known to survive without a direct or indirect way to tap the sun's energy. But such communities do exist, and they represent one of the most startling discoveries of 20th-century biology. They live in the deep ocean, under conditions that are both severe and variable (*American Scientist*, 1995).

This startling discovery contains clues to other realities that science should consider. The Prophet Muḥammad, upon him be peace and blessings, states that angels are created from light. We read in the Qur'ān that God created humankind from dried clay, and then made them *khalīfah* (vicegerent: one who comes after [to rule according to God's commandments]) for this planet. Many interpreters of the Qur'ān have concluded from this that the jinn once ruled the earth and were succeeded by human beings.

Starting from the clues above, it should be possible to conduct formal studies to determine the worth of such conclusions as the following:

God first created light (in the meaning of *nūr* in the Qur'ān), and He created living beings from it. The process of creation followed a gradual, regular accumulation of identities and/or a saltational sequence of abrupt leaps. Fire followed light in the "kneading" of the universe, and then came water and soil when it was the turn of the earth to come into being. God spread one existence through another, compounding and interweaving, and created living beings appropriate for each phase of creation. When the earth was in a state of smokeless fire, He created appropriate life forms, which the Qur'ān calls the jinn. When the soil became suitable for life, He created (appropriate) plants, animals, and humanity. He adorned every part and phase

of the universe with creatures, including living ones, appropriate for that part and phase.
Here it should be noted that even though the
conscious beings were brougt into existence at
different phases of creation, no kind of those
conscious beings, namely angels, other spiritual
beings, the jinn, and the humankind, has been
annihilated ever since, but all of the creatures
populate concurrently and some even sharing the same space/environment but different
dimension like humankind and the jinn.

Finally, just as He created innumerable
beings from light, ether, air, fire, water, and
soil, so too does He create Paradise or Hell
out of each of our words and deeds. In other
words, just as He causes a tree to grow from
a tiny seed through particles of soil, air, and
water, so too will He build the other world
out of the material of this world, including
Paradise and Hell, by adapting it for the other
world during the convulsions of the Day of
Judgment. (See also 2: 30, note 31-32.)

8. As mentioned before, the honor of humankind lies in their spiritual potential; this is what
causes it to have the greatest rank among all
created beings. God attributes it to Himself
by saying, "My Spirit." Spirit is the source of
both material and spiritual life, and therefore is
not something material; it is direct from God.
Just as God mentions such ordinary things
as earth, clay, and mud as being the material
origin of humankind and draws attention to
the baseness of the material dimension of their
existence, in order to present to view where the
real value of humanity lies, He mentions spirit

and attributes it to Himself. This also means,
as Bediüzzaman said, that the Almighty drew,
so to speak, an allegorical line before all His
Names and created humanity. That is, all of
God's Names which have given existence to
the whole universe are manifested in humanity
to certain, varying degrees. This is why, unlike
animals, human beings have consciousness,
will-power, conscience, a well-developed power
of learning, complex feelings, intellect, a power
of reasoning, an ego and ego-consciousness,
and the feeling of freedom and independence.

Human beings also have, unlike the angels,
a carnal soul and the capacity of spiritual progress as a result of the struggle they undergo.
In short, it is humankind that is the most
polished and perfect mirror to God. It is for
this reason that God expresses this dimension
of the existence of humanity as His breathing
into it out of His spirit. This point is clear in
2: 31-34; (notes 32-34). This expression can in
no way be interpreted to mean that God has
a body and a spirit. God addresses Himself to
the understanding capacity of human beings,
therefore He describes the most subtle matters and abstract truths through parables,
metaphors, similes, and personification and
the like. But in their description, the Qur'ān
sets forth for God's Names and Attributes the
most beautiful and highest parables and comparisons (16: 60), and we must never forget
that nothing is like Him (42: 11) and He is
absolutely different from everything else.

9. Iblīs is not among the angels; he belongs to
the jinn. For a detailed explanation, see 2: 34,
note 36.

٢٦٣ الجزء الرابع عشر 263

القرآن الكريم

—✦—

32. (God) said: "O Iblīs! What is the matter with you that you are not among those who have prostrated?"

33. (Iblīs) said: "I am not one to prostrate before a mortal, whom You have created from dried, sounding clay, from molded dark mud."

34. (God) said: "Then get you down out of it; surely You are one rejected (from My mercy).

35. "And cursing is upon you until the Day of Judgment (as recompense for you in the world)."

36. (Iblīs) said: "Then, my Lord, grant me respite till the Day when they will all be raised from the dead!"

37. He (God) said: "You are of the ones granted respite,

38. "(But) until the Day of the appointed time known (to Me) (i.e. the Last Day)."

39. (Iblīs said:) "My Lord![10] Because You have allowed me to rebel and go astray, I will indeed deck out to be appealing to them on the earth (the worldly, material dimension of human existence and the path of error), and I will surely cause them all to rebel and go astray,

40. "Except Your servants from among them, endowed with sincerity in faith and Your worship."

41. (God) said: "This (path of sincerity in faith) is a straight path that I have taken upon Myself (to lead to Me).

42. "My servants – you shall have no authority over any of them, unless it be such as follow you being rebellious (against Me, as you are)."[11]

43. And for all such (rebellious people), Hell is the promised place.

44. It has seven gates, with an appointed group of them for each gate.[12]

45. The God-revering, pious ones are surely in Gardens and water-springs,

46. (And it is said to them): "Enter you here in peace, perfectly secure!"

47. We strip away whatever there is in their bosoms of rancor and jealousy (which they may have felt against each other while in the world). As brothers face to face, (they take their ease) on couches raised.

48. No sense of fatigue ever touches them, nor are they ever asked to leave.

49. Inform, (O Messenger,) My servants that I surely am the All-Forgiving, the All-Compassionate,

50. And that My punishment – it is indeed the painful punishment.

51. Inform them about the guests of Abraham:

10. The obstinate unbelief of Satan is of great significance. He knows God and he knows that it is He Who creates, nourishes, maintains, and rears His creatures. He also knows that a Day will come when all conscious, responsible beings will be ordered to account for what they have done in the world. However, his knowledge did not suffice for him to overcome his ego, haughtiness, and obstinacy, so as to believe in God and to submit to His commands.

11. The Qur'ān describes this event for understanding the ontological nature of humankind, in considerably different words and expressions and from various viewpoints in many of its *sūrah*s. This is done because what is important in an event is its meaning and the lessons it teaches. This is why the Qur'ān presents to the view the characters and essence of the event in all the aspects that are fitting for the context of each chapter. This is why different words and expressions are required.

For other accounts of this event, similar in some ways while differing in others, see *sūrah* 2: 30–34, notes 30–36; *sūrah* 7: 11–18, notes 2–3.

12. The Qur'ān uses seven different names for the places or types of punishment in the Hereafter: *Jahannam* (Hell), *Nār* (Fire), *Saʿīr* (Blaze), *Jaḥīm* (Blazing Flame), *Ḥutamah* (Consuming Fire), *Saqar* (Scorching Fire), and *Laẓā* (Raging Flame). Most probably, these are the levels or degrees of punishment, each prepared for those who deserve it and each having a gate.

264   سُورَةُ الحِجْرِ   ٢٦٤

52. They presented themselves before him and bade him peace. Abraham said: "We are apprehensive of you."

53. They said: "Do not be apprehensive. We have brought you the glad tidings of a boy to be endowed with profound knowledge."

54. He said: "Do you bring me glad tidings when old age has overtaken me, then how can you bring me such glad tidings?"

55. They said: "We have brought you the glad tidings with truth, so be not of those who despair."

56. He said: "Who would despair of his Lord's mercy, other than those who are astray?"[13]

57. He said: "Then (after that) what is your concern, O you (heavenly) envoys?"

58. They said: "Indeed, we have been sent to a people who are all criminals,

59. "Except for the family of Lot – we are surely to save them all,

60. "Except his wife – about her God has decreed that she shall be among those who stay behind (and are destroyed)."

61. And when the envoys came to the family of Lot,

62. He said: "You are people unknown (here)."

63. They said: "No (do not be afraid)! We have come to you concerning that which they have persistently disputed (the inevitable consequence of their way of life).

64. "We have brought you the truth, and we are most certainly speaking the truth.

65. "So, set forth with your family in a part of the night, with yourself following them in the rear, and let no one among you turn round, but proceed whither you are ordered."

66. We made clear to him that decisive decree, that the root of those (sinful people) was to be cut off in the morning.

67. The people of the city came rejoicing at the news (that some handsome guests had arrived).

68. Lot said: "They are my guests; so do not put me to shame.

69. "Have fear of God, and do not disgrace me!"

70. They said: "Have we not forbidden you to offer protection and intercede for anyone in the world?"

13. As the Qur'ān mentions (11: 75) and as we have indicated elsewhere (5, note 26), the Prophet Abraham, upon him be peace, was exceptionally clement and tender-hearted, and constantly turning to God with all his heart. By saying, "Who would despair of his Lord's mercy, other than those who are astray?" he stresses God's particular mercy and favor for each of His creatures. As a manifestation of His being *ar-Rabbu'r-Raḥmān* (the All-Merciful Lord), He embraces all of His creatures together; but being *ar-Rabbu'r-Raḥīm* (the All-Compassionate Lord) He has particular mercy and favor for each of them. Everyone has their own particular relationship with God, and according to the nature and depth of this relationship, God favorably inclines toward and shows special mercy for them. As the All-Compassionate Lord (Sustainer, Upbringer, Protector) of each of them, God is always nearer to His creatures than they are to themselves. Everyone can build their special relationship with God and turn to Him without needing any intermediary, and no one needs to feel that He is like a "father." He is infinitely more compassionate toward His servants than their fathers, and perceiving Him to be like a father means reducing God to a mortal, helpless, material, needy being, while He is infinite in all His Attributes, All-Powerful, eternal; He is One who has no needs at all, and Who is exalted above having any human deficiencies.

قَالَ هَٰٓؤُلَآءِ بَنَاتِىٓ إِن كُنتُمۡ فَٰعِلِينَ ۝ لَعَمۡرُكَ إِنَّهُمۡ لَفِى سَكۡرَتِهِمۡ يَعۡمَهُونَ ۝ فَأَخَذَتۡهُمُ ٱلصَّيۡحَةُ مُشۡرِقِينَ ۝ فَجَعَلۡنَا عَٰلِيَهَا سَافِلَهَا وَأَمۡطَرۡنَا عَلَيۡهِمۡ حِجَارَةً مِّن سِجِّيلٍ ۝ إِنَّ فِى ذَٰلِكَ لَءَايَٰتٍ لِّلۡمُتَوَسِّمِينَ ۝ وَإِنَّهَا لَبِسَبِيلٍ مُّقِيمٍ ۝ إِنَّ فِى ذَٰلِكَ لَءَايَةً لِّلۡمُؤۡمِنِينَ ۝ وَإِن كَانَ أَصۡحَٰبُ ٱلۡأَيۡكَةِ لَظَٰلِمِينَ ۝ فَٱنتَقَمۡنَا مِنۡهُمۡ وَإِنَّهُمَا لَبِإِمَامٍ مُّبِينٍ ۝ وَلَقَدۡ كَذَّبَ أَصۡحَٰبُ ٱلۡحِجۡرِ ٱلۡمُرۡسَلِينَ ۝ وَءَاتَيۡنَٰهُمۡ ءَايَٰتِنَا فَكَانُوا۟ عَنۡهَا مُعۡرِضِينَ ۝ وَكَانُوا۟ يَنۡحِتُونَ مِنَ ٱلۡجِبَالِ بُيُوتًا ءَامِنِينَ ۝ فَأَخَذَتۡهُمُ ٱلصَّيۡحَةُ مُصۡبِحِينَ ۝ فَمَآ أَغۡنَىٰ عَنۡهُم مَّا كَانُوا۟ يَكۡسِبُونَ ۝ وَمَا خَلَقۡنَا ٱلسَّمَٰوَٰتِ وَٱلۡأَرۡضَ وَمَا بَيۡنَهُمَآ إِلَّا بِٱلۡحَقِّ وَإِنَّ ٱلسَّاعَةَ لَءَاتِيَةٌ فَٱصۡفَحِ ٱلصَّفۡحَ ٱلۡجَمِيلَ ۝ إِنَّ رَبَّكَ هُوَ ٱلۡخَلَّٰقُ ٱلۡعَلِيمُ ۝ وَلَقَدۡ ءَاتَيۡنَٰكَ سَبۡعًا مِّنَ ٱلۡمَثَانِى وَٱلۡقُرۡءَانَ ٱلۡعَظِيمَ ۝ لَا تَمُدَّنَّ عَيۡنَيۡكَ إِلَىٰ مَا مَتَّعۡنَا بِهِۦٓ أَزۡوَٰجًا مِّنۡهُمۡ وَلَا تَحۡزَنۡ عَلَيۡهِمۡ وَٱخۡفِضۡ جَنَاحَكَ لِلۡمُؤۡمِنِينَ ۝ وَقُلۡ إِنِّىٓ أَنَا ٱلنَّذِيرُ ٱلۡمُبِينُ ۝ كَمَآ أَنزَلۡنَا عَلَى ٱلۡمُقۡتَسِمِينَ ۝

---

71. Lot said: "Here are my daughters (whom you might lawfully take in marriage), if you have to be doing (something of that sort)!"

72. By your life (O Muḥammad), they moved blindly and wildly in their delirium (of perversion).

73. The awful blast seized them at the sunrise,

74. And We turned them (the sinful towns) upside down, and rained down on them stones of baked clay.

75. Surely in this there are signs (lessons and messages) for those who can read the signs (so as to understand the inner meaning of things and events).

76. They (the traces of those destroyed towns) stand by a road that still exists.

77. Surely in that there is a manifest sign for the believers (for the truth of God's decree, and the way He enjoins, and the call to it).[14]

78. And the people of al-Aykah were also wrongdoers (who associated partners with God).[15]

79. So We inflicted Our retribution on them (which they deserved), and both (of these sinful communities) lived by a highway plain to see.

80. And most certainly the people of al-Ḥijr denied the Messengers (by denying the Messenger sent to them).

81. So We presented to them Our signs (including miracles, and sent Our Revelations), but they turned away from them in aversion.

82. They hewed out dwellings in the mountains, feeling themselves secure (against any calamity).

83. But the awful blast seized them in the morning.

84. All (the wealth and power) that they acquired was of no avail to them.[16]

85. We did not create the heavens and the earth and all that is between them save with truth (meaningfully, and with definite purpose, and on solid foundations of truth); and the Last Hour is surely bound to come.[17] So, overlook (the faults of the people, O Messenger) with a gracious forbearance.[18]

86. Surely, your Lord is He Who is the Supreme Creator, the All-Knowing.

87. And, indeed We have granted you the Seven Doubly-Repeated (Verses) and, (built on it), the Grand Qur'ān.[19]

88. Do not strain your eyes toward what We have given some groups among them (the unbelievers) to enjoy (in the life of

this world), nor grieve over them (because of their attitude toward your mission); and lower your wings (of compassion and protection) for the believers.[20]

89. And say (to those coming to Makkah from neighboring towns): "Surely I, I am the plain warner (against a punishment to be sent down),"

90. Just as We have sent down on those who make divisions;

---

14. The Qur'ān narrates historical events from different perspectives, in all its different aspects according to the purpose it pursues in narrating them, and within the framework of the context. For the accounts of the heavenly envoys' visit to the Prophet Abraham, upon him be peace, and the destruction of Lot's people, which have already been mentioned, see *sūrah* 7: 80–84, note 18; *sūrah* 11: 69–83, notes 16–19.

15. Some commentators are of the opinion that the people of al-Aykah and the people of Midian were the names of the same people to whom the Prophet Shu'ayb was sent as Messenger and about whom information was given in 7: 85–93 (see note 19) and in 11: 84–95. However, the Qur'ān uses the phrase "their brother" for the Messengers sent to their people, meaning that both they and their people were of the same tribe. It uses the same phrase while recounting Shu'ayb's experience with the people of Midian (7: 85), but while narrating his experience with the people of al-Aykah, it does not (26: 177). The punishment that the peoples of Midian and al-Aykah were subjected to also seems to be different (7: 91; 11: 94; 26: 189). Based on these differences, other commentators are of the opinion that the people of Midian and al-Aykah were two separate branches of the same tribe. The territory of Madyan (Midian) lay to the north-west of Hijaz and south of Palestine on the coast of the Red Sea and the Gulf of 'Aqabah, with part of the territory stretching to the northern border of the Sinai Peninsula. Midian was the capital of the territory and al-Aykah was located a five-day journey from it. It is highly possible that al-Aykah was located in the present day 'Aqabah. Its people bore the same characteristics and committed the same crimes as the people of Midian. So Shu'ayb's experiences here were almost identical to what

took place between him and the Midianites. For a further account of the people of al-Aykah, see 26: 176–191.

16. For a more detailed account of the people of Ṣāliḥ see *sūrah* 7: 73–79, note 17; *sūrah* 11: 61–68.

17. God has definite purposes for the creation of the heavens and the earth. This is also true of their destruction that must take place in order to build the other world. In this world humankind and the jinn, the two kinds of conscious beings that have will-power and who are therefore responsible for their deeds, will be called to account for their worldly lives. So God's purposes for the creation of the heavens and the earth will be fulfilled completely only in the Hereafter.

The Majestic Lord and Ruler of this world has infinite Munificence and Mercy, infinite Splendor and Majesty. His Munificence requires infinite giving, His Mercy requires favoring worthy of Itself, and His Majesty and Splendor require chastising those who disrespect them. As only a minute fraction of the manifestations of such Attributes is established and manifested in this impermanent world and passing life, there must be a blessed realm where these manifestations can be fulfilled fully. Denying such a realm means denying the Mercy so evident to us; this is no different from denying the existence of the sun, which enlightens every day. Death without resurrection would turn compassion into torment, love into the affliction of separation, blessing into a vengeful curse, reason into an instrument of wretchedness, and pleasure into pain. Such events would cause Divine Mercy to vanish.

The Majestic Being, Who manifests the sovereignty of His being Lord in the universe's order, purpose, justice, and balance, will certainly show His favor to believers who seek the protection of His being their Lord and Sovereign, who believe in His Wisdom and Justice, and who act in conformity with these through faith and worship. There also must be a realm of punishment suitable for the Almighty's Majesty and Glory. This world's oppressors die with their oppressive power intact, while the oppressed die still subjected to humiliation. Such wrongs are necessarily deferred to a supreme tribunal; they are never ignored. Indeed, punishment is sometimes enacted even in this world. The torments endured by earlier disobedient and rebellious peoples show that we cannot escape whatever punishment God Almighty's Splendor and Majesty choose to apply.

The world is adorned with so many beautiful objects; the sun and the moon which serve as its lamps, the planet's surface teems with the finest varieties of sustenance – an overflowing feast of plenty, trees bearing fruit like so many dishes and renewed several times every year. All of this shows the existence of a great generosity and liberality.

Such inexhaustible treasures of Mercy require an everlasting abode of blissful repose that contains all desirable objects. They also require that those who enjoy them should dwell there eternally, without suffering the pain of cessation and separation. The end of pain is a sort of pleasure, and the end of pleasure is a sort of pain. As unlimited Generosity cannot allow such a thing, Paradise must be eternal and its inhabitants must live therein eternally. Unlimited Generosity and Liberality desire to bestow infinite bounty and kindness, which require infinite gratitude. Thus, those who are to receive the blessings and give continual thanks for this ongoing bestowal of bounty must live forever. A slight contentment, spoiled by its brevity or cessation, is incompatible with unlimited Generosity and Liberality.

The Lord of infinite compassion and mercy, Who most compassionately fulfills the least need of His lowliest creatures in the most unexpected fashion, Who answers the faintest cry of help of His most obscure creature, and Who responds to all petitions will never ignore the greatest desire and petition of the foremost among His creatures. The tender solicitude manifested in nurturing weak, young animals shows that the Sovereign Lord of the universe exercises His being Lord with infinite mercy. Is it conceivable that such Compassion and Mercy in the exercise of Lordship would refuse the prayer of the most valuable of all creation? Humankind petition for so universal a need – immortality and an eternal life of bliss – that all inhabitants of creation share in it and silently affirm: "Accept that prayer, O Lord, because we also desire it."

We see how the records of the lives of all spring flowers and fruits, the laws of their formation, and images of their forms are all inscribed within their minute seeds and preserved there. The following spring, those records are opened – a bringing to account as appropriate for them – and another vast world of spring emerges with absolute orderliness and wisdom. This shows the powerful and comprehensive exercise of the Divine Attribute of All-Preserving. Considering that the issue of such transient, commonplace, and insignificant things is preserved, how could our deeds not be preserved and recorded as a matter of high significance? God, Who is the All-Preserving and protects within absolute orderliness and equilibrium everything that exists, and sifts and takes account of their consequences, has the acts of His servants recorded, and He will not allow those acts of His noble vicegerent, who bears the Supreme Trust, to go unsifted, unaccounted, and unweighed in the balance of justice, unpunished or unrewarded as befits.

18. Based on this Islamic attitude, Fethullah Gülen writes:

> Be so tolerant that your heart becomes wide like the ocean. Become inspired with faith and love for others. Offer a hand to those in trouble, and be concerned about everyone.
>
> Applaud the good for their goodness, appreciate those who have believing hearts,

and be kind to believers. Approach unbelievers so gently that their envy and hatred melt away. Like a Messiah, revive people with your breath.

Remember that you travel the best road and follow an exalted guide, upon him be peace and blessings. Be mindful that you have his guidance through the most perfect and expressive Revelation. Be fair-minded and balanced in your judgment, for many people do not enjoy these blessings.

Return good for evil, and disregard discourteous treatment. An individual's character is reflected in their behavior. Choose tolerance, and be magnanimous toward the ill-mannered.

The most distinctive feature of a soul overflowing with faith is to love all types of love that are expressed in deeds, and to feel enmity for all deeds in which enmity is expressed. To hate everything is a sign of insanity or of infatuation with Satan.

Accept how God treats you. Make it the measure by which you treat others, so that you may represent the truth among them and be free from the fear of loneliness in either world.

Only those who do not use their reason, or who have succumbed to plain stupidity and desires of the flesh, are convinced that believing men and women might harm them. Apply to a spiritual master to stir up your heart, and fill your eyes with tears.

Judge your worth in the Creator's sight by how much space He occupies in your heart and your worth in people's eyes by how you treat them. Do not neglect the Truth even for a moment. And yet, "Be a man or woman among other men or women!"

Take note of and be attentive to any behavior that causes you to love others. Then remind yourself that behaving in the same way will cause them to love you. Always behave decently, and be alert.

Do not allow your carnal soul to be a referee in any contention, for it will always rule that everyone but you is sinful and unfortunate. Such a judgment, according to the saying of the most truthful, upon him be peace and blessings, signifies your

destruction. Be strict and implacable with your carnal soul, and be relenting and lenient toward others.

In sum: In order to preserve your credit, honor, and love, love for the sake of the Truth, hate for the sake of the Truth, and be open-hearted toward the Truth. (*Pearls of Wisdom*, 75–76)

19. The recitation of *al-Fātiḥah* (the first, opening chapter of the Qur'ān, which consists of seven verses) in all Prayers except the Funeral Prayer is obligatory; without it, the Prayer is not valid. It is obligatory in the first two *rak'ah*s of the Prescribed Prayers. It is also narrated that it was revealed twice, unlike other *sūrah*s. That is, it is a revealed, repeated recitation.

Al-Fātiḥah is like the seed of the Qur'ān or its essence. God's Messenger, upon him be peace and blessings, described it as the Mother of the Book (al-Bukhārī, "Kitāb at-Tafsīr," 1). Like a seed which contains all that a tree will grow into in an encapsulated form, this *sūrah* alludes to all the principles set forth in the Qur'ān (*İşârâtü'l-İ'caz*, 14).

The Qur'ān is so wonderfully comprehensive in style and meaning that a single *sūrah* may contain the whole ocean of the Qur'ān, in which the universe is contained. One verse may comprehend that *sūrah*'s treasury, as if most of the verses are really small *sūrah*s and most *sūrah*s little Qur'āns. This miraculous conciseness is a great gift of Divine Grace with respect to guidance and easiness, for although everyone always needs the Qur'ān, not all people can read it at all times. So that they are not deprived of its blessings, each *sūrah* may substitute for a small Qur'ān and each long verse for a short *sūrah*. This also serves to help understand the meaning of some Prophetic Traditions, for example, the fact that reciting *Sūrat al-Ikhlāṣ* three times or *Sūrat al-Kāfirūn* four times may gain one the merit of having recited the whole of the Qur'ān. Moreover, scholars agree that the Qur'ān is contained in *Sūrat al-Fātiḥah*, which is itself contained in the *Basmalah* (In the Name of God, the Merciful, the Compassionate).

The Qur'ān contains references to all the knowledge needed by humanity, such as explanations, aspects, and varieties of true knowledge, commands and prohibitions, promises and threats, encouragement and deterrence, restraint and guidance, stories and parables, Divine Knowledge and commands, "natural" sciences, and the rules and conditions of our personal, family, social, economic, spiritual, and otherworldly lives. Moreover, it gives people whatever they need, so that the phrase: "Take from the Qur'ān whatever you wish for whatever need you have," has been widely circulated among truth-seeking scholars. Its verses are so comprehensive that the cure for any ailment and the answer for any need can be found therein. This must be so, for the Book that is the absolute guide of all perfected people, who move forward each day on the way of God, must be of that quality (*The Words*, "the 25th Word," 413–416). What is important is to know how to approach and understand it and how to benefit from it.

20. The life of God's Messenger, upon him be peace and blessings, was so simple that once 'Umar, upon seeing him lying on a rough mat, could not help but weep and say: "O Messenger of God, kings sleep in soft, feather beds, while you lie on a rough mat. You are the Messenger of God and thereby deserve an easy life more than anyone else." God's Messenger answered: "Do you not agree that the luxuries of the world should be theirs and those of the Hereafter ours?" (al-Bukhārī, "Tafsīr," 287; Muslim, "Talaq," 31)

God's Messenger, like all Prophets, expected no reward for performing his mission. He suffered hunger, thirst, and every other hardship and persecutions. He was forced into exile and made the target of many assaults and traps both from within and without when he had emigrated. He bore all of these simply for the good pleasure of God and the good of humanity. Abū Hurayrah once saw him performing the Prayer in a seated position and asked if he were ill. The Messenger's reply caused Abū Huraryah to cry: "I am hungry, Abū Hurayrah. Hunger has left me no strength to stand up for the Prayer" (Abu Nu'aym, 7: 107; al-Hindī, 1: 199).

Even though most of his Companions became wealthier in later years, the Messenger and his family never changed their very simple lifestyle.

In addition to receiving no worldly benefit, as mentioned above, God's Messenger underwent much torture. He was beaten many times and left on the ground covered with dust, and only Fāṭimah, his daughter, ran to his aid. Once he was being beaten at the Ka'bah; Abū Bakr ran to help him, shouting to those beating him: "Will you kill a man because he says: 'My Lord is God?' " (al-Bukhārī, "Fadā'il as-Ṣaḥābah," 5; Ibn Hanbal, 2: 205) (*The Messenger of God*, 89–90).

So, the meanings of such statements as *Do not strain your eyes toward what We have given some groups among them (the unbelievers) to enjoy (in the life of this world)*, signify for the Messenger: We know that you never do so; rather, these verses address a warning to other believers. By "some groups" (*azwāj*), the verse actually refers to the social classes and class differences in un-Islamic societies.

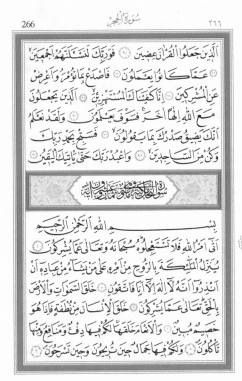

91. Those who have broken the Qur'ān into fragments (as they please).[21]

92. So, by your Lord, We will surely question them all

93. About what they have been doing.

94. So from now on, proclaim what you are commanded to convey openly and in an emphatic manner, and do not care (whatever) those who associate partners with God (say and do).[22]

95. We suffice you against all those who mock,

96. Those who adopt some deity along with God. In time they will come to know.

97. We certainly know that your breast is constricted by the (blasphemous) things that they say.

98. But glorify your Lord with His praise (proclaim that He is absolutely above having any partners, and that all praise belongs to Him exclusively) and be one of those who prostrate before Him (regularly in the Prayer).

99. And (continue to) worship your Lord until what is certain (death) comes to you.

---

21. People used to come to Makkah for several reasons such as Pilgrimage and trade. God's Messenger, upon him be peace and blessings, conveyed his Message to them also. Hoping to prevent them from believing, some Makkan unbelievers took clay tablets of the Qur'ānic verses which they regarded as product of magic or poetry and delivered them to those people.

22. Until this order came, the Messenger had been communicating the Divine Message secretly and privately. When this order came, he began to proclaim it openly and insistently.

Constant striving is an essential feature of the delivering of the Message, as well as an important element of the Prophetic method. A Prophet is, so to speak, obsessed with how to perform his duty. With that goal always uppermost in mind, he considers all circumstances and does everything permitted. Throughout his life, God's Messenger, upon him be peace and blessings, grieved for the misfortunes of humankind. He ceaselessly called people to God's way. During his years in Makkah, he walked the streets and visited the nearby annual fairs, always hoping to help a few people to convert. Insults, derision, and torture did not deter him even once.

SŪRAH 16

AN-NAḤL (THE BEE)

Makkah period

Revealed in Makkah, this *sūrah* consists of 128 verses. Its name is derived from verse 68, where bees are mentioned as another miraculous sign of God's Power, Knowledge, and Wisdom. It concentrates on the essentials of faith, the rejection of unbelief and of the association of partners with God, with many proofs in favor of faith, and encouragement to realize certain virtues, such as justice, doing good and generous deeds, as well as forbidding evil and vices.

In the Name of God, the All-Merciful, the All-Compassionate.

1. God's command (for the calamity to strike the unbelievers and their final destruction at the end of time) is bound to come, so (O unbelievers) do not wish it to be hastened (by asking the Messenger to bring it immediately in order only to deride and cast doubt on it). All-Glorified is He, and absolutely exalted above all that they associate with Him.

2. He sends down the angels with the Spirit (the life-giving Revelation) from His (absolutely pure, immaterial realm of) commands upon whom He wills of His servants (saying): "Warn people that there is no deity save Me, so keep from disobedience to Me in reverence for Me and piety."[1]

3. He has created the heavens and the earth in truth (meaningfully and with definite purpose, and on solid foundations of truth). Absolutely exalted is He above all that they associate (with Him).

4. He has created human from (so slight a beginning as) a mere drop of (seminal) fluid; and yet, he turns into an open, fierce adversary (selfishly disputing against the truth).

5. And the cattle He has created, from which you get warmth (of clothing) and other uses, and from them you get (food) to eat.

6. And in them there is beauty for you when you drive them home (in the evening) and when you take them out to pasture (in the morning).

1. Humankind, who have followed many so-called guides or leaders only to be led astray, have received true guidance through the Prophets. These servants of God were created for a special mission. Their lives resemble a beautiful symphony, perfectly harmonious and balanced. Their words are like sweet melodies that penetrate the soul. All of existence, animate or inanimate, listens to them. Trees and rocks would greet the Prophet Muḥammad, upon him be peace and blessings, just before and during his Prophethood, and he would answer them. In his well-known *Qaṣīdat al-Bur'ah*, Busirī says: "Trees answered his call, prostrating." When he called them, trees came to him. It was understood that the whole creation, animate or inanimate, has a definite meaning and purpose. Through his advent, existence became a "cosmos" out of "chaos," and each thing was perceived to become a voice that glorified God with praise. The extraordinary harmony in the universe displays God's Existence and Unity. Nothing is created in vain or without purpose (*The Messenger of God*, 31).

٢٦٧   الجزء الرابع عشر   267

وَتَحْمِلُ أَثْقَالَكُمْ إِلَى بَلَدٍ لَّمْ تَكُونُوا بَالِغِيهِ إِلَّا بِشِقِّ الْأَنفُسِ إِنَّ رَبَّكُمْ لَرَءُوفٌ رَّحِيمٌ ۝ وَالْخَيْلَ وَالْبِغَالَ وَالْحَمِيرَ لِتَرْكَبُوهَا وَزِينَةً وَيَخْلُقُ مَا لَا تَعْلَمُونَ ۝ وَعَلَى اللَّهِ قَصْدُ السَّبِيلِ وَمِنْهَا جَائِرٌ وَلَوْ شَاءَ لَهَدَاكُمْ أَجْمَعِينَ ۝ هُوَ الَّذِي أَنزَلَ مِنَ السَّمَاءِ مَاءً لَّكُم مِّنْهُ شَرَابٌ وَمِنْهُ شَجَرٌ فِيهِ تُسِيمُونَ ۝ يُنبِتُ لَكُم بِهِ الزَّرْعَ وَالزَّيْتُونَ وَالنَّخِيلَ وَالْأَعْنَابَ وَمِن كُلِّ الثَّمَرَاتِ إِنَّ فِي ذَٰلِكَ لَآيَةً لِّقَوْمٍ يَتَفَكَّرُونَ ۝ وَسَخَّرَ لَكُمُ اللَّيْلَ وَالنَّهَارَ وَالشَّمْسَ وَالْقَمَرَ وَالنُّجُومُ مُسَخَّرَاتٌ بِأَمْرِهِ إِنَّ فِي ذَٰلِكَ لَآيَاتٍ لِّقَوْمٍ يَعْقِلُونَ ۝ وَمَا ذَرَأَ لَكُمْ فِي الْأَرْضِ مُخْتَلِفًا أَلْوَانُهُ إِنَّ فِي ذَٰلِكَ لَآيَةً لِّقَوْمٍ يَذَّكَّرُونَ ۝ وَهُوَ الَّذِي سَخَّرَ الْبَحْرَ لِتَأْكُلُوا مِنْهُ لَحْمًا طَرِيًّا وَتَسْتَخْرِجُوا مِنْهُ حِلْيَةً تَلْبَسُونَهَا وَتَرَى الْفُلْكَ مَوَاخِرَ فِيهِ وَلِتَبْتَغُوا مِن فَضْلِهِ وَلَعَلَّكُمْ تَشْكُرُونَ ۝

---

7. They carry your loads to many a land which (otherwise) you would be unable to reach except with great hardship to yourselves. Indeed your Lord is All-Pitying, All-Compassionate.

8. And horses, mules and donkeys (has He created for you) to ride, as well as for ornament (the loveliness they add to your world); and (besides all that you see and know of,) He creates what you have no knowledge of.[2]

9. With God (being your Creator) rests the goal of the way (to which He will guide and which you must follow). And some (ways) are crooked (misleading those who follow them). But if God had willed (to impose His guidance without granting people freedom of choice), He would surely have guided you all together (on His way).

10. He it is Who sends down from the sky water; you drink thereof, and thereof (drink) the shrubs on which you pasture your cattle.

11. With it He causes to grow for you the crops, the olives, the date-palms, the grapes, and all (other) kinds of fruit. Surely in this is a sign (manifesting the truth) for people who reflect.

12. He has made the night and the day and the sun and the moon to be of service to you, and the stars are made subservient by His command. Surely in that are signs for people who reason and understand.

13. And whatsoever He has created for you on earth of varying colors (and diverse forms and qualities): surely in that is a sign for people who reflect and are mindful.

14. And He it is Who has made the sea to be of service (to you) so that you eat from it fresh meat, and draw out from it ornaments that you wear. And you see the ships plowing their course through it so that you may go forth in quest of His bounty and give thanks (to Him Who has created all this).

---

2. In parallel with the development of life, God creates new things for the use of humankind and to contribute to their life, ornamenting and enriching it. These include both plants and animals of which we are not aware at this time, but which may be discovered in later times, as well as the inventions and production of humankind, which God creates through our hands. This verse also implies that besides their many uses to human beings, plants and animals also serve them by arousing their sense of wonder and their capacity to appreciate beauty. The utility and beauty of the natural world should awaken the strongest feelings of dependence and indebtedness, which are elements of the gratitude human beings owe to the Creator of themselves and the world around them.

15. And He has cast firm mountains on the earth lest it should shake with you (with its movement), and rivers, and roads, so that you may find your way;

16. And (other) way-marks, and they (people) find their way by the stars.

17. Is He then Who creates to be likened to him who does not create? Will you not reflect and be mindful?

18. And should you attempt to count God's blessings, you could not compute them. God is indeed All-Forgiving, All-Compassionate (Who continues to provide for His servants despite their sins and even their denial of Him).

19. God knows whatever you keep concealed and whatever you disclose.

20. But those whom they invoke, apart from God, create nothing, rather they are themselves created.[3]

21. Dead (they are), not living (nor can they give life, being themselves in need of it). And they do not know when they will be raised to life.[4]

22. Your God is the One God, but those who disbelieve in the Hereafter – their hearts are in denial (of this most evident and essential truth, and the many other truths based on it): they are (too) arrogant (to accept dependence on the Supreme Being, and answerability to Him).[5]

23. Without doubt, God knows whatever they keep concealed and whatever they disclose; He does not love the arrogant.

24. When it is said to them: "What is it that your Lord (Who sustains, protects, and raises you) has sent down (on the Messenger)?" They say: "Fables of the ancients."

25. Hence, they will bear their own burdens (of sin) in full on the Day of Resurrection and some of the burdens of those whom they, being ignorant, caused to go astray. Look now! How evil is the burden they load upon themselves![6]

26. Those before them (like them, persistent in unbelief, wrongdoing, and evil) schemed (against the Messengers and the Divine Message they brought), so God struck what they built at its foundations, and the roof fell in upon them from above, and the doom came upon them without their having perceived whence it came.

3. The arguments that the Qur'ān puts forth are apparently straightforward, but have profound meanings. Since the Qur'ān aims at guiding people to God's way and since the overwhelming majority of people are always of average capacity, it addresses itself to their level of understanding. However, it never deprives the most knowledgeable and intellectual. This is one of the miraculous aspects of the Qur'ān.

Only one who can create can be a deity worthy of worship. We can clearly see that everything in the world is in flux, contained in time and space, and is changeable, and that all things have a beginning. The universe itself is also in a flux in time and space, and changeable dependent on certain laws. Therefore, anything with such attributes can only be created and must owe its existence to something other than itself. Something created cannot be a creator; rather it must have a creator. The creator obviously cannot be of the same kind as the created, nor can it be contained in time and space; therefore it must be eternal.

By means of the intellectual capacity God has granted us, human beings have been able to make great discoveries and inventions, yet we cannot create even a blade of grass. If humankind, despite being the most intelligent, knowledgeable, and powerful of all creations, due to the advantages with which we have been provided, cannot create even a blade of grass, and if we cannot give existence to an atom or element, then there is nothing that is contained in the universe that can be the creator. Therefore, something that is created, be it a human being, like Jesus, or an angel, or a "natural" force, or a spirit, or an idol, or anything else, cannot be a deity worthy of adoration and invocation.

Apart from this significant fact, we openly witness that whatever we are provided with in "nature" is created and granted to us, for almost nothing. Yet, as stated above, even if all the human beings in the world were to come together and unite their power, knowledge, and wealth, they would not be able to create even a single seed of wheat. And in order for that seed to grow into wheat, the sun, the soil, air, water, and the seed itself, as well as countless other conditions, must work together in a measured way. This means that the existence of something, no matter how small, depends on the existence of the whole universe. So, even though we have been granted everything for almost nothing, the price of every thing in the universe is nearly equal to that of the universe itself. Yet, still God gives all of these to us, for almost nothing. The more we need something, the more abundantly and more cheaply God grants it to us. He grants us air for nothing and also water; these are the two things that we need most in life. All these facts, so simple in appearance, yet so meaningful, decisively demonstrate the Existence and Oneness of God with all of His many Attributes and Names.

4. Whether a living being or not, anything deified other than God can only be dead when by itself; i.e. it is in need of another power in order to exist. In another place God declares: *Do they associate as partners with Him those who create nothing and themselves are created, and who have no power to give them any help, nor can help themselves? And if you call them in the direction of guidance, they do not follow you: It is the same for you whether you call to them or remain silent. Those whom you deify and call upon apart from God are subservient beings created by God just like yourselves. (If you think and claim otherwise) then call on them and let them answer you, if you are truthful!* (7: 191–194, and see the corresponding note 46).

In addition, the verse also refers to the persons such as the Prophets, saints, heroes, and other respected ones whom the polytheists deified. Many idols that the Makkan polytheists and earlier peoples worshipped, such as al-Lāt, al-Manāt, al-'Uzzā, Wad, Suwā, and Yaghūs, etc. were erected in memory of persons who had these names and who had once lived and been respected by their contemporaries. Later, these people came to be sanctified and worshipped. The verse emphasizes that, however great they are in reality or in people's sight, even such persons who are now dead and do not know when they will be raised to life, can in no wise be deities worthy of worship.

5. Denial of the Hereafter comes either from denial of the existence of the metaphysical realms beyond the reach of human senses, which usually arises from a person's arrogant confidence in their capacity of understanding and knowledge, or from an arrogant refusal to give account of their life before a superior being. This means a denial of the Hereafter usually entails a denial of the Supreme Being. The opposite is also true; that is, a denial of the Supreme Being entails the denial of the Hereafter. This indicates an important fact; the essentials of faith are in need of one another. Accepting one requires the acceptance of the others.

6. *Every soul earns only to its own account; and no burdened soul bears (and is made to bear) the burden of another* (6: 164), is a fundamental principle in Islamic law and tradition. This means that no one is responsible for another's sin or crime if they have nothing to do with it. However, according to the principle, *The one who causes is like the one who does it*, one who causes something good or bad has a responsibility and acquires a reward or punishment in accordance with their share in the deed. In this respect, God's Messenger, upon him be peace and blessings, pronounces the principle: "The one who establishes a good path in Islam receives the reward of those who follow it, without any decrease in their reward. Another who establishes an evil path in Islam is burdened with the sins of those who follow it, without any decrease in their burden" (Muslim, "Zakāh," 69; Ibn Mājah, "Muqaddimah," 203).

الجزء الرابع عشر ٢٦٩

ثُمَّ يَوْمَ الْقِيَـٰمَةِ يُخْزِيهِمْ وَيَقُولُ أَيْنَ شُرَكَآءِيَ الَّذِينَ كُنتُمْ تُشَآقُونَ فِيهِمْ ۚ قَالَ الَّذِينَ أُوتُوا الْعِلْمَ إِنَّ الْخِزْيَ الْيَوْمَ وَالسُّوٓءَ عَلَى الْكَافِرِينَ ۝ الَّذِينَ تَتَوَفَّىٰهُمُ الْمَلَـٰٓئِكَةُ ظَالِمِىٓ أَنفُسِهِمْ ۖ فَأَلْقَوُا السَّلَمَ مَا كُنَّا نَعْمَلُ مِن سُوٓءٍ ۚ بَلَىٰٓ إِنَّ اللَّهَ عَلِيمٌۢ بِمَا كُنتُمْ تَعْمَلُونَ ۝ فَادْخُلُوٓا أَبْوَٰبَ جَهَنَّمَ خَـٰلِدِينَ فِيهَا ۖ فَلَبِئْسَ مَثْوَى الْمُتَكَبِّرِينَ ۝ وَقِيلَ لِلَّذِينَ اتَّقَوْا مَاذَآ أَنزَلَ رَبُّكُمْ ۚ قَالُوا خَيْرًا ۗ لِّلَّذِينَ أَحْسَنُوا فِى هَـٰذِهِ الدُّنْيَا حَسَنَةٌ ۚ وَلَدَارُ الْءَاخِرَةِ خَيْرٌ ۚ وَلَنِعْمَ دَارُ الْمُتَّقِينَ ۝ جَنَّـٰتُ عَدْنٍ يَدْخُلُونَهَا تَجْرِى مِن تَحْتِهَا الْأَنْهَـٰرُ ۖ لَهُمْ فِيهَا مَا يَشَآءُونَ ۚ كَذَٰلِكَ يَجْزِى اللَّهُ الْمُتَّقِينَ ۝ الَّذِينَ تَتَوَفَّىٰهُمُ الْمَلَـٰٓئِكَةُ طَيِّبِينَ ۙ يَقُولُونَ سَلَـٰمٌ عَلَيْكُمُ ادْخُلُوا الْجَنَّةَ بِمَا كُنتُمْ تَعْمَلُونَ ۝ هَلْ يَنظُرُونَ إِلَّآ أَن تَأْتِيَهُمُ الْمَلَـٰٓئِكَةُ أَوْ يَأْتِىَ أَمْرُ رَبِّكَ ۚ كَذَٰلِكَ فَعَلَ الَّذِينَ مِن قَبْلِهِمْ ۚ وَمَا ظَلَمَهُمُ اللَّهُ وَلَـٰكِن كَانُوٓا أَنفُسَهُمْ يَظْلِمُونَ ۝ فَأَصَابَهُمْ سَيِّئَاتُ مَا عَمِلُوا وَحَاقَ بِهِم مَّا كَانُوا بِهِۦ يَسْتَهْزِءُونَ ۝

27. Then on the Day of Resurrection He will disgrace them and will say: "Where are (those beings whom you claimed) as partners with Me and for whose sake you used to oppose (the believers), defying and disobeying (My guidance)?" Those who (in their lifetime) were endowed with the Knowledge[7] declare: "Disgrace and evil are, this day, on the unbelievers:"

28. Those whose souls the angels take while they are still wronging themselves (by falsely associating partners with God and committing evils). (When they see the punishment), they offer full submission, (saying in an attempt to excuse themselves): "We did not (mean to) do any evil." (But they are answered:) "No! Surely God has full knowledge of what you were doing (and your intentions therein).

29. "So, go in through the gates of Hell to abide therein." How evil, indeed, is the dwelling of the arrogant (those too haughty to accept God's guidance).

30. Whereas it is said to those who keep from disobedience to God in reverence for Him and piety: "What is it that your Lord has sent down (on the Messenger)?" They answer: "That which is purely good and to our benefit (in both worlds)." For those devoted to doing good in this world, aware that God is seeing them, there is good, and the abode of the Hereafter is indeed better. How excellent, indeed, is the abode of the God-revering, pious!

31. Gardens of perpetual bliss which they will enter, through which rivers flow. Therein they will have whatever they may desire. Thus does God reward the God-revering, pious –

32. Those whose souls the angels take whilst they are in a pious state (free of evil, and worshipping none but God alone), saying: "Peace be upon you! Enter Paradise for what you have been doing."

33. Are they (the unbelievers and/or those who associate partners with God) but waiting for the angels to come to them (to take their souls or bring them a disaster), or for your Lord's command (to judge them and open Hell for them)? Even so did those before them. God did not wrong them but they did wrong themselves.

34. Then the evil consequences of what they used to do fell upon them, and that which they were mocking overwhelmed them.

7. As mentioned in many previous verses (2: 120, 145; 3: 7, 61, 66; 4: 157; 6: 100, 119, 144; 11: 46; 12: 68; 16: 25), unbelief and the association of partners with God are in no way connected to knowledge, while knowledge necessitates belief. Therefore, we should also point out that knowledge (al-ʿilm) and having some information are different from each other. Knowledge is a product, like milk, that is the result of many processes in the mind, like the imagination, conceptualization, reasoning, inquiry, verification, judging, adoption, conviction, and certainty. There is a kind of knowledge which is absolutely certain: it is the knowledge taught by the Divine Revelation. Islam accepts Revelation, intelligence (reason), sound sense, and scientific inquiry as being the means of knowledge.

A scholar should provide guidance for others in the way that a sheep feeds its young not in the way a bird does. A sheep feeds its lambs on milk, a fully-digested and processed substance, whereas a bird feeds its chicks on what it has half-chewed and then regurgitated. (For a quotation from Said Nursi, see sūrah 12, note 25.)

270　　　سُورَةُ النَّحْلِ　　　٢٧٠

وَقَالَ الَّذِينَ أَشْرَكُوا لَوْ شَآءَ اللَّهُ مَا عَبَدْنَا مِنْ دُونِهِ
مِنْ شَيْءٍ نَحْنُ وَلَا آبَآؤُنَا وَلَا حَرَّمْنَا مِنْ دُونِهِ مِنْ شَيْءٍ
كَذَٰلِكَ فَعَلَ الَّذِينَ مِنْ قَبْلِهِمْ فَهَلْ عَلَى الرُّسُلِ إِلَّا الْبَلَٰغُ
الْمُبِينُ ۝ وَلَقَدْ بَعَثْنَا فِي كُلِّ أُمَّةٍ رَّسُولًا أَنِ اعْبُدُوا اللَّهَ
وَاجْتَنِبُوا الطَّاغُوتَ فَمِنْهُمْ مَّنْ هَدَى اللَّهُ وَمِنْهُمْ مَّنْ حَقَّتْ عَلَيْهِ
الضَّلَالَةُ فَسِيرُوا فِي الْأَرْضِ فَانْظُرُوا كَيْفَ كَانَ
عَاقِبَةُ الْمُكَذِّبِينَ ۝ إِنْ تَحْرِصْ عَلَى هُدَىٰهُمْ فَإِنَّ اللَّهَ
لَا يَهْدِي مَنْ يُضِلُّ وَمَا لَهُمْ مِنْ نَاصِرِينَ ۝ وَأَقْسَمُوا بِاللَّهِ
جَهْدَ أَيْمَانِهِمْ لَا يَبْعَثُ اللَّهُ مَنْ يَمُوتُ بَلَىٰ وَعْدًا
عَلَيْهِ حَقًّا وَلَٰكِنَّ أَكْثَرَ النَّاسِ لَا يَعْلَمُونَ ۝ لِيُبَيِّنَ لَهُمُ
الَّذِي يَخْتَلِفُونَ فِيهِ وَلِيَعْلَمَ الَّذِينَ كَفَرُوا أَنَّهُمْ كَانُوا
كَاذِبِينَ ۝ إِنَّمَا قَوْلُنَا لِشَيْءٍ إِذَا أَرَدْنَاهُ أَنْ نَقُولَ لَهُ كُنْ
فَيَكُونُ ۝ وَالَّذِينَ هَاجَرُوا فِي اللَّهِ مِنْ بَعْدِ مَا ظُلِمُوا
لَنُبَوِّئَنَّهُمْ فِي الدُّنْيَا حَسَنَةً وَلَأَجْرُ الْآخِرَةِ أَكْبَرُ لَوْ كَانُوا
يَعْلَمُونَ ۝ الَّذِينَ صَبَرُوا وَعَلَى رَبِّهِمْ يَتَوَكَّلُونَ ۝

------

35. Those who associate partners with God say: "Had God so willed, we would not have worshipped anything other than Him, neither we nor our forefathers; nor would we have declared anything unlawful without (a commandment from) Him." Even so did those who lived before them (and associated partners with God like them). But, then, is any duty laid upon the Messengers except to convey the Message clearly?

36. And assuredly, We have raised within every community a Messenger (to convey the primordial Message): Worship God alone, and keep away from false deities and powers of evil (who institute patterns of faith and rule in defiance of God). Among them (past generations) were people whom God guided, just as there were among them those for whom straying was their just due. Go about, then, on the earth and look! How was the outcome for those who denied (God's manifest signs and His Messengers)!

37. Though you long ardently for them (all humankind) to be rightly guided, God surely does not guide those whom He has led astray (as their just due).[8] And they have no helpers (to defend them against God).

38. And by God they swear their most solemn oaths, "God will never raise from the dead anyone who has died!" No! but it is a promise (that He has laid) upon Himself in truth, but most people do not know (being ignorant and lacking desire for knowledge of the truth).

39. (He will indeed fulfill that promise and resurrect them,) so that He will make clear to people the truth about what they differ on, and so that those who disbelieve will know that they were liars.

40. (Raising the dead to life, like giving them life in the first place, is easy for Us:) Our word for a thing when We will it is simply Our saying to it, "Be!" and it is.[9]

41. Those who emigrate (to another land) for God's cause after they have been oppressed on account of their faith, We will surely give them goodly residence in the world, and their reward in the Hereafter is certainly greater. If only they (all people) knew (how great that reward is)!

42. Those (they are) who have persevered in patience (through all adversities), and it is in their Lord that they put their trust.

8. The last two verses explicitly state that guidance is a gift from God, while misguidance is a person's due. God does not will misguidance for anybody, but people prefer misguidance under the influence of their carnal souls. So, such expressions should be viewed in the light of the following verses: *God leads the wrongdoers astray* (14: 27); *He thereby leads none astray save the transgressors* (2: 26); *Surely those who disbelieve and do wrong (to people by barring them from God's way, and to God and His Messengers and angels, and to all believers and all creatures bearing witness to the truth, and to their own conscience, by accusing them of lying and deception) – God will indeed not forgive them nor will He guide them to a road, except the road of Hell, to abide therein forever; and that is easy for God* (4: 168–169).

9. For the meaning of this and similar expressions, see *sūrah* 2: 117, note 101; *sūrah* 3: 47.

Here, we would add the following:

The Absolutely Powerful One creates things with absolute ease and speed and with no physical contact. He creates with a mere command. Moreover, although the All-Powerful Maker is infinitely near to creatures, they are infinitely distant from Him. Furthermore, despite His infinite Grandeur, He does not exclude even the most insignificant thing from the importance He attaches in designing and fashioning creation, nor does He deprive it of the beauty of His art. The perfect order which is observed in creation, despite the absolute facility witnessed in its being called into existence, testifies to this Qur'ānic truth. The following comparison explains how this is possible and serves to make it more easily comprehensible:

The sun, like a dense, solid mirror for the Divine Name of Light, is infinitely near to all things on earth; rather, it is nearer to them than their own selves, and has an effect on them in numerous ways, such as through its light and heat. By contrast, these things are millions of miles away, and they have no effect on the sun in any way, nor can they claim any nearness to

it. The presence of the sun with its light, heat, and image flooding in every transparent object, big or small, and its reflection in opaque, translucent things, the heat and color it gives to each, and how it affects things all go to prove this fact. The extent of its luminosity, i.e., the degree of its brightness, increases the capacity and comprehensiveness of its penetration. It is because of the greatness of its luminosity that even the tiniest things cannot hide or escape it. This means that the sun's immensity and "grandeur" do not exclude even the most insignificant particles, the tiniest things, from the sphere of its comprehension; rather everything is included in it. The sun manifests itself by God's leave in all things, from atoms to the planets, from droplets to the surface of vast oceans, with such ease and speed and over so comprehensive an area that if, supposing the impossible, we were to imagine that the sun could act of its own free will, then we would have to suppose that it performed all this with a mere command. An atom and a planet are equal before its manifestation. The heat and the light that it spreads over the entire surface of a vast ocean are also given with perfect order to the finest atom, in accordance with its capacity.

Thus, we can clearly see that the sun, which is a light-giving "bubble" in the "ocean" of the heavens and a small, solid mirror to the manifestation of the Absolutely Powerful One's Name of Light, displays examples of the principles of this truth. So, we believe, and everyone should believe, with complete certainty as though they have witnessed it, that the All-Majestic One, Who is the Light of Lights, the Illuminator of Light, the Determiner of Light, is all-present and all-seeing and infinitely near to all things through His Knowledge and Power, and other Attributes, and that things are infinitely distant from Him, and that He does things so easily and with no preparation. He creates with a mere command, and nothing, big or small, particular or universal, is excluded from the sphere of His Power, and His Greatness encompasses all things.

وَمَآ أَرْسَلْنَا مِن قَبْلِكَ إِلَّا رِجَالًا نُّوحِىٓ إِلَيْهِمْ فَسْـَٔلُوٓا أَهْلَ
الذِّكْرِ إِن كُنتُمْ لَا تَعْلَمُونَ ۞ بِالْبَيِّنَاتِ وَالزُّبُرِ وَأَنزَلْنَآ إِلَيْكَ
الذِّكْرَ لِتُبَيِّنَ لِلنَّاسِ مَا نُزِّلَ إِلَيْهِمْ وَلَعَلَّهُمْ يَتَفَكَّرُونَ ۞ أَفَأَمِنَ
الَّذِينَ مَكَرُوا السَّيِّئَاتِ أَن يَخْسِفَ اللَّهُ بِهِمُ الْأَرْضَ أَوْ يَأْتِيَهُمُ
الْعَذَابُ مِنْ حَيْثُ لَا يَشْعُرُونَ ۞ أَوْ يَأْخُذَهُمْ فِى تَقَلُّبِهِمْ
فَمَا هُم بِمُعْجِزِينَ ۞ أَوْ يَأْخُذَهُمْ عَلَىٰ تَخَوُّفٍ فَإِنَّ رَبَّكُمْ
لَرَءُوفٌ رَّحِيمٌ ۞ أَوَلَمْ يَرَوْا إِلَىٰ مَا خَلَقَ اللَّهُ مِن شَىْءٍ يَتَفَيَّؤُا ظِلَالُهُ
عَنِ الْيَمِينِ وَالشَّمَائِلِ سُجَّدًا لِلَّهِ وَهُمْ دَاخِرُونَ ۞ وَلِلَّهِ
يَسْجُدُ مَا فِى السَّمَوَاتِ وَمَا فِى الْأَرْضِ مِن دَابَّةٍ وَالْمَلَائِكَةُ
وَهُمْ لَا يَسْتَكْبِرُونَ ۞ يَخَافُونَ رَبَّهُم مِّن فَوْقِهِمْ وَيَفْعَلُونَ
مَا يُؤْمَرُونَ ۩ ۞ وَقَالَ اللَّهُ لَا تَتَّخِذُوٓا إِلَٰهَيْنِ اثْنَيْنِ إِنَّمَا هُوَ إِلَٰهٌ
وَاحِدٌ فَإِيَّايَ فَارْهَبُونِ ۞ وَلَهُ مَا فِى السَّمَوَاتِ وَالْأَرْضِ وَلَهُ
الدِّينُ وَاصِبًا أَفَغَيْرَ اللَّهِ تَتَّقُونَ ۞ وَمَا بِكُم مِّن نِّعْمَةٍ فَمِنَ اللَّهِ
ثُمَّ إِذَا مَسَّكُمُ الضُّرُّ فَإِلَيْهِ تَجْأَرُونَ ۞ ثُمَّ إِذَا كَشَفَ
الضُّرَّ عَنكُمْ إِذَا فَرِيقٌ مِّنكُم بِرَبِّهِمْ يُشْرِكُونَ ۞

---

43. We did not send before you (O Muhammad) any but men to whom We revealed – and if you (O people) do not know, then ask the people of expert knowledge (those who have knowledge of the Divine Revelations) —

44. (We sent them with) clear proofs of the truth and Scriptures. And on you We have sent down the Reminder (the Qur'ān) so that you may make clear to humankind whatever is sent down to them (through you of the truth concerning their present and next life), and that they may reflect.

45. Do they, who (in defiance of God's grace) devise evil schemes, feel safe and secure that God will not cause the earth to swallow them, or that the punishment will not come upon them without their perceiving whence it has come?

46. Or that He will not seize them in the midst of their strutting about (the land in pomp and show of dominion), and they are helpless to frustrate Him?

47. Or that He will not seize them with gradual wasting (of wealth and health giving them time to mend their ways)? For surely your Lord is All-Pitying, All-Compassionate.

48. Do they not see the things that God has created, how their shadows bend to the right and to the left, making prostration before God, and that in the humblest manner?

49. Before God prostrates itself whatever is in the heavens and whatever is on the earth of living creatures,[10] and the angels (likewise, for) they are not arrogant.

50. They (the angels) fear their Lord high above them (i.e., Who has absolute power over them), and they do what they are commanded.

51. God has said: "Do not take two (or more) deities: He is but One God. So be in awe of Me and Me alone, (and be saved from other fears bringing disgrace upon you)."

52. To Him belongs all that is in the heavens and on the earth, and to Him alone absolute obedience is always due. Will you, then, fear and obey in piety and due reverence other than God?

53. Whatever blessing you have, it is from God; and when harm touches you, it is to Him that you cry for help.

54. When thereafter He removes the harm from you, a party of you attribute partners to their Lord (Who alone sustains and provides for you, and saves you from misfortunes);

---

10. For the motion of the shadow and beings' prostration before God Almighty, see 13: 15, note 7.

55. And so deny with ingratitude the favors God has granted them. So enjoy (O polytheists, the favors We grant you) – in time you will come to know (the truth).

56. They assign, out of what We provide for them, a portion to the things (non-existent deities, misunderstood "causes," the real nature of) which they have no sure knowledge.[11] By God, you will certainly be questioned about what you used to fabricate.

57. And they assign daughters to God – All-Glorified is He (above having children) – and to themselves what they desire (sons)!

58. When any of them is given news of the birth of a girl, his face becomes overcast, and he is (as if choking inwardly) with suppressed anger.

59. He hides himself from the people because of the evil (as he wrongly supposes it) of what he has had news of. (So he debates within himself:) Shall he keep her with dishonor or bury her in earth? Look now! how evil is the judgment they make (concerning God, and how evil is the decision they debate)!

60. To those who do not believe in the Hereafter applies the most evil of attributes, and to God applies the most sublime attribute, and He is the All-Glorious with irresistible might, the All-Wise.

61. If God were to take people immediately to task for their wrongdoings, He would not leave on it (the earth) any living creature (as the wrongdoings of humankind would make the earth uninhabitable). But He grants them respite to a term appointed (by Him). When their term has come, they can neither delay it by a single moment, nor can they bring it forward.

62. They assign to God that which they dislike (for themselves); and all the

while their tongues utter the falsehood that ("if there would be another life as the Messenger claims,") the best reward (Paradise) would be theirs. No doubt theirs is (on the contrary, only) the Fire, and they will be hastened on into it.

63. By God, We certainly sent Messengers to the communities before you (O Messenger), but Satan decked out their deeds to be appealing to (the unbelievers among) them. And this day (too, when the Qur'ān is being revealed), he is their close friend, and theirs is a painful punishment (on Judgment Day).

64. And We have not sent down the Book on you except that you may explain to them all (the questions of faith and law) on which they differ, and as guidance and mercy for people who will believe and who have already believed.

11. This verse has several meanings:

- So as to order their lives some people ascribe creativity and the authority to things or beings which they assume to have (Divine) power, such as idols, persons, institutions, celestial bodies, spirits, and so on.
- They ascribe authority to make lawful what is unlawful or unlawful what is lawful concerning their livelihood to powers other than God; yet their livelihood has been granted to them by God.
- They assign to God, of the produce and cattle that He has created, a portion, and they say: "This is God's" – so they assert – "and this (the rest) is for the partners we associate with God" (6: 136).

وَاللَّهُ أَنزَلَ مِنَ السَّمَاءِ مَاءً فَأَحْيَا بِهِ الْأَرْضَ بَعْدَ مَوْتِهَا إِنَّ فِى

ذَٰلِكَ لَآيَةً لِّقَوْمٍ يَسْمَعُونَ ۝ وَإِنَّ لَكُمْ فِى الْأَنْعَامِ لَعِبْرَةً نُّسْقِيكُم

مِّمَّا فِى بُطُونِهِ مِنۢ بَيْنِ فَرْثٍ وَدَمٍ لَّبَنًا خَالِصًا سَآئِغًا لِّلشَّارِبِينَ ۝

وَمِن ثَمَرَاتِ النَّخِيلِ وَالْأَعْنَابِ تَتَّخِذُونَ مِنْهُ سَكَرًا وَرِزْقًا حَسَنًا

إِنَّ فِى ذَٰلِكَ لَآيَةً لِّقَوْمٍ يَعْقِلُونَ ۝ وَأَوْحَىٰ رَبُّكَ إِلَى النَّحْلِ أَنِ

اتَّخِذِى مِنَ الْجِبَالِ بُيُوتًا وَمِنَ الشَّجَرِ وَمِمَّا يَعْرِشُونَ ۝ ثُمَّ

كُلِى مِن كُلِّ الثَّمَرَاتِ فَاسْلُكِى سُبُلَ رَبِّكِ ذُلُلًا يَخْرُجُ مِنۢ

بُطُونِهَا شَرَابٌ مُّخْتَلِفٌ أَلْوَانُهُ فِيهِ شِفَآءٌ لِّلنَّاسِ إِنَّ فِى ذَٰلِكَ لَآيَةً

لِّقَوْمٍ يَتَفَكَّرُونَ ۝ وَاللَّهُ خَلَقَكُمْ ثُمَّ يَتَوَفَّىٰكُمْ وَمِنكُم مَّن يُرَدُّ

إِلَىٰ أَرْذَلِ الْعُمُرِ لِكَيْ لَا يَعْلَمَ بَعْدَ عِلْمٍ شَيْئًا إِنَّ اللَّهَ عَلِيمٌ قَدِيرٌ ۝

وَاللَّهُ فَضَّلَ بَعْضَكُمْ عَلَىٰ بَعْضٍ فِى الرِّزْقِ فَمَا الَّذِينَ فُضِّلُوا

بِرَآدِّى رِزْقِهِمْ عَلَىٰ مَا مَلَكَتْ أَيْمَانُهُمْ فَهُمْ فِيهِ سَوَآءٌ أَفَبِنِعْمَةِ

اللَّهِ يَجْحَدُونَ ۝ وَاللَّهُ جَعَلَ لَكُم مِّنْ أَنفُسِكُمْ أَزْوَاجًا

وَجَعَلَ لَكُم مِّنْ أَزْوَاجِكُم بَنِينَ وَحَفَدَةً وَرَزَقَكُم مِّنَ

الطَّيِّبَاتِ أَفَبِالْبَاطِلِ يُؤْمِنُونَ وَبِنِعْمَتِ اللَّهِ هُمْ يَكْفُرُونَ ۝

---

65. God sends down from the sky water and therewith revives the earth after its death. Surely in that there is a sign (manifesting the truth) for people ready to hear (and understand the discourses of the "Book of Creation" and the Revelation).[12]

66. And surely in the cattle (feeding on the pastures of the revived earth) there is a lesson for you: We give you from that which is within their bodies, (marvelously distinguished from) between the waste and blood, milk that is pure and palatable to those who drink.[13]

67. And there are (among the produce that God brings forth as nourishment for you on the revived earth) the fruits of the date-palm, and grapes: you derive from them intoxicants and good, wholesome nourishment. Surely in this is a sign for people who reason and understand.[14]

68. And your Lord inspired the (female) bee:[15] "Take for yourself dwelling-place in the mountains, and in the trees, and in what they (human beings) may build and weave.

69. "Then eat of all the fruits, and returning with your loads follow the ways your Lord has made easy for you." There comes forth from their bellies a fluid of varying color, wherein is health for human beings. Surely in this there is a sign for people who reflect.[16]

70. God has created you, then He takes your souls to Him. And among you are those who are deferred to the age of se-nility so they do not know, of what they once knew, anything at all. Surely God is All-Knowing, All-Powerful.

71. And God has favored some of you above others in provision. And yet, (while it is We Who provide them) those who are more favored do not consent to share their provision with those (slaves) whom their right hands possess so that they might be equal with them in this respect. How then do they deny God's grace and bounty, (and associate partners with Him)?

72. God has made for you, from your selves, mates (spouses), and has made for you children and grandchildren from your mates, and has provided you with good, wholesome things. Do they, then, believe in falsehood and deny the blessings of God?

12. It is God Who revives this vast earth when it is dead and dry, and therein manifests His Power by creating hundreds of thousands of species, each as extraordinary as humankind; these creatures manifest His all-embracing Knowledge in its infinite variations, within a complex intermingling of all their distinct forms. The dried, ossified roots and trunks of trees and plants, as also hibernating animals, are revived and restored exactly as they were. Animals, such as flies, and plants, flowers, and grass, which die leaving behind many seeds, are "recreated" in a form so similar as to be nearly identical to the original. The seeds, which outwardly appear so alike, grow over a short period, distinct and differentiated, and are brought to full vigor with extraordinary rapidity and facility, in absolute orderliness and harmony. Indeed, the Almighty Disposer of this world's affairs creates at every moment of time, on the finite, transient surface and in the depths of the earth, numerous signs, examples, and indications of revival after death, the Supreme Gathering and the Plain of Resurrection.

It is God Who, in addition to creating at every moment numerous signs, examples, and indications of the Resurrection and life after death, turns our attention toward everlasting happiness, assuring us of Resurrection in all of His heavenly decrees. So, both in these decrees and by causing "nature" to speak in numerous languages, He addresses our power of hearing as well. He shows the importance He attaches to humankind by creating them as the most comprehensive and subtle, the worthiest and most valued fruit on the Tree of Creation; He addresses humans, allowing them to get in touch with Him whenever and wherever they wish and without any intermediary.

13. The Qur'ān narrates the process of the production of milk in remarkable detail: the part-digestion of what is ingested as food, the absorption of it, and then a second process and refinement in the glands. Milk is a wholesome and agreeable product for living beings, yet it is a secretion, like other secretions and is non-essential for the life of the mother. Despite being a secretion produced from between the dung in the bowels and the blood in the veins, it is one of the most vital and useful foods for living beings. The Qur'ān's narration of the process of its production fourteen centuries ago is one of the countless proofs of its Divine origin.

14. This verse was revealed long before the prohibition of intoxicants (See 5: 90–91, note 18). However, by using the phrase of *good, wholesome nourishment* after intoxicants, the fact that an intoxicant is not *good, wholesome nourishment* is implied. Coming after the verse describing milk and how it is produced, the Qur'ān refers to intoxicants in correspondence to excrement and blood, while the phrase *good, wholesome nourishment* corresponds to milk, thereby preparing the minds for the prohibition of intoxicants. By calling on people to use their reason concerning this matter, it encourages them to think, and to be sensible and reasonable when choosing their food.

15. Almost from the very moment an animal is born, it seems to have been sent to this world having been trained in another, perfected in all its faculties. Within a few hours or days or months, it comes into full possession of its natural capacity to lead its life according to particular rules and conditions. A sparrow or a bee, for example, acquires, or, rather, is inspired with, the skill and ability to integrate into its environment in a matter of 20 days; for a human to achieve the same level of skill requires 20 years. This means that the basic obligation upon animals, i.e., their essential role, does not include seeking perfection through learning or progress through scientific knowledge; nor does it include "conscious" prayer and the petitioning for help by displaying their impotence. Their obligation or role in creation is to act within the bounds of their innate faculties, which is the mode of worship specified for them.

A human being, by contrast, is born with no knowledge of life or their environment and with a need to learn everything. Unable to entirely complete the conditions of life, even after 20 years, a human being needs to continue learning until the end of their life. They appear to have been sent to the world with much weakness and inability; it may take them as long as two years to learn just how to walk. Only after 15 years can they distinguish between good and evil, and by virtue of living in a society, attain a point where they can choose between what is beneficial and what is harmful to them.

Thus, the essential duty of human beings, the one intrinsic to their existence, is to seek perfection through learning and to proclaim their worship of God and their servanthood to Him through prayer and supplication. They should look for the answer to such questions as "Through whose compassion is my life so wisely administered? Through whose generosity am I being so affectionately trained? Through whose favors and benevolence am I being so solicitously nourished?" They should then pray and petition The Provider of Needs in humble awareness of their needs, even one in a thousand of which they are unable to satisfy unassisted. Their understanding and confession of their impotence and poverty will then become two wings on which to fly to the highest of ranks, that is, being a servant of God. (See *The Words*, "the 23rd Word," 331–332.)

16. For the diary of a honeybee, see Appendix 9.

274　سورة النحل　٢٧٦

73. And do they worship, apart from God, what has no ownership of any provision in the heavens and the earth with which to provide for them, nor have they (whom they falsely worship) any capacity (to take on, still less, discharge such a task)?

74. So do not invent similitudes for God (do not liken Him to others to associate partners with Him, for there is nothing similar to Him). Surely God knows and you do not know (the exact truth about Him and the exact nature of things).

75. God strikes a parable (of two men so that you may understand that true freedom lies in the service of God, because it frees

from servitude to all else): a man enslaved, unable to do anything of his own will, and a (free) man whom We have provided with a fair provision from Us, and he spends thereof secretly and openly. Are the two equal? All praise and gratitude are for God (for to Him alone belongs absolute ownership and disposition of the universe); but most of them do not know.

76. And God strikes a parable of two (other) men: one of them dumb, unable to control anything (unable to answer any call, unable to decide any matter or meet any need). He is a burden upon his master; wherever he directs him, he brings no good. Is he equal with one who enjoins right and justice and is himself on a straight path?

77. And to God belongs (absolute dominion and full knowledge of) the unseen of the heavens and the earth, and the matter of the Hour (of Doom) is (in relation with the Divine Power) but the twinkling of an eye, or even quicker. Surely God has full power over everything.[17]

78. God brought you forth from the wombs of your mothers when you knew nothing, and (in order that you might be perfected through learning) endowed you with hearing and eyes and hearts, that you may give thanks (from the heart and in speech, and in action by fulfilling His commandments).

79. Do they not consider the birds flying in the air subservient to God's command? None holds them but God (Who has endowed them with the power of flight). Surely in that there are signs (manifesting the truth) for people who will believe and who will deepen in faith.

17. The Divine Power is infinite, and an indispensable Attribute of the Supreme Being. It operates like a law, having the same relationship with everything, large or small, few or many, and directly upon the inner dimension of things, or the metaphysical domain, which is free of all obstacles and of particular differences. This domain is in direct contact with the Divine Power. Something big is as easy for the Divine Power to create as something small, and, therefore, it will be no more difficult for this Power to destroy the world in an instant and re-build it in a new form on the Last Day than it is for It to revive an insect in the spring.

80. And (among His blessings on you): God has made for you of your houses places of dwelling and rest; and He has made for you, from the hides of cattle, (another kind of) dwellings that you find light when you travel and when you stop to camp; and in their wool, fur, and hair (He has provided you with means for) furnishings and enjoyable comforts for an (appointed, transient) term.

81. And (among countless other blessings of His) He has made for you, out of the things He has created, shelter from the sun, and given you refuges in the mountains, and made (the means whereby you make) garments to protect you from heat (or cold), and garments (such as coats-of-mail) to protect you from your (mutual) violence. In this way He completes His favors on you so that you may submit to Him (and thereby receive the greatest favor of all).

82. Then if they (despite these blessings of God and His completing His favors upon them through this Revelation) turn away, what rests with you, (O Messenger,) is only to convey the Message fully and clearly.

83. They are fully aware of God's favors, but they refuse to acknowledge them (as such), and most of them are obstinate unbelievers (willfully and stubbornly associating partners with Him in belief and worship).

84. But a Day (will come) when We raise up a witness from among every community (to testify against them that God's Religion was communicated to them), and then those who were unbelievers will not be allowed (to speak their excuses), nor will they be allowed (it then being too late) to make amends.

85. When those who persist in wrongdoing (by associating partners with God and committing evils) see the punishment, it will not be lightened for them, nor will they be reprieved.

86. And when those who associate partners with God see their associate-deities (such as Prophets, saints, and heroes, whom they hold as partners with God in worship and absolute obedience), they will say "Our Lord! Those are our associate-deities whom we (held as partners with You, and) used to invoke apart from You. (They are the ones who led us astray.)" Whereupon (those beings) fling at them the retort: "You are indeed liars!"

87. On that Day they (those who associated partners with God) have offered submission to God, (which out of arrogance they used to withhold), and what they used to fabricate (by way of false deities to worship besides God) has failed them.

276   سورة النحل   ٢٧٦

بِسْمِ اللَّهِ الرَّحْمَٰنِ الرَّحِيمِ

ment in all matters), and devotion to doing good, and generosity towards relatives, and He forbids you indecency, wickedness, and vile conduct (all offenses against the Religion, life, personal property, chastity, and health of mind and body). He exhorts you (repeatedly) so that you may reflect and be mindful!

91. And fulfill God's covenant when you have made the covenant (and any commitment that you made among yourselves in God's Name), and do not break your oaths after having confirmed them; indeed you have made God your guarantor. Surely God knows all that you do.

92. And do not be like her who destroys her yarn that she herself made strong, betraying (thereby her own effort) – by making your oaths a means of deception among yourselves in order that you may be a community greater in numbers (in power and other worldly things) than another community.[19] In this God is only testing you, and on the Day of Resurrection, He will certainly make clear to you all that on which you used to differ.

93. Had God so willed, He would have made you all one single community (with the same faith and religion), but He (has granted you free will with the result that He) leads astray whomever He wills, and guides whomever He wills.[20] You will certainly be called to account for what you used to do.

88. Those who (themselves) disbelieved and barred (other) people from God's way – We add punishment to their punishment because they used to spread disorder and corruption.[18]

89. And on that Day We will raise up within every community a witness from among themselves (to testify) against them (that God's Religion was communicated to them), and We will bring you (O Messenger) as a witness against those (whom your Message has reached). We have sent down on you the Book as an exposition of everything (that pertains to guidance and error and to the knowledge of good and evil, and to happiness and misery in both worlds), and guidance and mercy and glad tidings for the Muslims (those who have submitted themselves wholly to God).

90. God enjoins justice (and right judg-

18. This verse refers to the leaders of unbelief, particularly those who both disbelieve and lead others to disbelieve, while also trying their hardest to prevent others from believing and following God's way. So, they also cause unrest and corruption in the society. It is because of this that in addition to punishment for their unbelief, they will also suffer punishment for barring others from God's way and causing unrest and corruption.

19. Any covenant which is made in God's Name means God's covenant. God's covenant consists of a "rope" of light woven from the threads of Divine Will, Wisdom, and Favoring, and functions as that which is responsible for order in the universe, and is able to establish peace, order, and harmony in the human life. It refers to the spiritual, moral, and social obligations that arise from one's belief in and worship of God (see *sūrah* 2: 27, note 24; *sūrah* 40, notes 47-48; *sūrah* 13: 20), and to all pledges or promises a person gives to another by naming God. It is aimed at justice, good judgment, devotion to doing good and mutual help in society, as well the eradication of all evil, indecency or all shameful deeds – such as fornication, adultery, homosexuality and all similar vices – and insolence and offense against one another. So, making a covenant with God calls for fulfilling all these obligations that arise from faith in Him, and fulfilling it is a sign of true guidance, while breaking this covenant means misguidance and transgression.

In social life, individuals, communities, and nations or states enter into different treaties with one another on certain conditions, and God Almighty orders loyalty to them. No individual or community, relying on their power or material superiority, should be able to break the treaties and betray the conditions. We are strictly forbidden from making our religion merely a means to take advantage of others in our relations and agreements. It is interesting to note that during the Prophet's time, the Quraysh were prone to break their treaties with other tribes when a more powerful party offered them an alliance. Such vices are almost the norm in international affairs today. Islam commands more rigorous ethical and moral standards; a covenant is binding before both humankind and God.

20. For God's leading whomever He wills astray, and guiding whomever He wills, see *sūrah* 2, note 10; 26-27, note 23; *sūrah* 6: 39, note 8.

Arabic text of the Qur'an.

reward in accordance with the best of what they used to do.

97. Whoever does good, righteous deeds, whether male or female, and is a believer, most certainly We will make him (or her) live a good life, and most certainly We will pay such as these their reward in accordance with the best of what they used to do.

98. So when you recite the Qur'ān (as a good, righteous deed), seek refuge in God from Satan rejected (from God's Mercy, because of his evil suggestions and whisperings during the recitation).

99. Surely he has no power over those who believe and put their trust in their Lord.

100. His power is only over those who make a confidant of him (seeking and heeding his suggestions and direction), and those who associate partners with God (in worship and obedience).

101. When We put a Revelation in place of another Revelation (in the course of perfecting the Religion and completing Our favor upon you), – and God knows best what He sends down – they say: "You are but a forger!" No, rather, most of them do not know.[21]

102. Say (to them, O Messenger): "(My Lord affirms): 'The Spirit of Holiness brings it down in parts from your Lord with truth (embodying the truth and with nothing false in it), that it may confirm those who believe (strengthening them in their faith and adherence to God's way), and as guidance, and glad tidings for the Muslims (those who have submitted themselves wholly to God)'."[22]

94. Do not make your oaths a means of deception and wrongdoing among yourselves, lest feet should slip (from the way of guidance) after having been firm (on it, and that others too may be misled by your misconduct); and you should taste the evil (consequences) of your barring from God's way. And (in the Hereafter) there is a mighty punishment for you.

95. And do not sell God's covenant for a trifling price (such as status and other worldly gains). Surely what is with God is the best for you, if you but knew.

96. Whatever is with you wastes away, but that which is with God is permanent. We will most certainly pay those who are persevering and patient (in fulfilling God's commandments, refraining from sins, and all the adversities in God's cause) their

21. For the doctrine of abrogation (*naskh*) referred to in this verse, see *sūrah* 2: 106, note 94; *sūrah* 13: 39, note 12.

22. For the Spirit of Holiness, see 2: 87, note 85. This most probably refers to Archangel Gabriel here, as Gabriel brought the Qur'ān from God to the Prophet Muḥammad, upon him be peace and blessings. His being mentioned as the Spirit of Holiness alludes to his purity of any blemish and the Qur'ān's being absolutely free from any defects or doubt.

278   سُوْرَةُ النَّحْلِ   ٢٧٨

(to the way of true prosperity), and for them is a painful punishment.

105. Only those fabricate lies who do not believe in God's Revelations; and those are the liars.

106. Whoever disbelieves in God after having believed – not he who is under duress, while his heart is firm in and content with faith, but the one who willingly opens up his heart to unbelief – upon them falls God's anger (His condemnation of them), and for them is a mighty punishment.

107. That is because they have chosen the present, worldly life in preference to the Hereafter, and because God does not guide the people of unbelief (to the way of true prosperity and Paradise).

108. Those are they upon whose hearts, hearing, and eyes God has set a seal, and those are they who are unmindful, heedless.

109. No doubt, in the Hereafter they will be the utter losers.

110. Yet surely your Lord turns with favor to those who emigrate after they have been subjected to persecutions (because of their faith) and thereafter exert themselves in God's cause and endure with patience (whatever befalls them) – indeed, in return for such (good deeds) your Lord is All-Forgiving, All-Compassionate.

103. Certainly We know that they say, "It is but a human being that teaches him." But the tongue of him to whom they falsely hint is outlandish, while this (Qur'ān) is in clear Arabic tongue.[23]

104. Surely those who do not believe in God's Revelations (and therefore persist in wrongdoing) – God does not guide them

23. In order to invent excuses, no matter how false they were, for their rejection of the Divine Message which the Prophet Muḥammad, upon him be peace and blessings, brought, the Makkan polytheists sometimes attributed the Qur'ān to the Messenger himself and sometimes to some other person whom they claimed had imparted it to the Messenger. But their claim was so baseless that not only did they contradict their own claim that the Messen-

ger had invented the Qur'ān himself, but also they did not take into consideration the simple fact that that other person to whom they were referring was not an Arab, and spoke another language. This has been the same throughout human history: those who have rejected the Divine Message constantly invent false and contradictory excuses for their rejection, and only manage to make themselves appear ridiculous.

111. (Be ever mindful of) the Day when every soul will come pleading for itself, and every soul will be repaid in full for what it did, and none of them will be wronged.

112. God strikes a parable of a township which was secure and at ease, with its provision coming to it in abundance from all quarters. But it showed ingratitude to God (its people disbelieved, attributed their apparent well-being to other than God and so fell into the habit of making up partners with Him in belief and worship, and daily life); and so God caused it to taste the garment of famine and fear because of what they habitually contrived.

113. For sure a Messenger from among themselves had come to them, but they denied him, and in consequence, the punishment seized them while they were doing wrong.

114. So (O people) partake as pure, lawful, and wholesome of what God has provided you, and give thanks for His bounty, if it is indeed Him that you worship.

115. He has made unlawful to you only carrion, and blood, and the flesh of swine, and that (the animal) which is offered in the name of other than God. Yet whoever is constrained by dire necessity to eat of them, provided he does not covet (what is forbidden) and does not exceed (the bounds of necessity) – (no sin shall be on him). Surely God is All-Forgiving, All-Compassionate.

116. And do not pronounce for what your tongues falsely describe: "This is lawful and this is forbidden," so that you fabricate falsehood in attribution to God. Surely those who fabricate falsehood in attribution to God do not prosper.

117. (Their lot is) a brief enjoyment (in this world), and theirs is a painful punishment (in the Hereafter).

118. And for those who are Jews We made unlawful what We have already related to you. We have never wronged them but they did habitually wrong themselves.[24]

يَوْمَ تَأْتِى كُلُّ نَفْسٍ تُجَادِلُ عَنْ نَفْسِهَا وَتُوَفَّىٰ كُلُّ نَفْسٍ مَّا عَمِلَتْ وَهُمْ لَا يُظْلَمُونَ ۝ وَضَرَبَ اللَّهُ مَثَلًا قَرْيَةً كَانَتْ ءَامِنَةً مُّطْمَئِنَّةً يَأْتِيهَا رِزْقُهَا رَغَدًا مِّن كُلِّ مَكَانٍ فَكَفَرَتْ بِأَنْعُمِ اللَّهِ فَأَذَاقَهَا اللَّهُ لِبَاسَ الْجُوعِ وَالْخَوْفِ بِمَا كَانُوا يَصْنَعُونَ ۝ وَلَقَدْ جَآءَهُمْ رَسُولٌ مِّنْهُمْ فَكَذَّبُوهُ فَأَخَذَهُمُ الْعَذَابُ وَهُمْ ظَالِمُونَ ۝ فَكُلُوا مِمَّا رَزَقَكُمُ اللَّهُ حَلَالًا طَيِّبًا وَاشْكُرُوا نِعْمَتَ اللَّهِ إِن كُنتُمْ إِيَّاهُ تَعْبُدُونَ ۝ إِنَّمَا حَرَّمَ عَلَيْكُمُ الْمَيْتَةَ وَالدَّمَ وَلَحْمَ الْخِنزِيرِ وَمَآ أُهِلَّ لِغَيْرِ اللَّهِ بِهِ فَمَنِ اضْطُرَّ غَيْرَ بَاغٍ وَلَا عَادٍ فَإِنَّ اللَّهَ غَفُورٌ رَّحِيمٌ ۝ وَلَا تَقُولُوا لِمَا تَصِفُ أَلْسِنَتُكُمُ الْكَذِبَ هَٰذَا حَلَالٌ وَهَٰذَا حَرَامٌ لِّتَفْتَرُوا عَلَى اللَّهِ الْكَذِبَ إِنَّ الَّذِينَ يَفْتَرُونَ عَلَى اللَّهِ الْكَذِبَ لَا يُفْلِحُونَ ۝ مَتَاعٌ قَلِيلٌ وَلَهُمْ عَذَابٌ أَلِيمٌ ۝ وَعَلَى الَّذِينَ هَادُوا حَرَّمْنَا مَا قَصَصْنَا عَلَيْكَ مِن قَبْلُ وَمَا ظَلَمْنَاهُمْ وَلَٰكِن كَانُوا أَنفُسَهُمْ يَظْلِمُونَ ۝

---

24. This verse has a connection with verse 114 above and the verses below; it explains why God forbade some pure, wholesome things to the Jews, even though they were believers. It refers to 4: 160–161, and 6: 146. So, see 4: 160–161; 6: 146, notes 31–32.

280   سورة النحل   ٢٨٠

ثُمَّ إِنَّ رَبَّكَ لِلَّذِينَ عَمِلُوا السُّوءَ بِجَهَالَةٍ ثُمَّ تَابُوا مِنۢ
بَعْدِ ذَٰلِكَ وَأَصْلَحُوٓا إِنَّ رَبَّكَ مِنۢ بَعْدِهَا لَغَفُورٌ رَّحِيمٌ ۝
إِنَّ إِبْرَٰهِيمَ كَانَ أُمَّةً قَانِتًا لِّلَّهِ حَنِيفًا وَلَمْ يَكُ مِنَ الْمُشْرِكِينَ
۝ شَاكِرًا لِّأَنْعُمِهِ ۚ اجْتَبَٰهُ وَهَدَٰهُ إِلَىٰ صِرَٰطٍ مُّسْتَقِيمٍ
۝ وَآتَيْنَٰهُ فِي الدُّنْيَا حَسَنَةً ۖ وَإِنَّهُ فِي الْآخِرَةِ لَمِنَ
الصَّٰلِحِينَ ۝ ثُمَّ أَوْحَيْنَآ إِلَيْكَ أَنِ اتَّبِعْ مِلَّةَ إِبْرَٰهِيمَ
حَنِيفًا ۖ وَمَا كَانَ مِنَ الْمُشْرِكِينَ ۝ إِنَّمَا جُعِلَ السَّبْتُ عَلَى
الَّذِينَ اخْتَلَفُوا فِيهِ ۚ وَإِنَّ رَبَّكَ لَيَحْكُمُ بَيْنَهُمْ يَوْمَ
الْقِيَٰمَةِ فِيمَا كَانُوا فِيهِ يَخْتَلِفُونَ ۝ ادْعُ إِلَىٰ
سَبِيلِ رَبِّكَ بِالْحِكْمَةِ وَالْمَوْعِظَةِ الْحَسَنَةِ ۖ وَجَٰدِلْهُم
بِالَّتِي هِيَ أَحْسَنُ ۚ إِنَّ رَبَّكَ هُوَ أَعْلَمُ بِمَن ضَلَّ عَن سَبِيلِهِ
وَهُوَ أَعْلَمُ بِالْمُهْتَدِينَ ۝ وَإِنْ عَاقَبْتُمْ فَعَاقِبُوا بِمِثْلِ مَا
عُوقِبْتُم بِهِ ۖ وَلَئِن صَبَرْتُمْ لَهُوَ خَيْرٌ لِّلصَّٰبِرِينَ ۝ وَاصْبِرْ وَمَا
صَبْرُكَ إِلَّا بِاللَّهِ ۚ وَلَا تَحْزَنْ عَلَيْهِمْ وَلَا تَكُ فِي ضَيْقٍ مِّمَّا يَمْكُرُونَ
۝ إِنَّ اللَّهَ مَعَ الَّذِينَ اتَّقَوا وَّالَّذِينَ هُم مُّحْسِنُونَ ۝

---

119. Then indeed your Lord is – to those who do evil due to ignorance (an instance of defeat to the evil-commanding soul), and after that repent (soon as they realize what they have done is wrong) and mend their ways and conduct – indeed your Lord is All-Forgiving, All-Compassionate (with special mercy toward His penitent servants).

120. Abraham was an exemplary leader, (whose self-dedication to the good of his community made him) as if a community, sincerely obedient to God as a man of pure faith (free from any stain of unbelief and hypocrisy), and he was not of those who associate partners with God –[25]

121. Always thankful for His favors. He (God) chose him, and guided him to a straight path (to follow himself and guide others).

122. We granted him good in the world, and he is surely among the righteous in the Hereafter.

123. Thereafter, We have revealed to you (O Messenger): Follow the way of Abraham as one of pure faith (free from unbelief and hypocrisy), and he was never of those who associate partners with God.[26]

124. The Sabbath was ordained only for those who differed about it (not for all the communities that were to follow the way of Abraham).[27] Your Lord will assuredly judge between them on the Day of Resurrection concerning that on which they used to differ.

125. Call to the way of your Lord with wisdom and fair exhortation, and argue with them in the best way possible.[28] Your Lord surely knows best who has gone astray from His way, and He knows best who are the rightly guided.

126. If you have to respond to any wrong, respond (only) to the measure of the wrong done to you;[29] but if you endure patiently, it is indeed better for the patient.

127. Endure patiently; your endurance is only for God's sake and by His help; and do not grieve for them (because of their attitude toward your mission), nor be distressed because of what they scheme.

128. Surely God is with those who keep from disobedience to God in reverence for Him and piety and those devoted to doing good, aware that God is seeing them.

25. In addition to being the father of the great Messengers, including the Prophet Moses and the Prophet Jesus after him, the Prophet Abraham, upon him be peace, was also the father of the Quraysh through his son Ishmael, upon him be peace. Like the Jews and some Christians who claim that he was a Jew or Christian respectively, the Quraysh sometimes asserted that they were following the way of Abraham. The Qur'ān categorically rejects all such assertions. Abraham was neither a Jew, nor a Christian, nor a polytheist. He was a Messenger of God who absolutely believed in and preached His Oneness. He was extremely tender-hearted and was devoted to, and desired intensely, the guidance of all people. Having appeared among a polytheist nation, he alone revolted against all kinds of polytheism and proclaimed God's Existence, Oneness, and His absolute dominion of all the heavens and earth with whoever and whatever is in them. As a single person he preached the Divine Religion based on God's absolute Oneness and represented it. With all such aspects of his person and mission, and in particular with his wish for the good and guidance of all people, God Almighty appreciates him as being like a whole community. Bediüzzaman Said Nursi remarks: "One who aims at and endeavors for the good of their whole nation, is a nation."

26. For an exposition of the matters mentioned in these last four verses, see, 2: 124–135 and corresponding notes 102–111.

27. For the Sabbath and its breakers, see, 2: 65; 4: 47, and 7: 163–166 and corresponding notes.

28. The Almighty orders His Messenger to follow three ways in preaching His Message: calling to His way with wisdom, calling with fair exhortation, and arguing in the best way possible. As either or all of these three ways may be required to follow in calling everybody to God's way, either may be preferred to call certain people. People are usually of three groups: those who have knowledge and can think; the commonalty, who usually follow their "nature" and pursue their individual interests, and others who persist in unbelief. A preacher should call the first group with wisdom, addressing their intellect and explaining the evidence. He should advise the second group and exhort them to God's way in the best way possible, and argue with the third group mildly to win their hearts, trying not to increase them in unbelief and enmity.

29. For an exposition of responding to the extent of the wrong done to one, see *sūrah* 5: 45, note 10.

SŪRAH 17

AL-ISRĀ'
(THE NIGHT JOURNEY)

Makkah period

This *sūrah* consists of 111 verses. It derives its name from the first verse, where the Messenger's miraculous Night Journey from the Sacred Mosque in Makkah to the *Masjid al-Aqṣā* in Quds (Jerusalem) is related. God's Messenger, upon him be peace and blessings, was taken from there through the heavenly dimensions of existence and observed the greatest signs of God; this journey is known as *al-Mi'rāj* (the Ascension). Some commentators call this *Sūrah Banū Isrā'īl* (The Children of Israel) because it mentions the Children of Israel in verses 2–8 and 101–104. It was revealed in Makkah at the time of the *Mi'rāj*, toward the end of the Makkan period. It warns the unbe-

lievers and asks them to take a lesson from the history of the Children of Israel and other communities, explaining what leads to happiness and what leads to perdition. It states certain broad principles of morality and good conduct as the foundations of the laws which were to be legislated in Madīnah for the individual and collective life of the Muslims. The *sūrah* advises God's Messenger and the believers to endure patiently all that they encounter on God's way.

In the Name of God, the All-Merciful, the All-Compassionate.

1. All-Glorified is He Who took His servant for a journey[1] by night from the Sacred Mosque to the Farthest Mosque[2] the environs of which We have blessed, so that We might show him some of Our signs (of the truths concerning Our Divinity and Lordship). Surely He is the All-Hearing, the All-Seeing.[3]

2. We granted Moses the Book and made it a guidance for the Children of Israel, (commanding them): "Take, apart from Me, no guardian (one to rely on and to Whom affairs should be entrusted)."[4]

3. (They were among) the descendants of those whom We carried (in the Ark) with Noah. He surely was a servant greatly thankful.[5]

4. We decreed in the Book for the Children of Israel (as a consequence of their ingratitude and disobedience to the Book): "You will most certainly cause corruption and disorder in the land twice, and (elated with extreme arrogance) you will act with great insolence."

5. Hence, when the time of the first of the two came, We roused and sent against you some servants of Ours of great might (chosen by Us to punish you), and they ravaged the land, ransacking your homes. That was a promise to be executed.

6. Then We gave the turn back to you to prevail over them, and strengthened you with resources and children, and made you the more numerous in human power (than before).

7. If you do good (aware that God is seeing you), you do good to your own selves; and if you do evil, it is likewise to your own selves. And so, when the time (for the fulfillment) of the second decree comes, (We rouse new enemies against you) to disgrace you utterly and to enter the Temple as the others entered it before, and to destroy entirely all that they conquer.[6]

---

1. The initial verse of this *sūrah* is concerned with the miraculous night journey of God's Messenger from the Sacred Mosque in Makkah to the Masjid al-Aqsā in Jerusalem. The Messenger was taken from there through the dimensions of existence, reaching as high as the Presence of God. This second part of the journey is called the Ascension (*Mi'rāj*). For an explanation, see Appendix 10.

2. Why the Qur'an mentions the Bayt al-Maqdis in Jerusalem as Masjid al-Aqsā (The Farthest Mosque) is that at the time of the Revelation it was the farthest (sacred) mosque for the Muslims in Madīnah. The Muslims regard three mosques in the world as sacred, and may desire and travel to perform worship in these mosques because of the special reward involved in such a journey. They are Masjid al-Ḥarām (The Sacred Mosque in Makkah, in which the Ka'bah is situated), Masjid an-Nabī (The Prophet's Mosque in Madīnah), and Bayt al-Maqdis (Masjid al-Aqsā) in Jerusalem. These mosques are the fountainheads of the Divine Religion that is based on the absolute Oneness of God and was primarily preached and represented by the greatest Messengers of God, namely Abraham, Moses, Jesus, and Muḥammad, upon them all be peace. The word "farthest" also signifies greatness in degree. This *sūrah* was revealed in Makkah at a time when the Prophet's Mosque in Madīnah had not yet been built and the Ka'bah was full of idols; therefore the Muslims turned to that Masjid in Jerusalem for their prayers.

3. The pronoun in *Surely He is the All-Hearing, the All-Seeing*, which alludes to the furthest point of the Ascension indicated by the relevant verses from *Sūrah an-Najm* (53), refers either to Almighty God or to the Prophet, upon him be peace and blessings.

If it refers to the Prophet, according to the rules of eloquence and the relationship between the pronoun and its antecedent, the meaning is this: This journey, which is apparently particular, is in reality so comprehensive and signifies such a universal ascent that the Prophet, upon him be peace and blessings, heard and saw during it all the signs of the Lord and the wonders of His art. He perceived these, by sight and by hearing, as results of the manifestations of Divine Names in universal degrees as far as *the Lote-tree of the utmost boundary and the distance between the strings of two bows (put adjacent to each other) or even nearer* (for the meaning of these expressions, see 53: 9, 14 and the corresponding notes 4 and 6). Thus, through its conclusive phrase, the verse describes that particular journey as the key to understanding a (higher) journey that is universal and full of extraordinary events.

If the pronoun in *Surely He is the All-Hearing, the All-Seeing*, refers to God Almighty, the meaning is this: In order to call a servant of His on a journey to His Presence and entrust him with a duty, after sending him from Masjid al-Ḥarām to Masjid al-Aqsā, which is where the Prophets gather, and causing him to meet with them and showing that he is the absolute, indisputable heir of the principles of the religions of all the Prophets, He took that servant through both the external and inner dimensions of His dominion as far as *the Lote-tree of the utmost boundary and the distance between the strings of two bows (put adjacent to each other) or even nearer.*

The Prophet Muḥammad, God's most beloved servant, upon him be peace and blessings, was certainly a servant and that journey was a unique ascension. However, since he was given a Trust which is connected to the whole of the universe, and was accorded a light which would change the color of the universe, and also had with him a key which would open the door to eternal happiness, Almighty God describes Himself as the One Who hears and sees all things so that His world-embracing, comprehensive, and all-encompassing wisdom in the Trust, the light, and the key might be observed and understood.

Describing the Messenger as all-hearing and all-seeing in no way indicates that he became like God. Such an assertion amounts to unbelief and association of partners with God. What is meant here is that the Messenger heard and saw the greatest truths and signs of God's Divinity and Lordship in the universal degree; no other mortal had ever been able to do this nor would any mortal ever be able to attain this level. It also implies that the Messenger, upon him be peace and blessings, was honored with the universal manifestations of God's Names, the All-Hearing, the All-Seeing.

4. The transition from a mention of the Ascension to observations about the history of the Children of Israel is made here to underline the significant correspondence between their fate and the history of other communities. Since the history of the Children of Israel, from their appearance on the earth to their rise and their subsequent decline, is a complete history, constituting a complete example for all other communities, the Qur'ān frequently refers to it. Another reason why the Qur'ān frequently refers to the history of the Children of Israel is that they will continue to play important parts in the history of humankind, and that the Muslims in particular will have dealings with them until the end of time.

The Ascension is especially significant with respect to the mission of the Messenger, upon him be peace and blessings. As expounded in

note 1 above, the Messenger met with many previous Messengers during the Ascension, including especially the Prophet Moses, and in addition to observing the greatest signs of God concerning His Divinity and Lordship, he also proved to be His greatest sign for all the dimensions of existence. God's Messenger was also shown to be heir to the missions of all previous Prophets. Among the previous communities, it is primarily upon the Children of Israel, Moses' people, that God completed His favor, therefore from the perspective of the mission of Messengership, Moses most closely resembled the Prophet Muḥammad, upon him be peace and blessings. This is clear in the following verses of the Old Testament and the Qur'ān, respectively:

> The Lord said unto me (Moses): "What they have spoken is good. I will raise them up for them a Prophet like you from among their brethren, and will put My words in his mouth; and he shall speak to them all that I command him. And it shall be *that* whoever will not hear My words, which he speaks in My name, I will require *it* of him." (*Deuteronomy*, 18: 17–19)

It is clear from this verse that what is meant by "a Prophet like you from among their brothers" is a Prophet who will come from the line of Ishmael, since Ishmael is the brother of Isaac, the forefather of the Children of Israel. The only Prophet who came after the Prophet Moses and resembled him in many ways, for example, in the bringing of a new law and fighting with his enemies, is the Prophet Muḥammad, upon him be peace and blessings. The Qur'ān points to the same fact: *Surely We have sent to you (O people) a Messenger, a witness against you, just as We sent a Messenger to the Pharaoh* (73: 15).

5. By connecting the Children of Israel to the Prophet Noah, whom it mentions as a greatly thankful servant, the verse implies that Noah's being a thankful servant has a part in the Children of Israel being given the Book as a source of guidance. Thankfulness and efforts exerted in God's cause purely for His sake never go without return. It also warns that a com-

munity honored with God's Book as a source of guidance in life, which will also secure the afterlife, requires thankfulness; primarily this means that it is God Who grants all the blessings one has in life, and therefore one must believe in Him without associating any partners with Him, as well as worshipping Him alone. Thankfulness in no way benefits God, nor does ingratitude cause Him any loss. But thankfulness is indispensably important for a person and community to realize true humanity. As long as people thank God, He increases His favors on them. By contrast, if they become ungrateful, then God punishes them. This punishment is the natural consequence of ingratitude, as it means corruption in both individual and collective life.

6. The warnings mentioned with their reasons occur in several places in the Bible (*Leviticus*, 26: 14–39; *Deuteronomy*, 28: 15–68; *Psalms*, 106: 34–38, 40–41; *Isaiah*, 1: 4–5, 21–24; 2: 6, 8; 8: 7; 30: 9–10, 12–13; *Jeremiah*, 2: 5, 7, 20; 3: 6, 8–9; *Ezekiel*, 22: 3, 6–12, 14–16; *Matthew*, 23: 37; 24: 2; *Luke*, 23: 28–30).

For example, *Isaiah* 1: 4–5 writes about the corruption and its consequences:

Alas, sinful nation, a people laden with iniquity, a brood of evildoers, children who are corrupters! They have forsaken the Lord, they have provoked to anger the Holy One of Israel, they have turned away backward. Why should you be stricken again? You will revolt more and more. The whole head is sick, and the whole heart faints.

Jeremiah 5: 1, 7–9 reads:

Run to and fro through the streets of Jerusalem, see now and know; and seek in her open places if you can find a man, if there is *anyone* who executes judgment, who seeks truth, and I will I pardon her.... "How shall I pardon you for this? Your children have forsaken Me, and sworn by *those that* are not gods. When I had fed them to the full, then they committed adultery and assembled themselves by troops in the harlots' houses. They were *like* well-fed lusty stallions, everyone neighed after his neighbor's wife. Shall I not punish *them* for these *things*?" says

the Lord. "And shall I not avenge Myself on such a nation as this?

Jeremiah 5: 15–17 and 7: 33–34 tell about the people God would send against Israel and the extent of the destruction:

Behold, I will bring a nation against you from afar, O house of Israel," says the Lord. "It is a mighty nation, it is an ancient nation, a nation whose language you do not know, nor can you understand what they say. Their quiver *is* like an open tomb; they *are* all mighty men. And they shall eat up your harvest and your bread, *which* your sons and daughters should eat. They shall eat up your flocks and your herds; they shall eat up your vines and your fig trees; they shall destroy your fortified cities, in which you trust, with the sword.

The corpses of these people will be food for the birds of the heaven and for the beast of the earth. And no one will frighten *them away*. Then I will cause to cease from the cities of Judah and from the streets of Jerusalem the voice of mirth and the voice of gladness, the voice of the bridegroom and the voice of the bride. For the land shall be desolate.

During the time of the Prophet Samuel, in around 1020 BC, the Children of Israel were able to establish a unified state, under King Saul (Tālūt) (The Qur'ān, 2: 247–51) and during the time of the Prophets David and Solomon they reached the zenith of their power and magnificence. This lasted nearly one century, but after Solomon, upon him be God's peace, dissension and feuding broke out with the result that the state divided into two kingdoms, one Israel, with Samaria as its capital and comprising the northern part of Palestine and Transjordan, the other, Judah, comprising the southern part of Palestine and Edom with Jerusalem as its capital.

Polytheistic beliefs and moral corruption affected the kingdom of Israel more than the other and, despite the warnings of the Prophets and their great efforts at reformation, the people did not mend their ways. Eventually, the Assyrians launched a series of attacks and finally the ruthless Assyrian king Sargon put an end to the kingdom of Israel in 721 BC.

The kingdom of Judah was able to survive as an Assyrian tributary. However, the Babylonian king Nebuchadnezzar carried out a devastating attack on the kingdom in 586 BC and razed all the towns of the kingdom and sent the Jews into exile. Jerusalem and the Temple of Solomon were totally destroyed.

Some people in Judah continued to adhere to righteousness and did not cease to call others to it. Eventually, out of compassion and mercy, God came to their rescue and the Babylonian Empire collapsed. In 539 BC the Persian Emperor Cyrus conquered Babylonia and the following year he allowed the Children of Israel to return and settle once again in their homeland. This resulted in the reconstruction of the Temple of Solomon after great effort and the re-compilation and publication of the five books of the Old Testament by Ezra. While these occurred in the south and Jerusalem was restored, becoming once again the focal point of Judaic religion and culture, the Children of Israel of northern Palestine and Samaria did not benefit from Ezra's reform efforts. As a whole, the Children of Israel were not able to recover the magnificence of the reigns of David and Solomon, upon them be peace. They suffered serious setbacks through a succession of events and suffered invasions by Alexander the Great and the rise of the Greeks. But, deeply imbibed with the religious spirit inspired by Ezra, they were not daunted by the oppressive measures of these conquerors. Instead, their suffering led to the rise of the great resistance movement known as the Maccabean Revolt. They were able to set up their own independent, religious state, which lasted until 67 BC. The frontiers of the state gradually expanded, so that over the course of time it came to embrace the entire territory that had once been under the control of the two Israelite kingdoms of Judah and Israel.

Over the course of time, however, the moral and religious fervor that marked the Maccabean Revolt declined and was replaced by worldliness and a mechanical, superficial adherence to a mere show of religious rites. Serious divisions appeared among the Children of Israel, and some of them invited the Roman general Pompey to attack Palestine. Pompey returned to Palestine in 63 BC and put an end to the independence of the Children of Israel.

The Jewish religious leadership betrayed the Prophets Zechariah, John, and Jesus, upon them be peace, who appeared at around the same time and tried to reform them. The Prophet John was decapitated and his head was placed at the feet of the dancing maiden at whose behest this heinous crime had been committed. The Jews fiercely opposed the Prophet Jesus and persuaded the Roman Governor, Pontius Pilate, to have him put to death.

Not long after, a fierce conflict ensued between the Children of Israel and the Romans, culminating in an open rebellion by the Jews in 64 AD. When the Roman governor failed to crush the rebellion, a large-scale military operation was carried out by the Roman Empire. The rebellion was suppressed and in 70 AD Titus forcibly seized Jerusalem. A massacre followed in which 133,000 people lost their lives and a further 67,000 were made captive and enslaved. Additionally, thousands were conscripted to work in the mines in Egypt and thousands of others were dispatched to amphitheaters and coliseums in different parts of the Roman Empire to face either gladiators or wild beasts, who tore their bodies to pieces. All beautiful girls were offered up to the lust of the conquerors. Jerusalem, along with the Temple of Solomon, was razed to the ground. All this put an end to Jewish power in Palestine for about 1,800 years (Summarized from al-Mawdūdī, 5: 9–26).

282

سُورَةُ الإسْرَاء

٢٨٢

عَسَىٰ رَبُّكُمْ أَن يَرْحَمَكُمْ وَإِنْ عُدتُّمْ عُدْنَا وَجَعَلْنَا جَهَنَّمَ لِلْكَافِرِينَ
حَصِيرًا ۞ إِنَّ هَٰذَا الْقُرْآنَ يَهْدِي لِلَّتِي هِيَ أَقْوَمُ وَيُبَشِّرُ الْمُؤْمِنِينَ
الَّذِينَ يَعْمَلُونَ الصَّالِحَاتِ أَنَّ لَهُمْ أَجْرًا كَبِيرًا ۞ وَأَنَّ الَّذِينَ لَا يُؤْمِنُونَ
بِالْآخِرَةِ أَعْتَدْنَا لَهُمْ عَذَابًا أَلِيمًا ۞ وَيَدْعُ الْإِنسَانُ بِالشَّرِّ دُعَاءَهُ
بِالْخَيْرِ وَكَانَ الْإِنسَانُ عَجُولًا ۞ وَجَعَلْنَا اللَّيْلَ وَالنَّهَارَ آيَتَيْنِ
فَمَحَوْنَا آيَةَ اللَّيْلِ وَجَعَلْنَا آيَةَ النَّهَارِ مُبْصِرَةً لِتَبْتَغُوا فَضْلًا
مِّن رَّبِّكُمْ وَلِتَعْلَمُوا عَدَدَ السِّنِينَ وَالْحِسَابَ وَكُلَّ شَيْءٍ فَصَّلْنَاهُ
تَفْصِيلًا ۞ وَكُلَّ إِنسَانٍ أَلْزَمْنَاهُ طَائِرَهُ فِي عُنُقِهِ وَنُخْرِجُ لَهُ
يَوْمَ الْقِيَامَةِ كِتَابًا يَلْقَاهُ مَنشُورًا ۞ اقْرَأْ كِتَابَكَ كَفَىٰ
بِنَفْسِكَ الْيَوْمَ عَلَيْكَ حَسِيبًا ۞ مَّنِ اهْتَدَىٰ فَإِنَّمَا يَهْتَدِي
لِنَفْسِهِ وَمَن ضَلَّ فَإِنَّمَا يَضِلُّ عَلَيْهَا وَلَا تَزِرُ وَازِرَةٌ وِزْرَ
أُخْرَىٰ وَمَا كُنَّا مُعَذِّبِينَ حَتَّىٰ نَبْعَثَ رَسُولًا ۞ وَإِذَا أَرَدْنَا
أَن نُّهْلِكَ قَرْيَةً أَمَرْنَا مُتْرَفِيهَا فَفَسَقُوا فِيهَا فَحَقَّ عَلَيْهَا الْقَوْلُ
فَدَمَّرْنَاهَا تَدْمِيرًا ۞ وَكَمْ أَهْلَكْنَا مِنَ الْقُرُونِ مِن
بَعْدِ نُوحٍ وَكَفَىٰ بِرَبِّكَ بِذُنُوبِ عِبَادِهِ خَبِيرًا بَصِيرًا ۞

---

8. It is hoped that your Lord may show mercy to you, but if you return (to your sins), We will return (to Our punishment).[7] And We have made Hell a prison for the unbelievers.

9. This Qur'ān surely guides (in all matters) to that which is most just and right and gives the believers who do good, righteous deeds the glad tidings that for them there is a great reward.

10. And that for those who do not believe in the Hereafter, for them We have prepared a painful punishment.

11. Yet human (through his actions as well as his words) prays and calls for evil just as he prays and calls for good. Human is prone to be hasty.[8]

12. (As in the life of humankind, "days" and "nights" alternate in the world also.) We have made the night and the day two signs (manifesting the truth of God's Power, Knowledge, and absolute sovereignty, and His grace on you). We have obscured the sign of the night (made it dark) and We have made the sign of the day illuminating (therefore a means for you) to see,[9] that you may seek bounty from your Lord and that you may know the computation of (time) the years and the reckoning; We set out all things in clear detail.

13. Every human being's fate We have fastened around his neck, and We will bring forth for him on the Day of Resurrection a book which he will see spread open.

14. "Read your book! Your own self suffices you this day as a reckoner against you."[10]

15. Whoever takes the right way takes it for the good of his soul only; and whoever goes astray, goes astray but to its harm only. No soul, as bearer of burden, bears (and is made to bear) the burden of another. We would never punish (a person or community for the wrong they have done) until We have sent a Messenger (to give counsel and warning).

16. And when We finally will to destroy a township (that has deserved destruction), We leave those of its people lost in the pursuit of pleasures to their own devices, and so they transgress all limits therein. In consequence, the word (of punishment) is justified against it, and so We annihilate it, reducing it to nothing.

17. How many a generation have We (thus) destroyed after Noah! Your Lord suffices as one All-Aware and All-Seeing of the sins of His servants.

7. If the second punishment mentioned in the above verse is yet to come, and the first punishment refers to what the Assyrians and Babylonians and the Romans did, then this verse is in the continuation of the previous one and addresses all the Jews from 70 AD. If the second punishment is what Titus did in Palestine, then this verse addresses the Jews at the time of the Messenger and those to come. Islam, as the latest and most perfected form of God's Religion and which Prophet Muḥammad conveyed, was God's great mercy for them, and as mentioned in 2: 89, they had been asking for a victory in Madīnah over the tribes of Khazraj and Aws, who were then unbelievers, saying: "The Last Prophet will come and we will defeat and destroy you under his leadership." However, when there came to them the Messenger *whom they knew as they knew their own sons* (2: 146), they disbelieved in him," except a few. Despite this and their continuing refusal to believe in Islam, the Jews have lived their happiest years under Muslim governments, including, in particular, the Ottoman State. Finally, as God decreed, concerning the Jews, *Ignominy has been their portion wherever they have been found except for (when they hold on to) a rope from God or a rope from other peoples* (3: 112), by being much more obedient to the commandments of their religion, even if they were abrogated, than the Muslims are to Islam, and more respectful to their religious heritage, and, moreover, being backed up by many governments throughout the world, they were able to acquire power and influence in many parts of the world and to establish Israel in Palestine in 1948. No doubt, the future will reveal how long they can sustain this partial supremacy.

8. Unless God informs them, human beings cannot know what is ultimately to their advantage and what is to their disadvantage. The Qur'ān declares: *It may well be that you dislike a thing but it is good for you, and it may well be that you like a thing but it is bad for you. God knows, and you do not know* (2: 216). For this reason, people usually desire and call down on themselves (by their words and actions) what is evil for them, thinking that it is to their good.

They even pray to God for evil, knowingly or unknowingly, under the spell of their carnal souls and worldly ambitions. They also desire what they think of as an advance payment and dislike what they think of as a payment on credit. This is why they usually prefer a worldly advantage over eternal reward in the Hereafter, which is one of the primary reasons for their errors, including unbelief. The Qur'ān also draws the attention to this important point in several verses: *They choose the present, worldly life in preference to the Hereafter* (14: 3); *That is because they have chosen the present, worldly life in preference to the Hereafter* (14: 3). This is mostly because people are disposed to haste. Humankind are by nature hasty. Like other apparently negative attributes, such as greed, envy, and obstinacy, this attribute is ingrained in people so that they may channel it into virtues. The Messenger declares that haste comes from Satan and he advises that we should not postpone doing good and show celerity in good things, such as doing the Prescribed Prayers on time and helping the needy.

9. According to Ibn 'Abbās, the sign of the night refers to the moon, the sign of the day to the sun. Therefore, from the words *We have obscured the sign of the night*, we can understand that the moon once emitted light as the sun does and God took its light from it, causing it to darken, or obscuring it. Or we could infer that the solar system was a single mass, later dividing into the sun and its satellites. While the verse thus recounts the past of the moon, it also points to the future destiny of all heavenly bodies.

10. Everything exists in Divine Knowledge and is recorded. The Qur'ān calls this record "the Supreme Ever-Preserved Tablet" (85: 22; 13: 39, note 13). It explicitly states that nothing befalls us save that which God has decreed for us (9: 51); and no living creature moves on the earth, no bird flies on its two wings, but they are communities like us, and God has neglected nothing in the Book (the Qur'ān, the Supreme Ever-Preserved Tablet) (6: 38). Each thing is given a particular nature and identity, which constitutes its destined and determined

existence. Then, the Divine Power gives each nature and identity external or witnessed existence along with the dimensions or "tapes" of time and space, and branches into the worlds of the seen and unseen as the Tree of Creation.

The Supreme Ever-Preserved Tablet is a title for Divine Knowledge as related to creation. We can also call it the Original, Manifest Record. In the "process" of creation, this Record is duplicated. Its first, most comprehensive copy or duplication, which comprises the whole of creation, is called the "Tablet of Effacement (Canceling) and Confirmation" in the Qur'ān. While the Manifest Record relates to the origins of creatures and the principles and laws of creation, the Manifest Book or the Tablet of Effacement and Confirmation is the reality of time. Divine Power transfers things from the Manifest Record onto the Tablet of Effacement and Confirmation. In other words, Divine Power arranges things on the page of time or attaches them in turn to the string of time. Nothing changes on the Supreme Ever-Preserved Tablet; everything is fixed there, but in the "process" of creation, God effaces whatever He wills, and confirms and establishes whatever He wills (13: 39).

The second kind of duplication can be thought of as follows:

After birth, everyone is registered in their nation's registry of births. Then, according to the information in this state register, everyone is given an identity document. Similarly, everyone is registered on the Supreme Ever-Preserved Tablet with all their personal characteristics, special features, and future life-history, down to the smallest details. This original register of everyone is copied out by angels, and the part of it which relates to our life as a conscious, intelligent being is fastened around our neck as an invisible book, as mentioned in the verse. During our whole life, we enact whatever is in that book. However, this in no way means that Destiny or the pre-determination of a person's life-history compels them to behave in a certain way. It is better to think of it in the following way: you send someone to a place to do a job. You have previously procured whatever they will need during that journey and given them the necessary instructions to do the job. Since you

know in advance how they will behave on every step of their journey, you have recorded all the details of that future journey in a notebook and placed it in a secret pocket in the jacket of that person. They start out unaware of the notebook in their pocket and behave however they wish during the whole of their journey. Along with this person, you have dispatched two of your most reliable people to follow the first person wherever they go, to observe all their acts and to secretly record on video-tape whatever they do or say and however they act. On their return, you compare the video-tape recordings with the contents of the notebook hidden in their secret pocket and see that there is not the slightest difference between them. Afterwards, you call this person to account for the job they performed, whether or not it was in accordance with your instructions and either reward them, punish them, or forgive them.

As in the example above, God, Who knows everything in advance and is beyond all time and space, pre-records in registers the life-histories of all people to come to the world. The angels copy out the registers and fasten each person's record or register around their neck; this is what we call destiny or fate. God's fore-knowledge and recording of whatever a person will do throughout their whole life in no way compel that person to do these actions. Rather they act of their own free will, doing of their free will whatever they do. All of a person's life is recorded by two angels, whom we call the *Kirāmun Kātibūn* (Noble Scribes). On Judgment Day, the angels' recordings of a person's life will be presented to that person and they will be told to read their own book.

These two verses have another meaning. Everyone's life in this and the other world, their fate, and whatever they will encounter in both worlds are dependent on a person's own choice and actions. The original word translated as "fate" in verse 13 is *ṭā'ir*, meaning bird. The pre-Islamic Arabs would foretell the future from the manner and direction in which birds flew. The Qur'ān rejects such a superstition and concepts of good or bad omens, explicitly declaring that everyone's future is dependent on their own acts which they perform out of free choice.

بِسْمِ اللَّهِ الرَّحْمَنِ الرَّحِيمِ (Arabic Quranic text)

---

well as those ones – out of the free gifts of your Lord (in the world); the gift of your Lord is not confined.

21. See how We have made some of them excel others (in worldly gifts and in virtues); yet the Hereafter will certainly be greater in ranks and greater in excellence.[11]

22. Do not set up another deity besides God, or you will be sitting disgraced and forsaken.

23. Your Lord has decreed that you worship none but Him alone, and treat parents with the best of kindness. Should one of them, or both, attain old age in your lifetime, do not say "Ugh!" to them (as an indication of complaint or impatience), nor push them away, and always address them in gracious words.

24. Lower to them the wing of humility out of mercy, and say: "My Lord, have mercy on them even as they cared for me in childhood."

25. Your Lord best knows what is in your souls (in respect of all matters, including what you think of your parents). If you are righteous (in your thoughts and deeds), then surely He is All-Forgiving to those who turn to Him in humble contrition.[12]

26. And give his due to the relative, as well as the destitute and the wayfarer; and do not squander (your wealth) senselessly.

27. Surely squanderers are ever brothers of satans; and Satan is ever ungrateful to his Lord.

18. Whoever wishes for only the immediate gains (of this transitory life), We readily grant thereof as much as We please to whomever We will. Thereafter We consign him to Hell, wherein he will roast, disgraced and disowned.

19. But whoever wishes for the Hereafter and strives for it as it should be striven for, being a believer, then for those (who do so) their striving shall be recognized with thanks and reward.

20. Each do We supply – these ones as

---

11. Why does God not endow His servants equally? Why does He create some of them blind, disabled, or afflicted in other ways, and make some of His servants excel others in worldly things?

To begin with, God is Sovereign; He is the Lord of both the earthly and spiritual dominions of existence. He wills and creates whatever is in them and however He pleases: *Blessed and*

Supreme is He in Whose Hand is the Sovereignty; and He has full power over everything (67: 1). No one has any part in His Sovereignty, nor can anyone intervene in what He creates except as He wills and to the extent that He wills.

It is God Who has created every thing and every being and Who provides for them. It is God Who bestows our human nature upon us. We have given nothing to God but He has given us everything without our having deserved it. What claim or right do we have therefore over anything? We have no right to impute injustice to Him because injustice comes from not giving what is due. Nor can we question Him. We can ask such questions only to learn His wisdom in creating and providing for His servants in appearance unequally. He is absolutely free of injustice, since He is the Giver of everything that we have or use.

Secondly, we cannot know which conditions are for our own good, and everyone is responsible in proportion to their own capabilities. It is not possible for us to decide whether being wealthy or poor or sound or disabled is something that is good for us. The true criterion to decide on whether something is good or evil is the afterlife or what we will find in the Hereafter. God may deprive an individual of something they value, but grant that individual a manifold return for that loss in the Hereafter. By means of that loss, God makes us feel our need, our powerlessness, and our poverty in relation to Him. In this way, He makes us turn to Him with a weightier sincerity, a fuller heart, and so makes us worthier of His Blessing and Favor. Thus, our apparent loss is in reality a gain.

Thirdly, there are innumerable degrees in worldly things. If we observe and investigate all that is around us, we will certainly realize that there are many things or people different from us, inferior or worse in our judgment, with which we would not change places – just as there may be others with which we might, out of misguided thinking or envy of some kind, wish to change places. So everyone should accept their place with sincerity. Also, just as there are differences that arise with creation, they are also differences caused by human beings themselves. The differences that arise with creation are causes of the different professions one can follow in life; these are indispensable to the social life of humanity. Moreover, no one person excels all others in all respects, and everyone excels and is excelled by others in one or more respects.

Fourthly, material possessions should not be seen as necessarily good or bad in and of themselves. God sometimes bestows material security and happiness upon those who petition Him for such things, but sometimes He does not. The truth is that there is good in His bestowing what He bestows, be it wealth or poverty. For the faithful individual who does good deeds and is charitable with what has been given to them, wealth is a means of good. If, however, the individual is of weak faith and has strayed from the path of right action and charity, wealth becomes a means of evil. Similarly, for an individual who has deserted the path of right action, poverty may be a means of unbelief, determining that each day that person inwardly or outwardly rebels against God. Whoever does not submit heart, mind, and soul completely to God, whoever does not try sincerely to act upon the teachings of Islam, will find that whatever level of wealth they own will become a means of distress, a severe and demanding test: *Know that your possessions and your children are but a trial and temptation, and God is He with Whom there is a tremendous reward* (8: 28).

It is not poverty or richness itself which is good, rather it is the state of mind which has disciplined (and triumphed over) the carnal soul (*nafs*) and set its sights upon the eternal life. The surest way for a person to please God, therefore, is to understand that whatever God gives is given in order to perfect that person in the best way. Whatever a person's circumstances, they should strive to fulfill their duties toward the Creator and the created. The best attitude to adopt toward all the circumstances of this world, which is only a stopping-place on the way to our everlasting destination, is well-expressed in this brief poem:

> I accept, my Lord, whatever comes to me from You,
> For whatever comes to me from You is to my good;
> Whether a robe of honor comes or a shroud,
> Whether a sharp thorn or a sweet, fresh rose,
> If it comes with Your blessing, it comes to my good.

(Questions and Answers, 1: 158–160)

12. Paternal affection for children is one of the sublime realities of worldly life and, in turn, filial gratitude to them is a most urgent and strenuous duty. Parents sacrifice their lives lovingly for their children, and if this is so, what falls to a child who has not lost their humanity and become transformed into a monster of ingratitude, is to show sincere respect for them, to serve them willingly, and to try to gain their approval. With regard to filial respect and service, uncles and aunts are like parents.

We should be aware of how disgraceful and how unscrupulous it is to be tired of the existence of old parents and to desire and wait for their death. We should know this and understand what an injustice it is for us to desire the end of the lives of ones who have sacrificed their lives for us.

O you, who are immersed in earning your livelihood! Know that your disabled relative whom you regard as unbearable in your house is, in fact, the means of blessing and abundance. Never complain that you can scarcely make a living (that your means of subsistence are strained); for were it not for the blessing and abundance bestowed on you through them, you would have to face even more difficulties in making your living. This is an undeniable reality.

Indeed, as is witnessed by the whole of the existence, when the Generous, Majestic Creator, Who is infinitely merciful, compassionate, gracious, and munificent, sends children to the world, He sends them along with their sustenance, which He provides in abundance through the breasts of the mothers. In the same way, He sends in the form of blessing and unseen, immaterial abundance, the sustenance of the old, who are like children and even more worthy and needy of compassion than children. He does not load their sustenance onto mean, greedy people.

The truth expressed in the verses, *Surely God – it is He Who is the All-Providing, Lord of all might, and the All-Forceful* (51: 58); and *How many a living creature there is that does not carry its own provision (in store), but God provides for them, and indeed for you* (29: 60), is openly proclaimed by living creatures of all kinds through the language of their dispositions. So, not only the sustenance of old relatives, but also that of pets, like cats, which have been created as friends to human beings and usually live on food from human beings, is, again, sent in the form of a blessing.

A human being is the most esteemed, noble, and the most worthy-of-respect among all creatures; among human beings, the believers are the most perfect. Among the believers, helpless old people are those who are the most worthy and needy of respect and compassion. Among the old, close relatives deserve affection, love, and service more than others, and among relatives, one's parents are the most truthful confidants and the most intimate companions. So, if an animal becomes the means of blessing and abundance when it stays as a guest in a person's house, then we can conclude how invaluable a means of blessing and mercy parents are in a house and, additionally, as stated in the *hadīth*, *But for the old bent double (because of old age), calamities would be pouring down upon you* (al-'Ajlūnī, 2: 163), what an important means for the removal of calamities they are.

This being so, let us come to your senses! If our parents have been assigned a long life, certainly, we too, will grow old, and if we do not show due regard for our parents, then, according to the rule that one is rewarded or punished in accordance with one's action, then our children will not respect us either. Furthermore, if we consider our afterlife seriously, it is a precious provision for that life to gain the approval of our parents by serving them in this life. If we love the worldly life, again we should please them so that we too may lead a pleasant life. If, by contrast, we regard them as unbearable, if we break their easily-offended hearts, and if we desire their death, we will be the object of the Qur'ānic threat, *Such incur loss of both this world and the Hereafter* (22: 11). So, whoever wishes for the mercy of the All-Merciful must show mercy to those in their house who have been entrusted to them by God (*The Letters*, "the 21st Letter," 2: 53–56).

28. But if you must turn away from those (who are in need, because you are yourself in need, and) seeking mercy from your Lord in hopeful expectation, then (at least) speak to them gently and well-meaning.

29. Do not keep your hand bound to your neck (in niggardliness) nor stretch it without any restraint or else you will be left sitting reproached and denuded.

30. Surely your Lord God enlarges provision for whom He wills, and straitens it (for whom He wills). Indeed He is fully aware of His servants and sees them well.[13]

31. Do not kill your children for fear of poverty; it is We Who provide for them as well as for you. Killing them is surely a grave sin.[14]

32. Do not draw near to any unlawful sexual intercourse; surely it is a shameful, indecent thing, and an evil way (leading to individual and social corruption).[15]

33. Do not kill any soul, which God has forbidden, except for a just cause. If anyone has been killed wrongfully and intentionally, We have given his heir (as defender of his rights) the authority (to claim retaliation or damages or to forgive outright). But let him (the heir) not exceed the legitimate bounds in (retaliatory) killing. Indeed he has been helped (already and sufficiently by the provisions and procedures of the Law).[16]

34. And do not draw near to the property of the orphan except in the best way (such as to improve and increase it) until he comes of age and is strong; and fulfill the covenant: the covenant is surely subject to questioning (on the Day of Judgment you will be held accountable for your covenant).

35. Give full measure when you measure,

and weigh with a true, accurate balance. That is what is good and (to do so is) best in the long term.

36. Do not follow that of which you have no knowledge (whether it is good or bad), and refrain from groundless assertions and conjectures. Surely the hearing, the sight, and the heart – each of these is subject to questioning about it (you are answerable, and will be called to account for each of these on the Day of Judgment).[17]

37. Do not strut about the earth in haughty self-conceit; for you can never split the earth (no matter how hard you stamp your foot), nor can you stretch to the mountains in height (no matter how strenuously you seek to impress).

38. The evil of all this is abhorrent in the sight of your Lord.

13. Like everything else, provision for each person has also been (pre-)determined by God, and no one can obtain more than the provision that has been determined for them, nor can anybody die without having consumed their provision. Every living being's basic provision – the least amount of provision sufficient for its survival – is guaranteed by God, provided that being depends on Him in all respects. The procurement of any extra provision that will be needed because of certain conditions, like habits, depends on personal effort.

God does not forbid working or exerting effort, nor does He want His servants to be content with their basic provision. Rather He encourages the making of an effort, declaring, *Human has only that for which he labors* (53: 39), and wills that His servants should earn in lawful ways to spend in God's cause for the cause of Islam and for the good of people. He has created humankind as vicegerents to improve the earth, to share and distribute its provision justly, and to thank Him. One who earns lawfully, who is thankful and who helps others is much better in the sight of God than one who is content with the basic provision. Although asceticism is commended in order to keep one's lusts under control and to help advance toward spiritual perfection, lawful earning, spending for the livelihood of oneself and one's family and in God's cause, and being thankful, without indulging in luxuries, without going into extremes of consumption, and stimulating one's lusts, are better and more commendable than asceticism. What God forbids is greed, earning in unlawful ways, pursuing one's own interests only, hoarding wealth, miserliness, and not helping the needy. He also forbids taking the worldly life as the goal for working and earning.

Greed demonstrates its evil consequences throughout the world of animate beings, both at the level of species and at that of particular individuals. On the other hand, seeking one's lawful provision while putting one's trust in God is, by contrast, a means to achieve tranquility and demonstrates its good effects everywhere. For example, in the animal and human kingdoms only the young, who "demonstrate their trust in God through their weakness and helplessness," receive in full measure their rightful and delicious provision from the treasury of the Divine Compassion, Which sets the parents and some other elders at their service, while adult animals that leap greedily at their provision are able to obtain coarse food only at the cost of great effort. It is most pertinent to reflect on the fact that the more powerful wild animals get their food with greater difficulty and at greater intervals than others.

Greed is a source of humiliation and loss. There are so many instances of a greedy person being exposed to loss that the idea that "The greedy are subjected to disappointment and loss," can be found in many proverbs and is a universally accepted truth. That being the case, if we love wealth, we should seek it not with impatience, but with contentment, so that we may earn it abundantly.

Bediüzzaman Said Nursi writes:

All immorality and disturbances in human social life proceed mainly from two sources, from these two attitudes:

The first: Once my stomach is full, what do I care if others die of hunger?

The second: You work and I will eat.

The behavior that perpetuates these two attitudes is the prevalence of usury or interest on the one hand and the abandonment of the *Zakāh* on the other. The sole remedy for these two awful diseases can only be provided through implementing the *Zakāh* as a universal principle and duty, and banning interest. The *Zakāh* is an essential pillar, not only for individuals and particular communities, but for all of humankind, if they are to live a happy life. Humankind are usually divided into two classes; the elite and the commonalty. Only the obligation of the *Zakāh* can arouse compassion and generosity in the elite towards the commonalty and respect in the commonalty towards the elite. In the absence of the *Zakāh*, what will come to the commonalty from the elite is oppression and cruelty, and what will rise from the commonalty towards the elite is rancor and rebellion. That will give rise to a constant struggle and a constant opposition between the two classes, resulting finally in the confrontation of labor and capital, such as happened in Russia at the beginning of the century. (*The Letters*, "the 22nd Letter," 2: 74)

14. It is clear that Islam forbids the killing of children, whether after their birth or before it (abortion), for economic or other reasons. Birth control today is encouraged apparently for economic reasons, especially in poorer countries, but in truth this is done to prevent an increase in population in those countries. The growth of population can never be an obstacle to economic development nor does it cause poverty. On the contrary, population means a work force for a nation. All the rich countries of the world, such as Germany, England, France, Holland, Belgium, Italy, and the United States, have a high density of population. What people should do, as al-Mawdūdī says (5: 39, note 31), is not to waste their energy on the destructive task of reducing the number of mouths that have to be fed; instead, they should devote their energy to constructive tasks which will lead to an increase in the production of wealth.

15. The word translated as unlawful sexual intercourse is *zinā*, a word which signifies all sexual intercourse between a man and woman who are not husband and wife, and therefore denotes both "adultery" and "fornication" in English. The Qur'ān not only forbids any unlawful sexual intercourse, but also orders that all ways to it are blocked by saying *do not draw near*. So, just as a Muslim community or state is obliged to take all measures to prevent unlawful sexual intercourse in society, so too are individuals required to hold back from everything that may lead to it. Through the rules it has introduced and the spiritual and moral training it offers, Islam seeks to close the door to unlawful sexual intercourse, as well as other evils.

16. For Islam's view of life, the unjust taking thereof and retaliation, see *sūrah* 2: 178, note 131; 179, 194, note 140; *sūrah* 5: 31, 32, 45, note 10.

As well as murder or other unjust killing,

Islam also forbids suicide. A person is not their own master and has no right to treat themselves however they wish. Our bodies, souls, and lives belong to God and are sacred. Some people try to justify euthanasia. However, we should consider the fact that we are in the world to improve it according to God's laws and prepare for the other world, making it fertile ground for the other world; whatever misfortune a believer suffers, it causes one or some of their sins to be forgiven. The pain a believer suffers at death is also a means of forgiveness. God has endowed every person with the power to endure to a certain extent and when their pain comes to an unbearable point, they either faint or cease to feel. Therefore, Muslim jurists should approach the matter of euthanasia with great care in the light of Islam.

There are many ways in which one can exceed the legitimate bounds in retaliatory killing. For example, killing someone other than the actual killer or taking the life of another person in addition to the killer, subjecting the killer to torture, mutilating their corpse, and harming their relatives, are some examples of exceeding the bounds.

It is the legal authority to execute retaliation. People cannot attempt to restore their rights by themselves without first applying to the court.

17. Islam decrees that people should be guided by knowledge rather than conjecture and baseless assertions. The sources or means of knowledge are three: true reports (Divine Revelation and the authentic reports from the Messenger, upon him be peace and blessings, and the reports given by truthful persons), reason, and our five (sound) senses. A believer must accept the true report, but can study its meaning and draw certain conclusions from it, if they have the authority to do so. The data perceived by reason and the five senses may be either true or false and require further investigation.

Rejecting the Divine Revelation and the authentic reports that come from the Prophets means restricting the scope of knowledge and knowledge itself to what is obtained through reason, the five senses, and experiences which relate to the visible, sensed world. But there are so many dimensions of existence and almost innumerable things and beings outside the visible world, that restricting knowledge to this world in the name of scientific knowledge causes knowledge (or science) to either admit its ignorance of the other dimensions of existence or to remain agnostic. Also, science cannot deny these dimensions, simply because denial is a conclusion which should be based on investigation, therefore science must be able to prove the non-existence of the dimensions it denies. This is why, like atheism, rejecting the existence of beings that we cannot see such as Satan, angels, and the jinn, can in no way be a scientific attitude. It can merely be a baseless assertion or allegation, or even dogmatism.

Science can neither excuse itself by attributing the acceptance of such beings to belief. Islam states that belief should be based on, or at least corroborated by, knowledge and that it is in no way incompatible with knowledge. Therefore, accepting the existence of God and beings such as angels and jinn is not dogmatism, but rather a scientific attitude. There are scientific criteria that support the acceptance of their existence. First of all, even if our five senses cannot perceive these truths, God has actually given humankind other senses with which to be able to perceive them. More than 100,000 Prophets, who were able to use those senses, who never lied during their lives, and who were followed by innumerable people, as well as millions of saints, have informed us of their existence; in addition to these, millions of other people have had similar experiences. Secondly, denial of the Divine Revelation as a source of knowledge means accusing all the Prophets and saints, whose truthfulness has been witnessed and accepted, of being the meanest liars in human history, and designating their billions of followers as fools who blindly follow liars. Moreover, to cite just one example of truthfulness out of countless ones, both in the Qur'ān and the sayings of God's Messenger, upon him be peace and blessings, there are many predictions, most of which have proven true. The remaining ones are waiting for their due time to be proven true. There are indeed so many scientific facts which have been discovered or are being discovered in parallel with developments in science that these alone are sufficient to establish the truth of the Divine Revelation.

٢٨٥

285

ذَٰلِكَ مِمَّآ أَوۡحَىٰٓ إِلَيۡكَ رَبُّكَ مِنَ ٱلۡحِكۡمَةِ ۗ وَلَا تَجۡعَلۡ مَعَ ٱللَّهِ إِلَٰهًا ءَاخَرَ فَتُلۡقَىٰ فِى جَهَنَّمَ مَلُومًا مَّدۡحُورًا ۝ أَفَأَصۡفَىٰكُمۡ رَبُّكُم بِٱلۡبَنِينَ وَٱتَّخَذَ مِنَ ٱلۡمَلَٰٓئِكَةِ إِنَٰثًا ۚ إِنَّكُمۡ لَتَقُولُونَ قَوۡلًا عَظِيمًا ۝ وَلَقَدۡ صَرَّفۡنَا فِى هَٰذَا ٱلۡقُرۡءَانِ لِيَذَّكَّرُوا۟ وَمَا يَزِيدُهُمۡ إِلَّا نُفُورًا ۝ قُل لَّوۡ كَانَ مَعَهُۥٓ ءَالِهَةٌ كَمَا يَقُولُونَ إِذًا لَّٱبۡتَغَوۡا۟ إِلَىٰ ذِى ٱلۡعَرۡشِ سَبِيلًا ۝ سُبۡحَٰنَهُۥ وَتَعَٰلَىٰ عَمَّا يَقُولُونَ عُلُوًّا كَبِيرًا ۝ تُسَبِّحُ لَهُ ٱلسَّمَٰوَٰتُ ٱلسَّبۡعُ وَٱلۡأَرۡضُ وَمَن فِيهِنَّ ۚ وَإِن مِّن شَىۡءٍ إِلَّا يُسَبِّحُ بِحَمۡدِهِۦ وَلَٰكِن لَّا تَفۡقَهُونَ تَسۡبِيحَهُمۡ ۗ إِنَّهُۥ كَانَ حَلِيمًا غَفُورًا ۝ وَإِذَا قَرَأۡتَ ٱلۡقُرۡءَانَ جَعَلۡنَا بَيۡنَكَ وَبَيۡنَ ٱلَّذِينَ لَا يُؤۡمِنُونَ بِٱلۡأٓخِرَةِ حِجَابًا مَّسۡتُورًا ۝ وَجَعَلۡنَا عَلَىٰ قُلُوبِهِمۡ أَكِنَّةً أَن يَفۡقَهُوهُ وَفِىٓ ءَاذَانِهِمۡ وَقۡرًا ۚ وَإِذَا ذَكَرۡتَ رَبَّكَ فِى ٱلۡقُرۡءَانِ وَحۡدَهُۥ وَلَّوۡا۟ عَلَىٰٓ أَدۡبَٰرِهِمۡ نُفُورًا ۝ نَّحۡنُ أَعۡلَمُ بِمَا يَسۡتَمِعُونَ بِهِۦٓ إِذۡ يَسۡتَمِعُونَ إِلَيۡكَ وَإِذۡ هُمۡ نَجۡوَىٰٓ إِذۡ يَقُولُ ٱلظَّٰلِمُونَ إِن تَتَّبِعُونَ إِلَّا رَجُلًا مَّسۡحُورًا ۝ ٱنظُرۡ كَيۡفَ ضَرَبُوا۟ لَكَ ٱلۡأَمۡثَٰلَ فَضَلُّوا۟ فَلَا يَسۡتَطِيعُونَ سَبِيلًا ۝ وَقَالُوٓا۟ أَءِذَا كُنَّا عِظَٰمًا وَرُفَٰتًا أَءِنَّا لَمَبۡعُوثُونَ خَلۡقًا جَدِيدًا ۝

───────✦───────

39. All this is (part) of the Wisdom which your Lord has revealed to you (O Messenger). (As the source and basis of all wisdom), do not set up with God another deity, or you will be cast into Hell, blamed and disowned.[18]

40. Has, then, your Lord distinguished you (O unbelievers) by preferring for you sons, and taken for Himself from among the angels daughters? Most certainly you utter an awful, horrendous saying.

41. We have set out (the truths) in diverse ways in this Qur'ān, so that they may reflect and be mindful, but all this increases them (the unbelievers) only in their aversion (to truth).

42. Say: "If there were, as they assert, deities apart from Him, surely they would seek a way to the Master of the Supreme Throne (the dominion of the creation)."[19]

43. All-Glorified is He, and absolutely exalted, immeasurably high above all that they say.

44. The seven heavens and the earth, and whoever is therein, glorify Him. There is nothing that does not glorify Him with His praise (proclaiming that He alone is God, without peer or partner, and all praise and gratitude belong to Him exclusively),[20] but you cannot comprehend their glorification. Surely He is (despite what His servants have deserved from Him) All-Clement, All-Forgiving.

45. When you recite the Qur'ān, We place an invisible veil between you and those who do not believe in the Hereafter (and who, by making themselves deaf and blind to the creation's praise of its Creator, make themselves incapable of such belief).

46. And over their hearts We lay veils (made from their ill-intention, wrongdo-ing, and arrogance) that prevent them from grasping it (the Qur'ān), and in their ears, heaviness. When you make mention of your Lord in the Qur'ān as the One (the Unique Divine Being), they turn their backs in aversion.

47. We know best what they wish to hear when they listen to you and that, when they are secluded among themselves, these wrongdoers say (to one another): "You are following but a man bewitched."[21]

48. See what strange comparisons they invent about you. They have altogether strayed and are now unable to find a way (to the truth).

49. And they say: "What! is it when we have already become bones and particles of dust – is it then that we will be raised as a new creation?"

18. Islam aims to develop human beings from being potentially human to being truly human, thus perfecting them. It develops the human character in the best way. The parts of the Wisdom which the Qur'ān enumerates in verses 22–39, beginning and ending with the absolute prohibition of associating partners with God in any way in His Divinity and Lordship, are important in developing that character and raising members of a Muslim society. We can summarize them as follows:

- Do not set up another deity besides God.
- Your Lord has decreed that you worship none but Him alone.
- Treat parents with the best of kindness.
- Give their due to your relatives, as well as to the destitute and the wayfarer; and do not squander (your wealth) senselessly.
- Do not keep your hand bound to your neck (in niggardliness) nor stretch it without any restraint.
- Do not kill your children for fear of poverty.
- Do not draw near to any unlawful sexual intercourse.
- Do not kill any soul, which God has made forbidden, except in just cause.
- Do not draw near to the property of an orphan, except in the best way (such as to improve and increase it) until they come of age; and fulfill your commitments.
- Give full measure when you measure, and weigh with a true, accurate balance.
- Do not follow that of which you have no knowledge, (refraining from groundless assertions and conjectures).
- Do not strut about the earth in haughty self-conceit.
- Do not set up with God another deity or you will be cast into Hell, blamed and disowned.

Before proceeding to promulgate the laws that regulate the life of Muslim society, the Qur'ān aims to instruct the members of that society in such a way that the laws can be applied without resorting to force. Moreover, the Qur'ān raises the members of a Muslim society so perfectly that, at the time of the Prophet, before such laws existed, the believers requested him to pray to God Almighty for such laws to be promulgated. For example, before the Qur'ān ordered Muslim women to cover themselves, there had been applications to the Messenger requesting that women should cover themselves; the people at this time were convinced of the necessity of such a law. As another example, some also applied to the Messenger for the prohibition of alcohol before it was banned.

We should also point out here that all the injunctions above, which were revealed during the Makkah period of the Messenger's mission, end, with the exception of associating partners with God, by mentioning either the wisdom or reasoning in their revelation or with the words of encouragement or discouragement. When the same injunctions were revealed in Madīnah, where the Muslims were organized as a society, they usually ended in either promises or threats in return for following or disobeying them respectively, or the legal penalties that were to be given for committing the prohibitions.

For the meanings of wisdom in its special sense, see *sūrah* 2, notes 108 and 159.

19. It is the clearest fact that this universe, so harmonious, coherent, and balanced, and which obviously requires absolute, all-encompassing knowledge, will, and power, must have a creator and controller. Therefore, atheism is no more than a dogma, even the most incomprehensible dogma of all times.

As for associating partners with God in order to divide God's power and acts between different deities, one of its basic reasons is not knowing God with His Attributes. The perfect harmony, coherence, and balance observed in the universe clearly demonstrate that there cannot be more than one deity or lord with the same attributes. Having no beginning or end, and being eternal and uncontained by time and space are indispensable attributes of Divinity. Obviously, there cannot be two beings with these attributes existing at the same time. In addition, having a beginning and end requires coming into existence at a certain time as well as there being someone or something that brought this being into existence; yet, God eternally exists without having come into existence.

If, despite the clear facts which we have set out here, we were to conceive of more than one deity, then either these deities should be independent of the others or there must be one true god, the others being subordinate to him. In the former case, it is simply inconceivable that several independent, sovereign deities can always concur on all matters, and that the universe maintains its perfect harmony, coherence, and balance. Had there been a multiplicity of deities, there would have been clashes and discordance at every step. Moreover, it is sheer absurdity that there are several independent, sovereign deities with the same attributes of, for example, absolute knowledge, will, and power.

In the second case, while there is an independent, sovereign, all-knowing, all-willing, and all-powerful god, then it can be no more than a fantasy to conceive of subordinate gods. If there were such gods, they would desire and attempt to be lord of the universe or, at least, to have a part in the creation and administration of things. The order and operation of the universe also contradicts this. It is evident that everything in the universe is interconnected to everything else and all the forces in the universe are set to collaborate even just for a single blade of grass to come into existence and grow. In conclusion, there is nothing in the universe more manifest than the existence of the One, All-Knowing, All-Willing, All-Powerful, and All-Independent, Sovereign God, to Whom the Qur'ān introduces us.

20. The last two verses succinctly express what we have tried to explain in the note above. As Divinity must be and is absolutely free from how the polytheists conceive of it and God, the Sole Deity, is infinitely exalted above having any partners and similarity to the created, the universe, with all that is in it, declares this truth. Since it is the One God Who creates, sustains, maintains, and administers the whole universe with all that is in it, all praise is due to Him and so the whole of creation praises Him exclusively. While conscious, believing beings praise Him consciously – verbally, actively, and by heart – the bodies of all beings also praise Him through the satisfaction of their needs and contentment of their senses and faculties.

21. This verse explains the reason why God places an invisible veil between the Messenger and those who do not believe and lays veils over their hearts and heaviness in their ears. They did not listen to the Messenger's recitation of the Qur'ān to learn the truth; rather they listened to him with the hope of finding something to support their denial. Then they would come together in secret and consult among themselves as to how they could effectively refute the Prophet's Message and prevent people from believing in him.

286   سُورَةُ الإِسْرَاء   ٢٨٦

قُل كُونُوا حِجَارَةً أَوْ حَدِيدًا ۞ أَوْ خَلْقًا مِّمَّا يَكْبُرُ فِي صُدُورِكُمْ فَسَيَقُولُونَ مَن يُعِيدُنَا قُلِ الَّذِي فَطَرَكُمْ أَوَّلَ مَرَّةٍ فَسَيُنْغِضُونَ إِلَيْكَ رُءُوسَهُمْ وَيَقُولُونَ مَتَىٰ هُوَ قُلْ عَسَىٰ أَن يَكُونَ قَرِيبًا ۞ يَوْمَ يَدْعُوكُمْ فَتَسْتَجِيبُونَ بِحَمْدِهِ وَتَظُنُّونَ إِن لَّبِثْتُمْ إِلَّا قَلِيلًا ۞ وَقُل لِّعِبَادِي يَقُولُوا الَّتِي هِيَ أَحْسَنُ إِنَّ الشَّيْطَانَ يَنزَغُ بَيْنَهُمْ إِنَّ الشَّيْطَانَ كَانَ لِلْإِنسَانِ عَدُوًّا مُّبِينًا ۞ رَّبُّكُمْ أَعْلَمُ بِكُمْ إِن يَشَأْ يَرْحَمْكُمْ أَوْ إِن يَشَأْ يُعَذِّبْكُمْ وَمَا أَرْسَلْنَاكَ عَلَيْهِمْ وَكِيلًا ۞ وَرَبُّكَ أَعْلَمُ بِمَن فِي السَّمَاوَاتِ وَالْأَرْضِ وَلَقَدْ فَضَّلْنَا بَعْضَ النَّبِيِّينَ عَلَىٰ بَعْضٍ وَآتَيْنَا دَاوُدَ زَبُورًا ۞ قُلِ ادْعُوا الَّذِينَ زَعَمْتُم مِّن دُونِهِ فَلَا يَمْلِكُونَ كَشْفَ الضُّرِّ عَنكُمْ وَلَا تَحْوِيلًا ۞ أُولَٰئِكَ الَّذِينَ يَدْعُونَ يَبْتَغُونَ إِلَىٰ رَبِّهِمُ الْوَسِيلَةَ أَيُّهُمْ أَقْرَبُ وَيَرْجُونَ رَحْمَتَهُ وَيَخَافُونَ عَذَابَهُ إِنَّ عَذَابَ رَبِّكَ كَانَ مَحْذُورًا ۞ وَإِن مِّن قَرْيَةٍ إِلَّا نَحْنُ مُهْلِكُوهَا قَبْلَ يَوْمِ الْقِيَامَةِ أَوْ مُعَذِّبُوهَا عَذَابًا شَدِيدًا كَانَ ذَٰلِكَ فِي الْكِتَابِ مَسْطُورًا ۞

―――※―――

50. Say: "Whether you have become stone or iron,

51. "Or any other created substance which, in your minds, is greater (in its resistance to being given life)." Then they will say: "Who will bring us back to life?" Say: "He Who originated you in the first instance with a unique individuality." They will shake their heads at you (in amazement and derision) and say: "When will that be?" Say: "It may well be soon,

52. "On the Day when He will call you and you will answer with (words of) His praise, thinking that you have stayed (on the earth) but a little while."[22]

53. And say to My servants that they should always speak (even when disputing with others) that which is the best. Satan is ever ready to sow discord among them. For Satan indeed is a manifest enemy for humankind.

54. Your Lord knows you best (and what you deserve). If He so wills, He has mercy on you (which is sheer grace), and if He so wills, He punishes you (which is pure justice). We have not sent you (O Messenger) to be a guardian over them, responsible for them; (you are only a warner).[23]

55. And your Lord knows best all that are in the heavens and on the earth. Assuredly We have exalted some of the Prophets above others (some in an absolute sense, and others in some respects); and to David We granted the Psalms.[24]

56. Say: "Call upon those (the angels, human beings, the jinn) whom you pretend are deities apart from Him! They have no power to remove any affliction from you nor can they make any changes in your conditions."

57. Those whom they invoke themselves seek a means to approach their Lord, each trying to be nearer to Him, hoping for His mercy and fearing His punishment.[25] The punishment of your Lord is surely to be feared and avoided.

58. There is not a township but that We will have destroyed it before the Day of Resurrection (as a consequence of its people's way of life, and in accordance with the laws We have established for the lives of communities), or punished it with a severe punishment (such as dissension, corruption, and foreign invasion): all this is written down in the (eternal) Book.[26]

22. Concerning the arguments about the Resurrection, see Appendix 11.

23. No one, including even the Prophet, can judge or decide who will go to Paradise or Hell. It is God alone Who fully knows about all human beings, who among them deserves happiness or punishment in the other world. All that human beings can say, based on the teachings of the Qur'ān, is what kind of people deserve mercy and what kind deserve punishment. No one can know and say that a particular person will be treated with mercy or be punished.

Although God, being the All-Wise and the All-Just, has set conditions for going to Paradise and has clearly stated what kind of creed and deeds cause one to deserve Hell, no one can compel Him to do something nor claim, as the Mu'tazilites and Shī'ah do, that He is obliged to admit those who believe and do good deeds into Paradise, while the others go to Hell. Whereas He is not obliged to do anything, because He has absolute freedom to do what He wills. His admitting the believers into Paradise is out of His pure mercy, for no one can deserve Paradise with their own deeds, while His sending the unbelievers to Hell is pure justice. In viewing the judgments and acts of God, we must take into consideration all His Names and Attributes together.

24. This verse explains a Divine principle in choosing the Prophets. God knows best all that is in the heavens and on the earth with the characteristics and abilities of each, and He also knows best who is worthy of Prophethood. However, the Makkan polytheists tried to find excuses for their rejection of the Divine Message brought by the Prophet Muḥammad, upon him be peace and blessings. They falsely argued that the Messengership should have been given to Walīd ibn Mughīrah in Makkah or Abū Mas'ūd Urwah ibn Mas'ūd, the chief of the Thaqīf Tribe of Ṭāif (43: 31), although God knows best upon whom to place His Message (6: 124). They also argued that a Prophet should not need to eat or drink, nor walk in the streets – in short, that he should be an angel. The Qur'ān mentions such false objections and

answers them in several verses. By mentioning David in particular in this verse, the Qur'ān is saying that even a king with a splendid kingdom, who lived in a palace, and had several wives and children, can be chosen to be Prophet of God, whom He even exalted above many Prophets in certain respects. So, Muḥammad, as a human being who eats, drinks, and who is married, and not an angel, can be a Prophet; he can even be one who is the greatest of all.

This verse also hints at an important point concerning the evaluation of Prophethood and the Prophets. Both in the past and in the present some people have tended to see the Prophet only as a means of transmitting the Divine Revelation, without any distinction of character. Whereas, by beginning with an affectionate address to God's Messenger, *Your Lord knows best all that are in the heavens and on the earth*, the verse stresses that being a Prophet requires certain qualities and distinctions worthy of it, and that God knows best who is worthy of Prophethood and upon whom to place His Message.

By continuing, *Assuredly, We have exalted some of the Prophets above others (some in an absolute sense, and others in some respects)*, the verse suggests that God's Messenger is one of those exalted above others. Among the Prophets, Noah, Abraham, Moses, Jesus and Muḥammad, upon them be peace, are the greatest, and the Prophet Muḥammad, whose mission is universal and lasting until the Resurrection Day, is the greatest of all. It is worth quoting from Said Nursi here:

> The behavior and characteristics of the noble Prophet, upon him be peace and blessings, have been described in books of history and biographies. However, his spiritual persona and the sacred nature of his being are so sublime and illustrious that those of his qualities explained in books of history and biography fail to describe his high stature. For, according to the rule, "The cause is like the doer," from the time of the declaration of his Prophethood through to the present time (and, indeed, until the end of time) the rewards from the good deeds of every Muslim are added to

the accounts of the Prophet's perfections, upon him be peace and blessings. He also receives countless invocations of all the members of his community every day, as well as the mercy of God, which is infinite and which he draws in without measure. Furthermore, since he is the result and most perfect fruit of creation, and the beloved and interpreter of the Creator of the universe, his true nature and the truth of his perfections cannot be contained in the human qualities recorded in books of history and biography. Certainly, the stature of a blessed being who had the Archangels Gabriel and Michael, upon them be peace, as his aides-de-camp, one on each side, at the Battle of Badr, is not to be found within the incident of a man who haggled with a Bedouin in the marketplace over the price of a horse, calling Hudhayfah to be his witness in the deal.

Thus, in order not to fall into error, we must turn our attention away from the common human qualities of the holy Prophet, upon him be peace and blessings, to his true nature and illustrious spiritual persona in his rank of Messengership. Otherwise, we may risk showing him disrespect or entertain uncertainties about his persona. To understand this point, study the following analogy:

Suppose that a date-stone, planted under the ground, has sprouted and become a tall, fruitful tree, and is still continuing to grow taller and broader. Or that from a peacock egg duly incubated, a chick has hatched and grown into a beautiful peacock adorned by the Pen of Divine Power, and is still growing larger and more beautiful. Now there exist qualities, properties, and precisely balanced elements possessed by that date-stone and that egg. They are, however, not as striking and significant as those of the tree and the peacock that grew from them. While describing, therefore, the qualities of the date-stone and the egg, along with those of the tree and the peacock, it is important to appropriately distinguish the qualities of the date-stone and the egg from the palm-tree and peacock respectively, so that anyone reading or hearing the description may find it reasonable. Otherwise, if, for example, one claims to have got thousands of dates from a date-stone (and not from the tree) or commends the egg as (already) the prince of birds, people will be led to contradiction and denial.

The human nature of God's most noble Messenger, upon him be peace and blessings, may thus be likened to that date-stone or egg, but his true nature, illuminated with the Prophetic mission, is like the Tūbā Tree or the Royal Bird of Paradise. His true nature is, moreover, continually growing more and more perfect. That is why, when one is thinking of that exalted person while he was disputing with a Bedouin in the marketplace, one should turn the eye of one's imagination to the illustrious essential nature of the man who rode the Burāq and Rafraf during the Miʿrāj, who left Gabriel behind and reached the Divine Presence (See Appendix 10 for the Miʿrāj). Otherwise, one risks either showing insufficient respect to or failing to convince one's earthbound soul of his true nature. (The Letters, "the 19th Letter," 1: 110–111)

For the superiority of some Prophets to others (in some aspects or respects), see 4: 164, note 33.

25. This verse categorically rejects the claim to deification of any other being besides God, including the Prophets, angels, and saintly beings among humankind and the jinn, who themselves believe in God alone and try to do His commandments, seeking a means to approach Him, striving to be nearer to Him, hoping for His mercy and fearing His punishment. As for other beings, such as Satan, devils, the unbelieving jinn, and devilish people, to whom some have attributed Divinity, their bodies also obey God unconditionally, and they themselves will offer utter submission to God in the Hereafter and seek a means to obtain God's forgiveness.

26. For the Book and what is written down in it, see sūrah 6: 59, note 13; sūrah 13: 39, note 12; and in this sūrah, note 10.

بِسْمِ اللّٰهِ الرَّحْمٰنِ الرَّحِيْمِ

59. Nothing stops Us from sending the miracles (they demand as evidence in support of the Messenger's claim to be appointed by God) except that (many among the) former generations rejected them as false (and were destroyed). We had given the Thamūd the she-camel as a visible sign (miracle) but they did wrong in respect of her. We do not send (Our) Revelations except to warn (and to make them aware of a possible destruction, and the eternal punishment).

60. And (recall) when We said to you (by way of a warning), that your Lord encompasses all humankind (with His Knowledge and Power). We did not make the vision that We showed you (during the Ascension) but as a trial for humankind to mend their ways, and (in the same way We mentioned) in the Qur'ān the Accursed Tree (the tree in Hell absolutely outside the sphere of God's Mercy). And We warn them, exhorting them to be fearful and amend, but it increases them only in great insolence and rebellion.[27]

61. And (recall another instance of arrogance and insubordination) when We said to the angels: "Prostrate before Adam!" they prostrated, but *Iblīs* did not; he said: "Shall I prostrate myself before one whom You created of clay?"

62. He said: "Do You see this that You have honored above me? Indeed, if You grant me respite till the Day of Resurrection, I will certainly bring his descendants under my sway, all but a few!"

63. (God) said: "Go your way! Whoever

of them follows you – surely Hell will be the recompense of you all, a recompense most ample!

64. "Arouse with your (seductive) voice whomever you can from among them, and rally against them with your cavalry and foot soldiers, and be their partner in their wealth and children, and make promises to them. And Satan promises them nothing but deceit.[28]

65. "But as for My (sincere, devoted) servants – you will have no authority over them." And your Lord suffices as protecting guardian (as One on Whom to rely and to Whom all affairs are referred).

66. Your Lord (O humankind) is He Who causes the ships to sail for you through the sea, that you may seek of His bounty.[29] Surely He is ever Compassionate towards you.

27. When God's Messenger, upon him be peace and blessings, returned from the Ascension, he narrated to the Makkan people what he had witnessed during his miraculous journey. He had transcended the corporeal dimensions of existence and saw the forms that the creed, deeds, and words of people take on in the Hereafter. Although Paradise and Hell still exist as "seeds," they wait to be expanded into their eternal forms, which will take place during the Resurrection. People's creed, deeds, and words provide the building blocks for their places in Paradise or Hell. For example, a word of thanks or praise such as *al-hamdu li-l-lāh* (All praise is for God) is returned to the one who utters it as an apple in Paradise. People sometimes see in their dreams the similar forms that their creed, deeds, and words will take on in the Hereafter. So, during the Ascension, God's Messenger saw examples of these forms and of the people who have such creeds and do those deeds. The tree accursed in the Qur'ān, that is, the tree mentioned in the Qur'ān as being absolutely excluded from God's Mercy, is the Tree of *Zaqqūm* (37: 62–67; 44: 42–46; 56: 51–54). It is a bitter tree that will grow in Hell and of which the people of Hell will eat. Certainly, this is as a consequence of some deeds of the unbelievers, and constitutes one of the forms of torment in Hell. Far from providing sustenance, it gives pain and causes torment as food for the people of Hell.

The Messenger related to the Makkan people all that he had seen during the Ascension. Although the Messenger exhibited several clear and undeniable signs of his miraculous journey, the unbelievers contradicted him willfully and persisted knowingly in unbelief. Like all other miracles and truths, the Ascension, with all its aspects, proved to be a test for people. However, we should point out that the Almighty does not create miracles or test people so as to lead them astray. People stray because of their arrogance, willful obstinacy, and insistence on their way even in the face of the most manifest truths.

28. Satan seduces people in a variety of ways. As well as, in particular, whispering into people's hearts and with his voice, which those near to him can hear, he also seduces people with sounds like obscene music and calls for disobedience to God. In addition to his offspring, Satan has well-equipped armies, both from among the jinn and human beings, and he is a partner with people in the wealth gained through and spent in unlawful ways and in children who have not been brought up properly according to God's commands. He continually makes false, deceptive promises to people. He deceives them with long-term ambitions, worldly aims, and false expectations. (For the deception of Satan, see also 7: 17, note 2.)

29. God has created the sea both as a treasure of bounties and as a way to overseas bounties. In order to benefit from it, He has inspired people to build ships. As He employed His Messengers as both the conveyors of His Message and the vanguard of scientific and technological developments, initially He taught Prophet Noah to build a ship.

288 سُوْرَةُ الإِسْرَاء ٢٨٨

وَإِذَا مَسَّكُمُ الضُّرُّ فِي الْبَحْرِ ضَلَّ مَن تَدْعُونَ إِلَّا إِيَّاهُ فَلَمَّا
نَجَّلكُمُ إِلَى الْبَرِّ أَعْرَضْتُمْ وَكَانَ الْإِنسَانُ كَفُورًا ۞
أَفَأَمِنتُمْ أَن يَخْسِفَ بِكُمْ جَانِبَ الْبَرِّ أَوْ يُرْسِلَ عَلَيْكُمْ حَاصِبًا
ثُمَّ لَا تَجِدُوا لَكُمْ وَكِيلًا ۞ أَمْ أَمِنتُمْ أَن يُعِيدَكُمْ فِيهِ تَارَةً
أُخْرَى فَيُرْسِلَ عَلَيْكُمْ قَاصِفًا مِّنَ الرِّيحِ فَيُغْرِقَكُم بِمَا كَفَرْتُمْ
ثُمَّ لَا تَجِدُوا لَكُمْ عَلَيْنَا بِهِ تَبِيعًا ۞ وَلَقَدْ كَرَّمْنَا بَنِي آدَمَ
وَحَمَلْنَاهُمْ فِي الْبَرِّ وَالْبَحْرِ وَرَزَقْنَاهُم مِّنَ الطَّيِّبَاتِ
وَفَضَّلْنَاهُمْ عَلَى كَثِيرٍ مِّمَّنْ خَلَقْنَا تَفْضِيلًا ۞ يَوْمَ نَدْعُوا
كُلَّ أُنَاسٍ بِإِمَامِهِمْ فَمَنْ أُوتِيَ كِتَابَهُ بِيَمِينِهِ فَأُوْلَئِكَ
يَقْرَءُونَ كِتَابَهُمْ وَلَا يُظْلَمُونَ فَتِيلًا ۞ وَمَن كَانَ فِي
هَذِهِ أَعْمَى فَهُوَ فِي الْآخِرَةِ أَعْمَى وَأَضَلُّ سَبِيلًا ۞ وَإِن كَادُوا
لَيَفْتِنُونَكَ عَنِ الَّذِي أَوْحَيْنَا إِلَيْكَ لِتَفْتَرِيَ عَلَيْنَا غَيْرَهُ
وَإِذًا لَّاتَّخَذُوكَ خَلِيلًا ۞ وَلَوْلَا أَن ثَبَّتْنَاكَ لَقَدْ كِدتَّ
تَرْكَنُ إِلَيْهِمْ شَيْئًا قَلِيلًا ۞ إِذًا لَّأَذَقْنَاكَ ضِعْفَ الْحَيَاةِ
وَضِعْفَ الْمَمَاتِ ثُمَّ لَا تَجِدُ لَكَ عَلَيْنَا نَصِيرًا ۞

67. When distress afflicts you in the sea, all that you invoke (as powers to help you) fail you save Him only; yet when He brings you safe to land, you turn away from Him. Indeed human is ever ungrateful.

68. Do you then feel secure that He will not cause a part of the land to (fall on you and) engulf you, or send a sand-storm upon you? Then you will not find a protecting guardian for yourselves.

69. Or do you feel secure that He will not send you back (to the sea) another time, and send against you a raging tempest to drown you because you disbelieve in ingratitude? Then you find none to uphold you against Us.

70. Assuredly We have honored the children of Adam (with many distinctions): We have sustained their traveling on the land and the sea, and provided for them (their sustenance) out of pure, wholesome things, and preferred them above many of those whom We have created with particular preferment.

71. On the Day when We will call every human community with its leader: whoever (has followed a leader towards true faith and righteousness and accountability in the Hereafter) is given his Record (of his life) in his right hand – those will read their Record with contentment and they will not be wronged by even so much as a tiny hair.

72. Whoever is blind in this (world) (who has followed no guidance towards true faith and righteousness and accountability in the Hereafter), will be blind in the Hereafter, and even further astray from the way (that leads to Divine forgiveness and eternal contentment).[30]

73. They have indeed sought to tempt you (O Messenger) away from what We have revealed to you so that you may fabricate something else against Us. And then (had you done so), they would have taken you as a trusted friend.

74. And had We not made you wholly firm (in what We reveal to you), you might just have inclined to them a little bit.

75. In that case, We would have made you taste double punishment in life and double punishment after death, and you would have found none to help you against Us.[31]

30. As the Qur'ān explicitly states (6: 38), all beings created live in communities, and God, Who does not leave the bees without a queen bee nor the ants without a leader, does not leave humankind without a true leader. So, throughout history He sent to every community a Messenger and granted a Book to the leading ones among them, such as Abraham, Moses, Jesus, and Muḥammad, upon them be peace. After the Messengers, He sent Prophets in their footsteps, and after the Last Messenger – Muḥammad – He has created leading scholars and guides who have fulfilled the mission of the Prophets, except that they did not receive Revelation. This is because, unlike the previous Books, the Qur'ān has remained intact, without the least change or interpolation.

God has honored human beings with distinctive attributes and abilities, such as intellect, conscious nature, and heart (spiritual intellect). However, although the Divine Book is a leader (11: 17), every human being is not able to understand it properly or deduce from it the principles for the governance of human life in every age and all conditions. This is why God has favored some persons with perfect guidance, namely the Prophets, and those loyal to God, who are truthful in whatever they do and say, and the witnessing saints, who have seen the hidden Divine truths, the existence of which they bear witness to with their lives, and the righteous in all their deeds and sayings and those dedicated to setting everything right (4: 69). He has ordered us to pray to Him in every *rak'ah* of the daily Prescribed Prayers (in *Sūrat al-Fātiḥah*, 1: 6–7) to guide us to the Straight Path, as the Path of those whom He has favored; that is, those whom He has mentioned in 4: 69. So, what a person should do – if they do not have the necessary ability and purity to understand the Divine Book properly and infer from it and the Prophetic Sunnah the necessary rules to order their life according to God's Will and lead others – is not to be blind to the truth but to try to find a true leader. God has promised that He will guide those who strive for His sake to any of the paths that lead to the Straight Path (29:

69). Whoever tries to find this Path sincerely, will most certainly find what they seek.

31. God's Messenger, upon him be peace and blessings, submitted himself wholly to God and fulfilled his mission solely because God commanded him to. He never resorted to compromise in order to be successful and never deviated from his way.

When he began preaching his Message, he had to face severe opposition, but he confronted all the opposition with a smile on his lips. He stood firm, undeterred by criticism and coercion. When the locals realized that the threats had failed to frighten him and that the severest treatment of his person and his followers had not made them move even an inch, they played another trick on him – but that too was destined to failure.

A deputation of the leading Quraysh, his tribe, called upon the Prophet, upon him be peace and blessings, and tried to bribe him by offering all the worldly glory they could imagine. They said: "If you want to possess wealth, we will amass for you as much as you wish; if you aspire to win honor and power, we are prepared to swear allegiance to you as our overlord and king; if you have a fancy for beauty, you shall have the hand of the most beautiful maiden of your choice."

They wanted him to make a compromise, even if he did not abandon his mission. The terms were extremely tempting for any ordinary mortal, but they were of no significance in the eyes of the great Prophet, who replied:

> I want neither wealth nor power. I have been commissioned by God as a warner to humankind. I deliver His message to you. Should you accept it, you shall have felicity and joy in this life and eternal bliss in the life to come; should you reject the Word of God, surely God will decide between you and me.

On another occasion he said to his uncle, who, because of pressure from the leaders of Arabia, was trying to persuade him to abandon his mission: "O uncle! Should they place the sun in my right hand and the moon in my left, so as to make me renounce this mission, I will not do so. I will never give it up; either it will please God to make it triumph or I will perish in the attempt" (Ibn Hishām, 2: 285).

The unbelievers of the Prophet's time were the most refractory and bitterest unbelievers of all times, and so were the hypocrites. But the Messenger was never inclined to make a compromise; he never even contemplated the idea, by God's help and grace. In the words of Said Nursi:

> In his preaching of the Message and in his calling people to the truth, he displayed such steadfastness, firmness, and courage that, in spite of the antagonism of great powers and religions, and those of his own people and tribe, even of his uncle, he never showed even the slightest trace of hesitation, anxiety, or fear, and he successfully challenged the world; as a result, he made Islam superior to all other religions and systems. This proves that there is not and cannot be anyone like him

in his preaching of and calling to the message of the truth.

> He had such extraordinary strength, such wonderful certainty, such miraculous perseverance, and such elevated and world-enlightening conviction in his faith that none of the prevailing ideas and beliefs of that time, and none of the philosophies of the sages and teachings of the spiritual leaders, although they were all opposed and even hostile to him, were ever able to cause him any doubt, hesitation, or anxiety concerning his certainty, conviction, and assurance. Moreover, all saintly men throughout time, especially his Companions, have all benefited from his faith, which they admit to be of the highest degree. (*The Letters*, "the 19th Letter," 1: 267)

The verse also teaches that for people to be able to overcome all the plots of the unbelievers they are in dire need of God's help and support; without this no one can ever be successful.

٢٨٩ الجزء الخامس عشر

وَإِن كَادُوا لَيَسْتَفِزُّونَكَ مِنَ ٱلْأَرْضِ لِيُخْرِجُوكَ مِنْهَا وَإِذًا لَّا يَلْبَثُونَ خِلَـٰفَكَ إِلَّا قَلِيلًا ۝ سُنَّةَ مَن قَدْ أَرْسَلْنَا قَبْلَكَ مِن رُّسُلِنَا وَلَا تَجِدُ لِسُنَّتِنَا تَحْوِيلًا ۝ أَقِمِ ٱلصَّلَوٰةَ لِدُلُوكِ ٱلشَّمْسِ إِلَىٰ غَسَقِ ٱلَّيْلِ وَقُرْءَانَ ٱلْفَجْرِ إِنَّ قُرْءَانَ ٱلْفَجْرِ كَانَ مَشْهُودًا ۝ وَمِنَ ٱلَّيْلِ فَتَهَجَّدْ بِهِۦ نَافِلَةً لَّكَ عَسَىٰٓ أَن يَبْعَثَكَ رَبُّكَ مَقَامًا مَّحْمُودًا ۝ وَقُل رَّبِّ أَدْخِلْنِي مُدْخَلَ صِدْقٍ وَأَخْرِجْنِي مُخْرَجَ صِدْقٍ وَٱجْعَل لِّي مِن لَّدُنكَ سُلْطَانًا نَّصِيرًا ۝ وَقُلْ جَآءَ ٱلْحَقُّ وَزَهَقَ ٱلْبَاطِلُ إِنَّ ٱلْبَاطِلَ كَانَ زَهُوقًا ۝ وَنُنَزِّلُ مِنَ ٱلْقُرْءَانِ مَا هُوَ شِفَآءٌ وَرَحْمَةٌ لِّلْمُؤْمِنِينَ وَلَا يَزِيدُ ٱلظَّـٰلِمِينَ إِلَّا خَسَارًا ۝ وَإِذَآ أَنْعَمْنَا عَلَى ٱلْإِنسَـٰنِ أَعْرَضَ وَنَـَٔا بِجَانِبِهِۦ وَإِذَا مَسَّهُ ٱلشَّرُّ كَانَ يَـُٔوسًا ۝ قُلْ كُلٌّ يَعْمَلُ عَلَىٰ شَاكِلَتِهِۦ فَرَبُّكُمْ أَعْلَمُ بِمَنْ هُوَ أَهْدَىٰ سَبِيلًا ۝ وَيَسْـَٔلُونَكَ عَنِ ٱلرُّوحِ قُلِ ٱلرُّوحُ مِنْ أَمْرِ رَبِّي وَمَآ أُوتِيتُم مِّنَ ٱلْعِلْمِ إِلَّا قَلِيلًا ۝ وَلَئِن شِئْنَا لَنَذْهَبَنَّ بِٱلَّذِىٓ أَوْحَيْنَآ إِلَيْكَ ثُمَّ لَا تَجِدُ لَكَ بِهِۦ عَلَيْنَا وَكِيلًا ۝

---------❧---------

76. Indeed they have sought to estrange you from the land (of your birth) and drive you from it; but then, they themselves will not remain there, after you, except a little while.

77. (That has been Our) way with all those whom We sent (as Messengers) before you. You will not find any alteration in Our way.[32]

78. Establish the Prayer in conformity with its conditions, from the declining of the sun to the darkness of the night, and (be ever observant of) the recitation of the Qur'ān at dawn (the Dawn Prayer). Surely the recitation of the Qur'ān at dawn is witnessed (by the angels and the whole creation awakening to a new day).[33]

79. And in some part of the night rise from sleep and observe vigil therein

(through the Prayer and recitation of the Qur'ān) as additional worship for you;[34] your Lord may well raise you to a glorious, praised station (of nearness to Him and give you leave to intercede with Him, as He wills, on behalf of His servants, in the Hereafter).

80. And say: "My Lord! Cause me to enter in a manner sincere and faithful to the truth, and cause me to exit in a manner sincere and faithful to the truth, and grant me from Your Presence a sustaining authority!"[35]

81. And say: "The truth has come, and falsehood has vanished. Surely falsehood is ever bound to vanish by its very nature."

82. We are sending down the Qur'ān in parts – it is a healing and a mercy for the believers, though for the wrongdoers it increases them only in ruin.

83. When We favor human (an ungrateful one) with comfort and contentment, he draws aside and arrogantly keeps aloof (from any thought of Us), but when evil touches him, he is ever despairing.

84. Say: "Every one acts according to his own character (made up of his creed, worldview and disposition), and your Lord knows best who is better guided in his way."

85. They ask you about the spirit. Say: "The spirit is of my Lord's Command,[36] and of knowledge, you have been granted only a little."

86. (You are not, as the unbelievers allege, the author of the Qur'ān. It is only We Who reveal it entirely.) If We willed, We could certainly take away what We have revealed to you (by effacing it from the hearts and memory of you and those who have memorized it, and from any written record of it). Then you would find for yourself no protecting guardian against Us (to help you to claim or recover it) –

32. The verse alludes to and gives tidings of the Messenger's emigration to Madīnah. For the meaning and importance of emigration (*Hijrah*) for those who follow a sacred cause, see *sūrah* 19, note 10.

As emigration has a very important place in the preaching of the Divine Message and the missions and lives of those who carry it out, any people who force their Messenger to leave his native land are either destroyed or exposed to another calamity or defeated by the Messenger and his new followers. They cannot remain long in their former state. So, verse 76 gives the tidings that those who forced the Messenger to leave Makkah would be destroyed soon after his departure. And this happened. The leading opponents of Islam in Makkah were killed in the Battle of Badr two years after the Messenger's emigration, and Makkah was conquered six years later.

33. This verse alludes to the five daily Prescribed Prayers and the time of each prayer. The declining of the sun means that the sun has passed its zenith and therefore indicates the Noon Prayer. After the Noon Prayer comes the Afternoon Prayer. Immediately after sunset and after night has fully fallen, the Evening and Late Evening Prayers are performed respectively. The verse specifically mentions the Dawn or Morning Prayer because of its importance and draws attention to the recitation of the Qur'ān during this time. The Messenger, under Divine Revelation, used to lengthen his recitation in the Dawn Prayer. In addition, recitation at this time is more effective upon our hearts.

Although the Prayer was prescribed in the early days of Islam, it was only established as five daily Prayers at the Ascension. This *sūrah*, which begins with mention of this miraculous journey, contains this prescription.

Although the Qur'ān mentions some pillars of the Prayer, such as bowing and prostration, it does not specify all the pillars and other acts, nor does it describe how they must be performed. The Messenger performed the Prayer according to how God had taught him and he declared: "Establish the Prayer the way you see me establishing it" (al-Bukhārī, "Ṣalāh," 70; Muslim, "Nikāḥ," 5). So, like all other forms of worship, the way of establishing the Prayer is completely dependent on the Sunnah.

34. Each occasion of the Prayer is not only the opening of a significant turning-point but also a mirror to the Divine disposal of power and to the universal Divine bounties within that disposal. We are enjoined to perform the Prescribed Prayers at these defined times so as to give more adoration and glory to the All-Powerful One of Majesty and to give more thanks to Him for all the bounties that have been accumulated between any two occasions, which is the meaning of the Prescribed Prayers.

The consecutive divisions of day and night, the years and phases of each individual's life in the world are, as it were, an immense clock, the parts of which function like the wheels and cogs which calculate seconds, minutes and hours as they move. For example:

The time of *Fajr* (dawn or early morning) which is designated for the Morning Prayer, may be likened to the birth of spring, or the moment when sperm takes refuge in the protective womb, or to the first of the six consecutive "day"s during which the earth and the sky were created, and it recalls how God disposes His Power and acts at such times and events.

The time of *Ẓuhr* (just past midday) may be likened to the completion of adolescence, or the middle of summer, or the period of humankind's creation in the lifetime of the world. It too points to God's compassionate manifestations and abundant blessings in those events and periods of time.

The time of *'Aṣr* (afternoon) resembles autumn, old age, and the time of the Last Prophet, known as the Time of Happiness. It calls to mind the Divine acts and the favors of the All-Compassionate in them.

The time of *Maghrib* (sunset) reminds us of the decline of many creatures at the end of autumn, and the death of individual persons and, at the end of time, of humankind as a whole. It thus forewarns us of the destruction of the world at the beginning of Resurrection and also teaches us how to understand the manifestation of God's Majesty and in this way wakes us from a deep sleep of neglect.

The time of *'Ishā* (nightfall), calls to mind how the world of darkness veils all the objects of the daytime with its black shroud, and winter covers the surface of the dead earth with its white robe. It brings to mind, also, how the remaining works of the dead are completely forgotten, and points out to us the inevitable, complete decline of this world, which is a place of testing. Thus *'Ishā* proclaims the awesome acts of the All-Powerful One of Majesty.

As for night-time, if we bring to mind winter, the grave, and the Intermediate World, we are reminded how much our spirit is really in need of the Mercy of the All-Merciful One.

The *Tahajjud* Prayer, in the later, deeper part of the night, reminds and warns us how necessary this Prayer will be as a light in the darkness of the grave. In this way, by recalling the infinite bounties of the True Bestower that have been granted to humankind within the sequence of all these extraordinary events, it proclaims how worthy He is of praise and thanks.

The following morning is a time that points to the Resurrection or the morning that follows the destruction of the world. Just as it is reasonable, necessary, and certain that morning follows night, and spring comes after winter, so too will the morning of the Resurrection follow death.

We now understand that each appointed occasion for the five daily Prayers is itself the beginning of a vital turning-point and a reminder of greater revolutions or turning-points in the life of the universe. Through the incredible daily gifts of the Power of the Eternally Besought One, the times of the Prayers call to mind the miracles of Divine Power and the gifts of Divine Mercy found in every year, every age, and every epoch. So, the Prescribed Prayers, which are an innate need and the firm foundation of worship, and an unquestionable duty of humankind, are most appropriate and fitted for these times (See *The Words*, "the 9th Word," 58–59).

35. This prayer, taught to the Messenger by God, indicates that the time of the emigration to Madīnah is close at hand. According to some, God taught it when the Messenger approached Madīnah during the *Hijrah*. It was a practice and recommendation of the Messenger to say this prayer when entering and leaving a place. It also instructs us in what manner we should enter a place and leave it.

36. About the spirit, see Appendix 12.

الَا رَحْمَةً مِّنْ رَّبِّكَ إِنَّ فَضْلَهُ كَانَ عَلَيْكَ كَبِيرًا ۞ قُلْ لَّئِنِ
اجْتَمَعَتِ الْإِنْسُ وَالْجِنُّ عَلَى أَنْ يَأْتُوا بِمِثْلِ هَٰذَا الْقُرْآنِ لَا يَأْتُونَ
بِمِثْلِهِ وَلَوْ كَانَ بَعْضُهُمْ لِبَعْضٍ ظَهِيرًا ۞ وَلَقَدْ صَرَّفْنَا
لِلنَّاسِ فِي هَٰذَا الْقُرْآنِ مِنْ كُلِّ مَثَلٍ فَأَبَىٰ أَكْثَرُ النَّاسِ
إِلَّا كُفُورًا ۞ وَقَالُوا لَنْ نُّؤْمِنَ لَكَ حَتَّىٰ تَفْجُرَ لَنَا
مِنَ الْأَرْضِ يَنْبُوعًا ۞ أَوْ تَكُونَ لَكَ جَنَّةٌ مِّنْ نَّخِيلٍ
وَعِنَبٍ فَتُفَجِّرَ الْأَنْهَارَ خِلَالَهَا تَفْجِيرًا ۞ أَوْ تُسْقِطَ
السَّمَاءَ كَمَا زَعَمْتَ عَلَيْنَا كِسَفًا أَوْ تَأْتِيَ بِاللَّهِ وَالْمَلَائِكَةِ
قَبِيلًا ۞ أَوْ يَكُونَ لَكَ بَيْتٌ مِّنْ زُخْرُفٍ أَوْ تَرْقَىٰ فِي السَّمَاءِ وَلَنْ
نُّؤْمِنَ لِرُقِيِّكَ حَتَّىٰ تُنَزِّلَ عَلَيْنَا كِتَابًا نَّقْرَؤُهُ
قُلْ سُبْحَانَ رَبِّي هَلْ كُنْتُ إِلَّا بَشَرًا رَّسُولًا ۞ وَمَا مَنَعَ النَّاسَ
أَنْ يُّؤْمِنُوا إِذْ جَاءَهُمُ الْهُدَىٰ إِلَّا أَنْ قَالُوا أَبَعَثَ اللَّهُ بَشَرًا
رَّسُولًا ۞ قُلْ لَّوْ كَانَ فِي الْأَرْضِ مَلَائِكَةٌ يَمْشُونَ مُطْمَئِنِّينَ
لَنَزَّلْنَا عَلَيْهِمْ مِّنَ السَّمَاءِ مَلَكًا رَّسُولًا ۞ قُلْ كَفَىٰ بِاللَّهِ شَهِيدًا
بَيْنِي وَبَيْنَكُمْ إِنَّهُ كَانَ بِعِبَادِهِ خَبِيرًا بَصِيرًا ۞

87. But (you are one favored with) a great, special mercy from your Lord. His favor on you is great indeed.

88. Say: "Surely, if humankind and the jinn were to come together to produce the like of this Qur'ān, they will never be able to produce the like of it, though they backed one another up with help and support.

89. Assuredly We have set out in diverse ways for humankind in this Qur'ān all kinds of parables and comparisons (to help them understand the truth), yet most people refuse to accept anything save unbelief.

90. They say: "We will not believe in you (O Messenger) until you cause a spring to gush forth for us from this land (which is short of water);

91. "Or you have a garden of date-palms and grapes, and cause rivers to gush forth in their midst abundantly;

92. "Or you cause the heaven to fall upon us in pieces, as you have claimed (could happen), or bring God and the angels as a warrant (before our eyes proving the truth of your message);

93. "Or you have a house of gold, or you ascend to the heaven. But we will even then not believe in your ascension until you bring down upon us (from heaven) a book that we can read." Say, (O Messenger): "All-Glorified is my Lord (in that He is absolutely above what you conceive of Him)! Am I anything but a mortal sent as a Messenger?"

94. And what has kept people from believing when guidance has come to them, except that they said: "Has God sent a mortal man as the Messenger?"

95. Say: "If angels had been walking about on earth as their abode, We would surely have sent down upon them an angel from heaven as Messenger."

96. Say: "God suffices for a witness between me and you. Surely He is fully aware of His servants, and sees them well."

وَمَن يَهْدِ اللَّهُ فَهُوَ الْمُهْتَدِ وَمَن يُضْلِلْ فَلَن تَجِدَ لَهُمْ
أَوْلِيَاءَ مِن دُونِهِ وَنَحْشُرُهُمْ يَوْمَ الْقِيَامَةِ عَلَىٰ وُجُوهِهِمْ
عُمْيًا وَبُكْمًا وَصُمًّا مَأْوَاهُمْ جَهَنَّمُ كُلَّمَا خَبَتْ زِدْنَاهُمْ
سَعِيرًا ۝ ذَٰلِكَ جَزَاؤُهُم بِأَنَّهُمْ كَفَرُوا بِآيَاتِنَا وَقَالُوا أَإِذَا
كُنَّا عِظَامًا وَرُفَاتًا أَإِنَّا لَمَبْعُوثُونَ خَلْقًا جَدِيدًا ۝ أَوَلَمْ
يَرَوْا أَنَّ اللَّهَ الَّذِي خَلَقَ السَّمَاوَاتِ وَالْأَرْضَ قَادِرٌ عَلَىٰ أَن يَخْلُقَ
مِثْلَهُمْ وَجَعَلَ لَهُمْ أَجَلًا لَا رَيْبَ فِيهِ فَأَبَى الظَّالِمُونَ إِلَّا كُفُورًا
۝ قُل لَّوْ أَنتُمْ تَمْلِكُونَ خَزَائِنَ رَحْمَةِ رَبِّي إِذًا لَّأَمْسَكْتُمْ
خَشْيَةَ الْإِنفَاقِ وَكَانَ الْإِنسَانُ قَتُورًا ۝ وَلَقَدْ آتَيْنَا
مُوسَىٰ تِسْعَ آيَاتٍ بَيِّنَاتٍ فَاسْأَلْ بَنِي إِسْرَائِيلَ إِذْ جَاءَهُمْ
فَقَالَ لَهُ فِرْعَوْنُ إِنِّي لَأَظُنُّكَ يَا مُوسَىٰ مَسْحُورًا ۝ قَالَ
لَقَدْ عَلِمْتَ مَا أَنزَلَ هَٰؤُلَاءِ إِلَّا رَبُّ السَّمَاوَاتِ وَالْأَرْضِ
بَصَائِرَ وَإِنِّي لَأَظُنُّكَ يَا فِرْعَوْنُ مَثْبُورًا ۝ فَأَرَادَ أَن يَسْتَفِزَّهُم
مِّنَ الْأَرْضِ فَأَغْرَقْنَاهُ وَمَن مَّعَهُ جَمِيعًا ۝ وَقُلْنَا مِن بَعْدِهِ لِبَنِي
إِسْرَائِيلَ اسْكُنُوا الْأَرْضَ فَإِذَا جَاءَ وَعْدُ الْآخِرَةِ جِئْنَا بِكُمْ لَفِيفًا ۝

---

97. Whoever God guides, then he it is who is rightly guided; and whoever He leads astray, you shall find for them, apart from Him, no guardians (who might own and help them). We will raise to life and gather them together on the Day of Resurrection prone upon their faces, blind, dumb, and deaf. Their refuge is Hell – every time it (seems to them that its torment) is abating (because of their being inured to it), We increase them in (suffering in its) blazing flame.

98. That will be their recompense because they disbelieved in Our Revelations and signs (manifesting the truth) and said: "What! is it when we have already become bones and particles of dust – is it then that we will be raised as a new creation?"

99. Do they never consider that God Who has created the heavens and the earth, (the creation of which is something greater than the creation of human and never wearied Him) is able to create them (the dead) anew in their own likeness? And He has set a term for them about which there is no doubt; yet the wrongdoers refuse to accept anything save unbelief.

100. Say: "If you possessed the treasures of my Lord's Mercy, still you would surely hold them back for fear of spending (in God's cause and as subsistence for the needy)." Indeed human is ever grudging.

101. We certainly granted to Moses nine clear signs (miracles).[37] So ask the Children of Israel (what happened despite these miracles): when he came to them (and asked the Pharaoh to let the Children of Israel leave Egypt with him, and even after he showed to them these miracles), the Pharaoh said to him: "Certainly, O Moses, I certainly believe that you are one bewitched."

102. (Moses) said: "You know for certain that no one but the Lord of the heavens and the earth has sent down these (signs) as openings to discernment and insight. And certainly, O Pharaoh, I certainly believe that you are one doomed to loss."

103. Then the Pharaoh intended to terrify them from the land (of Egypt) and destroy them, but We caused him and all who were with him to drown.[38]

104. And after that We said to the Children of Israel: "Dwell now securely in the land (which God has decreed for you and commanded you to enter). But when the time (for the fulfillment) of the last decree comes, We will bring you as a mixed crowd (gathered from disparate nations).[39]

37. This, again, is in response to the Makkan polytheists' demands that the Messenger of God work miracles. God granted Moses nine miracles as clear signs of the truth of his message, but despite all these, Pharaoh and his people persisted in unbelief. Some of these miracles are mentioned in 7: 133: *We sent upon them floods and (plagues of) locusts and vermin, and frogs, and (water turning into) blood: distinct signs one after another.* The other three are: the Staff, Moses' white, radiant hand, and the defeat of the magicians' magic. Moses performed other miracles, such as making water gush forth from a rock by striking it with his staff, and bringing a cow back to life by striking it with a bone from its leg. However, the nine miracles mentioned in the verse are those that were shown to the Pharaoh and his people in particular. Despite these miracles, the Pharaoh and his people persisted in unbelief. So, the unbelievers were not sincere in their demand for miracles. They demanded them only in order to cause problems for the Prophets. They well knew that the Prophets were not lying when they declared their Prophethood. There were many irrefutable proofs that showed the sincerity of the Prophets; their truthfulness, trustworthiness, intelligence, and sinlessness are a few examples. However, when the people persisted in unbelief willfully, despite the miracles which they had demanded and which had been shown to them, they usually got what they deserved.

Being the last Divine Book valid until the Day of Judgment, and as a Book that serves us at a time when humankind have inclined greatly toward reason, sciences, and the exploration of the universe, the Qur'ān frequently and insistently calls on people to think, study, and reflect on the "natural" phenomena and the history of human communities. For this reason, except for a few times, like the Ascension and the splitting of the moon, God's Messenger did not work miracles that were visible to all during the Makkan period of his mission, the time when he preached the pillars of faith. Rather, he worked most of his miracles in Madīnah only in order to meet a need; these miracles were performed when there was no other way to solve a problem, such as the miraculous abundance of food or water, or a little food or water becoming sufficient for many people, and water flowing from his fingers. The Qur'ān is his greatest, lasting miracle, and the greatest of all the miracles performed by all the Prophets.

38. The Qur'ān is full of tidings of many future events, some of which it mentions explicitly, such as the victory of the Romans over the Sassanids (30: 2–3), and the conquest of Makkah by the believers (48: 27), and others which are implied. In verse 76 above, the Qur'ān threatens the Makkan polytheists who tried to drive the Messenger away from Makkah, saying: *Indeed they have sought to estrange you from the land (of your birth) and drive you from it; but then, they themselves will not remain there, after you, except a little while.*

It strengthened this threat by adding that God always punishes those who drive Prophets from their home by destroying them: *(That has been Our) way with all those whom We sent (as Messengers) before you. You will not find any means to change Our way* (77). Verse 103 substantiates the threat with an important example from history and hints that those who forced the Messenger to leave Makkah would soon be destroyed. This took place two years after the Messenger's emigration to Madīnah at the Battle of Badr, in which 70 of all leading Makkans were killed, and six years later, the Messenger conquered Makkah.

39. The original of the statement *when the time (for the fulfillment) of the last decree comes*, is exactly the same as that which is in verse 7 above, which expresses the second rise and decline of the Children of Israel (narrated in note 6 above). This must be referring to the last phase of the second decline, which ended in their dispersal throughout the world as the consequence of their own deeds and their coming together again in Palestine to establish a state in 1948. This concentration may continue for some time more, and the future will show what the Almighty will do with them.

However, as the word translated as the *last decree* also means the Last Day, the statement threatens them with a doom decreed after their coming together for the last time, and with the inevitable end that they will be questioned in the Hereafter for all that they did in the world. So, the verse is a miraculously succinct summary of the history of the Children of Israel.

105. It is with the truth that We have sent it down (this Qur'ān, embodying the truth and forever invulnerable to falsehood), and it is with the truth that it has come down. We have not sent you but as a bearer of glad tidings (of prosperity in return for faith and righteousness) and a warner (against the evil consequences of misguidance).

106. And (it is) a Qur'ān that We set forth in parts with clarity so that you may recite and convey it to people with deliberation (in order that they can absorb it), and We send it down in successive Revelations (each perfectly suited to its occasion and its wider purpose).

107. Say: "Believe in it or do not believe." Surely those who were endowed before it with knowledge (of the truth and Divine Revelation and teachings, and still follow that knowledge), fall down on their faces in prostration when the Qur'ān is recited to them.

108. They say: "All-Glorified is our Lord. Surely the promise of our Lord is ever bound to be fulfilled."

109. And they fall down on their faces, weeping, and it increases them in humility and a feeling of awe.[40]

110. Say: "Call upon Him as *Allāh* (God) or call upon Him as *ar-Rahmān* (the All-Merciful). By whichever Name you call upon Him, to Him belong the All-Beautiful Names.[41] And offer your Prayer neither in too loud a voice nor in a voice too low, but follow a middle course.[42]

111. And say: "All praise and gratitude are for God, Who has neither taken to Him a child, nor has a partner in the Sovereignty (the dominion and ownership of the whole creation), nor (being exalted above all want or insufficiency) has He a guardian against neediness and weakness. And exalt Him with His immeasurable greatness.

40. When those endowed with knowledge of the truth and Divine Revelation and teachings, whether from among the People of the Book or others, recite or listen to the Qur'ān, they immediately understand that it belongs to God, and cannot help but fall down on their faces in prostration before God. When they see that what God promised concerning the advent of Prophet Muḥammad, upon him be peace and blessings, and many other important events, like the sending of the Last Book, which came as the Qur'ān, were all fulfilled, they once more prostrate themselves before God in increasing humility and a feeling of awe before Him.

41. Almighty God has many Names that are included in the Qur'ān and which were taught by the Messenger. They are all the All-Beautiful Names in the sense that all of God's Titles and Attributes used to describe Him and His acts are absolutely free of any defect, because God is absolutely perfect and whatever He does and decrees is absolutely good and free of any flaw. *Allāh* (God) and *ar-Raḥmān* (the All-Merciful One) are His proper Names, names by which any other being cannot be called. For further explanations about Names, God and the All-Merciful, see *al-Fātiḥah*, notes 2–4.

42. One should neither raise the voice too loud nor keep it too low in one's invocations. The Qur'ān orders: *Remember and mention your Lord within yourself (in the depths of your heart), most humbly and in awe, not loud of voice, at morning and evening* (7: 205). In one's Prayer (the *Ṣalāh*), a person should recite loud enough so that they are distinctly able to hear their own recitation. It was a practice of the Prophet which we must follow that during the Morning, Evening and Late Evening or Nightfall Prayers, the Qur'ān is to be recited loud enough that those standing behind can hear, while the Noon and Afternoon Prayers should be recited in a voice that only the worshipper him/herself can hear.

SŪRAH 18

AL-KAHF (THE CAVE)

Makkah period

This sūrah was revealed in the Makkah period of the Messenger's mission, at a time when the polytheists had begun to escalate their opposition to the preaching of Islam. Searching for a way to stop this preaching the Makkans occasionally made contact with the People of the Book, in particular the Jews in Madīnah and neighboring lands in order to get from them questions they could put to the Messenger, upon him be peace and blessings. This sūrah apparently was revealed in response to questions about the People of the Cave, the story of Moses and al-Khadr, and Dhu'l-Qarnayn. It also contains the parable of two friends who owned vineyards. It is as if this sūrah has drawn a road map for us to follow in the preaching of Islam.

The sūrah takes its name from the ninth verse, where the People of the Cave are mentioned. It consists of 110 verses.

In the Name of God, the All-Merciful, the All-Compassionate.

1. All praise and gratitude are for God, Who has sent down on His servant the Book and has put no crookedness in it (so that it is free from contradiction and inconsistency, and anything offensive to truth and righteousness).

2. (He has made it) unerringly straight, to warn of a stern punishment from Him and give the believers who do good, righteous deeds the glad tidings that for them is an excellent reward (Paradise),

3. Abiding therein forever,

4. And to warn those who say: "God has taken to Him a child."[1]

---

1. It is clear that in the early years of Islam some among the Jews and Christians supported the Makkan polytheists in their hostilities. The previous sūrah ends by declaring that God has not taken to Himself a child, and this sūrah begins by declaring the same truth. By pronouncing that God has not taken to Himself a child, the Qur'ān is saying that God has no offspring and categorically rejects the polytheists who claim that He has taken angels for daughters, and the Christians who assert that Jesus is the son of God, and the claim of some Jews that Ezra is son of God.

As has been generally accepted by Qur'ānic commentators, the Companions of the Cave, whose exemplary story will be told in the following verses, were among the monotheist followers of Jesus. The fact that the sūrah begins by rejecting the notion of Divine fatherhood may be meant to underline the truth of this view.

293   الْجُزْءُ الْخَامِسَ عَشَر   ۲۹۳

> مَالَهُمْ بِهِ مِنْ عِلْمٍ وَلَا لِآبَآئِهِمْ كَبُرَتْ كَلِمَةً تَخْرُجُ مِنْ
> اَفْوَاهِهِمْ اِنْ يَقُولُونَ اِلَّا كَذِبًا ۞ فَلَعَلَّكَ بَاخِعٌ
> نَفْسَكَ عَلَى آثَارِهِمْ اِنْ لَمْ يُؤْمِنُوا بِهٰذَا الْحَدِيثِ اَسَفًا ۞
> اِنَّا جَعَلْنَا مَا عَلَى الْاَرْضِ زِينَةً لَهَا لِنَبْلُوَهُمْ اَيُّهُمْ اَحْسَنُ عَمَلًا
> ۞ وَاِنَّا لَجَاعِلُونَ مَا عَلَيْهَا صَعِيدًا جُرُزًا ۞ اَمْ حَسِبْتَ
> اَنَّ اَصْحَابَ الْكَهْفِ وَالرَّقِيمِ كَانُوا مِنْ اٰيَاتِنَا عَجَبًا ۞ اِذْ
> اَوَى الْفِتْيَةُ اِلَى الْكَهْفِ فَقَالُوا رَبَّنَا اٰتِنَا مِنْ لَدُنْكَ
> رَحْمَةً وَهَيِّئْ لَنَا مِنْ اَمْرِنَا رَشَدًا ۞ فَضَرَبْنَا عَلَى اٰذَانِهِمْ
> فِي الْكَهْفِ سِنِينَ عَدَدًا ۞ ثُمَّ بَعَثْنَاهُمْ لِنَعْلَمَ اَيُّ
> الْحِزْبَيْنِ اَحْصَى لِمَا لَبِثُوا اَمَدًا ۞ نَحْنُ نَقُصُّ عَلَيْكَ
> نَبَاَهُمْ بِالْحَقِّ اِنَّهُمْ فِتْيَةٌ اٰمَنُوا بِرَبِّهِمْ وَزِدْنَاهُمْ هُدًى ۞
> وَرَبَطْنَا عَلَى قُلُوبِهِمْ اِذْ قَامُوا فَقَالُوا رَبُّنَا رَبُّ السَّمٰوَاتِ
> وَالْاَرْضِ لَنْ نَدْعُوَ مِنْ دُونِهِ اِلٰهًا لَقَدْ قُلْنَا اِذًا شَطَطًا
> ۞ هٰؤُلَاءِ قَوْمُنَا اتَّخَذُوا مِنْ دُونِهِ اٰلِهَةً لَوْلَا يَأْتُونَ عَلَيْهِمْ
> بِسُلْطَانٍ بَيِّنٍ فَمَنْ اَظْلَمُ مِمَّنِ افْتَرٰى عَلَى اللّٰهِ كَذِبًا ۞

---

5. Of that they have no knowledge (on which to base such an assertion), nor did their forefathers. Dreadful as a word is (that assertion) coming out of their mouths.[2] Indeed they speak nothing but falsehood.

6. Yet it may be that you (O Muḥammad) will torment yourself to death with grief, following after them, if they do not believe in this Message.[3]

7. We have surely made whatever is on the earth as an ornament for it (appealing to humanity), so that We may try them (by demonstrating it to themselves) which of them is best in conduct.

8. Yet We surely reduce whatever is on it to a barren dust-heap, (and will do so when the term of trial ends).

9. Or do you reckon the People of the Cave and the Inscription[4] as something strange among Our signs (manifesting the truth, and too extraordinary to believe)?

10. (Events came to the point) when the young men[5] took refuge in the cave and said: "Our Lord! Grant us mercy from Your Presence and arrange for us in our affair what is right and good!"

11. Then We drew a veil over their ears (causing them to go into a deep sleep) in the cave for a number of years.

12. Then We raised them up, (and dividing into two groups, they discussed how long they had remained in that state). We willed to make known which of the two groups were (more conscious of time with the events in it, and therefore) better in computing the time-span during which they had remained (in this state).

13. It is We who relate to you their exemplary story with truth. They were young men who believed in their Lord, and We increased them in guidance (so they adhered to the truth more faithfully).

14. And We strengthened their hearts, (and a time came) when they rose up (against association of partners with God and other injustices in the society), and they proclaimed: "Our Lord is the Lord of the heavens and the earth, and we never invoke any deity apart from Him; if we did so, we would certainly have uttered an enormity (a monstrous unbelief).

15. "These people of ours have adopted deities other than Him: although they cannot bring any clear authority for them. And who is more in the wrong than he who fabricates falsehood against God?"

2. The original word translated as *forefathers* means fathers as well and also implies the Fathers of the Church who established the Christian creeds. The usage of *word* in *Dreadful as a word is (that assertion) coming out of their mouths*, also implies this. Those Fathers did not base their claim that Jesus was the son of God on any knowledge, and their followers have done nothing more than blindly imitating them. Their assertion is mere words uttered out of ignorance and myth-making.

As pointed out in note 1 above, the verses also reject the polytheists' assertion that God has taken angels for daughters.

3. A Prophet is, in a way, obsessed with how he is to perform his duty. To this end, he considers all circumstances and does everything permitted. Many Prophets lived and died with no one accepting their Message. However, they did not lose heart, weaken in resolve, or resort to means not permitted by God, like violence, terror, or deception, despite having to suffer every kind of hardship and torture of the most pitiless sort. Every Prophet conveyed God's Message to his people without becoming weary or daunted. The harsh reactions of people could not hinder a Prophet from his duty.

The communication of the Divine Message was the most essential characteristic of God's Messenger, upon him be peace and blessings. We are troubled whenever we are hungry or thirsty, or when we have difficulty in breathing; but he was troubled if a day passed when he could not find someone to whom he could convey the Divine Message. There was nobody left in Makkah whom he had not invited in public or in private to God's path. He had called some, like Abū Jahl, who was extremely stubborn, at least fifty times. He was so concerned about the guidance of people, and so physically pained by unbelief, that God advised him in this verse to take care of his health.

4. According to some of the interpreters of the Qur'ān, *ar-Raqīm* (translated here as Inscription) is the name of the district where the Cave is located. Others are of the opinion that it is the epitaph which was placed at the Cave as a monument to the People of the Cave.

5. The word used to mean young (*fatā*) has a special meaning and usage in Islamic literature. Its infinitive form *futuwwah*, meaning youth and chivalry, is a composite of virtues, such as energy, revolutionary vigor, heroism, generosity, munificence, modesty, chastity, trustworthiness, loyalty, mercifulness, knowledge, humility, and piety.

Futuwwah also signifies an altruistic character that enjoys helping others, wishing no one any harm. It is an important, indispensable dimension of good conduct and a significant aspect of humanity.

Derived from *fatā* meaning young man, *futuwwah* has become a symbol of rebellion against all kinds of evil and of sincere servanthood to God as the way to attain true freedom.

Some have summed up the descriptions made for *futuwwah* in the following cardinal virtues, in addition to those mentioned above:

- Forgiving when one is able to punish.
- Preserving mildness and acting mildly and gently when one is angry.
- Wishing well for all, including one's enemies, and doing good.
- Always being considerate of the well-being and happiness of others first, even when one is needy.

The signs of one being a *fatā* (young, chivalrous one) are that their spirit, which was created with the potential to accept Divine Unity and Islam, has utmost conviction of Divine Unity and urges them to live according to the requirements of this conviction, and that, without being captivated by carnal or bodily desires, they live a pure, spiritual life, always aiming to please God in all acts, thoughts, and feelings. It is not possible for one who cannot be saved from the temptations of their carnal soul, from Satan, from bodily appetites, and from a love of the world or attachment to worldly life, to climb up toward the peak of *futuwwah*. (See *Key Concepts*, 1: 81–83.)

294 سُوْرَةُ الْكَهْف ٢٩٤

وَإِذِ اعْتَزَلْتُمُوهُمْ وَمَا يَعْبُدُونَ إِلَّا اللّٰهَ فَأْوُوا إِلَى الْكَهْفِ يَنْشُرْ لَكُمْ رَبُّكُمْ مِنْ رَحْمَتِهِ وَيُهَيِّئْ لَكُمْ مِنْ أَمْرِكُمْ مِرْفَقًا ۝ وَتَرَى الشَّمْسَ إِذَا طَلَعَتْ تَزَاوَرُ عَنْ كَهْفِهِمْ ذَاتَ الْيَمِينِ وَإِذَا غَرَبَتْ تَقْرِضُهُمْ ذَاتَ الشِّمَالِ وَهُمْ فِي فَجْوَةٍ مِنْهُ ذَلِكَ مِنْ آيَاتِ اللّٰهِ مَنْ يَهْدِ اللّٰهُ فَهُوَ الْمُهْتَدِ وَمَنْ يُضْلِلْ فَلَنْ تَجِدَ لَهُ وَلِيًّا مُرْشِدًا ۝ وَتَحْسَبُهُمْ أَيْقَاظًا وَهُمْ رُقُودٌ وَنُقَلِّبُهُمْ ذَاتَ الْيَمِينِ وَذَاتَ الشِّمَالِ وَكَلْبُهُمْ بَاسِطٌ ذِرَاعَيْهِ بِالْوَصِيدِ لَوِ اطَّلَعْتَ عَلَيْهِمْ لَوَلَّيْتَ مِنْهُمْ فِرَارًا وَلَمُلِئْتَ مِنْهُمْ رُعْبًا ۝ وَكَذَلِكَ بَعَثْنَاهُمْ لِيَتَسَاءَلُوا بَيْنَهُمْ قَالَ قَائِلٌ مِنْهُمْ كَمْ لَبِثْتُمْ قَالُوا لَبِثْنَا يَوْمًا أَوْ بَعْضَ يَوْمٍ قَالُوا رَبُّكُمْ أَعْلَمُ بِمَا لَبِثْتُمْ فَابْعَثُوا أَحَدَكُمْ بِوَرِقِكُمْ هَذِهِ إِلَى الْمَدِينَةِ فَلْيَنْظُرْ أَيُّهَا أَزْكَى طَعَامًا فَلْيَأْتِكُمْ بِرِزْقٍ مِنْهُ وَلْيَتَلَطَّفْ وَلَا يُشْعِرَنَّ بِكُمْ أَحَدًا ۝ إِنَّهُمْ إِنْ يَظْهَرُوا عَلَيْكُمْ يَرْجُمُوكُمْ أَوْ يُعِيدُوكُمْ فِي مِلَّتِهِمْ وَلَنْ تُفْلِحُوا إِذًا أَبَدًا ۝

16. (Events developed to the point that they had to leave their society. They discussed what they should do and concluded:) "And now that you have withdrawn yourselves from them and all that they worship instead of God, then seek refuge in the Cave. Your Lord will lay out for you of His mercy, and He will arrange for you in your affair a comfort and support."

17. (They entered the Cave and fell into a deep sleep.) You would have seen the sun, when it rose, moving away from their Cave to the right, and when it set, turning away from them to the left, while they lay in a spacious hollow in the Cave. That was one of God's signs.[6] Whoever God guides, he alone is rightly guided; and whoever He leads astray, you will never be able to find for him any guardian to guide him to the right way.

18. You would have thought them awake though they were asleep. We caused them to turn over to the right and the left, and their dog lay outstretching its two forelegs on the threshold. Had you come upon them unprepared, you would certainly have turned away from them in flight, and would certainly have been filled with awe of them.[7/8]

19. Such being their state, We raised them up so they began to ask one another. One who spoke said: "How long have you stayed?" They (some among them) answered: "We have stayed a day, or part of a day." The others said: "Your Lord knows better how long you have stayed. Now (we must deal with our hunger. So) send one of you to the city with this coin of yours: let him see what food is most pure there (and so lawful), and bring a supply from it. But let him behave with utmost care and guarded courtesy and by no means make anyone aware of you.

20. "Indeed, if they should find you out, they will stone you to death or turn you back to their way of belief and life by force, then you will never attain prosperity ever hereafter."[9]

6. The position of the cave was such that God protected the young men from sunlight and protected their skin color from changing and their clothes from fading. Although they remained in the Cave for many years asleep, when they awoke, nothing about them had changed; they had not even grown beards. This shows that either they entered a death-like sleep or that God guarded their bodies against any changes; this situation, whichever scenario is correct, should be investigated by science, as there will be some beneficial factors hidden in this event. The fact that they remained asleep for a long time without suffering any alterations in their appearance is an exceptional sign of God.

7. It can be understood from this verse that their eyes were open. The Almighty caused them to turn from their right to their left and from their left to their right, preventing sores on the body, and eventual decay of both their bodies and their clothes. Such movement prevented their bodies from becoming weak and listless. A number of people lying down, yet with their eyes open, people who are repeatedly turning over in a cave in a mountainous area who are guarded by a dog, must present an awesome spectacle. It is highly probable that there were other factors that would cause fear in those who saw them.

8. Who were these young men and where did their experience take place? Before proceeding to answer this question, we should remember that the Qur'ān is not a history book and that it recounts past, exemplary events in the most proper way to guide people to the pillars of the Religion, to establish these pillars in the minds and hearts of people. It does not usually mention the names of the people involved, nor does it designate time and place. Similar events may well have taken place and may take place in other places at other times.

According to considerably more reliable narratives, as the message of Jesus, upon him be peace, spread across neighboring lands, six youths from the royal class of the Romans in Syria-Jordan region gave up idol-worship,

accepting God as the only Deity and their True Lord. It was the years when the followers of Jesus' faith were being subjected to great tortures and persecutions. The Emperor Trajan (98–117) had issued a decree that any follower of Jesus would be tried as a traitor and sentenced to death. He was visiting the region when these six youths openly and fearlessly proclaimed their faith in his presence, saying that the Lord of the heavens and the earth was their One and only True Lord. The emperor gave them three days' respite to revert to their old faith. But they managed to leave the city secretly in 112 AD. A shepherd from a neighboring village joined them, with his dog following them up to the cave despite their efforts to dissuade it. They took shelter in a deep cave with the dog sitting at its mouth. Soon they fell into a deep sleep.

There are different views about which cave it was in which they took shelter. In 1963, near the village Rajīb, 80 kilometers from Amman, the capital of Jordan, a cave was excavated. When this cave was discovered, Rafiq Wafā al-Dujānī wrote his book entitled *Iktishāfu Kahfi Ahl al-Kahf* (Discovery of the Cave of the People of the Cave). It was seen that the cave and its neighboring land correlates with the Qur'ānic description.

Due to the fact that the question about the People of the Cave arose from the Jews, some commentators, like Ibn Kathīr, present another opinion that the People of the Cave lived before the time of Jesus, even though similar events may have taken place after Jesus. There are several caves in the world, each of which is claimed to have belonged to the People of the Cave. As we pointed out above, the Qur'ān is not a history book and it usually recounts past, exemplary events for its main purposes. So what is important is that we should draw the intended lessons from them.

9. Since the Qur'ān is never concerned with events for their own sake, it does not go further in narrating what happened in the city. But the words used enable the reader to guess what might have happened.

This was at a time when Christianity had

long ago been accepted as the official creed of the Roman Empire, and the Christians were fiercely divided on the question of life after death. Many people refused to believe in the Hereafter, at least in the bodily resurrection. The Emperor was keen to find some means whereby he could persuade the people to give up this denial. He was so concerned about the matter that on one occasion he earnestly prayed to God to show a miraculous sign that would make people believe in the bodily resurrection and afterlife. It was under such circumstances that the People of the Cave awoke from their sleep. According to the narratives, the one who was sent to the city went to a shop to buy bread and paid for it with an ancient silver coin. There was an altercation as the man was trying to pay with a three-hundred year old coin, and this drew a crowd. The crowd, amazed, took the man to the governor. The things that he saw in the city confused the young man. Everything had changed. The city they had had to leave was now a Christian city, Christianity having been adopted as the official creed of the Empire. He reported his story to the governor (or, according to another account, to the Emperor Theodosius the Younger (418–450). Greatly amazed, the governor (or the Emperor) followed the young man to the Cave, followed by a crowd. Seeing that the words of the young man were true, they marveled at God's power and providence. At that point God took their souls from the Cave, and belief in revival after death, a matter over which the people had been disputing for many years, was firmly planted in the hearts of the people.

295

وَكَذَٰلِكَ أَعْثَرْنَا عَلَيْهِمْ لِيَعْلَمُوا أَنَّ وَعْدَ اللَّهِ حَقٌّ وَأَنَّ السَّاعَةَ
لَا رَيْبَ فِيهَا إِذْ يَتَنَازَعُونَ بَيْنَهُمْ أَمْرَهُمْ فَقَالُوا ابْنُوا
عَلَيْهِم بُنْيَانًا رَّبُّهُمْ أَعْلَمُ بِهِمْ قَالَ الَّذِينَ غَلَبُوا عَلَىٰ أَمْرِهِمْ
لَنَتَّخِذَنَّ عَلَيْهِم مَّسْجِدًا ۞ سَيَقُولُونَ ثَلَاثَةٌ رَّابِعُهُمْ
كَلْبُهُمْ وَيَقُولُونَ خَمْسَةٌ سَادِسُهُمْ كَلْبُهُمْ رَجْمًا بِالْغَيْبِ
وَيَقُولُونَ سَبْعَةٌ وَثَامِنُهُمْ كَلْبُهُمْ قُل رَّبِّي أَعْلَمُ بِعِدَّتِهِم
مَّا يَعْلَمُهُمْ إِلَّا قَلِيلٌ فَلَا تُمَارِ فِيهِمْ إِلَّا مِرَاءً ظَاهِرًا وَلَا
تَسْتَفْتِ فِيهِم مِّنْهُمْ أَحَدًا ۞ وَلَا تَقُولَنَّ لِشَايْءٍ إِنِّي
فَاعِلٌ ذَٰلِكَ غَدًا ۞ إِلَّا أَن يَشَاءَ اللَّهُ وَاذْكُر رَّبَّكَ
إِذَا نَسِيتَ وَقُلْ عَسَىٰ أَن يَهْدِيَنِ رَبِّي لِأَقْرَبَ مِنْ هَٰذَا
رَشَدًا ۞ وَلَبِثُوا فِي كَهْفِهِمْ ثَلَاثَ مِائَةٍ سِنِينَ وَازْدَادُوا
تِسْعًا ۞ قُلِ اللَّهُ أَعْلَمُ بِمَا لَبِثُوا لَهُ غَيْبُ السَّمَاوَاتِ وَالْأَرْضِ
أَبْصِرْ بِهِ وَأَسْمِعْ مَا لَهُم مِّن دُونِهِ مِن وَلِيٍّ وَلَا يُشْرِكُ فِي
حُكْمِهِ أَحَدًا ۞ وَاتْلُ مَا أُوحِيَ إِلَيْكَ مِن كِتَابِ رَبِّكَ
لَا مُبَدِّلَ لِكَلِمَاتِهِ وَلَن تَجِدَ مِن دُونِهِ مُلْتَحَدًا ۞

at random at (something related to) the Unseen. Still others will say: "They were seven, the dog being the eighth." Say (O Messenger): "My Lord knows their number better; it is but few that know (the truth about) them." So do not argue about them, and be content with what is obvious (to you through Revelation), nor ask any of them (who argue even among themselves) to give you an opinion about them.[12/13]

23. And do not say about anything (you intend), "I will do it tomorrow,"

24. Without (adding) "If God wills."[14] And remember and mention Him (straight-away) should you forget (to do so when expressing an intention for the future). And say: "I hope that my Lord will guide me to what is nearer to right conduct than this (forgetfulness of mine)."[15]

25. And they stayed in their Cave three hundred (solar) years, and added nine (for lunar years).

26. Say: "God knows better how long they stayed. To Him belongs (absolute domin-ion and full knowledge of) the unseen of the heavens and the earth.[16] How perfect His seeing and how perfect His hearing! And they have apart from Him no guard-ian, and He allots to no one a share in His absolute authority.

27. Recite (and teach) that which has been revealed to you from the Book of your Lord. There is none who can change His words (whatever the unbelievers may say or desire), and you will never find, apart from Him, any refuge.

21. And in this way We disclosed them to the people so that they might know that the promise of God is true, and that there can be no doubt about (the com-ing of) the Last Hour.[10] When they (the people) disputed about their affair, they said: "Build a structure over them (to hide them and leave them to their rest). Their Lord knows best about them." Those who prevailed (in the long-disputed matter) said: "We will most certainly build a place of worship over them."[11]

22. (Instead of reflecting on the lesson to be learnt from the People of the Cave, people concentrate their interest on the details of the event.) Some will say they were three, the dog being the fourth among them; and some will say they were five, the dog being the sixth – all guessing

10. The experience of the People of the Cave is significant in two important ways: One is that God has promised that He will make successful those who believe in Him sincerely and strive in His way, helping His Word to prevail, even if they are weak and oppressed at the beginning. This is a matter over which people have been disputing since the time of Adam and over which the People of the Cave rose against the ruler and his people. While the People of the Cave themselves remained in the Cave, their resistance on behalf of their faith ended in victory. The second point is, as in the case of the man whose experience is narrated in 2: 259, who remained dead for a hundred years and then was raised to life by God as a sign for the people (so that they might understand how He created them and how He will restore them to life after their death) that the experience of the People of the Cave became a manifest sign for the coming of the Last Hour and the Resurrection, over which there had been a fierce controversy until the time they awoke.

11. Despite this manifest sign, many did not refrain from doubting the Resurrection and the afterlife, and even disclosed their denial of, at least, their doubts about God by saying, "their Lord," not "our Lord." This shows that if one does not have a sincere intention to believe, one can refuse to believe, even in the face of miracles.

12. This verse shows that at the time of the revelation of this *sūrah* a number of stories were in circulation about the People of the Cave among the People of the Book – i.e., the Christians and the Jews who had provoked the Makkan polytheists to ask the Messenger about them. Rather than concentrating on the lessons this experience teaches, they only debated about its details, such as the number of the men and how long they had remained in the Cave. Those who said they were three, the dog being the fourth among them, or that they were five, the dog being the sixth, or that they were seven, the dog being the eighth, were the People of the Book. The verse using the tense denoting the near future should not mislead us. It points to the fact that people will keep arguing about their number as they argued following the death of the People of the Cave. The Qur'ān orders the believers to be intent primarily on the lessons given and not to ask anybody from among the People of the Book about these matters.

There is a subtle point here concerning the number of men in the cave in this Qur'ānic narrative. Naturally, it is not forbidden to investigate into details, without restricting the historical events to the details. Verse 19, which informs us of the men's conversation concerning how long they had remained in the Cave, mentions one person who asked about how long they had been there, with two different groups expressing their opinions. It uses the plural form in reference to these two groups. In Arabic, the plural is applicable to at least three persons. Therefore, we can conclude that there were two groups of at least three people, plus the man who posed the question, making at least seven People of the Cave, with the dog being the eighth. In addition, this last verse (22) does not criticize those who say they were seven, the dog being the eighth, for guessing at random at (something related to) the Unseen, while it does criticize the others who say they were three and those who say they were five.

13. By narrating the experience of the People of the Cave, the Qur'ān also dispels the false belief that the apparent complex of causal relationships, which people call "laws of nature," is unalterable. What we call the laws of nature are in fact the usual ways in which God lets things happen. He is not bound by any such laws. He can cause someone to remain asleep for hundreds of years and then rouse him, while preventing this long period from having any affect on that person's age, appearance, or health.

The Reasons Why God Has Created Natural Laws and Causes

In the next world, the realm of Power, God will execute His Will directly without the 'medium' of causes, so that everything will happen instantaneously. The Divine Name, the All-Wise, requires that in this world, which is the realm of Wisdom, Divine Power should operate from behind the veil of causes and laws. The following reasons may be given for this:

- Opposites are mingled in this world: truth with falsehood, light with darkness, good with evil, white with black, and so on. In this world, God tests humankind, in whose nature there are ingrained inclinations towards both good and evil, to mark out whether they will use their free will and other faculties in the way of truth and goodness or not, and in order that their potential may develop and that they may attain perfect humanity, Divine Wisdom has required that the veil of causes and laws should be drawn before the operations of Divine Power. If God had so willed, He could train the planets with His "Hands" in a way that is observable by us, or He could have them administered by angels whom we see openly, and we would then not be speaking of the laws of causes, such as gravity. Or, in order to communicate His Commandments, He could, without sending any Prophets, speak to each individual directly, or, in order to compel us to believe in His existence and Oneness, He could write His Name with stars on the skies. But in this case, human earthly existence would be meaningless.

- Like the two sides of a mirror, existence has two aspects or dimensions, one visible and material, the realm of opposites and (in most cases) imperfections, and the spiritual realm which is transparent, pure and perfect. There can be, in the material dimension, events and phenomena which appear disagreeable to human beings. Those who are unable to perceive the Divine Wisdom behind all things may go so far as to criticize the Almighty for those disagreeable events and phenomena. In order to prevent this, God has made natural laws and causes a veil to fall before His acts. For example, so that people should criticize neither God nor His angel of death for the loss of their beloved ones or for their own death, God has placed

between Himself and the phenomenon of death (among other "agents" or "causes") diseases and "natural" disasters.

Again, on account of the essential imperfection of this world of test and trial, people encounter and suffer from many deficiencies and shortcomings. In absolute terms, whatever God does or decrees is good, beautiful, and just. Injustice, ugliness, and evil arise from the errors and abuses of humankind. For example, a court may pass an unjust sentence on you; but you should know that Destiny permitted that judgment because of a crime which had remained hidden. Whatever befalls people is usually because of self-wronging, an evil they themselves have done. However, those who lack the sound reasoning and judgment necessary to understand the Divine Wisdom behind events and phenomena may attribute the apparent ugliness or evil, the imperfections and shortcomings that they experience, in this worldly life, directly to God. But God is absolutely free from any kind of defect or imperfection.

Therefore, to prevent people from ascribing to God the ugliness and evil they encounter in life, His Glory and Grandeur have required that natural causes and laws should be a veil before His acts, while belief in His Unity demands that any kind of creative power should not be ascribed to those causes and laws.

- If God Almighty were to act in the world directly, without the "medium" of causes and laws, humankind would not have been motivated and enabled to develop scientific knowledge and to live free from fears and anxieties. It is thanks to the fact that God acts from behind natural causes and laws that human beings are able to observe and study patterns in phenomena. Otherwise, each event would be perceived as a miracle. The regularity within the flux and mutability of events and phenomena makes them comprehensible to us, therefore awakening in us the desire to wonder and reflect; this is a principal factor in the establishment of sciences. It is for the same reason that we are able, to some degree, to plan and arrange our affairs in advance. Consider how complicated life would be if we had absolutely no idea whether or not the sun would rise tomorrow!

- God has absolute beauty and perfection; all His Names are absolutely beautiful without any defect. If He manifested His Names and Attributes directly, without the "medium" of causes and laws, we would not be able to endure them, and more than that, lost in these manifestations, we would not be able to know Him. It is impossible for us to know something that is infinite. It is only by putting a limit to a thing that we can recognize it. The Almighty manifests His Names and Attributes and His Perfections from behind causes and laws, and by degrees within the confines of time and space, so that the world and life might have a regularity with which we can build a connection by perceiving and reflecting. The gradual manifestation of the Divine Names and Attributes is also a reason for our curiosity and wonder about them.

These four constitute only some of the reasons why God acts through the "medium" of natural laws and causes.

14. Although human beings are free to make plans for the future and endowed with the necessary equipment to do what they plan, what they will do in the future, even in the present, is not dependent on their will power exclusively. There are many other factors that must be taken into consideration. No one knows whether they will be able to do what they have planned and intended. In fact, no one knows what lies in store even one minute later. Nor does anyone have the absolute power to do whatever they will. In addition, one does not know for sure whether what they intend to do is for their own good. So, we must do what we

should according to God's Will and commands, taking the necessary measures and making the required preparations, placing our trust in God, and then referring to Him whether our intention will be realized or not.

15. This part of the verse should not only be taken in connection with the previous one. Although it is evident that it demands that, in case we forget to refer the realization of our future intentions to His absolute Will, we should mention him when we remember, this verse should also be viewed in a more general sense in the light of the following, and other similar, Divine declarations:

And do not be like those who are oblivious of God and so God has made them oblivious of their own selves (59: 19).

Those who keep from disobedience to God in reverence for Him and piety: when a suggestion from Satan touches them – they are alert and remember God, and then they have clear discernment (7: 201).

Remember and mention your Lord within yourself (in the depths of your heart), most humbly and in awe, not loud of voice, at morning and evening. And do not be among the neglectful (7: 205).

16. According to some commentators, the People of the Cave took refuge in the Cave in 112 during the reign of Trajan. They argue that the Qur'ānic statement, *God knows better how long they stayed,* is a confirmation that they stayed 300 (solar) years, with 9 more for lunar years, that is, 300 solar or 309 lunar years, and that this is a statement answering those who put forth different opinions. However, God knows best the truth for *to Him belongs (absolute dominion and full knowledge of) the unseen of the heavens and the earth.* We must remain intent on the lessons to be drawn from historical events, and not become distracted by details the knowledge of which will not assist us in learning or applying those lessons.

296   سُوْرَةُ الْكَهْفِ   ٢٩٦

وَاصْبِرْ نَفْسَكَ مَعَ الَّذِيْنَ يَدْعُوْنَ رَبَّهُمْ بِالْغَدٰوةِ وَالْعَشِيِّ يُرِيْدُوْنَ وَجْهَهُ وَلَا تَعْدُ عَيْنَاكَ عَنْهُمْ تُرِيْدُ زِيْنَةَ الْحَيٰوةِ الدُّنْيَا وَلَا تُطِعْ مَنْ أَغْفَلْنَا قَلْبَهُ عَنْ ذِكْرِنَا وَاتَّبَعَ هَوٰىهُ وَكَانَ أَمْرُهُ فُرُطًا ۝ وَقُلِ الْحَقُّ مِنْ رَبِّكُمْ فَمَنْ شَاءَ فَلْيُؤْمِنْ وَمَنْ شَاءَ فَلْيَكْفُرْ إِنَّا أَعْتَدْنَا لِلظّٰلِمِيْنَ نَارًا أَحَاطَ بِهِمْ سُرَادِقُهَا وَإِنْ يَسْتَغِيْثُوْا يُغَاثُوْا بِمَاءٍ كَالْمُهْلِ يَشْوِي الْوُجُوْهَ بِئْسَ الشَّرَابُ وَسَاءَتْ مُرْتَفَقًا ۝ إِنَّ الَّذِيْنَ آمَنُوْا وَعَمِلُوا الصّٰلِحٰتِ إِنَّا لَا نُضِيْعُ أَجْرَ مَنْ أَحْسَنَ عَمَلًا ۝ أُولٰئِكَ لَهُمْ جَنّٰتُ عَدْنٍ تَجْرِيْ مِنْ تَحْتِهِمُ الْأَنْهَارُ يُحَلَّوْنَ فِيْهَا مِنْ أَسَاوِرَ مِنْ ذَهَبٍ وَيَلْبَسُوْنَ ثِيَابًا خُضْرًا مِنْ سُنْدُسٍ وَإِسْتَبْرَقٍ مُتَّكِئِيْنَ فِيْهَا عَلَى الْأَرَائِكِ نِعْمَ الثَّوَابُ وَحَسُنَتْ مُرْتَفَقًا ۝ وَاضْرِبْ لَهُمْ مَثَلًا رَجُلَيْنِ جَعَلْنَا لِأَحَدِهِمَا جَنَّتَيْنِ مِنْ أَعْنَابٍ وَحَفَفْنَاهُمَا بِنَخْلٍ وَجَعَلْنَا بَيْنَهُمَا زَرْعًا ۝ كِلْتَا الْجَنَّتَيْنِ آتَتْ أُكُلَهَا وَلَمْ تَظْلِمْ مِنْهُ شَيْئًا وَفَجَّرْنَا خِلَالَهُمَا نَهَرًا ۝ وَكَانَ لَهُ ثَمَرٌ فَقَالَ لِصَاحِبِهِ وَهُوَ يُحَاوِرُهُ أَنَا أَكْثَرُ مِنْكَ مَالًا وَأَعَزُّ نَفَرًا ۝

that scalds their faces. How dreadful a drink, and how evil a couch to rest on!

28. And keep yourself patient along with those who invoke their Lord morning and evening seeking His "Face" (His eternal, good pleasure and the meeting with Him in the Hereafter), and do not let your eyes pass from them, desiring the attraction of the life of this world, and pay no heed to him whose heart We have made unmindful of Our remembrance, who follows his lusts and fancies, and whose affair exceeds all bounds (of right and decency).[17]

29. And say: "The truth from your Lord (has come in this Qur'ān)." Then, whoever wills (to believe), let him believe; and whoever wills (to disbelieve), let him disbelieve. Surely We have prepared for the wrongdoers a Fire, its billowing folds encompassing them. If they beg for water they will be given water like molten metal

30. Surely for those who believe and do good, righteous deeds – We do not leave to waste the reward of any who do good deeds, aware that God is seeing them.

31. Those are they for whom are Gardens of perpetual bliss through which rivers flow; adorned therein with armbands of gold and they will dress in green garments of fine silk and rich brocade; they recline there upon thrones.[18] How excellent a reward, how lovely a couch to rest on!

32. Set forth to them the parable of two men: for one of them We had made two vineyards and surrounded both with datepalms, and placed between them a field of grain.

33. Each of the two vineyards yielded its produce, without failing in anything. We had also caused a stream to gush forth between the two.

34. So the man had fruit (in abundance), and one day he said to his companion while he was conversing with him: "I am more than you in wealth, and mightier in manpower (children and those working for me)."

17. God's Messenger, upon him be peace and blessings, nearly tormented himself to death with grief over those who rejected faith in the Qur'ān. People's prosperity in both worlds lay in faith in the Qur'ān and its rejection would bring their doom. So, without showing any trace of weariness, he called people to it. However, the chieftains in Makkah offered him to dissociate himself from the "lowly" believers in order to participate in his teaching circles. The Messenger categorically rejected such demands. This verse has come to condemn such demands and emphatically expresses that no follower of the Qur'ān can repulse a believer.

18. In the past, kings used to wear bracelets or armbands and garments of the finest silk and brocade. What people usually yearn for in the name of the worldly happiness is such royal prosperity. So the verse presents the enjoyment in Paradise in the terms of that prosperity, which is the greatest that people can imagine. However, the verse can also be taken with its literal meaning without forgetting that the garments described are particular to Paradise.

٢٩٧   ﴿الجزء الخامس عشر﴾   297

وَدَخَلَ جَنَّتَهُ وَهُوَ ظَالِمٌ لِّنَفْسِهِ قَالَ مَا أَظُنُّ أَن تَبِيدَ هَٰذِهِ
أَبَدًا ۞ وَمَا أَظُنُّ السَّاعَةَ قَآئِمَةً وَلَئِن رُّدِدتُّ إِلَىٰ رَبِّى لَأَجِدَنَّ
خَيْرًا مِّنْهَا مُنقَلَبًا ۞ قَالَ لَهُ صَاحِبُهُ وَهُوَ يُحَاوِرُهُ أَكَفَرْتَ
بِالَّذِى خَلَقَكَ مِن تُرَابٍ ثُمَّ مِن نُّطْفَةٍ ثُمَّ سَوَّاكَ رَجُلًا ۞
لَّٰكِنَّا هُوَ اللَّهُ رَبِّى وَلَا أُشْرِكُ بِرَبِّى أَحَدًا ۞ وَلَوْلَا إِذْ
دَخَلْتَ جَنَّتَكَ قُلْتَ مَا شَآءَ اللَّهُ لَا قُوَّةَ إِلَّا بِاللَّهِ إِن تَرَنِ
أَنَا أَقَلَّ مِنكَ مَالًا وَوَلَدًا ۞ فَعَسَىٰ رَبِّى أَن يُؤْتِيَنِ خَيْرًا مِّن جَنَّتِكَ
وَيُرْسِلَ عَلَيْهَا حُسْبَانًا مِّنَ السَّمَآءِ فَتُصْبِحَ صَعِيدًا زَلَقًا ۞ أَوْ يُصْبِحَ
مَآؤُهَا غَوْرًا فَلَن تَسْتَطِيعَ لَهُ طَلَبًا ۞ وَأُحِيطَ بِثَمَرِهِ فَأَصْبَحَ
يُقَلِّبُ كَفَّيْهِ عَلَىٰ مَا أَنفَقَ فِيهَا وَهِىَ خَاوِيَةٌ عَلَىٰ عُرُوشِهَا وَيَقُولُ
يَٰلَيْتَنِى لَمْ أُشْرِكْ بِرَبِّى أَحَدًا ۞ وَلَمْ تَكُن لَّهُ فِئَةٌ يَنصُرُونَهُ
مِن دُونِ اللَّهِ وَمَا كَانَ مُنتَصِرًا ۞ هُنَالِكَ الْوَلَايَةُ لِلَّهِ الْحَقِّ هُوَ
خَيْرٌ ثَوَابًا وَخَيْرٌ عُقْبًا ۞ وَاضْرِبْ لَهُم مَّثَلَ الْحَيَوٰةِ الدُّنْيَا
كَمَآءٍ أَنزَلْنَاهُ مِنَ السَّمَآءِ فَاخْتَلَطَ بِهِ نَبَاتُ الْأَرْضِ فَأَصْبَحَ
هَشِيمًا تَذْرُوهُ الرِّيَاحُ وَكَانَ اللَّهُ عَلَىٰ كُلِّ شَيْءٍ مُّقْتَدِرًا ۞

---

35. He went into his vineyard while wronging himself (in his vain conceit). He said: "I do not think that this will ever perish.

36. "Nor do I think that the Last Hour will ever come. Even if (it should come, and) I am brought back to my Lord, I will surely find something even better than this as a resort."[19]

37. His companion said to him, while he was arguing with him: "Do you (expressing such ingratitude) disbelieve in Him Who created you from earth, then from a mere drop of seminal fluid, then fashioned you into a perfect man?

38. "But (for my part I believe that) He is God, my Lord, and I do not associate with my Lord any partner.

39. "If only you had said, on enter-ing your vineyard, 'Whatever God wills (surely has and surely will come to pass); there is no strength (to achieve anything) save with God.' Though you see me with less wealth and offspring than you (I have no complaint at all, for it is God Who does as He wills, and He is All-Compassionate toward His servants).

40. "It may well be that my Lord will give me something better than your vineyard, and send on it (your vineyard) a calamity from heaven so that it becomes a barren waste.

41. "Or its water sinks deep into the ground so that you will never be able to seek it out."

42. And (as it happened) his produce was encompassed by ruin, and he set to wringing his hands with grief over all that he had spent on it, when it was now all ruined on its trellises, and he was saying: "Oh, would that I had never associated anyone with my Lord as partner!"

43. And he had, apart from God, none, no troop of men, to help Him, nor could he be of any help to himself.

44. For thus it is: all power to protect belongs to God, the All-True, Ever-Constant One. He is the best for reward, and the best for outcome.

45. And strike to them a parable of the present, worldly life: (it is) like water that We send down from the sky, and the vegetation of the earth mingles with it (flourishing abundantly). Then it turns into dry stubble which the winds scatter about. God is absolutely able to do all things.[20]

19. This is a very typical mood of many worldly people. They attribute whatever they have in the world to themselves. Because of this, they do not like anyone else, for example, the poor and the needy, to have any share in it. They are so puffed up by their worldly things that they deceive themselves into believing that God is their Lord in particular and He is ready to welcome them under any circumstances. Such people are usually ignorant upstarts with crude manners.

20. After the experience of the People of the Cave, the parable of the two men is significant in two points. One is that a religious movement, or faith movement, which is based on sincerity, altruism, self-sacrifice, and trust in God, usually requires donations from its followers. Even though those followers do not have considerable wealth, they prefer the continuation of the movement to a prosperous life. This movement usually encounters fierce opposition from those in power and the self-indulgent, capital-owning segment of society. With the sole aim of living a luxurious worldly life, those wealthy ones do not wish to accept a power above them that will interfere with their way of earning and spending and therefore prefer a life outside the fold of the Divine Religion. So great are their successes and attainments in their own eyes that they identify their prosperity with happiness in Paradise and cannot see any real reason to strive for Paradise in the Hereafter.

Another point to which the parable draws our attention is that among those who lead the faith movement, or rather those who have taken part in it in the later stages and who have not had to bear any misfortunes, there may appear some who have tasted the riches of the world and who are attached to the worldly life at the cost of the goals of the faith movement. Such people attribute their attainments to their own abilities consciously ignoring God as the sole Giver of all that one has. They forget thankfulness and gradually take a prosperous worldly life as the sole aim of their existence, remaining in oblivion of the other life. When they are reminded of Paradise, they are in a mood in which they see their worldly prosperity as being identical with Paradise and even worse, they regard themselves as the only ones who deserve Paradise. This is the stage where a civilization founded upon the pillars of the faith movement begins to decline. So, by telling the parable of the two men, the Qur'ān both urges the believers to spend in God's cause, for the sake of reforming themselves as well as the society, and warns both these and the other believers, who have managed to carry the movement to the stage of founding a civilization, against the corruption which comes with being defeated by the charms of the world.

المَالُ وَالْبَنُونَ زِينَةُ الْحَيَوٰةِ الدُّنْيَا ۖ وَالْبَٰقِيَٰتُ الصَّٰلِحَٰتُ خَيْرٌ عِنْدَ

رَبِّكَ ثَوَابًا وَخَيْرٌ أَمَلًا ۝ وَيَوْمَ نُسَيِّرُ الْجِبَالَ وَتَرَى الْأَرْضَ

بَارِزَةً وَحَشَرْنَٰهُمْ فَلَمْ نُغَادِرْ مِنْهُمْ أَحَدًا ۝ وَعُرِضُوا عَلَىٰ

رَبِّكَ صَفًّا ۖ لَّقَدْ جِئْتُمُونَا كَمَا خَلَقْنَٰكُمْ أَوَّلَ مَرَّةٍ ۚ بَلْ زَعَمْتُمْ

أَلَّن نَّجْعَلَ لَكُم مَّوْعِدًا ۝ وَوُضِعَ الْكِتَٰبُ فَتَرَى الْمُجْرِمِينَ مُشْفِقِينَ

مِمَّا فِيهِ وَيَقُولُونَ يَٰوَيْلَتَنَا مَالِ هَٰذَا الْكِتَٰبِ لَا يُغَادِرُ صَغِيرَةً

وَلَا كَبِيرَةً إِلَّا أَحْصَىٰهَا ۚ وَوَجَدُوا مَا عَمِلُوا حَاضِرًا ۗ وَلَا يَظْلِمُ

رَبُّكَ أَحَدًا ۝ وَإِذْ قُلْنَا لِلْمَلَٰئِكَةِ اسْجُدُوا لِآدَمَ

فَسَجَدُوا إِلَّا إِبْلِيسَ كَانَ مِنَ الْجِنِّ فَفَسَقَ عَنْ أَمْرِ

رَبِّهِ ۗ أَفَتَتَّخِذُونَهُ وَذُرِّيَّتَهُ أَوْلِيَاءَ مِن دُونِي وَهُمْ لَكُمْ

عَدُوٌّ ۚ بِئْسَ لِلظَّٰلِمِينَ بَدَلًا ۝ مَّا أَشْهَدْتُّهُمْ خَلْقَ السَّمَٰوَٰتِ

وَالْأَرْضِ وَلَا خَلْقَ أَنفُسِهِمْ وَمَا كُنتُ مُتَّخِذَ الْمُضِلِّينَ عَضُدًا

۝ وَيَوْمَ يَقُولُ نَادُوا شُرَكَاءِيَ الَّذِينَ زَعَمْتُمْ فَدَعَوْهُمْ فَلَمْ

يَسْتَجِيبُوا لَهُمْ وَجَعَلْنَا بَيْنَهُم مَّوْبِقًا ۝ وَرَأَى الْمُجْرِمُونَ النَّارَ

فَظَنُّوا أَنَّهُم مُّوَاقِعُوهَا وَلَمْ يَجِدُوا عَنْهَا مَصْرِفًا ۝

---

46. Wealth and children are an adornment of the present, worldly life, but the good, righteous deeds (based on faith and) which endure are better in the sight of your Lord in bringing reward and better to aspire for.

47. (Bear in mind) the Day when We set the mountains in motion, and you see the earth denuded, and We raise to life and gather them together (all those who are content with themselves, deluded by the charms of the world), leaving out none of them.

48. They are arrayed before your Lord (Whom they disgregarded in the world), all lined up (without discrimination of wealth or status as in the world, and they are told): "Now, indeed, you have come to Us (divested of all worldly things) as We created you in the first instance – though you used to suppose that We had not appointed for you a meeting with Us."

49. And the Record (of everyone's deeds) is set in place; and you will see the disbelieving criminals filled with dread because of what is in it, and they will say: "Alas, woe is ours! What is this Record? It leaves out nothing, be it small or great, but it is accounted!" They have found all that they did confronting them (in the forms thereof particular to the Hereafter). And Your Lord wrongs no one.

50. And (recall) when We said to the angels, "Prostrate before Adam!" and they all prostrated, but Iblīs did not; he was of the jinn (created before humankind, from smokeless, scorching fire), and transgressed against his Lord's command.[21] Will you, then, take him and his offspring for guardians (to rely on and refer your affairs to) rather than Me, when they are an enemy to you? How evil an exchange for the wrongdoers!

51. I did not make them (Iblīs and his offspring) witnesses to the creation of the heavens and the earth, nor of the creation of their own selves, nor did I (being absolutely beyond need) ever take as helpers those that lead (humankind) astray.[22]

52. The Day (will come when) He will say, "Now call upon all those whom you alleged to be My partners." Thereupon they will invoke them, but they will not respond to them, and We will place between them an unbridgeable gulf.

53. And the disbelieving criminals will see the Fire and know certainly that they are bound to fall into it, and they will find no way of escape from it.

21. This means that Satan was not of the angels, as the Qur'ān openly declares that the angels are sinless, always doing what they are commanded by God and never disobeying Him (16: 49–50; 66: 6). Satan belongs to the species of the jinn, which, like humankind, have free will and can either obey or disobey God.

If it is asked why God also ordered him to prostrate before Adam after having made the same order to the angels, the answer is: The prostration of the angels was an action signifying that they affirm the degree of knowledge and superiority of Adam and the fact that he deserves the vicegerency on the earth. Among the angels there are many which are charged with life on the earth and aiding humankind in many aspects of their lives. Therefore, their prostration also means that God commanded them to help humankind to perform their duty on the earth. Those angels are also the representatives of the earthly creatures in God's Presence, and humankind are the masters of these creatures. Satan, who belongs to the jinn, is an earthly creature and has duties toward humankind. When our Prophet, upon him be peace and blessings, took the oath of allegiance from the jinn in the valley of Baṭn an-Nakhlah, he wanted them to appear to his community either in their own form or in other agreeable forms, not in the forms of harmful animals like dogs and scorpions. He also warned his community, saying: "When you see any vermin in your house, say to it three times: 'For the sake of God, leave here!' For it may be from your jinn friends. If it does not leave, it is not from the jinn. Then you are permitted to kill it, if it is harmful." The jinn who gave allegiance to God's Messenger promised him: "If your community recites *basmalah* (the formula *In [and with] the Name of God, the All-Merciful, the All-Compassionate*) before anything they do,

and cover all their dishes, we will touch neither their food nor their drink." We do not know how they eat of our food or drink of our beverages. Another Tradition says: "(When you have relieved yourselves) do not clean yourselves with bones and dried pieces of dung, for they are among the foods of your jinn brothers." (at-Tirmidhī, "Ṭahārah," 14; al-Bukhārī, "Manāqib al-Anṣār," 32; Muslim, "Salām," 139, 140) All these Traditions show that there is an important relation between humankind and the jinn and this relationship is a requirement of human earthly life, which is why God also ordered Satan to prostrate before Adam. But he refused and, despite being eternally excluded from God's Mercy, he was granted respite until the Day of Judgment as a dimension of humankind's being tested on the earth, and he was given the ability to whisper to humankind in order to mislead them.

The verse also mentions Satan's offspring. This may mean either that Satan has a wife and begets children or, as mentioned in 17: 64, he has a share in the children of human beings, or both. Some human beings become like Satan.

22. What right do *Iblīs* and his offspring – satans (devils) – have to be taken as guardians, whom humankind should obey and refer their affairs to, seeing that they themselves are created beings in absolute need of God and not their own masters? Neither the satans of humankind nor of the jinn, in fact no created being, has the right to impose their rules and views upon others; such a being is not even their own master, does not play the least part in their coming into existence, the choice of their family, brothers and sisters, the place and date of their birth and death, or their color and physique, and therefore has no right to impose their rules and views upon others.

٢٩٩ الجزء الخامس عشر 299

وَلَقَدْ صَرَّفْنَا فِي هَٰذَا الْقُرْآنِ لِلنَّاسِ مِن كُلِّ مَثَلٍ وَكَانَ الْإِنسَانُ
أَكْثَرَ شَيْءٍ جَدَلًا ۞ وَمَا مَنَعَ النَّاسَ أَن يُؤْمِنُوا إِذْ جَاءَهُمُ
الْهُدَىٰ وَيَسْتَغْفِرُوا رَبَّهُمْ إِلَّا أَن تَأْتِيَهُمْ سُنَّةُ الْأَوَّلِينَ أَوْ
يَأْتِيَهُمُ الْعَذَابُ قُبُلًا ۞ وَمَا نُرْسِلُ الْمُرْسَلِينَ إِلَّا مُبَشِّرِينَ
وَمُنذِرِينَ ۚ وَيُجَادِلُ الَّذِينَ كَفَرُوا بِالْبَاطِلِ لِيُدْحِضُوا
بِهِ الْحَقَّ ۖ وَاتَّخَذُوا آيَاتِي وَمَا أُنذِرُوا هُزُوًا ۞ وَمَنْ أَظْلَمُ
مِمَّن ذُكِّرَ بِآيَاتِ رَبِّهِ فَأَعْرَضَ عَنْهَا وَنَسِيَ مَا قَدَّمَتْ يَدَاهُ ۚ
إِنَّا جَعَلْنَا عَلَىٰ قُلُوبِهِمْ أَكِنَّةً أَن يَفْقَهُوهُ وَفِي
آذَانِهِمْ وَقْرًا ۖ وَإِن تَدْعُهُمْ إِلَى الْهُدَىٰ فَلَن يَهْتَدُوا
إِذًا أَبَدًا ۞ وَرَبُّكَ الْغَفُورُ ذُو الرَّحْمَةِ ۖ لَوْ يُؤَاخِذُهُم
بِمَا كَسَبُوا لَعَجَّلَ لَهُمُ الْعَذَابَ ۚ بَل لَّهُم مَّوْعِدٌ لَّن يَجِدُوا مِن
دُونِهِ مَوْئِلًا ۞ وَتِلْكَ الْقُرَىٰ أَهْلَكْنَاهُمْ لَمَّا ظَلَمُوا وَجَعَلْنَا
لِمَهْلِكِهِم مَّوْعِدًا ۞ وَإِذْ قَالَ مُوسَىٰ لِفَتَاهُ لَا أَبْرَحُ حَتَّىٰ
أَبْلُغَ مَجْمَعَ الْبَحْرَيْنِ أَوْ أَمْضِيَ حُقُبًا ۞ فَلَمَّا بَلَغَا مَجْمَعَ
بَيْنِهِمَا نَسِيَا حُوتَهُمَا فَاتَّخَذَ سَبِيلَهُ فِي الْبَحْرِ سَرَبًا ۞

────── ❧ ──────

54. Assuredly We have set out in diverse ways for humankind in this Qur'ān all kinds of parables and comparisons (to help them understand the truth); but human is, above all else, given to contention.

55. What is there to keep people from believing when guidance has come to them, and from imploring their Lord for forgiveness – unless it be that they follow the way of the (sinful) people of the olden times as if wishing for their fate to come upon them or the punishment (which they did not believe in but asked their Prophet, in derision, to bring down upon them) come and confront them? (Then indeed they would have no opportunity to implore forgiveness and hope for relief).

56. We send the Messengers (not as bearers of punishment) but as bearers of glad tidings (of prosperity in return for faith and righteousness) and warners (against the evil consequences of misguidance). Whereas those who disbelieve contend on the basis of falsehood in order to refute the truth thereby; and they take My Revelations and that (the punishment) of which they are warned in mockery.

57. Who is more in the wrong than he who has been reminded of his Lord's Revelations and signs, yet turns away from them and forgets all that his hands have forwarded (to the reckoning in the future life). Surely over their hearts We have laid veils (made up of their ill-intention, wrongdoing, and arrogance, which caused them to lose the ability to believe,) so that they do not grasp (the Qur'ān with faith and understanding), and in their ears a heaviness (so they do not hear the Qur'ān). And if you call them to guidance, they will never even then accept guidance.

58. Your Lord is the All-Forgiving, having infinite Mercy. If He were to take them immediately to task for what they have earned, surely He would hasten on the punishment for them; but for them is an appointed time-limit, beyond which they will never find an escape (from God's punishment).

59. And (that was the case with) all those townships that We destroyed when they were given to wrong. We had surely appointed a time fixed for their destruction.

60. (Now relate to them, O Messenger, the experience of Moses): When Moses said to his (young) attendant: "I will not give up (journeying) until I reach the junction of the two seas, though I may march on for ages."

61. When they reached the junction of the two (seas), they forgot their fish, and it took its way amazingly through the sea as in an underground channel.

300   سُورَةُ الكَهْفِ   ٣٠٠

فَلَمَّا جَاوَزَا قَالَ لِفَتَىٰهُ ءَاتِنَا غَدَآءَنَا لَقَدْ لَقِينَا مِن سَفَرِنَا
هَٰذَا نَصَبًا ۝ قَالَ أَرَءَيْتَ إِذْ أَوَيْنَآ إِلَى ٱلصَّخْرَةِ فَإِنِّى نَسِيتُ
ٱلْحُوتَ ۝ وَمَآ أَنسَىٰنِيهُ إِلَّا ٱلشَّيْطَٰنُ أَنْ أَذْكُرَهُ وَٱتَّخَذَ سَبِيلَهُۥ
فِى ٱلْبَحْرِ عَجَبًا ۝ قَالَ ذَٰلِكَ مَا كُنَّا نَبْغِ فَٱرْتَدَّا عَلَىٰٓ ءَاثَارِهِمَا
قَصَصًا ۝ فَوَجَدَا عَبْدًا مِّنْ عِبَادِنَآ ءَاتَيْنَٰهُ رَحْمَةً مِّنْ عِندِنَا
وَعَلَّمْنَٰهُ مِن لَّدُنَّا عِلْمًا ۝ قَالَ لَهُۥ مُوسَىٰ هَلْ أَتَّبِعُكَ عَلَىٰٓ أَن
تُعَلِّمَنِ مِمَّا عُلِّمْتَ رُشْدًا ۝ قَالَ إِنَّكَ لَن تَسْتَطِيعَ مَعِىَ صَبْرًا
۝ وَكَيْفَ تَصْبِرُ عَلَىٰ مَا لَمْ تُحِطْ بِهِۦ خُبْرًا ۝ قَالَ سَتَجِدُنِىٓ إِن شَآءَ
ٱللَّهُ صَابِرًا وَلَآ أَعْصِى لَكَ أَمْرًا ۝ قَالَ فَإِنِ ٱتَّبَعْتَنِى فَلَا
تَسْـَٔلْنِى عَن شَىْءٍ حَتَّىٰٓ أُحْدِثَ لَكَ مِنْهُ ذِكْرًا ۝ فَٱنطَلَقَا
حَتَّىٰٓ إِذَا رَكِبَا فِى ٱلسَّفِينَةِ خَرَقَهَا قَالَ أَخَرَقْتَهَا لِتُغْرِقَ أَهْلَهَا
لَقَدْ جِئْتَ شَيْـًٔا إِمْرًا ۝ قَالَ أَلَمْ أَقُلْ إِنَّكَ لَن تَسْتَطِيعَ مَعِىَ
صَبْرًا ۝ قَالَ لَا تُؤَاخِذْنِى بِمَا نَسِيتُ وَلَا تُرْهِقْنِى مِنْ أَمْرِى
عُسْرًا ۝ فَٱنطَلَقَا حَتَّىٰٓ إِذَا لَقِيَا غُلَٰمًا فَقَتَلَهُۥ قَالَ أَقَتَلْتَ
نَفْسًا زَكِيَّةً بِغَيْرِ نَفْسٍ لَّقَدْ جِئْتَ شَيْـًٔا نُّكْرًا ۝

62. So when they had passed further on, Moses said to his attendant: "Bring us our morning meal; assuredly we have endured much fatigue in this journey of ours."

63. (The servant) said: "Would you believe it? When we betook ourselves to that rock for a rest, I forgot about (our cooked) fish – and none but Satan caused me to forget to mention it (to you) – and it took its way into the sea in an amazing way!"

64. (Moses) said: "That is what we have been seeking!" So they retraced their footsteps.

65. And they found (there) one of Our servants to whom We had granted a (special) mercy from Us and taught him special knowledge from Our Presence.[23]

66. Moses said to him: "May I follow you so that you may teach me something of the knowledge of guidance which you have been taught?"

67. He said: "You will never be able to have patience with being in my company.

68. "How could you be patient about something that you have never encompassed in your knowledge?"[24]

69. (Moses) said: "You will find me patient, if God so wills and allows me to, and I will not disobey you in anything."

70. (Al-Khadr) explained: "Well, if you go with me, do not ask me concerning anything (that I may do) until I myself make mention of it to you."

71. So they set forth[25] until, when they embarked on the boat, he (al-Khadr) made a hole in it. (Moses) said: "Have you made a hole in it in order to drown its people (who would be using it)? You have certainly done an awful thing!"

72. He said: "Did I not tell you that you would never be able to have patience with being in my company?"

73. (Moses) said: "Do not take me to task because I forgot, and do not overburden me in my affair (in what you ask of me)."

74. So they went on until, when they met a young boy, he (al-Khadr) killed him. (Moses) said: "Have you killed an innocent soul (not in lawful retaliation but) without his having killed anyone? Assuredly you have done a horrible thing!"

23. As we know, the Prophet Moses, upon him be peace, is one of the five greatest Messengers (42: 13) to whom God granted a Book as a guidance for all aspects of people's lives. As God's Last Messenger, upon him be peace and blessings, stated, once one from among Moses' community asked him if there was any of God's servants on whom He bestowed more knowledge than him. The Almighty informed him of the existence of one of His servants on whom He bestowed a special mercy and special knowledge from His Presence (al-Bukhārī, "Kitāb at-Tafsīr," 18).

This means that that servant's knowledge was not of the kind which everyone can possess. Even the Prophet Moses did not have it. In reports from the Prophet Muḥammad, upon him be peace and blessings, that servant was called al-Khadr or al-Khidr. Al-Khadr, which must have been a title he had been given, means the green one and signifies life. As quoted in note 2: 120 from Bediüzzaman Said Nursi, human life consists of five degrees, and al-Khadr possesses the second degree of life, which is free to some extent from the necessities of our life. He can be present in different places at the same time. The revival of the cooked fish implies al-Khadr's special mission and represents enduring life.

Existence does not consist in only the visible, material world. Beyond it, like the appearances in facing walls of mirrors, there are many other worlds or dimensions of existence, each inner one being more refined than the outer one before it. Although we accept that Moses and his attendant traveled on the earth until reaching a point where two seas met, this journey had a spiritual aspect and therefore was like a spiritual journey toward God. So the point Moses and his young servant reached signifies the junction of the material and spiritual worlds. The revival of the fish suggests that they had just entered the field of al-Khadr, where everything is enduringly alive in some way. This journey is truly a tiring one. In order to attain some of the knowledge that had been specially given to al-Khadr, Moses had to make this journey, a journey which corresponds to the spiritual journey to God Almighty.

According to some reports from God's Messenger, upon him be peace and blessings, the young, virtuous servant (fatā, for the meaning of which see note 5 in this sūrah) was Yūshā (Joshua), son of Nūn who would later succeed the Prophet Moses, upon them be God's peace.

24. These verses are stating that the knowledge taught to al-Khadr is not of the kind which had been taught to Moses up until that point. That was because the Prophet Moses was a Messenger whose mission was to guide or lead people in life according to God's commandments. That is, he was the leader or guide of (his) people living on the earth; he was responsible for their guidance and they were a people greatly varied in intelligence and understanding. Guiding people in life and teaching them how to live according to God's commandments in order to please Him is the greatest mission, and the knowledge inherent in this is the most valuable and important of all. As for al-Khadr, although it has not been established if he was a Prophet or a saintly person, God's referring to Himself using the first plural form of noun while mentioning him (one of Our servants to whom We had granted a mercy as a grace from Us and taught a special knowledge from Our Presence – verse 65 above) and al-Khadr's using the same form in explaining his actions (verse 81 below) and referring them to God (verse 82), suggest that, even though not in the special sense of the concept, he was also a Messenger or an envoy with special mission. However, he had knowledge on some special matters which we will examine in the following verses; these do not interest the majority of people and they are not compulsory to learn. For this reason, it was not a defect on the part of Moses that he did not have such knowledge, nor did the fact that al-Khadr had the knowledge mean that he was superior to Moses, upon him be peace. The Prophet Muḥammad, upon him be peace and blessings, sheds light on this matter,

saying: "Al-Khadr told Moses: 'I have a kind of knowledge that you do not have; and you have a kind of knowledge that I do not have.' " (al-Bukhārī, "Kitāb at-Tafsīr," 18).

25. It is highly interesting that there is no mention of Moses' young attendant after Moses met with al-Khadr, and that just the two of them made the mysterious journey. When we take into consideration Moses' experience in its totality and the identity of al-Khadr, along with the knowledge given to him, we can conclude that this journey did not take place in the corporeal realm. Many people can have dream-like experiences while awake, which is called *mushāhadah* (vision, witnessing). The spirit enters the incorporeal realm of "forms" or "ideas" or "symbols" (*'al-'Ālam al-Mithāl*) and has a vision of some truths. This vision resembles true dreams, with the exception that dreams are experienced while asleep, but people have such a vision or experience while awake. Like dreams, the *mushāhadah* is quite brief. Although there may be other people next to the one who is having such an experience or vision, they remain unaware of it. For this reason, while Moses and al-Khadr had this mysterious journey, Moses' young attendant did not accompany them, even though he was with them.

So, the journey that Moses and al-Khadr took resembles the spiritual vision we have just described. However, God favors even common believers with such visions. Therefore, Moses and al-Khadr may have made this mysterious journey in the incorporeal realm of forms or ideas with both their spirits and bodies; their bodies had temporarily gained the degree of refinement of the astral body or energetic form or envelope of the spirit, (for which see Appendix 12). There is resemblance between this journey and the Ascension of the Prophet Muḥammad, as well as that of Jesus' being taken from the world; the differences being that this journey may have been made in the world of ideas or forms. The Prophet Muḥammad, upon him be peace and blessings, made the Ascension in all the higher dimensions or worlds of existence with his spirit and his body, which became so refined as to be almost identical with the "astral" body of the spirit. After the Ascension, he preferred to return to the world to continue to guide people and to complete the preaching of Islam. As for the Prophet Jesus, upon him be peace, since his mission as a Messenger had ended, he was taken from the world with his spirit and body, which also became identical with the astral body of his spirit and remained in "heaven" where he had been elevated. (God knows best.)

قَالَ اَلَمۡ اَقُل لَّكَ اِنَّكَ لَن تَسۡتَطِيعَ مَعِيَ صَبۡرًا ۝ قَالَ اِن سَاَلۡتُكَ عَن شَيۡءٍ بَعۡدَهَا فَلَا تُصَاحِبۡنِي قَدۡ بَلَغۡتَ مِن لَّدُنِّي عُذۡرًا ۝ فَانطَلَقَا حَتَّىٰٓ اِذَآ اَتَيَآ اَهۡلَ قَرۡيَةٍ اسۡتَطۡعَمَآ اَهۡلَهَا فَاَبَوۡا اَن يُضَيِّفُوهُمَا فَوَجَدَا فِيهَا جِدَارًا يُرِيدُ اَن يَنقَضَّ فَاَقَامَهُ قَالَ لَوۡ شِئۡتَ لَتَّخَذۡتَ عَلَيۡهِ اَجۡرًا ۝ قَالَ هٰذَا فِرَاقُ بَيۡنِي وَبَيۡنِكَ سَاُنَبِّئُكَ بِتَاۡوِيلِ مَا لَمۡ تَسۡتَطِع عَّلَيۡهِ صَبۡرًا ۝ اَمَّا السَّفِينَةُ فَكَانَتۡ لِمَسَٰكِينَ يَعۡمَلُونَ فِي الۡبَحۡرِ فَاَرَدتُّ اَن اَعِيبَهَا وَكَانَ وَرَآءَهُم مَّلِكٌ يَاۡخُذُ كُلَّ سَفِينَةٍ غَصۡبًا ۝ وَاَمَّا الۡغُلَٰمُ فَكَانَ اَبَوَاهُ مُؤۡمِنَيۡنِ فَخَشِينَآ اَن يُرۡهِقَهُمَا طُغۡيَانًا وَكُفۡرًا ۝ فَاَرَدۡنَآ اَن يُبۡدِلَهُمَا رَبُّهُمَا خَيۡرًا مِّنۡهُ زَكَوٰةً وَاَقۡرَبَ رُحۡمًا ۝ وَاَمَّا الۡجِدَارُ فَكَانَ لِغُلَٰمَيۡنِ يَتِيمَيۡنِ فِي الۡمَدِينَةِ وَكَانَ تَحۡتَهُ كَنزٌ لَّهُمَا وَكَانَ اَبُوهُمَا صَالِحًا فَاَرَادَ رَبُّكَ اَن يَبۡلُغَآ اَشُدَّهُمَا وَيَسۡتَخۡرِجَا كَنزَهُمَا رَحۡمَةً مِّن رَّبِّكَ وَمَا فَعَلۡتُهُ عَنۡ اَمۡرِي ذٰلِكَ تَاۡوِيلُ مَا لَمۡ تَسۡطِع عَّلَيۡهِ صَبۡرًا ۝ وَيَسۡاَلُونَكَ عَن ذِي الۡقَرۡنَيۡنِ قُلۡ سَاَتۡلُوا عَلَيۡكُم مِّنۡهُ ذِكۡرًا ۝

---

75. He said: "Did I not tell you that you would never be able to have patience with being in my company?"

76. (Moses) said: "If I should ever question you about anything after this, keep me no more in your company. You have already received (full) excuse from me."

77. So they went on until when they came upon the people of a township, they asked its people for food, but they refused them hospitality. They found there a wall which was on the verge of tumbling down, and he (al-Khadr) restored it. (Moses) said: "If you had wished, you could have taken payment for it."

78. He (al-Khadr) said: "This is the parting of ways between me and you. I will tell you the meaning of what you were unable to bear patiently.

79. "As for the boat, it belonged to some destitute people who worked on the sea – and I wished to damage it, for there was a king after them who was seizing every boat by force.

80. "And as for the young boy, his parents were believers, and we feared lest he should oppress them with rebellion and unbelief.

81. "So we wished that their Lord would grant them in his place one better than him in purity and nearer in affection (to his parents).

82. "And as for the wall, it belonged to two orphan boys in the city, and beneath it was a treasure belonging to them. Their father had been a righteous man. So your Lord willed that they should come of age and bring forth their treasure as a mercy from your Lord. I did not do this (any of the actions that you witnessed) of my own accord. This is the meaning of all (those events) with which you were unable to have patience."[26/27]

83. And they ask you (O Messenger) about Dhu'l-Qarnayn.[28] Say: "I will recite to you a mention of him (quoting the Almighty)."

26. Any event which takes place in life has an apparent meaning and reason pertaining to the people involved in it, and a true meaning and reason pertaining to Divine Destiny. Destiny takes into consideration both the whole of creation and events from the time of Adam to the Last Day and each individual person and event at the same time. It never wrongs anybody; it always does justice and this justice usually dwells on mercy. Whatever good reaches one, it is because of the Divine Mercy, although a person has little share in it, but whatever one suffers is completely due to one's own errors. However, the Almighty forgives many of His servants' errors and never hastens to punish; He gives respite so that people may mend their ways. But if He punishes a servant, it is absolutely what that servant deserves. As Said Nursi reminds us, a court may pass a sentence on us because of a crime we did not commit and thus carry out an injustice, but Destiny allows this sentence to be passed on us because of another crime which we did, but which has remained unknown.

We understand from the Prophet Moses' experience with al-Khadr, upon them be peace, that the latter's mission is in connection with the inner, true meaning and reasons of events. But we judge according to the apparent reasons; this does not mean that we are not obliged to investigate the truth. But we cannot judge according to future expectations. Even if we have foreknowledge about something which will take place in the future, this cannot be a basis for our judgment. For this reason, those events may, as pointed out above, have taken place in the world of forms or ideas in which the Prophet Moses journeyed in the company of al-Khadr. According to the religious rules and laws that God has laid down for our worldly life, Moses was right to make his objections. But what al-Khadr did was not wrong; his mission pertained to the world of Destiny. God may have desired to teach Moses the true nature of Destiny and the true meaning of events, many of which people are unable to grasp. Whatever God does is absolute justice, and everyone gets what they deserve. Moreover, God is the All-Compassionate and overlooks many of His servants' errors (42: 30, 34).

27. By recounting the experience of the Prophet Moses with al-Khadr after the stories of the People of the Cave and the orchards of the two men, the Qur'ān is suggesting that for a faith movement, spiritual profundity and discovery of the inner meaning of existence and events are important.

28. There are different views about the identity of Dhu'l-Qarnayn. It is not of great importance who he really was in history. What is important is what the Qur'ān intends to teach by this narration.

Like al-Khadr, it is not certain whether Dhu'l-Qarnayn was a Prophet or not, but God's referring to Himself with the first plural form of noun while narrating His speech to him (verse 86 below), can be seen as an allusion to Dhu'l-Qarnayn having special mission. The expression of the Divine Revelation with the word "say" also suggests Messengership, if it is not used to mean inspiration, while when it is expressed with the verb "reveal" it can suggest Messengership, Prophethood, and sainthood. For example, God's revelation to a bee (16: 68) is Divine guidance and direction, while it is inspiration when it is sent to someone like Moses' mother, who was not a Prophet or Messenger (28: 7). However, what is clear concerning Dhu'l-Qarnayn is that, as reported by 'Ali, the fourth Caliph, he was a righteous servant of God who loved and was loved by God (Yazır, 5: 3279).

88. "But as for him who believes and does good, righteous deeds, for him there is recompense of the best, and we will speak to him an easy word of Our command (we will charge him with easy tasks)."

89. Then he followed another way,

90. Until, when he reached the rising-place of the sun and found it rising on a people for whom We had provided no shelter against it.

91. So it was (such was their state and the extent of Dhu'l-Qarnayn's power). We assuredly encompassed all concerning him in Our Knowledge.[30]

92. Then he followed another way,

93. Until, when he reached (a place) between two mountain-barriers, he found before them a people who scarcely understood a word.

94. They said: "O Dhu'l-Qarnayn! Gog and Magog[31] are causing disorder in this land. May we pay you a tribute so that you set a barrier between us and them?"

95. He said: "What my Lord has established me in (the power that He has granted me on this earth) is better (than what you offer). So help me with strength (manpower) and I will set a strong rampart between you and them.

96. "Bring me blocks of iron." Then, when he had filled up (the space between) the two steep mountain-sides, he said: "(Light a fire and) work your bellows!" At length, when he had made it (glow red like) fire, he said: "Bring me molten copper that I may pour upon it."

97. And they (Gog and Magog) were no longer able to surmount, nor were they able to dig their way through (the barrier).

84. We surely established him with power in the land, and for everything (that he rightly purposed) We granted him a way (the just means appropriate to just ends).

85. One such way he followed,

86. Until, when he reached the setting-place of the sun, he saw it setting in a spring of hot and black muddy water,[29] and nearby he found a people. We said: "O Dhu'l-Qarnayn! You can either punish them or you can treat them with kindness. (Which way will you choose?)"

87. He said: "As for him who does wrong (by disbelieving in Him or associating partners with Him and oppressing others) we will punish him and then he is brought back to his Lord, and He punishes him in an indescribable manner.

29. The Qur'ān, which was revealed fourteen centuries ago and is valid until Judgment Day, pursues four main purposes: it seeks to establish in minds and hearts the Existence and Unity of God, Prophethood, bodily Resurrection, and worship of God and justice. It addresses all times and places and is aimed at all levels of understanding. It is an accepted fact that the people of average understanding in every community in every age constitute its great majority. Therefore, in order to guide everyone to the truth and to its basic purposes, the Qur'ān considers the level of that majority, who usually follow their eye-perceptions. However, this never means that it ignores the existence of knowledgeable ones among humankind. So, it uses such styles that as an ordinary person with average intellect can benefit from the Qur'ān, so too can prominent scientists, no matter in which field of science they have expertise, also benefit from it. It sometimes uses symbolic language and frequently resorts to metaphors, allegories, comparisons, and parables. Those who are well-versed in knowledge (3: 7) know how to approach the Qur'ān and benefit from it and conclude that the Qur'ān is the Word of God.

So, by *the setting-place of the sun, he saw it setting in a spring of hot and black muddy water*, the Qur'ān means that Dhu'l-Qarnayn marched a long way toward the west and went as far as the point where he (probably) saw a sea or ocean, appearing like a spring. The description of the sea or ocean as *a spring of hot and black muddy water* suggests that he had reached that point in the hottest days of summer when vaporization was at its greatest.

The expressions *the setting-place of the sun* and *the rising-place of the sun* (verse 90 in the *sūrah*) also denote that Dhu'l-Qarnayn made long military trips toward the east and west.

30. The verses 89–91 mean that Dhu'l-Qarnayn went forth eastward and, conquering one land after another, he reached the farthest territory of the then civilized world. Those living in that territory were primitive people who had no clothes or buildings to protect them from

the sun. God Almighty does not inform us of how Dhu'l-Qarnayn treated them. However, it may be inferred from the verses that being a beloved servant of God and a just, righteous conqueror equipped with every kind of correct means to attain all correct ends, Dhu'l-Qarnayn may have invited them to the right path and they may have made some advances in the way of civilization. The observations of some Western writers on the changing power of Islam can give us a clue in this respect.

Below are given the impressions of the influence of Islam on native Africans written by a Westerner in the nineteenth century:

> As to the effects of Islam when first embraced by a Negro tribe, can there, when viewed as a whole, be any reasonable doubt? Polytheism disappears almost instantaneously; and magic, with its attendant evils, gradually dies away. The general moral elevation is most marked; the natives begin for the first time in their history to dress, and neatly. Squalid filth is replaced by some approach to personal cleanliness; hospitality becomes a religious duty; drunkenness, instead of the rule, becomes a comparatively rare exception... chastity is looked upon as one of the highest, and becomes, in fact, one of the commoner virtues. It is idleness that henceforward degrades, and industry that elevates, instead of the reverse. Offences are henceforward measured by a written code instead of the arbitrary caprice of a chieftain – a step, as everyone will admit, of vast importance in the progress of a tribe. The Mosque gives an idea of architecture at all events higher than any the Negro has yet had. A thirst for literature is created and that for works of science and philosophy as well as for commentaries on the Qur'ān (Ezzati, quoting from B. Smith, *Muḥammad and Muhammadism*, 111-112, 117-118, 231).

Isaac Taylor, in his speech delivered at the Church Congress of England about the effects and influence of Islam on people, said:

> When Muhammadanism (mislabeling for Islam by some Westerners as the result of an incorrect comparison of Islam with

Christianity – AÜ) is embraced, paganism, fetishism, infanticide and witchcraft disappear. Filth is replaced by cleanliness and the new convert acquires personal dignity and self-respect. Immodest dances and promiscuous intercourse of the sexes cease; female chastity is rewarded as a virtue; industry replaces idleness; license gives place to law; order and sobriety prevail; blood feuds, cruelty to animals and slaves are eradicated... Islam swept away corruption and superstitions. Islam was a revolt against empty polemics... It gave hope to the slave, brotherhood to mankind, and recognition to the fundamental facts of human nature. The virtues which Islam inculcates are temperance, cleanliness, chastity, justice, fortitude, courage, benevolence, hospitality, veracity and resignation... Islam preaches a practical brotherhood, the social equality of all Muslims. Slavery is not part of the creed of Islam. Polygamy is a more difficult question. Moses did not prohibit it. It was practiced by David and it is not directly forbidden in the New Testament. Muhammad limited the unbounded license of polygamy. It is the exception rather than the rule... In resignation to God's Will, temperance, chastity, veracity and in brotherhood of believers they (the Muslims) set us a pattern which we should do well to follow. Islam has abolished drunkenness, gambling and prostitution, the three curses of the Christian lands. Islam has done more for civilization than Christianity. The conquest of one-third of the earth to his (Muhammad's) creed was a miracle. (Ezzati, 235–237)

31. Gog and Magog (*Yajūj* and *Majūj* in the Qur'ān) are also mentioned in the Bible (*Genesis*, 10: 2; *Chronicles*, 1: 5; *Ezekiel*, 38: 2; 39: 6; *John*, 20: 8). They were wild tribes that probably inhabited the north-eastern region of Asia. They constantly carried out raids against civilized lands, overrunning the primitive people found on the way. The Mongols that invaded the Muslim lands and reached as far as the Central Europe in the 12th and 13th centuries were regarded as Gog and Magog by both the Muslims and the Europeans. The Qur'ān states that the strong rampart which Dhu'l-Qarnayn built would collapse and that those peoples would invade the civilized world once more before the end of time (18: 98; 21: 96). Reports from God's Messenger, upon him be peace and blessings, regard this invasion as one of the signs of the approach of the Last Hour. Bediüzzaman remarks that like the locusts that fly in great swarms and, then, after destroying crops and vegetables, disappear, Gog and Magog are wild peoples that invade the civilized world at times and then disappear (*Şualar* ["The Rays"], 453–454).

98. Dhu'l-Qarnayn said: "This is a mercy from my Lord. Yet when the time of my Lord's promise comes, He will level it down to the ground; and my Lord's promise is ever true."

99. On that day We will leave people to surge like waves on one another;[32] and the Trumpet will be blown, then We will gather them all together.

100. And on that Day We will place Hell before the unbelievers, plain to view,

101. Those whose eyes are veiled from My Book and any remembrance of Me, and who cannot bear to hear (them).

102. Do they who disbelieve reckon that they can (rightly and justifiably) take any of My servants as guardians (to own and protect them) besides Me? Surely We have prepared Hell to welcome the unbelievers.

103. Say: "Shall We inform you who are the greatest losers in respect of their deeds?

104. "Those whose endeavor has been wasted in this world (because it is directed only to this-worldly ends, and so it is bound to be wasted hereafter also) but who themselves reckon that they are doing good."[33]

105. They are those who disbelieve in the signs and Revelations of their Lord, and in the meeting with Him. Hence, their deeds have come to nothing, and on the Day of Resurrection We will not accord to them any weight.

106. That will be their recompense – Hell – because they have disbelieved and taken My signs and Revelations and My Messengers in mockery.

107. Surely for those who believe and do good, righteous deeds, their welcome is Gardens of the highest level of Paradise.

108. Therein will they abide, without desiring any change therefrom.

109. Say: "If all the sea were ink to write my Lord's words (the acts, decrees, and manifestations of all His Names and Attributes), the sea would indeed be exhausted before my Lord's words are exhausted, even if We were to bring the like of it in addition to it."

110. Say: "I am but a mortal like you, but it is revealed to me that your God is the One and Only God. So, whoever looks forward to meeting his Lord, let him do good, righteous deeds, and let him not associate any partner in the worship of His Lord."

32. It is clear that Dhu'l-Qarnayn made great conquests toward the west, east and northeast, throughout the civilized world as far as the "natural" limits, such as the sea, deserts and mountain ranges. By recounting his conquests after the narration of the Prophet Moses' journey with al-Khadr, which followed the stories of the People of the Cave and the orchards of the two men, the Qur'ān is referring to a "natural" outcome. What is more important than this is that a faith movement can and must be represented by perfect, righteous people. In particular, those who lead it after the Last Prophet, upon him be peace and blessings, must be true, perfect successors to the mission of the Messengers, except that they are not Prophets and they do not receive Revelation that came to the Prophets.

There have also been different opinions concerning where the rampart which Dhu'l-Qarnayn constructed was located. Some have suggested that it was built among the mountains in the range between the Caspian Sea and the Black Sea, while others suggested that the rampart was the Iron Gates near Bukhara, which stood between Transoxiana and Mongolia, and still others suggest that the rampart was the Great Wall of China.

What is of interest in this respect is that it was a barrier which kept the wild, aggressive masses or raiders of Gog and Magog from attacking the civilized world. For centuries there was no such barrier. However, if the latest assaults of Gog and Magog were not the Mongol invasion on the great part of the Muslim world and eastern Europe in the 13th century, then, as suggested by the Qur'ān (verse 99 in this *sūrah*, and 21: 96) and Prophetic reports, the civilized world will witness the greatest destruction of all human history at some time in the future. If we understand that the word *sadd* (barrier) in verse 94 also means a spiritual barrier, it is possible to think that prior to this latest destruction a spiritual barrier will have been erected before such an attack.

Some Prophetic Traditions say that memorizing (and reciting on every Friday) ten verses from the beginning or end of this *sūrah* may enable one to be safe from the corruption and evils of the *Dajjāl* (Anti-Christ in the Christian world), the man or a collective personality or movement expected to appear toward the end of time and will try to eradicate Islam from the social life of Muslims (Muslim, "Ṣalāt al-Musāfirīn," 257). So the stories narrated in this *sūrah* must have close relevance to or implications for the world-wide events that are expected before the end of time.

33. This verse contains a great threat and several warnings. First of all, if a person thinks that they are doing good, this does not mean that they are actually doing good. What is good is that which is acceptable to God and therefore what God has declared to be good. So, doing good depends on knowledge – that is, knowing what pleases God in every case and doing it in the way approved by Him. This requires either having the knowledge, insight, sagacity, and ability to distinguish good and evil in all cases, or in following a true guide who has these characteristics.

The first part of the verse has several meanings.

- Unbelievers and/or polytheists can do some useful things for the worldly life. But their being of use with respect to the afterlife depends on true belief. So, whatever unbelievers and/or polytheists do is bound to be wasted with respect to the afterlife.
- If there are true believers who form a formidable community and strive in God's cause, whatever unbelievers do to defeat them is bound to be in vain.
- Throughout history, unbelievers may at times have had the upper hand against the believers. However, the end always belongs to the believers.

SŪRAH 19

MARYAM (MARY)

Makkah period

This *sūrah* was revealed just before the majority of the Muslims in Makkah emigrated to Abyssinia to escape the persecutions of the Makkan polytheists in the 5th year of the Messenger's mission. In that time a monotheist king ruled Abyssinia. The Quraysh sent 'Abdullāh ibn Rabī'ah and 'Amr ibn al-'Āṣ to the king to attain the return of the refugees. The king questioned the Muslims about their faith and their view of the Prophet Jesus and his mother Virgin Mary. Ja'far ibn Abī Ṭālib, the head of the Muslim refugees, answered him by reciting the initial 35 verses of this *sūrah*.

The *sūrah* begins with the mention of John the Baptist and continues by relating facts about the Prophet Jesus and Virgin Mary. Then it mentions the Prophet Abraham, whose life was partly spent in emigrations, and hints that the way of God's Last Messenger, upon him be peace and blessings, would be no different from those of the previous Messengers, upon them be peace. Then it strongly criticizes the harsh reactions of the Makkan polytheists, and ends by giving the glad tidings to the believers that God will put love for them in the hearts of people and that many people will welcome Islam.

The *sūrah* takes its name after Virgin Mary, and consists of 98 verses.

In the Name of God, the All-Merciful, the All-Compassionate.

1. *Kāf. Hā. Yā. 'Ayn. Ṣād.*

2. A mention of your Lord's mercy to His servant Zachariah:

3. When he invoked his Lord with a call in secret,

4. Saying: "My Lord! My bones have grown feeble and my head glistens with gray hair from old age, and, my Lord, I

have never been unblessed in my prayer to You.

5. "I have fears about (how) my kinsmen (will act in respect of continuing my mission, and safeguarding the future of Mary), and my wife is barren. So bestow upon me a successor out of Your grace,

6. Who will be my heir (in my duty) and heir to (the straight way of) the House of Jacob; and make him, my Lord, one with whom You are well-pleased.[1]

7. (The angels called out to him on God's behalf:) "O Zachariah! We give you the glad tidings of a son whose name will be Yaḥyā (John). We have not given this name to anyone before."

8. He said: "My Lord! How shall I have a son when my wife is barren and I have already reached infirmity in old age?"

9. (The angel) answered: "Just so. Your Lord says: 'It is easy for Me – even as I created you before, when you had been nothing.' "

10. (Zachariah) prayed: "My Lord, appoint a sign for me." "Your sign," He said,

"is that you will not be able to speak to people for three nights."

11. So he came out to his people from the sanctuary, and signified to them (by gestures): "Glorify your Lord at daybreak and in the afternoon."

---

1. The Prophet Zachariah, upon him be peace, recited the prayer mentioned in these verses as he could not perceive of anyone among his kinsmen as able to succeed him in his duty of preaching God's Message, and safeguarding the future of Mary, whose guardianship he had undertaken.

While quoting a person's speech, God does not quote it word by word and in its literal sense; He is not narrating an event simply as a historian or an observer. He considers the intentions and feelings of the speaker and the parts of the speech that a person may not utter. In narrating an event, He considers it with its meaning, causes, and the lessons it provides, as well as with the circumstances under which it took place and the intentions, status, and positions of the principal actors in it. For this reason, we can find the same event or speech narrated in different words and from differ-

ent perspectives in the Qur'an, according to the subject that is being dealt with and which context in which it is found.

The Prophet Zachariah's prayer is mentioned in 3: 38 as: *My Lord, bestow upon me out of Your grace a good, upright offspring*, from which we understand that he asked for a successor from his own family and therefore asked for a son, as he had no children yet. One may wonder why Zachariah requested a successor from his own family; the answer is that *God knows best upon whom to place His Message* (6: 124), and *God made pure Adam and Noah and the House of Abraham and the House of 'Imrān, choosing them above all humankind, as descendants of one another* (3: 33–34). It is impossible that the Prophet Zachariah was not aware of this, and he knew that a successor of his progeny would be one who descended from Jacob's House. (See also 3: 34, note 7.)

305

12. (John was born and when he grew up, We commanded him:) "O John! Hold fast to the Book (the Torah) with (all your) strength!" And We granted him authority with sound, wise judgment (and true understanding of God's Law) while he was yet a little boy;

13. And (the gift of) compassion from Our Presence, and purity. He was very pious and righteous,

14. And dutiful towards his parents, and he was never unruly, rebellious.

15. So peace be upon him on the day he was born and the day of his death, and the day when he will be raised to life.

16. And make mention, in the Book, of Mary.[2] She withdrew from her family to a chamber (in the Temple) facing east (to devote herself to worship and reflection).

17. Thus she kept herself in seclusion from people. Then We sent to her Our spirit, and it appeared before her in the form of a perfect man.[3]

18. She said: "I seek refuge in the All-Merciful from you, if you are a pious, God-revering one."

19. He replied: "I am only a messenger of your Lord to be a means (for God's gift) to you of a pure son."

20. She said: "How shall I have a son, seeing no mortal has ever touched me, and I have never been unchaste?"

21. He said: "Just so. Your Lord says: 'It is easy for Me; and (you shall have a son) so

that We make him for humankind a sign (of Our Power on account of his birth) and a mercy from Us (on account of his being a Messenger). It is a matter already decreed.'"

22. So she conceived him, and then she withdrew with him to a distant place.

23. And the throes of childbirth drove her to the trunk of a date-palm. She said: "Would that I had died before this, and had become a thing forgotten, completely forgotten!"

24. (A voice) called out to her from beneath her: "Do not grieve! Your Lord has set a rivulet at your feet.

25. "And shake the trunk of the date-palm towards you: it will drop fresh, ripe dates upon you.[4]

2. The Qur'ān presents Mary as one of the two exemplary women who lived before the Prophet Muhammad, upon him be peace and blessings (66: 12). The Prophet Muhammad mentions her as one of the greatest four of all women, the other three being 'Āsya, the wife of the Pharaoh, Khadījah, the Prophet's first wife, and Fātimah, his daughter (al-Bukhārī, "Anbiyā," 45).

Mary was perfectly chaste, devout, and righteous. Her mother devoted her to the service of the Temple. She spent all her time in that service and worshipping God. She used to pray, prostrate, give thanks, and feel the inspiration of angels in her heart. God chose her as the virgin mother of the Prophet Jesus, who was distinguished among the Prophets with his superior spirituality. (Also see: 3: 35–37, 42–48)

3. As explained in Appendix 12, the spirit is the source of both physical and spiritual life. For this reason, it is used in the Qur'ān to describe both Revelation and the angel of Revelation (Gabriel). The designation of the angel as spirit is made because angels are spiritual.

Concerning the identity of the spirit who appeared before Mary in the form of a perfect man, the majority of interpreters of the Qur'ān are of the opinion that he was Archangel Gabriel, the angel of Revelation, upon him be peace. There are several arguments to support this, among these being that the Qur'ān mentions Gabriel as the Spirit of Holiness (16: 102) and the Trustworthy Spirit (26: 193). In verse 19 of the *sūrah*, the spirit presents himself as a messenger or envoy of the Lord. The Qur'ān also mentions Gabriel as a noble messenger (69: 40). The same event or other aspects of this event are told in *Sūrat Āl 'Imrān*, 3: 45–47. These verses mention angels, not a single angel. This means that Gabriel came to Mary to be a means of God's conveying to Mary the gift of a son, while other angels gave her the glad tidings of that son.

Despite the opinions of many interpreters of the Qur'ān concerning the identity of the spirit mentioned above, some hold the view that it may be another being mentioned in several places of the Qur'ān with the name of the Spirit, and about whose identity you will find an explanation in *sūrah* 70, note 1.

The Gospels report that Mary was later married to Joseph, the carpenter, and gave him sons and daughters. It is extremely difficult to accept such reports. It is much more likely that a chaste woman like Mary, who gave birth to a great Messenger without a father, would not have later married a man.

The verse indicates that spirit beings may assume visible forms. But the Qur'ān is not alluding to modern necromancy, which some "civilized" people practice by trying to contact the spirits of the dead, for these, in reality, are evil spirits masquerading as dead people. Rather, this form is the form known to certain saints, like Muhyi'd-Dīn ibn al-'Arabī, who could communicate with good spirits at will, make contact, and form relations with them.

4. While some of the commentators are of the opinion that the person who called out to Mary was the Spirit, while others argue that that person was the new-born child, and that the rivulet emerged suddenly, and the date-palm, which had already been dried up, grew green all at once and yielded fresh, ripe dates. We cannot deny such miracles could happen during the birth of a Prophet, as many miracles were reported to take place during the Prophet Muhammad's birth. Whichever of these views is right and whether this place suddenly became a restful place with a spring or not, we learn from 23: 50 that the place to which Mary retreated was a lofty, quiet setting with a spring flowing in it.

سُوْرَةُ مَرْيَمَ   ٣٠٦

فَكُلِى وَاشْرَبِى وَقَرِّى عَيْنًا فَإِمَّا تَرَيِنَّ مِنَ الْبَشَرِ أَحَدًا
فَقُوْلِى إِنِّى نَذَرْتُ لِلرَّحْمَٰنِ صَوْمًا فَلَنْ أُكَلِّمَ الْيَوْمَ إِنْسِيًّا
۞ فَأَتَتْ بِهِ قَوْمَهَا تَحْمِلُهُ ۚ قَالُوا يَامَرْيَمُ لَقَدْ جِئْتِ شَيْئًا
فَرِيًّا ۞ يَاأُخْتَ هُٰرُوْنَ مَا كَانَ أَبُوكِ امْرَأَ سَوْءٍ وَمَا
كَانَتْ أُمُّكِ بَغِيًّا ۞ فَأَشَارَتْ إِلَيْهِ ۖ قَالُوا كَيْفَ نُكَلِّمُ مَنْ
كَانَ فِى الْمَهْدِ صَبِيًّا ۞ قَالَ إِنِّى عَبْدُ اللَّهِ آتَانِىَ الْكِتَابَ
وَجَعَلَنِى نَبِيًّا ۞ وَجَعَلَنِى مُبَارَكًا أَيْنَ مَا كُنْتُ وَأَوْصَانِى
بِالصَّلَوٰةِ وَالزَّكَوٰةِ مَا دُمْتُ حَيًّا ۞ وَبَرًّا بِوَالِدَتِى وَلَمْ
يَجْعَلْنِى جَبَّارًا شَقِيًّا ۞ وَالسَّلَامُ عَلَىَّ يَوْمَ وُلِدْتُ وَيَوْمَ أَمُوتُ
وَيَوْمَ أُبْعَثُ حَيًّا ۞ ذَٰلِكَ عِيسَى ابْنُ مَرْيَمَ ۚ قَوْلَ الْحَقِّ الَّذِى فِيهِ
يَمْتَرُونَ ۞ مَا كَانَ لِلَّهِ أَنْ يَتَّخِذَ مِنْ وَلَدٍ ۖ سُبْحَانَهُ ۚ إِذَا قَضَى
أَمْرًا فَإِنَّمَا يَقُولُ لَهُ كُنْ فَيَكُونُ ۞ وَإِنَّ اللَّهَ رَبِّى وَرَبُّكُمْ
فَاعْبُدُوهُ ۚ هَٰذَا صِرَاطٌ مُسْتَقِيمٌ ۞ فَاخْتَلَفَ الْأَحْزَابُ مِنْ بَيْنِهِمْ ۖ
فَوَيْلٌ لِلَّذِينَ كَفَرُوا مِنْ مَشْهَدِ يَوْمٍ عَظِيمٍ ۞ أَسْمِعْ بِهِمْ وَأَبْصِرْ
يَوْمَ يَأْتُونَنَا ۖ لَٰكِنِ الظَّالِمُونَ الْيَوْمَ فِى ضَلَالٍ مُبِينٍ ۞

26. "So eat and drink, and be comforted. If you should see some person, say (through gesture): "I have vowed a fast of silence to the All-Merciful, so I cannot speak to any human being today."

27. She came to her people, carrying him. They exclaimed: "O Mary! Assuredly you have done an unexpected, strange thing!

28. "O sister of Aaron,[5] your father was never a wicked man, nor was your mother unchaste."

29. Mary pointed to him (the infant, signifying that they should ask him). They cried: "How can we talk to one in the cradle, an infant boy?"

30. (The infant) said: "Surely I am *'abdu 'l-Lāh* (a servant of God).[6] He (has already decreed that He) will give me the Book (the Gospel) and make me a Prophet.

31. "He has made me blessed (and a means of His blessings for people) wherever I may be, and He has enjoined upon me the Prayer (the *Ṣalāh*) and the Prescribed Purifying Alms (the *Zakāh*) (and to enjoin the same upon others) for as long as I live.

32. "And (He has made me) dutiful towards my mother, and He has not made me unruly, wicked.

33. "So peace be upon me on the day I was born and the day of my death, and the day when I will be raised to life."

34. Such was Jesus son of Mary: in the words of the truth about which they (the Jews and Christians) have been doubting (and disputing amongst themselves and with each other).

35. It is not for God to take to Himself a child. All-Glorified is He (in that He is absolutely above doing such things). When He decrees a thing, He does but say to it "Be!" and it is.

36. "Surely God is my Lord and your Lord, so worship Him. This is a straight path (to follow)."

37. And yet, the parties (the Jews and Christians) have differed among themselves (about him). Woe, then, to those who disbelieve because of the meeting of an awesome Day.

38. How well they will hear and how well they will see on the Day when they come before Us (the truth that they hide or push away will be clear to them)! But today (it will be of no avail to) the wrongdoers, (and they) will be in obvious loss.

5. It was a custom among the Children of Israel that they gave or linked their children to the names of renowned people or people were linked with one of their renowned ancestors. Mary was a descendent of Prophet Aaron, so people called her the sister of Aaron.

6. It can be expected that different opinions will emerge concerning a person who was born without a father from a chaste virgin. In this way, it was not long after his being withdrawn from the earth that some declared Jesus – God forbid! – God, while others claimed him as God's son, and that his virtuous mother was the mother of God, although they also reported that she married a man after Jesus' birth and gave him many children. By causing Jesus to speak while he was a baby in the cradle, the Almighty made him proclaim first that he was a servant of God, and forewarned against possible deviations. As in the basic formula of Islam preached by the Prophet Muḥammad that "I bear witness that there is no deity but God, and again I bear witness that Muḥammad is His servant and Messenger," Jesus stressed that he is, first of all, God's servant and then one of His Prophets.

وَاَنذِرْهُمْ يَوْمَ الْحَسْرَةِ اِذْ قُضِيَ الْاَمْرُ وَهُمْ فِي غَفْلَةٍ وَهُمْ لَا يُؤْمِنُونَ ۝ اِنَّا نَحْنُ نَرِثُ الْاَرْضَ وَمَنْ عَلَيْهَا وَاِلَيْنَا يُرْجَعُونَ ۝ وَاذْكُرْ فِي الْكِتَابِ اِبْرَاهِيمَ اِنَّهُ كَانَ صِدِّيقًا نَّبِيًّا ۝ اِذْ قَالَ لِاَبِيهِ يَا اَبَتِ لِمَ تَعْبُدُ مَا لَا يَسْمَعُ وَلَا يُبْصِرُ وَلَا يُغْنِي عَنكَ شَيْئًا ۝ يَا اَبَتِ اِنِّي قَدْ جَاءَنِي مِنَ الْعِلْمِ مَا لَمْ يَأْتِكَ فَاتَّبِعْنِي اَهْدِكَ صِرَاطًا سَوِيًّا ۝ يَا اَبَتِ لَا تَعْبُدِ الشَّيْطَانَ اِنَّ الشَّيْطَانَ كَانَ لِلرَّحْمَانِ عَصِيًّا ۝ يَا اَبَتِ اِنِّي اَخَافُ اَنْ يَمَسَّكَ عَذَابٌ مِّنَ الرَّحْمَانِ فَتَكُونَ لِلشَّيْطَانِ وَلِيًّا ۝ قَالَ اَرَاغِبٌ اَنْتَ عَنْ آلِهَتِي يَا اِبْرَاهِيمُ لَئِنْ لَّمْ تَنْتَهِ لَاَرْجُمَنَّكَ وَاهْجُرْنِي مَلِيًّا ۝ قَالَ سَلَامٌ عَلَيْكَ سَاَسْتَغْفِرُ لَكَ رَبِّي اِنَّهُ كَانَ بِي حَفِيًّا ۝ وَاَعْتَزِلُكُمْ وَمَا تَدْعُونَ مِنْ دُونِ اللهِ وَاَدْعُو رَبِّي عَسَى اَلَّا اَكُونَ بِدُعَاءِ رَبِّي شَقِيًّا ۝ فَلَمَّا اعْتَزَلَهُمْ وَمَا يَعْبُدُونَ مِنْ دُونِ اللهِ وَهَبْنَا لَهُ اِسْحَاقَ وَيَعْقُوبَ وَكُلًّا جَعَلْنَا نَبِيًّا ۝ وَوَهَبْنَا لَهُمْ مِنْ رَحْمَتِنَا وَجَعَلْنَا لَهُمْ لِسَانَ صِدْقٍ عَلِيًّا ۝ وَاذْكُرْ فِي الْكِتَابِ مُوسَى اِنَّهُ كَانَ مُخْلَصًا وَكَانَ رَسُولًا نَّبِيًّا ۝

———⟅⟆———

39. So warn people of the coming of the Day of anguish and regrets, when every-thing will have been decided, for (even now) they are in heedlessness, and they do not believe.

40. Surely it is We alone Who will inherit the earth and all who live on it; and to Us all will be brought back.

41. And make mention of Abraham in the Book. He was surely a sincere man of truth, a Prophet.

42. When he said to his father:[8] "O my father! Why do you worship that which neither hears nor sees, nor can in anything avail you?

43. "O my father! There has indeed come to me of knowledge (of truth) such as has never come to you, so follow me, and I will guide you to an even, straight path.

44. "O my father! Do not worship Satan (by obeying his suggestions to you to wor-ship idols)! Satan is ever rebellious against the All-Merciful.

45. "O my father! I am fearful lest a pun-ishment from the All-Merciful befall you, and then you will become a close friend of Satan (and an instrument in his hand)."

46. His father said: "Have you turned away from my deities, O Abraham? If you do not desist, I will surely cause you to be stoned! Now get away from me for a long while!"

47. He said: "Peace be upon you! I will pray to my Lord to forgive you. Surely He has ever been gracious to me.

48. "And I will withdraw from you (all), and from whatever you deify and invoke other than God. I pray to my Lord alone; I hope that I will not be unblessed in my prayer to my Lord."

49. After he had withdrawn from them and from all that they were worshipping other than God, We bestowed upon him Isaac and Jacob;[9] and each of them We made a Prophet.

50. We bestowed upon them (many other gifts) out of Our Mercy, and granted them a most true and lofty renown.[10]

51. And mention Moses in the Book. He was one chosen, endowed with perfect sincerity and purity of intention in faith and practicing the Religion, and was a Messenger, a Prophet.[11]

8. For Abraham's father, see 6: 74, note 14; 9: 114, note 24.

9. As is known, the Prophet Jacob was the son of Isaac and grandson of the Prophet Abraham, upon him be peace. Abraham had another son, Ishmael. The reason why the Qur'ān mentions Jacob here is that this *sūrah*, like the previous two, *al-Isrā'* and *al-Kahf*, makes frequent reference to the People of the Book – the Jews and Christians – in between the main topics. The Jews descended from the Prophet Jacob's twelve sons.

10. The Qur'ān mentions the Prophet Abraham, upon him be peace, here in particular in order to console the Muslims over their emigration to Abyssinia and to prepare their hearts for a possible, permanent emigration.

Emigration is an important phenomenon in human history. In addition to its general relevance to the establishment of civilizations, it has special significance in connection with the "holy ones," those dedicated to carrying the light throughout the world.

First of all, every individual is a traveler and therefore, in some sense, an emigrant. Their journey starts in the world of spirits and continues through the stations of their mother's womb, childhood, youth, old age and the grave, and from there to a completely new world. Although a person is one among millions of people, in essence, each individual is born alone, lives their own life, endures their own death, and is bound to be resurrected alone. Likewise, each of those people of high stature who throughout history have guided humankind started their sacred mission from a single being, then disseminated the light from the torch they carried, illuminating the minds and hearts of others, inculcating hope and faith in their followers and transforming lands once submerged in darkness into lands of light. And each one of these guides had to emigrate from one place to another for the sake of their cause.

Faith, emigration, and striving in God's cause are the three pillars of a single, sacred truth. They are the three "taps" of a fountain from which the water of life flows for people

to drink from, allowing them to convey their message without becoming wearied, and, when the opposition is too formidable to overcome, to set out for a new land regardless of their home, property, or family.

Every new idea or message has always been resisted wherever it has appeared, and those who have offered it have usually been welcomed in new places where their pasts were unknown. In every movement of revival, prior to emigration, there are two stages of great importance. In the first stage, a person with a cause develops their character, overflows with belief, and is inflamed by love, and surpassing their own self, grows into a passionate servant of the truth. They struggle, at this stage, against the temptations of the carnal soul to establish their authentic, spiritual character. This is called "the major or greater *jihad*" – *al-jihād al-akbar*. Then they rise, in the second stage, to radiate the lights of belief to the world around them. This stage is, in fact, the door to emigration.

Emigration should not, of course, be understood only in the material sense. Rather, a person experiences emigration throughout their life in the spiritual sense. Each inner intellectual or spiritual transformation, from indolence to action, from decay to self-renewal, from suffocation in the atmosphere of sinfulness to exaltation in the realm of the spirit, may be regarded as an emigration. It is my conviction that only those who have been able to actualize these inner emigrations can find in themselves the strength and resolution to leave their homes and families for the sake of a sublime ideal.

Emigration in its two dimensions, spiritual and material, was first represented by the great Prophets, Abraham, Lot, Moses, and Jesus, upon them be peace, who shone like suns on the horizon of humanity, and in its most comprehensive meaning and function, was realized by the greatest of them, namely the Prophet Muḥammad, who is the pride of mankind, upon him be peace and blessings. The door to emigration has since been open to all those who walk in his footsteps.

Emigration in the way of truth and for its sake is so sanctified that the community of holy ones around the Last Prophet, who sacrificed their possessions and souls for the sake of the cause they believed in, were praised by God as (and have since been called) "the Emigrants." We can see the importance of this in the fact that the beginning of the sacred era of this holy community was marked, not by the birth of the Prophet, or by the first Revelation, or by such victories as Badr or the conquest of Makkah, but by the emigration to Madīnah.

Every individual who has emigrated for the sake of a sublime ideal will always deeply feel the pressure of the ideal which urged them to emigrate and to design their life according to that ideal. Secondly, they will be freed from the criticism of some mistakes that they might have made in childhood or youth. While, in their own land, they are probably remembered and criticized for their past faults, and therefore have little influence upon people, in the land they have emigrated to they will be known for their spiritual brilliance, unadulterated ideas, pure intentions, and extraordinary sacrifices. For these and other reasons, it has almost always been the emigrants who change the flow of history and start new eras in the life of humankind.

Toynbee, the renowned British historian, mentions twenty-seven civilizations founded by nomadic or migrant peoples. No one can overcome such dynamic people. They are not accustomed to ease and comfort, they are ready to sacrifice everything worldly, they are used to every kind of hardship, and they are always ready to march wherever their cause requires them to go. (See *Towards the Lost Paradise*, 94–97.)

11. For the distinction between a Messenger and a Prophet, see *sūrah* 3: 81, note 16.

308   سورة مريم   ٣٠٨

وَنَادَيْنَاهُ مِن جَانِبِ الطُّورِ الْأَيْمَنِ وَقَرَّبْنَاهُ نَجِيًّا ۝ وَوَهَبْنَا لَهُ مِن
رَّحْمَتِنَا أَخَاهُ هَارُونَ نَبِيًّا ۝ وَاذْكُرْ فِي الْكِتَابِ إِسْمَاعِيلَ إِنَّهُ كَانَ
صَادِقَ الْوَعْدِ وَكَانَ رَسُولًا نَبِيًّا ۝ وَكَانَ يَأْمُرُ أَهْلَهُ بِالصَّلَاةِ
وَالزَّكَاةِ وَكَانَ عِندَ رَبِّهِ مَرْضِيًّا ۝ وَاذْكُرْ فِي الْكِتَابِ
إِدْرِيسَ إِنَّهُ كَانَ صِدِّيقًا نَبِيًّا ۝ وَرَفَعْنَاهُ مَكَانًا عَلِيًّا ۝
أُوْلَئِكَ الَّذِينَ أَنْعَمَ اللَّهُ عَلَيْهِم مِّنَ النَّبِيِّينَ مِن ذُرِّيَّةِ آدَمَ وَمِمَّنْ
حَمَلْنَا مَعَ نُوحٍ وَمِن ذُرِّيَّةِ إِبْرَاهِيمَ وَإِسْرَائِيلَ وَمِمَّنْ هَدَيْنَا وَاجْتَبَيْنَا
إِذَا تُتْلَى عَلَيْهِمْ آيَاتُ الرَّحْمَنِ خَرُّوا سُجَّدًا وَبُكِيًّا ۝ فَخَلَفَ مِن
بَعْدِهِمْ خَلْفٌ أَضَاعُوا الصَّلَاةَ وَاتَّبَعُوا الشَّهَوَاتِ فَسَوْفَ يَلْقَوْنَ
غَيًّا ۝ إِلَّا مَن تَابَ وَآمَنَ وَعَمِلَ صَالِحًا فَأُوْلَئِكَ يَدْخُلُونَ الْجَنَّةَ
وَلَا يُظْلَمُونَ شَيْئًا ۝ جَنَّاتِ عَدْنٍ الَّتِي وَعَدَ الرَّحْمَنُ عِبَادَهُ
بِالْغَيْبِ إِنَّهُ كَانَ وَعْدُهُ مَأْتِيًّا ۝ لَا يَسْمَعُونَ فِيهَا لَغْوًا إِلَّا سَلَامًا
وَلَهُمْ رِزْقُهُمْ فِيهَا بُكْرَةً وَعَشِيًّا ۝ تِلْكَ الْجَنَّةُ الَّتِي نُورِثُ مِنْ
عِبَادِنَا مَن كَانَ تَقِيًّا ۝ وَمَا نَتَنَزَّلُ إِلَّا بِأَمْرِ رَبِّكَ لَهُ مَا بَيْنَ
أَيْدِينَا وَمَا خَلْفَنَا وَمَا بَيْنَ ذَلِكَ وَمَا كَانَ رَبُّكَ نَسِيًّا ۝

———◈———

52. We called out to him from the right side of Mount Sinai[12] and drew him close for communication.

53. Out of Our Mercy, We granted him his brother Aaron to be a Prophet.

54. Also make mention of Ishmael in the Book. He was one always true to his promise, and was a Messenger, a Prophet.

55. He used to enjoin on his people the Prayer and the Prescribed Purifying Alms, and he was one favored and pleasing in his Lord's sight.

56. And mention Idrīs in the Book. He was surely a sincere man of truth, a Prophet.

57. And We raised him to a high station.[13]

58. Those are some of the Prophets – upon whom God bestowed His blessings (of Scripture, Prophethood, authority with

sound judgment, and wisdom) – from among the descendants of Adam and of those whom We carried (in the Ark) with Noah, and from among the descendants of Abraham and Israel (Jacob), and those whom We guided and chose. When the All-Merciful's Revelations were recited to them, they would fall down, prostrating and weeping.[14]

59. Then, there succeeded them generations who neglected and wasted the Prayer and followed (their) lusts, (abandoning the service of God's cause). They will meet perdition (as their just deserts).[15]

60. Except those who repent and come to faith and do good, righteous deeds. Such will enter Paradise and will not be wronged in anything.

61. Gardens of perpetual bliss which the All-Merciful has promised to His servants while unseen (beyond the perception and knowledge of the servants). His promise is ever sure of fulfillment.

62. They will hear therein no idle talk, but only peace (contentment and safety). And they will have their provision therein morning and evening.

63. That is the Paradise which We will cause those of Our servants who are God-revering, pious to inherit (as theirs forever).

64. (In response to an interval in the coming of Revelation, Gabriel explained:) We do not descend but by your Lord's command only. To Him belongs whatever is before us and whatever is behind us and whatever is between (all time and space and whatever we do at all times in all places). And your Lord is never forgetful (so do not fear that He forgets you).

12. On his way to Egypt from Midian, the Prophet Moses, upon him be peace, saw a fire as he was passing along the south of Mount Sinai. On drawing near to it, he heard a voice calling out to him, "O Moses, I am your Lord!" This voice came from the eastern side of the mountain; that is the right side according to where Moses was standing, as he was facing it.

13. The majority of the Qur'ān's interpreters are of the opinion that Idrīs was the Prophet who lived before Noah and was mentioned by Enoch in the Bible. According to the Bible, Enoch begat Methuselah when he was 65 years old, and walked with God after he begat Methuselah three hundred years. Then God took him. The Talmud adds that when people were corrupted before Noah, an angel of God came to Enoch, who had been living in seclusion, to bring him the Lord's order to teach people the way they should follow. People accepted his teachings, and he ruled them for 353 years with justice, during which God poured His bounties on people (H. Plano, *The Talmud Selections*, 18–21, quoted by al-Mawdūdī, 5: 163, note 33).

Many hold that the fact that Idrīs was raised to a high station means that God had granted him a high position. However, Bediüzzaman Said Nursi writes that life has five degrees, and the third degree is manifested in the lives of the Prophets Jesus and Idrīs, who live in heaven with their bodies. Their bodies are not bound by the necessities of human life and have acquired a sort of refinement and luminosity to the degree of astral bodies and an angelic type of life (*The Letters*, "the 1st Letter," 1: 2).

Writers such as Sayyid Hussain Nasr make a connection between Idrīs being raised to a high station (in heaven) with the theory that

he lived in Iraq and that astronomy made great developments during his lifetime. This astronomical knowledge was then transmitted by those who were on Noah's Ark, and was misused by the people in Iraq centuries later to worship celestial bodies. As is known, when the Prophet Abraham, upon him be peace, began his mission in Iraq, people were worshipping celestial bodies. Those writers also draw attention to the basic difference between the views of Islam and modern views of humanity and their relation with God. In the legend of Prometheus, which provides a basis for the modern view of humanity and their relation with God that developed in the West during and after the Renaissance, Prometheus was punished by the gods because he had stolen from the sacred fire to bring it to humanity. Whereas, God raised Idrīs, who was the father of astronomy and who brought Heaven's light or message to humanity, to heaven.

14. For similar verses for these and other Prophets, see 6: 87–89.

15. The verse draws attention to the fact that neglecting and wasting the Prayer, which causes or is accompanied by following some of the lusts which are mentioned in 3: 14 – women, children, treasures of gold and silver (hoarded money), cattle, plantations (and profits) – is the reason for the corruption of the generations that came after the Prophets. When we consider this verse along with verse 29: 45 – *Surely, the Prayer restrains from all that is indecent and shameful, and all that is evil* – the matter will be clearer. We should bear in mind that it is Satan who invites people to indecencies and evils (24: 21). The neglect of the Prayer, we can see then, is the primary cause for submission to Satan.

309   ٣٠٩

رَبُّ السَّمَوَاتِ وَالْأَرْضِ وَمَا بَيْنَهُمَا فَاعْبُدْهُ وَاصْطَبِرْ
لِعِبَادَتِهِ ۚ هَلْ تَعْلَمُ لَهُ سَمِيًّا ۞ وَيَقُولُ الْإِنْسَانُ أَءِذَا مَا مِتُّ
لَسَوْفَ أُخْرَجُ حَيًّا ۞ أَوَلَا يَذْكُرُ الْإِنْسَانُ أَنَّا خَلَقْنَاهُ
مِن قَبْلُ وَلَمْ يَكُ شَيْئًا ۞ فَوَرَبِّكَ لَنَحْشُرَنَّهُمْ وَالشَّيَاطِينَ
ثُمَّ لَنُحْضِرَنَّهُمْ حَوْلَ جَهَنَّمَ جِثِيًّا ۞ ثُمَّ لَنَنزِعَنَّ مِن
كُلِّ شِيعَةٍ أَيُّهُمْ أَشَدُّ عَلَى الرَّحْمَٰنِ عِتِيًّا ۞ ثُمَّ لَنَحْنُ أَعْلَمُ
بِالَّذِينَ هُمْ أَوْلَىٰ بِهَا صِلِيًّا ۞ وَإِن مِّنكُمْ إِلَّا وَارِدُهَا ۚ كَانَ عَلَىٰ
رَبِّكَ حَتْمًا مَّقْضِيًّا ۞ ثُمَّ نُنَجِّي الَّذِينَ اتَّقَوا وَّنَذَرُ الظَّالِمِينَ
فِيهَا جِثِيًّا ۞ وَإِذَا تُتْلَىٰ عَلَيْهِمْ ءَايَاتُنَا بَيِّنَاتٍ قَالَ الَّذِينَ
كَفَرُوا لِلَّذِينَ ءَامَنُوا أَيُّ الْفَرِيقَيْنِ خَيْرٌ مَّقَامًا وَأَحْسَنُ نَدِيًّا ۞
وَكَمْ أَهْلَكْنَا قَبْلَهُم مِّن قَرْنٍ هُمْ أَحْسَنُ أَثَاثًا وَرِءْيًا ۞ قُلْ مَن
كَانَ فِي الضَّلَالَةِ فَلْيَمْدُدْ لَهُ الرَّحْمَٰنُ مَدًّا ۚ حَتَّىٰ إِذَا رَأَوْا
مَا يُوعَدُونَ إِمَّا الْعَذَابَ وَإِمَّا السَّاعَةَ فَسَيَعْلَمُونَ مَنْ هُوَ شَرٌّ
مَّكَانًا وَأَضْعَفُ جُندًا ۞ وَيَزِيدُ اللَّهُ الَّذِينَ اهْتَدَوا هُدًى ۗ
وَالْبَاقِيَاتُ الصَّالِحَاتُ خَيْرٌ عِندَ رَبِّكَ ثَوَابًا وَخَيْرٌ مَّرَدًّا ۞

---

65. (He is) the Lord of the heavens and the earth and all that is between them; so worship Him alone, and be constant and patient in His worship. Do you know of any whose name is worthy to be mentioned along with His (as Deity and Lord to worship)?

66. And (despite this, that disbelieving) human says: "What? Once I am dead, will I then be brought forth alive?"

67. Does (that) human not bear in mind that We created him before when he was nothing?

68. And so, by your Lord, We will most certainly raise to life and gather them all together, as well as the satans (of humankind and jinn whom they used to follow,) before Us, and then We will most certainly heap them up on their knees in groups around Hell.

69. Then We will certainly pluck out from every group of the same belief the ones who were most obstinate in rebellion against the All-Merciful.

70. Indeed, We know best who deserves most (and before all others) to be thrown into Hell to roast therein.

71. There is no one among you, (O humankind,) who will not come to it. This is a fixed decree which your Lord has bound Himself to fulfill.

72. Then We will save those who keep from disobedience to Him in reverence for Him and piety, and We will leave in it the wrongdoers (who associate partners with God or deny Him), humbled on their knees.[16]

73. When Our Revelations, clear as evidence and in meaning are recited (and conveyed) to them, those who persistently disbelieve say to those who believe: "Which of the two parties (– you or us –) is superior in status with more impressive dwellings and more imposing as a company?"

74. And yet, how many a generation have We destroyed before them who were superior in respect of possessions and outward show!

75. Say: "Whoever is lost in error, no matter how much the All-Merciful adds (to their wealth and how long He prolongs their life-span), when they face what they were promised – whether it be punishment (here in this world) or the Last Hour – they will come to know who is worse in position and weaker in forces.

76. God strengthens in guidance those who have sought and found guidance. The righteous, good deeds of lasting merit are best in your Lord's sight for reward, and best for returns.[17]

16. The existence of Paradise increases the suffering of Hell, and the existence of Hell increases the happiness in Paradise. So, everyone will come to Hell so that the believers may witness its horror and be more thankful to God because He has not condemned them to its punishment. Those who deserve to be burned will be thrown into the Fire and left there, while the believers who have not been sentenced to burn will never enter it. Some of them will not even hear its sound (21: 102).

17. Human beings are inclined to show haste in making decisions based on current conditions. The Makkan polytheists argued that they had more beautiful and richly furnished houses, that they were greater and more esteemed in position, and more powerful in company, and therefore their way or belief must be true. The same argument has been put forward by many in the world in order to abase Islam. As Muslims, we sometimes make the same mistake by starting with the same argument in order to criticize Muslims. However, the primary criterion to judge and compare belief and unbelief or Islam and other religions is the afterlife. In the verses above, the Qur'ān refers to this point and draws attention to the fact that if Muslims really follow God's way in the footsteps of God's Messenger, upon him be peace and blessings, the superiority of unbelievers in number and possessions will cause their eventual doom. The Muslims were almost an unrivalled power in the world for nearly eleven centuries from the time of the Messenger. A few centuries of decline cannot be a criterion to make a true judgment. Those who will live long enough will see what the future will bring and the final judgment in the Hereafter will show the truth in all its clarity.

310   سورة مريم   ٣١٠

أَفَرَءَيْتَ الَّذِى كَفَرَ بِاٰيَـٰتِنَا وَقَالَ لَأُوتَيَنَّ مَالًا وَوَلَدًا ۝ أَطَّلَعَ الْغَيْبَ أَمِ اتَّخَذَ عِندَ الرَّحْمَـٰنِ عَهْدًا ۝ كَلَّا ۚ سَنَكْتُبُ مَا يَقُولُ وَنَمُدُّ لَهُۥ مِنَ الْعَذَابِ مَدًّا ۝ وَنَرِثُهُۥ مَا يَقُولُ وَيَأْتِينَا فَرْدًا ۝ وَاتَّخَذُوا مِن دُونِ اللّٰهِ اٰلِهَةً لِّيَكُونُوا لَهُمْ عِزًّا ۝ كَلَّا ۚ سَيَكْفُرُونَ بِعِبَادَتِهِمْ وَيَكُونُونَ عَلَيْهِمْ ضِدًّا ۝ أَلَمْ تَرَ أَنَّا أَرْسَلْنَا الشَّيَاطِينَ عَلَى الْكَافِرِينَ تَؤُزُّهُمْ أَزًّا ۝ فَلَا تَعْجَلْ عَلَيْهِمْ ۖ إِنَّمَا نَعُدُّ لَهُمْ عَدًّا ۝ يَوْمَ نَحْشُرُ الْمُتَّقِينَ إِلَى الرَّحْمَـٰنِ وَفْدًا ۝ وَنَسُوقُ الْمُجْرِمِينَ إِلَىٰ جَهَنَّمَ وِرْدًا ۝ لَا يَمْلِكُونَ الشَّفَاعَةَ إِلَّا مَنِ اتَّخَذَ عِندَ الرَّحْمَـٰنِ عَهْدًا ۝ وَقَالُوا اتَّخَذَ الرَّحْمَـٰنُ وَلَدًا ۝ لَّقَدْ جِئْتُمْ شَيْئًا إِدًّا ۝ تَكَادُ السَّمَـٰوَاتُ يَتَفَطَّرْنَ مِنْهُ وَتَنشَقُّ الْأَرْضُ وَتَخِرُّ الْجِبَالُ هَدًّا ۝ أَن دَعَوْا لِلرَّحْمَـٰنِ وَلَدًا ۝ وَمَا يَنبَغِى لِلرَّحْمَـٰنِ أَن يَتَّخِذَ وَلَدًا ۝ إِن كُلُّ مَن فِى السَّمَـٰوَاتِ وَالْأَرْضِ إِلَّا اٰتِى الرَّحْمَـٰنِ عَبْدًا ۝ لَّقَدْ أَحْصَىٰهُمْ وَعَدَّهُمْ عَدًّا ۝ وَكُلُّهُمْ اٰتِيهِ يَوْمَ الْقِيَـٰمَةِ فَرْدًا ۝

---

77. Have you ever considered the one who disbelieves in Our Revelations and says (in insolence): "(Whatever you say, I will continue just as I am, for) I will most certainly be given wealth and children"?

78. Has he gained knowledge of the Unseen, or has he made a (particular, private) covenant with the All-Merciful?

79. No indeed! But We will record what he says and saddle him (with its consequence) as an ever increasing punishment.

80. And We will inherit of him what he says, and he will come to us quite alone (bereft of wealth and children).[18]

81. They have taken deities apart from God so that they may be (a means of) might and glory for them.

82. No indeed! Those (whom they deified – beings such as angels, jinn, Prophets,

saints, and heroes, etc.) will deny their worship of them and turn against them as adversaries (on Judgment Day).

83. Do you not see that We send the satans upon the unbelievers (because of their unbelief), and they impel them (towards sin and every kind of evil) with strong impulsion?

84. Hence, be in no haste against them (so that their days and their persecutions of you might end sooner), for We but number for them a certain (fixed) number (of days, the time allotted for their respite).

85. A Day (will come) when We will gather the God-revering, pious ones as honored guests of the All-Merciful (in Paradise);

86. And drive the disbelieving criminals to Hell like thirsty cattle.

87. (Those who have taken deities so that they may intercede with God on their behalf should know that) none will have a right of intercession except such as have a covenant with the All-Merciful (by virtue of the quality of their faith and worship, and their nearness to Him).

88. As it is, some say: "The All-Merciful has taken to Himself a child."

89. Assuredly you have (in such an assertion) brought forth something monstrous –

90. The heavens are all but rent, and the earth split asunder, and the mountains fall down in ruins –

91. That they ascribe to the All-Merciful a child!

92. It is not for the All-Merciful to take to Himself a child.

93. There is none in the heavens and the earth but comes to the All-Merciful as a servant.[19]

94. Most certainly He knows and registers them, and has numbered them exactly, (having appointed for every being a

particular service or duty, and determined for each a life-span and provision);

95. And every one of them will appear before Him on the Day of Resurrection, quite alone (bereft of all worldly things, children and family, friends and helpers).

---

18. A person's possession of wealth and children is dependent on laws which the Almighty has established without discriminating between belief and unbelief. By using the phrase *No indeed!* in verse 79, the Qur'ān rejects the claim that insistence on unbelief brings wealth and children; it is not stating that unbelievers cannot have them. However, in addition to unbelief being totally wrong, insistence on unbelief because of one's wealth and children may cause one misfortunes in the world because of them. Furthermore, unbelief means Hell in the spirit, even when one is in material luxury. The apparent merry-making of unbelievers is no more than their trying to appease their inner unhappiness and purposeful self-deception. By contrast, belief and spiritual contentment cause one to experience Paradise in their heart, even if they are lacking material goods.

19. Everything is assigned a place in the grand scheme of the universe, which works in a magnificent way. The sun, the moon, stars, and all other heavenly bodies are knit together in a splendid system, following unalterable laws, and never deviating from their ordained course. So all of them are God's servants – those submitted to Him consciously or unconsciously – just as are the air, water, heat, stones, trees, and animals, for everything in existence obeys God by submitting to His laws. Even unbelievers and atheists are so as far as their bodily existence is concerned, for each part of their bodies follows the course God has established for it, from birth until death and dissolution. Moreover, they can never escape the sphere of God's Will and Power, even in the realm where they are allowed to exercise their free will. God has established what consequences they will meet by their actions. They do not play the least part in their coming into and departing from the world, and when, where and into what family they will be born. They can never determine their physical structure or color. So all things and beings in the universe can only live within the borders as God has determined them. Finally, everyone will appear before God in total submission on Judgment Day.

SŪRAH 20

ṬĀ. HĀ

Makkah period

This *surah* of 135 verses was revealed in Makkah. It begins with consoling God's Messenger, upon him be peace and blessings. As in nearly all of the Makkan *surah*s, it concentrates on the essentials of God's Religion which was preached by all the Prophets. It allots most space to the mission and experiences of the Prophet Moses, upon him be peace, because they are extremely significant for the preaching and future of Islam. It consoles the Muslims, who were suffering great persecutions at the hands of the Makkan polytheists, by mentioning Moses' victory over the magicians and the Pharaoh and also warns them against straying in belief in any way, presenting as an example the time the Children of Israel began to worship a golden calf made by one among them shortly after Moses went to Mount Sinai to receive the Torah.

Some commentators maintain that even though *Ṭā. Hā* is made up of two separate letters, it signifies *the Perfect Human Being*, while *Yā. Sīn* (the title of *surah* 36) signifies *human*.

In the Name of God, the All-Merciful, the All-Compassionate.

1. *Ṭā. Hā.*

2. We do not send down the Qur'ān on you so that you suffer distress (in your duty of conveying it to people);

3. But only as a reminder for him who holds some awe of God in his heart (and so has the potential to achieve faith).

4. A gradual sending down from Him Who has created the earth and the high heavens,

5. The All-Merciful, Who has established Himself on the Throne.[1]

6. To Him belongs whatever is in the heavens and whatever is on the earth, and

96. Surely those who believe and do good, righteous deeds, the All-Merciful will assign for them love (in the hearts of the inhabitants of the heaven and many on the earth, so that they will receive welcome throughout creation, no matter if they are weak and small in number now).

97. We make it (this Qur'ān) in your tongue and easy (to recite and understand) so that you may thereby give glad tidings to the God-revering, pious ones, and warn thereby a people given to contention.

98. And how many a generation We have destroyed before them! Can you feel (the existence) of a single one of them, or hear any whisper of them?

whatever is between them, and whatever is under the soil.

7. If you say something aloud (or keep it to yourself), He surely knows the secret as well as (whatever you may be keeping as) the more hidden.

8. God – there is no deity save Him; His are the All-Beautiful Names.[2]

9. Has the story of Moses come to you?[3]

10. (He was traveling with his family in the desert) when he saw a fire, and so said to his family: "Wait here! Indeed I perceive a fire far off. Perhaps I can bring you a burning brand from it, or find guidance by the fire."[4]

11. Then when he came near to it, he was called by name: "O Moses!

12. "Indeed it is I, I am your Lord. So take off your sandals, for you are in the sacred valley of Tuwā.[5]

---

1. For the Throne and God's establishing Himself on It, see *sūrah* 7: 54, note 13; and *sūrah* 11: 7, note 2. This verse, along with the three following it, emphasizes God's absolute dominion and Oneness as the Lord of creation.

2. For God's All-Beautiful Names, see *sūrah* 7: 180, note 44, and *sūrah* 17: 110, note 41.

3. Apart from references to the Prophet Moses in the *sūrah*s revealed earlier, the narrative in this *sūrah* from this verse to verse 98 is the earliest Qur'ānic explanation of the story of Moses as such.

4. This happened in the Sinai desert while Moses was returning with his family from Midian, where he had spent eight to ten years, to Egypt, or while he was in search of a suitable place to dwell. It was a cold night and they needed a fire to warm themselves and light to be able to continue their way. They must have been lost in the desert in the darkness of the night.

5. Taking off one's sandals or shoes is done in the Presence of God; the sacredness of the valley arises from the fact that it was where God's Presence was manifested to Moses. However, it should also be noted that, just as some parts of time have sacredness of their own – if this sacredness is not because of their being the time of certain types of worship – some places on earth may have some sacredness for some reasons beyond our comprehension – if this sacredness does not arise from their being the places of certain Divine manifestations.

As stated in *Sūrat al-Qaṣaṣ* (28), the Almighty called out to the Prophet Moses from behind a tree (28: 30). This type of Divine calling is one of the three types of Divine Revelation. The Qur'ān clarifies that God speaks to a human being either from behind a veil or by putting the meaning in the heart of the human being (as a special kind of Revelation) or by sending an angel (42: 51). A Prophet is sure that the one who speaks to him from behind a veil or puts a meaning in his heart is God. So the Qur'ān does not mention any reaction of Moses when God called out to him. A Prophet who will receive Revelation has already been prepared for it. The Qur'ān mentions that God granted Moses knowledge, insight, and good judgment years before he received this first Revelation and that he was one devoted to doing good as if seeing God (28: 14).

312   سُورَةُ طٰه   ٣١٢

وَأَنَا اخْتَرْتُكَ فَاسْتَمِعْ لِمَا يُوحَى ۝ إِنَّنِي أَنَا اللهُ لَا إِلَهَ إِلَّا
أَنَا فَاعْبُدْنِي وَأَقِمِ الصَّلَوٰةَ لِذِكْرِي ۝ إِنَّ السَّاعَةَ ءَاتِيَةٌ
أَكَادُ أُخْفِيهَا لِتُجْزَىٰ كُلُّ نَفْسٍ بِمَا تَسْعَى ۝ فَلَا يَصُدَّنَّكَ
عَنْهَا مَنْ لَّا يُؤْمِنُ بِهَا وَاتَّبَعَ هَوَىٰهُ فَتَرْدَىٰ ۝ وَمَا تِلْكَ
بِيَمِينِكَ يَامُوسَى ۝ قَالَ هِيَ عَصَايَ أَتَوَكَّؤُاْ عَلَيْهَا وَأَهُشُّ
بِهَا عَلَىٰ غَنَمِي وَلِيَ فِيهَا مَآرِبُ أُخْرَىٰ ۝ قَالَ أَلْقِهَا يَامُوسَى
۝ فَأَلْقَىٰهَا فَإِذَا هِيَ حَيَّةٌ تَسْعَى ۝ قَالَ خُذْهَا وَلَا تَخَفْ
سَنُعِيدُهَا سِيرَتَهَا الْأُولَىٰ ۝ وَاضْمُمْ يَدَكَ إِلَىٰ جَنَاحِكَ
تَخْرُجْ بَيْضَآءَ مِنْ غَيْرِ سُوٓءٍ ءَايَةً أُخْرَىٰ ۝ لِنُرِيَكَ مِنْ ءَايَاتِنَا
الْكُبْرَىٰ ۝ اذْهَبْ إِلَىٰ فِرْعَوْنَ إِنَّهُ طَغَىٰ ۝ قَالَ رَبِّ اشْرَحْ لِي
صَدْرِي ۝ وَيَسِّرْ لِي أَمْرِي ۝ وَاحْلُلْ عُقْدَةً مِّن لِّسَانِي ۝
يَفْقَهُواْ قَوْلِي ۝ وَاجْعَل لِّي وَزِيرًا مِّنْ أَهْلِي ۝ هَارُونَ أَخِي ۝
اشْدُدْ بِهِ أَزْرِي ۝ وَأَشْرِكْهُ فِي أَمْرِي ۝ كَيْ نُسَبِّحَكَ كَثِيرًا
۝ وَنَذْكُرَكَ كَثِيرًا ۝ إِنَّكَ كُنتَ بِنَا بَصِيرًا ۝ قَالَ قَدْ أُوتِيتَ
سُؤْلَكَ يَامُوسَى ۝ وَلَقَدْ مَنَنَّا عَلَيْكَ مَرَّةً أُخْرَىٰ ۝

---

13. "I have chosen you (to be My Messenger), so listen to what is revealed (to you).

14. "Surely it is I, I am God, there is no deity save Me. So worship Me, and establish the Prayer in conformity with its conditions for remembrance of Me.[6]

15. "Surely the Last Hour is bound to come (unexpectedly. It is so great a truth that) I all but keep it hidden so that every soul may strive for what it strives for (and achieve the just recompense for it).

16. "So do not let anyone who does not believe in it and (instead) follows his lusts and fancies, turn you from (believing in and preaching the truth about) it, lest you then perish![7]

17. "What is that in your right hand, Moses?"

18. He said: "It is my staff. I lean on it, and with it I beat down leaves for my flock, and I have some other uses for it."

19. (God) said: "Throw it down, O Moses!"

20. So he threw it down, and there and then it was a snake, slithering.

21. (God) said: "Take hold of it and do not fear! We will return it to its former state.

22. "Now, put your (right) hand under your armpit: it will come forth shining white, flawless, as another (miraculous) sign,

23. "So that We may show you some of Our greatest miraculous signs,

24. "Go to the Pharaoh, for he has indeed rebelled."

25. (Moses) said: "My Lord! Expand for me my breast.

26. "Make my task easy for me.

27. "Loose any knot from my tongue (to make my speaking more fluent),

28. "So that they may understand my speech clearly.

29. "And appoint a minister (helper) for me from my family:

30. "Aaron, my brother.

31. "Confirm my strength with him,

32. "And let him share my task;

33. "So that we may glorify You much,

34. "And mention and remember You abundantly.

35. "Surely You are ever seeing and watching us."[8]

36. (God) said: "Your request has already been granted, O Moses.

37. "And assuredly We did bestow Our favor upon you at another time before.

6. Mentioning the Prayer in addition to worship – although the Prayer is a kind of worship – is because of its importance as the chief way of worship.

7. Islam is the Divine Religion preached by all the Prophets, with slight differences in matters of law, according to time and conditions, a religion which was universally perfected through the Prophet Muḥammad, upon him be peace and blessings. It is based on four fundamentals, and it is upon these that the Qur'ān dwells. The first and most important of them is the belief in God's Existence and Oneness. It is this very fundamental which was first conveyed to the Prophet Moses, upon him be peace. Although belief in the Resurrection and the Hereafter is the fundamental of second-degree importance, the relationship of God as the Deity and Lord and His servants as the created and sustained require worship on the part of the servants, and therefore worship is mentioned after belief in God's Existence and Oneness in the verses above. Justice in human individual and collective life is a dimension of worship, and verse 16 alludes to it. Belief in the Resurrection and the Hereafter, which is the final or ultimate purpose of the existence of the world and humankind and human worldly life, is the second fundamental of Islam. The fourth fundamental is Prophethood, which is required by God's being the Lord of the whole creation and the fact that He created it. If God had not made Himself known to His conscious servants, informed them of His purpose for creating the universe and humankind and what He expects them to do, and if He had not appointed a leader to humanity to do all these, His creating them would have been unintelligible. So, God's purpose for creating the whole universe and humankind requires Prophethood or the sending of Prophets. In conclusion, God mentions these four fundamentals in the first Revelation He sent to the Prophet Moses, upon him be peace.

8. The Prophet Moses grew up in the Pharaoh's palace. Pharaoh was a title by which the kings of the native Copts in ancient Egypt were called. The Pharaoh to whom Moses was sent was the son of the Pharaoh in whose palace Moses grew up. As mentioned in several verses of the Qur'ān, this Pharaoh persecuted the Children of Israel. While trying to protect one of his people against an Egyptian, Moses accidentally caused the death of the latter and, on hearing that he was being sought by officials, he left for Midian. After having stayed there for eight to ten years, he most probably was returning to Egypt when he received the Divine Revelation. Now he was to go to the Pharaoh's palace with an extremely important and difficult task. So he asked his Lord to expand his breast to be able to show greater patience with whatever he would encounter from the Pharaoh and his clan, and to fully understand God's Religion and all that He would be pleased with. He also asked Him to increase his own power of speech and to allow his brother Aaron, a fluent speaker, to share his task as a Messenger. His purpose was to worship, exalt, glorify, and mention God as much as possible.

By saying *You are ever seeing and watching us*, the Prophet Moses presented his weakness and need of help as a servant to the Divine Court as a means of intercession.

إِذْ أَوْحَيْنَا إِلَىٰ أُمِّكَ مَا يُوحَىٰ ۞ أَنِ اقْذِفِيهِ فِي التَّابُوتِ فَاقْذِفِيهِ فِي الْيَمِّ فَلْيُلْقِهِ الْيَمُّ بِالسَّاحِلِ يَأْخُذْهُ عَدُوٌّ لِّي وَعَدُوٌّ لَّهُ وَأَلْقَيْتُ عَلَيْكَ مَحَبَّةً مِّنِّي وَلِتُصْنَعَ عَلَىٰ عَيْنِي ۞ إِذْ تَمْشِي أُخْتُكَ فَتَقُولُ هَلْ أَدُلُّكُمْ عَلَىٰ مَن يَكْفُلُهُ فَرَجَعْنَاكَ إِلَىٰ أُمِّكَ كَيْ تَقَرَّ عَيْنُهَا وَلَا تَحْزَنَ وَقَتَلْتَ نَفْسًا فَنَجَّيْنَاكَ مِنَ الْغَمِّ وَفَتَنَّاكَ فُتُونًا فَلَبِثْتَ سِنِينَ فِي أَهْلِ مَدْيَنَ ثُمَّ جِئْتَ عَلَىٰ قَدَرٍ يَا مُوسَىٰ ۞ وَاصْطَنَعْتُكَ لِنَفْسِي ۞ اذْهَبْ أَنتَ وَأَخُوكَ بِآيَاتِي وَلَا تَنِيَا فِي ذِكْرِي ۞ اذْهَبَا إِلَىٰ فِرْعَوْنَ إِنَّهُ طَغَىٰ ۞ فَقُولَا لَهُ قَوْلًا لَّيِّنًا لَّعَلَّهُ يَتَذَكَّرُ أَوْ يَخْشَىٰ ۞ قَالَا رَبَّنَا إِنَّنَا نَخَافُ أَن يَفْرُطَ عَلَيْنَا أَوْ أَن يَطْغَىٰ ۞ قَالَ لَا تَخَافَا إِنَّنِي مَعَكُمَا أَسْمَعُ وَأَرَىٰ ۞ فَأْتِيَاهُ فَقُولَا إِنَّا رَسُولَا رَبِّكَ فَأَرْسِلْ مَعَنَا بَنِي إِسْرَائِيلَ وَلَا تُعَذِّبْهُمْ قَدْ جِئْنَاكَ بِآيَةٍ مِّن رَّبِّكَ وَالسَّلَامُ عَلَىٰ مَنِ اتَّبَعَ الْهُدَىٰ ۞ إِنَّا قَدْ أُوحِيَ إِلَيْنَا أَنَّ الْعَذَابَ عَلَىٰ مَن كَذَّبَ وَتَوَلَّىٰ ۞ قَالَ فَمَن رَّبُّكُمَا يَا مُوسَىٰ ۞ قَالَ رَبُّنَا الَّذِي أَعْطَىٰ كُلَّ شَيْءٍ خَلْقَهُ ثُمَّ هَدَىٰ ۞ قَالَ فَمَا بَالُ الْقُرُونِ الْأُولَىٰ ۞

—⟨❧⟩—

38. "We inspired in your mother what she was to be inspired with, saying:

39. 'Place the child in a chest and cast it into the river, then the river will throw it up on the bank: one who is both My enemy and his enemy (the Pharaoh, who has decided to kill all the new-born sons of the Children of Israel) will take him up.' I cast over you (Moses) love from Me (protecting you, so love for you was aroused in the hearts of people who saw you), and so that you were brought up under My eyes.

40. "When your sister (on your mother's instruction, knowing the Pharaoh's household had taken you in) went and said: 'Shall I guide you to one who will nurse him?' Thus (– and it is We Who made none other capable of nursing you –) We returned you to your mother, so that she might re-

joice and forget her grief. And (much later on) you killed a man (not intending it), so We saved you from the (ensuing) trouble, and We tested you with trial (of different kinds and degrees only to perfect you). You stayed for years among the people of Midian, and then you attained to the (quality of mind and spirit) expected of and decreed for you, O Moses.

41. "And I have attached you to Myself (and so trained you to My service).

42. "Go, you and your brother, with My miraculous signs (with which I have provided you), and never slacken in remembrance of Me and reminding (others) of Me.

43. "Go, both of you, to the Pharaoh for he has exceedingly rebelled.

44. "But speak to him with gentle words, so that he might reflect and be mindful or feel some awe (of Me, and behave with humility)."[9]

45. They said: "Our Lord, we fear lest he act hastily in regard to us (not allowing us to complete our preaching), or become (more) tyrannical."

46. He said: "Do not fear! Surely I am with you, hearing and seeing.

47. "Go to him and say: 'We are indeed Messengers of your Lord (Who has created and sustains you), so let the Children of Israel go with us, and do not cause them to suffer (longer). Assuredly we have come to you with a clear proof from your Lord. And peace (success and safety and triumph) is upon him who follows His guidance.

48. 'It has surely been revealed to us that (only) punishment is upon him who denies and turns away (from God's call).' "

49. (When they had spoken to the Pharaoh as God had commanded them,) the Pharaoh said: "Who is this Lord of you two, O Moses?"

50. (Moses) said: "Our Lord is He Who creates everything and endows each thing with its particular character, and then guides (it to the fulfillment of the aim and purpose of its existence)."

51. (The Pharaoh) said: "Then, what is the case with the earlier generations (all of whom have passed away, how are they recompensed for their beliefs and deeds)?"

---

9. The tentative form of the phrase *so that he might ponder*, as well as similar phrases that frequently exist in the Qur'ān, never implies any doubt on God's part. It relates to the intention or hope with which the Messengers (and other addressees) should approach their task.

314

57. He said: "Moses, have you come to drive us from our land with your sorcery?

58. "Then, We will most certainly produce before you sorcery like it. So appoint a meeting between us and you, which neither we nor you will fail to keep, in an open, level place convenient (to both of us)."

59. (Moses) said: "The meeting will be on the Day of the Festival, and let the people assemble in the forenoon."[10]

60. The Pharaoh then left, and he (set out to) mobilize all his devices, then presented himself (at the appointed meeting).

61. Moses said to them (warning them before it was too late for them to be warned): "Woe to you! Do not fabricate lies against God (such as falsely describing His clear proofs as sorcery, falsely pretending that His Message to you aims at driving you out of your land, and by adopting other deities than Him), lest He ruin you with a severe scourge. Whoever fabricates a lie is doomed."

62. (Moses' warning having influenced some among the sorcerers and the Pharaoh's men,) they began to debate their affair among themselves, holding a secret counsel.

63. (The Pharaoh's men spoke to the sorcerers, and) they said: "These two men are surely sorcerers intent on driving you out of your land with their sorcery, and doing away with your exemplary way of life.

64. "So gather your devices, and then come in ordered ranks (as an organized, unified force), for the one who gains the upper hand today has surely triumphed."[11]

52. (Moses) answered: "My Lord holds the knowledge of them in a Record. My Lord never errs, nor forgets."

53. He Who has made the earth a cradle for you and traced out roads on it for you, and sends down water from the sky, and produces with it pairs of various plants.

54. Eat thereof, and feed your cattle. Surely in all this there are signs (manifesting the truth) for people of sound, unbiased thinking.

55. From it (earth) We create you, and into it are We returning you, and out of it will We bring you forth a second time.

56. We certainly showed the Pharaoh Our signs, all of them (including those We granted particularly to Moses), but he denied them and refused (to believe).

10. The Prophet Moses' decision is very significant. By appointing a time when almost all of the people would assemble on a special day, a day when they will be in different mood, he manifested his utmost confidence in his message and mission. In addition, he would deal a great blow to the Pharaoh and to his prestige and belief, and have the possibility to announce his message before all people with undeniable, visible proofs.

11. History is a telling of the recurring patterns and meanings in events at different times. The encounter told here is of the recurring battle between truth and falsehood, justice and tyranny. The Qur'an presents events in such a way that we not only follow clearly the line of events unfolding, but also understand the weight of meaning carried in them, their causes and outcomes, and the manners and motives of the people involved in them.

Islam never aims to debase or destroy people; instead it came to exalt them. For this reason, the Prophet Moses, upon him be peace, made an influential address to his opponents, warning them. Through the efforts of the Prophet Joseph, upon him be peace, God's true Religion – Islam – had begun to prevail in Egypt. Therefore, at the time the Prophet Moses began his mission, it could still be traced among the people there. As can be understood from the miracles granted to Moses – the miracle given to every Prophet was in relation to the branch of science and craft most developed at that time – chemistry and alchemy were of great import. Sorcerers were the leading scientists and intellectuals of the time. By addressing them (and other people) (verse 61), Moses, who knew Egypt very well, both did his principal task of conveying the Divine Message, and warned them against a possible calamity. His address had the expected influence on the sorcerers and caused a difference of opinion to arise among them. But, as always happens in history, the Pharaoh and his men intervened and attempted to eliminate this difference. They tried to encourage the sorcerers by saying that Moses and Aaron were sorcerers, like them, and alarmed and provoked them by saying that Moses intended to drive them out of their own land and abolish their way of life, and then went on to make alluring promises to them. We read this promise in 7: 113–114 and 26: 41–42: *Pharaoh promised: "(If you are the victors), you will indeed be among the near-stationed to me."*

قَالُوا يَا مُوسَىٰٓ إِمَّآ أَن تُلْقِىَ وَإِمَّآ أَن نَّكُونَ أَوَّلَ مَنْ أَلْقَىٰ ۝ قَالَ
بَلْ أَلْقُوا۟ فَإِذَا حِبَالُهُمْ وَعِصِيُّهُمْ يُخَيَّلُ إِلَيْهِ مِن سِحْرِهِمْ أَنَّهَا
تَسْعَىٰ ۝ فَأَوْجَسَ فِى نَفْسِهِۦ خِيفَةً مُّوسَىٰ ۝ قُلْنَا لَا تَخَفْ إِنَّكَ
أَنتَ الْأَعْلَىٰ ۝ وَأَلْقِ مَا فِى يَمِينِكَ تَلْقَفْ مَا صَنَعُوٓا۟ إِنَّمَا صَنَعُوا۟ كَيْدُ سَٰحِرٍ
وَلَا يُفْلِحُ السَّاحِرُ حَيْثُ أَتَىٰ ۝ فَأُلْقِىَ السَّحَرَةُ سُجَّدًا قَالُوٓا۟ ءَامَنَّا بِرَبِّ
هَٰرُونَ وَمُوسَىٰ ۝ قَالَ ءَامَنتُمْ لَهُۥ قَبْلَ أَنْ ءَاذَنَ لَكُمْ إِنَّهُۥ لَكَبِيرُكُمُ
الَّذِى عَلَّمَكُمُ السِّحْرَ فَلَأُقَطِّعَنَّ أَيْدِيَكُمْ وَأَرْجُلَكُم مِّنْ خِلَٰفٍ
وَلَأُصَلِّبَنَّكُمْ فِى جُذُوعِ النَّخْلِ وَلَتَعْلَمُنَّ أَيُّنَآ أَشَدُّ عَذَابًا وَأَبْقَىٰ
۝ قَالُوا۟ لَن نُّؤْثِرَكَ عَلَىٰ مَا جَآءَنَا مِنَ الْبَيِّنَٰتِ وَالَّذِى فَطَرَنَا
فَاقْضِ مَآ أَنتَ قَاضٍ إِنَّمَا تَقْضِى هَٰذِهِ الْحَيَوٰةَ الدُّنْيَآ ۝ إِنَّآ ءَامَنَّا بِرَبِّنَا
لِيَغْفِرَ لَنَا خَطَٰيَٰنَا وَمَآ أَكْرَهْتَنَا عَلَيْهِ مِنَ السِّحْرِ وَاللَّهُ
خَيْرٌ وَأَبْقَىٰ ۝ إِنَّهُۥ مَن يَأْتِ رَبَّهُۥ مُجْرِمًا فَإِنَّ لَهُۥ جَهَنَّمَ لَا يَمُوتُ
فِيهَا وَلَا يَحْيَىٰ ۝ وَمَن يَأْتِهِۦ مُؤْمِنًا قَدْ عَمِلَ الصَّٰلِحَٰتِ فَأُو۟لَٰئِكَ
لَهُمُ الدَّرَجَٰتُ الْعُلَىٰ ۝ جَنَّٰتُ عَدْنٍ تَجْرِى مِن تَحْتِهَا
الْأَنْهَٰرُ خَٰلِدِينَ فِيهَا ۚ وَذَٰلِكَ جَزَآءُ مَن تَزَكَّىٰ ۝

ers were thrown down, prostrate. They proclaimed: "We have come to believe in the Lord of Aaron and Moses!"

71. (The Pharaoh) said: "Do you believe in Him before I give you leave? I see that he (Moses) is your master who taught you sorcery! I will surely have your hands and feet cut off alternately, and have you crucified on the trunks of palm-trees, and you will certainly come to know which of us (– the Lord of Aaron and Moses or I –) is more severe in punishment and (whose punishment is) more lasting!"[13]

72. They said: "We will never prefer you above the clear proofs (manifesting the truth) that have come before us, and above Him Who originated us. So decree whatever you decree: you can decree only for the life of this world.

73. "We have surely come to believe in our Lord and (we hope) that He may forgive us our faults and that sorcery to which you compelled us. God is the Best (in giving reward), and the Most Permanent."

74. Whoever comes before his Lord as a disbelieving criminal, for him surely there will be Hell: he will neither die therein nor live.

75. Whereas he who comes before Him as a believer who did good, righteous deeds, for such are high ranks and lofty stations –

76. Gardens of perpetual bliss through which rivers flow, therein to abide. Such is the recompense of whoever attains to purity.

65. They (the sorcerers) said: "Moses, either you throw or we will be the first to throw!"

66. He said: "No, you throw first!" And there and then, by their sorcery, their ropes and their staffs seemed to him to be slithering.

67. Then Moses felt in his soul a bit apprehensive (that people may have been influenced by their sorcery).[12]

68. We said: "Do not fear! You surely, you are the uppermost.

69. "Throw that which is in your right hand: it will swallow up all that they have contrived. What they have contrived is only a sorcerer's artifice. And a sorcerer can never prosper whatever he may aim at."

70. And so (it happened, and) the sorcer-

12. When the sorcerers threw their ropes and staffs, it seemed to Moses as if hundreds of snakes were gliding on the ground. This caused some apprehension to arise in his heart. Such an apprehension is purely human and may arise even in a Prophet. In addition, like other human beings, a Prophet may be influenced by sorcery. *When they threw (whatever they held in their hands to make spells) they cast a spell upon the people's eyes (i.e. overawed and deluded them), and produced a mighty sorcery* (7: 116).

13. The Pharaoh's reaction is the reaction of all dictators throughout history. Nimrod and his men showed the same reaction before the Prophet Abraham, upon him be peace. When they were defeated in intellectual argument, they threw him into fire. The sorcerers who began to show their skills by declaring that they would triumph by the Pharaoh's honor and might (26: 44) were able to distinguish between sorcery and the truth. They saw that what the Prophet Moses did was not sorcery and that the Pharaoh's honor and might were of no avail, so they came to believe. Yet the Pharaoh refused to believe, even in the face of the truth which showed itself in utter clarity. The event had taken place before a crowd, so it was quite probable that some among those too would believe and some others would feel a light in the name of belief appearing in their heart. This was what the Pharaoh feared. He could not bear defeat and he felt that his sovereignty was at stake if people were to believe. So he resorted to threats and massacre.

This verse discloses another aspect of dictatorship. Dictators want people to do whatever they order them to do. They see themselves as the one and only authority to decide for people what to believe and what not to believe in as well as what and how to think and what and how not to think. That is, they try to command even their minds and hearts.

The miracles granted to each Prophet were of the same kind as the science and crafts which had developed in his time; each Prophet surpassed the level of that science and those crafts through the miracles he worked. Moses' experience with the Pharaoh also revealed that in addition to having outstanding virtues, the representatives and preachers of Islam also should excel others in knowledge.

316   سورة طه   ٣١٦

وَلَقَدْ أَوْحَيْنَآ إِلَىٰ مُوسَىٰٓ أَنْ أَسْرِ بِعِبَادِى فَاضْرِبْ لَهُمْ طَرِيقًا فِى الْبَحْرِ يَبَسًا لَّا تَخَٰفُ دَرَكًا وَلَا تَخْشَىٰ ۝ فَأَتْبَعَهُمْ فِرْعَوْنُ بِجُنُودِهِۦ فَغَشِيَهُم مِّنَ الْيَمِّ مَا غَشِيَهُمْ ۝ وَأَضَلَّ فِرْعَوْنُ قَوْمَهُۥ وَمَا هَدَىٰ ۝ يَٰبَنِىٓ إِسْرَٰٓءِيلَ قَدْ أَنجَيْنَٰكُم مِّنْ عَدُوِّكُمْ وَوَٰعَدْنَٰكُمْ جَانِبَ الطُّورِ الْأَيْمَنَ وَنَزَّلْنَا عَلَيْكُمُ الْمَنَّ وَالسَّلْوَىٰ ۝ كُلُوا۟ مِن طَيِّبَٰتِ مَا رَزَقْنَٰكُمْ وَلَا تَطْغَوْا۟ فِيهِ فَيَحِلَّ عَلَيْكُمْ غَضَبِى وَمَن يَحْلِلْ عَلَيْهِ غَضَبِى فَقَدْ هَوَىٰ ۝ وَإِنِّى لَغَفَّارٌ لِّمَن تَابَ وَءَامَنَ وَعَمِلَ صَٰلِحًا ثُمَّ اهْتَدَىٰ ۝ وَمَآ أَعْجَلَكَ عَن قَوْمِكَ يَٰمُوسَىٰ ۝ قَالَ هُمْ أُو۟لَآءِ عَلَىٰٓ أَثَرِى وَعَجِلْتُ إِلَيْكَ رَبِّ لِتَرْضَىٰ ۝ قَالَ فَإِنَّا قَدْ فَتَنَّا قَوْمَكَ مِنۢ بَعْدِكَ وَأَضَلَّهُمُ السَّامِرِىُّ ۝ فَرَجَعَ مُوسَىٰٓ إِلَىٰ قَوْمِهِۦ غَضْبَٰنَ أَسِفًا قَالَ يَٰقَوْمِ أَلَمْ يَعِدْكُمْ رَبُّكُمْ وَعْدًا حَسَنًا أَفَطَالَ عَلَيْكُمُ الْعَهْدُ أَمْ أَرَدتُّمْ أَن يَحِلَّ عَلَيْكُمْ غَضَبٌ مِّن رَّبِّكُمْ فَأَخْلَفْتُم مَّوْعِدِى ۝ قَالُوا۟ مَآ أَخْلَفْنَا مَوْعِدَكَ بِمَلْكِنَا وَلَٰكِنَّا حُمِّلْنَآ أَوْزَارًا مِّن زِينَةِ الْقَوْمِ فَقَذَفْنَٰهَا فَكَذَٰلِكَ أَلْقَى السَّامِرِىُّ ۝

---

77. We revealed to Moses: "Set forth with My servants by night, and (when you reach the sea's edge with the Pharaoh and his army in pursuit) strike for them a dry path with your staff through the sea, and you need have no fear of being overtaken (by the Pharaoh) or of drowning in the sea."

78. Then the Pharaoh pursued them with his armed hosts, and they were overwhelmed by the sea to their complete destruction.

79. The Pharaoh had led his people astray (and finally he led them to destruction); he did not guide them (either to the truth or to prosperity).[14]

80. O Children of Israel! We saved you from your enemy; and We made a covenant with you through Moses on the right side of Mount Sinai (and granted you the Torah); and We sent down on you manna and quails (to sustain you in the desert).

81. (We said:) Eat of the pure, wholesome things that We have provided for you but do not exceed the bounds therein (by wastefulness, ingratitude, unlawful earnings, and the like). Otherwise My wrath (condemnation) will justly fall upon you, and upon whoever My condemnation falls, he has indeed thrown himself into ruin.[15]

82. Yet I am surely All-Forgiving to whoever repents and believes and does good, righteous deeds, and thereafter keeps himself on the right path.

83. (When Moses came to Our appointment with him in Mount Sinai to receive the Torah, We asked him:) "Moses, what has caused you to leave your people behind in such haste?"

84. He replied: "They are following in my footsteps; and I have shown haste to come to You so that You may be well-pleased with Me."

85. (God) said: "Then (know that) We have put your people to a test in your absence, and the Sāmirī (Samaritan) has led them astray."[16]

86. So Moses returned to his people in anger and sorrow. He said: "My people! Did your Lord not make you a fair promise (that He would grant you the Torah for your happiness in both worlds and settle you in the land the environs of which He has blessed)? Did, then, the time appointed (for my absence) seem too long to you or did you desire that a condemnation from your Lord should fall upon you, that you broke your promise to me?"

87. They said: "We did not break our promise to you of our own accord (with intent), but we were loaded with (sinful) loads of ornaments of the people (of Egypt), and we threw them (to get rid of them), in the same way as the Sāmirī threw (them, into a fire)."

14. For the events which took place in the encounter of the Prophet Moses and the sorcerers and the Exodus, see 7: 127–135; 10: 75–90.

15. For details of the events and warnings and the subsequent events mentioned in verses 80 and 81, see *sūrah* 2: 51, 57, and 61, and the notes 67 and 73; *sūrah* 7: 142, note 30.

16. The Old Testament records that it was the Prophet Aaron who made the effigy of a calf for the Children of Israel to worship (*Exodus*, 32: 4, 24). Whereas the Prophet Aaron, upon him be peace, was the Prophet Moses' elder brother who shared his mission. He tried his best to prevent the calf-worship. The Qur'ān openly states that the one who made the calf is a man referred to as as-Sāmirī.

The article (*al-*) before Sāmirī and the suffix (ī) of the case ending suggest that the man was someone belonging to a place or tribe called Sāmir. Although some Orientalists and Christian writers, starting from the fact that Samaria was the capital of the Kingdom of Israel established in 925 BC, tried to accuse our Prophet, upon him be peace and blessings, of ignorance as if he were the author of the Qur'ān, the Bible itself contradicts them. We read in I *Kings*, 16: 24 that King Omri bought the hill Samaria from Shemer and built the city of Samaria on this hill, naming it after Shemer. So Samaria already existed before Moses as the name of a hill. The Sāmirī may well have been from that territory or they may have descended from the ancestry of Shemer. Another point to be considered is that the Sumerians lived in Iraq before the time of the Prophet Abraham. There were emigrations from this region to Egypt. For example, the Hyksos, who ruled Egypt during the time of the Prophet Joseph, had emigrated from Syria. So it is possible that the Sāmirī had descended from a Sumerian tribe that had immigrated to Egypt.

It is also possible that the personal name of the Sāmirī was "Aaron" and the later scribes of the Torah confused him with the Prophet Aaron.

The Bible contradicts itself in attributing the making of the calf to the Prophet Aaron. For we read in *Exodus*, 32: 27–28 that God ordered "every man to kill his brother (who had worshipped the calf), and every man his companion, and every man his neighbor, and the sons of Levi did, and there fell of the people that day about three thousand men." The Prophet Aaron was not among those who were killed. Again, according to *Exodus*, 32: 32–33, the Prophet Moses prayed to God to forgive his people or blot his name out of His book, and God answered that He would blot whoever had sinned against Him out of His book. It is clear in *Numbers*, 18: 5–7 that God did not blot Aaron's name out of His book, instead He favored him and his sons with the duty of being in charge of the sanctuary and the altar, that there may be no more wrath on the Children of Israel (al-Mawdūdī, 5: 217–218, note 69).

فَأَخْرَجَ لَهُمْ عِجْلًا جَسَدًا لَهُ خُوَارٌ فَقَالُوا هَٰذَآ إِلَٰهُكُمْ وَإِلَٰهُ مُوسَىٰ
فَنَسِىَ ۞ أَفَلَا يَرَوْنَ أَلَّا يَرْجِعُ إِلَيْهِمْ قَوْلًا وَلَا يَمْلِكُ لَهُمْ ضَرًّا
وَلَا نَفْعًا ۞ وَلَقَدْ قَالَ لَهُمْ هَٰرُونُ مِن قَبْلُ يَٰقَوْمِ إِنَّمَا فُتِنتُم
بِهِ ۖ وَإِنَّ رَبَّكُمُ ٱلرَّحْمَٰنُ فَٱتَّبِعُونِى وَأَطِيعُوٓا أَمْرِى ۞ قَالُوا
لَن نَّبْرَحَ عَلَيْهِ عَٰكِفِينَ حَتَّىٰ يَرْجِعَ إِلَيْنَا مُوسَىٰ ۞ قَالَ
يَٰهَٰرُونُ مَا مَنَعَكَ إِذْ رَأَيْتَهُمْ ضَلُّوٓا ۞ أَلَّا تَتَّبِعَنِ ۖ
أَفَعَصَيْتَ أَمْرِى ۞ قَالَ يَبْنَؤُمَّ لَا تَأْخُذْ بِلِحْيَتِى وَلَا
بِرَأْسِىٓ ۖ إِنِّى خَشِيتُ أَن تَقُولَ فَرَّقْتَ بَيْنَ بَنِىٓ إِسْرَٰٓءِيلَ وَلَمْ
تَرْقُبْ قَوْلِى ۞ قَالَ فَمَا خَطْبُكَ يَٰسَٰمِرِىُّ ۞ قَالَ
بَصُرْتُ بِمَا لَمْ يَبْصُرُوا بِهِ فَقَبَضْتُ قَبْضَةً مِّنْ أَثَرِ
ٱلرَّسُولِ فَنَبَذْتُهَا وَكَذَٰلِكَ سَوَّلَتْ لِى نَفْسِى ۞ قَالَ
فَٱذْهَبْ فَإِنَّ لَكَ فِى ٱلْحَيَوٰةِ أَن تَقُولَ لَا مِسَاسَ ۖ وَإِنَّ لَكَ
مَوْعِدًا لَّن تُخْلَفَهُ ۖ وَٱنظُرْ إِلَىٰٓ إِلَٰهِكَ ٱلَّذِى ظَلْتَ عَلَيْهِ
عَاكِفًا ۖ لَّنُحَرِّقَنَّهُ ثُمَّ لَنَنسِفَنَّهُ فِى ٱلْيَمِّ نَسْفًا ۞ إِنَّمَا
إِلَٰهُكُمُ ٱللَّهُ ٱلَّذِى لَآ إِلَٰهَ إِلَّا هُوَ ۚ وَسِعَ كُلَّ شَىْءٍ عِلْمًا ۞

88. And then he brought out for them a calf shaping to it (from the molten ornaments) a body (which made a sound like) mooing. Then they said (some of them to others): "This is your deity and the deity of Moses, but he has forgotten."

89. Did they not see at all that (even) it could not return to them a word (for answer), and had no power to harm or benefit them?

90. And assuredly Aaron had said to them before Moses' return, (warning them:) "O my people! You are only being tested through this (idol to prove the quality of your understanding and faith). Truly Your Lord is the All-Merciful (Who is most forgiving), so follow me and obey my order!"

91. But they said: "We will by no means cease to worship it until Moses comes back to us."

92. (Having returned, and unaware of Aaron's warning, Moses) said: "O Aaron! What prevented you, when you saw them gone astray,

93. "From following me? Have you, then, disobeyed my order?"[17]

94. Aaron said: "O son of my mother! Do not seize me by my beard, nor by my head! I was afraid lest you should say: 'You have caused division among the Children of Israel, and paid no heed to my orders!' "[18]

95. (Moses turned to the Sāmirī and) said: "What is the matter with you, O Sāmirī, (that you did such a monstrous thing)?"

96. He answered: "I have seen something which they were unable to see, and so I took a handful (of dust) from the trail of the messenger (the archangel Gabriel) and cast it into the molten ornaments: thus did my soul prompt me to act."[19]

97. (Moses) said: "Be gone, then! (The sentence) upon you is that in this present life you say 'Touch me not!' (to warn people against proximity to you), and surely there is for you a promise (of punishment) that you cannot evade. Now look to this deity of yours to whose worship you have become devoted: we will most certainly burn it, and scatter whatever remains of it over the sea!

98. "(O my people!) Your only deity is God, other than Whom there is no deity. He encompasses all things in His Knowledge."

17. Before leaving for Mount Sinai, the Prophet Moses, upon him be peace, appointed Aaron as his deputy among his people, saying: *Take my place among my people (act to reform them and set things right), and do not follow the way of those who provoke disorder and corruption* (7: 142).

18. As we have stated elsewhere before (i.e., 7, note 35; 15, note 11; 19, note 1), while narrating an event in different places, the Qur'ān deals with the aspects of the event that concern the topic discussed. So it reports here only part of Aaron's answer to Moses, *I was afraid lest you should say: "You have caused division among the Children of Israel, and paid no heed to my orders!"* This does not mean that Aaron did nothing else. As reported in *sūrah* 7: 150, he did his best to prevent the fundamental error into which his people had lapsed, but they nearly killed him. So Aaron, aware of the delicacy of the situation, did not proceed, in order to avoid causing a division among them which would most probably have amounted to bloodshed. He waited for Moses' return, as he knew he had gone for a short, definite period.

19. How should we understand these words of the Sāmirī?

The people of ancient Egypt were farmers and worshipped cattle in addition to other major deities. The Children of Israel had been influenced by this. This influence manifested itself as devotion to this statue of the calf, to the extent that the Qur'ān describes it as *Because of their unbelief, they were made to drink into their hearts (love of) the calf (with then no place left therein for faith)* (2: 93). They were also inclined toward idol-worship or adopting figures as deities, as manifested by their asking the Prophet Moses to make them an idol when they found a people worshipping idols along their way in the desert after departing from Egypt: *And We led the Children of Israel across the sea, and then they came upon a people who were devoted to the worship of some idols that they had (particular to themselves). They said: "O Moses! Make for us a deity even as they have deities!"* (7: 138).

Some people have exceptional abilities or characteristics, such as telepathy, necromancy, ability to make contact with the jinn and the ability to act as a medium. They can bring about some accomplishments which may seem extraordinary to others and they themselves like to add some mystery to their accomplishments. Because of their haughtiness and self-admiration that arise from these accomplishments, God Almighty makes their abilities a means of gradual perdition for them.

The Sāmirī had the ability of smelting ore and making statues. He intentionally made an effigy of a calf to lead the Children of Israel astray and caused it to produce a sound by means of some holes located in the effigy.

The Qur'ān introduces the matter of the calf as a trial and temptation for the Children of Israel. By saying, *I have seen something which they were unable to see, and so I took a handful (of dust) from the trail of the messenger (the archangel Gabriel) and cast it into the molten ornaments*, is merely a lie the Sāmirī made up to excuse himself for what he did. He must have attempted to also add a spiritual and mysterious dimension to some abilities he had or that he thought he had.

318 سُورَةُ طه ٣١٨

كَذَٰلِكَ نَقُصُّ عَلَيْكَ مِنْ أَنۢبَآءِ مَا قَدْ سَبَقَ ۚ وَقَدْ ءَاتَيْنَٰكَ
مِن لَّدُنَّا ذِكْرًا ۞ مَّنْ أَعْرَضَ عَنْهُ فَإِنَّهُۥ يَحْمِلُ يَوْمَ ٱلْقِيَٰمَةِ
وِزْرًا ۞ خَٰلِدِينَ فِيهِ ۖ وَسَآءَ لَهُمْ يَوْمَ ٱلْقِيَٰمَةِ حِمْلًا ۞
يَوْمَ يُنفَخُ فِى ٱلصُّورِ ۚ وَنَحْشُرُ ٱلْمُجْرِمِينَ يَوْمَئِذٍ زُرْقًا ۞
يَتَخَٰفَتُونَ بَيْنَهُمْ إِن لَّبِثْتُمْ إِلَّا عَشْرًا ۞ نَّحْنُ أَعْلَمُ بِمَا
يَقُولُونَ إِذْ يَقُولُ أَمْثَلُهُمْ طَرِيقَةً إِن لَّبِثْتُمْ إِلَّا يَوْمًا ۞
وَيَسْـَٔلُونَكَ عَنِ ٱلْجِبَالِ فَقُلْ يَنسِفُهَا رَبِّى نَسْفًا ۞ فَيَذَرُهَا قَاعًا
صَفْصَفًا ۞ لَّا تَرَىٰ فِيهَا عِوَجًا وَلَآ أَمْتًا ۞ يَوْمَئِذٍ يَتَّبِعُونَ
ٱلدَّاعِىَ لَا عِوَجَ لَهُۥ ۖ وَخَشَعَتِ ٱلْأَصْوَاتُ لِلرَّحْمَٰنِ فَلَا تَسْمَعُ إِلَّا هَمْسًا ۞
يَوْمَئِذٍ لَّا تَنفَعُ ٱلشَّفَٰعَةُ إِلَّا مَنْ أَذِنَ لَهُ ٱلرَّحْمَٰنُ وَرَضِىَ لَهُۥ قَوْلًا ۞
يَعْلَمُ مَا بَيْنَ أَيْدِيهِمْ وَمَا خَلْفَهُمْ وَلَا يُحِيطُونَ بِهِۦ عِلْمًا ۞
وَعَنَتِ ٱلْوُجُوهُ لِلْحَىِّ ٱلْقَيُّومِ ۖ وَقَدْ خَابَ مَنْ حَمَلَ ظُلْمًا ۞
وَمَن يَعْمَلْ مِنَ ٱلصَّٰلِحَٰتِ وَهُوَ مُؤْمِنٌ فَلَا يَخَافُ ظُلْمًا وَلَا
هَضْمًا ۞ وَكَذَٰلِكَ أَنزَلْنَٰهُ قُرْءَانًا عَرَبِيًّا وَصَرَّفْنَا
فِيهِ مِنَ ٱلْوَعِيدِ لَعَلَّهُمْ يَتَّقُونَ أَوْ يُحْدِثُ لَهُمْ ذِكْرًا ۞

---

99. Thus do We relate to you (O Messenger) some of the exemplary events which happened in the past. Indeed We have granted you a Reminder (a Book of knowledge and instructions) from Our Presence.

100. Whoever turns away from it, certainly bears a burden on the Day of Resurrection,

101. Forever carrying it. How evil a burden is theirs on the Day of Resurrection!

102. That Day the Trumpet will be blown, and We will raise to life and gather the disbelieving criminals white-eyed (with terror and fatigue);

103. They whisper among themselves: "You stayed in the world only ten (days)."

104. It is We Who have full knowledge of what they talk about, when the most

perceptive among them say, "You stayed only one day."

105. They ask you (O Messenger) about (what will happen to) the mountains (on Doomsday). Say: "My Lord will blast them into scattered dust.

106. "And He will leave it (the earth) as a desolate waste.

107. "You will see in it neither curve nor ruggedness."

108. On that Day, all will follow the summoning Voice straightforwardly without any deviation, and all voices will be humbled for the All-Merciful, and you will hear nothing but a hushed murmur.

109. On that Day, intercession is not of any avail except his to whom the All-Merciful gives permission and with whose words He is well-pleased.

110. He knows what lies before His servants (especially on Judgment Day) and whatever (of intentions, or speech, or actions) they have left behind, whereas they cannot comprehend Him with their knowledge.

111. And (on that Day) all faces are humbled before the All-Living, the Self-Subsisting One (by Whom all else subsist). And assuredly he has failed whose load is wrongdoing.

112. Whereas whoever does good, righteous deeds, being a believer, need have no fear of being wronged or deprived (of his just recompense).

113. And thus have We sent it down as a *qur'ān* (a discourse) in Arabic and set out in it warnings in diverse contexts and from diverse perspectives, so that they may keep from disobedience to Us in reverence for Us and piety, or that it may prompt them to remembrance and heedfulness.

فَتَعَالَى اللهُ الْمَلِكُ الْحَقُّ وَلَا تَعْجَلْ بِالْقُرْآنِ مِنْ قَبْلِ أَنْ يُقْضَى إِلَيْكَ وَحْيُهُ وَقُلْ رَبِّ زِدْنِي عِلْمًا ۝ وَلَقَدْ عَهِدْنَا إِلَى آدَمَ مِنْ قَبْلُ فَنَسِيَ وَلَمْ نَجِدْ لَهُ عَزْمًا ۝ وَإِذْ قُلْنَا لِلْمَلَائِكَةِ اسْجُدُوا لِآدَمَ فَسَجَدُوا إِلَّا إِبْلِيسَ أَبَى ۝ فَقُلْنَا يَا آدَمُ إِنَّ هَذَا عَدُوٌّ لَكَ وَلِزَوْجِكَ فَلَا يُخْرِجَنَّكُمَا مِنَ الْجَنَّةِ فَتَشْقَى ۝ إِنَّ لَكَ أَلَّا تَجُوعَ فِيهَا وَلَا تَعْرَى ۝ وَأَنَّكَ لَا تَظْمَأُ فِيهَا وَلَا تَضْحَى ۝ فَوَسْوَسَ إِلَيْهِ الشَّيْطَانُ قَالَ يَا آدَمُ هَلْ أَدُلُّكَ عَلَى شَجَرَةِ الْخُلْدِ وَمُلْكٍ لَا يَبْلَى ۝ فَأَكَلَا مِنْهَا فَبَدَتْ لَهُمَا سَوْآتُهُمَا وَطَفِقَا يَخْصِفَانِ عَلَيْهِمَا مِنْ وَرَقِ الْجَنَّةِ وَعَصَى آدَمُ رَبَّهُ فَغَوَى ۝ ثُمَّ اجْتَبَاهُ رَبُّهُ فَتَابَ عَلَيْهِ وَهَدَى ۝ قَالَ اهْبِطَا مِنْهَا جَمِيعًا بَعْضُكُمْ لِبَعْضٍ عَدُوٌّ فَإِمَّا يَأْتِيَنَّكُمْ مِنِّي هُدًى فَمَنِ اتَّبَعَ هُدَايَ فَلَا يَضِلُّ وَلَا يَشْقَى ۝ وَمَنْ أَعْرَضَ عَنْ ذِكْرِي فَإِنَّ لَهُ مَعِيشَةً ضَنْكًا وَنَحْشُرُهُ يَوْمَ الْقِيَامَةِ أَعْمَى ۝ قَالَ رَبِّ لِمَ حَشَرْتَنِي أَعْمَى وَقَدْ كُنْتُ بَصِيرًا ۝

114. Absolutely Exalted is God, the Supreme Sovereign, the Ultimate Truth and Ever-Constant. Do not show haste (O Messenger) with (the receiving and memorizing of any Revelation included in) the Qur'an before it has been revealed to you in full, but say: "My Lord, increase me in knowledge."

115. Assuredly We had made a covenant with Adam (and forbidden him to approach a tree in the Garden), but he acted forgetfully. We did not find resolve in him (at that moment).

116. And when We said to the angels, "Prostrate before Adam," they all prostrated. But *Iblīs* did not; he refused.

117. So We said: "O Adam, surely this is an enemy to you and your wife; so let him not drive the two of you out of the Garden, lest you become distressed.

118. "Surely it is provided for you that you shall not go hungry therein nor become naked,

119. "And that you shall not go thirsty therein nor suffer the sun's heat."

120. But Satan made an evil suggestion to him, saying: "O Adam, shall I lead you to the tree of everlasting life and a kingdom that will never decay?"

121. They both ate of it, so their shameful parts (and all the seemingly evil impulses in their creation) were apparent to them, and both began to cover themselves with leaves from the Garden. Adam disobeyed his Lord and fell into error.

122. Thereafter his Lord chose him (for His favor), accepted His repentance, and bestowed His guidance upon him.

123. He said: "Go down from there, the two of you, all together (with Satan, and henceforth you will live a life,) some of you being the enemies of others. If there comes to you from Me a guidance (like a Book through a Messenger), then whoever follows My guidance (and turns to Me with faith and worship), will not go astray, nor will he be unhappy.

124. "But as for him who turns away from My remembrance (and from the Book), his will be a suffocated life, and We will raise him up blind on the Day of Resurrection."[20]

125. He says: "My Lord, why have You raised me up blind, while I used to be seeing (in my life of the world)?"

20. For the incidents and truths described from verse 115 on, see *sūrah* 2: 30–39, notes 30–44; *sūrah* 7: 11–27, notes 3–4. Here we can add the following points:

- The prohibition of approaching a tree in the Garden was not a prohibition included in the Sharī'ah or the Religious Law. It was a prohibition and instruction concerning the life of Adam and his spouse. It is clear that the purpose of such a prohibition was, on their part, to avoid suffering from hunger, nakedness, thirst, and the heat of the sun. So the consequence of or recompense for not heeding this prohibition would be exposure to this kind of suffering.

- The verses reveal that the desire for eternity, passionate desire for the opposite sex (especially for women on the part of men), and the worldly kingdom are, at least, among the most alluring lusts or appetites for human beings, so much so that they cause human beings many sufferings.

- The Qur'ān mentions Adam as being chosen and forgiven just after their lapse in order to prevent us from harboring any negative feelings towards Adam. It also teaches that we should immediately repent and pray for forgiveness as soon as we have sinned or lapsed.

- The Bible unfortunately blames Eve more than Adam for their lapse (*Genesis*, 3: 1–6). According to the Bible, Eve incited Adam to eat from the forbidden tree. This caused the Jews and Christians to see women as being accursed creatures for many centuries. By contrast, the Qur'ān tells us that Satan approached Adam and deceived him. This reveals an important truth that it is generally men who have been responsible for the deviation of women from the right path, not the other way round.

126. (God) says: "Just so. Our Revelations came to you but you disregarded them, so today you will be disregarded."

127. Thus do We recompense him who is wasteful (of his God-given faculties) and commits excesses, and does not believe in his Lord's Revelations. And indeed, the punishment in the Hereafter is more severe and most enduring.

128. Is it not a guidance for them how many a generation We have destroyed before them, in whose ruined dwelling-places they walk about (in the present)? Surely in that there are signs (manifesting the truth) for people of discernment.

129. Had it not been for a decree already issued by your Lord,[21] and for a term already appointed (by Him), the judgment (against them) would certainly have been given and executed.

130. Therefore, be patient (O Messenger) with whatever they say and glorify your Lord with praise before sunrise and before sunset, and glorify Him during some hours of the night – as well as glorifying (Him) at the ends of the day – so that you may obtain God's good pleasure and be contented (with what God has decreed for you).

131. Do not strain your eyes toward what We have given some groups among them to enjoy (in this worldly life), the splendor of the present, worldly life, so that We may test them thereby. The provision of Your Lord (the favors He has bestowed upon you here and will bestow in the Hereafter) is better and more lasting.

132. Order your family and community to establish the Prayer, and be diligent in its observance. We do not ask you to provide for Us; rather it is We Who provide for you. (So all your worship is for your own benefit.) And the (desired) outcome is in favor of piety and righteousness.

320   سورة طه   ٣٢٠

قَالَ كَذَٰلِكَ أَتَتْكَ ءَايَـٰتُنَا فَنَسِيتَهَا وَكَذَٰلِكَ ٱلْيَوْمَ تُنسَىٰ ۞
وَكَذَٰلِكَ نَجْزِى مَنْ أَسْرَفَ وَلَمْ يُؤْمِنۢ بِـَٔايَـٰتِ رَبِّهِ وَلَعَذَابُ ٱلْـَٔاخِرَةِ
أَشَدُّ وَأَبْقَىٰٓ ۞ أَفَلَمْ يَهْدِ لَهُمْ كَمْ أَهْلَكْنَا قَبْلَهُم مِّنَ ٱلْقُرُونِ
يَمْشُونَ فِى مَسَـٰكِنِهِمْ إِنَّ فِى ذَٰلِكَ لَـَٔايَـٰتٍ لِّأُوْلِى ٱلنُّهَىٰ ۞ وَلَوْلَا
كَلِمَةٌ سَبَقَتْ مِن رَّبِّكَ لَكَانَ لِزَامًا وَأَجَلٌ مُّسَمًّى ۞ فَٱصْبِرْ عَلَىٰ
مَا يَقُولُونَ وَسَبِّحْ بِحَمْدِ رَبِّكَ قَبْلَ طُلُوعِ ٱلشَّمْسِ وَقَبْلَ غُرُوبِهَا وَمِنْ
ءَانَآئِ ٱلَّيْلِ فَسَبِّحْ وَأَطْرَافَ ٱلنَّهَارِ لَعَلَّكَ تَرْضَىٰ ۞ وَلَا تَمُدَّنَّ
عَيْنَيْكَ إِلَىٰ مَا مَتَّعْنَا بِهِۦٓ أَزْوَٰجًا مِّنْهُمْ زَهْرَةَ ٱلْحَيَوٰةِ ٱلدُّنْيَا
لِنَفْتِنَهُمْ فِيهِ وَرِزْقُ رَبِّكَ خَيْرٌ وَأَبْقَىٰ ۞ وَأْمُرْ أَهْلَكَ بِٱلصَّلَوٰةِ
وَٱصْطَبِرْ عَلَيْهَا لَا نَسْـَٔلُكَ رِزْقًا نَّحْنُ نَرْزُقُكَ وَٱلْعَـٰقِبَةُ
لِلتَّقْوَىٰ ۞ وَقَالُوا۟ لَوْلَا يَأْتِينَا بِـَٔايَةٍ مِّن رَّبِّهِۦٓ أَوَلَمْ تَأْتِهِم
بَيِّنَةُ مَا فِى ٱلصُّحُفِ ٱلْأُولَىٰ ۞ وَلَوْ أَنَّا أَهْلَكْنَاهُم بِعَذَابٍ
مِّن قَبْلِهِۦ لَقَالُوا۟ رَبَّنَا لَوْلَآ أَرْسَلْتَ إِلَيْنَا رَسُولًا فَنَتَّبِعَ ءَايَـٰتِكَ
مِن قَبْلِ أَن نَّذِلَّ وَنَخْزَىٰ ۞ قُلْ كُلٌّ مُّتَرَبِّصٌ فَتَرَبَّصُوا۟
فَسَتَعْلَمُونَ مَنْ أَصْحَـٰبُ ٱلصِّرَٰطِ ٱلسَّوِىِّ وَمَنِ ٱهْتَدَىٰ ۞

———❧———

133. And they say: "If only he brought us a sign (a miracle) from his Lord!" Has there not come to them (as a sufficient miracle) a Clear Proof of (the truth) in what is (to be found) in the former Scriptures?[22]

134. Had We destroyed them with a punishment before it (before the Proof came to them), they would surely have said: "Our Lord! If only You had sent us a Messenger, we would have followed Your Revelations before we were humiliated and disgraced."

135. Say: "Everyone (we and you) is in an expectation (of what the future will bring), so continue to expect! You will soon come to know who have been the followers of the even path and who have been rightly guided (and therefore whose expectations have proved true).

21. The decree is that which was proclaimed during Adam's descent from the Garden: *There shall be for you on the earth (where you have already been appointed as vicegerent) a habitation and provision until an appointed time* (7: 24).

22. Is it not a sufficient miracle for them that there has come to them a Messenger who was predicted by the former Divine Scriptures and whose features are found in them? That Messenger, though an illiterate one, has come to them with a Book which contains all the truths concerning correct belief and worship, and eternal principles for a good life, which are all to be found in the former Divine Scriptures. This Book also explains what happened to the peoples who asked their Messengers for similar miracles.

SŪRAH 21

AL-ANBIYĀ'
(THE PROPHETS)

Makkah period

This *surah* of 112 verses was revealed toward the end of the Makkan period of the Messenger's mission. It explains the "even path" mentioned at the end of *Surah Ṭā-Hā*. It gives answers to the objections made by the Makkan polytheists to the creeds of Islam, and provides support for these creeds, as well as relating some episodes from the lives of a number of earlier Prophets. It concludes by stating that, with its essentials of faith, worship, morality, and individual and collective life, Islam is the Religion which God has appointed for humankind and which He has conveyed to them through all the Prophets.

In the Name of God, the All-Merciful, the All-Compassionate.

1. Their reckoning has drawn near for humankind, yet they do not pay heed to it, being lost in worldly things and heedlessness.[1]

2. Whenever a new Revelation comes to them from their Lord to warn and enlighten them, they only listen to it in a playful manner,

3. With hearts set on passing pleasures; yet those who lead in wrongdoing, especially by associating partners with God, confer among themselves in great secret: "Is this (not) but a mortal like you? Will you, then, yield to sorcery while you see it patently?"

4. (The Messenger) says (in response): "My Lord knows every word spoken in the heaven and on the earth. He is the All-Hearing, the All-Knowing."

5. (Confused about which source they should attribute the Qur'an to) they say,

"No, but Muḥammad offers some jumbles of dream images he has. No, but he fabricates all this! No, but he is a poet. If he is true in his claim, then let him come to us with a sign (a miracle), just as the previous Messengers were sent with miracles!"

6. Not one of the peoples before them that We destroyed believed (even though the Messengers came to them with miracles). Will then these believe?

7. We did not send as Messengers before you (O Muḥammad) any but men to whom We revealed. So (O people) ask those who have expert knowledge (of the Divine Revelations), if you do not know.

8. Nor did We make them bodies not needing food so that they would not eat like others, nor were they immortals.

9. We promised them help and victory and We kept Our promise: We saved them and all whom We willed (– the believers),[2] and We destroyed those who wasted their God-given faculties and committed excesses.

10. Now We send down to you (O people of Makkah and O all humankind,) a Book which contains what you must heed in life for your honor and happiness. Will you not, then, reason and understand?

---

1. Knowledge of the Last Day rests only with God, and the Last Day may come unexpectedly at any time. If we look at how many centuries have passed since this warning was given concerning the Last Hour, which has not yet come, compared with the life of the world and humankind on the earth, the period is very brief. A person who says in the late afternoon that evening is near is telling the truth. Secondly, reckoning for everybody begins just after their death, and nothing is nearer to one than death.

2. See *sūrah* 37: 171–173; *sūrah* 10: 103.

11. How many a community that did the greatest wrong (by associating partners with God) and thereby wronged itself have We shattered, and raised up another people after them.

12. When they felt Our mighty punishment coming, they at once attempted to flee from it.

13. "Do not attempt to flee, but return to all that (ease and comfort) in which you had been lost without scruples, and to your homes, that you may be appealed to by the poor and needy, or to take your valuable counsels!

14. They could only cry: "Oh, woe to us! We were indeed wrongdoers!"

15. That cry of theirs did not cease until We made them like reaped corn, and a heap of ashes.

16. We have not created the heavens and the earth and all that is between them as a play and game for Us.

17. If We had willed to find a pastime (without creating the heavens and the earth with all that is in and between them), We would indeed have found it in Our Presence, if We were going to do so!

18. No, but We hurl the truth against falsehood, and it breaks the latter's head, and see, it vanishes. So woe to you for all the falsehood you attribute to God.

19. To Him belongs whoever is in the heavens and the earth. And those (the angels) who are with Him, never disdain to worship Him, nor do they ever weary.

20. They glorify Him by night and day (proclaiming that He is absolutely exalted above any shortcoming or need of partners or doing pointless things), and never show tiredness and never lose zeal.

21. What! have those polytheists (given up hope of heaven and) adopted deities from the earth, (do they believe) that they (those deities) can raise up the dead?

22. But the fact is that had there been in the heavens and the earth any deities other than God, both (of those realms) would certainly have fallen into ruin. All-Glorified is God, the Lord of the Supreme Throne, in that He is absolutely above all that they attribute to Him.

23. He cannot be called to account for whatever He does, but their false deities (they have adopted from among conscious beings) are accountable.

24. What! have they adopted deities other than Him? Say: "If so, present your proof! But look, here is the Book those who are in my company follow, and there are the Books those who came before me followed: (what is stressed in all of them is that there is no deity other than Him.)" Whereas they have nothing to do with knowledge so that they might know the truth, and this is why they turn away from it in aversion.

وَمَا أَرْسَلْنَا مِن قَبْلِكَ مِن رَّسُولٍ إِلَّا نُوحِي إِلَيْهِ أَنَّهُ لَا إِلَٰهَ إِلَّا أَنَا۠ فَاعْبُدُونِ ۝ وَقَالُوا اتَّخَذَ الرَّحْمَٰنُ وَلَدًا سُبْحَانَهُ ۚ بَلْ عِبَادٌ مُّكْرَمُونَ ۝ لَا يَسْبِقُونَهُ بِالْقَوْلِ وَهُم بِأَمْرِهِ يَعْمَلُونَ ۝ يَعْلَمُ مَا بَيْنَ أَيْدِيهِمْ وَمَا خَلْفَهُمْ وَلَا يَشْفَعُونَ إِلَّا لِمَنِ ارْتَضَىٰ وَهُم مِّنْ خَشْيَتِهِ مُشْفِقُونَ ۝ وَمَن يَقُلْ مِنْهُمْ إِنِّي إِلَٰهٌ مِّن دُونِهِ فَذَٰلِكَ نَجْزِيهِ جَهَنَّمَ ۚ كَذَٰلِكَ نَجْزِي الظَّالِمِينَ ۝ أَوَلَمْ يَرَ الَّذِينَ كَفَرُوا أَنَّ السَّمَاوَاتِ وَالْأَرْضَ كَانَتَا رَتْقًا فَفَتَقْنَاهُمَا ۖ وَجَعَلْنَا مِنَ الْمَاءِ كُلَّ شَيْءٍ حَيٍّ ۖ أَفَلَا يُؤْمِنُونَ ۝ وَجَعَلْنَا فِي الْأَرْضِ رَوَاسِيَ أَن تَمِيدَ بِهِمْ وَجَعَلْنَا فِيهَا فِجَاجًا سُبُلًا لَّعَلَّهُمْ يَهْتَدُونَ ۝ وَجَعَلْنَا السَّمَاءَ سَقْفًا مَّحْفُوظًا ۖ وَهُمْ عَنْ آيَاتِهَا مُعْرِضُونَ ۝ وَهُوَ الَّذِي خَلَقَ اللَّيْلَ وَالنَّهَارَ وَالشَّمْسَ وَالْقَمَرَ ۖ كُلٌّ فِي فَلَكٍ يَسْبَحُونَ ۝ وَمَا جَعَلْنَا لِبَشَرٍ مِّن قَبْلِكَ الْخُلْدَ ۖ أَفَإِن مِّتَّ فَهُمُ الْخَالِدُونَ ۝ كُلُّ نَفْسٍ ذَائِقَةُ الْمَوْتِ ۗ وَنَبْلُوكُم بِالشَّرِّ وَالْخَيْرِ فِتْنَةً ۖ وَإِلَيْنَا تُرْجَعُونَ ۝

---

well-pleased, and they themselves quake for reverent awe of Him.

29. If any of them were to attempt to say, "I am a deity besides Him," We would recompense him with Hell. Thus do We recompense all such wrongdoers.

30. Do those who disbelieve ever consider that the heavens and the earth were at first one piece, and then We parted them as separate entities; and that We have made every living thing from water?[3] Will they still not come to believe?

31. We have set up firm mountains in the earth lest it should shake them with its movement, and We have made thereon broad paths, so that they might find their way.

32. And We have established the heaven as a canopy well-secured (against collapse and the ascension of devils). Yet they turn away from all such signs (of truth manifested) in the universe.

33. It is He Who has created the night and the day and the sun and the moon. Every one (of such celestial bodies) floats[4] in its orbit.

34. We never granted everlasting life to any human being before you (O Messenger); so if you die, will they live forever?

35. Every soul (person)[5] is bound to taste death, and We try you through the bad and the good things (of life) by way of testing (so that your real character and rank may reveal itself). In fact, you are on the way to return to Us, (to finally be brought to Our Presence).

25. We never sent any Messenger before you except that We revealed to him that there is no deity but Me, so worship Me alone.

26. Yet some say, "The All-Merciful has taken to Himself a child." All-Glorified is He (in that He is absolutely above doing such things). Rather, those (the angels, whom they regard as God's offspring) are but His honored servants.

27. They speak only what He has spoken to them and allows them to speak, and they act by His command.

28. He knows what lies before them and what lies after them (what lies in their future and in their past, what is known to them and what is hidden from them); and they cannot intercede for any but His believing servants, those with whom He is

3. Every verse of the Qur'ān has both outer and inner meanings, and limits, and a point of comprehension, as well as boughs, branches, and twigs. Each phrase, word, letter, and diacritical point has many aspects. Each person who hears it receives their share through a different door.

To learned people who have not studied modern sciences, *one piece* in the verse means that when the heavens were clear and without clouds, and the earth was dry, lifeless, and incapable of giving birth, God opened the heavens with rain and the soil with vegetation, and created all living beings through some sort of marriage and impregnation by means of water. They understand that everything is the work of such an All-Powerful One of Majesty, and that the surface of the earth is merely His small garden, and all the clouds that veil the surface of the sky are sponges for watering it. They prostrate themselves before the greatness of His Power.

To exacting scholars, it means: "In the beginning, the heavens and the earth were a formless mass, each consisting of matter as if "dough," without produce or creatures. The All-Wise Creator separated them and rolled them out and, giving each a comely shape and beneficial form, made them the origins of multiform, adorned creatures." These scholars are filled with admiration at His Wisdom's comprehensiveness.

Modern scientists understand that the solar system was like a cloud of gases or was fused like a mass of "dough." Then the All-Powerful and Self-Subsistent One rolled it out and placed the planets in their respective positions. Or the mass of gases began to cool due to the extremely speedy movement. The Almighty left the sun where it was and brought the earth here. Spreading soil over its surface, watering it with rain, and illuminating it with sunlight, He made the world inhabitable and placed us on it. These scientists are saved from the swamp of naturalism, and declare: "I believe in God, the One, the Unique."

Another meaning this verse presents to modern scientists is: The universe was only in the form of ether, a pervasive matter (which some regard as hydrogen, one of the two atoms that are needed to make up water). God made ether a source of atoms from which He created all things, and He has placed everything in this "ocean" of the ether (See *The Words*, "the 25th Word," 411–412, "the 31st Word," 587–588).

4. The verbs *SaBaḤa* and *JāRa* (36: 38), meaning floating and running in the water respectively, and the terms which the Qur'ān uses for the movement of celestial bodies suggest that space is not empty, but rather is filled with some pervasive matter. Bediüzzaman Said Nursi emphasizes that space consists of ether and refers to it as "the ocean of heaven" (*The Words*, "the 31st Word," 587–588).

5. The term *nafs* (soul, self) is used in the Qur'ān in various, but similar, complementary meanings. First, it means the self of a person or a thing. In this meaning, it is also used for God (3: 28; 5: 116).

Its second meaning is the substance and essence which is the source of physical life in a human being or the dimension or aspect of the spirit which is the basis of animal and human physical life (6: 93).

In its third meaning, as the basis of the human physical or worldly life, it is the essence or substance which is aware of the needs of life, which demands and tastes pleasures and encourages a person to meet those needs and experience those pleasures. In a sense, it is the substance which incites a person to commit evil (12: 53). It can and must be trained. When trained, it can be elevated from being a substance which commands evils or being an evil-commanding soul to the rank of being a soul at rest with faith in and worship of God (89: 27–28).

In its other and most comprehensive meaning, it is human nature or the individual person (4: 1).

324 سُورَةُ الْأَنْبِيَاء ٣٢٢

وَإِذَا رَآكَ الَّذِينَ كَفَرُوٓا إِن يَتَّخِذُونَكَ إِلَّا هُزُوًا أَهَٰذَا الَّذِى يَذْكُرُ ءَالِهَتَكُمْ وَهُم بِذِكْرِ الرَّحْمَٰنِ هُمْ كَٰفِرُونَ ۞ خُلِقَ الْإِنسَٰنُ مِنْ عَجَلٍ سَأُوْرِيكُمْ ءَايَٰتِى فَلَا تَسْتَعْجِلُونِ ۞ وَيَقُولُونَ مَتَىٰ هَٰذَا الْوَعْدُ إِن كُنتُمْ صَٰدِقِينَ ۞ لَوْ يَعْلَمُ الَّذِينَ كَفَرُوا حِينَ لَا يَكُفُّونَ عَن وُجُوهِهِمُ النَّارَ وَلَا عَن ظُهُورِهِمْ وَلَا هُمْ يُنصَرُونَ ۞ بَلْ تَأْتِيهِم بَغْتَةً فَتَبْهَتُهُمْ فَلَا يَسْتَطِيعُونَ رَدَّهَا وَلَا هُمْ يُنظَرُونَ ۞ وَلَقَدِ اسْتُهْزِئَ بِرُسُلٍ مِّن قَبْلِكَ فَحَاقَ بِالَّذِينَ سَخِرُوا مِنْهُم مَّا كَانُوا بِهِ يَسْتَهْزِءُونَ ۞ قُلْ مَن يَكْلَؤُكُم بِالَّيْلِ وَالنَّهَارِ مِنَ الرَّحْمَٰنِ بَلْ هُمْ عَن ذِكْرِ رَبِّهِم مُّعْرِضُونَ ۞ أَمْ لَهُمْ ءَالِهَةٌ تَمْنَعُهُم مِّن دُونِنَا لَا يَسْتَطِيعُونَ نَصْرَ أَنفُسِهِمْ وَلَا هُم مِّنَّا يُصْحَبُونَ ۞ بَلْ مَتَّعْنَا هَٰٓؤُلَآءِ وَءَابَآءَهُمْ حَتَّىٰ طَالَ عَلَيْهِمُ الْعُمُرُ أَفَلَا يَرَوْنَ أَنَّا نَأْتِى الْأَرْضَ نَنقُصُهَا مِنْ أَطْرَافِهَآ أَفَهُمُ الْغَٰلِبُونَ ۞

36. When those who persistently disbelieve see you, they make you but a target of mockery, (saying to each other): "Is this the one who speaks against your deities?" (They cannot bear to hear their false deities denied.) And yet it is they themselves who deny the Book of the All-Merciful (Who has created them and embraces them with mercy, without recognizing this as a crime).

37. Humankind are by nature impatient as if made of haste, (this is why they ask derisively when the punishment with which they are threatened will come). I will soon show you the truth of My threats, so do not ask Me to hasten it.

38. But they insistently ask, "After all, when will this threat be fulfilled? (Answer us, O you who believe in it,) if you are people of truth!"

39. If only those who persistently disbelieve knew the time when they will be unable to ward off the Fire from their faces, and from their backs, and they will never be helped against it!

40. But it will come upon them all of a sudden and dumbfound them. They will not be able to avert it, nor will they be given respite to escape it.

41. Indeed, Messengers were mocked before you (O Muhammad), but the very thing, because of which the people used to mock them, overwhelmed those who scoffed at the Messengers (to humiliate them).

42. Say: "Who could protect you by night and day from the All-Merciful, if He wills to punish you?" And yet, they turn away from the Book of their Lord in aversion.

43. Or do they really have deities apart from Us to defend them? They (those alleged deities) are not even able to help themselves, nor can they get any help and friendship from Us.

44. The truth is that We have provided for those (polytheist sinners) and their forefathers to enjoy life, so that they have lived for a long time in ease and safety. (This is why they think that they will live forever in prosperity.) Whereas do they not see how We deal with the earth, reducing it of its outlying parts? [6] So, can they really be the victors?

6. For reducing the earth of its outlying parts, see 13: 41, note 14.

قُلْ إِنَّمَآ أُنذِرُكُم بِالْوَحْيِ وَلَا يَسْمَعُ الصُّمُّ الدُّعَآءَ إِذَا مَا يُنذَرُونَ ۝ وَلَئِن مَّسَّتْهُمْ نَفْحَةٌ مِّنْ عَذَابِ رَبِّكَ لَيَقُولُنَّ يَٰوَيْلَنَآ إِنَّا كُنَّا ظَٰلِمِينَ ۝ وَنَضَعُ ٱلْمَوَٰزِينَ ٱلْقِسْطَ لِيَوْمِ ٱلْقِيَٰمَةِ فَلَا تُظْلَمُ نَفْسٌ شَيْـًٔا وَإِن كَانَ مِثْقَالَ حَبَّةٍ مِّنْ خَرْدَلٍ أَتَيْنَا بِهَا وَكَفَىٰ بِنَا حَٰسِبِينَ ۝ وَلَقَدْ ءَاتَيْنَا مُوسَىٰ وَهَٰرُونَ ٱلْفُرْقَانَ وَضِيَآءً وَذِكْرًا لِّلْمُتَّقِينَ ۝ ٱلَّذِينَ يَخْشَوْنَ رَبَّهُم بِٱلْغَيْبِ وَهُم مِّنَ ٱلسَّاعَةِ مُشْفِقُونَ ۝ وَهَٰذَا ذِكْرٌ مُّبَارَكٌ أَنزَلْنَٰهُ أَفَأَنتُمْ لَهُۥ مُنكِرُونَ ۝ وَلَقَدْ ءَاتَيْنَآ إِبْرَٰهِيمَ رُشْدَهُۥ مِن قَبْلُ وَكُنَّا بِهِۦ عَٰلِمِينَ ۝ إِذْ قَالَ لِأَبِيهِ وَقَوْمِهِۦ مَا هَٰذِهِ ٱلتَّمَاثِيلُ ٱلَّتِىٓ أَنتُمْ لَهَا عَٰكِفُونَ ۝ قَالُوا۟ وَجَدْنَآ ءَابَآءَنَا لَهَا عَٰبِدِينَ ۝ قَالَ لَقَدْ كُنتُمْ أَنتُمْ وَءَابَآؤُكُمْ فِى ضَلَٰلٍ مُّبِينٍ ۝ قَالُوٓا۟ أَجِئْتَنَا بِٱلْحَقِّ أَمْ أَنتَ مِنَ ٱللَّٰعِبِينَ ۝ قَالَ بَل رَّبُّكُمْ رَبُّ ٱلسَّمَٰوَٰتِ وَٱلْأَرْضِ ٱلَّذِى فَطَرَهُنَّ وَأَنَا۠ عَلَىٰ ذَٰلِكُم مِّنَ ٱلشَّٰهِدِينَ ۝ وَتَٱللَّهِ لَأَكِيدَنَّ أَصْنَٰمَكُم بَعْدَ أَن تُوَلُّوا۟ مُدْبِرِينَ ۝

45. Say: "I warn you only on the strength of the Revelation (in which there is no doubt). But the deaf do not hear the call, however much they are warned."

46. And yet, if but a breath of your Lord's punishment touches them,[7] they are sure to cry: "Oh, woe to us! We were indeed wrongdoers!"

47. We will set up balances of absolute justice on the Day of Resurrection, and no person will be wronged in the least. Even though it be a deed so much as the weight of a grain of mustard seed, We will bring it forth to be weighed. We suffice as reckoners.

48. We granted Moses and Aaron the Criterion (the Book distinguishing between truth and falsehood,) and made it a (guiding) light and reminder for the God-revering, pious.

49. They stand in great awe of their Lord though unseen (and beyond their perception), and tremble with the thought of the Last Hour.

50. And this one (the Qur'ān), too, is a Reminder full of blessings which We are sending down. Will you then reject it?

51. Indeed We had, before this, granted Abraham discretion and his particular consciousness of truth, and We knew him very well (in all aspects of his character).

52. He said to his father and his people: "What are these images to which you pay such sincere devotion?"

53. They said: "We have found our forefathers worshipping them."

54. "So, it is certain that," said he, "both of you, you and your forefathers, have been in obvious error."

55. They asked: "Is it the truth that you are proclaiming to us or are you jesting?"

56. He answered: "No, but your Lord is the Lord of the heavens and the earth, Who has originated them each with particular features, and I am one to bear witness to this truth."

57. And (he made a decision:) "By God, I will most certainly devise a plan against your idols as soon as you have turned your backs and gone away!"

7. Bediüzzaman Said Nursi cites this verse as one of the typical examples of the Qur'ān's miraculous eloquence. To indicate the severity of God's punishment, the clause points to the least amount or slightest degree of it. As the entire clause expresses this slightness, all of its parts should reinforce that meaning.

The words "If but" (*la-in*) signify uncertainty and therefore imply slightness (of punishment). The verb *massa* means to touch slightly, also signifying slightness. *Nafḥatun* (a breath) is merely a puff of air. By both its meaning and being used without the definite article and therefore indicating indefiniteness, this word again underlines the slightness. The partitive *min* implies a part or a piece, thus indicating paucity. The word *'adhāb* (punishment) is light in meaning compared to *nakāl* (exemplary chastisement) and *'iqāb* (heavy penalty), and denotes a light punishment. The use of *Rabb* (Lord, Provider, Sustainer), suggesting affection, instead of (for example) Overwhelming, All-Compelling, or Ever-Able to Requite, also expresses slightness.

Therefore, when so slight a breath of punishment has such an affect, we should ponder how severe Divine chastisement might be. We see in this short clause the way its parts are related to each other and complement their meaning. This example demonstrates the Qur'ān's choice of words and the wisdom in choosing them (*The Words*, "the 25th Word," 392).

326   سُورَةُ الأَنبِيَاءِ   ٣٢٦

فَجَعَلَهُمْ جُذَاذًا إِلَّا كَبِيرًا لَّهُمْ لَعَلَّهُمْ إِلَيْهِ يَرْجِعُونَ ۝ قَالُوا مَن فَعَلَ هَٰذَا بِآلِهَتِنَا إِنَّهُ لَمِنَ الظَّالِمِينَ ۝ قَالُوا سَمِعْنَا فَتًى يَذْكُرُهُمْ يُقَالُ لَهُ إِبْرَاهِيمُ ۝ قَالُوا فَأْتُوا بِهِ عَلَىٰ أَعْيُنِ النَّاسِ لَعَلَّهُمْ يَشْهَدُونَ ۝ قَالُوا أَأَنتَ فَعَلْتَ هَٰذَا بِآلِهَتِنَا يَا إِبْرَاهِيمُ ۝ قَالَ بَلْ فَعَلَهُ كَبِيرُهُمْ هَٰذَا فَاسْأَلُوهُمْ إِن كَانُوا يَنطِقُونَ ۝ فَرَجَعُوا إِلَىٰ أَنفُسِهِمْ فَقَالُوا إِنَّكُمْ أَنتُمُ الظَّالِمُونَ ۝ ثُمَّ نُكِسُوا عَلَىٰ رُءُوسِهِمْ لَقَدْ عَلِمْتَ مَا هَٰؤُلَاءِ يَنطِقُونَ ۝ قَالَ أَفَتَعْبُدُونَ مِن دُونِ اللَّهِ مَا لَا يَنفَعُكُمْ شَيْئًا وَلَا يَضُرُّكُمْ ۝ أُفٍّ لَّكُمْ وَلِمَا تَعْبُدُونَ مِن دُونِ اللَّهِ أَفَلَا تَعْقِلُونَ ۝ قَالُوا حَرِّقُوهُ وَانصُرُوا آلِهَتَكُمْ إِن كُنتُمْ فَاعِلِينَ ۝ قُلْنَا يَا نَارُ كُونِي بَرْدًا وَسَلَامًا عَلَىٰ إِبْرَاهِيمَ ۝ وَأَرَادُوا بِهِ كَيْدًا فَجَعَلْنَاهُمُ الْأَخْسَرِينَ ۝ وَنَجَّيْنَاهُ وَلُوطًا إِلَى الْأَرْضِ الَّتِي بَارَكْنَا فِيهَا لِلْعَالَمِينَ ۝ وَوَهَبْنَا لَهُ إِسْحَاقَ وَيَعْقُوبَ نَافِلَةً وَكُلًّا جَعَلْنَا صَالِحِينَ ۝

──────────────◈──────────────

58. And then he broke all of them to pieces except the one biggest in their sight, so that they might be able turn back to it (to ask what had happened)!

59. "Who has done all this to our deities?" they exclaimed. "Indeed, he is one of the worst wrongdoers!"

60. Some said: "We heard a young man make mention of them, who is called Abraham."

61. They said: "Then bring him before the people's eyes, so that they may bear witness against him!"

62. "Abraham," they asked, "is it you who has done this to our deities?"

63. He answered: "Rather, (some doer) must have done it – this is the biggest of them. Ask them, if they are able to speak!"

64. So they turned to their conscious nature which awoke to truth, and said (among themselves): "You (we), it is you (we) who are the wrongdoers!"

65. But afterwards, (under the influence of the same factors causing them to disbelieve) they relapsed into their former way of believing, and said to Abraham: "You know very well that these (images) cannot speak."

66. (Abraham) said: "Then, do you worship, instead of God, that which cannot benefit you in any way, nor harm you?

67. "Shame on you and on all that you worship instead of God! Will you not reason and understand?"

68. They exclaimed: "Burn him and so protect your deities, if you really mean to do something!"

69. "O fire," We ordered, "Be cool and peaceful for Abraham!"[8]

70. They had schemed to destroy him but We frustrated them, making them the worst of losers.

71. We saved him and Lot (who believed in him), guiding them to the land (of Damascus, including Palestine) in which We have produced many blessings for all peoples.

72. We bestowed upon him Isaac, and as an additional gift, Jacob (for grandson); and each We made righteous.

8. This verse contains three subtle points:

First: Like every element in nature, fire performs a duty under God's command. It did not burn Abraham, for God commanded it not to do so.

Second: One type of heat burns through coldness. Through the phrase *Be peaceful*, God Almighty commanded the cold: "Do not burn him." An interpreter of the Qur'ān remarks: "If He had not said '*Be peaceful!*', it would have burned him with its coldness." Fire can simultaneously burn and be cold. Science has discovered a fire called "white heat" which does not radiate its heat. Instead, by attracting the surrounding heat, it causes the surrounding area to become cold enough to freeze liquids and in effect burns them through its cold. (Hell, which contains all degrees and sorts of fire, must also have this intense cold.)

Third: Just as there is an immaterial substance like faith and an armor like Islam, which will remove the effects of Hellfire and prevent them from harming us, there must be a physical substance that will protect against and prevent the effects of fire. As the fire did not burn Abraham's body or clothes, people can make a similar armor to protect them against fire.

Thus the verse suggests:

O nation of Abraham. Be like Abraham, so that your garments may be your guard against the fire, your greatest enemy, in both worlds. Coat your spirit with faith, and it will be your armor against Hellfire. Moreover, earth contains substances that will protect you from fire's evil. Search for them, extract them, and coat yourselves with them.

As an important step in their progress, humankind discovered a fire-resistant substance. But see how elevated, fine, and beautiful a garment this verse indicates, one which will be woven on the loom of purity of faith in and submission to God, and which will not be torn for all eternity (See *The Words*, "the 20th Word," 273).

وَجَعَلْنَاهُمْ أَئِمَّةً يَهْدُونَ بِأَمْرِنَا وَأَوْحَيْنَا إِلَيْهِمْ فِعْلَ الْخَيْرَاتِ وَإِقَامَ الصَّلَوٰةِ وَإِيتَاءَ الزَّكَوٰةِ وَكَانُوا لَنَا عَابِدِينَ ۝ وَلُوطًا آتَيْنَاهُ حُكْمًا وَعِلْمًا وَنَجَّيْنَاهُ مِنَ الْقَرْيَةِ الَّتِي كَانَتْ تَعْمَلُ الْخَبَائِثَ إِنَّهُمْ كَانُوا قَوْمَ سَوْءٍ فَاسِقِينَ ۝ وَأَدْخَلْنَاهُ فِي رَحْمَتِنَا إِنَّهُ مِنَ الصَّالِحِينَ ۝ وَنُوحًا إِذْ نَادَىٰ مِنْ قَبْلُ فَاسْتَجَبْنَا لَهُ فَنَجَّيْنَاهُ وَأَهْلَهُ مِنَ الْكَرْبِ الْعَظِيمِ ۝ وَنَصَرْنَاهُ مِنَ الْقَوْمِ الَّذِينَ كَذَّبُوا بِآيَاتِنَا إِنَّهُمْ كَانُوا قَوْمَ سَوْءٍ فَأَغْرَقْنَاهُمْ أَجْمَعِينَ ۝ وَدَاوُدَ وَسُلَيْمَانَ إِذْ يَحْكُمَانِ فِي الْحَرْثِ إِذْ نَفَشَتْ فِيهِ غَنَمُ الْقَوْمِ وَكُنَّا لِحُكْمِهِمْ شَاهِدِينَ ۝ فَفَهَّمْنَاهَا سُلَيْمَانَ وَكُلًّا آتَيْنَا حُكْمًا وَعِلْمًا وَسَخَّرْنَا مَعَ دَاوُدَ الْجِبَالَ يُسَبِّحْنَ وَالطَّيْرَ وَكُنَّا فَاعِلِينَ ۝ وَعَلَّمْنَاهُ صَنْعَةَ لَبُوسٍ لَكُمْ لِتُحْصِنَكُمْ مِنْ بَأْسِكُمْ فَهَلْ أَنْتُمْ شَاكِرُونَ ۝ وَلِسُلَيْمَانَ الرِّيحَ عَاصِفَةً تَجْرِي بِأَمْرِهِ إِلَى الْأَرْضِ الَّتِي بَارَكْنَا فِيهَا وَكُنَّا بِكُلِّ شَيْءٍ عَالِمِينَ ۝

73. And We made them leaders guiding people by Our command, and We revealed to them to do good deeds, and to establish the Prayer in conformity with its conditions, and pay the Prescribed Purifying Alms. They were Our servants devoted to worshipping us with all sincerity.

74. And Lot too (We made a leader), to whom We granted authority with sound, wise judgment, and (revealed) knowledge, and We saved him from the people of the land who were given to deeds of corruption. Truly, they were a wicked people lost in transgression.

75. We embraced him in Our Mercy; surely he was among the righteous.

76. And Noah, too. He had called out to Us long before (Abraham), and We answered his prayer and saved him and (those of) his family and people (who believed in him) from the tremendous distress.

77. We helped him to safety from the people who denied Our Revelations. Truly, they were a wicked people, so We caused them all to drown.

78. (Among those whom We made leaders were) David and Solomon. The two were once judging a case regarding a field into which the sheep of some other people had strayed at night. We were watching and witnessing their judgment.

79. We made Solomon understand the case more clearly. We granted each of them authority with sound, wise judgment and knowledge (pertaining to the mission and in accordance with the time and conditions of each).[9] And We subdued the mountains, as well as birds, to glorify Us along with David.[10] It is We Who do all these things.

80. And We taught him the art of making iron coats-of-mail so that they might fortify you from the violence of war. So, are you (really people who are) thankful?

81. And in Solomon's service We put the stormy wind, running at his command to carry him to the land in which We have produced blessings (for people).[11] We have full knowledge of everything (with their true nature and all their aspects).

9. According to the reports, Solomon, upon him be peace, judged that the owner of the field should temporarily possess the sheep and benefit from their milk, wool, and new-born lambs. In the meanwhile, the field was to be entrusted to the owner of the sheep to cultivate it and restore to its former condition. David, upon him be peace, approved this judgment.

The verse is silent about David's judgment. The sentence, *We granted each of them sound judgment and knowledge (pertaining to the mission and in accordance with the time and conditions of each)*, removes any misunderstanding concerning him. But it suggests that Solomon's judgment was more to the point.

A Prophetic Tradition recorded in *Ṣaḥīḥ al-Bukhārī* ("I'tiṣām," 21) establishes a judicial principle: "If a judge does his best to arrive at the right judgment, he gets two rewards when he gives a correct verdict and one reward when he errs." The verse supports this and makes it clear that both of the two judges, who give two different verdicts in the same case, get a reward, provided both sincerely do their best to judge rightly in a matter about which there is no clear, specific judgment in the Qur'ān and the Sunnah.

10. The verse points out that Almighty God gave David's glorifications such strength and such a resonant and pleasing tone that they brought ecstasy to the mountains. Like a huge sound system, each mountain formed a circle around the chief reciter – David – and repeated his glorifications. This is a reality, for every mountain with caves can "speak." If you declare before a mountain: "All praise be to God," the mountain will echo it back. Since God Almighty has granted this ability to mountains, it can be developed.

God endowed David with both Messengership and the Caliphate in an exceptional form. Thus, He made this seed of ability flourish as a miracle with that comprehensive Messengership and magnificent sovereignty, causing the great mountains to follow him like soldiers, students, or disciples. Under his direction and in his tongue, they glorified the All-Majestic Creator and repeated whatever he said.

At present, due to advancements in communication, a great commander can disperse a large army through the mountains to repeat his declaration "God is the Greatest" at the same time, and make the mountains speak and ring with the words. If an ordinary commander can do this, a magnificent commander of Almighty God can get them actually to utter and recite God's glorifications. Moreover, each mountain has a collective personality and corporate identity, and offers glorifications and worship particular to it. Just as each one through echoes glorifies in the tongue of humankind, it also glorifies the All-Majestic Creator in its own particular tongue (*The Words*, "the 20th Word," 271).

11. Solomon covered the distance it would normally take two months to walk in two strides by flying through the air (34: 12). This suggests that humanity can and should strive to travel through the air. Almighty God is saying here: "One of My servants did not obey his carnal desires, and I mounted him on the air. If you give up laziness and benefit properly from certain of My laws in nature, you too can mount it" (*The Words*, "the 20th Word," 267–268).

328   سُورَةُ الأنبِيَاء   ٣٢٨

وَمِنَ الشَّيَاطِينِ مَن يَغُوصُونَ لَهُ وَيَعْمَلُونَ عَمَلًا
دُونَ ذَٰلِكَ وَكُنَّا لَهُمْ حَافِظِينَ ۞ وَأَيُّوبَ إِذْ نَادَىٰ رَبَّهُ
أَنِّي مَسَّنِيَ الضُّرُّ وَأَنتَ أَرْحَمُ الرَّاحِمِينَ ۞ فَاسْتَجَبْنَا لَهُ
فَكَشَفْنَا مَا بِهِ مِن ضُرٍّ وَآتَيْنَاهُ أَهْلَهُ وَمِثْلَهُم
مَّعَهُمْ رَحْمَةً مِّنْ عِندِنَا وَذِكْرَىٰ لِلْعَابِدِينَ
۞ وَإِسْمَاعِيلَ وَإِدْرِيسَ وَذَا الْكِفْلِ كُلٌّ مِّنَ
الصَّابِرِينَ ۞ وَأَدْخَلْنَاهُمْ فِي رَحْمَتِنَا إِنَّهُم مِّنَ
الصَّالِحِينَ ۞ وَذَا النُّونِ إِذ ذَّهَبَ مُغَاضِبًا فَظَنَّ
أَن لَّن نَّقْدِرَ عَلَيْهِ فَنَادَىٰ فِي الظُّلُمَاتِ أَن لَّا
إِلَٰهَ إِلَّا أَنتَ سُبْحَانَكَ إِنِّي كُنتُ مِنَ الظَّالِمِينَ
۞ فَاسْتَجَبْنَا لَهُ وَنَجَّيْنَاهُ مِنَ الْغَمِّ وَكَذَٰلِكَ
نُنجِي الْمُؤْمِنِينَ ۞ وَزَكَرِيَّا إِذْ نَادَىٰ رَبَّهُ
رَبِّ لَا تَذَرْنِي فَرْدًا وَأَنتَ خَيْرُ الْوَارِثِينَ ۞ فَاسْتَجَبْنَا لَهُ
وَوَهَبْنَا لَهُ يَحْيَىٰ وَأَصْلَحْنَا لَهُ زَوْجَهُ إِنَّهُمْ كَانُوا يُسَارِعُونَ
فِي الْخَيْرَاتِ وَيَدْعُونَنَا رَغَبًا وَرَهَبًا وَكَانُوا لَنَا خَاشِعِينَ ۞

---

82. And of the jinn and satans (devils) were some who dived for him (to extract precious stones from the sea) and did other works besides,[12] and We were keeping watch over them (to prevent them from disobeying him).[13/14]

83. And (mention) Job (among those whom We made leaders): he called out to his Lord, saying: "Truly, affliction has visited me (so that I can no longer worship You as I must); and You are the Most Merciful of the merciful."

84. We answered his prayer and removed all the afflictions from which he suffered; and restored to him his household and the like thereof along with them as a mercy from Us and, as a reminder to those devoted to Our worship.[15/16]

85. (Mention also) Ishmael, Idrīs, and Dhu 'l-Kifl[17] (among the leaders). All were men of fortitude and patience.

86. We embraced them in Our Mercy. They were among the people of utmost righteousness.

87. And (also mention) Dhu 'n-Nūn (Jonah). He departed in anger (from his people, who persistently disbelieved and paid no attention to his warnings), and he was certain that We would never straiten (his life for) him. But eventually he called out in the veils of darkness (formed of the belly of the fish, the sea, and dark, rainy night): "There is no deity but You, All-Glorified are You (in that You are absolutely above having any defect). Surely I have been one of the wrongdoers (who have wronged themselves)."

88. We answered His call, too, and We saved him from distress. Thus do We save the believers.[18]

89. (Mention also) Zachariah. Once he called out to his Lord, saying: "My Lord! Do not let me leave the world without an heir, for You are the Best of the inheritors."

90. We answered his call, too, and bestowed upon him John, and cured his wife for him (so she was able) to bear a child. Truly, these (three) used to hasten to do good deeds as if competing with each other, and invoke Us in hopeful yearning and fearful anxiety. And they were utterly humble before Us.

12. They made for him sanctuaries and figures (of inanimate objects) and carvings, as well as basins like ponds and boilers built into the ground (34: 13).

13. The verse states that the Prophet Solomon, upon him be peace, made the jinn, devils, and evil spirits obey him. He prevented their evil and used them for beneficial work. This verse suggests that the jinn, conscious beings and earth's most important inhabitants after humankind, may serve us and can be contacted. Devils also may be made to serve, either willingly or unwillingly. God Almighty made them obey a servant who obeyed His commands. The verse also implies: "O humankind! I made jinn and devils, including their most evil ones, obey a servant who obeyed Me. If you submit yourself to My commands, most creatures, including the jinn and devils, may be subjugated to you."

These verses mark the highest point in the occult or supernatural sciences that deal with paranormal events, which appear as a blend of art and science. They urge us to subjugate and employ such beings through the Qur'ān so that we may be saved from their evil.

The Qur'ān, however, does not allude to modern necromancy, which some "civilized" people practice by trying to contact the spirits of the dead, for these, in reality, are evil spirits masquerading as the dead persons. Rather, it is the form known to certain saints, like Muhyi'd-dīn ibn al-'Arabī, who could communicate with good spirits at will, and make contact and form relations with them.

14. It is very difficult to find in the present Bible any sound concept or true knowledge of Divinity, Prophethood, afterlife, Divine Destiny in its relation with human free will, and spiritual existence. And in addition to some other Prophets, the Bible attributes some sinful acts to the Prophets David and Solomon (see *II Samuel*, 11, and *I Kings*, 11: 1–8).

David is a Prophet who was given a Divine Scripture (the Psalms) and who is praised in the Qur'ān for his sincere and profound devotion to God (38: 17–20). Even though he was a king, he lived a simple life, making his living through his own labor. He had such a great awareness of God that he cried a great deal and fasted every other day. Our Prophet recommended this type of fasting to some Companions who asked what the most rewarding type of supererogatory fasting was (al-Bukhārī, "Tahajjud," 7, "Ṣawm," 59; Muslim, "Ṣiyām," 182).

It is also absolutely inconceivable for the Prophet Solomon that he committed the grievous sins attributed to him.

If the Qur'ān had not been revealed, we would not be sure whether the previous Prophets really were sincere, devout, and thankful servants of God. The Qur'ān frees Jesus from his followers' mistaken deification of him and from his own people's denial of his Prophethood, explaining that God had no sons and daughters. It also clears the Israelite and non-Israelite Prophets of their supposed "sins" that are mentioned in the Bible. It presents Jesus as a spirit from God that was breathed into the Virgin Mary, Abraham as an intimate friend of God, Moses as one who spoke to God, David as a sincere servant of God, a Messenger and Caliph, and Solomon as a king and a Prophet who prayed to Him humbly. Despite being the greatest and most powerful king that ever lived, the Prophet Solomon, upon him be peace, remained a humble servant of God until his death.

15. Truthfulness, trustworthiness, the ability to communicate God's commands, intelligence, and sinlessness are essentials of Prophethood. These are the attributes possessed by every Prophet.

All Muslim theologians also agree that Prophets have no bodily or mental defects. Just as they were extraordinarily attractive in personality and conduct, they were also graceful and charming in outward appearance. They were perfect in bodily structure.

Prophets must be free from all bodily defects, for their appearance should not repel others. In explaining the Divine wisdom of God's Messenger living for 63 years, Said Nursi writes:

Believers are religiously obliged to love and respect God's Messenger to the utmost degree, and follow his every command without feeling any dislike for any aspect of him. For this reason, God did not allow him to live to the troublesome and often humiliating period of old age, and sent him to the "highest abode" when he was 63 years old. (*The Letters* 2, 84–85)

So, just as it is a baseless assertion that the Prophet Moses had a speech impediment, some allegations about Job's distress are also baseless. As can be deduced from the Qur'ānic verses, and as mentioned in the Bible (*Job*, 2: 7), he was afflicted with a skin disease, which caused painful sores from the soles of his feet to the top of his head. But the allegations that worms lived in his sores or abscesses, and that the resulting offensive odor caused people to leave him are completely groundless. If people really left him, this might have been due to his later poverty. In the beginning, a rich, thankful servant of God; later on, he lost his wealth and children or his family left him. As a Prophet, he could not have had a repulsive or disgusting appearance; his face, at least, must have been exempt from sores. Nor could his body have emitted an offensive smell. Contrary to the Biblical account that he cursed the day of his birth (*Job*, 3: 1) and God openly (*Job*, 7: 20-21), and justified himself rather than God (*Job*, 32: 2), the Prophet Job bore his afflictions for years without any objection. He prayed: *Affliction has visited me, and You are the Most Merciful of the merciful* (21: 83). God answered his prayer and removed his affliction, and restored to him his household (that he had lost) and the like thereof along with them.

16. While afflicted with numerous wounds for a long time, the Prophet Job, upon him be peace, feared that his duty of worship would suffer, and so he prayed, not for the sake of his own comfort, but for the sake of his worship of God: *Affliction has visited me, and You are the Most Merciful of the merciful* (21: 83). God Almighty accepted this sincere, disinterested, and devout supplication in the most miraculous fashion. He granted Job perfect good health and made manifest in him all kinds of compassion.

Job's supplication has some important lessons for us to take note of:

Corresponding to the physical wounds and sicknesses of Job, upon him be peace, we have spiritual sicknesses. If our inner being were to be turned outward, we would appear more wounded and diseased than Job. For each sin that we commit and each doubt that enters our mind inflicts wounds on our heart and our spirit.

The wounds of Job, upon him be peace, were of such a nature that they threatened his brief worldly life, but our inner wounds threaten our infinitely long, everlasting life. We need the supplication of Job thousands of times more than he did himself.

Sin, penetrating to the heart, darkens it until it extinguishes the light of faith. Each sin has a path leading to unbelief. Unless that sin is swiftly obliterated by seeking God's forgiveness, it grows from a worm into a snake that gnaws on the heart.

Secondly, life is refined, perfected, and strengthened by means of disasters and illnesses, and fulfils its own purpose. Life led monotonously on the couch of ease and comfort is almost identical with non-existence.

Thirdly, this worldly realm is the field of testing, the abode of service. It is not the place of pleasure and being rewarded for things done in it in God's cause. So sicknesses and misfortunes – as long as they do not affect faith and are patiently endured – conform fully to service and worship, and even strengthen it. Since such misfortunes make each hour's worship equivalent to that of a day, one should offer thanks instead of complaining.

Worship consists in fact of two kinds, positive and negative. What is meant by positive is obvious. As for negative worship, this is when one afflicted with misfortune or sickness perceives their own weakness and helplessness, and turning to their Compassionate Lord, seeks refuge in Him, meditating upon Him, petitioning Him, and thus offering a pure form of worship that no hypocrisy can penetrate. If he or she endures patiently, thinks of the reward attendant on misfortune and offers thanks, then each hour that passes will count as a whole day spent in worship. Their brief life becomes much longer. There are even cases where a single minute is counted as being equal to a whole day's worship.

The power of patience given to a person by God Almighty is adequate for every misfortune, unless it has been squandered on baseless fears. But through the predominance of delusion, one's neglect and imagining that this transient life is eternal, a person squanders their power of patience on the past and the future. When their patience that has been squandered is not equal to the misfortunes of the present, then they begin to complain. It is as if – God forbid! – they were complaining about God Almighty to people.

In short, just as gratitude increases Divine bounty, so too does complaint increase misfortune, removing all occasion for compassion.

Fourthly, the truly harmful misfortune is that which affects the Religion. One should at all times seek refuge at the Divine Court from misfortune in matters of the Religion and cry out for help. But misfortunes that do not affect the Religion are not in reality misfortunes. Some of them are warnings from the All-Merciful One. If a shepherd throws a stone at his sheep when they trespass on another's pasture, they understand that the stone was intended as a warning to save them from a perilous action; full of gratitude they turn back. So too, there are many apparent misfortunes that are Divine warnings and admonishments, some others that cause sins to be forgiven, and still others that awaken people from the sleep of neglect, reminding them of their human helplessness and weakness, thus affording them a form of peace. Illness that is deemed as a variety of misfortune is indeed not a misfortune, as has already been said, but rather a favor from God and a means of purification.

The Prophet Job, upon him be peace, did not pray for the comfort of his soul, but rather sought cures for the purpose of worship, because disease was preventing his remembrances of God with his tongue and his meditation upon God in his heart. We too should make our primary intent, when making that supplication, the healing of the inward and spiritual wounds that arise from sinning.

As far as physical diseases are concerned, we may seek refuge from them when they hinder our worship. But we should seek refuge in a humble and supplicating fashion, not protesting and being plaintive. If we accept God as our Lord, then we must resign ourselves to all that He gives us as a manifestation of His Lordship. To sigh and complain in a manner that suggests we object to the Divine Destiny and Decree is a form of criticizing Divine Destiny, an accusation leveled against God's compassion. One who finds fault with God's mercy will inevitably be deprived of it. A person who when afflicted with misfortune responds to it with protest and complaint, only compounds their misfortune. (Summarized from *Lem'alar* ["The Gleams"], 8–11.)

17. It is not possible to say anything definite about the identity of the Prophet *Dhu 'l-Kifl*, upon him be peace. Abu'l-'Alā al-Mawdūdī points out that *Dhu 'l-Kifl* is not a name, but a title like the title *Dhu 'n-Nūn* that was used for the Prophet Jonah, meaning "the Companion of the Fish." According to him, *Dhu 'l-Kifl* means a man of great portion and was used for him because of his exalted personality and lofty degree in the Hereafter. Like al-Mawdūdī, Professor Suad Yıldırım in Turkey is of the opinion that he might be the Prophet Ezekiel, who was among the Children of Israel driven out of Jerusalem to Babylon. He lived and performed his mission of calling people to God in the land of the Chaldeans by the river Chebar, roughly between 594–572 BC.

18. The supplication of the Prophet Yūnus (Jonah), son of Mattā, upon our Prophet and him be peace, is the most powerful supplication, a most effective means for the acceptance of prayer by God. The gist of the story of Jonah, upon him be peace, is as follows:

He was cast into the sea and swallowed by a large fish. The sea was stormy, the night turbulent and dark, and his hope was exhausted. But it was while he was in such a situation that his supplication became a swift means of salvation. The secret of the power of his supplication was this:

In that situation all causes were suspended, for Jonah could only be saved by one whose command would subdue the fish and the sea, and the night and the sky. The night, the sea, and the fish were united against him. Only one whose command might subdue all three of these could bring him to the shore of salvation. Even if the entirety of creation had become his servants and helpers, it would have been of no avail. For causes have no real, creative effect. Since Jonah saw with the eye of certainty that there was no refuge other than in the Creator of causes, and clearly perceived God's special mercy for every being in the light of his faith in the Divine Oneness, his supplication was suddenly able to subdue the night, the sea, and the fish. Through his substantial faith in God's Oneness and absolute Sovereignty throughout the universe, the belly of the fish became a submarine for him, and the surging sea, which in its awesomeness resembled an erupting volcano, became a serene plain, the site of a pleasant excursion. Again, through the light of his faith, the sky's surface was cleared of all clouds and the moon appeared over his head, like a lamp. In the end he reached the shore of salvation, and observed God's favor clearly.

Now we are in a situation one hundred times more awesome than that in which Jonah, upon him be peace, first found himself. Our night is the future. When we look upon our future with the eye of neglect, it is a hundred times darker and more fearful than his night. Our sea is this earth revolving in space. Each wave of this sea bears on it thousands of corpses, and is thus a thousand times more frightening than his sea. Our fish is the malicious desires of our carnal soul, which strives to destroy the foundation of our eternal life. This fish is a thousand times more harmful than his. For his fish could destroy a hundred-year lifespan, whereas ours seeks to destroy an eternal life. This being our true state, we should, in imitation of Jonah, upon him be peace, take refuge directly in the Creator of causes, Who is our Lord, and should say:

There is no god but You, All-Glorified are You! Surely I have been one of the wrongdoers, and understand with full certainty that it is only He who can repel from us the harm of the future, this world, and the temptations of our carnal souls, united against us because of our neglect and misguidance. For the future is subject to His command, the world to His authority, and our soul to His direction. (Summarized from *Lem'alar* ["The Gleams"], 5–7)

19. The conclusion of the verse is not contrary to the first part of Zachariah's supplication, rather it confirms it. God Almighty usually acts from behind the veil of causality in this world, which is the realm of wisdom and testing. So the meaning is: "I fully believe that You are the Best of the inheritors, so I expect You to favor me with a righteous heir," and it is similar to Job's asking for God's mercy by concluding his supplication: "You are the Most Merciful of the merciful."

وَالَّتِي أَحْصَنَتْ فَرْجَهَا فَنَفَخْنَا فِيهَا مِن رُّوحِنَا وَجَعَلْنَاهَا
وَابْنَهَا ءَايَةً لِّلْعَالَمِينَ ۝ إِنَّ هَٰذِهِ أُمَّتُكُمْ أُمَّةً
وَاحِدَةً وَأَنَا۠ رَبُّكُمْ فَاعْبُدُونِ ۝ وَتَقَطَّعُوٓا أَمْرَهُم
بَيْنَهُمْ كُلٌّ إِلَيْنَا رَاجِعُونَ ۝ فَمَن يَعْمَلْ مِنَ
الصَّالِحَاتِ وَهُوَ مُؤْمِنٌ فَلَا كُفْرَانَ لِسَعْيِهِ وَإِنَّا لَهُۥ
كَاتِبُونَ ۝ وَحَرَامٌ عَلَىٰ قَرْيَةٍ أَهْلَكْنَاهَآ
أَنَّهُمْ لَا يَرْجِعُونَ ۝ حَتَّىٰٓ إِذَا فُتِحَتْ يَأْجُوجُ
وَمَأْجُوجُ وَهُم مِّن كُلِّ حَدَبٍ يَنسِلُونَ ۝
وَاقْتَرَبَ الْوَعْدُ الْحَقُّ فَإِذَا هِيَ شَاخِصَةٌ أَبْصَارُ
الَّذِينَ كَفَرُوا۟ يَٰوَيْلَنَا قَدْ كُنَّا فِي غَفْلَةٍ مِّنْ
هَٰذَا بَلْ كُنَّا ظَالِمِينَ ۝ إِنَّكُمْ وَمَا تَعْبُدُونَ
مِن دُونِ اللَّهِ حَصَبُ جَهَنَّمَ أَنتُمْ لَهَا وَارِدُونَ ۝ لَوْ
كَانَ هَٰٓؤُلَآءِ ءَالِهَةً مَّا وَرَدُوهَا وَكُلٌّ فِيهَا خَالِدُونَ ۝
لَهُمْ فِيهَا زَفِيرٌ وَهُمْ فِيهَا لَا يَسْمَعُونَ ۝ إِنَّ الَّذِينَ
سَبَقَتْ لَهُم مِّنَّا الْحُسْنَىٰٓ أُوْلَٰٓئِكَ عَنْهَا مُبْعَدُونَ ۝

---

91. And (mention) that blessed woman who set the best example in guarding her chastity.[20] We breathed into her out of Our Spirit,[21] and We made her and her son a miraculous sign (of Our Power and matchless way of doing things) for all the worlds.

92. So, this community of yours (which all the Messengers and their followers have formed) is one single community of the same faith, and I am your Lord (Who creates, sustains, and protects you);[22] so worship Me alone.

93. But people have broken up and differed among themselves as regards the Religion. But they are all bound to return to Us (to account for all that they did).

94. Whoever does any deed of good and righteousness, being a true believer, his endeavor will not be left unrewarded in ingratitude. We are keeping the record of every good deed of his in his favor (without the least being neglected).

95. It is inconceivable that a community, the destruction of which We have decreed (because of their unbelief and irremediable sins), could return to faith, (nor a community which We destroyed should not come back to Us and then be returned to the world again so that they could believe and do good deeds).[23]

96. Eventually, a day will come when Gog and Magog will be let loose, and they will rush down from every mound.

97. And the true promise of the Last Hour has been close at hand, and look, the eyes of those who obstinately disbelieve stare in horror fixedly, exclaiming: "Woe to us! Indeed we have lived in heedlessness and forgetfulness of this. Ah! We truly have been wrongdoers (who have, most of all, wronged our own selves)!"

98. "You and all the things you deify and worship apart from God are but firewood for Hell. You are bound to arrive in it."

99. If those (false objects of their worship) had truly been deities, they would not arrive in it. Every one of them will abide therein.

100. Moaning will be their lot in it, and (nothing to their benefit) will they be able to hear therein (as a recompense for their willful deafness to the Divine Revelation in the world).

101. But surely those for whom the decree of ultimate good has already gone forth from Us, they will be kept away from it (Hell).

20. Why the Qur'ān mentions Mary along with the Prophets, even though she was not a Prophet, is because of Mary's exceptional greatness and honor, and for the purpose of introducing Jesus in his real (human) identity.

21. For God's breathing out of His Spirit into Mary to conceive of Jesus, and into the "body" of Adam, which He shaped out of clay, so that he might come to the world, and the meaning of His breathing out of His Spirit, see 4: 171, note 34; 15: 29, note 8.

22. Having discussed many Prophets with the suffering each had to bear and of which they were then relieved by God, and by discussing the distinguished aspect of the character and mission of each, the Qur'ān declares that the Prophet Muḥammad, upon him be peace and blessings, did not bring a different religion, and thus all the Prophets and their followers, from the first day of human history on the earth to the Last Day, constitute a single community with God being their Lord, Who alone must be worshipped. The basic foundation of this faith and the basic point of unity among the believers, which is the main dynamic against disunities among them, is believing in God as the only Deity, Lord and Sovereign of the whole creation, including, of course, humanity, and worshipping Him alone.

23. The verse has all of the three meanings given. While verse 94 mentions a believing servant, this verse talks about a community. This suggests that corruption is like a contagious disease and individuals usually go astray in imitation of others in a community. Total destruction comes as a result of the corruption that encompasses almost the whole or at least the majority of a community. This shows the importance of social reform or improvement.

24. For Gog and Magog and their invasion of the civilized world just before the end of time, see 18: 98–99, note 30–31.

102. They will not even hear the slightest sound of it, and they will abide in that which their souls desire, (enjoying it to the full).

103. Even the greatest shock (of the second blowing of the Trumpet) will not cause them any worry, and the angels welcome them, with the greeting: "This is your day, the day which you were promised."

104. The Day when We will roll up the heaven as written scrolls are rolled up. We will bring the creation back into existence as easily as We originated it in the first instance.[25] This is a binding promise on Us, and surely We fulfill whatever We promise.

105. We (recorded in the Supreme Ever-Preserved Tablet and then) wrote down in the Psalms after the Torah that My righteous servants will inherit the earth.[26]

106. Surely in this (Qur'ān) there is the explanation (of every truth necessary) for God's servants devoted to worshipping Him.

107. We have not sent you (O Muhammad) but as an unequalled mercy for all the worlds.[27]

108. Say: "It is revealed to me that your God is the One and Only God. Will you, then, become Muslims (those wholly submitted to Him)?"

109. If they still turn away, say: "I have conveyed to you all that I must convey, and warned you all alike. But I do not know if that with which you are threatened (whether it be the destruction or the Last Judgment,) is near or far.

110. "Truly, He knows all that is spoken openly, just as He knows all that you keep concealed (including your secret intentions).

111. "I do not know but the respite given to you may be a trial for you (– a respite so that you may fully display your deserving His punishment), and enjoyment for a while."

112. (The Messenger) said (in conclusion): "My Lord, judge (between me and those unbelievers) with truth (and allow the truth to be fully manifested). Our Lord is the All-Merciful, the One Whose help is ever sought against all that you falsely attribute (to Him and me)."

25. God revives this vast earth when it is dead and dry, thereby displaying His Power via quickening countless species of creation, each as extraordinary as humankind. He shows His all-embracing Knowledge in these creatures' infinite variations within the complex inter-mingling of all their distinct forms. God turns His servants' attention toward the eternal happiness, assuring them of Resurrection in His heavenly decrees, and makes visible the splendor of His being their Lord and Nurturer. He causes all His creatures to collaborate with each other, turning within the orbit of His Command and Will, causing them to help each other in submission to Him.

He shows our value by creating us as the Tree of Creation's most comprehensive, sub-tle, worthy, and valued fruit; by addressing us directly; and by subjugating all things to us. Could One so Compassionate and Powerful, Wise and All-Knowing not bring about the Resurrection, assemble His creatures, and restore us to life? Could He not institute His Supreme Court or create the Heaven and Hell? Such ideas are inconceivable.

Indeed, the Almighty Disposer of the affairs of this world continually creates on its finite, transient surface numerous signs, examples, and indications of the Supreme Gathering and the Place where this will take place. Each spring we see countless animal and plant species assembled in a few days and then scattered. All tree and plant roots, as well as certain animals, are revived and restored exactly as they were. Other animals are re-created in nearly identical forms. Seeds that appear so alike quickly grow into distinct and differentiated entities, after being brought to full vigor with extraordinary rapidity and ease in absolute orderliness and harmony. How could anything be difficult for the One Who does this? How could He Who has created the heavens and the earth in "six days" be unable to resurrect humankind with a single blast?

Suppose a gifted writer could write count-less books on a vast sheet of paper in just an hour, without error or omission, fully and in the best style. If someone then told you that he could rewrite his own book from memory, even if it had fallen into the water and had become lost, how could anyone say that he could not do so? Or think of a sovereign who, to show his power or warn his subjects, removes mountains at a command, turns his country around, and transforms the sea into dry land. Then imagine that a great boulder blocks the path of guests traveling to his reception. If someone says that the sovereign will remove the boulder at a com-mand, would you say that he could not do so? Or imagine someone assembles a great army, and you are told that he will recall it to parade in battalions by a trumpet blast after dismissing them to rest? If the battalions formed in disci-plined rows, would you respond with unbelief? If you did, your error would be enormous (*The Words*, "the 10th Word," 96).

26. For the Supreme Ever-Preserved Tablet, see *sūrah* 6: 59, note 13; *sūrah* 13: 39, note 13; *sūrah* 17, note 10.

This verse will be more understandable when it is considered along with 24: 55: *God has promised those of you who believe and do good, righteous deeds that He will most certainly empower them as vicegerents on the earth (in the place of those who are in power at present), even as He empowered those (of the same qualities) that preceded them, and that, assuredly, He will firmly establish for them their religion, which He has (chosen and) approved of for them, and He will replace their present state of fear with security (so that they can practice their religion freely and fully and in peace). They worship Me alone, associating none with Me as partners (in belief, worship, and the authority to order their life).* The righteous servants promised to finally inherit the world will be those who combine righteousness with devotion to worshipping God exclusively, as will be mentioned in the verse to come.

27. This verse expounds the mission of our Prophet in all clarity. This mission has two cardinal aspects, one for the creation and life of the whole universe, and the other for the people from his time until the Last Hour.

With respect to the former aspect of his

mission, the Prophet Muḥammad, upon him be peace and blessings, is both the seed of the Tree of Creation and its most illustrious and perfect fruit, one about whom God declares, "But for you, I would not have created the worlds" (al-'Ajlūnī, 2: 232), and the mirror or means for God's manifestation of His being the All-Merciful or His favors of Mercy to reach the whole creation. In Sufi terminology, he is the first and foremost or greatest Universal Man. With respect to the second, religious aspect of his mission, he is the means for the individuals and communities following him to attain eternal happiness, and the owner of the most comprehensive rank of intercession in the Hereafter. In other words, he is the mirror or means for God's particular favors of His being the All-Compassionate to reach each creature. There is no other way than his to lead to eternal salvation.

SŪRAH 22

AL-ḤAJJ
(THE PILGRIMAGE)

Madīnah period

I t is commonly accepted that this *sūrah* began to be revealed in Makkah and was completed in Madīnah. It has 78 verses.

The *sūrah* criticizes the Makkan polytheists for their blind, willful insistence on associating partners with God and demonstrates the contradictions in their creeds. It warns new believers, who might waver and be unwilling to persevere through some of the hardships that accepting a new faith naturally entails. Also, the *sūrah* allows the believers to set up armed resistance to the continuing harassment of the Makkans and their threats to the security of the Muslims in Madīnah.

In the Name of God, the All-Merciful, the All-Compassionate.

1. O humankind! Keep from disobedience to your Lord in reverence for Him and piety and get under His protection. (Never forget that) the violent convulsion of the Last Hour is an awesome thing.

2. On the Day when you all see it, every suckling mother will utterly forsake her infant in dread, and every pregnant female will cast off her burden. You will see all people as if gone out of their senses, while, in fact, they are in their senses. This is because God's punishment is extremely severe.

3. Among people there are such as dispute about God without any true knowledge and follow every corrupt, rebellious, and mischievous satan.

4. It is decreed about him (Satan) that whoever takes him for a guardian, surely he leads him astray, and guides him to the punishment of the Blaze.

5. O humankind! If you are in doubt about the Resurrection, (consider that) We created you from earth (in the beginning while there was nothing of your existence as humankind), and the material origin of every one of you is earth. Then (We have created you) from a drop of (seminal) fluid, then from a clot clinging (to the womb wall), then from a (chew of) lump in part shaped and in part not shaped, and differentiated and undifferentiated, and so do We clarify for you (the reality of the Resurrection).[1] And We cause what We will (to come into the world) to rest in the wombs for an appointed term, then We bring you out as (dependent) infants, then (We provide what is necessary and appropriate) so that you may attain your age of full strength. Among you some are caused to die (during this period of

growth and afterwards), and some are kept back to the most miserable state of old age, ceasing to know anything after once having known some things. (As another proof for the Resurrection and a sign to comprehend it,) you see earth dry and lifeless, and suddenly, when We send down the (known, blessed) water on it, it stirs and swells and grows every pleasant pair of vegetation.

---

1. For the full stages of the development of the human embryo which the Qur'ān taught us fourteen centuries ago, and which the modern science of embryology has recently discovered, also see 23: 12–14.

As in several other verses (i.e., 21: 104, and see the corresponding note 25), the Qur'ān brings the first creation to our attention as an analogy for the Resurrection. It also mentions, as a sign and proof of it, the creation of a human being, starting with the elements in earth, air, and water and continuing with the developmental stages in the mother's womb. It must certainly be much easier for reason to accept that a being who once was not a thing completely unknown in existence, and then was created in stages from materials that bear no resemblance to it, will, by the same Creative Power, be raised to life again after death.

6. And so, God is He Who is the Ultimate Truth and Ever-Constant, and He gives life to the dead, and He has full power over everything.

7. And the Last Hour is sure to come – there is no doubt about it. And God will surely raise up all who are in the graves.

8. And yet, among people there are some who dispute about God without having any true knowledge or any true guidance[2] or an enlightening (Divine) Book.

9. They keep on disputing arrogantly to lead people astray from God's way.[3] For such there is disgrace in the world, and on the Day of Resurrection We will cause them to taste the punishment of the scorching Fire.

10. "This punishment is the outcome of what you have (committed and) forwarded with your own hands, and never does God do the least wrong to His servants."

11. Among people there are also many a one who worships God on the borderline (of faith) in expectation of only worldly gains. If any good befalls him, he is satisfied with it, but if a trial afflicts him, he turns away utterly, reverting back to unbelief. He (thereby) incurs loss of both this world and the Hereafter. This indeed is the obvious loss.

12. He invokes, apart from God, that which can neither harm nor benefit him. That indeed is straying very far away.

13. He even invokes the being that is far more likely to cause harm than benefit: what evil a patron, and what evil an associate!

14. Surely God will admit those who be-

lieve and do good, righteous deeds into the Gardens through which rivers flow. Surely God does whatever He wills.

15. Whoever thinks that God will not help the Messenger to victory in the world and to prosperity in the Hereafter, then let him move heaven and earth to prevent His help: let him stretch out a rope to heaven (to prevent God's help and Revelation from reaching him), and then sever that rope to descend without being broken into pieces. Then let him see whether the schemes he makes will be of any avail to him, and (whether he can) do away with what enrages him.

2. The verse cites three sources that one should base oneself on to have correct knowledge of God. These are: (i) knowledge obtained through the study of and reflection on the creation in the light of the Revelation and through the disciplines of the spiritual way; and (ii) true guidance, by which it is referred to the Divine Revelation or inspiration, or the guidance of any of those mentioned in 4: 69; and (iii) the Divine Book, which illuminates minds and hearts.

3. Zamakhsharī, the author of al-Kashshāf, writes that those who are mentioned in verses 8 and 9 as disputing about God are the corrupt, rebellious, and mischievous devils mentioned in verse 3, and the disputers in verse 3 are those who follow them.

٣٣٣　　　الجزء السابع عشر　　　333

وَكَذَٰلِكَ أَنزَلْنَٰهُ ءَايَٰتٍۭ بَيِّنَٰتٍ وَأَنَّ ٱللَّهَ يَهْدِى مَن يُرِيدُ ۝
إِنَّ ٱلَّذِينَ ءَامَنُوا۟ وَٱلَّذِينَ هَادُوا۟ وَٱلصَّٰبِـِٔينَ وَٱلنَّصَٰرَىٰ
وَٱلْمَجُوسَ وَٱلَّذِينَ أَشْرَكُوٓا۟ إِنَّ ٱللَّهَ يَفْصِلُ بَيْنَهُمْ يَوْمَ ٱلْقِيَٰمَةِ ۚ
إِنَّ ٱللَّهَ عَلَىٰ كُلِّ شَىْءٍ شَهِيدٌ ۝ أَلَمْ تَرَ أَنَّ ٱللَّهَ يَسْجُدُ لَهُۥ مَن فِى
ٱلسَّمَٰوَٰتِ وَمَن فِى ٱلْأَرْضِ وَٱلشَّمْسُ وَٱلْقَمَرُ وَٱلنُّجُومُ
وَٱلْجِبَالُ وَٱلشَّجَرُ وَٱلدَّوَآبُّ وَكَثِيرٌ مِّنَ ٱلنَّاسِ ۖ
وَكَثِيرٌ حَقَّ عَلَيْهِ ٱلْعَذَابُ ۗ وَمَن يُهِنِ ٱللَّهُ فَمَا لَهُۥ مِن مُّكْرِمٍ ۚ
إِنَّ ٱللَّهَ يَفْعَلُ مَا يَشَآءُ ۩ ۝ هَٰذَانِ خَصْمَانِ ٱخْتَصَمُوا۟
فِى رَبِّهِمْ ۖ فَٱلَّذِينَ كَفَرُوا۟ قُطِّعَتْ لَهُمْ ثِيَابٌ مِّن نَّارٍ يُصَبُّ
مِن فَوْقِ رُءُوسِهِمُ ٱلْحَمِيمُ ۝ يُصْهَرُ بِهِۦ مَا فِى بُطُونِهِمْ
وَٱلْجُلُودُ ۝ وَلَهُم مَّقَٰمِعُ مِنْ حَدِيدٍ ۝ كُلَّمَآ أَرَادُوٓا۟ أَن
يَخْرُجُوا۟ مِنْهَا مِنْ غَمٍّ أُعِيدُوا۟ فِيهَا وَذُوقُوا۟ عَذَابَ ٱلْحَرِيقِ ۝
إِنَّ ٱللَّهَ يُدْخِلُ ٱلَّذِينَ ءَامَنُوا۟ وَعَمِلُوا۟ ٱلصَّٰلِحَٰتِ جَنَّٰتٍ
تَجْرِى مِن تَحْتِهَا ٱلْأَنْهَٰرُ يُحَلَّوْنَ فِيهَا مِنْ أَسَاوِرَ
مِن ذَهَبٍ وَلُؤْلُؤًا ۖ وَلِبَاسُهُمْ فِيهَا حَرِيرٌ ۝

---

many among human beings?[5] Whereas many others are deservedly condemned to punishment. Whoever God humiliates can have none to give him honor. Assuredly, God does whatever He wills.[6]

19. These are two opposing groups (– those who prostrate to God and those who do not. Though there may be differences of approach within either group), they contend about (the truth concerning) their Lord. As for those who disbelieve (by categorically denying Him or associating partners with Him in His Attributes or authority as the Lord), garments of fire are certain to be cut out for them, with boiling water being poured down over their heads,

20. With which all that is within their bodies, as well as their skins, is melted away.

21. For them are also goads and maces of iron.

22. Whenever in their anguish they attempt to come out of the Fire, they will be returned into it (and told): "Taste the punishment of the scorching Fire!"

23. (On the other hand,) God will admit those who believe and do good, righteous deeds into the Gardens through which rivers flow; adorned therein with armbands of gold and pearls, and their garments therein will be of silk.[7]

16. It is in the face of such rage and malice that We send down the Qur'ān in messages clear in meaning and content and as manifest signs of the truth; and God guides whomever He wills.

17. Those who truly believe (in God and follow Muḥammad), and those who have become Jews, and the Sabaeans, and the Christians, and the Magians, and those who associate partners with God (without having any relation with a Divinely-inspired religion)[4] – God will certainly judge between them on the Day of Resurrection. God is witness over everything.

18. Do you ever consider that all who are in the heavens and all who are on the earth prostrate themselves to God, and so do the sun, the moon, the stars, the mountains, the trees, and the beasts, and so do

4. This verse mentions three cardinal groups of faith. The first group are the true believers who follow the Prophet Muḥammad, upon him be peace and blessings. They are also the true heirs to all the previous Prophets.

The second group is comprised of four sub-groups. They are:

Those who are Jews, i.e., those who have reduced their God-revealed Religion into a national or tribal religion and God into a god that belongs exclusively to a single race. They have also denied eternal life and reduced eternal happiness to worldly happiness in the so-called "promised land." Moreover, they have altered the Divine Law.

The Sabaeans were either those who claimed to follow the Prophet John or those who worshipped celestial bodies and claimed to follow the religion of the Prophets Seth and Enoch. Both groups lived in northern Iraq.

The Christians mentioned here are those who, although they followed the Prophet Jesus, upon him be peace, sullied the faith of Jesus by attributing a son to God or by claiming that Jesus was God incarnate and attributed divinity to the Virgin Mary and the Spirit who functioned as a means for God's gift of a son reaching Mary. They also imported some other pagan doctrines into their religion.

The Magians refer to the fire-worshippers in Persia. They believed in the two gods of light or good and dark or evil. They claimed to be the followers of Zoroaster.

The Qur'ān regards those who are Jews and Christians as the People of the Book. God's Messenger and the Companions, based on this verse, also treated the Sabaeans and Magians as People of the Book.

The third group consists of the polytheists who do not follow any Divine Book or Prophet and, though many among them believe in God in some way as the Creator of the universe, they have adopted and worshipped many deities, usually represented by idols or statues.

5. The reason why many among human beings are specifically mentioned, even though they are included in all those who are on the earth, is that all human beings prostrate to God in the sense that they cannot escape God's laws of "nature" or creation and the operation of the universe in many respects, such as their coming into and leaving the world, the operation of their bodies, the appointment of their families and races, and their physique, etc. However, many among human beings prostrate before God of their free volition – they believe in Him and worship and live according to His commandments.

6. God is absolutely free in His will and acts. However, in His judgments about human beings, He considers their choices, acts, and intentions. As we have regularly pointed in these notes, as far as God's absolute Will and its relation to human will and the judgments about human beings are concerned, the verses, *The earth belongs indeed to God, and He makes it an inheritance for whom He wills of His servants* (7: 128); and *My righteous servants will inherit the earth* (21: 105), constitute a good example. We understand that God's will takes the choice and free acts of human beings into consideration when He decrees about them.

7. For a similar verse and its explanation, see 18: 31, note 17.

334

سُوْرَةُ الْحَجّ   ٣٣٤

وَهُدُوٓا إِلَى الطَّيِّبِ مِنَ الْقَوْلِ وَهُدُوٓا إِلَى صِرَاطِ الْحَمِيدِ
۞ إِنَّ الَّذِينَ كَفَرُوا وَيَصُدُّونَ عَن سَبِيلِ اللهِ وَالْمَسْجِدِ
الْحَرَامِ الَّذِى جَعَلْنَاهُ لِلنَّاسِ سَوَآءً الْعَاكِفُ فِيهِ
وَالْبَادِ وَمَن يُرِدْ فِيهِ بِإِلْحَادٍ بِظُلْمٍ نُّذِقْهُ مِنْ عَذَابٍ
اَلِيمٍ ۞ وَإِذْ بَوَّأْنَا لِإِبْرَٰهِيمَ مَكَانَ الْبَيْتِ أَن لَّا تُشْرِكْ
بِى شَيْئًا وَطَهِّرْ بَيْتِىَ لِلطَّآئِفِينَ وَالْقَآئِمِينَ وَالرُّكَّعِ
السُّجُودِ ۞ وَأَذِّن فِى النَّاسِ بِالْحَجِّ يَأْتُوكَ رِجَالاً
وَعَلَىٰ كُلِّ ضَامِرٍ يَأْتِينَ مِن كُلِّ فَجٍّ عَمِيقٍ ۞
لِّيَشْهَدُوا مَنَافِعَ لَهُمْ وَيَذْكُرُوا اسْمَ اللهِ فِىٓ أَيَّامٍ
مَّعْلُومَاتٍ عَلَىٰ مَا رَزَقَهُم مِّنۢ بَهِيمَةِ الْأَنْعَامِ فَكُلُوا
مِنْهَا وَأَطْعِمُوا الْبَآئِسَ الْفَقِيرَ ۞ ثُمَّ لْيَقْضُوا
تَفَثَهُمْ وَلْيُوفُوا نُذُورَهُمْ وَلْيَطَّوَّفُوا بِالْبَيْتِ
الْعَتِيقِ ۞ ذَٰلِكَ وَمَن يُعَظِّمْ حُرُمَاتِ اللهِ فَهُوَ خَيْرٌ
لَّهُ عِندَ رَبِّهِ وَأُحِلَّتْ لَكُمُ الْأَنْعَامُ إِلَّا مَا يُتْلَىٰ عَلَيْكُمْ
فَاجْتَنِبُوا الرِّجْسَ مِنَ الْأَوْثَانِ وَاجْتَنِبُوا قَوْلَ الزُّورِ ۞

---

material and spiritual filth) for those who will go round it in devotion, and those who will stand in prayer before it, and those who will bow down and prostrate themselves in worship."

27. Publicly proclaim the (duty of) Pilgrimage for all humankind, that they come to you on foot and on lean camels, coming from every far-away point,

28. So that they may witness all (the spiritual, social, and economic) benefits in store for them, and offer during the known, appointed days the sacrificial cattle that He has provided for them by pronouncing God's Name over them. Eat of their meat and feed the distressed, the poor.

29. Thereafter let them tidy themselves up (by having their hair cut, removing their *iḥrām* (Hajj attire), taking a bath, and clipping their nails, etc.), and fulfill the vows (if they have made any, and complete other acts of the Pilgrimage), and go round the Most Ancient, Honorable House in devotion.[9]

30. All that (is what God ordained concerning the *Hajj*). So whoever venerates God's sanctities will find it to be the best for him in his Lord's sight. Cattle have been made lawful for you (for sacrifice and food) except what has already been mentioned to you (as unlawful). So, shun the loathsome evil of idol-worship and shun all words of falsehood (never say or consider or legislate anything contrary to revealed commandments concerning the lawful and the unlawful),[10]

24. They have been guided to (believe in and declare) the purest of words,[8] and they have been guided to the path of the All-Praiseworthy One, (saying and doing only what is praiseworthy).

25. Those who disbelieve and bar (others) from God's way and (the believers from visiting) the Sacred Mosque, which We have set up as a place of worship for all (believing) people alike, both for those who dwell therein (in Makkah) and for those who come from abroad – whoever seeks a deviation from the right course therein by deliberate wrongdoing, We cause him to taste a painful punishment.

26. Remember when We assigned to Abraham the site of the House (Ka'bah) as a place of worship, (directing him): "Do not associate any partners with Me in any way, and keep My House pure (from any

8. What is meant in this verse is that such people believe in and declare, *There is no deity but God*, and they only speak pure speech or say pure words, such as a declaration of faith, mentioning God, giving advice for God's sake, reciting the Qur'ān, etc. They refrain from any idle, useless, or unbefitting talk.

9. The last two verses mention certain prescribed acts of the *Ḥajj*, some of which have already been mentioned in 2: 196–203.

On arriving at the *mīqāt* (any of the stations designated for entering the state of *ihrām*), pilgrims should shave themselves, clip their fingernails, perform *ghusl* or *wuḍū'*, and put on some perfume. Men don their special *Ḥajj* attire, which is also called *ihrām*, as it is a symbol of entering the state of *ihrām*. There is no special attire for women. Pilgrim candidates should offer a prayer of two-*rak'ah* and declare their intention to do *Ḥajj* or *Umrah*, or *Ḥajj* and *Umrah* together. Wearing *ihrām* and declaring one's intention to do *Ḥajj* or *Umrah* are essential elements of the Pilgrimage rites, and the rites are invalid without these two elements.

While in the state of *ihrām*, pilgrims must avoid sexual intercourse and whatever leads to it, wrangling and useless bickering, marriage ceremonies or attending marriage ceremonies, for men wearing any clothes that have been stitched or shoes that cover the feet above the ankles, covering their heads and (for both men and women) faces (women), wearing perfume, cutting their hair or nails, hunting on land, killing any animals, and cutting trees or grass within the sacred precincts of Makkah.

Before sunrise on the first day of *Īd al-Adḥā* (the Festival of Sacrifice), pilgrims who have already performed the duties of *wakfah* (staying for some time) in 'Arafāt on the afternoon of the ninth day of *Dhu 1-Hijjah* (Eve of the Day of the Festival) and in al-Muzdalifah on the following night should return to Mina after collecting pebbles at al-Muzdalifah. After sunrise, they must throw seven pebbles at *Jamrat al-'Aqabah*. Then they offer their sacrifice, have their hair cut, remove their *ihrām*, and return to their everyday life – with the exception of having sexual intercourse with their spouse.

They then go to the *Ka bah* to perform the obligatory *Ṭawāf* of Visiting, an essential part of the *Ḥajj*. Performing this *ṭawāf* on the first day of *Īd al-Adḥā* is recommended, but one can perform it during the following two days. After this *ṭawāf*, if both of the pilgrims (husband and wife) have already had their hair cut and have removed their *ihrām*, then sexual intercourse becomes permissible. If the pilgrims are doing *Ḥajj Tamattu'* (combining the *Ḥajj* and *Umrah* with a break in between), they must perform a *sa y* after this *ṭawāf*. Those who are doing the *Ḥajj Qiran* (combining the *Umrah* and *Ḥajj* in one state of *ihrām*) or *Ifrād* (the *Ḥajj* only) do not have to make this second *sa y* if they did the *ṭawāf* and *sa y* upon arrival in Makkah.

The pilgrims must now return to Mina and spend the three days of *Īd al-Adḥā* there. After midday on the second and third day (*Dhu 1-Hijjah* 11 and 12), they throw seven pebbles at each of three *Jamrah*s, beginning with *Jamrat al-Ūlā* and then *Jamrat al-Wusṭā* and *Jamrat al-'Aqabah*. They exalt God at each throwing and, after throwing pebbles at the first two *Jamrah*s, they pray for themselves, their parents, and their relatives, as well as for all Muslims. If they want to stay in Mina on the fourth day of *Īd al-Adḥā*, they throw pebbles at the *Jamrah*s before noon.

After returning to Makkah, those pilgrims who will be returning to their native land must perform the Farewell *Ṭawaf*. Afterwards, they should go to the Zamzam well and drink as much of its water as possible. Then they go to al-Multazim, rub their face and chest against it, taking hold of the curtain that covers the Ka'bah, pray, and supplicate.

10. This verse refers to the commandments that forbid the eating of carrion, blood that has spilled out of the animal, i.e. other than that which has been left in the veins of the organs, such as the liver and spleen, the flesh of swine, and that which is profane having been slaughtered in the name of other than God and without having God's Name pronounced over it (See 6:

145; 16: 115). The animals or kinds of meat that are forbidden are not only these. The forbidden things mentioned in these two verses pertain only to domestic animals – sheep and cattle. Based on the Revelation, God's Messenger informed us of the other animals that we are forbidden to eat.

Alongside the Qur'ān, the Sunnah of the Messenger is another basic source of the Divine commandments in Islam. It includes everything connected to religious commandments – everything that the Messenger actually said or did, or those actions which he approved of among his Companions. The Sunnah serves as a source of legislation by enjoining and prohibiting, and it lays down the principles related to establishing all religious obligations and necessities, and determines what is lawful or unlawful. It should never be forgotten that the Sunnah is also based on Divine Revelation. The Messenger *does not speak on his own, out of own desire; that (which he conveys to you) is but a Revelation that is revealed to him* (53: 3-4).

In response to a question whether *wudū'* could be performed with sea-water, the Messenger declared: "A sea is that of which the water is clean and the dead animals are lawful to eat" (Abū Dāwūd, "Ṭahārah," 41; at-Tirmidhī, "Ṭaharah," 52). This has provided a basis for many rulings. One is that the Qur'ān generally forbids eating animals that have died naturally and that were not killed according to Islamic rules. The Sunnah, however, elaborates on this general rule (commandment) by allowing the consumption of sea animals that have died in the water.

For the same point, see also 6: 145, note 31.

31. Being believers of pure faith in God, without associating any partners with Him. Whoever associates any partners with God, it is as if he fell down from heaven, and thereupon the wild birds of prey snatch him away, or the wind blows him away into a distant, abysmal ditch (causing him to be shattered into pieces).[10]

32. That (is the truth itself). And whoever venerates the public symbols and rituals set up by God (such as *Jumu'ah* and *'Id* Prayers, call to the Prayer, Sacrifice, and the rites of the Pilgrimage), surely it is because of the true piety and God-consciousness of their hearts.

33. There are benefits for you in them (the sacrificial animals offering of which in God's cause is among Islam's public symbols and rituals,) until the appointed term (of their sacrifice). Then their being carried for sacrifice (during the *Ḥajj*) ends in the sacred precincts of the Most Ancient, Honorable House.

34. For every believing community We have laid down sacrifice as an act of worship to be performed at a certain time and place. So they must pronounce God's Name over what We have provided for them of cattle (while offering it). And (bear in mind that) your God is the One and Only God, so to Him alone submit yourselves wholly. And give glad tidings to the deeply devoted, humble servants –

35. Those whose hearts tremble with awe whenever God is mentioned, who are always patient with whatever ill befalls them, who always establish the Prayer in conformity with its conditions, and who spend (in God's cause and for the needy) out of whatever We provide for them.

36. And the cattle, (including especially the camels) – We have appointed their sacrifice as among the public symbols and rituals set up by God for you, in which

there is much good for you. When they (the camels) are lined up in standing position for sacrifice, pronounce God's Name over them. When they fall down on their sides and fully die ready to be eaten, eat of their meat and feed the poor such as (beg not but) live in contentment and such as beg with due humility. (It is for the purposes and benefits mentioned, and based on the principles mentioned) that We have put the sacrificial animals in your service, so that you may give thanks to God.[11]

37. (Bear in mind that) neither their flesh nor their blood reaches God, but only piety and consciousness of God reach Him from you. (It is for the purposes and benefits mentioned, and based on the principles mentioned) that We have put them in your service so that you must exalt God because He has guided you (to correct be-

lief and worship and obedience to Him). Give glad tidings to those devoted to doing good, aware that God is seeing them.

38. Surely God defends strongly those who believe. Certainly God does not love any treacherous, ungrateful one.

---

11. Considering the extremely eloquent simile the verse contains, we can elaborate on it as follows:

Being believers of pure faith in God, without associating any partners with Him. Whoever associates any partners with God, it is as if he fell down from heaven (the heights or peak of true humanity), *and thereupon the wild birds of prey* (of all misguiding human or satanic forces) *snatch him away* and employ him each for its own benefit, *or the wind* (of lusts, fancies, and events) *blows him away into a distant, abysmal ditch* of misguidance *(causing him to be shattered into pieces).*

12. These verses lay down the principles of offering animals as sacrifice and remove some misunderstandings that were widely circulated in the pre-Islamic era concerning them.

Offering a sacrifice (a sheep, a goat, and for seven people a camel, a cow, or an ox) is incumbent (*wājib*) upon every adult Muslim who has the *niṣāb* (required) amount of wealth. The difference between having to pay the *Zakāh* and performing a sacrifice is that the *Zakāh* must be paid if the person has had the goods or money for one year, while a sacrifice must be offered if the person has had it for only one day. The sacrifice must be made on any of the first three days of *Ῑd al-Aḍḥā*.

Sacrifice during Hajj. Pilgrims doing the *Ḥajj Qirān* and *Ḥajj Tamattu‘*, who miss any necessary act (e.g., throwing pebbles, putting on *iḥrām* from a *mīqāt*, or doing *sa ̔y*), or violate any major *iḥrām* restriction or the sanctity of *Ḥarām* (sacred precincts of) Makkah, must make a sacrifice.

Sacrificial Animals. The most common sacrificial animal is a sheep or a goat. Cattle and camels also can be offered as a sacrifice.

Pilgrims must sacrifice a camel if they perform *ṭawāf* in a state of major ritual impurity (*junub*), or while they are menstruating or having post-childbirth bleeding, if they have had sexual intercourse with their spouse after spending *Dhu ̔l-Ḥijjah* 9 (Eve) in ‘Arafāt, but before shaving or clipping the hair, or have vowed to sacrifice a camel.

Conditions for Sacrifice. A sacrificial animal should satisfy the following conditions:

If it is a sheep, it must be one year old, or as fat and healthy as a one-year-old sheep if it is more than six months old. A camel must be at least five years old, a cow two years old, and a goat one year old.

The animal should be healthy and without defect (i.e., it must not be one-eyed, have a limp, be mangy, very thin, or weak).

Time of Offering. The sacrifice must be made at a specific time, as follows:

Whether one is performing the *Ḥajj* or not, a sacrifice must be offered on any of the first three days of *Ῑd al-Aḍḥā*.

A sacrifice made to fulfill a vow, atone for sins, or perform a supererogatory act of worship may be offered at any time during the year.

Place of Offering. A sacrifice that will be offered during the *Ḥajj*, whether it is necessary (*wājib*) or voluntary, must be offered within Makkah's sacred precincts.

Who Must Sacrifice the Animal. The one who kills the animal must be a Muslim or belong to the People of the Book (a Christian or a Jew). He must say *Bismillāh* before making the sacrifice, for the meat of an animal slaughtered by an atheist, an agnostic, an apostate, or one who intentionally does not say *Bismillāh* cannot be eaten.

Eating the Meat of the Sacrificial Animal. God commands Muslims to eat the meat of animals that have been sacrificed: *Eat of their meat and feed the poor such as (beg not but) live in contentment and such as beg with due humility* (22: 36). It is advisable to eat one-third, to give one-third to the poor, and one-third to one's friends and relatives. Apparently, this command applies to both the obligatory and supererogatory sacrifice. However, one cannot eat the meat of any animal sacrificed in fulfillment of a vow, for all of the meat must be distributed among the poor and needy.

The skin of a sacrificed animal may be used as a rug or in some other way, after it is tanned, or given away to a charity. It cannot, however, be sold.

336　　　سُورَةُ الحَجِّ　　　٣٣٦

بِسْمِ اللَّهِ

أُذِنَ لِلَّذِينَ يُقَاتَلُونَ بِأَنَّهُمْ ظُلِمُوا ۚ وَإِنَّ اللَّهَ عَلَىٰ نَصْرِهِمْ
لَقَدِيرٌ ۞ الَّذِينَ أُخْرِجُوا مِن دِيَارِهِم بِغَيْرِ حَقٍّ إِلَّا أَن يَقُولُوا
رَبُّنَا اللَّهُ ۗ وَلَوْلَا دَفْعُ اللَّهِ النَّاسَ بَعْضَهُم بِبَعْضٍ
لَّهُدِّمَتْ صَوَامِعُ وَبِيَعٌ وَصَلَوَاتٌ وَمَسَاجِدُ يُذْكَرُ فِيهَا
اسْمُ اللَّهِ كَثِيرًا ۗ وَلَيَنصُرَنَّ اللَّهُ مَن يَنصُرُهُ ۗ إِنَّ اللَّهَ لَقَوِيٌّ عَزِيزٌ
۞ الَّذِينَ إِن مَّكَّنَّاهُمْ فِي الْأَرْضِ أَقَامُوا الصَّلَوٰةَ وَآتَوُا
الزَّكَوٰةَ وَأَمَرُوا بِالْمَعْرُوفِ وَنَهَوْا عَنِ الْمُنكَرِ ۗ وَلِلَّهِ عَاقِبَةُ
الْأُمُورِ ۞ وَإِن يُكَذِّبُوكَ فَقَدْ كَذَّبَتْ قَبْلَهُمْ قَوْمُ
نُوحٍ وَعَادٌ وَثَمُودُ ۞ وَقَوْمُ إِبْرَاهِيمَ وَقَوْمُ لُوطٍ ۞ وَأَصْحَابُ
مَدْيَنَ ۖ وَكُذِّبَ مُوسَىٰ فَأَمْلَيْتُ لِلْكَافِرِينَ ثُمَّ أَخَذْتُهُمْ ۖ
فَكَيْفَ كَانَ نَكِيرِ ۞ فَكَأَيِّن مِّن قَرْيَةٍ أَهْلَكْنَاهَا
وَهِيَ ظَالِمَةٌ فَهِيَ خَاوِيَةٌ عَلَىٰ عُرُوشِهَا وَبِئْرٍ مُّعَطَّلَةٍ
وَقَصْرٍ مَّشِيدٍ ۞ أَفَلَمْ يَسِيرُوا فِي الْأَرْضِ فَتَكُونَ لَهُمْ
قُلُوبٌ يَعْقِلُونَ بِهَا أَوْ آذَانٌ يَسْمَعُونَ بِهَا ۖ فَإِنَّهَا لَا تَعْمَى
الْأَبْصَارُ وَلَٰكِن تَعْمَى الْقُلُوبُ الَّتِي فِي الصُّدُورِ ۞

───────◈───────

39. The believers against whom war is waged are given permission to fight in response, for they have been wronged. Surely, God has full power to help them to victory –

40. Those who have been driven from their homeland against all right, for no other reason than that they say, "Our Lord is God." Were it not for God's repelling some people by means of others, monasteries and churches and synagogues and mosques, where God is regularly worshipped and His Name is much mentioned, would surely have been pulled down (with the result that God is no longer worshipped and the earth becomes uninhabitable). God most certainly helps whoever helps His cause. Surely, God is All-Strong, All-Glorious with irresistible might.

41. They are the believers who, if We give them authority on earth, without doubt establish the Prayer in conformity with its conditions, pay the Prescribed Purifying Alms fully, and enjoin and promote what is right and good and forbid and try to prevent the evil. With God rests the outcome for all matters.[13]

42. If they are denying you (O Messenger, you know that) before them the people of Noah, the Ād and the Thamūd also denied (the Messengers sent to each.)

43. And so too did the people of Abraham and the people of Lot;

44. And the dwellers of Midian, and Moses too was denied (by the Pharaoh and his clan). Every time I granted respite to the unbelievers and then seized them (when they persisted in unbelief and injustices), how awesome was My disowning them!

45. How many a township have We destroyed because it was given up to wrongdoing: so they all lie in ruins, with their roofs caved in, wells and fountains deserted, and towering, lofty castles collapsed.

46. Do they never travel about the earth (and view all these scenes with an eye to learn lessons) so that they may have hearts with which to reason (and arrive at truth), or ears with which to hear (God's call)? For indeed it is not the eyes that have become blind, it is rather the hearts in the breasts that are blind.[14]

13. Almost all scholars are in agreement that verse 39, which was revealed during the first year after the *Hijrah*, is the first verse in the Qur'ān concerning fighting on the part of the believers. It was revealed to permit the believers to fight in self-defense against those who waged war against them. Along with the following two verses, it propounds the reason for and wisdom in this permission being granted, as well as the result expected of the believers in case of victory, and it contains certain warnings by allusion.

It is interesting that the verses permitting the believers to fight and the verses of 2: 190–195 which order them to fight when inevitable, occur in the Qur'ān in the same context as the *Ḥajj*. This suggests that what lies behind both this permission and the order in verses 2: 190–195 is a putting an end to association of partners with God in Makkah, and particularly in the Ka'bah, purifying it of all idols and idol-worship. The association of partners with God in any way is what lies at the bottom of the disorder on earth and verse 2: 193 propounds the final end in communicating God's Religion: there should no longer be any disorder and corruption arising from the association of partners with God, and the authority to organize life should be recognized as belonging to God. In addition to the *Ḥajj* being a sign of the purification of the Ka'bah from idols and idol-worship, and as the place of the final dominion of God's Religion, it is also the consummation of all the ways or forms of worship that are to be found within Islam. Moreover, it symbolizes the ordering of worldly life according to the requirements of the afterlife, and is a rehearsal of the events in the Hereafter.

These verses also remind us of the following facts and principles that are concerned with the permission to fight:

Warfare is not an essential of Islam. God wills that there be none other than Him to be worshipped. Only His authority is absolute and no other power has the right to exercise absolute authority over His creatures. His Messengers come to people to convey this message. Throughout human history worldly powers that have exercised authority over people in a wrongful way or that have caused injustice and sedition in the world have declined to give a positive response to God's call. Worse than that, they have tried to prevent others from accepting it and have gone as far as to torture and kill those who convey God's Message and those who have accepted it. The Last Messenger, upon him be peace and blessings, and his followers also encountered the same ruthless reaction and were forced to leave their native homeland without being allowed to take any of their property. They were not even allowed to live peacefully and in safety in Madīnah and were frequently molested. They were also thwarted in all their attempts to visit Makkah and the Ka'bah. It was in such circumstances that the believers were given permission to fight in self-defense.

So long as irreligious, tyrannical forces prevail in a land, believers will not be allowed to order their lives according to God's commandments. Nor will they be allowed to believe in and worship the One and Only God, to enjoy their freedom of faith and their practice of their faith. The verse is clear in this respect: *Those who have been driven from their homeland against all right for no other reason than that they say, "Our Lord is God."* Such forces will not be content with the usurpation of this basic human right. They will close down or destroy all buildings in which God is worshipped. History is a clear witness to this.

If the believers are to enjoy authority on the earth, they must never behave like the tyrannical forces described. They must fulfill the duty of worshipping God, which prevents them from all kinds of evil and leads to their spiritual and moral perfection. They must also pay the Prescribed Purifying Alms, which will purify their hearts of a love for wealth, and which eliminates any class differences in society, thus establishing social justice, balance, and peace. Moreover, they will support, promote, and spread all good acts, and try to prevent all evil ones. This means that believers can never have worldly or personal aims in fighting, such as the conquest or colonization of lands, the subjugation of peoples, the attainment of wealth, or the usurpation of the property of others.

14. The word translated here as "to reason (and arrive at truth)" is *'aql*. Literally, it means taking refuge, holding fast to something, fasten, and preserve. As a faculty, it is described as the spiritual power which preserves human through knowledge, and prevents them from being dragged along the ways of perdition.

However, the Qur'ān uses the word *'aql* not as a separate faculty, but as a function or act of the heart. Thus, the verb is used in two forms, (*'A-Qa-La-ya'qilu-*) *'aqlan* and *ta'aqqul*. This means thinking, deducing, or inferring, arriving at a conclusion, by using one's heart.

In Qur'ānic terminology, "heart" signifies the spiritual aspect of the heart, which is the center of all emotions and (intellectual and spiritual) faculties, such as perception, consciousness, sensation, reasoning, and will-power.

An individual's real nature is found in their heart. It is in relation to this intellectual and spiritual aspect of existence that one is able to know, perceive, and understand. The spirit is the essence and inner dimension of this faculty; the soul (*nafs*) is its mount.

It is one's heart that God addresses and that undertakes responsibilities; it is the heart that is elevated through true guidance or debased through deviation, and which is honored or humiliated. The heart is also the "polished mirror" in which Divine knowledge is reflected.

The heart or spiritual intellect, if we may call it thus, has an intrinsic connection with its biological counterpart. The nature of this connection has been discussed by philosophers and Muslim sages for centuries. Of whatever nature this connection may be, it is beyond doubt that there is a close connection between the biological heart and the "spiritual" one, which is a Divine faculty, the center of true humanity, and the source of all human feelings and emotions.

In the Qur'ān, religious sciences, morals, literature, and Sufism, the word "heart" signifies the spiritual heart. Belief, knowledge and love of God, and spiritual delight are the objectives to be achieved through this Divine faculty.

God considers one's heart. He treats human beings according to the quality of their hearts, as the heart is the stronghold of many elements vital to the believer's spiritual life and humanity: reason, knowledge, knowledge of God, intentions, belief, wisdom, and nearness to God Almighty. If the heart is alive, all of these elements and faculties are alive; if the heart is diseased, it is difficult for those elements and faculties to remain sound.

Belief is the life of the heart; worship is the blood that flows in its veins; reflection, self-supervision, and self-criticism are the foundations of its permanence. The heart of an unbeliever is dead; the heart of a believer who does not worship is dying; and the heart of a believer who worships but does not engage in self-reflection, self-control, or self-criticism is exposed to many spiritual dangers and diseases (*Key Concepts*, 22–27).

A heart has two windows opening on the outer world: the spiritual ear and eye. It is the heart which hears the Divine messages with its ear, and which sees God's signs with its eye. If a heart is blinded or dead, even if a person sees and hears with their eyes and ears, they are blind and deaf spiritually and in the sight of God. (Also see *sūrah* 2: 7, note 7; *sūrah* 6: 36, note 7; *sūrah* 10: 100, note 21.)

وَيَسْتَعْجِلُونَكَ بِالْعَذَابِ وَلَن يُخْلِفَ اللَّهُ وَعْدَهُ ۚ وَإِنَّ يَوْمًا عِندَ رَبِّكَ كَأَلْفِ سَنَةٍ مِّمَّا تَعُدُّونَ ۝ وَكَأَيِّن مِّن قَرْيَةٍ أَمْلَيْتُ لَهَا وَهِيَ ظَالِمَةٌ ثُمَّ أَخَذْتُهَا وَإِلَيَّ الْمَصِيرُ ۝ قُلْ يَا أَيُّهَا النَّاسُ إِنَّمَا أَنَا لَكُمْ نَذِيرٌ مُّبِينٌ ۝ فَالَّذِينَ آمَنُوا وَعَمِلُوا الصَّالِحَاتِ لَهُم مَّغْفِرَةٌ وَرِزْقٌ كَرِيمٌ ۝ وَالَّذِينَ سَعَوْا فِي آيَاتِنَا مُعَاجِزِينَ أُولَٰئِكَ أَصْحَابُ الْجَحِيمِ ۝ وَمَا أَرْسَلْنَا مِن قَبْلِكَ مِن رَّسُولٍ وَلَا نَبِيٍّ إِلَّا إِذَا تَمَنَّىٰ أَلْقَى الشَّيْطَانُ فِي أُمْنِيَّتِهِ فَيَنسَخُ اللَّهُ مَا يُلْقِي الشَّيْطَانُ ثُمَّ يُحْكِمُ اللَّهُ آيَاتِهِ ۗ وَاللَّهُ عَلِيمٌ حَكِيمٌ ۝ لِّيَجْعَلَ مَا يُلْقِي الشَّيْطَانُ فِتْنَةً لِّلَّذِينَ فِي قُلُوبِهِم مَّرَضٌ وَالْقَاسِيَةِ قُلُوبُهُمْ ۗ وَإِنَّ الظَّالِمِينَ لَفِي شِقَاقٍ بَعِيدٍ ۝ وَلِيَعْلَمَ الَّذِينَ أُوتُوا الْعِلْمَ أَنَّهُ الْحَقُّ مِن رَّبِّكَ فَيُؤْمِنُوا بِهِ فَتُخْبِتَ لَهُ قُلُوبُهُمْ ۗ وَإِنَّ اللَّهَ لَهَادِ الَّذِينَ آمَنُوا إِلَىٰ صِرَاطٍ مُّسْتَقِيمٍ ۝ وَلَا يَزَالُ الَّذِينَ كَفَرُوا فِي مِرْيَةٍ مِّنْهُ حَتَّىٰ تَأْتِيَهُمُ السَّاعَةُ بَغْتَةً أَوْ يَأْتِيَهُمْ عَذَابُ يَوْمٍ عَقِيمٍ ۝

47. They challenge you to hasten the coming upon them of God's punishment (with which they are threatened). Let them know that God never fails to fulfill His promise; but a day with your Lord is like a thousand years in your reckoning.[15]

48. (Let them not hasten you to bring on them Our punishment.) How many a township that was given up to wrongdoing have I given respite to, but then seized them (when they persisted in unbelief and injustices); and to Me is the homecoming.

49. Say (O Messenger): "O people! (I am not a man who can do whatever he wills, nor whatever you wish;) I am only a plain warner sent to you."

50. So those who believe and do good, righteous deeds – for them is a forgiveness (to bring unforeseen blessings) and an honorable, generous provision (in the Hereafter).

51. As to those who strive against Our Revelations, seeking to frustrate and void them, they are the companions of the Blazing Flame.

52. Never did We send a Messenger or a Prophet before you but that when he recited (God's Revelations to the people) Satan would make insinuations (about these Revelations, prompting people to misconstrue them in many wrong senses, rather than the right one). But God abrogates whatever insinuations Satan may make, and then He confirms and establishes His Revelations. God is All-Knowing, All-Wise.

53. He makes Satan's insinuations a trial for those in the center of whose hearts there is a sickness (that extinguishes their power of understanding and corrupts their character), and who have hardened hearts. The wrongdoers have certainly veered far from the truth and are in wide schism.

54. While those who have been granted knowledge (of the truth) know (with a greater certainty) that whatever God reveals is the truth itself, and they believe in it and their hearts submit to Him in utmost humility. God most certainly guides to a straight path those who believe with sincerity.

55. Whereas those who persistently disbelieve will not cease to be in doubt about it (the Revelation) until the Last Hour comes upon them suddenly, or there comes to them the punishment of a barren day (when every hope would turn into despair, and after which there will be no night to rest in).

15. This verse touches on certain important facts from the perspectives of astrophysics and the sociology of history.

First of all, it draws attention to the relativity of time. A time or duration which people see as being long may be very short in the sight of God. In addition, God does not consider time as people do. He is not contained by time or space, and His Wisdom that directs things and events considers each thing and event both as an individual entity in and as an indispensable part of the general fabric of creation and history. As each thing in the universe has an intrinsic relationship not only with every other thing individually, but also with the whole universe at the same time, so too is each event in human history interrelated with every other event individually and with the whole of history. Human beings cannot grasp this relationship in its entire web; they cannot know the past perfectly, grasp the present completely, nor guess the future well. Besides, the wheel of both the universe and history does not revolve according to the desires of human beings.

Secondly, a day for humanity is the time it takes the earth to make a single rotation around itself. The earth has another day, which consists in its revolution around the sun. This day lasts 365 days according to the reckoning of a day by humanity. So too does every other planet and all systems, like the solar system, have a day that is peculiar to each. This means that the concept of a day differs according to the planets and the systems.

Thirdly, God has laid out certain laws concerning human social life. He judges a community according to the creeds, world-view, and conduct of, at least, the majority. Thus, there are eras and ages in human history and eras of foundation, rising, fall, and decline for communities and civilizations. Thus, we can consider the whole life of a state or community or civilization as a day; the most important changes in the history of humanity usually occur once in 1,000 years. This verse also alludes to this fact.

338

سُوْرَةُ الْحَجّ

٣٣٨

الْمُلْكُ يَوْمَئِذٍ لِلَّهِ يَحْكُمُ بَيْنَهُمْ فَالَّذِينَ ءَامَنُوا وَعَمِلُوا
الصَّالِحَاتِ فِى جَنَّاتِ النَّعِيمِ ۝ وَالَّذِينَ كَفَرُوا وَكَذَّبُوا
بِـَٔايَاتِنَا فَأُولَٰئِكَ لَهُمْ عَذَابٌ مُّهِينٌ ۝ وَالَّذِينَ هَاجَرُوا
فِى سَبِيلِ اللَّهِ ثُمَّ قُتِلُوٓا أَوْ مَاتُوا لَيَرْزُقَنَّهُمُ اللَّهُ
رِزْقًا حَسَنًا وَإِنَّ اللَّهَ لَهُوَ خَيْرُ الرَّازِقِينَ ۝ لَيُدْخِلَنَّهُم
مُّدْخَلًا يَرْضَوْنَهُ وَإِنَّ اللَّهَ لَعَلِيمٌ حَلِيمٌ ۝ ذَٰلِكَ
وَمَنْ عَاقَبَ بِمِثْلِ مَا عُوقِبَ بِهِ ثُمَّ بُغِىَ عَلَيْهِ
لَيَنْصُرَنَّهُ اللَّهُ إِنَّ اللَّهَ لَعَفُوٌّ غَفُورٌ ۝
ذَٰلِكَ بِأَنَّ اللَّهَ يُولِجُ الَّيْلَ فِى النَّهَارِ وَيُولِجُ النَّهَارَ
فِى الَّيْلِ وَأَنَّ اللَّهَ سَمِيعٌ بَصِيرٌ ۝ ذَٰلِكَ بِأَنَّ اللَّهَ
هُوَ الْحَقُّ وَأَنَّ مَا يَدْعُونَ مِن دُونِهِ هُوَ
الْبَاطِلُ وَأَنَّ اللَّهَ هُوَ الْعَلِىُّ الْكَبِيرُ ۝
أَلَمْ تَرَ أَنَّ اللَّهَ أَنزَلَ مِنَ السَّمَاءِ مَاءً فَتُصْبِحُ الْأَرْضُ
مُخْضَرَّةً إِنَّ اللَّهَ لَطِيفٌ خَبِيرٌ ۝ لَهُ مَا فِى السَّمَاوَاتِ وَمَا
فِى الْأَرْضِ وَإِنَّ اللَّهَ لَهُوَ الْغَنِىُّ الْحَمِيدُ ۝

56. On that Day the absolute authority belongs to God exclusively. He judges (all people and makes a distinction) between them. Consequently, those who believe and do good, righteous deeds will be in Gardens of bounty and blessings.

57. As for those who disbelieve and deny Our Revelations, for them there will be a shameful, humiliating punishment.

58. Those who emigrate in God's cause, and then are killed (for God's cause) or die – God will most certainly provide for them with a good, wholesome sustenance. Surely God is He Who is the Best to be sought as provider with the ultimate rank of providing.

59. He will most certainly admit them into a place with which they will be pleased. Surely God is All-Knowing, All-Clement.

60. So it will be. And whoever responds to the wrong done to him to the extent of the wrong, and then is again subjected to oppression, God will most certainly help him. Assuredly, God is All-Pardoning, (Who overlooks the faults of His servants), All-Forgiving.[16]

61. So (will He do), because God makes the night pass into the day and makes the day pass into the night, and God is All-Hearing, All-Seeing.[17]

62. So (will He do), because God is He

Who is the Absolute Truth and all that they (the unbelievers) deify and invoke instead of (or apart from) Him is sheer falsehood, and God is He Who is the All-Exalted, the All-Great.

63. Do you not consider that God sends down from the sky water, and behold, the earth turns green. Surely, God is All-Subtle (penetrating to the most minute dimensions of all things and accomplishing what He wills by ways that are not quite tangible), All-Aware.

64. To Him belongs all that is in the heavens and all that is on the earth. And surely God is He Who is the All-Wealthy and Self-Sufficient (absolutely independent of the whole creation), the All-Praiseworthy (Who provides for all of them as their Lord).[18]

16. Islam allows retaliation in the case of wrong as a principle of law, for justice requires that inviolate values demand equal respect and retaliation (2: 194). However, in many of its verses (i.e., 2: 237; 41: 34; 42: 40; and 42: 43), the Qur'ān advises an individual to forgive an evil done to them, even to repel it with what is better, and warns against exceeding the limits in retaliation (17: 33).

However, we should remember here that an individual is urged to forgive any wrong done to them, but no one can forgive any wrong done to a community or its sacred values. As the community or government has no authority to forgive in the name of an individual, neither can an individual forgive in the name of the community. But the Qur'ān also warns a community against exceeding the limits in repelling an attack and warns it to remain within the limits of piety (2: 194).

What verse 60, which is being discussed here, means by *God will most certainly help him* is similar to that found in verse 33 of Sūrah 17: *If anyone has been killed wrongfully and intentionally, We have given his heir (as defender of his rights) the authority (to claim retaliation or damages or to forgive outright). But let him (the heir) not exceed the legitimate bounds in (retaliatory) killing. Indeed he has been helped (already and sufficiently by the provisions and procedures of the Law)* (17: 33). In the case of a community being attacked, it also means that God helps it against the attacker, as He helped the believers in the Battle of Badr by sending angels, or in other ways (8: 9–12).

As for the verse concluding by mentioning God's being All-Pardoning and All-Forgiv-

ing, it is similar to: *Whoever is constrained by dire necessity (and driven to what is forbidden), without purposely inclining to sin – surely God is All-Forgiving, All-Compassionate* (5: 3). This means that even if any act that is done in the name of retaliation is an evil in and of itself, if the continuation of human life through justice requires it, God will forgive the person who does it.

17. Something similar to this idea exists in Sūrat Āl 'Imrān (3: 27).Thus, it also has the same meaning as exists in that verse and is to be considered together with the verse that comes just before it (26): *Say: "O God, Master of all dominion! You give dominion to whom You will, and take away dominion from whom You will, and You exalt whom You will, and abase whom You will; in Your hand is all good; surely You have full power over everything."* We can also view this together with the verse: *Such (historic, eventful) days – We deal them out in turns among people so that God may mark out those who (truly) believe and select from among you such as bear witness to the truth (with their lives)* (3: 140). God rules over the universe and just as He makes night and day follow each other and brings about the brightness of the day after the darkness of night, He also changes the dark night of the oppressed into a bright day for them and the bright day of the oppressors into a dark night for them. Every night is followed by a day and every winter is followed by spring.

18. For a mention of God's acts or disposals in the world of humankind and the worlds of other creatures or other parts of the universe, see 7: 57–58, note 14.

65. Do you not consider that God has made all that is on earth to be of service to you, and the ships that run upon the sea by His command? And He holds the heaven so that it may not fall upon the earth unless by His leave. Surely God is for humankind All-Pitying, All-Compassionate.

66. It is He Who has given you life, then He causes you to die, then He will bring you to life again. However, humankind are really ungrateful.

67. For every community We have appointed a whole system of worship which they are to observe. So do not let those (who follow their own systems) draw you into disputes concerning this matter, but continue to call people to your Lord. You are most certainly on the straight way leading to pure guidance.[19]

68. If they argue with you, say only: "God knows well what you are doing. (To me are accounted my deeds, and to you, your deeds. You are quit of all that I do, and I am quit of all that you do.)"

69. God will judge between you on the Day of Resurrection concerning what you used to differ on.

70. Do you not know that surely God knows whatever there is in the heavens and on the earth (including whatever takes place in them). They are all recorded in a Book. This (keeping the record of them all) is indeed easy for God.

71. And yet, they worship, apart from God, things for which He has sent down no warrant, nor are they are based on true knowledge (when they claim that there can be partners with Him). The wrongdoers will have no helper (to protect them from God's punishment).

72. When Our Revelations, clear as evidence and in meaning are recited (and conveyed) to them, you perceive utter repugnance and denial on the faces of those who disbelieve; they would almost pounce upon those who convey Our Revelations to them. Say: "Then, shall I tell you of something worse than what you now regard as repugnant? The Fire! God has promised it to those who disbelieve. How evil a destination to arrive at!

19. The Religion with which all the Prophets came is the same and is in agreement in the essentials of faith or creeds, worship, principles of good morality, and the prescriptions of the lawful and unlawful. However, there are differences in some secondary matters that are open to changes according to time and conditions. This is what is meant by the verse:

> For each (community to which a Messenger was sent with a Book) have We appointed a clear way of life and a comprehensive system (containing the principles of that way and how to follow it). And if God had so willed, He would surely have made you a single community (following the same way of life and system surrounded by the same conditions throughout all history); but (He willed it otherwise) in order to test you by what He granted to you (and thereby made you subject to a law of progress). Strive, then, together as if competing in good works. To God is the return of all of you, and He will then make you understand (the truth) about what you have differed on (5: 48).

There are also differences in the way of observing worship. The system of worship prescribed by God for the Islam conveyed by the Last Messenger, upon him be peace and blessings, is the last and perfected one (5: 3), as it is universal and meant for all people. The verse, *We have set you on a way of life (shari'ah) based on the Religion, so follow it, and do not follow the desires and caprices of those who do not know (the Divine Guidance)* (45: 18), is related to both verse 5: 48 and this one. So Muslims should not allow others to draw them into disputes concerning this matter. Their system of worship and way of life are perfect. What the Messenger and his followers are expected to do is to continue to call people to God with all their strength.

340 سُورَةُ الحجّ ٣٤٠

بِسۡمِ ٱللّٰهِ ٱلرَّحۡمٰنِ ٱلرَّحِيمِ

يَـٰٓأَيُّهَا ٱلنَّاسُ ضُرِبَ مَثَلٌ فَٱسۡتَمِعُواْ لَهُۥٓ إِنَّ ٱلَّذِينَ تَدۡعُونَ مِن دُونِ ٱللّٰهِ لَن يَخۡلُقُواْ ذُبَابًا وَلَوِ ٱجۡتَمَعُواْ لَهُۥ وَإِن يَسۡلُبۡهُمُ ٱلذُّبَابُ شَيۡـًٔا لَّا يَسۡتَنقِذُوهُ مِنۡهُ صَعُفَ ٱلطَّالِبُ وَٱلۡمَطۡلُوبُ ۝ مَا قَدَرُواْ ٱللّٰهَ حَقَّ قَدۡرِهِۦٓ إِنَّ ٱللّٰهَ لَقَوِيٌّ عَزِيزٌ ۝ ٱللّٰهُ يَصۡطَفِى مِنَ ٱلۡمَلَـٰٓئِكَةِ رُسُلًا وَمِنَ ٱلنَّاسِ إِنَّ ٱللّٰهَ سَمِيعٌۢ بَصِيرٌ ۝ يَعۡلَمُ مَا بَيۡنَ أَيۡدِيهِمۡ وَمَا خَلۡفَهُمۡ وَإِلَى ٱللّٰهِ تُرۡجَعُ ٱلۡأُمُورُ ۝ يَـٰٓأَيُّهَا ٱلَّذِينَ ءَامَنُواْ ٱرۡكَعُواْ وَٱسۡجُدُواْ وَٱعۡبُدُواْ رَبَّكُمۡ وَٱفۡعَلُواْ ٱلۡخَيۡرَ لَعَلَّكُمۡ تُفۡلِحُونَ ۝ وَجَٰهِدُواْ فِى ٱللّٰهِ حَقَّ جِهَادِهِۦ هُوَ ٱجۡتَبَىٰكُمۡ وَمَا جَعَلَ عَلَيۡكُمۡ فِى ٱلدِّينِ مِنۡ حَرَجٍ مِّلَّةَ أَبِيكُمۡ إِبۡرَٰهِيمَ هُوَ سَمَّىٰكُمُ ٱلۡمُسۡلِمِينَ مِن قَبۡلُ وَفِى هَـٰذَا لِيَكُونَ ٱلرَّسُولُ شَهِيدًا عَلَيۡكُمۡ وَتَكُونُواْ شُهَدَآءَ عَلَى ٱلنَّاسِ فَأَقِيمُواْ ٱلصَّلَوٰةَ وَءَاتُواْ ٱلزَّكَوٰةَ وَٱعۡتَصِمُواْ بِٱللّٰهِ هُوَ مَوۡلَىٰكُمۡ فَنِعۡمَ ٱلۡمَوۡلَىٰ وَنِعۡمَ ٱلنَّصِيرُ ۝

73. O humankind! A parable is struck, so pay heed to it: Those whom, apart from God, you deify and invoke will never be able to create even a fly, even if all of them were to come together to do so. And if a fly snatches away anything from them, they cannot recover that from it. Powerless indeed is the seeker, and (so is) the sought!

74. They have no true judgment of God, such as His being God requires. God is certainly All-Strong, All-Glorious with irresistible might.

75. God chooses Messengers from among the angels as well as from among humankind (so they are all created beings having no share in Divinity at all.) Surely God is All-Hearing, All-Seeing.

76. He knows what lies before them and what lies after them (what lies in their future and in their past, what is known to them and what is hidden from them). To God are all affairs ultimately referred, (and whatever He wills occurs).

77. O you who believe! Bow down and prostrate yourselves, (thus performing the Prayer), and fulfill all your other duties of worship to your Lord, and do (all the oth-er commands of your Religion, which are all) good, so that you may prosper.[20]

78. Strive in God's cause and purely for His sake (against His enemies to raise His Word, and against Satan and your carnal, evil-commanding souls,) in a manner worthy of that striving.[21] He has chosen you (especially for this task)[22] and has not laid any hardship on you in the Religion.[23] This is the way of your father Abraham. God named you Muslims previously,[24] and in this Book, that the (most noble) Messenger may be a witness for you (as to the ways you follow), and that you may be the witnesses for people. So establish the Prayer in conformity with its conditions, pay the Prescribed Purifying Alms, and hold fast to God. He is your Owner and Guardian. How excellent a Guardian and an Owner He is, how excellent a Helper.

20. This is the only way in which one may hope to prosper, particularly in the other world. However, all duties of worship and commands of the *Sharī'ah* are in order to thank God for His bounties that He has already bestowed on us; they are not performed to receive His future rewards. But purely out of His Compassion, God has made them a reason to forgive us and to admit us into Paradise. Even if we were to spend every second of our life worshipping Him, we would not be able to pay our duty of thanksgiving for, say, our eyes. We should not restrict God's favors to what we are provided with. Nature, with everything in it, life, the family, the environment, love, compassion, belief, and many other things are also included in His favors. Our basic necessities of life are given to us for free, while others are virtually free. So no one can prosper in the other world unless God has mercy on us, and His admitting us into Paradise is purely out of His Compassion. He has made faith and the fulfillment of our duties of worship a reason for us to receive His compassion.

21. For the meaning and types of striving made in God's cause and for His sake (*jihād*), see 2: 218, note 147.

22. Al-Mawdūdī notes:

Of all humanity, the believers were chosen for the task mentioned in the present verse. The same point is also made in other places in the Qur'ān: *We have made you a middle-way community, that you may be witnesses for the people (as to the ways they follow), and that the (most noble) Messenger may be a witness for you* (2: 143). (For an explanation of this verse, see 2, note 113 in this study.) *You are the best community ever brought forth for (the good of) humankind, enjoining and actively promoting what is right and good and forbidding and trying to prevent the evil, and (this you do because) you believe in God* (3: 110).

It is perhaps pertinent to point out here that this is one of several verses which establish the excellence of the Prophet's Companions. The verse also makes clear how wrong those people who are prone to launch attacks on the Com-panions are. It is quite obvious that this verse directly identifies the Companions as those chosen by God, and furthermore it indirectly extols other members of the *Ummah* (al-Mawdūdī, 6: 71, note: 129).

23. Islam contains nothing that hinders the growth of culture and civilization (in ways approved by God); it does not restrain human practical life, nor obstruct intellectual progress. Neither does it have any shackles forged by theologians, priests, and lawyers, as were imported into previous religions. Its principles of faith are quite clear, and its commandments for worship and life are both meaningful and practical. It also contains special dispensations for those who should be excused. It avoids all complicated rituals or systems of taboos, which impose undue restrictions on everyday human life.

24. *And when Abraham, and Ishmael with him, raised the foundations of the House (they were praying): "Our Lord! Accept (this service) from us. Surely You are the All-Hearing, the All-Knowing. Our Lord! Make us Muslims, submissive to You, and of our offspring a community Muslim, submissive to You...."* (2: 127–28).

Abraham bequeathed and enjoined this submission to his sons (Ishmael and Isaac) and (to his grandson) Jacob, saying: "My sons, God has chosen for you (from different ways of faith and life) the Religion (of Islam, based on submission to Him and absolutely free from any kind of associating partners with Him). Therefore, make sure that you do not die except as Muslims (those submitted to Him exclusively)." Or were you (O Children of Israel, of Jacob) witnesses when death came to Jacob (so that you might claim that he bequeathed and enjoined a religion otherwise than as Abraham did, to give yourselves an excuse for refusing Islam,) when he said to his sons: "What will you worship after me?" They answered: "We will worship your God and the God of your fathers, Abraham, Ishmael, and Isaac, One God; we are Muslims submitted to Him" (2: 132–33).

SŪRAH 23

AL-MU'MINŪN
(THE BELIEVERS)

Makkah period

This *sūrah* takes its title "the believers" from the mention of the believers who are praised for their moral superiority at the very beginning of the *sūrah*. It was revealed in Makkah when the persecution perpetrated by the Makkan unbelievers was increasing. It consists of 118 verses.

The *sūrah* begins by mentioning certain moral characteristics of the believers. This is followed by stating the signs inherent in the creation of humankind and the universe in order to draw attention to God's Existence and Unity. Then significant episodes from the experiences of several previous Messengers and their peoples are given in order to emphasize that there was nothing untypical about the reactions of the Makkan unbelievers, and also that the teachings that the Prophet Muhammad, upon him be peace and blessings, conveyed were the same as those communicated by the earlier Messengers. By recounting the experiences of some of the earlier Messengers, the Qur'ān also aims to stress that the final victory will always belong to the believers. Then, the *sūrah* reminds us of certain important principles concerning human life. The *sūrah* concludes by warning the unbelievers that they will face a severe reckoning in the Hereafter.

In the Name of God, the All-Merciful, the All-Compassionate.

1. Prosperous indeed are the believers.

2. They are in their Prayer humble and fully submissive (being overwhelmed by the awe and majesty of God).

3. They always turn away from and avoid whatever is vain and frivolous.

4. They are in a constant effort to give alms and purify their own selves and wealth.

5. They strictly guard their private parts, and their chastity and modesty,

6. Save from their spouses or (as a permission for men) those (bondsmaids) whom their right hands possess, for with regard to them they are free from blame.

7. But whoever seeks beyond that, such are they who exceed the bounds (set by God).[1]

8. They are faithful and true to their trusts (which either God or society or an individual places in their charge) and to their pledges (between them and God or other persons or society).

9. They are ever mindful guardians of their Prayers (including all the rites of which they are constituted).

10. Those (illustrious ones) are the inheritors,

11. Who will inherit the highest floor of Paradise. Therein they will abide forever.[2]

12. We created humankind (in the very beginning) from a specially sifted extract of clay.[3]

13. Then We have made it into a fertilized ovum in a safe lodging.

14. Then We have created of the fertilized ovum a clot clinging (to the womb wall), and (afterwards in sequence) We have created of the clinging clot a (chew of) lump, and We have created of (a chew of) lump bones, and We have clothed the bones in flesh. Then We have caused it

to grow into another creation. So Blessed and Supreme is God, the Creator Who creates everything in the best and most appropriate form and has the ultimate rank of creativitiy.[4]

15. Then, after all this, you are bound to die.

16. Thereafter, you will, on the Day of Resurrection, certainly be raised up.

17. Indeed, We have created above you seven heavens, one layer upon the other, and seven paths (for angels to move, God's commands to descend, and acts of conscious beings to ascend, along). Never are We unaware of creation and what We create (with all aspects of their lives).[5]

---

1. These last three verses lay down important principles concerning one's family life:

Islam emphasizes chastity and modesty, but it never orders celibacy or monasticism. It allows people to satisfy their desires and needs in a legitimate manner.

A man must guard his private parts except from his wife and slave-girls whom he rightfully possesses, while a woman must do the same except from her husband.

The verse, *Whoever seeks beyond that, such are they who exceed the limits (set by God)*, forbids all forms of sexual relations, except the two specified in the previous verse, including homosexuality, lesbianism, and sex with animals. Imam Malik and Imam Shafi'ī also consider masturbation a way of seeking something beyond what is lawful.

Some commentators of the Qur'ān cite this verse to support prohibition of *mut'ah*, (temporary marriage). As a matter of fact, a *mut'ah* is neither a normal, lawful marriage nor a relationship with a slave-girl whom one possesses. None of the laws with regard to lawful marriage, such as divorce, the waiting period (*'iddah*), or maintenance (*nafaqah*) apply to it. In *mut'ah* there is no divorce; once you pay the set amount of money and the assigned time ends

there are no rights, no duties, no inheritance laws, nor a divorce process. The only law is that the woman waits for a period of 45 days before she enters into another *mut'ah*, while the man can have an immediate one, even while he is married or in another *mut'ah*.

Although the argument of the commentators that these verses ban *mut'ah* is weighty, it is recorded in the *hadīth* collections that *mut'ah* was categorically and decisively forbidden in Madīnah (Muslim, "Nikah," 22). This *sūrah* was revealed during the Makkan period of the Prophet's mission. Despite this decisive prohibition, only a few Companions, who might not have heard of its prohibition by the Messenger, continued to think it was lawful. But they confined its lawfulness to highly exceptional circumstances. Ibn 'Abbās, who is recorded as one of those Companions, clarified himself and said: "I meant something similar to what God meant when He allowed the meat of dead animals and pork to be eaten in extreme necessity" (al-Jaṣṣāṣ, 2: 147).

Many of the Shī'ite scholars, the scholars of the sect which accepts the lawfulness of *mut'ah*, have contradicting opinions and report contradicting traditions concerning it. One of their highly authentic *hadīth* books, *Uṣūl* al-Kāfī, 5: 462, has a hadīth that states that a mut'ah for a virgin girl is not recommended, because of the shame it will bring upon her parents. Imam Abī 'Abdullāh (Ja'far al-Ṣādiq) proclaims: "Do not enter a mut'ah with a believing woman, because you will humiliate her by so doing" (Kitāb at-Tadhhīb, 1: 253; al-Istibṣār, 3: 143). In another narration, it is stated that a mut'ah can only be entered into with a believing woman (al-Kāfī, 5: 454), while in yet another it is stated that a mut'ah is not allowed with a Muslim woman, but only with Jewish or Christian women. In Biḥār al-Anwār (103: 340), it is also stated that it is unlawful to enter into a mut'ah with a person who is married or able to marry.

Imam 'Alī is one of the leading Companions who declared that mut'ah is unlawful (al-Bukhārī, "Nikāḥ," 31; Muslim, "Nikāḥ," 29–31). The Shī'ite scholars also recorded that 'Alī declared its unlawfulness, although they attributed this to taqiyyah (dissimulation) (Kitāb at-Tadhhīb, 7: 253; al-Istibṣār, 3: 142).

It would not be correct to say that it was 'Umar who forbade mut'ah. What 'Umar did was to enforce the prohibition (Ibn Mājah, "Nikāḥ," 44: 196).

2. Verses 1–9 expound the qualities of true believers. These qualities serve as evidence in support of the claim that one is a true believer, and that the believers who have these qualities will inevitably prosper in both worlds. God's Messenger, upon him be peace and blessings, declared: "There are ten verses that have been revealed to me that if anyone follows them, he will certainly enter Paradise." Then he recited the first ten verses of this sūrah (at-Tirmidhī, "Kitāb at-Tafsīr," 24).

3. The verse implies: We created humankind (in the very beginning) from a specially sifted extract of clay and subsequently, create each human being from mineral, vegetable and animal elements produced in extracts of clay and which constitute the sustenance to form the male sperm and female egg.

4. The literal translation of the phrase here rendered as the Creator Who creates every-thing in the best and most appropriate form and has the ultimate rank of creativit is "the Best of the creators." Phrases such as the Best of the creators or the Most Merciful of the merciful or the Best of the providers do not suggest the existence of other creators or merciful ones or providers comparable with God. Rather, they point to the ultimate or perfect ranks of the manifestations of the attributes of creating, showing mercy, and providing. Thus, these phrases mean that He is the Majestic Creator having the ultimate rank or all-beautiful degree of creating, and a Merciful One having the ultimate or perfect rank of mercifulness, and a Provider with the ultimate or perfect rank of providing.

Secondly, such phrases as the Best of the creators do not suggest a plurality of creators. Rather, they mean that God is the Creator Who creates everything in the best and most appropriate fashion. Verses like He Who makes excellent everything that He creates (32: 7), have the same meaning.

Thirdly, such phrases as the Best of the creators, the Best of the judges, and the Best of the providers do not compare the acts and Attributes of God that are manifested in the universe with those of creatures, who manifest only their shadowy reflections. Whatever beings have is a gift from God (We see because God is the All-Seeing, and hear because He is the All-Hearing.) All (relative) perfections shared by humanity, angels, and jinn are only indistinct shadows in relation to His, which are beyond compare.

People, especially the misguided, cannot have true judgment of God as His right (in being God) requires, and they are usually forgetful of Him. For example, a private respects his corporal, but is oblivious of the king when he thanks the corporal for anything. Such a private should be warned: "The king is greater than your corporal, so you must thank the king." Actually, everything ultimately comes from the king; the corporal is only an envoy. The king's majestic command cannot be compared with that of the corporal. The only purpose for the warning, which contains a comparison, is to warn the private, who prefers the corporal in gratitude against forgetting the gratitude he owes to the king.

Similarly, the means by which something is achieved, as well as nature and causes make heedless people blind to the True Bestower of Bounties. They attribute the bounties which they receive to means and nature, and give creativity to causes, as if they were the real sources, and praise and thank them. This is a path to associating others with God, and so the Qur'ān warns: Almighty God is much greater and a far better Creator and Provider (actually meaning that He is the sole Creator and Provider). Regard Him and thank Him.

Finally, comparisons may be made between actually existent, possible, or even imagined things. People may imagine infinite grades in the essence of the Divine Names and Attributes. Almighty God is, however, of the highest, most perfect, and most beautiful of all grades that His Names and Attributes are imagined to have. The universe bears witness to this. His description of all His Names as the best or all-beautiful, as in: *His are the All-Beautiful Names* (20: 8), underlines this fact (*The Words*, "the 32nd Word," 631–632).

5. The phrase, *creation and what We create (with all aspects of their lives),* clearly demonstrates that creation is based on absolute Knowledge, Will, and Power. So, it certainly has a purpose and meaning and bears countless messages. No so-called deities, nature, material causes, or any notions such as coincidence and necessity have any part in either its coming into existence or its continuance.

وَأَنزَلْنَا مِنَ السَّمَاءِ مَاءً بِقَدَرٍ فَأَسْكَنَّاهُ فِي الْأَرْضِ وَإِنَّا عَلَى
ذَهَابٍ بِهِ لَقَادِرُونَ ۞ فَأَنشَأْنَا لَكُم بِهِ جَنَّاتٍ مِّن نَّخِيلٍ وَأَعْنَابٍ
لَّكُمْ فِيهَا فَوَاكِهُ كَثِيرَةٌ وَمِنْهَا تَأْكُلُونَ ۞ وَشَجَرَةً تَخْرُجُ
مِن طُورِ سَيْنَاءَ تَنبُتُ بِالدُّهْنِ وَصِبْغٍ لِّلْآكِلِينَ ۞ وَإِنَّ لَكُمْ
فِي الْأَنْعَامِ لَعِبْرَةً نُّسْقِيكُم مِّمَّا فِي بُطُونِهَا وَلَكُمْ فِيهَا مَنَافِعُ
كَثِيرَةٌ وَمِنْهَا تَأْكُلُونَ ۞ وَعَلَيْهَا وَعَلَى الْفُلْكِ تُحْمَلُونَ
۞ وَلَقَدْ أَرْسَلْنَا نُوحًا إِلَى قَوْمِهِ فَقَالَ يَا قَوْمِ اعْبُدُوا اللَّهَ
مَا لَكُم مِّنْ إِلَٰهٍ غَيْرُهُ أَفَلَا تَتَّقُونَ ۞ فَقَالَ الْمَلَأُ الَّذِينَ كَفَرُوا
مِن قَوْمِهِ مَا هَٰذَا إِلَّا بَشَرٌ مِّثْلُكُمْ يُرِيدُ أَن يَتَفَضَّلَ عَلَيْكُمْ وَلَوْ شَاءَ اللَّهُ
لَأَنزَلَ مَلَائِكَةً مَّا سَمِعْنَا بِهَٰذَا فِي آبَائِنَا الْأَوَّلِينَ ۞ إِنْ هُوَ
إِلَّا رَجُلٌ بِهِ جِنَّةٌ فَتَرَبَّصُوا بِهِ حَتَّى حِينٍ ۞ قَالَ رَبِّ
انصُرْنِي بِمَا كَذَّبُونِ ۞ فَأَوْحَيْنَا إِلَيْهِ أَنِ اصْنَعِ الْفُلْكَ
بِأَعْيُنِنَا وَوَحْيِنَا فَإِذَا جَاءَ أَمْرُنَا وَفَارَ التَّنُّورُ فَاسْلُكْ فِيهَا
مِن كُلٍّ زَوْجَيْنِ اثْنَيْنِ وَأَهْلَكَ إِلَّا مَن سَبَقَ عَلَيْهِ الْقَوْلُ
مِنْهُمْ وَلَا تُخَاطِبْنِي فِي الَّذِينَ ظَلَمُوا إِنَّهُم مُّغْرَقُونَ ۞

─────────⟐─────────

18. We send down from the sky water with a measure set by Us, and lodge it in the earth. We are most certainly able to withdraw it.[6]

19. And with it We cause to grow for you gardens of date-palms and vines, wherein are abundant, diverse fruits for you, and from which you eat and obtain some of your livelihood.

20. As well as a tree that grows from and in the lands around Mount Sinai,[7] yielding oil and a kind of relish for all to eat.

21. And in the cattle (feeding on the grass God brings forth with the water He sends down) there is a lesson for you. We give you to drink of that (milk) which is within their bodies; and you have many other benefits in them, and from them you obtain food.

22. And on them (on land) and on the ships (in the sea) you are carried.

23. Indeed, We sent Noah to his people as Messenger, and he said: "O my people! Worship God alone: you have no deity other than Him. Will you not, then, keep from disobedience to Him in reverence for Him and piety?"

24. The leading ones who disbelieved from among his people reacted, saying (among themselves and to each other): "This is but a mortal like you. He only wishes to gain superiority over you. Had God willed (to send us a Messenger to convey His Message), He would surely have sent down angels (to communicate His Message). Further, we have never heard of anything like this in the case of our forefathers of old.

25. "He is but a man in whom there is madness, so watch him for a while (to see) whether he will recover."

26. Noah prayed: "My Lord, help me because they have denied me!"

27. Thereupon We revealed to him: "Build the Ark (which We have described to you) under Our eyes and in accordance with Our instructions to be revealed (to you). Then finally, when Our command comes to pass and the boiler starts boiling over, take on board a pair of each kind of animal, as well as your family, except those of them against whom Our sentence (of destruction) has already been passed. Do not plead with Me for those people who have persisted in wrongdoing. They are bound to be drowned.

6. In several verses, the Qur'ān draws attention to water. This verse may be understood to mean both the seasonal rainfall and the water which God lodged in the earth during the creation of the universe. God provided the earth with water in a known, measured quantity that would suffice the needs of the earth for all time to come. The water that was so provided accumulated in the recesses of the earth, giving rise to seas, gulfs and subterraneous water. It is this accumulation of water which is kept rotating through the varying seasons and with the winds. The original source of water continues to be distributed through the rain, from snow-clad mountains, rivers, springs, and wells. This very accumulation of water enters into the process of creation and into the composition of a variety of things. Then it also becomes part of the wind and eventually returns to the same original water source. Thus, from the beginning of time until the present the total quantity of water has neither increased nor decreased in the world, not by as much as a single drop.

The distribution of water through the rains is dependent on the Divine Will and there are changes in that distribution owing to many instances of Divine Wisdom. In addition, since we cannot know exactly the time of rain before its signs appear, and rain is one of the most important embodiments of Divine mercy, the Almighty occasionally reminds us how great a blessing rain is through drought, and calls us to pray for it.

What is even more astonishing is that water is composed of two gases, namely hydrogen and oxygen, which were released only once in such a quantity and in the right proportions, allowing a vast quantity of water to be produced; this continues to fill the seas and oceans, with no fresh supply being added to it. So who is it that prevents hydrogen and oxygen from intermingling, even though both gases are found in the world? Who is it who prevents this mixture from happening, with the result being that not a drop of water has been added to the original reservoir of water? We also know that water evaporates into the air. Again, who is it that prevents the two gases from separating after this evaporation? Do atheists, materialists, and naturalists have any answers to these questions? Or can all this be satisfactorily explained by those who believe in a multiplicity of deities, who believe that there are separate deities for the wind and water, and for the heat and cold? (Extracted in part from al-Mawdūdī, 6: 90, note 17.) For another astonishing feature of water, see 2: 74, note 78.

7. The tree mentioned here is the olive tree. The Qur'ān mentions it as a tree growing in the lands around Mount Sinai; Mount Sinai must have been its natural habitat or the place where the best olives were produced, at least at the time when the verse was revealed.

فَإِذَا اسْتَوَيْتَ أَنتَ وَمَن مَّعَكَ عَلَى الْفُلْكِ فَقُلِ الْحَمْدُ
لِلَّهِ الَّذِي نَجَّانَا مِنَ الْقَوْمِ الظَّالِمِينَ ۝ وَقُل رَّبِّ أَنزِلْنِي مُنزَلًا
مُّبَارَكًا وَأَنتَ خَيْرُ الْمُنزِلِينَ ۝ إِنَّ فِي ذَٰلِكَ لَآيَاتٍ وَإِن كُنَّا
لَمُبْتَلِينَ ۝ ثُمَّ أَنشَأْنَا مِن بَعْدِهِمْ قَرْنًا آخَرِينَ ۝
فَأَرْسَلْنَا فِيهِمْ رَسُولًا مِّنْهُمْ أَنِ اعْبُدُوا اللَّهَ مَا لَكُم
مِّنْ إِلَٰهٍ غَيْرُهُ أَفَلَا تَتَّقُونَ ۝ وَقَالَ الْمَلَأُ مِن قَوْمِهِ الَّذِينَ كَفَرُوا
وَكَذَّبُوا بِلِقَاءِ الْآخِرَةِ وَأَتْرَفْنَاهُمْ فِي الْحَيَاةِ الدُّنْيَا مَا هَٰذَا إِلَّا
بَشَرٌ مِّثْلُكُمْ يَأْكُلُ مِمَّا تَأْكُلُونَ مِنْهُ وَيَشْرَبُ مِمَّا تَشْرَبُونَ ۝ وَلَئِنْ أَطَعْتُم
بَشَرًا مِّثْلَكُمْ إِنَّكُمْ إِذًا لَّخَاسِرُونَ ۝ أَيَعِدُكُمْ أَنَّكُمْ إِذَا مِتُّمْ وَكُنتُمْ تُرَابًا
وَعِظَامًا أَنَّكُم مُّخْرَجُونَ ۝ هَيْهَاتَ هَيْهَاتَ لِمَا تُوعَدُونَ ۝ إِنْ هِيَ إِلَّا
حَيَاتُنَا الدُّنْيَا نَمُوتُ وَنَحْيَا وَمَا نَحْنُ بِمَبْعُوثِينَ ۝ إِنْ هُوَ إِلَّا رَجُلٌ افْتَرَىٰ عَلَى
اللَّهِ كَذِبًا وَمَا نَحْنُ لَهُ بِمُؤْمِنِينَ ۝ قَالَ رَبِّ انصُرْنِي بِمَا
كَذَّبُونِ ۝ قَالَ عَمَّا قَلِيلٍ لَّيُصْبِحُنَّ نَادِمِينَ ۝
فَأَخَذَتْهُمُ الصَّيْحَةُ بِالْحَقِّ فَجَعَلْنَاهُمْ غُثَاءً فَبُعْدًا لِّلْقَوْمِ
الظَّالِمِينَ ۝ ثُمَّ أَنشَأْنَا مِن بَعْدِهِمْ قُرُونًا آخَرِينَ ۝

---

28. "Then, when you are seated in the Ark, you and those who are with you, say: 'All praise and gratitude are for God, Who has saved us from the wrongdoing people.'

29. "And pray: 'My Lord, let me land in a blessed place (in peace and safety and) with blessings from You. You are the Best to cause people to land in peace and safety'."[8]

30. Surely in that (exemplary story) are signs (manifesting the truth); and for sure We are ever trying (people).[9]

31. Then, after them, We brought forth another generation.

32. In time, We sent among them a Messenger from among themselves (with the message): "Worship God alone; you have no deity other than Him. Will you not, then, keep from disobedience to Him in reverence for Him and piety?"

33. The leading ones from among his people – who disbelieved, and denied the meeting of the Hereafter, and to whom We granted ease and comfort in the life of this world – said: "This is but a mortal like you, eating of what you eat of, and drinking of what you drink of.

34. "If you obey a mortal like yourselves, then you will surely be the losers.

35. "Does he promise you that, after you have died and become mere dust and bones, you will be brought forth (to a new life)?

36. "Far-fetched, utterly far-fetched, is what you are promised.

37. "There is no life beyond our present, worldly life. Some of us die (while others

are born,) and so life continues; and we are not raised from the dead.

38. "He is nothing but a man, fabricating falsehood in attribution to God; and we are not (going to) to believe in him."

39. Eventually, the Messenger invoked: "My Lord, help me because they deny me!"

40. (God) said: "In a little while, they are sure to be regretful."

41. So in consequence, the awful blast seized them as a judgment of God rightly fitted to their deserts, and We made them like the waste of dead plants carried by a flood and left on the coast once the water recedes. So away with the wrongdoing people!

42. Then, after them, We brought forth new generations (in succession).

8. For a detailed account of the events mentioned concerning the Prophet Noah's mission, particularly the boiling over of the boiler, and the Ark, see 11: 25–48 and the corresponding notes 10–14.

9. One of the most important instances of wisdom in God's putting people to test is that human beings need to be educated, matured, and perfected, and that by developing their minds and hearts and by developing their potential, they can rise from being potential humans to being true, perfected human beings. Through the testing of humankind, life is purified, it grows and is enriched. In short, through this testing, human beings reach the rank or position of being able to perform the function of vicegerency on the earth. In this testing, without the guidance of the Religion that God conveyed through the Prophets to guide humankind, success is not possible. However, the Religion is also a means of this testing.

344

مَا تَسْبِقُ مِنْ أُمَّةٍ أَجَلَهَا وَمَا يَسْتَأْخِرُونَ ۞ ثُمَّ أَرْسَلْنَا رُسُلَنَا
تَتْرَا كُلَّمَا جَاءَ أُمَّةً رَسُولُهَا كَذَّبُوهُ فَأَتْبَعْنَا بَعْضَهُمْ بَعْضًا
وَجَعَلْنَاهُمْ أَحَادِيثَ فَبُعْدًا لِقَوْمٍ لَا يُؤْمِنُونَ ۞ ثُمَّ أَرْسَلْنَا
مُوسَى وَأَخَاهُ هَارُونَ بِآيَاتِنَا وَسُلْطَانٍ مُبِينٍ ۞ إِلَى فِرْعَوْنَ
وَمَلَئِهِ فَاسْتَكْبَرُوا وَكَانُوا قَوْمًا عَالِينَ ۞ فَقَالُوا أَنُؤْمِنُ
لِبَشَرَيْنِ مِثْلِنَا وَقَوْمُهُمَا لَنَا عَابِدُونَ ۞ فَكَذَّبُوهُمَا فَكَانُوا مِنَ
الْمُهْلَكِينَ ۞ وَلَقَدْ آتَيْنَا مُوسَى الْكِتَابَ لَعَلَّهُمْ يَهْتَدُونَ ۞
وَجَعَلْنَا ابْنَ مَرْيَمَ وَأُمَّهُ آيَةً وَآوَيْنَاهُمَا إِلَى رَبْوَةٍ ذَاتِ قَرَارٍ
وَمَعِينٍ ۞ يَا أَيُّهَا الرُّسُلُ كُلُوا مِنَ الطَّيِّبَاتِ وَاعْمَلُوا صَالِحًا إِنِّي
بِمَا تَعْمَلُونَ عَلِيمٌ ۞ وَإِنَّ هَذِهِ أُمَّتُكُمْ أُمَّةً وَاحِدَةً وَأَنَا
رَبُّكُمْ فَاتَّقُونِ ۞ فَتَقَطَّعُوا أَمْرَهُمْ بَيْنَهُمْ زُبُرًا كُلُّ حِزْبٍ بِمَا
لَدَيْهِمْ فَرِحُونَ ۞ فَذَرْهُمْ فِي غَمْرَتِهِمْ حَتَّى حِينٍ ۞ أَيَحْسَبُونَ أَنَّمَا
نُمِدُّهُمْ بِهِ مِنْ مَالٍ وَبَنِينَ ۞ نُسَارِعُ لَهُمْ فِي الْخَيْرَاتِ بَلْ لَا يَشْعُرُونَ
۞ إِنَّ الَّذِينَ هُمْ مِنْ خَشْيَةِ رَبِّهِمْ مُشْفِقُونَ ۞ وَالَّذِينَ هُمْ بِآيَاتِ
رَبِّهِمْ يُؤْمِنُونَ ۞ وَالَّذِينَ هُمْ بِرَبِّهِمْ لَا يُشْرِكُونَ ۞

---

43. (What happened to all those generations proves that) no community can ever hasten on the end of its term, nor can they delay it (once it has been decided by God because of their beliefs and life-styles).[10]

44. We sent Our Messengers one after the other (each to a generation). Whenever their Messenger came to a community, they denied him, and in consequence We caused each community to follow the other to its doom, and reduced them to mere tales of the past. So away with a people who do not believe!

45. After all those Messengers (sent to the past generations that are now all extinct,) We sent Moses and his brother Aaron as Messengers with Our clear signs (miracles to support them) and a manifest authority (from Us),

46. To the Pharaoh and his chiefs. But they grew arrogant in the face of them, and demonstrated that they were a haughty, self-exalting people.

47. They said: "Shall we believe in two mortals like ourselves, when their people (the people of Moses and Aaron) are serving us in humility and obedience?"

48. They denied them, and they too eventually became of those who were destroyed.

49. (After their destruction) We granted Moses the Book so that his people might follow the right way.

50. We made the Son of Mary and his mother a miraculous sign (of Our Lordship and Power), and We provided for them ref-

uge on a lofty ground of comfort and security with a (water) spring.

51. O you Messengers! Partake of (God's) pure and wholesome bounties, and always act righteously. I have full knowledge of all that you do.

52. This community of yours is one single community of the same faith, and I am your Lord (Who creates, sustains, and protects you), so hold Me alone in fear and keep your duty to Me in piety.

53. But people, having broken up into groups, differed among themselves as regards the Religion, each group proudly rejoicing in the portion they have.

54. So (if they, despite all the evidence We have put forth in support of the truth of the Message that you, O Messenger, are conveying to them, still refuse to accept it), leave

them alone, immersed in their ignorance and heedlessness until an appointed time.

55. Do they think that by all the wealth and children We provide for them,

56. We but hasten to lavish on them all kinds of good? No, but they do not perceive (the reality of the matter).

57. While as for those who live in awe because of deep reverence for their Lord,

58. Who have renewed, ever-strengthening faith in their Lord's signs and Revelations,

59. Who never associate partners with their Lord,

---

10. For an explanation of this verse, see 7: 34, note 10.

وَالَّذِينَ يُؤْتُونَ مَا آتَوا وَّقُلُوبُهُمْ وَجِلَةٌ أَنَّهُمْ إِلَىٰ رَبِّهِمْ رَاجِعُونَ ۝ أُولَٰئِكَ يُسَارِعُونَ فِي الْخَيْرَاتِ وَهُمْ لَهَا سَابِقُونَ ۝ وَلَا نُكَلِّفُ نَفْسًا إِلَّا وُسْعَهَا وَلَدَيْنَا كِتَابٌ يَنطِقُ بِالْحَقِّ وَهُمْ لَا يُظْلَمُونَ ۝ بَلْ قُلُوبُهُمْ فِي غَمْرَةٍ مِّنْ هَٰذَا وَلَهُمْ أَعْمَالٌ مِّن دُونِ ذَٰلِكَ هُمْ لَهَا عَامِلُونَ ۝ حَتَّىٰ إِذَا أَخَذْنَا مُتْرَفِيهِم بِالْعَذَابِ إِذَا هُمْ يَجْأَرُونَ ۝ لَا تَجْأَرُوا الْيَوْمَ إِنَّكُم مِّنَّا لَا تُنصَرُونَ ۝ قَدْ كَانَتْ آيَاتِي تُتْلَىٰ عَلَيْكُمْ فَكُنتُمْ عَلَىٰ أَعْقَابِكُمْ تَنكِصُونَ ۝ مُسْتَكْبِرِينَ بِهِ سَامِرًا تَهْجُرُونَ ۝ أَفَلَمْ يَدَّبَّرُوا الْقَوْلَ أَمْ جَاءَهُم مَّا لَمْ يَأْتِ آبَاءَهُمُ الْأَوَّلِينَ ۝ أَمْ لَمْ يَعْرِفُوا رَسُولَهُمْ فَهُمْ لَهُ مُنكِرُونَ ۝ أَمْ يَقُولُونَ بِهِ جِنَّةٌ بَلْ جَاءَهُم بِالْحَقِّ وَأَكْثَرُهُمْ لِلْحَقِّ كَارِهُونَ ۝ وَلَوِ اتَّبَعَ الْحَقُّ أَهْوَاءَهُمْ لَفَسَدَتِ السَّمَاوَاتُ وَالْأَرْضُ وَمَن فِيهِنَّ بَلْ أَتَيْنَاهُم بِذِكْرِهِمْ فَهُمْ عَن ذِكْرِهِم مُّعْرِضُونَ ۝ أَمْ تَسْأَلُهُمْ خَرْجًا فَخَرَاجُ رَبِّكَ خَيْرٌ وَهُوَ خَيْرُ الرَّازِقِينَ ۝ وَإِنَّكَ لَتَدْعُوهُمْ إِلَىٰ صِرَاطٍ مُّسْتَقِيمٍ ۝ وَإِنَّ الَّذِينَ لَا يُؤْمِنُونَ بِالْآخِرَةِ عَنِ الصِّرَاطِ لَنَاكِبُونَ ۝

---

60. Who do whatever they do and give whatever they give in charity and for God's cause, with their hearts trembling at the thought that they are bound to turn to their Lord (remaining anxious, for they are unsure whether God will accept from them and be pleased with them)[11] –

61. It is those (illustrious ones) who hasten to do all kinds of virtuous deeds, and they are in a virtuous competition with one another in doing them.

62. (No one, especially those unbelievers, should think that there is something superhuman required of humanity. For) We do not burden any soul except within its capacity, and with Us is a record that speaks the truth (about the deeds, thoughts, and intentions of each individual). They will in no wise be wronged.

63. The fact is that the hearts of those unbelievers are utterly ignorant and heedless of all this, and apart from this, they have some evil deeds that they habitually commit (which prevent them from seeing and accepting the truth),

64. Until the time when We seize (them) with the punishment – those of them who have been lost in the pursuit of pleasures. They will then begin to groan for help.

65. "Stop groaning for help today; you are not to receive any help from Us!

66. "You know that My Revelations used to be recited to you, but you used to turn on your heels in aversion,

67. "Behaving arrogantly, and talking nonsense (about the Messenger and the Religion he conveys) in your nightly conversations."

68. Have they ever pondered over this Word (of God) or has there come to them something (completely novel in human history) which never came to their forefathers of old?

69. Or is it that they are unaware of their Messenger, and so they disavow him?

70. Or do they say that there is madness in him? No, he has brought them the truth, but most of them are disdainful of the truth.

71. Were the truth to follow their desires and caprices, the heavens and the earth and all those who live in them would certainly have gone to ruin. But We have brought to them whatever they must heed in life for their honor and happiness, and they turn away from that which will bring them honor and happiness.[12]

72. Or do you (O Messenger) ask them

for any payment? Whereas the reward of your Lord is the best and to everyone's good. He is the Provider, with the ultimate rank of providing and the Best to be sought as provider.

73. And certainly, you are calling them to a Straight Path.

74. Whereas, those who do not believe in the Hereafter are ever astray from the Path.

---

11. This is the state of a true believer. As stated in a *hadīth*, a true believer prays, fasts, and pays the *Zakāh*, and yet fears whether God will accept their deeds or not, forgive them and be pleased with them) (at-Tirmidhī, "Kitāb at-Tafsīr," 4; Ibn Mājah, "Kitāb az-Zuhd," 20). One of the best examples in this regard is 'Umar ibn al-Khaṭṭāb. Despite his great care in practicing Islam and his outstanding services in God's cause, he said, close to the time of his death: "If I am reckoned on the Day of Judgment as one whose good and evil deeds are equal, that will be enough for me." Hasan al-Baṣrī also says: "A believer obeys and yet remains fearful, whereas a hypocrite disobeys and is fearless" (al-Mawdūdī, 6: 108–109, note 54).

12. Almost all the unbelievers throughout history who opposed the Messengers or the truth which they brought from God did not base their opposition on any truth. For God is the Absolute Truth, and whatever He orders or establishes is the truth itself. The clearest example of this is the universe with whatever is in it.

We clearly see that as a whole, and in all its individual parts, the universe displays an evident order and an extraordinary concord. Everything in it is so exactly measured and proportioned that it announces *there is no deity but God*; it is He Who has set this measure and made all things in proportion and exactly commensurate with one another.

The mutual relationship between all things and the faultless artistry displayed in each, the connection among and between all things, such as, say, the eyes of a honeybee and an ant, and the sun and the solar system, demonstrate that the One Who created the sky with the stars is the same as He Who created the honeybee and the ant and their cells. In the language of all its creatures, the universe bears witness to the fact that *there is no deity but God*.

A compound's minutest particles or atoms, as well as the compounds one within another, are placed according to such delicate calculations that, for example, all the atoms or particles in the eye are interrelated with the other atoms of the eye and with all bodily systems and cells. If an atom were misplaced, existence would not be possible, or an abnormality or anomaly would be the result. We know that when just a single cell in the human body, out of nearly one hundred thousand billion cells, malfunctions, as in cancer, the result can be the death of the entire body.

A species' comprehensive disposition and the wide distribution of certain species, such as birds and fish, indicate that the Creator of one living being is the Creator of the entire species. The Pen which draws the lines of an individual's face and thus identifies or individualizes that person has to be able to see all the faces at the same time in order to make each one unique. Otherwise, individualization would be impossible. This requires that the Creator of an individual be the Creator of the human family and the species.

Everything is measured in exact proportions. Also, for the simplest example, as the fact that almost everyone has had a glimpse or clue of the future in dreams indicates, a universal Destiny, a Determining Power with absolute Knowledge, Will, and Wisdom that predetermines everything prevails in the universe. This negates chance. Again, all seeds and fully grown plants or trees indicate this universal Destiny or Determining Power. Due to this all-inclusive Destiny, everything is perfectly ordered and serves predetermined, evident purposes according to the form, characteristics, and capacities of each thing. Consider the human body, with all its characteristics and limbs. Each one has been built and shaped according to its purpose, thus signifying the Destiny that has determined these purposes and structure. According to Destiny's plan, the Power puts into "writing" the meanings established and kept by the Knowledge. The Destiny that has preplanned all things and the Destiny that records the life-histories of all things indicate the necessary existence of Him, Whose Pen of Destiny and Decree has drawn the outlines of all things.

All these facts are only some of the innumerable universal facts that demonstrate the Existence and Unity of a single, unique Creator, Orderer, and Ruler, as well as proving that it is not possible for different hands to interfere in the universe, whether for its existence or for its maintenance. Everyone should acknowledge that it is much easier for one creator to create everything than for many creators to create one thing. The interference of many blind hands in creating something only increases the blindness. For example, if the creation of a honeybee were not attributed to the Power of a Necessarily Existent Being, everything that exists must have participated in its existence. The creation of a minute particle or a hair, if attributed to many agents, like material causes, would be as difficult as the creation of a mountain. A commander can organize and direct a military company much better than the soldiers themselves or multiple commanders could. Apparent material causes have no consciousness or will, and most are subject to nominal (not material) "laws" that are perceived only after the effects have been brought about. Compared to their causes, effects are extraordinary and display splendid artistry. For example, a cell's formation and its relation with all other cells and the body are so complex that it requires much more knowledge, skill, comprehensive will, and power to create it than can be found in all the members of creation. Only a Creator with boundless Power can be the real agent. Material causes and means are only excuses that allow hu-

man beings to contemplate that there is some space for human agency. We speak about the material causes and means because most people cannot discern the beauty and wisdom behind events, and they complain of and object to God. To divert such complaints from God, causes are placed as an intervening veil (between people and God's acts). However, those who see the real beauty and wisdom in events know the truth of what is going on. In short, God's Dignity and Grandeur require apparent causes and means to prevent complaints and to hide, from those who reason superficially, the Hand of Power's involvement in certain seemingly insignificant or vile things and affairs. At the same time, God's Unity and Glory require that these apparent causes have no part in either the creation or disposition of things. In fact, what we call "laws" are manifestations of the Divine Knowledge, Command, and Will.

Humankind are the most capable part of creation, the most eminent of causes that is equipped with consciousness and free will. However, our role, even in our own actions, is very small. This being the case, what part can inanimate objects have in creating and operating the universe?

In short, the existence and maintenance of the universe clearly show that everything is based on an absolute truth which comes from the One Who is the Absolute Truth. If the truth, which is responsible for the magnificent order, harmony, and proportion in the universe, were to follow the desires, caprices, or even the intellect of humanity, then the entire universe would long ago have gone to ruin. When humankind attempt to order their own life, we see that only disorder and chaos ensue, as witnessed by history. Harmony, happiness, order, and proportion require universal knowledge; this must encompass the entire universe, with all its parts and humanity in all its aspects, down to the being of every person, as well as all of time, with the past, present, and future. It is clear that human beings cannot do this.

346   سُورَةُ الْمُؤْمِنُونَ   ٣٤٦

وَلَوْ رَحِمْنَاهُمْ وَكَشَفْنَا مَا بِهِم مِّن ضُرٍّ لَّلَجُّوا فِي طُغْيَانِهِمْ يَعْمَهُونَ ۞ وَلَقَدْ أَخَذْنَاهُم بِالْعَذَابِ فَمَا اسْتَكَانُوا لِرَبِّهِمْ وَمَا يَتَضَرَّعُونَ ۞ حَتَّىٰ إِذَا فَتَحْنَا عَلَيْهِم بَابًا ذَا عَذَابٍ شَدِيدٍ إِذَا هُمْ فِيهِ مُبْلِسُونَ ۞ وَهُوَ الَّذِي أَنشَأَ لَكُمُ السَّمْعَ وَالْأَبْصَارَ وَالْأَفْئِدَةَ قَلِيلًا مَّا تَشْكُرُونَ ۞ وَهُوَ الَّذِي ذَرَأَكُمْ فِي الْأَرْضِ وَإِلَيْهِ تُحْشَرُونَ ۞ وَهُوَ الَّذِي يُحْيِي وَيُمِيتُ وَلَهُ اخْتِلَافُ اللَّيْلِ وَالنَّهَارِ أَفَلَا تَعْقِلُونَ ۞ بَلْ قَالُوا مِثْلَ مَا قَالَ الْأَوَّلُونَ ۞ قَالُوا أَإِذَا مِتْنَا وَكُنَّا تُرَابًا وَعِظَامًا أَإِنَّا لَمَبْعُوثُونَ ۞ لَقَدْ وُعِدْنَا نَحْنُ وَآبَاؤُنَا هَـٰذَا مِن قَبْلُ إِنْ هَـٰذَا إِلَّا أَسَاطِيرُ الْأَوَّلِينَ ۞ قُل لِّمَنِ الْأَرْضُ وَمَن فِيهَا إِن كُنتُمْ تَعْلَمُونَ ۞ سَيَقُولُونَ لِلَّهِ قُلْ أَفَلَا تَذَكَّرُونَ ۞ قُلْ مَن رَّبُّ السَّمَاوَاتِ السَّبْعِ وَرَبُّ الْعَرْشِ الْعَظِيمِ ۞ سَيَقُولُونَ لِلَّهِ قُلْ أَفَلَا تَتَّقُونَ ۞ قُلْ مَن بِيَدِهِ مَلَكُوتُ كُلِّ شَيْءٍ وَهُوَ يُجِيرُ وَلَا يُجَارُ عَلَيْهِ إِن كُنتُمْ تَعْلَمُونَ ۞ سَيَقُولُونَ لِلَّهِ قُلْ فَأَنَّىٰ تُسْحَرُونَ ۞

──────────⦂◉⦂──────────

75. If We have mercy on them and remove from them the harm afflicting them, for sure they will persist in their rebellion, blindly wandering on.

76. For indeed We have seized them with the punishment (of famine), and yet, they have not bowed down to their Lord, nor do they invoke Him humbly.

77. Finally We open to them a gate of severe punishment and look, they are plunged into utter despair and sorrow.[13]

78. He it is Who has made for you (the faculty of) hearing, and eyes, and hearts.[14] Scarcely do you give thanks.

79. He it is Who has brought forth and made you grow up on earth, and to Him you will be gathered.

80. He it is Who gives life and causes to die, and the alternation of night and day (with their periods shortening and lengthening) occurs in obedience to Him (and for the purposes He has established). Will you not, then, reason and understand (that there cannot be another deity besides God)?

81. (Instead of using their reason), they only speak as the former (disbelieving) peoples spoke.

82. They say, "What! after we have died and become dust and bones, will we then be raised from the dead?

83. "We were already promised such things, we and our forefathers. These are no more than the fables of the ancients."

84. Say: "To whom belongs the earth and whoever is on it? (Tell me,) if you have any knowledge?"

85. They could not help but acknowledge: "To God."[15] Say: "Will you not, then, reflect and be mindful?"[16]

86. Say: "Who is the Lord of the seven heavens and the Lord of the Supreme Throne (He Who rules the whole universe and sustains all that live in it)?"

87. They could not help but acknowledge: "These belong to God, too." Say: "Will you not, then, keep from disobedience to God in reverence for Him and piety?"

88. Say: "In Whose Hand is the absolute ownership and dominion of all things, and He protects and grants asylum, whereas against Him no asylum is available, and Himself never needs protection? (Tell me,) if you have any knowledge."

89. They could not help but acknowledge: "God exclusively." Say: "How, then, can you be so deluded?"[17]

13. As reported in al-Bukhārī ("Kitāb al-Istisghā," 2), when God's Messenger, upon him be peace and blessings, encountered severe and harsh opposition, he prayed to God: "O God, help me against them with a seven-year famine as You helped Joseph with a seven-year famine." As a result, a severe famine took hold of the Makkans, to the extent that they had to eat carrion. Verses 75 and 76 refer to this famine, while verse 77 refers to death as the gate opened on or the way that leads to the severe punishment of the Hereafter.

14. Hearing and seeing are two important senses with which people perceive the outer world and from which they learn. What they receive from the outer world is made into knowledge by the heart (fuād), which in English may also be rendered as "the mind." The Qur'ān uses the power of hearing as a singular noun, while the power of seeing and that of the heart are plural nouns. The reason why the Qur'ān uses the singular for the power of hearing while the others are plural is that it refers to the Revelation, or God, as the source of knowledge that comes via the ears. Whereas, the visual perceptions people have and their way of understanding and interpreting them through the hearts or minds may differ from person to person, and the objects of seeing and the material to be used by the hearts to form knowledge are infinitely abundant.

15. Any person who is concerned with true knowledge and the power of thinking cannot help but acknowledge that the universe with whatever is in it has been created and belongs to God exclusively as His creation, unless one is prejudiced and purposeful refractory, and unless there are some other factors such as arrogance, wrongdoing, and self-centeredness which prevent them from believing.

16. If it is God Who has created the earth and whoever is on it, and Who has absolute authority over them as their Master and Lord, then why will He not bring them back to life after their death if He so wills? Is the One Who has created the earth and whoever is on it, One Who has absolute power to create something from nothing and One who deals death, not able to restore the dead to life?

17. At first glance, it seems as if all these questions are asked to those who have some knowledge of the One God Who creates and governs the universe, but who still associate partners with Him in ordering their lives. However, the answers demanded are dependent on knowledge. This means that true knowledge – knowledge acquired through an objective study of the universe – must inevitably conclude that there is only One God Who creates and governs the entire universe, and has absolute authority over everything. So what falls to human beings is to submit to Him in governing their lives, too. As true knowledge acknowledges this, anyone who listens to the message of the universe and the voice of their conscience will also acknowledge the same truth. But if they are deluded by false hopes, carnal desires, arrogance and selfishness, ignorance, ideological or quasi-religious prejudices or predispositions, people may follow ways that mislead them.

94. "Then, do not include me, my Lord, among those wrongdoing people!"

95. Surely We are absolutely able to let you witness the fulfillment of what We have promised them to suffer (and save you from).

96. (But whatever they may say or do) repel the evil (done to you and committed against your mission) with the best (of what you can do).[18] We know best all that they falsely attribute to Us.

97. And say: "My Lord! I seek refuge in You from the promptings and provocations of the satans (of the jinn and humankind especially in my relations with people, while I am performing my mission).

98. "I seek refuge in You, O my Lord, lest they be present with me."

99. (Those who persist in their evil ways will not cease from their false attributions to God, and from their harsh reaction to you) until when death comes to one of them, and then he implores: "O my Lord! Please, let me return to life,

100. "That I may act righteously with respect to whatever I have left undone in the world." No, never! It is merely a word that he utters over and over again. Before those (who are dead) is an intermediate world (of the grave, where they will stay) until the Day when they will be raised up.[19]

101. Then, when the Trumpet (of Resurrection) is blown, there will no longer be any ties of kinship among them (which will be of any avail), nor will they ask about one another (as everyone will be too engrossed in their own plight to think of others).

102. (Balances are set up) and those whose scales (of good deeds) are heavy – they are the prosperous.

90. The fact is that We have conveyed to them the truth but for sure they are the liars (in their assertions, denial of the pillars of faith, and against their own selves).

91. God has never taken to Himself a child, nor is there any deity along with Him; otherwise each deity would surely have sought absolute independence with his creatures under his authority, and they would surely have tried to overpower one another. All-Glorified is God, in that He is far above what they attribute to Him,

92. The Knower of the Unseen and the witnessed (all that lies in the hidden and visible realms and beyond and within the reach of any created being's perception), and absolutely exalted is He above all that they associate with Him as partners.

93. Say: "My Lord, if You let me witness the fulfillment of what they have been promised (to suffer),

103. While those whose scales (of good deeds) are light – they will be those who have ruined their own selves, in Hell abiding.

104. The Fire will scorch their faces, their lips being displaced and their jaws protruding.

18. As this order pertains to the way of repelling the evil done to a Muslim personally, it also pertains to how the Muslims must respond to the evils committed while they are practicing Islam and trying to communicate it to others. We cannot act with feelings of vengeance; we cannot follow our desires and act in the way we wish. Whatever we do must be for the purpose of serving the cause of Islam in the best possible way and for winning the hearts of others in its favor.

19. The grave is an intermediate world between this world and the next. The dead stay there until the Day of Resurrection. The Messenger says that the grave is either a garden from among the Gardens of Paradise or a pit from among the pits of Hell (at-Tirmidhī, "Ṣifat al-Qiyāmah," 26). The deeds of human beings take forms in the world of the grave peculiar to it, and the dead live a life resembling either Paradise or Hell, each according to their rank.

After burial, the spirit waits in the intermediate world between this one and the Hereafter. Although the body decomposes, its essential particles (called *'ajb adh-dhanab*, which literally means coccyx, in a *hadīth*) do not rot. We do not know whether *'ajb adh-dhanab* is a person's genes or something else. Regardless of this ambiguity, however, the spirit continues its relations with the body through it. God will make this part, which is formed of the body's essential particles, atoms, or all its other particles already dispersed in the soil, conducive to eternal life during the final destruction and rebuilding of the universe. He also will use it to re-create us on the Day of Judgment.

The intermediate world is the realm where the spirit feels the "breath" of the bliss of Paradise or the punishment of Hell. If we led a virtuous life in the world, our good deeds (e.g., prayers, recitations, acts of charity) will appear as amiable fellows. Also, windows onto heavenly scenes will be opened for us and our grave will become like a garden of Paradise. However, if some of our sins still remain unpardoned, regardless of how virtuous we were, we may suffer some punishment in the intermediate world until we become deserving of Paradise. Unbelievers who indulged in sin will be met by their deeds, which will assume the forms of bad fellows and vermin. They will see scenes of Hell, and their graves will become like a pit of Hell.

Martyrs enjoy a higher degree of life in the grave than non-martyrs who have died. Since martyrs have sacrificed their life in His way, they do not feel the pangs of death or know that they are dead. Instead, they consider themselves as having been transferred to a better world and they enjoy perfect happiness. On the other hand, the dead are aware that they are dead (although their spirits are eternal) and those who believed and did righteous deeds among them experience a lesser degree of pleasure in the intermediate life than that enjoyed by martyrs.

Death is a change of residence and a discharge from worldly duties; the spirit is set free. Death is not annihilation into non-existence. This degree of life has been established clearly by facts that have been repeatedly observed; for example, the spirits of some godly persons appear in their human (material) forms and are seen by those who have insight into hidden truths. Another proof is the deceased's ability to communicate with us while we are dreaming or awake.

Almost everyone, with the exception of the Prophets, who are sinless, may suffer in the grave to a certain extent, because of the sins which were not forgiven while they were in the world. However, just as any suffering in the world serves as a means of forgiveness for the believers, any suffering in the grave also causes some of their sins to be forgiven. If there are still sins that have been left unpardoned, the suffering that this person will have to experience in the other worlds of the Hereafter, such as the Supreme Gathering Place, the Balance, which is the world where the records of people's deeds will be laid open and dealt out, the Bridge, and the Heights (see 7: 46, note 12) will serve as purgatory.

110. "You used to take them in mockery, so much so that your hostilities to them caused you to forget My remembrance, and you simply persisted in laughing at them.

111. "But look, today I have rewarded them for what they endured patiently, so that they are those who are the triumphant."

112. (God) says: "For how many years did you stay on earth?"

113. They say: "We stayed for a day or part of a day. Ask of those who are able to keep count of this."

114. Says He: "You stayed but for a short while, if only you had known (how short it was to be and acted accordingly)!

115. "Or did you think that We created you in vain (so that you should devote all your time to play and entertainment), and that you would not be brought back to Us?"

116. Absolutely exalted is God, the Supreme Sovereign, the Absolute Truth and Ever-Constant. There is no deity but He, the Lord of the Supreme Throne of Nobility and Munificence.[20]

117. Whoever asserts the existence of another deity to worship along with God, for which it is inconceivable for him to have any evidence, will certainly be questioned by his Lord. Surely the unbelievers will not prosper.

118. Say: "O my Lord, forgive me and have mercy on me (always treat me with Your forgiveness and mercy), for You are the Best of the merciful."

105. "Were not My Revelations recited to you, and you used to deny them?"

106. They will say: "Our Lord! Our wretchedness (which we ourselves provoked upon ourselves) prevailed over us, and we were people lost in error.

107. "Our Lord! Take us out of this (suffering). Then, if we ever revert to evil, we will indeed be wrongdoers."

108. "Away with you into it! No longer address Me!"

109. "There was among My servants a party who would pray, 'Our Lord! We have believed, so forgive us, and have mercy on us, for You are the Best of the merciful.'

20. For the Supreme Throne, see *sūrah* 2: 28, note 28; *sūrah* 7: 54, note: 13; *sūrah* 17: 42, note 19.

SŪRAH 24

AN-NŪR (THE LIGHT)

Madīnah period

Sūrat an-Nūr was revealed in the sixth year of the *Hijrah* after the campaign against the tribe of Banū al-Muṣṭaliq. It is composed of 64 verses. In the context of declaring the chastity and innocence of 'Â'ishah, the Prophet's wife, in the face of an ugly campaign of slander against her, it lays down the punishments for illicit sexual intercourse and slander. The *sūrah* also contains rules concerning relations between the sexes, and members of a family and society, as well as discussing the relationships between the Prophet and his wives and other believers. It makes clear certain ethical values that are to be observed in social life, as well as indicating rules concerned with the apparel of women.

In the Name of God, the All-Merciful, the All-Compassionate.

1. (This is) a *sūrah* which We have sent down and made obligatory (the observance of the rules therein); and in it We have sent down clear explanations (of the truth about belief and unbelief) and instructions (concerning human life), so that you may reflect and be mindful.

2. The fornicatress and the fornicator[1] – flog each of them with a hundred stripes;[2/3] and do not let pity for them hold you back from carrying out God's law, if you truly believe in God and the Last Day;[4] and let a group of believers witness their punishment.[5]

3. A fornicator (one notorious for indulgence in illicit sexual relations) is not to marry other than a fornicatress (a woman notorious for indulgence in illicit sexual relations) or an idolatress, and fornicatress – only a fornicator or an idolater is to take her in wedlock. Acting the other way is forbidden to the believers.[6]

4. Those who accuse chaste, honorable women (of illicit sexual relations) but do not produce four male witnesses (who will witness that they personally saw the act being committed): flog them with eighty stripes, and do not accept from them any testimony ever after. They are indeed transgressors,

5. Except those of them who repent thereafter and mend their ways. For surely God is All-Forgiving, All-Compassionate.[7]

6. As for those who accuse their own wives of adultery but have no witnesses except themselves, such a person must testify four times swearing by God in each oath that he is indeed speaking the truth.

7. And the fifth time, that God's curse be upon him if he is lying.

8. But the punishment will be averted from the wife if she testifies four times by swearing by God in each oath that the man is surely telling a lie,

9. And the fifth time, that the wrath (condemnation) of God be upon her if the man is speaking the truth.[8]

10. Were it not for God's grace and favor on you, and His mercy, and that God is One Who opens a way to repentance and returns it with liberal forgiveness and additional reward, and All-Wise, (you could not resolve your problems justly and wisely).[9]

---

1. The Qur'ān uses the same term, zinā, for both fornication and adultery. Whether the partners are married or unmarried, the Qur'ān considers every kind of illicit sexual intercourse as being zinā. However, it distinguishes between the punishments to be inflicted.

Adultery and fornication are considered sins in all religions. The Bible orders the death sentence for both the adulterer and the adulteress (Leviticus, 20: 10; Deuteronomy, 22: 22). However, the Qur'ānic definition of adultery is very different from the Biblical definition. Zinā, according to the Qur'ān, is the involvement of a man and a woman, whether married or not, in an extramarital affair. The Bible only considers the extramarital affair of a married woman to be adultery (zinā) (Leviticus, 20: 10; Deuteronomy, 22: 22; Proverbs, 6: 20–35; 7: 1–27).

According to the Biblical definition, if a married man sleeps with an unmarried woman, this is simply a case of fornication. A man's sleeping with an unmarried woman is not considered a crime at all, irrespective of whether the man has a wife or not. The Talmud's command related to this case is:

If a man seduces a virgin who is not pledged to be married to another and sleeps with her, he must pay the bride-price, and she shall be his wife. If her father absolutely refuses to give her to him, he must still pay the bride-price for virgins (Exodus 22: 16-17), which is fifty shekels of silver to be paid to the virgin's father (Deuteronomy. 22: 28-29). However, if the virgin is a daughter of a priest (rabbi), the man is to be hanged until dead, whereas the girl is to be burned alive. (Everyman's Talmud, 319–320)

The Judaic commandment is almost identical with the Hindu code. But, in Hinduism, if the girl belongs to a higher caste and the man is of a lower one, the girl should be driven away from her home and the limbs of the man amputated (Dharma Shastra, ch. 8, 365–366). If the girl is a Brahmin, the punishment is to burn the man alive (Ibid., 377).

According to the Bible (Judaic Law), the crime of adultery is committed only when a man sleeps with a married woman. In this case the man is considered an adulterer, whether he is married or not, and the woman is considered an adulteress. In short, adultery is any illicit sexual intercourse involving a married woman. The extramarital affair of a married man is not itself a crime in the Bible. The reason why this is so, according to Encyclopedia Judaica, is that the wife was considered to be the husband's possession and adultery constituted a violation of his exclusive right to her; the wife, as the husband's possession had no such rights on him (Jeffrey H. Togay, "Adultery," Encyclopaedia Judaica, 2, col. 313. Also, see Judith Plaskow, Standing Again at Sinai: Judaism from a Feminist Perspective, 170–177.)

That is, if a man has sexual intercourse with a married woman, he is violating the property of another man and thus he should be punished.

To the present day in Israel, if a married man indulges in an extramarital affair with an unmarried woman, his children by that woman are considered to be legitimate. But, if a married woman has an affair with another man, whether married or not, her children by that man are illegitimate and are forbidden to marry any other Jews, except converts and other bastards. This ban is handed down to the children's descendants for ten generations, until the taint of adultery has presumably weakened (Lesley Hazleton, *Israeli Women, The Reality Behind the Myths*, 41–42).Other Biblical legal provisions pertaining to unlawful sexual relations are as follows:

If a man sleeps with a woman who is a slave girl promised to another man, but who has not been ransomed or given her freedom, there must be due punishment. Yet they are not to be put to death, because she has not been freed. (*Leviticus*, 19: 20)

If a man happens to meet in a town a virgin pledged to be married and he sleeps with her, you shall take both of them to the gate of that town and stone them to death – the girl because she was in a town and did not scream for help, and the man because he violated another man's wife. You must purge the evil from among you. But if out in the country a man happens to meet a girl pledged to be married and rapes her, only the man who has done this shall die. (*Deuteronomy*, 22: 23–26)

In Christianity, although the Old Testament is accepted along with the New Testament as being canonical Scripture, if sexual relations take place between an unmarried man and an unmarried woman, it is certainly a sin, but it is not a cognizable offence. However, if either or both of the partners are married, their sexual relations are considered as being a cognizable offence. Nonetheless, what makes the act a sin is the violation of the marriage contract, rather than the mere fact of unlawful sex. The only legal consequence of such an act is that the wife of the guilty man might secure a separation from him by charging her husband with infidelity. The same is also true of a man whose wife has engaged in sexual relations outside of her marriage covenant. In addition, the husband also has the right to claim damages from the man who subjected his wife to adultery.

The modern Western legal enactments in regard to this question are based on Christian concepts. According to these laws, fornication is regarded at most as a blemish, but not a cognizable offence unless one party has resorted to the use of force. As for having sexual intercourse with someone else's married partner, the aggrieved party can file for a divorce from the offending party.

Islam regards the act of any unlawful sexual intercourse as a crime in itself. If such an act is committed by a married person, the offence becomes more severe. The severity is due to the fact that a married person still resorts to unlawful means to satisfy their sexual urges while they can satisfy it by lawful means, i.e. within their marriage.

Unlawful sex is viewed by Islam as a crime which, if no measures are taken to curb it, strikes at the very root of human personality, family and society. Both the survival of the human race and the continuity of human collective existence make it imperative that the sexual relations between men and women are confined to their lawful forms alone. Just as eating and drinking are not indulged in for their own sake by a healthy individual, but rather for the continuation of life, so too, the sexual urge has been granted to humankind to continue their existence on earth. Therefore, the pleasure in its satisfaction is a sort of advance payment, not the goal in itself. In order to protect humankind from the harmful effects of unlawful sex, Islam does not confine itself to legal sanctions alone. It also seeks, through the spiritual, moral, and social values it promotes and the principles it has laid down, to almost completely close the door to adultery and fornication, while leaving some room for human free will. Human beings are tried in this world so as to develop their inborn capacities and to improve the world according to the standards God has established, and thereby earn a degree of perfection worthy of the eternal life of bliss (Mostly from al-Mawdūdī, 6: 149–159).

In addition to inculcating in our hearts the love and fear of God at one and the same time, and to giving us an awareness of the eternal life, which will be lived in either Paradise or Hell, and to perfecting its followers both spiritually and morally, Islam takes every step to make marriage easy and convenient so that lineages will not be confounded through unlawful sex. Also, if either party to the marriage finds the other incompatible, they may resort to divorce.

Islam also seeks to remove factors which prompt or provoke people into illegitimate sexual relations or which provide opportunities for engaging in it. It forbids all kinds of obscenity, as well as free mixing of the sexes, ordering women to cover themselves and forbidding them to parade their charms in public. It also orders both sexes to lower their gaze when they encounter one another.

Islam aims to purify individual persons and society. The person and society it seeks to encourage and enable is like a healthy body; one who engages in crimes like unlawful sex, murder, theft and robbery, like a gangrenous organ or a cancer in the body, is a harm and danger to individual persons and to society. Just as one seeks first prevention and then treatment for every ailment of the body, so too Islam seeks to prevent crime, and for what has not been prevented it prescribes and applies a particular method of responding. (For a detailed discussion of Islamic penal law, see *sūrah* 2, note: 131; *sūrah* 4, note: 6.)

2. The punishment legislated for a man or woman who fornicates is a hundred stripes. The original word used for stripe is *jaldah*, derived from *jild*, which means skin. So all linguists and commentators on the Qur'ān consider it to mean that the effect of flogging must be confined to the skin and therefore not cut the flesh. The whip to be used should be an average one, neither too thick nor too thin, and the act of flogging should be of average intensity. Caliph 'Umar, may God be pleased with him, used to direct the flogger: "Strike in such manner that your armpit is not revealed" (al-Jassās, 3: 45).

Other conditions for flogging can be found in books of Islamic law.

3. As pointed out above, the punishment of a hundred lashes is given to unmarried persons who are guilty of unlawful sexual intercourse. This is evident from the relevant Qur'ānic verses, including the one discussed here. The first verses concerning unlawful sex are those found in *Sūrat an-Nisā': Such of your women as have committed indecency (adultery), there must be four male witnesses of you who (having seen them in the act) will testify against them (within one succeeding month in towns and six succeeding months in the rural areas). If they do bear witness, then confine those women to their houses until death takes them away or God opens some way for them. When two of you have committed it, then punish them both by scolding and beating; but if they are remorseful and repent, and make amends, then withdraw from them. Assuredly, God is He Who accepts repentance and returns it with liberal forgiveness, All-Compassionate* (4: 15–16).

When these two verses were revealed as a step toward the decisive banning and prevention of any kind of unlawful sex, Islam prescribed that the partners guilty of such acts should be scolded and beaten and that women should be kept in their houses to prevent prostitution. The statement *or God opens some way for them*, implied that a new legislation would come. This new legislation was the command to lash the unmarried partners with a whip 100 times. The punishment for the married was established by the Sunnah.

Islam has laid down certain conditions for establishing the fact of the crime of *zinā* (adultery and fornication), which is then liable to punishment. These conditions can also be found in relevant books. For example, see al-Mawdūdī, 6: 166–173.

4. God warns believers against any misplaced compassion that would prevent them from enforcing the punishments He has legislated. No one can ever be more compassionate toward any creature than its Creator.

It is true that everything in the universe speaks of compassion and promises compassion, and because of this the universe can be considered to be a symphony of compassion. Human beings have a responsibility to show compassion to all beings; this is a requirement of being human. The more a person displays compassion, the more exalted they become, while the more they resort to wrongdoing, oppression, and cruelty, the more they are disgraced and humiliated, and bring shame upon their kind.

We heard from the Prophet how compassion enabled a prostitute to enter the way to Paradise because, out of compassion, she gave water to a poor dog dying of thirst, whilst another woman was condemned to enter the way leading to the torments of Hell because she tormented a cat, neither feeding it nor letting it feed itself until it died of hunger (al-Bukhārī, "al-Anbiyā," 54).

However, compassion, like everything else, must be balanced. We can see an example of how such a balance works in the water we drink. Oxygen and hydrogen, when mixed in the proper ratio, form one of the substances most vital to life. However, when this ratio changes, each element resumes its original combustible identity. Likewise, it is of great importance to apportion the amount of compassion and to know who deserves it. Compassion for a wolf sharpens its appetite, and not being content with what it has received, it demands even more. Compassion for a rebel makes them more aggressive, encouraging them to offend against others. It would not be appropriate to have compassion for one who takes sadistic pleasure in poisoning others. So we must place compassion in the right place and never claim to be more compassionate than the All-Compassionate One.

If someone alters God's laws in consideration of the culprit's social position, this is surely the very worst kind of offence. The Messenger declared: "O people! One of the reasons why some communities before you perished is that when a respectable person of the community committed theft, people spared him, and punished others because of their weaknesses" (al-Bukhārī, "Ḥudūd," 11; Muslim, "Ḥudūd," 8).

5. The punishment for zinā should be carried out publicly at least before four persons. The main advantage to doing so is that it prevents those in authority from acting with undue harshness or leniency. Such a stipulation secures the enforcement of the punishment as required by the Law. It also arouses in the culprit a feeling of shame and helps to deter them from repeating the same crime, as well as serving as a lesson for others.

6. A believing man or woman cannot marry a woman or man who is known for indulging in zinā – i.e., one who has been punished for this crime and thereafter has not repented or mended their ways, who is morally dissolute and ignores the evil involved in this crime. Acting the other way cannot be compatible with faith. So it is obvious that this injunction applies to those who persist in their evil ways, not those who repent and mend their ways after some lapse. Hence, if someone who committed unlawful sexual intercourse in the past later on marries, this does not mean that the relationship between the spouses is unlawful. It is dependent on whether or not the offender has truly repented and refrains from committing the same crime again.

This verse in no way suggests that a sexually deviant Muslim can marry a polytheist, or that such a marriage is legitimate. Rather, the purpose of the verse is to stress that unlawful sex is an extremely evil act and that a Muslim guilty of it is no longer worthy of having matrimonial relations with people of good character in the Muslim society; choosing a person notorious for sexual immorality as a marriage partner is a sin and is forbidden.

7. This commandment applies also to cases where a woman accuses a man of unlawful sex. The severity of the punishment as well as the requirement of four witnesses, while two witnesses are considered sufficient in all other criminal and civil suits, show the importance of the matter and aim at preventing idle talk and gossip about people's honor and chastity. Islam severely condemns both unlawful sex and the ungrounded accusation of others. Even if one observes someone actually indulging in unlawful sex, one should not publicize it. This prevents corruption from spreading. If four persons observe the act or one (a husband or wife) can get four witnesses (to observe the act), they may report the matter to the author-

ities concerned, but should not publicize it. Islam aims at ensuring both pure persons and a pure society.

It should also be noted here that from a legal point of view everyone is innocent until conclusive proof to the contrary has been produced; so too must every woman be considered chaste and honorable.

If one repents and mends one's ways after having accused a chaste woman of unlawful sex without producing four witnesses to the unlawful act, this person is no longer regarded as a transgressor. However, this does not void the prescribed punishment of 80 stripes, and any testimony will not be accepted from such a person ever again. God's forgiveness and compassion apply only to one's being sinful in His sight, not to legal matters.

8. This procedure is called *li'ān* (oath of condemnation and mutual cursing.) When a man accuses his wife of adultery, he must testify four times and swear by God. The fifth time he must invoke God's curse upon himself if he is lying.

If a man accuses his wife or disowns the paternity of a child, the wife has the right to seek the intervention of the court and have her husband make such an oath. In this respect, her rights are the same as her husband's.

A few cases of *li'ān* took place during the time of the Messenger, upon him be peace and blessings. He first mentioned the command God had given to the husband and added: "Are you aware that God's punishment in the Hereafter is much more grievous than the one in this life?" The husband answered in the affirmative, yet the wife totally denied the charge, so the Messenger invited both to make an oath. First the husband rose and four times swore that his accusation was true. While he was

doing this, the Messenger repeatedly warned him: "God knows that one of you is certainly a liar. Will neither of you repent?" Before the husband went on to state that if he was lying, God's wrath (condemnation) should fall upon him, those present told him: "Fear God. Punishment in this life is lighter than that in the next. This fifth oath will incur God's punishment on you." The husband took the fifth oath without hesitation.

The wife underwent the same procedure. Before the fifth oath, she hesitated a little, but concluded: "I will not bring lasting dishonor to my tribe." So saying, she took the final oath.

The Messenger effected a separation between them and resolved that the child whom she had recently conceived would be known as her child, not as the child of her husband (al-*Bukhārī*, "Kitāb at-Tafsīr, Sūrat an-Nūr," 3). The husband and the child could not inherit from each other. The child and its mother would inherit from each other. Yet no one would be able to accuse her of being unchaste or her child of being illegitimate.

If the husband who accused his wife of adultery refrains from taking the oaths, he will be imprisoned until he confesses that he has leveled a false charge and when he does, he will be punished with the punishment of false accusation (*qadhf*), which is mentioned in verse 4 above. If the wife declines to take the oaths, she is imprisoned until she takes the oaths or confesses that she has committed adultery. If she confesses, she undergoes the punishment for adultery.

9. This verse reminds us that the Religion (and law) God has chosen for us and conveyed to us through His Messenger has been based on God's liberal Forgiveness, Bountifulness, Compassion, and Wisdom.

350

سورة النور

۳٥۰

إِنَّ الَّذِينَ جَاءُوا بِالْإِفْكِ عُصْبَةٌ مِّنكُمْ لَا تَحْسَبُوهُ شَرًّا لَّكُم بَلْ هُوَ خَيْرٌ لَّكُمْ لِكُلِّ امْرِئٍ مِّنْهُم مَّا اكْتَسَبَ مِنَ الْإِثْمِ وَالَّذِى تَوَلَّى كِبْرَهُ مِنْهُمْ لَهُ عَذَابٌ عَظِيمٌ ۝ لَّوْلَا إِذْ سَمِعْتُمُوهُ ظَنَّ الْمُؤْمِنُونَ وَالْمُؤْمِنَاتُ بِأَنفُسِهِمْ خَيْرًا وَقَالُوا هَذَا إِفْكٌ مُّبِينٌ ۝ لَّوْلَا جَاءُو عَلَيْهِ بِأَرْبَعَةِ شُهَدَاءَ فَإِذْ لَمْ يَأْتُوا بِالشُّهَدَاءِ فَأُوْلَئِكَ عِندَ اللَّهِ هُمُ الْكَاذِبُونَ ۝ وَلَوْلَا فَضْلُ اللَّهِ عَلَيْكُمْ وَرَحْمَتُهُ فِي الدُّنْيَا وَالْآخِرَةِ لَمَسَّكُمْ فِى مَا أَفَضْتُمْ فِيهِ عَذَابٌ عَظِيمٌ ۝ إِذْ تَلَقَّوْنَهُ بِأَلْسِنَتِكُمْ وَتَقُولُونَ بِأَفْوَاهِكُم مَّا لَيْسَ لَكُم بِهِ عِلْمٌ وَتَحْسَبُونَهُ هَيِّنًا وَهُوَ عِندَ اللَّهِ عَظِيمٌ ۝ وَلَوْلَا إِذْ سَمِعْتُمُوهُ قُلْتُم مَّا يَكُونُ لَنَا أَن نَّتَكَلَّمَ بِهَذَا سُبْحَانَكَ هَذَا بُهْتَانٌ عَظِيمٌ ۝ يَعِظُكُمُ اللَّهُ أَن تَعُودُوا لِمِثْلِهِ أَبَدًا إِن كُنتُم مُّؤْمِنِينَ ۝ وَيُبَيِّنُ اللَّهُ لَكُمُ الْآيَاتِ وَاللَّهُ عَلِيمٌ حَكِيمٌ ۝ إِنَّ الَّذِينَ يُحِبُّونَ أَن تَشِيعَ الْفَاحِشَةُ فِي الَّذِينَ آمَنُوا لَهُمْ عَذَابٌ أَلِيمٌ فِي الدُّنْيَا وَالْآخِرَةِ وَاللَّهُ يَعْلَمُ وَأَنتُمْ لَا تَعْلَمُونَ ۝ وَلَوْلَا فَضْلُ اللَّهِ عَلَيْكُمْ وَرَحْمَتُهُ وَأَنَّ اللَّهَ رَؤُوفٌ رَّحِيمٌ ۝

---

11. Surely those who invented and spread the slander (against 'Ā'ishah, the Messenger's wife) are a band from among you. However, do not deem this incident an evil for you; rather, it is good for you.[10] (As for the slanderers:) every one of them has accumulated sin in proportion to his share in this guilt, and he who has the greater part of it[11] will suffer a tremendous punishment.

12. When you heard of it, why did the believing men and women not think well of one another[12] and declare: "This is obviously a slander"?

13. Why did they not produce four witnesses (in support of the accusation)? Now that they have not produced witnesses, it is indeed they who are the liars in God's sight.

14. Were it not for God's grace and favor upon you, and His mercy in the world and the Hereafter, a mighty punishment would certainly have afflicted you (who got involved in circulating rumors) on account of what you indulged in.

15. Just think how you welcomed it with your tongues from one another and uttered with your mouths something about which you had no knowledge. You deemed it a trifle whereas in God's sight it was most grave.

16. Why did you not say, when you heard of it, "It is not for us to speak of this. All-Glorified are You (O God)! This is an awesome slander."

17. God admonishes you lest you ever repeat anything like this, if you are (truly)] believers.

18. He clearly expounds to you His instructions and the signposts of His way. God is All-Knowing, All-Wise.

19. Those who love that indecency should spread among those who believe, surely for them is a painful punishment in the world and the Hereafter. God knows (the exact truth and nature of all matters), but you do not know.

20. Were it not for God's grace and favor upon you, and His mercy, and that God is All-Pitying, All-Compassionate (especially towards His believing servants, what terrible consequences would such evils have caused in your community)!

10. By the 5th year of the *Hijrah*, the Islamic movement led by the Messenger had reached a point where all its opponents realized that they would no longer be able to uproot it by sheer force. The hostile tribes had formed a united front under the leadership of the Quraysh and had besieged Madīnah with a massive army at the Battle of the Trench, which took place in the 5th year of the *Hijrah*. When they had to retreat after a four-week siege, the Messenger declared: "From this moment on we will march upon them; they will no longer be able to attack us" (al-Bukhārī, "Maghazī," 29).

The Islamic movement derived its main force from its spiritual and moral values and the unblemished character of its followers. So, led in particular by the Hypocrites in Madīnah, the enemy began to resort to vicious and unfair campaigns against the Muslims. Such conspiracies first manifested themselves on the occasion of the Messenger's marriage to Zaynab bint al-Jahsh, the divorced wife of Zayd ibn Ḥārithah, who was the Messenger's emancipated slave; this event is mentioned in *Sūrat al-Ahzāb* (33: 36–38) and will be dealt with when that *sūrah* is looked at. The concerted efforts to blemish the absolutely pure character of God's Messenger, upon him be peace and blessings, proved of no avail; so this time, they slandered 'Ā'ishah, the pure and beloved wife of the Messenger.

On the return from an expedition to the Banū Muṣṭaliq in the 6th year of the *Hijrah*, 'Ā'ishah, who had accompanied the Messenger during that expedition, was inadvertently left behind when the Muslim army moved from the place where it had camped. After having spent several hours alone, she was found by Ṣafwān ibn al-Mu'aṭṭal, one of the Emigrants who had participated in the Battle of Badr and whose duty was to make sure that nothing and no one got left behind. 'Ā'ishah got on his cam-

el and they rejoined the army at the next bivouac. This gave occasion to the enemies to raise a malicious scandal, which was led by 'Abdullāh ibn Ubayy ibn Salūl, the chief of the hypocrites in Madīnah.

As long as the Muslims preserve their moral and spiritual strength and solidarity, whatever the enemy does to defeat them will only end in bringing good to the Muslims. So incidents that seem to be evil in the beginning prove to be good for them. The incident of slander against 'Ā'ishah, the Mother of Believers, proved to be an occasion on which the Muslims were once more able to realize the source of their real power, to increase their solidarity, to gain further experience and knowledge in order to lead the movement onwards, as well as coming to know what they should think of their brothers and sisters in the Religion and how they should behave toward each other. This incident also served for many new laws to be revealed concerning the mutual relations of Muslims.

11. This refers to 'Abdullah ibn Ubayy ibn Salūl, the chief of the hypocrites.

12. This expression may also be translated as "When you heard of it, why did the believing men and women not think well of *their own folk*?" A believer is a mirror to another believer. Since belief is a light that illuminates a believer's mind and heart, and which shows them how they should react in the face of events, it also prevents a believer from performing evil and obscene acts; thus, every believer should think well of another believer. A believer cannot think of other believers in a way that is different from how they think of themselves. All believers form a single body; every believer is an embodiment of the values represented by other believers.

351

يَا أَيُّهَا الَّذِينَ آمَنُوا لَا تَتَّبِعُوا خُطُوَاتِ الشَّيْطَانِ وَمَن يَتَّبِعْ خُطُوَاتِ
الشَّيْطَانِ فَإِنَّهُ يَأْمُرُ بِالْفَحْشَاءِ وَالْمُنكَرِ وَلَوْلَا فَضْلُ اللَّهِ
عَلَيْكُمْ وَرَحْمَتُهُ مَا زَكَى مِنكُم مِّنْ أَحَدٍ أَبَدًا وَلَكِنَّ اللَّهَ
يُزَكِّي مَن يَشَاءُ وَاللَّهُ سَمِيعٌ عَلِيمٌ ۝ وَلَا يَأْتَلِ أُولُو الْفَضْلِ مِنكُمْ
وَالسَّعَةِ أَن يُؤْتُوا أُولِي الْقُرْبَى وَالْمَسَاكِينَ وَالْمُهَاجِرِينَ فِي سَبِيلِ اللَّهِ
وَلْيَعْفُوا وَلْيَصْفَحُوا أَلَا تُحِبُّونَ أَن يَغْفِرَ اللَّهُ لَكُمْ وَاللَّهُ
غَفُورٌ رَّحِيمٌ ۝ إِنَّ الَّذِينَ يَرْمُونَ الْمُحْصَنَاتِ الْغَافِلَاتِ الْمُؤْمِنَاتِ
لُعِنُوا فِي الدُّنْيَا وَالْآخِرَةِ وَلَهُمْ عَذَابٌ عَظِيمٌ ۝ يَوْمَ تَشْهَدُ عَلَيْهِمْ
أَلْسِنَتُهُمْ وَأَيْدِيهِمْ وَأَرْجُلُهُم بِمَا كَانُوا يَعْمَلُونَ ۝
يَوْمَئِذٍ يُوَفِّيهِمُ اللَّهُ دِينَهُمُ الْحَقَّ وَيَعْلَمُونَ أَنَّ اللَّهَ هُوَ الْحَقُّ الْمُبِينُ
۝ الْخَبِيثَاتُ لِلْخَبِيثِينَ وَالْخَبِيثُونَ لِلْخَبِيثَاتِ وَالطَّيِّبَاتُ
لِلطَّيِّبِينَ وَالطَّيِّبُونَ لِلطَّيِّبَاتِ أُولَئِكَ مُبَرَّؤُونَ مِمَّا يَقُولُونَ
لَهُم مَّغْفِرَةٌ وَرِزْقٌ كَرِيمٌ ۝ يَا أَيُّهَا الَّذِينَ آمَنُوا
لَا تَدْخُلُوا بُيُوتًا غَيْرَ بُيُوتِكُمْ حَتَّى تَسْتَأْنِسُوا وَتُسَلِّمُوا عَلَى
أَهْلِهَا ذَلِكُمْ خَيْرٌ لَّكُمْ لَعَلَّكُمْ تَذَكَّرُونَ ۝

---

21. O you who believe! Do not follow in the footsteps of Satan. Whoever follows in the footsteps of Satan, (let him know well that) Satan insistently calls to all that is indecent and shameful, and all that is evil. Were it not for God's bounty on you, and His mercy, not one of you would have ever attained purity; but God purifies whomever He wills. God is All-Hearing, All-Knowing.[13]

22. Let not those among you who are favored with resources swear that they will no longer give to the kindred, the needy, and those who have emigrated in God's cause, (even though those wealthy ones suffer harm at the hands of the latter). Rather let them pardon and forbear. Do you not wish that God should forgive you? God is All-Forgiving, All-Compassionate.

23. Those who falsely accuse chaste women, who are unaware of devious ways of corruption and are believers, are cursed in the world and the Hereafter, and for them is a mighty punishment.

24. On the Day when their own tongues and hands and feet will all bear witness against them in regard to what they were doing.

25. On that Day God will pay them in full their just due, and they will come to know that God is the Absolute Truth (from Whom nothing is hidden and Who makes all truth manifest).

26. (In principle,) corrupt women are for corrupt men, and corrupt men for corrupt women, just as good, pure women are for good, pure men, and good, pure men for good, pure women. (On account of their purity and chastity coming from faith) the latter are innocent of all that evil tongues may impute to them. For them there is a forgiveness and an honorable, generous provision.

27. O you who believe! Do not enter dwellings other than your own until you have ascertained the permission of their residents and have greeted them with peace. Your doing so is what is good and appropriate for you, so that you may be mindful (of good manners and proper courtesy).

13. No one, even if they are God's Messengers, can attain purity – purity in thought, belief, intention, and action – merely on the basis of their own abilities and efforts. At best what a person can do is to sincerely desire purity and to work to this end. God is aware of anyone who has sincere intentions and who is trying to attain purity, and it is He Who enables people to attain purity and remain pure. Humanity is prone to evil, indecency, and error, and can easily be defeated by Satan and their carnal souls. Therefore, all of us are indebted to God alone for any of our good thoughts and deeds. It is for this reason that for the fourth time in the *sūrah* God reminds us of the fact that, were it not for His grace, and favor, and mercy on us, we would have been doomed. Once the Messenger, upon him be peace and blessings, declared: "No one can enter Paradise by virtue of their own deeds." When asked if this was true for him as well, he replied that had it not been for God's Mercy Which embraced him, he could not enter either (al-Bukhārī, "Riqāq," 18).

352

سُوۡرَةُ النُّوۡرِ

٣٥٢

> فَإِن لَّمْ تَجِدُوا فِيهَا أَحَدًا فَلَا تَدْخُلُوهَا حَتَّىٰ يُؤْذَنَ لَكُمْ وَإِن قِيلَ لَكُمُ ٱرْجِعُوا فَٱرْجِعُوا هُوَ أَزْكَىٰ لَكُمْ وَٱللَّهُ بِمَا تَعْمَلُونَ عَلِيمٌ ۝ لَّيْسَ عَلَيْكُمْ جُنَاحٌ أَن تَدْخُلُوا بُيُوتًا غَيْرَ مَسْكُونَةٍ فِيهَا مَتَٰعٌ لَّكُمْ وَٱللَّهُ يَعْلَمُ مَا تُبْدُونَ وَمَا تَكْتُمُونَ ۝ قُل لِّلْمُؤْمِنِينَ يَغُضُّوا مِنْ أَبْصَٰرِهِمْ وَيَحْفَظُوا فُرُوجَهُمْ ذَٰلِكَ أَزْكَىٰ لَهُمْ إِنَّ ٱللَّهَ خَبِيرٌ بِمَا يَصْنَعُونَ ۝ وَقُل لِّلْمُؤْمِنَٰتِ يَغْضُضْنَ مِنْ أَبْصَٰرِهِنَّ وَيَحْفَظْنَ فُرُوجَهُنَّ وَلَا يُبْدِينَ زِينَتَهُنَّ إِلَّا مَا ظَهَرَ مِنْهَا وَلْيَضْرِبْنَ بِخُمُرِهِنَّ عَلَىٰ جُيُوبِهِنَّ وَلَا يُبْدِينَ زِينَتَهُنَّ إِلَّا لِبُعُولَتِهِنَّ أَوْ ءَابَآئِهِنَّ أَوْ ءَابَآءِ بُعُولَتِهِنَّ أَوْ أَبْنَآئِهِنَّ أَوْ أَبْنَآءِ بُعُولَتِهِنَّ أَوْ إِخْوَٰنِهِنَّ أَوْ بَنِىٰٓ إِخْوَٰنِهِنَّ أَوْ بَنِىٰٓ أَخَوَٰتِهِنَّ أَوْ نِسَآئِهِنَّ أَوْ مَا مَلَكَتْ أَيْمَٰنُهُنَّ أَوِ ٱلتَّٰبِعِينَ غَيْرِ أُو۟لِى ٱلْإِرْبَةِ مِنَ ٱلرِّجَالِ أَوِ ٱلطِّفْلِ ٱلَّذِينَ لَمْ يَظْهَرُوا عَلَىٰ عَوْرَٰتِ ٱلنِّسَآءِ وَلَا يَضْرِبْنَ بِأَرْجُلِهِنَّ لِيُعْلَمَ مَا يُخْفِينَ مِن زِينَتِهِنَّ وَتُوبُوٓا إِلَى ٱللَّهِ جَمِيعًا أَيُّهَ ٱلْمُؤْمِنُونَ لَعَلَّكُمْ تُفْلِحُونَ ۝

---

28. Then if you find no one in them, do not enter them until you have permission to enter. If you are asked to go back, then go back (without feeling offended). It is a purer way for you. God has full knowledge of all that you do.[14]

29. There is no blame on you if you enter dwellings that are uninhabited which are of use to you. (But always bear in mind that) God knows whatever you reveal (of acts or intentions) and whatever you keep concealed.

30. Tell the believing men that they should restrain their gaze (from looking at the women whom it is lawful for them to marry, and from others' private parts), and guard their private parts and chastity.[15] This is what is purer for them. God is fully aware of all that they do.

31. And tell the believing women that they (also) should restrain their gaze (from looking at the men whom it is lawful for them to marry, and from others' private parts), and guard their private parts,[16] and that they should not display their charms except that which is revealed of itself;[17] and let them draw their veils over their bosoms,[18] and (tell them) not to display their charms to any save their husbands, or their

fathers (and grandfathers and both paternal and maternal uncles), or the fathers of their husbands, or their sons, or the sons of their husbands (both their own and stepsons and grandsons), or their brothers (and foster- and step-brothers), or the sons of their brothers, or the sons of their sisters, or the Muslim women and the women of good conduct with whom they associate, or those (slave-girls) their right hands possess, or the male attendants in their service free of sexual desire, or children that are as yet unaware of femininity. Nor should they stamp their feet (i.e. act in such a manner as to) draw attention to their charms (and arouse the passion of men). And O believers, turn to God all together in repentance that you may attain true prosperity.

14. In the pre-Islamic age of *Jāhiliyyah*, people would barge into each other's house without asking for permission and greeting the residents with peace, but only saying: "Good morning" or "Good evening!" Islam ruled that everyone has a right to privacy in their own house and that no one could enter another's house without ascertaining the prior consent of the inmates. Islam also ruled that the proper way to greet one another is to say, "Peace be upon you." One is required to ask for permission to enter even the houses of one's relatives. The Messenger, upon him be peace and blessings, stated that a person should ask for permission no more than three times. If there is no response, the would-be visitor should leave.

Islam also forbade peeping into the houses of others, looking into them from the outside, and reading other people's letters without permission. It is also unlawful to listen to conversations which take place in another's house.

15. This means not only that one should be mindful of one's chastity, but also that they should avoid exposing their private parts. The parts of the body that are forbidden for men to expose are between the navel and the knee. A man should not expose this part of his body before anyone except his wife. They should also avoid being naked, even when they are alone, out of respect for the angels (at-Tirmidhī, "Adab," 42).

16. A woman should not expose any part of her body other than her hands and feet before men with whom she can marry. According to the majority of scholars, she must cover her face, except for her eyes. She is not obliged to cover her face while performing the rites of the *Hajj* or in places like court or during a marriage contract. Nor can a woman wear such thin, tight or transparent clothes that her body is exposed, revealing its shape. As for the parts of the body which she is obliged to keep covered before other women of faith, good char-

acter and chastity, these consist of the lower body, between the navel and the knee. She should also cover herself in the presence of women of loose morals, just as she must cover before men whom she can marry.

17. What is meant by the *charm*s that must not be displayed are the parts of the woman's body on which she wears ornaments, such as ears, wrists, and ankles. As these should not be displayed in the presence of others than those mentioned in the verse, especially when adorned, women should also not show any adornments which they use to make them look attractive, such as eye-catching dresses, jewelry, and cosmetics.

Scholars interpret the statement, *that which is revealed of itself*, to mean that women should not intentionally display their beauty and charms. But sometimes it may happen that the outer garment, for example, is blown up by the wind, causing something to be exposed. However, a believing woman must take precautions against such occasions. Some scholars hold that what is meant by this statement – *that which is revealed of itself* – is garments like a veil, gloves, and head-cover, and the parts of the body which a woman is allowed to keep uncovered, namely, her hands, feet and eyes, and her face, in cases of necessity, and the adornment which she wears on them.

18. In the pre-Islamic age of *Jāhiliyyah*, women wore head-bands to keep their tied hair up in a bun at the rear of their head, thus revealing their neck and the upper part of their bosoms. With this verse, the Qur'ān ordered them to wear their hair-covering in such a way that it covered their head and bosoms. When this order was communicated to the believing women in the Messenger's time, they immediately cast away their transparent clothes and veils and made veils of thick material, wearing them in a way that fully covered their head and bosoms (Abū Dāwūd, "Kitāb al-Libās," 32).

وَأَنكِحُوا الْأَيَامَىٰ مِنكُمْ وَالصَّالِحِينَ مِنْ عِبَادِكُمْ وَإِمَائِكُمْ إِن يَكُونُوا فُقَرَاءَ يُغْنِهِمُ اللَّهُ مِن فَضْلِهِ وَاللَّهُ وَاسِعٌ عَلِيمٌ ۝ وَلْيَسْتَعْفِفِ الَّذِينَ لَا يَجِدُونَ نِكَاحًا حَتَّىٰ يُغْنِيَهُمُ اللَّهُ مِن فَضْلِهِ وَالَّذِينَ يَبْتَغُونَ الْكِتَابَ مِمَّا مَلَكَتْ أَيْمَانُكُمْ فَكَاتِبُوهُمْ إِنْ عَلِمْتُمْ فِيهِمْ خَيْرًا وَآتُوهُم مِّن مَّالِ اللَّهِ الَّذِي آتَاكُمْ وَلَا تُكْرِهُوا فَتَيَاتِكُمْ عَلَى الْبِغَاءِ إِنْ أَرَدْنَ تَحَصُّنًا لِّتَبْتَغُوا عَرَضَ الْحَيَاةِ الدُّنْيَا وَمَن يُكْرِههُّنَّ فَإِنَّ اللَّهَ مِن بَعْدِ إِكْرَاهِهِنَّ غَفُورٌ رَّحِيمٌ ۝ وَلَقَدْ أَنزَلْنَا إِلَيْكُمْ آيَاتٍ مُّبَيِّنَاتٍ وَمَثَلًا مِّنَ الَّذِينَ خَلَوْا مِن قَبْلِكُمْ وَمَوْعِظَةً لِّلْمُتَّقِينَ ۝ اللَّهُ نُورُ السَّمَاوَاتِ وَالْأَرْضِ مَثَلُ نُورِهِ كَمِشْكَاةٍ فِيهَا مِصْبَاحٌ الْمِصْبَاحُ فِي زُجَاجَةٍ الزُّجَاجَةُ كَأَنَّهَا كَوْكَبٌ دُرِّيٌّ يُوقَدُ مِن شَجَرَةٍ مُّبَارَكَةٍ زَيْتُونَةٍ لَّا شَرْقِيَّةٍ وَلَا غَرْبِيَّةٍ يَكَادُ زَيْتُهَا يُضِيءُ وَلَوْ لَمْ تَمْسَسْهُ نَارٌ نُّورٌ عَلَىٰ نُورٍ يَهْدِي اللَّهُ لِنُورِهِ مَن يَشَاءُ وَيَضْرِبُ اللَّهُ الْأَمْثَالَ لِلنَّاسِ وَاللَّهُ بِكُلِّ شَيْءٍ عَلِيمٌ ۝ فِي بُيُوتٍ أَذِنَ اللَّهُ أَن تُرْفَعَ وَيُذْكَرَ فِيهَا اسْمُهُ يُسَبِّحُ لَهُ فِيهَا بِالْغُدُوِّ وَالْآصَالِ ۝

---

32. Marry those among you who are single (whether men or women) and those of your male and female slaves that are righteous (and fit for marriage). If they are poor, God will grant them sufficiency out of His bounty. God is All-Embracing in His mercy, All-Knowing.[19]

33. Let those who cannot afford to marry keep themselves chaste until God grants them sufficiency out of His bounty.[20] And if any of those whom your right hands possess desire to enter into a contract with you to purchase their freedom, make this contract with them if you know that they are honest (and able to earn without begging and be good, free citizens).[21] Help them out of God's wealth which He has granted you. And do not compel your slave-girls to prostitution in order to seek the (fleeting) benefits of the life of this world while they desire to remain chaste. If anyone compels them to prostitution, then God will be All-Forgiving, All-Compassionate to them after they are subjected to such compulsion.

34. Indeed, We have sent down to you Revelations which show the truth clearly and illuminate your way, and examples (from the histories) of those who have passed away before you, and an instruction for the God-revering, pious.

35. God is the Light of the heavens and the earth. The example of His Light is like a niche wherein is a lamp; the lamp is in a crystal, and the crystal shining as if a pearl-like radiant star, lit from the oil of a blessed olive tree that is neither of the east nor of the west. The oil would almost give light of itself though no fire touches it: light upon light. God guides to His Light whom He wills. God strikes parables for people. God has full knowledge of all things.[22]

36. (This light can best be obtained and those guided to it are found) in some houses (that are usually concealed from people's eyes and) for which God has provided a way for them to be built and appreciated, and for His Name to be mentioned and invoked therein; in them glorify Him in the morning and evening,

19. This is not a compulsory order; as marriage depends on the choice of an individual. However, if a person wants to marry, but cannot afford it, those responsible for them among their relatives or, in case of their being without relatives, the state should arrange their marriage.

20. God's Messenger, upon him be peace and blessings, said: "O young people! Those among you who can afford to marry should do so, for it will help you to keep your gaze averted and enable you to preserve your chastity. Whoever cannot afford to marry, let him fast, for fasting blunts sexual passion" (Bukhārī, "Kitāb an-Nikāḥ." 2) He also said: "There are three types of Muslims whom God binds Himself to help: he who marries to preserve his chastity; he who enters into contract to purchase his freedom and sincerely intends to pay the amount; and he who goes out on God's way for *jihād*" (at-Tirmidhī, "Fadāil al-Jihād," 20).

21. Such type of agreements also pertain to prisoners of war.

Here I deem it useful to quote from Fethullah Gülen concerning the outlining aspects of an Islamic social system:

What is of great significance in such commandments is that the duties entrusted to modern states are those that Islam refers to society and classifies, in order of importance, as "absolutely necessary, relatively necessary, and commendable to carry out." The Qur'ān includes the following passages: *O you who believe! Come in full submission to God, all of you (2: 208); O you who believe! Spend (in God's cause) out of the pure, wholesome things you have earned and of what We have produced for you from the earth (2: 267); Such of your women as have committed indecency (adultery), you must have four male witnesses of you who (having seen them in the act) will testify against them (4: 15); God commands you to deliver trusts (including public and professional duties of service) to those entitled to them; and when you judge between people, to judge with justice (4: 58); O you who believe! Be upholders and standard-bear-*

ers of justice, bearing witness to the truth for God's sake, even though it be against your own selves, or parents or kindred (4: 135); And if they (the enemies) incline to peace, incline to it also, and place your trust in God (8: 61); O you who believe! If some transgressor brings you news (that requires taking action), verify it carefully (before you believe and act upon it), lest you harm a people in ignorance and then become regretful for what you have done (49: 6); If two parties of believers fall to fighting, make peace between them (and act promptly) (49: 9). In short, the Qur'ān addresses the entire community and assigns it almost all the duties that are entrusted to modern states.

People cooperate with one another by sharing these duties and establishing the essential institutions that are necessary to perform them. The government is composed of these institutions. Thus, Islam recommends a government that is based on a social contract. People elect the administrators and establish a council to debate common issues. Also, the society as a whole participates in auditing the administration. Particularly during the rule of the first four Caliphs (632–661), the fundamental principles of government mentioned above were fully observed. The political system was transformed into a sultanate after the death of 'Ali, the fourth Caliph, due to internal conflicts and the global conditions of the time. Unlike during the caliphate, power in the sultanate was passed on through the sultan's family. However, even though elections were no longer held, societies maintained the other principles.

Islam is an inclusive religion. It is based on the belief in one God as the Creator, Lord, Sustainer, and Administrator of the universe. Islam is the religion of the whole universe. That is, the entire universe obeys the laws laid down by God, so everything in the universe is "Muslim" and obeys God by submitting to His laws. Even a person who refuses to believe in God or follows another religion has perforce to be a

Muslim as far as their physical existence is concerned. Throughout their entire life, from the embryonic stage to the body's dissolution into dust after death, every tissue of their muscles, and every limb of their body follows the course prescribed for each by God's law. Thus, in Islam, God, nature, and humanity are neither remote from each other nor are they alien to each other. It is God Who makes Himself known to humanity through nature and humanity itself, and nature and humanity are the two books of creation through which each word of God is known. This leads humankind to look upon everything as belonging to the same Lord, to whom it itself belongs, so that it regards nothing in the universe as alien. (A Muslim's) sympathy, love, and service do not remain confined to the people of any particular race, color, or ethnicity. The Prophet summed this up with the command, "O servants of God, be brothers (and sisters)!"

A separate, but equally important point is that Islam recognizes the Divinely-inspired religions that predated it. It accepts all the Prophets and Books sent to different peoples in different epochs of history. Not only does it accept them, but it also regards belief in them as being an essential principle of being a Muslim. In this way, Islam acknowledges the basic unity of all religions. A Muslim is at the same time a true follower of Abraham, Moses, David, Jesus, and of all the other Hebrew Prophets. This belief explains why both Christians and Jews enjoyed their religious rights under the rule of Islamic governments throughout history.

The Islamic social system seeks to form a virtuous society and thereby gain God's approval. It recognizes right, not force, as the foundation of social life. Hostility is unacceptable. Relationships must be based on belief, love, mutual respect, assistance, and understanding instead of conflict and the pursuit of personal interests. Social education encourages people to pursue lofty ideals and to strive for perfection, not just to run after their own desires. The pur-

suit of what is right demands unity, virtues bring mutual support and solidarity, and belief secures brother- and sisterhood. Encouraging the soul to attain perfection brings happiness in both worlds. (A Comparative Approach, *SAIS Review*, vol. XXI, no. 2, 136–137)

22. This verse is one of the ambiguous, allegorical verses of the Qur'ān. It has deep meanings about which many interpretations have been made.

First, it should be remembered that the Essence of God or the Divine Being Himself cannot be known, as there is nothing comparable to Him, and He is infinitely beyond whatever we conceive of Him. Because of this, the Qur'ān presents us His acts, and creates allegories to give some "knowledge (*ma'rifah*)" of Him with His Attributes, and Names. Acts lead to the Names, and the Names to the Attributes.

As we know, light appears of itself and causes other objects to become apparent. It also signifies existence, illumination, and knowledge in contrast to non-existence, darkness, and ignorance. So, the verse suggests that God is the only One Who exists of and by Himself, absolutely independent of all others. Whatever exists other than He depends on Him to come into existence and subsist.

Secondly, (the) Light is one of the Names of God. All the lights in the universe are manifestations of this Name. So, the verse means that it is God Who has created light and illuminates everything in the universe.

Thirdly, as is implied at the conclusion of the verse, knowledge is light and is the source of intellectual enlightenment. All knowledge has its source in God's Knowledge. With respect to God, His Existence and Knowledge are, in one respect, identical. Even if there were none to be aware of Him, He knows Himself. Some Muslim scholars, like Bediüzzaman Said Nursi, are of the opinion that existence ends in or issues from His Knowledge. So, as pointed out above, knowledge is light. It is also through knowledge that one can attain true faith which illuminates hearts. So *true* knowledge provides guidance for people, and its main source is Revelation. True enlightenment is possible through Revelation, and any information that goes against the Revelation is darkness and causes darkness.

As mentioned above, the Essence of God cannot be known, as He is incomparable to anything in the universe, and He is infinite or unlimited. We can only obtain some knowledge of Him through His works or acts, which are manifested from behind the veil of causality or the "laws of nature," which are in fact the titles of His ways of acting or executing the events of the universe, and the universe itself. So, the metaphor of the glass, lamp, and crystal stands for this veil.

The metaphor indicates modern electricity and electrical lamps; modern interpreters of the Qur'ān in particular think that this verse suggests electricity. Actually, as we know, energy is comprehended through its effects and electric energy is used for illumination through a bulb. The glass, lamp, crystal, or pearl-like radiant star, when taken together, bring to mind the image of an electric lamp. As electric energy is seen and illuminates by means of light bulbs, the Divine Light manifest Itself through Its effects and by means of the veil mentioned above in the same way. Energy can serve as an example of having some knowledge of the Divine Light.

In the past, light was mostly obtained from lamps lit by olive oil, and the brightest lamp was that which was lit from the oil of an olive tree that grew in an open and elevated place, receiving the rays of the sun not only in the morning, but in the afternoon and throughout the day. So, the statement, *neither of the east nor of the west* implies the intensity of the light obtained from a lamp lit from the oil of such olive trees, as it is not restricted by any direction. It also suggests that God's Light does not emit from matter or belong to the universe. It is meta-universal or meta-physical, and therefore glows forth of itself without needing fire to kindle it. Likewise, the Revelation as the source of knowledge and Islam, which it has formed, belong to none other than God. These are a pure light from God which illuminates the minds and hearts of humankind.

354

سُورَةُ النُّورِ

٣٥٤

رِجَالٌ لَا تُلْهِيهِمْ تِجَارَةٌ وَلَا بَيْعٌ عَن ذِكْرِ اللَّهِ وَإِقَامِ الصَّلَوٰةِ وَإِيتَآءِ الزَّكَوٰةِ يَخَافُونَ يَوْمًا تَتَقَلَّبُ فِيهِ الْقُلُوبُ وَالْأَبْصَارُ ۞ لِيَجْزِيَهُمُ اللَّهُ أَحْسَنَ مَا عَمِلُوا وَيَزِيدَهُم مِّن فَضْلِهِ وَاللَّهُ يَرْزُقُ مَن يَشَآءُ بِغَيْرِ حِسَابٍ ۞ وَالَّذِينَ كَفَرُوٓا أَعْمَالُهُمْ كَسَرَابٍۭ بِقِيعَةٍ يَحْسَبُهُ الظَّمْآنُ مَآءً حَتَّىٰٓ إِذَا جَآءَهُ لَمْ يَجِدْهُ شَيْـًٔا وَوَجَدَ اللَّهَ عِندَهُۥ فَوَفَّىٰهُ حِسَابَهُۥ وَاللَّهُ سَرِيعُ الْحِسَابِ ۞ أَوْ كَظُلُمَاتٍ فِى بَحْرٍ لُّجِّىٍّ يَغْشَىٰهُ مَوْجٌ مِّن فَوْقِهِۦ مَوْجٌ مِّن فَوْقِهِۦ سَحَابٌ ظُلُمَاتٌۢ بَعْضُهَا فَوْقَ بَعْضٍ إِذَآ أَخْرَجَ يَدَهُۥ لَمْ يَكَدْ يَرَىٰهَا وَمَن لَّمْ يَجْعَلِ اللَّهُ لَهُۥ نُورًا فَمَا لَهُۥ مِن نُّورٍ ۞ أَلَمْ تَرَ أَنَّ اللَّهَ يُسَبِّحُ لَهُۥ مَن فِى السَّمَٰوَٰتِ وَالْأَرْضِ وَالطَّيْرُ صَآفَّٰتٍ كُلٌّ قَدْ عَلِمَ صَلَاتَهُۥ وَتَسْبِيحَهُۥ وَاللَّهُ عَلِيمٌۢ بِمَا يَفْعَلُونَ ۞ وَلِلَّهِ مُلْكُ السَّمَٰوَٰتِ وَالْأَرْضِ وَإِلَى اللَّهِ الْمَصِيرُ ۞ أَلَمْ تَرَ أَنَّ اللَّهَ يُزْجِى سَحَابًا ثُمَّ يُؤَلِّفُ بَيْنَهُۥ ثُمَّ يَجْعَلُهُۥ رُكَامًا فَتَرَى الْوَدْقَ يَخْرُجُ مِنْ خِلَٰلِهِۦ وَيُنَزِّلُ مِنَ السَّمَآءِ مِن جِبَالٍ فِيهَا مِنۢ بَرَدٍ فَيُصِيبُ بِهِۦ مَن يَشَآءُ وَيَصْرِفُهُۥ عَن مَّن يَشَآءُ يَكَادُ سَنَا بَرْقِهِۦ يَذْهَبُ بِالْأَبْصَٰرِ ۞

37. Men (of great distinction) whom neither commerce nor exchange (nor any other worldly preoccupations) can divert from the remembrance of God, and establishing the Prayer in conformity with all its conditions, and paying the Prescribed Purifying Alms; they are in fear of a Day on which all hearts and eyes will be overturned.[23]

38. God will reward them in accordance with the best of what they have ever done, and give them yet more out of His bounty (i.e. more than they deserve). God provides beyond all measure for whom He wills.[24]

39. As for the unbelievers, all their deeds are like a mirage in the desert, which the thirsty one supposes to be water until he comes up to it, only to find that it was nothing; instead he finds God near it, and He settles his account in full. God is swift at settling the account.

40. Or their deeds are like veils of darkness covering up an abysmal sea down into its depths, covered up by a billow, above which is a billow, above which is a cloud: veils of darkness piled one upon another, so that when he stretches out his hand, he can hardly see it. For whomever God has appointed no light, no light has he.[25]

41. Do you not see that all that is in the heavens and the earth, and the birds flying in patterned ranks with wings spread out glorify God. Each knows the way of its prayer and glorification. God has full knowledge of all that they do.

42. To God belongs the sovereignty of the heavens and the earth; and to God is the homecoming.

43. Do you not see that God gently drives the clouds, then joins them together, (completing the formation of a circuit between them,)[26] and then turns them into a thick mass, and consequently you see rain-drops issue out of their midst. He sends down hail out of snow-laden mountains (of clouds) from the sky, and smites with it whom He wills and averts it from whom He wills. The flash of the lightning almost takes away the sight.[27]

---

23. Although many commentators of the Qur'ān have interpreted the word *houses* in verse 36 to mean mosques, understanding it to mean the houses which believers construct where they mention God, study His religion, and serve His cause is more appropri-

ate. The term *houses* is used in the indefinite form. Mosques are not indefinite, so they are not concealed from people's eyes. Furthermore, *God's providing for them a way to be built and appreciated, and for His Name to be mentioned and invoked therein* suggest that they are or will be built at a time when the believers are closely watched and face great pressure to enjoy their Religion and serve God's cause. In addition, believers assemble in mosques five times a day to glorify God, not only in the morning and evening. In the houses mentioned in this verse, distinguished believers dedicated to God's cause, who are not diverted by their worldly occupations nor buying and selling from God's remembrance, come together to glorify God and uplift His Name.

When these verses are considered in the light of what God said to Moses and Aaron in 10: 87, then their true meaning will be clearer:

> We revealed to Moses and his brother: "Appoint houses for your people in Egypt (as places of refuge and coming together in God's cause), and (as a whole community) make your homes places to turn to God, and establish the Prescribed Prayer in conformity with all its conditions. And (O Moses,) give glad tidings to the believers!"

24. Since God is the All-Independent, the One Who does whatever He wills, He is never obliged to do anything according to people's deeds and wishes, including rewarding good or punishing evil. However, because of His absolute Justice, He rewards people who believe and do good deeds that are acceptable by Him, and punishes the others who disbelieve and do evil deeds. In other words, He treats people as they deserve. But He is also the All-Compassionate, All-Forgiving, and All-Providing. So, He overlooks and forgives His servants many of their sins, and rewards the believers with more than they deserve. This does not mean that He treats all the believers in the same way. Believers vary in degrees, according to the depth of their faith, the multiplicity of their deeds, their sincerity in faith and their performance of good deeds, their purity of intention, their depth of devotion, and their contribution to God's cause. As all such factors cause variations in God's rewards to them, God is also free to reward whom He wills as He wills, once He has given to each their due.

25. The parables or comparisons presented here illustrate the state of unbelievers. Their deeds, although seeming to bring them some benefit in the world for some time, will increase them in nothing but loss and suffering both in the world and in the Hereafter. In addition, so long as there are believers whose minds and hearts have been enlightened by God's Light and who strive for His cause sincerely, whatever the unbelievers do to stop them and prevent the spread of this Light, the believers will ultimately be victorious. What the unbelievers call enlightenment is only darkness upon darkness, so they are wrapped up by veils of darkness, and cannot find their way to true salvation and success.

26. For an explanation of this statement, see 15: 22, note 6.

27. This verse explains the curious Divine disposals in sending rain and hail from accumulated clouds, which are among the Divine Lordship's miracles and the most curious manifestations of His Mercy. While the cloud's atoms are scattered in the atmosphere, they come together to form a cloud at the command of God, just like a dispersed army assembles at the sound of the trumpet. Then, like small troops coming from different directions to form an army, God joins the clouds together to enable the completion of an electric circuit between them. He causes those piled-up clouds, charged with rain or snow or hail, to pour down the water of life to all living beings on earth.

Rain does not fall by itself. Rather, it is sent down because it comes for certain purposes and according to need. When the atmosphere is clear and no clouds can be seen, the mountain-like forms of clouds, gathered like a great cloud, assemble because the One Who knows all living beings and their needs gathers them together to send down the rain. These events suggest several Divine Names: the All-Powerful, All-Knowing, All-Disposer of Things, All-Arranger, All-Upbringing, All-Helper, and Reviver.

355

بِقَلِّبُ اللهُ الَّيْلَ وَالنَّهَارَ إِنَّ فِى ذَلِكَ لَعِبْرَةً لِأُولِى الْأَبْصَارِ ۝ وَاللهُ خَلَقَ كُلَّ دَابَّةٍ مِّنْ مَّاءٍ فَمِنْهُمْ مَّنْ يَّمْشِى عَلَى بَطْنِهِ وَمِنْهُمْ مَّنْ يَّمْشِى عَلَى رِجْلَيْنِ وَمِنْهُمْ مَّنْ يَّمْشِى عَلَى أَرْبَعٍ يَخْلُقُ اللهُ مَا يَشَاءُ إِنَّ اللهَ عَلَى كُلِّ شَيْءٍ قَدِيرٌ ۝ لَقَدْ أَنْزَلْنَا آيَاتٍ مُّبَيِّنَاتٍ وَاللهُ يَهْدِى مَنْ يَّشَاءُ إِلَى صِرَاطٍ مُّسْتَقِيمٍ ۝ وَيَقُولُونَ آمَنَّا بِاللهِ وَبِالرَّسُولِ وَأَطَعْنَا ثُمَّ يَتَوَلَّى فَرِيقٌ مِّنْهُمْ مِّنْ بَعْدِ ذَلِكَ وَمَا أُولَئِكَ بِالْمُؤْمِنِينَ ۝ وَإِذَا دُعُوا إِلَى اللهِ وَرَسُولِهِ لِيَحْكُمَ بَيْنَهُمْ إِذَا فَرِيقٌ مِّنْهُمْ مُّعْرِضُونَ ۝ وَإِنْ يَّكُنْ لَّهُمُ الْحَقُّ يَأْتُوا إِلَيْهِ مُذْعِنِينَ ۝ أَفِى قُلُوبِهِمْ مَّرَضٌ أَمِ ارْتَابُوا أَمْ يَخَافُونَ أَنْ يَحِيفَ اللهُ عَلَيْهِمْ وَرَسُولُهُ بَلْ أُولَئِكَ هُمُ الظَّالِمُونَ ۝ إِنَّمَا كَانَ قَوْلَ الْمُؤْمِنِينَ إِذَا دُعُوا إِلَى اللهِ وَرَسُولِهِ لِيَحْكُمَ بَيْنَهُمْ أَنْ يَّقُولُوا سَمِعْنَا وَأَطَعْنَا وَأُولَئِكَ هُمُ الْمُفْلِحُونَ ۝ وَمَنْ يُطِعِ اللهَ وَرَسُولَهُ وَيَخْشَ اللهَ وَيَتَّقْهِ فَأُولَئِكَ هُمُ الْفَائِزُونَ ۝ وَأَقْسَمُوا بِاللهِ جَهْدَ أَيْمَانِهِمْ لَئِنْ أَمَرْتَهُمْ لَيَخْرُجُنَّ قُلْ لَّا تُقْسِمُوا طَاعَةٌ مَّعْرُوفَةٌ إِنَّ اللهَ خَبِيرٌ بِمَا تَعْمَلُونَ ۝

44. God turns about the night and the day. Surely in that is a lesson for those who have the power of seeing.

45. God has created every living creature from water.[28] Among them are such as move on their bellies, and such as move on two legs, and such as move on four. God creates whatever He wills. Surely, God has full power over everything.

46. Assuredly We have sent down Revelations which show the truth clearly and illuminate your way. God guides whom He wills to a straight path.

47. They say, "We have believed in God and in the Messenger, and We have promised obedience (to both)," but then, after that a party among them turn away (contradicting their declaration by their attitudes and actions). Such are not believers.

48. When they are called to God and His Messenger so that the Messenger may judge between them, see how a party among them turn away in aversion.

49. If the right be on their side, they come willingly in acceptance of it.

50. Is there a sickness in their hearts (that corrupts their will and character)? Or have they fallen prey to doubts? Or do they fear that God and His Messenger will deal unjustly with them? No, the truth is that they themselves are wrongdoers.

51. The only utterance of the (true) believers, when they are called to God and His Messenger so that the Messenger may judge between them, is: "We have heard and we obey." Such are those who are the prosperous.[29]

52. Whoever obeys God and His Messenger, and is overwhelmed by awe of God and keeps from disobedience to Him in reverence for Him and piety, such indeed are those who are the triumphant.

53. They (the hypocritical ones) swear by God most solemnly that if you should ever order them, they would most certainly go forth (to fight in God's cause). Tell them: "Do not swear. What is expected of you is obedience of the proper kind, well-known. (So you should do what other believers do and therefore will go forth when commanded to do so without gestures indicating exaggeration and affectation)." God is fully aware of all that you do.

28. One meaning of this verse is that the primary material in creation is something fluid – ether, hydrogen, or a large cloud, a huge nebula, or a mass of hot gas, or something else. God made ether a source of atoms from which He created all things, and He has placed everything in the "ocean" of ether. Another meaning is that water itself was caused by two gases. Its vapors rise from the ground, condense, and then return as rain to form or prepare a suitable environment for life.

For further explanation, see *sūrah* 2: 74, note 78; *sūrah* 21: 30, note 3; *sūrah* 23: 18, note 5.

29. For similar injunctions about believing in and obeying God and the Messenger and wholeheartedly submitting to his judgments, see: 4: 60–65. Verse 65 in particular is significant in this respect: *But no! By your Lord, they will not (truly) believe until they make you the judge regarding any dispute between them, and then find not the least vexation within themselves over what you have decided, and surrender in full submission.*

The Prophet's Mosque in Madīnah toward the end of the 19th century. (A painting by R. Yazdani, reproduced from a photo from the Yıldız Sarayı Archives in Istanbul.)

356   ٣٥٦

سُورَةُ النُّورِ

قُلْ أَطِيعُوا اللَّهَ وَأَطِيعُوا الرَّسُولَ فَإِن تَوَلَّوْا فَإِنَّمَا عَلَيْهِ
مَا حُمِّلَ وَعَلَيْكُم مَّا حُمِّلْتُمْ وَإِن تُطِيعُوهُ تَهْتَدُوا وَمَا عَلَى
الرَّسُولِ إِلَّا الْبَلَاغُ الْمُبِينُ ۝ وَعَدَ اللَّهُ الَّذِينَ آمَنُوا مِنكُمْ
وَعَمِلُوا الصَّالِحَاتِ لَيَسْتَخْلِفَنَّهُمْ فِي الْأَرْضِ كَمَا اسْتَخْلَفَ الَّذِينَ
مِن قَبْلِهِمْ وَلَيُمَكِّنَنَّ لَهُمْ دِينَهُمُ الَّذِي ارْتَضَى لَهُمْ وَلَيُبَدِّلَنَّهُم
مِّن بَعْدِ خَوْفِهِمْ أَمْنًا يَعْبُدُونَنِي لَا يُشْرِكُونَ بِي شَيْئًا وَمَن
كَفَرَ بَعْدَ ذَٰلِكَ فَأُولَٰئِكَ هُمُ الْفَاسِقُونَ ۝ وَأَقِيمُوا الصَّلَاةَ
وَآتُوا الزَّكَاةَ وَأَطِيعُوا الرَّسُولَ لَعَلَّكُمْ تُرْحَمُونَ ۝ لَا تَحْسَبَنَّ
الَّذِينَ كَفَرُوا مُعْجِزِينَ فِي الْأَرْضِ وَمَأْوَاهُمُ النَّارُ وَلَبِئْسَ
الْمَصِيرُ ۝ يَا أَيُّهَا الَّذِينَ آمَنُوا لِيَسْتَأْذِنكُمُ الَّذِينَ مَلَكَتْ
أَيْمَانُكُمْ وَالَّذِينَ لَمْ يَبْلُغُوا الْحُلُمَ مِنكُمْ ثَلَاثَ مَرَّاتٍ مِّن قَبْلِ
صَلَاةِ الْفَجْرِ وَحِينَ تَضَعُونَ ثِيَابَكُم مِّنَ الظَّهِيرَةِ وَمِن بَعْدِ
صَلَاةِ الْعِشَاءِ ثَلَاثُ عَوْرَاتٍ لَّكُمْ لَيْسَ عَلَيْكُمْ وَلَا عَلَيْهِمْ
جُنَاحٌ بَعْدَهُنَّ طَوَّافُونَ عَلَيْكُم بَعْضُكُمْ عَلَىٰ بَعْضٍ
كَذَٰلِكَ يُبَيِّنُ اللَّهُ لَكُمُ الْآيَاتِ وَاللَّهُ عَلِيمٌ حَكِيمٌ ۝

54. Say: "Obey God and obey the Messenger."[30] But, (O people), if you turn away from the Messenger, (then be aware that) what rests with him is only what he has been charged with and what rests with you is only what you have been charged with. However, if you obey, you will be guided (to the truth). What rests with the Messenger is but to convey the Message fully and clearly.

55. God has promised those of you who believe and do good, righteous deeds that He will most certainly empower them as vicegerents on the earth (in the place of those who are in power at present), even as He empowered those (of the same qualities) that preceded them, and that, assuredly, He will firmly establish for them their Religion, which He has (chosen and) approved of for them, and He will replace their present state of fear with security (so that they can practice their Religion freely and fully and in peace). They worship Me alone, associating none with Me as partners (in belief, worship, and the authority to order their life). Whoever turns ungrateful after that, such indeed are the transgressors.

56. Establish the Prayer in conformity with its conditions and pay the Prescribed Purifying Alms, and obey the Messenger so that you may be shown mercy (to be granted a good, virtuous life in the world and eternal happiness in the Hereafter.)[31]

57. Do not suppose that those who disbelieve can frustrate (Our will) on the earth. Their final refuge is the Fire: how evil a destination to arrive at!

58. O you who believe! Let (even) those whom your right hands possess (as slaves), as well as those of you (your children) who have not yet reached puberty, ask for your permission (before they come into your private room) at three times (of the day) – before the Morning Prayer, and when you lay aside your garments in the middle of the day for rest, and after the Night Prayer. These are your three times of privacy. Beyond these occasions, there is no blame on you nor on them if they come in without permission – they are bound to move about you, some of you attending on others. Thus God makes clear for you (the instructions in) the Revelations. God is All-Knowing, All-Wise.

30. This statement, like similar ones (e.g., verse 47 above), establishes that the Messenger commands and forbids on matters other than those included in the Qur'ān, and therefore refers to the Sunnah as a separate source of Islamic commandments. Otherwise, it would have said: "Obey God and the Messenger," without repeating the order *obey* before the Messenger.

(For a detailed explanation, see 4: 59, note 13.)

31. Establishing the Prayer, paying the Prescribed Purifying Alms and obeying the Messenger absolutely in all the aspects of his mission (adherence to the Sunnah) are the most important conditions to fulfill in order to deserve God's promise mentioned in the preceding verse and to deserve the promised state.

The Prophet's Mosque and Madīnah toward the end of the 19th century. (A painting by R. Yazdani, reproduced from a photo from the Yıldız Sarayı Archives in Istanbul.)

٣٥٧

الجزء الثامن عشر

357

وَإِذَا بَلَغَ الْأَطْفَالُ مِنكُمُ الْحُلُمَ فَلْيَسْتَأْذِنُوا كَمَا
اسْتَأْذَنَ الَّذِينَ مِن قَبْلِهِمْ كَذَلِكَ يُبَيِّنُ اللَّهُ
لَكُمْ ءَايَاتِهِ وَاللَّهُ عَلِيمٌ حَكِيمٌ ۝ وَالْقَوَاعِدُ مِنَ النِّسَاءِ
الَّتِي لَا يَرْجُونَ نِكَاحًا فَلَيْسَ عَلَيْهِنَّ جُنَاحٌ أَن يَضَعْنَ ثِيَابَهُنَّ
غَيْرَ مُتَبَرِّجَاتٍ بِزِينَةٍ وَأَن يَسْتَعْفِفْنَ خَيْرٌ لَّهُنَّ وَاللَّهُ
سَمِيعٌ عَلِيمٌ ۝ لَّيْسَ عَلَى الْأَعْمَى حَرَجٌ وَلَا عَلَى الْأَعْرَجِ
حَرَجٌ وَلَا عَلَى الْمَرِيضِ حَرَجٌ وَلَا عَلَى أَنفُسِكُمْ أَن تَأْكُلُوا
مِن بُيُوتِكُمْ أَوْ بُيُوتِ ءَابَائِكُمْ أَوْ بُيُوتِ أُمَّهَاتِكُمْ
أَوْ بُيُوتِ إِخْوَانِكُمْ أَوْ بُيُوتِ أَخَوَاتِكُمْ أَوْ بُيُوتِ أَعْمَامِكُمْ
أَوْ بُيُوتِ عَمَّاتِكُمْ أَوْ بُيُوتِ أَخْوَالِكُمْ أَوْ بُيُوتِ خَالَاتِكُمْ
أَوْ مَا مَلَكْتُم مَّفَاتِحَهُ أَوْ صَدِيقِكُمْ لَيْسَ عَلَيْكُمْ
جُنَاحٌ أَن تَأْكُلُوا جَمِيعًا أَوْ أَشْتَاتًا فَإِذَا دَخَلْتُم
بُيُوتًا فَسَلِّمُوا عَلَى أَنفُسِكُمْ تَحِيَّةً مِّنْ عِندِ اللَّهِ
مُبَارَكَةً طَيِّبَةً كَذَلِكَ يُبَيِّنُ اللَّهُ
لَكُمُ الْآيَاتِ لَعَلَّكُمْ تَعْقِلُونَ ۝

59. And when your children reach puberty, let them ask you for permission (whenever they want to enter your private room), even as those (who have already reached the same age) before them ask for it. Thus God makes clear for you (the instructions in) His revelations. God is All-Knowing, All-Wise.

60. The women advanced in years, having passed the age of child-bearing and no longer feel any sexual desire, incur no sin if they cast off their outer garments without making display of their charms. But even so, it is better for them to abstain from this. God is All-Hearing, All-Knowing.

61. There is no blame on the blind nor any blame on the lame nor any blame on the sick (for eating only to satisfy their need without causing any harm and waste, in the house of any healthy, well-off person), and neither on yourselves that (in case of need and without prior invitation), you eat in your spouse's and children's houses, or your fathers' houses, or your mothers' houses, or your brothers' houses, or your sisters' houses, or your paternal uncles' houses, or your paternal aunts'

houses, or your maternal uncles' houses, or your maternal aunts' houses, or in the houses for which you are responsible, or the house of any of your close friends (who should be happy to see you feeling free to eat at their home). There is no blame on you if you eat together or separately. But when you enter any of these houses, greet one another with a blessed, pure and good salutation appointed by God. Thus God makes clear for you (the instructions in) His Revelations, that you may reason and understand.[32]

---

32. When thinking about this instruction, we may consider the importance Islam gives to mutual helping, solidarity, and brother/sisterhood which it seeks to establish among Muslims.

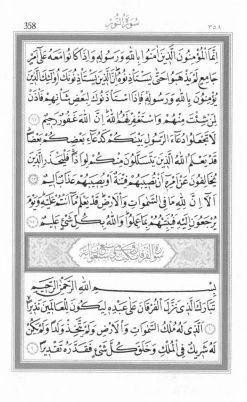

358   سُوْرَةُ النُّوْرِ   ٣٥٨

to whomever of them you will, and ask God for forgiveness on their behalf. Surely, God is All-Forgiving, All-Compassionate.[33]

63. Do not treat the Messenger's summoning and praying for you as your summoning and praying for one another. Indeed, God knows well those of you who surreptitiously sneak away, taking cover behind one another. So, let those who go against the Messenger's order beware lest a bitter trial[34] befall them or a painful punishment afflict them.

64. Beware: to God belongs whatever is in the heavens and the earth. He knows well where you stand (and what you are about). And (to Him belongs) the Day when you are brought back to Him, then He will make them understand all that they did (in the world). God has full knowledge of everything.

62. Only those are true believers who believe in God and His Messenger, and who, when they are with him for a collective cause, do not leave unless they have obtained his permission. Surely those who ask for your permission, it is they who truly believe in God and His Messenger. So, if they ask you for permission for some affair of their own, give permission

33. Whenever Muslims or those among them who are concerned are summoned to a collective cause, they should never fail to respond to the call nor depart without the permission of the ruler/leader or administrator. Should any of them have a reason for departing, the reason must be a genuine, valid one, and again they should not depart without permission. The administrator or leader is fully entitled to grant

or deny permission that has been asked for, at his discretion.

34. The trial to befall those who oppose the orders of the Messenger and, after him, of his successors, has many forms or aspects, such as the yoke of unjust and oppressive rulers, dissension or disorder and civil war, moral degeneration, and the loss of power.

SŪRAH 25

AL-FURQĀN
(THE CRITERION)

Makkah period

This *sūrah* takes its name from the word *al-Furqān* (the Criterion, the Book that distinguishes between truth and falsehood) in the first of its 77 verses. The *sūrah* was revealed in the mid-Makkan period. It negates the doubts that were voiced by the Makkan polytheists concerning the Divine origin of the Qur'ān, and the Prophethood of Muḥammad, upon him be peace and blessings. It also propounds the moral excellence of the believers *vis-à-vis* their enemies, and states that the Divine Message elevates its followers intellectually, morally, and spiritually.

In the Name of God, the All-Merciful, the All-Compassionate.

Blessed and Supreme is He Who sends down the Criterion in parts on His servant so that he may be a warner to all conscious beings (against the consequences of misguidance).

He to Whom belongs the sovereignty of the heavens and the earth, and He has taken to Himself no child, nor has He any partner (in His dominion or any aspect of His being God), and He creates everything and determines its destiny.[1]

---

1. As explained in several places in this study (*sūrah* 4: 79, note 18; *sūrah* 6: 59, note 13; *sūrah* 7: 173, note 43; *sūrah* 11: 6, note 1; *sūrah* 13: 39, note 13; *sūrah* 17: 14, note 10, and Appendix 7), there are various aspects of destiny. Here destiny means a certain, exact measure, and a form and size, and the potentials, attributes, characteristics, and functions that are particular to a being, and the limits of its growth, and development, as well as all other details that pertain to it and its life.

وَاتَّخَذُوا مِن دُونِهِ اٰلِهَةً لَّا يَخْلُقُونَ شَيْئاً وَهُمْ يُخْلَقُونَ
وَلَا يَمْلِكُونَ لِأَنفُسِهِمْ ضَرّاً وَلَا نَفْعاً وَلَا يَمْلِكُونَ
مَوْتاً وَلَا حَيَوٰةً وَلَا نُشُوراً ۞ وَقَالَ الَّذِينَ كَفَرُوٓا
إِنْ هٰذَآ إِلَّآ إِفْكٌ افْتَرَىٰهُ وَأَعَانَهُ عَلَيْهِ قَوْمٌ اٰخَرُونَ
فَقَدْ جَآءُو ظُلْماً وَزُوراً ۞ وَقَالُوٓا أَسَاطِيرُ الْأَوَّلِينَ
اكْتَتَبَهَا فَهِيَ تُمْلَىٰ عَلَيْهِ بُكْرَةً وَأَصِيلاً ۞ قُلْ أَنزَلَهُ
الَّذِي يَعْلَمُ السِّرَّ فِي السَّمٰوَاتِ وَالْأَرْضِ إِنَّهُ كَانَ غَفُوراً
رَّحِيماً ۞ وَقَالُوا مَالِ هٰذَا الرَّسُولِ يَأْكُلُ الطَّعَامَ
وَيَمْشِي فِي الْأَسْوَاقِ لَوْلَآ أُنزِلَ إِلَيْهِ مَلَكٌ فَيَكُونَ مَعَهُ
نَذِيراً ۞ أَوْ يُلْقَىٰ إِلَيْهِ كَنزٌ أَوْ تَكُونُ لَهُ جَنَّةٌ يَأْكُلُ
مِنْهَا وَقَالَ الظَّالِمُونَ إِن تَتَّبِعُونَ إِلَّا رَجُلاً مَّسْحُوراً ۞ انظُرْ
كَيْفَ ضَرَبُوا لَكَ الْأَمْثَالَ فَضَلُّوا فَلَا يَسْتَطِيعُونَ سَبِيلاً ۞
تَبَارَكَ الَّذِي إِن شَآءَ جَعَلَ لَكَ خَيْراً مِّن ذٰلِكَ جَنَّاتٍ تَجْرِي
مِن تَحْتِهَا الْأَنْهَارُ وَيَجْعَل لَّكَ قُصُوراً ۞ بَلْ كَذَّبُوا
بِالسَّاعَةِ وَأَعْتَدْنَا لِمَن كَذَّبَ بِالسَّاعَةِ سَعِيراً ۞

------

3. Yet some choose to take, apart from God, deities that create nothing but are themselves created, and have no power to avert harm from, or bring benefit to, even themselves (so that they can give harm or bring benefit to their worshippers), and they have no power over death, nor over life, nor over resurrection.[2]

4. Those who disbelieve say: "This (Qur'ān) is but a fabrication which he (Muḥammad) himself has invented, and some others have helped him with it, so they have produced a wrong and a falsehood."

5. They also say: "(It consists of) only fables of the ancients which he has got written. They are being read to him in early mornings and evenings (while people are at home)."[3]

6. Say: "(It is a Book full of knowledge revealing many secrets such as no human being could in any wise discover by himself:) He Who knows all the secrets contained in the heavens and the earth sends it down (to teach you some of these secrets and guide you in your life so that you may attain happiness in both worlds). He surely is All-Forgiving, All-Compassionate."

7. Again, they say: "What sort of Messenger is this? He eats food and goes about in market-places (like any other mortal). Why is an angel not sent down to him so that he may act as a warner in his company (and help him to persuade the people)?"

8. Or: "Why is a treasure not cast down upon him from the heaven (so that he should no longer need to go about in market-places to earn a living)?" Or: "Why does he not have a garden (granted to him miraculously) to obtain his food from?" And so these wrongdoers say (to the believers): "You are following only a man bewitched!"

9. See how strangely they invent comparisons about you. They have so strayed and are no longer able to find a way (to the truth). excuse

10. Blessed and Supreme is He Who, if He wills, can grant you (O Messenger) better than all that (they propose): gardens through which rivers flow, and grant you palaces.

11. But they deny the Last Hour (and this is why they invent such pretexts for their denial of your call. However,) We have prepared a Blaze for whoever denies the Last Hour.

2. All creatures, including human beings, even though they are endowed with better developed faculties and potentials than other creatures, are essentially weak. Human beings have no power to decide whether they will come into existence or not, maintain their lives, nor are they able to decide on their physical attributes or choose the date and place of their birth or death; they cannot decide who will be part of their families or not, nor are they able to determine what is harmful or beneficial to them. Neither do they have control over the operation of the heavens and the earth, not even of their own bodies, nor can they control their vital needs, such as hunger, thirst, and sleep. Even if all humans were to come together and were supported by all other beings, they would not be able to create even a blade of grass.

If humankind are weak and limited to such degree, then there is no other kind of mortal being that can be their owner, creator, or governor. Only One Who has absolute knowledge of the universe in its entirety, with whatever is in it, including the relation of everything with everything else and with the universe as a whole, and a knowledge of each being with all its particularities and needs, and Who has absolute power to create, while Himself is not created, and to give or avert harm and benefit, and to deal out death, give life and raise the dead, can be the creator, owner, and governor of all beings, including humankind.

3. Such baseless allegations are no different from those which the orientalists raise against the Qur'ān. The only difference is that those who made these allegations during the Prophet's time were more honest than their contemporary counterparts. Unlike the orientalists, they never claimed that the Messenger, upon him be peace and blessings, had acquired the essence of his teaching from Bahīrā, whom he met in his childhood during his travels. Nor did they assert that he was taught by the Christian or Jewish scholars during these same travels. They were well aware that the Messenger made these journeys during his childhood and youth along with the caravans, and they also knew that those who were with him would have refuted such claims. In addition, the Messenger declared his Messengership many years after his travels. Among the many false objections they raised, they also claimed that at times when people were at home, some relatively more knowledgeable people in Makkah would secretly recite to him from some old books so that he might have these ideas written down, subsequently conveying these to other people during the day. No one ever believed these baseless allegations. Even those who fabricated them did not truly believe them, and soon started to make many other allegations.

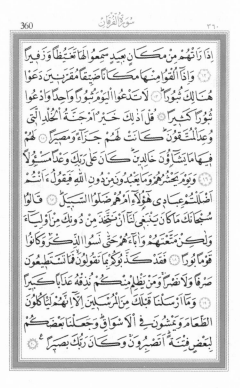

12. When the Blaze sees them (even) from a far-off place, they will hear it raging and roaring.[4]

13. And when they are flung, chained together, into a narrow place in it, they will pray there for extinction.

14. (They will then be told) "Today, you will not pray to die only once, instead, you will pray to die many times, (but it will be of no avail)."

15. Say (O Messenger): "Is this or is the Garden of life everlasting, which has been promised to the God-revering, pious, better to prefer?" It will be for them a reward and a final destination.

16. For them there will be therein all that they desire, themselves abiding (in it).[5] This is a promise which your Lord has bound Himself to fulfill.

17. A Day (will come) when God will gather them together (all the unbelievers) and all those whom they worship (apart from God: angels, Prophets, saints, and others, and idols), and He will ask them: "Was it you who led these servants of Mine astray or did they themselves stray away from the right way?"

18. They will say: "All-Glorified You are! It was not for us to take for friends other than You (so they had no right to take us as such and make us objects of their worship). But (the truth is that, out of Your grace) You lavished on them and their forefathers ease in life, but they (being ungrateful) forgot all remembrance of You (and paid no heed to the warning Message Your Messengers brought to them). They were people (corrupt and) doomed to perdition."

19. (God will say:) "So they have denied you (who falsely worship them) in all that you assert regarding them, and you can neither ward off (your due punishment) nor obtain any help (from those you falsely deified and worshipped while in the world)." (O people!) Whoever commits the greatest wrong (by associating partners with God), We will cause him to taste a great punishment.

20. (O Messenger!) We never sent any Messengers before you but they surely ate food and went about in the market-places (to meet their needs). We cause you (O humankind) to be a means of testing for one another. Will you show good patience and perseverance (in the face of Our decrees and remain steadfast in Our way)? Your Lord is All-Seeing.

4. Although some commentators take the phrase *the Blaze sees them* for a metaphorical description, it may well be literal and mean that Hell is not devoid of life and consciousness. In verse 65 of *Sūrat al-'Ankabūt* (29) it is stated that *the abode of the Hereafter is truly alive*. We cannot measure that life in the terms and scales known to us in this world. For this world is the abode of Wisdom, where God operates from behind the veil of matter and causality. But the Hereafter will be the abode of Power, where God will operate without any veil.

As reported by at-Ṭabarānī from Abū Umāmah, the Messenger declared: "Whoever attributes to me any word which I did not say should prepare himself for his place between the two eyes of Hell." When asked whether Hell had eyes, he recited this verse and added: "If it did not have eyes, how could it see?" (Yazır, 5: 3576)

5. Paradise is the abode of absolute purity and the believers will enter it after attaining purity by passing through all the realms of the Hereafter. These realms will serve as a means of purification until they are fit for Paradise. So they will desire there only the things that one who is absolutely pure is expected to desire and which are to be found in Paradise in accordance with God's approval.

وَقَالَ الَّذِينَ لَا يَرْجُونَ لِقَآءَنَا لَوْلَآ أُنزِلَ عَلَيْنَا الْمَلَـٰٓئِكَةُ أَوْ نَرَىٰ رَبَّنَا ۗ لَقَدِ اسْتَكْبَرُوا فِىٓ أَنفُسِهِمْ وَعَتَوْ عُتُوًّا كَبِيرًا ۞ يَوْمَ يَرَوْنَ الْمَلَـٰٓئِكَةَ لَا بُشْرَىٰ يَوْمَئِذٍ لِّلْمُجْرِمِينَ وَيَقُولُونَ حِجْرًا مَّحْجُورًا ۞ وَقَدِمْنَآ إِلَىٰ مَا عَمِلُوا مِنْ عَمَلٍ فَجَعَلْنَـٰهُ هَبَآءً مَّنثُورًا ۞ أَصْحَـٰبُ الْجَنَّةِ يَوْمَئِذٍ خَيْرٌ مُّسْتَقَرًّا وَأَحْسَنُ مَقِيلًا ۞ وَيَوْمَ تَشَقَّقُ السَّمَآءُ بِالْغَمَـٰمِ وَنُزِّلَ الْمَلَـٰٓئِكَةُ تَنزِيلًا ۞ الْمُلْكُ يَوْمَئِذٍ الْحَقُّ لِلرَّحْمَـٰنِ ۚ وَكَانَ يَوْمًا عَلَى الْكَـٰفِرِينَ عَسِيرًا ۞ وَيَوْمَ يَعَضُّ الظَّالِمُ عَلَىٰ يَدَيْهِ يَقُولُ يَـٰلَيْتَنِى اتَّخَذْتُ مَعَ الرَّسُولِ سَبِيلًا ۞ يَـٰوَيْلَتَىٰ لَيْتَنِى لَمْ أَتَّخِذْ فُلَانًا خَلِيلًا ۞ لَّقَدْ أَضَلَّنِى عَنِ الذِّكْرِ بَعْدَ إِذْ جَآءَنِى ۗ وَكَانَ الشَّيْطَـٰنُ لِلْإِنسَـٰنِ خَذُولًا ۞ وَقَالَ الرَّسُولُ يَـٰرَبِّ إِنَّ قَوْمِى اتَّخَذُوا هَـٰذَا الْقُرْءَانَ مَهْجُورًا ۞ وَكَذَٰلِكَ جَعَلْنَا لِكُلِّ نَبِىٍّ عَدُوًّا مِّنَ الْمُجْرِمِينَ ۗ وَكَفَىٰ بِرَبِّكَ هَادِيًا وَنَصِيرًا ۞ وَقَالَ الَّذِينَ كَفَرُوا لَوْلَا نُزِّلَ عَلَيْهِ الْقُرْءَانُ جُمْلَةً وَاحِدَةً ۚ كَذَٰلِكَ لِنُثَبِّتَ بِهِ فُؤَادَكَ ۖ وَرَتَّلْنَـٰهُ تَرْتِيلًا ۞

---

21. Those who (being unbelievers) do not expect to meet Us (in the Hereafter) say: "Why are no angels sent down on us or (why) do we not see our Lord?" Assuredly they are far too arrogant of themselves (demanding what is impossible for them), and exceed all bounds (in their presumption).

22. The Day when they see the angels – there will be no good tidings on that Day for the disbelieving criminals, and they will cry out to the angels in fear: "Keep away, away from us!"

23. And We will turn to deal with all the (supposedly good) deeds that they did (in the world), and will reduce them all to dust particles scattered about.

24. Whereas the companions of Paradise will, on that Day, have appointed for them the best abode and the fairest place of repose.

25. On that Day the heaven will split asunder with the clouds (covering it) and the angels will be made to descend in a majestic descending.

26. The sovereignty on that Day will absolutely and belong to the All-Merciful, (which He will exercise then with no intermediary veil of cause and effect).[6] It will be a hard day for the unbelievers.

27. On that Day the wrongdoer will bite at his hands, saying (with remorse) "Oh, would that I had taken a way in the company of the Messenger.

28. "Oh, woe is me! Would that I had not taken so-and-so for a friend!

29. "Indeed, he led me astray from the Reminder (the Qur'ān) once it had come to me. Satan has proved to be a betrayer of humankind."

30. And the Messenger says: "My Lord! Surely my people have made this Qur'ān something worthy of no attention."

31. So for every Prophet We have made an enemy (band) from among the disbelieving criminals committed to accumulating sins. But Your Lord is sufficient as a guide (to truth and the right course of action) and a helper (against the plots and practices of your enemies).

32. Those who disbelieve say (by way of yet another false argument for unbelief): "Why has the Qur'ān not been sent down on him all at once?" (We send it down in parts) so that We may (impress it on your mind and) establish your heart with it, and We are conveying it distinctly and gradually, (one part supporting the other, and providing guidance and instruction for emerging occasions).

6. The attributive Name of God that is used in this verse and which has been translated as the All-Merciful is *ar-Raḥmān*. As explained while interpreting the *Basmalah* at the very beginning of this study, it is not possible to render *ar-Raḥmān* in its exact meaning in another language. It implies God's all-inclusive, universal manifestation throughout the universe and, although derived from *raḥmah* (mercy) and implying One Who gives life, maintains, provides, and equips all beings with the necessary capacities, it also refers to God as the All-Majestic One and is therefore the origin of God's Attributes of Majesty, such as the All-Compelling, the All-Overwhelming, the All-Glorious with irresistible might, and the One Who punishes. For this reason, His punishing is also included in His Mercy. God's pure mercy, which is required to reward, forgive, and pity, is necessitated by or is the manifestation of His being *ar-Raḥīm* (the All-Compassionate). This explains why the All-Merciful is preferred in this verse. In the Hereafter, God will manifest Himself first of all as *ar-Raḥmān* (the All-Merciful), the All-Majestic One Who both rewards and punishes out of mercy. As *ar-Raḥmān*, He will exercise His Will in the Hereafter without the veil of cause and effect or any law (as He exercises it in the world). For this reason, it is said that the Hereafter is the abode of Power, while the world is the abode of Wisdom.

362   سُوْرَةُالْفُرْقَانِ   ٣٦٢

وَلَا يَأْتُونَكَ بِمَثَلٍ إِلَّا جِئْنَاكَ بِالْحَقِّ وَأَحْسَنَ تَفْسِيرًا ۝ الَّذِينَ يُحْشَرُونَ عَلَى وُجُوهِهِمْ إِلَىٰ جَهَنَّمَ أُوْلَئِكَ شَرٌّ مَّكَانًا وَأَضَلُّ سَبِيلًا ۝ وَلَقَدْ ءَاتَيْنَا مُوسَى الْكِتَابَ وَجَعَلْنَا مَعَهُ أَخَاهُ هَرُونَ وَزِيرًا ۝ فَقُلْنَا اذْهَبَا إِلَى الْقَوْمِ الَّذِينَ كَذَّبُوا بِآيَاتِنَا فَدَمَّرْنَاهُمْ تَدْمِيرًا ۝ وَقَوْمَ نُوحٍ لَّمَّا كَذَّبُوا الرُّسُلَ أَغْرَقْنَاهُمْ وَجَعَلْنَاهُمْ لِلنَّاسِ ءَايَةً وَأَعْتَدْنَا لِلظَّالِمِينَ عَذَابًا أَلِيمًا ۝ وَعَادًا وَثَمُودَ وَأَصْحَابَ الرَّسِّ وَقُرُونًا بَيْنَ ذَلِكَ كَثِيرًا ۝ وَكُلًّا ضَرَبْنَا لَهُ الْأَمْثَالَ وَكُلًّا تَبَّرْنَا تَتْبِيرًا ۝ وَلَقَدْ أَتَوْا عَلَى الْقَرْيَةِ الَّتِي أُمْطِرَتْ مَطَرَ السَّوْءِ أَفَلَمْ يَكُونُوا يَرَوْنَهَا بَلْ كَانُوا لَا يَرْجُونَ نُشُورًا ۝ وَإِذَا رَأَوْكَ إِن يَتَّخِذُونَكَ إِلَّا هُزُوًا أَهَذَا الَّذِي بَعَثَ اللهُ رَسُولًا ۝ إِن كَادَ لَيُضِلُّنَا عَنْ ءَالِهَتِنَا لَوْلَا أَن صَبَرْنَا عَلَيْهَا وَسَوْفَ يَعْلَمُونَ حِينَ يَرَوْنَ الْعَذَابَ مَنْ أَضَلُّ سَبِيلًا ۝ أَرَأَيْتَ مَنِ اتَّخَذَ إِلَهَهُ هَوَاهُ أَفَأَنتَ تَكُونُ عَلَيْهِ وَكِيلًا ۝

---

33. And also, they never come to you with any (false) argument (to taunt and provoke you) but that We provide you with the truth (to counter their false arguments) and a better exposition (which enables and deepens understanding).[7]

34. Those who will be gathered in Hell upon their faces: such represent the evil side in standing and are further astray from the right way.

35. (Examples from history:) Assuredly We granted to Moses the Book and appointed his brother Aaron with him as a helper.

36. Then We said: "Go both of you to the people who deny Our signs (in the universe and within their own selves that demonstrate Our Existence and Oneness). Then (after they had been warned), We destroyed them utterly.

37. And the people of Noah – when they denied (Noah and thereby meant to deny) the Messengers, We drowned them, and made them a sign (of warning and instruction) for humankind. We have kept ready a painful punishment for the wrongdoers.

38. And the Ād and Thamūd, and the people of ar-Rass,[8] and many other generations that lived between these (and the people of Noah).

39. To each (of them) did We explain the truth in diverse ways and warning examples (from history), and each (of them) did We annihilate utterly.

40. And they (in Makkah who now persist in unbelief) have surely come across the land (of the Prophet Lot) upon which was rained a rain of evil. Have they, then, never seen it (with an eye to take heed)? No, they have no expectation of being raised after death (and so they pay no heed to any warning).

41. Whenever they see you (O Messenger), they take you for nothing but a mockery, (saying): "Is this the one whom God has sent as Messenger?

42. "Indeed, he would almost have led us astray from our deities, had we not persevered in our attachment to them." But in time when they see the (promised) punishment, they will come to know who it was that strayed too far from the right way.

43. Do you ever consider him who has taken his lusts and fancies for his deity?[9] Would you then be a guardian over him (and thereby assume responsibility for guiding him)?

7. Although the Qur'ān was revealed in parts over 23 years for different needs and purposes, it has such a perfect harmony that it is as if it were revealed all at once.

Although the Qur'ān was revealed over 23 years on different occasions, its parts are so mutually supportive that it is as if it were revealed all at once.

Although the Qur'ān came in answer to different and repeated questions, its parts are so united and harmonious with each other that it is as if it were the answer to a single question.

Although the Qur'ān came to judge diverse cases and events, it displays such a perfect order that it is as if it were a judgment delivered on a single case or event.

Although the Qur'ān was revealed by Divine courtesy in styles varied to suit innumerable people from different levels of understanding, moods, and temperament, its parts exhibit so beautiful a similarity, correspondence, and fluency that it is as if it were addressing one degree of understanding and temperament.

Although the Qur'ān speaks to an infinite variety of people who are remote from each other in time, space, and character, it has such a simple way of explanation, pure style, and clear description that it is as if it were addressing only one homogenous group, with each different group thinking that it is being addressed uniquely and specifically.

Although the Qur'ān was revealed with various purposes for the gradual guidance of different peoples, it has such a perfect straightforwardness, sensitive balance, and such a beautiful order that it is as if it were pursuing only one purpose (*The Words*, "the 25th Word," 433).

8. We have no definite knowledge about the identity of the people of ar-Rass. *Ar-rass* means a well. Some scholars are of the opinion that it was the name of a river. Some others point out that a town of that name exists to this day in the central Arabian province of al-Qasīm. It seems to have been inhabited by descendants of the Nabataean tribe of the Thamūd (at-Tabarī) (*The Message of the Qur'ān*, 554, note 33). Another opinion is that those people were called the people of ar-Rass because they threw the Messenger sent to them down a well.

9. Deifying one's lusts and fancies means pursuing one's lusts and fancies at all costs and making the satisfaction of them the goal of one's life. The greatest obstacle to believing in God or being attached to His Religion is one's carnal soul prompting them to pursue the satisfaction of their lusts whether lawfully or unlawfully. God's Messenger, upon him be peace and blessings, warned: "Of all the false deities that are worshipped under the sky, the worst in God's sight is one's carnal, evil-commanding soul" (at-Ṭabarānī, vol. 8, *hadīth no*: 7502).

أَمْ تَحْسَبُ أَنَّ أَكْثَرَهُمْ يَسْمَعُونَ أَوْ يَعْقِلُونَ ۚ إِنْ
هُمْ إِلَّا كَالْأَنْعَامِ ۖ بَلْ هُمْ أَضَلُّ سَبِيلًا ۞ أَلَمْ تَرَ إِلَىٰ
رَبِّكَ كَيْفَ مَدَّ الظِّلَّ وَلَوْ شَاءَ لَجَعَلَهُ سَاكِنًا ثُمَّ جَعَلْنَا
الشَّمْسَ عَلَيْهِ دَلِيلًا ۞ ثُمَّ قَبَضْنَاهُ إِلَيْنَا قَبْضًا يَسِيرًا ۞
وَهُوَ الَّذِي جَعَلَ لَكُمُ اللَّيْلَ لِبَاسًا وَالنَّوْمَ سُبَاتًا وَجَعَلَ النَّهَارَ
نُشُورًا ۞ وَهُوَ الَّذِي أَرْسَلَ الرِّيَاحَ بُشْرًا بَيْنَ يَدَيْ رَحْمَتِهِ
وَأَنْزَلْنَا مِنَ السَّمَاءِ مَاءً طَهُورًا ۞ لِنُحْيِيَ بِهِ بَلْدَةً مَيْتًا
وَنُسْقِيَهُ مِمَّا خَلَقْنَا أَنْعَامًا وَأَنَاسِيَّ كَثِيرًا ۞ وَلَقَدْ صَرَّفْنَاهُ
بَيْنَهُمْ لِيَذَّكَّرُوا فَأَبَىٰ أَكْثَرُ النَّاسِ إِلَّا كُفُورًا ۞ وَلَوْ شِئْنَا
لَبَعَثْنَا فِي كُلِّ قَرْيَةٍ نَذِيرًا ۞ فَلَا تُطِعِ الْكَافِرِينَ وَجَاهِدْهُمْ
بِهِ جِهَادًا كَبِيرًا ۞ وَهُوَ الَّذِي مَرَجَ الْبَحْرَيْنِ هَذَا عَذْبٌ فُرَاتٌ
وَهَذَا مِلْحٌ أُجَاجٌ وَجَعَلَ بَيْنَهُمَا بَرْزَخًا وَحِجْرًا مَحْجُورًا ۞
وَهُوَ الَّذِي خَلَقَ مِنَ الْمَاءِ بَشَرًا فَجَعَلَهُ نَسَبًا وَصِهْرًا وَكَانَ
رَبُّكَ قَدِيرًا ۞ وَيَعْبُدُونَ مِنْ دُونِ اللَّهِ مَا لَا يَنْفَعُهُمْ
وَلَا يَضُرُّهُمْ وَكَانَ الْكَافِرُ عَلَىٰ رَبِّهِ ظَهِيرًا ۞

---

44. Or do you think that most of them (really) hear or reason and understand? They are but like cattle, (following only their instincts). No, they are more heedless of the right way (and therefore in greater need of being led than cattle).

45. Have you considered your Lord – how He spreads the shade? If He willed, He would surely make it stationary, but We have made the sun its pilot.

46. And then (as the sun rises), We gradually draw it back up towards Us.[10]

47. And He it is Who has made the night a garment for you, and sleep a rest. And He has made the day a time of rising to life and going about (for daily livelihood).

48. And He it is Who sends forth the (merciful) winds as glad tidings in advance of His mercy. And We cause pure water to descend from the sky,

49. So that We may revive through it a dead land and give it for drink to many beings among Our creation, beasts as well as humans.

50. Assuredly We distribute it among them (without depriving any) so that they may remember and so be mindful. But most of humankind obstinately refuse to do anything except showing ingratitude.

51. Had We so willed, We could certainly have raised up a warner in every township.

52. (But We have willed instead that you are the last Messenger whose mission is universal.) So pay no heed to (the desires of) the unbelievers, but engage in a mighty striving against them by means of it (the Qur'ān).

53. And He it is Who has let flow forth the two large bodies of water, one sweet and palatable and the other salty and bitter; and He has set a barrier and an insurmountable, forbidding ban that keeps them apart.[11]

54. And He it is Who from a fluid has created human and made it (a male and female and, through them,) into a population through descent and marriage. And Your Lord is All-Powerful.[12]

55. And yet they (the polytheists) worship, apart from God, that which can neither benefit them nor harm them. The unbeliever is ever prone to make cause (i.e. to back everyone and every movement) against his Lord.

10. These verses, up to verse 50, draw attention to God's acts in the universe as evidence of His Existence, Oneness, His absolute authority over creation, and revival after death.

As we know, the lengthening and shortening of shadows depends on the movement and position of the earth in respect to the sun. If there were no shadows, or if shadows were stationary, no life or vegetation would be possible on the earth. Life on earth requires the heat and light of the sun, but constant exposure to its heat and light would destroy everything. For a further explanation about shadows, see 13: 15, note 7; 16: 49.

The statement *We gradually draw it back towards Us*, expresses the fact that nothing disappears into non-existence. Every thing and every event end "in" God or return "to" Him.

As explained when interpreting the verses of *sūrah* 7: 55–58 (note 14), the Qur'ān mentions the "natural" phenomena along with sociological events and those that pertain to human spiritual life in such a way that one provides an example for the other. So, behind the apparent meaning of these verses concerning shadows and the sun as their pilot, there is the suggestion that the dark shadow of ignorance and unbelief depends on the sun of guidance in their lengthening and shortening. As this sun rises, the shadows of ignorance and unbelief vanish away gradually (not abruptly). So, if Muslims desire these shadows to disappear, they should support the sun of guidance, which has appeared finally and universally in the person of the Prophet Muḥammad, upon him be peace and blessings.

11. Wherever a large river flows into the sea we can encounter the phenomenon described here. There are springs of sweet water at several locations in different seas where the sweet water remains separate from the salty water. Seydi Ali Reis, a Turkish admiral of the 16th century, mentions in his work *Mir'āt al-Mamālik* one such place in the Persian Gulf. He writes that he found springs of sweet water under the salty water of the sea and drew drinking water from them for his fellow sailors (al-Mawdūdī, 7: 32, note 68).

The French marine-scientist Jacques Cousteau discovered that the Mediterranean Sea and the Atlantic Ocean have different chemical and biological constitutions. After conducting undersea investigations in the Straits of Gibraltar to study this phenomenon, he concluded that unexpected fresh water springs issue from the southern and northern coasts of Gibraltar. These waters gush forth toward each other at an angle of 45°, forming a reciprocal dam that acts like the teeth of a comb. Due to this fact, the Mediterranean and the Atlantic Ocean cannot intermingle.

In addition to this meaning, commentators on the Qur'ān also derive from this verse a meaning that is applicable to all the pairs of "seas" or realms, i.e., the spiritual and material, the figurative and actual, the realms of the human spirit and the carnal self, and of the Lordship and servanthood. Also included are the spheres of belief and unbelief, righteousness and transgression, necessity and contingency, as well as this world and the Hereafter (including this visible, corporeal world and all unseen worlds).

12. Just as sweet water can exist side by side with salty, bitter water, humankind also form a population by the combination of the two sexes – male and female. They are similar in nature and composition, but different in psychology and certain physiological features. It is by the union of these two that God has produced ties of kindred, creating love and compassion toward one another, and multiplied human populations.

364   سُورَةُ الفُرْقَانِ   ٣٦٤

وَمَآ أَرْسَلْنَٰكَ إِلَّا مُبَشِّرًا وَنَذِيرًا ۝ قُلْ مَآ أَسْـَٔلُكُمْ عَلَيْهِ
مِنْ أَجْرٍ إِلَّا مَن شَآءَ أَن يَتَّخِذَ إِلَىٰ رَبِّهِۦ سَبِيلًا ۝ وَتَوَكَّلْ
عَلَى ٱلْحَىِّ ٱلَّذِى لَا يَمُوتُ وَسَبِّحْ بِحَمْدِهِۦ وَكَفَىٰ بِهِۦ بِذُنُوبِ
عِبَادِهِۦ خَبِيرًا ۝ ٱلَّذِى خَلَقَ ٱلسَّمَٰوَٰتِ وَٱلْأَرْضَ
وَمَا بَيْنَهُمَا فِى سِتَّةِ أَيَّامٍ ثُمَّ ٱسْتَوَىٰ عَلَى ٱلْعَرْشِ
ٱلرَّحْمَٰنُ فَسْـَٔلْ بِهِۦ خَبِيرًا ۝ وَإِذَا قِيلَ لَهُمُ ٱسْجُدُوا۟
لِلرَّحْمَٰنِ قَالُوا۟ وَمَا ٱلرَّحْمَٰنُ أَنَسْجُدُ لِمَا تَأْمُرُنَا وَزَادَهُمْ
نُفُورًا ۩ ۝ تَبَارَكَ ٱلَّذِى جَعَلَ فِى ٱلسَّمَآءِ بُرُوجًا وَجَعَلَ
فِيهَا سِرَٰجًا وَقَمَرًا مُّنِيرًا ۝ وَهُوَ ٱلَّذِى جَعَلَ ٱلَّيْلَ وَٱلنَّهَارَ
خِلْفَةً لِّمَنْ أَرَادَ أَن يَذَّكَّرَ أَوْ أَرَادَ شُكُورًا ۝ وَعِبَادُ
ٱلرَّحْمَٰنِ ٱلَّذِينَ يَمْشُونَ عَلَى ٱلْأَرْضِ هَوْنًا وَإِذَا خَاطَبَهُمُ ٱلْجَٰهِلُونَ
قَالُوا۟ سَلَٰمًا ۝ وَٱلَّذِينَ يَبِيتُونَ لِرَبِّهِمْ سُجَّدًا وَقِيَٰمًا ۝
وَٱلَّذِينَ يَقُولُونَ رَبَّنَا ٱصْرِفْ عَنَّا عَذَابَ جَهَنَّمَ إِنَّ عَذَابَهَا
كَانَ غَرَامًا ۝ إِنَّهَا سَآءَتْ مُسْتَقَرًّا وَمُقَامًا ۝ وَٱلَّذِينَ إِذَآ
أَنفَقُوا۟ لَمْ يُسْرِفُوا۟ وَلَمْ يَقْتُرُوا۟ وَكَانَ بَيْنَ ذَٰلِكَ قَوَامًا ۝

───≫───

56. Yet, We have not sent you (O Messenger) but as a bearer of glad tidings and a warner (you are not accountable for their straying and sinning).

57. Say: "I ask of you no wage for this (conveying of the Message to you), except that whoever so wills may take a way leading to his Lord."[13]

58. Put your trust in the All-Living Who does not die, and glorify Him with His praise (proclaiming that He is absolutely above having any partners and that all praise is due to Him). He suffices as One Who is ever aware of the sins of His servants –

59. He Who has created the heavens and the earth and all that is between them in six days, and then established Himself on

the Supreme Throne.[14] That is the All-Merciful (with absolute Will, Power, and Knowledge), so ask Him about it (the truth about Him and creation) as All-Aware, (and ask Him for whatever you will ask for).

60. When they are told: "Prostrate before the All-Merciful (to express your submission to Him)," they say: "What is the All-Merciful? Shall we prostrate before whatever you command us?" Your call but increases them in (their haughty) aversion.

61. Blessed and Supreme is He Who has set in the sky great constellations, and placed in it a (great, radiant) lamp[15] and a shining moon.

62. It is He Who has appointed the night and the day to succeed one another, providing a sign for whoever desires to reflect and so be mindful, or desires to be thankful.

63. The (true) servants of the All-Merciful are they who move on the earth gently and humbly, and when the ignorant, foolish ones address them (with insolence or vulgarity as befits their ignorance and foolishness), they response with (words of) peace, (without engaging in hostility with them);

64. And (those true servants of the All-Merciful are they) who spend (some of) the night (in worship) prostrating before their Lord and standing;

65. And who entreat (whether after the Prayers or at other times): "Our Lord! Ward off from us the punishment of Hell; its punishment is surely constant anguish:

66. "How evil indeed it is as a final station and permanent abode!";

67. And who, when they spend (both for their own and others' needs), are neither wasteful nor niggardly, and (are aware that) there is a happy mean between those (two extremes);[16]

13. One of the basic purposes for God's sending the Prophets and Islam's order for *jihād* and communicating Islam to people is to show people the way that leads to God and to remove the obstacles on this way or those between God and those who want to reach Him.

14. For an explanation of this sentence, see 2: 28, note 28; 7: 54, note 13; 11: 7, note 2.

15. By depicting the sun as a lamp, the Qur'ān opens a window on a specific meaning: This world is a palace, and its contents are the food and necessities of life for humanity and other living things. The sun is a lamp that illuminates this palace. By making the Maker's magnificence and the Creator's favors comprehensible in this way, the sentence provides a proof for God's Unity and declares the sun (which some polytheists of that time viewed as the most significant and brightest deity) to be a lifeless object, a lamp subdued for the benefit of living beings.

Thus, this verse deals with the sun and moon not in their own name, but in the Name of their Creator and in a way that turns our attention to the Creator's Unity as well as His acts and His favors to humankind. The vividness and extraordinariness of the styles of the Qur'ān sometimes entranced the Bedouins with just one phrase; they would then prostrate before even becoming a Muslim. Once *So from now on, proclaim what you are commanded to convey openly and in an emphatic manner* (15: 94), (whose original Arabic consists of only 3 words), engendered this very reaction. When asked if he had become a Muslim, the man thus affected, answered: "No. I prostrate before the eloquence of the phrase" (*The Words*, "the 25th Word," 400; al-Ālūsī, 14: 85).

16. Spending must be either to meet a necessity or a need or to satisfy a desire for lawful beauty. Eating to maintain life is a necessity; eating to be full – provided that one avoids excess – is a need; eating pleasant food satisfies one's desire for beauty. Spending in order to meet a necessity is obligatory; meeting a need is commendable, while satisfying one's desire for beauty may be harmless, according to the general conditions of the community and one's income. Spending in order to obtain an easy life while the majority of the Muslims are in need is wasteful.

Spending on unlawful things, no matter the amount, and over-spending on lawful things, in the sense that one spends more than one can afford or aspires to a luxurious life are also included under the idea of wastefulness. As for niggardliness, this means spending too little on the necessities and needs of oneself and one's family, even though one has sufficient funds, and the refusal to spend on charity or for the cause of Islam.

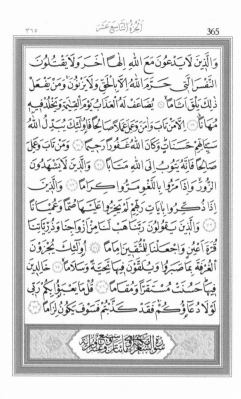

68. And who invoke no other deity along with God, and do not kill any soul – which God has made forbidden – except by right (for just cause and after due process), and do not commit unlawful sexual intercourse. Whoever commits any of these will face a severe penalty.

69. His punishment will be greater on the Day of Resurrection, and he will abide in it in ignominy,[17]

70. Except he who gives up his way in repentance and believes (without associating partners with God), and does good, righteous deeds – such are those whose (past) evil deeds God will efface and record virtuous deeds in their place (and whose faculties which enabled the evil deeds He will change into enablers of virtuous deeds). God is All-Forgiving, All-Compassionate.

71. Whoever repents and does good, righteous deeds (and who has therefore shown that he has renounced his evil ways for good) – such a one has surely turned to God with true repentance.

72. And (those true servants of the All-Merciful are they) who do not take part in and bear witness to any vanity or falsehood, (and who will not deem anything true unless they know it to be so for certain), and when they happen to pass by anything vain and useless, pass by it with dignity;

73. And who, when they are reminded of the Revelations of their Lord (and His signs in the creation as well as in their inner world, as a basis of advice or teaching or discussion), do not remain unmoved as though deaf and blind;

74. And who say: "Our Lord! Grant us that our spouses and offspring may be a means of happiness for us, and enable us to lead others in piety (to become a means of the promotion of piety and virtue)."

75. Such (illustrious) ones will be rewarded with the loftiest mansion (in Paradise) for their steadfastness (in spite of adversities, for their obedience to God in spite of all persecutions), and they will be met therein with a greeting of welcome and peace.

76. Therein to abide. How good it is as a final station and permanent abode.

77. Say: "My Lord would not care for you were it not for your prayer.[18] Now that you have denied (His Message), the inescapable punishment will cleave to you."

17. It is certain that God does not forgive that partners be associated with Him. He will punish eternally only those who deny Him or associate partners with Him. However, less than that He forgives to whomever He wills (whomever He has guided to repentance and righteousness either out of His pure grace or as a result of the person's choosing repentance and righteousness by his free will) (4: 48). Killing a person unjustly and committing unlawful sexual intercourse are sins that are not as grave as the association of partners with God.

Considering that this *sūrah* was revealed in Makkah, the penalty mentioned in verse 68 for the crimes in question may refer to their punishment in this world, rather than in the Hereafter. If He so wills, God may punish the association of partners with Him in the world in many ways, such as sending afflictions, defeats, diseases, total destruction, and disasters. (The penalties for killing a person unjustly and that for indulging in unlawful sexual intercourse in the world were later established in Madīnah. For these punishments, see *sūrah* 2: 178–179, note 131; 194–95, note 140; *sūrah* 5: 45, note 10; *sūrah* 22: 60, note 16; *sūrah* 24: 2–3, note 1–6. However, punishment in the Hereafter for these cardinal crimes is always greater.

Repentance does not ward off the punishment inflicted by the worldly law, while God may forgive the repentant in the Hereafter.

18. Faith requires prayer as a means of attainment and perfection, and our essence desperately needs it.

If people say that they pray many times, yet still their prayers go unanswered, despite the assurance given in the verse, *Pray to Me, I will answer you* (40: 60), we should point out that an answered prayer does not necessarily mean its acceptance. There is an answer for every prayer. However, accepting a prayer and giving what is requested depends upon the All-Mighty's Wisdom. Suppose an ill child asks a doctor for a certain medicine. The doctor may give what is asked for, or prescribe something better, or nothing at all. It all depends upon how the medicine will affect the child. Similarly the All-Mighty, Who is the All-Hearing and the All-Seeing, answers His servant's prayer and changes loneliness into the pleasure of His company. But His answer does not depend on the individual's fancies; rather, according to His Wisdom, He gives what is requested, what is better, or nothing at all.

Moreover, prayer is a form of worship and worship is rewarded mainly in the Hereafter. In essence, prayer is not performed for worldly purposes; rather worldly purposes are the cause for prayer. For example, praying for rain is a kind of worship occasioned by the lack of rain. If rain is the prayer's only aim, the prayer is unacceptable, for it is not sincere or intended to please God. Sunset determines the time for the evening prayer, while solar and lunar eclipses occasion two particular kinds of worship. Since such eclipses are two manifestations of the Divine Majesty, the All-Mighty calls His servants to perform a form of worship particular to these occasions. The prayer recited has nothing to do with causing the eclipse to end; the time this will occur has already been established through astronomical calculations. The same argument applies to drought and other calamities, for all such events occasion certain kinds of prayer. It is at such times that we are most aware of our innate weakness, and thus feel the need to take refuge in the high Presence of the Absolutely Powerful One through prayer and supplication. If a calamity is not alleviated, despite many prayers, we should not say that our prayer has not been accepted. Rather, we should say that the time for prayer has not yet ended. God removes the calamity because of His endless Grace and Munificence. The end of that event marks the end of that special occasion for prayer.

We must pursue God's good pleasure through worship, affirm our innate poverty and weakness in our prayer, and seek refuge with Him through prayer. We must not try to interfere in His Lordship but rather let God do as He wills and rely on His Wisdom. In addition, we should not doubt His Mercy.

Every creature offers its own kind of praise and worship to God. What reaches the Court of God from the universe is, in fact, a kind of prayer.

Some creatures, like plants and animals, pray through the language of their potential, thus achieving a full form and then displaying and showing certain Divine Names (e.g., a plant's seeds grow naturally into plants, and the semen and eggs of animals grow naturally into animals.) Since they have this potential, their natural disposition to mature is, in essence, a prayer. By doing so, they affirm the manifestation of such Divine Names as the All-Sustaining and the All-Forming.

Another kind of prayer is performed in the language of natural needs. All living beings ask the Absolutely Generous One to meet their vital needs, as they cannot do so alone. Yet another kind of prayer is done in the language of complete helplessness. A living creature in straitened circumstances takes refuge in its Unseen Protector with a genuine supplication, and turns to its All-Compassionate Lord. These three kinds of prayer are always acceptable, unless somehow impeded.

The fourth type of prayer is the one engaged in by human beings. This type falls into two categories: active and by disposition, and verbal and with the heart. For example, acting in accordance with causes is an active prayer. We try to gain God's approval by complying with causes, for causes alone cannot produce the result – only God can do that. For example, plowing the soil is an active prayer, for this is nothing less than knocking at the door of the treasury of God's Compassion. Such a prayer is usually acceptable, for it is an application to the Divine Name the All-Generous. Going to a doctor is also a prayer, as it means applying to the Divine Name, the All-Healing. It is God Who heals. We should not be content with plowing the soil or going to a doctor, but should combine our activities with verbal prayer.

The second type of prayer, recited by the tongue and the heart, is the ordinary one. This means that we ask God from the heart for something we cannot reach and put it into words. The most important aspect and finest and sweetest fruit of this type of prayer is that we know that God hears us, that He is aware of the contents of our heart, that His Power extends everywhere, that He can satisfy every desire, and that He comes to our aid out of mercy for our weakness and inadequacy.

We should never abandon prayer, for it is the key to the Treasury of Compassion and the means of obtaining access to the Infinite Power. We should hold on to It and ascend to the highest rank of humanity and, as creation's most favored and superior member, include the prayer of the entire universe in our prayer. We should say, on behalf of all beings: *From You alone do we seek help* (1: 5), and become a beautiful pattern for all of creation. (See *The Words*, "the 23rd Word," 333–334).

SŪRAH 26

ASH-SHU'ARĀ' (THE POETS)

Makkah period

This *sūrah* of 227 verses takes its name from the word *shu'arā* (poets) in verse 224. It rejects the Makkans' claim that the Messenger was a poet and that the Qur'ān is the work of a poet (the Makkans used to associate poets with the jinn, and viewed them as akin to soothsayers). The *sūrah* was revealed in the mid-Makkan period, when the unbelievers launched a campaign of fierce opposition to the Divine Message, using one pretext or another. It answers these pretexts, and sets forth the signs for the truth of the Message which abound in the universe and in the history of preceding communities.

In the Name of God, the All-Merciful, the All-Compassionate.

1. *Ṭā. Sīn. Mīm.*

2. These are the Revelations of the Book clear in itself and clearly showing the truth.

3. It may be that you (O Messenger) will torment yourself to death because they refuse to believe.

4. If We will, We can send down a (compelling) sign on them from heaven, so that they are forced to bow their necks before it (in humility).[1]

5. Whenever a new Revelation comes to them from the All-Merciful (to warn and enlighten them), they but turn away from it in aversion.

6. So they have obstinately denied (this Message). But soon they will come to understand what it was that they were mocking.

7. Have they not considered the earth, how many of every noble kind We have caused to grow therein in pairs?

8. Surely in this there is a sign, but most of them are not believers.

9. And surely your Lord is indeed the All-Glorious with irresistible might (able to punish whoever goes against His Glory), the All-Compassionate (especially towards His believing servants).

10. (Remember) when your Lord called Moses, saying: "Go to the wrongdoing people,

11. "The people of the Pharaoh. Will they not give up their way in fear of Me and take the way of piety?"

12. Moses replied: "My Lord! I fear that they will deny me,

13. "And my breast will be constricted (so that I fail to show the necessary perseverance and tolerance), and my tongue will

not be free (to convey Your Message with the right fluency), so appoint Aaron as a Messenger beside me.

14. "They also have a charge of crime against me,[2] so I fear that they will kill me (and not let me convey Your Message)."

15. (God) said: "Not so, indeed! Go forth, then, the two of you, with Our miraculous signs (with which I have provided you).[3] We will surely be with you all (you and them), listening attentively (to all that is to happen between you).

16. "So go, both of you, to the Pharaoh and say: 'We have come with a message from the Lord of the worlds (He Who has created and sustains everything):

17. 'Let the Children of Israel go with us!' "

18. (When Moses delivered his message, the Pharaoh) said: "Did we not bring you up among us (in our palace) when you were a child? And you spent many years of your life among us!

19. "Then you committed that heinous deed of yours which you did,[4] (proving thereby that) you are indeed one of the ungrateful."

---

1. If God willed, He could, for example, write His Name on the surface of the heavens with stars or, as He caused Mount Sinai to tower above the Children of Israel to compel them to keep their covenant (2: 63), He could compel people to believe in some way. However, the signs He provides in creation and the lives of humankind, as well as through the Prophets, are perfectly sufficient for one who is not overcome by arrogance, wrongdoing, misjudgment, and carnal desires; if God were to provide a more obvious sign, this would mean negating human free will and nullifying the purpose of the tests we are put through.

God has endowed human beings with distinguishing faculties and honored us with free will. He has also created us with a disposition to believe and worship. Moreover, just as the whole universe and our physical composition provide multiple signs for the Existence and Unity of God, each human being has many experiences throughout their life that also give certainty to their conscience about this same, cardinal truth. In addition, God sent numerous Prophets throughout history, the character and life of each of whom, along with the many

miracles God created at their hand, were an undeniable sign for the truth of the Message from God. In short, God opens all the doors to faith for human reason and conscience. However, He never compels human beings to believe, because this would be in contradiction to the dignity of free will. Unbelief arises not from there being a lack of sufficient signs, but rather from human arrogance, wrongdoing, misjudgment, and an attachment to the world and worldly benefits, or carnal desires. This is clear in the history of many peoples who refused to believe, even when the miracle they asked their Prophet to perform had been shown to them, and who were subsequently destroyed as a result. (For example, see 7: 73–79.)

2. This verse is referring to the time (see 28: 15) when Moses accidentally killed an Egyptian, which prompted him to leave Egypt for Midian.

3. For these signs, see *sūrah* 7: 106–108, 130–135.

4. This is a reference to the unintentional killing, by Moses of a Copt, who had fought with an Israelite (28: 15).

20. (Moses) said: "I committed that deed unintentionally when I did not know (it would end in the way it did.)

21. "Then I fled[5] from you when I feared (living together with) you (any longer), but (since then) my Lord has granted to me sound, wise judgment, and has made me one of His Messengers.

22. "As for that favor you taunt me with: (it is owed to the fact) that you have enslaved the Children of Israel."

23. (The Pharaoh) said: "What (and who) is that, 'the Lord of the worlds'?"

24. (Moses) answered: "The Lord (Creator, Sustainer, and sole Ruler) of the heavens and the earth and all that is between them, if you would but (let yourselves be) convinced!"

25. (The Pharaoh) said to those around him: "Do you not hear (what he is saying)?"

26. (Moses) continued: "Your Lord, and the Lord of your forefathers."

27. (The Pharaoh) exclaimed: "See! This Messenger of yours who has been sent to you is assuredly a madman."

28. (Moses) went on: "He is the Lord of the east and the west and all that is between them, if you would but reason and understand!"

29. (The Pharaoh) threatened: "If you, (O Moses,) take any deity other than me (to worship, to offer your prayer and sacrifices to, and to seek help from), I will most certainly make you one of those imprisoned."[6]

30. (Moses) said: "Even if I have brought you something clear (which demonstrates that I am speaking the truth)?"

31. (The Pharaoh) answered: "Then, produce it if you are truthful (in your claim)!"

32. Thereupon Moses threw down his staff, and it was manifestly a serpent.

33. And he drew forth his (right) hand (from his armpit where he had put it), and thereupon it was shining white to those looking on.

34. (The Pharaoh) said to the chiefs around him: "This is indeed a learned, skillful sorcerer,

35. "Who seeks to drive you out from your land by his sorcery. What, then, do you advise (me to do)?"

36. They said: "Put him and his brother off for a while, and (in the meantime) send forth heralds to all cities,

37. "To bring to your presence every learned, skillful sorcerer."

38. So the sorcerers were assembled (to contend with Moses) at the appointed time on a day (made) well-known (to all),[7]

39. And it was said to the people: "Will you not assemble (and attend also)?

5. *Firār*, which literally means to run away from or flee, is used in Muslim Sufi literature to denote the journey from the created to the Creator, and thereby escaping the confinement of self-adoration to "melt away" in the rays of the Truth. The verse *flee to God* (51: 50), which points to a believer's journeying in heart and in spirit, refers to this action of the heart, the spiritual intellect.

The further people are from the suffocating atmosphere of corporeality and the carnal dimension of their existence, the closer they are to God, and the more respect they have for themselves. Let us hear from the Prophet Moses, upon him be peace, a loyal devotee at the door of the Truth, how one fleeing to and taking shelter in God is rewarded: *Then I fled from you when I feared (living together with) you (any longer), but (since then) my Lord has granted to me the power of judgment (and the ability to distinguish between truth and falsehood, right and wrong, and to act accordingly) and has made me one of His Messengers.* The Prophet Moses states that the way to spiritual contentment and meeting with God, the way to the Divine vicegerency and nearness to Him proceeds through a stage of fleeing.

Ordinary people flee from the tumults of life and the ugliness of sin, taking refuge in God's forgiveness and favor. They declare or ponder on the meaning of: *My Lord, always treat us with Your forgiveness and mercy, for You are the Best of the merciful* (23: 118). They seek God's shelter in total sincerity, saying: "I take refuge in You from the evil that I have done" (at-Tirmidhī, "Dawa'āt," 15).

Those distinguished by their piety and nearness to God flee from their own lesser qualities to the Divine Attributes; they flee from feeling with their outward senses to discerning and observing with the heart; they flee from ceremonial worship to its innermost dimension and from carnal feelings to spiritual sensations. This is what is referred to in: "O God, I take refuge in Your approval from Your wrath, and in Your forgiveness from Your punishment" (Muslim, "Ṣalāh," 222).

The most advanced in knowledge and love of God and in piety flee from the Attributes to the Divine Being or Essence, and from the Truth to the Truth Himself. They say: "I take refuge in You from You" (*ibid.*), and are always in awe of God. (See *Key Concepts*, 1: 13–14.)

6. The Pharaoh claimed that he was the greatest lord of all those under his rule (79: 24). He ruled over them however he wished. Yet, when the Prophet Moses, upon him be peace, proclaimed that God was the Lord of all creation, including the Pharaoh himself and his men and their ancestors, the Pharaoh felt that his rule had been challenged. So, as every dictator does, he resorted to threats. Although Moses proclaimed God as the Lord (Creator, Sustainer, and Ruler) of all creation, at this point the Pharaoh claimed divinity. He must have understood that Divinity and Lordship cannot be considered separately and only one who has divinity can be lord. However, despite his claim of divinity, both the Pharaoh himself and the Copts worshipped many deities (7: 127). So he must have used deity in the sense that he was the sole lord and master of Egypt, where he deemed himself to have absolute authority.

Lordship demands obedience, while Divinity demands worship. Since God is the Deity of all creation, One Who has absolute, perfect Knowledge, Will, and Power, and Who deserves to be worshipped exclusively, being entitled to receive all kinds of sacrificial offerings and Whose help is sought, absolute Lordship also belongs to Him. As He has supreme authority and sovereignty over the universe as its Lord, (its Creator, Sustainer, and Ruler,) One Who has full knowledge of the universe as a whole and of each particular thing or being, and absolute Will and Power to be able to do anything He wills, absolute sovereignty in the human realm also belongs to Him. However, while all other beings, except the jinn and humans obey Him absolutely, because they have no free will, human beings and the jinn are allowed some space for the exercise of their free will.

7. See *sūrah* 20: 59.

40. "We are expecting that the sorcerers will triumph and we will follow them (in their religion)."[8]

41. So then the sorcerers came forth (for the encounter) and said to the Pharaoh: "We shall surely have a reward, if we are the victors, shall we?"

42. (The Pharaoh) answered: "Yes, indeed. And you will then be among those near-stationed to me."

43. Moses said to them (the sorcerers): "Throw whatever you are going to throw!"

44. So they threw their ropes and staffs, saying: "By the might and glory of Pharaoh, we will surely be the victors."

45. Thereafter, Moses threw his staff, and behold, it swallowed up their false devices.

46. The sorcerers threw themselves down, prostrating,

47. And they said: "We have come to believe in the Lord of the worlds,

48. "The Lord of Moses and Aaron!"

49. (The Pharaoh) said: "What! Do you believe in Him before I give you permission? For sure he is your chief who has taught you sorcery. But in time you will certainly come to know. I will most certainly have your hands and feet cut off alternately, and then I will most certainly have you crucified all together."

50. They responded: "There is no hurt (in what you threaten us with). For surely to our (true and everlasting) Lord we are bound to return."

51. "We ardently desire that our Lord will forgive us our sins for we are the first to believe."

52. (Events developed to the point that) We revealed to Moses: "Set forth with My servants by night: surely, you will be pursued."

53. Then the Pharaoh sent heralds to the cities (to mobilize his troops),

54. (Saying:) "Those people are indeed a paltry band;

55. "And (forgetting their lack in numbers and power), they have offended against us (and so provoked our wrath).

56. "As for us, we are assuredly a numerous host, ever on guard."[9]

57. Thus did We drive them out of (all that they had enjoyed of) gardens and springs,

58. And treasures, excellent dwellings, and noble status.

59. Things happened thus, and We made the Children of Israel survive them and inherit (the same kind of bounties).[10]

60. At sunrise, the Pharaoh set off in pursuit of them.

9. The Pharaoh's propaganda indicates the deep-rooted fears that he was trying to hide under the guise of fearlessness. On the one hand, he was mobilizing forces from all corners of the country, and on the other, he was stating that the Children of Israel were powerless. In fact, he was trying to prevent people from seeing that a mighty king like himself was afraid of a people whom he and his forefathers had been persecuting over the ages.

10. This is a reference to the final victory of a tyrannized people – the Children of Israel – and to their founding a great state and civilization during the time of the Prophets David and Solomon, upon them be peace. While this verse refers to how events finally ended, the succeeding verses proceed to narrate the story of the Pharaoh and his army, and the Prophet Moses and his people, intended as an example for humanity.

369

فَلَمَّا تَرَآءَا الْجَمْعَانِ قَالَ أَصْحَابُ مُوسَىٰٓ إِنَّا لَمُدْرَكُونَ ۞ قَالَ كَلَّآ إِنَّ مَعِيَ رَبِّى سَيَهْدِينِ ۞ فَأَوْحَيْنَآ إِلَىٰ مُوسَىٰٓ أَنِ اضْرِب بِّعَصَاكَ الْبَحْرَ فَانفَلَقَ فَكَانَ كُلُّ فِرْقٍ كَالطَّوْدِ الْعَظِيمِ ۞ وَأَزْلَفْنَا ثَمَّ الْآخَرِينَ ۞ وَأَنجَيْنَا مُوسَىٰ وَمَن مَّعَهُۥٓ أَجْمَعِينَ ۞ ثُمَّ أَغْرَقْنَا الْآخَرِينَ ۞ إِنَّ فِى ذَٰلِكَ لَآيَةً ۖ وَمَا كَانَ أَكْثَرُهُم مُّؤْمِنِينَ ۞ وَإِنَّ رَبَّكَ لَهُوَ الْعَزِيزُ الرَّحِيمُ ۞ وَاتْلُ عَلَيْهِمْ نَبَأَ إِبْرَٰهِيمَ ۞ إِذْ قَالَ لِأَبِيهِ وَقَوْمِهِۦ مَا تَعْبُدُونَ ۞ قَالُوا۟ نَعْبُدُ أَصْنَامًا فَنَظَلُّ لَهَا عَاكِفِينَ ۞ قَالَ هَلْ يَسْمَعُونَكُمْ إِذْ تَدْعُونَ ۞ أَوْ يَنفَعُونَكُمْ أَوْ يَضُرُّونَ ۞ قَالُوا۟ بَلْ وَجَدْنَآ ءَابَآءَنَا كَذَٰلِكَ يَفْعَلُونَ ۞ قَالَ أَفَرَءَيْتُم مَّا كُنتُمْ تَعْبُدُونَ ۞ أَنتُمْ وَءَابَآؤُكُمُ الْأَقْدَمُونَ ۞ فَإِنَّهُمْ عَدُوٌّ لِّىٓ إِلَّا رَبَّ الْعَالَمِينَ ۞ الَّذِى خَلَقَنِى فَهُوَ يَهْدِينِ ۞ وَالَّذِى هُوَ يُطْعِمُنِى وَيَسْقِينِ ۞ وَإِذَا مَرِضْتُ فَهُوَ يَشْفِينِ ۞ وَالَّذِى يُمِيتُنِى ثُمَّ يُحْيِينِ ۞ وَالَّذِىٓ أَطْمَعُ أَن يَغْفِرَ لِى خَطِيٓـَٔتِى يَوْمَ الدِّينِ ۞ رَبِّ هَبْ لِى حُكْمًا وَأَلْحِقْنِى بِالصَّٰلِحِينَ ۞

----

61. When the two hosts came in view of each other, the companions of Moses said: "We are certainly overtaken!"

62. He replied: "Certainly not. My Lord is surely with me; He will guide me (to deliverance)."[11]

63. We revealed to Moses: "Strike the sea with your staff." Thereupon the sea split, and each part became like a towering mountain.

64. We brought the others (the Pharaoh and his host) close to the same spot.

65. And We saved Moses and all those who were with him.

66. Afterwards, We caused the others to drown.[12]

67. Surely in that (which took place between Moses and Pharaoh) there is a sign (a great, important lesson). Most of them (the Pharaoh's people) were not believers.

68. And surely your Lord is indeed the All-Glorious with irresistible might (able to punish whoever goes against His Glory), the All-Compassionate (especially towards His believing servants).[13]

69. Now recite to them this exemplary history of Abraham.

70. When he said to his father and his people: "What is it that you worship?"[14]

71. They said: "We worship idols; and (even though they are made of wood and stone) we are ever devoted to them (as they are our deities)."

72. (Abraham) said: "Do they hear you when you invoke them?

73. "Or do they benefit you (when you worship them) or harm (you when you do not)?

74. They replied: "But we found our forefathers doing the same."[15]

75. (Abraham) said: "So, have you considered what you have been worshipping?

76. "You and all your forefathers that have passed (before you)?

77. "I see that they (all that you worship) are enemies to me,[16] but the Lord of the worlds is not.

78. "He Who has created me and so guides me (to whatever is to my benefit in both this world and the next).

79. "And He it is Who gives me food and drink;

80. "And Who, when I fall ill, heals me.

81. "And Who will make me die and then will give me life again.

82. "And Who, I hope, will forgive me my faults on Judgment Day."[17]

83. "My Lord! Grant me true, wise judgment, and join me with the righteous.

11. When the Prophet Muḥammad, upon him be peace and blessings, hid himself and his friend, Abū Bakr, in the Cave of Thawr during his emigration to Madīnah, those who pursued him from among the Makkans approached as close as the entrance of the cave. Worried about the life of the Messenger, Abū Bakr told him: "O Messenger of God, we have been overtaken." The Messenger replied: "Do not grieve, God is surely with us" (9: 40). The reactions of both God's Last Messenger and the Prophet Moses, upon them be peace, are in essence the same, yet there are significant and subtle differences between them.

The Prophet Moses spoke on his own behalf, which shows that he had absolute leadership over his community, while the Prophet Muḥammad spoke on behalf of himself and his companion. This signifies that he shared his leadership with his community. This is why the Qur'ān addresses the whole community of Muslims when the matter concerns the performance of public responsibilities carried out by modern states. Sharing responsibilities, mutual help, solidarity, and consultation are essential in Islam. The Prophet Muḥammad's words also show Abū Bakr's greatness and closeness to the Messenger.

Secondly, the Prophet Moses spoke of God as "my Lord," which suggests that his relationship with God was particular to himself. Whereas, the Prophet Muḥammad spoke of Him as God, the proper Name of the Divine Being, a Name which contains the meaning of all of His other Names. So the Prophet Muḥammad's relationship with Him was universal and representative of all conscious beings. This also shows that his mission is universal.

Thirdly, the Prophet Moses used the (near) future tense in order to express God's expected help, but the Prophet Muḥammad used the present tense, saying: *God is surely with us*. This difference implies that the Prophet Muḥammad's relationship with God and his expectations of God are eternal.

Finally, it should not be forgotten that this comparison is between two of the greatest Messengers of God, and concerns the mission and particular greatness of each.

12. For a more detailed account of the events narrated here, see 7: 103–137; 10: 75–93; 20: 9–79.

13. These last two verses refer back to verses 8 and 9, and express the same truth in the same words. They threaten those who stubbornly persist in unbelief and wrongdoing and try to prevent the spreading of God's Message, while they console and encourage the believers. The fact that the unbelievers are usually greater in number should not mislead us. So long as the believers are steadfast in God's cause and help His cause, the final happy end will belong to them both in this world and absolutely in the Hereafter. For nothing can prevent God from punishing whom He wills, while at the same time He is All-Compassionate towards the believers.

14. For Āzar, Abraham's father, his people, and their faith, see 6: 74, note 16; 9: 114, note 25.

15. This is typical human nature. It is really very difficult for human beings to abandon established ideas and customs. People tend not to think too much about whether or not what they are doing is rational or is based on some truth. Islam brings freedom to human thinking, saves the human mind from prejudice and blind imitation, and explains the truth in all its clarity, aiming at removing all obstacles that can be placed before free human choice. A. Cressy Morrison, former-head of the New York Academy of Sciences, draws attention to this aspect of human nature:

> . . . all the nearly exact requirements of life could not be brought about on one planet at one time by chance. The size of the Earth, the distance from the Sun, the temperature and the life-giving rays of the Sun, the thickness of the Earth's crust, the quantity of water, the amount of carbon dioxide, the volume of nitrogen, the emergence of man and his survival—all point to order out of chaos, to design and purpose, and to the fact that, according to the inexorable laws of mathematics, all these could not occur by chance simultaneously on one planet once in a billion times. When the

facts are so overwhelming, and when we recognize, as we must, the attributes of our minds which are not material, is it possible to flaunt the evidence and take the one chance in a billion that we and all else are the result of chance?

There are 999,999,999 chances to one against a belief that all things happen by chance. Science will not deny the facts as stated; the mathematicians will agree that the figures are correct. Now we encounter the stubborn resistance of the human mind, which is reluctant to give up fixed ideas. The early Greeks knew the Earth was a sphere, but it took two thousand years to convince (Western) men that this fact is true.

New ideas encounter opposition, ridicule and abuse, but truth survives and is verified. (Morrison, 99–100)

16. These idols are enemies in that when one worships them, their worship brings ruin in both worlds, and they deny this worship of them and turn against that person on the Day of Judgment.

17. Everyone, even the Prophets, is in need of God's Mercy and Forgiveness. God's Messenger, upon him be peace and blessings, used to pray:

O God, I ask You for contentment af-

ter misfortune, a peaceful life after death, the pleasure of observing Your Face, and the desire to meet You. I take refuge in You from wronging others and from being wronged, from showing animosity and being subject to animosity, and from erring or committing unforgivable sins. If You leave me to myself, You leave me in weakness, need, sinfulness, and error. I depend only on Your Mercy, so forgive all my sins, for only You can do so. Accept my repentance, for You are the Oft-Relenting, All-Compassionate. (Ibn Ḥanbal, 5: 191)

This invocation does not mean that God's Messenger sinned; instead, it shows His deep devotion to God and his consciousness of responsibility. He regarded himself as an ordinary servant of God. Once he said: "No one can enter Paradise by virtue of their own deeds (without God's Mercy)." When asked if this was true for himself as well, he replied that God's Mercy embraced him (al-Bukhārī, "Riqāq," 18).

God's Messenger asked God to forgive him at least seventy times a day. It is a great characteristic of a Prophet that he regards himself as being fallible. Other people can never state that a Prophet ever sinned, because sinlessness is one of the essentials of Prophethood, but at the same time all the Prophets were notable for their humility.

92. They will be asked: "Where are all those (idols or revered human beings, or angels, or the jinn) that you used to worship

93. "Apart from God? Can they be of any help to you, or even to themselves?"

94. Then they will be hurled into the Flame headlong, one upon another – they (the idols), and the rebellious (who worship them).

95. And so too the hosts of Iblīs, all together.

96. Blaming one another therein, they (the rebellious) will say (to the others):

97. "By God, assuredly, we were lost in obvious error,

98. "When we held you as equals (in worship and obedience) to the Lord of the worlds.

99. "It is none but the criminals (the leaders in associating partners with God) who led us astray.

100. "And now we have none to intercede (on our behalf),

101. "Nor any intimate friend.

102. "If only we had a second chance (in the world), so that we might be among the believers!"

103. Surely in that (which took place between Abraham and his people) there is a sign (a great, important lesson). Most of them were not believers.

104. And surely your Lord is indeed the All-Glorious with irresistible might (able to punish whoever goes against His Glory), the All-Compassionate (especially towards His believing servants).

105. The people of Noah denied (Noah and thereby meant to deny all) the Messengers.

106. (Recall) when their brother Noah said to them (by way of timely warning): "Will you not keep from disobedience to

84. "And grant me a most true and virtuous renown among posterity.[18]

85. "And make me one of the inheritors of the Garden of bounty and blessing.[19]

86. "And forgive my father, for he is among those who have gone astray.[20]

87. "And do not disgrace me on the Day when all people will be raised up to life.

88. "The Day when neither wealth will be of any use, nor offspring,

89. "But only he (will prosper) who comes before God with a sound heart (free of all kinds of unbelief, hypocrisy, and associating partners with God)."

90. And Paradise (on that Day) will be brought near for the God-revering, pious;

91. And the Blazing Flame will be laid open before those who rebelled (against God) and went astray.[21]

God in reverence for Him and seek refuge with His protection?

107. "Surely I am a Messenger to you, trustworthy.

108. "So keep form disobedience to God in reverence for Him, and obey me.

109. "I ask of you no wage for that (for conveying God's Message); my wage is due only from the Lord of the worlds."[22]

110. "So keep from disobedience to God in reverence for Him, and obey me."

111. They responded: "Shall we believe in you, when the lowliest (among the people) follow you!"[23]

---

18. The Qur'ān declares that God granted the prophets Zachariah, John, Jesus, Abraham, Moses, and Aaron a most true and virtuous renown among people (19: 50). This means that He made them (and all other Prophets) exceptional examples to follow in belief, thought, and conduct. The example they left continued to benefit later generations by inspiring them to do good. By virtue of this, the Prophets continue to increase their rewards, because "one who causes (enables something) is like one who does it." God's Messenger declared: "Those who establish a good path in Islam receive the reward of those who follow it, without any decrease in their reward. Those who establish an evil path in Islam are burdened with the sins of those who follow it, without any decrease in their burden" (Muslim, "Zakāh," 69).

19. The reason why we ask to be an inheritor of Paradise is that: (1) Inheritance is the easiest way of earning, a way which requires no labor, so asking to inherit Paradise means that we are saying, "I ask You, O my Lord, to place me in Paradise out of Your pure grace, because I cannot deserve it by my deeds." (2) There is a place pre-assigned for everyone in both Paradise and Hell. If one dies and enters Hell, the people of Paradise inherit that person's place.

20. The Prophet Abraham, upon him be peace, prayed for Āzar because he had promised his father that he would prayer for him (19: 47). But when God informed him that Āzar was an enemy of God, condemned to eternal punishment because he had associated partners with God, Abraham stopped praying for him (9: 114). God declared: *It is not for the Prophet and those who believe to ask God for the forgiveness of those who associate partners with God even though they be near of kin, after it has become clear to them that those (polytheists) are condemned to the Blazing Flame* (9: 113).

21. Paradise and Hell are two fruits growing on the tip of a branch that extends from the Tree of Creation far into eternity, two opposite destinations along the chain of beings. These destinations are located on opposite ends of the chain: the degraded one on the lower end, and the luminous sublime one on the upper end.

Paradise and Hell are two storerooms for the flow of worldly events and the products of the earth, all made by its conscious inhabitants. They are two pools that collect the flow of two streams, one stream carrying the wicked and foul while the other carries the good and pure. Paradise is the place where Divine Favor and Mercy manifest themselves, whereas Hell is the place where Divine 'Wrath' and Awe are exhibited. The All-Merciful and the All-Majestic One manifests Himself (through His Names and Attributes) wherever He wills. The existence of the fruit is as evident as the existence of the branch; the existence of the destination is as evident as the existence of the chain, the existence of the storeroom is as evident as that of the product, the pool is as evident as the stream, and the place of manifestation is as evident as the existence of (Divine) Mercy and Wrath. (See *The Letters*, "the First Letter," 6–8.)

22. Trustworthiness and communication of God's Message are two of the essentials of Messengership, the others being truthfulness, intelligence, sinlessness, and freedom from all bodily and mental defects. These are present in every Messenger.

Truthfulness is the cornerstone of Messengership. No lies or deceit, whether explicit or implicit, were ever uttered by them. The second attribute of Messengership is *amānah*, an Arabic word meaning trustworthiness and which is derived from the same root as *mu'min* (believer). Being a believer implies being a trustworthy person. All Prophets were the best believers and therefore perfect exemplars of trustworthiness. To stress this principle, God summarizes the stories of five Prophets in this *sūrah* using the same statements: *Surely I am a Messenger to you, trustworthy* (107, 125, 143, 162, 178).

Mu'min is also a Divine Name, for God is the ultimate *Mu'min*, the source of security and reliability. We put our trust in, confide in, and rely upon Him. He distinguished the Prophets by their trustworthiness, and our connection to Him through the Prophets is based entirely on their trustworthiness and reliability.

The third attribute of Messengership is communication of the Divine Message. God manifested His Mercy and Compassion for humankind through the Messengers. They expected no reward for performing their mission. They suffered hunger, thirst, and every other hardship. Many of them were forced into exile and were made the target of many assaults and traps, and still many others were killed. They bore all of these simply for the good pleasure of God and the good of humankind.

Messengers never thought of material gain, spiritual reward, or even Paradise – they strove only for God's good pleasure and to see humanity guided to the truth. Imam Busīrī expresses in vivid language the altruism, sincerity, and patience of God's Messenger, upon him be peace and blessings: "Mountains would desire to run on either side of him in heaps of gold, but he refused."

Those who feel responsible for serving the cause of Islam in every age must be trustworthy and communicate God's Message without expecting any reward from others.

23. For a detailed explanation of the attitude of the leaders among the people of Noah, see *sūrah* 11: 27, note 8.

قَالَ وَمَا عِلْمِي بِمَا كَانُوا يَعْمَلُونَ ۝ إِنْ حِسَابُهُمْ إِلَّا عَلَىٰ رَبِّي لَوْ تَشْعُرُونَ ۝ وَمَا أَنَا بِطَارِدِ الْمُؤْمِنِينَ ۝ إِنْ أَنَا إِلَّا نَذِيرٌ مُبِينٌ ۝ قَالُوا لَئِنْ لَمْ تَنْتَهِ يَا نُوحُ لَتَكُونَنَّ مِنَ الْمَرْجُومِينَ ۝ قَالَ رَبِّ إِنَّ قَوْمِي كَذَّبُونِ ۝ فَافْتَحْ بَيْنِي وَبَيْنَهُمْ فَتْحًا وَنَجِّنِي وَمَنْ مَعِيَ مِنَ الْمُؤْمِنِينَ ۝ فَأَنْجَيْنَاهُ وَمَنْ مَعَهُ فِي الْفُلْكِ الْمَشْحُونِ ۝ ثُمَّ أَغْرَقْنَا بَعْدُ الْبَاقِينَ ۝ إِنَّ فِي ذَٰلِكَ لَآيَةً وَمَا كَانَ أَكْثَرُهُمْ مُؤْمِنِينَ ۝ وَإِنَّ رَبَّكَ لَهُوَ الْعَزِيزُ الرَّحِيمُ ۝ كَذَّبَتْ عَادٌ الْمُرْسَلِينَ ۝ إِذْ قَالَ لَهُمْ أَخُوهُمْ هُودٌ أَلَا تَتَّقُونَ ۝ إِنِّي لَكُمْ رَسُولٌ أَمِينٌ ۝ فَاتَّقُوا اللَّهَ وَأَطِيعُونِ ۝ وَمَا أَسْأَلُكُمْ عَلَيْهِ مِنْ أَجْرٍ إِنْ أَجْرِيَ إِلَّا عَلَىٰ رَبِّ الْعَالَمِينَ ۝ أَتَبْنُونَ بِكُلِّ رِيعٍ آيَةً تَعْبَثُونَ ۝ وَتَتَّخِذُونَ مَصَانِعَ لَعَلَّكُمْ تَخْلُدُونَ ۝ وَإِذَا بَطَشْتُمْ بَطَشْتُمْ جَبَّارِينَ ۝ فَاتَّقُوا اللَّهَ وَأَطِيعُونِ ۝ وَاتَّقُوا الَّذِي أَمَدَّكُمْ بِمَا تَعْلَمُونَ ۝ أَمَدَّكُمْ بِأَنْعَامٍ وَبَنِينَ ۝ وَجَنَّاتٍ وَعُيُونٍ ۝ إِنِّي أَخَافُ عَلَيْكُمْ عَذَابَ يَوْمٍ عَظِيمٍ ۝ قَالُوا سَوَاءٌ عَلَيْنَا أَوَعَظْتَ أَمْ لَمْ تَكُنْ مِنَ الْوَاعِظِينَ ۝

112. (Noah) said: "What knowledge could I have about what they were engaged in doing (before they became believers)?

113. "Indeed their reckoning rests with none but my Lord; if only you could understand!²⁴

114. "And it is not expected of me that I should repel the believers.

115. "I am but a plain warner (responsible for no other duty than the duty to warn)."

116. They said: "If you do not desist, O Noah, you will certainly be stoned to death in utter abjection."

117. (After ages of struggle)²⁵ he said (in supplication): "My Lord! Indeed, my people have denied me.

118. "So judge between me and them a conclusive (and everlasting) separation, and save me and the believers in my company."

119. So We saved him and those who were with him in the laden Ark.

120. And then, following their rescue, We caused the rest to drown.²⁶

121. Surely in that (which took place between Noah and his people) there is a sign (a great, important lesson). Most of them were not believers.

122. And surely your Lord is indeed the All-Glorious with irresistible might (able to punish whoever goes against His Glory), the All-Compassionate (especially towards His believing servants).

123. The 'Ād denied (Hūd and thereby meant to deny all) the Messengers.

124. (Recall) when their brother Hūd said to them (by way of timely warning): "Will you not keep from disobedience to God in reverence for Him and seek refuge with His protection?

125. "Surely I am a Messenger to you, trustworthy.

126. "So keep from disobedience to God in reverence for Him and obey me.

127. "I ask of you no wage for that (for conveying God's Message); my wage is only due from the Lord of the worlds.

128. "Will you continue to build on every high spot monumental buildings for fun and show;

129. "And make for yourselves great castles (as if) hoping that you might live for ever;

130. "And when you strike and seize (others and their goods), strike and seize in the style of tyrants?

131. "So keep from disobedience to God in reverence for Him and obey me.

132. "Keep from disobedience to Him

Who has amply provided you with (all that) you are well-aware of;

133. "Amply provided you with flocks and herds and children,

134. "And gardens and springs.

135. "Indeed I fear for you the punishment of an awesome Day."

136. They responded: "It is all the same to us whether you preach or are not of those who preach.

---

24. That is, a believer cannot be a lowly person. What the Prophet Noah, upon him be peace, is saying here is: "You may regard them as the lowliest of people because of some of the deeds they had done before believing, but I cannot have any knowledge about these deeds. Furthermore, belief removes all that was left in the past. Nor can I question any of their deeds. Nor can I know whether they believe in me for some ulterior motives, such as gaining material advantages. Furthermore, I am not responsible for judging their intentions. It is God alone Who knows everybody's intention and will take them to account." The Prophet Noah could only judge the people according to what they said, not what was truly in their hearts, nor in their past.

25. The Prophet Noah, upon him be peace, remained among his people for 950 years (29: 14).

26. For a detailed account of the Ark and the fate of Noah and his people, see *sūrah* 11: 25–48 and the corresponding notes 8-14.

سُورَةُ الشُّعَرَاء

٣٧٢

﷽

إِنْ هَٰذَآ إِلَّا خُلُقُ الْأَوَّلِينَ ۝ وَمَا نَحْنُ بِمُعَذَّبِينَ ۝ فَكَذَّبُوهُ فَأَهْلَكْنَاهُمْ إِنَّ فِي ذَٰلِكَ لَآيَةً وَمَا كَانَ أَكْثَرُهُم مُّؤْمِنِينَ ۝ وَإِنَّ رَبَّكَ لَهُوَ الْعَزِيزُ الرَّحِيمُ ۝ كَذَّبَتْ ثَمُودُ الْمُرْسَلِينَ ۝ إِذْ قَالَ لَهُمْ أَخُوهُمْ صَالِحٌ أَلَا تَتَّقُونَ ۝ إِنِّي لَكُمْ رَسُولٌ أَمِينٌ ۝ فَاتَّقُوا اللَّهَ وَأَطِيعُونِ ۝ وَمَا أَسْأَلُكُمْ عَلَيْهِ مِنْ أَجْرٍ إِنْ أَجْرِيَ إِلَّا عَلَىٰ رَبِّ الْعَالَمِينَ ۝ أَتُتْرَكُونَ فِي مَا هَٰهُنَا آمِنِينَ ۝ فِي جَنَّاتٍ وَعُيُونٍ ۝ وَزُرُوعٍ وَنَخْلٍ طَلْعُهَا هَضِيمٌ ۝ وَتَنْحِتُونَ مِنَ الْجِبَالِ بُيُوتًا فَارِهِينَ ۝ فَاتَّقُوا اللَّهَ وَأَطِيعُونِ ۝ وَلَا تُطِيعُوا أَمْرَ الْمُسْرِفِينَ ۝ الَّذِينَ يُفْسِدُونَ فِي الْأَرْضِ وَلَا يُصْلِحُونَ ۝ قَالُوا إِنَّمَا أَنتَ مِنَ الْمُسَحَّرِينَ ۝ مَا أَنتَ إِلَّا بَشَرٌ مِّثْلُنَا فَأْتِ بِآيَةٍ إِن كُنتَ مِنَ الصَّادِقِينَ ۝ قَالَ هَٰذِهِ نَاقَةٌ لَّهَا شِرْبٌ وَلَكُمْ شِرْبُ يَوْمٍ مَّعْلُومٍ ۝ وَلَا تَمَسُّوهَا بِسُوءٍ فَيَأْخُذَكُمْ عَذَابُ يَوْمٍ عَظِيمٍ ۝ فَعَقَرُوهَا فَأَصْبَحُوا نَادِمِينَ ۝ فَأَخَذَهُمُ الْعَذَابُ إِنَّ فِي ذَٰلِكَ لَآيَةً وَمَا كَانَ أَكْثَرُهُم مُّؤْمِنِينَ ۝ وَإِنَّ رَبَّكَ لَهُوَ الْعَزِيزُ الرَّحِيمُ ۝

137. "This (what we do) is the pattern of conduct of (all our) predecessors.

138. "And (so) we are not going to be subject to any punishment."

139. So they denied him and, in consequence, We destroyed them. Surely in that (which took place between Hūd and his people) there is a sign (a great, important lesson). Most of them were not believers.

140. And surely your Lord is indeed the All-Glorious with irresistible might (able to punish whoever goes against His Glory), the All-Compassionate (especially towards His believing servants).

141. The Thamūd denied (Ṣāliḥ and thereby meant to deny all) the Messengers.

142. (Recall) when their brother Ṣāliḥ said to them (by way of timely warning): "Will you not keep from disobedience to God in reverence for Him and seek refuge with His protection?

143. "I am indeed a Messenger to you, trustworthy.

144. "So keep from disobedience to God in reverence for Him and obey me.

145. "I ask of you no wage for that (for conveying God's Message); my wage is only due from the Lord of the worlds.

146. "(Do you think) you will be left secure forever in what is here before us,

147. "Amidst gardens and springs,

148. "Cornfields and date-palms with heavy bunches (of dates);

149. "And that you will (continue to) skillfully hew dwellings out of mountains?

150. "So keep from disobedience to God in reverence for Him and obey me;

151. "And do not follow the commands of those who are wasteful (of God-given faculties) and commit excesses,

152. "Those who cause disorder and corruption on the earth, without setting things right."

153. They responded: "You are only one of those who are bewitched.

154. "You are but a mortal like us, so produce a sign if you are truthful (in your claim of Messengership)."

155. (Ṣāliḥ) said: "This is a she-camel,[27]

one day is for her to drink and one day is for you to get water.

156. "Do not touch her with evil lest the punishment of an awesome Day should seize you."

157. But (after a time, being unable to put up with it any longer,) they cruelly slaughtered her, and then became regretful,

158. For the (shocking) punishment seized them. Surely in that (which took place between Ṣāliḥ and his people) there is a sign (a great, important lesson). Most of them were not believers.

159. And surely your Lord is indeed the All-Glorious with irresistible might (able to punish whoever goes against His Glory), the All-Compassionate (especially towards His believing servants).

---

27. For the she-camel, see *sūrah* 7: 73, note 17; *sūrah* 11: 64.

كَذَّبَتْ قَوْمُ لُوطٍ الْمُرْسَلِينَ ۞ إِذْ قَالَ لَهُمْ أَخُوهُمْ لُوطٌ أَلَا تَتَّقُونَ
۞ إِنِّي لَكُمْ رَسُولٌ أَمِينٌ ۞ فَاتَّقُوا اللَّهَ وَأَطِيعُونِ ۞ وَمَا أَسْأَلُكُمْ
عَلَيْهِ مِنْ أَجْرٍ إِنْ أَجْرِيَ إِلَّا عَلَى رَبِّ الْعَالَمِينَ ۞ أَتَأْتُونَ
الذُّكْرَانَ مِنَ الْعَالَمِينَ ۞ وَتَذَرُونَ مَا خَلَقَ لَكُمْ رَبُّكُمْ
مِنْ أَزْوَاجِكُمْ بَلْ أَنْتُمْ قَوْمٌ عَادُونَ ۞ قَالُوا لَئِنْ لَمْ تَنْتَهِ يَا لُوطُ
لَتَكُونَنَّ مِنَ الْمُخْرَجِينَ ۞ قَالَ إِنِّي لِعَمَلِكُمْ مِنَ الْقَالِينَ ۞ رَبِّ
نَجِّنِي وَأَهْلِي مِمَّا يَعْمَلُونَ ۞ فَنَجَّيْنَاهُ وَأَهْلَهُ أَجْمَعِينَ ۞
إِلَّا عَجُوزًا فِي الْغَابِرِينَ ۞ ثُمَّ دَمَّرْنَا الْآخَرِينَ ۞ وَأَمْطَرْنَا
عَلَيْهِمْ مَطَرًا فَسَاءَ مَطَرُ الْمُنْذَرِينَ ۞ إِنَّ فِي ذَلِكَ لَآيَةً وَمَا
كَانَ أَكْثَرُهُمْ مُؤْمِنِينَ ۞ وَإِنَّ رَبَّكَ لَهُوَ الْعَزِيزُ الرَّحِيمُ ۞
كَذَّبَ أَصْحَابُ الْأَيْكَةِ الْمُرْسَلِينَ ۞ إِذْ قَالَ لَهُمْ شُعَيْبٌ أَلَا تَتَّقُونَ
۞ إِنِّي لَكُمْ رَسُولٌ أَمِينٌ ۞ فَاتَّقُوا اللَّهَ وَأَطِيعُونِ ۞ وَمَا أَسْأَلُكُمْ
عَلَيْهِ مِنْ أَجْرٍ إِنْ أَجْرِيَ إِلَّا عَلَى رَبِّ الْعَالَمِينَ ۞ أَوْفُوا الْكَيْلَ
وَلَا تَكُونُوا مِنَ الْمُخْسِرِينَ ۞ وَزِنُوا بِالْقِسْطَاسِ الْمُسْتَقِيمِ ۞
وَلَا تَبْخَسُوا النَّاسَ أَشْيَاءَهُمْ وَلَا تَعْثَوْا فِي الْأَرْضِ مُفْسِدِينَ ۞

160. The people of Lot denied (Lot and thereby meant to deny all) the Messengers.

161. (Recall) when their brother Lot said to them (by way of timely warning): "Will you not keep from disobedience to God in reverence for Him and seek refuge with His protection?

162. "I am indeed a Messenger to you, trustworthy.

163. "So keep from disobedience to God in reverence for Him and obey me.

164. I ask of you no wage for that (for conveying God's Message); my wage is only due from the Lord of the worlds.

165. "What! do you, of all the world's people, come to men (with lust),

166. "And leave aside what your Lord has created (and made lawful) for you in your wives? No, indeed! you are a people exceeding all bounds (of decency)."

167. They responded: "If you do not desist, you will most certainly be cast out (from our land)."

168. (Lot) said: "I am indeed one who abhors your practice."

169. (And he prayed:) "My Lord! Save me and my family[28] from (the consequences of) what they have been doing."

170. So We saved him and his family, all of them,

171. Except an old woman, who was among those who stayed behind (and were destroyed).[29]

172. Then We annihilated the others.

173. We poured upon them a (destructive) rain (of stones). How evil was the rain of those who had been warned![30]

174. Surely in that (which took place between Lot and his people) there is a sign (a great, important lesson). Most of them were not believers.

175. And surely your Lord is indeed the All-Glorious with irresistible might (able to punish whoever goes against His Glory), the All-Compassionate (especially towards His believing servants).

176. The dwellers of al-Aykah[31] denied (Shu‘ayb and thereby meant to deny all) the Messengers.

177. (Recall) when Shu‘ayb said to them (by way of timely warning): "Will you not keep from disobedience to God in rever-

ence for Him and seek refuge with His protection?

178. "I am indeed a Messenger to you, trustworthy.

179. "So keep from disobedience to God in reverence for Him and obey me.

180. "I ask of you no wage for that (for conveying God's Message); my wage is only due from the Lord of the worlds.

181. "Give full measure (in all your dealings) and be not one of those who (by cheating and giving less) cause loss to others.

182. "And weigh with a true, accurate balance.

183. "Do not wrong people by depriving them of what is rightfully theirs, and do not go about acting wickedly in the land, causing disorder and corruption.

---

28. Lot prayed for himself and his family only because his family had accepted his Message and submitted to God (51: 36).

29. The verse refers to Lot's wife, who did not believe in him and who sided with the wicked people (11: 81).

30. For other accounts of the Prophet Lot, upon him be peace, and his people, see *sūrah* 7: 80–84, note 18; *sūrah* 11: 77–83, note 18; *sūrah* 15: 61–77.

31. For the identity of the people of al-Aykah, see *sūrah* 15, note 15.

184. "Keep from disobedience to Him in reverence for Him Who has created you and all the earlier generations."

185. They responded: "You are only one of those who are bewitched.

186. "You are but a mortal like us, and we have become convinced that you are certainly one of the liars.

187. "So cause lumps from the sky to fall down upon us, if you are truthful in your claim (of Messengership)."

188. (Shu'ayb) said: "My Lord knows well all that you do." (Thus he referred their matter to God.)

189. So they denied him and in consequence, the punishment of the Day of the Overshadowing seized them.[32] It surely was the punishment of an awesome day.

190. Surely in that (which took place between Shu'ayb and his people) there is a sign (a great, important lesson). Most of them were not believers.

191. And surely your Lord is indeed the All-Glorious with irresistible might (able to punish whoever goes against His Glory), the All-Compassionate (especially towards His believing servants).

192. This (Qur'ān) is indeed the Book of the Lord of the worlds being sent down by Him (in parts).

193. The Trustworthy Spirit[33] brings it down

194. On your heart, so that you may be one of the warners (entrusted with the Divine Revelation),

195. In clear Arabic tongue.

196. It has certainly been (prefigured) in the previous Scriptures.

197. Is it not an evidence enough for them that the scholars of the Children of Israel know it (to be so)?

198. But even if We had sent it down on any of the non-Arabs,

199. And he had recited it to them, they would still not have believed in it.[34]

200. Thus (because of their willful persistence in unbelief and injustices) have We caused it (the Qur'an) to pass unheeded through the hearts of the disbelieving criminals:

201. (Despite irrefutable proofs of its truth,) they will not believe in it until they see the painful punishment.[35]

202. So it will come on them all of a sudden, when they are unaware (and incapable of awareness) of its coming.

203. Then they say: "Are we to be granted some respite (so that we might reform ourselves?"

204. (This being so,) do they still wish for Our punishment to be hastened?[36]

205. Have you considered that, if We let them enjoy life for many (more) years (– something they will desperately wish for when they face the punishment),

206. And the punishment they were promised comes upon them after that,

---

32. There is nowhere in the Qur'ān or the Ḥadīth that explains the identity of the Overshadowing. It might have been a dark cloud hovering over al-Aykah and from which a "rain of calamity" poured upon them; or it might be a reference to the dark shadows which accompany volcanic eruptions and earthquakes.

33. The Trustworthy Spirit is Archangel Gabriel, as explicitly stated in *Whoever is an enemy to Gabriel (should know that) it is he who brings down the Qur'ān on your heart by the leave of God* (2: 97). God mentions him here as trustworthy in order to stress that there can be no doubt about the authenticity and genuineness of the Qur'ān. As clearly seen in the verses above about the Messengers and verses 221–226 which follow and state that the jinn or devils can never have an effect on the Prophet Muḥammad, upon him be peace and blessings, this *sūrah* dwells on the trustwor-thiness of the Messengers and the fact that there is nothing that can in any way interfere with Divine Revelation.

34. The Makkans sometimes claimed that the Prophet Muḥammad himself composed the Qur'ān. But all their assertions were only pretexts in order not to believe. Even if one of the non-Arabs had brought it in such a clear and eloquent Arabic, they would still not have believed and would have come up with new pretexts.

35. This refers to death for every unbeliever and a calamity in the world for some communities and the world's final destruction of all the unbelievers who will witness it.

36. The unbelievers did not believe that any punishment with which they were threatened would ever come upon them, so with derision they told the Messenger to bring the punishment without delay.

207. It will be of no avail to them at all (that their lives of enjoyment were prolonged).

208. We have never destroyed any township except that it had warners (sent to it),

209. To remind and admonish them. We have never been unjust.

210. It is not the satans who have brought down this (Book).

211. It is neither (permitted nor proper) for them, nor is it within their power (to do that).

212. Indeed they are utterly debarred even from hearing it (during its Revelation).[37]

213. Hence, never take to you any other deity to invoke besides God, lest you should become of those condemned to the punishment.

214. And (O Messenger) warn your nearest kinsfolk.[38]

215. Spread your wings (to provide care and shelter) over the believers who follow you (in practicing God's commandments in their lives).

216. But if they disobey you (your kinsfolk by refusing your call, or those who have newly believed by not giving up their former way of life), then say (to them): "I am free of (responsibility for) what you do."[39]

217. And (taking no account of any earthly power in performing your mission) put your trust in the All-Glorious with irresistible might (able to do whatever He wills), the All-Compassionate (especially towards His believing servants),[40]

218. He Who sees you when you rise (in the Prayer, and in readiness to carry out Our commands),

219. As well as your strenuous efforts in prostration among those who prostrate (to

be able to fulfill your duty of servanthood and help the believer to reform their lives).

220. Surely, He is the All-Hearing, the All-Knowing.

221. (O people!) Shall I inform you upon whom the satans descend?

222. They descend upon everyone addicted to inventing falsehoods, addicted to sinning.

223. They (the satans) give ear eagerly (to the conversations of the angels, and whisper to every forger lost in sin as if they received something), but they (both the satans and their sinful agents) are liars in most of their words.[41]

224. As for poets, only the misguided follow them.

225. Do you not see that they roam confusedly through all the valleys (of falsehoods, thoughts, and currents).

226. And they say what they themselves do not do.[42]

227. Except those who believe and do good, righteous deeds, and remember God much, and vindicate themselves when they have been wronged.[43] The wrongdoers will come to know by what a (great) reverse they will be overturned.

---

37. Whatever may be claimed about the revelation of the Qur'ān, the satans were never allowed to listen to a single word of it from the moment Archangel Gabriel received the Revelation from God and conveyed it to God's Messenger until the Messenger had fully grasped and memorized it. For further information about attempts by the satans or devils to ascend to heaven and their being expelled, see 15: 18, note 5; 67: 5, note 4.

38. That the Messenger was sinless does not mean that he was not responsible for carrying out God's commands and avoiding His prohibitions. Moreover, there is no special consideration or dispensation for either the Messenger or his family. Rather, the Messenger is the first of those responsible for carrying out God's commandments, and he began communicating God's Message with his family. In addition, he always employed the members of his family and clan in the most dangerous tasks and never showed them any undue favor. This is a very important lesson and warning for Muslim leaders and administrators.

When this verse was revealed, God's Messenger invited his nearest relatives over for a meal. 'Ali later narrated the incident:

God's Messenger invited his relatives to his house. After the meal, he addressed them: "God has commanded me to warn my nearest relatives. You are my tribe of the nearest kindred. I will not be able to do anything for you in the Hereafter unless you proclaim that there is no deity but God." At the end of his speech, he asked who would support him. At that time, I was a boy with puny legs and arms. When no one responded, I put aside the pitcher in my hand and declared: "I will, O Messenger of God!" The Messenger repeated the call three times, and each time only I answered him. (Ibn Hanbal, 1: 159)

Once the Messenger climbed Mount Ṣafā and, calling every clan of the Quraysh by name, conveyed to them God's Message and warned them against His punishment (Muslim, "al-Īmān," 355).

God's Messenger himself suffered hunger, thirst, and every other hardship. He was forced into exile and made the target of many assaults and ambushes. He bore all of these simply for the good pleasure of God and the good of humanity. Abu Hurayrah once saw him praying in a sitting position and asked if he were ill. The Messenger's reply caused Abu Huraryah to weep: "I am hungry, Abu Hurayrah. Hunger has left me no strength to stand up for prayer" (Muslim, "Ashribah," 140).

Even though most of his Companions became wealthier in later years in Madīnah, the Messenger and his family never changed their very simple lifestyle. Fāṭimah, his only surviving child, did all of the housework for her family herself. Once when captives were distributed in Madīnah, she asked her father for a maid. He replied:

O my daughter. I can give you nothing before I satisfy the needs of the people of the Suffah. However, let me teach you something that is better for you than having a servant. When you go to bed, say: "Glory be to God, All praise be to God, God is the Greatest" 33 times. (Some Traditions say that the last phrase should be recited 34 times.) This is better for your next life. (al-Bukhārī, "Faḍā'il as-Ṣaḥābah," 9)

One day he saw her wearing a bracelet (or a necklace) and warned her: "O my daughter, do you want people to say of my daughter that she is wearing a ring of Hellfire? Take it off immediately!" Fāṭimah sold it and bought a slave for the money she received and emancipated him (an-Nasā'ī, "Zīnah," 39).

39. The acts, lifestyles, and conduct of a leader's family members and relatives in particular, and also those of his followers may be either in the leader's favor or against him. Every evil action on their part makes the position of the leader difficult in the face of the masses. For this reason, a leader cannot defend their evil acts through kinship. Rather, the leader must declare being quit of their evil acts.

40. It is worth noting that this *sūrah* begins by declaring that God is the All-Glorious with irresistible might and the All-Compassionate (verse 9), and continues by relating the experiences of some Messengers, concluded with the pronouncement of the same two Divine Names. Once again, it mentions them and calls God's Messenger to rely on Him Who has these Names. This implies that God is able to punish whoever goes against His Glory, while He is All-Compassionate toward the believers and therefore protect the Messenger against his opponents. It also suggests that believers should be honored and mighty in the face of the unbelievers and compassionate toward one another.

41. Satans or the jinn try to rise to the heaven in order to listen to hear the conversations of the angels, but are prevented. However, they whisper some things to their agents among human beings as if they received something. In addition, since they are more refined in matter than humans, their time-dimension is different and they move much more swiftly in time and space than humans can. This is why they can acquire some information which humans cannot. They add many lies to that information and whisper them to those who can hear them – fortune-tellers, mediums, magicians, etc. – in order to deceive and mislead them and others and separate people, particularly spouses, from each other. This is expressed in a *hadīth* recorded by al-Bukhārī in his *Ṣaḥīḥ*. When asked about magicians and fortunetellers, God's Messenger answered that they were nothing. When he was told that they sometimes told the truth, the Messenger explained: "The jinn whisper this truth to their friends, and they forge a story out of it by adding many falsehoods to it" (al-Bukhārī, "Bad'u'l-Khalq," 6).

42. In the pre-Islamic age of ignorance, people believed that poets had some contact with evil spirits. The Makkan polytheists sometimes claimed that God's Messenger was one of these poets and therefore had received the Qur'ān from these spirits. God declares that the Messenger is absolutely free of any contact with evil spirits and that the Qur'ān is entirely His Word. The Messenger was one without any sin, while those who had contact with evil spirits were people lost in sin. Like the satans who whispered to them, those who had contact with them were also liars, but the Messenger was absolutely truthful in every word he uttered. The poets who had contact with satans wandered aimlessly in every valley of (literary) trends, played with words, followed every false thought and philosophy, dragged along by their impulses, lacked consistency, and they did not observe any established true standard in their sayings, thoughts, or actions. However, just as the Messenger had nothing to do with such acts or behavior, the Qur'ān is also absolutely above having anything to do with utterances of poets. Moreover, while it was the misguided, that is, the Makkan polytheists who opposed the Messenger, and who followed the poets, the Companions who believed in and followed the Messenger were of high character and conduct and had laudable virtues. Also, the poets related acts that they did not perform or act upon. There was no consistency between their sayings and their actions. Whereas the Messenger and his Companions preached what they practiced and practiced what they preached.

43. This verse makes four exceptions to the general condemnation of poets. The poets who (i) believe in the essentials of faith; (ii) do good, righteous deeds required by their faith; (iii) never forget God, perform their Prayers, and mention Him much; and (iv) without ever using their literary ability for sinful ends or for any goals disapproved by Islam, support truth and defend it whenever it is attacked. Whenever necessary, they use their poetic talent to defend Islam and Muslims, and oppose oppression and the oppressors.

376   سُورَةُ النَّمْل   ٣٧٦

بِسْمِ اللهِ الرَّحْمٰنِ الرَّحِيمِ

(Arabic Qur'anic text)

though they were the most powerful rulers of their time. It expounds many truths that prove God's Oneness and the Hereafter and, through a number of questions, it establishes the falsehood of polytheism.

In the Name of God, the All-Merciful, the All-Compassionate.

1. *Ṭā. Sīn.* These are the Revelations of the Qur'ān, (and) a Book clear in itself and clearly showing the truth;[1]

2. Guidance and glad tidings for the believers,

3. Who establish the Prayer in conformity with its conditions and pay the Prescribed Purifying Alms, and in the Hereafter they have certainty of faith.

4. As for those who do not believe in the Hereafter, We have surely decked out their deeds to be appealing to them (because of their unbelief),[2] and so they wander in anxiety (about their worldly lives with deadened hearts).

5. Those are the ones for whom is the worst of punishment (in the world and in the Hereafter), and they will be the greatest losers in the Hereafter (as they will be left with no good deeds forwarded for acceptance).[3]

6. And to you (O Messenger) the Qur'ān is being conveyed from the Presence of One All-Wise, All-Knowing.[4]

7. (Remember and recount to them) when Moses (while traveling in the desert saw a fire and) said to his family: "I perceive a fire far off. (Wait here,) I will bring you from there some information (about where we are and the way we should take), or bring you at least a burning brand so that you may (kindle a fire and) warm yourselves."

8. When he came to it, he was called: "Blessed is he who is at the fire and those

SŪRAH 27

AN-NAML (THE ANT)

Makkah period

Revealed in the middle Makkan period, this *sūrah* has 93 verses, and derives its name from the word *al-naml* (the ant) in verse 18. It emphasizes that only those who accept the truths expounded in the Qur'ān and order their lives according to God's commandments can truly benefit from this Revelation. One of the basic obstacles to adopting the way of the Qur'ān is the denial of the Hereafter, which usually makes one irresponsible and a slave to one's carnal desires. This *sūrah* gives examples from history of those who stubbornly resisted God's Message and those who accepted it – the Prophet Solomon and the Queen of Sheba, even who are around it; and All-Glorified is God (above having any resemblance with the created), the Lord of the worlds.[5]

9. "O Moses! It is I, God, the All-Glorious with irresistible might, the All-Wise.

10. "Now, throw down your staff." (He threw it, and) when he saw it slithering as if a snake, he turned his back to flee. "O Moses, have no fear. The Messengers (those who enjoy nearness to Me and therefore absolute security) do not (have any reason to) feel fear in My Presence.

11. "Only those who have done wrong (should fear). But if (they repent and) substitute good in place of evil – surely I am All-Forgiving, All-Compassionate.

12. "Put your (right) hand into your bosom: it will come forth shining white without flaw. It is (one) among the nine signs (miracles[6] for you to show) to the Pharaoh and his people. Surely, they are a transgressing people."

13. But when Our signs came to them in plain sight and clear enough to have opened their eyes to truth, they said: "This is clearly nothing but sorcery."

---

1. The Qur'ān mentions a Manifest Record (36: 12), and in several of its verses (such as 6: 59, 10: 61, and 11: 6) refers to a Manifest Book (for explanations of both, see 6: 59, note 13; 13: 39, note 13; 17: 14, note 10). In its several other verses (5: 11; 12: 1; 26: 2; 28: 2), it refers to a Book clear in itself and which clearly shows the truth.

The Manifest Record is the Original Register which comprises the originals of everything to come into existence and every event to happen, in the Divine Knowledge, together with the causes and laws to accompany them. As for the Manifest Book, it is the Book of Creation manifesting whatever of the Manifest Record or the Original Register which the Divine Will wants to bring into the realm of creation, and in which everything in creation, down to the sayings and deeds of every human being and jinn, is being recorded. It may be said that the Qur'ān, which is referred to as the Book clear in itself and which clearly shows the truth, is identical with the Manifest Record with respect to the eternal existence of both in God's Knowledge, and with the Manifest Book with respect to their existence in the realm of creation. However, the Qur'ān is also different from both. It is different from the Manifest Record with respect to the fact that while the Manifest Record exists in the Divine Knowledge or is even identical with It in one respect, the Qur'ān is also re-

lated with the Divine Speech. As for its difference from the Manifest Book, the Qur'ān issues or has been revealed from God's Attribute of Speech, and is a Book which is read, and stored in writing. Whereas, the Manifest Book is the Book of Creation that emanates from the Divine Attributes of Will and Power. (God knows the best.)

2. That God decks out one's deeds to be appealing one means that, as a result of the laws and rules He has established for human life and of the nature of unbelief, those who do not follow God's Religion are usually haughty and approve of their own deeds. Whereas true believers are always self-critical, fearful about whether they are able to accomplish whatever needs to be done in order to obtain God's approval.

Some verses state that Satan decks out their deeds to be appealing to the unbelievers. What Satan does is that it whispers to humans and invites them to do an evil deed which he tries to persuade them it is good. He has no power to compel them to do something.

3. In the Hereafter, people will find themselves at different levels, as they are in the world, according to their level of belief or unbelief, their good or bad deeds, their sincerity in carrying out these deeds, their sacrifices along God's way or their efforts to bar people from this

way. Because of this, both Paradise and Hell will have stations for people at each level.

4. Because of this, the Qur'ān is an embodiment of perfect wisdom and knowledge.

5. As stated in *Sūrat al-Qaṣaṣ* (28), God Almighty called out to Moses from behind a tree (28: 30). We explained in note 5 to *sūrah* 20 that this type of Divine calling is one of the three types of Divine Revelation. The Qur'ān clarifies that God addresses human beings either from behind a veil or by putting the meaning into the heart (as a special kind of Revelation) or by sending an angel (42: 51). In order not to provide any grounds for anthropomorphism, as well as to mark the significance of the particular event, the Qur'ān uses the expression, *All-Glorified is God, the Lord of the worlds*, meaning that God is absolutely above having any resemblance with the created.

The valley in which this event took place was the "sacred valley of Tuwā" in Sinai (for the sacredness of this valley, see 20: 12, note 5). God blessed the Prophet Moses (who was at the fire when this event took place) with Messengership and His speech to him, and also his family (who were around the fire) because of Moses, upon him be peace. He also blessed the region around this place, which is the land of Damascus, including Palestine; here He has produced many blessings for all people (7: 137; 17: 1; 21: 71, 81). He has also blessed the Prophets and their followers who have lived in this region (as well as in other regions).

6. For the nine signs, see 7: 133; 17: 101, note 37.

377

14. They rejected them out of mere iniquity and self-exaltation, although their consciences were convinced of their being true. So see how was the outcome for those given in to spreading disorder and corruption.

15. (On the other hand, We saved the Children of Israel whom the Pharaohs had persecuted for centuries, and granted them great triumph. And in time,) We granted David and Solomon (special) knowledge. Both used to thank and praise God, saying: "All praise and gratitude are for God, Who has favored us more than many of His believing servants."[7]

16. Solomon succeeded David. He would say (citing in gratitude God's favors to him): "O people! We have been taught the language of birds[8] and we have been granted (some portion) of everything (which God provides for His servants). Surely this is a conspicuous favor.

17. One day his hosts of jinn, and of men, and of birds were assembled before Solomon (upon his command), and were led forth under full control

18. Until, when they reached a valley of ants, one of the ants said: "O you ants! Get into your dwellings lest Solomon and his army crush you unawares."

19. Smiling at her words (in humble contentment with God's favors to him), he said: "My Lord! Inspire and guide me so that I may thank You for Your favor which

You have bestowed on me and on my parents, and so that I may act righteously in a manner that will please You; and include me (out of Your mercy) among Your righteous servants."

20. (On another occasion) he inspected the birds and said: "How is it that I cannot see the hoopoe? Or is he among the absentees?

21. "I will certainly inflict a severe punishment on him or maybe even kill him unless he comes to me with a convincing reason (for his absence)."

22. Before long the hoopoe came up and said: "I have obtained (some important information) which you do not have, and have come to you from Sheba[9] with reliable news.

7. David and Solomon, upon them be peace, were among the great Messengers of God, each of whom God distinguished with many special favors. First of all, both were message-bearing Prophets. God granted Caliphate to David and kingdom to Solomon. Both were granted special knowledge, wisdom, sound judgment, and the ability to distinguish between right and wrong (21: 79). Mountains and birds glorified God with David; he was taught how to smelt iron and make armor, while Solomon was able to employ the jinn and the devils, and able to understand the language of the birds and ants, as well as the ability to travel on wind. Despite all these blessings, these Prophets remained perfectly humble. David earned his living by manual labor. They attributed to God whatever they enjoyed. So they recognized that their being more favored, as compared with many of God's believing servants, was not a blessing that they had deserved or some privilege to rejoice in and be proud of; rather, they perceived it as a means of their being tested, that required praise and thankfulness.

8. The verses: *We have been taught the language of birds* (27: 16) and *The birds assembled* (38: 19) indicate that Almighty God bestowed on the Prophet Solomon the knowledge of language of the birds and the language of their abilities (how they could be of benefit), as well as pointing out David's glorification of God with the birds. Given this, and also taking into account that the earth is the laden table of the All-Merciful, set up in our honor, most animals and birds that benefit from this table may serve us. God uses small animals, as honeybees and silkworms, through the guidance of His special inspiration, to benefit humankind.

If we could discover how to use other birds and animals, many species might be employed for important tasks, just as domestic animals are. Thus, the verses mentioned show the ultimate aim in subjugating and benefiting from birds. By specifying the greatest aim in this field, the verses urge humankind toward it.

In the same verses, God Almighty indicates:

> So that his sinlessness as a Prophet and his justice as a sovereign might not be damaged, I subjugated to one of your fellow men, who was totally submitted to Me, the enormous creatures in My Kingdom and made them speak. I put most of My hosts and animals at his service. I have entrusted to each of you the Supreme Trust that the heavens and earth avoided undertaking, and have endowed you with the potential to rule on the earth according to My commands. Therefore, you should yield to the One in Whose Hand are the reins of all creatures. This will cause His creatures to yield to you, so that you may use them in the Name of the One Who holds their reins and rise to a position worthy of your potential. Most birds may be an intimate friend or an obedient servant, like Solomon's hoopoe. They may entertain you and drive you with zeal toward the perfections and attainments of which you are capable, rather than causing you to fall from the position required by your humanity, as vain amusements do. (*The Words*, "the 20th Word," 272)

9. Sheba (Saba') was the famous trading nation of southern Arabia, where they ruled for almost 1,000 years from around 1100 BC to around 115 BC. Their capital was Ma'ārib, located 55 miles north-east of San'ā, the present capital of Yemen. They controlled the trade between East Africa, India, the Far East and Arabia with Egypt, Syria, Greece, and Rome. In addition to this, they had an excellent irrigation system which dotted the length and breadth of the country with dams. Their land was unusually fertile and lush. These explain their affluence. Greek historians called them the richest nation of the world (al-Mawdūdī, 7: 151, note 29).

378

سُوْرَةُ النَّمْل

٣٧٨

اِنِّىْ وَجَدْتُ امْرَاَةً تَمْلِكُهُمْ وَاُوْتِيَتْ مِنْ كُلِّ شَىْءٍ وَلَهَا عَرْشٌ
عَظِيْمٌ ۞ وَجَدْتُهَا وَقَوْمَهَا يَسْجُدُوْنَ لِلشَّمْسِ مِنْ دُوْنِ اللّٰهِ
وَزَيَّنَ لَهُمُ الشَّيْطَانُ اَعْمَالَهُمْ فَصَدَّهُمْ عَنِ السَّبِيْلِ فَهُمْ
لَا يَهْتَدُوْنَ ۞ اَلَّا يَسْجُدُوْا لِلّٰهِ الَّذِىْ يُخْرِجُ الْخَبْءَ فِى
السَّمٰوٰتِ وَالْاَرْضِ وَيَعْلَمُ مَا تُخْفُوْنَ وَمَا تُعْلِنُوْنَ ۞ اَللّٰهُ
لَا اِلٰهَ اِلَّا هُوَ رَبُّ الْعَرْشِ الْعَظِيْمِ ۩ ۞ قَالَ سَنَنْظُرُ اَصَدَقْتَ اَمْ كُنْتَ
مِنَ الْكَاذِبِيْنَ ۞ اِذْهَبْ بِكِتَابِىْ هٰذَا فَاَلْقِهْ اِلَيْهِمْ ثُمَّ تَوَلَّ عَنْهُمْ
فَانْظُرْ مَاذَا يَرْجِعُوْنَ ۞ قَالَتْ يَا اَيُّهَا الْمَلَؤُا اِنِّىْ اُلْقِىَ اِلَىَّ كِتَابٌ
كَرِيْمٌ ۞ اِنَّهُ مِنْ سُلَيْمٰنَ وَاِنَّهُ بِسْمِ اللّٰهِ الرَّحْمٰنِ الرَّحِيْمِ ۞ اَلَّا
تَعْلُوْا عَلَىَّ وَاْتُوْنِىْ مُسْلِمِيْنَ ۞ قَالَتْ يَا اَيُّهَا الْمَلَؤُا اَفْتُوْنِىْ فِىْ
اَمْرِىْ مَا كُنْتُ قَاطِعَةً اَمْرًا حَتّٰى تَشْهَدُوْنِ ۞ قَالُوْا نَحْنُ
اُولُوْا قُوَّةٍ وَّاُولُوْا بَأْسٍ شَدِيْدٍ وَّالْاَمْرُ اِلَيْكِ فَانْظُرِىْ مَاذَا
تَاْمُرِيْنَ ۞ قَالَتْ اِنَّ الْمُلُوْكَ اِذَا دَخَلُوْا قَرْيَةً اَفْسَدُوْهَا
وَجَعَلُوْا اَعِزَّةَ اَهْلِهَا اَذِلَّةً وَكَذٰلِكَ يَفْعَلُوْنَ ۞ وَاِنِّىْ
مُرْسِلَةٌ اِلَيْهِمْ بِهَدِيَّةٍ فَنَاظِرَةٌ بِمَ يَرْجِعُ الْمُرْسَلُوْنَ ۞

23. "I found there a woman ruling over them, one who has been granted everything (that a ruler is expected to have), and who has a mighty throne.

24. "However, I found her and her people prostrating to the sun rather than God. Satan has decked out their deeds to be appealing to them, and thus has barred them from the (unique straight) way, so they are not rightly guided,

25. "So that they do not prostrate before God, Who brings to light what is hidden in the heavens and the earth (Who brings into the light of existence all things and beings in the heavens and the earth from the veil of non-existence), and knows what you keep secret and what you disclose.

26. "God – there is no deity but He, the Lord of the Mighty Throne."[10]

27. (Solomon) said: "We will see whether you are speaking the truth or are one of the liars.

28. "Go with this letter of mine, and drop it to them; then draw back from them and see how they will deal with it among themselves, and return."[11]

29. She (the Queen, when the letter reached her) said: "O you nobles! See, an honorable letter has been cast to me.

30. "It is from Solomon, and it is: 'In the Name of God, the All-Merciful, the All-Compassionate.

31. 'Do not act towards me in defiance, but come to me in submission.'

32. "O you nobles! Let me have your counsel in this matter. (You know well that) I never conclude a decision on a matter unless you are present with me."

33. They said: "We dispose great power and we dispose great daring but the decision is yours, so consider what you will command."

34. She said: "When kings enter a country, they cause destruction and corruption in it, and make the noble (ones of its inhabitants) abased. This is what they really do.

35. "Now I will send them a present and see with what (answer) the envoys return."

10. Deluded by Satan and defeated by their carnal desires, many people stray from the Straight Path and live their entire life in misguidance. They cannot find the greatest and clearest truth, a truth even a bird knows with certainty. The Qur'ān draws attention to this fact in another verse as well: *(He [Cain] did not know what to do with the dead body of his brother.) Then God sent forth a raven, scratching in the earth, to show him how he might cover the corpse of his brother. So seeing he cried: "Oh, alas for me! Am I then unable even to be like this raven, and so find a way to cover the corpse of my brother?" And he became distraught with remorse* (5: 31).

Said Nursi reminds us of this fact in many places in his works. For example:

> Furthermore, our nature and spiritual being demonstrate that we have been created to worship God. As for our physical powers and ability to live here, we are worse off than sparrows. But in respect to our knowledge, understanding our needs, and supplication and worship, which are necessary for our spiritual life and the life of the Hereafter, we are the king and commander of all animate creatures.
>
> O my soul. If you consider this world as your major goal and work for it, you will remain only a soldier with no more control over your affairs than a sparrow. But if you move toward the Hereafter, considering this world to be a field to be sown, a preparation for the other world, and act accordingly, you become the ruler of the animal kingdom, a supplicant of Almighty God, and His favored or indulged guest in this world. You can choose either option. So ask for guidance and success in His way from the Most Merciful of the merciful. (*The Words*, "the 5th Word," 29–30)
>
> Your potential makes you superior to all

animals. But even a sparrow can do a better job than you when it comes to satisfying your daily needs. Why do you not understand that your duty as a human being is to work for the real, everlasting life? You are not an animal! Most of your worldly concerns are trivial and useless matters from which you derive no benefit. And yet, leaving aside the most essential things, you spend your time acquiring useless information as if you had thousands of years to live.

> As for the worldly, physical dimension of your being, you cannot compete with a bee or a sparrow, are weaker than a fly or a spider, and cannot achieve what they can. As for the second aspect of your being, however, you can surpass the mountains, the earth, and the heavens, for you can bear a burden that they cannot. Thus, your acts have a greater impact than theirs. When you do something good or build something, it reaches only as far as your hand and your strength. But your evil and destructive acts are aggressive and widespread.
>
> We have been created in the best pattern. If we concentrate on this worldly life we are far lower than a sparrow, although we have far more developed faculties than any animal. (So our duty in the world is to find God, know Him and worship Him alone). (*The Words*, "the 23rd Word," 335–336)

11. Although we ought to believe in a person's verbal declaration, the hoopoe damaged his reputation for reliability by committing a grievous fault. He deserted the army without permission. The Qur'ān orders that any statement of a transgressor be tested (one known for his or her transgressions of the limits set by God) without attempting to do anything based on their statement (49: 6).

36. When he (the envoy with the present) came to Solomon, he (Solomon) said: "Do you mean to help me with wealth? What God has granted me (of Prophethood, kingdom, and wealth) is much more and better than all that He has given you. It is only (people such as) you who would rejoice in this gift of yours.

37. "Go back to them (who sent you, and inform them that, if they do not come to us in submission), we will certainly come upon them with hosts which they have no power to resist. We will assuredly drive them from there in disgrace, and they will be humbled."[12]

38. (The Queen, having received his message, decided to visit Solomon in Jerusalem. Knowing of her journey,) Solomon said (to his council): "O you nobles! Who among you can bring me her throne before they come to me in submission?"

39. One strong and cunning among the jinn said: "I can bring it to you before you rise from your council. Surely I have the strength and skill to do so and I am trustworthy."

40. And one who had some knowledge of the Book said: "I can bring it to you in the twinkling of your eye." When Solomon saw the throne set in his presence, he said: "This is out of the pure grace of my Lord that He may try me whether I give thanks or act with ingratitude. Whoever gives thanks gives thanks only for (the good of) his own soul; and whoever acts with ingratitude – (let him be aware that) my Lord is surely All-Wealthy and Self-Sufficient, All-Munificent."[13]

41. He said: "Disguise her throne, and let us see whether she is able to find guidance or remains one of those who are not guided."[14]

42. When she (the Queen) arrived, she was asked: "Is your throne like this?" She

said: "It is as if it were the same. We were given knowledge (about the magnificence of Solomon's rule and his extraordinary power) before all this (we have seen here), and we have already decided to submit."

43. That she had been worshipping other than God kept her back (from the Straight Path); for she belonged to a disbelieving people.[15]

44. It was said (to her): "Enter the palace." When she saw it, she thought it was a pool of water and bared her calves (in order to hold her robes above the water). He (Solomon) said: "This is a palace paved with crystal." (Having now concluded that Solomon must truly be a Prophet,) she said: "My Lord, surely I have wronged myself (by worshipping false gods). But now I submit myself, in Solomon's company, to God, the Lord of the worlds."[16/17]

12. The Qur'ān never condones the mobilization of armies on others or the occupation of their territories for worldly reasons. It also forbids bloodshed, killing, and usurpation. In short, it condemns every kind of imperialism. What it reports from the Queen of Sheba in verse 34 is of this import. So, Solomon's threat to the Shebans was not a threat of warlike aggression. It is quite clear in the verses that as a Messenger, Solomon was never proud of his wealth or kingdom, and never had an eye on the wealth or lands of others. His only concern was to see that the true faith was embraced by more people to attain true felicity in both worlds or that others should submit to the system based on righteousness and justice in all its dimensions. Everybody should enjoy freedom from the shackles of servitude to human-made systems of oppression, and the obstacles put between them and their only Creator and Sustainer by those systems should be removed so that they can make a free choice.

13. The verse describes the wonderful event of how the Queen of Sheba's throne was brought to Solomon's court. The verse suggests that things can be transported over long distances, either bodily or in their images. In fact, God Almighty bestowed this as a miracle upon Solomon, who was honored with kingship as well as Divine Messengership, so that he could maintain his sinlessness and justice by being personally informed of all regions in his extensive realm, see his subjects' conditions, and hear their troubles.

That means that if we rely on Almighty God and appeal to Him in the language of our potentials, as the Prophet Solomon did in the language of his sinlessness, and if our acts conform to His laws in the universe and with what attracts His favor, the world may become like a town for us. The Queen's throne was in Yemen, yet it was seen in (Jerusalem in the region of) Damascus either physically or as an image, as were the forms of the people around it, who were seen and heard.

This verse suggests the transportation of forms and the transmission of sounds over long distances. In effect, it says: "O rulers. If you wish to realize perfect justice, try to see and know your realm in all its details, as Solomon did. Only by rising to such a level can a just ruler, who cherishes his subjects, be saved from being held accountable. Only in this manner may he realize perfect justice." What God Almighty is saying here is:

> O humankind. I bestowed on My servant a vast realm. In order for him to realize perfect justice throughout it, I allowed him to know whatever was happening therein. Since I have created every individual with a capacity to rule according to My commands, I have also given him, as a requirement of My Wisdom, the potential to scan the face of earth and comprehend whatever is in it. Even if every individual cannot reach this point, humankind as a species may realize it. If they cannot achieve it physically, they can do it spiritually, like the saints. Therefore, you may benefit from this great blessing. Come on and let Me see you do it. Fulfill your duties of worship. Strive in such a way that you turn the surface of the earth into a garden; so that you can see every part of it, and hear the sounds from every corner. *Heed the decree of the All-Merciful: He it is Who has made the earth subservient to you (as if a docile animal), so go about through its shoulders (uplands) and eat of His provision; but (be ever mindful that) to Him will be the Resurrection.* (67: 15)
>
> Thus the verse mentioned above marks the ultimate point in the transmission of images and sounds, which constitutes one of the latest and most significant developments in science and technology, and encourages humanity toward that furthest point. (*The Words*, "the 20th Word," 270)

The Prophet Solomon, upon him be peace, was a Prophet and a king. Since he fully submitted to God's Will, he only cared for absolute justice and the good of people in both worlds. Therefore, he used whatever ability and favors God had bestowed on him in His way and for the people's good. But other kings and/ or governments, including the modern "democratic" ones that champion justice and fundamental human rights and freedoms, have used throughout history and continue to use at the present time, all the powers they have, much in the way the Queen of Sheba described in the verse 34: *When kings enter a country, they cause destruction and corruption in it, and make the noble (ones of its inhabitants) abased. This is what they really do.*

14. The Queen and her people worshipped the sun, thus her throne may have been decorated with images or figures that belonged to and demonstrated her faith. The Prophet Solomon, upon him be peace, wanted to disguise it, most probably by obliterating the images on it and decorating it with inscriptions and images associated with the Divine Religion. By doing so, Solomon aimed at her conversion.

15. The Queen worshipped the sun not as the result of willful choice or stubbornness on her part, but only as a tradition. She was born into an unbelieving nation and grew up as one who saw the sun being worshipped. Yet, she did not have such a character that would insist on misguidance due to reasons such as arrogance, submission to carnal desires, and stubbornness. When she became aware of the rule of the Prophet Solomon, she began to grasp the truth.

16. What the Queen witnessed concerning the character, manners, and rule of Solomon sufficed for her to conclude that Solomon could be nothing but a Messenger of God and to understand all that he had derived from his faith and mission. This is the reason why she did not hesitate to accept the true faith and became a Muslim.

17. The Biblical account of the story of Solomon and the Queen of Sheba (*2 Chronicles*, 9: 1-12) is different from that found in the Qur'ān in many respects.

However, the rabbinical traditions of the Jews relate the story in terms and details that more closely resemble the Qur'ānic version, except for the fact that there are also calumnies against Solomon, upon him be peace, in the rabbinical texts.

The Qur'ān has restored both Solomon and all other Israelite Prophets, against whom many similar accusations are found in the Bible, to their rightful honored positions.

380

٣٨٠

وَلَقَدۡ أَرۡسَلۡنَآ إِلَىٰ ثَمُودَ أَخَاهُمۡ صَٰلِحًا أَنِ ٱعۡبُدُوا۟ ٱللَّهَ فَإِذَا هُمۡ فَرِيقَانِ يَخۡتَصِمُونَ ۝ قَالَ يَٰقَوۡمِ لِمَ تَسۡتَعۡجِلُونَ بِٱلسَّيِّئَةِ قَبۡلَ ٱلۡحَسَنَةِ لَوۡلَا تَسۡتَغۡفِرُونَ ٱللَّهَ لَعَلَّكُمۡ تُرۡحَمُونَ ۝ قَالُوا۟ ٱطَّيَّرۡنَا بِكَ وَبِمَن مَّعَكَ قَالَ طَٰٓئِرُكُمۡ عِندَ ٱللَّهِ بَلۡ أَنتُمۡ قَوۡمٌ تُفۡتَنُونَ ۝ وَكَانَ فِى ٱلۡمَدِينَةِ تِسۡعَةُ رَهۡطٍ يُفۡسِدُونَ فِى ٱلۡأَرۡضِ وَلَا يُصۡلِحُونَ ۝ قَالُوا۟ تَقَاسَمُوا۟ بِٱللَّهِ لَنُبَيِّتَنَّهُۥ وَأَهۡلَهُۥ ثُمَّ لَنَقُولَنَّ لِوَلِيِّهِۦ مَا شَهِدۡنَا مَهۡلِكَ أَهۡلِهِۦ وَإِنَّا لَصَٰدِقُونَ ۝ وَمَكَرُوا۟ مَكۡرًا وَمَكَرۡنَا مَكۡرًا وَهُمۡ لَا يَشۡعُرُونَ ۝ فَٱنظُرۡ كَيۡفَ كَانَ عَٰقِبَةُ مَكۡرِهِمۡ أَنَّا دَمَّرۡنَٰهُمۡ وَقَوۡمَهُمۡ أَجۡمَعِينَ ۝ فَتِلۡكَ بُيُوتُهُمۡ خَاوِيَةً بِمَا ظَلَمُوٓا۟ إِنَّ فِى ذَٰلِكَ لَءَايَةً لِّقَوۡمٍ يَعۡلَمُونَ ۝ وَأَنجَيۡنَا ٱلَّذِينَ ءَامَنُوا۟ وَكَانُوا۟ يَتَّقُونَ ۝ وَلُوطًا إِذۡ قَالَ لِقَوۡمِهِۦٓ أَتَأۡتُونَ ٱلۡفَٰحِشَةَ وَأَنتُمۡ تُبۡصِرُونَ ۝ أَئِنَّكُمۡ لَتَأۡتُونَ ٱلرِّجَالَ شَهۡوَةً مِّن دُونِ ٱلنِّسَآءِ بَلۡ أَنتُمۡ قَوۡمٌ تَجۡهَلُونَ ۝

---

45. And certainly We sent to the Thamūd their brother Ṣāliḥ (with the message): "Worship God alone." (When he conveyed the Message) they split into factions in dispute with each other.

46. He (Ṣāliḥ) said (to them): "O my people! Why do you seek to hasten the coming (upon you) of evil instead of good? Why do you not seek God's forgiveness for your sins so that you may be shown mercy (to be granted a good, virtuous life in the world and eternal happiness in the Hereafter)?"

47. They said: "We augur ill of you and those who are with you." (Ṣāliḥ) answered: "What you describe as augury is (something ordained) by God. But the truth is that you are a people who are being tried."[18]

48. There were nine ringleaders in the city, causing disorder and corruption in the land and not setting things right.

49. They said, swearing in God's Name: "We will certainly swoop on him and his family by night suddenly and kill them all. Then we will assuredly say to his heirs that we did not witness the destruction of his family (nor of Ṣāliḥ himself); indeed we speak the truth."

50. And so they devised a scheme, and indeed We put Our will into force (to give them their just deserts), while they were not aware.

51. So see how was the end of their scheme! We utterly destroyed them and their people all together.

52. Those then are their houses, all lying in utter ruins because they were lost in wrongdoing. Surely in this is a sign (an important lesson) for a people seeking knowledge.[19]

53. And We saved those who believed and kept from disobedience to God in reverence for Him and piety.

54. We also sent Lot as Messenger. He warned his people: "Will you do that abhorrent indecency in plain view (of one another)?

55. "What' do you come with lust to men in place of women? You are indeed an ignorant people with no sense (of decency and right and wrong)."

18. The peoples to whom Messengers were sent usually accused the Messengers of causing them evils. God sent the Messengers (i) to illuminate the way for humankind; (ii) to guide them to the service of God; (iii) to teach them God's laws; (iv) to be examples for them to follow in their lives; (v) to establish balance between the material and spiritual life, the reason and the soul, this world and the next, and indulgence and abstinence; (vi) to be God's witnesses so that people will not be able to plead ignorance in the Hereafter (*The Messenger of God*, 23–32). They were the perfect teachers and educators. A human being is like raw material that needs to be worked on. They have the potential to develop. The Messengers developed this potential so that they were able to rise to the rank of perfection. Testing is an indispensable dimension and requirement of this education. Therefore, God tests people in many ways and on many matters; we may perceive these as being good or bad.

When a Messenger came to a people, they were tested in different ways. The Qur'ān declares: *And We did not send a Prophet to a township but We seized its people with distress and hardship so that they might (wake from heedlessness and) be humble (invoking Us for forgiveness and turning to the truth)* (7: 94). This is also true for a human being or a community that has newly accepted God's Religion. Nevertheless, many people in history have accused their Prophets of being the cause of these evils, while they attributed to themselves whatever good they were favored with, as pointed out in verse 7: 131: *But whenever prosperity came their way, they would say: "This is but our due and by our deserving," and whenever evil befell them, they would attribute it to the evil auspices (they alleged) of Moses and whoever was in his company. Beware! their auspice (whether evil or good) was decreed by God, but most of them did not know (being ignorant of true knowledge).*

Ṣāliḥ's answer is the same as that in verses (17: 13–14): *Every human being's fate We have fastened around his neck, and We will bring forth for him on the Day of Resurrection a book which he will see spread open. "Read your book! Your own self suffices you this day as a reckoner against you."* For a detailed explanation, see the corresponding note 10.

19. For other accounts of the story of Ṣāliḥ and his people, see 7: 73–79; 11: 61–68; 26: 141–159.

بِسۡمِ اللّٰهِ الرَّحۡمٰنِ الرَّحِیۡمِ

فَمَا كَانَ جَوَابَ قَوۡمِهِ إِلَّا أَنۡ قَالُوۤا أَخۡرِجُوۤا اٰلَ لُوۡطٍ مِّنۡ قَرۡیَتِكُمۡ إِنَّهُمۡ أُنَاسٌ یَّتَطَهَّرُوۡنَ ۞ فَأَنۡجَیۡنٰهُ وَأَهۡلَهُۤ إِلَّا امۡرَأَتَهُ قَدَّرۡنٰهَا مِنَ الۡغٰبِرِیۡنَ ۞ وَأَمۡطَرۡنَا عَلَیۡهِمۡ مَّطَرًا فَسَآءَ مَطَرُ الۡمُنۡذَرِیۡنَ ۞ قُلِ الۡحَمۡدُ لِلّٰهِ وَسَلٰمٌ عَلٰى عِبَادِهِ الَّذِیۡنَ اصۡطَفٰى آللّٰهُ خَیۡرٌ أَمَّا یُشۡرِكُوۡنَ ۞ أَمَّنۡ خَلَقَ السَّمٰوٰتِ وَالۡأَرۡضَ وَأَنۡزَلَ لَكُمۡ مِّنَ السَّمَآءِ مَآءً فَأَنۡبَتۡنَا بِهٖ حَدَآئِقَ ذَاتَ بَهۡجَةٍ مَّا كَانَ لَكُمۡ أَنۡ تُنۡۢبِتُوۡا شَجَرَهَاۤ ءَإِلٰهٌ مَّعَ اللّٰهِ بَلۡ هُمۡ قَوۡمٌ یَّعۡدِلُوۡنَ ۞ أَمَّنۡ جَعَلَ الۡأَرۡضَ قَرَارًا وَّجَعَلَ خِلٰلَهَاۤ أَنۡهٰرًا وَّجَعَلَ لَهَا رَوَاسِیَ وَجَعَلَ بَیۡنَ الۡبَحۡرَیۡنِ حَاجِزًا ءَإِلٰهٌ مَّعَ اللّٰهِ بَلۡ أَكۡثَرُهُمۡ لَا یَعۡلَمُوۡنَ ۞ أَمَّنۡ یُّجِیۡبُ الۡمُضۡطَرَّ إِذَا دَعَاهُ وَیَكۡشِفُ السُّوۤءَ وَیَجۡعَلُكُمۡ خُلَفَآءَ الۡأَرۡضِ ءَإِلٰهٌ مَّعَ اللّٰهِ قَلِیۡلًا مَّا تَذَكَّرُوۡنَ ۞ أَمَّنۡ یَّهۡدِیۡكُمۡ فِیۡ ظُلُمٰتِ الۡبَرِّ وَالۡبَحۡرِ وَمَنۡ یُّرۡسِلُ الرِّیٰحَ بُشۡرًۢا بَیۡنَ یَدَیۡ رَحۡمَتِهٖ ءَإِلٰهٌ مَّعَ اللّٰهِ تَعٰلَى اللّٰهُ عَمَّا یُشۡرِكُوۡنَ ۞

---

56. But his people's only reply was nothing but to say (to one another): "Expel Lot's family (as well as himself) from your land. They are a people who make themselves out to be pure!"

57. Then We saved him and his family except his wife. We decreed that she should be among those who stayed behind (and were destroyed).

58. We poured upon them a (destructive) rain (of stones). How evil was the rain of those who had been warned.[20]

59. Say: "All praise and gratitude are for God and peace be upon those of His servants whom He has chosen (and made pure)." Is God better or all that they associate as partners (with Him)?

60. Or He Who has created the heavens and the earth, and sends down for you water from the sky? –We cause to grow with it gardens full of loveliness and delight: it is not in your power to cause their trees to grow. Is there another deity besides God? No, but they are a people who veer away (from truth). –

61. Or He Who has made the earth as a fixed abode, and has caused rivers to flow in its fissures, and has set for it firm mountains, and has placed a barrier between the two large bodies of water?[21] Is there another deity besides God? No, but most of them do not know.

62. Or He Who answers the helpless one in distress when he prays to Him, and removes the affliction from him, and (Who) has made you (O humankind) vicegerents of the earth (to improve it and rule over it according to God's commandments)? Is there another deity besides God? How little you reflect!

63. Or He Who guides you through the veils of the darkness of land and sea, and Who sends forth the (merciful) winds as a glad tiding in advance of His mercy? Is there another deity besides God? Absolutely exalted is He above all that they associate with Him as partners.

20: For other accounts of the story of the Prophet Lot and his people, see 7: 80–84; 11: 77–83; 15: 58–76; 21: 74–75; 26: 160–174.

21. For an explanation of the barrier between the two large bodies of water, see 25: 53, note 11.

382   سُوۡرَةُ النَّمۡل   ٣٨٢

أَمَّنۡ يَبۡدَؤُاْ الۡخَلۡقَ ثُمَّ يُعِيدُهُۥ وَمَن يَرۡزُقُكُم مِّنَ السَّمَآءِ وَالۡأَرۡضِ ءَإِلَـٰهٌ مَّعَ اللَّهِ قُلۡ هَاتُواْ بُرۡهَـٰنَكُمۡ إِن كُنتُمۡ صَـٰدِقِينَ ۝ قُل لَّا يَعۡلَمُ مَن فِى السَّمَـٰوَٰتِ وَالۡأَرۡضِ الۡغَيۡبَ إِلَّا اللَّهُ وَمَا يَشۡعُرُونَ أَيَّانَ يُبۡعَثُونَ ۝ بَلِ ادَّٰرَكَ عِلۡمُهُمۡ فِى الۡأَخِرَةِ بَلۡ هُمۡ فِى شَكٍّ مِّنۡهَا بَلۡ هُم مِّنۡهَا عَمُونَ ۝ وَقَالَ الَّذِينَ كَفَرُوٓاْ أَءِذَا كُنَّا تُرَٰبًا وَءَابَآؤُنَآ أَئِنَّا لَمُخۡرَجُونَ ۝ لَقَدۡ وُعِدۡنَا هَـٰذَا نَحۡنُ وَءَابَآؤُنَا مِن قَبۡلُ إِنۡ هَـٰذَآ إِلَّآ أَسَـٰطِيرُ الۡأَوَّلِينَ ۝ قُلۡ سِيرُواْ فِى الۡأَرۡضِ فَانظُرُواْ كَيۡفَ كَانَ عَـٰقِبَةُ الۡمُجۡرِمِينَ ۝ وَلَا تَحۡزَنۡ عَلَيۡهِمۡ وَلَا تَكُن فِى ضَيۡقٍ مِّمَّا يَمۡكُرُونَ ۝ وَيَقُولُونَ مَتَىٰ هَـٰذَا الۡوَعۡدُ إِن كُنتُمۡ صَـٰدِقِينَ ۝ قُلۡ عَسَىٰٓ أَن يَكُونَ رَدِفَ لَكُم بَعۡضُ الَّذِى تَسۡتَعۡجِلُونَ ۝ وَإِنَّ رَبَّكَ لَذُو فَضۡلٍ عَلَى النَّاسِ وَلَـٰكِنَّ أَكۡثَرَهُمۡ لَا يَشۡكُرُونَ ۝ وَإِنَّ رَبَّكَ لَيَعۡلَمُ مَا تُكِنُّ صُدُورُهُمۡ وَمَا يُعۡلِنُونَ ۝ وَمَا مِنۡ غَآئِبَةٍ فِى السَّمَآءِ وَالۡأَرۡضِ إِلَّا فِى كِتَـٰبٍ مُّبِينٍ ۝ إِنَّ هَـٰذَا الۡقُرۡءَانَ يَقُصُّ عَلَىٰ بَنِىٓ إِسۡرَٰٓءِيلَ أَكۡثَرَ الَّذِى هُمۡ فِيهِ يَخۡتَلِفُونَ

---

64. Or He Who originates creation in the first instance and then reproduces it,[22] and Who provides you from the heaven and the earth? Is there another deity besides God? Say: "Produce your evidence, if you are truthful!"

65. Say: "None in the heavens and on the earth knows the Unseen (all that lies in the hidden realms and beyond any created being's perception), but only God knows it. Neither do they (or their false deities) know when (the world will be destroyed and) they will be raised to life (after their death)."[23]

66. No, indeed. Their knowledge does not attain to the Hereafter (as they have desired only the worldly life and wasted their faculties of learning in pursuit of worldly knowledge).[24] No, indeed, for (despite being informed about it through Revelation) they remain in doubt about it. No, indeed, for they remain blind to (all the arguments about) it.

67. Those who obstinately persist in unbelief say: "What! is it when we have already become dust – is it then that we and our forefathers will be brought forth (to a new life)?

68. "We have certainly been threatened with this before, we and our forefathers. This is nothing but fables of the ancients!"

69. Say: "Go about the earth and see how was the outcome for the disbelieving criminals!"

70. Do not grieve over them (because of their negative response toward your mission), nor be distressed because of all that they scheme (to void your mission and bar people from God's way).

71. They also say: "(So tell us) when is this threat to be fulfilled, if you are truthful?"

72. Say: "It may well be that something of that which you ask to be hastened has already drawn quite near behind you."

73. Indeed your Lord is most Bountiful to humankind but most of them do not give thanks.[25]

74. Your Lord certainly knows whatever their bosoms conceal and whatever they disclose.[26]

75. There is nothing hidden (from them as from all creatures) in the heaven or on the earth but is in a Manifest Book.[27]

76. Surely this Qur'ān explains to the Children of Israel most of the matters on which they differ.[28]

22. Life is the greatest evidence of God's Unity and the source of His bounty, a most subtle manifestation of His Compassion, and the most hidden and delicate embroidery of His art. Life is so mysterious and subtle that even the life of plants, the simplest level of life, and the awakening of a seed's life-force at the beginning of a plant's life, is still not fully understood. Although such an event is now considered to be commonplace, it has remained a mystery from the time of Adam, for the human mind remains unable to fathom the nature of life.

Life, in both its outer or material and inner or immaterial aspects, is pure. The Divine Power creates life directly without the participation of causes, while It employs natural causes to create everything else. God creates everything but life behind the veil of natural causes so that human beings, unable to discern Divine Wisdom in some events, do not attribute to Him that which they consider unpleasant.

A. C. Morrison writes:

> Life is a sculptor and shapes all living things; an artist that designs every leaf of every tree, that colors the flowers, the apple, the forest, and the plumage of the bird of paradise. Life is a musician and has taught each bird to sing its love song, the insects to call each other in the music of their multitudinous sounds.
>
> Life has given to man alone mastery over combined sound vibrations and has furnished the material for their production.
>
> Life is an engineer, for it has designed the legs of the grasshopper and the flea, the coordinated muscles, levers and joints, the tireless beating heart, the system of electric nerves of every animal, and the complete system of circulation of every living thing.
>
> Life is a chemist that gives taste to our fruits and spices and perfume to the rose. Life synthesizes new substances which Nature has not yet provided to balance its processes and to destroy invading life... Life's chemistry is sublime, for not only does it set the rays of the Sun to work to change water and carbonic acid into wood and sugar, but, in doing so, releases oxygen so that animals may have the breath of life.
>
> Life is a historian, for it has written its history page by page, through the ages, leaving its record in the rocks, an autobiography which only awaits correct interpretation.
>
> Life protects its creations by the abundance of food in the egg and prepares many of its infants for active life after birth, or by conscious motherhood, storing food in preparation for her young. Life produces life—giving milk to meet immediate needs, foreseeing this necessity and preparing for events to come.
>
> Matter has never done more than its laws decree. The atoms and molecules obey the dictates of chemical affinity, the force of gravity, the influences of temperature, and electric impulses. Matter has no initiative, but life brings into being marvelous new designs and structures.
>
> What life is no man has yet fathomed; it has no weight or dimensions... Nature did not create life; fire-blistered rocks and a saltless sea did not meet the necessary requirements. Gravity is a property of matter; electricity we now believe to be matter itself; the rays of the Sun and stars can be deflected by gravity and seem to be akin to it. Man is learning the dimensions of the atom and is measuring its locked-up power, but life is illusive, like space. Why?
>
> Life is fundamental and is the only means by which matter can attain understanding. Life is the only source of consciousness and it alone makes possible knowledge of the works of God which we, still half blind, yet know to be good. (Morrison, 31–36)

Like life, death also demonstrates God's Existence and Unity. For example, by showing the sun's image, light and reflection, bubbles on a mighty river, sparkling in the sun, as well as transparent objects glistening on the face of the earth, testify to the existence of the sun. Despite the bubbles' occasional disappearance (e.g., when they pass under a bridge), the splendid continuation of the manifestations of the sun and the uninterrupted display of its light on successive bubbles proves that the images of the sun, the lights that appear and disappear, sparkle and die away and are then renewed, come from an enduring, perpetual, single sun that manifests itself from on high. Therefore, by their appearance, these sparkling bubbles demonstrate the sun's existence, and by disappearing and ceasing to exist, they display its continuation and unity.

In the same way, beings in continuous flux testify through their existence and life to the necessary Existence and Oneness of the Necessarily Existent Being. They testify to His Unity, Permanence, and Eternity through their decay and death. Beautiful, delicate creatures that are renewed and recruited along with the alternation of day and night, summer and winter, and the passage of time show the Existence, Unity, and Permanence of an Everlasting One with a continuous display of beauty. Their decay and death, together with the apparent causes for their lives, demonstrates that the (material or natural) causes are only veils. This fact decisively proves that these arts, inscriptions, and manifestations are the constantly renewed arts, changing inscriptions, and moving mirrors of an All-Beautiful One of Majesty.

23. The absolute knowledge of the Unseen or all that lies behind human perception is with God only. Those who have some partial knowledge of it, such as the Prophets, can have it only through being taught by God. This point is of great significance concerning God's Existence and Unity and absolute sovereignty over creation. Even humankind, who are equipped with the greatest faculties to learn, cannot acquire perfectly accurate knowledge of the past, of what is happening in the present, and of the future. Moreover, human capacity is also insufficient to have full, accurate knowledge of itself. It is unable to conclude even where its benefit or harm lies. In addition, as declared in the previous verse, every living being needs provision and it is God Who provides us with it. It is clear that nothing, including humankind, has determined its own needs and how they should be met. There must be One Who has full knowledge of every being, with all its needs and how they can be met, and Who has full power to design the "natural" environment as a food store from which living beings can procure their provision. All these facts explain why human beings cannot order their life exactly as it should be ordered, based on ab-

solute justice and for their benefit, even in this world. When the afterlife is taken into consideration, they are completely unable to decide what they should do. So there must be One Who has full and accurate knowledge of every member of humankind, of where their benefit and harm lie, of the past, present, and future, and of the hidden reality underlying the observable and unobservable dimensions of existence and events, and of the future, eternal life. In short, like every other being, a human being is in absolute need of God. As it is God Who informs humankind of all these things through Messengership, they have an absolute need for the Messengers and the Divine Books.

24. See 53: 29–30.

25. If God gives people respite, despite their stubborn insistence on associating partners with Him and their wrongdoings, this is because of His bountifulness to humankind. Although they must appreciate this and thank Him in return (by acknowledging His bounties and living in faith and obedience to Him), they insist on unbelief and disobedience.

26. That is, His postponing their punishment is not because He is unaware of their state, for He knows even what they keep concealed in their bosoms. Also, there may be hearts which are apt to believe, so they should be given a certain respite. Moreover, He is fully aware of whatever schemes they conceive of. Again, those things which human beings keep concealed in their bosoms are not always the same as that which they disclose. But God knows whatever lies in their bosoms and whatever they disclose. So whatever God decrees and does is absolutely what is required to be decreed and done and full of wisdom.

27. For the Manifest Book, see this *sūrah*, verse 1, note 1, and 6: 59, note 13; 13: 39, note 13.

28. The Children of Israel and, following them, the Christians, have differed in many matters such as Divinity, the Prophet Solomon, Mary and Jesus, and many other things concerning other Prophets. The Qur'ān has clarified the truth, particularly in matters which are of particular significance concerning faith and its essentials.

وَاِنَّهُ لَهُدًى وَرَحْمَةٌ لِّلْمُؤْمِنِيْنَ ۞ اِنَّ رَبَّكَ يَقْضِيْ بَيْنَهُمْ بِحُكْمِهٖ ۚ وَهُوَ الْعَزِيْزُ الْعَلِيْمُ ۞ فَتَوَكَّلْ عَلَى اللّٰهِ ۖ اِنَّكَ عَلَى الْحَقِّ الْمُبِيْنِ ۞ اِنَّكَ لَا تُسْمِعُ الْمَوْتٰى وَلَا تُسْمِعُ الصُّمَّ الدُّعَاءَ اِذَا وَلَّوْا مُدْبِرِيْنَ ۞ وَمَا اَنْتَ بِهَادِي الْعُمْيِ عَنْ ضَلٰلَتِهِمْ ۖ اِنْ تُسْمِعُ اِلَّا مَنْ يُّؤْمِنُ بِاٰيٰتِنَا فَهُمْ مُّسْلِمُوْنَ ۞ وَاِذَا وَقَعَ الْقَوْلُ عَلَيْهِمْ اَخْرَجْنَا لَهُمْ دَآبَّةً مِّنَ الْاَرْضِ تُكَلِّمُهُمْ ۙ اَنَّ النَّاسَ كَانُوْا بِاٰيٰتِنَا لَا يُوْقِنُوْنَ ۞ وَيَوْمَ نَحْشُرُ مِنْ كُلِّ اُمَّةٍ فَوْجًا مِّمَّنْ يُّكَذِّبُ بِاٰيٰتِنَا فَهُمْ يُوْزَعُوْنَ ۞ حَتّٰى اِذَا جَآءُوْ قَالَ اَكَذَّبْتُمْ بِاٰيٰتِيْ وَلَمْ تُحِيْطُوْا بِهَا عِلْمًا اَمَّا ذَا كُنْتُمْ تَعْمَلُوْنَ ۞ وَوَقَعَ الْقَوْلُ عَلَيْهِمْ بِمَا ظَلَمُوْا فَهُمْ لَا يَنْطِقُوْنَ ۞ اَلَمْ يَرَوْا اَنَّا جَعَلْنَا الَّيْلَ لِيَسْكُنُوْا فِيْهِ وَالنَّهَارَ مُبْصِرًا ۚ اِنَّ فِيْ ذٰلِكَ لَاٰيٰتٍ لِّقَوْمٍ يُّؤْمِنُوْنَ ۞ وَيَوْمَ يُنْفَخُ فِي الصُّوْرِ فَفَزِعَ مَنْ فِي السَّمٰوٰتِ وَمَنْ فِي الْاَرْضِ اِلَّا مَنْ شَآءَ اللّٰهُ ۚ وَكُلٌّ اَتَوْهُ دَاخِرِيْنَ ۞ وَتَرَى الْجِبَالَ تَحْسَبُهَا جَامِدَةً وَّهِيَ تَمُرُّ مَرَّ السَّحَابِ ۚ صُنْعَ اللّٰهِ الَّذِيْ اَتْقَنَ كُلَّ شَيْءٍ ۚ اِنَّهُ خَبِيْرٌ بِمَا تَفْعَلُوْنَ ۞

ing to) believe in Our Revelations and signs (in the outer world as well as in their inner world), and are (therefore) ready to submit (to the truth).

82. When the time for the fulfillment of the word (of punishment) about them comes, We will bring forth for them a living creature from the earth who will speak to them – that people have no certainty of faith in Our signs and Revelations.[29]

83. A Day (will come) when We will raise up and gather from every community a host of those who denied Our Revelations and signs (which establish the truth of all the essentials of faith), and they will be set in array (and driven to the place of reckoning)

84. Until they arrive there, when He will say to them: "Did you deny My Revelations and signs even without having full, certain knowledge about them? If that is not so, what else were you doing?"

85. The word (of punishment) will be fulfilled against them because they did wrong (including especially associating partners with God). They will then not (be able to) speak (a single word of excuse and defense).

86. Have they not noticed that We have made the night so that they may rest in it, and the day sight-giving (for them to work in)? Surely in this are signs for people who will believe.

87. On the Day when the Trumpet is blown[30] all who are in the heavens and all who are on the earth will be stricken with shock and terror, except those whom God wills to exempt. All will come to His Presence, utterly humbled.

---

77. And most certainly it is guidance (in all matters) and mercy (full of blessings) for the believers.

78. Indeed your Lord will judge between them (the believers and the unbelievers) according to His decree. He is the All-Glorious with irresistible might, the All-Knowing.

79. So put your trust in God. You surely stand on the truth, which is clear and doubtless.

80. Indeed you cannot make the dead hear nor can you make the deaf hear the call once they have turned their backs, going away.

81. Nor can you guide the blind out of their error. You can make none hear save those who (being unprejudiced, are willing to) believe in Our Revelations and

88. You see the mountains, thinking them to be firmly fixed, but in reality they (are in constant motion) and pass by (with the movement of the earth) like the passing of the clouds. (And so will they be crumbled on Doomsday so as to take on the form particular to the other world.) This is the pattern of God Who has perfected everything. He is fully aware of all that you do.

---

29. Some Traditions have been reported about this verse and especially the moving creature to be brought forth near the end of time. Several opinions have been expressed. The gist of the matter is as follows: Particularly through scientific developments, God will display His signs in the outer world and within people themselves, until it is clear to people that the Qur'ān is true. That is, with all their features, humankind and the universe will appear as an assemblage of proofs for the truth of whatever the Qur'ān declares, but immersed in the satisfaction of their carnal desires and deluded by the achievements with which God will favor them, people will stubbornly insist on unbelief and wrongdoing. They will most probably cause a species of small (microscopic) animals or moving things (mechanical beings) of some other kinds to grow and harm themselves. It will become clear that, whether people believe it or not, all this is because of unbelief, wrongdoing, and leading an immoral, dissipated life.

30. For the Trumpet and its being blown, see 2, note 31; 6: 73, note 13; 39: 68, note 22. The Trumpet will be blown twice. The blowing mentioned in this verse is the second one which will cause the dead to be raised from their graves, look around in shock and terror, and rush toward God's Presence utterly humbled. As for those whom God will exempt from the terror of that Day when the Trumpet will be blown, see 21: 101–103, and the verse 89 below in this *sūrah*. They will be those who will come on the Judgment Day with good (free from sins) and for whom the decree of ultimate good has already gone forth from God. However, all, without exception, will be brought into His Presence, but the distinguished servants of utmost sincerity will be exempted from being questioned (37: 128).

89. Whoever comes (on Judgment Day) with good (and purified of sin) will have better than its worth, and such will be safe from any shock and terror on that Day.

90. But whoever comes with (unforgivable) evil, such will be flung down upon their faces into the Fire. "Are you recompensed for anything but what you used to do?"

91. (Say, O Messenger:) "I am ordered only to worship the Lord of this city (Makkah, where the first house of worship dedicated to God was built, and) which He has made sacred and to Whom all things belong. And I am ordered to be of the Muslims (those who submit to Him in all His orders).

92. And (I am ordered) to recite the Qur'ān

(to convey His messages). Whoever, therefore, chooses to follow the right way, follows it but for (the good of) his soul. And if any wills to go astray, say: "I am but one of the Messengers sent to warn."

93. Also say: "All praise and gratitude are for God. Soon He will show you His signs (which will prove that whatever He has decreed is true), and you will come to know them." Your Lord is never heedless and unmindful of whatever you do.

SŪRAH 28

AL-QAṢAṢ
(THE NARRATIVE)

Makkah period

This *sūrah* of 88 verses was revealed in Makkah. It takes its title from the word *qaṣaṣ* in verse 25. It is again concerned with the Prophet Moses' life and mission, and also contains glad tidings for God's Messenger and the believers.

The history of the Children of Israel is an example in and of itself for the history of humankind and civilizations. Moreover, more than any other Prophets, the Prophet Moses, upon him be peace, resembled God's Messenger in many ways (e.g., bringing a new law and fighting against his enemies). This is why the Qur'ān mentions him frequently.

The following verses of the Old Testament, which promise the coming of the Prophet Muḥammad, upon him be peace and the blessings of God, and draw the attention to the resemblance between him and the Prophet Moses, upon him be peace:

> The Lord said to me (Moses): "What they have spoken is good. I will raise up for them a Prophet like you among their brethren, and will put My words in his mouth, and he shall speak to them all that I command him. And it shall be *that* whoever will not hear My words, which he speaks in My name, I will requite *it* of him." (*Deuteronomy*, 18: 17–19)

It is clear from these verses that *a Prophet like you among their brethren* means a Prophet from Ishmael's line, for Ishmael was the brother of Isaac, the forefather of the Children of Israel. The only Prophet who came after Moses and resembled him in many ways is the Prophet Muḥammad, upon him be peace and blessings. The Qur'ān indicates this in the following verse: *Surely We have sent to you (O people) a Messenger, a witness against you (one who will testify in the Hereafter as to your deeds in response to God's Message), just as We sent a Messenger to the Pharaoh* (73: 15).

In the Name of God, the All-Merciful, the All-Compassionate.

1. *Ṭā. Sīn. Mīm.*

2. These are the Revelations of the Book clear in itself and clearly showing the truth.

3. We now convey to you with truth some of the exemplary events which took place between Moses and the Pharaoh, for people who will believe.

4. The Pharaoh turned into an arrogant tyrant in the land (of Egypt) and divided its people into castes. One group of them he humiliated and oppressed, slaughtering their sons and letting live their womenfolk (for further humiliation and suffering). He surely was one of those spreading disorder and corruption.

5. But We willed to bestow Our favor upon those who were humiliated and oppressed in the land, and make of them exemplary leaders (to guide people on the way to God and in their lives), and make them inheritors (of the glory of the Pharaoh and the land in which We produced blessings for people).

وَنُمَكِّنَ لَهُمْ فِى الْأَرْضِ وَنُرِىَ فِرْعَوْنَ وَهَامَانَ وَجُنُودَهُمَا مِنْهُم مَّا كَانُوا يَحْذَرُونَ ۞ وَأَوْحَيْنَا إِلَىٰ أُمِّ مُوسَىٰ أَنْ أَرْضِعِيهِ فَإِذَا خِفْتِ عَلَيْهِ فَأَلْقِيهِ فِى الْيَمِّ وَلَا تَخَافِى وَلَا تَحْزَنِى إِنَّا رَادُّوهُ إِلَيْكِ وَجَاعِلُوهُ مِنَ الْمُرْسَلِينَ ۞ فَالْتَقَطَهُ آلُ فِرْعَوْنَ لِيَكُونَ لَهُمْ عَدُوًّا وَحَزَنًا إِنَّ فِرْعَوْنَ وَهَامَانَ وَجُنُودَهُمَا كَانُوا خَاطِئِينَ ۞ وَقَالَتِ امْرَأَتُ فِرْعَوْنَ قُرَّتُ عَيْنٍ لِى وَلَكَ لَا تَقْتُلُوهُ عَسَىٰ أَن يَنفَعَنَا أَوْ نَتَّخِذَهُ وَلَدًا وَهُمْ لَا يَشْعُرُونَ ۞ وَأَصْبَحَ فُؤَادُ أُمِّ مُوسَىٰ فَارِغًا إِن كَادَتْ لَتُبْدِى بِهِ لَوْلَا أَن رَّبَطْنَا عَلَىٰ قَلْبِهَا لِتَكُونَ مِنَ الْمُؤْمِنِينَ ۞ وَقَالَتْ لِأُخْتِهِ قُصِّيهِ فَبَصُرَتْ بِهِ عَن جُنُبٍ وَهُمْ لَا يَشْعُرُونَ ۞ وَحَرَّمْنَا عَلَيْهِ الْمَرَاضِعَ مِن قَبْلُ فَقَالَتْ هَلْ أَدُلُّكُمْ عَلَىٰ أَهْلِ بَيْتٍ يَكْفُلُونَهُ لَكُمْ وَهُمْ لَهُ نَاصِحُونَ ۞ فَرَدَدْنَاهُ إِلَىٰ أُمِّهِ كَىْ تَقَرَّ عَيْنُهَا وَلَا تَحْزَنَ وَلِتَعْلَمَ أَنَّ وَعْدَ اللَّهِ حَقٌّ وَلَكِنَّ أَكْثَرَهُمْ لَا يَعْلَمُونَ ۞

---

6. And to establish them in the land with power, and let the Pharaoh and Hāmān[1] and their hosts experience what they feared from them (the people they had oppressed).

7. We inspired the mother of Moses, saying: "Suckle him (for a time, without anxiety for his life), then when you have cause to fear for him, put him in the river, and do not fear or grieve. We will surely return him to you and make him one of our Messengers."

8. Then the family of Pharaoh picked him up only to be an adversary and a source of grief for them. Indeed the Pharaoh, Hāmān and their hosts were habitually in the wrong (sinful in their treatment of people and especially of the Children of Israel).

9. The Pharaoh's wife said (to him): "(Here is a child that will be) a means of happiness for me and for you. Do not kill him. Maybe he will prove useful for us, or we may adopt him as a son." They were unaware (of how the events were being prepared and how their outcome would turn to be in the end).

10. A void grew in the heart of the mother of Moses, and she would almost have disclosed all about him (in the hope that he would be returned to her) had We not strengthened her heart so that she might have faith (in Our promise).

11. She said to his sister: "Follow him (secretly)." So she watched him from afar, while the others were not aware.

12. We had forbidden wet-nurses for him from before (so that he refused the milk of the nurses called by the Queen to suckle him). Then his sister (who was able to get into the palace) said: "Shall I guide you to a family that will nurse him for you and they will take care of him?"

13. And thus We returned him to his mother, so that she might rejoice and forget her grief, and that she might certainly know that God's promise was true. But most people do not know this.

1. Hāmān must be, rather than a proper name, Hā-Amen, the title given to the high priest in the cult of Amon that was prevalent in ancient Egypt. He held a rank second to that of the Pharaoh and served as his chief adviser (Asad, 590, note 6) .

Another argument is that Maurice Bucaille claims that the name Hāmān occurs in some ancient Egyptian inscriptions, notably one at the Hofmuseum in Vienna (now the Naturhistorisches Museum Wien) (*Aegyptische Inschriften*, I34, p. 130), and is listed in Ranke's dictionary of Egyptian personal names as *Vorsteher der Steinbrucharbeiter*, "head of the stone quarry workers" (http://en.wikipedia.org/wiki/Haman_%28Islam%29).

2. After God established the Prophet Joseph, upon him be peace, in Egypt together with the family of Jacob, the Children of Israel attained high ranks there. God appointed among them Prophets and high-ranking administrators, and made them free people, masters of their own affairs (5: 20). Thus, the Pharaoh and his chiefs feared that they might recover their former state, expel them from their offices of government or even from Egypt, and abolish their state-religion and their way of life (20: 63). This is why they slaughtered their sons and spared their women to employ them and force them to marry the native Copts. They must have been practicing a form of genocide.

386   سُوۡرَةُ الۡقَصَص   ٣٨٦

وَلَمَّا بَلَغَ أَشُدَّهُ وَاسۡتَوَىٰٓ ءَاتَيۡنَٰهُ حُكۡمًا وَعِلۡمًا ۚ وَكَذَٰلِكَ نَجۡزِى الۡمُحۡسِنِينَ ۞ وَدَخَلَ الۡمَدِينَةَ عَلَىٰ حِينِ غَفۡلَةٍ مِّنۡ أَهۡلِهَا فَوَجَدَ فِيهَا رَجُلَيۡنِ يَقۡتَتِلَانِ هَٰذَا مِن شِيعَتِهِۦ وَهَٰذَا مِنۡ عَدُوِّهِۦ ۖ فَاسۡتَغَٰثَهُ الَّذِى مِن شِيعَتِهِۦ عَلَى الَّذِى مِنۡ عَدُوِّهِۦ فَوَكَزَهُۥ مُوسَىٰ فَقَضَىٰ عَلَيۡهِ ۖ قَالَ هَٰذَا مِنۡ عَمَلِ الشَّيۡطَٰنِ ۖ إِنَّهُۥ عَدُوٌّ مُّضِلٌّ مُّبِينٌ ۞ قَالَ رَبِّ إِنِّى ظَلَمۡتُ نَفۡسِى فَاغۡفِرۡ لِى فَغَفَرَ لَهُۥٓ ۚ إِنَّهُۥ هُوَ الۡغَفُورُ الرَّحِيمُ ۞ قَالَ رَبِّ بِمَآ أَنۡعَمۡتَ عَلَىَّ فَلَنۡ أَكُونَ ظَهِيرًا لِّلۡمُجۡرِمِينَ ۞ فَأَصۡبَحَ فِى الۡمَدِينَةِ خَآئِفًا يَتَرَقَّبُ فَإِذَا الَّذِى اسۡتَنصَرَهُۥ بِالۡأَمۡسِ يَسۡتَصۡرِخُهُۥ ۚ قَالَ لَهُۥ مُوسَىٰٓ إِنَّكَ لَغَوِىٌّ مُّبِينٌ ۞ فَلَمَّآ أَنۡ أَرَادَ أَن يَبۡطِشَ بِالَّذِى هُوَ عَدُوٌّ لَّهُمَا قَالَ يَٰمُوسَىٰٓ أَتُرِيدُ أَن تَقۡتُلَنِى كَمَا قَتَلۡتَ نَفۡسًۢا بِالۡأَمۡسِ ۖ إِن تُرِيدُ إِلَّآ أَن تَكُونَ جَبَّارًا فِى الۡأَرۡضِ وَمَا تُرِيدُ أَن تَكُونَ مِنَ الۡمُصۡلِحِينَ ۞ وَجَآءَ رَجُلٌ مِّنۡ أَقۡصَا الۡمَدِينَةِ يَسۡعَىٰ قَالَ يَٰمُوسَىٰٓ إِنَّ الۡمَلَأَ يَأۡتَمِرُونَ بِكَ لِيَقۡتُلُوكَ فَاخۡرُجۡ إِنِّى لَكَ مِنَ النَّٰصِحِينَ ۞ فَخَرَجَ مِنۡهَا خَآئِفًا يَتَرَقَّبُ ۖ قَالَ رَبِّ نَجِّنِى مِنَ الۡقَوۡمِ الظَّٰلِمِينَ ۞

———— ❧ ————

14. When Moses reached his full manhood and grew to maturity, We granted him sound, wise judgment, and special knowledge. Thus do We reward those devoted to doing good as if seeing God.

15. (One day he left the palace where he was living and) he entered the city at a time when he was unnoticed by its people, and found therein two men fighting, one of his own people and the other of their enemies (the native Copts). The one from his people called on him for help against the other, who was from their enemies. So Moses struck him with his hand and caused his

death (unintentionally). He said: "This (enmity and fighting) is of Satan's doing. Surely he is manifestly a misleading enemy."

16. He said (in supplication): "My Lord! Indeed I have wronged myself, so forgive me." So He forgave him. Surely He is the One Who is the All-Forgiving, the All-Compassionate (especially toward His believing, repentant servants).

17. "My Lord!" Moses said, "Forasmuch as You have blessed me with favors, I will never be a supporter of the guilty."[3]

18. Now in the morning he was in the city, apprehensive and watchful. And the man who had sought his help on the day before (turned up) and cried out to him again for help. Moses said to him: "You are indeed, obviously, an unruly hothead."

19. But then, when he was about to fall upon the man who was an enemy of them both, he (the Israelite who thought that Moses would attack him because he had chided him severely) said: "Moses, do you intend to kill me as you killed a person yesterday? You want only to become a tyrant in this land; you do not want to be of those who set things right!"

20. Then a man (from the royal court) came running from the farthest end of the city (where the court was) and said: "Moses, now the chiefs are deliberating upon your case to kill you, so leave the city. I am surely one of your sincere well-wishers."

21. So he left the city, apprehensive and looking around. He said (in supplication): "My Lord, save me from these wrongdoing, oppressive people!"

---

3. Some commentators of the Qur'ān have taken this pledge of Moses, upon him be peace, to also mean that he decided to leave the Pharaoh's palace forever in order to avoid doing anything which would be of help to the Pharaoh, as his government was a tyrannical one. God orders in the Qur'an: *And do not incline towards those who do wrong (against God by associating partners with Him and against people by violating their rights), or the Fire will touch you. For you have no guardians and true friends apart from God, (but if you should incline towards those who do wrong,) you will not be helped (by Him)* (11: 113).

٣٨٧

387

وَلَمَّا تَوَجَّهَ تِلْقَاءَ مَدْيَنَ قَالَ عَسَىٰ رَبِّيٓ أَن يَهْدِيَنِي سَوَآءَ السَّبِيلِ
۞ وَلَمَّا وَرَدَ مَآءَ مَدْيَنَ وَجَدَ عَلَيْهِ أُمَّةً مِّنَ النَّاسِ يَسْقُونَ
وَوَجَدَ مِن دُونِهِمُ امْرَأَتَيْنِ تَذُودَانِ قَالَ مَا خَطْبُكُمَا
قَالَتَا لَا نَسْقِي حَتَّىٰ يُصْدِرَ الرِّعَآءُ وَأَبُونَا شَيْخٌ كَبِيرٌ ۞ فَسَقَىٰ
لَهُمَا ثُمَّ تَوَلَّىٰٓ إِلَى الظِّلِّ فَقَالَ رَبِّ إِنِّي لِمَآ أَنزَلْتَ إِلَيَّ مِنْ
خَيْرٍ فَقِيرٌ ۞ فَجَآءَتْهُ إِحْدَىٰهُمَا تَمْشِي عَلَى اسْتِحْيَآءٍ
قَالَتْ إِنَّ أَبِي يَدْعُوكَ لِيَجْزِيَكَ أَجْرَ مَا سَقَيْتَ لَنَا
فَلَمَّا جَآءَهُ وَقَصَّ عَلَيْهِ الْقَصَصَ قَالَ لَا تَخَفْ نَجَوْتَ مِنَ
الْقَوْمِ الظَّالِمِينَ ۞ قَالَتْ إِحْدَىٰهُمَا يَٰٓأَبَتِ اسْتَأْجِرْهُ إِنَّ
خَيْرَ مَنِ اسْتَأْجَرْتَ الْقَوِيُّ الْأَمِينُ ۞ قَالَ إِنِّيٓ أُرِيدُ أَنْ
أُنكِحَكَ إِحْدَى ابْنَتَيَّ هَٰتَيْنِ عَلَىٰٓ أَن تَأْجُرَنِي ثَمَانِيَ حِجَجٍ
فَإِنْ أَتْمَمْتَ عَشْرًا فَمِنْ عِندِكَ وَمَآ أُرِيدُ أَنْ أَشُقَّ
عَلَيْكَ سَتَجِدُنِيٓ إِن شَآءَ اللَّهُ مِنَ الصَّالِحِينَ ۞ قَالَ
ذَٰلِكَ بَيْنِي وَبَيْنَكَ أَيَّمَا الْأَجَلَيْنِ قَضَيْتُ
فَلَا عُدْوَانَ عَلَيَّ وَاللَّهُ عَلَىٰ مَا نَقُولُ وَكِيلٌ ۞

❧

22. As he headed towards Midian (the nearest territory independent of Egyptian rule), he said: "I hope my Lord will guide me on the right way (so as to avoid capture by Egyptian forces)."

23. When he arrived at the wells of Midian, he found there a group of people watering their flocks, and he found, apart from them, two women (maidens) holding back their flock. He said: "What is the matter with you?" The two (women) said: "We do not water our flock until the shepherds take their flocks away. (It is we who do this work because) our father is a very old man."

24. So Moses watered their flock for them, and then he withdrew to the shade and said (in supplication): "My Lord! Surely I am in need of whatever good you may send down to me."

25. Thereafter one of the two (maidens) approached him, walking bashfully,[4] and said: "My father invites you, so that he may reward you for watering our flock for us." So when he came to him[5] and told him the whole of his story, he said: "Wor-

ry no longer! You are now safe from the wrongdoing, oppressive people."

26. One of the two daughters said: "Father, employ him, for the best whom you could employ should be one strong and trustworthy (as he is)."

27. (The father) said to Moses: "I want to marry one of these two daughters of mine to you if you serve me for eight years (according to the lunar calendar). But if you should complete ten years, that would be an act of grace from you. I do not mean to impose any hardship on you. You will find me, God willing, one of the righteous."[6]

28. (Moses) answered: "So let it be between me and you. Whichever of the two terms I fulfill, let there be no ill-will against me. God is a Guarantor over what we say."

4. 'Umar ibn al-Khaṭṭāb, the Second Caliph, may God be pleased with him, commented on this sentence: "She came, walking modestly, with her face covered with a part of outer garment, unlike immodest women who are prone to loiter at night, who unabashedly find their way everywhere, and who are ever ready to go out" (al-Ālūsī, 19: 64).

5. Although there are some opinions that the old man who entertained Moses as a guest was the Prophet Shu'ayb, upon him be peace, many scholars such as 'Abdullāh ibn 'Abbās, Ḥasan al-Baṣrī, and Sa'īd ibn al-Jubayr, and commentators on the Qur'ān such as Ibn Jarīr aṭ-Ṭabarī and Ibn Kathīr, do not hold the same view. The Bible and Jewish sources are also not certain about his identity. What is certain is that he was a believing, righteous man.

6. This verse suggests that the man who employed Moses was an insightful one. He must have realized what a valuable, promising man Moses was. He must also have realized that he would need a period of spiritual education for the mission that he would serve in the future. His offer should be considered from this perspective. Once God's Messenger said that every Prophet, including himself, pastured animals for some time (Al-Bukhārī, "Ijārah," 2).

29. When Moses fulfilled the term and was traveling with his family (in the desert) he perceived a fire from the direction of the Mount (Sinai). He said to his family: "Wait here! For I perceive a fire far off; I may bring you from there some information (about where we are and the way we should take), or a burning brand from the fire so that you may (kindle a fire and) warm yourselves."

30. When he came to the fire, he was called from the right bank of the valley in the blessed ground, from the tree: "O Moses! Surely it is I, I am God, the Lord of the worlds.[7]

31. "Throw down your staff. (He threw it, and) when he saw it slithering as if a snake, he turned his back to flee. "O Moses, come forward and have no fear. You (chosen as a Messenger) are indeed of those who are secure.[8]

32. Put your (right) hand into your bosom: it will come forth shining white without flaw, and now hold your arms close to yourself free of awe (and ready to receive My command). These are two evidences (of your Messengership) from your Lord (for you to demonstrate) to the Pharaoh and his chiefs. Surely, they are a transgressing people."

33. (Moses) said: "My Lord! I killed a person among them, so I fear that they will kill me (and not let me convey Your Message).

34. "And my brother Aaron – he is one more eloquent in speech than me, so (appointing him also as a Messenger) send him with me as a helper to confirm my truthfulness, for indeed I fear that they will deny me."

35. He said: "We will strengthen you through your brother and will invest both of you with power and authority;[9] and they will not be able to reach you (with any harm they intend) from awe of Our signs (miracles). You two, and all who follow you, will be the victors."

---

7. For an explanation of what is related in this verse, see 27: 8, note 5.

8. See also 27: 10–11.

9. As stated in the continuation of the verse, this must refer to the miracles granted to the Prophet Moses, the calamities that God caused to visit the Pharaoh and his people, one after the other, like Moses' other miracles (see 7: 133–134). It may also be referring to those who fill believe in and follow them.

فَلَمَّا جَآءَهُم مُّوسَىٰ بِـَٔايَٰتِنَا بَيِّنَٰتٍ قَالُوا۟ مَا هَٰذَآ إِلَّا سِحْرٌ مُّفْتَرًى وَمَا سَمِعْنَا بِهَٰذَا فِىٓ ءَابَآئِنَا ٱلْأَوَّلِينَ ۝ وَقَالَ مُوسَىٰ رَبِّىٓ أَعْلَمُ بِمَن جَآءَ بِٱلْهُدَىٰ مِنْ عِندِهِۦ وَمَن تَكُونُ لَهُۥ عَٰقِبَةُ ٱلدَّارِ إِنَّهُۥ لَا يُفْلِحُ ٱلظَّٰلِمُونَ ۝ وَقَالَ فِرْعَوْنُ يَٰٓأَيُّهَا ٱلْمَلَأُ مَا عَلِمْتُ لَكُم مِّنْ إِلَٰهٍ غَيْرِى فَأَوْقِدْ لِى يَٰهَٰمَٰنُ عَلَى ٱلطِّينِ فَٱجْعَل لِّى صَرْحًا لَّعَلِّىٓ أَطَّلِعُ إِلَىٰٓ إِلَٰهِ مُوسَىٰ وَإِنِّى لَأَظُنُّهُۥ مِنَ ٱلْكَٰذِبِينَ ۝ وَٱسْتَكْبَرَ هُوَ وَجُنُودُهُۥ فِى ٱلْأَرْضِ بِغَيْرِ ٱلْحَقِّ وَظَنُّوٓا۟ أَنَّهُمْ إِلَيْنَا لَا يُرْجَعُونَ ۝ فَأَخَذْنَٰهُ وَجُنُودَهُۥ فَنَبَذْنَٰهُمْ فِى ٱلْيَمِّ فَٱنظُرْ كَيْفَ كَانَ عَٰقِبَةُ ٱلظَّٰلِمِينَ ۝ وَجَعَلْنَٰهُمْ أَئِمَّةً يَدْعُونَ إِلَى ٱلنَّارِ وَيَوْمَ ٱلْقِيَٰمَةِ لَا يُنصَرُونَ ۝ وَأَتْبَعْنَٰهُمْ فِى هَٰذِهِ ٱلدُّنْيَا لَعْنَةً وَيَوْمَ ٱلْقِيَٰمَةِ هُم مِّنَ ٱلْمَقْبُوحِينَ ۝ وَلَقَدْ ءَاتَيْنَا مُوسَى ٱلْكِتَٰبَ مِنۢ بَعْدِ مَآ أَهْلَكْنَا ٱلْقُرُونَ ٱلْأُولَىٰ بَصَآئِرَ لِلنَّاسِ وَهُدًى وَرَحْمَةً لَّعَلَّهُمْ يَتَذَكَّرُونَ ۝

---

36. When Moses came to them (the Pharaoh and his chiefs) with Our manifest signs, they said: "This (that you show as miracles to prove your Messengership) is nothing but sorcery contrived. And we never heard this (the call[10] to Him Whom you call the Lord of the worlds) in the time of our forefathers of old."

37. (Moses) said: "My Lord knows best who has come with the true guidance from Him, and to whom the ultimate abode of happiness will belong (both in the world and in the Hereafter). Surely, the wrongdoers do not prosper, (nor attain their goals)."

38. The Pharaoh (turned to the chiefs and) said: "O you nobles! I do not know that you have another deity than me.[11] Well, then, O Hāmān, kindle (the furnace) for me to bake bricks, and make me a lofty tower so that I may have a look at the God of Moses, though I surely think that he is a liar."

39. He grew arrogant in the land, he and his hosts, against all right, and they thought that they would never be brought back to Us (for judgment).

40. So We seized him and his hosts, and cast them into the sea. Then see how was the outcome for the wrongdoers!

41. We have made them leaders (exemplary patterns) of misguidance calling (those who would follow them) to the Fire. And (even though they employ many in their service in this world) on the Day of Resurrection they will not be helped.

42. We have caused a curse to pursue them in this world (and increase them in sin because of their being leaders in misguidance misleading those who followed them), and on the Day of Resurrection they will be among the spurned (those utterly deprived of God's Mercy).

43. And indeed, after We had destroyed those earlier (wrongdoing) generations, We granted Moses the Book (the Torah) as lights of discernment and insight for people, and as guidance and mercy, so that they might reflect and be mindful.

---

10. See 20: 47–53; 26: 23–29.

11. For the Pharaoh's claim of divinity, see 26: 29, note 6.

44. (All that We have told you about Moses and the Book granted to him is a Revelation We reveal to you, O Muḥammad, for) you were not present on the spot lying to the western side (of the valley) when We decreed the Commandment (the Torah) to Moses, nor were you a witness (to what happened there).

45. But (after them) We brought into being many generations and long indeed were the ages that passed over them. (The information you give about them is also that which We reveal to you, just as what you tell about what happened concerning Moses in Midian is also a Revelation. For) neither did you dwell among the people of Midian so that you are conveying to them (the Makkan people) Our Revelations (about what Moses did in Midian). Rather, We have been sending Messengers (to convey Our Revelations).

46. And neither were you present on the side of the Mount Sinai when We called out (to Moses), but (We reveal all this to you) as a mercy from your Lord so that you may warn a people to whom no warner has come before you, so that they may reflect and be mindful.

47. (We have sent you as Messenger) lest they say when a disaster befalls them (either in the world or in the Hereafter) because of what they themselves with their own hands have forwarded, "Our Lord! If only you had sent a Messenger to us, we would have followed Your Revelations and been among the believers."

48. And yet, now that the truth has come to them from Us (through a Messenger), still they say (by way of an excuse for their denial of it), "Why has he not been granted the like of what Moses was granted (all at

once)?"[12] Did they not previously refuse to believe in what had been granted to Moses?[13] They said: "Both are sorcery, each supporting the other." They also said: "In each we are unbelievers."

49. Say (to them): "Then bring another Book from God which would offer better guidance than either of these two so that I may follow it, if you are truthful (in your claim that they are both sorcery)."

50. If they cannot respond, then know that they are merely following their whims and caprices. Who can be more astray than he who follows his lusts and fancies deprived of all guidance from God. God surely does not guide people given to wrongdoing and injustice.

---

12. This is referring to the objection made by the Makkan polytheists: "Why has the Qur'ān not been sent down to him all at once?" (25: 32) The Torah was granted to Moses as a complete book.

13. The Makkan polytheists rejected the Messengership, the Revelations and all the Divinely-revealed Books, as it is stated in: *Those who disbelieve say: "We will not believe in this Qur'ān, nor in any (Message) that came before it"* (34: 31).

وَلَقَدْ وَصَّلْنَا لَهُمُ الْقَوْلَ لَعَلَّهُمْ يَتَذَكَّرُونَ ۞ اَلَّذِينَ

اٰتَيْنَاهُمُ الْكِتَابَ مِنْ قَبْلِهٖ هُمْ بِهٖ يُؤْمِنُونَ ۞ وَاِذَا

يُتْلٰى عَلَيْهِمْ قَالُوٓا اٰمَنَّا بِهٖٓ اِنَّهُ الْحَقُّ مِنْ رَّبِّنَآ اِنَّا كُنَّا

مِنْ قَبْلِهٖ مُسْلِمِينَ ۞ اُولٰٓئِكَ يُؤْتَوْنَ اَجْرَهُمْ مَّرَّتَيْنِ

بِمَا صَبَرُوْا وَيَدْرَؤُنَ بِالْحَسَنَةِ السَّيِّئَةَ وَمِمَّا رَزَقْنَاهُمْ

يُنْفِقُونَ ۞ وَاِذَا سَمِعُوا اللَّغْوَ اَعْرَضُوْا عَنْهُ وَقَالُوْا لَنَآ

اَعْمَالُنَا وَلَكُمْ اَعْمَالُكُمْ سَلَامٌ عَلَيْكُمْ لَا نَبْتَغِي الْجَاهِلِينَ

۞ اِنَّكَ لَا تَهْدِي مَنْ اَحْبَبْتَ وَلٰكِنَّ اللهَ يَهْدِي مَنْ

يَّشَاءُ وَهُوَ اَعْلَمُ بِالْمُهْتَدِينَ ۞ وَقَالُوٓا اِنْ نَّتَّبِعِ الْهُدٰى مَعَكَ

نُتَخَطَّفْ مِنْ اَرْضِنَا اَوَلَمْ نُمَكِّنْ لَّهُمْ حَرَمًا اٰمِنًا يُجْبٰٓى اِلَيْهِ ثَمَرَاتُ

كُلِّ شَيْءٍ رِّزْقًا مِّنْ لَّدُنَّا وَلٰكِنَّ اَكْثَرَهُمْ لَا يَعْلَمُونَ ۞ وَكَمْ اَهْلَكْنَا

مِنْ قَرْيَةٍ بَطِرَتْ مَعِيشَتَهَا فَتِلْكَ مَسَاكِنُهُمْ لَمْ تُسْكَنْ مِنْ بَعْدِهِمْ

اِلَّا قَلِيلًا وَكُنَّا نَحْنُ الْوَارِثِينَ ۞ وَمَا كَانَ رَبُّكَ مُهْلِكَ

الْقُرٰى حَتّٰى يَبْعَثَ فِيٓ اُمِّهَا رَسُوْلًا يَتْلُوْا عَلَيْهِمْ اٰيَاتِنَا

وَمَا كُنَّا مُهْلِكِي الْقُرٰٓى اِلَّا وَاَهْلُهَا ظَالِمُونَ ۞

---

51. Assuredly We have conveyed to them the Word (one verse after the other, and one chapter after the other for their good) so that they may reflect and be mindful.

52. Those to whom We granted the Book before it do believe in it.[14]

53. When it is recited to them, they say: "We believe in it. Surely it is the truth from our Lord. Even before this We were such as submitted (to the Divine Will)."

54. These will be granted their reward twice over because they have remained steadfast (in following their religion free of falsehood and so keeping themselves above all prejudices to believe in and follow the Qur'ān and Muḥammad); and they repel evil with good and out of what We have provided for them (of wealth, knowledge, power, etc.) they spend (in God's cause and for the needy, and purely for the good pleasure of God).

55. When they hear any vain (useless or aggressive) talk, they turn away from it, without reciprocating it, and say (to those who are engaged in it): "To us are accounted our deeds, and to you, your deeds. Peace be upon you! We do not seek to mix with the ignorant (those unaware of God, true guidance and right and wrong)."

56. You cannot guide to truth whomever you like but God guides whomever He wills. He knows best who are guided (and amenable to guidance).

57. They say: "Should we follow this Guidance in your company, we would be annihilated in our land." Have We not established them in a secure sanctuary to which, as a provision from Us, products of all kinds are brought? But most of them do not know (that it is We Who protect and provide for them, and assume that it is their worshipping idols that attracts other Arab tribes to Makkah for trade and that protects them from being attacked by those tribes).

58. How many a township have We destroyed that exulted insolently on account of their affluence. Those are their dwellings – except for few people for a short time only, they have never been dwelt in after them. It is always We Who are the inheritors (Who remain as the Ever-Living when all else have passed away).

59. Yet Your Lord never destroys townships without first raising up in their mother-town a Messenger who conveys to them Our messages. We never destroy townships, save that their people are wrongdoers (who associate partners with God and are given to many injustices).

---

14. This does not mean that all the People of the Book actually believed in the Qur'ān. This verse refers to some among the People of the Book who believed in it during the Makkan period of the mission of the Prophet Muḥammad, upon him be peace and blessings.

60. Whatever thing you are granted (of the world) is but for the passing enjoyment of the present, worldly life and its adornment. Whereas what God keeps for you (as the reward for your good deeds and which He will give you in excess of your deserving) is much better and more enduring. Will you not reason and understand?

61. Is, then, he to whom We have given a fair promise (forgiveness and Paradise) which he will obtain, like him whom We have let enjoy for a time the good things of the present, worldly life, but who will be, on the Day of Resurrection, among those who are arraigned (for punishment)?

62. On that Day God will call to them and say: "Where now are those (beings, things, and powers) that you alleged to be My partners?"

63. Those (who led others to associate partners with God, and) against whom God's judgment of punishment has been realized will say: "Our Lord! Those whom we led astray, we led them astray just because we ourselves were astray (– they imitated us out of their free will, we never coerced them to it). Now in Your Presence we declare our innocence (of their taking us for partners with You). It was not us that they worshipped. (Rather, they worshipped their own carnal souls.)"

64. And it will be said (to those who associated them as partners with God): "Call for help now upon your associate-deities!" And they will call upon them, but they will not answer them, and they will see the punishment in front of them. If only they had followed the right guidance!

65. On that Day God will call to them (once more) and ask: "How did you respond to the Messengers?"

66. That Day (all ways and means of finding) information will be darkened to them, and they will not (even) be able to ask one another.

67. But as for those who repent and believe and do good, righteous deeds, they may well hope to be among the prosperous.

68. Your Lord creates whatever He wills and chooses and decrees (for His servants) whatever way of life He wills. They have no freedom of choice (in respect of what God has chosen and commanded). All-Glorified is He, and infinitely Exalted above their association of partners with Him.

69. Your Lord knows whatever their bosoms conceal and whatever they disclose.

70. He is God, there is no deity but He (only He is owed worship). (As all beauties, perfections, accomplishments, and favors are essentially from Him,) for Him are all praise and gratitude at the beginning and at the end (of every accomplishment, both in the world and in the Hereafter). His alone is judgment and authority, and to Him you are being brought back.

قُلْ اَرَءَيْتُمْ اِنْ جَعَلَ اللّٰهُ عَلَيْكُمُ الَّيْلَ سَرْمَدًا اِلٰى يَوْمِ الْقِيٰمَةِ مَنْ اِلٰهٌ غَيْرُ اللّٰهِ يَاْتِيْكُمْ بِضِيَاءٍ اَفَلَا تَسْمَعُوْنَ ۝ قُلْ اَرَءَيْتُمْ اِنْ جَعَلَ اللّٰهُ عَلَيْكُمُ النَّهَارَ سَرْمَدًا اِلٰى يَوْمِ الْقِيٰمَةِ مَنْ اِلٰهٌ غَيْرُ اللّٰهِ يَاْتِيْكُمْ بِلَيْلٍ تَسْكُنُوْنَ فِيْهِ اَفَلَا تُبْصِرُوْنَ ۝ وَمِنْ رَّحْمَتِهٖ جَعَلَ لَكُمُ الَّيْلَ وَالنَّهَارَ لِتَسْكُنُوْا فِيْهِ وَلِتَبْتَغُوْا مِنْ فَضْلِهٖ وَلَعَلَّكُمْ تَشْكُرُوْنَ ۝ وَيَوْمَ يُنَادِيْهِمْ فَيَقُوْلُ اَيْنَ شُرَكَآءِىَ الَّذِيْنَ كُنْتُمْ تَزْعُمُوْنَ ۝ وَنَزَعْنَا مِنْ كُلِّ اُمَّةٍ شَهِيْدًا فَقُلْنَا هَاتُوْا بُرْهَانَكُمْ فَعَلِمُوْا اَنَّ الْحَقَّ لِلّٰهِ وَضَلَّ عَنْهُمْ مَّا كَانُوْا يَفْتَرُوْنَ ۝ اِنَّ قَارُوْنَ كَانَ مِنْ قَوْمِ مُوْسٰى فَبَغٰى عَلَيْهِمْ وَاٰتَيْنٰهُ مِنَ الْكُنُوْزِ مَآ اِنَّ مَفَاتِحَهٗ لَتَنُوْٓاُ بِالْعُصْبَةِ اُولِى الْقُوَّةِ اِذْ قَالَ لَهٗ قَوْمُهٗ لَا تَفْرَحْ اِنَّ اللّٰهَ لَا يُحِبُّ الْفَرِحِيْنَ ۝ وَابْتَغِ فِيْمَآ اٰتٰىكَ اللّٰهُ الدَّارَ الْاٰخِرَةَ وَلَا تَنْسَ نَصِيْبَكَ مِنَ الدُّنْيَا وَاَحْسِنْ كَمَآ اَحْسَنَ اللّٰهُ اِلَيْكَ وَلَا تَبْغِ الْفَسَادَ فِى الْاَرْضِ اِنَّ اللّٰهَ لَا يُحِبُّ الْمُفْسِدِيْنَ ۝

saying: "Where now are those (beings, things, and powers) that you alleged to be My partners?"

75. And We will take out from every community a witness (the Messenger sent to them), and will say (to those who rejected the Messengers): "Produce your evidence (for your claim that God has partners)!" Then they will know that all truth rests with God and that it is only God Who has the absolute right (to Divinity and Lordship); and all (the false deities) that they fabricated besides God will fail them.

76. Qārūn (Korah) was one of Moses' people, but he betrayed and oppressed them.[15] We had granted him such great treasures that their very keys alone were too heavy a burden for a company of strong people. Even his people warned him: "Do not exult in your wealth; surely God does not love those who exult.

77. "But seek, by means of what God has granted you, the abode of the Hereafter (by spending in alms and other good causes), without forgetting your share (which God has appointed) in this world.[16] Do good to others as God has done good to you (out of His pure grace). Do not seek corruption and mischief in the land, for God does not love those who cause corruption and make mischief."

71. Say: "Have you ever considered that if God should make the night perpetual over you until the Day of Resurrection, is there a deity other than God who can bring you light? Will you not, then, give ear (to the truth and take heed)?"

72. Say: "Have you considered that if God should make the day perpetual over you until the Day of Resurrection, is there a deity other than God who can bring you the night, that you may rest in it? Will you not, then, see (the truth and take heed)?"

73. It is out of His Mercy that He has made for you the night and the day so that you may rest (during the night) and seek after His bounty (during the day), and that you may give thanks (to Him for both).

74. A Day will come and He will call to those who associate partners with Him,

15. The story of Qārūn (in the Bible, Korah) is another of the arguments against the Makkan unbelievers' excuse that, if they were to follow the Qur'ān in the Messenger's company they would be utterly annihilated in their land (verse 57). Those who made this excuse were wealthy traders, the rich money-lenders, and interest-accumulators of Makkah. Their only concern was to maximize their monetary earnings and maintain their luxurious life. As for the common people, many among them looked up to the rich as their role models. They wished to become like them and lead a similar life.

Qārūn, despite being an Israelite, had allied himself with the Pharaoh and become one of his closest courtiers. Since he was also one of the three most vocal opponents of Moses, upon him be peace, the Qur'ān mentions him along with the Pharaoh and Hāmān as those who oppressed people and of those to whom Moses was sent with God's signs (miracles) and a clear authority (40: 23–24). This shows that Qārūn had betrayed his people and become an agent of the enemy who wanted to destroy the Children of Israel. Due to his treachery, he had attained a very high position in the Pharaoh's court.

16. God has appointed for every living being a certain share of providence in the world, which will be enough for the maintenance of that being's life. It comes to trees and plants by itself, as they have no consciousness, will, or power to obtain it. Babies receive it almost without any effort, as they too are powerless. As a conscious living being grows in strength and self-reliance, it has to work to earn its provision. What is important for human beings is that they must earn it by lawful ways. Islam, even though it does not forbid possessing wealth, advises a moderate life. It orders a certain amount of wealth (the *Zakāh*) to be spent in God's cause and for the needy, and encourages the rich to spend more in charity and on other good causes. It also commands emphatically that money be earned through lawful ways and spent on lawful things.

394   سورة القصص   ٣٩٤

قَالَ إِنَّمَآ أُوتِيتُهُ عَلَىٰ عِلْمٍ عِندِىٓ أَوَلَمْ يَعْلَمْ أَنَّ ٱللَّهَ قَدْ أَهْلَكَ مِن قَبْلِهِ مِنَ ٱلْقُرُونِ مَنْ هُوَ أَشَدُّ مِنْهُ قُوَّةً وَأَكْثَرُ جَمْعًا ۚ وَلَا يُسْـَٔلُ عَن ذُنُوبِهِمُ ٱلْمُجْرِمُونَ ۝ فَخَرَجَ عَلَىٰ قَوْمِهِۦ فِى زِينَتِهِۦ ۖ قَالَ ٱلَّذِينَ يُرِيدُونَ ٱلْحَيَوٰةَ ٱلدُّنْيَا يَـٰلَيْتَ لَنَا مِثْلَ مَآ أُوتِىَ قَـٰرُونُ إِنَّهُۥ لَذُو حَظٍّ عَظِيمٍ ۝ وَقَالَ ٱلَّذِينَ أُوتُوا۟ ٱلْعِلْمَ وَيْلَكُمْ ثَوَابُ ٱللَّهِ خَيْرٌ لِّمَنْ ءَامَنَ وَعَمِلَ صَـٰلِحًا وَلَا يُلَقَّىٰهَآ إِلَّا ٱلصَّـٰبِرُونَ ۝ فَخَسَفْنَا بِهِۦ وَبِدَارِهِ ٱلْأَرْضَ فَمَا كَانَ لَهُۥ مِن فِئَةٍ يَنصُرُونَهُۥ مِن دُونِ ٱللَّهِ وَمَا كَانَ مِنَ ٱلْمُنتَصِرِينَ ۝ وَأَصْبَحَ ٱلَّذِينَ تَمَنَّوْا۟ مَكَانَهُۥ بِٱلْأَمْسِ يَقُولُونَ وَيْكَأَنَّ ٱللَّهَ يَبْسُطُ ٱلرِّزْقَ لِمَن يَشَآءُ مِنْ عِبَادِهِۦ وَيَقْدِرُ ۖ لَوْلَآ أَن مَّنَّ ٱللَّهُ عَلَيْنَا لَخَسَفَ بِنَا ۖ وَيْكَأَنَّهُۥ لَا يُفْلِحُ ٱلْكَـٰفِرُونَ ۝ تِلْكَ ٱلدَّارُ ٱلْأَخِرَةُ نَجْعَلُهَا لِلَّذِينَ لَا يُرِيدُونَ عُلُوًّا فِى ٱلْأَرْضِ وَلَا فَسَادًا ۚ وَٱلْعَـٰقِبَةُ لِلْمُتَّقِينَ ۝ مَن جَآءَ بِٱلْحَسَنَةِ فَلَهُۥ خَيْرٌ مِّنْهَا ۖ وَمَن جَآءَ بِٱلسَّيِّئَةِ فَلَا يُجْزَى ٱلَّذِينَ عَمِلُوا۟ ٱلسَّيِّـَٔاتِ إِلَّا مَا كَانُوا۟ يَعْمَلُونَ ۝

---

78. He said: "All this has been given to me only by virtue of a certain knowledge that I have."[17] Did he not know that God had destroyed among the generations before him men who were greater than him in power, and greater in wealth amassed? In fact, the criminals committed to accumulating sins are not asked about their sins (before they are destroyed so that they can defend themselves).

79. (Korah) showed off before his people in all his pomp. Those who cared only for the life of this world said: "Ah, if we but had the like of what Korah has been given! Indeed he is one of tremendous good fortune!"

80. But those who had been granted (true) knowledge[18] said: "Woe to you! God's reward for any who believes and does good, righteous deeds is better by far. But none save the patient (who persevere through adversities, in obedience to God and avoidance of sins) can ever attain to it."

81. Then We caused the earth to swallow him and his dwelling. There was then no host to help him against God, nor (for all his possessions) was he himself able to come to his own aid.

82. And on the morrow, those who had longed to be in his place the day before began to say: "Woe to us! (We had forgotten that) God enlarges provision for whom He wills of His servants, and straitens it (for whom He wills). Had God not been gracious to us, He would have made us too swallowed up. Woe to us! (for we had forgotten that) the unbelievers do not prosper."

83. As for the abode of the Hereafter, We will assign it to those who do not seek arrogant power on earth nor cause corruption and disorder. The (truly desirable) outcome is for the God-revering, pious.

84. Whoever comes to God with a good deed will have better than it, and whoever comes with an evil deed – those who do evil deeds will not be recompensed save only for what they have done.[19]

17. This is a typical attitude of human ingratitude and arrogance. Human beings usually attribute their accomplishments to themselves, to some advantage in knowledge, power, intelligence, and abilities. In consequence, all such advantages and indeed all that God has granted to human beings and their accomplishments therewith become the means to an eternal loss.

18. It is of great significance that the Qur'ān implies that those who seek the worldly life are only people of ignorance. In another verse (53: 29–30), it introduces them as having very little knowledge, which is only related to the world: *Withdraw from those who turn away from Our Book and remembrance, and desire nothing but the life of this world. Such is their sum of knowledge.* In both that verse and verse 80 in this *sūrah*, knowledge is used with the definite article; it indicates the revealed knowledge. So what the Qur'ān accepts as knowledge is, first of all, revealed knowledge – God-given knowledge about Divinity and knowledge of the Religion. Those who have this knowledge desire God and what He has prepared for them in the Hereafter.

19. Another verse reads: *Whoever comes to God with a good deed will have ten times as much, and whoever comes with an evil deed, will be recompensed with only the like of it; and they will not be wronged* (6: 160). However, the reward of a good deed is not restricted to only ten times as much. God multiplies for whom He wills as much as He wills, both out of His grace and according to the sincerity of the one who does good and according to the time and conditions in which it was done.

---

85. Surely He Who has entrusted you (O Messenger) with the (duty of conveying) the Qur'ān, will certainly bring you round to the fulfillment of the promise (– you will be returned in victory to the home you were compelled to abandon).[20] Say: "My Lord knows best who has the (true) guidance and who is lost in obvious error."

86. You did not expect that this Book would be revealed to you; but it is being revealed to you as a mercy from your Lord, so do not lend any support to the unbelievers.

87. And never let them divert you away from conveying God's Revelations after they have been sent down to you. Call (people) to your Lord, and do not be of those who associate partners with God.

88. Do not call upon another deity along with God.[21] There is no deity but He. Everything is perishable (and so perishing) except His "Face" (His eternal Self and what is done in seeking His good pleasure).[22/23] His alone is judgment and authority, and to Him you are being brought back.

---

20. Different comments have been made on this verse. However it must be related to God's promise to *those who are humiliated and oppressed in the land*, and therefore to verse 5 of this sūrah: *But We willed to bestow Our favor upon those who were being humiliated and oppressed in the land, and make of them exemplary leaders (to guide people on the way to God and in their lives), and make them inheritors (of the glory of the Pharaoh and the land in which We produced blessings for people). And to establish them in the land with power....* When this sūrah was revealed, the Muslims in Makkah were being brutally persecuted. Therefore, the verse implies that the Messenger and the Muslims will be forced to leave Makkah and return to it in victory, which means that the Qur'ān will be completed to be their guide for the whole of life in its totality.

21. Such statements which address a prohibition to God's Messenger in no way mean that he might be tempted to lend some support to the unbelievers, or to let them drive him away from conveying God's Revelations, or to call upon another deity alongside God. Rather, they stress the importance of the matter mentioned and describe the way he and his successors should follow in fulfilling their mission. For the Messenger in particular they also mean: "You are never expected to do that."

22. The meaning of the word here literally translated as *His Face* is "God Himself as One with infinite Mercy, Who sees, hears, and speaks, and to Whom every being turns for its needs." God can never be conceived of as One Who resembles created beings. So words such as *hand* or *face* should be dealt with as figurative expressions for some among His Attributes. When used for human beings, *face* is the part of the body from which the person looks out to others and to which communication from others is addressed. It therefore represents the person. For the Divine Being, *face* means that "He is One with infinite mercy Who turns to the creation with seeing, hearing, mercy, and provision, to Whom every being can turn for the fulfillment of its needs."

23. *A question*: Does *Everything is perishable (and so perishing), except His Face* (28: 88) also include Paradise and Hell, and their inhabitants?

Answer: Many qualified scholars, saints, and people of deep perception and insight have discussed this subject. Some maintain that the inhabitants of the permanent world are not included, while others hold that these people will also enter annihilation, albeit for such a brief period that they will not feel it. Although some others argue that all existence – except God – will perish permanently, this cannot be, for the Divine Essence and God's Attributes and Names are permanent. Thus, permanent beings in the World of Permanence cannot experience absolute annihilation, for they are the manifestations of God's permanent Attributes and Names and the mirrors in which they are reflected.

I now would like to briefly mention two points concerning the subject:

First point: The All-Mighty is absolutely All-Powerful, and so creation and destruction are equally easy for Him. He can annihilate or re-create all of creation in an instant. In addition, absolute non-existence cannot exist, for there is an encompassing Knowledge. As everything is contained or has a kind of existence or an ideal form within the infinite Divine Knowledge, there is no room for non-existence. Within the encompassing circle of Divine Knowledge, relative non-existence is, in essence, a nominal veil reflecting the manifestations of Divine Knowledge.

Some people of profound understanding have called such ideal forms of existence "archetypes." Based on this, going into non-existence means taking off an outer dress (the body) and returning to the circle of spiritual existence, or existence in Divine Knowledge. In other words, that which perishes by leaving its physical body puts on a spiritual body and, leaving the circle where (Divine) Power operates, enters the circle of (Divine) Knowledge.

Second point: As nothing can exist by itself, everything's existence depends on God. Since a thing exists as a manifestation of the permanent Divine Names, it has a permanent, sublime reality due to its reflecting the Divine Name that caused its existence. The verse: *Everything is perishable, except His Face* (28: 88) also serves as a sword that cuts away from people all that is not God (e.g., the world, the flesh, and life's vanities). Thus, whatever people have or do for God's sake is not included in the meaning of this verse.

In sum, if people find God and act only for His sake, there will be nothing left to be included in the meaning of *Everything is perishable, except His Face*. So if they want to make their deeds eternal and be rewarded with permanent happiness, they must seek God and live for His sake and good pleasure. (See *The Letters*, "the 15th Letter," 80–82.)

SŪRAH 29

AL-'ANKABŪT
(THE SPIDER)

Makkah period

This *sūrah*, comprising 69 verses, was revealed in Makkah at a time when the believers were being subject to severe persecutions. It takes its name from the word *al-'ankabūt* ("the spider") in verse 41, implying the frailty of false beliefs and encouraging the believers to show patience and resistance. The *sūrah*, which also threatens the rebellious polytheists with an evil end, puts forth irrefutable arguments for God's Oneness and the afterlife.

In the Name of God, the All-Merciful, the All-Compassionate.

1. *Alif. Lām. Mīm.*

2. Do people reckon that they will be left (to themselves at ease) on their mere saying, "We believe," and will not be put to a test?

3. We certainly tested those who preceded them. (This is Our unchanging way) so that God will certainly mark out those who prove true (in their profession of faith) and He will certainly mark out those who prove false.[1]

4. Or do those who do evil deeds (and persecute the believers) reckon that they can frustrate Us and escape Our punishment? How evil is the judgment they have reached!

5. Whoever looks forward to meeting with God: the term set by God (for His meeting) will certainly come. He is the All-Hearing, the All-Knowing.[2]

6. And whoever strives hard (against his carnal, evil-commanding soul and Satan to be a good Muslim and to resist all persecutions in God's cause) strives for the good of his own soul only. Surely God is Self-Sufficient in absolute independence of all the worlds.

---

1. See 2: 155–157 and the corresponding notes 121, and 122.

2. God is He Who hears whatever people utter openly or within themselves, and He knows them fully in every state, all their intentions and deeds, and with all that they reveal and all that they keep concealed. Nothing escapes Him. Mentioning God in this verse with these two Names is both a glad tiding to those who are sincere in their belief and expectations, and a warning to those who are not sincere, as well as to the unbelievers.

7. Those who believe and (in striving hard to be good Muslims) do good, righteous deeds, We will most certainly blot out from them their evil deeds, and will most certainly reward them in accordance with the best of what they used to do.

8. (As the requirement for being good Muslims) We have enjoined on human to be kind and good to his parents; but if they endeavor to make you associate with Me anything as partner, about whose being so you impossibly have no knowledge, do not obey them. To Me is your return, so I will make you understand what you were doing (and call you to account for it).

9. Those who believe and do good, righteous deeds, We will most certainly include them among the righteous (who enter Paradise).

10. Among the people are such as say, "We believe in God," but when (such a person) is subjected to persecution (for his confession of faith) in God, he construes persecution at the hands of people as God's punishment (and rejects his faith); but if a victory comes from your Lord (to the believers), (such people) will most certainly say, "Surely we have always been with you." Or (do they think that) God is not fully aware of what is in the bosoms of all creatures (that He created)?

11. God will most certainly mark out those who truly believe and He will most certainly mark out the hypocritical ones.

12. Those who disbelieve say to those who believe: "If you follow our way (of religion and life), we will take your sins upon us, yet they cannot take upon them any-

thing of their sins. They are liars indeed.

13. They will most certainly have to bear their own burdens, and other burdens together with their own;[3] and most certainly they will be called to account on the Day of Resurrection for what they were busy fabricating (against God and other truths of faith).

14. Indeed, We sent Noah to his people (as Messenger), and he remained among them a thousand years save fifty years, and in the end the Flood overtook them as they were wrongdoers (who persisted in associating partners with God and committing grave injustices).

---

3. The burdens these people will have to bear besides their own are the burdens of those whom they have misled (16: 25), and of those who follow the evil path they have established. God's Messenger, upon him be peace and blessings, declared: "Those who establish a good path in Islam receive the reward of those who follow it, without any decrease in their (own) reward. Those who establish an evil path in Islam are burdened with the sins of those who follow it, without any decrease in their (own) burden" (Muslim, "Zakāh," 69; Ibn Mājah, "Muqaddimah," 203).

فَأَنجَيْنَاهُ وَأَصْحَابَ السَّفِينَةِ وَجَعَلْنَاهَا آيَةً لِّلْعَالَمِينَ ۞

وَإِبْرَاهِيمَ إِذْ قَالَ لِقَوْمِهِ اعْبُدُوا اللَّهَ وَاتَّقُوهُ ذَٰلِكُمْ خَيْرٌ

لَّكُمْ إِن كُنتُمْ تَعْلَمُونَ ۞ إِنَّمَا تَعْبُدُونَ مِن دُونِ اللَّهِ أَوْثَانًا وَتَخْلُقُونَ

إِفْكًا إِنَّ الَّذِينَ تَعْبُدُونَ مِن دُونِ اللَّهِ لَا يَمْلِكُونَ

لَكُمْ رِزْقًا فَابْتَغُوا عِندَ اللَّهِ الرِّزْقَ وَاعْبُدُوهُ

وَاشْكُرُوا لَهُ إِلَيْهِ تُرْجَعُونَ ۞ وَإِن تُكَذِّبُوا فَقَدْ

كَذَّبَ أُمَمٌ مِّن قَبْلِكُمْ وَمَا عَلَى الرَّسُولِ إِلَّا الْبَلَاغُ

الْمُبِينُ ۞ أَوَلَمْ يَرَوْا كَيْفَ يُبْدِئُ اللَّهُ الْخَلْقَ ثُمَّ يُعِيدُهُ

إِنَّ ذَٰلِكَ عَلَى اللَّهِ يَسِيرٌ ۞ قُلْ سِيرُوا فِي الْأَرْضِ

فَانظُرُوا كَيْفَ بَدَأَ الْخَلْقَ ثُمَّ اللَّهُ يُنشِئُ النَّشْأَةَ

الْآخِرَةَ إِنَّ اللَّهَ عَلَىٰ كُلِّ شَيْءٍ قَدِيرٌ ۞ يُعَذِّبُ مَن يَشَاءُ

وَيَرْحَمُ مَن يَشَاءُ وَإِلَيْهِ تُقْلَبُونَ ۞ وَمَا أَنتُم بِمُعْجِزِينَ فِي

الْأَرْضِ وَلَا فِي السَّمَاءِ وَمَا لَكُم مِّن دُونِ اللَّهِ مِن وَلِيٍّ وَلَا

نَصِيرٍ ۞ وَالَّذِينَ كَفَرُوا بِآيَاتِ اللَّهِ وَلِقَائِهِ أُولَٰئِكَ

يَئِسُوا مِن رَّحْمَتِي وَأُولَٰئِكَ لَهُمْ عَذَابٌ أَلِيمٌ ۞

---

15. Yet We saved him and those who were together with him on the Ark, and We made this event as an exemplary sign (full of lessons) for all the people (to come after).

16. And Abraham, too, (We sent as Messenger). He said to his people (in conveying this message): "Worship God alone and keep from disobedience to Him in reverence for Him and piety. Doing so is the best for you, if you would know (the truth of the matter).

17. "You worship only idols instead of God, and thus you invent a mere falsehood (by deifying some things and beings such that it is impossible for them to be Deity). Surely those (beings whom you deify and make statutes of, and idols)[4] that you worship instead of God do not have power to provide for you; so seek all your provision from God, and worship Him and be thankful to Him. To Him you are being brought back."

18. If you deny Our Messenger, know that many communities before you denied (the Messengers sent to them, but their denial was of no avail to them). What rests with the Messenger is no more than to convey the Message fully and clearly.

19. Have they not considered how God originates creation in the first instance, and then reproduces it? This is indeed easy for God.

20. Say: "Go about on the earth and see how God originated creation. Then God will bring forth the other (second) creation (in the form of the Hereafter).[5] Surely God has full power over everything.

21. (He will bring forth the Hereafter, where) He punishes whom He wills and has mercy on whom He wills.[6] To Him you are being returned.

22. You cannot frustrate Him (in the execution of His Will even if you penetrate the depths) in the earth or in the heaven. And you have none to protect you, and none to help you, except God.[7]

23. Those who disbelieve in the signs of God (in the universe and in themselves) and His Revelations, and in the meeting with Him (in the Hereafter), they have no hope and expectation of a share in My Mercy. (God has forbidden them Paradise.) And for them there is a painful punishment.[8]

4. The pronoun used in the verse and translated as *those* is the pronoun used for living
beings. So this shows that, as in all the polytheistic societies, the idols or statutes usually
represented some beings whom people respected and then exalted and deified, such as angels, the jinn, Prophets, heroes, or statesmen.
The Prophet Abraham, upon him be peace,
meant both those beings represented by idols
and the idols themselves. Later generations began to forget the beings whose statutes were
made for deification, and rather came to deify
and worship the statutes themselves. However, besides some beings, people would person-
ify many powers or things, such as spirits and
"forces of nature," and attribute God's power
or acts to many false deities or adopt many deities, to each of which they would assign a Divine act or power. We should note that paganism or idol-worship has not ceased. It continues in many explicit or implicit forms.

5. For an explanation of this statement and
the statement, *God originates creation in the
first instance, and reproduces it*, in the previous verse, see 21: 104, note 25. While this verse
(20) is about the initial creation of the entire
universe and resurrection after death, the previous one must be the uninterrupted and ever-renewed process of creation (see 55: 29,
note 11) and the instances of death (in winter) and revival (in spring), which take place
every year.

6. This verse indicates God's absolute Will,
Justice and special Compassion, as explained
in several places (*sūrah* 4: 79, note 18; *sūrah*
15, note 17; *sūrah* 17: 54, note 23; *sūrah* 24: 38,
note 25).

7. This verse both awakens the fear of humankind in order to discourage them from rebellion against God and embraces them, calling
them to God by reminding that it is only God
Who can protect and help them in any case.

8. The verses 18–23 are implicit allusions to
the Makkan unbelievers and to all humankind
through Abraham's account. From here on, the
Qur'ān will proceed by relating Abraham's encounter with his people.

398   سُوْرَةُ العَنكَبُوْت   ٣٩٨

فَمَا كَانَ جَوَابَ قَوْمِهِ إِلَّا أَن قَالُوا اقْتُلُوهُ أَوْ
حَرِّقُوهُ فَأَنجَاهُ اللَّهُ مِنَ النَّارِ إِنَّ فِي ذَٰلِكَ لَآيَاتٍ لِّقَوْمٍ
يُؤْمِنُونَ ۝ وَقَالَ إِنَّمَا اتَّخَذْتُم مِّن دُونِ اللَّهِ أَوْثَانًا مَّوَدَّةَ
بَيْنِكُمْ فِي الْحَيَاةِ الدُّنْيَا ثُمَّ يَوْمَ الْقِيَامَةِ يَكْفُرُ بَعْضُكُم
بِبَعْضٍ وَيَلْعَنُ بَعْضُكُم بَعْضًا وَمَأْوَاكُمُ النَّارُ
وَمَا لَكُم مِّن نَّاصِرِينَ ۝ فَآمَنَ لَهُ لُوطٌ وَقَالَ
إِنِّي مُهَاجِرٌ إِلَىٰ رَبِّي إِنَّهُ هُوَ الْعَزِيزُ الْحَكِيمُ ۝
وَوَهَبْنَا لَهُ إِسْحَاقَ وَيَعْقُوبَ وَجَعَلْنَا فِي ذُرِّيَّتِهِ
النُّبُوَّةَ وَالْكِتَابَ وَآتَيْنَاهُ أَجْرَهُ فِي الدُّنْيَا وَإِنَّهُ
فِي الْآخِرَةِ لَمِنَ الصَّالِحِينَ ۝ وَلُوطًا إِذْ قَالَ لِقَوْمِهِ
إِنَّكُمْ لَتَأْتُونَ الْفَاحِشَةَ مَا سَبَقَكُم بِهَا مِنْ أَحَدٍ مِّنَ
الْعَالَمِينَ ۝ أَئِنَّكُمْ لَتَأْتُونَ الرِّجَالَ وَتَقْطَعُونَ السَّبِيلَ
وَتَأْتُونَ فِي نَادِيكُمُ الْمُنكَرَ فَمَا كَانَ جَوَابَ
قَوْمِهِ إِلَّا أَن قَالُوا ائْتِنَا بِعَذَابِ اللَّهِ إِن كُنتَ مِنَ
الصَّادِقِينَ ۝ قَالَ رَبِّ انصُرْنِي عَلَى الْقَوْمِ الْمُفْسِدِينَ ۝

―――――――⟨⟩―――――――

24. But the response of his (Abraham's) people was only to say: "Kill him, or burn him," but God saved him from the fire (that they kindled to burn him). Surely in this are signs (important lessons) for people who will believe and who will deepen in faith.

25. He (Abraham) said to them: "You have taken to yourselves idols to worship instead of God, for no other reason than to have a bond of love and attachment between you only in the life of this world. But then, on the Day of Resurrection you will deny one another (disowning any relation between you), and curse one another.[9] Your final refuge will be the Fire, and you will have no helpers.

26. Lot believed in him, and he (Abraham) said: "I am emigrating to my Lord (leaving my land and people for a place where I can practice my Religion). Surely, He is the All-Glorious with irresistible might (whomever He helps cannot be debased, and whomever He preserves does not fail), the All-Wise (in whatever He does and decrees there are many instances of wisdom).

27. We bestowed upon him (a son) Isaac and (a grandson) Jacob, and caused Prophethood and the revelation of the Book to continue among his offspring, and We granted him his reward in this world also;[10] and he surely is among the righteous in the Hereafter.

28. And Lot too (We sent as Messenger). He said (to his people in conveying this message): "Indeed you (the men of this whole community) commit an indecency such as no people in all the world have ever done before you.

29. (After such severe warnings of God) will you continue to come to men with lust, waylay (travelers) on the road (especially male travelers), and commit shameful deeds in your assemblies? The response of his people was only that they said (mocking and challenging him): "Bring down upon us the punishment of God with which you threaten us, if you are truthful!"

30. He (Lot) said (in supplication): "My Lord, help me against these people given to spreading corruption."

9. The disavowal mentioned in the verse is similar to that found in the verses: *No indeed! Those (whom they deified – beings such as angels, the jinn, Prophets, saints, and heroes, etc.) will deny their worship of them and turn against them as adversaries (on Judgment Day)* (19: 82).

At that time those who were followed (in the world as the elders, heads, or leaders and who were loved as God is loved), will disown those who followed them and declare themselves innocent of their evil deeds; they will see the punishment and that the relations between them are cut off (2: 166).

And the curse is like that which is mentioned in the verse: *He (God) says: "Enter in company with the communities of the jinn and humankind that went before you into the Fire!" Every time a community enters the Fire, it curses its fellow-community (that went before it) – so much so that, when they all have gathered there one after another, those who came later say of those who came earlier: "Our Lord! Those are the ones who led us astray: give them, therefore, double suffering through fire!" He (God) says: "For each is double (since those who went earlier both strayed themselves and led others astray, and those who came later both strayed themselves and imitated the others blindly), but you do not know." Then the preceding ones among them say to the succeeding ones: "You are in no wise superior to us, so taste the punishment for all (the sins) that you were busy earning (through your belief and deeds)!"* (7: 38–39)

10. God put the Prophet Abraham, upon him be peace, through tremendous tests, and he fulfilled them all, bearing many hardships purely for God's good pleasure. So God made him a leader for people and also appointed leaders among his offspring (2: 124). He absolutely purified his household (3: 33), and granted them (including the progeny of Ishmael proceeding from him, as well as that of Isaac) a mighty dominion in both the material and spiritual realm (4: 54). God also granted Abraham a good, blessed life in the world after his emigration for His sake (16: 122).

٣٩٩ · اَلْجُزْءُ الْعِشْرُوْنَ   399

وَلَمَّا جَآءَتْ رُسُلُنَآ اِبْرٰهِيمَ بِالْبُشْرٰى قَالُوٓا اِنَّا
مُهْلِكُوٓا اَهْلِ هٰذِهِ الْقَرْيَةِ اِنَّ اَهْلَهَا كَانُوا ظٰلِمِيْنَ ۝
قَالَ اِنَّ فِيْهَا لُوْطًا ۚ قَالُوْا نَحْنُ اَعْلَمُ بِمَنْ فِيْهَا ۖ
لَنُنَجِّيَنَّهٗ وَاَهْلَهٗٓ اِلَّا امْرَاَتَهٗ ۖ كَانَتْ مِنَ الْغٰبِرِيْنَ ۝
وَلَمَّآ اَنْ جَآءَتْ رُسُلُنَا لُوْطًا سِيْٓءَ بِهِمْ وَضَاقَ بِهِمْ
ذَرْعًا وَّقَالُوْا لَا تَخَفْ وَلَا تَحْزَنْ ۖ اِنَّا مُنَجُّوْكَ وَاَهْلَكَ
اِلَّا امْرَاَتَكَ ۖ كَانَتْ مِنَ الْغٰبِرِيْنَ ۝ اِنَّا مُنْزِلُوْنَ
عَلٰٓى اَهْلِ هٰذِهِ الْقَرْيَةِ رِجْزًا مِّنَ السَّمَآءِ بِمَا كَانُوْا
يَفْسُقُوْنَ ۝ وَلَقَدْ تَّرَكْنَا مِنْهَآ اٰيَةً بَيِّنَةً لِّقَوْمٍ
يَّعْقِلُوْنَ ۝ وَاِلٰى مَدْيَنَ اَخَاهُمْ شُعَيْبًا ۙ فَقَالَ يٰ
قَوْمِ اعْبُدُوا اللّٰهَ وَارْجُوا الْيَوْمَ الْاٰخِرَ وَلَا تَعْثَوْا فِي
الْاَرْضِ مُفْسِدِيْنَ ۝ فَكَذَّبُوْهُ فَاَخَذَتْهُمُ الرَّجْفَةُ
فَاَصْبَحُوْا فِيْ دَارِهِمْ جٰثِمِيْنَ ۝ وَعَادًا وَّثَمُوْدَا۟ وَقَدْ
تَّبَيَّنَ لَكُمْ مِّنْ مَّسٰكِنِهِمْ ۖ وَزَيَّنَ لَهُمُ الشَّيْطٰنُ
اَعْمَالَهُمْ فَصَدَّهُمْ عَنِ السَّبِيْلِ وَكَانُوْا مُسْتَبْصِرِيْنَ ۝

———❦———

31. And so, when Our (heavenly) envoys came to Abraham with the glad tidings (of the birth of Isaac),[11] they said to him: "We are going to destroy the people of that township. For its people are wrongdoers (who exceed all bounds in indecency)."

32. He said: "But Lot is there." They said: "We know very well who is there. We will certainly save him and his family (by allowing them to leave the place), except his wife, who (as has been decreed) is among those who will stay behind (and be destroyed)."

33. And when Our messengers came to Lot, he was troubled on their account and felt himself powerless to protect them. They said: "Do not be worried, nor be grieved. We are going to save you and your family except your wife who (as has been decreed) is among those who will stay behind (and be destroyed).

34. "We are going to bring down on the people of this township a scourge from the sky because they have persistently been transgressing (all bounds of decency and equity)."

35. Assuredly We have left behind a clear sign for a people who will reason and understand.

36. And to Midian We sent their brother Shu‘ayb (as Messenger), and he said (to them in conveying this message): "O my people! Worship God alone and be prepared for the Last Day (in certain expectation that you will be asked to account for all your deeds in the world), and do not go about acting wickedly in the land, causing disorder and corruption."

37. But they denied him, and in consequence a shocking catastrophe seized them, so that they lay prostrate (and lifeless) in their dwellings.

38. And the Ād and Thamūd – (their fate) is manifest to you from their dwellings (still lying in ruins). Satan decked out their (evil) deeds to be appealing to them, and so debarred them from the right way,[12] though they were intelligent (enough to see the truth).

---

11. See *sūrah* 11: 69–71.

12. Satan can only try to kindle an inclination to evil within a person's heart and to convince them that the deed to which they have been aroused is a good thing. He has no power to force a person to do something. A person follows his call out of their free will and under the influence of their carnal desires or material interests or because of arrogance or certain racial, ideological, or religious prejudices. A person's being able to see the truth is not usually enough for them to follow the truth, unless they are saved from the influence of such deviating factors.

400

وَقَارُونَ وَفِرْعَوْنَ وَهَامَانَ وَلَقَدْ جَاءَهُمْ مُّوسَى
بِالْبَيِّنَاتِ فَاسْتَكْبَرُوا فِى الْأَرْضِ وَمَا كَانُوا سَابِقِينَ ۞
فَكُلًّا أَخَذْنَا بِذَنبِهِ فَمِنْهُم مَّنْ أَرْسَلْنَا عَلَيْهِ حَاصِبًا
وَمِنْهُم مَّنْ أَخَذَتْهُ الصَّيْحَةُ وَمِنْهُم مَّنْ خَسَفْنَا بِهِ الْأَرْضَ
وَمِنْهُم مَّنْ أَغْرَقْنَا وَمَا كَانَ اللَّهُ لِيَظْلِمَهُمْ وَلَٰكِن
كَانُوا أَنفُسَهُمْ يَظْلِمُونَ ۞ مَثَلُ الَّذِينَ اتَّخَذُوا
مِن دُونِ اللَّهِ أَوْلِيَاءَ كَمَثَلِ الْعَنكَبُوتِ اتَّخَذَتْ
بَيْتًا وَإِنَّ أَوْهَنَ الْبُيُوتِ لَبَيْتُ الْعَنكَبُوتِ
لَوْ كَانُوا يَعْلَمُونَ ۞ إِنَّ اللَّهَ يَعْلَمُ مَا يَدْعُونَ
مِن دُونِهِ مِن شَيْءٍ وَهُوَ الْعَزِيزُ الْحَكِيمُ ۞ وَتِلْكَ
الْأَمْثَالُ نَضْرِبُهَا لِلنَّاسِ وَمَا يَعْقِلُهَا إِلَّا الْعَالِمُونَ
۞ خَلَقَ اللَّهُ السَّمَاوَاتِ وَالْأَرْضَ بِالْحَقِّ إِنَّ فِى ذَٰلِكَ
لَآيَةً لِّلْمُؤْمِنِينَ ۞ اتْلُ مَا أُوحِيَ إِلَيْكَ مِنَ الْكِتَابِ وَأَقِمِ
الصَّلَاةَ إِنَّ الصَّلَاةَ تَنْهَى عَنِ الْفَحْشَاءِ وَالْمُنكَرِ
وَلَذِكْرُ اللَّهِ أَكْبَرُ وَاللَّهُ يَعْلَمُ مَا تَصْنَعُونَ ۞

39. And Korah, Pharaoh, and Hāmān – indeed Moses came to them with clear proofs of the truth, but they were arrogant and oppressive in the land. Yet they could not outrun (Our punishment).

40. Each of them (of the communities mentioned) We seized in their sins. Of them are those upon whom We sent a hurricane (of stones), and of them are those whom the awful blast seized, and of them is him whom We caused to be swallowed by the earth, and of them those whom We caused to drown.[13] God would never wrong them, but it was they who wronged themselves.

41. The parable of those who take to them other than God for guardians (to entrust their affairs to) is like a spider: it has made for itself a house, and surely the frailest of houses is the spider's house.[14] If only they knew this!

42. God surely knows what they deify and invoke apart from Him and that their doing so is not based on any truth. He is the All-Glorious with irresistible might (Who never accepts any partner in Divinity, Lordship, and Sovereignty), the All-Wise (in Whose creation and rule there are many instances of wisdom).

43. Those parables – We strike them for people (so that they may see the truth and mend their ways). But none reasons to understand (their true meaning and purpose) save the knowledgeable.

44. He has created the heavens and the earth with truth (meaningfully and for definite, wise purposes, and on solid foundations of truth). Surely in this is a sign for the believers.[15]

45. Recite and convey to them what is revealed to you of the Book, and establish the Prayer in conformity with its conditions. Surely, the Prayer restrains from all that is indecent and shameful, and all that is evil. Surely God's remembrance is the greatest (of all types of worship and not restricted to the Prayer). God knows all that you do.

13. Those upon whom God sent a hurricane of stones were the tribe of Ād, who were destroyed in a sandstorm which lasted seven nights and eight days (7: 72; 11: 58; 23: 27; 26: 120; 69: 7), and the people of Lot, upon whom an evil rain of stones was sent (7: 84; 11: 82–83; 15: 73–74). Those whom the awful blast seized were the tribe of Thamūd (7: 78; 11: 67; 15: 83; 69: 6), and the peoples of Shu'ayb (7: 91; 11: 94; 26: 189). The one whom God caused to be swallowed by the earth was Korah (28: 81), and those whom God caused to drown were the people of Noah (7: 64; 11: 42–44) and Pharaoh, Hāmān, and their hosts (10: 90; 20: 77–78; 26: 65–66).

14. This comparison has, in fact, two meanings: (1) Whoever relies on something other than God is as if relying on or taking refuge in a spider's web. (2) A spider's web is formed of numerous fine threads, yet it easily catches weak creatures, such as flies; the unbelievers can easily hunt people who are as weak as a fly in spirit and will-power. The traps they build have many threads to catch their victims, such as addiction to comfort, love of position and money, lusts, ego-centeredness, racial prejudices, etc.

15. The Qur'ān reiterates that only those who believe or are disposed to believe can grasp the meaning and purposes in creation and God's signs in it. This is of great significance because of the following examples:

The value of the iron (or other material) from which a work of art is made differs from the value of the art expressed in it. The art's worth is far more than its material. An antique may fetch as much as a million dollars, while its material is not even worth a few cents. If taken to an antiques market, it may be sold for its true value, because of the skill involved and the fame of the artist. If taken to a blacksmith, it will only attain its scrap value.

Similarly, each person is a unique, priceless work of God Almighty's art. We are the most delicate and graceful miracles of His Power, beings created to manifest all His Names and inscriptions as unique specimen of the universe. If we are illuminated with faith, these meaningful inscriptions become visible. Believers manifest these inscriptions through their connection with their Maker, for the Divine art contained in each person is revealed through such affirmations as: "I am the work of the Majestic Maker, the creature and object of His Mercy and Munificence." As a result, and because we gain value in proportion to how well we reflect this art, we move from insignificance (in material terms) to beings ranked above all creatures. We address God, we are His guests on earth, and we are qualified for Paradise.

But if unbelief is ingrained in us, all of the Divine Names' manifestations are veiled by darkness and thus non-expressive. If the Artist is unknown, how can the aspects that express the value of His art be identified? Thus, the most meaningful instances of that sublime art and elevated inscription are concealed. In material terms, unbelievers attribute such art and inscription to trivial causes, nature, and chance, thereby reducing them to plain glass instead of sparkling diamonds. They are no more significant than any other material entity, self-condemned to a transient and suffocating life, and no better than the most impotent, needy, and afflicted animal that eventually will become dust. Unbelief thus spoils our nature by changing our diamond into coal.

Just as faith illuminates human beings and reveals all the messages inscribed in their being by the Eternally-Besought-of-All, it also illuminates the universe and removes darkness from the past and future. It displays all things and beings in their true worth coming from their connection with their Maker. But unbelief shows them only as physical entities moving toward eternal non-existence. (See *The Words*, "the 23rd Word," 328)

46. Do not argue with those who were given the Book save in the best way, unless it be those of them who are given to wrongdoing (and therefore not accessible to courteous argument).[16] Say (to them): "We believe in what has been sent down to us and what was sent down to you, and your God and our God is one and the same. We are Muslims wholly submitted to Him."

47. It is in this way (upon the principle of submission to God and as a confirmation of all the previous Books and Prophets) that We have sent down the Book to you. So those who were given the Book before (and are sincere with respect to the Divine Revelation) believe in it, and among those (people of Makkah, also) there are some who believe in it. None could oppose and reject Our Revelations except unbelievers (those who knowingly cover them with falsehood).

48. You did not (O Messenger) read of any book before it (the revelation of this Qur'ān), nor did you write one with your right (or left) hand. For then those who have ever sought to disprove the truth might have a reason to doubt (it).

49. It (the Qur'ān) is indeed self-evident, enlightening Revelations (revealed by God and so able to impress themselves) in the hearts of those endowed with knowledge. None oppose and reject them except wrongdoers (those who cannot determine with justice and so act arrogantly in response to them).

50. They say: "Why have no miraculous signs been sent down on him from his Lord?" Say: "The miraculous signs are but

at the Will and in the Power of only God. I am but a plain warner (with no freedom and power to be able to do whatever I wish)."

51. Is it not enough for them (as a miraculous sign) that We have sent down to you the Book which is recited to them? Surely in it there is great mercy and (instructive) reminder for a people who believe.

52. Say: "God suffices as a witness between me and you. He knows whatever is in the heavens and on the earth. As for those who believe in the falsehood and disbelieve in God (by rejecting His Revelation and Messenger), they are the losers (who have ruined themselves)."

---

16. This verse, which must have been revealed during the migration to Abyssinia, teaches Muslims how they should behave toward the People of the Book. In fact, this manner is the general way in which the Muslims must behave in their relationship with the followers of other faiths. They must convey Islam with gentle words and in a mild manner. If, however, those addressed show a harsh reaction, then the Muslims must avoid disputation with them (see 16: 125, note 29; 22: 67–68).

402   سُوۡرَةُ الۡعَنۡكَبُوۡتِ   ٩۰٢

وَيَسۡتَعۡجِلُوۡنَكَ بِالۡعَذَابِ وَلَوۡلَاۤ اَجَلٌ مُّسَمًّى لَّجَآءَهُمُ الۡعَذَابُ
وَلَيَاۡتِيَنَّهُمۡ بَغۡتَةً وَّهُمۡ لَا يَشۡعُرُوۡنَ ۞ يَسۡتَعۡجِلُوۡنَكَ بِالۡعَذَابِ
وَاِنَّ جَهَنَّمَ لَمُحِيۡطَةٌ بِالۡكٰفِرِيۡنَ ۞ يَوۡمَ يَغۡشٰىهُمُ الۡعَذَابُ
مِنۡ فَوۡقِهِمۡ وَمِنۡ تَحۡتِ اَرۡجُلِهِمۡ وَيَقُوۡلُ ذُوۡقُوۡا مَا كُنۡتُمۡ تَعۡمَلُوۡنَ
۞ يٰعِبَادِيَ الَّذِيۡنَ اٰمَنُوۤا اِنَّ اَرۡضِىۡ وَاسِعَةٌ فَاِيَّايَ فَاعۡبُدُوۡنِ
۞ كُلُّ نَفۡسٍ ذَآئِقَةُ الۡمَوۡتِ ثُمَّ اِلَيۡنَا تُرۡجَعُوۡنَ ۞ وَالَّذِيۡنَ
اٰمَنُوۡا وَعَمِلُوا الصّٰلِحٰتِ لَنُبَوِّئَنَّهُمۡ مِّنَ الۡجَنَّةِ غُرَفًا تَجۡرِىۡ مِنۡ تَحۡتِهَا
الۡاَنۡهٰرُ خٰلِدِيۡنَ فِيۡهَا ؕ نِعۡمَ اَجۡرُ الۡعٰمِلِيۡنَ ۞ الَّذِيۡنَ صَبَرُوۡا وَعَلٰى
رَبِّهِمۡ يَتَوَكَّلُوۡنَ ۞ وَكَاَيِّنۡ مِّنۡ دَآبَّةٍ لَّا تَحۡمِلُ رِزۡقَهَا
اللّٰهُ يَرۡزُقُهَا وَاِيَّاكُمۡ وَهُوَ السَّمِيۡعُ الۡعَلِيۡمُ ۞ وَلَئِنۡ سَاَلۡتَهُمۡ
مَّنۡ خَلَقَ السَّمٰوٰتِ وَالۡاَرۡضَ وَسَخَّرَ الشَّمۡسَ وَالۡقَمَرَ لَيَقُوۡلُنَّ
اللّٰهُ فَاَنّٰى يُؤۡفَكُوۡنَ ۞ اللّٰهُ يَبۡسُطُ الرِّزۡقَ لِمَنۡ يَّشَآءُ مِنۡ
عِبَادِهٖ وَيَقۡدِرُ لَهٗ ؕ اِنَّ اللّٰهَ بِكُلِّ شَىۡءٍ عَلِيۡمٌ ۞ وَلَئِنۡ سَاَلۡتَهُمۡ
مَّنۡ نَّزَّلَ مِنَ السَّمَآءِ مَآءً فَاَحۡيَا بِهِ الۡاَرۡضَ مِنۡ بَعۡدِ مَوۡتِهَا لَيَقُوۡلُنَّ
اللّٰهُ ؕ قُلِ الۡحَمۡدُ لِلّٰهِ ؕ بَلۡ اَكۡثَرُهُمۡ لَا يَعۡقِلُوۡنَ ۞

---∾---

53. They challenge you to hasten the punishment (with which they are threatened by God). Had it not been for the term appointed by God, the punishment would have come upon them (already).[17] And it will come upon them all of a sudden, when they are unaware.

54. They challenge you to hasten the punishment (with which they are threatened by God). Surely Hell will encompass the unbelievers (with the reasons for them to enter it,[18] and is bound to have them in it).

55. On that Day the suffering will overwhelm them from above them and from beneath their feet, and (God) will say to them: "Taste now what you used to do (in the world)!"

56. O My servants who believe (but are prevented from living according to your belief)! My earth is vast, so worship Me alone.[19]

57. Every soul is bound to taste death,[20] and then to Us you will be brought back.

58. Those who believe and do good, righteous deeds, We will most certainly lodge them in high, lofty mansions in Paradise through which rivers flow, therein to abide. How excellent is the reward of those who always do good deeds!

59. They are patient (in the face of the adversities they suffer for the sake of worshipping God only), and in their Lord they put their trust (expecting no support from any other power or authority).

60. How many a living creature there is that does not carry its own provision (in store), but God provides for them,[21] and indeed for you. He is the All-Hearing, the All-Knowing.[22]

61. If you ask them, "Who is it that has created the heavens and the earth, and made the sun and the moon subservient to His order (thereby sustaining life)?" they will most certainly say, "God." How then are they (who oppose this Revelation) turned away from the truth and make false claims?

62. God enlarges provision for whom He wills of His servants, and straitens it (for whom He wills). Surely God has full knowledge of everything.

63. If you ask them, "Who is it that sends down water from the sky, and revives with it the earth after its death?" they will most certainly say, "God." Say (you, also): "All praise and gratitude are for God." But most of them do not reason (to know the truth and distinguish it from falsehood).

17: For an explanation and similar verses, see 7: 34, note 10; 10: 98, note 20; 18: 58.

18. That is, unbelief and evil deeds are the reasons for entering Hell, and the unbelievers are bound to go into it. Secondly, as faith bears in itself the seed of Paradise, unbelief bears the seed of Hell and is in fact a manifestation of Hell in the heart of the unbelievers.

19. That is, you can search for and emigrate to another place where you can worship Me without associating any partners with Me.

20. For comment, see 21: 35, note 5.

21. For an explanation of God's providing for creatures, see 11: 6, note 1.

22. That is, you have no reason to fear for your sustenance when you emigrate to another land in order to be able to live according to your faith. There are many creatures that do not store up their provision for the future nor carry it with them. Just as God provides for them, He also provides for you and will continue to do so, because He hears all the petitions made to Him and knows all the needs of His creatures.

But when He brings them safe to land, see, they begin again to associate partners with God![25]

66. And so let them show ingratitude for all that We have granted them, and so let them give themselves up to the enjoyment of the worldly life; but they will come to know.

67. Do they not consider that We have established (them in) a secure sanctuary while people are ravaged all around them? (How then) do they believe in falsehood and (show such ingratitude as) to disbelieve in God's greatest blessing (of the Qur'ān and Islam)?

68. Who is more in the wrong than he who fabricates falsehood in attribution to God or denies the truth when it has come to him? Is there not a dwelling in Hell for the unbelievers?!

69. Those (on the other hand) who strive hard for Our sake, We will most certainly guide them to Our ways (that We have established to lead them to salvation). Most assuredly, God is with those devoted to doing good, aware that God is seeing them.

64. The present, worldly life is nothing but a pastime and play,[23] but the abode of the Hereafter is truly alive.[24] If they but knew.

65. When they embark on a ship (and find themselves in danger), they call upon God sincerely believing in Him alone (as the only Deity, Lord, and Sovereign).

---

23. For more on "the present, worldly life," see 6, note 5.

24. For the liveliness of the abode of the Hereafter, see 25: 12, note 4.

25. This reality is not only restricted to when one encounters a danger in the sea. The danger at sea is a metaphor used for perilous conditions one finds oneself in. Almost everyone

experiences this several times in their life. In such conditions people, whether they be atheists, agnostics, or polytheists, discover God in the depth of their conscience, and call upon God only, without even remembering other so-called deities or powers. So their denial of God or associating partners with Him is the denial of their inner profession of God and implies self-contradiction.

SŪRAH 30

AR-RŪM
(THE BYZANTINE ROMANS)

Makkah period

This *sūrah* of 60 verses was revealed about six or seven years before the *Hijrah*. It takes its name from the Byzantine Romans mentioned in the second verse. The Byzantines were Christians who had a Divine Scripture and who believed in God without worshipping idols. This is why the Muslims in Makkah felt close to them, while the pagan Quraysh sympathized with the Persians, who they thought would vindicate their opposition to belief in One God. At a time when the Muslims were a very small minority subject to persecution in Makkah, this *sūrah* consoled them by predicting the unexpected victory of the Romans against the Persians only nine years after a great defeat. Through this prediction, the *sūrah* also implies the future victory of the Muslims, which was soon to occur. In addition, this *sūrah* puts forward a multitude of evidence in favor of faith in One God and the Hereafter and against associating partners with Him.

In the Name of God, the All-Merciful, the All-Compassionate.

1. *Alif. Lām. Mīm.*

2. The Byzantine Romans have been defeated,

3. In the lands close-by, but they, after their defeat, will be victorious

4. Within a few (nine) years – to God belongs the command (the absolute judgment and authority) both before and after (any event) – and at the time (when the Romans are victorious), the believers will rejoice,

5. Because of God's help leading them to victory. He helps whom He wills to victory. He is the All-Glorious with irresistible might, the All-Compassionate (especially towards His believing servants).

404 سُورَةُ الرُّومِ ٤٠٤

وَعْدَ اللَّهِ لَا يُخْلِفُ اللَّهُ وَعْدَهُ وَلَٰكِنَّ أَكْثَرَ النَّاسِ
لَا يَعْلَمُونَ ۝ يَعْلَمُونَ ظَاهِرًا مِّنَ الْحَيَوٰةِ الدُّنْيَا وَهُمْ عَنِ
الْآخِرَةِ هُمْ غَافِلُونَ ۝ أَوَلَمْ يَتَفَكَّرُوا فِي أَنفُسِهِم مَّا
خَلَقَ اللَّهُ السَّمَوَٰتِ وَالْأَرْضَ وَمَا بَيْنَهُمَا إِلَّا بِالْحَقِّ وَأَجَلٍ مُّسَمًّى
وَإِنَّ كَثِيرًا مِّنَ النَّاسِ بِلِقَآئِ رَبِّهِمْ لَكَافِرُونَ ۝ أَوَلَمْ يَسِيرُوا فِي
الْأَرْضِ فَيَنظُرُوا كَيْفَ كَانَ عَاقِبَةُ الَّذِينَ مِن قَبْلِهِمْ
كَانُوا أَشَدَّ مِنْهُمْ قُوَّةً وَأَثَارُوا الْأَرْضَ وَعَمَرُوهَا أَكْثَرَ
مِمَّا عَمَرُوهَا وَجَآءَتْهُمْ رُسُلُهُم بِالْبَيِّنَاتِ فَمَا كَانَ اللَّهُ
لِيَظْلِمَهُمْ وَلَٰكِن كَانُوا أَنفُسَهُمْ يَظْلِمُونَ ۝ ثُمَّ
كَانَ عَاقِبَةَ الَّذِينَ أَسَاءُوا السُّوأَىٰ أَن كَذَّبُوا بِآيَاتِ اللَّهِ
وَكَانُوا بِهَا يَسْتَهْزِئُونَ ۝ اللَّهُ يَبْدَؤُا الْخَلْقَ ثُمَّ يُعِيدُهُ ثُمَّ
إِلَيْهِ تُرْجَعُونَ ۝ وَيَوْمَ تَقُومُ السَّاعَةُ يُبْلِسُ الْمُجْرِمُونَ ۝ وَلَمْ
يَكُن لَّهُم مِّن شُرَكَائِهِمْ شُفَعَاءُ وَكَانُوا بِشُرَكَائِهِمْ كَافِرِينَ
۝ وَيَوْمَ تَقُومُ السَّاعَةُ يَوْمَئِذٍ يَتَفَرَّقُونَ ۝ فَأَمَّا الَّذِينَ
آمَنُوا وَعَمِلُوا الصَّالِحَاتِ فَهُمْ فِي رَوْضَةٍ يُحْبَرُونَ ۝

───◈───

6. (This is) God's promise. God never fails His promise, but most people do not know this (as they have no true knowledge about God).[1]

7. They only know (what reaches to their senses from) the outward aspect of the life of this world, but they are heedless and unaware of (what lies beyond it and) the Hereafter.

8. Do they not reflect upon themselves (even once)? God has not created the heavens and the earth and all that is between them save with truth (meaningfully and for definite, wise purposes, and on solid foundations of truth), and for an appointed term. But surely many among the people are in unbelief about the meeting with their Lord.

9. Have they never traveled about the earth and seen what was the outcome for those before them (who also obstinately disbelieved in Our signs)? They were greater than them in power. They cultivated the soil and mined it (for minerals and water resources), and built it up more and better than these have done. And in time their Messengers came to them with clear proofs of the truth (which they rejected to their own doom). God would never wrong them, but it was they themselves who were wronging themselves.

10. In consequence, the outcome for those who were lost in evil was evil, as they denied God's Revelations and signs, and were mocking them.

11. God originates creation in the first instance, and then reproduces it,[2] (and will bring it back in the Hereafter), and then you will be returned to Him.

12. When the Last Hour stands forth and the Judgment is established, the disbelieving criminals will be plunged into despair.

13. They will have no intercessors in the beings whom they associate (as partners with God), and they will no longer believe in their being partners with God.

14. When the Last Hour stands forth (and the Judgment is established) – on that Day all people will be separated from one another.

15. As for those who believe and do good, righteous deeds, they will be honored and made happy in a delightful Garden.

1. These verses contain important predictions. Some saintly scholars have arrived at many predictions based on these. For example, as reported by Abū Ḥayyān, a commentator from al-Andalusia, in his *Baḥr al-Muḥīṭ*, Abū al-Ḥakam ibn al-Barrajān predicted the recovery of Jerusalem by the Muslims from the Crusaders in 1187 with its exact date. However, what is clear to everybody in these verses is that the Byzantine Romans who were defeated by the Persians would be victorious over them within nine years and in the same year, the Muslims would rejoice because of the victory which would be granted to them by God (Yazır, 6: 3802–3803).

In 615, when some Muslims were forced, by the persecution that they faced in Makkah, to migrate to Abyssinia the Persians gained a victory over the Romans in the war that had begun in 613. The victory was so great that the total destruction of the Byzantine Empire seemed imminent. The *sūrah* decisively pronouced that within nine years from that time, the Romans would defeat the Persians. The war continued and the Persians advanced as far as Constantinople (present-day Istanbul), the capital of the Byzantines, in 617. No one thought that the Byzantines would be able to turn defeat into victory so soon in the future; when these verses were revealed, the pagan Makkans made fun of them and of the Muslims for believing in them.

However, in 622, just nine years after the beginning of this war, the tide began to turn in favor of the Byzantines. In that year, God's Messenger also emigrated to Madīnah. In 624, again nine years after the decisive victory of the Persians, the Byzantines gained the first victory over them and destroyed the birthplace of Zoroaster in Azerbaijan. It was in this year also that the Muslims were victorious in the Battle of Badr against the polytheist Makkans. When the Byzantines completely routed the Persians in 627, the Muslims won the Battle of the Trench, and the next year they signed the treaty of Hudaybiyah, which the Qur'an describes as a manifest victory (48: 1); this proved to be a door opening to the free expansion of Islam. This same year witnessed the imprisonment and death of the Persian king, and the Messenger's entering Makkah for a minor pilgrimage.

2. For God's origination of creation and then bringing it forth anew or reproducing it, see 21: 104, note 25; 55: 29, note 11. Also see 29: 19–20, note 5.

الجزء الحادى والعشرون   405

وَأَمَّا الَّذِينَ كَفَرُوا وَكَذَّبُوا بِآيَاتِنَا وَلِقَآئِ الْآخِرَةِ
فَأُوْلَٰئِكَ فِي الْعَذَابِ مُحْضَرُونَ ۝ فَسُبْحَانَ اللَّهِ حِينَ تُمْسُونَ
وَحِينَ تُصْبِحُونَ ۝ وَلَهُ الْحَمْدُ فِي السَّمَوَاتِ وَالْأَرْضِ وَعَشِيًّا
وَحِينَ تُظْهِرُونَ ۝ يُخْرِجُ الْحَيَّ مِنَ الْمَيِّتِ وَيُخْرِجُ الْمَيِّتَ
مِنَ الْحَيِّ وَيُحْيِ الْأَرْضَ بَعْدَ مَوْتِهَا وَكَذَٰلِكَ تُخْرَجُونَ
۝ وَمِنْ آيَاتِهِ أَنْ خَلَقَكُم مِّن تُرَابٍ ثُمَّ إِذَا أَنتُم
بَشَرٌ تَنتَشِرُونَ ۝ وَمِنْ آيَاتِهِ أَنْ خَلَقَ لَكُم مِّنْ
أَنفُسِكُمْ أَزْوَاجًا لِّتَسْكُنُوا إِلَيْهَا وَجَعَلَ بَيْنَكُم
مَّوَدَّةً وَرَحْمَةً ۚ إِنَّ فِي ذَٰلِكَ لَآيَاتٍ لِّقَوْمٍ يَتَفَكَّرُونَ
۝ وَمِنْ آيَاتِهِ خَلْقُ السَّمَوَاتِ وَالْأَرْضِ وَاخْتِلَافُ أَلْسِنَتِكُمْ
وَأَلْوَانِكُمْ ۚ إِنَّ فِي ذَٰلِكَ لَآيَاتٍ لِّلْعَالِمِينَ ۝ وَمِنْ آيَاتِهِ
مَنَامُكُم بِاللَّيْلِ وَالنَّهَارِ وَابْتِغَاؤُكُم مِّن فَضْلِهِ ۚ إِنَّ فِي ذَٰلِكَ لَآيَاتٍ
لِّقَوْمٍ يَسْمَعُونَ ۝ وَمِنْ آيَاتِهِ يُرِيكُمُ الْبَرْقَ خَوْفًا
وَطَمَعًا وَيُنَزِّلُ مِنَ السَّمَاءِ مَاءً فَيُحْيِ بِهِ الْأَرْضَ
بَعْدَ مَوْتِهَا ۚ إِنَّ فِي ذَٰلِكَ لَآيَاتٍ لِّقَوْمٍ يَعْقِلُونَ ۝

---

have grown into a human population scattered widely.

21. And among His signs is that He has created for you, from your selves, mates, that you may incline towards them and find rest in them, and He has engendered love and tenderness between you. Surely in this are signs for people who reflect.

22. And among His signs is the creation of the heavens and the earth, and the diversity of your languages and colors. Surely in this are signs indeed for people who have knowledge (of the facts in creation and who are free of prejudices).

23. And among His signs is your sleeping at night and in the day, and your seeking (livelihoods) out of His bounty. Surely in this are signs for people who listen (to the God's messages in creation and His provision for all creatures).

24. And among His signs is His displaying before you the lightning, giving rise to both fear (of being struck) and hopeful expectation (of rain), and that He sends down water from the sky, and revives with it the earth after its death. Surely in this are signs for people who will reason and understand.

16. But those who disbelieve and deny Our Revelations and the final meeting (with Us) in the Hereafter, such will be arraigned for punishment (in Hell).

17. So glorify God when you enter the evening and when you enter the morning;

18. – And (proclaim that) all praise and gratitude in the heavens and on the earth are for Him – and in the afternoon and when you enter the noon time.[3]

19. He brings forth the living out of the dead, and brings the dead out of the living, and revives the earth after its death. It is in the way (that He revives the dead earth that) you will be brought forth from the dead.[4]

20. And among His signs is that He created you from earth, and (since) then you

3. Although glorifying God or proclaiming His being absolutely free of any defects or having partners is not restricted to certain times, most commentators suggest that these two last verses specify the times of the daily Prayers. For the meaning of these times and their specification, see 17: 78–79, notes 33–34.

Glorification is knowing and declaring God to be above having any attributes that are never fit for Him such as having defects, partners, begetting or being begotten, and union (i.e. with any creature) and incarnation (i.e. taking any form of presentation or representation of Himself). Praising Him means knowing and declaring Him with the Attributes belonging and fitting for Him, and thanking Him.

It is God Who has created the heavens and the earth and all that is in and between them, and Who has put many things in them at the service of humankind; all praise and thanks are due to Him. Moreover, all that is in the heavens and on the earth praises and gives thanks to Him, each in its own language or the tongue of its disposition.

4. This verse, which mentions concrete events in nature, also implies that God sometimes bring up a believer born into an unbelieving family and an unbeliever born into a believing family, and that He may finally cause a believer to apostatize because of their sins, and an unbeliever to enter the fold of Islam purely out of His grace or due to some of that person's good acts. While mentioning God's raising of the dead as analogous to reviving the dead earth, it also suggests that God's reviving a disbelieving "dead" person (6: 122) is analogous to His reviving the dead earth. For such implied analogies in the Qur'an, see 7: 55–58, note 14.

406   سورة الروم   ٤٠٦

وَمِنْ ءَايَٰتِهِۦٓ أَن تَقُومَ ٱلسَّمَآءُ وَٱلْأَرْضُ بِأَمْرِهِۦ ثُمَّ إِذَا دَعَاكُمْ
دَعْوَةً مِّنَ ٱلْأَرْضِ إِذَآ أَنتُمْ تَخْرُجُونَ ۝ وَلَهُۥ مَن فِى ٱلسَّمَٰوَٰتِ
وَٱلْأَرْضِ كُلٌّ لَّهُۥ قَٰنِتُونَ ۝ وَهُوَ ٱلَّذِى يَبْدَؤُا۟ ٱلْخَلْقَ ثُمَّ
يُعِيدُهُۥ وَهُوَ أَهْوَنُ عَلَيْهِ وَلَهُ ٱلْمَثَلُ ٱلْأَعْلَىٰ فِى ٱلسَّمَٰوَٰتِ
وَٱلْأَرْضِ وَهُوَ ٱلْعَزِيزُ ٱلْحَكِيمُ ۝ ضَرَبَ لَكُم مَّثَلًا مِّنْ
أَنفُسِكُمْ هَل لَّكُم مِّن مَّا مَلَكَتْ أَيْمَٰنُكُم مِّن شُرَكَآءَ
فِى مَا رَزَقْنَٰكُمْ فَأَنتُمْ فِيهِ سَوَآءٌ تَخَافُونَهُمْ كَخِيفَتِكُمْ
أَنفُسَكُمْ كَذَٰلِكَ نُفَصِّلُ ٱلْأَيَٰتِ لِقَوْمٍ يَعْقِلُونَ ۝ بَلِ ٱتَّبَعَ
ٱلَّذِينَ ظَلَمُوٓا۟ أَهْوَآءَهُم بِغَيْرِ عِلْمٍ فَمَن يَهْدِى مَنْ أَضَلَّ
ٱللَّهُ وَمَا لَهُم مِّن نَّٰصِرِينَ ۝ فَأَقِمْ وَجْهَكَ لِلدِّينِ حَنِيفًا فِطْرَتَ
ٱللَّهِ ٱلَّتِى فَطَرَ ٱلنَّاسَ عَلَيْهَا لَا تَبْدِيلَ لِخَلْقِ
ٱللَّهِ ذَٰلِكَ ٱلدِّينُ ٱلْقَيِّمُ وَلَٰكِنَّ أَكْثَرَ ٱلنَّاسِ
لَا يَعْلَمُونَ ۝ مُنِيبِينَ إِلَيْهِ وَٱتَّقُوهُ وَأَقِيمُوا۟ ٱلصَّلَوٰةَ
وَلَا تَكُونُوا۟ مِنَ ٱلْمُشْرِكِينَ ۝ مِنَ ٱلَّذِينَ فَرَّقُوا۟ دِينَهُمْ
وَكَانُوا۟ شِيَعًا كُلُّ حِزْبٍ بِمَا لَدَيْهِمْ فَرِحُونَ ۝

--- ❧ ---

25. And among His signs is that the heaven and the earth stand firm (subsisting) by His Command.[5] In the end, when He calls you forth from the earth (with a single, particular summons), then (at once) you will come forth.

26. To Him belongs all that is in the heavens and on the earth. All are obedient to Him in humble service.[6]

27. He it is Who originates creation in the first instance and then reproduces it (in the world) and will bring it back (in the Hereafter): and that (reproduction and bringing back) is easier for Him.[7] Whatever attribute of sublimity there is (like existence, life, power, knowledge, munificence, and might, etc.) in the heavens and the earth, it is His in the highest degree, and He is the All-Glorious with irresistible might, the All-Wise.

28. He strikes a parable from your selves: Do you recognize for those, over whom you hold possession and authority (slaves or animals), a share in what We have provided for you, so that you and they have equal shares in it, and do you hold them in fearful respect as you hold each other in fearful respect?[8] Thus We set out in detail the signs (of Our Oneness) for people who will reason and understand.

29. No indeed! Those who do (the greatest) wrong (by associating partners with God) follow only their own desires and caprices, without (basing on any) knowledge. Who has power to guide him whom God has led astray (on account of following merely his lusts and fancies)? And such have none to help them (to salvation).

30. So set your whole being upon the Religion (of Islam) as one of pure faith (free from unbelief, polytheism, and hypocrisy). This is the original pattern belonging to God on which He has originated humankind. No change can there be in God's creation. This is the upright, ever-true Religion, but most of the people do not know.[9]

31. (Set your whole being, you and the believers in your company, on the upright, ever-true Religion) turning in devotion to Him alone, and keep from disobedience to Him in reverence for Him and piety, and establish the Prayer in conformity with its conditions; and do not be of those who associate partners (with Him),

32. Those who have made divisions in their religion (whereas they must accept it in its totality), and become split into different factions (following different guides to falsehood), each party rejoicing in what (portion) it has.

5. God is the All-Powerful Being Who can do whatever He wills by a mere command of "Be!" However, in the corporeal realm He acts from behind the veil of cause and effect or regular patterns of events – that is, His exercise of His decrees or will in the corporeal realm gives rise in our minds to some notions that we call "natural laws." So, this statement means that the heaven and earth stand firm and subsist by the laws issuing from the pure realm of His commands that originate from His Attributes of Power and Will.

6. On the obedience of all beings to God, see 3: 83, note 16.

7. Everything is equally easy for God. So the use of *easier* in the verse is in the view of, or according to, the understanding and perception of human beings. Reproduction or bringing something back is certainly easier than the original creation. So, this verse addresses those who see the final destruction of the world and its re-building as impossible, and means that if one can invent or originate something, one can reproduce it even more easily. Therefore, destroying the world and re-creating it can in no way be difficult for God, Who originated it.

8. This comparison is highly significant. Basically, whatever we possess belongs to God, and our share in its acquisition is minimal. For example, in order to produce a single apple, there must be an apple seed, which the whole human-kind would not be able to make even if they were to come together, and almost the whole universe (including the sun, air, water, and earth) must cooperate in a perfectly measured way. None of these are in our power to create or control. Our share in an apple is only our labor that we use to produce it and it is God Who has endowed us with the necessary power, ability, and with our body. Our share in any machine we make is no greater than this. The basic material we use in making it and its utility in production or manufacture, as well as the physical and/or chemical "laws" that are involved in its production, belong solely to God. Moreover, it is He Who has endowed us with the ability to learn and to make things. Despite this clear fact, we never accept that others have some share in our right to possession and use of such machine or instruments. But God is the sole Creator and Owner of everything in the universe including us, without anyone else having any partnership in their creation or ownership. However, by accepting many other powers, such as angels, or some important persons, or "nature," or "natural powers and laws," or even their own selves, many people associate partners with Him in Divinity or authority regarding the rule of the universe and the ordering of human life. This is the greatest of wrongdoings, injustices, and expressions of ignorance.

9. For an explanation of this verse, see Appendix 13.

وَإِذَا مَسَّ النَّاسَ ضُرٌّ دَعَوْا رَبَّهُم مُّنِيبِينَ إِلَيْهِ ثُمَّ إِذَآ أَذَاقَهُم مِّنْهُ رَحْمَةً إِذَا فَرِيقٌ مِّنْهُم بِرَبِّهِمْ يُشْرِكُونَ ۝ لِيَكْفُرُوا بِمَآ ءَاتَيْنَاهُمْ فَتَمَتَّعُوا فَسَوْفَ تَعْلَمُونَ ۝ أَمْ أَنزَلْنَا عَلَيْهِمْ سُلْطَانًا فَهُوَ يَتَكَلَّمُ بِمَا كَانُوا بِهِ يُشْرِكُونَ ۝ وَإِذَآ أَذَقْنَا النَّاسَ رَحْمَةً فَرِحُوا بِهَا وَإِن تُصِبْهُمْ سَيِّئَةٌ بِمَا قَدَّمَتْ أَيْدِيهِمْ إِذَا هُمْ يَقْنَطُونَ ۝ أَوَلَمْ يَرَوْا أَنَّ اللَّهَ يَبْسُطُ الرِّزْقَ لِمَن يَشَاءُ وَيَقْدِرُ إِنَّ فِي ذَلِكَ لَآيَاتٍ لِّقَوْمٍ يُؤْمِنُونَ ۝ فَـَٔاتِ ذَا الْقُرْبَى حَقَّهُ وَالْمِسْكِينَ وَابْنَ السَّبِيلِ ذَلِكَ خَيْرٌ لِّلَّذِينَ يُرِيدُونَ وَجْهَ اللَّهِ وَأُوْلَٰٓئِكَ هُمُ الْمُفْلِحُونَ ۝ وَمَآ ءَاتَيْتُم مِّن رِّبًا لِّيَرْبُوَا۟ فِيٓ أَمْوَالِ النَّاسِ فَلَا يَرْبُوا عِندَ اللَّهِ وَمَآ ءَاتَيْتُم مِّن زَكَاةٍ تُرِيدُونَ وَجْهَ اللَّهِ فَأُوْلَٰٓئِكَ هُمُ الْمُضْعِفُونَ ۝ اللَّهُ الَّذِي خَلَقَكُمْ ثُمَّ رَزَقَكُمْ ثُمَّ يُمِيتُكُمْ ثُمَّ يُحْيِيكُمْ هَلْ مِن شُرَكَآئِكُم مَّن يَفْعَلُ مِن ذَٰلِكُم مِّن شَيْءٍ سُبْحَانَهُ وَتَعَالَى عَمَّا يُشْرِكُونَ ۝ ظَهَرَ الْفَسَادُ فِي الْبَرِّ وَالْبَحْرِ بِمَا كَسَبَتْ أَيْدِي النَّاسِ لِيُذِيقَهُم بَعْضَ الَّذِي عَمِلُوا لَعَلَّهُمْ يَرْجِعُونَ ۝

---

33. When affliction befalls people, they invoke their Lord turning to Him in contrition; then, no sooner does He favor them with a taste of mercy from Him than some of them associate partners with their Lord, (Who has created them, and sustains and cares for them).

34. Thus (do they behave) with disbelieving ingratitude for all that We have granted them. Then: Enjoy (for a while the worldly favors He has granted you), but in time you will come to know!

35. Or have We sent down on them a document of authority which speaks in favor of their associating partners with Him?

36. When We favor people with a taste of mercy, they rejoice in it (without thinking of Him Who bestows it). But if an evil befalls them because of what they themselves have committed, look how they lose all hope!

37. Have they never considered that God enlarges provision for whom He wills, and straitens it (for whom He wills). Surely in this are signs for people who will believe and who will deepen in faith.

38. And so give their due[10] to relatives, as well as to the destitute and the wayfarer. That is best for those who seek God's "Face" (His approval and good pleasure); and those are they who are the prosperous.

39. Whatever you give to people in usurious hope that it may return to you increased through the goods of (other) people, will bring no increase in God's sight. Whereas whatever you give in charity seeking God's "Face" (His approval and good pleasure) – for those there is increase (of recompense) multiplied.[11]

40. God is He Who creates you, then He sustains you (by providing for you), and then He causes you to die and then He will bring you to life again. Are there any among the partners you associate (with God) that do anything of that? All-Glorified He is, and infinitely Exalted above what they associate (with Him).

41. Corruption and disorder have appeared on land and in the sea because of what the hands of people have (done and) earned (of evil deeds). Thus He causes them to taste the consequence of some of what they have done, so that they may (take heed, repent and reform, and so) return (to the right way).[12]

10. It is highly significant that the Qur'ān uses the word "their due" for the portion one must give to the needy out of one's wealth. It means that since it is God Who provides for everybody, the portion the wealthy must give to the needy essentially belongs to the needy. God gives this portion to the wealthy for the poor; by ordering the wealthy to give, He both opens a door through which they can earn merits for their eternal life and establishes a bridge between people in the society, thus creating means of mutual assistance and solidarity. So whoever does not give to the needy the portion they should give has usurped their due.

11. Islam never aims to favor hypocrisy and hypocrites. So before establishing a law, first it trains and prepares hearts and minds in its favor or against it. This is why the Prophet's Companions could easily accept any commandment when it was revealed. To this end, Islam followed a gradual way in establishing its legal code. In Makkah, it prepared hearts and minds for its future injunctions. For example, in 17: 22–39, it propounded many rules only as moral values; many of these would later become laws in Madīnah. It also followed a gradual way in prohibiting such established vices as drinking alcohol and transactions involving interest. This verse is the first to be revealed on the way to the decisive prohibition of transactions involving interest, with the aim of encouraging Muslims to avoid it. Some people would give gifts or similar things to others, particularly the merchants and money-lenders; this was not done with a pure intention, but with the hope or aim that it might come back to them, increased in value. That is, those who took these "gifts" would use them in their trade for profitable transactions, and return the "gifts" with the extra amount or value to the original owner.

12. All the social convulsions and evils, unjust wars, pestilences, environmental pollution, and similar catastrophes arise from human rebellion against God and His Religion. God has established human life on the fact that this human rebellion causes such calamities. The basic wisdom behind this is that humankind will be awakened to the truth and, giving up their wrong ways, turn to God in faith and obedience. But, unfortunately, the number of people who perceive this is quite limited. Especially scientific materialism and materialist philosophy make this perception almost impossible and refer every such thing to "nature" and self-becoming.

408   سُورَةُ الرُّومِ   ٤٠٨

قُل سِيرُوا فِى الأَرْضِ فَانظُرُوا كَيْفَ كَانَ عَاقِبَةُ الَّذِينَ مِن قَبْلُ كَانَ أَكْثَرُهُم مُّشْرِكِينَ ۞ فَأَقِمْ وَجْهَكَ لِلدِّينِ الْقَيِّمِ مِن قَبْلِ أَن يَأْتِىَ يَوْمٌ لَّا مَرَدَّ لَهُ مِنَ اللَّهِ يَوْمَئِذٍ يَصَّدَّعُونَ ۞ مَن كَفَرَ فَعَلَيْهِ كُفْرُهُ وَمَنْ عَمِلَ صَالِحاً فَلِأَنفُسِهِمْ يَمْهَدُونَ ۞ لِيَجْزِىَ الَّذِينَ آمَنُوا وَعَمِلُوا الصَّالِحَاتِ مِن فَضْلِهِ إِنَّهُ لَا يُحِبُّ الْكَافِرِينَ ۞ وَمِنْ آيَاتِهِ أَن يُرْسِلَ الرِّيَاحَ مُبَشِّرَاتٍ وَلِيُذِيقَكُم مِّن رَّحْمَتِهِ وَلِتَجْرِىَ الْفُلْكُ بِأَمْرِهِ وَلِتَبْتَغُوا مِن فَضْلِهِ وَلَعَلَّكُمْ تَشْكُرُونَ ۞ وَلَقَدْ أَرْسَلْنَا مِن قَبْلِكَ رُسُلاً إِلَى قَوْمِهِمْ فَجَاؤُوهُم بِالْبَيِّنَاتِ فَانتَقَمْنَا مِنَ الَّذِينَ أَجْرَمُوا وَكَانَ حَقّاً عَلَيْنَا نَصْرُ الْمُؤْمِنِينَ ۞ اللَّهُ الَّذِى يُرْسِلُ الرِّيَاحَ فَتُثِيرُ سَحَاباً فَيَبْسُطُهُ فِى السَّمَاءِ كَيْفَ يَشَاءُ وَيَجْعَلُهُ كِسَفاً فَتَرَى الْوَدْقَ يَخْرُجُ مِنْ خِلَالِهِ فَإِذَا أَصَابَ بِهِ مَن يَشَاءُ مِنْ عِبَادِهِ إِذَا هُمْ يَسْتَبْشِرُونَ ۞ وَإِن كَانُوا مِن قَبْلِ أَن يُنَزَّلَ عَلَيْهِم مِّن قَبْلِهِ لَمُبْلِسِينَ ۞ فَانظُرْ إِلَى آثَارِ رَحْمَتِ اللَّهِ كَيْفَ يُحْيِى الْأَرْضَ بَعْدَ مَوْتِهَا إِنَّ ذَلِكَ لَمُحْيِ الْمَوْتَى وَهُوَ عَلَى كُلِّ شَيْءٍ قَدِيرٌ ۞

---

of His bounty. He does not love the unbelievers.

46. Among His signs is that He sends forth the merciful winds as glad tidings so that He may favor you with a taste of His mercy, and that ships may sail by His command (according to the laws He has established), and that you may seek of His bounty, and that (in recognition of all these favors of His) you may give thanks (to Him).

47. Indeed We sent before you (O Messenger, other) Messengers each to his own people, and they came to them with clear proofs (of the truth of God's Unity and Sovereignty). Then, We took retribution from those who disbelieved and were committed to accumulating sins. We have bound Ourselves to rescue the believers.

48. God is He Who sends forth the merciful winds, so that they set clouds to move, and He spreads them in the heaven in the manner that He wills, and makes them aggregated particles, and there! you see rain issuing from their midst. When He has caused it to fall on such of His servants as He wills, they rejoice,

49. Even though a short while before, just before it was sent down upon them, they had been in despair.

50. Look, then, at the imprints of God's Mercy – how He revives the dead earth after its death: certainly then it is He Who will revive the dead (in a similar way). He has full power over everything.[13]

42. Say: "Travel about on the earth and see what was the outcome for those who lived before you. Most of them were (obstinately given to) associating partners (with God)."

43. Set, then, your whole being on the upright, ever-true Religion before there comes a Day which God will not remove (from them) and none can prevent Him from bringing it. On that Day they will be sundered apart.

44. Whoever disbelieves, his unbelief is charged against him. Whereas those who (believe and) do good, righteous deeds, they make provision for themselves (of a happy, everlasting life),

45. That He (God) will reward those who believe and do good, righteous deeds out

13. The Qur'ān puts forward various arguments concerning the Resurrection. For example, to impress upon the human heart the wonder of what the Almighty will accomplish in the Hereafter, and to prepare the human mind to accept and understand it, the Qur'ān presents the wonder of what He accomplishes here in the world. It gives examples of God's comprehensive acts in the macro-cosmos and, at times, presents His overall disposal of the macro-, normo-, and micro-cosmoses (the universe, humanity, and atoms, respectively). Verse 13: 2 is an example of this.

The Qur'ān presents the phenomenon of the universe's creation, which it defines as the first origination (56: 62), while describing the raising of the dead as the second origination (53: 47) to establish the Resurrection. It also directs our attention to our own origin for this same end (22: 5; 23: 13–16).

In making analogies between the Resurrection and God's deeds in this world, the Qur'ān sometimes alludes to the deeds God will do in the Hereafter in such a way that we are convinced of them, drawing analogies to what we observe here. It also shows His similar deeds in the world and makes comparisons between them and the Resurrection. One example is 36: 78–81.

The Qur'ān likens the Resurrection to the earth's springtime rejuvenation or revival following its death in winter. As well as innumerable instances of death and revival or replacement that are constantly witnessed in nature and in our own bodies, an overall death and revival is repeated every year. During winter, a white "shroud" covers much of the earth. Nature already has turned pale and shows fewer traces of life. Trees seem to be no more than hard bones. Grass fades away, flowers wither, migrating birds leave, and insects and reptiles disappear.

But winter is not eternal, for it is followed by a general revival. When the weather becomes warm, trees begin to bud and, wearing their finery, present themselves to the Eternal Witness. The soil swells, and grass and flowers start to blossom everywhere. Seeds that fell into the ground the previous autumn have germinated and, having annihilated themselves, begin to grow into new forms of life without suffering the least confusion. All of these new things are similar (but not identical) to those that came into being the previous year. In short, nature appears before us in all its splendor and finery. The raising of the dead on the Day of Judgment will be very much like this (41: 39; 71: 17–18; 75: 36–40).

54. God is He Who creates you in a state of weakness, and then gives you strength after weakness, and then, after a period of strength, ordains weakness (of old age) and grey hair. He creates however He wills. He is the All-Knowing, the All-Powerful.

55. When the Last Hour stands forth and the Judgment is established, the disbelieving criminals swear that they stayed in the world no longer than a short while (of the day). Thus were they habitually turned away from the truth, (having always depended on their sense-perceptions, false reasoning and defective knowledge).

56. But those who were endowed with knowledge (of the truth) and faith say: "For certain, you have stayed until the Day of Raising according to how God decreed in His Book (of Creation and Life). And now this is the Day of Raising but you were (persistent in) refusing true knowledge (about it).

57. On that Day their excuses will be of no avail to the wrongdoers (who denied God or associated partners with Him), nor will they be allowed to make amends (and offer regrets to escape the punishment).

58. Assuredly We have set forth for humankind in this Qur'ān all kinds of parables and comparisons (to help them understand the truth). Even though you bring them a miracle (of the kind they demand), those who (pay no heed to these parables and comparisons and obstinately) disbelieve will certainly say (to the believers): "You are only seeking a false way."

59. Thus does God seal the hearts of those who have no (attachment to) knowledge.

60. So be patient; surely God's promise (that He will help the believers to victory) is true. And do not let those who lack certainty (of this truth) shake your firmness.[14]

51. But if We send forth a scorching wind (against their land) and they see it (being dust-laden) as yellow, they begin, straight after that (joy), to show disbelieving ingratitude (as if God were obliged to always treat them with mercy and it were not God Who provides for them).

52. Indeed you cannot make the dead hear, nor can you make the deaf hear the call when they have turned their backs, going away.

53. Nor can you guide the blind out of their error. None can you make hear save those who (being capable of reflection without prejudice) believe in Our Revelations and signs (in the outer world as well as in their inner world), and are (therefore) ready to submit (to the truth).

---

14. *The sūrah* began with God's promise that He would help the believers to victory and that they would rejoice. It ends with reiteration of this promise, strengthening the determination of the Messenger and the believers in the face of the harsh reactions of the unbelievers.

SŪRAH 31

LUQMĀN

Makkah period

This *sūrah* of 34 verses was revealed in Makkah. It begins by affirming the wisdom of the Qur'ān, and offers pearls of wisdom narrated by Luqmān. It also mentions some virtues of the believers, presents evidence of God's Power and Oneness, emphasizes the essential need of human beings for God's Religion, and ends by stating that some matters are bound to remain unknown to humankind.

In the Name of God, the All-Merciful, the All-Compassionate.

1. *Alif. Lām. Mīm.*

2. These are the Revelations of the Book full of wisdom,

3. A guidance and mercy for those devoted to doing good, aware that God is seeing them.

4. They establish the Prayer in conformity with its conditions, and pay what is due to the needy out of their belongings, and in the Hereafter they have certainty of faith.

5. Those stand on true guidance (originating in this Book) from their Lord; and they are those who are the prosperous.

6. Among the people is one who pays for idle tales and diverting talk to lead people astray from (the Qur'ān, which is) God's way, without knowledge, and makes a mockery of it (the Qur'ān). For such (a man) there is a shameful, humiliating punishment.

7. When our Revelations are recited to such a one, he turns away in arrogance as if he had not heard them, as if there were heaviness in his ears. So give him the glad tidings of a painful punishment.

8. As against this, those who believe and do good, righteous deeds, for them are Gardens of bounty and blessing,

9. To abide therein. This is a promise of God in truth. He is the All-Glorious with irresistible might, the All-Wise.

10. He has created the heavens without pillars you can see;[1] and He has set up firm mountains on earth lest it should shake you with its movement, and dispersed thereon all kinds of living creatures. We also send down water from the sky, and cause every noble kind of vegetation rich (in color, scent, flavor, and fruit) to grow on earth in pairs.

11. This is God's creation; now show Me what is there that others bebides Him have created. No indeed, but the wrongdoers (who deny God or associate partners with Him) are lost in obvious error.

---

1. For an explanation of this statement, see 13: 2, note 1.

وَلَقَدْ آتَيْنَا لُقْمَٰنَ ٱلْحِكْمَةَ أَنِ ٱشْكُرْ لِلَّهِ ۚ وَمَن يَشْكُرْ فَإِنَّمَا يَشْكُرُ لِنَفْسِهِ ۖ وَمَن كَفَرَ فَإِنَّ ٱللَّهَ غَنِىٌّ حَمِيدٌ ۝ وَإِذْ قَالَ لُقْمَٰنُ لِٱبْنِهِ وَهُوَ يَعِظُهُ يَٰبُنَىَّ لَا تُشْرِكْ بِٱللَّهِ ۖ إِنَّ ٱلشِّرْكَ لَظُلْمٌ عَظِيمٌ ۝ وَوَصَّيْنَا ٱلْإِنسَٰنَ بِوَٰلِدَيْهِ حَمَلَتْهُ أُمُّهُۥ وَهْنًا عَلَىٰ وَهْنٍ وَفِصَٰلُهُۥ فِى عَامَيْنِ أَنِ ٱشْكُرْ لِى وَلِوَٰلِدَيْكَ إِلَىَّ ٱلْمَصِيرُ ۝ وَإِن جَٰهَدَاكَ عَلَىٰٓ أَن تُشْرِكَ بِى مَا لَيْسَ لَكَ بِهِۦ عِلْمٌ فَلَا تُطِعْهُمَا ۖ وَصَاحِبْهُمَا فِى ٱلدُّنْيَا مَعْرُوفًا ۖ وَٱتَّبِعْ سَبِيلَ مَنْ أَنَابَ إِلَىَّ ۚ ثُمَّ إِلَىَّ مَرْجِعُكُمْ فَأُنَبِّئُكُم بِمَا كُنتُمْ تَعْمَلُونَ ۝ يَٰبُنَىَّ إِنَّهَآ إِن تَكُ مِثْقَالَ حَبَّةٍ مِّنْ خَرْدَلٍ فَتَكُن فِى صَخْرَةٍ أَوْ فِى ٱلسَّمَٰوَٰتِ أَوْ فِى ٱلْأَرْضِ يَأْتِ بِهَا ٱللَّهُ ۚ إِنَّ ٱللَّهَ لَطِيفٌ خَبِيرٌ ۝ يَٰبُنَىَّ أَقِمِ ٱلصَّلَوٰةَ وَأْمُرْ بِٱلْمَعْرُوفِ وَٱنْهَ عَنِ ٱلْمُنكَرِ وَٱصْبِرْ عَلَىٰ مَآ أَصَابَكَ ۖ إِنَّ ذَٰلِكَ مِنْ عَزْمِ ٱلْأُمُورِ ۝ وَلَا تُصَعِّرْ خَدَّكَ لِلنَّاسِ وَلَا تَمْشِ فِى ٱلْأَرْضِ مَرَحًا ۖ إِنَّ ٱللَّهَ لَا يُحِبُّ كُلَّ مُخْتَالٍ فَخُورٍ ۝ وَٱقْصِدْ فِى مَشْيِكَ وَٱغْضُضْ مِن صَوْتِكَ ۚ إِنَّ أَنكَرَ ٱلْأَصْوَٰتِ لَصَوْتُ ٱلْحَمِيرِ ۝

---

12. We surely granted wisdom[2] to Luqmān[3] and said: "Give thanks to God." Whoever gives thanks to God, gives thanks but for (the good of) his own soul; and whoever is ungrateful, surely God is the All-Wealthy and Self-Sufficient (absolutely independent of the whole creation), All-Praiseworthy.

13. (Remember) when Luqmān said to his son by way of advice and instruction: "My dear son! Do not associate partners with God. Surely associating partners with God is a tremendous wrong."

14. We have enjoined on human in respect of his parents: his mother bore him in strain upon strain, and his weaning was in two years. (So, O human,) be thankful to Me and to your parents. To Me is the final homecoming.

15. But if they strive with you to make you associate with Me something of which you certainly have no knowledge (and which is absolutely contrary to the Knowledge), do not obey them. Even then, treat them with kindness and due consideration in respect of (the life of) this world. Follow the way of him who has turned to Me with utmost sincerity and committed himself to seeking My approval. Then, (O all human beings,) to Me is your return, and then I will make you understand all that you were doing (and call you to account).

16. "My dear son! Whether good or evil, if a deed should have the weight of only a mustard-seed, and though it be kept hidden in a rock, in the heavens or in the earth, God brings it to light (for judgment). Surely God is All-Subtle (penetrating to the most minute dimensions of all things), All-Aware.

17. "My dear son! Establish the Prayer in conformity with its conditions, enjoin and promote what is right and good and forbid and try to prevent the evil, and bear patiently whatever may befall you. Surely (all of) that is among greatly meritorious things requiring great resolution to fulfill.

18. "Do not turn your face from people in scornful pride, nor move on earth haughtily. Surely God does not love anyone proud and boastful.

19. "Be modest in your bearing, and subdue your voice. For certain the most repugnant of voices is braying of donkeys."

2. For an explanation of wisdom, see *sūrah* 2: 129, note 108, and 269, note 159.

3. Luqmān is one of the three persons – the other two being Dhu'l-Qarnayn and 'Uzayr – mentioned in the Qur'ān about whom it is not clear whether they were Prophets or not. Luqmān was widely known in Arabia before the advent of Islam for his wisdom and spiritual maturity. Some traditions say that he was from Abyssinia and lived in Egypt (al-Mawdūdī, *Tafhīm*, "*Sūrah* Luqmān," note 17). According to some other traditions, he was the nephew of the Prophet Ayyūb (Job) and lived long enough to see the Prophet Dāwūd (David) and Yūnus (Jonah), upon them be peace (Yazır, 6: 3842).

412   سُوْرَةُ لُقْمَن   ٤١٢

وَلَمْ تَرَوْا أَنَّ اللَّهَ سَخَّرَ لَكُمْ مَّا فِى السَّمَوَاتِ وَمَا فِى الْأَرْضِ
وَأَسْبَغَ عَلَيْكُمْ نِعَمَهُ ظَاهِرَةً وَبَاطِنَةً وَمِنَ النَّاسِ مَنْ يُجَادِلُ فِى
اللَّهِ بِغَيْرِ عِلْمٍ وَلَا هُدًى وَلَا كِتَابٍ مُّنِيرٍ ۞ وَإِذَا قِيلَ لَهُمُ
اتَّبِعُوا مَا أَنزَلَ اللَّهُ قَالُوا بَلْ نَتَّبِعُ مَا وَجَدْنَا عَلَيْهِ آبَاءَنَا ۚ أَ
وَلَوْ كَانَ الشَّيْطَانُ يَدْعُوهُمْ إِلَى عَذَابِ السَّعِيرِ ۞ وَمَن يُسْلِمْ
وَجْهَهُ إِلَى اللَّهِ وَهُوَ مُحْسِنٌ فَقَدِ اسْتَمْسَكَ بِالْعُرْوَةِ الْوُثْقَىٰ وَإِلَى
اللَّهِ عَاقِبَةُ الْأُمُورِ ۞ وَمَن كَفَرَ فَلَا يَحْزُنكَ كُفْرُهُ إِلَيْنَا مَرْجِعُهُمْ
فَنُنَبِّئُهُم بِمَا عَمِلُوا إِنَّ اللَّهَ عَلِيمٌ بِذَاتِ الصُّدُورِ ۞ نُمَتِّعُهُمْ قَلِيلًا
ثُمَّ نَضْطَرُّهُمْ إِلَى عَذَابٍ غَلِيظٍ ۞ وَلَئِن سَأَلْتَهُم مَّنْ خَلَقَ السَّمَوَاتِ
وَالْأَرْضَ لَيَقُولُنَّ اللَّهُ قُلِ الْحَمْدُ لِلَّهِ بَلْ أَكْثَرُهُمْ
لَا يَعْلَمُونَ ۞ لِلَّهِ مَا فِى السَّمَوَاتِ وَالْأَرْضِ إِنَّ
اللَّهَ هُوَ الْغَنِيُّ الْحَمِيدُ ۞ وَلَوْ أَنَّ مَا فِى الْأَرْضِ مِن شَجَرَةٍ
أَقْلَامٌ وَالْبَحْرُ يَمُدُّهُ مِن بَعْدِهِ سَبْعَةُ أَبْحُرٍ مَّا نَفِدَتْ
كَلِمَاتُ اللَّهِ إِنَّ اللَّهَ عَزِيزٌ حَكِيمٌ ۞ مَّا خَلْقُكُمْ
وَلَا بَعْثُكُمْ إِلَّا كَنَفْسٍ وَاحِدَةٍ إِنَّ اللَّهَ سَمِيعٌ بَصِيرٌ ۞

20. Do you not see that God has made all that is in the heavens and all that is on the earth of service to you, and lavished on you His favors, outward and inward? And yet, among people are those who dispute about God without having any true knowledge or any true guidance or an enlightening Divine Book.[4]

21. When such people are told to follow what God has sent down, they say: "No, but we follow that (the traditions, customs, beliefs, and practices) which we found our forefathers in.." What! even if Satan is inviting them to the punishment of the Blaze (by suggesting to them the way of their forefathers)?

22. (The truth is that) whoever submits his whole being to God and is devoted to doing good, aware that God is seeing him, he has indeed taken hold of the firm, unbreakable handle. With God rests the outcome for all matters.

23. Then whoever disbelieves, let his unbelief not grieve you. To us is their final return and We will make them understand all that they did (and call them to account for it). Surely God has full knowledge of what lies hidden in the bosoms.

24. We will (continue to) provide for them to enjoy themselves for a short while (in this life), then We will compel them to a harsh punishment.

25. If you should ask them who has created the heavens and the earth, they would certainly say, "God." Say: "All praise and gratitude are for God," (seeing that even those who associate partners with God feel compelled to acknowledge Him as the Creator; that recognition indeed destroys the foundations of polytheism).[5] But most of them do not know (what that recognition of theirs implies).

26. To God belongs whatever is in the heavens and on the earth (over which He has full and exclusive authority, and therefore He alone is to be worshipped but none other). God is He Who is the All-Wealthy and Self-Sufficient (absolutely independent of the whole creation), All-Praiseworthy (to Whom all praise and thanks belong and are due).

27. If all the trees on the earth were pens, and all the sea (were ink), with seven more seas added thereto, the words of God (Hic decrees, the acts of all His Names and Attributes manifested as His commandments, and the events and creatures He creates) would not be exhausted in the writing. Surely God is the All-Glorious with irresistible might (Whom none can frustrate and Whom nothing can tire), the All-Wise.

28. Your creation and your resurrection are but as (the creation and resurrection) of a single soul.[6] Surely God is All-Hearing, All-Seeing.

4. On knowledge and guidance, see 22: 8, note 2.

5. Being the Creator means owning the creation, having the sole authority to judge and administrate, and deserving worship. Moreover, as there is only One Creator, He does in no way need to have a partner in administrating what He has created, or to share His authority over it. So, this single reality destroys the foundations of any other ideology or system which offers partnership with God in His being the sole Deity deserving worship and obedience, in His Lordship and sovereignty over the creation. Even though certain modern systems of thought and scientific materialism try to find a source for creation, such efforts are only ideological and artificial. In fact, they must acknowledge the existence of the One Creator, and I believe that they acknowledge this, consciously or unconsciously, yet they stubbornly insist on saying otherwise. Some think that acknowledging the Creator is the easy way out. But denial of Him means trying to escape reality and taking shelter in that which is psychologically easier. It is also a device of human presumption and arrogance, to avoid a properly rooted moral responsibility and to conform to the cultural temperament of the age, which boasts of unrestricted human autonomy in all spheres of life – something that is neither real nor credible, and whose consequences for the moral, socio-economic and physical environment that we inhabit are proving catastrophic..

6. The Eternal Divine Power is essential to the Divine Essence; it is an indispensable attribute of Divinity. Any limitation of capacity is inconceivable of God, for this would presuppose the existence of two opposites in the Infinite Being. Since this is impossible, and since impotence cannot occur in the Divine Essence, nothing can interfere with the Divine Power. Since impotence cannot be existent in the Divine Power, It can have no degrees, for such degrees of a thing's existence, attributes and potentialities come about only through the intervention of opposites. Degrees of temperature occur because of the intervention of cold, and degrees of beauty exist because of the intervention of ugliness. This is true of all qualities in the universe. Contingent things and beings contain opposites, for they do not exist essentially of themselves and no undiluted quality is essential to their existence. As the world of contingencies contains degrees and graduations, it is subject to change and transformation.

Since the Eternal Divine Power contains no degrees, it is equally easy for It to create or bring into existence particles and galaxies. Resurrecting all of humankind is as easy for the Divine Power as reviving one person, and creating the whole of spring is as easy as creating one flower. If creation or resurrection were ascribed to causes, creating a flower would be as difficult as creating spring. But if there is only One Creator, for Him, creating all things is as easy as creating one thing.

As an analogy, the sun is one being, but is universal through its effects on each and every thing on the earth. Everything functions as if it were a throne for the sun. The sun is manifested in all objects with all its attributes, and so encompasses all that confronts it; with all or many of its attributes it is manifested in one single object and in all objects simultaneously, and so is present with many or all of its attributes in each and every item.

The Most Holy Being is absolutely transcendent and free of matter, time, and space, and is exalted above and exempt from any restriction, as well as from the darkness of density and compactness. His Attributes are all-embracing. Nothing can escape or hide from His manifestation with all His Attributes, particularly His universal Will, absolute Power, and all-encompassing Knowledge. Nothing is difficult for Him.

The sun's unrestricted light and immaterial reflection make it nearer to every thing and every being than itself, although everything is far from it. In the same way, the All-Powerful One is infinitely near to everything and infinitely able to do anything He wills concerning them. (See *The Words*, "the 16th and 29th Word," 210–211, 542–545.)

413

الجزء الحادى والعشرون   ٤١٣

أَوَلَمْ تَرَوْا أَنَّ اللَّهَ يُولِجُ الَّيْلَ فِي النَّهَارِ وَيُولِجُ النَّهَارَ فِي الَّيْلِ وَسَخَّرَ الشَّمْسَ وَالْقَمَرَ كُلٌّ يَجْرِي إِلَى أَجَلٍ مُّسَمًّى وَأَنَّ اللَّهَ بِمَا تَعْمَلُونَ خَبِيرٌ ۝ ذَلِكَ بِأَنَّ اللَّهَ هُوَ الْحَقُّ وَأَنَّ مَا يَدْعُونَ مِن دُونِهِ الْبَاطِلُ وَأَنَّ اللَّهَ هُوَ الْعَلِيُّ الْكَبِيرُ ۝ أَلَمْ تَرَ أَنَّ الْفُلْكَ تَجْرِي فِي الْبَحْرِ بِنِعْمَتِ اللَّهِ لِيُرِيَكُم مِّنْ آيَاتِهِ إِنَّ فِي ذَلِكَ لَآيَاتٍ لِّكُلِّ صَبَّارٍ شَكُورٍ ۝ وَإِذَا غَشِيَهُم مَّوْجٌ كَالظُّلَلِ دَعَوُا اللَّهَ مُخْلِصِينَ لَهُ الدِّينَ فَلَمَّا نَجَّاهُمْ إِلَى الْبَرِّ فَمِنْهُم مُّقْتَصِدٌ وَمَا يَجْحَدُ بِآيَاتِنَا إِلَّا كُلُّ خَتَّارٍ كَفُورٍ ۝ يَا أَيُّهَا النَّاسُ اتَّقُوا رَبَّكُمْ وَاخْشَوْا يَوْمًا لَّا يَجْزِي وَالِدٌ عَن وَلَدِهِ وَلَا مَوْلُودٌ هُوَ جَازٍ عَن وَالِدِهِ شَيْئًا إِنَّ وَعْدَ اللَّهِ حَقٌّ فَلَا تَغُرَّنَّكُمُ الْحَيَاةُ الدُّنْيَا وَلَا يَغُرَّنَّكُم بِاللَّهِ الْغَرُورُ ۝ إِنَّ اللَّهَ عِندَهُ عِلْمُ السَّاعَةِ وَيُنَزِّلُ الْغَيْثَ وَيَعْلَمُ مَا فِي الْأَرْحَامِ وَمَا تَدْرِي نَفْسٌ مَّاذَا تَكْسِبُ غَدًا وَمَا تَدْرِي نَفْسٌ بِأَيِّ أَرْضٍ تَمُوتُ إِنَّ اللَّهَ عَلِيمٌ خَبِيرٌ ۝

سُورَةُ السَّجْدَةِ وَهِيَ ثَلَاثُونَ آيَةً

———✦———

show you some of His signs? Surely in that are signs (to know Him for His Munificence, Knowledge, Power, Wisdom, and way of acting) for all who are greatly patient (in adversity) and greatly grateful (for His favors).

32. When the waves overwhelm them like a canopy (of dark clouds), they call upon God sincerely believing in Him alone (as the only Deity, Lord, and Sovereign). But when He brings them safe to land, some of them are lukewarm, wavering between faith and unbelief. None opposes and rejects Our signs (knowingly) unless he is perfidious, ungrateful.

33. O humankind! Keep from disobedience to your Lord in reverence for Him and piety, seeking His protection, and fear a Day when no parent will be able to avail his child, nor a child avail his parent in anything. God's promise (of the Last Judgment) is certainly true. So do not let the present, worldly life delude you, nor let any deluder (including especially Satan) delude you (in your conceptions) about God.

34. With God alone rests the knowledge of the Last Hour (when it will come). He sends down rain (just at the time and place He alone knows), and He alone knows what is in the wombs. No soul knows what it will reap tomorrow, and no soul knows in what place it will die.[7] Surely God is All-Knowing, All-Aware.

29. Do you not consider that God makes the night pass into the day and makes the day pass into the night, (and so makes each grow longer or shorter), and that He has made the sun and the moon subservient to His command (at your service), each running its course for a term appointed (by Him)? And surely God is fully aware of all that you do.

30. That (is so) because God is He Who is the Absolute Truth and Ever-Constant (Whose decrees and deeds are all true and in absolute accord with one another), and all that they invoke (as deities) apart from Him is sheer falsehood. And because God is He Who is the All-Exalted, the All-Great.

31. Do you not consider that the ships run on the sea by God's favor, that He may

7. This verse explains five things of which God alone has exact knowledge. Although the time of rain can be guessed to a certain extent, it is no more than a guess that can be made after the signs of the rain have appeared, and therefore it is not foreknowledge. The statement referring to what is in the wombs does not merely relate to the sex of the embryo in the womb, but also to its future physical traits, inborn capacities, and character, and to the question of whether it will be born, and if it is born, what role it will play in life, etc.

As pointed out in note 3 to 3: 3, it is of great significance that the Qur'ān praises the believers first of all for their faith in the Unseen (ghayb). This means that existence is not restricted to what is sensed and observed. This corporeal realm is, according to the measures particular to it, the manifestation of the unseen and unobservable, and it is only one of the numerous realms. The truth or full reality of every phenomenon in this world lies in the world of the Unseen. So, by mentioning five things included in the Unseen in this verse, the Qur'ān draws our attention to God's absolute, all-encompassing Knowledge *vis-à-vis* the restricted knowledge of humankind. Human existence is restricted in many respects. A person has no dominion over the operation of even their own body, let alone over the world as a whole. They cannot prevent themselves from getting hungry and thirsty; they have no part in determining their parents, or the time and place of their birth, nor their physique or physical structure, nor do they know when and where they will die. In addition, they have no knowledge of the future and, in most cases, cannot acquire true knowledge of the past or even of the present. But just as the creation is a whole with all its parts interrelated, time and space also comprise a whole whose parts are linked to one another. Every event in the human realm is not independent of those who do it, of the time or the place when and where it takes place, or even of the past and the future. So how can a being who is deprived of the exact knowledge of itself, of the other members of its kind, of the time and space with all its parts, of its environment with its relation to the other parts of the universe, claim to order or have authority over its life, as well the lives of others, or dare to give order to the world according to its own will? As this is the truth of the matter, it is only God Who has full knowledge of everything, of all of time and place and every being with all its relations to others, to time and space; it is only God Who can have and Who has the right to order the life of all creatures.

414   سورة السجدة   ٤١٤

بِسْمِ اللهِ الرَّحْمٰنِ الرَّحِيمِ

الٓمٓ ۝ تَنْزِيلُ الْكِتَابِ لَا رَيْبَ فِيهِ مِنْ رَبِّ الْعَالَمِينَ ۝ أَمْ يَقُولُونَ افْتَرَاهُ بَلْ هُوَ الْحَقُّ مِنْ رَبِّكَ لِتُنْذِرَ قَوْمًا مَا أَتَاهُمْ مِنْ نَذِيرٍ مِنْ قَبْلِكَ لَعَلَّهُمْ يَهْتَدُونَ ۝ اللهُ الَّذِي خَلَقَ السَّمَاوَاتِ وَالْأَرْضَ وَمَا بَيْنَهُمَا فِي سِتَّةِ أَيَّامٍ ثُمَّ اسْتَوَىٰ عَلَى الْعَرْشِ مَا لَكُمْ مِنْ دُونِهِ مِنْ وَلِيٍّ وَلَا شَفِيعٍ أَفَلَا تَتَذَكَّرُونَ ۝ يُدَبِّرُ الْأَمْرَ مِنَ السَّمَاءِ إِلَى الْأَرْضِ ثُمَّ يَعْرُجُ إِلَيْهِ فِي يَوْمٍ كَانَ مِقْدَارُهُ أَلْفَ سَنَةٍ مِمَّا تَعُدُّونَ ۝ ذٰلِكَ عَالِمُ الْغَيْبِ وَالشَّهَادَةِ الْعَزِيزُ الرَّحِيمُ ۝ الَّذِي أَحْسَنَ كُلَّ شَيْءٍ خَلَقَهُ وَبَدَأَ خَلْقَ الْإِنْسَانِ مِنْ طِينٍ ۝ ثُمَّ جَعَلَ نَسْلَهُ مِنْ سُلَالَةٍ مِنْ مَاءٍ مَهِينٍ ۝ ثُمَّ سَوَّاهُ وَنَفَخَ فِيهِ مِنْ رُوحِهِ وَجَعَلَ لَكُمُ السَّمْعَ وَالْأَبْصَارَ وَالْأَفْئِدَةَ قَلِيلًا مَا تَشْكُرُونَ ۝ وَقَالُوا أَإِذَا ضَلَلْنَا فِي الْأَرْضِ أَإِنَّا لَفِي خَلْقٍ جَدِيدٍ بَلْ هُمْ بِلِقَاءِ رَبِّهِمْ كَافِرُونَ ۝ قُلْ يَتَوَفَّاكُمْ مَلَكُ الْمَوْتِ الَّذِي وُكِّلَ بِكُمْ ثُمَّ إِلَى رَبِّكُمْ تُرْجَعُونَ ۝

---❦---

SŪRAH 32

AS-SAJDAH (PROSTRATION)

Makkah period

This *sūrah*, which consists of 30 verses, was revealed in Makkah. It takes its name from verse 15, which states that the believers prostrate upon hearing the Revelations. It discusses the Divine origin of the Qur'ān, and mentions the creation of humankind to draw the attention to the second creation in the other world, and to the end of both those who believe and disbelieve in God's signs and Revelations. It also tells how the Children of Israel were guided through a similar Divine Book given to the Prophet Moses, upon him be peace. The *sūrah* ends with glad tidings for the believers concerning the rewards awaiting them in the Hereafter.

In the Name of God, the All-Merciful, the All-Compassionate.

1. *Alif. Lām. Mīm.*

2. (This is) the Book which, it is beyond all doubt, is being sent down in parts from the Lord of the worlds.

3. Or do they say: he (Muḥammad) has fabricated it? No, rather it is the truth from your Lord, that you may warn a people to whom no warner has come before you (during a long interlude during which no Messengers appeared), so that they may be guided (to find and follow the Straight Path).[1]

4. God is He Who has created the heavens and the earth and what is between them in six days, then established Himself on the Supreme Throne. You have, apart from Him, no guardian (to whom you might refer the ultimate meaning and outcome of your affairs), nor any intermediary (who, without His leave, can cause anything of use to reach you).[3] Will you not reflect and be mindful?

5. He directs the affair from heaven to the earth; then the affair ascends to Him in a day the measure of which is a thousand years of what you reckon.[4]

6. Such is He, the Knower of the Unseen and the witnessed (all that lies in the hidden and visible realms and beyond and within the realm of any created being's perception), the All-Glorious with irresistible might, the All-Compassionate:

7. He Who makes excellent everything that He creates; and He originated the creation of humankind from clay.

8. Then He made his reproduction dependent upon an extraction of humble fluid.[5]

9. Then He fashioned him in due proportions, and breathed into him out of His

Spirit;[6] and He appointed for you (the faculty of) hearing, and eyes, and hearts (for understanding, feeling and insight). Scarcely do you give thanks!

10. Yet they say: "What! when we have been (dead and) lost in the earth, will we then be created anew?" No, (they do not really regard being created anew as impossible; rather,) they are unbelievers in the meeting with their Lord.[7]

11. Say: "The Angel of Death who is charged with taking your souls will take your souls; then you will be returned to your Lord."[8]

---

1. Deducing from *We would never punish (a person or community for the wrong they have done) until We have sent a Messenger (to give counsel and warning)* (17: 15), some Muslim scholars hold that one who has not heard the Name of God or the teachings of Islam will be "excused," unless they are a wrongdoing, unjust person. God, as He wills, rewards such people for the good they have done, and they enjoy the blessings of Paradise.

There are other scholars, however, who are of the opinion that humankind is created with a capacity to find the Creator through the use of reason, even though they do not know His Names or Attributes. They can also find Him in their conscience. A Bedouin once came to the Prophet and explained how he had attained faith: "Camel droppings point to the existence of a camel. Footprints on the sand tell of a traveler. The heaven with its stars, the earth with its mountains and valleys, and the sea with its waves – do they not point to the Maker, All-Powerful, Knowing, Wise, and Caring?" As he had attained faith in God through logical deduction, we cannot underrate the role of reason and thinking in faith. Thus, the exemption from punishment stated in 17: 15 means that unless a Messenger has been sent no one will be held responsible for neglecting the other pillars of faith and for not living a life according to Islam. God uses Messengers to convey His injunctions distinguishing what is good and evil, and does not leave human beings to stray into error because of fallible human judgment and experience.

2. On the creation of the heavens and the earth in six days and God's establishing Himself on the Supreme Throne, see 2: 29, note, 28; 7: 54, note 11.

3. *Shafī'* (translated as intermediary) means one who intercedes, and is usually taken to mean one who pleads with God on behalf of people. However, it is clear in this verse that this phrase is only concerned with worldly affairs. It is also clear that the pagans who did not believe in the Hereafter would never think of intercession in connection with the afterlife. Therefore, this phrase here means any intermediary agent or principle that acts between humankind and the origin of anything that is of use to them. Humans had adopted some of their so-called deities to act as intermediaries between God and themselves for their worldly affairs. The verse categorically rejects such a belief as this, as well as the creative effect of any material or immaterial cause in the creation or government of the universe. The material causes and what we call "natural forces and laws" are only titles we give to the executions of His orders by God, or the works of His Names. It is God Who creates, administers, maintains, and provides.

4. The sun is nearer to us than ourselves. Its light manifests itself in and penetrates the "heart" of everything in the world, unless a hindrance intervenes. Similarly, God, free of all restrictions of matter, time, and space, is infinitely nearer to us than ourselves, but we are infinitely distant from Him. So this verse expresses God's infinite nearness to us *vis-à-vis* our infinite distance from Him. It also implies the fact that we can get near to Him only by His making us near.

Secondly, the origin of everything and every affair or event in the world is the pure, heavenly realm. So what is meant by *heaven* in this verse is not the sky, but the pure, spiritual realms where God acts and executes His will without any veil or material cause. All decrees concerning the world issue from these realms.

Thirdly, as stated in note 13 to 7: 54, the Qur'ān uses the word *day* not only in the sense of our normal day, but also as time unit and period. While this verse mentions a day to be the equivalent of 1,000 years by our reckoning, another verse mentions a day that measures 50,000 years (70: 4). This shows that the concept of *day* is relative. The world does not consist only in our world or the visible universe. Rather there are worlds or dimensions within one another. Just as time or the length of a day is different in the world of dreams, so too is it also different in the worlds of spirit and imagination and that of immaterial forms, in other spiritual realms.

Fourthly, the verse may also be referring to the fact that periods of 1,000 years are usually turning points in human history. (Also see 55: 29, note 11.)

5. Maurice Bucaille comments on this verse:

> The Arabic word, translated here by the word 'quintessence (extraction)', is *sulālah*. It signifies 'something which is extracted, the issue of something else, the best part of a thing.' In whatever way it is translated, it refers to a part of a whole.
>
> The fertilization of the egg and reproduction are produced by a cell that is very elongated: its dimensions are measured in ten thousandths of a millimeter. In normal conditions (it is estimated that in one cubic centiliters of sperm there are 25 million spermatozoon that, under

normal conditions, have an ejaculation of several cubic centimeters), only one single cell among several tens of millions produced by a man will actually penetrate the ovule; a large number of them are left behind and never complete the journey that leads from the vagina to the ovule, passing through the uterus and Fallopian tubes. It is therefore an infinitesimally small part of the extract from a liquid whose composition is highly complex that actually fulfills its function.

> In consequence, it is difficult not to be struck by the agreement between the text of the Qur'ān and the scientific knowledge we possess today of these phenomena (*The Bible, the Qur'an and Science*).

6. For God's breathing out of His Spirit, see 2:31–34, notes 32–34; 15: 29, note 8.

7. Those who live a dissipated life driven by their carnal desires and who are lost in accumulating sins cannot look forward to being taken to account for their lives. This is what lies behind their denial of the Hereafter.

8. Verse 39: 42 says that God takes the souls, while verses 6: 61 and 16: 28 say that God's envoys and the angels take them, respectively. We learn from this verse that the Angel of Death does this task. These verses do not, of course, contradict each other. It is ultimately God Who makes people die, but out of wisdom, He has charged the Angel of Death with this task, and he has aides.

Another point to be mentioned is that sometimes God Himself takes the souls of some of His servants, and sometimes the Angel of Death does this task, without sending in his helpers. This is according to the spiritual rank of the person, or whether they are a believer or not, a hypocrite, or a sinful believer.

وَلَوْ تَرَىٰٓ إِذِ ٱلْمُجْرِمُونَ نَاكِسُوا۟ رُءُوسِهِمْ عِندَ رَبِّهِمْ رَبَّنَآ أَبْصَرْنَا وَسَمِعْنَا فَٱرْجِعْنَا نَعْمَلْ صَٰلِحًا إِنَّا مُوقِنُونَ ۝ وَلَوْ شِئْنَا لَءَاتَيْنَا كُلَّ نَفْسٍ هُدَىٰهَا وَلَٰكِنْ حَقَّ ٱلْقَوْلُ مِنِّى لَأَمْلَأَنَّ جَهَنَّمَ مِنَ ٱلْجِنَّةِ وَٱلنَّاسِ أَجْمَعِينَ ۝ فَذُوقُوا۟ بِمَا نَسِيتُمْ لِقَآءَ يَوْمِكُمْ هَٰذَآ إِنَّا نَسِينَٰكُمْ وَذُوقُوا۟ عَذَابَ ٱلْخُلْدِ بِمَا كُنتُمْ تَعْمَلُونَ ۝ إِنَّمَا يُؤْمِنُ بِـَٔايَٰتِنَا ٱلَّذِينَ إِذَا ذُكِّرُوا۟ بِهَا خَرُّوا۟ سُجَّدًا وَسَبَّحُوا۟ بِحَمْدِ رَبِّهِمْ وَهُمْ لَا يَسْتَكْبِرُونَ ۩ ۝ تَتَجَافَىٰ جُنُوبُهُمْ عَنِ ٱلْمَضَاجِعِ يَدْعُونَ رَبَّهُمْ خَوْفًا وَطَمَعًا وَمِمَّا رَزَقْنَٰهُمْ يُنفِقُونَ ۝ فَلَا تَعْلَمُ نَفْسٌ مَّآ أُخْفِىَ لَهُم مِّن قُرَّةِ أَعْيُنٍ جَزَآءًۢ بِمَا كَانُوا۟ يَعْمَلُونَ ۝ أَفَمَن كَانَ مُؤْمِنًا كَمَن كَانَ فَاسِقًا لَّا يَسْتَوُۥنَ ۝ أَمَّا ٱلَّذِينَ ءَامَنُوا۟ وَعَمِلُوا۟ ٱلصَّٰلِحَٰتِ فَلَهُمْ جَنَّٰتُ ٱلْمَأْوَىٰ نُزُلًۢا بِمَا كَانُوا۟ يَعْمَلُونَ ۝ وَأَمَّا ٱلَّذِينَ فَسَقُوا۟ فَمَأْوَىٰهُمُ ٱلنَّارُ كُلَّمَآ أَرَادُوٓا۟ أَن يَخْرُجُوا۟ مِنْهَآ أُعِيدُوا۟ فِيهَا وَقِيلَ لَهُمْ ذُوقُوا۟ عَذَابَ ٱلنَّارِ ٱلَّذِى كُنتُم بِهِۦ تُكَذِّبُونَ ۝

---

12. If you could but see those disbelieving criminals when they hang their heads before their Lord (pleading): "Our Lord! Now we have seen and heard (the truth and are ready to be obedient). So return us (to the world): we will certainly do good, righteous deeds. Now we are certain (of the truth)."

13. (That is no more than a vain desire.) If We had so willed, We would have given every soul its guidance (the route to salvation particular to it); but (many choose unbelief, and) the word from Me has proven true that I would most certainly fill Hell with the jinn and humankind, all together.[9]

14. "So, (you who willingly chose and followed the way of unbelief in the world despite Our warnings,) taste the punishment because you acted in oblivious heedlessness of (the appointment I gave you for) this Day. We are (now) oblivious and heedless of you. Taste the abiding punishment for what you used to do."

15. Only they (truly) believe in Our signs and Revelations who, when they are mentioned of them (by way of advice and instruction), fall down in prostration, and glorify their Lord with His praise, and they do not behave with haughtiness.

16. Their sides forsake their beds at night, calling out to their Lord in fear (of His punishment) and hope (for His forgiveness, grace, and good pleasure), and out of what We have provided for them (of wealth, knowledge, power, etc.,) they spend (to provide sustenance for the needy and in God's cause, purely for the

good pleasure of God and without placing others under obligation).

17. No soul knows what joyous means of happiness are kept hidden (reserved) for them as a reward for what they have being doing.

18. Is, then, he who is a believer like him who is a transgressor? They are not equal.

19. As for those who believe and do good, righteous deeds, for them are Gardens of Refuge and Dwelling, as a welcome (from God, in return) for what they have been doing.

20. But as for those who transgress (the bounds set by God in belief and action), their refuge and dwelling is the Fire. Every time they desire to come out of it, they will be returned to it and they will be told, "Taste the punishment of the Fire which you used to deny."

9. As beings endowed with free will and special mechanisms, the jinn and humankind are responsible for their free choices. Because of this, God does not compel them to choose a certain way in their lives. Therefore, in the same way as He does not impose guidance on them, He also has explained to them the causes of guidance and misguidance. For example, He decreed and declared that He would not guide those lost in wrongdoing and injustice (3: 86; 5: 51; 6: 144; 9: 19, etc.) and in transgression (5: 108; 9: 24, etc.), and those who have willfully chosen the way of unbelief (5: 67; 9: 37, etc.).

That is, a stubborn and prejudiced insistence on unbelief, wrongdoing, injustice, and transgression prevent one from believing. He also declared that those with whom He would fill Hell would be Satan, his progeny, and his followers (38: 85). Just as He has created humankind with a disposition to belief and equipped them with necessary mechanisms, He has also sent Messengers to every nation throughout history to call them to His way and to warn them of the consequences of their evil acts, and showed them openly the way to the truth with perfectly clear signs.

21. However (before that supreme punishment) We will most certainly make them taste the lower kinds of punishment (in the world), so that they may (repent their ways) and return.

22. Who is more in wrong than he who has been reminded (repeatedly) of his Lord's Revelations and signs, yet turns away from them in aversion. We will surely requite the criminals (committed to accumulating sins).

23. And We surely granted Moses the Book (as We are sending you the Qur'ān), so be not in doubt of its reaching you (from your Lord, and your final meeting with Him in the Hereafter). And We made it (the Book We granted to Moses) a guidance for the Children of Israel.

24. And so long as they remained patient (in adversity they met on the path of God) and they had certainty of faith in Our Revelations, We appointed from amongst them leaders guiding by Our command (in accordance with Our ordinances).

25. Surely your Lord will judge between them on the Day of Resurrection concerning the matters on which they (subsequently) differed (and about which they continue to be at variance).[10]

26. Is it not (enough as a means of) guidance for them (the unbelievers) how many a generation We have destroyed before them, amidst whose dwelling places they travel? Surely in this are signs. Will they still not listen (and pay heed to warnings revealed directly and in these signs)?

27. Do they not consider that We drive the rain to the dry land (bare of vegetation), and bring forth with it crops, of which their

cattle and they themselves eat? Will they still not see (the truth)?

28. Instead, they say (throwing out a challenge): "When will this judgment take place (which will cause everything to appear in all clarity), if you are truthful (in your threats)?"

29. Say: "On the day of the judgment (when everything will appear in all clarity),[11] their faith (then) will be of no use to those who disbelieve (now), nor will they be reprieved.

30. So withdraw from them (do not care what they do and say), and wait (for the judgment to come); they too are waiting.

---

10. The Qur'ān's method of guidance is extremely significant. While verse 24 implies the future victory of the Muslims at a time when they were persecuted in Makkah, verse 25 implicitly warns them of certain internal conflicts that might later ensue among them. Both the implied good tidings and the implicit warning are certainly true for all similar periods.

11. This day is the day when death or an inescapable calamity or war, in which they will be killed, will come upon them.

417

[Arabic Qur'anic text, Sūrah 33, verses 1–6]

بِسْمِ اللهِ الرَّحْمٰنِ الرَّحِيْمِ

—❦—

SŪRAH 33

AL-AHZĀB
(THE CONFEDERATES)

Madīnah period

This *sūrah* of 73 verses was revealed in the 5th year of the Madīnah period, and derives its name from verse 20, where the word *ahzāb* (the confederates) occurs, referring to the allied enemy forces that besieged Madīnah. The *sūrah* concentrates on the Battle of the Trench, which ensued from that siege, and the campaign against the Banū Qurayzah that followed the battle. In addition, the *sūrah* introduces laws pertaining to marriage and divorce, new regulations concerning the law of inheritance, Islamic family life, and the relation between the Prophet and his wives and the Islamic community. It also abolishes a form of adoption that had been an established custom in the pre-Islamic period.

In the Name of God, the All-Merciful, the All-Compassionate.

1. O (most illustrious) Prophet! Keep your duty to God in utmost reverence for Him and piety, and pay no heed to (the offers of) the unbelievers and hypocrites. Surely God is All-Knowing, All-Wise.[1]

2. Follow what is revealed to you from your Lord. Surely God is fully aware of all that you do.

3. And put your trust in God. God suffices as One on Whom to rely (and to Whom to refer all affairs).

4. God has not made for any man two hearts within his body (one to be assigned for belief in and worship of Him and the other for belief in and worship of others). Nor has He made your wives whom you declare to be (unlawful to you) as your mothers' back (to mean you divorce them[2]) your mothers (in fact). Nor has He made your adopted sons your sons (in fact).[3] Those are only expressions you utter with your mouths. Whereas God speaks the truth and He guides to the right way.

5. Call them (the children you have adopted) after their (real) fathers: doing so is more equitable in the sight of God. If you do not know who their fathers are, then (they are) your brothers in religion and your protégés (so observe the duties of brotherhood between you and them). However, there is no blame on you because of the mistakes you may make unintentionally (in naming them), but what your hearts have premeditated (matters greatly). God is All-Forgiving, All-Compassionate.

6. The Prophet has a higher claim on the believers than they have on their own selves, and (seeing that he is as a father to them), his wives are (as) their mothers.[4] Those who are bound by blood have a greater right (in inheritance and charity) upon one

another according to God's Book than other believers and the Emigrants – except that you must (nevertheless) act with kindness toward your friends (and bequeath some of your goods to them).[5] That is what is written in the Book (of God's Decree).

---

1. The Muslims had to suffer many hardships after the Battle of Uhud. A group from the Adal and al-Qārah tribes, who were apparently from the same ancestral stock as the Quraysh and who lived near Makkah, came to God's Messenger and, declaring that they had accepted Islam, asked for some teachers to be given to them. The Messenger, upon him be peace and blessings, selected six Companions to go with them. Upon reaching the land of the Hudhayl tribe, the group halted and the Companions settled down to rest. Suddenly, a group of Hudhaylī tribesmen fell upon them and martyred four of them, handing Hubayb ibn 'Adiyy and Zayd ibn Dasīnah over to the Quraysh for execution. In the same year, 40 (according to another report, 70) Muslim teachers were requested by the chief of the Banū 'Āmir to teach the Qur'ān to a tribe from Najd and were martyred near the Well of Ma'ūnah.

The following year, God's Messenger, upon him be peace and blessings, was informed that the tribe of Banū Asad were making preparations for war against Madīnah, and dispatched an army of 150 soldiers to combat them, under the command of Abū Salamah.

The Jewish Banū Nadīr tribe was originally the sworn ally of the Muslims in Madīnah. However, its members secretly intrigued with the Makkan pagans and the Madīnan hypocrites. They even tried to kill the Messenger while he was visiting them, breaking the laws of hospitality and their treaty. The way in which this happened is as follows: the Messenger asked them to abandon their strategic position, about three miles south of Madīnah, and they agreed to do so. But when 'Abdullāh ibn Ubayy, the chief of the Hypocrites, promised to help them in case of war, the Banū Nadīr reneged on their agreement. The Muslim army then besieged them in their fortresses. The Banū Nadīr, seeing that neither the Makkan polytheists nor the Madīnan hypocrites cared enough to help them, abandoned the city. They were dismayed, but their lives were spared. Given ten days to leave, along with their families and all they could carry, most of them joined their brethren in Syria and others in Khaybar (Ibn Hishām, 3: 47–49, 190–192).

While returning from Uhud, Abū Sufyān challenged the Muslims to meet them at Badr in the following year (Ibid., 3: 94). However, when God's Messenger reached Badr with an army of 1,500 fighters, there was no enemy to meet him. They stayed there for eight days, waiting for the threatened encounter. When there was no sign of the Quraysh army, they returned to Madīnah. This campaign was called Badr as-Sughrā (Badr the Minor).

In 627, God's Messenger, upon him be peace and blessings, was told that the desert tribes of Anmār and Sa'labah had decided to attack Madīnah. He went to Dhāt ar-Riqa' with 400 fighters and, hearing that the enemy tribes had fled, returned to Madīnah. (Ibid, 3: 213). In the same year, the Messenger marched upon the people of Dūmat al-Jandal, who had lived on the border between Arabia and Syria. These people had previously attacked Muslim tradesmen and robbed them. When the Muslim army came upon them, they fled and the territory came under Muslim control.

It was in these difficult days that a group from the leaders of the Quraysh under the leadership of Abū Sufyan came to Madīnah and, together with 'Abdullāh ibn Ubayy ibn Salūl, the leader of the hypocrites, offered the Messenger their support if he would not oppose their worship of their idols and declare that these idols had a right of intercession with God? The Messenger categorically rejected this offer. This verse was revealed in connection with this event (az-Zamakhsharī).

2. This refers to a pre-Islamic custom among the pagan Arabs. A husband would say to his wife, "You are henceforth as my mother's back to me," and thus removed himself from conjugal relations with his wife. This was the equivalent of an irrevocable divorce, but a woman thus divorced could not marry again. The Qur'ān's forceful disapproval here was the first step to abolishing this custom, soon followed by its explicit abolition in *Sūrat al-Mujādilah*.

3. In the pre-Islamic period adopted and foster children were regarded as enjoying the same legal status as biological children. This custom had other implications, notably that the adopted child held the same status within the forbidden degrees of marriage as a biological child. Islam abolished this practice and declared that adoption has no legal effect. (A father may not marry his natural son's former wife, nor a son his natural father's former wife. The extension of that prohibition to adopted children is the specific occasion of the abolition of the custom.)

4. The relationship described in the verse is of course a spiritual relationship with no legal implications, with the exception that the Prophet's wives were eternally forbidden to other believers. As reported in al-Bukhārī ("Īmān," 8) and Muslim ("Īmān," 70), the Prophet, upon him be peace and blessings, said: "None of you is a true believer unless I am dearer to him than his father, and his children, and all humankind." A believer must prefer the Prophet to their own person and to all other people in all matters, including love and protection; they must put the decisions of the Prophet above their own.

5. Following the *Hijrah*, God's Messenger, upon him be peace and blessings, had joined the believers in brotherhood, declaring one from among the Emigrants as brother to one from among the Helpers (the Muslims of Madīnah), to the degree that they could even inherit from one another. This verse abolished this practice, but it reiterated the brotherhood in faith among the believers. However, it allowed believers to bequeath some proportion (to a maximum, as stipulated by the Prophet, of one-third of the whole) of their wealth in lawful ways, including, of course, to help their brothers and sisters in faith.

418

سُوْرَةُ الْاَحْزَابِ

٤١٨

وَإِذْ اَخَذْنَا مِنَ النَّبِيِّنَ مِيْثَاقَهُمْ وَمِنْكَ وَمِنْ نُوحٍ وَإِبْرٰهِيْمَ
وَمُوْسٰى وَعِيْسَى ابْنِ مَرْيَمَ وَاَخَذْنَا مِنْهُمْ مِيْثَاقًا غَلِيْظًا ۞
لِيَسْئَلَ الصَّادِقِيْنَ عَنْ صِدْقِهِمْ وَاَعَدَّ لِلْكٰفِرِيْنَ عَذَابًا اَلِيْمًا
۞ يَا اَيُّهَا الَّذِيْنَ اٰمَنُوا اذْكُرُوا نِعْمَةَ اللهِ عَلَيْكُمْ اِذْ جَاءَتْكُمْ
جُنُوْدٌ فَاَرْسَلْنَا عَلَيْهِمْ رِيْحًا وَجُنُوْدًا لَّمْ تَرَوْهَا وَكَانَ اللهُ
بِمَا تَعْمَلُوْنَ بَصِيْرًا ۞ اِذْ جَاءُوْكُمْ مِّنْ فَوْقِكُمْ وَمِنْ اَسْفَلَ مِنْكُمْ
وَإِذْ زَاغَتِ الْاَبْصَارُ وَبَلَغَتِ الْقُلُوْبُ الْحَنَاجِرَ وَتَظُنُّوْنَ بِاللهِ
الظُّنُوْنَا ۞ هُنَالِكَ ابْتُلِيَ الْمُؤْمِنُوْنَ وَزُلْزِلُوْا زِلْزَالًا شَدِيْدًا ۞
وَإِذْ يَقُوْلُ الْمُنٰفِقُوْنَ وَالَّذِيْنَ فِيْ قُلُوْبِهِمْ مَّرَضٌ مَّا وَعَدَنَا اللهُ
وَرَسُوْلُهُ اِلَّا غُرُوْرًا ۞ وَإِذْ قَالَتْ طَائِفَةٌ مِّنْهُمْ يَا اَهْلَ يَثْرِبَ
لَا مُقَامَ لَكُمْ فَارْجِعُوْا وَيَسْتَأْذِنُ فَرِيْقٌ مِّنْهُمُ النَّبِيَّ يَقُوْلُوْنَ اِنَّ
بُيُوْتَنَا عَوْرَةٌ وَمَا هِيَ بِعَوْرَةٍ اِنْ يُّرِيْدُوْنَ اِلَّا فِرَارًا ۞ وَلَوْ
دُخِلَتْ عَلَيْهِمْ مِّنْ اَقْطَارِهَا ثُمَّ سُئِلُوا الْفِتْنَةَ لَاٰتَوْهَا
وَمَا تَلَبَّثُوا بِهَا اِلَّا يَسِيْرًا ۞ وَلَقَدْ كَانُوْا عَاهَدُوا اللهَ
مِنْ قَبْلُ لَا يُوَلُّوْنَ الْاَدْبَارَ وَكَانَ عَهْدُ اللهِ مَسْئُوْلًا ۞

───────◈───────

7. And (remember) when We took from the Prophets their covenant, and from you (O Muḥammad), and from Noah, Abraham, Moses, and Jesus son of Mary. We took from them a solemn covenant

8. So that He may question the truthful concerning their truthfulness (and all that which was entrusted to them);[6] and He has prepared a painful punishment for the unbelievers.

9. O you who believe! Remember God's favor on you when hosts (of the enemy) came down on you, and We sent against them a fierce, (freezing) wind and (heavenly) hosts that you could not see. And God saw all that you did.[7]

10. (Remember) when they came upon you from above you (from the east) and from below you (from the west), and when (your) eyes turned dull and (your) hearts came up to the throats; and (those of weak faith among) you were harboring vain thoughts about God.[8]

11. There (amid those circumstances) the believers were tried, and shaken with a mighty shock.

12. And (remember) when the hypocrites and those in whose hearts was a disease (at just that point in the situation) were saying: "God and His Messenger promised us nothing but delusion."[9]

13. And when a group among them said: "O people of Yathrīb![10] You cannot withstand the enemy (here), therefore go back (to your homes)!" And a party among them asked for leave of the Prophet, saying, "Surely our houses are exposed (to attack)," though they were not exposed (indeed). They desired nothing but to flee.

14. Now if they (and their houses) had been invaded from all sides (of the city) and they had been asked to betray (their faith), they would certainly have done so with but little hesitation.

15. Yet before that they had (in swearing allegiance to God's Messenger) made a covenant with God, that they would never turn their backs (in the face of the enemy). Covenants with God will certainly be accounted for.

6. The covenant which God took from the Prophets, except the Messengers, was that which is in the verse: *And when God took compact with the Prophets: "That I have given you a Book and Wisdom; then there will come to you a Messenger confirming what is with you – you shall certainly believe in him and you shall certainly help him"* (3: 81). But this verse mentions another covenant which was taken in particular from the five greatest of all the Prophets and Messengers, namely the Prophet Muḥammad, upon him be peace and blessings, and the Prophets Noah, Abraham, Moses, and Jesus, upon them be peace. When it is considered that these five Messengers were also those to whom God granted the Sharī'ah – the collection of all the Divine laws to govern human life in the world – which enabled God's Religion to be applied in full and allowed it to be observed without giving way to any deviations (42: 13), this covenant must be understood as their conveying and establishing God's Message fully and realizing the eternal unity of all the believers, as declared in the verse: *So, this community of yours (which all the Messengers and their followers have formed) is one single community of the same faith, and I am your Lord (Who creates, sustains, and protects you); so worship Me alone* (21: 92).

As for questioning the truthful concerning (that which was entrusted to) their truthfulness, there are two aspects, as in the verses: *And (remember) when God will say: "Jesus son of Mary, is it you who said to people: 'Take me and my mother for deities besides God?"* and he will answer: "All-Glorified You are (in that You are absolutely above having a partner, as from any need or deficiency whatever)! It is not for me to say what I had no right to! Had I said it, You would already have known it. You know all that is within myself, whereas I do not know what is within Yourself. Surely You and You alone have knowledge of the Unseen (of all that lies beyond the reach of any created being's perception)"* (5: 116); and *So We will surely question those to whom Messengers were sent (as to how they responded to them), and We will surely question those sent with Our Message (concerning their duty of conveying it and how their peoples reacted to it)* (7: 6). So *the truthful* refers both to the Prophets and to the believers who gave allegiance to them and remained true to their allegiance.

7. In 627, a leading group of the expelled Banū Naḍīr Jews went to Makkah. They met with the Quraysh, urging them to continue fighting with the Muslims, and promised their help and support. These Jews then went to the Ghaṭafān and Qays Aylān tribes and, promising them help, encouraged them to fight against the Messenger (Ibn Hishām, 3: 225–226). These intrigues resulted in a great anti-Muslim confederacy of Makkan polytheists, the desert tribes of central Arabia, the Jews (both those already expelled from and those still resident) in Madīnah, and the hypocrites. The last two constituted a fifth column within Madīnah.

When God's Messenger, upon him be peace and blessings, received intelligence of this anti-Muslim gathering of confederates, he consulted his Companions. It was their unanimous view that they should remain in Madīnah and fight from there. Salmān al-Fārisī suggested digging a trench around the city. It took six days of intense labor to dig this trench. The Messenger divided the Muslims into groups of ten and told them to compete with each other. It was a hard task, there was not much time, winter was about to come in, and there was great hunger. Yet all the Companions worked enthusiastically. In order to not feel the hunger, each fastened a rock around his stomach. The Messenger dug alongside them and fastened two rocks around his stomach. He kept strict control of the city so that no news of the preparation should reach the enemy.

The enemy forces advanced against Madīnah in the hope of destroying the Muslims on an open battlefield. However, this new strategy that they faced was the first blow. Numbering around 20,000, the enemy forces camped near the trench. The Madīnans had no more than 3,000 soldiers. Moreover, the Jewish Banū Qurayzah and the hypocrite fifth columnists had already contacted the enemy.

The Messenger once again displayed his sagacity: he kept the soldiers within the city and stationed them so that they could both defend the city and safeguard their homes against possible attacks of the Banū Qurayzah.

While the war was continuing with exchanges of arrows and stones, the Messenger engaged in diplomatic attempts to split the allied enemy forces. He was able to do that and dissension grew among them (Ibn Hishām, 3: 240–242).

The Messenger, protected by Mount Sal that lay behind the city, had ordered a narrow point to be made in the trench, as he expected that leading Qurayshī horsemen would try to cross there. This is how it happened, for some of the most renowned Qurayshī warriors tried to cross to engage in hand-to-hand combat with the Muslim fighters. 'Ali, the Messenger's cousin and son-in-law, killed three of them, which discouraged the enemy from any new attempts.

The siege lasted 27 days. The Muslims suffered greatly from hunger, cold, unending barrages of arrows and stones, attempts and concentrated assaults to cross the trench, and betrayals and intrigues within Madīnah. The Qur'ān describes this situation in the verses that follow.

After almost four weeks, during which the enemy was disheartened by their failure and the believers proved their steadfastness and loyalty, there was a piercing blast of cold wind from the east. God also sent hosts of angels. (For God's sending angels and its purpose, see 3: 124–127; 8: 9–10, 12.) The enemy's tents were torn up, their fires were extinguished, and sand and rain beat their faces. Terrified by the portents against them, they soon gave up.

The Battle of the Trench was the last Qurayshī attempt to destroy Islam and the Muslims.

8. Some thought that the unbelievers would be victorious and invade Madīnah; others that Islam would be wiped out; and still others that pre-Islamic unbelief would come back, or entertained other negative thoughts.

9. As the Qur'ān promised in several of its verses that Islam would be victorious and prevail over all other faiths, the Messenger also made similar promises from the very first day of his message. Even during the digging of the trench, he said: "I have been given the keys to Persia. God is the Greatest. I have been given the keys to Byzantium" (Ibn Hishām, 3:235–236; al-Bidāyah, 4: 123).

10. God's Messenger changed the name of Yathrīb into Madīnah after the *Hijrah*. By continuing to call Madīnah Yathrīb, the hypocrites were displaying their inward unbelief and hope for the failure of the Messenger's mission.

419 الجزء الحادي والعشرون ٤١٩

قُل لَّن يَنفَعَكُمُ الْفِرَارُ إِن فَرَرْتُم مِّنَ الْمَوْتِ أَوِ الْقَتْلِ وَإِذًا لَّا تُمَتَّعُونَ إِلَّا قَلِيلًا ۝ قُلْ مَن ذَا الَّذِى يَعْصِمُكُم مِّنَ اللَّهِ إِنْ أَرَادَ بِكُمْ سُوٓءًا أَوْ أَرَادَ بِكُمْ رَحْمَةً وَلَا يَجِدُونَ لَهُم مِّن دُونِ اللَّهِ وَلِيًّا وَلَا نَصِيرًا ۝ قَدْ يَعْلَمُ اللَّهُ الْمُعَوِّقِينَ مِنكُمْ وَالْقَآئِلِينَ لِإِخْوَانِهِمْ هَلُمَّ إِلَيْنَا وَلَا يَأْتُونَ الْبَأْسَ إِلَّا قَلِيلًا ۝ أَشِحَّةً عَلَيْكُمْ فَإِذَا جَآءَ الْخَوْفُ رَأَيْتَهُمْ يَنظُرُونَ إِلَيْكَ تَدُورُ أَعْيُنُهُمْ كَالَّذِى يُغْشَىٰ عَلَيْهِ مِنَ الْمَوْتِ فَإِذَا ذَهَبَ الْخَوْفُ سَلَقُوكُم بِأَلْسِنَةٍ حِدَادٍ أَشِحَّةً عَلَى الْخَيْرِ أُوْلَٰٓئِكَ لَمْ يُؤْمِنُوا فَأَحْبَطَ اللَّهُ أَعْمَالَهُمْ وَكَانَ ذَٰلِكَ عَلَى اللَّهِ يَسِيرًا ۝ يَحْسَبُونَ الْأَحْزَابَ لَمْ يَذْهَبُوا وَإِن يَأْتِ الْأَحْزَابُ يَوَدُّوا لَوْ أَنَّهُم بَادُونَ فِى الْأَعْرَابِ يَسْأَلُونَ عَنْ أَنبَآئِكُمْ وَلَوْ كَانُوا فِيكُم مَّا قَاتَلُوٓا إِلَّا قَلِيلًا ۝ لَّقَدْ كَانَ لَكُمْ فِى رَسُولِ اللَّهِ أُسْوَةٌ حَسَنَةٌ لِّمَن كَانَ يَرْجُوا اللَّهَ وَالْيَوْمَ الْآخِرَ وَذَكَرَ اللَّهَ كَثِيرًا ۝ وَلَمَّا رَأَ الْمُؤْمِنُونَ الْأَحْزَابَ قَالُوا هَٰذَا مَا وَعَدَنَا اللَّهُ وَرَسُولُهُ وَصَدَقَ اللَّهُ وَرَسُولُهُ وَمَا زَادَهُمْ إِلَّا إِيمَانًا وَتَسْلِيمًا ۝

------------◈------------

16. Say: "Flight will be of no avail to you if you flee from death or being killed (in battle). However you fare, you are not allowed to enjoy life more than a little while (only until your appointed time)."

17. Say: "Who is there that can hinder God from it, if He wills evil for you, or if He wills mercy for you?" They will not find for themselves, apart from God, either guardian or helper.

18. God certainly knows those of you who are bent on diverting (others from fighting), as well as those who (being hypocrites) say

to their brothers, "(Give up risking your life, so) come and join with us," and they do not join the struggle (of battle) except only a little,

19. Being very miserly (in joining you and reluctant to help you in God's cause). So when (danger threatens in battle and) fear comes, you see them (O Messenger) looking to you (for help), their eyes rolling (in terror) like the eyes of one who swoons to death. But once (the battle subsides and) fear departs, they assail you with sharp tongues, being avaricious for (a share in) the goods thereof (the gainings of victory). Those have never (truly) believed, and therefore God has caused their deeds to come to nothing. That is ever easy for God.

20. (They are so fearful that) they think that the Confederates have not (really) retreated. Should the Confederates come once more, they would much rather be among the Bedouins in the deserts and ask for news about you (than remain in Madīnah and face the battle). Even if they were among you, they would fight only a little.

21. Assuredly you have in God's Messenger an excellent example to follow, for whoever looks forward to God and the Last Day, and remembers and mentions God much.[11]

22. When the (true) believers saw the Confederates before them, they said: "This is what God and His Messenger promised us, and God is true and so is His Messenger. This has but increased them in faith and submission.[12]

---

11. Islam being the universal Religion encompasses human life in its totality, and God's Messenger set a perfect example to follow in all aspects of life. He set this example as a spiritual guide, a teacher of minds, a perfect model of morality, an educator, a president, a commander, a diplomat, and a husband, father, friend, neighbor, and as an individual human being among other human beings. The French historian Lamartine writes:

Never had a man set himself, voluntarily or involuntarily, a more sublime aim, since this aim was superhuman: to subvert superstitions which had been interposed between man and his Creator, to render God unto man and man unto God; to restore the rational and sacred idea of divinity amidst the chaos of the material and disfigured gods of idolatry then existing. Never has a man undertaken a work so far beyond human power with so feeble means, for he had in the conception as well as in the execution of such a great design no other instrument than himself, and no other aid, except a handful of men living in a corner of desert. Finally, never has a man accomplished such a huge and lasting revolution in the world, because in less than two centuries after its appearance, Islam, in faith and arms, reigned over the whole of Arabia, and conquered in God's name Persia, Khorasan, Western India, Syria, Abyssinia, all the known continent of Northern Africa, numerous islands of the Mediterranean, Spain, and a part of Gaul.

If greatness of purpose, smallness of means, and astounding results are the three criteria of human genius, who could dare to compare any great men to Muḥammad? The most famous men created arms, laws, and empires only. They founded, if anything at all, no more than material powers which often crumbled away before their eyes. This man moved not only armies, legislation, empires, peoples, and dynasties, but millions of men in one-third of the then inhabited world; and more than that, he moved the altars, the gods, the religions, the ideas, the beliefs and the souls. On the basis of a Book, every letter of which has become law, he created a spiritual nationality which has blended together peoples of every tongue and of every race. He has left to us as the indelible characteristic of this Muslim nationality, the hatred of false gods and the passion for the One and immaterial God. This avenging patriotism against the profanation of Heaven formed the virtue of the followers of Muhammad: the conquest of one-third of the Earth to his creed was his miracle. The idea of the Unity of God, proclaimed amidst the exhaustion of fabulous theogonies, was in itself such a miracle that upon its utterance from his lips it destroyed all the ancient temples of idols and set on fire one-third of the world. His life, his meditations, his heroic revilings against the superstitions of his country, and his boldness in defying the furies of idolatry; his firmness in enduring them for thirteen years at Mecca, his acceptance of the role of public scorn and almost of being a victim of his fellow-countrymen: all these and,

finally his incessant preaching, his wars against odds, his faith in his success and his superhuman security in misfortune, his forbearance in victory, his ambition which was entirely devoted to one idea; his endless prayer, his mystic conversations with God, his death and his triumph after death; all these attest not to an imposture but to a firm conviction. It was his conviction which gave him the power to restore a creed. This creed was two-fold, the unity of God and the immateriality of God; the former telling what God is; the latter telling what God is not. Philosopher, orator, apostle, legislator, warrior, conqueror of ideas, restorer of rational dogmas, of a cult without images; the founder of twenty terrestrial states and of one spiritual state, that is Muhammad. As regards all standards by which human greatness may be measured, we may well ask: Is there any man greater than he? (*Histoire de la Turquie*, 2: 276–277.)

12. Since the hypocrites pursued only worldly gains and judged everything according to apparent circumstances, when they found themselves besieged in the center of Islam, they thought that the promises of God and His Messenger concerning the future successes of Islam were a delusion. However, the true believers were well aware of the way in which God acts and of the fact that God did not promise them success without them having to do anything in return. They knew that God would not leave them at ease merely because they had professed, "We have believed," without putting them to a test. He certainly tested those who had preceded them. This was His unchanging way and was done so that He might mark out with certainty those who proved to be true in their profession of faith and so that He might mark out with certainty the liars (29: 2–3). He would certainly test them with something of fear and hunger, and loss of wealth, lives and benefits. The good tidings were for those who, when they were visited by an affliction, said: *"Surely we belong to God (as His creatures and servants) and surely to Him we are bound to return"* (2: 155–157), and they acted accordingly. He would certainly reward those who succeeded in the test and made them victorious. The Battle of the Trench once more showed that God and His Messenger are always true to their promises.

420 سورة الأحزاب ٢٠

بِسْمِ اللّٰهِ الرَّحْمٰنِ الرَّحِيمِ

مِنَ الْمُؤْمِنِينَ رِجَالٌ صَدَقُوا مَا عَاهَدُوا اللّٰهَ عَلَيْهِ فَمِنْهُمْ
مَنْ قَضَىٰ نَحْبَهُ وَمِنْهُمْ مَنْ يَنْتَظِرُ وَمَا بَدَّلُوا تَبْدِيلًا
لِيَجْزِيَ اللّٰهُ الصَّادِقِينَ بِصِدْقِهِمْ وَيُعَذِّبَ الْمُنَافِقِينَ إِنْ شَاءَ أَوْ يَتُوبَ
عَلَيْهِمْ إِنَّ اللّٰهَ كَانَ غَفُورًا رَحِيمًا ۞ وَرَدَّ اللّٰهُ الَّذِينَ كَفَرُوا
بِغَيْظِهِمْ لَمْ يَنَالُوا خَيْرًا وَكَفَى اللّٰهُ الْمُؤْمِنِينَ الْقِتَالَ
وَكَانَ اللّٰهُ قَوِيًّا عَزِيزًا ۞ وَأَنْزَلَ الَّذِينَ ظَاهَرُوهُمْ مِنْ
أَهْلِ الْكِتَابِ مِنْ صَيَاصِيهِمْ وَقَذَفَ فِي قُلُوبِهِمُ الرُّعْبَ فَرِيقًا
تَقْتُلُونَ وَتَأْسِرُونَ فَرِيقًا ۞ وَأَوْرَثَكُمْ أَرْضَهُمْ وَدِيَارَهُمْ
وَأَمْوَالَهُمْ وَأَرْضًا لَمْ تَطَؤُوهَا وَكَانَ اللّٰهُ عَلَىٰ كُلِّ شَيْءٍ
قَدِيرًا ۞ يَا أَيُّهَا النَّبِيُّ قُلْ لِأَزْوَاجِكَ إِنْ كُنْتُنَّ تُرِدْنَ
الْحَيَاةَ الدُّنْيَا وَزِينَتَهَا فَتَعَالَيْنَ أُمَتِّعْكُنَّ وَأُسَرِّحْكُنَّ
سَرَاحًا جَمِيلًا ۞ وَإِنْ كُنْتُنَّ تُرِدْنَ اللّٰهَ وَرَسُولَهُ وَالدَّارَ
الْآخِرَةَ فَإِنَّ اللّٰهَ أَعَدَّ لِلْمُحْسِنَاتِ مِنْكُنَّ أَجْرًا عَظِيمًا ۞
يَا نِسَاءَ النَّبِيِّ مَنْ يَأْتِ مِنْكُنَّ بِفَاحِشَةٍ مُبَيِّنَةٍ يُضَاعَفْ لَهَا
الْعَذَابُ ضِعْفَيْنِ وَكَانَ ذَٰلِكَ عَلَى اللّٰهِ يَسِيرًا ۞

---

23. Among the believers are men (of highest valor) who have been true to their covenant with God: among them are those who have fulfilled their vow (by remaining steadfast until death), and those who are awaiting (its fulfillment). They have never altered in any way.

24. In consequence God will reward the truthful ones for having been true to their covenant, and punish the hypocrites if He wills or turn to them in lenience and accept their repentance (if they repent).

Surely God is All-Forgiving, All-Compassionate.[13]

25. God repulsed those who disbelieved still in their rage without gaining any good. God sufficed for the believers in the fighting. Surely God is All-Strong, All-Glorious with irresistible might.

26. And He brought down from their strongholds those of the People of the Book who had supported them (the Confederates in their attack on Madīnah), and cast fright in their hearts: some of them you killed, and others you took as prisoners of war.

27. And He made you heirs to their lands, their habitations, and their possessions, and a land (Khaybar) on which you never yet set foot. God has indeed full power over everything.[14]

28. O (most illustrious) Prophet! Say to your wives: "If you desire the present, worldly life and its charms, then come and let me make the necessary provision for you (in return for divorce),[15] and release you with a handsome release.

29. But if you desire God and His Messenger, and the abode of the Hereafter, then it is a fact that God has prepared a tremendous reward for those among you who act in a good manner, aware that God is seeing them."[16]

30. O wives of the Prophet! If any of you were to commit a manifestly sinful deed, the punishment would be doubled for her. That is easy for God.

---

13. The verse subtly implies that God's punishment depends on His Will: if He so wills, He punishes those who deserve it, but He may pardon them as well. But if any of His servants turn to Him with true repentance, He accepts their repentance. The conclusion of the verse mentioning God as All-Forgiving, All-Compassionate emphasizes His forgiveness and there-

fore encourages His sinful servants and even the hypocrites to turn to Him in true faith and repentance and mend their ways with the hope of being forgiven.

14. After the Confederates who had held Madīnah under siege for four weeks were routed and returned to their homes, God's Messenger, upon him be peace and bless-

ings, focused on the Banū Qurayzah, who had betrayed their agreement with the Messenger and allied with the Quraysh during the war. According to the agreement, they should have defended the city against any foreign attack, along with the Muslims. They also had given asylum to Banū Nadīr's leaders, like Huyayy ibn Akhṭāb, who had been expelled from Madīnah and continued to conspire against the Muslims.

No sooner had the Messenger returned from this battle than he ordered his Companions to march upon the Banū Qurayzah upon God's order (al-Bukhārī, "Maghazī," 30). He had his tent pitched opposite their fortresses. He would have forgiven them if they had asked, but they preferred to resist. The Messenger besieged them for 25 days. At last they asked for surrender terms. (Ibn Hishām, 3: 101, 249–251).

15. When a husband divorces his wife, just as he cannot take back anything of the bridal-due he gave her during marriage (4: 20), he is also obliged to make provision for her according to his standards of living during her waiting period – three full menstrual cycles – appointed by God (2: 228, 241).

16. The Prophet Muhammad, upon him be peace and blessings, personifies the roles of perfect father and husband. He was so kind and tolerant with his wives that they could not envisage their lives without him, nor did they want to live away from him.

The Messenger discussed matters with his wives, although he did not need their advice, as he was directed by Revelation. However, he wanted to teach his nation that Muslim men were to give women every consideration. This was quite a radical idea in his time, as it is today in many parts of the world. He began teaching his people through his own relationship with his wives (al-Bukhārī, "Shurūṭ," 15).

When the Muslim people of Madīnah began to extricate themselves from the utter poverty that they had been suffering for years, a few of his wives (who numbered four at that time) asked him: "Couldn't we live a bit better, like other Muslims do?"

The Messenger reacted by going into retreat. He excused himself, saying: "I cannot afford what they want" (Muslim, "Ṭalaq," 34, 35).

It is not easy to merit being together with the Messenger in this world and the Hereafter. Others might save themselves by simply fulfilling their obligations, but those who were at the very center of Islam had to devote themselves fully to the cause of Islam, so that no weakness would appear at the center. There were advantages in being the Prophet's wife, but these advantages brought responsibilities and potential risks. The Messenger was preparing them as exemplars for all present and future Muslim women. He was especially worried that they might enjoy the reward for their good deeds in this world, and thereby be included in: *You consumed in your life of the world your (share of) pure, wholesome things, and enjoyed them fully (without considering the due of the Hereafter, and so have taken in the world the reward of all your good deeds)* (46: 20).

Thus, these special women were put to a great test. The Messenger allowed them to choose his poor home or the world's luxury. If they chose the world, he would give them what he could afford to and then dissolve his marriage with them. If they chose God and His Messenger, they had to be content with their lives. This was a peculiarity of his family. Since this family was unique, its members had to be unique. The head of the family was chosen, as were the wives and children.

The Messenger first called 'Ā'isha and said: "I want to discuss something with you. You had better talk with your parents before making a decision." Then he recited the verses mentioned above. Her decision was exactly what would be expected from the truthful daughter of a truthful father: "O Messenger of God, do I need to talk with my parents? By God, I choose God and His Messenger" (Muslim, "Ṭalaq," 35).

'Ā'isha herself tells us what happened next: "The Messenger received the same answer from all his wives. No one expressed a different opinion. They all said what I had said."

421

وَمَن يَقْنُتْ مِنكُنَّ لِلَّهِ وَرَسُولِهِ وَتَعْمَلْ صَالِحًا نُّؤْتِهَا أَجْرَهَا مَرَّتَيْنِ وَأَعْتَدْنَا لَهَا رِزْقًا كَرِيمًا ۝ يَا نِسَاءَ النَّبِيِّ لَسْتُنَّ كَأَحَدٍ مِّنَ النِّسَاءِ إِنِ اتَّقَيْتُنَّ فَلَا تَخْضَعْنَ بِالْقَوْلِ فَيَطْمَعَ الَّذِي فِي قَلْبِهِ مَرَضٌ وَقُلْنَ قَوْلًا مَّعْرُوفًا ۝ وَقَرْنَ فِي بُيُوتِكُنَّ وَلَا تَبَرَّجْنَ تَبَرُّجَ الْجَاهِلِيَّةِ الْأُولَىٰ وَأَقِمْنَ الصَّلَاةَ وَآتِينَ الزَّكَاةَ وَأَطِعْنَ اللَّهَ وَرَسُولَهُ إِنَّمَا يُرِيدُ اللَّهُ لِيُذْهِبَ عَنكُمُ الرِّجْسَ أَهْلَ الْبَيْتِ وَيُطَهِّرَكُمْ تَطْهِيرًا ۝ وَاذْكُرْنَ مَا يُتْلَىٰ فِي بُيُوتِكُنَّ مِنْ آيَاتِ اللَّهِ وَالْحِكْمَةِ إِنَّ اللَّهَ كَانَ لَطِيفًا خَبِيرًا ۝ إِنَّ الْمُسْلِمِينَ وَالْمُسْلِمَاتِ وَالْمُؤْمِنِينَ وَالْمُؤْمِنَاتِ وَالْقَانِتِينَ وَالْقَانِتَاتِ وَالصَّادِقِينَ وَالصَّادِقَاتِ وَالصَّابِرِينَ وَالصَّابِرَاتِ وَالْخَاشِعِينَ وَالْخَاشِعَاتِ وَالْمُتَصَدِّقِينَ وَالْمُتَصَدِّقَاتِ وَالصَّائِمِينَ وَالصَّائِمَاتِ وَالْحَافِظِينَ فُرُوجَهُمْ وَالْحَافِظَاتِ وَالذَّاكِرِينَ اللَّهَ كَثِيرًا وَالذَّاكِرَاتِ أَعَدَّ اللَّهُ لَهُم مَّغْفِرَةً وَأَجْرًا عَظِيمًا ۝

31. But if any of you devoutly obeys God and His Messenger and does good, righteous deeds, We will give her reward doubly; and We have prepared for her an honorable, generous provision (in Paradise).

32. O wives of the Prophet! You are not like any of the other women, provided that you keep from disobedience to God in reverence for Him and piety (and therefore act with awareness of your special status). So (even more than other believing women) do not be complaisant in your speech (when addressing men), lest he in whose heart is a disease should be moved to desire, but speak in an honorable way.

33. And (prefer to) remain in your homes (unless there is a need. If you do go out for a need) do not go out flaunting your charms as (women used to do) in the former times of Ignorance. And establish the Prayer in conformity with its conditions, and pay the Prescribed Purifying Alms, and obey God and His Messenger (in whatever they command). God only wills to remove from you, O members of the (Prophet's) household,[17] all that may be loathsome, and to purify you to the utmost of purity.

34. Keep in mind and study what is recited in your homes of God's Revelations and the Wisdom (which especially includes the Sunnah of His Messenger). Surely God is All-Subtle (penetrating down into the innermost part of people's heart and mind), All-Aware.

35. Surely all men and women who submit to God (whose submission is attested by their words and deeds), and all truly believing men and truly believing women, and all devoutly obedient men and devoutly obedient women, and all men and women honest and truthful in their speech (and true to their words in their actions), and all men and women who persevere (in obedience to God through all adversity), and all men and women humble (in mind and heart before God), and all men and women who give in alms (and in God's cause), and all men and women who fast (as an obligatory or commended act of devotion), and all men and women who guard their chastity (and avoid exposing their private parts), and all men and women who remember and mention God much – for them God has prepared forgiveness (to bring unforeseen blessings) and a tremendous reward.

17. As declared in a *hadīth*, Fāṭimah, the Messenger's daughter, and her husband 'Alī ibn Abī Ṭālib (the fourth Caliph), and their sons Ḥasan and Ḥusayn are also included in the Prophet's household (Muslim, "Faḍāil aṣ-Ṣaḥābah," 37, 61).

36. When God and His Messenger have decreed a matter, it is not for a believing man and a believing woman to have an option insofar as they themselves are concerned.[18] Whoever disobeys God and His Messenger has evidently gone astray.

37. (Remember) when you (O Messenger) said to him whom God has favored (with guidance to Islam and close companionship with the Prophet), and whom you have favored (with kind treatment, special consideration, and emancipation): "Retain your wife in marriage and fear God (concerning your treatment of her)." You were hiding within yourself what God (had already decreed and) would certainly bring to light: you were feeling apprehensive of people (that they might react in a way harmful to their faith), while God has a greater right that you should fear Him (lest you err in the implementation of His commands). So, when Zayd had come to the end of his union with her (and she had completed her period of waiting after the divorce), We united you with her in marriage, so that there should be no blame (or legal impediment) for the believers in respect of (their marrying) the wives of those whom they called their sons (though they really were not), when the latter have come to the end of their union with them. And God's command must be fulfilled.[19]

38. There is no hindrance for the Prophet with respect to what God has ordained and made lawful for him. This was God's way with those (Prophets) who passed before. The command of God is a decree determined (in due measures for every thing, event, and individual).

39. (The Prophets are those) who convey God's Messages and feel great awe of Him; and they hold none but God in awe. God suffices as One Who reckons and settles the accounts (of His servants).

40. O believers, (know) that Muḥammad is not the father of any man among you, but he is the Messenger of God and the Seal of the Prophets.[20] God has full knowledge of everything.

41. O you who believe, remember and mention God much;

42. And glorify Him (in that He is absolutely above all defects and having partners) in the morning and in the evening (day and night).[21]

43. He it is Who (in return for your remembrance of Him) bestows His special blessings upon you, with His angels (praying and asking His forgiveness for you), that He may lead you out of (all kinds of intellectual, spiritual, social, economic, and political) darkness into light (and keep them firm therein). He is All-Compassionate toward the believers.

18. This means absolute submission to the Islamic Law, and the rule of the Law. Since the Islamic Law is primarily based on the rules established by God in the Qur'ān and the Sunnah of the Messenger, everyone is equal before it, and no one can impose their own decisions or ideas upon others. So Islam has brought absolute equality and freedom to humankind and saved them from submission or slavery to the choices and decisions of others. It is God Who creates human beings and is therefore their owner. Human beings cannot even claim ownership over themselves, as it is not they who have created themselves or who maintain or provide for themselves. Servanthood or submission to God means freedom from all kinds of slavery to the created powers, including the human carnal soul, which always calls humankind to the evil that is opposed to their duty.

19. The Messenger's actions and norms of conduct constitute, like his sayings, the second source of the Islamic Law or constitution. His Companions inherited and transmitted whatever they observed while he was living among them, while his wives narrated and conveyed the rules and norms of the Islamic personal and family life. This heavy responsibility required that he should have wives of different temperaments, upbringing, and character. A great many of the religious matters and rules were narrated by these women, known as the Pure Wives.

Zayd ibn Hārithah was the Messenger's emancipated slave and servant, whom he called "my son" according to the customs of the time before adoption was legally abolished. The Messenger, upon him be peace and blessings, had requested that Zaynab bint Jahsh, a "noble-born" lady from the Messenger's clan, be married to this former slave to show in action that people should not judge others by their color or social status. However, their marriage did not last long. Zayd, realizing her wife's sublime character, admitted that he was spiritually and intellectually inferior to her. So, he eventually divorced her. As stated in: *We united you with her in marriage*, God ordered His Messenger to marry Zaynab. This was extremely difficult for the Messenger to do, because, according to the prevailing customs, "adopted" children were treated as if they were real children, and Zayd, as mentioned above, was his emancipated slave and servant. But God willed that this custom be abolished and first put it into effect through His Messenger. The Messenger apprehended that the people might draw incorrect conclusions and think unbecoming things about him if he were to perform such an action, and this would therefore harm their faith. But such a grounded "legal" fiction was to be eternally abolished, and God willed that such an established custom be abolished through His Messenger's actions, because only then would it be able to have the desired effect upon the people. So, the Messenger had no alternative other than to obey God's decree, as he always did.

20. The verse implies that those of superior rank and responsibility feel a fatherly affection toward those who work under them. If they are spiritual leaders, Prophets, or saints, for example, their compassion and affection will far exceed that of a father. As the people will see them as a father, they may consider it improper for such people to marry one of their women. To remove this illusion, the Qur'ān tells us that: "Divine Mercy causes the Prophet to have great affection for you. Due to his position as your leader, you are like his children. But as he is not your biological father, he can marry one of your women. His calling you 'my sons' does not mean you are legally his sons."

The verse also contains an implicit prediction, which, of course, proved to be true. It is that God's Messenger, upon him be peace and blessings, would not have a male child who would survive and succeed him. He would be succeeded by a female child and his progeny would continue through her. As known, the Messenger's line continued through Fātimah, his beloved daughter, who alone survived him from among his children.

21. All words of praise and glorification of God – extolling Him with His Perfect Attributes

of Power and Majesty, Beauty and Sublimity, and declaring that He is absolutely above having any defects or negative attributes shared by the creation, or above doing useless things, whether one utters these words vocally or says them silently in one's heart – are known as *dhikr* (remembrance of God). So, glorification of Him is also included in the meaning of *dhikr*. In addition to this, reading, reflecting, and studying to gain knowledge of God, speaking about Him to others are also included in the concept of *dhikr*.

In a *hadīth qudsī* (a Tradition whose meaning God directly inspired in the heart of the Messenger), the Messenger narrated: "God says: 'I am to My servant as he expects of Me, I am with him when he remembers Me. If he remembers Me in his heart, I remember him to Myself; if he remembers Me in an assembly, I mention him in an assembly better than his; if he draws nearer to Me a hand's span, I draw nearer to him an arm's length; if he draws nearer to Me an arm's length, I draw nearer to him a fathom's length; and if he comes to me walking, I rush to him with (great) speed' " (al-Bukhārī, "Tawḥīd," 50; Muslim, "Dhikr," 2).

God has bestowed a special distinction upon those who remember Him. The Messenger, upon him be peace and blessings, said: "The devotees have surpassed all." They asked: "Who are these exceptional people, O Messenger of God?" He replied: "They are men and women who remember God unceasingly" (Muslim, "Dhikr," 2). These are the people who are truly alive. Abū Mūsā reported from the Messenger: "The likeness of the house where God is mentioned and the one where He is not is like that of a living person to a dead person" (al-Bukhārī, Da'awāt," 66). Mujāhid, one of the earliest interpreters of the Qur'ān, explained: "A person cannot be one of 'those men and women who remember God much,' unless he or she remembers God at all times, standing, sitting, or lying in bed (as stated in 3: 191)."

Joining the assemblies or circles of *dhikr* is commendable, as shown by the following hadīth: Ibn 'Umar reported: "The Prophet, upon him peace and blessings, said: 'When you pass by a garden of Paradise, avail yourselves of it.' The Companions asked: 'What are the gardens of Paradise, O Messenger of God?' The Prophet, upon him be peace and blessings, replied: 'The assemblies or circles of *dhikr*. There are some angels of God who go about looking for such assemblies of *dhikr*, and when they find them they surround them' " (Muslim, "Dhikr," 39).

٤٢٣

423

٢٢ الجزء الثاني والعشرون

بِسْمِ اللَّهِ الرَّحْمَنِ الرَّحِيمِ

47. And (so) give the believers the glad tidings that surely for them is a great bounty from God (in addition to what they may have merited by their faith and good deeds).

48. And pay no heed to (the offers of) the unbelievers and the hypocrites, and do not mind the sufferings they cause you, and put your trust in God. God suffices as the One to rely on and to Whom affairs should be referred.

49. O you who believe! When you have made a marriage contract with any of the believing women (including those belonging to the People of the Book), and then divorce them before you have touched them, you have no reason to ask them to observe any waiting-period for you. Make some provision for them and release them in fair manner.[23]

50. O (most illustrious) Prophet! We have made lawful for you your wives to whom you have already paid their bridal-due, as well as those whom your right hands possess from among the captives of war that God has granted you, and the daughters of your paternal uncles and paternal aunts, and the daughters of your maternal uncles and maternal aunts,[24] who have emigrated (to Madīnah) for God's cause as you did; and any believing woman who offers herself to the Prophet (freely, without demanding any bridal-due) if the Prophet wants to marry her – a rule (of privilege) for you exclusively, not for the believers (in general) – We have (already decreed and) made known what We have enjoined on them with regard to their wives and those whom their right hands possess.[25] (This exceptional privilege[26] is) in order that there may not be any hindrance to you (in fulfilling your mission because of marriage relationships).[27] God is All-Forgiving, All-Compassionate.

44. On the Day when they meet Him, their greeting (from those who welcome them will be), "Peace" (the promise of eternal security from punishment). And He has prepared for them an honorable, generous reward.

45. O (most illustrious) Prophet! We have surely sent you (with the mission of Messengership) as a witness (to the truth through your life, and through your testimony on Judgment Day for your community concerning their deeds), and as a bearer of glad tidings (of prosperity in return for faith and righteousness) and a warner (against the consequences of misguidance);

46. And as one who calls (all humankind and the jinn) to God by His leave, and a light-diffusing lamp (enlightening minds and hearts, and showing the way to those who follow that light).[22]

22. The Qur'ān describes the sun as a lamp and the moon as a shining object (reflecting light) placed in the heavens (on this description and its meaning, see 25: 61, note 15). This verse presents God's Messenger, upon him be peace and blessings, through the simile of a light-diffusing (shining) lamp. This implies that the Prophet Muḥammad, upon him be peace and blessings, is a sun in the heaven of humankind and the jinn, enlightening their worlds and through which they can find their way. The fact that the Qur'ān uses for the Messenger the word (lamp) used for the sun, as well as the phrase light-diffusing or shining which it uses for the moon, suggests that the Messenger has a very bright light, and although he has absorbed this light, it is in fact from God, Who is the Source of all lights. As is known, the moon derives its light from the sun. The Messenger is like the sun with respect to his radiance and the moon with respect to the source of his light.

23. If the divorce mentioned in the verse takes place before any marriage-portion or bridal due has been determined, the husband must make provision according to his means. If it takes place after a bridal-due has already been appointed, half of what has been appointed should be given to the divorced woman. However, the woman can make remission and forgo it or the man can make remission and pay the full amount. (See 2: 236–237.)

24. In Judaism, a man can marry his nieces, while in Christianity, he cannot marry any relatives within seven degrees, but Islam allows marriage with one's cousins, but forbids marriage with one's nephews or nieces.

25. On these injunctions, see: 2: 221; 4: 3–4, notes 2–3.

26. Because of his mission, there are some exceptional rules for the Prophet, upon him be peace and blessings. Unlike other believing men, he was allowed to marry a believing woman who would come to him without demanding any bridal due. While all other Muslim men could marry the daughters of their uncles and aunts, whether they had emigrated or not, the Prophet was allowed to marry any among them provided they had emigrated. There were other exceptions that were just pertinent to the Messenger, for example: The *Tahajjud* Prayer (in the last third or later part of the night) was prescribed for the Prophet until his death; this is only supererogatory for other Muslims. Like other Prophets, his inheritance could not be shared by his "heirs" but was used as alms for the Muslim Community. Eating of the *Zakāh* was forbidden to him and his family, while all other needy Muslims could partake of it. The permission for him to marry as many as nine women was also exceptional for him, while other Muslims can only have four women together in marriage. While all other Muslim men can marry until their death, God's Messenger was prohibited to marry after some point in his life, as stipulated in verse 52 of this *surah*.

27. These special conditions were not introduced due to a need for women, but rather merely because of the role women played in the fulfillment of the Messenger's mission. Islam has rules for women and many of those rules can only be learned from women teachers and could be put to the Messenger only by women who had close relationships with him. So the reasons behind the Messenger's several marriages, while differing from case to case, all have to do with his role as the leader of the new Muslim community, and his responsibility to guide his followers toward the norms and values of Islam.

The Messenger, upon him be peace and blessings, married his first wife, fifteen years older than him, when he was 25 years old, fifteen years before his Prophethood began. He lived with her for almost 25 years, and after her death, he lived for nearly six years without a wife. Given the cultural and moral climate in which he lived, not to mention his youth and other factors, he nevertheless enjoyed a sound reputation for chastity, integrity, and trustworthiness. As soon as he was called to the Prophethood, he acquired enemies who made all sorts of charges. However, not even his fiercest enemies attacked his reputation, for doing so would have caused them to be ridiculed and discredited immediately. It is important to realize that his life was founded upon chastity and self-discipline from the outset, and remained thus. All his other marriages began when he was 53 years old, an age when very little real interest and desire for marriage remains, especially in Arabia where people grow old relatively earlier, and when especially in those days people's average life-expectancy was much lower.

Some marriages were contracted for specific reasons, such as:

* The Prophet's wives were young, middle-aged, and elderly. The accurate requirements and norms of Islamic family life for every age could be learnt within the Prophet's household better and then conveyed to other Muslims through his wives.

* Each wife was from a different clan or tribe, which allowed the Prophet to establish bonds of kinship and affinity throughout Arabia. This caused a profound attachment to him to spread Islam among the diverse peoples of the new *Ummah*, and also brought about and secured equality and brother/sisterhood among both in practical matters and in terms of the Religion.

* Both before and after the Prophet's death, each wife proved to be of great benefit and service. They conveyed and interpreted Islam to their people in all its inner and outer experiences, as well as the qualities, manners, and faith of the man who was the living embodiment of the Qur'ān in *every* aspect of his life. In this way, all of their people learned the Qur'ān, the Traditions, *tafsīr* (Qur'ānic interpretation and commentary), and *fiqh* (understanding of the Qur'an and Sunnah as law). Thus, through his wives these people became fully aware of Islam's essence and spirit.

* These marriages allowed the Prophet, upon him be peace and blessings, to establish kinship ties throughout Arabia, and thus to move freely wherever he wished and to be accepted as a member in each family. In addition, everyone so connected to him felt that they could approach him personally for guidance on any issue. The entire tribe also benefited from this connection; they considered themselves fortunate and took pride in their new relationship. For example, such relationships were established for the Umayyads (through Umm Habībah), the Hashimites (through Zaynab bint Jahsh), and the Banū Makhzm (through Umm Salamah).

* It is also a highly notable fact that all the Prophet's wives (except 'Ā'ishah and Māriyah) were divorcees or widows, thus underlying the importance and care that needs to be given to lone women in Islamic society, as against the then prevalent norm of casting them off.

ترجِي مَن تَشَاءُ مِنْهُنَّ وَتُؤْوِي إِلَيْكَ مَن تَشَاءُ وَمَنِ ابْتَغَيْتَ مِمَّنْ
عَزَلْتَ فَلَا جُنَاحَ عَلَيْكَ ذَلِكَ أَدْنَى أَن تَقَرَّ أَعْيُنُهُنَّ وَلَا يَحْزَنَّ
وَيَرْضَيْنَ بِمَا آتَيْتَهُنَّ كُلُّهُنَّ وَاللَّهُ يَعْلَمُ مَا فِي قُلُوبِكُمْ
وَكَانَ اللَّهُ عَلِيمًا حَلِيمًا ۞ لَا يَحِلُّ لَكَ النِّسَاءُ مِن بَعْدُ وَلَا أَن
تَبَدَّلَ بِهِنَّ مِنْ أَزْوَاجٍ وَلَوْ أَعْجَبَكَ حُسْنُهُنَّ إِلَّا مَا مَلَكَتْ يَمِينُكَ
وَكَانَ اللَّهُ عَلَى كُلِّ شَيْءٍ رَقِيبًا ۞ يَا أَيُّهَا الَّذِينَ آمَنُوا
لَا تَدْخُلُوا بُيُوتَ النَّبِيِّ إِلَّا أَن يُؤْذَنَ لَكُمْ إِلَى طَعَامٍ غَيْرَ
نَاظِرِينَ إِنَاهُ وَلَكِنْ إِذَا دُعِيتُمْ فَادْخُلُوا فَإِذَا طَعِمْتُمْ
فَانتَشِرُوا وَلَا مُسْتَأْنِسِينَ لِحَدِيثٍ إِنَّ ذَلِكُمْ كَانَ يُؤْذِي
النَّبِيَّ فَيَسْتَحْيِي مِنكُمْ وَاللَّهُ لَا يَسْتَحْيِي مِنَ الْحَقِّ وَإِذَا
سَأَلْتُمُوهُنَّ مَتَاعًا فَاسْأَلُوهُنَّ مِن وَرَاءِ حِجَابٍ ذَلِكُمْ
أَطْهَرُ لِقُلُوبِكُمْ وَقُلُوبِهِنَّ وَمَا كَانَ لَكُمْ أَن تُؤْذُوا
رَسُولَ اللَّهِ وَلَا أَن تَنكِحُوا أَزْوَاجَهُ مِنْ بَعْدِهِ أَبَدًا
إِنَّ ذَلِكُمْ كَانَ عِندَ اللَّهِ عَظِيمًا ۞ إِن
تُبْدُوا شَيْئًا أَوْ تُخْفُوهُ فَإِنَّ اللَّهَ كَانَ بِكُلِّ شَيْءٍ عَلِيمًا ۞

51. You can put off whomever among them (who offer themselves to you freely) you please, and accept to yourself whomever you please, as you can defer the turn of visiting any of them (your wives) you please, and take to you whomever you please.[28] There is no blame on you if you give precedence to one whom you deferred before. It will make it more likely that they are pleased, and do not grieve (when they are deferred), and that all of them will be content with your treatment of them. God knows (O people) whatever is in your hearts. God is indeed All-Knowing, All-Clement.

52. Other women (than those just mentioned and those already married to you[29]) will not be lawful for you to take; nor, (seeing that they – your wives – have preferred God and His Messenger over the charms of the world) are you allowed to change them for other wives, even though their fineness should please you, except those whom your right hands possess. God is ever watchful over everything.

53. O you who believe! Do not enter the Prophet's rooms (in his house) unless you have been given leave, (and when invited) to a meal, without waiting for the proper time (when the meal is to be served). Rather, when you are invited, enter (his private rooms) at the proper time; and when you have had your meal, disperse. Do not linger for mere talk. That causes trouble for the Prophet, and he is shy of (asking) you (to leave). But God does not shy away from (teaching you) the truth. When you ask something of them (his wives), ask them from behind a screen. Your doing so is purer for your hearts and for their hearts. It is not for you to cause hurt to God's Messenger as it is unlawful for you ever to marry his widows after him. That (marrying his widows) would be an enormity in God's sight.

54. Whether you reveal something or keep it secret, (know) that surely God has full knowledge of everything.

28. It is possible that this verse has both of the meanings given (i.e., it is related to both the Prophet's treatment of the women who would offer themselves to him, and the rotation in the conjugal attentions due to his wives.) Islam orders a husband who has more than one wife to be just in his relations with them and to observe a strict rotation in the conjugal attentions due to his wives. Since this is difficult, it advises one to be content with one wife (4: 3). However, since the Messenger had many wise purposes for his marriages, some of which have been mentioned in the previous note, he was not obliged to observe this responsibility. But, as reported by 'Ā'ishah in the books of *Hadīth* Abū Dāwūd, "Nikāḥ," 39; at-Tirmidhī, "Nikāḥ," 42), he showed no negligence in observing it during his life. Although the verse allows him freedom to prefer or defer any of his wives in visiting, it also offers him a way not to grieve any of them and make all of them happy. If he had postponed visiting any of them, he could give her precedence the next time.

29. This prohibition is related to other women than those mentioned in verse 50. However, since the verse was revealed when the Messenger already had nine wives, it also forbids him to marry again. This implies that the purposes for his marriages have already been fulfilled.

55. There is no blame on them (the wives of the Prophet, if they speak without a screen) with their fathers (including grandfathers and uncles both paternal and maternal), or their sons (including grandsons), or their brothers, or their brothers' sons, or the sons of their sisters, or the Muslim women and women of good conduct with whom they associate, or those (bondsmaids) whom their right hands possess. Keep, (O wives of the Prophet,) from disobedience to God in reverence for Him and piety (observing this command as well as all of His other commands). God is indeed a witness over everything.

56. Surely God and His angels bless the Prophet (He always treats him with His special mercy, with the angels praying to Him to grant him the highest station of praise with Him and for the decisive victory of his Religion). O you who believe, invoke the blessings of God on him, and pray to God to bestow His peace on him, greeting him with the best greeting. (Love and follow him with utmost sincerity and faithfulness, and give yourselves to his way with perfect submission.)[30]

57. Those who affront God and His Messenger (through disrespect for Him in words and acts and for His Messenger and Islamic values), God certainly curses them (excludes them from His mercy) in this world and the Hereafter, and has prepared for them a shameful, humiliating punishment.[31]

58. And those who affront believing men and believing women without their having done any wrong to deserve it, they have surely burdened themselves with calumny and a blatant sin.[32]

59. O (most illustrious) Prophet! Tell your wives and your daughters, as well as the women (wives and daughters) of the believers, to draw over themselves some part of their outer garments (when outside their homes and when before men whom

they are not forbidden to marry because of blood relation).[33] This is better and more convenient for them to be recognized (and respected for their decency and decorum) and not harrassed.[34] God is indeed All-Forgiving, All-Compassionate.[35]

60. Assuredly, if the hypocrites and those in whose hearts there is a sickness, and those scare-mongers in the City (given to spreading false rumors to cause disturbance in the heartland of the Islamic Community) do not desist, We will most certainly urge you against them, and then they will not be able to remain in it as your neighbors except a little while only,

61. Excluded from God's Mercy for ever, and wherever they may be found they will be seized, and killed one and all.[36]

62. (That was) the way of God with those who passed before. You will never find any change in God's way.

30. Calling God's blessings and peace upon God's Messenger at least once in a lifetime is incumbent upon every Muslim. Doing so at each mention of his name is a highly recommended act. According to the Shāfi'ī and Ḥanbalī schools, it is obligatory in the last sitting of every Prayer (Ṣalāh) after tashahhud, without which the Prayer is not acceptable. According to other schools, it is a sunnah.

Calling God's blessings and peace upon the Messenger is a link between him and the believers. His responsibility was extremely grave and he is always concerned with the Muslims individually and collectively, even after his death. So calling God's blessings and peace upon him as a religious duty was not restricted to his lifetime. By doing so we are also praying for ourselves, because we are both building an important connection with him and petitioning God through him to help us with our religious responsibilities.

Upon the injunction of the Messenger, we must include his family and even his progeny in calling God's blessings and peace upon him.

That the injunction of calling God's blessings and peace upon him stays in effect even after his death until the Last Day signifies that praying for the dead is a valid religious act and may be of help for them.

31. The original word (which we have translated as affront) is adhā. It is mainly used to express any words that hurt another's feelings. So the verse is warning us about any unbecoming words that we may utter concerning God and His Messenger, and Islamic values. The verse also forbids any disrespectful act toward God and His Messenger, and Islamic values.

32. If one says something about a believer with which the believer will not be pleased, this is backbiting, which the Qur'an decisively forbids. If one says something about a believer that is untrue, this is a calumny. In addition to forbidding such talk about the believers, the verse also forbids any unbecoming talk or act that will hurt a believer.

Before the injunction of flogging with a hundred stripes (24: 2), the Qur'an had ordered the punishment of fornicators by scolding and beating (4: 16). However, this was abrogated by the injunction of flogging them. Therefore, hurting a believer with unbecoming words is forbidden in any case. Thus, the permission to hurt or affront them that this verse gives in case of their having done some wrong concerns any acts that the law may punish in this way. Such a punishment can only be implemented by legal authorities.

While the Qur'an forbids affronting any believer without their having done any wrong that would deserve such an affront, it decisively forbids offending God's Messenger without specifying any exception and regards offending him as if one has offended Almighty God. This shows the Messenger's sinlessness and that he is exalted above any blemish.

33. The verse means that women must cover their heads and upper parts of their bodies. The majority of scholars conclude that they must also cover their faces except the eyes. As understood from the Traditions, this was the practice during the Messenger, upon him be peace and blessings, and the Companions (Abū Dāwūd, "Libās," 32, "Menāsik," 34; Imam Mālik, "Ḥajj," 16).

34. There are two important instances of wisdom in ordering Muslim women to cover themselves. Muslim women are women who deserve respect and who are protected from any offense or harassment. The veil both shows that they are Muslims, decent, and free (not bondsmaids), and demands protection against any harassment. Although no one can claim that a woman who does not wear a veil desires to attract the attention of men to herself, it is an undeniable and frequently witnessed reality that a woman who displays her charms often exposes herself to unwanted attention.

35. Despite all contrary assertions in the modern world, God, Who relates the injunction of veiling for women to His infinite forgiveness and compassion, explicitly declared that it is from compassion for women.

36. This is, as will be pointed out in the following verse, the end that the hypocrites must inevitably come to, as a consequence of the sedition they cause in society.

426   سورة الأحزاب   ٤٢٦

يَسْـَٔلُكَ ٱلنَّاسُ عَنِ ٱلسَّاعَةِ قُلْ إِنَّمَا عِلْمُهَا عِندَ ٱللَّهِ وَمَا يُدْرِيكَ لَعَلَّ ٱلسَّاعَةَ تَكُونُ قَرِيبًا ۝ إِنَّ ٱللَّهَ لَعَنَ ٱلْكَٰفِرِينَ وَأَعَدَّ لَهُمْ سَعِيرًا ۝ خَٰلِدِينَ فِيهَآ أَبَدًا لَّا يَجِدُونَ وَلِيًّا وَلَا نَصِيرًا ۝ يَوْمَ تُقَلَّبُ وُجُوهُهُمْ فِى ٱلنَّارِ يَقُولُونَ يَٰلَيْتَنَآ أَطَعْنَا ٱللَّهَ وَأَطَعْنَا ٱلرَّسُولَا۠ ۝ وَقَالُوا۟ رَبَّنَآ إِنَّآ أَطَعْنَا سَادَتَنَا وَكُبَرَآءَنَا فَأَضَلُّونَا ٱلسَّبِيلَا۠ ۝ رَبَّنَآ ءَاتِهِمْ ضِعْفَيْنِ مِنَ ٱلْعَذَابِ وَٱلْعَنْهُمْ لَعْنًا كَبِيرًا ۝ يَٰٓأَيُّهَا ٱلَّذِينَ ءَامَنُوا۟ لَا تَكُونُوا۟ كَٱلَّذِينَ ءَاذَوْا۟ مُوسَىٰ فَبَرَّأَهُ ٱللَّهُ مِمَّا قَالُوا۟ وَكَانَ عِندَ ٱللَّهِ وَجِيهًا ۝ يَٰٓأَيُّهَا ٱلَّذِينَ ءَامَنُوا۟ ٱتَّقُوا۟ ٱللَّهَ وَقُولُوا۟ قَوْلًا سَدِيدًا ۝ يُصْلِحْ لَكُمْ أَعْمَٰلَكُمْ وَيَغْفِرْ لَكُمْ ذُنُوبَكُمْ وَمَن يُطِعِ ٱللَّهَ وَرَسُولَهُ فَقَدْ فَازَ فَوْزًا عَظِيمًا ۝ إِنَّا عَرَضْنَا ٱلْأَمَانَةَ عَلَى ٱلسَّمَٰوَٰتِ وَٱلْأَرْضِ وَٱلْجِبَالِ فَأَبَيْنَ أَن يَحْمِلْنَهَا وَأَشْفَقْنَ مِنْهَا وَحَمَلَهَا ٱلْإِنسَٰنُ إِنَّهُۥ كَانَ ظَلُومًا جَهُولًا ۝ لِّيُعَذِّبَ ٱللَّهُ ٱلْمُنَٰفِقِينَ وَٱلْمُنَٰفِقَٰتِ وَٱلْمُشْرِكِينَ وَٱلْمُشْرِكَٰتِ وَيَتُوبَ ٱللَّهُ عَلَى ٱلْمُؤْمِنِينَ وَٱلْمُؤْمِنَٰتِ وَكَانَ ٱللَّهُ غَفُورًا رَّحِيمًا ۝

---

63. People ask you about the Last Hour (when it will befall). Say: "Knowledge of it rests with God alone." For all you know, the Last Hour may well be near.

64. Surely God has cursed (eternally excluded from His Mercy) the unbelievers, and has prepared for them the Blaze,

65. To abide therein forever. They will find neither guardian nor helper.

66. On the Day when their faces are turned over and over in the Fire, they will exclaim, "Oh, woe to us! Would that we had obeyed God and obeyed the Messenger!"

67. And they will say: "Our Lord! Surely we obeyed our chiefs and our great ones, and they caused us to follow a misleading path.

68. "Our Lord! Cause them to suffer the punishment doubled, and curse them with a mighty curse (so that they are utterly excluded, absolutely and eternally, from Your Mercy)!"

69. O you who believe! Do not be like those (among the Children of Israel) who affronted Moses, and (be mindful that) God proved him to be innocent of all that they alleged against him. He was of great honor in God's sight.[37]

70. O you who believe! Act in reverence for God and piously, without doing anything to incur His punishment, and always speak words true, proper and straight to the point,

71. That He will make your deeds good and upright and forgive you your sins. Whoever obeys God and His Messenger has surely attained to a mighty triumph.

72. We offered the Trust to the heavens, and the earth, and the mountains, but they shrank from bearing it, and were afraid of it (fearful of being unable to fulfill its responsibility), but human has undertaken it. He is indeed prone to doing great wrong and misjudging, and acting out of sheer ignorance.[38]

73. (As a consequence of the choice of each individual) God will punish the hypocrites, men and women, and those men and women who associate partners with God, and He will turn to the believing men and women with forgiveness (and compassion in return for their repentance for any wrong they do). God is indeed All-Forgiving, All-Compassionate.

37. This warning came with respect to the Messenger's marriage with Zaynab, the Mother of Believers. Hypocrites and some with weak faith spoke unbecomingly about this event and about the Messenger in connection with it. The same kinds of offending words were uttered about the Prophet Moses, upon him be peace. Just as the Prophet Moses was absolutely free of any such offences alleged against him, God's Messenger, upon him be peace and blessings, is also absolutely free of any similar allegations. As stated in verses 57 and 58 and note 31 and 32 above, any offensive word uttered against the Messenger is as if uttered against God, for he is infallible and free of any blemish.

38. For the meaning of the Trust, see Appendix 14.

37. By concluding with the emphasis on God's being All-Forgiving and All-Compassionate, this verse is stating that out of His Forgiveness and Compassion God will support the believers and enable them to follow the Straight Path because they have chosen that Path and try to follow it. He will also accept their repentance when they repent for their sins, and forgive them their shortcomings in following His Path. The verse also encourages the hypocrites and those who associate partners with God not to sink into despair and to give up their way to turn to God.

SŪRAH 34

AS-SABA' (SHEBA)

Makkah period

Revealed in Makkah in the initial years of the revelation of Islam, this *sūrah* of 54 verses derives its name from verse 15 in which the civilization of *Saba'* (Sheba) is mentioned. That civilization was founded in Yemen and was famous for its cities rich in greenery, dams, and trade. A Queen of this country, who was mentioned in *Sūrat an-Naml* along with her experiences with the Prophet Solomon, upon him be peace, became a Muslim (for detailed information, see 27: 22–44, notes 10–17). This *sūrah* dwells for the most part on the pillars of faith, such as the Divine Oneness, the afterlife, and Prophethood. By mentioning the civilization of *Saba'* with its magnificence and tragic end, and the favors God granted to the Prophets David and Solomon, upon them be peace, this *sūrah* warns us that God's favors come as a result of following His commandments for human life and continually thanking Him in return for His favors. Thanking means acknowledging that all of one's achievements belong to God, feeling gratitude in return for them, and obeying His commandments.

In the Name of God, the All-Merciful, the All-Compassionate.

1. All praise and gratitude are for God to Whom belongs whatever is in the heavens and whatever is on the earth (for it is He Who has created them and sustains them); and for Him are all praise and gratitude in the Hereafter (as it is He alone Who will found it as an eternal abode for His servants). He is the All-Wise, the All-Aware.

2. He knows whatever enters into the earth and whatever comes out of it, and whatever descends from the heaven and whatever ascends to it. He is the All-Compassionate, the All-Forgiving.

3. The unbelievers say: "The Last Hour will not come upon us." Say: "No indeed! By my Lord – and He is the Knower of the unseen – it most certainly will come upon you." Not an atom's weight of whatever there is in the heavens or in the earth escapes Him, nor is there anything smaller than that, or greater, but it is (recorded) in a Manifest Book.[1]

4. (That is so, in order) that He may reward those who believe and do good, righteous deeds. It is they for whom there is forgiveness (to bring unforeseen blessings) and an honorable, generous provision.

5. Whereas those who strive against Our

Revelations, seeking to frustrate and void (them), for those (who have thus distanced themselves from their Lord) is a painful punishment of loathsome kind (earned by their own loathsome deeds).

6. Those to whom the knowledge (of the truth) has been granted are well aware that what is sent down to you from your Lord (the Qur'ān) is the truth (and what

it declares of the afterlife is therefore true also), and that it guides to the Path of the All-Glorious with irresistible might, the All-Praiseworthy.

7. But those who disbelieve say (in ridicule): "Shall we show you a man who will inform you that after you have been scattered entirely to dust, you will, even then, be raised in a new creation?

---

1. On the Manifest Book, see 6: 59, note 13; 13: 39, note 13; 17: 14, note 10; 27: 1, note 1.

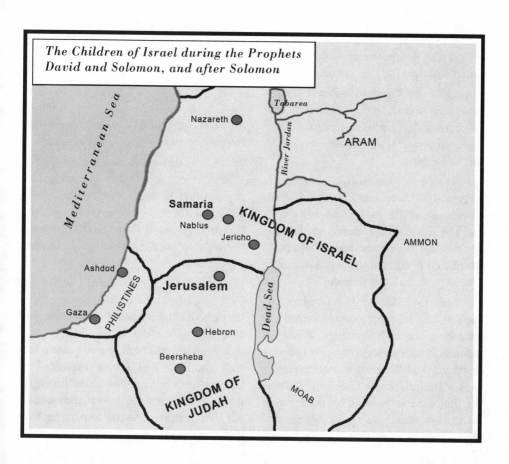

The Children of Israel during the Prophets David and Solomon, and after Solomon

428

سُورَةُ سَبَأٍ   ٤٢٨

أَفْتَرَىٰ عَلَى اللَّهِ كَذِبًا أَمْ بِهِ جِنَّةٌ ۗ بَلِ الَّذِينَ لَا يُؤْمِنُونَ بِالْآخِرَةِ فِي الْعَذَابِ وَالضَّلَالِ الْبَعِيدِ ۝ أَفَلَمْ يَرَوْا إِلَىٰ مَا بَيْنَ أَيْدِيهِمْ وَمَا خَلْفَهُمْ مِنَ السَّمَاءِ وَالْأَرْضِ ۚ إِنْ نَشَأْ نَخْسِفْ بِهِمُ الْأَرْضَ أَوْ نُسْقِطْ عَلَيْهِمْ كِسَفًا مِنَ السَّمَاءِ ۚ إِنَّ فِي ذَٰلِكَ لَآيَةً لِكُلِّ عَبْدٍ مُنِيبٍ ۝ وَلَقَدْ آتَيْنَا دَاوُودَ مِنَّا فَضْلًا ۖ يَا جِبَالُ أَوِّبِي مَعَهُ وَالطَّيْرَ ۖ وَأَلَنَّا لَهُ الْحَدِيدَ ۝ أَنِ اعْمَلْ سَابِغَاتٍ وَقَدِّرْ فِي السَّرْدِ ۖ وَاعْمَلُوا صَالِحًا ۖ إِنِّي بِمَا تَعْمَلُونَ بَصِيرٌ ۝ وَلِسُلَيْمَانَ الرِّيحَ غُدُوُّهَا شَهْرٌ وَرَوَاحُهَا شَهْرٌ ۖ وَأَسَلْنَا لَهُ عَيْنَ الْقِطْرِ ۖ وَمِنَ الْجِنِّ مَنْ يَعْمَلُ بَيْنَ يَدَيْهِ بِإِذْنِ رَبِّهِ ۖ وَمَنْ يَزِغْ مِنْهُمْ عَنْ أَمْرِنَا نُذِقْهُ مِنْ عَذَابِ السَّعِيرِ ۝ يَعْمَلُونَ لَهُ مَا يَشَاءُ مِنْ مَحَارِيبَ وَتَمَاثِيلَ وَجِفَانٍ كَالْجَوَابِ وَقُدُورٍ رَاسِيَاتٍ ۚ اعْمَلُوا آلَ دَاوُودَ شُكْرًا ۚ وَقَلِيلٌ مِنْ عِبَادِيَ الشَّكُورُ ۝ فَلَمَّا قَضَيْنَا عَلَيْهِ الْمَوْتَ مَا دَلَّهُمْ عَلَىٰ مَوْتِهِ إِلَّا دَابَّةُ الْأَرْضِ تَأْكُلُ مِنْسَأَتَهُ ۖ فَلَمَّا خَرَّ تَبَيَّنَتِ الْجِنُّ أَنْ لَوْ كَانُوا يَعْلَمُونَ الْغَيْبَ مَا لَبِثُوا فِي الْعَذَابِ الْمُهِينِ ۝

8. "Does he fabricate something false in attribution to God or is there a madness in him?" No! (The truth is that) those who disbelieve in the Hereafter are in torment (of mind and heart) and lost far in error.

9. Do they never consider that it is the heaven and the earth that are (extended) before and after them (so they are entirely and inescapably enclosed within His Kingdom)? If We so will, We can cause the earth to swallow them, or cause lumps of the heaven to fall down upon them. Surely in this is a sign for every servant of God who (being sincere in quest of the truth) will turn (to Him) in contrition.

10. Assuredly We graced David with a great favor from Us: "O mountains! Sing the praises of God with him, and likewise you birds!"[2] And We also made iron supple for him;

11. (So that he was enabled to obey the command): "Make long coats-of-mail (to cover more of the body) and order with care the sequence (of actions in the process)". And (O family and followers of David,) do good, righteous deeds. Surely I see very well all that you do."[3]

12. And to Solomon We (subjugated) the wind: its morning course covered the distance of a month's journey (at normal pace), and its evening course, a month's journey.[4] And We caused molten copper to flow for him (like a fountain).[5] Among the jinn were some who, by the leave of his Lord, worked under him. Whoever of them swerved away from Our command

(by disobeying him), We would make him taste the punishment of a fiery blaze.[6]

13. They made for him whatever he wished – sanctuaries, and figures (of inanimate objects), and carvings, as well as basins like ponds and boilers built into the ground. "Work, O family of David, in thankfulness to Me!" Few are the truly thankful among My servants.

14. Then, when We executed Our decree for his death, nothing showed them (the jinn who had been laboring at the tasks he assigned to them) that he was dead, except that a termite had been gnawing away his staff (until it broke). Then when he fell to the ground, it became clear to the jinn that if they had known the Unseen, they would not have continued in the tormenting toil that humiliated them.[7]

2. For an explanation, see 21: 79, note 10.

3. This is both an order to give thanks in return for God's favors and a warning to use all of God's favors, such as the ability to make coats-of-mail out of iron, within the limits established by God and for lawful purposes.

4. See 21: 81, note 11. Despite the fact that conditions usually change, the wind kept its speed every day both in the morning and in the evening for Solomon.

5. The verses: *We also made iron supple for him* (10); and *We caused molten copper to flow for him (like a fountain)* (12) indicate that softening iron and melting copper to use in making different tools are two of God's greatest bounties for humankind, revealed through two of His Messengers. It also points to the virtues of those two Messengers. Softening iron, melting copper, and extracting minerals is the origin, source, and basis of all material industries. These favors were granted to two great Prophets, who ruled according to God's commandments, and these have become the basis of most industries that serve our needs today.

By endowing two of His Prophets, who were both spiritual and temporal leaders, with craftsmanship and industry, God urges people toward craftsmanship and industry. In these verses, God Almighty suggests:

> I endowed two servants of Mine who obeyed My religious commandments with such skill that one could cast iron into any mold and then use it as an important source of strength for his rule, and the other could make many things out of molten copper. Since these are possible and since iron and copper have great significance for your social life, such wisdom and skill will be bestowed on you if you obey My commands of creation, My laws of nature. Eventually you will attain it. (*The Words*, "the 20th Word," 269)

By softening iron and smelting copper, people have achieved great industrial progress and material power. These verses direct our attention toward this truth. These verses not only warned earlier peoples, who did not appreciate its importance, they also warn the idle people of today.

6. Since the jinn are created from fire, it is understood that they are punished with something from fire.

7. It is understood that a termite had been gnawing away Solomon's staff from within it. It must have taken it a long time to gnaw away a staff so that it would break. If the jinn had known the Unseen (beyond the reach of a created being's perception), they could have been aware of this. This verse may also be referring figuratively to the fact that Solomon's kingdom had for long been being "gnawed away" from within it by some secret organizations. The jinn had not been aware of this either.

لَقَدْ كَانَ لِسَبَإٍ فِى مَسْكَنِهِمْ ءَايَةٌ جَنَّتَانِ عَن يَمِينٍ وَشِمَالٍ كُلُوا۟ مِن رِّزْقِ رَبِّكُمْ وَٱشْكُرُوا۟ لَهُۥ بَلْدَةٌ طَيِّبَةٌ وَرَبٌّ غَفُورٌ ۝ فَأَعْرَضُوا۟ فَأَرْسَلْنَا عَلَيْهِمْ سَيْلَ ٱلْعَرِمِ وَبَدَّلْنَٰهُم بِجَنَّتَيْهِمْ جَنَّتَيْنِ ذَوَاتَىْ أُكُلٍ خَمْطٍ وَأَثْلٍ وَشَىْءٍ مِّن سِدْرٍ قَلِيلٍ ۝ ذَٰلِكَ جَزَيْنَٰهُم بِمَا كَفَرُوا۟ وَهَلْ نُجَٰزِىٓ إِلَّا ٱلْكَفُورَ ۝ وَجَعَلْنَا بَيْنَهُمْ وَبَيْنَ ٱلْقُرَى ٱلَّتِى بَٰرَكْنَا فِيهَا قُرًى ظَٰهِرَةً وَقَدَّرْنَا فِيهَا ٱلسَّيْرَ سِيرُوا۟ فِيهَا لَيَالِىَ وَأَيَّامًا ءَامِنِينَ ۝ فَقَالُوا۟ رَبَّنَا بَٰعِدْ بَيْنَ أَسْفَارِنَا وَظَلَمُوٓا۟ أَنفُسَهُمْ فَجَعَلْنَٰهُمْ أَحَادِيثَ وَمَزَّقْنَٰهُمْ كُلَّ مُمَزَّقٍ إِنَّ فِى ذَٰلِكَ لَءَايَٰتٍ لِّكُلِّ صَبَّارٍ شَكُورٍ ۝ وَلَقَدْ صَدَّقَ عَلَيْهِمْ إِبْلِيسُ ظَنَّهُۥ فَٱتَّبَعُوهُ إِلَّا فَرِيقًا مِّنَ ٱلْمُؤْمِنِينَ ۝ وَمَا كَانَ لَهُۥ عَلَيْهِم مِّن سُلْطَٰنٍ إِلَّا لِنَعْلَمَ مَن يُؤْمِنُ بِٱلْءَاخِرَةِ مِمَّنْ هُوَ مِنْهَا فِى شَكٍّ وَرَبُّكَ عَلَىٰ كُلِّ شَىْءٍ حَفِيظٌ ۝ قُلِ ٱدْعُوا۟ ٱلَّذِينَ زَعَمْتُم مِّن دُونِ ٱللَّهِ لَا يَمْلِكُونَ مِثْقَالَ ذَرَّةٍ فِى ٱلسَّمَٰوَٰتِ وَلَا فِى ٱلْأَرْضِ وَمَا لَهُمْ فِيهِمَا مِن شِرْكٍ وَمَا لَهُۥ مِنْهُم مِّن ظَهِيرٍ ۝

---

15. Indeed, there was a sign (a meaningful lesson) for the people of Sheba to take from their abode[8] –two (lovely, vast expanses of) gardens, on the right and on the left. "Eat of the provision your Lord has granted you, and give thanks to Him: a land most wholesome and a Lord All-Forgiving."

16. But they turned away (from thanksgiving to the sins of luxury and heedless self-indulgence). So We sent upon them the flood of (waters released from) the dams, and converted their two (lovely) gardens into a couple of gardens yielding bitter produce, tamarisks, and sparse lote-trees.

17. Thus We recompensed them for their (sins originating in persistent) ingratitude. Do We ever punish any but the ingrate?

18. We had set between them and the lands We blessed (Palestine and Damascus, with great blessings for their people) many towns within sight of one another, and We had established the journey distances (between them for ease and safety): "Travel therein by night or by day in security!"

19. But (this comfort and security spoiled them, and) they said: "Our Lord! Make the distances between our travel-stages longer!"[9], and they wronged themselves (by committing sins). So We caused them to become one of the legends (to circulate among later generations about the distant past), and dispersed them around in numerous fragments.[10] Surely in that are signs (important lessons) for all who are greatly patient and perseverant (in obedience to God and in adversity for His sake), and greatly thankful (for His favors).

20. Iblīs certainly found his conjecture (about humankind) true in what they (the people of Sheba) did. (He called them, and) they followed him, all but a group of true believers.[11]

21. And yet, he had no authority over them (to compel them to do anything),[12] except in that (by testing humankind through him) We distinguish those who truly believe in the Hereafter from those who are in doubt concerning it. Your Lord keeps watch and record of all things.

22. Say: "Call upon those (things or beings) whom you fancy to be deities besides God: they have no ownership or authority over an atom's weight (of anything) either in the heavens or on the earth (so that they could benefit you therewith or avert from you any harm), nor do they have any share in (governing), nor does He (God) have any aide from among them.

8. On the people of Sheba, see 27, note 9, and note 10 below.

9. This was like the demand of the Children of Israel for the produce of the soil when they were provided with manna and quails by God in the desert (2: 57). They said: *"Moses, we will no longer be able to endure one sort of food. Pray for us to your Lord, that He may bring forth for us of all that the soil produces – its green herbs, and its cucumbers, and its corn, and its lentils, and its onions." He (Moses) responded: "Would you have in exchange what is meaner for what is better?"* (2: 61) (For an explanation, see 2, notes 72–73). They were not content with what God had provided for them, and instead of thanking God, spoiled by richness, they indulged in sins.

10. The people of Sheba ruled in southern Arabia for almost 1,000 years from around 1100 BC to around 115 BC. Their capital was Ma'ārib. They controlled the trade between East Africa, India, the Far East, and Arabia with Egypt, Syria, Greece, and Rome. In addition to this, they had an excellent irrigation system that dotted the length and breadth of the country with dams. Their land was unusually fertile and lush. Between their lands and Syria there were cities that were closely located to each other and travelers could travel in this vast area in security. As understood from the relationship between the Prophet Solomon, upon him be peace, and the Queen of Sheba in his time (27: 22–44), the Divine Religion found way to their land, although they had previously worshipped the sun. However, they went astray later and their prosperous life drove them to sins without repentance. They did not give heed to the warnings of the Prophets sent to them. In the end they deserved a severe punishment. The dams and the irrigation systems collapsed and their cities and fertile lands were overwhelmed by floods, and changed into wastelands. The people were scattered throughout Arabia in small groups, and the civilization of Sheba came to exist only in tales that circulated among people.

11. For the conjecture of Iblīs concerning humankind, see 15: 39–40: *(Iblīs said:) "Because You have allowed me to rebel and go astray, I will indeed deck out to be appealing to them on the earth (the worldly, material dimension of human existence and the path of error), and I will surely cause them all to rebel and go astray, except Your servants from among them, endowed with sincerity in faith and Your worship."*; 4: 119: *"I will surely lead them astray"*; and 7: 17: *"...Then I will come upon them from before them and from behind them, and from their right and from their left. And You will not find most of them thankful."*

12. For similar statements and an explanation, see 14: 22; 15: 42, note 10.

23. Besides, no intercession (for the fulfillment of any demand and for the accomplishment of any deed) is of any avail before Him, except that it be made for him (and by him) whom He permits.[13] Yet, when the dread and awe (the angels, whose intercession those polytheists hope for, feel before God's commands) is removed from their hearts, (other angels) ask: "What has your Lord commanded?" They answer: "The truth (that which is always and unalterably true)."[14] He is the All-Exalted, the All-Great.

24. Say: "Who is it that provides for you out of the heavens and the earth?" Say: "It is God! Surely then, either we (who believe in His Oneness as the Deity, Lord, and Supreme Sovereign) or you (who associate partners with Him in His Divinity, Lordship, and Sovereignty) follow the right guidance or are in obvious error."

25. Say: "(If you consider us to be committing a wrong in believing in and worshipping the One God, then know that) you will not be called to account for what we have done, nor will we be called to account for what you do."

26. Say: "Our Lord will bring us all together and then He will judge between us with truth and separate us. He is One Who judges between people with truth and separates them, the All-Knowing."[15]

27. Say: "Show me those beings that you have joined with Him as partners (so that I may see whether any among them deserve worship!) No! (You cannot do it because it is impossible!) But He alone is God, the All-Glorious with irresistible might (Who never needs and admits any partnership), the All-Wise (Whose Divine Wisdom rejects partnership with Him)."

28. We have not sent you but to all humankind as a bearer of glad tidings (of prosperity for faith and righteousness) and a warner (against the consequences

of misguidance). But most of humankind do not know (this, nor do they appreciate what a great blessing it is for them).

29. They say: "When is this promise (of judgment) to be fulfilled, if you are truthful (in your claim)?"

30. Say: "You have the promise of a Day which you can neither delay by a single moment nor advance."

31. Those who disbelieve say: "We will not believe in this Qur'ān, nor in any (Message) that came before it." If you could but see when such wrongdoers are made to stand before their Lord, throwing back blame at one another! Those who (in the world) were oppressed (and did not oppose being oppressed, humiliated, and misled) say to those who acted in arrogance and oppressed others: "Had it not been for you, we would have been true believers."

13. The polytheists claimed that they believed in the idols and some beings such as angels, thinking that they might intercede with God for the fulfillment of their desires. The verse categorically rejects this.

14. The angels are God's servants whom He employs in many tasks. As explained in note 31 to 2: 30, no event in the universe can be thought of without the function of the angels. There are angels that represent or are responsible for every event in the universe and every species on the earth. They also look on God's acts with wonder and admiration and present to Him the glorification and worship each species of creature makes in the language of their disposition. Angels are of different ranks. So, the ones who the verse tells us are asked about what God has commanded must be those of greater ranks. They receive God's commands, and when the dread and awe they feel while they are receiving those commands, other angels ask them what God has commanded. All angels carry out whatever God orders them (21: 27). So they cannot do anything of their own accord and cannot intercede with God or pray to Him for anybody they wish.

15. The manners in the verses 24, 25, and 26 are the manners to be preferred in communicating the truth to others. Although God's Messenger clearly follows the right guidance and he is certain of this, he is ordered to say, *either we or you follow the right guidance or are in a manifest error*, instead of *we follow the right guidance and you are in a manifest error*. In verse 25, he allows that, in the polytheists' view, the believers may be people who are in the wrong, but he does not accuse the polytheists, whom he is addressing, of any sins. And, in verse 26, he refers the matter to God's judgment.

الجُزْءُ الثَّانِي وَالْعِشْرُوْنَ

قَالَ الَّذِينَ اسْتَكْبَرُوا لِلَّذِينَ اسْتُضْعِفُوا أَنَحْنُ صَدَدْنَاكُمْ
عَنِ الْهُدَىٰ بَعْدَ إِذْ جَاءَكُمْ بَلْ كُنتُم مُّجْرِمِينَ ۞ وَقَالَ الَّذِينَ
اسْتُضْعِفُوا لِلَّذِينَ اسْتَكْبَرُوا بَلْ مَكْرُ الَّيْلِ وَالنَّهَارِ إِذْ تَأْمُرُونَنَا
أَن نَّكْفُرَ بِاللَّهِ وَنَجْعَلَ لَهُ أَندَادًا وَأَسَرُّوا النَّدَامَةَ لَمَّا
رَأَوُا الْعَذَابَ وَجَعَلْنَا الْأَغْلَالَ فِي أَعْنَاقِ الَّذِينَ كَفَرُوا هَلْ
يُجْزَوْنَ إِلَّا مَا كَانُوا يَعْمَلُونَ ۞ وَمَا أَرْسَلْنَا فِي قَرْيَةٍ
مِّن نَّذِيرٍ إِلَّا قَالَ مُتْرَفُوهَا إِنَّا بِمَا أُرْسِلْتُم بِهِ كَافِرُونَ ۞
وَقَالُوا نَحْنُ أَكْثَرُ أَمْوَالًا وَأَوْلَادًا وَمَا نَحْنُ بِمُعَذَّبِينَ ۞
قُلْ إِنَّ رَبِّي يَبْسُطُ الرِّزْقَ لِمَن يَشَاءُ وَيَقْدِرُ وَلَٰكِنَّ أَكْثَرَ
النَّاسِ لَا يَعْلَمُونَ ۞ وَمَا أَمْوَالُكُمْ وَلَا أَوْلَادُكُم بِالَّتِي
تُقَرِّبُكُمْ عِندَنَا زُلْفَىٰ إِلَّا مَنْ آمَنَ وَعَمِلَ صَالِحًا فَأُولَٰئِكَ لَهُمْ
جَزَاءُ الضِّعْفِ بِمَا عَمِلُوا وَهُمْ فِي الْغُرُفَاتِ آمِنُونَ ۞ وَالَّذِينَ
يَسْعَوْنَ فِي آيَاتِنَا مُعَاجِزِينَ أُولَٰئِكَ فِي الْعَذَابِ مُحْضَرُونَ ۞
قُلْ إِنَّ رَبِّي يَبْسُطُ الرِّزْقَ لِمَن يَشَاءُ مِنْ عِبَادِهِ وَيَقْدِرُ لَهُ وَمَا
أَنفَقْتُم مِّن شَيْءٍ فَهُوَ يُخْلِفُهُ وَهُوَ خَيْرُ الرَّازِقِينَ ۞

---

32. The arrogant oppressors retort to those who were oppressed: "What! did we (forcibly) bar you from following the guidance after it had reached you? No, but you yourselves were the criminals (committed to accumulating sins)?"

33. Those who were oppressed and humiliated say to the arrogant (who oppressed them): "No! Rather, (it was your) scheming night and day (that kept us away from the guidance); you were constantly commanding us to blaspheme against God and set up rivals to Him." When they all face the punishment, they will be unable to express their remorse. We will put fetters around the necks of those who disbelieved (and keep them in the Fire). Will they have been recompensed for anything other than what they used to do?

34. We never sent a warner to any township but those of its people who had been lost in the pursuit of pleasures without scruples reacted, saying: "Surely we are unbelievers in that with which you have been sent."

35. And they said: "We are more abundant (than you) in wealth and children and so we are not (the ones) to be punished (as you tell us to happen in the Hereafter)."

36. Say: "Surely my Lord God enlarges provision for whom He wills, and straitens it (for whom He wills); but most of humankind do not know."

37. And it is neither your wealth nor your children which will bring you near to Us; but only one who believes and does good, righteous deeds (can come near to Us), and it is those whose reward for their deeds is multiplied, and they will dwell in high, lofty mansions (of Paradise), secure (from any suffering).

38. Whereas those who strive hard against Our Revelations, seeking to frustrate them, such will be arraigned for punishment (in Hell).

39. Say: "Surely God enlarges provision for whom He wills of His servants, and straitens it (for whom He wills). Whatever you spend (in God's cause and in alms), He will replace it. He is the Best to be sought as provider with the ultimate rank of providing."

432　سُورَةُ سَبَإ　٤٣٢

بِسْمِ اللّٰهِ الرَّحْمٰنِ الرَّحِيمِ

[Arabic Qur'anic text of Sūrah Sabā, verses, enclosed in decorative border]

---

40. And a Day (will come and) He will gather them (those who strive against Our Revelations and those beings or things they worshipped in the world) all together, and will ask the angels, "Was it you that those used to worship (within your knowledge and to your pleasure)?"

41. They will answer: "All-Glorified You are (in that You are absolutely above having partners). You alone are our Guardian (Whom We worship,) having no such relation with them." Rather, they were worshipping the jinn; most of them believed in them (the jinn as beings deserving worship)."[16]

42. So on this Day you will have no power over one another to benefit or harm. And We will say to those who have persistently committed wrong (by following misleading paths): "Taste the punishment of the Fire, (the existence of) which you used to deny!"

43. When Our Revelations clear as evidence and in meaning are recited to them (the Makkan polytheists), they say: "This is but a man who wants to bar you from what your forefathers used to worship." They also say (of the Qur'ān): "This is nothing but a fabrication falsely attributed to God." Those who disbelieve say of the truth when it has reached them (in willful defiance of its clarity): "This is clearly nothing but sorcery."

44. But We did not grant them any Book which they studied (so that they should dare pretend to be able to discriminate between true and false scripture). Nor did We send them a warner before you (so that they should dare pretend to be able to distinguish you as being a fabricator and a sorcerer).

45. Many of those who lived before them also denied the truth. These have not attained a tenth of what We granted to those (of knowledge, as well as power and means); and yet they denied My Messengers – then how awesome was My disowning them!

46. Say: "I exhort you to one thing: Pull yourselves together and draw aside purely for God's sake, together with another person or alone, and then reflect (on this issue, leaving aside all your prejudices). There is no madness in your companion (God's Messenger). He is but a warner to you (sent) prior to a severe punishment."

47. Say: "(I ask of you no wage, yet, even so) whatever you may think I might ask you for by way of wage, it is yours. My wage is only due from God. He is indeed a witness over everything."

48. Say: "Surely my Lord sends down the truth, hurling it (against falsehood to destroy it). (My Lord:) He alone is the All-Knowing of the whole of the unseen (all that is beyond human perception)."

16. During history, most of the pagans have worshipped angels they have regarded as good spirits from whom benefit is expected, and the jinn as evil spirits against whom protection is sought. However, since in many cases these people have gone astray under the influence of the jinn, they have been actually worshipping the jinn while they have thought they have been worshipping the angels; they have been misled by the jinn. Most of them have also attributed divinity to the jinn, as they have regarded them as beings that are capable of causing harm and therefore are to be worshipped in order to be protected from their evil.

49. Say: "The truth has come (and manifested itself); and falsehood cannot originate (anything even if its followers try to keep it going), nor can it restore anything (of that which it has lost)."

50. Say: "Were I to go astray, it would be to my own harm (and due to my own self). And if I am rightly guided, it is by virtue of what my Lord is revealing to me. Surely He is All-Hearing, All-Near."

51. If you could but see when they quake with dread (of death), with no escape, and are seized from a position very near.[17]

52. They say: "We have believed in it (the Qur'ān)!" But how can they hope to attain to faith and salvation from a position so far away,[18]

53. (Seeing that) they certainly disbelieved in it before. They have been aiming at the Unseen (the Hereafter) from far away[19] (with words all untrue and without any basis in true knowledge).

54. And a barrier has been placed between them and what they had appetite for (while in the world), as was done with the likes of them before. Surely they were (lost) in hopeless doubt.

---

17. This statement expresses, in relation with the previous verse, which says God is All-Near, God's infinite nearness to human beings. He is nearer to us than our own selves. A living being is seized at the time of death from within its own self.

18. This means that at the time of death a human being is extremely near to the Hereafter and far away from the world. There is no longer any chance of escape or return, so it is no more possible for an unbeliever, who has lived very far away from faith, to attain to faith.

19. This signifies that a human being is extremely far away from the world at the time of death when they are on the verge of being transferred to the Hereafter. It also implies that while in the world they are far away from the Hereafter. This distance signifies the distance between unbelief and the Hereafter and arises from unbelief itself.

SŪRAH 35

AL-FĀṬIR
(THE ALL-ORIGINATING)

Makkah period

Revealed in the mid-Makkan period of Islam, this *sūrah* of 45 verses takes its name from the first verse where God Almighty is introduced as *al-Fāṭir* (the All-Originating). It is also called *Sūrat al-Malāʾikah*. The main topics dealt with in the *sūrah* are God's Oneness, the Hereafter, and the Messengership of Muḥammad, upon him peace and blessings. The *sūrah* presents proofs for these three pillars of faith and draws attention to the bounties of God.

In the Name of God, the All-Merciful, the All-Compassionate.

1. All praise and thanks are for God, the Originator of the heavens and the earth (each with particular features and ordered principles), Who appoints the angels as messengers (conveying His commands) having wings, two, or three, or four (or more).[1] He increases in creation what He wills.[2] Surely God has full power over everything.

2. Whatever God opens up for human beings out of (the treasures of) His Mercy, none is able to withhold; and whatever He withholds, none is able to release. He is the All-Glorious with irresistible might (Whom none can prevent Him from doing what He wills), the All-Wise (in Whose every act there are many instances of wisdom).

3. O humankind! Remember and reflect on God's favors upon you. Is there any Creator, other than God, that provides for you from the heaven and the earth? There is no deity but He: How then are you turned away from the truth and make false claims?

---

1. On the existence of the angels and their being the conveyors of God's commands and messages, see 2, notes 31, 36, 40; 11: 83, note 19; 15: 27, note 7.

What the verse means by the angels' wings is their speed, power, and the tasks they carry out. Their wings are not restricted to four. God's Messenger says that during his Ascension he saw the Archangel Gabriel with 600 wings, and that Gabriel told him that he had seen Isrāfīl with 12,000 wings, a single one of which filled up the space between the heavens and the earth (al-Qurṭubī).

2. This means that God's process of creation is continuous with expansion in scope, range, and variety. It also means that He not only creates to satisfy a purpose, but also for perfection. Because of this, He creates whatever He creates in the best, and the most beautiful and purposeful form and fashion.

434　　سُوۡرَةُ فَاطِرٍ　　٤٣٤

وَإِن يُكَذِّبُوكَ فَقَدْ كَذَّبَتْ رُسُلٌ مِّن قَبْلِكَ وَإِلَى اللَّهِ تُرْجَعُ الْأُمُورُ ۝ يَآأَيُّهَا النَّاسُ إِنَّ وَعْدَ اللَّهِ حَقٌّ فَلَا تَغُرَّنَّكُمُ الْحَيَوةُ الدُّنْيَا وَلَا يَغُرَّنَّكُم بِاللَّهِ الْغَرُورُ ۝ إِنَّ الشَّيْطَانَ لَكُمْ عَدُوٌّ فَاتَّخِذُوهُ عَدُوًّا إِنَّمَا يَدْعُواْ حِزْبَهُ لِيَكُونُواْ مِنْ أَصْحَابِ السَّعِيرِ ۝ الَّذِينَ كَفَرُواْ لَهُمْ عَذَابٌ شَدِيدٌ وَالَّذِينَ ءَامَنُواْ وَعَمِلُواْ الصَّالِحَاتِ لَهُم مَّغْفِرَةٌ وَأَجْرٌ كَبِيرٌ ۝ أَفَمَن زُيِّنَ لَهُ سُوۤءُ عَمَلِهِ فَرَءَاهُ حَسَنًا فَإِنَّ اللَّهَ يُضِلُّ مَن يَشَآءُ وَيَهْدِي مَن يَشَآءُ فَلَا تَذْهَبْ نَفْسُكَ عَلَيْهِمْ حَسَرَاتٍ إِنَّ اللَّهَ عَلِيمٌ بِمَا يَصْنَعُونَ ۝ وَاللَّهُ الَّذِي أَرْسَلَ الرِّيَاحَ فَتُثِيرُ سَحَابًا فَسُقْنَاهُ إِلَى بَلَدٍ مَّيِّتٍ فَأَحْيَيْنَا بِهِ الْأَرْضَ بَعْدَ مَوْتِهَا كَذَٰلِكَ النُّشُورُ ۝ مَن كَانَ يُرِيدُ الْعِزَّةَ فَلِلَّهِ الْعِزَّةُ جَمِيعًا إِلَيْهِ يَصْعَدُ الْكَلِمُ الطَّيِّبُ وَالْعَمَلُ الصَّالِحُ يَرْفَعُهُ وَالَّذِينَ يَمْكُرُونَ السَّيِّئَاتِ لَهُمْ عَذَابٌ شَدِيدٌ وَمَكْرُ أُوْلَٰئِكَ هُوَ يَبُورُ ۝ وَاللَّهُ خَلَقَكُم مِّن تُرَابٍ ثُمَّ مِن نُّطْفَةٍ ثُمَّ جَعَلَكُمْ أَزْوَاجًا وَمَا تَحْمِلُ مِنْ أُنثَىٰ وَلَا تَضَعُ إِلَّا بِعِلْمِهِ وَمَا يُعَمَّرُ مِن مُّعَمَّرٍ وَلَا يُنقَصُ مِنْ عُمُرِهِ إِلَّا فِي كِتَابٍ إِنَّ ذَٰلِكَ عَلَى اللَّهِ يَسِيرٌ ۝

---

them is a forgiveness (to bring unforeseen blessings), and a noble, generous reward.

8. Is one whose evil deeds is decked out to be appealing to him so that he considers it as good (like him who follows God's guidance)? God leads astray whom He wills and guides whom He wills.[3] So do not let yourself perish in bitter regrets on their behalf (because they refuse faith). Surely God has full knowledge of all that they do.

9. God is He Who sends forth the merciful winds, so that they set clouds to move, and We drive them towards a dead land and (thereby) We revive the earth after its death (with the rain carried in the clouds by the wind). Even so will the Resurrection be.

10. Whoever seeks might and glory should know that all might and glory is for God (so let him seek from Him alone). To Him ascends only the pure word (as the source of might and glory), and the good, righteous action (accompanying it) raises it.[4] But those who are devising evil actions, for them there is a severe punishment, and their devising is bound to come to nothing.

11. (O humankind:) God created you from earth (in the beginning, and the material origin of every one of you is also earth), and then from a drop of (seminal) fluid, and then He has fashioned you in pairs (as either of the two sexes, making you mates of one another). And no female carries or gives birth, save with His knowledge. No one long-lived has been granted a long life, nor another one not so long-lived has been appointed a shorter life but is recorded in a Book. Surely that is easy for God.

❧

4. If they deny you (O Messenger), even so Messengers were denied before you. (So do not grieve:) to God all affairs are ultimately referred (and whatever He wills occurs).

5. O humankind! (Know well that) God's promise (of the Last Judgment) is surely true; so do not let the present, worldly life delude you, nor let any deluder (including especially Satan) delude you in (your conceptions) about God.

6. Surely Satan is an enemy to you, so treat him as an enemy (do not follow him, and be alert against him). He calls his party (of followers) but that they may become companions of the Blaze.

7. Those who persist in unbelief, for them is a severe punishment. As for those who believe and do good, righteous deeds, for

3. God has two kinds of Will. One is His (pre-eternal) Decree concerning the creation, including responsible, conscious beings. This Will, called *Mashīah*, is absolute with regard to things and unconscious beings, while It takes into consideration the (future) will of responsible, conscious beings. That is, God knows beforehand in what way those beings will use their free will and decrees accordingly. God's other Will (*Irādah*) entails what He demands from His servants and denotes those things with which He is pleased. In this verse, *God leads astray whom He wills* means that He lets go astray those who choose to follow Satan and the promptings of their carnal soul, with the result that they follow their fancies and personal ideas and commit evil deeds that, though not based on true knowledge, seem just to them. As for *He guides whom He wills*, this denotes those who choose to resist the tempta-tions of Satan and their carnal soul, and instead follow the guidance that God sends through His Messengers and they see as good whatever God decrees as so.

4. The pure word is, first of all, the Declaration of the Divine Oneness, namely *There is no deity but God*. Declarations of other pillars of faith and all other pure, truthful words are based on this Word. Without the good, righteous actions that it requires, this declaration remains only an assertion. Only good, righteous actions make it wholly acceptable in God's sight and cause it to yield pure, wholesome fruit (14: 25). Other pure words and declarations approved by God likewise become acceptable in God's sight by means of the good actions that are called for. In addition, any assertion or declaration becomes true faith and is established in the heart through the good actions that are required by it.

435

وَمَا يَسْتَوِى الْبَحْرَانِ هَٰذَا عَذْبٌ فُرَاتٌ سَآئِغٌ شَرَابُهُ وَهَٰذَا
مِلْحٌ أُجَاجٌ وَمِن كُلٍّ تَأْكُلُونَ لَحْمًا طَرِيًّا وَتَسْتَخْرِجُونَ حِلْيَةً
تَلْبَسُونَهَا وَتَرَى الْفُلْكَ فِيهِ مَوَاخِرَ لِتَبْتَغُوا مِن فَضْلِهِ
وَلَعَلَّكُمْ تَشْكُرُونَ ۞ يُولِجُ الَّيْلَ فِى النَّهَارِ وَيُولِجُ النَّهَارَ
فِى الَّيْلِ وَسَخَّرَ الشَّمْسَ وَالْقَمَرَ كُلٌّ يَجْرِى لِأَجَلٍ مُّسَمًّى
ذَٰلِكُمُ اللّٰهُ رَبُّكُمْ لَهُ الْمُلْكُ وَالَّذِينَ تَدْعُونَ مِن دُونِهِ
مَا يَمْلِكُونَ مِن قِطْمِيرٍ ۞ إِن تَدْعُوهُمْ لَا يَسْمَعُوا دُعَآءَكُمْ
وَلَوْ سَمِعُوا مَا اسْتَجَابُوا لَكُمْ وَيَوْمَ الْقِيَٰمَةِ يَكْفُرُونَ
بِشِرْكِكُمْ وَلَا يُنَبِّئُكَ مِثْلُ خَبِيرٍ ۞ يَٰٓأَيُّهَا النَّاسُ أَنتُمُ الْفُقَرَآءُ
إِلَى اللّٰهِ وَاللّٰهُ هُوَ الْغَنِىُّ الْحَمِيدُ ۞ إِن يَشَأْ يُذْهِبْكُمْ
وَيَأْتِ بِخَلْقٍ جَدِيدٍ ۞ وَمَا ذَٰلِكَ عَلَى اللّٰهِ بِعَزِيزٍ
وَلَا تَزِرُ وَازِرَةٌ وِزْرَ أُخْرَىٰ وَإِن تَدْعُ مُثْقَلَةٌ إِلَىٰ حِمْلِهَا
لَا يُحْمَلْ مِنْهُ شَىْءٌ وَلَوْ كَانَ ذَا قُرْبَىٰٓ إِنَّمَا تُنذِرُ الَّذِينَ
يَخْشَوْنَ رَبَّهُم بِالْغَيْبِ وَأَقَامُوا الصَّلَوٰةَ وَمَن
تَزَكَّىٰ فَإِنَّمَا يَتَزَكَّىٰ لِنَفْسِهِ وَإِلَى اللّٰهِ الْمَصِيرُ ۞

---

12. Nor are the two seas (large bodies of water) alike: this one is sweet and palatable, and pleasant to drink, but that one, salty and bitter. You obtain from both fresh meat (for your nourishment), and precious stones to wear as ornament. And you see ships plowing through (both kinds of water), so that you may seek of His bounty, and that you may give Him thanks.[5]

13. He makes the night pass into the day and He makes the day pass into the night (and so makes each grow longer or shorter); and He has made the sun and the moon subservient to His command, each running its course for a term appointed. Such is God, your Lord: His is the Sovereignty (the absolute ownership and dominion of all things). Whereas those whom you deify and invoke, apart from Him, own not so much as the pellicle of a date-stone.

14. If you invoke them, they do not hear your call; and even if they heard, they would not able to respond to you. And on the Day of Resurrection they will disown your having associated them (with God). And none can inform you (and thereby lead you to understand the truth) like One All-Aware.

15. O humankind! You are all poor before God and in absolute need of Him, whereas He is the All-Wealthy and Self-Sufficient (absolutely independent of the creation), the All-Praiseworthy (as your Lord, Who provides for you and all other beings, supplying all your needs).[6]

16. If He so wills (in order for the fulfillment of His purpose for creation), He can put you away and bring a new generation (in your place, who will acknowledge their poverty and praise God in return for His favors).

17. That is surely no great matter for God.

18. And no soul, as bearer of burden, bears (and is made to bear) the burden of another; and if one weighed down by his burden calls to (another for help to) carry it, nothing of it will be carried by that other, even if he be his near of kin.[7] You can warn (in a profitable way) only those who stand in awe of their Lord though unseen (beyond their perception), and establish the Prayer in conformity with its conditions. And whoever is purified (of his wrong ideas or actions), is only purified for the good of his own soul. And to God is the homecoming.

5. The Qur'ān draws our attention to the two types of seas (and similar large bodies of water) in some other verses (e.g., 25: 53). The material origin of the universe is one single matter, namely ether (see 11, note 2; 41, note 5); and all things in the universe are made of basically four substances: hydrogen, oxygen, carbon, and nitrogen. Despite the simplicity of origin, there is almost an infinite variety of creatures in the universe. Moreover, all human beings are created, originally, from earth. The biological origin of every human being – male sperm and female ovum – is also made of the same substances, and all parents are nourished with the same. But there is a world of difference between human beings in many aspects. This infinite variety in apparent similarity clearly demonstrates God and His absolute freedom, and based on many instances of wisdom.

6.   His is power, by which we are powerful.
    We are well-known by His Name or fame.
    We go beyond peaks and continue on our way;
    We overcome all difficulties with facility.
    We possess nothing worldly but are absolutely rich,
    And are dignified and respectable through His Dignity.
    We follow the way of reflection, so
    Whatever exists is a source of knowledge of God for us.

(Key Concepts, 1: 172)

Your perception and acknowledgment of your essential poverty leads you to the Divine Name the All-Merciful, by Which you find inexhaustible treasure. Your perception and acknowledgment of your essential helplessness leads you to the Divine Name the All-Powerful, by Which you find the real source of power. You can purify yourself by perceiving that your existence lies in acknowledging your essential non-existence. Considering yourself self-existent, you fall into the darkest pit of non-existence. In other words, relying on your personal existence and thus ignoring the Real Creator causes your ephemeral personal existence to be drowned in the infinite darkness of non-existence. But if you abandon pride and egoism and recognize that you are only a mirror in which the Real Creator manifests Himself, you attain infinite existence. One who discovers the Necessary Being, the manifestations of Whose Names cause all things to come into existence, is counted as having found everything. *(The Words*, "the 26th Word," 493)

7. In the same way that no one is held responsible for the crime of another, no one can take upon themselves the sin of another. This is inconceivable both from the viewpoint of the Religion (and law), and because of the fact that every one will be concerned only with their own soul in the Hereafter. So, the doctrine of Original Sin, with which all humankind is supposedly burdened because of the "lapse" of Adam and Eve, is completely groundless and contrary to this basic principle of the Religion (and law) (namely, responsibility and the corresponding recompense are not transferable). Secondly, as no one can be burdened with the burden of another, nor absolved of any crime or sin they have committed through the suffering of another, the Christian doctrine of atonement is baseless. Moreover, God did not compel Adam and Eve to eat of the forbidden tree in order to incarnate into or create out of Him a human son, nor did or would He then condemn Jesus to suffer great pains and to taste death, even if temporarily. That too is completely contrary to Divinity as taught by the Divine Religion(s).

436　سُورَةُ فَاطِرٍ　٤٣٦

وَمَا يَسْتَوِى الْأَعْمَى وَالْبَصِيرُ ۞ وَلَا الظُّلُمَاتُ وَلَا النُّورُ ۞
وَلَا الظِّلُّ وَلَا الْحَرُورُ ۞ وَمَا يَسْتَوِى الْأَحْيَاءُ وَلَا الْأَمْوَاتُ اِنَّ
اللّٰهَ يُسْمِعُ مَنْ يَشَاءُ وَمَا أَنْتَ بِمُسْمِعٍ مَنْ فِي الْقُبُورِ ۞ اِنْ
أَنْتَ اِلَّا نَذِيرٌ ۞ اِنَّا أَرْسَلْنَاكَ بِالْحَقِّ بَشِيرًا وَنَذِيرًا وَإِنْ
مِنْ أُمَّةٍ اِلَّا خَلَا فِيهَا نَذِيرٌ ۞ وَإِنْ يُكَذِّبُوكَ فَقَدْ كَذَّبَ
الَّذِينَ مِنْ قَبْلِهِمْ جَاءَتْهُمْ رُسُلُهُمْ بِالْبَيِّنَاتِ وَبِالزُّبُرِ
وَبِالْكِتَابِ الْمُنِيرِ ۞ ثُمَّ أَخَذْتُ الَّذِينَ كَفَرُوا فَكَيْفَ
كَانَ نَكِيرٍ ۞ أَلَمْ تَرَ أَنَّ اللّٰهَ أَنْزَلَ مِنَ السَّمَاءِ مَاءً
فَأَخْرَجْنَا بِهِ ثَمَرَاتٍ مُخْتَلِفًا أَلْوَانُهَا وَمِنَ الْجِبَالِ جُدَدٌ بِيضٌ
وَحُمْرٌ مُخْتَلِفٌ أَلْوَانُهَا وَغَرَابِيبُ سُودٌ ۞ وَمِنَ النَّاسِ
وَالدَّوَابِّ وَالْأَنْعَامِ مُخْتَلِفٌ أَلْوَانُهُ كَذٰلِكَ اِنَّمَا يَخْشَى
اللّٰهَ مِنْ عِبَادِهِ الْعُلَمَاءُ اِنَّ اللّٰهَ عَزِيزٌ غَفُورٌ ۞ اِنَّ
الَّذِينَ يَتْلُونَ كِتَابَ اللّٰهِ وَأَقَامُوا الصَّلَاةَ وَأَنْفَقُوا
مِمَّا رَزَقْنَاهُمْ سِرًّا وَعَلَانِيَةً يَرْجُونَ تِجَارَةً لَنْ تَبُورَ ۞
لِيُوَفِّيَهُمْ أُجُورَهُمْ وَيَزِيدَهُمْ مِنْ فَضْلِهِ اِنَّهُ غَفُورٌ شَكُورٌ ۞

───────❧───────

19. The blind and the seeing are not equal;

20. Nor are the depths of darkness and the light.

21. Nor the shade and the scorching heat.

22. And nor are equal the living and the dead. Surely God makes hear whomever He wills; and you are not one to make hear those who are in the graves.[8]

23. You are only a warner (not accountable for their being guided).

24. Surely We have sent you as Messenger with the truth, as a bearer of glad tidings (of prosperity in return for faith and righteousness) and a warner (against the consequences of misguidance); and there has never been a community but a warner lived among them.

25. If they deny you, even so denied those before them (to whom a Messenger was sent). Their Messengers came to them with the clear proofs (of their Messengership), Scriptures (full of wisdom and advice), and the Book enlightening (their mind and hearts, and) illuminating (their way.)[9]

26. Then I have seized those who insisted on unbelief. How awesome was My disowning them!

27. Do you not see that God sends down water from the sky? Then We bring forth with it produce of various colors (shapes and taste); and in the mountains are streaks of white and red, of various colors (due to the flora or the variety of stone and rock), as well as raven-black;

28. And likewise human beings, and beasts, and cattle, diverse are their colors. Of all His servants, only those possessed of true knowledge stand in awe of God.[10] Surely God is All-Glorious with irresistible might, All-Forgiving.

29. Those who recite God's Book (and thereby glorify, praise, and exalt God, and declare His absolute Oneness),[11] and establish the Prayer in conformity with its conditions, and spend out of what We have provided for them (in God's cause and for the needy) secretly and openly, hope for a trade which will never perish.

30. For God will pay them their rewards in full, and give them yet more out of His bounty. Surely He is the All-Forgiving, the All-Responsive (to the gratitude of His creatures).

8. The comparisons in the verses 19-22 implicitly refer to the difference between faith and unbelief with their characteristics and consequences, and between the believers and unbelievers. Faith means seeing, insight, light, knowledge, life or being alive, while unbelief is blindness, darkness with many depths, ignorance, and being dead. So faith gives a believer serenity, tranquility, and peace of heart, while unbelief is the cause of stress, discontent, and unhappiness.

9. That is, some of the Messengers like the Prophet David came with Scriptures full of wisdom and advice, and some like the Prophets Noah, Abraham, Moses, Jesus, and Muḥammad (upon them be peace) with the enlightening Book. In addition, the Book also contained what there was in the Scriptures.

10. That is, only those who are unbiased and unprejudiced can have true knowledge or the knowledge of the truth. The sign of one having such knowledge is sincere faith in and awe of God. Such people can truly and deeply understand what all such phenomena in creation really mean and cannot help but feel deep respect for God and the need and desire to worship Him.

11. Glorifying God means believing, acknowledging, and declaring that God is absolutely free from and exalted above having any defects and attributes particular to the creation, such as begetting and being begotten, dying, feeling any need and therefore having partners or helpers. In short, glorifying means knowing and declaring what God is not and cannot be. Praising God means believing, acknowledging, and declaring that God has all attributes of perfection and therefore deserves praise, thanks and worship. In other words, praising means knowing and declaring what and who God is, and mentioning Him as such, with the attributes of perfection that are exclusively His. Exalting God means believing, acknowledging, and declaring that God is infinitely and absolutely great and there can be none comparable with Him, and that He is infinitely beyond what we can conceive of Him. We glorify, praise, and exalt Him and declare His absolute Oneness after the daily Prayers.

وَالَّذِيٓ أَوْحَيْنَآ إِلَيْكَ مِنَ الْكِتَابِ هُوَ الْحَقُّ مُصَدِّقًا لِّمَا
بَيْنَ يَدَيْهِ ۚ إِنَّ اللَّهَ بِعِبَادِهِ لَخَبِيرٌ بَصِيرٌ ۞ ثُمَّ أَوْرَثْنَا
الْكِتَابَ الَّذِينَ اصْطَفَيْنَا مِنْ عِبَادِنَا ۖ فَمِنْهُمْ ظَالِمٌ لِّنَفْسِهِ
وَمِنْهُم مُّقْتَصِدٌ وَمِنْهُمْ سَابِقٌ بِالْخَيْرَاتِ بِإِذْنِ اللَّهِ ۚ
ذَٰلِكَ هُوَ الْفَضْلُ الْكَبِيرُ ۞ جَنَّاتُ عَدْنٍ يَدْخُلُونَهَا يُحَلَّوْنَ
فِيهَا مِنْ أَسَاوِرَ مِن ذَهَبٍ وَلُؤْلُؤًا ۖ وَلِبَاسُهُمْ فِيهَا حَرِيرٌ
۞ وَقَالُوا الْحَمْدُ لِلَّهِ الَّذِي أَذْهَبَ عَنَّا الْحَزَنَ ۖ إِنَّ رَبَّنَا
لَغَفُورٌ شَكُورٌ ۞ الَّذِي أَحَلَّنَا دَارَ الْمُقَامَةِ مِن فَضْلِهِ
لَا يَمَسُّنَا فِيهَا نَصَبٌ وَلَا يَمَسُّنَا فِيهَا لُغُوبٌ ۞ وَالَّذِينَ
كَفَرُوا لَهُمْ نَارُ جَهَنَّمَ لَا يُقْضَىٰ عَلَيْهِمْ فَيَمُوتُوا وَلَا يُخَفَّفُ
عَنْهُم مِّنْ عَذَابِهَا ۚ كَذَٰلِكَ نَجْزِي كُلَّ كَفُورٍ ۞ وَهُمْ
يَصْطَرِخُونَ فِيهَا رَبَّنَا أَخْرِجْنَا نَعْمَلْ صَالِحًا غَيْرَ الَّذِي كُنَّا
نَعْمَلُ ۚ أَوَلَمْ نُعَمِّرْكُم مَّا يَتَذَكَّرُ فِيهِ مَن تَذَكَّرَ وَجَاءَكُمُ
النَّذِيرُ ۖ فَذُوقُوا فَمَا لِلظَّالِمِينَ مِن نَّصِيرٍ ۞ إِنَّ اللَّهَ
عَالِمُ غَيْبِ السَّمَاوَاتِ وَالْأَرْضِ ۚ إِنَّهُ عَلِيمٌ بِذَاتِ الصُّدُورِ ۞

---

31. That which We reveal to you of the Book is the truth, confirming (the Divine origin of and the truths that are still contained by) the Revelations prior to it. Surely God is fully aware of His servants and sees (them) well.

32. Then (after every Messenger), We have made those of Our servants whom We chose heirs to the Book (to preserve and teach it, and secure its practice in daily life). However, among them are those who (in fulfilling their duty as heirs to the Book) wrong their own selves (on account of certain failings and sins), and among them are those who follow a moderate way, and among them are those who, by God's leave, are foremost in doing good deeds. That (the inheriting of the Book) is the great favor.

33. (So) Gardens of perpetual bliss they will enter, therein adorned with armbands of gold and pearls, and their garments therein will be of silk.[12]

34. And they will say: "All praise and gratitude are for God, Who has removed grief from us (such as we had suffered until we were admitted here). Surely Our Lord is All-Forgiving, All-Responsive (to the gratitude of His creatures),

35. Who, out of His grace, has made us settle in the abode of eternal residence, wherein no toil touches us, and wherein no weariness afflicts us."[13]

36. As for those who disbelieve, for them is the fire of Hell: they will not be sentenced to death so that they can die (and so be relieved), nor will its suffering be lightened for them. Thus do We recompense every ungrateful one who disbelieves.

37. And therein they will cry aloud: "O our Lord! Take us out, we will do good, (righteous deeds), not (the wrong) we used to do before." "Did We not grant you a life long enough for whoever would reflect and be mindful to reflect and be mindful? In addition, a warner came to you (to warn against this punishment). Taste then (the consequences of your heedlessness); for the wrongdoers have none to help them (against it)."

38. Surely God is the Knower of the unseen of the heavens and the earth. And He surely has full knowledge of what lies hidden in the bosoms (so that He treats you according to your beliefs and intentions).

12. For an explanation, see 18: 31, note 17.

13. The Qur'ān often distinguishes three groups of people, namely the unbelievers (including hypocrites) who are condemned to punishment in Hell, the believers whose good excels their evils, and the believers who are foremost in doing good deeds (e.g., 56: 7–11). So some commentators have concluded that verse 32 makes the same classification, and means by *those who wrong their own selves*, as the Qur'ān does in many of its verses, the unbelievers and hypocrites, and by *those who follow a moderate way* the believers who have mixed their righteous deeds with evil ones (see 9: 102). Hence, those who have been promised Gardens of perpetual bliss in the following verse (33) are those who are foremost in doing good deeds, and for the second group *it may be that God will return their repentance with forgiveness* (9: 102).

However, as pointed out by some commentators, this verse is about the inheritance of the Qur'ān and those whom God has specially chosen among His servants for this duty. Inheritance of the Qur'ān (the Book) means to preserve, teach, and practice it in daily life (5: 44). So, since this inheritance has special importance, this verse emphasizes it and distinguishes among those among the Muslims or the Community of Muḥammad, upon him peace and blessings, chosen for this duty. They are not, however, all of the same quality and degree. Among them are those who wrong their own selves on account of certain failings and sins (not by unbelief, hypocrisy, and the association of partners with Him, of course), and those who follow a moderate way, i.e., those who cannot dedicate themselves fully to this duty, and those who, fully dedicated, outstrip all others. So, as long as they serve the Qur'ān and continue to learn and teach it and practice it in daily life, all these three groups will be forgiven by God and admitted to Paradise.

God's Messenger, upon him be peace and blessings, bequeathed the Qur'ān and his household, including his progeny, to his Community (Muslim, "Faḍāil as-Ṣaḥābah," 37). This means that, first of all, his household and progeny must and will serve the Qur'ān. However, this Tradition also gives the glad tiding that those who serve the Qur'ān, even though they do not belong to his progeny by blood, are (spiritually) included in them, as is Salmān al-Fārisī. For the Messenger declared: "Salmān is from us, from the Prophet's Household" (Canan, 12: 370).

438　　سُوۡرَةُ فَاطِر　　٤٣٨

هُوَ الَّذِي جَعَلَكُمْ خَلَائِفَ فِي الْأَرْضِ ۚ فَمَنْ كَفَرَ فَعَلَيْهِ كُفْرُهُ ۖ وَلَا يَزِيدُ الْكَافِرِينَ كُفْرُهُمْ عِنْدَ رَبِّهِمْ إِلَّا مَقْتًا ۖ وَلَا يَزِيدُ الْكَافِرِينَ كُفْرُهُمْ إِلَّا خَسَارًا ۝ قُلْ أَرَأَيْتُمْ شُرَكَاءَكُمُ الَّذِينَ تَدْعُونَ مِن دُونِ اللَّهِ أَرُونِي مَاذَا خَلَقُوا مِنَ الْأَرْضِ أَمْ لَهُمْ شِرْكٌ فِي السَّمَاوَاتِ أَمْ آتَيْنَاهُمْ كِتَابًا فَهُمْ عَلَىٰ بَيِّنَتٍ مِّنْهُ ۚ بَلْ إِن يَعِدُ الظَّالِمُونَ بَعْضُهُم بَعْضًا إِلَّا غُرُورًا ۝ إِنَّ اللَّهَ يُمْسِكُ السَّمَاوَاتِ وَالْأَرْضَ أَن تَزُولَا ۚ وَلَئِن زَالَتَا إِنْ أَمْسَكَهُمَا مِنْ أَحَدٍ مِّن بَعْدِهِ ۚ إِنَّهُ كَانَ حَلِيمًا غَفُورًا ۝ وَأَقْسَمُوا بِاللَّهِ جَهْدَ أَيْمَانِهِمْ لَئِن جَاءَهُمْ نَذِيرٌ لَّيَكُونُنَّ أَهْدَىٰ مِنْ إِحْدَى الْأُمَمِ ۖ فَلَمَّا جَاءَهُمْ نَذِيرٌ مَّا زَادَهُمْ إِلَّا نُفُورًا ۝ اسْتِكْبَارًا فِي الْأَرْضِ وَمَكْرَ السَّيِّئِ ۚ وَلَا يَحِيقُ الْمَكْرُ السَّيِّئُ إِلَّا بِأَهْلِهِ ۚ فَهَلْ يَنظُرُونَ إِلَّا سُنَّتَ الْأَوَّلِينَ ۚ فَلَن تَجِدَ لِسُنَّتِ اللَّهِ تَبْدِيلًا ۖ وَلَن تَجِدَ لِسُنَّتِ اللَّهِ تَحْوِيلًا ۝ أَوَلَمْ يَسِيرُوا فِي الْأَرْضِ فَيَنظُرُوا كَيْفَ كَانَ عَاقِبَةُ الَّذِينَ مِن قَبْلِهِمْ وَكَانُوا أَشَدَّ مِنْهُمْ قُوَّةً ۚ وَمَا كَانَ اللَّهُ لِيُعْجِزَهُ مِن شَيْءٍ فِي السَّمَاوَاتِ وَلَا فِي الْأَرْضِ ۚ إِنَّهُ كَانَ عَلِيمًا قَدِيرًا ۝

──────⟨❦⟩──────

39. He it is Who has made you vicegerents on the earth.[14] So whoever disbelieves (in ingratitude, rejecting this truth and attributing God's deeds to others than Him), his unbelief is charged against him. The unbelief of the unbelievers does not increase them in the sight of their Lord in anything but abhorrence; and the unbelief of the unbelievers does not increase them in anything but loss.

40. Say: "Have you considered those (beings and things) that you associate with God and, apart from God, invoke? Show me what it is that they have created of the earth. Or do they have a share in the (process of creation in the) heavens?" Or

have We granted those people a Book so that they are (in associating partners with God) based on a clear evidence from it? No! Rather, the wrongdoers promise each other nothing but delusion.

41. Surely God alone upholds the heavens and the earth, lest they cease to be. If they should start to fail, there is none that could uphold them (if He were to let them fail. That He does not let them fail, despite all the wrongdoing of His servants, is because) He is All-Clement (showing no haste to punish the errors of His servants), All-Forgiving.

42. They swore by God with their most solemn oaths that if a warner came to them, they would most certainly follow his guidance more than any of the communities (to whom a warner came). Yet, now that a warner has come to them, it has increased them in nothing but aversion;

43. Growing in arrogance in the land and devising evil schemes. But an evil scheme overwhelms none but its own authors. So, can they expect anything other than the pattern of (events and outcomes that overtook) the people of old times (whom God destroyed)? You will never find in God's way any change; you will never find in God's way any alteration.[15]

44. Have they never traveled about the earth that they may see what was the outcome for those before them (who obstinately disbelieved in Our signs)? They were greater than them in power. By no means is God One Whom anything whatever in the heavens or on earth can frustrate (in His decrees). Surely He is All-Knowing, All-Powerful.

---

14. On vicegerency, see 2: 31, note 32.

15. This means that the way in which God Almighty treats people in return for following the same path is evident. God never makes a mistake, never forgets, is never ne-

glectful, and never can be bribed; He always does what is true and wise. His decree can never be turned away from its goal, nor postponed, nor evaded. His way is always straight (11: 56).

45. If God were to take people to task for whatever wrong they commit (and accumulate to their account), He would not leave on earth any living creature. But He grants them respite to a term appointed (by Him). When the end of their term falls, (He treats each as He wills according to his deserts), for surely He sees His servants well.

SŪRAH 36

YĀ. SĪN (YĀ. SĪN)

Makkah period

This *sūrah*, which consists of 83 verses, was revealed in the mid-Makkan period. It takes its name from the first verse, the shortest in the Qur'ān, and which, according to some, implicitly means a human being. It deals, using diverse arguments, with three of the pillars of faith, namely the Divine Oneness, afterlife, and Prophethood. God's Messenger, upon him be peace and blessings, declared that this *sūrah* is the heart of the Qur'ān (at-Tirmidhī, "Thawāb al-Qur'ān," 7) because it stirs up "dead" hearts to awaken them to life. He also advised its recitation over one who is at one's death-bed.

In the Name of God, the All-Merciful, the All-Compassionate.

1. *Yā. Sīn.*

2. By the Wise Qur'ān,

3. You are indeed one of the Messengers (commissioned to convey God's Message);

4. Upon a straight path.

5. (This is) the Book which is being sent down by the All-Glorious with irresistible might, the All-Compassionate,

6. So that you may warn a people whose (near) forefathers were not warned, and who are therefore heedless (of the truth and falsehood).

7. The word (of God's judgment) has assuredly proved true against most of them (humankind from the very first day),[1] for they do not believe.

8. We have surely put chains around the necks (of the unbelievers among your people), right up to their chins, so that their heads are forced up.[2]

9. And We have set a barrier before them and a barrier behind them, and (thus) We have covered them (from all sides), so that they cannot see.[3]

10. So, it is alike to them whether you warn them or do not warn them; (although it is your mission to warn them and you do it without any neglect) they will not believe.[4]

11. You can (profitably) warn only him who (is unprejudiced and) follows the Message and feels awe of the All-Merciful though unseen (beyond their perception). To him, then, give the glad tiding of forgiveness and an honorable, generous provision.

12. Surely it is We Who will bring the dead to life; and We record what they send ahead (to the Hereafter) and what they leave behind (of good and evil). Everything We have written down and kept in a Manifest Record.[5]

---

1. For an explanation, see 32: 13, note 9.

2. This is an allegory that alludes to people being purposefully prejudiced and too haughty to believe. It also signifies that they never think about their selves, their being, and their physical composition, that which would enable them to come to recognize God's signs in them and believe.

3. The comparison here symbolizes the condition in which stubborn unbelievers finds themselves. As they are too arrogant to reflect on their existence in an unprejudiced way, so too they fail to observe the universe around them in any way that is beneficial. They are, as if in veils of darkness, blind to their environment which is full of signs pointing to God's Existence and Oneness. Their blindness comes from arrogance and the fact that their hearts are so dead that they have lost the ability to believe. So, even if they study "nature" and are specialists in many sciences, this information increases them only in ignorance about God and the ultimate truth on which the universe is based.

4. Whether people believe or not, Messengers are charged with communicating God's Message with all its proofs. This is so that *in order that he who was to perish should perish by a clear evidence (of his deserving perishing because he followed falsehood), and he who survived might survive by a clear evidence (of his deserving survival because of his devotion to the truth)* (8: 42), and so that people may have no excuse before God in the Hereafter. The Messengers did not only communicate it verbally, they also practiced it fully in their lives and embodied it. That is, they proved its truth practically or with their very lives.

God informs the Messenger beforehand that some will not believe in order to console him and to inform him that he should concentrate primarily on those who are not prejudiced, whose hearts are not dead, and who therefore are not spiritually blind and deaf.

5. On the meaning of the Manifest Record and the difference between writing down and keeping people's deeds in it and recording them during their lifetimes, see 6: 59, note 13; 13: 39, note 13; 17: 14, note 10.

13. Set out to them, by way of a parable, the (story of the) people of that township, when the Messengers came there;[6]

14. When We first sent them two (Messengers) and they denied them, We reinforced them with a third, and they said: "Surely we are Messengers sent to you (with God's Message)."

15. They said: "You are but mortals like us. The All-Merciful has never sent down anything (by way of Book, as you claim). You are only telling lies."

16. (The Messengers) said: "Our Lord knows that we certainly are Messengers sent to you.

17. "And what rests with us is but to convey (God's Message) fully and clearly; (we do not compel faith)."

18. They said: "We augur ill of you. If you do not desist, we will most certainly stone you, and a painful punishment will most certainly afflict you at our hands."

19. (The Messengers) said: "What you describe as augury lies with you. What? (Do you consider it an ill augury) to be reminded (of the truth) and admonished? No, indeed! Rather, you are a people committing excesses and wasteful of your God-given faculties."

20. A man came running from the farthest end of the city[7] and said: "O my people! Follow those who have been sent (to you as Messengers of God).

21. "Follow those who ask of you no wage (for their service), and are themselves rightly guided.

22. "And what reason do I have that I should not worship Him Who originated me with a nature particular to me, and to Whom you all (as well as I) are being brought back (to give an account of our lives)?

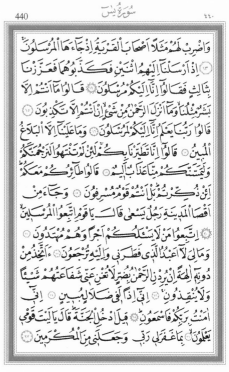

23. "Shall I take, apart from Him, deities whose intercession (that you claim they can make on our behalf) will not avail me anything, if the All-Merciful should will a harm for me, nor can they bring deliverance?

24. "I would indeed, if I were to do so, be in obvious error.

25. "But surely, I have believed in (the Lord Who is, in fact,) the Lord of you all, so listen to me (heedfully)!"

26. (But they killed him, and this word of welcome) was said to him: "Enter Paradise!"[8] He said: "Would that my people knew,

27. "That my Lord has forgiven me and made me one of those honored (with particular favors)!"

6. Although there are different views about which land this is and who the Messengers sent to them are, the Qur'ān and the Hadith are silent in this respect. So, what is of importance is the instruction the Qur'ān gives by this exemplary event. It is not possible to accept the speculations that the land or city was Antioch and the Messengers were the disciples sent by Jesus. Verse 29 informs us that the city was consequently destroyed with a blast, as the lands of many ancient peoples who rejected the Messengers were, whereas it has not been historically established that Antioch suffered such destruction after Jesus, upon him be peace. Even though some commentators have viewed the destruction mentioned metaphorically, the style and wording of the verses is similar to those the Qur'ān uses for the destruction of many ancient peoples.

7. These same words are used of the man who informed the Prophet Moses, upon him be peace, of the plans to seize him (28: 20). As suggested by verse 28: 20, this man belonged to the palace and kept his faith secret. So, the man who came to the aid of the Messengers may well have been one who belonged to the leading group, one who had already believed in the Messengers and kept his faith secret until then.

8. Many among the commentators hold that the Paradise mentioned here is the Paradise where God will admit His believing, righteous servants in the Hereafter. So the verse informs us that this valiant man, who gave full support to the Messengers and was consequently martyred, will be admitted to Paradise, where he will be specially favored. However, it may well be that by Paradise the verse also refers to his Paradise-like place in the Intermediate World (of the grave) (*Barzakh*).

وَمَآ أَنزَلْنَا عَلَىٰ قَوْمِهِۦ مِنۢ بَعْدِهِۦ مِن جُندٍ مِّنَ ٱلسَّمَآءِ وَمَا

كُنَّا مُنزِلِينَ ۞ إِن كَانَتْ إِلَّا صَيْحَةً وَٰحِدَةً فَإِذَا هُمْ

خَٰمِدُونَ ۞ يَٰحَسْرَةً عَلَى ٱلْعِبَادِ مَا يَأْتِيهِم مِّن رَّسُولٍ إِلَّا

كَانُوا۟ بِهِۦ يَسْتَهْزِءُونَ ۞ أَلَمْ يَرَوْا۟ كَمْ أَهْلَكْنَا قَبْلَهُم

مِّنَ ٱلْقُرُونِ أَنَّهُمْ إِلَيْهِمْ لَا يَرْجِعُونَ ۞ وَإِن كُلٌّ لَّمَّا جَمِيعٌ

لَّدَيْنَا مُحْضَرُونَ ۞ وَءَايَةٌ لَّهُمُ ٱلْأَرْضُ ٱلْمَيْتَةُ أَحْيَيْنَٰهَا وَأَخْرَجْنَا

مِنْهَا حَبًّا فَمِنْهُ يَأْكُلُونَ ۞ وَجَعَلْنَا فِيهَا جَنَّٰتٍ مِّن نَّخِيلٍ

وَأَعْنَٰبٍ وَفَجَّرْنَا فِيهَا مِنَ ٱلْعُيُونِ ۞ لِيَأْكُلُوا۟ مِن ثَمَرِهِۦ

وَمَا عَمِلَتْهُ أَيْدِيهِمْ أَفَلَا يَشْكُرُونَ ۞ سُبْحَٰنَ ٱلَّذِي

خَلَقَ ٱلْأَزْوَٰجَ كُلَّهَا مِمَّا تُنۢبِتُ ٱلْأَرْضُ وَمِنْ أَنفُسِهِمْ

وَمِمَّا لَا يَعْلَمُونَ ۞ وَءَايَةٌ لَّهُمُ ٱلَّيْلُ نَسْلَخُ مِنْهُ ٱلنَّهَارَ

فَإِذَا هُم مُّظْلِمُونَ ۞ وَٱلشَّمْسُ تَجْرِى لِمُسْتَقَرٍّ لَّهَا ذَٰلِكَ

تَقْدِيرُ ٱلْعَزِيزِ ٱلْعَلِيمِ ۞ وَٱلْقَمَرَ قَدَّرْنَٰهُ مَنَازِلَ حَتَّىٰ

عَادَ كَٱلْعُرْجُونِ ٱلْقَدِيمِ ۞ لَا ٱلشَّمْسُ يَنۢبَغِى لَهَآ أَن تُدْرِكَ

ٱلْقَمَرَ وَلَا ٱلَّيْلُ سَابِقُ ٱلنَّهَارِ وَكُلٌّ فِى فَلَكٍ يَسْبَحُونَ ۞

---

28. We did not send down upon his people after him any hosts (of angels) from heaven (to destroy them): it is not Our way to send down such.

29. It was but a single blast only, and see! they were extinguished.[9]

30. Ah! Alas for the servants (of God who fail to serve Him)! Every time there has come to them a Messenger, they have but mocked him.

31. Have they not considered how many a generation We have destroyed before them; they never return to them (nor to their life of the world).

32. Instead, every generation, all without exception, will be arraigned before us (for judgment).[10]

33. A clear sign for them (of God's Oneness and Lordship) is the dead earth: We revive it and bring forth from it grain, and (following the necessary preparatory processes) they eat of it.

34. And We have set therein gardens of palms and vines, and We have caused springs to gush forth in it;

35. So that they may eat of the fruit of all (that He produces) – and they did not make it with their own hands. Will they not, then, give thanks?

36. All-Glorified is He (in that He is absolutely exalted above having any peer or partner), Who has created the pairs all together out of what the earth produces, as well as out of themselves, and out of what they do not know.[11]

37. A(nother) clear sign for them is the night: We withdraw the day from it, and see, they are plunged in darkness.

38. And the sun runs the course appointed for it for a term to its resting-place for the stability of it(s system).[12] This is the measured determining of the All-Glorious with irresistible might (to Whose omnipotent ordering the whole universe is submitted), the All-Knowing.

39. And for the moon We have determined mansions till it returns like an old shriveled palm-leaf.

40. It is not for the sun to overtake the moon, nor does the night outstrip the day. All (the celestial bodies and systems) float in an orbit (determined for each).

9. Although some verses (3: 124–125; 8: 9; 33: 9) state that God Almighty sent hosts of angels and invisible hosts from the heaven, they came for positive, important purposes, namely, to encourage and reinforce the believers in their struggle against the disbelieving, unjust peoples, and to acclaim their victory. God does not send hosts to destroy wicked, criminal people; rather He destroys them with a catastrophe. The three angels He sent before the destruction of the people of the Prophet Lot, upon him be peace, were not "a host" and had other purposes, like giving Abraham the glad tiding of the birth of Isaac. Lot's people were destroyed with a blast and a rain of stones, even though God employed these angels in that task, as it is His way to employ angels in every event in the universe.

10. The last two verses decisively reject any doctrine or assertion such as reincarnation that claims sinful people will continue to return to the world in new, different bodies until they have purified their souls. Instead of returning, the verses explicitly state that they will be brought before God to be judged. The verses also reject the Shi'ite doctrine of raj'ah, which asserts that some oppressive people – especially those who oppressed the members of the Messenger's household – and their victims will be returned to the world before the end of time so that the latter can take vengeance on their oppressors.

11. Everything animate or inanimate has a pair; we can see opposition and complementarity in all created things and beings, whether in physical or chemical or moral or psychological qualities. Recent discoveries of complementarity/opposition among sub-atomic particles may be an instance of the kind of pairs that we do not see directly; there will be many other instances of "pairing" of which we remain ignorant.

12. The original of this statement is comprised of 4 words. The phrase translated as "the course appointed for it for a term to its resting-place for the stability of it(s system)" is li-mustaqarrin lahā. Mustaqarr means course or orbit, stability and the place and time of sta-

bility; the preposition li indicates both reason or aim ("for"), the course of a movement ("in or along"), and destination ("to" or "towards"). So the phrase li-mustaqarrin lahā points out four facts concerning the sun or its system: It moves for a certain (appointed) term, along a course appointed for it, to its resting-place, for the sake of the stability of the system. We understand from the statement in its context that the sun is not motionless and has a vital function in the universal order.

In recent decades, solar astronomers have been able to observe that the sun is not in fact motionless. It quivers and shakes and continually rings like a well-hit gong. These vibrations of the sun reveal vital information about the sun's deep interior, its hidden layers, and this information affects calculations of the age of the universe. Also, knowing exactly how the sun spins internally is important in testing Einstein's theory of general relativity. Like so many other significant findings in astronomy, this discovery about the sun was totally unexpected. Having discovered the quivering and ringing sun, some astronomers have commented that it is as if the sun were a symphony orchestra, with all the instruments being played simultaneously. All the vibrations combine at times to produce a net oscillation on the solar surface that is thousands of times stronger than any individual vibration (Bartusiac, M., 61–68).

Commenting on this Qur'ānic verse several decades before this totally unexpected discovery in astronomy, Said Nursi wrote in Muḥakemat ("Reasonings"), 68–69:

> As the word tajrī ("runs") points to a style, the phrase li-mustaqarrin lahā ("the course appointed for it for a term to its resting-place for the stability of it(s system)" demonstrates a reality. The sun, like a vessel built of gold, travels and floats in the ocean of the heavens comprised of ether and defined in a ḥadīth as a stretched and tightened wave. Although it quivers and shakes in its course or orbit, since people see it moving, the Qur'ān uses the word travel or float. However, since the origin of the force of gravity is

movement, the sun moves and quivers in its orbit. Through this vibration, which is the wheel of its figurative movement, its satellites are attracted to it and preserved from falling and scattering. When a tree quivers, its fruit fall. But when the sun quivers and shakes, its fruit – its satellites – are preserved from falling.

Again, wisdom requires that the sun should move and travel on its mobile throne – its course or orbit – accompanied by its soldiers – its satellites. For the Divine Power has made everything moving and condemned nothing to absolute rest or motionlessness. Divine Mercy allows nothing to be condemned to inertia that is the cousin of death. So, the sun is free, it can travel provided it obeys the laws of God and does not disturb the freedom of others. So, it may actually be traveling, or its traveling may also be figurative. However, what is important according to the Qur'ān is the universal (or solar system's) order, the wheel of which is the sun and its movement. Through the sun, the stability and orderliness of the system are ensured.

442　سورة يس　۴۴۲

بِسْمِ اللّٰهِ الرَّحْمٰنِ الرَّحِيمِ

past when committed by former peoples), so that you may be shown mercy (a good, virtuous life in the world and eternal happiness in the Hereafter)."

46. Yet there does not come to them a clear sign from among the signs of their Lord (a Revelation from among His Revelations), but they turn away from it (being averse to the admonition given therein).

47. And when they are told: "Spend (for the needy) out of what God has provided for you," those who disbelieve say to those who believe, "Shall we then feed those whom God would feed if He willed? You are but in obvious error."

48. And they say (intending mockery): "So, when is this promise (of Resurrection and Judgment), if you are truthful?"

49. They should await only a single blast that will seize them unawares even as they are disputing (heedlessly among themselves about their worldly concerns).[15]

50. Then they will not be able even to make a bequest (so suddenly will the blast seize them), nor return to their families.

51. And the Trumpet will be blown, and see, out of the graves they rush forth to their Lord.

52. They will cry: "Woe to us! Who has raised us from our place of sleep?[16] (We have come to know that) this is what the All-Merciful promised, and that the Messengers spoke the truth!"

53. It is but one single blast, and see, they will all have been (raised and) arraigned together before Us (for judgment).

54. On that Day, no soul will be wronged in the least, and you will not be recompensed for anything but what you used to do.

---

41. A(nother) sign for them is that We bear their generations on the ship laden (with them and their cargo, and yet sustained in the water, without sinking).

42. And We have created for them the like of it (for land travel) on which they ride.[13]

43. If We will, We cause them to drown, and there is no help for them (against Our will), nor can they be saved (from drowning)

44. Unless by a mercy from Us and (Our allowing them) to enjoy life for some more time until a term (determined).[14]

45. When they are told: "Beware of and guard against what lies before you and what lies behind you (of unforgivable sins and punishment they will bring in the world or the Hereafter, and brought about in the

13. Many of the commentators have understood that what is meant by "the ship laden" in verse 41 is the Prophet Noah's Ark. Although this meaning may be included in the verse, when considered together with this verse (42) and similar ones such as 40: 80 and 43: 12, we can conclude that it mentions the ships as means of transportation on the sea and other means and animals of transport both on the sea and on the earth.

14. The term is either the end of life (pre-)determined for each person by God or the respite granted to the wrongdoers so that they may give up their way and accept the true guidance.

15. This verse draws attention to the fact that the unbelievers, especially those who are wealthy among them, are usually engaged in disputes over worldly matters in utter heedlessness of God's admonitions. This causes many calamities, such as wars and social convulsions, to afflict them in the world, and the Last Hour will also come upon them when they are involved in such disputes.

16. This statement reveals two facts concerning life in the grave. One is that compared with the dread of the Resurrection and the Place of the Supreme Gathering, and the punishment in Hell, the suffering in the grave will be like a sleep tormented by nightmares. The other is: 'Ali, the Fourth Caliph, may God be pleased with him, says that the life of the world is sleep, and people wake up when they die. So, from the perspective of the truths of faith and the truths concerning creation and life, the worldly life is like dream. When people die, their seeing and perception will be much keener (50: 22). Compared with the eternal life in the other world, the life in the grave is like a dream during sleep. All the truths will be manifested in all their clarity in the Hereafter.

443

إِنَّ أَصْحَابَ الْجَنَّةِ الْيَوْمَ فِى شُغُلٍ فَاكِهُونَ ۝ هُمْ وَأَزْوَاجُهُمْ فِى ظِلَالٍ عَلَى الْأَرَائِكِ مُتَّكِئُونَ ۝ لَهُمْ فِيهَا فَاكِهَةٌ وَلَهُم مَّا يَدَّعُونَ ۝ سَلَامٌ قَوْلاً مِّن رَّبٍّ رَّحِيمٍ ۝ وَامْتَازُوا الْيَوْمَ أَيُّهَا الْمُجْرِمُونَ ۝ أَلَمْ أَعْهَدْ إِلَيْكُمْ يَا بَنِى آدَمَ أَن لَّا تَعْبُدُوا الشَّيْطَانَ إِنَّهُ لَكُمْ عَدُوٌّ مُّبِينٌ ۝ وَأَنِ اعْبُدُونِى هَذَا صِرَاطٌ مُّسْتَقِيمٌ ۝ وَلَقَدْ أَضَلَّ مِنكُمْ جِبِلّاً كَثِيراً أَفَلَمْ تَكُونُوا تَعْقِلُونَ ۝ هَذِهِ جَهَنَّمُ الَّتِى كُنتُمْ تُوعَدُونَ ۝ اصْلَوْهَا الْيَوْمَ بِمَا كُنتُمْ تَكْفُرُونَ ۝ الْيَوْمَ نَخْتِمُ عَلَى أَفْوَاهِهِمْ وَتُكَلِّمُنَا أَيْدِيهِمْ وَتَشْهَدُ أَرْجُلُهُم بِمَا كَانُوا يَكْسِبُونَ ۝ وَلَوْ نَشَاءُ لَطَمَسْنَا عَلَى أَعْيُنِهِمْ فَاسْتَبَقُوا الصِّرَاطَ فَأَنَّى يُبْصِرُونَ ۝ وَلَوْ نَشَاءُ لَمَسَخْنَاهُمْ عَلَى مَكَانَتِهِمْ فَمَا اسْتَطَاعُوا مُضِيّاً وَلَا يَرْجِعُونَ ۝ وَمَن نُّعَمِّرْهُ نُنَكِّسْهُ فِى الْخَلْقِ أَفَلَا يَعْقِلُونَ ۝ وَمَا عَلَّمْنَاهُ الشِّعْرَ وَمَا يَنبَغِى لَهُ إِنْ هُوَ إِلَّا ذِكْرٌ وَقُرْآنٌ مُّبِينٌ ۝ لِّيُنذِرَ مَن كَانَ حَيّاً وَيَحِقَّ الْقَوْلُ عَلَى الْكَافِرِينَ ۝

worship Satan? Indeed he is a manifest enemy to you.

61. "And that you should worship Me alone. This is a straight path (for you to follow).

62. "Yet he has assuredly caused great multitudes of you to go astray. Should you not reason and take heed?

63. "This is Hell, with which you were threatened (repeatedly).[18]

64. "Enter it this Day to roast because you persistently disbelieved."

65. That Day We will set a seal upon their mouths, and their hands will speak to Us, and their feet will bear witness to what they earned (in the world).[19]

66. If We had so willed, We could certainly have blotted out their eyes, and they would rush around for the right path. How then would they be able to see their way?[20]

67. If We had so willed, We could have fixed them in their places (immobilized where they are), unable to go forward or turn back.

68. Whomever We cause to live long, We may also reverse him in nature (so that he returns to weakness after strength, to ignorance after knowledge, to forgetting after remembering). So will they not reason and take heed?

69. We have not taught him (the Messenger) poetry; further, it is not seemly for him.[21] This is but a Reminder (teaching and admonishing), a Qur'ān recited and conveyed (from God), clear in itself and clearly showing the truth.

70. So that the Messenger may warn with it those who are (truly) alive (and thus can reason, and see, and hear the truth), and that the word (of Divine judgment after evidence and admonition) may be completed against the unbelievers.

55. Surely the companions of Paradise will on that Day be in happy occupations enjoying the blessings (of Paradise that God will grant them abundantly out of His grace, in return for their good deeds).

56. They and their spouses are in pleasant shade (safe from any troubling weather), reclining on thrones.

57. They will have therein the fruit (of their good deeds in the world), and they will have whatever they call for.[17]

58. "Peace!" is the word (of welcome for them and of safety from any trouble) from the Lord All-Compassionate (toward His believing servants).

59. "And you, O disbelieving criminals! Get you apart this Day!

60. "Did I not make a covenant with you, O children of Adam, that you should not

17. The original of the statement *enjoying the blessings (of Paradise that God will grant them abundantly out of His grace, in return for their good deeds)* in verse 55 above is *fākihūn*, literally meaning "enjoying the fruits." A similar meaning is given in this verse, where the word *fākihāh* (literally, fruit) is mentioned. This shows one of the miraculous aspects of the Qur'ān's style. That is, verse 54 has mentioned that people will be recompensed for what they do in the world. As is known, fruit denotes the ultimate result of a tree's life or, metaphorically, the result of an effort. So, verses 55 and 57 signify that people's deeds in the world are sown in the field of the Hereafter like seeds. Each good seed will grow into a tree with many fruits, by God's grace, according to its worth, varying from person to person, according to the degree of its righteousness and the sincerity with which it is done. The blessings of Paradise will be those "fruits." But, out of pure grace, God will grant them much more than they deserve, so they will have whatever they desire and call for.

18. The Qur'ān repeatedly threatens us with Hell and warns against it. God made the first warning when Satan refused to prostrate before Adam after Adam's creation, and he was allowed to try to seduce humankind until the end of time: *My servants – you shall have no authority over any of them, unless it be such as follow you being rebellious against God, as you are). And for all such (rebellious people), Hell is the promised place* (15: 42–44).

The Qur'ān makes many similar reiterations. It is the Book of not only law, prayer, wisdom, worship, and servanthood to God, but also commands and invitations, invocations and reflection, glad tidings and warnings. It is a holy book containing books for all of our spiritual needs; a heavenly book that, like a sacred library, contains numerous booklets from which all the saints, eminently truthful people, all purified and discerning scholars, and those well-versed in knowledge of God have derived their own specific ways, and which illuminate each way and answer their followers' needs. It is because of this and the fact that all the teachings of the Qur'ān need reiteration to explain and establish them in people's mind and hearts that the Qur'ān has many reiterated statements. However, in most cases they are of the kind that explain truths from various perspectives and in different styles according to different conditions, times, cases, and audience. The Qur'ān calls this style *taṣrīf*.

19. This verse has two meanings or two aspects in its meaning. One is that since the Hereafter will be the abode where everything will be alive (29: 64; 25: 12, note 4), the body parts of people will act as a witness in favor or against them. Second, the beliefs and deeds of everyone are reflected on their parts of the body, and people of special insight can even discern them in the world.

20. This verse means that God has equipped humankind with the ability and necessary organs to see the truth. But the disbelieving people have lost this ability and made these organs functionless, and so it is as if they are blind and cannot find the right path.

21. In addition to the Qur'ān's judgment about poets (and poetry) in 26: 224–227 and the relevant explanations in notes 42 and 43, we can add here what follows concerning why poetry is not seemly for God's Messenger, upon him be peace and blessings:

Since the wise Qur'ān encompasses infinite brilliant and exalted truths, it is free from and superior to the fancies of much poetry. The Qur'ān of miraculous expression is not in strict verse because, despite its perfect order and arrangement, it expounds the Book of the Universe's beauty and order in its well-ordered styles, therefore, its freedom from (poetic) constraints allows each verse to connect with other verses in an encompassing context. Such connections give the meaning of its different verses a relationship to one another.

Thus, there are thousands of Qur'āns within the Qur'ān, each being adopted by a different path or school in Islam. For example, *Sūrat al-Ikhlās* contains a treasury of knowledge of Divine Unity provided by 36 ways of reading *Sūrat al-Ikhlas* (see 112, note 4). This is comparable to the way each star, apparently at random, extends (as if from a center) a line of connection to every other star in the surrounding area. More clearly, these verses are interrelated to one another in the same way that all cells and organs in a body are interrelated with one another. Such a network indicates the hidden relation between all creatures. This is the same relationship as that found among the verses of the Qur'ān. So it cannot design itself according to the human system of poetry. Reflect on the perfect order in apparent disorder, and learn something. Understand one meaning of: *We have not taught him poetry; further, it is not seemly for him.*

Understand also from the meaning of *it is not seemly for him* that poetry tends to adorn insignificant and dull facts with grandiose images and fancies to make them attractive. But the Qur'ānic truths are so great and elevated, so brilliant and splendid, that even the greatest and most brilliant poetic images appear dull and insignificant (*The Words*, "the 13th Word," 156–157).

71. Have they not considered how (as signs of Our Lordship), out of what Our Hands have originated and fashioned, We have created for them cattle, and so they are their owners?

72. We have subdued them to them, so that among them (they find) their mounts and from them they obtain food.

73. And they have many other benefits in them and (diverse) things to drink. Will they not then give thanks?

74. Yet they have taken deities for worship apart from God, (expecting) that they may receive help (from them).

75. They (the false deities) are unable to help them; rather, they (the worshippers) are a (supportive) host for them (the false deities, and all will be arraigned for punishment on the Day of Judgment).[22]

76. So do not let their (slanderous) words (against God and you) grieve you (O Messenger). Surely We know whatever they keep concealed (of speech or deeds) and whatever they disclose.

77. Has human not considered that We have created him from (so slight a beginning as) a drop of (seminal) fluid? Yet, he turns into an open, fierce adversary (selfishly disputing against the truth).

78. And he coins a comparison for Us, having forgotten his own origin and creation, saying, "Who will give life to these bones when they have rotten away?"

79. Say: "He Who produced them in the first instance will give them life. He has full knowledge of every (form and mode and possibility of) creation (and of everything He has created He knows every detail in every dimension of time and space)."[23]

80. He Who has made for you fire from the green tree, and see, you kindle fire with it.[24]

81. Is not He Who has created the heavens and the earth able to create (from rotten bones) the like of them (whose bones have rotted under the ground)?[25] Surely He is; He is the Supreme Creator, the All-Knowing.

82. When He wills a thing to be, He but says to it "Be!" and (in the selfsame instant) it is.

83. So, All-Glorified is He in Whose Hand is the absolute dominion of all things,[26] and to Him you are being brought back.

22. Polytheists take many deities hoping that those so-called gods may help them with their worldly affairs. Among them are idols, devils, some invisible forces such as "good" or "evil" spirits, angels, some powerful or saintly peoples, and Prophets, etc. However, they do not think and understand that it is they themselves who raise them to the position of divinity and serve them as a host. They and their idols carved out of stone or wood, devils, and the cruel tyrants or powerful persons rebellious against God will be brought up for punishment on the Day of Judgment.

23. That is, God has innumerable ways of creating, so He can create and re-create in any way He wills. Moreover, He has full knowledge of everything He has created. He never forgets anything. So, can He Who created in the first instance out of nothing when there was nothing to copy, from which He would be able to draw knowledge – can He not re-create?

24. This verse has a very subtle meaning. It explains how God can give life to a rotten bone, and suggests that God produces unexpected things from their opposites, or from the things from which it seems to us impossible their opposites could be produced. According to the classical commentators, what is meant by the green tree mentioned here – a fresh tree in which there is still water – are the trees of Markh and 'Afār, which grow in the Arabian desert and from which people kindle fire. The verse, according to some contemporary commentators, also refers to petroleum. As is known, petroleum is formed from rotten plants, which were once green. In the past, people in countries such as Azerbaijan used petroleum that flowed on the earth without knowing that it was petroleum. It is possible that there may have been a relationship between this and fire-worship. It is also a fact that the Saudi Arabia, which was once rich in greenery, is now a country rich in petroleum. In short, God creates as He wills things from their opposites.

25. That is, He creates every human being from so simple a matter as a drop of seminal fluid. He also creates many things from almost nothing. It is also He Who has created the heavens and the earth, the creation of which is something greater than the creation of humanity (40: 57). So He can create or recreate the like of human beings from rotten bones. God's Messenger, upon him be peace and blessings, said that an essential matter in the human body does not rot. God will re-create a human being from this matter.

26. The original of "the absolute dominion of all things" is *malakūt*. As the real existence and origin of a word lies in its invisible meaning, while the word composed of letters serves merely to represent it, the existence of every thing and every event in the universe lies in its immaterial essence, which is pure and unrestricted by matter. This essential existence has degrees of manifestation. One of the pure, immaterial realms where a manifestation of certain degree takes place is called the Realm of the Pure Sovereignty (*Malakūt*). While God acts in the material, visible world from behind the veil of causality (on the reason why He does so, see 18: 22, note 13), He acts in the Realm of Pure Sovereignty without any veils. So, His saying or ordering in this realm is identical with His creating, which is immediate. This act of creation generally takes place in or is transferred into the material world in a gradual process. However, it is also so swift in this world that we feel as if it happened in a single moment.

In order to be able to grasp God's creation or making of everything with a single command, we can consider the operating system of computers and "verbal" writing with computers. The operating system of computers consists in commands and the words made by pressing on keys are manifested on the screen. Like this, God's creation or making consists in commands or, in other words, the Divine Speech operates like the Power or the Power operates through the Speech. (God knows best.)

SŪRAH 37

AS-ṢĀFFĀT
(THOSE ALIGNED IN RANKS)

Makkah period

This *sūrah* of 182 verses was revealed in the last stage of the middle Makkan period when God's Messenger, upon him be peace and blessings, and His Companions were heavily persecuted. It derives its name from the first verse. It begins by mentioning some of the angels that are responsible for certain duties and goes on to mention the jinn, rejecting the pagan assertion that they are the daughters of God. The *sūrah* then emphasizes the afterlife and the Last Judgment. Afterwards, certain episodes of the lives of some Messengers are mentioned and victory for the believers is promised.

In the Name of God, the All-Merciful, the All-Compassionate.

1. By those (the angels) who align themselves in ranks;

2. (Some) driving away with reproof,

3. (And others) reciting the Reminder (revealed from God).[1]

4. Most surely your Lord is One;

5. The Lord of the heavens and the earth and all that is between them, and the Lord of all the easts.[2]

6. We have indeed adorned the lowest heaven (the heaven of the world) with an ornament – the stars;

7. And for guard against every devil persistent in haughty rebellion.

8. They cannot hear anything from the High Assembly (of the angels of the heavens) – and (whenever they attempt to hear) become targets of missiles from all directions;

9. Repelled, and for them is a perpetual punishment –

10. Excepting one who snatches something by stealth, and is pursued (and destroyed) by a piercing shooting-star.[3]

11. So ask them (the polytheists): "Are they more formidable in structure or those that We have created (the heavens and the angels in them). Indeed, We have created them (human beings) from a sticky clay.

12. You find all God's acts wonderful, and their denial strange, but they continue to mock (God's Message and His Messenger).

13. And when they are reminded (of Divine truths and admonished by His Revelations), they pay no heed.

14. When they see an extraordinary evidence (of the truth, a miracle), they take it in mockery (and call others to do the same).

15. And they say, "This is clearly nothing but sorcery.

16. "What! after we have died and become dust and bones, will we then be raised from the dead?

17. "And also our forefathers of old?!"

18. Say: "Yes, indeed, and most humiliated you will be."

19. It will be only a single scaring cry, and then behold, they are staring (in dread),

20. And saying: "Woe to us! This is the Day of Judgment!"

21. (And it is said): "This is the Day of Judgment and Distinction (between truth and falsehood, between the righteous and the sinful – the Day) that you used to deny."

22. (God commands the angels:) "Gather together all those who committed the greatest wrong (by obstinately associating partners with God), and their (devilish) comrades, and all that they used to worship (of idols, and the rebellious among humankind and the jinn),

23. "Apart from God, and lead them to the path of the Blazing Flame!

24. "And arrest them there, for they must be questioned (concerning their deeds in the world).

---

1. The most commonly accepted opinion concerning the angels mentioned in these verses is that they are the angels accompanying Archangel Gabriel, who was charged with gradually bringing the Qur'ān to God's Messenger, upon him be peace and blessings. Those angels aligned themselves in ranks along the way while Gabriel, upon him be peace, brought the Revelation to the Messenger, and some of them drove away the devils that tried to grasp parts of the Revelation. Some stood around the Messenger for the same purpose. Among those were the aids of Gabriel, who conveyed Revelations to the Messenger (see 72: 28). There are many Revelations that have not been included in the Qur'ān but came to explain it and constitute the basis of the Sunnah. There are also angels who glorify God in ranks, and recite the Revelation or parts from the Qur'ān, sometimes to or around the Messenger. (For verses with similar meanings, see 2: 97; 26: 194; 80: 16; 72: 28; 37: 166.)

2. This verse emphasizes the fact that it is God Who has absolute authority and control over the whole universe. By *the easts*, it indicates the spherical shape of planets and their rotations; the plural "easts" indicating many dimensions: any point on the earth is east with respect to what is west of it, therefore the concept of "east" is different at every point on the earth, thus forming an ensemble of easts. Moreover, there are 180 points where the sun rises in one hemisphere, that is, the sun rises at one place only two days in the year, thus making 360 points throughout the earth. Therefore, this verse is also indicative of the meridians as well as of infinite dimensions, of the relativity of space and the spherical shape of planets, as well as the rotation of the earth.

3. Particularly in the pre-Islamic era, soothsaying or fortune-telling was very widespread among the Arabs, as it is today throughout the world. Devils attempted to ascend to the heavens and listen to the angels' conversations about the Divine truths and some future events, and if they could grasp something, they would convey it to the soothsayers and fortune-tellers with whom they had relationships, adding many untrue things as well. They made the same attempts when the Revelation began to be revealed to God's Messenger, upon him be peace and blessings. But God did not permit them to do so, and if any among them snatched away something from the angels, they were destroyed with missiles. The devils never give up their attempts to ascend to the heavens, but in every attempt they are repelled and if some are able to obtain something from the angels, they are then destroyed. (For similar verses and explanations, see 15: 16–18, note 5; 26: 212; 67: 5, note 4; 72: 9.)

446

سُورَةُ الصَّآفَّاتِ

٤٢٦

مَا لَكُمْ لَا تَنَاصَرُونَ ۞ بَلْ هُمُ الْيَوْمَ مُسْتَسْلِمُونَ ۞ وَأَقْبَلَ بَعْضُهُمْ عَلَىٰ بَعْضٍ يَتَسَآءَلُونَ ۞ قَالُوٓا إِنَّكُمْ كُنتُمْ تَأْتُونَنَا عَنِ الْيَمِينِ ۞ قَالُوا بَل لَّمْ تَكُونُوا مُؤْمِنِينَ ۞ وَمَا كَانَ لَنَا عَلَيْكُم مِّن سُلْطَانٍ بَلْ كُنتُمْ قَوْمًا طَاغِينَ ۞ فَحَقَّ عَلَيْنَا قَوْلُ رَبِّنَا إِنَّا لَذَآئِقُونَ ۞ فَأَغْوَيْنَاكُمْ إِنَّا كُنَّا غَاوِينَ ۞ فَإِنَّهُمْ يَوْمَئِذٍ فِي الْعَذَابِ مُشْتَرِكُونَ ۞ إِنَّا كَذَٰلِكَ نَفْعَلُ بِالْمُجْرِمِينَ ۞ إِنَّهُمْ كَانُوٓا إِذَا قِيلَ لَهُمْ لَآ إِلَٰهَ إِلَّا اللَّهُ يَسْتَكْبِرُونَ ۞ وَيَقُولُونَ أَئِنَّا لَتَارِكُوٓا آلِهَتِنَا لِشَاعِرٍ مَّجْنُونٍ ۞ بَلْ جَآءَ بِالْحَقِّ وَصَدَّقَ الْمُرْسَلِينَ ۞ إِنَّكُمْ لَذَآئِقُوا الْعَذَابِ الْأَلِيمِ ۞ وَمَا تُجْزَوْنَ إِلَّا مَا كُنتُمْ تَعْمَلُونَ ۞ إِلَّا عِبَادَ اللَّهِ الْمُخْلَصِينَ ۞ أُو۟لَٰٓئِكَ لَهُمْ رِزْقٌ مَّعْلُومٌ ۞ فَوَاكِهُ وَهُم مُّكْرَمُونَ ۞ فِي جَنَّاتِ النَّعِيمِ ۞ عَلَىٰ سُرُرٍ مُّتَقَابِلِينَ ۞ يُطَافُ عَلَيْهِم بِكَأْسٍ مِّن مَّعِينٍ ۞ بَيْضَآءَ لَذَّةٍ لِّلشَّارِبِينَ ۞ لَا فِيهَا غَوْلٌ وَلَا هُمْ عَنْهَا يُنزَفُونَ ۞ وَعِندَهُمْ قَاصِرَاتُ الطَّرْفِ عِينٌ ۞ كَأَنَّهُنَّ بَيْضٌ مَّكْنُونٌ ۞ فَأَقْبَلَ بَعْضُهُمْ عَلَىٰ بَعْضٍ يَتَسَآءَلُونَ ۞ قَالَ قَآئِلٌ مِّنْهُمْ إِنِّي كَانَ لِي قَرِينٌ ۞

---

25. "But, what is the matter with you that you do not help one another (to escape punishment)?"

26. Instead, on that Day they will be in utter submission (without the least sign of arrogance).

27. And they turn to one another, exchanging words (of blame) with one another.

28. They (the ones led) say (to the leaders): "It was you who used to come to us affecting (pretending to be our well-wishers and claiming falsehood to be the truth)."

29. They (the leaders) say: "No! Rather, you yourselves were not believers, (with no inclination and intention to believe).

30. "And we had no power over you (to compel you to disbelieve). But you yourselves were a rebellious people.

31. "So our Lord's word (of punishment) has come true against us. (In justice) we are bound to taste it.

32. "So then, (though without power to compel, if) we did mislead you (and cause you to rebel), for surely we ourselves had been lost in error."

33. So, on that Day they will be associated together in (suffering) the punishment.

34. That is how We will deal with the disbelieving criminals.

35. For when they were told that there is no deity but God, they would grow arrogant and reject it.

36. And they would say, "Are we to give up our deities for the sake of a mad poet?"

37. No! Rather he has brought (you) the truth and confirms those (Messengers) sent (before him).

38. You are surely bound to taste the painful punishment (on account of your attitude and actions),

39. And you will not be recompensed but for what you were doing.

40. But not so God's servants endowed with sincerity in faith and practicing the Religion.

41. For those there is (in Paradise) a provision specially prepared:

42. Fruits (as the reward of their life in the world); and they will be highly honored,

43. In Gardens of bounty and blessing;

44. Sitting on thrones, face to face,

45. A cup will be passed round among them with a drink from a pure, gushing spring;

46. Clear, delightful for those who drink it;

47. Free from any headiness or harm, and they will not suffer intoxication from it.

48. And with them will be pure, chaste-eyed spouses (whose glances are fixed on them only), most beautiful of eye;

49. (As free from any ugliness, and) un-touched, as if they were hidden (ostrich) eggs.

50. They will turn to one another, indulging in friendly talk.

51. One of them speaks thus: "I had a close companion,

52. "Who used to ask me, 'Are you really one of those who confirm the truth (of what the Messenger teaches us about the Last Judgment)?

53. 'Will we, when we die and have become dust and bones – will we then really be (raised and) put under judgment?' "

54. He (the speaker) will say: "Would you like to look (into Hell to see him)?"

55. He will look down and see him in the midst of the Blazing Flame.

56. He will say: "By God, you would nearly have caused me to perish:

57. "Had it not been for the grace of my Lord, I would certainly have been among those arraigned (in the Flame for punishment)."

58. (Then, turning to his companions, he will say:) "We are not to experience death any more, are we?

59. "Except the former death (that we experienced in leaving the world), and we are not to be punished.

60. "(Then) this is most certainly the supreme triumph."

61. For the like of this, then, let those who will labor (to a goal) labor.

62. Is this what is good as a welcome or the tree of *Zaqqūm*?

63. We have made it (that tree) a means of trial[4] and punishment for the wrongdoers (who associate partners with God).

64. It is a tree growing in the heart of the Blazing Flame.

65. Its fruits are like the heads of satans.[5]

66. So, most surely, they will eat of it and fill up their bellies with it.

67. Then, for them will be boiling water (to mix with the *zaqqūm* in their bodies).

68. And afterwards, they are bound to return to the Blazing Flame again.[6]

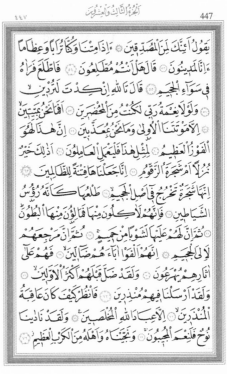

447

69. Assuredly they found their forefathers on the wrong path.

70. And yet, they rush (after them) in their footsteps.

71. Indeed, most of those (communities) that lived before them went astray,

72. Though We had sent among them warners (with Our guidance).

73. So see how was the outcome for those who were warned (but paid no heed),

74. Except God's servants, endowed with sincerity in faith and practicing the Religion.

75. And Noah (just such a servant and warner) had called upon Us (for help),[7] and how excellent We are in answering (prayer)!

76. We saved him and (his true followers among) his family and people from the mighty distress.

4. On the tree of *Zaqqūm* and its being a means of trial, see 17: 60, note 27.

5. We usually liken beautiful beings to angels, as the women who saw the Prophet Joseph, upon him be peace, likened him to an honorable angel (12: 31); and we liken ugly beings to devils. However, there may be many other points of resemblance between the fruit of the tree of *Zaqqūm* and the heads of devils. For example, this tree will grow from the seeds sown by the evil deeds committed by the people in Hell, deeds that were prompted by Satan. The Qur'ān mentions deeds – such as taking intoxicants, playing games of chance, offering sacrifices for anything having the meaning of an idol or at the places consecrated for offerings to other than God, and polytheistic divination by shooting arrows and other similar ways (like drawing lots and throwing dice) – as loathsome evil of Satan's doing (5: 90). So, it is quite natural that such deeds will grow into satan-like trees and yield fruit that resembles the heads of devils.

6. After eating, one needs water. The people of Hell will eat of the fruit of the tree of *Zaqqūm* and come out of the Blazing Flame into another area of Hell to drink. But their drink will be boiling water that will be mixed with the fruits of *Zaqqūm*, and it will cut up their bowels (47: 15). Then, they will have to return to the Flame as their dwelling, and their punishment will go on in this strain.

The Qur'ānic descriptions concerning Paradise and Hell cannot be taken as being metaphors. Paradise with all its blessings and Hell with all its elements of punishment will be the outcome of people's beliefs and deeds in the world. So people will live in them with both their spirit, their carnal souls, and bodies – the carnal souls of the people of Paradise will be perfectly purified – in resemblance with the worldly life, but in a way that is particular to the other world.

It may be asked: What do the human carnal soul or selfhood and the defective, changing, unstable, and pain-stricken body

have to do with eternity and Paradise? The spirit's elevated pleasures must surely be enough. Why should a bodily resurrection take place for bodily pleasures? The answer is:

Soil, despite its darkness and density when compared to water, air, and light, is the means and source of all works of Divine art. Therefore, it is somehow superior in meaning over other elements. Human selfhood or the carnal soul, despite its density is comprehensive, and provided it is purified, it is able to gain some kind of superiority over the other senses and faculties. Likewise, the body is a most comprehensive and diverse mirror for the manifestations of the Divine Names, and has been equipped with instruments to weigh and measure the contents of all Divine treasures. For example, if the tongue's sense of taste were not the origin of all the varieties of food and drink, we could not experience, recognize, or measure them. Furthermore, the body also contains the instruments needed to experience and recognize most of the manifestations of the Divine Names, as well as the faculties for experiencing the most diverse and infinitely varied pleasures.

The Maker of the universe wants to make known all the treasures of His Mercy and all the manifestations of His Names, as well as enabling us to experience all His bounties. Given this, as the world of eternal happiness is a mighty pool into which the flood of this life flows, as it is a vast exhibition of what the loom of the universe produces, as it is the everlasting store of the crops produced in the field of this (material) world, it will resemble this world and life to some degree. The All-Wise Maker, the All-Compassionate Just One will give pleasures particular to each bodily organ as wages for their duty, service, and worship. To think otherwise would be contrary to His Wisdom, Justice, and Compassion. (*The Words*, "the 28th Word," 515–516)

7. For Noah's prayer, see *sūrah* 54: 10; *sūrah* 71: 26.

448

سُورَةُ الصَّآفَّاتِ

﴿وَجَعَلْنَا ذُرِّيَّتَهُ هُمُ الْبَاقِينَ ۞ وَتَرَكْنَا عَلَيْهِ فِي الْآخِرِينَ ۞ سَلَامٌ عَلَىٰ نُوحٍ فِي الْعَالَمِينَ ۞ إِنَّا كَذَٰلِكَ نَجْزِي الْمُحْسِنِينَ ۞ إِنَّهُ مِنْ عِبَادِنَا الْمُؤْمِنِينَ ۞ ثُمَّ أَغْرَقْنَا الْآخَرِينَ ۞ وَإِنَّ مِنْ شِيعَتِهِ لَإِبْرَاهِيمَ ۞ إِذْ جَاءَ رَبَّهُ بِقَلْبٍ سَلِيمٍ ۞ إِذْ قَالَ لِأَبِيهِ وَقَوْمِهِ مَاذَا تَعْبُدُونَ ۞ أَئِفْكًا آلِهَةً دُونَ اللَّهِ تُرِيدُونَ ۞ فَمَا ظَنُّكُمْ بِرَبِّ الْعَالَمِينَ ۞ فَنَظَرَ نَظْرَةً فِي النُّجُومِ ۞ فَقَالَ إِنِّي سَقِيمٌ ۞ فَتَوَلَّوْا عَنْهُ مُدْبِرِينَ ۞ فَرَاغَ إِلَىٰ آلِهَتِهِمْ فَقَالَ أَلَا تَأْكُلُونَ ۞ مَا لَكُمْ لَا تَنْطِقُونَ ۞ فَرَاغَ عَلَيْهِمْ ضَرْبًا بِالْيَمِينِ ۞ فَأَقْبَلُوا إِلَيْهِ يَزِفُّونَ ۞ قَالَ أَتَعْبُدُونَ مَا تَنْحِتُونَ ۞ وَاللَّهُ خَلَقَكُمْ وَمَا تَعْمَلُونَ ۞ قَالُوا ابْنُوا لَهُ بُنْيَانًا فَأَلْقُوهُ فِي الْجَحِيمِ ۞ فَأَرَادُوا بِهِ كَيْدًا فَجَعَلْنَاهُمُ الْأَسْفَلِينَ ۞ وَقَالَ إِنِّي ذَاهِبٌ إِلَىٰ رَبِّي سَيَهْدِينِ ۞ رَبِّ هَبْ لِي مِنَ الصَّالِحِينَ ۞ فَبَشَّرْنَاهُ بِغُلَامٍ حَلِيمٍ ۞ فَلَمَّا بَلَغَ مَعَهُ السَّعْيَ قَالَ يَا بُنَيَّ إِنِّي أَرَىٰ فِي الْمَنَامِ أَنِّي أَذْبَحُكَ فَانْظُرْ مَاذَا تَرَىٰ قَالَ يَا أَبَتِ افْعَلْ مَا تُؤْمَرُ سَتَجِدُنِي إِنْ شَاءَ اللَّهُ مِنَ الصَّابِرِينَ ۞﴾

77. And We caused his offspring to endure (on the earth).

78. And We left for him among later-comers (until the end of time this greeting and remembrance of him and his Message):

79. "Peace be upon Noah among all beings."[8]

80. Thus do We reward those devoted to doing good as if seeing God.

81. Surely he was one of Our truly believing servants.

82. As for the others (who opposed him), We caused them to drown.

83. Abraham was surely one who followed the same way as his.

84. He had turned to his Lord with a heart sound and pure (from any trace of insincerity of faith).

85. (Remember) when he said to his father and his people, "What is that you worship?

86. "Is it a fabrication that you pursue, worshipping deities apart from God?

87. "So, what do you think about the Lord of the worlds (that you dare to do so)?"

88. Then (when invited to participate in the religious ceremonies of the people on a festival day) he cast a glance at the stars;

89. And he said: "Indeed I am sick."[9]

90. So they (the others) turned away from him and departed.

91. Thereupon he approached their deities,

and said, "Will you not eat (of the offerings put before you)?

92. "What is the matter with you that you do not speak?"

93. Then he fell upon them, striking them with his right hand (with all his strength).

94. Then, the other people headed towards him hurriedly.

95. He said: "Do you worship things that you yourselves have carved,

96. "While it is God Who has created you and all that you do?"[10]

97. They (consulted among themselves and) said: "Build him a pyre and throw him into the blazing flames!"

98. So they intended a scheme against him (to destroy him), but We made them the ones brought low.[11]

99. And he said: "Now I am going to my Lord (to quit my homeland purely for His sake, in the full conviction that) He will guide me (to a land where I will be able to worship Him freely).

100. (And he prayed): "My Lord, Grant me (the gift of a child who will be) one of the righteous."

101. So We gave him the glad tidings of a boy (who was to grow as one) mild and forbearing.

102. Then, when (his son) grew alongside him to the age of striving (for the necessities of life), he said: "O my dear son! I have seen in my dream that I should offer you in sacrifice. So think about this and tell me your view!" He said (unhesitatingly): "O my dear father! Do as you are commanded.[12] You will find me, by God's will, one of those who show steadfast patience (in obeying God's commands)."[13]

---

8. The Prophet Adam, upon him be peace, was the first human being (together with his wife Eve) on the earth and the first Prophet. Though he conveyed God's Message for the first time, his mission was, in one respect, restricted to his children. However, when the Prophet Noah, upon him be peace, came, humankind had already multiplied and divided into many tribes. So he came to a community that consisted of many divisions, in order to unify them upon God's Message and struggled against polytheism and injustices. Despite his efforts that lasted 950 years, few believed in him and the others were punished by God with the Flood. Humankind began a new life after this event. This shows how refractory and corrupt the people were during Noah's time and how difficult Noah's mission was. Had it not been for Noah and his continuous endeavors to reform people, the world would have been destroyed at that time. So all the later generations of both humankind, the jinn and all the other beings in the world are indebted to the Prophet Noah, upon him be peace, because of the continuity of existence in the world. It is because of this that Noah deserves and receives greetings with peace, good reputation, and thanks from all the existent beings in the world. The Qur'ān uses this kind of greeting for him only. Though it also sends greetings to the Messengers whom it will mention below, it does not mention the phrase *among all beings*.

9. Abraham was not physically sick, but the grief that he felt due to his people's falsehood was preying on his mind and soul. So he was determined to tell them the truth in a convincing way. Once, to avoid participating in their ceremonies, he told them he was unwell and, after they left, smashed their idols. The people thought that he was really sick, but what he had meant was that he was extremely uneasy because of their worshipping idols.

10. This means: It is God Who creates us and enables us to do things. He has given us will and power so that we are able to will something and do it. However, it is He Who creates and gives external existence to what we do. Our performing an action does not mean that that action must come about. Were it not for His creation, we could do nothing. We are doers or agents, while God is the Creator. If we had no ability to do something and God did not create our actions, then our having free will would be meaningless and we would have no responsibility for our deeds.

11. For a more detailed account of this event, see 21: 51–70.

12. This explicitly shows that what Abraham dreamed as a Prophet was a revealed Divine order.

13. Though the present versions of the Bible record that the son God ordered Abraham to sacrifice was Isaac (*Genesis*, 22: 2), this son

was actually Ishmael, the elder brother of Isaac. The Qur'ān describes the boy here with the terms *mildness* and *forbearance* (37: 101; 21: 85), but presents Isaac as a knowledgeable boy, thus emphasizing he was one with profound knowledge (15: 53). Isaac was born of Sārah, when she was too old to give birth to a child (11: 71–72; *Genesis*, 21). Ishmael was born of Hagar and, upon God's command, Abraham left them in the place where Makkah is now located. Years later he built the Ka'bah with Ishmael. His attempt to sacrifice Ishmael upon God's order took place in Mina, in Makkah, where sacrifices are offered during the Pilgrimage.

The verse of the Bible (*Genesis*, 22: 2) which states that God ordered Abraham to sacrifice Isaac contradicts several other verses. This verse mentions that when this order was given to Abraham, Isaac was his only son. Whereas, according to *Genesis*, 21: 5, when Isaac was born, Abraham was 100 years old,

and according to *Genesis*, 16: 16, Ishmael was born when Abraham was 86 years old. So according to the Bible, when Isaac came into the world, Ishmael was a young man of 14 years. This clearly shows that when Abraham was ordered to sacrifice his "only son" he was being ordered to sacrifice Ishmael. And the Qur'ānic verse that follows (113) makes it very clear that Isaac was born years after Ishmael. So this agreement between the Qur'ān and the Bible, together with their agreement on the fact that when God ordered Abraham to sacrifice his son he had only one son, are enough to make the truth plain.

The most compelling piece of non-textual evidence that God ordered Abraham to sacrifice Ishmael, not Isaac, is that this momentous event, the child-sacrifice being replaced with a ram, is celebrated in Islam – there is evidence that it was celebrated also in pre-Islamic Arabia by the descendants of Ishmael – but has no place among the festivals of the Jews.

449

فَلَمَّآ أَسْلَمَا وَتَلَّهُ لِلْجَبِينِ ۝ وَنَادَيْنَاهُ أَن يَا إِبْرَاهِيمُ ۝ قَدْ
صَدَّقْتَ الرُّءْيَا إِنَّا كَذَٰلِكَ نَجْزِي الْمُحْسِنِينَ ۝ إِنَّ هَٰذَا لَهُوَ
الْبَلَاءُ الْمُبِينُ ۝ وَفَدَيْنَاهُ بِذِبْحٍ عَظِيمٍ ۝ وَتَرَكْنَا عَلَيْهِ فِي
الْآخِرِينَ ۝ سَلَامٌ عَلَىٰ إِبْرَاهِيمَ ۝ كَذَٰلِكَ نَجْزِي الْمُحْسِنِينَ
۝ إِنَّهُ مِنْ عِبَادِنَا الْمُؤْمِنِينَ ۝ وَبَشَّرْنَاهُ بِإِسْحَاقَ نَبِيًّا مِنَ
الصَّالِحِينَ ۝ وَبَارَكْنَا عَلَيْهِ وَعَلَىٰ إِسْحَاقَ وَمِن ذُرِّيَّتِهِمَا
مُحْسِنٌ وَظَالِمٌ لِنَفْسِهِ مُبِينٌ ۝ وَلَقَدْ مَنَنَّا عَلَىٰ مُوسَىٰ
وَهَارُونَ ۝ وَنَجَّيْنَاهُمَا وَقَوْمَهُمَا مِنَ الْكَرْبِ الْعَظِيمِ
۝ وَنَصَرْنَاهُمْ فَكَانُوا هُمُ الْغَالِبِينَ ۝ وَآتَيْنَاهُمَا
الْكِتَابَ الْمُسْتَبِينَ ۝ وَهَدَيْنَاهُمَا الصِّرَاطَ الْمُسْتَقِيمَ
۝ وَتَرَكْنَا عَلَيْهِمَا فِي الْآخِرِينَ ۝ سَلَامٌ عَلَىٰ مُوسَىٰ
وَهَارُونَ ۝ إِنَّا كَذَٰلِكَ نَجْزِي الْمُحْسِنِينَ ۝ إِنَّهُمَا مِنْ
عِبَادِنَا الْمُؤْمِنِينَ ۝ وَإِنَّ إِلْيَاسَ لَمِنَ الْمُرْسَلِينَ ۝ إِذْ قَالَ
لِقَوْمِهِ أَلَا تَتَّقُونَ ۝ أَتَدْعُونَ بَعْلًا وَتَذَرُونَ أَحْسَنَ
الْخَالِقِينَ ۝ اللَّهَ رَبَّكُمْ وَرَبَّ آبَائِكُمُ الْأَوَّلِينَ ۝

---

103. Then when both had submitted to God's will, and Abraham had laid him down on the side of his forehead,

104. (At just that moment,) We called out to him: "O Abraham!

105. "You have already fulfilled the dream (which tested your loyal obedience to the command; so you no longer have to offer your son in sacrifice.) Thus do We reward those devoted to doing good as if seeing God."

106. Behold, all this was indeed a trial, clear.

107. And We ransomed him with a sacrifice tremendous in worth.[14]

108. And We left for him among later-comers (until the end of time this greeting and remembrance of him and his Message):

109. "Peace be upon Abraham."

110. Thus do We reward those devoted to doing good as if seeing God.

111. Surely he was one of Our truly believing servants.

112. We gave him the glad tidings of Isaac to be a Prophet among the righteous.

113. We showered Our blessings on both him (Ishmael) and on Isaac; and among the offspring of both there have been those devoted to doing good, aware that God is seeing them, and those who have plainly been wronging themselves (by sinning).

114. We assuredly bestowed Our favor also upon Moses and Aaron;

115. And We saved them and their people from the mighty distress (of slavery and persecution).

116. And We helped them, so they became the victors.

117. And We granted them both (Moses and Aaron) the clear Book[15] (which explained the matters that had been secret, and which the people needed for the happiness of their life in both worlds).

118. We showed them the Straight Path (enabling them to follow it in every matter without any deviance).

119. And We left for them among later-comers (until the end of time, this greeting and remembrance of them and their Message):

120. "Peace be upon Moses and Aaron."

121. Thus do We reward those devoted to doing good as if seeing God.

122. Surely those two were among Our truly believing servants.

123. And surely Ilyās (Elijah) was one of the Messengers.

124. (Remember) when he said to his people: "Will you not keep from disobedience to God in reverence for Him and piety?

125. "Will you continue to invoke Ba'l[16] (as deity) and forsake the Creator Who creates everything in the best and most appropriate form and has the ultimate rank of creativity –

126. "God, your Lord and the Lord of your forefathers?"

---

14. God never wills that human beings should be offered as a sacrifice, although it is a virtue for human beings to sacrifice themselves for His sake for lawful ends and in lawful ways. There are many instances of wisdom involved in God's order to the Prophet Abraham, upon him be peace, to offer his son as a sacrifice. Abraham had a very great character endowed with great potential that allowed him to be the origin of a holy line of Prophets. He was very compassionate, generous, and sincerely submitted to God. He was very concerned for the happiness of his people, both in the world and, more particularly, in the Hereafter. However, in order for this potential to be developed, God puts a person, even if that person is a Prophet, through trials. Succeeding in these trials requires that there should not be any obstacles in the heart that prevent one from getting near to God. These obstacles (see 3: 14) may be women (or men, for a woman), children, treasures of gold and silver (hoarded money), branded horses (or, in the modern form, cars), cattle, and plantations, posts and positions. So true believers in God can feel love for such things only because of their love of God and according to their relation with God. They cannot give their heart to any of them. *God has not made for any man two hearts within his body (one to be assigned for belief in and worship of Him and the other to belief in and worship of others)* (33: 4). So God tested Abraham with severe commandments and terrible ordeals (such as being thrown into a fire, the destruction of the people of Lot, who was his relative, being obliged to leave his homeland and family, and being ordered to sacrifice his son Ishmael), all of which he fulfilled thoroughly. *"Indeed I will make you an imām for all people." He (Abraham) pleaded: "(Will You appoint imāms) also from my offspring?"*

He (his Lord) answered: "(I will appoint from among those who merit it. But) My covenant does not include the wrongdoers" (2: 124).

By unhesitatingly obeying God's order, both Abraham and Ishmael were greatly rewarded. God made Abraham an imām (leader) for human beings and the father of many great Messengers to come after him. He rewarded Ishmael by making him the origin of a holy line, which finally gave birth to the greatest of creation, the Prophet Muḥammad, upon him be peace and blessings.

15. Although the Book was given to Moses, upon him be peace, due to the fact that his brother Aaron shared his task (20: 32), the verse mentions the Book as being granted to both of them.

16. Ba'l literally means master, lord, or chief. The ancient Semitic peoples called one of their deities by this name and worshipped him together with "his wife," Ashtaroth. During the period of the Judges, many among the Children of Israel began to worship them: "And they forsook the Lord God of their fathers, who had brought them out of the land of Egypt, and they followed other gods from *among* the gods of the people who *were* all around them, and they bowed down to them; and they provoked the Lord to anger. They forsook the Lord and served Baal and the Ashtoreths" (*Judges*, 2: 12–13). This deviance re-appeared after the death of the Prophet Solomon, upon him be peace. The Prophet Ilyās, who is also mentioned in the Qur'ān, 6: 85 and thought to be the Biblical Elijah, grew up at the same time, during the reign of King Ahab in Israel who was notorious for his injustices, (1 Kings, 17–21) and King Jehoram in Judah (2 Chronicles, 21). He struggled against this deviance, immoralities, and injustices.

450　سُوْرَةُ الصَّافَّات　٤٥٠

فَكَذَّبُوهُ فَإِنَّهُمْ لَمُحْضَرُونَ ۝ إِلَّا عِبَادَ اللَّهِ الْمُخْلَصِينَ
۝ وَتَرَكْنَا عَلَيْهِ فِى الْآخِرِينَ ۝ سَلَامٌ عَلَى إِلْ يَاسِينَ
۝ إِنَّا كَذَلِكَ نَجْزِى الْمُحْسِنِينَ ۝ إِنَّهُ مِنْ عِبَادِنَا الْمُؤْمِنِينَ
۝ وَإِنَّ لُوطًا لَّمِنَ الْمُرْسَلِينَ ۝ إِذْ نَجَّيْنَاهُ وَأَهْلَهُ أَجْمَعِينَ
۝ إِلَّا عَجُوزًا فِى الْغَابِرِينَ ۝ ثُمَّ دَمَّرْنَا الْآخَرِينَ
۝ وَإِنَّكُمْ لَتَمُرُّونَ عَلَيْهِم مُّصْبِحِينَ ۝ وَبِالَّيْلِ أَفَلَا تَعْقِلُونَ
۝ وَإِنَّ يُونُسَ لَمِنَ الْمُرْسَلِينَ ۝ إِذْ أَبَقَ إِلَى الْفُلْكِ الْمَشْحُونِ
۝ فَسَاهَمَ فَكَانَ مِنَ الْمُدْحَضِينَ ۝ فَالْتَقَمَهُ الْحُوتُ وَهُوَ مُلِيمٌ
۝ فَلَوْلَا أَنَّهُ كَانَ مِنَ الْمُسَبِّحِينَ ۝ لَلَبِثَ فِى بَطْنِهِ إِلَى يَوْمِ
يُبْعَثُونَ ۝ فَنَبَذْنَاهُ بِالْعَرَاءِ وَهُوَ سَقِيمٌ ۝ وَأَنبَتْنَا عَلَيْهِ
شَجَرَةً مِّن يَقْطِينٍ ۝ وَأَرْسَلْنَاهُ إِلَى مِائَةِ أَلْفٍ أَوْ يَزِيدُونَ
۝ فَآمَنُوا فَمَتَّعْنَاهُمْ إِلَى حِينٍ ۝ فَاسْتَفْتِهِمْ أَرَبِّكَ الْبَنَاتُ
وَلَهُمُ الْبَنُونَ ۝ أَمْ خَلَقْنَا الْمَلَائِكَةَ إِنَاثًا وَهُمْ شَاهِدُونَ
۝ أَلَا إِنَّهُم مِّنْ إِفْكِهِمْ لَيَقُولُونَ ۝ وَلَدَ اللَّهُ وَإِنَّهُمْ
لَكَاذِبُونَ ۝ أَصْطَفَى الْبَنَاتِ عَلَى الْبَنِينَ ۝

---

to leave the land of sinners and) saved him and his family all together,

135. Except an old woman among those who stayed behind;

136. Then We annihilated the others.

137. Indeed, you pass by them (the ruins of their dwellings) at morning-time (during your travels for trade),

138. And by night. Will you not, then, use your reason and take heed?

139. And surely Jonah was one of the Messengers.

140. (Remember) when he left like a runaway slave for a ship fully laden.[18]

141. And then he (agreed to) cast lots, and he was one of those who lost;

142. (They threw him into the sea, and) the big fish swallowed him, while he was accused (by his conscience).

143. Had it not been that he was one who always glorified God, (declaring Him absolutely above having any defects and partners),[19]

144. He would certainly have remained in its belly (serving as his grave) until the Day when all will be raised (from the dead).

145. But We caused him to be cast forth on a desert shore, sick as he was;

146. And caused a gourd plant to grow over him.

127. But they denied him, and so they are surely bound to be arraigned (for judgment).

128. Except God's servants, endowed with sincerity in faith and practicing the Religion.

129. And We left for him among latercomers (until the end of time this greeting and remembrance of him and his Message):

130. "Peace be upon Il-Yāsīn."[17]

131. Thus do We reward those devoted to doing good as if seeing God.

132. Surely he was one of Our truly believing servants.

133. And surely Lot was one of the Messengers.

134. (Remember) when We (ordered him

147. And We sent him once again to (his people, numbering) a hundred thousand, rather they tended to increase.

148. And they believed in him (this time), and so, (sparing them,) We allowed them to enjoy life for a term allotted to them.

149. So ask them, (O Messenger,) whether your Lord has daughters while sons are allotted for them?

150. Or that We created the angels female and they were witnesses?

151. Beware, it is surely one of their fabrications that they say,

152. "God has begotten." Most certainly they are liars.

153. He has (made gender-discrimination and so) chosen daughters in preference to sons, has He?

---

17. It is generally accepted that Ilyās was also pronounced as Il-Yāsīn, or it may be that Il-Yāsīn is another name by which the Prophet Ilyās, upon him be peace, was called.

18. For a detailed explanation of Jonah's story, see sūrah 10, note 20.

19. As a Messenger of God, the Prophet Jonah, upon him peace, always praised and glorified God. In particular, he glorified Him in the belly of the fish. For his glorification in the bely of the fish and its meaning, see sūrah 21: 87, note 18.

154. What is the matter with you? How can you judge so?

155. Will you not still reflect and be mindful?

156. Or do you have a clear authority (of evidence)?

157. If so, produce your book (which), if you are truthful in your claim, (must have come from God)!

158. And they have concocted a kin-relationship between Him and the jinn (to excuse their worshipping the jinn); whereas the jinn know quite well that they (are created and sustained by God and) are bound to be arraigned (before Him for judgment).[20]

159. All-Glorified is He, absolutely exalted above such as they attribute to Him.

160. But God's servants endowed with sincerity in faith and practicing the Religion do not do so.

161. For sure you and those that you worship,

162. Cannot cause any to deviate concerning God,

163. Except those who have willfully adopted the way to the Blazing Flame.

164. (The angels whom they assert to be God's daughters say): "There is none among us but has his duty and position assigned,

165. "And surely we are those ranged in ranks (ever-expecting God's commands);

166. "And most certainly we are the ones glorifying Him (declaring Him to be above having any defects and partners)."

167. They (the polytheists) surely used to say:

168. "If only We had had a Reminder of the like those who lived before us had,

169. "Then we would certainly have been God's servants endowed with sincerity in faith and practicing the Religion."

170. Yet (now the Qur'ān has come to them) they disbelieve in it; so they will come to know.

171. Indeed Our word (of promise) has already gone forth in respect of Our servants sent with Our Message (of guidance and warning):

172. That they would surely be helped to victory,

173. And that surely Our host (the host of the true believers), they are certainly the victors.

174. So turn aside from them for a little while, (do not care what they do and say);

175. And watch them and see (to what end their denial will lead them), as they also will see it.

176. Or do they seek to hasten on Our punishment (that it befall them immediately)?

177. But when it descends encompassing them, then evil will be the morning of those who have been warned.

178. And ignore what they say and do for a little while.

179. And watch them and see (what the ultimate end of all people will be), as they also will see it.

180. All-Glorified is your Lord, the Lord of might and glory, exalted above all that they attribute (to Him).

181. And peace be upon the Messengers.

182. And all praise and gratitude are for God, the Lord of the worlds.

---

20. As implied in *sūrah* 2: 30, the jinn preceded humankind on the earth and ruled it, so they were all aware of the Divine Message. God's Messenger, upon him be peace and blessings, was also sent to the jinn. This is why they know well what kind of relations there must be and what is between God and His creatures.

452   سُورَة ص   ٤٥٢

بِسْمِ اللَّهِ الرَّحْمَٰنِ الرَّحِيمِ

ص وَالْقُرْآنِ ذِي الذِّكْرِ ۝ بَلِ الَّذِينَ كَفَرُوا فِي عِزَّةٍ وَشِقَاقٍ ۝
كَمْ أَهْلَكْنَا مِن قَبْلِهِم مِّن قَرْنٍ فَنَادَوا وَّلَاتَ حِينَ مَنَاصٍ ۝ وَعَجِبُوا
أَن جَاءَهُم مُّنذِرٌ مِّنْهُمْ ۖ وَقَالَ الْكَافِرُونَ هَٰذَا سَاحِرٌ كَذَّابٌ ۝
أَجَعَلَ الْآلِهَةَ إِلَٰهًا وَاحِدًا ۖ إِنَّ هَٰذَا لَشَيْءٌ عُجَابٌ ۝ وَانطَلَقَ الْمَلَأُ
مِنْهُمْ أَنِ امْشُوا وَاصْبِرُوا عَلَىٰ آلِهَتِكُمْ ۖ إِنَّ هَٰذَا لَشَيْءٌ يُرَادُ ۝ مَا سَمِعْنَا
بِهَٰذَا فِي الْمِلَّةِ الْآخِرَةِ إِنْ هَٰذَا إِلَّا اخْتِلَاقٌ ۝ أَؤُنزِلَ عَلَيْهِ
الذِّكْرُ مِن بَيْنِنَا ۚ بَلْ هُمْ فِي شَكٍّ مِّن ذِكْرِي ۖ بَل لَّمَّا يَذُوقُوا عَذَابِ ۝
أَمْ عِندَهُمْ خَزَائِنُ رَحْمَةِ رَبِّكَ الْعَزِيزِ الْوَهَّابِ ۝ أَمْ لَهُم مُّلْكُ
السَّمَاوَاتِ وَالْأَرْضِ وَمَا بَيْنَهُمَا ۖ فَلْيَرْتَقُوا فِي الْأَسْبَابِ ۝ جُندٌ
مَّا هُنَالِكَ مَهْزُومٌ مِّنَ الْأَحْزَابِ ۝ كَذَّبَتْ قَبْلَهُمْ قَوْمُ
نُوحٍ وَعَادٌ وَفِرْعَوْنُ ذُو الْأَوْتَادِ ۝ وَثَمُودُ وَقَوْمُ لُوطٍ
وَأَصْحَابُ الْأَيْكَةِ ۚ أُولَٰئِكَ الْأَحْزَابُ ۝ إِن كُلٌّ إِلَّا كَذَّبَ الرُّسُلَ
فَحَقَّ عِقَابِ ۝ وَمَا يَنظُرُ هَٰؤُلَاءِ إِلَّا صَيْحَةً وَاحِدَةً مَّا لَهَا
مِن فَوَاقٍ ۝ وَقَالُوا رَبَّنَا عَجِّل لَّنَا قِطَّنَا قَبْلَ يَوْمِ الْحِسَابِ ۝

───── ❦ ─────

SŪRAH 38

ṢĀD

Makkah period

This *sūrah* of 88 verses derives its name from the abbreviated or single letter *ṣād* in the first verse. It was revealed in the mid-Makkan period of Islam, after the conversion of 'Umar ibn al-Khaṭṭāb, may God be pleased with him. It warns those who oppose the preaching of the Messenger, upon him be peace and blessings. It calls for obedience to the Messenger, and gives examples from the experiences of earlier Messengers.

In the Name of God, the All-Merciful, the All-Compassionate.

1. *Ṣād.* (I swear) by the glorious Qur'ān bearing the Reminder (with guidance to

the truth and warning, that you are one who has been sent to convey God's Religion).

2. However, those who disbelieve are lost in self-glory and opposition.

3. We destroyed before them many generations (who likewise willfully persisted in unbelief and opposition). (In the end) they called out for help but only when it was too late for the punishment (they had earned) to be canceled.

4. They deem it strange that a warner from among them has come to them, and the unbelievers say: "This man is but a sorcerer, a fraud (who makes fabrications in attribution to God).

5. "What! has he made all the deities into One God. This is a very strange thing, indeed!"

6. The leaders among them went about inciting one another: "Move on, and remain constant to your deities. Surely that (to which this man calls) is the very thing that is certainly intended (deliberately plotted by him and those who follow him).[1]

7. "We have not heard of this in recent ways of faith. This is surely nothing but a concoction.[2]

8. "From among all of us has the Reminder been sent down on him?" No! Rather, (on account of their self-glory) they are lost in doubts concerning My Reminder. No indeed! they have not yet tasted My punishment (so that they might abandon their arrogance and recognize the truth).[3]

9. Or do they own and control the treasures of the Mercy of your Lord, the All-Glorious with irresistible might, the All-Bestowing, (that they presume to object to your being chosen as the Messenger)?

10. Or do they own the sovereignty of the heavens and the earth and all that is between them? Then let them ascend to the heavens by ropes (and see if they can prevent the Message from being sent to you).

11. They are no more than a routed band of (disunited) parties there (awaiting a defeat as certain as the defeat of the hordes of old times who rejected the Messengers and were utterly abased).

12. Before them the people of Noah denied (their Messenger), and the Ād, and the Pharaoh with formidable strongholds.

13. And also the Thamūd, and the people of Lot, and the people al-Aykah. Those are the hordes (of old times).

14. Not one of them but denied the Messengers (sent to them), and therefore My retribution was their just, inevitable due.

15. These wait but for a single blast, which will tolerate no delay (to give them respite).

16. Yet, they say: "Our Lord! Hasten on to us our share before the Day of Reckoning!"

---

1. Like the leading ones among the people of Noah who reacted to his call, saying, *"He only wishes to gain superiority over you"* (23: 24), the leading polytheists of Makkah claimed that what God's Messenger intended by his call and those who followed him was leadership and high position in Makkah.

2. When 'Umar became Muslim, the leading clique of the Quraysh became furious. They thought that the Messenger and those who followed him desired leadership in Makkah and therefore felt their position was threatened by his call. Led by Abū Jahl, they went to Abū Ṭalib, the Messenger's uncle, and suggested that the Messenger continue to follow his own Religion but give up preaching it. God's Messenger, upon him be peace and blessings, responded to this proposal: "O my uncle! I know and call them to such a word that should they pronounce it, not only the other Arabs but other peoples will follow them." Unable to dispute that word, they asked what it was. The Messenger replied: "There is no deity but God." They reacted very strongly: "We have not heard of this in recent ways of faith. This is surely nothing but a concoction" (at-Tirmidhī, "Tafsīr," 39).

3. Although Divine punishments coming in the world cause some to recognize the truth, most of the unbelievers recognize it usually at death or when the punishment comes in the form of an overall destruction. However, this recognition is of no use to them, just as their recognition during the final destruction of the world will not benefit them in the least.

453

اِصۡبِرۡ عَلٰى مَا يَقُوۡلُوۡنَ وَاذۡكُرۡ عَبۡدَنَا دَاوُدَ ذَا الۡاَيۡدِ اِنَّهٗٓ اَوَّابٌ ۝
اِنَّا سَخَّرۡنَا الۡجِبَالَ مَعَهٗ يُسَبِّحۡنَ بِالۡعَشِيِّ وَالۡاِشۡرَاقِ ۝
وَالطَّيۡرَ مَحۡشُوۡرَةً ؕ كُلٌّ لَّهٗٓ اَوَّابٌ ۝ وَشَدَدۡنَا مُلۡكَهٗ وَاٰتَيۡنٰهُ
الۡحِكۡمَةَ وَفَصۡلَ الۡخِطَابِ ۝ وَهَلۡ اَتٰىكَ نَبَؤُا الۡخَصۡمِ ۘ اِذۡ تَسَوَّرُوا
الۡمِحۡرَابَ ۝ اِذۡ دَخَلُوۡا عَلٰى دَاوُدَ فَفَزِعَ مِنۡهُمۡ قَالُوۡا لَا تَخَفۡ ۚ خَصۡمٰنِ
بَغٰى بَعۡضُنَا عَلٰى بَعۡضٍ فَاحۡكُمۡ بَيۡنَنَا بِالۡحَقِّ وَلَا تُشۡطِطۡ وَاهۡدِنَآ
اِلٰى سَوَآءِ الصِّرَاطِ ۝ اِنَّ هٰذَآ اَخِيۡ ۟ لَهٗ تِسۡعٌ وَّتِسۡعُوۡنَ نَعۡجَةً وَّلِيَ
نَعۡجَةٌ وَّاحِدَةٌ ۟ فَقَالَ اَكۡفِلۡنِيۡهَا وَعَزَّنِيۡ فِى الۡخِطَابِ ۝ قَالَ لَقَدۡ
ظَلَمَكَ بِسُؤَالِ نَعۡجَتِكَ اِلٰى نِعَاجِهٖ ؕ وَاِنَّ كَثِيۡرًا مِّنَ الۡخُلَطَآءِ لَيَبۡغِىۡ
بَعۡضُهُمۡ عَلٰى بَعۡضٍ اِلَّا الَّذِيۡنَ اٰمَنُوۡا وَعَمِلُوا الصّٰلِحٰتِ وَقَلِيۡلٌ مَّا هُمۡ ؕ
وَظَنَّ دَاوُدُ اَنَّمَا فَتَنّٰهُ فَاسۡتَغۡفَرَ رَبَّهٗ وَخَرَّ رَاكِعًا وَّاَنَابَ ۩ ۝
فَغَفَرۡنَا لَهٗ ذٰلِكَ ؕ وَاِنَّ لَهٗ عِنۡدَنَا لَزُلۡفٰى وَحُسۡنَ مَاٰبٍ ۝ يٰدَاوُدُ
اِنَّا جَعَلۡنٰكَ خَلِيۡفَةً فِى الۡاَرۡضِ فَاحۡكُمۡ بَيۡنَ النَّاسِ بِالۡحَقِّ
وَلَا تَتَّبِعِ الۡهَوٰى فَيُضِلَّكَ عَنۡ سَبِيۡلِ اللّٰهِ ؕ اِنَّ الَّذِيۡنَ يَضِلُّوۡنَ
عَنۡ سَبِيۡلِ اللّٰهِ لَهُمۡ عَذَابٌ شَدِيۡدٌۢ بِمَا نَسُوۡا يَوۡمَ الۡحِسَابِ ۝

---

17. Bear patiently all that they say, and remember Our servant David, powerful (in his glorification of God, in knowledge, in kingdom, and in fighting). Surely he was one ever turning to God in penitence.

18. We subdued the mountains to glorify (their Lord) along with him in the afternoon and bright morning;

19. And the birds assembled; all were turned to Him (in devotion and glorification).

20. We strengthened his kingdom, and granted him wisdom and decisive speech (to inform, and convince, and lead).

21. Now, has the report of the litigants come to you, when they climbed over the wall into the royal chamber?

22. When they entered in upon David, and so he was taken aback by them. They said: "Do not be alarmed! (We are) two litigating parties; one party trespassed against the right of the other. So judge between us with truth; do not be unjust; and guide us to the level path."

23. (One of them explained the case): "This is my brother: He has ninety-nine ewes, and I have but one. Then he said, 'Make it over to me,' and he overpowered me in (force of) speech."

24. David said: "He has undoubtedly wronged you in demanding your single ewe to add to his own ewes. Truly many are the partners in business who trespass against the right of one another, except such as believe and do good, righteous deeds, and how few they are!" David came to understand that We had tried him, so he appealed to his Lord for forgiveness, and fell down in prostration, and turned to God in contrition.

25. So We forgave him that. Indeed he enjoyed nearness to Us and an excellent place of final return.

26. "O David! We have appointed you a vicegerent in the land (to rule according to Our commandments); so judge among people with the truth and do not follow personal inclination, lest it leads you astray from the path of God. Surely, those who wander astray from God's path – for them there is a severe punishment because they have forgotten the Day of Reckoning.[4]

4. The gist of the trial under which God put David must be as follows:

All the Messengers were sent to convey God's Message to people. However, each had a particular mission within this general mission according to the demands of the time and conditions and was therefore equipped with a special capacity peculiar to him. For example, God appointed the Prophet Abraham a leader (*imām*), and David a vicegerent (*khalīfah*), and Solomon a king (*malik*), upon them be peace. However, before they were commissioned for such particular duties, each had to pass through a strenuous trial. God tested the Prophet Abraham with severe commandments and terrible ordeals (such as being thrown into a fire, the destruction of the people of Lot, who was his relative, and being ordered to sacrifice his son Ishmael), and after Abraham fulfilled all these tests thoroughly, He appointed him an *imām*, (one who leads people in all matters). He put the Prophet David to the test mentioned in verses 21–24 in this *sūrah*, and when David succeeded, He appointed him a *khalīfah* (vicegerent: one who judges and governs according to God's commandments). He also tried the Prophet Solomon, as will be mentioned in verse 34 in this *sūrah*, and when Solomon was successful, He made him a king invested with very great power. We should point out that imamate, caliphate (vicegerency), and kingdom are all particular missions within the comprehensive mission of Messengership. We can conclude from this fact that any trial through which a particular Messenger had to pass was particular to the mission for which he had been chosen. So, the trial to which God put the Prophet David, upon him be peace, was concerning judging between people.

Whether the litigants who entered the presence of David by climbing the high walls of his royal chamber were angels who appeared in the form of human beings or not, what David thought he had been mistaken about must be his pronouncing a judgment before listening to both sides. When he listened to the one who complained about his brother (brother-in-religion or partner-in-business), either David felt in himself that this man must be truthful or some other sign convinced him that the man was speaking the truth, or perhaps his judgment was based on the compassion David felt towards him; in any case, David pronounced the judgment before listening to the other side. Then he came to understand that God had tested him and he thought he had made a mistake. Since he was a Messenger ever-turning to God in sincere devotion, he again turned to Him in contrition and asked for forgiveness. God forgave him, which meant that David had passed the test and then He appointed David as a vicegerent.

Verse 20 states that God favored David with, in addition to other blessings, the power of speech to clarify all matters distinctly and convince his audience. It is very significant that the one making a complaint about his brother had said that the other had overpowered him in speech (verse 23). So, through this trial, God must have been warning David against powerful speech while judging between people. God's Messenger, upon him be peace and blessings, draws our attention to this point: "I am a mortal man like you. You come to me to judge the matters between you. It is possible that some of you are more convincing than the others, and I judge in his favor according to what I hear. (So everyone should speak the truth). Because if I judge in someone's favor as against the right of his brother, let him know that I have assigned for him a brand of Hell's fire" (al-Bukhārī, "Shahādah," 27; Muslim, "'Aqdiyah," 5).

454

سُورَةُ ص

٤٥٤

وَمَا خَلَقْنَا السَّمَاءَ وَالْأَرْضَ وَمَا بَيْنَهُمَا بَاطِلاً ذَلِكَ ظَنُّ الَّذِينَ
كَفَرُوا فَوَيْلٌ لِلَّذِينَ كَفَرُوا مِنَ النَّارِ ۝ أَمْ نَجْعَلُ الَّذِينَ آمَنُوا وَعَمِلُوا
الصَّالِحَاتِ كَالْمُفْسِدِينَ فِي الْأَرْضِ أَمْ نَجْعَلُ الْمُتَّقِينَ كَالْفُجَّارِ ۝
كِتَابٌ أَنْزَلْنَاهُ إِلَيْكَ مُبَارَكٌ لِيَدَّبَّرُوا آيَاتِهِ وَلِيَتَذَكَّرَ أُولُوا
الْأَلْبَابِ ۝ وَوَهَبْنَا لِدَاوُدَ سُلَيْمَانَ نِعْمَ الْعَبْدُ إِنَّهُ أَوَّابٌ ۝
إِذْ عُرِضَ عَلَيْهِ بِالْعَشِيِّ الصَّافِنَاتُ الْجِيَادُ ۝ فَقَالَ إِنِّي أَحْبَبْتُ
حُبَّ الْخَيْرِ عَنْ ذِكْرِ رَبِّي حَتَّى تَوَارَتْ بِالْحِجَابِ ۝ رُدُّوهَا عَلَيَّ فَطَفِقَ
مَسْحًا بِالسُّوقِ وَالْأَعْنَاقِ ۝ وَلَقَدْ فَتَنَّا سُلَيْمَانَ وَأَلْقَيْنَا عَلَى كُرْسِيِّهِ
جَسَدًا ثُمَّ أَنَابَ ۝ قَالَ رَبِّ اغْفِرْ لِي وَهَبْ لِي مُلْكًا لَا يَنْبَغِي لِأَحَدٍ
مِنْ بَعْدِي إِنَّكَ أَنْتَ الْوَهَّابُ ۝ فَسَخَّرْنَا لَهُ الرِّيحَ تَجْرِي بِأَمْرِهِ
رُخَاءً حَيْثُ أَصَابَ ۝ وَالشَّيَاطِينَ كُلَّ بَنَّاءٍ وَغَوَّاصٍ ۝ وَآخَرِينَ
مُقَرَّنِينَ فِي الْأَصْفَادِ ۝ هَذَا عَطَاؤُنَا فَامْنُنْ أَوْ أَمْسِكْ بِغَيْرِ
حِسَابٍ ۝ وَإِنَّ لَهُ عِنْدَنَا لَزُلْفَى وَحُسْنَ مَآبٍ ۝ وَاذْكُرْ
عَبْدَنَا أَيُّوبَ إِذْ نَادَى رَبَّهُ أَنِّي مَسَّنِيَ الشَّيْطَانُ بِنُصْبٍ وَعَذَابٍ
۝ ارْكُضْ بِرِجْلِكَ هَذَا مُغْتَسَلٌ بَارِدٌ وَشَرَابٌ ۝

―――― ❧ ――――

27. We have not created the heavens and the earth and all that is between them in vain (so that people should think themselves at liberty to act each according to his own desires and inclinations). That is the mere conjecture of those who disbelieve. Woe to those who disbelieve because of the Fire!

28. Or (do they think that) We treat those who believe and do good, righteous deeds the same as those who provoke disorder and corruption on earth, or (that) We treat the pious, God-revering ones the same as the shameless, dissolute ones?

29. This is a Book, which We send down to you, full of blessings, so that they (all conscious, responsible beings) may ponder its verses and that the people of discernment may reflect on it and be mindful.

30. We granted to David (who was per-

fectly righteous in his Caliphate) Solomon. How excellent a servant Solomon was! Surely he was one ever-turning (to God) in penitence.[5]

31. Once, in the afternoon, there were brought before him nobly-bred horses (trained for fighting in God's cause, steady when standing, swift when running).

32. (Having watched them for some time,) he said: "Indeed my love for these horses is (not on their own behalf, but) because they serve for the remembrance of my Lord (and conveying His Name to other lands)." And the horses were hidden by the veil of distance.

33. (He commanded): "Bring them back to me." Then, he rubbed down their legs and their necks.[6]

34. Indeed, We tried Solomon and placed a lifeless body upon his throne. Afterwards, he turned (to God) in contrition.

35. He prayed: "My Lord, forgive me, and bestow on me a kingdom which will not suit anyone after me.[7] Surely You are the All-Bestowing."

36. We (accepted his prayer and) subdued the wind to his service, so that it coursed gently by his command wherever he willed;[8]

37. And of the satans (devils) (We made subservient to him) every builder (on earth) and diver (to extract precious stones from the sea);[9]

38. And others (of the rebellious jinn) linked together in fetters.[10]

39. "This is Our gift, so either bestow (from it), or withhold (from it), without reckoning (that it may diminish or that you will be held to account for it).

40. Surely he enjoyed nearness to Us and an excellent place of final return.

41. And remember Our servant Job, when

he called out to his Lord: "Surely Satan has caused me to be afflicted with distress and great suffering."[11]

42. (We told him:) "Strike the ground with your foot: here is cool water to wash with and to drink.[12]

---

5. The Qur'ān mentions the basic function or duties of a Messenger in the verse 2: 151 as follows:

As We have sent among you a Messenger of your own, reciting to you Our Revelations, and purifying you (of false beliefs and doctrines, and sins, and all kinds of uncleanness), and instructing you in the Book and the Wisdom, and instructing you in whatever you do not know.

The term Imamate is used in the sense of guiding people to truth in all matters, especially in purely religious ones, and leading them in life, Caliphate is used in the sense of judging, particularly among people with the truth, while Kingdom is used in the sense of enjoying temporal authority or rulership in the highest degree; these are all included in the duties of Messengership when time and conditions necessitate them. Imamate does not require caliphate and kingdom, nor is every caliph or king or sovereign an *imām* in all matters. Caliphate and kingdom require people's resignation and allegiance. So neither the caliphate nor the kingdom that are referred to by the Qur'ān are the same as absolutism. It is significant that God's Messenger, upon him be peace and blessings, emigrated to Madīnah after he took the allegiance of the Muslims in Madīnah and there felt the need to renew this allegiance before attempting certain important tasks. In addition, he never neglected to consult with his Companions, the citizens of the Muslim state in his time, in all social and political issues. Islam insists upon the necessity of consultation or an advisory government and freedom of opinion in all social and political matters. In the history of the Children of Israel, the period of founding a government or having caliphs or kings began after or upon the Children of Israel's demand to have a commander-king to fight against their enemies (2: 246–247). In their history, the Prophet Moses was a Mes-

senger-Imām, David was a Messenger-Caliph, and Solomon was a Messenger-King.

6. The Prophet Solomon, upon him be peace, was a Prophet-king. But nothing of the world, even those nobly bred horses, kept and trained for fighting in God's cause, ever prevented him from remembrance of God, because remembrance of God is the most important thing. He loved everything for God's sake or because of his love for God. So these three verses, which come after the verse that states Solomon was one ever-turning to God in devotion, emphasize Solomon's deep devotion to God despite his being a powerful king.

7. When we consider the trial by which the Prophet Solomon, upon him be peace, was tried from the perspective of the subsequent prayer of Solomon and the fact that, as explained in note 4 above, a Messenger is put through a test with respect to the particular aspect of his mission of Messengership, in addition to taking into account a Prophetic Tradition related to that event, we can conclude that the trial through which the Prophet Solomon passed must be concerned with his kingdom.

The Prophet Abraham, upon him be peace, prayed to God to grant him a son (37: 100). God accepted his prayer and granted him Ishmael when he was an old man. Then Abraham was tried by being ordered to offer Ishmael in sacrifice. When he succeeded in this, God granted him Isaac and many grandsons. The Prophet Abraham showed that his desire for a son was due to his desire for the continuation of his mission. The Prophet Zachariah, upon him be peace, also prayed for a son (19: 5–6), and he was also tried by seeing his son, the Prophet John, killed before his eyes. The greater a favor is, the greater the responsibility and suffering it brings. As pointed out by some, the Prophet Solomon desired his kingdom to continue through his offspring, and as reported from God's Messenger, to have sons who would struggle for God's sake (al-Bukhārī, "Anbiyā," 40). This was, of course, because he desired to earn uninterrupted spiritual rewards through his offspring and so that the Divine Sovereignty in the human realm might continue without lessening. However, God's will was different. How and by whom people should be governed depend on what kind of a government and ruler they deserve due to their spiritual, moral, and intellectual level in adherence to Islam. So the lifeless body placed upon his throne might be the body of one of his sons or his son whom he desired to succeed him. Whereupon the Prophet Solomon prayed to God that He might grant him such a kingdom that through it he could serve Him to the extent that all his progeny would have served if they had succeeded him, and no one else would be able to serve Him through the kingdom to that degree. Since this meant that there would be agreeable competition in serving God and since he was perfectly sincere in his prayer – he desired such a kingdom purely for God's service – his prayer was accepted.

8. For similar statements and an explanation, see *sūrah* 21: 81, note 11; *sūrah* 34: 12.

9. See *sūrah* 21: 82, note 12; *sūrah* 34: 13.

10. These fetters must be of a kind peculiar to the jinn.

11. On the suffering of Job and his supplication to God, see *sūrah* 21: 83–84, notes 15–16.

For any event to take place, for a thing to come into and go out of existence, and for a blessing or an affliction to visit a person, there are two causes: one apparent and visible, material, the other real and invisible. The former

cause relates to the material world with the beings in it and human beings themselves, while the latter relates to God. God allows something good or evil to visit a person either because of that person's belief or unbelief, or good or evil intention and deeds, or purely as a blessing or harm for them, either to test them or to make them rise to higher ranks. Like all other apparent, material causes, Satan is also a cause for human beings to do something. Like all other material causes, he also has no creative effect in anything that takes place. So, the Prophet Job's attributing his affliction to Satan as a cause can be seen to be either like the Prophet Moses' qualifying enmity and fighting which led to someone's death as of Satan's doing, or that Satan and other jinn may cause some illnesses in the human body. The second alternative needs medical research.

Another point that should be mentioned here is that although the Prophets are sinless, this does not prevent them from seeing themselves as having faults or lapsing, or from asking God for forgiveness. Since they are extremely sensitive to their duties and their relationship with God, they asked for God's forgiveness much more than other people. God's Messenger, upon him be peace and blessings, says: "I ask for God's forgiveness and turn to Him in repentance (according to al-Bukhārī, "Da'awāt," 3) more than seventy times (or according to Muslim, "Dhikr," 41) a hundred times a day."

12. The Prophet Job, upon him be peace, must have suffered from a skin disease. When he struck the ground with his foot, God caused a spring to gush forth. When he washed himself with it and drank of it, his disease was healed, by God's leave.

ووَهَبْنَا لَهُ أَهْلَهُ وَمِثْلَهُم مَّعَهُمْ رَحْمَةً مِّنَّا وَذِكْرَىٰ لِأُولِى الْأَلْبَابِ ۞ وَخُذْ بِيَدِكَ ضِغْثًا فَاضْرِب بِّهِ وَلَا تَحْنَثْ إِنَّا وَجَدْنَاهُ صَابِرًا نِّعْمَ الْعَبْدُ إِنَّهُ أَوَّابٌ ۞ وَاذْكُرْ عِبَادَنَا إِبْرَاهِيمَ وَإِسْحَاقَ وَيَعْقُوبَ أُولِي الْأَيْدِي وَالْأَبْصَارِ ۞ إِنَّا أَخْلَصْنَاهُم بِخَالِصَةٍ ذِكْرَى الدَّارِ ۞ وَإِنَّهُمْ عِندَنَا لَمِنَ الْمُصْطَفَيْنَ الْأَخْيَارِ ۞ وَاذْكُرْ إِسْمَاعِيلَ وَالْيَسَعَ وَذَا الْكِفْلِ وَكُلٌّ مِّنَ الْأَخْيَارِ ۞ هَٰذَا ذِكْرٌ وَإِنَّ لِلْمُتَّقِينَ لَحُسْنَ مَآبٍ ۞ جَنَّاتِ عَدْنٍ مُّفَتَّحَةً لَّهُمُ الْأَبْوَابُ ۞ مُتَّكِئِينَ فِيهَا يَدْعُونَ فِيهَا بِفَاكِهَةٍ كَثِيرَةٍ وَشَرَابٍ ۞ وَعِندَهُمْ قَاصِرَاتُ الطَّرْفِ أَتْرَابٌ ۞ هَٰذَا مَا تُوعَدُونَ لِيَوْمِ الْحِسَابِ ۞ إِنَّ هَٰذَا لَرِزْقُنَا مَا لَهُ مِن نَّفَادٍ ۞ هَٰذَا وَإِنَّ لِلطَّاغِينَ لَشَرَّ مَآبٍ ۞ جَهَنَّمَ يَصْلَوْنَهَا فَبِئْسَ الْمِهَادُ ۞ هَٰذَا فَلْيَذُوقُوهُ حَمِيمٌ وَغَسَّاقٌ ۞ وَآخَرُ مِن شَكْلِهِ أَزْوَاجٌ ۞ هَٰذَا فَوْجٌ مُّقْتَحِمٌ مَّعَكُمْ لَا مَرْحَبًا بِهِمْ إِنَّهُمْ صَالُو النَّارِ ۞ قَالُوا بَلْ أَنتُمْ لَا مَرْحَبًا بِكُمْ أَنتُمْ قَدَّمْتُمُوهُ لَنَا فَبِئْسَ الْقَرَارُ ۞ قَالُوا رَبَّنَا مَن قَدَّمَ لَنَا هَٰذَا فَزِدْهُ عَذَابًا ضِعْفًا فِي النَّارِ ۞

---

43. We granted him his household and the like thereof along with them as a mercy from Us, and as a reminder (with guidance and instruction) for the people of discernment.

44. (We also told him): "Take in your hand a bundle of rushes and strike with it: do not break your oath."[13] Surely, We found him full of patience and constancy. How excellent a servant! He was surely one ever-turning to God in penitence.

45. And remember Our servants Abraham and Isaac and Jacob, endowed with power (in obedience to God and doing good deeds), and insight (to discern the truth in things and events).

46. We made them perfectly pure and sincere by virtue of a characteristic most pure: their constant remembrance of the Abode (of the Hereafter).

47. They are in Our sight among the perfectly purified, chosen ones, the truly good.

48. And also remember Ishmael and al-Yasa'a (Isaiah),[14] and Dhu'l-Kifl.[15] Every one of them is of the truly good.

49. All this is a remembrance (of the excellence of those We have mentioned and an instruction for people). For the God-revering, pious there is an excellent abode of return:

50. Gardens of perpetual bliss whose gates are wide-open to them,

51. In which they will recline (on thrones), calling therein for many a fruit and drink.

52. And with them will be pure, chaste-eyed spouses, well-matched, (whose glances are fixed on them only).

53. This is what you are promised for the Day of Reckoning.

54. This is certainly Our provision (for you) with no diminishing (nor end) in it.

55. All this (for the God-revering, pious); but for the rebellious is an evil abode of return:

56. Hell, where they will enter to roast: how evil a cradle.

57. This (then is for them), so let them taste it: boiling water and intensely-cold, dark fluid.

58. And paired with that, another (torment) of similar nature.

59. "(O rebellious ones!) Here is the crowd of people who rushed blindly into sin in your company (while in the world, and now they will rush into the Fire together with you)!" (The rebellious ones cry out:) "No welcome for them! They will indeed enter the Fire to roast."

60. They (who had blindly followed) say:

"No! rather for you, there is no welcome for you! It is you who forwarded this for us (from the world)!" Then, how evil a place to abide in!

61. And they say (in supplication): "Our Lord! Whoever forwarded this for us, increase him in punishment doubled in the Fire!"

---

13. While he was ill, the Prophet Job, upon him be peace, swore by God that if God would restore him to health, he would punish his wife with lashes because she had committed an error. God revealed to him that he could fulfill his vow by striking her with a bundle of (as many) rushes (as the amount of the lashes with which he swore to punish her). There is such a rule in the Sharī'ah: Should the culprit be so ill that there is no reasonable chance of recovery, or if they are too old, they should be hit only once with a branch with as many twigs as the amount of the lashes with which the culprit should be punished, or with a broom with the same number of straws, so as to meet the formal requirements of the Law.

14. Al-Yasa'a, who is also mentioned in 6: 86, is most probably Isaiah in the Bible. He succeeded the Prophet Ilyās (Elijah) and put up a fierce struggle against worshipping the idol Ba'al in Israel. However, after his death, idol-worship and evils re-appeared in Israel and this was followed by attacks from the Assyrians. After a series of attacks, the ruthless Assyrian king Sargon put an end to the kingdom of Israel in 721 BC.

15. On Dhu'l-Kifl, see 21: 85, note 17.

62. And (the rebellious ones) say: "What is it with us that we cannot see the men (the poor and weak believers) whom we used to count among the wicked,

63. "Whom we used to take in mockery? Or is it that (they are here with us, but) our eyes have missed them (just as we turned our eyes from them in contempt in the world)?"

64. Such will in truth be the mutual wrangling of the people of the Fire.

65. Say: "I am but a warner. There is no deity save God, the One (with no-one and nothing like or comparable to Him), the All-Overwhelming (with absolute sway over all that exists).

66. The Lord of the heavens and the earth and all that is between them, the All-Glorious with irresistible might, the All-Forgiving.

67. Say: "This (Qur'ān) is a supreme message.

68. "You turn away from it in aversion.

69. "I had no knowledge of the High Assembly (in the heavens) when they were arguing.[16]

70. "I (follow only what is revealed to me and) it is revealed to me that I am but a plain warner."

71. (Remember) when your Lord said to the angels: "I am creating a mortal (man) out of clay (to set him on the earth as vicegerent).

72. "When I have fashioned him fully and breathed into Him out of My Spirit,[17] then fall down prostrating before him (as a sign of respect for him and his superiority)."

73. So the angels prostrated, all of them together,[18]

74. But Iblīs did not (in defiance of God's explicit order to him); he grew arrogant and displayed himself as an unbeliever.

75. (God) said: "O Iblīs! What prevents you from prostrating before the being whom I have created with My two Hands?[19] Are you too proud (to bow down before any created being in defiance of My command), or are you (of those who think themselves) so high in honor (that they cannot be ordered to prostrate before anyone)?"

76. (Iblīs) answered: "I am better than him. You have created me from fire and him You have created from clay."[20]

77. (God) said: "Then get you down out of it; surely You are one eternally rejected (from My Mercy).

78. And My curse is on you until the Day of Judgment."

79. He said: "My Lord, grant me respite

till the Day when they are raised (from the dead)!"

80. (God) said: "You are of the ones granted respite

81. "Until the Day of the Time Appointed."[21]

82. (Iblīs) said: "Then (I swear) by Your Glory, I will certainly cause them all to rebel and go astray,

83. "Except Your servants among them, endowed with sincerity in faith and worshipping You."

---

16. This statement emphasizes that the Messenger had no means to knowledge of the events that take place in the heavens among the angels or between God and the angels, except by Revelation. For example, he could not have had any knowledge of the things that took place between God and the angels and Iblīs (Satan) concerning the creation and appointment of humankind as vicegerent on the earth, which will be mentioned in the verses to come.

17. On God's breathing into humankind out of His Spirit, see 15: 29, note 7.

18. On the vicegerency of humankind and the angels' prostrating before them, see 2: 30–34, notes 30–35.

19. In 36: 71, God says that He has originated many things and beings with *His Hands*. However, in this verse He states that He has created humanity with *both of His Hands*. Hand signifies power. Mentioning *two Hands* in this verse has two important meanings: one is that God has created humankind in the perfect form as the best pattern of creation; the other is that humankind has two dimensions in its existence, spiritual and material. Verse

71 refers to humankind's material origin (clay), while verse 72 refers to its real value, which lies in the spiritual dimension of its existence.

20. According to *Iblīs*, honor and goodness lie in physical origin or matter. His attitude is typical of materialism and a lack of correct understanding. He saw only the material origin of humankind and ignored their spiritual dimension that originated in being breathed into out of God's Spirit.

The other point to mention here is that *Iblīs* judged God's order according to his own knowledge and understanding, and opposed His explicit order based on his own judgment. He demonstrated that, out of arrogance, he would fulfill God's orders only when they conformed with his desire or understanding, not because he believed all of these orders to be truth in themselves and that therefore they must be obeyed. So are those who act in the same way aware who it is that they follow and whose pupils they are?

21. This time is the overall destruction of the world, a time until which human beings will continue to carry the responsibility of carrying out God's orders.

84. (God) said: "(Whatever I do and command is) the truth itself, and the truth I speak:

85. "I will most certainly fill Hell with you (and your kind), and those (of humankind) who follow you, all together."

86. Say (O Messenger): "I ask of you no wage for this (conveying the Qur'ān to you), and I am not of those who claim to be what they are really not and make fabrications of their own.

87. "This (Qur'ān) is only a Reminder (with guidance and admonishment) for all conscious beings.

88. You will most certainly come to know of what it informs after a time (as appointed for you).

SŪRAH 39

AZ-ZUMAR
(THE COMPANIES)

Makkah period

Revealed in the mid-Makkan period when the persecutions to the believers had escalated, this *sūrah* of 75 verses derives its name from the word *zumar* (companies) that occurs in verses 71 and 73. It expounds the signs of God's Oneness in the natural world and emphasizes the absurdity of associating partners with Him. It hints at emigration for the believers who were suffering great difficulties in worshipping God in their homeland. It declares that there will be no compromise between believing in God's Oneness and associating partners with Him. It reminds us of the other world where people will see the outcome of their deeds in this world.

In the Name of God, the All-Merciful, the All-Compassionate.

1. (This is) the Book being sent down in parts from God, the All-Glorious with irresistible might, the All-Wise.

2. We have sent down to you the Book with the truth (embodying it, and with nothing false in it), so worship God, sincere in your faith in Him and practicing the Religion purely for His sake.

3. Beware! it is to God alone that all sincere faith, worship, and obedience are due. Yet, those who take, apart from Him, others (angels, the jinn, or humans) for guardians and confidants (to entrust their affairs to) say: "We worship them for no other reason than they may bring us nearer to God." God will judge between

them (between those who worship and obey God exclusively and those who associate partners with Him) concerning all on which they differ. God does not guide anyone who is a determined liar and ingrate.

4. Had God willed to take to Himself a child, He could certainly have chosen whatever He willed out of all that He has created. All-Glorified is He (in that He is exalted above having any children). He is God, the One, the All-Overwhelming (with absolute sway over all that exists).

5. He has created the heavens and the earth with truth (meaningfully and for definite purpose, and on solid foundations of truth). He wraps the night around the day and He wraps the day around the night (until one covers the other completely).[1] And He has made the sun and the moon subservient (to His command), each running its course for a term appointed (by Him). Be aware! He is the All-Glorious with irresistible might (able to punish those who oppose Him), the All-Forgiving (Who forgives those who turn to Him in repentance).

---

1. This is a very fine simile, which alludes both to the earth's being rounded and to differences of the times of sunrise and sunset. Like a turban wrapped around the head until it is completely covered, God wraps lines of night and day around each other round the earth until one covers the other completely.

458

سُوۡرَةُ الزُّمَرِ

٤٥٨

خَلَقَكُمۡ مِّنۡ نَّفۡسٍ وَّاحِدَةٍ ثُمَّ جَعَلَ مِنۡهَا زَوۡجَهَا وَأَنۡزَلَ لَكُمۡ مِّنَ الۡأَنۡعَامِ ثَمَانِيَةَ أَزۡوَاجٍ يَخۡلُقُكُمۡ فِىۡ بُطُوۡنِ أُمَّهَاتِكُمۡ خَلۡقًا مِّنۡۢ بَعۡدِ خَلۡقٍ فِىۡ ظُلُمَاتٍ ثَلَاثٍ ذٰلِكُمُ اللّٰهُ رَبُّكُمۡ لَهُ الۡمُلۡكُ لَآ إِلٰهَ إِلَّا هُوَ فَأَنّٰى تُصۡرَفُوۡنَ ۞ إِنۡ تَكۡفُرُوۡا فَإِنَّ اللّٰهَ غَنِىٌّ عَنۡكُمۡ وَلَا يَرۡضٰى لِعِبَادِهِ الۡكُفۡرَ وَإِنۡ تَشۡكُرُوۡا يَرۡضَهُ لَكُمۡ وَلَا تَزِرُ وَازِرَةٌ وِّزۡرَ أُخۡرٰى ثُمَّ إِلٰى رَبِّكُمۡ مَّرۡجِعُكُمۡ فَيُنَبِّئُكُمۡ بِمَا كُنۡتُمۡ تَعۡمَلُوۡنَ إِنَّهُ عَلِيۡمٌۢ بِذَاتِ الصُّدُوۡرِ ۞ وَإِذَا مَسَّ الۡإِنۡسَانَ ضُرٌّ دَعَا رَبَّهُ مُنِيۡبًا إِلَيۡهِ ثُمَّ إِذَا خَوَّلَهُ نِعۡمَةً مِّنۡهُ نَسِىَ مَا كَانَ يَدۡعُوۡا إِلَيۡهِ مِنۡ قَبۡلُ وَجَعَلَ لِلّٰهِ أَنۡدَادًا لِّيُضِلَّ عَنۡ سَبِيۡلِهِ قُلۡ تَمَتَّعۡ بِكُفۡرِكَ قَلِيۡلًا إِنَّكَ مِنۡ أَصۡحَابِ النَّارِ ۞ أَمَّنۡ هُوَ قَانِتٌ ءَانَآءَ الَّيۡلِ سَاجِدًا وَّقَآئِمًا يَّحۡذَرُ الۡأٰخِرَةَ وَيَرۡجُوۡا رَحۡمَةَ رَبِّهِ قُلۡ هَلۡ يَسۡتَوِى الَّذِيۡنَ يَعۡلَمُوۡنَ وَالَّذِيۡنَ لَا يَعۡلَمُوۡنَ إِنَّمَا يَتَذَكَّرُ أُولُوا الۡأَلۡبَابِ ۞ قُلۡ يٰعِبَادِ الَّذِيۡنَ ءَامَنُوا اتَّقُوۡا رَبَّكُمۡ لِلَّذِيۡنَ أَحۡسَنُوۡا فِىۡ هٰذِهِ الدُّنۡيَا حَسَنَةٌ وَأَرۡضُ اللّٰهِ وَاسِعَةٌ إِنَّمَا يُوَفَّى الصّٰبِرُوۡنَ أَجۡرَهُمۡ بِغَيۡرِ حِسَابٍ ۞

6. He has created you from a single human self, and then He has made from it its mate,[2] and He has sent down for you eight in pairs of cattle.[3] He creates you in the wombs of your mothers, one act and phase of creation after another,[4] in three veils of darkness.[5] This is God, your true Lord (Who creates and sustains you): To Him belongs the sovereignty (absolute ownership and dominion of everything). There is no deity but He. How, then, are you turned about (to different kinds of belief)?

7. If you disbelieve in Him (in ingratitude), yet surely God is absolutely independent of you. He is not pleased with ingratitude and unbelief from His servants; whereas, if you give thanks (and believe), He is pleased with it from you. And no soul, as bearer of burden, bears (and is made to bear) the burden of another. Then, to your Lord is your return so that He will make you understand all that you were doing (and call you to account). Surely He has full knowledge of what lies hidden in the bosoms.

8. When an affliction befalls human, he calls upon his Lord turning to Him (in contrition); then when He bestows a favor upon him, he forgets for what he prayed to Him before, and sets up rivals to God so that he (himself goes astray and) misleads (others) from His way. Say (to such a one): "Enjoy life in your unbelief for a while! You are for sure one of the companions of the Fire."

9. Is he who worships God devoutly in the watches of the night prostrating and standing, who fears the Hereafter and hopes for the mercy of his Lord (to be likened to that other)? Say: "Are they ever equal, those who know and those who do not know?"[6] Only the people of discernment will reflect on (the distinction between knowledge and ignorance, and obedience to God and disobedience,) and be mindful.

10. Say (quoting Me): "O My servants who believe: Keep from disobedience to your Lord in reverence for Him and piety. For those devoted to doing good in this world, aware that God is seeing them, there is good (by way of recompense). And God's earth is vast (enabling worship).[7] Those who are patient (persevering in adversity, worshipping God, and refraining from sins) will surely be given their reward without measure."

2. For an explanation, see 4: 1, note 1.

3. Eight in pairs (see 6: 143–144): two of sheep, two of goats, and, likewise, of camels there are two, and of oxen there are two. The phrase God *"has sent them down"* means that they are among the bounties of God that He has bestowed out of the treasures He maintains. Elsewhere (15: 21), He states: *There is not a thing but the stores (for its life and sustenance) are with Us, and We do not send it down except in due, determined measure.*

4. *One act and phase of creation after another* refers to the stages an embryo passes through in the womb. They are explained in 22: 5: *Then (We have created you) from a drop of seminal fluid, then from a clot clinging (to the womb wall), then from a lump in part shaped and in part not shaped, and differentiated and undifferentiated;* and in 23: 14: *Then We have created of the fertilized ovum a clot clinging (to the womb wall), and (afterwards in sequence) We have created of the clinging clot, a (chewed) lump, and We have created of the (chewed) lump bones, and We have clothed the bones in flesh. Then We have caused it to grow into another creation.*

5. Three veils of darkness must be the anterior abdominal wall, the uterine wall, and the amniochorionic membrane. Although there are other interpretations of this statement, the one presented here seems the most logical to modern embryologists from an embryological point of view.

6. Though the verse declares a general truth that knowledge and ignorance cannot be alike and those who know and those who do not know are never equal, here it draws particular attention to the fact that those who have true knowledge of God and act accordingly and those who are devoid of knowledge of Him and therefore either disbelieve in Him or associate partners with Him cannot be equal. Any knowledge based on knowledge of God is true knowledge, and in both worlds beneficial to those who have it. However, anyone who lacks (true) knowledge of God, and cannot find a point of confirmation in their heart through which any knowledge that they obtain from the outer world and their inner world adds to or strengthens their faith, is ignorant. Even if they have absorbed thousands of branches of science, their ignorance is only compounded by that science. (Also see 33: 72, note 38.)

7. This statement exists in the Qur'ān to remind us of the importance of emigration for God's sake and to encourage the believers toward it or to prepare their hearts for it. (See 4: 97; 29: 56.)

٤٥٩

459

قُلْ إِنِّيٓ أُمِرْتُ أَنْ أَعْبُدَ اللَّهَ مُخْلِصًا لَّهُ الدِّينَ ۞ وَأُمِرْتُ لِأَنْ أَكُونَ أَوَّلَ
الْمُسْلِمِينَ ۞ قُلْ إِنِّيٓ أَخَافُ إِنْ عَصَيْتُ رَبِّي عَذَابَ يَوْمٍ عَظِيمٍ ۞ قُلِ
اللَّهَ أَعْبُدُ مُخْلِصًا لَّهُ دِينِي ۞ فَاعْبُدُوا مَا شِئْتُم مِّن دُونِهِ ۗ قُلْ
إِنَّ الْخَاسِرِينَ الَّذِينَ خَسِرُوٓا أَنفُسَهُمْ وَأَهْلِيهِمْ يَوْمَ الْقِيَامَةِ ۗ أَلَا
ذَٰلِكَ هُوَ الْخُسْرَانُ الْمُبِينُ ۞ لَهُم مِّن فَوْقِهِمْ ظُلَلٌ مِّنَ النَّارِ
وَمِن تَحْتِهِمْ ظُلَلٌ ۚ ذَٰلِكَ يُخَوِّفُ اللَّهُ بِهِ عِبَادَهُ ۚ يَا عِبَادِ فَاتَّقُونِ
۞ وَالَّذِينَ اجْتَنَبُوا الطَّاغُوتَ أَن يَعْبُدُوهَا وَأَنَابُوٓا إِلَى
اللَّهِ لَهُمُ الْبُشْرَىٰ ۚ فَبَشِّرْ عِبَادِ ۞ الَّذِينَ يَسْتَمِعُونَ الْقَوْلَ فَيَتَّبِعُونَ
أَحْسَنَهُ ۚ أُولَٰئِكَ الَّذِينَ هَدَاهُمُ اللَّهُ ۖ وَأُولَٰئِكَ هُمْ أُولُو الْأَلْبَابِ
۞ أَفَمَنْ حَقَّ عَلَيْهِ كَلِمَةُ الْعَذَابِ أَفَأَنتَ تُنقِذُ مَن فِي النَّارِ ۞
لَٰكِنِ الَّذِينَ اتَّقَوْا رَبَّهُمْ لَهُمْ غُرَفٌ مِّن فَوْقِهَا غُرَفٌ مَّبْنِيَّةٌ تَجْرِي مِن
تَحْتِهَا الْأَنْهَارُ ۖ وَعْدَ اللَّهِ ۖ لَا يُخْلِفُ اللَّهُ الْمِيعَادَ ۞ أَلَمْ تَرَ أَنَّ
اللَّهَ أَنزَلَ مِنَ السَّمَاءِ مَاءً فَسَلَكَهُ يَنَابِيعَ فِي الْأَرْضِ ثُمَّ
يُخْرِجُ بِهِ زَرْعًا مُّخْتَلِفًا أَلْوَانُهُ ثُمَّ يَهِيجُ فَتَرَاهُ مُصْفَرًّا ثُمَّ
يَجْعَلُهُ حُطَامًا ۚ إِنَّ فِي ذَٰلِكَ لَذِكْرَىٰ لِأُولِي الْأَلْبَابِ ۞

11. Say: "I am commanded to worship God, sincere in faith in Him and practicing the Religion purely for His sake.

12. "And I am commanded to be the first and foremost in being Muslim (in faith in and submission to what I am commanded to convey to you)."

13. Say: "I fear, if I disobey my Lord, the punishment of an awesome Day."

14. Say: "I worship God, sincere in my faith in Him and practicing the Religion purely for His sake.

15. "(As for those of you who reject my call,) worship then whatever you will apart from Him (you are forewarned of the consequences)!" Say: "Surely the losers are those who will ruin themselves and their families on the Day of Resurrection." Beware! this indeed is the obvious loss.

16. For them will be dark layers of the Fire above them, and dark layers below them. With this does God warn off His servants. O My servants, keep from disobedience to Me in reverence for Me and piety and so deserve My protection.

17. As for those who keep away from false deities and powers of evil (instituting patterns of faith and rule in defiance of God) – away from worshipping them, and turn toward God in penitence, for

them are glad tidings, so give the glad tidings to My servants,

18. Who, when they hear speech, follow the best of it (in the best way possible, and even seek what is better and straighter).[8] Those are the ones whom God has guided, and those are the ones who are people of discernment.

19. Is he, against whom the word of (God's) punishment has been justified and realized (to be likened to one who will be rewarded with Paradise)? Could you, then, deliver one who is in the Fire?

20. But those who keep from disobedience to God in reverence for Him and piety, for them are lofty mansions built one above another, beneath which rivers flow. (This is) God's promise. God never fails to fulfill His promise.

21. Have you not considered that God sends down water from the sky, and leads it into springs in the earth to flow therein; then He causes to grow with it produce of various colors; then it withers so that you see it grow yellow; then He makes it break and fade away. In this, for sure, is a reminder for people of discernment.

---

8. Humankind, by their primordial nature, seeks what is good and right. When a person encounters what is good and right and what is evil and wrong, they prefer what is good and right. When one is between what is good and right and what is better or righter, one tends to follow the latter. It is virtuousness to follow what is better or even the best, but one in a congregation or community should not force others or seek to see in them what is better and more right.

22. Is he (who derives lessons from God's acts in the universe and so) whose breast God has expanded to Islam, so that he follows a light from his Lord (– is such a one to be likened to one whose heart is closed up to any remembrance of God and therefore to Islam)? So woe to those whose hearts are hardened against the remembrance of God (and who learn nothing from His signs and Revelations)! Those are lost in obvious error.

23. God sends down in parts the best of the words as a Book fully consistent in itself, and whose statements corroborate, expound and refer to one another. The skins of those who stand in awe of their Lord tingle at (the hearing and understanding of) it. Then, their skins and their hearts come to rest in the Remembrance of God (the Qur'ān). This is God's guidance, by which He guides whomever He wills. And whoever God leads astray, there is no guide for him.[9]

24. Is he who (thrown into the Fire upon his face with his hands chained around his neck,) tries to guard himself with his face (by trying to keep it away) from the evil punishment on the Day of Resurrection (to be likened to one who will be safe from the punishment that Day)? It will be said to the wrongdoers: "Taste (this Day) what you used to earn (in the world)!"

25. Those before them denied (the Revelation), and so the punishment came upon them without their having perceived from where it came.

26. Thus God made them taste disgrace in the life of this world, but the punishment of the Hereafter is greater. If only they had known!

27. Assuredly We have struck for humankind in this Qur'ān all kinds of parables and comparisons, so that they may reflect and be mindful.

28. It is a Qur'ān in Arabic with no crookedness (free from any contradiction and anything offensive to truth and righteousness and reason), so that they may keep from disobedience to God in reverence for Him and piety to deserve His protection.

29. God strikes a parable: a man in (the employment of) many partners who continuously dispute with one another, and another man employed by one person: are those two equal in likeness? All praise and gratitude are for God (the only Sovereign Lord of the creation). But most people have no knowledge (of the meaning of this truth).[10]

30. You will surely die (one day), and surely they (too) will die.

31. Then, on the Day of Resurrection, you will stand in the Presence of your Lord as litigants.

9. Through its style, recitation, the issues it deals with, and its promises and threats, the Qur'ān causes the person who reads or listens to it to tremble. It arouses in hearts deep veneration for both itself and its Author – God the Almighty. In addition to this majesty, it is also so pleasing to all the senses and faculties that it inspires calm and serenity. It satisfies hearts and minds and solves all intellectual and spiritual problems. So, anyone unprejudiced and who has tendency toward belief in God cannot help but feel struck by the Qur'ān.

Like the Qur'ān and its Author, God's nearest servants – the Prophets and the saints – also have some sort of majesty and grace each according to their degree. However, their majesty, which first strikes others about them, envelops a welcoming grace. So, everyone feels awe in their first encounter with a Prophet or a saint, and then it is their grace that attracts them. This perception and feeling struck by the Qur'ān and satisfaction with it is a great favor and guidance of God. One who feels no awe or satisfaction in the face of the Qur'ān is the very one that has lost the innate capacity to believe.

10. If all things are not attributed to the Almighty in creation and administration, an infinite number of deities, all essentially opposite, but simultaneously identical, must be recognized. Due to the interrelation of all things and the essential quality of Divinity, their number would increase in proportion to the number of particles and compounds found in creation.

For example, a deity who creates a honeybee or a grape should be able to rule and influence all elements in the universe, as a honeybee or a grape is a miniature of creation. So there is only room for a Single Necessarily Existent One. If things are attributed to themselves, each minute particle would be a deity – a deity having all the Names and Attributes of God Almighty, for having these Names and Attributes is a requirement of being a deity.

A single fruit grown by many people requires as many tools as does growing a tree with abundant fruit. Similarly, the instruments, machines, and factories needed to equip an army would be the same if only a single soldier were to be equipped. The difference is only qualitative, and the difficulty that arises from being produced by many people will make its production almost impossible. So the universe rejects more than one creator and administrator, and its testimony to its Single Creator is more manifest, radiant, clearer, and expressive than its testimony to its own existence. Even if one were to deny the existence of the universe, as the Sophists did, the existence of the One, Who is powerful over all things, cannot be denied.

In short: If innumerably multiple things are not attributed to one source, then, in addition to having to attribute one thing to innumerably multiple things, there would be a multitude of difficulties (as many as there are things) in explaining the matter. So, the apparent, extraordinary ease of creating so many species distributed worldwide must therefore come from the Oneness of their Creator.

32. Who, then, is more in the wrong than he who fabricates falsehood against God, and denies the truth when it comes to him? Is there not in Hell a dwelling for the unbelievers?!

33. As for him who has come with the truth and him who has confirmed it, those are the God-revering, pious ones.

34. For them is whatever they desire in the Presence of their Lord.[11] That is the reward of those devoted to doing good, aware that God is seeing them.

35. For God will blot out from them (even) the worst of what they once did, and pay them their reward in accordance with the best of what they used to do.[12]

36. Is not God sufficient for His servant? Yet they seek to frighten you with those (whom they deify and worship) apart from God. Whoever God leads astray, there is no guide for him.

37. And whomever God guides, there is no one who can lead him astray. Is not God All-Glorious with irresistible might, Able to Requite?

38. Indeed, if you ask them who has created the heavens and the earth, they will certainly say, "God." Say: "Have you, then, ever considered what it is that you invoke apart from God? If God wills some harm for me, are they the ones that can remove His harm (from me), or if He wills for me a mercy, are they the ones that can withhold it?" Say: "God is sufficient for me. In Him

do those who trust (and know the worth and meaning of putting one's trust) put their trust.

39. Say: "O my people! Do all that may be within your power, surely I (too) am doing (the work asked of me). In time you will come to know

40. Who they are upon whom (in the world) there will come a punishment that will abase them, and upon whom a lasting punishment will descend (in the Hereafter)."

---

11. For an explanation, see 25: 16, note 5.

12. God will blot out their former unbelief or associating partners with God and reward them according to their best deeds in Islam.

God will blot out the major sins they may have committed before they attained true piety and righteousness and the consciousness of God's constantly seeing them, and He will reward them for their best deeds that they do thereafter.

462　　سُورَةُ الزُّمَرِ　　٢٦٢

إِنَّا أَنزَلْنَا عَلَيْكَ الْكِتَابَ لِلنَّاسِ بِالْحَقِّ فَمَنِ اهْتَدَىٰ فَلِنَفْسِهِ وَمَن ضَلَّ فَإِنَّمَا يَضِلُّ عَلَيْهَا وَمَا أَنتَ عَلَيْهِم بِوَكِيلٍ ۝ اللَّهُ يَتَوَفَّى الْأَنفُسَ حِينَ مَوْتِهَا وَالَّتِي لَمْ تَمُتْ فِي مَنَامِهَا فَيُمْسِكُ الَّتِي قَضَىٰ عَلَيْهَا الْمَوْتَ وَيُرْسِلُ الْأُخْرَىٰ إِلَىٰ أَجَلٍ مُّسَمًّى إِنَّ فِي ذَٰلِكَ لَآيَاتٍ لِّقَوْمٍ يَتَفَكَّرُونَ ۝ أَمِ اتَّخَذُوا مِن دُونِ اللَّهِ شُفَعَاءَ قُلْ أَوَلَوْ كَانُوا لَا يَمْلِكُونَ شَيْئًا وَلَا يَعْقِلُونَ ۝ قُل لِّلَّهِ الشَّفَاعَةُ جَمِيعًا لَّهُ مُلْكُ السَّمَاوَاتِ وَالْأَرْضِ ثُمَّ إِلَيْهِ تُرْجَعُونَ ۝ وَإِذَا ذُكِرَ اللَّهُ وَحْدَهُ اشْمَأَزَّتْ قُلُوبُ الَّذِينَ لَا يُؤْمِنُونَ بِالْآخِرَةِ وَإِذَا ذُكِرَ الَّذِينَ مِن دُونِهِ إِذَا هُمْ يَسْتَبْشِرُونَ ۝ قُلِ اللَّهُمَّ فَاطِرَ السَّمَاوَاتِ وَالْأَرْضِ عَالِمَ الْغَيْبِ وَالشَّهَادَةِ أَنتَ تَحْكُمُ بَيْنَ عِبَادِكَ فِيمَا كَانُوا فِيهِ يَخْتَلِفُونَ ۝ وَلَوْ أَنَّ لِلَّذِينَ ظَلَمُوا مَا فِي الْأَرْضِ جَمِيعًا وَمِثْلَهُ مَعَهُ لَافْتَدَوْا بِهِ مِن سُوءِ الْعَذَابِ يَوْمَ الْقِيَامَةِ وَبَدَا لَهُم مِّنَ اللَّهِ مَا لَمْ يَكُونُوا يَحْتَسِبُونَ ۝

---

is the sole Authority over the universe in need of nothing) have they taken to themselves, apart from God, intercessors (whom they suppose capable of intervening for their souls or even in the operation of the universe)? Say: "Why – even though they have no share in the dominion of anything, nor (like idols) any sense or intelligence?

44. Say: "To God exclusively belongs the whole authority to intercede, (whether He grants any being permission to intercede with Him or not).[14] To Him alone belongs the sovereignty of the heavens and the earth. Then, to Him you will be returned."

45. When God as One (and only God) is mentioned, the hearts of those who do not believe in the Hereafter recoil in aversion; but when those (whom they worship) apart from Him are mentioned, they are surely gladdened.

46. Say: "O God, Originator of the heavens and the earth, the Knower of the Unseen and the witnessed! You it is Who will judge among Your servants concerning that on which they differ."

47. Even if those who do the greatest wrong (by associating partners with God and refusing to believe in the Hereafter) could possess all that is on the earth and its like besides, they would certainly offer it as ransom to escape from the evil punishment on the Day of Resurrection. Something will confront them from God, which they never reckoned.

---

41. Surely We have sent down the Book to you with the truth for humankind (embodying the truth, and with no falsehood in it). So, whoever chooses to go right, it is for his own soul's good; and whoever chooses to go astray, goes astray but to its own harm. You are not one appointed as a guardian over them (to assume their responsibility for going right).

42. God takes the spirits at the time of the death of (the souls), and in their sleep those (of the ones) that have not died. Thus He withholds (the spirits of) those for whom He has decreed death, and the rest He sends back (to their bodies to live on) for a term appointed by Him. Surely in that are signs (important lessons) for people who reflect and are mindful.[13]

43. What! (Failing to recognize that God

13. This verse draws our attention to a number of important facts, including the following:

- It is not the human spirit but the human soul that dies. The soul (*nafs*) is, in one respect, the human being itself and therefore encompasses the spirit, and in another, it is the center or mechanism of worldly life. As for the spirit, it is the source of both bodily and spiritual life. It has an existence independent of the body, and continues to live after death.

- The human soul has various dimensions. These dimensions are mentioned by the scholars as the human spirit, the animal spirit, and the vegetable spirit. The human spirit also has dimensions which are described as the spirit that believes in and worships God (the spirits of the believers) and the spirit common to all people, which thinks, learns, loves, etc.

- Death and sleep are identical in that during both God takes the spirit. However, at death, God does not return the spirit to the body, thus causing the soul to die, while during sleep He takes the spirit, but returns it if He has not ordained death for the soul. So, at death the spirit leaves the body completely, but during sleep it does not leave it completely and therefore continues its relation with the body. If the body still has some degree of animal life during sleep, it is because there is still a relation, however weak it is, between the body and the spirit during sleep.

- Death is when the spirit leaves the body completely and begins another kind of life, which is called the intermediate life (of the grave) between this world and the Hereafter. The conditions of this life are determined by the person's belief and deeds in the world. The spirit still has a relation with its body through the part of it that does not rot under the soil.

14. For a similar meaning of intercession, see *sūrah* 34: 23, note 13. Here there is also a reference to appealing to God to accept our prayers for some of His servants to be placed with Him.

وَبَدَا لَهُمْ سَيِّئَاتُ مَا كَسَبُوا۟ وَحَاقَ بِهِم مَّا كَانُوا۟ بِهِۦ يَسْتَهْزِءُونَ ۝ فَإِذَا مَسَّ ٱلْإِنسَـٰنَ ضُرٌّ دَعَانَا ثُمَّ إِذَا خَوَّلْنَـٰهُ نِعْمَةً مِّنَّا قَالَ إِنَّمَآ أُوتِيتُهُۥ عَلَىٰ عِلْمٍۭ بَلْ هِىَ فِتْنَةٌ وَلَـٰكِنَّ أَكْثَرَهُمْ لَا يَعْلَمُونَ ۝ قَدْ قَالَهَا ٱلَّذِينَ مِن قَبْلِهِمْ فَمَآ أَغْنَىٰ عَنْهُم مَّا كَانُوا۟ يَكْسِبُونَ ۝ فَأَصَابَهُمْ سَيِّئَاتُ مَا كَسَبُوا۟ وَٱلَّذِينَ ظَلَمُوا۟ مِنْ هَـٰٓؤُلَآءِ سَيُصِيبُهُمْ سَيِّئَاتُ مَا كَسَبُوا۟ وَمَا هُم بِمُعْجِزِينَ ۝ أَوَلَمْ يَعْلَمُوٓا۟ أَنَّ ٱللَّهَ يَبْسُطُ ٱلرِّزْقَ لِمَن يَشَآءُ وَيَقْدِرُ إِنَّ فِى ذَٰلِكَ لَءَايَـٰتٍ لِّقَوْمٍ يُؤْمِنُونَ ۝ قُلْ يَـٰعِبَادِىَ ٱلَّذِينَ أَسْرَفُوا۟ عَلَىٰٓ أَنفُسِهِمْ لَا تَقْنَطُوا۟ مِن رَّحْمَةِ ٱللَّهِ إِنَّ ٱللَّهَ يَغْفِرُ ٱلذُّنُوبَ جَمِيعًا إِنَّهُۥ هُوَ ٱلْغَفُورُ ٱلرَّحِيمُ ۝ وَأَنِيبُوٓا۟ إِلَىٰ رَبِّكُمْ وَأَسْلِمُوا۟ لَهُۥ مِن قَبْلِ أَن يَأْتِيَكُمُ ٱلْعَذَابُ ثُمَّ لَا تُنصَرُونَ ۝ وَٱتَّبِعُوٓا۟ أَحْسَنَ مَآ أُنزِلَ إِلَيْكُم مِّن رَّبِّكُم مِّن قَبْلِ أَن يَأْتِيَكُمُ ٱلْعَذَابُ بَغْتَةً وَأَنتُمْ لَا تَشْعُرُونَ ۝ أَن تَقُولَ نَفْسٌ يَـٰحَسْرَتَىٰ عَلَىٰ مَا فَرَّطتُ فِى جَنۢبِ ٱللَّهِ وَإِن كُنتُ لَمِنَ ٱلسَّـٰخِرِينَ ۝

---

fell upon them. So also will the evil results of what they have earned fall upon these (new generations) who do wrong. And they will never be able to frustrate (Our will).

52. Do they still not know that God enlarges provision for whom He wills, and restricts it (for whom He wills). Surely in that are signs (of the clear truth) for people who will believe and who will deepen in faith.

53. Say: "(God gives you hope): 'O My servants who have been wasteful (of their God-given opportunities and faculties) against (the good of) their own souls! Do not despair of God's Mercy. Surely God forgives all sins. He is indeed the All-Forgiving, the All-Compassionate.' "[16]

54. Turn to your Lord in penitence and submit to Him wholly before the punishment comes upon you (when it will be too late, and acknowledgment of faith will no longer avail you); for after (that) you will not be helped.[17]

55. Follow in the best way possible what has been sent down to you from your Lord, before the punishment comes upon you all of a sudden, without your being aware (of its coming);

56. Lest any soul should say, "Alas for me for that I have fallen short of my duty to God, and I was indeed among those who used to mock (at the truth)!"

48. The evil deeds they earned (to their account) will become obvious to them, and what they used to mock (God's promised punishment) will overwhelm them.

49. When an affliction befalls human he calls upon Us (to save him). Then, when We (from sheer grace) have bestowed a favor upon him from Us, he says: "I have been given this only by virtue of a certain knowledge that I have." No, indeed. Rather, this (favor bestowed on human) is a trial, but most of them do not know.

50. Those who lived before them (and adopted the same attitude and followed a similar way) said it (too);[15] but all that they achieved (in the world) was of no avail to them.

51. The evil results of what they earned

15. This is a reference to Korah. See 28: 78, note 17.

16. This verse, first of all, contains great good tidings, in that it declares that there is no unforgivable sin. That is, even if one who disbelieves in God or associates partners with Him, or whether one is an atheist or materialist, repents and comes to belief, God forgives him or her. Second, God forgives any sinful one He wills, unless one disbelieves in Him (or in any other pillar of faith) or associates partners with Him (4: 48). However, although He can forgive whom He wills, He has made His forgiving dependent on repentance and the mending of one's ways, as will be pointed out in succeeding verses. So this verse, which contains the greatest promise in the Qur'ān, is followed by successive warnings. This is one of the most meaningful examples of the Qur'ānic method of warning and encouraging, and it admonishes people against abandoning themselves to evil ways and instills confidence in them about God's infinite Compassion.

17. The last two verses establish three essential principles concerning faith:

- God may forgive whom He wills, but in practice, He has made forgiveness dependent on repentance and mending one's ways.

- For eternal salvation, belief and submission are necessary. There is a difference between being a believer and being a Muslim. There are two aspects to being a Muslim. One is that if one sincerely confirms the essentials of faith, one is a believer and expected to carry out the rules of Islam. A true believer and Muslim is one who sincerely confirms the essentials of faith and fulfills the commandments of Islam. The other aspect is that one is a Muslim according to law if one does not pronounce anything contrary to faith and performs some Islamic acts, such as, in particular, performing the Jumu'ah Prayer in a mosque and paying the Prescribed Purifying Alms (*Zakāh*). Although such a person may be a hypocrite, they must be treated as a Muslim by law.

- The punishment mentioned in verse 54 may be either the punishment in the Hereafter or one which will cause repentance to be of avail no longer (40: 85). When the decisive signs of death appear or when God's punishment, after many warnings (such as of the kind that came upon many bygone peoples), comes, repentance for unbelief or associating partners with God and coming to belief are not acceptable.

464   سُوْرَةُ الزُّمَرِ   ٢٦٢

بَلَى قَدْ جَاءَتْكَ ءَايَـٰتِى فَكَذَّبْتَ بِهَا وَاسْتَكْبَرْتَ

tribution to God with their faces darkened by grief and ignominy. Is there not in Hell a dwelling for those (too) arrogant (for faith)!

61. But God will save (from Hell) those who keep from disobedience to God in reverence for Him and piety by virtue of what they have achieved (in following God's way). Evil will never touch them, nor will they grieve.[18]

62. God is the Creator of all things, and He is the Guardian (with power of disposition) over all things.

63. His are the keys of (the treasures of) the heavens and the earth. So those who disbelieve in God's Revelations and signs (of the truth) – such are they who are the losers.[19]

64. Say: "(That being the truth) do you still call me to worship other than God, O ignorant ones?"

65. Indeed it has been revealed to you as well as to those (Messengers) sent before you: "Should you associate partners with God, your labor will most certainly come to nothing and you will most certainly be among the losers.

66. Rather, worship God alone, and be among the thankful."[20]

67. They have no true judgment of God, such as His being God requires, and (such is His Power and Sovereignty that) the whole earth will be in His Grasp on the Day of Resurrection, and the heavens will be rolled up in His Right Hand.[21] All-Glorified is He, and absolutely exalted above what they associate with Him.

---

57. Or (lest it) should say (by way of invalid excuse): "If only God had guided me, I would surely have been among the God-revering, pious!"

58. Or (lest it) should say when it sees the punishment, "If only I had a second chance (to live), so that I could be among those devoted to doing good, aware that God is seeing them!"

59. (But God will answer): "No, indeed! My Revelations and signs (of the truth) did come to you, but you denied them, and grew in arrogance (so as not to confirm them), and you proved yourself to be one of the unbelievers."

60. On the Day of Resurrection you will see those who fabricated falsehood in at-

18. There are both believers and unbelievers, that is, good and evil people, the righteous and sinful, side by side in the world. Similarly, good and evil are both intrinsic to humankind and exist together. So a true, fruitful education requires not only encouragement, arousing desire, and promises, but also discouragement, warning and threats. This is the way of the Qur'ān. It encourages humankind to do good and promises God's reward, triumph, and eternal happiness, as well as warning and threatening the punishment of God. As seen in the verses that follow verse 53, the Qur'ān discourages people from sinning with the most powerful statements immediately after making them exuberant with the greatest hope and encouragement.

19. God has two different sets of laws, those that govern the universe, including the aspects of human life independent of humankind, (which are God's signs of the truth and which we wrongly call the "laws of nature" – these are the subject matter of the natural sciences), the other being the Religion. Both require obedience. Results for the latter usually are deferred to the Hereafter, while the returns of obedience or disobedience to the former usually come in this life. For example, the reward for patience is success, while the punishment for indolence is privation. Industry brings wealth, and steadfastness brings victory. So being a sincere believing Muslim requires obe-dience to both of these laws. When Muslims, in addition to their failures in the religious life, neglect to fulfill the requirements of obedience to God's laws of life and the universe (God's signs of the truth), they become losers in the world relatively to those unbelievers who have obeyed them. However, those (unbelievers) who reject God's Revelations (which are also God's signs of the truth) will be eternal losers, as they will lose in the Hereafter.

20. Whatever we have is a favor from God, so true humanity requires being always thankful to Him. One's humanity lies in thankfulness for any good one receives, and acknowledgment of one's defects, failures, errors, and sins, and being repentant of them, trying to improve oneself. In Qur'ānic terminology, unbelief and thanklessness are derived from the same root word. So thanklessness leads to unbelief, while thankfulness gives rise to belief.

21. As it is clear in *And His is the Sovereignty on the day when the Trumpet is blown, the Knower of the Unseen and the witnessed. He is the All-Wise, the All-Aware* (6: 73); the *Grasp* and *Right Hand* allude to God's absolute power and dominion over the whole universe. God acts in the world from behind the nominal veil of causality out of wisdom, but He will exercise His absolute dominion over the whole universe on the Day of Judgment without any veil.

465

اللہ کی آیات عربی

68. The Trumpet will be blown, and so all who are in the heavens and all who are on the earth will fall dead, except those whom God wills to exempt. Then it will be blown for the second time, and see, they have all stood upright, looking on (in anticipation).[22]

69. And the earth (altered from what it was) will be bright and clearly visible throughout by the Light of its Lord,[23] and the Record (of the deeds of responsible beings endowed with free will) will be laid out, and the Prophets and the Witnesses will be brought forward, and it will be judged among them (conscious, responsible beings) with truth (concerning that on which they used to differ),[24] and they will not be wronged.

70. And every soul will be paid in full

whatever (good or evil) it has done (in the world); and indeed He knows best all that they do.

71. Those who disbelieve (and die unbelievers) will be led to Hell in companies. Until when they arrive there, its doors will immediately be opened and its keepers will ask them: "Did there not come to you Messengers from among you, reciting to you the Revelations of your Lord and warning you of this Day that you were to encounter?" They will answer: "Yes, indeed!" But the word of (God's) punishment upon the unbelievers[25] is fulfilled.

72. They will be told: "Enter through the doors of Hell, to abide therein." How evil is the dwelling of those (too) arrogant (to believe).

73. Those who keep from disobedience to their Lord in reverence for Him and piety will be led to Paradise in companies. Until when they arrive there, its doors will be opened (as sheer grace from God), and its keepers will welcome them saying: "Peace be upon you! Well you have faired and are purified (from the foul residues of sin, and delivered from all suffering), so enter it (Paradise) to abide!"

74. And they say: "All praise and gratitude are for God, Who has fulfilled His promise to us, and has made us inheritors of this land (of bliss), so that We may dwell in Paradise as we please!" Then: how excellent is the reward of the doers (of good deeds in obedience and devotion to God)!

22. The Qur'ān mentions three results of blowing the Trumpet. (1) *The Trumpet will be blown, and so all who are in the heavens and all who are on the earth will fall dead, except those whom God wills to exempt* (39: 68). (2) *Then it will be blown for a second time, and see, they have all stood upright, looking on* (39: 68). (3) *On the Day when the Trumpet is blown all who are in the heavens and all who are on the earth will be stricken with shock and terror, except those whom God wills to exempt. All will come to His Presence, utterly humbled* (27: 87). *And the Trumpet will be blown, and see, out of the graves they rush forth to their Lord* (36: 51).

If we consider the results of blowing the Trumpet, we may conclude that it will be blown three times. However, the second part of this verse says that *it will be blown for the second time, and see, they have all stood upright*, and verse 36: 51 states that upon blowing the Trumpet, *the dead will rush forth to their Lord out of their graves*. We learn from verse 27: 87 that *when the Trumpet is blown, all who are in the heavens and all who are on the earth will be stricken with shock and terror, except those whom God wills to exempt, and all will come to His Presence, utterly humbled*. So it is understood from verses 27: 87, 36: 51 and the second part of this verse (39: 68), that the dead will be raised from their graves, most of people will stricken with terror, and all will rush to their Lord upon the same blowing of the Trumpet. In conclusion, we can say that the Trumpet will be blown twice.

As for those whom God wills to exempt from falling dead as a result of the blowing of the Trumpet, it is not clear who they will be. However, if we take into account verses 37: 58–59 and 44: 56 which state that the believers taste death only once while the unbelievers taste it twice (40: 11), they may be the spirits of the believers who have already died. The true knowledge always rests with God, the All-Knowing.

23. On the Day of Resurrection the earth is changed into another earth, and the heavens also, they all appear before God, the One, the All-Overwhelming (14: 48). That is, there will be nothing hidden, all truth will come to be known clearly, and everyone will clearly see the consequences of their deeds.

24. The Prophets will come forward to testify that they conveyed God's Message and how their people responded to their call. And some pure and righteous ones (the witnesses) will be brought forward to testify concerning the communication of God's Message by the Prophets and the people's reaction to it. (See 4: 41; 7: 6.)

25. The *word of punishment* against the unbelievers which the Qur'ān refers to in several of its verses (e.g. 27: 82, 85) is the word the Almighty pronounced when He decreed that humankind would live on the earth: *But those who disbelieve and deny Our signs (the verses of the revealed Book of guidance as well as the signs in both their inner world and the outer world establishing My Existence and Unity and other pillars of faith), they will be the companions of the Fire; they will abide therein* (2: 39).

75. And you (O Messenger) will see the angels surrounding the Supreme Throne (of God), glorifying their Lord with His praise. It has been judged among them with truth and justice, and it will be said (by all the people of Paradise): "All praise and gratitude are for God, the Lord of the worlds!"

SŪRAH 40

AL-MU 'MIN (THE BELIEVER)

Makkah period

This *sūrah* of 85 verses takes its name from verse 28 which mentions, from among the clan of the Pharaoh, a distinguished believer who supported the Prophet Moses. The *sūrah* is also called *al-Ghāfir* (the All-Forgiving), the Divine Name mentioned in verse 3. It was revealed after *Sūrat az-Zumar* (the preceding *sūrah*) at a time when the Makkan polytheists increased their persecutions against the believers to the point that they were plotting to kill God's Messenger, upon him be peace and blessings. The *sūrah* reproaches them for their reaction, which was as harsh as the Pharaoh's reaction to Moses, upon him be peace, and reminds both them and the believers of the fact that, however harsh and strong their reaction to the Divine Message might be, the triumph of the believers is inevitable. The *sūrah* also narrates at length how an important believer from among the clan of the Pharaoh, who had hidden his faith, appeared and supported Moses at a very critical point.

In the Name of God, the All-Merciful, the All-Compassionate.

1. Ḥā. Mīm.

2. (This is) the Book being sent down in parts from God, the All-Glorious with irresistible might, the All-Knowing.

3. The Forgiver of sins and the Accepter of repentance, and yet severe in retribution, and limitless in His bounty. There is no deity but He. To Him is the homecoming.[1]

4. None dispute concerning God's Revelations and signs (in creation, human life and history) but those who obstinately disbelieve. But let not their strutting about the land in pomp and apparent domination deceive you.

5. Before them the people of Noah denied (God's Revelations and signs), and so did the communities who came after them (and who have been mentioned in the Qur'ān). Every community plotted against the Messenger sent to them to capture him (then kill or expel him), and they struggled (against God's Message) with falsehood,

so as to render the truth void thereby; but then I seized them, and (see) how was My retribution!

6. And thus your Lord's word has proven true against the unbelievers, that surely they are companions of the Fire.

7. Those (angels) who bear the Supreme Throne (of God), and the others around it² glorify their Lord with His praise;³ and they believe in Him (as the Unique Deity, Lord, and Sovereign of all creation), and ask for His forgiveness for those (among His creation) who believe, saying: "Our Lord! You embrace all things with mercy and knowledge (having perfect knowledge of every creature's need and answering that need with mercy), so forgive those who repent (of their sins) and follow Your way, and protect them from the punishment of the Blazing Flame.

---

1. This is a perfectly balanced argument that encourages people to believe and do good, righteous deeds as well as refraining from unbelief or associating partners with God or any transgression. The verse gives great hope by mentioning that God forgives sins and accepts repentance, and thus calls people to repent and mend their ways. It also discourages people from committing any unforgivable sin, such as disbelieving or associating partners with God, unless one repents of it and believes. Then, by mentioning that God is limitless in His bounty and the only God, to Whose Presence all humankind will finally return, it exhorts them to believe and do good, righteous deeds in order that they may receive abundant provision from God (see 39: 61, note 18) in both worlds.

2. On the nature and duties of angels, see 2: 30, note 31; on God's Supreme Throne: 7: 54, note 13; 11: 7, note 2; 17: 42, note 20, and 69: 17, note 7. Bearing the Supreme Throne means, in one respect, carrying out the Divine orders issued from His absolute Sovereignty over the universe. As for those who are around the Supreme Throne mentioned in the verse, they must be the angels who have greater nearness to God in rank.

3. For glorifying God with His praise, see 35: 29, note 11. The verse alludes that those (angels) bearing God's Supreme Throne carry out His orders in such perfection that they prove that God is absolutely above having any defects and partners and that He is One to Whom praise is absolutely due.

رَبَّنَا وَأَدْخِلْهُمْ جَنَّاتِ عَدْنٍ الَّتِي وَعَدْتَهُمْ وَمَنْ صَلَحَ
مِنْ ءَابَآئِهِمْ وَأَزْوَجِهِمْ وَذُرِّيَّتِهِمْ إِنَّكَ أَنْتَ الْعَزِيزُ
الْحَكِيمُ ۝ وَقِهِمُ السَّيِّئَاتِ وَمَن تَقِ السَّيِّئَاتِ يَوْمَئِذٍ
فَقَدْ رَحِمْتَهُ وَذَلِكَ هُوَ الْفَوْزُ الْعَظِيمُ ۝ إِنَّ
الَّذِينَ كَفَرُوا يُنَادَوْنَ لَمَقْتُ اللَّهِ أَكْبَرُ مِن مَّقْتِكُمْ
أَنفُسَكُمْ إِذْ تُدْعَوْنَ إِلَى الْإِيمَانِ فَتَكْفُرُونَ ۝ قَالُوا
رَبَّنَا أَمَتَّنَا اثْنَتَيْنِ وَأَحْيَيْتَنَا اثْنَتَيْنِ فَاعْتَرَفْنَا
بِذُنُوبِنَا فَهَلْ إِلَى خُرُوجٍ مِّن سَبِيلٍ ۝ ذَلِكُم بِأَنَّهُ إِذَا دُعِيَ
اللَّهُ وَحْدَهُ كَفَرْتُمْ وَإِن يُشْرَكْ بِهِ تُؤْمِنُوا فَالْحُكْمُ
لِلَّهِ الْعَلِيِّ الْكَبِيرِ ۝ هُوَ الَّذِي يُرِيكُمْ ءَايَتِهِ وَيُنَزِّلُ
لَكُم مِّنَ السَّمَاءِ رِزْقًا وَمَا يَتَذَكَّرُ إِلَّا مَن يُنِيبُ ۝ فَادْعُوا
اللَّهَ مُخْلِصِينَ لَهُ الدِّينَ وَلَوْ كَرِهَ الْكَافِرُونَ ۝ رَفِيعُ الدَّرَجَاتِ
ذُو الْعَرْشِ يُلْقِي الرُّوحَ مِنْ أَمْرِهِ عَلَى مَن يَشَاءُ مِنْ عِبَادِهِ
لِيُنذِرَ يَوْمَ التَّلَاقِ ۝ يَوْمَ هُم بَارِزُونَ لَا يَخْفَى عَلَى
اللَّهِ مِنْهُمْ شَيْءٌ لِّمَنِ الْمُلْكُ الْيَوْمَ لِلَّهِ الْوَاحِدِ الْقَهَّارِ ۝

8. "Our Lord! Admit them into the Gardens of perpetual bliss which You have promised them, and those who are righteous from among their forebears, and their spouses, and their offspring. Surely You are the All-Glorious with irresistible might, the All-Wise.

9. "And protect them from (doing) evil deeds (and the consequences thereof on the Day of Judgment). Whoever You protect from evils on that Day, You have surely had mercy on him; and that is the supreme triumph."

10. As for those who obstinately disbelieve (and die unbelievers), it is proclaimed to them (while they are in Hell): "God's 'abhorrence' of you is greater than your (present) abhorrence of yourselves and each other (because of your being

the cause of the punishment you suffer), for you used to be called to faith but you persistently refused to believe."[4]

11. They will say: "Our Lord! You have made us die twice, and given us life twice,[5] so (we have become fully convinced of the truth of all that You have informed us of, and) we acknowledge our sins (of unbelief). Is there, then, any way to get out (so that we may believe and do good, righteous deeds)?"

12. "That (your being in Hell) is so because when the One God alone is invoked, you obstinately refuse to believe, but when partners are associated with Him, you believe.[6] Then (whatever you do), the judgment rests with God, the All-Exalted, the All-Great."

13. He it is Who shows you His signs (in the universe as well as within yourselves, your life, and in history, which demonstrate His Oneness), and sends down provision for you from the heaven. But none reflect and are mindful save those who (being without prejudice) turn to God in penitence.

14. So (O believers,) invoke God alone, sincere in your faith in Him and practicing the Religion purely for His sake, however hateful this may be to the unbelievers.

15. He is exalted above all degrees, Owner of the Supreme Throne. He conveys the Spirit (the life-giving Revelation, from the immaterial realm) of His command to whom He wills of His servants, so as to warn (conscious, responsible beings) of the Day of Meeting (when His servants will meet Him).

16. The Day when they will come forth (from death), with nothing of them being hidden from God. Whose is the absolute Sovereignty on that Day? It is God's, the One, the All-Overwhelming (with absolute sway over all that exist).

4. The unbelievers will abhor themselves because it is they themselves who caused themselves to suffer the punishment of Hell. However, unbelief or associating partners with God is so great an offense to God, to the whole universe which testifies about God and the other pillars of faith and innumerable believers, from the beginning of conscious life to the Day of Judgment, that it incurs God's "wrath" and "abhorrence," which is much greater than the unbelievers' abhorrence of themselves. So, this verse actually expresses the hideousness of unbelief and associating partners with God.

5. Death means the detachment of the spirit from the body or that the body and spirit exist separately from each other. Before everyone comes to the world, the particles that are destined to constitute their body exist in God's Knowledge and are scattered throughout "nature." The Qur'ān calls this condition death (2: 28; see note 27). Then God gives life to a body in the womb by "breathing" into it its spirit. This is the first instance of giving life. Thereafter, every soul, or the living self composed of the spirit and body, tastes death by God's taking the spirit from the body either by Himself or employing the Angel of Death or the aids of this angel (see 32: 11, note 8). God will revive every dead person on the Day of Resurrection. That is, He will restore the bodies according to the conditions of the afterlife and return the spirits to them. This is the second instance of life. The Qur'ān states that the believers taste death only once (37: 58; 44: 56), so we can conclude that the believers will die once, but will be given life twice. However, this verse narrates to us that God will cause the people of Hell to die twice and He will revive them twice. So the death and revival mentioned in this verse concerning the people of Hell must be somehow different. When we consider verse 39: 68, which states, *The Trumpet will be blown, and so all who are in the heavens and all who are on the earth will fall dead, except those whom God wills to exempt. Then it will be blown for the second time, and see, they have all stood upright, looking on (in anticipation)* (see also note 22 on this verse), we can understand that the spirits of the unbelievers will die at the first sound of the Trumpet, and then be revived again to their restored bodies. In conclusion, the first death they taste is their departure from the world, and the second death is their spiritual death. The believers' spirits will be exempt from this. Therefore, by saying that God causes the people of Hell to die twice, the verse is referring to their departure from the world and their spiritual death during the final destruction of the world, and by His giving them life twice, it is referring to the revival of their spirit and their being raised from the dead on the Resurrection Day. God knows the best.

6. This means that the excuse that the people of Hell will put forward in Hell (mentioned in the previous verse) is baseless. Their unbelief does not arise from their ignorance of the truth, but from their intentional rejection of it for other reasons.

468   سُوۡرَةُ الۡمُؤۡمِنِ   ٤٦٨

أَلۡيَوۡمَ تُجۡزَىٰ كُلُّ نَفۡسٍۭ بِمَا كَسَبَتۡ لَا ظُلۡمَ الۡيَوۡمَ إِنَّ اللَّهَ
سَرِيعُ الۡحِسَابِ ۝ وَأَنذِرۡهُمۡ يَوۡمَ الۡأٓزِفَةِ إِذِ الۡقُلُوبُ
لَدَى الۡحَنَاجِرِ كَاظِمِينَ مَا لِلظَّٰلِمِينَ مِنۡ حَمِيمٍ وَلَا شَفِيعٍ
يُطَاعُ ۝ يَعۡلَمُ خَآئِنَةَ الۡأَعۡيُنِ وَمَا تُخۡفِي الصُّدُورُ ۝ وَاللَّهُ
يَقۡضِي بِالۡحَقِّ وَالَّذِينَ يَدۡعُونَ مِن دُونِهِۦ لَا يَقۡضُونَ بِشَيۡءٍ إِنَّ اللَّهَ
هُوَ السَّمِيعُ الۡبَصِيرُ ۝ أَوَلَمۡ يَسِيرُوا۟ فِي الۡأَرۡضِ فَيَنظُرُوا۟
كَيۡفَ كَانَ عَٰقِبَةُ الَّذِينَ كَانُوا۟ مِن قَبۡلِهِمۡ كَانُوا۟ هُمۡ
أَشَدَّ مِنۡهُمۡ قُوَّةً وَءَاثَارًا فِي الۡأَرۡضِ فَأَخَذَهُمُ اللَّهُ
بِذُنُوبِهِمۡ وَمَا كَانَ لَهُم مِّنَ اللَّهِ مِن وَاقٍ ۝ ذَٰلِكَ بِأَنَّهُمۡ
كَانَت تَّأۡتِيهِمۡ رُسُلُهُم بِالۡبَيِّنَٰتِ فَكَفَرُوا۟ فَأَخَذَهُمُ اللَّهُ
إِنَّهُۥ قَوِيٌّ شَدِيدُ الۡعِقَابِ ۝ وَلَقَدۡ أَرۡسَلۡنَا مُوسَىٰ
بِـَٔايَٰتِنَا وَسُلۡطَٰنٍ مُّبِينٍ ۝ إِلَىٰ فِرۡعَوۡنَ وَهَٰمَٰنَ وَقَٰرُونَ
فَقَالُوا۟ سَٰحِرٌ كَذَّابٌ ۝ فَلَمَّا جَآءَهُم بِالۡحَقِّ مِنۡ
عِندِنَا قَالُوا۟ اقۡتُلُوٓا۟ أَبۡنَآءَ الَّذِينَ ءَامَنُوا۟ مَعَهُۥ وَاسۡتَحۡيُوا۟
نِسَآءَهُمۡ وَمَا كَيۡدُ الۡكَٰفِرِينَ إِلَّا فِي ضَلَٰلٍ ۝

---

17. On that Day every soul will be recompensed for what it has earned; no wrong (will be done to any) on that Day. God is Swift at reckoning.

18. Warn them of the Day that draws near, when the hearts will come right up to the throats, choking them. The wrongdoers will have no intimate friend, nor any intercessor who will be heeded.

19. God knows the treacheries of the eyes and all that the bosoms conceal.

20. God judges with truth, whereas those whom they invoke apart from Him do not judge at all. Surely God is He Who is the All-Hearing, the All-Seeing.[7]

21. Have they never traveled about the earth that they may see what was the outcome for those (who obstinately disbelieved in Our signs) before them? They were greater than them in power and in the marks (they left) on the land. Then God seized them for their sins, and they had none to protect them against God.

22. That was because the Messengers sent to them came to them with clear proofs of the truth, but they obstinately disbelieved; and so God seized them. Surely He is All-Strong, Severe in retribution.

23. We surely sent Moses with clear signs from Us (including miracles to support him), and a manifest authority,

24. To the Pharaoh, and Hāmān, and Korah, but they said: "(This man is) a sorcerer, a liar!"

25. When he brought them the truth from Our Presence (so clearly that they could not deny it), they said: "Kill the sons of those who believe (in his Message) along with him and let live their womenfolk (for further humiliation and suffering)." But the scheming of unbelievers is but bound to fail.

---

7. In judgment, hearing and seeing are essential. One who can judge justly is expected to see or hear (from reliable sources) everything concerning the case that one is judging. It is only God Who has full sight and hearing of everything. So only He has right to judge and only He can judge with perfect justice. Judgment also requires knowledge of right and wrong. Again it is only God Who has full knowledge of everything and therefore full knowledge of right and wrong. So absolute judgment belongs to Him exclusively.

26. The Pharaoh said (to his chiefs): "Let me kill Moses, and let him call upon his Lord! I fear lest he alter your religion (replacing it with his), or lest he provoke disorder in the land."

27. Moses said: "Indeed I seek refuge in my Lord, Who is your Lord as well, from every haughty one who disbelieves in the Day of Reckoning."

28. (At just that moment) a believing man from among the household of the Pharaoh, who until then had concealed his faith, (came forward and) said: "Would you kill a man only because he declares, 'My Lord is God!', when he has indeed come to you with clear proofs from your Lord? If he be a liar, then his lie will be (reckoned) against him; but if he is true (in his proclamations), then something of what he threatens you with will befall you. Surely God does not guide (either to truth or to any achievement) one who (transgressing all bounds) is wasteful (of his God-given faculties), and deceitful.

29. "O my people! You enjoy the dominion today, being uppermost in the land; but who could help us against the punishment of God, should it come to us?" The Pharaoh said (to his people): "I would show you only what I see (as needing to be done), and I guide you only to the right way (to follow)."

30. But he who believed said: "O my people! I do indeed fear for you the like of the day (of disaster) of the communities (that, before you, also denied the Messengers sent to them);

31. "The like of what befell the people of

Noah, the 'Ād, and the Thamūd, and others that came after them; and God never wills any wrong for (His) servants.

32. "O my people! I do indeed fear for you the Day of the Summons (the Day when people will vainly be calling out to one another for help, and cursing one another in distress);[8]

33. "The Day when you will (strive in vain desperation) to turn and flee (from the Fire), having none to protect you from (the punishment of) God. Whomever God leads astray, there is no guide.

---

8 For such and other kinds of calling out between people in the Hereafter, see 7: 44–50; 34: 31–33; 37: 21–33.

470   سُوْرَةُ الْمُؤْمِنِ   ٤٧٠

وَلَقَدْ جَاءَكُمْ يُوسُفُ مِنْ قَبْلُ بِالْبَيِّنَاتِ فَمَا زِلْتُمْ فِي شَكٍّ
مِّمَّا جَاءَكُمْ بِهِ حَتَّى إِذَا هَلَكَ قُلْتُمْ لَنْ يَبْعَثَ اللّٰهُ مِنْ بَعْدِهِ
رَسُولًا كَذَلِكَ يُضِلُّ اللّٰهُ مَنْ هُوَ مُسْرِفٌ مُّرْتَابٌ ۞ الَّذِينَ
يُجَادِلُونَ فِي آيَاتِ اللّٰهِ بِغَيْرِ سُلْطَانٍ أَتَاهُمْ كَبُرَ مَقْتًا
عِنْدَ اللّٰهِ وَعِنْدَ الَّذِينَ آمَنُوا كَذَلِكَ يَطْبَعُ اللّٰهُ عَلَى كُلِّ
قَلْبِ مُتَكَبِّرٍ جَبَّارٍ ۞ وَقَالَ فِرْعَوْنُ يَا هَامَانُ ابْنِ لِي
صَرْحًا لَعَلِّي أَبْلُغُ الْأَسْبَابَ ۞ أَسْبَابَ السَّمَاوَاتِ فَأَطَّلِعَ
إِلَى إِلَهِ مُوسَى وَإِنِّي لَأَظُنُّهُ كَاذِبًا وَكَذَلِكَ زُيِّنَ
لِفِرْعَوْنَ سُوءُ عَمَلِهِ وَصُدَّ عَنِ السَّبِيلِ وَمَا كَيْدُ
فِرْعَوْنَ إِلَّا فِي تَبَابٍ ۞ وَقَالَ الَّذِي آمَنَ يَا قَوْمِ
اتَّبِعُونِ أَهْدِكُمْ سَبِيلَ الرَّشَادِ ۞ يَا قَوْمِ إِنَّمَا
هَذِهِ الْحَيَاةُ الدُّنْيَا مَتَاعٌ وَإِنَّ الْآخِرَةَ هِيَ دَارُ
الْقَرَارِ ۞ مَنْ عَمِلَ سَيِّئَةً فَلَا يُجْزَى إِلَّا مِثْلَهَا وَمَنْ
عَمِلَ صَالِحًا مِنْ ذَكَرٍ أَوْ أُنْثَى وَهُوَ مُؤْمِنٌ فَأُولَئِكَ
يَدْخُلُونَ الْجَنَّةَ يُرْزَقُونَ فِيهَا بِغَيْرِ حِسَابٍ ۞

──────⟨❧⟩──────

34. "And (reflect that) Joseph brought
to you the manifest truths before, but
you never ceased to doubt as to what he
brought you. But when he finally died,
you said that God would no longer send
a Messenger after him.[9] Thus God leads
astray one who (transgressing all bounds)
is wasteful (of his God-given faculties),
persistently doubting (without good reason) –

35. "Those who dispute concerning God's
signs and Revelations without any authority that has reached them. It is grievous and loathsome in the sight of God and
those who believe. Thus God impresses (a
seal) on every haughty, tyrant's heart."

36. The Pharaoh said: "O Hāmān! Build
me a lofty tower so that I may attain the
ways,

37. "The ways of (peering into) the skies,
and that I may have a look at the God of
Moses, even though I am sure that he is a
liar." Thus were his evil deeds decked out
to be appealing to the Pharaoh, and he was
debarred from the (right) way. And the
scheme of the Pharaoh ended in nothing
but destruction.

38. And the one who believed said (continuing his warnings): "O my people! Follow me so that I may guide you to the
way of right guidance.

39. "O my people! The life of this world is
but a (passing) enjoyment, while the Hereafter – that is indeed the home of permanence.

40. "Whoever does an evil is not recompensed except with the like of it; whereas
whoever does good, righteous deeds –
whether man or woman – and is a believer,
such will enter Paradise, being provided
there without measure.

---

9. That is, the Copts were not sincere in their
attitude toward the Messengers. They did not
believe in the Prophet Joseph, upon him be
peace, during his lifetime, but when he died, at
least they seemed, at the cost of contradicting
themselves, to acknowledge his Messengership
and paid him so great, extraordinary respect
that later generations made this an excuse
for their denial of any new Messenger sent
by God.

وَيَٰقَوْمِ مَالِىٓ أَدْعُوكُمْ إِلَى ٱلنَّجَوٰةِ وَتَدْعُونَنِىٓ إِلَى ٱلنَّارِ ۞ تَدْعُونَنِى لِأَكْفُرَ بِٱللَّهِ وَأُشْرِكَ بِهِۦ مَالَيْسَ لِى بِهِۦ عِلْمٌ وَأَنَا۠ أَدْعُوكُمْ إِلَى ٱلْعَزِيزِ ٱلْغَفَّٰرِ ۞ لَاجَرَمَ أَنَّمَا تَدْعُونَنِىٓ إِلَيْهِ لَيْسَ لَهُۥ دَعْوَةٌ فِى ٱلدُّنْيَا وَلَا فِى ٱلْأَخِرَةِ وَأَنَّ مَرَدَّنَآ إِلَى ٱللَّهِ وَأَنَّ ٱلْمُسْرِفِينَ هُمْ أَصْحَٰبُ ٱلنَّارِ ۞ فَسَتَذْكُرُونَ مَآ أَقُولُ لَكُمْ وَأُفَوِّضُ أَمْرِىٓ إِلَى ٱللَّهِ إِنَّ ٱللَّهَ بَصِيرٌۢ بِٱلْعِبَادِ ۞ فَوَقَىٰهُ ٱللَّهُ سَيِّـَٔاتِ مَا مَكَرُوا۟ وَحَاقَ بِـَٔالِ فِرْعَوْنَ سُوٓءُ ٱلْعَذَابِ ۞ ٱلنَّارُ يُعْرَضُونَ عَلَيْهَا غُدُوًّا وَعَشِيًّا وَيَوْمَ تَقُومُ ٱلسَّاعَةُ أَدْخِلُوٓا۟ ءَالَ فِرْعَوْنَ أَشَدَّ ٱلْعَذَابِ ۞ وَإِذْ يَتَحَآجُّونَ فِى ٱلنَّارِ فَيَقُولُ ٱلضُّعَفَٰٓؤُا۟ لِلَّذِينَ ٱسْتَكْبَرُوٓا۟ إِنَّا كُنَّا لَكُمْ تَبَعًا فَهَلْ أَنتُم مُّغْنُونَ عَنَّا نَصِيبًا مِّنَ ٱلنَّارِ ۞ قَالَ ٱلَّذِينَ ٱسْتَكْبَرُوٓا۟ إِنَّا كُلٌّ فِيهَآ إِنَّ ٱللَّهَ قَدْ حَكَمَ بَيْنَ ٱلْعِبَادِ ۞ وَقَالَ ٱلَّذِينَ فِى ٱلنَّارِ لِخَزَنَةِ جَهَنَّمَ ٱدْعُوا۟ رَبَّكُمْ يُخَفِّفْ عَنَّا يَوْمًا مِّنَ ٱلْعَذَابِ ۞

41. "O my people! How is it with me that I call you to salvation when you call me to the Fire!

42. "You call me so that I should dis-believe in God and associate with Him partners about whose partnership I have no sure knowledge; and I call you to the All-Glorious with irresistible might (Able to destroy whoever rebels against Him), the All-Forgiving (Who forgives whoever turns to Him in repentance).

43. "Without doubt you call me but to one who has no title (to be called to) in the world, or in the Hereafter; our return will be to God, and those who (transgressing all bounds) are wasteful (of their God-given faculties) – they will be companions of the Fire.

44. "Soon you will remember all that I now am telling you. As for me, I com-mit my affair to God (in full submission). Surely God sees the servants well."

45. So God preserved him from the evils they schemed (against him),[10] while a most evil punishment overwhelmed the clan (the court and military aristocracy) of the Pharaoh:

46. The Fire: they are exposed to it morn-ing and evening; and when the Last Hour comes in (and the Judgment is established,

it is ordered): "Admit the clan of the Pha-raoh into the severest punishment."[11]

47. See, how they will dispute with each other in the Fire; so the weak ones (who blindly obeyed the leaders of unbelief) will say to those who acted arrogantly and oppressed (others): "Surely we were your followers; now can you therefore rid us of (even) a portion of the Fire?"

48. Those who were arrogant (and op-pressed others) will say: "We are all to-gether in this (Fire)! God has indeed judged between the servants (and all must face a reckoning and meet their deserts)."

49. Those who are in the Fire will cry to the keepers of Hell: "Call upon your Lord that He may lighten the punishment for us for one day (at least)."[12]

10. As can be understood from the verses, the believer who appeared at a most critical point to support Moses against the plots of the Pharaoh must have been a powerful person among the chiefs and governing elite of the Pharaoh. He had successfully concealed his faith. Then, at the time when the Pharaoh was about to order an attempt on the life of Moses he came forward and gave full support to Moses. He acted like an aide to Moses alongside Aaron, and because of his status, Pharaoh could not cause him any harm, and their secret plots came to nothing due to God's help. In the end, Pharaoh, his governing elite and the army drowned in the sea, while Moses and his people successfully left Egypt.

11. This verse explicitly establishes that the punishment in the grave, the intermediate world between this and the next, is real. This punishment is also related to burning in the Fire. However, the punishment of the Fire for the Pharaoh and his family in the grave is in the form of being exposed to it in the morning and evening, while in Hell it will be in the form of continuous burning.

12. According to some commentators, "one day" means some little portion of time.

472   سُوۡرَةُ الۡمُؤۡمِنِ   ٤٧٢

قَالُوٓا۟ أَوَلَمۡ تَكُ تَأۡتِيكُمۡ رُسُلُكُم بِٱلۡبَيِّنَـٰتِ ۖ قَالُوا۟ بَلَىٰ ۚ قَالُوا۟ فَٱدۡعُوا۟ ۗ وَمَا دُعَـٰٓؤُا۟ ٱلۡكَـٰفِرِينَ إِلَّا فِى ضَلَـٰلٍ ۝ إِنَّا لَنَنصُرُ رُسُلَنَا وَٱلَّذِينَ ءَامَنُوا۟ فِى ٱلۡحَيَوٰةِ ٱلدُّنۡيَا وَيَوۡمَ يَقُومُ ٱلۡأَشۡهَـٰدُ ۝ يَوۡمَ لَا يَنفَعُ ٱلظَّـٰلِمِينَ مَعۡذِرَتُهُمۡ ۖ وَلَهُمُ ٱللَّعۡنَةُ وَلَهُمۡ سُوٓءُ ٱلدَّارِ ۝ وَلَقَدۡ ءَاتَيۡنَا مُوسَى ٱلۡهُدَىٰ وَأَوۡرَثۡنَا بَنِىٓ إِسۡرَٰٓءِيلَ ٱلۡكِتَـٰبَ ۝ هُدًى وَذِكۡرَىٰ لِأُو۟لِى ٱلۡأَلۡبَـٰبِ ۝ فَٱصۡبِرۡ إِنَّ وَعۡدَ ٱللَّهِ حَقٌّ وَٱسۡتَغۡفِرۡ لِذَنۢبِكَ وَسَبِّحۡ بِحَمۡدِ رَبِّكَ بِٱلۡعَشِىِّ وَٱلۡإِبۡكَـٰرِ ۝ إِنَّ ٱلَّذِينَ يُجَـٰدِلُونَ فِىٓ ءَايَـٰتِ ٱللَّهِ بِغَيۡرِ سُلۡطَـٰنٍ أَتَىٰهُمۡ ۙ إِن فِى صُدُورِهِمۡ إِلَّا كِبۡرٌ مَّا هُم بِبَـٰلِغِيهِ ۚ فَٱسۡتَعِذۡ بِٱللَّهِ ۖ إِنَّهُۥ هُوَ ٱلسَّمِيعُ ٱلۡبَصِيرُ ۝ لَخَلۡقُ ٱلسَّمَـٰوَٰتِ وَٱلۡأَرۡضِ أَكۡبَرُ مِنۡ خَلۡقِ ٱلنَّاسِ وَلَـٰكِنَّ أَكۡثَرَ ٱلنَّاسِ لَا يَعۡلَمُونَ ۝ وَمَا يَسۡتَوِى ٱلۡأَعۡمَىٰ وَٱلۡبَصِيرُ وَٱلَّذِينَ ءَامَنُوا۟ وَعَمِلُوا۟ ٱلصَّـٰلِحَـٰتِ وَلَا ٱلۡمُسِىٓءُ ۚ قَلِيلًا مَّا تَتَذَكَّرُونَ ۝

50. (The keepers) will say: "Did not the Messengers sent to you come to you with clear proofs (of the truth)?" They will say, "Yes, indeed." (The keepers then) will say: "Then call (as you like)!" But the call of unbelievers is bound to be in vain.

51. Most certainly we help Our Messengers, and those who believe, in the life of this world and on the Day when the Witnesses will stand forth (to testify concerning people's response to the Messengers)[13] –

52. The Day when their excuses will not avail the wrongdoers, and for them there is curse (they will be eternally excluded from God's mercy), and for them there is the evil abode.

53. Most certainly We did grant to Moses the guidance, and We made the Children of Israel inheritors of the Book (after Moses),

54. As guidance (for all to follow in their life) and a reminder (with teaching and admonition) for the people of discernment (among them).

55. So be patient (O Messenger, with whatever they do), for surely God's promise (that He always helps His Messengers and the believers) is true; and ask forgiveness for your sins,[14] and glorify your Lord with His praise[15] in the afternoon and morning hours.

56. Those who dispute concerning the signs and Revelations of God without any authority that has reached them,[16] (do so because) in their bosoms is a craving for superiority, which they will not attain. But take refuge in God (from their schemes). Surely He is the All-Hearing, the All-Seeing.

57. Surely the creation of the heavens and the earth is something greater than the creation of human, but most of humankind do not know (this truth).[17]

58. Not equal are the blind and the seeing, nor (are equal) those who believe and do good, righteous deeds, and the doers of evil. Little do you reflect and be mindful!

13. See *sūrah* 4: 41; *sūrah* 39: 69, note 24.

14. Infallibility is an indispensable attribute of Prophethood. So all the Prophets are infallible in the sense that they do not sin or disobey God's orders. Here God reminds the believers of an important fact to which we must be attentive on the way to Him. What falls on those who believe in God, and who endeavor to attain the level of ordering their life according to the rules that are established in His Book, is to be patient, ask for His forgiveness for their sins, and as will be stated in the verse, to be occupied with His glorification and praise.

15. On the meaning of glorifying God and praising Him, see 35: 29, note 11.

16. In several other verses, such as verse 35 of this *sūrah*, the Qur'ān draws attention to the fact that those who talk about God's signs and Revelations must have a warrant or authority that has reached them. That is, God's signs and Revelations are matters that concern Him and His Religion. So talking about God requires definite knowledge of Him, which can only be acquired through Revelation and the Messengers. Talking about God's Religion requires expert knowledge about it, and its first and foremost source is, again, God and the Revelation. Therefore, those who dispute about God and His Religion without basing their information on sufficient, expert knowledge from the Qur'ān and God's Messenger, upon him be peace and blessings, are included in the threats found in these verses.

17. This verse has several implications, such as follows:

• Many human beings see their revival in the Hereafter as being impossible. However, their creation is no easier than their revival. More than that, God has created the heavens and the earth, and He will destroy and re-create them on the Day of Resurrection. Their creation is not easier than the creation of humankind. So it is in no way difficult for the One Who has created the heavens and the earth to revive or re-create human beings.

• Humans have no right to assume superiority before God's signs and Revelations. They are completely powerless before God, Who has created the heavens and the earth, so what is expected of them is to submit to Him in awareness of their weakness and the limitless greatness of God. The heavens are full of conscious spiritual beings who are much more powerful than human beings. Despite this and despite their immense size, the heavens and the earth have willingly submitted to God's orders. What is wrong with humans that they pretend superiority before God's signs and Revelations?

• God has made humankind His vicegerent on the earth and has endowed them with many capabilities so that they can realize great, astonishing achievements. However, the greatest of those achievements are as nothing compared to God's creation of the heavens and the earth with all that are in them. So their achievements must never lead human beings to be boastful and assume superiority in the face of God's signs and Revelations. Rather, they must submit to God's orders and live according to them.

إِنَّ السَّاعَةَ لَآتِيَةٌ لَّا رَيْبَ فِيهَا وَلَٰكِنَّ أَكْثَرَ النَّاسِ لَا يُؤْمِنُونَ ۝ وَقَالَ رَبُّكُمُ ادْعُونِي أَسْتَجِبْ لَكُمْ إِنَّ الَّذِينَ يَسْتَكْبِرُونَ عَنْ عِبَادَتِي سَيَدْخُلُونَ جَهَنَّمَ دَاخِرِينَ ۝ اللَّهُ الَّذِي جَعَلَ لَكُمُ اللَّيْلَ لِتَسْكُنُوا فِيهِ وَالنَّهَارَ مُبْصِرًا إِنَّ اللَّهَ لَذُو فَضْلٍ عَلَى النَّاسِ وَلَٰكِنَّ أَكْثَرَ النَّاسِ لَا يَشْكُرُونَ ۝ ذَٰلِكُمُ اللَّهُ رَبُّكُمْ خَالِقُ كُلِّ شَيْءٍ لَّا إِلَٰهَ إِلَّا هُوَ فَأَنَّىٰ تُؤْفَكُونَ ۝ كَذَٰلِكَ يُؤْفَكُ الَّذِينَ كَانُوا بِآيَاتِ اللَّهِ يَجْحَدُونَ ۝ اللَّهُ الَّذِي جَعَلَ لَكُمُ الْأَرْضَ قَرَارًا وَالسَّمَاءَ بِنَاءً وَصَوَّرَكُمْ فَأَحْسَنَ صُوَرَكُمْ وَرَزَقَكُم مِّنَ الطَّيِّبَاتِ ذَٰلِكُمُ اللَّهُ رَبُّكُمْ فَتَبَارَكَ اللَّهُ رَبُّ الْعَالَمِينَ ۝ هُوَ الْحَيُّ لَا إِلَٰهَ إِلَّا هُوَ فَادْعُوهُ مُخْلِصِينَ لَهُ الدِّينَ الْحَمْدُ لِلَّهِ رَبِّ الْعَالَمِينَ ۝ قُلْ إِنِّي نُهِيتُ أَنْ أَعْبُدَ الَّذِينَ تَدْعُونَ مِن دُونِ اللَّهِ لَمَّا جَاءَنِيَ الْبَيِّنَاتُ مِن رَّبِّي وَأُمِرْتُ أَنْ أُسْلِمَ لِرَبِّ الْعَالَمِينَ ۝

---

59. The Last Hour is certainly bound to come; there is no doubt in it: Yet, most of humankind do not believe.[18]

60. Your Lord has said: "Pray to Me, (and) I will answer you."[19] Those who are too haughty to worship Me will enter Hell abased.

61. God it is Who has made the night for you, that you may rest in it, and the day, clear and sight-giving (to work). Indeed God has grace and bounty for humankind, but most of them do not give thanks.

62. Such is God, your Lord (Who creates you, and maintains and provides for you), the Creator of all things. There is no deity but He. How then are you turned away from the truth (and adopt false deities to worship)?

63. Thus it is: those who obstinately reject God's signs and Revelations are turned away from the truth.

64. God is He Who has made the earth as a fixed abode, and the heaven as a canopy, and has formed you and perfected your forms, and He provides you with pure, wholesome things. Then Blessed and Supreme is God, the Lord of the worlds.

65. He is the All-Living, there is no deity but He, so pray to Him, being sincere in your faith in Him and practicing the Religion purely for His sake. All praise and gratitude are for God, the Lord of the worlds.

66. Say: "I have been forbidden to worship those whom you invoke apart from God when clear proofs (of the truth) have come to me from my Lord, and I have been ordered to submit myself wholly to the Lord of the worlds."

---

18. The last two verses imply that good and evil can be distinguished perfectly only in the Hereafter. So, without the Hereafter, neither good nor evil receive the just and full recompense due to them. This is contrary to morality. That is why belief in the Hereafter is one of the most basic foundations of morality and a sound social life. But only those who believe and therefore can see, or those who have not blinded themselves to the truth, can perceive this.

19. On prayer and God's answering it, see sūrah 25: 77, note 18.

474   سورة المؤمن   ٤٧٤

هُوَ الَّذِى خَلَقَكُم مِّن تُرَابٍ ثُمَّ مِن نُّطْفَةٍ ثُمَّ مِنْ عَلَقَةٍ ثُمَّ يُخْرِجُكُمْ طِفْلًا ثُمَّ لِتَبْلُغُوٓا أَشُدَّكُمْ ثُمَّ لِتَكُونُوا شُيُوخًا وَمِنكُم مَّن يُتَوَفَّىٰ مِن قَبْلُ وَلِتَبْلُغُوٓا أَجَلًا مُّسَمًّى وَلَعَلَّكُمْ تَعْقِلُونَ ۝ هُوَ الَّذِى يُحْىِۦ وَيُمِيتُ فَإِذَا قَضَىٰٓ أَمْرًا فَإِنَّمَا يَقُولُ لَهُۥ كُن فَيَكُونُ ۝ أَلَمْ تَرَ إِلَى الَّذِينَ يُجَٰدِلُونَ فِىٓ ءَايَٰتِ اللَّهِ أَنَّىٰ يُصْرَفُونَ ۝ الَّذِينَ كَذَّبُوا بِالْكِتَٰبِ وَبِمَآ أَرْسَلْنَا بِهِۦ رُسُلَنَا فَسَوْفَ يَعْلَمُونَ ۝ إِذِ الْأَغْلَٰلُ فِىٓ أَعْنَٰقِهِمْ وَالسَّلَٰسِلُ يُسْحَبُونَ ۝ فِى الْحَمِيمِ ثُمَّ فِى النَّارِ يُسْجَرُونَ ۝ ثُمَّ قِيلَ لَهُمْ أَيْنَ مَا كُنتُمْ تُشْرِكُونَ ۝ مِن دُونِ اللَّهِ قَالُوا ضَلُّوا عَنَّا بَل لَّمْ نَكُن نَّدْعُوا مِن قَبْلُ شَيْئًا كَذَٰلِكَ يُضِلُّ اللَّهُ الْكَٰفِرِينَ ۝ ذَٰلِكُم بِمَا كُنتُمْ تَفْرَحُونَ فِى الْأَرْضِ بِغَيْرِ الْحَقِّ وَبِمَا كُنتُمْ تَمْرَحُونَ ۝ ادْخُلُوٓا أَبْوَٰبَ جَهَنَّمَ خَٰلِدِينَ فِيهَا فَبِئْسَ مَثْوَى الْمُتَكَبِّرِينَ ۝ فَاصْبِرْ إِنَّ وَعْدَ اللَّهِ حَقٌّ فَإِمَّا نُرِيَنَّكَ بَعْضَ الَّذِى نَعِدُهُمْ أَوْ نَتَوَفَّيَنَّكَ فَإِلَيْنَا يُرْجَعُونَ ۝

---

67. He it is Who has created you from earth, then from a drop of (seminal) fluid, then from a clot clinging (to the womb wall), then He brings you forth (into the world) as an infant, then (arranges that) you attain your (age of) full strength, thereafter that you (live long enough to) become old – though there are some of you who are caused to die before (reaching old age) – and that you reach a term appointed by Him, so that you may reason and understand (the truth).

68. He it is Who gives life and causes to die; and when He decrees a thing to be, He does but say to it "Be!" and it is.

69. Have you not considered those who dispute concerning God's signs and Revelations, how they are turned about (to different kinds of belief)?

70. They have denied the Book (the Qur'ān) and whatever (of guidance and wisdom) We have sent Our Messengers with. So in time they will come to know;

71. When the chains are around their necks, and fetters (around their legs): they will be dragged,

72. In the boiling water, then in the Fire they will be burned.

73. Then it is said to them: "Where are those to whom you ascribed Divinity (or Lordship or absolute Sovereignty)

74. "Apart from God? (Where are now those whose help you expected?)?" They will say: "They have failed us – or rather, we were not invoking before any (real) thing (which had part in Divinity or Lordship or absolute Sovereignty)." Thus does God lead astray the unbelievers (those who willfully disregard the truth and refuse to believe in it).

75. "That (His leading you astray and your punishment) is because you arrogantly exulted on the earth without (sense of the bounds of) right, and because you were arbitrary in your exulting.

76. "Now enter through the gates of Hell to abide therein. How evil, indeed, is the dwelling of those (too) haughty (to acknowledge the truth)."

77. So, be patient (O Messenger) for God's promise is true. Whether We let you witness some of what We have promised them, or whether We cause you to die (before it befalls them), still it is to Us that they will return.

وَلَقَدْ أَرْسَلْنَا رُسُلًا مِّن قَبْلِكَ مِنْهُم مَّن قَصَصْنَا عَلَيْكَ وَمِنْهُم مَّن لَّمْ نَقْصُصْ عَلَيْكَ وَمَا كَانَ لِرَسُولٍ أَن يَأْتِيَ بِآيَةٍ إِلَّا بِإِذْنِ اللَّهِ فَإِذَا جَاءَ أَمْرُ اللَّهِ قُضِيَ بِالْحَقِّ وَخَسِرَ هُنَالِكَ الْمُبْطِلُونَ ۝ اللَّهُ الَّذِي جَعَلَ لَكُمُ الْأَنْعَامَ لِتَرْكَبُوا مِنْهَا وَمِنْهَا تَأْكُلُونَ ۝ وَلَكُمْ فِيهَا مَنَافِعُ وَلِتَبْلُغُوا عَلَيْهَا حَاجَةً فِي صُدُورِكُمْ وَعَلَيْهَا وَعَلَى الْفُلْكِ تُحْمَلُونَ ۝ وَيُرِيكُمْ آيَاتِهِ فَأَيَّ آيَاتِ اللَّهِ تُنكِرُونَ ۝ أَفَلَمْ يَسِيرُوا فِي الْأَرْضِ فَيَنظُرُوا كَيْفَ كَانَ عَاقِبَةُ الَّذِينَ مِن قَبْلِهِمْ كَانُوا أَكْثَرَ مِنْهُمْ وَأَشَدَّ قُوَّةً وَآثَارًا فِي الْأَرْضِ فَمَا أَغْنَى عَنْهُم مَّا كَانُوا يَكْسِبُونَ ۝ فَلَمَّا جَاءَتْهُمْ رُسُلُهُم بِالْبَيِّنَاتِ فَرِحُوا بِمَا عِندَهُم مِّنَ الْعِلْمِ وَحَاقَ بِهِم مَّا كَانُوا بِهِ يَسْتَهْزِئُونَ ۝ فَلَمَّا رَأَوْا بَأْسَنَا قَالُوا آمَنَّا بِاللَّهِ وَحْدَهُ وَكَفَرْنَا بِمَا كُنَّا بِهِ مُشْرِكِينَ ۝ فَلَمْ يَكُ يَنفَعُهُمْ إِيمَانُهُمْ لَمَّا رَأَوْا بَأْسَنَا سُنَّتَ اللَّهِ الَّتِي قَدْ خَلَتْ فِي عِبَادِهِ وَخَسِرَ هُنَالِكَ الْكَافِرُونَ ۝

---

78. Indeed We sent Messengers before you; among them are those (the exemplary histories of) whom We have already related to you, and among them are those (the exemplary histories of) whom We have not related to you. It is not for a Messenger to bring forth a miracle except by God's leave. Then, when God's command is issued, it is judged with truth and justice, and those inventors of vain falsehoods (who associate partners with God and strive to disprove the truth) are brought to loss and ruin.

79. God is He Who has made the cattle (for your service), so that you use some of them for riding – and from them you obtain food.

80. And you have (many other) benefits in them – that you may attain by them some need in your breasts, and you are borne on them (over land) and on ships (over water).[20]

81. He shows you His signs (so that they are manifest to your senses and understanding). Then which of God's signs do you deny?

82. Have they not traveled about the earth that they might see what was the outcome for those before them (who obstinately disbelieved in Our signs)? They were more in numbers than these, and greater in power and the marks (that they left) on the land, but all that they had earned availed them nothing (in the face of God's displeasure).

83. When their Messengers came to them with manifest truths, they chose to remain in pleasure and pride only in the (narrow, superficial) knowledge they had (about the worldly life and the means to enjoy it), and what they used to mock (God's promised punishment) overwhelmed them.[21]

84. Then when they saw Our mighty punishment, they exclaimed: "We have come to believe in God as One and rejected all that we used to associate (with Him)!"

85. But their faith when they actually saw Our mighty punishment could not avail them: (that is) God's way (of dealing with humankind, a way) which has always been in effect for His servants. And so the unbelievers have lost altogether.

20. The term cattle includes sheep, goats, cows, oxen, and camels. All of them are edible, and camels are also used for riding. They are especially useful for traveling great distances. The females of these animals provide us with milk, while the skin of all can be used. In addition, the wool or hair of some, such as sheep, goats, and camels, is also useful. People benefit from camels as mounts in many ways – such as carrying their goods on them and traveling on them. In the past camels were also used in battle. Also see *sūrah* 36: 72–73.

21. This verse apparently alludes to modern times. Modern people are content with the worldly life and spend their whole life in pursuing the means for deriving the greatest possible pleasure from worldly life. They admire accomplishments in science and technology and use them only for the worldly pleasures, in complete ignorance and negligence of the other life. Seeking worldly pleasures causes ruthless competition in using material resources and never-ending conflicts, including world wars. These events are obviously God's mighty punishments. However, it seems that, being immersed in scientific materialism, modern people do not take lessons from these events.

SŪRAH 41

FUṢṢILAT
(DISTINCTLY SPELLED OUT)

Makkah period

This *sūrah* of 54 verses was revealed in Makkah after the conversion of Hamzah, the Prophet's uncle, and before the conversion of 'Umar, may God be pleased with him. It derives its name from the word *fuṣṣilat* in the third verse, which means, "arranged in sequence and distinctly spelled out." It is also called *Ḥā. Mīm Sajdah*. It mentions some attributes of the Qur'ān and some of the purposes for its revelation. It also describes the nature of Prophethood and Revelation. It draws attention to the proofs of Divine Oneness in the universe, the tragic end of some ancient peoples who denied God's Revelation, and the rewards given to the believers.

In the Name of God, the All-Merciful,
the All-Compassionate.

1. Ḥā. Mīm.

2. (This is) the Book being sent down in parts from the All-Merciful (Who embraces all beings with His Mercy), the All-Compassionate (Who has special mercy for the believers).

3. A Book whose communications have been spelled out distinctly and made clear, and whose verses are in ordered sequence, a Qur'ān (Recitation) in Arabic for a people who have knowledge (and so can appreciate excellence in the use of the language).

4. (Being sent) as a bearer of glad tidings (of the recompense for faith and righteousness), and a warner (against the consequences of misguidance).[1] Yet most of them (the Makkan people) turn away, and they do not give ear to it (being inwardly averse, and deaf to its excellence).

5. They say: "Our hearts are wrapped in coverings against what you call us to, and in our ears is heaviness, and between us and you is a veil. So take action (such as is in your power), as we are taking action (such as we wish to take)."

6. Say: "I am but a mortal like you. But it is revealed to me that your God is the One and Only God. So take the straight path to Him (in correct belief and obedience), and ask His forgiveness (for your sins)." Woe to those who associate partners (with Him),

7. Those who do not spend out of their wealth (in alms for the poor and needy), and they are unbelievers in the Hereafter.

8. Whereas those who believe and do good, righteous deeds, surely for them is a reward constant and beyond measure.

9. Say: "Is it that you (associate partners with and therefore) disbelieve in the One Who created the earth in two days,[2] and (on account of that unbelief) set up rivals to Him (as deities, lords, and objects of worship)?" That is the Lord of the worlds.

10. He has set in it (the earth) firm mountains rising above it, and bestowed blessings therein, and determined its provisions in due measure (to be obtained) in four periods, in a way to meet the vital necessities of all things and beings, that seek their provision from Him.

11. And He directed (His Knowledge, Will, Power, and Favor) to the heaven when it was as a cloud (of gases), and ordered it and the earth, "Come both of you, willingly or unwillingly!" They said: "We have come in willing obedience."[3]

---

1. Verses 2–4 mention some attributes of the Qur'ān, as follows:

(1) It cannot be imitated. (2) It is a Book. (3) It was sent down in parts. (4) In addition to His other Attributes, God's Mercy and Compassion are reflected in the Qur'ān, and therefore it is a mercy for all creation and especially for the believers. (5) Its verses are arranged in sequence without any confusion and distinctly spelled out. (6) It is a Book that is and should be distinctly recited. (7) It is in Arabic and therefore Arabic is an essential aspect of it. (8) Particularly those people who have sufficient knowledge of language can easily discern its aspects as a Book. (9) It gives glad tidings of a bright future and eternal happiness to those who believe and do good, righteous deeds. (10) It warns the misguided against the consequences of their way (Suat Yıldırım, 476).

The Qur'ān being revealed in Arabic is not incompatible with its message being universal. It was in Makkah in the very early period of his mission that God's Messenger declared that his message was meant for everyone: *"O humankind! Surely I am to you all the Messenger of God, of Him to Whom belongs the sovereignty of the heavens and the earth"* (7: 158); *Say: "God: a witness between me and you; and to me is being revealed this Qur'ān so that I may warn you thereby, and whomever it may reach"* (6: 19).

2. As stated in *sūrah* 7, note 11, the concept of day (*yawm*) in the Qur'ān is a relative unit of time. So it may mean here two stages or eras, one referring to the parting of the primeval matter of creation into heaven and earth (21: 30), and the other, to the fashioning of the earth and preparing it for life (13: 3; 79: 30–33).

3. Some modern researchers (i.e., Nurbaki, 13–24) understand from this verse the following:

The Qur'ān indicates that there is some difficulty in the co-operation between the earth and sky. As is known, the molecules and atoms in the atmosphere try to escape into space while the earth tries to attract and hold them. For the formation of an atmosphere, the motions that lead to the force of escaping molecules have to be counterbalanced by the gravitational attraction of the earth. This is an almost impossibly difficult condition to fulfill. From the standpoint of geophysics, these extremely difficult conditions require the preservation of three important balances: (i) atmospheric temperature, (ii) proportionate gravitational attraction on the part of the earth, and (iii) the non-violation of this balance by various radiant energies arriving from space. The Qur'ān expresses all these facts by the phrases, *Come both of you, willingly or unwillingly!* That the almost impossible conditions have been fulfilled only by God's Power is indicated by the statement, *They said: "We have come in willing obedience."*

12. So He fashioned them (the clouds of gaseous elements which then existed in the place of the heaven) seven heavens in two days and inspired in each heaven its tasks. And We adorned the lowest heaven (the heaven of the world) with lamps (stars), and guard (against every satan who would attempt to steal away information of the Unseen from angels).[4] That is the measured determination of the All-Glorious with irresistible might, the All-Knowing.[5]

13. If they turn away in aversion, say (to them): "I have warned you of a punishment striking like the lightning (that struck the tribes of) Ād and Thamūd.

14. When the Messengers (sent to each) came to them (with all evidence of truth) from every approach, preaching: "Worship none but God alone!" they said: "Had it been the will of our Lord (to send us Messengers to warn us), He would certainly have sent down angels. So we disbelieve in what (you claim) you have been sent with."

15. Now, as for the Ād: They acted arrogantly and oppressively in the land against all right, and said: "Who can be superior to us in power?" Did they not see that God, Who created them, is superior to them in power? And they persisted in rejecting Our manifest signs and Revelations.

16. So then We sent upon them a furious windstorm through days of disaster, and so We made them taste the punishment of disgrace in the life of this world, while the punishment of the Hereafter is more humiliating. And they will not be helped (to evade it).

17. As for the (tribe of) Thamūd: We showed them (the straight path of) guidance but they preferred blindness over guidance. So

then the lightning-like punishment of humiliation seized them because of what they had been earning for themselves.

18. And We saved those who believed and who, in awe of God and reverence for Him, habitually avoided sin.

19. And (remind of) the day when the enemies of God will be raised up (from their graves) and gathered for the Fire: they will be driven (to the place of reckoning) in arrays,

20. Until when they reach it, their ears, and their eyes, and their skins will bear witness against them as to all that they did habitually.

---

4. For an explanation, see *sūrah* 15: 16–18, note 5; *sūrah* 37: 6–7, note 3; and *sūrah* 67: 5, note 4.

5. For the creation of the heavens and the earth, and the meaning of seven heavens, see 2: 29, note 28.

478

٤٧٨

وَقَالُوا لِجُلُودِهِمْ لِمَ شَهِدتُّمْ عَلَيْنَا قَالُوا أَنطَقَنَا اللَّهُ الَّذِى
أَنطَقَ كُلَّ شَيْءٍ وَهُوَ خَلَقَكُمْ أَوَّلَ مَرَّةٍ وَإِلَيْهِ تُرْجَعُونَ ۞
وَمَا كُنتُمْ تَسْتَتِرُونَ أَن يَشْهَدَ عَلَيْكُمْ سَمْعُكُمْ وَلَا
أَبْصَارُكُمْ وَلَا جُلُودُكُمْ وَلَٰكِن ظَنَنتُمْ أَنَّ اللَّهَ لَا يَعْلَمُ
كَثِيرًا مِّمَّا تَعْمَلُونَ ۞ وَذَٰلِكُمْ ظَنُّكُمُ الَّذِى ظَنَنتُم بِرَبِّكُمْ
أَرْدَىٰكُمْ فَأَصْبَحْتُم مِّنَ الْخَاسِرِينَ ۞ فَإِن يَصْبِرُوا فَالنَّارُ مَثْوًى
لَّهُمْ وَإِن يَسْتَعْتِبُوا فَمَا هُم مِّنَ الْمُعْتَبِينَ ۞ وَقَيَّضْنَا لَهُمْ قُرَنَآءَ
فَزَيَّنُوا لَهُم مَّا بَيْنَ أَيْدِيهِمْ وَمَا خَلْفَهُمْ وَحَقَّ عَلَيْهِمُ الْقَوْلُ فِى
أُمَمٍ قَدْ خَلَتْ مِن قَبْلِهِم مِّنَ الْجِنِّ وَالْإِنسِ إِنَّهُمْ كَانُوا خَاسِرِينَ ۞
وَقَالَ الَّذِينَ كَفَرُوا لَا تَسْمَعُوا لِهَٰذَا الْقُرْآنِ وَالْغَوْا فِيهِ لَعَلَّكُمْ
تَغْلِبُونَ ۞ فَلَنُذِيقَنَّ الَّذِينَ كَفَرُوا عَذَابًا شَدِيدًا وَلَنَجْزِيَنَّهُمْ
أَسْوَأَ الَّذِى كَانُوا يَعْمَلُونَ ۞ ذَٰلِكَ جَزَآءُ أَعْدَآءِ اللَّهِ النَّارُ
لَهُمْ فِيهَا دَارُ الْخُلْدِ جَزَآءً بِمَا كَانُوا بِآيَاتِنَا يَجْحَدُونَ ۞
وَقَالَ الَّذِينَ كَفَرُوا رَبَّنَا أَرِنَا الَّذَيْنِ أَضَلَّانَا مِنَ الْجِنِّ
وَالْإِنسِ نَجْعَلْهُمَا تَحْتَ أَقْدَامِنَا لِيَكُونَا مِنَ الْأَسْفَلِينَ ۞

————❦————

saved from it, or do not ask), still they are not of those who will be shown favor (and saved).

25. (In return for their preferring unbelief and sinfulness over belief and piety) We have assigned them comrades (of satanic disposition, not right-minded) who deck out their past (deeds) and their present (intentions) to be appealing to them. And the word (the sentence of punishment passed) on the communities of the jinn and humankind before them (who were self-righteous in the same way) has also been their due. Surely they are the losers.

26. Those who disbelieve say: "Do not listen to this Qur'ān, and speak random noise (during its recitation) so that you may prevail over it."

27. But We will certainly make those who disbelieve taste a severe punishment, and certainly recompense them for the worst of what they keep doing.[8]

28. That is the recompense of God's enemies – the Fire. Therein they will have the everlasting abode, as a deserving recompense for rejecting Our signs and Revelations obstinately.

29. Those who disbelieve will say (as they enter the Fire): "Our Lord! Show us those of both the jinn and humankind that led us astray, that we may trample them underfoot and they will be of the most humiliated!"

21. They will ask their skins, "Why have you borne witness against us?" They will answer: "God Who makes everything speak has made us speak."[6] It is He Who has created you in the first instance, and to Him you are being brought back.

22. You did not seek to veil yourselves (when sinning) without ever considering that your ears or your eyes or your skins would one day bear witness against you. Moreover, you supposed that God did not know most of what you did habitually.[7]

23. It is that supposition of yours which you entertained about your Lord that has tumbled you down into perdition, and so you have come to be among the losers.

24. If they endure it (or do not endure it), still the Fire will be an everlasting dwelling for them. If they ask for favor (to be

6. As pointed out in the verse *The abode of the Hereafter is truly alive* (29: 64), and as explained in note 4 to 25: 12, the Qur'ān states that everything in the Abode of Hereafter will be alive. So every part of a human being will bear witness for or against them. The restriction of testifying to the skin in verse 21 is because the skin is the boundary between a living creature and the world around it, it is also the physical interface between the creature and other creatures and the world. Hence it is the location of all contact, good or bad in kind. If, as here implied, it is also the medium where all such contact is recorded (we know in this life only the extremes of contact that leave scars on the skin), then the skin is an ideal witness.

7. Saying *you thought that God did not know* most of what *you used to do*, instead of *you supposed that God did not know* whatever *you used to do*, means that they believed in God as the Supreme Being with knowledge, but they acted recklessly as if they did not accept that God had no knowledge of most of what they used to do or that they did not really believe in the all-encompassing nature of God's Knowledge.

8. The worst of what the unbelievers do is certainly unbelief, so first of all, God will punish them for unbelief. The verse aims to strongly discourage the unbelievers.

٤٧٩   479

إِنَّ الَّذِينَ قَالُوا رَبُّنَا اللّٰهُ ثُمَّ اسْتَقَامُوا تَتَنَزَّلُ عَلَيْهِمُ الْمَلَٰئِكَةُ أَلَّا تَخَافُوا وَلَا تَحْزَنُوا وَأَبْشِرُوا بِالْجَنَّةِ الَّتِي كُنتُمْ تُوعَدُونَ ۝ نَحْنُ أَوْلِيَآؤُكُمْ فِي الْحَيَوٰةِ الدُّنْيَا وَفِي الْأَخِرَةِ وَلَكُمْ فِيهَا مَا تَشْتَهِىٓ أَنفُسُكُمْ وَلَكُمْ فِيهَا مَا تَدَّعُونَ ۝ نُزُلًا مِّنْ غَفُورٍ رَّحِيمٍ ۝ وَمَنْ أَحْسَنُ قَوْلًا مِّمَّن دَعَآ إِلَى اللّٰهِ وَعَمِلَ صَالِحًا وَقَالَ إِنَّنِى مِنَ الْمُسْلِمِينَ ۝ وَلَا تَسْتَوِى الْحَسَنَةُ وَلَا السَّيِّئَةُ ادْفَعْ بِالَّتِى هِىَ أَحْسَنُ فَإِذَا الَّذِى بَيْنَكَ وَبَيْنَهُ عَدَاوَةٌ كَأَنَّهُ وَلِىٌّ حَمِيمٌ ۝ وَمَا يُلَقَّاهَآ إِلَّا الَّذِينَ صَبَرُوا وَمَا يُلَقَّاهَآ إِلَّا ذُو حَظٍّ عَظِيمٍ ۝ وَإِمَّا يَنزَغَنَّكَ مِنَ الشَّيْطَانِ نَزْغٌ فَاسْتَعِذْ بِاللّٰهِ إِنَّهُ هُوَ السَّمِيعُ الْعَلِيمُ ۝ وَمِنْ آيَاتِهِ الَّيْلُ وَالنَّهَارُ وَالشَّمْسُ وَالْقَمَرُ لَا تَسْجُدُوا لِلشَّمْسِ وَلَا لِلْقَمَرِ وَاسْجُدُوا لِلّٰهِ الَّذِى خَلَقَهُنَّ إِن كُنتُمْ إِيَّاهُ تَعْبُدُونَ ۝ فَإِنِ اسْتَكْبَرُوا فَالَّذِينَ عِندَ رَبِّكَ يُسَبِّحُونَ لَهُۥ بِالَّيْلِ وَالنَّهَارِ وَهُمْ لَا يَسْـَٔمُونَ ۝

———⌖———

30. As for those who say, "Our Lord is God," and then follow the Straight Path (in their belief, thought, and actions) without deviation, the angels descend upon them from time to time (in the world as protecting comrades and in the Hereafter, with the message): "Do not fear or grieve, but rejoice in the glad tidings of Paradise which you have been promised.

31. "We are your well-wishing comrades and helpers in the Hereafter, as we have been in the life of the world. You will have therein all that your souls desire, and you will have therein all that you ask for.

32. "A welcoming gift from the One All-Forgiving, All-Compassionate."[9]

33. Who is better in speech than one who calls to God and does good, righteous deeds, and says: "Surely I am of the Muslims (wholly submitted to Him)?"

34. Goodness and evil can never be equal. Repel evil with what is better (or best).[10] Then see: the one between whom and you there was enmity has become a bosom friend.

35. And none are ever enabled to attain to it (such great virtue) save those who are patient (in adversities and against the temptations of their souls and Satan), and none are ever enabled to attain to it save those who have a great part in human perfections and virtues.

36. And if a prompting from Satan should stir in you (when carrying out your mission or during worship or in your daily life), seek refuge in God immediately. He is the One Who is the All-Hearing, the All-Knowing.

37. And the night and the day, and the sun and the moon (all the phenomena and objects you see in the universe) are among His signs (guiding to His absolute Oneness). Do not prostrate in adoration of the sun or the moon, but prostrate in adoration of God, Who has created them, if indeed it is Him that you worship.

38. If they are too arrogant (to worship Him alone), it is a fact that those who are in the Presence of your Lord (the angels and His sincere servants among humankind and the jinn), glorify Him alone by night and day and are tireless (therein).

---

9. Since Paradise is a place of absolute purity and those who will enter it will enter fully purified, Paradise will be full of pure blessings with which its residents will be totally content.

10. That is, repel falsehood with the truth; do not give harm in return for harm, and follow the right way and take the right means to attain a right goal. This is a basic principle of Islamic conduct and of preaching Islam. In addition, a Muslim individual is expected to forgive what has been done to them individually and to respond with what is the best in conduct.

39. And among His signs is this: you see the earth lying low and barren; but when We send down water upon it, it stirs and swells (with life). He Who revives it is certainly the One Who will bring the dead to life. Surely He has full power over everything.

40. Surely those who deviate from the right way concerning Our signs (in nature and life) and Revelations[11] are not hidden from Us. Who is in better state – the one who is thrown into the Fire or the one who comes secure on the Day of Resurrection? Do what you will, surely He sees well all that you do.

41. Those who disbelieve in this Reminder (the Qur'ān) when it comes to them (are among those who will be thrown into the Fire). For it is surely a glorious, unconquerable Book.

42. Falsehood can never have access to it, whether from before it or from behind it (whether by arguments and attitudes based on modern philosophies or by attacks from the past based on earlier Scriptures;[12] (it is) the Book being sent down in parts from the One All-Wise, All-Praiseworthy (to Whom all praise and gratitude belong).

43. What is said to you (O Messenger) is but that which was said (by the unbelievers) to the Messengers before you. Your Lord is indeed One Who disposes forgiveness, and Who disposes painful retribution.

44. If We had made it a Qur'ān in a foreign tongue, they (who now reject it) would certainly have said: "If only its communications had been spelled out distinctly and made clear! Why a foreign tongue, and an Arab (to speak it to Arabs)?" Say: "(It is not a Book whose power or purpose is confined by language.) For those who believe, it is a guidance and healing (for their hearts and minds, and all their senses). But as for those who do not believe, in their ears is

heaviness, and it is imperceptible to them. They are (like people who are being) called from far off (so the call does not reach their hearing and sight).

45. Assuredly We granted Moses the Book, and discordant views arose about it (just as your people, O Messenger, say different things concerning the Book We are revealing to you). Had it not been for a decree already issued by your Lord (postponing the final, decisive judgment until an appointed term), it would indeed have been judged between them.[13] They are (nevertheless) in doubting uncertainty about it (about the Qur'ān and their attitude to it).

46. Whoever does good, righteous deeds, it is for his own soul's good, and whoever does evil, it is to its harm. Your Lord never does the least wrong to His servants.

11. Deviation from the right way concerning God's signs in nature and life can occur in many ways. For example, making any of these signs, the sun, the moon, the stars, or any human being or the jinn – an object of worship, or using them as the means of denying God as the Creator and Ruler of them, as the modern materialistic scientific approach does, are two such ways. Deviation concerning the Revelations or the Divine Scriptures can also occur in numerous ways. Some of these ways are by distorting their meaning, misusing them for worldly benefits, making alterations in them, interpreting them arbitrarily without being based on sound knowledge.

12. If you look at the Qur'ān from a sound heart, you will see that its six sides are so brilliant and transparent that no darkness and misguidance, doubt and suspicion, or decep-

tion can penetrate it. Nor is there a fissure through which such things could infiltrate into the sphere of its purity. Above it is the stamp of miraculousness, beneath it proof and evidence, behind it its point of support – pure Divine Revelation, before it happiness in this world and the next, on its right questioning human reason about its truth and ensuring its confirmation, and on its left calling the human conscience to testify to its truth and securing its submission. Inside the Qur'ān is the pure guidance of the All-Merciful One, and outside is the light of faith. (See *The Words*, "the 22nd Word," 321.)

13. The decree in question is that which is found in 2: 36, and 7: 24: *There shall be for you on the earth (where you have already been appointed as vicegerent) a habitation and provision until an appointed time.*

٤٨١

481

إِلَيْهِ يُرَدُّ عِلْمُ السَّاعَةِ وَمَا تَخْرُجُ مِن ثَمَرَاتٍ مِّنْ أَكْمَامِهَا وَمَا تَحْمِلُ مِنْ أُنثَى وَلَا تَضَعُ إِلَّا بِعِلْمِهِ وَيَوْمَ يُنَادِيهِمْ أَيْنَ شُرَكَآءِي قَالُوٓا۟ آذَنَّاكَ مَا مِنَّا مِن شَهِيدٍ ۝ وَضَلَّ عَنْهُم مَّا كَانُوا۟ يَدْعُونَ مِن قَبْلُ وَظَنُّوا۟ مَا لَهُم مِّن مَّحِيصٍ ۝ لَّا يَسْـَٔمُ الْإِنسَانُ مِن دُعَآءِ الْخَيْرِ وَإِن مَّسَّهُ الشَّرُّ فَيَـُٔوسٌ قَنُوطٌ ۝ وَلَئِنْ أَذَقْنَاهُ رَحْمَةً مِّنَّا مِنۢ بَعْدِ ضَرَّآءَ مَسَّتْهُ لَيَقُولَنَّ هَٰذَا لِي وَمَآ أَظُنُّ السَّاعَةَ قَآئِمَةً وَلَئِن رُّجِعْتُ إِلَىٰ رَبِّي إِنَّ لِي عِندَهُ لَلْحُسْنَىٰ فَلَنُنَبِّئَنَّ الَّذِينَ كَفَرُوا۟ بِمَا عَمِلُوا۟ وَلَنُذِيقَنَّهُم مِّنْ عَذَابٍ غَلِيظٍ ۝ وَإِذَآ أَنْعَمْنَا عَلَى الْإِنسَانِ أَعْرَضَ وَنَـَٔا بِجَانِبِهِ وَإِذَا مَسَّهُ الشَّرُّ فَذُو دُعَآءٍ عَرِيضٍ ۝ قُلْ أَرَءَيْتُمْ إِن كَانَ مِنْ عِندِ اللَّهِ ثُمَّ كَفَرْتُم بِهِ مَنْ أَضَلُّ مِمَّنْ هُوَ فِي شِقَاقٍ بَعِيدٍ ۝ سَنُرِيهِمْ آيَاتِنَا فِي الْآفَاقِ وَفِي أَنفُسِهِمْ حَتَّىٰ يَتَبَيَّنَ لَهُمْ أَنَّهُ الْحَقُّ أَوَلَمْ يَكْفِ بِرَبِّكَ أَنَّهُ عَلَىٰ كُلِّ شَيْءٍ شَهِيدٌ ۝ أَلَآ إِنَّهُمْ فِي مِرْيَةٍ مِّن لِّقَآءِ رَبِّهِمْ أَلَآ إِنَّهُ بِكُلِّ شَيْءٍ مُّحِيطٌ ۝

47. To Him alone is referred the knowledge of the Last Hour. And no fruits emerge from their sheaths, and no female conceives or gives birth, but with His Knowledge. And on the Day He will call out to them: "Where now are those (you alleged and proclaimed as) partners to Me?" They will surely say: "We proclaim to You that there is none among us who can testify (to that false claim)."

48. And those whom (they made as deities and) invoked before will surely fail them; so they will know for certain that there is no escape for them.

49. Human never tires of asking for (what he presumes is) his own good, but if evil befalls him, then he gives up all hope and loses heart.[14]

50. And assuredly if We (by Our grace) let him taste a mercy from Us after a hardship that has visited him, he certainly says: "This is but my due (and I can dispose it as I please), and I do not consider that the Last Hour will ever come (so that I should be called to account for it). Even if (it should come, and) I should be brought back to my Lord, I will surely find with Him the best (because I judge myself to always be deserving what is the best)." Without doubt We will make those who disbelieve understand all that they do (and call them to account), and without doubt We will make them taste a harsh punishment.

51. When We bestow favors upon human, he retreats and draws aside (from his Lord), and when evil befalls him, then he has recourse to long supplications.

52. Say: "Tell me if it (the Qur'ān) is from God and after (knowing that) you have disbelieved in it, then who is more astray than one who is in wide schism (separating himself from the truth)?"

53. We will show them Our manifest signs (proofs) in the horizons of the universe and within their own selves, until it will become manifest to them that it (the Qur'ān) is indeed the truth.[15] Is it not sufficient (as proof) that your Lord is a witness over all things (just as He is witnessed to by all things)?[16]

54. Beware! They are in (willful) doubt about the meeting with God (because they vainly expect to escape accounting for their deeds, and therefore decline to believe in the Qur'ān). Beware! He is One Who encompasses all things (in His Knowledge and Power).

14. This is typical of one who does not believe in God as the Creator of all good and evil, and in Divine Destiny. Since such a person concentrates on the worldly life in pursuit of its enjoyments and attributes everything to their own knowledge and abilities according to the "law" of cause and effect, when they feel that there is no longer any means to attain something, they become utterly desperate. Whereas a believer never loses hope because they believe that it is God Who also creates the means to attain something and He can always create new means when one fails. A believer also knows for certain that God is the Creator of all things, including good and evil, and that evil is an outcome of their own choice. So when they cannot attain something, they either think that they have made a mistake in trying to attain it or that God does not will them to have it because it is not good for them to attain it.

15. This sentence has several implications, such as follows:

* The polytheists of Makkah will certainly witness that the tidings of the Qur'ān and the Messenger for the future will prove true. Also, all other future events will establish the truth of the Qur'ān and the call of the Messenger, so that the Makkan unbelievers will confess it.

* The developments of "natural" sciences and the sciences that study human physiology will prove the essentials of Islamic faith, especially God's Existence and Oneness. So almost all human beings will have to confess the truth of the Qur'ān and the Messengership of the Prophet Muḥammad, upon him be peace and blessings.

* In addition to sciences, future history, worldwide, will clearly show that the Qur'ān is the truth, and the promise stated in 24: 55 will prove to be true for the believers toward the end of time, as it proved for the believers during the Messenger's time.

16. That is, God sees, hears and is aware of all things and events. He is also witnessed by all things and events as their Sole Creator, Deity, Lord (Sustainer, Protector), Provider, and Sovereign. In every thing and event there are manifest signs pointing to Him with His Names and Attributes. For one whose heart is not dead or sealed, whose eyes are not blinded, and whose ears are not deafened to the truth because of prejudices, sins, wrongdoing, and arrogance, He is more manifest than anything else.

SŪRAH 42

ASH-SHŪRĀ (CONSULTATION)

Makkah period

Revealed in Makkah, this *sūrah* of 53 verses derives its name from the word "consultation" in verse 38. Consultation is one of the most important principles of Islamic social life. This *sūrah* concentrates on Revelation and the fact that all the Messengers came with and preached the same truths. It warns those who resist against them and gives glad tidings to the believers.

In the Name of God, the All-Merciful, the All-Compassionate.

1. Ḥā. Mīm.

2. 'Ayn. Sīn. Qāf.

3. Just so: He reveals to you as (He did) to those (whom He chose as Messengers) before you, (being as He is) God, the All-Glorious with irresistible might, the All-Wise.

4. His is whatever is in the heavens and whatever is on the earth. And He is the All-Exalted, the Supreme.

5. The heavens are all but rent asunder from above them (because of the majesty of Revelation); and the angels glorify their Lord with His praise, and pray for (His establishing a way of guidance for) those on the earth and for forgiveness (of those who follow it). Beware, surely God is He Who is the All-Forgiving, the All-Compassionate.[1]

6. As for those who take for themselves others besides God for guardians and confidants, (to whom they entrust their affairs, thereby associating partners with Him): God is ever watchful over them, (preserving a record of their deeds). You are not a

guardian over them (responsible for their conduct).

7. And just so: (as We revealed these truths to the Messengers before you) We reveal to you a Qur'ān (a Recitation) in Arabic so that you may warn the mother-city and all those around it,[2] and warn of the Day of Assembly, about (the coming of) which there is no doubt. One party will be in Paradise, and one party in the Blaze.[3]

8. If God had so willed, He would surely have made them a single community (of the same faith and way of life), but He admits whom He wills into His Mercy. As for the wrongdoers, they have neither a guardian (to protect them), nor a helper.[4]

9. What? Have they taken for themselves others beside God for guardians and confidants (to whom they entrust their affairs,

thereby associating partners with Him)? Rather, God is He Who is the true Guardian, and He will revive the dead, and He has full power over everything.

10. "Whatever you differ on, the final judgment about it is with God. Such is God, my Lord: in Him I put my trust, and to Him I turn in devotion:

---

1. These initial verses concern the Revelation. As a term, it means God's communication of His Messages to His Prophets and Messengers in a special way, the exact nature of which we cannot know. As will be mentioned in verse 51 in this *sūrah* and as was explained before in *sūrah* 20, note 5, Revelation takes place in three ways. God speaks or communicates a message to a Prophet either from behind a veil, or by putting the meaning in the heart of the Prophet (as a special kind of Revelation), or by sending an angel. A Prophet is sure that the one who speaks to him from behind a veil or puts a meaning in his heart is God.

It is because of the weight and majesty of Revelation that the heavens are nearly rent asunder from above while it is being conveyed to the Prophet. Their being nearly rent asunder from above implies that Revelation issues from the "realm" that is more sublime or higher; there are paths along which God's Revelation is carried, along which the angels move, and the acts of conscious beings ascend to God (23: 17). The sublimity and height are, of course, not of a material or physical kind. And as explained in *sūrah* 37: 1-3, note 1, some other angels accompanied Archangel Gabriel, who brought the Qur'ān gradually to God's Messenger, upon him be peace and blessings. Those angels aligned themselves in ranks along the way of Gabriel, upon him be peace, and drove away the devils that tried to grasp something of the Revelation. Some from among them, as the aides of Gabriel, brought

Revelations to the Messenger that was not of the Qur'ān. Muslim scholars call the Revelations that constitute the Qur'ān "the Revelation recited." The Revelations which they call "the Revelation not recited" and are not included in the Qur'ān, came either to explain the Qur'ān or to lay new commandments and guide the Messenger and the believers in emerging matters. The Sunnah as the verbal declarations, acts, and confirmations of God's Messenger is based on these Revelations. The Messenger says: "Beware! I have been given the Book and its like together with it" (Abū Dāwūd, "Sunnah," 5).

2. God's Messenger, upon him be peace and blessings, was ordered to begin his mission with his nearest relatives (26: 214), and then to warn all the Makkan people (in this verse) and all the Arab people (in this verse and 41: 3,) and then all conscious beings (all humankind and the jinn) (38: 87; 21: 107).

3. The second part of the verse is of the same import as verses 103 and 105 in *Sūrah Hūd*: *That is a day when all humankind will be gathered together.... Among those (gathered together) some are wretched and some happy.*

4. For an explanation, see: 5: 48, note 11. In addition, God admits into His Mercy (owns and protects them, especially from eternal punishment) those who are not wrongdoers. As for the wrongdoers (those who deny God or associate partners with Him and commit injustices in life), He excludes them from His Mercy.

11. The Originator of the heavens and the earth (each with particular features and on ordered principles); He has made for you, from your selves, mates, and from the cattle mates (of their own kind): by this means He multiplies you (and the cattle). There is nothing whatever like Him.[5] He is the All-Hearing, the All-Seeing.

12. His are the keys of (the treasures of) the heavens and the earth. He enlarges provision for whom He wills, and straitens it (for whom He wills). Surely He has full knowledge of everything.

13. Of the Religion (that He made for humankind and revealed through His Messengers throughout history), He has laid down for you as way of life what He willed to Noah, and that which We reveal to you, and what We willed to Abraham, and Moses, and Jesus, (commanding): "Establish the Religion and do not divide into opposing groups concerning it."[6] What you call people to is hard and distressful for those who associate partners with God. God chooses whom He wills and brings them together (in faith and in obedience) to Himself, and He guides to Himself whoever turns to Him in devotion.

14. And they (who follow the previous ways) were not divided (into opposing groups) until after the knowledge came to them (of the way they must follow and what that entailed, and only) because of envious rivalry and insolence among themselves. Had it not been for a decree already issued by your Lord, (granting people respite and postponing the final, decisive judgment) until an appointed term, it would indeed have been judged between them. Surely those who (succeeded those

opposing groups and) inherited the Book, are in doubting uncertainty about it.[7]

15. So (O Messenger) call people to that (the way of life God has laid down for you). Pursue what is exactly right (in every matter) as you are commanded (by God). Do not follow their lusts and fancies (who follow other ways, including the followers of the previous Scriptures), and say: "I believe in whatever Book God has sent down; and I am commanded to bring about equity among you (without discrimination of race or rank by birth or by wealth or by power). God is our Lord and your Lord. To us are accounted our deeds, and to you, your deeds: (let there be) no contention between us and you: God will bring us all together (and settle any difference between us and you). To Him is the homecoming."[8]

5. This short statement emphasizes that God is not of the same kind as those who have been created, and therefore He is beyond all human concepts of Him. So He has no mates, nothing is like Him, nor does He beget nor is He begotten. Nothing – neither matter, nor space, nor time – can restrict or contain Him. And this is why His Attributes – His Hearing, Seeing, Knowledge, Will, Power, Creating, and so on – are also beyond anything we can conceive.

6. This verse has many implications, such as the following:

- The religion God has made and appointed for humankind during history is one and the same. It has the same essentials of faith, worship, conduct, and morality.

- Among the Prophets God chose some as Messengers and among the Messengers He chose five as being of a particular degree: Noah, Abraham, Moses, Jesus, and Muḥammad, upon them all be peace and blessings. He established for each principles of conduct in life, in addition to the pillars of faith, worship, and morality. These principles, which form a way of life (Law), are the same in essence, though there are some differences among them in secondary matters, as we can understand from verse 5: 48 (see that verse and the corresponding note 11). When the Last Messenger, upon him be peace and blessings, came, his Law encompassed all the previous Laws with certain changes (in regard to how the Islamic Law treated the previous ones, see 2: 106, note 95).

- In Islamic terminology, the Law is *Sharī'ah* and it is used for the practical aspect of the Religion.

- The verse uses the word *will* for the Laws ordained for Noah, Abraham, Moses, and Jesus, but the verb *reveal* for the Last Messenger. *Will* implies strong advice and giving special importance to certain things. So concerning the way of life willed to Noah, Abraham, Moses, and Jesus, some matters had special importance according to the time and conditions particular to each. However, the use of *reveal* for the way of life enjoined on the Last Messenger implies that all aspects of it – including those which exist in the Qur'ān and those established by the Sunnah of the Messenger – were revealed by God and are of universal importance.

- The verse first mentions the Prophet Noah and continues to talk about the Last Messenger and then the other great Messengers. This is because the Prophet Noah is the first Messenger to whom a comprehensive Law to govern life was willed, and the Last Messenger is the greatest of all and the way of life revealed to him is universal and inclusive of all the previous ones. We see a similar order in 33: 7: *And (remember) when We took from the Prophets their covenant, and from you (O Muḥammad), and from Noah, Abraham, Moses, and Jesus the son of Mary. We took from them a solemn covenant*. This verse first mentions all the Prophets, particularly mentioning the five greatest among them beginning with the last one, due to his being the greatest among them and also because God's Religion gained universality with him.

- Preserving and obeying the Law is indispensable for establishing the Religion and preserving it from distortions, changes, and corruptions. The Law has the same meaning for the Religion as the skin has for the human body. The main reason why the Religion lost its originality and purity after the Prophets Noah, Abraham, Moses, and Jesus is that people either ignored or neglected the Law, or changed it, or disobeyed it. Negligence of or disobedience to the Law is also one of the basic reasons for the internal divisions among the communities of the Messengers after them and for the deviations witnessed concerning the essentials of faith.

7. This verse mainly concerns the People of the Book, the followers of Moses and Jesus, upon them be peace. Their being in doubt about their Book means that some of them are really in doubt about its being a Divine Book and/or about some passages being really from God, while some others doubt whether it has been preserved and transmitted to them in its originality, and still others have other uncertainties about it. For the decree already issued by God, see *sūrah* 2: 36; *sūrah* 7: 24.

8. This verse is of similar import to verse 3: 64: *Say (to them, O Messenger): "O People of the Book, come to a word common between us and you, that we worship none but God, and associate none as partner with Him, and that none of us take others for Lords, apart from God." If they (still) turn away, then say: "Bear witness that we are Muslims (submitted to Him exclusively)."* See the corresponding note 12.

16. And as for those who contend about God (defying His Lordship or struggling against His Religion) after His call has been accepted (and His Religion recognized as true), their contention is void in their Lord's sight, and (His) wrath (condemnation) is upon them, and for them is a severe punishment.

17. God is He Who has sent down the Book with truth and the Balance, (setting out the truth and what is right in all matters). And for all you know, the Last Hour may well be near.

18. Those who do not believe in it (derisively) ask it to be hastened; whereas those who believe hold it in awe, and know that it is true (certain to come). Be aware! those who dispute concerning the Last Hour have indeed gone far astray.

19. God is All-Gracious to His servants. He grants provision to whom He wills (in the manner and degree that He wills); and He is the All-Strong, the All-Glorious with irresistible might.

20. Whoever desires (and strives to gain) the harvest of the Hereafter, We increase him in his harvest; and whoever desires the harvest of the world, We grant him out of that, and he has no portion in the Hereafter.[9]

21. Or do they have partners with God who have prescribed for them in the Religion what God has not allowed (and so they judge and act however they wish)? Had it not been for a decree (already issued by God, postponing the final, decisive judgment) between people, it would

indeed have been judged between them. Surely for the wrongdoers there is a painful punishment.

22. You will see the wrongdoers (who presume to lay down a way of life in the name of religion other than God's) full of fear on account of what they have earned, and it will inevitably befall them. As for those who believe and do good, righteous deeds, they will be in the luxuriant meadows of the Gardens. They will have whatever they wish prepared in God's Presence. That indeed is the great favor.

---

9. The last two verses explain two important principles in the provision of living beings. The one is that God creates all living beings and determines their needs and the way in which they are provided for. The other is that He gives those who aim at the Hereafter more than they deserve, but gives those who aim at the world some amount of the worldly provision with no portion at all in the Hereafter. This implies that it is not possible for one who is greedy for worldly provisions to obtain everything in the world and feel content with it. So one should not aim for the world, but rather focus on the harvest of the Hereafter, while not neglecting working for one's livelihood (see 28: 77, note 16).

23. That it is of which God gives the glad tidings to His servants who believe and do good, righteous deeds. Say: "I ask of you no wage for it (for conveying God's Religion to you which will bring you this favor), but (I ask of you for) love for my near relatives (on account of my mission)."[10] Whoever scores a good deed, We increase him in good in respect of it. Surely God is All-Forgiving, All-Responsive (to gratitude).

24. What? Do they say that he (the Messenger) has fabricated a falsehood in attribution to God? If He so wills, He can seal up your heart (so you would not be able to recite to them anything of Revelation. But what you convey to them is the Revelations from Us.) And God blots out falsehood and affirms the truth to be true by His decrees. Surely, God has full knowledge of what lies hidden in the bosoms.

25. He is the One Who accepts repentance from His servants and excuses evil deeds, and He knows all that you do.

26. He responds with acceptance to (the worship and supplication of) those who believe and do good, righteous deeds, and grants them more out of His bounty (than they asked for). However, as to the unbelievers, for them is a severe punishment.

27. If God were always to provide for (all of) His servants in great abundance, they would certainly have transgressed all bounds on the earth, but He sends it down in due measure as He wills. Surely He is fully aware of His servants, and sees them well.

28. He it is Who sends down the rain useful in all ways to rescue (them) after they have lost all hope, and spreads out His mercy far and wide (to every being). He it is Who is the Guardian, and the All-Praiseworthy.

29. Among His manifest signs is the creation of the heavens and the earth, and that He has dispersed in both of them living creatures. And He has full power to gather them together when He wills.[11]

30. Whatever affliction befalls you, it is because of what your hands have earned,[12] and yet He overlooks many (of the wrongs you do). .

31. You cannot frustrate in the earth (God's will). You have, apart from God, neither a guardian (to whom you can entrust your affairs) nor a helper.

10. All love is essentially for God, and all other loves should be on account of Him, and even love for the Messenger is essentially on account of God. Otherwise love for any other being, without considering God or that being's relationship with God, may lead to perdition, like the love of the Christians for Jesus, which has caused them to deify him, and the love of many Shi'ites for 'Ali, which has led many of them to disparage the majority of other Companions. The reason why God's Messenger asked his community to love his near relatives, including his household in particular ('Ali, Fāṭimah, Ḥasan, and Ḥusayn – his grandsons from Fāṭimah and 'Ali) was because of the great service they and their descendants would provide for Islam until the Judgment Day.

11. According to many classical interpreters of the Qur'ān, such as Mujāhid, and contemporary interpreters, such as Fethullah Gülen, it is more appropriate to understand from this verse that there are corporeal, even conscious creatures like those on the earth in some other parts of the heavens. In the future, humankind may travel as far as those parts, and at any point of the heavens or on the earth they may meet up with those creatures.

12. In principle, everyone gets what they deserve. However, an affliction that befalls a believer because of their sins or faults causes, if the believer repents, that sin to be forgiven and a new door to a new reward to be opened. However, those who suffered the greatest sufferings have been the Prophets and their true successors in serving God's cause. The afflictions befalling sinless people cause them to be continuously promoted to higher and higher ranks.

486   سورة الشورى   ٤٨٦

وَمِنْ ءَايَٰتِهِ ٱلْجَوَارِ فِى ٱلْبَحْرِ كَٱلْأَعْلَٰمِ ۞ إِن يَشَأْ يُسْكِنِ ٱلرِّيحَ فَيَظْلَلْنَ رَوَاكِدَ عَلَىٰ ظَهْرِهِۦٓ إِنَّ فِى ذَٰلِكَ لَءَايَٰتٍ لِّكُلِّ صَبَّارٍ شَكُورٍ ۞ أَوْ يُوبِقْهُنَّ بِمَا كَسَبُواْ وَيَعْفُ عَن كَثِيرٍ ۞ وَيَعْلَمَ ٱلَّذِينَ يُجَٰدِلُونَ فِىٓ ءَايَٰتِنَا مَا لَهُم مِّن مَّحِيصٍ ۞ فَمَآ أُوتِيتُم مِّن شَىْءٍ فَمَتَٰعُ ٱلْحَيَوٰةِ ٱلدُّنْيَا وَمَا عِندَ ٱللَّهِ خَيْرٌ وَأَبْقَىٰ لِلَّذِينَ ءَامَنُواْ وَعَلَىٰ رَبِّهِمْ يَتَوَكَّلُونَ ۞ وَٱلَّذِينَ يَجْتَنِبُونَ كَبَٰٓئِرَ ٱلْإِثْمِ وَٱلْفَوَٰحِشَ وَإِذَا مَا غَضِبُواْ هُمْ يَغْفِرُونَ ۞ وَٱلَّذِينَ ٱسْتَجَابُواْ لِرَبِّهِمْ وَأَقَامُواْ ٱلصَّلَوٰةَ وَأَمْرُهُمْ شُورَىٰ بَيْنَهُمْ وَمِمَّا رَزَقْنَٰهُمْ يُنفِقُونَ ۞ وَٱلَّذِينَ إِذَآ أَصَابَهُمُ ٱلْبَغْىُ هُمْ يَنتَصِرُونَ ۞ وَجَزَٰٓؤُاْ سَيِّئَةٍ سَيِّئَةٌ مِّثْلُهَا فَمَنْ عَفَا وَأَصْلَحَ فَأَجْرُهُۥ عَلَى ٱللَّهِ إِنَّهُۥ لَا يُحِبُّ ٱلظَّٰلِمِينَ ۞ وَلَمَنِ ٱنتَصَرَ بَعْدَ ظُلْمِهِۦ فَأُوْلَٰٓئِكَ مَا عَلَيْهِم مِّن سَبِيلٍ ۞ إِنَّمَا ٱلسَّبِيلُ عَلَى ٱلَّذِينَ يَظْلِمُونَ ٱلنَّاسَ وَيَبْغُونَ فِى ٱلْأَرْضِ بِغَيْرِ ٱلْحَقِّ أُوْلَٰٓئِكَ لَهُمْ عَذَابٌ أَلِيمٌ ۞ وَلَمَن صَبَرَ وَغَفَرَ إِنَّ ذَٰلِكَ لَمِنْ عَزْمِ ٱلْأُمُورِ ۞ وَمَن يُضْلِلِ ٱللَّهُ فَمَا لَهُۥ مِن وَلِىٍّ مِّنۢ بَعْدِهِۦ وَتَرَى ٱلظَّٰلِمِينَ لَمَّا رَأَوُاْ ٱلْعَذَابَ يَقُولُونَ هَلْ إِلَىٰ مَرَدٍّ مِّن سَبِيلٍ ۞

enduring for those who believe and put their trust in their Lord;

37. Those who avoid the major sins and indecent, shameful deeds (which are indeed to be counted among major sins),[14] and when they become angry, even then they forgive (rather than retaliate in kind).

38. And those who answer the call of their Lord and obey Him (in His orders and prohibitions), and establish the Prayer in conformity with its conditions; and whose affairs are by consultation among themselves;[15] and who spend out of what We provide for them (to provide sustenance for the needy, and in God's cause);

39. And those who, when an unjust aggression is inflicted on (any or all of) them, defend themselves and one another (to end the aggression).

40. The recompense of an evil deed can only be an evil equal to it; but whoever pardons and makes reconciliation, his reward is due from God. Surely He does not love the wrongdoers.[16]

41. But whoever defends himself and restores his right (in the lawful way) after he has been wronged – against such there is no route (of blame and retaliation).

42. The route (of blame and retaliation) is only against those who wrong people and behave rebelliously on earth, offending against all right. For such there is a painful punishment.

43. But indeed whoever shows patience and forgives (the wrong done to him), surely that is a very meritorious thing, a matter of great resolution.

44. Whoever (due to his choice) God leads astray, he will no longer have any guardian (to help and support him). You will see the wrongdoers, when they see the punishment, saying: "Is there any way back (to the world for us to become righteous people)?"

32. And among His manifest signs are the ships running through the sea like (floating) hills.

33. If He so wills, He calms the wind and so they lie motionless on its surface. Surely in that are signs for all who are greatly patient and perseverant (in adversity for His sake), and greatly thankful (for His favors).[13]

34. Or He causes them (the ships) to sink because of what they (the travelers) have earned; and yet He overlooks many (of their wrongs).

35. Those who dispute concerning Our signs and Revelations should know that they have no (escape, nor any) place of refuge.

36. Whatever thing you are granted is but for the passing enjoyment of the present, worldly life, but what God keeps for you in the Hereafter is much better and more

13. When an affliction befalls believers, they show patience; when they are favored with something good, they give thanks to God. In either case they gain reward.

14. For the major sins, see: 4: 31, note 11. "Indecent, shameful deeds" generally denote deeds such as fornication, adultery, prostitution, and homosexuality.

15. Consultation is the first requirement for reaching the right decision. Decisions reached without due reflection or proper consultation usually come to nothing. Individuals who depend only on themselves are disconnected from others and unconcerned with the opinions of others; such people, even if they happen to be geniuses, are at considerable risk of error, as compared to those who exchange opinions and arguments (See *Pearls of Wisdom*, 77–78).

The advisory system is so important in Islam that God praises the first, exemplary Muslim community as a community whose affairs were conducted through consultation. This becomes even clearer when we realize that this first community was led by the Prophet, who never spoke out of caprice or on his own accord, but only spoke about what was revealed to him by God (53: 2–3); God considers consultation so important that He ordered His Messenger to practice it with his Companions (3: 159). Even after the Muslims' reverse at the Battle of Uhud (in 625), due to some of the Companions' disobedience of the Prophet's orders, God told him to engage in consultation. The Prophet and his rightly-guided successors always followed the principle of consultation.

Consultation settles many affairs among Muslims. Judges who cannot decide cases employ consultation to reach a verdict, based on the Qur'ān and the Sunnah, thus making it similar to *ijtihād* (deducing new laws through reasoning based on the Qur'ān and Sunnah) and *qiyās* (analogy). Furthermore, any punishment of a secondary nature that is not explicitly mentioned in the Qur'ān and the Sunnah can be pronounced after consulting authoritative Muslim jurists.

16. The Qur'ān insists on justice, the equality of rights, and that inviolate values demand equal respect and retaliation. So the Qur'ān allows one to reciprocate any wrong done to one if retaliation is possible (For an explanation, see *sūrah* 2: 178–179, 194, notes 131, 140; *sūrah* 5: 31, 45, notes 6, 10). However, since a person wronged can easily be tempted to exceed the limits in retaliation, in the places where the Qur'ān mentions the permission of retaliation as a legal principle it also warns against exceeding the limits and draws attention to the beauty and importance of forgiveness, exhorting individuals to forgive any wrongdoing inflicted on them (see *sūrah* 22: 60, note 16).

وَتَرَىٰهُمْ يُعْرَضُونَ عَلَيْهَا خَٰشِعِينَ مِنَ الذُّلِّ يَنظُرُونَ مِن طَرْفٍ خَفِىٍّ وَقَالَ الَّذِينَ ءَامَنُوٓا إِنَّ الْخَٰسِرِينَ الَّذِينَ خَسِرُوٓا أَنفُسَهُمْ وَأَهْلِيهِمْ يَوْمَ الْقِيَٰمَةِ أَلَآ إِنَّ الظَّٰلِمِينَ فِى عَذَابٍ مُّقِيمٍ ۝ وَمَا كَانَ لَهُم مِّنْ أَوْلِيَآءَ يَنصُرُونَهُم مِّن دُونِ اللَّهِ وَمَن يُضْلِلِ اللَّهُ فَمَا لَهُۥ مِن سَبِيلٍ ۝ اسْتَجِيبُوا لِرَبِّكُم مِّن قَبْلِ أَن يَأْتِىَ يَوْمٌ لَّا مَرَدَّ لَهُۥ مِنَ اللَّهِ مَا لَكُم مِّن مَّلْجَإٍ يَوْمَئِذٍ وَمَا لَكُم مِّن نَّكِيرٍ ۝ فَإِنْ أَعْرَضُوا فَمَآ أَرْسَلْنَٰكَ عَلَيْهِمْ حَفِيظًا إِنْ عَلَيْكَ إِلَّا الْبَلَٰغُ وَإِنَّآ إِذَآ أَذَقْنَا الْإِنسَٰنَ مِنَّا رَحْمَةً فَرِحَ بِهَا وَإِن تُصِبْهُمْ سَيِّئَةٌ بِمَا قَدَّمَتْ أَيْدِيهِمْ فَإِنَّ الْإِنسَٰنَ كَفُورٌ ۝ لِّلَّهِ مُلْكُ السَّمَٰوَٰتِ وَالْأَرْضِ يَخْلُقُ مَا يَشَآءُ يَهَبُ لِمَن يَشَآءُ إِنَٰثًا وَيَهَبُ لِمَن يَشَآءُ الذُّكُورَ ۝ أَوْ يُزَوِّجُهُمْ ذُكْرَانًا وَإِنَٰثًا وَيَجْعَلُ مَن يَشَآءُ عَقِيمًا إِنَّهُۥ عَلِيمٌ قَدِيرٌ ۝ وَمَا كَانَ لِبَشَرٍ أَن يُكَلِّمَهُ اللَّهُ إِلَّا وَحْيًا أَوْ مِن وَرَآئِ حِجَابٍ أَوْ يُرْسِلَ رَسُولًا فَيُوحِىَ بِإِذْنِهِۦ مَا يَشَآءُ إِنَّهُۥ عَلِىٌّ حَكِيمٌ ۝

﹏﹏﹏

45. You will see them brought before it (Hell), in fear and humbled by disgrace, and looking around with furtive look. And those who believe will say: "Those are the real losers who have ruined their own selves and their families on the Resurrection Day." Be aware: the wrongdoers are in an enduring punishment.

46. And they will surely have no guardians to help them apart from God (only He is the Guardian with power to help His servants, as He wills). Whoever God leads astray, he can no longer have a way (to guidance and eternal happiness).

47. Answer the call of your Lord before there comes to you a Day which God will not remove (from them) and none can prevent Him from bringing it. You will have no refuge on that Day nor power of denial (of any of your sins or of your identity).

48. But (do not grieve) if they turn away in aversion (from your call, O Messenger): We have not sent you (as a Messenger) so as to be their keeper (to prevent their misdeeds or carry accountability for them). What rests with you is but to convey (God's Message) fully. Indeed, when We favor human with a taste of mercy, he rejoices in it (without ever thinking to express gratitude to Him Who favored him). But if an evil befalls them because of what their hands have forwarded, surely then human is ungrateful.

49. To God belongs the sovereignty of the heavens and the earth. He creates whatever He wills. He grants to whom He wills daughters and grants to whom He wills sons.

50. Or He mingles them, both sons and daughters (granted to whom He wills); and He leaves barren whom He wills. Surely He is All-Knowing, All-Powerful.

51. It is not for any mortal that God should speak to him unless it be by Revelation or from behind a veil, or by sending a messenger (angel) to reveal, by His leave, whatever He wills (to reveal).[17] Surely He is All-Exalted, All-Wise.

17. Every human being has potential to be addressed by God. However, in order to use this potential, one has to have attained to a certain degree of spiritual and intellectual purity. The Prophets had the highest degree of this purity. God's special speaking to the Prophets is called *wahy* (Revelation). Revelation occurs in three ways. One is that God suddenly puts the meaning in the Prophet's heart and he knows that this meaning is from God. This is the first way mentioned in the verse as *by Revelation*.

The second way or form is that God speaks to a human being from behind a veil, as He spoke to the Prophet Moses in the Valley of Tuwā from behind a tree, or on Mount Sinai where Moses heard God's speech from behind a veil, the identity of which we do not know. The third way is that God sends an angel to convey His Message to the Prophet.

The Qur'ān was revealed to God's Messenger in this way. The archangel Gabriel brought it to him. The Messenger saw him and heard his speech.

A person can also receive God's Message in dreams. If a Prophet receives such a message in dream, it is Revelation. An ordinary person can also have true dreams through which he or she can receive some meaning from the Almighty. Such dreams sometimes require interpretation but sometimes are clear enough not to need an interpretation. The meanings or messages an ordinary believer receives in true dreams are called "glad heralds" in a Prophetic Tradition (al-Bukhārī, "Ta'bīr," 5).

God also reveals to or inspires in animals (16: 88). This is either an intrinsic, constant knowledge deposited in them or constant orientation or direction by God (see Appendix 9).

SŪRAH 43

AZ-ZUKHRUF (ORNAMENTS)

Makkah period

Consisting of 89 verses, this *sūrah* was revealed in Makkah toward the closing years of the Makkan period, when the polytheists were concocting plots to assassinate the Messenger of God. It takes its name from verse 35, where the word *zukhruf* occurs. It concentrates on some of the fundamentals of faith, namely God's Oneness, Divine Messengership, and the afterlife, and rejects certain false beliefs of ignorance, such as attributing daughters to God. It mentions certain episodes from the life of Prophets Abraham and Moses, upon them be peace, in order to urge polytheists to give up associating partners with God. Finally, it warns them against the end that awaits them in the Hereafter.

In the Name of God, the All-Merciful, the All-Compassionate.

1. *Ḥā. Mīm.*

2. By the Book clear in itself and clearly showing the truth,

3. We have made it a Recitation (a Qur'ān) in Arabic so that you may reason (and understand it and the wisdom in its revelation).

4. Surely it is in the Mother Book with Us, exalted, firm, and decisive.[1]

5. Shall We take away this Reminder from you (and leave you to your own devices), because you are a people wasteful (of your God-given faculties and committing excesses)?

6. How many a Prophet have We sent to convey Our Message among the former peoples,

52. And thus (in the ways mentioned) We have revealed to you a spirit of Our command (the life-giving Message, the Qur'ān). You would not (otherwise) have known what the Book was (with all the knowledge it contains and the way of life it establishes), and what faith was (as described by the Book and with all its principles, requirements, and implications). But We have made it a light by which We guide whom We will of Our servants. And certainly you, (by God's guidance) guide (people) to a straight path –

53. The path of God, to Him belongs whatever is in the heavens and whatever is on the earth. Be aware: all affairs are ultimately referred to God.

7. And there never came to them a Prophet but they mocked him.

8. So We destroyed peoples mightier than these in prowess, and the illustrative histories of those (destroyed peoples) have already have been related.

9. If you ask them who has created the heavens and the earth, they most certainly say (in answer), "The One All-Glorious with irresistible might, the All-Knowing, has created them;"

10. He Who has made the earth a cradle for you, and has set on it roads for you so that you may find your way.

---

1. The Mother Book is also called the Supreme Ever-Preserved Tablet (85: 22; for the nature and meaning of the Supreme Ever-Preserved Tablet, see: 6: 59, note 13; 13: 39, note 13; 17: 14, note 10). The Qur'ān originally exists in the Mother Book, which exists with God. The Qur'ān is so high and exalted, firm and unfathomable in the Mother Book that no one is ever able to reach and understand it. However, God revealed it to the Messenger as a Book in the Arabic language so that people might be able to read and study it and understand why it has been revealed. That is, the Almighty has a very important and sublime purpose for sending it down as a Book that is comprehensible to human reason, and we must reflect on this purpose and act accordingly. Since the Qur'ān was revealed from the Mother Book, which is in a form that is infinitely high and impenetrable by human reason, it is described as "The Divine Condescension to the Human Mind."

Truly, the Qur'ān of miraculous exposition teaches and explains many profound and subtle truths in a way so direct and clear that it is familiar to the general way of seeing things, and does not offend general human sentiments. Nor does it present itself against generally held opinions. Just as one chooses to use appropriate words when addressing a child, so too does the Qur'ān choose a style that is suitable to the level of those whom it addresses, and speaking in allegories, parables, and comparisons, makes the most difficult Divine truths and mysteries, which even the minds of the most profound philosophers will not otherwise be able to comprehend, understandable by ordinary people, literate or illiterate.

٤٨٩ الجزء الخامس والعشرون 489

بِسْمِ اللّٰه (Arabic Qur'an text)

وَالَّذِى نَزَّلَ مِنَ السَّمَآءِ مَآءً بِقَدَرٍ فَأَنشَرْنَا بِهِ بَلْدَةً مَّيْتًا كَذَٰلِكَ تُخْرَجُونَ ۝ وَالَّذِى خَلَقَ الْأَزْوَاجَ كُلَّهَا وَجَعَلَ لَكُم مِّنَ الْفُلْكِ وَالْأَنْعَامِ مَا تَرْكَبُونَ ۝ لِتَسْتَوُۥا عَلَىٰ ظُهُورِهِ ثُمَّ تَذْكُرُوا نِعْمَةَ رَبِّكُمْ إِذَا اسْتَوَيْتُمْ عَلَيْهِ وَتَقُولُوا سُبْحَانَ الَّذِى سَخَّرَ لَنَا هَـٰذَا وَمَا كُنَّا لَهُۥ مُقْرِنِينَ ۝ وَإِنَّا إِلَىٰ رَبِّنَا لَمُنقَلِبُونَ ۝ وَجَعَلُوا لَهُۥ مِنْ عِبَادِهِ جُزْءًا إِنَّ الْإِنسَانَ لَكَفُورٌ مُّبِينٌ ۝ أَمِ اتَّخَذَ مِمَّا يَخْلُقُ بَنَاتٍ وَأَصْفَىٰكُم بِالْبَنِينَ ۝ وَإِذَا بُشِّرَ أَحَدُهُم بِمَا ضَرَبَ لِلرَّحْمَٰنِ مَثَلًا ظَلَّ وَجْهُهُۥ مُسْوَدًّا وَهُوَ كَظِيمٌ ۝ أَوَمَن يُنَشَّؤُا فِى الْحِلْيَةِ وَهُوَ فِى الْخِصَامِ غَيْرُ مُبِينٍ ۝ وَجَعَلُوا الْمَلَٰئِكَةَ الَّذِينَ هُمْ عِبَادُ الرَّحْمَٰنِ إِنَاثًا أَشَهِدُوا خَلْقَهُمْ سَتُكْتَبُ شَهَادَتُهُمْ وَيُسْـَٔلُونَ ۝ وَقَالُوا لَوْ شَآءَ الرَّحْمَٰنُ مَا عَبَدْنَاهُم مَّا لَهُم بِذَٰلِكَ مِنْ عِلْمٍ إِنْ هُمْ إِلَّا يَخْرُصُونَ ۝ أَمْ آتَيْنَاهُمْ كِتَابًا مِّن قَبْلِهِ فَهُم بِهِ مُسْتَمْسِكُونَ ۝ بَلْ قَالُوا إِنَّا وَجَدْنَا آبَآءَنَا عَلَىٰ أُمَّةٍ وَإِنَّا عَلَىٰ آثَارِهِم مُّهْتَدُونَ ۝

────────❧────────

11. And Who sends down water from the sky in a measure, and We raise a dead land to life with it. Even so will you be (raised from the dead and) brought forth (from your graves).

12. And Who has created all the pairs (of all things),[2] and has enabled for you ships and cattle on which you ride,

13. So that you sit secure on their backs, then remember and reflect on the favor of your Lord, and when you settle securely on them, say: "All-Glorified is He Who has subjugated this to our use. We were never capable (of accomplishing this by ourselves).

14. "And surely, to our Lord we are indeed bound to return."[3]

15. Yet they attribute to Him (fatherhood of) some among His servants. Human is indeed ungrateful, obviously.

16. What! has He taken to Himself daughters out of all that He creates, and "honored" you with sons?

17. When any of them is given the news of the birth of what he accepts as appropriate for the All-Merciful, his face darkens, choking with anger.

18. "What! (Am I to have a daughter –) one who is brought up in adornments, and unable to be clear in disputation?"

19. And yet they have judged the angels, who are themselves the servants of the All-Merciful, to be females (whom they judge to be of little value, and yet regard as His daughters). Did they witness their creation? This testimony of theirs will be recorded, and they will be called to account (for this falsehood in the Hereafter).

20. They also say: "If the All-Merciful had so willed, we would not have worshipped them (our deities, including angels)." They have no knowledge whatever of that (the relationship of Divine Will and human will and actions). Indeed, they only judge and speak according to their own fancies and interests.

21. Or did We give them a Book before this (Qur'ān) and so they are holding fast to it (and worshipping their false deities by its authority)?

22. Not at all! (Indeed, their only argument is that) they say: "We have found our forefathers following a certain religion, and we are led in their footsteps."

---

2. For creation in pairs, see *sūrah* 36: 36, note 11.

3. Reciting this statement of praise and glorification when seated on any mount was a practice of the Prophet, upon him be peace and blessings,, and therefore is incumbent upon us as a Sunnah act.

23. In just that way, We never sent a warner to a township before you but those of its people who had been lost in the pursuit of pleasures without scruples reacted, saying: "We have found our forefathers following a religion, and we certainly follow in their footsteps."

24. He (who was sent to warn them) said: "What! even though I have come to you with better guidance[4] than what you have found your forefathers following?" They said: "Surely we are unbelievers in that with which you have been sent."

25. So then We took Our retribution on them. So look: how was the outcome for those who denied (God's Messengers)?

26. And (remember) when Abraham (who rejected following the way of his forefathers blindly) said to his father and his people: "I am indeed free of all that you worship.

27. "I worship only Him Who has originated me with a particular nature, and He will guide me (to the truth and to eternal happiness)."

28. And He left it as a Word to endure among those who would come after him, so that they may return (from worshipping false deities to the worship of One God).

29. Indeed I have allowed these (people of Makkah), as I had allowed their forefathers, to enjoy their lives until when the truth and a Messenger came to them, making the truth clear, (and embodying it in every element of his life and character).

30. But now the truth has come to them, they say: "This is sorcery and we are unbelievers in it."

31. They also say: "If only this Qur'ān had been sent down on a man of leading position of the two (chief) cities!"[5]

32. Is it they who distribute the mercy of your Lord (so that they may appoint whom they wish as Messenger to receive the Book)? (Moreover, how do they presume to value some above others only because of their wealth or status, when) it is also We Who distribute their means of livelihood among them in the life of this world, and raise some of them above others in degree, so that they may avail themselves of one another's help? But your Lord's mercy (in particular Prophethood) is better than what they amass (in this life).

33. And were it not that all people would become one community (around unbelief),[6] We might well have provided for everyone who disbelieves in the All-Merciful roofs of silver for their houses, and (silver) stairways on which to go up,

4. The Religion with which any Messenger came was completely true and the best in guidance, while any religion or faith based on associating partners with God or denial of Him is essentially false and devoid of any guidance. However, there may be some true elements in any false religion or doctrine. So the reason why the warners used *better guidance* was both by way of argumentation and persuasion, as well as referring to those elements of truth that can be found in any religion.

5. This typical objection explains the standards for greatness of people bereft of Divine guidance. According to them, greatness lies in wealth, position, and posts. However, in God's sight the most honored and greatest are those who are the most advanced in piety and righteousness (49: 13).

By the chief cities Makkah and Tā'if are meant.

6. This should not be taken to mean that people may realize a peaceful unity in unbelief and lead a peaceful life without any dissension or conflict. The original word for community is *ummah*, which means a community based around a certain belief or doctrine. So what the verse draws our attention to is the danger and possibility of all people tending toward unbelief because of an easy life.

وَلِبُيُوتِهِمْ أَبْوَابًا وَسُرُرًا عَلَيْهَا يَتَّكِئُونَ ۝ وَزُخْرُفًا ۚ وَإِنْ كُلُّ ذَٰلِكَ لَمَّا مَتَاعُ الْحَيَاةِ الدُّنْيَا ۚ وَالْآخِرَةُ عِنْدَ رَبِّكَ لِلْمُتَّقِينَ ۝ وَمَنْ يَعْشُ عَنْ ذِكْرِ الرَّحْمَٰنِ نُقَيِّضْ لَهُ شَيْطَانًا فَهُوَ لَهُ قَرِينٌ ۝ وَإِنَّهُمْ لَيَصُدُّونَهُمْ عَنِ السَّبِيلِ وَيَحْسَبُونَ أَنَّهُمْ مُهْتَدُونَ ۝ حَتَّىٰ إِذَا جَاءَنَا قَالَ يَا لَيْتَ بَيْنِي وَبَيْنَكَ بُعْدَ الْمَشْرِقَيْنِ فَبِئْسَ الْقَرِينُ ۝ وَلَنْ يَنْفَعَكُمُ الْيَوْمَ إِذْ ظَلَمْتُمْ أَنَّكُمْ فِي الْعَذَابِ مُشْتَرِكُونَ ۝ أَفَأَنْتَ تُسْمِعُ الصُّمَّ أَوْ تَهْدِي الْعُمْيَ وَمَنْ كَانَ فِي ضَلَالٍ مُبِينٍ ۝ فَإِمَّا نَذْهَبَنَّ بِكَ فَإِنَّا مِنْهُمْ مُنْتَقِمُونَ ۝ أَوْ نُرِيَنَّكَ الَّذِي وَعَدْنَاهُمْ فَإِنَّا عَلَيْهِمْ مُقْتَدِرُونَ ۝ فَاسْتَمْسِكْ بِالَّذِي أُوحِيَ إِلَيْكَ ۖ إِنَّكَ عَلَىٰ صِرَاطٍ مُسْتَقِيمٍ ۝ وَإِنَّهُ لَذِكْرٌ لَكَ وَلِقَوْمِكَ ۖ وَسَوْفَ تُسْأَلُونَ ۝ وَسْأَلْ مَنْ أَرْسَلْنَا مِنْ قَبْلِكَ مِنْ رُسُلِنَا أَجَعَلْنَا مِنْ دُونِ الرَّحْمَٰنِ آلِهَةً يُعْبَدُونَ ۝ وَلَقَدْ أَرْسَلْنَا مُوسَىٰ بِآيَاتِنَا إِلَىٰ فِرْعَوْنَ وَمَلَئِهِ فَقَالَ إِنِّي رَسُولُ رَبِّ الْعَالَمِينَ ۝ فَلَمَّا جَاءَهُمْ بِآيَاتِنَا إِذَا هُمْ مِنْهَا يَضْحَكُونَ ۝

34. And (silver) doors for their houses, and (silver) couches on which to recline,

35. And also adornments of gold (and other jewelry).[7] Yet all this is nothing but a (fleeting) enjoyment of the present, worldly life. And the Hereafter with your Lord is only for the God-revering, pious.

36. Whoever willfully ignores the remembrance of the All-Merciful (and lives as if He did not exist always watching him), We assign to him a devil,[8] who becomes his closest comrade.

37. Such devils certainly bar them from the way (of truth). Yet they think (in themselves) that they are rightly guided.[9]

38. But in the end, when such a one comes to Us (on Judgment Day), he says (to his comrade): "Ah, would that between me and you were the distance of the two easts.[10] How evil a comrade!"

39. "It is of no avail to you at all today (this remorse after death). For you did wrong (in the world), and you will suffer the punishment together."

40. (Although this is the truth and clear to you, O Messenger,) can you make the deaf hear or guide the blind and him who is lost in obvious error?

41. And whether We take you away from among them, and then We take retribution on them;

42. Or We let you see (in your lifetime) the fulfillment of what We have promised them: (either way) We have full power over them.

43. So hold fast to what is revealed to you. Surely you are on a straight path (in all matters).[11]

44. Indeed, it (the Qur'ān) is a Reminder for you and for your people, in which lie your honor and happiness (in both worlds). And you (all people) will be questioned (about how it was understood, and how lived).

45. And ask (their true followers about) those of Our Messengers whom We sent before you: Did We ever enable deities to be worshipped apart from the All-Merciful?[12]

46. Assuredly We sent Moses to the Pharaoh and his chiefs with Our clear signs (miracles demonstrating Our being the sole Deity and Lord to be worshipped), and he said: "I am a Messenger of the Lord of the worlds."

47. But when he came to them with Our clear signs (miracles), they then ridiculed them.

7. Verses 33–35 warn against the fact that luxury may lead people to self-adoration, indulgence in worldly appetites, and ingratitude to God, and therefore unbelief.

8. The devil mentioned in the verse, as in verses 41: 25 and 19: 83, may be of the jinn or humankind. In any case, both human and jinn "devils," or satanic devils are always standing close to unbelievers or those who willfully ignore God's Existence and awareness of whatever they do, living a life according to their own desires. So, the Turkish proverb, "Tell me who your friend is, I will tell you what kind of person you are," is very apt.

9. Right or true guidance is the guidance of the Qur'ān. So, however rightly-guided those who follow other ways may regard themselves to be, they have in reality strayed far from the truth. The Qur'ān severely warns such people in 18: 103–104: Say: "Shall We inform you who are the greatest losers in respect of their deeds? Those whose endeavor has been wasted in this world (because it is directed only to this-worldly ends, and so it is bound to be wasted hereafter also) but who themselves reckon that they are doing good." (See corresponding note 32.)

10. This phrase is highly typical, and suggests that the earth is sphere. As we know, the point where the sun sets in a hemisphere is in fact the same point where it rises in another, and so the setting of the sun is a relative fact. What is meant is the distance between the east and the west – the distance impossible to cross.

11. These verses came at a time when the believers were extremely weak and unprotected in Makkah and the leaders of the Quraysh were plotting to assassinate the Messenger of God, upon him be peace and blessings. If the Messenger had died, God would have inflicted total retribution upon the polytheists of Makkah. However, He took him away from among them by letting him emigrate to Madīnah to perfect Islam and complete His favor upon the believers, and He inflicted His retribution upon their most obstinate leaders in the Battle of Badr, letting His Messenger witness the fulfillment of His promise both to him and others. So, as stated in verse 43, what befalls the believer is always to hold fast to God's Religion in the footsteps of His Messenger in perfect conviction and confidence of its truth and the absolute Power of God, and to leave to Him the fulfillment of the result.

12. The All-Merciful (ar-Raḥmān) is the attributive Name that is particular to the Divine Being and exclusive (1: 1, note 4; 17: 110).

492   سورة الزخرف   ٢٩٢

وَمَا نُرِيهِم مِّنْ آيَةٍ إِلَّا هِيَ أَكْبَرُ مِنْ أُخْتِهَا وَأَخَذْنَاهُم
بِالْعَذَابِ لَعَلَّهُمْ يَرْجِعُونَ ۝ وَقَالُوا يَا أَيُّهَ السَّاحِرُ ادْعُ لَنَا
رَبَّكَ بِمَا عَهِدَ عِندَكَ إِنَّنَا لَمُهْتَدُونَ ۝ فَلَمَّا كَشَفْنَا عَنْهُمُ
الْعَذَابَ إِذَا هُمْ يَنكُثُونَ ۝ وَنَادَىٰ فِرْعَوْنُ فِي قَوْمِهِ قَالَ
يَا قَوْمِ أَلَيْسَ لِي مُلْكُ مِصْرَ وَهَـٰذِهِ الْأَنْهَارُ تَجْرِي مِن تَحْتِي
أَفَلَا تُبْصِرُونَ ۝ أَمْ أَنَا خَيْرٌ مِّنْ هَـٰذَا الَّذِي هُوَ مَهِينٌ
وَلَا يَكَادُ يُبِينُ ۝ فَلَوْلَا أُلْقِيَ عَلَيْهِ أَسْوِرَةٌ مِّن ذَهَبٍ
أَوْ جَاءَ مَعَهُ الْمَلَائِكَةُ مُقْتَرِنِينَ ۝ فَاسْتَخَفَّ قَوْمَهُ
فَأَطَاعُوهُ إِنَّهُمْ كَانُوا قَوْمًا فَاسِقِينَ ۝ فَلَمَّا آسَفُونَا
انتَقَمْنَا مِنْهُمْ فَأَغْرَقْنَاهُمْ أَجْمَعِينَ ۝ فَجَعَلْنَاهُمْ سَلَفًا
وَمَثَلًا لِّلْآخِرِينَ ۝ وَلَمَّا ضُرِبَ ابْنُ مَرْيَمَ مَثَلًا إِذَا قَوْمُكَ
مِنْهُ يَصِدُّونَ ۝ وَقَالُوا أَآلِهَتُنَا خَيْرٌ أَمْ هُوَ مَا ضَرَبُوهُ
لَكَ إِلَّا جَدَلًا بَلْ هُمْ قَوْمٌ خَصِمُونَ ۝ إِنْ هُوَ إِلَّا عَبْدٌ
أَنْعَمْنَا عَلَيْهِ وَجَعَلْنَاهُ مَثَلًا لِّبَنِي إِسْرَائِيلَ ۝ وَلَوْ نَشَاءُ
لَجَعَلْنَا مِنكُم مَّلَائِكَةً فِي الْأَرْضِ يَخْلُفُونَ ۝

---

48. We displayed to them sign after sign, each greater than the other, and We seized them with (diverse forms of) punishment[13] so that they might turn back (from the way they followed).

49. (Whenever We seized them with a punishment) they would say (to Moses): "O Sorcerer! Pray for us to your Lord by the covenant He has made with you (that He will remove affliction from us if we believe); for we will surely accept the right guidance."

50. But when We removed the punishment from them, they then broke their promise.

51. The Pharaoh made this proclamation among his people: "O my people! Does not the dominion of Egypt belong to me, as well as these rivers flowing beneath me? Will you not see the truth?

52. "And, am I not better than this man, who is despicable and can scarcely express himself clearly?

53. "(If he is true in his claim) why are bracelets of gold not dropped upon him (from the sky), or why do there not come with him angels (to support him in his cause)?"

54. Thus did he make fools of his people and demeaned them, and they obeyed him. Assuredly they were a people given to transgression.[14]

55. So finally when they incurred Our condemnation, We took retribution on them, and We caused them to drown all together.

56. So We made them a thing of the past,

and a precedent (in entering the Fire), and an example to later generations.

57. And when (Jesus) the son of Mary has been presented as an example (of God's Power and Oneness and to refute his being deified by many Christians), your people turn from it in disdain;

58. And they say, "Are our deities better or is he?" They put it to you only for disputation. Indeed, they are a people addicted to contentiousness.[15]

59. Surely he (Jesus) was not other than a servant (worshipping God), whom We favored (with Messengership), and We made him a miraculous example for the Children of Israel (to follow and mend their ways).

60. If We had so willed, We could have made some from among you angels, succeeding each other on the earth.[16]

13. For the kinds of punishment with which God seized the Pharaoh and his people, see 7: 130–133.

14. As can be understood from the verses, the Pharaoh began to really fear the Prophet Moses and worried about what would happen. So in order to secure his throne, he sent out heralds among the people to strengthen their obedience to him. He reminded them of his absolute dominion over Egypt, implying that the people led their lives in his land only by his generosity. They could only be his servants. Moreover, he tried to disgrace Moses in their eyes by reminding them that he belonged to an inferior class – the Children of Israel, who had long been serving them. He also claimed that Moses could not express himself clearly, although this was not true. There was no impediment in Moses' speech, as some have thoughtlessly claimed (see *sūrah* 20, note 8; *sūrah* 21: 84, note 15). The Pharaoh fooled his people, and they blindly obeyed him, though for years they had been witnessing the truth clearly. Their obedience was not because they believed in the proclamations of the Pharaoh, but rather because they were a people given to a dissipated life-style and who recognized no rules to guide their behavior. They also feared the Pharaoh, as he could take their lives. So they followed him and shared with him his rebellion against God and his cruel treatment of Moses and his followers.

15. Many leading polytheists of Makkah tended to use the fact that Jesus was deified by many Christians as a pretext for their polytheism, and their worship of angels in particular. But when the Qur'ān clarified Jesus' identity, making it clear that he was only a human being

who worshipped God, they did not like this and desired to continue to use the fact that many Christians deified him as an alleged argument for their polytheism. They even said: "We worship angels, while Christians worship a human being. So our deities are better than theirs."

16. This is also stated to refute the deification of angels. The Qur'ān warns that being a human, Jesus was able to revive some of the dead and give life to some clay figures, but he did those things by God's permission, and he was a human being who had been created, one responsible for worshipping God, which he did. The polytheists of Makkah thought that only angels could do the extraordinary things that Jesus and other Prophets did with God's permission. In fact, the believers among human beings are more virtuous and exalted in rank than the angels; the distinguished ones among them, such as the Prophets, are greater than the greatest among the angels. The ordinary ones among the believers are greater than their counterparts among the angels. Human beings have a will, i.e. freedom of choice, which the angels do not possess. So the angels cannot elevate their rank. Thus it was that God willed humankind, not the angels, to inhabit the earth as vicegerents to improve it and live on it according to His Will, and He chose the Prophets from among them. Therefore, there is no need to look for virtue and achievement in other creatures, as it is humankind that has been endowed with the potential to attain the greatest virtues and achievements any created being can attain. And this fact categorically refutes the deification of the angels and the worship of them by human beings.

وَإِنَّهُ لَعِلْمٌ لِّلسَّاعَةِ فَلَا تَمْتَرُنَّ بِهَا وَاتَّبِعُوْنِ هٰذَا صِرَاطٌ مُّسْتَقِيمٌ ۞ وَلَا يَصُدَّنَّكُمُ الشَّيْطَانُ اِنَّهُ لَكُمْ عَدُوٌّ مُّبِيْنٌ ۞ وَلَمَّا جَاءَ عِيْسٰى بِالْبَيِّنَاتِ قَالَ قَدْ جِئْتُكُمْ بِالْحِكْمَةِ وَلِاُبَيِّنَ لَكُمْ بَعْضَ الَّذِيْ تَخْتَلِفُوْنَ فِيْهِ فَاتَّقُوا اللّٰهَ وَاَطِيْعُوْنِ ۞ اِنَّ اللّٰهَ هُوَ رَبِّيْ وَ رَبُّكُمْ فَاعْبُدُوْهُ هٰذَا صِرَاطٌ مُّسْتَقِيمٌ ۞ فَاخْتَلَفَ الْاَحْزَابُ مِنْ بَيْنِهِمْ فَوَيْلٌ لِّلَّذِيْنَ ظَلَمُوْا مِنْ عَذَابِ يَوْمٍ اَلِيْمٍ ۞ هَلْ يَنْظُرُوْنَ اِلَّا السَّاعَةَ اَنْ تَأْتِيَهُمْ بَغْتَةً وَهُمْ لَا يَشْعُرُوْنَ ۞ اَلْاَخِلَّاءُ يَوْمَئِذٍ بَعْضُهُمْ لِبَعْضٍ عَدُوٌّ اِلَّا الْمُتَّقِيْنَ ۞ يَاعِبَادِ لَا خَوْفٌ عَلَيْكُمُ الْيَوْمَ وَلَا اَنْتُمْ تَحْزَنُوْنَ ۞ اَلَّذِيْنَ اٰمَنُوْا بِاٰيَاتِنَا وَكَانُوْا مُسْلِمِيْنَ ۞ اُدْخُلُوا الْجَنَّةَ اَنْتُمْ وَاَزْوَاجُكُمْ تُحْبَرُوْنَ ۞ يُطَافُ عَلَيْهِمْ بِصِحَافٍ مِّنْ ذَهَبٍ وَاَكْوَابٍ وَفِيْهَا مَا تَشْتَهِيْهِ الْاَنْفُسُ وَتَلَذُّ الْاَعْيُنُ وَاَنْتُمْ فِيْهَا خَالِدُوْنَ ۞ وَتِلْكَ الْجَنَّةُ الَّتِيْ اُوْرِثْتُمُوْهَا بِمَا كُنْتُمْ تَعْمَلُوْنَ ۞ لَكُمْ فِيْهَا فَاكِهَةٌ كَثِيْرَةٌ مِّنْهَا تَأْكُلُوْنَ ۞

—❧—

61. Surely he (Jesus) (brought into the world without a father, and granted such miracles as reviving the dead) is a means to the knowledge of the Last Hour, so do not feel any doubt concerning it and follow Me (to attain eternal happiness in the other life). This is a straight path.

62. And never let Satan debar you (from the Straight Path). Surely he is a manifest enemy.

63. When Jesus came with manifest truths (and miracles), he said: "I have come to you with the Wisdom (the truths and essentials of faith and good life), and so that I may make clear to you some of what you differ on (matters that require clarification for your good in both worlds). So keep from disobedience to God in reverence for Him and piety, and obey me.

64. "Surely God is He Who is my Lord as well as your Lord, so worship Him (alone). This is a straight path."

65. However, parties (that arose and held differing views concerning him and his teachings) fell into disagreement among themselves. Then woe to those who do the greatest wrong (by corrupting his teachings) because of the punishment of a painful Day.

66. Do they (who persist in unbelief and evil deeds) wait but for the Last Hour – (waiting) that it come upon them all of a sudden, being unaware and indifferent toward it?

67. Those who are intimate friends (in the world) will be enemies one to another on that Day, except the God-revering, pious. (They will hear:)

68. "O My servants! You will have no fear today, nor will you grieve!

69. "(You) who have believed in My signs and Revelations, and have submitted to Me wholly (as Muslims).

70. "Enter Paradise, you and your (believing) spouses, made contented."

71. Trays of gold and goblets will be passed round them; and there will be therein all that souls desire, and eyes delight in,[17] "and you will abide therein.

72. "That is the Paradise which is made your inheritance[18] in return for what you used to do (in the world).

73. "In it there is for you fruit (of all kinds) in abundance, to eat therefrom."

---

17. See 41: 31–32, note 9.

18. For inheriting Paradise, see 26: 85, note 19.

494　　سُورَةُ الزُّخْرُفِ　　٤٩٤

اِنَّ الْمُجْرِمِيْنَ فِيْ عَذَابِ جَهَنَّمَ خَالِدُوْنَ ۞ لَا يُفَتَّرُ عَنْهُمْ وَهُمْ فِيْهِ مُبْلِسُوْنَ ۞ وَمَا ظَلَمْنَاهُمْ وَلَكِنْ كَانُوْا هُمُ الظَّالِمِيْنَ ۞ وَنَادَوْا يَامَالِكُ لِيَقْضِ عَلَيْنَا رَبُّكَ قَالَ اِنَّكُمْ مَّاكِثُوْنَ ۞ لَقَدْ جِئْنَاكُمْ بِالْحَقِّ وَلَكِنَّ اَكْثَرَكُمْ لِلْحَقِّ كَارِهُوْنَ ۞ اَمْ اَبْرَمُوْا اَمْرًا فَاِنَّا مُبْرِمُوْنَ ۞ اَمْ يَحْسَبُوْنَ اَنَّا لَا نَسْمَعُ سِرَّهُمْ وَنَجْوٰىهُمْ بَلٰى وَرُسُلُنَا لَدَيْهِمْ يَكْتُبُوْنَ ۞ قُلْ اِنْ كَانَ لِلرَّحْمٰنِ وَلَدٌ فَاَنَا اَوَّلُ الْعَابِدِيْنَ ۞ سُبْحَانَ رَبِّ السَّمٰوٰتِ وَالْاَرْضِ رَبِّ الْعَرْشِ عَمَّا يَصِفُوْنَ ۞ فَذَرْهُمْ يَخُوْضُوْا وَيَلْعَبُوْا حَتّٰى يُلٰقُوْا يَوْمَهُمُ الَّذِيْ يُوْعَدُوْنَ ۞ وَهُوَ الَّذِيْ فِي السَّمَآءِ اِلٰهٌ وَفِي الْاَرْضِ اِلٰهٌ وَهُوَ الْحَكِيْمُ الْعَلِيْمُ ۞ وَتَبَارَكَ الَّذِيْ لَهُ مُلْكُ السَّمٰوٰتِ وَالْاَرْضِ وَمَا بَيْنَهُمَا وَعِنْدَهُ عِلْمُ السَّاعَةِ وَاِلَيْهِ تُرْجَعُوْنَ ۞ وَلَا يَمْلِكُ الَّذِيْنَ يَدْعُوْنَ مِنْ دُوْنِهِ الشَّفَاعَةَ اِلَّا مَنْ شَهِدَ بِالْحَقِّ وَهُمْ يَعْلَمُوْنَ ۞ وَلَئِنْ سَاَلْتَهُمْ مَّنْ خَلَقَهُمْ لَيَقُوْلُنَّ اللّٰهُ فَاَنّٰى يُؤْفَكُوْنَ ۞ وَقِيْلِهِ يَارَبِّ اِنَّ هٰؤُلَآءِ قَوْمٌ لَا يُؤْمِنُوْنَ ۞ فَاصْفَحْ عَنْهُمْ وَقُلْ سَلَامٌ فَسَوْفَ يَعْلَمُوْنَ ۞

———✥———

74. But the disbelieving criminals will abide in the punishment of Hell.

75. It will not be abated for them, and therein they are in despair (of any mercy and hope of escape).

76. We have not wronged them, but they are the wrongdoers (who ever wronged themselves).

77. They will call out (to the chief keeper of Hell): "O Mālik! Let your Lord make an end of us!" He says: "You are bound to remain (therein)!"

78. We have brought you the truth, assuredly, but most of you are averse to the truth.

79. Or are they settling on some plan (against you, O Messenger)? But We have already settled a "plan" (against them).

80. Or do they think that We do not hear their secrets (that they whisper only to themselves,) and their private counsels? Indeed We do, and Our messengers (angels) are by them, recording.

81. Say: "If the All-Merciful had a child, I would be the first to worship."

82. All-Glorified is the Lord of the heavens and the earth, the Lord of the Supreme Throne,[19] (exalted) above all that they attribute (to Him in ignorance and falsehood).

83. So leave them plunging about in play and amusement until the Day which they have been promised.

84. And He it is Who is God in the heaven (exclusively deserving of worship), and God on the earth (exclusively deserving of worship). He is the All-Wise, the All-Knowing.

85. Blessed and Supreme is He to Whom belongs the sovereignty of the heavens and the earth, and all that is between them; and with Him is the knowledge of the Last Hour. And to Him you are on the way to return.

86. Those whom they (deify and then) invoke apart from God have no power and permission to intercede (with God in either world); only those who bear witness to the truth (of God's absolute Oneness in Divinity, Lordship, and Sovereignty), and who have knowledge (of the truth, will have it).

87. If you ask them who has created them, they will certainly say, "God." How then are they turned away from the truth and make false claims?

88. (God certainly hears His Messenger when) he says: "O my Lord! Surely those are a people who do not believe."

89. Yet forbear and pardon them, and (when you go your way,) say, "Peace (be upon you)!" In time, they will come to know.

---

19. For the Supreme Throne, see 7: 54, note 13.

SŪRAH 44

AD-DUKHĀN (THE SMOKE)

Makkah period

This *sūrah* of 59 verses was revealed in Makkah toward the end of the Makkan period. It derives its name from the word *dukhān* (smoke) in verse 10. It warns the obstinate enemies of the Messenger of the punishments that might come upon them and reminds them of how and why the Pharaoh and his army were drowned in the sea. It also concentrates upon the Qur'ān's Divine authorship, on God's being the unique Creator and Lord of the whole universe, and therefore the Only One to be worshipped. It concludes with mention of the final end of the believers and their enemies.

In the Name of God, the All-Merciful, the All-Compassionate.

1. *Ḥā. Mīm.*

2. By the Book clear in itself and clearly showing the truth.

3. We sent it down on a night full of blessings; surely We have ever been warning (humankind since their creation).

4. In that night every affair is identified and made distinct for wise purposes,

5. As a command issued from Our Presence; surely We have ever been sending Messengers (from among the angels and human beings to convey Our decrees and guide),

6. As a mercy from your Lord – surely He is the All-Hearing, the All-Knowing[1] –

7. The Lord of the heavens and the earth and all that is between them, if you would but seek certainty (about the Messenger and the Book he brings).

8. There is no deity but He, giving life and causing to die; your Lord and the Lord of your forefathers.[2]

9. Yet (they do not desire certainty; instead) they are in an irrecoverable doubt, lost in the playthings of the worldly life.

10. Then watch (O Messenger) for the day when the sky will bring forth a visible smoke,

11. Which will engulf the people, (causing them to exclaim): "This is a painful punishment.[3]

12. "Our Lord! Remove this punishment from us, for now we are true believers."

13. How is a reminder possible for them (such that their profession of faith could be true), seeing that there has come to them a Messenger making the truth clear (and embodying it in every element of his life and character),

14. But they turn away from him and say (of him): "One taught by others, a madman."[4]

15. We will hold back the punishment for a little (while), but you will turn back (to your former ways of unbelief, whose outcome is a punishment everlasting) –

16. On the day when We will seize with the mightiest grasp.[5] We will indeed take retribution.

17. Before them, assuredly We tried the people of the Pharaoh, when there came to them a noble Messenger,

18. Saying: "Deliver to me the servants of God![6] I am a trustworthy Messenger sent to you (by God).

---

1. When we consider these verses together with *Sūrat al-Qadr* (no. 97), we can conclude that they mention God's unchanging practice from the beginning of the universe. This practice has two aspects, one for the life of all creatures, the other for the guidance of humankind and the jinn. Although we do not, and cannot, know its exact nature, all things and affairs or events have, in God's Knowledge, an eternal existence. This is the existence of things and events in their totality or universality. God wills an individual thing to come into existence or an individual event to take place and He decrees for it its own particular identity. We can describe this process as each thing and event being identified with its particular nature by the Divine Destiny (as referred to in verse 15: 21: *There is not a thing but the stores [for its life and sustenance] are with Us, and We do not send it down except in due, determined measure*). Destiny transfers this event or thing to the realm of Divine Power, and Divine Power creates it according to the measures determined by Destiny. This creation is called *fatr* – origination according to or on a certain system, and the totality of the attributes given to a particular thing or being is called its *fitrah*.

As we can deduce from the verses discussed, each year has a particular identity and importance in the total history of the universe in general, and that of humankind in particular, and there is a special night during each year in which every thing or being that God has willed to come into existence and every event to take place during that year is identified or particularized and transferred from Divine Knowledge to the disposal of the Divine Power. As can be understood from other relevant verses, such as 97: 1 and 2: 185, where it is stated that the Qur'ān was sent down on the Night of Destiny (or Power and Measure), and during the holy month of Ramaḍān, this night is the Night of Destiny (or Power and Measure). Since this night is in the Holy Month of Ramaḍān, according to the lunar year, which is 11 days shorter than the solar year, any night of the solar year will be this night once every 354 years. (We should always bear in mind that all of the explanations concerning God are in respect to us, or from our perspective, and according to our measures in our relation with Him. As for God Himself, He is beyond all restrictions and measures of time and space.)

What the verses mean as far as the warning and guidance of human beings is concerned is that throughout history God sent Messengers and sent down or revealed Scriptures. The Qur'ān was sent down in two ways, one in its totality, and the other in parts. Interpreters of the Qur'ān say that the Qur'ān was sent in its totality from the Supreme Ever-Preserved Ever-Tablet to the heaven of the world, or *Bayt al-Maʿmūr*. We do not know the nature of this *Bayt* (House) and how the Qur'ān was sent down to it or to the heaven of the world. However, in the light of the verses discussed here (1–6 in this *sūrah*), it can be said that as every Divine Book was identified with its particular nature in its totality, or transferred in its totality from God's Knowledge or the Supreme Ever-Preserved Tablet or the Mother Book (see *sūrah* 43: 4; *sūrah* 6: 59, note 13; *sūrah* 13: 39, note 13; *sūrah* 17: 14, note 10; *sūrah* 85: 22), the Qur'ān was also identified in its totality in, or transferred from, the same original source on the Night of Destiny (or Power and Measure).

As can be understood from verse 97: 4, the Messengers that are mentioned in verse 5 as being sent are both the angels responsible for the events that occur in the universe and those events that occur in the life of all beings, including those angels charged with bringing the Divine Book to the Prophets (namely Gabriel and his aides), and the human Messengers sent for the guidance of humankind.

Verse 6 states that whatever God decrees is a mercy for beings, including humankind. It is a manifestation of His being either *ar-Rahmān* (the All-Merciful) or *ar-Rahīm* (the All-Compassionate). (For the meaning of these titles, and the difference between them, see *sūrah* 1, notes 4–5.)

2. The descriptions of God Almighty in verses 7 and 8 signify that there is nothing in the universe that creates, maintains, and causes to die, and therefore there is no thing or being that deserves to be worshipped and there is no thing or being that can give orders by which one should arrange one's life.

3. When the Makkan polytheists obstinately insisted on their polytheism and cruel treatment of God's Messenger and the believers, the Messenger, upon him be peace and blessings, prayed to God to help him by sending something like the drought that had afflicted the Egyptians during the time of the Prophet Joseph, so that they might come to belief. God accepted his prayer and a severe drought and hunger overtook the Makkans. Because of this, they felt as if the sky was full of smoke or mist.

As stated in certain Prophetic Traditions, the smoke also refers to another punishment of God that will afflict nearly all the unbelieving people and make the believers feel as if they have caught influenza toward the end of time, and this will be a sign of the approach of the Last Hour. So too it may indicate the "smoke" of philosophical and scientific materialism that has engulfed many people in the world and to some extent affected the believers also, or the "smoke" produced by modern weaponry and the side-effects of world wars, or similar punishments that will manifest themselves in the future.

4. This and similar slanders were uttered against God's Messenger by his severest opponents in Makkah, and they have been repeated by many orientalists and materialists in modern times.

5. The verses flow in such a way that the "smoke" is indicated in all the meanings mentioned above in note 3. So the day mentioned in this verse and the seizure may well be referring to the Battle of Makkah where almost all the leading enemies of the Messenger were killed, as well as to the greatest calamities and wars that will occur toward the end of time, and finally to the Judgment Day when the unbelievers will be thrown into Hell.

6. The Prophet Moses, upon him be peace, meant the Children of Israel by *the servants of God*, and reminded the Pharaoh and his people that they had wrongfully enslaved them, although they were only God's servants, who, as all people are, were sent to the world with freedom by their Creator – God.

496   سُوۡرَۃُ الدُّخَانِ   ٤٩٦

وَأَن لَّا تَعۡلُوۡا عَلَى اللّٰهِ إِنِّیۡ ءَاتِیۡکُم بِسُلۡطٰنٍ مُّبِیۡنٍ ۝ وَإِنِّیۡ عُذۡتُ بِرَبِّیۡ وَرَبِّکُمۡ أَن تَرۡجُمُوۡنِ ۝ وَإِن لَّمۡ تُؤۡمِنُوۡا لِیۡ فَاعۡتَزِلُوۡنِ ۝ فَدَعَا رَبَّهٗۤ أَنَّ هٰۤؤُلَآءِ قَوۡمٌ مُّجۡرِمُوۡنَ ۝ فَأَسۡرِ بِعِبَادِیۡ لَیۡلًا إِنَّکُم مُّتَّبَعُوۡنَ ۝ وَاتۡرُکِ الۡبَحۡرَ رَهۡوًا إِنَّهُمۡ جُندٌ مُّغۡرَقُوۡنَ ۝ کَمۡ تَرَکُوۡا مِن جَنّٰتٍ وَعُیُوۡنٍ ۝ وَزُرُوۡعٍ وَمَقَامٍ کَرِیۡمٍ ۝ وَنَعۡمَةٍ کَانُوۡا فِیۡهَا فٰکِهِیۡنَ ۝ کَذٰلِکَ وَأَوۡرَثۡنٰهَا قَوۡمًا ءَاخَرِیۡنَ ۝ فَمَا بَکَتۡ عَلَیۡهِمُ السَّمَآءُ وَالۡأَرۡضُ وَمَا کَانُوۡا مُنظَرِیۡنَ ۝ وَلَقَدۡ نَجَّیۡنَا بَنِیۤ إِسۡرَآءِیۡلَ مِنَ الۡعَذَابِ الۡمُهِیۡنِ ۝ مِن فِرۡعَوۡنَ إِنَّهٗ کَانَ عَالِیًا مِّنَ الۡمُسۡرِفِیۡنَ ۝ وَلَقَدِ اخۡتَرۡنٰهُمۡ عَلَىٰ عِلۡمٍ عَلَى الۡعَالَمِیۡنَ ۝ وَءَاتَیۡنٰهُم مِّنَ الۡءَایٰتِ مَا فِیۡهِ بَلٰٓؤٌا مُّبِیۡنٌ ۝ إِنَّ هٰۤؤُلَآءِ لَیَقُوۡلُوۡنَ ۝ إِنۡ هِیَ إِلَّا مَوۡتَتُنَا الۡأُوۡلَىٰ وَمَا نَحۡنُ بِمُنشَرِیۡنَ ۝ فَأۡتُوۡا بِءَابَآئِنَاۤ إِن کُنتُمۡ صٰدِقِیۡنَ ۝ أَهُمۡ خَیۡرٌ أَمۡ قَوۡمُ تُبَّعٍ وَالَّذِیۡنَ مِن قَبۡلِهِمۡ أَهۡلَکۡنٰهُمۡ إِنَّهُمۡ کَانُوۡا مُجۡرِمِیۡنَ ۝ وَمَا خَلَقۡنَا السَّمٰوٰتِ وَالۡأَرۡضَ وَمَا بَیۡنَهُمَا لٰعِبِیۡنَ ۝ مَا خَلَقۡنٰهُمَاۤ إِلَّا بِالۡحَقِّ وَلٰکِنَّ أَکۡثَرَهُمۡ لَا یَعۡلَمُوۡنَ ۝

———⟨≈⟩———

19. "And do not exalt yourself in proud defiance against God (by disobeying His order and so rejecting my Messengership). Surely I have come to you with an evident authority.

20. "I have sought refuge in my Lord, Who is surely also your Lord, from your stoning me to death.

21. "If you will not believe in me, then keep away from me (let me go)!"

22. Then he called upon his Lord: "These are indeed a guilty people committed to accumulating sins."

23. Then (his Lord commanded him): "Set forth with My servants by night. You are sure to be pursued.

24. "And now leave the sea in quiet (as it was when it divided for you), for they are a host destined to be drowned."

25. How many were the gardens and springs that they left behind;

26. And cornfields, and excellent dwellings, and elevated, honored situations;

27. And other comforts of life, in which they used to take delight!

28. Just so! And We made another people heirs (to the bounties they enjoyed).[7]

29. And neither the heaven nor the earth shed tears over them, nor were they given a respite (when the punishment became due on them).

30. And indeed We delivered the Children of Israel from the humiliating persecutions

31. Of the Pharaoh. He was indeed a haughty tyrant committing excesses.

32. And with knowledge (deliberately and for a purpose known to Us) We chose them (the Children of Israel) over all other peoples (in their time).

33. And (as a favor) We granted them many signs (miracles), in which there was a manifest trial.[8]

34. Yet these (Makkan polytheist) people say with emphasis:

35. "There is nothing beyond our first death,[9] and we will not be raised again.

36. "If you are truthful (in claiming that the dead will be raised to a new life), then bring back our forefathers."

37. What? Are they better (in wealth and power), or were the people of Tubbaʿ[10] and the others (that We destroyed) before them? We destroyed them, for they were disbelieving criminals committed to accumulating sins.[11]

38. We have not created the heavens and the earth and all that is between them in play and fun.

39. We have created them only with truth (for meaningful purposes, and on solid foundations of truth), but most people do not know.

7. For detailed account of Moses' experiences with the Pharaoh and his men, see *sūrah* 20: 43–79; *sūrah* 26: 10–68; *sūrah* 28: 36–40.

8. God's treatment of a people is for their good and is directed toward their education. This sometimes requires rewards and sometimes punishment. Both rewarding and punishment contain favors and tribulations which require gratitude and patience. The Children of Israel had been oppressed by the dynasty of the Pharaohs for many years, and this had caused them to develop many complexes and an attitude of slavery. So, in order that they should arouse themselves to freedom and evolve the character needed to live as a free people according to God's commandments, God favored them with many miracles both in Egypt and after the Exodus. However, as every favor and extraordinary blessing do, those miracles also contained a trial. Just as every miracle undeniably convinces people of the Divine truths proclaimed by the Prophets, denial of them brings ruinous punishment.

9. For the first death and whether there will be a second one, see Appendix 11, and *sūrah* 40: 11, note 4.

10. Tubba' was the title used for the rulers of Himyar, who lived in Yemen. The people of Himyar were a tribe of the Sheba who ruled in south Arabia for almost 1,000 years from around 1100 BC to around 115 BC. (For the people of Sheba, see *sūrah* 27, note 9, *sūrah* 34, note 10.) The dynasty of Tubba' came to power in 115 BC in Yemen and survived until 300 AD. Their story circulated among the Arabs as a legend.

11. The verse means that it is highly likely that any people who do not believe in the Hereafter will lapse into all kinds of sins. This will happen because they are devoid of any spiritual sanctions that would keep them away from evil. Belief in the Hereafter or the Resurrection is very important for individual and collective life for many reasons, as listed below:

Children are one-fourth of humanity. They cannot comprehend death, which must seem to them an awful tragedy, except via the idea of Paradise, which spiritually strengthens their weak, fragile natures. It gives them the hope to live joyfully, despite the vulnerability of their na-

ture, which can so readily burst into tears. Keeping Paradise in mind, they may say: "My little sister or friend has died and has become a bird in Paradise. She is playing there and enjoying a better life."

The elderly make up another one-fourth of humankind. They can endure death only by believing in the afterlife, which consoles them somewhat for the imminent extinction of this life to which they are so attached, for their exclusion from their lovely world. The hope of eternal life allows them to counter the pain and despair arising from the anticipation of death and separation, despite their fragile temperament and spirit.

Young people are the mainspring and foundation of social life. Only the thought of Hell enables them to control the stormy energy of feelings and passions and their tempestuous spirits from destructiveness and oppression by diverting them into serving the collective interest. Without this fear, and drunk on the energy of youth, they would follow the principle of "might makes right" and give free rein to their passions. This would turn the world into a hell for the weak and powerless, and lower human life to the level of beasts.

The family is the inclusive core of our worldly life, our most fundamental resource, and the paradise, home, and castle of our worldly happiness. Every person's home is their own miniature world. The vitality and happiness of our homes and families depend upon sincere and devoted respect, true kindness, and self-denying compassion. All of this, in turn, depends upon eternal friendship and companionship, an immortal bond, as well as the belief that feelings between parents and children, brothers and sisters, and husbands and wives, will be everlasting.

If the Resurrection's reality and truth and all the consequences thereof are removed from the human state, the meaning of being human – so exalted, vital, and important within creation – is lowered to that of a carcass fed upon by microbes. Let those concerned with humanity's orderly life, morals, and society focus on this matter. If the Resurrection is denied, with what will they fill the resulting void and how will they cure the deep wounds? (*The Words*, "the Tenth Word," 109–110)

45. Like molten brass; it will boil in their bellies,

46. Like the boiling of hot water.

47. "(O angels of Hell!) Take him (the sinful one) and drag him into the midst of the Blazing Flame!

48. "Then pour over his head boiling water as punishment.

49. "Taste! (Only in your own judgment) were you mighty, honorable, and noble.

50. "And this (what you are suffering now) is that which you used to doubt!"

51. Whereas the God-revering, pious ones will be in a position absolutely secure (from any evil),

52. Amid gardens and springs (of Paradise);

53. Dressed in fine silk and silk brocade, (seated) face to face.

54. Just so it will be. And We will assign for them maidens pure, most beautiful of eye.

55. There they call for every kind of fruit in security (from any harm).

56. They will not taste death therein, except the first death (of leaving the world); and He has preserved them from the punishment of the Blazing Flame;

57. As a grace from your Lord. That is the supreme triumph.

58. So (to enable you for that triumph) We have made this Qur'ān easy to understand by revealing it in your tongue, so that they may remember and be mindful (and order their lives according to it).

59. Then wait (O Messenger, and watch (how they react and how they fare); they too are waiting (to see how your mission will fare).

40. Surely the Day of Judgment and Distinction (between the truth and falsehood and the righteous and the sinful) is the time appointed for them all;

41. The Day when no guardian will be of any avail to one supported and protected, and none will be helped;

42. Save those on whom God will have mercy.[12] Surely He is the All-Glorious with irresistible might (Whose punishment no one can escape), the All-Compassionate (especially toward His believing servants).

43. (Here is) the tree of Zaqqūm,[13]

44. The food of him addicted to sinning,

---

12. Such people are the God-revering, pious ones, who believe in all of God's signs and Revelations, and have submitted to Him wholly (in Islam) (43: 67, 69).

13. For the tree of Zaqqūm, see: 17: 60, note 27.

SŪRAH 45

AL-JĀTHĪYAH
(KNEELING DOWN)

Makkah period

This *surah* of 37 verses was revealed toward the end of the Makkan period. It takes its name from the word *al-jāthiyah* in verse 28. In its initial verses, the *surah* draws attention to God's signs in the universe for the believers, for those who seek certainty, and for those who use their reason. Then it cites many of God's favors to humankind so that they may reflect and accept the guidance of the Qur'ān. It continues to recount some events from the history of the Children of Israel. Finally, it presents the end that awaits both believers and unbelievers.

In the Name of God, the All-Merciful, the All-Compassionate.

1. Ḥā. Mīm.

2. (This is) the Book being sent down in parts from God, the All-Glorious with irresistible might, the All-Wise.

3. In the heavens and on the earth there are indeed (clear) signs for the believers (pointing to God's Existence, Oneness, and Lordship);

4. And in your creation and His scattering (innumerable kinds of) living creatures (through the earth) there are (clear) signs for a people who seek certainty of faith (in His existence, Oneness, and Lordship).

5. And in the alternation of night and day (with their periods shortening and lengthening), and in the provision (rain) God sends down from the sky and reviving thereby the earth after its death, and in His turning about of the winds — (in all this) there are (clear) signs for a people who are able to reason and understand.[1]

6. Those are the Revelations of God that We recite to you (through Gabriel) with truth. In what other statement, if not in God and His Revelations, will they, then, believe?[2]

7. Woe to everyone addicted to inventing falsehoods, addicted to sinning:

8. He hears God's Revelations recited to him, and yet he persists in unbelief haughtily as if he had not heard them. So give him the glad tidings of a painful punishment.[3]

9. When he has come to some knowledge of Our signs (whether in the universe or in the Qur'ān), he takes them in mockery.[4] For such there is a humiliating punishment.

10. In front of them there is Hell; and all that they have earned (of this world) will be of no avail whatever to them, and

nor will those whom (apart from God and in defiance of Him) they have taken as guardians (to entrust their affairs to). For them there is a mighty punishment.

11. This (Qur'ān) is the guidance, and for those who disbelieve in the signs and Revelations of their Lord there is a painful punishment of loathsome kind (brought on by their loathsome deeds).

12. God it is Who has made the sea to be of service to you by making it subservient (to His command) so that the ships may run through it by His command, and that you may seek of His bounty, and that (in return) you may give thanks.

13. He has also made of service to you whatever is in the heavens and whatever is on the earth, all is from Him (a gift of His Grace). Surely in this there are (clear) signs for a people who reflect.

---

1. Verse 3 states that what is manifest to the eye through the universe is enough to enable faith, for believers see the heavens and the earth replete with manifest signs for God's Existence, Oneness, and Lordship. However, verse 4 calls us to study the parts of creation or the universe. When we study our existence and the existence and life of animals on the earth, our faith is strengthened and develops into certainty. Bediüzzaman Said Nursi reminds us that to strengthen our faith we should reflect generally on the outer world (the heavens and the earth), but be more detailed and penetrating when we study our own creation and structure.

The 3rd verse uses the word *believers*; this is different from the usage of the phrase *those who believe*. This form denotes those who have attained faith and in whose hearts faith has been established. The phrase *those who believe* refers to those who have acknowledged faith. When the Qur'ān uses the verb *believe* in the simple present tense, which in Arabic denotes actions expressed in English by both the present continuous and simple present tense, it signifies that one is journeying in faith. This journeying continues until it has been established in the heart. However, this faith continues to be strengthened and becomes certainty (*yaqīn*). Certainty also has degrees: these are certainty arising from knowledge, certainty coming from observation, and certainty arising from direct experience. According to many, certainty of the truths of faith arising from direct experience can be attained in the Hereafter. Since journeying or developing in certainty continues throughout life, the Qur'ān usually uses it in the verbal form and in the (Arabic) simple present tense. The 4th verse here also uses the verbal form in this tense. So, the more we study ourselves and other creatures on the earth, the more we are certain of the truths of faith.

As for verse 5, it calls people to approach some important phenomena in the life of the universe with their reason or intellect and urge them to reflect on them, reason them out, and try to understand them with their meaning and functions in the complex web of creation and life. Such an approach to and study of these phenomena lead people who can use their reason in the proper way to be able to distinguish between truth and falsehood and between what is good and to their benefit and what is evil and to their harm. This is a more advanced rank that one can attain through certainty of faith. Without faith and certainty, reason alone cannot raise one to the rank where this distinction can be made. The person who has risen to the rank where reason or intellect enlightened by certainty of faith can be used in the proper way can easily perceive that whatever the Qur'ān says is absolutely true, and they do not see any conflict between the Revelation or the reported knowledge (the Qur'ān and the Sunnah) and reason, or between the Religion and science (not scientism). If there should sometimes seem to be a conflict, this kind of reason or intellect can correctly reconcile it. Said Nursi refers to this fact when he says, "If reported knowledge and reason conflict, reason is preferred, provided the reason is the kind of reason (fully enlightened by the Revelation)" (*Muhakemat*, 13).

By referring to the believers (believing individuals), the 3rd verse implies that an individual can have a general view of the universe that enables them to attain faith. By contrast, the 4th and 5th verses mention people who seek certainty and people who use their reason respectively, thus suggesting that a detailed study of existence and existential phenomena is important in reaching certainty and using reason properly.

We should point out here that acknowledgment and profession are essential to faith, unless there is an absolute, religiously accepted obstacle. Although certainty is a deeper degree in faith, it cannot be faith (*īmān*) unless acknowledgment and profession accompany it. For there have been many whose conscience has been convinced of the truths of faith, yet they have knowingly and obstinately refused to believe. The verse, *They rejected them out of mere iniquity and self-exaltation, although their consciences were convinced of their being true* (27: 14), refers to this.

2. The original (Qur'ānic) word translated as sign, Revelation, and verse is *āyah*. This means that both the heavens and the earth and all the phenomena they contain are manifest signs for the truths of faith. The Qur'ānic verses or Revelations are verbal expressions of the signs of the universe. In other words, every Qur'ānic word (*sūrah*, verse, sentence, phrase, word, and letter) has a counterpart in the universe. If the universe is a palace, the Qur'ān is, in addition to its many other aspects, the book that describes it. It is because of this that Muslim scholars say that the universe is the Book Created or the Book of Creation, and the Qur'ān is the Book Revealed or the Book of Revelation. So, the study of the universe or creation, which has given rise to many sciences, cannot be separated from the study of the Qur'ān. This is why there is no conflict between the Qur'ān and established scientific facts. One who can accurately understand the universe or the principles of sciences can understand the main essentials of the Religion. The same is true for history and historical events and for understanding them correctly. In the future, sciences will make greater and greater advances. So as Muslims, we should be ahead of others in the study of creation, history, and historical events, and thus can discover the correlation between the Qur'ān and the universe and history, and present the Qur'ān and Islam in the tongue of sciences or the Book of Creation, and history or events.

3. Despite every thing and every phenomenon in the universe being a clear sign of God's Existence, Oneness, Creativity, Lordship, and of His other Attributes, such as Power, Knowledge, Wisdom, and Will, despite the Qur'ān translating them to us in the most convincing way, and despite God's Messenger and all other previous Prophets having clearly established this fact through their character and miracles, there are those who claim otherwise and insist on unbelief; this is the greatest of slanders and sins. Moreover, such a person easily falls into sin, and therefore such a person earns a painful punishment.

4. This verse refers both to those who have some knowledge of the creational phenomena in the universe or of some scientific facts, and to those who have some knowledge of the Qur'ān and Islam. Since they are defeated by their arrogance and sinfulness, they tend to resort to the weapon of mocking the Qur'ān and Islam or some of their principles or tenets as a despicable means, and therefore prepare for themselves a humiliating punishment.

قُل لِّلَّذِينَ ءَامَنُوا يَغۡفِرُوا لِلَّذِينَ لَا يَرۡجُونَ أَيَّامَ ٱللَّهِ لِيَجۡزِيَ قَوۡمًۢا بِمَا كَانُوا يَكۡسِبُونَ ۝ مَنۡ عَمِلَ صَٰلِحًا فَلِنَفۡسِهِۦ وَمَنۡ أَسَآءَ فَعَلَيۡهَا ثُمَّ إِلَىٰ رَبِّكُمۡ تُرۡجَعُونَ ۝ وَلَقَدۡ ءَاتَيۡنَا بَنِىٓ إِسۡرَٰٓءِيلَ ٱلۡكِتَٰبَ وَٱلۡحُكۡمَ وَٱلنُّبُوَّةَ وَرَزَقۡنَٰهُم مِّنَ ٱلطَّيِّبَٰتِ وَفَضَّلۡنَٰهُمۡ عَلَى ٱلۡعَٰلَمِينَ ۝ وَءَاتَيۡنَٰهُم بَيِّنَٰتٍ مِّنَ ٱلۡأَمۡرِ فَمَا ٱخۡتَلَفُوٓا إِلَّا مِنۢ بَعۡدِ مَا جَآءَهُمُ ٱلۡعِلۡمُ بَغۡيًۢا بَيۡنَهُمۡ إِنَّ رَبَّكَ يَقۡضِى بَيۡنَهُمۡ يَوۡمَ ٱلۡقِيَٰمَةِ فِيمَا كَانُوا فِيهِ يَخۡتَلِفُونَ ۝ ثُمَّ جَعَلۡنَٰكَ عَلَىٰ شَرِيعَةٍ مِّنَ ٱلۡأَمۡرِ فَٱتَّبِعۡهَا وَلَا تَتَّبِعۡ أَهۡوَآءَ ٱلَّذِينَ لَا يَعۡلَمُونَ ۝ إِنَّهُمۡ لَن يُغۡنُوا عَنكَ مِنَ ٱللَّهِ شَيۡـًٔا وَإِنَّ ٱلظَّٰلِمِينَ بَعۡضُهُمۡ أَوۡلِيَآءُ بَعۡضٍ وَٱللَّهُ وَلِىُّ ٱلۡمُتَّقِينَ ۝ هَٰذَا بَصَٰٓئِرُ لِلنَّاسِ وَهُدًى وَرَحۡمَةٌ لِّقَوۡمٍ يُوقِنُونَ ۝ أَمۡ حَسِبَ ٱلَّذِينَ ٱجۡتَرَحُوا ٱلسَّيِّـَٔاتِ أَن نَّجۡعَلَهُمۡ كَٱلَّذِينَ ءَامَنُوا وَعَمِلُوا ٱلصَّٰلِحَٰتِ سَوَآءً مَّحۡيَاهُمۡ وَمَمَاتُهُمۡ سَآءَ مَا يَحۡكُمُونَ ۝ وَخَلَقَ ٱللَّهُ ٱلسَّمَٰوَٰتِ وَٱلۡأَرۡضَ بِٱلۡحَقِّ وَلِتُجۡزَىٰ كُلُّ نَفۡسِۭ بِمَا كَسَبَتۡ وَهُمۡ لَا يُظۡلَمُونَ ۝

---

of the Religion; and it was only after all this knowledge came to them that they differed through envious rivalry and insolence among themselves. Surely your Lord will judge among them on the Day of Resurrection concerning that on which they used to differ.

18. Thereafter (in this conclusive Revelation) We have set you on a way of life (*Shari'ah*) based on the Religion,[6] so follow it and do not follow the lusts and fancies of those who do not know (the Divine Guidance).

19. They surely cannot be of any avail to you as against God. And surely the wrongdoers (who, out of their caprices, follow ways other than that on which God has set you) are guardians of one another. Whereas God is the Guardian of the God-revering, pious.

20. This (Qur'ān which teaches the way of life God has prescribed) is perception and insight (into the truth) for humankind, and guidance and mercy for people who seek certainty of faith.

21. What? Do those who commit evil deeds think that We hold them equal with those who believe and do good, righteous deeds – equal in respect of their life and their death? How evil is their judgment!

22. God has created the heavens and the earth in truth (for meaningful purpose, on solid foundations of truth and embodying it), and so that every soul may be recompensed for what it has earned (in this world), and they will not be wronged.

⤙❧⤚

---

14. Tell those who believe that they should pardon those who do not hope for the coming of the Days of God (when He will make them understand what their unbelief means),[5] seeing that He will recompense people for what they have earned.

15. Whoever does a good, righteous deed, it is for (the good of) his own soul; and whoever does an evil, it is against it. Thereafter (in all events) it is to your Lord that you will be brought back.

16. We did for sure grant to the Children of Israel the Book, and the authority to judge (by the Book), and Prophethood; and We provided them with pure, wholesome things, and exalted them above all other peoples (of their time).

17. And We granted them clear proofs concerning the affairs and commands

5. The believers should not act in the manner of their opponents, lowering themselves to their ranks to respond to their attacks in like manner. Rather, they should preserve their dignity.

6. Some think and claim that the *Sharī'ah* consists in the assembly of the Islamic (social, economic, and political) laws. However, these laws were laid down in Madīnah, and this *sūrah* was revealed in Makkah. *Sūrah Shūrā* (no. 42), which mentions the *Sharī'ah* in its 13th verse, was also revealed in Makkah. So the *Sharī'ah* is the practical aspect of the Religion of Islam, and also includes the rules of worship.

500 سُورَةُ الْجَاثِيَةِ ٥٠٠

أَفَرَءَيْتَ مَنِ اتَّخَذَ إِلَٰهَهُ هَوَىٰهُ وَأَضَلَّهُ اللَّهُ عَلَىٰ عِلْمٍ وَخَتَمَ عَلَىٰ سَمْعِهِ وَقَلْبِهِ وَجَعَلَ عَلَىٰ بَصَرِهِ غِشَٰوَةً فَمَن يَهْدِيهِ مِنۢ بَعْدِ اللَّهِ أَفَلَا تَذَكَّرُونَ ﴿٢٣﴾ وَقَالُوا مَا هِيَ إِلَّا حَيَاتُنَا الدُّنْيَا نَمُوتُ وَنَحْيَا وَمَا يُهْلِكُنَا إِلَّا الدَّهْرُ وَمَا لَهُم بِذَٰلِكَ مِنْ عِلْمٍ إِنْ هُمْ إِلَّا يَظُنُّونَ ﴿٢٤﴾ وَإِذَا تُتْلَىٰ عَلَيْهِمْ ءَايَٰتُنَا بَيِّنَٰتٍ مَّا كَانَ حُجَّتَهُمْ إِلَّا أَن قَالُوا ائْتُوا بِـَٔابَآئِنَا إِن كُنتُمْ صَٰدِقِينَ ﴿٢٥﴾ قُلِ اللَّهُ يُحْيِيكُمْ ثُمَّ يُمِيتُكُمْ ثُمَّ يَجْمَعُكُمْ إِلَىٰ يَوْمِ الْقِيَٰمَةِ لَا رَيْبَ فِيهِ وَلَٰكِنَّ أَكْثَرَ النَّاسِ لَا يَعْلَمُونَ ﴿٢٦﴾ وَلِلَّهِ مُلْكُ السَّمَٰوَٰتِ وَالْأَرْضِ وَيَوْمَ تَقُومُ السَّاعَةُ يَوْمَئِذٍ يَخْسَرُ الْمُبْطِلُونَ ﴿٢٧﴾ وَتَرَىٰ كُلَّ أُمَّةٍ جَاثِيَةً كُلُّ أُمَّةٍ تُدْعَىٰ إِلَىٰ كِتَٰبِهَا الْيَوْمَ تُجْزَوْنَ مَا كُنتُمْ تَعْمَلُونَ ﴿٢٨﴾ هَٰذَا كِتَٰبُنَا يَنطِقُ عَلَيْكُم بِالْحَقِّ إِنَّا كُنَّا نَسْتَنسِخُ مَا كُنتُمْ تَعْمَلُونَ ﴿٢٩﴾ فَأَمَّا الَّذِينَ ءَامَنُوا وَعَمِلُوا الصَّٰلِحَٰتِ فَيُدْخِلُهُمْ رَبُّهُمْ فِي رَحْمَتِهِ ذَٰلِكَ هُوَ الْفَوْزُ الْمُبِينُ ﴿٣٠﴾ وَأَمَّا الَّذِينَ كَفَرُوا أَفَلَمْ تَكُنْ ءَايَٰتِي تُتْلَىٰ عَلَيْكُمْ فَاسْتَكْبَرْتُمْ وَكُنتُمْ قَوْمًا مُّجْرِمِينَ ﴿٣١﴾ وَإِذَا قِيلَ إِنَّ وَعْدَ اللَّهِ حَقٌّ وَالسَّاعَةُ لَا رَيْبَ فِيهَا قُلْتُم مَّا نَدْرِي مَا السَّاعَةُ إِن نَّظُنُّ إِلَّا ظَنًّا وَمَا نَحْنُ بِمُسْتَيْقِنِينَ ﴿٣٢﴾

---❦---

23. Do you ever consider him who has taken his lusts for his deity,[7] and whom God has (consequently) led astray though he has knowledge (of guidance and straying), and sealed his hearing and his heart, and put a cover on his sight? Who, then, can guide him after God (has led him astray)? Will you not then reflect and be mindful?

24. And they say: "There is nothing but only our life in this world. Some of us die while others continue to live; and nothing causes us to perish but Time (the processes of decline and decay)." But they have no (sure and true) knowledge about this (the real nature and meaning of life and death, and the life after it). They merely follow their conjectures.

25. When Our Revelations, clear as evidence and in meaning are recited (and conveyed) to them, they have no argument except to say: "Bring back our forefathers, if you are truthful in your claim."

26. Say: "God gives you life, then causes you to die, then He will gather you together for the Day of Resurrection, about (the coming of) which there is no doubt. But most people do not know (being content with narrow conjectures and ignorant suppositions).

27. To God belongs the sovereignty of the heavens and the earth.[8] On the Day when the Last Hour stands forth (and the Judgment is established), on that Day those who invented and followed falsehood will be ruined in loss;

28. And you will see every community gathered together and kneeling down (in fear). Every community will be called to its record of deeds (to account for whatever it did in the world). "This Day you will be recompensed for what you used to do.

29. "This is Our Book (the record of your deeds that We prepared), speaking the truth against you. Assuredly We have had transcribed what you used to do (in the world)."

30. Then: as for those who believed and did good, righteous deeds, their Lord will admit them into (Paradise, which is the embodiment of) His mercy. That is the obvious triumph.

31. As for those who disbelieved (there will be this reproach): "Were My Revelations not recited to you (indeed, recited repeatedly) but you in arrogance scorned them, and proved yourselves a guilty people committed to accumulating sins?

32. "When it was proclaimed that God's promise is true and that there is no doubt about the coming of the Last Hour, you said: 'We can make no sense of the Last Hour; we think it is only a supposition. We are by no means convinced (of it)'."

---

7. For an explanation, see 25: 43, note 9.

8. These verses clearly state that belief in God requires believing in the other pillars of faith. Aware of this fact, the materialists, to whom the verses refer, deny God's Existence. However, although denial is a conclusion and therefore has to be based on evidence, their denial is based on no evidence at all, and therefore is a mere assertion with no true knowledge. However, the whole universe with whatever is in it clearly proves the Existence of God. Anyone whose heart, eyes, and ears have not been sealed because of prejudices, desires, conceit, wrongdoing, or any other causes of unbelief cannot help but admit this truth. However, as stated in verse 23 above, no one can do anything for one whose senses have been sealed.

33. The evil deeds they committed have (now) become obvious to them, and what they used to mock (God's promised punishment) has overwhelmed them.

34. And it will be said: "We are oblivious of you today (so do not hope for forgiveness and favor), as you were oblivious of the encounter of this day of yours, and your (lasting) refuge will be the Fire, and you have no helpers.

35. "That is because you used to take all the signs and Revelations of God in mockery, and the life of the world deluded you." And so this Day they will not be taken out of it (the Fire), and (no plea will be accepted from them to return to the world and so) they can no longer make amends.

36. And all praise and gratitude are for God, the Lord of the heavens and the Lord of the earth, the Lord of the worlds.

37. And to Him belongs grandeur and sovereignty in the heavens and the earth, and He is the All-Glorious with irresistible might, the All-Wise.

SŪRAH 46

AL-AḤQĀF
(WIND-SHAPED DUNES)

Makkah period

Revealed toward the end of the Makkan period, this *sūrah* of 35 verses takes its name from the word *al-'aḥqāf* in verse 21, which means the sand hills, but is also the name of a place in the south of the Arabian peninsula. It warns all those who obstinately persist in their evil ways and defiance against the Religion of Truth by reminding them of the tragic end of the people of 'Ād. It presents some of the concrete proofs of the Messengership of the Prophet Muḥammad, upon him be peace and blessings. It also mentions the conversion to Islam of some jinn who listened to some parts from the Qur'ān, and who then went on to try to guide their people.

In the Name of God, the All-Merciful, the All-Compassionate.

1. Ḥā. Mīm.

2. (This is) the Book being sent down in parts from God, the All-Glorious with irresistible might, the All-Wise.

3. We have not created the heavens and the earth and all that is between them save with truth (for meaningful purposes, and on solid foundations of truth), and for an appointed term. But those who disbelieve turn away from that (Day of Judgment)[1] about which they are warned.

4. Say: "Do you not consider what those are whom (you deify and) invoke apart from God? Show me what they have created of the earth. Or do they have a share in (the

creation and maintenance of) the heavens? Bring me a Book (revealed) before this one (the Qur'ān) or some remnant of knowledge (accurately preserved and transmitted),[2] if you are truthful (in your claims)."

5. Who is more astray than one who invokes, apart from God, such as will not make any answer to him until the Day of Resurrection, and are (self-evidently) unconscious and heedless of their invocation?

1. This means that Judgment Day is both the end of the term God appointed for this (material) universe, one of the truths on which creation is based, and one of the important purposes for the creation of the earth.

2. The Qur'ān never makes it a cause of polemics that true knowledge is what God has revealed or the revealed knowledge. It always challenges its opponents to bring forth accurate or certified knowledge for their denial. Denial has two forms or kinds, one is "acceptance of non-existence" or willful rejection, and the other being mere "non-acceptance." The latter is doubt. It can be removed through evidence, provided it is not a willful attitude. If it is a willful attitude, then it becomes a judgment. As for the former, it is a conclusion, a judgment, which must be based on evidence or knowledge. For example, claims such as: there is no God, or God has never sent a Prophet or a Book, or there is no afterlife, or God has some partners, or things are formed by themselves, or causes have brought it about, or nature requires it (to be so) – all of such claims are conclusion and judgment, and therefore must be based on evidence and knowledge. Any assertion or conclusion

that is not based on evidence and knowledge is to be rejected. However, in whatever form it is, (willful) denial cannot be based on any knowledge and evidence, and is arbitrary negation, repudiation, rejection, and therefore it has no weight. Muslims must follow the Qur'ān in their response to the trends of denial, and accept the Revelation as the first and certain source of knowledge, without feeling any discomfiture.

Any claim of objectivity in this subject is in essence non-objectivity. Objective reasoning means impartial judgment, but "impartial" judgment means siding with the opponents or deniers and following temporary unbelief. Because it starts from the proposition: Let us not accept the Existence of God, or of Revelation, or of afterlife, and so on. So it is temporary unbelief and siding with unbelief. Therefore, what a denier should do is to falsify all the evidence upon which the pillars of faith are founded. This is impossible. While a single proof is enough for the establishment of the existence of something, proving its non-existence is not possible at all. In conclusion, there is and can be no evidence on which denial is based, and it is a mere conjecture, a baseless assertion.

502   سُورَةُ الأحْقَاف   ٥٠٢

وَإِذَا حُشِرَ ٱلنَّاسُ كَانُوا لَهُمْ أَعْدَآءً وَكَانُوا بِعِبَادَتِهِمْ كَافِرِينَ ۞ وَإِذَا تُتْلَىٰ عَلَيْهِمْ ءَايَٰتُنَا بَيِّنَٰتٍ قَالَ ٱلَّذِينَ كَفَرُوا لِلْحَقِّ لَمَّا جَآءَهُمْ هَٰذَا سِحْرٌ مُّبِينٌ ۞ أَمْ يَقُولُونَ ٱفْتَرَىٰهُ قُلْ إِنِ ٱفْتَرَيْتُهُ فَلَا تَمْلِكُونَ لِي مِنَ ٱللَّهِ شَيْئًا هُوَ أَعْلَمُ بِمَا تُفِيضُونَ فِيهِ كَفَىٰ بِهِ شَهِيدًۢا بَيْنِي وَبَيْنَكُمْ وَهُوَ ٱلْغَفُورُ ٱلرَّحِيمُ ۞ قُلْ مَا كُنتُ بِدْعًا مِّنَ ٱلرُّسُلِ وَمَآ أَدْرِي مَا يُفْعَلُ بِي وَلَا بِكُمْ إِنْ أَتَّبِعُ إِلَّا مَا يُوحَىٰ إِلَيَّ وَمَآ أَنَا۠ إِلَّا نَذِيرٌ مُّبِينٌ ۞ قُلْ أَرَءَيْتُمْ إِن كَانَ مِنْ عِندِ ٱللَّهِ وَكَفَرْتُم بِهِۦ وَشَهِدَ شَاهِدٌ مِّنۢ بَنِيٓ إِسْرَٰٓءِيلَ عَلَىٰ مِثْلِهِۦ فَـَٔامَنَ وَٱسْتَكْبَرْتُمْ إِنَّ ٱللَّهَ لَا يَهْدِي ٱلْقَوْمَ ٱلظَّٰلِمِينَ ۞ وَقَالَ ٱلَّذِينَ كَفَرُوا لِلَّذِينَ ءَامَنُوا لَوْ كَانَ خَيْرًا مَّا سَبَقُونَآ إِلَيْهِ وَإِذْ لَمْ يَهْتَدُوا بِهِۦ فَسَيَقُولُونَ هَٰذَآ إِفْكٌ قَدِيمٌ ۞ وَمِن قَبْلِهِۦ كِتَٰبُ مُوسَىٰٓ إِمَامًا وَرَحْمَةً وَهَٰذَا كِتَٰبٌ مُّصَدِّقٌ لِّسَانًا عَرَبِيًّا لِّيُنذِرَ ٱلَّذِينَ ظَلَمُوا وَبُشْرَىٰ لِلْمُحْسِنِينَ ۞ إِنَّ ٱلَّذِينَ قَالُوا رَبُّنَا ٱللَّهُ ثُمَّ ٱسْتَقَٰمُوا فَلَا خَوْفٌ عَلَيْهِمْ وَلَا هُمْ يَحْزَنُونَ ۞ أُو۟لَٰٓئِكَ أَصْحَٰبُ ٱلْجَنَّةِ خَٰلِدِينَ فِيهَا جَزَآءًۢ بِمَا كَانُوا يَعْمَلُونَ ۞

---

6. When all people are raised from the dead and gathered together for judgment, they (whom they invoked) will be enemies to them, and will disown their worshipping them.

7. When Our Revelations, clear as evidence and in meaning are recited (and conveyed) to them, those who disbelieve say of the truth when it reaches them: "This is clearly nothing but sorcery."[3]

8. Or do they say, "He (the Messenger) has fabricated it (the Qur'ān)?" Say: "If I have fabricated it, you have no power at all to help me against God. He knows best all that you are busy inventing concerning it (the Qur'ān). He suffices for a Witness between me and you. He is the All-Forgiving, the All-Compassionate.

9. "I am no novelty (either in my person or in the message I have brought) among the Messengers, and (being human) I do not know (unless God informs me) what (will happen in the future in the world and therefore what will) be done to me and to you. I only follow what is revealed to me, and I am only a plain warner."

10. Say: "Do you ever consider that if this Qur'ān is from God, and you disbelieve in it while (many) a witness from among the Children of Israel (those who had knowledge of Revelation) had already testified to the like of it and (also) believed, whereas you are too arrogant to believe: (is this not plain deviation and wrong?) Surely God does not guide the wrongdoing people."[4]

11. Those who disbelieve say of those who believe (as another pretext for their rejection of faith in the Qur'ān): "If it (the Qur'ān) had been something good and useful, those people would not have preceded us in accepting it." And as they (having refused it) have not found guidance through it, they say: "This is a fabrication from ancient times."

12. (They say so despite the fact that) before this there was the Book of Moses as a guide and mercy (for the Children of Israel); and this (Qur'ān) is a Book confirming (the truth in the earlier Scriptures) and revealed in Arabic to warn those who commit wrong, and as a good tiding for those devoted to doing good, aware that God is seeing them.

13. Surely those who profess, "Our Lord is God," and then follow the Straight Path (in their belief, thought, and actions), they will have no fear, nor will they grieve.

14. They are the companions of Paradise, abiding therein as a reward for what they used to do.

3. Their claim that the Qur'ān is sorcery is in fact an admission that it is not part of ordinary human speech and is something extraordinary.

4. As a continuation of the argument put forward in the previous verse, this verse means that God's Messenger is saying: "I am no novelty and different among the Messengers. Many came before me with Books similar to the Qur'ān in the teachings they contained. One of these Books was the Torah, which was granted to Moses. And many knowledgeable ones among the Children of Israel believed in it. But you, having no exact knowledge of Divine Books and Messengership, venture to disbelieve in its like – the Qur'ān. Then is this not plain deviation, wrong, and misjudgment?"

وَوَصَّيْنَا الْإِنسَانَ بِوَالِدَيْهِ إِحْسَانًا حَمَلَتْهُ أُمُّهُ كُرْهًا وَوَضَعَتْهُ كُرْهًا وَحَمْلُهُ وَفِصَالُهُ ثَلَاثُونَ شَهْرًا حَتَّى إِذَا بَلَغَ أَشُدَّهُ وَبَلَغَ أَرْبَعِينَ سَنَةً قَالَ رَبِّ أَوْزِعْنِي أَنْ أَشْكُرَ نِعْمَتَكَ الَّتِي أَنْعَمْتَ عَلَيَّ وَعَلَىٰ وَالِدَيَّ وَأَنْ أَعْمَلَ صَالِحًا تَرْضَاهُ وَأَصْلِحْ لِي فِي ذُرِّيَّتِي إِنِّي تُبْتُ إِلَيْكَ وَإِنِّي مِنَ الْمُسْلِمِينَ ۝ أُولَٰئِكَ الَّذِينَ نَتَقَبَّلُ عَنْهُمْ أَحْسَنَ مَا عَمِلُوا وَنَتَجَاوَزُ عَن سَيِّئَاتِهِمْ فِي أَصْحَابِ الْجَنَّةِ وَعْدَ الصِّدْقِ الَّذِي كَانُوا يُوعَدُونَ ۝ وَالَّذِي قَالَ لِوَالِدَيْهِ أُفٍّ لَّكُمَا أَتَعِدَانِنِي أَنْ أُخْرَجَ وَقَدْ خَلَتِ الْقُرُونُ مِن قَبْلِي وَهُمَا يَسْتَغِيثَانِ اللَّهَ وَيْلَكَ آمِنْ إِنَّ وَعْدَ اللَّهِ حَقٌّ فَيَقُولُ مَا هَٰذَا إِلَّا أَسَاطِيرُ الْأَوَّلِينَ ۝ أُولَٰئِكَ الَّذِينَ حَقَّ عَلَيْهِمُ الْقَوْلُ فِي أُمَمٍ قَدْ خَلَتْ مِن قَبْلِهِم مِّنَ الْجِنِّ وَالْإِنسِ إِنَّهُمْ كَانُوا خَاسِرِينَ ۝ وَلِكُلٍّ دَرَجَاتٌ مِّمَّا عَمِلُوا وَلِيُوَفِّيَهُمْ أَعْمَالَهُمْ وَهُمْ لَا يُظْلَمُونَ ۝ وَيَوْمَ يُعْرَضُ الَّذِينَ كَفَرُوا عَلَى النَّارِ أَذْهَبْتُمْ طَيِّبَاتِكُمْ فِي حَيَاتِكُمُ الدُّنْيَا وَاسْتَمْتَعْتُم بِهَا فَالْيَوْمَ تُجْزَوْنَ عَذَابَ الْهُونِ بِمَا كُنتُمْ تَسْتَكْبِرُونَ فِي الْأَرْضِ بِغَيْرِ الْحَقِّ وَبِمَا كُنتُمْ تَفْسُقُونَ ۝

—❧—

15. Now (among the good deeds) We have enjoined on human is the best treatment towards his parents. His mother bore him in pain, and in pain did she give him birth. The bearing of him and suckling of him (until weaned) is thirty months,⁵ until when he has reached his full manhood⁶ and reached forty years of age, he says: "My Lord! Arouse me that I may be thankful for all Your favors (life, health, sustenance, faith, and submission, and more) that You have bestowed on me and on my parents, and that I may do good, righteous deeds with which You will be pleased, and grant me righteous offspring (so that they treat me righteously, as I treat my parents). I have turned to You, and I am one of those who have submitted to You."

16. Those are they from whom We will accept (their good deeds in a manner to reward them in accordance with) the best of what they ever did, and whose evil deeds We will overlook, (and include them) among the companions of Paradise. This is a true promise which they have been given (here in the world).

17. But (there is many a one) who says to his parents (who call him to righteousness and faith): "Uff to you both! (I am fed up with you!) Do you threaten me that I will be brought forth from the dead (to a new life and judgment), while so many generations have passed away before me (and so far not a single person has been raised)?" And they both pray to God for help (in the guidance of their child, and say to him): "Woe to you! Believe! God's promise is certainly true!" But he says: "All this is nothing but fables of the ancients!"

18. Such are they upon whom the word (of God's punishment) is rightly due (as included) among the (similar) communities of the jinn and humankind before them. Surely they are the ones ruined in loss.

19. For all (individuals and groups) there will be degrees of their own, according to what they have done, and so God will pay them fully for their deeds, and they will not be wronged.

20. On that Day, those who disbelieve will be brought to the Fire (and they will be told): "You consumed in your worldly life your (share of) pure, wholesome things, and enjoyed them fully (without considering the due of the Hereafter, and so have taken in the world the reward of all your good deeds).⁷ So this Day you are recompensed with the punishment of abasement because of your scornful arrogance on the earth against all right, and because of your transgressing (the bounds set by God)."

5. Verse 2: 233 says that, (if they wish) mothers can suckle their children for two whole years, and verse 31: 14 expresses the same, that his weaning was in two years. So when the statement that the pregnancy and nursing of a child consists of 30 months is considered together with these verses, it is understood that the shortest period of bearing a child is 6 months. That is, a mother can give birth to a healthy baby in 6 months. So if a wife gives birth at the end of the sixth month of her pregnancy, she cannot be regarded as having committed the crime of adultery.

6. The age of full manhood or full (physical) maturity is, in the first stage, 15-20 or so years. The middle stage is 30-33 years, and the age when one is supposed to reach full intellectual and spiritual maturity is 40 years. It is rare that people change their belief and way of life after forty.

7. As stated in a Prophetic Tradition, there is a place pre-assigned for everyone in both Paradise and Hell. If one dies and enters Hell, the people of Paradise inherit one's place in Paradise. So God has pre-assigned for everyone pure, wholesome things to consume. If one does not believe in the Hereafter and chooses to consume all one's share of pure, wholesome things in the world, God grants them from these in return for their good deeds. Such a one will have no share in the Hereafter. The verse also says that God never allows any good deed to go to waste. He rewards an unbeliever in the world for their good deeds. A believer should aim at the Hereafter, without neglecting working for livelihood in the world.

504   سُورَةِ الاَحْقَافِ   ٥٠٤

وَاذْكُرْ أَخَا عَادٍ إِذْ أَنذَرَ قَوْمَهُ بِالأَحْقَافِ وَقَدْ خَلَتِ
النُّذُرُ مِن بَيْنِ يَدَيْهِ وَمِنْ خَلْفِهِ أَلَّا تَعْبُدُوا إِلَّا اللَّهَ إِنِّي أَخَافُ
عَلَيْكُمْ عَذَابَ يَوْمٍ عَظِيمٍ ۞ قَالُوا أَجِئْتَنَا لِتَأْفِكَنَا عَنْ آلِهَتِنَا فَأْتِنَا بِمَا
تَعِدُنَا إِن كُنتَ مِنَ الصَّادِقِينَ ۞ قَالَ إِنَّمَا الْعِلْمُ عِندَ اللَّهِ وَأُبَلِّغُكُم
مَّا أُرْسِلْتُ بِهِ وَلَكِنِّي أَرَاكُمْ قَوْمًا تَجْهَلُونَ ۞ فَلَمَّا رَأَوْهُ عَارِضًا
مُّسْتَقْبِلَ أَوْدِيَتِهِمْ قَالُوا هَذَا عَارِضٌ مُّمْطِرُنَا بَلْ هُوَ مَا اسْتَعْجَلْتُم
بِهِ رِيحٌ فِيهَا عَذَابٌ أَلِيمٌ ۞ تُدَمِّرُ كُلَّ شَيْءٍ بِأَمْرِ رَبِّهَا فَأَصْبَحُوا
لَا يُرَى إِلَّا مَسَاكِنُهُمْ كَذَلِكَ نَجْزِي الْقَوْمَ الْمُجْرِمِينَ ۞
وَلَقَدْ مَكَّنَّاهُمْ فِيمَا إِن مَّكَّنَّاكُمْ فِيهِ وَجَعَلْنَا لَهُمْ سَمْعًا
وَأَبْصَارًا وَأَفْئِدَةً فَمَا أَغْنَى عَنْهُمْ سَمْعُهُمْ وَلَا أَبْصَارُهُمْ
وَلَا أَفْئِدَتُهُم مِّن شَيْءٍ إِذْ كَانُوا يَجْحَدُونَ بِآيَاتِ اللَّهِ وَحَاقَ بِهِم
مَّا كَانُوا بِهِ يَسْتَهْزِئُونَ ۞ وَلَقَدْ أَهْلَكْنَا مَا حَوْلَكُم
مِّنَ الْقُرَى وَصَرَّفْنَا الْآيَاتِ لَعَلَّهُمْ يَرْجِعُونَ ۞ فَلَوْلَا
نَصَرَهُمُ الَّذِينَ اتَّخَذُوا مِن دُونِ اللَّهِ قُرْبَانًا آلِهَةً
بَلْ ضَلُّوا عَنْهُمْ وَذَلِكَ إِفْكُهُمْ وَمَا كَانُوا يَفْتَرُونَ ۞

───※───

21. Make mention of (Hūd) the brother of Ād: he warned his people in al-Aḥqāf – as indeed warners came and went before and after him (to warn their peoples) – saying: "Worship none but God alone. I surely fear for you the punishment of an awesome day."

22. They said: "Have you come to us to turn us away from our deities? If you are truthful in your claims, then bring us what you are threatening us with."

23. He said: "The knowledge (of when it will come) is only with God. I convey to you that with which I have been sent as a Messenger, but I see you are a people acting ignorantly."

24. Then (as the events unfolded) they saw that (which they were threatened with) as a dense cloud in the sky advancing towards their valleys, and they said: "This is a cloud bringing us rain." No; it is what you have (derisively) asked to be hastened: a wind bearing a painful punishment,

25. Bound to devastate everything by the command of its Lord. And so they became such that nothing was to be seen except their dwellings. Thus do We recompense the guilty people committed to accumulating sins.

26. We had, assuredly, given them such power and prosperity (on the earth) that We have not given to you (O Quraysh), and We had endowed them with hearing and eyes and hearts (all the means of perception, outward and inward). But neither their ears, nor their eyes, nor their hearts, availed them anything, as they obstinately rejected God's signs and Revelations, and what they used to mock overwhelmed them.

27. We have, assuredly, destroyed many townships that are around you, and (before that) We had set out the signs and Revelations in diverse ways, so that they might turn back (from their wrong ways).

28. So, why did those whom they took for deities apart from God as a means of nearness (to God) not help them (against God's punishment)? Rather, they failed them. That was (the end result of) their falsehood and all that they used to fabricate (of slanders against God).

وَإِذْ صَرَفْنَا إِلَيْكَ نَفَرًا مِّنَ الْجِنِّ يَسْتَمِعُونَ الْقُرْآنَ فَلَمَّا حَضَرُوهُ
قَالُوا أَنصِتُوا فَلَمَّا قُضِيَ وَلَّوْا إِلَى قَوْمِهِم مُّنذِرِينَ ۝ قَالُوا يَا قَوْمَنَا
إِنَّا سَمِعْنَا كِتَابًا أُنزِلَ مِن بَعْدِ مُوسَى مُصَدِّقًا لِّمَا بَيْنَ يَدَيْهِ يَهْدِي إِلَى
الْحَقِّ وَإِلَى طَرِيقٍ مُّسْتَقِيمٍ ۝ يَا قَوْمَنَا أَجِيبُوا دَاعِيَ اللَّهِ وَآمِنُوا بِهِ
يَغْفِرْ لَكُم مِّن ذُنُوبِكُمْ وَيُجِرْكُم مِّنْ عَذَابٍ أَلِيمٍ ۝
وَمَن لَّا يُجِبْ دَاعِيَ اللَّهِ فَلَيْسَ بِمُعْجِزٍ فِي الْأَرْضِ وَلَيْسَ لَهُ مِن دُونِهِ
أَوْلِيَاءُ أُولَئِكَ فِي ضَلَالٍ مُّبِينٍ ۝ أَوَلَمْ يَرَوْا أَنَّ اللَّهَ الَّذِي خَلَقَ
السَّمَوَاتِ وَالْأَرْضَ وَلَمْ يَعْيَ بِخَلْقِهِنَّ بِقَادِرٍ عَلَى أَن يُحْيِيَ الْمَوْتَى بَلَى إِنَّهُ
عَلَى كُلِّ شَيْءٍ قَدِيرٌ ۝ وَيَوْمَ يُعْرَضُ الَّذِينَ كَفَرُوا عَلَى النَّارِ أَلَيْسَ هَذَا
بِالْحَقِّ قَالُوا بَلَى وَرَبِّنَا قَالَ فَذُوقُوا الْعَذَابَ بِمَا كُنتُمْ تَكْفُرُونَ
۝ فَاصْبِرْ كَمَا صَبَرَ أُولُوا الْعَزْمِ مِنَ الرُّسُلِ وَلَا تَسْتَعْجِل لَّهُمْ
كَأَنَّهُمْ يَوْمَ يَرَوْنَ مَا يُوعَدُونَ لَمْ يَلْبَثُوا إِلَّا سَاعَةً مِّن
نَّهَارٍ بَلَاغٌ فَهَلْ يُهْلَكُ إِلَّا الْقَوْمُ الْفَاسِقُونَ ۝

29. We directed a company of the jinn towards you in order that they might listen to the Qur'ān (while you were reciting of it). When they were present for it, they said (to one another): "Be silent and listen!" When the recitation finished, they returned to their community as warners.[8]

30. They said: "O our people! We have listened to a Book which has been sent after Moses, confirming (the Divine origin of and the truths that are still contained by) the Revelations prior to it:[9] It guides towards the truth and towards a straight road (in all matters).

31. "O our people! Respond (affirmatively) to him who calls to God, and believe in him. God will forgive you your sins (which you have committed so far), and save you from a painful punishment.

32. "Whoever does not respond (affirmatively) to him who calls to God, he cannot frustrate (God's will) on the earth, and no guardian will he have apart from God (once God has disowned him):[10] those (who seek to do so) are in obvious error."

33. Have they (the unbelievers) not considered that surely God, Who has created the heavens and the earth, and never wearied with their creation, is able to bring the dead to life? Certainly He is; He has full power over everything.

34. On the Day when those who disbelieve are brought to the Fire (they will be asked): "Is this not true?" They will say: "Yes, most certainly, by our Lord!" He (God) will say: "Taste the punishment in which you used to disbelieve!"

35. So, be patient (O Messenger), (with their rejection of faith and with whatever they do), just as those of greatest steadfastness and resolution among the Messengers[11] were patient, and do not seek to hasten (the judgment on) them. The Day when they see what they are threatened with, (they will feel) as if they had not stayed (in the world) save a short while of the day only. The message has been conveyed. Will, then, any be destroyed save the people who transgress the bounds (in belief and action)?

8. This happened in Batn an-Nakhlah outside Makkah while God's Messenger was doing Prayer on his return to Makkah from his journey to Ṭā'if.

9. As can be understood from the reference of the jinn that the Qur'ān was revealed after Moses, without mentioning Jesus and the Gospel, they were among the followers of the faith of Moses and the Torah.

10. After this event, the jinn came to the Messenger in groups one after the other.

The word jinn literally means something hidden or veiled from sight. The jinn are a species of invisible beings. A short Qur'ānic chapter (72) is named after them. The Prophet Muḥammad, upon him be peace and blessings, was sent to them too, and many among them believed in him.

The jinn are conscious beings charged with Divine obligations. Recent discoveries in biology make it clear that God created beings particular to each realm in the universe (See 2: 30,

note 31). The jinn were created before Adam. and Eve, and were responsible for cultivating and improving the world. Although God later superseded them with us, He did not exempt them from religious obligations.

Like angels, the jinn move extremely fast and are not bound by the time and space constraints within which we normally move. However, since the spirit is more active and faster than the jinn, a person who lives at the level of the spirit's life, and who can transcend what we know as the limits of matter and the confines of time and space, can be quicker and more active than them (see 27: 38–40). (For detailed information about the jinn and their relation with humankind, see *Essentials of the Islamic Faith*, 69–73.)

11. According to many scholars, basing their conclusions on verse 42: 13, those Messengers are Noah, Abraham, Moses, Jesus, and finally, the Prophet Muḥammad, upon them be peace and blessings.

SŪRAH 47

MUHAMMAD

Madīnah period

One of the earliest Revelations in Madīnah, this *sūrah* of 38 verses is named after Muḥammad, who is mentioned in the second verse. It deals with such matters as fighting, the treatment of prisoners of war, the distribution of the spoils of war, and the final end that awaits the believers and unbelievers.

In the Name of God, the All-Merciful, the All-Compassionate.

1. Those who disbelieve and bar (people) from God's way – God will render all their deeds vain.[1]

2. While those who believe and do good, righteous deeds, who believe in what has been sent on Muḥammad – and it is the truth from their Lord – He will blot out from them their evil deeds (which will otherwise prevent their achievement of their goals in both worlds), and set their hearts fully aright and improve their conditions (both in this world and the next).[2]

3. That is because those who disbelieve follow falsehood (in their beliefs, thoughts, and actions), while those who believe follow the truth from their Lord.[3] Thus God expounds to people what they are like.

4. So, when you meet those who disbelieve in war, smite at their necks (without giving them opportunity to defeat you). At length, when you have sufficiently suppressed them, (without continuing fighting) bind a firm bond of captivity on them. Then set them free either as a favor without demanding anything in return, or for ransom (which may consist of a reciprocal

exchange of prisoners of war), so that warfare may abandon weapons and come to an end. That (is God's command). Had God so willed, He would certainly exact retribution from them (Himself), but (He orders you to fight) in order to try you by means of one another. As for those who are killed in God's cause, He will never render their deeds vain.

5. (Rather,) He will guide them (to the realization of their goal in both worlds) and set their conditions right for them,[4]

6. And He will admit them into Paradise that He has made known to them.

7. O you who believe! If you help God('s cause by striving in His cause), He will help you and make your feet firm (so that you are steadfast in His cause and ultimately victorious).

8. But those who disbelieve: collapse and perdition are their lot, and He will render all their deeds vain.

9. This is because they are averse to that which God has sent down, and so He causes their deeds to go to waste.

10. Have they not traveled about the earth and seen how the outcome was for those who came before them (and persisted in associating partners with Him, and in all kinds of transgression)? God brought utter devastation upon them, and the unbelievers (now) the like of their fate awaits.

11. This is because God surely is the Guardian of those who believe, but those who disbelieve have no guardian (acceptable in God's sight and who can help them against Him).

---

1. That is, all their efforts to prevent the spread of Islam will be in vain. Secondly, although their good deeds may bring profit to them in the world, but this will signify nothing in the Hereafter because they did not aim at the afterlife and pursued only the goods of the worldly life.

2. Sincere faith and doing good, righteous deeds as required by faith cause one to have a sound, sincere, and satisfied heart. God leads such a person to right decisions, proper thoughts, and good actions, which in turn cause that person to deepen in faith and sincerity. The virtuous circle that is formed in this way will lead the believers to attain their (Islamic) goals in the world and eternal happiness in the Hereafter.

3. The falsehood mentioned here is any system of belief, thought, or action that is based not on the Revelation, but on human desires and fancies that do not conform to or contradict God's ways of acting in the universe, which we improperly call "laws of nature," and the moral laws He has established for life in the world. Whereas the truth is the system of belief, thought, and action that is based on the Divine Revelation, and therefore in conformity with the laws God has established for the operation of the universe and human life on the earth. So, as we have sometimes mentioned, God has two collections of laws, one to govern human life and the universe, the other for religious life. Both require obedience. Obedience or disobedience to the former gives its results mainly in this world, while obedience or disobedience to the latter yields its results both in this world and in the Hereafter, but more in the Hereafter. Believers must obey both of them.

4. This verse mainly refers to the conditions of those killed in God's cause, though it has some reference to the world also. That is, God never lets the sacrifices made in His cause go to waste. Such actions contribute to the realization of the goal of those who perform them in the world. Martyrdom is among the greatest of sacrifices made in God's cause. Martyrs aim to uplift God's Word and gain God's approval and good pleasure, God enables the uplifting of His Word, becomes pleased with martyrs, saves them from suffering in the worlds of the Hereafter, and forgive them.

12. God will admit those who believe and do good, righteous deeds into Gardens through which rivers flow. As for those who disbelieve, they take their enjoyment and consume (God's bounties) just as cattle consume, (without considering Who has given them to them, and what they are expected to do in return, and with no sense of the life to come); and the Fire will be their dwelling (fitting for them).

13. How many a township there has been, greater in power (and more abundant in wealth) than your township, which has driven you out, (O Messenger). We destroyed them and they had no helper (against Us).

14. Is, then, the one who is (standing) upon a clear evidence from his Lord like him whose evil deeds are decked out to be appealing to him, and (those who) follow their lusts and fancies?

15. A likeness of Paradise which the God-revering, pious are promised is this: in it are rivers of water incorruptible (in taste, smell, and color); and rivers of milk whose taste never changes; and rivers of wine[5] delicious for the drinkers; and rivers of pure, clear honey. And in it there are also fruits of every kind for them, as well as forgiveness from their Lord (to bring unforeseen blessings).[6] (Are those who will enjoy all this) like those who will abide in the Fire and be given boiling water to drink, so that it rends their bowels?

16. Among them (the people of Madīnah) are some who give ear to you, but when they go out from your presence, they ask (with arrogance and derision) those who have been given (some) knowledge (of the truths of the Religion): "What has he said just now?" Those are they whose hearts God has sealed, and who follow their lusts and fancies.

17. As for those who have accepted God's

إِنَّ ٱللَّهَ يُدْخِلُ ٱلَّذِينَ ءَامَنُوا۟ وَعَمِلُوا۟ ٱلصَّٰلِحَٰتِ جَنَّٰتٍ تَجْرِى مِن تَحْتِهَا ٱلْأَنْهَٰرُ وَٱلَّذِينَ كَفَرُوا۟ يَتَمَتَّعُونَ وَيَأْكُلُونَ كَمَا تَأْكُلُ ٱلْأَنْعَٰمُ وَٱلنَّارُ مَثْوًى لَّهُمْ ۝ وَكَأَيِّن مِّن قَرْيَةٍ هِىَ أَشَدُّ قُوَّةً مِّن قَرْيَتِكَ ٱلَّتِىٓ أَخْرَجَتْكَ أَهْلَكْنَٰهُمْ فَلَا نَاصِرَ لَهُمْ ۝ أَفَمَن كَانَ عَلَىٰ بَيِّنَةٍ مِّن رَّبِّهِۦ كَمَن زُيِّنَ لَهُۥ سُوٓءُ عَمَلِهِۦ وَٱتَّبَعُوٓا۟ أَهْوَآءَهُم ۝ مَّثَلُ ٱلْجَنَّةِ ٱلَّتِى وُعِدَ ٱلْمُتَّقُونَ ۖ فِيهَآ أَنْهَٰرٌ مِّن مَّآءٍ غَيْرِ ءَاسِنٍ وَأَنْهَٰرٌ مِّن لَّبَنٍ لَّمْ يَتَغَيَّرْ طَعْمُهُۥ وَأَنْهَٰرٌ مِّنْ خَمْرٍ لَّذَّةٍ لِّلشَّٰرِبِينَ وَأَنْهَٰرٌ مِّنْ عَسَلٍ مُّصَفًّى ۖ وَلَهُمْ فِيهَا مِن كُلِّ ٱلثَّمَرَٰتِ وَمَغْفِرَةٌ مِّن رَّبِّهِمْ ۖ كَمَنْ هُوَ خَٰلِدٌ فِى ٱلنَّارِ وَسُقُوا۟ مَآءً حَمِيمًا فَقَطَّعَ أَمْعَآءَهُمْ ۝ وَمِنْهُم مَّن يَسْتَمِعُ إِلَيْكَ حَتَّىٰٓ إِذَا خَرَجُوا۟ مِنْ عِندِكَ قَالُوا۟ لِلَّذِينَ أُوتُوا۟ ٱلْعِلْمَ مَاذَا قَالَ ءَانِفًا ۚ أُو۟لَٰٓئِكَ ٱلَّذِينَ طَبَعَ ٱللَّهُ عَلَىٰ قُلُوبِهِمْ وَٱتَّبَعُوٓا۟ أَهْوَآءَهُمْ ۝ وَٱلَّذِينَ ٱهْتَدَوْا۟ زَادَهُمْ هُدًى وَءَاتَىٰهُمْ تَقْوَىٰهُمْ ۝ فَهَلْ يَنظُرُونَ إِلَّا ٱلسَّاعَةَ أَن تَأْتِيَهُم بَغْتَةً ۖ فَقَدْ جَآءَ أَشْرَاطُهَا ۚ فَأَنَّىٰ لَهُمْ إِذَا جَآءَتْهُمْ ذِكْرَىٰهُمْ ۝ فَٱعْلَمْ أَنَّهُۥ لَآ إِلَٰهَ إِلَّا ٱللَّهُ وَٱسْتَغْفِرْ لِذَنۢبِكَ وَلِلْمُؤْمِنِينَ وَٱلْمُؤْمِنَٰتِ ۗ وَٱللَّهُ يَعْلَمُ مُتَقَلَّبَكُمْ وَمَثْوَىٰكُمْ ۝

guidance, He strengthens them in guidance (through deeper knowledge and submission), and gives them piety and protection from sinning.

18. Do they (who persist in unbelief and evil deeds) wait but for the Last Hour – (waiting) that it come upon them all of a sudden? Now indeed its portents have already come.[7] But how can it benefit them to take admonition when the Last Hour has (already) come upon them?

19. Then, know (bear in mind) that there is no deity but God, and ask forgiveness for your lapses,[8] and for the believing men and believing women. God knows from which (inner) state and (social) condition to which state and condition you do and will move, and in which state and condition you will be steady.

5. Wine as one of the blessings of Paradise is used metaphorically to denote the perfection of the pleasure that the drinks of Paradise will give.

6. Everything in the Hereafter will be particular to the conditions of that world. But as stated in verse 2: 25, everything will resemble in name, shape, and color its counterparts in this world, but this resemblance will be only in name, shape, and color so that its inhabitants will not lose their appetite because of being presented with an unknown food. Their taste and smell or the pleasure they will give will be completely particular to that world, and every time these bounties will be presented to the people of Paradise, they will be renewed.

7. Only God knows the exact time of the Last Hour, but it has many portents which show that its coming is certain and near. The advent of God's Messenger as the Last and universal Messenger or the Seal of the Prophets, upon him be peace and blessings, was the first and greatest portent of its coming.

8. For the sinlessness of the Prophets and the Messenger's asking forgiveness for his "faults," see 48: 2, and the corresponding note 2.

وَيَقُولُ الَّذِينَ ءَامَنُوا لَوْلَا نُزِّلَتْ سُورَةٌ فَإِذَآ أُنزِلَتْ سُورَةٌ مُّحْكَمَةٌ
وَذُكِرَ فِيهَا الْقِتَالُ رَأَيْتَ الَّذِينَ فِي قُلُوبِهِم مَّرَضٌ يَنظُرُونَ إِلَيْكَ
نَظَرَ الْمَغْشِيِّ عَلَيْهِ مِنَ الْمَوْتِ فَأَوْلَى لَهُمْ ۞ طَاعَةٌ وَقَوْلٌ
مَّعْرُوفٌ فَإِذَا عَزَمَ الْأَمْرُ فَلَوْ صَدَقُوا اللَّهَ لَكَانَ خَيْرًا لَّهُمْ
۞ فَهَلْ عَسَيْتُمْ إِن تَوَلَّيْتُمْ أَن تُفْسِدُوا فِي الْأَرْضِ وَتُقَطِّعُوا
أَرْحَامَكُمْ ۞ أُوْلَئِكَ الَّذِينَ لَعَنَهُمُ اللَّهُ فَأَصَمَّهُمْ وَأَعْمَى
أَبْصَارَهُمْ ۞ أَفَلَا يَتَدَبَّرُونَ الْقُرْءَانَ أَمْ عَلَى قُلُوبٍ أَقْفَالُهَا
۞ إِنَّ الَّذِينَ ارْتَدُّوا عَلَى أَدْبَارِهِم مِّن بَعْدِ مَا تَبَيَّنَ
لَهُمُ الْهُدَى الشَّيْطَانُ سَوَّلَ لَهُمْ وَأَمْلَى لَهُمْ ۞
ذَلِكَ بِأَنَّهُمْ قَالُوا لِلَّذِينَ كَرِهُوا مَا نَزَّلَ اللَّهُ
سَنُطِيعُكُمْ فِي بَعْضِ الْأَمْرِ وَاللَّهُ يَعْلَمُ إِسْرَارَهُمْ
۞ فَكَيْفَ إِذَا تَوَفَّتْهُمُ الْمَلَائِكَةُ يَضْرِبُونَ وُجُوهَهُمْ
وَأَدْبَارَهُمْ ۞ ذَلِكَ بِأَنَّهُمُ اتَّبَعُوا مَا أَسْخَطَ اللَّهَ
وَكَرِهُوا رِضْوَانَهُ فَأَحْبَطَ أَعْمَالَهُمْ ۞ أَمْ حَسِبَ الَّذِينَ
فِي قُلُوبِهِم مَّرَضٌ أَن لَّن يُخْرِجَ اللَّهُ أَضْغَانَهُمْ ۞

20. Those who believe (look forward to a new *surah* conveying knowledge of Divine truths and God's new commandments being sent down, and) say: "If only a new *surah* were sent down!" But when a decisive *surah* has been sent down in which fighting is mentioned (clearly as a commanded duty), you see those in whose hearts there is sickness looking at you with a look of one swooning to death. That is, in fact, what is expected of them!

21. (Whereas, what true believers are expected to do in response to any Divine order is) obedience and a proper word. So, if they were true to God when the command has been resolved upon (and it calls them to do what their pledge to God requires them), it would certainly be good for them.

22. But is it to be expected of you (O hypocritical ones), that you break your promise and turn away (from God's commandments), and cause disorder and corruption in the land, and sever the ties of kinship?

23. Such are they whom God has cursed (excluded from His mercy), and so He has made them deaf and blinded their eyes (to the truth).

24. Do they not meditate earnestly on the Qur'ān, or are there locks on the hearts (that are particular to them so that they are as if deaf and blind, and incapable of understanding the truth)?[9]

25. Surely those who have turned back as apostates after (God's) guidance has become clear to them, Satan has seduced them; he has implanted in them long-term worldly ambitions.

26. This is because they have said to those who are averse to what God has sent down: "We will obey you in some issues." God knows their secrets.[10]

27. So, how (will it be) when the angels take their souls at death, striking their faces and their backs?

28. This is because they have followed what incurs God's wrath (condemnation), and are averse to what pleases Him, and so He has caused all their (previous good) deeds to go to waste.

29. Or do those in whose hearts is sickness think that God will not bring to light their spite (against the Divine Religion and its followers)?

9. The persons mentioned are the hypocritical ones among the believers. Hypocrisy arises from a sickness in the center of the heart which dries up the source of spiritual life, extinguishing the power of understanding, and corrupting character (See: 2: 10). The main reason for the "spiritual" sense of hearing being lost in deafness or the "spiritual" sense of seeing being lost in blindness is this sickness in the heart: *For indeed it is not the eyes that have become blind, it is rather the hearts in the breasts that are blind* (22: 46). So verse 24 in this *sūrah* also interprets the verse before it, explaining why God makes the ears deaf and the eyes blind. The locks on the heart must be those put on the senses or faculties of the heart, such as hearing, seeing, thinking, and understanding, etc. (Also see the verse 26 and the corresponding note 10 below.)

10. Obedience to the carnal soul in its desires and nursing long-term worldly ambitions cause one to fear death, to falter in carrying out. God's commandments, particularly those related to fighting. And this causes the death of the heart (spiritual intellect) and the blindness of the eye of the heart and the deafness of the ear of the heart. This verse explains the true reason for the spiritual death mentioned in the previous verses. It also gives information about the secret agreements against the believers that were made between the hypocrites in Madīnah and the unbelievers (of Makkah), who are also described in verse 9 above as being averse to what God sends down.

وَلَوْ نَشَآءُ لَأَرَيْنَاكَهُمْ فَلَعَرَفْتَهُمْ بِسِيمٰهُمْ وَلَتَعْرِفَنَّهُمْ فِىْ لَحْنِ الْقَوْلِ ۚ وَاللّٰهُ يَعْلَمُ اَعْمَالَكُمْ ۝ وَلَنَبْلُوَنَّكُمْ حَتّٰى نَعْلَمَ الْمُجٰهِدِيْنَ مِنْكُمْ وَالصّٰبِرِيْنَ ۙ وَنَبْلُوَا۟ اَخْبَارَكُمْ ۝ اِنَّ الَّذِيْنَ كَفَرُوْا وَصَدُّوْا عَنْ سَبِيْلِ اللّٰهِ وَشَآقُّوا الرَّسُوْلَ مِنْ بَعْدِ مَا تَبَيَّنَ لَهُمُ الْهُدَى ۙ لَنْ يَّضُرُّوا اللّٰهَ شَيْـًٔا ۚ وَسَيُحْبِطُ اَعْمَالَهُمْ ۝ يٰٓاَيُّهَا الَّذِيْنَ اٰمَنُوْٓا اَطِيْعُوا اللّٰهَ وَاَطِيْعُوا الرَّسُوْلَ وَلَا تُبْطِلُوْٓا اَعْمَالَكُمْ ۝ اِنَّ الَّذِيْنَ كَفَرُوْا وَصَدُّوْا عَنْ سَبِيْلِ اللّٰهِ ثُمَّ مَاتُوْا وَهُمْ كُفَّارٌ فَلَنْ يَّغْفِرَ اللّٰهُ لَهُمْ ۝ فَلَا تَهِنُوْا وَتَدْعُوْٓا اِلَى السَّلْمِ ۖ وَاَنْتُمُ الْاَعْلَوْنَ ۖ وَاللّٰهُ مَعَكُمْ وَلَنْ يَّتِرَكُمْ اَعْمَالَكُمْ ۝ اِنَّمَا الْحَيٰوةُ الدُّنْيَا لَعِبٌ وَّلَهْوٌ ۚ وَاِنْ تُؤْمِنُوْا وَتَتَّقُوْا يُؤْتِكُمْ اُجُوْرَكُمْ وَلَا يَسْـَٔلْكُمْ اَمْوَالَكُمْ ۝ اِنْ يَّسْـَٔلْكُمُوْهَا فَيُحْفِكُمْ تَبْخَلُوْا وَيُخْرِجْ اَضْغَانَكُمْ ۝ هٰٓاَنْتُمْ هٰٓؤُلَآءِ تُدْعَوْنَ لِتُنْفِقُوْا فِىْ سَبِيْلِ اللّٰهِ ۚ فَمِنْكُمْ مَّنْ يَّبْخَلُ ۚ وَمَنْ يَّبْخَلْ فَاِنَّمَا يَبْخَلُ عَنْ نَّفْسِهٖ ۚ وَاللّٰهُ الْغَنِيُّ وَاَنْتُمُ الْفُقَرَآءُ ۚ وَاِنْ تَتَوَلَّوْا يَسْتَبْدِلْ قَوْمًا غَيْرَكُمْ ثُمَّ لَا يَكُوْنُوْٓا اَمْثَالَكُمْ ۝

---

30. Had We so willed, We would have shown them to you, and you would have known them by their marks (visible on their faces). But you certainly know them by the false tone and rhythm of their speech. God knows (O humankind) your deeds (and why and how you do them).

31. And We will most certainly try you so that We may mark out those among you who strive hard (in God's cause with their persons and their wealth), and those who are steadfast (on His Path and patient through adversities), and try your accounts (of deeds).[11]

32. Those who disbelieve and bar (people) from God's way, and defy the Messenger after (God's) guidance has become clear to them – they will never be able to harm (the cause of) God, and He will cause their deeds to go to waste.

33. O you who believe! Obey God (in all His commandments) and obey the Messenger (in his execution of God's commandments and in his own directives), and do not let your deeds go to waste.[12]

34. Those who disbelieve and bar (people) from God's way, and then die unbelievers, God will never forgive them.

35. So (when in warfare with the enemy) do not be faint of heart and cry out for peace (which will bring you humiliation) when you have the upper hand. (Always bear in mind that) God is with you, and He will never diminish the reward of your good deeds.

36. The present, worldly life is nothing but a play and a pastime. If you truly believe and keep from disobedience to Him in reverence for Him and piety, He will grant you your rewards, and will not ask of you your wealth.

37. If He should ask it of you and press you (to give it), you would covet and withhold, and He would bring out your (suppressed) resentments.[13]

38. You are surely those called upon to spend (of your wealth) in God's cause; yet among you are some who are niggardly. But whoever is niggardly is niggardly only to the depriving of his own soul. God is the All-Wealthy and Self-Sufficient (absolutely independent of any need), and you are the poor (in need of Him). If you turn away (from true faith and piety), He will substitute in your stead another people; then they will not be like you.

11. That is, God will distinguish between and judge His servants' deeds, whether they are right or wrong and recompense each type of deed.

12. Letting one's deeds go to waste occurs through ostentation, hypocrisy, apostatizing, opposing God and His Messenger, and through doing something that will annul a good deed, such as speaking during Prayer.

13. God has implanted in humankind numerous urges, some of which are apparently evil. However, a proper education causes these to be channeled into virtues. For example, enmity is channeled into enmity towards one's own carnal soul in order to train it, and jealousy into emulating others in their virtues. In fact, these urges have been given to humankind for this end, that is, to channel them into virtues that will cause one to grow spiritually and morally.

SŪRAH 48

AL-FATḤ (VICTORY)

Madīnah period

This *sūrah* was revealed in Madīnah in the sixth year after the *Hijrah* on the occasion of the Treaty of Hudaybiyah between the Muslim city-state of Madīnah and the Makkan polytheists. It has 29 verses and is named after the word *al-fatḥ* (victory) in the first verse. It mentions this victory, then criticizes the attitudes of the hypocrites, and continues with further promises to the Muslims, and ends by mentioning certain important virtues of the Muslim Community.

In the Name of God, the All-Merciful, the All-Compassionate.

1. We have surely granted you a manifest victory (which is a door to further victories),[1]

2. That God may forgive you (O Messenger) your lapses of the past and those to follow,[2] and complete His favor on you,[3] and guide you (to steadfastness) on a straight path (leading to God's being pleased with You and eternal happiness);[4]

3. And that God may help you to a glorious, mighty achievement –

4. He it is Who sent down His (gift of) inner peace and reassurance into the hearts of the believers, so that they might add faith to their faith. To God belong the hosts of the heavens and the earth;[5] and God is All-Knowing, All-Wise –

5. And that He may admit the believing men and believing women into Gardens through which rivers flow, therein to abide, and may blot out from them their evil deeds. That is a supreme triumph in God's sight;

6. And that He may punish the hypocritical men and the hypocritical women, and the men and the women who associate partners with God, who always entertain evil thoughts about God.[6] Theirs will be the evil

turn of fate. God has destined them to a severe punishment, eternally excluded them from His Mercy, and prepared Hell for them. How evil a destination to arrive at!

7. To God belong the hosts of the heavens and the earth. God is All-Glorious with irresistible might, All-Wise.

8. Surely We have sent you as Messenger as a witness (to the truth of Islam and the falsehood of other ways, and as a witness in both worlds to people's deeds), and as a bearer of glad tidings (of prosperity in return for faith and righteousness) and a warner (against the consequences of misguidance);

9. And in order that you (O humankind and jinn) believe in God and His Messenger (and support His cause), and hold God in the highest regard, and glorify Him in the early morning and in the evening (i.e., day and night).

1. This verse is about the Treaty of Hudaybiyah. After the Battle of the Trench (33: 9–25; notes 7–12), the Messenger told his Companions that he had had a vision (dream) that they would shortly enter the Holy Mosque in Makkah in security. His Companions, especially the Emigrants, were delighted. During that year, the Prophet set out for Makkah with 1,400–1,500 people in pilgrim dress.

Informed of this event, the Quraysh armed themselves and the neighboring tribes to keep the Muslims out of Makkah. The Muslims halted at Hudaybiyah, 12 miles away from Makkah. Exchanges of envoys took place.

Finally, God's Messenger, upon him be peace and blessings, sent 'Uthmān ibn al-'Affān to the Quraysh, a man who had powerful relatives among the Quraysh. Although 'Uthmān came to negotiate, the Makkans imprisoned him. When he did not return at the expected time, rumors circulated that he had been killed. At this point, the Messenger, sitting under a tree, took an oath from his Companions that they would hold together and fight to the death.

In that moment of tension, a cloud of dust appeared in the distance. This turned out to be a Makkan delegation, led by Suhayl ibn 'Amr. After negotiations, a treaty was concluded.

Under this treaty, the Messenger and his followers could not make the pilgrimage in this year but could do so the following year, at which time the Makkans would vacate the city for 3 days. The treaty also stipulated a 10-year truce, that people or tribes could join or ally themselves with either side they wished, and that Qurayshī subjects or dependents who had defected to Madīnah would be returned. This last condition was not reciprocal, and thus was opposed in the Muslim camp. However, it really was of little importance. The Muslims sent back to Makkah were not likely to renounce Islam; on the contrary, they would be agents of change within Makkah.

The Qur'ān called the Treaty of Hudaybiyah "a manifest victory." This proved true for several reasons, among them the following:

• By signing this treaty after years of con-

flict, the Quraysh admitted that the state of Madīnah was their equal. Seeing the Makkans deal with the Prophet as an equal and a president, a rising tide of converts flowed toward Madīnah from all over Arabia.

• Many Qurayshīs would benefit from the resulting peace by finally reflecting on what was really happening. Such leading Qurayshīs as Khālid ibn Walīd, 'Amr ibn al-'Ās, and 'Uthmān ibn Talhah, all famous for their military and political skills, came to accept Islam.

• The Quraysh used to regard the Ka'bah as their exclusive property, and made its visitors pay them a tribute. By not subjecting the Muslims' deferred pilgrimage to this condition, the Quraysh unwittingly ended their monopoly. The Bedouin tribes now realized that the Quraysh had no right to claim exclusive ownership.

• At the time, there were Muslim men and women living in Makkah. Not everyone in Madīnah knew who they were. Had a fight taken place in Makkah, the victorious Muslim army might have unintentionally taken the lives of some Muslims. This would have caused great personal anguish, as well as the martyrdom or identification of the Muslims who had been keeping their faith secret. The treaty prevented such a disaster.

• The Prophet performed the minor pilgrimage the following year. The declaration, *There is no deity but God, and Muhammad is God's Messenger*, rang throughout Makkah. The Quraysh, camped on the hill of Abū Qubays, heard this portent of Islam's coming triumph. This was, in fact, God's fulfilling the vision He had given to His Messenger.

• The treaty allowed the Messenger, upon him be peace and blessings, to enter into diplomatic relations with others. Their neighbors, as well as other Arab tribes, were impressed with the Islamic state's growing strength. The Messenger also sent letters to neighboring kings and chiefs, calling them to accept Islam.

• The Muslims spread across Arabia and communicated Islam's Message. While during 19 years, from the beginning of the Messenger's mission to the Treaty of Hudaybiyah, only a few thousand people had accepted Islam, within two years after the Treaty more than 5,000 people had converted.

- During the period of armistice, the Muslims won new victories, such as the conquest of al-Khaybar.

- The Muslims faithfully observed the terms of the treaty. However, a tribe allied to the Makkans did not. The Banū Bakr attacked the Banū Khudā'ah, who were allied with the Prophet. So in December 629, the Messenger marched a 10,000-man army against Makkah, and captured it with almost no resistance on the first day of January. The Ka'bah was purified of idols and, over the next couple of days, the Makkans accepted Islam.

So, this verse proved to be another manifest miracle of the Qur'ān.

2. Before proceeding to explain the sinlessness of the Prophets, we should point out that, as will be stated in the last verse, the sins mentioned here are the sins committed by the believers, not the Messenger himself. As in many other verses, God addresses the believers through the person of the Messenger, upon him be peace and blessings. However, the Messenger also has a share in this address. It should be understood in the light of the following explanation:

Infallibility in the sense of sinlessness is a necessary attribute of the Prophets. Their infallibility is an established fact, based on reason and tradition. This quality is required for several reasons.

- First, the Prophets came to convey the Message of God. If we liken this Message to pure water or light (13: 17; 24: 35), the Archangel Gabriel (who brought it) and the Prophet (who conveyed it) also must be absolutely pure. If this were not so, their impurity would pollute the Message. Every falling off is an impurity, a dark spot, in the heart. The hearts or souls of Gabriel and the Prophet are like polished mirrors

that reflect the Divine Revelation to people, a cup from which people quench their thirst for the pure Divine water.

Any black spot on the mirror would absorb a ray of that light; a single drop of mud would make the water unclear. As a result, the Prophets would not be able to deliver the complete Message. But they delivered the Message perfectly, as stated in 5: 3 and 67.

- Second, the Prophets taught their people all the commands and principles of faith and conduct. In order for people to learn their Religion in its pristine purity and truth, and as perfectly as possible so that they can secure their happiness and prosperity in both worlds, the Prophets must present and also represent the Revelation without fault or defect. This is their function as guides and good examples to be followed (33: 21; 60: 4, 6). A Prophet can do or say only that which has been sanctioned by God. If he could not, he would have to repent even beyond his current lifetime.

- Third, the Qur'ān commands believers to obey the Prophet's orders and prohibitions, without exception, and emphasizes that it is not fitting for a believer, man or woman, to have any doubts about a judgment on a matter when it has been decided by God and His Messenger (33: 36). It also warns believers that what falls to them when God and His Messenger have given a judgment is only to say: "We have heard and obeyed" (24: 51). Absolute obedience to a Prophet means that all of his commands and prohibitions are correct and beyond reproach.

Then, how should we evaluate some verses that mention the forgiveness of a Prophet?

Prophethood is such a great favor that all Prophets bore extreme hardship while fulfilling the duty of thanksgiving, and always worried about not worshipping God sufficiently. The Prophet Muḥammad often implored God as follows: "Glory be to You, We have not been able to know You as Your knowledge requires, O Known One. Glory be to You, We have not been able to worship You as Your worship requires, O Worshipped One."

The Qur'ānic verses that are sometimes understood (mistakenly) to reprimand certain Prophets for some faults or to show that they have sought God's forgiveness for some sin should be considered in this light. Moreover, God's forgiveness does not always mean that a sin has been committed. The Qur'ānic words *'afw* (pardon) and *maghfirah* (forgiveness) also signify a special favor and kindness, as well as Divine dispensation, in respect to lightening or overlooking a religious duty, as in the following verses:

> *Whoever is constrained by dire necessity (and driven to what is forbidden), without purposely inclining to sin – surely God is All-Forgiving, All-Compassionate.* (5: 3)

> *If you ... can find no water, then betake yourselves to pure earth, passing with it lightly over your face and hands (and forearms up to and including the elbows). Assuredly God is One Who grants remission, All-Forgiving.* (4: 43)

In addition, sins (lapses in respect with the Prophets) and pardoning have different types and degrees. These are: disobeying religious commandments, and forgiveness thereof; disobeying God's laws of creation and life, and forgiveness thereof; and disobeying the rules of good manners or courtesy, and forgiveness thereof. A fourth type, which is not a sin, involves not doing something as perfectly as possible, as required by the love of and nearness to God. Some Prophets may have done this, but such acts cannot be considered sins according to the common definition.

3. See *sūrah* 5: 3, note 1.

4. As with the address in the first part of the verse concerning the forgiveness of sins, this address also is, as will be seen in the verse 20, to the believers through the person of the Messenger, though the Messenger has also a share in it with respect to his rank as Messenger and being one who is nearest to God, and therefore with respect to his relation with God.

5. Some of the hosts of the heavens and the earth are angels and all the forces and laws in the universe which modern science improperly calls "natural forces and laws."

6. The verse mentions hypocrites before polytheists. This is because the harm the former cause to the Muslims is worse than that of the latter, and therefore they will be in the lowest level of the Fire (4: 145). Entertaining evil thoughts about God means having any evil thought that is unbecoming about God. Here it particularly means the thought that God will not help the believers and make Islam triumphant, and therefore whatever He has promised is – God forbid! – a lie.

إِنَّ الَّذِينَ يُبَايِعُونَكَ إِنَّمَا يُبَايِعُونَ اللَّهَ يَدُ اللَّهِ فَوْقَ أَيْدِيهِمْ فَمَنْ نَكَثَ فَإِنَّمَا يَنْكُثُ عَلَىٰ نَفْسِهِ وَمَنْ أَوْفَىٰ بِمَا عَاهَدَ عَلَيْهُ اللَّهَ فَسَيُؤْتِيهِ أَجْرًا عَظِيمًا ۝ سَيَقُولُ لَكَ الْمُخَلَّفُونَ مِنَ الْأَعْرَابِ شَغَلَتْنَا أَمْوَالُنَا وَأَهْلُونَا فَاسْتَغْفِرْ لَنَا يَقُولُونَ بِأَلْسِنَتِهِمْ مَا لَيْسَ فِي قُلُوبِهِمْ قُلْ فَمَنْ يَمْلِكُ لَكُمْ مِنَ اللَّهِ شَيْئًا إِنْ أَرَادَ بِكُمْ ضَرًّا أَوْ أَرَادَ بِكُمْ نَفْعًا بَلْ كَانَ اللَّهُ بِمَا تَعْمَلُونَ خَبِيرًا ۝ بَلْ ظَنَنْتُمْ أَنْ لَنْ يَنْقَلِبَ الرَّسُولُ وَالْمُؤْمِنُونَ إِلَىٰ أَهْلِيهِمْ أَبَدًا وَزُيِّنَ ذَٰلِكَ فِي قُلُوبِكُمْ وَظَنَنْتُمْ ظَنَّ السَّوْءِ وَكُنْتُمْ قَوْمًا بُورًا ۝ وَمَنْ لَمْ يُؤْمِنْ بِاللَّهِ وَرَسُولِهِ فَإِنَّا أَعْتَدْنَا لِلْكَافِرِينَ سَعِيرًا ۝ وَلِلَّهِ مُلْكُ السَّمَاوَاتِ وَالْأَرْضِ يَغْفِرُ لِمَنْ يَشَاءُ وَيُعَذِّبُ مَنْ يَشَاءُ وَكَانَ اللَّهُ غَفُورًا رَحِيمًا ۝ سَيَقُولُ الْمُخَلَّفُونَ إِذَا انْطَلَقْتُمْ إِلَىٰ مَغَانِمَ لِتَأْخُذُوهَا ذَرُونَا نَتَّبِعْكُمْ يُرِيدُونَ أَنْ يُبَدِّلُوا كَلَامَ اللَّهِ قُلْ لَنْ تَتَّبِعُونَا كَذَٰلِكُمْ قَالَ اللَّهُ مِنْ قَبْلُ فَسَيَقُولُونَ بَلْ تَحْسُدُونَنَا بَلْ كَانُوا لَا يَفْقَهُونَ إِلَّا قَلِيلًا ۝

---

10. Those who swear allegiance to you (O Messenger), swear allegiance to God only. God's "Hand" is over their hands.[7] Whoever then breaks his oath, breaks his oath only to his own harm; and whoever fulfills what he has covenanted with God, He will grant him a tremendous reward.

11. Those of the Bedouins (dwellers of the desert) who (did not respond to your call to participate in the Minor Pilgrimage Campaign and) stayed behind will say to you (by way of excuse): "Our possessions and families kept us busy, so ask God for our forgiveness." They speak with their tongues that which is not in their hearts. Say (to them): "Who is there that can intervene on your behalf with God if He wills harm for you or if He wills a benefit for you? (Whatever excuse you offer, bear in mind that) God is fully aware of all that you do."[8]

12. Indeed you thought that the Messenger and the believers would never return to their families (from the Campaign), and this thought was decked out to be appealing in your hearts, and you entertained an evil thought (that God would not help the believers and they would be defeated). You (in thinking so have proved yourselves to be and you) are a people useless and doomed to perish.

13. Whoever does not believe (and trust) in God and His Messenger: then We have surely prepared a Blaze for the unbelievers.

14. To God belongs the sovereignty of the heavens and the earth: He forgives whom He wills and punishes whom He wills. God is All-Forgiving, All-Compassionate.[9]

15. When you (O believers) set forth for (the campaign during which they think that you are sure) to take gains of war, those who stayed behind (aforetime) will say: "Let us go with you." They desire to alter God's decree. Say (to them): "You will by no means come with us. That (decision) regarding you is what God declared before." Then they will say: "Rather, you are jealous of us." But the fact is that they are lacking in discernment and understanding, except a very little.[10]

7. This statement has two important meanings. As obedience to the Messenger means the same as obedience to God (4: 80), and his throwing at the enemy means the same as God's throwing (8: 17), the Messenger's hand being over the hand which he grasps in allegiance represents God's Hand. (For God 'hand' or any other such term is metaphorical.) The other meaning is that God helps those who swear allegiance to the Messenger. So, here 'hand' signifies Power.

8. This and the following verse are concerned with the desert Arabs who did not answer the call of the Messenger to participate in the 'Umrah (Minor Pilgrimage) Campaign they made in the 6th year after the *Hijrah*, thinking that the Quraysh would exterminate the Muslims and they would no longer be able to turn back to Madīnah.

9. This verse is significant in understanding God's forgiving and punishing. First of all, He does whatever He wills and so cannot be questioned concerning His will and acts. However, He never does anything unjust, he forgives many of the sins of His servants unless they disbelieve and/or associate partners with Him, and shows special compassion to them. So, the conclusion of the verse with the mention of His being the All-Forgiving and All-Compassionate (One Who has particular compassion for His servants) is a great consolation and source of hope for the servants who tremble before His Majesty. This is stressed in the first part of the verse.

10. After the Treaty of Hudaybiyah, the believers took several tribes under control, and conquered Khaybar. Once the hypocritical desert Arabs saw the Muslims conquering all their enemies, they wanted to participate in the Campaign of Khaybar with the hope of gaining spoils. However, God decreed that only those who had taken part in the Campaign of the Minor Pilgrimage could participate in this campaign. So they were left devoid of the war-gains that they had so craved.

512   سُوۡرَةُ الۡفَتۡحِ   ٥١٢

قُلْ لِّلْمُخَلَّفِيْنَ مِنَ الْاَعْرَابِ سَتُدْعَوْنَ اِلٰى قَوْمٍ اُولِيْ بَأْسٍ شَدِيْدٍ تُقَاتِلُوْنَهُمْ اَوْ يُسْلِمُوْنَ ۚ فَاِنْ تُطِيْعُوْا يُؤْتِكُمُ اللّٰهُ اَجْرًا حَسَنًا ۚ وَاِنْ تَتَوَلَّوْا كَمَا تَوَلَّيْتُمْ مِّنْ قَبْلُ يُعَذِّبْكُمْ عَذَابًا اَلِيْمًا ۝ لَيْسَ عَلَى الْاَعْمٰى حَرَجٌ وَّلَا عَلَى الْاَعْرَجِ حَرَجٌ وَّلَا عَلَى الْمَرِيْضِ حَرَجٌ ۗ وَمَنْ يُّطِعِ اللّٰهَ وَرَسُوْلَهٗ يُدْخِلْهُ جَنّٰتٍ تَجْرِيْ مِنْ تَحْتِهَا الْاَنْهٰرُ ۚ وَمَنْ يَّتَوَلَّ يُعَذِّبْهُ عَذَابًا اَلِيْمًا ۝ لَقَدْ رَضِيَ اللّٰهُ عَنِ الْمُؤْمِنِيْنَ اِذْ يُبَايِعُوْنَكَ تَحْتَ الشَّجَرَةِ فَعَلِمَ مَا فِيْ قُلُوْبِهِمْ فَاَنْزَلَ السَّكِيْنَةَ عَلَيْهِمْ وَاَثَابَهُمْ فَتْحًا قَرِيْبًا ۝ وَّمَغَانِمَ كَثِيْرَةً يَّأْخُذُوْنَهَا ۗ وَكَانَ اللّٰهُ عَزِيْزًا حَكِيْمًا ۝ وَعَدَكُمُ اللّٰهُ مَغَانِمَ كَثِيْرَةً تَأْخُذُوْنَهَا فَعَجَّلَ لَكُمْ هٰذِهٖ وَكَفَّ اَيْدِيَ النَّاسِ عَنْكُمْ ۚ وَلِتَكُوْنَ اٰيَةً لِّلْمُؤْمِنِيْنَ وَيَهْدِيَكُمْ صِرَاطًا مُّسْتَقِيْمًا ۝ وَّاُخْرٰى لَمْ تَقْدِرُوْا عَلَيْهَا قَدْ اَحَاطَ اللّٰهُ بِهَا ۗ وَكَانَ اللّٰهُ عَلٰى كُلِّ شَيْءٍ قَدِيْرًا ۝ وَلَوْ قَاتَلَكُمُ الَّذِيْنَ كَفَرُوْا لَوَلَّوُا الْاَدْبَارَ ثُمَّ لَا يَجِدُوْنَ وَلِيًّا وَّلَا نَصِيْرًا ۝ سُنَّةَ اللّٰهِ الَّتِيْ قَدْ خَلَتْ مِنْ قَبْلُ ۖ وَلَنْ تَجِدَ لِسُنَّةِ اللّٰهِ تَبْدِيْلًا ۝

---

16. Say to those of the dwellers of the desert who stayed behind: "Soon you will be called (to fight) against a people of great military power, then either you will fight against them or they will submit to God and become Muslims. If you obey, God will grant you a handsome reward, but if you turn away as you turned away before, He will punish you with a painful punishment."[11]

17. There is no blame on the blind nor any blame on the lame nor any blame on the sick (for staying away from a war in God's cause). Whoever obeys God and His Messenger (in the religious duties he is charged with and can carry out), God will admit him into Gardens through which rivers flow. But whoever turns away, He will punish him with a painful punishment.

18. God was assuredly well-pleased with the believers when they swore allegiance to you under the tree. He knew what was in their hearts (of sincere intention and loyalty to God's cause), and therefore He sent down (the gift of) inner peace and reassurance on them, and rewarded them with a near victory,

19. And much in gains of war that they will take.[12] And God is All-Glorious with irresistible might, All-Wise.

20. God has promised you abundant gains of war that you will take later,[13] and these He granted you as present reward (for your obedience and purity of intention).[14] And He has restrained the hands of (other hostile) people from you so that it may be a sign for the believers (concerning

the truth of their way and God's promises to them), and that He may guide you to (steadfastness on) a straight path.

21. And there are yet other (gains) which you have not been able to acquire but God has encompassed (in His Knowledge and Power, and will grant you). Surely God has full power over everything.

22. If the unbelievers (of Makkah) had fought against you (instead of signing the treaty with you at Hudaybiyah), they would certainly have turned their backs in flight, then they would have found no protecting guardian or helper (to rescue them).

23. It is God's way that has continued (ever so) from the past:[15] you will never find any change in God's way.

11. There are many predictions in this *surah*, such as:

- God would help the believers and favor them with great victories;

- those who stayed behind from the Campaign of Minor Pilgrimage would try to excuse themselves with false pretexts;

- they would desire to participate in the campaign against Khaybar that was to take place following the Treaty of Hudaybiyah with the aim of taking gains of war;

- the Muslims would have to fight against powerful tribes or states in the future;

- the Muslims would take abundant war-gains in battles to come in the future;

- the Messenger and his Companions would visit the Ka'bah in safety, thus completing the Minor Pilgrimage the year after they had intended;

- God would complete His favor upon the Messenger;

- Islam would continue to flourish so powerfully and speedily that it would amaze both the Muslims and others.

All of these predictions came true within a very short time.

The people mentioned in this verse must be one of the Arab polytheistic tribes in the Hijāz or neighboring regions; some of these tribes are mentioned in *Sūrat at-Tawbah*. The Muslims had to give them two alternatives, they would either have to be resigned to fighting or become Muslims. Most probably it refers to the Thaqīf and Hawāzin tribes against whom God's Messenger, upon him be peace and blessings,

had to fight after the Conquest of Makkah in order to stop their attacks.

12. The verse mentions the allegiance that the 1,400–1,500 believers swore to the Messenger at Hudaybiyah. When rumors circulated that 'Uthmān ibn 'Affān, who had been sent to Makkah to negotiate the Muslims' intention to make Minor Pilgrimage, had been killed, God's Messenger, upon him be peace and blessings, called the believers in his company to swear allegiance to him to defend themselves even if they might be killed. They had come with the intention to visit the Ka'bah and to make a Minor Pilgrimage. However, when they met with the unexpected reaction and felt their cause to be under great threat, they united around the Messenger as if a single body. They had no other intention than to serve God's cause in order to gain His approval and good pleasure. God was well pleased with the purity of intention and faithfulness in their hearts. So He favored them with a victory in the near future; i.e., the conquest of Khaybar and abundant war-gains.

13. The abundant war-gains promised are the gains that the Muslims were to acquire in the battles they had to fight after the Battle of Khaybar.

14. The present reward granted to the Muslims was the war-gains that they acquired at the Battle of Khaybar.

15. This way is what is stated in (4: 141): . . . *and never will God allow the unbelievers to find a way (to triumph) over the (true) believers,* and in (3: 139): . . . *you are always the superior side if you are (true) believers.*

وَهُوَ الَّذِي كَفَّ أَيْدِيَهُمْ عَنكُمْ وَأَيْدِيَكُمْ عَنْهُم بِبَطْنِ
مَكَّةَ مِنْ بَعْدِ أَنْ أَظْفَرَكُمْ عَلَيْهِمْ وَكَانَ اللَّهُ بِمَا تَعْمَلُونَ
بَصِيرًا ۞ هُمُ الَّذِينَ كَفَرُوا وَصَدُّوكُمْ عَنِ الْمَسْجِدِ الْحَرَامِ
وَالْهَدْيَ مَعْكُوفًا أَن يَبْلُغَ مَحِلَّهُ وَلَوْلَا رِجَالٌ مُّؤْمِنُونَ وَنِسَاءٌ
مُّؤْمِنَاتٌ لَّمْ تَعْلَمُوهُمْ أَن تَطَئُوهُمْ فَتُصِيبَكُم مِّنْهُم مَّعَرَّةٌ
بِغَيْرِ عِلْمٍ لِّيُدْخِلَ اللَّهُ فِي رَحْمَتِهِ مَن يَشَاءُ لَوْ تَزَيَّلُوا لَعَذَّبْنَا
الَّذِينَ كَفَرُوا مِنْهُمْ عَذَابًا أَلِيمًا ۞ إِذْ جَعَلَ الَّذِينَ كَفَرُوا
فِي قُلُوبِهِمُ الْحَمِيَّةَ حَمِيَّةَ الْجَاهِلِيَّةِ فَأَنزَلَ اللَّهُ سَكِينَتَهُ
عَلَى رَسُولِهِ وَعَلَى الْمُؤْمِنِينَ وَأَلْزَمَهُمْ كَلِمَةَ التَّقْوَى
وَكَانُوا أَحَقَّ بِهَا وَأَهْلَهَا وَكَانَ اللَّهُ بِكُلِّ شَيْءٍ عَلِيمًا
۞ لَّقَدْ صَدَقَ اللَّهُ رَسُولَهُ الرُّؤْيَا بِالْحَقِّ لَتَدْخُلُنَّ الْمَسْجِدَ
الْحَرَامَ إِن شَاءَ اللَّهُ آمِنِينَ مُحَلِّقِينَ رُءُوسَكُمْ وَمُقَصِّرِينَ
لَا تَخَافُونَ فَعَلِمَ مَا لَمْ تَعْلَمُوا فَجَعَلَ مِن دُونِ ذَٰلِكَ فَتْحًا
قَرِيبًا ۞ هُوَ الَّذِي أَرْسَلَ رَسُولَهُ بِالْهُدَى وَدِينِ
الْحَقِّ لِيُظْهِرَهُ عَلَى الدِّينِ كُلِّهِ وَكَفَى بِاللَّهِ شَهِيدًا ۞

---

24. And He it is Who restrained their hands from you and your hands from them in the valley of Makkah after He had granted you victory over them.[16] Surely God sees well all that you do.

25. (God defeated them because) they are the ones who have disbelieved and who barred you from (visiting) the Sacred Mosque and (prevented) the offerings from reaching their destination. And had there not been (in Makkah) believing men and believing women whom you did not know and therefore might have trodden down, and thus something undesired might have afflicted you on their account (for what you did) unknowingly, (God would not have restrained your hands from fighting. But He restrained your hands) so that He might admit to His mercy whom He wills (by sparing the believers in Makkah and enabling many among the Makkans to embrace Islam in time). If they (the believers and unbelievers in Makkah) had been clearly separated, We would certainly have punished those among them who disbelieved with a painful punishment.

26. When those who disbelieved harbored in their hearts fierce zealotry (coming from egotism, tribalism, and feuding), the zealotry particular to the Age of Ignorance, God sent down His (gift of) inner peace and reassurance on His Messenger and on the believers, and bound them to the Word of faith, piety, and reverence for God. They were most worthy of it and en-

titled to it. And God has full knowledge of everything.

27. God has assuredly confirmed the vision for His Messenger as true (and will certainly fulfill it) in reality:[17] you will certainly enter the Sacred Mosque, if God wills,[18] in full security, with your heads shaven or your hair cut short,[19] and you will have nothing to fear. But He always knows what you do not know, and (therefore, without allowing you to enter the Mosque this year,) granted you a near victory before this.[20]

28. He it is Who has sent His Messenger with the Divine guidance and the Religion of truth that He may make it prevail over all religions.[22] God suffices for a witness (for the truth of His promise and the mission of His Messenger).

16. This victory is that which happened when the Makkans could not do anything to the Muslims who had come for Minor Pilgrimage, and they returned safe and sound to their families, despite the expectations of the hypocrites. In addition, the Makkans had to recognize Madīnah as an equal city-state to them, and the Muslims secured the Minor Pilgrimage for the following year. The truce signed also paved the way for them to communicate Islam in circumstances of peace and, in consequence, numerous people converted. All these developments ended two years later in the conquest of Makkah, the decisive bloodless victory of Islam.

17. For this vision, see note 1 in this *sūrah*.

18. *If God wills*, has three meanings here:

• Your entering the Sacred Mosque, like all other events in the universe and in your lives, will take place by God's Will, not by your will or that of the Makkan polytheists. So do not ask the Messenger why you have not been able to enter this year.

• The verse teaches us that whatever we intend or have decided to do in the future, we must always refer it to God's Will and say, "We will do or intend to do that if it is God's will." (See 18: 23.)

• Some may die before it is time for them to enter the Mosque or will not be able to join the Muslims who will go to visit it.

19. During the Pilgrimage, men either have their heads totally shaven or their hair cut short as a mark of the completion of the Pilgrimage, whether it be major or minor. Having heads shaven is more rewarding. Women only have some of their hair cut short. So this statement means that the Muslims will complete their Minor Pilgrimage in full security and the Messenger's vision will come true.

20. This victory must be the Treaty of Hudaybiyah, which in time proved to be a manifest victory. (See above, verse 1, note 1.)

21. For an explanation, see 9: 33, note 9.

29. Muḥammad is the Messenger of God; and those who are in his company are firm and unyielding against the unbelievers, and compassionate among themselves. You see them (constant in the Prayer) bowing down and prostrating, seeking favor with God and His approval and good pleasure. Their marks are on their faces, traced by prostration.[22] This is their description in the Torah; and their description in the Gospel: like a seed that has sprouted its shoot, then it has strengthened it, and then risen firmly on its stem, delighting the sowers (with joy and wonder); (thereby) it fills the unbelievers with rage at them (the believers).[23] God has promised all those among them who believe and do good, righteous deeds forgiveness (to bring unforeseen blessings) and a tremendous reward.

---

22. That is, the fact that they are believers is discernible in their faces. Their faith is reflected in their manner of life and their outward aspect, including particularly their faces.

23. Although it is difficult to find these descriptions in the present versions of the Torah and Gospel, the following quotations show that they definitely existed in their originals:

> The Lord came from Sinai, and dawned on them from Seir; He shone forth from Mount Paran. And he came with ten thousands of saints; from His right hand *came* a fiery law for them. Yes, He loves the people; all His saints *are* in Your hand; they sit down at Your feet; *everyone* receives Your words. (*Deuteronomy*, 33: 2–3)

> And He said, "The kingdom of God is as if a man should scatter seed on the ground, and should sleep by night and rise by day, and the seed should sprout and grow, he himself does not know how. For the earth yields crops by itself; first the blade, then the head. But when the grain ripens, immediately he puts in the sickle, because the harvest has come. Then he said, "To what shall we liken the kingdom of God? or with what parable shall we picture it? *It is like* a mustard seed which, when it is sown on the ground, is smaller than all the seeds on the earth; but when it is sown, it grows up and becomes greater than all herbs, and shoots out large branches, so that the birds of the air may nest under its shade. And with many such parables He spoke the word to them as they were able to hear it. (*Mark*, 4: 26–33)

SŪRAH 49

AL-ḤUJURĀT
(THE PRIVATE APARTMENTS)

Madīnah period

Revealed in Madīnah and consisting of 18 verses, this *sūrah* takes its name from the word *ḥujurāt* (private apartments) that occurs in verse 4. It is concerned with how the believers must behave toward the Messenger and among themselves. It lays down important principles concerning how to deal with any report we receive, internal fighting in a Muslim community, assessments of individuals, and the avoidance of racism. It also focuses on the difference between true faith and submitting to a Muslim authority (or being Muslim outwardly or in the sight of law).

In the Name of God, the All-Merciful, the All-Compassionate.

1. O you who believe! Do not be forward in the Presence of God and His Messenger.[1] Keep from disobedience to God in piety and reverence for Him, so that you may deserve His protection. Surely God is All-Hearing, All-Knowing.

2. O you who believe! Do not raise your voices above the voice of the Prophet, nor speak loudly when addressing him, as you would speak loudly to one another, lest your good deeds go in vain without your perceiving it.[2]

3. Those who lower their voices in the presence of God's Messenger, those are they whose hearts God has tested and proven for piety and reverence for Him. For them there is forgiveness (to bring unforeseen rewards) and a tremendous reward.

4. Those who call out to you from behind the private apartments (which you share with your wives), most of them do not reason and understand (and are therefore lacking in good manners).

1. Whatever God and His Messenger will and decree on a matter, believers must accept and obey it. Believers must always take the Qur'ān and the Sunnah as the standard to which they must conform in their thoughts and actions. In addition, they must show utmost respect to God and His Messenger, upon him be peace and blessings.

2. Obedience to the Messenger in all his verdicts means obedience to God, and faith in and obedience to God require unconditional obedience to the Messenger. In addition, as any purposeful disrespect to him amounts to unbelief, it may cause one's all good deeds to go in vain. This is so both during the Prophet's life and after his death. There are some acts that, though they do not amount to unbelief in themselves, carry the risk of causing unbelief. Raising one's voice or any other action that does not arise from purposeful disrespect does not mean unbelief, yet it can cause the good deed done by way of speech or action to go in vain. (See also *sūrah* 24: 62–63 and the corresponding notes 33 and 34.)

وَلَوْ أَنَّهُمْ صَبَرُوا حَتَّى تَخْرُجَ إِلَيْهِمْ لَكَانَ خَيْرًا لَّهُمْ وَاللَّهُ عَفُورٌ رَّحِيمٌ ۝ يَا أَيُّهَا الَّذِينَ آمَنُوا إِن جَاءَكُمْ فَاسِقٌ بِنَبَإٍ فَتَبَيَّنُوا أَن تُصِيبُوا قَوْمًا بِجَهَالَةٍ فَتُصْبِحُوا عَلَى مَا فَعَلْتُمْ نَادِمِينَ ۝ وَاعْلَمُوا أَنَّ فِيكُمْ رَسُولَ اللَّهِ لَوْ يُطِيعُكُمْ فِي كَثِيرٍ مِّنَ الْأَمْرِ لَعَنِتُّمْ وَلَٰكِنَّ اللَّهَ حَبَّبَ إِلَيْكُمُ الْإِيمَانَ وَزَيَّنَهُ فِي قُلُوبِكُمْ وَكَرَّهَ إِلَيْكُمُ الْكُفْرَ وَالْفُسُوقَ وَالْعِصْيَانَ أُولَٰئِكَ هُمُ الرَّاشِدُونَ ۝ فَضْلًا مِّنَ اللَّهِ وَنِعْمَةً وَاللَّهُ عَلِيمٌ حَكِيمٌ ۝ وَإِن طَائِفَتَانِ مِنَ الْمُؤْمِنِينَ اقْتَتَلُوا فَأَصْلِحُوا بَيْنَهُمَا فَإِن بَغَتْ إِحْدَاهُمَا عَلَى الْأُخْرَىٰ فَقَاتِلُوا الَّتِي تَبْغِي حَتَّىٰ تَفِيءَ إِلَىٰ أَمْرِ اللَّهِ فَإِن فَاءَتْ فَأَصْلِحُوا بَيْنَهُمَا بِالْعَدْلِ وَأَقْسِطُوا إِنَّ اللَّهَ يُحِبُّ الْمُقْسِطِينَ ۝ إِنَّمَا الْمُؤْمِنُونَ إِخْوَةٌ فَأَصْلِحُوا بَيْنَ أَخَوَيْكُمْ وَاتَّقُوا اللَّهَ لَعَلَّكُمْ تُرْحَمُونَ ۝ يَا أَيُّهَا الَّذِينَ آمَنُوا لَا يَسْخَرْ قَوْمٌ مِّن قَوْمٍ عَسَىٰ أَن يَكُونُوا خَيْرًا مِّنْهُمْ وَلَا نِسَاءٌ مِّن نِّسَاءٍ عَسَىٰ أَن يَكُنَّ خَيْرًا مِّنْهُنَّ وَلَا تَلْمِزُوا أَنفُسَكُمْ وَلَا تَنَابَزُوا بِالْأَلْقَابِ بِئْسَ الِاسْمُ الْفُسُوقُ بَعْدَ الْإِيمَانِ وَمَن لَّمْ يَتُبْ فَأُولَٰئِكَ هُمُ الظَّالِمُونَ ۝

---

5. If (instead of shouting to you to come out to them) they had been patient until you came out to them, it would certainly have been better for them (in respect of the manners due to you from them). However, God is All-Forgiving, All-Compassionate (especially toward His believing servants, and may forgive ill-manners arising from ignorance).[3]

6. O you who believe! If some transgressor brings you news (that requires taking action), verify it carefully (before you believe and act upon it), lest you harm a people in ignorance and then become regretful for what you have done.[4]

7. Always bear in mind that God's Messenger is among you (so that you have a duty to refer decisions to him).[5] If he were to follow you in many affairs of public concern, you would surely be in trouble

(and suffer loss).[6] But God has endeared the faith to you (O believers) and made it appealing to your hearts, and He has made unbelief, transgression, and rebellion hateful to you. Those are they who are rightly guided (in belief, thought, and action),

8. As a grace from God and a favor. God is All-Knowing, All-Wise.

9. If two parties of believers fall to fighting, make peace between them (and act promptly). But if one of them aggressively encroaches the rights of the other, then fight you all against the aggressive side until they comply with God's decree (concerning the matter). If they comply, then make peace between them with justice and be scrupulously equitable. Surely God loves the scrupulously equitable.

10. The believers are but brothers, so make peace between your brothers and keep from disobedience to God in reverence for Him and piety (particularly in your duties toward one another as brothers), so that you may be shown mercy (granted a good, virtuous life in the world as individuals and as a community, and eternal happiness in the Hereafter).[7]

11. O you who believe! Let not some people among you deride another people, it may be that the latter are better than the former; nor let some women deride other women, it may be that the latter are better than the former. Nor defame one another (and provoke the same for yourselves in retaliation), nor insult one another with nicknames (that your brothers and sisters dislike). Evil is using names with vile meaning after (those so addressed have accepted) the faith (– doing so is like replacing a mark of faith with a mark of transgression). Whoever (does that and then) does not turn to God in repentance, (giving up doing so), those are indeed wrongdoers.

3. The type of treatment toward God's Messenger mentioned in the last two verses is different from the type condemned in the first three verses. The former is concerned with any ill manner arising from ignorance, while the latter is about disrespect to the Messenger and treating oneself as being at par with him and holding one's views as of equal value with his. While the latter may cause one's good deeds to go in vain and to perish, the former is forgivable. However, such actions, so explicitly condemned by this verse, should not be repeated.

4. The principle laid down in this verse after the commands concerning behavior toward the Messenger requires attention in many respects, such as follows:

- In another verse (17: 36), God orders: *Do not follow that of which you have no knowledge (whether it is good or bad), and refrain from groundless assertions and conjectures. Surely the hearing, the sight, and the heart – each of these is subject to questioning about it (you are answerable, and will be called to account, for each of these on the Day of Judgment).* So a Muslim cannot judge anything without confirmed or true knowledge about it. Especially in matters requiring responsibility and concerning social relationships, Muslims must be very careful that they are acting on certain knowledge. This knowledge must be based either on eyewitness reports, or on true, verified reports and never arise from conjecture, individual opinions, or false reports. As will be decreed in verse 12 below, a Muslim cannot have an ill opinion of another Muslim.

- One who, even if a believer, lies, has been proved to be a slanderer, and has been witnessed to commit any of the decisively prohibited actions cannot be listened to in a court, and the report of such a person is not acceptable.

- Based on this verse, the scholars of the *Hadith* developed a very important and significant science, called the Science of *jarḥ* and *taʿdīl* – the science of establishing whether one who reports any of the Prophetic sayings, actions, and confirmations is reliable or not. This must be true for all matters, especially those concerning social relationships and court trials.

- One is regarded as trustworthy until such a transgression as lying, slander, or the committing of any decisively prohibited action has been established.

5. Also, in particular, see 4: 59, 64-65, 83, note 13.

6. This does not mean that God's Messenger should not consult with his Companions in the matters of government. Rather, consultation is essential to Islamic government and it was enjoined on the Messenger (3: 159). If we consider that this command was reiterated just after the Battle of 'Uhud and one of the reasons for the temporary setback in that battle followed from the Messenger's (reluctant) acceptance of the decision to go out to face the enemy that arose from consultation, but which was opposed to his view, the importance of consultation will become clearer (See 3: 159, note 31). However, if there is something contrary to the basic principles of faith and action, it cannot be put forward for discussion, and if the Messenger has definitely decided on a subject, it should not be discussed.

7. The last two verses mean that all the believers are brothers and sisters, who are dutiful to one another in this relationship. It hints that there may be quarrels, even fighting, among brothers, which may sometimes arise from rivalry and jealousy. Even if they quarrel and fight with one another, they are still brothers and sisters, and brotherhood and sisterhood require peace. If, despite the fact that there cannot be enmity among them, two parties of believers dispute or fight with each other, the other believers, who are brothers and sisters to them, must reconcile them immediately and make peace between them as required by such a relationship. When they are reconciled and have made peace, they must be meticulous in acting according to the precepts of justice. Since quarrels among brothers and sisters usu-

ally break out because of rivalry and jealousy; therefore, dispensing justice with great care is particularly important.

Brotherhood (and sisterhood) is very important for both the individual and social life of the believers. In particular, their prosperity in the world and superiority against their enemies depend on faith and this relationship. If they clash with one another and divide into rival groups, it is inevitable that they will weaken and be defeated by their enemies. For this reason, both the Qur'ān and God's Messenger, upon him be peace and blessings, have greatly stressed the importance of brotherhood and sisterhood. God's Messenger used to demand the allegiance of the believers on the conditions that they had to perform the Prescribed Prayers, paying the Prescribed Purifying Alms, and be well wishers of the believers. He also said: "Cursing a Muslim is a transgression, and fighting with him amounts to unbelief" (al-Bukhārī, "Īmān," 36). Again, he said: "A Muslim is a brother of another Muslim. He never wrongs him nor makes him devoid of his support. There is no greater offense for a Muslim than despising his Muslim brother" (al-Bukhārī, "Adab," 57–58; Muslim, "Birr," 28–34). He also said: "Believers are like a single body in loving, and showing mercy to one another. (Just as the whole body suffers from any suffering in any part of the body,) so too, will all believers suffer because of the suffering of a believer" (al-Bukhārī, "Adab," 122; Muslim, "Birr," 66). (For the importance of brotherhood and how it can be realized and preserved, see Said Nursi, Lem'alar, "20. Lem'a.")

بِسْمِ اللَّهِ الرَّحْمَنِ الرَّحِيمِ

يَا أَيُّهَا الَّذِينَ آمَنُوا اجْتَنِبُوا كَثِيرًا مِنَ الظَّنِّ إِنَّ بَعْضَ الظَّنِّ إِثْمٌ وَلَا تَجَسَّسُوا وَلَا يَغْتَب بَّعْضُكُم بَعْضًا أَيُحِبُّ أَحَدُكُمْ أَن يَأْكُلَ لَحْمَ أَخِيهِ مَيْتًا فَكَرِهْتُمُوهُ وَاتَّقُوا اللَّهَ إِنَّ اللَّهَ تَوَّابٌ رَّحِيمٌ ۝ يَا أَيُّهَا النَّاسُ إِنَّا خَلَقْنَاكُم مِّن ذَكَرٍ وَأُنثَى وَجَعَلْنَاكُمْ شُعُوبًا وَقَبَائِلَ لِتَعَارَفُوا إِنَّ أَكْرَمَكُمْ عِندَ اللَّهِ أَتْقَاكُمْ إِنَّ اللَّهَ عَلِيمٌ خَبِيرٌ ۝ قَالَتِ الْأَعْرَابُ آمَنَّا قُل لَّمْ تُؤْمِنُوا وَلَكِن قُولُوا أَسْلَمْنَا وَلَمَّا يَدْخُلِ الْإِيمَانُ فِي قُلُوبِكُمْ وَإِن تُطِيعُوا اللَّهَ وَرَسُولَهُ لَا يَلِتْكُم مِّنْ أَعْمَالِكُمْ شَيْئًا إِنَّ اللَّهَ غَفُورٌ رَّحِيمٌ ۝ إِنَّمَا الْمُؤْمِنُونَ الَّذِينَ آمَنُوا بِاللَّهِ وَرَسُولِهِ ثُمَّ لَمْ يَرْتَابُوا وَجَاهَدُوا بِأَمْوَالِهِمْ وَأَنفُسِهِمْ فِي سَبِيلِ اللَّهِ أُولَئِكَ هُمُ الصَّادِقُونَ ۝ قُلْ أَتُعَلِّمُونَ اللَّهَ بِدِينِكُمْ وَاللَّهُ يَعْلَمُ مَا فِي السَّمَاوَاتِ وَمَا فِي الْأَرْضِ وَاللَّهُ بِكُلِّ شَيْءٍ عَلِيمٌ ۝ يَمُنُّونَ عَلَيْكَ أَنْ أَسْلَمُوا قُل لَّا تَمُنُّوا عَلَيَّ إِسْلَامَكُم بَلِ اللَّهُ يَمُنُّ عَلَيْكُمْ أَنْ هَدَاكُمْ لِلْإِيمَانِ إِن كُنتُمْ صَادِقِينَ ۝ إِنَّ اللَّهَ يَعْلَمُ غَيْبَ السَّمَاوَاتِ وَالْأَرْضِ وَاللَّهُ بَصِيرٌ بِمَا تَعْمَلُونَ ۝

12. O you who believe! Avoid much suspicion, for some suspicion is a grave sin (liable to God's punishment);[8] and do not spy (on one another),[9] nor backbite (against one another). Would any of you love to eat the flesh of his dead brother?[10] You would abhor it! Keep from disobedience to God in reverence for Him and piety. Surely God is One Who truly returns repentance with liberal forgiveness and additional reward, All-Compassionate (particularly towards His believing servants).

13. O humankind! Surely We have created you from a single (pair of) male and female, and made you into tribes and families so that you may know one another (and so build mutuality and co-operative relationships, not so that you may take pride in your differences of race or social rank, and breed enmities). Surely the noblest, most honorable of you in God's sight is the one best in piety, righteousness, and reverence for God. Surely God is All-Knowing, All-Aware.[11]

14. (Some of) the dwellers of the desert say: "We believe." Say (to them): "You have not believed. Rather, (you should) say, 'We have submitted (to the rule of Islam),' for faith has not yet entered into your hearts."[12] But, if you obey God and His Messenger, He will not hold back anything of the reward of your (good) deeds.[13] Surely God is All-Forgiving, All-Compassionate.

15. Only those are the believers who have truly believed in God (as the Unique Deity, Lord, and Sovereign), and (believed in) His Messenger (including all that he has brought from God), then have never since doubted (the truth of what they have testified to), and who strive hard with their wealth and persons in God's cause. Those are they who are truthful and honest (in their profession of faith).

16. (If those desert dwellers still insist on thinking themselves true believers,) say: "What? Would you teach God (how truly you are devoted to) your Religion, while God knows all that is in the heavens and all that is on the earth?" God has full knowledge of everything.

17. They impress it on you as their favor to you that they have submitted (to the rule of Islam and thereby put you under an obligation to them). Say: "Do not count your being Muslims as a favor to me (nor seek to put me under an obligation. The Religion does not belong to me, but to God only.) It is indeed God Who has conferred

a favor upon you inasmuch as He has shown you the way to faith – if you are truthful (in your profession of being Muslims, those who have submitted to God)."

18. Surely God knows the unseen of the heavens and the earth (all that is beyond human perception and knowledge in them). And God sees well all that you do.

---

8. The *sūrah*, which has begun and continues with mention of the things injurious to the social relationships in a Muslim community, now mentions the most common ones among them such as derision, defamation, calling others by offensive nicknames, and the ill-opinion or evil suspicion of Muslims. So the suspicion that the verse condemns as a grave sin and prohibits is the evil suspicion of Muslims. If we avoid suspicion as much as possible, we can preserve ourselves from that suspicion which is sinful. Ill-opinion or evil suspicion of a Muslim brother and sister means one's evil suspicion of oneself. Muslims are mirrors to one another, so whoever has an evil suspicion of a Muslim is merely reflecting his or her own inner state. Verse 24: 12 states that a Muslim's opinion of other Muslims is in fact their opinion of themselves.

Islam absolutely orders that we cherish the good opinion of God and His Messenger. God declares: "Toward My servant I am how My servant thinks of Me" (al-Bukhārī, "Tawhīd", 15; Muslim, "Tawbah," 1).

9. The Qur'ān decisively prohibits spying into and disclosing the secrets and private lives of people, and orders keeping secret any defect and sinful act one has seen in a Muslim. Neither can a Muslim government spy on people to see whether they are committing a sin or crime, unless a decisive proof has been established that they are committing something against the public peace and others. Likewise, spying into houses, opening and reading letters that belong to others, and listening to the conversations of other people are all wrong.

10. Said Nursi writes:

This statement reprimands the backbiter with six degrees of reprimand and restrains them from this sin with six degrees of severity:

- The *hamzah*, marking the interrogative (and here translated as *would*) at the beginning of the sentence reaches into all the words of the verse, so that each of them carries an interrogative accent.

- Thus, at the very beginning the *hamzah* in itself asks, "Do you have no intelligence, with which you ask and answer, so that you fail to perceive how abominable this thing is?"

- The second word, *love*, asks through *hamzah*, "Is it that your heart, with which you love or hate, is so spoiled that you love a most repugnant thing like backbiting?"

- Third, the phrase, *any of you*, asks, "What has happened to your sense of the nature and responsibility of society and civilization that you dare to accept something so poisonous to social life?"

- Fourth, the phrase, *to eat the flesh*, asks, "What has happened to your sense of humanity that you are tearing your friend to pieces with your teeth like a wild animal?"

- Fifth, the phrase, *of his brother*, asks, "Do you have no human tenderness, no sense of kinship, that you sink your teeth into some innocent person to whom you are tied by numerous links of brotherhood? Do you have no intelligence that you bite into your own limbs with your teeth, in such a senseless fashion?"

- Sixth, the word, *dead*, asks, "Where is your conscience? Is your nature so corrupt that you commit such a disgusting act as eating the flesh of your dead brother who deserves much respect?"

According, then, to the total meaning of the verse and the indications of each of these words, slander and backbiting are repugnant to the intelligence, and to the heart, to humanity and conscience, to human nature, the

Religion, and social brotherhood/sisterhood. You see, then, that the verse condemns backbiting in six degrees in a very concise and exact manner and restrains people from it in six miraculous ways.

Backbiting is a shameful weapon and most commonly used by people of enmity, envy, and obstinacy; no self-respecting, honorable human being would ever demean themselves by resorting to such a vile weapon.

Backbiting consists in speaking about an absent person in a way that would repel and annoy them if they were present and were to hear. If the words uttered are true, that is backbiting; if they are not, this is both backbiting and slander and, therefore, is a doubly loathsome sin.

Backbiting can be permissible in a very few, particular circumstances:

- A person who has been wronged can present a formal complaint to some officer, so that with their help a wrong may be righted and justice restored.

- If a person contemplating co-operation or marriage with another comes to hold counsel with you, and you say to them, disinterestedly and purely for the sake of their benefit, and in order to counsel them properly, without any further motive, "Do not do that business with that person; it will be to your disadvantage."

- If a person says only by way of factual description, not to expose to disgrace or notoriety, "That crippled one went to such and such a place."

- If the person being criticized is an open and unashamed sinner; that is, far from being ashamed of it, they take pride in the sins they commit; if they take pleasure in their wrongdoing and commit sins openly.

In these particular cases, backbiting may be permissible, provided it is done disinterestedly and purely for the sake of truth and in the collective interest. Otherwise, backbiting is like a fire that consumes good deeds in the manner of a flame eating up wood.

If one has engaged in backbiting or listened to it willingly, one should seek God's forgiveness, saying, "O God, forgive me and the one whom I backbit", and when he meets the person about whom they spoke ill, they should say to them: "Forgive me!" (*The Letters*, "the 22nd Letter," 2: 76–78).

11. Racism is one of the severest problems of our age. When God's Messenger, upon him be peace and blessings, was raised as a Prophet, the attitudes behind racism were prevalent in Makkah in the guise of tribalism. The Quraysh considered themselves (in particular) and Arabs (in general) as being superior to all other people. God's Messenger came with this Divine message and proclaimed it, explaining: *No Arab is superior to a non-Arab, and no white person is superior to a black person* (Ibn Ḥanbal, 5: 441); and *If a black Abyssinian Muslim is to rule over Muslims, he should be obeyed* (Muslim, "'Imārah," 37).

God's Messenger eradicated color-based racism and discrimination so successfully that, for example, 'Umar once said of Bilāl, who was black: "Bilāl is our master, and was emancipated by our master Abū Bakr" (Ibn Ḥajar, 1: 165). Once Abū Dharr got so angry with Bilāl that he insulted him: "You son of a black woman!" Bilāl came to God's Messenger and reported the incident in tears. The Messenger reproached Abū Dharr: "Do you still have a sign of *Jāhiliyyah*?" Full of repentance, Abū Dharr lay on the ground and said: "I won't raise my head (meaning he wouldn't get up) unless Bilāl puts his foot on it to pass over it." Bilāl forgave him, and they were reconciled (al-Bukhārī, "Īmān," 22). Zayd ibn Ḥārithah, a black slave emancipated by God's Messenger, was his adopted son before the Revelation banned such adoption. The Prophet married him to Zaynab bint Jahsh, one of the noblest (and non-black) Arab and Muslim women. In addition, he chose Zayd as the commander of the Muslim army that was sent against the Byzantine Empire, even though it included such leading Companions as Abū Bakr, 'Umar, Ja'far ibn Abī Ṭālib (the cousin of God's Messenger), and Khālid ibn Walīd (even then famed for his genius as a military commander) (Muslim, "Faḍā'il aṣ-Ṣaḥābah," 63). The Prophet appointed Zayd's son Usāmah to command the army he formed just before his death. Included therein were such leading Companions as Abū Bakr, 'Umar, Khālid, Abū 'Ubaydah, Talhah, and Zubayr. This established in the Muslims' hearts and minds that superiority is not by birth or color or blood, but by righteousness and devotion to God.

During his caliphate, 'Umar paid Usāmah a higher salary than his own son, 'Abdullāh. When his son asked why, 'Umar replied: "My son, I do so because I know God's Messenger loved Usāmah's father more than your father, and Usāmah more than you" (Ibn Sa'd, 4: 70).

12. Being a Muslim has three aspects. One is believing in all the essentials of the Islamic faith and submitting to God and His Messenger wholeheartedly by carrying out the commandments of Islam. This is being a sincere Muslim. The second is accepting the sovereignty of the Islamic government or being a Muslim according to the law. This requires a verbal declaration of faith, joining the Muslim congregation in the Prayer, and paying the Prescribed Purifying Alms (az-Zakāh), and not doing openly anything that will invalidate the declaration of faith. Such a person may be a hypocrite, but is treated as a Muslim by law. The third is only submission to the Islamic government. The Bedouins mentioned in the verse were Muslims of the third type.

13. This has three meanings:

- If you truly believe and obey God and His Messenger, He will not diminish anything in the reward of your deeds both in the world and, especially, in the Hereafter.

- If you continue to obey God and His Messenger in submission to the Muslim state, you will never be left unrewarded for your services in the world.

- If a virtuous non-believer who is not too prejudiced and arrogant to believe does good deeds pleasing to God and does not wrong others, God usually rewards or favors them with faith. A man asked God's Messenger: "Will our good deeds in *Jāhiliyyah* be rewarded?" The Messenger replied: "God bestowed Islam on you because of those deeds of yours" (al-Bukhārī, "Adab," 16; Muslim, "Īmān," 194).

SŪRAH 50

QĀF

Makkah period

Revealed in Makkah, most probably in the fourth or fifth year of the Makkan period, this *sūrah* of 45 verses takes its name after the letter *Qāf* in the first verse. It mentions many phenomena in the universe that indicate God, and then concentrates on the afterlife. It also presents episodes from the lives of peoples who were destroyed in earlier times. God's Messenger frequently read this *sūrah* during the Prayers of the religious festive days and sometimes during the Morning Prayer.

In the Name of God, the All-Merciful, the All-Compassionate.

1. *Qāf*.[1] By the Qur'ān most sublime. (We have indeed, in spite of what they say, sent it to you to warn people that they will be raised from the dead to account for their lives.)

2. But they deem it strange that a warner from among them has come to them, and the unbelievers say: "This is something strange!

3. "When we have died and become dust (you say, we will be raised from the dead)? That is a far-fetched return!"

4. We know for certain whatever the earth corrodes of them (to the most minute particle); with Us there is a book recording and preserving (incorruptibly).[2]

5. Rather, they have denied the truth when it has come to them (and done so willfully and persistently), so they are in a dire state (utterly confused about how to explain their rejection, and about how to prevent the acceptance of others).

6. But do they, then, never observe the sky above them (to ponder Our Knowledge and Power; and reflect) how We have constructed it and adorned it, and that there are no rifts in it?

7. And the earth – We have spread it out, and set therein firm mountains, and caused to grow thereon every lovely pair of vegetation.

8. (All this is a means of) insight and reminder for every servant (of God) willing to turn to Him in contrition.

9. And We send down from the sky blessed water with which We cause to grow gardens and grain to harvest,

10. And tall and stately date-palms with ranged clusters,

11. As provision for the servants. And We

revive with it a dead land: even so will the dead be raised and come forth (from their graves).

12. Before them the people of Noah denied, and the companions of ar-Rass, and the Thamūd;

13. And the ʿĀd, and the Pharaoh,[3] and the people among whom Lot was sent as Messenger;[4]

14. And the companions of al-Aykah, and the people of Tubbaʿ.[5] Every one of them denied the Messengers and My threat was duly fulfilled.

15. What! did We show failure and weariness in the first creation (that We will not be able to repeat creation after its destruction)? Rather, (knowing that it could never be so) they are in a tangle (of thought and argument) about a new creation (after destruction of the old).

---

1. Information was given in note 1 to the first verse of *Sūrat al-Baqarah* about *Ḥurūf al-Muqattaʿāt*, the disjunctive, individual, or abbreviated letters that come at the beginning of some *sūrah*s. *Qāf* is one of them. It can additionally be said here that *Qāf* implies elevation and may be referring to the Qur'ān.

2. The unbelievers claim that the dead bodies are mixed into the dust, and become dust, and that it is therefore inconceivable that it can be known and distinguished to whom which particles (of dust) belong and so it is impossible to reconstruct individual bodies. But the Qur'ān answers that God knows everything down to the particles, and every event in the universe down to the motion of the particles. They are recorded in a book that is recording and preserving and is protected from any interference.

3. The verse mentions the Pharaoh alone, without any reference to his aristocracy and people. This is because as a dictator the Pharaoh was responsible for their denial and was almost as sinful as all of them put together.

4. The original of this sentence is *the brothers of Lot*. In many verses, the Qur'ān presents the Messengers as brothers of their people because each was chosen from among his people and therefore was of the same race as them and spoke the same language. Stressing this point here for Lot and his people is to remind us that any relationship with a Messenger that is not based on faith can never save one from perishing unless one believes.

5. See, on the companions of al-Aykah, 15: 78, note 15, and the people of Tubbaʿ, 44: 37, note 10.

وَلَقَدْ خَلَقْنَا الْإِنْسَانَ وَنَعْلَمُ مَا تُوَسْوِسُ بِهِ نَفْسُهُ وَنَحْنُ أَقْرَبُ إِلَيْهِ مِنْ حَبْلِ الْوَرِيدِ ۝ إِذْ يَتَلَقَّى الْمُتَلَقِّيَانِ عَنِ الْيَمِينِ وَعَنِ الشِّمَالِ قَعِيدٌ ۝ مَا يَلْفِظُ مِنْ قَوْلٍ إِلَّا لَدَيْهِ رَقِيبٌ عَتِيدٌ ۝ وَجَاءَتْ سَكْرَةُ الْمَوْتِ بِالْحَقِّ ذَلِكَ مَا كُنْتَ مِنْهُ تَحِيدُ ۝ وَنُفِخَ فِي الصُّورِ ذَلِكَ يَوْمُ الْوَعِيدِ ۝ وَجَاءَتْ كُلُّ نَفْسٍ مَعَهَا سَائِقٌ وَشَهِيدٌ ۝ لَقَدْ كُنْتَ فِي غَفْلَةٍ مِنْ هَذَا فَكَشَفْنَا عَنْكَ غِطَاءَكَ فَبَصَرُكَ الْيَوْمَ حَدِيدٌ ۝ وَقَالَ قَرِينُهُ هَذَا مَا لَدَيَّ عَتِيدٌ ۝ أَلْقِيَا فِي جَهَنَّمَ كُلَّ كَفَّارٍ عَنِيدٍ ۝ مَنَّاعٍ لِلْخَيْرِ مُعْتَدٍ مُرِيبٍ ۝ الَّذِي جَعَلَ مَعَ اللَّهِ إِلَهًا آخَرَ فَأَلْقِيَاهُ فِي الْعَذَابِ الشَّدِيدِ ۝ قَالَ قَرِينُهُ رَبَّنَا مَا أَطْغَيْتُهُ وَلَكِنْ كَانَ فِي ضَلَالٍ بَعِيدٍ ۝ قَالَ لَا تَخْتَصِمُوا لَدَيَّ وَقَدْ قَدَّمْتُ إِلَيْكُمْ بِالْوَعِيدِ ۝ مَا يُبَدَّلُ الْقَوْلُ لَدَيَّ وَمَا أَنَا بِظَلَّامٍ لِلْعَبِيدِ ۝ يَوْمَ نَقُولُ لِجَهَنَّمَ هَلِ امْتَلَأْتِ وَتَقُولُ هَلْ مِنْ مَزِيدٍ ۝ وَأُزْلِفَتِ الْجَنَّةُ لِلْمُتَّقِينَ غَيْرَ بَعِيدٍ ۝ هَذَا مَا تُوعَدُونَ لِكُلِّ أَوَّابٍ حَفِيظٍ ۝ مَنْ خَشِيَ الرَّحْمَنَ بِالْغَيْبِ وَجَاءَ بِقَلْبٍ مُنِيبٍ ۝ ادْخُلُوهَا بِسَلَامٍ ذَلِكَ يَوْمُ الْخُلُودِ ۝ لَهُمْ مَا يَشَاءُونَ فِيهَا وَلَدَيْنَا مَزِيدٌ ۝

—❧—

16. Assuredly, it is We Who have created human, and We know what suggestions his soul makes to him. We are nearer to him than his jugular vein.

17. Remember that the two recording angels (appointed to record his speech and deeds), seated on the right and on the left, receive and record.

18. Not a word does he utter but there is a watcher by him, ever-present.

19. And the stupor of death comes in truth (being the established decree of God for life). That is, (O human,) what you were trying to escape.

20. And (in time) the Trumpet will be blown. That is the Day when God's threat will be fulfilled.

21. And every person will come (before the Supreme Court) with one (angel) driving, and one (angel) bearing witness.

22. "Indeed you were in heedlessness of this, and now We have removed from you your veil, so your sight today is sharp."

23. And the one (the witnessing angel) who accompanies him says: "This is (his record) that I keep ready with me."

24. (The sentence is pronounced): "You two, throw into Hell everyone persistent in unbelief, obstinate (in rejecting the truth),

25. "Who impedes the doing of good (preventing himself and others), and who exceeds all bounds (of right and decency), and who is lost in doubts and implants doubts (in others);

26. "Who sets up another deity beside God: so cast him into the severe punishment."

27. His companion (the devil who accompanied him in the world and seduced him into evil) will say: "Our Lord! I did not cause him to rebel and transgress, but he himself was far astray."

28. God will say: "Do not dispute (with each other) in My Presence. I had warned you (of this Day) before.

29. "And the decree[6] from Me will not be changed, and I am in no wise one who wrongs (My) servants."

30. On that Day We will say to Hell, "Are you filled (to the full)?", and it will say, "Are there (yet) more (to come)?"[7]

31. And Paradise will be brought near for the God-revering, pious; not (any longer) is it far.

32. "This is what was promised for you –

for everyone who was penitent, careful in keeping his duties (to God).

33. "Everyone who stood in awe of the All-Merciful though unseen (beyond their perception), and has come with a heart contrite and devout.

34. "Now enter it in peace (secure from any trouble or distress). That is the Day of immortality."

35. Therein will be for them everything that they desire, and in Our Presence there is yet more.[8]

---

6. This decree states that God will put into Hell those who follow Satan and disbelieve or associate partners with God (17: 63; 32: 13). For the disputes which will take place in Hell between Satan or the devils and the people of Hell and between the disbelieving wrongdoers and those who follow them, see: 38: 85; 34: 31–33; 37: 50–57; 40: 47–52.

7. Everything will be alive in the Hereafter (29: 64), so Hell will speak there (25: 12, note

4). This question and answer is to emphasize that Hell can comprehend all those who have deserved it. For it will finally be filled to the limit (32: 13).

8. God Almighty declares: "I have prepared for My righteous servants in Paradise such blessings that neither eyes have seen them, nor ears heard them, nor minds ever conceived of them" (al-Bukhārī, "Tawḥīd," 35; Muslim, "Jannah," 4-5).

36. How many a generation We have destroyed before them who were mightier than these in prowess, and overran other lands. But was there any place of escape (for them when God's punishment became due: is there ever?)

37. Surely in that is a warning reminder for anyone who has a heart (that is truly alive), and who gives ear (to the one conveying this reminder), with eyes able to see well.

38. We assuredly created the heavens and the earth and all that is between them in six days, and nothing of fatigue touched us.[9]

39. So (with confident reliance on Our promise and Power) bear with patience whatever they say and glorify your Lord with His praise before the rising of the sun and before its setting;

40. And during (some part of) the night,

too, glorify Him, and after the prostrations.[10]

41. And wait with ears able to hear for the Day when the Caller will call out from a place near;[11]

42. The Day when they will hear the Blast in truth (as a predetermined decree of God that must happen). That is the Day of the coming forth (when the dead will be raised from their graves).

43. Surely it is We Who give life and cause to die, and to Us is the homecoming.

44. That Day the earth will be rent asunder away from them, and they, hurrying out of it (will come to the gathering). That will be a gathering easy for Us.

45. We know best whatever they say, and you (O Messenger) are not one to compel them (to faith). So remind and warn by the Qur'ān him who fears My threat.

---

9. This statement categorically rejects the Biblical assertion that God needed to rest on the seventh day, an assertion that nullifies the idea of an omnipotent God.

10. In verse 39 the Morning Prayer, the Noon and the Afternoon Prayers, and in verse 40 the Evening and Late Evening Prayers are ordered. Glorification after the prostrations refers to the supererogatory Prayers after the prescribed ones (except the Morning and Afternoon

Prayers), and saying words of glorification (*Subḥān Allāh*), praise (*al-ḥamdu li 'llāh*), and exaltation (*Allāhu akbar*). The Messenger earnestly advised utterance of these phrases 33 times each after each Prescribed Prayer.

11. The Caller is the Archangel Isrāfīl who will blow the Trumpet. What is meant from a place near is that everyone in the world will hear the sound of the Trumpet as if it were being blown just next to them.

SŪRAH 51

ADH-DHĀRIYĀT (THE SCATTERERS)

Makkah period

Revealed in Makkah when the Quraysh's persecutions of the believers began, this *sūrah* of 60 verses derives its name from the word *adh-dhāriyāt* (those that scatter) in the first verse. It concentrates on the afterlife and God's Oneness, and warns the unbelievers, reminding them what happened to many previous peoples who had obstinately persisted in unbelief and wrongdoing.

In the Name of God, the All-Merciful, the All-Compassionate.

1. By those that (like winds) scatter far and wide;

2. And those that (like clouds) bear heavy burdens:

3. And those (like ships) that run with gentle ease;

4. And those (angels) who distribute by command (of God, His provision of rain and innumerable other blessings):[1]

5. What you are promised is most certainly true:

6. The Last Judgment is bound to take place.

1. In these verses God Almighty takes the attention to all the material causes and/or forces He employs in carrying out His orders on the earth, in the air, and in the sea (i.e., throughout the universe), and therefore swears by the angels responsible for them. As explained in *sūrah* 2, note 31, whatever takes place in the universe takes place through the angels that are responsible for that action. The angels are of different classes or ranks. They receive God's commands and by His command they distribute God's provision and other blessings.

7. By the heaven full of braided pathways (for the movement of angels and celestial objects, for the sending down of God's commands, and for the ascent of the diverse supplications of conscious beings by speech or act or need):

8. Surely you are in contradicting views (about the Qur'ān and how to describe it).

9. Whoever has been deluded from it (the Qur'ān) is (first) self-deluded (turning away from the right way in thought, belief, and action).[2]

10. Be away from God's mercy the liars building on conjecture,

11. Who are quite heedless (of truth) in an abyss of ignorance.

12. They ask: "When is the Day of Judgment?"

13. The Day when they will be tormented over the Fire.

14. "Taste your torment (that you have brought upon yourselves). This is what you (in mockery) would ask to be hastened!"

15. As for the God-revering, pious: they will be in Gardens and springs,

16. Taking whatever their Lord grants them. For they were, before that, devoted to doing God's commands, aware that God was seeing them.

17. They used to sleep but little by night (almost never missing the *Tahajjud* Prayer).

18. And in the hour of early dawn, they would implore God's forgiveness.

19. And in their wealth the poor (who had to beg) and the destitute (who did not beg out of shame) had due share (a right they gladly honored).

20. On the earth there are (clear) signs (of God's Oneness as Lord and Sovereign) for those who seek certainty;

21. And also in your own selves. Will you then not see (the truth)?

22. And in the heaven there is your provision, and what you are promised.[3]

23. Then, by the Lord of the heaven and the earth, this (promise) is as much (a fact conveyed to you) as that you speak.

24. Has there come to you report of Abraham's honored guests?

25. They presented themselves before him and bade him peace. He said (in returning their greeting) "Peace!" (and thought:) A people unknown.

26. He withdrew to his household and brought a (roast of) fatted calf.

27. He placed it before them, and said: "Will you not eat?"

28. (When he saw that they did not eat)

he became apprehensive of them.[4] They said: "Do not be apprehensive!" They gave him the glad tidings of (the birth of) a son to be endowed with profound knowledge.

29. Then his wife came forward, groaning, and struck her forehead, saying: "How shall I bear a child, (being) a barren old woman?"

30. They said: "Thus has your Lord decreed. Surely He is the All-Wise, the All-Knowing."

---

2. There is a unity in the multiplicity in creation. As all other things and beings differ, so do human beings differ from one another in many ways. All other things and beings, despite their infinite multiplicity, obey the One and Single God, Lord, and Sovereign, and this is why there is a magnificent accord in the universe. So the beings (humankind and the jinn) endowed with free will and responsible for their choices must believe in and obey the same One and Single God if they desire accord in their individual and social lives. This does not mean that they must be uniform and standardized in their opinions.

There are many fields in which a difference of views and choices is necessary, but there are some other fields in which they must be unified. For example, they must believe in One God and must be united in belief in the other essentials of faith; and they must worship the same One and Single God, obeying His laws in ordering their lives. Some of these laws are essential to human life, regardless of time and place, and are therefore immutable, while others are changeable according to time, place, and conditions.

3. That is, whatever we have as provision is God's favor, and because of its sublimity and worth, the Qur'ān states that it has descended from the heaven. In addition, since the earth is revived with rain after its death and everything we obtain from the earth needs rain, the Qur'ān sometimes uses rain to mean provision. As for what is meant by *what you are promised*, it is everything that God will grant as a reward for the good deeds of His servants, including, in particular, Paradise. Since these rewards are also purely God's favors, they are sublime and therefore have their source in the heaven, or since the heaven suggests sublimity, the Qur'ān tells us that their source is the heaven.

4. If a guest held back from eating the food offered to him, it meant that he had an evil intention.

قَالَ فَمَا خَطْبُكُمْ أَيُّهَا الْمُرْسَلُونَ ۞ قَالُوٓا إِنَّآ أُرْسِلْنَآ إِلَىٰ قَوْمٍ مُّجْرِمِينَ ۞ لِنُرْسِلَ عَلَيْهِمْ حِجَارَةً مِّن طِينٍ ۞ مُّسَوَّمَةً عِندَ رَبِّكَ لِلْمُسْرِفِينَ ۞ فَأَخْرَجْنَا مَن كَانَ فِيهَا مِنَ الْمُؤْمِنِينَ ۞ فَمَا وَجَدْنَا فِيهَا غَيْرَ بَيْتٍ مِّنَ الْمُسْلِمِينَ ۞ وَتَرَكْنَا فِيهَآ ءَايَةً لِّلَّذِينَ يَخَافُونَ الْعَذَابَ الْأَلِيمَ ۞ وَفِي مُوسَىٰٓ إِذْ أَرْسَلْنَاهُ إِلَىٰ فِرْعَوْنَ بِسُلْطَانٍ مُّبِينٍ ۞ فَتَوَلَّىٰ بِرُكْنِهِ وَقَالَ سَاحِرٌ أَوْ مَجْنُونٌ ۞ فَأَخَذْنَاهُ وَجُنُودَهُ فَنَبَذْنَاهُمْ فِي الْيَمِّ وَهُوَ مُلِيمٌ ۞ وَفِي عَادٍ إِذْ أَرْسَلْنَا عَلَيْهِمُ الرِّيحَ الْعَقِيمَ ۞ مَا تَذَرُ مِن شَيْءٍ أَتَتْ عَلَيْهِ إِلَّا جَعَلَتْهُ كَالرَّمِيمِ ۞ وَفِي ثَمُودَ إِذْ قِيلَ لَهُمْ تَمَتَّعُوا حَتَّىٰ حِينٍ ۞ فَعَتَوْا عَنْ أَمْرِ رَبِّهِمْ فَأَخَذَتْهُمُ الصَّاعِقَةُ وَهُمْ يَنظُرُونَ ۞ فَمَا اسْتَطَاعُوا مِن قِيَامٍ وَمَا كَانُوا مُنتَصِرِينَ ۞ وَقَوْمَ نُوحٍ مِّن قَبْلُ ۚ إِنَّهُمْ كَانُوا قَوْمًا فَاسِقِينَ ۞ وَالسَّمَآءَ بَنَيْنَاهَا بِأَيْدٍ وَإِنَّا لَمُوسِعُونَ ۞ وَالْأَرْضَ فَرَشْنَاهَا فَنِعْمَ الْمَاهِدُونَ ۞ وَمِن كُلِّ شَيْءٍ خَلَقْنَا زَوْجَيْنِ لَعَلَّكُمْ تَذَكَّرُونَ ۞ فَفِرُّوا إِلَى اللَّهِ ۖ إِنِّي لَكُم مِّنْهُ نَذِيرٌ مُّبِينٌ ۞ وَلَا تَجْعَلُوا مَعَ اللَّهِ إِلَٰهًا ءَاخَرَ ۖ إِنِّي لَكُم مِّنْهُ نَذِيرٌ مُّبِينٌ ۞

---

31. He (Abraham) said: "Then (after that), what is your concern, O you (heavenly) envoys?"

32. They said: "Indeed, we have been sent to a people who are all criminals,

33. "So that We may send upon them stones of baked clay,

34. "Marked out in your Lord's Presence for (the destruction of) the people wasteful (of their God-given faculties and) committing excesses."

35. We brought out such as were therein of the believers;

36. But We did not find there any but a single house of Muslims (those wholly submitted to God).

37. We left there a clear sign (of the truth of God's Messages) for those who fear the painful punishment."[5]

38. And in (the exemplary history of) Moses too (there is a clear sign): We sent him as Messenger to the Pharaoh with an evident authority.

39. But the Pharaoh turned away (from Our Message), together with his hosts, and said: "(Moses is either) a sorcerer or a madman."

40. So We seized him and his hosts, and hurled them into the sea. And he was self-accused, remorseful (too late, when he was drowning).

41. And in (the illustrative history of the tribe of) 'Ād also (there is a clear sign), when We sent upon them the devastating wind.

42. It spared nothing that it reached, but made it like ashes.

43. And in (the illustrative history of the tribe of) Thamūd also (there is a clear sign), when they (were given respite and) it was said to them: "Enjoy life for a little while!"

44. But they rebelled against their Lord's decree, so the thunderbolt (along with the blast) seized them, even while they were looking on.

45. They were not able to rise up (still less escape the punishment), nor were able to receive help.

46. (And We had destroyed) the people of Noah before. They were a people transgressing (God's bounds).

47. And the heaven,[6] We have constructed it mightily, and it is surely We Who have vast power, and keep expanding it.[7]

48. And the earth, We have spread it out, and how excellent We are in spreading it out (like a cradle).

49. And all things We have created in pairs, so that you may reflect and be mindful.

50. "So, flee to (refuge in) God. I am surely a plain warner to you from Him.

51. "And do not set up another deity besides God. I am surely a plain warner to you from Him."

---

5. For further explanations, see 11: 69–83; 15: 51–77 and the corresponding notes.

6. After the accounts of some past, exemplary events, this verse is a continuation of verse 22.

7. The expansion of the universe, of which the Qur'ān informed us centuries ago, is the most imposing discovery of modern science. Today it is a firmly established concept and the only debate centers around the way this is taking place.

52. Similarly, no Messenger came to the peoples who lived before them but they said of him (in like manner): "A sorcerer or a madman."

53. Have they bequeathed this to one another (by way of response)? They were indeed a rebellious people.

54. So, turn away from disputing with them, and you are not to be blamed (for doing so).

55. But remind and warn, for reminding and warning are of benefit to the believers.[8]

56. I have not created the jinn and humankind but to (know and) worship Me (exclusively).[9]

57. I demand of them no provision, nor do I demand that they should feed Me.

58. Surely God – it is He Who is the All-Providing, Lord of all might, and the All-Forceful.

59. So surely those who commit the greatest wrong (namely, not believing in and worshipping God or associating partners with Him in worship), will have their share (of the punishment) like the share of their fellows (of old who were destroyed). Then, let them not ask Me to hasten it.

60. Then, woe to those who disbelieve because of their Day with which they are threatened.

---

8. Dispute is of no use in communicating the Message. What is important and should be done is to communicate and preach the truth in the proper style. The other thing that should be pointed out here is that in preaching the truth or the Divine Message the believers should not be neglected, thinking that they already believe, and their needs should be taken into consideration. Everyone needs reminding.

9. This verse expresses the Divine purpose for creation. While all other beings and things worship and obey God willy-nilly, only the jinn and humankind, endowed with free will, have the capacity to worship and obey or not to worship and obey Him. Yet, as it is God Who creates and maintains, He alone deserves worship. It is also He Who will ask conscious beings to account for their lives, and this is why God alone must be worshipped. Worshipping and obeying the One God will also secure justice and accord in the lives of the jinn and humankind. Worshipping God entails knowledge and love of Him. Bediüzzaman Said Nursi writes:

Belief in God is creation's highest aim and most sublime result, and humanity's most exalted rank is knowledge of Him that is contained in this belief. The most radiant happiness and sweetest bounty for the jinn and humanity is love of God contained within knowledge of God. The purest joy of the human spirit and the sheerest delight of the human heart is spiritual ecstasy contained within the love of God. All true happiness, pure joy, sweet bounties, and unclouded pleasures are contained within knowledge and love of God. Those who truly know and love God can receive infinite happiness, bounties, enlightenment, and understand infinite mysteries. Those who do not are afflicted with infinite spiritual and material misery, pain, and fear. If any person were allowed to rule this world, despite his or her being powerless, miserable, and unprotected amid other purposeless people in this world, what would the true worth of this be?

People who do not recognize their Owner and discover their Master are miserable and bewildered. But those who do, taking refuge in His Mercy and relying on His Power, see this desolate world transformed into a place of rest and felicity, a place of exchange for the Hereafter. (*The Letters*, "the 20th Letter," 2: 2)

SŪRAH 52

AṬ-ṬŪR (MOUNT (SINAI))

Makkah period

Revealed in Makkah, this *sūrah* of 49 verses derives its name from the word *aṭ-Ṭūr* (the Mount) in the first verse. It deals with the confused reactions of the Makkan polytheists to the revelation of the Qur'ān and how they made themselves look ridiculous. It emphasizes the truth of Judgment Day and that the unbelievers will be punished while the believers will be rewarded with Paradise. It also draws attention to the destruction that may come upon those who obstinately resist the truth.

In the Name of God, the All-Merciful, the All-Compassionate.

1. By the Mount (Sinai),

2. And by a Book inscribed,

3. In parchments outstretched,

4. And by *Bayt al-Maʿmūr* (the House continuously frequented),

5. And by the canopy (of heaven) raised high,

6. And by the sea kept filled (and ready to overflow),

7. The punishment of your Lord will certainly take place.[1]

8. There is none that can avert it.

9. On that Day the heaven will be convulsed violently;

10. And the mountains will move away with an awesome movement.

11. Woe, then, on that Day to those who deny (God's Message and the Messengers) –

12. Those who are habitually playing, absorbed (in vanities):

13. On that Day they will be forcefully thrust into the fire of Hell.

14. "This is the Fire which you used to deny.

1. The Qur'ān draws attention to many important phenomena in the universe, human life, and history in order to emphasize the inevitable advent of the Last Day. In the same way as the creation of the universe, the changes and convulsions it has experienced, and the changes of the days, months, seasons, years, and centuries all bear witness to the coming of the Last Day, so too do the revealed Books throughout human history inform us of its decisive occurrence. Science also testifies to this (See Ali Ünal, *The Resurrection and the Afterlife*, 57–94) So, by the Mount, the Qur'ān refers to both Mount Sinai, where the Prophet Moses received the Torah, and another mount (an-Nūr) where the Prophet Muḥammad began to receive the Qur'ān. By the Books inscribed, it refers to the revealed Books of God, like the Torah and the Qur'ān.

The Books inscribed may also signify the records of deeds where the deeds of human beings are recorded and which will be unrolled on Judgment Day. *Bayt al-Maʿmūr* refers both to the Ka'bah, which has continuously been visited by human beings and angels, and also its counterpart in the heavenly realm that is continuously visited and circumambulated by angels. It also refers to the revelation of the Qur'ān, in that according to some, the Qur'ān was first sent down on it in its entirety (See *sūrah* 44, note 1). The heaven will be rent asunder on the Last Day and all the seas or the mass of water on the earth will be made to boil over. So, all the phenomena referred to in these six verses allude to the Last Day, and because of this, the oaths sworn in them conclude with the declaration of its inevitable and already destined advent.

أَفَسِحْرٌ هَٰذَآ أَمْ أَنتُمْ لَا تُبْصِرُونَ ۝ اصْلَوْهَا فَٱصْبِرُوٓا
أَوْ لَا تَصْبِرُوا سَوَآءٌ عَلَيْكُمْ إِنَّمَا تُجْزَوْنَ مَا كُنتُمْ تَعْمَلُونَ ۝
إِنَّ ٱلْمُتَّقِينَ فِى جَنَّٰتٍ وَنَعِيمٍ ۝ فَٰكِهِينَ بِمَآ ءَاتَىٰهُمْ رَبُّهُمْ
وَوَقَىٰهُمْ رَبُّهُمْ عَذَابَ ٱلْجَحِيمِ ۝ كُلُوا وَٱشْرَبُوا هَنِيٓـًٔا بِمَا كُنتُمْ
تَعْمَلُونَ ۝ مُتَّكِـِٔينَ عَلَىٰ سُرُرٍ مَّصْفُوفَةٍ ۖ وَزَوَّجْنَٰهُم بِحُورٍ عِينٍ
۝ وَٱلَّذِينَ ءَامَنُوا وَٱتَّبَعَتْهُمْ ذُرِّيَّتُهُم بِإِيمَٰنٍ أَلْحَقْنَا بِهِمْ
ذُرِّيَّتَهُمْ وَمَآ أَلَتْنَٰهُم مِّنْ عَمَلِهِم مِّن شَىْءٍ ۚ كُلُّ ٱمْرِئٍ بِمَا كَسَبَ
رَهِينٌ ۝ وَأَمْدَدْنَٰهُم بِفَٰكِهَةٍ وَلَحْمٍ مِّمَّا يَشْتَهُونَ ۝
يَتَنَٰزَعُونَ فِيهَا كَأْسًا لَّا لَغْوٌ فِيهَا وَلَا تَأْثِيمٌ ۝ وَيَطُوفُ عَلَيْهِمْ
غِلْمَانٌ لَّهُمْ كَأَنَّهُمْ لُؤْلُؤٌ مَّكْنُونٌ ۝ وَأَقْبَلَ بَعْضُهُمْ عَلَىٰ
بَعْضٍ يَتَسَآءَلُونَ ۝ قَالُوٓا إِنَّا كُنَّا قَبْلُ فِىٓ أَهْلِنَا مُشْفِقِينَ
۝ فَمَنَّ ٱللَّهُ عَلَيْنَا وَوَقَىٰنَا عَذَابَ ٱلسَّمُومِ ۝ إِنَّا كُنَّا مِن قَبْلُ
نَدْعُوهُ ۖ إِنَّهُ هُوَ ٱلْبَرُّ ٱلرَّحِيمُ ۝ فَذَكِّرْ فَمَآ أَنتَ بِنِعْمَتِ رَبِّكَ
بِكَاهِنٍ وَلَا مَجْنُونٍ ۝ أَمْ يَقُولُونَ شَاعِرٌ نَّتَرَبَّصُ بِهِ رَيْبَ
ٱلْمَنُونِ ۝ قُلْ تَرَبَّصُوا فَإِنِّى مَعَكُم مِّنَ ٱلْمُتَرَبِّصِينَ ۝

---

15. "Is this sorcery (for you used to deride the Revelation as sorcery), or is it that you do not see (so that, for you, it is something illusory)?

16. "Suffer the heat of it now! Bear it patiently, or do not bear it patiently, it is all the same to you. You are only being recompensed for all that you used to do (in the world)."

17. The God-revering, pious ones will surely be in Gardens and bliss,

18. Enjoying all that their Lord will grant them (by His grace and in recompense for their good deeds); and their Lord has protected them from the punishment of the Blazing Flame.

19. "Eat and drink to your hearts' content for all that you used to do (in the world)."

20. They will recline on thrones arranged;

and We have assigned for them maidens pure, beautiful of eye.

21. Those who have believed and their offspring have followed them in faith, We will unite them with their offspring (even though the faith of the latter may not be of the same degree as that of the former), and We will not decrease the reward of their deeds in anything (because of their being united with their offspring). Every person will enjoy according to what he has earned.[2]

22. And We will provide them with fruit and meat, one meal after the other, such as they desire.

23. There they will pass among one another a cup wherein is (a drink inciting) no false, foolish talk nor sin.

24. And there will go round them boy-servants attending upon them, (so pure) as hidden pearls.

25. Some of them will move closer to others, asking (about their affairs in the world and how they were admitted to Paradise).

26. They say: "We used to be, when amongst our families, indeed most apprehensive before (most careful and alert for the guidance and eternal life of our family members).

27. "Then God bestowed His favor upon us, and protected us from the punishment of the scorching fire penetrating through the skin.

28. "We used to worship and invoke Him alone before. Surely He is the All-Benign, the All-Compassionate (especially to His believing servants)."

29. So (O Messenger, continue to) preach and remind; by God's grace, you are not a soothsayer, nor a madman.

30. Or do they say (of him): "A poet (jinn-possessed). We await for him some calamity ahead"?

31. Say: "Wait on, for I am waiting with you (though I hope for a different outcome)."

---

2. God will unite the parents with their believing offspring in Paradise, even though the faith and deeds of their offspring may not be of the same rank as them. This will be another blessing for the believers. However, everyone will not enjoy Paradise to the same degree, even though they will be together in the same place. Each person will enjoy it according to the degree of their own faith and deeds.

The verse also hints that, as pointed out in 56: 10–14, particularly at the beginning of a new movement of faith, those who attain the faith first are generally more valued in God's sight and will be the foremost in enjoying Paradise. They have outstripped others in believing and supported God's cause at a time when supporting it was the most difficult, without considering any worldly advantage, and therefore suffered greater hardships than those who followed.

36. Or did they create the heavens and the earth (so that their sovereignty belongs to them)? No indeed. Rather, they have no certain knowledge (about creation, humankind, and the basic facts concerning them).

37. Or are the treasures of your Lord at their disposal (so that they provide for creation however they will, and choose whomever they will as Messenger and send down to him whatever Book they will)? Or have they been given authority over them (so that they can prevail upon God to send them a Message and Messenger that suits their interests)?

38. Or do they have a ladder by which (having climbed to heaven) they overhear (the secrets of heaven, confirming their stand against the Messenger and the Qur'ān)? Then let their eavesdropper produce some clear authority (to prove what he claims to have heard).

39. Or (do you in your absurdity attribute to Him children, so that) for Him there are daughters (whom you yourselves foolishly disdain), while for you there are sons?

40. Or is it that you (O Messenger) ask them for wage (for conveying God's Religion to them) so that they are crushed under debt?

41. Or do they have the knowledge of the Unseen (and the Supreme Ever-Preserved Tablet) so that they write down the decrees (determining all events, and stipulating a way of life for others to follow)?

42. Or do they intend a plot (to entrap you so as to defeat your mission)? Yet it is those who disbelieve who are entrapped (in so plotting, because they deny themselves God's blessings in both worlds).

43. Or do you have a deity other than God (to whom, in vain, you look to sustain, and

32. Do their minds urge them to such (absurd falsehoods), or are they a people (in the habit of being) rebellious and outrageous?

33. Or do they say: "He forges it (and then attributes the Qur'ān to God)?" No indeed. Rather, (they make such claims because) they have no will to believe.

34. (If they really believe such a Book can be forged) then, let them produce a Discourse like it, if they are truthful (in their claims).

35. Or were they created without anything being before them (or out of something different than the basic material of all creation, so that they know things others do not), or are they the creators (of themselves, so that they can maintain themselves and are free in their acts)?

help, and protect you)? All-Glorified is He (in that He is absolutely exalted) above what they associate as partners with Him.

44. (So obstinate are they in rejecting the truth that) if they saw a piece of the sky falling down (on them), they would say, "This is (only) a heap of clouds!" (For they cannot conceive that it may be a punishment for their obstinate denial).

45. So, leave them until they meet their Day when they will be struck dead.

46. The Day when their scheming will avail them nothing, nor will they be helped.

47. And surely for those who commit the greatest wrong (through unbelief or associating partners with God and resisting the conveying of His Religion), there is another punishment besides that, but most of them do not know.[3]

48. So wait patiently for your Lord's judgment, for you are under Our Eyes (under Our care and protection); and glorify your Lord with His praise when you rise up (to pray);

49. And in the night-time also glorify Him, and at the retreat of the stars.

---

3. The Day mentioned in verse 45 may be referring either to the day when the leaders of unbelief will be struck dead in the world in a war (as the leaders of the Quraysh were killed in the Battle of Badr) or in another catastrophe, or to the overall destruction of the world.

So *another punishment* mentioned in verse 47 is both the kind of punishment they will be made to suffer in the world so that they may repent, and the punishment in the grave that they will suffer until the Day of Resurrection.

٥٢٥   الجزء السابع والعشرون   525

بِسْمِ اللّٰهِ الرَّحْمٰنِ الرَّحِيْمِ
وَالنَّجْمِ اِذَا هَوٰى ۙ مَا ضَلَّ صَاحِبُكُمْ وَمَا غَوٰى ۙ وَمَا يَنْطِقُ عَنِ
الْهَوٰى ۚ اِنْ هُوَ اِلَّا وَحْيٌ يُّوْحٰى ۙ عَلَّمَهُ شَدِيْدُ الْقُوٰى ۙ ذُوْ مِرَّةٍ
فَاسْتَوٰى ۙ وَهُوَ بِالْاُفُقِ الْاَعْلٰى ۙ ثُمَّ دَنَا فَتَدَلّٰى ۙ فَكَانَ
قَابَ قَوْسَيْنِ اَوْ اَدْنٰى ۚ فَاَوْحٰى اِلٰى عَبْدِهٖ مَا اَوْحٰى ۙ مَا كَذَبَ
الْفُؤَادُ مَا رَاٰى ۙ اَفَتُمٰرُوْنَهُ عَلٰى مَا يَرٰى ۚ وَلَقَدْ رَاٰهُ نَزْلَةً
اُخْرٰى ۙ عِنْدَ سِدْرَةِ الْمُنْتَهٰى ۙ عِنْدَهَا جَنَّةُ الْمَأْوٰى ۙ اِذْ يَغْشَى
السِّدْرَةَ مَا يَغْشٰى ۙ مَا زَاغَ الْبَصَرُ وَمَا طَغٰى ۙ لَقَدْ رَاٰى مِنْ
اٰيٰتِ رَبِّهِ الْكُبْرٰى ۙ اَفَرَءَيْتُمُ اللّٰتَ وَالْعُزّٰى ۙ وَمَنٰوةَ
الثَّالِثَةَ الْاُخْرٰى ۙ اَلَكُمُ الذَّكَرُ وَلَهُ الْاُنْثٰى ۙ تِلْكَ اِذًا
قِسْمَةٌ ضِيْزٰى ۚ اِنْ هِيَ اِلَّا اَسْمَاءٌ سَمَّيْتُمُوْهَا اَنْتُمْ وَاٰبَاؤُكُمْ مَّا
اَنْزَلَ اللّٰهُ بِهَا مِنْ سُلْطَانٍ ۚ اِنْ يَّتَّبِعُوْنَ اِلَّا الظَّنَّ وَمَا تَهْوَى
الْاَنْفُسُ ۚ وَلَقَدْ جَاءَهُمْ مِّنْ رَّبِّهِمُ الْهُدٰى ۙ اَمْ لِلْاِنْسَانِ مَا تَمَنّٰى
فَلِلّٰهِ الْاٰخِرَةُ وَالْاُوْلٰى ۩ وَكَمْ مِّنْ مَّلَكٍ فِى السَّمٰوٰتِ لَا تُغْنِى
شَفَاعَتُهُمْ شَيْئًا اِلَّا مِنْ بَعْدِ اَنْ يَّأْذَنَ اللّٰهُ لِمَنْ يَّشَاءُ وَيَرْضٰى

❧

SŪRAH 53

AN-NAJM (THE STAR)

Makkah period

Revealed in Makkah, this *sūrah* of 62
verses derives its name from the word
an-Najm (the star) in the first verse.
God's Messenger, upon him be peace and blessings, recited it in its entirety to both the believers and the Makkan polytheists at the Ka'bah.
It warns the polytheists of their attitude to the
Qur'ān. It reminds them that all their beliefs
are based on mere surmises, while those who
follow the Straight Path are those believe in
and worship the One God, Who is the Owner of the whole universe. It also stresses that
the Religion God's Messengers communicates
is not a new, invented one in human history,
and it threatens the polytheists with Judgment
Day, which is bound to come.

In the Name of God, the All-Merciful,
the All-Compassionate.

1. By the star when it goes down,

2. Your Companion (the Messenger) has
neither gone astray nor adopted a wrong
way (in belief and action).

3. He does not speak on his own, out of
his own desire;

4. That (which he conveys to you) is but a
Revelation that is revealed to him.[1]

5. One of forceful might (Gabriel) has
taught it;

6. One firm, with ability to penetrate and
perfect in spirit, rose with all his splendor[2]

7. When he was in the highest part of the
horizon.[3]

8. Then, he drew near and came close,

9. So he was (so near that there was left
only the distance between) the strings of
two bows (put adjacent to each other) or
even nearer (than that).

10. And He revealed to His servant what
He revealed.[4]

11. The heart did not contradict what he
saw (with his eyes).[5]

12. Will you then dispute with him concerning what he saw?

13. Assuredly he saw him during a second
descent,

14. By the Lote-tree of the utmost boundary,[6]

15. Near it is the Garden of Refuge and
Dwelling.

16. Meanwhile that was covering the
Lote-tree which was covering it.[7]

17. The sight (of the Messenger) did not
swerve (so that he looked elsewhere and
saw something different), nor did it go
wrong (so that he might have seen an illusion).

18. Indeed, he saw one among the greatest signs of His Lord.[8]

19. (As compared to that) have you considered al-Lāt and al-'Uzzā?

20. And the other, the third (idol), al-Manāt: (what things are these that you concoct)?

21. What? For you the males and for Him the females?

22. That is an unfair division indeed![9]

23. They (your false deities) are nothing but made-up names that you and your forefathers have invented; God sent no authority for them. They follow only conjecture and that which they themselves lust after. But now there has certainly come to them guidance from their Lord (Who has created them, and sustains them).

24. Or will human attain whatever he craves?[10]

25. But (whatever human desires, be it to serve his higher good, or to serve his carnal appetites) to God belong the after(life) and the former (life).[11]

26. How many an angel there is in the heavens (even supposing they would intercede for a human) whose intercession does not avail at all except after God has given permission to whomever He wills (to intercede on behalf of whomever He wills) and is pleased with.

---

1. As mentioned in the introductory words about this *sūrah* above, God's Messenger recited it in its entirety to both the believers and the polytheists at the Ka'bah. The polytheists were trying to find excuses for their rejection of the Qur'ān and the Messenger, and discussing how they should brand them. So the verses remove all the doubts and confusion that they were trying to form around the Divine origin of the Qur'ān and the Messengership of the Prophet Muḥammad, upon him be peace and blessings.

In many verses God swears by objects in the universe. This *sūrah* begins with an oath by the star. This has many implications. By *the star*, it refers to all celestial objects and, by swearing by it when it goes down, it implies that no celestial object can be a deity to worship (See 6: 76, note 16). As is known, the Makkan polytheists also worshipped some celestial objects, including, in particular, the star of Sirius (verse 49 in this *sūrah*). It also implies that, since the time when the star goes down is the time when day breaks, the day or sun of truth (Islam) is about to rise. The Ascension of God's Messenger, some aspects of which are mentioned in this *sūrah*, may also be symbolized by this.

The word translated as star also means passage, and according to some, it also refers to the Qur'ān's being revealed in passages. So the verse means, *By the passage(of the Qur'ān) when it goes down (is sent down).*

2. The verses possibly refer to important phenomena that are connected to one another. The one described in the verse may be referring to both the Archangel Gabriel and the Prophet Muḥammad, upon them be peace. The meaning given in the interpretation is referring to Gabriel. In its reference to the Messenger, the meaning of the verse is: *And by receiving the Qur'ān, the Messenger has attained full perfection and the greatest position.*

3. Gabriel used to come to God's Messenger in different forms. The Messenger, upon him be peace and blessings, saw him in his original form twice, first when he descended from Mount Nūr after receiving the first Revelation, and then, as mentioned in verse 13, during the Messenger's return from the Ascension. So this verse refers to his first sight of him. When it is taken to refer to the Messenger, it implies his greatness.

4. These verses, like the verses above, are

about both Gabriel's bringing the Revelation to the Messenger, and the Messenger's meeting with God during the Ascension, an event that happened beyond all concepts of modality. In the former case, verse 8 means that Gabriel "went down" from his position in the heaven and came close to the Messenger who was on the earth. In the latter case, it means that God manifested His nearness to the Messenger and attracted him toward Him, and the Messenger ascended toward Him, high enough to meet with Him. This meeting, which signifies the Messenger's unparalleled nearness to God, is expressed in verse 9 as the "nearness between the strings of two bows put adjacent to each other." This comparison points to the insurmountable boundary between the realm of contingency (creation) and the infinite "realm" of Absolute Necessity (the Creator). God's Messenger, upon him be peace and blessings, reached the highest point that a created being can. During the Ascension, God prescribed the five daily Prayers, so these verses also suggest the importance of the Prescribed Prayer. For this reason, the Prayer contains the meaning of the Ascension and is regarded as the ascension of every believer who performs it. A believer can realize ascension according to their capacity in the Prayer, an occasion on which a believer is nearest to God.

5. The original of the word translated as "the heart" is *fuād*. It is the center or central sense of the (spiritual) heart. The heart has senses of hearing and seeing, and what perceives or comprehends a perception received by the heart through its senses of hearing and seeing is *fuād*.

6. This tree signifies the insurmountable infinite boundary between the "realm" of Absolute Necessity (Divinity), and the realm of contingency (the created).

7. What covered the Lote-tree was God's Light and His overflowing radiance.

8. It is not certain what this greatest sign was. God had His Messenger travel in the highest dimensions of creation during the Ascension

so that he could see some of His signs (17: 1). It is understood that these signs are of the kind that they can only be perceived through seeing, and the greatest of creation, upon him be peace and blessings, was favored with their sight. Human language is inadequate to express these signs in such a way that we would be able to perceive them.

9. Al-Lāt, al-'Uzzā, and al-Manāt were three of the "greatest" idols of the Makkan polytheists. It is very interesting that these three idols were regarded as females and had female names. Since they were images or representations of some angels or angelic powers in the sight of the polytheists and since the polytheists regarded the angels as females or daughters of God, they called them by female names. But they despised females and did not desire to have daughters, yet they attributed females to God. As explained in note 25 to 4: 117, the reason why they chose their deities from among the females was because they did not want these to have any authority over them, moreover, they tended to seek to lord it over even their deities and to use them for the realization of their worldly ambitions.

10. For example, will humans choose whomever or whatever they desire as deities, and will they want God to accept angels as intermediaries with Him on their part, and is this something that God will accede to?

11. It is God Who has created the universe and humankind. No one has any choice in whether they come to the world or not, when and where they are born, or in what family they will come to the world, when they will depart from the world, nor in the determination of their color, race, physical body, or sex. So it is also God Who has established the conditions of life in the world and the law of causality (what happens to humans as a result of their actions), and it is also He Who has established what deed will bring a reward or punishment in the Hereafter. In sum, human beings have not been given an absolute freedom or absolute autonomy.

526   سُورَةُ النَّجْمِ   ٥٢٦

اِنَّ الَّذِينَ لَا يُؤْمِنُونَ بِالْاٰخِرَةِ لَيُسَمُّونَ الْمَلَٰٓئِكَةَ تَسْمِيَةَ الْاُنْثٰى ۝ وَمَا لَهُمْ بِهٖ مِنْ عِلْمٍ اِنْ يَتَّبِعُونَ اِلَّا الظَّنَّ وَاِنَّ الظَّنَّ لَا يُغْنِى مِنَ الْحَقِّ شَيْئاً ۝ فَاَعْرِضْ عَنْ مَنْ تَوَلّٰى عَنْ ذِكْرِنَا وَلَمْ يُرِدْ اِلَّا الْحَيٰوةَ الدُّنْيَا ۝ ذٰلِكَ مَبْلَغُهُمْ مِنَ الْعِلْمِ اِنَّ رَبَّكَ هُوَ اَعْلَمُ بِمَنْ ضَلَّ عَنْ سَبِيلِهٖ وَهُوَ اَعْلَمُ بِمَنِ اهْتَدٰى ۝ وَلِلّٰهِ مَا فِى السَّمٰوَاتِ وَمَا فِى الْاَرْضِ لِيَجْزِىَ الَّذِينَ اَسَآءُوْا بِمَا عَمِلُوْا وَيَجْزِىَ الَّذِينَ اَحْسَنُوْا بِالْحُسْنَى ۝ اَلَّذِينَ يَجْتَنِبُونَ كَبَآئِرَ الْاِثْمِ وَالْفَوَاحِشَ اِلَّا اللَّمَمَ اِنَّ رَبَّكَ وَاسِعُ الْمَغْفِرَةِ هُوَ اَعْلَمُ بِكُمْ اِذْ اَنْشَاَكُمْ مِنَ الْاَرْضِ وَاِذْ اَنْتُمْ اَجِنَّةٌ فِى بُطُونِ اُمَّهَاتِكُمْ فَلَا تُزَكُّوْا اَنْفُسَكُمْ هُوَ اَعْلَمُ بِمَنِ اتَّقٰى ۝ اَفَرَاَيْتَ الَّذِى تَوَلّٰى ۝ وَاَعْطٰى قَلِيلاً وَّاَكْدٰى ۝ اَعِنْدَهُ عِلْمُ الْغَيْبِ فَهُوَ يَرٰى ۝ اَمْ لَمْ يُنَبَّاْ بِمَا فِى صُحُفِ مُوسٰى ۝ وَاِبْرٰهِيمَ الَّذِى وَفّٰى ۝ اَلَّا تَزِرُ وَازِرَةٌ وِّزْرَ اُخْرٰى ۝ وَاَنْ لَيْسَ لِلْاِنْسَانِ اِلَّا مَا سَعٰى ۝ وَاَنَّ سَعْيَهُ سَوْفَ يُرٰى ۝ ثُمَّ يُجْزٰهُ الْجَزَآءَ الْاَوْفٰى ۝ وَاَنَّ اِلٰى رَبِّكَ الْمُنْتَهٰى ۝ وَاَنَّهُ هُوَ اَضْحَكَ وَاَبْكٰى ۝ وَاَنَّهُ هُوَ اَمَاتَ وَاَحْيَا ۝

---

27. It is those who do not believe in the Hereafter who name the angels (whom they regard as God's daughters) with feminine names.

28. They have no knowledge of this. They follow nothing other than conjecture, and conjecture can never substitute for anything of the truth.

29. So withdraw from those who turn away from Our Book and remembrance, and desire nothing but the life of this world.

30. Such is their sum of knowledge (limited by desires of the moment, and the falsehoods they have inherited unthinkingly and become used to, limited to the outer surface of things). Surely your Lord knows best him who has gone astray, and He knows best him who goes right (following the Straight Path of his Lord).

31. To God belongs all that is in the heavens and all that is on the earth, and (since He knows best him who has gone astray and him who follows the right path) He will recompense those who do evil with what they have done, and recompense those who do good with the best reward.

32. Those who avoid the major sins and indecent, shameful deeds (which are in fact included in the major sins), only falling into small fault,[12] – surely your Lord is of extensive forgiveness. He knows you well when He originates you from (the particles of) earth, and when you are hidden (fetuses) in the wombs of your mothers. So do not hold yourselves pure (sinless; it is vain self-justification). He knows best him who keeps from disobedience to God in reverence for Him and piety.

33. Have you considered him who turns away (from your call)?

34. He has given (the needy) a little, then he is stern (in not giving).

35. Does he have knowledge of the Unseen, and so he sees (what is to happen in the future)?

36. Or has he not been informed of all (that is to follow and) was in the Scrolls of Moses,

37. And of Abraham who discharged his due (fulfilling all his duties to perfection)?

38. That no soul, as bearer of burden, is made to bear the burden of another.

39. And that human has only that for which he labors,

40. And his labor will be brought forth to be seen.[13]

41. And afterward he will be repaid for it with fullest payment.

42. And in your Lord everything ends.

43. And He it is Who (by His Will, Power, and creation) enables to laugh and to weep.

44. And He it is Who causes to die and gives life.

---

12. For the major sins, see 2: 194, note 140; 4: 31, note 11, and for the indecent, shameful deeds, see: 4: 25, note 9. Indecent acts, such as illegal sexual intercourse and homosexuality are in fact included in the major sins. They are mentioned separately because God especially warns us against them. In order to better understand this verse and the meaning of *small faults*, it should be considered together or in the light of the verse: *They are also the ones who, when they have committed a shame-ful deed or wronged themselves (through any kind of sinful act to bring harm to themselves), immediately remember God and implore Him to forgive their sins – for who will forgive sins save God? – and do not persist knowingly in whatever (evil) they have committed (3: 135).*

13. *The day when every soul will find whatever good it has done brought forward, and whatever evil it has done.... (3: 30).*

45. And He creates the pairs, the male and the female,

46. From a drop of (seminal) fluid when it is emitted.

47. And He has taken on Himself the other bringing forth;

48. And He it is Who grants abundant wealth and suffices (all need by His providing).

49. And surely He it is Who is the Lord of Sirius.[14]

50. And He destroyed the former (tribe of) 'Ād,[15]

51. And the (tribe of) Thamūd; He spared no (disbelieving criminal) among them;

52. And the people of Noah before; surely they were further in wrongdoing and further in rebellion.

53. (He also destroyed) the overthrown cities (of Lot's people);

54. So that there covered them that which covered.

55. Then which of the gifts of your Lord do you dispute about?[16]

56. And this (Messenger) is a warner like the warners of old.

57. That (the Last Hour) which is bound to draw near has drawn near.

58. None besides God can disclose it (or remove the dread and suffering it entails).

59. Do you then deem this Discourse (which enables your eternal salvation) strange?

60. And do you laugh and not weep (in consideration of your recalcitrance and sinfulness),

61. Moreover entertain yourselves (with fun and games)?

62. Rather: prostrate before God (in submission) and worship Him (so that He may protect you from the dread and suffering of the Last Hour).

---

14. Sirius is the brightest star in the sky. Many Arabs worshipped it during the Time of Ignorance and attributed to it celestial events, such as rain. The Qur'ān categorically rejects this and states that it is God Who has created Sirius, Who makes it last, and gives it its light.

15. The former tribe of 'Ād were the people of the Prophet Hūd. The latter 'Ād were those descending from the believers who had survived the destruction.

16. Justice is indisputably good in itself and absolutely necessary for human life. So the destruction of several peoples who were obstinate in wrongdoing was their just due; it is a gift or bounty of God to humankind.

SŪRAH 54

AL-QAMAR (THE MOON)

Makkah period

This *sūrah* of 55 verses, revealed five years before the *Hijrah*, derives its name from the word *al-Qamar* (the moon) in the first verse. It mentions the splitting of the moon by a gesture of God's Messenger, and contains, in order to both warn the unbelievers and console the believers, the brief accounts of the people of Noah and of 'Ād and Thamūd and that of the peoples of Lot and the Pharaoh. The splitting of the moon by a gesture of God's Messenger alludes to God's absolute authority over the universe, as well as to the fact that it is God Who really controls and maintains the universe behind all apparent causes, and it points to the inevitable end of the world.

In the Name of God, the All-Merciful, the All-Compassionate.

1. The Last Hour has drawn near, and the moon has split.[1]

2. Whenever they see a miracle, they turn from it in aversion and say: "This is sorcery like many others, one after the other."

3. And they have denied (Prophethood and whatever sign the Prophet has shown them), and followed their lusts and caprices. Yet every matter has its appointed time (and so they will come to know the truth).

4. And for certain there have already come to them reports (of the Hereafter and former peoples) wherein is ample warning to deter (them from their ways).

5. All this (which is included in the Qur'ān) is consummate wisdom, but warnings do not avail (such people).

6. (Seeing that they reject your call) withdraw from them. The Day will come when the caller will call[2] (all the people) to something exceptionally terrible.

1. The amazing and wonderful phenomenon of the splitting of the Moon, which took place at Minā five years before the *Hijrah*, caused by a gesture of God's Messenger, upon him be peace and blessings, was a manifest miracle of the Messenger, and a clear sign of the truth that the Resurrection, of which the Messenger was giving the news, would take place. The great sphere of the moon had split into two distinct parts in front of the very eyes of the people present. The two parts had separated and receded so far apart from one another that, to the onlookers, one part had appeared on one side of the mountain and the other on the other side of it. Then, in an instant, the two had rejoined. The unbelievers described it as a magical illusion and persisted in their denial. Such people neither believe as a result of admonition, nor learn the lessons from history, nor affirm faith after witnessing manifest signs with their eyes.

The verse states that the moon split when the Last Hour approached. This is because the time from the advent of the Prophet Muḥammad, upon him be peace and blessings, to the destruction of the world is known as the End of Time. The Messenger himself says that his time in the life of the world is as the late afternoon in a day (al-Bukhārī, "Ijārah," 8).

Some ask why this miracle was not recorded and transmitted in the history of other peoples. Although there are serious studies showing that it was seen by some in such countries as India, and that it was recorded, we deem it useful to mention the following points concerning the event as an answer to the question.

- Such objections arise from considering the splitting of the moon as if it were a natural event, whereas it was a miracle. A miracle is created by God to decisively prove the Prophethood of His Messengers to his opponents, so it is not necessary that others should see it. So this miracle was primarily shown to the Makkan polytheists and occurred before a group of people to convince them of Muḥammad's Prophethood. It happened momentarily at a time of night when people were sleeping; such obstacles

as mist, clouds, and time differences may have prevented others from seeing it.

- The obstinacy of the Prophet Muḥammad's disbelieving contemporaries is well-known and recorded. When the Qur'ān announced this incident of the moon splitting, not one unbeliever dared contradict it. If they had not seen this event, they would have used this verse as a pretext to attack the Prophet more formidably. However, neither the biographies of the Prophet nor history books report anything that even suggests that they denied the occurrence of this event. Their reaction was only to say that it was sorcery of the Prophet's doing. They declared the event to be sorcery, and added further that if the Makkan caravans in other places had seen it, then it had truly happened; otherwise, the Prophet had bewitched them. When the caravans arrived the following morning from Yemen and other places and announced that they had seen this miracle, the unbelievers replied: "The sorcery of Abu Ṭālib's orphan has affected even the heavens!" (Since the miracle was created for the Makkan polytheists, the Almighty allowed their caravans to see it as well.)

- The majority of the foremost scholars, after carrying out meticulous research, such as Sa'du'd-Dīn at-Taftazānī, concluded that the splitting of the Moon is *mutawātir*. That is, it has been transmitted down the generations by one truthful group after another, and that the transmitters form such a vast community that they would be unable to agree on a lie. It is as certain as Haley's comet, which appeared 1,000 years before (its last appearance in 1986), or the existence of an island we have not seen.

- Prophets work miracles to prove their claim of Prophethood and to convince deniers, not to compel belief. Thus, every miracle is shown to convince those who heard the claim of Prophethood. If they somehow forced everyone to see or believe in them, the Wisdom of the All-Wise One, the Divine purpose for creating us with free will and sending religion, which entails that the ground be prepared for willing acceptance, would be violated.

Thus if the All-Wise Creator had left the moon in two pieces for several hours, so that everyone could see it and record it in their historical records, it would have been regarded as only another astronomical event instead of a miracle unique to Muḥammad's Messengership or an evidence of his Prophethood.

- Some argue that if this event had really occurred, it would have been mentioned in Chinese, Japanese, and Native American historical accounts. But how could they have seen it for, in addition to other obstacles, it was barely sunset in such European countries as Spain, France, and England (all enveloped in mists of ignorance), daytime in America, and morning in China and Japan.
- This miracle is not an ordinary incident that happened due to particular causes or randomly, enabling us to criticize it based on the law of cause and effect. Rather, the All-Wise Creator of the sun and the moon made it an extraordinary event to confirm His Messenger's Prophethood and support his claim.

Out of all the evidence of the occurrence of this miracle, we will mention only six, as these six have the strength of a six-fold consensus:

- The Companions of the Prophet, all people of justice and truthfulness, agreed that it took place.
- All exacting Qur'ānic interpreters agreed that the moon split upon a gesture of the Prophet Muḥammad's finger.
- All truthful narrators and scholars of Hadīth narrated this incident through various authentic channels of transmission.
- All people of truth and sainthood, as well as of inspiration and spiritual discovery, testify that this event took place.
- All foremost theologians and learned scholars confirm this event, despite other differences of opinions.
- Muḥammad's community, which an authentic Prophetic Tradition states can never agree on an error, accepts its occurrence.

These six proofs clearly establish the splitting of the moon.

Some modern commentators claim that the verse refers to the fact that the moon will split before the destruction of the world. However, the second verse rejects this assertion. The signs to appear before the destruction of the world will decisively prove that the Last Hour has come and this is the time when the world will be destroyed. But the second verse clearly says that the unbelievers reacted to the splitting of the moon by claiming that it was sorcery, and they showed the same reaction to many similar signs. Hasan al-Baṣrī and 'Aṭa' ibn ar-Rabāḥ, who asserted that the moon would split before the destruction of the world, did not deny the occurrence of this miracle as evidence of the Prophethood of Muḥammad, upon him be peace and blessings, in Makkah.

It is stated in some verses (e.g. 17: 59) that God did not allow His Messenger to work a miracle because the former peoples had denied the miracles they had asked their Messenger to show them, and so deserved their destruction. However, the splitting of the moon was not a miracle that the unbelievers had asked the Messenger to work so that they would believe in him. The Messenger showed them this miracle to prove his Prophethood (The Letters, "the 19th Letter," 1: 265–272).

2. The caller and the call signify the Trumpet Call for the revival of the dead and gathering them on the Plain of the Supreme Gathering.

7. With eyes downcast, they will come forth from their graves as if they were locusts scattered abroad (in confusion),

8. Hastening (in obedience) toward the caller. The unbelievers will say: "This is a hard day."

9. Before them the people of Noah denied: they denied Our servant, and said: "This is a madman!" and he was rebuked (with insolence and prevented from preaching).

10. So he prayed to his Lord, saying: "I have been overcome, so help me!"

11. So We opened the gates of the sky, with water outpouring;

12. And We caused the earth to gush forth with springs, so the waters (of the sky and the earth) combined for (the fulfillment of) a matter already ordained.

13. And We carried him on a (construction of) wooden planks and nails,

14. Running (through the water) under Our Eyes as a reward for one who had (wrongfully) been rejected with ingratitude.

15. And indeed We left it (the Ark) as a sign (of the truth),³ then is there any that remembers and takes heed?

16. But see how (severe) was My punishment and (how true) My warnings!

17. And indeed (by revealing it through human language) We have made the Qur'ān easy for remembrance (of God, and taking heed), then is there any that remembers and takes heed?⁴

18. The (tribe of) 'Ād also denied (their Messenger), then see how (severe) was My punishment and (how true) My warnings:

19. We sent upon them a furious windstorm through certain time of enduring disaster;

20. Tearing people away as if they were trunks of uprooted palm-trees.

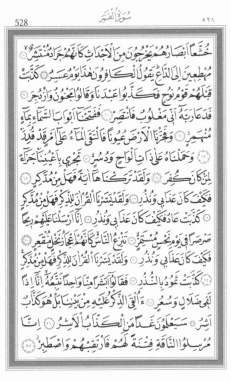

21. So see how (severe) was My punishment and (how true) My warnings!

22. And indeed (by revealing it through human language) We have made the Qur'ān easy for remembrance (of God and for taking heed). Then, is there any that remembers and takes heed?

23. The (tribe of) Thamūd also denied all the warnings (given to them).

24. They said: "What! a mortal from among us, all alone – shall we follow him? Then indeed we would be lost in a strange error and madness!

25. "Is the Remembrance and Reminder (sent down) upon him from among us? No. Rather, he is a presumptuous liar (one claiming superiority over us)."

26. (We told their Messenger): "Soon they will know who is the presumptuous liar.

27. "We will surely send the she-camel as a trial for them (in response to their insistently asking you to show a miracle). So watch them (and observe what they do), and bear patiently (with their misconduct toward you).

---

3. This shows that the remains of Noah's Ark were still present and could be seen when this *sūrah* was revealed. Imam al-Bukhārī, Ibn Jarīr at-Ṭabarī, Ibn Abī Ḥātem and 'Abdu'r-Razzāq report from Qatādah that the Muslims who conquered Iraq saw it on al-Jūdī (for Mount al-Jūdī, see note 14 to 11: 48). It may also suggest that it will continue to remain so that people will be able to find it as a lesson.

4. That is, God revealed the Qur'ān through human language so that people could understand it. Although the Qur'ān has unfathomable depths of meaning, it has such styles that it satisfies everyone, from the most ordinary to the most advanced in sciences. What is necessary for everybody is to recognize the essentials of faith and a good life, so even the most ordinary people can derive from the Qur'ān what they must believe in and what they must do in order to gain eternal happiness, and can take from it the necessary lessons. However, this in no way means that everybody can understand all of the Qur'ān perfectly by only reading it or by studying a translation of it.

28. "And inform them that the water is to be shared between her and them; each sharer will be present by the water when it is their turn to drink."[5]

29. But (without observing the turn) they (schemed to slaughter the she-camel and) called their comrade (one of the nine ring-leaders); and so he ventured (upon the evil deed), and slaughtered her cruelly.

30. And see how (severe) was My punishment and (how true) My warnings:

31. We sent upon them a single Blast, and they became like dried chippings of shrubs used as cattle-fodder.

32. And indeed (by revealing it through human language) We have made the Qur'ān easy for remembrance (of God and for taking heed). Then, is there any that remembers and takes heed?

33. And the people of Lot also denied all the warnings (given to them).

34. We sent a hurricane of stones upon them, save the family of Lot: We saved them by early dawn,

35. As a grace from Us. Thus do We reward those who give thanks.

36. Lot had indeed forewarned them of Our striking down, but they disputed the warnings.

37. They had harassed him (with frequent coming-and-going) to abuse his guests,[6] and so We blotted out their eyes: taste My punishment and (the consequences of) My warnings!

38. The punishment decreed assuredly overtook them early in the morning.

39. So taste My punishment and (the consequences of) My warnings!

40. And indeed (by revealing it through human language) We have made the Qur'ān easy for remembrance (of God and for taking heed). Then, is there any that remembers and takes heed?

41. And warnings certainly came also to the clan of the Pharaoh,

42. Who denied all Our messages and signs (including the miracles showed to them), and in the end We seized them after the manner of One All-Glorious with irresistible might, All-Omnipotent.

43. Now are the unbelievers of yours (O Makkans) better and more powerful than those (whose histories We have recounted)? Or is there an exemption (from punishment written) for you in the Scriptures?

44. Or do they say, "We are a host united and invincible"?

45. (But let them know that) the hosts

will all be routed, and they will turn their backs and flee.[7]

46. Indeed, the Last Hour is their appointed time (for their complete recompense), and the Last Hour will be more grievous and more bitter.

47. The disbelieving criminals will be in utter loss away (from Paradise) and burning in the Blazes.

48. On that Day they will be dragged in the Fire on their faces: "Taste the touch of Hell!"

49. Surely We have created each and every thing by (precise) measure.

---

5. For the she-camel and the water to be shared, see *sūrah* 7: 73–77, note 17, *sūrah* 11: 64–65, and *sūrah* 26: 155–157.

6. For the guests of the Prophet Lot and the destruction of his people, see *sūrah* 11: 69–83, *sūrah* 15: 51–77, and *sūrah* 26: 160–175, and the corresponding notes. The Old Testament also records that the eyes of the people who rushed to Lot's house to abuse his guests, guests who were in fact angels in the appearance of human beings, were blinded (*Genesis*, 19: 9–11).

7. When this verse was revealed, the Muslims were few in number and weak in Makkah. Some of them had had to migrate to Abyssinia to escape the persecutions. But it was no more than 10 years before their powerful enemies were utterly defeated in the Battle of Badr. Seventy of their leaders were killed and the others fled the battlefield, leaving many prisoners of war.

50. And Our commanding is not other than a single (command), like the twinkling of an eye.[8]

51. We have destroyed many peoples like you (in wrongdoing, some of whose stories We have recounted and some not). Then, is there any that will remember and take heed (and so believe in God and follow His Religion)?

52. And everything that they did exists (recorded) in (their) notebooks (of deeds).

53. Everything small or great is written down.

54. And the God-revering, pious ones will be in Gardens and by rivers;

55. In the assembly of honor composed of the loyal and truthful in the Presence of the One All-Omnipotent Sovereign.

8. For a similar Qur'ānic statement and explanation, see 36: 82–83, note 26.

SŪRAH 55

AR-RAHMĀN
(THE ALL-MERCIFUL)

Makkah period

Revealed in Makkah, this sūrah of 78 verses derives its name from ar-Rahmān (the All-Merciful), which constitutes the first verse. Throughout it is mentioned that the manifestations of God are a result of His being the All-Merciful. As explained in note 4 on Sūrat al-Fātihah, the term the All-Merciful designates the Divine Being as the One with infinite mercy Who embraces all of creation with mercy, grace, and favor, including humankind, without any discrimination between believers and unbelievers, as the One Who gives life, maintains, provides, and equips all with the capacities necessary for each. God has created the universe out of, and as the manifestation of, the mercy embodied by His Name the All-Merciful.

In the Name of God, the All-Merciful, the All-Compassionate.

1. The All-Merciful

2. He has taught the Qur'ān (to humankind and, through them, the jinn);[1]

3. He has created human;

4. He has taught him speech.[2]

5. The sun and the moon are by an exact calculation (of the All-Merciful).[3]

6. And the stars and the trees both prostrate (before God in perfect submission to His laws).

7. And the heaven – He has made it high (above the earth), and He has set up the balance.

8. So that you may not go beyond (the limits with respect to) the balance.

9. And observe the balance with full eq-uity, and do not fall short in it.[4]

10. And the earth – He has laid it down and furnished for living beings.

11. Therein are fruits (of various kinds), and date-palms with sheathed clusters;

12. And also corn, with leaves and stalk (for use as fodder), and scented herb.

13. Then, (O humankind and jinn) which of the favors of your Lord will you deny?[5]

14. He has created human from sounding clay like the potter's;

15. And He has created the jinn from a smokeless (fusing flame of) fire.[6]

16. Then, (O humankind and jinn) which of the favors of your Lord will you deny?

17. He is the Lord of the two easts and the Lord of the two wests.[7]

18. Then, (O humankind and jinn) which of the favors of your Lord will you deny?

---

1. The Qur'ān, as the greatest manifestation of God's Mercy, is the embodiment of the Straight Path that leads to happiness in both the world and the Hereafter. It is by means of the Qur'ān that we have knowledge about God and what He asks us to do in order that He may be pleased with us. The purpose of the creation of the universe and humankind has been universally disclosed in the Qur'ān. This *sūrah* reminds us of God's favors and asks *Which of the favors of your Lord will you deny?* When God's Messenger recited it to the jinn, they responded: "We do not deny any of Your favors. All praise and gratitude are for You." In appreciation of this, the Messenger narrated this to his Companions (at-Tirmidhī, "Tafsīr ar-Raḥmān," 55).

The fact that the Qur'ān was taught signifies that the Qur'ān consists of knowledge throughout. Like the petals of a rose, knowl-edge of everything exists in it in degrees and everyone can attain this knowledge from it, according to their capacity, purity of intention, and degree of submission to it.

2. Teaching the Qur'ān, creating humankind, endowing them with the ability to speak, and teaching them how to speak by inspiring lan-guage in them are among the greatest bless-ings of God and manifestations of His being the All-Merciful. Speech is a very compli-cated process, which takes place at the same

instant as thought. Through speech people make themselves known. How languages have come into being and been diversified is a mystery. No one knows how this happened, although there are many different theories. However, God declares that He made all things known to Adam and taught him their names (1: 31). Therefore, language is also a direct gift from God.

3. A. Cressy Morrison writes:

The earth rotates on its axis in twenty-four hours or at the rate of about one thou-sand miles an hour. Suppose it turned at the rate of a hundred miles an hour. Why not? Our days and nights would then be ten times as long as now. The hot sun of summer would then burn up over vegeta-tion each long day and every sprout would freeze in such a night. The sun, the source of life (on the earth), has a surface tem-perature of 12.000 degrees Fahrenheit, and our earth is just far enough away so that this "eternal fire" warms us just enough and not too much. It is marvelously stable, and during millions of years has varied so little that life as we know it has survived... The earth travels around the sun at the rate of eighteen miles each second. If the rate of revolution had been, say, six miles or forty miles each second, we would be too far from or too close to the sun for our form of life to exist.

Stars vary in size, as we all know. One is so large that if it were our sun, the orbit of the earth would be millions of miles inside its surface. Stars vary in the type of radiation. Many of their rays would be deadly to every known form of life. The intensity and volume of this radiation is anywhere from less than that of our sun to ten thousand times as great.... But our sun is about right for our life among millions of others which are not.

The earth is tilted at an angle of twenty-three degrees. This gives us our seasons. If it had not been tilted, the poles would be in eternal twilight. The water vapor from the ocean would move north and south, piling up continents of ice and leaving possibly a desert between the equator and the ice. Glacial rivers would erode and roar through canyons into the salt-covered bed of the ocean to form temporary pools of brine. The weight of the unbelievably vast mass of ice would depress the poles, causing our equator to bulge or erupt or at least show the need of a new waistline belt. The lowering of the ocean would expose vast new land areas and diminish the rainfall in all parts of the world, with fearful results.

The moon is 240.000 miles away, and the tides twice a day are usually a gentle reminder of its presence. Tides of the ocean ran as high as sixty feet in some places, and even the crust of the earth is twice a day bent outward several inches by the moon's attraction. All seems so regular that we do not grasp to any degree the vast power that lifts the whole area of the ocean several feet and bends the crust of the earth, seemingly so solid. If our moon was, say, fifty thousand miles away instead of its present respectable distance, our tides would be so enormous that twice a day all the lowland of all the continents would be submerged by a rush of water so enormous that even the mountains would soon be eroded away, and probably no continent could have risen from the depths fast enough to exist today. The earth would crack with the turmoil and the tides in the air would create daily hurricanes.

(In short,) there must be in nature some form of intelligent direction. If this be true, then there must be a purpose. (Morrison, 13–18)

4. By mentioning balance in three successive verses, the Qur'ān shows the importance attached to it. It clearly states that there is a very sensitive balance in creation and the relationships among its parts. The wonderful accord observed in the universe and its maintenance is due to this most sensitively computed balance. It is also indispensable to human life, both individually and socially. Its social manifestation is justice. With respect to human education and perfection, this balance requires that everything is given its due importance in life, that the basic faculties or impulses of anger, desire or appetite, and reason are trained, disciplined, and employed in order to develop them into the virtues of chivalrous courage, moderation and chastity, and wisdom (for a detailed explanation, see *sūrah* 2, notes 23, 39, and 113).

5. This verse points out that not only humankind but also the jinn have a share in the benefits in the favors mentioned previously and in those which will be mentioned in the verses to come.

6. The Qur'ān has many references to the creation of humankind from clay, which signifies their lowly material origin and the fact that the body is composed of elements coming from earth, air, and water. This also implies that the real worth of human beings lies in the immaterial dimensions of their existence.

The last two verses may also be referring to the initial origin of humankind and the jinn and the phases the earth passed through during the process of its creation or formation. As stated in note 7 in *sūrah* 15, the process of creation may have followed a gradual, regular accumulation of identities and/or a saltational sequence of abrupt leaps. He spread one existence through another, compounding and interweaving, and created living beings appropriate for each phase of creation. When the earth was in a state of smokeless fire, He created appropriate life forms, which the Qur'ān calls the jinn. They ruled the earth before humankind. When the soil became suitable for the present, visible forms of life, He created (appropriate) plants and animals, and eventually humans.

Verse 14 also suggests that in the beginning the earth was dry and barren and therefore not suitable for life. Then God revived it, stirring it up for life by means of the rain He sent down from the direction of the sky. This is continuously repeated every year. So as with the first human being on the earth, the particles to form each human body also initially come from the dried, lifeless earth.

7. This verse, first of all, emphasizes the fact that it is God Almighty Who has absolute authority and control over the whole universe. By *the two easts* and *two wests*, the Qur'ān may be suggesting the rising and setting points of the sun on the longest and shortest days of the year, between which there are 178 such points, which is what verse 37: 5 refers to. It may also suggest that the sun rises in one hemisphere while it sets in another, thus having two points of rising and setting throughout the whole world. Moreover, it also indicates that the sun rises and sets in the same place two days in a year.

19. He has let flow forth the two large bodies of water, they meet together

20. (But) between them is a barrier, which they do not transgress (and so they do not merge).[8]

21. Then, (O humankind and jinn) which of the favors of your Lord will you deny?

22. There come forth from them pearl and coral.

23. Then (O humankind and jinn) which of the favors of your Lord will you deny?

24. His are the ships constructed (by God's inspiration and running) through the sea (with sails unfurled), lofty like mountains.[9]

25. Then, (O humankind and jinn) which of the favors of your Lord will you deny?

26. All that is on the earth is perishable;

27. But there remains forever the "Face" of your Lord, the One of Majesty and Munificence.[10]

28. Then, (O humankind and jinn) which of the favors of your Lord will you deny?

29. All that are in the heavens and on the earth entreat Him (in their needs). Every (moment of every) day He is in a new manifestation (with all His Attributes and Names as the Divine Being).[11]

30. Then, (O humankind and jinn) which of the favors of your Lord will you deny?

31. We will (in time) settle your affairs, O you two most honorable classes of creatures (of the earth endowed with important faculties and therefore having heavy responsibilities)![12]

32. Then, (O humankind and jinn) which of the favors of your Lord will you deny?

33. O you assembly of jinn and humankind! If you are able to pass through and beyond the spherical regions of the heavens and the earth, then pass through. You will not pass through except with an authority (spiritual or scientific).[13]

34. Then, (O humankind and jinn) which of the favors of your Lord will you deny?

35. There will be sent on you both, a flame of fire (to burn) and a smoke (to choke), then you will not help each other (to safety or refuge).[14]

36. Then, (O humankind and jinn) which of the favors of your Lord will you deny?

37. And finally when the heaven is rent asunder, and it becomes rosy like red hide – !

38. Then, (O humankind and jinn) which of the favors of your Lord will you deny?[15]

39. On that Day neither humans nor jinn will be questioned about their sins (to know whether they are sinful or not).

40. Then, (O humankind and jinn) which of the favors of your Lord will you deny?

41. The disbelieving criminals will be known by their marks (especially on their faces), and seized by the forelocks and the feet.

8. For an explanation, see 25: 53, note 11.

9. It is God Who has created the seas, equipping water with the power of lifting solid objects, and Who has taught humankind how to construct ships.

10. The sun's images reflected in bubbles floating on a river and the sea, as well as in transparent things on the earth, bear witness to the sun. These images disappear when the sun sets or a river enters a tunnel, and new ones appear when the sun rises or the river emerges from the tunnel. These phenomena testify to the permanence of the light of the sun and demonstrate that these images are the reflection of a single sun. Their existence proves the sun's existence; their disappearance and re-appearance show that there is only one permanent sun.

Similarly, along with the alternation of day and night, seasons and years, beautiful beings are renewed, and fine creatures are replaced as they "set," while their likes "rise." Thus the existence of creatures proves the existence of the Necessarily Existent Being, while their disappearance, along with the causes of their existence and their replacement with new creatures bear witness to His Permanence, Eternity, and Oneness.

The disappearance of causes and their effects, along with the succession of years and centuries and their being followed by similar things, testify that the causes and their effects are created for subtle purposes. All of those fine beings coming in succession are creatures of the All-Majestic, All-Gracious, and Beautiful One, all of Whose Names are beautiful and holy. Such activity testifies that they are His changing works, moving mirrors, and successive stamps and seals. (See *al-Mathnawī an-Nūriyah*, "The First Treatise," 13–14.)

As nothing can exist by itself, everything's existence depends absolutely on God. Since it exists as a manifestation of the permanent Divine Names, it has a permanent, sublime reality that emanates from its reflection of the Divine Name that caused it to be. So this verse is a sword that liberates people from that which is not God (e.g., the world, the flesh, and life's

vanities). Thus whatever people have or do for God's sake is not included in the meaning of this verse.

If people find God and act only for His sake, there will be nothing left to be included in the meaning of *All that is on the earth is perishable*. So if they want to make (themselves eternal and) to have their deeds rewarded with permanent happiness, they must seek God and live for His sake and good pleasure. (See *The Letters*, "the 15th Letter," 82.)

11. Following classical Newtonian physics and under the spell of developments in science, physicists of the 19th century claimed that they could explain every phenomenon in the universe. E. Dubois Reymond, at a meeting held in memory of Leibniz in the Prussian Academy in 1880 was a bit more humble: "There have remained seven enigmas in the universe, three of which we have as yet been unable to solve: The essential nature of matter and force, the essence and origin of movement and the nature of consciousness. Three of the remaining that we can solve, although with great difficulties, are: The origin of life, the order in the universe and the apparent purpose for it, and the origin of thought and language. As for the seventh, we can say nothing about it. It is individual free will" (A. Adivar, 282).

The sub-atomic world threw all scientists into confusion. This world and the "quantum cosmology" which it introduced, rather than being a heap or assemblage of concrete things, is made up of five elements: the mass of the electron in the field where an action occurs (M), the mass of the proton (m), the electrical charge which these two elements carry, the energy quanta (h) – the amount of the energy remaining during the occurrence of the action – and the unchanging speed of light (c). These five elements of the universe can be reduced even further to action or energy waves traveling through space in tiny packets or quanta. Since the quanta required for an action are peculiar to it and exist independently of the quanta required for the previous action, it becomes impossible to predict the exact state of the universe. If the universe is in T_1 state now, it cannot be predicted that it will be the same at time T_2. Paul Renteln, assistant professor of physics at California State University, writes (*American Scientist*, Nov.-Dec., 1991, p. 508):

> Modern physicists live in two different worlds. In one world we can predict the future position and momentum of a particle if we know its present position and momentum. This is the world of classical physics, including the physics described by Einstein's theory of gravity, the general theory of relativity. In the second world it is impossible to predict the exact position and momentum of a particle. This is the probabilistic, subatomic world of quantum mechanics. General relativity and quantum mechanics are the two great pillars that form the foundation of 20th-century physics, and yet their precepts assume two different kinds of universe.

The real nature of this sub-atomic world and the events taking place in it make it impossible to construct a theory to describe them, because they cannot be observed. One reason for their unobservability is that, as Renteln writes in an attempt to propose a theory which he calls quantum gravity to reconcile the two different worlds of classical and quantum physics, "the events take place at a scale far smaller than any realm yet explored by experimental physics. It is only when particles approach to within about 10^{-35} meters that their gravitational interactions have to be described in the same quantum-mechanical terms that we adopt to understand the other forces of nature. This distance is 1,024 times smaller than the diameter of an atom – which means that the characteristic scale of quantum gravity bears the same relation to the size of an atom as an atom bears to the size of the solar system. To probe such small distances would require a particle accelerator 1,015 times more powerful than the proposed Superconducting Supercollider.

Later research suggests that the electron is more of an energy field cloud that fluctuates around a nucleus. The nucleus itself seems to be composed of two smaller constituents – protons and neutrons. However, in the 1960s, physicists Murray Gell-Mann and George Zweig confirmed in experiments that protons and neutrons were made up of even more elementary particles, which Gell-Mann called "quarks." Quarks cannot be seen, not just because they are too small, but also because they do not seem to be quite "all there."

Quarks are better described as swirls of dynamic energy, which means that solid matter is not, at its fundamental level, solid at all. Anything you hold in your hand and which seems solid, is really a quivering, shimmering, lacy lattice of energy, pulsating millions of times every second as billions of fundamental particles gyrate and spin in an eternal dance. At its most fundamental level, everything is energy held together by forces of incredible power.

This is not all that makes us unable to predict even the nearest future of the universe. According to Werner Heisenberg's theories, at the time when we can know either where a particle is or how fast it is traveling, we cannot know both. This is because the very act of measuring the particle alters its behavior. Measuring the particle's speed changes its position, and measuring its position changes its speed. However, unpredictability in the sub-atomic world does not change anything in our everyday, predictable world. Everything works according to the basic laws of classical Newtonian physics (*Groping in the Light*, 1990, pp. 11–17).

Why is this so and how should our view of the world and events be? Scientists who believe in the Existence of God and His creation of the universe suggest that creation was not a single event. That is, God did not create the universe as a single act and then leave it to operate according to the laws He established. Rather, creation is a continuous act (*creatio continua*). In other words, roughly like the movement of energy or electricity and its illuminating our world by means of bulbs, existence continuously comes from God and returns to and perishes in Him. Through the manifestation of all His Names, God continuously creates, annihilates and re-creates the universe. Some medieval Muslim scholarly saints, such as Muhyi'd-Dīn ibn al-'Arabī and Jalālu'd-Dīn ar-Rūmī, called these pairs of acts the continuous cycle of coming into existence and dying. Because of the incredible speed of this movement, the universe appears to be uniform and continuous. Ar-Rūmī likens this to the spinning of a staff on one end of which there is fixed a light. When spun at speed, the light on the end of the staff appears to be a circle of light. Modern researchers liken it to the projection of a film onto the screen. A film-strip is composed of numerous frames, but the film is projected onto the screen, appearing as an undivided, complete frame. So, the universe incessantly undergoes appearance and disappearance, or perishing and re-creation, but we have the impression that it continues to exist without any interruption.

In consequence, all creatures incessantly need God throughout their entire life – when they come into existence and in order to continue to exist. So God Almighty constantly manifests Himself with All His Attributes and Names, which have their source in His Essential Qualities as God. All the creatures exist because He creates; they meet their needs because He is the All-Providing and the All-Munificent; they continue to exist because He is Self-Subsisting and the All-Maintaining.

(For another important meaning of this verse, see note 12 below.)

12. The original of the word "moment" in the verse 29 is *yawm*, the first meaning of which is day. So the whole of creation consists of two days, one being the entire lifetime of this visible universe, the other being the Hereafter. So when the word *yawm* is taken to mean a day, the second part of verse 29 suggests that God manifests Himself with all His Attributes and Names in the world in a manner particular to this world, and He will manifest Himself in the other world peculiar to it. In this world, which is the world of wisdom, creatures live a life according to its conditions, and humankind and the jinn, the responsible beings, sow here to reap in the Hereafter. But in the other world,

He will take them to account for their deeds in the world and recompense them accordingly. This world is the world of labor, while the other is the world of remuneration.

13. This verse states that it is possible to travel and even go beyond the regions or layers of the heavens and the earth. God's Messenger achieved this both in his body and spirit, which we call the Ascension, and showed that it is possible for every one to do it in spirit. The verse also suggests that it can be possible to make this journey by means of an authority (scientific knowledge). However, it may not be possible to go beyond the heavens by means of science. However, the verse may also be suggesting that the immaterial dimensions of existence can "scientifically" be discovered and established. The word *aqṭār*, which we have translated as spherical regions, means regions or layers with a diameter, and therefore spherical regions.

14. God does not allow any jinn that have ill intentions to ascend to the heavens to take something from the conversation of the angels; rather he destroys them (*sūrah* 15: 16–18, note 5; *sūrah* 26: 212, note 37; *sūrah* 37: 10, note 3; *sūrah* 67: 5, note 4). However, saintly people can ascend the heavens in spirit. The verse may also be predicting modern firearms, bombs, and missiles.

15. Although people do not like death, it is liberation from the sufferings of the world, and a door to the eternal life where people will receive remuneration for their deeds in the world. Moreover, like God's Justice, His Compassion will also manifest Itself with all Its infinity in the Hereafter. So the advent of the Last Hour will be a blessing or favor in this respect; its announcement is also a blessing for people in that it urges them to self-criticism. The thought of getting what one deserves, with no action being concealed, prevents people from committing evil actions. (For a detailed explanation of the benefits of belief in the afterlife, see 44: 37, note 11.)

532

سُورَةُ الرَّحْمٰن

٥٣٢

يُعْرَفُ الْمُجْرِمُونَ بِسِيمَاهُمْ فَيُؤْخَذُ بِالنَّوَاصِى وَالْأَقْدَامِ ۝ فَبِأَىِّ ءَالَآءِ رَبِّكُمَا تُكَذِّبَانِ ۝ هٰذِهِ جَهَنَّمُ الَّتِى يُكَذِّبُ بِهَا الْمُجْرِمُونَ ۝ يَطُوفُونَ بَيْنَهَا وَبَيْنَ حَمِيمٍ ءَانٍ ۝ فَبِأَىِّ ءَالَآءِ رَبِّكُمَا تُكَذِّبَانِ ۝ وَلِمَنْ خَافَ مَقَامَ رَبِّهِ جَنَّتَانِ ۝ فَبِأَىِّ ءَالَآءِ رَبِّكُمَا تُكَذِّبَانِ ۝ ذَوَاتَآ أَفْنَانٍ ۝ فَبِأَىِّ ءَالَآءِ رَبِّكُمَا تُكَذِّبَانِ ۝ فِيهِمَا عَيْنَانِ تَجْرِيَانِ ۝ فَبِأَىِّ ءَالَآءِ رَبِّكُمَا تُكَذِّبَانِ ۝ فِيهِمَا مِن كُلِّ فَاكِهَةٍ زَوْجَانِ ۝ فَبِأَىِّ ءَالَآءِ رَبِّكُمَا تُكَذِّبَانِ ۝ مُتَّكِئِينَ عَلَىٰ فُرُشٍ بَطَآئِنُهَا مِنْ إِسْتَبْرَقٍ وَجَنَى الْجَنَّتَيْنِ دَانٍ ۝ فَبِأَىِّ ءَالَآءِ رَبِّكُمَا تُكَذِّبَانِ ۝ فِيهِنَّ قَاصِرَاتُ الطَّرْفِ لَمْ يَطْمِثْهُنَّ إِنسٌ قَبْلَهُمْ وَلَاجَآنٌّ ۝ فَبِأَىِّ ءَالَآءِ رَبِّكُمَا تُكَذِّبَانِ ۝ كَأَنَّهُنَّ الْيَاقُوتُ وَالْمَرْجَانُ ۝ فَبِأَىِّ ءَالَآءِ رَبِّكُمَا تُكَذِّبَانِ ۝ هَلْ جَزَآءُ الْإِحْسَانِ إِلَّا الْإِحْسَانُ ۝ فَبِأَىِّ ءَالَآءِ رَبِّكُمَا تُكَذِّبَانِ ۝ وَمِن دُونِهِمَا جَنَّتَانِ ۝ فَبِأَىِّ ءَالَآءِ رَبِّكُمَا تُكَذِّبَانِ ۝ مُدْهَآمَّتَانِ ۝ فَبِأَىِّ ءَالَآءِ رَبِّكُمَا تُكَذِّبَانِ ۝ فِيهِمَا عَيْنَانِ نَضَّاخَتَانِ ۝ فَبِأَىِّ ءَالَآءِ رَبِّكُمَا تُكَذِّبَانِ ۝

42. Then, (O humankind and jinn) which of the favors of your Lord will you deny?

43. This is Hell, which the disbelieving criminals deny.

44. They will go round between it(s fire) and hot, boiling water.

45. Then, (O humankind and jinn) which of the favors of your Lord will you deny?

46. But for him who lives in awe of his Lord and of the standing before his Lord (in the Hereafter), there will be two Gardens.[16]

47. Then, (O humankind and jinn) which of the favors of your Lord will you deny?

48. Having in them trees with thick, spreading branches.

49. Then, (O humankind and jinn) which of the favors of your Lord will you deny?

50. In them both are two flowing springs.

51. Then, (O humankind and jinn) which of the favors of your Lord will you deny?

52. In them both are all kinds of fruit in pairs.[17]

53. Then, (O humankind and jinn) which of the favors of your Lord will you deny?

54. Reclining upon beds lined with silk brocade, and the fruits of the two Gardens within reach.

55. Then, (O humankind and jinn) which of the favors of your Lord will you deny?

56. In them are pure, chaste-eyed spouses (whose glances are fixed on their spouses only), whom no man or jinn has touched before.

57. Then, (O humankind and jinn) which of the favors of your Lord will you deny?

58. Like rubies and coral (they will seem, in rare beauty and radiance).

59. Then, (O humankind and jinn) which of the favors of your Lord will you deny?

60. Is the recompense of excellence (in obedience to God) other than excellence?

61. Then, (O humankind and jinn) which of the favors of your Lord will you deny?

62. And besides these two, there are yet two other Gardens.[18]

63. Then, (O humankind and jinn) which of the favors of your Lord will you deny?

64. Dark green throughout,

65. Then, (O humankind and jinn) which of the favors of your Lord will you deny?

66. In them both are springs gushing forth.

67. Then, (O humankind and jinn) which of the favors of your Lord will you deny?

68. In them both are fruits, and date-palms and pomegranates.

69. Then, (O humankind and jinn) which of the favors of your Lord will you de-ny?

---

16. These people are mentioned in the next chapter of the Qur'ān, *Sūrat al-Wāqi'ah*, as those who are the foremost in faith and good deeds, and serving God's cause, and therefore made near to God by God Himself.

17. Concerning the pairs of fruit, some say there will be fruits of the same kind as those in the world and fruits peculiar to Paradise. How-ever, if we consider that verse 50 mentions two springs, and verse 54 below mentions the fruits of the two Gardens, we can put forward the opinion that one of the springs and one of the pairs of fruit will belong to one of the Gardens, and the other to the other. However, it is God Who knows the exact nature of both.

18. These two Gardens will be granted to the people of happiness and prosperity who will be given their Records in their right hands.

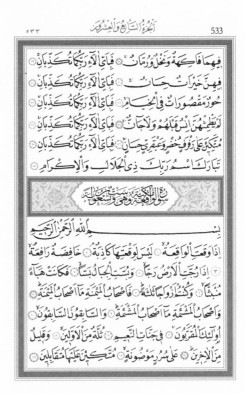

70. In them both are maidens good in character and beautiful.

71. Then, (O humankind and jinn) which of the favors of your Lord will you deny?

72. Pure maidens assigned for them in secluded pavilions.

73. Then, (O humankind and jinn) which of the favors of your Lord will you deny?

74. Whom no man or jinn has touched before.

75. Then, (O humankind and jinn) which of the favors of your Lord will you deny?

76. (The people of those Gardens) reclining on green cushions and rich, beautiful mattresses.

77. Then, (O humankind and jinn) which of the favors of your Lord will you deny?

78. Blessed and Supreme is the Name of your Lord, the One of Majesty and Munificence.

SŪRAH 56

AL-WĀQI'AH
(THE EVENT TO HAPPEN)

Makkah period

This *sūrah* of 96 verses was revealed in Makkah and takes its name from the word *al-wāqi'ah* in the first verse. It mentions some events that will take place during the destruction of the world, and the three groups that people will form in the Hereafter, according to their belief and deeds in the world. It also presents some proofs of God's Existence and Oneness and some characteristics of the Qur'ān.

In the Name of God, the All-Merciful, the All-Compassionate.

1. When the Event to happen happens,

2. There is no denying its happening –

3. Abasing some and exalting others;

4. When the earth is shaken with a violent shock;

5. And the mountains are shattered and crumble

6. So they become dust scattered;

7. You (all conscious, responsible beings) will be sorted out into three groups

8. Thus: the people of the Right (the people of happiness and prosperity, who receive their Records in their right hands): how happy and prosperous are the people of the Right!

9. And the people of the Left (the people of wretchedness, who will receive their Records in their left hands): how wretched are the people of the Left!

10. And the foremost (in faith and good deeds, and serving God's cause) will be the foremost (in receiving and enjoying God's mercy).

11. Those are the ones near-stationed to God,[1]

12. In Gardens abounding in bounty and blessings.

13. A good many of them are from among the first (to have embraced God's Religion);

14. And a few from the later (generations).[2]

15. (They will be seated) on lined thrones (encrusted with gold and precious stones),

16. Reclining upon them, facing one another.

---

1. Nearness to God means transcending corporeality and acquiring perfected spirituality, and thereby proximity to God. It depends on true faith and can be acquired by doing whatever God has decreed as good and right. The obligatory and supererogatory religious duties, done with the due consciousness that is their due, are like wings of light that carry one toward the "skies" of infinitude. A traveler to God enters new corridors leading to eternity on the wings of supererogatory duties, and is aware of being rewarded with new Divine gifts, which engender an even greater desire to do both the obligatory and the supererogatory duties. One awakened to this truth feels in their conscience the love of God in direct proportion to their love of God. God declares:

My servant cannot come near to Me through anything else more lovable to Me than doing the obligatory religious duties. However, by doing supererogatory duties he comes nearer to Me, and when he comes nearer to Me, I will be his eyes to see with, his ears to hear with, his hands to grasp with, and his legs to walk on (al-Bukhārī, "Riqāq," 38). That is, such a believer is directed to act by the Divine Will.

2. As suggested in 52: 21 and explained in note 2 to this verse, particularly at the begin-

ning of a new movement of faith launched by the Prophets and their true successors, those who attain faith first of all are generally more valued in God's sight and will be the foremost in enjoying Paradise. They have outstripped others in believing and supporting God's cause at a time when supporting it was the most difficult, and therefore suffered greater hardships than those that followed. They are usually more sincere in their faith and more devoted to God and His cause. A few people can reach their rank from among the later generations. This is also indicated in verse 9: 100, which gives the greatest rank to the first among the Emigrants and the Helpers. God's Messenger said that the best among his Community are his Companions, and then those who appeared among the first generation to follow them and those among the second generation. This is, of course, when one's virtues are considered in general terms. There may always be in later generations those that outstrip the virtuous ones of the preceding generations in certain particular virtues. But in general terms, the best of all generations are the Prophet's Companions, and then the second generation who followed them and the third generation who followed the latter.

17. There will go round them immortal youths,[3]

18. With goblets, and ewers, and a cup from a clear-flowing spring,

19. From which no aching of the head ensues, nor intoxication of the mind;

20. And with fruits such as they choose,

21. And with the flesh of fowls such as they desire;

22. And (there will be) pure maidens, most beautiful of eye,

23. Like pearls kept hidden (in their shells).

24. A reward for all (the good) that they used to do.

25. They will hear there neither vain talk nor accusing speech;

26. (They will hear) only speech (wishing) peace and security after peace and security.

27. And the people of the Right (the people of happiness and prosperity who will receive their Records in their right hands): how happy and prosperous are the people of the Right!

28. Amidst cherry trees laden with fruit,

29. And banana trees with fruit piled high,

30. And shade long-extended,

31. And water gushing (and flowing constantly),

32. And fruits (of every other kind) abounding,

33. Never cut off, nor forbidden;

34. And (with them will be their) spouses ennobled with beauty and spiritual perfection:[4/5]

35. We have brought them into being in a new creation;

36. And We have made them virgins,

37. Full of love for their husbands, and equal in age,[6]

38. For the people of the Right (the people of happiness and prosperity):

39. A good many of them are from among the first (to have embraced God's Religion);

40. And a good many are from the later (generations).

41. And the people of the Left (who will be given their Records in their left hands): how wretched are the people of the Left!

42. In the midst of scorching wind and hot, boiling water,

43. And the shadow of black smoke,

44. (A shadow) neither cooling nor refreshing.

45. Indeed, before that, they were lost in excess of pleasures (without moral scruples);

46. And would persist in committing the

greatest sin (of unbelief or associating partners with God and denying the afterlife).

47. And would say: "What? After we have
died and become dust and bones, will we
indeed be raised from the dead?

48. "And also our forefathers of old?"

49. Say: "Those of old and those of later
times

50. "Will all be brought together at an appointed time on a Day well-known."

3. These youths will be the children who died
before reaching puberty. According to many
scholars, the children of unbelievers will also
be admitted into Paradise and serve the people
of Paradise (al-Qurṭubī).

4. These are the women who died as Muslims
and will be admitted into Paradise. They will
be together with their spouses, who will be
admitted into Paradise like them.

5. All the blessings of Paradise mentioned so
far, as well as the sufferings of Hell that will
be cited below, are in the indefinite form. This
signifies that although all those blessings and
sufferings are cited in the Qur'ān in terms,

and will be presented in Paradise in forms, that
we are acquainted with here in this world, they
will be different in character or nature; their
nature will be peculiar to the other world. It is
impossible for us to imagine them in their true
nature (see 2: 25, and note 21).

6. Equality of age means either that the spouses
will be equal in age with one another, or that
men will be of the same age as one another
and the women as one another. A Prophetic
Tradition says that men will be 33 years old and
women 18 years old in Paradise, where there
will be no aging (at-Tirmidhī, "Sifat al-Jannah,"
12; Ibn Hanbal, 2: 295).

51. Then: O you who have strayed (from the Straight Path), who deny (the afterlife),

52. You will surely eat of the tree of *Zaqqūm*;

53. And you fill up your bellies with it.

54. Thereafter you will drink of hot, boiling water;

55. You will drink as the camel raging with thirst drinks.

56. This will be their welcome on the Day of Judgment.

57. It is We Who have created you. So will you not confirm as truth (what We convey to you as truth)?[7]

58. Have you considered the semen that you emit?

59. Is it you who create it, or are We[8] the Creator?

60. It is also We Who decree death among you[9] – and We cannot be overcome,

61. So that We may replace you (with new generations like you), and bring you about in a new mode and form of existence you do not know.[10]

62. For certain you know the first creation (how you are brought into the world), then should you not reflect on (and anticipate the second creation)?

63. Have you ever considered the seed you sow (in the ground)?

64. Is it you who cause it to grow, or is it We Who make it grow?[11]

65. If We so willed, We would surely make it into chaff, and then you would not cease to exclaim:

66. "We are indeed in a great loss (with our money, time, and efforts gone to waste).

67. "Rather, we are left utterly deprived (of our livelihood)."

68. Have you ever considered the water that you drink?

69. Is it you who send it down from the cloud or is it We Who send it down?

70. If We so willed, We would make it bitter and salty. Then, should you not give thanks?[12]

71. Have you ever considered the fire that you kindle?

72. Is it you who bring into being the tree for it, or is it We Who bring it into being?[13]

73. We have made it something for reflection (on Our handiwork and Our grace in making the creation useful and beautiful), and a comfort (especially) for the dwellers (and wayfarers) in the desert.

74. Therefore, glorify the Name of your Lord, the Supreme (declaring His being absolutely above having any defects and partners).

75. I swear by the locations of the stars (and their falling),

76. – It is indeed a very great oath, if you but knew.[14] –

---

7. That is, We have created you, and maintain you in the world, and will cause you to die. We also know you and whatever you do and have it recorded. Again, We have not created you in vain; you are responsible beings. So why do you not confirm Our declaration that We will raise you from the dead for a new, eternal life?

8. The use of plural form of the pronoun and the verb for the Divine Being is to stress His Grandeur and absolute dominion of the creation.

9. That is, you do not die at random, or at the behest of another power, or as a natural end of your life. We have decreed death and cause you to die as a meaningful dimension of your life until eternity.

10. Through death, God continuously renews and refreshes the world and prepares a new, eternal world. So death, being a change of worlds only, discharges us from life's hardships, which gradually become harder through old age. It releases us from worldly life, which is a turbulent, suffocating, narrow dungeon of space, and admits us to the wide circle of the Eternal Beloved One's Mercy, where we will enjoy a pleasant and everlasting life without suffering. God makes our other world out of our deeds in this world, so we must send there good deeds in order to be worthy of a happy life there.

11. It is clear that the growth of a seed sown under earth requires the ability of the seed to germinate and grow, and the cooperation with it in the right proportions of the earth, the sun, the air, and rain. This cooperation can evidently be created only by a Knowledge Which knows all of these elements and how they should cooperate for a seed to grow, and a Will Which decrees this cooperation, and a Power Which is able to accomplish all of that. No one other than the Absolutely Knowledgeable, Willing, and Powerful One can do that. And

such a Being has no need of partners, and His having partners is absolutely inconceivable.

12. Whatever God grants us is pure blessing and grace. So we must always be thankful to Him, and if He sometimes grants us less than our need and even deprives us of our necessary provision, we must never complain about Him; rather we must complain to Him of our own selves. God may sometimes grant less in order to test us and sometimes to remind us of the importance of provision for us and that it is He Who provides for us. It even sometimes occurs that He grants us less to punish us for our sins that have caused the deprivation and to warn us to repent and mend our ways. So whatever He decrees for us is for our own good, and therefore requires thanksgiving.

13. The origin of almost all kinds of fuel, including petrol is wood and/or plants, either directly or indirectly, through decay under the ground. This verse particularly refers to the trees of Markh and 'Afār, which grow in the Arabian desert and from which people kindle fire (see 36: 80, note 24).

14. Modern interpreters of the Qur'ān assert that by the locations of the stars, the Qur'ān alludes to the white holes (quasars) and black holes in the sky. These are the locations of stars that have to date been found in the universe. Quasars store incredible amounts of energy, enough to form galaxies (assemblages of billions of stars). As for the black holes, they form as a result of the collapse of a star. They cannot be seen but are recognized by the fact that they devour all radiation and stars that pass nearby, and cause an indirect emission of gamma rays and X-rays, and by the fact that time is suddenly dilated in its vicinity. These star locations are regions of gravitational shock or collapse and of equilibrium in the universe.

77. Most certainly it is a Qur'ān (recited) most honorable,

78. In a Book well-guarded.[15]

79. None except the purified ones can reach it (to obtain the knowledge it contains. And none except those cleansed of material and spiritual impurities should touch it).[16]

80. It is a Book being sent down in parts from the Lord of the worlds.

81. Is it this Discourse that you hold in low esteem?

82. And do you make your share of it denying it?

83. Then, how is it you do not – when the soul comes up to the throat (of a dying human),

84. While you are looking on –

85. And while We are nearer to him (the dying human) than you are, but you do not see (that) –

86. Then, how is it you do not – if you are not bound to Us in dependence (subject to Our will) –

87. (How is it that) you do not restore the soul (of that dying human), if you are truthful (in your claim)?

88. Now, if he (that dying human) is of those near-stationed to God,

89. Then (there is for him) comfort in eternal relief (from all kinds of hardships and pains), and abundance, and a Garden of bounty and blessing.

90. If he is of the people of the Right (the people of happiness and prosperity who will receive their Records in their right hands),

91. Then "Peace be upon you" (will be what you will always hear) from the people of the Right.

92. But if he is one of those who denied (Our Message and Our Messengers), who strayed (from the Straight Path),

93. Then his entertainment is boiling water

94. And roasting in a Blazing Flame.

95. Surely this (Qur'ān) is certain truth.

96. So glorify the Name of your Lord, the Supreme (affirming that He is exalted above any falsehood).

---

15. This Book is the Supreme Ever-Preserved Tablet (85: 22). For this Tablet, see 6: 59, note 13; 13: 39, note 13; 17: 14, note 10.

16. This verse expresses both a reality and an order. In expressing a reality, it means that none except the purified ones (the angels and the human beings whom God has purified, such as the Prophets) can reach the well-guarded Book (the Supreme Ever-Preserved Tablet) to attain any knowledge that is contained in it. Such beings as devils cannot reach It. When-ever they make any attempt to ascend through the heavens they are expelled (see 15: 18, note 5; 26: 212, note 37; 67: 5, note 4). In expressing an order, it means that none except those who have purified themselves from any material impurity by taking minor or major ablution, and those purified from the spiritual impurity of unbelief and the association of partners with God should touch the Qur'ān. Both the syntax of the verse and the words used equally give both meanings.

SŪRAH 57

AL-ḤADĪD (IRON)

Madīnah period

Revealed in Madīnah, most probably four or five years after the *Hijrah*, this *sūrah* has 29 verses and takes its name from the word *al-ḥadīd* in verse 25. It deals with God's absolute sovereignty, the necessity of sacrifice in God's cause, and the passing nature of worldly pleasures. It promises the Muslims victory and the unbelievers defeat, and reiterates that belief in the previous Prophets requires believing in Prophet Muḥammad as the last, universal Prophet.

In the Name of God, the All-Merciful, the All-Compassionate.

1. Whatever is in the heavens and the earth glorifies God;[1] and He is the All-Glorious with irresistible might, the All-Wise.

2. To Him belongs the sovereignty of the heavens and the earth. He gives life and causes to die. He has full power over everything.

3. He is the First, the Last, the All-Outward, and the All-Inward. He has full knowledge of everything.[2]

---

1. That is, all things, with their existence, their lives, maintenance, and functions, show that God is absolutely above having any defects or any partners in His Divinity, Lordship, and Sovereignty. Even the bodies of the unbelievers show this reality. As explained in note 31 to 2: 30, for every species of creation there is an angel that governs them and represents them in God's Presence, and presents to the Divine Court their glorifications and prayers made through their disposition. And, as stated in 17: 44, every thing and being glorify and praise God in a language that we do not understand.

2. A *ḥadith* explains this part of the verse as follows:

My God, You are the First, there is none that precedes You; You are the Last, there is none that will outlive You; You are the All-Outward, there is none that encompasses You; and You are the All-Inward, there is none that is more penetrating than You (Muslim, "Dhikr," HN: 2713).

God is eternal with everything before or after Him. He is uncontained in time and place. The visible existence is the manifestation of His Names, and the origin or source of all creation, which is invisible and spiritual, is also contained in His Knowledge. So, God encompasses all creation in His Knowledge and Power, and He Himself is eternal.

هُوَ الَّذِي خَلَقَ السَّمَوَاتِ وَالْأَرْضَ فِي سِتَّةِ أَيَّامٍ ثُمَّ اسْتَوَى عَلَى الْعَرْشِ
يَعْلَمُ مَا يَلِجُ فِي الْأَرْضِ وَمَا يَخْرُجُ مِنْهَا وَمَا يَنْزِلُ مِنَ السَّمَاءِ وَمَا يَعْرُجُ
فِيهَا وَهُوَ مَعَكُمْ أَيْنَ مَا كُنْتُمْ وَاللَّهُ بِمَا تَعْمَلُونَ بَصِيرٌ ۞ لَهُ مُلْكُ
السَّمَوَاتِ وَالْأَرْضِ وَإِلَى اللَّهِ تُرْجَعُ الْأُمُورُ ۞ يُولِجُ الَّيْلَ فِي النَّهَارِ
وَيُولِجُ النَّهَارَ فِي الَّيْلِ وَهُوَ عَلِيمٌ بِذَاتِ الصُّدُورِ ۞ آمِنُوا بِاللَّهِ
وَرَسُولِهِ وَأَنْفِقُوا مِمَّا جَعَلَكُمْ مُسْتَخْلَفِينَ فِيهِ فَالَّذِينَ آمَنُوا
مِنْكُمْ وَأَنْفَقُوا لَهُمْ أَجْرٌ كَبِيرٌ ۞ وَمَا لَكُمْ لَا تُؤْمِنُونَ بِاللَّهِ
وَالرَّسُولُ يَدْعُوكُمْ لِتُؤْمِنُوا بِرَبِّكُمْ وَقَدْ أَخَذَ مِيثَاقَكُمْ إِنْ كُنْتُمْ
مُؤْمِنِينَ ۞ هُوَ الَّذِي يُنَزِّلُ عَلَى عَبْدِهِ آيَاتٍ بَيِّنَاتٍ لِيُخْرِجَكُمْ
مِنَ الظُّلُمَاتِ إِلَى النُّورِ وَإِنَّ اللَّهَ بِكُمْ لَرَءُوفٌ رَحِيمٌ ۞ وَمَا
لَكُمْ أَلَّا تُنْفِقُوا فِي سَبِيلِ اللَّهِ وَلِلَّهِ مِيرَاثُ السَّمَوَاتِ وَالْأَرْضِ
لَا يَسْتَوِي مِنْكُمْ مَنْ أَنْفَقَ مِنْ قَبْلِ الْفَتْحِ وَقَاتَلَ أُولَئِكَ أَعْظَمُ
دَرَجَةً مِنَ الَّذِينَ أَنْفَقُوا مِنْ بَعْدُ وَقَاتَلُوا وَكُلًّا وَعَدَ اللَّهُ
الْحُسْنَى وَاللَّهُ بِمَا تَعْمَلُونَ خَبِيرٌ ۞ مَنْ ذَا الَّذِي يُقْرِضُ اللَّهَ
قَرْضًا حَسَنًا فَيُضَاعِفَهُ لَهُ وَلَهُ أَجْرٌ كَرِيمٌ ۞

4. He it is Who has created the heavens and the earth in six days, then He established Himself on the Throne.[3] He knows whatever goes into the earth (such as rain and seeds), and whatever comes forth out of it (such as moisture, plant and animal life-forms), and whatever descends from the heaven (such as rain, light, and angels), and whatever ascends into it (such as vapor, and supplications). And He is with you wherever you may be. And God sees well all that you do.

5. To Him belongs the sovereignty of the heavens and the earth. To God are all matters ultimately referred, (and whatever He wills occurs).

6. He makes the night pass into the day and He makes the day pass into the night (and so makes each grow longer or shorter). And He has full knowledge of whatever lies (hidden) in the bosoms.

7. Believe in God and His Messenger, and spend (in God's cause) out of all that He has entrusted to you – those among you who believe and spend (in God's cause), for them there is a great reward.

8. What is the matter with you that you do not believe in God (as His being God requires), when the Messenger calls you to believe in your Lord (Who has created and sustains you), and He has indeed taken your pledge,[4] if you are true believers.

9. He it is Who sends down to His servant Revelations clear as evidence and in meaning in order to lead you out of all kinds of darkness into the light. Surely God is All-Pitying, All-Compassionate toward you.

10. What is the matter with you that you do not spend in God's cause, when God's is the inheritance of the heavens and the earth.[5] Not equal among you are those who spend before the victory comes and fight (for God's sake, and those who do not): they are greater in rank than those who spend after the victory comes and fight later. However to all God has promised what is the best (Paradise). God is fully aware of all that you do.[6]

11. Whoever lends God a goodly loan, God will increase it manifold (to his credit), and he will have an honorable, generous reward (in addition).[7]

3. For an explanation of this statement, see: 7: 54, note 13.

4. This pledge was that they would obey the commands of God and His Messenger, and spend in God's cause, whether in ease or hardship, support and promote good, prohibit and try to prevent evil, and strive in God's way without fearing the censure of anyone.

5. Whether we spend in God's cause or not, God Almighty is the ultimate heir to whatever we have, as it is He Who has granted us whatever we have. He is the real Owner of everything. He has whatever we do, spend or do not spend, recorded, so that He will recompense us for it.

6. Although both types of people mentioned in the verse may be admitted into Paradise on account of their faith and good deeds, everyone will enjoy Paradise according to the degree of their faith, loyalty to God and His cause, and the value of their good deeds.

7. Spending in God's cause is like lending God a loan. God returns it multiplied and, in addition, with extra reward.

12. On that Day you will see the believing men and the believing women (led swiftly toward Paradise), with their light shining forth before them and on their right hands.[8] "Glad tidings for you today! Gardens through which rivers flow, (into which you will enter) to abide therein. This is indeed the supreme triumph."

13. On that Day the hypocritical men and the hypocritical women will say to those who believe: "Wait for us that we may have some light from your light." It will be said: "Turn back (if you can, to the world where such light was to be obtained), and seek light (through your deeds you did there)." Just then a wall of separation will be put between them, with a gate therein (through which the hypocrites, so as to increase their regret, will observe the state of the believers). The inner side of the wall (which will separate the believers from the hypocrites) – there will be in it the mercy (of eternal happiness), and outside it there will be the punishment (of eternal doom)

14. They (the hypocrites) will call out to the believers: "Were we not with you (in the world)?" They will reply: "True! But you (willfully) put yourselves in the way of temptation, and hesitated and doubted (waiting on events to choose which side to be on and not assuming yourselves to stand by the truth of Islam), and false expectations (that God's Religion would one day be defeated) deluded you, until God's decree (of death) came to you; and the deluder (Satan) deluded you (with wrong conceptions) about God.

15. "And this Day no ransom will be taken from you, nor from those who disbelieved. Your final refuge is the Fire; that is your harbor suited to you. How evil a destination to arrive at!"

16. Has not the time yet come for those who believe that their hearts should soften with humility and submit (to God to strive in His cause) in the face of God's Remembrance (the Qur'ān) and what has come down of the truth (the Divine teachings)? And (has not the time yet come) that they should not be like those who were given the Book before? A long time has passed over them (after they received the Book) and so their hearts have hardened; and many among them (have been) transgressors.

17. Know that God revives the earth after its death (and He may revive the decaying hearts in the same way). We have indeed made clear the signs and Revelations (to enable such revival and) that you may reason and understand.

18. Those men and women who give alms (by spending out of their wealth in both the prescribed and supererogatory duties of alms-giving), and lend to God a goodly loan (by spending either in His cause or for the needy), it will be increased manifold to their credit, and they will have an honorable, generous reward in addition.[9]

---

8. This is the light that the believers send forth from the world through their good deeds. The more deeds there are and the more sincerely they are done, the greater and brighter is the light that they will produce. As understood from the verse, the believers will advance toward Paradise on the right side, while, as will be understood from the following verse, the hypocrites (and the unbelievers), who will receive their records of deeds in their left hands, will advance toward Hell on the left side and be left behind because of being enveloped by the darkness produced by their unbelief, hypocrisy, and evil deeds.

9. Verse 16 is a warning against the hardening of hearts toward the Divine teachings and God's Remembrance, and toward striving for God's cause. One of the most important reasons of this hardening is growing familiarity with the Revelation and the revealed Divine teachings, and the passage of time after it. Another important reason is committing sins (transgression) through indifference to God's warnings. So it is necessary to continuously be alert against such a hardening and always to seek means for the softening of the heart. As pointed out in verses 17 and 18, just as God revives any land after its death with rain, and this is repeated every year, He may also revive dead or dead-like hearts with clear Revelations provided we remain loyal to God and His Religion by carrying out God's commands and avoiding transgression, and spending in His cause.

وَالَّذِينَ ءَامَنُوا بِاللَّهِ وَرُسُلِهِ أُوْلَٰٓئِكَ هُمُ الصِّدِّيقُونَ

وَالشُّهَدَآءُ عِندَ رَبِّهِمْ لَهُمْ أَجْرُهُمْ وَنُورُهُمْ وَالَّذِينَ كَفَرُوا

وَكَذَّبُوا بِـَٔايَٰتِنَآ أُوْلَٰٓئِكَ أَصْحَٰبُ الْجَحِيمِ ۝ اعْلَمُوٓا أَنَّمَا الْحَيَوٰةُ

الدُّنْيَا لَعِبٌ وَلَهْوٌ وَزِينَةٌ وَتَفَاخُرٌ بَيْنَكُمْ وَتَكَاثُرٌ فِي

الْأَمْوَٰلِ وَالْأَوْلَٰدِ كَمَثَلِ غَيْثٍ أَعْجَبَ الْكُفَّارَ نَبَاتُهُۥ ثُمَّ يَهِيجُ

فَتَرَىٰهُ مُصْفَرًّا ثُمَّ يَكُونُ حُطَٰمًا وَفِي الْأَخِرَةِ عَذَابٌ شَدِيدٌ

وَمَغْفِرَةٌ مِّنَ اللَّهِ وَرِضْوَٰنٌ وَمَا الْحَيَوٰةُ الدُّنْيَآ إِلَّا مَتَٰعُ

الْغُرُورِ ۝ سَابِقُوٓا إِلَىٰ مَغْفِرَةٍ مِّن رَّبِّكُمْ وَجَنَّةٍ عَرْضُهَا

كَعَرْضِ السَّمَآءِ وَالْأَرْضِ أُعِدَّتْ لِلَّذِينَ ءَامَنُوا بِاللَّهِ وَرُسُلِهِۦ

ذَٰلِكَ فَضْلُ اللَّهِ يُؤْتِيهِ مَن يَشَآءُ وَاللَّهُ ذُو الْفَضْلِ

الْعَظِيمِ ۝ مَآ أَصَابَ مِن مُّصِيبَةٍ فِي الْأَرْضِ وَلَا فِي أَنفُسِكُمْ إِلَّا فِي

كِتَٰبٍ مِّن قَبْلِ أَن نَّبْرَأَهَآ إِنَّ ذَٰلِكَ عَلَى اللَّهِ يَسِيرٌ ۝ لِّكَيْلَا تَأْسَوْا

عَلَىٰ مَا فَاتَكُمْ وَلَا تَفْرَحُوا بِمَآ ءَاتَىٰكُمْ وَاللَّهُ لَا يُحِبُّ

كُلَّ مُخْتَالٍ فَخُورٍ ۝ الَّذِينَ يَبْخَلُونَ وَيَأْمُرُونَ

النَّاسَ بِالْبُخْلِ وَمَن يَتَوَلَّ فَإِنَّ اللَّهَ هُوَ الْغَنِيُّ الْحَمِيدُ ۝

19. Those who believe in God and His Messengers (those whose actions prove their profession of faith) – they are, in the sight of their Lord, the loyal and truthful (to God in whatever they do and say), and the witnesses (who have borne testimony to the truth with their lives). They have their (particular) reward and their (particular) light. But those who disbelieve and deny Our manifest signs and Revelations – they will be companions of the Blazing Flame.

20. Know that the present, worldly life[10] is but a play, vain talk and ostentation, and mutual boasting among you, and competing in wealth and children – it is like when rain comes down and the vegetation grown by it pleases the farmers, (but) then it dries up and you see it turn yellow, then it becomes straw; and in the Hereafter there is a severe punishment, but also (there is) forgiveness from God and His good pleasure (which are everlasting); whereas the present, worldly life is but a transient enjoyment of delusion.

21. And (rather than competing for the things of this world) race with one another to forgiveness from your Lord, and to a Garden the vastness of which is as the vastness of heaven and earth, prepared for those who truly believe in God and His Messengers. That is God's bounty, which He grants to whom He wills. God is of tremendous bounty.[11]

22. No affliction occurs on the earth (such

as drought, famine, and earthquakes) or in your own persons (such as disease, damage in your property, and loss of loved ones), but it is recorded in a Book before We bring it into existence – doing so is surely easy for God –[12]

23. So that you may not grieve for what has escaped you, nor exult because of what God has granted you: God does not love anyone proud and boastful –[13]

24. Those who act niggardly (in spending of what God has granted them) and urge others to be niggardly: whoever turns away (from carrying out God's command to spend in His cause and for the needy), then surely God is All-Wealthy and Self-Sufficient (absolutely independent of all His creatures), All-Praiseworthy (as your Lord, Who provides for you and the needs of all other beings).

10. The expression translated as *the present, worldly life* also means the basic elements or attributes of the present life. So by this expression the Qur'ān denotes, rather than the world, the life that pertains to the bodily or material dimension of human existence. Otherwise the world is the field to be sown for harvest in the Hereafter, and is also the place where God's Names are manifested.

11. Verse 3: 133 says: *And hasten, as if competing with one another, to forgiveness from your Lord, and to a Garden as spacious as the heavens and the earth, prepared for the God-revering, pious.* The promise in that verse is to those who keep their duties to God and avoid all kinds of sins out of piety and reverence for God. So we can conclude that those who truly believe in God and His Messengers, whom this verse mentions, are the God-revering, pious ones – those who believe and keep their duties to God and avoid sins out of reverence for Him.

An important point in both verses to be noted is that forgiveness precedes Paradise because Paradise is the place of perfect purity, and no one can enter Paradise without God's forgiveness. So before entering Paradise, God will clean or purify the people of Paradise of all their sins out of pure grace, and the hardships they will have to suffer from resurrection to the gates of Paradise will also serve as a means of purification.

12. That is, recording such acts out of His Eternal Knowledge and keeping them record-ed, and then bringing them into existence by His Power for many wise purposes – such as to punish the sinful as they deserve or to warn them against their end or to forgive the sins of believers or to promote the sinless to higher ranks – is absolutely easy for God.

The verse also includes a consolation for people in affliction. Provided the intended lesson has been learned, when we consider any misfortune in the light of Divine Destiny, or as an application of Divine Destiny, we may find rest and not feel the need to complain about it. The verse to come corroborates this.

13. We have free will, are enjoined to follow religious obligations, and cannot ascribe our sins to God. We have free will so that our rebellious carnal soul does not consider itself free of the consequences of its sins by ascribing them to Destiny. Destiny exists so that pious people do not ascribe their good acts to themselves and thereby become proud. Destiny exists so that the successful and the wealthy are not proud of their success and wealth.

Past and (present) misfortune should be considered in the light of Destiny so that we do not grieve for what has befallen us and what we have not been able obtain. The future, along with sins and questions of responsibility, should be referred to human free will. That is, we should do whatever we should in order for a desired result, and avoid neglect, faults, and sins. This reconciles the extremes of fatalism and denial of the role of Destiny in our actions.

540   سُورَةُ الْحَدِيدِ   ٥٤

لَقَدْ أَرْسَلْنَا رُسُلَنَا بِالْبَيِّنَاتِ وَأَنزَلْنَا مَعَهُمُ الْكِتَابَ وَالْمِيزَانَ
لِيَقُومَ النَّاسُ بِالْقِسْطِ ۖ وَأَنزَلْنَا الْحَدِيدَ فِيهِ بَأْسٌ شَدِيدٌ
وَمَنَافِعُ لِلنَّاسِ وَلِيَعْلَمَ اللَّهُ مَن يَنصُرُهُ وَرُسُلَهُ بِالْغَيْبِ ۚ إِنَّ
اللَّهَ قَوِيٌّ عَزِيزٌ ۝ وَلَقَدْ أَرْسَلْنَا نُوحًا وَإِبْرَاهِيمَ وَجَعَلْنَا فِي
ذُرِّيَّتِهِمَا النُّبُوَّةَ وَالْكِتَابَ ۖ فَمِنْهُم مُّهْتَدٍ ۖ وَكَثِيرٌ مِّنْهُمْ
فَاسِقُونَ ۝ ثُمَّ قَفَّيْنَا عَلَىٰ آثَارِهِم بِرُسُلِنَا وَقَفَّيْنَا بِعِيسَى
ابْنِ مَرْيَمَ وَآتَيْنَاهُ الْإِنجِيلَ وَجَعَلْنَا فِي قُلُوبِ الَّذِينَ
اتَّبَعُوهُ رَأْفَةً وَرَحْمَةً وَرَهْبَانِيَّةً ابْتَدَعُوهَا مَا كَتَبْنَاهَا
عَلَيْهِمْ إِلَّا ابْتِغَاءَ رِضْوَانِ اللَّهِ فَمَا رَعَوْهَا حَقَّ رِعَايَتِهَا ۖ
فَآتَيْنَا الَّذِينَ آمَنُوا مِنْهُمْ أَجْرَهُمْ ۖ وَكَثِيرٌ مِّنْهُمْ فَاسِقُونَ ۝
يَا أَيُّهَا الَّذِينَ آمَنُوا اتَّقُوا اللَّهَ وَآمِنُوا بِرَسُولِهِ يُؤْتِكُمْ
كِفْلَيْنِ مِن رَّحْمَتِهِ وَيَجْعَل لَّكُمْ نُورًا تَمْشُونَ بِهِ وَيَغْفِرْ لَكُمْ ۚ
وَاللَّهُ غَفُورٌ رَّحِيمٌ ۝ لِّئَلَّا يَعْلَمَ أَهْلُ الْكِتَابِ أَلَّا
يَقْدِرُونَ عَلَىٰ شَيْءٍ مِّن فَضْلِ اللَّهِ ۙ وَأَنَّ الْفَضْلَ بِيَدِ
اللَّهِ يُؤْتِيهِ مَن يَشَاءُ ۚ وَاللَّهُ ذُو الْفَضْلِ الْعَظِيمِ ۝

25. Assuredly We have sent Our Messengers with manifest truths (and clear proofs of their being Messengers), and We have sent down with them the Book and the Balance so that (relations among) humankind may live by equity. And We have sent down iron[14] in which is stern might and benefits for humankind, so that God may mark out those who help (the cause of) God and His Messengers, though they do not see Him. Surely God is All-Strong, All-Glorious with irresistible might.[15]

26. We certainly sent as Messengers Noah and Abraham, and established in their line Prophethood and the Book. Among them (their offspring) there have been those who have followed the right guidance, but many among them have been transgressors.

27. Thereafter, We sent, following in their footsteps, others of Our Messengers, and We sent Jesus son of Mary, and granted him the Gospel, and placed in the hearts of those who followed him tenderness and mercy. And monasticism: they innovated it – We did not prescribe it to them – only to seek God's good pleasure, but they have not observed it as its observance requires.[16] So We have granted those among them who have truly believed their reward, but many among them have been transgressors.

28. O you who believe! Keep from disobedience to God in reverence for Him and piety, and truly believe in His Messenger (Muḥammad). He will grant you twofold of His mercy (one for your believing in all the previous Prophets and one for the Last Prophet), and He will appoint for you a light to move (on the Straight Path in this world, leading to Paradise in the Hereafter), and He will forgive you. God is All-Forgiving, All-Compassionate.[17]

29. (This is told you so) that the people of the Book should know that they cannot determine or restrict anything of God's grace, (and neither they nor Muslim believers will be able to attain anything of it unless they believe in Muḥammad together with all the previous Prophets), and that all grace is in God's Hand, He grants it to whom He wills. God is of tremendous grace.

14. Sending down iron means the same as sending down cattle in 39: 6; iron is one of God's great bounties which He has bestowed out of the treasures He has with Him, as stated in 15: 21: *There is not a thing but the stores (for its life and sustenance) are with Us, and We do not send it down except in due, determined measure.*

15. This verse is very significant in assessing a sound society and government. The Messengers are the God-appointed leaders of humankind, who always guided them to the truth and led them in all aspects of life throughout human history. The Book is the compilation of knowledge, instructions, and laws essential to their happiness in both worlds. The Balance is the criterion to attain what is right in belief, thinking, and action, and also to realize justice in human individual and social life (see: 55: 7–9, note 4). Iron, other than being perhaps the most important and necessary matter for technology and fighting in God's way to eradicate injustice and uphold God's Word, symbolizes force or power in human social life. Without the Book, iron (force) destroys justice and brings about injustice. Without the Balance, iron misuses the Book according to its own benefits. Without iron, the Book and Balance are not sufficient to form a good society and government. Said Nursi remarks: "Principles of wisdom and laws of truth have no effect upon ordinary people unless the former are combined with the state's laws and the latter with power" (*The Letters*, "Seeds of the Truth," 2: 306).

16. Islam does not approve of monasticism. It is said that there is no monasticism in Islam. Monasticism for the Muslim Community is striving in God's cause. Islam does not approve of holding aloof from people and life in order to attain self-perfection. Rather it calls its followers to be among people and to work for their welfare and consider self-perfection along with the perfection of others. Even though some members of Islamic Sufi orders have practiced retreat or seclusion for self-training and perfection, they have done so only for a short restricted period and considered being among people to work for their perfection as being the greatest rank.

17. Although some interpreters have thought that this verse addresses the people of the Book, it is addressed to the Muslims, though not excluding the former in order to urge them to believe in the Last Prophet, upon him be peace and blessings. While the Jews refuse to believe in the Messengers Jesus and Muḥammad, who came after the Messengers sent to them, and the Christians refuse to believe in God's Last Messenger, Muḥammad, the Muslims believe in all the Prophets. So the later deviations of the people of the Book should never cause the Muslims to have any negative opinion of any of the previous Messengers and their true followers.

SŪRAH 58

AL-MUJĀDILAH
(THE PLEADING WOMAN)

Madīnah period

Consisting of 22 verses, this *sūrah* was revealed in Madīnah, most probably after the Battle of the Trench in the fifth year after *Hijrah*. It derives its name from the first verse, where a woman's plea to the Messenger to solve a problem between her and her husband is recounted. It decisively abolishes the pre-Islamic custom of a form of divorce that took effect when a man said to his wife, "You are henceforth like my mother's back to me." It denounces the hypocrites for their holding secret counsels against the Messenger, and forbids the believers from taking as guardians those whom God has condemned to eternal punishment. It orders that support be given to God's Religion.

In the Name of God, the All-Merciful, the All-Compassionate.

1. God has indeed heard (and accepted) the words of the woman who pleads with you concerning her husband and refers her complaint to God. God hears the dialogue between you.[1] Surely God is All-Hearing, All-Seeing.[2]

2. Those among you who declare their wives to be unlawful for them by using of them the expression "Be as my mother's back to me," (should know that) their wives are not their mothers. Their mothers are none other than the women who gave them birth. Such men certainly utter a word abhorred (by the Sharī'ah) and a falsehood. Yet God is surely All-Pardoning (He overlooks the faults of His servants), All-Forgiving.

3. Those who declare their wives unlawful for them (by using of them that abhorred expression) and thereafter wish to go back on the words they have uttered must free a slave before they (the spouses) touch each other. This is what you are urged to do. And God is fully aware of what you do (so do not seek to evade this act of penance and expiation for your wrong).

4. Whoever does not find (means to do that), let him fast two (lunar) months consecutively before they (the spouses) touch each other. And he that is not able to do so, (his penance shall be) to feed sixty destitute ones (two meals). This is in order that you perfect your faith in God and His Messenger (so that you believe in the truth of whatever God has enjoined and His Messenger conveyed to you, and live accordingly). These are the bounds of

God. And for the unbelievers there is a painful punishment.

5. Those who oppose God and His Messenger (in the observance of God's bounds) will certainly be abased (in the world) even as those (who did likewise) before them were abased. We have certainly sent down clear Revelations (to guide you to happi-ness in both worlds). And for the unbeliev-ers there is a humiliating punishment.[3]

6. On the day when God will raise them all from the dead, and make them truly understand all that they did (in the world, and call them to account): God has had it written down, though they have forgotten it. God is witness over everything.

---

1. There is reference here to a pre-Islamic custom among the pagan Arabs. A husband would say to his wife, "You are henceforth as my mother's back to me," thus forbidding himself from conjugal relations with her. This meant an irrevocable divorce, but a woman thus divorced was not allowed to remarry. In *Sūrat al-Ahzāb* (verse 4), which was revealed before this *sūrah*, the Qur'ān took the first step towards abolishing this custom (it was called *zihār*), and declared that a woman, whose husband had pronounced her to be as his mother's back, was in no way his mother in reality. Aws ibn Sāmit from the Aws tribe among the Muslims of Madīnah was angry with his wife for some reason, and declared that she was as unlawful to him as his mother's back. Afterwards, he regretted having done so, but according to custom, he was not able to return to his wife. So his wife, Hawlah bint Tha'labah, appealed to God's Messenger and told him about the case. She added that her children had grown up and she lived alone with her husband. So if her husband left her, she would have been left alone without anyone to protect her, and she added that her husband would agree to re-accept her as his wife. During her conversation with the Messenger, God revealed this and the following verses concerning the same subject, decisively and permanently abolishing the pagan custom.

2. The verse concludes: "God is All-Hearing, All-Seeing." God hears everything, even the conversation between a woman and the Messenger about a particular, personal, private matter between herself and her husband. A woman is generally more compassionate than a man, and is a source of care and tenderness that inspires self-sacrifice. As a requirement of His being All-Compassionate, Almighty God heard her complaint and considered it a matter of great importance through His Name, the Truth. In that He expresses a universal principle in relation to a particular event, we may realize that the One Who hears and sees and weighs a particular, minor incident must hear and see all things. One Who claims Lordship over the universe must be aware of the troubles of any creature who has been wronged and hear its cries. One who cannot do so cannot be Lord. Thus God being All-Hearing, All-Seeing establishes these two mighty truths. (See *The Words*, "the 25th Word," 446.)

3. The verse is clear enough in warning that the communities that oppose God and His Messenger(s) in their ordering of life, those who do not observe the rules they have laid down, will inevitably suffer abasement (manifested as total or partial destruction through "natural" calamities, internal or external wars, famine, drought, and pestilence, etc.), and what awaits those who obstinately reject them in the Hereafter is a much more humiliating and shameful punishment (in Hell).

542　　　سُورَةُ الْمُجَادَلَة　　　٥٩٢

أَلَمْ تَرَ أَنَّ اللَّهَ يَعْلَمُ مَا فِي السَّمَوَاتِ وَمَا فِي الْأَرْضِ مَا يَكُونُ
مِنْ نَجْوَى ثَلَاثَةٍ إِلَّا هُوَ رَابِعُهُمْ وَلَا خَمْسَةٍ إِلَّا هُوَ سَادِسُهُمْ
وَلَا أَدْنَى مِنْ ذَلِكَ وَلَا أَكْثَرَ إِلَّا هُوَ مَعَهُمْ أَيْنَ مَا كَانُوا
ثُمَّ يُنَبِّئُهُمْ بِمَا عَمِلُوا يَوْمَ الْقِيَامَةِ إِنَّ اللَّهَ بِكُلِّ شَيْءٍ
عَلِيمٌ ۞ أَلَمْ تَرَ إِلَى الَّذِينَ نُهُوا عَنِ النَّجْوَى ثُمَّ يَعُودُونَ لِمَا نُهُوا عَنْهُ
وَيَتَنَاجَوْنَ بِالْإِثْمِ وَالْعُدْوَانِ وَمَعْصِيَتِ الرَّسُولِ وَإِذَا جَاءُوكَ حَيَّوْكَ بِمَا
لَمْ يُحَيِّكَ بِهِ اللَّهُ وَيَقُولُونَ فِي أَنْفُسِهِمْ لَوْلَا يُعَذِّبُنَا اللَّهُ بِمَا نَقُولُ
حَسْبُهُمْ جَهَنَّمُ يَصْلَوْنَهَا فَبِئْسَ الْمَصِيرُ ۞ يَا أَيُّهَا الَّذِينَ
آمَنُوا إِذَا تَنَاجَيْتُمْ فَلَا تَتَنَاجَوْا بِالْإِثْمِ وَالْعُدْوَانِ وَمَعْصِيَتِ
الرَّسُولِ وَتَنَاجَوْا بِالْبِرِّ وَالتَّقْوَى وَاتَّقُوا اللَّهَ الَّذِي إِلَيْهِ
تُحْشَرُونَ ۞ إِنَّمَا النَّجْوَى مِنَ الشَّيْطَانِ لِيَحْزُنَ الَّذِينَ آمَنُوا
وَلَيْسَ بِضَارِّهِمْ شَيْئًا إِلَّا بِإِذْنِ اللَّهِ وَعَلَى اللَّهِ فَلْيَتَوَكَّلِ
الْمُؤْمِنُونَ ۞ يَا أَيُّهَا الَّذِينَ آمَنُوا إِذَا قِيلَ لَكُمْ تَفَسَّحُوا فِي الْمَجَالِسِ فَافْسَحُوا
يَفْسَحِ اللَّهُ لَكُمْ وَإِذَا قِيلَ انْشُزُوا فَانْشُزُوا يَرْفَعِ اللَّهُ الَّذِينَ آمَنُوا
مِنْكُمْ وَالَّذِينَ أُوتُوا الْعِلْمَ دَرَجَاتٍ وَاللَّهُ بِمَا تَعْمَلُونَ خَبِيرٌ ۞

7. Have you not considered that God knows whatever is in the heavens and whatever is on the earth? There is not a secret counsel between three persons but He is the fourth of them, nor between five but He is the sixth of them, nor less than that nor more but He is with them wherever they may be. Thereafter He will make them truly understand all that they do (and call them to account) on the Day of Resurrection. Surely God has full knowledge of everything.

8. Have you not considered those who were forbidden to hold secret counsels, and yet reverted to what they had been forbidden, and held secret meetings to commit sins (such as drinking alcohol, gambling, and evading the Prayer), and for (urging one another to) offensiveness and disobedience to the Messenger (in his commands and prohibitions). (It is these very people who) when they come to you, salute you with a salutation that God has never taught you and with which He has never saluted you,[4] and say to one another (in derision): "Why does God not punish us for what we say (if Muḥammad is truly His Prophet)?" Hell will suffice them, they will enter it to roast. How evil a destination to arrive at!

9. O you who believe! If you hold secret counsels, do not hold secret counsels to commit sins, or for (urging one another to) offensiveness and disobedience to the Messenger; but rather hold counsels for godliness, and righteousness, and piety.[5] Keep from disobedience to God in reverence for Him and piety, to Whom you will be gathered.

10. Secret counsels (held for other reasons) are only (a provocation) from Satan, in order that he may cause grief to the believers; yet he cannot harm them in anything unless by God's leave; and in God let the believers put their trust.

11. O you who believe! When you are told, "Make room in the assemblies (for one another and for new comers)," do make room. God will make room for you (in His Grace and Paradise). And when you are told, "Rise up (and leave the assembly)," then do rise up. God will raise (in degree) those of you who truly believe (and act accordingly), and in degrees those who have been granted the knowledge (especially of religious matters).[6] Surely God is fully aware of all that you do.

4. Generally the disbelieving Jews and hypocrites in Madīnah, instead of saying the words of greeting as ordered by God (24: 61), used to and pronounce the word *salām* ("peace") in a manner to make it indistinguishable from *sām* (death). They also vented their spite by using ambiguous expressions in their conversations. They either used words with double meanings, one innocent and the other offensive, or changed the pronunciation of the expressions used by the Companions (see 2: 104, note 94). The verse refers to their enmity and that of the hypocrites which were displayed in such ways.

5. Believers always pursue godliness and piety, and therefore God's approval and good pleasure. So, if believers come together privately or publicly, they do so only to discuss and solve matters in godliness and piety, and their conversations are conducted around these values. And as pointed out in 4: 114, *No good is there in most of their secret counsels except for him who exhorts to a deed of charity, or kind equitable dealings and honest affairs, or setting things right between people. Whoever does that seeking God's good pleasure, We will grant to him a tremendous reward.*

6. Merit is not to be sought only in sitting in the assembly of a scholar or spiritual guide. Merit lies in faith and knowledge. So one should seek the assemblies of scholars and/or guides only with the intention of visiting them for God's sake and with their permission, and only in order to increase in faith and knowledge. When (true) knowledge, which leads one to greater piety, a better religious life, and from which others benefit, is added to faith, God will exalt its owner in many ranks.

593   543

بِسْمِ اللّٰهِ الرَّحْمٰنِ الرَّحِيْمِ

12. O you who believe! When you intend to consult the Messenger in private, offer something in alms (to the needy) before your consultation. That is better for you and purer. Yet if you do not find (means to do so), then God is surely All-Forgiving, All-Compassionate.

13. Is it that you are afraid of offering something in alms before your consultation (with him)? (If so) and you have not done it, and God has turned to you in forgiveness, then establish the Prayer in conformity with its conditions, and pay the Prescribed Purifying Alms, and obey God and His Messenger. God is fully aware of all that you do.[7]

14. Have you not considered those who take for confidants and guardians a people whom God has condemned to punishment? They are neither of you (O believers) nor of the others (whom they take for confidants and guardians). They swear to a lie (that they are of you), while they know (it to be a lie).

15. God has prepared for them a severe punishment. Evil indeed is that which they do habitually.

16. They take their oaths as a covering (to screen their misdeeds and themselves from accusation), and bar (people) from God's way. Therefore there is for them a humiliating punishment.

17. Neither their wealth nor their children will avail them anything against God.

They are companions of the Fire: they will abide therein.

18. The Day when God will raise them all from the dead, they will swear to Him as (now) they swear to you. They fancy that they will have some standing (through their oaths). Be aware: they are but liars.

19. Satan has subdued them and so caused them to forget remembrance of God. Those are the party of Satan. Be aware: the party of Satan, they are the losers (the self-ruined).

20. Those who oppose God and His Messenger – surely those will be among the most abased.

21. God has decreed: "I will most certainly prevail, I and My Messengers." Surely God is All-Strong, All-Glorious with irresistible might.

7. It is clear that this verse was revealed to train and educate the believers in their relations with the Messenger, upon him be peace and blessings. Some people frequently appealed to the Messenger in private concerning their affairs, some with the hope of nearness to him, and still some others in order to appear to be near to him. Since the Messenger refused nobody, this caused him a lot of trouble, and since most of those who appealed to him were from among the wealthy, it caused grief for the poor. In order to train and educate the believers and make them more sincere in their relationship with the Messenger, and to purify their hearts, the Qur'ān ordered them to spend something in charity before their appeal to him. When this order had the desired effect, God annulled it. However, it still retains its spirit, meaning, and importance in educating people in their relationship with the leaders of Muslims.

22. You never find a people who truly believe in God and the Last Day loving toward those who oppose God and His Messenger, even if they be their (own) parents, or their children, or their brothers (and sisters), and their clan.[8] Those (are they) in whose hearts God has inscribed faith and has strengthened them with a spirit from Him (which is the source of their spiritual vigor and intellectual enlightenment). And He will admit them into Gardens through which rivers flow, therein to abide. God is well-pleased with them and they are well-pleased with Him. Those are the party of God. Be aware: the party of God are those who are the prosperous.

---

8. As pointed out by Hamdi Yazır in interpreting this verse, this Qur'ānic statement should be understood in the light or considered together with 60: 8–9. God never forbids the believers to be good and beneficial to others, even if they are unbelievers and hypocrites. He always orders goodness and justice. So what is forbidden in this verse concerning love is that a believer cannot love an unbeliever or the followers of other false religions because of their unbelief or false belief. The believers cannot prefer blood relations over the relationship created by faith. This means that the Qur'ān categorically rejects racism. It also forbids loving and taking for friends those who fight against the Muslims because of their Religion and who try to violate the most fundamental rights of human beings, notably the right to believe in God and obey His commands.

SŪRAH 59

AL-ḤASHR
(THE GATHERING)

Madīnah period

Revealed in Madīnah, most probably in the fourth year after the *Hijrah*, this *sūrah* consists of 24 verses. It takes its name from the word *ḥashr* in verse 2, which means gathering people to dispatch somewhere. The *sūrah* deals with the Muslims' encounter with the Jewish tribe of Banū Naḍīr, and mentions the conspiracies of the hypocrites in alliance with some Jews. It gives instructions on the distribution of the war-gains obtained from the enemy without fighting. It also advises the believers to always be God-revering and pious, and describes God with some of His Attributes.

In the Name of God, the All-Merciful, the All-Compassionate.

1. Whatever is in the heavens and whatever is on the earth glorifies God. He is the All-Glorious with irresistible might, the All-Wise.

2. He it is Who drove out those who disbelieve from among the People of the Book from their (fortified) homes as the first

instance of gathering (them for punishment and banishing from the heartland of Islam). You did not think that they would go forth (so easily), just as they thought that their strongholds would protect them against God. But (the will of) God came upon them from where they had not reckoned (it could come): He cast dread into their hearts. And so they were wrecking their homes by their own hands, as well as by the hands of the believers.[1] Learn a lesson, then, O people of insight.

3. Had it not been that God had decreed banishment for them, He would certainly have punished them (with death and expropriation) in this world. And for them in the Hereafter there is the punishment of the Fire.

---

1. When God's Messenger, upon him be peace and blessings, emigrated to Madīnah, he signed a pact with the Jewish tribes living there. The pact stipulated that the Jews would remain neutral in the hostilities between the Muslims and the pagan Quraysh, but if there were to be an attack on Madīnah, they would defend the city together with the Muslims. But the Jewish tribes were reluctant to honor their agreements. During the Battle of Badr, they favored the Makkan polytheists; after Badr, they openly encouraged the Quraysh and other Arab tribes to unite against the Muslims. They also collaborated with the hypocrites, who were apparently an integral part of the Muslim body-politic. To sabotage the spread of Islam, they began to fan the flames of old animosities between the Aws and Khazraj, the two tribes of Madīnan Muslims. Ka'b ibn Ashraf, the chief of the Banū Nadīr, went to Makkah and recited stirring elegies concerning the Makkans killed at Badr to provoke the Quraysh into renewed hostile action. He also slandered the Muslims and satirized God's Messenger in his poems.

The violation by the Jewish tribes of their obligations according to the treaty exceeded all reasonable limits. A few months after Badr, a Muslim woman was treated indecently by some Jews of Banū Qaynuqa', the most anti-Muslim Jewish tribe. During the ensuing fight, a Muslim and a Jew were killed. When God's Messenger reproached them for this conduct and reminded them of their treaty obligations, the Jews threatened him: "Don't be misled by your encounter with a people who have no knowledge of warfare. You were lucky. But if we fight you, you will know that we are men of war."

Finally, God's Messenger had to attack the Jewish Banu Qaynuqa'; he defeated them and banished them from the outskirts of Madīnah.

As for the Jewish Banū Nadīr tribe, its members also secretly intrigued with the Makkan pagans and the Madīnan hypocrites to destroy the Muslim community once and for all. They even tried to kill the Prophet while he was visiting them. God's Messenger asked them to leave their strategic position, about three miles south of Madīnah, and depart from the city. They would be allowed to return every year to gather the produce of their date groves. But when 'Abdullāh ibn Ubayy, the chief of the hypocrites, promised them help in case of war, the Banū Nadīr disagreed. They had great faith in their strongly built houses and other strongholds.

The Muslim army then besieged them in their fortresses. The Banū Nadīr, seeing that neither the Makkan polytheists nor the Madīnan hypocrites cared enough to help them, had to leave the city. They were dismayed, but their lives were spared. They were given ten days to remove themselves, their families, and all they could carry. Most of them joined their brethren in Syria and others in Khaybar (Ibn Hishām, 3: 47-49, 190-192).

545

ذٰلِكَ بِأَنَّهُمْ شَاقُّوا اللّٰهَ وَرَسُولَهُ وَمَنْ يُشَاقِّ اللّٰهَ فَإِنَّ اللّٰهَ شَدِيدُ الْعِقَابِ ۝ مَا قَطَعْتُمْ مِنْ لِينَةٍ أَوْ تَرَكْتُمُوهَا قَائِمَةً عَلٰى أُصُولِهَا فَبِإِذْنِ اللّٰهِ وَلِيُخْزِيَ الْفَاسِقِينَ ۝ وَمَا أَفَاءَ اللّٰهُ عَلٰى رَسُولِهِ مِنْهُمْ فَمَا أَوْجَفْتُمْ عَلَيْهِ مِنْ خَيْلٍ وَلَا رِكَابٍ وَلٰكِنَّ اللّٰهَ يُسَلِّطُ رُسُلَهُ عَلٰى مَنْ يَشَاءُ وَاللّٰهُ عَلٰى كُلِّ شَيْءٍ قَدِيرٌ ۝ مَا أَفَاءَ اللّٰهُ عَلٰى رَسُولِهِ مِنْ أَهْلِ الْقُرٰى فَلِلّٰهِ وَلِلرَّسُولِ وَلِذِي الْقُرْبٰى وَالْيَتَامٰى وَالْمَسَاكِينِ وَابْنِ السَّبِيلِ كَيْ لَا يَكُونَ دُولَةً بَيْنَ الْأَغْنِيَاءِ مِنْكُمْ وَمَا آتَاكُمُ الرَّسُولُ فَخُذُوهُ وَمَا نَهَاكُمْ عَنْهُ فَانْتَهُوا وَاتَّقُوا اللّٰهَ إِنَّ اللّٰهَ شَدِيدُ الْعِقَابِ ۝ لِلْفُقَرَاءِ الْمُهَاجِرِينَ الَّذِينَ أُخْرِجُوا مِنْ دِيَارِهِمْ وَأَمْوَالِهِمْ يَبْتَغُونَ فَضْلًا مِنَ اللّٰهِ وَرِضْوَانًا وَيَنْصُرُونَ اللّٰهَ وَرَسُولَهُ أُولٰئِكَ هُمُ الصَّادِقُونَ ۝ وَالَّذِينَ تَبَوَّؤُوا الدَّارَ وَالْإِيمَانَ مِنْ قَبْلِهِمْ يُحِبُّونَ مَنْ هَاجَرَ إِلَيْهِمْ وَلَا يَجِدُونَ فِي صُدُورِهِمْ حَاجَةً مِمَّا أُوتُوا وَيُؤْثِرُونَ عَلٰى أَنْفُسِهِمْ وَلَوْ كَانَ بِهِمْ خَصَاصَةٌ وَمَنْ يُوقَ شُحَّ نَفْسِهِ فَأُولٰئِكَ هُمُ الْمُفْلِحُونَ ۝

4. This is because they defied and opposed God and His Messenger. Whoever deifies and opposes God, then surely God is severe in retribution.

5. Whatever (of their) palm-trees you may have cut down or left them standing on their roots,² it was by God's leave and so that He might disgrace the transgressors.

6. What of theirs God bestowed as gains of war on His Messenger – and you did not spur any horse or riding-camel for it, but God gives His Messenger mastery over whomever He wills. God has full power over everything –

7. What God has bestowed on His Messenger as gains of war from the peoples of the townships: (one-fifth of) it belongs to God, and to the Messenger, and his near kinsfolk, and orphans, and the destitute, and the wayfarer (lacking means to sustain a journey), so that it should not become a fortune circulating among the rich among you.³ Whatever the Messenger gives you accept it willingly, and whatever he forbids you, refrain from it. Keep from disobedience to God in reverence for Him and piety. Surely God is severe in retribution.

8. It is also for the poor Emigrants, who have been driven from their homes and their property, seeking favor with God and His approval and good pleasure, and who help (the cause of) God and His Messenger. Those are they who are truthful (in their profession of faith and loyalty to its commands).

9. Those who, before their coming, had their abode (in Madīnah), preparing it as a home for Islam and faith, love those who emigrate to them for God's sake, and in their hearts do not begrudge what they have been given, and (indeed) they prefer them over themselves, even though poverty be their own lot.⁴ (They too have a share in such gains of war.) Whoever is guarded against the avarice of his own soul – those are the ones who are truly prosperous.

2. God allowed the Muslims to cut down the trees during their siege of the Banū Nadīr to facilitate the operation. However, except for such strict military exigencies, the Prophet continually forbade the destruction of trees and crops. The Qur'ān's special mention of this incident during the fighting against the Banū Nadīr must refer to this extraordinary exemption.

3. For an explanation of this distribution, see 8: 41, note 8. The principle laid out in the last sentence – *it should not become a fortune circulating among the rich among you* – is very important and is a basic characteristic of Islamic economy and social justice. Islam orders people to strive and be industrious, it does not commend begging. However, it is a fact that due to human facilities and capacities, people vary in their earning power and their wealth. But in Islam there should be no extremely rich people while there are destitute people. So through ordinances, such as prescribed and recommended alms as a recompense for fasts that have been broken willingly or that cannot be fulfilled due to extreme old age or permanent illnesses, for the oaths broken, and unlawful actions such as saying to one's wife "You are henceforth as my mother's back to me," (see 58: 1, note 1), it seeks as broad a distribution of wealth as possible, so that the standard of life will be balanced in the community.

4. These verses tell (and remind) us what praiseworthy qualities the *Muhājirūn* (Emigrants) and the *Anṣār* (the Helpers – the Madīnan Muslims) had and their degree in those qualities.

546

وَالَّذِينَ جَآءُو مِنۢ بَعۡدِهِمۡ يَقُولُونَ رَبَّنَا اغۡفِرۡ لَنَا وَلِإِخۡوَٰنِنَا
الَّذِينَ سَبَقُونَا بِالۡإِيمَٰنِ وَلَا تَجۡعَلۡ فِي قُلُوبِنَا غِلًّا لِّلَّذِينَ
ءَامَنُوا رَبَّنَآ إِنَّكَ رَءُوفٌ رَّحِيمٌ ۝ أَلَمۡ تَرَ إِلَى الَّذِينَ نَافَقُوا
يَقُولُونَ لِإِخۡوَٰنِهِمُ الَّذِينَ كَفَرُوا مِنۡ أَهۡلِ الۡكِتَٰبِ لَئِنۡ
أُخۡرِجۡتُمۡ لَنَخۡرُجَنَّ مَعَكُمۡ وَلَا نُطِيعُ فِيكُمۡ أَحَدًا أَبَدًا
وَإِن قُوتِلۡتُمۡ لَنَنصُرَنَّكُمۡ وَاللَّهُ يَشۡهَدُ إِنَّهُمۡ لَكَٰذِبُونَ
۝ لَئِنۡ أُخۡرِجُوا لَا يَخۡرُجُونَ مَعَهُمۡ وَلَئِن قُوتِلُوا لَا يَنصُرُونَهُمۡ
وَلَئِن نَّصَرُوهُمۡ لَيُوَلُّنَّ الۡأَدۡبَٰرَ ثُمَّ لَا يُنصَرُونَ ۝ لَأَنتُمۡ
أَشَدُّ رَهۡبَةً فِي صُدُورِهِم مِّنَ اللَّهِ ذَٰلِكَ بِأَنَّهُمۡ قَوۡمٌ لَّا
يَفۡقَهُونَ ۝ لَا يُقَٰتِلُونَكُمۡ جَمِيعًا إِلَّا فِي قُرًى مُّحَصَّنَةٍ
أَوۡ مِن وَرَآءِ جُدُرٍ بَأۡسُهُم بَيۡنَهُمۡ شَدِيدٌ تَحۡسَبُهُمۡ جَمِيعًا
وَقُلُوبُهُمۡ شَتَّىٰ ذَٰلِكَ بِأَنَّهُمۡ قَوۡمٌ لَّا يَعۡقِلُونَ ۝ كَمَثَلِ
الَّذِينَ مِن قَبۡلِهِمۡ قَرِيبًا ذَاقُوا وَبَالَ أَمۡرِهِمۡ وَلَهُمۡ عَذَابٌ
أَلِيمٌ ۝ كَمَثَلِ الشَّيۡطَٰنِ إِذۡ قَالَ لِلۡإِنسَٰنِ اكۡفُرۡ فَلَمَّا كَفَرَ
قَالَ إِنِّي بَرِيٓءٌ مِّنكَ إِنِّيٓ أَخَافُ اللَّهَ رَبَّ الۡعَٰلَمِينَ ۝

10. And all those who come after them (and follow in their footsteps) pray: "O Our Lord! Forgive us and our brothers (and sisters) in Religion who have preceded us in faith, and let not our hearts entertain any ill-feeling against any of the believers. O Our Lord! You are All-Forgiving, All-Compassionate (especially toward Your believing servants).⁵

11. Have you not considered those who are hypocrites: they say to their brothers who disbelieve from among the People of the Book: "If you are driven away (from Madīnah), we will certainly go out with you, and we will never obey anyone against you. If war is waged against you, we will most certainly help you." God bears witness that they are indeed liars.⁶

12. For if they are indeed driven away, they will never go out with them, and if war is waged against them, they will never help them. Even supposing they would help them (in such an eventuality), they would most certainly turn their backs in flight, and so they would not receive help (from anywhere, and be destroyed because of their manifest treachery to the Muslims).

13. The dread they have of you in their hearts is more intense than their fear of God. This is because they are a people who are devoid of understanding and so cannot grasp the truth.

14. They will never fight against you as a united body (in alliance with the Hypocrites, with the Jews of Khaybar and others), unless it be from within fortified strongholds or from behind high walls. Severe is their belligerent discord among themselves (except when not opportunistically allied in warfare against you). You think of them as one body, but in fact their hearts are at odds with one another: This is because they are a people who do not reason (and come to an understanding of the situations they face).

15. Just like those (the Jews of the Banū Qaynuqaʿ) who, a short time before them (the Jews of the Banū Naḍīr), tasted the evil result of their own doings – and (in the Hereafter) for them there is (also) a painful punishment.

16. (The hypocrites have deceived them) just like Satan, when he says to human, "Disbelieve (in God)!" Then when he disbelieves, he says (to human): "Surely I am quit of you, for surely I fear God, the Lord of the worlds!"⁷

5. Caliph 'Umar understood from these verses that the spoils gained without fighting are for all the Muslims, including the Emigrants, the Helpers, and those succeeding them in later centuries. His view received a general welcome from other Companions.

6. As explained in note 1 above, when God's Messenger asked the Jewish Banū Nadīr tribe to leave their strategic position, about three miles south of Madīnah, and depart from the city, 'Abdullāh ibn Ubayy ibn Salūl, the chief of the hypocrites, promised to help the Banū Nadīr in case of war. However, when the Muslim army besieged them in their fortresses, neither the Makkan polytheists nor the Madīnan hypocrites dared to help them.

7. The hypocrites promised help to the Jews of the Banū Nadīr and provoked them to fight against the Messenger. But when fighting began, the hypocrites did nothing. Their manners are like the manner of Satan. He makes promises to humans, calls them to disbelieve or commit sins, but when they have done whatever he has urged them to do, he withdraws and derides them. Actually, he has no power to do anything to fulfill his promises. Before the Battle of Badr began, he told the Makkan army: *"Today no power among humankind can overcome you, and for sure I am your supporter."* But when the two hosts came within sight of each other, he turned on his heels to run away and said: *"Indeed I am quit of you; surely I see that which you do not see. Indeed, I fear God"* (8: 48). He had perceived that the Muslim army was supported by angels and in fear of receiving harsh blows he preferred to take flight. His words *"Surely I am quit of you,"* and *"for surely I fear God,"* were only excuses for his flight.

17. So the end of both (Satan and those whom he has deceived, and the hypocrites and those whom they have betrayed) is that they will find themselves in the Fire to abide therein. That is the recompense of the wrongdoers.

18. O you who believe! Keep from disobedience to God in reverence for Him and piety to deserve His protection, and let every person consider what he has forwarded for the morrow. Keep from disobedience to God in reverence for Him and piety. Surely God is fully aware of all that you do.

19. And do not be like those who are oblivious of God and so God has made them oblivious of their own selves.[8] Those, they are the transgressors.

20. Not equal are the companions of the Fire and the companions of Paradise. The companions of Paradise, they are the triumphant.

21. If We had sent down this Qur'ān on a mountain, you would certainly see it humble itself, splitting asunder for awe of God. Such parables We strike for humankind so that they may reflect (on why the Qur'ān is being revealed to humankind and how great and important their responsibility is).

22. God is He save Whom there is no deity; the Knower of the unseen (all that lies beyond sense-perception) and the witnessed (the corporeal realm). He is the All-Merciful, the All-Compassionate.

23. God is He save Whom there is no deity; the Sovereign, the All-Holy and All-Pure, the Supreme Author of peace and salvation and the Supreme Author of safety and security Who bestows faith and removes all doubt, the All-Watchful Guardian, the All-Glorious with irresistible might, the All-Compelling of supreme majesty, the One Who has exclusive right to all greatness. All-Glorified is God in that He is absolutely exalted above what they associate with Him.

24. He is God, the Creator, the All-Holy Maker, the All-Fashioning. To Him belong the All-Beautiful Names.[9] Whatever is in the heavens and on the earth glorifies Him, (declaring Him to be absolutely above having any defects). He is the All-Glorious with irresistible might, the All-Wise.[10]

8. This verse is telling those who are oblivious of God and the believers: You are oblivious and unaware of yourselves. You do not want to remember death although you always consider others mortal. You hold back when confronting hardship and rendering service, but believe that you should be the first to be rewarded when it is time to collect the wages. You do not like obeying God in your lives and follow your lusts and caprices, and so are oblivious of the purpose for your worldly life. To purify yourselves of this, carry out your responsibilities, be prepared for death, and forget whatever reward you might obtain in the world. You should never forget why you are here in the world and what you should do, and for what end you are heading. You should know your true leader and follow him. Otherwise, (a Day will come and) it will be said: *"We are oblivious of you today (so do not hope for forgiveness and favor), as you were oblivious of the encounter of this day of yours, and your (lasting) refuge will be the Fire, and you have no helpers (45: 34).*

9. For God's Beautiful Names, see 7: 180, note 44; 17: 110, note 41.

10. It is a *sunnah* to recite the last three verses after the Early Morning and Evening Prayers.

SŪRAH 60

AL-MUMTAHANAH
(THE WOMAN TO BE TESTED)

Madīnah period

Revealed in Madīnah between the Treaty of Hudaybiyah and the conquest of Makkah, this *sūrah* has 13 verses. It derives its name from the 10th verse, which commands that women who have declared their conversion to Islam and emigrated to Madīnah should be tested as to whether they are true. The *sūrah* also deals with what the Muslims' relations with their disbelieving enemies should be.

In the Name of God, the All-Merciful, the All-Compassionate.

1. O you who believe! Do not take My enemies and your enemies for friends, offering them love and affection, while they have disbelieved in the truth that has come to you and driven the Messenger and yourselves away (from your homes) only because you believe in God, your Lord (Who has created you and sustains you). If you (now) have set forth (from your homes) to strive in My way and to seek My approval and good pleasure, (then do not take them for friends). You reveal to them your secret in secrecy out of your love and friendship, but I am better aware (than yourselves) of what you do in secret as well as of what you disclose. Whoever does so among you has surely strayed from the right way.[1]

2. Should they gain the upper hand over you, they will be to you as enemies (not friends), and stretch forth their hands and tongues against you with malice, and they long for you to disbelieve.

3. Your relatives, not even your own children, will be of any benefit to you on the Day of Resurrection. God will distinguish and part you from each other (according to how you believed and acted in the world).[2] God sees well all that you do.

4. Indeed you have had an excellent example to follow in Abraham and those in his company, when they said to their (idolatrous) people (who were their kin): "We are quit of you and whatever you worship besides God. We have rejected you (in your polytheism), and there has arisen between us and you enmity and hate forever until you believe in God alone (as the only One to be worshipped)." (So it was) except for Abraham's saying to his father: "I most surely will plead for God's forgiveness for

you, though I have no power at all to do anything for you against God."[3] (And their prayer was): "O Our Lord! It is in You that We have put our trust, and it is to You that we turn in utmost sincerity and devotion, and to You is the homecoming.

5. "O Our Lord! Do not make us a prey to those who disbelieve (lest, in overcoming us they think their unbelief to be true and increase therein). And forgive us, our Lord (– especially those of our sins that may cause us to fall prey to those who disbelieve). You are the All-Glorious with irresistible might, the All-Wise."

---

1. When the Treaty of Hudaybiyah was violated by the attack of the Banū Bakr, an ally of the Makkan polytheists, on the Banu Khudā'ah, an ally of the Muslims, and by some of the latter being killed, God's Messenger, upon him be peace and blessings, began to prepare for war. As always, he kept the affair quite secret and no one, including his wives and closest friends, knew where the campaign would be. However, an Emigrant named Khaṭīb ibn Abī Balta'ah guessed the intention of God's Messenger. He sent a letter to the Quraysh, informing them of the Messenger's preparations. The Messenger was told of this through a Revelation, and ordered 'Ali, Zubayr ibn al-'Awwām and Miqdād ibn 'Amr to take the letter from the woman to whom Khaṭīb had entrusted it. They did this successfully. When questioned why he had written this letter, Khaṭīb excused himself by saying that he had family members in Makkah and desired their protection. Since this was not an ill-intended treachery and Khaṭīb was one who had proved that he was a sincere Muslim by participating in the Battle of Badr, the Messenger forgave him (Ibn Hishām, 2: 39–42). The verse is about this incident and intends to warn the Muslims against similar events.

2. See 2: 166; 6: 94; 80: 37.

3. This saying of Abraham, upon him be peace, should be considered and evaluated together with 9: 114: *The prayer of Abraham for the forgiveness of his father was only because of a promise which he had made to him. But when it became clear that he was an enemy of God, he (Abraham) dissociated himself from him. Abraham was most tender-hearted, most clement.*" For the identity of Abraham's father, see 9: 114, note 25.

6. You certainly have in them an excellent example to follow for everyone who looks forward to God and the Last Day. Whoever turns away: then (let him know that) God is He Who is the All-Wealthy and Self-Sufficient (absolutely beyond need), the All-Praiseworthy.

7. (When you obey God in His commands and prohibitions), it may be that God will bring about love and friendship between you and those of them with whom you are in enmity.[4] God is All-Powerful, and God is All-Forgiving, All-Compassionate.

8. God does not forbid you, as regards those who do not make war against you on account of your Religion, nor drive you away from your homes, to be kindly to them, and act towards them with equity. God surely loves the scrupulously equitable.

9. God only forbids you, as regards those who make war against you on account of your Religion and drive you away from your homes, or support others to drive you away, to take them for friends and guardians. Whoever takes them for friends and guardians, those are the wrongdoers.

10. O you who believe! When believing women come to you as emigrants, test them,[5] (though only) God knows best their faith. Then, if you have ascertained that they are believers,[6] do not return them to the unbelievers. They are not (being believers) lawful (as wives) for the unbelievers nor are the unbelievers lawful (as husbands) for them. But return to them (the unbelievers) whatever they expended (by way of bridal-due when they wed those women).[7] And there will be no blame on you (O believers) if you marry them when you have given them their bridal-due. Also, (on the other side) do not continue to retain disbelieving women in marriage,

and ask for the return of whatever you expended as their bridal-due (if they remain among or join the unbelievers), just as the disbelieving men (whose wives have emigrated to you after embracing Islam) have the right to demand the return of whatever they spent. That is God's judgment and His law; He lays down the law and judges between you. God is All-Knowing, All-Wise.

11. If anything of the bridal-dues of your (former) disbelieving wives (who remain among or have joined the unbelievers) has passed to the unbelievers, and afterwards you have your turn (of victory) over them, then pay to those whose wives have gone away the equivalent of what they expended (as bridal-due).[8] And keep from disobedience to God in reverence for Him and piety, in Whom you are believers.

4. The events that are described here began after the Treaty of Hudaybiyah. The Muslims obeyed God's commands strictly, relayed to them by God's Messenger, until it became clear that they were invincible. In the atmosphere of peace brought about by the Treaty, many among the polytheists found opportunity to consider Islam clearly. They were finally awakened to the truth and Islam spread widely among the Arab tribes. After the conquest of Makkah in particular, nearly all the tribes embraced Islam.

5. Under the terms of the Treaty of Hudaybiyah, people or tribes could join or ally themselves with whomever they wished – the pagan Quraysh or the Muslims in Madīnah; any Makkan men who defected to Madīnah would be returned. The Quraysh took this stipulation to include also married women. So when several Makkan women embraced Islam after the Treaty and emigrated to Madīnah, their return to Makkah was demanded. However, since the word "men" was used in the stipulation mentioned, the Messenger responded that the stipulation included only the men, not women, and rejected the demand. This verse is concerned with these women, and of course includes all women who take refuge in a Muslim land claiming that they have become Muslims and left their husbands on account of their religion.

6. In order to establish whether they were believers, they were asked to swear by God. It is clear that this is a procedure of legal form and effect. It is because of this that God reminds us that it is only He who can determine whether they are true believers.

7. Since a former husband who is not Muslim is not responsible for the breaking of the marriage contract and it is the (newly Muslim) wife who is considered to be responsible, she has to refund the bridal-due that she received at the time of the marriage contract. If the woman is unable to do that, the Muslim community (or state on behalf of the community) is obliged to indemnify the former husband.

8. If the unbelievers did not return what the Muslim husbands had spent on their (former disbelieving) wives as dowry, the Muslims were to compensate this out of what the (former disbelieving) husbands had spent on their wives who had converted to Islam. Or if the Muslims were to gain war-spoils from the unbelievers, the Muslim husbands were to be compensated out of this.

12. O Prophet! When the believing women (who have professed Islam) come to you to swear allegiance to you – that they will never associate partners with God in any way, and will not steal, and will not commit any illegal sexual intercourse, and will not kill their children, and will not indulge in slander (such as attributing any of their children to other than their own father) that they have willfully devised, and that they will not disobey you in anything that is proper[9] – then accept their allegiance and ask God for their forgiveness. Surely God is All-Forgiving, All-Compassionate.

13. O you who believe! Do not take for friends and guardians a people who have incurred God's condemnation and punishment: (people) who are bereft of any hope in the Hereafter (because of what their wickedness has earned), just as the unbelievers are bereft of any hope of (ever seeing again) those in the graves.

---

9. The stipulations are important in understanding the place of women in the Age of Ignorance and for what purposes they were employed at that time, i.e. before Islam. It may be said that the same is true in almost every age of ignorance.

SŪRAH 61

AṢ-ṢAFF (THE RANKS)

Madīnah period

The name of this *sūrah* is derived from verse 4 where the word *ṣaff* (ranks) is used in praise of the Muslims who fought in ranks, coming together as though they were a firm and solid building. This *sūrah* consists of 14 verses. It was revealed just before or just after the Battle of Uhud. It stresses the importance of striving hard in the cause of God after faith, and the unity between professed belief and actual behavior.

In the Name of God, the All-Merciful, the All-Compassionate.

1. All that is in the heavens and all that is on the earth glorifies God. He is the All-Glorious with irresistible might, the All-Wise.

2. O you who believe! Why do you say what you do not do (as well as what you will not do)?

3. Most odious it is in the sight of God that you say what you do not (and will not) do.[1]

4. God surely loves those who fight in His cause in ranks as though they were a firm and solid structure.

5. And (remember) when Moses said to his people: "O my people! Why do you affront me[2] while you know indeed that I am the Messenger of God sent to you?" And so, when they swerved from the right way, God made their hearts swerve from the truth. God does not guide the transgressing people.

---

1. The last two verses severely condemn saying one thing and doing another; i.e. breaking one's promise, lying, and showing oneself to be different from what one really is. These are things that are incompatible with faith and which are signs of hypocrisy.

2. For Moses' being affronted by his people, see *sūrah* 2: 51, 55, 60, 67, 71; *sūrah* 4: 153; *sūrah* 5: 20, 26; *sūrah* 7: 138, 141, 148, 151; *sūrah* 20: 86, 98, and *Exodus*, 5: 20, 21; 14: 11-13; 16: 2-16; 17: 3-4, *Numbers*: 11: 1-15; 14: 1-10; ch. 16; 20: 1-5.

6. And Jesus son of Mary said: "O Children of Israel! Surely I am the Messenger of God sent to you, confirming (whatever of the truth is contained in) the Torah which was revealed before me,[3] and bringing the glad tidings of a Messenger to come after me, whose name is Ahmad."[4] But when he came to them (the whole of humankind including the later generations of the Children of Israel) with the manifest signs (of his being God's Messenger), they said: "This (which he preaches and does) is clearly (nothing but) sorcery."

7. Who is more in wrong than him who fabricates falsehood in attribution to God, when he is being invited to Islam (which is what the promised Messenger is conveying to them?) God surely does not guide the wrongdoing people.

8. They long to extinguish God's light[5] with (a breath from) their mouths (as if it entailed no more than extinguishing a candle with a breath), but God will surely perfect His light, however hateful (it may be) to the unbelievers.

9. He it is Who has sent His Messenger with the guidance and the Religion of truth (based on truth, and embodying it) that He may make it prevail over all religions, however hateful it may be to those who associate partners with God.[6]

10. O you who believe! Shall I direct you to a bargain (a deal) that will save you from a painful punishment?

11. That you believe in God and His Messenger, and strive hard in God's cause with your wealth and persons. Doing so is what is to your own good, if you but knew it.

12. So that He may forgive you your sins and admit you into Gardens through which

rivers flow, and into delightful dwellings in Gardens of perpetual bliss. That is the supreme triumph.

13. And yet another (blessing) which you love: Help from God and a near victory soon to come (which will lead to further victories). Give glad tidings to the believers.[7]

14. O you who believe! Be helpers of God('s cause and Messenger), even as Jesus son of Mary said to his disciples: "Who will be my helpers (on this way) to God?" The disciples said: "We are the helpers (in the cause) of God." And so it happened that some of the Children of Israel believed (in him and his Message) and others disbelieved (thus becoming two groups). So We strengthened those who believed against their enemies, and they became the uppermost.

3. Jesus did not come with a new religion or message from God. He communicated the same message as all the previous Prophets had done, and

the Sharī'ah of Moses; the only difference was that he made lawful for them certain things that had been forbidden to them (3: 50). He also made clear to them some of the matters in which they differed (43: 63). For Jesus and other dimensions of his Messengership, see *sūrah* 3: 48–51, notes 8–9; *sūrah* 5: 46–47, 110, 116–118; *sūrah* 19: 30–34.

4. Every Prophet gave the glad tidings of the Messenger to come after him and declared his faith in him. (For the mission of the Messengers and the preceding Messenger's giving the tiding of the advent of the one to follow, see 3: 81, note 15; and why God sent a Messenger with a Book after the others, see 5: 48, note 11.)

So, it is natural that Jesus gave the glad tidings of the Prophet Muḥammad, upon them be peace. It is also clear in the Gospel *John* that the Children of Israel had been expecting another Prophet besides Jesus:

> Now this is the testimony of John, when the Jews sent priests and Levites from Jerusalem to ask him, "Who are you?" He confessed, and did not deny; but confessed, "I am not the Christ." And they asked him, "What then? Are you Elijah?" He said, "I am not." "Are you that Prophet?" And he answered, "No." Then said they to him, "Who are you, that we may give an answer to those who sent us. What do you say about yourself?" He said: "I *am* the voice of one crying in the wilderness: 'Make straight the way of the Lord,' as the prophet Isaiah said." (*John*, 1: 19–23)

As understood from this passage, the Children of Israel had been expecting the coming of the Christ (Messiah), Elijah, and another Prophet (*that prophet*) who must have been known and who was expected by everyone at that time.

As explained in Appendix 1, this prediction is supported by several references. Paráklētos (differently rendered as *Counselor*, *Helper*, or *Comforter* in different versions of the New Testament) is in fact a corruption of *Períklytos* (the "Much-Praised"). Its Aramaic counterpart is Mawhamana, which means Aḥmad. Aḥmad and Muḥammad are derived from the same root verb, "Ḥa-Mi-Da" meaning to praise. However, Aḥmad also means one who praises. In many Prophetic Traditions, it is stated that one of the Prophet Muḥammad's names is Aḥmad, and this is mentioned by Ḥasan ibn Thābit, a famous poet during the Prophet's time, in one of his poems. So the Prophet Muḥammad was also known and mentioned as Aḥmad during his own lifetime. Though the name Aḥmad had not been known and used before him among the Arabs, this name became widely known and used during his time. It is of interest that Bediüzzaman Said Nursi records that the Prophet Muḥammad was mentioned in the Torah also with the name Munhamanna, meaning Muḥammad, the praised one. (For other predictions of the Prophet Muḥammad in the Old and New Testaments, see Appendix 1.)

Concerning the Prophet Muḥammad's mission regarding the People of the Book, and their relationship with him, the Qur'ān states: *They follow the (most illustrious) Messenger, the unlettered Prophet, whom they find described (with all his distinguishing features) in the Torah and the Gospel (that are) with them. He enjoins upon them what is right and good and forbids them what is evil; he makes pure, wholesome things lawful for them, and bad, corrupt things unlawful. And he relieves them of their burdens (remaining of their own Law) and the restraints that were upon them. So those who believe in him (with all sincerity), honor and support him, and help him, and follow the Light (the Qur'ān) which has been sent down with him – those, they are the truly prosperous* (7: 157).

5. It is clear that God's light is Islam, which removes "the veil of darkness" from the surface of the entire universe, a veil put there by other systems or false religions or philosophies; Islam illuminates minds, hearts, and the ways of humanity in all spheres of life and from birth to eternity.

6. For an explanation, see 9: 33, note 9.

7. The bargain and the glad tidings mentioned in the verses are stated in 9: 111 thus: *God has bought from the believers their selves and wealth because Paradise is for them. They fight in God's cause, and they kill or are killed. This is a promise with which God has bound Himself in the Torah and in the Gospel and in the Qur'ān. Who could be more faithful to his covenant than God? So (O believers) glad tidings to you because of the bargain you have made with Him! That indeed is the supreme triumph.*

SŪRAH 62

AL-JUMU'AH
(FRIDAY)

Madīnah period

This *sūrah* of 11 verses takes its name from verse 9, in which the *Jumu'ah* Congregational Prayer is made obligatory. It was revealed in the early part of the Madīnan period of the mission of God's Messenger. It orders the believers to hasten toward the remembrance of God when they are called on Friday (the day of *Jumu'ah*). It also mentions some fundamentals of the mission of God's Messenger, and criticizes the Jews who claimed that they alone were God's friends.

In the Name of God, the All-Merciful, the All-Compassionate.

1. All that is in the heavens and all that is on the earth glorifies God, the Absolute Sovereign, the All-Holy and All-Pure, the All-Glorious with irresistible might, the All-Wise.

2. He it is Who has sent among the unlettered ones[1] a Messenger of their own, reciting to them His Revelations, and purifying them (of false beliefs and doctrines, and sins, and all kinds of uncleanness), and instructing them in the Book and the Wisdom, whereas before that they were indeed lost in obvious error.

3. And (with the same mission, He has sent him) to other peoples than them who have not yet joined them (in faith). He is the All-Glorious with irresistible might, the All-Wise.

4. That is God's grace. He grants it to whom He wills. Surely God is of tremendous grace.

5. The parable of those entrusted to carry the Torah, who subsequently do not carry it out in practice, is that of a donkey carrying a load of books (it transports what it does not understand). How evil is the example of those who (ignore what their Book teaches and) deny God's Revelations (sent down for them and containing news of the Last Messenger)! God does not guide the wrongdoing people.

6. Say: "O you who are Jews! If you claim that you are the favorites of God to the exclusion of all other people, then wish for death, if you are truthful (in your claim)."

7. But they will never wish for it because of what they have forwarded (to the Hereafter of sins and offenses) with their own

hands. God has full knowledge of the wrongdoers.

8. Say: "Death, from which you flee, will surely meet you in any case. Then you will be returned to the Knower of the Unseen and the witnessed, and He will make you understand all that you were doing (and call you to account).

---

1. The Jews are a people to whom the Divine Book (the Torah) was given. Most of them knew how to read and write during the Prophet's time. But as will be pointed out in verse 5 below, although they were instructed in the Torah, they acted as if they were unaware of the value of what they had been entrusted with, just as a donkey laden with books does not understand the value of its load. On the other hand, the Arabs who were unlettered in the sense that they had not been given the Book or that most of them did not know how to read and write, greatly appreciated the Book sent to them through the Prophet Muḥammad, upon him be peace and blessings, and made it the guide for their lives.

9. O you who believe! When the call is made for the Prayer on Friday, then move promptly to the remembrance of God (by listening to the sermon and doing the Prayer), and leave off business (and whatever else you may be preoccupied with). This is better for you, if you but knew.[2]

10. And when the Prayer is done, then disperse in the land and seek (your portion) of God's bounty, and mention God much (both by doing the Prayer and on other occasions), so that you may prosper (in both worlds).

11. Yet (it happened that) when they saw (an opportunity for) business or pastime, they broke away for it and left you standing (while preaching the sermon). Say: "What is with God is better (for you) than pastimes and business.[3] God is the Best to be sought as provider with the ultimate rank of providing."

---

2. The Friday Congregational Prayer is obligatory and a major Islamic symbol. God's Messenger declared that God seals the heart of one who misses it three consecutive times without a valid excuse (Abū Dāwūd, "Ṣalāh," 215; at-Tirmidhī, "Ṣalāh," 359). There are also elements in the Friday Prayer that concern the Muslim community's political freedom and condition, and it cannot be offered alone.

This prayer is offered during the time of the Noon Prayer, and the normal Noon Prayer is not performed on Friday. Every free, adult, sane, and resident Muslim male who can attend must attend, unless they have a valid reason not to do so. It is not obligatory upon women, children, those with valid excuses (e.g., illness, lack of security, extreme cold), and travelers.

A sermon must be made before the Friday Prayer. (The remembrance of God in the verse includes both the sermon and the Prayer itself.)

The imām gives the sermon from a pulpit while standing. He begins by praising God and calling God's blessings and peace upon God's Messenger and his family. Next, he gives a sermon in which he exhorts Muslims to good deeds, discourages them from evil, advises them, and seeks to enlighten them mentally and spiritually and to guide them. He should not make the sermon too lengthy. After this part of the sermon, he sits for a short while and then, standing up, praises God, calls for God's blessings and peace upon God's Messenger and his family, and prays for all Muslims. The congregation must listen carefully and silently.

The Friday Prayer consists of two rak'ahs. It is a sunnah to offer four rak'ahs before it, just like the four rak'ahs offered before the Noon Prayer. After the Prayer, another (supererogatory) prayer of four rak'ahs is recommended.

Particularly the scholars of the Ḥanafī School of Law have had some doubts about the Friday Prayer's validity due to the (political) conditions of the Muslim community. Muslims are under the general control of non-Muslims (literally and explicitly, or by indirect means), and so do not have the absolute freedom to offer their Jumu'ah Congregational Prayer and/or give the sermon in the manner that would make the Prayer and sermon valid. Therefore, to be certain that the performance of the prescribed Noon Prayer has been carried out correctly, they have ruled that another Prayer of four rak'ahs, just like the prescribed Noon Prayer, along with the intention of offering a later noon prayer, should be offered after the four-rak'ah supererogatory Prayer. They also advise following this with another supererogatory Prayer of two rak'ahs with the intention of offering the sunnah Prayer for that time.

3. This verse alludes to an event that took place during the time of the Prophet, upon him be peace and blessings. There had been a famine in Madīnah when a long-expected caravan arrived from Syria. The Messenger was giving the Jumu'ah sermon, and on hearing the trumpet sound to proclaim the coming of the caravan, most of the congregation left the mosque. So the verse warns all Muslims to be attentive to the remembrance of God during the Prayer.

SŪRAH 63

AL-MUNĀFIQŪN (THE HYPOCRITES)

Madīnah period

Revealed in Madīnah, most probably in the 6th year after the Hijrah, this sūrah has 11 verses, and takes its name from the word al-munāfiqūn (hypocrites) in the first verse. It reveals the inner world of the hypocrites and their plots against Islam. It orders the believers not to cling to the passing delights of the world and to remain free of hypocrisy.

In the Name of God, the All-Merciful, the All-Compassionate.

1. When the hypocrites come to you, they say: "We bear witness that you are indeed God's Messenger." God knows that you are indeed His Messenger, and God bears witness that the hypocrites are certainly lying (they do not believe in the truth of what they say).[1]

2. They make their oaths a shelter (to hide their inner unbelief and protect themselves in the Muslim community), and so divert themselves (and seek to bar others) from God's way. Evil indeed is what they habitually do.

3. That is because they declared faith but thereafter (inwardly) disbelieved, so a seal has been set on their hearts so that they do not grasp the truth (and cannot recover the ability to reach to it).

4. When you see them, their outward form pleases you, and (their posture and speech are attractive and effective so that) you give ear to their words when they speak. (In reality) they are like blocks of wood propped up and (draped over) in striped cloaks.[2] They think (being themselves treacherous) every shout (they hear) to be against them. They are the enemies themselves, so beware of them. May God destroy them (they are liable to destruction by God)! How they are turned away from the truth (and pursue evil purposes)!

1. The hypocrites who emphatically bore witness to the Messengership of God's Messenger in his presence, upon him be peace and blessings, were lying, saying what they did not believe in or what was contrary to their hearts. They did so in order to hide their hypocrisy and unbelief in their hearts. One who declares something true to be true frequently, emphatically, and without any reason incurs doubt and should be doubted.

2. This description also implies the hypocrites' manner of sitting. Due to the inferiority complex that they had developed through constant hypocrisy, they sat reclining on cushions in a manner as if they were extremely important persons. The verse also draws attention to their manner of dressing, and hints at the secret organizations of hypocrisy. Hypocrisy is always the same, and hypocrites are of the same character in different ages.

THE HYPOCRITES

554

سُورَةُ الْمُنَافِقُونَ ٥٥٤

بِسْمِ اللّٰهِ الرَّحْمٰنِ الرَّحِيمِ

5. When it is said to them, "Come, and let the Messenger of God ask forgiveness for you (from God)," they turn away their faces, and you see them drawing back in arrogance.[3]

6. It is alike for them whether you ask forgiveness for them or do not ask forgiveness for them: God will never forgive them (so that they may return to guidance and hope for happiness in both worlds). God surely does not guide transgressors (whose hearts are infected with irremediable hypocrisy).

7. It is they who say (to their comrades): "Do not spend on those (impoverished Muslims) who are with God's Messenger, so that they may disperse (from around him)." But the treasures of the heavens and the earth belong to God (Who provides

for whom He wills as He wills, so the hypocrites have no power to withhold anything from those impoverished Muslims). But the hypocrites do not grasp this (being incapable of truth).

8. They say: "For certain, if we return to Madīnah, those with more status and power will drive out from it the weaker and lowlier ones." But all glory and might belong to God, and (by His leave) to His Messenger and the believers. But (being incapable of knowledge of the truth) the hypocrites do not know this.[4]

9. O you who believe! Let not your wealth nor your children (distract and) divert you from the remembrance of God. Those who do so, they are the losers.

10. And spend (in God's cause and for the needy) out of whatever We provide for you before death comes to any of you and he says: "My Lord! If only You would grant me respite for a short while, so that I may give alms, and be one of the righteous!"

11. But never will God grant respite to a soul when its appointed term has come. God is fully aware of all that you do.

3. In fact, the hypocrites were expected to come to the Messenger to beg his pardon and ask for God's forgiveness because of their continuous scheming, and their plots that were revealed each time. Not only did they not do this, they even arrogantly refused the call to approach the Messenger, upon him be peace and blessings, so that he might pray to God for their forgiveness.

4. When God's Messenger, upon him be peace and blessings, emigrated to Madīnah, the Arab peoples of al-Aws and al-Khazraj of Madīnah were preparing to crown 'Abdullāh ibn Ubeyy ibn Salūl as their king. So Ibn Ubayy never forgave the Messenger and, though he accepted Islam outwardly, he was always a fierce enemy of the Prophet and Islam. He collaborated with the Makkan polytheists and Madīnan Jews, and tried to bring about dissension among the Muslims. The events described in these verses happened during the return from the military expedition against the Banū Mustaliq in the 5th year of *Hijrah*. Availing himself of a quarrel that had broken out between two Muslims, one from Madīnah and the other from Makkah (an emigrant), when the army had halted halfway for a rest, he tried to instigate the *Anṣār* (Helpers) against the *Muhājirūn* (Emigrants). But the sagacity of the Messenger, who ordered the army to march without halting until they reached Madīnah, was enough to extinguish the fire of dissension before it was kindled.

Verse 8 emphasizes that all glory and real power rest with God and then with the Messenger and the believers because of their faith in and submission to God. So the believers must always seek these with God and by being good, sincere Muslims.

بِسْمِ اللهِ الرَّحْمٰنِ الرَّحِيمِ

(Arabic Qur'anic text of Sūrah 64)

SŪRAH 64

AT-TAGHĀBUN
(GAIN AND LOSS)

Madīnah period

This *sūrah* of 18 verses was revealed in Madīnah. It takes its name from the phrase in verse 19, *yawm at-taghābun* (the day of loss for some and gain for some). The *sūrah* concentrates on faith in God and the Hereafter, doing one's duty to God in reverence for Him, and on sincerity, contentment, and obedience to God, and spending in His cause.

In the Name of God, the All-Merciful, the All-Compassionate.

1. Whatever is in the heavens and whatever is on the earth glorifies God. To Him belongs the sovereignty (absolute ownership and dominion of everything) and for Him are all praise and gratitude; and He has full power over everything.

2. He it is Who has created you, but among you are those who are unbelievers, and among you are those who are believers. God sees well all that you do.[1]

3. He has created the heavens and the earth with truth (meaningfully and for definite purpose, and on solid foundations of truth), and has formed you, and made your forms so well. And to Him is the homecoming.

4. He knows all that is in the heavens and on the earth, and knows all that you keep concealed as well as all that you disclose. God has full knowledge of whatever lies hidden in the bosoms (of His creatures).

5. Have there not come to you the illustrative histories of those who disbelieved before, and therefore tasted the evil results of their deeds? And (in the Hereafter) there is for them a painful punishment.

6. This is because the Messengers (appointed for them) came to them consistently with manifest truths (and clear proofs of their being Messengers), but (consistently) they said, "Shall a mere mortal guide us?", and so they disbelieved and turned away (from the warning and hope offered to them). God was independent (of any need of them: it was they who needed to believe in and obey Him). God is All-Wealthy and Self-Sufficient (on Whom the whole creation is dependent), All-Praiseworthy.

7. Those who disbelieve claim that they will never be raised from the dead. Say: "Yes indeed, by my Lord, you will certainly be raised from the dead, then you will certainly be made to understand all that you did (in the world and called to account for it)." That is easy for God.

8. Believe, then, (O humankind) in God and His Messenger, and the light (i.e. the Qur'ān) that We send down! God is fully aware of all that you do.

9. On the Day when He will assemble you all for the Day of Assembly – that will be the day of loss for some (the unbelievers) and gain for some (the believers). Whoever believes in God and does good, righteous deeds, He will blot out from them their evil deeds (which they sometimes happen to commit), and admit them into Gardens through which rivers flow, therein to abide forever. That is the supreme triumph.

---

1. It is God Who creates everything and every event, including the actions of human beings. Whatever He creates is in fact beautiful in that it is His creation. His creation of humankind is also beautiful. He creates every human being with the capacity and ability to believe, but some humans misuse this capacity and ability, choosing to disbelieve. Since in the world people are judged outwardly according to their verbal profession and actions, some may be regarded and treated as believers although they are inwardly unbelievers. However, God sees fully whatever everybody does and knows them with their inner worlds, and therefore He will judge them as they really are. So the verse contains a warning for the hypocritical ones and calls everybody to sincerity in belief and action.

2. Everything in the world occurs according to certain laws God has established, and whatever a person meets as a consequence of whatever they do is also according to these laws. It is God Who has established and created both the causes and the effects. However, He is never dependent on these laws and, if He so wills, He can create or bring about different things or nothing as a result of the same cause, or He can annul a law for whomever He wills. So, though things usually occur according to certain laws God has established and we should consider these laws in our life, we should never hold back from praying to God because we think that these laws are absolute and whatever we do we cannot escape its consequences. Those who know that God has this power and believe in Him accordingly, or those who believe in God in perception of how He acts, submit to Him wholly and find peace and rest in their hearts in this life. For the same meaning, see 57: 22–23: *No affliction occurs on the earth (such as drought, famine, and earthquakes) or in your own persons (such as disease, damages in your property, and loss of loved ones), but it is recorded in a Book before We bring it into existence – doing so is surely easy for God. So that you may not grieve for what has escaped you, nor exult because of what God has granted you: God does not love anyone proud and boastful.* Also see notes 12 and 13 concerning these verses.

10. But as for those who disbelieve and deny Our Revelations, they will be the companions of the Fire, therein to abide: how evil a destination to arrive at!

11. No affliction befalls except by God's leave. Whoever believes in God (truly and sincerely), He guides his heart (to true knowledge of His eternal Will and how He acts with regard to the life of His creatures, and so leads him to humble submission to Him, and to peace and serenity).[2] God has full knowledge of all things.

12. Obey God and obey the Messenger.[3] If you turn away (from that command, know that) what rests with Our Messenger is only to convey the Message fully and clearly.

13. God, there is no deity but He: so in God let the believers put their trust.

14. O you who believe! Among your spouses and children there may be enemies for you, so beware of them. Yet, if you pardon, forbear, and forgive (their faults toward you and in worldly matters), then (know that) God is All-Forgiving, All-Compassionate.[4]

15. Your worldly possessions and your children are but a source of temptation and trial (for you); and God it is with Whom is a tremendous reward.

16. Keep, then, from disobedience to God in reverence for Him and piety as far as you can,[5] and listen attentively and submit (to His commands), and obey Him, and spend (in His cause and for the needy) as it is to the betterment of your souls. Whoever is guarded against the avarice of his soul, those are they who are truly prosperous.[6]

17. If you lend God a goodly loan,[7] He will increase it manifold to you and will forgive you. God is All-Responsive (to gratitude), All-Clement (forbearing before many of the faults of His servants).

18. (And He is) the Knower of the unseen and the witnessed, the All-Glorious with irresistible might, the All-Wise.

3. The repetition of *obey* in the imperative mood for the Messenger indicates that the Messenger is also authorized to command or forbid, and that Muslims must do what he says.

Obedience to God means unconditional obedience to what has been revealed in the Qur'ān. Obedience to the Messenger means following his way of life (Sunnah) as closely as possible and obeying what has been enjoined and prohibited in the Qur'ān and by the Messenger. The Sunnah is a comprehensively detailed account of the life of God's Messenger, who said: "Take care! I have been given the Book and its like [i.e. my Sunnah] together with it" (Abū Dāwūd, "Sunnah," 5).

The Sunnah defines what is stated in general terms by referring to particular instances, and it defines the general principle underlying statements in the Qur'an that are in themselves specific and particular. Also, the Sunnah (like the Qur'ān which it embodies) is also concerned with moral guidance, so the Sunnah provides inspiration and the horizons for moral and spiritual instruction in all spheres of life, as well as providing the inspiration and horizons (limits) within which Islamic legislation may be affected. Everything it teaches, every legal ruling, and every piece of moral instruction, derived from the Sunnah, remains within the framework, the spirit, the "color" and temperament, of the Qur'ān.

As stated in 8: 20 as well, Muslims must not turn away from the Messenger. Therefore, willful disobedience to the Sunnah, even belittling or criticizing it, is to approach heresy or apostasy.

4. Spouses are dutiful toward each other, and parents have intrinsic love for and duties toward their children. However, the love of spouses for each other and the love of parents for their children should be regulated according to the commandments of the Religion. Love of family may sometimes bar a man from his religious duties or cause him to behave toward them and work for them and their future without considering their duties toward God and their afterlife. Whereas true love necessitates that parents should first consider the afterlife and religious duties of their children. They should consider their worldly welfare within the framework of the Religion. Unfortunately, many spouses and parents neglect this cardinal principle and they misuse their love and compassion for each other and for their children. In addition to this, some spouses and children may put pressure upon each other and their parents to act without considering the religious commandments and cause each other or themselves to lose in the Hereafter. This is in fact enmity. So the Qur'ān draws the attention of spouses to this fact and warns them. However, despite such enmity, parents should be careful, patient, and tolerant in their mutual relations and their approach to the conduct of their children. They can be forbearing and pardon their mutual faults toward each other and the faults of their children toward themselves. (This is what is expected from parents, but children must be extremely careful about observing the rights of their parents.) They should also overlook any faults concerning worldly matters and be able to act as educators concerning religious matters. They should always give precedence to religious matters over worldly ones.

The next verse concisely expresses this truth.

5. This statement is not contradictory with *Keep from disobedience to God in reverent piety with all the reverence that is due to Him* (3: 102), nor does the former abrogate the latter. God should be revered and obeyed as He should because His position as God requires this. In fact, every position requires respect and obedience to the extent of its greatness. However, each human being has a capacity for respect and obedience particular to them; they cannot go beyond this. But as we cannot know the limits of our capacity, we must try to revere and obey God as His being God requires us to do to the utmost of our capacity.

6. This verse explains how people can be saved from the enmity of their spouses or children and be successful in the trial of their worldly possessions and children.

7. See *sūrah* 57: 11, note 7.

الجزء الثامن والعشرون   557

بِسْمِ اللَّهِ الرَّحْمَٰنِ الرَّحِيمِ

يَٰٓأَيُّهَا ٱلنَّبِيُّ إِذَا طَلَّقْتُمُ ٱلنِّسَآءَ فَطَلِّقُوهُنَّ لِعِدَّتِهِنَّ وَأَحْصُوا۟ ٱلْعِدَّةَ وَٱتَّقُوا۟ ٱللَّهَ رَبَّكُمْ لَا تُخْرِجُوهُنَّ مِنۢ بُيُوتِهِنَّ وَلَا يَخْرُجْنَ إِلَّآ أَن يَأْتِينَ بِفَٰحِشَةٍ مُّبَيِّنَةٍ وَتِلْكَ حُدُودُ ٱللَّهِ وَمَن يَتَعَدَّ حُدُودَ ٱللَّهِ فَقَدْ ظَلَمَ نَفْسَهُۥ لَا تَدْرِى لَعَلَّ ٱللَّهَ يُحْدِثُ بَعْدَ ذَٰلِكَ أَمْرًا ۝ فَإِذَا بَلَغْنَ أَجَلَهُنَّ فَأَمْسِكُوهُنَّ بِمَعْرُوفٍ أَوْ فَارِقُوهُنَّ بِمَعْرُوفٍ وَأَشْهِدُوا۟ ذَوَىْ عَدْلٍ مِّنكُمْ وَأَقِيمُوا۟ ٱلشَّهَٰدَةَ لِلَّهِ ذَٰلِكُمْ يُوعَظُ بِهِۦ مَن كَانَ يُؤْمِنُ بِٱللَّهِ وَٱلْيَوْمِ ٱلْءَاخِرِ وَمَن يَتَّقِ ٱللَّهَ يَجْعَل لَّهُۥ مَخْرَجًا ۝ وَيَرْزُقْهُ مِنْ حَيْثُ لَا يَحْتَسِبُ وَمَن يَتَوَكَّلْ عَلَى ٱللَّهِ فَهُوَ حَسْبُهُۥٓ إِنَّ ٱللَّهَ بَٰلِغُ أَمْرِهِۦ قَدْ جَعَلَ ٱللَّهُ لِكُلِّ شَىْءٍ قَدْرًا ۝ وَٱلَّٰٓـِٔى يَئِسْنَ مِنَ ٱلْمَحِيضِ مِن نِّسَآئِكُمْ إِنِ ٱرْتَبْتُمْ فَعِدَّتُهُنَّ ثَلَٰثَةُ أَشْهُرٍ وَٱلَّٰٓـِٔى لَمْ يَحِضْنَ وَأُو۟لَٰتُ ٱلْأَحْمَالِ أَجَلُهُنَّ أَن يَضَعْنَ حَمْلَهُنَّ وَمَن يَتَّقِ ٱللَّهَ يَجْعَل لَّهُۥ مِنْ أَمْرِهِۦ يُسْرًا ۝ ذَٰلِكَ أَمْرُ ٱللَّهِ أَنزَلَهُۥٓ إِلَيْكُمْ وَمَن يَتَّقِ ٱللَّهَ يُكَفِّرْ عَنْهُ سَيِّـَٔاتِهِۦ وَيُعْظِمْ لَهُۥٓ أَجْرًا ۝

---◆---

SŪRAH 65

AT-TALĀQ (DIVORCE)

Madīnah period

This *sūrah* of 12 verses was revealed in Madīnah. It takes its name from its subject matter as well as from the first verse, where the verb *TalLaQa* ("to divorce") occurs. It contains rules additional to those mentioned in *Sūrat al-Baqarah* concerning divorce, the waiting period, alimony, and habitation.

In the Name of God, the All-Merciful, the All-Compassionate.

1. O (most illustrious) Prophet![1] When you (Muslims) intend to divorce women, divorce them considering their waiting-period

(as appointed in Law), and reckon the period (with due care), keeping from disobedience to God, your Lord, in reverence for Him and piety. (While the divorce is taking effect, during their waiting-period) do not drive them out from their houses (where they have lived with their husbands), nor shall they themselves leave, except in case they have committed an open indecency.[2] These are the bounds set by God. Whoever exceeds the bounds set by God has surely wronged his own self. You do not know: it may be that afterward God will enable some new situation (to come about between the concerned parties).[3]

2. Then, when they reach the end of their waiting-term, either retain them in a fair manner and in observance of their rights, or (the waiting-period having ended) part with them in a fair manner and in observance of their rights. And (as the commended way, in either case) call upon two (Muslim) men of probity from among you as witnesses, and establish the testimony for God (with due consciousness of your responsibility to Him). Anyone who believes in God and the Last Day is exhorted to act so. Whoever keeps from disobedience to God in reverence for Him and piety, He enables a way out for him (of every difficulty),

3. And provides for him from where he does not reckon. Whoever puts his trust in God, He is sufficient for him (for all his needs). God surely executes what He decrees; assuredly God has appointed a measure for everything.[4]

4. Those of your women who have passed the age of monthly courses (or those who for some reason do not have monthly periods) – if you are in uncertainty about it – their waiting-period is three (lunar) months. As for the women who are pregnant (whether divorced or widows), their

waiting-period is until they deliver their burden. Whoever keeps from disobedience to God in reverence for Him and piety, He makes his affair easy for him.

5. All that (which has been said) is God's commandment which He has sent down to you. Whoever keeps from disobedience to God in reverence for Him and piety, He blots out from him his evil deeds, and vastly enlarges reward for him.[5]

---

1. While all the other Prophets are mentioned in the Qur'ān with their names, the Qur'ān usually addresses God's Messenger by his mission. This is done in order to refer to the fact that his mission has the greatest importance and that his position is unequaled among the Prophets. According to a rule of Arabic grammar, mentioning something (a position, reputation, or an attribute) without specifying to whom it belongs, means that he who possesses this possesses it in the greatest degree. Therefore, this implies that God's Messenger (the Prophet Muḥammad), upon him be peace and blessings, is the greatest representative of the office of Prophethood.

2. Islam orders that if a man wishes to divorce his wife he should do so during the time when she is not in the course of a monthly period and he has had no intercourse with her. The wife is then to wait for three monthly courses, during which the husband is obliged to provide for her and cannot force her to leave the home. They can turn to each other during this period. If they do so, they do not have to renew the marriage contract. If they turn to each other after the end of this period, they have to renew it. This divorce can occur for a second time, but if it is repeated for the third time, they can no longer turn to each other, unless the woman marries another man and divorces him or is divorced by him. For other ordinances concern-

ing divorce, see *sūrah* 2: 228–232, 234, notes 152–154; *sūrah* 33: 49, note 23.

3. That is, there may be reconciliation between the divorced spouses and they may reassume their marital relations before the final divorce occurs. This statement is a warning to observe the bounds set by God. If we observe them strictly, God may bring about a new thing that will please us. So we must submit to God and carry out His orders without transgressing the limits set by Him.

4. That is, God has established certain causes, conditions, and limits, and a certain frame and therefore a certain result for everything. Nothing occurs beyond the limits He has established.

5. Blotting out evil deeds means forgiving the minor sins that may have been committed in obeying God's commandments. It is as stated in: *If you avoid the major sins which you have been forbidden, We will blot out from you your minor evil deeds and make you enter by a noble entrance (to an abode of glory)* (4: 31). So it may be inferred that disobedience to the orders and prohibitions of the Qur'ān concerning divorce and the waiting-period in these verses, within the framework of *taqwā* (piety and reverence for God), is a major sin. It may also be inferred that a believer should be careful concerning all of God's commandments (orders and prohibitions).

558

سُورَةُ الطَّلَاقِ   ٥٥٨

أَسْكِنُوهُنَّ مِنْ حَيْثُ سَكَنتُم مِّن وُجْدِكُمْ وَلَا تُضَآرُّوهُنَّ لِتُضَيِّقُوا
عَلَيْهِنَّ وَإِن كُنَّ أُوْلَاتِ حَمْلٍ فَأَنفِقُوا عَلَيْهِنَّ حَتَّى يَضَعْنَ حَمْلَهُنَّ
فَإِنْ أَرْضَعْنَ لَكُمْ فَـَٔاتُوهُنَّ أُجُورَهُنَّ وَأْتَمِرُوا بَيْنَكُم بِمَعْرُوفٍ
وَإِن تَعَاسَرْتُمْ فَسَتُرْضِعُ لَهُ أُخْرَى ۞ لِيُنفِقْ ذُو سَعَةٍ مِّن
سَعَتِهِ وَمَن قُدِرَ عَلَيْهِ رِزْقُهُ فَلْيُنفِقْ مِمَّآ ءَاتَىٰهُ اللَّهُ لَا يُكَلِّفُ اللَّهُ
نَفْسًا إِلَّا مَآ ءَاتَىٰهَا سَيَجْعَلُ اللَّهُ بَعْدَ عُسْرٍ يُسْرًا ۞ وَكَأَيِّن مِّن قَرْيَةٍ
عَتَتْ عَنْ أَمْرِ رَبِّهَا وَرُسُلِهِ فَحَاسَبْنَٰهَا حِسَابًا شَدِيدًا وَعَذَّبْنَٰهَا عَذَابًا
نُّكْرًا ۞ فَذَاقَتْ وَبَالَ أَمْرِهَا وَكَانَ عَٰقِبَةُ أَمْرِهَا خُسْرًا ۞ أَعَدَّ اللَّهُ
لَهُمْ عَذَابًا شَدِيدًا فَاتَّقُوا اللَّهَ يَٰٓأُوْلِي الْأَلْبَٰبِ الَّذِينَ ءَامَنُوا قَدْ أَنزَلَ اللَّهُ
إِلَيْكُمْ ذِكْرًا ۞ رَّسُولًا يَتْلُوا عَلَيْكُمْ ءَايَٰتِ اللَّهِ مُبَيِّنَٰتٍ لِّيُخْرِجَ
الَّذِينَ ءَامَنُوا وَعَمِلُوا الصَّٰلِحَٰتِ مِنَ الظُّلُمَٰتِ إِلَى النُّورِ وَمَن يُؤْمِنۢ بِاللَّهِ
وَيَعْمَلْ صَٰلِحًا يُدْخِلْهُ جَنَّٰتٍ تَجْرِي مِن تَحْتِهَا الْأَنْهَٰرُ خَٰلِدِينَ
فِيهَآ أَبَدًا قَدْ أَحْسَنَ اللَّهُ لَهُ رِزْقًا ۞ اللَّهُ الَّذِي خَلَقَ سَبْعَ
سَمَٰوَٰتٍ وَمِنَ الْأَرْضِ مِثْلَهُنَّ يَتَنَزَّلُ الْأَمْرُ بَيْنَهُنَّ لِتَعْلَمُوٓا أَنَّ اللَّهَ
عَلَىٰ كُلِّ شَيْءٍ قَدِيرٌ وَأَنَّ اللَّهَ قَدْ أَحَاطَ بِكُلِّ شَيْءٍ عِلْمًا ۞

6. House them (the divorced women during their waiting-period in a part of the house) where you dwell and provide for them, according to your means; and do not harass them so as to straiten conditions for them (thus forcing them to leave). If they are pregnant, maintain them until they deliver their burden; and if (after delivery and the waiting-period has ended) they suckle (the baby) for you, give them their due payment. Take counsel with each other (about the matter and payment for suckling) according to customary good and religiously approvable practice. If you find yourselves making difficulties (and so unable to come to an agreement), then let another (woman) suckle (the baby) on behalf of him (the baby's father, who must settle the expense).

7. Let him who has abundant means spend accordingly; and whoever is granted his provision in (narrower) measure, let him spend out of what God has granted him. God does not charge a soul with a duty except in what He has (already) granted it (of capacity to discharge that duty). God will bring about, after hardship, ease.

8. How many a township has turned in arrogance from the commandment of its Lord and His Messengers, and so We called them to account with a severe reckoning (by exposing them to awesome calamities), and punished them with a dire punishment.[6]

9. So they tasted the evil result of their own doings and the outcome of their doings was ruin.

10. God has prepared for them a severe punishment (in addition, in the Hereafter). So keep from disobedience to God in reverence for Him and piety to deserve His protection, O people of discernment who have believed! Indeed God has sent down to you a Reminder (this Book of guidance to what is true, instructing you in what is for your good and what is against it).

11. (And as its embodiment, He has also sent you) a Messenger reciting (and so conveying) to you God's signs and Revelations which show the truth clearly and illuminate your way, so that He may lead you out of all kinds of darkness into the light, and keep you firm therein. Whoever (truly and sincerely) believes in God and does good, righteous deeds, He will admit him into Gardens through which rivers flow, therein to abide forever. God has indeed granted him an excellent provision (as faith and good deeds in this world and Paradise in the Hereafter).

12. God is He Who has created seven heavens and of the earth the like of them; His commands (concerning the creation and its operation, and the life of the inhabitants of the heavens and earth) descend through them,[7] so that you may know for certain that surely God has full power over everything, and that God indeed encompasses all things in (His) Knowledge.

---

6. This, as well as the following verse, is, in one respect, the summation of what befell the Jews, Christians, and Muslims when they broke with God's commandments in their daily lives.

7. The earth and the heavens are like two countries under one government that conduct important relations and transactions. For example, *He directs the affair from heaven to the earth; then the affair ascends to Him in a day the measure of which is a thousand years of what you reckon* (32: 5; and see note 4). Moreover, the earth needs the light, heat, blessings, and forms of mercy (like rain) sent from the heavens. Also, as all Revealed religions confirm, angels and spirit beings descend to the earth for certain purposes. Thus, we may deduce that the inhabitants of the earth can ascend to the heavens.

People can travel to the heavens via their mind, vision, and imagination. Freed from or purified of their carnal and material being's gross heaviness, the spirits of Prophets and saints travel in such realms; our Prophet traveled through all the realms of the heavens with his spirit and body, which gained the refinement of spirit; this is what we call the Ascension (*Miʿrāj*); and God lifted up Jesus with both his spirit and body to the heaven. The spirits of ordinary people do so after death, and then are returned to the intermediate realm (between this world and the next). Since those who are "lightened" and have acquired "subtlety" and spiritual refinement travel there, certain inhabitants of the earth may go to the heavens if they are clothed in an "ideal" body, energetic envelope, or immaterial body or form, and are light and subtle like spirits. And also humankind can physically travel to the heaven.

The earth, despite its small size and insignificance when compared with the heavens, is the heart and center of the universe with respect to its meaning and art, for it is our cradle and dwelling place. Moreover, it exhibits all the miracles of the Divine Names and concentrates and reflects God's infinite activity as the Master, Sustainer, Trainer, and Ruler of all beings. It is also the center and pivot of the endless Divine creativity displayed in infinite liberality, particularly in the numerous small plant and animal species, as well as in the microcosm of samples of all that is found in the Hereafter's truly vast worlds: the speedily operating workshop for eternal textiles, the fast-changing place of copies of eternal scenes, and the narrow, temporary field and tillage that rapidly produces seeds for the permanent Gardens (in the Hereafter).

Due to this immaterial greatness and importance with respect to art, the wise Qur'ān puts the earth on a par with the heavens, although it is like the tiny fruit of a huge tree when compared with the heavens. It places the earth on one side of the scales and the heavens on the other, and repeatedly says, the "Lord of the heavens and the earth" (mentioning both together).

SŪRAH 66

AT-TAḤRĪM (PROHIBITION)

Madīnah period

Revealed in Madīnah seven or eight years after the *Hijrah*, this *sūrah* of 12 verses takes its name from the infinitive form of the verb *ḤarRaMa* (forbid, make something unlawful) that occurs in the first verse. It warns against any disrespect toward God's Messenger, upon him be peace and blessings, and that righteousness lies not in belonging to a certain family but in one's faith and good deeds. It also calls believers to repentance for their misdeeds.

In the Name of God, the All-Merciful, the All-Compassionate.

1. O (most illustrious) Prophet! Why do you forbid (yourself) what God has made lawful to you? You seek to please your wives.[1] And God is All-Forgiving, All-Compassionate.

2. God has already decreed for you (O believers) on the breaking of your oaths (of not fulfilling what is not just and right, and the expiation thereof).[2] God is your Guardian, and He is the All-Knowing, the All-Wise.

3. (It so happened that) the Prophet confided something to one of his wives, and when she divulged it (to another), and God acquainted him of it, he made known part of it, and missed out part. And when he informed her of it, she asked: "Who has told you this?" He said: "He informed me Who is the All-Knowing, the All-Aware."[3]

4. If you two (wives of the Prophet) turn to God in repentance (then that is indeed what you should do); for the hearts of both of you swerved (from what is right). But if you back each other up against him, (be mindful that) God Himself is His Guardian, and that Gabriel, and the righteous ones among the believers, and all the angels besides, are his helpers.[4]

5. It may happen that his Lord, if he should divorce you (O wives of the Prophet), will give him in your place wives better than you – submissive to God (*muslimah*), true in faith (*mu'minah*), devout in obedience to God, penitent, dedicated to worship and fasting – widows or virgins.[5]

6. O you who believe! Guard yourselves and your families (through the enabling discipline of Islamic faith and worship) against a Fire whose fuel is human beings and stones. Over it are angels stern and strict (in executing the command to punish), who do not disobey God in whatever He commands them, and carry out what they are commanded (to carry out).

7. "O you who disbelieve! Do not offer excuses for yourselves this Day! You are only being recompensed for what you used to do (in the world)."[6]

1 Although there are some reports about what the Messenger had forbidden himself, that God had made lawful to him, the gist is as follows:

The Messenger was extremely kind. He was particularly kind toward his wives. In order not to cause any trouble for anybody, he had to bear many hardships. God established exceptional rules for him, particularly in relation to his family life, so that there would not be any undue problems for him (in fulfilling his mission) (33: 50). Therefore, the statement *Why do you forbid (yourself) what God has made lawful to you?* expresses a consolatory warning. It is interesting that both this verse and verse 33: 50, which contains exceptional rules for the Messenger, end with the phrase, *God is All-Forgiving, All-Compassionate.* This means that God had willed ease for him and was particularly compassionate toward him.

2. See *sūrah* 2: 224–225; 5: 89.

3. This explicitly shows that the Revelations that the Messenger received did not consist only of what is in the Qur'ān. In addition to the Qur'ān, he received many other Revelations, and declared: "Take care! I have been given the Book and its like together with it" (Abū Dāwūd, "Sunnah," 5).

4. This verse teaches us four important things:

*   Doing something which will affront the Messenger causes one's heart to swerve, as declared in 61: 5: *And (remember) when Moses said to his people: "O my people! Why do you affront me while you know indeed that I am the Messenger of God sent to you?" And so, when they swerved from the right way, God made their hearts swerve from the truth. God does not guide the transgressing people.*

*   Any disloyalty from inside a home or country is usually more dangerous than that from outside.

*   Whatever scheme is made against God's Messenger, God will absolutely protect him; Gabriel, who brings him God's Revelation, those who are advanced in righteousness among the believers, and all other angels are also his helpers. So no one can cause any harm to him or his mission.

*   Even being a wife of a Prophet is not enough to save one unless one believes and does good deeds. Rather, according to the rule, responsibility is proportionate to authority or blessing; the greater the favor God blesses one with, the greater the responsibility. (Also see 33: 29–32.)

5. This is the second warning in the Qur'ān to the wives of God's Messenger (for the first one, see 33: 29–33, and for the Messenger's relationship with his wives, see 33, note 16). This verse does not mean that his wives did not have the praiseworthy qualities mentioned. Rather, it reminds that as both Muslim women and especially as the wives of the Messenger, who should set an example for all other believing women, they should have these qualities in the highest degree and retain them.

6. This verse, which addresses the unbelievers, contains a severe warning for the Muslims also. It warns that any disobedience to God and His Messenger and doing things that will affront them may – God forbid! – drive them to unbelief and therefore to the Fire in the Hereafter. So, they must also be on the alert against sins.

560   سُوۡرَةُ التَّحۡرِیمِ   ٥٦

يَـٰٓأَيُّهَا الَّذِينَ ءَامَنُوا تُوبُوٓا إِلَى اللَّهِ تَوۡبَةً نَّصُوحًا عَسَىٰ رَبُّكُمۡ
أَن يُكَفِّرَ عَنكُمۡ سَيِّـَٔاتِكُمۡ وَيُدۡخِلَكُمۡ جَنَّـٰتٍ تَجۡرِى مِن
تَحۡتِهَا الۡأَنۡهَـٰرُ يَوۡمَ لَا يُخۡزِى اللَّهُ النَّبِىَّ وَالَّذِينَ ءَامَنُوا مَعَهُۥ
نُورُهُمۡ يَسۡعَىٰ بَيۡنَ أَيۡدِيهِمۡ وَبِأَيۡمَـٰنِهِمۡ يَقُولُونَ رَبَّنَآ
أَتۡمِمۡ لَنَا نُورَنَا وَاغۡفِرۡ لَنَآ إِنَّكَ عَلَىٰ كُلِّ شَىۡءٍ قَدِيرٌ ۝ يَـٰٓأَيُّهَا
النَّبِىُّ جَـٰهِدِ الۡكُفَّارَ وَالۡمُنَـٰفِقِينَ وَاغۡلُظۡ عَلَيۡهِمۡ وَمَأۡوَىٰهُمۡ
جَهَنَّمُ وَبِئۡسَ الۡمَصِيرُ ۝ ضَرَبَ اللَّهُ مَثَلًا لِّلَّذِينَ كَفَرُوا
امۡرَأَتَ نُوحٍ وَامۡرَأَتَ لُوطٍ كَانَتَا تَحۡتَ عَبۡدَيۡنِ مِنۡ
عِبَادِنَا صَـٰلِحَيۡنِ فَخَانَتَاهُمَا فَلَمۡ يُغۡنِيَا عَنۡهُمَا مِنَ اللَّهِ
شَيۡـًٔا وَقِيلَ ادۡخُلَا النَّارَ مَعَ الدَّاخِلِينَ ۝ وَضَرَبَ اللَّهُ
مَثَلًا لِّلَّذِينَ ءَامَنُوا امۡرَأَتَ فِرۡعَوۡنَ إِذۡ قَالَتۡ رَبِّ
ابۡنِ لِى عِندَكَ بَيۡتًا فِى الۡجَنَّةِ وَنَجِّنِى مِن فِرۡعَوۡنَ وَعَمَلِهِۦ
وَنَجِّنِى مِنَ الۡقَوۡمِ الظَّـٰلِمِينَ ۝ وَمَرۡيَمَ ابۡنَتَ عِمۡرَٰنَ الَّتِىٓ
أَحۡصَنَتۡ فَرۡجَهَا فَنَفَخۡنَا فِيهِ مِن رُّوحِنَا وَصَدَّقَتۡ
بِكَلِمَـٰتِ رَبِّهَا وَكُتُبِهِۦ وَكَانَتۡ مِنَ الۡقَـٰنِتِينَ ۝

---

8. O you who believe! Turn to God in sincere and reforming repentance.[7] It is hoped[8] that your Lord will blot your evil deeds from you and admit you into Gardens through which rivers flow, on a Day when God will not disgrace nor disappoint the Prophet and those who believe in his company. Their (the believers') light will shine and spread before them and on their right hands, as they are saying: "Our Lord! Perfect our light (by Your grace so that we may reach Paradise), and forgive us.[9] Surely You have full power over everything!"

9. O Prophet! Strive hard against the unbelievers and the hypocrites (as occasion and conditions require), and be stern against them.[10] Their final refuge is Hell: how evil a destination to arrive at!

10. God presents the wife of Noah and the wife of Lot as an example for those who disbelieve. They were married to two of Our righteous servants yet betrayed them (by rejecting the Messages they brought from God and collaborating with the unbelievers). But they (their husbands) availed them nothing against God and it was said to them: "Enter the Fire with all those who enter it!"[11]

11. And God presents the wife of the Pharaoh as an example for those who believe. She prayed: "My Lord! Build for me a home in Paradise in nearness to You, and keep and save me from the Pharaoh and his conduct, and save me from the wrong-doing people."[12]

12. And also Mary, the daughter of 'Imrān,[13] who kept herself chaste (body and soul), so We breathed into it out of Our Spirit,[14] and who affirmed the truth of the words of her Lord (His Revelations – commandments, promises and warnings – to His Messengers), and His Books, and she was of those devoutly obedient to God.

7. 'Ali, the Prophet's cousin and son-in-law and the fourth Caliph, describes a sincere, reforming repentance as follows:

In order that your repentance can be a sincere, reforming, and valid one, you should (1) sincerely feel remorse for the sin you have committed, (2) fulfill all the obligatory religious duties and make up the missed ones, (3) return any right you have usurped to its owner, (4) beg the pardon of those you have offended, (5) resolve not to commit again the sin you have committed, and (6) make your carnal soul taste the difficulty of obedience to God as you have caused it to taste the pleasure of sinning (Yazır, Zamakhsharī).

8. God is never obliged to accept repentance, but a repentant one should sincerely hope that He will accept it and forgive them.

9. This means that human beings are fallible and except for the Prophets, almost everyone goes to the other world with some sins. In addition, their good deeds will not be enough for them to provide the light that they will need in order to reach Paradise from the very moment they will be resurrected. So they pray to God to complete their light purely out of His grace (also see *sūrah* 57: 12, 19). They will also need forgiveness in order to be saved from the darkness of their sins. The hypocrites will not be able to advance toward Paradise and will be enveloped by the darkness of their hypocrisy (57: 13).

10. For an explanation, see *sūrah* 9: 73, note 15; 123, note 28.

11. This is the final judgment against them and also a reference to their condition in the grave.

12. Some reports say that the name of the Pharaoh's wife was Āsyā. The prayer the Qur'ān quotes from her explains her sincere and deeply established faith in and devotion to God, and her keeping away from the wrongdoings of the Pharaoh and the rebellion of his people against God. Some interpreters infer from "his deeds" that God also saved her from intercourse with the Pharaoh. The Pharaoh may have been (sexually) impotent and had no offspring, as many Pharaoh-like tyrants have been throughout history. This carries the implication that their tyrannical rule will not last long.

13. See *sūrah* 3: 33–34, note 7.

14. God not only breathed into Mary to conceive of Jesus a "spirit" from Him, but also breathed it into the "body" He fashioned out of clay so that Adam might come to the world. For the meaning of God's breathing out of His Spirit, see 4: 171, note 34; 15: 29, note 8. Even though the verse attributes the breathing into Mary to God, this is because it is God Who creates every act of every being. In fact, it was the Archangel Gabriel or another, angel-like Spirit (see 19: 17, note 3).

SŪRAH 67

AL-MULK
(THE SOVEREIGNTY)

Makkah period

This *sūrah* of 30 verses was revealed in Makkah. It derives its name from the first verse where the word *al-mulk* (sovereignty) occurs. The basic points the *sūrah* deals with are the testimony of the universe to God's Oneness, the end of the unbelievers who pay no heed to God's Messages, God's favors to humankind, and human dependence on God in both worlds.

In the Name of God, the All-Merciful, the All-Compassionate.

1. Blessed and Supreme is He in Whose Hand is the Sovereignty; and He has full power over everything.

2. He Who has created death and life,[1] so that He may try you (and demonstrate to yourselves) which of you is better in deeds; and He is the All-Glorious with irresistible might (Whose will none can frustrate), the All-Forgiving (Who forgives many of His servants' sins so that they learn from being tested).

3. He Who has created seven heavens[2] in harmony. You do not see any fault or incongruity in the creation of the All-Merciful. Look yet again: can you see any rifts?

4. Then look again and yet again, (and however often you do so, with whatever instruments to aid your looking) your sight will fall back to you dazzled (by the splendor of God's creation), and awed and weakened (being unable to discern any flaw to support any excuse for claiming that there could be any sharing in the dominion of the universe).[3]

5. And, indeed, We have adorned the lowest heaven (the heaven of the world) with lamps (stars), and made (out of) them missiles to drive away devils; and for them We have prepared (in the Hereafter) the punishment of the Blaze.[4]

6. And also for those who disbelieve in their Lord is the punishment of Hell. How evil a destination to arrive at!

7. When they are cast into it, they will hear its raucous breath (by which they are sucked in) as it boils up,

8. Almost bursting with fury. Every time a group is cast into it,[5] its keepers will ask them: "Did no warner ever come to you?"

9. They will say: "Yes, indeed, a warner came to us but we denied (him) and said (to him): "God has never sent down anything, you are only in a great error."

10. They will say: "If only we had listened (to him) or reasoned (and distinguished what was to our benefit from what was to our harm, and acted accordingly), we

would not (now) be among the companions of the Blaze."

11. Thus will they acknowledge their sins, but God's mercy will (then) be far from the companions of the Blaze!

12. As for those who stand in awe of their Lord though unseen (beyond their perception), for them there is forgiveness (to bring unforeseen blessings), and a great reward.

---

1. Death is not the end of a life or the removal of life from living things or beings. Rather it is something that is created, like life. God creates death in a living thing or being and so that thing or being dies. Since God's creation is at all times beautiful, death is also beautiful. This is because all human beings have an intrinsic feeling of eternity, and so feel imprisoned in the narrow confines of the material world and yearn for eternity. Whoever is aware of their conscious nature will hear it pronouncing eternity, over and over again. If we were given the whole universe, we would still hunger for the eternal life for which we have been created. This natural inclination toward eternal happiness comes from an objective reality: the existence of eternal life and our desire for it. Death is the door that opens on eternity.

Those who believe and live righteous lives are greeted with opened windows from the places reserved for them in Paradise. The Prophet Muḥammad, upon him be peace and blessings, stated that the souls of the righteous are drawn out as gently as flowing water from a pitcher. Better than that, martyrs do not feel the agony of death and do not even know that they are dead. Instead, they consider themselves as being transferred to a better world and enjoy perfect happiness.

Although death seems to bring decomposition, extinguish life, and destroy pleasure, in fact it represents a Divine discharge from the heavy duties of worldly life. It is no more than a change of residence, a transference of the body, an invitation to and the beginning of everlasting life. It releases us from the hardships of this worldly life, which is a turbulent, suffocating, narrow dungeon that gradually becomes harder with old age and illness, and admits us to the infinitely wide circle of the mercy of Eternal, Beloved One. There we may enjoy the everlasting company of our beloved ones and the consolation of a happy, eternal life.

The world is continually enlivened through acts of creation and death. Death leads to a more perfect life. The dying of plants, the simplest level of life, proves itself a work of Divine artistry, like their lives, but one that is more perfect and better designed. When the seed of a fruit dies in the soil, it seems to decompose and rot away. But in reality, it undergoes a perfect chemical process, passing through predetermined stages of re-formation, and ultimately grows again into an elaborate, new tree. So a seed's death is really the beginning of a new tree, a new, more perfect and elaborate life. Since the death of fruit, vegetables, and meat in our stomachs causes them to rise to the degree of human life, in this sense their death can be regarded as more perfect than their lives. Since the dying of plants is so perfect and serves so great a purpose, our deaths, given that we are the highest form of life, must be much more perfect and serve a still greater purpose. Once we have gone underground, we certainly will be brought into eternal life.

2. See *sūrah* 2: 29, note 28.

3. The universe is like a magnificent palace, a well-ordered factory, a well-planned city, all of whose elements or parts are interrelated with one another and with the whole of it, all at the same time, and which work together for great purposes. Even over long distances, elements hasten to help each other when needed and do not get lost. For example, the sun and the moon, day and night, and summer and winter work with plants to help animals and to help convey their food to them, which they take from the treasury of Mercy. Animals hasten to help human beings. For example, honeybees and silkworms take honey and silk from the treasury of the All-Merciful and prepare them for the use of humankind. Particles of soil, air, and water help fruit and vegetation, each of which has a differ-

ent taste and quality of nourishment. In turn, they help the body's cells in perfect orderliness and for great purposes.

This perfect, purposeful, and well-arranged mutual helping is manifested by all of those things, especially inanimate objects. It is also an evident proof and clear argument that they are servants of an All-Wise Sustainer, workers controlled by a Munificent Manager, who all work by His command and leave, and by His Power and Wisdom.

On the surface of this planet, we observe acts of ever-original and purposeful creation. These occur in infinite abundance together with beautiful and perfect artistry; with absolute ease and in perfect order and arrangement; at incredible speed with no loss of proportion, firmness, or substantiality; and in an infinite distribution of species together with each individual's infinite beauty. These acts occur with the greatest economy or lowest cost imaginable, yet every individual is priceless, distinguished perfectly from everything else while having the highest correspondence and similarity between and among species, despite the vast distances of time and space. They are in balance with an absolute variety, a perfect individualization of characters and features, though generated from similar or even the same materials, structural principles, and organization. Each thing is enough to manifest the stamp of the One and Single Creator and Lord. Perfect artistry despite abundance, perfect order despite absolute ease, perfect measure, proportion, and firmness despite incredible speed, perfect individualization despite world-wide distribution, the highest price and value despite the greatest economy, perfect distinction despite absolute integration and similarity – all point to the One, Single Creator and Lord, Who has absolute Will, Power, and Knowledge (*Mathnawī an-Nūriyah*, 51–52).

4. As stated in *sūrah* 65, note 7, the earth and the heavens are interconnected like two countries under one government, and there are journeys between them. Important necessities for the earth are sent from the heavens, pure spirits travel to the heavens, and evil spirits, in imitation of pure ones, attempt to travel to the heavenly abode. Physically, these are subtle beings made of smokeless fire. However, they

will certainly be repulsed and repelled, for by nature they are evil and unclean. As the silence and tranquility, the order and serene regularity of the heavens, and their vastness and radiance show, their inhabitants are not like those of the earth; they are all obedient to God and do whatever He commands them. There is nothing to cause quarrels or disputes among them because they are innocent, their realm is vast, their nature is pure, and their stations are fixed. So when devils or evil spiritual beings attempt to ascend to the heavens, the pure inhabitants there are mobilized to repel them.

Without a doubt, there must be a sign or reflection in the visible, material world of this important interaction and contest. For the wisdom of the sovereignty of Divine Lordship requires that the Lord should put a sign, an indication, for conscious beings, particularly for humankind, whose most important duty is observing, witnessing, supervising, and acting as a herald to His significant disposals in the realm of the Unseen. This is just as He has made the rain and the sun's heat a sign for them to explain, in physical terms, His countless miracles in spring, and has also made apparent (natural) causes as the indications of the wonders of His art, so that He may call the inhabitants of the visible, material world to witness them, indeed to attract the attentive gaze of all the inhabitants of the vast heavens and the earth to that amazing exhibition. That is, He displays the vast heavens as a castle or a city arrayed with towers on which sentries are posted, so that those inhabitants of the heavens and earth may reflect on the majesty of His Lordship.

Since wisdom requires the announcement of this elevated contest, there will surely be a sign for it. However, other than the fact that some stars are being used as "missiles" against the devils, no event among those of the atmosphere and heavens seems to be appropriate to this announcement. For it is evident how suitable these stellar events are for the repulsion of the devils, events that resemble missiles and rockets fired from the formidable bastions of high castles. Furthermore, unlike other events that take place in the heavens, no other function is known for such stellar events. In addition, this function has been widely recognized since the time of Adam, and witnessed by those who know the reality of things and events.

Like angels and other creatures, there are also many different varieties of stars. Some are extremely small, and some are extremely large. Everything that shines in the sky can be called a star. One sort of star is that which the Majestic Creator, the Gracious Maker, has created as a sort of jewel on the face of the sky or like the shining fruit of a vast tree. He has also made them places of excursion or mounts or dwelling-places for His angels. He has made one sort of small star a missile to drive off devils and kill them. Thus, firing these shooting stars to repulse devils may have three meanings:

The first: It is a sign that there is a contest (among conscious beings) in the vastest sphere of existence.

The second: It indicates that in the heavens there are watchful guards and obedient inhabitants, i.e., Divine forces, who do not like the earthly evil-doers to mix with and eavesdrop on them.

The third: The spying devils, who are representatives of the foulness and wickedness of the earth, attempt to soil the clean and pure realm of the heavens inhabited by pure beings, and spy on the conversations of their inhabitants in the name of evil spirits (disbelieving jinn and their human companions who try to mislead people, particularly through sorcery, mediumship, and soothsaying). Shooting stars are fired to prevent these and to repulse them from the doors of the heavens. (See *The Words*, "the 15th Word," 192–199.)

What Does a Meteor Shower Signify?

The Perseid meteor shower observed almost every year suggests that those meteors are shot for certain, important purposes, for they surprise the observers by showing great diversity. The observations made in, for example, 1993, demonstrate the fact that the structure of the shower is yet little understood.

According to information given by the International Meteor Organization about the events of the 1993 shower (*Astronomy*, October 1993), the first results posted for the night of 11/12 August came from Japan. Up to 20:30 (all times UT), 11 August, the meteor rates were found to be normal. A zenithal hourly rate (ZHR) of 40 meteors per hour (m/h) was tentatively assigned to the shower at this time.

Preliminary data from European observers indicated that the rates had gradually increased to ZHR of order 100 m/h between 20:00, 11 August and 01:00, 12 August. Observers in France reported a noticeable increase in rates after 00:30, 12 August, with the rate being about twice that of 'normal.' The rates continued to climb between 01:00 and 03:00. A preliminary ZHR of 200–250 was ascribed to this period. The rates appeared to reach a maximum between 03:00 and 03:30. The ZHR at maximum was estimated to be of the order of 500. Observations from the Canary Islands indicated that the rates began to decline after 04:00.

Higher than normal rates were also reported by many observers in the United States and Japan. As observed by Martin Beech in *Astronomy*, p. 11, the results clearly indicated that the shower did not behave as predicted. Speculation about a possible meteor storm proved incorrect. Another unexpected feature in 1993 was the high number of bright fireballs observed. Observers reported something like five times the normal level of Perseid fireballs on the night of 11/12 August. The Perseid shower once again demonstrated how difficult it is to predict meteor shower activity.

A. Cressy Morrison (p, 100) mentions, as a typical human characteristic, the reluctance to give up fixed ideas and the stubborn resistance to accepting unfamiliar truths. The early Greeks knew that the earth was spherical, but it took two thousand years to convince (the Western) men that this fact was true. New ideas encounter opposition, ridicule and abuse, but truth survives and is verified. Neither scientific studies nor developments in science can offer any excuse not to accept God. What we observe in nature and what we obtain from it must encourage us to know Him more closely and see the strong bridge between science and religion, the world and the Hereafter, and between reason and spirit.

5. See *sūrah* 8: 37; 39: 71.

562

13. Whether you keep concealed what you intend to say or speak it out loud, He surely has full knowledge of all that lies in the bosoms.

14. Is it conceivable that One Who creates should not know?[6] He is the All-Subtle (penetrating to the most minute dimensions of all things), the All-Aware.

15. He it is Who has made the earth subservient to you (as if a docile animal), so go about through its shoulders (uplands) and eat of His provision;[7] but (be ever mindful that) to Him will be the Resurrection.

16. And yet, are you secure that He Who is above everything will not cause the earth to swallow you up then, when it is in a state of commotion?

17. Or are you secure that He Who is above everything will not send against you a dead-ly sand-storm? Then you will know how My warning is.

18. Indeed, those before them denied (the truth and were destroyed). So (reflect on) how awesome was My disowning them!

19. Have they never considered the birds above them, flying in lines with wings they spread out and fold in? Nothing holds them up except the All-Merciful. He indeed sees everything very well.

20. Who is there that will be an "army" for you, (a means of strength and support) to help you (to survive or succeed), apart from the All-Merciful? The unbelievers are surely in nothing but delusion.

21. Who is there that can provide for you if He should withhold His provision? No, but they persist in disdain and aversion (in obstinate flight from truth and reality).

22. (Now consider:) Is one who goes prone upon his face (with no breadth or depth to his line of sight, barely seeing what is touching his face) better guided, or one who goes upright (with a clear line of sight to what is ahead of him) on a straight path?

23. Say: "He it is Who has brought you into being and endowed you with hearing, and eyes, and hearts. How little you give thanks!

24. Say: "He it is Who has multiplied you on the earth, and (it is) to Him you will be gathered (to give account of your life on that earth).

25. They say (questioning with derision): "When is this promise (of gathering) to be fulfilled, if you are truthful (in your claim)?"

26. Say: "The knowledge (of that, and true and full knowledge of all things) is with God. And I am but a plain warner."

6. This is of high significance. Humans who manufacture something prepare a manual to describe how it must be used and we use it according to that guide. This means that one who manufactures it knows it best and that only one who truly knows can manufacture it. So God being the All-Knowing creates and being the Creator knows all that He creates. Thus we must conclude that One Who knows and creates is entitled to and should control and govern it, because only the One Who creates and knows can govern what He creates in the best way. However, it shows the injustice and ignorance of humankind that while they claim authority over what they make or manufacture, they deny God's authority over what He creates.

7. The phrase, *going about through the shoulders of the earth* means that although it is impossibly difficult to travel on the shoulders of a horse or camel, the earth is more compliant to humankind than a trained camel or horse. In addition, the verse implies that God's provision exists more on the shoulders of the earth (the mountains and uplands) and the plains among them. So the verse calls humanity to explore the mountains for the provision God has created in them.

is there that can bring to you (a source to replace it of) gushing water?"

---

8. The last verses contain a strong argument for God's Existence and Oneness, silencing the opponents. "We have believed in God and do rely on Him. If, supposing the inconceivable, we were mistaken, what harm will we suffer? But if we are true and you deny a truth, which is the greatest and most important truth of life and being, then who will be able to save you from the consequence of your denial, which is eternal punishment?"

SŪRAH 68

AL-QALAM (THE PEN)

Makkah period

This *sūrah* of 52 verses is one of the earliest Revelations in Makkah. It takes its name from the word *al-qa-lam* (the Pen) in the opening verse. It categorically refutes some allegations of the polytheists against God's Messenger and proves the office of Prophethood. It cites the perfect character of the Messenger as the most visible and undeniable proof of his Prophethood. It warns against the evil consequences of ingratitude and unbelief, and promises the believers a happy, eternal life in the Hereafter.

In the Name of God, the All-Merciful, the All-Compassionate.

1. *Nūn.* By the Pen and what they write with it line by line.[1]

2. You are not, by the grace of your Lord, a madman.

3. And yours for sure is a reward constant and beyond measure.

4. You are surely of a sublime character and do act by a sublime pattern of conduct.[2]

5. Soon you will see and they will see

27. But then, when they see it close at hand, the faces of those who disbelieve turn black with grief, and it will be said to them (who had been so mocking): "This is what you were calling for (derisively)."

28. Say: "Have you ever considered (this): whether God destroys me and those in my company or He has mercy on us (and enables us to attain victory), then who is there that can protect the unbelievers from a painful punishment?"

29. Say: "He is the All-Merciful. In Him We believe and in Him we put our trust, so you will soon come to know who it is that is lost in obvious error."[8]

30. Say: "Have you ever considered (this): If your water should vanish underground (leaving you with no source of water), who

6. Which of you is afflicted with madness.

7. Surely your Lord is He Who knows best who is astray from His way, and He knows best those who are rightly guided.

8. So pay no heed to (the desires of) those who persistently deny (God's Message).

9. They wish you to compromise (with them in matters of faith), so they would compromise (with you).

10. Pay no heed to any contemptible oathmaker (who swears much with no consid-eration of truth, and no will to act on his word),

11. A defamer, circulating slander (in all directions),

12. Who hinders the doing of good, transgressor of all bounds (of sense or decency), one addicted to sinning;

13. Cruel and ignoble, and in addition to all that, morally corrupt

14. Because he has wealth and many sons.

15. When Our Revelations are recited to him, he says: "Fables of the ancients."

---

1. Endowing humankind with the capacity of speech is one of God's greatest blessings. The greatest expression is the Qur'ān, which is also God's greatest blessing on humankind (55: 1–4). God also draws attention to the fact that He has taught humans to write with the pen (96: 4). One of the basic reasons for which the Qur'ān has come down to us unchanged is that God's Messenger had it written down by scribes, verse by verse. Writing is the most important means of both storing and transmitting information. So due to this great importance, God swears by the Pen – especially the pens with which the Qur'ān was written down – and what is written with the pen – especially the Qur'ān. *Nūn* is one of the abbreviated or isolated letters, concerning which see *sūrah* 2, note 1. In addition to its other meanings or implications, *nūn* may be referring to the inkpot or similar equipment used in writing. In addition, the Qur'ān calls the Prophet Jonah *Dhu 'n-Nūn* (the owner of *Nūn*) in 21: 87 and verses 48–50 of this *sūrah* also mention him. So according to some, *Nūn* also refers to the fish which swallowed up the Prophet Jonah, upon him be peace.

2. The sublime character of God's Messenger and the praiseworthy qualities he had in the greatest degree are known to history and to everybody. Including his most fierce opponents in his time, no one, except some blind, willfully prejudiced orientalists, has ever been able to say anything that could taint his pure person. For an account of his most sublime qualities, see *The Messenger of God: Muḥammad,* pp., 279–309.

With his every act and word he represented the Qur'ān. As his wife 'A'ishah said, he was a perfect embodiment of the Qur'ān. So the verse also points to this fact and means that every word and act of his is an embodiment of a Qur'ānic principle.

564   سُورَةُ الۡقَلَمِ   ٦٦٢

بِسْمِ اللّٰهِ الرَّحْمٰنِ الرَّحِيمِ

[Arabic Qur'anic text of verses]

سَنَسِمُهُ عَلَى الْخُرْطُومِ ۞ إِنَّا بَلَوْنَاهُمْ كَمَا بَلَوْنَا أَصْحَابَ الْجَنَّةِ إِذْ أَقْسَمُوا

لَيَصْرِمُنَّهَا مُصْبِحِينَ ۞ وَلَا يَسْتَثْنُونَ ۞ فَطَافَ عَلَيْهَا طَائِفٌ مِّن رَّبِّكَ

وَهُمْ نَائِمُونَ ۞ فَأَصْبَحَتْ كَالصَّرِيمِ ۞ فَتَنَادَوْا مُصْبِحِينَ ۞ أَنِ اغْدُوا

عَلَى حَرْثِكُمْ إِن كُنتُمْ صَارِمِينَ ۞ فَانطَلَقُوا وَهُمْ يَتَخَافَتُونَ ۞ أَن لَّا

يَدْخُلَنَّهَا الْيَوْمَ عَلَيْكُم مِّسْكِينٌ ۞ وَغَدَوْا عَلَى حَرْدٍ قَادِرِينَ ۞ فَلَمَّا رَأَوْهَا

قَالُوا إِنَّا لَضَالُّونَ ۞ بَلْ نَحْنُ مَحْرُومُونَ ۞ قَالَ أَوْسَطُهُمْ أَلَمْ أَقُل لَّكُمْ

لَوْلَا تُسَبِّحُونَ ۞ قَالُوا سُبْحَانَ رَبِّنَا إِنَّا كُنَّا ظَالِمِينَ ۞ فَأَقْبَلَ بَعْضُهُمْ

عَلَى بَعْضٍ يَتَلَاوَمُونَ ۞ قَالُوا يَا وَيْلَنَا إِنَّا كُنَّا طَاغِينَ ۞ عَسَى رَبُّنَا

أَن يُبْدِلَنَا خَيْرًا مِّنْهَا إِنَّا إِلَى رَبِّنَا رَاغِبُونَ ۞ كَذَٰلِكَ الْعَذَابُ

وَلَعَذَابُ الْآخِرَةِ أَكْبَرُ لَوْ كَانُوا يَعْلَمُونَ ۞ إِنَّ لِلْمُتَّقِينَ عِندَ رَبِّهِمْ

جَنَّاتِ النَّعِيمِ ۞ أَفَنَجْعَلُ الْمُسْلِمِينَ كَالْمُجْرِمِينَ ۞ مَا لَكُمْ كَيْفَ تَحْكُمُونَ

۞ أَمْ لَكُمْ كِتَابٌ فِيهِ تَدْرُسُونَ ۞ إِنَّ لَكُمْ فِيهِ لَمَا تَخَيَّرُونَ ۞ أَمْ لَكُمْ

أَيْمَانٌ عَلَيْنَا بَالِغَةٌ إِلَى يَوْمِ الْقِيَامَةِ إِنَّ لَكُمْ لَمَا تَحْكُمُونَ ۞ سَلْهُمْ أَيُّهُم

بِذَٰلِكَ زَعِيمٌ ۞ أَمْ لَهُمْ شُرَكَاءُ فَلْيَأْتُوا بِشُرَكَائِهِمْ إِن كَانُوا صَادِقِينَ

۞ يَوْمَ يُكْشَفُ عَن سَاقٍ وَيُدْعَوْنَ إِلَى السُّجُودِ فَلَا يَسْتَطِيعُونَ ۞

―――――❧―――――

16. We will brand him on the nose (to mark indelibly his disgrace).

17. For sure We try them (with drought as they rely on their wealth and children We have granted them and reject Our call), just as We tried the owners of the garden. They swore that they would assuredly harvest its produce the next day.

18. They made no allowance (in their oaths, being oblivious of the rights of the needy and oblivious of God's will).

19. Then a visitation from your Lord encompassed it while they were sleeping.

20. So by morning it had become bleak.

21. So they cried out to one another having risen for the morning:

22. "Hurry to your cultivated land if you mean to harvest (its produce)!"

23. So they set out, confiding to one another:

24. "(Take care) that no destitute enter there on you today."

25. So early they went, firmly resolved in intent (to collect the harvest and not share it with the destitute).

26. But when they saw it, they said: "We have assuredly arrived at the wrong place!"

27. (Then when they realized that it was indeed their garden:) "No, rather we are made destitute!"

28. The one more equitable among them said: "Did I not say to you: Will you not glorify God?"[3]

29. They said: "All-Glorified is our Lord! Indeed we have done wrong (by regarding ourselves as self-sufficient and not dependent on Him)."

30. Then they approached one another, reproaching themselves.

31. They said: "Oh, woe to us! We were habituated to arrogance and rebellion.

32. "It may be that our Lord will grant us something better than this instead. Surely to our Lord do we turn with hope."

33. That is (an example of) the punishment (such as the ingrate rebellious may be made to endure in the world); and certainly the punishment of the Hereafter is greater, if they but knew!

34. For the God-revering, pious there are Gardens of bounty and blessing with their Lord.

35. Do We ever treat those who have submitted to God like the disbelieving criminals (who have submitted only to their own lusts and fancies)?

36. What is the matter with you (that you can judge so)? How can you judge (that all are valued alike in God's sight whether they are Muslims or not)?

37. Or do you have a Book (revealed by God) that you read

38. Wherein you find that you will indeed have whatever you prefer (to have)?

39. Or do you have a covenant with Us confirmed by Us on oath as binding until the Day of Resurrection, that you will have whatever you judge (should be yours)?

40. Ask them (seeing that they do not have such a covenant) which of them will vouch for that?

41. Or do they have partners (with God who guarantee them whatever they wish for themselves)? Then let them produce their partners if they are truthful (in their claim).

42. On the Day when the truth will be manifest and they are in trouble, and being called to prostrate, they will be incapable of it:

---

3. That is: Why do you not acknowledge Him as Lord, Who alone sustains and provides all that we are and have? Why do you not hold Him in awe, Who does not admit any partner in His authority and is not pleased with arrogance and wrongdoing?

43. Downcast will be their eyes, with abasement overwhelming them. Assuredly they were called to prostrate while they were yet safe and whole (in this world, but they did not).

44. So leave Me with such as deny this Word (the Qur'ān). We will lead them on to perdition step by step from where they do not know.

45. But I grant respite to them (so that they may mend their ways). My scheme (all that is willed for them) is firm and unfailing.

46. Or is it that you ask them for a wage (in return for your calling them to Our Word), and so they are weighed down with debt?

47. Or is the Unseen within their reach that they write down (prescribing and stipulating what is to come, and how they are to be judged)?

48. So wait patiently for your Lord's judgment, and do not be like the companion of the fish,[4] when he called out choking inwardly (with distress).[5]

49. If there had not reached him grace from his Lord (Who accepted his repentance), he would indeed have been cast forth on the desert shore, being reproached.[6]

50. But his Lord chose him and enabled him to be among the specially chosen, righteous servants.

51. Those who disbelieve would (if they could) strike you down with their looks because of hatred and enmity, when they hear the Reminder, and they say: "Surely he is a madman."

52. But it is not other than a Reminder for all beings.

---

4. The companion of the fish is the Prophet Jonah, upon him be peace. For a detailed explanation of his story, see 10: 98, note 20; 21: 87–88, note 18; 37: 139–148.

5. He called out in the abdomen of the fish: "There is no deity but You, All-Glorified You are (in that You are absolutely above having any defect). Surely, I have been one of the wrongdoers (who have wronged themselves)"

(21: 87). For the meaning of this, see sūrah 21, note 18.

6. Verses 37: 143-145 say: Had it not been that he was one who glorified (God, declaring Him absolutely above having any defects and partners), he would certainly have remained in its belly (serving as his grave) until the Day when all will be raised (from the dead). But We caused him to be cast forth on a

desert shore, sick as he was. Whereas this verse says that if there had not reached him grace from his Lord, he *would indeed have been cast forth on the desert shore, being reproached.* There is no contradiction between these verses. Verse 37: 143 says that if the Prophet Jonah, upon him be peace, had not been one who *always* glorified God, he would have remained in the belly of the fish until the Day of Resurrection. His being one who always glorified God caused him to be cast forth. This verse says that if he had not glorified God *in the belly of the fish*, he would have been cast forth, being reproached. His special glorification in the belly of the fish caused him to be cast forth, forgiven, preserved on desert land and returned to his people, who accepted his message.

SŪRAH 69

AL-ḤĀQQAH
(THE SURE REALITY)

Makkah period

Revealed in the early years of the Qur'ānic Revelation in Makkah, this *sūrah* of 52 verses takes its name from the word *al-ḥāqqah* (the Sure Reality) in the first verse, implying the Day of Resurrection and Judgment. It warns those who associated partners with God and indulged in committing sins, reminding them of what befell some early wrongdoing communities, and draws attention to the Day of Resurrection and Judgment. It also offers evidence to establish the Divine origin of the Qur'ān and the Prophethood of Muḥammad, upon him be peace and blessings.

In the Name of God, the All-Merciful, the All-Compassionate.

1. The Sure Reality.

2. What is the Sure Reality?!

3. And what enables you to perceive[1] what the Sure Reality is?

4. The (tribes) of Thamūd and 'Ād denied the Sudden, Mighty Strike.[2]

5. Now as for the (tribe of) Thamūd – they were destroyed by the overwhelming (catastrophe).

6. And the (tribe of) 'Ād – they were destroyed with a furious, roaring windstorm,

7. Which God made to prevail against them for seven nights and eight days, uninterruptedly,[3] so that you could have seen people lying overthrown in it, as though they were hollow trunks of palm-trees.

8. Now do you see any of them remaining?

---

1. The phrase *What enables you to perceive* denotes that the thing being asked about is unusual and that it is impossible for anyone to perceive it unless God makes it known.

2. The Sure Reality (which will undoubtedly take place and make every truth perfectly clear) signifies the Day of the Resurrection and Judgment with all the events that will take place during it. The *Sudden, Mighty Strike* implies the event of the Last Day or the destruction of the world.

3. For the peoples of 'Ād and Thamūd, see *sūrah* 7: 65–79, notes 16–17, *sūrah* 11: 50–68, and *sūrah* 26: 123–158. The Qur'ān uses several words for the punishment that struck the Thamūd, such as the awful blast (11: 67), a shocking catastrophe (7: 78), and the lightning-like punishment of humiliation (41: 17). These are aspects of the punishment that the Qur'ān describes, being suited to the subject and style of the *sūrah* where they are mentioned. In *sūrah* 29: 40, the Qur'ān sums up the kinds of punishment with which God destroyed many peoples.

566 سُورَةُ ٱلْحَاقَّةِ ٥٦٦

وَجَاءَ فِرْعَوْنُ وَمَن قَبْلَهُ وَٱلْمُؤْتَفِكَـٰتُ بِٱلْخَاطِئَةِ ۞ فَعَصَوْا رَسُولَ رَبِّهِمْ فَأَخَذَهُمْ أَخْذَةً رَّابِيَةً ۞ إِنَّا لَمَّا طَغَا ٱلْمَآءُ حَمَلْنَـٰكُمْ فِى ٱلْجَارِيَةِ ۞ لِنَجْعَلَهَا لَكُمْ تَذْكِرَةً وَتَعِيَهَآ أُذُنٌ وَٰعِيَةٌ ۞ فَإِذَا نُفِخَ فِى ٱلصُّورِ نَفْخَةٌ وَٰحِدَةٌ ۞ وَحُمِلَتِ ٱلْأَرْضُ وَٱلْجِبَالُ فَدُكَّتَا دَكَّةً وَٰحِدَةً ۞ فَيَوْمَئِذٍ وَقَعَتِ ٱلْوَاقِعَةُ ۞ وَٱنشَقَّتِ ٱلسَّمَآءُ فَهِىَ يَوْمَئِذٍ وَاهِيَةٌ ۞ وَٱلْمَلَكُ عَلَىٰٓ أَرْجَآئِهَا ۚ وَيَحْمِلُ عَرْشَ رَبِّكَ فَوْقَهُمْ يَوْمَئِذٍ ثَمَـٰنِيَةٌ ۞ يَوْمَئِذٍ تُعْرَضُونَ لَا تَخْفَىٰ مِنكُمْ خَافِيَةٌ ۞ فَأَمَّا مَنْ أُوتِىَ كِتَـٰبَهُۥ بِيَمِينِهِۦ فَيَقُولُ هَآؤُمُ ٱقْرَءُوا۟ كِتَـٰبِيَهْ ۞ إِنِّى ظَنَنتُ أَنِّى مُلَـٰقٍ حِسَابِيَهْ ۞ فَهُوَ فِى عِيشَةٍ رَّاضِيَةٍ ۞ فِى جَنَّةٍ عَالِيَةٍ ۞ قُطُوفُهَا دَانِيَةٌ ۞ كُلُوا۟ وَٱشْرَبُوا۟ هَنِيٓـًٔا بِمَآ أَسْلَفْتُمْ فِى ٱلْأَيَّامِ ٱلْخَالِيَةِ ۞ وَأَمَّا مَنْ أُوتِىَ كِتَـٰبَهُۥ بِشِمَالِهِۦ فَيَقُولُ يَـٰلَيْتَنِى لَمْ أُوتَ كِتَـٰبِيَهْ ۞ وَلَمْ أَدْرِ مَا حِسَابِيَهْ ۞ يَـٰلَيْتَهَا كَانَتِ ٱلْقَاضِيَةَ ۞ مَآ أَغْنَىٰ عَنِّى مَالِيَهْ ۞ هَلَكَ عَنِّى سُلْطَـٰنِيَهْ ۞ خُذُوهُ فَغُلُّوهُ ۞ ثُمَّ ٱلْجَحِيمَ صَلُّوهُ ۞ ثُمَّ فِى سِلْسِلَةٍ ذَرْعُهَا سَبْعُونَ ذِرَاعًا فَٱسْلُكُوهُ ۞ إِنَّهُۥ كَانَ لَا يُؤْمِنُ بِٱللَّهِ ٱلْعَظِيمِ ۞ وَلَا يَحُضُّ عَلَىٰ طَعَامِ ٱلْمِسْكِينِ ۞

---

9. And there was the Pharaoh, and many other communities before him,[4] and the cities overthrown (where Lot's people lived): all of them indulged in the unpardonable sins.

10. And they rebelled against their Lord's Messenger (sent to each to warn them), and so He took hold of them with a severe seizing.

11. It was We Who, when the water (of the Flood in the time of Noah) burst beyond limits, carried you (i.e. your believing ancestors) in the on-moving Ark,

12. So that We might make it a reminder for you (to be transmitted from generation to generation), and that heeding ears might take it in and retain it.

13. And when (the Last Hour comes and) the Trumpet is blown[5] with a single blast,

14. And the earth, and the mountains (on it) are removed and burst within, and are crushed with a single crushing.

15. It is on that Day that the Event to happen[6] will happen.

16. And the sky split asunder, and so, on that Day it will be most frail,

17. And the angels will be at its ends;[7] and above them, eight will bear the Throne of your Lord on that Day.[8]

18. On that Day you will be arraigned for judgment, and no secret of yours will remain hidden.

19. Then as for him who is given his Record[9] in his right hand, he will say: "Here, take and read my Record!

20. "I surely knew that (one day) I would meet my account."

21. And so he will be in a state of life pleasing to him,

22. In a lofty Garden,

23. With clusters (of fruit) within easy reach.

24. "Eat and drink to your hearts' content for all that you sent ahead in advance in days past (in anticipation of this Day)."

25. But as for him whose Record is given in his left hand, he will say: "Ah, would that I had never been given my Record,

26. "And that I had known nothing of my account!

27. "Oh, would that death had been (and nothing thereafter had followed).

28. "My wealth has availed me nothing,

29. "And all my authority (my power over all that I had) has gone from me!"

30. (And the command will come): "Lay hold of him and shackle him (by the neck, the hands, and the feet)!

31. "Then in the Blazing Flame let him to roast.

32. "Then, fasten him with a chain the length of which is seventy cubits."[10]

33. For he surely did not believe in God, the Supreme,

34. And did not urge to the feeding of the destitute.

---

4. By *many other communities* before that of the Pharaoh the Qur'ān is referring to Noah's people (see 7: 59–64; 11: 25–48; 23: 23–29; 26: 105–121; 71: 1–28, and the corresponding notes), the people of Shu'ayb (7: 85–93; 11: 84–95; 15: 78–79; 26: 176–189, and the corresponding notes), and the companions of ar-Rass (25: 38, note 8). There were, no doubt, other communities not mentioned in the Qur'ān, who were also destroyed for their wrongdoings.

5. For the Trumpet and its being blown, see *sūrah* 2, note 31; *sūrah* 6: 73, note 14, and *sūrah* 39: 68, note 22.

6. *The Event to happen* is a title of a Qur'ānic chapter (56). It also implies what will take place on the Day of Resurrection.

7. This statement may be considered together with verse (25: 25): *On that Day the heaven will split asunder with the clouds (covering it) and the angels will be made to descend in a majestic descending.*

8. As explained in *sūrah* 7, note 13, the Supreme Throne of God (*'Arsh*), the exact nature of which we cannot know, signifies God's absolute authority over the universe. Deducing from Bediüzaman's description of water as the *'arsh* (throne) of mercy and earth as the throne of life, we can say that the *'Arsh* (Throne) indicates primarily God's Attributes of Knowledge, Will, Power, and Providence, and His Names originating in them, such as the All-Knowing, the All-Willing, the All-Powerful, and the All-Providing. As it encompasses the whole universe, it is also composed of God's Names the First, the Last, the Outward, and the Inward. These are His most prominent Attributes and Names relating to the creation and actual rule of the universe. And as pointed out in *sūrah* 2, note 30, no event in the universe is conceivable without the operative intervention of the angels. The Qur'ān mentions many types of angels (37: 1–3; 77: 1–4, 79: 1–5, 82: 11). So those who bear God's Throne may be Archangels whom He employs in the rule of the universe for some wise purposes and for the majesty of His rule, particularly those who are endowed with the greatest manifestation of the Attributes of God mentioned. According to some, based on a Prophetic Tradition recorded in *ad-Durr al-Manthūr* by as-Suyūtī, there are four beings that bear the Throne during the life of the world, and there will be eight on the Resurrection Day. According to Muhyi'd-Dīn ibn al-'Arabī and Ibn Maysarah al-Jīlī, these are the Prophets Muhammad, Abraham and Adam, and the angels Riḍwān (the chief guard of Paradise), Mālik (the chief guard of Hell), Gabriel, Mikā'il (Michael), and Isrā'fil (Yazır, 8: 5325–5326).

9. For this Record, see 17: 13–14, note 10.

10. As Hamdi Yazır suggests in interpreting this verse (8: 5334), this chain of seventy cubits may be the result of the sins committed by a sinful unbeliever throughout their seventy years of life. So in addition to its apparent meaning, the verse may be referring to the average human life-span in the world or to the years spent (after puberty) in unbelief and sins. Each year will be a link of the chain in Hellfire.

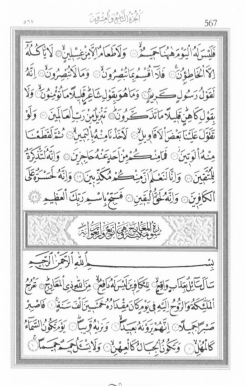

35. And so, he will have none to befriend him this Day,

36. Nor any food except foul pus.[11]

37. None eat it except the sinful (those guilty of denying God or associating partners with Him and oppressing people).

38. No indeed! I swear by all that you can see,

39. And all that you cannot see,[12]

40. It surely is the speech (conveyed to you by) an illustrious, noble Messenger.

41. And not a poet's speech (composed in a poet's mind). How little is what you believe! (It is so limited by the poverty of your souls and hearts.)

42. Nor is it a soothsayer's speech (pretending to foretell events). How little it is that you reflect and be mindful! (It is so limited by the poverty of your minds.)

43. (No indeed!) It is a Revelation being sent down in parts from the Lord of the worlds.

44. If he (the Messenger) had dared to fabricate some false sayings in attribution to Us,

45. We would certainly have seized him with might,

46. Thereafter We would certainly have cut his life-vein.

47. Then not one from among you could have shielded and saved him from Us.

48. And it is a sure Reminder (bringing hope and guidance) for the God-revering, pious.

49. We are most certainly aware that among you are some who deny (it).

50. It will surely be a bitter regret for the unbelievers.[13]

51. And this (the whole Qur'ān) is surely certain truth.

52. So glorify the Name of your Lord, the Supreme.[14]

---

11. Since both the people of Paradise and the people of Hell prepare their eternal future with their deeds in the world, this foul pus must be the product of their denial of God or association of partners with God, and their oppressing the poor and denying them any help.

12. This oath is very important in that neither the truth nor creation consists in what is observable and perceivable by humanity. Moreover, the basic truth lying behind all that we observe

and perceive is unobservable and imperceptible through our senses. It is because of this that the Qur'ān begins praising the believers by saying that they believe in the Unseen. With this oath, the Qur'ān draws attention to this fact and to the fact that the most fundamental and essential truths should not be looked for in the observable realm of creation. The truth of the Resurrection and the Final Judgment and that of the eternal life presented in the previous verses and the truth of the Revelation and its communication by the Messenger are among such truths.

13. The unbelievers will see that the Qur'ān is the truth from God; they will realize what a future it has prepared for the believers both in the world and especially in the Hereafter, and what a great loss its rejection has brought, and those who have rejected it will greatly regret doing so.

14. We must declare God as the Lord of supreme authority over creation without any partner. This also refers to the majesty and supremacy of the Qur'ān. This order teaches us how we should thank, praise, exalt, and glorify God and in what circumstances we should do this.

———✥———

SŪRAH 70

AL-MA 'ĀRIJ (THE STAIRS OF ASCENT)

Makkah period

From the early years of the Revelation of the Qur'an in Makkah, this *sūrah* of 44 verses takes its name from the word *al-ma'ārij* (the stairs of ascent) in the third verse. Its central concern is the rejection of the Makkan polytheists' denial of the afterlife and of the Prophethood of Muḥammad, upon him be peace and blessings.

In the Name of God, the All-Merciful, the All-Compassionate.

1. A questioner (in mocking denial of the Day of Resurrection) has asked about the punishment certain to befall,

2. (And prepared for) the unbelievers; none can ward it off (from them).

3. (It is) from God, Whose are the stairs of ascent.

4. The angels and the Spirit ascend to Him (thereby), in a day the measure of which is fifty thousand years (of your normal worldly years).[1]

5. So (O Messenger) endure (their insolence) with becoming patience.

6. They see it (the punishment) as far off (beyond their reason),

7. But We see it as (certain to come and) near at hand.

8. The Day when the sky will be like molten metal;

9. And the mountains will be like multicolored tufts of wool.

10. And no loyal friend will ask after his friend,

---

1. "Reaching" God requires traversing great "distances" and ascending innumerable steps. So the stairs of ascent to God and the measure of the day as being fifty thousand years imply both our distance from Him despite His infinite nearness to Us and His indescribable "elevation" and transcendence (see also *sūrah* 32: 5, note 4). The *day* may also be referring to the Day of Judgment. In this case, its measure suggests the great distances between the stations or worlds of the Hereafter, and the dread and hardships the people of Hell will suffer while they are being driven through these stations and worlds to Hell. In this case, such a great distance constitutes a great threat. As explained in several places in this study, the angels are dutiful in conveying God's commands throughout the universe. They also convey the worship and life-functions of all creatures before the Presence of God. So, by the stairs of ascent and a day measuring fifty thousand years, the verse may be referring to this fact. The Spirit mentioned in verse 4 is either Gabriel or another angel-like being that is greater than the angels. According to Imam Ghazzālī, he is an angel (or angel-like being) whom God employs in breathing an individual's spirit into that individual's body. Bediüzzaman Said Nursi maintains that there is a spirit representing every thing, every being. So the Spirit may be the being responsible for all the spirits.

568　　　سُورَةُ المَعَارِجَ　　　٥٦٨

وَيَقْصُرُونَهُمْ يَوَدُّ الْمُجْرِمُ لَوْ يَفْتَدِى مِنْ عَذَابٍ يَوْمِئِذٍ بِبَنِيهِ ۝ وَصَاحِبَتِهِ وَأَخِيهِ ۝ وَفَصِيلَتِهِ الَّتِى تُؤْوِيهِ ۝ وَمَن فِى الْأَرْضِ جَمِيعًا ثُمَّ يُنجِيهِ ۝ كَلَّا إِنَّهَا لَظَى ۝ نَزَّاعَةً لِّلشَّوَى ۝ تَدْعُواْ مَنْ أَدْبَرَ وَتَوَلَّى ۝ وَجَمَعَ فَأَوْعَى ۝ إِنَّ الْإِنسَانَ خُلِقَ هَلُوعًا ۝ إِذَا مَسَّهُ الشَّرُّ جَزُوعًا ۝ وَإِذَا مَسَّهُ الْخَيْرُ مَنُوعًا ۝ إِلَّا الْمُصَلِّينَ ۝ الَّذِينَ هُمْ عَلَى صَلَاتِهِمْ دَائِمُونَ ۝ وَالَّذِينَ فِى أَمْوَالِهِمْ حَقٌّ مَّعْلُومٌ ۝ لِّلسَّائِلِ وَالْمَحْرُومِ ۝ وَالَّذِينَ يُصَدِّقُونَ بِيَوْمِ الدِّينِ ۝ وَالَّذِينَ هُم مِّنْ عَذَابِ رَبِّهِم مُّشْفِقُونَ ۝ إِنَّ عَذَابَ رَبِّهِمْ غَيْرُ مَأْمُونٍ ۝ وَالَّذِينَ هُمْ لِفُرُوجِهِمْ حَافِظُونَ ۝ إِلَّا عَلَى أَزْوَاجِهِمْ أَوْ مَا مَلَكَتْ أَيْمَانُهُمْ فَإِنَّهُمْ غَيْرُ مَلُومِينَ ۝ فَمَنِ ابْتَغَى وَرَاءَ ذَلِكَ فَأُوْلَئِكَ هُمُ الْعَادُونَ ۝ وَالَّذِينَ هُمْ لِأَمَانَاتِهِمْ وَعَهْدِهِمْ رَاعُونَ ۝ وَالَّذِينَ هُم بِشَهَادَاتِهِمْ قَائِمُونَ ۝ وَالَّذِينَ هُمْ عَلَى صَلَاتِهِمْ يُحَافِظُونَ ۝ أُوْلَئِكَ فِى جَنَّاتٍ مُّكْرَمُونَ ۝ فَمَالِ الَّذِينَ كَفَرُواْ قِبَلَكَ مُهْطِعِينَ ۝ عَنِ الْيَمِينِ وَعَنِ الشِّمَالِ عِزِينَ ۝ أَيَطْمَعُ كُلُّ امْرِئٍ مِّنْهُمْ أَن يُدْخَلَ جَنَّةَ نَعِيمٍ ۝ كَلَّا إِنَّا خَلَقْنَاهُم مِّمَّا يَعْلَمُونَ ۝

---

11. Though they will be in sight of each other. Every disbelieving criminal will yearn to ransom himself from the punishment of that Day even by his sons,

12. And his wife and his brother,

13. And all his kinsfolk who sheltered him,

14. And whoever else is on the earth, all of them, so that he might then save himself.

15. By no means! It is a furiously flaming fire,

16. Tearing away the skin.

17. It will call to itself those who turn their backs (on the call to faith) and turn away (from worship of God),

18. And amass wealth and withhold it (from spending in God's cause and for the needy).

19. Surely human has been created with a restless, impatient disposition.[2]

20. Fretful when evil visits him;

21. And niggardly when good visits him.

22. Except those who are devoted to the Prayer.

23. Those who are constant in their Prayer.

24. And those in whose wealth there is a right acknowledged (by them)

25. For such as have no means other than begging, and such as are denied help (because, having self-respect, they cannot beg and are thought to be well-off).

26. And those who affirm as true the Day of Judgment.

27. And those who are fearful of their Lord's punishment (and live accordingly).

28. Indeed, their Lord's punishment is that of which no one can ever feel secure.

29. And those who strictly guard their private parts, and their chastity and modesty,

30. Save from their spouses or (as a permission for men) those (bondsmaids) whom their right hands possess, for with regard to them they are free from blame.

31. But whoever seeks beyond that, such are those who exceed the bounds (set by God).[3]

32. And those who are faithful to their trusts (which either God or society or an individual places in their charge) and to their pledges (between them and God or other persons or society).

33. And those who are upholders (of right and justice) by bearing true witness and without avoiding giving testimony.

34. And those who safeguard their Prayers (including all the rites of which they are constituted).

35. Those will be in Gardens, high-honored.

36. What is the matter with those who disbelieve, that (with the intent of mockery) they hasten on toward you with staring eyes fixed on you,

37. From the right and from the left, in crowds?

38. Does every one of them covet admission into the Garden of bounty and blessing (regarding himself as supremely deserving Paradise without the effort of faith)?[4]

39. By no means! We have surely created them out of that (simple matter) which they know very well,

---

2. Each person has two aspects: one angelic, pure, and spiritual, and the other one turned to the elements, plants, and animals; all people are "children of the world." We have been equipped with lust (e.g., for the opposite sex, children, income, wealth, and comfort) and anger (to protect ourselves and our values), and intellect. By nature we are fallible, forgetful, neglectful, fond of disputing, obstinate, selfish, jealous, and much more. Since our free will distinguishes us from other conscious beings, such as angels, these powers, faculties, and negative-seeming feelings are not restricted. However, to attain individual and collective happiness in both worlds and to rise to higher ranks of humanity, we should restrict these powers according to certain precepts and channel them into virtues. For example, obstinacy can be channeled into steadfastness in defense of right and truth, and jealousy into approvable competition in doing good things. Impatience and restlessness can be channeled into the virtue of alertness to danger, preemptive preparation against it, or the virtue of prompt-

ness, non-hesitation when there is occasion and opportunity to do good.

Our human nature is no more than our struggle against the negative and/or negative-seeming aspects of our character, restricting or channeling them into virtues, and acquiring distinction with good qualities so that we may become good, worshipful servants of God and useful members of society. The Messenger of God said: "The most perfect in faith among the believers are the most perfect in conduct" (Ibn Hanbal, 2: 250); "A human can cross with good conduct the distances which he cannot with acts of worship and adoration" (al-Haythamī, 8: 24).

3. See *sūrah* 23, note 1.

4. While the Messenger was reciting the Qur'ān at the Ka'bah, some leading polytheists would come and sit around him in separate circles and stare at him with enmity. They would mock the believers, who were lowly (in worldly wealth and status), and say: "If there is Paradise and people will enter it, then it is more fitting that it should be we who will enter it, not you."

---

40. So, I swear by the Lord of the points of sunrise and sunset, that surely We are able[5]

41. To replace them with (others) better than them (in respect of faith in God and in their worship of Him), and We are not to be frustrated (in doing what We will).

42. So leave them plunging in their falsehoods and amusements until the Day that they have been promised.

43. The Day when they come forth from their graves in haste as if they were hurrying to a goal,

44. Downcast will be their eyes, abasement overwhelming them. That is the Day that they have been repeatedly promised.

---

5. These verses emphasize the helplessness of humankind before God and His full power and authority over every point of space and time with whatever takes place therein.

SŪRAH 71

NŪḤ (NOAH)

Makkah period

From the early years of the Revelation of the Qur'an in Makkah, this *sūrah* of 28 verses takes its name from the word *Nūḥ* (Noah). It records how the Prophet Noah, upon him be peace, conveyed God's Message to his people and how harshly they reacted against it. The *sūrah* ends with Noah's appeal to God after ages of harshness, derision and persecution he endured at the hands of his people.

In the Name of God, the All-Merciful, the All-Compassionate.

1. We sent Noah as Messenger to his people (and commanded him): "Warn your people before a painful punishment comes to them."

2. He said: "O my people! I am indeed a plain warner to you (and I urge you:)

3. "Worship God alone and keep from disobedience to Him in reverence for Him and piety, and obey me,

4. "So that He may forgive you your sins (which you have committed so far) and grant you respite until a term appointed by Him (instead of destroying you because of your sins). The term appointed by God, when it comes, is never deferred. If you but knew!"[1]

5. (After long ages spent in conveying God's Message, he turned to his Lord in prayer and)[2] he said: "My Lord, I have surely called my people night and day;

6. "But my call has only caused them to flee more and more (from accepting the truth).

7. "And every time I have called them so that You may forgive them, they have thrust

their fingers in their ears, and wrapped themselves up in their garments, and grown obstinate and more and more arrogant (in refusing my call).

8. "Then I have called them in a loud (emphatic) manner;

9. "Then again, I have called them in public, and I have spoken to them confidentially in private.

10. "I have said: 'Ask your Lord for forgiveness, for surely He has always been All-Forgiving.

---

1. For God's sparing and reprieving people over a term appointed by Him, see *sūrah* 10: 98, note 20. The term mentioned here is the final term, which normally is never altered, neither delayed nor brought forward. However, if a person or people persist in doing things that incur God's punishment, then God may punish and destroy them, as He has destroyed many peoples throughout history. This is also included in God's Destiny, which relates to both cause and effect. If they had paid heed to God's Message conveyed to them by His Messengers, upon them be peace, they would not have been destroyed and would have lived until the final term appointed for them by God.

570   سورة نوح   ٥٧٠

يُرْسِلِ السَّمَآءَ عَلَيْكُم مِّدْرَارًا ۞ وَيُمْدِدْكُم بِأَمْوَالٍ وَبَنِينَ
وَيَجْعَل لَّكُمْ جَنَّاتٍ وَيَجْعَل لَّكُمْ أَنْهَارًا ۞ مَا لَكُمْ لَا تَرْجُونَ
لِلَّهِ وَقَارًا ۞ وَقَدْ خَلَقَكُمْ أَطْوَارًا ۞ أَلَمْ تَرَوْا كَيْفَ خَلَقَ
اللَّهُ سَبْعَ سَمَٰوَاتٍ طِبَاقًا ۞ وَجَعَلَ الْقَمَرَ فِيهِنَّ نُورًا وَجَعَلَ الشَّمْسَ سِرَاجًا
وَاللَّهُ أَنبَتَكُم مِّنَ الْأَرْضِ نَبَاتًا ۞ ثُمَّ يُعِيدُكُمْ فِيهَا وَيُخْرِجُكُمْ إِخْرَاجًا ۞
وَاللَّهُ جَعَلَ لَكُمُ الْأَرْضَ بِسَاطًا ۞ لِّتَسْلُكُوا مِنْهَا سُبُلًا فِجَاجًا
۞ قَالَ نُوحٌ رَّبِّ إِنَّهُمْ عَصَوْنِي وَاتَّبَعُوا مَن لَّمْ يَزِدْهُ مَالُهُ وَوَلَدُهُ
إِلَّا خَسَارًا ۞ وَمَكَرُوا مَكْرًا كُبَّارًا ۞ وَقَالُوا لَا تَذَرُنَّ
آلِهَتَكُمْ وَلَا تَذَرُنَّ وَدًّا وَلَا سُوَاعًا وَلَا يَغُوثَ وَيَعُوقَ وَنَسْرًا
۞ وَقَدْ أَضَلُّوا كَثِيرًا وَلَا تَزِدِ الظَّالِمِينَ إِلَّا ضَلَالًا ۞ مِّمَّا
خَطِيئَاتِهِمْ أُغْرِقُوا فَأُدْخِلُوا نَارًا فَلَمْ يَجِدُوا لَهُم مِّن دُونِ
اللَّهِ أَنصَارًا ۞ وَقَالَ نُوحٌ رَّبِّ لَا تَذَرْ عَلَى الْأَرْضِ مِنَ الْكَافِرِينَ
دَيَّارًا ۞ إِنَّكَ إِن تَذَرْهُمْ يُضِلُّوا عِبَادَكَ وَلَا يَلِدُوا إِلَّا فَاجِرًا
كَفَّارًا ۞ رَّبِّ اغْفِرْ لِي وَلِوَالِدَيَّ وَلِمَن دَخَلَ بَيْتِيَ مُؤْمِنًا
وَلِلْمُؤْمِنِينَ وَالْمُؤْمِنَاتِ وَلَا تَزِدِ الظَّالِمِينَ إِلَّا تَبَارًا ۞

---

earth like a plant (in a mode of growth particular to you).[6]

18. 'Thereafter He will return you into it, and He will bring you forth from it in resurrection.

19. 'God has made for you the earth a wide expanse,

20. 'So that you may move on it along the ways through mountains and valleys.' "

21. Noah (turned to his Lord, and) said: "My Lord! They have disobeyed me and followed those whose wealth and children[7] have increased them only in loss and self-ruin.

22. "And they have made tremendous schemes (to prevent my call and people's acceptance of it).

23. "And they have said: 'Do not abandon your deities; do not ever abandon (in particular) Wadd, nor Suwā', nor Yaghūth, and Ya'ūq, and Nasr!'

24. "And they have indeed led many astray. And (O God,) increase not these wrongdoers in anything but further straying (by way of just punishment for all that they have done)."

25. And because of their (unforgivable) sins, they were drowned (in the Flood), and were made to enter a (punishing) Fire; and so they found none who could help them against God.

26. Noah also said: "My Lord! Do not leave on the earth any from among the unbelievers dwelling therein!

27. "If You do leave them, they will lead Your servants astray, and they will beget none but shameless and dissolute thankless unbelievers.[8]

28. "My Lord! Forgive me and my parents, and everyone who joins my household as a believer, and all the believing men and believing women, and do not increase the wrongdoers in anything but ruin."[9]

11. 'He will release (the rain-bearing clouds in) the sky over you, with abundance of rain;

12. 'And will strengthen you by increasing you in wealth and children, and make for you gardens, and make for you running waters.[3]

13. 'What is the matter with you that you do not want to see majesty in God (to worship Him),

14. 'Seeing that He has created You in different, successive stages?[4]

15. 'Do you not see how God has created the seven heavens in harmony?

16. 'And He has set up within them the moon as a light (reflected), and has set up the sun as a lamp.[5]

17. 'And God has caused you to grow from

2. The Prophet Noah, upon him be peace, is one of the first five greatest Messengers (42: 13, note 6). He stayed among his people for 950 years and conveyed God's Message to his people (29: 14).

3. Turning to God with sincere repentance and asking for forgiveness is a door that opens on God's blessings. Whoever complains of anything – such as drought, a lack of wealth or children, or barren fields, etc. – is advised by Hasan al-Baṣrī to repent and ask God for forgiveness for their sin. They then must do whatever (lawful) they must in order to attain to their goal.

4. See *sūrah* 22: 5, and 23: 12–14.

5. It is worth noticing that the verse mentions the moon and the sun not as in a (single) heaven, but in or within the seven heavens. This may be a clue to what the Qur'ān means by *seven heavens*. However, some hold that there is no difference between the moon being mentioned in a single heaven or within seven heavens, since what is meant is that all the heavens are of the same substance and in full harmony with each other.

6. The verse alludes to the first origin of the father of humanity from the elements of the earth – soil, air, and water – and also the material origin of every human being, which are the same elements that are made into particular biological entities in human body. As Hamdi Yazır points out, the word *nabātan*, which comes at the end of the verse as an adverbial complement to "grow," denotes the particular way of human creation and growth. So, the verse allows no room for any inclination toward the Darwinian theory of evolution.

7. There is no direct link between faith and worship and God's allocation of provision in the form of income or children. The granting of wealth and children is quite different from His opening the door of His blessings as a result of one's repentance and asking for forgiveness, as mentioned in note 3 above. As pointed out in several places before, besides His laws in the form of the Religion, God has also laws of life. Prosperity in both worlds requires obedience to both of these laws. Obedience to the former (the Religion) adds to the success coming as a result of obedience to the latter (Divine laws of life). So if believers obey the latter in addition to sincere adherence to the Religion, they always and inevitably prevail over unbelievers. In any case, we should always bear in mind that whatever blessing we are given, it is a means of testing us and requires certain things, such as thanking God, spending wealth on religiously lawful things and in God's cause, for the needy, and for educating our children so that they can be good servants of God.

8. The words of this prayer of a Messenger who had been calling his people to Divine guidance for 950 years, show how obstinately wicked, ungrateful and misled those unbelievers were who were drowned in the Flood.

9. For other accounts of the story of Noah and his people, in all its diverse aspects, see: 7: 59–72; 10: 71–73; 11: 25–48; 23: 23–30; 26: 105–122; 29: 14–15; 37: 75–80; 54: 9–16, and the corresponding notes.

571

SŪRAH 72

AL-JINN (THE JINN)

Makkah period

This *sūrah* of 28 verses was revealed in Makkah. It takes its name from the word *al-jinn* (the jinn) in the first verse and recounts how some of the jinn heard God's Messenger reciting the Qur'ān and came to believe. The *sūrah* also emphasizes God's absolute Oneness and the Messengership of Muḥammad, upon him be peace and blessings, and those jinn's acceptance of both.

In the Name of God, the All-Merciful, the All-Compassionate.

1. Say (O Messenger): "It has been revealed to me that a company of the jinn gave ear (to my recitation of the Qur'ān),[1]

then (when they returned to their people) they said: 'We have indeed heard a wonderful Qur'ān,

2. 'Guiding to what is right in belief and action and so we have believed in it; and we (affirm that we) will not associate any as partner with our Lord.

3. 'And that He – exalted is the majesty of our Lord – has taken neither consort nor child.

4. 'And that the foolish among us uttered an enormity against God.

5. 'And that (we were mistaken when) we thought that humankind and the jinn would never speak a falsehood against God.

6. '(But we have come to see that) there have indeed been men from among humankind who took refuge in some men from among jinn, and so (the former) increased them (the latter) in conceit, rebellion and wrongdoing.[2]

7. 'And they (those men) have thought, as you have thought, that God would never raise anyone (as Messenger from among them).

8. 'But now when we sought to reach heaven, we found it filled with stern guards and flaming fires (shooting-stars).[3]

9. 'We used to be established in position to overhear (its inhabitants); but now whoever attempts to listen finds a flaming fire in wait for him.

10. 'We (being prevented from overhearing) did not know whether evil is intended for those who live on the earth or their Lord wills for them right guidance and good.[4]

11. 'There are among us such as are righteous (in conduct and apt to believe) and there are those who are otherwise. We have been sects with divergent paths.

12. 'We have come to know that we can by no means frustrate God (in His will on the earth), nor can we frustrate Him by flight.

13. 'And when we heard the guidance (embodied in the Qur'ān), we (immediately) believed in it. Whoever believes in his Lord has no fear of loss (of being wronged in return for his faith and for the good deeds required by faith), or disgrace.

---

1. While God's Messenger was returning from Ṭā'if to Makkah in great sorrow, God caused some jinn to hear his recitation of the Qur'ān and they believed and returned to their people as bearers of its message. This is narrated in *Sūrat al-Ahqāf*, 46: 29–32. Another time, when the Messenger was going to the fair at 'Uqaz with a few Companions, another company of the jinn heard his recitation during the Early Morning Prayer. This latter incident is the one being related here. The other group of the jinn (who listened to the Messenger during his return from Ṭā'if) belonged to the nation of Moses, upon him be peace. As can be understood from the following verses, the jinn who heard the Messenger's recitation during the Morning Prayer were polytheists who attributed to God wife and children. They too became believers and, like the other jinn, returned to their people and conveyed the Qur'ān's message.

For the nature of the jinn, see *sūrah* 46, note 10.

2. Men in particular from among the Arab people of the (pre-Islamic) Age of Ignorance used to take refuge from any possible evil in men from among the jinn, whom they supposed to have authority over the valleys or the ruins where they stopped on their journeys. Moreover, people would appeal to the jinn to cure some diseases or to prophesy their future or plans. There have always been people who have been able to make some type of contact with the jinn, and there are people who appeal to the jinn. This causes the jinn to be overproud and to mislead those who appeal to or contact them.

3. As mentioned in *sūrah* 15: 17–18, note 5, and *sūrah* 67: 5, note 4, shooting stars are fired to prevent the jinn from reaching the heaven or to repulse them from its doors.

Contact between fortune-tellers and the jinn and/or devils has a certain function in certain sort of fortune-telling. The spying devils, who are the representatives of the foulness and wickedness on the earth, attempt to soil the clean and pure realm of the heavens that are inhabited by pure beings, and spy on the talk of their inhabitants in the name of some disbelieving jinn and their human companions who try to mislead people, particularly through sorcery, mediumship, and soothsaying. God allowed them to grab some snatches of information from their talks before the advent of His Last Messenger. However, just prior to his advent, He shut the gates of the heaven to them completely. When they try to reach the heaven, they find it filled with strong guards who hurl missiles at them. If anyone from among them is able to grab something, they are pursued (and destroyed) by a shooting star dispatched by the angels on guard there.

4. The verse suggests: "But now seeing that the Recitation which we heard guides to right, we have come to know that their Lord wills good and right for the inhabitants of the earth by shutting the gates of the heaven to us."

572

٥٧٢

وَأَنَّا مِنَّا الْمُسْلِمُونَ وَمِنَّا الْقَاسِطُونَ فَمَنْ أَسْلَمَ فَأُوْلَئِكَ تَحَرَّوْا رَشَدًا ۞ وَأَمَّا الْقَاسِطُونَ فَكَانُوا لِجَهَنَّمَ حَطَبًا ۞ وَأَنْ لَّوِ اسْتَقَامُوا عَلَى الطَّرِيقَةِ لَأَسْقَيْنَاهُم مَّاءً غَدَقًا ۞ لِنَفْتِنَهُمْ فِيهِ وَمَن يُعْرِضْ عَن ذِكْرِ رَبِّهِ يَسْلُكْهُ عَذَابًا صَعَدًا ۞ وَأَنَّ الْمَسَاجِدَ لِلَّهِ فَلَا تَدْعُوا مَعَ اللَّهِ أَحَدًا ۞ وَأَنَّهُ لَمَّا قَامَ عَبْدُ اللَّهِ يَدْعُوهُ كَادُوا يَكُونُونَ عَلَيْهِ لِبَدًا ۞ قُلْ إِنَّمَا أَدْعُوا رَبِّي وَلَا أُشْرِكُ بِهِ أَحَدًا ۞ قُلْ إِنِّي لَا أَمْلِكُ لَكُمْ ضَرًّا وَلَا رَشَدًا ۞ قُلْ إِنِّي لَن يُجِيرَنِي مِنَ اللَّهِ أَحَدٌ وَلَنْ أَجِدَ مِن دُونِهِ مُلْتَحَدًا ۞ إِلَّا بَلَاغًا مِّنَ اللَّهِ وَرِسَالَاتِهِ وَمَن يَعْصِ اللَّهَ وَرَسُولَهُ فَإِنَّ لَهُ نَارَ جَهَنَّمَ خَالِدِينَ فِيهَا أَبَدًا ۞ حَتَّى إِذَا رَأَوْا مَا يُوعَدُونَ فَسَيَعْلَمُونَ مَنْ أَضْعَفُ نَاصِرًا وَأَقَلُّ عَدَدًا ۞ قُلْ إِنْ أَدْرِي أَقَرِيبٌ مَّا تُوعَدُونَ أَمْ يَجْعَلُ لَهُ رَبِّي أَمَدًا ۞ عَالِمُ الْغَيْبِ فَلَا يُظْهِرُ عَلَى غَيْبِهِ أَحَدًا ۞ إِلَّا مَنِ ارْتَضَى مِن رَّسُولٍ فَإِنَّهُ يَسْلُكُ مِنْ بَيْنِ يَدَيْهِ وَمِنْ خَلْفِهِ رَصَدًا ۞ لِيَعْلَمَ أَن قَدْ أَبْلَغُوا رِسَالَاتِ رَبِّهِمْ وَأَحَاطَ بِمَا لَدَيْهِمْ وَأَحْصَى كُلَّ شَيْءٍ عَدَدًا ۞

18. All places of worship (and all parts of the body with which one prostrates[6]) are for God, and all worship is due to Him alone, so do not worship anyone along with God.

19. Yet, when God's servant rises to pray, they (the polytheists) are all but upon him in swarms (with loud, derisive shouting to prevent his recitation of the Qur'ān being heard).

20. Say: "I worship only my Lord and do not associate anyone as partner with Him."

21. Say: "It is not in my power to cause you harm or bring you good by guiding you (to the Straight Path)."

22. Say: "No one could ever protect me from God (if I were to disobey Him), nor could I find a refuge except in Him.

23. "(What I can and must do is) only to convey (the truth) from God and His Messages." And whoever disobeys God and His Messenger, for him there is surely the fire of Hell, to abide therein forever.

24. (Let them continue to see you as few in number and weak and therefore belittle you, but) when they see what (the Fire) they are promised, they will come to know who is really weaker in helpers and fewer in number.

25. Say: "I do not know whether (your coming face to face with) what you are promised is near, or whether my Lord sets for it a distant term."[7]

26. (He alone is) the Knower of the Unseen (what lies beyond human perception), and He does not disclose His Unseen to anyone

27. Except to a Messenger whom He has chosen (and is well-pleased with – He informs him of the Unseen as much as He wills –); and He dispatches a watchful

14. 'And among us are some who have wholly submitted to God, just as there are among us some who have deviated into disobedience to God. Whoever has submitted to God wholly, then such have sought and attained to right guidance (in belief and action).

15. 'But as for those who have deviated into disobedience to God, they have become firewood for Hell.'"

16. If they (humankind and the jinn) followed the (Right) Road (of Islam, without deviation), We would certainly grant them water (and provision) in abundance;[5]

17. We try them in that (which We grant them). Whoever turns away from his Lord's Reminder (His Book of instruction), He will drive him into an ever-growing punishment (enveloping him in its severity).

guard before him (between him and his audience) and a watchful guard behind him (between him and the origin of the Revelation);

28. In order that He may establish that they (the Messengers) have for certain conveyed the messages of their Lord. He encompasses all that they have (of the Revelation), and He has recorded everything one by one.[8]

---

5. This verse has almost the same meaning as (7: 96): *If the peoples of those townships had but believed and, in order to deserve His protection, had kept from disobedience to God in reverence for Him and piety, We would surely have opened up for them blessings out of heaven and earth.*

6. Imam Bukhārī relates ("Adhān," 133, 134, 137) that God's Messenger enumerated the parts of the body that must touch the ground during prostration: "I have been ordered to prostrate on seven bodily parts: the forehead (and he also pointed to his nose), the hands, the knees, and the ends of the feet."

7. Like the verse 71: 25, this verse establishes the punishment or reward in the intermediate world (of the grave); here it is done decisively. What is promised for the obstinate enemies of God is Hellfire, as stated in verse 23 above. The exact time of Judgment Day is known exclusively to God and never changes. But this verse particularly refers it to God's Will, which emphasizes the fact that the unbelievers will encounter the punishment promised to them when they die.

8. This same fact is also indicated in the initial verses of *Sūrat al-Sāffāt* (37). Angels accompanied the Archangel Gabriel when he conveyed the Revelation to God's Messenger, upon him be peace and blessings. They aligned themselves in ranks along the route by which Gabriel carried the Revelation to the Messenger, and some of them drove away the devils that were trying to grab something of the Revelation. Among those angels were also those who stood around the Messenger while other angels were conveying to him God's messages concerning the invisible world or the future. These three last verses also emphasize that the Revelation which came to the Messenger and which he conveyed to the people was perfectly preserved from the time it was entrusted to Gabriel by God until it was conveyed to the people (er-Rāzī, al-Qurṭubī, aṭ-Ṭabatabāī).

SŪRAH 73

AL-MUZZAMMIL
(THE ENWRAPPED ONE)

Makkah period

This *sūrah* of 20 verses, revealed in early period in Makkah, takes its name from the word *al-muzzammil* (the enwrapped one) in the first verse. However, there are some reports that its last verse was revealed in Madīnah, although some scholars are of the opinion that it came at some later date in Makkah. It strongly advises Prayer at night, patience, and reliance upon God. It warns the unbelievers against the Day of Judgment.

In the Name of God, the All-Merciful, the All-Compassionate.

1. O you enwrapped one!¹

2. Rise to keep vigil at night, except a little,

3. Half of it, or lessen it a little;

4. Or add to it (a little); and pray and recite the Qur'ān calmly and distinctly (with your mind and heart concentrated on it).

5. We will surely charge you with a weighty Word (and with applying it in your daily life and conveying it to others).

6. Rising and praying at night impresses (mind and heart) most strongly and (makes) recitation more certain and upright.

7. For by day you do have extended preoccupations.

8. And keep in remembrance the Name of your Lord (and mention It in your Prayer), and devote yourself to Him whole-heartedly.

9. The Lord of the east and the Lord of the west; there is no deity but He, so take Him alone for one to rely on and to entrust your affairs to.

10. And endure patiently all that they say (against you), and stay aloof from their way (and part from them) in a becoming manner (not as they treat you; rather with forbearance and good advice).

11. And leave Me to deal with those who enjoy God's worldly blessings and yet obstinately persist in denying (Our Revelations), and grant them respite for a little while.

12. We have (in store for the likes of them) heavy fetters and a Blazing Flame,

13. And food that chokes, and a painful punishment.²

14. On that Day the earth and the mountains will be violently shaken, and the mountains will be as a heap of slipping sand.

15. Surely We have sent to you (O people) a Messenger, a witness against you (one who will testify in the Hereafter as to your deeds in response to God's Message), just as We sent a Messenger to the Pharaoh.

16. But the Pharaoh rebelled against the Messenger, and so We seized him with a calamitous grasp.

17. Then how will you, if you persist in unbelief, guard yourselves against a Day which will turn the children gray-headed?

18. The sky will cleft open thereby. His promise (of Resurrection and Judgment) is certainly to be fulfilled.

19. This is a reminder and admonition, and so let him, who wills, take a path to his Lord.

---

1. This address is directed to God's Messenger, upon him be peace and blessings. As understood from the verses to come, God's Messenger lay down in his house enwrapped in his cloak or blanket because of his grief over the fact that the Makkan polytheists were labeling him as a sorcerer and a madman.

2. Concerning the kinds of torment in the Hereafter mentioned in the last two verses, Fakhru'd-Dīn ar-Rāzī says: "These four kinds of torment can well be interpreted as spiritual torments. Fetters symbolize the carnal soul's remaining shackled to its physical attachments and bodily pleasures. Since the carnal soul has acquired acquaintance with such pleasures and loved them in the world, when it departs from the body, it increases in agonies and worries, and its former acquaintance with and attachment to these become obstacles preventing it from entering the realm of peace and purity. Then those spiritual shackles generate spiritual fires, burning to the degree that the carnal soul was inclined towards such pleasures, along with the impossibility of attaining them; all this gives rise to a sensation of spiritual burning. This is the second step in the torment, which the verse describes as 'a blazing flame.' Then the carnal soul tries to swallow the choking agonies of deprivation and the pangs of separation (from the objects of its worldly enjoyment). This is the 'food that chokes.' And, finally, it remains deprived of being illuminated by the Divine light and joining the community of the blessed ones. This is the greatest torment and is depicted as the 'painful punishment.' But these explanations of mine should not be misunderstood. I do not mean that the meaning of these verses is restricted to what I have stated. Rather, I mean that these verses mention four steps of torment in the Hereafter which will be suffered both spiritually and physically."

Nevertheless, as he does with many verses concerning the pleasures and torments of the Hereafter, Muhammad Asad does not quote ar-Rāzī's last sentence (which states that the four steps of torment will be suffered in the Hereafter both physically and spiritually); this gives the false impression that ar-Rāzī has restricted these steps of torment to spiritual torment only. It is a fact that both the blessings the people of Paradise will enjoy and the torments the people of Hell will suffer will be the consequences of their faith and deeds in the world. But they are not restricted to spiritual torment. Where the human self or soul (*nafs*) exists, things are not only spiritual. When we consider that even in the world it is the human soul which suffers from what happens to the body, not the body itself, we can easily understand that the pleasure and torment in the Hereafter cannot be thought of as being only spiritual. But we cannot know the exact nature of physical or bodily existence there.

20. Surely your Lord knows that you (O Messenger) rise and keep vigil sometimes nearly two-thirds of the night or (other times) a half of it or a third of it, and so do some of those who are in your company as believers. God determines the measure of the night and day (which He has created). He knows that you (O believers) are unable to sustain (such long vigils every night) and He has turned to you in mercy: so recite (when you do the Prayer) from the Qur'ān what is easy for you (to sustain as regular practice). He knows there will be those among you who are sick, and others going about the land seeking of God's bounty, and still others fighting in God's cause. Recite from it, then, as much as is easy (for you).[3] But establish the Prayer in conformity with its conditions as prescribed, pay the Prescribed Purifying Alms (*the Zakāh*), and lend God a good loan (by spending in His cause and for the needy). Whatever of good you forward (to your future, eternal life) for your own selves, you will find it with God, better and greater in reward (than all that you have left behind in the world and much increased in value). And seek God's forgiveness (in all circumstances and eventualities).[4] God is All-Forgiving, All-Compassionate (especially toward His believing, penitent servants).

---

3. The Night Prayer (*aṣ-Ṣalāt at-Tahajjud*) was enjoined on the Messenger in the early years of his Messengership. The Messenger kept such long vigils that his feet swelled up. Some of the believers followed him in keeping long vigils, although it was not obligatory upon them. But it was difficult for them to pray for two-thirds of the night, or half the night, or even one-third of the night, and so in Madīnah God eased this burden. Although the *Tahajjud* Prayer is not obligatory upon Muslims, it is a highly recommended Prayer. It is sometimes said that those who have dedicated themselves to God's cause should observe it.

4. This verse draws attention to and emphasizes the importance of observing the prescribed commandments of Islam. Due observance of them may compensate for the loss that is caused by some faults or minor sins and the faults that come from negligence in the recommended religious acts. The verse *sūrah* 58: 13, *Is it that you are afraid of offering something in charity before your consultation (with him)? (If so) and you have not done it, and God has turned to you in forgiveness, then establish the Prayer in conformity with its conditions, and pay the Prescribed Purifying Alms, and obey God and His Messenger. God is fully aware of all that you do*, is of the same import. And as pointed out in *sūrah* 71, note: 3, asking for God's forgiveness is a door that opens on almost every blessing of God. As we are fallible in nature, we should always seek His forgiveness.

SŪRAH 74

AL-MUDDATHTHIR
(THE CLOAKED ONE)

Makkah period

B eing one of the earliest Revelations to the Messenger, this *sūrah* has 56 verses and derives its name from the word *al-muddaththir* in the first verse, meaning "the cloaked and solitary one." It outlines almost all the fundamentals of faith and the basic truths pertaining to humankind with which the Qur'ān is closely concerned.

In the Name of God, the All-Merciful, the All-Compassionate.

1. O you cloaked one (who has preferred solitude)!¹

2. Arise and warn!²

3. And declare your Lord's (indescribable and incomparable) greatness.

4. And keep your clothing clean!³

5. Keep away from all pollution.

6. Do not consider your fulfillment of these orders as a kindness (to God and people).

7. And for the sake of your Lord be patient (in fulfilling your duty toward God and people).

8. Then, when the Horn is sounded,

9. That Day will be a day of hardship,

10. For the unbelievers, not easy.

11. Leave Me (to deal) with him whom I created alone,

12. And I enabled for him abundant wealth,

13. And children around him as means of power;

14. And I have granted him all means and status for a comfortable life.

15. And yet, he desires that I should give more.

16. By no means! Surely he has been in obstinate opposition to Our Revelations.

17. I will oblige him to a strenuous climb.⁴

---

1. After the first Revelation in the Cave of Hirah, the Revelation did not come for some time. During this break God's Messenger usually preferred solitude in his home, and waited for the new Revelation to come. One day when he was walking outside, he saw Gabriel in his original form, "sitting between the heaven and the earth." This marked the end of the intermission and the Revelation that began to come with this *sūrah* continued without cessation.

2. God's Messenger was both a warner (against all kinds of misguidance and transgression) and one who gave good tidings in return for correct belief and good deeds. So the command "warn" also suggests giving glad tidings. However, especially in the beginning, warning took priority.

3. This verse is about the absolute purity of the garments and should be considered together with the third verse as a preparation for the Prayer, which is ordered in the following verses. Or, if we take into account that the Qur'ān likens righteousness and piety to a garment (7: 26), in addition to its outward meaning, this verse may also signify deepening or growing in devotion to God.

However, these orders should not be regarded as only pertaining to the Messenger; they are directed to all believers.

4. This refers to the difficulties that this man would encounter in the world and the torment awaiting him in the Hellfire. The man (Walīd ibn Mughīrah) mentioned here did not cease to lose his wealth and children after the revelation of these verses until he died.

إِنَّهُۥ فَكَّرَ وَقَدَّرَ ۞ فَقُتِلَ كَيْفَ قَدَّرَ ۞ ثُمَّ قُتِلَ كَيْفَ قَدَّرَ ۞ ثُمَّ نَظَرَ ۞ ثُمَّ عَبَسَ وَبَسَرَ ۞ ثُمَّ أَدْبَرَ وَاسْتَكْبَرَ ۞ فَقَالَ إِنْ هَٰذَا إِلَّا سِحْرٌ يُؤْثَرُ ۞ إِنْ هَٰذَا إِلَّا قَوْلُ ٱلْبَشَرِ ۞ سَأُصْلِيهِ سَقَرَ ۞ وَمَا أَدْرَىٰكَ مَا سَقَرُ ۞ لَا تُبْقِي وَلَا تَذَرُ ۞ لَوَّاحَةٌ لِّلْبَشَرِ ۞ عَلَيْهَا تِسْعَةَ عَشَرَ ۞ وَمَا جَعَلْنَآ أَصْحَٰبَ ٱلنَّارِ إِلَّا مَلَٰٓئِكَةً وَمَا جَعَلْنَا عِدَّتَهُمْ إِلَّا فِتْنَةً لِّلَّذِينَ كَفَرُوا۟ لِيَسْتَيْقِنَ ٱلَّذِينَ أُوتُوا۟ ٱلْكِتَٰبَ وَيَزْدَادَ ٱلَّذِينَ آمَنُوٓا۟ إِيمَٰنًا وَلَا يَرْتَابَ ٱلَّذِينَ أُوتُوا۟ ٱلْكِتَٰبَ وَٱلْمُؤْمِنُونَ وَلِيَقُولَ ٱلَّذِينَ فِى قُلُوبِهِم مَّرَضٌ وَٱلْكَٰفِرُونَ مَاذَآ أَرَادَ ٱللَّهُ بِهَٰذَا مَثَلًا كَذَٰلِكَ يُضِلُّ ٱللَّهُ مَن يَشَآءُ وَيَهْدِى مَن يَشَآءُ وَمَا يَعْلَمُ جُنُودَ رَبِّكَ إِلَّا هُوَ وَمَا هِىَ إِلَّا ذِكْرَىٰ لِلْبَشَرِ ۞ كَلَّا وَٱلْقَمَرِ ۞ وَٱلَّيْلِ إِذْ أَدْبَرَ ۞ وَٱلصُّبْحِ إِذَآ أَسْفَرَ ۞ إِنَّهَا لَإِحْدَى ٱلْكُبَرِ ۞ نَذِيرًا لِّلْبَشَرِ ۞ لِمَن شَآءَ مِنكُمْ أَن يَتَقَدَّمَ أَوْ يَتَأَخَّرَ ۞ كُلُّ نَفْسٍۭ بِمَا كَسَبَتْ رَهِينَةٌ ۞ إِلَّآ أَصْحَٰبَ ٱلْيَمِينِ ۞ فِى جَنَّٰتٍ يَتَسَآءَلُونَ ۞ عَنِ ٱلْمُجْرِمِينَ ۞ مَا سَلَكَكُمْ فِى سَقَرَ ۞ قَالُوا۟ لَمْ نَكُ مِنَ ٱلْمُصَلِّينَ ۞ وَلَمْ نَكُ نُطْعِمُ ٱلْمِسْكِينَ ۞ وَكُنَّا نَخُوضُ مَعَ ٱلْخَآئِضِينَ ۞ وَكُنَّا نُكَذِّبُ بِيَوْمِ ٱلدِّينِ ۞ حَتَّىٰٓ أَتَىٰنَا ٱلْيَقِينُ ۞

---

18. He pondered and he calculated (how he could disprove the Qur'ān in people's sight).

19. Be away from God's mercy, how he calculated!

20. Yea, may God preserve him from the evil eye![5] how he calculated!

21. Then he looked around (in the manner of one who will decide on a matter about which he is asked).

22. Then he frowned and scowled.

23. Then he turned his back and (despite inwardly acknowledging the Qur'ān's Divine origin), grew in arrogance,

24. And he said: "This is nothing but sorcery (of a sort transmitted from sorcerers) from old times.

25. "This is nothing but the word of a mortal."

26. I will make him enter a pit of Hell.

27. What enables you to perceive what that pit is?

28. It leaves none (but entirely burns everyone of those thrown into it), nor does it spare anyone (so that they might die and escape).

29. It scorches up the skin.

30. Over it there are nineteen (keepers).

31. We have appointed none but angels as keepers of the Fire, and We have not caused their number to be anything but a trial for those who disbelieve, that those who were granted the Book before may become certain (that Muḥammad, who explains everything revealed to him without any hesitation in the face of all antagonism and derision, is God's Messenger), and those who believe may grow more firm in faith; and that both they who were granted the Book before and the believers may feel no doubt at all; and those in whose hearts there is a sickness and the unbelievers may say: "What does God mean by this description?" Thus God leads astray whom He wills, and guides whom He wills. None knows your Lord's hosts except He. All this is but a reminder to the mortals (so that they may take heed and act accordingly).[6]

32. No indeed (the Qur'ān is not as the unbelievers claim)! By the moon,

33. And by the night when it retreats,

34. And by the morning when it shines forth,[7]

35. Surely it (the Qur'ān) is of the greatest (of God's signs);

36. A warning for humankind,

37. For everyone of you, whether he goes forward (by choosing faith and good deeds) or hangs back (because his choice of unbelief and sin pulls him away from the Straight Path).

38. Every person is held in pledge for what he earns (through his deeds),

39. Except the people of the Right (the people of happiness and prosperity who receive their Records in their right hands. God will forgive them and reward them with much more than they earned).[8]

40. Dwelling in Gardens (whose beauty cannot be perceived while in the world), they will put questions to one another

41. About the disbelieving criminals, (and convey the answers they give):

42. "What has brought you into the pit?"

43. They will reply: "We were not of those who prayed (who turn to God in sincere worship);

44. "Nor did we use to feed the destitute.

45. "We used to plunge (in falsehood and sin) together with those who plunged (in it).

46. "And we used to deny the (coming of the) Day of Judgment.

47. "Until what is certain to come did come upon us."

---

5. The original of the initial phrases in the last two verses, namely *Be away from God's mercy*, and *Yea, may God preserve him from the evil eye!*, is *QuTiLa*. It has both meanings. However, its usage in the meaning of *May God preserve him from the evil eye!*, is figurative, even derisive, and means: How badly he did it!

6. The unbelievers who rejected the afterlife and therefore any fact or Qur'ānic expression concerning it, scoffed at the idea that there are 19 keepers over the Fire, saying that they could easily defeat such a number. So God explained that these 19 are angels, not human beings. However, those unbelievers considered angels as "the daughters of God" and therefore did not hold their power in awe. Another verse (66: 6) describes them: *Over it are angels stern and strict (in executing the command to punish), who do not disobey God in whatever He commands them, and carry out what they are commanded (to carry out).* So this otherworldly fact became a means of trial for them. God has many other hosts about which we do not know. The Qur'ān mentions such facts, in addition to some other purposes, as a reminder and explanation for humans, especially unbelievers, who tend to perceive God and the facts concerning Him in human terms.

7. Swearing by *the moon* and *the night when it retreats* and *the morning when it shines forth* implies that the daylight and the sun of God's guidance are about to replace the moon and the night in the history of humanity.

8. Believing in God and obedience to Him in His commandments are among God's rights upon human beings, so everyone is held in pledge by God as they are duty-bound to fulfill this right of God upon them. Those who fulfill this duty are released, while others are kept in Hell. The Qur'ān classifies people into three, according to whether they have fulfilled this duty or not and according to the degree of its fulfillment (see 56: 7–10). In addition to the two groups mentioned in this *sūrah* (namely, the people of the Right and the disbelieving criminals [the people of the Left]), there are those foremost in faith and good deeds, and in serving God's cause; they will be the foremost (in receiving and enjoying God's mercy). Since they are the nearest to God and constant in faith and good deeds, and as they will therefore be exempt from being tried in the Supreme Court in the Hereafter (37: 128), they are not mentioned in the verses discussed.

576

and take heed unless God wills; He is the Lord of righteousness and piety, and the Lord of forgiveness.[9]

9. That is, all success depends on God's absolute Will and forgiveness. But He wills success and forgiveness for those who revere Him and act righteously and piously.

SŪRAH 75

AL-QIYĀMAH (RESURRECTION)

Makkah period

This *sūrah* of 40 verses is concerned with death as the "doom" of every individual, and with events that will take place during the final overall destruction of the world and revival of all the dead. It was revealed in Makkah. It takes its name from the word *al-qiyāmah* (Resurrection) in the first verse.

In the Name of God, the All-Merciful, the All-Compassionate.

1. I swear by the Day of Resurrection,

2. And I swear by the self-accusing human soul;[1]

3. Does human think that We will never assemble his bones (to resurrect him)?

4. Yes indeed, We are able to make complete his very fingertips.[2]

5. But human (by willful choice) denies what lies ahead of him (the other life, because he desires to live only as he pleases).

6. He asks: "When is the Day of Resurrection?"

7. When the eyesight is confounded (through fear),

8. And the moon is darkened,

9. And the sun and the moon are joined together,

10. On that Day human will say: "Where is the escape?"

11. By no means! No refuge (to flee to)!

48. And so, of no benefit to them will be the intercession of any who are entitled to intercede, (even if they are allowed to intercede).

49. What, then, is the matter with them that they turn away in aversion from the Reminder (the Qur'ān),

50. As though they were frightened wild donkeys

51. Fleeing from a lion!

52. Indeed, every one of them desires that he should be given a Book (particular to him) opened out.

53. By no means! Indeed, they do not (believe in and, therefore, do not) fear the Hereafter.

54. By no means! This (Qur'ān) is a reminder and admonition (sufficient for all).

55. So, whoever wills receives admonition and takes heed.

56. Yet they will not receive admonition

12. To your Lord the journey's end will be on that Day.

13. Human will be made understand on that Day all (the good and evil) that he has forwarded (to his afterlife while in the world), and all (the good and evil) that he has left behind.[3]

14. Indeed, human will be an eye-witness (providing evidence) against himself,

15. Even though he puts forth his excuses.[4]

16. O Prophet!) Move not your tongue to hasten it (for safekeeping in your heart).

17. Surely it is for Us to collect it (in your heart) and enable you to recite it (by heart).

18. So when We recite it, follow its recitation;

19. Thereafter, it is for Us to explain it.[5]

---

1. For the meaning of human soul (*nafs*), see *sūrah* 3, note 37; *sūrah* 21, note 5.

Self-training, or the training of the soul, has been accepted as an extremely important element of the Divine Religion. This training, according to some schools in Islam, has ten stages, and according to others and some Qur'ānic allusions seven stages:

If the soul lives only a life of ease in the swamp of carnal appetites, it is the evil-commanding soul (*nafs al-ammārah*); if it falters time and again while following the way of the Religion to attain piety and righteousness, but each time that it falters it criticizes itself and turns to its Lord, then it is the self-accusing soul (*nafs al-lawwāmah*). The soul which always resists evil in devotion to God and is favored with certain Divine gifts in proportion to its purity is called the soul receiving inspiration (*nafs al-mulhimah*). When it reaches the point where it has a relation with its Lord in perfect devotion and sincerity and when its consciousness is at rest, it is the soul at rest (*nafs al-muṭmainnah*). If it has reached the station where it abandons all its choices and is a representative of Divine will, it is the soul pleased with God (*nafs ar-rāḍiyah*). When its greatest aim is acquiring God's good pleasure and approval and when it is always acting to this end in consideration of, "I am pleased with You, so be pleased with me," then it is the soul with which God is pleased (*nafs al-marḍiyyah*). Finally, the soul which has been perfectly purified of all sins and evil morals and has the capacity to be completely adorned with the full manifestations of Divine Qualities and Prophetic will-power and reso-

lution is called the soul perfected or the soul pure (*nafs az-zakiyyah* or *nafs aṣ-ṣāfiyah*).

2. The fingertips are the physical extremities of the body, and it is also important that the identity of a person can be determined through their fingerprints. So what this verse is saying is that every human being will be revived in all their particularities, down to their fingertips. The uniqueness of the fingertips of each human being became widely known only centuries after the revelation of the Qur'an.

3. On the Day of Resurrection people will rejoice in the good they did and the evil they did not do while in the world, and they will regret the evil they did and the good that they left undone.

4. That is, as pointed out in 32: 20 and 36: 65, on the Day of Resurrection, the parts of the human body will testify as to what they saw or heard or experienced.

5. The last four verses seem to have no relation with those before or after them. They are concerned with the revelation of the Qur'ān to God's Messenger and his manner of receiving it. The Messenger, upon him be peace and blessings, showed great concern in receiving and committing to heart the Qur'ān during its revelation, and therefore tried to repeat and memorize it. He was also very concerned about fully understanding the meaning. These verses, like 20: 114, which is almost of the same import, assure him that God will enable him to memorize it and understand its meaning. As for the reason why these verses exist between the verses concerning the Day of Resurrection, the Messenger may have shown special care in memorizing them during their revelation.

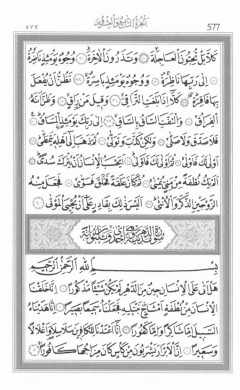

---

meaning of life) when it (the last breath) comes up to the throat,

27. And it is said, "Is there a wizard (that could save him)?"

28. While he (who is dying) is certain that it is the (moment of) parting.

29. And (in the agony of death) one leg is intertwined with the other;

30. To your Lord is, on that Day, the driving.

31. He did not affirm the truth (of the Divine Message conveyed to him), nor did he do the Prayer;

32. Rather, he denied and turned away.

33. Thereafter he went back to his family in gleeful conceit.

34. So: well have you deserved (this doom), well have you deserved (it).

35. Again, well have you deserved it and well deserved.

36. Does human think that he is to be left to himself (to go about as he pleases)?

37. Was he not once a mere drop of semen poured forth?

38. Then he became a clot clinging (to the womb wall), and He created and fashioned (him) in due proportions.

39. Then He made of him a pair, male and female.

40. Is not He (Who does that, equally) able to bring the dead back to life?

20. Yes indeed! but you (people) love and prefer what is before you (the present, worldly life),[6]

21. And abandon that which is to come later (the Hereafter).

22. Some faces on that Day will be radiant (with contentment),

23. Looking up toward their Lord.

24. And some faces on that Day will be despondent,

25. Knowing that a crushing calamity is about to be inflicted on them.

26. No indeed! (No doubt remains for the

---

6. This is another passage to follow *Does human think that We will never assemble his bones (to resurrect him)?* (verse 3), and so

means: Yes indeed, We are able to make complete his very fingertips, (reviving him wholly), but you . . . .

SŪRAH 76

AL-INSĀN (HUMAN)

Makkah period

This *sūrah* of 31 verses was revealed in Makkah and takes its name from the word *al-insān* (human) in the first verse. It is about human perfectibility, the virtues of good believers and the reward they will get in the Hereafter. It also contains advice for the Messenger and hence for the believers dedicated to his cause.

In the Name of God, the All-Merciful, the All-Compassionate.

1. Did there pass (– and surely there did pass –) over human a stretch of time when he was a thing not mentioned and remembered (as human)?[1]

2. We have surely created human from a small quantity of mingled fluids, moving him from one state to another, and (finally) We have made him one hearing and seeing (so that he may hear God's Message and see His signs).

3. And We have shown him the right way, whether he be grateful (and follow this way) or ungrateful (and follow the way opposed to the right one).[2]

4. We have surely prepared for the thankless unbelievers chains, and fetters, and a Blaze.

5. The virtuous and godly will surely drink from a cup with heavenly wine flavored with heavenly additives.

---

1. This does not mean that human did not exist at all during that stretch of time. Rather, as implied in *sūrah* 2: 28 and explained in the note 27, each member of humankind has some sort of existence in the world of atoms or particles. In other words, since it has already been evident in God's Knowledge and determined by Destiny which particles among the innumerable particles of the world will constitute the body of which person, those particles, however widely distributed in air, water, and earth, had long been appointed to constitute the body of the particular individual, even though that individual was not known or mentioned as (a) human being.

Humankind is the fruit of the Tree of Creation and therefore contained its seed. So the Tree of Creation has grown out of the seed of humankind. In other words, as a tree is the grown or developed form of its seed, humankind carries in its body and being the nature and all original elements of other existents. What meaning a seed bears with respect to a tree, humankind has it with respect to the universe. Science should concentrate on this point while investigating how life began on earth and how humankind was originated.

2. God has created human with a disposition and capacity to believe in God and follow His way, and endowed him accordingly with the necessary faculties. This is His guidance based on or originating in His creation, as pointed out in 30: 30: *So set your whole being upon the true religion (of Islam) as one of pure faith (free from unbelief, polytheism, and hypocrisy). This is the original pattern belonging to God on which He has originated humankind. No change can there be in God's creation. This is the upright, ever-true Religion, but most of the people do not know.* (See also Appendix 13.) Out of His special compassion, He also sent them Messengers and showed them His way. Further than that, He made following His way very easy for them through the character and leadership of those Messengers. He declares: *Messengers (have been sent as) bearers of glad tidings and warners, so that people might have no argument against God after the Messengers (had*

come to them). And God is All-Glorious with irresistible might, All-Wise (4: 165). This is His showing His right way. However, He has created humankind as distinct from other creatures and endowed them with free will, and so He does not compel them to choose and follow His way. He has left it to their free choice – being grateful and choosing His way, or being ungrateful and choosing their own way. But He has also informed humankind explicitly of the consequence of their choice.

So, humankind divides into two main groups after God's guidance is conveyed to them: those who accept God's guidance and follow it, and those who reject it. Every one will be treated in the Hereafter according to their choice. However, there is another group made up of those to whom the Divine guidance has not been conveyed or who have not been able to find it due to certain circumstances. They are the ones mentioned in 4: 98: *Except those truly oppressed among the men, and the women, and the children altogether without means and not guided to a way (to emigrate, and including those who, in their lifetime, have not had a means to be guided to faith.) For those (while their circumstances are unchanged, it is expected that) God will not hold them accountable and will excuse them. Assuredly God is One Who excuses much, All-Forgiving* (4: 98–99).

God will treat them in the Hereafter as He wills. However, it is greatly hoped that He will not punish particularly those among them who believe in God and do not oppress others and commit certain major sins such as murder, adultery, and usurpation of others' rights that are abhorrent to human conscience.

سُورَةُ الْإِنْسَان

578

عَيْنًا يَشْرَبُ بِهَا عِبَادُ اللَّهِ يُفَجِّرُونَهَا تَفْجِيرًا ۞ يُوفُونَ بِالنَّذْرِ وَيَخَافُونَ يَوْمًا كَانَ شَرُّهُ مُسْتَطِيرًا ۞ وَيُطْعِمُونَ الطَّعَامَ عَلَىٰ حُبِّهِ مِسْكِينًا وَيَتِيمًا وَأَسِيرًا ۞ إِنَّمَا نُطْعِمُكُمْ لِوَجْهِ اللَّهِ لَا نُرِيدُ مِنكُمْ جَزَاءً وَلَا شُكُورًا ۞ إِنَّا نَخَافُ مِن رَّبِّنَا يَوْمًا عَبُوسًا قَمْطَرِيرًا ۞ فَوَقَاهُمُ اللَّهُ شَرَّ ذَٰلِكَ الْيَوْمِ وَلَقَّاهُمْ نَضْرَةً وَسُرُورًا ۞ وَجَزَاهُم بِمَا صَبَرُوا جَنَّةً وَحَرِيرًا ۞ مُتَّكِئِينَ فِيهَا عَلَى الْأَرَائِكِ لَا يَرَوْنَ فِيهَا شَمْسًا وَلَا زَمْهَرِيرًا ۞ وَدَانِيَةً عَلَيْهِمْ ظِلَالُهَا وَذُلِّلَتْ قُطُوفُهَا تَذْلِيلًا ۞ وَيُطَافُ عَلَيْهِم بِآنِيَةٍ مِّن فِضَّةٍ وَأَكْوَابٍ كَانَتْ قَوَارِيرَا ۞ قَوَارِيرَ مِن فِضَّةٍ قَدَّرُوهَا تَقْدِيرًا ۞ وَيُسْقَوْنَ فِيهَا كَأْسًا كَانَ مِزَاجُهَا زَنجَبِيلًا ۞ عَيْنًا فِيهَا تُسَمَّىٰ سَلْسَبِيلًا ۞ وَيَطُوفُ عَلَيْهِمْ وِلْدَانٌ مُّخَلَّدُونَ إِذَا رَأَيْتَهُمْ حَسِبْتَهُمْ لُؤْلُؤًا مَّنثُورًا ۞ وَإِذَا رَأَيْتَ ثَمَّ رَأَيْتَ نَعِيمًا وَمُلْكًا كَبِيرًا ۞ عَالِيَهُمْ ثِيَابُ سُندُسٍ خُضْرٌ وَإِسْتَبْرَقٌ وَحُلُّوا أَسَاوِرَ مِن فِضَّةٍ وَسَقَاهُمْ رَبُّهُمْ شَرَابًا طَهُورًا ۞ إِنَّ هَٰذَا كَانَ لَكُمْ جَزَاءً وَكَانَ سَعْيُكُم مَّشْكُورًا ۞ إِنَّا نَحْنُ نَزَّلْنَا عَلَيْكَ الْقُرْآنَ تَنزِيلًا ۞ فَاصْبِرْ لِحُكْمِ رَبِّكَ وَلَا تُطِعْ مِنْهُمْ آثِمًا أَوْ كَفُورًا ۞ وَاذْكُرِ اسْمَ رَبِّكَ بُكْرَةً وَأَصِيلًا ۞

──────⌘──────

6. A spring from which God's (virtuous and godly) servants will drink (their fill), causing it to gush abundantly.[3]

7. (They are those who) fulfill the vow (the promises and responsibilities that they undertake), and who fear a Day whose evil is extensive and encompassing (everyone that deserves it).

8. They give food, however great be their need for it, with pleasure to the destitute, and to the orphan, and to the captive, (saying):[4]

9. "We feed you only for God's sake; we desire from you neither recompense nor thanks (we desire only the acceptance of God).

10. "We are surely fearful of a Day from our Lord, (a Day) of frowning and severity (toward the guilty)."

11. So God will surely preserve them from the evil of that Day and enable them to find radiance and joy.

12. He will reward them for all that they endure: a Garden (of Paradise) and garments of silk.

13. Reclining therein on thrones. They will find therein neither (burning) sun nor severe cold.

14. And its shade will come down low over them, and its clusters of fruit hang down low within their reach.

15. And they will be served with vessels of silver and goblets like crystal,

16. Crystal-clear, made of silver – they themselves determine the measure of the drink (as they wish.)[5]

17. And there they will be given to drink of a cup flavored with ginger (of Paradise),

18. (Filled from) a spring therein called *Salsabīl* (as it flows smoothly and continuously as they wish).

19. There will go round them youths of perpetual freshness;[6] when you see them you would think them scattered pearls.

20. And wherever you have a look therein, you will see unimaginable delight and a great kingdom.

21. Upon those (servants) will be garments of fine green silk and brocade, and they will be adorned with armbands of silver;[7] and their Lord will favor them with the service of a pure drink.

22. "This is what has been (prepared) for you as a reward, and your endeavor has been recognized and accepted."

23. It is We Who send down the Qur'ān on you (O Messenger) in parts,

24. So wait patiently for your Lord's judgment, and pay no heed to (the desires and caprices of) any of them who is a willful sinner or a thankless unbeliever.

---

3. The last two verses may be considered together with 37: 45–47; 47: 15, and 56: 18–19.

4. This virtue is essential and common to godliness and true piety. See 2: 177; 3: 92.

5. That is, therein will be for them everything that they desire, and in God's Presence there is yet more (50: 35).

6. On these youths, see *sūrah* 56, note 3.

7. On these garments and armbands, see *sūrah* 18, note 18.

579

بِسْمِ اللهِ الرَّحْمٰنِ الرَّحِيمِ

25. And remember and mention the Name of your Lord (in worship) in the early morning and in the afternoon.

26. And during part of the night prostrate to Him, and glorify Him a long part of the night.[8]

27. Those (sinful unbelievers) love and prefer that which is in advance (the present, worldly life), and neglect a grievous Day ahead of them.

28. It is We Who have created them and made firm their composition, and whenever We will, We can change their structure and character entirely.

29. All this is an admonition and reminder, and so let him who wills, take a path to his Lord.

30. You cannot will unless God wills.[9] Surely God is All-Knowing, All-Wise.

31. He admits whom He wills into His mercy; and as to the wrongdoers, He has prepared for them a painful punishment.

---

8. In many verses (e.g., 11: 114; 17: 78; 20: 130), the Qur'ān orders mentioning God or His Name, glorifying Him, and prostrating to Him. These orders are generally understood and interpreted as commanding prayer to God. Accordingly, in the last two verses in this *sūrah*, it orders mentioning His Name in the early morning (meaning the Dawn Prayer), and from noon until the evening (meaning the Noon/Afternoon Prayer). And it orders prostrating before Him *during part of the night* (meaning the Evening, the Late Evening or Early Night Prayer), and glorifying Him *a long part of the night* (meaning the Tahajjud Prayer). Five daily services of Prayer were ordered during the Ascension in the 11th year

of the Makkan period of Islam. Until then, as it is understood from the relevant verses, the Prayer was performed at three times – in the morning before the sunrise, at any time from noon until the evening, and in the early part of night. The *Tahajjud* Prayer (the Prayer in the second part of night before dawn) was also stressed.

Understanding mentioning our Lord's Name as meaning the Morning and Afternoon Prayer, and prostration as meaning the early night Prayer, and glorification as meaning the *Tahajjud* Prayer may indicate that we should prolong *qirā'ah* (recitation of the Qur'ān) in the Morning and Noon/Afternoon Prayers, that prostration is more important in the Evening and Late Evening Prayers, and glorification in the *Tahajjud Prayer*. God knows the best.

9. For the meaning of this statement and the relation between God's absolute Will and human free will, see: *sūrah* 2, notes 10, 23; *sūrah* 3, note 30; *sūrah* 4, note 18; *sūrah* 6, note 9; *sūrah* 11, note 1; and note 2 on this *sūrah*, and Appendix 7. To summarize what has been said so far:

God's Will is absolute and encompasses human free will. From one perspective, the Divine Will is identical with the Divine Knowledge. God knows (beforehand) what people freely will to do and all that they do is within God's Knowledge. The actions of humankind are within God's Knowledge and Wisdom.

That is, in order for their will to be a cause of their deeds, God's all-encompassing Wisdom also has a part in it. This verse's concluding with mentioning God as All-Knowing and All-Wise, points to this fact. It is God Who has endowed humankind with free will, and humankind always need God to be able to use their free will and accomplish what they will. God has designed human life and established the reality of deeds and all that a person meets in consequence of their deeds. No one can go beyond this encompassing design. God never compels a person to do a particular deed; the human experience of free choice of action is quite real, and it must be so, for everyone is responsible and accountable for their actions.

SŪRAH 77

AL-MURSALĀT
(THE COMPANIES SENT)

Makkah period

Revealed in the early years of the Makkan period of the mission of God's Messenger, upon him be peace and blessings, this *sūrah* of 50 verses takes its name from the word *al-mursalāt* (the companies sent) in the first verse. It mentions the functions of some classes of angels in certain universal events, focusing attention on the Power of God, the truth of the Resurrection and the afterlife, and warning against the denial of this truth.

In the Name of God, the All-Merciful, the All-Compassionate.

1. By the companies (of angels) sent one after another for some good results,

2. And then moving as fast and forcefully as tempests.

3. And by those enfolding the Scrolls of Revelation,

4. And serving (for right and wrong) to be separated with all clarity,

5. And so bringing down the Revelation,

6. In order that some may have the means to ask for forgiveness and that some may be warned,

7. Surely what you are promised is bound to take place,[1]

8. When the stars are effaced,

9. And when the sky is rent asunder,

10. And when the mountains are blown away (as dust),

11. And when the time for the Messengers (to bear witness for or against their communities) is appointed.

12. For what day has the term (of all this) been set?

13. For the Day of Judgment and Distinction (between people according to how they believed and acted in the world).

14. What enables you to perceive what the Day of Judgment and Distinction is?

15. Woe on that Day to those who deny (the Day)!

16. Did We not destroy the ancient peoples (who denied)?

17. So do We make the later generations (of the same standing) follow them (in being destroyed).

18. For thus do We deal with the disbelieving criminals.

19. Woe on that Day to those who deny!

---

1. Angels have very important functions or duties in both our lives and the operation of the universe around them. The Qur'ān mentions the angels with the duties they fulfill and in the groups that fulfill those duties. For example, see 37: 1–3; 79: 1–5. However, we usually live unaware of them and their universal duties. In these initial verses God focuses our attention on them, particularly those of them conveying the Revelation to the Messengers and thus playing a role in the separation of right from wrong, and the separation of those who serve right from those who serve wrong. God concludes the oaths He makes by those angels by emphasizing that the Day of Resurrection will most certainly come.

580

سُوۡرَةُ الۡمُرۡسَلَاتِ   ٥٨

الَمۡ نَخۡلُقُكُّم مِّن مَّآءٍ مَّهِينٍ ۞ فَجَعَلۡنَٰهُ فِى قَرَارٍ مَّكِينٍ ۞ اِلَىٰ قَدَرٍ مَّعۡلُومٍ ۞ فَقَدَرۡنَا فَنِعۡمَ الۡقَٰدِرُونَ ۞ وَيۡلٌ يَوۡمَئِذٍ لِّلۡمُكَذِّبِينَ ۞ اَلَمۡ نَجۡعَلِ الۡأَرۡضَ كِفَاتًا ۞ اَحۡيَآءً وَّأَمۡوَاتًا ۞ وَجَعَلۡنَا فِيهَا رَوَاسِىَ شَامِخَاتٍ وَّأَسۡقَيۡنَٰكُم مَّآءً فُرَاتًا ۞ وَيۡلٌ يَوۡمَئِذٍ لِّلۡمُكَذِّبِينَ ۞ اِنطَلِقُوٓاۡ اِلَىٰ مَا كُنتُم بِهِۦ تُكَذِّبُونَ ۞ اِنطَلِقُوٓاۡ اِلَىٰ ظِلٍّ ذِى ثَلَٰثِ شُعَبٍ ۞ لَّا ظَلِيلٍ وَّلَا يُغۡنِى مِنَ اللَّهَبِ ۞ اِنَّهَا تَرۡمِى بِشَرَرٍ كَالۡقَصۡرِ ۞ كَأَنَّهُۥ جِمَٰلَتٌ صُفۡرٌ ۞ وَيۡلٌ يَوۡمَئِذٍ لِّلۡمُكَذِّبِينَ ۞ هَٰذَا يَوۡمُ لَا يَنطِقُونَ ۞ وَلَا يُؤۡذَنُ لَهُمۡ فَيَعۡتَذِرُونَ ۞ وَيۡلٌ يَوۡمَئِذٍ لِّلۡمُكَذِّبِينَ ۞ هَٰذَا يَوۡمُ الۡفَصۡلِ جَمَعۡنَٰكُمۡ وَالۡأَوَّلِينَ ۞ فَإِن كَانَ لَكُمۡ كَيۡدٌ فَكِيدُونِ ۞ وَيۡلٌ يَوۡمَئِذٍ لِّلۡمُكَذِّبِينَ ۞ اِنَّ الۡمُتَّقِينَ فِى ظِلَٰلٍ وَّعُيُونٍ ۞ وَفَوَٰكِهَ مِمَّا يَشۡتَهُونَ ۞ كُلُواۡ وَاشۡرَبُواۡ هَنِيٓئًا بِمَا كُنتُمۡ تَعۡمَلُونَ ۞ اِنَّا كَذَٰلِكَ نَجۡزِى الۡمُحۡسِنِينَ ۞ وَيۡلٌ يَوۡمَئِذٍ لِّلۡمُكَذِّبِينَ ۞ كُلُواۡ وَتَمَتَّعُواۡ قَلِيلًا اِنَّكُم مُّجۡرِمُونَ ۞ وَيۡلٌ يَوۡمَئِذٍ لِّلۡمُكَذِّبِينَ ۞ وَإِذَا قِيلَ لَهُمُ ارۡكَعُواۡ لَا يَرۡكَعُونَ ۞ وَيۡلٌ يَوۡمَئِذٍ لِّلۡمُكَذِّبِينَ ۞ فَبِأَىِّ حَدِيثٍ بَعۡدَهُۥ يُؤۡمِنُونَ ۞

---

20. (How and why do you dare to deny?) Did We not create you from a humble fluid?

21. Then We placed it in a firm, secure place (to remain)

22. For a known, pre-ordained term (of gestation).

23. Thus have We determined (everything related to your existence), and how excellent We are in determining!

24. Woe on that Day to those who deny!

25. Have We not made the earth a receptacle

26. Both for the living and the dead?

27. And set therein mountains firm, lofty in stature, and given you to drink the sweet water (gushing out of them).

28. Woe on that Day to those who deny!

29. "Move towards that (Fire) which you used to deny!

30. "Move towards the shadow (of black smoke ascending) in three columns.[2]

31. It will neither give (cooling) shade nor will it be of any avail against the flame.

32. It (the Fire) will throw out sparks like castles,

33. (Scattered abroad) as if they were yellow camels.[3]

34. Woe on that Day to those who deny!

35. This will be a Day when they (the deniers) will not utter a word;

36. Nor will they be allowed to offer excuses.[4]

37. Woe on that Day to those who deny!

38. "This is the Day of Judgment and Distinction (between people, according to how they believed and acted in the world). We have assembled you and the earlier ones (from earlier communities who were also deniers).

39. "So if you have a scheme (to save yourselves from My punishment), then apply it (against Me)!"

40. Woe on that Day to those who deny!

41. Surely the God-revering, pious will be amidst pleasant shade and springs;

42. And fruit of whatever kinds they desire.

43. "Eat and drink to your hearts' content for all that you used to do (in the world)."

44. Thus do We reward those who are devoted to doing good, aware that God is seeing them.

45. Woe on that Day to those who deny!

46. Consume (the riches of the world) and enjoy your life but for a little while, for you are criminals, committed to accumulating sins!

47. Woe on that Day to those who deny!

48. When they are told, "Bow down (before God in humility and worship Him)!" they do not bow down.

49. Woe on that Day to those who deny!

50. In what other Word, beyond this (Qur'ān), will they believe?

---

2. It is worth attention that the smoke of Hellfire will ascend in three columns. This becomes more meaningful when we consider that the Qur'ān uses light in singular and darkness in plural as depths or veils of darkness (in Arabic the smallest number of the plural form is three). This may be an indication to the fact that in history, the association of partners with God and systems of oppression have usually been based on three "columns." While describing the deeds of unbelievers, the Qur'ān says that *their deeds are like veils of darkness covering up an abysmal sea down into its depths, covered up by a billow, above which is a billow, above which is a cloud: veils of darkness piled one upon another so that when he stretches out his hand, he can hardly see it* (24: 40). It may also allude to the result of misuse of the three cardinal faculties given to humans, namely intellect, anger, and lusts, and of the three powers upon which a government is based, namely execution, judgment, and legislation, and from another perspective, power, capital, and knowledge or education, or power, justice, and law (see 57: 25, note 15). For example, the Qur'ān says that the Prophet Moses was sent to the Pharaoh, Korah, and Hāmān (29: 39; 40: 24). This must be one of the reasons for, as an instance of wisdom, the fact that during the *Hajj*, the pilgrims throw stones at three devils (the major, the middle, and the minor).

3. The sparks of Hellfire being as big as or being likened to castles and camels may be an allusion to the worldly things that those condemned to Hellfire love passionately. What is most valuable for the desert people is camel, while those who live in towns lost in pleasures are addicted to having lofty castles.

4. According to several verses, the people condemned to Hell will utter words of different import. For example, from Hell they will address God and the believers in Paradise (23: 105–106); they will address the chief guard of Hell (Mālik) (43: 77); on their way to Hell they will address the believers in order to try to get some of their light (57: 13–14); they will reproach themselves in the Place of Supreme Gathering (36: 52; 37: 20); they will dispute among themselves (34: 31–33), etc. So it can be concluded that everything will not take place in the same strain on the Day of Judgment. It will be a Day during which there will be many other "days;" this verse does not contradict others that state that the unbelievers will utter some things and attempt to offer vain excuses.

SURAH 78

AN-NABA'
(THE TIDINGS)

Makkah period

Revealed in Makkah and composed of 40 verses, this *sūrah* takes its name from the word *an-naba'* (important tidings) in the second verse. It is concerned with the Day of Resurrection, and focuses attention on some manifestations of God's Power in the universe.

In the Name of God, the All-Merciful, the All-Compassionate.

1. What are they asking each other about?

2. About the awesome tidings,

3. About which they are in disagreement.[1]

4. No indeed! (They have no need to disagree or question one another about it:) Soon they will come to know!

5. Again, no indeed! Soon they will come to know!

6. Have We not made the earth as a cradle,[2]

7. And the mountains as masts?[3]

8. And We have created you in pairs.

9. And We have made your sleep for rest.

10. And We have made the night as a cloak (covering both you and the world).

11. And We have made the day for seeking livelihood.

12. And We have built above you seven firm heavens.

13. And We have set up (therein) a lamp blazing and resplendent.[4]

14. And We send down out of the rain-clouds water in abundance,

15. So that We may produce with it grain and plants,

16. And gardens dense and luxuriant.

17. Now assuredly, the Day of Judgment and Distinction is a time appointed (as the result of all that takes place in this world).

18. The Day when the Trumpet is blown and you all come forth in hosts.[5]

19. And the heaven is opened (for the descent of angels), and becomes as if gates (so that the world of angels and the world of humankind join each other).

20. And the mountains are set in motion and so become as if they had never existed.

21. Surely Hell lies as a place for surveillance,

22. For the (disbelieving) rebellious, (and) a destined home (which they prepared for themselves while in the world),

23. Wherein they will remain for ages.

24. There they will taste neither coolness nor any drink,

25. Except boiling water and pus,

26. As a recompense fitting (for their sins).

27. For they used not to expect to be called to account (for their deeds);

28. And denied Our Revelations (and all Our other signs in the universe) with willful, obstinate denial.

29. And every thing (that they did) We wrote down as a record.

30. So: "Taste (the fruit of your deeds), and We will not increase you except in suffering."

---

1. The disagreement of the unbelievers about the Resurrection was not about whether they denied it or not, but about their approach to denial of it. Some of them had irreconcilable doubts about it (27: 66), some deemed it as inconceivable (23: 36), and some obstinately rejected whatever of the truth and essentials of faith they were told (67: 21). So the initial verses tell us that, when God's Messenger conveyed to the people of Makkah some truths about the Day of Resurrection and warned them, those who were denying the truths inquired of one another in an attempt to find some argument to back up their denials, and with this interest in mind, sometimes came to the Messenger or the believers, and sometimes went to the Jews or Christians around and asked them questions. They then proceeded to discuss how they should react against these truths and offered different views.

2. The eleven verses from here to verse 17 present some manifestations of the Divine Power in the universe and, by drawing attention to them, establish the truth of the Day of Resurrection. What these verses say is that the universe, with whatever is in it and whatever event takes place, and human life with all its aspects, clearly show that nothing is without meaning or purpose. Rather, all these things indicate another, very important fact, which is their outcome, or indeed their raison d'être. That is, this world is an antecedent of the other world.

3. This verse means:

I have made mountains like masts and stakes for your earth. Ordinary people see mountains as if they have been driven in-

to the ground and, thinking of the benefits and bounties thereof, thank the Creator. Poets imagine the earth as a land upon which the dome of the heaven has been pitched, in a sweeping arc, as a mighty blue tent adorned with lamps. Perceiving the mountains that surround the base of the heaven as tent pegs, they worship the Majestic Creator in amazement.

The literary people of the deserts imagine the earth as a vast desert, and its mountain chains as many nomads' tents. They perceive these as if the soil were stretched over high posts and the pointed tips of the posts had raised the "cloth" of the soil, the home for countless creatures. They prostrate in amazement before the Majestic Creator, Who placed and set up such imposing and mighty things so easily. Geographers with a literary bent view the earth as a ship sailing in the ocean of air or ether, and the mountains as masts that give balance and stability to the ship. Before the All-Powerful One of Perfection, Who has made the earth like a well-built orderly ship on which He makes us travel through the universe, they declare: "Glory be to You. How magnificent Your creation is."

Philosophers or historians of culture see the earth as a house, the pillar of whose life is animal life that, in turn, is supported by air, water, and soil (the conditions of life). Mountains are essential for these conditions, for they store water, purify the atmosphere by precipitating noxious gases, and preserve the ground from becoming a swamp and being overrun by the sea. Mountains also are treasuries for other necessities of human life. In perfect reverence, they praise the Maker of Majesty and Munificence, Who has made these great mountains the pillars for the earth, the house of our life, and appointed them as keepers of the treasures necessary for our life.

Naturalists say: "The earthquakes and tremors, which are due to certain underground formations and fusions, were stabilized with the emergence of mountains. This event also stabilized the axis and orbit of the earth. Thus, its annual rotation is not affected by earthquakes. Its wrath and anger is quieted by coursing through mountain vents." They come to believe and declare: "There is a wisdom in everything God does." (The Words, "the 25th Word," 410–411)

4. The Messenger talks, in the language of the Qur'ān, of a Sovereign "in Whose realm the moon flies round a moth like a fly, while the moth (the earth) flutters round a lamp, and the lamp (the sun) is merely one of thousands of lamps in one of thousands of guest-houses belonging to that Sovereign. He speaks of such a wonderful world and predicts such a revolution that, compared to it, if the earth were a bomb and were to explode, this would not cause amazement.

"The Qur'ān mentions certain facts of creation to make known the Divine Essence, Attributes, and Names. It explains the meaning of the Book of the Universe to make known its Creator. Therefore, it considers creation for the sake of knowledge of its Creator. Modern science, which considers creation only for its own sake, usually addresses scientists. The Qur'ān, however, addresses all of humanity. Since it uses creation as evidence and proof in order to guide humanity, most of whom are common people, its evidence should be easily understandable. Guidance requires that unimportant things only be touched upon, and that subtle points be made understandable via parables.

"For example, it calls the sun "a lamp." It does not mention the sun for its own sake, but rather because it is the "mainstay" of the order and the center of our world's system, and order and system are two ways of learning about the Creator. By depicting the sun as a lamp, it also reminds people that the world is like a palace illuminated by the sun, and that its contents (e.g., beauties, provisions, and other necessities) are prepared for humankind and other living creatures. In this way it teaches and inspires understanding of, and the need for gratitude for, the Creator's Mercy and Bounty" (The Words, "the 19th Word," 250, 254–255). (Also see 25: 61, note 15.)

5. See 6: 73, note 14; 39: 68, note 22.

582   سُوۡرَۃُ النَّبَأِ   ٥٨٢

اِنَّ لِلْمُتَّقِیْنَ مَفَازًا ۙ حَدَآئِقَ وَاَعْنَابًا ۙ وَّکَوَاعِبَ اَتْرَابًا ۙ وَّکَاْسًا دِهَاقًا ۙ لَا یَسْمَعُوۡنَ فِیۡهَا لَغْوًا وَّلَا کِذَّابًا ۚ جَزَآءً مِّنْ رَّبِّکَ عَطَآءً حِسَابًا ۙ رَّبِّ السَّمٰوٰتِ وَالْاَرْضِ وَمَا بَیْنَهُمَا الرَّحْمٰنِ لَا یَمْلِکُوۡنَ مِنْهُ خِطَابًا ۚ یَوۡمَ یَقُوۡمُ الرُّوۡحُ وَالْمَلٰٓئِکَةُ صَفًّا ۙ لَّا یَتَکَلَّمُوۡنَ اِلَّا مَنْ اَذِنَ لَهُ الرَّحْمٰنُ وَقَالَ صَوَابًا ۙ ذٰلِکَ الْیَوۡمُ الْحَقُّ ۚ فَمَنْ شَآءَ اتَّخَذَ اِلٰی رَبِّهٖ مَاٰبًا ۙ اِنَّآ اَنْذَرْنٰکُمْ عَذَابًا قَرِیۡبًا ۚ یَّوۡمَ یَنْظُرُ الْمَرْءُ مَا قَدَّمَتْ یَدٰهُ وَیَقُوۡلُ الْکٰفِرُ یٰلَیۡتَنِیۡ کُنْتُ تُرٰبًا ۙ

سُوۡرَۃُ النَّازِعٰتِ مَکِّیَّةٌ وَّ اٰیَاتُهَا سِتٌّ وَّ اَرْبَعُوۡنَ

بِسْمِ اللّٰهِ الرَّحْمٰنِ الرَّحِیْمِ

وَالنّٰزِعٰتِ غَرْقًا ۙ وَّالنّٰشِطٰتِ نَشْطًا ۙ وَّالسّٰبِحٰتِ سَبْحًا ۙ فَالسّٰبِقٰتِ سَبْقًا ۙ فَالْمُدَبِّرٰتِ اَمْرًا ۘ یَوۡمَ تَرْجُفُ الرَّاجِفَةُ ۙ تَتْبَعُهَا الرَّادِفَةُ ۙ قُلُوۡبٌ یَّوۡمَئِذٍ وَّاجِفَةٌ ۙ اَبْصَارُهَا خَاشِعَةٌ ۘ یَقُوۡلُوۡنَ ءَاِنَّا لَمَرْدُوۡدُوۡنَ فِی الْحَافِرَةِ ۙ ءَاِذَا کُنَّا عِظَامًا نَّخِرَةً ۙ قَالُوۡا تِلْکَ اِذًا کَرَّةٌ خَاسِرَةٌ ۘ فَاِنَّمَا هِیَ زَجْرَةٌ وَّاحِدَةٌ ۙ فَاِذَا هُمْ بِالسَّاهِرَةِ ۙ

---

31. For the God-revering, pious there will surely be triumph:

32. Gardens and vineyards,

33. And youthful, full-breasted maidens of equal age.[6]

34. And a cup full to the brim.

35. They will hear therein neither vain talk nor falsehood.

36. (All this as) a reward from your Lord, a gift according to (His) reckoning in full satisfaction.[7]

37. The Lord of the heavens and the earth and (all) that is between them, the All-Merciful. No one will have the power to address Him.

38. On that Day the Spirit[8] and the angels stand in ranks. No one will speak except him whom the All-Merciful allows,[9] and he speaks what is right.

39. That Day (of Judgment) is the Day absolutely true (on which the truth will prevail). So whoever wills, then, let him take a way of return to his Lord.

40. We have surely warned you against a punishment near at hand. On that Day a person will look at what he has forwarded (from the world) with his own hands, and the unbeliever will say: "Oh, would that I were mere dust (instead of being a responsible being with consciousness and free will)!"

---

6. Some biased persons from other religions accuse Islam of promising a paradise full of carnal pleasures. Islam considers humans with their complete nature, not as a body only or carnal soul, nor as a spirit only. Islam considers all of these and has laid down the necessary rules for each. So it neither orders monasticism nor sets human desires free. It employs human desires for human perfection. So Paradise will be a place where both the human spirit and the carnal soul (which will have been trained and purified) will be satisfied with the (pure) pleasures particular to each.

Question: What does the defective, changing, unstable, and pain-stricken body have to do with eternity and Paradise? The spirit's elevated pleasures must be enough. Why should a bodily resurrection take place for bodily pleasures?

Answer: Soil, despite its darkness and density when compared to water, air, and light, is the means and source of all works of Divine art. Therefore it is somehow superior in meaning over other elements. Your selfhood, despite its density and due to its being comprehensive and provided it is purified, gains some kind of superiority over your other senses and faculties. Likewise, your body is a most comprehensive and rich mirror for the Divine Names' manifestations, and has been equipped with instruments to weigh and measure the contents of all Divine treasuries. For example, if the tongue's sense of taste were not the origin of as many measures as the varieties of food and drink, it could not experience, recognize, or measure them. Furthermore, your body also contains the instruments needed to experience and recognize most of the Divine Names' manifestations, as well as the faculties for experiencing the most various and infinitely different pleasures.

The universe's conduct and humanity's comprehensive nature show that the Maker of the universe wants to make known all His Mercy's treasuries and all His Names' manifestations, and to make us experience all His bounties by means of the universe. Given this, as the world of eternal happiness is a mighty pool into which the flood of the universe flows, a vast exhibition of what the loom of the universe produces, and the everlasting store of crops produced in the field of this (material) world, it will resemble the universe to some degree. The All-Wise Maker, the All-Compassionate Just One, will give pleasures particular to each bodily organ as wages for their duty, service, and worship. To think otherwise would be contrary to His Wisdom, Justice, and Compassion.

Question: A living body is in a state of formation and de-formation, and so is subject to disintegration and is non-eternal. Eating and drinking perpetuate the individual; sexual relations perpetuate the species. These are fundamental to life in this world but must be irrelevant and unnecessary in the world of eternity. Given this, why have they been included among Paradise's greatest pleasures?

Answer: A living body declines and dies because the balance between what it needs

to maintain and takes in is disturbed. From childhood until the age of physical maturity, it takes in more than it lets out and grows healthier. Afterwards, it usually cannot meet its needs in a balanced way, and death comes in. In the world of eternity, however, the body's particles remain constant and are immune to disintegration and re-formation. In other words, this balance remains constant.

Like moving in perpetual cycles, a living body gains eternity together with the constant operation of the factory of bodily life for pleasure. In this world, eating, drinking, and marital sexual relations arise from a need and perform a function. Thus a great variety of excellent (and superior) pleasures are ingrained in them as immediate wages for the functions performed. In this world of ailments, eating and marriage lead to many wonderful and various pleasures. Thus Paradise, the realm of perfect happiness and pleasure, must contain these pleasures in their most elevated form. Adding to them otherworldly wages (as pleasures) for the duties performed in the world by them and the need felt for them here in the form of a pleasant and otherworldly appetite, they will be transformed into an all-encompassing, living source of pleasure that is appropriate to Paradise and eternity. (*The Words*, "the 28th Word," 515–517)

(For other explanations of blessings of Paradise, see *sūrah* 2: 25, note 21; *sūrah* 73: 13, note 2; and for equality of age, see *sūrah* 56: 37, note 6.

7. The punishment for rebellious unbelievers will be a recompense fitting and in accordance with their sins (verses 22, 26, 30), but the reward for the God-revering, pious will be according to God's reckoning out of His Grace and to their full satisfaction.

8. On the Spirit, see *sūrah* 70, note 1.

9. This statement also annotates the second sentence in the previous verse: *No one will have the power to address Him.*

SŪRAH 79

AN-NĀZI'ĀT
(THOSE WHO FLY OUT)

Makkah period

Revealed in Makkah, this *sūrah* of 46 verses takes its name from the word *an-nāzi'āt* (those angels who fly out) in the first verse. It reminds us of death, warns against those who deny the afterlife, and draws attention to the Pharaoh, whose power could not save him from God's punishment. It also mentions some acts of God in the universe and establishes the truth of the afterlife.

In the Name of God, the All-Merciful, the All-Compassionate.

1. By those (angels) who immediately fly out and plunge (with God's command), and plunge (into fulfilling it);

2. By those (angels) who move gently and eagerly (because of the command they have received);

3. By those (angels) who swiftly float (through space to fulfill God's command);

4. And so hasten along as if in a race;

5. And thus fulfill the commands (in the operation of the universe),

6. (The Last Hour will have come) on the Day when a blast (of the Trumpet) will convulse (the world);

7. Followed by the succeeding one.

8. Hearts on that Day will be throbbing in distress;

9. Their eyes downcast.

10. Yet, they (the unbelievers) say: "Will we really be restored to our former state (of life)?

11. "Will we when we have become bones rotten and crumbled away?"

12. They say (in derision): "Then, that would be a return with loss!"

13. It will indeed be but a single cry,

14. And then, they will all have been awakened to life on the plain (of Supreme Gathering).

٥٨٣　　　الجزء الثلاثون　　　583

> هَلْ أَتَىٰكَ حَدِيثُ مُوسَىٰ ۝ إِذْ نَادَاهُ رَبُّهُ بِالْوَادِ الْمُقَدَّسِ طُوًى ۝ اذْهَبْ إِلَىٰ فِرْعَوْنَ إِنَّهُ طَغَىٰ ۝ فَقُلْ هَل لَّكَ إِلَىٰ أَن تَزَكَّىٰ ۝ وَأَهْدِيَكَ إِلَىٰ رَبِّكَ فَتَخْشَىٰ ۝ فَأَرَاهُ الْآيَةَ الْكُبْرَىٰ ۝ فَكَذَّبَ وَعَصَىٰ ۝ ثُمَّ أَدْبَرَ يَسْعَىٰ ۝ فَحَشَرَ فَنَادَىٰ ۝ فَقَالَ أَنَا رَبُّكُمُ الْأَعْلَىٰ ۝ فَأَخَذَهُ اللَّهُ نَكَالَ الْآخِرَةِ وَالْأُولَىٰ ۝ إِنَّ فِي ذَٰلِكَ لَعِبْرَةً لِّمَن يَخْشَىٰ ۝ أَأَنتُمْ أَشَدُّ خَلْقًا أَمِ السَّمَاءُ بَنَاهَا ۝ رَفَعَ سَمْكَهَا فَسَوَّاهَا ۝ وَأَغْطَشَ لَيْلَهَا وَأَخْرَجَ ضُحَاهَا ۝ وَالْأَرْضَ بَعْدَ ذَٰلِكَ دَحَاهَا ۝ أَخْرَجَ مِنْهَا مَاءَهَا وَمَرْعَاهَا ۝ وَالْجِبَالَ أَرْسَاهَا ۝ مَتَاعًا لَّكُمْ وَلِأَنْعَامِكُمْ ۝ فَإِذَا جَاءَتِ الطَّامَّةُ الْكُبْرَىٰ ۝ يَوْمَ يَتَذَكَّرُ الْإِنسَانُ مَا سَعَىٰ ۝ وَبُرِّزَتِ الْجَحِيمُ لِمَن يَرَىٰ ۝ فَأَمَّا مَن طَغَىٰ ۝ وَآثَرَ الْحَيَاةَ الدُّنْيَا ۝ فَإِنَّ الْجَحِيمَ هِيَ الْمَأْوَىٰ ۝ وَأَمَّا مَنْ خَافَ مَقَامَ رَبِّهِ وَنَهَى النَّفْسَ عَنِ الْهَوَىٰ ۝ فَإِنَّ الْجَنَّةَ هِيَ الْمَأْوَىٰ ۝ يَسْأَلُونَكَ عَنِ السَّاعَةِ أَيَّانَ مُرْسَاهَا ۝ فِيمَ أَنتَ مِن ذِكْرَاهَا ۝ إِلَىٰ رَبِّكَ مُنتَهَاهَا ۝ إِنَّمَا أَنتَ مُنذِرُ مَن يَخْشَاهَا ۝ كَأَنَّهُمْ يَوْمَ يَرَوْنَهَا لَمْ يَلْبَثُوا إِلَّا عَشِيَّةً أَوْ ضُحَاهَا ۝

---

15. Has the report of Moses come to you?

16. When His Lord called out to him in the sacred Valley of Tuwa':

17. "Go to the Pharaoh, for he has exceedingly rebelled.

18. "And say to him: 'Would you (do you have intent or inclination to) attain to purity?

19. 'Then I will guide you to your Lord so you stand in awe of Him (and behave with humility).' "

20. He (went to the Pharaoh and) showed him the great sign (the miracle of the Staff).

21. But the Pharaoh denied (his Messengership) and defied (him).

22. Thereafter he turned away and set out to struggle (with him).

23. Then he gathered (his men and hosts), and made a proclamation,

24. Saying: "I am your Supreme Lord!"

25. And so God seized him and made an example of him, of punishment in the later and the earlier (life).

26. For sure, in this there is certainly a lesson for anyone who has awe of and therefore humility before God.[1]

27. (O humankind!) Are you harder to create or is the heaven? He has built it.[2]

28. He has raised its vault and put it in an order.

29. And He obscured its night and brought out its light of day.[3]

30. And after that He has spread out the earth in the egg-shape[4] (for habitability).

31. Out of it He has brought forth its waters and its herbage;

32. And the mountains He has set firm:

33. (All this) as a means of life for you and your animals.

34. But when the great overwhelming event comes;

35. On that Day human will recall (and understand) for what he strove.

36. And the Blazing Flame will come into view for all who see.

37. And so, whoever rebelled (against God),

38. And preferred the life of this world,

39. The Blazing Flame will be his (final) refuge.

40. But as for him who lived in awe of his Lord, being ever conscious of His seeing him and of the standing before Him (in the Hereafter), and held back his carnal soul from lusts and caprices,

41. Surely Paradise will be his (final) refuge.

42. They ask you (O Messenger) about the Last Hour: "When will it come to anchor?"

43. But how could you have knowledge about its time,

44. With your Lord alone rests (the exact knowledge) of its term.

45. You are only a warner to those who are in awe of it.

46. It will be, on the Day they see it, as if they had remained (in the world) but for the afternoon (of a day) or its morning.

---

1. For the details of Moses' story, see 20: 9–79; 28: 3–42.

2. As noted in 30: 27, note 7; 31: 28, note 6; and 40: 57, note 17, nothing is difficult for God. To put it more properly, difficulty is not an attribute that can be conceived of for God, for everything is absolutely easy for Him in the same degree. So the comparison in the verse is from the perspective of humankind, asking which is more difficult for them to conceive of.

3. In the beginning the heaven was in darkness, or there was no light-emitting object in it. So after fashioning the heaven, God placed light-emitting objects in it, such as the sun and the other stars and He removed its darkness. This verse also means that He has made some celestial objects, including the earth, which have both darkness (night) and light (day), alternately.

4. Surely at the time when the Qur'ān was revealed, people had no idea that the earth was an ellipse, nor was it a known fact until recently.

584

SŪRAH 80

'ABASA (HE FROWNED)

Makkah period

Revealed in Makkah in the early years of Islam, this *sūrah* of 42 verses takes its name from the verb *'ABaSa* (he frowned) in the first verse. It stresses that everyone, whatever their family origin and whatever their social status, is equal with respect to the communication of God's Message. It invites people to reflect on some works of God's Power and warns against the Day of Resurrection.

In the Name of God, the All-Merciful,
the All-Compassionate.

1. He (a disbelieving, haughty man) frowned and turned away,

2. Because (while he was talking with the Messenger) the blind man approached him.

3. What would inform you (O haughty one) but that he might grow in purity (by doing good deeds)?

4. Or that he might grow mindful (of God's Message), and the reminder benefit him?

5. As for him who deems himself to be independent (not needy of Divine guidance because of pride in his wealth and status),

6. You (O Messenger) attend to him (so that he may accept Islam and reform),

7. Though you are not accountable if he does not grow in purity (through acceptance of faith and fulfilling its obligations and responsibilities).

8. But as for him who came to you eagerly,

9. And he was in awe of God,

10. You divert your attention from him (to the other).[1]

11. No indeed! It surely is a reminder and an admonition (that suffices for all who come to it with an open heart).

12. So whoever wills receives admonition and takes heed.

13. (It is recorded) in scrolls greatly honored,

14. Exalted (in God's sight) and perfectly purified (of falsehood, vanity, and inconsistency);

15. (Borne) by the hands of angel-envoys,

16. Noble and virtuous.[2]

17. Human is ruined – for how thankless and disbelieving he is!

18. (Does he never consider) from what thing He has created him?

19. From a drop of (seminal) fluid; He has created him and fashioned him in measured proportions (for his shape and for his life).

20. Thereafter He has made the path (to God) easy for him,

21. Thereafter He causes him to die and buries him.

22. Thereafter, when He wills, He raises him again to life.

23. No indeed! Human has not fulfilled what God enjoined on him.

24. Then, let human consider his food (and so reflect on his Lord's Mercy and the truth of Resurrection),

25. That We pour down the water in abundance;

26. Then We split the earth in clefts;

27. And so We enable grain to grow therein,

28. And grapes, and edible plants,

29. And olive-trees and date-palms,

30. And gardens dense with foliage,

31. And (diverse other) fruits and herbage,

32. As a means of livelihood for you and your livestock.

33. But when the piercing Cry (heralding the Resurrection) sounds;

---

1. Particularly in the early period of conveying Islam, God's Messenger, upon him be peace and blessings, thought that if the leaders of the Quraysh accepted Islam, the other people would more easily enter it. So without ever neglecting others, he preached Islam to the leaders with great eagerness. One day when he was busy with one of those leaders, 'Abdullāh ibn Umm Maktūm, a blind Muslim, came to the Messenger in order to listen to him and benefit from him. However, since the Messenger was busy with the other, who stated that in what the Messenger proclaimed he found nothing harmful (al-Muwatta', "Tafsīr al-Qur'ān," 8;

at-Tirmidhī, "Tafsīr Sūrah 80,"), he delayed attending to the blind man for a little while. And the other man frowned at the poor, blind one standing near him, and left. The verses were revealed on this occasion.

2. As stated in some verses and pointed out in the corresponding notes (i.e., 32: 11, note 8; 37: 1–3, note 1), like other Archangels, such as Azrā'il (the Angel of Death), Gabriel also has aides. So the scrolls referred to in verses 13–14 are the heavenly pages on which the Qur'ānic Revelations are recorded, and the envoys are the aides of Gabriel who accompanied him while carrying them to the Messenger.

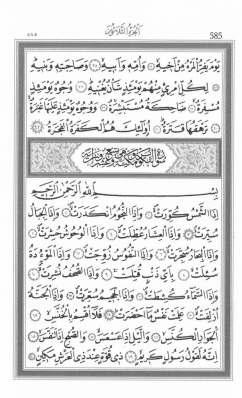

SŪRAH 81

AT-TAKWĪR
(THE FOLDING UP)

Makkah period

Revealed in Makkah in the early years of Islam, this *sūrah* of 29 verses takes its name from the verb *kuwwirat* (folded up) in the first verse. It draws attention to the Hereafter by mentioning certain events that will occur during the final destruction of the world and the rebuilding thereof. It also establishes the Divine origin and authenticity of the Qur'ān and the Messengership of God's Messenger, upon him be peace and blessings.

In the Name of God, the All-Merciful, the All-Compassionate.

1. When the sun is folded up (and darkened);[1]

2. And when the stars fall (losing their luster);

3. And when the mountains are set moving;

4. And when (highly prized) pregnant camels are left untended;

5. And when the wild beasts (as also the domesticated ones) go forth from their places of rest (in terror of the destruction of the world, and then, following their revival, are gathered together before God, for the settlement of their accounts);[2]

6. And when the seas rise up boiling;

7. And when the souls are coupled (the righteous men with pure, righteous spouses, and the evil ones with their evil spouses and with devilish companions);[3]

8. And when the female infant, buried alive, is questioned

34. On that Day when a person flees from his brother,

35. And from his mother and father,

36. And from his spouse and his children;

37. Everyone on that Day has concern of his own enough to make him heedless (of anything else).

38. Some faces will on that Day be radiant with happiness

39. Smiling, rejoicing at good tidings.

40. And some faces will on that Day be dust-stained;

41. Veiled in darkness:

42. Those are the unbelievers, shameless and dissolute.

9. For what crime she was killed;[4]

10. And when the scrolls (of the deeds of every person) are laid open;[5]

11. And when the heaven is torn away (with all the truths becoming manifest);[6]

12. And when the Blazing Flame is kindled (to fierce heat);

13. And when Paradise is brought near (for the God-revering, pious to enter);

14. Every person will (then) come to know what he has prepared (for himself).

15. Oh, I swear by the stars which re-cede (disappearing in the sun's light),

16. And rise in their course, and then set (disappearing again);

17. And by the night as it inclines to depart,

18. And the morning as it breathes,

19. That this (which informs you of all the events mentioned) is the Word (brought) by an honored messenger (Gabriel),

20. Endowed with power, with high rank and esteem before the Lord of the Supreme Throne;

---

1. Besides the brilliant metaphor contained in *folded up* (or "rolled" or "wrapped up"), the verse alludes to several related events: First, by drawing back non-existence, ether, and the skies respectively, like veils, Almighty God brought a brilliant lamp (the sun) out of the treasury of His Mercy to illuminate and be displayed to the world. After the world is destroyed, He will again wrap it in its veils and remove it.

Second, the sun is an official of God charged with spreading its light and giving heat, and with winding light and darkness alternately round the world's head, like a turban. Each evening it gathers up and conceals its light. Sometimes it does little work because a cloud veils it; sometimes it withdraws from working because the moon draws a veil over its face and closes its account book for a short, fixed time. At some future time, this official will resign from its post. Even if there is no cause for its dismissal, due to the two black spots growing on its face, as they have begun to do, the sun will obey the Divine command to draw back the light it sends to the earth and wrap it around its own head. God will also order it: "You no longer have any duty toward the earth. Now, go to Hell and burn those who, by worshipping you, have insulted an obedient official with disloyalty as if you had claimed divinity." Through its black-spotted face, the sun exhibits the meaning of:

When the sun is folded up. (See *The Words*, "the 25th Word," 445.)

2. For an explanation, see 6: 38, note 8. Although animals are not responsible for any religious commands, they are responsible for and ruled by God's law of the operation of the world (*ash-Shari'at at-takwīnī*). So they will be called to account for having or not having observed this law in relation with themselves. Also, human beings will be questioned about their treatment of them.

3. See 4: 57; 37: 22; 43: 36; 44: 54.

4. Many pagan Arabs buried their daughters alive during the pre-Islamic era of Ignorance (16: 58–59). Women were despised, not only in pre-Islamic Arabia, but almost throughout the world, including in Roman and Sassanid lands. The Qur'ān openly declares that people will be questioned concerning this.

After God's Messenger, upon him be peace and blessings, had declared his Messengership, a Companion told him what he had done with his daughter:

O Messenger of God, I had a daughter. One day I told her mother to dress her, for I was taking her to her uncle. My poor wife knew what this meant, but could do nothing but obey and weep. She dressed the girl, who was very happy that she was going to see her uncle. I took her near a well, and told her to look down into it. While she was looking into the well, I kicked her into it. While she was rolling down, she was shouting: "Daddy, Daddy!"

As he was recounting this, the Messenger sobbed (as if he had lost one of his nearest kinsfolk) (Dārimī, *Sunan*, "Muqaddimah," 7–8).

Hearts had become hard. Pits were dug in the desert for innocent girls to be buried in. Human beings were more brutal and cruel than hyenas. The powerful crushed the weak. Brutality was taken for humanity, cruelty received approval, the bloodthirsty were exalted, bloodshed was considered a virtue, and adultery and fornication were more common than legal marriage. The family structure had been destroyed.

This dark period was followed by Islam and all the evils were eradicated. People who had once been extremely cruel were transformed into such compassionate people that they inquired what was the penalty to be paid for accidentally trampling locusts. (For details, see *The Messenger of God*.) Islam also forbade abortion, particularly after the seventh week of pregnancy unless there were pressing medical reasons. This verse also includes this.

5. This verse implies: At the time of the Resurrection, everyone's deeds will be revealed on written pages. At first glance, this appears rather strange and incomprehensible. But as indicated by this *sūrah*, just as the renewal of spring parallels another resurrection, the "laying open of the scrolls" has a very clear parallel. Every fruit-bearing tree and flowering plant has its properties, functions, and deeds. It performs its worship particular to itself. All of its deeds and the record of its life are inscribed in each seed that will emerge the next spring in another plot of soil. In the language of shape and form, the trees or flowering plants grow from seeds that were buried the previous autumn, eloquently indicating the original tree's or flowering plant's life and deeds, and spread out the pages of their deeds through their branches, twigs, leaves, blossoms, and fruits. He Who says: *When the scrolls are laid open* is the same Being Who, before our eyes, achieves these feats in a very wise, prudent, efficient, and subtle way. Such a way is dictated by His Names the All-Wise, All-Preserving, All-Sustaining and Training, and All-Subtle.

6. See: 25: 25; 39: 67; 40: 16; 69: 18.

21. One obeyed (by his aides), and trust-worthy (in fulfilling God's orders, most particularly conveying the Revelation).

22. Your companion (the Messenger who has spent his life among you) is not a madman;

23. Indeed he saw him (Gabriel) on the clear horizon.[7]

24. He is not niggardly (in conveying to you Revelation and knowledge) of the Unseen (what lies beyond the reach of your perception).

25. Nor is it (this Qur'ān) the Word of any devil excluded from God's Mercy.

26. Then, where are you going?

27. It is nothing other than a Reminder (and instruction) for all conscious beings;

28. For any of you who wills to take a straight path (and follow it without deviance).

29. But you cannot will (to do so) unless God wills,[8] the Lord of the worlds.

---

7. See *sūrah* 53: 7, note 3; *sūrah* 74: 1, note 1.

8. See *sūrah* 76, note 9.

SŪRAH 82

AL-INFIṬĀR
(THE CLEAVING OPEN)

Makkah period

Revealed in Makkah, this *sūrah*, which consists of 19 verses, derives its name from the infinitive form (*infiṭār*) of the verb *infaṭara* (to be cleft open) in the first verse. It draws attention to the Hereafter by mentioning certain important events during the final destruction of the world and calls to faith in and obedience to God in His absolute Oneness.

In the Name of God, the All-Merciful, the All-Compassionate.

1. When the heaven is cleft open;

2. And when the stars fall in disorder and are scattered;

3. And when the seas burst forth (spilling over their bounds to intermingle);

4. And when the graves are overturned (and pour out their contents);

5. Everyone will come to understand all (the good and evil) that he has forwarded (to his afterlife while in the world), and all (the good and evil) that he has left behind (undone).

6. O human! What is it that deludes you concerning your Lord, the All-Munificent?

7. He Who has created you, fashioned you, and proportioned you (in measures perfect for the purpose of your creation);

8. Having constituted you in whatever form He has willed.

9. No indeed! But (being deluded) they deny the Last Judgment (in the other world);

10. Yet there are angel-guardians (watching) over you –

11. Noble and honorable, recording,

12. Who know what you do.[1]

13. The virtuous and godly ones will indeed be in (the Gardens of) perpetual bliss;

14. While the (disbelieving) shameless, dissolute ones will indeed be in the Blazing Flame.

15. They will enter it to roast (therein) on the Day of Judgment.

16. They will never be absent from it.

17. What enables you to perceive what the Day of Judgment is?

18. Again: What is it that enables you to perceive what the Day of Judgment is?[2]

19. The Day on which no soul has power to do anything in favor of another. The command on that day will be God's (entirely and exclusively).

---

1. Verse 50: 17 states that for each person there are two angels appointed to watch over them and record all that they do. The one on the right side records one's good deeds, while the other (on the left side) records the evil ones.

2. Concerning this type of question, see 69: 3, note 1.

SŪRAH 83

AL-MUṬAFFIFĪN
(DEALERS IN FRAUD)

Makkah period

Revealed in Makkah, this *sūrah* of 36 verses derives its name from the word *muṭaffifīn* (dealers in fraud) in the first verse. It explains and enjoins honesty in dealings and presents some aspects of the afterlife.

In the Name of God, the All-Merciful, the All-Compassionate.

1. Woe to those who deal in fraud;

2. Those who, when they are to receive their due from others, demand that it be in full;

3. But when they measure or weigh out for others, they make it less (than the due).

4. Do those (people) not know that they are bound to be raised from the dead,

5. For an awesome Day,

6. The Day when all humankind will rise (from their graves and) stand before the Lord of the worlds?

7. No indeed! The record of the shameless dissolute one is surely in *sijjīn* (a lowly register, portending eternal punishment).

8. What enables you to perceive what *sijjīn* is?

9. A register inscribed indelibly and sealed.

10. Woe on that Day to those who deny –

11. Those who deny the Day of Judgment!

12. Which none denies except everyone exceeding the bounds (set by God), everyone addicted to sinning,

13. Who, when Our Revelations are conveyed to him, says: "Fables of the ancients!"

14. By no means! But what they themselves have earned has rusted upon their hearts (and prevents them from perceiving the truth).

15. By no means! Assuredly they will on that Day be veiled from (the mercy of) their Lord.

16. Then they will certainly enter in the Blazing Flame to roast.

17. Thereafter they will be told: "This is what you used to deny (while in the world)."

18. No indeed! The record of the virtuous

and godly ones is surely in *'illiyyīn* (a lofty register, portending elevated stations).

19. What enables you to perceive what *'illiyyin* is?

20. It is a register inscribed indelibly and sealed.

21. Those who are near-stationed to God will attest to it.

22. The virtuous and godly ones will certainly be in (Gardens of) bounty and blessing;

23. On thrones, looking around (at the blessings of Paradise).

24. You will recognize on their faces the brightness of bliss.

25. They will be served to drink pure wine[1] under the seal (of Divine sanction and preservation).

26. Its seal is a fragrance of musk. And to that (blessing of Paradise), then, let all those who aspire (to things of high value) aspire as if in a race (with each other).

---

1. For wine, see *sūrah* 47: 15, note 5.

27. Its admixture will be from *tasnīm* (the most delightful drink out of the loftiest spring of Paradise).

28. A spring from which those near-stationed to God drink.

29. Those who disbelieved and were committed to accumulating sins used to laugh at those who believed;

30. Whenever they passed by them, they winked at one another (in derision).

31. And when they returned to their families, they would return full of quips (about how they mocked the believers).

32. When they saw those (who believed), they would say: "Look: those have indeed gone astray."

33. Yet they were not appointed as keepers over them (that they should presume to pass judgment on them).

34. So on this Day (of Judgment), those who believed will laugh at the unbelievers.

35. On thrones, looking on (at the condition of the unbelievers in Hell).

36. (Now see:) Are the unbelievers being paid for what they used to do?

SŪRAH 84

AL-INSHIQĀQ (THE SPLITTING ASUNDER)

Makkah period

Revealed in Makkah, this *sūrah*, which warns people concerning God's supreme Power and emphasizes that it is extremely easy for Him to resurrect them, has 25 verses. It derives its name from the infinitive form (*inshiqāq*) of the verb *inshaqqa* (to split asunder) in the first verse.

In the Name of God, the All-Merciful, the All-Compassionate.

1. When the heaven is split asunder,

2. Obeying its Lord, as is expected indeed, and it always does so;

3. And when the earth is flattened out,

4. And casts forth whatever is in it and becomes empty,

5. Obeying its Lord, as is expected indeed, and it always does so;

6. O human! You are ever toiling toward your Lord in a labor to be re-encountered (before His judgment).

7. Then, as for him who will be given his Record in his right hand,

8. Surely he will be reckoned with by an easy reckoning,

9. And will return in joy to his household (prepared for him in Paradise).[1]

10. But as for him who will be given his Record (in his left hand) from behind his back,

11. He will surely pray for destruction,

12. And enter the Flame to roast.

13. For indeed he used to be in joyous conceit among his household (in his earthly life).[2]

---

1. If the good deeds of the believers outweigh their evil acts, their evil acts will be forgiven and they will receive an easy reckoning. If somebody is called to a severe account, as stated in a Prophetic Tradition, it will mean his doom (al-Bukhārī, " 'Ilm," 35; Muslim, "Jannah," 80).

2. The contrast between the state of a believer and an unbeliever is highly significant. An unbeliever condemned to eternal punishment is one who is conceited and joyful among his household in the world. He rejoices in his worldly possessions, of which he is proud, and is indifferent to his Creator and His commands. When he sees the punishment in the Hereafter, he will pray for eternal destruction. Whereas a believer who is to be rewarded with eternal bliss in the other world is one who is, as is stated in 52: 26, very careful and alert among his family for their guidance and eternal life. So he will rejoice in the Hereafter in the reward he has been given.

٥٨٩   589

الجزء الثلثون

بِسْمِ اللَّهِ الرَّحْمَٰنِ الرَّحِيمِ

14. He thought that he would never return (to God for judgment).

15. No indeed! Rather, his Lord was ever seeing him.

16. So I swear by the afterglow of sunset,

17. And the night, and all that it enshrouds
(by degrees),

18. And the moon, as it grows full,

19. You will most certainly move on from
one state to another (congruous with it).[3]

20. What, then, is the matter with them
that they do not believe,

21. And when the Qur'ān is recited to
them, they do not prostrate in submission
(to its Message)?

22. Rather: those who disbelieve deny (it
and its Message).

23. And God has full knowledge of what
they harbor (in their hearts).[4]

24. So give them the glad tidings of a
painful punishment.

25. Except for those who believe and do
good, righteous deeds: for them there is a
reward constant and beyond measure.

---

3. This verse, which in the original consists of
three words, has a very wide range of meaning.
As the things by which God swears (the sunset's afterglow, the night and what it enshrouds
by degrees, and the full moon) denote a transition from one state and stage to another, this
verse expresses the states and stages that every
individual and community and all of humanity move through. This is so in both this world
and the next one. The world is in such a continuous movement and change. When Islam begins to be conveyed in a community in the footsteps of God's Messenger, upon him be peace
and blessings, the believers start to rise toward
higher and higher stages and better and better
states, though some setbacks may be suffered,

and the movement of their opponents becomes
downward. This verse implies both. The stages
and states traveled though are each a result of
the former and a cause for the latter, so there
is congruity between them. This same upward
or downward movement is also true for individuals. There is congruity or interrelation between the states and stages through which an
individual moves.

4. That is, their denial of the Qur'ān and its
Message is not because that there is a fault in
the Qur'ān or that its Message lacks sufficient
proof to affirm it. Rather, they persist in unbelief because of evil intentions and worldly
ambitions or some other selfish motives, and
therefore deny the Qur'ān and its Message.

SŪRAH 85

AL-BURŪJ
(THE CONSTELLATIONS)

Makkah period

Revealed in Makkah, this *sūrah* of 22 verses derives its name from the word *al-burūj* (the constellations) in the first verse. It calls the believers to patience in the face of the persecutions they have suffered, and reminds them that those who resisted the Messengers of God perished; it suggests that the opponents of the Qur'ān will not succeed.

In the Name of God, the All-Merciful, the All-Compassionate.

1. By the heaven with its constellations,[1]

2. And by the Promised Day,

3. And by the one who witnesses and that which is witnessed.[2]

4. Ruined were the people of the ditch,[3]

5. Of the fire kept burning with fuel.

6. When they were seated over it,

7. And were themselves witnesses of what they did to the believers.

8. They detested them for no other reason than that they believed in God, the All-Glorious with irresistible might, the All-Praiseworthy,

9. (They believed in) Him, to Whom belongs the sovereignty of the heavens and the earth. God is indeed a witness over everything.

10. Those who persecute the believing men and the believing women and then do not repent, for them there surely is the punishment of Hell, for them there is the punishment of burning fire.

11. But those who believe and do good, righteous deeds, for them there are Gardens through which rivers flow. That is the great triumph.

---

1. For the constellations, see *sūrah* 15: 16–18, note 5.

2. The verses that follow are concerned with the persecutions carried out against the believers, and the end that awaits the persecutors, as well as the reward that the persecuted believers will receive. So, by swearing by the heaven with constellations, God suggests that, as stated in 15: 16–18, just as the devils attempting to ascend the heaven are repulsed from it, so too will the devilish people persecuting the believers ultimately be repulsed, and receive their due on the Promised Day (of Judgment). So, the phrase, *one who witness-*

es refers to the believers and the Messenger in particular, i.e., those who witness the evil deeds of the wrongdoing unbelievers and who will witness their trial and punishment on the Judgment Day. The phrase, *that which is witnessed* means the persecutions the believers suffer and those who carry them out, and the punishment dealt to the persecutors in the Hereafter.

3. What is common for all the traditions about the people of the ditch is that they were tyrants who dug deep ditches to burn alive those believers who refused to renounce their Religion.

590

12. Surely the grip of your Lord is indeed severe.

13. He it is Who originates and brings forth anew.[4]

14. And He is also the All-Forgiving, the All-Loving;

15. The Lord of the Throne, the All-Sublime.

16. One Who freely does whatever He wills.

17. Has there come to you the report of the hosts –

18. The Pharaoh and the (tribe of) Thamūd (whom God seized and punished severely)?

19. Yet those who disbelieve (among your people) persist in denying (the Divine Message).

20. But all the while God encompasses them from all sides.

21. Indeed it is a glorious Qur'ān (– a sublime Book revealed and recited),

22. In a Preserved Tablet[5] (guarded from every accursed devil, and secure from any falsehood).

---

4. The verse implies that it is God Who surrounds all creation with His Knowledge and Power, and every creature is under His absolute dominion. So no one can escape His grip.

5. For the Supreme Ever-Preserved Tablet, see 6: 59, note 13; 13: 39, note 13; 17: 14, note 10.

SŪRAH 86

AT-ṬĀRIQ
(THAT WHICH COMES AT NIGHT)

Makkah period

Revealed in Makkah, this *sūrah* of 17 verses derives its name from the word *aṭ-ṭāriq* (that which comes at night) in the first verse. It concentrates on the Resurrection.

In the Name of God, the All-Merciful, the All-Compassionate.

1. By the heaven and that which comes at night.

2. What enables you to perceive what it is that comes at night?

3. It is the bright piercing star.

4. There is not a soul but over it is a guardian.[1]

5. Let human, then, consider from what he has been created.[2]

6. He has been created from some of a lowly fluid gushing forth.

7. It proceeds (as a result of incitement) between the (lumbar zone in the) vertebra and the ribs.[3]

8. Surely He (Who has created human from a lowly fluid) is able to restore him (to life after his death)

9. On the Day when all things (that remained or were kept) secret will be made manifest;

10. And he will have no power, nor a helper (against God's punishment).

11. I swear by the heaven ever-revolving (with whatever is in it and recurring patterns of rainfall),

12. And by the earth, bursting (with the growth of plants):

13. Surely it (the Qur'ān) is a decisive Word distinguishing (between truth and falsehood).

14. It is not (a word) in jest.

15. They (who reject it) are busy making schemes;

16. And I am "making a scheme."[4]

17. So let the unbelievers remain at will; let them continue to remain at will for a little while.

---

1. There are angels accompanying each person (13: 11), two of which record their deeds by God's command (50: 17; 82: 10–12). God is the Unique Guardian over all those angels and the One Who knows whatever a person thinks, conceives of, and does (50: 16). The verse carries all these meanings.

2. According to some interpreters of the Qur'ān, the star piercing through the darkness is a metaphor for God's Messenger, or the Qur'ān and the Divine guidance that was sent to him. It is a light that pierces through the darkness of falsehood and shows the right path. In its light humankind can discover the truth of creation and their own true nature. They also come to realize that humankind has not been created in vain. Humankind has very important duties in the world and, as will be stated in the next verse, all their deeds are re-

corded. So they should consider the simple matter from which they are created and see that their real value does not lie in this. They attach due importance to the One Who has created them from such a simple, lowly substance and yet elevated them as the most important of His creatures.

3. This verse refers to both the mechanism of ejection of the seminal fluid and the zone from which it is emitted. This is a relatively recent discovery of biology, yet the Qur'ān informed us of it many centuries ago.

4. Such expressions in the Qur'ān occur in reciprocation. God's making a scheme means that the way He lays out for the Messenger and the believers to follow will finally triumph over all other systems and bring all schemes against it to nothing.

SŪRAH 87

SŪRAT AL-A 'LĀ
(THE MOST HIGH)

Makkah period

Revealed in Makkah, this *sūrah* of 19 verses derives its name from the word *al-a 'lā* (the Most High) in the first verse. It concentrates on God's Power and Unity and the Revelation, and contains some advice on observing the proper conditions and manners for preaching and admonition.

In the Name of God, the All-Merciful, the All-Compassionate.

1. Glorify the Name of your Lord, the Most High,

2. Who creates and fashions in due proportions,

3. And Who determines (a particular life, nature, and goal for each creature), and guides (it toward the fulfillment of that goal);

4. And Who brings forth herbage,

5. Then turns it to dark-colored, rotten stubble.[1]

6. (For the guidance of humankind,) We will establish the Qur'ān in your heart and have you recite (it to others), so you will not forget (anything of it)[2]

7. Except what God wills.[3] Surely He knows all that is manifest and all that is hidden (including your outward and inward states).

8. We will guide you to the easiest path (in all your affairs).

9. So remind and instruct (them in the truth), in case reminder and instruction may be of use.[4]

10. He who stands in awe of God will be mindful of the instruction.

11. But the most wicked one remains aloof from it;

12. He who will enter the Great Fire (of Hell) to roast.

13. He will neither die therein (to be saved from punishment) nor live.

14. Prosperous indeed is he who purifies himself (of sins, and of his wealth by spending from it in God's cause and for the needy);

15. And who mentions the Name of his Lord and does the Prayer.[5]

16. But you (O humankind) are disposed to prefer the life of this world;

17. While the Hereafter is better and more lasting.[6]

18. This is surely contained in the former Scrolls.

19. The Scrolls of Abraham and Moses.[7]

1. Interpreters of the Qur'ān find references to coal and oil in this verse, because the original words that have been translated as rotten stubble connote manure, charcoal, and the heaps carried by a flood.

2. See 20: 114; 75: 16–19, note 5.

3. Many interpreters of the Qur'ān rightly take this exception as being related to the rule of abrogation stated in 2: 106: *We do not abrogate any verse or omit it (leaving it to be forgotten) but We bring one better than it or the like of it (more suited to the time and conditions in the course of perfecting the Religion and completing Our favor upon you). Do you not know (and surely you do know) that God has full power over everything?* The verse does not mean that there is something of the Qur'ān that God caused the Messenger to forget. This exception is like the exception in verse 11: 108: see the corresponding note 24. It came to stress that everything depends on God's absolute Will.

4. The Qur'ān says that instruction and reminding will be of use to the believers (51: 55) and one who stands in awe of God will receive instruction and admonition (this occurs in the next verse in this *sūrah*), and the Messenger is told to withdraw from those who decisively turn away from God's Book and remembrance, and who aim at and desire nothing but the life of this world (53: 29). So, an instructor or preacher should observe whether instructing or preaching will be of use, and in what circumstances and to whom it will be of use. However, it should also be pointed out that instruction and preaching will not be rendered useless, particularly when done by sincere people like the Prophets. So the verse also implies that we should try to give constructive instructions and preaching.

5. According to some Prophetic Traditions, in the last two verses there is an allusion to the alms-giving to be performed before the *'Īd al-Fitr* (the religious festival of the end of Ramadān), and the congregational prayer on that day, which would be prescribed in Madīnah (at-Tabarī, ar-Rāzī, and al-Qurtubī in the interpretation of this verse).

6. The Hereafter is incomparably good and eternal. The reason why the verse uses *better and more lasting* is for the sake of comparison with the worldly life.

7. What is told in verses 14-17 is also contained is the former Divine Scriptures. Mentioning only the Scrolls given to Abraham and Moses, upon them be peace, is to attract our attention toward their high standing among the earlier Revelations. Some Traditions say that before the Torah, the Prophet Moses was given a Scroll of ten pages (as-Suyūtī from Ibn Mirdawayh and Ibn Asākīr).

SŪRAH 88

AL-GHĀSHIYAH
(THE OVERWHELMING)

Makkah period

Revealed in Makkah, this *sūrah* of 26 verses derives its name from the word *al-ghāshiyah* (the overwhelming, meaning the Resurrection Day) in the first verse. It draws attention to the hardships and punishment the unbelievers will suffer in the Hereafter and the bliss with which the believers will be favored. It also calls on us to reflect on some manifestations and evidence of God's Power and Wisdom.

In the Name of God, the All-Merciful, the All-Compassionate.

1. Has the account of the Overwhelming come to you?

2. Some faces will on that Day be downcast,

3. Having toiled (in the world) only to weariness (with no portion in the Hereafter).

4. They will enter the hot, burning Fire to roast;

5. They will be given to drink from a boiling spring.

6. No food will there be for them but a poisonous thorny plant:

7. It will neither nourish nor avail against hunger.

8. And some faces on that Day will be in delight,

9. Well-pleased with (the fruit of) their endeavor (in the world),

10. In a lofty Garden,

11. Wherein they will hear no idle talk.[1]

---

1. It is interesting that one of the first blessings of the lofty Garden will be that there is no idle talk in it. This means that Paradise is not a place where its inhabitants will be entertained as the worldly people are used to amuse themselves in the world. Every blessing of Paradise is pure and noble in character, as its inhabitants will be purified, noble persons. The verse also implies a warning against idle talk and meaningless amusements in the world.

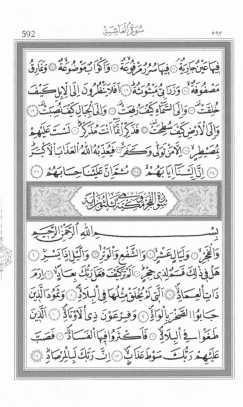

23. But whoever turns away (averse to re-minder and exhortation), and disbelieves (in what is conveyed to him),

24. God will punish him with the greatest punishment (of Hell).

25. Indeed to Us is their return;

26. Thereafter it is for Us to call them to account.

SŪRAH 89

AL-FAJR (THE DAWN)

Makkah period

This *sūrah*, revealed in Makkah, has 30 verses. It takes its name from the word *al-fajr* (dawn) in the first verse. It draws attention to the painful end that befell some ancient peoples who denied God's Mes-sengers and the Message they brought. It also explains some basic traits of human nature and the wisdom of God's testing His servants. It ends by reminding us of what kind of an eter-nal life awaits the believers and unbelievers.

In the Name of God, the All-Merciful, the All-Compassionate.

1. By the dawn,

2. And ten nights,[1]

3. And the even and the odd,[2]

4. And the night as it journeys on (to-wards an end).[3]

5. Is there not in that a solemn oath for one endowed with reason (to reflect upon, so that it may guide him to the truth and keep him away from evils)?

6. Have you not considered how your Lord dealt with the (tribe of) 'Ād,

7. (The people of) Iram with many-col-umned (i.e. monumental) buildings,

8. The like of which had not been created in the land?

---

12. Therein will be a flowing spring,

13. Therein couches raised high,

14. And goblets placed ready,

15. And cushions arrayed,

16. And rich carpets spread out.

17. Do they not consider the camels, how they are created?

18. And the heaven, how it has been raised high?

19. And the mountains, how they have been set firm?

20. And the earth, how it has been spread out?

21. And so remind and exhort (them), for you are one (whose duty is) to remind and exhort.

22. You are not one to dictate (faith) to them.

9. And with (the tribe of) Thamūd, who hewed rocks in the valley (to make dwellings)?[4]

10. And with the Pharaoh, who had formidable strongholds?

11. (All of) these rebelled (and transgressed all bounds) in the lands (where they lived);

12. And increased manifold disorder and corruption therein.

13. Therefore your Lord let loose on them a scourge of punishment (coming in different forms).[5]

14. Your Lord is ever on the watch (over human and tests him in the blessings with which He favors him).

---

1. By *ten nights*, the verse is referring to the last ten nights of the holy Month of Ramadān or the first ten nights of Dhu'l-Hijjah, the month of the Pilgrimage, or both. In each of these ten nights the time during which God is worshipped has a special importance and reward, and this time period is followed by the religious festival. So the dawn in the first verse, in addition to referring to the dawn of every new day, may be implying in particular the dawn of these festivals. In addition to these meanings, the ten nights and the dawn also imply that no matter how long they may be, the dark periods in the life of an individual or in the life of a society usually end in a new, happy day. The verses also allude to the fact that, as pointed out in *Sūrat al-Muzzammil* (73: 2–6), devotions at night have a special efficacy in human spiritual endeavor, and give rise to a spiritual awakening (dawn).

2. In addition to other possible meanings, such as the months in the (Muslim) lunar calendar that end in either an even or odd number, and

the fact that the last third of the holy Month of Ramadan sometimes consists of ten days and sometimes nine days, this expression also implies all of creation enshrouded by the night and over which the day breaks.

3. Night has its own characteristics and runs its own course. But however long it may be, it will certainly come to an end, and the sun will rise and spread its light. So when God's light (of Islam) begins to show over the horizon of humankind, it means that the end of night is near for both individuals and communities.

4. On the peoples of 'Ād and Thamūd, see *sūrah* 7: 65–79, notes 16–17, *sūrah* 11: 50–68, *sūrah* 26: 123–58.

5. On the kinds of punishment that visited the tribe of 'Ād, see *sūrah* 7: 72, *sūrah* 11: 58, *sūrah* 23: 27, *sūrah* 26: 120, *sūrah* 69: 77, and the tribe of Thamūd, see *sūrah* 7: 78, *sūrah* 11: 67, *sūrah* 15: 83, *sūrah* 69: 5, and the Pharaoh, see *sūrah* 10: 90, *sūrah* 20: 77–78, *sūrah* 26: 65–66.

19. And you consume inheritance (belonging to you or others) with greed (without distinction of the lawful and unlawful);

20. And you love wealth with a boundless ardor for it and for hoarding.

21. No indeed! When the earth is pounded to dust with pounding after pounding;

22. And your Lord comes (unveils His Power and Majesty), and the angels in row upon row;

23. And on that Day Hell is brought (forward); on that Day human will come to understand (what being favored with bounties meant and how he should have responded), but what will that understanding (then) avail him?

24. He will say: "Would that I had forwarded (some good deeds) for my life (to come)!"

25. None can punish as He will punish on that Day;

26. And none can bind as He will bind (on that Day).

27. (But to the righteous God will say:) "O you soul at rest (content with the truths of faith and God's commands and His treatment of His creatures)!

28. "Return to your Lord, well-pleased (with Him and His treatment of you), and well-pleasing to Him.

29. "Enter, then, among My servants (fully content with servanthood to Me)!

30. "And enter my Paradise!"

15. And so, human – when his Lord tries him by bestowing favors on him – says: "My Lord has honored me."

16. But whenever He tries him by straitening his means of livelihood, then he says, "My Lord has humiliated me."[6]

17. No indeed! You (O people) do not treat the orphan with kindness and generosity;

18. And do not urge one another to feed the destitute.[7]

---

6. That is, in the former case (verse 15), he deems himself worthy of the favors God bestows on him, and does not consider that he is tried to see whether he will be thankful. In the later case (verse 16), he imputes to God injustice, and does not consider that he is being tried for patience, in preparation for the reward to be given in return.

7. Being rich or poor is not and should not be

considered as a cause of honor or shame. God's granting abundant or scant bounties is a means of testing for humans. In any case, what a human being should do is to admit that whatever they have is from God as a bounty and therefore thank Him, and especially in circumstances of poverty, show patience, without complaint. Honor or virtue lies in thanking the All-Munificent Lord, and helping the needy.

SŪRAH 90

AL-BALAD (THE CITY)

Makkah period

This *sūrah*, which was revealed in Makkah, has 20 verses. It derives its name from the word *al-balad* (the city) in the first verse. Most interpreters hold that the city the verse is referring to is Makkah. Reminding us of God's favors upon humankind and of His Power, the *sūrah* invites people to help one another and prepare for the next life.

In the Name of God, the All-Merciful, the All-Compassionate.

1. I swear by this (sacred) city (Makkah) –

2. And you (O Messenger) are a dweller in this city –

3. And by him (Abraham) who begets, and him (Muḥammad) whom he begot;

4. We have assuredly created human in (a life of) trial and hardship.[1]

5. Does human think that no one has power over him?

6. He says: "I have consumed abundant wealth!"

7. Does he, then, think that no one ever sees him?[2]

---

1. Verses 117–119 of *Sūrah Ṭā. Hā* say that by being expelled from the original Garden where Adam and Eve had settled, humankind descended into a life full of afflictions, including hunger, thirst, cold, and heat. There are of course other hardships humans are bound to suffer in the world. Moreover, those who set their heart on a lofty ideal usually suffer great hardships and persecutions. Those who are exposed the most to such hardships and persecutions are the Prophets, and then come other believers, each according to the strength of their faith and their degree of nearness to God. However, life is purified, perfected, and bears fruit through these afflictions and tri-

als. Inertia or an easy life is a close equivalent to death.

2. Wealth may cause its owner to boast of it and see in himself a great power. There are many wealthy people who boast of spending wealth, but since they spend it on fleeting enjoyments of the world or for fame or show, it will contribute nothing to them in God's sight and be of no use to them in the Hereafter. Whereas, as it is God Who determines the livelihood of everyone and endows people with the necessary capacity, power, and healthy organs to earn their livelihood, what humans should do is to thank God and spend out of their wealth as God has commanded.

en their Records in their right hands on Judgment Day).

19. But those who disbelieve in Our Revelations – they are the people of wretchedness (who will be given their Records in their left hands),

20. On them is Fire closed over.

---

3. The ascent signifies the road to human perfection and therefore to God. The next five verses define some steps of this ascent.

SŪRAH 91

ASH-SHAMS (THE SUN)

Makkah period

This *sūrah* of 15 verses was revealed in Makkah. It takes its name from the word *ash-shams* (the sun) in the first verse. It brings to our attention a basic feature of humankind, namely its being created with a disposition or capacity to do both good and evil. However, it calls them to faith and good deeds, and warns against evil deeds ending in destruction by giving the lucid example of the tribe of Thamūd.

In the Name of God, the All-Merciful, the All-Compassionate.

1. By the sun and its brightness;

2. And the moon as it follows it (reflecting its light);

3. And the day as it reveals it (the sun);

4. And the night as it enshrouds it;[1]

5. And the heaven and that (All-Magnificent One) Who has built it;

6. And the earth and that (All-Magnificent One) Who has spread it;[1]

7. And the human selfhood and that (All-Knowing, All-Powerful, and All-Wise One) Who has formed it to perfection;

8. And Who has inspired it with the con-

8. Have We not made for him a pair of eyes,

9. And a tongue and two lips,

10. And shown him the two ways (one to follow and one to avoid)?

11. Yet he makes no effort to make the ascent.

12. What enables you to perceive what the ascent is?[3]

13. It is the freeing of a bondsman (a slave or a captive);

14. Or feeding, on a day of privation,

15. An orphan near of kin,

16. Or a poor wretch in misery;

17. And being, besides, of those who believe and exhort one another to patience and exhort one another to pity and compassion.

18. Those are they who are the people of happiness and prosperity (who will be giv-

science of what is wrong and bad for it and what is right and good for it:[2]

9. He is indeed prosperous who has grown it in purity (away from self-aggrandizing rebellion against God);

10. And he is indeed lost who has corrupted it (in self-aggrandizing rebellion against God).[3]

11. The (tribe of) Thamūd denied (the Divine Message and their Messenger, and displayed their denial) in their arrogant rebellion,

12. (Especially) when (finally) the most wicked among them (instigated by his people) rushed forward.

13. The Messenger of God (Ṣāliḥ) said (warning them, and reminding them again of the terms of their pledge): "It is the she-camel of God, and observe her turn in drinking."[4]

14. But they denied him and slaughtered her, and so their Lord crushed them for their sin, and leveled them (with the ground);

15. And He (being the All-Knowing and All-Powerful and All-Just) does not fear the outcome (of events).

---

1. Spreading the earth means making its surface suitable for settlement and life. The fact that it is spread out does not contradict the fact that it is spherical.

2. God has endowed the human self or ego with necessary potentials, and equipped it with a capacity to be able to realize the goal of its existence. He has also created it with a disposition to guarding against the Divine prohibitions, and taught it through Revelation how it should guard against them, and appointed some (the Messengers) to guide it to that goal.

3. There are essential differences between humans and animals. The primary difference lies in the observable fact that when animals are born, it is as if they have been taught and trained in another world. They begin to walk almost as soon as they are born and quickly adapt to their surroundings, as if they were acquainted with them beforehand. However, a human (on average) needs almost a whole year to learn how to walk, and then spends the rest of life learning how to live, and how to discriminate between what is beneficial and what is harmful. This shows that learning and progress are fundamental to human life.

Humans are very complicated beings. We resemble seeds, for in each of us is the potential to engender and attain perfection. A seed is endowed by the Divine Power with great potential and is destined to put this potential into effect. If that seed abuses its potential and attracts harmful substances, soon it will rot away in its confined space. If it uses its potential properly, however, it will emerge from these narrow confines and grow into a fruit-bearing tree. In addition, its tiny and particular nature will come to represent a great and universal truth.

Our essence has also been equipped by the Divine Power with great potential. If we use our potential and intellectual and spiritual faculties in this narrow world under the soil of the worldly life only to satisfy the fancies of our carnal, evil-commanding soul or selfhood, we will become corrupt, like a rotten seed, and merely to enjoy a fleeting pleasure during this short life. Thus we will depart from this world with a heavy spiritual burden on our unfortunate souls.

But if we germinate the seed of our potential under the "soil of spirituality" with the "water of faith and worship," and if we use our spiritual faculties for their true purposes, we will grow into an eternal, majestic tree, the branches of which extend into eternity. We will yield fruit of virtue in the world and eternal happiness in the next world. We will be favored in Paradise with infinite perfection and countless blessings.

All this means that we have been sent to the world to be perfected through knowledge and faith. And due to our special position among other beings, we have been entrusted with improving the earth through knowledge and faith and establishing justice on it. This imposes on us duties toward our Creator and other beings. (Also see Appendix 14.)

4. See *sūrah* 7: 73–77, note 17, *sūrah* 11: 61–68, and *sūrah* 26: 141–159.

595

SŪRAH 92

AL-LAYL (THE NIGHT)

Makkah period

This *sūrah* of 21 verses was revealed in Makkah. It takes its name from the word *al-layl* (the night) in the first verse. It urges humans to do the things that will earn their salvation, and to avoid the things that will earn their perdition.

In the Name of God, the All-Merciful, the All-Compassionate.

1. By the night as it enshrouds (the earth in its darkness);

2. And the day as it rises bright;

3. And that (All-Magnificent One) Who has created the male and the female:

4. Surely your endeavor is diverse (in character and ends).

5. Then, as for him who gives (out of his wealth for God's good pleasure), and keeps from disobedience to Him in reverence for Him and piety,

6. And affirms the best (in creed, action, and the reward to be given),

7. We will make easy for him the path to the state of ease (salvation after an easy reckoning).

8. But as for him who is niggardly and regards himself as self-sufficient in independence of Him,

9. And denies the best (in creed, action, and the reward to be given),

10. We will make easy for him the path to hardship (punishment after a hard reckoning).

11. And his wealth will not avail him when he falls to ruin.

12. It is surely for Us to bestow guidance;

13. And to Us belong the Hereafter as well as the former (life).

14. And so I warn you of a Fire blazing fiercely.

15. None will enter it to roast but the most wicked,

16. Who denies (My Message) and turns away.

17. And far removed from it (the Fire) will be he who keeps farthest away from dis-

obedience to God in greater reverence for Him and piety;

18. Who spends his wealth (in God's cause and for the needy), so that he may grow in purity;

19. Without anyone who has favored him so that he should spend in return for it, or

expecting any reward in return for what he spends.

20. (Rather, he spends) only in longing for the good pleasure of his Lord, the Most High.

21. He will certainly be contented (he with his Lord and his Lord with him).[1]

---

1. This alludes to the rank of being well-pleased with God and well-pleasing to Him (see 89: 28). For this rank, please refer to *Key Concepts*, 1: 104–115.

SŪRAH 93

AD-DUHĀ (THE FORENOON)

Makkah period

This *sūrah* of 11 verses was revealed in Makkah. It takes its name from the word *ad-duhā* (the forenoon) in the first verse. It consoles the Messenger, and mentions some of God's favors upon him.

In the Name of God, the All-Merciful, the All-Compassionate.

1. By the forenoon,

2. And the night when it has grown dark and most still,

3. Your Lord has not forsaken you, nor has He become displeased with you.[1]

---

1. The oaths taken on some of the phenomena in the world have a definite relationship with the verse or verses following them. For example, as God's pleasure and displeasure with His servants may mean a bright day or darkness for them, so can happy and sorrowful moments in the life of a person correspond to daytime and night respectively. There may of course be many other instances of such correlations to be found in such oaths and the facts or truths expressed in the verses that follow them.

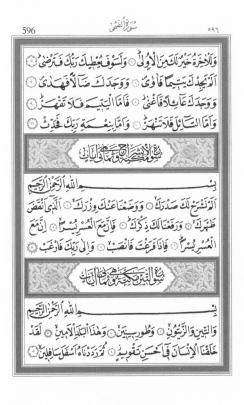

and his promotion still continues through the good deeds every one of his community performs, as he was the person to establish the Religion of Islam in its last and universal form. The verse also gives the good tidings that Islam is always on the way to completion in his own time, and any Islamic movement in his footsteps that comes after him will be on the way to success. Moreover, the Hereafter will be in every way better for both God's Messenger and all the Muslims than this world.

3. That is, you will attain the rank of being well-pleased with God and His being well-pleased with you, (which was specially assigned to you). In this verse there is a reference to the fact that in the Hereafter God's Messenger will be given the universal authority of intercession, and he will intercede on behalf of all humankind in the Supreme Place of Gathering, and more particularly, he will intercede for his community. He was one who never lived for his own comfort, but always lived for the sake of the happiness of others (al-Bukhārī, "Tawḥīd," 36, Anbiyā'," 3; Muslim, "Īmān," 320).

4. At the time God's Messenger, upon him be peace and blessings, was born, his father had died a few months before, and he lost his mother when he was only six years old.

5. This refers both to the life of God's Messenger before his Messengership and to his every moment compared to a next one, being related to verse 4 above. Verses 42: 52–53 say: *And thus (in the ways mentioned) We have revealed to you a spirit of Our command (the life-giving Message, the Qur'ān). You would not (otherwise) have known what the Book was (with all the knowledge it contains and the way of life it establishes), and what faith was (as described by the Book and with all its principles, requirements, and implications). But We have made it a light by which We guide whom We will of Our servants. And certainly you, (by God's guidance) guide (people) to a straight path – the path of God, to Him belongs whatever is in the heavens and whatever is on the earth. Be aware: all affairs are ultimately referred to God. So although God's*

4. Assuredly, what comes after will be better for you than what has gone before.[2]

5. And assuredly He will increasingly grant you his favors one after another and you will be contented.[3]

6. Did He not find you an orphan and give shelter (to you)?[4]

7. And find you unguided (by God's Messengership), and guide (you)?[5]

8. And find you in want, and make you self-sufficient?

9. Therefore, do not oppress the orphan;

10. Nor chide and drive away the petitioner.[6]

11. And as for the favor of your Lord, proclaim it![7]

---

2. This means that God's Messenger was continually promoted to higher and higher ranks,

Messenger never and in any way went astray from the Straight Path in creed, even before his Messengership, he did not receive the Revelation during that time and was not guided through it or God's Messengership.

6. God's Messenger, upon him be peace and blessings, never repelled anyone who asked him for something. He was so willing to help all that Imam Buṣīrī says: "If he had not had to say 'No!' when seated in the Prayer, he would

never have uttered the word 'No!'" (Every Muslim has to say "I bear witness that there is *no* deity but God," when seated during the Prayer.) Although giving to whoever asks for something is a noble attitude, it does not mean that we must give to every supplicant regardless of what they ask for, or our means to give or the consequences of doing so.

7. This order relates in particular to conveying God's Message to people.

SŪRAH 94

AL-INSHIRĀH (THE EXPANSION)

Makkah period

This *sūrah* of 8 verses was revealed in Makkah after the previous *sūrah*. It takes its name from the verb *nashrah* (from the root *SHaRaḤa* which means to expand) in the first verse. The *sūrah* mentions some of God's favors upon the Messenger and exhorts him to carry out his sacred mission.

In the Name of God, the All-Merciful, the All-Compassionate.

1. Have We not expanded for you your breast,[1]

2. And eased you of the burden,

3. Which weighed so heavily on your back;[2]

4. And (have We not) exalted for you your renown?[3]

5. Then, surely, with hardship comes ease;

6. Surely, with hardship comes ease.

7. Therefore, when you are free (from one task), resume (another task);

8. And seek and strive to please your Lord.[4]

---

1. The Prophet Moses, having received the Divine command to go to the Pharaoh to convey God's Message, prayed to God and the first thing for which he prayed was for the expansion of his breast (20: 25). He did this so that he would be able to show greater patience with whatever he would encounter from the Pharaoh and his clan, and so that he could fully understand God's Religion and all that He would be pleased with (see *sūrah* 20, note 8).

So, literally meaning growing larger and deeper, spreading and expanding, the expansion of the breast (*inbisaṭ* in Islamic terminol-

ogy) signifies the relaxing of one's heart to the extent allowed by the Sharī'ah, so that one can embrace everybody and make them pleased or contented with one's gentle words and pleasant manners. In the context of one's relationship with God Almighty, it denotes a spiritual state that is a combination of fear and hope for those who are at the beginning of journeying on the way to God, and for those near to God, like the Prophets, it signifies the exhilaration that comes from knowledge of God. Those who have attained this state are awed by being in the Presence of God, and feel exhilarated by the breezes of delight and joy blowing in His Presence. They are awed while inhaling, and feel delight when exhaling.

As pointed out in the description above, expansion can be dealt with in two categories: our relationship with the created and our relationship with the Creator. With respect to our relationship with the Creator, expansion means that we feel both awe and exhilaration from being in God's Presence; and with respect to our relationship with the created, it means that we live in a society as a member of it, that we are generous, sincere, and respectful to everyone, and that we treat people according to their level of understanding.

The noble Prophet, upon him be peace and blessings, was sincere with those around him. He spoke according to his listeners' level of understanding, and sometimes even made wise and meaningful jokes. Although he suffered inwardly from the unbelief, injustice, and sins that he witnessed, and even though he was anxious for the end and afterlife of all people, he always smiled and behaved pleasantly. So the verse means that despite the great inner suffering he felt because of the deviation of his people, and despite the harsh treatments he received from them, God enabled him to tolerate all this. The Prophet always received solace from God and felt exhilaration because of His continuous Presence. (For further explanations, see *Key Concepts*, 1: 115–116.)

2. As pointed out in 33: 72, the supreme trust of selfhood (ego) is a great burden for the human being to carry; it is of such a weight that the heavens, and the earth, and the mountains shrank from bearing it (see the corresponding note 38). It was God's Messenger, upon him be peace and blessings, who felt this weight more than all other people. Moreover, as a Messenger of God, God had sent down on him a weighty Word, i.e., the Qur'ān, and charged him with conveying it to others (73: 5). This is such a weighty Word that, in the words of God, if by a Divine Discourse the mountains were to be set in motion, or the earth were to be cleft, or the dead be made to speak, all

would do so by the Qur'ān, not by any other Divine or non-Divine word (13: 31). So, naturally, the Messenger should have felt weighed down under such a burden. However, by expanding his breast and endowing him with the capacity to bear all hardships and by helping him to carry out his mission, God eased him of this burden.

3. The name of the Messenger is mentioned along with God in the proclamations of faith: *There is no deity but God, and Muḥammad is His Messenger. I bear witness that there is no deity but God, and I also bear witness that Muḥammad is His servant and Messenger.* The Prophet Muḥammad, upon him be peace and blessings, is the person most loved, and most correctly loved, by people. He is a person about whom thousands of poems, articles, and books have been written. God has sent His blessings and peace on him for 14 centuries, His angels and millions and millions of people have been calling for the same for 14 centuries; this will continue to happen until the Last Day. Even the enemies of the Prophet Muḥammad have admitted that he is the greatest of creation, the person who has influenced human history more than any other. No one has ever deified him, and God has always purified him of the slanders of his biased foes. See Lamartine's tribute to him quoted in *sūrah* 33, note 11. However, the Prophet Muḥammad never misused the glory and fame he had won, he always lived as if he were an ordinary man among the people, and remained the most modest of all during his entire life. So his glory and fame served his cause.

4. The last two verses teach us how time should be used. Changing one's task provides a rest and refreshes one's zeal and power. Especially when an intellectual task is followed by a bodily one, the mind feels relaxed. Daily Prayers refresh the mind and the spirit amidst one's daily occupations. But whatever we do, we must do it to please God and therefore we should be occupied with lawful deeds and refrain from doing that which has been forbidden by Him.

SŪRAH 95

AT-TĪN (THE FIG)

Makkah period

This *sūrah* of 8 verses was revealed in Makkah. It takes its name from the noun *at-tīn* (the fig) in the first verse. It stresses the common ground for all the Divine religions and the fact that dignity and salvation for humankind lie in belief and doing good deeds.

In the Name of God, the All-Merciful, the All-Compassionate.

1. By the fig and the olive,

2. And Mount Sinai,

3. And this City secure:[1]

4. Surely We have created human of the best stature as the perfect pattern of creation;

5. Then We have reduced him to the lowest of the low,

---

1. The fig and olive, two highly prized fruits, also symbolize, as indicated in *sūrah* 23: 20, the eastern part of the Mediterranean where many of the Prophets lived. In particular, the three great predecessors of the Prophet Muḥammad, namely the Prophets Abraham, Moses, and Jesus, lived in these lands, though Abraham was born and started his mission in Iraq. It is well known that the mountain where Jesus gave his famous sermon is Mount Zaytūn (Olive). Mount Sinai is the mountain where Moses received the Torah. Makkah is indicated by the phrase "this City secure" (see *sūrah* 106). These verses resemble a verse in the Old Testament: *The Lord came from Sinai, and dawned on them from Seir; He shone forth from Mount Paran (Deuteromony*, 33: 2).

This verse of the Bible refers to the Prophethood of Moses, Jesus, and Muḥammad respectively, upon them be peace. Sinai is the place where the Prophet Moses spoke to God and received the Torah. Seir, a place in Palestine, is where the Prophet Jesus received Divine Revelation. The last place mentioned, Paran, is the place where God revealed His will to humankind for the last time through His Revelation to Prophet Muḥammad, upon him be peace and blessings.

Paran, mentioned in the Old Testament (*Genesis*, 21: 14–21), is the area in the desert where, upon the order of God, Hagar was left by her husband Abraham, upon him be peace, to live with her son Ishmael. They found a well of water there. As stated explicitly in the Qur'ān (14: 35–37), and as is well known, Abraham left Hagar and Ishmael in the valley of Makkah, which was then an uninhabited place, within the mountain ranges of Paran, and the well of water is the famous Well of *Zamzam*.

6. Except those who believe and do good, righteous deeds, so there is for them a reward constant and beyond measure.[2]

7. What, then, (O human,) causes you, after all (these realities), to deny the Last Judgment?

8. Is not God the Best of judges and the Most Powerful of sovereigns?

---

2. The universe, an integral, composite entity, the parts of which are fully interrelated and interlinked, and which is composed of many worlds or realms, both immaterial and material, may be likened to a tree. Particularly in Oriental traditions, this metaphor has been used and some Muslim sages, such as Muhyi'd-Dīn ibn al-'Arabī, have even written books concerning this matter under the title of "The Tree of Creation." All creatures constituting this Tree

come into existence through the manifestations of the Divine Names – they exist because God eternally exists and makes them exist, they subsist because God is the Self-Subsisting and the All-Maintaining, the living among them see and hear because God is the All-Seeing and the All-Hearing, they are provided for because God is the All-Providing, and so on. So the universe as a whole is a mirror that reflects its Creator.

As everybody knows, a tree grows from a seed or a stone. The whole future life of the tree, the program of its life, is pre-recorded encoded in this seed. With the sowing of the seed in the ground, the life of the tree proceeds through certain stages and ultimately yields its fruit, which contains the seed as the embodiment of the whole past life of the tree.

Thus the human being is both the seed and fruit of the Tree of Creation. Whatever there is in the Tree can also be found in the human being. Laws, such as the law of germination and the law of growth, which the Creator has established for the seed to germinate and grow into a tree, play the same role for the tree as the spirit does for humans. So in one dimension of their nature, humans resemble angels or spiritual beings, or they have pure, angelic aspects. In addition to what the angels have, humans have free will and a more developed intellect. In another dimension of their nature, which relates to their being the children of the world, humans have been equipped with some basic powers or drives or faculties. They experience the lust and animal drives that are essential to maintain their worldly life – lust for the opposite sex, offspring, money, earning, and the comforts of life, and wrath or the power of anger to protect themselves and their values, and the faculty of intellect or reason. Moreover, humans are, by nature, fallible, forgetful, neglectful, fond of disputing, obstinate, selfish, and jealous, and much more. These all seem to be negative characteristics but, as will be explained below, they have been given to human beings to serve their moral and spiritual progress.

There is another important point to note concerning the difference between humans and other beings. While animals, for example, come or are sent into the world as if they have already been taught whatever they need in life, and while they adapt to life in a very brief time, for example, a few days or weeks, humans come into the world without any knowledge and it takes them a long time to adapt to life and to learn what is necessary. So humans are bound to progress or develop through learning, and to develop their potential. Thus the above-mentioned powers, faculties, and negative-seeming feelings given to them have not been restricted in creation.

If, however, humans obey their urges without any consideration of right and wrong and do not discipline their animal drives according to some standards, then these urges and drives can become the source of innumerable vices. If undisciplined, anger can cause great crimes, such as murder, all kinds of injustices and the violations of the rights of others; lust can lead humans to consume whatever they find, to earn in any way they find convenient, to commit many crimes, such as theft, usurpation, to enter into illicit sexual relations and to attempt to hide the consequences with abortion and infanticide. The faculty of reason or intellect, if it is not used according to certain standards, can be a means for such deceitful practices as demagogy, lying and sophistry, and for hypocrisy, unbelief and many different types of associating partners with God. This faculty, which has enabled human beings to realize admirable scientific and technological successes and developments in recent centuries, has also brought many disasters unparalleled in human history, such as continual wars, the creation of machines for killing and destruction on an unbelievable scale, and an increase in environmental pollution. In short, because of their unrestricted urges or powers, humans, if undisciplined, can be an agent of destruction and make life and the world into a prison for themselves. This happens when they have been reduced to the lowest of the low.

However, in order to attain true humanity by climbing to higher ranks, and to obtain happiness in their individual and collective lives, in the world and in the Hereafter, humans should restrict the urges or powers given to them according to certain precepts and channel the apparently negative characteristics into virtues. Moreover, humans are not beings composed of only body and intellect. They have also a spirit, which requires satisfaction, without which they can never find true happiness. So the control of all these is possible through learning, faith, regular worship, and the struggle against their carnal soul and using their will in the correct way. By restricting or training the power of lust or the animal drive, they can acquire chastity and moderation. By restricting or training the power of anger, they can acquire chivalry and gallantry, and by restricting or training the power of intellect, they can acquire true wisdom. Channeling the apparently negative feelings or aspects of their nature can lead to a positive result; obstinacy, for example, can be channeled into steadfastness in the cause of right and truth, and jealousy into a competitiveness in doing good things. So true humanity lies in true spiritual satisfaction and acquiring distinction with these virtues or good qualities, and thus becoming a good, worshipping servant of God and a useful member of society.

SŪRAH 96

AL-'ALAQ (THE CLOT)

Makkah period

This *sūrah* of 19 verses derives its name from the word *al-'alaq* (clinging clot – the fertilized female ovum or zygote) that occurs in the second verse. Its initial five verses are the first part of the Qur'ān that was revealed to God's Messenger while he was secluded in the Cave of Hirah on Mount Nūr. The Archangel Gabriel came and told the Messenger to read. When the Messenger, who most probably thought that he was expected to read actual script, answered that he did not know how to read, the angel squeezed the Messenger to himself until he had almost lost all his strength and repeated the order, "Read!" This was repeated three times, and after the third time, the Messenger asked: "What will I read?" Then the angel conveyed the initial five verses of the *sūrah*. This *sūrah* implies the importance of knowledge, reading, and writing, and warns that people go astray by regarding themselves as being self-sufficient. It also threatens against denying God's Message.

In the Name of God, the All-Merciful, the All-Compassionate.

1. Read in and with the Name of your Lord, Who has created –

2. Created human from a clot clinging (to the wall of the womb).[1]

3. Read, and your Lord is the All-Munificent,

4. Who has taught (human) by the pen –

5. Taught human what he did not know.

6. No indeed, (despite all His favors to him), human is unruly and rebels,

7. In that he sees himself as self-sufficient, independent (of his Lord).

8. But to your Lord surely is the return (when everyone will account for their life).

9. Have you considered the one who would impede and forbid

10. A servant (of God) when he prays?

11. Have you considered if he is (and surely he is) on the right way;

12. Or exhorts others to righteousness and piety?

13. Have you considered if he himself denies the truth and turns away (from it)?

14. Does he (who would impede the servant in his Prayer) not know that God sees (all that people do)?

15. No indeed! If he does not desist, We will certainly seize and drag him by the forelock,

16. A lying, sinful forelock!

17. Then let him summon (to his help his) council,

18. We will summon the guards of Hell.[2]

19. By no means! Pay no heed to him (in his attempt to prevent the Prayer), but prostrate and draw near (to God).

---

1. It is quite significant that the first command of God to His Messenger, the unlettered Prophet, was "read," when there was as yet no Book to be read. Although this also implies that the Messenger would be revealed a Book to read from memory, the name of which derives from the verb "read," in particular it meant that there is another book or, rather, there are two books, counterparts to the Book which was to be revealed. These two books are the universe and human. A believer should approach the study of the universe and humanity without prejudice. It is also significant that the verses of the Qur'ān and the phenomena in the universe and those in human nature, material and psychological, are both called *āyah* – a sign. The imperative "Read!" is followed, not by a direct object or an adverb, but by "in and with the Name of your Lord, Who has created." This signifies:

- "Reading" the universe – studying it as a book that has chapters, paragraphs, sentences, words, and letters that are interrelated and interlinked – a study that has procedures peculiar to itself, like, for example, observation and experiment.

- The word translated as Lord is *Rabb*, and has meanings such as "educator, upbringer, sustainer, giver of a certain pattern, and the giver of a particular nature to each entity." Human nature includes free will, whereas every other entity acts according to the primordial nature assigned to it, what modern science refers to by using the words "nature" and the "laws of nature." What humans are commanded to do is to discover these "laws."

- Every act of a human being, including scientific studies, should be performed in the Name of God, and therefore be an act of worship. That is, the only limit which the Qur'ān or Islam puts on science. Any act so performed cannot be against God's commandments. For example, in the pursuit of scientific knowledge as worship, no one can cause harm to humankind, nor put that knowledge in the form of a deadly weapon in the hands of an irresponsible minority. If performed only in the Name of God, by people conscious of always being supervised by God and who will be called to account before a Supreme Tribunal for all their actions in the world, science can change the world into a Garden of Eden.

As humans study the universe and perceive its meaning and content, they come to know more deeply the beauty and splendor of the Creator's system and the infinitude of His Might. Thus, it is incumbent upon human beings to penetrate the manifold meanings of the universe, discover the Divine laws of "nature" and establish a world where science and faith complement one another so that humanity will be able to attain true bliss in both worlds. Otherwise, as Bertrand Russell says, "Unless human increases in wisdom (and faith) as much as in knowledge, the increase of knowledge will be an increase of sorrow" (*Impact of Science on Society*, 121). "Science teaches man to fly in

the air like birds, and to swim in the water like fishes, but man, without faith, cannot know how to live on the earth." (Quoted by Joad in *Counter Attack from the East*, 28).

Thus, as Seyyed Hossein Nasr emphasizes (*Man and Nature*, 1976, London, pp. 94–95), the revelation given to humankind is inseparable from the cosmic revelation, which is also a book of God. Islam, by refusing to separate humanity from nature and the study of nature from gnosis (metaphysical knowledge), or its metaphysical dimension, has preserved an integral view of the universe and sees in the arteries of the cosmic and natural order the flow of Divine grace. From the bosom of nature human beings seek to transcend nature and nature can be an aid in this process, provided they learn to contemplate it as a mirror reflecting a higher reality. This is the reason why one finds an elaborate hierarchy of knowledge in Islam, integrated by the principle of Divine Unity – "natural," juridical, social, and theological sciences and also metaphysical ones – and why so many Muslim scientists, like Ibn Sinā (Avicenna), Nāṣiru'd-Dīn at-Tūsī, Ak Shamsaddin, and Ibrāhīm Ḥaqqi of Erzurum, in addition to being well-versed in religious sciences, were either practicing Sufis or were intellectually affiliated to the Sufi schools of Islam. A man like Ibn Sinā could be a physician and Peripatetic philosopher and yet expound his Oriental philosophy that sought knowledge through illumination. Nāṣiru'd-Dīn al-Tūsī was the leading mathematician and astronomer of his day and the author of an outstanding treatise on the metaphysical dimension of Islam. Ibn Jarir aṭ-Ṭabarī, who is one of the outstanding figures in Islamic jurisprudence, history, and Qur'ānic interpretation, wrote eleven centuries ago about how the winds fertilize clouds to make rain fall.

2. Though God is the All-Powerful, in need of nothing, of no support, He has, out of His Wisdom, guards of Hell, who are many times more powerful than any council and who will drag the people of Hell into their final resting place. The mention of the guards of Hell here is to answer, in their own language, the stubborn leaders of the polytheists, who perceive the council of the city as being on their side.

598

2. What enables you to perceive what the Night of Destiny and Power is?

3. The Night of Destiny and Power is better than a thousand months.

4. The angels and the Spirit descend in it by the permission of their Lord with His decrees for every affair;

5. (It is) a sheer mercy and security (from all misfortunes, for the servants who spend it in devotions in appreciation of its worth). (It is) until the rising of the dawn.[1]

---

1. As explained in *sūrah* 44, note 1, everything and event has eternal existence in God's Knowledge. Since He is absolutely uncontained by time and space, there are no divisions of the past, the present, and the future in His Knowledge, in Which all time is a point or the present. Creating means that He gives external existence to the "archetypes" in His Knowledge according to the measures of the world to which the things belong. His will for things and events in the material world is that they follow a process in order to come into being.

When God wills for an individual thing to come into existence or an individual event to take place, He decrees it to be with its own particular identity. We can describe this as each thing and event being identified with its particular nature by the Divine Destiny, as referred to in verse 15: 21. Destiny transfers this event or thing from the realm of Knowledge to the realm of Divine Power, and Divine Power creates it according to the measures determined by Destiny. (We should always bear in mind that all of the explanations concerning God are in respect to us or from our perspective and according to our measures in our relationship with Him.)

Thus each year must have a particular identity and importance for the acts of the Divine Destiny and Power during the whole history of the universe in general, and for humankind in particular, and there is a special night during each year in which every thing or being that God has willed to come into existence and every event that has been willed to take place during

---

SŪRAH 97

AL-QADR
(DESTINY and POWER)

Makkah period

This *sūrah* of 5 verses takes its name from the word *al-qadr* (power, destiny, measure, worth) in the first verse. It is about the *Laylat al-Qadr* (the Night of Destiny, Power, and Measure), which occurs in the third part of the holy month of Ramaḍān. Spending this blessed night in devotions is of great worth.

In the Name of God, the All-Merciful, the All-Compassionate.

1. We have surely sent it (the Qur'ān) down in the Night of Destiny and Power.

that year is identified or particularized and transferred from the Divine Knowledge to the disposal of the Divine Power. As understood from other relevant verses, such as 2: 185, which states that the Qur'ān was sent down in Ramaḍān, this night is the Night of Destiny, Power, and Measure. Since this night is in Ramaḍān according to the lunar year, which is 11 days shorter than the solar year, any night in the solar year can be this night, once every 354 years.

The Qur'ān is sent down in one of two ways, one in its totality, the other in parts. Interpreters of the Qur'ān say that the Qur'ān was sent in its totality from the Supreme Ever-Preserved Tablet to the heaven of the world or *Bayt al-Maʿmūr*. We do not know the nature of this *Bayt* (House) and of the Qur'ān's being sent down to it or to the heaven of the world. However, in the light of verses 44: 1–6, it can be said that as every Divine Book was identified with its particular nature in its totality by Destiny in, or transferred in its totality from, God's Knowledge or the Supreme Ever-Preserved Tablet or Mother Book (see 6: 59, note 13; 13: 39, note 13; 17: 14, note 10; 43: 4, note

1), the Qur'ān was also identified in its totality in, or transferred from, the same original source on the Night of Destiny, Power, and Measure.

The angels, who are called messengers in 44: 5, are responsible for the affairs in the universe and also in the life of all beings. Among them are those charged with bringing the Divine Revelation to the Prophets, namely Gabriel and his aides. They receive God's decrees and set out to carry them out. They also descend with God's special grace, mercy, and security during the Night of Destiny, Power, and Measure.

As for the Spirit, as explained in *sūrah* 70, note 1, he must be an angel-like being. According to Imām al-Ghazzālī, he is an angel (or angel-like being) whom God employs in breathing each person's spirit into their body. Bediüzzaman Said Nursi maintains that there is a spirit representing every thing, every being. So the Spirit may be the being responsible for all the spirits, who represents their worship and presents it to God. During the Night of Destiny, Power, and Measure, he may be descending to breathe peace, liveliness, and exhilaration into the believers who keep vigil. (God knows best.)

SŪRAH 98

AL-BAYYINAH (THE CLEAR EVIDENCE)

Madīnah period

Revealed in Madīnah and consisting of 8 verses, the *sūrah* takes its name from the word *al-bayyinah* (the clear evidence) in the first verse. It draws attention to the fact that God's Messenger is the clear evidence for the truth of the Message that he brought, and that the unbelievers among both the polytheists and the People of the Book denied him and Islam, even when they had clearly witnessed the truth of this evidence. So people have been divided into two main groups: those who believe and do good, righteous deeds, and those who reject belief.

In the Name of God, the All-Merciful, the All-Compassionate.

1. Those who reject faith (in the Qur'ān and God's Messenger) from among the People of the Book and the polytheists would not abandon (the way they were supposed to follow) and deviate (into the way of unbelief) until there had come to them the Clear Evidence,[1] –

2. A Messenger from God,[2] reciting and conveying (to them teachings absolutely free from any falsehood) from purified pages (which only those cleansed of material and spiritual impurities may touch),[3]

3. In which are right, ever-true ordinances (concerning belief, thought, and action).

4. Those who were given the Book before did not split into parties until after the Clear Evidence (of the truth) came to them.

5. But they were not enjoined anything other than that they should worship God, sincere in faith in Him and practicing the Religion purely for His sake, as people of pure faith, and establish the Prayer in accordance with its conditions, and pay the Prescribed Purifying Alms; and that is the upright, ever-true Religion.[4]

6. Surely those who disbelieve (after the Clear Evidence has come to them) –from among the People of the Book and from among the polytheists– will be in the fire of Hell (a seed of which they bear in their hearts), abiding therein. They are the worst of creatures.

7. And those who believe and do good, righteous deeds – they are the best of creatures.

8. Their reward is with their Lord: Gardens of perpetual bliss through which rivers flow, abiding therein forever. God is well-pleased with them, and they are well-pleased with Him. That is for him who stands in awe of his Lord.

---

1. The polytheists who rejected God's Messenger and the Message he brought well knew that the Prophet Muḥammad, upon him be peace and blessings, was a truthful one, and that what he claimed was true. But despite the clarity of the Evidence for both himself and the Message he brought, the unbelievers rejected him for selfish reasons, such as tribal rivalry, obstinacy, conceit, and fear of losing their interests, and therefore they deserved eternal Divine condemnation. Just like them, those who rejected Islam and God's Messenger from among the People of the Book – the Jews and Christians – also preferred unbelief for base reasons such as jealousy, rivalry, racist considerations, and the like, although they had been waiting for a Prophet to come whose signs they found in their Books, and they knew well that Muḥammad was that Prophet.

The verse also indicates that unbelief in Islam and the Prophet Muḥammad, upon him be peace and blessings, means for the People of the Book unbelief in their own Books.

2. God's Messenger – the Prophet Muḥammad, upon him be peace and blessings, is one of the two greatest and clearest proofs for the truth of Islam, the other being the Qur'ān. His absolute truthfulness and trustworthiness, his pure personality distinguished by the most noble and praiseworthy virtues, his conquest of minds and hearts despite his being unlettered, his formation of a community called al-Aṣḥāb (the Companions) and that was com-

posed of the most virtuous people in history after the Prophets, his foundation of a state from tribes that had been trapped in unending feuds, his changing the path of human history in so short a time as 23 years; his sermons, sayings, prayers, and the criteria he established for the best individual and collective life; his being loved by his Companions and all the succeeding generations of his community to the extent that they have willingly sacrificed themselves for his way; his laying the foundations of the greatest civilization in history, which raised numerous scholars, scientists, saints, and literary people; his predictions, none of which have been contradicted over time – all these and many other aspects of his life, person, achievements, and mission decisively show that God's Messenger is one of two greatest and most comprehensive proofs for both himself, his Messengership, and the Message he brought from God.

3. The purity of the pages on which the Qur'ān is written comes from the purity of the Qur'ān. So the Qur'ān can only be touched by those purified from material and spiritual impurities. That is, unbelievers, polytheists, and the believers in need of ritual purity, cannot touch it. Also see sūrah 56: 79, note 16.

4. This summarizes God's Religion, which He conveyed through all His Messengers. This Religion is Islam. For the last two verses, also see 3: 19, note 4.

SŪRAH 99

AZ-ZILZĀL
(THE EARTHQUAKE)

Madīnah period

This *sūrah* of 8 verses was revealed in Madīnah. It takes its name from the word *zilzāl* (violent earthquake) in the first verse. It is concerned with some important events that will take place on the Day of Resurrection.

In the Name of God, the All-Merciful, the All-Compassionate.

1. When the earth quakes with a violent quaking destined for it,

2. And the earth yields up its burdens;

3. And human cries out, "What is the matter with it?" –

4. On that day it will recount all its tidings,

5. As your Lord has inspired it to do so.[1]

6. On that day all humans will come forth in different companies, to be shown their deeds (that they did in the world).[2]

7. And so, whoever does an atom's weight of good will see it;

8. And whoever does an atom's weight of evil will see it.[3]

---

1. The verses are, both in wording and meaning, possibly relating major events during the final destruction and re-building of the world, or they may be referring to earthquakes in general. During the final destruction of the world, the earth will be shaken with a violent shock (56: 4) by a violent blast of the Trumpet (79: 6). The mountains will be as a heap of slipping sand (73: 14), and the earth flattened out (84: 3), casting forth whatever is in it and becoming empty (84: 4). In other words, the graves are overturned and bring out their contents (82:

4). So during that destruction, whatever is in the earth – mines, treasures, and dead bodies – will be thrown out. Then, the first blast of the Trumpet will be followed by a second one (79: 7), and the dead will be revived and hasten toward the Plain of Gathering (50: 44; 70: 43). The unbelievers will witness the destruction of the world, and they will be greatly shaken also by the second blow of the Trumpet and revival.

The earth's recounting all its tidings must be figurative concerning the final destruction of the world. That is, it will cast out whatever is in it and the unbelievers will come to understand the truth of Doomsday, and everything about it will be revealed to them. They will also come to see the truth of whatever God's Messengers brought from God. However, after the Resurrection, the earth may relate all the deeds done on it during the worldly life by God's making it speak, as He will also make the human bodily organs speak against the humans (*sūrah* 41: 20–21, note 6).

Whatever a human being suffers is usually the result of their sins and faults, their rebellion against God in His commandments or laws of the Religion and life. So an earthquake, though it usually causes some treasures to be revealed and thermal sources to form, informs humans of and warns them against their sins and faults. As understood from some Qur'ānic verses (17: 44; 41: 21), even inanimate objects have some life, or they have a spirit particular to themselves that represents them. So they are directly affected by the deeds of humans. It is therefore not wrong to interpret these five verses of this *sūrah* as referring also to all earthquakes that take place throughout the world.

2. Everyone will go to the Supreme Court or Tribunal alone and be questioned about their deeds (6: 94; 18: 48). They will also be sorted out into the people of Paradise and the people of Hell. The people of Paradise will be in two main groups: those who are the nearest to God, and the others. In one stage or part of the Day of Resurrection, people will be called in groups, each after its leader (17: 71). The verse encompasses all these meanings.

3. Whatever a person does not go unnoticed by God. He has whatever people do recorded. And both in the world and in the Hereafter, everyone will see and receive the consequences of their deeds. This is the basic principle. The believers will receive the reward of their (religiously) good deeds in the Hereafter, though God does not leave them unrewarded, even in the world. But the unbelievers will receive the reward of their good deeds only in the world, and the recompense for their evil deeds is generally postponed to the Hereafter, even though they sometimes suffer for some of their deeds in the world. In the Hereafter, every person will be shown all their deeds, down to the smallest ones. However, as God overlooks and forgives many of people's evils in the world, except unbelief and the association of partners with Him, He will also forgive some evils of His believing servants in the Hereafter.

SŪRAH 100

AL-'ĀDIYĀT
(THE CHARGERS)

Madīnah period

This *sūrah* of 11 verses was probably revealed in Madīnah. It gets its name from the word *al-ādiyāt* (chargers) in its first verse. After it praises the vanguards of Islam, it draws attention to some negative attitudes that exist in human beings, particularly in unbelievers, and warns that God is fully aware of whatever people do.

In the Name of God, the All-Merciful, the All-Compassionate.

1. By the chargers that run panting,

2. Striking sparks of fire,

3. Rushing to make sudden raids at morn,

4. Raising thereby clouds of dust,

5. Storming thereby into a host, cleaving it:[1]

6. Surely human is ungrateful to his Lord;[2]

7. And to this he himself is a sure witness;[3]

8. And most surely he is violent in love of wealth.

9. Does he think he will not come to know when all that is in the graves is raised and brought out,

10. And all that is in the breasts is laid open and made out?

11. Surely their Lord on that Day will be fully aware of them.

---

1. The verses are concerned with Muslim warriors on horseback. According to Ikrimah, a classical commentator who lived in the first century of Islam, the second verse refers to arms of war. So modern commentators, such as Hamdi Yazır, maintain that the verses also imply firearms, especially modern tanks and other armored weaponry.

2. Although the oaths in the initial verses are of positive import, this verse mentions a negative aspect of human nature. This is because the verse condemns those who do not appreciate God's favor of guidance upon humankind as embodied in Islam. So the initial verses praise the Muslim warriors who respond to the wrongdoing enemy forces attacking them for reasons of religious intolerance or in betrayal of their agreements with them.

3. That is, the uncorrupted conscience of human beings, who cannot but admit God's favor of guidance that comes in the form of Islam, bears witness to their purposeful ingratitude and rebellion against God. Moreover, the life, attitudes, and acts of an ungrateful person attest to their demonstration of ingratitude to God. Humans themselves, as well as certain parts of their bodies, will bear witness against their ingratitude on the Day of Resurrection.

600

SŪRAH 101

AL-QĀRI'AH
(THE SUDDEN, MIGHTY STRIKE)

Makkah period

This *sūrah* of 11 verses was revealed in Makkah. It takes its name from the word *al-qāri'ah* (the sudden, mighty strike) in its first verse. It is about the dreadful occurrences on the Day of Resurrection and the end of good and evil.

In the Name of God, the All-Merciful, the All-Compassionate.

1. The sudden, mighty strike!

2. What is the sudden, mighty strike?

3. What enables you to perceive what the sudden, mighty strike is?

4. The day (when it occurs) humans will be like moths scattered about;

5. And the mountains will be like carded wool.[1]

6. And then, the one whose scales are heavy (with faith and good deeds),

7. He will be in a life of contentment.

8. Whereas the one whose scales are light (as devoid of faith and accepted good deeds),

9. He will have his home in a bottomless pit,

10. What enables you to perceive what it is?

11. It is a fire burning fiercely.

---

1. These verses relate some of the dreadful events that will take place during the destruction of the world. The following verses focus attention on the result of the deeds of people in the world.

SŪRAH 102

AT-TAKĀTHUR
(RIVALRY IN WORLDLY
INCREASE)

Makkah period

This *surah* of 8 verses was revealed in Makkah. It is named after the word *at-takāthur* (rivalry in worldly increase) in its first verse. It warns against competition in and boasting about the possession of ever more worldly things.

In the Name of God, the All-Merciful, the All-Compassionate.

1. Competing in increase of worldly goods (seeking and then boasting of the acquisition of things, wealth, pedigree, and posterity) distracts you (from the proper purpose of life),

2. Until you come to the graves.

3. No indeed! You will surely come to understand (when death comes to you).

4. Again, no indeed! You will surely come to understand it (when you are raised from the dead).

5. No indeed! If only you knew with certainty of knowledge (then you would not disorder priorities).

6. You will most surely see the Blazing Flame!

7. Then (when you go to the other world), you will most surely see it with the eye of certainty.

8. And on that Day you will most surely be questioned as to all the favors (bestowed on you).[1/2]

---

1. That is, there are certain duties concerning all the worldly things bestowed on you. You should not be proud because of them and their abundance. Rather, you should thank God because He has given them to you, and earn and spend your wealth lawfully, and do so primarily with the intention of using it in God's way, and bring up your children as good believers.

2. This *surah* has a similar meaning to verse 57: 20: *Know that the present, worldly life is but a play, vain talk and ostentation, and mutual boasting among you, and competing in wealth and children – it is like when rain comes down and the vegetation grown by it pleases the farmers, (but) then it dries up and you see it turn yellow, then it becomes straw; and in the Hereafter there is a severe punishment, but also (there is) forgiveness from God and His good pleasure (which are everlasting); whereas the present, worldly life is but a transient enjoyment of delusion.*

3. Except those who believe and do good righteous deeds, and exhort one another to truth, and exhort one another to steadfast patience (in the face of misfortunes, and suffering in God's way, and in doing good deeds, and not committing sins).[2]

---

1. *Al-ʿAsr* has various meanings, such as time, day and night together, the afternoon, the last part of time, etc. It also implies being full of things and ready to be emptied. Our Prophet says that he is the Prophet of *al-ʿasr*, meaning the afternoon (al-Bukhārī, "Ijārah," 8, 9). If we consider all these meanings, we can say that by *al-ʿasr*, the *sūrah* is referring to time from the beginning to end, as far as the events it contains are concerned, and draws attention in particular to the last part, during which God's Last Messenger was sent with the last, universal Message of God. It also implies the latest period of this part when extremely important events do and will take place.

2. See also *sūrah* 95: 4–6, note 2.

SŪRAH 103

AL-ʿASR
(TIME HEAVY WITH EVENTS)

Makkah period

This *sūrah* of 3 verses, revealed in Makkah, takes its name from the word *al-ʿasr* in the first verse. This short *sūrah* contains the basic teachings of the Qurʾān in a compacted form. Imam Shāfiʿī said: "If no other *sūrah*s had been revealed, this short one would have been enough for the happiness of people in both worlds" (Yazır). When the Companions joined in a gathering, they did not usually leave there without reciting this *sūrah* (al-Bayhaqī, 6: 501).

In the Name of God, the All-Merciful, the All-Compassionate

1. By Time (especially the last part of it, heavy with events),[1]

2. Most certainly, human is in loss,

SŪRAH 104

AL-HUMAZAH
(SLANDERER)

Makkah period

This *sūrah* of 9 verses was revealed in Makkah. Its name is taken from the word *al-humazah* (slanderer) in its first verse. It warns against slandering and defaming, and seeing oneself as above other people because of one's wealth (or other worldly things).

In the Name of God, the All-Merciful, the All-Compassionate.

1. Woe to every one who slanders and vilifies,

2. Who (sees himself above others because he) has amassed wealth and (without expending it in God's cause and for the needy) counts it (in greedy love for it).

4. By no means! He will most certainly be hurled into the Consuming Disaster.

5. What enables you to perceive the Consuming Disaster?

6. It is God's fire, set ablaze,

7. Which penetrates deep into hearts (and burns within, as it burns outside).

8. Surely it shall be closed over upon them.

9. In extended columns.

SŪRAH 105

AL-FĪL (THE ELEPHANT)

Makkah period

This *sūrah* of 5 verses was revealed in Makkah. It takes its name from the word *al-fīl* (the elephant) that occurs in its first verse. Describing what befell the Abyssinian army of Abrahah, which attacked Makkah in order to destroy the Ka'bah in 571, fifty days before the birth of God's Messenger, it warns against active opposition to God's Religion.

In the Name of God, the All-Merciful, the All-Compassionate.

1. Have you considered how your Lord dealt with the people of the Elephant?[1]

2. Did He not bring their evil scheme to nothing?

3. He sent down upon them flocks of birds (unknown in the land),

4. Shooting them with bullet-like stones of baked clay (an emblem of the punishment due to them),

5. And so He rendered them like a field of grain devoured and trampled.[2]

---

1. This verse draws attention to what befell the Abyssinian army that attacked Makkah in an attempt to destroy the Ka'bah under the command of Abrahah ibn Sabāh. The army had a number of war elephants. Abrahah had erected a great temple in San'ā, hoping to attract the Arab pilgrims from Makkah to his own territory.

2. Unusual events come as signs of a new turning point in human history. The Makkans were not strong enough to defend Makkah and the Ka'bah against the army of Abrahah. They left Makkah for the surrounding mountains. So its real owner – God – defended it on the eve of the birth of God's Messenger, upon him be peace and blessings. He sent down on the army flocks of birds. As can also be understood from the word *ababīl* translated here as birds, these were a species unknown in the Ḥijaz. . They were birds of different colors that carried stones of backed clay, one in their mouth and two in their claws. The stones penetrated deep into the bodies of Abrahah's soldiers, entering from the head and slicing through their organs. This was a clear miracle (ar-Rāzī, Ibn Kathīr [*Tafsīr*], Hamdi Yazır). This event became so famous in Arabian history that the year when it took place came to be known as the Year of the Elephant.

In the Name of God, the All-Merciful, the All-Compassionate.

1. (At least) for (God's constant) favor of concord and security to the Quraysh,

2. Their concord and security in their winter and summer journeys,

3. Let them worship the Lord of this House (the Ka'bah),

4. Who has provided them with food against hunger, and made them safe from fear.[1]

---

1. The verse shows the acceptance of Abraham's prayer: *And (remember) once Abraham prayed: "My Lord! Make this (untilled valley) a land of security, and provide its people with the produce of earth, such of them as believe in God and the Last Day." He (his Lord) answered: "(I will bestow provision upon both believers and unbelievers. But) whoever is thankless and disbelieves, I will provide for him to enjoy himself for a short while, then I will compel him to the punishment of the Fire – how evil a destination to arrive at!"* (2: 126)

SŪRAH 106

QURAYSH

Makkah period

This *sūrah* of 4 verses was revealed in Makkah. It takes its name from the word *al-Quraysh* (the name of the tribe living then in Makkah) in its first verse. It mentions God's important favors upon them. As God defended and protected them against foreign assaults, making Makkah a secure land, He also fed them against hunger. Because of the existence of the Ka'bah, pilgrims came to Makkah, and the Makkan people received respect from other tribes. This respect increased after the event of the Elephant mentioned in the previous *sūrah*. The trade caravans they dispatched to Syria in winter and to Yemen in summer traveled in security.

SŪRAH 107

AL-MĀ'ŪN (ASSISTANCE)

Makkah period

This *sūrah* of 7 verses was revealed in Makkah. It is named after the word *al-mā'ūn* (assistance) that occurs in the 7th verse. It emphasizes sincerity in faith and worship, and the importance of mutual assistance in society. Also, it warns against hypocrisy.

In the Name of God, the All-Merciful, the All-Compassionate.

1. Have you considered one who denies the Last Judgment?

2. That is the one who repels the orphan,

3. And does not urge the feeding of the destitute.

4. And woe to those worshippers (denying the Judgment),

5. Those who are unmindful in their Prayers,[1]

6. Those who want to be seen and noted (for their acts of worship),

7. Yet deny all assistance (to their fellow-men).

---

1. The last two verses, together with the succeeding ones, threaten hypocritical people. These hypocrites see no good in the Prayer and do not fear God when they do not pray. If they sometimes pray, they are proud of it. They are careless about whether they pray on time and how they pray. They do not pursue God's good pleasure and approval in their Prayers; rather they expect some worldly advantages from them.

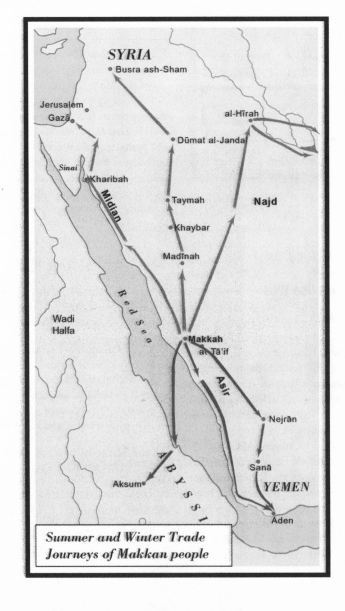

Summer and Winter Trade Journeys of Makkan people

SŪRAH 108

AL-KAWTHAR
(ABUNDANT GOOD)

Makkah period

Revealed in Makkah and having 3 verses, this *sūrah* takes its name from *al-kawthar* (unceasing, abundant good) in its first verse. It gives God's Messenger the good tidings that he will be favored with unceasing, abundant blessings, and that those who oppose him and qualify him as one with no posteri-

ty will be cut off from every good, as well as from posterity.

In the Name of God, the All-Merciful, the All-Compassionate

1. We have surely granted you (unceasing) abundant good;[1]

2. So pray to your Lord, and sacrifice (for Him in thankfulness).[2]

3. Surely it is the one who offends you who is cut off (from unceasing good, including posterity).[3]

---

1. By *(unceasing) abundant good*, the verse means that God's Messenger will be successful in his cause and, in return, be favored with great blessings both in the world and in the Hereafter. So the word includes the future successes and conquests of Islam, his community's unparalleled love for the Messenger and their calling God's blessings and peace on him and praying for him continually. In addition, God's Messenger, upon him be peace and blessings, will also be given the right to intercede for all humans in the Hereafter and be raised to the rank of being praised. Again, his Religion will prevail over all other religions and religion-like systems. Both the Messenger and the members of his Community will be favored with great blessings in Paradise.

The *(unceasing) abundant good* also implies that God's Messenger will have ever-multiplying descendants who will serve his cause ardently. In truth, there is no posterity that approaches his in number, virtue, or serving God's cause.

2. The Prayer the Messenger is ordered to perform by this verse must be the Forenoon (*Duḥā*) Prayer, which, like the *Tahajjud* Prayer, is obligatory for the Messenger and supererogatory for other Muslims. However, the verse also suggests the Prayer of the Religious Day of Sacrifice (*'Id* Prayer), which is done in the forenoon. It was ordered in Madīnah as a nec-

essary act of worship for all Muslims. There are two *'Id* prayers in Islam: *'Id al-Fiṭr* (marking the end of Ramaḍān and lasting for three days) and *'Id al-Aḍḥā* (beginning on the tenth of *Dhu 'l-Ḥijjah*, and lasting for four days). By sacrifice the verse means that while God's Messenger offered sacrifices in thankfulness to God in Makkah, offering a sacrifice during the Religious Festival of Sacrifice was enjoined upon the Muslims as a necessary act of worship in Madīnah. The Muslims who have the required amount of wealth should sacrifice cattle (a sheep or a goat for one person, or a camel, a cow, or an ox up to seven people). Offering a sacrifice is incumbent (*wājib*) upon every adult Muslim who has the *niṣāb* (the required amount of wealth). The difference between having to pay the *Zakāh* and sacrificing is that the *Zakāh* must be paid if the required amount of wealth has been in the possession of the person for one year, while a sacrifice must be offered if the person has had the required or sufficient amount of wealth for only one day. The sacrifice must be made on any of the first three days of *'Id al-Aḍḥā*.

3. The verse, which apparently means that the one who satirizes God's Messenger will be cut off from posterity, also suggests that, until the Last Day, those who are like such a one in thought or deed will also be cut off (sooner or later) from posterity, and the anti-Islamic systems they establish or support will not last long.

SŪRAH 109

AL-KĀFIRŪN
(THE UNBELIEVERS)

Makkah period

This *surah* of 6 verses was revealed in Makkah. It takes its name from the word *al-kāfirūn* in the first verse. *Kāfir* means one who rejects faith in one, some, or all the principles of faith that must be believed in in order to be a believing Muslim. The *surah* tells the Messenger and all other Muslims to be sure, determined, and steadfast in their faith against the unbelievers and that they should not compel the unbelievers to accept faith.

In the Name of God, the All-Merciful, the All-Compassionate.

1. Say: "O you unbelievers (who obstinately reject faith)!

2. "I do not worship that which you worship.[1]

3. "Nor are you worshipping what I worship.[2]

4. "Nor will I ever worship that which you worship.

5. "And nor will you ever worship what I worship.

6. "You have your religion (with whatever it will bring you), and I have my religion (with whatever it will bring me).

---

1. This verse is a declaration that there can be no reconciliation between faith in God and other so-called, invented deities.

2. The unbelievers to whom the verse is addressed or whom God's Messenger is addressing are those who are so obstinate in rejecting the faith that God informed His Messenger that they would never believe. (See 2: 6; 36: 7.)

SŪRAH 110

AN-NAṢR (HELP)

Madīnah period

This *surah* of 3 verses was revealed in Madīnah some three months before the death of God's Messenger. It is about God's completion of His favor upon His Messenger during his life and therefore the end of the Messenger's duty of Messengership. Therefore, it suggests his imminent death. It also implies a warning to the believers that they, because they have been victorious, should be even more alert against avoiding sins and indulging in worldly amusements.

In the Name of God, the All-Merciful, the All-Compassionate.

1. When God's help comes and victory (which is a door to further victories),[1]

2. And you see people entering God's Religion in throngs,

3. Then glorify your Lord with His praise, and ask Him for forgiveness, for He surely is One Who returns repentance with liberal forgiveness and additional reward.[2/3]

---

1. On many occasions, God promised His Messenger help and victory and openly declared that He and His Messenger would prevail. For example: While the Messenger and his followers suffered great persecutions at the hands of the Makkan polytheists, He declared: *Most certainly We help Our Messengers, and those who believe, in the life of this world and on the Day when the Witnesses will stand forth (to testify concerning people's response to the Messengers)* (40: 51). In Madīnah, during the days of the Battle of Uhud in the 3rd year of the *Hijrah*, He declared: *And yet another (blessing) which you love: Help from God and a near victory soon to come (which will lead to further victories). Give glad tidings to the believers* (61: 13). And after the Battle of the Trench, that took place in the 5th year of the *Hjirah*, He promised: *God has decreed: "I will most certainly prevail, I and My Messengers." Surely God is All-Strong, All-Glorious with irresistible might* (58: 21). However, since humans are tested in the world in order to prepare for their life in the other world, He made His help and victory dependent upon the believers' helping His cause: *O you who believe! If you help God('s cause by striving in His way), He will help you and make your feet firm (so that you are steadfast in His cause and ultimately victorious)* (47: 7). So, with God's help victory was secured, and this meant that the believers had helped His cause and carried out their duties in a way that pleased Him.

This verse marks an important aspect of the Qur'ān's miraculousness and its Divine authorship. For no one other than God can speak so certainly about the future. As seen in the few examples above, God clearly declared that He would complete His favor on His Messenger and lead him and the believers to victory, which He did.

2. The order to glorify God with His praise and to ask Him for forgiveness is a warning to the believers that they should never fall into the perilous error of attributing victory to themselves, and that they should always be careful to avoid indulging in sins after a victory. The victory is not their achievement, rather it is God Who bestows victory on His servants. Moreover, we can put up with hardships and persecutions, but it is more difficult to be firm and unyielding against the temptations of the carnal soul, particularly in times of ease that come after years of privation and persecution. This we can clearly see in a typical attitude of the Messenger. While the Muslim army was returning to Madīnah after they had defeated the enemy, the Messenger of God said to them: "We are returning from the lesser *jihād* to the greater one." The Companions asked what the greater *jihad* was, and he explained that it was fighting with the carnal soul (al-'Ajlūnī, *Kashf al-Khafa'*, 1: 424).

Secondly, we may have made some mistakes and committed sins on the way to victory. Therefore, we should also seek forgiveness for these. The Qur'ān gives great importance to seeking forgiveness from God, and since we are fallible, we should always implore God for forgiveness. Imploring Him for forgiveness also severs the roots of evil and greatly helps us not to indulge in sins.

3. As pointed out by 'Abdullāh ibn 'Abbās, a great Companion well-versed in the interpretation of the Qur'ān, this *sūrah* informs us that the time for God's Messenger to leave the world has approached. The Messengers were sent to convey God's Message, and God's Messenger had completed his mission, so there was no longer any reason for him to stay in the world. This also reminds us that humans have duties in the world, and when a person no longer has anything to do in the world or when they can no longer serve God and His cause any more, there is no reason for them to stay in the world any longer.

'Ā'ishah, the beloved wife of God's Messenger, tell us about the last moments of the Messenger:

> I was with him during his last moments. Whenever he was ill, he would ask me to pray for him and, expecting my prayer to be accepted through the blessing of his auspicious hand, I would hold his hand and pray. During his last illness, I wanted to do the same and pray, when he suddenly withdrew his hand and said: "To *ar-Rafīq al-A'lā*!" (The All-Exalted Friend, meaning God Almighty) (al-Bukhārī, "Maghazī," 78; Muslim, "Salām," 50, 51).

SŪRAH 111

TABBAT (RUIN)

Makkah period

Revealed in Makkah in the early period of the Makkan era of the Prophet Muhammad's mission, this *sūrah* of 5 verses takes its name from the verb *TabBa* (be ruined) in the first verse. It promises and foretells the perishing of Abū Lahab and his wife Umm Jamīl, implying the perdition of similar enemies of Islam.

In the Name of God, the All-Merciful, the All-Compassionate.

1. May both hands of Abū Lahab be ruined, and are ruined are they![1]

2. His wealth has not availed him, nor his gains.

3. He will enter a flaming Fire to roast;

4. And (with him) his wife, carrier of firewood (and of evil tales and slander),

5. Around her neck will be a halter of strongly twisted rope.[2]

---

1. Abū Lahab was one of the Prophet Muhammad's uncles. Abū Lahab, meaning the father of flame, is a nickname that was given to him while he was a child because of the rosy glow on his cheeks. He was one of the fiercest enemies of the Messenger and Islam. Since he was an uncle of the Messenger, he knew him very well and therefore was expected to believe in him. But he stubbornly rejected him and actively opposed him. He cursed him, saying: *May your hands ruin*, meaning "May you be left with no good at all and perish!" So because of his limitless enmity, the Qur'ān designated him as the Father of the Flame, signifying that he was one destined to be among those who would suffer the greatest torment in Hellfire, and foretold that he would perish without accepting faith and be left without any good. It happened just as the Qur'ān foretold. He died in great sorrow when he learned that the Makkan army had been badly defeated at the Battle of Badr. Because of his illness, which was very contagious, no one dared to approach his body to bury it. After a few days, they dug a pit and, pushing his body with long cudgels into it, buried it with stones they threw over his corpse from some distance away.

2. Abū Lahab's wife, Arwā Umm Jamīl, was no less than her husband in her enmity to the Messenger. She scattered thorns along the Messenger's way and in front of his house. She also slandered him and the Message he brought, with a view to kindling flames of hatred and enmity against him and his followers. So the Qur'ān announces the type of punishment that she would be given in Hell. She will both burn in the Hellfire and carry the wood of her fire around her neck, the part of her body where she wore precious necklaces.

SŪRAH 112

AL-IKHLĀS
(PURITY OF FAITH)

Makkah period

This *sūrah* of 4 verses was revealed in Makkah. It takes its name from the subject matter; for this reason it is also called *Sūrat at-Tawḥīd* (Declaration of God's Absolute Unity).

In the Name of God, the All-Merciful, the All-Compassionate.

1. Say: "He, God, the One of Absolute Unity.[1]

2. "God, the Eternally-Besought-of-All (Himself in no need of anything).

3. "He begets not, nor is He begotten.[2]

4. "And comparable to Him there is none."[3/4]

---

1. As pointed out by Fakhru'd-Dīn ar-Rāzī, a great interpreter of the Qur'ān, God is called by three Names in this verse: *He*, *God*, and *the One of Absolute Unity*. "He" denotes the Divine Being in His Essence, Who is indescribable, known by none but Himself only, not designated by any Attributes and Names. "God" is the Divine Being Who manifests Himself with and is recognized by His Attributes and Names, Who encompasses all the Attributes and Names by Which the Divine Being is called. "The One of Absolute Unity" negates all false notions and concepts about the Divine Being. "He" is the term used by those nearest to the Divine Being; they appeal to Him as He. "God" is the term used by the people of the Right, the people of happiness and prosperity (who will be given their records in their right hands), while "the One of Absolute Unity" comes in this verse in connection with the people of the Left, the people of wretchedness (who will be given their Records in their left hands), who have incorrect concepts of God, who deny Him or associate different partners with Him.

There are some differences between God's being One (*Wāḥid*) and the One of Absolute Unity (*Aḥad*). God's being One (*Wāḥid*) means the manifestation of God's Names, which give existence to all things and beings, and are responsible for their life, throughout the entire universe. God's being "the One of Absolute Unity" (*Aḥad*) means God's concentration of the manifestations of His Names on individual things or beings. In order to understand the difference more clearly, consider this analogy:

The sun encompasses innumerable things in its light. This can serve to understand God's Oneness. But to hold the totality of its light in our minds, we would need a vast conceptual and perceptual power. So lest the sun be forgotten, each shining object reflects its properties (light and heat) as best it can and so manifests the sun. This is an analogy for God's being the One of Absolute Unity. As related to the manifestation of God's Oneness, the whole universe is a mirror to God. While as related to the manifestation of His being the One of Absolute Unity, each (shining) being is a mirror of Him.

Bediüzzaman Said Nursi notes that faith in God's Unity has two degrees: believing superficially that God has no partners, and that the universe belongs only to Him (such believers may be susceptible to deviation and confusion); and firm conviction that God is One, that everything belongs to Him exclusively, and that only He creates, maintains, provides, causes to die, etc. Such believers see His seal and observe His stamp on all things. Free from doubt, they feel themselves always and everywhere in His Presence. Their conviction cannot be diluted by deviation or doubt.

2. Declaring that God begets not, and nor is He begotten is such an evident principle for the Divine Being that it is mentioned here to refute all creeds that attribute sons or daughters to God. It primarily and categorically refutes the pagans' attribution to Him of the angels as daughters and the Christians' seeing Him as the Father of Jesus, or their attributing Jesus to Him as a son.

3. The Divine Religion, which had been revealed to Prophets of various peoples was the same in essence, but over the course of time its message had been misinterpreted and it had become mixed up with superstitions and had degenerated into magical practices and meaningless rituals. The concept of God, the very core of the Religion, had become debased by (a) the anthropomorphic tendency of turning God into a being with a human shape and passions, (b) by the deification of angels, (c) by the association of other personalities with the Godhead of the One and only God (as in Hinduism and Christianity), (d) by making the Prophets or some godly persons into incarnations of God (e.g., Jesus Christ in Christianity, the Buddha in Mahayana Buddhism, Krishna and Rama in Hinduism), and (e) by the personification of the Attributes of God as separate Divine persons (e.g., the Christian Trinity of the Father, the Son, and the Holy Ghost and the Hindu Trimutri of Brahma, Vishnu, and

Shiva). The holy Prophet of Islam, Muḥammad (upon him be peace and blessings), rejected all such theological trends and restored the concept of God to its pristine purity as the only Creator, Sustainer, and Master of all of creation (*Rabbul-ʿālamīn wa-ilāhuhum wa-malikuhum*).

Tawḥīd is the highest conception of deity, the knowledge of which God has sent to humankind in all ages through His Prophets. It was this same knowledge that all the Prophets, including Moses, Jesus, and the Prophet Muḥammad, upon them all be peace, brought to humankind. People became guilty of polytheism or idol-worship after the death of their Prophets only because they had deviated from the pure teachings of the Prophets. They relied upon their own faulty reasoning, false perceptions, and biased interpretations in order to satisfy their lusts, which they would have been unable to do with a *Tawḥīd*-based system, in which they would have had to obey the commandments of the One Supreme God.

"The foremost in the Religion," ʿAli ibn Abī Ṭālib, the Fourth Caliph, is reported to have said, "God's knowledge, the perfection of His knowledge, is to testify to Him, the perfection of testifying to Him is to believe in His Oneness, the perfection of believing in His Oneness is to regard Him as pure and the perfection of His purity is to deny all kinds of negative attributes about Him." He is infinite and eternal; He is self-existent and self-sufficient. As stated in this *sūrah*: *He, God, the One of Absolute Unity; the Eternally-Besought-of-All (Himself in no need of anything); He begets not, nor is He begotten; and comparable to Him there is none.* Vision perceives Him not, and He perceives all vision. Nothing whatsoever (is there) like Him; and He (alone) is the All-Hearing and All-Seeing. Again, in the words of Ali, "He is a Being, but not through the phenomenon of coming into being. He exists, but not from non-existence. He is with everything, but not by a physical nearness. He is different from everything, but not by a physical separation. He acts, but without the accompaniment of movements and instruments. He is the One, the only One Who is such that there is none with whom He keeps company or whom He misses when absent" (*an-Nahj al-Balāghah*, "1ˢᵗ Sermon").

4. This short *sūrah*, which God's Messenger describes as equivalent to one-third of the Qur'ān, has six sentences, three positive, and three negative, which prove and establish six aspects of Divine Unity and reject and negate six types of associating partners with God. Each sentence has two meanings: one a priori (functioning as a cause or proof) and the other a posteriori (functioning as an effect or result). That means that the *sūrah* actually contains 36 *sūrah*s, each made up of a combination of six sentences and each having many aspects. One is either a premise or a proposition, and the others are arguments supporting it.

For example:

Say: He is God, because He is the One of Absolute Unity, because He is the Eternally-Besought-of-All, because He begets not, because He is not begotten, because comparable to Him there is none.

Also:

Say: Comparable to Him there is none, because He begets not, because He is not begotten, because He is the Eternally-Besought-of-All, because He is the One of Absolute Unity, because He is God.

Also:

He is God, therefore He is the One of Absolute Unity, therefore He is the Eternally-Besought-of-All, therefore He begets not, therefore He is not begotten, and therefore comparable to Him there is none.

And so on. In this way, there are thousands of Qur'āns within the Qur'ān.

SŪRAH 113

AL-FALAQ (THE DAYBREAK)

Madīnah period

Revealed in Madīnah, and consisting of 5 verses, this *sūrah* gets its name from the word *al-falaq* (the daybreak) in the first verse. It teaches us how to seek refuge in God from every evil to which we may be exposed.

In the Name of God, the All-Merciful, the All-Compassionate.

1. Say: "I seek refuge in the Lord of the daybreak

2. "From the evil of what He has created,

3. "And from the evil of the darkness (of night) when it overspreads,[1]

4. "And from the evil of the witches who blow on knots (to cast a spell),[2]

5. "And from the evil of the envious one when he envies."

---

1. As darkness figuratively implies evil, a person can be a target of evil in the darkness more easily than during the daytime. Also, evil beings, like disbelieving jinn, usually come out when darkness overspreads and becomes intense. So the verses warn us against the evil that may be done to us secretly and to which we may be exposed in darkness, and which may be done by invisible beings. The contrast in the verses is very beautiful in how they order us to seek refuge in God as the Lord of the daybreak from the evil of darkness. Daybreak means light, and the light reveals secret schemes; Islam is God's light which removes the veils of darkness from everything.

2. Particularly since ancient times, it has generally been women who were occupied with casting spells or sorcery; that is why this verse fo-

cuses on such women. Just as God's Messenger declared that the evil eye is an undeniable fact, so too is sorcery an undeniable reality. Those who deny that there are such things as spells and sorcery do so either because they do not believe in anything metaphysical or what they suppose to be connected with the Religion, or because they are unaware of the realities beyond the physical realm. The Qur'ān speaks about (and severely condemns) the sorcery that is practiced to cause a rift between spouses (2: 102). According to Islam, sorcery and casting spells are as sinful as unbelief. While breaking a spell is a good, meritorious deed, it must not be adopted and practiced as a profession. Although our Messenger met with jinn, preached Islam to them, and took their allegiance, he never explained how they were to be contacted or how to cast or break a spell. However, he taught how

jinn approach us and seek to control us, how to protect ourselves against their evil, and how to protect ourselves against the evil eye.

The safest way to protect ourselves against evil spirits or things like sorcery is to sustain a strong loyalty to God and His Messenger. This requires following the principles of Islam strictly. In addition, we should never give up praying, for prayer is a weapon against hostility, protects us from harm, and helps us to attain our goals. The Messenger advises us to recite this and the following *sūrah* in order to be protected against such evils and to be saved from them. (For detailed explanation for the matter, see *The Essentials of the Islamic Faith*, 69–87)

This verse also implies seeking refuge with God from the evils planned and practiced secretly and by secret enemies, such as foreign agents or intelligence services.

SŪRAH 114

AN-NĀS (HUMANKIND)

Madīnah period

This *sūrah* of 6 verses was revealed in Madīnah. Its name comes from the word *an-nās* (humankind), which recurs throughout. It teaches us how to seek refuge in God from the secret devices of Satan and similar beings.

In the Name of God, the All-Merciful, the All-Compassionate.

1. Say: "I seek refuge in the Lord of humankind,

2. "The Sovereign of humankind,

3. "The Deity of humankind,

4. "From the evil of the sneaking whisperer (the Satan),

5. "Who whispers into the hearts of humankind,

6. "Of jinn and humankind."[1]

---

1. This *sūrah* teaches us to be most alert to the temptations and secret devices of Satan and Satan-like people (see 6: 112). With all the means at their disposal, they will do their utmost to lead us astray from God's way into their own evil ways, to commit sins, to bring about dissension among us, and to do other things to cause us harm both in the world and the Hereafter. The best way to be protect-

ed against their devices and temptations is to believe in God as our Lord (Creator, Sustainer, Master) and Absolute Sovereign, Who has the absolute right to rule us, and Who, as the sole Deity, has the exclusive right to be worshipped. Then, we must act according to this faith. (For some of the ways in which Satan approaches us *in order to lead us astray*, see *sūrah* 7: 17, note 2.)

THE PROPHET MUḤAMMAD IN THE BIBLE

All the previous Prophets predicted the Prophet Muḥammad, upon him be peace and blessings. We can still find indications to his coming in the Torah, the Psalms and the Gospels. Here are some examples:

- The Lord said unto me (Moses): "What they have spoken is good. I will raise them up for them a Prophet like you from among their brethren, and will put My words in his mouth; and he shall speak to them all that I command him. And it shall be that whoever will not hear My words, which he speaks in My name, I will require it of him." (*Deuteronomy*, 18: 17–19)

It is clear from these verses that what is meant by "a Prophet like you among their brethren," is a Prophet who will come from the line of Ishmael, since Ishmael is the brother of Isaac, who is the forefather of Moses' people, the Children of Israel. The only Prophet who came from the line of Ishmael after Moses and resembled him in many ways, for example, in the bringing of a new law and fighting with his enemies, is the Prophet Muḥammad, upon him be peace and blessings. Also, the verse of the Bible "But since then there has not arisen in Israel a prophet like Moses, whom the Lord knew face to face," (*Deuteronomy*, 34: 10) clearly states that no Prophet like Moses did ever appear among the Israelites. The Qur'ān (73: 15) points to the same fact: *Surely We have sent to you (O people) a Messenger, a witness against you, just as We sent a Messenger to the Pharaoh* (73: 15).

The sentence, "I will put my words in his mouth; and he shall speak to them all that I command him," in the verses from Deuteronomy quoted above, means that the promised Prophet will be unlettered and speak whatever is revealed to him. God restates the same in the Qur'ān (53: 3–4): *He does not speak on his own, out of his own desire; that (which he conveys to you) is but a Revelation that is revealed to him.*

- The Lord came from Sinai, and dawned on them from Seir; He shone forth from Mount Paran. (*Deuteromony*, 33: 2)

refers to the Prophethood of Moses, Jesus, and Muḥammad respectively, upon them be peace. Sinai is the place where the Prophet Moses spoke to God and received the Torah. Seir, a place in Palestine, is where the Prophet Jesus received Divine Revelation. As for Paran, it is mentioned in the Torah (*Genesis*, 21: 19–21) as the area in the desert where Hagar was left by her husband Abraham, upon him be peace, to live with her son, Ishmael, upon the order of God. The well of Zamzam appeared in it. As is stated explicitly in the Qur'ān (14: 35–37), Abraham left Hagar and Ishmael in the valley of Makkah, which was then an uninhabited place within the mountain ranges of Paran.

- The verse in Deuteronomy, continues:

  And he came with ten thousands of saints; from His right hand came a fiery law for them.

This verse refers to the promised Prophet, Muḥammad, upon him be peace and blessings, who would have numerous Companions of the highest degree of sainthood. The law is his *Sharīʿah*, its being depicted as fiery alludes to the fact that the promised Prophet would be allowed to fight against his enemies.

- Surely God said to Abraham: "Hagar will certainly bear children. There will appear from her sons one whose hand will be above all, and the hands of all others will be opened to him in reverence."

Although it does not exist word for word in the present versions of the Bible, it is recorded by ʿAli al-Qārī in his *Sharh ash-Shifā*, 1: 743. However, we read in the Torah, the following verses:

> Yet I will also make a nation of the son of the bondwoman, because he *is* your seed (*Genesis*, 21: 13). (Hagar,) arise, lift up the lad and hold him with your hand; for I will make him a great nation. (21: 18)

These verses explicitly refer to the descendants of Ishmael. They were made into a great nation only after the Prophethood of Muḥammad, upon him be peace and blessings.

- Again, the present versions of the Bible record that the son God ordered Abraham to sacrifice was Isaac (*Genesis*, 22: 2). However, as discussed and proved in *sūrah* 37, note: 13 based on the Bible itself, this son was actually Ishmael, the elder brother of Isaac. So, the following verses which *Genesis* records God said to Abraham after his fulfilling the test of sacrificing his son must be referring also to the descendants and community of Muḥammad, upon him be peace and blessings, and so corroborates the quotations above from ʿAli al-Qārī:

> ....because you have done this thing, and have not withheld your son, your only *son*– blessing I will bless you, and multiplying I will multiply your descendants as the stars of the heaven and as the sand which *is* on the seashore; and your descendants shall possess the gates of their enemies. In your seed all the nations of the earth shall be blessed, because you have obeyed My voice. (*Genesis*, 22: 16-18)

- Behold my servant, whom I uphold; My elect one in whom My soul delights; I have put My spirit upon him: he will bring forth justice to the Gentiles. He will not cry out, nor raise his voice, nor cause his voice to be heard in the street. A bruised reed he will not break, and smoking flax he will not quench: he will bring forth justice for truth. He will not fail nor be discouraged, till he has established justice in the earth: and the coastlands will wait for his law. (*Isaiah*, 42: 1-4)

Although these verses in Isaiah are taken by Christians to be "prophecies" of the Jesus of the Gospels, the predictions they contain refer to the Prophet Muḥammad and Islam. For Jesus did not bring a law, nor did he claim to establish Christianity on earth and set justice in the earth, so that the coastlands should wait for his law. In law he followed the Old Testament, with the exception that he made a few things unlawful in the Old Testament lawful by God's order. And it is the Gospels which report from Jesus that he was not sent but unto the lost sheep of the house of Israel (*Matthew*, 15: 24). He also clearly told his twelve disciples: "Go not into the way of the Gentiles, and do not enter a city of the Samaritans: But go rather to the lost sheep of the house of Israel."

(*Matthew*, 10: 5-6). In addition, these verses have great resemblance with the following verse which 'Abdullāh ibn 'Amr ibn al-'Ās, who made extensive studies of earlier Divine books, 'Abdullah ibn Salām, who was the first to embrace Islam from amongst the famous Jewish scholars, and the renowned scholar Ka'b ibn al-Akhbār from amongst the foremost scholars of the Israelites, said they had seen in the Torah:

> O Prophet, certainly We have sent you as a witness, a bearer of glad tidings, a warner and a protection for the unlettered. You are My servant; I have named you "the Reliant on God," who are not harsh and stern, and not clamorous in the market-places; who do not repel the evil with evil, but instead pardon and forgive. God will certainly not take away his life until He straightens a crooked nation by means of him (by causing them) to proclaim "There is no deity but God." (al-Bukhārī, "Buyū'," 50; Ibn Hanbal, 2: 174)

> • Jesus said to them, "Have you never read in the Scriptures: The stone which the builders rejected has become the chief cornerstone. This was the Lord's doing, and it is marvelous in our eyes? Therefore I say to you, the kingdom of God will be taken from you, and given to a nation bringing the fruits of it. And whoever falls on this stone will be broken: but on whomsoever it falls, it will grind him to powder. (*Matthew*, 21: 42–44)

The "chief cornerstone" mentioned in the verses cannot be the Prophet Jesus for the verses refer to the crushing victories that the followers of the "chief cornerstone" will win against their enemies. No people were ever broken to pieces or crushed because they resisted Christianity. Christianity gained ground against the Roman Empire only after it had made significant compromises with Roman rites and ways of life. The Western dominion over the world came after scientific thought's triumph over the medieval Christian dogmatic view of nature, and was realized in the form of colonialism. By contrast, Islam ruled almost half of the "Old World" for many centuries as a religion in its original purity and its enemies were many times defeated before it. In its struggle with other religions, Islam has always been successful. It is, again, Islam which is on the rise as both a pure, authentic religion and as a way of life, and which is the hope of salvation for humanity. More than that, the Prophet Jesus himself alludes to this fact by stating explicitly that the kingdom of God will be taken away from the people to whom he was sent and given to a people who will produce its fruit.

Second, in a telling detail recorded in a *hadīth* in al-Bukhari and Muslim, the Prophet Muḥammad, upon him be peace and blessings, describes himself as the "cornerstone" completing the building of Prophethood.

> • Nevertheless I tell you the truth: It is to your advantage that I go away; for if I do not go away, the Helper (Paraklit) will not come to you; but if I depart, I will send him to you. And when he has come, he will convict the world of sin, and of righteousness, and of judgment. (*John*, 16: 7-8)

In these verses, the Prophet Muḥammad is originally referred to as the *Paraklit*. According to Webster's New World Dictionary, Paraklit derives from the word *parakle-tos*, meaning "intercessor, advocate, pleader." However Abidin Pasha, a nineteenth-century scholar from Yanya, Greece, who knew Greek very well and whose works on Greek literature were highly praised by Greek authorities, writes that its real Greek origin means

Aḥmad, the one who is much praised. (al-Jisrī, 59). Truly, *Paráklētos* is derived from the Greek word *Períklytos* and means Aḥmad. The Qur'ān also states that Jesus predicted the Prophet Muḥammad with the name Aḥmad, a synonym of Muḥammad (61: 6). Christians assert that Jesus used Paraklit for the Holy Spirit. However, what is the Holy Spirit's exact connection with interceding, pleading or advocating, which refer to principal attributes of the Prophet Muḥammad, even if we accept that the word derives from *parakletos*? In addition, Gospel translators prefer to replace "Paraklit" with different terms. For example, they translate it as "Counselor" (New International Version by International Bible Society, placed and distributed by Gideon's International), "Helper" (American Bible Society), "Comforter" (the Company of the Holy Bible), and other such terms. None of those who have claimed that it refers to the Holy Spirit has ever established whether the Holy Spirit has come down and done what Jesus said it would do. In addition, Jesus gives good tidings of the one to come not only as Paraklit but also as "the prince (ruler) of this world" and "the Spirit of truth," along with many other functions, which must belong to a Prophet and not to a "spirit," as seen in the following verses:

> When the Helper (Paraklit) comes, ... the Spirit of truth who proceeds from the Father, he will testify of me. (*John*, 15: 26)
>
> I still have many things to say to you, but you cannot bear *them* now. And when he, the Spirit of truth, has come, he will guide you into all truth: for he will not speak on his own *authority*; but whatever he hears he will speak: and he will tell you things to come. He will glorify me: for he will take of what is mine and declare *it* to you. (*John*, 16: 12–14)
>
> I will no longer talk much with you, for the ruler of this world is coming, and he has nothing in me. (*John*, 14: 30)

It is interesting that the titles with which the Prophet Muḥammad is called have mostly been "the Pride of the World" and "the Prince of the World." It was also the Prophet Muḥammad, upon him be peace and blessings, who testified to Jesus, brought glory to him by declaring his Prophethood against the denial of the Jews and false deification of him by Christians, and restoring his religion to its pristine purity through the Book he brought.

> • Now this is the testimony of John, when the Jews sent priests and Levites from Jerusalem to ask him, "Who are you?" He confessed, and did not deny; but confessed, "I am not the Christ." And they asked him, "What then? Are you Elijah?" He said, "I am not." "Are you that Prophet?" And he answered, "No." Then said they to him, "Who are you, that we may give an answer to those who sent us. What do you say about yourself?" He said: "I am the voice of one crying in the wilderness: 'Make straight the way of the Lord,' as the prophet Isaiah said." (John, 1: 19–23)

As understood from this passage, the Children of Israel had been expecting the coming of the Christ (Messiah), Elijah, and another Prophet (*that prophet*) who must have been known and who was expected by everyone at that time. So *that Prophet* expected was obviously, and appeared as, the Prophet Muḥammad, upon him be peace and blessings. For no other Prophet appeared after Jesus, upon him be peace. It cannot be the Prophet John, because he had already been chosen as Prophet before Jesus announced his mission.

APPENDIX 2

ISLAM AND WAR AND THE MAIN FACTORS
IN THE SPREAD OF ISLAM

S ome have criticized Islam because it recognizes war and even commands it in order to put an end to the domination of injustice and tyranny, to rescue the oppressed and to establish a tolerant social–political environment where Islam can be practiced freely and everyone is free to practice their religion. The criticism is wholly unjust insofar as, though not in so many words, it seems to be arguing that Islam introduced war into human history. The criticism is wholly inappropriate when voiced by those who would call themselves Christians: although there is not a specific commandment in the Gospels to permit or prohibit war – the Gospels are silent and present no rules for war and its proper conduct and containment – wars within and by Christendom have been much bloodier and wider in scope, and more ruthless in their intensity. Indeed, Christianity was misused to provide, for Western powers in previous centuries, a cover and means for the colonization of two-thirds of the world's peoples and resources. The criticism is wholly inappropriate when voiced by the Jews, for their history, like that of the Christians, is also full of wars, as the Old Testament is explicit in ordering war. As for other religions such as those in south, east and south-eastern Asia: they lack rules to govern the collective life, and so are more comparable to esoteric philosophies, and yet their followers have not refrained from waging war. The modern secular world has least right of all to criticize Islam (or indeed any other religion) for allowing war, since it has caused more bloodshed and destruction in the past hundred years than during the whole of human history before it.

Part of the very meaning of the word *islām* is peace, therefore Islam prefers peace, desires it and seeks to establish it throughout the world. However, war is a reality of human history, a manifestation in the collective life of humankind of the inner condition of those who have not been able to attain excellence in mind, heart (spirit) and conduct. Or it is a manifestation of the war between the spirit and the carnal soul, or between Satan and the perfectibility of human nature. What is important and necessary therefore is, rather than turning away from the reality in a vainly idealistic manner, to establish rules to make war just, in respect of both its motives and purposes, and its means and conduct, so that the harm of it is contained, and the good in it may benefit the people in general. War may then be, not something in itself desirable, but capable of serving (rather than perverting) a desirable end – like disciplining and training the body to improve its strength or skill, or doing a necessary operation to save someone's health, or administering upon a criminal the due punishment for the sake of deterrence and the health of the moral environment. Precisely such disciplining of the means and ends of war is what Islam has done.

The verse does not order war, but allows it on condition that it be in God's cause and for defensive purposes. It also enjoins that the limits set by God must not be exceeded.

Those limits are related to both the intention and the practice. For example, Islam does not permit war for motives such as conquest or plunder, or to quench a lust for revenge, or for the sake of some material advantage or to satisfy racist persuasions. Islam does not seek to compel anyone to change their faith. On the contrary, it seeks an environment where all are free to accept faith freely. Islam has also set limitations on the conduct of relations before, during and after conflict; for example:

- Do not betray any agreements you have entered into.
- Do not plunder.
- Do not commit injustices or use torture.
- Do not touch the children, the womenfolk, the elderly, or other non-combatants of the enemy.
- Do not destroy orchards or tilled lands.
- Do not kill livestock.
- Treat with respect the religious persons who live in hermitages or convents and spare their edifices. (Ibn al-Athīr, 3: 227)

We should also point out here that people have embraced Islam in very large numbers over very many centuries and in very diverse conditions (from the heights of political and military superiority to the depths of military collapse and subjection), while few have left it to accept another faith. In part because of the psychological difficulty this success has provoked in those who do not wish it, and in part because of prejudices derived from ignorance about Islam combined with dogmatic conviction about their own cultural superiority, some Westerners have claimed that Islam is a religion of the sword and was spread by the force of the sword. However, this claim has been refuted by Western unbiased scholarly researchers who have managed to defeat such cultural prejudice. One of them writes:

> Many have sought to answer the question of why the triumph of Islam was so speedy and complete? Why have so many millions embraced the religion of Islam and scarcely a hundred ever recanted? Some have attempted to explain the first overwhelming success of Islam by the argument of the Sword. They forget Carlyle's laconic reply. "First get your sword." You must win men's hearts before you can induce them to imperil their lives for you; and the first conquerors of Islam must have been made Muslims before they were made fighters on the Path of God.
>
> In all these explanations the religion itself is left out of the question. Decidedly, Islam itself was the main cause for its triumph. Islam not only was at once accepted (by many peoples and races in) Arabia, Syria, Persia, Egypt, Northern Africa and Spain, at its first outburst; but, with the exception of Spain, it has never lost its vantage ground; it has been spreading ever since it came into being. Admitting the mixed causes that contributed to the rapidity of the first swift spread of Islam, they do not account for the duration of Islam. There must be something in the religion itself to explain its persistence and spread, and to account for its present hold over so large of a proportion of the dwellers on the earth... Islam has stirred an enthusiasm that has never been surpassed. Islam has had its martyrs, its self-tormentors, its recluses, who have renounced all that life offered and have accepted death with a smile for the sake of the faith that was in them. (Ezzati, quoting from Stanley Lane-Poole, *Study in a Mosque*, 86–89)

Islam has spread because of its religious content and values, and "its power of appeal and ability to meet the spiritual and material needs of people adhering to cultures totally alien to their Muslim conquerors." Among other important factors are the tolerance that Islam has shown to the people of other religions, the absence of an ecclesiastic hierarchy, intellectual freedom, the equity and justice that Islam enjoins and that Muslims have striven for throughout the centuries, the ethical values that Islam propagates, and its inclusiveness and universalism, its humanity and brotherhood. In addition, the activism of the Sufis, the moral superiority of Muslim tradesmen, the principle of "enjoining the good," and the dynamism and magnificence of Islamic civilization, contributed to the spread of Islam.

The qualities that principally attracted people to Islam were and are still:

- the simplicity of its doctrines based on the strictest and purest Divine Unity;
- the rationality of Islamic teachings;
- the harmony between Islamic ideals and values and natural human conscience;
- the inclusiveness and comprehensiveness of Islam as a way of life covering all aspects of individual and collective being, physical, mental, and spiritual, and the consequent harmony between religion and life lived within its compass and jurisdiction;
- the lack of formalism and mediation in its rites and doctrines;
- the vividness, dynamism, and resilience of the Islamic creed, its creativity and universality, and its compatibility with established scientific facts;
- the internal cohesion and harmony of the Islamic principles, and the practicability and practice thereof in everyday life;
- the shortcomings of other religious systems.

A. J. Arberry has pointed out that the reason for the spread of Islam is Islam itself and its religious values (*Aspects of Islamic Civilization*, 12). He states: "The rapidity of the spread of Islam, noticeably through extensive provinces which had long been Christian, is a crucial fact of history.... The sublime rhetoric of the Qur'ān, that inimitable symphony, the very sounds of which move men to tears and ecstasy...." He continues: "This, and the urgency of the simple message carried, holds the key to the mystery of one of the greatest cataclysms in the history of religion. When all military, political and economic factors have been exhausted, the religious impulse must still be recognized as the most vital and enduring."

Brockelman, who is usually very unsympathetic and partial, also recognizes the religious values of Islam as the main factor for the spread of Islam and suggests that Islamic monotheism to a considerable extent is the basis of the proselytizing power of Islam (*History of the Islamic Peoples*, 37). Rosenthal makes the point as follows:

> The more important factor for the spread of Islam is the religious law of Islam (i.e. the *Sharī'ah*, which is an inclusive, all-embracing, all-comprehensive way of thinking and living) which was designed to cover all manifestations of life. (*Political Thought in Medieval Islam*, 21)

The tolerance of Islam is particularly relevant to an explanation of why it spread. Toynbee praises this tolerance towards the Peoples of the Book, after comparing it with the attitude of the Christians towards Muslims and Jews in their lands (*An Historian Approach to Religion*, 246). Trevor Ling attributes the spread of Islam to the credibility of its principles, its tolerance, persuasiveness, and other attractive elements (*A History of Religion*, 330). Makarios, Orthodox Patriarch of Antioch in the seventeenth century, compared the harsh treatment received by the Russians of the Orthodox Church at the hands of the Roman Catholic Poles with the tolerant attitude towards Orthodox Christians shown by the Ottoman Government, and he prayed for the Sultans (Ling, 331). (For all these and several other quotations, see Ezzati, 2–35.)

That is by no means the only example of the followers of other religions preferring Islamic rule to that of their co-religionists. The Orthodox Christians of Byzantium openly expressed their preference for the Ottoman turban in Istanbul to the hats of the Catholic cardinals. Hans Barth wrote that the Muslim Turks allowed the followers of different religions to perform their religious duties and rituals, and that the Christian subjects of the Ottoman Sultan were more free to live their own lives than the Christians who lived under the rule of any rival Christian sect (*Le Droit du Croissant*, 143). Popescu Ciocanel pays tribute to the Muslim Turks by stating that it was lucky for the Romanian people that they lived under the government of the Turks rather than that of the Russians or Austrians as, otherwise, "no trace of the Romanian nation would have remained (*Revue du Monde Musulman*)." (For both quotations, see Djevad, 71–72, 91)

A historical episode recounted by Balādhurī, a famous Muslim historian, tells how pleased the native peoples were with their Muslim conquerors :

> When Heraclius massed his troops against the Muslims, and the Muslims heard that they were coming to meet them, they refunded the inhabitants of Hims the tribute they had taken from them, saying: "We are too busy to support and protect you. Take care of yourselves." But the people of Hims replied: "We like your rule and justice far better than the state of oppression and tyranny in which we were. The army of Heraclius we shall indeed, with your help, repulse from the city." The Jews rose and said: "We swear by the Torah, no governor of Heraclius shall enter the city of Hims unless we are first vanquished and exhausted." Saying this, they closed the gates of the city and guarded them. The inhabitants of other cities – Christians and Jews – that had capitulated did the same. When by Allah's help the unbelievers were defeated and the Muslims won, they opened the gates of their cities, went out with the singers and players of music, and paid the tribute. (Ezzati, 144)

MORE ON ISLAM AND WAR

W hen considered together with other relevant verses of the Qur'ān, the verses 1-6 in *sūrah* 9 present significant principles concerned with the Islamic view of war. In summary:

- The purpose of war is not to kill people. On the contrary, Islam, which attaches great value to life and regards the killing of one innocent person as being the same as killing all of humankind, and the saving the life of one person as being the same as saving the lives of all humankind, aims at the survival of humanity and at helping them to find the truth through education.

- Even in warfare, Islam is ready to make peace and a treaty with the opposing side.

- A Muslim government remains faithful to any treaty it has made until the end of its term.

- If the opposing side betrays the agreement, the Muslim government must publicly and officially declare to the other side that the agreement is no longer valid. Even though it can declare war as soon as the agreement loses its validity, it should grant them a respite so that a new evaluation of the situation can be made.

- If the opposing side continue their hostilities and do not change their attitude, even after the end of the term granted, this means that a state of war has begun.

- In order to force the enemy to cease hostilities or to defeat them in war, the Muslims must be powerful and remain steadfast. However, the Muslims must always observe the rules of war that are mentioned in Appendix 2 above.

- It should be borne in mind that the expressions in *sūrah* 9, verse 5 are aimed at people who employ violence and who, as can also be inferred from the conclusion of the following verse, do not recognize any rule or law and do not understand any language other than war. Like some commandments of the Islamic Penal Law, these expressions are of a deterrent character. The second part of the verse, which mentions repentance and the fact that God is All-Forgiving and All-Compassionate, reveals the main purpose of the verse. In addition, this verse also aims at removing from Makkah and Madīnah the violent, polytheist outlaws and therefore is significant with respect to the security of the center of Islam.

- It is never the goal of Islam to kill people and conquer lands through war. Therefore, when the enemy side is inclined toward peace and making a treaty, the Muslims should also be inclined this way. They should also give asylum to those who seek it and, without harming in any way the wealth or persons of the asylum seekers, convey them to a place of safety.

- War is a legal matter between nations. Islam is, above all else, a religion that arranges the relationship between God and humankind, and this relationship is based on sincere faith. Therefore, its main adherents are the sincere believers. However, as a part of its basic mission, Islam also orders human individual and social life. This is the legal side of Islam. In legal terms, a Muslim is one who professes faith and attends the Muslim congregation of Prayer, and who pays the Prescribed Purifying Alms as the fulfillment of the financial duty of being a Muslim citizen. It is possible that such a person may be not a believer but a hypocrite. But one who professes faith and attends the Muslim congregation of Prayer and who pays the Prescribed Alms is legally regarded as a Muslim. So, when an individual or a group of persons at war with Muslims profess faith, the state of war must end. No one is compelled to believe. One who professes faith and lives in a Muslim society is expected to see the truth and become a sincere believer. This is why, even if we know that one who professes faith is in fact a hypocrite, they must be treated as a Muslim as long as they do not declare unbelief.

• Islam will never apologize to any other religion, ideology, or system for granting permission to fight. On the contrary, all other religions, ideologies, and systems have a debt of apology and gratitude to Islam. Islam, aiming at universal peace and accepting the reality of human history, realizes that ensuring peace sometimes requires fighting. As declared in the Qur'ān, *(Though killing is something you feel aversion to) disorder (rooted in rebellion against God and recognizing no laws) is worse than killing* (2: 191); and *disorder (coming from rebellion to God and recognizing no laws) is even more grave and more sinful than killing* (2: 217), the conditions that give rise to war and disorder are more grievous than killing itself and therefore war, although not inherently a good thing, is permissible if it will remove these conditions.

Only to cite the realities: Since Christianity introduced no rules for the conduct of war, the wars in Christendom have been much bloodier and more ruthless. It can also be said that, the Crusades included, in previous centuries Christianity provided or was misused as a means for the colonization of two-thirds of the world by the Western powers. Graham Fuller and Ian Lesser (Graham E. Fuller, Ian O. Lesser, 41-42) records that the Christians killed by Muslims during fourteen centuries of Islamic history were fewer in number than the Muslims killed by Christians in the twentieth century alone. Christianity began its assaults on Islam while the latter was still a small conclave in Madīnah. In the 8th year of the *Hijrah*, the first generation of Muslims had to face a Byzantine army of 100,000 soldiers in Mu'tah with only 3,000 warriors. One year later, the Messenger had to muster all his power against them; this battle was recorded in history as the Tabuk Campaign and is one of the subjects of *sūrah* 9. Three years later the Muslim and Byzantine forces once more faced off in Yarmuk, a battle which ended in the decisive defeat of the Byzantines.

As for Judaism, a few quotations from the Old Testament are enough to see what position it adopts concerning war and compare this position with that of Islam:

> Then Sihon and all his people came out against us to fight at Jahaz. And the Lord our God delivered him over to us; so we defeated him, his sons, and all his people. We took all his cities at that time, and we utterly destroyed the men, women, and little ones of every city; we left none remaining. We took only the livestock as plunder for ourselves, with the spoil of the cities which we took.... So the Lord our God also

delivered into our hands Og king of Bashan, with all his people, and we attacked him until he had no survivors remaining. And we took all his cities at that time; there was not a city which we did not take from them; sixty cities, all the region of Argob, the kingdom of Og in Bashan.... We utterly destroyed them, as we did to Sihon king of Heshbon, utterly destroying the men, women, and children of every city. But all the livestock and the spoil of the cities we took as booty for ourselves. (*Deuteronomy*, 2: 32–35; 3: 3–7)

As for modern times, we only want to mention some facts to clarify the point: Islam has never had the least part in tens of millions of deaths in the communist revolutions, the suppression of freedom movements in several parts of the world at the cost of millions of lives, and in the adventures in several poor countries, costing more than millions of lives during the wars and many more indirectly since. It is not Islam which caused the death of more than 70 million people, mainly civilians, and forced countless millions more to remain homeless, widowed and orphaned, during and after the two world wars. It is not Islam which gave rise to totalitarian regimes such as Communism, Fascism, and Nazism, and raised war-mongers like Hitler, Stalin, and Mussolini. Islam is not responsible for using scientific knowledge to make nuclear and other weapons of mass destruction. Islam was not responsible for the extermination of tens of millions of natives in many parts of the world, for world-wide colonialism which lasted centuries, and for the slave trade, which cost the lives of tens of millions of people. It is not Islam, nor Muslim peoples even, that are responsible for the establishment of the despotic governments that rule over some Muslim countries and for their oppression, injustice, and bloody regimes. Nor is it Islam which is responsible for modern terrorism, mafia organizations, and for the world-wide smuggling of weapons and drugs.

APPENDIX 4

THE STATUS OF WOMEN IN ISLAM

I t is not necessary to argue in an apologetic manner, contrasting the plight of wom-
en in the pre-Islamic era or in the modern world of today, that in Islam women are
accorded recognition, rights, and privileges that they have not enjoyed under other systems. It becomes clear enough, without apology, if the issue is studied as a whole,
rather than partially. Broadly speaking, the rights and responsibilities of a woman are
equal to those of a man but they are not necessarily identical with them. Equality and
identity are not the same, and should not be confused. No two people, leaving aside gender differences, are the same: for there to be justice, those differences need to be recognized and affirmed without being made into a pretext for improper discrimination.

Human beings are not created identical but they are created equal. With that distinction in mind, there is no excuse for any argument that would represent woman as inferior to man. There is no ground for the presumption that she is less important because
her rights are not in every respect identical to those of the man. But the woman is not
a duplicate of the man, and accordingly there is a difference in rights and responsibilities. The fact that Islamic law gives to the woman equal – but not identical – rights
shows that it recognizes the woman's being a woman, with proper respect for both the
difference in constitution and personality and the sameness of her need for social and
political dignity.

It will be worthwhile at this point to take a summary look at the rights of woman under Islamic law.

- Woman is recognized as a full and equal partner with the man in the procreation
  of humankind. He is the father; she is the mother, and both are essential for life.
  Her role is not less vital than his. Within this partnership she has an equal share of
  respect and dignity; indeed, as a mother, she gets greater respect and care from the
  children, in accordance with the Prophet's injunction: "Paradise is under the feet of
  mothers" (an-Nasā'ī, "Jihād," 6).
- An adult woman is equal to an adult man in carrying responsibilities, some individual some shared with others, and she is equal in the recompense due for her actions.
  She is acknowledged as an independent legal personality, in possession of the moral and intellectual qualities, and the spiritual aspirations, that are characteristic of
  human beings. The woman's human nature is neither inferior to nor different from
  that of a man. Both are members of one another.
- She is equal to man in the seeking of education, of knowledge. The seeking of
  knowledge is enjoined upon Muslims as such, without distinction of gender. Almost
  fourteen centuries ago, the Prophet Muḥammad, upon him be peace and God's
  blessings, declared that the pursuit of knowledge (necessary for every believer) is
  incumbent on every Muslim, (male and female) (Ibn Mājah, "Muqaddimah," 17).

- She is entitled to the same freedom of expression as man. Her sound opinions are taken into consideration and may not be disregarded merely because she is a woman. It is reported in the Qur'ān that women not only expressed their opinion freely but also argued and participated in serious discussion with the Prophet himself (e.g. 58: 1-4; 60: 10-12). There are many hadiths that record similar occasions, and in subsequent history, we know that women objected in public to what Caliphs declared from the pulpit in the mosque.

- Historical records show that women participated in public life with the early Muslims, especially in times of emergencies.

- A woman has equal rights in law to enter into contracts, to initiate and run commercial enterprise, to earn and possess wealth independently. Her life, her property, her honor are as sacred as those of man. If she commits any offense, her penalty is no less or more than a man's in a similar case. If she is wronged or harmed, she gets due compensation equal to what a man in the same situation would get (2: 178; 4: 92-93).

- The law and religion of Islam envisaged the measures necessary to safeguard these rights and put them into practice as integral articles of faith. The faith does not tolerate those who are inclined to prejudice against woman or discriminate unjustly on the basis of the difference between man and woman. Again and again, the Qur'ān reproaches those who used to believe woman to be inferior to man: 16: 57-59, 62; 42: 49-50; 43: 15-19; 53: 21-23.

- Apart from recognition of woman as an independent human being, acknowledged as equally essential for the survival of humanity, Islamic law (derived from the Qur'ān) has stipulated a share of inheritance for female heirs – as is explained in *Sūrat an-Nisā'*, note 5.

- Woman enjoys certain privileges of which man is deprived. She is exempt within the household from all financial liabilities. As a mother, she enjoys more recognition and higher honor in the sight of God (31: 14-15; 46: 15). As a wife she is entitled to demand of her prospective husband a suitable dowry that will be her own. She is entitled to support and maintenance by the husband. She does not have to work or share with her husband the family expenses. She is free to retain, after marriage, whatever she possessed before it, and the husband has no right whatsoever to any of her belongings. As a daughter or sister she is entitled to support and maintenance by her father and brother respectively. That is her privilege. If she wishes to work or be self-supporting and participate in handling the family responsibilities, she is free to do so, provided her integrity and honor are safeguarded.

- The faith of Islam does not differentiate between men and women as far as relationship to God is concerned, as both are promised the same reward for good conduct and the same punishment for evil conduct. Women's standing behind men in the Prayer is neither intended nor understood as a mark of inferiority. The woman, as already mentioned, is exempt from attending congregational Prayers. But if she does attend she stands in separate rows made up exclusively of women. The order of rows in the Prayer is introduced to help everyone to concentrate on their prayer without distraction. The Prayer includes actions and movements – standing and sitting shoulder to shoulder, bowing, prostration, etc. If men mix with women in the same rows, it is possible that something disturbing or distracting may occur to the minds of those praying, alien to the purpose of the occasion, and a manifest obstacle to the duty to meditate.

Finally, there is no significance in the fact that the Qur'ān usually uses masculine pronouns when addressing or referring to the community. It is a feature of almost all languages that the masculine pronoun is used for a group formed of both men and women. This may be related to the fact that throughout history in most societies most of the time the man has carried a "degree" of responsibility (for the household and for the collective affairs of the community) "above" that of the woman, and this is undoubtedly a consequence of having different duties and functions centered around maintaining the family and caring for the children, the next generation of the community. (For explanations for other aspects of the matter, see 2, note 161.)

THE PROPHET MUHAMMAD AMONG HIS PEOPLE

The Prophet Muḥammad, upon him be peace and blessings, was born in the heart of a desert; his father had died some time before his birth, and he lost his mother when he was six years old. Consequently, he was deprived even of the scant training and upbringing which an Arab child of the time normally got. Education never touched him; he was unlettered and unschooled.

The Prophet, upon him be God's peace and blessings, did not leave Makkah to go outside the Arabian peninsula except for two brief journeys. The first was with his uncle Abū Tālib when he was still a youth in his early teens. The other was in his mid-thirties when he accompanied a caravan carrying the goods of Khadījah, a widow who was forty when she married her at 25, and with whom he lived for almost twenty years, until her death. Because of his being unlettered, he had no opportunity to read any of the religious texts of the Jews or Christians, nor did he become acquainted with these texts. Makkah was an idolatrous city both in its ideas and customs, into which neither Christian nor Jewish religious thought had penetrated. Even the *ḥanīf*s (people who followed some things of the pure religion of Abraham in an adulterated and unclear form) among the Arabs of Makkah, who rejected the worship of idols, were influenced by neither Judaism nor Christianity. Nothing of Jewish or Christian thought appears to have been reflected in the poetic heritage left us by the literary men of the time. Had the Prophet made any effort to become acquainted with Jewish or Christian thought, this would have been noticed. We observe moreover that the Prophet did not take part, before his Prophethood, in the intellectual forms of poetry and rhetoric which were popular among the people at that time.

Prior of his Prophethood, there is no mention of any distinction of the Holy Prophet, upon him be peace and blessings, over the rest of the people except in his moral commitments, his trustworthiness, honesty, truthfulness, and integrity. He never told a lie; even his worst enemies never accused him of lying on any occasion during his life. He used to talk politely and never used obscene or abusive language. He had a charming personality and excellent manners with which he captivated the hearts of those who came into contact with him. In his dealings with people he always followed the principles of justice, altruism, and fair-play. He never deceived anyone and never broke his promise. He remained engaged in trade and commerce for years, but he never entered into any dishonest transaction. Those who dealt with him in business had full confidence in his integrity. The entire nation called him *"Al-Amīn"* (the Truthful and the Trustworthy). Even his enemies would deposit their precious belongings with him for safe custody and he scrupulously fulfilled their trust. He was the very embodiment of modesty in the midst of a society which was immodest to the core. Born and bred among a people who regarded drunkenness and gambling as virtues, he never touched alcohol and never indulged in gambling. Surrounded on all sides by heartless people, he himself had a heart overflowing with the milk of human kindness. He would help orphans, widows, and the poor; he was hospitable to travelers. He harmed no one; rather, he exposed himself to hardships for the sake of others. He kept aloof from the feuds in his tribe, and was foremost in bringing about reconciliation. He did not bow before any other created thing and did not partake of the offerings made to idols, even in his childhood. He hated all kinds of worship devoted to creatures and beings other than God. In brief, the towering and radiant personality of this gentle man in the midst of such a benighted and dark environment may be likened to a beacon of light illuminating a pitch-dark night, or to a diamond shining out amongst a heap of stones.

Suddenly a remarkable change came over his person. His heart became illuminated by the Divine Light. He went to the people, and addressed them in the following strain:

The idols which you worship are a mere sham. Cease to worship them from now on. No mortal being, no star, no tree, no stone, no spirit, is worthy of human worship. Therefore, do not bow your heads in worship before them. The entire universe with everything that it contains belongs to God Almighty. He alone is the Creator, the Nourisher, the Sustainer, and, consequently, the real Sovereign before Whom all should bow down and to Whom all should pray and render obedience. Thus, worship Him alone and obey His commands. Theft and plunder, murder and rapine, injustice and cruelty – all the vices in which you indulge are crimes in the eyes of God. Leave your evil ways. Speak the truth. Be just. Do not kill anyone; whoever slays a soul unjustly, it will be as if he had slain all of humanity; and whoever saves the life of one, it will be as if he had saved the life of all of humanity.

Do not steal from anyone. Take your lawful share. Give that which is due to others in a just manner.

Do not set up another god with God, or you will sit condemned and forsaken. Be good to your parents whether one or both of them attains old age with you, do not say to them even "uff" nor chide them, but speak to them with respectful words, and lower to them the wing of humbleness out of mercy. Give your kinsfolk their rights and give to the needy, and the traveler, and never squander. Do not slay your children from fear of poverty or other reasons. Do not approach adultery; surely it is an indecency, an evil way. Do not approach the property of orphans and the weak. Fulfill the covenant, because it will be questioned. Fill up the measure when you measure, and weigh with a true balance. Do not pursue that of which you have no knowledge; the hearing, the sight, and the heart will be questioned about it. Do not walk on the earth exultantly; certainly you will never tear the earth open, nor attain the mountains in height. Say to each other words that are kindly, for surely Satan provokes strife between you because of the use of strong words. Do not turn your cheek in scorn and anger toward people nor walk with impudence in the land. God does not love the braggart. Be modest in your bearing and subdue your voice. Let not some people deride another people, who may be better than they are in God's sight. And do not find fault with one another, nor revile one another with nicknames. Shun most of suspicion, for suspicion is a sin. And do not spy, nor backbite other people. Be staunch followers of justice and witnesses for God, even though it be against yourselves, or your parents and kinsfolk, whether the person be rich or poor. Do not follow caprices, which cause you to swerve. Be steadfast witnesses for God in equity, and do not let your hatred of any people seduce you so that you do not deal justly. Restrain your rage and pardon the offences of your fellow-people. The good deed and the evil deed are not alike, so repel the evil deed with the one which is good, then the person with whom you have enmity will become as though a loyal friend. The recompense for evil committed wittingly is like evil; but whoever pardons and makes amends with the evil-doer with kindness and love, their reward falls upon God. Do not drink alcohol and do not play games of chance; they are both forbidden by God.

You are human beings and all human beings are equal in the eyes of God. None is born with the slur of shame on their face; nor has anyone come into the world with the mantle of honor hung around their neck. Those who are God-revering and pious, true in words and deeds alone are high and honored. Distinctions of birth and glory of race are no criteria of greatness and honor. There is an appointed day after your death when you will have to appear before a supreme court. You will be called to account for all your deeds, good or bad, and you will not then be able to hide anything. The whole record of your life will be an open book to God. Your fate will be determined by your good or bad actions. In the court of the True Judge – the All-Knowing God – the question of improper recommendation and favoritism does not arise. You will not be able to bribe Him. No consideration will be given to your pedigree or parentage. True faith and good deeds alone will stand you in good stead at that time. Those who have performed these fully will take their abode in the Heaven of eternal happiness, while the one devoid of them will be cast in the fire of Hell.

For forty years the Prophet, upon him be peace and blessings, lived as an ordinary individual amongst his people. In that long period he was not known as a statesman, a preacher, or an orator; none had heard him imparting wisdom or knowledge, as he began to do thereafter. He had never been seen discoursing upon the principles of metaphysics, ethics, law, politics, economy, or sociology. Not only was he not a general, he was not even known as an ordinary soldier. He had uttered no words about God, the Angels, the revealed Books, the early Prophets, the bygone nations, the Day of Judgment, life after death, Hell or Heaven. No doubt he possessed an excellent character and charming manners, and he was well-behaved; yet he did not think of himself different from others. He was known among his acquaintances as a sober, calm, gentle, and trustworthy citizen of good nature, but when he appeared with the new message, he was completely transformed.

In the face of these historical facts, facts which can never be challenged, there are two alternatives: either one can claim that the Prophet Muḥammad, upon him be peace and blessings, is – God forbid! the greatest liar and meanest trickster of all times or one must accept that he is a Messenger and Prophet of God. Even Satan and the Messenger's bitterest enemies of his time never dared to voice the first claim; nor can anyone else dare to do so. Therefore, there is no alternative but that everyone with reason should acknowledge Muḥammad's Messengership and Prophethood (Mostly from al-Mawdūdī, *Towards Understanding Islam*, 56–65).

THE QUR'ĀN'S CHALLENGE AND SOME
ASPECTS OF ITS MIRACULOUSNESS

At a time in history when eloquence was most highly prized, the Qur'ān of miraculous exposition was revealed. Just as God Almighty had endowed Moses and Jesus, upon them be peace, with the miracles which were most suitable to their times, He used eloquence as the most notable aspect of the Qur'ān, the chief miracle of the Prophet Muḥammad, upon him be peace and blessings. At the time that the Qur'ān was revealed, it first challenged the literary figures of the Arabian peninsula, and then all the people throughout the ages and at every level of knowledge and understanding until the Judgment Day in the following manner:

- If you think that a human being wrote the Qur'ān, then let one of your people who are unlettered as is Muḥammad produce something similar.
- If he or she cannot do this, let a learned one or a literary one try to do the same.
- If he or she cannot do this either, then send your most famous writers or scholars and let them come together and produce the like of the Qur'ān.
- If they cannot, let them work together and call upon all their history, "deities," scientists, philosophers, sociologists, theologians, and writers to produce something similar.
- If they cannot, let them try – leaving aside the miraculous and inimitable aspects of its meaning – to produce a work of equal eloquence in word order and composition, regardless of what they produce is true or not.
- If you cannot produce the like of it in equal length, then produce only the like of its 10 chapters.
- If you cannot do this, then produce only one chapter.
- If you cannot do that, produce only a short chapter.

Those self-conceited people could not argue verbally with the Qur'ān and chose rather to fight it with their swords, a perilous and difficult course. If such intelligent people could have argued verbally with the Qur'ān they would not have chosen the perilous, difficult course as they did, risking losing their property and lives. It is only because they could not rise to the challenge that they had to choose this more dangerous way.

The Qur'ān is miraculous in many aspects. Here we will indicate only some of them:

- There is an extraordinary eloquence and stylistic purity in the Qur'ān's word order and composition. Just as a clock's hands complete and are fitted to one another in precise orderliness, so too does every word and sentence – indeed the entire Qur'ān – complete and fit with every other.
- It is in this way that each of the Qur'ānic verses is not only part of a larger entity; it is also a whole in itself and has an independent existence. There is an intrinsic relation among all the verses of the Qur'ān and between one verse and all the others. In

the words of Bediüzzaman Said Nursi, "The verses of the Qur'ān are like stars in the sky among which there are visible and invisible ropes and relationships. It is as if each of the verses of the Qur'ān has an eye which sees most of the verses, and a face which looks towards them, so that it extends to them the immaterial threads of relationship to weave a miraculous fabric. A single *sūrah* can contain the whole "ocean" of the Qur'ān in which the whole of the universe is contained. A single verse can comprehend the treasury of that *sūrah*. It is as if most of the verses are each a small *sūrah*, and most of the *sūrah*s each a little Qur'ān."

- In many places, like in *Sūrat al-Ikhlāṣ* (Sincerity) which comprises six verses or sentences, each sentence has two meanings: one *a priori* (functioning as a cause or proof) with the other being *a posteriori* (functioning as an effect or result). This means that the *sūrah* contains 36 *sūrah*s, each made up of six sentences. One is a premise or a proposition, while the others are arguments supporting it. (See *sūrah* 112, note 4.)

- The Qur'ān has a unique, original style that is both novel and convincing. Its style, which always preserves its originality, freshness, and "bloom of youth," does not imitate and cannot be imitated.

- The Qur'ān's wording is extraordinarily fluent and pure. Not only is it extraordinarily eloquent when expressing meaning, it is also wonderfully fluent and pure in wording and word arrangement. One proof of this is that it never bores even when recited thousands of times. The more you read it the more it gives pleasure. A child can easily memorize it. Even fatally ill people who get easily annoyed by a few words of ordinary speech, feel relief and comfort upon hearing the Qur'ān. For people at their death-bed, the Qur'ān gives their ears and minds great taste and pleasure.

- The Qur'ān feeds the heart, gives power and wealth to the mind, functions as water and light for the spirit, and cures the illnesses of the soul. Reciting or listening to the pure truth of the Qur'ān and its guidance does not fatigue the mind, but rather refreshes and broadens it.

- The Qur'ān's expressions contain a superiority, power, sublimity, and magnificence. Its fluent, eloquent pure composition and word order, as well as its eloquent meanings, and original and unique style, give it an unsurpassed excellence in explaining things. Truly, in all categories of expression and address – deterrence and threats, in praise, censure and restraint, in proof and demonstration, and in teaching and explanation, and in silencing and overcoming arguments – its expositions are of the highest degree.

- As pointed out in a *hadith* (Ibn Ḥibbān, 1:146; al-Munāwī, 3: 54), each verse has external and internal meanings, limits and a point of comprehension, as well as boughs, branches, and twigs. Each phrase, word, letter, and even every diacritical point has many aspects. Each person who hears a verse receives their share of understanding within their capabilities through a different door. In addition to providing resources to exacting jurists, the treasuries of the meanings of the Qur'ān provide enlightenment for those seeking knowledge of God, ways for those trying to reach God, paths for perfected human beings, and schooling of mind and heart for truth-seeking scholars. The Qur'ān has always guided them and illuminated their ways. It deals with humankind and our duty, the universe and its Creator, the heavens and the earth, this world and the next, and the past, future, and eternity. It explains all essential matters related to our creation and life, from the correct ways to eat and sleep to issues of Divine Decree and Will, from the universe's creation in six days to the functions of the winds. For human beings it is a book of law, prayer, wisdom, worship, and servanthood to God, it contains commands and invitations, invocations and reflections. It is a holy book containing comprehensive guidance for all of our spiritual needs; a heavenly book that, like a sacred library, contains numerous booklets from which all saints, eminent truthful people, all purified and discerning scholars, and those well-versed in knowledge of God, have derived their own specific ways, and which illuminate each way and answer the needs of its followers. The Qur'ān contains references to all knowledge that is needed by humankind. Moreover, it gives people whatever they need, so that the expression *Take from the Qur'ān whatever you wish, for whatever need you have*, has been widely circulated among exacting scholars.

- The Qur'ān is always fresh, and its freshness is maintained as if it were revealed anew in every epoch. As an eternal discourse addressing all human beings, regardless of time or place and level of understanding, it should – and does – have a never-fading freshness. The wise Qur'ān informs all people, regardless of time, place, or level of understanding about God, Islam, and faith. Therefore, it has to teach each group and level in an appropriate manner. People are very diverse, yet the Qur'ān has sufficient levels for all. It addresses all levels of understanding, regardless of time and place.

- The Qur'ān's conciseness is like offering up the ocean contained in a pitcher. Out of mercy and courtesy for ordinary human minds, it demonstrates the most comprehensive and universal principles and general laws through a particular event on a particular occasion.

- The Qur'ān has an extraordinarily comprehensive aim, subject-matter, meaning, style, beauty, and subtlety. When studied well, its *sūrah*s and verses, particularly the opening sections of the *sūrah*s and the beginning and end of each verse, clearly show that there is no trace of confusion. And this is despite the fact that it contains a variety of modes of speech, all categories of elevated style, all examples of good morals and virtues, all principles of natural science, all indices of knowledge of God, all the beneficial rules of individual and social life, and all the laws that enlighten creation's exalted reasons and purposes.

- The Qur'ān gives news of the past, and it has many categories of predictions. It contains information concerning people of the past and gives news of people of the future. From one viewpoint, the Qur'ān is full of explicit and implicit predictions. It also speaks about the Unseen Divine truths, and the realities of the Hereafter. It is impossible to contradict its accounts of historical events, therefore, whatever it predicts either has come true or will come true when its time is due. It was impossible for God's Messenger to know the histories of the Prophets and their peoples. But, based on Divine Revelation and with utmost confidence in his mission, he conveyed both the histories of bygone nations and many predictions concerning future important events. This is a challenge to all ages and peoples, including historians and other researchers, and is one of the undeniable proofs of His Prophethood and the Divine origin of the Qur'ān.

GOD WILLS GOOD FOR HUMANKIND BUT
HUMANKIND INCURS EVIL

From one perspective, the Qur'ān anatomizes the spirit or character of humankind. In human life, the periods of health and prosperity are greater in number and last much longer than those of illness and misfortune. Despite this, people complain greatly when some misfortune visits them; it is as if all their lives have passed in hardship and affliction, and they now feel as if the days of health and prosperity will never come again. Yet, when they are relieved of their misfortune or when they recover from an illness, they are exultant beyond all measure and in self-glorification forget to thank God, as if they had not suffered at all. One of the most important reasons why humans act in such a way is that they are unaware of the wisdom in and Divine reasons for illnesses and misfortunes or health and prosperity.

God Almighty always wills good for humanity. In other words, He always gives us mercy, good, and grace. Even in misfortunes that arise as a result of unforgivable corruption or wrongdoing, there are many aspects of good for people, including for believers in particular. But human beings, by misusing their free will, either prevent that grace, good, and mercy from reaching them or transform these things into evil. Let us give an illustration here. Water is inherently a good thing – it quenches our thirst and provides moisture for our crops. Yet, if we were to dive into the water without measuring its depth or considering whether there may be currents, or without knowing how to swim, then water becomes a means of evil. In the same way fire can be made into an evil if we allow it to burn a finger because of ignorance or carelessness. Factors such as haste, thoughtlessness, ignorance, inexperience, and not taking due care can all transform something which is good for a person into an evil. Consequently, all the evils that befall humankind are caused by ourselves, by our mistakes and errors.

Here it can be argued: Huge numbers of people are born into misfortune of one kind or another, having had no part in causing it – in any meaningful sense of causing (i.e. being responsible, answerable for) it. It may be that collectively, over a large span of generations, human beings cause all the misfortunes that beset some of them; but the fact is that many misfortunes are suffered individually by people who themselves, individually, did not earn them by their intentions or actions – some indeed suffer long before they attain the age of legal responsibility.

It is true that individuals have no part into the misfortune they are born into and which has been caused by earlier generations. However, the Divine Religion views the world and misfortunes from the perspective of the afterlife, and we are here in the world to gain this eternal life. So God tests us here so that we acquire the state appropriate for this life. He tests us according to His blessings upon us. More blessings mean more responsibility. As God gives us more bounties and blessings, our responsibility grows. For example, almsgiving is compulsory for the wealthy, not the poor; while those who have the required power and equipment are required to go to war when necessary, while the disabled, blind, or sick do not have to bear arms in God's cause.

The Prophet Jesus says: "If your right eye causes you to sin, pluck it out and cast *it* from you; for it is more profitable for you that one of your members perish, than for your whole body to be cast into hell. And if your right hand causes you to sin, cut it off and cast *it* from you; for it is more profitable for you that one of your members perish, than for your whole body to be cast into hell (*Matthew*, 5: 27-30). When viewed from this perspective, we cannot know what circumstances into which we are born are to our good or to our harm. God knows, and we do not know. We cannot know if being rich or poor, or healthy or sick, or sound or disabled is better for us. And, the Qur'an tells us that it may be that we dislike a thing although it is good for us, and love a thing although it is bad for us. God knows but we know not (2: 216). This means that we cannot regard as misfortune any circumstances into which we are born.

Evil is destruction, and humankind have great capacity for destruction. Destruction is related to non-existence, and the non-existence of something is possible even if just one component is missing. But all the good that comes to humanity is from God. Good relates to existence and the existence of something is not possible even if only one of the components does not exist. For example, a person can survive and be healthy on condition that all the cells of their body – numbering more than 60 trillion – are healthy. If only one cell is deformed, it can lead to the death of a person. So the health of a body is dependent on the health of its components. Furthermore, for something to exist time is required, while its destruction can take place within a minute. A lazy child, by igniting a match, can burn to ashes in an hour a building that took a hundred days for a team of people to build. What all this means is that human beings have little capacity to accomplish good. As has been pointed out in the example of bread in *Surah* 9, note 23, in order to obtain bread, which is a vital food for humans, a person needs soil, air, water, the sun, a seed of wheat which has the capacity to germinate and grow into wheat, and the ability and power to grow wheat, all of which are provided by God. So whatever good a person has, it is from God, while whatever evil befalls them, it is from themselves.

It can be said that the human free will works in the direction of evil, while it is God Who causes people to will good and enables them to do it. The human carnal soul always wills evil and to commit sins, but God always wills good and makes people succeed in willing good, provided that they refrain from characteristics such as haughtiness, wrong view-points, ill intentions and ill-disposition, evil suspicions, prejudices, wrong judgment, and subjection to carnal appetites. In order to help them to refrain from such ills, God has sent Prophets, revealed Books, and established a special way of thinking, belief, and conduct in the name of religion.

As a consequence, a person should know and acknowledge that whatever evil befalls them is because of their errors and sins, and therefore they should turn to God in repentance, mending their ways and correcting their errors. They should neither fall into despair nor complain about others or Destiny. When they recover from an illness or are relieved of any misfortune, they should attribute this blessing to God alone, and accept that, like illnesses and misfortunes, health and prosperity are also a test for them. They should be thankful to God, without taking any credit for themselves, refraining from making errors and sinning. Both of these attitudes – turning to God in repentance and mending one's ways when visited by illness or misfortune, and thanking God in times of health and prosperity – require patience. Patience which is shown in resisting the temptations of the carnal soul and in avoiding sins, and which is displayed when enduring misfortunes without complaint causes one to acquire piety; patience and perseverance in thanking and worshipping God elevates one to the rank of being loved by God.

Another point to mention here is that a person should attribute to themselves whatever misfortune or evil befalls them, but when another believer has been visited by misfortune, others should not think ill of them; rather they should take into consideration that God has caused this person to be able to attain a higher spiritual rank through misfortune or evil. The greatest of humankind, such as the Prophets and saints did not remain immune from illnesses and other misfortunes. Nearness to God is a cause of misfortune, as God always keeps people pure by means of misfortune. As the Prophets and saints always thanked God in patience when a misfortune visited them, they were promoted to a higher rank as heroes of patience and thankfulness. The Messenger, upon him be peace and blessings, declares: "Those who are most visited by misfortunes are the Prophets, then come others who are near to God, each according to his nearness." (at-Tirmidhī, "Zuhd," 57) A Companion came to the Messenger and said: "O Messenger of God, I love you very much." The Messenger replied: "Then be prepared for poverty" (at-Tirmidhī, "Zuhd," 36). When another one said that he loved God very much, the Messenger replied: "Then be prepared for misfortunes." That is why it is said: "Nearness to the Sultan is a burning fire." This is another subtle point that merits much reflection.

ON THE EXISTENCE AND UNITY OF GOD

I t is very easy to explain existence when one attributes it to One Divine Being. If you try to explain existence by attributing it to various origins, insurmountable barriers are encountered. If you attribute existence to One Divine Being, you can then see that the whole universe is as easy to create as a honeybee, and that a honeybee is as easy to create as fruit. If, by contrast, you ascribe it to multiple origins, creating a honeybee is as difficult as creating the universe, and creating fruit will be as difficult as creating all the trees in the universe. This is because a single being, with a single movement, can produce an effect that deals with a whole. If that effect or treatment is expected of multiple beings, it will only be obtained, if at all, with extreme difficulty and after much controversy. Which is easier or more difficult: managing an army under a single commander or letting the soldiers make their own decisions, employing a builder to construct a building or letting the stones arrange themselves, the revolution of many planets around a single sun or vice versa?

When all things are attributed to One Divine Being, they do not have to be created from absolute non-existence, for creation means giving external, material existence to things that already exist in the Divine Knowledge. It is like putting in words the meaning in one's mind, or applying a substance to make letters written in invisible ink visible. However, if things, most of which are lifeless, ignorant, and unconscious, or, if alive, powerless and lacking in sufficient knowledge, are ascribed to themselves, or to their causes, which are lifeless, ignorant, and unconscious, then these things have to be created from absolute non-existence. This is impossible. The ease with which One Divine Being does this makes the existence of things as easy as is necessary; the difficulty in the latter is beyond measure. The existence of a living being requires that the atoms forming it, which are spread throughout the soil, water, and air, should come together. Therefore, each atom would have to have universal knowledge and absolute will. Anything with such knowledge and will would be independent of any partner and would not need to acknowledge any such partner. Nowhere in the universe is there any sign of such things or partners to be found. Creating the heavens and the earth requires a perfect, infinite power that has no partner. Otherwise, this power would have to be limited by a finite power, which is inconceivable. An infinite power does not need partners and is not obliged to admit of such even if they were to exist (which they do not).

Tawḥīd, that is the Principle of Divine Unity and Oneness, can be clearly observed throughout the universe. Whoever takes a look at themselves and their environment can easily discern that everything depends upon this basic principle of God-revealed Religion. Parts of the human body, for example, are in close cooperation with one another, and each cell is so interconnected with the whole body, making it impossible not to conclude that He Who has created the single cell is also He Who has created the whole body. Likewise, the elements comprising the universe are interrelated and in harmony with one another and the universe as a whole. One cannot help but believe that the entire universe, from the particles to the galaxies, has been brought into existence by the same Creator, and furthermore that the motion of atoms observed in a molecule is the same as that observed in the solar system. Everything originates from "one" and eventually will return to "one." The tree, for instance, which grows out of a seed or a stone, will result finally in a seed or stone. This visible evidence explains why an orderliness and harmony are observed in the whole universe; it operates in strict obedience to the One Who has established that order. In other words, it is directly operated by the Creator, the One, the All-Powerful, and the All-Knowing. Otherwise, as pointed out in the Qur'ān: *God has never taken to Himself a child, nor is there any god along with Him; otherwise each god would surely have sought absolute independence with his creatures under his authority, and they would surely have tried to overpower one another* (23: 91); and: *The fact is that had there been in the heavens and the earth any gods other than God, both (of those realms) would certainly have fallen into ruin* (21: 22).

Tawḥīd is the highest conception of deity, the knowledge of which God has sent to humankind in all ages through His Prophets. It was this same knowledge which all the Prophets, including Moses, Jesus, and the Prophet Muḥammad (God's blessings and peace be upon them all), brought to humankind. Humankind were guilty of polytheism or idol-worship after the demise of their Prophets. They misinterpreted the religion, mixed it with superstition, and let it degenerate into magical practices and meaningless rituals. The concept of God, the very core of religion, was debased by anthropomorphism, the deification of angels, the association of others with God, the attempt to elevate Prophets or godly people as 'incarnations' of God, and personification of His Attributes through separate deities.

The followers of *Tawḥīd* must not be narrow-minded. Their belief in One God, the Creator of the heavens and the earth, the Master of the east and the west, and the Sustainer of the universe, leads them to view everything as belonging to the same Lord, to Whom they belong as well. Thus, they consider nothing as alien. Their sympathy, love, and service are not confined to any particular race, color, or group; they come to understand the Prophetic saying: "O servants of God, be brothers (and sisters)!"

The followers of *Tawḥīd* know that only God has true power, that only He can benefit or harm them, fulfill their needs, cause them to die, or wield authority and influence. This conviction makes them indifferent to and independent and fearless of all powers other than those of God. They never bow in homage to any of God's creatures.

The followers of *Tawḥīd*, although humble and mild, never abase themselves by bowing before anyone or anything except God. They never aim at any advantage by their worship, even if that advantage is Paradise. They seek only to please God and obtain His approval. They know that the only way to success and salvation is to acquire a pure soul and righteous behavior. They have perfect faith in God, Who is above all needs, related to none, absolutely just, and without partner in His exercise of Divine Power. Given this belief, they understand that they can succeed only through right living and just action, for no influence or underhanded activity can save them from ruin.

However, some believe that they have atoned for their sins, while others assert that they are God's favorites and thus immune to punishment. Still others believe that their idols or saints will intercede with God on their behalf, and so make offerings to their deities in the belief that such bribes give them license to do whatever they want. Such false beliefs keep them entangled in sin and evil, and their dependence on such deities causes them to neglect their need for spiritual purification and for living a pure and good life.

The followers of *Tawḥīd* do not become hopeless or disappointed. Their firm faith in God, Master of all treasures of the earth and the heavens, and Possessor of limitless grace, bounty, and infinite power, imparts to their hearts extraordinary consolation, grants them contentment, and keeps them filled with hope. In this world they might meet with rejection at all doors, nothing might serve their ends, and all means might desert them. But faith in and dependence on God, which never leave them, give them the strength to go on struggling. Such a profound confidence can come only from belief in One God. Such a belief produces great determination, patient perseverance, and trust in God. When such believers decide to devote their resources to fulfilling the Divine commands in order to secure God's good pleasure and approval, they are sure that they have the support and backing of the Lord of the universe.

Tawḥīd inspires bravery, for it defeats the two factors that make people cowardly: fear of death and love of safety, and the belief that someone other than God can somehow be bribed into postponing one's death. Belief in the Islamic creed that "there is no deity but God" purges the mind of these ideas. The first idea loses its influence when people realize that their lives, property, and everything else really belong to God, for this makes them willing to sacrifice whatever they have for God's approval. The second idea is defeated when people realize that no weapon, person, or power can kill them, for only God has this power. No one can die before their appointed time, even if all of the world's forces combine to do so. Nothing can bring death forward or push it back, even for one instant. This firm belief in One God and dependence upon Him makes followers of *Tawḥīd* the bravest of people.

Tawḥīd creates an attitude of peace and contentment, purges the mind of subtle passions and jealousy, envy and greed, and prevents one from resorting to base and unfair means for achieving success.

FROM THE DIARY OF A HONEYBEE

Today I am at the beginning of my life, a white egg, hardly bigger than a full stop.

This is my fourth day; I am a larva today. I have about 1,300 meals every day during my growth. I feed on a sort of jelly that is extremely rich in vitamins and proteins, prepared by my elder sisters in the hive. I gain five times my weight every day. The temperature around me must be 35°C, and this is maintained by my elder sisters, too.

This is my seventh day. Instead of jelly, I begin to feed on a food prepared with honey and pollen.

This is the ninth day in my life; the ceiling of my cell has been covered with wax. My elder sisters tell me that I will weave a silk cocoon around me tomorrow and become a pupa.

I am growing speedily; almost two weeks have passed since my birth. I look more like a bee.

Today I am on the twentieth day of my life; I am a perfectly-formed honeybee with a head that has antennae to touch and smell, five eyes – three of which are located on the upper part of my head with the other two larger ones on the side of my head – a tongue to suck water and nectar, jaws, legs, wings, and a sting to defend myself. My abdomen has been arranged in such a way that it can both digest and secrete. I begin to work according to a strict division of labor in the hive. My first job is cleaning, which I am told that I will do for two days. Then I will be promoted to nurse, looking after the larvae of four to six days. A secretion gland will begin to work in my body. I will feed the larvae with the pollen to be offered to me by my elders.

Days are passing, and today I am twenty-six days old. I begin to make jelly and offer it to the larvae, which eat 1,300 meals a day.

I am aging, having reached the half of my life. I have left behind one month and I am a cook, making honey from the nectar my elders have collected from the flowers. The honey is composed of water, sucrose, and glucose and is very rich in vitamins. It contains enzymes to digest carbohydrates.

Thousands of bees die every day in the comb while thousand others are born. This happens in such an orderly way that no confusion is apparent. In our community, the queen bee lays the eggs. She must lay around 2,000 eggs every day. While we – the female bees – are feeding her, she lets us taste from a substance she produces. We go round the comb and allow all our sisters to taste that substance, which enforces a kind of birth control. On the day when we do not taste of this substance, we begin to lay eggs. Since those eggs are not fertilized, only male bees hatch out. Male bees have no task other than inseminating the queen bee. Their number is quite limited.

I am on the thirty-fifth day of my life, and a new factory has started to work in my body. Located in the back, lower part of my abdomen, this factory produces wax. We collect the wax with the hairs on our middle legs and chew it in order to mould it into the cells of the comb. The cells are hexagonal in shape; this is the ideal shape to ensure the greatest amount of storage for the least amount of wax. Also, a hexagonal form has the greatest resistance to external pressure.

35 thousand cells are made from half a kilo of wax and 10 kilograms of honey are stored in these. We need 3.5 kilos of honey to make half a kilo of wax. While making the cells, we take gravity into account. For example, the cells where the female worker bees lie are horizontal, forming a vertical layer, while the cells where the queen bee lies are vertical, parallel to the surface of the earth. The cells where male bees grow are larger than those of the females.

This is my thirty-seventh day. I am extremely excited because I will leave the hive to fly around it and to obtain knowledge of the outer world. Unlike birds, we do not flap our wings. When we fly, our wings move automatically in such a way that they make 250 complete turns per second, as well as curving along certain lines so that we are able to adjust our bodies to the air current. The wings make a figure of 8 shape in the air. In proportion to the size of our wings, our bodies are heavy (unlike birds). Our bodies grow progressively heavier as we collect nectar from flowers. Despite this, we can fly as fast as 15 kilometers an hour. Not only is a bee's flight miraculous; the way we land is awe-inspiring as well. Unlike birds, we do not need to decrease our speed before we land. Thanks to God for the tips of our legs, we can immediately alight wherever we want in mid-flight.

I am thirty-eight days old. I am one of the guards controlling the entrance of the hive. No one, not even bees from other hives, are allowed to enter our hive. Bees recognize one another by smell. The smell of each community of honeybees is different. The entrance of a hive is also marked by the smell unique to that community.

This is the forty-first day of my life and I am old enough to begin to collect nectar from flowers. The factories in my body that produce royal jelly and wax have ceased production. From now on, I will spend my days collecting nectar. Flowers attract us by their colors and smells. The flowers are structured in such a way that it is as if they have been built as landing platforms. When we land on a flower, we use our tongues to reach into the source of the nectar in its center. At the same time, the pollen from the flowers clings to the hairs on our bodies, making us look like a thorny twig. We leave some of this pollen on other flowers we visit and thereby assist in the pollination of flowers. We do not visit flowers at random. We continue to visit the same kind of flowers in the same environment as the first flower we visited that day.

A bee can visit as many as 20,000 flowers in one day. We store the nectar in our stomach and the pollen in sacs located on our back legs. Since flying home is made more difficult by the weight of our load, we follow a direct route when returning to the hive; this is known as a bee line. Even if we pass through places unknown to us, we always follow this direct route. It is extremely easy for a bee to establish a bee line. The place and position of the sun tells us the direction. The change of the sun's position does not hinder us. We can easily calculate the exact place and position of the sun at any time of the day. We use atmospheric polarization and find the place of the sun by means of any light that comes from anywhere in the sky.

Having collected nectar for twenty days, I have completed my task in life. Today I am at the end of my life, a span of two months. During all the twenty days that have passed I have flown more than 2,000 kilometers and have produced 50 grams of honey. This amount should not be considered as trivial, for the population of a hive makes 200,000 flights a day, producing one kilo of honey. If all the human beings in the world, proud of their knowledge and abilities, were to come together and combine all their skills, they could not produce even a single gram of honey.

It is clear that it is impossible for any being other than God Almighty, Who is the All-Knowing, All-Powerful, All-Willing, even for what some call nature or natural forces or matter, to create the bee and organize her life; all of these are blind, lifeless, ignorant, they have no will at all and cannot create. It is God Almighty Who has created me, organized my life, and enabled me to fulfill so great tasks. (Summarized from *The Diary of a Honeybee* by Ümit Şimşek, İstanbul.)

THE ASCENSION (*Mİ 'RĀJ*) OF THE PROPHET MUḤAMMAD

D uring his entire life-time, God's Messenger, upon him be peace and blessings, was in continual search for unadulterated minds and hearts to which he could impart God's Message. He may have offered his Message only a few times to those like Abu Bakr and 'Umar, but he must have offered it to Abu Jahl and his like at least fifty times. Each time he appeared before them, he would say: "Proclaim, 'There is no deity but God', and be saved!" He would visit the places where people gathered and carry the fragrance of the same words, "Proclaim, 'There is no deity but God', and be saved!"

Fairs used to be held periodically in places around Makkah such as 'Arafāt, Mina, Muzdalifah and 'Aqabah, which attracted many people not native to Makkah. The Messenger would visit these fairs for the purpose of preaching Islam, and his effort, as well as the measure of success he had in persuading people to listen, angered the polytheists of Makkah.

A time came when reactions, which had begun as indifference, then turned to derision and mocking, then to persecution, torture, and boycotting of the Muslims, reached an unbearable point and there was no hope for further conversions among the Makkan polytheists. God's Messenger, upon him be peace and blessings, took Zayd ibn Hārithah with him and went to Tāif. Unfortunately, there, too, he was faced with violent anger and terror. The children of Tāif, positioned on either side of the road, threw stones at him. There was not a square inch on his body that was not hit by the stones. However, he finally succeeded in leaving the town and reached a tree in a vineyard, under which he took shelter, bleeding profusely. He held up his hands and supplicated:

> O God, unto You do I complain of my frailty, lack of resources, and lack of significance before those people. O Most Merciful of the merciful, You are the Lord of the oppressed and You are my Lord. To whom do You abandon me? To that stranger who looks askance and grimaces at me? Or to that enemy to whom You have given mastery over me? If, however, Your indignation is not against me, I am not worried. But Your grace is a much greater thing for me to wish for. I seek refuge in the Light of Your "Face," which illuminates all darkness and by which the affairs of this life and the Hereafter have been rightly ordered, lest Your wrath alight upon me, or Your indignation descend upon me. I expect Your forgiveness so that You may be pleased with me, and there is no other resource nor any power but what is in You.

While he was lying in the Sacred Mosque one night, some time after he had returned from this painful trip, he was taken from there to Masjid al-Aqsā in Jerusalem and thence through the heavenly dimensions of existence where he observed the greatest signs of God. That is, he observed the greatest truths and signs concerning God's Divinity and Lordship, and the original truths of the fundamentals of faith and worship and all existence in archetypal forms. He also witnessed the original meanings of all events and things in the physical world, as well as the forms they take and their results that pertain to the other world. The Prescribed Prayer was also enjoined on him and his community and was established as five times daily.

The Ascension is one of the greatest miracles of the Prophet Muḥammad, upon him be peace and blessings. The Prophet realized a spiritual perfection and full refinement through faith and worship and as a reward God took him to His holy Presence. Escaping from the imprisonment of "natural" laws and material causes and rising beyond the limits of bodily existence, the Prophet, upon him be peace and blessings, crossed distances swiftly and transcended all dimensions of existence until he reached the holy Presence of God.

MULTI-DIMENSIONAL EXISTENCE AND THE ASCENSION

In order to clarify subtle matters and abstract truths we usually make use of comparisons, and we compare such matters and truths to concrete things in the material world. For such comparisons to be possible and potentially worthwhile, there must be some similarity between the things that are compared to each other. However, since both the Prophet's journeying from Makkah to Jerusalem (the Night Journey) and his Ascension (*al-Miʿrāj*) through the dimensions of existence are miracles without equal or like in the material world, the method of comparison cannot be applied. These events can only be known and understood by God's teaching. Nevertheless, the names of the "vehicles" mentioned in the Prophetic Traditions with respect to both the Night Journey and the Ascension – *Burāq* (derived from *barq*, meaning lightning) – and the very name of the journeying through the dimensions of existence *Miʿrāj* (meaning stairway), allude to the fact that we can refer to certain scientific truths to make this miracle understandable by the "restricted" human mind.

Atomic physics has changed many notions in physics and established that the material world is a dimension or an appearance of existence. Alongside this world, there are many other worlds or dimensions of existence, each having its own peculiarities. Einstein put forward the notion that time is only one of the dimensions of existence. Science has not yet reached a final conclusion about existence and new findings and developments continually change our understanding. Therefore, especially today, it would be irrational to question the event of the Ascension.

In the Ascension, the Prophet Muḥammad, upon him be peace and blessings, must have moved with the speed of the spirit and he traveled through all time and space and all dimensions of existence in a very short period. People may have difficulty in understanding how a mortal, physical being can make such a journey and observe all existence with its past and future. In order to understand this subtle matter, consider this analogy: Imagine that you are standing with a mirror in your hand, with everything reflected on the right representing the past, while everything reflected on the left represents the future. The mirror can reflect one direction only since it cannot show both sides at the same time as you are holding it. If you wish to reflect both directions at the same time, you will have to rise high above your original position, so that left and right are united into one and nothing remains to be called first or last, beginning or end. As in this comparison, the Messenger traveled through the dimensions of existence, including time and space, and reached a point from where he could penetrate all time as a single point in which the past, present and future are united.

During that heavenly journey, the Messenger met with the previous Prophets, saw angels and beheld the beauties of Paradise and the terrors of Hell. He also observed the essential realities of all the Qur'ānic issues and the meanings of and wisdom in all the acts of worship. He went as far as the realms where even the greatest of angels, Gabriel, cannot reach and was honored with vision of God's "Face," free from any qualitative or quantitative dimensions or restrictions. Then, in order to bring humanity out of the darkness of material existence into the illuminated realm of faith and worship, through which they could realize a spiritual ascension each according to their capacity, he returned to the world where he was made subject to all kinds of persecution.

THE WISDOM OF THE ASCENSION

A ruler holds two kinds of conversation and interviews and has two modes of address and favor. One is when he converses with an ordinary subject or citizen about a particular matter or need by means of a direct, private line of communication, such as a telephone. The other is that under the title of supreme sovereignty, being the ruler of the whole country, he chooses an envoy, one whose office is concerned with the matter, to publish and promulgate his royal decree, and this decree carries the authority and weight of his majesty.

Similarly, the Master of the whole of existence has two kinds of conversing and speaking, and two manners of favoring. One is particular and private, the other, universal and general. The particular and private one occurs in the mirror of the heart by means of one's particular relationship with the Lord. Everyone may receive a manifestation of the light and conversation of the Master of creation in accordance with their capacity and the character of their spiritual journeying in traversing the degrees toward sainthood and their ability to receive the manifestations of Divine Names and Attributes. That is why there are innumerable degrees in sainthood. The second is that, by virtue of having a comprehensive nature and being the most enlightened fruit of the Tree of Creation, humankind are potentially able to reflect all the Divine Names manifested in the universe in the mirror of their spirit. But not everyone can realize this. Almighty God manifests all His Beautiful Names and Attributes only in the greatest of humanity at the greatest level and most comprehensively, as it is only that greatest one who is able to receive them. It was this form of manifestation that occurred in Muḥammad, upon him be peace and blessings.

THE REALITY OF THE ASCENSION

The Ascension is the journey of the Prophet Muḥammad, upon him be peace and blessings, through the degrees of perfection. That is, Almighty God has various Names or Titles manifested in the arrangement and disposition of creatures, and the diverse works of His Lordship (His upbringing, training, sustaining, and providing) are displayed as the results of the execution of His absolute authority in the invention and administration of creatures in the levels of the heavens where He executes His Lordship according to the different conditions of each level.

Thus, in order to show those works of His Lordship to His special servant and thereby make him a being encompassing all human perfections and receiving all Divine manifestations, i.e., one who can view all the levels of the universe and announce the sovereignty of His Lordship, and who can proclaim the things of which He approves and unveil the enigmatic meaning of creation, God Almighty mounted him on *Burāq* (a mount of Paradise) and had him travel through the heavens like lightning, promoting him to higher and higher ranks, and causing him to observe the Divine Lordship from mansion to mansion and from sphere to sphere, showing him the Prophets, his brothers, whose abodes are in the heavens of those spheres, one after the other. Finally, He raised him to the station of *the distance between the strings of two bows (put adjacent to each other) or even nearer* (for the meaning of which, see 53: 9, and the corresponding note 4), and honored him with the special manifestation of all of His Names to the fullest degree.

THE FRUITS OR BENEFITS OF THE ASCENSION

Out of numerous fruits of the Ascension, we will mention only five.

The First Fruit

The vision of the truths from which the pillars of faith originate and of the angels, Paradise and the Hereafter, became the cause of such a treasure of eternal light, such a gift for the universe and humankind, that it has freed the universe from being perceived and experienced as a disordered heap doomed to destruction. This gift showed that, in reality, the universe is the harmonious collection of the sacred "inscriptions" of the Eternally Besought-of-All and lovely mirrors where the Grace and Beauty of the Single One are reflected. This vision has pleased and delighted the universe and all conscious beings. Again, through that light and gift, this vision has freed humankind from the confused state of misguidance in which they were seen as wretched, helpless and destitute beings, entangled in innumerable needs and hostilities and doomed to permanent annihilation, and showed that, in reality, each human being is of the most fair composition and the best pattern of creation, one who, being a miracle of the Power of the Eternally Besought-of-All and a comprehensive copy of the collection of His "inscriptions," is addressed by the Sovereign of Eternity, and one who is His private servant to appreciate His perfections, His friend to behold His Beauty in amazement, and His beloved and His honored guest designated for Paradise. This fruit of the Ascension implant infinite joy and enthusiasm in those who are truly human.

The Second Fruit

The Ascension brought to humankind and the jinn the essentials of Islam as a gift, including primarily the prescribed five daily Prayers, which contain all the things pleasing to the Ruler of Eternity, Who is the Maker of creatures, the Owner of the universe, and the Lord of the worlds. People are inevitably curious to perceive what it is that pleases Him, and their perceiving it brings an indescribable happiness. For everyone is desirous of knowing the wishes of a renowned benefactor or a benevolent ruler; they say: "We wish we had a means of communication so that we could talk to him directly! We wish we knew what he asks of us! We wish we knew what things we have done that are pleasing to Him!" God has the possession of all creatures, and the grace, beauty, and perfections shared by all creatures are but a dim shadow in relation to His Beauty, Grace, and Perfection. You may understand to what degree human beings, who need Him in infinite ways and receive His endless bounties every moment, should be curious about and desirous of perceiving His will and the things pleasing to Him.

It was as a fruit of the Ascension that, having left "seventy thousand veils" behind, the Prophet Muḥammad, upon him be peace and blessings, heard of the things pleasing to the Creator and Sustainer of the universe directly, and brought them with absolute certainty to humankind as a gift.

People are extremely eager to learn facts about the moon or indeed any other planet. They send explorers there to find out and then tell them about it. They are ready to make great sacrifices for this end. But the moon travels in the domain of such a Master that it flies around the earth like a fly. The earth flies around the sun like a moth. As for the sun, it is only a lamp among thousands of other lamps and functions like a candle in a guest-house of the Majestic Master of the Kingdom. Thus, these are the acts and qualities of the Majestic Being and the wonders of His art and the treasures of His Mercy in the eternal world that the Prophet Muḥammad, upon him be peace and blessings, saw during the Ascension and then told humankind about. You may understand how contrary to reason and wisdom it would be if humankind were not to listen to this person with utmost curiosity and in perfect amazement and love.

The Third Fruit

The Prophet Muḥammad, upon him be peace and blessings, saw the hidden treasure of eternal happiness during the Ascension and brought its keys to humankind and jinn as a gift. Through the Ascension he saw Paradise with his own eyes, observed the everlasting manifestations of the Mercy of the Majestic All-Merciful One, and perceived eternal happiness with absolute certainty, and then he brought to humankind and jinn the glad tidings that there is eternal happiness (in an everlasting world).

It is indescribable what great happiness this aroused in the mortal, wretched human beings and the jinn who had regarded themselves as being condemned to permanent annihilation; such glad tidings were given to them at a time when all creatures were emitting heart-rending cries at the thought of being in a flux amidst the convulsions of death and decay in an unstable world, of diving into the ocean of non-existence and eternal separation through the flow of time and the motion of the atoms. Consider how a person would rejoice if they learned that they were to be given a palace by the king in the vicinity of his residence just at the time of their execution. Add to this the instances of joy and happiness to the number of all humankind and jinn, and then you may be able to measure the value of these glad tidings.

The Fourth Fruit

As the Prophet Muḥammad, upon him be peace and blessings, himself received the fruit of the vision of God's All-Beautiful "Face," he brought it to humankind and jinn as a gift that every believer may be honored with the same vision. You can understand how delicious, fine, and beautiful that fruit is when you make the following comparison:

Anyone with a heart loves a beautiful, perfect, and benevolent one. This love increases in proportion to the extent of the beauty, perfection, and benevolence of the being and mounts to the degree of adoration and self-sacrifice. Whereas, when compared to God's Attributes, all the beauty, perfection, and benevolence shared by the whole of the creation are nothing more than a few flashes of the sun when compared to the sun itself. You may understand from this what a pleasant, beautiful, rejoicing, and blissful fruit it is that one deserves the sight of the Majestic One of perfection, Who is worthy of infinite love in the abode of eternal happiness; such a sight can only inspire infinite eagerness.

The Fifth Fruit

It was understood through the Ascension that each human being is a valuable fruit of the universe and a darling beloved of the Maker of the universe. Though outwardly an insignificant creature, a weak animal, and an impotent conscious being, each person has risen to a position so far above all other creatures that it is the cause of pride for us. The joy and happiness we receive from this is indescribable. If you tell an ordinary private that he has been promoted to the rank of field-marshal, he will feel infinite joy. While being a mortal, helpless, reasoning, and articulating animal knowing only the blows of decay and separation, we were told unexpectedly through the Ascension:

As you may realize all your heart's desires in an everlasting Paradise, enveloped by the Mercy of an All-Merciful, All-Compassionate, and All-Magnificent One, and in recreation, in traveling with the speed of imagination and in the broad sphere of the spirit and the mind, you also may see His Most Beautiful "Face" in an eternal happiness. (Summarized from *The Words*, "the 31st Word," by Said Nursi.)

ARGUMENTS FOR THE RESURRECTION

Concerning the Resurrection the following six questions may be asked:

One: Why will the world be destroyed? Is its destruction necessary?

Two: Is he who will destroy it, and the builder who will rebuild it, capable of doing this?

Three: Is the destruction of the world possible?

Four: If it is possible, will it really be destroyed?

Five: Is the rebuilding of the world possible?

Six: If possible, will it actually be rebuilt?

It is possible to destroy the world, and there is a necessary cause for its destruction. He Who will destroy and rebuild it is capable of that, and it will certainly take place, and it will surely be rebuilt. Our arguments are as follows:

FIRST ARGUMENT

The spirit is undoubtedly eternal, and the proofs of the existence of angels and other spirit beings (for the existence and characteristics of angels and other invisible beings, see *sūrah* 2, note 31, 36, 40; *sūrah* 11, note 19; *sūrah* 15: 27, note 7) are proofs of the eternity of the spirit. We are too close to the souls of the dead, who are waiting in the *Barzakh*, the intermediate world between this and the next to go to the Hereafter, to require any proof of their existence. It is commonly known that some can communicate with them, whilst almost everyone encounters them in true dreams. (For arguments concerning the eternity of the spirit, see Appendix 12.)

SECOND ARGUMENT

It is necessary that an eternal world of happiness should be established and the Majestic One Who will establish this world is certainly capable of doing that. The destruction of the world is possible and will certainly occur. Moreover, the resurrection of everything is also possible and, with equal certainty, will take place.

There is a purpose and necessary cause for the foundation of an eternal world of happiness; the following ten points indicate the existence and necessity of this purpose and cause:

First Point

The whole of creation displays a perfect harmony and a purposeful order, and in every aspect of the universe signs of a will are manifest. It is impossible not to discern, through the testimony of its fruits or results, in each thing and event, an intention and will, and in each composition an instance of wisdom and choice. If this creation were not meant to produce eternal happiness, then its harmony and order would be a deceptive appearance, and the meanings, relations and connections that are the spirit of the order would come to nothing – for it is eternal happiness which causes this order to be established and the world to be so in its present state.

Second Point

The creation of the universe displays perfect wisdom embodied in benefits and purposes. Indeed, the Divine Wisdom, being the representation of eternal favor, announces the coming of eternal happiness in the language of the benefits and purposes in the whole universe. If, then, there was no eternal happiness, it would require the denial of all the benefits and purposes observed in every thing and event in the universe.

Third Point

As pointed out by the intellect, wisdom, experience and deductive reasoning, nothing superfluous or vain occurs in creation, and this indicates the existence of eternal happiness. The Majestic Maker of the universe chooses the best and easiest way in creation, and apportions hundreds of duties and thousands of purposes to any creature, no matter how insignificant it may appear. Since there is no waste and nothing is in vain, there will surely be eternal happiness. Eternal non-existence would make everything futile, and everything would be a waste. The absence of waste in all creation, and in humankind in particular, demonstrates that humankind's endless spiritual potential, their limitless aspirations and ideas, and their inclinations will never go to waste. Their basic inclination towards perfection indicates the existence of perfection, and their desire for happiness proclaims that they are definitely destined for eternal happiness. If this was not so, then all the basic spiritual features and sublime aspirations which constitute their true nature would be for nothing.

Fourth Point

The alternation of day and night, spring and winter, atmospheric changes, the renewal of the human body each year, and awakening and rising every morning after sleep, all indicate a complete rising and renewal. Just as in time, seconds forecast the coming of the minute, the minute predicts the hour, and the hour anticipates the day, so, too, do the dials of God's great clock – the earth – point, in succession, to the day, the year, a person's lifetime and the ages through which the world passes. As they show that morning follows night, and spring winter, they intimate that the morning of the Resurrection will follow the death of the whole of creation.

As the daily, seasonal and annual changes, going to sleep and awakening the next morning, and the revivals and renewals which occur during a person's life can all be regarded as a kind of death and resurrection, so too is the revival of nature every spring a promise of the final resurrection. Hundreds of thousands of different kinds of resurrection take place in the realm of animals and plants each spring; some animals come to "life" after hibernation, while trees burst into leaf and flower. Thus, the All-Wise Creator reminds us of the Resurrection to come.

Each human being is equal in value and comprehensiveness to any other animate species because the light of the human intellect has endowed people with comprehensive aspirations and ideas that encompass the past and future. In other species, the nature of the individuals is particular, their value is local, their view restricted, their qualities limited, their pleasure and pain is instantaneous. Humankind, on the other hand, have a sublime nature and are of the greatest value; their perfection is limitless and spiritual pleasures and suffering are more lasting. It can be concluded from these facts that the kinds of resurrection experienced by other species in nature indicate that every human being will be completely resurrected on the Day of Judgment.

Fifth Point

Humankind have been endowed with unlimited potential. This potential develops into unrestricted abilities, which give rise to countless inclinations. These inclinations generate limitless desires and these desires are the source of infinite ideas and concepts. All these together indicate the existence of a world of eternal happiness beyond this material world. Their innate inclination towards eternal happiness makes one sure that this world of happiness will be established.

Sixth Point

The all-encompassing Mercy of the All-Merciful Maker of the universe requires that there be a world of eternal happiness. Were it not for such a world of happiness, which is the chief grace of God for human beings, they would unceasingly lament due to the pain of eternal separation, and acts of favor would turn into vengeance, and Divine Compassion would be negated. Divine Mercy, however, is found throughout the whole of creation, and is more evident than the sun. Observe love, affection, and intellect, which are the three manifestations of Divine Compassion. If human life were to result in eternal separation, with unending pangs of parting, then that gracious love would turn into the greatest affliction. Affection would turn into a most painful affliction, and that light-giving intellect would become an unmitigated evil. Divine Compassion, however, (because it is Compassion) would never inflict the agony of eternal separation upon true love.

Seventh Point

All the pleasure-giving experiences known in the universe, all the beauty, perfection, attractions, ardent yearnings, and feelings of compassion are spiritual articulations and manifestations of the Majestic Creator's Favor, Mercy, and Munificence made known to the intellect. Since there is a truth, a reality in this universe, there most certainly is true Mercy. And since there is true Mercy, there will be eternal happiness.

Eighth Point

The human conscience, which is humanity's conscious nature, reflects eternal happiness, and whoever hearkens to this conscience will hear it pronouncing eternity over and over again. If a human being were given the whole universe, it would not compensate them for a lack of eternity – people have an innate longing for eternity; it is this for which we have been created. This means that humankind's natural inclination towards eternal happiness comes from an objective reality, which is the existence of eternity and humankind's desire for it.

Ninth Point

The Prophet Muḥammad, upon him be peace and blessings, who spoke the truth and whose words have been confirmed over the centuries, preached the coming of everlasting life and eternal happiness, and it was his words which promised this. In his message, he concentrated almost as much upon the Resurrection as he did upon the Divine Unity, referring to the consensus of all the Prophets, peace be upon them all, and the unanimous agreement of all the saints.

Tenth Point

The Qur'ān, as well as all other Divine Books, announces the Resurrection and the coming of eternal happiness. It unveils the mystery of creation and offers many rational arguments in support of the Resurrection.

THIRD ARGUMENT

Just as the necessity of the Resurrection cannot be doubted, so too it is without question that the One Who will bring it about is eminently able to do so. He is absolutely powerful over everything. The greatest things and the smallest are the same in relation to His Power. He creates the spring with as much facility as He creates a flower. He is so powerful that the whole of creation, with its planets, stars, worlds, particles, and substances bear witness to His Power and Majesty. No one, then, has the right to doubt that He will be able to raise the dead for the Last Judgment. His Power is such that each century He causes a new environment to come into existence; He renews the world every year or rather, He creates a new world every day. He hangs many transient worlds upon the string of time as centuries, years, or even days pass, for a perfect, definite purpose. He does all these things, and He also displays the perfection of His Wisdom and the beauty of His art by causing the earth to wear the garment of spring, as if it were a single flower which He has decorated with the embellishments of hundreds of thousands of resurrections. Since He is able to do this, how is it then possible for anyone to doubt that He is able to cause the Resurrection to happen and to replace this world with another? (For the infinite capability of Divine Power, see 31: 28 and the corresponding note 6.)

FOURTH ARGUMENT

It has been established that there is a necessity for the Resurrection, and the One Who will raise the dead is able to do this. The whole world is exposed to the Resurrection and there are four matters relating to this subject as follows:

First: It is possible for this world to come to an end.

Second: The world will actually come to an end.

Third: The possibility exists for the destroyed world to be rebuilt again in the form of the Hereafter.

Fourth: The destroyed world will actually be resurrected and re-built.

First Matter

The death of all of creation is possible. If something is subject to the law of development, then it will certainly evolve to a final end. If something develops to this final end, then that means it will have a limited lifetime, and if something has a limited lifetime, then a "natural" end is certain to be fixed for it. Lastly, if something is destined for a fixed end, then it will inevitably die, and since humankind are a microcosm and nothing prevents us from dying, so too, the whole universe, which can be regarded as a macro-human being, cannot be saved from perishing. Accordingly, it will perish and be brought to life again on the morning of the Last Day. Just as a living tree, which is a miniature of the universe, is not able to save itself from annihilation, so too will "the branches of creatures" which have grown from "the Tree of Creation" pass away. If the universe is not destroyed by an external destructive event, which could occur by the leave of the Eternal Will, then a day, as also predicted by science, will certainly come when this macro-human being will go into the throes of death. It will give a sharp cry, and what is described in these Qur'ānic verses will take place:

When the sun is folded up (darkened); and when the stars fall (losing their luster; and when the mountains are set moving (81: 1–3).

When the heaven is cleft open; And when the stars fall in disorder and are scattered; And when the seas burst forth (spilling over their bounds to intermingle) (82: 1-3).

A Subtle but Important Point

Water freezes, and loses its essential liquid form; ice changes into water and loses its essential state as a solid; the essence of something becomes stronger at the expense of its material form; the spirit weakens as the flesh becomes more substantial, and the flesh weakens as the spirit becomes more illuminated. Thus, the solid world is being gradually refined by the mechanism of life to the advantage of the afterlife. The Creative Power breathes life into dense, solid, and inanimate substances as a result of astonishing activities and refines that solid world to the advantage of the coming world through the light of life.

A truth never perishes, no matter how weak it is. As the truth flourishes and expands, the form containing it grows weaker and is refined. The spiritual truth which actually constitutes the essence of something is inversely proportional to the strength of its form, in other words, as the form grows denser, the truth becomes weaker, and as the form grows weaker, the truth obtains more strength. This law is common to all creatures that are destined to develop and evolve. We can conclude from this argument that the corporeal world, which is a form containing the great truth of the universe, will break into pieces by leave of the Majestic Creator and be rebuilt more beautifully.

One day, the meaning expressed by the Qur'ānic verse, *On the Day when the earth is changed into another earth, and the heavens (also), they all appear before God, the One, the All-Overwhelming* (14: 48), will be realized. Finally, it is without a doubt that the death of the world is possible.

Second Matter

The world will certainly die. It is indicative of the inevitable death of the world that its inhabitants are replaced by new ones every day, every year, and in every age. Those who have been welcomed into this worldly guesthouse bid us farewell some time later and are followed by newcomers, a fact which testifies to the final death of the world itself.

If you would like to imagine the death of this world as indicated by the relevant Qur'ānic verses, look at how minutely and precisely the constituent parts of the universe have been connected to one another. Consider how sublimely and delicately they have been organized into a system, so that if a single heavenly body were to be given the order "Leave your axis!" the whole universe would be thrown into its death throes. Stars would collide, planets would be scattered and the sound of the exploding spheres would fill space. Mountains would be set in motion and the earth would be flattened. This is what the Eternal Power will actually do to bring about the next life, upsetting the universe, to separate the elements of Paradise from those of Hell.

Third Matter

The universe can be resurrected after its death because, first of all, the Divine Power is in no way defective. Secondly, there is a strong necessity for this resurrection, and, moreover, it is possible. Consequently, if there is a strong necessity that something should occur, and if that thing is possible, then it comes to be regarded as being something that will inevitably occur.

Another Significant Point

A close examination of what goes on in the universe will make it clear that within it are two opposed elements that have spread everywhere and become rooted. The result of the opposition of these elements, like good and evil, benefit and harm, perfection and defect, light and darkness, guidance and misguidance, belief and unbelief, obedience and rebellion, fear and love, is that they clash with one another in the universe. The universe manifests, through such a continuous conflict of opposites, the incessant alterations and transformations necessary to produce the elements of a new world. These opposed elements will eventually lead in two different directions to eternity, materializing as Paradise and Hell. The Eternal World will be made up of the essential elements of this transitory world, and these elements will then be given permanence. Paradise and Hell are in fact two opposite fruits which grow on the two branches of the Tree of Creation; they are the two results of the chain of creation. They are the two cisterns which are being filled by the two streams of things and events, and the two poles to which beings are flowing in waves. They are the places where Divine Grace and Divine

Punishment manifest themselves, and they will be filled up with their particular inhabitants when the Divine Power shakes up the universe with a violent motion.

People are being tested here so that their potential can develop and their abilities manifest themselves. This emergence of abilities causes the appearance of relative truths in the universe. In other words, the All-Beautiful Names of the Majestic Maker manifest their inscriptions and make the universe a missive of the Eternally Besought-of-All. It is also by virtue of this testing that the diamond-like essences of sublime souls are separated from the coal-like matter of the base ones.

For whatever sublime purposes God has willed creation to take place (we are aware of some of these purposes and of others we are unaware) He also willed the change and alteration of this world for the same purposes. He mixed together opposites and made them confront one another; He kneaded them together like dough, and made the universe subject to the law of alteration and to the principle of perfection. The time will arrive when the trial or testing comes to an end, and the Pen of Divine Destiny will have written what it has to write. The Divine Power will have completed its work, all the creatures will have fulfilled their duties and services, and the seeds will have been sown in the field of the afterlife. The earth will have displayed the miracles of Divine Power, and this transitory world will have hung all the eternal scenes upon the picture-rail of time, while the eternal Wisdom and Favor of the Majestic Maker will require that the results of the test be announced, the truths of the manifestations of the Divine Beautiful Names and the missives of the Pen of Divine Destiny be unveiled, the duties performed by the creatures be repaid, the truths of the meanings expressed by the words of the book of the universe be seen, the fruit of potential be yielded, a supreme court be established, and the veil of natural causes be removed so that everything is submitted directly to the Divine Will and Power. On that Day, the Majestic Creator will destroy the universe in order to eternalize it, and He will separate the opposites from one another. This separation will result in the appearance of Paradise with all its beauty and splendor, and of Hell with all its awfulness; the People of Paradise will be welcomed with the words, *Peace be upon you! Well you have faired and are purified (from the foul residues of sin, and delivered from all suffering), so enter it (Paradise) to abide!* (39: 73) whilst the people of Hell will be threatened with the words, *And you, O disbelieving criminals! Get you apart this Day!* (36: 59).

The Eternal All-Wise One will give, through His perfect Power, an everlasting, unchanging existence to the inhabitants of both these dwelling-places. They will never grow old, nor will their bodies suffer any disintegration or decomposition because there will be nothing to cause any changes that lead to disintegration.

Fourth Matter

We have stated in the previous Matter that it is possible for the earth to be resurrected after its death. After being destroyed, the One Who created this world will undoubtedly create it again more beautifully, and will convert it into one of the mansions of the Hereafter. In the same way that the Holy Qur'ān, with all its verses containing so many rational proofs, and the other Divine Scriptures are unanimously agreed upon this matter, so too are the Attributes of the All-Majestic One pertaining to His Majesty and those pertaining to His Grace, and all His Beautiful Names clear indications of the occurrence of the Resurrection. Furthermore, He has promised that He would bring about the Resurrection and the Great Gathering through all His heavenly decrees which He sent to His Prophets, and He will certainly carry out His promise. This is an undeniable truth, which is agreed upon by all the Prophets; the Prophet Muḥammad, upon him be peace and blessings, is the foremost in confirming it with the strength of his thousand miracles, as are the saints and righteous scholars. Lastly, the universe predicts it with all the scientific proofs contained in it (From *The Words*, "the 29th Word"). (For the Resurrection, see also *sūrah* 15: 85, note 17.)

THE SPIRIT, ITS IDENTITY AND ARGUMENTS
FOR ITS EXISTENCE

The interpreters of the Qur'ān have disagreed about what is meant by "spirit" in the verse 17: 85: *They ask you about the spirit. Say: "The spirit is of my Lord's Command, and of knowledge, you have been granted only a little."* Some are of the opinion that it means Revelation, while others assert that it is the essence of living existence or the source of life, movement, consciousness, feelings, and senses in living beings. If we consider that it is the spirit in a human being which is, as well as being the source of life, the essence that learns, is educated, and believes or denies, and that Revelation is the source or means of spiritual liveliness, we can conclude that Revelation is the life of spirit. The Qur'ān declares: "O you who believe! Respond to God and to the Messenger when the Messenger calls you (in the Name of God) to that which gives you life" (8: 24).

God has two laws, one issuing from His Attribute of Speech, and manifested as the Divine Revelation or Religion. The other issues from His Attributes of Will and Power, and is manifested as what we call the "laws of nature" and life. The spirit is also a manifestation of God's Attributes of Will and Power. It is a living law endowed with consciousness and a real, sensible existence. Bediüzzaman Said Nursi writes:

The spirit is a law with consciousness and a real, sensible existence: Divine Power has clothed it in an energetic envelope within a body of sensory organs. This spirit, which exists in humankind, is a counterpart to the "laws of nature and life." Both are unchanging (unless God wills otherwise for certain wise purposes) and permanent, and both have issued from the world of Divine Commands. If the Eternal Power had clothed the laws with perceptible existence and consciousness, each would have been a spirit; and if the human spirit were stripped of life and consciousness, it would become an immaterial law (*The Letters*, "Seeds of Truth").

Although science is not yet ready to accept it, there are many worlds in the universe, as well as there being subdivisions in the world – like the worlds of plants, animals, and human beings (the plant kingdom, animal kingdom, and human kingdom) and the world of jinn; these worlds lie one within the other or above and enveloping one another. Of these worlds, the visible, material world is that in which we live, the world which addresses itself to our senses. From the tiniest particles to the greatest galaxies, this world is the realm where God Almighty gives life, fashions, renews, changes, and causes to die. The sciences concern themselves with the phenomena of this world.

The sciences attribute almost every phenomenon in the physical world to natural laws. But these laws have no directly perceptible existence. Therefore, attributing creativity to those laws which are only nominal principles deduced from what is going on in nature is the same as denying the existence of the spirit, and is mere prejudice or bias, and deliberate denial. Like the laws that seem to operate in the universe, the spirit is a law that issues from the world of Divine Laws or Commands. Nevertheless, unlike these other laws, the human spirit is a living, conscious law.

Above this visible, material world is the immaterial world of Divine Laws or Commands. In order to have some knowledge of this world, we can consider, for example, how a book, or a tree, or a human being comes into existence. The most important part of a book's being is found in its meaning; for example, a book can be bound, or can be in audio form, or even found on-line. The physical entity of "a book" has no meaning in and of itself; it is the meaning of the book, the ideas that cause it to exist. Another example: that thing that stimulates a seed to germinate under the earth and grow into a tree is the essence of life and the law of germination and growth with which the seed has previously been endowed. We can observe the germination of the seed and the subsequent development of the seedling into a tree with the naked eye. If it were not for the essence of life and the laws of germination and growth, which, even if invisible or unobservable, govern the birth and growth of a new living thing, there would be no plants in the world.

We conclude the existence of all these laws from the almost never-changing repetition of all these processes. Likewise, by observing the "natural" phenomena around us, we can also deduce the existence of many other laws, like gravity and repulsion, freezing and vaporization.

Thus, like the laws we have thus mentioned and many others, the spirit is a law issuing from the world of Divine Commands. Nevertheless, unlike the other laws, the human spirit is a living, conscious law. If the spirit were to be stripped of life and consciousness, it would become a law; if on the other hand, the laws were to be given life and consciousness, they would each become a spirit.

THE SPIRIT CANNOT BE DEFINED OR PERCEIVED THROUGH MODERN SCIENTIFIC INFORMATION

While matter or anything in the material world is composed of atoms and atoms are made up of more minute particles, the spirit is a simple entity. Since it is simple, it does not disintegrate. We cannot see it as we see a material thing; we recognize it through its manifestations in the material world. Although we accept its existence and observe its manifestations, we cannot know its nature. Yet our ignorance of the nature of a thing does not mean that that thing does not exist.

IT IS THE SPIRIT WHICH SEES, HEARS, ETC.

We see with our eyes. In other words, our eyes are simply instruments with which we see. The main center of sight is in the brain. However, it is not the brain itself which sees, as seeing and hearing are conscious perceptions. The brain has no consciousness or perceptiveness. We do not say "My brain sees," but rather, "I see." It is we who see or hear or sense. But who is this being that we call "I"? Is it something composed of a brain, a heart, and other organs and limbs? Why can we not move when we die, although all our organs and limbs are still there? How does a factory work? Does it work by itself or does some other thing, for example, electrical energy, cause it to work? Any defect in the machinery, or some other problem at the factory which causes a disruption between the electrical energy source and the factory is enough to reduce a large highly-productive factory into a pile of useless metal. Can this relationship between the factory and electrical energy be, in one way, comparable to that between the spirit and the body?

When the connection of the body with the spirit is cut – what we call death – the body is reduced to something which we do not want to hang on to, even for a few hours, as it will soon rot and decompose.

THE SPIRIT IS A CONSCIOUS, POWERFUL THING, WHICH IS APT TO LEARN AND WHICH THINKS, SENSES, AND REASONS, CONTINUALLY DEVELOPING

Of course, the spirit is not the same as electrical power. It is a conscious, powerful thing which is able to learn and which thinks, senses, and reasons, continually developing, usually in parallel with the physical development of the body, both mentally and spiritually, through learning, reflection, belief, and worship. It is also the spirit which determines the character, nature, or identity of an individual, i.e. what makes one person different or distinguishable from others. Although all human beings, from the first to the last, are essentially made up of the same elements, they all differ from one another in character, nature, and features. Thus, the only thing that can determine this difference is the spirit.

THE SPIRIT COMMANDS THE INNER FACULTIES OF THE HUMAN BEING

Similarly, human conscience, so long as it remains sound, does not lie. If it is not deluded by the human carnal soul or desires, it is deeply aware of the Existence of God and finds peace in belief in and worship of Him. Thus, it is the spirit which directs or commands the human conscience, as well as the other faculties. The spirit seeks the world from which it has come and yearns for its Creator. Unless it is stunted and perverted by sin, the spirit will find the Creator and in Him it will attain true happiness.

THE SPIRIT HAS DEEP RELATIONSHIPS TO THE PAST AND FUTURE

Animals have no concept of time; in accordance with the primordial nature God has assigned to them, they live only for the present time and they feel neither the pain of the past nor anxiety about the future. But the human is deeply influenced by the pain of past events and misfortunes and is anxious about their future. This is because their spirit is a conscious, sentient entity.

The spirit is never satisfied with this mortal, fleeting world. A person's accomplishments or worldly possessions, such as money, rank, and the satisfaction of worldly desires never suffice for the happiness of the spirit. Rather, worldly possessions only increase dissatisfaction and unhappiness. The spirit is only at ease when there is belief in God, and worship and remembrance of Him.

Humankind have a very strong desire for eternity. The source of this desire cannot be the physical dimension of their existence. Physically, we are mortal and the feeling of eternity and the desire for it cannot issue from mortal existence. Rather, this desire or feeling originates in the eternal dimension of our existence, and it is the spirit which constitutes this dimension. It is the spirit which causes a human being to sigh: "I am mortal but I do not desire what is mortal. I am impotent but I do not desire what is impotent. What I desire is an eternal beloved (who will never desert me) and I yearn for an eternal world."

THE SPIRIT ESTABLISHES ITS CONNECTION WITH THE MATERIAL WORLD THROUGH THE BODY

The spirit is a simple entity which issues from the world of Divine Commands. In order to be manifested and function in the material, visible world, it needs material things. As the body is unable to get in touch with the world of symbols or immaterial forms, the spirit cannot establish any contact with this world without the mediation of the heart, the brain, and other organs and limbs of the body.

The spirit functions, as we have just said, through all the nerves, cells, and other elements of the body. Therefore, if something goes wrong with a system or organ in the body, the relation of the spirit with that system or organ is disconnected and the spirit can no longer command it. If the failure or "illness" that has caused the disconnection is serious enough to sever the relationship of the spirit with the entire body, then what we call death occurs.

Although some coarse, meaningless movements can be observed in the hands or fingers as a result of stimulation to certain areas of the brain, these movements are like some confused, meaningless sounds produced by pressing the keys of a piano at random. Or rather, these movements are autonomous responses of the body to stimulation, which come about as the result of the autonomous working of the body. Therefore, in order for the body to produce meaningful movements, the spirit must be present, as it has consciousness and free will.

IT IS THE SPIRIT WHICH DETERMINES THE FEATURES OF ONE'S FACE

The spirit manifests itself for the most part in the face. One's face is a window that opens onto one's inner world. Through all the features, one's face can disclose one's character.

Psychologists assert that almost all movements, down to the most natural reflex like coughing, reveal a person's character. However, the face is such a clear way to discover character, ability, and personality that a science, known as physiognomy, sprang up from its study. Physiognomy is judging the character of a person from the features of the face. What determines the features of the face? It is the spirit.

As is known, the cells of the body are continuously renewed. Every day millions of cells die and are replaced by new ones. Biologists say that all of the cells that make up the body are renewed every six months. Despite this continuous renewal, the main features of the face remain unchanged. We can recognize individuals through the unchanging features of the face. In the same way, one's fingerprints also remain unchanged. Neither the renewal of the cells of the fingers nor injuries nor bruises to the fingers can cause the fingerprints to change. It is again the spirit, with its characteristics peculiar to itself, that secures the stability of one's distinguishing features.

IT IS THE SPIRIT WHICH RECEIVES MORAL, SPIRITUAL, AND INTELLECTUAL EDUCATION, AND WHICH CAUSES DIFFERENCES IN CHARACTER AMONG PEOPLE

The body undergoes constant change throughout its life. Until a certain period, this change is involved in physical growth and development, making the body stronger and better. However, this growth stops at a certain point and decay sets in. Yet, as far as the spirit is concerned, a human being can continuously grow in knowledge, unlike the physical changes where eventually everything tends to decline. A human being can also continuously develop or may decay spiritually and intellectually, or, yet again, while developing or decaying they may stop at any point and then change their direction. This means that the moral, spiritual, and intellectual education of a person does not depend on their bodily changes. Also, the moral, spiritual, and intellectual differences among human beings have nothing to do with their physical structure. All human beings are composed of the same physical or material elements. What is it then that causes the moral and intellectual differences among them? What part of a human being receives the moral and intellectual education and what part of them is trained physically? Does physical training bear any relation to learning and moral and intellectual education? Can we say that the more a person is trained physically and the more they are physically developed, the more they become developed in learning and morality? If we cannot say this is so and if physical training or development has nothing to do with a person's scientific, moral, and intellectual level, why then do we not accept the existence of the spirit and how can we attribute learning, moral, and intellectual education to some biochemical processes in the brain? Are those processes swifter in some people than in others? If this is so, are some more developed intellectually because those processes are swifter or are the processes swifter because some study and are more developed intellectually? Also, what relation do those processes have with one's spiritual and moral education and development or corruption? How can we explain the differences that regular worship brings to a person's face? Why are the faces of some believers more radiant than those of unbelievers and sinners?

IT IS THE SPIRIT WHICH FEELS AND BELIEVES OR DISBELIEVES

Furthermore, a person is a being who has innumerable, complex feelings. They love or hate, rejoice or grieve, feel happy or sad, hope or despair, cherish ambitions and dreams, and feel relieved or bored... Also, they like or dislike, appreciate or disdain, and fear or become timid or become encouraged and feel enthusiastic, and they repent, become excited, and long for things. If we look through a dictionary, we can come across hundreds of words used to express human feelings. And there are great differences among human beings with respect to their feelings as well. Moreover, they are able to reflect on the events that happen around them or on the beauty of creation and thus develop in learning. People are also able to make comparisons and reason, and therefore come to believe in the Creator of all things. Then, through worship and following His commandments, humans are able to develop morally and spiritually, becoming more perfect human being. So, how else can we explain all these phenomena than by acknowledging that there is a part of humanity called the spirit? Can we attribute these to chemical processes in the brain?

THE SPIRIT IS THE BASIS OF HUMAN LIFE

In this world, matter is refined in favor of life. A lifeless body, no matter how large, like a mountain, is lonely, passive, and static. But, life enables a body the size of a bee, for example, to interact with nearly the whole world, allowing it to go as far as to say: "This world is my garden and flowers are my partners." The smaller a living body is, the more active, astonishing, and powerful its life is. A bee, a fly or even a microorganism is no different, in this respect, than an elephant. Also, the more refined matter is, the more active and powerful the body. For example, when wood burns, it produces flames and carbon. When heated, water vaporizes. We come across electrical energy in the atomic or subatomic world. We cannot see electrical energy, but we are aware of how powerful it is through its manifestations. This means that existence does not consist of the visible, material world. Rather, this world is only the apparent, mutable, and unstable dimension of existence. Behind it lies the pure invisible dimension, which uses matter to be seen and known. Thus, the essence of life, the spirit, belongs to that dimension and is therefore pure and invisible.

THE SPIRIT HAS ITS OWN COVER OR ENVELOPE

The body is not the cover of the spirit. Rather, the spirit has its own cover or envelope and when it leaves the body at death, it is not left naked, without a cover. This cover is like the "negative" of the material body and is called by various names, such as the envelope of light, the ethereal figure of the human individual, the energetic form, the second body, the astral body, the double, or the ghost (Mostly summarized from *The Essentials*, 41–49).

APPENDIX 13

ISLAM: GOD'S ORIGINAL PATTERN
ON WHICH HE HAS CREATED HUMANKIND

God created the universe so that He could be known and recognized in all His Names and Attributes, and so His creation includes one creature with free will: humankind. Of all creatures, (in addition to the jinn), only human beings can manifest the Divine Name the All-Willing, and more than any other species, His Names the All-Knowing, and the All-Speaking. That is, humanity excels other creatures in having free will, greater knowledge, and a more articulate and sophisticated mode of communication. God then endowed us with the knowledge of things ("names"), and made us His vicegerent to rule on the earth according to His laws. As having free will means that one must make choices, each person's life consists of choosing between what is right and wrong.

God endowed humankind with three principal faculties fundamental to our survival and carrying out our function as His vicegerent: *desire* for such things as the opposite sex, offspring, livelihood, and possessions; *anger* or resolve in defense and struggle; and *reason* or intellect. We are tested in this worldly life so that we may be able to develop our potential, and become intellectually and spiritually perfected, in order to deserve eternal happiness. For this reason, and in order that we may be able to progress materially, spiritually, and scientifically, God did not restrict these faculties, but has established standards to use them within proper limits so that we may be able to rise to perfection.

According to Islam, human happiness lies in disciplining our faculties in order that we may produce a harmonious and peaceful individual and collective life. If these faculties remain undisciplined, they may drive people to pursue immorality, illicit sexual relationships, unlawful livelihoods, tyranny, injustice, deception, falsehood, and other vices. To prevent the ensuing chaos and suffering, we must submit to an authority that guides and regulates our collective affairs. Since one person should not accept the authority of another just like themselves and cannot be forced to do so, and since all human beings are unable to find the exact criteria and rules for human individual and collective happiness in both worlds, humankind need a universal intellect and guidance from beyond human reason and experience, to whose authority all may assent freely. That guidance is the Religion revealed and perfected by God through His Prophets: Islam.

All Prophets came with the same essentials of faith: belief in God's Existence and Unity, the world's final destruction, Resurrection and Final Judgment, Prophethood and all Prophets without distinction between them in believing, all Divine Scriptures, angels, and Divine Destiny and Decree (including human free will). They called people to worship the One God, preached and promoted moral virtue, and condemned vice.

Differences in particular rules and injunctions were connected with the scientific-intellectual development level and the social, economic and political relationships that existed at that time, and it is also because of this that all Prophets prior to the Prophet Muḥammad, upon him be peace and God's blessing, were sent to their own people and for their own time. The Prophet Muḥammad, however, came at a time when humankind were on the threshold of a new era when there would no longer be need for a new Prophet, and therefore was sent to the whole of humankind until the Last Day. With the Prophet Muḥammad, Islam, the Religion which God chose for humankind and sent with every Prophet, was perfected and gained a universal form. Thus to be a Muslim means believing in all previous Prophets and the original previous Scriptures.

Faith or belief, the essence of religion, is not just a simple brief affirmation based on imitation. Rather, it has degrees and stages of expansion or development, just as a tree's seed is gradually transformed into a fully-grown, fruit-bearing tree. Faith contains so many truths pertaining to God's Names and the realities contained in the universe that the most perfect human knowledge and virtue are faith with all its degrees and stages of development, and knowledge of God that originates in faith based on argument and investigation. Such faith has as many degrees and grades of manifestation as the number of Divine Names. Those who attain the degree of certainty of faith coming from direct observation of the truths on which faith is based, can study the universe as a kind of Divine Scripture.

Another degree of faith is known as certainty coming from the direct experience of its truths. This depends on God's consciousness, regular worship, strict obedience to God's orders and prohibitions, and reflection, and those who possess it can challenge the world. So, Muslims' foremost duty is to attain the greatest degree of faith that they can, and to communicate it to others.

Faith engenders different kinds of worship, the basic ones of which are the Prescribed Prayers, Fasting, the Prescribed Purifying Alms, and the Pilgrimage, and requires obeying prohibitions (e.g., avoiding killing, all kinds of unlawful sexual relations, intoxicants, gambling, usury, and deception). Those seeking to strengthen their faith and attain higher ranks of perfection should be careful of acts of their hearts and intellects (e.g., contemplation, reflection, invocation, the recitation of God's Names, self-criticism, perseverance, patience, thankfulness, self-discipline, and perfect reliance upon God). Moral virtues are the fruits of religious life.

Islam also regulates our collective life. By means of faith and worship, as well as its intellectual, moral, and spiritual principles, Islam educates us in the best possible way. In addition, it uses its socio-economic principles and the virtues it emphasizes, such as solidarity, mutual assistance, and altruism, to establish an ideal society free of dissension, corruption, anarchy, and terror, one that allows everyone to obtain happiness both in this world and in the Hereafter. Its penal law is principally directed toward preserving individual and collective happiness.

The Qur'ān, the universe, and humankind are three manifestations of one truth. Therefore, in principle, there can be no contradiction or incompatibility between the truths of the Qur'ān, described as the Revealed Universe and issuing from the Divine Attribute of Speech, and truths derived from the objective study of its counterpart, described as the Created Qur'ān, and issuing from the Divine Attributes of Power and Will. If there sometimes appear to be contradictions, they arise from an incorrect approach to either the Qur'ān or the universe and humankind, or to both at the same time. An Islamic civilization true to its authentic, original roots and dynamics contains no contradiction between science (the objective study of the natural world) and the Religion (the guide for the personal and collective effort to seek God's good pleasure). True faith is not a dogmatic commitment based on blind imitation, but rather it should appeal to our reason and heart, and combine reason's affirmation and the heart's inward experience and conviction.

Islam is primarily based on *Tawḥīd*, absolute faith in God's Oneness without any partners whatsoever in His Divinity, Lordship, and Sovereignty. Given this, the universe is an integral whole of interrelated and cooperative parts in which a splendid coordination, harmony, and order are displayed, both throughout the universe and within each living organism. This harmony and order come from the Oneness of the One Who created them and Who is absolute, without partner, peer, or like. The universe operates according to the laws God established for it, and therefore is literally Muslim – absolutely submitted to God. Thus its operations are stable, orderly, and harmonious.

So, Islam is the Religion of all creation, which every thing and every being follows willingly or unwillingly. In this sense, even unbelievers are Muslims, as far as the functioning of their bodies is considered. In addition, as stated in a *hadith*, the Messenger declares that every human being is born in the original nature or pattern of Islam and is prone to accept Islam as Religion in their life. However, under the influence of a person's family, environment, and the education they receive, they may adopt another religion, another way of life. But if they can remain free of prejudices and the misguiding influence of their inclinations, bodily desires, worldly ambitions, the delusions or drives of their carnal self, and especially preserve their primordial, moral purity, they can find Islam or be rewarded by God with Islam.

THE TRUST HUMAN HAS UNDERTAKEN

Although the Trust mentioned in the verse 33: 72 includes the Divine Religion which humankind must follow in life, it is not restricted to it. Not only humankind, but also the jinn are responsible for following the Divine Religion. Some commentators are of the opinion that the Trust is human free will or the faculty of volition. This is also included in the meaning of the Trust, but we should bear in mind that the jinn also have been endowed with free will. So, what is meant by the Trust is, first of all, the human ego.

God has absolutely no limits at all. So something absolute and unlimited cannot be determined in such a way that its essential nature can be comprehended. For example, light undetermined by darkness cannot be known or perceived. However, light can be determined if a real or hypothetical boundary line of darkness is drawn. In the same way, the Divine Attributes and Names (e.g., Knowledge, Power, Wisdom, and Compassion) cannot be determined, for they are all-encompassing and have no limits nor anything similar. Thus, what they are essentially cannot be known or perceived. A hypothetical boundary is needed for them to become known.

God Almighty, so to speak, has drawn a hypothetical line before His Names and Attributes and created ego, reflecting in it all His Names and Attributes. Since absolute Independence is the most essential quality of Divinity, ego finds in itself the same quality. It imagines within itself a fictitious lordship, power, and knowledge, and so posits a boundary line, hypothesizes a limit to God's all-encompassing Attributes, and says: "This is mine, and the rest is His." Ego thus makes a division.

Through this imagined lordship, ego can and must understand the Lordship of the Creator of the universe. By means of its own apparent ownership, it can understand the real Ownership of its Creator, saying: "As I am the owner of this house, the Creator is the Owner of this creation." Through its partial knowledge, ego comes to understand His Absolute Knowledge. Through its defective, acquired art, it can intuit the Exalted Fashioner's primary, originative art. For example, ego says: "I built and arranged this house, so there must be One Who made and arranged this universe." So, ego is the key to the Divine Names and Attributes and also to solving the enigma of creation.

However, ego has two aspects or faces. One face looks toward its Creator and therefore to good. With this aspect, it only receives what is given; it cannot create. It is not the origin of the good and virtues God creates in or through it. The other face looks toward evil. Here ego is active and the source and doer of all evils.

Essentially, as stated above, ego is like a measure, a mirror, or an instrument for seeing or finding out. Its real nature is only indicative – like a letter that has no meaning by itself – and indicates the meaning of things other than itself. Its lordship is completely hypothetical, and its own existence is so weak and insubstantial that it cannot bear or support anything on its own. Rather, ego is a kind of scale or measure showing the degrees and quantities of what is measured. The Necessarily Existent Being's absolute, all-encompassing, and limitless Attributes can become known through it.

Ego must realize that it is God's servant and that it is to serve the One other than itself and that its essential nature has only an indicative function. It must understand that it bears the meaning of the One rather than that of itself and that it can be meaningful only when it points to that One upon Whom its existence depends. Its existence and life depend upon that One's creativity and Existence. Its feeling of ownership is illusory, for it enjoys only an apparent, temporary ownership by the real Owner's permission and it only has a shadow-like reality. It is a contingent entity, an insignificant shadow manifesting the true and necessary Reality. Its function of serving as a measure and balance for its Creator's Attributes and essential Qualities is a conscious willing service.

Those who know and realize that this is the reality of their essential nature or the human ego act accordingly: these are included in: *He is indeed prosperous who has grown it in purity (away from self-aggrandizing rebellion against God)* (91: 9). Such people truly carry out the trust and, through their ego, see what the universe really is and what duties it performs. They also find that their ego confirms the information they have gathered about the universe. As a result, this information will retain the quality of light and wisdom for them, and will not be changed into darkness and futility. When ego has performed its duty in this way, it renounces its claim to lordship and hypothetical ownership (mere devices of measurement) and proclaims: His is the sovereignty and ownership of all beings, and to Him are due all praise and thanks. His is the Judgment and rule, and to Him we are returning. Thus it achieves true worship and attains the rank of the best pattern of creation.

But if ego forgets the Divine purpose of its creation, abandons the duty of its nature, and views itself as a self-existing being independent of the Creator, it betrays the Trust. Thus it supposes itself to be a permanent reality that has, as its duty, the quest for self-satisfaction. It falsely assumes that it owns its being and is the real lord and master of its own domain. Those who see ego in this way fall into the class of those warned and threatened by: *And he is indeed lost who has corrupted it (in self-aggrandizing and rebellion against God)* (91: 10). This development is responsible for all the varieties of polytheism, evil, and deviation that have caused the heavens, earth, and the mountains to be terrified of assuming the Trust – lest they might be led to associate partners with God, because such an ego grows and swells until it gradually permeates all parts of a human being. Like some huge monster, it completely swallows such people so that they and their faculties consist of nothing more than an ego. Eventually, the ego of the human race gives strength to the individual ego through mere individualism and national racism. This causes the ego, swollen by support from the ego of race, to contest, like Satan, the Majestic Maker's commands. Finally, taking itself as a yardstick, it compares everyone and everything with itself, divides God's Sovereignty between them and other causes, and begins to associate partners with God in the most grievous manner. It is such people that are being referred to in: *Surely associating partners with God is indeed a tremendous wrong* (31: 13).

This betrayal causes the ego to sink into absolute ignorance. Even if it has absorbed thousands of branches of science, its ignorance is only compounded by its knowledge. Whatever glimmers of knowledge of God that it may have obtained from the universe through its senses or reflective powers have been extinguished, for it can no longer find within itself anything with which to confirm, polish, and maintain them. Whatever comes to the ego is stained with the colors within it. Even if pure wisdom comes, it becomes absolutely futile within an ego stained by atheism, polytheism, or other forms of denying the All-Mighty. If the whole universe were full of shining indications of God, a dark point in that ego would hide them from view, as though they were invisible.

We will now shed some light on the truth of this subject. Consider the following: From Adam's time until the present, two great currents or lines of thought have spread their branches in all directions and in every class of humanity, just like two tall trees. One is the line of Prophethood and Religion; the other is that of mere human thinking. Whenever they agree and unite (whenever human thinking joins the Religion in obedience and service to it), humankind have experienced brilliant happiness in individual and collective life. But whenever they have followed separate paths, truth and goodness have accumulated on the side of Prophethood and the Religion, whereas error, evil, and deviation have been drawn to the side of human thinking.

Human thinking, whenever it has split from the Religion, has taken the form of a tree of *Zaqqūm* that spreads its dark veils of ascribing partners to God and of all other innumerable kinds of misguidance. On the branch of empowered reason, which is one of the three cardinal faculties with which human beings are endowed, it has yielded the fruits of materialism and naturalism for the intellect's consumption. On the branch of empowered anger and passion, it has produced such tyrants as the Nimrod and the Pharaoh who tyrannize people. On the branch of empowered animal desires and appetites, it has produced the fruits of "goddesses," idols and those who have claimed Divine status for themselves. This line has shown the "lowest of the low" into which humankind can fall.

In contrast, the blessed line of Prophethood, which takes the form of the *Tūbā* tree of worship, has borne the fruit of Prophets, Messengers, saints, and the righteous in the garden of earth and on the branch of empowered reason. On the branch of empowered anger, the branch of defense against and repelling of evil, it has yielded the fruits of virtuous and just rulers. On the branch of empowered animal desires or appetites, which have taken the form of empowered attractiveness, it has borne the fruits of generous, benevolent persons of good character and modest bearing throughout history. As a result, this line has demonstrated how humankind are the perfect fruit of creation.

Prophethood considers that the aim and function of human beings is to be molded by the Divine values and to achieve good character. Prophets believed that people should perceive their weakness and seek refuge with Divine Power and rely on Divine Strength, realize their insufficiency and essential poverty and trust in Divine Mercy, know their need and seek help from Divine Wealth, see their faults and plead for pardon through Divine Forgiveness, and perceive their inadequacy and glorify Divine Perfection.

According to human thinking that has been deviated, power is approved. "Might is right" is the norm. Its maxims are: "All power to the strongest;" "Survival of the fittest;" "Winner takes all;" and "In power there is right." It has given moral support to tyranny, encouraged dictators, and urged oppressors to claim Divinity. By ascribing the beauty in "works of art" to the works themselves, and not to the Maker and Fashioner's pure, sacred Beauty, it says: "How beautiful it is," not: "How beautifully it is made," and thus considers each as an idol worthy of adoration.

A GLOSSARY OF GOD'S ALL-BEAUTIFUL NAMES

God has many All-Beatiful Names. He is and should be called by them. The following are those of them that are most famous and mentioned either in the Qur'ān or by God's Messenger in his speeches.

Allāh: Translated as God, *Allāh* is the proper Name of the Divine Being Who creates and administers His creatures, individually and as a whole, Who provides, brings up, sustains, protects, guides each and all, Who causes to perish and revives each and all, Who rewards or punishes, etc. All His Attributes are Attributes of absolute perfection, and He is absolutely free from any and all defect. He is Unique and Single, having no like or resemblance and nothing is comparable to Him. He is absolutely beyond any human conception: "Eyes comprehend Him not, but He comprehends all eyes (6: 103)." God is the Unique, Single Being with the exclusive right to be worshipped and to be made the sole aim of life. He is loved in and of Himself. Everything is dependent on Him and subsists by Him. Every truth has its source in Him. Knowledge of God (in the sense of the Arabic *'ilm*) is impossible in respect of His Being or Essence (*Dhāt*). Because there is none like or comparable unto Him, it is therefore impossible to grasp or comprehend His Essence. However, we can recognize God or have some knowledge of Him (in the sense of the Arabic *ma'rifah*) through His works, acts, Names, Attributes and Essential Qualities (*shu'ūn*). Awareness of His works (what we see in the world, His creation) leads us to become aware of His acts, and that awareness leads us to His Names and Attributes which, in turn, lead us to His Essential Qualities, and thence to awareness of the One Who has these Qualities.

(Al-)'Adl: The All-Just

(Al-)'Afuww: The All-Pardoning (Who overlooks the faults of His servants); The One Who grants remission; The One Who excuses much.

(Al-)Ahad: The Unique One of Absolute Unity (Who is beyond all kinds of human conceptions of Him and absolutely free from having any partners, likes, parents, and sons or daughters; One Who manifests His certain particular Names on an individual thing or being to give that thing or being their unique individuality)

Ahkamu 1-Hākimīn: The Best of judges (and the Most Powerful of sovereigns)

Ahlu 1-maghfirah: The Lord of forgiveness

Ahlu 't-taqwā: The Lord of righteousness and piety

Ahsanu 1-Khāliqīn: The Creator Who creates everything in the best and most appropriate form and has the ultimate rank of creativity

(Al-)Ākhir: The Last (Who eternally exists while all other beings are perishable)

(Al-)'Alīm: The All-Knowing

Ālimu 1-ghaybi wa 'shshahādah: The Knower of the unseen (all that lies beyond sense-perception) and the witnessed (the sensed realm)

(Al-)'Aliyy: The All-Exalted

(Al-)Amān: The One in Whose Refuge Is Sought

(Al-)'Atūf: The All-Affectionate

(Al-)Awwal: The First (Whom there is none that precedes)

(Al-)'Azīz: The All-Glorious with irresistible might (Whom no force can prevent from doing what He wills)

(Al-)Badī': The All-Originating with nothing preceding Him to imitate

Badī'u's-samāwāti wa 1-arḍ: The Originator of the heavens and the earth with nothing preceding Him to imitate

(Al-)Bāith: The One Who restores life to the dead

(Al-)Bāqī: The All-Permanent

(Al-)Bārī: The All-Holy Creator (Who is absolutely free from having any partners and Who makes every being perfect and different from others)

(Al-)Barr: The All-Benign

(Al-)Bāsiṭ: The All-Expanding

(Al-)Baṣīr: The All-Seeing

(Al-)Bāṭin: The All-Inward, (Who encompasses the whole existence from within in His Knowledge, and there is none that is more penetrating than Him)

(Al-)Burhān: The All-Proving and Demonstrating

(Ad-)Dārr: The Creator of evil and harm

(Ad-)Dayyān: The Supreme Ruler and All-Requiting (of good and evil)

Dhu 1-'Arsh: The Owner (Lord) of the Supreme Throne

Dhu 1-Faḍl: The One (or Lord) of grace and bounty

Dhu 1-Jalāl wa 1-ikrām: The One of Majesty and Grace

Dhu 1-Ma'ārij: The One Having Stairs of Ascent (to Him)

Dhu 1-Quwwah: The Lord of all might

Dhu ṭ-Ṭawl: The One limitless in His bounty

Fāliqu 1-ḥabb wa 'n-nawā: The splitting of the grain and the fruit-stone (so that they germinate by His command)

Fāliqu 1-iṣbāḥ: The Splitting of the dawn (from the darkness of night)

(Al-)Fard: The All-Independent, Single One (free from having any equals or likes in His Essence and Attributes)

(Al-)Fāṭir: The All-Originating (with a unique individuality)

Fāṭiru 's-samāwāti wa 1-arḍ: The Originator of the heavens and the earth (each with particular features)

(Al-)Fattāḥ: The One Who judges between people with truth and separates them

(Al-)Ghaffār: The One Who forgives much

(Al-)Ghafūr: The All-Forgiving

Ghālibun alā emrihī: The One Who always prevails in whatever be His Will

(Al-)Ghaniyy: The All-Wealthy and Self-Sufficient

(Al-)Habīb: The All-Loving and Loved

(Al-)Hādī: The All-Guiding

(Al-)Hafiyy: The All-Gracious

(Al-)Hafīz: The All-Preserving and Keeping recorded (everything and every deed of His servants)

(Al-)Hakam: The All-Judging (who settles the matters between people)

(Al-)Hakīm: The All-Wise (in Whose every act and decree there are many instances of wisdom)

(Al-)Halīm: The All-Clement (showing no haste to punish the errors of His servants)

(Al-)Hamīd: The All-Praiseworthy (as the Lord Who creates, provides, and rears)

(Al-)Hannān: The All-Kind and Caring

(Al-)Haqq: The Ultimate Truth and Ever-Constant

(Al-)Hasīb: The All-Sufficing as One Who reckons and settles the accounts (of His servants);

(Al-)Hayy: The All-Living

(Al-)Jabbār: The All-Compelling of supreme majesty (Who subdues wrong and restores right)

(Al-)Jalīl: The All-Majestic

(Al-)Jāmi': The One Having All Excellences in the Infinite Degree; the All-Gathering

(Al-)Jamīl: The All-Gracious

(Al-)Kabīr: The All-Great

(Al-)Kāfī: The All-Sufficing

(Al-)Karīm: The All-Munificent

(Al-)Khabīr: The All-Aware

(Al-)Khāfid: The All-Abasing (whomever He wills)

(Al-)Khāliq: the Creator (Who determines measure for everything and brings it into existence out of nothing)

(Al-)Khallāq: The Supreme Creator

Khayru 'l-fāṣilīn: The Best Judge between truth and falsehood

Khayru 'l-Hākimīn: The Best of judges

Khayru 'r-Rāziqīn: The One Who is the Best to be sought as provider with the ultimate rank of providing

(Al-)Laṭīf: The All-Subtle (penetrating to the most minute dimensions of all things)

(Al-)Mahmūd: The All-Praised

(Al-)Majīd: The All-Sublime

(Al-)Malik: The Sovereign

(Al-)Māni': The All-Preventing and Withdrawing

Māliku 'l-mulk: The absolute Master of all dominion

Mālik-i Yawm ad-Dīn: The absolute Master of the Day of Judgment

(Al-)Mannān: The All-Bounteous and Favoring

(Al-)Ma'rūf: The One Known (with His works); The All-Recognized

(Al-)Matīn: The All-Forceful

(Al-)Mu'āfī: The Giver of health

(Al-)Mu'akhkhir: The One Who leaves behind

(Al-)Mubdī: The All-Initiating

(Al-)Mubīn: The One Whom nothing is hidden and Who makes all truth manifest

(Al-)Mughnī: The All-Enriching

(Al-)Muhaymin: The All-Watchful Guardian

(Al-)Muhīṭ: The All-Encompassing

(Al-)Muhṣī: The All-Counting and Recording

(Al-Muhsin: The All-Benevolent

(Al-)Muhyī: The One Who revives, Who gives life to the dead

(Al-)Mu'īd: The All-Returning and Restoring

(Al-)Mu'īn: The All-Helping and Supplying

(Al-)Mu'izz: The All-Exalting and Honoring

(Al-)Mujīb: The All-Answering (of prayers) and Meeting (of needs)

(Al-)Mu'min: The Supreme Author of safety and security Who bestows faith and removes all doubt

(Al-)Mumīt: The One Causing to Die; the All-Dealer of death

(Al-)Mundhir: The All-Informing and Warning

(Al-)Muntaqim: The Ever-Able to requite

(Al-)Muqaddim: The One Who causes to precede and places before

(Al-)Muqaddir: The All-Determining

(Al-)Muqīt: The All-Aiding and Sustaining

(Al-)Muqsiṭ: The All-Dealing of Justice

(Al-)Muqtadir: The All-Omnipotent, the Ever-Able (to do whatever He wills)

(Al-)Murīd: The All-Willing

(Al-)Mūsī: The All-Expanding (of the universe and sustenance for His creatures)

(Al-)Muṣawwir: The All-Fashioning

(Al-)Musta'ān: The One Whose Help Is Ever Sought

(Al-)Muta'āl: The All-Transcending

(Al-)Mutakabbir: The One Who has exclusive right for all greatness

(Al-)Mudhill: The All-Abasing

(Al-)Mu'ṭī: The All-Granting

(An-)Nāfi': The All-Favoring and Giving of Benefit

(An-)Naṣīr: The All-Helping and Giving Victory

(An-)Nūr: The All-Light (see 24: 35 and the note to it)

(Al-)Qāim: The All-Observing and Controlling

(Al-)Qābiḍ: The All-Constricting

(Al-)Qadīr: The All-Powerful

(Al-)Qāhir: The All-Omnipotent (Who has full sway over all that exists)

(Al-)Qahhār: The All-Overwhelming (with absolute sway over all that exists).

(Al-)Qarīb: The All-Near

(Al-)Qawiyy: The All-Strong

(Al-)Qayyūm: The Self-Subsisting (by Whom all subsist)

(Al-)Quddūs: The All-Holy and All-Pure (Who is absolutely free of any defect and keeps the universe clean)

(Ar-)Rabb: The Lord (God as the Creator, Provider, Trainer, Upbringer, and Director of all creatures)

Rabbu 1-'ālamīn: The Lord of the worlds

(Ar-)Rāfi': The All-Exalting

Rafī'u 'd-darajāt: The All-Exalted above all degrees

(Ar-)Rahīm: The All-Compassionate (Who has particular compassion for each of His creatures in their maintenance, and for His believing servants especially in the other world)

(Ar-)Rahmān: The All-Merciful (Who has mercy on the whole existence and provides for them without making a distinction between believers and unbelievers)

(Ar-)Raqīb: The All-Watchful

(Ar-)Rashīd: The All-Guide to what is correct

(Ar-)Raūf: The All-Pitying

(Ar-)Razzāq: The All-Providing

(As-)Sabūr: The All-Patient (Whom no haste induces to rush into an action)

Sādiqu 1-wa'd: The All-True to His Promise

(As-)Salām: the Supreme Author of peace and salvation

(As-)Samad: The Eternally-Besought-of-All (Himself is needy of nothing).

(As-)Samī': The All-Hearing

(As-)Sāni': The Maker

(As-)Sattār: The All-Veiling (of His servants' shortcomings and sins)

Sarī'u 1-hisāb: The One Who is Most Swift in reckoning

Shadīdu 1-'iqāb: The One Who is Most Severe in retributing

(Ash-)Shāfī: The All-Healing

(Ash-)Shāhīd: The All-Witnessing

(Ash-)Shakūr: The All-Responsive (to the gratitude of His creatures)

(As-)Subhān: The All-Glorified

(As-)Sultān: The Absolute, Eternal Authority

(At-)Tawwāb: The One Who accepts repentance and returns it with liberal forgiveness and additional reward

(Al-)Wājid: The Ever-Present and All-Finding

(Al-)Wadūd: The All-Tender and Excusing; The All-Loving and All-Beloved

(Al-)Wahhāb: The All-Bestowing

(Al-)Wāhid: The One (having no partners and equals; One Who manifests all His Names on the whole of the universe or a species or on a whole)

(Al-)Wakīl: The One to rely on and to Whom affairs should be entrusted

(al-)Wālī: The All-Governing

(Al-)Waliyy: The Guardian, the Protecting Friend (to rely on)

(Al-)Wārith: The One Who survives all beings and inherits them

(Al-)Wāsi': The All-Embracing (in His Mercy and Knowledge)

(Az-)Zāhir: The All-Outward (Who encompasses the whole existence from outside, and there is none that encompasses Him)

A GLOSSARY OF NAMES

(The Prophet) Muḥammad, upon him be peace and blessings (571 Makkah–632 Madīnah): God's Last Prophet and Messenger, with whom God's Religion – al-Islām – was universally perfected and conveyed. Born in Makkah in 571, and raised as a Messenger in 610. After 13 harsh years in Makkah, he emigrated to Madīnah. He was made the target of hostilities from hypocrites within Madīnah and pagan tribes from outside. He also had to encounter the Jewish tribes and the Byzantine empire. Within a very short period he carried his mission to a decisive victory and submitted his soul to God in 632.

'Abdu'llāh ibn 'Abbās (d., 687): A Companion of the Prophet (upon him be peace and blessings), was the most outstanding scholar of Qur'ānic interpretation in his time and one of the leading jurists. He was very sagacious.

'Abdu'llāh ibn 'Amr ibn al-'Āṣ (d., 684): One of the great scholars among the Companion. He was noted for his devotion and learning and prepared one of the first collections of *Hadīth*.

'Abdu'llāh ibn Jubayr (d., 625): A Companion of the Prophet, participated in the battles of Badr and Uhud. In the latter battle, in which he was martyred, he was the commander of the archers.

'Abdu'llāh ibn Mas'ūd (d., 653): One of the most learned Companions of the Prophet, upon him be peace and blessings. He was noted especially for his nearness to the Prophet and juristic caliber.

'Abdu'llāh ibn Ubayy ibn Salūl (d., 630): He was the head of the hypocrite block in Madīnah, and the foremost in enmity towards the Prophet.

'Abdu'llāh ibn 'Umar (d., 692): A famous Companion and son of 'Umar, the second Caliph, was famous for his piety and for transmitting many Traditions from the Prophet.

'Abdu'l-Qādir al-Jilānī (d. 1166): One of the most celebrated Sufi masters. A student of jurisprudence and Hadith, he became known as the "spiritual axis" of his age and the "the greatest succor." He wrote *Kitāb al-Ghunyah*, *Futūḥ al-Ghayb*, and *Al-Fatḥ ar-Rabbānī*.

'Abdu'r-Raḥmān ibn 'Awf (d., 652): One of the earliest converts to Islam and one of the ten whom the Prophet informed would be admitted to Paradise. He was a prosperous merchant who acquired great wealth of which he spent generously in God's cause.

Abū Bakr (aṣ-Ṣiddīq) (573–634): One of the first four to embrace Islam and greatest and closest Companions of the Prophet Muḥammad, upon him be peace and blessings. The first caliph after the Prophet. He has always been remembered with his attachment of the Prophet and support to him, truthfulness, and simple life.

Abū'd-Dardā', 'Uwaymir ibn Mālik (d., 652): A distinguished Companion who contributed to the collection of the Qur'ān, and was known for his bravery as well as his piety and religious devotion.

Abū Dharr al-Ghifārī, Jundub ibn Junādah (d., 652): A prominent Companion and among the earliest converts to Islam. He was known for his piety, austerity, and straightforwardness.

Abū Hurayrah, Abdu'r-Raḥmān (d., 679): A Companion of the Prophet who transmitted a very large number of Traditions.

Abū Lahab: Abū Lahab was One of the Prophet Muḥammad's uncles. Abū Lahab, meaning the father of flame, is a nickname that was given to him while he was a child because of the rosy glow on his cheeks. He was one of the fiercest enemies of the Messenger and Islam. He died from great sorrow because of the defeat of the pagan Quraysh at the battle of Badr.

Abū Ṭālib, ‘Abd Manāf ibn ‘Abdu’l-Muṭṭalib (d., 620): An uncle of the Prophet and the father of the fourth Caliph, ‘Ali. Even though he did not embrace Islam, he continued to provide protection for the Prophet against his enemies.

Abū Yazīd al-Bistāmī (d. 873): One of the most famous Sufi (Muslim spiritual masters) and saints

(The people of) Ād: An ancient people known throughout Arabia for their legendary prosperity. The region called al-Ahqāf that is situated between Hijaz, Yemen, and Yamāmah was their native land. The Prophet Hūd, upon him be peace, was sent to them, and since they persisted in associating partners with God and other forms of wrongdoing, they were destroyed with a sandstorm which lasted seven nights and eight days.

‘Adīy ibn Ḥātim (d., 687): A Companion who took a prominent part in the military expeditions against the apostates during the caliphate of Abū Bakr.

Ahl al-Bayt: The household. As a term, it refers to the household of the Prophet Muhammad, upon him be peace and blessings, including Fāṭimah, his daughter, and her husband ‘Ali, and their sons Ḥasan and Ḥusayn.

Ahl al-Kitāb: The People of the Book. Any people who have been given a Divine Book. The Qur’ān tends to use this term particularly for the Jews and Christians. The term also included the Sabeans and the Magians.

Ahl al-Kitāb wa’s-Sunnah: The People of the Book and the Sunnah. They are the Muslims who strive to follow exactly the teachings of the Qur’ān and the way of the Prophet Muhammad, upon him be peace and blessings, as reported by his Companions.

Aḥmad: Another name of the Prophet Muhammad, upon him be peace and blessings. The Prophet Jesus, upon him be peace, prophesied his coming with this name.

Aḥmad ibn Ḥanbal (d., 855): The founder of one of the four Sunnī schools of law in Islam. He valiantly suffered persecution for the sake of his religious conviction. His *Musnad* is famous, which contained about 40.000 Traditions that he collected.

‘Āisha bint Abī Bakr (? – 676): Daughter of Abu Bakr as-Siddīq, may God be pleased with him, and wife of the Prophet Muhammad, upon him be peace and blessings. She was one the foremost scholars among the Companions. She had numerous narrations from the Messenger.

(al-)Ālūsī, Maḥmūd ibn ‘Abdu’llāh al-Husaynī (d., 1854): One of the leading commentators of the Qur’ān, a jurist, and a Sufi. His commentary *Rūḥ al-Ma‘ānī* is an encyclopedic work which continues to command considerable respect.

‘Ammār ibn Yāsir (d., 657): One of the early converts to Islam and the greatest of the Companions. He served the cause of Islam selflessly and lived a moderate life. He was appointed the governor of Kūfah by ‘Umar, the second Caliph.

Anas ibn Mālik (d., 712): A distinguished Companion who had the honor of serving the Prophet for many years. He was among the Companions who made numerous narrations from the Prophet, upon him be peace and blessings.

‘Arafāt: The pilgrimage site, about 25 km east of Makkah where the pilgrims have to stay from midday to sunset on the eve of the ‘Īd al-Aḍḥā (the Festive Day of Sacrifice)

‘Ali ibn Abī Ṭālib (606–661): One of the first four to embrace Islam and greatest companions of the Prophet Muhammad, upon him be peace and blessings, and his cousin and son-in-law. The last of the four rightly guided caliphs. He has been renowned for his profound knowledge, deep spirituality, great courage and sacrifices for God’s cause, and eloquence.

(al-)‘Arīm: The dam which the people of Sheba built and whose traces still exist in Yemen

Āsyā: The wife of the Pharaoh, who rejected the Prophet Moses and his call. She is one of the four greatest women of all times, the other three being: Maryam (Mary), the mother of the Prophet Jesus, upon him be peace; Khadījah, the first wife of the Prophet Muhammad, upon him be peace and blessings; Fāṭimah, the daughter of the Prophet Muḥammad, may God be pleased with them.

al-Aykah*:* The region which was located in the present day ʿAqabah. In ancient times a pagan people lived there, and the Prophet Shuʿayb was sent to them. However, they denied him and were ultimately destroyed with an "awful blast."

(The Prophet) Ayyūb (Job)*:* A Prophet of Islam who was renowned for his patience and constancy.

(The Battle of) Badr*:* The first decisive encounter between the Muslims of Madīnah and the pagan tribe of the Quraysh of Makkah in 624 C.E., and 2 A.H. The Muslims won the battle, which proved to be the turning point and one of the greatest victories in Muslim history, perhaps even the greatest.

Bakkah: Another, rarely used name for Makkah

Banū Isrāīl: The Children of Israel – the Children of the Prophet Jacob. The Qurʾān uses this term as an honorific title. By referring to the Jews as the children of a Prophet (Isrāīl, the Prophet Jacob, a pure servant of God), the Qurʾān means that they are expected to believe in the Prophet Muḥammad as well and so fulfill their covenant with God. This usage also establishes an important principle of good manners, especially in calling people to the Straight Path, that one should address people with the titles they like to be addressed with.

Banū Kaynuqaʿ, Banū Nadīr, and **Banū Quraydah**: The three Jewish tribes of Madīnah. When God's Messenger emigrated to Madīnah, he concluded an agreement with all of them, but none of them remained faithful to their agreement, and favored and supported the Makkan polytheists and the hypocrites in Madīnah against the Muslims. In the end, all of them had to leave Madīnah.

(al)-Bayhaqī, Abū Bakr Aḥmad ibn al-Ḥusayn (d., 1066): An erudite scholar of *Hadīth* and a prominent scholar of the Shafiʿī school of law. The author of some well-known books such as *as-Sunan al-Kubrā* ("A Compendium

of The Prophet's Traditions"), *Dalāʾil an-Nubuwah* ("The Proofs of the Prophethood of Muḥammad"), and *Shuʿab al-Īmān* ("The Aspects of Faith").

(al-)Bayt al-Maʿmūr*:* A House in the heaven whose nature we do not know and where the angels pray

(al-)Bayt al-Maqdis (Masjid al-Aqṣā): The famous *masjid* (mosque) in al-Quds (Jerusalem). It was the first *qiblah* during the Messenger's time. Then God ordered turning towards the Kaʿbah in Makkah. Al-Bayt al-Maqdis is the third in virtue or degree among the places of worship in the world, the first being the Masjid al-Ḥarām in Makkah and the second being Masjid an-Nabiyy in Madīnah

Bediüzzaman Said Nursi (1877-1960): One of the greatest Muslim thinkers and scholars of the 20th century. He wrote about the truhts and essentials of the Islamic faith, the meaning and importance of worship, morality, and the meaning of existence. He is very original in his approaches. *Sözler* ("The Words"), *Mektubat* ("The Letters"), *Lemʿalar* ("The Gleams"), and *Şualar* ("The Rays") are among his famous works.

Bilāl ibn Rabāḥ al-Ḥabashī (d., 641): He was a "black" slave in the house of one of the fiercest enemies of Islam in Makkah when he embraced Islam. He suffered great persecutions. He was a *muʾadhdhin* (caller to Prayer) of the Prophet, upon him be peace and blessings.

(al)-Bukhārī, Muḥammad ibn Ismaʾīl (d., 870). The most famous traditionist of Islam, whose work is one of the six most authentic collections of *Hadīth*, generally considered to be the soundest book after the Book of God.

(al-)Busīri, Muḥammad ibn Saʿīd (1211–1295): An Egyptian saintly scholar, calligrapher and poet. He has poems in which he expressed his deep love for the Messenger and his Companions. *Al-Qasīda al-Burdah* is the most famous of them.

(ad-)Dārimī, ʿAbduʾllāh ibn ʿAbduʾr-Raḥmān (d., 869): One of the outstanding scholars of *Hadīth* whose *Musnad* is highly regarded.

(The Prophet) Dāwūd (David): A Messenger of God. He was the Caliph of the Israelite state. The *Zabūr* (Psalms) was given to him.

Dhu'l-Kifl: As generally accepted, he is the Israelite Prophet Ezekiel. He was among the Children of Israel driven out of Jerusalem to Babylon. He lived and performed his mission of calling people to God in the land of the Chaldeans by the river Chebar, roughly between 594–572 BC.

Dhu'l-Qarnayn: A beloved servant of God who made great conquests in His Name. It is not certain whether he was a Prophet or not.

Dhu'n-Nūn: The Companion of the Fish. This is a title of the Prophet Yūnus (Jonah), upon him be peace.

Fāṭimah (614?–632): Daughter of the Prophet Muḥammad, upon him be peace and blessings, from Khadījah, and wife of 'Ali ibn Abī Ṭālib. She is one of the four greatest women of all times, and the Prophet's progeny has descended from her.

Fir'awn (the Pharaoh): The title of the kings of the Coptic Egyptians; the king to whom and whose people the Prophets Moses and Aaron were sent, and who rejected them. He was finally drowned in the sea with his army.

(al-)Firdaws: The highest level of Paradise

Gülen, M. Fethullah (1941–): A well-known scholar, intellectual, writer, and poet from modern Turkey. He has more than forty books, many of which are among the best-sellers in Turkey. Known also for his activities of education and endeavors to promote tolerance and dialogue among the civilizations and followers of different religions.

(al-)Ḥākim an-Naysābūrī, Muḥammad ibn 'Abdu'llāh ibn Hamdawayh (d., 1014): Known both for having memorized a very large number of Traditions and for enriching the field of *Hadīth* by his works, especially by *al-Mustadrak 'alā'ṣ-Ṣaḥīḥayn* ("An Addition to the Two Most Authentic Books of Hadīth" – al-Bukhārī and Muslim), containing the Traditions which are as authentic as those found in al-Bukhārī and Muslim but not found in them.

Ḥamzah ibn 'Abdu'l-Muṭṭalib (d., 625): An uncle of the Prophet, and one of the leaders of the Quraysh, who embraced Islam before *Hijrah*, and became a major source of strength for it. He fought valiantly in the Battle of Badr and was martyred in the Battle of Uhud and is regarded as one of the greatest heroes of Islam.

(al-)Ḥasan al-Baṣrī (d., 728): One of the most distinguished scholars of the *Tābiūn* (the generation succeeding the Companions). In addition to his profound knowledge, he was also known for his piety and righteousness.

Hijāz: The region along the western seaboard of Arabia, in which Makkah, Madīnah, Jiddah, and Ṭā'if are situated

Hirā': The cave in Jabal an-Nūr (the Mount Nūr) where the first Revelation came to God's Messenger in 610 C.E.

Hārūt & Mārūt: The two angels sent by God to the Children of Israel during their exile in Babylon, who taught them about something of occult sciences so that they could be protected against sorcery and similar evils

Hārūn (Aaron): The brother of the Prophet Moses whom God chose as a Messenger and sent as his associate helper against the Pharaoh

Ḥawwā: Eve, wife of Adam, upon him be peace.

(al-)Ḥijr: The north-west of Arabia where the people of Thamūd lived in ancient times. The Prophet Ṣāliḥ was sent to them. Their main city was *Madā'in Ṣāliḥ*, situated along the route of the famous Hijāz railway. Some remnants of this city can still be found.

Hubal: The chief idol of the pagan people of Makkah when the Messenger began his mission. It was an image of a man, and was said to have been originally brought to Arabia from Syria.

(The Prophet) Hūd: The Messenger sent to the people of Ād.

Ḥudhayfah ibn al-Yamān (d., 656): A Companion of the Prophet, upon him be peace and blessings, (peace be on him) who played an important role in the early Islamic conquests. The Prophet entrusted to him many secrets.

(The Battle of) Ḥunayn: The battle that took place after the conquest of

Makkah between the Muslims and the tribes of Hawāzīn and Thaqīf. The Muslims won the battle and soon afterwards the conquered tribes became Muslims.

Ibn al-'Arabī, Abu Bakr ibn Muhammad ibn 'Abdu'llāh (d., 1148): One of the important commentators of the Qur'ān and Mālikī jurisprudents; the author of *Ahkâm al-Qur'ān* ("Judgments of the Qur'ān").

Ibn Kathīr, Ismā'īl ibn 'Umar (d., 1373): A famous traditionist, historian and jurist and the author of one of the best-known commentaries on the Qur'an titled *Tafsīru 1-Qur'āni 1-Azīm.*

Ibn Mājah, Ebū 'Abdu'llāh Muhammad ibn Yazīd el-Qazvinī (d., 273): The compiler of the one of the six most authentic books of Hadīth. He was also well-versed in Qur'ānic sciences and commentary.

Ibn Qayyim al-Jawziyah, Muhammad ibn Abī Bakr (d., 1350): A famous, all-round scholar; a disciple of ibn Taymiyah and is considered among the best representatives of his school of thought.

Ibn Sinā, Abū 'Ali (Avicenna) (980–1037): One of the foremost philosophers, mathematicians, and physicians of the golden age of Islamic tradition. In the west he is also known as the "Prince of Physicians" for his famous medical text *al-Qānūn* "Canon." In Latin translations, his works influenced many Christian philosophers, most notably Thomas Aquinas.

(The Prophet) Ibrāhīm (Abraham): One of the five greatest Messengers of God. God sent him to Chaldeans, who lived in modern day Iraq in around 2100 B.C. The Prophet Abraham, upon him be peace, later settled in Palestine. He made travels to Makkah, then an uninhabited valley, and settled there his wife Hagar and his son Ishmael. He built the Ka'bah with Ishmael, whom God also chose as a Messenger.

(The Prophet) Ilyās: Most probably he Prophet Elijah whom God sent to the Children of Israel during the reign of King Ahab in Israel who was notorious for his injustices. He

struggled against deviances in belief, immoralities, and injustices.

Imam Abū Hanīfah, Nu'mān ibn Thābit (d. 768): Founded the Hanafī School of Law and one of the greatest Muslim scholars of jurisprudence and deducers of new laws from the Qur'ān and Sunnah. He also was well-versed in theology.

Imam Abu'l-Hasan al-Ash'arī, 'Ali ibn Ismā'īl (d., 330): Born in al-Basra and died in al-Baghdād. One of the most prominent scholars of *Ahl al-Sunnah wa 1-Jamā'ah.* Besides theology, he was also well-versed in Islamic jurisprudence and Qur'ānic commentary. Among his famous books are *Kitāb al-Fuṣūl* ("A Book of Explanation and Distinction"), *Kitāb an-Nawādir* ("A Book of Rarities"), and *Kitāb al-Īmān* ("A Book of Faith").

Imam al-Ghazzālī, Abū Hamīd Muhammad (d. 1111): A major theologian, jurist, and sage who was considered a reviver (of the religious sciences and Islam's purity and vitality) during his time. Known in Europe as Algazel, he was the architect of Islam's later development. He left behind many books, the most famous being *Ihyā' al-'Ulūm ad-Dīn* ("Reviving the Religious Sciences").

Imam (al-)Māturidī, Abū Mansūr Muhammad ibn Muhammad (d., 853): One of the most outstanding scholars of *Ahl al-Sunnah wa 1-Jamā'ah.* Besides *al-Kalām* (Theology), he was also well-versed in the Qur'ānic commentary. Among his well-known books are *Kitāb at-Tawhīd* ("A Book of Faith in God's Oneness"), *ar-Risālah fī l-'Aqāid* ("An Epistle of Islamic Creed"), and *Ta'wīlāt al-Qur'ān* ("An Interpretatiton of the Qur'ān").

Imam Nasāī, Abū 'Abdu'r-Rahmān Ahmad ibn Shu'ayb (d., 915). The compiler of the one of the six most authentic books of hadīth. He made long travels and were taught by several scholars. Besides his compilation of hadīth, he also wrote *Musnad 'Ali* ("A Book of the Traditions Narrated by 'Ali"), *Musnad Mālik* ("A Book of the Traditions Narrated by Mâlik") and *Du'āfā wa 1-Matrūkīn* ("The Weak and Rejected Ones among the Narrators of Hadīth").

Imam ash-Shafi'ī, Muḥammad ibn Idrīs (d. 820): Founded the Shafi'ī School of Law. He was well-versed in Islamic jurisprudence, Hadith (the Prophet's sayings and actions), language, and poetry. He wrote *Al-Umm* ("The Foundation"), *ar-Risālah* ("A Book of Methodology"), and *Aḥkām al-Qur'ān* ("Judgments of the Qur'ān").

Imam Rabbānī, Aḥmad Fārūq al-Sarhandī (d. 1624): Accepted by many as "reviver of the second millennium" especially in Islamic spirituality. Born in Sarhand (India) and well-versed in Islamic sciences, he removed many corrupt elements from Sufism. He taught Shah Alamgir or Awrangzeb (d. 1707), who had a committee of scholars prepare the most comprehensive compendium of the Ḥanafī Law.

(al-)Injīl: The Divine Book revealed to the Prophet Jesus, upon him be peace; the Gospel

Iram: The Capital city of the ancient people of 'Ād in Yemen. It was famous for its many-columned (i.e. monumental) buildings.

(The Prophet) 'Īsā: Jesus son of Mary, upon him be peace

(The Prophet) Ishāq: The Prophet Isaac, son of the Prophet Abraham, upon them be peace

(The Prophet) Ismā'īl: The Prophet Ishmael, the older son of the Prophet Abraham, upon them be peace

Isrāīl: Israel – a title of the Prophet Jacob, upon him be peace, meaning a pure servant of God. The Qur'ān usually refers to the Jews as the Children of Isrāīl.

(al-)Jabriyyah: The school of the (fatalists) which denies human free will

Ja'far aṣ-Ṣādiq ibn Muḥammad al-Bāqir (d., 765): The great grandson of Imam Ḥusayn, son of 'Ali, the fourth Caliph. A distinguished scholar in religious sciences and also known for his piety and righteousness. The Twelve-Imam Shi'ites regard him as their sixth *imam*.

(al-)Jāmi', Nūru'd-Dīn 'Abdu'r-Raḥmān ibn Aḥmad (1414–1492): Commonly recognized as the last great classical poet of Persia, and a saint; composed numerous lyrics, as well as many works in prose. His *Salaman*

and Absal is an allegory of profane and sacred love. Some of his other works include *Haft Awrang*, *Tuhfat al-Aḥrār*, *Laylā wu Majnūn*, *Fātiḥat ash-Shabāb*, *Lawāa'iḥ*, *ar-Durrah al-Fākhirah*.

(al-)Jaṣṣāṣ, Abū Bakr Aḥmad ibn 'Ali ar-Rāzī (d., 980): An eminent jurist of the Ḥanafi school of law in his time. He is celebrated for his Qur'ānic commentary, *Aḥkām al-Qur'ān*, which is an erudite commentary on the Qur'ān from a legal perspective.

Jibrīl: The Archangel Gabriel, who brings the Revelation to a Messenger. It is described in the Qur'an a spirit of holiness, and as a noble, honored messenger, mighty, having a high, secured position with the Lord of the Supreme Throne, obeyed by other angels, and trustworthy.

(al-)Jīlī, 'Abdu'l-Karīm ibn Ibrāhīm (1365–1417?): The writer of the famous book, *al-Insān al-Kāmil* ("The Universal Man"). He was from Baghdād. In his Sufi teachings he generally followed Muhyi'd-Dīn ibn al-'Arabī.

Junayd al-Baghdādī (d. 910): One of the most famous early Sufis. He enjoyed great respect and was known as "the prince of the knowers of God."

al-Jurjānī Sayyid Sharif (d., 1413): One of the leading theologians of the 15th century. He visited Istanbul in 1374, and, upon his return in 1377, he was given a teaching appointment in Shiraz. *Sharh al-Mawaqif* is his most famous work.

(al-)Ka'bah: The Ka'bah: the cubic stone building in Makkah visited by the Muslims to do the Pilgrimage; it is the first building, at least the first building for the Divine worship built in the world.

Khabbāb ibn al-Arat (d., 657): A Companion and one of the early converts to Islam, who was mercilessly persecuted by the opponents of Islam in Makkah.

Khadījah bint Khuwaylid, Umm al-mu'minīn (d., 620): The first wife of God's Messenger, upon him be peace and blessings, the first of the Mothers of Believers. The Messenger married her when he was 25 years old and she was 40. He lived with her almost 25 years. She is one of the four greatest women of all times (for the others see the entry for *Āsyā*). She gave birth to several sons and daughters including Kāsim, Fātimah, Zaynab, Umm Kulthum, and Ruqayyah.

(al-)Khadr*: Khadr is the one with whom the Qur'an recounts (18: 60-82) the Prophet Moses made a travel to learn something of the spiritual realm of existence and the nature of God's acts in it. It is controversial whether he was a Prophet or a saint with special mission. It is believed that he enjoys the degree of life where one feels no need for the necessities of normal human life.

Khaybar*: A famous town north of Madīnah; it was conquered by the Muslims under the command of the Messenger in 629 C.E., 7 A.H.

(al-)Lāt*: It was one of the four chief idols of the pagan Quraysh tribe in pre-Islamic Makkah and Thaqīf tribe in Tā'if, and among the most famous idols in pre-Islamic Arabia

(al-)Layth ibn Sa'd (d., 791): A famous scholar of *Hadīth* and *Fiqh* and a foremost jurist of Egypt in his time.

(The people of) Lūt (Lot): The people who lived in the region lying to the southeast of the Dead Sea and notorious for sexual deviations (homosexuality), which they adopted as a general way of life. The Prophet Lot, upon him be peace, was sent to them but they rejected him and his call. They were utterly destroyed together with their cities – Sodom, Gomorrah, Admah, Zeboim, and Zo'ar – where they lived.

(al-)Majūs*: Fire worshippers, Magians

(al-)Madīnah*: The blessed city where the Prophet Muhammad, upon him be peace and blessings, emigrated, and the first city-state of the Muslims

Madyan (Midian): The territory which lay to the north-west of *Hijāz* and south of Palestine on the coast of the Red Sea and the Gulf of 'Aqabah. Initially their people were Muslims, but later contaminated their pure faith with polytheism, and their economic life with corruption and dishonesty. They rejected the Prophet Shu'ayb and his call, and consequently they were destroyed.

Makkah*: The holy city in Arabia where the Ka'bah exists. The Prophet Ishmael, upon him be peace, and his descendants launched the building of Makkah, and the Prophet Muhammad, upon him be peace and blessings, began his mission there.

Mālik ibn Anas (d., 795): A famous second Islamic century traditionist and jurist of Madīnah, and the founder of one of the four Sunni schools of law in Islam. His *al-Muwatta'*, a collection of Traditions as well as legal opinions of the jurists of Madīnah, is one of the earliest extant works of *Hadīth* and *Fiqh*.

(al-)Manāt*: One of the four chief idols in pre-Islamic *Hijāz*

Maqām Ibrāhīm*: The Station of Abraham – (the place of) the stone on which the Prophet Abraham, upon him be peace, reportedly stood while building the Ka'bah, and before which it is a necessary act of the *Hajj* to offer a Prayer of two rak'ahs after every seven circumambulations around the Ka'bah.

(al-)Marwah*: One of the two hills, the other being as-Safā' near the Ka'bah between which the pilgrims perform the rite of *Sa'y* (speedy walking)

Maryam*: Virgin Mary – the blessed mother of the Prophet Jesus, upon him be peace; she is one of the four greatest women of all times

(al-)Mash'ar al-Harām*: The site just near al-Muzdalifah. In Muzdalifah the pilgrims stay for some time and pray to God at dawn on the first of the '*Īd* days of Sacrifice.

(al-)Masīh*: The Christ – Jesus son of Mary

al-Masjid al-Aqsā: See al-Bayt al-Maqdis

(al-)Masjid al-Harām: The Grand Masjid in Makkah which surround the Ka'bah

(al-)Masjid an-Nabiyy: The Mosque of the Prophet. The Mosque in Madīnah which was built just following the Messenger's emigration to Madīnah

Minā*: A place five miles to 'Arafāt to Makkah, where the pilgrims offer their sacrifices and stay during the first three days of *'Īd al-Aḍḥā*

Mu'ādh ibn Jabal (d., 639): A Companion known for his knowledge of Law; he was among those who undertook the collection of the Qur'ān and was appointed by the Prophet as a judge in Yemen.

Muḥammad Bahāu'd-Dīn Shah an-Naqsh-band (d. 1389): One of the most prominent Islamic spiritual masters and founder of the Sufi Naqshbandiyyah order. Among his books are *Risālat al-Wāridah*, *al-Awrād al-Bahā'iyyah*, *Hayātnāmah*, and *Tanbīh al-Ghāfilīn*.

Muhammed Lutfi Efendi (1868–1956): One of the Sufi masters who lived in Erzurum. He has a *Divan* containing many beautiful, lyrical poems.

Muhyi'd-Dīn ibn al-'Arabī (1165-1240): One of the greatest and most famous Sufi masters. His doctrine of the Transcendental Unity of Existence, which most have mistaken for monism and pantheism, made him the target of unending polemics. He wrote many books, the most famous of which are *Fuṣūṣ al-Ḥikam* and *al-Futuḥāt al-Mkakiyyah*.

(The Prophet) Mūsā (Moses): One of the five greatest Messengers of God, who was sent to the Children of Israel and given the Torah to guide them and bring them out of Egypt

Muslim ibn al-Ḥajjāj an-Naysābūrī (d., 875): One of the greatest scholars of *Hadīth*, whose work is one of the six most authentic collections of *Hadīth* and ranks second in importance only to that of al-Bukharī

(al-)Mu'tazilah: The school of the Muslim "rationalists" which accorded creative effect to human will and agency, concluding that it is human beings who create their actions

(al-)Muzdalifah: A site between *al-'Arafāt* and *Minā* where the pilgrims while returning from *'Arafāt*, have to stop and stay for the whole night or some part of it (the night), between the 9th and 10th of *Dhul-Hijjah* and to perform the Evening and Late Evening Prayers together

(an-)Naṣārā: Those who call themselves the followers of Jesus; the Christians

(The Prophet) Nūḥ (Noah): One of the five greatest Messengers, and the second father of humankind; the Prophet of the Flood

Qārūn: Korah. A wealthy man from the Children of Israel who rebelled against God and collaborated with the Pharaoh. God made him and all his wealth swallowed by the earth.

(al-)Quraysh: The Makkan, most esteemed Arab tribe to which God's Messenger belonged

(al-)Qurṭubī, Muḥammad ibn Aḥmad (d., 1273): One of the most distinguished commentators of the Qur'ān. His *al-Jāmi' li Ahkām al-Qur'ān* ("A Compendium of the Judgments of the Qur'ān) is not only one of the best commentaries on the legal verses of the Qur'ān but also one of the best *tafsīr* works.

Rabi'ah al-'Adawiyyah (717–801): Born in Basra. As a child, after the death of her parents, she was sold into slavery. After years of service to her slavemaster, Rabī'ah began to serve only the Beloved with her actions and thoughts. Since she was no longer useful to the slave-owner, Rabī'ah was then set free to continue her devotion to the Beloved.

(ar-)Rāzī, Muḥammad ibn 'Umar Fakhru'd-Dīn (d., 1210): One of the most famous commentators of the Qur'ān and the most outstanding scholars of his time who was well-versed in both religious and rational sciences. *Mafātīh al-Ghayb* is the name of his monumental commentary on the Qur'ān.

(ar-)Rūmī, Jalālu'd-Dīn (1207–1273): One of the most renowned figures of the Islamic Sufism. Founder of the Mawlawī Order of the whirling dervishes, famous for his *Mathnawī*, an epic of the religious life in six volumes. For Western readers, ar-Rūmī is a powerful voice among the poets of Sufism.

(as-)Sābiūn: A people of the Book who lived in Iraq and deviated into worshipping heavenly bodies in course of time

Sa'd ibn Abī Waqqās (d., 670): One of the ten who were promised Paradise while alive, of the heroes of early Islam who took part in many battles during the life of the Prophet. The commander of the Muslim armies in the Qadisiyah wars leading to the conquest of Iran.

Saʿd ibn Muʿādh (d. 627): A Madīnan Companion and one of the leaders of the Aws tribe. He fought valiantly in many battles and was martyred in the Battle of *Khandaq* (or Trench).

Saʿdī ash-Shirazī (1215?–1292): The greatest didactic poet of Persia, author of the *Gulistān* ("Rose-Garden") and the *Bustān* ("Orchard"), who also wrote many fine odes and lyrics.

(aṣ-)Ṣafā: One of the two hills, the other being Marwah near the Kaʿbah between which the pilgrims perform the rite of *Saʿy* (speedy walking)

Saʿīd ibn al-Musayyib (d., 713): A foremost scholar and jurist of the generation succeeding the Companions. One of the seven recognized jurists of Madīnah, he was known for his knowledge of *Hadīth* and *Fiqh* as well as for his piety and devotion.

(The Prophet) Ṣāliḥ: The Prophet sent to the tribe of *Thamūd* who lived in al-Ḥijr, the north-west of Arabia

(ash-)Shāfiʿī, Muḥammad ibn Idrīs (d., 820): The founder of the Shāfiʿī school of Islam. The first to write about the methodology of Islamic law. He has also a *Dīwān*, a collection of poems.

Shams at-Tabrizī: In Konya, Rūmī became a religious teacher and then a Sufi at the age of 39, when he met Shamsuʾd-Dīn at-Tabrizī. A-Tabrizī was to have a profound influence upon ar-Rūmī and to vivify, like a veritable sun, the growth of his latent spiritual and literary genius.

(ash-)Shaybānī, Muḥammad ibn al-Hasan (d., 804): A famous Iraqī jurist and disciple of Abū Ḥanīfah. His Siyar al-Kabīr is first book ever written about the international law and relations. He is reckoned as one of the founders of the Ḥanafī school of law.

(The Prophet) Shuʿayb: A Prophet. He was sent to the peoples of Madyan (Midian) and al-Aykah, but they rejected him, so God destroyed them.

(The Prophet) Sulaymān (Solomon): Son of the Prophet David and one of the Prophets sent to the Children of Israel, and their first king; the most powerful of the kings who have ever lived. He was a very humble servant of God despite his great power. In addition to many miracles and miraculous achievements, he was distinguished by his ability, by leave of God, to subjugate jinn and satans to his command and employ them in diverse tasks.

(as-)Suyūṭī Jalāluʾd-Dīn (1446–1506): A great scholar well-versed in *Hadīth*, jurisprudence, and history. He was also a Sufi and interpreter of the Qurʾān. He authored works in virtually all Islamic sciences.

(aṭ-)Ṭabarānī, Sulaymān ibn Aḥmad ibn Ayyūb (d., 971): Specialized in *Hadīth*. His works cover the fields of *Hadīth*, *Tafsīr* and *Kalām* (Theology). His *Muʿjam al-Kabīr* ("The Great Encyclopedia of Hadīth"), *Muʿjam al-Awṣaṭ* ("The Medium Encyclopedia of Hadīth"), and *Muʿjam aṣ-Ṣaghīr* ("The Small Encyclopedia of Hadīth") are well-known.

(aṭ-)Ṭabarī, Muḥammad ibn Jarīr (d., 923): A distinguished historian, jurist and Qurʾān-commentator. His major extant works include his commentary *Jāmiʿuʾl-Bayān fī Tafsīr al-Qurʾān* ("A Comprehensive Collection of Words in Expounding the Qurʾān") and *Tārīkh al-Umam waʾl-Mulūk* ("The History of Nations and Rulers").

(at-)Taftazānī, Saʿduʾd-Dīn (d., 1390): A famous scholar of logic, rhetoric, grammar, theology, and jurisprudence of Samarqand during the rule of Timur. His *Sharh al-ʿAqāid an-Nasafiyyah* ("An Exposition of the Book of Creed by an-Nasafī") is among the basic works of the Muslim theology.

Ṭalḥah ibn ʿUbayduʾllāh (d., 656): One of the ten Companions whom the Prophet declared to be among the People of Paradise. He was among the earliest converts to Islam, and was noted for his bravery and generosity.

Ṭālūt: King Saul. He led his army against the army of Jālūt (Goliath).

(at-)Tawrāh: The Divine Book (of law) given to the Prophet Moses by God; the Torah

(The people of) Thamūd: An ancient Arab people who lived in al-Ḥijr in the north-west of Arabia. Their main city, Madāʾin Ṣāliḥ, was situated along the route of the famous Hijāz railway. The Prophet Ṣāliḥ came to them with God's Message but their, like many other ancient peoples, rejected him and his Message and persisted in wrongdoing. Finally God destroyed them.

(ath-)Thawrī, Sufyān ibn Sa'īd ibn Masrūq (d., 778): Considered an authority in different branches of Islamic learning, especially *Hadīth*. His works include *al-Jāmi' al-Kabīr* and *al-Jāmi' aṣ-Ṣaghīr*, both of which are included in *Hadīth*.

(at-)Tirmidhī, Muḥammad ibn 'Īsā (d., 892): A famous traditionist whose collection of Traditions, *Kitāb as-Sunan* ("The Book of the Prophetic Traditions") is considered one of the six most authentic collections of *Hadīth*.

(aṭ-)Ṭūr: A mountain. Mount Sinai, on which the Prophet Moses received the revelation of the Torah from God

(The Battle of) Uhud: The battle which took place between the Muslims and the pagan Quraysh of Makkah at the foot of Mount Uhud, three miles from the Prophet's Mosque in Madīnah in the 3rd year of *Hijrah*

'Umar ibn al-Khaṭṭāb al-Fārūq (582–644): One of the ten Companions to whom Paradise was promised while they were in the world. Famous for his keen insight into the spirit of Islam, and his legendary justice and very simple life as the Caliph. He succeeded Abū Bakr as-Siddīq in Caliphate.

Umm Salamah, Hind bint Suhayl, Umm al-mu'minīn (d., 681): One of the wives of the Prophet, who reported several hundred Traditions from him.

Usāmah ibn Zayd ibn Hārithah (d., 674): One of the young Companions much loved by God's Messenger. Son of Zayd, the only Companion mentioned in the Qur'ān with his name, and emancipated slave of the Messenger. The Messenger entrusted the command of the army he collected just before his death to dispatch against the Byzantines to Usāmah while he was still at a very young age.

'Uthmān ibn 'Affān Dhu'n-Nūrayn (576–656): One of the first Companions who emb-

raced Islam and of the ten whom the Messenger informed would enter Paradise. Since the Messenger gave him two of His daughters in marriage (the second one after the first died), he has been called Dhu'n-Nūrayn (the possessor of two lights). He was especially renowned for his generosity and modesty. He succeeded 'Umar in Caliphate.

Uways al-Qaranī (d., 656): One of outstanding figures of the generation succeeding the Companions. Some regard him as the greatest Muslim saint of the first Islamic century.

(al-)Uzzā: One of the four chief idols worshipped in Hijāz before Islam

(The Prophet) Yaḥyā (John the Baptist): Son of the Prophet Zachariah – a Messenger of God highly praised in the Qur'ān for his devotions, chastity, sound judgment, profound knowledge, piety, righteousness, and dutifulness to his parents. He was killed by the Jews.

Yaḥyā ibn Mu'ādh (d., 871): A great Sufi and a disciple of Ibn Karrām, left his native town of Rayy and lived for a time in Balkh, afterwards proceeding to Nishapur where he died. A certain number of poems are attributed to him.

Ya'jūj wa Ma'jūj (Gog and Magog): Wild tribes that have invaded the civilized world many times and are expected to appear as the last time before the destruction of the world

(The Prophet) Ya'qūb (Jacob): a Messenger of God, son of the Prophet Isaac and grandson of the Prophet Abraham, upon them be peace. He was also known as Israel. His twelve sons each became head of their own tribe and these were known as the twelve tribes of Israel.

Yathrib: One of the names of Madīnah before Islam

(The Prophet) Yūsuf (Joseph): Son of the Prophet Jacob, a Messenger of God who was envied by his brothers and sold to the Egyptian court as a slave. Then he became a minister in the court and was deputed to the king.

(The Prophet) Yūnus (Jonah): A Messenger of God who was sent to Nineveh (on the left bank of the Tigris, opposite the city of Mosul, in Iraq) to preach against their wickedness and call them to the worship of God. The people of Nineveh at first rejected him, and he left the city but was swallowed by a fish in the sea. God saved him from the belly of the sea, and returned him to his people, who had embraced God's Religion when they had seen God's punishment coming.

(Az-)Zabūr: The Book given to the Prophet David, upon him be peace; the Psalms

(The Prophet) Zakariyā (Zachariah): A Messenger of God who appeared in the Children of Israel just before the advent of the Prophet Jesus. He was killed by the Jews.

Yahūdī: Jew. The term describes one who belongs to Yahūda – Judah in the Old Testament. Judah – *Yehudah* in Hebrew – is the name of one of the two kingdoms which emerged with the division of Prophet Solomon's kingdom after

his death, and takes this name from Judah, one of the sons of Jacob. According to another opinion, *Yahūdī* means one who follows the Law established by Judah, an Israelite jurist who lived in the second century after Jesus. The Jews themselves name their religion – Judaism – after Judah.

Zaynab bint Jahsh, Umm al-mu'minīn (d., 641) One of the Messenger's wives, who first married to Zayd ibn Hārithah. But the marriage broke up whereafter the Messenger married her. She is well-known for her generosity.

(az-)Zubayr ibn al-'Awwām (d., 656): Among the heroes of the earliest period of Islam; one of the most prominent Companions, and one of those ten about whom the Prophet gave the glad tidings of Paradise.

A GLOSSARY OF TERMS

(al-)Abad: Eternity in the future

(al-)Azal: Eternity in the past

(al-)'Abd: The servant; the servant of God by creation; the servant of God who believes in and worships Him

(al-)'Adhāb: Punishment. The Qur'ān uses seven different names for the places or types of punishment in the Hereafter: *Jahannam* (Hell), *Nār* (Fire), *Sa'īr* (Blaze), *Jahīm* (Blazing Flame), *Hutamah* (Consuming Fire), *Saqar* (Scorching Fire), and *Lazā* (Raging Flame). Most probably, these are the levels or degrees of punishment, each prepared for those who deserve it and each having a gate.

(al-)Adhān: The call to the Prayer. It is as follows: *Allāhu akbar* (God is the All-Great: 4 times); *Ashhadu an lā ilāha illa 'llāh* (I bear witness that there is no deity but God: twice); *Ashhadu anna Muhammadan Rasūlu 'llāh* (I bear witness that Muhammad is the Messenger of God: twice); *Hayya 'alā's-salāh* (Come on, to the Prayer: twice), *Hayya 'alā 'l-falāh* (Come on, to salvation: twice); *Allāhu akbar* (God is the All-Great: twice); *Lā ilāha illa 'llāh* (There is no deity but God: once).

(al-)'Afw: Pardoning, granting remission; excusing

(al-)'Ahd: covenant; contract

'Ahdu 'llāh: God's covenant. It is the promise that God has taken from His servants that they should believe in Him and worships Him alone. Besides this cardinal one, God has made different covenants with His Prophets and many peoples in different times.

Ahl al-Bayt: The household. As a term, it refers to the household of the Prophet Muhammad, upon him be peace and blessings, including Fātimah, his daughter, and her husband 'Ali, and their sons Hasan and Husayn.

Ahl al-Kitāb: The People of the Book. Any people who have been given a Divine Book. The Qur'ān tends to use this term particularly for the Jews and Christians. The term also included the Sabeans and the Magians.

Ahl al-Kitāb wa's-Sunnah: The People of the Book and the Sunnah. They are the Muslims who strive to follow exactly the teachings of the Qur'an and the way of the Prophet Muhammad, upon him be peace and blessings, as reported by his Companions.

(al-)Ākhirah: The next one; afterlife, the Hereafter. The other world where conscious, responsible being will be called to account for their beliefs and deeds in the world and recompensed for them.

(al-)Ahzāb: Parties, confederates. It is particularly used for the remnants of the ancient, destroyed peoples who lived in Arabia during the revelation of the Qur'ān, and for the confederate forces composed of different tribes that besieged Madīnah and fought the Muslims in the Battle of the Trench in 627 C.E., 5 A.H.

(al-)Ākif: One who abides in devotion to God

(al-)Akhlāq: The science and principles of good conduct and morality. The most distinguishing characteristic of Islam and, when loyal to that characteristic, of the community of Muhammad, upon him be peace and blessings, is that it is far from all kinds of extremism. Islam represents the middle way in all aspects of life. For example, it is neither spiritualism nor materialism, neither realism nor idealism, neither capitalism nor socialism, neither individualism nor étatism, neither absolutism nor anarchism, neither this-worldly and hedonist, nor purely other-worldly or monastic. As it is unique in its worldview and social, economic and political aspects, it is also unique in the

moral education it gives to individuals. Islam aims to develop human beings from being potentially human to being truly human, thus perfecting them. It develops the human character in the best way. The parts of the Wisdom which the Qur'ān enumerates in verses 22–39, beginning and ending with the absolute prohibition of associating partners with God in any way in His Divinity and Lordship, are important in developing that character and raising members of a Muslim society.

(al-)'Ālam (pl. *'ālamūn*): World, worlds. The word comes from *'alam, 'alāmah,* meaning something by which another thing is known. Thus, in this perspective, every individual thing or set of things, from the tiniest sub-atomic particles to the largest nebulae and galaxies, is a "world" and indicates God. The plural form (*'ālamūn*) is particularly used for conscious beings, giving the sense that everything that is created is as if conscious, and signifying that its pointing to God's Existence, Unity and Lordship is extremely clear for conscious beings.

(al-)Alaq: The clot clinging (to the wall of the female womb)

(al-)'amal: Action, deed

(al-)'amal aṣ-ṣāliḥ: Good, righteous deed

(al-)Amānah: The trust. Any responsibility or all the duties which either God or society or individual places in someone's charge; the Supreme Trust which only humankind has undertaken, so in this sense it refers to the human ego.

(al-)Amīr: The leader; the commander

(al-)Amr: Command; authority; affair

Amr bi 'l-Ma 'rūf: Enjoining and actively promoting what is good and right (in appropriate ways)

(al-)Anṣār: The Helpers. It is particularly used for the Muslims of Madīnah who helped the emigrant Muslims of Makkah in the process of the latter's settling down in Madīnah.

(al-)'Arāf: The Heights (between Paradise and Hell upon which the believers who still have sins unpardoned and therefore will be retained to be forgiven so that they can enter Paradise)

(al-)'Arsh: Throne; the Supreme Throne of God. As the Qur'ān addresses all levels of understanding through all ages, it tends to present certain abstract truths, like those pertaining to Divinity, with concrete expressions and uses metaphors and comparisons. It presents the *Kursiyy* (Seat: see 2: 256) as if it were a platform or seat, and the *'Arsh* as if it were a throne and God were the ruler of the universe seated on His throne, governing all creation. *'Arsh* is the composition of God's Names the First, the Last, the Outward, and the Inward. Also, deducing from Said Nursi's description of water as the *'arsh* (throne) of mercy and earth, the throne of life, we can say that the *'Arsh* (Throne) implies God's full control of and authority over the universe. Elements such as water and earth are things that conduct God's decrees or media by which they are manifested and executed.

(al-)'Aṣabiyyat (al-Jāhiliyyah): Tribal or racial attachment; racism. Islam eradicated any blood and color-based discrimination and condemned it as an attitude arising from sheer ignorance and carnality.

Asbāb an-nuzūl: Occasions on which verses of the Qur'ān were revealed

Aṣḥāb al-Kahf: The young people from the royal class of the Romans in Syria-Jordan region who gave up idol-worship and believed in God as the only Deity and Lord, and had to take shelter in a cave. They stayed in the cave in a death-like sleep for 300 years, and then woke up as a sign of resurrection.

Aṣḥāb al-Uḥdūd: A tyrannical people who dug ditches and burnt the believers alive in them.

'Aṣḥāb al-Yamīn (al-Maymanah): The people of the Right, the people of happiness and prosperity (who will be given their Records in their right hands in the Hereafter)

'Aṣḥāb ash-Shimāl (al-Mash 'amah): The people of the Left, the people of wretchedness (who will be given their Records in their left hands in the Hereafter)

(al-)Ashhur al-Ḥurum: The months of Dhu'l-Qa'dah, Dhu'l-Hijjah, Muharram and

Rajab (the 11ᵗʰ, 12ᵗʰ, 1ˢᵗ, and 7ᵗʰ months of the lunar year) during which warfare, killing, and pillage are prohibited.

(al-)Asmā' al-Ḥusnā: The All-Beautiful Names (of God). These Names are either included in the Qur'ān or were taught by God's Messenger, and God is and should be called by them.

(al-)Asmā' wa'ṣ-Ṣifāt: God's Names and Attributes. Besides His Names, God has Attributes. Some Attributes are essential to His being God. They are Existence, Having No Beginning, Permanence, Oneness, Being Unlike the Created, and Self-Subsistence. God has another kind of Attributes called the Positive Attributes which describe God as what He is. They are Life, Knowledge, Will, Power, Hearing, Seeing, Speech, and Bringing into Existence. These Attributes are the origin of the Names such as Giver of life and the All-Reviver, the All-Knowing, the All-Willing, the All-Powerful, the All-Hearing, the All-Seeing, the All-Speaking, and the Creator, etc. Having such absolute, unrestricted Attributes and All-Beautiful Names means that their manifestation is "inevitable." One Who exists in and of Himself, and Whose Existence is absolutely perfect, will manifest Himself, as "required" by His very "nature." Thus, the universe is the collection of the manifestations of God's Attributes and Names, and those manifestations are focused on humankind. God has a third kind of Attributes which describe what God is not. They are almost endless. For example, God is not One Who begets and begotten, One Who has any partners, One who has any need, etc.

(al-)'Asr: Time; afternoon; the last part of time replete with important events

(al-)'Awrah: Parts of the body that are not supposed to be exposed to others. For men this is from the navel to the knee. For the women it is all of her body except the hands, feet, and face.

(al-)Āyah: Manifest sign; miracle; lesson to be taken from an event; each of the Qur'ān's independent sentences between two points (verse)

Āyātun bayyināt: signs or messages clear in meaning and content (as evidence of the truth)

(al-)Āyat al-Kursīyy: The verse of the Divine Seat of dominion. It is the verse of 255 of *Sūrat al-Baqarah* which makes God known with some of His Names and Attributes.

Ayyāmu 'llāh: Days of God (momentous historical events such as destructions of communities, turning-points in history, and eschatological events)

(al-)Baghy: envious rivalry and insolence (which the Qur'ān stresses as the cardinal reason for the internal conflicts in a community)

(al-)Balā': Trial, testing. Although it usually comes in the form of disaster, God tries people with both good and evils. When He tries with good such as success, wealth, high position, and physical beauty, it requires gratitude to God and attributing it to Him. When He tries with evils such as a misfortune, illness or poverty, it requires patience without complaint. This, however, does not mean that one stricken by an evil should not try to escape from it. Being tried with evil is usually the result of a sin. Therefore, it also requires repentance, seeking forgiveness, and reformation.

(al-)Baqā: Permanence, persistence

(al-)Barāah: Disavowal, proclamation of disavowal; ultimatum

(al-)Barzakh: A barrier (between the dead and the other world), the intermediate world of the grave (between this world and the next)

(al-)Baṣāir: "Lights" of discernment and insight

al-Bashīr: A bearer of glad tidings; a Messenger who bears glad tidings (of prosperity in return for faith and righteousness)

(al-)Baṣīrah: Discernment, insight, sagacity

(al-)Basmalah: Bismi 'llāhir-Raḥmāni 'r-Raḥīm: In (and with) the Name of God, the All-Merciful, the All-Compassionate

(al-)Ba'th: Revival; sending a Messenger (to "revive" people); restoration of the dead to life; resurrection

(al-)Bāṭin: What is inward; the inward or internal dimension of something; the metaphysical dimension of existence

(al-)Bāṭil: What is false; falsehood; any system of belief, thought, or action that is based not on the Revelation, but on human desires and fancies that do not conform to but do contradict God's Religion and ways of acting in the universe

(al-)Bay'ah – (al-)Bī'ah: An allegiance sworn by the citizens etc. to their Imam (Muslim Ruler) to be obedient to him according to the Religion of Islam

Bay'at ar-Riḍwān: The oath and pledge taken by God's Messenger from his Companions under a tree at al-Ḥudaybiyah in the year of 6 A.H. (628 C.E.) to fight the Quraysh in case of necessity

(al-)Bayān: Intelligent speech, as opposed to sounds which have no power of expression or meaning

Baytu 'llāh: God's House (the Ka'bah)

(al-)Bayyinah: The Clear Proof

(al-)Bayyināt: All evidence of the truth; clear signs or documents of the truth; miracles

Bi-ghayri 'l-ḥaqq; as a sinful act (or attitude) that can never be right and just; against all right

Bi 'l-ḥaqq: With the truth (embodying it, and with nothing false in it); all meaningfully, and for meaningful purposes, and on solid foundations of the truth

(al-)Bukhl: Niggardliness, meanness

(al-)Birr: Godliness, virtue; a high degree in faith and practice of Islam, especially having acquired the spiritual refinement that enables one to spend in God's cause or to give others of what one loves

(al-)Burūj: The constellations, (which are the names of some fixed star-groups)

(ad-)Dābbah: Any living, moving creature

(ad-)Dābbat min al-Arḍ: A living creature which God will bring forth from the earth towards the end of time. It will speak to the disbelieving, criminal people or make them to

understand that they have no certainty of faith in God's signs and Revelations.

(ad-)Dahr: "The Time," processes of progress and decline

(ad-)Dajjāl: An impostor or impostors who will appear towards the end of time to mislead humanity; the *Dajjāl* who will appear in the Muslim world is generally called *as-Sufyān.*

(aḍ-)Ḍāl: One who has gone astray; the straying.

(aḍ-)Ḍalāl(ah): Straying from the Straight Path. It refers to a broad range of straying from the Path – from the slightest lapse of a believer to complete deviation from the Straight Path. As a term, it denotes returning to unbelief after belief and exchanging unbelief for belief (2: 108), associating partners with God either in His Essence or His Attributes or acts (4: 116), and rejecting faith in all or any of the pillars of faith.

(ad-)Dawlah: As a Qur'ānic term, it means fortune. The Qur'ān declares: What God has bestowed on His Messenger as war-gains from the peoples of the townships: (one-fifth of) it belongs to God, and to the Messenger, and his near kinsfolk, and orphans, and the destitute, and the wayfarer (lacking means to sustain a journey), so that it should not become *dawlatan* (a *fortune*) circulating among the rich among you.

(adh-)Dhanb: Sin in various degrees. Sin and pardoning have different types and degrees. These are: disobeying religious commandments, and forgiveness thereof; disobeying God's laws of creation and life, and forgiveness thereof; and disobeying the rules of good manners or courtesy (*adab*), and the forgiveness thereof. A fourth type, which is not a sin, involves not doing something as perfectly as possible, which is required by the love of and nearness to God. Some Prophets may have done this, but such acts cannot be considered sins according to our common definition of that word.

(adh-)Dhikr: Remembrance; recollection; mentioning; reminder; recitation of one or some

of God's Names. It is also used to refer to a Divine Book.

(ad-)Dīn: The collection of moral, spiritual, and worldly principles, system, and way of conduct; judging; rewarding and punishing; way; law; constitution; servanthood and obedience; and peace and order.

(ad-)Du'ā': Prayer and supplication. It has kinds and degrees: The first kind is the prayer of all organisms, plant, animal and human, through the natural disposition of their bodies and their functioning in line with their duties in creation. The second kind is that which is uttered by all organisms, plant, animal and human, in the tongue of vital needs. The third kind of prayer is that which is done by human beings. This falls into two categories: The first category is the active prayer. It means complying with the laws that God has set for life. For example, a farmer's plowing the soil is knocking on the door of Divine providence. A patient's going to the doctor's is appealing to God for cure. This kind of prayer is usually accepted. The second category is the verbal prayer that we do.

(ad-)Dunyā: The world. It has three aspects. The first aspect is that world is the realm where God's Names are manifested and therefore, whatever is there and whatever takes place in it is a mirror to God with His Attributes and Names. The second aspect is that the world is the tillage for the Hereafter. The building-blocks to make up one's Paradise or Hell in the Hereafter are the seeds of one's belief or unbelief and the deeds that one sows here. The third aspect of the world is that which looks to our carnal desires, passions, lusts, and ambitions. It is this aspect that the Qur'ān condemns, as these consist of games, pastimes, greed (hoarding things), and competing in having more goods; in short, the source of all vice and evil.

(al-)Fahshā, (al-)Fāhishah (pl. al-fawāhīsh): Indecency; any whose abominable character is self-evident. In the Qur'an all extra-marital sexual relationships, sodomy, nudity, false accusation of unchastity are specifically reckoned as shameful deeds.

al-Falāḥ: Prosperity. It has many degrees and types according to the needs and aspirations of people and the degrees of their spiritual enlightenment. For example, some want to be saved from eternal punishment, while others desire Paradise. There are still some who aim at the higher ranks in Paradise and others who aspire to obtain God's good pleasure.

(al-)Faqīh: a person who is an expert on Islamic jurisprudence (Law); one who has correct and profound comprehension of Islam who can give an authoritative legal opinion or judgment regarding Islamic matters.

(al-)Farḍ: Any obligatory religious act

(al-)Farā'iḍ: Plural of al-fard. It is also used to mean the science of sharing inheritance.

Farḍ 'Ayn: Any act which is obligatory on every Muslim who is mature, healthy, and sane

Farḍ Kifāyah: A collective duty of the Muslim community so that if some people carry it out no Muslim is considered blameworthy, but if no one carries it out all incur a collective guilt.

(al-)Fasād: Disorder and corruption – one which appears as a result of following a path other than God's

(al-)Fāsiq: A transgressor of the bounds set by God; one who commits any of the major sins

(al-)Fatā: A youth, usually a chivalrous young man who has dedicated himself to God's cause

(al-)Fatḥ: The Victory which functions as a door to further victories

(al-)Fatwā: A legal verdict given on a religious basis

(al-)Fayy: Gains of war obtained without fighting

(al-)Fidyah: Compensation for a missed or wrongly practiced religious act of worship or order usually in the form of money or foodstuff or offering (animal)

(al-)Fiqh: Correct and profound comprehension (of Islam); the science of Islamic Jurisprudence

(al-)Fisq: Transgression of the bounds set by God; committing of any of the major sins

(al-)Fitnah: Disorder and corruption rooted in rebellion against God and recognizing no laws. It denotes associating partners with God and adopting that as a life-style, spreading unbelief and apostasy, committing major sins with willful, insolent abandon, open hostilities to Islam, destroying collective security or causing public disorder, and oppression; the term *fitnah* covers all of these.

(al-)Fitrah: The original Divine pattern or system governing the universe; the totality of the attributes God has given to a particular thing or being; the Divine Religion (Islam) as the translation of the Divine pattern or system

(al-)Fujūr: Shameless, sinful act

(al-)Furqān: The Criterion to distinguish between truth and falsehood, and the knowledge, insight, and power of judgment to put it into effect; an inner sense or faculty of insight, discernment, inspiration, and power of judgment to distinguish between right and wrong

(al-)Futuwwah: Youth and chivalry as a composite of virtues, such as energy, revolutionary vigor, heroism, generosity, munificence, modesty, chastity, trustworthiness, loyalty, mercifulness, knowledge, humility, and piety

(al-)Ghaḍab: Wrath. When used for God's wrath, it denotes punishment and condemnation.

(al-)Ghāfil: Heedless, unmindful

(al-)Ghaflah: Heedlessness, unawareness

(al-)Ghanīmah: Gains of war obtained through fighting

al-Ghayb: The (absolutely or relatively) Unseen or unsensed; beyond the reach of human perception

(al-)Ghiybah: Backbiting

(al-)Ghurūr: Deception, delusion

(al-)Ghusl: The full ritual washing of the body with water alone to be pure for the prayer. To do *Ghusl:* (1) Wash your private parts; (2) Do *wuḍū*; (3) Wash your entire body from the top to bottom and from right to left

Hablu 'llāh: The rope of God, usually used to denote the Qur'ān or Islam

(al-)Ḥadd (pl. *Ḥudūd*): Any bound God set and ordered His creatures not to transgress.

It is also used for the cardinal penalties Islam laid down in return for cardinal offenses such as killing, unlawful sexual relations, usurpation, theft, causing disorder and corruption in the society, and drinking intoxicants.

(al-)Ḥadīth: Communication, narration, word or saying. As a term, it denotes the record of whatever the Prophet (upon him be peace and blessings) said, did, or tacitly approved. According to some scholars, the word *ḥadīth* also covers reports about the sayings and deeds, etc., of the Companions of the Prophet in addition to those of the Prophet himself. The whole body of Traditions is termed *Ḥadīth* and the science which deals with it is called *ʿIlm al-Ḥadīth.*

Ḥadīth qudsī: A saying of God narrated by His Messenger but not included in the Qur'ān

(al-)Hady: Cattle brought to the sacred precincts of Makkah to sacrifice during the days of ʿĪd al-Aḍḥā

(al-)Ḥajj: Major Pilgrimage which the Muslims do in Makkah during *Dhu 'l-Ḥijjah*, the last month of the lunar year. It is one of the five pillars of Islam, a duty one must perform during one's life-time if one has the financial resources for it. In addition to *ṭawāf* and *saʿy*, there are a few other requirements but especially staying for some time in al-ʿArafāt (*al-waqfah*) from the mid-day to sunset on 9th of *Dhu 'l-Ḥijjah*.

(al-)Halāk: Destruction, ruin

(al-)Halāl: Religiously lawful

Ḥamalat al-ʿArsh: The eight beings (angels?) that bear God's Throne (the greatest of beings who carry out God's order in the universal order)

al-Ḥamd: All praise and gratitude that is due to and for God

(al-)Ḥanīf: One who has a sincere, sound faith in God and worships God with purity of intention

al-Ḥaqq: The truth, what is ever constant and true

(al-)Ḥarām: Religiously forbidden or unlawful; sacred and inviolable; any sacred and inviolable thing

(al-)Ḥasanah: Good; reward

(al-)Ḥashr: Gathering together; the raising of the dead and gathering them on the Plain of the Supreme Gathering on Judgment Day

(al-)Ḥawā: The fanciful inclinations and lusts of the human carnal soul

(al-)Ḥayā': Bashfulness, and refraining from saying or doing anything improper or indecent; seeking to avoid displeasing God out of awe of Him

(al-)Ḥayāh: Life. Human life has five degrees: (1) Our life which depends on certain conditions and the fulfillment of certain needs. (2) The life of al-Khadr and Ilyās (Elijah) which is free to some extent from the necessities of our life. (3) The life of the Prophets Jesus and Enoch. These two Prophets live in heaven free of the necessities of human life in their "astral" bodies. (4) The life of martyrs – those who are killed in God's cause. They do not feel the pangs of death and know themselves to be transferred into a better world where they enjoy the blessings of God. (5) The life of the dead. Death means one's being discharged from worldly duties with the spirit set free.

(al-)Ḥayāt ad-dunyā: The present, worldly life or the life of this world (see *ad-dunyā*)

(al-)Hidāyah: True or right guidance; following God's Path in belief, thought, and action

(al-)Hijrah: Emigration. The emigration of God's Messenger from Makkah to Madīnah in 622 C.E.

(al-)Ḥikmah: Wisdom. Knowledge of creation, life, right and wrong, and of the Divine system prevailing in the universe, so as to enable persuasive, convincing answers for such questions as "Who am I? What is the purpose for my existence in this world? Who has sent me to this world and why? Where did I come from and where am I heading? What does death ask of me?" It also signifies the true nature of and purpose behind the things and events in the universe, including especially in human life. The Qur'an is the source of knowledge in all these vital matters. The Sunnah of the Prophet, upon him be peace and blessings, being the system or principles by which to understand and practice the Qur'an in daily life, comes to mind first of all when speaking of "the Wisdom."

(al-)Ḥubb (al-maḥabbah): Love. God declares: *Say (O Messenger): "If you indeed love God, then follow me, so that God will love you and forgive you your sins." God is All-Forgiving, All-Compassionate* (3: 31).

(Muṣālaḥat) Ḥudaybiyah: The Treaty of Hudaybiyah. Almost a year after the Battle of the Trench in 627 C.E., 5 A.H., the Messenger left for Makkah for a minor pilgrimage with his 1.400 and so Companions. However, the Quraysh did not let them do the pilgrimage. After negotiations, a treaty was signed at al-Ḥudaybiyah 12 miles away from Makkah.

(al-)Ḥukm (pl. al-aḥkām): Authority; authority with knowledge and sound judgment; judgment; verdict; legal ordinance(s)

(al-)Ḥusn: Good, beautiful

(al-)Ḥuṭamah: The Consuming Fire. One of the degrees or places of Divine Punishment in the Hereafter (see *al-adhāb*)

(al-)'Ibādah: Worship, devotion; humble worshipping or devotion to God

Iblīs: The chief Satan. The jinn who persistently disobeyed God and was eternally rejected from His Mercy. It was allowed to try to tempt human for wise purposes God has appointed for human earthly life

(al-)'Iddah: The waiting period that a woman is required to observe for a new marriage after divorce or because of the husband's death. It is three menstrual courses for divorced women and four months and ten days for the women who have lost their husbands.

(al-)Ifk: Slander, calumny; ungrounded accusation

(al-)Iḥrām: The special Pilgrimage attire and the state in which pilgrims are held for some time during which they must wear that attire and perform the prescribed rituals of the Pilgrimage and observe certain prohibitions such as abstention from all sex acts, from the use of perfume, from hunting or killing animals, cutting the beard or shaving the head,

cutting the nails, plucking blades of grass, and cutting green trees

(al-)Ifsād: cause or provoke disorder and corruption

(al-)Ihkām: Making firm and explicit in meaning

(al-)Ihsān: Highest level of obedience in worship; devotion to doing good and doing it as if seeing God or in the awareness of God's seeing His servants; kindness, kind treatment

(al-)Ijmā': Consensus of Muslim *faqīh*s (jurisprudents) on a ruling for a new issue

(al-)Ijtihād: A *faqīh*'s exerting the sum total of their capacity in order to deduce rulings or laws on new issues from the basic sources of law, namely the Qur'ān, Sunnah, and *Ijmā'*

(al-)Ikhlāṣ: Believing in God sincerely and without associating any partners with Him; purity of intention in faith and practicing the Religion only for God's sake

(al-)Ikhtilāf: Differences of view and attitude; differences in intelligence, ability, ambition, and desire etc. in life and character; being at variance and in conflict with one another

(al-)Ilā': The oath taken by a husband that he will not approach his wife for a certain period. If this continues for longer than four months, then it is considered a divorce. Backing on this vow requires atonement.

(al-)Ilāh: Deity

(al-)'Ilm: Knowledge. (True) knowledge based on the Revelation. Knowledge is a product, like milk, that is the result of many processes in the mind, like the imagination, conceptualization, reasoning, inquiry, verification, judging, adoption, conviction, and certainty. Islam accepts Revelation, intelligence (reason), sound sense, and scientific inquiry as being the means of knowledge.

(al-)Imām: Leader in the Prayer; leader of the Muslims especially in religious matters

(al-)Imām al-Mubīn: The Manifest Record; the Record in which the future lives of all things and beings including all the principles governing those lives and all their deeds and the reasons or causes therefor are kept pre-recorded

(al-)Īmān: Undoubted belief or faith (in whatever God wants to be believed in). Like unbelief, belief or faith is an acknowledgment and an act of confirmation by the heart. Faith does not consist in a simple acceptance or confession. Just as there are many stages or degrees in the growth of a tree from its seed until it is in its fully-grown, fruit-bearing state, and just as there are countless degrees and ranks in the manifestations of the sun from its manifestations of light and heat in all things on the earth up to its reflection on the moon and then back to itself, so too does faith have almost uncountable degrees and ranks, from a simple acknowledgment of reason and confirmation of the heart, up to degrees of penetration in all the parts and faculties of the body that control and the degrees that direct the entire life of a person – from the faith of a common person to that of the greatest of the Messengers.

(al-)Indhār: Warning

(al-)Infāq: Spending of whatever God provides (of wealth, knowledge, power, etc.) in God's cause or to those in need purely for the good pleasure of God and without placing others under obligation

(al-)Injīl: The Divine Book which God gave to the Prophet Jesus, upon him be peace

(al-)Insān (pl. *an-nās*): Human, humankind

(al-)Inshā': Producing, bringing about, building

(al-)Inshirāh: The expansion of the breast so that one can fully understand God's Religion, feel exhilaration coming from knowledge of Him, and show patience with whatever one encounters in God's way

(al-)Inzāl: A sending down of the Qur'ān or the Qur'ānic verses

Iqāamat aṣ-Ṣalāh: The offering of the Prayer perfectly (in conformity with all its conditions)

(al-)Irādah: Will-power (by which a person can direct his or her thoughts and actions). *Al-Irādah* is also an Attribute of God, denoting His absolute Will. It has another meaning, which is decree, command.

(al-)Irshād: Guiding to spiritual and intellectual excellence

(al-)'Ishā': The Night or Late Evening Prayer

(al-)Islāḥ: Setting things right; reformation; mending one's way

(al-)Islām: The Divine Religion which God has appointed for humankind and revealed through all His Prophets. It was lastly and universally revealed through and conveyed by the Prophet Muhammad, upon him be peace and blessings.

(al-)Ism: Name; the word by which a thing or person is known

(al-)Isrā': The (miraculous) Night Journey (which the Prophet Muhammad, upon him be peace and blessings, made from Makkah to Masjid al-Aqsā' in Jerusalem)

(al-)Isrāf: Being wasteful of God-giving faculties and committing excesses

(al-)Istibrā: Ensuring that the drops of urine have ceased, and that one's heart is content according to one's general habit, either by walking, coughing, lying down or any other method

(al-)Istidrāj: Leading to perdition by degrees

(al-)Istifā: Choosing and making pure and distinguished

(al-)Istighfār: Imploring God for forgiveness of one's misdeeds or sins

(al-)Istihsān: Adoption of what is good and beneficial in legislation

(al-)Istinjā: Cleaning the private parts after urinating or passing stool, preferably using water and toilet paper

(al-)Istiqāmah: Straightforwardness (as avoiding all deviation and extremes, and as following in the footsteps of the Prophet

(al-)Istisqā': Invoking God for rain at the time of a drought

(al-)Istishāb: Law Maintaining without change what has already been approved

(al-)Istiwā: Literally: *a plant or a tree* rising firmly on its stem; *a human being* reaching his or her full man/womanhood and growing to maturity: God directing His Will, (Power, and Favor) to something

Istiwā alā'l-'Arsh: God or a sovereign establishing oneself on the throne

Istiwā ila's-samāi: God directing (His Knowledge, Will, Power, and Favor) to the heaven

(al-)'Isyān: Disobeying, defiance, rebellion

(al-)Itā'ah: Obedience

(al-)I'thār: Altruism, preferring others to oneself, thinking of the needs and desires of others to one's own; giving precedence to the common interests of the community over one's own; devoting oneself to the lives of others in complete forgetfulness of all concerns of one's own

(al-)Ithm: Blatant sin

(al-)I'tidā: Exceeding the bounds (set by God); offending

al-I'tikāf: Retreat in the mosques for the purpose of worship; especially the practice of spending some time in *Ramadān* in a mosque in devotion to God

(al-)Itmi'nān: Being at rest; contentment; full conviction and satisfaction

(al-)Ittiqā: Keeping one's duties to God and avoiding all kinds of sins in reverence for God and piety; attaining reverent piety toward God and His protection (against any kind of straying and its consequent punishment in this world and the Hereafter)

(al-)Jahālah: Ignorance; a lack of knowledge and behaving like one devoid of knowledge; an instance of being defeated to the evil-commanding carnal soul

Jahannam: Hell; the place where the disbelieving criminals will go in the Hereafter

(al-)Jāhiliyyah: Any doctrine or worldview and way of life based on rejection or disregard of heavenly guidance communicated to humankind through the Prophets and Messengers of God; the attitude of treating human life – either wholly or partly – as independent of the directives of God

(al-)Jamrah: One of the three stone-built pillars situated at Minā in Makkah, which repre-

sent Satan. The pilgrims throw pebbles at them during the three *Íd* days during the Pilgrimage

(al-)Janābah: The state of major ritual impurity caused by coitus, discharge of semen, menses, and post-childbirth bleeding. People who are in this state cannot pray, circumambulate the Ka'bah (*ṭawāf*), enter a mosque or place of worship unless necessary, or touch the Qur'an or any of its verses except with a clean cloth or something similar.

(al-)Jannah: Paradise; the heavenly realm of blessings where in the Hereafter God will admit those who believe and do good, righteous deeds

Jannatu 'l-Ma 'wā: The Heavenly Garden of Refuge and Dwelling

Jannāt 'Adn: Heavenly Gardens of perpetual bliss

Jannatu 'l-Khuld: The Heavenly Garden of Immortality

Jannātu 'n-na 'ím: Heavenly Gardens of bounty and blessing

(al-)Jibt: Any false deity

(al-)Jihād: Striving, doing one's utmost to achieve something; striving in God's cause with one's possessions and person

(al-)Jinn: A species of invisible, conscious, and responsible beings created from smokeless "fire" penetrating through the body

(al-)Jizyah: The tax of protection and exemption from military service which non-Muslim citizens of a Muslim state are required to pay

(al-)Jumu 'ah: Friday. The Friday Congregational Prayer is obligatory on every free, adult, sane, and resident Muslim male. It is offered during the time of the Noon Prayer, and the normal Noon Prayer is not performed on Friday.

(al-)Kabāir: The major sins. They are those in return for committing which God or His Messenger threatens a severe punishment in the Hereafter, and for some of which there is (also) a prescribed punishment in the world.

(al-)Kafālah: The pledge given by somebody to a creditor to guarantee that the debtor will be present at a certain specific place to pay their debt or fine, or to undergo a punishment etc.

(al-)Kaffārah: Atonement, expiation; the prescribed way of making amends for wrong actions, particularly missed obligatory actions

(al-)Kāfir (pl. *al-Kuffār):* Unbeliever; one who denies any of the things which must be believed in although the truths of faith have been thoroughly and convincingly conveyed to them

(al-)Kalālah: One who dies leaving behind no lineal heirs

(al-)Kalām: Speech; an Attribute of God; any of God's Words manifested as a Scripture

(al-)Kalimah: Word; any of God's words. God has two kinds of words, one issuing from His Attribute of Speech, the other from His Power. His words that issue from His Attribute of Speech are His Scriptures that He sent to some of His Messengers. His words that issue from His Attribute of Power are all of His works.

(al-)Kalimat al-Khabīthah: A corrupt word (is like a corrupt tree uprooted from upon the earth, having no constancy).

(al-)Kalimat at-Tayyibah: A good or pure word. A good word is like a good tree – its roots holding firm (in the ground) and its branches in heaven; it yields its fruit in every season due by its Lord's leave.

(al-)Kasb: Earning; earning reward or punishment in return for one's belief and doing

(al-)Kawthar: Unceasing, abundant good

(al-)Khabīth: The corrupt

(al-)Khalīfah: Vicegerent or one who exercises the authority delegated to them by their principal, and does so in the capacity of their deputy and agent; one having the status or duty of *khilāfah* (see *al-Khilāfah*); caliph

(al-)Khalq: Creating; creation

(al-)Khamr: Anything that acts as an agent of intoxication

(al-)Khāshi ': One humbled by one's deep reverence and awe of God

(al-)Khayr: What is better; property one has

(al-)Khilāfah: Succession; vicegerency; the status or duty of improving the earth on the basis of knowledge of things and the laws of creation (which we wrongly call the "laws of nature"), and ruling on the earth according to the dictates of God, thus establishing justice

(al-)Kharāj: Tax imposed on the revenue out of land taken from non-Muslim citizens of an Islamic state

Khātam al-Anbiyā': A title of the Prophet Muḥammad, upon him be peace and blessings, in the meaning of the seal (last) of the Prophets

(al-)Khāsir: A loser, one ruined in loss

(al-)Khawf: Fear; fear leading one to abstain not only from all that is forbidden, but also from those deeds from which it is advisable to refrain

(al-)Khizy: Disgrace

(al-)Khuld: Immortality

(al-)Khuluq: Conduct; pattern of conduct; morality, good morals

(al-)Khums: *Literally* one-fifth. One-fifth of the gains of war or any buried treasure dug out which must be paid to the state

(al-)Khushū': Humility, and deep reverence and awe

(al-)Khutbah: Sermon; the sermon given during the Friday Congregational Prayer; a sermon given during the marriage ceremony

(al-)Kitāb: Book; any of the Divine Books given or revealed to some among the Messengers of God

(al-)Kitāb al-A'māl: A record of one's deeds in the world to be displayed in the Hereafter

(al-)Kitāb al-Mubīn: The Divine Book, particularly the Qur'an clear in itself and clearly showing the truth; the Manifest Book in which the lives of all things and beings are recorded in detail

(al-)Kufr: Literally meaning concealing and covering, it denotes rejection of and unbelief in any of the pillars of faith and the established religious commandments

(al-)Kursī: The platform on which the 'Arsh (the Throne) is set up (see *al-'Arsh*); when

used for God, it must signify His Knowledge, Will, Power, and Sovereignty.

(al-)La'nah: Cursing; God's cursing denotes rejecting from His Mercy and condemning to punishment

(al-)Lawḥ al-Maḥfūẓ: The Supreme Ever-Preserved Tablet (or Record) where the Divine principles that determine the archetypal "plan and program" of the creation, and the future lives of all beings including all their deeds are kept recorded. In one respect, it is identical with the *Imām al-Mubīn*.

(al-)Lawḥ al-Maḥw wa 'l-Ithbāt: The Tablet of Effacement (Canceling) and Confirmation or the metaphorical page of time along which God manifests or hangs whatever He wills and decrees of the beings and/or things and events recorded on the Supreme Ever-Preserved Tablet

Laylat al-Qadr: The Night of Power and Destiny. Any of the last ten nights of the Month of *Ramaḍān* during which the Divine Destiny identifies all the things and events to come into existence or happen in the new one year each with its particular nature and entrusts to the Divine Power

(al-)Li'ān: An oath which is taken by both the wife and the husband when he accuses his wife of committing illegal sexual intercourse (*sūrah* 24: 6-9)

(al-)Mā': Water; rain; the seminal fluid; ether filling the space

(al-)Maghfirah: Forgiveness

(al-)Mahr: The bridal-due. It signifies the amount of payment that is settled between the spouses at the time of marriage, and which the husband is required to make to his bride.

(al-)Maḥram: The group of people who are unlawful for a woman to marry due to marital or blood or milk relationships

(al-)Makrūh: Disliked and Disapproved of, but not prohibited by God

(al-)Mala': Council; board of ministers or leaders in a community

(al-)Malau 'l-a'lā: The heavenly high assembly (of angels)

(al-)Malak (pl: *al-Malāikah*): The spiritual beings of light endowed with great might, who absolutely obey God and carry out His commands. Angels have different kinds or species but are not differentiated as male or female. There is nothing to cause quarrels or disputes among them because they are innocent, their realm is vast, their nature is pure, and their stations are fixed. Each of the heavenly bodies is a place of worship for the angels.

(al-)Malakūt: The spiritual and transcendental dimension of existence; God's absolute dominion of the creation where His Power operates without the medium of matter and material causes

(al-)Mālik: Master

(al-)Manāsik: All the rites of the *Hajj*

(al-)Mansūkh: Any command or verdict abrogated or canceled; a statement utterly canceled and removed or abrogated in regard with its meaning or the command it contains or both

(al-)Maqām al-Maḥmūd: The highest station or rank of being praised by God and the whole body of believers as particular to the Prophet Muḥammad, upon him be peace and blessings, by virtue of which he will be honored with the permission to intercede on behalf of all people on the Plain of Supreme Gathering

(al-)Ma'rifah: Knowledge of God; the appearance and development of knowledge of God in one's conscience, or knowing God by one's conscience or heart

(al-)Ma'ruf: Any norm of behavior or practice generally accepted by a community and not opposed to the basic principles of Islam

Maṣāliḥ al-mursalah: Law Taking what is suited to the public benefit and discarding what is harmful

Māshā'allāh: Whatever God wills (occurs); What excellent things God wills and does!

(al-)Mashī'ah: Will. God's absolute Will for the creation and direction of the universe and guidance of people

(al-)Mashwarah: Consultation

(al-)Masīḥ: The Christ – Jesus son of Mary

(al-)Masjid: The building where the Prayer is offered in congregation; the parts of human body with which one prostrates

(al-)Matā': Enjoyment of the worldly life

(al-)Mathal: Parable, comparison, example

(al-)Mawlā: Lord; emancipated slave; master; guardian; friend

(al-)Miḥrāb: The Prayer niche of a mosque, in front of which the imam stands when leading the congregational prayers

(al-)Millah: The way of belief and life; life-style

(al-)Minnah: Favoring; favoring and putting under obligation

(al-)Mīqāt: The specific places where pilgrims or people intending to perform *Hajj* or *'Umrah* must declare their intention to do so and enter the state of *iḥrām*

(al-)Mi'rāj: The Ascension. The miraculous journeying of the Prophet Muḥammad, upon him be peace and blessings, through the realms of existence beyond the limit of forms

(al-)Miskīn (pl. *al-masākīn*): A destitute one in greater distress than the ordinary poor people and yet whose sense of self-respect prevents them from begging and whose outward demeanor fails to give the impression that they are deserving of help

(al-)Mīthāq: A solemn binding

(al-)Mīzān: The balance, the equilibrium

(al-)Muadhdhin (or *muezzin*): The person who calls the *adhān* – who makes the call to the Prayer

(al-)Mubārak: Blessed; provided with blessings

(al-)Mubīn: Clear in itself and clearly showing (the truth)

(al-)Muḥaddith: An Islamic scholar of *Ḥadīth*

(al-)Muhājir: One who emigrates to another land for God's sake; a Companion of the Prophet who emigrated to *Madīnah* before the conquest of Makkah

(al-)Muḥāsabah: Self-criticism or self-interrogation

(al-)Muhkam: Firm and valid; any of the verses of the Qur'ān that are explicit in meaning and content and consist the core of the Qur'ān and foundations of the Islamic belief and life. They also serve as principles to understand the whole of the Qur'ān and understanding the Qur'ān (see *al-mutashābih*)

(al-)Munkar: Evil; anything disapproved of by God, as well as by common sense and public view

(al-)Mustakbir: An oppressive, arrogant one

(al-)Mutashābih: The allegorical, multifaceted (verses of the Qur'ān). They are those which, having more than one meaning, contain relative truths which can be understood by considering the relevant verses and referring to the *muhkam* ones.

(al-)Muhsanāt: The chaste, Muslim, free Muslim women

(al)Muhsin: One who tries to do well whatever they do and is devoted to doing good aware that God sees them

al-Mu'jizah: Any extraordinary, supernatural achievement God creates at the hand of a Prophet

(al-)Mujrim: (Disbelieving) criminal lost in accumulating sin

(al-)Mukhlas: One endowed with sincerity and purity of intention in faith and practicing the Religion for God's sake

(al-)Mukhlis: One sincere in their faith in the Only One God and pure of intention in practicing the Religion only for God's sake

(al-)Mujāhid: One who strives to be a good Muslim and in God's cause with their wealth and person

(al-)Mujtahid: One who exerts the sum total of their capacity in order to deduce rulings or laws on new issues from the basic sources of law, namely the Qur'ān, Sunnah, and *Ijmā'*.

(al-)Mulk: Sovereignty; absolute ownership and dominion

(al-)Mu'min: The Believer. A person who has faith in whatever must be believed in and is a righteous and obedient servant of Him

(al-)Munāfiq: One who is a believer outwardly or professes faith while being an unbeliever inwardly and in reality; hypocrite

(al-)Munīb: A servant of God who, sincere in quest of the truth, turns to Him in contrition

(al-)Muqarrab: Those foremost in faith and practicing the Religion and inner-stationed to God

(al-)Murāqabah: (Self-)supervising and controlling, and living in the consciousness of being controlled (by God)

(al-)Murtad: Apostate; one who has become an unbeliever after having believed

(al-)Mursal: A Prophet sent or charged with calling to God's Religion; an angel sent to the world with a special mission

(al-)Musallī: One who regularly does the prescribed Prayers

(al-)Mushaf: A copy of the Qur'ān

(al-)Mushrik: A polytheist: a person who commits *Shirk* (see *Shirk*) – who associates partners with God in His Divinity, and Lordship, and Sovereignty or in any of these

(al-)Muslih: One who sets things right; one who mends their way

(al-)Muslim: One who believes in whatever is to be believed in and practices Islam in their daily life in submission to God; *law* one who professes faith and, as a citizen of a Muslim state, joins a Muslim congregation in the Prayer and pays the *Zakāh*

(al-)Musrif: One, having wasted their God-given faculties, commits excesses; one given to wastefulness

(al-)Mustad'af: One bereft of any means to find the true guidance; one bereft of any means to carry out the required religious obligation like emigrating in God's cause

(al-)Mutraf: Self-indulgent; lost in pursuit of pleasures without moral limit or consideration

(al-)Muttaqī: One trying to keep their duties to God required by both the Religion and the Divine laws of life and avoid the forbidden things in reverence for God and piety

(al-)Mudtarr: In strained circumstances

(an-)Nabiyy: Prophet; one who receives Revelation from God and has the duty of communicating it to people. The last of the Prophets is the Prophet Muḥammad, upon him be peace and blessings.

(an-)Nadhīr: Warner. Basically, a Prophet who gave the glad tidings of prosperity in return for faith and righteousness (see *al-Bashīr*) and warned of evil consequences of all kinds of misguidance.

(an-)Nāfilah: Any optional or supererogatory good deed, which when done brings reward and when not done causes no sin

(an-)Nafl (al-anfāl): Any worldly reward coming as the result of services rendered in God's cause; war-gains

(an-)Nafs: The self of a living being; the faculty (soul) which is the source or mechanism of the worldly life possessed by humankind and the jinn. Self-training, or the training of the soul, has been accepted as an extremely important element of the Divine Religion. This training, according to some schools in Islam, has ten stages, and according to others and some Qur'ānic allusions seven stages: If the soul lives only a life of ease in the swamp of carnal appetites, it is the evil-commanding, carnal soul (*an-nafs al-ammārah*); if it falters time and again while following the way of the Religion to attain piety and righteousness, but each time that it falters it criticizes itself and turns to its Lord, then it is the self-accusing soul (*an-nafs al-lawwāmah*). The soul which always resists evil in devotion to God and is favored with certain Divine gifts in proportion to its purity is called the soul receiving inspiration (*an-nafs al-mulhimah*). When it reaches the point where it has a relation with its Lord in perfect devotion and sincerity and when its consciousness is at rest, it is the soul at rest (*an-nafs al-muṭmainnah*). If it has reached the station where it abandons all its choices and is a representative of Divine will, it is the soul pleased with God (*an-nafs ar-rāḍiyah*). When its greatest aim is acquiring God's good pleasure and approval and when it is always acting to this end in consideration of, "I am pleased with You, so be pleased with me," then it is the soul with which God is pleased (*an-nafs al-marḍiyyah*). Finally, the soul which has been perfectly purified of all sins and evil morals and has the capacity to be completely adorned with the full manifestations of Divine Qualities and Prophetic willpower and resolution is called the soul perfected or the soul pure (*an-nafs az-zakiyyah* or *an-nafs aṣ-ṣāfiyah*).

(an-)Najāḥ: Delivery, being saved, salvation

Nahy 'ani'l-munkar: Forbidding and trying to prevent evil (in appropriate ways)

(an-)Nār: Fire; the Fire – Hellfire

(an-)Nās: Humankind

(an-)Naskh: Abrogation. Canceling a legal verdict or commandment, or removal of a statement

(an-)Nāsikh: A new legal verdict or command in place of an abrogated one; a new statement in place of another canceled or removed

(an-)Naṣr: Help leading to victory

(an-)Nifāq: Hypocrisy; profession of faith while being an unbeliever in heart; underground and secret activities to undermine an Islamic order

(an-)Nikāḥ: Marriage according to God's law; marriage contract

(an-)Ni'mah: Favor and blessing; any favor or blessing of God, prominently His favor of guidance

(an-)Nisāb: Minimum amount of property liable to payment of the *Zakāh* or animal sacrifice or *Sadaqat al-fiṭr* (payment made to the needy before the Prayer of *Īd al-Fiṭr)*

(an-)Nubuwwah: Prophethood.

(an-)Nūr: Light. It is not exactly identical with the energy coming from the sun (*ḍiyā'*) or another light-giving object. It is as if more substantial than the known light and having precedence to light in the process of creation. The Qur'ān uses it in spiritual sense in many of its verses.

(an-)Nusuk: All forms of devotion and worship

(an-)Nuṭfah: a drop of seminal fluid

(an-)Nuzūl: The coming down of the Qur'ān from God

(al-)Qadar wa 'l-Qaḍā: The Divine Destiny and Decree; the Divine Destiny and its enforcement

(al-)Qāḍī: Judge

(al-)Qalb: The heart; the spiritual intellect; the center of all emotions and (intellectual and spiritual) faculties, such as perception, consciousness, sensation, reasoning, and will-power

Qālū balā: They said, "Yes!" – the event (mentioned in 33: 72) describing the human profession of God's Lordship in spirit or conscience or in a dimension of existence unknown to us with its exact nature

(al-)Qarḍ al-ḥasan: A goodly loan (to God), signifying any expenditure made in God's cause or for the needy purely for God's sake

(al-)Qasam: The oath which especially God swears by certain phenomena (in the Qur'ān)

(al-)Qawwām or *qayyim:* Protector and maintainer; one who is responsible for administering or supervising the affairs of either an individual or an organization, for protecting and safeguarding them and taking care of their needs

(al-)Qiblah: The direction to face in the Prayer. For the Muslims it is the direction of the Sacred Mosque of the Ka'bah in Makkah.

al-Qiṣāṣ: Inviolate values (especially in the sense of basic human rights) being of the same value and demanding retribution, a principle which gives rise to retaliation in law

al-Qitāl: Fighting, war, warfare

(al-)Qiyām: The standing position during the Prayer; "rising" to make an evaluation and adopt a new attitude or position; maintenance

(al-)Qiyāmah: The overall destruction of the world and subsequent resurrection and re-building of the world

(al-)Qiyās: Analogy

(al-)Qunūt: Humble, devoutly obedience; supplication in the Prayer, particularly in the standing position just before the *rukū'* (bowing down) in the third *rak'ah* (cycle) of the

Witr Prayer following the Late-Evening or Night Prayer

al-Qur'ān: The Qur'ān; the last Book of God which He revealed to the Prophet Muhammad, upon him be peace and blessings as His last and universal Message to conscious, responsible beings

al-Qurūn al-'Ūlā: The earliest generations and ages in human history until the Prophet Abraham or Moses, upon them be peace

(al-)Qu'ūd: Sitting position during the Prayer

(ar-)Rabb: Lord, master; the Lord (God as the Creator, Provider, Trainer, Upbringer, and Director of all creatures)

(ar-)Rajā': Expectation, waiting for what one wholeheartedly desires to be

(ar-)Rak'ah: A unit or cycle of the Prayer

(ar-)Raḥm: Mercy; womb; blood relations

(ar-)Raḥmah: Mercy, compassion, grace

(ar-)Rajīm: Rejected (from God's Mercy)

Ramaḍān: The 9th month of the (Islamic) lunar calendar which the Muslims spend fasting

(ar-)Rasūl: The Prophet given a Scripture and charged with conveying God's Revelations

(ar-)Ribā: Interest

(ar-)Riḍā: Resignation, willing submission to God's treatments; being pleased with God and pleasing to Him

(ar-)Riḍwān: God's good pleasure; God's being pleased with one

(ar-)Risālah: Messengership (see *ar-Rasūl*); message (Divine Message)

(ar-)Rizq: Provision, anything with which God provides

(ar-)Rubūbiyah: Lordship; God's being the Lord of all creatures

(ar-)Rūḥ: The spirit; the center or source of conscious life which continues to live after a person dies; the Revelation; the spiritual, angelic being responsible for or representing all spirits

Rūḥu 'l-Quds: The Spirit of Holiness; the Spirit of extraordinary purity, cleanliness, and blessing *(ar-)Rushd:* Integrity and maturity in thought and action, and right conduct and correct behavior

(as-)Sabīl: Road, path, way, a means to an end *(fī sabīli 'llāh:* in God's cause)

(as-)Sābiqūn: The foremost in faith and good deeds, and serving God's cause

(as-)Sābirūn: The patient and steadfast

(as-)Sabr: Patience; steadfastness in carrying out the obligations and refraining from prohibitions, resisting the temptations to sin of the evil-commanding, carnal soul and Satan, enduring any disaster, and showing no haste in pursuing those of one's hopes or plans that require a stretch of time to achieve

(as-)Sabt: The Sabbath; Saturday of every week which the Children of Israel must consecrate for rest and worship

(as-)Sab'u 'l-Mathānī (Sab'an mina 'l-Mathānī): Another name for *Sūrat al-Fātihah*, meaning the Seven Doubly-Repeated Verses.

(as-)Sadaqah: Anything given away in alms or done supererogatorily for the good pleasure of God

Sadaqat al-fitr: The obligatory payment made to the needy in *Ramadān* until the Prayer of *Īd al-Fitr*

Sadd az-zarā'i: Blocking corruption and what is unlawful

(as-)Safīh: A foolish one, devoid of common sense and reasoning

(as-)Sahābī (pl. al-Ashāb): A Companion of the Prophet Muhammad, upon him be peace and blessings, who saw and heard him at least once and died as a believer

(as-)Sajdah: Prostration; it signifies utmost and most sincere submission

(as-)Sakīnah: Inner peace and reassurance, perfect calmness due to the Presence of God being made clear and apparent

(as-)Salāh: The Prayer; the cardinal form of worship Muslims do for the good pleasure of God

(as-)Salām: Peace, wish of peace and security from all kinds of deviations and sufferings

Salāt al-Khawf: The Prayer of Fear; the Prescribed Prayer done shortened during a journey or when in a state of fear or insecurity, including times of war or disaster, such as fire and flood

Salāt al-Musāfir: The Prayer of Journey; the Prescribed Prayer done shortened during a journey

(as-)Sālih: Good and righteous, sound

(as-)Sawm: Fasting; total abstinence from food, liquid, and any sexual pleasure (either from sexual relations or self-satisfaction) from dawn to sunset with the intention of worshipping God as His order

(as-)Sa'y: Labor, working, striving; slight running or speedy walking between the hills of as-Safā and al-Marwah as a rite of *Hajj* and *Umrah*

(ash-)Shafā'ah: Intercession. Expecting God's help or favor through an intermediary agent either in the world or in the Hereafter. On Judgment Day, intercession is made on behalf of one and by one whom God permits

(ash-)Shahwah: Passion, passionate attachment, lust

(ash-)Shahādah: What is observable or sensed; witnessing and bearing witness; martyrdom

(ash-)Shāhid: Witness; one who observes and bears witness to; one who sees the hidden Divine truths and testifies to them with their lives; one who testifies for or against

(ash-)Shahīd: Witness; one who observes and bears witness to; martyr (one who sacrifices one's life in God's cause and thereby proves the truth of God's way

(ash-)Shākir: A thankful one

(ash-)Sharī'ah: The way God has laid down for His creatures to follow in their daily lives; the practical aspect of the Religion of Islam; the body of all Islamic injunctions or laws, based on the Qur'ān and the Sunnah, and then further developed by jurists to apply Islamic concepts to daily life

(ash-)Sharī'at at-Takwīniyyah: The body of God's laws related to the lives of all creatures and the creation and operation of the universe

(ash-)Shaytān: The jinn who persistently disobeyed God and was eternally rejected from His Mercy. It was allowed to try to tempt human for wise purposes God has appointed for human earthly life. There are many similar *shaytān*s among the jinn and human beings who try to tempt others from God's Straight Path.

(ash-)Shi'ār (pl. *ash-sha'āir):* Emblem or public symbol. The call to the Prayer, Prayer in congregation, most particularly the congregational prayers of *Jumu'ah* and the two *'Īd*s, *Hajj* with its rituals, mosques, sacrifice, etc., are (as well as having their religious meaning for the individual and the community) among the public symbols that identify Islam and the Muslim community.

(as-)Sidq: Truthfulness

(ash)-Shirk: Associating partners with God in His Divinity, and Lordship, and Sovereignty or in any of these

(ash-)Shu'r: Perception, awareness

(ash-)Shūrā: Consultation. It is among the most important requirements for reaching the right decision, and one of the essentials of Islamic constitution.

(ash-)Shukr: Thankfulness, gratitude, gratefulness

(as-)Siddīq: The sincere and truthful; loyal and faithful; following the Straight Path without deviation

Sidrat al-Muntahā: The Lote-tree of the furthest limit; the boundary between the realm of Divinity and the realm of creation

(as-)Sīrah: Conduct, personality; the personality and life story of God's Messenger, upon him be peace and blessings

(as-)Sirāt: The path having ups and downs, wide in some of it parts and narrow in others, difficult to walk on. The path over Hell to lead to Paradise with ups and downs, one having walls on its sides, and doors and windows opening on the outside. If this Prophetic

description is figurative, it means that we cannot know its real identity.

(as-)Sirāt al-Mustaqīm: The only Straight Path to God, which the Prophet Muhammad, upon him be peace and blessings, demonstrated to humankind and the jinn, and was manifested by way of the Qur'an and Sunnah.

Subhāna'llāh: All-Glorified is God (in that He is absolutely exalted above having any defects, needs, and partners); I glorify God.

(as-)Suffah: A shaded place in al-Masjid an-Nabī in Madīnah where poor people used to take shelter during the Messenger's time

Ashāb as-Suffah: About three or four hundred Companions who stayed in *as-Suffah* and spent most of their time in the company of the Messenger, upon him be peace and blessings

(as-)Sulh: Reconcilitaion, peace

(as-)Suhuf (pl. of *as-Sahīfah):* Scrolls given to some Messengers by God

(as-)Sunnah: The way of God's Messenger. It is the Traditions recording every act, word, and confirmation of the Messenger. It is the second source of Islamic legislation (the Qur'ān being the first one). All scholars of religious sciences and sometimes even natural scientists use it to establish the principles of their disciplines and to solve difficulties. The Qur'ān and authentic prophetic Traditions enjoin Muslims to follow the Sunnah. In addition to being an independent source of legislation, it also defines what is stated in general terms in the Qur'ān by referring to particular instances, and it defines the general principle underlying statements in the Qur'ān that are in themselves specific and particular. Besides, the Sunnah (like the Qur'ān which it embodies) is also concerned with moral guidance, so the Sunnah provides inspiration and the horizons for moral and spiritual instruction in all spheres of life, as well as providing the inspiration and horizons (limits) within which Islamic legislation may be effected.

Sunnah Prayers: They are the Prayers considered recommended in view of the fact that God's Messenger either performed them often and/or made statements about their meritorious character and urged the Muslims to do them.

Sunnatu 'llāh: God's unchanging way and practice from the beginning of the universe. It has two aspects, one for the life of all creatures, the other for the guidance of humankind and jinn. History mirrors *Sunnatu 'llāh*.

(aṣ-)Ṣūr: The Trumpet which will be blown by the archangel Isrāfīl. We do not know the exact nature of the Trumpet and what is really meant by its being blown. It will be blown twice, and when it is blown the first time, the entire order of the universe will be disrupted, and on its second blowing, all the dead will be raised in a completely fresh world and order.

(as-)Sūrah: An independent chapter of the Qur'ān.

(at-)Ta'aqqul: Reasoning and reflecting to make a conclusion and be able to distinguish between what is right and wrong and what is beneficial and harmful

(at-)Tabarrī: Disowning, to be quit of; declaring to longer have any relation with

(at-)Tābiūn: Successors; the generation succeeding the Companions of the Prophet Muḥammad, upon him be peace and blessings

(at-)Tablīgh: Conveying a message to others as best as possible; conveying Islam or God's Message to people to the extent that, left to their (carnal) soul and conscience they can make a free choice between belief and unbelief

(at-)Tabshīr: Giving the good tidings of; making appealing

(The Campaign of) Tabuk: The military campaign which the Muslims under the command of God's Messenger made to Tabuk near the Jordan boundary of Arabia in the 9th year of *Hijrah* in order to counter the Byzantine offensive. The Qur'ān relates it in *Sūrah* 9 especially from the perspective that it served for a decisive separation between faith and hypocrisy in *Madīnah*, and the believers proved their loyalty to God's cause.

(at-)Tabyīn: Clarifying, making clear

(at-)Tadabbur: Pondering deeply

(at-)Taḍarru': Humble turning (to God); humble devotion and supplication

(at-)Tadhakkur: Reflecting and being mindful

(at-)Tafaqquh: Discerning and understanding, penetrating the essence of a matter and grasping it

(at-)Tafakkur: Reflecting deeply and systematically

(at-)Tafriqah: Splitting into factions or parties

(at-)Tafṣīl: Propounding in detail; spelling out distinctly, making clear, and putting in ordered sequence

(at-)Tafsīr: Expounding, usually referring to expounding studies of the Qur'ān

(aṭ-)Ṭāghūt: The power or powers of evil who institute patterns of belief and rule in defiance of God

(aṭ-)Ṭahārah: Purification, cleansing. Purity of soul or spiritual purification can be accomplished through sincere faith in and submission to God and freedom from egotism and arrogance. Bodily purification occurs through *tayammum*, *wuḍū'*, and *ghusl*, according to conditions and types of contamination. Clothes and other things are usually purified by washing.

(at-)Tahajjud: A Sunnah Prayer done before dawn.

(at-)Taḥmīd: Praising; praising God in that one knows and declares Him with the Attributes belonging and fitting for Him, and thanking Him.

(at-)Tajallī al-Wāḥidiyah: God's manifestation of His Names on the whole of the universe or a species or on a whole; His universal manifestation with all of His Names related to the universe

(at-)Tajallī al-Aḥadiyah: God's particular manifestation on an individual thing or being with one or some of His Names

(at-)Takbīr: Saying *Allahu Akbar* (God is the All-Great); declaring God to be immeasurably and incomparably great

(at-)Takdhīb: Denial, contradiction

(aṭ-)Ṭalāq: Divorce

(at-)Tanzīl: Sending down (the Qur'ān) in parts

(at-)Taqdīs: Declaring that God alone is all-holy and to be worshipped as God and Lord. It also means calling God's blessings upon saintly people, saying: May God exalt His holiness.

(at-)Taqwā: Reverent piety towards God; refraining from sins in reverence for God and piety and receiving His protection against deviations and His punishment

(at-)Tartīl: Reciting calmly and distinctly

(at-)Tasbīḥ: Glorifying God; proclaiming that God is absolutely free from any defect and doing anything meaningless and useless, and that He is absolutely above having any likes and partners, and sons and daughters, and bearing any resemblance with the created. The word of tasbīḥ is Subḥāna 'llāh

(at-)Tashahhud: Giving testimony; a declaration of the Muslim faith at the sitting position in the Prayer, saying: I bear witness that there is no deity but God, and again I witness that Muḥammad is His servant and Messenger

(at-)Taskhīr: Subjugation; subjugating to one's will and putting under one's service

(at-)Taṣrīf: Setting out the signs (of God's Existence and Unity and other truths of faith) in diverse ways from different perspectives

(aṭ-)Ṭawāf: The rite of going round the Ka'bah

(at-)Tawakkul: Reliance on or putting one's trust (in God)

(at-)Tawbah: Turning to God in repentance

(at-)Tawbat an-Naṣūḥ: A sincere, reforming repentance. 'Ali, the Prophet's cousin and son-in-law and the fourth Caliph, describes a sincere, reforming repentance as follows: In order that your repentance can be a sincere, reforming, and valid one, you should (1) sincerely feel remorse for the sin you have committed, (2) fulfill all the obligatory religious duties and make up the missed ones, (3) return any right you have usurped to its owner, (4) beg the pardon of those you have offended, (5) resolve not to commit again the sin you have committed, and (6) make your carnal soul taste the difficulty of obedience to God as you have caused it to taste the pleasure of sinning.

(at-)Tawḥīd: God's Oneness and Unity; believing in and declaring God's Oneness and Unity; the belief and world-view Islam teaches. By saying God is One (Wāḥid), we mean that He is the Single Divine Being, and that no one or thing is like or comparable to Him. By His Unity or saying that He is One of absolute Unity, and Unique One (Aḥad), we mean that He is beyond all human conceptions and without partners (i.e., parents, sons, or daughters). Believing in God's Oneness entails accepting Him as the sole Deity and Lord of humankind, and so their sole Object of Worship. That in turn means recognizing Him as having the exclusive authority to make things lawful or unlawful.

(at-)Tawḥīd al-'Ubūdiyah: Total devotion, submission and subjection to God and declaring that none other than God deserves worship

(at-)Tawḥīd ar-Rubūbiyah: God's being and affirming Him as the sole Creator, Provider, Upbringer, Trainer, Sustainer, Nourisher, Lord and Master of all creatures

(at-)Tawḥīd al-Ulūhiyah: Believing that there is no deity but God and only God has the sole and exclusive right to be worshipped

(at-)Ta'wīl: Referring a word, an attitude, or an action to or explaining it with one of its probable meanings; expounding something read or seen or heard with other than what first comes to the mind and with a rational knowledge that is not instantly comprehended. Ta'wīl implies the preference of one of the probable meanings.

(at-)Tayammum: Purification for the Prayer using clean dust, earth or stone, when water for Ghusl or Wuḍū' is either unavailable or would be detrimental to health. It is done by striking the hands lightly on some clean earth and passing the palms over the face once, and striking the pure earth again with one's palms and rubbing the right and left arms alternately from the fingertips to the elbows.

(at-)Tayyib: Pure and wholesome (in composition and religiously)

(at-)Tazkiyah: Purification (of false beliefs and doctrines, sins, and all kinds of filth)

(at-)Tilāwah: Studying the Qur'an in order to understand it in the way it should be understood; reciting the Qur'ān; reciting the Qur'ān and conveying its meaning and message to others

(aṭ-)Ṭughyān: Rebellion, insubordination

(al-)Ubūdiyah: Servanthood; worshipful servanthood to God

(al-)Ukhuwwah: Brotherhood and sisterhood

Ulu 'l-absār: Those having the power of "seeing" and discernment

Ulu 'l-albāb: People of discernment

Ulu 'l-amr: Those entrusted with directing Muslims in matters of common concern; those who are in charge or in authority, or who are leaders

(al-)Ulūhiyah: God's being the Deity (of the whole creation)

(al-)Ummah: A community following the same way (of belief and life-style)

Ummat Muḥammad: Community of Muḥammad, the whole body of the Muslims

Umm al-mu'minīn: Mother of the believers. A title given to each wives of the Prophet Muḥammad, upon him be peace and blessings

(al-)Ummī: Unlettered, illiterate; following no Book revealed by God; *Prophet* one who neither reads nor writes (and has therefore remained preserved from any traces of the existing written culture and is free from any intellectual and spiritual pollution)

(al-)Umrah: Minor Pilgrimage: an Islamic rite and consists of *al-iḥrām*, and *aṭ-ṭawāf*, and *as-saʿy*

(al-)Urf: A generally accepted and established social practice and norm of conduct, one which is not opposed to Islam

(al-)Wājib: What is incumbent or necessary

(al-)Waʿd: Promise

(al-)Waʿīd: Threat

(al-)Waḥy: Divine Revelation; God's conveying His Message to a Prophet in a special way. It occurs in three ways. One is that God suddenly puts the meaning in the Prophet's heart and the Prophet knows that this meaning is from God. The second way or form is that God speaks to a Prophet from behind a veil. The third way is that God sends an angel to convey His Message to the Prophet.

(al-)Wajh: Face; Face as representing the person himself/herself; good pleasure and approval

(al-)**Wakīl:** *An authorized representative acting on behalf of someone; one chosen to direct the affairs of another*

(al-)Walāyah: Guardianship; friendship; mastership; the relationship of mutual support between the Islamic state and its citizens, and between the citizens themselves; special nearness to God

(al-)Waliyy (pl. *al-awliyāʾ):* Guardian; intimate friend; confidant; master; one enjoying special nearness to God

(al-)Warāthah: Inheritance

(al-)Wārith: Heir, inheritor

(al-)Wāsi: Guardian (of a child, an incompetent person); executor (of an estate or will)

(al-)Wasiyyah: Testament, will

(al-)Witr: Odd number; *Witr rakʿahs* are odd numbers of *rakʿahs* such as 1, 3, 5, etc. – usually 1 or 3 – which are performed after the last Prayer at night

(al-)Wuḍūʾ: Ablution. It requires washing the face from the top of the forehead to the chin and as far as each ear, and the hands and arms up to the elbow; and wiping with wet hands a part of the head, and washing the feet up to and including the ankle. It has also some other acts that are Sunnah to perform.

(al-)Yahūd: The Jews. In Muslim history, the Jews are usually referred to as *Yahūdī*, meaning one who belongs to Yahūda –Judah in the Old Testament. Judah – *Yehudah* in Hebrew – is the name of one of the two kingdoms which emerged with the division of the Prophet Solomon's kingdom after his death, and takes this name from Judah, one of the

sons of Jacob. According to another opinion, *Yahūdī* means one who follows the Law established by Judah, an Israelite jurist who lived in the second century after Jesus. The Jews themselves name their religion – Judaism – after Judah. The Qur'ān uses the term *Yahūdī* for the most rigid enemies of Muslims among the Children of Israel and those who regard and call themselves as *Yahūdī* among them.

(al-)Yaqīn: Certainty of faith; having no doubt about the truth of a matter and arriving at accurate, doubt-free knowledge. This knowledge can come from either Revelation or study and verification. *Yaqīn* has three degrees: first, that which comes from knowledge (*'ilm al-yaqīn*); second, that which depends on seeing and observation (*'ayn al-yaqīn*); and third, that which comes from direct experience (*ḥaqq al-yaqīn*).

(al-)Yawm: Day. The Qur'ān uses the word "day" not only in the sense of our normal day, but also as time unit and period.

Yawm ad-Dīn: The Day of Judgment

Yawm al-Faṣl: Another name of the Day of Judgment meaning the Day of Judgment and Distinction (between people)

Yawm al-Jazā': Another name of the Day of Judgment meaning the Day of Recompense

Yawm al-Qiyāmah: The Day of Destruction of the World and Resurrection

(az-)Zakāh: The Prescribed Purifying Alms. It is among the five pillars of Islam and refers to the mandatory amount that a Muslim must pay out of his property. A Muslim who has money beyond a certain quantity is to pay the *Zakāh*. It is to be used in eight categories for welfare of the society that are mentioned in the Qur'ān.

Zakāt al-Fiṭr: See Sadaqat al-fiṭr

(Az-)Zaqqūm: An extremely bitter and thorny tree that grows at the bottom of Hellfire and of which the people of Hell will eat

Ẓihār: A husband's saying to his wife, "You are henceforth as my mother's back to me," meaning divorce. This was a custom among the pagan Arabs. When a husband said this to his wife, he meant he would remove himself from conjugal relations with his wife. This was the equivalent of an irrevocable divorce, but a woman thus divorced could not marry again. Islam decisively prohibited and abolished this custom.

(az-)Zinā: Any sexual intercourse between a man and woman who are not husband and wife, thus denoting both "adultery" and "fornication" in English. The Qur'ān not only forbids any unlawful sexual intercourse, but also orders that all ways to it must be blocked.

(az-)Zuhd: Renouncing worldly pleasures and resisting carnal desires for God's good pleasure

(az-)Ẓālim: Wrongdoer. One who does something not at the proper time and place and in the wrong way, thus causing "darkness" and wronging one's own self; having a very wide area of usage, the term includes from one who does little wrong to another who commits the unforgivable sin of associating partners with God (or denying Him).

(az-)Ẓulm: Wrongdoing. Doing something not at the proper time and place and in the wrong way, thus causing (spiritual) darkness and wronging one's own self who does it. Having a very wide area of usage, in the terminology of the Qur'ān, *ẓulm* includes a wide of range of wrong actions from deviancy in a small matter to the unforgivable sin of associating partners with God (or denying Him).

SUBJECT INDEX

GOD

BASIC POINTS CONCERNING GOD'S ACTS WITH RESPECT TO CONSCIOUS, RESPONSIBLE BEINGS: 6: 18, 61–62, 149; 7: 194–198; 10: 104, 109; 50: 16

GOD AND HIS ONENESS: 3: 18; 4: 171; 6: 103; 7: 194–198; 42: 11

GOD AND THE MULTIFARIOUS MANIFESTATIONS OF HIS ATTRIBUTES AND NAMES: 2: 186; 6: 133; 10: 104; 18: 109; 24: 35; 26: 78–82; 28: 88; 40: 3, 15; 48: 4, 7; 53: 43–53; 55: 26, 27, 29, 78; 74: 56

GOD AS THE (ALL-HOLY) CREATOR (WITH NOTHING TO IMITATE PRECEDING HIM), AND THE ALL-GOVERNING: 2: 117; 6: 72–73, 95, 101–102; 7: 54: 10: 34; 20: 50; 29: 19; 30: 11, 27; 31: 28; 54: 50; 85: 12–16: 87: 2–5

GOD AS THE ABSOLUTE TRUTH AND EVER-CONSTANT, AND THE SOVEREIGN OVER THE UNIVERSE: 3: 189; 6: 3, 12–13, 73, 18, 61, 62, 114; 5: 54; 10: 109; 11: 123; 13: 2; 14: 2; 16: 52; 22: 62; 24: 25; 25: 2; 28: 68, 70; 31: 25; 39: 19, 67; 40: 20; 42: 49–50; 85: 9; 95: 8

GOD AS THE ALL-PROVIDING: 6: 14; 10: 31; 39: 63; 42: 12

GOD AS THE LORD (THE CREATOR, REARER, UPBRINGER, PROVIDER, AND RULER) OF THE WHOLE CRE-ATION: 1: 1; 2: 21–22; 26: 24–28, 78–82; 27: 25–26; 37: 5; 39: 81–82; 44: 7–8; 45: 36–37; 55: 1–7, 10–12, 14–15, 17, 19–20, 22, 24, 26–27, 29, 31, 33, 35, 37, 39, 41, 43–44, 46, 48, 50, 52, 54, 56, 58, 60, 62, 64, 66, 68, 70, 72, 74, 76

GOD IS ABSOLUTELY FREE FROM ANY DEFECT AND NEED AND FROM HAVING ANY CHILDREN, PARTNERS, AND AIDES: 2: 21–22, 116; 4: 36, 171–173; 6: 14, 101; 7: 194–198; 16: 60, 74; 17: 111; 18: 5; 19: 88–96; 21: 16–18; 25: 2; 34: 22; 37: 149–157; 39: 81–82; 42: 11; 112: 3–4

GOD, HIS KNOWLEDGE, AND HIS BEING THE WITNESS OVER ALL THINGS: 6: 19, 59; 10: 61; 13: 8–10; 21: 4; 34: 2–3; 39: 46; 41: 47; 67: 13, 14, 26

GOD'S ABSOLUTE DOMINION OF THE UNIVERSE: 6: 62, 72–73, 7: 54; 11: 123; 13: 2; 16: 49, 52; 28: 70; 40: 20

GOD'S ACTS OR EXECUTION OF HIS WILL IN "NATURE": 2: 29, 117; 6: 72–73, 95, 97, 99, 101–102; 10: 31, 34; 13: 2; 20: 50; 29: 19; 30: 11, 27; 31: 28; 54: 50; 87: 2–5

GOD'S BEING WITH HIS ESSENTIAL ATTRIBUTES: 2: 34, 255; 39: 84–85; 57: 1–6; 59: 22–24; 112: 1–4

GOD'S COVENANT: 2: 24; 16: 91; 36: 60–61

GOD'S PUNISHMENT: 2: 7; 8: 33; 33: 24

GOD'S SPECIAL TREATMENT OF BELIEVERS: 3: 123–126, 150; 8: 26, 30; 9: 111; 28: 5–6; 33: 43

GOD'S TREATMENT OF HIS SERVANTS: 2: 185–186; 3: 128; 4: 40; 6: 17, 54, 62, 149; 7: 194–198; 9: 105, 115; 10: 44, 107; 13: 11; 14: 7–8, 12; 16: 90; 27: 10–11, 73–74; 32: 4; 40: 3; 53: 31; 61: 8; 67: 20–21; 68: 35; 72: 16; 74: 56; 76: 30–31; 113: 1–5; 114: 1–6

GOD'S UNIVERSAL OR GENERAL ACTS WITH RESPECT TO HIS CONSCIOUS, RESPONSIBLE BEINGS: 2: 21–22, 26, 29; 3: 103; 140–141; 6: 141–142; 6: 60; 26: 78–82; 31: 27–28; 42: 49–50; 53: 43–53; 67: 23–24; 71: 7; 73: 17; 91: 15; 92: 12–13; 96: 2–5

GOD'S UNIVERSAL PROVIDING: 10: 31; 11: 6; 42: 12

GOD'S WILL: 35: 8

SOME RULES CONCERNING PEOPLE'S RELATIONSHIP WITH GOD: 3: 31; 7: 180; 16: 60, 74; 18: 24; 31: 33; 59: 19

THE WHOLE CREATION IS UNDER GOD'S ABSOLUTE SWAY AND OBEYS AND GLORIFIES HIM WITH HIS PRAISE: 16: 49; 17: 44; 57: 1; 59: 1; 61: 1; 62: 1; 64: 1

WHAT AND WHOM GOD DOES NOT LOVE: 2: 205, 206; 3: 57; 4: 36, 148; 5: 87; 16: 23; 22: 38; 57: 22–23

WHAT AND WHOM GOD LOVES: 2: 222; 3: 76, 148, 146; 61: 4

THE ALL-MERCIFUL AND THE ALL-COMPASSIONATE: 2: note 4–5; 25: 26; 55: 1–7, 10–12, 14–15, 17, 19–20, 22, 24, 26–27, 29, 31, 33, 35, 37, 39, 41, 43–44, 46, 48, 50, 52, 54, 56, 58, 60, 62, 64, 66, 68, 70, 72, 74, 76 (notes 1–18); 67: 3–4, 19, 20–21, 29

ARGUMENTS FOR GOD'S ONENESS AND FAITH IN HIM

ARGUMENTS FROM THE EARLIER DIVINE SCRIPTURES: 21: 24; 45: 6

ARGUMENTS IN HUMAN SELF AND LIFE: 6: 98; 10: 31, 67; 13: 41; 16: 70, 72, 78–81; 17: 70; 22: 18–24; 21: 44; 25: 54; 30: 54; 35: 11, 15, 18; 39: 6, 36; 42: 11; 67: 23–24, 28–29

ARGUMENT OF CREATING: 6: 72–73; 13: 16; 15: 85; 21: 30; 42: 29

ARGUMENT OF GIVING LIFE AND DEATH, AND REVIVING: 2: 28, 164; 16: 65; 30: 34; 30: 40

WORKS OF REFERENCE

The works referred to in this study, either with their titles or the names of the authors sometimes in full and sometimes abbreviated, due to considerations of space, are given below in the left-hand column. The explanations of the Qur'ān commentators referred to in the notes are found, unless otherwise indicated, in the context of the particular author's commentary on the relevant verse. Since there may be different editions of a book, especially a classical one, which edition has been utilized in this work is not mentioned. Likewise, the books of Hadīth referred to in the notes are also given with their titles and the names of their compilers. The works which exist in easily identifiable editions are stated with the place and date of publication.

All references to the Bible are from *The Holy Bible*, New King James Version, 1982 by Thomas Nelson, Inc.

Abū Dāwūd	Abū Dāwūd Sulayman ibn al-Ash'ath as-Sijistānī, *Kitāb as-Sunan*. Beirut, 1994.
Abū'l-Baqā	Abu'l-Baqā, *Kulliyāt*, Beirut, 1993.
Abū Nu'aym	Aḥmad ibn 'Abdu'llāh, *Hilyat al-Awliya' wa Ṭabaqāt al-Aṣfiya'*, Beirut.
A Comparative	Fethullah Gülen, "A Comparative Approach to Islam and Democracy," *SAIS Review*, vol, XXI, no. 2 (Summer–Fall 2001).
Ahmed Cevdet Paşa	Ahmed Cevdet Paşa, *Kısas-ı Enbiya ve Tavārih-i Hulefa*, İstanbul, Bedir Yayınevi, 1976.
'Ali al-Qārī	'Ali al-Qārī, *al-Asrār al-Marfū'ah fī Akhbār al-Mawdū'ah*, Beirut.
(al-)'Ajlūnī	Ismā'il ibn Muḥammad al-'Ajlūnī, *Kashf al-Khafā' wa Muzil al-Ilbās*, Beirut.
(al-)Ālūsī	Shihābü'd-dīn Maḥmūd al-Ālūsī, *Rūḥ al-Maānī*, Beirut 1987.
Asad	Muḥammad Asad, *The Message of the Qur'ān*, Gibraltar, Dar al-Andalus, 1980.
(al-)Asqalānī	Ibn Hajar al-Asqalānī, *al-Isābah fī Tamyīz as-Ṣahābah*, Dāru'l-Beyân, Cairo, 1988.
(al-)Bayhaqī	Abū Bakr Aḥmad ibn al-Ḥusayn al-Bayhaqī, *Shu'ab al-Īmān*.
(al-)Bidāyah	Ibn al-Kathīr Abū'l-Fidā' Isma'īl Ibn al-Kathīr, *al-Bidāyah wa 'n-Nihāyah*, Beirut.
(al-)Bukhārī	Abū 'Abdu'llāh Muḥammad ibn Ismā'īl al-Bukhārī, *al-Jāmi' aṣ-Ṣaḥīḥ*, Beirut, Dār al Ma'rifah.
Çetin	Abdurrahman Çetin, *Kur'an İlimleri ve Kur'an-ı Kerim Tarihi*, Istanbul, Dergâh Yayınevi, 1982.
(ad-)Dārimī	Abū Muḥammad 'Abdu'llāh ibn 'Abdu'r-Rahmān ad-Dārimī, *as-Sunan*, Cairo.
Djevad	Ahmed Djevad, *Eski Türkler*, İstanbul, Yağmur Yayınevi, 1978.
Ezzati	Abul-Fazl Ezzati, *An Introduction to the History of the Spread of Islam*, London, News and Media Ltd., 1978.

(al-)Haythami	Nūru'-d-Dīn Abu'l-Hasan 'Ali al-Haythami, *Majma' az-Zawā'id wa Manba' al-Fawā'id*, Beirut.
(al-)Hindī	al-Muttaqī al-Hindī, *Kanz al-'Ummāl*, Beirut, 1985.
Ibn al-Athīr	'Izzu'd-Dīn Abu'l-Hasan 'Ali ibn Muḥammad al-Jazarī, *al-Kāmil fī't-Tārīkh*, Beirut.
Ibn Ḥanbal	Aḥmad ibn Ḥanbal, *al-Musnad*, Beirut.
Ibn Ḥibbān,	Abū Hātim Muḥammad ibn Ḥibbān, *Sahīhu ibn Ḥibbān*, Beirut.
Ibn Hishām	Muḥammad Ibn Hishām, *as-Sīrat an-Nabawiyyah*, Beirut, Shirkat al-Maktabat ve Matbaat al Ḥalabī.
Ibn Jarīr aṭ-Ṭabarī	Abū Ja'far Muḥammad ibn Jarīr aṭ-Ṭabarī, *Jami' al-Bayān fī Tafsīr al-Qur'an*, Beirut.
Ibn al-Kathīr	Abu'l-Fidā' Isma'īl Ibn al-Kathīr, *Tafsīr al-Qur'ān al-'Aẓīm*, İstanbul, 1984.
Ibn Mājah	Abū 'Abdu'llāh Muḥammad ibn Yazīd al-Qazwīnī, *as-Sunan*, Dār al-Iḥyā at-Turāth al 'Arabī.
Ibn Sa'd	Abū 'Abdu'llāh Muḥammad, *at-Tabaqāt al-Kubrā*, Beirut, Dār aṣ-Ṣādir.
İşârâtü'l-İ'caz	Bedüzzaman Said Nursi, *İşârâtü'l-İ'caz*, İstanbul, Tenvir Neşriyat.
(al-)Jassās	Abū Bakr Aḥmad ibn 'Ali ar-Rāzī al-Jassās, *Aḥkām al-Qur'ān*, Beirut.
Karaman	Hayreddin Karaman, *Fıkıh Usulü*, İstanbul, İrfan Yayınevi, 1975.
Key Concepts	Fethullah Gülen, *Key Concepts in the Practice of Sufism*, trans., New Jersey, the Light Inc. 2005.
Kur'an'dan İdrake	Fethullah Gülen, *Kur'an'dan İdrake Yansıyanlar*, İstanbul, Zaman, 2000.
Lem'alar	Bediüzzaman Said Nursi, *Lem'alar*, İstanbul, Işık Yayınları, 2004.
M. Asım Köksal	M. Asım Köksal, *İslâm Tarihi*, İstanbul, Şamil Yayınevi, 1981.
(al-)Mawdūdī	Sayyid Abul A'lā al-Mawdūdī, *Towards Understanding the Qur'ān*, translated and edited by Zafar Ishaq Ansari, London.
al-Munāwī	Shamsu'd-Dīn Muḥammad 'Abdu'r-Ra'ūf al-Munāwī, *Fayḍ al-Qadīr*, Beirut.
Mutahhari	Murtaza Matahhari, *Woman and Her Rights*, http://www.al-islam.org/WomanRights/index.html.
Mathnawī	Bediüzzaman Said Nursi, *Epitomes of Light (Mathnawī an-Nūriyah)*, trans., İzmir, Kaynak Yayınları, 1999.
Morrison	A. Cressy Morrison, *Man Does not Stand Alone*, New York, 1945.
Muhakemat	Bediüzzaman Said Nursi, *Muhakemat*, İstanbul, Tenvir Neşriyat, 1988.
Muslim	Abū'l-Husayn Muslim ibn Hajjāj al-Qushayrī, *al-Jāmi' aṣ-Ṣahīh*, Beirut.
(al-)Muwatta'	Mālik ibn Anas, *al-Muwatta'*, Cairo.
(an-)Nahj al-Balāghah	'Ali ibn Abī Tālib, *an-Nahj al-Balāghah*, Qum, Center of Islamic Studies.
(an-)Nasā'ī	Abū 'Abdu'r-Raḥmān 'Aḥmad ibn Shu'ayb an-Nasā'ī, *as-Sunan*, Beirut.
Nurbaki,	Dr. Haluk Nurbaki, *Verses from the Glorious Qur'ān and Facts of Science*, Ankara, TDV, 1989.
Pearls of Wisdom	Fethullah Gülen, *Pearls of Wisdom*, trans., New Jersey, the Light Inc. 2005
(al-)Qurṭubī	Muḥammad ibn Aḥmad al-Qurṭubī, *al-Jāmi' li-Aḥkāmi'l-Qur'ān*, Beirut.
Rāghib al-Isfahānī	Rāghib al-Isfahānī, *al-Mufradāt fī Gharīb al-Qur'ān*, Beirut.
(ar-)Rāzī	Muḥammad ibn 'Umar Fakhru'd-Dīn ar-Rāzī, *Mafātīh al-Ghayb*, Beirut.

(aṣ-)Ṣābūnī	Muḥammad ʿAli aṣ-Ṣābūnī, *Mukhtaṣar Tafsīr Ibn Kathīr*, Beirut.
aṣ-Ṣāliḥ	Ṣubḥi as-Ṣāliḥ, *Kurʾan Ilimleri ve Kurʾan-ı Kerim Tarihi*, trans. Konya, Hibaş Yayınevi.
Sherif Muḥammad	Sherif Muḥammad, *To Clarify an Important Point*, http://www.jannaḥ.org/sisters/compare.html.
Sözler	Bediüzzaman Said Nursî, *Sözler*, İstanbul, Işık Yayınları, 2004.
Özek et al.	A. Özek, N. Uzunoğlu, T. R. Topuzoğlu, M. Maksutoğlu, *The Holy Qurʾan with English Translation*, İstanbul, İlmî Neşriyat, 1992.
Suat Yıldırım	Suat Yıldırım, *Kurʾan-ı Hakim ve Açıklamal Meali*, İstanbul, Işık Yayınları, 2002.
(as-)Suyūṭī	Jalālu'd-Dīn as-Suyūṭī, *ad-Durr al-Manthūr*, Beirut.
Ṣualar	Bediüzzaman Said Nursi, *Ṣualar*, İstanbul, Tenvir Neşriyat.
(aṭ-)Ṭabarānī	Sulaymān ibn Aḥmad ibn Ayyūb aṭ-Ṭabarānī, *al-Muʾjam al-Kabīr*, Beirut.
(aṭ-)Ṭabarī	Abū Jaʿfar Muḥammad ibn Jarīr aṭ-Ṭabarī, *Tārikh al-Umam wa 'l-Mulūk*, Beirut.
(aṭ-)Ṭabāṭabāī	ʿAli ibn Husayn at-Ṭabāṭabāī, *al-Mīzān fī Tafsīr al-Qurʾan*, Tehran, Dār al-Kutub al Islāmiyyah.
Tefhim	Sayyid Abul Aʿlā al-Mawdūdī, *Tefhîmü 'l-Kurʾan*, İstanbul, İnsan Yayınları, 1987.
Tereddütler	Fethullah Gülen, *Asrın Getirdiği Tereddütler*, İzmir, Nil A.Ş. 1988.
The Essentials	Fethullah Gülen, *The Essentials of the Islamic Faith*, trans., New Jersey, the Light Inc. 2005.
The Letters	Bediüzzaman Said Nursî, *The Letters*, trans., London, Truestar, 1995.
The Lost Paradise	Fethullah Gülen, *Towards the Lost Paradise*, trans. İzmir, 1995.
The Messenger	Fethullah Gülen, *The Messenger of God: Muḥammad – An Analysis of the Prophet's Life*, trans., New Jersey, the Light Inc. 2005.
(at-)Tirmidhī	Abū ʿĪsā Muḥammad ibn ʿĪsā at-Tirmidhī, *Sunan*, Beirut.
The Words	Bediüzzaman Said Nursi, *The Words (The Reconstruction of Islamic Belief and Thought)*, trans. H. Akarsu, New Jersey, the Light Inc. 2005.
Yazır	Elmalılı Hamdi Yazır, *Hak Dini Kurʾan Dili*, İstanbul, Eser Yayınevi.
Yıldırım	Suat Yıldırım, *Kurʾan-ı Kerim ve Kurʾan İlimlerine Giriş*, İstanbul, Ensar Yayınevi, 1983.
(az-)Zamakhsharī	Abū'l-Qāsim Jāru'llāh Mahmūd ibn ʿUmar az-Zamakhsharī, *al-Kashshāf an Haqāiq at-Tanzīl wa ʿUyūn al Aqāwīl fī Wucūh at-Taʾwīl*, Egypt.

ISBN 978-1-59784-000-2